Pocket

PCRef

by

Thomas J. Glover
Millie M. Young

Thirteenth Edition

Sequoia Publishing, Inc.
Littleton, Colorado U.S.A.

This Book belongs to:
NAME:
HOME ADDRESS:
HOME PHONE:
WORK PHONE:
BUSINESS ADDRESS:
In case of accident or serious illness, please notify: Name: Phone Number:

Pocket PCRef, 13th Edition, 2nd Printing, September 2007

Sequoia Publishing, Inc.
9903 Titan Court, Suite 16, Dept 101
Littleton, Colorado 80125
(303) 932-1400   (888) 932-1500
Web Site: http://www.sequoiapublishing.com

ISBN 1–885071–40–X

Table of Contents

No longer included in this book:

Preface

Due to lack of space for additional material, Pocket PCRef, 12th Edition (published in 2002) is the last version of Pocket PCRef to be released as a 3.2"x5.4" shirt pocket reference book. From this date forward, Pocket PCRef has been resized to a 4"x6" format and will have identical content to TechRef (the large print version of Pocket PCRef). We have also decided to make the edition numbers (13 Edition) the same between Pocket PCRef and TechRef in order to avoid confusion. For TechRef, that means that Edition numbers 8 through 12 will be skipped.

Sequoia Publishing, Inc. and the authors have made a serious effort to provide accurate information in this book. However, the probability exists that there are errors and misprints. Sequoia Publishing, Inc. and the authors do not represent the information as being exact and make no warranty of any kind with regard to the content of Pocket PCRef or TechRef. Sequoia Publishing, Inc. and the authors shall not be held liable for any errors contained in Pocket PCRef or TechRef or for incidental or consequential damages in connection with any use of the material herein.

The publishers would appreciate being notified of any errors, omissions, or misprints which may occur in this book. *__Your suggestions for future editions would also be greatly appreciated.__* See the copyright page for address, telephone, and website contact information.

The information in this manual was collected from numerous sources and if not properly acknowledged, Sequoia Publishing, Inc. and the authors would like to express their appreciation for those contributions. Registered trademarks or Trade Names are included in the following table:

Trademark or Trade Name	Owner
ASCII	American Standard Code for Information Interchange
Commodore 64	Commodore Computers
Epson	Epson America
Hayes	Microcomputer Products, Inc
HP, HP-IB	Hewlett-Packard
Laserjet	Hewlett-Packard
IBM, AT, XT, PC, PS2, PC Convertible, PC Jr., PC- DOS	International Business Machine
ISO	International Organization for Standardization

Trademark or Trade Name	Owner
Macintosh, Apple IIc, Apple	Apple Computer, Inc.
Microsoft, MS-DOS, Microsoft Windows	Microsoft Corporation

Acknowledgments

This book would not have been possible without the efforts and endless patience of our families and many co-workers. Our deepest love and thanks to all of you.

Our deepest gratitude to Dave Derby, co-owner of Sequoia Publishing, for his technical editing, suggestions, and effort in tracking down the true meaning of Keyboard Scan Codes (a task no less difficult than tracking down the true meaning of life!).

Many thanks to the following people:

Richard Young for his relentless pursuit of the perfect DOS, CPU and Glossary Chapters. (Richard knows the true meaning of life and he has assured us that it has nothing to do with any of these!).

Trish Glover for virtually all of the graphics in this book.
Carrie Glover for work on the Startup Programs and Processes
Bob Olson for help with the XP Commands Chapter

Trish Derby, Bunny Derby, Angel Derby, Donna Baumgarten and Liz Kinney for their help in compiling and verifying the Phone Book.

Donna Baumgarten for her efforts in the never ending task of updating the Hard drive, CDROM, Optical, Tape and floppy drive sections. She also contributed to the Errors Chapter and Phone Book.

Thanks to Millie who taught me the true meanings of courage, dedication and perseverance and in her spare time she wrote the DOS Chapter.

Thank you never seems to be enough when you're saying it to the ones you care about the most! My beautiful wife Mary is the light of my life and helps me survive the daily insanities of the publishing business . . .Thank you and I love you. She compiled the UNIX Command Reference, indexed and proofed and is now officially a geek!

And last but not least, a very special thank you to our children Eric, Dena, Trish, Carrie and David for their love and understanding. You have all made us proud.

Thomas

It is amazing to me, what one person can accomplish when that accomplishment is based on the faith another person has in you. I share only in a small part of this book, the DOS Commands section, and though that may seem insignificant to some, it is a major accomplishment to this novice in the computer world. To the man I love, my gentle and patient husband Richard and our understanding offspring, Elizabeth, Christopher, and Stephanie, none of this would have been possible without you. And, especially to my mentor and friend Thomas, who doesn't know the meaning of limitations. To all of you who have had great faith in me and have allowed this humble sparrow to soar as an eagle, I give my sincerest thanks.

Millie

Products by Sequoia Publishing, Inc.

Bells Guide, 1st Edition · · · · · · · · · · · · · · · · · · · ISBN 1-886734-11-9

DeskRef, 3rd Edition · ISBN 0-885071-44-2
   (DeskRef is the large print version of Pocket Ref)

Handyman In~Your~Pocket, 1st Edition · · · · · · · ISBN 1-885071-29-9

Pocket Partner, 3rd Edition · · · · · · · · · · · · · · · · ISBN 1-885071-51-5

Pocket PCRef, 13th Edition · · · · · · · · · · · · · · · · · ISBN 1-885071-40-X

Pocket Ref, 3rd Edition · ISBN 1-885071-33-7

Measure for Measure, 1st Edition · · · · · · · · · · · · ISBN 1-889796-00-X

Seldovia, Alaska: An Historical Portrait of Herring Bay
    · · · ISBN 1-889796-03-4

TechRef, 13th Edition · ISBN 1-885071-46-9
   (TechRef is the large print version of Pocket PCRef)

Troubleshooting Your Contracting Business to Cause Success
    · · · · ISBN 1-889796-04-2

WinRef 98-95 In~Your~Pocket · · · · · · · · · · · · · · · ISBN 1-885071-22-1

Coming Winter 2004

BoatRef, 1st Edition · ISBN 1-885071-52-3

Be A Cop, 1st Edition · ISBN 1-885071-49-3

Out of Print Publications by Sequoia Publishing, Inc.

Highpoint Adventures

How to Ski the Blues and Blacks Without Getting Black and Blue

MegaRef, DOS software version of Pocket Ref

Troubleshooting Tools

Introduction to Troubleshooting

This chapter consists of a series of sections that relate to PC and Windows problem resolution. The sections are listed in the sequence that would normally be followed during the startup and running of the computer. This chapter is intended to provide a technician with basic tools, utilities, and techniques that will aid in the repair of a computer system. It is NOT designed to be a comprehensive troubleshooting flow chart

Troubleshooting Dos and Don'ts
If you are repairing someone's computer, be sure to interview the computer owner to determine as closely as possible the exact symptoms. Also determine if the computer is still under warranty as that may restrict the type of work you can do on the computer.
A static free work space is imperative! Keep the environment humid and dust free, wear ESD wrist straps, use antistatic floor mats, use antistatic tools and containers, and do not wear clothing that helps creates static. I personally work in my stocking feet during repairs to help insure a good static ground through damp socks and feet.
When working on a system, always make sure that all hardware related to the computer (box, monitor, modems, routers, hubs, etc) is powered through a battery backup (UPS). A power outage during a software update procedure will seriously complicate the repair process.
Never work inside the computer box when it is plugged into the AC power source. Even if the computers power switch has been turned off, the motherboard can still be hot. You can physically damage components that are installed or removed if the system still has live power.
Intermittent hardware problems can sometimes be quickly resolved by swapping out individual components with known good components. This is particularly true of monitors, power supplies, memory chips, and CPU's since reconfiguration is not required when the replacement is completed.
When taking "hot" measurements of voltage or current, us only one hand during the test. With two hands, you are in danger of being a short circuit.
When troubleshooting specific error codes, error text, viruses, parasites, spyware, trojans, and worms, one of your most valuable weapons is the internet search engine. Search engines from Google.com, Yahoo.com, MSN.com, AltaVista.com, and Microsoft.com provide a vast warehouse of information on diagnosing and repairing these types of problems.

System Will Not Power Up

	No lights or fan noise from either the monitor or computer box.
1	Verify power switches are turned on at the computer, monitor, control panel, surge protector and battery backup. If no power at these points, use an AC voltmeter to verify that the wall outlet is live.
2	If computer has lights and fan noise but the monitor does not appear to have power, try to reestablish power and then try swapping out the monitor.
3	On the back of the computer near the power cord port, verify that the small power toggle switch is turned ON (the "I" should be depressed, not the "O").
4	On the back of the computer also near the power cord port, verify that the voltage selector slide switch is set to 115V. If not, unplug computer and move switch from 230V to 115V (unless of course, the house power you are using is supposed to be 230V).
5	If the monitor has power but the computer does not and you have followed Steps 1 and 2, start looking inside the computer case. Unplug the computer, remove the computer case cover and verify that the main 20 pin power supply connector (and the 4 pin 12V connector if this is a Pentium 4 motherboard) is plugged into the motherboard. Also verify that at least one hard drive power plug is connected to a hard drive.
6	If all of these internal connectors were correct, then unplug all power connectors from components in the computer EXCEPT one hard drive. Reconnect the computer to AC power. Using a paper clip or short piece of wire, TEMPORARILY short between the green wire (pin 14) and the adjacent black wire (pin 15) of the main 20 pin power supply plug (see page 533 for a picture of the connector if needed.) If the power supply fan starts running, the power supply is probably good.
7	If the power supply did not start, unplug the single hard drive that was left connected in the Step 6 and connect that power plug to a different hard drive and perform the test in Step 6 again. If the power supply started this time, the hard drive was the problem.
8	If the power supply did start in Step 6, isolate which component is causing the problem by reconnect each of them (one at a time) and performing the Step 6 test again.
9	If the power supply starts but you still suspect the is a power supply problem then start the system and use a voltmeter to check each individual voltage output on every connector. See plug voltages starting on page 532. If any of the voltages are substantially higher or lower than what they are supposed to be, replace the power supply to see if the problem goes away. If everything checks out but the problem persists, it is caused by something else in the computer.
10	***Power Supply Testing Hints:*** If you need to test power supplies regularly, the procedures in Step 8 can take a lot of time. It is suggested that instead of using a voltmeter, purchase a "Power Supply Tester". Much simpler, much quicker and relatively inexpensive.

	No lights or fan noise from either the monitor or computer box.
11	Motherboard monitoring software typically monitors power supply voltages. If you suspect an intermittent power supply problem, try installing a program like **Motherboard Monitor** from www.3degs.net to monitor the system.

Start Problems Before Windows Launch

	Power lights on and monitor is known to be good
1	Power on, no video, multiple beeps are heard: Check that the video card is seated properly as unseating is a common problem. If it is seated correctly, listen to the beep code sequence (for example a sequence of 3 beeps then 1 beep then 2 beeps). Look at the motherboard and chips to see if you can determine which BIOS the system uses then look up the meaning of the beep code in Chapter 2 (page 23.)
2	Power on, video works, multiple beeps are heard: Follow same procedure as Step 1.
3	Power on, video works, system hangs at some point before Windows launches: Determine BIOS POST code if available and look up the meaning of the POST code in Chapter 2. If the POST code is not listed in Chapter 2 (page 23), go online with a search engine and search for the code and instructions for problem correction.
4	Power on, video works, errors occur before Windows launches: Start the CMOS Setup program with the correct key sequence for the computer (see page 11.) If everything appears normal in the CMOS Setup, select Load Setup Defaults, Save Settings and then reboot. If the system now boots normally but the problem reappears in several days, replace the CMOS motherboard battery.
5	If BIOS/CMOS errors continue and are critical or fatal errors, start the process of removing all cards (keep track of which slots they were removed from) and all drives (except 1 hard drive and 1 CD-ROM drive). Restart the system in it's simplest configuration, determine that the problem is not present, shut down the system, reinstall one of the removed components, restart and check for the problem, and so on until you locate the component that is causing the problem.
6	In some situations, it may be difficult to tell if the error is occurring before or during Windows launch. In these cases, it may be simpler to remove the boot drive, install a blank hard drive, install a clean Windows OS and check to see if the problem still exists. If it does still exist, it means the problem is not Windows related.
7	If the system powers up but you receive an error message that states "No boot disk found" or "Non system disk", be sure to make sure there is not a floppy disk, L120 or Zip Disk in one of the drives. Depending on how your system is configured, the computer might be trying to boot from one of those disks instead of the hard drive.

Troubleshooting

How to Access your PC's CMOS Setup

Most PC's of the past 20 years have a built in setup program for the systems BIOS. Unfortunately, the motherboard and BIOS manufacturers never agreed to a standardized way of activating the setup program. The table below is a list of most of the common keystrokes used to access setup programs. The Keystrokes should be pressed during the POST process of bootup, i.e. as soon as something starts to display when you turn on the computer. If you wait until the Windows splash screen displays, it is probably too late. In many systems, one of the text lines that displays early in the boot process will tell you what key combination to use to access Setup.

If the Setup screen has been password protected and you can't locate the password, you will need to reset the CMOS. Most systems have a jumper on the motherboard that will clear the CMOS and reset it to factory specs: turn the system power off, jump the jumper, turn the system power on. Remove the jumper and restart. It is recommended that you check your motherboard User Guide for specific instructions before attempting this procedure. When you reboot the system, you will have to enter CMOS Setup and reenter all of the user preferences.

Keystrokes to Activate System CMOS	BIOS or Computer Brand
Control + Alt + Enter	Dell (old)
Control + Alt + Escape	Phoenix & Phoenix BIOS, Dell, AST Advantage, Tandon
Control + Alt + F11 after boot into the DOS prompt	ThinkPad with Phoenix BIOS
Control + Alt + F3 after boot into the DOS prompt	ThinkPad (Old)
Control + Alt + Insert after Control + Alt + Delete	IBM PS2 BIOS, IBM ThinkPad (old), Zenith, Phoenix (old)
Control + Alt + S	Phoenix BIOS (old version), Packard Bell 386 & 486
Control + Alt + Shift + Del key on the numeric keypad	Olivetti PC Pro
Control + Alt + "+"	Off brand
Control + Alt + ?	PS/2 (75 & 90)
Control + Escape	Off brand
Control + Insert	PS/2
Control + S	Phoenix (old)

Keystrokes to Activate System CMOS	BIOS or Computer Brand
Control + Shift + Escape	Tandon 386
Delete key (repeatedly during boot if necessary)	AMI BIOS, Award BIOS, Dell
Escape key	DTK BIOS, Toshiba
F1 Key	Phoenix Bios, Toshiba, late model PS/1, HP, ThinkPad, IBM Aptiva
F1 Key, hold down while booting	IBM BIOS ThinkPad (newer), EC Versa Notebooks
F1 + Fn Key	Dell Latitude
F2 Key	Phoenix Bios, NEC, Dell, ThinkPad (old), Gateway
F10 Key	Compaq (newer)
Fn Key + Escape	Gateway
Insert Key	IBM PS/2 with special partition
Page Up Key or Page Down Key	Off brands
Reset Button	Dell (rare; press button twice)
Tab Key	Emachine
Hold down suspend/resume switch while powering on	ThinkPad (old)
Boot to DOS in Safe Mode, then Control + Alt + Esc	Phoenix Bios (old), Gateway
Boot to DOS in Safe Mode, then Control + Alt + S	Phoenix Bios (old), Gateway
Booting system with aSetup or Diagnostics disk. The setup program is actually stored in a small, non-DOS drive partition.	Old XT, 286, 386, and some 486 systems, Older Phoenix Bios., Older Compaqs (setup was actually contained on a small drive partition. If corrupt, you have to boot from a setup floppy)
Software: from Windows, run the HWSetup program or from DOS, run the TSetup program.	Toshiba

How to Start Windows in Safe Mode

Safe Mode is a Windows troubleshooting mode that is especially useful in removing certain viruses, parasites, and spyware as well as resolving hardware, device driver and configuration errors.

In Safe Mode, Windows <u>does not</u> load protected mode device drivers, autoexec.bat, config.sys, the [Boot] and [386Enh] sections of system.ini, or any Load= or Run= entries in the win.ini file. Windows <u>does</u> load the floppy driver, real mode drivers, shell= and drivers= entries in system.ini and the default Standard VGA video driver (640x480).

If you select Safe Mode without networking, you will not have internet access through the ethernet card.

To exit Safe Mode, simply shutdown or restart as you would normally.

How to Start Windows in Safe Mode	
Program	**Description**
Windows 95	1. Power on, tap F5 key after the memory count and before "Starting Windows 95" message
	2. Power on, tap F8 key after the memory count and before "Starting Windows 95" message, select "Safe Mode" from the menu.
	3. If Windows does not start, it will attempt to enter safe mode automatically.
Windows 98 Windows ME	1. Power on, tap F8 key after the memory count (or in some cases as soon as you see the black and white screen with a cursor showing), select "Safe Mode"Power on, then select "Safe Mode" from the menu.
	2. If Windows does not start, it will attempt to enter safe mode automatically.
	3. Power on, boot to Normal Mode, do Start> Run> msconfig. Under the Advanced tab, check "Enable Startup Menu", click Ok, then restart the system (which will now automatically launch Safe Mode.) Be sure to uncheck the "Enable Startup Menu" box after your troubleshooting is completed.
	4. On some systems, holding down the <Ctrl> key when you power on the system will activate the Startup Menu so you can select Safe Mode.
	5. On some systems, insert a non-system floppy disk in the floppy drive, when the message "Non-system disk or disk error" appears, press the F8 key TWICE. This will access the Startup Menu.
Windows 2000	1. Power on, tap F8 key after the memory count (or in some cases as soon as you see the black and white screen with a cursor showing), select "Safe Mode"Power on, then select "Safe Mode" from the menu.
Windows XP	1. Power on, tap F8 key after the memory count (or in some cases as soon as you see the black and white screen with a cursor showing), select "Safe Mode"Power on, then select "Safe Mode" from the menu.
	2. Power on, boot to Normal Mode, do Start> Run> msconfig. Under the BOOT.INI tab, check "/ SAFEBOOT", click Ok, then restart the system (which will now automatically launch Safe Mode.) Be sure to uncheck the "/ SAFEBOOT" box after your troubleshooting is completed.

How to Create a Boot Floppy for Windows XP

This procedure creates a boot floppy disk for NTFS or FAT partitions on a Windows XP system that has a hard drive with a faulty boot sequence. Specifically, this type of boot floppy may be used as a troubleshooting tool to possibly boot systems with the following problems: damaged boot sector, damaged MBR (master boot record), incorrect Ntbootdd.sys driver, or missing or damaged Ntldr or Ntdetect.com file. Microsoft also states that this may allow you to boot from the shadow of a broken mirror but that issue will require a modification of the Boot.ini file. Obviously, this type of boot floppy could be a valuable disaster recovery tool and should be created for every Windows XP system. This is NOT a standalone boot floppy like Windows ME and earlier systems could use. Complete the following steps:

1. In Windows XP, format a floppy disk. This must be done in XP.

2. Copy the Ntldr and Ntdetect.com files from the I386 folder of the Windows XP Setup CD-ROM to the floppy. Note that you could also copy these files from any XP computer running exactly the same version of XP as the system you want to boot.

3. Copy the Boot.ini file from the XP computer you want to boot or create a plain text file manually using the following example (this will work only for a single-partition IDE drive with XP installed in the \Windows folder of the hard drive):

```
[boot loader]
timeout=30
default=multi(0)disk(0)rdisk(0)partition(1)\WINDOWS
[operating systems]
multi(0)disk(0)rdisk(0)partition(1)\WINDOWS="Microsoft Windows XP"
```

4. Start the computer with the floppy disk.

Notes:
1. If the computer boots from a SCSI hard drive, you will need to alter the Boot.ini example show above by replacing both instances of multi(0) with scsi(0) AND copy the appropriate SCSI device driver to the Setup floppy and rename the driver to Ntbootdd.sys. Change the disk(0) entries to match the SCSI ID of the boot hard drive. For example, if the drive id ID2, change the entry to disk(2).
2. You cannot use this boot disk to resolve incorrect or damaged device drivers that are installed in the system folder of the hard drive or boot issues that occur once Windows has started to launch (i.e. the Windows XP Osloader startup screen has launched.)
3. This procedure will not work for RISC-based computers.
4. This procedure was compiled from Microsoft Knowledge Base Article 305595.

Start Problem During and After Windows Launch

The rest of this chapter deals with software tools to help you troubleshoot problems during and after Windows launch. This also includes diagnosing hardware problems if you are able to launch Windows. There are obviously tens of thousands of diagnostic and utility programs available today; the programs in the sections below are simply my favorites and most of the software is either free or very inexpensive (<$50). Software has been grouped into the following categories:

Windows Resources and Download Sites

Computer Hardware and Software Audit

Password Problems

Windows Startup Programs & Services

Virus, Worm, Trojan, Parasite, and Spyware

Diagnose Hardware Problems

Create a Bootable XP CD-ROM or Floppy Disk

System General Utilities & Tweaking

Network and Wireless

Internet and Browser

Drive and Storage Utilities

Windows Resources and Download Sites

Windows Resources and Download Sites	
Web Site	Description
Download.com	Software downloads; www.download.com
MajorGeeks	Software downloads; www.majorgeeks.com
SnapFiles	Software downloads; www.snapfiles.com
SofoTex	Software downloads; www.sofotex.com
SourceForge	Software downloads; http://sourceforge.net
TomsHardware	Hardware reviews; www.tomshardware.com

Computer Hardware and Software Audit

Computer Hardware and Software Audit	
Program	Description
AIDA32	PC audit and benchmark tool; Free; www.majorgeeks.com
Belarc Advisor	PC audit tool to document installed hardware and software; Free personal use; www.belarc.com
WCPUID	Displays CPU info; Free; www.h-oda.com

Password Problems

Password Problems	
Program	**Description**
123 Password Recovery	Recovers passwords stored under the ***** mask. Free and commercial versions; www.webattack.com/get/123pwrecovery.shtml
LOphtCrack	Password recovery tool; Free trial and >$650; www.blazingtools.com/bpk.html
NTPassword	Utility to overwrite NT/2K/XP Administrator password in order to regain entry to a system; Free; http://home.eunet.no/~pnordahl/ntpasswd/bootdisk.html
RockXP	Recover Windows Product Key Codes and passwords; Free; www.snapfiles.com/get/rockxp.html

Windows Startup Programs & Services

Windows XP provides a Startup Manager called msconfig which is accessed through Start> Run> msconfig. Be very careful when changing settings in any Startup Manager as you can quickly disable the operating system. Start> Run> services.msc provides quick access to all services running on the system and they can be started/stopped as well as changing the startup mode Automatic/Manual/Disabled.

Windows Startup Programs & Services	
Program	**Description**
ProcessExplorer	Explore process from Task Manager; Free; www.sysinternals.com
StartRight	Controls the start order of Windows programs; Free; http://jackass.arsware.ort
StartUp Control Panel	Sophisticated startup program manager; Free; www.mlin.net
StartupCop	Startup manager; Free & $15; www.pcmag.com

Virus, Worm, Trojan, Parasite, and Spyware

See also Chapter 3, Startup Programs, Processes and Task Manager (page 47) for additional information on this topic.

The internet has done many wonderful things for the world today but with all good things, there is always a dark side. This section deals with malicious software that has been created to vandalize, terrorize and frustrate everyone who uses computers today. The following is a brief summary of malicious software that we are confronted with today:

Virus - a piece of program code that is designed to make copies of itself and spread by attaching to a host. While some viruses are very malicious and destroy data, most are simply annoying. The predominant destructive effect of viruses comes from their uncontrolled self-reproduction. An excellent web site that review antivirus programs is www.software-antivirus.com

---

Worm - a self contained, self-replicating program similar to a virus but does not require a host to propagate itself. These programs can install backdoors on your system that allow spammers to use your computer in spam attacks.

Trojan - a self contained program that presents itself as a good program but is, in fact, a malicious program. A trojan is similar to a virus but, unlike a worm, it does not move by itself from machine to machine. The program must be intentionally moved to another machine and then run.

Parasite - an unsolicited commercial software application that works through your browser to install itself on your computer without your knowledge. After installation, the program functions in one of the following groups:

Spyware - spies on your web surfing habits and relays that information back to an outside host.

Adware - a form of spyware that collects information on the user and then displays advertising in the users browser.

Antivirus - Based on reviews from www.software-antivirus.com	
Program	Description
Kaspersky	Top rated program; $50; www.kaspersky.com
Panda	Very good rating; $70; www.pandasecurity.com
NOD32	Very good rating; $65; www.nod32.com.au/nod32/home/home.htm
Command	Good rating; $20; www.authentium.com/products/avmatrix/index.htm
McAfee VirusScan Online Scan	Good rating; $29; www.mcafee.com
F-prot for DOS	Good rating; Free; www.f-prot.com
F-Secure	Fair rating; $78; www.f-secure.com
PC-cillin 2002	Fair rating; $50; www.trendmicro.com
AVG	Poor rating; Free; www.grisoft.com
eTrust EZ	Poor rating; $30; www2.my-etrust.com
McAfee VS Pro	Poor rating; $35; www.mcafee.com
Norman Virus Control	Poor rating; www.norman.com
Norton 2003	Poor rating; $50; www.symantec.com
Sophos	Poor rating; www.sophos.com

Anti Parasite, Spyware, and Adware These are our favorites, there are more than 100 programs available	
Program	Description
AdAware	Very good; Free; www.lavasoftusa.com
HijackThis	Tool to list things installed in a browser; Free; www.spychecker.com
PestPatrol	Very good; $40; www.pestpatrol.com
Spybot Search and Destroy	Very good; Free; www.safer-networking.org/en/index.html
SpySweeper	Good; Free Trial, $30; www.webroot.com
SpyHunter	Good; Free Trial, $30; www.enigmasoftwaregroup.com
SpyRemover	Good; Free Trial, $30; www.itcompany.com/remover.htm
SpywareBlaster	Prevents spyware from being installed on your system, it does not scan and clean; Free; www.javacoolsoftware.com

Firewalls	
Program	**Description**
Smoothwall	Express; Free; http://smoothwall.org
Zone Alarm	Free version and commercial version with extra features. www.zonealarm.com

Diagnose Hardware Problems

Diagnose Hardware Problems	
Program	**Description**
Burnin64	Burn in and test AMD 64-bit systems; $19; www.3degs.com
HotCPU	CPU temperature monitor and tester; Free & $20; www.3degs.net
Memtest86	Memory chip tester; Free; www.memtest86.com
MotherboardMonitor	Monitor and view motherboard information; Free; www.3degs.com
MotherboardMonitor5	Monitor and view motherboard information and display in system tray; Free; www.livewiredev.com

Create a Bootable XP CD-ROM or Floppy

Create a bootable XP CD-ROM	
Program	**Description**
Bart PE	Creates a bootable Windows XP CD-ROM or DVD; Free Trial or $60; www.nu2.nu/pebuilder

System General Utilities & Tweaking

System General Utilities & Tweaking	
Program	**Description**
Clip Control	Changes the functionality of the capslock key; Free; www.anticapslock.com
Disk Jockey File Viewer	Windows file manager; $80; www.clear-simple.com
DupDetector	Finds duplicate and near duplicate images by opening and reading image pixel data; Shareware; www.prismaticsoftware.com
Duplicate File Finder	Finds duplicate files on a drive; $15; www.funduc.com/dupfiles.htm
Easy Cleaner	Registry cleaner; Free; personal.inet.fi/business/toniarts/
RegScrubXP	Cleans junk out of Win2K/XP registry; Free; www.majorgeeks.com
ResourceBuilder	Windows tweaking; Free; www.tgtsoft.com
ResourceHacker	Windows tweaking; Free; www.users.on.net/johnson/resourcehacker
ZTree	Windows file manager; $30; www.ztree.com

Network and Wireless

Networks and Wireless	
Program	**Description**
Air Snare	Wireless intrusion detection, see who is on a wireless network; Free; http://home.comcast.net/~jay.deboer/airsnare/
Air Snort	Recovers wireless encryption keys, requires Linux; Free; http://airsnort.shmoo.com/
Cute FTP	FTP client; $40; www.cuteftp.com
DSLReports (website)	Many internet and network tools and testers; small fee for priority service; www.dslreports.com
IPChicken	IP Address echo; Free; www.ipchicken.com
NeoTrace	Traceroute program that provides more feedback about failed connections; Free & $30; www.download.com
PeerFTP	Peer to Peer ftp (share files between users, large file transfer); Free and $20; www.clientbackup.com
SmartFTP	FTP client; Free & $30; www.smartftp.com
Sygate	Single PC firewall; $40; www.sygate.com
Tiny Personal Firewall	Single PC firewall; $49; www.tinysoftware.com
WepKey	Sophisticated WEP Key Generator for wireless; Free Trial; www.clariondeveloper.com/wepgen
ZoneAlarm	Single PC firewall; Free and

Internet and Browsers

Internet and Browsers	
Program	**Description**
Firefox	IE replacement for everything except Windows Updates; Free; www.mozilla.org
Anonymizer	Surf the web anonymously, blocks IP's, wireless blocker; $30; www.anonymizer.com
Clean Cache	Internet Explorer: cleans internet tracks, including browser cache, cookies, history, typed URL's, index.dat and more; Free; www.buttuglysoftware.com
Clean MO Cache	Firefox and Mozilla: cleans internet tracks, including browser cache, cookies, history, typed URL's, index.dat and more; Free; www.buttuglysoftware.com
Download Accelera-tor Plus	Speed up downloads and download more than 2 files at a time; Free; www.speedbit.com
Favorg.zip	Custom internet favorites icons for Favico; $?; www.pcmag.com
I Protect You	Controls which Web sites can be visited and which programs can have Internet access; Free; www.softforyou.com
Megaproxy	Surf the web anonymously; Free trial, $40/yr; www.megaproxy.com
NetNanny	Internet access monitor and filter; $40; www.netnanny.com
NetTransport	Download multiple threads; Shareware; www.xi-soft.com
SpamBayes	Spam filter for Outlook; Free; www.spambayes.sourceforge.net
SpoofStick	Identifies the actual site a user is connected to in both IE and Firefox; Free; www.corestreet.com/spoofstick

Drive & Storage Utilities

Disk Drive Utilities	
Program	**Description**
Aloha Bob PC Relocator	Performs a "hands-off" relocation of installed software from one computer to another; $30 to $70; www.eisenworld.com/ProductsHome.asp
Backup4All	Configurable backups to CD and DVD using zip compression; $20 to $45; www.backup4all.com
Circle Virtual CD	Creates virtual CD's on a hard drive, better access times and makes CD copies; Free; www.circleofone.com
Cryptainer LE	Encrypt up to 20meg of files creates a virtual drive; Free; www.cypherix.co.uk/cryptainerle/
Drive Fitness Test	IBM-Hitachi drive fitness test for SCSI and IDE drive; Free; www.ibm.com/us/
DVD Shrink	Copy DVD disks; Free; www.dvdshrink.org
Eraser	Hard drive security erase; Free; http://sourceforge.net
PhotoRecovery	Recover lost images from most digital camera media; $40; www.LC-tech.com
Retrospect	Backup software; $40; www.dantz.com
VirtualCD	Creates virtual CD's on your hard drive for better access times; $40; www.virtualcd-online.com

My Favorite Non-Troubleshooting Free Programs

My Favorite Non-Troubleshooting Programs	
Program	**Description**
AbiWord	Microsoft Word alternative; Free; www.abisource.com
Audacity	Sound editor; Free; http://audacity.sourceforge.net
AVID Free DV	Video and Audio editor; Free; www.avid.com/index.fl.asp
Cute PDF Writer	PDF creator from almost any printable document; Free; www.acrosoftware.com
Gimp	Photoshop alternative; Free; www.gimp.org
IconArt	Create icons and mouse cursors; Free; www.conware.org
ImageBrowserArctic	Image browser; Free; www.uticasoft.com
MyAlbum	Digital image cataloger; Free; http://pmeindre.free.fr/MyAlbum.html
PhotoPlus	Photoshop alternative; Free; www.freeserifsoftware.com
Pixia	Photoshop alternative; Free; park18.wakwak.com/~pixia
WeatherWatcher	View current weather conditions; Free; www.bardon.com/winu.htm

ClearType   XP Only

Microsoft's "ClearType" delivers improved font display quality over traditional forms of font smoothing or anti-aliasing. ClearType improves readability on color LCD displays with a digital interface, such as those in laptops and high-quality flat panel displays. Readability on CRT screens can also be somewhat improved.

To turn on ClearType, go to the web site below for visual examples on your system and then follow instructions:

    http://www.microsoft.com/typography/cleartype/tuner/1.htm

You can manually turn ClearType on and off with the following:

1. Right click on your desktop->Select the "Appearance" tab
2. Select the "Effects" button
3. Check the box "Use the following method to smooth edges of screen fonts"
4. From the drop down box, Select "Standard" or "ClearType"

Disable Microsoft Instant Messenger

If you don't use Instant Messenger programs, remove or disable them since they consume system resources, add a level of security risk and can significantly slow down your system startup. To disable the Microsoft Instant Messenger, perform the following:

1. Select Start->Select Run->Type gpedit.msc
2. Select "Computer Configuration"->Select "Administrative Templates"
3. Select "Windows Components"->Select "Windows Messenger"
4. ENABLE "Do not allow Windows Messenger to be run"
   ENABLE "Do not automatically start Windows Messenger initially"

Disable Error Reporting

If you are tired of getting the Error Report window for a problem program, turn of the Error Reporting!

1. Start "Control Panel" or Start->Settings->"Control Panel"
2. Select "System"-> Select the "Advanced" tab
3. Select the "Error Reporting" button at the bottom of the window.
4. Select "Disable error reporting"

Disable Dr. Watson

There is no need to have this active unless a programmer/tech from the problem programs company is working with you to resolve a problem.

1. Select Start->Select Run->Type c:\windows\system32\drwtsn32.exe
2. In the Dr. Watson window, uncheck "Create Crash Dump File"

Turn off the CD or DVD drive AutoPlay feature

When you insert a CD or DVD into a drive, this stops it from automatically running the disk.

1. Open "My Computer"->Right Click on the drive you are changing

Troubleshooting

2. Select "Properties"->Select the "AutoPlay" tab
3. In the Drop Down box, select the type of file then select an action.

Desktop Shortcut to Lock your Computer
This little trick provides an instant lockdown of your computer

1. Right Click on your desktop->Select "New"->Select "Shortcut"
2. In the Field labeled "Type the location of the item", type in the following line exactly as shown:
   C:\WINDOWS\system32\rundll32.exe user32.dll, LockWorkStation
3. In the Field labeled "Type a name for this shortcut", type in the shortcut name as you want it to appear on your desktop. Select "Finish"
4. If you want to change the icon used for the shortcut, right click on the new icon, Select "Change Icon", and then choose a different icon.

Block the AIM Port at your router
Tired of your employees or kids using the AOL Instant Messenger? Try blocking Port 5190 at your DSL router.

`<fatal error: Computer will self destruct in five minutes..//`

Chapter 2

Error Codes

Error Codes

BIOS Audio Error Codes

A variety of tests are executed automatically when computers are first turned on. Initially, the "Power-On Self Test" (POST) is run. It provides error or warning messages whenever a faulty component is encountered. Typically, two types of messages are issued: **Audio Beep Codes** and **Display Error Messages. Audio Beep Codes** consist of a series of beeps that identify a faulty component. In the case of an IBM computer, if it is functioning normally, you will hear one short beep when the system is turned on. However, if a problem is detected, a series of beeps or no beeps will occur. The type and number of beeps define the problem. Audio Beep Codes for some of the major BIOS manufacturers are included below. If the system has problems but completes the POST process, then additional errors may be reported in the form of **Display Error Messages**. The list of **Display Error Messages** is quite extensive and only the IBM PC/XT/PS2 messages are included in this book.

American Megatrends BIOS (AMI)

Beeps	AMI BIOS Error Description
Fatal Errors	
1	DRAM refresh failed
2	Parity circuit failed
3	Base 64K or CMOS RAM failed
4	System timer failed
5	Processor failed
6	Keyboard controller or gate A20 error
7	Virtual mode exception error
8	Display memory write/read test failed
9	ROM BIOS checksum failed
10	CMOS RAM shutdown register failed
11	Cache memory bad, do not enable cache
1 long, 2 short	Video system failure
2 short	POST Failure, hardware test failed
Continuous beep	Memory or video problem
Nonfatal errors	
1 long, 3 short	Conventional/extended memory failed
1 long, 8 short	Display and retrace failed

Award Software BIOS

Beeps	Award Software BIOS Error Description
1 long, 2 short	Video card failure
1 long, 3 short	Bad video RAM or no card
Endless beep	Memory error
High pitch beep while running	CPU overheated
Any other beeps are probably RAM problems; no other audio errors	

AST BIOS

Beeps	AST BIOS Error Description
1 short	CPU failure
2 short	Keyboard controller buffer failure
3 short	Keyboard controller reset failure
4 short	Keyboard communication failure
5 short	Keyboard input failure
6 short	System board chipset failure
9 short	BIOS ROM checksum error
10 short	System timer test failure
11 short	ASIC failure
12 short	CMOS RAM shutdown register failure
1 long	D.M.A. controller 0 failure
1 long, 1 short	D.M.A. controller 1 failure
1 long, 2 short	Video vertical retrace failure
1 long, 3 short	Video memory test failure
1 long, 4 short	Video adapter failure
1 long, 5 short	Memory failure of 64kb
1 long, 6 short	Interrupt vectors unload able
1 long, 7 short	Video Error
1 long, 8 short	Failure in the video memory

Compaq BIOS

Beeps	Compaq BIOS Error Description
1 short	System booted correctly – no error
1 long, 1 short	BIOS ROM checksum error
2 short	Unknown general error
1 long, 2 short	Video adapter error
1 l,1s,1l,1s,pause,1l,1s,1s	AGP video card error
1 continuous long	Memory error
1 short, 2 long	RAM error

Dell Computer Corporation BIOS

Beeps	Dell Computer Corp BIOS Error Description
1-3	Video memory test failure
1-1-2	Testing CPU register
1-1-3	CMOS write/read test failed
1-1-4	ROM BIOS checksum bad
1-2-1	Programmable interval timer failed
1-2-2	D.M.A. initialization failed
1-2-3	D.M.A. page register write/read bad
1-3-1	RAM refresh verification failed
1-3-2	Testing first 64K RAM
1-3-3	First 64K RAM chip or data line bad, multi-bit
1-3-4	First 64K RAM odd/even logic bad
1-4-1	Address line fault in first 64K RAM
1-4-2	Parity error detected in first 64K RAM

Beeps	Dell Computer Corp BIOS Error Description
2-1-1	Bit 0 fault in first 64K RAM
2-1-2	Bit 1 fault in first 64K RAM
2-1-3	Bit 2 fault in first 64K RAM
2-1-4	Bit 3 fault in first 64K RAM
2-2-1	Bit 4 fault in first 64K RAM
2-2-2	Bit 5 fault in first 64K RAM
2-2-3	Bit 6 fault in first 64K RAM
2-2-4	Bit 7 fault in first 64K RAM
2-3-1	Bit 8 fault in first 64K RAM
2-3-2	Bit 9 fault in first 64K RAM
2-3-3	Bit 10 fault in first 64K RAM
2-3-4	Bit 11 fault in first 64K RAM
2-4-1	Bit 12 fault in first 64K RAM
2-4-2	Bit 13 fault in first 64K RAM
2-4-3	Bit 14 fault in first 64K RAM
2-4-4	Bit 15 fault in first 64K RAM
3-1-1	Slave D.M.A. register bad
3-1-2	Master D.M.A. register bad
3-1-3	Master interrupt mask register bad
3-1-4	Slave interrupt mask register bad
3-2-2	Interrupt vector loading in progress
3-2-4	Keyboard controller test failed
3-3-1	CMOS RAM power bad; calculating checksum
3-3-2	CMOS configuration validation in progress
3-3-4	Video memory test failed
3-4-1	Video initialization failed
3-4-2	Video retrace failure
3-4-3	Search for video ROM in progress
none	Screen operable, running with video ROM
none	Monochrome monitor operable
none	Color monitor (40 column) operable
none	Color monitor (80 column) operable
4-2-1	Timer tick interrupt test in progress or bad
4-2-2	Shutdown test in progress or bad
4-2-3	Gate A20 bad
4-2-4	Unexpected interrupt in protected mode
4-3-1	RAM test in progress or high address line bad FFFF
4-3-3	Interval timer channel 2 test or bad
4-3-4	Time-of-Day clock test or bad
4-4-1	Serial port test or bad
4-4-2	Parallel port test or bad
4-4-3	Math coprocessor test or bad
4-4-4	Cache test failure
5-1-2	BIOS update error; no RAM in system
5-1-3	BIOS update error; external video card detected
5-1-4	BIOS execution error
6-1-2	I/O controller failure

Beeps	Phoenix BIOS Ver. 4 Error Description
1-3-1	Start chipset registers with original values
1-3-2	Set in POST flag error
1-3-3	Start CPU registers error
1-4-1	Start cache with initial values
1-4-3	Initialize I/O
2-1-1	Start power management
2-1-2	Load alternative registers with initial POST values
2-1-3	Go to UserPatch0
2-2-1	Initialize timer
2-2-3	BIOS ROM checksum error
2-3-1	Timer component error
2-3-3	8237DMA-Controller error
2-4-1	Programmable interrupt controller error
3-1-1	Test DRAM refresh error
3-1-3	Test 8742 Keyboard Controller error
3-2-1	ES segment register error; set at 4GB
3-3-1	Autosize DRAM error
3-3-3	Clear 512K base memory error
3-4-1	RAM failure on address line XXXX
3-4-3	RAM failure on data bits xxxx of low byte of memory bus
4-2-1	RAM error with databitxxx
4-2-2	Test CPU bus-clock frequency error
4-3-1	CMOS RAM read/write failure
4-3-4	Chipset error
4-4-1	Shadow system BIOS ROM error
4-4-2	Reinitialize cache error
4-4-3	Cache autosize error
5-1-1	Configure advanced chipset registers error
5-1-2	Load alternate registers with CMOS values
5-2-4	CPU speed error
5-3-4	Interrupt vectors error
	Initialize BIOS interrupts
	ROM copyright notice error
	PCI Options ROMs manager
	Video configuration error
	PCI bus and devices error
	Video Adapter initialization
	Shadow video BIOS ROM
	Copyright notice error
	Display CPU type and speed
	Keyboard error
	Test for unexpected interrupts error
	Display "Press F2 to enter setup" prompt
	RAM error between 512K and 640K
	Expanded memory error
	Extended memory address line error
	Jump to UserPatch1

Beeps	Dell Computer Corp BIOS Error Description
6-1-3	Keyboard controller failure
6-1-4	CMOS register test failure
6-2-1	BIOS shadowing failure
6-2-2	Pentium speed determination failure
6-2-3	No SIMM installed

IBM Corporation BIOS

Beeps	IBM Corp BIOS Error Description
1 short	Successful Post, no errors
2 short	Initialization error - serial, parallel, floppy, ROM, or D.M.A.
1 long, 1 short	System Board
1 long, 2 short	Video adapter or video memory failed
1 long, 3 short	Video adapter failed, EGA
3 long	3270 keyboard card failure
None	Power supply or system board
Continuous	Power supply or system board
Repeating short	Power supply or system board

IBM Thinkpad BIOS

Beeps	IBM Thinkpad BIOS Error Description
1 Beep Unreadable	System board/LCD connector failure
1 Beep; "Unable to access boot source" message	System board/boot device failure
1 long, 2 short	Video adapter problem
1 long, 4 short	Battery voltage low
1 beep per second	Battery voltage low
2 short with error code	POST error message
2 short	System board failure
Non-stop beeping	System board failure

Mylex and Eurosoft BIOS

Beeps	Mylex and Eurosoft BIOS Error Description
1	Always present to indicate start of beep coding
2	Video adapter bad or not detected
3	Keyboard controller error
4	Keyboard error
5	8259 Programmable Interrupt Controller (PIC) 1 Er
6	8259 PIC 2 error
7	D.M.A. page register failure
8	RAM refresh error
9	RAM data test failed
10	RAM parity error occurred
11	8237 D.M.A. controller 2 failed
12	CMOS RAM failure
13	8237 D.M.A. controller 2 failed
14	CMOS RAM battery failure

Beeps	Mylex and Eurosoft BIOS Error Description
15	CMOS RAM checksum error
16	RIOS ROM checksum error

Mylex 386

Beeps	Mylex 386 BIOS Error Description
1 long	Boot Normally
2 long	Video Adapter Error
1 long, 1 short, 1 long	Keyboard controller error
1 long, 2short, 1 long	Keyboard error
1 long, 3 short, 1 long	PIC 0 error
1 long, 4 short, 1 long	PIC 1 error
1 long, 5 short, 1 long	D.M.A. page register error
1 long, 6short, 1 long	RAM refresh error
1 long, 7 short, 1 long	RAM data error
1 long, 8 short, 1 long	RAM parity error
1 long, 9 short, 1 long	D.M.A. controller 1 error
1 long, 10 short, 1 long	CMOS RAM error
1 long, 11 short, 1 long	D.M.A. controller 2 error
1 long, 12 short, 1 long	CMOS RAM battery error
1 long, 13 short, 1 long	CMOS checksum error
1 long, 14 short, 1 long	BIOS ROM checksum failure

Phoenix BIOS - 3 Code Version

Beeps	Phoenix BIOS Ver. 3 Error Description
none/1-1-2	Faulty CPU/motherboard. CPU register test in progress
1-1-3	CMOS write/read test failed; faulty motherboard
1-1-4	ROM BIOS checksum bad; faulty BIOS
1-2-1	Programmable interval timer failed
1-2-2	D.M.A. initialization failed
1-2-3	D.M.A. page register write/read bad
1-3-1	RAM refresh verification failed
none/1-3-2	Testing first 64K RAM
1-3-3	First 64K RAM chip or data line fault, multi-bit
1-3-4	First 64K RAM odd/even logic bad
1-4-1	Address line bad first 64K RAM
1-4-2	Parity error detected in first 64K RAM
1-4-3	EISA fail-safe timer test in progress
1-4-4	EISA s/w NMI port 462 test in progress
2-1-1	Bit 0 fault in first 64K RAM
2-1-2	Bit 1 fault in first 64K RAM
2-1-3	Bit 2 fault in first 64K RAM
2-1-4	Bit 3 fault in first 64K RAM
2-2-1	Bit 4 fault in first 64K RAM
2-2-2	Bit 5 fault in first 64K RAM
2-2-3	Bit 6 fault in first 64K RAM
2-2-4	Bit 7 fault in first 64K RAM

2-3-1	Bit 8 fault in first 64K RAM
2-3-2	Bit 9 fault in first 64K RAM
2-3-3	Bit 10 fault in first 64K RAM
2-3-4	Bit 11 fault in first 64K RAM
2-4-1	Bit 12 fault in first 64K RAM
2-4-2	Bit 13 fault in first 64K RAM
2-4-3	Bit 14 fault in first 64K RAM
2-4-4	Bit 15 fault in first 64K RAM
3-1-1	Slave D.M.A. register bad
3-1-2	Master D.M.A. register bad
3-1-3	Master interrupt mask register bad
3-1-4	Slave interrupt mask register bad
none/3-2-2	Interrupt vector loading in progress
3-2-4	Keyboard controller test failed
none/3-3-1	CMOS RAM power bad; calculating checksum
none/3-3-2	CMOS configuration validation in progress
3-3-4	Video memory test failed
3-4-1	Video initialization failed
3-4-2	Video retrace failure
none/3-4-3	Search for video ROM in progress
none	DDNIL bit scan failed
none	Screen operable, running with video ROM
none	Monochrome monitor operable
none	Color monitor (40 column) operable
none	Color monitor (80 column) operable
4-2-1	Timer tick interrupt test in progress or bad
4-2-2	Shutdown test in progress or bad
4-2-3	Gate A20 bad
4-2-4	Unexpected interrupt in protected mode
4-3-1	RAM test in progress or high address line bad FFFF
4-3-2	Timer 2 faulty
4-3-3	Interval timer channel 2 test or bad
4-3-4	Time-of-Day clock test or bad
4-4-1	Serial port test or bad
4-4-2	Parallel port test or bad
4-4-3	Math coprocessor test or bad
4-4-4	Cache test failure (Dell)
low-1-1-2	System board select bad (MCA only)
low-1-1-3	Extended CMOS RAM bad (MCA only)

Phoenix BIOS 4.0

Beeps	Phoenix BIOS Ver. 4 Error De
1	One short beep before boot - not an error
1-2	Search for option ROMs. One long, two shor failure
1-1-1-3	Faulty CPU or motherboard. Check real mo
1-1-2-1	Acquire CPU type
1-1-2-3	System hardware error

Error Codes

Error Codes

Beeps	Phoenix BIOS Ver. 4 Error Description
2-3-2-3	Enable external and CPU caches
2-3-3-2	SMI handler
2-3-3-3	External cache size display error
2-3-4-1	Shadow message display
2-3-4-3	Display non-disposable segments
2-4-1-1	Display error messages
2-4-1-3	Configuration errors
2-4-2-1	Real-Time clock error
2-4-2-3	Keyboard error
2-4-4-1	Hardware interrupt vectors
2-4-4-3	Coprocessor error
3-1-1-1	Disable onboard I/O ports
3-1-1-3	Detect and install external RS232 ports
3-1-2-1	Detect and install external parallel ports
3-1-2-3	Reinitialize onboard I/O ports
3-1-3-1	BIOS data area initialization
3-1-3-3	Extended BIOS Data area initialization
3-1-4-1	Floppy controller initialization
3-2-1-1	Hard disk controller initialization
3-2-1-2	Local bus hard disk controller initialization
3-2-1-3	Jump to UserPatch2
3-2-2-1	Disable A20 address line
3-2-2-3	Large ES segment register – Clear
3-2-3-1	Search for option ROMs
3-2-3-3	Shadow options ROMs
3-2-4-1	Setup Power Management
3-2-4-3	Enable hardware interrupts
3-3-1-1	Set time of day
3-3-1-3	Key lock error
3-3-3-1	Erase F2 prompt
3-3-3-3	Scan for F2 keystroke
3-3-4-1	Enter SETUP
3-3-4-3	in-POST flag error
3-4-1-1	Check for errors
3-4-1-3	POST complete
3-4-2-1	One Beep
3-4-2-3	Optional Check Password
3-4-3-1	Clear global descriptor table
3-4-4-1	Clear parity checkers
3-4-4-3	Check backup and virus reminders
4-1-1-1	Boot with INT 19
4-2-1-1	Interrupt handler error
4-2-1-3	Interrupt error – unknown
4-2-2-1	Interrupt error pending
4-2-2-3	Initialize option ROM error
4-2-3-1	Shutdown error
4-2-3-3	Extended block move

Beeps	Phoenix BIOS Ver. 4 Error Description
4-2-4-1	Shutdown 10 error
4-2-4-3	Keyboard controller failure error
4-3-1-3	Initialize chipset
4-3-1-4	Initialize refresh counter
4-3-2-1	Forced Flash
4-3-2-2	BIOS ROM okay
4-3-2-4	RAM Test needed
4-3-3-1	Do OEM initialization
4-3-3-2	Initialize interrupt controller
4-3-3-3	Read in bootstrap code
4-3-3-4	Initialize vectors
4-3-4-2	Initialize boot device
4-3-4-3	Boot code read okay

Terminal POST Errors derives a beep code from the test point error as follows:
1. 8-bit code is broken down into four 2-bit groups
2. Each group is made one-based (1 through 4) by adding 1
3. Short beeps are generated for the number in each group.
For example: Test point 01AH = 00 01 10 10 = 1-2-3-3 beeps
The BIOS outputs the test point error to I/O address 80h.

Quadtel BIOS

Beeps	Quadtel BIOS Error Description
1 beep	POST ran okay and detected no error. System will now boot.
2 beeps	POST detected a configuration error, or a CMOS RAM change since the last time you ran Setup. Check the CMOS battery and rerun Setup.
1 long, 2 short	Faulty video configuration (no or bad video card installed), or bad ROM on a peripheral controller card (address range C0000 through FFFF)
1 long, 3+shorts	Faulty peripheral controller, such as VGA. Usually, the display shows a descriptive message. Check the setup of peripheral controllers.

Tandon BIOS

Beeps	Tandon BIOS Error Description
long-short-long-short	8254 counter timer failure
short-long-short	RAM refresh failure
long-long-long	System RAM failure
short-short-short	BIOS RAM checksum failure
long-long	No video adapter is installed
long-long-long-long	Video adapter failure

BIOS POST Error Codes

Award BIOS Error Codes (Phoenix Tech)

When a PC computer is turned on, the BIOS tests and configures the various components in the computer through a process called POST (Power-On Self Test). If errors are detected, it tries to display an error message on the screen, generates an audio error beep code, and finally generates a POST code.

Award BIOS Screen Messages (© Phoenix Tech)

Message	Award BIOS Screen Message Descriptions
BIOS ROM checksum error	- System halted - The checksum of the BIOS code in the BIOS chip is incorrect, indicating the BIOS code may have become corrupt. Contact your system dealer to replace the BIOS
CMOS battery failed	The CMOS battery is no longer functional. Contact your system dealer for a replacement battery
CMOS checksum error	- Defaults loaded - Checksum of CMOS is incorrect, so the system loads the default equipment configuration. A checksum error may indicate that CMOS has become corrupt. This error may have been caused by a weak battery. Check the battery and replace if necessary.
CPU at nnnn	Displays the running speed of the CPU.
Display switch is set incorrectly	The display switch on the motherboard can be set to either monochrome or color. This message indicates the switch is set to a different setting than indicated in Setup. Determine which setting is correct, and then either turn off the system and change the jumper, or enter Setup and change the VIDEO selection.
Press ESC to skip memory test	The user may press Esc to skip the full memory test.
Floppy disk(s) fail	Cannot find or initialize the floppy drive controller or the drive. Make sure the controller is installed correctly. If no floppy drives are installed, be sure the Diskette Drive selection in Setup is set to NONE or AUTO.
HARD DISK initializing - Please wait a moment	Some hard drives require extra time to initialize.
Hard Disk Install Failure	Cannot find or initialize the hard drive controller or the drive. Make sure the controller is installed correctly. If no hard drives are installed, be sure the Hard Drive selection in Setup is set to NONE.
Hard disk(s) diagnosis fail	The system may run specific disk diagnostic routines. This message appears if one or more hard disks return an error when the diagnostics run.
Keyboard error or no keyboard present	Cannot initialize the keyboard. Make sure the keyboard is attached correctly and no keys are pressed during POST. To purposely configure the system without a keyboard, set the error halt condition in Setup to HALT ON ALL, BUT KEYBOARD. The BIOS then ignores the missing keyboard during POST.
Keyboard is locked out - Unlock the key	This message usually indicates that one or more keys have been pressed during the keyboard tests. Be sure no objects are resting on the keyboard.

Message	Award BIOS Screen Message Descriptions
Memory Test:	This message displays during a full memory test, counting down the memory areas being tested.
Memory test fail	If POST detects an error during memory testing, additional information appears giving specifics about the type and location of the memory error.
Override enabled - Defaults loaded	If the system cannot boot using the current CMOS configuration, the BIOS can override the current configuration with a set of BIOS defaults designed for the most stable, minimal-performance system operations.
Press TAB to show POST screen	System OEMs may replace the Phoenix Technologies' Award BIOS POST display with their own proprietary display. Including this message in the OEM display permits the operator to switch between the OEM display and the default POST display.
Primary master hard disk fail	POST detects an error in the primary master IDE hard drive.
Primary slave hard disk fail	POST detects an error in the secondary master IDE hard drive.
Resuming from disk, Press TAB to show POST screen	Phoenix Technologies offers a save-to-disk feature for notebook computers. This message may appear when the operator re-starts the system after a save-to-disk shut-down. See the Press Tab & message above for a description of this feature.
Secondary master hard disk fail	POST detects an error in the primary slave IDE hard drive.
Secondary slave hard disk fail	POST detects an error in the secondary slave IDE hard drive.

Award BIOS POST Codes (© Phoenix Tech)

Code (Hex)	Name	Award BIOS POST Code Descriptions
co	Turn off Chipset Cache	OEM Specific-Cache control
1	Processor Test 1	Processor status (1FLAGS) Verification.Tests the following processor status flags: carry, zero, sign, overflow.
2	Processor Test 2	Read/Write/Verify all CPU registers except SS, SP, and BP with data pattern FF and 00.
3	Initialize Chips	• Disable NMI, PIE, AIE, UEI, SQWV. • Disable video, parity checking, D.M.A. • Reset math coprocessor. • Clear all page registers, CMOS shutdown byte. • Initialize timer 0,1, and 2, including set EISA timer to a known state. • Initialize D.M.A. controllers 0 and 1. • Initialize interrupt controllers 0 and 1. • Initialize EISA extended registers.
4	Test Memory Refresh Toggle	RAM must be periodically refreshed to keep the memory from decaying. This refresh function is working properly.
5	Blank video, Initialize keyboard	Keyboard controller initialization.

Code (Hex)	Name	Award BIOS POST Code Descriptions
6	Reserved	
7	Test CMOS Interface and Battery Status	Verifies CMOS is working correctly, detects bad battery.
BE	Chipset Default Initialization	Program Chipset registers with power on BIOS defaults.
CI	Memory presence test	OEM Specific-Test to size on-board memory.
C5	Early Shadow	OEM Specific-Early Shadow enable for fast boot.
C6	Cache presence test	External cache size detection.
8	Setup low memory	• Early chip set initialization. • Memory presence test. • OEM chip set routines. • Clear low 64K of memory. • Test first 64K memory.
9	Early Cache Initialization	Cyrix CPU initialization. Cache initialization.
A	Setup Interrupt Vector Table	Initialize first 120 interrupt vectors with SPURIOUS_INT_HDLR and initialize INT 00h-1Fh according to INT_TBL.
B	Test CMOS RAM Checksum	Test CMOS RAM checksum, if bad, or insert key pressed, load defaults.
C	Initialize Video Interface	• Detect type of keyboard controller (optional). • Set NUM_LOCK status.
D	Initialize Video Interface	• Detect CPU clock. • Read CMOS location 14h to find out type of video in use. • Detect and Initialize Video Adapte4r.
E	Test Video Memory	• Test video memory, write sign-on message to screen. • Setup shadow RAM, enable shadow according to Setup.
F	Test D.M.A. Controller 0	BIOS checksum test. Keyboard detect and initialization.
10	Test D.M.A. Controller 1	Test D.M.A. Controller 1.
11	Test D.M.A. Page Registers	Test D.M.A. Page Registers.
12-13	Reserved	
14	Test Timer Counter 2	Test 8254 Timer 0 Counter 2.
15	Test 8259-1 Mask Bits	Verify 8259 Channel 1 masked interrupts by alternately turning off and on the interrupt lines.
16	Test 8259-2 Mask Bits	Verify 8259 Channel 2 masked interrupts by alternately turning off and on the interrupt lines
17	Test Stuck 8259 as Interrupt Bits	Turn off interrupts then verify no interrupt mask register is on.
18	Test 8259 Interrupt Functionality	Force an interrupt and verify the interrupt occurred.
19	Test Stuck NMI	Verify NMI can be cleared.
1A	Display CPU clock.	Display CPU clock.
1B-1E	Reserved	

Error Codes

Code (Hex)	Name	Award BIOS POST Code Descriptions
1F	Set EISA Mode	• If EISA non-volatile memory checksum is good, execute EISA initialization. • If not, execute ISA tests an clear • EISA mode flag. • Test EISA Configuration Memory • Integrity (checksum & communication interface).
20		
21-2F		
30		

Phoenix BIOS V4 Error Messages

PhoenixBIOS and the contents of the above table are trademarks and copyrights owned by Phoenix Technologies Ltd. During POST, the BIOS can display the following error messages:

Code	Phoenix BIOS Ver. 4 Error Description
0200	Failure Fixed Disk: drive is not working or not configured properly. Check to see if the disk is attached properly, then run setup and check that the fixed-disk type is correctly identified.
0210	Stuck Key: Stuck key on the keyboard
0211	Keyboard Controller Failed: May require replacing keyboard controller
0213	Keyboard locked - Unlock key switch
0220	Monitor type does not match CMOS - Run SETUP
0230	Shadow RAM Failed at offset: nnnn (of the 64k block at which the error was detected)
0231	System RAM Failed at offset: nnnn (of the 64k block at which the error was detected)
0232	Extended RAM Failed at offset: nnnn. Extended memory not working or not configured properly at offset nnnn.
0250	System battery is dead - Replace and run SETUP (CMOS battery)
0251	System CMOS checksum bad - Default configuration used: CMOS has been corrupted or modified incorrectly, perhaps by an application program that changes data stored in CMOS. The BIOS has forced install of Default Setup Values. If you want these changed, enter Setup. Also check the CMOS system battery.
0260	System timer error: requires repair of the system board.
0270	Real time clock error: Clock fails hardware test, may require board repair.
0271	Check date and time settings: BIOS found date or time out of range and reset the Real-Time Clock. Legal date range is 1991 to 2099
0280	Previous boot incomplete - default configuration used: Previous POST did not complete successfully and POST loads default values and offers to run Setup. This can be caused by the incorrect setting of wait states, check Setup and reboot the system.
0281	Memory Size found by POST differed from CMOS
02B0	Diskette drive A error: Floppy drive(s) are present but fail the BIOS POST test. Check Setup to see if diskette type is correct and check that cables are attacked correctly.
02B1	**Diskette drive B error** - see 02B0
02B2	**Incorrect Drive A type - run Setup**

Code	Phoenix BIOS Ver. 4 Error Description
02B3	**Incorrect Drive B type - run Setup**
02D0	**System cache error - Cache disabled** - RAM cache failed and BIS disabled the cache. On older boards, check the cache jumpers. You may need to replace the cache. A disabled cache will slow system performance considerably.
02F0	**CPU ID:** CPU socket number for Multi-Processor error.
02F4	**EISA CMOS not writeable**: ServerBIOS2 test error: cannot write to EISA CMOS
02F5	**D.M.A. Test Failed**: ServerBIOS2 test error: cannot write to extended D.M.A. registers
02F6	**Software NMI Failed**: ServerBIOS2 test error: Cannot generate software NMI (Non-Maskable Interrupt).
02F7	**Fail-Safe Timer NMI Failed**: ServerBIOS2 test error, Fail-Safe Timer takes too long.
	device **Address Conflict**: address conflict for the specified *device*.
	Allocation Error for: *device* - Run ISA or EISA Configuration Utility to resolve resource conflict for the specified *device*.
	CD ROM Drive - Drive identification
	Entering SETUP . . . - Starting Setup program
	Failing Bits: nnnn - The hex number nnnn is a map of the bits at the RAM address which failed the memory test. Each 1 in the map indicates a failed bit. See errors 230, 231, 232 above for offset address of the failure in System, Extended, or Shadow memory
	Fixed Disk n - Fixed disk n (0 to 3) identified
	Invalid System Configuration Data - Problem with NVRAM (CMOS) data
	I/O device IRQ conflict
	PS/2 Mouse Boot Summary Screen: shows installed
	nnnn kB Extended RAM Passed - Where nnnn is the amount of RAM in kilobytes successfully tested
	nnnn Cache SRAM Passed - Where nnnn is the amount of system cache in kilobytes successfully tested
	nnnn kB Shadow RAM Passed - Where nnnn is the amount of shadow RAM in kilobytes successfully tested.
	nnnn kB System RAM Passed - Where nnnn is the amount of system RAM in kilobytes successfully tested.
	One or more I20 Block Storage Devices were excluded from the Setup Boot Menu. There was not enough room in the IPL table to display all installed I₂O block-storage devices.
	Operating system not found - Operating system cannot be located on either drive A: or drive C:. Enter Setup and see if fixed disk and drive A: are properly identified
	Parity Check 1 nnnn - Parity error found in the system bus. BIOS attempts to locate the address and display it on the screen. If it cannot locate the address, it displays ????. Parity is a method for checking errors in binary data. A parity error indicates that some data has been corrupted.
	Parity Check 2 nnnn - Parity error found in the I₂O bus. BIOS attempts to locate the address and display it on the screen. If it cannot locate the address, it displays ????.

Code	Phoenix BIOS Ver. 4 Error Description
	Press <F1> to resume, <F2> to Setup, <F3> for previous - Displayed after any recoverable error message. Press <F1> to start the boot process or <F2> to enter Setup and change the settings. Press <F3> to display the previous screen (usually an initialization error of an Option ROM, i.e., an add-on card). Write down and follow the information shown on the screen.
	Press <F2> to enter Setup - Optional message displayed during POST. Can be turned off in Setup.
	PS/2 Mouse: mouse type identification message
	Run the I₂O Configuration Utility - One or more unclaimed block storage devices have the Configuration Request bit set in the LCT. Run an I₂O Configuration Utility such as the SAC utility.
	System BIOS shadowed - shows that the system BIOS copied to shadow RAM
	UMB upper limit segment address: nnnn - Displays the address nnnn of the upper limit of Upper Memory Blocks, indicating released segments of the BIOS which can be reclaimed by a virtual memory manager.
	Video BIOS shadowed - Video BIOS successfully copied to shadow RAM.

IBM XT/AT Class Error Codes

IBM is a registered trademark of the International Business Machine Corp.

Code	IBM XT/AT Class Error Code Descriptions
01x	Undetermined problem errors
02x	Power supply errors
1xx	System board error
101	Interrupt failure
102	Timer failure
103	Timer interrupt failure
104	Protected mode failure
105	Last 8042 command not accepted
106	Converting logic test
107	Hot NMI test
108	Timer bus test
109	Direct memory access test error
121	Unexpected hardware interrupts occurred
131	Cassette wrap test failed
152	System board error: defective battery
161	System Options Error-(Run SETUP) [Battery failure]
162	System options not set correctly-(Run SETUP)
163	Time and date not set-(Run SETUP)
164	Memory size error-(Run SETUP)
165	Adaptor error
199	User indicated configuration not correct
2xx	Memory (RAM) errors
201	Memory test failed
202	Memory address error
203	Memory address error
3xx	Keyboard errors

Code	IBM XT/AT Class Error Code Descriptions
301	Keyboard did not respond to software reset correctly or a stuck key failure was detected. If a stuck key was detected, the scan code for the key is displayed in hexadecimal. For example, the error code 49 301 indicates that key 73, the PgUp key failed (49Hex = 73Dec)
302	User indicated error from the keyboard test or AT system unit keylock is locked
303	Keyboard or system unit error
304	Keyboard or system unit error; CMOS does not match system
4xx	Monochrome monitor errors
401	Monochrome memory test, horizontal sync frequency test, or video test failed
408	User indicated display attributes failure
416	User indicated character set failure
424	User indicated 80X25 mode failure
432	Parallel port test failed (monochrome adapter)
5xx	Color monitor errors
501	Color memory test failed, horizontal sync frequency test, or video test failed
508	User indicated display attribute failure
516	User indicated character set failure
524	User indicated 80X25 mode failure
532	User indicated 40X25 mode failure
540	User indicated 320X200 graphics mode failure
548	User indicated 640X200 graphics mode failure
6xx	Diskette drive errors
601	Diskette power on diagnostics test failed
602	Diskette test failed; boot record is not valid
606	Diskette verify function failed
607	Write protected diskette
608	Bad command diskette status returned
610	Diskette initialization failed
611	Time-out - diskette status returned
612	Bad NEC - diskette status returned
613	Bad D.M.A. - diskette status returned
621	Bad seek - diskette status returned
622	Bad CRC - diskette status returned
623	Record not found - diskette status returned
624	Bad address mark - diskette status returned
625	Bad NEC seek - diskette status returned
626	Diskette data compare error
7xx	8087 or 80287 math coprocessor errors
9xx	Parallel printer adapter errors
901	Parallel printer adapter test failed
10xx	Reserved for parallel printer adapter
11xx	Asynchronous communications adapter errors
1101	Async communications adapter test failed
12xx	Alternate asynchronous communications adapter errors
1201	Alternate asynchronous communications adapter test failed
13xx	Game control adapter errors
1301	Game control adapter test failed

Error Codes

Code	IBM XT/AT Class Error Code Descriptions
1302	Joystick test failed
14xx	Printer errors
1401	Printer test failed
1404	Matrix printer failed
15xx	Synchronous data link control (SDL) Comm adapter errors
1510	8255 port B failure
1511	8255 port A failure
1512	8255 port C failure
1513	8253 timer 1 did not reach terminal count
1514	8253 timer 1 stuck on
1515	8253 timer 0 did not reach terminal count
1516	8253 timer 0 stuck on
1517	8253 timer 2 did not reach terminal count
1518	8253 timer 2 stuck on
1519	8273 port B error
1520	8273 port A error
1521	8273 command/read time-out
1522	Interrupt level 4 failure
1523	Ring Indicate stuck on
1524	Receive clock stuck on
1525	Transmit clock stuck on
1526	Test indicate stuck on
1527	Ring indicate not on
1528	Receive clock not on
1529	Transmit clock not on
1530	Test indicate not on
1531	Data set ready not on
1532	Carrier detect not on
1533	Clear to send not on
1534	Data set ready stuck on
1536	Clear to send stuck on
1537	Level 3 interrupt failure
1538	Receive interrupt results error
1539	Wrap data mis-compare
1540	D.M.A. channel 1 error
1541	D.M.A. channel 1 error
1542	Error in 8273 error checking or status reporting
1547	Stray interrupt level 4
1548	Stray interrupt level 3
1549	Interrupt presentation sequence time-out
16xx	Display emulation errors (327x, 5520, 525x)
17xx	Fixed disk errors
1701	Fixed disk POST error
1702	Fixed disk adapter error
1703	Fixed disk drive error
1704	Fixed disk adapter or drive error
1780	Fixed disk 0 failure

Code	IBM XT/AT Class Error Code Descriptions
1781	Fixed disk 1 failure
1782	Fixed disk controller failure
1790	Fixed disk 0 error
1791	Fixed disk 1 error
18xx	I/O expansion unit errors
1801	I/O expansion unit POST error
1810	Enable/Disable failure
1811	Extender card wrap test failed (disabled)
1812	High order address lines failure (disabled)
1813	Wait state failure (disabled)
1814	Enable/Disable could not be set on
1815	Wait state failure (disabled)
1816	Extender card wrap test failed (enabled)
1817	High order address lines failure (enabled)
1818	Disable not functioning
1819	Wait request switch not set correctly
1820	Receiver card wrap test failure
1821	Receiver high order address lines failure
19xx	3270 PC attachment card errors
20xx	Binary synchronous communications (BSC) adapter errors
2010	8255 port A failure
2011	8255 port B failure
2012	8255 port C failure
2013	8253 timer 1 did not reach terminal count
2014	8253 timer 1 stuck on
2016	8253 timer 2 did not reach terminal count or timer 2 stuck on
2017	8251 Data set ready failed to come on
2018	8251 Clear to send not sensed
2019	8251 Data set ready stuck on
2020	8251 Clear to send stuck on
2021	8251 hardware reset failed
2022	8251 software reset failed
2023	8251 software "error reset" failed
2024	8251 transmit ready did not come on
2025	8251 receive ready did not come on
2026	8251 could not force "overrun" error status
2027	Interrupt failure - no timer interrupt
2028	Interrupt failure - transmit, replace card or planar
2029	Interrupt failure - transmit, replace card
2030	Interrupt failure - receive, replace card or planar
2031	Interrupt failure - receive, replace card
2033	Ring indicate stuck on
2034	Receive clock stuck on
2035	Transmit clock stuck on
2036	Test indicate stuck on
2037	Ring indicate stuck on
2038	Receive clock not on

Code	IBM XT/AT Class Error Code Descriptions
2039	Transmit clock not on
2040	Test indicate not on
2041	Data set ready not on
2042	Carrier detect not on
2043	Clear to send not on
2044	Data set ready stuck on
2045	Carrier detect stuck on
2046	Clear to send stuck on
2047	Unexpected transmit interrupt
2048	Unexpected receive interrupt
2049	Transmit data did not equal receive data
2050	8251 detected overrun error
2051	Lost data set ready during data wrap
2052	Receive time-out during data wrap
21xx	Alternate binary synchronous communications adapter errors
2110	8255 port A failure
2111	8255 port B failure
2112	8255 port C failure
2113	8253 timer 1 did not reach terminal count
2114	8253 timer 1 stuck on
2115	8253 timer 2 did not reach terminal count or timer 2 stuck on
2116	8251 Data set ready failed to come on
2117	8251 Clear to send not sensed
2118	8251 Data set ready stuck on
2119	8251 Clear to send stuck on
2120	8251 hardware reset failed
2121	8251 software reset failed
2122	8251 software "error reset" failed
2123	8251 transmit ready did not come on
2124	8251 receive ready did not come on
2125	8251 could not force "overrun" error status
2126	Interrupt failure - no timer interrupt
2128	Interrupt failure - transmit, replace card or planar
2129	Interrupt failure - transmit, replace card
2130	Interrupt failure - receive, replace card or planar
2131	Interrupt failure - receive, replace card
2133	Ring indicate stuck on
2134	Receive clock stuck on
2135	Transmit clock stuck on
2136	Test indicate stuck on
2137	Ring indicate stuck on
2138	Receive clock not on
2139	Transmit clock not on
2140	Test indicate not on
2141	Data set ready not on
2142	Carrier detect not on
2143	Clear to send not on

Code	IBM XT/AT Class Error Code Descriptions
2144	Data set ready stuck on
2145	Carrier detect stuck on
2146	Clear to send stuck on
2147	Unexpected transmit interrupt
2148	Unexpected receive interrupt
2149	Transmit data did not equal receive data
2150	8251 detected overrun error
2151	Lost data set ready during data wrap
2152	Receive time-out during data wrap
22xx	Cluster adapter errors
24xx	Enhanced graphics adapter errors
29xx	Color matrix printer errors
2901	
2902	
2904	
33xx	Compact printer errors
IBM is a registered trademark of the International Business Machine Corporation.	

Error Codes

HTTP Internet Errors and Codes

The following are information and error codes used in HTTP1.1 and are fully explained in RFC2616 of the World Wide Web Consortium. See http://www.w3.org for additional information.

Information Status Codes (rarely used outside of server logs)

Code	Description
100	Continue, everything is working
101	Switching Protocols, everything is working

Successful Transactions Codes (primarily written to server logs)

Code	Description
200	Request was fulfilled, everything is OK
201	POST request was completed successfully, new resource created.
202	Request has been accepted for processing unknown type, not done.
203	Request probably completed but may be partially fulfilled
204	Request completed but no content (resource is empty)
205	Request completed, reset content (clear cache)
206	Request canceled before completion, partial content received.

Warning & Redirection Transaction Codes

Code	Description
300	Request is ambiguous, multiple choices available
301	Requested resource has been permanently moved to a new URL. This is usually accompanied by an automatic connection to the new URL.
302	Requested resource found but it is located at a different URL. This typically occurs when a trailing "slash" is omitted. Moved temporarily.
304	Browser has found data in the cache and unmodified data was not returned. Not modified, information is up-to-date.
305	Send request through selected proxy server.
307	Requested resource temporarily redirected.

Client Error Codes (invalid client request; URL= a sites address)

Code	HTTP Client Error Code Descriptions
400	Bad File Request: Incorrect syntax in the URL prevents the request from being understood by Server. Common error, check the URL carefully, especially if it is long.
401.1	Unauthorized: Login failed due to failed credentials for the server.
401.2	Unauthorized: Login failed due to server configuration; usually an invalid WWW-Authenticate header field.
401.3	Unauthorized: Client does not have access to requested page or file.
401.4	Unauthorized: Authentication failed due to client verification filter installed on the Server.
401.5	Unauthorized: Authentication failed due to a ISAPI or CGI client verification program installed on the Server.
402	Invalid Chargeto field: the requested operation requires money and a valid Chargeto field was not specified.

Code	HTTP Client Error Code Descriptions
403.x	Forbidden Request: User does not have read privileges or you are not allowed to have pages sent to you. The Server understood the request but based on privileges it is refusing to comply with the request.
403.1	Forbidden Request: Attempted to run a program from a directory that does not allow programs to be executed.
403.2	Forbidden Request: Read Access forbidden
403.3	Forbidden Request: Write Access forbidden
403.4	Forbidden Request: Secure Sockets Layer (SSL) is required; use HTTPs:// instead of HTTP://
403.5	Forbidden Request: Secure Sockets Layer 128 is required and client browser does not support SSL128.
403.6	Forbidden Request: Client IP address rejected due to access restriction list stored at Server.
403.7	Forbidden Request: Secure Sockets Layer (SSL) Certificate on client is required to authenticate client.
403.8	Forbidden Request: Access to requested Site is denied due to Server being down or lack of client permissions.
403.9	Forbidden Request: Server cannot process request due to heavy traffic, i.e. too many users are connected.
403.10	Forbidden Request: Invalid configuration on the Web Server.
403.11	Forbidden Request: Authentication failed due to incorrect password; re-enter password or change password.
403.12	Forbidden Request: Access denied due to client certificate map.
403.13	Forbidden Request: Access denied due to revoked Client certificate.
403.14	Forbidden Request: Virtual directory listing denied.
403.15	Forbidden Request: Client Access Licenses exceeded due to too many clients accessing the Web Site; retry later.
403.16	Forbidden Request: Access denied due to invalid or untrusted Client certificate.
403.17	Forbidden Request: Access denied due to invalid or expired Client certificate.
404	Not Found: The document or web page you are requesting no longer exists or the URL is not correct. Common error.
404.1	Web site not found due to identification configuration settings.
405	Method Not Allowed: The method specified in the Request Line is not allowed because a list of valid methods was not identified by the request.
406	Not Acceptable: The Server cannot generate a response due to requirements specified or not specified by the requestor.
407	Proxy Authentication Required: This is an "unauthorized" message similar to 401 because the Client must first authenticate itself with the Proxy.
408	Request Timeout: The Server timed out (stopped) while waiting for a Client request.
409	Conflict: The request could not be completed due to a conflict with the state of the resource.
410	Gone: The requested resource is permanently no longer available. Similar error code to 404.
411	Length Required: Content length is required by the Server, repeat request with valid content length.
412	Precondition Failed: Client has placed preconditions on the request and the Server has evaluated the field to false.

Error Codes

Code	HTTP Client Error Code Descriptions
413	Request Entity Too Large: The Server is refusing to process a Clients request because the entity is too large. In some cases the Server may actually close the connection.
414	Request-URI Too Long: The Server is refusing to process a Clients request because the URI is too long. (rare)
415	Unsupported Media Type: The Server is refusing to process a request because the request is in a format that is not supported.
416	Requested Range Not Satisfiable: The portion of the resource requested is not available or out of range.
417	Expectation Failed: HTTP request header expect specifier could not be met.
500	Internal Error: An internal Server software error has prevented the document from being sent to you.
500.12	Application restarting: there is a problem with the requested page.
500.13	Server too busy: requested page cannot be displayed
500.15	Requests for Global.asa not allowed, requested page cannot be displayed.
501	Not Implemented: The Server does not recognize the requested method.
502	Server Temporarily Overloaded or Bad Gateway: Try later when traffic is lower.
503	Service Unavailable: Your ISP or internet connection is down or temporarily overloaded. Wait a few minutes and try again. If the problem persists, call your ISP.
504	Gateway timeout: A Server somewhere in the pathway has not responded in time and the request for information has been closed. This can be caused by Server problems, network problems or client problems.
505	HTTP Version Not Supported: The Server does not support the protocol version that was used in the request message.

Unnumbered Errors

Bad file request: An online form contains a technical error and your browser cannot decipher the form. Notify the webmaster.

Connection refused by host: You have probably entered an incorrect password or you do not have permission to access the requested page.

Failed DNS lookup: The Domain Name System is unable to look up the address for a given website name. This can be caused by a variety of problems such as your ISP's DNS Server being down. Basically, try clicking your Reload button or try again at a later time.

File contains no data: The web site has no pages, try again later.

Host unavailable: The web server is down, try again later. Try clicking your reload or refresh button.

Host unknown: The web server is down or it is possible that the site has move or you have lost your internet connection.

Network connection refused by the server: The web server is busy or overloaded, try again later.

Unable to locate host: The web server is down or you have lost your internet connection.

Unable to locate server: The web server is no longer available or out of business. It is possible that you have entered the address incorrectly, try again.

Chapter 3

<fatal error: Computer
will self destruct in
five minutes..//

Start Up Programs
and Processes

The Good, The Bad and The Ugly

This chapter contains a quick reference to approximately 5,000 programs and their corresponding names that would show up as a "Process" in your computers Task Manager (Ctrl-Alt-Delete, then Task Manager) or in the "Startup Item" or "Command" fields of your Windows System Configuration Utility (msconfig in WinXP). If you are using a Windows operating system other than XP, msconfig is not available to you and you will need to use a third party program to examine and modify programs that launch at startup. The following are a few of the many startup editing programs available today (2004 pricing):

- Startup Control Panel by MLin; www.mlin.net, Free
- TuneUp Utilities by TuneUp Software; www.tune-up.com, $40
- WinTasks Professional by LIUtilities; www.liutilities.com, $40

Please note that unless specifically indicated, all of the files listed in the main table in the "Program" column are ".exe" files (executables).
The listing included in this chapter covers only a small fraction of the more than 15,000 programs, tasks and processes currently in use. We have categorized each of the entries based on the following ratings:

Rating	Description
Good	Critical operating system programs, antivirus, antispyware, antiadware, drivers
Bad	Virus, worm, trojan, parasite, spyware, adware
Ugly	Resource hogs, buggy or misbehaved software, performance killers
User	User preference, files required to use specific programs

This chapter does <u>NOT</u> include any information on removal of the "Bad" or "Ugly" programs nor does it contain any information that will help you decide what User programs to use or not use. It is simply designed to be a quick reference to help you determine *what* programs are currently running on your computer and whether they likely to be Good or Bad. Do not simply start deleting the program with the indicated name because there may be a good file with the same name that is simply stored in a different location. For example, look at the section for "Explorer"; if you delete the Windows OS file named Explorer.exe in the c:\windows folder, your computer will be in serious trouble there can be bad program files named Explorer.exe that are simply in a different folder. This type of information is particularly useful to a troubleshooter when trying to resolve system problems. The following three steps will help you obtain additional information:

Step 1: Detailed information on virtually all processes and startup programs is usually available at one of the following extensive web sites:

> *Answers that Work*
> http://www.answersthatwork.com/
>
> *Startup Inspector for Windows*
> http://www.windowsstartup.com/wso/browse.php
>
> *Pacmans Portal (Paul Collins)*
> http://www.pacs-portal.co.uk/startup_index.htm
>
> *SYSINFO.ORG*
> http://www.sysinfo.org/startuplist.php

Our sincerest gratitude goes to the creators and managers of the above web sites. These extensive and detailed sites are free to use by anyone and are a tremendous asset to everyone, especially technicians in the PC computing world.

Step 2: If the process or startup program cannot be identified or if you need additional information that was not included in one of the above sites, do a search on www.google.com for the exact name of the executable file name, e.g. type in "svchost.exe" in the Google search field and you will locate over 90,000 records containing information about the Microsoft process named svchost. Additional useful search engines include AltaVista.com and Yahoo.com.

Step 3: If you determine that the particular program is a virus, worm, trojan, parasite, spyware, or adware, obtain removal instructions and removal software from antivirus and spyware software companies. See Chapter 1 - Troubleshooting on page 16 for additional information.

Warning: Resolving problems with any software, especially virus, worm, trojan, parasite, spyware, or adware programs can be a very complex process and you can very quickly damage your computers operating system to a point where your computer will no longer boot. Uses extreme caution and follow instructions very carefully when editing your computers registry.

If you find errors in concerning entries in the main table, we appreciate being notified. See page 2 for contact information.

Program	Description	Good/Bad
764	pmc Adult dialer	Bad
@tour_ww[1]	@tour_ww adult dialer	Bad
_backup	Swf32 Symfan virus	Bad
_x-Finder	Adult dialer	Bad
~ djqzxu3zYF···	^ djqZxu Gaobot.gen!poly virus	Bad
~CAB001	Regcheck Cyberspy virus	Bad
0	Zonavirus Kitro.d virus	Bad
00THotKey	Toshiba	User
1111a	load32 Dumaru.ah virus	Bad
12popup	12Ghosts Popup-Killer	User
1on1	1on1 Adult dialer	Bad
1ST	1st Impression's	User
1xconfig	Shuttle Technology	User
2portalmon	2Wire Homeportal	User
2hray	Image Converter Plus	User
3capplink	US Robotics	User
3CDMINIC	3Com DMI Atent	User
3cmlink/3cpipe-3c1807bp	3Com WinModem	User
3CmlinkW	US Robotics WinModem	Good
3CMLnkW	3Com WinModem	User
3D Text.scr	3D Text Screensaver	User
3DeepCTL	3Deep LightSurf Tech	User
3dfxCmn.dll	3dfx Interactive Voodoo	User
3dfxMan	3dfx Interactive Voodoo	User
3dfxv2ps.dll	3dfx Interactive Voodoo	User
3ddemon	Permedia 2/2 & Oxygen	User
3dm	3ware IDE RAID	Good
3dmoused	Primax 3D Mouse	User
3gdctl	Terratec sound card	User
4DMAIN	Fellowes Wheelman Mouse	User
4t-min	4t Tray Minimizer	User
5-2-46-112	5-2-46-112 Adult dialer	Bad
7SUwlaQ5P7eg	trojan cleaner program	Bad
802.11 WLAN	Atheros integrated chipset	User
8x8_init	Pinnacle PCTV Initialize 8x8	User
9	KAZAACut Kitro.d virus	Bad
a	IE redirector	Bad
a2guard	a2 antitrojan	Good
A3dInit	Aureal A3D soundcard	User
A4Proxy	Anonymity 4 Proxy	User
Aaar	see IWAR	Bad
Aasd	see IWAR	Bad
AbbeyNewsReader	Abbey FineReader OCR	User
Abilon	Abilon RSS Aggregator	User
abiteq	ABIT motherboard monitor	User
ABMTSR	Scanner Adburn Fast Start	User
AboutTime	AboutTime time sync	User
ABReceiver	Bufallo Airstation WiFi	User
AbsoluteControl	Absolute Control	User
Absr	Backdoor.Autoupder virus	Bad
absr	ABsr Autoupder virus	Bad
abyssws	Abyss web server	User
Acao	see IWAR	Bad
AcBtnMgr_X63	Lexmark X63 Button Manager	User
AcBtnMgr_x73	Lexmark X73 Button Manager	User
AcBtnMgr_x83	Lexmark X83 Button Manager	User
accelerate	Webroot Accelerate	User
ACCOUNT_DETAILS.DOC...Quaters.a virus	Bad
AccountLogon	Account Logon	User
AcctMgr	Symantec Norton Antivirus	User
acertmb	Aspire Time Machine	Good
achron	Achronomaton	User
AcMonitor_x73	Lexmark X73 Button Monitor	User
AcMonitor_x83	Lexmark X83 Button Monitor	User
Acombo3d	Mouse Driver	User
aconti	Aconti Adult dialer	Bad
acoustic	Philips Acoustic Edge	User
AcroFd32	Adobe Acrobat Reader	User
AcroTray	Adobe Acrobat Assistant	User
ACSd	AOL Connectivity Service	User
actalert	ByFuCA Active Alert Adult dialer	Bad
ActionAgent	Dell OpenManage	User
ACTIVATOR	kernel system Handex.aw virus	Bad
Activation	Microsoft Activation Module	Good
ACTIVEDS	Dynazip Activet.t virus	Bad
ActiveEyes	TFI Technology ActiveEyes	User
ActiveMenu	HP Wild Tangent games	User
activeplus	MSN Messenger Plus!	User
ActualTitleButtonsCenter···	Actual Title Buttons	User
ACU	Atheros WiFi Startup	User
ACUMon	Cisco	User
AD	AutoDialogs	User
AD2KCClient	Iomega Active Disk	User
adaware	Adaware lptt01 parasite	Bad
adaware	Adaware ml097e parasite	User
adaware	foobin lptt01 parasite	Bad
adaware	foobin ml097e parasite	User
Ad-aware	Lavasoft Ad-Aware	User
adblck	Browser Pal foistware	Bad
ADC	XemiComputers Desktop Calendar	User
AddClass	AddClass parasite	Bad
AdDestroyer	AdDestroyer	User
Addrbook	Novell Groupwise Address Book	User
AdFree	BioNet Systems NetNanny	User
ADGJDET	Creative Labs Jet Detection	User
ADIMonEx	DSL Monitor	User
Adiras	Adiras ADSL USB modem	Good
ADMAGIC	svchost Smibag virus	Bad
Admin··	NetDisk Administrator	User
admib32	ADM Library SDbot virus	Bad
ADMUNCH	Ad Muncher	User
Adobe	Adobe virus	Bad
Adobe Gamma Loader	Adobe Gamma	User
adobes	AdobeA FLOOD RA virus	Bad
adp	adp spyware	Bad
adpn	ATM Control MMS.a virus	Bad
adscleanertrial	AdsCleaner	User
ADSerivce	Iomega Active Disk	User
Adsgone	AdsGone	User
ADSL Autoconnect	ADSL Autoconnect	User
ADSS	Access Denied Security Server	Bad
AdSub	Subtract the Ads	User
Adtray	After Dark screen saver	User
Adult_Chat	Adult_Chat Adult dialer	Bad
Adult_Chat1	Adult_Chat1 Adult dialer	Bad
AdultX	AdultX Adult dialer	Bad
ADUserMon	Iomega Active Disk User Monitor	User
Advapi	Advapi Netdevil.12 virus	Bad
Advchk	Symante Advanced Tools Check	User
adw30	After Dark screen saver	User
Ad-watch	Lavasoft Ad-Aware Plus	User
AEDiction	Bulgarian/English Dictionary	User
AEJCT32	Avatar Shark Eject	Ugly
AELaunch	Philips AE Launch	User
afolders	notification area folder access	User
After Dark	Berkeley Systems After Dark	User
Agent	Cyberlink Power VCR II 3.0	User
AgentSvr	Microsoft Agent Server	Good
AgfaCLnk	Agfa camera memory stick access	User
agpart11	Online truck finder	User
agpwiz	Creative AGP Wizard	User
agquickp	ActivCard Quick Password	User
AGRemind	Forget Me Not calendar	User
AGSMMSG	IBM AMR modem driver	User
AGSatellite	AudioGalaxy AG Satellite	User
Agtexe16	Atomica	User
AgtServ	Atomica reference software	User
ahfp	Advanced Hide Folders	User
AhnSD	AhnLab v3 Antivirus	User
AHQInit	Creative Labs Audio HeadQuarters	User
Ahqrun	Creative Labs Audio HeadQuarters	User
AHQTbl	Creative Labs Audio HeadQuarters	User
AHQTbU	Creative Labs Audio HeadQuarters	User
AICLIENT	Tangram Asset Insight	Good
aiepk	Another IE Popup Killer	User
aiepk2	see aiepk	User
AIM	AOL Instant Messenger	User
AIM reminder	AIM reminder Buddy virus	Bad
aim95	Configuration LOADCFG SDBOT	Bad
aimaol	m097e RapidBlaster parasite	Bad
aimaol	m097e RapidBlaster parasite	Bad
AimingClick	Aiming Tech Aiming Click	User
AirCFG	D-Link Air Utility	User
airplus	D-Link AirPlus	User
AIRSVCU	Media Manager Indexer	User
Akiller	Advertising Killer	User
AlarmApp	Palm Desktop	User
AlarmClock	Alarm Clock	User
Alchem	Ipinsite parasite	Bad
Alcohol	Alcohol 120% autorun	User
Alcxmntr	Realtek AC97 sound driver	User
alert	MSI PC Alert	User
AlertSvc	Norton AntiViruse Alert Service	User
Alevir	Alevir OPASERV.A virus	Bad
Alexa	Alexa Toolbar	User
AlexClock	System Clock	User
ALG	MS Application Layer Gateway Sv	Good
ALiSndMg	ALi AC97 Sound driver	User
AllerCat	AllerCat	User
allSnap	Top level window alignment	User
almqdray	Acer Notebook Manager	User
ALogServ	McAfee VirusScan	User
alpha100	Coco Holo Software AlphaCuts	User
ALUNotify	Symantec LiveUpdate Notification	User
AlwaysOnTopMaker	Always On Top Maker	User
am32	Action Manager 32	User
AMON	Eset NOD 32 Antivirus	User
amon	Tiny Personal Firewall	Good
AMOUJMAIN	A4Tech mouse driver	User
Amra	see IWAR	Bad
AMSNDMGR	Internet Explorer KWBOT.R virus	Bad
Angel	Utopia Angel	User
Anncilist	MS Announcement Listener	User
Anntext	Capree Pagekeeper	User
AnonTns	Anonymizer Total Net Shield	User
Ante Browse Trust	HideStyle toolbar	Bad
AntiCash	AntiCash	User
antikey	Anti-Keylogger Check	User
AntiPopUp	AntiPopUp	User
Antispy	antivirus parasite	Bad
AnVir	AnVir	User
anvshell	ASUS video card options	User
AnyDVD	AnyDVD	User

Program	Description	Good/Bad
AOL Dial	AOL Dialer	User
AOLFix	QHOSTS trojan virus	Bad
AOLTray	AOL System Tray icon	User
aornum	iWon Prize Machine spyware	Bad
Aornum/Aornumsp/Ornum	iWon	Bad
AOTray	AOpen soundcard	User
ApacheMonitor	Apache Web Server	User
APASServ	Sunbelt Auto-Start	User
apc_tray	APC UPS	User
AptnEx	Aptis Pointing Device Driver	Good
APoint	see AptnEx	
App	WAXPOW virus	Bad
AppExtCB	AppExtender	Bad
ApplicationWarp	System memory manager	User
AppServices	Iomega Zip drive	User
Apropos	POP! - PeopleOnPage	Bad
Apropos_Client_Loader	AproposMedia adware	Bad
Aptezbp	IBM Aptiva EZ Buttons	User
APVXDWIN	Panda AntiVirus	User
Apwheel	Aptis wheel mouse	User
aritima	ARITIMA virus	Bad
Armon32/Armon32s	Inverse Tech Access Ramp Monitor	User
arr	MS-Connect adult dialer	Bad
arr	MS-RunKey dialer hijacker	Bad
ARUpdate	AdRoarUpdate adware	Bad
ARUpld32	Visual Networks Browsing History	Bad
AS	Active Speed	User
asd	Active ShutDown	User
ASDAPI	LoadPowerProfile CABRO virus	Bad
ASDSCSVC	ARCServe Discovery Service	User
AService	Run Alert	User
AseScanner	Spyware Scanner	User
ashDisp	Avast 4.0 Home Edition	User
ashmaisv	Avast! Antivirus	User
ashserv	Avast! Antivirus	User
asistant	NEC SuperScript printer monitor	User
ASMon	Absolute StartUp Monitor	User
asp4setp	Aureal Vortex soundcard	User
asp4tray	see asp4setp	
ASPNet_State	Microsoft ASP State Service	User
ASPNET_WP	Microsoft ASP.NET	User
ASSISTANT	Excite Assistant	User
AST	TROJANDOWNLOADER.WIN32.VB.AH virus	Bad
astart	ASUS TweakEnable	User
AStart	TROJANDOWNLOADER.WIN32.VB.AH virus	Bad
Astart32	Avast32 Antivirus	User
Astray	Voyetra Ultimate MP3/CD Manager	User
Astro	Astro Quicken updates	User
Astrotoolbar	Gateway Quick Controls	User
AsusProb	ASUS Probe	User
asutype	As-U-Type 2.5	User
ASWATC32	AutoSpell	User
ASWDP	MLS Pulse	User
aswnk	ASWnk adult dialer	Bad
AtClock	AtClock	User
ATDialler1/ATDialler2/ATDialler3	Freeserve Connection dialler	User
AtHoc	AtHoc Toolbar	User
ATI2wxx	ATI Tech graphics card driver	User
ATI2evxx/ATIevxx	ATI External Event Utility	User
ATI2mdxx	ATI 2D Mode Component	User
ATI2plab	ATI Tech graphics card driver	User
ATI2ptxx	see ATI2plab	Good
Ati2ptxx/Atiptaxx	ATI video card controls	User
ati2s9ag	ATI SmartGart	User
ATI2dvag/ATIcwd32/Ati2cwad	ATI VGA card driver	User
Atigart	ATI GART Set-Up Utility	User
ATIKey32/atiptkad	ATI hotkey programming	Ugly
ATIptaab	ATI graphics card display driver	User
ATIptaxx	ATI Task Bar Icon	User
AtiQIPcl	ATI DVD decoding	User
Atira	KOTIRA virus	Bad
ATIRW	ATI Remote Control	User
ATISched	ATI Scheduler	User
ATITask	ATI Task Bar	User
Atitkad	ATI Task Application	User
ATIUPDATE5	DEBESKI.A virus	Bad
ATIX10	remote control sensor icon	User
atmdlusr	US Robotics Micro Attune Download	User
atmdlusr	adware	User
atmsg	Miramar Systems PC Maclan	User
ATnotes	AT Notes	User
atomica	Atomica	User
ATOMICTIME	Atomic Time	User
AtomTime	AtomTime Pro	User
Atrack	Symantec Alert Tracker	User
ats	Atomic Time Server	User
Attune_ce	Aveo Attune Client Engine	Ugly
attune_ce	adware	Bad
attune_cu	adware	Bad
attune_di	adware	Bad
attune_st	adware	Bad
atuner	GeForce graphics card aTuner	User
ATWatch	Anti-Trojan Watch	User
atwtusb	Aiptek Graphics Tablet USB interface	User
Au	W32.Beagle.B@mm virus	Bad
au	BEAGLE.B virus	Bad
au30setp/asp4tray/asp4setb	Aureal Vortex soundcard Tray	User
AUagent	Zilab AU Agent	User
aucchp n	Adaptec USB CardBus Safe-Eject	User
Aucompat	GEMA virus	Bad
audevicemgr	Sony Ericsson PCSuite	User
AUEKXRZ	SPYBOT virus	Bad
aupd	spyware	Bad
AUpdate	Symantec Automatic LiveUpdate	User
aupdate	spyware	Bad
Ausvc	Backdoor Autoupdater virus	Bad
ausvc	AUTOUPDER virus	Bad
AutoAct	AutoAct Startup	User
autobar	HP hotkey buttons	User
AutoChk-	imagineLAN ConfigSafe	User
AutoConnect	Auto Connect	User
Autodet	EasySync Pro	User
Autolaunch	Iomega Drag'n'Drop Autolaunch	User
AUTOREG	MaxtorReg	User
autorun-	QBCD Autorun	User
AUTOSIZER	AutoSizer	Good
AUTOSTART	HP JetSpeed Autostart	User
autopd	virus	Bad
autoupd (1)	Raxco Auto Update	User
AutoUpdate	AT&T Red Update	User
AutoUpdate	PeopleonPage foistware	Bad
av	SINKIN virus	Bad
AVBgle	NETSKY.O virus	Bad
AVConsol	McAfee AntiVirus Console	User
Aveagent	TrendMicro AntiVirus	User
Avgamsvr	AVG AntiVirus	Good
AVGCC	AVG Antivirus 7.0 Control Center	User
AVGCC32	Grisoft AVG Control Center	User
AVGCtrl	H+BEDV AntiVir	User
AVGEMC	Grisoft AVG Antivirus 7.0	User
avgnsvr	Grisoft AVG Antivirus 7.0	User
AVGNT	Antivir Personal Edition	User
AVGREGCL	Gristoft AVG Antivirus 7.0	User
AVGServ9	Gristoft AVG Antivirus 7.0	User
AVGuard	W32.Netsky.G@mm virus	Bad
avguard	NETSKY.O virus	Bad
avgw	AVG Antivirus 7.0	Good
Avimgt	GEMA virus	Bad
Avimgt32	GEMA virus	Bad
AVIRCHK	DASMIN virus	Bad
AvirMail	AvirMail	User
AVKWCTL9X	eScan antivirus	User
Avmaisrv	Avast32 AntiVirus	User
avpcc	Kaspersky Labs AntiVirus	User
avpguard	NETSKY.J virus	Bad
AvpM	Kaspersky Labs AntiVirus	User
Avprotect9x	NETSKY.L virus	Bad
AVprotect9x	NETSKY.M virus	Bad
AVSched32	H+BEDV AntiVir	User
Avserve	W32.Sasser.Worm virus	Bad
avserve	SASSER virus	Bad
Avserve2	W32.Sasser.B.Worm virus	Bad
avserve2	SASSER.B or SASSER.C viruses	Bad
AVSynMgr	McAfee VirusScan Sync Mgr	User
Avsynmgr32	Trojan Framer virus	Bad
Avsynmgr32e	FRAMAR virus	Bad
Avsynmgr32n	FRAMGO virus	Bad
Avsynmgr32S	VOLAC or VOLAC.DR viruses	Bad
Avtray	Command AntiVirus	User
AVupdate	MERKUR virus	Bad
AVWUPD32	AntiVir update	User
avxinit	BitDefender or Bullguard antivirus	User
avxlive	BitDefender or Bullguard antivirus	User
awhost32	Symantec PCAnywhere	User
AWMonitor	Active Words	User
AZARE10S.PLT	Desktop Plant	User
B3DUpdate	Brillian Digital B3D Projector	User
Babylon	Babylon Translator	User
Backzip	Avatar Software	User
back32_service	virus	Bad
BACKTIME	Timed Backups manager Startup	User
BACKWE-1	Western Digital Data LifeGuard	User
BackWeb	adware	User
BACKWEB-137903	adware	Bad
backweb-4448364	Packard Bell ActivSurf	User
backWeb-728897	Kodak Software Updater	User
BackWeb-8876480/idmconf	Logitech Desktop Messenger	User
Backwork	Backwork	User
bacpi10a	PowerKey	User
bacstray	BroadcomAdvanced Control Suite	User
BADDATE	virus	Bad
bagent	Quicken Scheduled Updates	User
Bandwidth Monitor Pro	Bandwidth Monitor Pro	User
banish	Oslis/Winproxy Banish!	User
bargainbuddy	spyware	Bad

Program	Description	Good/Bad
Bargains	Exact Bargain Buddy Advertising	Bad
bargains	spyware	Bad
Barthel	People PC	Ugly
BasicUpdate.dll.vbs	BISCUIT.A virus	Bad
batmgr	Battery Scope	User
Battery Doubler	Battery Doubler	User
batterybar	Battery Bar	User
BatteryLife	Asus Power Gear	User
BatzBack.scr	BACKZAT virus	Bad
Bbeagle	W32.Beagle.A@mm virus	Bad
bbeagle	BEAGLE.A virus	Bad
bboy	MUMU.B virus	Bad
bbSysTray	Philips CD-RW Blue Button	User
bbui	AOL DSL	User
BBCTicker	BBC Ticker	User
bbwiz	Broadband Wizard	User
BCDetect	Creative Labs BCDetect	User
Bcmdmmsg	Broadcom Modem Messaging	User
BCMSMMsg	Broadcom Soft Modem Msg Applet	User
BcTool	GIBE virus	Bad
bctweak	Creative Labs Blaster Control	User
bcwipetm	BCWipe	User
BDEtsecurinstall	B3d Projector	User
bdinit	BitDefender Live Init	User
Bdmcon	BitDefender Antivirus	User
bdnagent	BitDefender Antivirus Updater	Good
bdss	Veritas Backup Exec Server	User
bdswitch	BD Switch Agent	User
BE	CompuSec	User
bearshare	BearShare	User
Belt	adware	Bad
benadrilalert	dialer	Bad
besch	Veritas Backup Exec Scheduler	User
BEngine	Veritas Backup Exec Job Engine	Good
BENSer	Veritas Backup Exec Naming Service	Good
BESrv	Veritas Backup Exec Server	User
BestCrypt	Jesico Best Crypt Auto Open	User
Bfrecv	Bitware modem software	User
bgsmsnd	Printer Driver	User
bgswitch	Background Switcher	User
biblaster	Browswer Hijack Blaster	User
BHOCop	ZDNet BHO Cop	User
BHODemon	BHO Demon	User
bible	LITMUS virus	Bad
bigbadvirus	RANDEX.F virus	Bad
BigBen	Big Ben	User
BIGFIX	BigFix	User
Billmind	Intuit Quicken Billminder	User
Bingdian.vbs	BINGD virus	Bad
BIOS1	OPASERV.T virus	Bad
Bios32	virus	Bad
BitDefender_P2P_Startup	BitDefender Antivirus	User
BJCFD	Broadjump Foundation Client	User
BkupExec	Veritas Backup Exec Agent	User
blackd	BlackICE PC Protection	User
blackice	BlackICE PC Protection	User
blads	Tweak-XP	User
Blengine	ClickSpring PurityScan	Bad
blengine	adware	Bad
blocker	Ad Blocker	User
BlockTracker	Block Tracker	User
bliss	dialer	Bad
blstapp	Creative Labs Blaster Control	User
bluefritz!	AVM BlueFritz	User
BMExtreme	BM Extreme	User
BMLauncher	Bookmark Central	User
BMouse	Kensington ValuMouse Scroll	User
Bmqnzkg	W32.Randex.BE virus	Bad
bmqnzkg	RANDEX.BE virus	Bad
Bmui	RingCentral Inc Buzma	User
BMupdate	Bookmark Central	User
bmz	adware	Bad
Bndt32	LACON virus	Bad
Boclean	NSClean ROClean	User
BODMom	Caddais Backup On Demand	User
BOMB32	McAfee Nuts & Bolts	User
boot	ELEM virus	Bad
bootconf	coolwwwsearch.com hijacker	Bad
bootconf	coolwwwsearch.com hijacker	Bad
BootLoader.vbs	WATERWORKS virus	Bad
BOOT5T~1	Boot Status	User
BootWarn	Norton AntiVirus Boot Warning	User
bpc	spyware	Bad
bpcable	Big Pond Cable	User
Bpcpost	MS TV Viewer Post Setup	User
bpk	Blazing Tools Perfect Keylogger	Bad
bpsinstall	parasite	Bad
bpudfmon	Microsolutions Backpack UDF	User
bpumTray	Telstra Big Pond Toolbar	User
BQTray	BurnQuick	User
Brad32	Total Virus Defense Network Suite	User
Brasil	OPASERV.E virus	Bad

Program	Description	Good/Bad
BRASIL.PIF	OPASERV.E virus	Bad
BRIDGE	3Com Winmodem	User
BridgeDeCor	BridgeDeCor	User
BRITRAY	Brindys Software 8nTray	User
Brojac3	Brojac Impulsa	User
browseraid	foistware	User
Brpkmon	Brother printer driver	User
bs2.dll.DllRun	adware	Bad
BSCLIP	B's Clip	User
Bsoft	parasite	User
BT	Busstister	User
BTStackServer	Widcomm Bluetooth Stack COM Srvr	User
Bttnserv	see CPQEAUI	User
BTTray	Widcomm Bluetooth Tray App	User
BtUsrBdg	Mitsumi USP Bluetooth Adapter	User
Buddyizer	AOL Buddyizer	User
bugwatcher	Bugwatcher Service	User
buildownload	Bullguard Antivirus	Good
bullguard	Bullguard Antivirus	User
bundle	parasite	Bad
ButtonKey	Button Key	User
buzof	Basta Computing Buzof	User
BVT	Backdoor.Autoupder virus	Bad
Bwd	AUTOUPDER virus	Bad
BWCfgLoader	adware and homepage hijacker	Bad
BWMeter	Desksoft.com BW Meter	User
bwprmmon	BitWare Print Monitor	User
bxservice	Systweak Boost XP Service	User
c:archiv~1win.com	CUYDOC virus	Bad
C:PROGRA~1Avast4ashmaisrv	Avast! 4 Home Edition	User
C4ULnch	Change Highlighter for webpages	User
ca	Microsoft EZ Firewall	User
Cabchk	GEMA virus	Bad
Cabchk32	GEMA virus	Bad
CABCInstall	CABC content delivery	User
Cacheman	Outer Technologies Cacheman	User
CacheMgr	Sophos Antivirus Remote Update	Good
CacheSentry	Cache Sentry	User
cads	Cyber Sentinel internet filtering	User
CAgent	Abbny Community Agent	Ugly
CahootWebcard	Cahoot Webcard	User
caKe	CAKE virus	User
caKe	CAKE virus	User
CalCheck	ULaad Photo Xprs Calendar Chkr	Ugly
Calendarium	Calendarium	User
CALLSOFTPRO	TOSC International Call Soft	User
CallWaiting	US Robotics Internet Call No-	User
calrem	Cal Reinder Shortcut	User
CamCheck	NuCam CamCheck	User
Canada	Canada Dialler	Bad
canary	CANARY virus	User
canary-std	Canary	User
CapCalAgent	Capacity Calibration Agent	User
capexp	Capture Express 2000	User
CapFax	BVRP Phone Tools	User
capinmonitor	CAPI Monitor	User
Capon	Canon Printer Driver	Good
CAPS	Anti-Caps Lock	User
CaptainHook	Novell Secure Login v3.x	User
Card1Phone1.liStarter	UI Starter	User
CArpServ	Conexant internal modem speaker	User
cart322	GAOBOT.DJ virus	Bad
cat	dialer	Bad
Cateye	Quick Heal Online	User
Cavapsvc	GAOBOT.AO virus	Bad
CAZNO	CAZNO virus	Bad
CBRSS	SPYBOT virus	Bad
CBSysTray	Backup Solutions	User
CBWAttn	Bitware	User
CBWHost	Bitware	User
cc	adware and homepage hijacker	Bad
ccApp	Norton Security Common Client App	User
ccApp32	GAOBOT.GET virus	Bad
CCD	Broadjump CorrectConnect Engine	User
ccdoctor	Rational ClearCase	User
ccEvtMgr	Norton Security Common Client	User
CCleaner	Crap Cleaner	User
CCMON	CAPI Call Monitor System Tray	User
CConnect	CorrectConnect	User
ccProxy	Norton Security Common Client	User
CCProxy	YoungZSoft CCProxy In Conn Sharing	User
ccPwdSvc	Norton Security Common Client	User
ccPvpSvc	Norton Security Common Client	User
ccRegVfy	Norton Security Common Client	User
ccSetMgr	Norton 2004 Security	User
CD_Load	Cydoor Desktop Media	Bad
CD_Load	adware	Bad
Cdac11ba	MacroVision SafeCast Copy Procton	User
cdaEngine0400.dll	Wild Tangent CDA	User
CDANTSRV	C-Dilla License Management	User
cdawman	CD Anywhere	User
Cdcompat	GEMA virus	Bad
cdesk	Cool Desk	User

Start Up & Tasks

Program	Description	Good/Bad	Program	Description	Good/Bad
cdf	Broadjump Client Foundation	User	cmd32	LOADCFG or SDBOT viruses	Bad
cdi	CD Interceptor	User	CmdServ	HOLAR.A virus	Bad
cdm	adult dialer	Bad	cme	spyware	Bad
CDock	Compaq Docking Monitor	User	cmesseng	Qchex.com Check Messenger	User
CDTray	HP CD Tray	User	Cmesys	Gator GAIN	User
CDUpdater	adult dialer	Bad	CMEsys	spyware	Bad
Center	ASUS WiFi card Control Ctr	User	CMEupd	spyware	Bad
CFD	Broadjump App Client Fndtn	User	CMGrdian	McAfee AntiVirus	User
cffrem	Corel Colleagues & Contracts	User	Cmluc	Client Manager	User
Cfgdll32	W32 Randex.BD virus	Bad	Cmmon32	MS Connection Manager Monitor	User
CfgDll32	RANDEX.BD virus	Bad	CMMPU	C-Media MPU-401 Emulator	User
cfgintpr	Tiny Prsnl Firewall Config Interpreter	User	cmonitor	DC300 Monitor	User
CFGSAFE/AUTOCHK	ConfigSafe	User	CMPDPSRV	ViewAhead Tech Print Driver Plus	User
cfgwiz	NortonAntiVirus 2002	User	CNBABE	spyware	Bad
Cfgwiz32	Configuration Wizard	User	CNF UPD	SPYBOT.GEN virus	Bad
cfinst	Intel TMA Distribution	User	cnf.bat	REMABL virus	Bad
cFosDNT	cFos DSL modem driver and GUI	User	CNFGLD32	SDBOT virus	Bad
cfservice	GFI LANguard System Integrity	User	Cnfgldr	SDBOT virus	Bad
cftrb32	SOBIG.D virus	Bad	CNFRM	W32.Mimail.D@mm virus	Bad
CG16eh	Norton Crash Guard Deluxe	User	cnfrm	MIMAIL.D or MIMAIL.G viruses	Bad
CGMenu	Norton CrashGuard Monitor	User	cnfrm33	MIMAIL.D or MIMAIL.G viruses	Bad
cgserver	Eicon Networks Call Guard Server	User	cnqmax	RANDEX.P virus	Bad
cgtask	LALA.B virus	Bad	CnxDSLTb...	Conexant DSL TaskBar App	User
ch	Copy Handler	User	Code	adult com	Bad
ChamClock	Chameleon Clock	User	codedcolor	CodedColor	User
ChangeWallpaper	Wallpaper Cycle	User	color	SiS Color	User
ChannelUp	ee IWAR	Bad	coloreal	Brightens Color on Monitor	User
ChannelUp	adware	Bad	ComboButton	Maxtor OneTouch Detection	User
charmapx	System Startup	User	comcfg	TOADCOM.A virus	Bad
Chcenter	IMSI Hijaak	User	comctl_32	downloader	Bad
Cheatle	SHOOI.B virus	Bad	COMDLGEX	McAfee Nuts & Bolts	User
CheckIt86	Smith Micro CheckIt 86	User	comet	CC2KUL malware	Bad
checkp3	Mail Checker	User	COMIP	COM-IP Virtual Modem Driver	User
china.bat	WCUP virus	Bad	command	QQPASS.E virus	Bad
CHKADMIN	Compaq Network Mgmt System	User	Command	BUDDY virus	Bad
ChkFont	Ulead Photo Express Check Fonts	User	COMMANDER	IomegaWare	User
ChkMail	ASUS Check Mail	User	Commandr	Logitech Browser Launcher	User
CHKNET	MS LAN Mgr Enhanced Workstation	Ugly	Companion	FetPhone CommCenter	Ugly
ChkRAS	NetZero	User	Companion	AOL Companion	Ugly
Choke-blahh	CHOKE virus	Bad	COMPAQ-RBA	Compaq Message Server	Ugly
chostes	BANPAES.C virus	Bad	COMSMD	3Com Tray Icon	User
CHotKey/MK9805	Chicony to program hotkeys	User	ComSocks	Linkbyte ComSockets Internet Proxy	User
chrono	Chronograph Atomic Time Clock	User	configdir	POLYBOT virus	Bad
CiDaemon	MS Index Server	User	config	Linksys Wireless Cnnctn Config	User
cihost	LINST virus	Bad	config.com	TAPLAK virus	Bad
Cjbp2ps	Lexmark LXP2PS MFC	User	Config32	LGS/Telegraphics Internet Mouse	User
CiJxP2PS	Compaq Printer Utility	User	configdr	AGOBOT.CC virus	Bad
CISRVR	Compaq Internet Setup	User	confsrv	NTL Gearbox	User
CISRVR	MS Content Index Service	User	ConMgr	Earthlink Connection Manager	User
Cissi	W32.Cissi.A@mm virus	Bad	connect2party	adult dialer	Bad
CiSvc	MS Content Index Service	User	ConnectState	Nokia PC Suite	User
CitiVAN	Citibank CitiVAN	User	connmngmntbox	Nokia PC Suite	User
citrusac	Citrus Alarm Clock	User	consol32	hijacker	Bad
Cjstcom	Canon Bubble Jet Status Monitor	User	Control	hijacker	Bad
Cjstlst	Canon Bubble Jet Printer Monitor	User	ControlUtility	Dell Wireless Control Utility	User
CJSTRxx	Canon Bubble Jet Status Monitor	User	cookie	ANalog X Cookie Wall	User
CKA	Symantec Norton System Works	User	CookieCop	PC Magazine Cookie Cop 2	User
CleanCache	Cache Cleanup	User	Cookiejar	Jason's Toolbox Cookie Jar	User
clch	Clean Ram	User	CookiePatrol	PestPatrol Cookie Patrol	User
Clear Tweak	Microsoft Clear Tweak	User	Cool	DONK.B virus	Bad
Clickoff	Clickoff	User	CoolMon	CoolMon	User
clickr-1	Click Radio Tuner	User	coolsystemsinfo	Cool Beans System Info	User
ClickT-1	Click Tray Calendar	User	CopConsolidator	Cookie Cop	User
CLICONFIG	OPASERV.T virus	Bad	CopernicPerUserTaskMgr	Copernic Pro	User
Client	Samurize	User	copykfg	Resume Copy	User
CLIENT/client01	DigiGuide	User	copystart	Copyshop 2000	User
clipc	Clip Cache	User	coresrv	Used by trojans and worms	Bad
ClipMt5x	Thomsoft Clip Mate 5.x	User	corona	CORONEX.A virus	Bad
CLIPMT60	Thomsoft Clip Mate 6.0	User	couponica	adware	Bad
ClipMt5x	see CLIPMT60	User	CP35EBTN	Laptop One-Touch Buttons	User
ClipMt62	see CLIPMT60	User	cpad	Verizon Control Pad	User
CLIPOM-2	Mike Lin Clipomatic	User	CPAi...	Kookaburra Software Cookie Pal...	User
Clipomatic	Mike Lin Clipomatic	User	CPBrWtch	Dritek/Compal ATR10 Easy Btn	User
clipsize	ClipSize 2.4	User	CPCTRAY	Powerquest Second Chance	User
ClipSrv	MS Clipboard DDE Server	User	CPD	McAfee VirusScan 6	User
ClipSync	Zita Farm Ltd ClipSync	User	CPDClnt/CPD	McAfee ConSeal Private Dsktp Frwl	Ugly
ClipTrak	Clip Trak	User	CPLBCL53	LManager	User
ClipTrakker	Clip Trakker	User	CPLBTS88	Toshiba Easy Button	User
clisvc95	SMS Client Service	User	CPortPatch	Dell Patch	User
clmpanel	CLM Front Panel	User	cpqa1000	Compaq A1000 Settings Utility	User
CLOCK	Clock	User	CPQAcDc	Compaq PowerCon	User
CLOCKWISE	R J Software Clockwise	User	CPQAlert	Compaq Alerter	User
CloCkX	Bc Bohdan Rylko ClocX 1.4	User	CPQCalib	Compaq PowerCon	User
CloneCDTray	Clone CD Tray	User	CpqDfwAg	Compaq diagnostics	User
ClrSchP038	see STCLOADER	User	cpqdiaga	Compaq System DLF	User
clrschp038	adware	Bad	cpqdm	Compaq DMI	User
clrsrn	parasite	Bad	CPQEAUI	Compaq EasyAccess Btn Support	User
CIShield	Panda Antivirus Client Shield	User	CPQEK	Compaq EasyAccess Btn Support	User
ClvrKeys	CleverKeys	User	Cpqinet	Compaq CPQInet Runtime Service	User
cma	Desksite CMA	User	cpqik	Compaq Ink Agent	User
CMAgent	Cybermedia Inc Oil Change	Ugly	cpqki	Compaq PK Daemon	User
cmail.dll, Rundll32	CrisMin hijacker	Bad	Cpqnpcss	Compaq Internet Service	User
Cmanager	SBC Connection Manager	User	cpqscp	Compaq System Tray	User
CMCp16	Cybermedia First Aid 98	Ugly	cpqset	HP default settings	User
cmd32	P2P.TANKED virus	Bad			

Program	Description	Good/Bad
cpr	adware downloader	Bad
cpsdv	AGOBOT.EW virus	Bad
Cpucool	CPU Cool	User
cpuidle	CPU Idle	User
cpumgr	PANDEM.G virus	Bad
Cpunumber	Compaq Pentium 3 Srl Num Blocker	Good
Cpusave	GEMA virus	Bad
Cpusave32	GEMA virus	Bad
cracked_windows1	Cracked Windows	User
Crashmon	CyberMedia First Aid Crash Mon	Ugly
Craubo	Paragon Encrypted Disk	User
CREATE~1	Roxio Easy CD Creator 5	User
CreateCD	Roxio Easy CD Creator	User
CreateCD50	Creator v5	User
createsw	FTP_EMAIL virus	Bad
Creative	PROLIN virus	Bad
CricketJr40	Cricket Jr 4x	User
CRunner	Control Runner	User
cs	Calendarscope	User
cseinst	Fortis Secure Layer Configuration	User
CSInject	Symantec Norton Clean Sweep	User
Csinrsm32/CsinsmNT	Norton Clean Sweep Install Mon	User
Csksvr	LinkByte ComSocks Service	User
Csrrs	GAOBOT.AO virus	Bad
csrsc	virus	Bad
Csrss	Trojan.Gutta virus	Bad
csrss	MS Client Server Runtime SubSys	Good
csrss	NETSKY.AB virus	Bad
Csrss	search page hijacker	Bad
csrss	HALE virus	Bad
csrss	SOKACAPS virus	Bad
csrss	GUTTA virus	Bad
csrss	AHLEM.A virus	Bad
CSS_1630	Authentium Command AntiVirus	User
CSS_1631	CSS Central	User
CSS-AVS	Authentium CSS AVScheduler	User
cssrs	WORM_ABOGOT.FX virus	Bad
cssrs	WORM_ABOGOT.FX virus	Bad
Csss	BALICK virus	Bad
csta	Clean Space	User
CSUSEM32	Symantec Clean Sweep	User
CSysTime	RANDEX.S virus	Bad
ct	HP Learning Adventure	User
CTAvTray	Creative Tech SoundBlaster Live	User
CTB	spyware	Bad
CTCMSGo	Creaative MediaSource Go	User
CTDetect	Creative Labs DVD Detect	User
CTDVDDet	Creative Labs DVD Audio Startup	User
CTEaxSpl	CTStartup	User
Ctfmon	W32.Mydoom.B@mm virus	Bad
CTFMon	MS Text Services & Speech	User
ctfmon32	parasite	Bad
CTHELPER	WINDVD Patch	User
CTin10	BANCOS.E virus	Bad
ctistartup	Interel Callview	User
CTLauncher	Creative Labs Creative Launcher	User
CTLTray	Soundblaster Audigy Task Tray	User
CTMIX32	Creative mixer	User
CTNMRun	Creative Labs Nomad Detector	User
CTNotify	Creative Tech Disc Detector	User
ctpdsrvr	pdp Server	User
CTRegRun	Creative Soundblaster Card Rgstrtn	User
CTSRReg	Creative Speed Racer	User
CTsvcCDA	Creative Tech Creative Services	Ugly
CTsysVol	Creative Soundblaster Card Audigy	User
ctuclwin	Central Tweaking Unit	User
Cuagent	Authentium Command AntiVirus	User
cujo	BUGBEAR virus	Bad
CursorXP	Stardock CursorXP	User
Cusrvc	Novell Client Update Service	Ugly
CuteMX	CuteMX	User
cvpnd	Cisco VPN Client	User
Cvshost	GAOBOT.AO virus	Bad
cwbckver	IBM Client Access Check Version	User
cwbinhlp	IBM Client Access Help Update	User
CwbSvStr	IBM Client Access Service	User
cxp	Clock XP	User
CYB2K	CYBERsitter 2000/2001	User
cyberbud	CyberBuddy	User
cyberchk	Belkin	User
CyberWolf	KICKIN.A virus	Bad
d	Adult dialer	Bad
DO66UUTY	Twain Driver	User
D4	Dimension 4 Synchronization	User
D4NG3.vbs	BISCUIT.A virus	Bad
D5MediaServer	Gateway D5 Streaming Media Srvr	User
daconfig	3Com NIC Diagnostics	User
DAD8	Corel Desktop App Director 8	User
DadApp	Dell AccessDirect Applet	User
dadapp	Dell SW Utility	Good
DadTray	Dell AccessDirect Tray	User
dadx	Corel Desktop App Director	User
daemon/tp4serv	Track Point Server	User
Daemon14	Microsoft Strategic Commander	User
DAEMON32	MS Sidewinder Game Controllers	User
DAMon	Dell Alert Monitor	User
Dancer	Dancer	User
DAP	SpeedBit Ltd Download Accelerator	User
dashboard	Codename Dashboard	User
DataKeeper	PowerQuest DataKeeper	User
DATALA~1	Nokia DataLayer	User
DataLayer	Nokia Data Layer Module	User
DataLinkLauncher	Timex Data Link USB Launcher	User
datcheck	KEYPANIC virus	Bad
DateMakerIntl	dialer	Bad
dateManager	Gator Adware Date Manager	Bad
datemanager	spyware/adware	Bad
DATray	Ken Foster Desktop Architect	User
DAupdate	Double Agent Update	User
DavCData	MS HTTP-DAV Common Data	User
dayplan	Daily Planner	User
DAYTODAY	RoboMagic Software Day Today	User
dbnetlib	DONK.L virus	Bad
DbServer	Graves AppAware Loader	User
DC1300	DC1300 Monitor	User
DcDaemon	Dazel Delivery Agent	User
dcemgr	TUMAG virus	Bad
DcFsSvc	Kodak DC File System Driver	User
dcomx	CIREBOT virus	Bad
dd	Double Desktop	User
dd_clock	DigiDay Clock	User
DDCActiveMenu	adware	Bad
DDCMan	Wild Tangent Dig Dist Chnl Mgr	Ugly
DDCMan	adware	Bad
ddeproc	spyware	Bad
DDHelp	MS DirectDraw Helper for DirectX	User
ddhelp32	BIONET.318 virus	Bad
DDialler	adult dialer	Bad
DeadAIM	Dead AIM	User
Deam	see IWAR	Bad
DebugW32	GUBED virus	Bad
DeeEnEs	URL.link	Bad
DefAlert	Symantec Definitions Alert	User
defragment	parasite	Bad
DEFSCANGUI	spyware	Bad
DefWatch	Norton Corp Ed Defn Watch Svc	User
DelayDelayrun	John Hysted time conflict prevention	Good
DellDMI	Dell DMI Service Provider	User
DELLMMKB	Dell Touch	User
dellsc	Dell Solution Center	User
delmsbb	adware	Bad
deltray	M-Audio Analog Recording Interface	User
DeltTray	M-Audio Recording Sys Driver	User
desires	adult dialer	Bad
Desk##	ATI Technologies Hydravision	User
DESKCOLOR	Desk Color	User
Deskflag	DeskFlag	User
Deskshop	Discover Deskshop	User
DesktopCalendar	Desktop Calendar	User
desktopmgr	Research In Motion handheld sync	User
DESKTOPX	DesktopX	User
Deskup	IomegaWare driver icons	User
Detector	LG Scanner USB Monitor	User
DevDetect	Device Detector	User
DevDtct2	Olympus Device Detector 2	User
Devgulp	Compaq Digital Dashboard	User
Devidr	Creative Labs	Ugly
Devidr16	Creative Labs Sound Cards	User
Devidr32	Creative Ring3 NT	User
devidr32	virus	Bad
DFSSvc	MS WinNT Dist File Sys Svc	User
DGDRHE~1	Hermes Messenger	User
DHCP	FatPipe	User
dhcpagnt	Intel DSL Modem Driver	Good
DiAgent	Creative Diagnostics Agents	User
DIAL	trojan	Bad
DialoutEZTray	Tactical Software Dial Out/EZ	User
die and either ttg or secure or mdll or secure.bat	SUMTAX virus	Bad
DigiWMix	Digigram VX Pocket PC-card	User
Digstream	Disney Internet Group Streaming	User
DIIhost	GAOBOT.AO virus	Bad
dino3	adware	Bad
DirectCD	Roxio DirectCD	Ugly
directs	BEAGLE family of viruses	Bad
Directvdsl	DirectTV DSL Modem	User
Directx	SDBOT.D virus	Bad
DirectX	BLAXE or LOGPOLE viruses	Bad
DirectXset	BROWNEY.A virus	Bad
Dirkey	Dirkey	User
disknap	Dell Disknap	User
Display	APC UPS Status	User
DISTASST	Adobe Distiller Assistant 3.01	User
Dit	Drive Icon and Label Utility	User
DiTask	Eicon Networks Modem Status	User
DivX	NALDEM or MASTAK virus	Bad
Difgucxr	W32.Gluber.B@mm virus	Bad
DKService	Executive Software Diskeeper	Good

Program	Description	Good/Bad
dkware	Dkware lprt01	Bad
dkware	Dkware ml097e	Bad
DI	Trojan Horse Virus	Bad
Dlatray	HP DirectCD tray icon	User
dlbabmgr	Dell AIO Printer A940	User
dlder	spyware	Bad
Dlg	EVRP Digital Line Detection	User
DLGCHBW	Western Digital Data LifeGuard	User
DLGI	DataLifeGuard LifeLine Lite	User
dlink	Network Setup	User
DLLCmd32	HP Configure Live Menu	User
DLLHost	MS Dist Component Object Model	Good
dllhost	Gilat SOM Enumerator	Good
dllmem32	KWBOT.E virus	Bad
Dlm	Trojan Horse Virus	Bad
dlm	Adult dialer	Bad
dlm	Adult dialer	Bad
DLT	Dell Legacy Translator	User
dluca	Adult dialer	Bad
dluca	DLUCA.C virus	Bad
dm_mgr	JITTAR virus	Bad
DMAdmin	MS Logical Disk Mgr Admin Svc	User
DMCenter	Diamond Multimedia InControl Tools	User
dmcpl	RUSTY virus	Bad
DMHKey	Diamond Multimedia InControl Tools	User
dmildr	Dell OpenManage Client	User
DMISL	Intel Desktop Mgmt Intrface Svc Layer	User
DMISLAPP	see DMISL	
dmserver	adware	Bad
DMX6Fire	TerraTec DMX 6Fire 2496 Ctrl Pnl	User
Dnar	dialer	Bad
DNETC	Distributed.net Client	User
dnetc	virus	Bad
DiodicMage	Download Mage	User
DockApp	Dell Docking Monitor	User
Doctor	DOTOR virus	Bad
dontpanicdemodp	Panicware Don't Panic	User
dopus	DOpus	User
Dos32	GAOBOT.AO virus	Bad
dosrun32	GAOBOT.AO virus	Bad
downlo-1	Digital River eBot	User
download	spyware	Bad
DownloadPlus	parasite	Bad
DownloadWizard	Digital River eBot	User
DownloadWonder	Forty Software Download Wonder	User
dp-******	adware	Bad
DPAgnt	Digital Persona Agent	User
dpcnav	DirectTV DirecWay	User
dpcstart	DirectTV DirecWay	User
Dpi	Delfin Project PromulGate	User
dpi	adware	Bad
DP-K13w13	KaZaA	User
Dpmw32	Novell Client	User
Dpps2	Panicware Don't Panic	User
Dr.DivX	ALADINZ.G virus	Bad
Dragdiag	Alcatel Speedtouch USB Diagnostics	User
DragStrip	DragStrip	User
drempels	Drempels Desktop	User
DrgToDsc	Roxio Drag-to-Disc	User
DriBat32	KE-9801 Multimedia Keyboard	User
DriveCrypt	DriveCrypt Startup	User
DRIVES-1	Nero DriveSpeed	User
driveselect	Drive Select	User
drv	SOBER virus	Bad
drvddll	BEAGLE.X virus	Bad
drvlsnr	Compaq/ADI SoundMax Audio Ctrl	User
drvr32h	virus	Bad
drvrquery32	BOOHOO virus	Bad
drvsys	W32.Beagle.W@mm virus	Bad
drvsys	BEAGLE.W virus	Bad
Drwebscd	Dr. Web Antivirus	Good
dsa	hijacker	Bad
dsclock	DS Clock	User
Dsentry	Dell DVD Sentry	User
dseraser	Absolute Shield/Evidence Eliminator	
DSHMap	Intel AnyPoint Internet Sharing	User
Dskcompat	GEMA virus	Bad
DSLagent	Eicon USB ADSL modems	User
DSLaunch	Yamaha DS-XG Soundcard Driver	User
dslmon	Sagem Broadband modem	User
Dssagent	Broderbund ads, updates, etc	User
dssagent	spyware	Bad
DTemp	DaleSoft DTemp	User
DTHtml	MagicTune	User
dtiorm98	Iomega Backup Scheduler	User
DTLoader	MiniStars Effective Desktop Loader	User
dtxservice	PROGENT virus	Bad
DUC20	No-IP DUC	User
DUKControl	Direct Updated	User
DUMeter	Hagel Tech DU Meter	User
DumpRep	MS Win Error Dump Reporting	Ugly

Program	Description	Good/Bad
DVDBitSet	HP DVD Bit Set	User
Dvdcompat	GEMA virus	Bad
Dvldr32	DELODER.A virus	Bad
Dvp95	F-Secure & Command Antivirus	User
DVPAPI9X	Command Antivirus	User
Dvpinit	Command Antivirus	User
Dvprpt	Command Antivirus	User
dvsync	daVinci DVSync	User
DvzIncMsgr	Dataviz Documents to Go	User
DvzMsgr	Dataviz Documents to Go	Ugly
dw	DownloadWare	Bad
dw	DownloadWare	Bad
DW (1)	Medialoads	User
DW (2)	MS Application Error Reporting	Ugly
Dwe	DownloadWare	Bad
dwMon	InstallShield Digital Wizard Mon	User
DWRCS	DameWare Dev Mini Remot Ctrl	User
DX3DPndr	GIBE.B virus	Bad
Dxdcompat	GEMA virus	Bad
Dxdllreg	MS DirectX DLL Register	User
Dxsty	GEMA virus	Bad
Dxupdate	MAFEG virus	Bad
DynDns	DynDNS Updater	User
dynubas	Dynu Basic Client	User
E_AICN03	Epson Stylus Color 580	User
E_S0EIC1	Epson Stylus Photo 820 printer	User
e_s0hic1	Epson Stylus C82 Printer	User
E_s10ic1	Epson Status Monitor 3	User
E_s10ic2	see E-S10ic1	User
E_S4I2D1	see E-S10ic1	User
E_S4I2G1	Epson Stylus CX5400 Printer	User
E_Srcv02/E_Srcv03	Epson Status Monitor 2	User
E2S4Outlook	Easy2Sync	User
EA2Check	AJSystems.com Express Assist	User
EabServr	Compaq Easy Access Buttons	User
eaclean	Compaq Easy Access	User
EANTHO~1	spyware	Bad
EasyAV	NETSKY.S or NETSKY.T viruses	Bad
easyclip	Lotus Organizer EasyClip	User
EasyDates_nl	Adult dialer	Bad
EasyGoBackRT	Useful'n Healty Sltns EasyGoBack	User
easykey	EasyKey	User
EasyShare	Kodak EasyShare	User
EasyTune	Easy Tune III	User
easywww2	virus	Bad
EasyZapperMonitor	Harmony Monitor	User
EatMenu	EAT Menu	User
EAUSBKBD	Compaq Easy Access Button	User
EBAYTBAR	spyware	Bad
Eber	see IWAR	
Eboard	eMachines eBoard	User
Ebot	Digital River eBot	Ugly
Ebrr	Epson Bi-Directional Request Router	
ecard	YODI virus	User
EchoCtrl	C-Media Echo Control	User
ectasckscheduler	Nokia PC Suite	User
eDexter	eDexter	User
EditPad	EditPad Lite	User
editpad	parasite	Bad
editpad	parasite	Bad
Edrserv32	Novell GroupWise 5.5	User
Edsdiv32	Novell GroupWise 5.5	User
ee	Evidence Eliminator	User
efaxs	parasite	Bad
efaxs	parasite	Bad
Efpap	Easy File & Folder Protector	User
efpeadm	eTrust EZ Firewall	User
Ekiller	Exit Killer	User
ElbyCheck	Elaborate Bytes AG Clone CD/DVD	User
Element.txt	ELEM virus	Bad
elf	hacker program	Bad
Elmenv	Via1 ech eLicense	User
elsavect	ChipGuard	User
EM_Exec	Logitech MouseWare	User
em2	Easy Message	User
EMA	Time Management	User
email95	email Notify v1.22	User
emptemp2	Empty Temp 2	User
Emsw	Alset Help Express	User
emsw	spyware	Bad
En406t0ct	Efficient SpeedStream DSL Modem	User
enbiei	BLASTER.F virus	Bad
ENCMONTR	Encompass	User
EnergizerFileSaver	Energizer FileSaver	User
ENGSS	Status Monitor XE	User
EngUtil	Roxio Engine Compatibility Utility	User
Erins	see IWAR	Bad
EnterNet	Efficient Networks Access Mgr	User
eOneMng	eOne Manager	User
epf	EPFolder	User
EPOAgpentnaimag32	McAfee ePolicy Orchestrator	User
ePrompter	ePrompter	User

Program	Description	Good/Bad
Epscansv	Epson Scan Server	User
EPSON_PhotoStarter	Epson PhotoStarter	User
EPSONCardMonitor1.0	Epson CardMonitor	User
eraser	ScanSoft OmniPage Pro Reminder	User
Ereg	ScanSoft OmniPage Pro Reminder	User
eros	adult dialer	Bad
ErPhn2	EasySync Pro	User
ErTray	XTNDConnect	User
E-S0BIC1	Epson Stylus C62	User
esb	Easy Start Button	User
eschlp	BLASTER.T virus	Bad
escorcher	spyware	Bad
esftp	eSftp	User
ESPWatch	Aladdin eSafe Protect	User
essd	ESS Solo Soundcard	User
ESSOLO	ESSOLO	User
EssSpk	Ess Technologies V92 Modems	User
ET4Tray	Easy Tune IV	User
etdintrv	Entrust Scotia On Line Recovery	User
etoolbar	EarthLin ToolBar 2.0	User
Euea	see IWAR	Bad
eusebe	ICH Synth	User
EventMgt	Dell Event Agent	User
EventMgr	Microtek ScanWizard Event Mgr	User
eventsentry_gui	Event Sentry Tray Icon	User
EvLsten	Event Listener	User
evntsc	Application Scheduler	User
Evntsvc	RealOne Player	User
EWALLET	BMO MasterCard Wallet	User
exe	parasite	Bad
Execdll32	W32.Randex.AZ virus	Bad
EXECDLL32	RANDEX.AZ virus	Bad
execfg4	ELECTRON virus	Bad
Exiflaquickdcr/QuickDCF	Exif Launcher	User
Exlaunch	Oracle Platform	User
expander	HiJaak Expander	User
expl32	RATSOU virus	Bad
Expl32	HACKTAK virus	Bad
Explore	GAOBOT.V8V virus	Bad
Explore	W32.Gaobot.ADW virus	Bad
explore	Adult dialer	Bad
Explore	NETBUS, HAWAWI viruses	Bad
explore	GRAYBIRD.G virus	Bad
explore	hijacker	Bad
Explore	GAOBOT.ADW virus	Bad
explored	GAOBOT.RF virus	Bad
Explorer	MS Desktop, Taskbar, etc	Good
explorer	ZCREW virus	Bad
Explorer	IRC.FLOOD.G virus	Bad
explorer	parasite	Bad
explorer	parasite	Bad
Explorer	CLICKER-C virus	Bad
explorer	virus	Bad
Explorer	GRAYBIRD virus	Bad
explorer	virus	Bad
Explorer	YODO virus	Bad
Explorer.scr	BENJAMIN.A virus	Bad
EXPLORER.SCR	BENJAMIN virus	Bad
EXPLORER32	KWBOT or KWBOT.Y viruses	Bad
EXPLORERE	YAHA.AB virus	Bad
explores	GAOBOT.BT virus	Bad
expup	hijacker	Bad
Exshow	Kensington MouseWorks	User
Exshow95	Kensington Expert Mouse driver	User
ExtraDNS	ExtraDNS	User
EyeballChat	Eyeball Chat	User
EyeOnSite	EyeOnSite	User
ezagent	EzVCR	User
EZDESK	EZDesk	User
ezdsmain	Comp Assoc eTrus EX Deskshield	User
EzEjMnApp	IBM Easy Eject	User
ezlwy.bat	REOW virus	Bad
eZmmod	spyware	Bad
ezsmart	StorageSoft EZ-SMART	User
ezSP_Px/exSP_PxEngine	Easy Systems Japan Drag'n Drop	User
EZTimeSync	EZTimeSync	User
EZulaMain	eZula TOPText	Bad
eZulaMain	spyware	Bad
eZuluMain	spyware	Bad
F1AutoSync	FusionOne MightyPhone	User
F1Tray	FusionOne MightyPhone	User
f607	URAT.B virus	Bad
FA_GD32	Cybermedia First Aid 98 Win Grdian	User
FAMEH32	F-Secure Antivirus & Internet Firewall	Ugly
		Good
fan	Toshiba Fan	User
FAPIEXE	Thoght Comm FaxTalk Msngr Pro	User
Fast	adware	Bad
Fast	MS PowerToys	User
FAST2	AMS Network Fast Defrag 2 Std	User
Fastboot	MS Fast Cache	User
fastdown	Adult dialer	Bad
FastFolder	Fast Folder	User

Program	Description	Good/Bad
fastfown	Adult dialer	Bad
FAWGrd32	Cybermedia First Aid 98	Ugly
FaxCtrl	Right Fax Print-to-Fax	User
Faxsvc	Microsoft Fax	User
FB_PNU	NICHELLO.A virus	Bad
FBDirect	Visioneer Scanner	Ugly
Fbmount	McAfee Mount Safe & Sound	User
FBZPaper	Ember Blaze Changer	User
fc	AnalogX FastCache	User
feedreader	Feed Reader	User
feelitdm	Feel It Device Manager	User
FeyenoordNetTracker	Feyenoord News Tracker	User
ffolder	Folder Cache	User
FGKEY	Folder Guard	User
fhtisxk	XtraKeys	User
FileBx	File Box Extender	User
FileEx	File-Ex	User
filez	adult dialer	Bad
Flltgrd2	Filterguard	User
FindFast	MS Office Find Fast	Ugly
Findfast	Resource hog, remove	Bad
FindService	Actual Names Browse Proxy	User
finetrowser	FineBrowser	User
Firedaemon	Backdoor.NT Hack virus	Bad
FirewallSvr	W32.Netsky.X @mm virus	Bad
FirewallSvr	NETSKY.X or NETSKY.Y viruses	Bad
FirstReboot	Hercules Audio tool	User
FlashEnc	EasyDisk USP Pen Device	User
flashget	FlashGet	User
Flashrisk	DataCaching	User
flatbed	Twain Driver	User
Flexicd	MS Win 95 Power Toys	User
fljzsshc	adware	Bad
FLooDeR	FLOODNET virus	Bad
fps.vbs	BYRON virus	Bad
Flshstat	Toshiba FlashPath Status Mon	User
flydesk	spyware	Bad
Fmctrl	Genius SM-Live Control Panel	User
FMEMPRO	FreeMem Pro	User
fmnwebassist	adware	Bad
FNDlg	FileNotes	User
FNESSE32	Toshiba FN Keys	User
fnldr	parasite	Bad
FolderShield	Folder Shield	User
fontfix	FontFix	User
fontfix	virus	Bad
fonts.hta	hijacker	Bad
fonts.hta	hijacker	Bad
FONTVIEW	OPASERV.T virus	Bad
foobar2000	Foobar 2000	User
fooding	NETSKY.J virus	Bad
ForbesAlerts	Forbes Business News Alerts	User
FotoStation Easy AutoLaunch	FotoStation Easy AutoLaunch	Ugly
FourthDay	The Fourth Day	User
FoxHot	Foxmail 4.1	User
Foxmail	Foxmail	User
fpassist	Free PDF Assistant	User
FP-CHECK	FProt Update Checker	User
FpDisp4/FpDisp4a/FpDisp5a	FinePrint Dispatcher	User
Fppdisi1/Fppdis1a/Fppdis2a	FinePrint pdfFactory	User
FPUK	foistware	Bad
fpwinldr	Smart Stuff FoolProof Security	User
Fquick32	QuickStartup	User
freedom	Zero Knowledge Freedom	User
FreeMem	FreeMem Pro	User
FreeRam XP Pro 1.40	FreeRAM XP Pro	User
FriFax32	FRITZ!fax	User
FriFon32	FRITZ!fon	User
fmtgate	FrontGate MX	User
frsk	adware	Bad
FRW	ConSeal Signal9	User
frxmkins	ATI 3D Studio MAX/VIZ driver	User
frzstate	Hyper Technologies Deep Freeze	User
FS20	EMS Project Free Surfer Companion	User
fs30	Free Surfer	User
Fsb	W32.HllW.Yero.Worm virus	Bad
F-Sched	FRISK FP-Scheduler	User
fserv	Farsighter Server	Bad
fsg	spyware	Bad
FSG_4104	Gator Trickler	User
fsg-ag_3102	spyware	Bad
FSMA32	F-Secure Management Agent	User
fsp	Folder Shield	User
FSScrCtl	Screen Saver Control	User
F-StopW	F-Secure Software On-Access F-PROT	User
FSW	parasite	Bad
ftc	Gilat FTc	User
FTCtrl32	Though Comm FaxTalk Msgr Pro	User
FTP_Back	BMail Installation	User
FTPQueue	Ipswitch FTP Queuing	User
Ftpsched	Ipswitch WS FTOP Pro	User
FTPServer	FTP Server	User
fvlaunch	Find Virus Launch Program	User
FVProtect	W32.Netsky.P@mm virus	Bad

Start Up & Tasks

Program	Description	Good/Bad
FVProtect	NETSKY.P virus	Bad
fwenc	Check Point SecuRemote VPN Client	User
FWLink	foistware	Bad
fwrastrc	Friendly Technologies free ISP	User
FxRedir	Canon MultiPASS Fax Redirector	User
FxSSvc	MS Fax Service	User
g2svc	GoToMyPC	User
G6FTPSrv	Bullet Proof FTP Server	User
gaim	Gaim	User
gain_trickler_3202	spyware	Bad
game	Adult dialer	Bad
GameChannel	Wild Tangent Web Driver	Ugly
GameI.III	Rage3D Tweak	User
gatesmc	Sygate Personal Firewall	User
gator	spyware	Bad
gator	spyware	Bad
GBMenu	GoBack	User
gbot	JUNTADOR.K virus	Bad
GBPoll	Roxio GoBack Polling Service	User
GBTray	Roxio GoBack	User
Gdrive	IBM GDrive	Ugly
GDriver	IBM GDrive	User
Gear511	Wester Wireless Network Card	User
Gearsec	GEAR Software Security Svc	User
GEDZAC	GEMEL virus	Bad
GemStRmW	GemPlus Smart Card Reader	User
general	parasite	Bad
general	parasite	Bad
gesfm32	RANDEX.C virus	Bad
GETRIGHT	Headlight Software GetRight	User
getsmile	Get Smile	User
GFXACC	GIBE virus	Bad
gg	Gadu-Gadu	User
ggsearch	GG Search Tool	User
GhostStartService/GHOSTS~2	Norton Ghost Start Service	User
GhostStartTrayApp	Norton Ghost System Tray Icon	User
ghrone	Ghrone Clock	User
gigabit	W32 Beagle.U@mm virus	Bad
gigabit	BEAGLE.U virus	Bad
GigaByte	SHODI.B virus	Bad
Girder	Girder3	User
GISIONLog	BT ISDN Cnctn Event Recorder	Ugly
Glidew32	Glide	User
Gmouse	Gmouse	User
GMT	Gator GAIN	Bad
GMT	spyware	Bad
GMT16	RANDEX.AT virus	Bad
gnetmouse	Genius NetScroll Mouse Driver	User
Go	spyware	Bad
GoogleDCC	Google Compute Client	User
GoSync	Zita Farm Ltd GoSync	Bad
Gotit	TITOG virus	Bad
gozilla	TITOG virus	Bad
GPGtray	Privacy Guard	User
GpStart	Serif Graphics Plus	User
gra	System Resource Information	User
GrabClipSave	GrabClipSave	User
Grasiele.VBS	LEMBRA virus	Bad
GREENMARK	Chronos ALiUSBfix	User
GrpCnv	MS Win Program Group Converter	User
GrpWise	Novell GroupWise	User
GSDOGST	virus	Bad
gshp.vbs	hijacker	Bad
Gsicon	Eicon Networks ADSL Modem Mon	User
GSOrganizer	Golden Section Organizer	User
gspotbot	SPIGOT.C virus	Bad
gssomatic	hijacker	Bad
Gsyno	FHLP-BeWan GazelDisplay	User
gtwatch	Mustec Scanner	User
GuidaTVMonitor	Guida TV Monitor	User
guide	Guidescope	User
GuruNet	GuruNet	User
G-vGA	Gigabyte VGA Utility	User
GWHotkey	BillP Studios Keyboards	User
GWMdmMsg	Gateway Modem Messaging App	User
GWMdmPf	Gateway 450/500 Internal modem	User
gwreg	SourcePath	User
Gwremind	Greetings Workshop	Ugly
gwum	Gigabyte Utility Manager	User
H_menu	H-Menu 5.0	User
HalAsst	Zabaware Ultra Hal Assistant	User
hallowelt	GAOBOT.RS or GAOBOT.SA viruses	Bad
hampanel	HaMFrontPanel	Bad
Hamster	Classic Hamster	User
hardcopy	Hardcopy	User
hare	HARE virus	Bad
HAWK_32	HawkEye IV Control Panel	User
HAWK_95	HawkEye	User
hbagent	Handy Backup 3.9	User
HBinst	HotBar	Bad
HBinst	adware/spyware	Bad
HBinst	adware/spyware	Bad
HBSrv	HotBar	Bad
hc	Compaq HC Reminder	User
HCDetect	MS Home Click	User
hcontrol	ASUS Hotkeys	User
hcwPri.ill	HCW PVR Reset	User
HDDHealth	HDD Health	User
HDDTemperaturePro	HDD Temperature Pro	User
HDE	McAfee Icon Animation	User
hdi	Hard Drive Indicator	User
HDtray	Philips Edge Soundscard Ctrl Panel	User
hearit95	Moon Valley Icon Hearit 95	Ugly
hearit98	see hearit95	Ugly
HeldUp	HeldUp	Bad
helpctl	GASLIDE virus	Bad
helper.dll, Rundll32	hijacker	Bad
HelpExp	Attune Help Express	Bad
HelpSVC	MS Help Center Service	User
HERASER	Internet History Eraser	User
Hf	Hide Folders	User
hfxp	Hide Folders XP	User
HGCCTL95	E-Color Colorific	Ugly
HgrServer	GRAYBIRD.C virus	Bad
hib32	Hibernation	User
hid	RATSOU.B virus	Bad
hidden32 (path) explorer	ZCREW.B virus	Bad
HideOutlook	R2 Studios Hide Outlook	Ugly
Hiderun and svhost and pro.gif	BOOHOO virus	Bad
HIDServ	Human Interface Device Audio Svc	User
histkill	HistoryKill	User
hit	Adult dialer	Bad
hk2re	Hook99 Startup	User
HKCMD	Intel Hotkey Command Module	User
hkcontrol	Hotkeycontrol XP	User
hkey	GAOBOT.AFW virus	Bad
HKServ	Sony Hotkey Server	Good
HKSS	Compaq HotKey Support	User
HKWnd	Sony Hotkey Client	Good
hmonitor	Hardware Sensors Monitor	User
Hndsync	Pocket Real Estate Sync Data	User
Holiday Lights	Tiger Technologies Holiday Lights	User
Holu	see IWAR	Bad
HomeAlarm	Chameleon Clock	User
HookSys	SurfinGuard Pro	User
HostsToggle	HostsToggle	User
Hot_Kiss	adult dialer	Bad
Hotc	Hot Corners	User
hotide	HotIDE	User
hotkey	Solo 5300 Display Driver	User
HotkeyApp	Acer Launch Manager	User
HOTKEYS	Hotkeys	User
Hotkeyz	HotKeyz	User
hotpix	adult dialer	Bad
hotpop	Hotmail Popper	User
HotSync	Palm Inc HotSync Manager	User
HotTray	eFax Messenger Plus	User
hotwerlove	adult dialer	Bad
HoverDesk	HoverDesk	User
hp_finder	HP LogiFinder	User
hpccopy	HP ScanJet Copy Utility	User
hpcdtray	HP CD-DVD/HP CD Writer	User
Hpcron	HP Simple Trax	User
hpdrv	Recovery Monitor	User
HPfkg02/HPfbkg03-	HP DeskJet Printer Driver	User
HPFSched	HP DeskJet Printer Driver	User
HPgS2Wnd/HPgS2Wnf	HP Share-to-Web	Ugly
HPHAxMON	HP Printer Media Card Reader	User
HPHipm07/HPHipm09/HPHipm11 ...HP	PML Driver	User
HPHmon03/HPHMon04/HPHMon05 ..	HP Card Reader	User
hphome.js	hijacker	Bad
hphupd04/hphupd05	HP Photosmart	User
HPI_Monitor	HP Digital Camera	User
HPJETDSC	JetDiscovery	User
HPLamp	HP Scanner Utility	User
hplampc	HP Scanner Lamp	User
Hpmblbwa	HP Scan Button Task	User
hpmdibwx	see hpmblbwa	User
HpmmKbd	HP Keyboard driver	User
HPNRA	HP Network Registry Agent	User
HPObkg01	see HPOjvdix	User
HPObnz08	HP PSC Printer driver	User
HPObrt07	HP COM Device Object	User
HPObrt01	HP Scan Button Monitor	User
hpodev07	HP Device Objects Server	User
hpodib08	HP Scan Button Monitor	User
HPOevm07/HPOevm08	HP Image Editor	User
HPOhmr08	HP All-in-One Printer Driver	User
HPOipm07	HP Photosmart	User
HPOJStart	HP OfficeJet Driver	Ugly
HPOjvdix	HP OfficeJet Software Suite	Ugly
HPOmich	HP OfficeJet Software Suite	Ugly
hpoopm07	HP Port Monitor	User
HPOsol08	HP Multifunction Printer Driver	User
HPOsts07/HPOsts08	HP OfficeJet Status Monitor	User
HPObxo1	see HPOjvdix	User
HPOst01	HP Photo and Imaging	User
HPPDirector	HP LaserJet Director Device Mon	Ugly
HPPPT	HP Parallel Port Test	User
HPPPTA	HP Parallel Port Driver	User

Start Up & Tasks

Program	Description	Good/Bad	Program	Description	Good/Bad
HPPROPTY	HP LaserJet Printer Toolbox	User	idwlog	IDW Logging Tool	User
HPPwrSav	HP Power Save	User	lebool6	Keving McAleavy IECleanAux	User
hpqcmon	HP CamMonitor	User	iebs	trojan and adware	Bad
hpdtrap08	HP Digital Imaging Monitor	User	iedll	hijacker	Bad
HprSnap/HprSnap5	HyperSnap Screen Capture	User	IEDriver	adware	Bad
HPRTRY09	HP 2200C Toolbox	User	IEexplore	SDBOT.H virus	Bad
HPScanFix	HP ScanPatch	User	IEExec	ALADINZ.N virus	Bad
HPSjbmgr	HP ScanJet Background Manager	User	IEfeatures	POPMON.A virus	Bad
HPSJvxd	HP Scan Monitor	User	IEHost	adware	Bad
hpsplmwa	HP ScanPicture	User	iemaximizer	IE New Window Maximizer	User
hpstart.wsf	HP Start	User	ienavigator	IE Navigator 2.0	User
hpsysdrv	Recovery Tracker	User	IEPrivacyKeeper	IE Privacy Keeper	User
hptasks	HP Display Settings	User	iesar	hijacker	Bad
HpTvNow	HP TV Now	User	ietsr	Keving McAleavy IEClean	User
HPW8Tbx	HP DeskJet Printer Toolbox	User	IEWERSV	Winpup	Bad
HPWrIRC	HP Status Window	User	Iexplore	OBLIVION.B virus	Bad
HPWuSchd/HPWuSchd2	HP Windows Updates Scheduler	Ugly	IEXPLORE	LOADCFG or SDBOT viruses	Bad
HPZeng03	HP Printer Driver	User	Iexplore	Backdoor.Apexdoor virus	Bad
HPZipm12	HP Printer Driver	User	iexplore	MS Internet Explorer	User
HPzstatx	HP Printer Status Monitor	Ugly	iexplore	LOADCFG or SDBOT viruses	Bad
Hpztsb01/HPztsb02/HPztsb03/HPztsb04/HPztsb05/HPztsb06/Hpztsb07/HPztsb08/HPztsb09 HP DeskJet Spooling Task		User	iexplore	BOXER virus	Bad
			iexplore	APHEXDOOR virus	Bad
htpatch	SIS AGP Patch	User	iexplore	virus	Bad
https	MOEGA.D virus	Bad	iexplore	KILL.AV.B virus	Bad
Hvid	GEMA virus	Bad	iexplore	downloader trojan	Bad
HWDOCTOR	Windond Hrdwr Mon Prdct Utlity	User	iexplore	EVIVINC virus	Bad
HWINFO*	PUROL virus	Bad	iexplore	LOVGATE viruses	Bad
Hwinst	Gilat Internet Satellite Sys	Good	iexplore	GASLIDE virus	Bad
hxdef	LOVEGATE.R virus	Bad	iexplore	RANDEX.AD virus	Bad
Hxdl	Alset HelpExpress	User	iexplore32	PWSTEAL.ABCHILP virus	Bad
HXDL	spyware	Bad	iexplorer	SPEX or SPEX.B viruses	Bad
HXIUL	Alset HelpExpress	Ugly	iexplorer	parasite	Bad
I_26dadCC	CorelCENTRAL 10	User	iexplorer	LORSIS virus	Bad
i1154n4	BEAGLE viruses	Bad	iexplorer	REUR.B virus	Bad
i386	MYPOWER virus	Bad	iexplorer	CULT.C virus	Bad
I3Explorer	SDBOT.H virus	Bad	iexplorer	CUL virus	Bad
i8kfangui	Graphical Interface	User	IEXPLORER	GAOBOT.AZ virus	Bad
ia99	spyware	Bad	iexplorer0	EVIVNC virus	Bad
iaanotif	Intel IAA Evnt Mon User Notification	User	iexplorer0	THREADSYS virus	Bad
iaas	see IWAR		iexplorera	GAOBOT.AP virus	Bad
IAM	Internet Answering Machine		iexpres	POLDO.B virus	Bad
IAMAPP	Symantec Personal Firewall Engine	User	IFSplash	i-FORCE	User
IAMNET-1	Internet Answering Machine		IGFxTray	Intel Graphics tray	User
IAMSETUP	Internet Answering Machine		iglmtray	TZET virus	Bad
IAMSETUP	see IAMSETUP		ILLC	homepage hijacker	Bad
IAP	Dell OpenManage	User	iL75P2PS	Printer Utility	User
IASHLPR	OPASERV.T virus	Bad	IKEService	PGP	Good
ibackup	Iomega Automatic Backup	User	IKEYMAIN	A4Tech iKey Works	User
IBMBAY2N	IBM Ultra Bay Hot Swap CPL Loader	User	iM_Tray	iM Start Center	User
ibmmessages	IBM Messages	User	IMAGE32	McAfee Image & Restore	User
ibmpmsvc	IBM Power Management	User	imagefox	ImageFox 2.0	User
ibot4	GASTER virus	Bad	Imagemgr32	GEMA virus	Bad
Ibtna	Install Buddy	User	IMAPi	MS Image Mastering API Svc	User
iClean	IE Clean	User	IMApp	IncrediMail	Ugly
iclient	Zone Labs Integrity Client	User	imekrig	Input Method Editor	User
ICLOAD95	Sophos Antivirus Sweep 95	User	Imgicon	Iomega Zip Drive	User
iclogin	IC Login	User	ImgStart	Iomega Zip Drive	User
ICMon	Sophos Antivrs InterChk Actvty Mon	User	IMJPMIG	Input Method Editor	User
ICO	Mouse Suite 98 Daemon	User	imonitor	Remote Update Monitor	User
icon	parasite	Bad	IMonNt	Intel Active Monitor	User
Icon347D1603	MS Winter Fun Wallpaper Changer	User	IMonTray	Intel Active Monitor	User
iconclnt	APC PowerChute Tray Icon	User	ImSchet	MS Input Message Editor	User
ICONDESK	Hides Desktop Icons	User	InCD	Ahead Software InCD	User
iconfc7322861	Connected TaskBar Icon	User	InCDsrv	Ahead Software InCD	User
iconfig	Shuttle Tech USB Device Driver	User	Incinerator.dll	IOLO Tech Sys Mechanic Update	User
IconMgr	colorific.com E-Color	User	IncMail	IncrediMail	User
iconoid	Iconoid	User	incredimail	IncrediMail	User
iconsaver	IconSaver	User	indexcleaner	MRU Blaster	User
icq	ICQ Messaging	User	IndexSearch	ScanSoft PaperPort	User
ICQLite	ICQ Lite	User	INETDG2	Hummingbird Comm Inet Daemon	User
ICQNet	Mirabilis ICQ	User	inetinfo	MS Internet Information Service	User
ICQpro	NETSPY virus	User	inetman	DONK.O virus	Bad
icsdclt.dll	Internet Connection Sharing	User	inetp60.dll	BrowserAid	User
Icserver	Intel Intercast Viewer	User	inetsw95	MS Personal Web Server	User
ICSMGR	MS Internet Sharing Protocol	User	inetwizard	Compaq Internet	User
icw	Internet Call Waiting	User	Info32s	GEMA virus	Bad
ICWConn1	Internet Connection Wizard	User	infus	Adult dialer	Bad
iD_Bank	Rainbow Innovations iD_Bank	User	Infuzer	Troden Development Corp Infuzer	User
iD2CertMover	Handelsbanken iD2 CSP Certificate	User	infwin	parasite	Bad
ID8525	ID8525 virus and hijacker	Bad	INISvc	ANARCH virus	Bad
id85255	ID8525 virus and hijacker	Bad	InkMonitor	Epson Ink Monitor	User
ida	Internet Download Accellerator	User	InkSaver	Strydent Software Ink Saver	User
IDCom	ID Commander	User	InkWatch	Canon In Watch	User
ide	ASSASIN.F virus	Bad	InoRpc	eTrust Antivirus/InoculateIT	User
IDEllbr32	XILON virus	Bad	InoRTRx	eTrust Antivirus/InoculateIT	User
Identify	iDentify	User	InoTask	eTrust Antivirus/InoculateIT	User
idesktop	Immersion TouchWare Desktop	User	insight	Nielson NetRatings	User
idetect	Clasys Ltd INTERNET Turbo	Bad	InstallAnalDemos.js	Install Anal Demos	User
IDETOOL	Via Tech IDETool	User	InstallSpy	InstallSpy	User
idhost	parasite	Bad	InstallStub	Plaxo Update	User
IDMan	Internet Download Manager	User	INSTAN-1	Instant Access	User
			InstantAccess	Xerox Textbridge OCR	Ugly
			InstantDrive	InstantDrive	User
			instantpleasure	adult dialer	Bad
			instantpleasurexxx	adult dialer	Bad
			instapp	HotSync Install Tool Manager	User

Program	Description	Good/Bad
instit.bat	OPASERV.H virus	Bad
INSTIT.BAT	OPASERV.H virus	Bad
Int*****	Adult dialer	Bad
intcp32	RANDEX.UG virus	Bad
Intdel	spyware	Bad
intdel_2	Inet Delivery	Bad
IntelProcNumUtility	Intel Product Number Utility	User
Interdll	spyware	Bad
Internat	MS Multilanguage Support	User
Internat	POINTEX virus	Bad
Internat	MAGICALL virus	Bad
Internetcolor	LightSurf Tech True Internet Color	Bad
Internetfeatures	POPMON.A virus	User
INTERNETFEATURES	POPMON.A virus	Bad
Internrt	PEEPER or CARUFAX.A viruses	Bad
interwarm	Storm Alert InterWARN	User
Intmngr	GEMA virus	Bad
Intreat	W32.HLLW.Doomjuice virus	Bad
intreat	DOOMJUICE virus	Bad
Intreat	LEMIR.E virus	Bad
intspvc	DINFOR.D virus	Bad
Iomon98	PC-Cillin 98	User
Iosdt	IOSDT Trojan virus	Bad
IOWatch	Iomega Watch	User
ip	iProtect You	User
ipclient	monitor and disgnostic tool	Bad
iphider	ICQ Anti-Bomb Software	User
Ipinst	Gilat Internet Satellite Sys	Good
ipmon	RECERV or R3C.B viruses	Bad
ipmon32	Verizon IP Insight Monitor	User
iPodManager	Apple iPod Manager	User
iPodService	Apple iPod Hardware Mngmnt Svc	User
iPodSrv	Apple iPod	User
iPodWatcher	Apple iPod	User
ipsecdialer	Cisco Systems VPN Client	User
IPSecMon	MS L2TP/IPSec VPN Client	User
ipstack	AGOBOT.CS virus	Bad
Iqrobot/Remind	HP Registration Reminder	Ugly
Ir	AutoStart IR	User
ir_ftp	IRFTP virus	Bad
IrelKE	MS L2TP/IPSec VPN Client	User
irmon	MS Infrared Monitor	User
irprops.cpl	Bluetooth Authentification Agent	User
irun	MITGLIEDER.D virus	Bad
irun4	BEAGLE.J virus	Bad
irunjve	MITGLIEDER.F virus	Bad
irwftp	BANCOS.H virus	Bad
is	Micro Logic Info Select	User
isafe	ZoneAlarm Security Suite	User
isass	see LSASS	
isass	OPTIX PRO viruses	Bad
ISATRAY	MS Firewall Client	User
Isdbdc	Compaq Presario Task	User
iservc	FIZZER virus	Bad
Ispdbeg	Service Config	User
ispynow	iSpyNow	User
isrped.vbs	GAGGLE.D virus	Bad
ISS_Srvr	Intel AnyPoint	User
ISStart	Logitech Gallery Repair	User
ISTSvc	Integrated Search Tech IE Toolbar	Bad
Itoishware	toishware	User
ISWizard	Digital Wizard	User
it_cpg-1	InterTrust Quick Start	User
iTIMER	Ratsoft Internet Timer	User
iTimeSync	Internet Time Synchronisation	User
Itk	In The Know	User
itLoad	Praize Messenger	User
iTouch/Commandr	iTouch	User
ItsD7	Its Deductible 7 PopUp	User
ItsDeductible	Its Deductible PopUp	User
iTunesHelper	Apple iTunes Helper	User
IVIVSCHED	InVirsible Scheduler	User
IVPSvMgr	Toshiba IVP Service Manager	Ugly
iw	Internet Washer	User
iw	manages temporary browser files	User
iw	manages temporary browser files	Bad
iwar	Purity Scan	Bad
iWareStart	eWare Startup	User
IWatch	AVM ISDNWatch Monitor	User
IWC9n	NovaStor Instant Write Ctrl Ctr	User
IXApplet	Camio Viewer	User
IzyMail (1)	IzySoft IzyMail Server	User
IzyMail (2)	DigiForal WebMail Gateway Srvr	User
jajc	Just Another Jabber Client	User
jammer	Agnitum Jammer	User
JAMMER2ND	NETSKY.Z virus	Bad
janis.com	POPS virus	Bad
JavaFun	marketing software	Bad
JavaRun	marketing software	Bad
Javaw	Sun Corporation Java	User
Jdbgmgr	Microsoft Debugger Registrar	User
jdbgmrg	DASMIN.A virus	Bad
jdbgmrg	DASMIN.C virus	Bad
Jiffybar	Get Paid While Online	User
JobHisInit	Ricoh Network Printers	User
JogServ2	Jog Dial	User

Program	Description	Good/Bad
JUCheck	Sun Java Update Checker	Ugly
JUSched	Sun Java Runtime Update Scheduler	Ugly
jushed32	parasite	User
jv16t_network	jV16 PowerTools	User
K2ps_full	JUNTADOR.K virus	Bad
K6CPU	Authenticates CPU as K6	User
K9	Launch K9	User
kak.hta	KAKWORM virus	Bad
Kalibump	Kalibump	User
kaspersky	MIMAIL.T virus	Bad
Kasperskyaveng	NETSKY.V virus	Bad
KatMouse	KatMouse	User
kav	Kaspersky Antivirus 5.0	User
kazaa	KaZaA	User
kazaa	parasite	Bad
KazaaFasterDownload	KaZaa Booster	User
kazaalite	Kazaalite	User
Kazza	OPTIXPRO.12C virus	Bad
KBD	Multimedia Keyboard Manager	User
KbdTray	Logitech Keyboard Driver	User
KBOOST	Typing Satellite	User
kcpgek	Compaq Easy Access	User
Keenvalue	spyware	Bad
KEM	Logitech SetPoint	User
KEMailKb	Internet Access Keyboard	User
Kem32	BADTRANS virus	Bad
kern32	BADTRANS.A virus	Bad
Kem32/Kernel32/Krnl32	BADTRANS virus	Bad
kernel.com	OPTIXPRO.12 virus	Bad
kernel.dll	NETDEVIL.8 virus	Bad
Kernel.dll	REDLOF.M virus	Bad
kernel.dll	viruses such as BABYLNOIA	Bad
kernel32	KICKIN.A virus	Bad
kernel32	TENDOOLT virus	Bad
kernel32.com	ESTRELLA virus	Bad
kernel32.dll	NETDEVIL.15 virus	Bad
kernel32.dll	Microsoft Windows	Good
kernel32.pif	MOKS virus	Bad
kernel32.win	GAGGLE.D virus	Bad
Kernell.dll	DESTINY virus	Bad
Kernelw32	INDOR.E virus	Bad
keyacc32	Keyserver KeyAccess	Good
KeybdMgr	Netropa Hotkeys	User
KeyCount	Key Count	User
Keyhost	hijacker	User
keylogger	spyware	Bad
KeyMan	Cherry Key Manager	User
KeyMap	Kesmai Keymap	User
Keymgr	DONK.M virus	Bad
Keynote	Keynote	User
KeyPatrol	Key Patrol	User
KEYSTATE	Toshiba Key State	User
KeyText	MJMSoft Design Key Text 2000	User
KeyTickk	Key Tick	User
keyword	hijacker	Bad
kgzgjkpcw	SDBOT.T virus	Bad
KHooker	SiS Keyboard Daemon	User
KHost	KonTiki Secure Delivery Plug In	User
KICKMON	KeepItClean	User
Killer	Innovative Tech Popup Killer	User
KillProcess	KillProcess	User
Kinberlink	Kinberlink	User
kirbyalarm	Kirby Alarm	User
KlipFolio	Klip Folio	User
kmaestro	Key Maestro	User
k-mania	Kleptomania	User
kmw_run	Kensingron MouseWorks	User
kmw_show	Kensington MouseWorks	User
kn0x	HOBBIT.F virus	Bad
knowbase	Know Base	User
KodakCCS	Kodak DC File Sys Driver	User
KonniSymbol	Konni Symbol Autostart	User
kontiki	Kontiki Delivery Manager	User
kpp	Kazaa Lite	User
Krnl32	W32.HLLW.Epon@mm virus	Bad
krnl32	EPON virus	User
Krnlmod	Keylogger	User
KWallet	Key Wallet	User
komixer	kX Audio Driver	User
KYEScan	Genius Kyescan scanner	User
L3tx	W32.Dizamu.Y@mm virus	Bad
l32x	DUMARU viruses	Bad
Lamapp - N/A	see lamapp	Ugly
LanLight	LanLight	User
LanNSvc	RANDEX.AAS virus	Bad
Lans32w	LANSource WinPort	Ugly
LanSpeed2	LanSpeed2	User
LinTalk	LinTalk	User
LASOAds	ZeroAds	User
lastchance	LastChance	User
LASTinst	Gilat Internet Satellite Sys	Good
lasvr32	FEMOT.D virus	Bad
launch	Traceless 2003	User
Launch	MailScan Dispatcher	Good
LAUNCH32	SMS Application Launcher	User
LaunchAp	Acer Launch Manager	User

Program	Description	Good/Bad	Program	Description	Good/Bad
Launcher	Webshots	User	LSPmonitor	foistware	Bad
launcher	spyware	Bad	LSPmonitor	foistware	Bad
LaunchPD	ATI Tech Multimedia Ctr Launch Pad	User	LSvr	foistware	Bad
Lconfig - N/A	see config	Ugly	LTCM000C	Xircom PCI 56K Modem Driver	User
Lcl	parasite	Bad	LTDaemon	Lucent Chipset Modem	User
LDMConf	Logitech Desktop Messenger	Ugly	LTDMgr	foistware	Bad
LEDTRAY	LED Tray	User	Lt.moh	Modem On Hold	User
LeechGet	see leechget	User	ltmsg	LT WinModem	User
Leerlaufprozess - N/A	German MS System Idle Process	User	Ltsmrmsg	Lucent Softmodem Mssging Applet	User
LetsSearch	foistware	Bad	Ltsstart	Lotus QuickStart 97	Ugly
LetterBox	LetterBox 4.3.4	User	LuComServer/Lucoms~1	LiveUpdate Engine COM Module	User
lexbac	DOWNLOAD virus	Bad	Lvcomsr	Logitech QuickCam Lunar Almanack	User
Lexbces	SODABOT virus	User	Lvcmic	Logitech QuickCam Camera Driver	User
LexMVS	Lexmark MarkVision Server	User	LwbWheel/MOUSE32A	IBM Mouse Suite	User
LEXPLORE	Lexmark Printer Port Scanner	User	LWernon/lwtest	Wingman Profiler Joystick	User
Lexpps	Lexmark Printer Port Scanner	User	LWPEvntM	Wingman Profiler Evnt Mngr	User
LexStart	Lexmark Printer Driver	Ugly	lxbabmgr	Lexmark Scan and Fax	User
LFCK	Connection Keeper	User	LXbbbmgr	Lexmark X74/X75 Button Manager	User
lfsndnmng	LightningFAX Enterprise Fax Srvr	User	LXBBbMon	Lexmark X74/X75 Button Monitor	User
Lgrpsp32	REDIST.O virus	User	LXDBOXCP	Lexmark DOS-Printing Control	User
lgwakeup	Logitech Wakeup	User	lxmstart	virus	Bad
libupdate	BIONET viruses	Bad	LxSupMon	Lexmark Status Update Monitor	User
libupdate32	BIONET.405 virus	Bad	m1mmpti	Mpact Mediaware	User
libupdte	BIONET.316 virus	Bad	m3tray	Movielink	User
Lights	MS Modem Monitor Applet	User	MacExp	MacroExpress	User
li-multi****	Adult dialer	Bad	MacLic	DataVIz Conversions Plus	User
LineSpeedMeter	Line Speed Meter v3.0	User	MacName	DataVIz Conversions Plus	User
Linksts	Ascecom ISDN Modem Card DriverUgly	Ugly	Macros	Gui Macro magic	User
linksts	tray icon	User	MAD	MS System Attendant Service	User
Linux.vbs	LOVELETTER.AS virus	Bad	Magic	Magic Mail Monitor	User
ListProAlarms	List Pro Alarms	User	MAGICDSK	Magic DeskTop	User
li-thund****	Adult dialer	Bad	MagicKRD	Samsung MagicKeyboard Utility	User
LIU/Rubicon	Logitech Internet Update	User	MagicKey	Enable Belkin Wireless Keyboard	User
LiveJournal/U	LiveJournal	User	Magtime	Magtime	User
Livenote	Asus LiveNote	User	MagnifyingGlass	Magnifying Glass	User
LiveUpdate	Openwares LiveUpdate	User	Mail_Check	PANOIL.C virus	Bad
li-vita****	Adult dialer	Bad	mailbell	MailBell	User
Llass	INOR-A virus	User	maildefense	MailDefense	User
Llsched	LapLink Scheduler	User	MAILMA	Mailmoa	User
LMGICON	see imgicon	Ugly	mailshield	Lyris MailShield Desktop	User
lmgui	Murphy Shield	User	MAILWA~1	MailWasher	User
LMonitor	Live Monitor	User	MailWasher	MailWasher Pro	User
lms2cenu	SECONDTHOUGHT virus	Bad	MAIN	SypCop ScanCheck	User
LMSTATUS	Lexmark Status Monitor	User	Main	SuperCool Compress Backup	User
Lmsxxe	Xerox XE8 LM Status	User	Maja	W32.Netsky.H@mm virus	Bad
ln32h.dll	parasite	Bad	maja	NETSKY.H virus	User
lnchbrd	Darwin LaunchBoard	User	Manage	see WINSERVN	User
LnchMate	LaunchMate	User	manage	adware	Bad
load win64.drv	parasite	Bad	Manager	Task Manager	User
load32	NIBU, DUMAU viruses	Bad	mapicon	ADSL Diagnostic Tools	User
loadcfg32	LOADCFG or SDBOT virus	Bad	MAPISp32	Win Messaging Subsys Spooling	User
loaded	Adult dialer	Bad	max	spyware	Bad
Loader	Clearsearch, IGetNet	Bad	MBM4	Motherboard Monitor 4	User
loader	hijacker	Bad	MBM5	Motherboard Monitor 5	User
LoadPoints.vbs	hijacker	Bad	mboxverfy	Mailbox Verifier	User
loadtp	SmartStuff Fool Proof Loader	User	mbrprobe	MBProbe	User
loadkk	KeyKey.com KK Loader	User	MC	Kittyfeet MouseCount	User
LoadQM	MSN Queue Manager	Ugly	McAgent	McAfee Agent	User
LOADWB	Stardock Load Windows Blinds	User	MCamBoot	Vista Imaging MultiCAM Initializer	User
LoadWC	MS Load WebCheck	User	mcat	parasite	Bad
LoadWC	MS BrowserWebCheck	User	MChanger	Media Changer	User
Locator	Remote Procedure Call Locator	User	MCL	Command Line Utility	User
Logi_MWX	Logitech MouseWare	User	MCMNHDLR	Security Ctr & VirusScan Online	User
Logi_MwX	Logitech Utility	User	MCP****	ASOXY virus	Bad
Logitech.Pen.Traylcon	Logitech Personal Digital Pen	User	mcpserver	Stardock Master Control	User
LogiTray	Logitech Image Studio Tray	User	McShield	McAfee OnAccess Scanner	User
logon	hijacker	Bad	Mcstvbi	McAfee VirusScan Console	User
logonmonitor.vbs	Network Drive Map	User	McUpdate	McAfee VirusScan AutoUpdate	User
logonstudio	WinCustomize LogonStudio	User	mcursrt	McAfee Security Center	User
Logviewer	Linksys Router Access Logs	Ugly	MCVSEscan	McAfee VirusScan Email Scan	Ugly
Logwatch95/Logwatt	Computer Associates Fixer	User	MCVSFTSN	McAfee VirusScan Online	User
lockinstop	Lock 'n Stop Personal Firewall	User	MCVSFTE	McAfee VirusScan	User
lookupsys	trojan	Bad	McVSShld	McAfee ActiveShield	User
lopsearch	lop.com	Bad	MCW	Monitor Calibration Wizard	User
Lorena	MAPSON.C virus	Bad	md	Adult dialer	Bad
lover.vbe	ZSYANG.B virus	Bad	md	hijacker	Bad
Lpr123	password stealer trojan	Bad	MDM	MS Machine Debug Manager	User
Ls	hijacker and dialer	Bad	Mdm.vbs	WHITEHO or TRAPPY viruses	User
LS3EXEC	LanSafe III Executive	User	MDShetPe	Aztech Modem Icon	User
lsas	COM+ System Applications	User	mdmsetup	Aztech Modem Driver	User
lsass	Windows Explorer	User	MDTools	MD Tool	User
lsass	RATSU.B virus	Bad	Meca	FLDMEDIA-A virus	Bad
lsass	RANDEX.ATR virus	Bad	media	FLDMEDIA-A virus	Bad
LSASS	NIMOS virus	User	Media Player	HAWAWI virus	User
Lsass (1)	Local Security Authentication Srvr	Good	media_driver	TIEG virus	User
Lsass (2)	W32.Sasser.E Worm virus	Bad	MEDIACTR	KBD MediaCenter	User
lsasssa	CIADOR.122 virus	Bad	MediaDet	Creative Labs Disc Detector	Ugly
lsasss	W32.Sasser.E Worm virus	Bad	MediaKey	MediaKey	User

Program	Description	Good/Bad	Program	Description	Good/Bad
Mediam~1	Media Monitor	User	More log	adware	Bad
mediaman	foistware	Bad	morfitwebentrance	homepage hijacker	Bad
members-area	Adult dialer	User	morpheus	Morpheus MusicCity Network	User
MemCheck	V_Comm Mijenix Fix-It Utilities	User	MOSearch	Microsoft Office XP Fast Search	Ugly
memoptimizer	TuneUp Memory Optimizer	User	mosearch	creates caching of Office files	Bad
memore	KILLAV.C virus	Bad	MoStat	Wurld Media spyware	Bad
Memory32	UEN Software PassMan	User	MotiveSB	Motive SmartBridge sys tray	Ugly
MemoryMeter	spyware	Bad	Motmon	Dell Resolution Assistant, Motive	User
memturbo	MemTurbo	User	Mouse32A	Azona Mouse 32A	User
MenuSnap	Rietta Solutions MenuSnap	User	mouseinfo	Microsoft Mouse information	User
mercury	David Harris Mercury	User	mousetips	Tips, mouse	User
messageblock	Message Blocker	User	MovieNetworks	Adult dialer, 900 phone number	Bad
messenger	KUTEX virus	Bad	Movieplace	malware	Bad
messenger	trojan virus	Bad	Mozilla	Mozilla Web browser	User
metalrock	TASTYFED virus	Bad	MP3Dancer	Animated dancer on desktop	User
mexplore	YAHA.AE virus	Bad	mp3serch	executable version	Bad
mfin32	adware	Bad	mpbtn	AT&T Motive SmartBridge	User
MFindexer/MFINDE-1	CorelMedia Folders Indexer	User	mpf	McAfee Personal Firewall	Good
MFNTCTL	MightyFAX Controller	User	MPFAgent	McAfee Personal Firewall	Good
Mgabg	Matrox BIOS Guard	User	MpfTray	McAfee Personal Firewall	Good
mgactrl	Matrox Control Center	User	MPFTray/mpf	McAfee Personal Firewall	Good
mgadiag	Matrox Diagnostic	User	MPGSRV32	LITMUS virus	Bad
mgagdesk	Matrox QuickDesk	User	mpisvc	MIPSV virus	Bad
mgasetup	MGA CD Install	User	Mplayer	HOLAR.C virus	Bad
mgavrtcl	McAfee VirusScan Online	Good	Mplayer	HOLAR.C virus	Bad
mgavrtc/mgavrtb	McAfee VirusScan Online	User	MplSetup	Ricoh network printers	User
mgavrtb	McAfee VirusScan Online	Good	mpm	Mypring Mileage, battery stat	User
MGUI	BullGuard AntiVirus	User	MPower	MindBead Mpower free up RAM	User
mhdogst	virus	Bad	MPREXE	MS Multiple Provider Router	Good
MHINT	Cybermedia Link Sweep	Bad	MPREXE	OPASERV.T virus	Bad
MI-HOTKEY/MK9805	Internet Keyboards	User	MpHTML	VAGRNROCKER virus	Bad
MHPRMINF	Microsoft Greetings Reminder	User	mprmmon	Chromatic Research MPact2	User
MicroLog	MICROLOG.A virus	Bad	MPSERVER	MultiPASS Background	User
microsoft	GAOBOT.JB virus	Bad	MPService	Canon MultiPass Service	User
Microsoft	GAOBOT.AFJ virus	Bad	mptask	LALA or DOWNLOADER.DBN.B or AOT	
microsoft420	MENACE.B virus	Bad		viruses	Bad
microsoftscanreg	FRAMRIV.A virus	Bad	MPTBox	Canon MultiPass Toolbar	Ugly
Migrate.dll	Microsoft RUNDLL32	Good	mptcloaxs	RANDEX.CT virus	Bad
MimpHost	MouseImp Pro	User	mqbkup	OPASERV.K virus	Bad
MINIBUG	displays ads inside Weatherbug	Bad	mqbkup	OPASERV.K virus	Bad
MINIFERT	Backweb	Bad	mrowyekdc	GOTORM virus	Bad
Minilog	Zone Alarm Internet Firewall	User	mrtalk	Media Ring Talk	User
MININOTE	Fookes Software Mini Note Tab	User	MRTMsg	Intuit Maint Release Task Mgr	Ugly
minitb2	Netopia Inc Timbuktu Pro	User	mrublaster	MRU-Blaster Silent Clean	User
Mini-XP	Minimizer XP	User	MS SPOOL32	ASASSIN virus	Bad
miranda32	Miranda IM	User	ms32sys	virus	Bad
MIRC32	SPYBUZZ virus	Bad	ms7531	homepage hijacker	Bad
misitray	miroVIDEO Tray Tool	User	MSA****.TMP	homepage hijacker	Bad
Mixer	C-Media Mixer	Ugly	msagent	NEGASMS.A virus	Bad
mixghost	Mac Ghost	User	msapp	RSBOT virus	Bad
MK	MemoKit	User	mster	RETSAM virus	Bad
MK9805	see C-HotKey	User	mswindows	GAOBOT.AFJ virus	Bad
mlfbuddy	Matador	User	MSBB	180Solutions.com	Bad
MM_Server	MusicMatch Jukebox	User	msbb	spyware	Bad
Mm_Tray	MusicMatch Jukebox	User	Msblast	BLASTER virus	Bad
Mmaker	IRCBOT.C virus	Bad	msblast	BLASTER.B virus	Bad
MMC	Microsoft Management Console	Good	MSBNTray	MS Broadband Network Utility	User
Mmext	MinMax Extender	User	mscache	spyware	Bad
mmhid.dll	Human Interface Device Server	User	mscon32	PALYH.A virus	Bad
MMHotKey	Turbo-Media Multimedia Keyboard	User	mscedit32	SDBOT.P virus	Bad
MMKbd	Samsung Internet Keyboard	User	mschost	BLASTER.K virus	Bad
MMKeybd	One-Touch Multimedia Keyboard	User	Mscifapp	McAfee Privacy Service	User
MMManager	SunClock5	User	Msckin	Odyssess Mktg ClientMan	User
MMod	EZula	Bad	msclman	Odyssess Marketing	User
mmod	spyware/theftware	Bad	msclwan	spyware/malware	Bad
mmod	spyware/theftware	Bad	mscman	spyware/malware	Bad
mmtask	MusicMatch Jukebox	User	mscman	spyware/malware	Bad
Mmtask	adware	Bad	mscn	SafeChildNet	User
MMTASK	BACKDAT.A virus	Bad	mscrl	Adult dialer	Bad
MMTask.tsk	Microsoft multimedia	User	mscom32.com	BEASTY.H virus	Bad
MMTray	Morgan MultimediaMJPEG Codec	User	mscommand	KWBOT.P virus	Bad
MMTray2K	Morgan MultimediaMJPEG Codec	User	MSCONFG32	OPTIX.04.C virus	Bad
MMTrayLSI	Morgan MultimediaMJPEG Codec	User	mscvb32	OPTIX.04.C virus	Bad
MMUSBKB2	Netropa USB keyboard	User	mscvrt32	virus	Bad
mmx	ANALOGX virus	Bad	MSCVT	W32.HLLW.Slideshow virus	Bad
MndlSvr	Goldensoft CD Ghost	User	MSCVT	SLIDESHOW virus	Bad
MNMSrvc	Microsoft NetMeeting Remote	User	msdc32	Zebus	User
mngol	Adult dialer	Bad	msdm	MULDROP.352 virus	Bad
mnsvc	AUTOUPDER virus	Bad	msdm	spam relayer	Bad
mnsvcsp	virus	Bad	msdmxm	Adult dialer	Bad
mnyexpr	Microsoft Money Agent	User	msdos	adult content downloader	Bad
MobSync	Microsoft Synchronization Mgr	User	msdos	RECORY virus	Bad
mobsync32	FINERO virus	Bad	msdos423	MENACE.A virus	Bad
moffice	Logitec Typhoon Office mouse	User	msdos98	PWSEAL virus	Bad
MOH	NetWaiting Modem on Hold	User	mse	SOLAME.A virus	Bad
mon	Panasonic iPalm downloader	User	MsDTC/MsDTCw	MS Distributed Transaction Coord	User
moneyexpress	Microsoft Money Express	User			
monitor	Encompass Monitor	User			
Monitor	Scansoft Pagis Scheduler	User			
monitorbk	Belkin PCMCIA Monitor	User			
Monitormgt	GEMA virus	Bad			
Monserv	Alps USB Server	Good			
Mornwow	Norton CleanSweep	User			
moon	Moon Phase	User			
mope.scr	SINALA virus	Bad			
mopt	Memory Optimizer	User			

Start Up & Tasks

Program	Description	Good/Bad	Program	Description	Good/Bad
Msemu32	spyware/adware/hijacker	Bad	mssql32	RANDEX.AX virus	Bad
Msfind	parasite	Bad	msstart	LIVUP.C virus	Bad
MSFind32	W32.HLLW.Cayam@mm virus	Bad	MSStat	Memory Stick Monitor	User
msfind32	CAYAM virus	Bad	mssurfer	parasite	Bad
MSFramer	DOWNLOADER-BS virus	Bad	mssurfer	parasite	Bad
MSFramer	RANDEX.OL virus	Bad	Mssvc	Stealthdisk	User
Msg32	Nemesys Music	User	mssvc32	virus	Bad
msgdmf	parasite	Bad	mssvc	Microsoft Sound Volume Tool	User
MsgLoop	Crystal	Ugly	mssvr	toolbar	Bad
Msg32	KRYPGHOS virus	Bad	mssys	MYSS.B virus	Bad
MsgPlus	Microsoft Messenger Plus!	User	mssys	VANTA.A virus	Bad
MsgPlus!.dll	Microsoft Check Message Plus	User	Mstapi	trojan	Bad
Msgran	GRAMOS virus	Bad	mstask	OPASERV.N virus	Bad
Msgsrv16	DELF family of viruses	Bad	mstask32	YAHA.P virus	Bad
msgsrv32	Windows 32-bit VxD Msg Svr	Good	MSTasks	parasite	Bad
MSGSRV32	LITMUS virus	Bad	MSTasks	LOADCFG or SDBOT viruses	Bad
Msgsrv32 (1)	MS Windows 32-bit Msg Server	Good	MSTAT	Sony Memory Stick Monitor	User
Msgsrv32 (2)	W32.HLLW.Deadhat.B virus	Bad	MSTrig32	TANG virus	Bad
MSGSRV32	LITMUS virus	Bad	Mstray	WILKILL.A virus	Bad
msgsrv32	DEADHAT.B virus	Bad	msupdat	YAHA.AA virus	Bad
Msgsys	Intel LANDesk Mgmt Suite	User	msupdate	parasite related	Bad
MSGTAGStatus	MSGtag	User	msuser32	ANDROV virus	Bad
MSHT@	MAGISTR.A virus	Bad	msvc32	parasite variant	Bad
MSHTA	MS HTML Application Host	User	Msvchost	Trojan.Xombe/Downloader-GJ virus	Bad
Mshta ...filename.hta	Adult dialer	User	msvchost	XOMBE virus	Bad
msHtml	PESTDOOR.31 virus	Bad	msvcrmn32	Movielink	User
MSIExec	Microsoft Windows Installer	User	MSVXD	DATOM.A virus	Bad
msiexec16	OPTIX PRO family of viruses	Bad	mswavedll	CRYPTER-C virus	Bad
Msimn	MS Outlook Express 5/6	User	MSWheel	MS IntelliPoint/IntelliMouse	User
msinet	Cyber Patrol FitProcess	User	mswin	DUMBA virus	Bad
Msinfo	CoolWebSearch.com	Bad	MSWin32bck	GAOBOT.AA virus	Bad
MSinfo	Backdoor.IRC.Aladinz.M virus	Bad	Mswincfg32	CYBERSPY virus	Bad
msinfo	ALADINZ.M virus	Bad	Mswkwrh	Hacktool.Anavol virus	Bad
Msinit	BYMER virus	Bad	Msxpw	CITOR virus	Bad
MSInstall61	KWBOT.B virus	Bad	msynvr.com	BEASTY.G virus	Bad
msite18	adult content dialer	Bad	msys	parasite	Bad
msiwin64	GAOBOT.AFJ virus	Bad	msystem	adult content dialer	Bad
msjclh.com	PLUX virus	Bad	MtdAcq	Media Sniffer	User
MSKernel32.vbs	LOVELETTER virus	Bad	mtr2	KRYPTONIC GHOST virus	Bad
MSKSrvr	McAfee Spam Killer	User	mtv	Mood Logic TV	User
mslagent	SIMCUSS.B virus	Bad	mtx	MTX virus	Bad
mslat	LATINUS.SVR virus	Bad	muamger	Impact MicroAngelo On Display	User
mslaugh	BLASTER.E virus	Bad	Muamgr	Impact MicroAngelo 5.X	Ugly
msldr.com	virus	Bad	MultiMon	MultiMon	User
Mslg32	REDZED virus	Bad	MultiRes	MultiRes	User
msload	OPASERV.T virus	Bad	mum	Internode Usage	User
msload32	OBLIVION virus	Bad	MUPS	Belkin Bulldog Plus Service	User
msload32	OBLIVION virus	Bad	mugbme	Uptime	User
mslogon	parasite	Bad	Music01Server	J River Media Jukebox	User
mslogon	parasite	Bad	Musicr4.71	W32.Randex.Q virus	Bad
msmc	parasite variant	Bad	musirc4.71	RANDEX.Q virus	Bad
msmgr32	YAHA.AF virus	Bad	mwd	GRAPS virus	Bad
msmhn	adware/hijacker	Bad	mwincfg32	AGOBOT.BD virus	Bad
msmn	parasite variant	Bad	MWSnap	MWSnap	User
msmngr32	RANDON-R virus	Bad	MWSoemon	Email Plugin Outlook Express & IE	User
MSMGS	Backdoor.Freefors virus	Bad	mwsoemon	malware	Bad
msmgs	FREEFORS virus	Bad	mwsoemon	malware	Bad
MSMsgr	WinXP & MSN Messenger	User	mwsvm	search hijacker	Bad
MSMSGR	GAOBOT.BB virus	Bad	mwsvm	search hijacker	Bad
msmsgri32	RANDEX.D virus	Bad	MxHLp32	VAGRNOCKER virus	Bad
msmsgri32	RANDEX.D/ROXY family viruses	Bad	MXOaldr	Maxtor OneTouch Auto Loader	User
Msmsgs	MSN Messenger Service	User	MxRunner	Aladdin Systems	User
msnarrator	NARAT.A virus	Bad	mxtd	adult content dialer	Bad
msncncr	virus	Bad	MXTask	V Comm Mijenix Fit-It Utilities	Good
Msndc	MSN Quick View	User	matask	Ontrack Fix-It Utilities	Good
msnet	W32.Mockbot.a.Worm virus	Bad	myagtsvc	McAfee MyCIO Agent Service	User
msnet	SDBOT virus	Bad	MyAgtTry	McAfee VirusScan ASaP	User
msnet	MOCKBOT.A virus	Bad	MYCOME-1	adware	Bad
msnet	BOA virus	Bad	myfastupdate	My-Fast-Access	User
msngrblock	PATOO virus	Bad	MyFolders	My Folders	User
MSNIASVC	MSN Internet Access	User	MyPrivacy	OmniQuad My Privacy	User
msnmon	Microsoft BitDefender	User	mySB	My Start Button	User
MsnMsgr	MSN Messenger	User	MyTekSystray	MyTek System Tray	User
MSNService	CARPET.V virus	Bad	nabv32	TITOG.C virus	Bad
MSNShell	MSN Messenger	User	nad-	MetaProducts Net Activity Diagram viewer	User
msnv32	RANDEX.F virus	Bad	NADAEMON	NetActive NA Daemon	User
MSNVE	MSN Video Enhanced	User	NAG	iChoose	User
MSObject32.js	PUN virus	Bad	nagger	ePolicy Orchestrator Agent	User
MSOffice	Microsoft Office Toolbar	User	Naimag32/Naimas32	McAfee ePolicy Orchestrator	User
msoffice.hta	hijacker	Bad	NAS	ANTILAM.20.Q virus	Bad
msongn	parasite variant	Bad	Natal!.pif	OPASERV.AE virus	Bad
MSOOBD	MAGISTR.A virus	Bad	Natal.scr	OPASERV.AE virus	Bad
msosa	adult content dialer	Bad	natspeak	Dragon Naturally Speaking	User
MsPMSPSv	MS Win Media Device Mgr	User	NaturalColorLoad	Samsung Natural Color Load	User
MSprotect	DABYREV virus	Bad	NavAgent32	virus	Bad
Msrc	KRYPTONIC GHOST virus	Bad	NAVAPSvc	Norton Auto-Protect Service	User
MSREGE	ZINX virus	Bad	Navapw32 (1)	Norton Auto-Protect Service	User
msruncx32	SKUS virus	Bad	Navapw32 (2)	W32.JooA@mm virus	Bad
mss	malware	Bad	Navautoupdate	virus	Bad
MSSearch	Microsoft Search Service	User	NAVRPOWSER	Corel Reminder	User
msserv	HYD virus	Bad	naviscope	Naviscope	User
mssgs	trojan virus	Bad	NavPass	adult content dialer	Bad
MSSHVC	NUFFY.A virus	Bad	navpmc	trojan variant	Bad
msslut32	SLUTER-A virus	Bad	NAVSVC	virus	Bad
mssmgrd	SDBOT.JT virus	Bad	NBJ	Schedule Backup Program	User
Mssql	SDBOT virus	Bad	NbkCtrl	NovaSTOR Backup	User

Program	Description	Good/Bad	Program	Description	Good/Bad
ncd	Norton Change Directory	User	Nprotect	Symantec Norton Utilities	User
NCDialer	NetCruiser Dialer	User	nrcheck	virus	Bad
NclConf	Nokia Connection Monitor	User	Nrpr	NetRatings	Bad
nclip	Network Clipboard	User	nrpr	spyware	Bad
NCLTray	Nokia Connectivity Library	User	NSCHECK	spyware	Bad
ncoeenv	NuTCracker Setup Environment	User	Nsched32	Norton Program Scheduler	User
Ndd32	Symantec Norton Disk Doctor	User	nscntrl	adult content dialer	Bad
NDetect	Symantec NetDetect	User	nsdlua	adult content dialer	Bad
necmfk	NEC wireless keyboard driver	Good	Nsengine	NovaSTOR Backup	User
neo	Half.com Price Patrol	User	Nsl	AnalogX NetStat Live	User
NeroCheck	Ahead Nero CD Burning	User	NSPPTHLP	NetShow PowerPoint Helper	User
Net2fone	Net2Phone	User	nsrvnt	NERTE virus	Bad
NetAccel	NetAccelerator	User	nssys32	virus	Bad
NETADM7	BANCOS.F virus	Bad	nstask32	RANDEX.E virus	Bad
Netapi	NETDEVIL.14 virus	Bad	nstrue	RANDEX.E virus	Bad
Netapi	NETDEVIL.14 virus	Bad	NSupdate	adult content dialer	Bad
netchk	Netline	User	nsvif	adult content dialer	Bad
netconfig	NETCONF virus	Bad	NTCmd	SBPPT.D virus	Bad
Netd32	SOBOT.R virus	Bad	ntdll	BIONET.404 virus	Bad
NETD32	RANDEX.F virus	Bad	NTFSCLUP	ConfigSafe	User
netd32	RANDEX.F virus	Bad	nthost	virus	Bad
NetDDE	MS Dynamic Data Exchange	User	ntkml	CERVIVEC.A virus	Bad
netdet	Internet Usage Monitor	User	ntkrnlpt	NT Kernal Patch	User
NetDevSW	Toshiba NetWork Device Switch	User	NTOSA32	W32.HLLW.Anig virus	Bad
Netisp32.vbs	REDIST.C virus	Bad	NTOSA32	ANIG virus	Bad
Netlimiter	NetLimiter	User	ntrtc	Dell Non Standard Applications	User
netlink32	GAOBOT.WO virus	Bad	NtsAgent	EasySync Pro	User
NetMeeting	LOVEGATE.R virus	Bad	ntspcv	SDBOT.S virus	Bad
NetMeter	NetMeter	User	ntss	BESTPICS.A virus	Bad
NetMeter	spyware	Bad	NTVDM	MS WinNT Virtual DOS Machine	User
NetMon	W32.Mimail.M@mm virus	Bad	ntvdscm	TR/SCKEYLOG.SPY.20 virus	Bad
netmon	MIMAIL.M virus	Bad	Nuria	Nuria	User
NetPerSec	NetPerSec	User	NvCpl.dll	Nvidia Ctrl Panel Display Properties	User
Netropa	spyware	Bad	nvd32	parasite	Bad
NetRun	NetRun	User	Nvid32	GEMA virus	Bad
NETSCAPE	Netscape Messenger	User	Nvidex32	GEMA virus	Bad
Netscp	Netscape 7.x & 7.x Quick Launch	User	nvidia32	parasite variant	Bad
Netscp6	Netscape 6	User	nview.dll	NView	User
NETSERV	NETCONTROL virus	Bad	NVmax	Nvmax	User
netsvr	Optimum Online	User	NvMCTray.dll	Nvidia Media Center Library	User
NETSVC	GAOBOT/AGOBOT virus	Bad	NvMixerTray	Nvidia Sound Mixer	User
NETSWLL	NetSwitcher Tray Application	User	nvsvc	GAOBOT/AGOBOT virus	Bad
NETSWT-1	NetSwitcher Tray Application	User	NVSvc/NVSvc32	Nvidia Driver Helper Service	Ugly
NETTIME	NetTime	User	nwant33	Netword Agent	Bad
netturbo	ShareareOnline.com NetTurbo	User	nwclient	My Net Watchman	User
netwaiting	NetWaiting	User	NWDHCPOptions	Novell DHCP Patch Svc v4.81	User
netwatch	MIMAIL.C virus	Bad	nwiz	GAOBOT.ZX OR GABOT.ADV viruses	Bad
NetWatch (1)	Microsoft Net Watcher	User	Nwiz (1)	Nvidia nView Wizard	User
NetWatch (2)	W32.Mimail.C@mm virus	Bad	Nwiz (2)	W32.Gaobox.ZX virus	Bad
NetworkClient	LEMUR virus	Bad	nwiz /install	Nvidia nView Wizard	User
NeuroMedia	freeware	User	Nwpopup	Novell Netware	User
NEWDOT1.dll/NEWDOT-.2.dll ... NewDotNet		User	Nwrecmsg	Novell Broadcast Msg Handler	User
NEWSALRT	MSNBC news alert	User	NWTray	Novell system tray icon	User
newsgroup	RAPIDBLASTER parasite	Bad	nxdlghlp	Novatel Xplr Plus Dialog Tracker	User
NewsProxy	News Proxy	User	NZFProp	Netzip zip & unzip utility	User
NewsUpdNewsUpdate	Creative Labs News Update	Ugly	oahstifr	HyperText Studio	User
NewtKnow ...NewtnUpd.dll, runkey ... hijacker		Bad	OAKSTART	Speeds for timeout and startup	User
NF	Never Forget 2.0	User	OAKTASK	CD-RW taskbar	User
NHKSrv	Netropa Hotkey Server	User	Oato	see IWAR	Bad
NICTT	Wireless PCMCIA Adapter Driver	User	ObjectDock	Stardock Object Dock	User
niPCApp	CostAware	User	OCAudioini	One-click Audio Converter	User
nikLaus	NIKLAS virus	Bad	ocbtray	OWC Cardbus Tray	User
NILauncher	Net-It Launcher	User	OCRAware/OCRAwr32	Caere OmniPage OCR Aware	User
Ninit	Norton Uninstall Delux	User	OCTray32	CyberMedia/Ntwk Assoc Oil Chg	User
NISServer	Norton Internet Security Service	User	ocx32	ASTEF or RESPAN virus	Bad
nistime-32bit	clock synchronizer	User	ocxdll	virus	Bad
NISUM	Norton Internet Security Stats	User	od-matroxx	Adult dialer	Bad
NJG40	PWStead Bancos.D virus	Bad	od-stndxx	adult dialer	Bad
NJG40	BANCOS.D virus	Bad	od-teenxx	adult dialer	Bad
Njgal	KILO virus	Bad	Oecm	see IWAR	Bad
NKvMon	Nikon Monitor	User	Oeet	see IWAR	Bad
NkVwMon	Nikon View Monitor	User	Oeloader	foistware	User
NMCL32	Novell Messenger	User	OEMonitor	Neuro Speech	User
Nmonitor	Novell WIN2NCS	User	oemreset	OEM Cleanup	User
NMISSvc	Intel Network Mgmt Station Svc	User	offers	spyware	Bad
nmSvc	Covenant Eyes	User	ogrc	Kaspersky Labs Office Guard	User
nnloader	Norton Navigator Loader	User	Ohdd	see IWAR	Bad
nnsvc	NetNanny	User	ohttpd	Omnicron OmniHTTPd	User
NoAds	NoAds	User	Olehelp	parasite variant	Bad
nod32com	Eset NOD32	User	olehelp	BOOKMARKER family of viruses	Bad
Nod32krn	Nod32 Antivirus Version 2	Good	OLFSNT40	Symantec Fax Starter Edition P...	User
Nod32krnnod32kui	Nod32 Antivirus Version 2	Good	OLSysTray	QuickBooks Online Backup TaskB	User
nod32kui	Nod32 Antivirus Version 2	Good	OlympusCamedia	Camedia Master 2.5	User
NoeWinnt	ATAKA-E virus	Bad	OMF4	FREEMEGA virus	Bad
nomdchek	Intel Native Audio NomdCheck	User	omgstartup	OpenMG Jukebox-starts music	User
Nogofb	Symantec Norton Speed Disk	User	Omgtray	OpenMG Jukebox-Sony MiniDisc	User
nospamtoday	No Spam Today	User	oneeyetdoene	Eye Tide Launcher	User
nost_LM	Belin Loadout Manager	User	ONENOTEM	MS OneNote2003	User
NOTEPAD	RUSTY virus	Bad	OneTouch	Hewlett-Packard driver	User
notepad	parasite	Bad	OneTouchMonitor/OneTouchMon/OneTou-2	Visioneer system tray icon	User
Notesholder	Aklabs.com NotesHolder 1.32	User	Onflow	Onflow	User
Notify	Novell GroupWise Notify	User	onflow	Adware	Bad
NotifyAlert	Dell critical alert notification	Ugly	ONICTASK	Aladdin Systems Internet Cleanup	User
notmgr	Notmad Manager	User	online_party	adult content dialer	Bad
npdor/NPDOR9x	NPD Online Research	User			
npnzdad	spyware	Bad			
npnzdad	spyware	Bad			

Program	Description	Good/Bad
onlinetime	Online Timer	User
OnSrv	adware	Bad
Oocs	see IWAR	User
oodag	O&O Defrag v6.0 Professional	User
OODLed	O&O DriveLED	User
Opac	see IWAR	User
OPISTAT	OptiStat	User
opnste	adware	Bad
OPScan	Norton Out of Process Scan Svr Tsk	User
optimize	Internet Optimizer	User
optimize	adult content dialer	Bad
Opware12/Opware14/Opware16/Opware32	OmniPage Aware	User
oraboot	O'Reilly Utilities	User
org32	Lotus Organizer	User
OrgyCam	adult content dialer	Bad
Osa	resource hog	Bad
OSA/OSA9	MS Office Startup Application	Ugly
Osa9	resource hog	Bad
OSD	Netropa OnScreen Display	Ugly
OSDEx	Dually Dialog Box Assistant	User
Oses	see IWAR	User
osserver	Object Store Server	User
OssProxy	Netserfer/Marketscore Itml Accell	User
OSSPROXY	market research program	Bad
ostivity	Ostivity	User
otrxxh	CAROOL virus	User
Oubilette	encryption security function	User
outlook	MIMAIL.Q virus	Bad
outlook	Microsoft Outlook	User
Outlook (1)	W32.Mimail.Q virus	Bad
Outlook (2)	W32.Mimail.Q mm virus	Bad
outpost	Anghium Outpost Firewall	User
Overnet	Overnet	User
OWMngr	foistware	Bad
Oxigen	Oxigen ClientAdmin	User
P2P Networking	PeerEnabler P2P Networking	User
P3p4chk	GEMA virus	Bad
PacketHSvc	CompuServe Virtual Adapter Svc	User
PAgent	Spyware	Bad
PAGOO	Pagoo internet call waiting	User
Palm	Palm Desktop Software	User
PALNETAW-1	Paltalk Netaware	User
PandaAVEngine	NETSKY.R virus	Bad
Panorama	Panorama 32	User
PanPlus	Power Panel Plus	User
PanSeal	Sony Valo Recover	User
patch	NETBUS virus	Bad
PAV	PER Antivirus	User
PavFires	Panda Antivirus	User
pavmail	PER Antivirus	User
pavsched	Panda Antivirus	User
payload.dat	RANDEX.D virus	Bad
pc32	MASTAK virus	Bad
pcacceli	Smartalec PC Accelerator	User
PCAlert4	PC Alert 4	User
PCAMgt	Symantec CMS PC Anywhere Agent	User
PCBODYGUARD	Calluna PC Bodyguard	User
pcbooster	inKline Global PC Booster	User
PCCClient	PC-Cillin 2002 Antivirus	User
PCCIGuide	Trend Micro PC-Cillin	User
PCCIOMon	Trend Micro PC-Cillin Antivirus	User
PCClient	Trend Micro Internet Security Ste	User
pccntmon	Trend Micro OfficeScan NT Monitor	User
PccPfw	PC-Cillin 2003 personal firewall	User
pcfix2k	Splash Screen	User
PCHButton	Phoenix Tech Power Schemes Mgr	User
PCHbutton	Hewlett-Packard PCH Button	User
PCHSchd	MS PC Health Client Scheduling	User
Pcm25	PC Monitor	User
pcsidr	Cyber Armor Loader	User
PcSvc	Delfin Project PromulGate	User
PcSync	PC Sync	User
Pctptt	see PCTVoice	User
PCTSpk	www.PCTVoice	User
PCTVoice	PCTEL 2304WT V.92 MDC driver	User
PD	Popup Defender	User
PDDLGHLP	Ontrack Dialog Helper	User
PDEngine	Raxco Perfect Disk	User
PDesk	Matrox Powerdesk	User
PDEXPLO	Ontrack PowerDesk Pro	User
PDFClient	PDF Creator Client	User
pdfSaver9	PDF Xchange	User
PDirect	IGM Presentation Director	User
PDS	Intel Ping Discovery Service	User
PDVDServ	Remote Control	User
PeerGuardian_1.99b_pr14	Peer Guardian	User
Pelmiced	IBM Mouse Suite 98	User
PENGSS	Pro PCL Status Monitor	User
penis32	BLASTER virus	Bad
perf/wperf	Tiny Personal Firewall	User
PersFW	Kerio Tech Personal Firewall	User
PersFW (2)	Tiny Personal Firewall	User
pezdow1	Kodak Batch Transfer	User
PFDEnable	MaxBoost	User
pfppop??	Corel Perfect Print	User
PGMonitr	Delfin Project PromulGate	Bad
PgMonitr	adware	User
pgpsdkserv	SDK Service	User
pppservice	PGPnet Functions	User
pgptray	Network Associates PGP Tray	User
PH32	RANDEX.G virus	Bad
PHONEF??	Phone Free v6.2	User
PhoneCheck	Phone Check	User
PicApSrv	Sony Photo Suite	User
PicasaMediaDetector	LifeScape Media Detector	User
pickatag	Pick-a-tag	User
PICPRTR	View & Measure 3D CAD data	User
PIDLex	NIOVADOOR virus	Bad
PIDUNHK	Prodigy Internet Software	User
pinger	pinger	User
piolet	Toshiba Pinger	User
PipeCmd	Piolet File Sharing	User
Pixel32	SDBOT.D virus	Bad
Pixelpwr32	GEMA virus	Bad
Pixelsvr	GEMA virus	Bad
pjWebCam	GEMA virus	Bad
PKey_Pro	WebCam Automation Software	User
PLAuto	PrintKey Pro	User
	Casio Photo Loader Supervisory Tsk	User
PlayList	Roxio PlayList	User
pleapu	Powerleap CPU Control Panel	User
PlexTool	Plextor PlexTools Professional	User
PlgUni	McAfee QuickClean 2	User
plister	Paste Lister	User
PLNRnote	Sierra Event Planner Reminders	User
plucker-desktop	Plucker Desktop	User
plugin-<random>	adult content dialer	Bad
PLXSTART	Plextor Mgr 2000 Splash Screen	User
PLXTASK	Plextor CD-RW Control Panel	User
Powermarks	Powermarks	User
PMMON	Password Max	User
PMounter	Paragon Partition Mounter	User
pmr	foistware	Bad
pmremind	Brierbund Prntmstr Event Reminder	User
pmtshoot	Troubleshooting for power	User
pmxinit	PMXinit	User
pnetaware	PalNetaware	User
PNSetup	PopNot	User
pntask	LALA.C virus	Bad
PNTIOMon	Trend Micro PC-Cillin	User
POBOX	PO Box	User
PocketController	Soft Object Tech Pocket Ctrl Pro	User
Point32 (2)	Microsoft Intellipoint	User
Point32.dll (1)	Microsoft Intellipoint	User
Points Manager	Aitnet.com Points Manager	User
POL32ADM	Public Outlook Server	User
Pop3scan	Eset NOD32	User
POP3Trap	Trend Micro PC-Cillin	User
PopDown	PopDown Internet Explorer	User
PopFile	POPFile	User
PopFilter	Popup Ad Filter	User
PopMan	PopMan	User
PopNot	PopNot	User
PopOps	PopOps	User
popopen	PopOpen	User
POPPeeper	POP Peeper	User
Poppy	Poppy for Windows	User
POPProxy	Symantec Norton Email Protection	User
PopSrv**	foistware	Bad
poperv146	adware	User
PopSub	PopSubtract	User
PopTool	Popup Blocker	User
PopTray	PopTray	User
Populist	Populist	User
Popup	Popup Eliminator	User
Popup Eliminator	Popup Eliminator	User
PopUpKiller	PopUp Killer	User
PopUpStopperProfessional	PopUp Stopper Professional	User
PopUpWatch	PopUp Watch	User
PortAOL	AOL Pure Networks Port Magic	User
PORTC195	Samsung GW Port Controller	User
postcastserver	PostCast Server	User
pow	POW!	User
PowerDVD	Cyberlink PowerDVD	User
PowerKey	Acer Launch Manager	User
PowerMate	Griffin Tech PowerMate	User
powermenu	PowerMenu	User
powerpro	PowerPro	User
PowerReg Scheduler/PowerReg SchedulerV2	PopUp Stopper Professional	Leadertech
	PowerRegister Schdlr	User
powerstrip/PSTRIP	PowerStrip	User
POWPANEL	PowerPanel	User
powerprof.dll	Lowprof Power Profile	User
PPCleanDeleteAtReboot.bat	PPClean Remove at Boot	User
PPControl	PestPatrol Control Center	User
ppe	Pinnacle Sys PCI Prfrmnce Enhcr	User

Program	Description	Good/Bad
PPInupdt	Protector Plus	User
ppmemcheck	PPMemCheck	User
PPPGate	Softkik PPP	User
ppprotray	System Tray Control	User
ppstub	adware	Bad
PPTbc	Protector Plus	User
PPTD4ONT	Scansoft Paper Print to Desktop	User
PPVstop	Protector Plus	User
PPWebCap	Visioneer ScanSoft	User
pqhelper	search hijacker	Bad
PQINT	PowerQuest Startup Utility	User
PQTRAY	PaperQuote	User
PrcView	Symantec	User
PrecisionTime	Gator Corp	Bad
Prelenium	Millenium Keyboard Preload Chk	User
PresRdy	Hewlett-Packard Presentation Ready	User
Printer-Link	Usfor Ltd	User
printkey2000	Printkey 2000	User
printnov	PrintNow	User
PrinTray	Lexmark System Tray Icon	User
PrintScreen	Gadwin PrintScreen	User
PrivacyEraser	Privacy Eraser Pro	User
privoxy	Privoxy	User
prizesurfer	malware	Bad
Prkill	Ray Process Killer	User
prmt	spyware	Bad
prmt	spyware	Bad
Prmvr	adware	Bad
procdll	WEEDBOTZ.14 virus	Bad
procmon	BIONET ADA virus	Bad
ProDSL	Intel System Tray Icon	User
Profile.vbs	WHITEHO or TRAPPY viruses	Bad
Prognron	PEEPER virus	Bad
ProjSelector	Roxio Project Selector	User
PROMon	Intel PRO Monitor	User
PromptCast	PromptCast	User
PRONoMgr	Intel System Tray Icon	User
PropelAC	Propel Accelerator	User
ProPort	ProPort Startup	User
ProvenTactics	Proven Internet Marketing	User
Proxomitron	Web Proxy	User
Proyecto1	GRUEL virus	Bad
Proyecto1	GRUEL virus	Bad
Proyecto1	GRUEL virus	Bad
PRPCUI	Intel Speedstep	Good
PRT95MIN	Printscreen 95	User
ps	Punto Switcher	User
ps2	Hewlett-Packard	User
PSConSv	Symbian PSIWin 2.3 Conctn Srvr	User
psdeluxe	Print Screen Deluxe	User
PSDrvCheck	Pinnacle Driver Check	User
psexec.bat	BOXKOO virus	Bad
PSFree	Panicware Pop-Up Stopper Free Ed	User
PSHotLaunchVVL	PS Hot Launch WL	User
PsMFCard	Toshiba Power Save PCMCIA Slots	User
psn	Post-It Software Notes	User
Psn2Lite	see psn	User
PsnLite	see psn	User
Psnotes	see psn	User
psnotify	Pharos SignUp Vx	Good
PsPCCard	Toshiba Power Saving Tsk	User
pspcontr	Philips SpeechMike 6174	User
PsSound	Toshiba Sound Modes	User
Pssvo	MS Outlook 2000 patch	User
PStoreS	MS Protected Storage Server	User
pstrip	Power Strip 3.47	User
PSXLTRAY	Casio Pocket Sheet Sync	User
PT2	Powertweak	User
PTBSync	PTBSync	User
PTCTRL	see PT2	User
pttb	Puch the Freakin' Button	User
ptiphm.dll	Write Back caching should be used	User
ptipbrrdll	Promise RAID Controller	User
ptiseq.cpl	adware	Bad
PTReplicator	Karen's Tools Replicator	User
pts	Kodak Picture Transfer	User
PtSnoop	PCTEL Modems	User
PTSSvc	Kodak Picture Transfer Service	User
pttray	PowerTools	User
pttrun	Transmeta Crusoe Processor	User
PtuDfApp	Prassi abCD Interface Applicatn	Ugly
PTW	Prayer	User
puli	Interwise Push Client	User
pupdate	adware	Bad
pupstman	Ashampoo PowerUp XP & Deluxe	User
PUPSTTWK	Ashampoo	User
pupxpman	Ashampoo PowerUp XP	User
PUPXPTWK	Ashampoo PowerUp XP	User
PURGATIVE100	Purgative	User
PUSH6599	Relysis Episode MF6599 Scanner	User
PutA!!	OPASERV.I virus	Bad
PutA!!.com	OPASERV.Z virus	Bad
PVR	Pocket Voice Recorder	User
PWATCH	PowerMaster	User
Pwr32ctr	GEMA virus	Bad
Pwr32ctrl	GEMA virus	Bad
Pwr32mgt	GEMA virus	Bad
Pwrchute	PowerChute	User
Pwroff	GEMA virus	Bad
Pwrsave	Toshiba Power Save	User
PwrTray	Toshiba Power Mgmt Panel	User
PWSTray	MS Personal Web Server	User
PwUi	Proxycomm	User
QAgent	Intuit Background Dowloading Agent	Ugly
Qbdagent	Intuit QuickBooks v8 Dlvry Agent	User
Qbdagent2001	Intuit QuickBooks 2001 Dlvry Agent	Ugly
Qbdagent2002	Intuit QuickBooks 2002 Dlvry Agent	Ugly
Qbupdate	Intuit QuickBooks Update	User
Qctray	IBM Access Connection Wizard	User
Qcwlicon	IBM Thinkpad Laptop Sys Tray Icon	User
QDCSFS	Norton CleanSweep Fast & Safe	User
QdmStart	QDI Desktop Manager	User
Qeepit	Qeep It	User
QFSCHD100/QFSchdep	QuickHeal Scheduler	User
QHSTRT32	Quick Heal Startup	User
qhw	Microsoft QkRes2k	User
QkRes2k	Microsoft QkRes2k	User
QL	Hewlett-Packard QuickLink III	User
QLOEOader	Spam Filter	User
QQ	Tencent QQ	User
qsd	Quick Shutdown	User
Qsemsg	Quicken	User
QShelf2k	Microsoft Bookshelf	User
QSHLFED	Encarta Dictionary Quickshelf	User
QSORT	Qsort 2000	User
qsssfiej	homepage hijacker	Bad
qtask	Qtask Startup	User
qtopiatray	Sharp Zaurus PDA	User
QTRAYIME	Qcode	User
Qtstub	Quick Tax	User
QTTask	Apple QuickTime	User
qttasks	parasite	Ugly
QtzgAcer	Acer LManager	User
QtZiAcer	Acer LManager	User
Quat Task	M-Audio Quattro Control Panel	User
Quick95	Nisi G6 USB Graphics Tablet	User
QuickDCF	Exif Launcer	User
quicken	parasite variant	Bad
QuickFolders	ByteGenie Quick Folders	User
QuickLaunchEr	QuickLaunchEr	User
quicklink	Agfa PhotoWise QuickLink	User
quicknote	JC&MB Quicknote	User
QUICKRES	QuickRes	User
QuickResource	QuickResource	User
QUICKRUN	QuickRun	User
QUICKS~1	Open Office	User
quickset	Dell QuickSet	User
quickstart	Open Office	User
QUICKSYNC/quiksync3	Iomega QuikSync	User
quicktimeupdatehelper	QuickTime Update Completion	User
QuickTV	AVerMedia QuickTV	User
qushelfxx	Quick Shelf xx	User
QVP32	Inso Corp Quick View Plus	Ugly
QWDLLs	Intuit Quick Launch	User
r_server	Radmin	User
R3proxy	Fellowes Proxy	User
ra32	trojan	Bad
Rabbit	W32.Mimail.S@mm virus	Bad
rabbit	MIMAIL.S virus	Bad
RaboSessionMon	Rabo Session Monitor	User
radarfic	Radar Notifications	User
RadBoot	RadBoot	User
RAGE128TWEAK	ATI Rage 128 Video Cards	User
ragui	Remotely Anywhere GUI	User
raid_tool	VIA RAID Tool	User
raideutility	FastCheck Monitoring Utility	User
Rainlender	Rainlender	User
Rainmeter	Rainmeter	User
Ram Idle 98	Ram Idle Standard v5.0	User
RAM_XP	RAM Idle Pro	User
RAM_XP	TweakNow RAM Idle Profesional	User
RAMASST	LG DVD Writer	User
RAMBOOSTER	RamBooster	User
ramdef	Ram Def Xtreme	User
ramidle	RAM Idle	User
RAMpage	Sys Tray icon Available Memory	User
ramsys	Rays Lab Advanced Startup Mgr	User
RandomScreens	Logon UI Boot Randomizer	User
RAPAPP	BlackICE PC Protection	User
RapidRes	PC Magnification Settings	User
RASAutoU	Microsoft Remote Access Dialer	User
RAVEN_VLZS	spyware	Bad
RAVMOND	LOVGATE family of viruses	Bad
ravtray8	RAV Antivirus	User
ray	homepage hijacker	Bad
razertra	Razer Costumizer	User
rb32	homepage hijacker	Bad

Start Up & Tasks

Program	Description	Good/Bad
rb32	parasite	Bad
rb32	parasite	Bad
rbenh	parasite	Bad
rbserv	Mike Lin Start Rapid Backup Svc	User
RBSKQQBO	VBS.Vbswg2b.A@mm virus	Bad
Rcapi	RCAPI-Remote Cmn App Prog Intrfc	User
rcenterrll	Ring Central Fax	User
RcMan	Creative Labs Remote Center	User
rcrawler	Registry Crawler	User
RCSCHED	RC Schedule Check	User
RCScheduler	RegClass Expert Scheduler	User
RCSync	PrizeSurfer.com	Bad
RCSync	malware	Bad
readme	BEAGLE.V virus	Bad
RealEvent	Real Networks RealOne Player	User
realmon	Computer Assoc Realtime Monitor	User
RealPlay	Real Mrks RealPlyr or One Media	User
realplay	parasite	Bad
RealPopKiller	Real Pop Killer	User
Realsched	Real Networks RealOne Player	User
RealSched	Real Networks	Ugly
RealSPEED	Real Speed	User
Real-Tens	spyware	Bad
realupd	PARLAY virus	Bad
realupd	PAARLAY or MITGLIEDER.I viruses	Bad
recguard	Hewlett-Packard Recguard	User
reclip	Reclip Popup Clipboard	User
RecSche	Recording Scheduler	User
redflag	Red Flag	User
redirect*	hijacker	Bad
referee	MediaComm Referee	User
Refresh	Iomega Refresh	User
reg32	homepage hijacker	Bad
reg32	EReg	User
reg33	hijacker	Bad
reg33	NOUPDATE.B virus	Bad
REG33	parasite variant	Bad
REGCNT09	Card Monitor	User
Regcpm32	POLDO.B virus	Bad
REGCPM32	adult content dialer	Bad
regedit	DOOMJUICE.B virus	Bad
regedit	BRID.A virus	Bad
regedit ...data789.tmp	homepage hijacker	Bad
regedit /s %windir\c:\month number...	FORTNIGHT.D virus	Bad
regedit /s ...rad03FA6.tmp	...Hijack homepage	Bad
regedit /s ...win.dll	hijacker	Bad
regedit -s ..win.dll	SEEKER.K virus	Bad
regedit -s c:\ie.reg	hijacker	Bad
regedit -s spp.reg	search hijacker	Bad
regedit /s system.dll	homepage hijacker	Bad
regedit setupuser.log	parasite	Bad
regedit ... sp.dll	search hijacker	Bad
REGIST-1	Register Drop Center	User
register	Register MediaRing Talk	User
Registry	DOWNLOADER.CILE virus	Bad
RegistryController	RDF Converter Registry Control	User
regloadr	GAOBOT.AO virus	Bad
RegMech	Registry Mechanic	User
REGPROP/WMPADDIN.DLL ...AutoProp		User
Regprot	Diamont Comp Sys RegistryProt	User
regscan*	OPTIX LITE FIREWALL BYPASS virus	Bad
RegSeeker	RegSeeker	User
Regshave	Fuji Photo Film Registry Shaver	User
regsrv	OPTIXPRO.11 virus	Bad
Regsrv	BDS/OPTIXPRO.12 virus	Bad
Regsrv32.com	SOUTHGHOST virus	Bad
Regsrv32.com	SOUTHGHOST virus	Bad
regsv	search hijacker	Bad
REGSVC	MS Remote Registry Service	User
regsvc32	GAOBOT family of viruses	Bad
regsvc32	homepage hijacker	Bad
regsvc32	homepage hijacker	Bad
regsvr32	AsioReg	User
regsvr32 ...HREF.OCX	HREF.OCX xFX JumpStart	Good
regsvr32 veev****.dll	hijacker	Bad
regsvs	GAOBOT.YN virus	Bad
Regsysw	W32.Wilsef virus	Bad
Regsysw.com	WILSEF virus	Bad
RegTool	Pinnacle Sys Registration Studio 8	User
RegTwk	Rage 3d Tweak	User
REGVER	LATINUS.16 virus	Bad
relaunch	Philips Audio Applications Launcher	User
reload.vbs	LOVELETTER.AS virus	Bad
remark	MyBookmarks.com Remark	User
Remhelp	RemHelp	User
remin	Birthday Reminder 5.0	User
Remind32	Textbridge OCR Registm Reminder	Ugly
reminder	Reminder	User
RemindMe	RemindMe	User
RemoteAgent	Cyberlink Power Remote Agent	User
remotemaster	ASUS Remote Master	User
Remoterm	PCTV Remote	User
Removed	adware	Bad
RePEAtLD	REPEATLD virus	Bad
ReplayRadio	Replay Radio	User
RepliGoMon	Cerience RepliGo	User
RescueXP	WinRescue	User
ReserveModule	Timer Recording Manager	User
Residence	Picture Package VCD Maker	User
Restoration	Restore Lost Files	User
RestoreDesktop	Restore Desktop	User
restory	RETSAM virus	Bad
resumefix	Resume Fix Clocks	User
Resw	see IWAR	
RESWIN	21st Cent Ent Mania Win Restore	User
retime	GIPMA virus	Bad
retrieverscheduler	80-20 Retriever Scheduler	User
RetroRun	Dantz Develop Retrospect Backup	User
RevoRun	RevoTaskbar Application	User
Rexproxy	MS NetShow Real-Time Encdr Prxy	User
rexsymon	REX Synchronization	User
rfagent	Registry First Aid Agent	User
rfkampig	GIPMA virus	Bad
RFTRay	Logitech Rlty Fusion GameCam SE	User
RFTRay	Reality Fusion GamCam Video...	User
RH.DLL	adware	Bad
rIOPHosls.vBS	RICSYS virus	User
RivaTuner	nVidia Riva Tuner	User
rjhExtensions	rjhsoftware.com Extensions Orgnzr	User
Rlid	LIXY virus	User
RimCtrl	Cyberlink Remote Ctrl PowerDVD	User
Rnaapp	MS Windows Dial-Up Ntwkg App	User
RNDAL-	Real Networks RealOne Player	Ugly
RNDAL-	Real Networks Dynamic App Lnchr	User
RoboFormWatcher	Siber System AI Roboform	User
robotaskbaricon	RoboForm	User
RocketTime	Rocket Software Rocket Time	User
Root	GRUEL virus	Bad
Root	GRUEL virus	Bad
Root	GRUEL virus	Bad
rp32	Enterprise Intl ControlIT	User
Rpcss/Rpcss.dll	Remote Procedure Call Services	User
RPCX1sQ3	IRCBOT.B virus	Bad
RRAM	Release RAM	User
rrmedic	troubleshooting utility	User
Rscmpt	NVidia	User
rsMenu	Outlook & Casio PDA Synchronize	User
RsrcMtr	MS Windows Resource Meter	User
RssReader	PSS Reader	User
RState	Sybase Manage Anywhere Studio	User
RSVP	MS Resource Reservation Protocol	User
RtFixM32	Cybermedia First Aid 98	Ugly
rtos	trojan	Bad
rtunnel	Parradial RealTunnel	User
RTVScan	Symantec Real Time Virus Scan	User
RTVScN95	Symantec Real Time Virus Scan	User
ru	adult content dialer	Bad
RuLaunch	McAfee VirusScan 6.x	User
Run_od	GHOST.23 virus	Bad
run322	LANFILT virus	Bad
RUN32DLL	FTP ANA virus	Bad
Runapp32	NEODU/RK virus	Bad
Rund1132 qq.dll, Rundll32 ...QQPASS.F virus		User
Rundll16	w32.Gaobot.ZX virus	Bad
rundll-	TOPAZZOL virus	User
rundll32 kenel.dll, PowerProfileEnable	INMOTA virus	Bad
rundle2	JAVAKILLER virus	Bad
rundll32	LADE virus	Bad
Rundll (2)	PWSteal.Banpaes.D virus	User
rundll dnes.dll, DnDneCheckBindings - DNE-Deterministic NDIS		
rundll dnes.dll, DnDneCheckDUN13DNE-Deterministic NDIS Extender		User
Rundll powerprof.dll	LOXOSCAM virus	Bad
Rundll/Rundll32 (1)	Microsoft Run a DLL as an App	Good
RunDll16	SDBOT.F virus	Bad
Rundll16	virus	Bad
Rundll32	DOMWIS virus	Bad
Rundll32	MIROOT virus	Bad
Rundll32	DVLDR virus	Bad
rundll32	SANKER virus	Bad
rundll32 (2)	DVLDR virus	Bad
rundll32 (2)	SDBOT.A virus	Bad
rundll32 ...Bridge.dll	browser hijacker	Bad
rundll32 ...gvagfxj.dll	adware, spyware or virus	Bad
rundll32 ...drvupd.inl	spyware	Bad
rundll32 advpack.dll, DelModeRunDLL32 submit parasite related		Bad
Rundll32 BDSrHook.dll, Rundll32...	parasite	Bad
rundll32 bridge.dll, Load	browser hijacker	Bad
Rundll32 bs3.dll, DllRun	parasite variant	Bad

Program	Description	Good/Bad
RunDLL32 bsx5.dll	parasite variant	Bad
RunDLL32 bxxs5.dll, dllrun	parasite	Bad
rundll32 cnbabe.dll, dllstartup	toolbar spyware	Bad
Rundll32 CNBabe.dll, DllStartup	toolbar spyware	Bad
Rundll32 CNSMN.DLL, Rundll32	hijacker related	Bad
rundll32 ctrlpan.dll, Restore ControlPanel	parasite variant	Bad
rundll32 image.dll, Install	InstantAccess: adult content dialer	Bad
rundll32 inetp60.dll, DllRunServer	parasite variant	Bad
rundll32 internat.dll, LoadKeyboardProfile	parasite related	Bad
rundll32 msa32chk.dll	malware	Bad
rundll32 MSA64CHK.dll	parasite variant	Bad
rundll32 MSA64CHK.DLL, DllMostrar	adult content dialer	Bad
rundll32 msconfd.dll, Restore ControlPanel	BOOKMARKER virus	Bad
rundll32 mshtmpre.dll, MShmpre	browser hijacker	Bad
rundll32 MSIEFRA40.DLL, DllRunServer	hijacker variant	Bad
RUNDLL32 MSSIGN30.DLL ondll_reg	LOVEGATE.R virus	Bad
RUNDLL32 MSSIGN30.DLL ondll_reg	LOVEGATE family of viruses	Bad
rundll32 navupd.dll, Startup	NAVU virus	Bad
rundll32 NetDetGW Newdot~2	spyware variant	Bad
rundll32 NewdotNetStartup Newdot~2	spyware	Bad
RunDLL32 oo4.dll, DllRun	parasite variant	Bad
Rundll32 PwrMonit.dll	IBM's Battery Maximiser	Good
rundll32 QaBar.dll, ForceShowBar	parasite	Bad
RUNDLL32 reg.dll, ondll_reg	LOVEGATE virus	Bad
RUNDLL32 reg678.dll ondll_reg	LOVEGATE.F virus	Bad
rundll32 RSSToolbar.dll, DllRunMain	hijacker spyware	Bad
rundll32 sasync.dll, SyncWait	browser hijacker	Bad
rundll32 setupapi, InstallHinfSection...keymgr3.inf	parasite related	Bad
rundll32 setupapi, InstallHinfSection... oemsyspnp.inf	search hijacker	Bad
rundll32 shell32.dll, Control_RunDLL ...123456.cpl	KITRO.C virus	Bad
rundll32 stbupdt.DLL, DllRunMain	parasite	Bad
rundll32 stmctrl.dll, TaskBar	ISP Initializes DSL modem	Good
Rundll32 v128iitw.dll, STB_InitTweak	Drivers for STB Graphics Card	Good
rundll32 w3knet.dll, dllinitrun	spyware	Bad
rundll32.vbe	parasite variant	Bad
Rundll32 PowrProf.dll	Microsoft LoadPowerProfile	User
rundll32exe stlbdist.DLL, DllRunMain	hijacker	Bad
Rundll	SURDUX virus	Bad
rundlls	HABRACK virus	Bad
Rundllsystem32	NETDEVIL.B virus	Bad
runfc	CAMP URF virus	Bad
Runit	RUhit	User
RunOnce	Microsoft Run Once Wrapper	User
Runonce	MS Data Access Components v2.5	User
runpopfile	Run POP File	User
runppdrv	Paperport	User
runservice	eLicense	User
RunSysd32	Shane Groleau Desktop Sheild 2000	User
RuxDLL32	MAPSON.D virus	Bad
Rwon	adware	Bad
RxMon	Roxio Easy CD & DVD Creator 6	User
RxMon9x	Dell Resolution Assistant	User
S3hotkey	S3Hotkey	User
S3SysKey	S3 Inc Toshiba laptop graphics	User
S3Tray/S3Tray2	Taskbar for S3 Graphics	User
S4BAREQ2	parasite	Bad
S4F	S4F Internet Filter	User
s4helper	hijacker	Bad
sa	Spellex-Anywhere	User
sa3dsrv	Aureal A3D Interactive Audio	User
SABSERV	Sabreserver	User
Saea	see IWAR	User
SafeCfg	NetScreen Remote	User
SAFEIN~1	Safe Install	User
SafeOff	Safe Off	User
safesearch	parasite variant	Bad
Sage	Microsoft Plus! System Agent	User
SAHAgent	ShopAtHomeMeSelect.com	Bad
Sahagent	parasite	Bad
saiconfig	Saitek Auto Configure	User
SaiMon	SaiMon Joystick Driver	User
Sandicon	SandDisk	User
Sapisvr	MS Speech App Prgming Interface	User
saplpd	Print Locally from Sap Gui	User
saproxy	SA Proxy	User
SATARaid	Serial ATA RAID	User
SAUpdate	Quest ATT Broadband Update	User
SAVAgent	Sophos Antivirus	Good
Save	see SAVENOW	User
Save	spyware	Bad
Save	adware	Bad
SaveNow	spyware	Bad
savenow	spyware	Bad
SaveNow/Save	WhenU.com SaveNow	Bad
SaveStartDate	unidentified adware	Bad
SAVScan	Symantec Auto-Protect	User
SAYTIME	Say the Time 5.0	User
sbautoupdate	Spyware Blasters	User
SBDrv	Easy Front Panel Audio Drive	User
SBDrvDet	Creative Sound Card Driver Updates	User
SBHC	Gigatech SuperBar IE Plugin	Ugly
sbhc	parasite	Bad
Sbhost	SPYBOT.GEN virus	Bad
sbmx	soundMAX	User
browser	Slim Browser	User
SBServ	Symantec Script Blocking Svc	User
sbsetup	Rockwell RipTide Soundcard	User
SBWatchdog	spyware	Bad
SC	Second Copy 97	User
sc97	Second Copy 97	User
Scam32	SIRCAM virus	Bad
ScanDisk	GANDA.A virus	Bad
Scandisk.com	ESTRELLA virus	Bad
ScannerFinder	Microtek Scanner Finder	User
ScanPanelScnPanel	Artec Scan Panel	User
scanregiv	MASTERLOCK virus	Bad
ScanRegMgW	Microsoft Registry Checker	User
Scanregw	Scans System Registry	Good
Scanregw	STATOR virus	Bad
Scanregw	GWGHOST virus	Bad
SCard32	Towitoko SmartCard Readers	User
ScardSvr	MS Smart Card & Helper Svc	User
SCardSvr2	MOFEI.B virus	Bad
SCardSvr32	MOFEI.B virus	Bad
rundll32 SCardSvr32/Navpw32	W32.Femot.Worm virus	Bad
scbar	hijacker	Bad
SCCenter	Compaq Service Connection Ctr	Ugly
Schost	DONK virus	Bad
schost	KEYLOGGER.BC virus	Bad
SCHDPL32	MS Schedule Plus	User
scheck**	KETCH virus	Bad
schedhlp	Acronis Scheduler Service	User
Schedule	Schedule CM DiskCleaner	User
Scheduled_Maintenance	Scheduled Maintenance	User
scheduler	MRU-Blaster Scheduler	User
Scheduler	SUBWOOFER virus	Bad
SCHENGD	NovaStor NovaBACKUP Schdlr	User
schmaili	Schmaili	User
Schost	GAOBOT.AO virus	Bad
SCHWIZEX	ConfigSafe	User
SCIEClean	SecureClean	User
SCM	Microsoft Service Control Mgr	User
SCMan	SurfChoice	Bad
SCMon	Smart Connect Monitor	User
ScnPanel	Artec Scan Panel	User
scr.scr	OPASERV.T virus	Bad
Scrapad	Scrappad	User
Screens	Screens Startup	User
ScreenSaverDruid	ScreenSaver Druid	User
Scriptsentry	Jason's Toolbox Script Sentry	User
SCROLL	QTronix Scroll-In-Mouse v2.0	User
ScrSvr	OPASERV.N virus	Bad
ScrSvr	OPASERV.T virus	Bad
ScrSvr	OPASERV.T virus	Bad
Scrub2k/Scrub98/Scrub99/ScrubXP	Hewlett-Packard Scrubber App	Ugly
SCSetup	Smart Connect Setup	User
Scsi	SCSI Miniport Driver	Good
SCSIAccess	Alcohol Virtual SCSI Controller	User
scthemes	Screen Themes	User
sctray	Power Second Second Chance	User
SCVHOST	Backdoor.Sdbot.N virus	Bad
scvhost	GAOBOT family of viruses	Bad
scvhost	SOBOT.N virus	Bad
Scw64	Olympic Tech/A4 Tech 4D Mouse	User
sdaemon	Tropical Software	User
SDetect	Scanner Detector	User
Sdii	Microtek Scan Detector	User
SDJOIJE	SPYBOT.DR virus	Bad
Sdjoie	SPYBOT.B virus	Bad
sdplus	Shut Down Plus	User
SDSTAT/FLSHSTAT	FlashPath Status	User
SE	hijacker	Bad
Searl	see WINSERVN	User
Search	adware	Bad
searchnav	adware	Bad
searchnavversion	adware	Bad
SearchUpdate33	parasite	Bad
SecCopy	Second Copy 2003	User
secretmaker	Secret Maker	User
Secsys	Key Interceptor	Bad
secure2.bat	ZCREW.C virus	Bad
Secure32	Compaq Easy Access Buttons	User
secureitpro470p	SecureIT Pro	User
SECWIZ98	Security Wizard 98	User
SELFCERT	Friendly Web Quick Launch	User
sendmess	SEMES virus	Bad
Sensiva	Sensiva	User
senstrt	RNBO Start	Bad
SENTRY	Spyware	Bad
serials	worms and trojans	Bad

Program	Description	Good/Bad
serrdctl	Shared Modem Svc Client Evnt Vwr	User
Server	EASYSERV virus	Bad
Server	OPTIX.04.A virus	Bad
server	DELTAD.A virus	Bad
SERVER	BUSHTRO122 OR SMOKODOOR viruses	Bad
server	CHUPACABRA virus	Bad
Server.com	ESTRELLA virus	Bad
Server.txt.vbs	DELTAD.A virus	Bad
Server.txt.vbs	DELTAD.A virus	Bad
server.vbs	spyware	Bad
Server4PC	Technisat Server 4PC	User
Server5	trojan	Bad
service	ISRAZ.B virus	Bad
Service	GAOBOT.AO virus	Bad
Service	homepage hijacker	Bad
Service	Adware	Bad
service	FLOPCOPY virus	Bad
service	RANDEX.R virus	Bad
service5	GAOBOT.AF virus	Bad
service5	GAOBOT.AG virus	Bad
ServiceLayer	Nokia Connectivity Library	User
services	Netsky or Netsky.B virus	Bad
services	KAZPING virus	Bad
services	parasite variant	Bad
Services (1)	MS Services Control Manager	Good
Services	W32.Netsky@mm virus	User
Servicess	GAOBOT.AO virus	Bad
serv-u32	Serv-U	User
SERVUT-1	Serv-U Tray Icon	User
SEServe	Programmable Power Key Setup	User
SessMgr	MS Remote Desktop Help Mgr	User
setganma	Radeon Tweaker	User
Sethook	MediaFace Integration	User
SETI Driver	Shortcut to SETI Driver	User
SETI@home	SETI@home	User
Setigu-1	SetiQueue	User
SetiSpy	SetiSpy	User
SetPrinter	SetPrinter v2.0	User
setup	Windows Accelerator	User
Setup_32.1	EVILBOT.B virus	Bad
SetupIE.com	TAPLAK virus	Bad
setvol	Setvol	User
setvc	HUNTOCX virus	Bad
Sexy	Sexy virus	Bad
sexypicz	adult content dialer	Bad
sg	Ace Logix Startup Guard	User
SG2	Leadtek SpeedGear	User
sgmain	Spyware Guard	User
sgms	Screen Guard Message Scan	User
spgworm95	SyGate Service	User
SGTBox	Canon ScanGear Toolbox	User
SGTray	Veritas Storage Guard	User
Shakira_1997_Part_1_.Mpeg_.scr	MYLIFE.N virus	Bad
shambl3r	REMABL virus	Bad
shambl3r	REMABL virus	Bad
Shania.vbs	SHANIA virus	Bad
sharedprem	MAKECALL virus	Bad
SharpReader	Luke Hutteman SharpReader	User
Shell32	LEMIR.B virus	Bad
Shell32	BADSECTOR virus	Bad
Shellapi32	NETDEVIL virus	Bad
Shellfx	ANAKHA virus	Bad
shellexpl	CPIX and SHELDOR viruses	Bad
ShellMon	AOL 8.0/8.1	User
SHELLMSN	NETDEV.B virus	Bad
ShellPicture	ShellPicture	User
Shine	HAPPYLOW virus	Bad
Shine	HAPPYLOW virus	Bad
ShirusuiPad	Shirusu Pad	User
SHIZZLE	HOBBIT.C virus	Bad
ShopSafe	MBNA Banks ShopSafe	User
SHORTKEY	Insight Solutions ShortKeys	User
shost	YODO virus	Bad
Shove-it	Shove-It	User
SHOWBEHIND	Adware	Bad
showmode	G-Tek tech Cyber Trio	User
SHPC32	Lemark Printer Connectivity	User
SHSTAT	McAfee VirusScanNT 4.x	User
shutdown.inf	ShutDown 98	User
shutdownaware	ShutDown Aware	User
ShutDownPro	ShutDown Pro	User
Sibc	see IWAR	Bad
Sicom	NETLIP virus	Bad
SideACT	Best Software SideACT!	User
sidebar	Sidebar	User
Sidebar	search hijacker	Bad
SIGuardian	Palick SIGuardian	User
sigx	SigX	User
SilCfg	Sil0680 RAID Controller Card	User
silent/matcli	Compaq Knowledge Center	User
simcss	trojan	Bad
SimpleCheck	Simple Check	User
SimpLite-MSN	SimpLite-MSN	User
SimpPro	Secways Instant Msngr Encrypter	User
singapore	Spyware, adult dialer	Bad
Siren	Change Filenames	User
siService	GIANT Co Spam Inspector	User
SiSMon	SiS Monitor	User
SiSSwLED	SiS-Silicon Integrated Systems	User
sistem	MUZK virus	Bad
sistrai	PROVA virus	Bad
SiSTray	SiS-Silicon Integrated Systems	User
sistray	PROVA virus	Ugly
sistry	CEBE virus	Bad
SK9910DM	Gateway	User
Ska	NETBUS virus	Bad
SKDAEMON	Multifunction Keyboard Driver	User
skinkers	Howard the Weatherman	User
skynetave	SASSER.D virus	Bad
Skype	Skype	User
Slave	RA virus	Bad
Sleeper	Sleeper	User
SleepMgr	Sleep Manager	User
sleepwalker-smtp	sleepwalker SMTP	User
SIMP3 Server	Slimp3Server	User
SLINGS~1	Atomica Slingshot	User
slipaccel	SlipStream Web Accelerator	User
SLLights	SmartLink	User
SLMSS	see STCLOADER	User
slmss	search hijacker	Bad
SLPCap	Seiko Smart label	User
SLPMonX	Seiko Smart label	User
SLPService	Seiko Smart label	User
Slsched	System LifeGuard	User
SLServ	SmartLink Level Modem Svc	User
SM18G	Cypress Semiconductor	User
SM56Hlpr	Motorola Modem Drivers	User
SMAgent	Analog Devices SoundMAX	User
SMART	Ace Labs S.M.A.R.T. Vision 2.10	User
SmartAgt	drMON Smart Agent	User
SMARTC~1	Phoebus LLC sMaRTcaPs	User
Smartcertmover	SmartTrust Certificate Mover	User
SmartCtr	Lotus-IBM Lotus Smart Suite 97	User
smartfix	SmartFix	User
SmartProtectorPro	Smart Protector Pro	User
SmartUI	Scansoft SmartUI	User
SmaServ	Gilat Comm SkySurfer Mgmt Svc	User
Smasher	SMASHER virus	Bad
smax4	SoundMAX	User
SMax4PNP	SoundMAX	User
Smc - startgui	Sygate Personal Firewall	User
SMC/spfsmc	Sygate Personal Firewall	User
smctrlw	Control Panel	User
smjitray	Smith Micro	User
SMLoader	Smith Micro HotFax	User
SMLogSvc	MS Performance Logs & Alerts	User
Smreminder	Shockwave.com Shockmachine	Ugly
Sms	W32.HLLW.Deadfat/Vesser virus	Bad
sms	DEADFAT virus	Bad
smsrun16	MS Systems Mgmt Server	Good
Smss	MS Session Mgr SubSystem	User
smss	adware	Bad
smss	FLOOD.F virus	Bad
Smssnt	W32.HLLW.Gaobot.EE virus	Bad
SMSSvc	NEGASMS.A virus	Bad
Smsx	Security Tech Solutions SMSexpress	Ugly
SMT	BC Computing Win-Spy	Bad
Smtbrd32	Smart Board XP	User
smtpsever	QK SMTP Server	User
SMTray	Analog Devices SoundMAX	User
Snaglt32	TechSmith SnagIt v7	User
sncntr	adult content dialer	Bad
sndbdrv$104	parasite variant	Bad
Sndcompat	GEMA virus	Bad
sndloader	AGOBOT-BV virus	Bad
SNDMON	Symantec NetDriver Monitor	User
Sndsaver	GEMA virus	Bad
SNDSrvc	Symantec Network Driver Service	User
Sniffer	SystemSoft System Wizard Sniffer	User
Snipe	Merlin Auction Magic Snipe Tool	User
SNMP	SNMP Service	User
SNMPTrap	Microsoft SNMP	User
Snsicon	Second Nature	User
Snt	adult content dialer	Bad
soap	foistware	Bad
Sochost	GAOBOT.AO virus	Bad
sock32	SDBOT virus	Bad
SodaStartup	Soda Startup	User
Sodd	see IWAR	Bad
SOFFICE	StarOffice	User
SOFinst	Gilat Internet Satellite Sys	Good
Solocfg	Solo Antivirus	User
Solosent	Solo Sentry Antivirus	User
somatic	hijacker	Bad
Sony Tray	Image Transfer	User
SOS	PHILLIS virus	Bad
soundcontrl	GAOBOT.AFJ virus	Bad
Soundman	Realtek Avance Logic Sound Mgr	User
Soundmx	parasite	Bad
sp.req	search hijacker	Bad

Program	Description	Good/Bad
Sp00lsv	GRAYBIRD.E virus	Bad
sp32.dll	homepage hijacker	Bad
spamihilator	Spamihilator	User
spamkiller	McAfee SpamKiller	User
SpamMinder	Maysoft SpamMinder	User
spampal	SPAMPAL.ORG SpamPal	User
SpamSleuth	Spam Sleuth	User
spamweed	SpamWeed	User
SpClkDx	Speaking Clock Deluxe	User
SpdStart	Symantec Norton SpeedStart	User
spdstrm	DSL Monitor	User
SPEED UP	FastTrack Accelerator	User
speedfan	Speed Fan	User
speedKey	Microsoft IntelliType Pro	User
SpeedMgr	T-DSL Speed Manager	User
SpeedswitchXP	Speedswitch XP	User
speedtec	Montana Accel SpeedTec	User
speedy.bat	OPASERV.AO virus	Bad
SPEEDY.PIF	OPASERV.V virus	Bad
speedy.scr	OPASERV.Y virus	Bad
spfsmc	Sygate Firewall	User
Spguard	StartPage Guard	User
spidermin	DrWeb Antirus	Good
spinner	Spinner Plus	User
Splash	McAfee Splash Screen	User
SPLASHA	MS Media Manager	User
spoler	RANDEX.J virus	Bad
spollsv	LOVEGATE.R virus	Bad
spoo1sv	SOULJET virus	Bad
Spool32	SPY.EHKS.21 virus	Bad
spool	parasite	Bad
spool	parasite	Bad
Spool32	MS Spooler Sub Sys Process	Good
SPOOL32	YAB.A virus	Bad
spoolcrv.cpl	INSP1R.11 virus	Bad
spooll32	OPTIXPRO virus	Bad
spoolos	TORVEL virus	Bad
Spoolserv	DINFOR virus	Bad
spoolsrv	RANDEX.H virus	Bad
Spoolsrv	JOINER.C1 virus	Bad
SPOOLSRV	SPYBOT.P virus	Bad
Spoolsrv32	W32.HLLW.Gaobot.AG virus	Bad
SpoolSv	Microsoft Spooler Service	Good
Spoolsv	CIADOOR.B virus	Bad
Spoolsv	CIADOOR.B virus	Bad
Spoolsv	CIADOOR.B virus	Bad
SpoolSvc	STTB-A virus	Bad
spoolsvc	virus	Bad
spoolsvc32	SDBOT.BB virus	Bad
spoolsvv	search hijacker	Bad
spvic	Instant Chess	User
Spy	SETI Spy	User
SpyAgent4	SpyTech SpyAgent	User
Spyassault	malware	Bad
SpyBlaster	foistware	User
spyblocker	Spyblocker	User
Spybotsd	Spybot Search & Destroy	User
spybott	parasite	Bad
spybott	parasite	Bad
SpyBuddy	SpyBuddy	User
SPYHUNTER	SpyHunter	User
Spynuker	spyware	Bad
spystopper	SpyStopper	User
SpySweeper	SpySweeper	User
Spyware	spyware	Bad
Spywareguard	parasite	Bad
Spywareguard	parasite	Bad
SpywareNukerInstaller	spyware	Bad
SQInstaller	hijacker	Bad
Sqlexploit	SDBOT.D virus	Bad
SQLMangr	MS SQL Server Svc Manager	User
SQLServr	MS SQL Applications	User
sqstart	Sonique Quick Start	User
sqvynikp	Bayden Systems SlickRun	User
sr	spyware	Bad
SrchAsst	spyware	Bad
srmclean	srmclean	User
srmg	hijacker	Bad
srrpro	System Restore Remover Pro	User
SrsTray	SRS Applet	User
Srv32	OPASERV.J virus	Bad
Srv32	OPASERV.S virus	Bad
SrvAny	MS WinNT4/2000/XP/2003 Rsrc Kit	
SS	Smooth-Surfer	User
ss2-full	SurfSecret	User
Ssae	see IWAR	Bad
SSBkgdupdate	ScanSoft OmniPage Pro 14.0	User
ssbsch	Simply Safe Backup Scheduler	User
ssc_serv	SSC Service Utility	User
sscbitqu	ushii	Bad
SSDPSRV	MS Universal Plug and Play	User
SSFSch	Gilat Comm Sky Blaster Schdlr	User
sshtray	SSH Sentinel Agent	User
SSLFVIEW	Seiko Smart Label RFViewer	User
Ssloserv	Sony Smart Label Oserver	User
ssmmgr	Samsung LBP SM	User
sstray	nForce Tray Options	User
SSUpdate	parasite variant	Bad
SSUpdate	parasite variant	Bad
ssvchost	HELIOS.B virus	Bad
sswizard	X-Grabber	Bad
st01b	REPAD virus	Bad
sta	Smart Type Assistant	User
stardown	Star Downloader	User
start	hijacker	Bad
start.bat	ZCREW virus	Bad
start.bat	ZCREW virus	Bad
start.bat	ZCREW virus	Bad
StartCli	Shoreline Personal Call Manager	User
startcop	Start Up Cop	User
StartEAK	Compaq Easy Access Keyboard	User
starter	parasite	Bad
Starter (1)	CodeStuff Starter	User
Starter (2)	Creative Labs Ensoniq Mixer	User
StartGuard	StartGuard	User
STARTM	McAfee Nuts & Bolts Start Menu	User
StartMessager	Messenger Starter	User
StartNet	Buffalo StartNet	User
startpage	hijacker	Bad
StartRight	StartRight	User
STARTS	Start Surfing	User
STARTSTOP	TFI Technology StartStop	User
Startup Launcher	Startup Delayer	User
StartupCleaner	Startup Cleaner	User
StartupMgr	Whej Startup Manager	User
StartupMonitor	Mike Lin Run Startup Monitor	User
STATBAR	Resource Hog	Bad
StatBlaster	see STCLOADER	Bad
StateMgr	MS PC State Manager Stub	Good
statemgr	WinME default for Sys Restore	Good
StatnPerf	Stat 'n' Perf	User
status	Supastatus	User
StatusClient	Hewlett-Packard Status Client	User
StayCon	Stay Connected	User
STBWEBTV	TV Display on PC	User
STC	see STCLOADER	Bad
STCLOA-1	adware	Bad
Stcloader	2nd-thought.com IE Search Tlbr	Bad
stcloader	adware	Bad
STCPO	Sophos Sweep Antivirus	Good
Std	Stealthdisk	User
stdialup	SpeedTouch Dialup	User
stealth25	Stealth Anonymizer 2.5	User
Steam	Steam Half-Life Game	User
steven	Steven	User
STICKIES	Stickies	User
StickyNote	Sticky Note	User
stickypad	Green Eclipse Sticky Pad	User
Stimon	Microsoft Still Image Monitor	User
Stisvc	Microsoft Still Image Monitor	User
stmctrl.dll	Telecom Italia ADSL State Monitor	User
STMgr	Microsoft PC State Manager	User
Strne	Epson Background Monitor	User
StopDialer	Stop Dialers	User
Stopthepop	Sureshot Popup Killer	User
Stopzilla	STOPzilla	User
STRAY	STAMPIT-Tray	User
strngbox	STRAND virus	Bad
strokeit	Stroke It	User
stswin	All Aboard Status	User
stte	Irrlel Web Outfitter Tray	User
stray	parasite	Bad
stub	foistware	Bad
stub	Nullsoft	User
STUpdate	toolbar	Bad
StutFix	Compaq System Patch	User
StyleXP	StyleXP	User
SuiteSt	Lotus-IBM Lotus SuiteStart 97	User
SULFNBJ	PC_MAGISTR.DAM virus	Bad
Supercleaner	Super Cleaner	User
Support	Dell Support	Ugly
supporterb	Hewlett-Packard Internet Center	User
SURFBRD	Hewlett-Packard Internet Center	User
surfer	parasite variant	Bad
surfer	parasite variant	Bad
SurfingSaver	Surfing Saver	User
Surveyor	Compaq Survey Utility	User
Susp	malware	Bad
SVAplayer	spyware	Bad
svc	hijacker, parasite variant	Bad
Sved	DELF.F virus	Bad
Svch0st	Backdoor.Graybird virus	Bad
SVCH0ST	GRAYBIRD.D virus	Bad
Svchost	GAYBIRD.B virus	Bad
Svchost	GAYBIRD.B virus	Bad
Svchos1	W32.HLLW.Gaobot.DK virus	Bad
svchos1	GAOBOT.DK virus	Bad
svchos1	GAOBOT.R virus	Bad
svchost	GAOBOT.P virus	Bad
Svchost	Svchost virus	Bad
Svchost	Microsoft Service Host	Good
svchost	MIMAIL.L virus	Bad

Program	Description	Good/Bad
svchost	ASTEF or RESPAN virus	Bad
svchost	CONE.C virus	Bad
svchost	parasite	Bad
svchost	HOSTIDEL.B virus	Bad
svchost	HOSTIDEL.C virus	Bad
Svchost	JEEFO virus	Bad
svchost	HITON virus	Bad
SVCHOST	DARKER virus	Bad
svchost	virus	Bad
svchost	homepage hijacker	Bad
svchost	MORB or TARNO viruses	Bad
svchost	CONE.F virus	Bad
svchost	DEWIN.E virus	Bad
svchost	CONE.D virus	Bad
svchost	CONE.B virus	Bad
svchost	CONE or CONE.E viruses	Bad
svchost	ASTEF or RESPAN viruses	Bad
Svchost32	NETSKY.F virus	Bad
Svchost32	Backdoor.IRC.Zcrew virus	Bad
svchost32	parasite related	Bad
svchost32	MIMAIL.I ir MIMAIL.J viruses	Bad
svchost64	SDBOTER.G virus	Bad
svchosthlp	BLASTER.T virus	Bad
Svchosts	SDBOT.N virus	Bad
SVCHOSTS	virus	Bad
svchosts	SDBOT virus	Bad
svcinit	parasite related	Bad
svcinit	SINIT virus	Bad
svcinit	parasite related	Bad
svcpack	parasite related	Bad
svctt	Microsoft Webserver	User
svdhost	Orwell Monitoring 2003	User
svdhost32	GAOBOT.ZW virus	Bad
SVEHOST	SPYBOT.H virus	Bad
SVhost	Backdoor.Socksbot virus	Bad
svhost	MYDOOM.I virus	Bad
svhst	GAOBOT.YC virus	Bad
Svrload	Trojan Horse	Ugly
svshost	virus	Bad
svshost	virus	Bad
sw32	AGOBOT.BQ virus	Bad
swatch	SocketWatch	User
SWcoaler	homepage hijacker	Bad
Swcaller2	homepage hijacker	Bad
SWost	SMALL.GV virus	Bad
Sweboexec	Webshots Desktop	User
Sweeper	Internet Sweeper	User
Sweepsrv.sys	Sophos Swee Service	User
SwiftBtn	Manages Extra Lifebook Button...	User
SwinnSuitNetwork	spyware	Bad
SWINIT	Shockwave Init	User
Switch	Slphamega Switch Manager Pro	User
SWNetSup	Sophos AntiVirus Ntwk Support Svc	User
swoff	Switch Off	User
SwTdM	Puts Day of the Month on Desktop	User
SWTRAY/SWTrayV4	MS Sidewinder Game Controller	User
SWUpdate	Sophos AntiVirus Auto-Update Svc	User
Sxgdsenu	MIDI Driver	Good
Sxgtkbar	see Sxgdsenu	
sycfg34	GAOBOT.AN virus	Bad
svchost	LEOX.B virus	Bad
SyGate	SyGate Manager	User
symantec32	RANDEX family of viruses	Bad
SymAV	NETSKY.U virus	Bad
Symlcsvc	Symantec Norton Security Products	User
SymmTime	SymmTime	User
SymProxySvc	Symantec Transparent Prxy Srvr	User
SymTray	Symantec Norton Tray Manager	User
Symtdr	Symantec System Tray Integrator	User
Sync	WhenU spyware	Bad
syncagent	Ghost Keylogger	Bad
SyncClk	Compaq Synchronize Clock	User
Synchost	RIPJAC virus	Bad
Syncit	Sync-It	User
SynTPEnh	Synaptics TouchPad Enhancmnts	User
SynTPLpr	Synaptics TouchPad	Good
sys#	DEXTER.A virus	Bad
sys*.*.*	search hijacker	Bad
sys_alert	spyware	Bad
sys16	virus	Bad
Sys32Smm	virus	Bad
sys64dvr	SDBOT virus	Bad
SysAgent	SYSagent	User
SysAI	adware	Bad
sysbot	Spector	User
syscfg32	W32.Kwbot.S.Worm@mm virus	Bad
syscfg32	SDBOT.B virus	Bad
syscfg34	KWBOT.S virus	Bad
syscfg34	ELECTRON virus	Bad
syscfg35	KAZMOF.C virus	Bad
Syschk	GAIL.F virus	Bad
Syscm	adware	Bad
syscnfg	virus	Bad
syscnfg	virus	Bad

Program	Description	Good/Bad
syscnfg	virus	Bad
syscnfg	virus	Bad
SYSCNTR	dialer	Bad
syscon	parasite	Bad
syscon	parasite	Bad
sysconf	SDBOT virus	Bad
sysconf	GAOBOT.FQ virus	Bad
sysconf32	SDBOT virus	Bad
Syscpy	HOGLE virus	Bad
sysct	AOK virus	Bad
Sysdeb32	SYSBUG virus	Bad
sysdiag32	SDBOT.GEN virus	Bad
sysdll32	parasite related	Bad
sysdllwm.reg	parasite variant	Bad
SysDoc32	Symantec Norton System Doctor	Ugly
SysDown	HP/Compaq ProLiant Servers	User
sysfiler	RETSAM virus	Bad
syshelp	LOVEGATE virus	Bad
syshost	FRANCETTE virus	Bad
sysinfo	GAOBOT.FQ virus	Bad
sysinfo	BEDRILL virus	Bad
sysinfo	BEAGLE.V virus	Bad
SYSio32	adware	Bad
syslaunch	adware	Bad
syslaunch	adware	Bad
syslaunch	ADLCICKER.G virus	Bad
sysldr32	GAOBOT virus	Bad
Syslib	trojan	Bad
Sysload32	W32.Mimail.E@mm virus	Bad
Sysload32	W32.Mimail.E@mm virus	Bad
sysload32	MIMAIL.E virus	Bad
Syslog	parasite	Bad
Syslog	parasite	Bad
Syslog32	DONK family of viruses	Bad
SyslogRd	Logs Draytek Router Info	User
SysMap	MAPSIV virus	Bad
sysmd	foistware	Bad
SysMetrix	SysMetrix	User
SYSMON	System Monitor Aopen Mthrbrds	User
sysmon	BIZEX virus	Bad
Sysmon16	SDBOT virus	Bad
SysMonXP	W32.Netsky.Q@mm virus	Bad
SysMonXP	NETSKY.Q virus	Bad
sysnate	MEDIAS virus	Bad
sysnav32	hijacker	Bad
SysOps	MSNCORRUPT virus	Bad
SysReg	CCINVADER2 virus	Bad
SysReg	foistware	Bad
Sysres	LOGMOD virus	Bad
Syssafe	System Safety Monitor	User
SysService	DELF family of viruses	Bad
SysService32	KINDAL virus	Bad
SYSsftb	hijacker	Bad
systask32	THEUG virus	Bad
System	GATECRASH.A or .B viruses	Bad
System	GAOBOT.AO virus	Bad
System	DANI virus	Bad
system	NULLBOT virus	Bad
system	MITGLIEDER.C virus	Bad
system	NETSPY virus	Bad
system	viruses including CHILI, NULLBOT	Bad
system	BUSHTRO122 virus	Bad
system	REVIRD virus	Bad
System (1) n/a	MS Op Sys & All Kernal Threads	Good
System (2)	Trojan.Download.Revird virus	Bad
System 4820	TUXDER virus	Bad
System Idle Process n/a	MS Totals Idle Processor Time	Good
system..	OPTIXPRO.13.C virus	Bad
system.	OPTIXPRO.13.C virus	Bad
System.dat.vbs	BISCUIT.A virus	Bad
System32	viruses	Bad
System32	KWBOT.C virus	Bad
System32	LOGPOLE.C virus	Bad
System32Driver32	SUPOVA.2 virus	Bad
Systemcheck	LAVITS virus	Bad
SystemCONF98i	FROZEN BOT virus	Bad
SystemDll	LOXOSCAM virus	Bad
systeminit	hijacker	Bad
SystemRestorer	DULOAD.C virus	Bad
Systems	Keyboard Spectator	User
systems	TARNO.C virus	Bad
systems	TARNO.C virus	Bad
systemsearch.hta	TARNO.C virus	Bad
SystemTray	BIGFOOT virus	Bad
SystemUpd	Swampoo.com	User
Systemwiper	il System Wiper	User
Systimer	eAcceleration Corp	User
systoan	virus	Bad
Systools	RONOPER-G virus	Bad
Systra	LOVEGATE family of viruses	Bad
systray	FSERVE virus	Bad
systray	ALADINZ.P virus	Bad
SysTray	ALADINZ virus	Bad
systray	MUTEBOT virus	Bad
SysTray (1)	MS Windows System Tray	Good
Systray (2)	Backdoor.IRC.Mutebot virus	Bad

Start Up & Tasks

Program	Description	Good/Bad
Systray	KERGEZ.A virus	Bad
systray32	DABOOM virus	Bad
SysTray32	REPAD virus	Bad
systroy	IRC.ALADINZ.C virus	Bad
sysu	adware	Bad
Sysupd	foistware	Bad
Sysupd	SLACKBOT virus	Bad
Sysvupex	MEDIAS virus	Bad
SYSWIN96	We-Blocker	User
sysweb	SOBOT.GEN virus	Bad
Syswindow	COW virus	Bad
syswrun4x	MITGLIEDER.E virus	Bad
SYSZ	ALADINZ.P virus	Bad
Szchost	MERCURYCAS.A virus	Bad
SZMsgSvc	StopZilla!	User
SZNTSVC	StopZilla!	User
T g c m d	Tioga Software/Support.com	Ugly
TabLaunchpad	Tad Launchpad	User
Tablet	Wacom Technology	User
TabUserW	Wacom Technology	User
tad	Turtle Beach Santa Cruz	User
Tahni	Tahni Deskmate	User
Tahoma.vbs	homepage hijacker	Bad
TALKINGREMINDER	Sftwr River Sltns Talking Reminder	User
tamomous	mouseEt	User
Tapicfg	parasite related	Bad
TAPISRV	MS Telephony API Server	User
TapiTNA	Windows95 Power Toys	User
Tardis	Tardis	User
Task_Agent	iolo Task Agent	User
task32	virus	Bad
taskban	TaskBan	User
TaskBar	W32.Frethem.L@mm virus	Bad
TaskInfo	Taskinfo 2003	User
TaskMgr	MS Windows Task Manager	Good
Taskmgr	homepage hijacker	Bad
taskmgr#	SOWSAT.C and SOWSAT.J viruses	
taskmgr.exe	BEREB virus	Bad
taskmgr32#	SOWSAT.B virus	Bad
taskmgr	parasite	Bad
taskmgr	parasite	Bad
taskmon	MYDOOM.A and MYDOOM.J viruses	
TaskMon (1)	MS Windows Task Manager	User
TaskMon (2)	W32.Novarg.A@mm virus	Bad
TaskPanl	Earthlink E6 Task Panel	User
TASKPLUSO/TASKPL-1		Task Plus
taskplussetup	Task Plus	User
TaskSwitch	Microsoft PowerToys	User
tasksys.vbs	BYRON virus	Bad
TaskSystemDll	BACKZAT.G virus	Bad
TasKTray	foistware	Bad
tatss	adware	Bad
Taumon	Tau Monitor	User
tb_setup	HuntBar parasite toolbar	Bad
tb2init	Netopia Timbuktu Pro	User
Tbc	Titlebar Clock	User
tbcpro	Titlebar Clock	Ugly
TBCtray	Voyetra Turtle Beach	User
tbihouse	Aiptek HyperPen	User
TbNote	SPIS Ltd TurboNote	User
TBPanel	Gainward Graphics Card Config	User
tbtray	ThunderBird PCI Control Panel	User
TbUpdate	Bayswag2	User
tc	Time Calendar	User
tca	MooSoft The Cleaner	User
tcaudiag	3Com	User
TClock/TClock2/TCLOCKEX	Kazubon Tclock	User
tcm	MooSoft The Cleaner	User
TCPSvcs	MS TCP/IP Serivices Application	User
TDKSTART	Splash Screen for CD-RW	User
TDKTASK	Control Panel for CD-RW	User
Tdrp	see IWAR	Bad
TDS-3	Anti-Trojan Program	User
te	Acesoft Tracks Eraser Pro	User
teachbox	Teach In Box	User
teatimer	Spybot Search & Destroy	User
techbox	Tech-In-A-Box	User
Teskids	W32.Blaseter.C virus	Bad
teekids	BLASTER.C virus	Bad
telepath	US Robotics	User
TempCleaner	Toshiba Display Devices Hotkeys	User
TempTool	jv16 PowerTools	User
TEscKey	Toshiba Escape Key Handler	User
Test	DELF.B virus	Bad
testkey	SPYBOT.B virus	Bad
TextAloudMP3	TextAloud MP3	User
tfimemsr	Memory Optimization Program	User
TFncky	Toshiba Function Key Combos	User
TFNF5	Toshiba Function Keys	User
Tfswctrl	HP Drive Letter Assignment (DLA)	Ugly
tftp###	SPYBOT.B virus	Bad
TFuncKey	Toshiba Function Key Handler	User
tgdc	spyware	Bad
tgfix	SupportSoft	User
TGSHELL	see T g c m d	Ugly
THE WEATHER CHANNEL	Weather Chnl Desktop Weather	User
thebat	The Bat!	User
thehel1iawgrd32/Fawgrd32	Cybermedia Windows Guardian	User
THEWEA-1	Weather Chnl Dsktp Weather 3	User
THGuard	Monitors/Removes Trojans	User
ThirtyDayTimer	CoffeeCup Software	User
THotkey	Toshiba Laptop Fn Keys	User
thundertray	Thundertray	User
Timemanager	Time Manager	User
TIMEONLINE	Lightman Group TimeOnline	User
TIMER	TIMESE.AG virus	Bad
timesync	MS Input Message Editor	User
Timeup	TimeUp	User
TINTSETP	MS Input Message Editor	User
TintSvr	MS Telnet Server	User
tinyspell	Tinyspell	User
Tioman	Tioman	User
tisdnmon	TELES ISDN Monitor	User
TitlebarClock	TitleBar Clock	User
TiVoServer	TiVo Service	User
TConnect	Tiscali.co.uk	Ugly
T-Man	T-Man	User
tmchook	virus	Bad
TMEEJME	Toshiba Mobile Extensions	User
TMERzCtl	Toshiba Mobile Extensions	User
TMESBS32	Toshiba Mbl Extsn Slim Select Bay Svc	User
TMESrv31	Toshiba Mobile Extension Svc	User
TMListen	Trend Micro OfficeScan NT Listener	User
TMNTSrv	Trend Micro PC-Cillin Antivirus	User
TMOAgent	Trend Micro Outlook Agent	User
tmouse	Toshiba Mouse Control	User
TMProxy	Trend Micro Internet Security Ste	User
TMTMTSR	Thrust TSR	User
TMTMTST	Thrumaster	User
TNTCLK	TNT Graphic Cards	User
ToADlMon	T-Online Isp	User
ToolBox	CheckIt Toolbox	User
toolsclickstat	Iomega Clik Status Monitor	User
toscdspd	Alters CD/DVD Drive Speed	User
ToshHKCW	Toshiba hotkey	User
ToshibSu	Toshiba Laptop Setting	User
TosHKCW	Toshiba Wireless Hotkey	User
tosmem	Toshiba Laptops	User
TOTALCMD	Total Commander	User
TotRecSched	Total Recorder	User
TouchED	Toshiba TouchPad Control Panel	User
tp4ex	IBM TrackPoint	User
TP4Mon	IBM TrackPoint	User
tp4serv	Support for IBM ThinkPad	User
TP98	Config for IBM ThinkPad	User
TPHKMgr	IBM ThinkPad Hotkey Manager	User
TpKmapMn	Key Combos for ThinkPad Laptops	User
TPPaldr	DataStor TPP Auto Loader App	User
TPPstray	DataStor TPP System Tray	User
TpShocks	IBM Active Protection System	User
TPSMain	Toshiba Utility	User
TPTray	Notebook PC Touchpad Control	User
TPwrTray	Toshiba Power Management	Ugly
TrackerV3	TrackerV3	User
TRAHSGRD	McAfee Nuts & Bolts	User
tranicon	Transparent Icons	User
TransBar	Lets Taskbar be Transparent	User
TransText	TransText	User
Transparent0/TransparentW/TransparentB	Lets Icon Bckgrnds be Transparent	User
Tray	homepage hijacker	Bad
tray_helper	Tray Helper	User
trayapp	Novell iFolder	User
Traybar	TrayBar	User
TrayIcint	Microsoft System Tray Icon	Ugly
TRAYDATE	Date and Time in System Tray	User
traydevil	TrayDevil	User
TrayIcon	Display Tray Icon	User
trayInf	Tray Manager	User
Traymon	Netopia Intrnt Rcvr Tray Monitor	User
TrayMonitor	Stardock MacVision Tray Monitor	User
TrayPit	Tray Pilot Lite	User
TRAYSA-1	Mike Lin AAA Tray Saver	User
TraySaver	Mike Lin AAA Tray Saver	User
TrayServer	Stardock Tray Monitor	User
TRAYWND	LITMUS.002 virus	Bad
trickler_bis_GatorDM_4010	spyware	Bad
TridTray	Aztech	Ugly
Trillian	Trillian	User
Trjscan	Simply Super Trojan Remover	User
Trueimage	Acronis True Image	User
TRUG.vbs	TRUG.B virus	Bad
TSADBOT	Conducent/TimeSink	Bad
TSADBOT	spyware	Bad

Program	Description	Good/Bad	Program	Description	Good/Bad
TSADBOT	spyware	Bad	Usrsureconnect	US Robotics SureConnect ADSL Utlty	
TSIRCSrv	Laplink Gold 11	User	USRWLANG	US Robotics	User
TSIRCUsr	Laplink Gold 11	User	USSSrange	Ulead SmartSaver Pro	Ugly
tskdbg	FLOOD.E virus	Bad	UtilityPro	Rawhide Search Soltns Utility Pro	User
Tskmg	W32.HLLW.Warpigs.C virus	Bad	UtilMan	Microsoft Utility manager	User
tskmgr32	homepage hijacker	Bad	UTILsinet	Gilat Internet Satellite Sys	Good
TSMsger	Epson Scanner	User	v_ctl	3dfx Underground Tools	User
tstool	Starfish TrueSync Launcher	User	V38SHELL	ASUS Key	User
tsyn	TimeSync	User	VAGCTRL	Sony Vaio Laptop 10 Key Bay Use	User
TSysTray	Real Networks Real Jukebox	User	VAGCTRL	Central Command Vexira Antivirus	User
TTEST6	Christmas Music Player	Ugly	VAGINT	Central Command Vexira Antivirus	User
TTTimer	TerraTec Scheduler	User	vAppCon	Vital Application Console	User
Ttuh	see IWAP	User	VASCHD32	Virtual Access Scheduler	User
TUN	Total Uninstall	User	VAServ	Sony Vaio Action Setup	User
TurboTop	TurboTop	User	VBouncerInnerxxxx	malware	Bad
Tvm	hijacker variant	Bad	VBPTASK	FarStone RestoreIT!	User
tvmd	spyware	Bad	VCSPlay	Virtual CD	User
TvNow	TV Now	User	Vcatch	spyware and adware	Bad
TVTMD	spyware	Bad	VCDPlayer	Virtual CD	User
TVTool	TV Tool	User	vcdplayxx	Roxanie GameDrive & VirtualDriveUser	User
TVWakeUp	Microsoft Hidden TV Control	User	VCDTower	VCD Tower	User
twarnmsg	Toshiba Warning System	User	vchk	Command Antivirus	User
tweakdun	Tweak DUN	User	VCSPlay	H+H GmbH Virtual CD SDK Plyr	User
TWEAK-ME	Tweak-Me	User	VCSSecS	H+H GmbH Vrt CD SDK Scrty Svc	User
Tweakknow	RAM Idle Professional	User	VDTask	Farstone VirtualDrive	User
TweakUI.cpl	Microsoft TweakUI	User	VEEV296F.DLL	SafeGuard Popup Blocker Update	User
Tweak-xp	Tweak-XP	User	VELOZSYS	foistware	Bad
twinmos	USB Mass Storage Interface	User	ver_chk	Windows Version Check	User
Twunk_16	Twain Wrkg Grp 16-bit Thunking Srvr		versato	GTronix Keyboard hotbutton	User
twunk_64	homepage hijacker	User	Version	adware variant	Bad
Type32	Microsoft Intellitype	User	vet32/vet98	Computer Assoc Vet Start Up	User
Typeltin	Type It In	User	vet98	Cmptr Assoc Innoculate IT Antivirus	
TypePit	Type Pilot	User			Good
uability	UninstallAbility	User	vetmsg9x	Cmptr Assoc Innoculate IT Antivirus	
uc	adware and homepage hijacker	Bad			Good
UD	United Devices Agent	User	VetMsg9x/VetMsgNT	Cmptr Assoc Innoculate IT Antivirus	
uddater	LEOX virus	Bad	VetTray	Computer Assoc Vet Antivirus	User
UdServe	Executive Software Undelete	User	VGAProbe	ASUS SmartDoctor	User
UEPROC32	Norton Utilities	User	VHK	Volume Hotkey XP	User
Ufd	USB Flash Disk	User	vi	adult content dialer	Bad
uGIG	GINK virus	Bad	vi_grm	Trio 2x/3x Video Card Drivers	User
uICE	Universal Infrared Control Engine	User	Vidcompat	GEMA virus	User
Uidler	Uniloc Titleware Browser	User	vide_32	GAOBOT/AGOBOT virus	Bad
UIWatcher	Ashampoo Uninstaller Suite	User	videodrv	MIMAIL.A virus	User
ukvideo2	adult content dialer	Bad	videomgr	PANDEM.C virus	User
UltraMon	UltraMon	User	VidSvr	Microsoft Web TV	User
umxagent	Tiny Personal Firewall	User	vietatz	adult content dialer	Bad
umxldra	Tiny Personal Firewall	User	view	foistware	Bad
UMXLDRW	Tiny Personal Firewall	User	ViewMgr	spyware	Bad
Untitled.dks	PowerQuest DataKeeper	User	ViewPort	ATI Technologies HydraVision	User
untray	Command Antivirus	User	virscana	virus	Bad
UNWISE	Gadwin PrintScreen	User	VirtualBouncer	spyware	Bad
UPD	Totem	User	virtuald	Virtual Desktop	User
upd	adult content screen saver	Bad	VirtuaWin	Virtual Desktop	User
Update	Update Service	User	Virus_Cleaner	PANOL virus	Bad
Update	Handybits EasyCrypto	Good	Vision	PCTV Vision	User
Update	GAOBOT.AO virus	Bad	vistascan	VistaScan	User
update	foistware	Bad	VisualGuard	NETSKY family of viruses	Bad
UPDATE~1	parasite	Bad	VividGalut	web downloader	Bad
update911.js	hijacker	Bad	vmdfw	VirusMD Personal Firewall	User
UpdateMedia	foistware	Bad	VOBRegCheck	VOB/Pinnacle Instant Copy	User
updatemgr/UPDATE~1	Earthlink Update Manager	User	Volkey	Volume Control Settings	User
Updater	Auto-Updater	User	VPlus	ICQ.com Skin Manager	User
UpdateStats	see STCLOADER		vpngui	Cisco Systems VPN Client	User
updatewinlocator	toolbar	Bad	vpnservices	Symantec Raptor Mobile	User
Updmgr	KaZaA Popup Ad Creator	Bad	vpop3	Paul Smith VPOP3 Mail Server	User
updmgr	adware	Bad	VProperty	System Tray Icon	User
UpdReg	Creative Labs Registry Updater	User	VPTray	Symantec VirusProtect Shield	User
UpdTray	see NewsGui	User	vrmonnt	Hauri Antivirus	User
Uprootkit	backdoor.Up!RootKit virus	Bad	vrmont	Hauri Antivirus	Good
UPS	MS Uninterruptible Power Supply	User	vrtxctrl	Sonic A3D Control	User
	PowerChute v5.02	Good	vsaccess	UMAX VistaAccess	User
upscmd	Centralinn Intell UPS Commander	User	VSECCMR	McAfee VirusScan up to v4.x	User
UPSD	Belkin UPS Sentry Service	User	VSENMB	malware	Bad
UpTime	UpTime	User	VSHWin32	McAfee VirusScan	User
Uptimer4	Uptimer4	User	VSmon	Zone Labs Zone Alarm Firewall	User
uptodate	foistware	Bad	VSMon	Zone Labs True Vector	User
uptodate	foistware	Bad	vspdfprsrv	Visage PDF Printer	User
UrlFixer	URL Fixer	User	vsserv	BitDefender Antivirus	Good
Url95Svc	Norton Internet Security 2004	User	VSSTat	McAfee VirusScan	User
URLMap	Microsoft Money 2002	User	VSSvc	MS Volume Shadow Copy Svc	User
urlmon32.dll	EVIAN.C virus	User	VtlAgent	Lucent Tech My Vital Agent	User
Urt955Svc	Virtual LAN Assignmt Svc	User	vtpassid	Part of vYafta	User
USB	Installs USB Background Task	User	VTPreset	Savage Pro S3 Graphics	User
usbmmkbd	Hewlett-Packard Specialty Keys	User	vTuner	vYafta Tray	User
USBmonitor	Genie USB Monitor	User	vu_Brief	File Synchronization Program	User
usbshare	USB Sharing	User	Vx632v	W32.Dumaru.Y @mm virus	User
USBsircs	Sony Giga Pocket Remocon Driver	User	W32ALARM	World Watch Alarm Support	User
usbtapnp	System Tray Access	User	w32sup	adult content dialer	Bad
user32	PWSTEAL.PPORT virus	Bad	W30BSMgr	W32.Dumaru.Y @mm virus	Bad
Userinit	Microsoft Winlogon	Good	W75P2PS	Printer Utility	User
USRINIT	MADDIS.B virus	Bad	W95Mm	homepage hijacker install toolbar	Bad
USRmlnk!	US Robotics	User	wab	Address Book	User
USRmlnkA	US Robotics	Good			

Program	Description	Good/Bad
WallCal3	Wallpaper Calendar	User
Wallmast	WallMaster Pro	User
WALLPA-1	Wallpaper Changer	User
wallpaper	Compumatrix Wallpaper Changer	User
Wallpaper Changer 2	Wallpaper Changer	User
Wallpapertoy	Microsoft Wallpaper Changer	User
WanMPSvc	AOL Wan MiniPort Service	Ugly
WAOL	AOL	User
Waol-	parasite variant	Bad
Wapicc	see WINSERVN	Bad
Wapiit	see WINSERVN	Bad
Wapisu	see WINSERVN	Bad
Wapisvil	see WINSERVN	Bad
Wapisvsu	see WINSERVN	Bad
WAR-FTPD	Warez	User
WAR-FTPD	JGAA War FTP Daemon	User
Warm.scr	W32.Scold@mm virus	Bad
Warm.scr	SCOLD virus	Bad
warnet	G-Tek Tech Warner/CyberWarner	User
warnet	Warnet	User
washer	Webroot Windows Washer	User
washerie	Webroot Cache & Cookie Washer	User
washidx	Webroot Windows Washer	User
wast	Grokster ads updater	Bad
Watch	Direct Scan	User
WatchDog	Greatis RegRun 3 Security Suite	Good
Watchdog (1)	Scanner Light	User
Watchdog (2)	Compaq Internet Watchdog	User
wavepcmonitor	Bose Wave/PC Monitor	User
WaveTop	WaveTop	User
Wbiff	Wbiff	User
WBLoad	Stardock WindowBlinds Load Module	User
Wbsched	LJUtilities WinBackup Scheduler	User
Wcescomm	Microsoft ActiveSync Conn'th Mgr	User
WCESMgr	Microsoft ActiveSync	User
Wcmdmgr	Wild Tangent Automtd Support Engine	User
Wcmdmgrl	Wild Tangent Web Driver	User
Wcpcc	see WINSERVN	Bad
Wcpsvsu	see WINSERVN	Bad
Wcpsvtr	see WINSERVN	Bad
wd	Worm Detector	User
WDBtnMgr	WD Button Manager	User
wdinfo	adult content dialer	Bad
WDMIRROR	Worldox Document Mgmt	User
Wdrun32	GAOBOT.AO virus	Bad
WDVRCtrl	TV Capture Cart Driver Task	User
wdwctrl	DLUCA.R virus	Bad
Weather	AWS Convergence Technologies	User
Weatherbug	Tray Temperature	User
WeatherD	Weather Display	User
weatherpulse	weather Pulse	User
web	adult content dialer	Bad
web	parasite variant	Bad
web3trap	Trend Micro PC-Cillin Antivirus	User
webalize	hijacker	Bad
WebAssist	180Solutions.com n-Case	User
webassist	adware	Bad
WebCamRT	SpotLife Broadcast	Ugly
webcel	spyware	Bad
WebCheck.pif	CONE.C or CONE.F viruses	Bad
Webcolct	Logitech WebCollect	User
webdav	IRC DDoS virus	Bad
webdrive	Web Drive Tray	User
WebInstall	adware	Bad
WebInstall	adware	Bad
WebKey	JB Utilities WebKey	User
WebMon	WebMon	User
websaverlive	WebSaver Live!	User
WebScanX	McAfee Web & ActiveX Scanner	User
WebShotsTray/websgit1	Twofold Photos Webshots Desktop	User
WebTrap/WebTrapNT	Trend Micro PC-Cillin Antivirus	Ugly
Welcome	Welcome to Windows	User
wetsock	RoboMagic Wetsock	User
Wfb0x-	Leadtek WinFast Graphics Card	User
wf2kcpl.dll	WinFast2000 Load Default	User
WFGStartup	World Weather	User
Wflmgr32	Shell Novell Groupwise 5.5	User
WFShell	Citrix Systems WinFrame Shell	User
Wfwiz	Leadtek WinFast Schedule	User
WFXCTL32	Symantec TalkWorks Pro & WinFax	User
wfxload	Stardock WindowFX	User
WFxMod/WFxMod32	Symantec WinFax	User
Wfxsnt40	Symantec Fax Port Launcher	User
WFXSvc-	Symantec WinFax Pro Service	User
WFXSwtch	Delrina/Symantec WinFax App Port	User
WG511WLU	Netgear	User
WGFE95	Winguard Dr Solomon's Virex Antivirus	User
WGPRO32	McAfee WinGuage	User
WGWLocalManager	Flash-Network NetGain 2000	User
WgwMngr-	Flash-Network NetGain 2000	User
wh_exec	Wheel Mouse	User

Program	Description	Good/Bad
WHAgent	webHancer	Bad
whagent	spyware	Bad
whagent	spyware	Bad
whSurvey	webHancer	Bad
Whvlxd-	W32.LXD>Mirc virus	Bad
WillowRoad	Willow Road	User
WIN HOST PROCESS	KEYLOGGER.CLONE virus	Bad
win.hta	virus	Bad
Win????	DNSX virus	Bad
Win_vader.vbs	INVASION.A virus	Bad
WIN32	RATEGA virus	Bad
Win32	ISRAZ.A virus	Bad
win32	STARTPAGE virus	Bad
WIN32_I	Searchbarcash.com/CDT Inc	Bad
win32_i	parasite variant	Bad
win32_i	parasite variant	Bad
win32API	homepage hijacker	Bad
WIN32DLL.vbs	LOVELETTER virus	Bad
win32gb	adult content dialer	Bad
win32hlp	AMIVISION virus variant	Bad
win32nfo	adult content dialer	Bad
win32server.scr	HACARMY virus	Bad
Win32SL	Intel Dell's OpenManage DMI Svc Layer	User
win32us	adult content dialer	Bad
Win386	GOSUSUB virus	Bad
WINACTIVE	hijacker variant	Bad
WinActiveJ	ROTARRAN virus	Bad
winadm	Parents Friend	User
Winahlp	VAGRNBOCKER virus	Bad
winallap	DELF.E virus	Bad
winallapu	DELF.E virus	Bad
winamp.htm	hijacker	Bad
Winampa	Nullsoft Winamp	User
winampa	SPYBOTER.GEN virus	Bad
Winbackup	W32.Mertian@mm virus	Bad
winbackup	MERTIAN virus	Bad
winbait	RegRun WinBait	User
WinBar	WinBar	User
WIN-BUGSFIX	LOVELETTER virus	Bad
Wincfg32	SILVERFTP virus	Bad
WinCheck	PWS-CY virus	Bad
winchi-1-	WinChimes	User
WinCinemaMgr	InterVideo WinDVD	User
WINClock	unidentified mIRC virus	Bad
Wincmp32	ASYLUM virus	Bad
wincmp	trojan	Bad
wincooli	Windows ME Product Preview	Ugly
wincpu	virus	Bad
wincrt32	GAOBOT.BF virus	Bad
Windate	WinDates	User
Windates	rockinsoftware.com WinDates	User
WINDBKGND	McAfee Nuts & Bolts	User
winde	DLUCA virus	Bad
windefault	AFA Filter	User
windex	GAOBOT.BM virus	Bad
windex	GAOBOT.BZ virus	Bad
windfind	adult content dialer	Bad
WindII	TRYNOMA virus	Bad
WindII	TRYNOMA virus	Bad
WindII	STEALER virus	Bad
windII	GOP.F virus	Bad
windII32	ASTEF or RESPAN viruses	Bad
windII32	MSNPWS virus	Bad
WINDLL32XP-	SPBOTTER.GEN virus	Bad
windres32	GAOBOT.WX virus	Bad
window	MTGLEIDER.H OR _J virus	Bad
Windows	QQPASS.E virus	Bad
Windows	KAZMOR, BOBBINS, ALADINC.D virus	Bad
windows.vbs	homepage hijacker	Bad
windows_critical_update	ASTEF or RESPAN viruses	Bad
windows_update	LOHACK.B virus	Bad
WindowsAgent	GOP.G virus	Bad
WindowsUpd1	foistware	Bad
WindowsUpd2	foistware	Bad
Windowsupd4	adware	Bad
Windowz	RANDEX.AEV virus	Bad
WinDrivers	DULOAD.C virus	Bad
WINDRV	IRCINTER.A virus	Bad
windrv32	virus	Bad
windvd98	CULT.P virus	Bad
WinDVRCtrl	AOpen VA1000 TV Tuner Card	User
Winexec	foistware	Bad
Winexec32	REDIST.B virus	Bad
WinExec32	KAZWIN virus	Bad
WINFAH	Folding@home	User
Winfavorites1	adware	Bad
Winfi1e32	W32.Mertian@mm virus	Bad
Winfi1e32	MERITAN virus	Bad
WinGate	LOVGATE.G virus	Bad
WinGate	LOVGATE virus	Bad
winhelp	QQPASS.E virus	Bad
winhelp	LOVGATE.G virus	Bad

Program	Description	Good/Bad
WinHelp	LOVGATE.N or LOVGATE.O viruses	Bad
winhlp32	GAOBOT.AO virus	Bad
winhlp32	GAOBOT.SY virus	Bad
winhost	LOLAWEB.A virus	Bad
wini	OPTIZ.04.D virus	Bad
winicfg32	GAOBOT.GENPOLY virus	Bad
wininetd	WINET virus	Bad
wininfo	malware	Bad
Wininit	BYMER virus	Bad
wininit	WOLLF.16 virus	Bad
wininit32	XABOT virus	Bad
Wink*	KLEZ virus	Bad
wink66	We-Blocker	User
WinKer	MIRAB or SERVIDOR viruses	Bad
winkemal	LIAMED virus	Bad
winkey	Copernic WinKey	User
winkrnl386	ZEBKOXY virus	Bad
WinLED	Touch Manager	User
winlink32	GABOT.AAY virus	Bad
winload32	CULT.M virus	Bad
WINLODR.SCR	virus	Bad
winlogin	RANDEX.E virus	Bad
winlogin	RANDEX.K virus	Bad
winlogon	NETSKY family of viruses	Bad
winlogon	virus	Bad
winlogon	hijacker or adult content dialer	Bad
winlogon	TRODAL virus	Bad
WinLogon (1)	Microsoft Windows Logon App	Good
WinLogon (2)	W32.Netsky.C@mm virus	Bad
winlogon.scr	NETSKY.AA virus	Bad
winlogonn	RANDEX.FC virus	Bad
winman	malware	Bad
winmants	MANTAS virus	Bad
WinMatrixXP	WinMatrix XP	User
winmax	BANCOS.B virus	Bad
WinMBR	System Commander 7	User
WinMesgr	WinMessenger	User
Winmgm32	SOBIG and LALA.C viruses	Bad
WinMgr	MS Windows Mgmt Instrumentation	User
WinMgr32	W32.Mimail.P@mm virus	Bad
winmgr32	MIMAIL.P virus	Bad
winmgts	trojan	Bad
Winmsuit	ELSA WINman Suite	User
WinMuschi	dialer	Bad
winmsqladmin	Win My SQ Ladmin Tool	User
Winnet	CommonName Ltd.	Ugly
winnet	toolbar spyware	Ugly
WinntBB	DULOAD.C virus	Bad
Winoldap	Microsoft Windows Module	Good
WINPAT-1	WinPatrol Plus	User
WinPatrol	WinPatrol	User
WINPOPUP	WinPopup	User
WinPPPOverEthernet	Fine Point Tech WinPoET	User
winport32	SOBIG.F virus	Bad
winproc32	parasite	Bad
Winpro	CHUPACABRA virus	Bad
WinProxy	WinProxy	User
winpt	Windows Privacy Tracy	User
winpup32	ADCLICKER virus	Bad
winpup32	dialer	Bad
Winpup32	ADCLICKER virus	Bad
Winrar	parasite variant	Bad
winrar	parasite variant	Bad
winrarshell32	SALIRA virus	Bad
winrecon	WinRecon	User
Winreg	GAOBOT.AO virus	Bad
WINREG	ASSASIN.D virus	Bad
WINREG	DEWIN.A virus	Bad
winReg	YAHA.I or YAHA.J viruses	Bad
winregsrv	SYNRG virus	Bad
WinRet	Files Autoback	User
winroll	WinRoll	User
winrun	WINBUR.B virus	Bad
winrun	WINBUR.B virus	Bad
WinRunHelp.wrh	AIMVISION virus	Bad
WinScheduler	Intervideo WinScheduler	User
winsec	parasite variant	Bad
WinServ	EVILBOT.B virus	Bad
winserv	SHADOWTHIEF virus	Bad
winserv	IMISERV virus	Bad
WinServices	YAHA.K or YAHAM viruses	Bad
Winservn	ClickSpring PurityScan	Bad
winservn	homepage hijacker	Bad
Winservs	adware	Bad
Winservs	adware	Bad
WinSetup	EVILBOT.B virus	Bad
winsock2.2	SPYBOT virus	Bad
WinSOCKS	homepage hijacker	Bad
WinSocks5	GRAYBIRD.F virus	Bad
winsrv	OPASERV.T virus	Bad
Winsrv	ADUENT virus	Bad
Winsrvc	W32.Friendgreat.worm virus	Bad
WinSSK32	Sobig.E virus	Bad
winss32	SOBIG.E virus	Bad
winsta-1	foistware	Bad
winsta-1	foistware	Bad
WinStart	foistware	Bad
winstart	EARLYBIRD virus	Bad
WinStart.pif	CONE.E virus	Bad
WinStart001	iGetNet Internet Explorer Helper	Ugly
WinStart001	foistware	Bad
winstart32	PUROL virus	Bad
winstartup	malware	Bad
WinStrt16	CAKE virus	Bad
Winsvc32	homepage hijacker	Bad
Winsys	Win-Spy	User
winsys	BEAGLE.K virus	Bad
winsys32	GAOBOT.FL virus	Bad
Winsys32	CIGIVIP or RECDUS viruses	Bad
winsyslog	parasite	Bad
winsyst32	MOR5 virus	Bad
winsystem	WHITEBAIT virus	Bad
Wintask	NAVIDAD virus	Bad
Wintask	HIPO or LEMIR.F viruses	Bad
WinTasks	IL Utilities Win Taska	User
WinTidy	PC Magazine/Ziff Davis WinTidy	User
wintray	LEGUARDIEN.B virus	Bad
Wintms	WINTRIM virus	Bad
Wintsk32	YAHA.U virus	Bad
Wintsu	see WINSERVN	Bad
Wintsvcc	see WINSERVN	Bad
wintt	LOLAWEB.B virus	Bad
winuodps	GAOBOT.BH virus	Bad
WINUPD	adult content dialer	Bad
winupd	BEABLE.M or BEAGLE.N viruses	Bad
winupdate	LITMUS virus	Bad
winupdate	BMBOT virus	Bad
winupdate	BMBOT virus	Bad
winupdate	RADO virus	Bad
winupdates	GAOBOT.BC virus	Bad
winupdates	GAOBOT.BI virus	Bad
winupdgm	GAOBOT.AO virus	Bad
Winupdsdgm	GABOT.AO virus	Bad
winuplc	adware	Bad
WinVNC	WinVNC	User
Winwall	Winwall Autostart	User
winwan	parasite variant	User
winwan	parasite variant	User
winwd	Tropical Software PC Security	User
Winword	Microsoft Word	User
winy	adware	User
winz32	KWBOT.Z virus	Bad
winz32	SOBOT.Q virus	Bad
WireKeys	WireKeys	User
wiseupdt	Visioneer OneTouch	User
wizard	Creative Installation Wizard	User
wjview	Microsoft TVU	User
wjview ...websearch	Ebates Software popups	Bad
WkCalRem	MS Works Calendar Reminders	User
WKDetect	Microsoft Works	User
WKFUD	MS Works Marketing Feature	Ugly
WksCal	Microsoft Works Calendar	User
WksSb	Microsoft Works Portfolio	User
WkUFind	Microsoft Works 2002 Picture!t!	Ugly
wlancfg	MA111 Configuration Utility	User
wlancfg5	MA521 Configuration Utility	User
WlanMonitor	WLAN Monitor & Configuration	User
WLANSTA	WLAN Status Tray Applet	User
wlanutil	Configuration Utility	User
WlanUtility	Wireless LAN Utility	User
WL.PCCfg	WLAN Card Utility	User
WM	Novell Client Workstation Mgr	User
Wm95	Novell Client Workstation Mgr	User
WinMcAgt	MS Windows Media Encoder Agent	Ugly
WMexe	3Com	User
WMIAPSrv	MS Win Mgmt Adapter Svc	User
Wmiexe	MS Win Mgmt Instrumentation	Good
Wminf	GEMA virus	Bad
Wminfo	GEMA virus	Bad
WMIPrvSe	MS Win Mgmt Instrmntn Provider	Good
wmiprvsw	GABOT.AFC virus	Bad
Wmnvram	US Robotics/3 Com Drivers	User
WMP11Cfg	Wireless PCI Card Configuration	User
WMP54G	Connection Utility	User
WMPLAYER	Windows Media Player hijacker	Ugly
WMPlayer	Microsoft Windows Media Player	User
Wmplayer (2)	W32.HLLW.Gaobot.EF virus	Bad
wmsys32	BANPAES.B virus	Bad
WNAD	Sends popups	Bad
WNAD	spyware	Bad
WNConnect	My-Mainstreet.com Str Total Actng	Bad
WnCSMServer	AT&T WorldNet Internet Svc	User
Wnetlib	DONK.C virus	Bad
Wnsapoc	see WINSERVN	Bad
Wnsapisu	see WINSERVN	Bad
Wnsapisv	see WINSERVN	Bad
Wnscpsu	see WINSERVN	Bad
Wnscpsv	see WINSERVN	Bad
Wnsintit	see WINSERVN	Bad

Program	Description	Good/Bad
Wnsintsu	see WINSERVN	Bad
Wnsintsv	see WINSERVN	Bad
Wnstssv	see WINSERVN	Bad
WofE5	BADTRANS virus	Bad
wonderfl	Wonderful Icon	User
WordSpring	Write Source	User
WorkFlowTray	ScanSoft OmniPage Pro 14.0	User
WorkPlace	Work Pace 3.0	User
Workrave	Workrave	User
world_cup_.bat	WCUP virus	Bad
WorldTime	World Time	User
worm	DOOMHUNTER virus	Bad
WOWExec	see NTVDM	Bad
WPC11Cfg	Linksys Wireless Notebook Adapter	User
WPC54CFG	Linksys Wireless Notebook Adapter	User
wpctrl/wpctrlnt/wpctrl95	Portrait Studios PivotPro	User
WpCycleWin	Mplayer2	User
wperi/popfile.pl	POPFile	User
wposche-1	Webposition Gold 2	User
wpshrc	Compaq LBP-660 Laser Printer	User
WpsFlePsw	Canon LPB-550 Laser Printer	User
WQK	KLEZ virus	Bad
Wqk/Wqk.dll	KLEZ virus	Bad
WrCtrl	Tiny Software Win2k Pro	User
WrDialer	WinPoet DSL Dialer	User
WrDialer	dialer	Bad
wrexec	AOL PowerTools Watch Right	User
WScheduler	Windows Scheduler	User
wscript	VBSWG virus	Bad
Wscript _.ChkMgr32.vbs	NOTUP.A virus	Bad
Wscript _.Msexec32.vbs	GANT.B virus	Bad
wscript gpremier.vbs	GPREMIER virus	Bad
wscript MSupd32.vbs	CASER virus	Bad
Wscript UpdataFiles.vbs		SST.B virus
		Bad
Wscript WinStart.vbs	CIAN.C virus	Bad
wscript zshell.js	NETDEX.A virus	Bad
wserver	NETSKY.AC virus	Bad
WService	Graphics Tablet Driver Service	User
wsinspector	Windows Startup Inspector	User
wsript/Q152404.VBS	Scandisk When Startup NEC PC	Bad
wssdsu	MANIFEST virus	Bad
wssdtu	MANIFEST virus	Bad
wstart32	GAOBOT.CA virus	Bad
Wstat32	LOONBOT virus	Bad
wstimeb	NEC Printers	User
wstray	spyware	Bad
wswgd	Panasonic, Epson & NEC Printers	User
WSYS	STARR Key Logger	Bad
wsys	MANIFEST virus	Bad
wsys32	GAOBOT.TB virus	Bad
WTC32.scr	VOTE.B or VOTE.K viruses	Bad
Wted	see IWAR	Bad
Wtm	FileFreedom.net	User
WtoolsA/TB_Setup/WinTools/Wsup/WtoolsS	Trojan horse virus	
		Bad
Wtsit	see WINSERVN	Bad
Wtstr	see WINSERVN	Bad
WUALBoot	Microsoft Post Boot Auto-Update	User
Wuauclt	Microsoft AutoUpdate	User
WULoader	MS Win Critical Update Notification	User
wudate	AGOBOT.3.GEN virus	Bad
WULoader	MS Win Critical Update Loader	User
WUOLService9x	Novell ZenWorks	User
wupd	ALADINZ.M virus	Bad
wupdate	adware	Bad
Wugdated	W32.HLLW.Moega virus	Bad
wupdated	MOEGA family of viruses	Bad
WUpdater	KeenWare	Bad
wupdmgr32	DOS.AUTOCAT virus	Bad
wupdmgr32	DOS.AUTOCAT virus	Bad
Wupdt	Backdoor.Imiserv virus	Bad
wupdt	IMISERV virus	Bad
wupdt	wupdt	Bad
WUSB11B	Linksys	User
WUSB11cfg	Linksys	User
ww	WeatherWatcher	User
wwasher	Siemens WebWasher	User
WwDisp	WebRoots Window Washer	User
wweb32	WordWeb	User
wWin32.com	IMISERV virus	Bad
WWMon	Wildwire Monitor	User
WxEx	Weather Watcher Program	User
Wxpload	Wintime	User
wzhelper	BANSAP virus	Bad
Wzcpick	WinZip Computing	User
X1	X1 Keyword Search	User
X3DCTL	X3D Glasses Control	User
Xanadu	Foreignword Xanadu	User
XBoxe64	RANDEX.Y virus	Bad
xcommsrv	BitDefender virus scanner	User
xcommsvr	BitDefender virus scanner	User
XCOMMSVR	Bullguard	User
XCPCMenu	Lotus EasySync Pro	User
xdaemon	DELF.D virus	Bad
XEARTH	Xearth	User
Xfire	Ctrl Panel for Terratec Soundcard	User
xfr-	Intel File Transfer	User
Xiwin32	Xitami	User
xi	XtreamLok License Manager	User
X-LiteFWD	Xten SIP VOIP Phone App	User
xp_quickres	System Tray Software	User
xplore	adware	Bad
XPoint32	LCS/Telegraphics	User
XQXSetupStart	Xteq X-Setup	User
XStop95	Xstop 95	User
xstyles	SMALL.AJ virus	Bad
XTCfgLoader	Xupiter.com	Bad
XTCfgLoader	adware and homepage hijacker	Bad
xtmop	Operator	User
XupiterStartup	adware and homepage hijacker	Bad
Xupiterstartup2003	adware and homepage hijacker	Bad
XupiterToolbarLoader	adware and homepage hijacker	Bad
XWCTray	Xerox Control Center 2.0	User
XWheel	LCS/Telegraphics	User
XXXmpeg	adult content dialer	Bad
y	parasite variant	Bad
yac	YAC Listener	User
yahoo_toolbar	parasite	Bad
yahoo_toolbar	parasite	Bad
YAHOOPOPS	YahooPOPS	User
YankClip	Yankee Clipper III	User
Ypager	Yahoo Messenger	User
YPager	JUNTADOR.K virus	Bad
ystckAO32	adware	Bad
YTRAYMAGIC	YoconSoft YTrayMagic Lite	User
yredzdon	foistware	Bad
yz	VARDO virus	Bad
YzDock	Yz Dock	User
YzShadow	Yz Shadow	User
Zacker	GEMEL virus	Bad
zaplus	Zone Labs Zone Alarm Plus	User
ZAPro	Zone Labs Zone Alarm Pro	User
ZCast	NetZero	User
ZCfgSvc	Intel ProSET	User
ZDLM	Zinio DLM	User
zenrc32	Novell Remote Mgmt Agent	User
zentray	Novell ZenWorks	User
zg	ZipGeniu	User
ZingSpooler	ZingSpooler	User
ZipLoader32	OBLIVION virus	Bad
ZipLoader32	OBLIVION virus	Bad
ZipToA	Iomega Zip Drive "ATAPI Zip to A:"	User
ZISWin	Novell ZenWorks	User
Ziclient	Zone Labs Zone Lab Client	User
ZLH	Norman Antivirus	User
ZM32NT	Aladdin Systems ZipMagic	User
ZMover	Zmover	User
ZONEALARM	SDBOT.T virus	Bad
ZoneAlarm (1)	Zone Labs Zone Alarm	Good
Zonealarm (2)	Backdoor.Sbdot.T virus	Bad
zoom	ZoomOpen	User
ZoomOpen	ZoomOpen	User
ZPOINT32	USB Graphics/Writing Tablet Driver	User
ZPU	foistware	Bad
ZStatus	Zenographics Sys Tray Status Mon	User
ZUpdate	Adware Brilliant Digital	Bad
Zupdate	foistware	Bad
zzb	adware	Bad
zzb2	adware	Bad
zzgshp.vbs	homepage hijacker	Bad

Chapter 4

Networking

Networking

Bandwidth of Data Lines

The following table is a compilation of the various digital signals and carriers used in LAN's, WAN's, WLAN's, Modems and Internet Backbones

Maximum Data Rate	Digital Signal or Signal Carrier
13.271 Gbps	OC-255 (Optical Carrier), STS-255 (electrical)
9.953 Gbps	OC-192 (Optical Carrier), STS-192 (electrical)
4.976 Gbps	OC-96 (Optical Carrier), STS-96 (electrical)
2.488 Gbps	OC-48 (Optical Carrier), STS-48 (electrical)
2.325 Gbps	SciNet (vBNS Backbone)
1.866 Gbps	OC-36 (Optical Carrier), STS-36 (electrical)
1.244 Gbps	OC-24 (Optical Carrier), STS-24 (electrical)
1 Gbps	UltraFast or Gigabit Ethernet, 1000Base-xx
933.12 Mbps	OC-18 (Optical Carrier), STS-18 (electrical)
622.08 Mbps	OC-12 (Optical Carrier), STS-12, STM-4
565.148 Mbps	E5 (European)
480 Mbps	USB 2.0
466.56 Mbps	OC-9 (Optical Carrier)
400.352 Mbps	T5, DS5 (North America)
274.176 Mbps	E4 (European), T4, DS4
155.52 Mbps	OC-3 (Optical Carrier), STS-3 (electrical)
139.264 Mbps	DS4NA (3xDS3), E4 (European)
135 Mbps	T3D, DS3D
100 Mbps	Fast Ethernet, Category 5 Cable, CDDI (Copper Data Distribution Interface), FDDI (Fibre Distributed Data Interface), IEEE 802.11n Proposed Wireless LAN
54 Mbps	IEEE 802.11a and 802.11g Wireless LAN
53 Mbps	HSSI (High-Speed Serial Interface) cable
51.84 Mbps	OC-1 (Optical Carrier), STS-1 (electrical)
44.736 Mbps	T3, DS3 (North America)
34.368 Mbps	E3 (European), DS3
20 Mbps	Category 4 cable
16 Mbps	Fast Token Ring LANs
12 Mbps	USB 1.1 Full Speed
10Mbps	Thin Ethernet, Category 3 Cable, cable modem
8.448 Mbps	E2 (European)
6.312 Mbps	T2, DS2 (North America)
6.144 Mbps	Highest speed ADSL downstream (2 pair)
4 Mbps	Token Ring networks 802.5
3.152 Mbps	T1C, DS1C

Networking

Maximum Data Rate	Digital Signal or Signal Carrier
2.048 Mbps	E1 (European), DS1
11 Mbps	IEEE 802.11b Wireless LAN
10 Mbps	Category 3 cable
4 Mbps	Category 2 cable
2 Mbps	IEEE 802.11 Wireless LAN
2 Mbps	Bluetooth
up to 2 Mbps	UMTS (Universal Mobile Telecommunications System) wireless
1.544 Mbps	ADSL, T1, DS1 (all North America)
896 Kbps	High speed ADSL downstream
512 Kbps	Fast ADSL downstream
400 Kbps	Satellite (DirectPC)
384 Kbps	Standard ADSL downstream
384 Kbps	Enhanced Data GSM Environment (EDGE) wireless
256 Kbps	Fast ADSL upstream
256 Kbps	Average ADSL downstream
230.4 Kbps	AppleTalk networks
128 Kbps	Standard ADSL upstream
128 Kbps	ISDN, IDSL
56 Kbps to 114 Kbps	GPRS (General Packet Radio System) wireless
64 Kbps	ISDN (std)
64 Kbps	DS0, pulse code modulation
up to 56 Kbps	HSCSD (High Speed Circuit Switched Data) wireless
56 Kbps	K56FLEX, U.S. Robotics X2 modems, V.90
33.6 Kbps	K56FLEX, X2 modem, V42bis
28.8 Kbps	V.34, Rockwell V.Fast Class modems
20 Kbps	Level 1 cable, minimum cable data speed
19.2 Kbps	V.32terbo modem,
14.4 Kbps	V.32bis modem, V.17 Fax
9,600 to 14,400 Kbps	GSM wireless telephone
9600 bps	modem speed of the early 1990s
4800 bps	modem speed of the late 1980s
2400 bps	modem speed of the mid 1980s
1200 bps	modem speed of the early 1980s
300 bps	modem speed of the 1970s and earlier
60 bps	early teletype devices

Cable Modem ranges from 512Kbps to 52 Mbps

Wireless LAN Standards

IEEE 802.11 is the primary wireless LAN used in the USA today and is usually referred to "Wi-Fi" or "WLAN". WECA (Wireless Ethernet Compatibility Alliance) functions as a product certification agency to ensure that products from different manufacturers will operate with each other. Basically, this insures that a user can use any brand of client hardware with any brand of access point as long as they are WECA certified. The following table summarizes each of the wireless standards and provides information to help you determine which is the best fit for your network:

Wireless Standard	Data Speed/ Daba Band	Description
IEEE 802.11	2Mbps 2.4GHz	1 or 2 Mbps data rates using FHSS or DSSS modulation. WEP and WPA security. This original specification was extended to 802.11b
IEEE 802.11a	54Mbps 5GHz	Link speeds up to 54 Mbps, maximum usable throughput 25 Mbps, faster than 802.11b, shorter range than 802.11b, less crowded data band than 802.11b so there less interference with cordless phones and microwaves, uses OFDM modulation and is therefore not compatible with 802.11b or g. Eight available channels but range may be limited to only a few rooms and is more expensive than 802.11b or g. the 802.11b standard was actually implemented before 802.11a. WEP and WPA security.
IEEE 802.11b	11Mbps 2.4GHz	The defacto Wi-Fi standard for a long time but is being slowly replace by 802.11g (faster, less interference). Maximum link speed is 11Mbps and maximum useable throughput is 5 Mbps. 14 channels bus is slower than 802.11a and is less expensive and has better range and is compatible with 802.11g; uses DSSS and CCK modulation; hardware was certified in 1999 is very plentiful and inexpensive. Link range is up to 300 feet. WEP and WPA security.
IEEE 802.11d	802.11a 802.11b 802.11g	802.11 WLAN is not legal in some countries and 802.11d was created as a supplement to the MAC (Media Access Control) layer in order to allow worldwide use of 802.11. Essentially, the specification restricts power levels and adds features to access points.
IEEE 802.11e	802.11a 802.11b	Supplement to 802.11a, adds Quality-of-Service (QOS) features and multimedia support so that applications such as Voice over Wireless IP can be implemented.
IEEE 802.11f	802.11a 802.11b 802.11g	Supplement to add registration of access points within a network to facilitate roaming between different in a common coverage area. It essentially deals with fast hand-offs between the access points just like a cell phone has to hand-off the signal as it passes from cell to cell.

Wireless Standard	Data Speed/ Daba Band	Description
IEEE 802.11g	54Mbps 2.4GHz	The latest in Wi-Fi field; may replace 802.11b as the main Wi-Fi standard but it is also compatible with 802.11b, 14 channel (only 11 are legal in the USA, only 3 channels are non overlapping), uses OFDM (above 20Mbps) and CCK (below 20 Mbps) modulation, fewer problems with cordless phones and microwave ovens, 802.11g was approved in June, 1993, improved security enhancements; maximum link speed of 54 Mbps and maximum throughput of 20 Mbps; WEP and WPA security.
IEEE 802.11h	802.11a	Spectrum managed 802.11a; supplement to the MAC (Media Access Control) and PHY layers in order to comply with European regulations for 5GHz Wi-Fi; Europe requires products to have TPC (Transmission Power Control) to limit transmitter power to the minimum needed to reach the furthest user and DFS (Dynamic frequency Selection) to allow the access points to dynamically select the Wi-Fi channel in order to minimize interference with other systems.
IEEE 802.11i	802.11a 802.11b	Supplement to improve Wi-Fi security with new encryption key protocols suck as TKIP and AES.
IEEE 802.11j	802.11a	Japanese version of our 802.11a; designed to work in the 4.9 to 5.0 GHz band that is already in use in Japan.
IEEE 802.11k	--	Proposed standard involving client hardware feedback to Wi-Fi access points and switches.
IEEE 802.11m	802.11b 802.11g	Clean up of previously published 802.11 amendments.
IEEE 802.11n	100Mbps	New standard being developed to define "advanced radio technology" high speed Wi-Fi.
Bluetooth	2Mbps 2.45GHz	PDA and cell phone wireless standard that does not support TCP/IP; FHSS modulation; PPTP, SSL or VPN security schemes.
HomeRF	10Mbps 2.4GHz	Home use wireless network standard that is no longer in wide use; limited 150 foot range, good voice quality, good interference masking, FHSS modulation; security consists of independent IP addresses and 56-bit data encryption.
HiperLAN/1	20Mbps 5GHz	European-based only (ETSI), standard set in 1996, competitor of 802.11; range 150 feet, totally ad-hoc (no configuration, no controller); inexpensive.
HiperLAN/2	54Mbps 5GHz	European-based only, standard set in February 2000; high quality data, sound and video; competitor to 802.11a; good security with DES or 3DES, access terminal and wireless terminal can authenticate each other.

Networking

Common TCP/UDP Port Numbers

The Internet Assigned Numbers Authority (IANA) is the regulating agency that manages Protocol Numbers and Assignment Services for the Internet. TCP/UDP Port Numbers were originally documented through RFC-1700, which is now outdated. Ports are now managed through an online database that can be viewed at http://www.iana.org/assignments/port-numbers. The IANA assigns and manages ports 0 through 1023 (know as the "Well Known Ports") and manages the registration of ports 1024 through 49151 (known as "Registered Ports"). The Dynamic and/or Private Ports are those from 49152 through 65535. To the extent possible, these same port assignments are used with the UDP [RFC768].

WARNING: Unassigned port numbers should not be used. the IANA will assign the number for the port after your application has been approved. The Well Known Ports are assigned by the IANA and on most systems can only be used by system (or root) processes or by programs executed by privileged users.

The following table includes only the "Well Known Ports" and we have we have highlighted the very common ports gray within this primary set:

Port	Description	Port	Description	Port	Description
0	Reserved	36	Unassigned	67	Bootstrap Protocol Server
1	TCP Port Service Multiplexer	37	Time	68	Bootstrap Protocol Client
2	Management Utility	38	Route Access Protocol	69	Trivial File Transfer
3	Compression Process	39	Resource Location Protocol	70	Gopher
4	Unassigned	40	Unassigned	71	Remote Job Service
5	Remote Job Entry	41	Graphics	72	Remote Job Service
6	Unassigned	42	Host Name Server	73	Remote Job Service
7	Echo	43	Who Is	74	Remote Job Service
8	Unassigned	44	MPM FLAGS Protocol	75	any private dial out service
9	Discard	45	Message Processing Module [recv]	76	Distributed External Object Store
10	Unassigned	46	MPM [default send]	77	any private RJE service
11	Active Users	47	NI FTP	78	vettcp
12	Unassigned	48	Digital Audit Daemon	79	Finger
13	Daytime (RFC 867)	49	Login Host Protocol (TACACS)	80	World Wide Web HTTP
14	Unassigned	50	Remote Mail Checking Protocol	81	HOSTS2 Name Server
15	Unassigned [was netstat]	51	IMP Logical Address Maintenance	82	XFER Utility
16	Unassigned	52	XNS Time Protocol	83	MIT ML Device
17	Quote of the Day	53	Domain Name Server	84	Common Trace Facility
18	Message Send Protocol	54	XNS Clearinghouse	85	MIT ML Device
19	Character Generator	55	ISI Graphics Language	86	Micro Focus Cobol
20	File Transfer [Default Data]	56	XNS Authentication	87	any private terminal link
21	File Transfer [Control]	57	any private terminal access	88	Kerberos
22	SSH Remote Login Protocol	58	XNS Mail	89	SU/MIT Telnet Gateway
23	Telnet	59	any private file service	90	DNSIX Securit Attribute Token Map
24	any private mail system	60	Unassigned	91	MIT Dover Spooler
25	Simple Mail Transfer	61	NI MAIL	92	Network Printing Protocol
26	Unassigned	62	ACA Services	93	Device Control Protocol
27	NSW User System FE	63	whois++	94	Tivoli Object Dispatcher
28	Unassigned	64	Communications Integrator (CI)	95	SUPDUP
29	MSG ICP	65	TACACS-Database Service	96	DIXIE Protocol Specification
30	Unassigned	66	Oracle SQL*NET	97	Swift Remote Virtural File Protocol
31	MSG Authentication			98	TAC News
32	Unassigned			99	Metagram Relay
33	Display Support Protocol			100	[unauthorized use]
34	Unassigned			101	NIC Host Name Server
35	any private printer server			102	ISO-TSAP Class 0

Networking

Port	Description
103	Genesis Point-to-Point Trans Net
104	ACR-NEMA Digital Imag. & Comm. 300
105	CCSO name server protocol
105	Mailbox Name Nameserver
106	3COM-TSMUX
107	Remote Telnet Service
108	SNA Gateway Access Server
109	Post Office Protocol - Version 2
110	Post Office Protocol - Version 3
111	SUN Remote Procedure Call
112	McIDAS Data Transmission Protocol
113	Authentication Service
114	Deprecated June 2004
115	Simple File Transfer Protocol
116	ANSA REX Notify
117	UUCP Path Service
118	SQL Services
119	Network News Transfer Protocol
120	CFDPTKT
121	Encore Expedited Remote Pro.Call
122	SMAKYNET
123	Network Time Protocol
124	ANSA REX Trader
125	Locus PC-Interface Net Map Ser
126	NXEdit (previously assigned to Unisys Unatiry Login)
127	Locus PC-Interface Conn Server
128	GSS X License Verification
129	Password Generator Protocol
130	cisco FNATIVE
131	cisco TNATIVE
132	cisco SYSMAINT
133	Statistics Service
134	INGRES-NET Service
135	DCE endpoint resolution
136	PROFILE Naming System
137	NETBIOS Name Service
138	NETBIOS Datagram Service
139	NETBIOS Session Service
140	EMFIS Data Service
141	EMFIS Control Service
142	Britton-Lee IDM
143	Internet Message Access Protocol
144	Universal Management Architecture
145	UAAC Protocol
146	ISO-IP0

Port	Description
147	ISO-IP
148	Jargon
149	AED 512 Emulation Service
150	SQL-NET
151	HEMS
152	Background File Transfer Program
153	SGMP
154	NETSC
155	NETSC
156	SQL Service
157	KNET/VM Command/Message Protocol
158	PCMail Server
159	NSS-Routing
160	SGMP-TRAPS
161	SNMP
162	SNMPTRAP
163	CMIP/TCP Manager
164	CMIP/TCP Agent
165	Xerox
166	Sirius Systems
167	NAMP
168	RSVD
169	SEND
170	Network PostScript
171	Network Innovations Multiplex
172	Network Innovations CL/1
173	Xyplex
174	MAILQ
175	VMNET
176	GENRAD-MUX
177	X Display Manager Control Protocol
178	NextStep Window Server
179	Border Gateway Protocol
180	Intergraph
181	Unify
182	Unisys Audit SITP
183	OCBinder
184	OCServer
185	Remote-KIS
186	KIS Protocol
187	Application Communication Interface
188	Plus Five's MUMPS
189	Queued File Transport
190	Gateway Access Control Protocol
191	Prospero Directory Service
192	OSU Network Monitoring System
193	Spider Remote Monitoring Protocol
194	Internet Relay Chat Protocol
195	DNSIX Network Level Module Audit
196	DNSIX Session Mgt Module Audit Redir
197	Directory Location Service

Port	Description
198	Directory Location Service Monitor
199	SMUX
200	IBM System Resource Controller
201	AppleTalk Routing Maintenance
202	AppleTalk Name Binding
203	AppleTalk Unused
204	AppleTalk Echo
205	AppleTalk Unused
206	AppleTalk Zone Information
207	AppleTalk Unused
208	AppleTalk Unused
209	The Quick Mail Transfer Protocol
210	ANSI Z39.50
211	Texas Instruments 914C/G Terminal
212	ATEXSSTR
213	IPX
214	VM PWSCS
215	Insignia Solutions
216	Computer Associates Int'l License Server
217	dBASE Unix
218	Netix Message Posting Protocol
219	Unisys ARPs
220	Interactive Mail Access Protocol v3
221	Berkeley rlogin with SPX auth
222	Berkeley rshd with SPX auth
223	Certificate Distribution Center
224	masqdialer
225-241	Reserved
242	Direct
243	Survey Measurement
244	inbusiness
245	LINK
246	Display Systems Protocol
247	SUBNTBCST_TFTP
248	bhfhs
249-255	Reserved
256	RAP
257	Secure Electronic Transaction
258	Yak Winsock Personal Chat
259	Efficient Short Remote Operations
260	Openport
261	IIOP Name Service over TLS/SSL
262	Arcisdms
263	HDAP
264	BGMP
265	X-Bone CTL
266	SCSI on ST
267	Tobit David Service Layer
268	Tobit David Replica
269-279	Unassigned
280	http-mgmt

Port	Description	Port	Description	Port	Description
281	Personal Link	377	NEC Corporation	423	IBM Operations Planning and Control Start
282	Cable Port A/X	378	NEC Corporation	424	IBM Operations Planning and Control Track
283	rescap	379	TIA/EIA/IS-99 modem client	425	ICAD
284	corerjd	380	TIA/EIA/IS-99 modem server	426	smartsdp
285	Unassigned			427	Server Location
286	FXP Communication	381	hp performance data collector	428	OCS_CMU
287	K-BLOCK			429	OCS_AMU
288-307	Unassigned	382	hp performance data managed node	430	UTMPSD
				431	UTMPCD
309	EntrustTime	383	hp performance data alarm manager	432	IASD
310	bhmds			433	NNSP
311	AppleShare IP WebAdmin	384	A Remote Network Server System	434	MobileIP-Agent
312	VSLMP	385	IBM Application	435	MobilIP-MN
313	Magenta Logic	386	ASA Message Router Object Def.	436	DNA-CML
314	Opalis Robot			437	comscm
315	DPSI	387	Appletalk Update-Based Routing Pro.	438	dsfgw
316	decAuth			439	dasp Thomas Obermair
317	Zannet	388	Unidata LDM	440	sgcp
318	PKIX TimeStamp	389	Lightweight Directory Access Protocol	441	decvms-sysmgt
319	PTP Event			442	cvc_hostd
320	PTP General	390	UIS	443	http protocol over TLS/SSL
321	PIP	391	SynOptics SNMP Relay Port	444	Simple Network Paging Protocol
322	RTSPS	392	SynOptics Port Broker Port	445	Microsoft-DS
323-332	Unassigned	393	Meta5	446	DDM-Remote Relational Database Access
333	Texar Security Port	394	EMBL Nucleic Data Transfer	447	DDM-Distributed File Management
334-343	Unassigned	395	NETscout Control Protocol	448	DDM-Remote DB Access Using Secure Sockets
344	Prospero Data Access Protocol	396	Novell Netware over IP	449	AS Server Mapper
345	Perf Analysis Workbench	397	Multi Protocol Trans. Net.	450	Computer Supported Telecommunication Applications
346	Zebra server	398	Kryptolan		
347	Fatmen Server	399	ISO Transport Class 2 Non-Control over TCP	451	Cray Network Semaphore server
348	Cabletron Management Protocol	400	Workstation Solutions	452	Cray SFS config server
349	mftp	401	Uninterruptible Power Supply	453	CreativeServer
350	MATIP Type A	402	Genie Protocol	454	ContentServer
351	MATIP Type B	403	decap	455	CreativePartnr
352	DTAG (assigned long ago)	404	nced	456	macon-tcp
353	NDSAUTH	405	ncld	457	scohelp
354	bh611	406	Interactive Mail Support Protocol	458	apple quick time
355	DATEX-ASN	407	Timbuktu	459	ampr-rcmd
356	Cloanto Net 1	408	Prospero Resource Manager Sys. Man.	460	skronk
357	bhevent			461	DataRampSrv
358	Shrinkwrap	409	Prospero Resource Manager Node Man.	462	DataRampSrvSec
359	Network Security Risk Management Protocol	410	DECLadebug Remote Debug Protocol	463	alpes
361	Semantix			464	kpasswd
362	SRS Send	411	Remote MT Protocol	466	digital-vrc
363	RSVP Tunnel	412	Trap Convention Port	467	mylex-mapd
364	Aurora CMGR	413	Storage Management Services Protocol	468	proturis
365	DTK			469	Radio Control Protocol
366	ODMR	414	InfoSeek	470	scx-proxy
367	MortgageWare	415	BNet	471	Mondex
368	QbikGDP	416	Silverplatter	472	ljk-login
369	rpc2portmap	417	Onmux	473	hybrid-pop
370	codaauth2	418	Hyper-G	474	tn-tl-w1
371	Clearcase	419	Ariel 1	475	tcpnethaspsrv
372	ListProcessor	420	SMPTE	476	tn-tl-fd1
373	Legent Corporation	421	Ariel 2	477	ss7ns
374	Legent Corporation	422	Ariel 3	478	spsc
375	Hassle			479	iafserver
376	Amiga Envoy Network Inquiry Proto			480	iafdbase

Networking

Port	Description
481	Ph service
482	bgs-nsi
483	ulpnet
484	Integra Software Management Environment
485	Air Soft Power Burst
486	avian
487	saft Simple Asynchronous File Transfer
488	gss-http
489	nest-protocol
490	micom-pfs
491	go-login
492	Transport Independent Convergence for FNA
493	Transport Independent Convergence for FNA
494	POV-Ray
495	intecourier
496	PIM-RP-DISC
497	dantz
498	siam
499	ISO ILL Protocol
500	isakmp
501	STMF
502	asa-appl-proto
503	Intrinsa
504	citadel
505	mailbox-lm
506	ohimsrv
507	crs
508	xvttp
509	snare
510	FirstClass Protocol
511	PassGo
512	remote process execution;
513	remote login a la telnet;
514	cmd
515	spooler
516	videotex
517	like tenex link, but across machine
518	unknown
519	unixtime
520	extended file name server
521	ripng
522	ULP
523	IBM-DB2
524	NCP
525	timeserver
526	newdate
527	Stock IXChange
528	Customer IXChange
529	IRC-SERV
530	rpc
531	chat
532	readnews
533	for emergency broadcasts
534	MegaMedia Admin
535	iiop
536	opalis-rdv

Port	Description
537	Networked Media Streaming Protocol
538	gdomap
539	Apertus Technologies Load Determination
541	uucp-rlogin
542	commerce
543	Unknown
544	krcmd
545	appleqtcsrvr
546	DHCPv6 Client
547	DHCPv6 Server
548	AFP over TCP
549	IDFP
550	new-who
551	cybercash
552	deviceshare
553	pirp
554	Real Time Stream Control Protocol
555	Unknown
556	rfs server
557	openvms-sysipc
558	SDNSKMP
559	TEEDTAP
560	rmonitord
561	Unknown
562	chcmd
563	nntp protocol over TLS/SSL (was snntp)
564	plan 9 file service
565	whoami
566	streettalk
567	banyan-rpc
568	microsoft shuttle
569	microsoft rome
570	demon
571	udemon
572	sonar
573	banyan-vip
574	FTP Software Agent System
575	VEMMI
576	ipcd
577	vnas
578	ipdd
579	decbsrv
580	SNTP HEARTBEAT
581	Bundle Discovery Protocol
582	SCC Security
583	Philips Video-Conferencing
584	Key Server
585	IMAP4+SSL (use 993 instead)
586	Password Change
587	Submission
588	CAL
589	EyeLink
590	TNS CML
591	FileMaker, Inc. - HTTP Alternate (see Port 80)
592	Eudora Set
593	HTTP RPC Ep Map

Port	Description
594	TPIP
595	CAB Protocol
596	SMSD
597	PTC Name Service
598	SCO Web Server Manager 3
599	Aeolon Core Protocol
600	Sun IPC server
601	Reliable Syslog Service
602	XML-RPC over BEEP
603	IDXP
604	TUNNEL
605	SOAP over BEEP
606	Cray Unified Resource Manager
607	nqs
608	Sender-Initiated/Unsolicited File Transfer
609	npmp-trap
610	npmp-local
611	npmp-gui
612	HMMP Indication
613	HMMP Operation
614	SSLshell
615	Internet Configuration Manager
616	SCO System Administration Server
617	SCO Desktop Administration Server
618	DEI-ICDA
619	Compaq EVM
620	SCO WebServer Manager
621	ESCP
622	Collaborator
623	ASF Remote Management and Control Protocol
624	Crypto Admin
625	DEC DLM
626	ASIA
627	PassGo Tivoli
628	QMQP
629	3Com AMP3
630	RDA
631	IPP (Internet Printing Protocol)
632	bmpp
633	Service Status update (Sterling Software)
634	ginad
635	RLZ DBase
636	ldap protocol over TLS/SSL (was sldap)
637	lanserver
638	mcns-sec
639	MSDP
640	entrust-sps
641	repcmd
642	ESRO-EMSDP V1.3
643	SANity
644	dwr
645	PSSC
646	LDP
647	DHCP Failover
648	Registry Registrar Protocol (RRP)

Commom TCP Port Numbers (cont.)

Port	Description
649	Cadview-3d - streaming 3d models over the internet
650	OBEX
651	IEEE MMS
652	HELLO_PORT
653	RepCmd
654	AODV
655	TINC
656	SPMP
657	RMC
658	TenFold
659	Removed (2001-06-06)
660	MacOS Server Admin
661	HAP
662	PFTP
663	PureNoise
664	ASF Secure Remote Management and Control Protocol
665	Sun DR
666	doom Id Software
667	campaign contribution disclosures - SDR Technologies
668	MeComm
669	MeRegister
670	VACDSM-SWS
671	VACDSM-APP
672	VPPS-QUA
673	CIMPLEX
674	ACAP
675	DCTP
676	VPPS Via
677	Virtual Presence Protocol
678	GNU Generation Foundation NCP
679	MRM
680	entrust-aaas
681	entrust-aams
682	XFR
683	CORBA IIOP
684	CORBA IIOP SSL
685	MDC Port Mapper
686	Hardware Control Protocol Wismar
687	asipregistry
688	REALM-RUSD
689	NMAP
690	VATP
691	MS Exchange Routing
692	Hyperwave-ISP
693	connendp
694	ha-cluster
695	IEEE-MMS-SSL
696	RUSHD
697	UUIDGEN
698	OLSR
699	Access Network
700	Extensible Provisioning Protocol
701	Link Management Protocol (LMP)
702-703	Unassigned

Port	Description
704	errlog copy/server daemon
705	AgentX
706	SILC
707	Borland DSJ
708	Unassigned
709	Entrust Key Management Service Handler
710	Entrust Administration Service Handler
711	Cisco TDP
712	TBRPF
713-728	Unassigned
729	IBM NetView DM/6000 Server/Client
730	IBM NetView DM/6000 send/tcp
731	IBM NetView DM/6000 receive/tcp
732-740	Unassigned
741	netGW
742	Network based Rev. Cont. Sys.
743	Unassigned
744	Flexible License Manager
745-746	Unassigned
747	Fujitsu Device Control
748	Russell Info Sci Calendar Manager
749	kerberos administration
750-753	Unknown
754	send
755-756	Unassigned
758-765	Unknown
767	phone
768	Unassigned
769-776	Unknown
777	Multiling HTTP
778-779	Unassigned
780	Unknown
781-785	Unassigned
786	Unassigned (Removed 2002-05-08)
787	Unassigned (Removed 2002-10-08)
788-799	Unassigned
800-801	Unknown
802-809	Unassigned
810	FCP
811-827	Unassigned
828	itm-mcell-s
829	PKIX-3 CA/RA
830-846	Unassigned

Port	Description
847	dhcp-failover 2
848	GDOI
849-859	Unassigned
860	iSCSI
861-872	Unassigned
873	rsync
874-885	Unassigned
886	ICL coNETion locate server
887	ICL coNETion server info
888	AccessBuilder
889-899	Unassigned
900	OMG Initial Refs
901	SMPNAMERES
902	IDEAFARM-CHAT
903	IDEAFARM-CATCH
904-910	Unassigned
911	xact-backup
912	APEX relay-relay service
913	APEX endpoint-relay service
914-988	Unassigned
989	ftp protocol, data, over TLS/SSL
990	ftp protocol, control, over TLS/SSL
991	Netnews Administration System
992	telnet protocol over TLS/SSL
993	imap4 protocol over TLS/SSL
994	irc protocol over TLS/SSL
995	pop3 protocol over TLS/SSL (was spop3)
996	vsinet
997-1000	Unknown
1001-1009	Unassigned
1010	surf
1011-1024	Reserved
1080	Socks
8008	HTTP Alternate
8080	HTTP Alternate

Networking

Chapter 5

goto   halt

XP

Command List for
Windows XP & Windows 2000

DOS may be dead but the WinNT, Win2K and WinXP Command Lines are alive and well and healthier then ever! The Command Line looks like DOS, has the capacity to do batch files, has a DOS emulator (DOS Version 5) built in so that many DOS programs run quite nicely, has a large number of very powerful utilities, and has an expandable Command Window with scroll bars. The Command Line environment is an essential part of any technicians toolbox and should be studied in careful detail. Many of these commands are especially useful when used in conjunction with Filters and Redirection (pages 135 and 206).

The Command Line is started by a command interpreter named cmd.exe, which is in the \windows\system32 folder on WinXP and the \winnt\system32 folders on WinNT and Win2K. It can be started by typing "cmd" in the "Open:" field of the Start-Run menu or through Start-Programs (or All Programs)-Accessories. I personally prefer to have the icon on my desktop for quick access because I use it so often.

This chapter is a concise general reference of Command Line commands, listed in alphabetic order regardless of command type. Most of the Command descriptions, Syntax, Syntax Options, Examples and Notes have been extracted from the extensive help files, command references and Kowledge Base files on Microsofts web site and help files included in the Windows Operating Systems. We wish to thank Microsoft for providing the massive amout of documentation necessary to adequately compile this general command reference.

Over 160 commands are covered in this chapter, however, there are a significant number of additional commands that were not included due to space limitations. Omitted sections include CSCRIPT, FSUTIL, FTP Subcommands, NETSH, QUERY, and Terminal Services. As we continue to refine and compact the current commands, we will include new sections of the omitted command list.

Command descriptions in this chapter are based on the following notations and syntax:

Command Name

Short description of the command.
Syntax:
command parameter [option]................Optional arguments are enclosed in [ ] brackets
Examples:
test c:\abc.doc /s ....Program "test" acts on file "c:\abc.doc" using option /s

Syntax Options:

parameter·Required data, usually a path and filename

option1·····Optional argument such as "/s" in the above example

option2·····Options are also called switches and are usually preceded by a slash /

Notes:

- Additional information on the command or syntax

Help with the Syntax and Syntax Options is usually available by typing the command name followed by a /? or by typing help and then the command name, e.g. ipconfig /? or help ipconfig.

Commands included in this chapter:

Arp	Driverquery	Ipxroute	Perfmon	Set
Assoc	Echo	Irftp	Ping	Setlocal
At	Endlocal	Label	Popd	Shift
Atmadm	Erase	Lodctr	Print	Shutdown
Attrib	Eventcreate	Logman	Prncnfg	Sigverif
Batch files	Eventquery.vbs	Lpq	Prndrvr.vbs	Sort
Bootcfg	Eventtriggers	Lpr	Prnjobs.vbs	Start
Break	Evntcmd	Macfile	Prnmngr.vbs	Subst
Cacls	Exit	Mkdir (md)	Prnport.vbs	Systeminfo
Call	Expand	Mmc	Prnqctl.vbs	System File
Chcp	Fc	Mode	Prompt	Checker (sfc)
Chdir	Filter	More	Pushd	Taskkill
Chkdsk	commands	Mountvol	Rasdial	Tasklist
Chkntfs	Find	Move	Rcp	Tcmsetup
Cipher	Findstr	Msconfig	Recover	Telnet
Cls	Finger	MS-DOS	Redirection	commands
Cmd	Flattemp	subsystem	commands	Tftp
Cmstp	For	configuration	Reg	Time
Color	Format	commands	Regsvr32	Title
Comp	Fsutil	Msiexec	Relog	Tracerpt
Compact	Ftp	Msinfo32	Rem	Tracert
Contig	Ftype	Nbtstat	Rename	Tree
Convert	Getmac	Netstat	Replace	Type
Copy	Goto	Nslookup	Reset session	Typeperf
Cprofile	Gpresult	Ntcmdprompt	Rexec	Unlodctr
Date	Gpupdate	Ntsd	Rmdir	Ver
Defrag	Graftabl	Openfiles	Route	Verify
Del	Help	Pagefileconfig	Rsh	Vol
Dir	Helpctr	Path	Rsm	Vssadmin
Diskcomp	Hostname	Pathping	Runas	W32tm
Diskcopy	If	Pause	Sc	Winnt
DiskPart	Ipconfig	Pbadmin	Schtasks	Winnt32
Doskey	Ipseccmd	Pentnt	Secedit	Xcopy

ARP

View and change Address Resolution Protocol (ARP) cache entries, which contain one or more tables that are used to store IP addresses and their resolved Ethernet or Token Ring physical addresses. Each Ethernet or Token Ring network adapter installed on your computer is a separate table. *Internet Protocol (TCP/IP) must be installed as a component in the properties of a network adapter in Network Connections.*

Syntax:
arp [-a [InetAddr] [-N IfaceAddr]] [-g [InetAddr] [-N IfaceAddr]] [-d InetAddr[IfaceAddr]] [-s InetAddr EtherAddr [IfaceAddr]]

Examples:
arp –a *or* arp -a -N 10.0.0.99 *or* arp -s 10.0.0.80 00-AA-00-4F-2A-9C

Syntax Options:

Used without parameters, assoc displays a list of all the current file name extension associations.

InetAddr=Internet IP address in the form 10.0.0.99

IfaceAddr = Interface IP address in the form 10.0.0.99

EtherAdr = 6 byte physical address (hexadecimal)

-N parameter is case-sensitive.

Help is displayed when ARP is used without parameters.

-a [InetAddr] [-N IfaceAddr] : Displays current ARP cache tables for all interfaces. To display a specific IP address ARP cache entry use -a with the IP address. To display a specific interface ARP cache table use -a -N with the IP address assigned to the interface parameter.

-g [InetAddr] [-N IfaceAddr] : Identical to -a.

-d InetAddr [IfaceAddr] : Deletes an entry with a specific IP address, where InetAddr is the IP address. To delete a specific interface entry in a table use the assigned IP address as the IfaceAddr parameter. To delete all entries, use the asterisk (*) wildcard character in place of InetAddr.

-s InetAddr EtherAddr [IfaceAddr] : Adds a static entry to the ARP cache that resolves the IP address InetAddr to the physical address EtherAddr. To add a specific interface static ARP cache entry to the table use the IP address assigned to the interface as the IfaceAddr parameter.

Notes:

• Entries are removed if the TCP/IP protocol is stopped and started. Create permanent static ARP cache entries by using appropriate ARP commands in a batch file and use Scheduled Tasks at start up to run the batch file.

ASSOC

Displays or modifies file name extension associations.

Syntax:
assoc [.ext [= [filetype]]]

Examples:
assoc .txt *or* assoc .txt= *or* assoc I more *or* assoc>assoc.cfg

Syntax Options:

.ext··········Specifies the file name extension.

filetype······Specifies the file type with which you want to associate the specified file name extension.

Notes:

• A white space after the equal sign deletes the file type association for a file name extension.

• Use the ftype command to view current file types that have open command strings defined.

• Use the > redirection operator to redirect the output of assoc to a text file.

AT

At schedules commands and programs to run on a computer at a specified time and date. You can use at only when the Schedule service is running.

Schtasks is a more powerful superset command-line scheduling tool and includes all the functionality found in the at command-line utility. Use schtasks instead of at for all command-line scheduling tasks.

Syntax:

at [\\ComputerName] [{[ID] [/delete]|/delete [/yes]}]

at [[\\ComputerName] hours:minutes [/interactive] [{/every:date[,...]|/next:date[,...]}] command]

Examples:

at \\server5   *or*   at \\corp 3   *or*

at \\server5 00:00 /every:5,10,15,20,25,30 archive

Syntax Options:

Used without parameters, at lists scheduled commands.

\\ComputerName....Specifies a remote computer. Omit this parameter and at schedules the commands and programs on the local computer.

ID..............Specifies the identification number assigned to a scheduled command.

/delete.......Cancels a scheduled command. Omit ID and all of the scheduled commands on the computer are canceled.

/yes...........Answers yes to all queries from the system when you delete scheduled events.

hours:minutes ....Specifies when you want to run the command(in 24-hour notation, that is, 00:00 [midnight] through 23:59).

/interactive Allows command to interact with the desktop of the user logged on at the time command runs.

/every:......Runs command on every specified day or days of the week or month (for example, every Thursday, or the third day of every month).

date ....Specifies the date when you want to run the command. You can specify one or more days of the week (that is, type M,T,W,Th,F,S,Su) or one or more days of the month (that is, type 1 through 31). If you omit date, at uses the current day of the month.

/next:.........Runs command on the next occurrence of the day (for example, next Thursday).

command··Specifies the Windows command program (that is, .exe or .com file), or batch program (that is, .bat or .cmd file) that you want to run. When the command requires a path as an argument, use the absolute path (that is, the entire path beginning with the drive letter). If the command is on a remote computer, specify Universal Naming Convention (UNC) notation for the server and share name, rather than a remote drive letter.

Notes:

• To use AT, you must be a member of the local Administrators group.

• Scheduled commands are stored in the registry. As a result, you do not lose scheduled tasks if you restart the Schedule service.

• AT does not automatically load Cmd.exe, the command interpreter, before running commands. If you are not running an executable (.exe) file, you must explicitly load Cmd.exe at the beginning of the command as follows: cmd /c dir > c:\test.out

• When you schedule a command with at, especially a command that has command-line options, check that the command syntax is correct by typing at without command-line options. If incorrect, delete the command and retype it. If it is still incorrect, retype the command with fewer command-line options.

• Commands scheduled with at run as background processes with output not displayed. To redirect output to a file, use the redirection symbol (>). If you redirect output to a file, you need to use the escape symbol (^) before the redirection symbol, whether you are using at at the command line or in a batch file. For example, to redirect output to Output.text, type: at 14:45 c:\test.bat ^>c:\output.txt

• Current directory for the executing command is the systemroot folder.

• If you change computer system time, re-synchronize the at scheduler with the revised system time by typing at without command-line options.

• Connecting to network drives

• Do not use a redirected drive for scheduled jobs that access the network. Instead, use UNC paths for scheduled jobs. For example: at 1:00pm my_backup \\server\share

• Do not use the syntax where x: is a connection made by the user. For example: at 1:00pm my_ backup x:

• If you schedule an at command that uses a drive letter to connect to a shared directory, the assigned drive letter is not available at the command prompt. Include an at command to disconnect the drive when you are finished using the drive.

ATMADM

Monitors connections and addresses that are registered by the ATM Call Manager on an asynchronous transfer mode (ATM) network. You can use atmadm to display statistics for incoming and outgoing calls on ATM adapters.

Syntax:
atmadm [/c][/a] [/s]

Examples:
atmadm ©   *or*   atmadm /a   *or*   atmadm /s

Syntax Options:
Used without parameters, atmadm displays statistics for monitoring the status of active ATM connections.

©..............Displays call information for all current connections to the ATM network adapter installed on this computer.

/a ....Displays the registered ATM network service access point (NSAP) address for each adapter installed in this computer.

/s...............Displays statistics for monitoring the status of active ATM connections.

ATTRIB

Displays, sets, or removes the read-only, archive, system, and hidden attributes assigned to files or directories.

Syntax:
attrib [{+r|-r}] [{+a|-a}] [{+s|-s}] [{+h|-h}] [[Drive:][Path] FileName] [/s[/d]]

Examples:
attrib news86   *or*   attrib +r report.txt   *or*   attrib -r b:\public\jones*.* /s

Syntax Options:
Used without parameters, attrib displays attributes of all files in the current directory.

+[r,a,s,h] ···Sets the file attribute.

-[r,a,s,h] ····Clears the file attribute.

[Drive:][Path] FileName ··Specifies the location and name of the directory, file, or set of files for which you want to display or change attributes.

/s...............Applies attrib and any command-line options to matching files in the current directory and all of its subdirectories.

/d ....Applies attrib and any command-line options to directories.

Notes:

• You can use wildcard characters (that is, ? and *) with the FileName parameter to display or change the attributes for a group of files. If a file has the system or hidden attribute set, you must clear these attributes before you can change any other attributes for that file.

• The archive attribute (that is, +a) marks files that have changed since the last time they were backed up. The xcopy command uses archive attributes.

• The attrib command, with different parameters, is available from the Recovery Console.

Batch Files

Batch files(batch programs or scripts) simplify routine or repetitive tasks. A batch file is an unformatted, plain text file that contains one or more commands and has a .bat or .cmd file name extension. When you type the file name at the command prompt, Cmd.exe runs the commands sequentially as they appear in the file.

You can include any command in a batch file. Certain commands, such as for, goto, and if, enable you to do conditional processing of the commands in the batch file. Other commands allow you to control input and output and call other batch files.

See also the sections on Filter Commands and Redirection Operator.

Syntax:

For more information about commands that you can use in batch files see:

Call, Echo, Endlocal, For, Goto, If, Pause, Rem, Setlocal, Shift and Redirection

Examples:

In a batch file called Mybatch.bat: xcopy %1*.* %2

To run the file, at the command prompt type: mybatch.bat C:\folder1 D:\folder2

This copies the contents from Folder1 to Folder2, where %1 is replaced by the value Folder1 and %2 is replaced by the value Folder2

Syntax Options:

You can use batch parameters anywhere within a batch file to extract information about your environment settings.

Cmd.exe provides the batch parameter expansion variables %0 through %9. When you use batch parameters in a batch file, %0 is replaced by the batch file name, and %1 through %9 are replaced by the corresponding arguments that you type at the command line. To access arguments beyond %9, you need to use the shift command. The %* batch parameter is a wildcard reference to all the arguments, not including %0, that are passed to the batch file.

You can also use modifiers with batch parameters. Modifiers use current drive and directory information to expand the batch parameter as a partial or complete file or directory name. To use a modifier, type the percent (%) character followed by a tilde (~) character, and then type the appropriate modifier (that is, %~modifier).

The following table lists the modifiers you can use in expansion.

Modifier	Description
%~1	Expands %1 and removes any surrounding quotation marks ("").
%~f1	Expands %1 to a fully qualified path name.
%~d1	Expands %1 to a drive letter.
%~p1	Expands %1 to a path.
%~n1	Expands %1 to a file name.
%~x1	Expands %1 to a file extension.
%~s1	Expanded path contains short names only.
%~a1	Expands %1 to file attributes.
%~t1	Expands %1 to date and time of file.
%~z1	Expands %1 to size of file.
%~$PATH:1	Searches the directories listed in the PATH environment variable and expands %1 to the fully qualified name of the first one found. If the environment variable name is not defined or the file is not found, this modifier expands to the empty string.

The following table lists possible combinations of modifiers and qualifiers that you can use to get compound results.

Modifier	Description
%~dp1	Expands %1 to a drive letter and path.
%~nx1	Expands %1 to a file name and extension.
%~dp$PATH:1	Searches the directories listed in the PATH environment variable for %1 and expands to the drive letter and path of the first one found.
%~ftza1	Expands %1 to a dir-like output line.

Note: In the previous examples, you can replace %1 and PATH with other batch parameter values.

The %* modifier is a unique modifier that represents all arguments passed in a batch file. You cannot use this modifier in combination with the %~ modifier. The %~ syntax must be terminated by a valid argument value.

You cannot manipulate batch parameters in the same manner that you can manipulate environment variables. You cannot search and replace values or examine substrings. However, you can assign the parameter to an environment variable, and then manipulate the environment variable.

Notes:

• The standard error codes that most applications return are 0 if no error occurred and 1 (or higher value) if an error occurred. Please refer to your application help documentation to determine the meaning of specific error codes.

Configures, queries, or changes Boot.ini file settings.

bootcfg addsw

Adds operating system load options for a specified operating system entry.

Syntax:

bootcfg /addsw [/s Computer [/u Domain\User /p Password]] [/mm MaximumRAM] [/bv] [/so] [/ng] /id OSEntryLineNum

Examples:

bootcfg /addsw /mm 64 /id 2   *or*   bootcfg /addsw /so /id 3

Syntax Options:

/s Computer ··············Specifies the name or IP address of a remote computer (do not use backslashes). The default is the local computer.

/u Domain\User··········Runs the command with the account permissions of the user specified by User or Domain\User. The default is the permissions of the current logged on user on the computer issuing the command.

/p Password ···············Specifies the password of the user account that is specified in the /u parameter.

/mm MaximumRAM ·······Adds the /maxmem switch to the specified OSEntryLineNum and sets the maximum amount of RAM that the operating system can use.

/bv············Adds the /basevideo switch to the specified OSEntryLineNum, directing the operating system to use standard VGA mode for the installed video driver.

/so············Adds the /sos switch to the specified OSEntryLineNum, directing the operating system to display device driver names while they are being loaded.

/ng ···········Adds the /noguiboot switch to the specified OSEntryLineNum, disabling the Windows XP Professional progress bar that appears before the CTRL+ALT+DEL logon prompt.

/id OSEntryLineNum·······Specifies the operating system entry line number in the [operating systems] section of the Boot.ini file to which the operating system load options are added. The first line after the [operating systems] section header is 1.

bootcfg copy

Makes another operating system instance copy, for which switches can be added.

Syntax:

bootcfg /copy [/s Computer [/u Domain\User /p Password]] [/d Description] [/id OSEntryLineNum]

Examples:

bootcfg /copy /d "\ABC Server\" /id 1   *or*

bootcfg /copy /s srvmain /u maindom\hiropln /p p@ssW23 /d "Windows XP" /id 2

Syntax Options:

/s Computer ··············Specifies the name or IP address of a remote computer (do not use backslashes). The default is the local computer.

/u Domain\User··········Runs the command with the account permissions of the user specified by User or Domain\User. The default is the permissions of the current logged on user on the computer issuing the command.

/p Password ···············Specifies the password of the user account that is specified in the /u parameter.

/d Description···············Specifies the description for the new operating system entry.

/id OSEntryLineNum·······Specifies the operating system entry line number in the [operating systems] section of the Boot.ini file to copy. The first line after the [operating systems] section header is 1.

bootcfg dbg1394

Configures 1394 port debugging for a specified operating system entry.

Syntax:

bootcfg /dbg1394 {ON | OFF | EDIT} [/s Computer [/u Domain\User /p Password]] [/ch channel] /id OSEntryLineNum

Examples:
bootcfg /dbg1394 /id 2 *or* bootcfg /dbg1394 on /ch 1 /id 3
Syntax Options:

ON | OFF | EDIT ·············Specifies the value for 1394 port debugging.

Value ·······Description

ON·············Enables remote debugging support by adding the /dbg1394 switch to the specified OSEntryLineNum.

OFF·········Disables remote debugging support by removing the /dbg1394 switch from the specified OSEntryLineNum.

EDIT·······Allows changes to port and baud rate settings by changing the channel values associated with the /dbg1394 switch for the specified OSEntryLineNum.

/s Computer ·················Specifies the name or IP address of a remote computer (do not use backslashes). The default is the local computer.

/u Domain\User·············Runs the command with the account permissions of the user specified by User or Domain\User. The default is the permissions of the current logged on user on the computer issuing the command.

/p Password·················Specifies the password of the user account that is specified in the /u parameter.

/ch channel ·················Specifies the channel to use for debugging. Valid values are integers between 1 and 64. Do not use the /ch channel parameter if 1394 port debugging is being disabled.

/id OSEntryLineNum·······Specifies the operating system entry line number in the [operating systems] section of the Boot.ini file to which the 1394 port debugging options are added. The first line after the [operating systems] section header is 1.

bootcfg debug

Adds or changes the debug settings for a specified operating system entry.

Syntax:
bootcfg /debug {ON|OFF|EDIT} [/s Computer [/u Domain\User /p Password]] [/port {COM1|COM2|COM3|COM4}] [/baud {9600|19200|38400|57600|115200}] [/id OSEntryLineNum]

Examples:
bootcfg /debug on /port com1 /id 2 *or* bootcfg /debug edit /port com2 /baud 19200 /id 2
Syntax Options:

ON|OFF|EDIT ·················Specifies the value for debugging.

Value ·······Description

ON·············Enables remote debugging support by adding the /debug switch to the specified OSEntryLineNum.

OFF·········Disables remote debugging support by removing the /debug switch from the specified OSEntryLineNum.

EDIT·······Allows changes to port and baud rate settings by changing the values associated with the /debug switch for the specified OSEntryLineNum.

/s Computer ·················Specifies the name or IP address of a remote computer (do not use backslashes). The default is the local computer.

/u Domain\User·············Runs the command with the account permissions of the user specified by User or Domain\User. The default is the permissions of the current logged on user on the computer issuing the command.

/p Password....Specifies the password of the user account that is specified in the /u parameter.

/port {COM1|COM2|COM3|COM4} ·······Specifies the COM port to be used for debugging. Do not use the /port parameter if debugging is being disabled.

/baud {9600|19200|38400|57600|115200}·····Specifies the baud rate to be used for debugging. Do not use the /baud parameter if debugging is being disabled.

/id OSEntryLineNum·······Specifies the operating system entry line number in the [operating systems] section of the Boot.ini file to which the debugging options are added. The first line after the [operating systems] section header is 1.

Notes:

- If 1394 port debugging is required, use bootcfg /dbg1394.

bootcfg default

Specifies the operating system entry to designate as the default.

Syntax:

bootcfg /default [/s Computer [/u Domain\User /p Password]] [/id OSEntryLineNum]

Examples:

bootcfg /default /id 2   *or*   bootcfg /default /s srvmain /u maindom\hiropln /p p@ssW23 /id 2

Syntax Options:

/s Computer ················Specifies the name or IP address of a remote computer (do not use backslashes). The default is the local computer.

/u Domain\User ············Runs the command with the account permissions of the user specified by User or Domain\User. The default is the permissions of the current logged on user on the computer issuing the command.

/p Password ················Specifies the password of the user account that is specified in the /u parameter.

/id OSEntryLineNum ······Specifies the operating system entry line number in the [operating systems] section of the Boot.ini file to designate as default. The first line after the [operating systems] section header is 1.

bootcfg delete

Deletes an operating system entry in the [operating systems] section of the Boot.ini file.

Syntax:

bootcfg /delete [/s Computer [/u Domain\User /p Password]] [/id OSEntryLineNum]

Examples:

bootcfg /delete /id 1   *or*   bootcfg /delete /s srvmain /u maindom\hiropln /p p@ssW23 /id 3

Syntax Options:

/s Computer ················Specifies the name or IP address of a remote computer (do not use backslashes). The default is the local computer.

/u Domain\User ············Runs the command with the account permissions of the user specified by User or Domain\User. The default is the permissions of the current logged on user on the computer issuing the command.

/p Password ···Specifies the password of the user account that is specified in the /u parameter.

/id OSEntryLineNum ······Specifies the operating system entry line number in the [operating systems] section of the Boot.ini file to delete. The first line after the [operating systems] section header is 1.

bootcfg ems

Enables the user to add or change the settings for redirection of the EMS console to a remote computer. By enabling EMS, you add a "redirect=Port#" line to the [boot loader] section of the Boot.ini file and a /redirect switch to the specified operating system entry line. The EMS feature is enabled only on servers.

Syntax:

bootcfg /ems {ON|OFF|EDIT} [/s Computer [/u Domain\User /p Password]] [/port {COM1|COM2|COM3|COM4|BIOSSET}] [/baud {9600|19200|38400|57600|115200}] [/id OSEntryLineNum]

Examples:

bootcfg /ems on /port com1 /baud 19200 /id 2   *or*   bootcfg /ems on /port biosset /id 3

Syntax Options:

ON|OFF|EDIT ················Specifies the value for EMS redirection.

Value ·······Description

ON ··········Enables remote output for the specified OSEntryLineNum. Adds a /redirect switch to the specified OSEntryLineNum and a redirect=comX setting to the [boot loader] section. The value of comX is set by the /port parameter.

OFF ·········Disables output to a remote computer. Removes the /redirect switch from the specified OSEntryLineNum and the redirect=comX setting from the [boot loader] section.

EDIT ········Allows changes to port settings by changing the redirect=comX setting in the [boot loader] section. The value of comX is reset to the value specified by the /port parameter.

/s Computer ················Specifies the name or IP address of a remote computer (do not use backslashes). The default is the local computer.

/u ·············Domain\User·Runs the command with the account permissions of the user specified by User or Domain\User. The default is the permissions of the current logged on user on the computer issuing the command.

/p Password ··················Specifies the password of the user account that is specified in the /u parameter.

/port {COM1|COM2|COM3|COM4|BIOSSET}
Specifies the COM port to be used for redirection. BIOSSET directs EMS to get the BIOS settings to determine which port should be used for redirection. Do not use the /port parameter if remotely administered output is being disabled.

/baud {9600|19200|38400|57600|115200}
Specifies the baud rate to be used for redirection. Do not use the /baud parameter if remotely administered output is being disabled.

/id OSEntryLineNum ······Specifies the operating system entry line number to which the EMS option is added in the [operating systems] section of the Boot.ini file. The first line after the [operating systems] section header is 1. This parameter is required when the EMS value is set to ON or OFF.

bootcfg query

Queries and displays the [boot loader] and [operating systems] section entries from Boot.ini.

Syntax:

bootcfg /query [/s Computer [/u Domain\User /p Password]]

Examples:

bootcfg /query *or* bootcfg /query /s srvmain /u maindom\hiropln /p p@ssW23

Syntax Options:

/s Computer ················Specifies the name or IP address of a remote computer (do not use backslashes). The default is the local computer.

/u Domain\User···········Runs the command with the account permissions of the user specified by User or Domain\User. The default is the permissions of the current logged on user on the computer issuing the command.

/p Password ··················Specifies the password of the user account that is specified in the /u parameter.

bootcfg raw

Adds operating system load options specified as a string to an operating system entry in the [operating systems] section of the Boot.ini file.

Syntax:

bootcfg [/s Computer [/u Domain\User /p Password]] /raw OSLoadOptionsString [/id OSEntryLineNum]

Examples:

bootcfg /raw "/debug /sos" /id 2 *or*
bootcfg /raw /s srvmain /u maindom\hiropln /p p@ssW23 "/crashdebug " /id 2

Syntax Options:

/s Computer ················Specifies the name or IP address of a remote computer (do not use backslashes). The default is the local computer.

/u Domain\User···········Runs the command with the account permissions of the user specified by User or Domain\User. The default is the permissions of the current logged on user on the computer issuing the command.

/p Password ··················Specifies the password of the user account that is specified in the /u parameter.

OSLoadOptionsString·····Specifies the operating system load options to add to the operating system entry. These load options will replace any existing load options associated with the operating system entry. No validation of OSLoadOptions is done.

/id OSEntryLineNum·······Specifies the operating system entry line number in the [operating systems] section of the Boot.ini file to update. The first line after the [operating systems] section header is 1.

Notes:

• Bootcfg raw is used to add text to the end of an operating system entry, overwriting any existing operating system entry options. This text should contain valid OS Load Options such as /debug, /fastdetect, /nodebug, /baudrate, /crashdebug, and /sos. For example, the following command adds "/debug /fastdetect" to the end of the first operating system entry, replacing any previous operating system entry options: bootcfg /raw "/debug /fastdetect" /id 1

bootcfg rmsw

Removes operating system load options for a specified operating system entry.

Syntax:

bootcfg /rmsw [/s Computer [/u Domain\User /p Password]] [/mm] [/bv] [/so] [/ng] /id OSEntryLineNum

Examples:

bootcfg /rmsw /mm 64 /id 2   *or*   bootcfg /rmsw /so /id 3

Syntax Options:

/s Computer ················Specifies the name or IP address of a remote computer (do not use backslashes). The default is the local computer.

/u Domain\User···········Runs the command with the account permissions of the user specified by User or Domain\User. The default is the permissions of the current logged on user on the computer issuing the command.

/p Password ···············Specifies the password of the user account that is specified in the /u parameter.

/mm ·········Removes the /maxmem switch and its associated maximum memory value from the specified OSEntryLineNum. The /maxmem switch specifies the maximum amount of RAM that the operating system can use.

/bv···········Removes the /basevideo switch from the specified OSEntryLineNum. The /basevideo switch directs the operating system to use standard VGA mode for the installed video driver.

/so···········Removes the /sos switch from the specified OSEntryLineNum. The /sos switch directs the operating system to display device driver names while they are being loaded.

/ng···········Removes the /noguiboot switch from the specified OSEntryLineNum. The /noguiboot switch disables the Windows XP Professional progress bar that appears before the CTRL+ALT+DEL logon prompt.

/id OSEntryLineNum······Specifies the operating system entry line number in the [operating systems] section of the Boot.ini file from which the OS Load Options are removed. The first line after the [operating systems] section header is 1.

bootcfg timeout

Changes the operating system time-out value.

Syntax:

bootcfg /timeout TimeOutValue [/s Computer [/u Domain\User /p Password]]

Examples:

bootcfg /timeout 30   *or*   bootcfg /s srvmain /u maindom\hiropln /p p@ssW23 /timeout 50

Syntax Options:

TimeOutValue················Specifies the timeout value in the [boot loader] section. The value is the number of seconds the user has to select an operating system from the boot loader screen before NTLDR loads the default. If the value is 0, then NTLDR immediately starts the default operating system without displaying the boot loader screen.

/s Computer ················Specifies the name or IP address of a remote computer (do not use backslashes). The default is the local computer.

/u Domain\User ·············· Runs the command with the account permissions of the user specified by User or Domain\User. The default is the permissions of the current logged on user on the computer issuing the command.

/p Password ··· Specifies the password of the user account that is specified in the /u parameter.

BREAK

Windows XP does not use this command. It is accepted only for compatibility with MS-DOS files.

CACLS

Displays or modifies discretionary access control list (DACL) files.

Syntax:

cacls FileName [/t] [/e] [/c] [/g User:permission] [/r User [...]] [/p User:permission [...]] [/d User [...]]

Syntax Options:

FileName ·· Required. Displays DACLs of specified files.

/t ·············· Changes DACLs of specified files in the current directory and all subdirectories.

/e ·············· Edits a DACL instead of replacing it.

/c ·············· Continues to change DACLs, ignoring errors.

/g User:permission ·········· Grants access rights to the specified user. The following table lists valid values for permission.

Value	Description
n	None
r	Read
w	Write
c	Change (Write)
f	Full Control

/r User ······ Revokes access rights for the specified user.

/p User:permission ·········· Replaces access rights for the specified user. The following table lists valid values for permission.

Value	Description
n	None
r	Read
w	Write
c	Change (Write)
f	Full Control

/d User ······ Denies access for the specified user.

Notes:

• Use the following table to interpret the results:

Output	ACE applies to
OI	This folder and files
CI	This folder and subfolders
IO	The ACE does not apply to the current file/directory.
No output message	This folder only
(IO)(CI)	This folder, subfolders and files
(OI)(CI)(IO)	Subfolders and files only
(CI)(IO)	Subfolders only
(OI)(IO)	Files only

• You can use wildcards (that is, ? and *) to specify multiple files.

• You can specify more than one user.

CALL

Calls one batch program from another without stopping the parent batch program. The call command accepts labels as the target of the call. Call has no effect at the command-line when used outside of a script or batch file.

Syntax:

call [[Drive:][Path] FileName [BatchParameters]] [:label [arguments]]

Examples:

call checknew *or* call checknew %1 %2

Syntax Options:

[Drive:][Path] FileName ··Specifies the location and name of the .bat or .cmd extension batch program you want to call.

BatchParameters············Specifies any command-line information required by the batch program, including command-line options, file names, batch parameters (that is, %0 through %9), or variables (for example, %baud%).

:label·········Specifies the label to which you want a batch program control to jump. By using call with this parameter, you create a new batch file context and pass control to the statement after the specified label. The first time the end of the batch file is encountered (that is, after jumping to the label), control returns to the statement after the call statement. The second time the end of the batch file is encountered, the batch script is exited.

arguments Specifies any command-line information that you pass to the new instance of the batch program that begins at :label, including command-line options, file names, batch parameters (that is, %1 through %9), or variables (for example, %baud%).

Notes:

• Batch parameters can contain any information that you can pass to a batch program, including command-line options, file names, batch parameters (that is, %0 through %9), and variables (for example, %baud%).

• Do not use pipes and redirection symbols with call.

• You can create a batch program that calls itself, however, you must provide an exit condition. Otherwise, the parent and child batch programs can loop endlessly.

• With command extensions enabled (that is, the default), call accepts a label as the target of the call. The correct syntax is as follows: call :label arguments

CHCP

Displays the number of the active console code page, or changes the console's active console code page.

Syntax:

chcp [nnn]

Examples:

chcp *or* chcp 850

Syntax Options:

Used without parameters, chcp displays the number of the active console code page.

nnn ··········Specifies the code page. The following table lists each code page supported and its country/region or language:

Code page	Country/region or language
437	United States
850	Multilingual (Latin I)
852	Slavic (Latin II)
855	Cyrillic (Russian)
857	Turkish
860	Portuguese
861	Icelandic
863	Canadian-French
865	Nordic
866	Russian
869	Modern Greek

Notes:

- Only the original equipment manufacturer (OEM) code page installed with Windows XP appears correctly in a command prompt window that uses Raster fonts. Other code pages appear correctly in full-screen mode or command prompt windows that use TrueType fonts.

- You do not need to prepare code pages, as in MS-DOS.

- Programs that you start after you assign a new code page use the new code page, however, programs (except Cmd.exe) that you started before assigning the new code page use the original code page.

CHDIR (CD)

Displays the name of the current directory or changes the current folder.

Syntax:

chdir [[/d] [Drive:][Path] [..]] [[/d] [Drive:][Path] [..]]

cd [[/d] [Drive:][Path] [..]] [[/d] [Drive:][Path] [..]]

Examples:

chdir \reports   *or*   cd \reports   *or*   chdir c:\public\jones

Syntax Options:

Used with only a drive letter (for example, chdir C:), chdir displays the names of the current drive and folder.

/d ··············Changes the current drive or the current directory for a drive.

[drive:][Path] ···············Specifies the drive (that is, if it is different from the current drive) and directory to which you want to change.

[..] ············Specifies that you want to change to the parent folder.

Notes:

- With command extensions enabled (that is, the default), the current directory path matches the folder names exactly as they appear on your hard drive, using the same uppercase or lowercase folder-name format. For example, if the folder on your hard drive is called C:\Temp, CD C:\TEMP sets the current directory to C:\Temp to match the folder-name format of the folder on your hard drive.

- To disable command extensions for a particular process, type: cmd e:off

- When you disable command extensions, chdir does not treat white spaces as delimiters. As a result, you can change to a subdirectory name that contains a white space without having to surround [Path] in quotation marks. For example, the following path changes to the \Start menu subdirectory: cd \winnt\profiles\username\programs\start menu

- The root directory is the top of the directory hierarchy for a drive. To return to the root directory, type: cd\

- To change the default directory on a drive different from the one you are on, type one of the following: chdir [Drive:\[directory]]   or   cd [Drive:\[directory]]

- To verify the change to the directory, type one of the following:
cd [Drive:]   *or*   cd [Drive:]

- The chdir command, with different parameters, is available from the Recovery Console.

CHKDSK

Creates and displays a status report for a disk based on the file system. Chkdsk also lists and corrects errors on the disk.

Syntax:

chkdsk [volume:][[Path] FileName] [/f] [/v] [/r] [/x] [/i] [/c] [/l[:size]]

Examples:

chkdsk d: /f   *or*   chkdsk *.*

Syntax Options:

Used without parameters, chkdsk displays the status of the disk in the current drive.

volume: ·····Specifies the drive letter (followed by a colon), mount point, or volume name.

[Path] FileName ·············Specifies the location and name of a file or set of files that you want chkdsk to check for fragmentation. You can use wildcard characters (that is, * and ?) to specify multiple files.

/f ··············Fixes errors on the disk. The disk must be locked. If chkdsk cannot lock the drive, a message appears that asks you if you want to check the drive the next time you restart the computer. If you run chkdsk without the /f command-line option on an active partition, it might report spurious errors because it cannot lock the drive.

/v··············Displays the name of each file in every directory as the disk is checked.

/r··············Locates bad sectors and recovers readable information. The disk must be locked.

/x··············Use with NTFS only. Forces the volume to dismount first, if necessary. All open handles to the drive are invalidated. /x also includes the functionality of /f.

/l ··············Use with NTFS only. Performs a less vigorous check of index entries, reducing the amount of time needed to run chkdsk.

/c··············Use with NTFS only. Skips the checking of cycles within the folder structure, reducing the amount of time needed to run chkdsk.

/l[:size] ······Use with NTFS only. Changes the log file size to the size you type. If you omit the size parameter, /l displays the current size.

Notes:

• To run chkdsk on a fixed disk, you must be a member of the Administrators group.

• If you want chkdsk to correct disk errors, you cannot have open files on the drive. If files are open, the following error message appears: Chkdsk cannot run because the volume is in use by another process. Would you like to schedule this volume to be checked the next time the system restarts? (Y/N)

• If you choose to check the drive the next time you restart the computer, chkdsk checks the drive and corrects errors automatically when you restart the computer. If the drive partition is a boot partition, chkdsk automatically restarts the computer after it checks the drive.

• Chkdsk examines disk space and disk use for the file allocation table (FAT) and NTFS file systems. Chkdsk provides information specific to each file system in a status report. The status report shows errors found in the file system. You should use chkdsk occasionally on each disk to check for errors.

• Chkdsk corrects disk errors only if you specify the /f command-line option. Chkdsk must be able to lock the drive to correct errors. Because repairs usually change a disk's file allocation table and sometimes cause a loss of data, chkdsk sends a confirmation message similar to the following:

10 lost allocation units found in 3 chains.
Convert lost chains to files?

If you press Y, Windows saves each lost chain in the root directory as a file with a name in the format Filennnn.chk. When chkdsk finishes, you can check these files to see if they contain any data you need. If you press N, Windows fixes the disk, but it does not save the contents of the lost allocation units.

• If you do not use the /f command-line option, chkdsk sends a message if a file needs to be fixed, but it does not fix any errors.

• If you use chkdsk /f on a very large disk (for example, 70 gigabytes) or a disk with a very large number of files (for example, millions of files), chkdsk might take a long time (for example, over several days) to complete. The computer is not available during this time because chkdsk does not relinquish control until it is finished.

• If you specify the /f command-line option, chkdsk sends an error message if there are open files on the disk. If you do not specify the /f command-line option and open files exist, chkdsk might report lost allocation units on the disk. This could happen if open files have not yet been recorded in the file allocation table. If chkdsk reports the loss of a large number of allocation units, consider repairing the disk.

• Use the /r command-line option to find physical disk errors in the file system. For information about recovering physically damaged files with recover, see Related Topics.

• Bad sectors reported by chkdsk were marked as bad when your disk was first prepared for operation. They pose no danger.

- The following table lists the exit codes that chkdsk reports after it has finished.

Exit code	Description
0	No errors were found.
1	Errors were found and fixed.
2	Disk cleanup, such as garbage collection, was performed, or cleanup was not performed because /f was not specified.
3	Could not check the disk, errors could not be fixed, or errors were not fixed because /f was not specified.

- The chkdsk command, with different parameters, is available from the Recovery Console.

CHKNTFS

Displays or specifies whether automatic system checking is scheduled to be run on a FAT, FAT32, or NTFS volume when the computer is started.

Syntax:

chkntfs volume: [...]

chkntfs [/d]

chkntfs [/t[:time]]

chkntfs [/x volume: [...]]

chkntfs [/c volume: [...]]

Examples:

chkntfs /t   *or*   chkntfs /t:30   *or*   chkntfs /x e: f:

Syntax Options:

volume: [...] ·····················Required. Specifies the drive letter (followed by a colon), mount point, or volume name. Displays a message that identifies the file system of the specified volume. If automatic file checking is scheduled to be run, this parameter displays a message indicating whether the volume has been corrupted, which requires you to run chkdsk.

/d ·············Restores all chkntfs default settings, except the countdown time for automatic file checking. Default behavior is to check all volumes when the computer is started.

/t[:time] ······Changes the Autochk.exe initiation countdown time to the specified amount of time entered in seconds. If you do not specify :time, /t displays the current countdown time.

/x volume: [...] ·················Excludes the specified volume from being checked when the computer starts, even if the volume is marked as requiring chkdsk.

/c volume: [...] ·················Schedules the specified volume to be checked when the computer starts.

Notes:

- To run chkntfs, you must be a member of the Administrators group.

- Although you can set the Autochk.exe initiation countdown time to zero, you cannot cancel a potentially time-consuming automatic file check if you set it to zero.

CIPHER

Displays or alters the encryption of folders and files on NTFS volumes.

Syntax:

cipher [{/e|/d}] [/s:dir] [/a] [/i] [/f] [/q] [/h] [/k] [/u[/n]] [PathName [...]] |
[/r:PathNameWithoutExtension] | [/w:PathName]

Examples:

cipher /e monthlyreports\may   *or*   cipher /e /s:monthlyreports

Syntax Options:

Used without parameters, cipher displays the encryption state of the current folder and any files it contains.

/e ·············Encrypts the specified folders. Folders are marked so that files that are added to the folder later are encrypted too.

/d ···········Decrypts the specified folders. Folders are marked so that files that are added to the folder later are encrypted too.

/s: dir···········Performs the selected operation in the specified folder and all subfolders.

/a ···········Performs the operation for files and directories.

/i ···········Continues performing the specified operation even after errors occur. By default, cipher stops when it encounters an error.

/f ···········Forces the encryption or decryption of all specified objects. By default, cipher skips files that have been encrypted or decrypted already.

/q ···········Reports only the most essential information.

/h ···········Displays files with hidden or system attributes. By default, these files are not encrypted or decrypted.

/k ···········Creates a new file encryption key for the user running cipher. If you use this option, cipher ignores all of the other options.

/u ···········Updates the user's file encryption key or recovery agent's key to the current ones in all of the encrypted files on local drives (that is, if the keys have been changed). This option only works with /n.

/n ···········Prevents keys from being updated. Use this option to find all of the encrypted files on the local drives. This option only works with /u.

PathName Specifies a pattern, file, or folder.

/r:PathNameWithoutExtension···········Generates a new recovery agent certificate and private key, and then writes them to files with the file name specified in PathNameWithoutExtension. If you use this option, cipher ignores all of the other options.

/w:PathName ···········Removes data on unused portions of a volume. PathName can indicate any directory on the desired volume. If you use this option, cipher ignores all of the other options. /w removes data from portions of the volume it can access and have not been allocated to files or directories. It does not lock the drive, so other programs can obtain space on the drive, which cipher cannot erase. Because this option writes to a large portion of the hard volume, it might take a long time to complete and should only be used when necessary.

Notes:

• To prevent an encrypted file from becoming decrypted when it is modified, it is recommended that you encrypt both the file and the folder in which it resides.

• Cipher cannot encrypt files that are marked as read-only.

• You can use multiple folder names and wildcard characters.

• You must separate multiple parameters by at least one space.

CLS

Clears the Command Prompt window.

Syntax:

cls

Examples:

cls

CMD

Starts a new instance of the command interpreter, Cmd.exe.

Syntax:

cmd [[{/c|/k}] [/s] [/q] [/d] [{/a|/u}] [/t:fg] [/e:{on|off}] [/f:{on|off}] [/v:{on|off}] string]

Syntax Options:

Used without parameters, cmd displays Windows XP version and copyright information.

/c···········Carries out the command specified by string and then stops.

/k···········Carries out the command specified by string and continues.

/s···········Modifies the treatment of string after /c or /k.

/q ···········Turns the echo off.

/d ···········Disables execution of AutoRun commands.

/a ···········Creates American National Standards Institute (ANSI) output.

/u ···········Creates Unicode output.

/t:fg ··········Sets the foreground f and background g colors. The following tables lists valid hexadecimal digits that you can use as the values for f and g.

Value	Color
0	Black
1	Blue
2	Green
3	Aqua
4	Red
5	Purple
6	Yellow
7	White
8	Gray
9	Light blue
A	Light green
B	Light aqua
C	Light red
D	Light purple
E	Light yellow
F	Bright white

/e:on ········Enables command extensions.

/e:off ········Disables commands extensions.

/f:on ··········Enables file and directory name completion.

/f:off ··········Disables file and directory name completion.

/v:on··········Enables delayed environment variable expansion.

/v:off··········Disables delayed environment variable expansion.

string·········Specifies the command you want to carry out.

Notes:

• You can use multiple commands separated by the command separator && for string, but you must enclose them in quotation marks (for example, "command&&command").

• If you specify /c or /k, cmd processes the remainder of string and quotation marks are preserved only if all of the following conditions are met:
You do not use /s.
You use exactly one set of quotation marks.
You do not use any special characters within the quotation marks (for example: &( ) @ ^ |).
You use one or more white-space characters within the quotation marks.

• The string within quotation marks is the name of an executable file.

• If the previous conditions are not met, string is processed by examining the first character to verify whether or not it is an opening quotation mark. If the first character is an opening quotation mark, it is stripped along with the closing quotation mark. Any text following the closing quotation marks is preserved.

• If you do not specify /d in string, Cmd.exe looks for the following registry subkeys:
HKEY_LOCAL_MACHINE\Software\Microsoft\Command Processor\AutoRun\REG_SZ
HKEY_CURRENT_USER\Software\Microsoft\Command Processor\AutoRun REG_EXPAND_SZ

• If either one or both registry subkeys are present, they are executed before all other variables.

• Command extensions are enabled by default in Windows XP. You can disable them for a particular process by using /e:off. You can enable or disable extensions for all cmd command-line options on a computer or user session by setting the following REG_DWORD values:
HKEY_LOCAL_MACHINE\Software\Microsoft\Command Processor\EnableExtensions\REG_DWORD
HKEY_CURRENT_USER\Software\Microsoft\Command Processor\EnableExtensions\REG_DWORD

- Set the REG_DWORD value to either 0x1 (that is, enabled) or 0x0 (that is, disabled) in the registry by using Regedit.exe. User-specified settings take precedence over computer settings, and command-line options take precedence over registry settings.

- When you enable command extensions, the following commands are affected: assoc, call, chdir (cd), color, del (erase), endlocal, for, ftype, goto, if, mkdir (md), popd, prompt, pushd, set, setlocal, shift, start (also includes changes to external command processes)

- If you enable delayed environment variable expansion, you can use the exclamation character to substitute the value of an environment variable at run time.

- File and directory name completion is not enabled by default. You can enable or disable file name completion for a particular process of the cmd command with /f:{on|off}. You can enable or disable file and directory name completion for all processes of the cmd command on a computer or user logon session by setting the following REG_DWORD values:
HKEY_LOCAL_MACHINE\Software\Microsoft\Command Processor\CompletionChar\REG_DWORD
HKEY_LOCAL_MACHINE\Software\Microsoft\Command Processor\PathCompletionChar\REG_DWORD
HKEY_CURRENT_USER\Software\Microsoft\Command Processor\CompletionChar\REG_DWORD
HKEY_CURRENT_USER\Software\Microsoft\Command Processor\PathCompletionChar\REG_DWORD

- To set the REG_DWORD value, run Regedit.exe and use the hexadecimal value of a control character for a particular function (for example, 0x9 is TAB and 0x08 is BACK-SPACE). User-specified settings take precedence over computer settings, and command-line options take precedence over registry settings.

- If you enable file and directory name completion by using /f:on, use CTRL+D for directory name completion and CTRL+F for file name completion. To disable a particular completion character in the registry, use the value for white space [0x20] because it is not a valid control character.

- When you press CTRL+D or CTRL+F, cmd processes file and directory name completion. These key combination functions append a wildcard character to string (that is, if one is not present), build a list of paths that match, and then display the first matching path. If none of the paths match, the file and directory name completion function beeps and does not change the display. To move through the list of matching paths, press CTRL+D or CTRL+F repeatedly. To move through the list backwards, press the SHIFT key and CTRL+D or CTRL+F simultaneously. To discard the saved list of matching paths and generate a new list, edit string and press CTRL+D or CTRL+F. If you switch between CTRL+D and CTRL+F, the saved list of matching paths is discarded and a new list is generated. The only difference between the key combinations CTRL+D and CTRL+F is that CTRL+D only matches directory names and CTRL+F matches both file and directory names. If you use file and directory name completion on any of the built-in directory commands (that is, CD, MD, or RD), directory completion is assumed.

- File and directory name completion correctly processes file names that contain white space or special characters if you place quotation marks around the matching path.

- The following special characters require quotation marks: & < > [ ] { } ^ = ; ! ' + , ` ~ [white space]

- If the information that you supply contains spaces, use quotation marks around the text (for example, "Computer Name").

- If you process file and directory name completion from within string, any part of the [Path] to the right of the cursor is discarded (that is, at the point in string where the completion was processed).

CMSTP

Installs or removes a Connection Manager service profile.

Syntax:

Syntax 1: ServiceProfileFileName.exe /q:a /c:"cmstp.exe ServiceProfileFileName.inf [/nf] [/ni] [/ns] [/s] [/su] [/u]"

Syntax 2: cmstp.exe [/nf] [/ni] [/ns] [/s] [/su] [/u] "[Drive]:[Path]ServiceProfileFileName.inf"

Examples:
fiction.exe /c:"cmstp.exe fiction.inf /nf" *or*
fiction.exe /c:"cmstp.exe fiction.inf /s /su"

Syntax Options:
Used without optional parameters, cmstp installs a service profile with default settings appropriate to the operating system and to the user's permissions.

ServiceProfileFileName.exe ·········· Required for Syntax 1 but not valid for Syntax 2. Specifies, by name, the installation package that contains the profile that you want to install.

/q:a ········· Required for Syntax 1 but not valid for Syntax 2. Specifies that the profile should be installed without prompting the user. The verification message that the installation has succeeded will still appear.

[Drive:][Path]ServiceProfileFileName.inf
Required. Specifies, by name, the configuration file that determines how the profile should be installed. The [Drive:][Path] parameter is not valid for Syntax 1.

/nf ········· Specifies that the support files should not be installed.

/ni ········· Specifies that a desktop icon should not be created. This parameter is only valid for computers running Windows 95, Windows 98, Windows NT 4.0, or Windows Millennium Edition.

/ns ········· Specifies that a desktop shortcut should not be created. This parameter is only valid for computers running Windows 2000 or Windows XP.

/s ········· Specifies that the service profile should be installed or uninstalled silently (without prompting for user response or displaying verification message).

/su ········· Specifies that the service profile should be installed for a single user rather than for all users. This parameter is only valid for computers running Windows 2000 or Windows XP.

/u ········· Specifies that the service profile should be uninstalled.

Notes:
- /s is the only parameter that you can use in combination with /u.
- Syntax 1 is the typical syntax used in a custom installation application. To use this syntax, you must run cmstp from the directory that contains the ServiceProfileFileName.exe file.

COLOR

Changes the Command Prompt window foreground and background colors for the current session.

Syntax:
color [fb]

Examples:
color FC

Syntax Options:
Used without parameters, color restores the default Command Prompt window foreground and background colors.

fb ········· Sets the foreground f and background g colors. The following tables lists valid hexadecimal digits that you can use as the values for f and g.

Value	Color
0	Black
1	Blue
2	Green
3	Aqua
4	Red
5	Purple
6	Yellow
7	White
8	Gray
9	Light blue
A	Light green

Value	Color
B	Light aqua
C	Light red
D	Light purple
E	Light yellow
F	Bright white

Notes:

• To set the default Command Prompt window color, click the upper-left corner of the command prompt window, click Defaults, click the Colors tab, and then click the colors that you want to use for the Screen Text and Screen Background.

• You can use cmd /t:fb to change the Command Prompt window colors for the current session.

• If the foreground and background colors are the same, the color command sets ERRORLEVEL to one (1).

COMP

Compares the contents of two files or sets of files byte by byte. Comp can compare files on the same drive or on different drives, and in the same directory or in different directories. When comp compares the files, it displays their locations and file names.

Syntax:

comp [data1] [data2] [/d] [/a] [/l] [/n=number] [/c]

Examples:

comp c:\reports \\sales\backup\april *or*
comp \invoice*.txt \invoice\backup*.txt /n=10 /d

Syntax Options:

Used without parameters, comp prompts you to enter the files to compare.

data1 ········Specifies the location and name of the first file or set of files you want to compare. You can use wildcard characters (* and ?) to specify multiple files.

data2 ········Specifies the location and name of the second file or set of files you want to compare. You can use wildcard characters (* and ?) to specify multiple files.

/d ·············Displays differences in decimal format. (The default format is hexadecimal.)

/a ·············Displays differences as characters.

/l ·············Displays the number of the line on which a difference occurs, instead of displaying the byte offset.

/n=number Compares the first number of lines of both files, even if the files are different sizes.

/c·············Performs a comparison that is not case-sensitive.

Notes:

• The files that you compare can have the same file name, provided they are in different directories or on different drives. If you do not specify a file name for data2, the default file name for data2 is the same as the file name in data1. You can use wildcard characters (that is, * and ?) to specify file names.

• If you omit necessary components of either data1 or data2 or if you omit data2, comp prompts you for the missing information. If data1 contains only a drive letter or a directory name with no file name, comp compares all of the files in the specified directory to the file specified in data2. If data2 contains only a drive letter or a directory name, the default file name for data2 is the same as that in data1.

• During the comparison, comp displays messages to identify the locations of unequal information in the two files. Each message indicates the offset memory address of the unequal bytes and the contents of the bytes themselves (that is, in hexadecimal notation unless you specify the /a or /d command-line option). The message appears in the following format:

Compare error at OFFSET xxxxxxxx
file1 = xx
file2 = xx

- After 10 unequal comparisons, comp stops comparing the files and displays the following message: 10 Mismatches - ending compare

- You cannot compare files of different sizes unless you specify the /n command-line option. If the file sizes are different, comp displays the following message:
Files are different sizes   Compare more files (Y/N)?
Press Y to compare another pair of files. Press N to stop the comp command.
If you press Y in response to the prompt, comp includes any command-line options you specified on the command line in every comparison it makes, until you press N or retype the command.

- When comparing files of different sizes, use the /n command-line option to compare only the first portion of each file.

- If you use wildcard characters (* and ?) to specify multiple files, comp finds the first file matching data1 and compares it with the corresponding file in data2, if it exists. The comp command reports the results of the comparison, and then does the same for each file matching data1. When finished, comp displays the following message:
Compare more files (Y/N)?

- To compare more files, press Y. The comp command prompts you for the locations and names of the new files. To stop the comparisons, press N. When you press Y, comp prompts you for command-line options to use. If you don't specify any command-line options, comp uses the ones you specified before.

- If comp cannot find the file(s) you specify, it prompts you with a message to determine whether you want to compare more files.

COMPACT

Displays and alters the compression of files or directories on NTFS partitions.

Syntax:

compact [[{/c|/u}] [/s[:dir]] [/a] [/i] [/f] [/q] [FileName[...]]

Examples:

compact /c /s   *or*   compact /c /s *.*   *or*   compact /c /i /s:\

Syntax Options:

Used without parameters, compact displays the compression state of the current directory.

/c ················Compresses the specified directory or file.

/u ················Uncompresses the specified directory or file.

/s:dir ··········Specifies that the requested action (compress or uncompress) be applied to all subdirectories of the specified directory, or of the current directory if none is specified.

/a ···············Displays hidden or system files.

/i ················Ignores errors.

/f ···············Forces compression or uncompression of the specified directory or file. This is used in the case of a file that was partly compressed when the operation was interrupted by a system crash. To force the file to be compressed in its entirety, use the /c and /f parameters and specify the partially compressed file.

/q ···············Reports only the most essential information.

FileName ··Specifies the file or directory. You can use multiple file names and wildcard characters (* and ?).

Notes:

- The compact command, the command-line version of the NTFS file system compression feature, displays and alters the compression attribute of files and directories on NTFS partitions. The compression state of a directory indicates whether files added to the directory will be automatically compressed. When you set the compression state of a directory you do not necessarily change the compression state of files that are already there.

- You cannot use compact to read, write, or mount volumes that have been compressed using DriveSpace or DoubleSpace.

CONTIG

Defrag command for NTFS partitions: Free defrag command made by SysInternals.com that enables you to specify files and folders you want defragged instead of the entire drive.

Syntax:

CONTIG -a -s *.*

Examples:

CONTIG -a -s *.*   *or*   CONTIG -s *.*

Syntax Options:

-a -s ·············Analyses all files and folders on the selected drive and displays a fragmentation report

-s ·············Defrags all files and folders on the selected drive

Command Type and Version: External Command; WinXP, WinNT 4.0, will NOT run on Win9X

CONVERT

Converts FAT and FAT32 volumes to NTFS

Syntax:

convert [volume] /fs:ntfs [/v] [/cvtarea:FileName] [/nosecurity] [/x]

Examples:

convert e: /fs:ntfs /v

Syntax Options:

volume······Specifies the drive letter (followed by a colon), mount point, or volume name to convert to NTFS.

/fs:ntfs······Required. Converts the volume to NTFS.

/v··············Specifies verbose mode, that is, all messages will be displayed during conversion.

/cvtarea:FileName ··········For advanced users only. Specifies that the Master File Table (MFT) and other NTFS metadata files are written to an existing, contiguous placeholder file. This file must be in the root directory of the file system to be converted. Use of the /CVTAREA parameter can result in a less fragmented file system after conversion. For best results, the size of this file should be 1 KB multiplied by the number of files and directories in the file system, however, the convert utility accepts files of any size.

For more information about using the /cvtarea parameter, see "File Systems" at the Microsoft Windows XP Resource Kits Web site (http://www.microsoft.com/resources/documentation/windows/xp/all/proddocs/en-us/fsutil_file.mspx.)

Notes:

>>>Important<<<

• You must create the placeholder file using the fsutil file createnew command prior to running convert. Convert does not create this file for you. Convert overwrites this file with NTFS metadata. After conversion, any unused space in this file is freed.

• /nosecurity Specifies that the converted files and directory security settings are accessible by everyone. /x Dismounts the volume, if necessary, before it is converted. Any open handles to the volume will no longer be valid.

• You must specify that the drive should be converted when the computer is restarted. Otherwise, you cannot convert the current drive.

• If convert cannot lock the drive (for example, the system volume or the current drive), it offers to convert the drive the next time the computer restarts.

• The location of the MFT is different on volumes that have been converted from previous version of NTFS, so volume performance might not be as good on volumes converted from Windows NT.

• Volumes converted from FAT to NTFS lack some performance benefits compared to volumes initially formatted with NTFS. On converted volumes, the MFT might become fragmented. In addition, on converted boot volumes, NTFS permissions are not applied after the volume is converted.

COPY

Copies one or more files from one location to another.

Syntax:

copy [/d] [/v] [/n] [{/y|/-y}] [/z] [{/a|/b}] Source [{/a|/b}] [+ Source [{/a|/b}] [+ ...]] [Destination [{/a|/b}]]

Examples:

copy memo.doc letter.doc /a   *or*   copy robin.typ c:\birds   *or*   copy *.txt combin.doc

Syntax Options:

/d ·············· Allows the encrypted files being copied to be saved as decrypted files at the destination.

/v ·············· Verifies that new files are written correctly.

/n ·············· Uses a short file name, if available, when copying a file with a name longer than eight characters, or with a file extension longer than three characters.

/y ·············· Suppresses prompting to confirm that you want to overwrite an existing destination file.

/-y ············ Prompts you to confirm that you want to overwrite an existing destination file.

/z ·············· Copies networked files in restartable mode.

/a ·············· Indicates an ASCII text file.

/b ·············· Indicates a binary file.

Source ······ Required. Specifies the location from which you want to copy a file or set of files. Source can consist of a drive letter and colon, a folder name, a file name, or a combination of these.

Destination ·· Required. Specifies the location to which you want to copy a file or set of files. Destination can consist of a drive letter and colon, a folder name, a file name, or a combination of these.

Notes:

• You can copy an ASCII text file that uses an end-of-file character (that is, CTRL+Z) to indicate the end of the file.

• When /a precedes a list of files on the command line, it applies to all files listed until copy encounters /b. In this case, /b applies to the file preceding /b.

• When /a follows a list of files on the command line, it applies to all listed files until copy encounters /b. In this case, /b applies to the file preceding /b.

• The effect of /a depends on its position in the command-line string. When /a follows Source, copy treats the file as an ASCII file and copies data that precedes the first end-of-file character.

• When /a follows Destination, copy adds an end-of-file character as the last character of the file.

• /b directs the command interpreter to read the number of bytes specified by the file size in the directory. /b is the default value for copy, unless copy combines files.

• When /b precedes a list of files on the command line, it applies to all listed files until copy encounters /a. In this case, /a applies to the file preceding /a.

• When /b follows a list of files on the command line, it applies to all listed files until copy encounters /a. In this case, /a applies to the file preceding /a.

• The effect of /b depends on its position in the commandline string. When /b follows Source, copy copies the entire file, including any end-of-file character.

• When /b follows Destination, copy does not add an end-of-file character.

• If a write operation cannot be verified an error message appears. Although recording errors rarely occur with copy, you can use /v to verify that critical data has been correctly recorded. The /v command-line option also slows down the copy command, because each sector recorded on the disk must be checked.

• If /y is preset in the COPYCMD environment variable, you can override this setting by using /-y at the command line. By default, you are prompted when you replace this setting, unless the copy command is executed in a batch script.

• To append files, specify a single file for Destination, but multiple files for Source (using wildcard characters or file1+file2+file3 format).

• If the connection is lost during the copy phase (for example, if the server going offline severs the connection), copy /z resumes after the connection is reestablished. /z also displays the percentage of the copy operation that is completed for each file.

• You can substitute a device name for one or more occurrences of Source or Destination.

• When Destination is a device (for example, Com1 or Lpt1), /b copies data to the device in binary mode. In binary mode, copy /b copies all characters (that is, including special characters, such as CTRL+C, CTRL+S, CTRL+Z, and carriage return) to the device as data. However, if you omit /b, data is copied to the device in ASCII mode. In ASCII mode, special characters might cause Windows XP to combine files during the copying process. For more information, see "Combining files."

• If you do not specify a destination file, a copy is created with the same name, creation date, and creation time as the original file, placing the new copy in the current directory on the current drive. If the source file is on the current drive and in the current directory and you do not specify a different drive or directory for the destination file, the copy command stops and displays the following error message:

File cannot be copied onto itself
0 File(s) copied

• If you specify more than one Source, separating entries with a plus sign (+), copy combines the files into a single file. If you use wildcard characters (that is, * or ?) in Source, but you specify a single file name in Destination, copy combines all files matching the file name in Source and creates a single file with the file name specified in Destination. In either case, copy assumes the combined files are ASCII files unless you use /b.

• Copy does not copy files that are 0 bytes long. Use xcopy to copy these files.

• If you want to assign the current time and date to a file without modifying the file, use the following syntax: copy /b Source+,,
The commas indicate the omission of the Destination parameter.

• To copy all of a directory's files and subdirectories, use the xcopy command. For information about xcopy, see Related Topics.

• The copy command, with different parameters, is available from the Recovery Console.

Caution

• If you combine binary files, the resulting file might be unusable due to internal formatting.

• In the following example, copy combines each file that has a .txt extension with its corresponding .ref file. The result is a file with the same file name but with a .doc extension. Copy combines File1.txt with File1.ref to form File1.doc, and then copy combines File2.txt with File2.ref to form File2.doc, and so on. For example, type: copy *.txt + *.ref *.doc

• To combine all files with the .txt extension, and then combine all files with the .ref extension into one file named Combin.doc, type: copy *.txt + *.ref combin.doc

CPROFILE

Cleans specified profiles of wasted space and, if user-specific file associations are disabled, removes these associations from the registry. Profiles that are currently in use are not modified.

Syntax:

cprofile [/l] [/i] [/v] [FileList]

cprofile [/i] [/v] FileList

Syntax Options:

/l···············Cleans all local profiles. You can also specify a list of additional profiles in the FileList parameter.

/i···············Interactively prompts the user with each profile.

/v···············Displays information about the actions being performed.

FileList······A list of files from which you want to remove user-specific file associations. Separate each file in the list with a space. File names can contain wildcard characters.

Notes:

• Only administrators can run cprofile.

• A terminal server uses file associations to determine which application to use to access files of various types. File types are registered using Windows Explorer.

• Per-user file associations allow each user to have a different application associated with a specific file type. For example, one user could have .doc files associated with

Microsoft Word and another user could have .doc files associated with Windows WordPad.

• If user-specific file associations are enabled, cprofile only removes the unused space from the user profile. If user-specific file associations are disabled, cprofile also removes the corresponding registry entries.

Date

Displays the current system date setting.

Syntax:

date [mm-dd-yy] [/t]

Examples:

08.03.00 *or* 08-03-00 *or* 08/03/00 *or* date /t

Syntax Options:

Used without parameters, date displays the current system date setting and prompts you to type a new date.

mm-dd-yy ·Sets the date specified where mm is month, dd is day, and yy is year.

/t ·············Displays the current date without prompting you for a new date.

Notes:

• You must separate values for mm, dd, and yy with periods (.), hyphens (-), or slash marks (/).

• Valid mm values are 1 through 12.

• Valid dd values are 1 through 31.

• Valid yy values are 80 through 99, or 1980 through 2099.

• Windows XP changes the month and year automatically, whether the month has 28, 29, 30, or 31 days.

DEFRAG

Locates and consolidates fragmented boot files, data files, and folders on local volumes.

Syntax:

defrag volume

defrag volume [/a]

defrag volume [/a] [/v]

defrag volume [/v]

defrag volume [/f]

Syntax Options:

volume······The drive letter or a mount point of the volume to be defragmented.

/a ·············Analyzes the volume and displays a summary of the analysis report.

/v·············Displays the complete analysis and defragmentation reports.

When used in combination with /a, displays only the analysis report. When used alone, displays both the analysis and defragmentation reports.

/f ·············Forces defragmentation of the volume regardless of whether it needs to be defragmented.

Notes:

• A volume must have at least 15% free space for defrag to completely and adequately defragment it. Defrag uses this space as a sorting area for file fragments. If a volume has less than 15% free space, defrag will only partially defragment it.

• You cannot defragment volumes that the file system has marked as dirty, which indicates possible corruption. You must run chkdsk on a dirty volume before you can defragment it. You can determine if a volume is dirty by using the fsutil dirty query command.

• While defrag is analyzing and defragmenting a volume, it displays a blinking cursor. When defrag is finished analyzing and defragmenting the volume, it displays the analysis report, the defragmentation report, or both reports, and then exits to the command prompt.

• By default, defrag displays a summary of both the analysis and defragmentation reports if you do not specify the /a or /v parameters.

- You can send the reports to a text file by typing >filename.txt, where filename.txt is a file name you specify. For example: defrag volume /v >filename.txt

- To interrupt the defragmentation process, at the command line, press CTRL+C.

- Running the defrag command and Disk Defragmenter are mutually exclusive. If you are using Disk Defragmenter to defragment a volume and you run the defrag command at a command-line, the defrag command fails. Conversely, if you run the defrag command and open Disk Defragmenter, the defragmentation options in Disk Defragmenter are unavailable.

DEL (ERASE)

Deletes specified files.

Syntax:

del [Drive:][Path] FileName [...] [/p] [/f] [/s] [/q] [/a[:attributes]]

erase [Drive:][Path] FileName [...] [/p] [/f] [/s] [/q] [/a[:attributes]]

Examples:

del c:\test *or* del c:\test*.*

Syntax Options:

[Drive:][Path] FileName ··Specifies the location and name of the file or set of files you want to delete. Filename is required. You can use multiple file names. Separate file names with spaces, commas, or semicolons.

/p ··············Prompts you for confirmation before deleting the specified file.

/f ··············Forces deletion of read-only files.

/s··············Deletes specified files from the current directory and all subdirectories. Displays the names of the files as they are being deleted.

/q··············Specifies quiet mode. You are not prompted for delete confirmation.

/a ··············Deletes files based on specified attributes.

attributes···Specifies any of the following file attributes:

Attribute ····Description

r ··············Read-only

a ··············Archive

s··············System

h ··············Hidden

- ··············Prefix meaning "not"

Notes:

- Press Y to confirm the deletion, N to cancel the deletion and display the next file name (if you specified a group of files), or CTRL+C to stop the del command.

- If you disable command extensions, the /s command-line option displays the names of any files that were not found, instead of displaying the names of files that are being deleted (that is, the behavior is reversed).

- You can delete all of the files in a folder by typing del followed by [Drive:]Path. For example, the following command deletes all files in the \Work folder: del \work

- You can also use wildcards (that is, * and ?) to delete more than one file at a time. However, you should use wildcards cautiously with the del command to avoid deleting files unintentionally. For example, if you type the following command: del *.*
The del command displays the following prompt:
All files in directory will be deleted! Are you sure (Y/N)?
Press Y and then ENTER to delete all files in the current folder, or press N and then ENTER to cancel the deletion.

- Before you use wildcards with the del command to delete a group of files, you can use the same wildcards with the dir command to see a list of the names of all the files included in the group.

- *Warning: After you delete a file from your disk using del, you cannot retrieve it.*

- The del command, with different parameters, is available from the Recovery Console.

DIR

Displays a list of a directory's files and subdirectories.

Syntax:

dir [Drive:][Path][FileName] [...] [/p] [/q] [/w] [/d] [/a[[:]attributes]][/o[[:]SortOrder]]
[/t[[:]TimeField] [/s] [/b] [/l] [/n] [/x] [/c] [/4]

Examples:

dir /s/w/o/p *or* dir /s/w/o/p/a:-d *or* dir > prn *or* dir > \records\dir.doc

Syntax Options:

Used without parameters, dir displays the disk's volume label and serial number, followed by a list of directories and files on the disk, including their names and the date and time each was last modified. For files, dir displays the name extension and the size in bytes. Dir also displays the total number of files and directories listed, their cumulative size, and the free space (in bytes) remaining on the disk.

[Drive:][Path] ················ Specifies the drive and directory for which you want to see a listing.

[FileName] Specifies a particular file or group of files for which you want to see a listing.

/p ············ Displays one screen of the listing at a time. To see the next screen, press any key on the keyboard.

/q ············ Displays file ownership information.

/w ············ Displays the listing in wide format, with as many as five file names or directory names on each line.

/d ············ Same as /w but files are sorted by column.

/a [[:] attributes] ··············· Displays only the names of those directories and files with the attributes you specify. If you omit /a, dir displays the names of all files except hidden and system files. If you use /a without specifying attributes, dir displays the names of all files, including hidden and system files. The following list describes each of the values you can use for attributes. The colon (:) is optional. Use any combination of these values, and do not separate the values with spaces.

Value ······· Description

h ··············· Hidden files

s ··············· System files

d ··············· Directories

a ··············· Files ready for archiving

r ··············· Read-only files

-h ··············· Files that are not hidden

-s ··············· Files other than system files

-d ··············· Files only (not directories)

-a ··············· Files that have not changed since the last backup

-r ··············· Files that are not read-only

/o [[:]SortOrder] ··············· Controls the order in which dir sorts and displays directory names and file names. If you omit /o, dir displays the names in the order in which they occur in the directory. If you use /o without specifying SortOrder, dir displays the names of the directories, sorted in alphabetic order, and then displays the names of files, sorted in alphabetic order. The colon (:) is optional. The following list describes each of the values you can use for SortOrder. Use any combination of the values, and do not separate these values with white spaces.

Value ······· Description

n ··············· In alphabetic order by name

e ··············· In alphabetic order by extension

d ··············· By date and time, earliest first

s ··············· By size, smallest first

g ··············· With directories grouped before files

-n ··············· In reverse alphabetic order by name (Z through A)

-e ··············· In reverse alphabetic order by extension (.ZZZ through .AAA)

-d ··············· By date and time, latest first

-s ··············· By size, largest first

-g ··············· With directories grouped after files

/t [[:]TimeField] ················Specifies which time field to display or use for sorting. The following list describes each of the values you can use for TimeField.

Value ·······Description

c················Creation

a ·············Last access

w·············Last written

/s················Lists every occurrence, in the specified directory and all subdirectories, of the specified file name.

/b ·············Lists each directory name or file name, one per line, including the file name extension. /b does not display heading information or a summary. /b overrides /w.

/l·················Displays unsorted directory names and file names in lowercase. /l does not convert extended characters to lowercase.

/n ·············Displays a long list format with file names on the far right of the screen.

/x ·············Displays the short names generated for files on NTFS and FAT volumes. The display is the same as the display for /n, but short names are displayed after the long name.

/c················Displays the thousand separator in file sizes.

/4 ·············Displays four-digit year format.

Notes:

• You can use multiple filenames. Separate file names with spaces, commas, or semicolons. You can use wildcard characters (that is, ? and *) in FileName to display a group of files and to display a list of a subset of files and subdirectories.

• If you use /a with more than one value in attributes, dir displays the names of only those files with all the specified attributes. For example, if you use /a with r and -h for attributes by using either /a:r-h or /ar-h, dir displays only the names of read-only files that are not hidden.

• If you specify more than one SortOrder value, dir sorts the file names by the first criterion first, then by the second criterion, and so on. For example, if you use /o with the e and -s values for SortOrder by using either /o:e-s or /oe-s, dir sorts the names of directories and files by extension, with the largest first, and then displays the final result. The alphabetic sorting by extension causes file names with no extensions to appear first, then directory names, and then file names with extensions.

• When you use a redirection symbol (>) to send dir output to a file or a pipe (|) to send dir output to another command, use /a:-d and /b to list the file names only. You can use FileName with /b and /s to specify that dir is to search the current directory and its subdirectories for all file names that match FileName. Dir lists only the drive letter, directory name, file name, and file name extension, one path per line, for each file name it finds. Before you use a pipe for redirection, you should set the TEMP environment variable in your Autoexec.nt file.

• You can preset dir parameters by including set with the DIRCMD environment variable in your Autoexec.nt file. You can use any valid combination of dir parameters with set dircmd, including the location and name of a file.

• For example, to use the DIRCMD environment variable to set the wide display format (that is, /w) as the default format, type the following command in your Autoexec.nt file: set dircmd=/w

• For a single use of the dir command, you can override a parameter by using the DIRCMD environment variable. To do so, type the parameter that you want to override at the dir command prompt, preceding the parameter with a minus sign. For example: dir /-w

• To change the DIRCMD default settings, type: set=NewParameter

• The new default settings are effective for all subsequent dir commands until you use set dircmd again or until you restart your computer.

• To clear all default settings, type: set dircmd=

• To view the current settings of the DIRCMD environment variable, type: set
Set displays a list of environment variables and their settings.

• The dir command, with different parameters, is available from the Recovery Console.

DISKCOMP

Compares the contents of two floppy disks.

Syntax:

diskcomp [drive1: [drive2:]]

Examples:

If your computer has only one floppy disk drive (for example, drive A), and you want to compare two disks, type: diskcomp a: a:

Diskcomp prompts you to insert each disk, as needed.

Syntax Options:

Used without parameters, diskcomp uses the current drive for both disks that you want to compare.

drive1········Specifies the drive containing one of the floppy disks.

drive2········Specifies the drive containing the other floppy disk.

Notes:

• The diskcomp command works only with floppy disks. You cannot use diskcomp with a hard disk. If you specify a hard disk drive for drive1 or drive2, diskcomp displays the following error message:

Invalid drive specification
Specified drive does not exist
or is nonremovable

• If all tracks on the two disks being compared are the same, diskcomp displays the following message: Compare OK

• If the tracks are not the same, diskcomp displays a message similar to the following:
Compare error on
side 1, track 2

• When diskcomp completes the comparison, it displays the following message:
Compare another diskette (Y/N)?

• If you press Y, diskcomp prompts you to insert disks for the next comparison. If you press N, diskcomp stops the comparison.

• When diskcomp makes the comparison, it ignores a disk's volume number.

• If you omit the drive2 parameter, diskcomp uses the current drive for drive2. If you omit both drive parameters, diskcomp uses the current drive for both. If the current drive is the same as drive1, diskcomp prompts you to swap disks as necessary.

• If you specify the same floppy disk drive for drive1 and drive2, diskcomp does a comparison by using one drive and prompts you to insert the disks as necessary. You might have to swap the disks more than once, depending on the capacity of the disks and the amount of available memory.

• Diskcomp cannot compare a single-sided disk with a double-sided disk, nor a high-density disk with a double-density disk. If the disk in drive1 is not of the same type as the disk in drive2, diskcomp displays the following message: Drive types or diskette types not compatible

• Diskcomp does not work on a network drive or on a drive created by the subst command. If you attempt to use diskcomp with a drive of any of these types, diskcomp displays the following error message: Invalid drive specification

• When you use diskcomp with a disk that you made by using copy, diskcomp might display a message similar to the following: Compare error on side 0, track 0

• This type of error can occur even if the files on the disks are identical. Although copy duplicates information, it does not necessarily place it in the same location on the destination disk.

• The following table lists each exit code and a brief description.

Exit code	Description
0	Disks are the same
1	Differences were found
3	Hard error occurred
4	Initialization error occurred

• To process exit codes returned by diskcomp, you can use errorlevel on the if command line in a batch program.

DISKCOPY

Copies the contents of the floppy disk in the source drive to a formatted or unformatted floppy disk in the destination drive.

Syntax:

diskcopy [drive1: [drive2:]] [/v]

Examples:

diskcopy b: a:

Syntax Options:

Used without parameters, diskcopy uses the current drive for the source disk and the destination disk.

drive1········Specifies the drive containing the source disk.

drive2········Specifies the drive containing the destination disk.

/v··············Verifies that the information is copied correctly. This command-line option slows down the copying process.

Notes:

• Diskcopy works only with removable disks, such as floppy disks. You cannot use diskcopy with a hard disk. If you specify a hard disk drive for drive1 or drive2, diskcopy displays the following error message:
Invalid drive specification
Specified drive does not exist
or is nonremovable

• The diskcopy command prompts you to insert the source and destination disks and waits for you to press any key on the keyboard before continuing.

• After copying, diskcopy displays the following message:
Copy another diskette (Y/N)?
If you press Y, diskcopy prompts you to insert source and destination disks for the next copy operation. To stop the diskcopy process, press N.

• If you are copying to an unformatted floppy disk in drive2, diskcopy formats the disk with the same number of sides and sectors per track as are on the disk in drive1. Diskcopy displays the following message while it formats the disk and copies the files:
Formatting while copying

• If the source disk has a volume serial number, diskcopy creates a new volume serial number for the destination disk and displays the number when the copy operation is complete.

• If you omit the drive2 parameter, diskcopy uses the current drive as the destination drive. If you omit both drive parameters, diskcopy uses the current drive for both. If the current drive is the same as drive1, diskcopy prompts you to swap disks as necessary.

• Because diskcopy makes an exact copy of the source disk on the destination disk, any fragmentation on the source disk is transferred to the destination disk. Fragmentation is the presence of small areas of unused disk space between existing files on a disk.

• A fragmented source disk can slow down the process of finding, reading, or writing files. To avoid transferring fragmentation from one disk to another, use copy or xcopy to copy your disk. Because copy and xcopy copy files sequentially, the new disk is not fragmented.

• The following table lists each exit code and a brief description.

Exit code	Description
0	Copy operation was successful
1	Nonfatal read/write error occurred
3	Fatal hard error occurred
4	Initialization error occurred

• To process exit codes returned by diskcomp, you can use the errorlevel on the if command line in a batch program.

DISKPART

DiskPart.exe is a text-mode command interpreter that enables you to manage objects (disks, partitions, or volumes) by using scripts or direct input from a command prompt. Before you can use DiskPart.exe commands on a disk, partition, or volume, you must first list and then select the object to give it focus. When an object has focus, any DiskPart.exe commands that you type act on that object.

You can list the available objects and determine an object's number or drive letter by using the list disk, list volume, and list partition commands. The list disk and list volume commands display all disks and volumes on the computer. However, the list partition command only displays partitions on the disk that has focus. When you use the list commands, an asterisk (*) appears next to the object with focus. You select an object by its number or drive letter, such as disk 0, partition 1, volume 3, or volume C.

When you select an object, the focus remains on that object until you select a different object. For example, if the focus is set on disk 0, and you select volume 8 on disk 2, the focus shifts from disk 0 to disk 2, volume 8. Some commands automatically change the focus. For example, when you create a new partition, the focus automatically switches to the new partition.

You can only give focus to a partition on the selected disk. When a partition has focus, the related volume (if any) also has focus. When a volume has focus, the related disk and partition also have focus if the volume maps to a single specific partition. If this is not the case, then focus on the disk and partition is lost.

DiskPart commands

active

On basic disks, marks the partition with focus as active. This informs the basic input/output system (BIOS) or Extensible Firmware Interface (EFI) that the partition or volume is a valid system partition or system volume

Only partitions can be marked as active.

Important

DiskPart verifies only that the partition is capable of containing an operating system's startup files. DiskPart does not check the contents of the partition. If you mistakenly mark a partition as "active" and it does not contain the operating system's startup files, your computer might not start.

Syntax:

active

add disk

Mirrors the simple volume with focus to the specified disk.

Syntax:

add disk=n [noerr]

Syntax Options:

n ··············Specifies the disk to contain the mirror You can mirror only simple volumes. The specified disk must have unallocated space at least as large as the size of the simple volume you want to mirror.

noerr ·········For scripting only. When an error is encountered, specifies that DiskPart continue to process commands as if the error did not occur. Without the noerr parameter, an error causes DiskPart to exit with an error code.

assign ·······Assigns a drive letter or mount point to the volume with focus. If no drive letter or mount point is specified, then the next available drive letter is assigned. If the drive letter or mount point is already in use, an error is generated.

By using the assign command, you can change the drive letter associated with a removable drive.

You cannot assign drive letters to system volumes, boot volumes, or volumes that contain the paging file. In addition, you cannot assign a drive letter to an Original Equipment Manufacturer (OEM) partition or any GUID Partition Table (GPT) partition other than a basic MSDATA partition.

Syntax:

assign [{letter=d|mount=Path}] [noerr]

Syntax Options:

letter=d ·····The drive letter you want to assign to the volume.

mount=Path ··················The mount point path you want to assign to the volume.

noerr ·········For scripting only. When an error is encountered, specifies that DiskPart continue to process commands as if the error did not occur. Without the noerr parameter, an error causes DiskPart to exit with an error code.

break disk·Applies to dynamic disks only. Breaks the mirrored volume with focus into two simple volumes. One simple volume retains the drive letter and any mount points of the mirrored volume, while the other simple volume receives the focus so you can assign it a drive letter.

By default, the contents of both halves of the mirror are retained. Each half becomes a simple volume. By using the nokeep parameter, you retain only one half of the mirror as a simple volume, while the other half is deleted and converted to free space. Neither volume receives the focus.

Syntax:

break disk=n [nokeep] [noerr]

Syntax Options:

n ··············Specifies the disk that contains the mirrored volume.

nokeep······Specifies that only one of the mirrored volumes is retained; the other simple volume is deleted and converted to free space. Neither the volume nor the free space receive the focus.

noerr········For scripting only. When an error is encountered, specifies that DiskPart continue to process commands as if the error did not occur. Without the noerr parameter, an error causes DiskPart to exit with an error code.

clean········Removes any and all partition or volume formatting from the disk with focus. On master boot record (MBR) disks, only the MBR partitioning information and hidden sector information are overwritten. On GUID Partition Table (GPT) disks, the GPT partitioning information, including the Protective MBR, is overwritten. There is no hidden sector information.

Syntax:

clean [all]

Syntax Options:

all··············Specifies that each and every sector on the disk is zeroed, which completely deletes all data contained on the disk.

convert basic···················Converts an empty dynamic disk into a basic disk

Syntax:

convert basic [noerr]

Syntax Options:

noerr········For scripting only. When an error is encountered, specifies that DiskPart continue to process commands as if the error did not occur. Without the noerr parameter, an error causes DiskPart to exit with an error code.

convert dynamic··············Converts a basic disk into a dynamic disk

Syntax:

convert dynamic [noerr]

Syntax Options:

noerr········For scripting only. When an error is encountered, specifies that DiskPart continue to process commands as if the error did not occur. Without the noerr parameter, an error causes DiskPart to exit with an error code.

convert gptOn Itanium-based computers, converts an empty basic disk with the master boot record (MBR) partition style into a basic disk with the GUID partition table (GPT) partition style.

Important

The disk must be empty to convert it to a GPT disk. Back up your data and then delete all partitions or volumes before converting the disk.

Syntax:

convert gpt [noerr]

Syntax Options:

noerr········For scripting only. When an error is encountered, specifies that DiskPart continue to process commands as if the error did not occur. Without the noerr parameter, an error causes DiskPart to exit with an error code.

convert mbr····················On Itanium-based computers, converts an empty basic disk with the GUID Partition Table (GPT) partition style to a basic disk with the master boot record (MBR) partition style.

Important

The disk must be empty to convert it to an MBR disk. Back up your data and then delete all partitions or volumes before converting the disk.

Syntax:

convert mbr [noerr]

Syntax Options:

noerr·········For scripting only. When an error is encountered, specifies that DiskPart continue to process commands as if the error did not occur. Without the noerr parameter, an error causes DiskPart to exit with an error code.

create partition efi···········On Itanium-based computers, creates an Extensible Firmware Interface (EFI) system partition on a GUID Partition Table (GPT) disk. After the partition has been created, the focus is given to the new partition.

Syntax:

create partition efi [size=n] [offset=n] [noerr]

Syntax Options:

size=n·······The size of the partition in megabytes (MB). If no size is given, then the partition continues until there is no more space in the current region.

offset=n····The byte offset at which to create the partition. If no offset is given, the partition is placed in the first disk extent that is large enough to hold it.

noerr·········For scripting only. When an error is encountered, specifies that DiskPart continue to process commands as if the error did not occur. Without the noerr parameter, an error causes DiskPart to exit with an error code.

create partition extended Creates an extended partition on the current drive. After the partition has been created, the focus automatically shifts to the new partition. Only one extended partition can be created per disk. This command fails if you attempt to create an extended partition within another extended partition. You must create an extended partition before you can create logical drives.

Syntax:

create partition extended [size=n] [offset=n] [noerr]

Syntax Options:

size=n·······The size of the extended partition in megabytes (MB). If no size is given, then the partition continues until there is no more free space in the region. The size is rounded to the closest cylinder boundary. For example, if you specify a size of 500 MB, the partition would be rounded up to 504 MB.

offset=n····Applies to master boot record (MBR) disks only. The byte offset at which to create the extended partition If no offset is given, the partition will start at the beginning of the first free space on the disk. The offset is rounded to the closest cylinder boundary. For example, if you specify an offset that is 27 MB and the cylinder size is 8 MB, the offset is rounded to the 24 MB boundary.

noerr·········For scripting only. When an error is encountered, specifies that DiskPart continue to process commands as if the error did not occur. Without the noerr parameter, an error causes DiskPart to exit with an error code.

create partition logical·····Creates a logical drive in the extended partition. After the partition has been created, the focus automatically shifts to the new logical drive.

Syntax:

create partition logical [size=n] [offset=n] [noerr]

Syntax Options:

size=n·······The size of the logical drive in megabytes (MB). If no size is given, then the partition continues until there is no more free space in the current region.

offset=n····Applies to master boot record (MBR) disks only. The byte offset at which to create the logical drive. The offset is rounded up to completely fill whatever cylinder size is being used. If no offset is given, then the partition is placed in the first disk extent that is large enough to hold it. The partition is at least as long in bytes as the number specified by size=n. If you specify a size for the logical drive, it must be smaller than the extended partition.

noerr·········For scripting only. When an error is encountered, specifies that DiskPart continue to process commands as if the error did not occur. Without the noerr parameter, an error causes DiskPart to exit with an error code.

create partition msr ·········On Itanium-based computers, creates a Microsoft Reserved (MSR) partition on a GUID Partition Table (GPT) disk.

Caution

Be very careful when using the create partition msr command. Because GPT disks require a specific partition layout, creating Microsoft reserved partitions could cause the disk to become unreadable. On GPT disks that are used to start Windows XP 64-Bit Edition, the EFI System partition is the first partition on the disk, followed by the Microsoft Reserved partition. GPT disks used only for data storage do not have an EFI System partition; the Microsoft Reserved partition is the first partition.

Windows XP 64-Bit Edition does not mount Microsoft reserved partitions. You cannot store data on them and you cannot delete them.

Syntax:

create partition msr [size=n] [offset=n] [noerr]

Syntax Options:

size=n ·······The size of the partition in megabytes (MB). The partition is at least as long in bytes as the number specified by size=n. If no size is given, the partition continues until there is no more free space in the current region.

offset=n ····The byte offset at which to create the partition. The partition starts at the byte offset specified by offset=n. It is rounded up to completely fill whatever sector size is being used. If no offset is given, then the partition is placed in the first disk extent that is large enough to hold it.

noerr ·········For scripting only. When an error is encountered, specifies that DiskPart continue to process commands as if the error did not occur. Without the noerr parameter, an error causes DiskPart to exit with an error code.

create partition primary ···Creates a primary partition on the current basic disk After you create the partition, the focus automatically shifts to the new partition. The partition does not receive a drive letter. You must use the assign command to assign a drive letter to the partition.

Syntax:

create partition primary [size=n] [offset=n] [ID={byte|GUID}] [noerr]

Syntax Options:

size=n ·······The size of the partition in megabytes (MB). If no size is given, the partition continues until there is no more unallocated space in the current region. The size is rounded to the closest cylinder boundary. For example, if you specify a size of 500 MB, the partition would be rounded up to 504 MB. offset=n The byte offset at which to create the partition. If no offset is given, the partition will start at the beginning of the first free space on the disk. For master boot record (MBR) disks, the offset is   rounded to the closest cylinder boundary. For example, if you specify an offset that is 27 MB and the cylinder size is 8 MB, the offset is rounded to the 24 MB boundary. ID={byte|GUID} Intended for Original Equipment Manufacturer (OEM) use only.

Caution

Creating partitions with this parameter might cause your computer to crash or be unable to start up. Unless you are an OEM or an IT professional experienced with GPT disks, do not create partitions on GPT disks using the ID=byte | GUID parameter. Instead, always use the create partition efi command to create EFI System partitions, the create partition msr command to create Microsoft Reserved partitions, and the create partition primary command (without the ID=byte | GUID parameter) to create primary partitions on GPT disks.

For MBR disks, you can specify a partition type byte, in hexadecimal form, for the partition. If no partition type byte is specified on an MBR disk, the create partition primary command creates a partition of type 0x6. Any partition type byte can be specified with the ID=byte | GUID parameter. DiskPart does not check the partition type byte for validity, nor does it perform any other checking of the ID parameter.

For GPT disks you can specify a partition type GUID for the partition you want to create:

EFI System partition: c12a7328-f81f-11d2-ba4b-00a0c93ec93b

Microsoft reserved partition: e3c9e316-0b5c-4db8-817d-f92df00215ae

MSDATA partition: ebd0a0a2-b9e5-4433-87c0-68b6b72699c7

LDM Metadata partition on a dynamic disk: 5808c8aa-7e8f-42e0-85d2-e1e90434cfb3

LDM Data partition on a dynamic disk: af9b60a0-1431-4f62-bc68-3311714a69ad

If no partition type GUID is specified, the create partition primary command creates an MSDATA partition. Any partition type can be specified with the ID={byte | GUID} parameter. DiskPart does not check the partition GUID for validity, nor does it perform any other checking of the ID parameter.

noerr   For scripting only. When an error is encountered, specifies that DiskPart continue to process commands as if the error did not occur. Without the noerr parameter, an error causes DiskPart to exit with an error code.

create volume raid

Creates a RAID-5 volume on the specified dynamic disks After you create the volume, the focus automatically shifts to the new volume.

Syntax:

create volume raid [size=n] [disk=n[,[n,]] [noerr]

Syntax Options:

size=n·······The amount of disk space, in megabytes (MB), that the volume will occupy on each disk. If no size is given, the largest possible RAID-5 volume will be created. The disk with the smallest available contiguous free space determines the size for the RAID-5 volume and the same amount of space is allocated from each disk. The actual amount of usable disk space in the RAID-5 volume is less than the combined amount of disk space because some of the disk space is required for parity.

disk=n·······The dynamic disks on which to create the volume. An amount of space equal to size=n is allocated on each disk.

noerr·········For scripting only. When an error is encountered, specifies that DiskPart continue to process commands as if the error did not occur. Without the noerr parameter, an error causes DiskPart to exit with an error code.

create volume simple

Creates a simple volume After you create the volume, the focus automatically shifts to the new volume.

Syntax:

create volume simple [size=n] [disk=n] [noerr]

Syntax Options:

size=n·······The size of the volume in megabytes (MB). If no size is given, the new volume takes up the remaining free space on the disk.

disk=n·······The dynamic disk on which to create the volume. If no disk is given, the current disk is used.

noerr·········For scripting only. When an error is encountered, specifies that DiskPart continue to process commands as if the error did not occur. Without the noerr parameter, an error causes DiskPart to exit with an error code.

create volume stripe ·······Creates a striped volume on the specified disks. After you create the volume, the focus automatically shifts to the new volume.

Syntax:

create volume stripe [size=n] [disk=n[,[n,]] [noerr]

Syntax Options:

size=n·······The amount of disk space, in megabytes (MB), that the volume will occupy on each disk. If no size is given, the new volume takes up the remaining free space on the smallest disk and an equal amount of space on each subsequent disk.

disk=n·······The dynamic disks on which to create the volume. An amount of space equal to size=n is allocated on each disk.

noerr·········For scripting only. When an error is encountered, specifies that DiskPart continue to process commands as if the error did not occur. Without the noerr parameter, an error causes DiskPart to exit with an error code.

delete disk Deletes a missing dynamic disk from the disk list.

Syntax:

delete disk [noerr] [override]

Syntax Options:

noerr·········For scripting only. When an error is encountered, specifies that DiskPart continue to process commands as if the error did not occur. Without the noerr parameter, an error causes DiskPart to exit with an error code.

override ···· Enables DiskPart to delete all simple volumes on the disk. If the disk contains half of a mirrored volume, the half of the mirror on the disk is deleted. The delete disk override command fails if the disk is a member of a RAID-5 volume.

delete partition ················ On a basic disk, deletes the partition with focus. You cannot delete the system partition, boot partition, or any partition that contains the active paging file or crash dump (memory dump).

Caution

Deleting a partition on a dynamic disk can delete all offline dynamic volumes on the disk, thus destroying any data and converting the disk to a basic disk. To delete a dynamic volume, always use the delete volume command instead.

Partitions can be deleted from dynamic disks, but they should not be created. For example, it is possible to delete an unrecognized GUID Partition Table (GPT) partition on a dynamic GPT disk. Deleting such a partition does not cause the resulting free space to become available. This command is particularly intended to allow reclamation of the space on a corrupted offline dynamic disk in an emergency situation where the clean command cannot be used.

Syntax:

delete partition [noerr] [override]

Syntax Options:

noerr ········· For scripting only. When an error is encountered, specifies that DiskPart continue to process commands as if the error did not occur. Without the noerr parameter, an error causes DiskPart to exit with an error code.

override ···· Enables DiskPart to delete any partition regardless of type. Typically, DiskPart only allows you to delete known data partitions.

delete volume ················· Deletes the selected volume. You cannot delete the system volume, boot volume, or any volume that contains the active paging file or crash dump (memory dump).

Syntax:

delete volume [noerr]

Syntax Options:

noerr ········· For scripting only. When an error is encountered, specifies that DiskPart continue to process commands as if the error did not occur. Without the noerr parameter, an error causes DiskPart to exit with an error code.

detail disk ·Displays the properties of the selected disk and the volumes on that disk.

Syntax:

detail disk

detail volume (Displays the disks on which the current volume resides.)

Syntax:

detail volume

exit (Exits the DiskPart command interpreter.)

Syntax:

exit

extend

Extends the volume with focus into next contiguous unallocated space. For basic volumes, the unallocated space must be on the same disk as, and must follow (be of higher sector offset than) the partition with focus. A dynamic simple or spanned volume can be extended to any empty space on any dynamic disk Using this command, you can extend an existing volume into newly created space.

If the partition was previously formatted with the NTFS file system, the file system is automatically extended to occupy the larger partition. No data loss occurs. If the partition was previously formatted with any file system format other than NTFS, the command fails with no change to the partition.

You cannot extend the current system or boot partitions.

Syntax:

extend [size=n] [disk=n] [noerr]

Syntax Options:

size=n ········ The amount of space, in megabytes (MB), to add to the current partition. If you do not specify a size, the disk is extended to take up all of the next contiguous unallocated space.

disk=n ········ The dynamic disk on which to extend the volume. An amount of space equal to size=n is allocated on the disk. If no disk is specified, the volume is extended on the current disk.

noerr ········ For scripting only. When an error is encountered, specifies that DiskPart continue to process commands as if the error did not occur. Without the noerr parameter, an error causes DiskPart to exit with an error code.

help ········ Displays a list of the available commands.

Syntax:

help

import

Imports a foreign disk group into the local computer's disk group. The import command imports every disk that is in the same group as the disk that has focus.

Syntax:

import [noerr]

Syntax Options:

noerr ········ For scripting only. When an error is encountered, specifies that DiskPart continue to process commands as if the error did not occur. Without the noerr parameter, an error causes DiskPart to exit with an error code.

list disk ········ Displays a list of disks and information about them, such as their size, amount of available free space, whether the disk is a basic or dynamic disk, and whether the disk uses the master boot record (MBR) or GUID partition table (GPT) partition style. The disk marked with an asterisk (*) has focus.

Syntax:

list disk

list partition

Displays the partitions listed in the partition table of the current disk. On dynamic disks, these partitions may not correspond to the dynamic volumes on the disk. This discrepancy occurs because dynamic disks contain entries in the partition table for the system volume or boot volume (if present on the disk) and a partition that occupies the remainder of the disk in order to reserve the space for use by dynamic volumes.

Syntax:

list partition

list volume

Displays a list of basic and dynamic volumes on all disks.

Syntax:

list volume

online

Brings an offline disk or volume with focus online.

Syntax:

online [noerr]

Syntax Options:

noerr ········ For scripting only. When an error is encountered, specifies that DiskPart continue to process commands as if the error did not occur. Without the noerr parameter, an error causes DiskPart to exit with an error code.

rem ········ Provides a way to add comments to a script.

Syntax:

rem

Examples:

rem These commands set up 3 drives.
create partition primary size=2048
assign d:

```
create partition extend
create partition logical size=2048
assign e:
create partition logical
assign f:
remove
```

Removes a drive letter or mount point from the volume with focus. If the all parameter is used, all current drive letters and mount points are removed. If no drive letter or mount point is specified, then DiskPart removes the first drive letter or mount point it encounters. The remove command can be used to change the drive letter associated with a removable drive. You cannot remove the drive letters on system, boot, or paging volumes. In addition, you cannot remove the drive letter for an OEM partition, any GPT partition with an unrecognized GUID, or any of the special, non-data, GPT partitions such as the EFI system partition.

Syntax:

remove [{letter=d|mount=Path [all]}] [noerr]

Syntax Options:

letter=d ····· The drive letter to be removed.

mount=Path ···················· The mount point path to be removed.

all ············· Removes all current drive letters and mount points.

noerr ········· For scripting only. When an error is encountered, specifies that DiskPart continue to process commands as if the error did not occur. Without the noerr parameter, an error causes DiskPart to exit with an error code.

rescan ······· Locates new disks that may have been added to the computer.

Syntax:

rescan

retain

Prepares an existing dynamic simple volume to be used as a boot or system volume.

On an x86-based computer, creates a partition entry in the master boot record (MBR) on the dynamic simple volume with focus. To create an MBR partition, the dynamic simple volume must start at a cylinder aligned offset and be an integral number of cylinders in size.

On an Itanium-based computer, creates a partition entry in the GUID partition table (GPT) on the dynamic simple volume with focus.

Note

• The retain command is intended for use only during Unattended Setup or by Original Equipment Manufacturers (OEMs).

Syntax:

retain

select disk

Selects the specified disk and shifts the focus to it.

Syntax:

select disk=[n]

Syntax Options:

n ·············· The disk number of the disk to receive focus. If no disk number is specified, the select command lists the disk that currently has the focus. You can view the numbers for all disks on the computer by using the list disk command.

select partition ················Selects the specified partition and gives it focus. If no partition is specified, the select command lists the current partition with focus. You can view the numbers of all partitions on the current disk by using the list partition command.

Syntax:

select partition=[{n|d}]

Syntax Options:

n ·············· The number of the partition to receive the focus.

d ·············· The drive letter or mount point path of the partition to receive the focus.

XP Command: DISKPART   **123**

select volume·················Selects the specified volume and shifts the focus to it. If no volume is specified, the select command lists the current volume with focus. You can specify the volume by number, drive letter, or mount point path. On a basic disk, selecting a volume also gives the corresponding partition focus. You can view the numbers of all volumes on the computer by using the list volume command.

Syntax:

select volume={[{n|d}]}

Syntax Options:

n ···············The number of the volume to receive the focus.

d ···············The drive letter or mount point path of the volume to receive the focus.

DiskPart scripting············Using DiskPart, you can create scripts to automate disk-related tasks, such as creating volumes or converting disks to dynamic. Scripting these tasks is useful if you are deploying Windows by using Unattended Setup or Sysprep, which do not support creating volumes other than the boot volume

To start a DiskPart script, at the command prompt, type: DiskPart /S scriptname.txt

Where scriptname.txt is the name of the text file that contains your script.

To redirect DiskPart's scripting output to a file, type: DiskPart /S scriptname.txt > logfile.txt

Where logfile.txt is the name of the text file where DiskPart writes its output.

When DiskPart starts, the DiskPart version and computer name are displayed at the command prompt. By default, if DiskPart encounters an error while attempting to perform a scripted task, DiskPart stops processing the script and displays an error code (unless you specified the noerr parameter). However, DiskPart always returns errors when it encounters syntax errors, regardless of whether you used the noerr parameter. The noerr parameter enables you to perform useful tasks such as using a single script to delete all partitions on all disks regardless of the total number of disks.

The following table lists the DiskPart error codes:

Error	Description
0	No errors occurred. The entire script ran without failure.
1	A fatal exception occurred. There may be a serious problem.
2	The parameters specified for a DiskPart command were incorrect.
3	DiskPart was unable to open the specified script or output file.
4	One of the services DiskPart uses returned a failure.
5	A command syntax error occurred. The script failed because an object was improperly selected or was invalid for use with that command.

DOSKEY

Calls Doskey.exe, which recalls Windows XP commands, edits command lines, and creates macros.

Syntax:

doskey {/reinstall | /listsize=size | /macros:[{all | exename}] | /history | /insert | /overstrike | /exename=exename | /macrofile=FileName | macroname=[text]}

Examples:

doskey /macros > macinit   or   doskey /macrofile=macinit   or   doskey /history > tmp.bat

Syntax Options:

/reinstall ····Installs a new copy of Doskey.exe. Clears the command history buffer.

/listsize=size ···················Specifies the maximum number of commands in the history buffer.

/macros·····Displays a list of all doskey macros. You can use a redirection symbol (>) with /macros to redirect the list to a file. You can abbreviate /macros to /m.

all···············Displays doskey macros for all executables.

exename···Displays doskey macros for the specified executable.

/history·····Displays all commands stored in memory. You can use a redirection symbol (>) with /history to redirect the list to a file. You can abbreviate /history as /h.

{/insert | /overstrike} ·······Specifies whether new text you type is to replace old text. If you use /insert, new text that you type on a line is inserted into old text (that is, as if you pressed the INSERT key). If you use /overstrike, new text replaces old text. The default setting is /overstrike.

/exename=exename ·······Specifies the program (that is, executable) in which the doskey macro runs.

/macrofile=FileName ·······Specifies a file containing macros that you want to install.

macroname=[text] ··········Creates a macro that carries out the commands specified by text. Macroname specifies the name you want to assign to the macro. Text specifies the commands you want to record. If text is left blank, macroname is cleared of any assigned commands.

Notes:

• Doskey.exe is always available for all character-based, interactive programs (such as program debuggers or file transfer programs), and maintains a command history buffer and macros for each program that it starts. You cannot use doskey command-line options from a program. You must run doskey command-line options before you start a program. Program key assignments override doskey key assignments.

• To recall a command, you can use any of the following keys after starting Doskey.exe. If you use Doskey.exe within a program, that program's key assignments take precedence.

Key	Description
UP ARROW	Recalls the command you used before the one displayed.
DOWN ARROW	Recalls the command you used after the one displayed.
PAGE UP	Recalls the oldest command you used in the current session.
PAGE DOWN	Recalls the most recent command you used.

• With Doskey.exe, you can edit the current command line. If you use Doskey.exe within a program, that program's key assignments take precedence and some Doskey.exe editing keys might not work.

• The following table lists doskey editing keys and their functions.

Key or Key combination	Description
LEFT ARROW	Moves the insertion point back one character.
RIGHT ARROW	Moves the insertion point forward one character.
CTRL+LEFT ARROW	Moves the insertion point back one word.
CTRL+RIGHT ARROW	Moves the insertion point forward one word.
HOME	Moves the insertion point to the beginning of the line.
END	Moves the insertion point to the end of the line.
ESC	Clears the command from the display.
F1	Copies one character from the same column in the template to the same column in the Command Prompt window. (The template is a memory buffer that holds the last command you typed.)
F2	Searches forward in the template for the next key you type after pressing F2. Doskey.exe inserts the text from the template up to, but not including, the character you specify.
F3	Copies the remainder of the template to the command line. Doskey.exe begins copying characters from the position in the template that corresponds to the position indicated by the insertion point on the command line.
F4	Deletes characters from the current insertion point position up to a character you specify. To use this editing key, press F4 and type a character. Doskey.exe deletes the characters from the current insertion point position to the first letter specified.
F5	Copies the template into the current command line.
F6	Places an end-of-file character (that is, CTRL+Z) at the current insertion point position.

Key or Key combination	Description
F7	Displays all commands for this program stored in memory in a pop-up box. Use the UP ARROW key and the DOWN ARROW key to select the command you want, and press ENTER to run the command. You can also note the sequential number in front of the command and use this number in conjunction with the F9 key.
ALT+F7	Deletes all commands stored in memory for the current history buffer.
F8	Displays all commands in the history buffer that start with the characters in the current command.
F9	Prompts you for a history buffer command number, then displays the command associated with the number you specify. Press ENTER to run the command. To display all the numbers and their associated commands, press F7.
ALT+F10	Deletes all macro definitions.

• Certain character-based, interactive programs, such as program debuggers or file transfer programs (FTP), automatically use Doskey.exe. To use Doskey.exe, a program must be a console process and use buffered input. Program key assignments override doskey key assignments. For example, if the program uses the F7 key for some function, you cannot get a doskey command history in a pop-up window.

• With Doskey.exe you can maintain a command history for each program you start, repeat and edit previous commands at the program's prompt, and start doskey macros created for the program. If you exit and then restart a program from the same Command Prompt window, the command history from the previous program session is available.

• You must run Doskey.exe before you start a program. You cannot use doskey command-line options from a program's command prompt, even if the program has a shell command.

• If you want to customize how Doskey.exe works with a program and create doskey macros for that program, you can create a batch program that modifies Doskey.exe and starts the program.

• If you press the INSERT key, you can type text on the doskey command line in the middle of old text without replacing the old text. However, after you press ENTER, Doskey.exe returns your keyboard to replace mode. You must press INSERT again to return to insert mode.

• The insertion point changes shape when you use the INSERT key to change from one mode to the other.

• You can use Doskey.exe to create macros that carry out one or more commands. The following table lists special characters you can use to control command operations when you define a macro.

Character	Description
$G or $g	Redirects output. Use either of these special characters to send output to a device or a file instead of to the screen. This character is equivalent to the redirection symbol for output (>).
GG or gg	Appends output to the end of a file. Use either of these special double characters to append output to an existing file instead of replacing the data in the file. These double characters are equivalent to the append redirection symbol for output (>).
$L or $l	Redirects input. Use either of these special characters to read input from a device or a file instead of from the keyboard. This character is equivalent to the redirection symbol for input (<).
$B or $b	Sends macro output to a command. These special characters are equivalent to using the pipe (|) on a command line.
$T or $t	Separates commands. Use either of these special characters to separate commands when you create macros or type commands on the doskey command line. These special characters are equivalent to using the ampersand (&) on a command line.
$$	Specifies the dollar-sign character ($).

Character	Description
$1 through $9	Represent any command-line information you want to specify when you run the macro. The special characters $1 through $9 are batch parameters, which make it possible for you to use different data on the command line each time you run the macro. The $1 character in a doskey command is similar to the %1 character in a batch program.
$*	Represents all the command-line information you want to specify when you type the macro name. The special character $* is a replaceable parameter that is similar to the batch parameters $1 through $9, with one important difference: everything you type on the command line after the macro name is substituted for the $* in the macro.

• To run a macro, type the macro name starting at the first position on the command line. If the macro was defined with $* or any of the batch parameters $1 through $9, use a white space to separate parameters. You cannot run a doskey macro from a batch program.

• If you always use a particular command with specific command-line options, you can create a macro that has the same name as the command. To specify whether you want to run the macro or the command, follow these guidelines:

• To run the macro, begin typing the macro name immediately after the command prompt, with no space between the prompt and the command name.

• To run the command, insert one or more white spaces between the command prompt and the command name.

• To delete a macro, type: doskey macroname=

DRIVERQUERY

Displays a list of all installed device drivers and their properties. This is a good command to document your computer drivers.

Syntax:
driverquery [/s Computer] [/u Domain\User /p Password] [/fo {TABLE | LIST | CSV}] [/nh] [/v] [/si]

Examples:
driverquery or driverquery /fo csv or driverquery /nh or driverquery /s ipaddress

Syntax Options:
/s Computer ....Specifies the name or IP address of a remote computer (do not use backslashes). The default is the local computer.

/u Domain\User ....Runs the command with the account permissions of the user specified by User or Domain\User. The default is the permissions of the current logged on user on the computer issuing the command.

/p Password ....Specifies the password of the user account that is specified in the /u parameter.

/fo {TABLE | LIST | CSV} Specifies the format to display the driver information. Valid values are TABLE, LIST, and CSV. The default format for output is TABLE.

/nh ....Omits the header row from the displayed driver information. Valid when the /fo parameter is set to TABLE or CSV.

/v ....Specifies that detailed driver information be displayed.

/si ....Displays digital signature information for both signed and unsigned device drivers.

ECHO

Turns the command-echoing feature on or off, or displays a message.

Syntax:
echo [{on|off}] [message]

Examples:
The following example is a batch program that includes a three-line message preceded by and then followed by a blank line:
echo off
echo.
echo This batch program

echo formats and checks
echo new disks
echo.

If you want to turn echo off and you do not want to echo the echo command, type an at sign (@) before the command as follows: @echo off

You can use the if and echo commands on the same command line. For example:
if exist *.rpt echo The report has arrived.

Syntax Options:

Used without parameters, echo displays the current echo setting.

{on|off} ······Specifies whether to turn the command-echoing feature on or off.

message···Specifies text you want to display on the screen.

Notes:

• The echo message command is useful when echo is turned off. To display a message that is several lines long without displaying other commands, you can include several echo message commands after the echo off command in your batch program.

• If you use echo off, the command prompt does not appear on your screen. To display the command prompt, type echo on.

• To echo a blank line on the screen, type: echo.

• To display a pipe (|) or redirection character (< or >) when you are using echo, use a caret character immediately before the pipe or redirection character (for example, ^>, ^<, or ^|). If you need to use the caret character (^), type two (^^).

ENDLOCAL

Ends localization of environment changes in a batch file, restoring environment variables to their values before the matching setlocal command.

Syntax:

endlocal

Examples:

You can localize environment variables in a batch file. For example:
@echo off
rem This program starts the superapp batch program on the network,
rem directs the output to a file, and displays the file
rem in Notepad.
setlocal
path=g:\programs\superapp;%path%
call superapp>c:\superapp.out
endlocal
start notepad c:\superapp.out

Notes:

• You must use endlocal in a script or batch file. If you use endlocal outside of a script or batch file, it has no effect.

• There is an implicit endlocal command at the end of a batch file.

• With command extensions enabled (that is, the default), the endlocal command re-stores the state of command extensions (that is, enabled or disabled) to what it was be-fore the matching setlocal command was executed.

ERASE

Deletes one or more files. SEE DEL COMMAND

EVENTCREATE

Enables an administrator to create a custom event in a specified event log. Custom events cannot be written to the security log.

Syntax:

eventcreate [/s Computer [/u Domain\User [/p Password]] {[/l {APPLICATION | SYS-TEM}][/so SrcName]} /t {ERROR | WARNING | INFORMATION | SUCCESSAUDIT | FAILUREAUDIT} /id EventID /d Description

Examples:
eventcreate /t error /id 100 /l application /d "Create event in application log"   or
eventcreate /t information /id 1000 /so winmgmt /d "Create event in WinMgmt source"

Syntax Options:

/s Computer ················pecifies the name or IP address of a remote computer (do not use backslashes). The default is the local computer.

/u Domain\User···············uns the command with the account permissions of the user specified by User or Domain\User. The default is the permissions of the current logged on user on the computer issuing the command.

/p Password ················Specifies the password of the user account that is specified in the /u parameter.

/l {APPLICATION | SYSTEM} ···········Specifies the name of the event log where the event will be created. The valid log names are APPLICATION and SYSTEM.

/so SrcName ················Specifies the source to use for the event. A valid source can be any string and should represent the application or component that is generating the event.

/t {ERROR | WARNING | INFORMATION | SUCCESSAUDIT | FAILUREAUDIT}
Specifies the type of event to create. The valid types are ERROR, WARNING, INFOR-MATION, SUCCESSAUDIT, and FAILUREAUDIT.

/id EventID Specifies the event ID for the event. A valid ID is any number from 1 to 65535.

/d Description ················Specifies the description to use for the newly created event.

EVENTQUERY.VBS

Lists the events and event properties from one or more event logs.

Syntax:

eventquery[.vbs] [/s Computer [/u Domain\User [/p Password]]] [/fi FilterName] [/fo {TA-BLE | LIST | CSV}] [/r EventRange [/nh] [/v] [/l [APPLICATION] [SYSTEM] [SECURITY] ["DNS server"] [UserDefinedLog] [DirectoryLogName] [*]]

Examples:
eventquery /l system   *or*   eventquery /l mylog   *or*   eventquery /l application /l system

Syntax Options:

/s Computer ················Specifies the name or IP address of a remote computer (do not use backslashes). The default is the local computer.

/u Domain\User···············Runs the script with the account permissions of the user specified by User or Domain\User. The default is the permissions of the current logged on user on the computer issuing the command.

/p Password ················Specifies the password of the user account that is specified in the /u parameter.

/fi FilterName ················Specifies the types of events to include in or exclude from the query. To find events with either value, Type and ID can be used together in a single syntax statement by using the or operator. The following are valid filter names, operators, and values.

Name	Operator	Value
Datetime	eq, ne, ge, le, gt, lt	mm/dd/yy(yyyy), hh:mm:ssAM(/PM)
Type	eq, ne, or	{ERROR	INFORMATION	WARNING	SUCCESSAUDIT	FAILUREAUDIT}
ID	eq, ne, or, ge, le, gt, lt	Any valid positive integer.
User	eq, ne	Any valid string.
Computer	eq, ne	Any valid string.
Source	eq, ne	Any valid string.
Category	eq, ne	Any valid string

/fo {TABLE | LIST | CSV} Specifies the format to use for the output. Valid values are table, list, and csv.

/r EventRange ················Specifies the range of events to list.

Value	Description
N	Lists N most recent events.

-N···········Lists N oldest events.

N1-N2······Lists the events from N1 to N2.

/nh ···········Suppresses column headers in the output. Valid only for table and csv formats.

/v···········Specifies that verbose event information be displayed in the output.

/l [APPLICATION] [SYSTEM] [SECURITY] ["DNS server"] [UserDefinedLog] [DirectoryLogName] [*]] ···········Specifies the log(s) to monitor. Valid values are Application, System, Security, "DNS server", a user-defined log, and Directory log. "DNS server" can be used only if the DNS service is running on the computer specified by the /s parameter. To specify more than one log to monitor, reuse the /l parameter. The wildcard (*) can be used and is the default.

Notes:

• To run this script, you must be running CScript. If you have not already set the default Windows Script Host to CScript, type:
    cscript //h:cscript //s //nologo

EVENTTRIGGERS

Displays and configures event triggers on local or remote machines.

eventtriggers create

Creates a new event trigger that monitors and acts upon the occurrence of log events of given criteria.

Syntax:

eventtriggers[.exe] /create [/s Computer [/u Domain\User [/p Password]]] /tr TriggerName [/l [APPLICATION] [SYSTEM] [SECURITY] ["DNS Server"] [LOG] [DirectoryLogName] [*]] {[/eid ID]|[/t {ERROR | INFORMATION | WARNING | SUCCESSAUDIT | FAILUREAUDIT}] | [/so Source]} [/d Description] /tk TaskName [/ru {[Domain\User | "System"} [/rp Password]]

Examples:

eventtriggers /create /s srvmain /u maindom\hiroln /p p@ssW23 /tr "Low Disk Space" /eid 4133 /t warning /tk \\server\share\diskcleanup.cmd

Syntax Options:

/s Computer ···········Specifies the name or IP address of a remote computer (do not use backslashes). The default is the local computer.

/u Domain\User ···········Runs the command with the account permissions of the user specified by User or Domain\User. The default is the permissions of the current logged on user on the computer issuing the command.

/p Password ···········Specifies the password of the user account that is specified in the /u parameter.

/tr TriggerName ···········Specifies a friendly name to associate with the event trigger.

/l [APPLICATION] [SYSTEM] [SECURITY] ["DNS Server"] [LOG] [DirectoryLogName] [*]] Specifies the event log(s) to monitor. Valid types include: Application, System, Security, DNS server, Log, and Directory log. The wildcard (*) can be used and is the default value.

/eid ID ·······Specifies a specific event ID for which the event trigger should monitor. Valid values are any valid integer. Cannot be used in conjunction with the /type or /so parameters.

/t {ERROR | INFORMATION | WARNING | SUCCESSAUDIT | FAILUREAUDIT} Specifies an event type for which the event trigger should monitor. Valid values include: ERROR, INFORMATION, WARNING, SUCCESSAUDIT, and FAILUREAUDIT. Cannot be used in conjunction with the /id or /so parameters.

/so Source Specifies an event source for which the event trigger should monitor. Valid values are any string. Cannot be used in conjunction with the /id or /type parameters.

/d Description···········Specifies a detailed description of the event trigger. Valid values are any string.

/tk TaskName···········Specifies the task/command/line to execute when the event trigger conditions are met.

/ru {[Domain\]User | "System"} ·············· Runs the tasks with the permission of the speci-
fied user account. By default, the task runs with the permissions of the user logged on
to the computer running SchTasks.

Value ······· Description

[Domain\]User ················Specifies a user account.

"System" or "" ···············Specifies the NT Authority\System account, which is used by the
operating system.

/rp Password ···················Specifies the password of the user account that is specified in
the /ru parameter. If you omit this parameter when specifying a user account,
SchTasks.exe prompts you for the password and obscures the text you type. Tasks
run with with permissions of the NT Authority\System account do not require a password and SchTasks.exe does not prompt for one.

eventtriggers delete

Deletes an event trigger from a system by event trigger ID.

Syntax:

eventtriggers[.exe] /delete [/s Computer [/u Domain\User [/p Password]]] /tid {ID|*}

Examples:

eventtriggers /delete /tid 1 /tid 2 /tid 4 /tid 6   or

eventtriggers /delete /s srvmain /u maindom\hiropln /p p@ssW23 /tid.*

Syntax Options:

/s Computer ················Specifies the name or IP address of a remote computer (do not
use backslashes). The default is the local computer.

/u Domain\User ···········Runs the command with the account permissions of the user
specified by User or Domain\User. The default is the permissions of the current logged
on user on the computer issuing the command.

/p Password ·················Specifies the password of the user account that is specified in
the /u parameter.

/tid {ID|*} ···Specifies the event trigger(s) to be deleted by "Event Trigger ID". The (*) wild-
card can be used.

eventtriggers query

Queries and displays a system's event trigger properties and settings.

Syntax:

eventtriggers[.exe] /query [/s Computer [/u Domain\User [/p Password]]] [/fo {TA-
BLE|LIST|CSV}] [/nh] [/v]

Examples:

eventtriggers /query   or   eventtriggers /query /s srvmain

Syntax Options:

/s Computer ················Specifies the name or IP address of a remote computer (do not
use backslashes). The default is the local computer.

/u Domain\User ···········Runs the command with the account permissions of the user
specified by User or Domain\User. The default is the permissions of the current logged
on user on the computer issuing the command.

/p Password ·················Specifies the password of the user account that is specified in
the /u parameter.

/fo {TABLE|LIST|CSV} ····Specifies the format to use for the query output. Valid values are
TABLE, LIST, and CSV. The default format for output is TABLE.

/nh ···········Suppresses column header in the output. Valid when the /fo parameter is set
to TABLE or CSV.

/v···············Specifies that detailed information be displayed in the output.

Notes:

• When specified without an operation, eventtriggers returns a list of event triggers. To
see a list of event triggers, type: eventtriggers

• Output similar to the following appears:

• Trigger ID Event Trigger Name   Task

- 1 Disk Cleanup   c:\windows\system32\cleanmgr.exe

- In the case that an event fails to execute, eventtriggers creates a log file called TriggerConsumer.log in the \windows\system32\wbem\logs directory containing a message that the event failed to trigger.

EVNTCMD

Configures the translation of events to traps, trap destinations, or both based on information in a configuration file.

Syntax:

evntcmd [/s ComputerName] [/v VerbosityLevel] [/n] FileName

Examples:

#pragma ADD System "Eventlog" 2147489653   or
#pragma ADD System "Eventlog" 2147489653 2 180

Syntax Options:

/s ComputerName ·········Specifies, by name, the computer on which you want to configure the translation of events to traps, trap destinations, or both. If you do not specify a computer, the configuration occurs on the local computer.

/v VerbosityLevel ············Specifies which types of status messages appear as traps and trap destinations are configured. This parameter must be an integer between 0 and 10. If you specify 10, all types of messages appear, including tracing messages and warnings about whether trap configuration was successful. If you specify 0, no messages appear.

/n ···············Specifies that the SNMP service should not be restarted if this computer receives trap configuration changes.

FileName ··Specifies, by name, the configuration file that contains information about the translation of events to traps and trap destinations you want to configure.

Notes:

- If you want to configure traps but not trap destinations, you can create a valid configuration file by using Event to Trap Translator, which is a graphical utility. If you have the SNMP service installed, you can start Event to Trap Translator by typing evntwin at a command prompt. After you have defined the traps you want, click Export to create a file suitable for use with evntcmd. You can use Event to Trap Translator to easily create a configuration file and then use the configuration file with evntcmd at the command prompt to quickly configure traps on multiple computers.

- The syntax for configuring a trap is as follows: #pragma ADD EventLogFile EventSource EventID [Count [Period]]

- The text #pragma must appear at the beginning of every entry in the file.

- The parameter ADD specifies that you want to add an event to trap configuration.

- The parameters EventLogFile, EventSource, and EventID are required. The parameter EventLogFile specifies the file in which the event is recorded. The parameter EventSource specifies the application that generates the event. The EventID parameter specifies the unique number that identifies each event. To find out what values correspond to particular events, start Event to Trap Translator by typing evntwin at a command prompt. Click Custom, and then click Edit. Under Event Sources, browse the folders until you locate the event you want to configure, click it, and then click Add. Information about the event source, the event log file, and the event ID appear under Source, Log, and Trap specific ID, respectively.

- The Count parameter is optional, and it specifies how many times the event must occur before a trap message is sent. If you do not use the Count parameter, the trap message is sent after the event occurs once.

- The Period parameter is optional, but it requires you to use the Count parameter. The Period parameter specifies a length of time (in seconds) during which the event must occur the number of times specified with the Count parameter before a trap message is sent. If you do not use the Period parameter, a trap message is sent after the event occurs the number of times specified with the Count parameter, no matter how much time elapses between occurrences.

- *The syntax for removing a trap is as follows:* #pragma DELETE EventLogFile EventSource EventID

- The text #pragma must appear at the beginning of every entry in the file.

- The parameter DELETE specifies that you want to remove an event to trap configuration.

- The parameters EventLogFile, EventSource, and EventID are required. The parameter EventLogFile specifies the log in which the event is recorded. The parameter EventSource specifies the application that generates the event. The EventID parameter specifies the unique number that identifies each event.

- *The syntax for configuring a trap destination is as follows:*
- #pragma ADD_TRAP_DEST CommunityName HostID
- The text #pragma must appear at the beginning of every entry in the file.
- The parameter ADD_TRAP_DEST specifies that you want trap messages to be sent to a specified host within a community.
- The parameter CommunityName specifies, by name, the community in which trap messages are sent.
- The parameter HostID specifies, by name or IP address, the host to which you want trap messages to be sent.

- *The syntax for removing a trap destination is as follows:*
- #pragma DELETE_TRAP_DEST CommunityName HostID
- The text #pragma must appear at the beginning of every entry in the file.
- The parameter DELETE_TRAP_DEST specifies that you do not want trap messages to be sent to a specified host within a community.
- The parameter CommunityName specifies, by name, the community in which trap messages are sent.
- The parameter HostID specifies, by name or IP address, the host to which you do not want trap messages to be sent.

EXIT

Exits the current batch script or the Cmd.exe program (that is, the command interpreter) and returns to the program that started Cmd.exe or to the Program Manager.

Syntax:

exit [/b] [ExitCode]

Syntax Options:

/b ·············Exits the current batch script.

ExitCode···Specifies a numeric number.

Notes:

- If you use /b outside of a batch script, it will exit Cmd.exe.
- If you use /b, Cmd.exe sets the ERRORLEVEL to the specified ExitCode. If you exit Cmd.exe, Cmd.exe sets the process exit code with the specified ExitCode.

EXPAND

Expands one or more compressed files. This command is used to retrieve compressed files from distribution disks. (Also available through the Recovery Console.)

Syntax:

expand [-r] Source [Destination]

expand -d source.cab [-f:files]

expand source.cab -f:files Destination

Syntax Options:

-r ·············Renames expanded files.

-d ·············Displays a list of files in the source location. Does not expand or extract the files.

-f:files·······Specifies the files in a cabinet (.cab) file you want to expand. You can use wildcards (* and ?).

Source ······Specifies the files to expand. Source can consist of a drive letter and colon, a directory name, a file name, or a combination. You can use wildcards (* and ?).

Destination·····················Specifies where files are to be expanded. If Source is multiple files and -r is not specified, Destination must be a directory. Destination can consist of a drive letter and colon, a directory name, a file name, or a combination.

FC

Compares two files and displays the differences between them.

Syntax:

fc [/a] [/b] [/c] [/l] [/lbn] [/n] [/t] [/u] [/w] [/nnnn] [drive1:][path1]filename1 [drive2:][path2]filename2

Examples:

To make an ASCII comparison of two text files that are named Monthly.rpt and Sales.rpt and display the results in abbreviated format, type:
fc /a monthly.rpt sales.rpt
To make a binary comparison of two batch files named Profits.bat and Earnings.bat, type:
fc /b profits.bat earnings.bat
The results similar to the following appear:

```
00000002: 72 43
00000004: 65 3A
0000000E: 56 92
00000012: 6D 5C
00000013: 0D 7C
00000014: 0D 0A
00000015: 0A 0D
0000001E: 43 7A
0000001F: 09 0A
00000022: 72 44
...

...
000005E0: 00 61
000005E1: 00 73
000005E2: 00 73
000005E3: 00 69
000005E4: 00 67
000005E5: 00 6E
000005E6: 00 6D
000005E7: 00 65
000005E8: 00 6E
```

FC: Earnings.bat longer than Profits.bat
If the Profits.bat and Earnings.bat files are identical, fc displays the following message:
FC: no differences encountered
To compare every .bat file in the current directory with the file New.bat, type:
fc *.bat new.bat
To compare the file New.bat on drive C with the file New.bat on drive D, type:
fc c:new.bat d:*.bat
To compare each batch file in the root directory on drive C to the file with the same name in the root directory on drive D, type:
fc c:*.bat d:*.bat

Syntax Options:

/a ··············Abbreviates the output of an ASCII comparison. Instead of displaying all of the lines that are different, fc displays only the first and last line for each set of differences.

/b ··············Compares the files in binary mode. Fc compares the two files byte by byte and does not attempt to resynchronize the files after finding a mismatch. This is the default mode for comparing files that have the following file extensions: .exe, .com, .sys, .obj, .lib, or .bin.

/c ··············Ignores the case of letters.

/l ··············Compares the files in ASCII mode. Fc compares the two files line by line and attempts to resynchronize the files after finding a mismatch. This is the default mode for comparing files, except files with the following file extensions: .exe, .com, .sys, .obj, .lib, or .bin.

/lbn ··········Sets the n number of lines for the internal line buffer. The default length of the line buffer is 100 lines. If the files that you are comparing have more than this number of consecutive differing lines, fc cancels the comparison.

/n ···········Displays the line numbers during an ASCII comparison.

/t ···········Prevents fc from converting tabs to spaces. The default behavior is to treat tabs as spaces, with stops at each eighth character position.

/u ···········Compares files as Unicode text files.

/w ···········Compresses white space (that is, tabs and spaces) during the comparison. If a line contains many consecutive spaces or tabs, /w treats these characters as a single space. When used with the /w command-line option, fc ignores (and does not compare) white space at the beginning and end of a line.

/nnnn ·······Specifies the number of consecutive lines that must match before fc considers the files to be resynchronized. If the number of matching lines in the files is less than nnnn, fc displays the matching lines as differences. The default value is 2.

[drive1:][path1]filename1 Specifies the location and name of the first file you want to compare. Filename1 is required.

[drive2:][path2]filename2 Specifies the location and name of the second file you want to compare. Filename2 is required.

Notes:

• When you use fc for an ASCII comparison, fc displays differences between two files in the following order:
Name of the first file
Lines from filename1 that differ between the files
First line to match in both files
Name of the second file
Lines from filename2 that differ
First line to match
/b displays mismatches found during a binary comparison as follows:
xxxxxxxx: yy zz

• The value of xxxxxxxx specifies the relative hexadecimal address for the pair of bytes, measured from the beginning of the file. Addresses start at 00000000. The hexadecimal values for yy and zz represent the mismatched bytes from filename1 and filename2, respectively.

• You can use wildcards (that is, * and ?) in filename1 and filename2. If you use a wildcard in filename1, fc compares all the specified files to the file specified by FileName. If you use a wildcard in filename2, fc uses the corresponding value from filename1.

• When comparing ASCII files, fc uses an internal buffer (large enough to hold 100 lines) as storage. If the files are larger than the buffer, fc compares what it can load into the buffer. If fc does not find a match in the loaded portions of the files, it stops and displays the following message: Resynch failed. Files are too different.

• When comparing binary files that are larger than available memory, fc compares both files completely, overlaying the portions in memory with the next portions from the disk. The output is the same as that for files that fit completely in memory.

Filter Commands

Filter Commands are used within other commands to read input, transform the input, and then write output. These commands are commonly used in conjunction with the redirection pipe (|). See also the Redirection Commands section on page 206.

Syntax:

To send input from a file to a filter command, use a less than sign (<). If you want the filter command to get input from another command, use a pipe (|).

Examples:

find "sequoia"< c:\ customer.txt············find text string "sequoia" in the designated .txt file
find "sequoia"< customer.txt > newcust.txt·····same find as above but saves them in newcust.txt

more < customer.txt········displays contents of txt file one command window at a time
dir c:\ data | more····displays a directory of data one command window at a time

sort "sequoia" < customer.txt ···············display a sorted list from customer.txt
sort "sequoia" < customer.txt > newcust.txt···sort as above and store results in newcust.txt file

Syntax Options:

find············Search through command output and files for specific characters

more ········Displays the contents of a file or the output of a command in one Command Prompt window at a time. Press any key to display next window and press CTRL+C to stop viewing.

sort ··········Alphabetized files and command output.

FIND

Searches for a specific string of text in a file or files. After searching the specified file or files, find displays any lines of text that contain the specified string.

Syntax:

find [/v] [/c] [/n] [/i] "string" [[Drive:][Path]FileName[...]]

Examples:

find "Pencil Sharpener" pencil.ad   or   for %f in (*.bat) do find "PROMPT" %f

Syntax Options:

/v·············Displays all lines that do not contain the specified string.

/c·············Counts the lines that contain the specified string and displays the total.

/n ·············Precedes each line with the file's line number.

/i·············Specifies that the search is not case-sensitive.

"string" ·····Required. Specifies the group of characters that you want to search for. You must enclose string in quotation marks (that is, "string").

[Drive:][Path] FileName ··Specifies the location and name of the file in which to search for the specified string.

Notes:

• If you do not use /i, find searches for exactly what you specify for string. For example, the find command treats the characters "a" and "A" differently. If you use /i, however, find is not case-sensitive and treats "a" and "A" as the same character.

• If the string you want to search for contains quotation marks, you must use two quotation marks for each quotation mark contained within the string (that is, "StringContaining""QuotationMarks").

• If you omit a file name, find acts as a filter, taking input from the standard input source (usually the keyboard, a pipe, or a redirected file) and then displaying any lines that contain string.

• You can type parameters and command-line options for the find command in any order.

• You cannot use wildcards (that is, * and ?) in file names or extensions that you specify with the find command. To search for a string in a set of files that you specify with wildcards, you can use the find command in a for command.

• If you use /c and /v in the same command line, find displays a count of the lines that do not contain the specified string. If you specify /c and /n in the same command line, find ignores /n.

• The find command does not recognize carriage returns. When you use find to search for text in a file that includes carriage returns, you must limit the search string to text that can be found between carriage returns (that is, a string that is not likely to be interrupted by a carriage return). For example, find does not report a match for the string "tax file" wherever a carriage return occurs between the word "tax" and the word "file."

FINDSTR

Searches for patterns of text in files using regular expressions.

Syntax:

findstr [/b] [/e] [/l] [/r] [/s] [/i] [/x] [/v] [/n] [/m] [/o] [/p] [/offline] [/g:file] [/f:file] [/c:string] [/d:dirlist] [/a:ColorAttribute] [strings] [[Drive:][Path] FileName [...]]

Examples:

findstr "hello there" x.y   *or*   findstr /c:"hello there" x.y   *or*   findstr Windows proposal.txt

Syntax Options:

/b ·············Matches the pattern if at the beginning of a line.

/e ··············Matches the pattern if at the end of a line.

/l ···············Uses search strings literally.

/r ···············Uses search strings as regular expressions. Findstr interprets all metacharacters as regular expressions unless you use /l.

/s ···············Searches for matching files in the current directory and all subdirectories.

/i ················Specifies that the search is not to be case-sensitive.

/x ···············Prints lines that match exactly.

/v ···············Prints only lines that do not contain a match.

/n ···············Prints the line number before each line that matches.

/m ··············Prints only the file name if a file contains a match.

/o ···············Prints seek offset before each matching line.

/p ···············Skips files with non-printable characters.

/offline ·······Processes files with offline attribute set.

/f:file ··········Reads file list from the specified file.

/c:string ·····Uses specified text as a literal search string.

/g:file ·········Gets search strings from the specified file.

/d:dirlist ·····Searches a comma-delimited list of directories.

/a:ColorAttribute ·············Specifies color attributes with two hexadecimal digits.

strings·······Specified text to be searched for in FileName.

[Drive:][Path] FileName [...] ···················Specifies a file or files to search.

Notes:

• Findstr is capable of finding the exact text you are looking for in any ASCII file or files. However, sometimes you have only part of the information that you want to match, or you want to find a wider range of information. In such cases, findstr has the powerful capability to search for patterns of text using regular expressions.

• Regular expressions are a notation for specifying patterns of text, as opposed to exact strings of characters. The notation uses literal characters and metacharacters. Every character that does not have special meaning in the regular expression syntax is a literal character and matches an occurrence of that character. For example, letters and numbers are literal characters. A metacharacter is a symbol with special meaning (an operator or delimiter) in the regular-expression syntax.

• The following table lists the metacharacters that findstr accepts.

Character	Value
.	Wildcard: any character
*	Repeat: zero or more occurrences of previous character or class
^	Line position: beginning of line
$	Line position: end of line
[class]	Character class: any one character in set
[^class]	Inverse class: any one character not in set
[x-y]	Range: any characters within the specified range
\x	Escape: literal use of metacharacter x
\<xyz	Word position: beginning of word
xyz\>	Word position: end of word

• The special characters in regular expression syntax are most powerful when you use them together. For example, the following combination of the wildcard character (.) and repeat (*) character match any string of characters: .*

• Use the following expression as part of a larger expression that matches any string beginning with "b" and ending with "ing": b.*ing

FINGER

Displays information about a user or users on a specified remote computer (typically a computer running UNIX) that is running the Finger service or daemon. The remote computer specifies the format and output of the user information display.

Syntax:

finger [-l] [User] [@host] [...]

Examples:

finger user1@users.microsoft.com   **or**   finger @users.microsoft.com

Syntax Options:

Used without parameters, finger displays help.

-l ....Displays user information in long list format.

User ....Specifies the user about which you want information. If you omit the User parameter, finger displays information about all users on the specified computer.

@host ....Specifies the remote computer running the Finger service where you are looking for user information. You can specify a computer name or IP address.

Notes:

• Multiple User@host parameters can be specified.

• You must prefix finger parameters with a hyphen (-) rather than a slash (/).

• This command is available only if the Internet Protocol (TCP/IP) protocol is installed as a component in the properties of a network adapter in Network Connections

• Windows 2000 and Windows XP do not provide a finger service.

FLATTEMP

Enables or disables flat temporary folders.

Syntax:

flattemp {/query l /enable l /disable}

Syntax Options:

/query ....Queries the current setting.

/enable ......Enables flat temporary directories.

/disable .....Disables flat temporary directories.

Notes:

• Once each user has a unique temporary directory, use flattemp /enable to enable flat temporary directories.

• The default method for creating temporary folders for multiple users (usually pointed to by the TEMP and TMP environment variables) is to create subfolders in the \Temp folder, using the logonID as the subfolder name. For example, if the TEMP environment variable points to C:\Temp, the temporary folder assigned to the user logonID 4 is C:\Temp\4. Using flattemp, you can point directly to the \Temp folder and prevent subfolders from forming. This is useful when you want the user temporary folders to be contained in home directories, whether on a Terminal server local drive or on a network share drive. You should use this command only when each user has a separate temporary folder.

• You must have administrative privileges to run flattemp.

• You might encounter application errors if the user's temporary directory is on a network drive. This occurs when the network share becomes momentarily inaccessible on the network. Because the temporary files of the application are either inaccessible or out of synchronization, it responds as if the disk has stopped. Moving the temporary directory to a network drive is not recommended. The default is to keep temporary directories on the local hard disk. If you experience unexpected behavior or disk-corruption errors with certain applications, stabilize your network or move the temporary directories back to the local hard disk.

• Flattemp settings are ignored if you disable using separate temporary folders per-session. This option is set in Terminal Services Configuration.

FOR

Runs a specified command for each file in a set of files.

Syntax:

for {%variablel%%variable) in (set) do command [CommandLineOptions]

Examples:

for %%variable in (set) do command [CommandLineOptions]   **or**   for %f in (*.doc *.txt) do type %f

Syntax Options:

{%variable|%%variable}··Required. Represents a replaceable parameter. Use %variable to carry out for from the command prompt. Use %%variable to carry out the for command within a batch file. Variables are case-sensitive and must be represented with an alpha value, such as %A, %B, or %C.

(set) ·········· Required. Specifies one or more files, directories, range of values, or text strings that you want to process with the specified command. The parentheses are required.

command··Required. Specifies the command that you want to carry out on each file, directory, range of values, or text string included in the specified (set).

CommandLineOptions ····Specifies any command-line options that you want to use with the specified command.

Notes:

- You can use the for command within a batch file or directly from the command prompt.
- The following attributes apply to the for command:

The for command replaces %variable or %%variable with each text string in the specified set until the command processes all of the files.

For variable names are case-sensitive, global, and no more than 52 total can be active at any one time.

To avoid confusion with the batch parameters %0 through %9, you can use any character for variable except the numerals 0 through 9. For simple batch files, a single character such as %%f works.

You can use multiple values for variable in complex batch files to distinguish different replaceable variables.

- The set parameter can represent a single group of files or several groups of files. You can use wildcards (that is, * and ?) to specify a file set. The following are valid file sets:
(*.doc)
(*.doc *.txt *.me)
(jan*.doc jan*.rpt feb*.doc feb*.rpt)
(ar??1991.* ap??1991.*)

- When you use the for command, the first value in set replaces %variable or %%variable, and then the specified command processes this value. This continues until all of the files (or groups of files) that correspond to the set value are processed.

- In and do are not parameters, but you must use them with for. If you omit either of these keywords, an error message appears.

- If command extensions are enabled (that is, the default), the following additional forms of for are supported:

Directories only

- If set contains wildcards (* and ?), the specified command executes for each directory (instead of a set of files in a specified directory) that matches set. The syntax is:

for /D {%% | %}variable in (set) do command [CommandLineOptions]

Recursive

- Walks the directory tree rooted at [Drive:]Path, executing the for statement in each directory of the tree. If no directory is specified after /R, the current directory is assumed. If set is just a single period (.), it only enumerates the directory tree. The syntax is:

for /R [[Drive :]Path] {%% | %}variable in (set) do command [CommandLineOptions]

Iterating a range of values

- Use an iterative variable to set the starting value (start#) and then step through a set range of values until the value exceeds the set ending value (end#). /L will execute the iterative variable by comparing start# with end#. If start# is less than end# the command will execute. When the iterative variable exceeds end# the command shell exists the loop. You can also use a negative step# to step through a range in decreasing values. For example,

(1,1,5) generates the sequence 1 2 3 4 5 and (5,-1,1) generates the sequence (5 4 3 2 1). The syntax is:

    for /L {%% | %}variable in (start#,step#,end#) do command
    [CommandLineOptions]

Iterating and file parsing

• Use file parsing to process command output, strings and file content. Use iterative variables to define the content or strings you want to examine and use the various ParsingKeywords options to further modify the parsing. Use the ParsingKeywords token option to specify which tokens should be passed as iterator variables. Note that when used without the token option, /F will only examine the first token.

• File parsing consists of reading the output, string or file content, breaking it up into individual lines of text and then parsing each line into zero or more tokens. The for loop is then called with the iterator variable value set to the token. By default, /F passes the first blank separated token from each line of each file. Blank lines are skipped. The different syntaxes are:

• for /F ["ParsingKeywords"] {%% | %}variable in (filenameset) do command [CommandLineOptions]

• for /F ["ParsingKeywords"] {%% | %}variable in ("LiteralString") do command [CommandLineOptions]

• for /F ["ParsingKeywords"] {%% | %}variable in ('command') do command [CommandLineOptions]

• The filenameset argument specifies one or more file names. Each file is opened, read and processed before going on to the next file in filenameset. To override the default parsing behavior, specify "ParsingKeywords". This is a quoted string that contains one or more keywords to specify different parsing options.

• If you use the usebackq option, use one of the following syntaxes:

• for /F ["usebackqParsingKeywords"] {%% | %}variable in ("filenameset") do command [CommandLineOptions]

• for /F ["usebackqParsingKeywords"] {%% | %}variable in ('LiteralString') do command [CommandLineOptions]

• for /F ["usebackqParsingKeywords"] {%% | %}variable in (`command`) do command [CommandLineOptions]

• The following table lists the parsing keywords that you can use for ParsingKeywords.

Keyword	Description
eol=c	Specifies an end of line character (just one character).
skip=n	Specifies the number of lines to skip at the beginning of the file.
delims=xxx	Specifies a delimiter set. This replaces the default delimiter set of space and tab.
tokens=x,y,m-n	Specifies which tokens from each line are to be passed to the for body for each iteration. As a result, additional variable names are allocated. The m-n form is a range, specifying the mth through the nth tokens. If the last character in the tokens= string is an asterisk (*), an additional variable is allocated and receives the remaining text on the line after the last token that is parsed.
usebackq	Specifies that you can use quotation marks to quote file names in filenameset, a back quoted string is executed as a command, and a single quoted string is a literal string command.

Variable substitution

• Substitution modifiers for for variable references have been enhanced. The following table lists optional syntax (for any variable I).

Variable with modifier	Description
%~I	Expands %I which removes any surrounding quotation marks ("").
%~fI	Expands %I to a fully qualified path name.

Variable with modifier	Description
%~dI	Expands %I to a drive letter only.
%~pI	Expands %I to a path only.
%~nI	Expands %I to a file name only.
%~xI	Expands %I to a file extension only.
%~sI	Expands path to contain short names only.
%~aI	Expands %I to the file attributes of file.
%~tI	Expands %I to the date and time of file.
%~zI	Expands %I to the size of file.
%~$PATH:I	Searches the directories listed in the PATH environment variable and expands %I to the fully qualified name of the first one found. If the environment variable name is not defined or the file is not found by the search, this modifier expands to the empty string.

• The following table lists modifier combinations that you can use to get compound results.

Variable with combined modifiers	Description
%~dpI	Expands %I to a drive letter and path only.
%~nxI	Expands %I to a file name and extension only.
%~fsI	Expands %I to a full path name with short names only.
%~dp$PATH:I	Searches the directories listed in the PATH environment variable for %I and expands to the drive letter and path of the first one found.
%~ftzaI	Expands %I to an output line that is like dir.

• In the above examples, you can replace %I and PATH by other valid values. A valid for variable name terminates the %~ syntax.

• By use uppercase variable names such as %I, you can make your code more readable and avoid confusion with the modifiers, which are not case-sensitive.

• You can use the for /F parsing logic on an immediate string, by wrapping the filenameset between the parentheses in single quotation marks (that is, 'filenameset'). Filenameset is treated as a single line of input from a file, and then it is parsed.

• You can use the for /F command to parse the output of a command by making the filenameset between the parenthesis a back quoted string. It is treated as a command line, which is passed to a child Cmd.exe and the output is captured into memory and parsed as if it were a file.

FORMAT

Formats the disk in the specified volume to accept Windows files.

Syntax:
format volume [/fs:file-system] [/v:label] [/q] [/a:UnitSize] [/c] [/x]

format volume [/v:label] [/q] [/f:size]

format volume [/v:label] [/q] [/t:tracks /n:sectors]

format volume [/v:label] [/q]

format volume [/q]

Examples:
format a: *or* format a: /q *or* format a: /v:DATA

Syntax Options:
volume······Specifies the mount point, volume name, or drive letter of the drive you want to format. If you do not specify any of the following command-line options, format uses the volume type to determine the default format for the disk.

/fs:file-system·················Specifies the file system to use FAT, FAT32, or NTFS Floppy disks can use only the FAT file system.

/v:label·······Specifies the volume label. If you omit the /v command-line option or use it without specifying a volume label, format prompts you for the volume label after the formatting is completed. Use the syntax /v: to prevent the prompt for a volume label. If you format more than one disk by using one format command, all of the disks will be given the same volume label.

/a:UnitSize : Specifies the allocation unit size to use on FAT, FAT32, or NTFS volumes. If you do not specify UnitSize, it is chosen based on volume size. The following table lists valid values for UnitSize.

Value	Description
512	Creates 512 bytes per cluster.
1024	Creates 1024 bytes per cluster.
2048	Creates 2048 bytes per cluster.
4096	Creates 4096 bytes per cluster.
8192	Creates 8192 bytes per cluster.
16K	Creates 16 kilobytes per cluster.
32K	Creates 32 kilobytes per cluster.
64K	Creates 64 kilobytes per cluster.

/q··············Performs a quick format. Deletes the file table and the root directory of a previously formatted volume but does not perform a sector by sector scan for bad areas. You should use the /q command-line option to format only previously formatted volumes that you know are in good condition.

/f:size········Specifies the size of the floppy disk to format. When possible, use this command-line option instead of the /t and /n command-line options. Windows accepts the following value for size: .

1440 or 1440k or 1440kb or 1.44 or 1.44m or 1.44mb
   1.44-MB, double-sided, quadruple-density, 3.5-inch disk

/t:tracks·····Specifies the number of tracks on the disk. When possible, use the /f command-line option instead of this command-line option. If you use the /t command-line option, you must also use the /n command-line option. These two command-line options provide an alternative method of specifying the size of the disk being formatted. You cannot use the /f command-line option with the /t command-line option.

/n:sectors··Specifies the number of sectors per track. When possible, use the /f command-line option instead of this command-line option. If you use the /n command-line option, you must also use the /t command-line option. These two command-line options provide an alternative method of specifying the size of the disk being formatted. You cannot use the /f command-line option with the /n command-line option.

/c···············NTFS only. Files created on the new volume will be compressed by default.

/x···············Causes the volume to dismount, if necessary, before it is formatted. Any open handles to the volume will no longer be valid.

Notes:

• The format command, with different parameters, is available from the Recovery Console.

• You must be a member of the Administrators group to format a hard drive.

• The format command creates a new root directory and file system for the disk. It can also check for bad areas on the disk, and it can delete all data on the disk. To be able to use a new disk, you must first use this command to format the disk.

• After formatting a floppy disk, format displays the following message:
Volume label (11 characters, ENTER for none)?

• The volume label can be a maximum of 11 characters (including spaces). If you do not want your disk to have a volume label, just press ENTER. When you use the format command to format a hard disk, format displays a message of the following form before attempting to format the hard disk:

WARNING, ALL DATA ON nonremovable DISK
DRIVE x: WILL BE LOST!
Proceed with Format (Y/N)?_

• To format the hard disk, press Y; if you do not want to format the disk, press N. You must have Administrator rights to format a hard disk.

- FAT file systems restrict the number of clusters to no more than 65526. FAT32 file systems restrict the number of clusters to between 65527 and 4177917.

- NTFS compression is not supported for allocation unit sizes above 4096.

- When formatting is complete, format displays messages showing the total disk space, any space marked as defective, and the space available for your files.

- You can speed up the formatting process by using the /q command-line option. Use this command-line option only if there are no bad sectors on your hard disk.

- You should not use the format command on a drive prepared by using the subst command. You cannot format disks over a network.

- The following table lists each exit code and a brief description of its meaning.

Exit code	Description
0	The format operation was successful.
1	Incorrect parameters were supplied.
4	A fatal error occurred (any error other than 0, 1, or 5).
5	The user pressed N in response to the prompt "Proceed with Format (Y/N)?" to stop the process.

- You can check these exit codes by using the errorlevel condition with the if batch command.

FTP

Transfers files to and from a computer running a File Transfer Protocol (FTP) server service such as Internet Information Services. Ftp can be used interactively or in batch mode by processing ASCII text files.

Syntax:

ftp [-v] [-d] [-i] [-n] [-g] [-s:FileName] [-a] [-w:WindowSize] [-A] [Host]

Examples:

ftp ftp.example.microsoft.com *or* ftp -A ftp.example.microsoft.com

Syntax Options:

-v ··············Suppresses the display of FTP server responses.

-d ··············Enables debugging, displaying all commands passed between the FTP client and FTP server.

-i ···············Disables interactive prompting during multiple file transfers.

-n ··············Suppresses the ability to log on automatically when the initial connection is made.

-g ··············Disables file name globbing. Glob permits the use of the asterisk (*) and question mark (?) as wildcard characters in local file and path names. For more information, see http://www.microsoft.com/resources/documentation/windows/xp/all/proddocs/en-us/ftp__glob.mspx

-s:FileName ··················Specifies a text file that contains ftp commands. These commands run automatically after ftp starts. This parameter allows no spaces. Use this parameter instead of redirection (<).

-a ··············Specifies that any local interface can be used when binding the FTP data connection.

-w:WindowSize ··············Specifies the size of the transfer buffer. The default window size is 4096 bytes.

-A ··············Logs onto the FTP server as anonymous.

Host ·········Specifies the computer name, IP address, or IPv6 address of the FTP server to which to connect. The host name or address, if specified, must be the last parameter on the line.

Notes:

- You must prefix ftp parameters with a hyphen (-) rather than a slash (/).

- Ftp command-line parameters are case-sensitive.

- This command is available only if the Internet Protocol (TCP/IP) protocol is installed as a component in the properties of a network adapter in Network Connections

- Ftp can be used interactively. After it is started, ftp creates a subenvironment in which you can use ftp commands. You can return to the command prompt by typing the quit command. When the ftp subenvironment is running, it is indicated by the ftp > command prompt.

- Ftp supports the use of IPv6 when the IPv6 protocol is installed.

FTYPE

Displays or modifies file types used in file name extension associations.

Syntax:

Ftype [FileType[=[OpenCommandString]]]

Examples:

ftype *or* ftype FileType *or* ftype FileType=

Syntax Options:

Used without parameters, ftype displays the file types that have open command strings defined.

FileType····Specifies the file type you want to display or change.

OpenCommandString·····Specifies the open command to use when opening files of this type.

Notes:

- Within an OpenCommandString, ftype substitutes the following variables:
  %0 or %1 are replaced with the file name that you want to open.
  %* is replaced with all of the parameters.
  %~n is replaced with all of the remaining parameters, starting with the nth parameter, where n can be any number from 2 to 9.
  %2 is replaced with the first parameter, %3 with the second, and so on.

GETMAC

Returns the media access control (MAC) address and list of network protocols associated with each address for all network cards in each computer, either locally or across a network.

Syntax:

getmac[.exe] [/s Computer [/u Domain\User [/p Password]]] [/fo {TABLE | LIST | CSV}] [/nh] [/v]

Examples:

getmac /fo table /nh /v *or* getmac /s srvmain *or* getmac /s srvmain /u maindom\hiropln

Syntax Options:

/s Computer ·················Specifies the name or IP address of a remote computer (do not use backslashes). The default is the local computer.

/u Domain\User ··············Runs the command with the account permissions of the user specified by User or Domain\User. The default is the permissions of the current logged on user on the computer issuing the command.

/p Password ·················Specifies the password of the user account that is specified in the /u parameter.

/fo {TABLE | LIST | CSV} Specifies the format to use for the query output. Valid values are TABLE, LIST, and CSV. The default format for output is TABLE.

/nh ··········Suppresses column header in output. Valid when the /fo parameter is set to TABLE or CSV.

/v··············Specifies that the output display verbose information.

Notes:

- Getmac can be useful either when you want to enter the MAC address into a network analyzer or when you need to know what protocols are currently in use on each network adapter in a computer.

GOTO

Within a batch program, directs Windows XP to a line identified by a label. When the label is found, it processes the commands that begin on the next line.

Syntax:

goto label

Examples:
The following batch program formats a disk in drive A as a system disk. If the operation is successful, the goto command directs Windows XP to the :end label:

echo off
format a: /s
if not errorlevel 1 goto end
echo An error occurred during formatting.
:end
echo End of batch program.

Syntax Options:

label·········Specifies the line in a batch program that you want to go to.

Notes:

• If command extensions are enabled (that is, the default) and you use the goto command with a target label of :EOF, you transfer control to the end of the current batch script file and exit the batch script file without defining a label. When you use goto with the :EOF label, you must insert a colon before the label. For example: goto :EOF

• You can use spaces in the label parameter, but you cannot include other separators (for example, semicolons or equal signs). The goto command uses only the first eight characters of a label. For example, the following labels are equivalent and resolve to :hithere0:

:hithere0
:hithere01
:hithere02

• The label value you specify must match a label in the batch program. The label within the batch program must begin with a colon (:). Windows XP recognizes a batch program line beginning with a colon (:) as a label and does not process it as a command. If a line begins with a colon, any commands on that line are ignored. If your batch program does not contain the label that you specify, the batch program stops and displays the following message:

Label not found

GPRESULT

Displays Group Policy settings and Resultant Set of Policy (RSOP) for a user or a computer.

Syntax:

gpresult [/s Computer [/u Domain\User /p Password]] [/user TargetUserName] [/scope {user|computer}] [/v] [/z]

Examples:

gpresult /user targetusername /scope computer   *or*
gpresult /s srvmain /u maindom\hiropln /p p@ssW23

Syntax Options:

/s Computer ·······················Specifies the name or IP address of a remote computer. (Do not use backslashes.) The default is the local computer.

/u Domain\User···············Runs the command with the account permissions of the user that is specified by User or Domain\User. The default is the permissions of the current logged-on user on the computer that issues the command.

/p Password ·····················Specifies the password of the user account that is specified in the /u parameter.

/user TargetUserName ···Specifies the user name of the user whose RSOP data is to be displayed.

/scope {user | computer}·Displays either user or computer results. Valid values for the /scope parameter are user or computer. If you omit the /scope parameter, gpresult displays both user and computer settings.

/v··············Specifies that the output display verbose policy information.

/z··············Specifies that the output display all available information about Group Policy. Because this parameter produces more information than the /v parameter, redirect output to a text file when you use this parameter (for example, gpresult /z >policy.txt).

Notes:

• Group Policy is the primary administrative tool for defining and controlling how programs, network resources, and the operating system operate for users and computers in
an organization. In an Active Directory environment, Group Policy is applied to users or
computers on the basis of their membership in sites, domains, or organizational units.

• Because you can apply overlapping levels of policies to any computer or user, the Group
Policy feature generates a resulting set of policies at logon. Gpresult displays the resulting
set of policies that were enforced on the computer for the specified user at logon.

GPUPDATE

Refreshes local and Active Directory-based Group Policy settings, including security settings. This command supersedes the now obsolete /refreshpolicy option for the secedit command. A syntax error generages a summary page.

Syntax:

gpupdate [/target:{computer|user}] [/force] [/wait:value] [/logoff] [/boot]

Examples:

gpupdate *or* gpupdate /target:computer *or* gpupdate /force /wait:100 *or* gpupdate
/boot

Syntax Options:

/target:{computer|user} ···Processes only the Computer settings or the current User set-
tings. By default, both the computer settings and the user settings are processed.

/force ·······Ignores all processing optimizations and reapplies all settings.

/wait:value Number of seconds that policy processing waits to finish. The default is 600
seconds. 0 means "no wait"; -1 means "wait indefinitely."

/logoff·······Logs off after the refresh has completed. This is required for those Group Policy client-side extensions that do not process on a background refresh cycle but that
do process when the user logs on, such as user Software Installation and Folder Redirection. This option has no effect if there are no extensions called that require the user
to log off.

/boot ·········Restarts the computer after the refresh has completed. This is required for
those Group Policy client-side extensions that do not process on a background refresh
cycle but that do process when the computer starts up, such as computer Software Installation. This option has no effect if there are no extensions called that require the
computer to be restarted.

GRAFTABL

Enables the ability to display an extended character set in graphics mode.

Syntax:

graftabl [xxx] [/status]

Examples:

graftabl 437 *or* graftabl 850

Syntax Options:

xxx ············Specifies the code page for which you want the appearance of extended characters in graphics mode defined. The following table lists each valid code page identification number and its Country/Region or language.

Value	Country/Region
437	United States
850	Multilingual (Latin I)
852	Slavic (Latin II)
855	Cyrillic (Russian)
857	Turkish
860	Portuguese
861	Icelandic
863	Canadian-French
865	Nordic
866	Russian
869	Modern Greek

/status·······Identifies the code page that graftabl is using.

Notes:

- Graftabl does not change the console input code page. Graftabl affects only the monitor display of extended characters of the code page you specify. To change the code page you are using, use the mode or chcp command.

- Understanding graftabl exit codes

- The following table lists each exit code and a brief description of it.

Exit code	Description
0	Character set was loaded successfully. No previous code page was loaded.
1	An incorrect parameter was specified. No action was taken.
2	A file error occurred.

- You can use the errorlevel parameter on the if command line in a batch program to process exit codes returned by graftabl.

HELP

Provides online information about system commands (that is, non-network commands).

Syntax:

{help [command]|[command]/?}

Examples

help xcopy *or* xcopy /?

Syntax Options:

Used without parameters, help lists and briefly describes every system command.

command··Specifies the name of the command about which you want information.

Notes:

- There are two ways to get online Help for a command. You can type help command, or you can type command /?. /? is slightly faster.

HELPCTR

Starts Help and Support Center.

Syntax:

helpctr [/url [URL]] [/mode [URL]] [/hidden] [/fromstarthelp]

Examples:

HelpCtr /mode *or*
"hcp://CN=Microsoft%20Corporation,L=Redmond,S=Washington,C=US/Remote%20Assistance/RAClientLayout.xml" /url

Syntax Options:

Used without parameters, helpctr displays the Help and Support Center home page.

/url [URL]··Specifies the Uniform Resource Locator (URL) that you want to display within Help and Support Center.

/mode [URL] ··················Specifies an Extensible Markup Language (XML) Definition file that complies with the Launch_Description.dtd schema, which controls the context, layout and content of Help and Support Center.

/hidden······Starts Help and Support Center without displaying the user interface. This command can load a topic. You use this command for remotely administered script execution.

/fromstarthelp··················Starts a new instance of Help and Support Center.

Notes:

- When you use /url or /mode, you can use quotation marks around the URL (that is, "URL"). If a space exists within URL, replace it by typing %20 (that is, "URL%20Address").

HOSTNAME

Displays the host name portion of the full computer name of the computer. (Internet Protocol (TCP/IP) protocol must be installed as a component in the properties of a network adapter in Network Connections.)

Syntax:

hostname

Examples:

hostname

IF

Performs conditional processing in batch programs.

Syntax:

if [not] errorlevel number command [else expression]

if [not] string1==string2 command [else expression]

if [not] exist FileName command [else expression]

If command extensions are enabled, use the following syntax:

if [/i] string1 CompareOp string2 command [else expression]

if cmdextversion number command [else expression]

if defined variable command [else expression]

Examples:

- If the file Product.dat cannot be found, the following message appears:
- if not exist product.dat echo Can't find data file
- If an error occurs during the formatting of the disk in drive A, the following example displays an error message:

:begin
@echo off
format a: /s
if not errorlevel 1 goto end
echo An error occurred during formatting.
:end
echo End of batch program.

- If no error occurs, the error message does not appear.

- You cannot use the if command to test directly for a directory, but the null (NUL) device does exist in every directory. As a result, you can test for the null device to determine whether a directory exists. The following example tests for the existence of a directory:

if exist c:\mydir\nul goto process

Syntax Options:

not ············Specifies that the command should be carried out only if the condition is false.

errorlevel number ···········Specifies a true condition only if the previous program run by Cmd.exe returned an exit code equal to or greater than number.

command··Specifies the command that should be carried out if the preceding condition is met.

string1==string2 ··············Specifies a true condition only if string1 and string2 are the same. These values can be literal strings or batch variables (for example, %1). You do not need to use quotation marks around literal strings.

exist FileName ···············Specifies a true condition if FileName exists.

CompareOp ·····················Specifies a three-letter comparison operator. The following table lists valid values for CompareOp.

Operator	Description
EQU	equal to
NEQ	not equal to
LSS	less than
LEQ	less than or equal to
GTR	greater than
GEQ	greater than or equal to

/i················Forces string comparisons to ignore case. You can use /i on the string1==string2 form of if. These comparisons are generic, in that if both string1 and string2 are both comprised of all numeric digits, the strings are converted to numbers and a numeric comparison is performed.

cmdextversion number ···Specifies a true condition only if the internal version number associated with the Command Extensions feature of Cmd.exe is equal to or greater than number. The first version is 1. It is incremented by one when significant enhancements are added to the command extensions. The cmdextversion conditional is never true when command extensions are disabled (by default, command extensions are enabled).

defined variable ··············Specifies a true condition if variable is defined.

expression Specifies a command-line command and any parameters to be passed to the command in an else clause.

Notes:

• If the condition specified in an if command is true, the command that follows the condition is carried out. If the condition is false, the command in the if clause is ignored, and executes any command in the else clause, if one has been specified.

• When a program stops, it returns an exit code. You can use exit codes as conditions by using the errorlevel parameter.

• If you use defined variable, the following three variables are added: %errorlevel%, %cmdcmdline%, and %cmdextversion%.

• %errorlevel% expands into a string representation of the current value of errorlevel, provided that there is not already an environment variable with the name ERRORLEVEL, in which case you get the ERRORLEVEL value instead. The following example illustrates how you can use errorlevel after running a batch program:

```
goto answer%errorlevel%
:answer0
echo Program had return code 0
:answer1
echo Program had return code 1
goto end
:end
echo done!
```

• You can also use the CompareOp comparison operators as follows:
if %errorlevel% LEQ 1 goto okay

• %cmdcmdline% expands into the original command line passed to Cmd.exe prior to any processing by Cmd.exe, provided that there is not already an environment variable with the name cmdcmdline, in which case you get the cmdcmdline value instead.

• %cmdextversion% expands into the a string representation of the current value of cmdextversion, provided that there is not already an environment variable with the name CMDEXTVERSION, in which case you get the CMDEXTVERSION value instead.

• You must use the else clause on the same line as the command after the if. For example:
IF EXIST filename. (del filename.) ELSE (echo filename. missing.)

• The following code does not work because you must terminate the del command by a new line:
IF EXIST filename. del filename. ELSE echo filename. missing

• The following code does not work because you must use the else clause on the same line as the end of the if command:
IF EXIST filename. del filename.
ELSE echo filename. missing

• If you want to format it all on a single line, use the following form of the original statement:
IF EXIST filename. (del filename.) ELSE echo filename. missing

IPCONFIG

Displays all current TCP/IP network configuration values and refreshes Dynamic Host Configuration Protocol (DHCP) and Domain Name System (DNS) settings.

Syntax:

ipconfig [/all] [/renew [Adapter]] [/release [Adapter]] [/flushdns] [/displaydns] [/registerdns] [/showclassid Adapter] [/setclassid Adapter [ClassID]]

Examples:

ipconfig *or* ipconfig /all *or* ipconfig /renew "Local Area Connection" *or* ipconfig /flushdns

Syntax Options:

Used without parameters, ipconfig displays the IP address, subnet mask, and default gateway for all adapters.

/all···········Displays the full TCP/IP configuration for all adapters. Without this parameter, ipconfig displays only the IP address, subnet mask, and default gateway values for each adapter. Adapters can represent physical interfaces, such as installed network adapters, or logical interfaces, such as dial-up connections.

/renew [Adapter]···········Renews DHCP configuration for all adapters (if an adapter is not specified) or for a specific adapter if the Adapter parameter is included. This parameter is available only on computers with adapters that are configured to obtain an IP address automatically. To specify an adapter name, type the adapter name that appears when you use ipconfig without parameters.

/release [Adapter]··········Sends a DHCPRELEASE message to the DHCP server to release the current DHCP configuration and discard the IP address configuration for either all adapters (if an adapter is not specified) or for a specific adapter if the Adapter parameter is included. This parameter disables TCP/IP for adapters configured to obtain an IP address automatically. To specify an adapter name, type the adapter name that appears when you use ipconfig without parameters.

/flushdns ···Flushes and resets the contents of the DNS client resolver cache. During DNS troubleshooting, you can use this procedure to discard negative cache entries from the cache, as well as any other entries that have been added dynamically.

/displaydns····Displays the contents of the DNS client resolver cache, which includes both entries preloaded from the local Hosts file and any recently obtained resource records for name queries resolved by the computer. The DNS Client service uses this information to resolve frequently queried names quickly, before querying its configured DNS servers.

/registerdns····Initiates manual dynamic registration for the DNS names and IP addresses that are configured at a computer. You can use this parameter to troubleshoot a failed DNS name registration or resolve a dynamic update problem between a client and the DNS server without rebooting the client computer. The DNS settings in the advanced properties of the TCP/IP protocol determine which names are registered in DNS.

/showclassid Adapter······Displays the DHCP class ID for a specified adapter. To see the DHCP class ID for all adapters, use the asterisk (*) wildcard character in place of Adapter. This parameter is available only on computers with adapters that are configured to obtain an IP address automatically.

/setclassid Adapter [ClassID]················Configures the DHCP class ID for a specified adapter. To set the DHCP class ID for all adapters, use the asterisk (*) wildcard character in place of Adapter. This parameter is available only on computers with adapters that are configured to obtain an IP address automatically. If a DHCP class ID is not specified, the current class ID is removed.

Notes:

• The ipconfig command is the command-line equivalent to the winipcfg command, which is available in Windows Millennium Edition, Windows 98, and Windows 95. Although Windows XP does not include a graphical equivalent to the winipcfg command, you can use Network Connections to view and renew an IP address. To do this, open Network Connections, right-click a network connection, click Status, and then click the Support tab.

• This command is most useful on computers that are configured to obtain an IP address automatically. This enables users to determine which TCP/IP configuration values have been configured by DHCP, Automatic Private IP Addressing (APIPA), or an alternate configuration.

• If the Adapter name contains any spaces, use quotation marks around the adapter name (that is, "Adapter Name").

• For adapter names, ipconfig supports the use of the asterisk (*) wildcard character to specify either adapters with names that begin with a specified string or adapters with names that contain a specified string. For example, Local* matches all adapters that start with the string Local and *Con* matches all adapters that contain the string Con.

• This command is available only if the Internet Protocol (TCP/IP) protocol is installed as a component in the properties of a network adapter in Network Connections

• Whenever an IP change is made to a DNS entry (in Win9X or WinNT 4.0), you will have to reboot the machine to get the new address or use the /flushdns switch to dump the cached DNS entries.

IPSECCMD

Configures Internet Protocol Security (IPSec) policies in a directory service or in a local or remote registry. Ipseccmd is a command-line alternative to the IP Security Policies Microsoft Management Console (MMC) snap-in. Ipseccmd has three modes: dynamic mode, static mode, and query mode.

ipseccmd dynamic mode

You can use Ipseccmd dynamic mode to add anonymous rules to the existing IPSec policy by adding them to the IPSec security policies database. The rules added will be present even after the IPSEC Services service is restarted. The benefit of using dynamic mode is that the rules you add coexist with domain-based IPSec policy. Dynamic mode is the default mode for Ipseccmd.

Syntax:

To add a rule, use the following syntax: ipseccmd [\\ComputerName] -f FilterList [-n NegotiationPolicyList] [-t TunnelAddr] [-a AuthMethodList] [-1s SecurityMethodList] [-1k MainModeRekeySettings] [-1p] [-1f MMFilterList] [-1e SoftSAExpirationTime] [-soft] [-confirm] [{-dialup | -lan}]

To delete all dynamic policies, use the following syntax: ipseccmd -u

Examples:

ipseccmd -f 0+* -n ah[md5]   *or*   ipseccmd -f 10.2.1.1=10.2.1.13 -t 10.2.1.13 -n ah[sha] -1p -c

Syntax Options:

\\ComputerName ············Specifies the computer name of a remote computer to which you want to add a rule.

-f FilterList·Required for first syntax. Specifies one or more filter specifications, separated by spaces, for quick mode security associations (SAs). Each filter specification defines a set of network traffic affected by this rule.

-n NegotiationPolicyList ··Specifies one or more security methods, separated by spaces, for securing traffic defined by the filter list.

-t TunnelAddr ················Specifies the tunnel endpoint for tunnel mode as either an IP address or a DNS domain name.

-a AuthMethodList ·········Specifies one or more authentication methods, separated by spaces.

-1s SecurityMethodList ···Specifies one or more key exchange security methods, separated by spaces.

-1k MainModeRekeySettings ···············Specifies main mode SA rekey settings.

-1p ···Enables master key perfect forward secrecy.

-1f MMFilterList ···············Specifies one or more filter specifications for main mode SAs, separated by spaces.

-1e SoftSAExpirationTime·····················Specifies the expiration time for soft SAs in seconds.

-soft ·········Enables soft SAs.

-confirm ····Specifies that a confirmation prompt appears before the rule or policy is added.

{-dialup | -lan}··················Specifies whether the rule applies only to remote access or dial-up connections or whether the rule applies only to local area network (LAN) connections.

-u ·············Required for the second syntax. Specifies that all dynamic rules are deleted.

Notes:

• Ipseccmd cannot be used to configure rules on computers running Windows 2000.

XP Command: IPSECCMD   **151**

- If you do not specify the ComputerName parameter, the rule is added to the local computer.

- If you use the ComputerName parameter, you must use it before all other parameters, and you must have administrator permissions on the computer to which you want to add the rule.

- For the -f parameter, a filter specification is one or more filters that are separated by spaces and defined by the format:
SourceAddress/SourceMask:SourcePort=DestAddress/DestMask:DestPort:Protocol

- SourceMask, SourcePort, DestMask, and DestPort are optional. If you omit them, the mask of 255.255.255.255 and all ports are used for the filter.

- Protocol is optional. If you omit it, all protocols are used for the filter. If you specify a protocol, you must specify the port or precede the protocol with two colons (::). (See the first example for dynamic mode.) The protocol must be the last item in the filter. You can use the following protocol symbols: ICMP, UDP, RAW, or TCP.

- You can create mirrored filters by replacing the equals sign (=) with a plus sign (+).

- You can replace SourceAddress/SourceMask or DestAddress/DestMask with the values in the following table.

Value	Description
0	My address or addresses
*	Any address
DNSName	DNS domain name. If the DNS name resolves to multiple addresses, it is ignored.
GUID	A globally unique identifier (GUID) of a local network interface in the form {12345678-1234-1234-1234-123456789ABC}. Specifying a GUID is not supported when the -n parameter is used in static mode.

- You can enable the default response rule by specifying the filter specification of default.

- You can specify a permit filter by surrounding the filter specification with parentheses. You can specify a blocking filter by surrounding the filter specification with brackets ([ ]).

- If you are using Internet address class-based subnet masks (the subnet masks are defined along octet boundaries), you can use wildcard notation to specify subnet masks. For example, 10.*.*.* is the same as 10.0.0.0/255.0.0.0 and 10.92.*.* is the same as 10.92.0.0/255.255.0.0.

- Filter examples

To create mirrored filters to filter TCP traffic between Computer1 and Computer2, type:
Computer1+Computer2::TCP

To create a filter for all TCP traffic from the subnet 172.31.0.0/255.255.0.0, port 80, to the subnet 10.0.0.0/255.0.0.0, port 80, type:
172.31.0.0/255.255.0.0:80=10.0.0.0/255.0.0.0:80:TCP

To create a mirrored filter that permits traffic between the local IP address and the IP address 10.2.1.1, type: (0+10.2.1.1)

- For the -n parameter, one or more negotiation policies are separated by spaces and follow one of the following forms:
esp[EncrypAlg,AuthAlg]RekeyPFS[Group]
ah[HashAlg]
ah[HashAlg]+esp[EncrypAlg,AuthAlg]
where EncrypAlg can be none, des, or 3des, AuthAlg can be none, md5, or sha, and HashAlg can be md5 or sha.

- The configuration esp[none,none] is not supported.

- The sha parameter refers to the SHA1 hash algorithm.

- The Rekey parameter is optional, and it specifies the number of kilobytes (indicated by placing a K after the number) or the number of seconds (indicated by placing an S after the number) that precede a rekeying of the quick mode SA. To specify both rekey parameters, separate the two numbers with a slash (/). For example, to rekey the quick mode SA every hour and after every 5 megabytes of data, type: 3600S/5000K

- The PFS parameter is optional, and it enables session key perfect forward secrecy. By default, session key perfect forward secrecy is disabled.

- The Group parameter is optional, and it specifies the Diffie-Hellman group for session key perfect forward secrecy. For the Low(1) Diffie-Hellman group, specify PFS1 or P1. For the Medium(2) Diffie-Hellman group, specify PFS2 or P2. By default, the group value for session key perfect forward secrecy is taken from the current main mode settings.

- If you do not specify negotiation policies, the default negotiation policies are the following:

esp[3des,sha]
esp[3des,md5]
esp[des,sha]
esp[des,md5]

- If you omit the -t parameter, IPSec transport mode is used.

- For the -a parameter, one or more authentication methods are separated by spaces and are in one of the following forms:

preshare:"PresharedKeyString"
kerberos
cert:"CAInfo"

- The PresharedKeyString parameter specifies the string of characters of the preshared key. The CAInfo parameter specifies the distinguished name of the certificate as displayed in the IP Security Policies snap-in when the certificate is selected as an authentication method for a rule. The PresharedKeyString and CAInfo parameters are case-sensitive. You can abbreviate the method by using the first letter: p, k, or c. If you omit the -a parameter, the default authentication method is Kerberos.

- For the -1s parameter, one or more key exchange security methods are separated by spaces and defined by the following format:

EncrypAlg-HashAlg-GroupNum

where EncrypAlg can be des or 3des, HashAlg can be md5 or sha, and GroupNum can be 1 for the Low(1) Diffie-Hellman group or 2 for the Medium(2) Diffie-Hellman group. If you omit the -1s parameter, the default key exchange security methods are 3des-sha-2, 3des-md5-2, des-sha-1, and des-md5-1.

- For the -1k parameter, you can specify the number of quick mode SAs (indicated by placing a Q after the number) or the number of seconds (indicated by placing an S after the number) to rekey the main mode SA. To specify both rekey parameters, you must separate the two numbers with a slash (/). For example, to rekey the main mode SA after every 10 quick mode SAs and every hour, type: 10Q/3600S

- If you omit the -1k parameter, the default values for main mode rekey are an unlimited number of quick mode SAs and 480 minutes.

- Master key perfect forward secrecy is disabled by default.

- For the -1f parameter, the syntax for specifying main mode filter specifications is the same as for the -f parameter, except that you cannot specify permit filters, blocking filters, ports, or protocols. If you omit the -1f parameter, the main mode filters are automatically created based on the quick mode filters.

- If you omit the -1e parameter, the expiration time for soft SAs is 300 seconds. However, soft SAs are disabled unless you include the -soft parameter.

- Confirmation is available for dynamic mode only.

- If you specify neither the -dialup parameter nor the -lan parameter, the rule applies to all adapters.

ipseccmd static mode

You can use Ipseccmd static mode to create named policies and named rules. You can also use static mode to modify existing policies and rules, provided they were originally created with Ipseccmd. The syntax for static mode combines the syntax for dynamic mode with parameters that enable it to work at a policy level.

Syntax:

ipseccmd DynamicModeParameters -w Type[:Location] -p PolicyName[:PollInterval]
-r RuleName [{-x | -y}] [-o]

Examples:
ipseccmd -f 0+SecuredServer1 0+SecuredServer2 -a k p:"corpauth" -w ds -p "Default Domain Policy":30 -r "Secured Servers"

Syntax Options:

DynamicModeParameters ....Required. Specifies a set of dynamic mode parameters for an IPSec rule as described earlier.

-w Type[:Location] ....Required. Specifies that the policies and rules are written to the local registry, to the registry of a remote computer, or to an Active Directory domain.

-p PolicyName[:PollInterval]..................Required. Specifies the name of the policy and how often, in minutes, the policy is checked for changes. If PolicyName contains any spaces, use quotation marks around the text (that is, "Policy Name").

-r RuleName ....Required. Specifies the name of the rule. If RuleName contains any spaces, use quotation marks around the text (that is, "Rule Name").

[{-x | -y}] ....Specifies whether the local registry policy is assigned. The -x parameter specifies that the local registry policy is assigned. The -y parameter specifies that the local registry policy is unassigned.

-o ....Specifies that the rule or policy should be deleted.

Notes:

• For the -w parameter, the Type is either reg to specify the registry of the local computer or a remote computer or ds to specify Active Directory.

• If you specify reg for the Type parameter but you do not use the Location parameter, the rule is created for the registry of the local computer.

• If you specify reg for the Type parameter and you specify the name of a remote computer for the Location parameter, the rule is created for the registry of the remote computer you specify.

• If you specify ds for the Type parameter but you do not use the Location parameter, the rule is created for the Active Directory domain of which the local computer is a member.

• If you specify ds for the Type parameter and you specify an Active Directory domain for the Location parameter, the rule is created for the specified domain.

• For the -p parameter, if a policy with this name already exists, the rule you specify is added to the policy. Otherwise a policy is created with the name you specify. If you specify an integer for the PollInterval parameter, the polling interval for the policy is set to that number of minutes.

• For the -r parameter, if a rule with that name already exists, the rule is modified to reflect the parameters you specify in the command. For example, if you include the -f parameter for an existing rule, only the filters of that rule are replaced. If no rule exists with the name you specify, a rule with that name is created.

• For the -o parameter, all aspects of the specified policy are deleted. Do not use this parameter if you have other policies that point to the objects in the policy you want to delete.

• Static mode usage differs from dynamic mode usage in one respect. Using dynamic mode, you indicate permit and blocking filters in FilterList, which you identify using the -f parameter. Using static mode, you indicate permit and blocking filters in NegotiationPolicyList, which you identify using the -n parameter. In addition to the parameters described for NegotiationPolicyList under dynamic mode, you can also use the block, pass, or inpass parameters in static mode. The following table list these parameters and a description of their behavior.

Parameter	Description
block	The rest of the policies in NegotiationPolicyList are ignored, and all of the filters are made blocking filters.
pass	The rest of the policies in NegotiationPolicyList are ignored, and all of the filters are made permit filters.
inpass	Inbound filters will allow initial communication to be unsecured, but responses will be secured using IPSec.

ipseccmd query mode

You can use Ipseccmd query mode to display data from the IPSec security policies database.

Syntax:

ipseccmd [\\ComputerName] show {{[filters] | [policies] | [auth] | [stats] | [sas]} | all}

Examples:

ipseccmd show filters policies **or** ipseccmd \\Server1 show all

Syntax Options:

\\ComputerName ·············· Specifies, by name, the remote computer for which you want to display data.

show ········ Required. Indicates that Ipseccmd should run in query mode.

filters ········ Displays main mode and quick mode filters.

policies ····· Displays main mode and quick mode policies.

auth ········ Displays main mode authentication methods.

stats ········ Displays statistics about Internet Key Exchange (IKE) and IPSec.

sas ·········· Displays main mode and quick mode security associations (SAs).

all ············· Displays all of the above types of data.

Notes:

- Ipseccmd cannot be used to display IPSec data for computers running Windows 2000.

- If you do not use the ComputerName parameter, information about the local computer is displayed.

- If you use the ComputerName parameter, you must use it before all other parameters, and you must have administrator permissions on the computer for which you want to display information.

IPXROUTE

Displays and modifies information about the routing tables used by the IPX protocol.

Syntax:

ipxroute servers [/type=x]

ipxroute ripout network

ipxroute resolve {guid | name} {guid | AdapterName}

ipxroute board=n [def] [gbr] [mbr] [remove=xxxxxxxxxxxx]

ipxroute config

Examples:

ipxroute config

Syntax Options:

Used without parameters, ipxroute displays the default settings for packets that are sent to unknown, broadcast, and multicast addresses.

servers [/type=x] ·············· Displays the Service Access Point (SAP) table for the specified server type. x must be an integer. For example, /type=4 displays all file servers. If you do not specify /type, ipxroute servers displays all types of servers, listing them by server name.

ripout network ·················· Discovers if network is reachable by consulting the IPX stack's route table and sending out a rip request if necessary. Network is the IPX network segment number.

resolve {guid | name} {guid | AdapterName}
Resolves the name of the guid to its friendly name, or the friendly name to its guid.

board=n ····· Specifies the network adapter for which to query or set parameters.

def ·········· Sends packets to the ALL ROUTES broadcast. If a packet is transmitted to a unique Media Access Card (MAC) address that is not in the source routing table, ipxroute sends the packet to the SINGLE ROUTES broadcast by default.

gbr ·········· Sends packets to the ALL ROUTES broadcast. If a packet is transmitted to the broadcast address (FFFFFFFFFFFF), ipxroute sends the packet to the SINGLE ROUTES broadcast by default.

mbr ·········· Sends packets to the ALL ROUTES broadcast. If a packet is transmitted to a multicast address (C000xxxxxxxx), ipxroute sends the packet to the SINGLE ROUTES broadcast by default.

remove=xxxxxxxxxxxx ···· Removes the given node address from the source routing table.

config ········ Displays information about all of the bindings for which IPX is configured.

IRFTP

Sends files over an infrared link.

Syntax:

irftp [Drive:\] [[Path] FileName] [/h]

irftp /s

Examples:

irftp C:\MyWorkFiles\MyWorkDoc.doc /h   or

irftp C:\MyWorkFiles\MyWordDoc1.doc C:\MyWorkFiles\MyWordDoc2.doc /h

Syntax Options:

Used without parameters or used with /s, irftp opens the Wireless Link dialog box, where you can select the files that you want to send without using the command line.

Drive:\ ·······Specifies the drive that contains the files that you want to send over an infra-red link.

[Path] FileName ···············Specifies the location and name of the file or set of files that you want to send over an infrared link. If you specify a set of files, you must specify the full path for each file.

/h ·············Specifies hidden mode. When hidden mode is used, the files are sent without displaying the Wireless Link dialog box.

/s···············Opens the Wireless Link dialog box, so that you can select the file or set of files that you want to send without using the command line to specify the drive, path, and file names.

Notes:

• Before using this command, verify that the devices that you want to communicate over an infrared link have infrared functionality enabled and working correctly, and that an infrared link is established between the devices.

LABEL

Creates, changes, or deletes the volume label (that is, the name) of a disk.

Syntax:

label [Drive:][label]

label [/MP][volume][label]

Examples:

label a:sales-july

Syntax Options:

Used without parameters, label changes the current volume label or deletes the existing label.

Drive: ········Specifies the drive letter (followed by a colon) of the disk you want to name.

label··········Specifies the name for the volume.

/MP ··········Specifies that the volume should be treated as a mount point or volume name.

volume······Specifies the drive letter (followed by a colon), mount point, or volume name. If a volume name is specified, the /MP parameter is unnecessary.

Notes:

• Windows displays the volume label as part of the directory listing. If a volume serial number exists, Windows displays this number as well.

• Label command messages

• If you do not specify a label when you use the label command, label displays a message in the following format:

Volume in drive A is xxxxxxxxxxx
Volume Serial Number is xxxx-xxxx
Volume label (11 characters, ENTER for none)?

• The "Volume Serial Number" part of the message is not displayed if the disk has no serial number.

- You can type the volume label you want or press ENTER to delete the current label. If a disk has a label and you press ENTER for none, label prompts you with the following message:

- Delete current volume label (Y/N)?Press Y to delete the label; press N to keep the label.

- Limitations on volume label names

- A volume label can contain as many as 32 characters for NTFS volumes and as many as 11 characters for FAT volumes and can include spaces but no tabs.

- FAT volume labels cannot contain any of the following characters:

* ? / \ | . , ; : + = [ ] < > "
This limitation does not apply to NTFS volumes.

- For FAT volumes, volume labels are stored as uppercase regardless of whether they contain lowercase letters. NTFS volume labels retain and display the case used when the label was created.

LODCTR

Registers new Performance counter names and Explain text for a service or device driver, and saves and restores counter settings and Explain text.

Syntax:

lodctr [\\ComputerName] FileName [/s:FileName] [/r:FileName]

Examples:

lodctr /s:"perf backup1.txt"

Syntax Options:

[\\ComputerName] FileName Registers the Performance counter name settings and Explain text provided in initialization file FileName. If you do not specify the ComputerName, lodctr uses the local computer by default.

/s:FileName ·················Saves Performance counter registry settings and Explain text to file FileName.

/r:FileName ·················Restores Performance counter registry settings and Explain text from file FileName.

Notes:

- If the information that you supply contains spaces, use quotation marks around the text (for example, "Computer Name").

Caution

If you use the lodctr /r command, you will overwrite all Performance counter registry settings and Explain text, replacing them with the configuration defined in the file specified.

LOGMAN

Manages and schedules performance counter and event trace log collections on local and remote systems.

Syntax Verbs:

Logman [create {counter | trace} collection_name] [start collection_name] [stop collection_name] [delete collection_name] [query {collection_name|providers}] [update collection_name]

Examples:

Date formats in the following examples are for US local time only.

- To create daily counter collection queries with begin and end times, repeat collections, version control numbers, counter paths and sample intervals, type:

Logman create counter daily_perf_log -b 7/27/2000 13:00:00 -e 7/27/2000 15:00:00 -r -v mmddhhmm -c "\Processor(_Total)\% Processor Time" "\Memory\Available bytes" -si 00:15 -o "c:\perflogs\daily_log"

- To create daily collection queries with begin and end times, repeat collections, output file collections, version control numbers, counter paths and sample intervals, type:

Logman create counter daily_perf_log -b 7/27/2000 13:00:00 -e 7/27/2000 15:00:00 -r -o "c:\perflogs\daily_log" -v mmddhhmm -c "\Processor(_Total)\% Processor Time" "\Memory\Available bytes" -si 00:15

• To create daily collection queries using the config file, instead of the command line file, type:

Logman -config file daily_perf.txt

• To create daily trace collection queries with begin and end times, repeat collections, version control numbers, provider names, input and output file collections, type:

Logman create trace daily_kernel_trace_log -b 7/27/2000 13:00:00 -e 7/27/2000 15:00:00 -r -v mmddhhmm -p "Windows Kernel Trace" 0xFFFFFFFF -rf 100 -o "c:\perflogs\daily_nt_trace"

• To create daily trace collection queries with begin and end times, repeat collections, version control numbers, Guid and logger names, input and output file collections, type:

Logman create trace daily_lsass_trace_log -b 7/27/2000 13:00:00 -e 7/27/2000 15:00:00 -r -v mmddhhmm -p "Local Security Authority(LSA) " 0x00000001 -rf 30:00 -o " c:\perflogs\daily_lsass_trace"

• To create daily counter collection queries with begin and end times, repeat collections, version control numbers, counter paths, sample intervals, SQL formats and output file collections, type:

Logman create counter daily_perf_log -b 7/27/2000 13:00:00 -e 7/27/2000 15:00:00 -r -v mmddhhmm -c "\Processor(_Total)\% Processor Time" "\Memory\Available bytes" -si 00:15 -f sql -o perfdb!daily_log

• To start daily collections with sample intervals, account names and passwords, type:
Logman start daily_perf_log -s \\%computer_name% -u admin "adminpassword"

• To start manual data collections, type:
Logman start daily_perf_log

• To stop data collections, type:
Logman stop daily_perf_log

• To delete data collections, type:
Logman delete daily_perf_log

• To display the status of collection queries, type the following commands:
Logman query
Logman query daily_perf_log

Syntax Options:

create {counter | trace} collection_name
   Creates collection queries for either counter or trace collections. You can use command line options to specify settings.

start collection_name······Starts the data collection query collection_name. Use this option to change from scheduled collections to manual ones. Use the update parameter in the command line with begin-time (-b), end-time (-e), or repeat-time (-rt) to reschedule collections.

stop collection_name······Stops the data collection query collection_name. Use this option to change from scheduled collections to manual ones. Use the update parameter in the command line with begin-time (-b), end-time (-e), or repeat-time (-rt) to reschedule collections.

delete collection_name···Deletes the data collection query collection_name. If the collection_name does not exist, you will receive an error.

query {collection_name|providers}········If no collection_name or providers are given, the status of all existing collection queries are displayed. Use collection_name to display the properties of a specific collection. To display the properties on remote computers, use the -s remote computer option in the command line. Use providers as your keyword in place of collection_name to display the registered providers installed on your local system. To list registered providers installed on the remote system, use the -s option in the command line.

update collection_name··Updates collection queries for counter and trace collections. For counter collections, modifications to the query will stop, and then restart the collections. For trace collections, use the following parameters in the command line to query without stopping the collection: -p provider [(flags[,flags ...])]] Level, - max n, - o PathName, -ft mm:ss, or -fd.

Syntax Options:

[-s computer_name] [-config FileName] [-b M/d/yyyy h:mm:ss[AM | PM]] [-e M/d/yyyy h:mm:ss[AM | PM]] [-m [start] [stop]] [-[-]r] [-o {Path | DSN!counter_log}] [-f {bin | bincirc | csv | tsv | SQL}] [-[-]a] [-[-]v {(nnnnn | mmddhhmm}]] [-[-] rc [FileName]] [-[-] max {value}] [-[-]cnf [[[hh:]mm:]ss] [-c {Path [path ...] | -cf FileName}] [-si [[hh:]mm:]ss] [-ln logger_name] [-ets] [-[-] rt] [-p {GUID | provider [(flags [,flags...])]}] Level | -pf File-Name}] [-[-] ul] [-bs value] [-ft [[hh:]mm:]ss] [-nb min max] [-fd logger name] [-[-]u user password] [-rf [[hh:]mm:]ss] [-y] [-mode {trace_mode [trace_mode ...]}]]

Syntax Options:

-s computer_name·········Specifies that create, start, stop, delete, query, or update commands will be performed on the remote system. By default, the local system is used for commands.

-config FileName ············Specifies the pathname of the settings file that contains command line parameters.

-b M/d/yyyy h:mm:ss[AM | PM] ···········Specifies begin-time for collections in a 24-hour format. You can also specify begin-time for collections in a 12-hour format by adding AM or PM in the command line. By default, the current day and time is used unless otherwise specified. Use the manual start option to start the collection immediately.

-e M/d/yyyy h:mm:ss[AM | PM] ···········Specifies end-time for collections in a 24-hour format. You can also specify end-time for collections in a 12-hour format by adding AM or PM in the command line. By default, the current day and time is used unless otherwise specified. Use the manual stop and then the repeat option to specify a stop time before the actual current time, or you will receive an error message.

-m start stop···················Specifies that collections start and stop manually by using the start and stop parameters in the command line. You cannot use the -m start and -b, or the -m stop and -e, or -rf parameters together in your command line for the same query.

-r·············Repeats the collection every day at the time periods specified by the -b and -rf options, or the -b and -e options. This command is only valid for begin- and end-times specified on the same day, month, and year.

—r·············Turns off the repeat option.

-o {Path | DSN!counter_log}·················Specifies the pathname of the output file that collects performance counter and trace data, or the location of the SQL database and dataset. To specify SQL using the DSN!counter_log format, use the -f option in the command line. By default, the collection log file name is the collection query name suffixed by either .blg for performance counters, or .etl for trace data.

-f {bin | bincirc | csv | tsv | SQL} ···········Specifies the file format used for collecting performance counter and trace data. You can use binary, circular binary, comma and tab separated, or SQL database formats when collecting performance counters. You must use the -o option in the command line with the DSN!counter_log option. For SQL database formats, the Database System Name (DSN) must be predefined, and privileges granted to write to the database. The dataset counter_log is created in the database, and is specified by the DSN. Defaults to binary.

-a ··············Use this option to append the file.

—a ············Turns off the append command option, and reverts to the overwrite mode.

-v {nnnnn | mmddhhmm} Attaches the version control information to the end of the output file and path name. Use numeric nnnnn format, or date format mmddhhmm (month, day, 24-hour, minute) for version control.

—v ············Turns off the version option.

-rc FileName ··················Specifies to run this command after the file is closed either at the end, or during the collection period. Use the -rf option in conjunction with -cnf to close the files during the collection periods. Using the -stop option will not turn off this command. Commands always run in the foreground.

—rc············Turns off the run this command option.

-max valueSpecifies the maximum size of the collected log file in megabytes. If the log file exceeds the maximum size, the collection will stop. For a SQL database, the maximum size is the number of records to be written.

—max·······Turns off the maximum size limit option. This is the default option.

-cnf [[hh:]mm:]ss ···············Creates a new file when output files exceed a maximum size, or when the time specified elapses. You must include the -v option when executing this command. By default, only one log file is created during each collection.

—cnf ········Turns off the create-new-file option.

-c {Path [path ...] | -cf FileName} ···········Specifies the performance counter path to log, or specifies the pathname of the log file that lists these counters. To list multiple counter paths, separate the command line by a space, or use the -cf option to list counter paths in an input file, one per line.

The general format for counter paths is as follows:

[\\Computer]\object[parent/instance#index]\counter] where: The parent, instance, index, and counter components of the format may contain either a valid name or a wildcard character. The computer, parent, instance, and index components are not necessary for all counters.

You determine the counter paths to use based on the counter itself. For example, the LogicalDisk object has an instance index, so you must provide the #index or a wildcard. Therefore, you could use the following format: \LogicalDisk(*/*#*)*

In comparison, the Process object does not require an instance index. Therefore, you could use the following format: \Process(*)\ID Process

The following is a list of the possible formats:

\\machine\object(parent/instance#index)\counter

\\machine\object(parent/instance)\counter

\\machine\object(instance#index)\counter

\\machine\object(instance)\counter

\\machine\object\counter

\object(parent/instance#index)\counter

\object(parent/instance)\counter

\object(instance#index)\counter

\object(instance)\counter

\object\counter

If a wildcard character is specified in the parent name, all instances of the specified object that match the specified instance and counter fields will be returned.

If a wildcard character is specified in the instance name, all instances of the specified object and parent object will be returned if all instance names corresponding to the specified index match the wildcard character.

If a wildcard character is specified in the counter name, all counters of the specified object are returned.

Partial counter path string matches (for example, pro*) are not supported.

-si [[hh:]mm:]ss ···············Specifies sample intervals for performance counter collection in hours, minutes, and seconds. Default is 15-seconds.

-ln logger_name···············Specifies a user-defined name for the event trace logging session. By default, the collection name is used as the logger name.

-ets ··········Creates and starts an event trace session with the options specified on the command line. You can use this optional parameter with the create trace, update, query, and delete parameters.

-rt ···········Specifies that the event trace session run in real-time mode, and not log to a file. By default, the data logs to a file.

—rt ···········Turns off the real-time logging option.

-p {GUID | provider [(flags[,flags ...])] Level] | -pf {FileName} Specifies the providers (trace data collectors) to use for trace data collection. Use logman query providers to find the pname (named providers) from the registered provider list. Use the -pf option to list multiple providers. The -pf option identifies the input file containing the provider names. The provider names are enclosed by quotation marks ("), or with GUIDs enclosed by braces, flag masks, and integers (enable level). The flags are either in hexadecimal (OXFFFF) or (flag, flag) format.

-ul ···········Specifies that the event trace session is run in user mode. If you use the -ul option, only one provider can be enabled for the event trace session.

—ul ···········Specifies that the user mode is turned off, and the event trace session is run in kernel mode.

-bs value ··· Specifies the buffer size in n kilobytes for trace data collections.

-ft [[hh:]mm:]ss ············ Specifies the flush timer interval in minutes and seconds for trace data collections.

-nb min max ··············· Specifies the minimum and maximum number of buffers for trace data collection. Minimum default is the number of processors on the system plus two. Maximum default is at 25.

-fd logger_name ············ Flushes all the active buffers of an existing event trace session to a disk. Use this command in conjunction with the -ln option.

-u user password ·········· Specifies the account name and password the collection query uses on local or remote systems. To start collecting data for collection queries, log Performance Logs and Alerts to the remote system. You can use * as your password in the command line to produce a prompt for the password.

—u ············ Resets the account name to the Performance Logs and Alerts service account.

-rf [[hh:]mm:]ss ············· Specifies that collections run for a set period of time.

-y ············ Overwrites the settings for collection name, and then applies new ones without querying the end user.

-mode {trace_mode [trace_mode ...]} ··· Specifies advanced options for trace sessions only where trace_mode can be either globalsequence, localsequence or pagedmemory. Globalsequence specifies that the event tracer add a sequence number to every event it receives irrespective of which trace session received the event. Localsequence specifies that the event tracer add sequence numbers for events received at a specific trace session. When the localsequence option is used, duplicate sequence numbers can exist across all sessions but will be unique within each trace session. Pagedmemory specifies that the event tracer use paged memory rather than the default non-paged memory pool for its internal buffer allocations.

Notes:

• Valid options for the command-line verbs create update, start, stop, delete, and query are:

-s remote machine name
-[-]u Domain/username password

• Valid options for create and update, and common options for counter and trace are:

-y
-b M/d/yyyy h:mm:ss [AM|PM]
-e M/d/yyyy h:mm:ss [AM|PM]
-rf hh:mm:ss
-m start stop
-f bin|bincirc
-[-]r
-o PathName
-[-]a
-[-]v nnnnn|mmddhhmm
-[-]rc command pathname
-[-]max n
-[-]cnf hh:mm:ss

• Common options for counters only are:
-f bin|bincirc|csv|tsv|SQL
-o PathName | DSN!counter_log

• Common options for create counter are:
-c counterpath | -cf input file
-si [[hh:]mm:]ss

• These options update the counter, and will stop and start collections.

• Options for update for trace collection are:
- max n
- o PathName
-ft mm:ss
-fd

• These options will query trace collections without stopping the collections.

• Valid options with counters only are:
-f bin|bincirc|csv|tsv|SQL
-o PathName | DSN!counter_log

- Valid options with create counter commands are:
counterpath | -cf input file
-si hh:mm:ss

- Valid options for create trace commands are:
-ln logger name
-[-]rt
-p Guid | provider (flags[,flags ...]) level | -pf FileName
-[-]ul
-bs n
-ft mm:ss
-nb min max
-fd logger name
-ets

- Using the -config option
The contents of the setting file used with the -config option should have the following format:
[command_option]
value

- where command_option is a command line option and value specifies its value. For example:
[create]
counter logx
[-s]
mysystem
[-u]
mypassword

- Using the -mode option
You should only use this option if you are an advanced user.

- Managing Performance monitor

- You can only use Logman to manage systems running Windows 2000 or Windows XP.

LPQ

Displays the status of a print queue on a computer running Line Printer Daemon (LPD).

Syntax:

lpq -S ServerName -P PrinterName [-l]

Syntax Options:

Used without parameters, lpq displays command-line help for the lpq command.

-S ServerName ·············· Required. Specifies, by name, the computer that hosts the print queue whose status you want to display.

-P PrinterName ·············· Required. Specifies, by name, the printer for the print queue whose status you want to display.

-l ·············· Specifies that you want to display details about the status of the print queue.

LPR

Sends a file to a computer running Line Printer Daemon (LPD) in preparation for printing.

Syntax:

lpr [-S ServerID] -P PrinterName [-C BannerContent] [-J JobName] [{-o | -o l}] [-d] [-x] FileName

Syntax Options:

Used without parameters, lpr displays command-line help for the lpr command.

-S ServerID ·············· Specifies, by name or IP address, the computer that hosts the printer on which you want to print the file. You do not need to provide this parameter if the printer is attached to the local computer.

-P PrinterName ·············· Required. Specifies, by name, the printer on which you want to print the file.

-C BannerContent ·········· Specifies the content to print on the banner page of the print job. If you do not include this parameter, the name of the computer from which the print job was sent appears on the banner page.

-J JobName ·················Specifies the print job name that will be printed on the banner page. If you do not include this parameter, the name of the file being printed appears on the banner page.

{-o l -o l}····Specifies the type of file that you want to print. The parameter -o specifies that you want to print a text file. The parameter -o l specifies that you want to print a binary file (for example, a PostScript file).

-d ··············Specifies that the data file must be sent before the control file. Use this parameter if your printer requires the data file to be sent first. For more information, see your printer documentation.

-x ··············Specifies that the lpr command must be compatible with the Sun Microsystems operating system referred to as SunOS for releases up to and including 4.1.4_u1.

FileName ··Required. Specifies, by name, the file to be printed.

Notes:

• To find the name of the printer, open the Printers and Faxes folder. To open Printers and Faxes, click Start, click Control Panel, click Printers and Other Hardware, and then click Printers and Faxes.

MACFILE

Use the macfile commands at the command prompt to manage File Server for Macintosh servers, volumes, directories, and files. You can automate administrative tasks by including a series of commands in batch files and starting them manually or at predetermined times.

To modify directories in Macintosh-accessible volumes

Syntax:

macfile directory [/server:\\ComputerName] /path:Directory [/owner:OwnerName] [/group:GroupName] [/permissions:Permissions]

Examples:

macfile directory /path:"e:\statistics\may sales" /permissions:11111011000

Syntax Options:

/server:\\ComputerName Specifies the server on which to change a directory. If omitted, the operation is performed on the local computer.

/path:Directory ·············Required. Specifies the path to the directory that you want to change. The directory must exist. Macfile directory does not create directories.

/owner:OwnerName·······Changes the owner of the directory. If omitted, the owner remains unchanged.

/group:GroupName········Specifies or changes the Macintosh primary group that is associated with the directory. If omitted, the primary group remains unchanged.

/permissions:Permissions ····················Sets permissions on the directory for the owner, primary group, and world (everyone). An 11-digit number is used to set permissions. The number 1 grants permission and 0 revokes permission (for example, 11111011000). The position of the digit determines which permission is set, as described in the following table. If omitted, permissions remain unchanged.

Position	Sets Permission for
First	OwnerSeeFiles
Second	OwnerSeeFolders
Third	OwnerMakeChanges
Fourth	GroupSeeFiles
Fifth	GroupSeeFolders
Sixth	GroupMakeChanges
Seventh	WorldSeeFiles
Eighth	WorldSeeFolders
Ninth	WorldMakeChanges
Tenth	The directory cannot be renamed, moved, or deleted.
Eleventh	The changes apply to the current directory and all subdirectories.

Notes:

• If the information that you supply contains spaces or special characters, use quotation marks around the text (for example, "Computer Name").

• Use macfile directory to make an existing directory in a Macintosh-accessible volume available to Macintosh users. The macfile directory command does not create directories. Use File Manager, the command prompt, or the macintosh new folder command to create a directory in a Macintosh-accessible volume before you use the macfile directory command. To join a Macintosh file's data and resource forks

Syntax:

macfile forkize [/server:\\ComputerName] [/creator:CreatorName] [/type:TypeName] [/datafork:FilePath] [/resourcefork:FilePath] /targetfile:FilePath

Examples:

macfile forkize /resourcefork:c:\cross\mac\appcode /type:APPL /creator:MAGNOLIA /targetfile:D:\Release\Treeapp

Syntax Options:

/server:\\ComputerName Specifies the server on which to join files. If omitted, the operation is performed on the local computer.

/creator:CreatorName ·····Specifies the creator of the file. The Macintosh Finder uses the /creator command-line option to determine the application that created the file.

/type:TypeName ············Specifies the type of file. The Macintosh Finder uses the /type command-line option to determine the file type within the application that created the file.

/datafork:FilePath ··········Specifies the location of the data fork that is to be joined. You can specify a remote path.

/resourcefork:FilePath·····Specifies the location of the resource fork that is to be joined. You can specify a remote path.

/targetfile:FilePath···········Required. Specifies the location of the file that is created by joining a data fork and a resource fork, or specifies the location of the file whose type or creator you are changing. The file must be on the specified server.

Notes:

• If the information that you supply contains spaces or special characters, use quotation marks around the text (for example, "Computer Name").

To change the logon message and limit sessions

Syntax:

macfile server [/server:\\ComputerName] [/maxsessions:{Number | unlimited}] [/loginmessage:Message]

Examples:

macfile server /maxsessions:5 /loginmessage:"Log off from Server for Macintosh when you are finished."

Syntax Options:

/server:\\ComputerName Specifies the server on which to change parameters. If omitted, the operation is performed on the local computer.

/maxsessions:{Number | unlimited}·······Specifies the maximum number of users who can simultaneously use File and Print Servers for Macintosh. If omitted, the maxsessions setting for the server remains unchanged.

/loginmessage:Message ·Changes the message Macintosh users see when logging on to the File Server for Macintosh server. The maximum number of characters for the logon message is 199. If omitted, the loginmessage message for the server remains unchanged. To remove an existing logon message, include the /loginmessage parameter, but leave the Message variable blank

Notes:

• If the information that you supply contains spaces or special characters, use quotation marks around the text (for example, "Computer Name").

To add, change, or remove Macintosh-accessible volumes

Syntax:

macfile volume {/add | /set} [/server:\\ComputerName] /name:VolumeName /path:Directory [/readonly:{true | false}] [/guestsallowed:{true | false}] [/password:Password] [/maxusers:{Number | unlimited}]

macfile volume /remove [/server:\\ComputerName] /name:VolumeName

Examples:
   macfile volume /add /name:"US Marketing Statistics" /guestsallowed:false /path:e:\Stats

Syntax Options:

{/add | /set}·················Required when you are adding or changing a
   Macintosh-accesible volume. Adds or changes the specified volume.

/server:\\ComputerName Specifies the server on which to add, change, or remove a volume. If omitted, the operation is performed on the local computer.

/name:VolumeName······Required. Specifies the volume name to be added, changed, or
   removed.

/path:Directory ···············Required and valid only when you are adding a volume. Specifies the path to the root directory of the volume to be added.

/readonly:{true | false}·····Specifies whether users can change files in the volume. Type
   true to specify that users cannot change files in the volume. Type false to specify that
   users can change files in the volume. If omitted when adding a volume, changes to
   files are allowed. If omitted when changing a volume, the readonly setting for the volume remains unchanged.

/guestsallowed:{true | false} ··················Specifies whether users who log on as guests can
   use the volume. Type true to specify that guests can use the volume. Type false to specify that guests cannot use the volume. If omitted when adding a volume, guests
   can use the volume. If omitted when changing a volume, the guestsallowed setting for
   the volume remains unchanged.

/password:Password·······Specifies a password that will be required to access the volume.
   If omitted when adding a volume, no password is created. If omitted when changing a
   volume, the password remains unchanged.

/maxusers:{Number | unlimited}············Specifies the maximum number of users who can
   simultaneously use the files on the volume. If omitted when adding a volume, an unlimited number of users can use the volume. If omitted when changing a volume, the
   maxusers value remains unchanged.

/remove ····Required when you are removing a Macintosh-accesible volume. Removes
   the specified volume.

Notes:

• If the information that you supply contains spaces or special characters, use quotation
marks around the text (for example, "Computer Name").

MKDIR

Creates a directory or subdirectory.

Syntax:

   mkdir [Drive:]Path

   md [Drive:]Path

Examples:

   mkdir \Taxes\Property\Current *or* mkdir \Taxes *or* mkdir Property *or* mkdir Current

Syntax Options:

   Drive: ·······Specifies the drive on which you want to create the new directory.

   Path ··········Required. Specifies the name and location of the new directory. The maximum
   length of any single path is determined by the file system.

Notes:

• When you enable command extensions (that is, the default), you can use a single
mkdir command to create intermediate directories in a specified path.

MMC

Opens Microsoft Management Console (MMC). Using the mmc command-line options, you
can open a specific MMC console, open MMC in author mode, or specify that the 32-bit or
64-bit version of MMC is opened..

Syntax:

   mmc Path\filename.msc [/a] [/64] [/32]

Syntax Options:

Path\filename.msc ·········Starts MMC and opens a saved console. You need to specify the complete path and file name for the saved console file. If you do not specify a console file, MMC opens a new console.

/a ··············Opens a saved console in author mode. Used to make changes to saved consoles.

/64 ···········Opens the 64-bit version of MMC (MMC64). Use this option only if you are running Windows XP 64-Bit Edition.

/32 ···········Opens the 32-bit version of MMC (MMC32). When running Windows XP 64-Bit Edition, you can run 32-bit snap-ins by opening MMC with this command-line option.

Notes:

• Using the Path\filename.msc command-line option

• You can use environment variables to create command lines or shortcuts that do not depend on the explicit location of console files. For instance, if the path to a console file is in the system folder (for example, mmc c:\winnt\system32\console_name.msc), you can use the expandable data string %systemroot% to specify the location (mmc %systemroot%\system32\console_name.msc). This can be useful when you need to delegate tasks to people in your organization who are working on different computers.

• Using the /a command-line option

• When consoles are opened with this option, they are opened in author mode, regardless of their default mode. This does not permanently change the default mode setting for files. When you omit this option, MMC opens console files according to their default mode settings.

• After you open MMC or a console file in author mode, you can open any existing console by clicking Open on the Console menu.

• You can use the command line to create shortcuts for opening MMC and saved consoles. A command-line command works with the Run command on the Start menu, in any command-prompt window, in shortcuts, or in any batch file or program that calls the command.

MODE

Displays system status, changes system settings, or reconfigures ports or devices. To configure a serial communications port

Syntax:

mode comm[:] [baud=b] [parity=p] [data=d] [stop=s] [to={on|off}] [xon={on|off}]
[odsr={on|off}] [octs={on|off}] [dtr={on|off|hs}] [rts={on|off|hs|tg}] [idsr={on|off}]

Syntax Options:

Used without parameters, mode displays all the controllable attributes of the console and the available COM devices. Because you can use mode to perform many different tasks, the syntax you need to use to carry out each task is different.

comm[:]····Specifies the number of the asynchronous-communications (COM) port.

baud=b ·····Specifies the transmission rate in bits per second. The following table lists valid abbreviations for b and its related rate.

Value	Rate
11	110 baud
15	150 baud
30	300 baud
60	600 baud
12	1200 baud
24	2400 baud
48	4800 baud
96	9600 baud
19	19,200 baud

parity=p ····Specifies how the system uses the parity bit to check for transmission errors. The following table lists valid p values. The default value is e. Not all computers support the values m and s.

Value	Description
n	none
e	even
o	odd
m	mark
s	space

data=d ······Specifies the number of data bits in a character. Valid values for d are in the range 5 through 8. The default value is 7. Not all computers support the values 5 and 6.

stop=s ·······Specifies the number of stop bits that define the end of a character: 1, 1.5, or 2. If the baud rate is 110, the default value is 2. Otherwise, the default value is 1. Not all computers support the value 1.5.

to={on|off}·Specifies whether infinite time-out processing is on or off. The default is off.

xon={on|off} ····················Specifies whether the xon or xoff protocol for data-flow control is on or off.

odsr={on|off} ··················Specifies whether output handshaking that uses the Data Set Ready (DSR) circuit is on or off.

octs={on|off}··················Specifies whether output handshaking that uses the Clear To Send (CTS) circuit is on or off.

dtr={on|off|hs} ···············Specifies whether the Data Terminal Ready (DTR) circuit is on or off, or set to handshake.

rts={on|off|hs|tg}············Specifies whether the Request To Send (RTS) circuit is set to on, off, handshake, or toggle.

idsr={on|off} ··················Specifies whether the DSR circuit sensitivity is on or off.

To display the status of all devices or of a single device

Syntax

mode [device] [/status]

Syntax Options:

device·······Specifies the name of the device for which you want to display the status.

/status·······Requests the status of any redirected parallel printers. You can abbreviate the /status command-line option as /sta.

Notes:

• Used without parameters, mode displays the status of all devices installed on your system.

To redirect output from a parallel port to a serial communications port

Syntax

mode lptn[:]=comm[:]

Examples:

To set up your system so that it sends parallel-printer output to a serial printer, you must use the mode command twice. The first time, use mode to configure the serial port. The second time, use mode to redirect parallel-printer output to the serial port you specified in the first mode command.

For example, if your serial printer operates at 4800 baud with even parity and is connected to the COM1 port (the first serial connection on your computer), type:

mode com1 48,e,,,b
mode lpt1=com1

If you redirect parallel-printer output from LPT1 to COM1 but then decide that you want to print a file by using LPT1, type the following command before you print the file:

mode lpt1

This command prevents the redirection the file from LPT1 to COM1.

Syntax Options:

lptn············Required. Specifies the parallel port. Valid values for n are in the range 1 through 3.

comm [:]····Required. Specifies the serial port. Valid values for m are in the range 1 through 4.

Notes:

- You must be a member of the Administrators group to redirect printing.

To select, refresh, or display the numbers of the code pages for the console

Syntax

mode device codepage select=yyy

mode device codepage [/status]

Syntax Options:

device ······· Required. Specifies the device for which you want to select a code page. CON is the only valid name for a device.

codepage select= ··········Required. Specifies which code page to use with the specified device. You can abbreviate codepage and select as cp and sel, respectively.

yyy ············Required. Specifies the number of the code page to select. The following table lists each code page supported and its Country/Region or language.

Value	Country/Region
437	United States
850	Multilingual (Latin I)
852	Slavic (Latin II)
855	Cyrillic (Russian)
857	Turkish
860	Portuguese
861	Icelandic
863	Canadian-French
865	Nordic
866	Russian
869	Modern Greek

codepage··Required. Displays the numbers of the code pages, if any, that are selected for the specified device.

/status······Displays the numbers of the current code pages selected for the specified device. You can abbreviate /status to /sta. Whether or not you specify /status, mode codepage displays the numbers of the code pages that are selected for the specified device.

To change the size of the command prompt screen buffer

Syntax

mode con[:] [cols=c] [lines=n]

Syntax Options:

con[:]········Required. Indicates that the change is to the command prompt window.

cols=c ·······Specifies the number of characters (columns) wide in the command prompt screen buffer.

lines=n ······Specifies the number of lines deep in the command prompt screen buffer.

To set the keyboard typematic rate

Syntax

mode con[:] [rate=r delay=d]

Syntax Options:

con[:]········Required. Refers to the keyboard.

rate=r·······Specifies the rate at which a character is repeated on the screen when you hold down a key.

delay=d·····Specifies the amount of time that must elapse, after you press and hold down a key, before the character output starts to repeat.

Notes:

• The typematic rate is the rate at which a character repeats when you hold down the key for that character. The typematic rate has two components, the rate and the delay. Some keyboards do not recognize this command.

• Using rate=r : Valid values are in the range 1 through 32. These values are equal to approximately 2 to 30 characters per second, respectively. The default value is 20 for IBM AT-compatible keyboards, and 21 for IBM PS/2-compatible keyboards. If you set the rate, you must also set the delay.

• Using delay=d : Valid values for d are 1, 2, 3, and 4 (representing 0.25, 0.50, 0.75, and 1 second, respectively). The default value is 2. If you set the delay, you must also set the rate.

MORE

Displays one screen of output at a time.

Syntax:

command | more [/c] [/p] [/s] [/tn] [+n]

more [[/c] [/p] [/s] [/tn] [+n]] < [Drive:] [Path] FileName

more [/c] [/p] [/s] [/tn] [+n] [files]

Examples:

To view the file named Clients.new that you want to view on your screen, type either of the following two commands:

more < clients.new

type clients.new | more

The more command displays the first screen of information from Clients.new, and then the following prompt appears:

— More —

You can then press the SPACEBAR to see the next screen of information.

To clear the screen and remove all extra blank lines before displaying the file Clients.new, type either of the following two commands:

more /c /s < clients.new

type clients.new | more /c /s

The more command displays the first screen of information from Clients.new, and then the following prompt appears:

— More —

To display the file one line at a time, press ENTER.

To display the next page, press the SPACEBAR.

To display the next file listed on the command line, type f.

To quit more, type q.

Add commands to the more prompt as shown in this example:

— More [Options: psfq=<space><ret>] —

To display the current line number, type =. The current line number is added to the more prompt as shown in this example:

— More [Line: 24] —

To display a specific number of lines, type p. More prompts you for the number of lines to display as follows:

— More — Lines:

Type the number of lines to display and press ENTER. More displays the specified number of lines.

To skip a specific number of lines, type s. More prompts you for the number of lines to skip as follows:

— More — Lines:

Type the number of lines to skip, and then press ENTER. More skips the specified number of lines and displays the next screen of information.

Syntax Options:

[Drive:] [Path] FileName ·Specifies the file to display.

command··Specifies a command for which you want to display the output.

/c················Clears screen before displaying page.

/p ···············Expands form-feed characters.

/s···············Changes multiple blank lines to one blank line.

/tn ·············Changes tabs to the number of spaces specified by n.

+n ·············Displays first file beginning at the line specified by n.

files·········Specifies list of files to display. Separate file names with a space.

Notes:

• The more command, with different parameters, is available from the Recovery Console.

• The following commands are accepted at the more prompt (— More —).

Key	Action
SPACEBAR	Display next page
ENTER	Display next line
f	Display next file
q	Quit
?	Show available commands
=	Show line number
p n	Display next n lines
s n	Skip next n lines

• When using the redirection character (<), you must specify a file name as the source. When using the pipe (|), you can use such commands as dir, sort, and type.

MOUNTVOL

Creates, deletes, or lists a volume mount point. Mountvol is a way to link volumes without requiring a drive letter.

Syntax:

mountvol [Drive:]Path VolumeName

mountvol [Drive:]Path /d

mountvol [Drive:]Path /L

mountvol Drive: /s

Syntax Options:

[Drive:]Path···········Specifies the existing NTFS directory folder where the mount point will reside.

VolumeName···········Specifies the volume name that is the target of the mount point. The volume name is of the form \\?\Volume{GUID}\, where {GUID} is a globally unique identifier (GUID) (for example, \\?\Volume\{2eca078d-5cbc-43d3-aff8-7e8511f60d0e}\).

/d ···········Removes the volume mount point from the specified folder.

/L ···········Lists the mounted volume name for the specified folder.

/s ···········Itanium-based computers only. Mounts the EFI System Partition on the specified drive.

Notes:

• If you are running out of drive letters to use, mount your local volumes with no drive letters.

• If you need to expand your volume space without reformatting or replacing a hard drive, you can add a mount path to another volume.

• The benefit is that if you use one volume with several mount paths, you can access all local volumes using a single drive letter (such as C:). You need not remember which volume corresponds to which drive letter, although you can mount local volumes and still have them assigned to drive letters.

MOVE

Moves one or more files from one directory to the specified directory.

Syntax:

move [{/yl/-y}] [Source] [target]

Examples:

move \data*.xls \second_q\reports\

Syntax Options:

/y···········Suppresses prompting to confirm you want to overwrite an existing destination file.

/-y ············Causes prompting to confirm you want to overwrite an existing destination file.

Source ·····Specifies the path and name of the file or files to move. If you want to move or rename a directory, Source should be the current directory path and name.

target ·······Specifies the path and name to move files to. If you want to move or rename a directory, target should be the desired directory path and name.

Notes:

• The /y command-line option might be preset in the COPYCMD environment variable. You can override this with /-y on the command line. The default is to prompt on overwrites unless the copy command is being executed from within a batch script.

• Moving encrypted files to a volume that does not support Encrypting File System (EFS) results in an error. Decrypt the files first or move the files to a volume that does support EFS.

MSCONFIG

View or change the programs that start when Windows boots up. External Command in Windows XP only; execute this program from Start-Run, NOT from the Command Window. MSCONFIG is a very powerful troubleshooting tool and will be explained in more detail in the Troubleshooting Chapter.

Syntax:
  MSCONFIG
Examples:
  MSCONFIG
Syntax Options:
  None

MSIEXEC

Provides the means to install, modify, and perform operations on Windows Installer from the command line.

To install or configure a product
Syntax:
  msiexec /i {package|ProductCode}
Examples:
  msiexec /i A:\Example.msi
Syntax Options:
  /i·················Installs or configures a product.
  package····Specifies the name of the Windows Installer package file.
  ProductCode··················Specifies the globally unique identifier (GUID) of the Windows Installer package.
Notes:
  • Windows Installer command-line options are not case-sensitive.

To use the administrative installation option
Syntax:
  msiexec /a package
Syntax Options:
  /a ·············Applies the administrative installation option.
  package····The name of the Windows Installer package file.

To repair a product
Syntax:
  msiexec /f [p][o][e][d][c][a][u][m][s][v]{package|ProductCode}
Examples:
  msiexec /fpecms Example.msi
Syntax Options:
  /f ·············Enables one or more of the command-line options listed in the following table.

Command	Description
p	Reinstalls only if file is missing.
o	Reinstalls if file is missing or if an older version is installed.
e	Reinstalls if file is missing or an equal or older version is installed.
d	Reinstalls if file is missing or a different version is installed.
c	Reinstalls if file is missing or the stored checksum does not match the calculated value.
a	Forces all files to be reinstalled.
u	Rewrite all required user-specific registry entries.
m	Rewrites all required computer-specific registry entries.
s	Overwrites all existing shortcuts.
v	Runs from source and re-caches the local package.
package	Name of the Windows Installer package file.
ProductCode	Globally unique identifier (GUID) of the Windows Installer package.

Notes:

- This option ignores any property values that you type at the command line.
- The default parameter for this command-line option is /fpecms.

To uninstall a product

Syntax

msiexec /x {package|ProductCode}

Examples:

msiexec /x Example.msi

Syntax Options:

/x·············uninstalls a product.

package····Name of the Windows Installer package file.

ProductCode··················Globally unique identifier (GUID) of the Windows Installer package.

To advertise a product

Syntax:

msiexec /j [{ulm}] package

msiexec {ulm} package /t TransformList

msiexec {ulm} package /g LanguageID

Examples:

msiexec /jm Example.msi *or* msiexec /jm Example.msi

Syntax Options:

/j···············Advertises a product.

u ···············Advertises to the current user.

m ···············Advertises to all users of the computer.

package····Specifies the Windows Installer package file.

/g LanguageID ···············Identifies the language.

/t TransformList···············Applies transform to advertised package.

Notes:

- This option ignores any property values that you type at the command line.
- If you want to install the application with elevated privileges, use /jm.

To set logging level

Syntax:

msiexec /L [i][w][e][a][r][u][c][m][p][v][+][!]LogFile.txt

Examples:

msiexec /i Example.msi /Lime logfile.txt

Syntax Options:

/L ···············Specifies the path to the log file.

i ·············Logs status messages.

w ·············Logs nonfatal warnings.

e ·············Logs all error messages.

a ·············Logs startup of actions.

r ·············Logs action-specific records.

u ·············Logs user requests.

c ·············Logs initial user interface parameters.

m ·············Logs out-of-memory.

p ·············Logs terminal properties.

v ·············Logs verbose output. To use v, specify /L*v.

+ ·············Appends to existing file.

! ·············Flushes each line to the log.

* ·············Logs all information except for the v option. This is a wildcard.

LogFile.txt·Name and path of the text log file.

Notes:
• To include the v option in a log file using the wildcard flag, type /L*v at the command prompt.

• The Windows Installer log file options can also be used with the uninstall and repair processes.

To apply a patch

Syntax:
msiexec /p PatchPackage

Syntax Options:
/p ·············Applies a patch.

PatchPackage ·············Specific patch.

Notes:
• To apply a patch to an administrative installation package, use:
msiexec /p PatchPackage /a Example.msi

To install a transform using the command line

Syntax:
msiexec /i packageTRANSFORMS=TransformList

Syntax Options:
/i·············Installs or configures a product.

package····Specifies the Windows Installer package file.

TRANSFORMS= ·············Property that is used to specify what transform (.mst) files should be applied to the package.

TransformList·············List of paths separated by semicolons.

To advertise a product using a transform with the command line

Syntax:
msiexec /j[u][m] package /t TransformList

Syntax Options:
/j·············Advertises a product. This option ignores any property values entered on the command line.

u ·············Advertises to the current user.

m ·············Advertises to all users of this computer.

package····Name of the Windows Installer package file.

/t ·············Applies transform to advertised package.

TransformList·············List of paths separated by semicolons.

To set the user interface level

Syntax:

msiexec /q{n|b|r|f|n+|b+|b-}

Examples:

msiexec /qb Example.msi

Syntax Options:

/qn ···········Displays no user interface.

/qb ···········Displays a basic user interface.

/qr ···········Displays a reduced user interface with a modal dialog box displayed at the end of the installation.

/qf ···········Displays the full user interface with a modal dialog box displayed at the end.

/qn+ ·········Displays no user interface, except for a modal dialog box displayed at the end.

/qb+ ·········Displays a basic user interface with a modal dialog box displayed at the end.

/qb- ·········Displays a basic user interface with no modal dialog boxes.

Notes:

• /qb+- is not a supported user interface level. The modal box is not displayed if the user cancels the installation.

• Windows Installer command-line options are not case-sensitive.

To display copyright information for the Windows Installer

Syntax:

msiexec {/?|/h}

Syntax Options:

{/?|/h} ·······Displays the Windows Installer version and copyright information.

To call the system API DllRegisterServer to self-register modules passed on the command line

Syntax:

msiexec /y module

Examples:

msiexec /y my_file.dll

Syntax Options:

/y···············Calls the system API DllRegisterServer to self-register modules passed on the command line.

module······Specifies the file name of module.

Notes:

• This option is used only for registry information that cannot be added using the registry tables of the .msi file.

To call the system API DllUnRegisterServer to unregister modules passed on the command line

Syntax:

msiexec /z module

Examples:

msiexec /z my_file.dll

Syntax Options:

/z···············Calls the system API DllUnRegisterServer to unregister modules passed on the command line.

module······File name of module.

Notes:

• This option is used only for registry information that cannot be added using the registry tables of the .msi file.

MSINFO32

Displays a comprehensive view of your hardware, system components, and software environment.

Syntax:

msinfo32 [/?] [/pch] [/nfo FileName] [/report FileName] [/computer ComputerName] [/showcategories] [/category categoryID] [/categories categoryID]

Examples:

msinfo32 /showcategories or msinfo32 /categories +all -loadedmodules

Syntax Options:

FileName ··Specifies the file to be opened. This can be an .nfo, .xml, .txt, or .cab file.

/pch··········Displays the history view.

/nfo FileName ················Saves the exported file as an .nfo file.

/report FileName ············Saves the exported file as a .txt file.

/computer ComputerName····················Starts System Information for the specified remote computer.

/showcategories··············Starts System Information with all available category IDs displayed.

/category categoryID·······Starts System Information with the specified category selected. Use /showcategories to display a list of available category IDs.

/categories categoryID····Starts System Information with only the specified category or categories displayed. It also limits the output to the selected category or categories. Use /showcategories to display a list of available category IDs.

Notes:

• Some System Information categories contain large amounts of data. You can use the start /wait command to optimize reporting performance for these categories.

NBTSTAT

Displays NetBIOS over TCP/IP (NetBT) protocol statistics, NetBIOS name tables for both the local computer and remote computers, and the NetBIOS name cache. Nbtstat allows a refresh of the NetBIOS name cache and the names registered with Windows Internet Name Service (WINS).

Syntax:

nbtstat [-a RemoteName] [-A IPAddress] [-c] [-n] [-r] [-R] [-RR] [-s] [-S] [Interval]

Examples:

nbtstat -a CORP07 or nbtstat -A 10.0.0.99 or nbtstat -n or nbtstat -c or nbtstat -R

Syntax Options:

Used without parameters, nbtstat displays help.

-a RemoteName ·············Displays the NetBIOS name table of a remote computer, where RemoteName is the NetBIOS computer name of the remote computer. The NetBIOS name table is the list of NetBIOS names that corresponds to NetBIOS applications running on that computer.

-A IPAddress ·················Displays the NetBIOS name table of a remote computer, specified by the IP address (in dotted decimal notation) of the remote computer.

-c ··············Displays the contents of the NetBIOS name cache, the table of NetBIOS names and their resolved IP addresses.

-n ··············Displays the NetBIOS name table of the local computer. The status of Registered indicates that the name is registered either by broadcast or with a WINS server.

-r ···············Displays NetBIOS name resolution statistics. On a Windows XP computer that is configured to use WINS, this parameter returns the number of names that have been resolved and registered using broadcast and WINS.

-R··············Purges the contents of the NetBIOS name cache and then reloads the #PRE-tagged entries from the Lmhosts file.

-RR·············Releases and then refreshes NetBIOS names for the local computer that is registered with WINS servers.

-s ··············Displays NetBIOS client and server sessions, attempting to convert the destination IP address to a name.

-S ·············· Displays NetBIOS client and server sessions, listing the remote computers by destination IP address only.

Interval ······ Redisplays selected statistics, pausing the number of seconds specified in Interval between each display. Press CTRL+C to stop redisplaying statistics. If this parameter is omitted, nbtstat prints the current configuration information only once.

Notes:

• Nbtstat command-line parameters are case-sensitive.

• The following table describes the column headings that are generated by nbtstat.

Heading	Description
Input	The number of bytes received.
Output	The number of bytes sent.
In/Out	Whether the connection is from the computer (outbound) or from another computer to the local computer (inbound).
Life	The remaining time that a name table cache entry will live before it is purged.
Local Name	The local NetBIOS name associated with the connection.
Remote Host	The name or IP address associated with the remote computer.

• The last byte of a NetBIOS name converted to hexadecimal. Each NetBIOS name is 16 characters long. This last byte often has special significance because the same name might be present several times on a computer, differing only in the last byte. For example, is a space in ASCII text.

• Type ····· The type of name. A name can either be a unique name or a group name.

• Status ··· Whether the NetBIOS service on the remote computer is running (Registered) or a duplicate computer name has registered the same service (Conflict).

• State ····· The state of NetBIOS connections.

• The following table describes the possible NetBIOS connection states.

State	Description
Connected	A session has been established.
Associated	A connection endpoint has been created and associated with an IP address.
Listening	This endpoint is available for an inbound connection.
Idle	This endpoint has been opened but cannot receive connections.
Connecting	A session is in the connecting phase and the name-to-IP address mapping of the destination is being resolved.
Accepting	An inbound session is currently being accepted and will be connected shortly.
Reconnecting	A session is trying to reconnect (it failed to connect on the first attempt).
Outbound	A session is in the connecting phase and the TCP connection is currently being created.
Inbound	An inbound session is in the connecting phase.
Disconnecting	A session is in the process of disconnecting.
Disconnected	The local computer has issued a disconnect and it is waiting for confirmation from the remote system.

• This command is available only if the Internet Protocol (TCP/IP) protocol is installed as a component in the properties of a network adapter in Network Connections

NETSTAT

Displays active TCP connections, ports on which the computer is listening, Ethernet statistics, the IP routing table, IPv4 statistics (for the IP, ICMP, TCP, and UDP protocols), and IPv6 statistics (for the IPv6, ICMPv6, TCP over IPv6, and UDP over IPv6 protocols).

Syntax:

netstat [-a] [-e] [-n] [-o] [-p Protocol] [-r] [-s] [Interval]

Examples:
   netstat -e -s *or* netstat -s -p tcp udp *or* nbtstat -o 5 *or* nbtstat -n -o

Syntax Options:
   Used without parameters, netstat displays active TCP connections.

-a ·············Displays all active TCP connections and the TCP and UDP ports on which the computer is listening.

-e ·············Displays Ethernet statistics, such as the number of bytes and packets sent and received. This parameter can be combined with -s.

-n ·············Displays active TCP connections, however, addresses and port numbers are expressed numerically and no attempt is made to determine names.

-o ·············Displays active TCP connections and includes the process ID (PID) for each connection. You can find the application based on the PID on the Processes tab in Windows Task Manager. This parameter can be combined with -a, -n, and -p.

-p Protocol ·Shows connections for the protocol specified by Protocol. In this case, the Protocol can be tcp, udp, tcpv6, or udpv6. If this parameter is used with -s to display statistics by protocol, Protocol can be tcp, udp, icmp, ip, tcpv6, udpv6, icmpv6, or ipv6.

-s ·············Displays statistics by protocol. By default, statistics are shown for the TCP, UDP, ICMP, and IP protocols. If the IPv6 protocol for Windows XP is installed, statistics are shown for the TCP over IPv6, UDP over IPv6, ICMPv6, and IPv6 protocols. The -p parameter can be used to specify a set of protocols.

-r ·············Displays the contents of the IP routing table. This is equivalent to the route print command.

Interval······Redisplays the selected information every Interval seconds. Press CTRL+C to stop the redisplay. If this parameter is omitted, netstat prints the selected information only once.

Notes:
 • Parameters used with this command must be prefixed with a hyphen (-) rather than a slash (/).

 • Netstat provides statistics for the following:
Proto
The name of the protocol (TCP or UDP).
Local Address
The IP address of the local computer and the port number being used. The name of the local computer that corresponds to the IP address and the name of the port is shown unless the -n parameter is specified. If the port is not yet established, the port number is shown as an asterisk (*).
Foreign Address
The IP address and port number of the remote computer to which the socket is connected. The names that corresponds to the IP address and the port are shown unless the -n parameter is specified. If the port is not yet established, the port number is shown as an asterisk (*).

 • (state) Indicates the state of a TCP connection. The possible states are as follows:
CLOSE_WAIT
CLOSED
ESTABLISHED
FIN_WAIT_1
FIN_WAIT_2
LAST_ACK
LISTEN
SYN_RECEIVED
SYN_SEND
TIMED_WAIT

 • For more information about the states of a TCP connection, see RFC 793.

 • This command is available only if the Internet Protocol (TCP/IP) protocol is installed as a component in the properties of a network adapter in Network Connections

NSLOOKUP

Displays information that you can use to diagnose Domain Name System (DNS) infrastructure. Before using this tool, you should be familiar with how DNS works.

Syntax:

nslookup [-SubCommand ...] [{ComputerToFind| [-Server]}]

Examples:

nslookup -querytype=hinfo -timeout=10

Syntax Options:

The Nslookup command-line tool is available only if you have installed the TCP/IP protocol.

-SubCommand ... ···········Specifies one or more nslookup subcommands as a command-line option. For a list of subcommands, see Related Topics.

ComputerToFind···········Looks up information for ComputerToFind using the current default DNS name server, if no other server is specified. To look up a computer not in the current DNS domain, append a period to the name.

-Server······Specifies to use this server as the DNS name server. If you omit -Server, the default DNS name server is used.

{help|?} ·····Displays a short summary of nslookup subcommands.

Notes:

• If ComputerToFind is an IP address and the query is for an A or PTR resource record type, the name of the computer is returned. If ComputerToFind is a name and does not have a trailing period, the default DNS domain name is appended to the name. This behavior depends on the state of the following set subcommands: domain, srchlist, defname, and search.

• The command-line length must be less than 256 characters.

• Nslookup has two modes: interactive and noninteractive. If you need to look up only a single piece of data, use noninteractive mode. For the first parameter, type the name or IP address of the computer that you want to look up. For the second parameter, type the name or IP address of a DNS name server. If you omit the second argument, nslookup uses the default DNS name server.

• If you need to look up more than one piece of data, you can use interactive mode. Type a hyphen (-) for the first parameter and the name or IP address of a DNS name server for the second parameter. Or, omit both parameters and nslookup uses the default DNS name server. Following are some tips about working in interactive mode:

• To interrupt interactive commands at any time, press CTRL+B.

• To exit, type exit.

• To treat a built-in command as a computer name, precede it with the escape character (\).

• An unrecognized command is interpreted as a computer name.

• If the lookup request fails, nslookup prints an error message. The following table lists possible error messages.

Error message	Description
Timed out	The server did not respond to a request after a certain amount of time and a certain number of retries. You can set the time-out period with the set timeout subcommand. You can set the number of retries with the set retry subcommand.
No response from server	No DNS name server is running on the server computer.
No records	The DNS name server does not have resource records of the current query type for the computer, although the computer name is valid. The query type is specified with the set querytype command.
Nonexistent domain	The computer or DNS domain name does not exist.
Connection refused -or- Network is unreachable	The connection to the DNS name server or finger server could not be made. This error commonly occurs with ls and finger requests.
Server failure	The DNS name server found an internal inconsistency in its database and could not return a valid answer.
Refused	The DNS name server refused to service the request.
Format error	The DNS name server found that the request packet was not in the proper format. It may indicate an error in nslookup.

Perform backup operations at a command prompt or from a batch file using the ntbackup command followed by various parameters.

Syntax:

ntbackup backup [systemstate] "@bks file name"} [/J {"job name"}] [/P {"pool name"}] [/G {"guid name"}] [/T { "tape name"}] [/N {"media name"}] [/F {"file name"}] [/D {"set description"}] [/DS {"server name"}] [/IS {"server name"}] [/A] [/V:{yes|no}] [/R:{yes|no}] [/L:{f|s|n}] [/M {backup type}] [/RS:{yes|no}] [/HC:{on|off}] [/SNAP:{on|off}]

Examples:

Example 1

The following example performs a normal backup named "My Job 1" of the remote share \\iggy-multi\c$. This example pulls a tape from the Backup media pool, and name the tape "Command Line Backup 1." The description of the backup job is "Command Line Functionality." The backup is verified after the backup job is complete, access is not restricted to the owner/administrator, the logging level is set to summary only, Remote Storage data is not backed up, and hardware compression is enabled.
ntbackup backup \\iggy-multi\c$ /m normal /j "My Job 1" /p "Backup" /n "Command Line Backup 1" /d "Command Line Functionality" /v:yes /r:no /l:s /rs:no /hc:on

Example 2

The following example performs a copy backup named "My Job 2" of the local drive D:\. The backed up files and folders are appended to the tape named "Command Line Backup 1." All other options default to those specified in the Backup program.
ntbackup backup d:\ /j "My Job 2" /a /t "Command Line Backup 1" /m copy

Example 3

The following example performs a backup using the backup type that is specified in the Backup program. It uses the backup selection file named Commandline.bks, located in the C:\Program Files\Windows NT\ntbackup\data\ directory to choose which files to backup. The backup job is named "My Job 3" and it overwrites the tape named "Command Line Backup 1" with the new name "Command Line Backup 2."
ntbackup backup "@C:\Program Files\Windows NT\ntbackup\data\commandline.bks" /j "My Job 3" /t "Command Line Backup 1" /n "Command Line Backup 2"

Example 4

The following examples show how to perform a backup to a file from the command line. All three examples use the Backup program's default values for the backup type, verification setting, logging level, hardware compression, and any other restrictions. The first example shows how to backup \\iggy-multi\d$ to the file D:\Backup.bkf. The second example shows how to append the same backup to the same file. The third example shows how to overwrite the file with the same backup. In all three examples a complete UNC name could be substituted for the drive letter (that is, instead of d:\backup.bkf, the user could specify \\iggy-multi\d$\backup.bkf as the backup destination).
ntbackup backup \\iggy-multi\d$ /j "Command Line Backup 4" /f "D:\backup.bkf"
ntbackup backup \\iggy-multi\d$ /j "Command Line Backup 5" /f "D:\backup.bkf" /a
ntbackup backup \\iggy-multi\d$ /j "Command Line Backup 6" /f "D:\backup.bkf" /a

Syntax Options:

systemstate··············Specifies that you want to back up the System State data. When you select this option, the backup type will be forced to normal or copy

@bks file name·············Specifies the name of the backup selection file (.bks file) to be used for this backup operation. The at (@) character must precede the name of the backup selection file. A backup selection file contains information on the files and folders you have selected for backup. You have to create the file using the graphical user interface (GUI) version of Backup.

/J {"job name"}·············Specifies the job name to be used in the log file The job name usually describes the files and folders you are backing up in the current backup job as well as the date and time you backed up the files.

/P {"pool name"}···········Specifies the media pool from which you want to use media. This is usually a subpool of the Backup media pool, such as 4mm DDS. If you select this you cannot use the /A, /G, /F, or /T command-line options.

/G {"guid name"}···········Overwrites or appends to this tape. Do not use this switch in conjunction with /P.

/T {"tape name"}···········Overwrites or appends to this tape. Do not use this switch in conjunction with /P.

/N {"media name"} ·········Specifies the new tape name. You must not use /A with this switch.

/F {"file name"} ···········Logical disk path and file name. You must not use the following switches with this switch: /P /G /T.

/D {"set description"} ······Specifies a label for each backup set

/DS {"server name"}·······Backs up the directory service file for the specified Microsoft Exchange Server.

/IS {"server name"}·········Backs up the Information Store file for the specified Microsoft Exchange Server.

/A ··············Performs an append operation. Either /G or /T must be used in conjunction with this switch. Do not use this switch in conjunction with /P.

/V:{yes|no} Verifies the data after the backup is complete.

/R:{yes|no} Restricts access to this tape to the owner or members of the Administrators group

/L:{f|s|n} ····Specifies the type of log file: f=full, s=summary, n=none (no log file is created).

/M {backup type} ···········Specifies the backup type. It must be one of the following: normal, copy, differential, incremental, or daily

/RS:{yes|no}···············Backs up the migrated data files located in Remote Storage. The /RS command-line option is not required to back up the local Removable Storage database (that contains the Remote Storage placeholder files). When you backup the %systemroot% folder, Backup automatically backs up the Removable Storage database as well.

/HC:{on|off} ··············Uses hardware compression, if available, on the tape drive.

/SNAP:{on|off}·············Specifies whether or not the backup is a volume shadow copy

/M {backup type} ···········Specifies the backup type. It must be one of the following: normal, copy, differential, incremental, or daily

Notes:

• You cannot restore files from the command line using the ntbackup command.

• The following command-line options default to what you have already set using the graphical user interface (GUI) version of Backup unless they are changed by a command-line option: /V /R /L /M /RS /HC. For example, if hardware compression is turned on in the Options dialog box in Backup, it will be used if /HC is not specified on the command line. However, if you specify /HC:off at the command line, it overrides the Option dialog box setting and compression is not used.

• If you have Windows Media Services running on your computer, and you want to back up the files associated with these services, see "Running Backup with Windows Media Services" in the Windows Media Services online documentation. You must follow the procedures outlined in the Windows Media Services online documentation before you can back up or restore files associated with Windows Media Services.

• You can only back up the System State data on a local computer You cannot back up the System State data on a remote computer

• If you are using Removable Storage to manage media, or you are using the Remote Storage to store data, then you should regularly back up the files that are in the following folders:

• Systemroot\System32\Ntmsdata

• Systemroot\System32\Remotestorage

• This ensures that all Removable Storage and Remote Storage data can be restored.

NTCMDPROMPT

Runs the command interpreter Cmd.exe, rather than Command.com, after running a TSR or after starting the command prompt from within an MS-DOS application.

Syntax:

ntcmdprompt

Examples:

ntcmdprompt

Notes:

• When Command.com is running, some features of Cmd.exe, such as the doskey display of command history, are not available. If you would prefer to run the Cmd.exe command interpreter after you have started a TSR or started the command prompt from within an application based on MS-DOS, you can use the ntcmdprompt command. However, keep in mind that the TSR may not be available for use when you are running Cmd.exe. You can include the ntcmdprompt command in your Config.nt file or the equivalent custom startup file in an application's program information file (PIF).

NTSD

Ntsd is included as a courtesy to software developers. Only system developers should use this command. For more information, see the help file included with NTSD.

OPENFILES

Queries or displays open files. Also queries, displays, or disconnects files opened by network users. "openfiles disconnect" Disconnects one or more remote users connected to open shared files.

Syntax:

openfiles.exe /disconnect [/s Computer [/u Domain\User [/p Password]]] {[/id OpenFileID]|[/a UserName]|[/o OpenMode]} [/se SessionName] [/op OpenFile Name]

Syntax Options:

/s Computer ·················· Specifies the name or IP address of a remote computer. (Do not use backslashes.) The default is the local computer.

/u Domain\User ·············· Runs the command with the account permissions of the user specified by User or Domain\User. The default is the permissions of the current logged on user on the computer issuing the command.

/p Password ·················· Specifies the password of the user account that is specified in the /u parameter.

/id OpenFileID ·············· Disconnects the file opened with the specified numeric OpenFileID on the computer specified by the /s parameter. Use openfiles.exe /query to learn the file ID. The wildcard (*) can be used to disconnect all open files on the specified computer.

/a UserName ················· Disconnects all open files that were accessed by the specified user on the computer specified by the /s parameter. The wildcard (*) can be used to disconnect all open files on the specified computer.

/o OpenMode ················ Disconnects all open files with the specified OpenMode on the computer specified by the /s parameter. The OpenMode parameter includes the Read/Write and Read modes. The wildcard (*) can be used to disconnect all open files on the specified computer.

/se SessionName ·········· Disconnects all open files that were created by the specified session on the computer specified by the /s parameter. The wildcard (*) can be used to disconnect all open files on the specified computer.

/op OpenFileName ········ Disconnects the open file that was created with the specified OpenFileName on the computer specified by the /s parameter. The wildcard (*) can be used to disconnect all open files on the specified computer.

Examples:

openfiles.exe /disconnect /id 1   or   openfiles.exe /disconnect /a

openfiles query

Queries and displays all open files.

Syntax:

openfiles.exe /query [/s Computer [/u Domain\User [/p Password]]] [/fo {TABLE | LIST | CSV}] [/nh] [/v]

Examples:

openfiles.exe /query *or* openfiles.exe /query /fo table /nh *or* openfiles.exe /query /fo list /v

Syntax Options:

/s Computer ·················Specifies the name or IP address of a remote computer. (Do not use backslashes.) The default is the local computer.

/u Domain\User ···········Runs the command with the account permissions of the user specified by User or Domain\User. The default is the permissions of the current logged on user on the computer issuing the command.

/p Password ·················Specifies the password of the user account that is specified in the /u parameter.

/fo {TABLE | LIST | CSV} Specifies the format to use for the query output. Valid values are TABLE, LIST, and CSV. The default value for output is TABLE.

/nh ···········Suppresses column header in the output. Valid only when the /fo parameter is set to TABLE or CSV.

/v···············Specifies that verbose task information be displayed in the output.

PAGEFILECONFIG.VBS

Enables an administrator to display and configure a system's paging file Virtual Memory settings.

"pagefileconfig change" changes a system's existing paging file Virtual Memory settings.

Syntax:

pagefileconfig[.vbs] /change [/s Computer [/u Domain\User [/p Password]]] {[/i InitialPageFileSize]|[/m MaximumPageFileSize]} /vo {VolumeLetter|*} [/vo {VolumeLetter2|*} [...]]

Examples

pagefileconfig.vbs /change /m 400 /vo c: *or*

pagefileconfig.vbs /change /s srvmain /u maindom\hiropln /m 400 /vo c:

Syntax Options:

/s Computer ·················Specifies the name or IP address of a remote computer (do not use backslashes). The default is the local computer.

/u Domain\User ···········Runs the script with the account permissions of the user specified by User or Domain\User. The default is the permissions of the current logged on user on the computer issuing the command.

/p Password ·················Specifies the password of the user account that is specified in the /u parameter.

/i InitialPageFileSize ······Specifies the new initial size (in MB) to use for the paging file specified.

/m MaximumPageFileSize ···················Specifies the new maximum size (in MB) to use for the paging file specified.

/vo {VolumeLetter|*}·······Specifies the volume or volumes of the paging file settings to be changed. The volume is specified by a letter followed by a colon (for example, "C:").

pagefileconfig create

Creates or adds an additional paging file to a system.

Syntax:

pagefileconfig.vbs /create [/s Computer [/u Domain\User [/p Password]]] /i InitialPageFileSize /m MaximumPageFileSize /vo {VolumeLetter|*} [/vo {VolumeLetter2|*} [...]]

Examples:

pagefileconfig.vbs /create /i 140 /m 300 /vo d: or

pagefileconfig.vbs /create /s srvmain /u maindom\hiropln /i 150 /m 300 /vo d:

Syntax Options:

- **/s Computer**··············Specifies the name or IP address of a remote computer (do not use backslashes). The default is the local computer.
- **/u Domain\User**··············Runs the script with the account permissions of the user specified by User or Domain\User. The default is the permissions of the current logged on user on the computer issuing the command.
- **/p Password**··············Specifies the password of the user account that is specified in the /u parameter.
- **/i InitialPageFileSize**······Specifies the new initial size (in MB) to use for the paging file specified.
- **/m MaximumPageFileSize**··············Specifies the new maximum size (in MB) to use for the paging file specified.
- **/vo {VolumeLetter|*}**·······Specifies the volume or volumes of the paging file settings to be created. The volume is specified by a letter followed by a colon (for example, "C:").

pagefileconfig delete

Deletes a paging file from a system.

Syntax:

pagefileconfig.vbs /delete [/s Computer [/u Domain\User [/p Password]]] /vo {VolumeLetter|*} [/vo {VolumeLetter2|*} [...]]

Examples:

pagefileconfig.vbs /delete /vo d: or   pagefileconfig.vbs /delete /s srvmain /u maindom\hiropln /vo d:

Syntax Options:

- **/s Computer**··············Specifies the name or IP address of a remote computer (do not use backslashes). The default is the local computer.
- **/u Domain\User**··············Runs the script with the account permissions of the user specified by User or Domain\User. The default is the permissions of the current logged on user on the computer issuing the command.
- **/p Password**··············Specifies the password of the user account that is specified in the /u parameter.
- **/vo {VolumeLetter|*}**·······Specifies the volume or volumes of the paging file settings to be deleted. The volume is specified by a letter followed by a colon (for example, "C:").

pagefileconfig query

Queries and displays a system's paging file Virtual Memory settings.

Syntax:

pagefileconfig.vbs /query [/s Computer [/u Domain\User [/p Password]]] [/fo {TABLE | LIST | CSV}]

Examples:

pagefileconfig.vbs /query   or   pagefileconfig.vbs /query /fo table

Syntax Options:

- **/s Computer**··············Specifies the name or IP address of a remote computer (do not use backslashes). The default is the local computer.
- **/u Domain\User**··············Runs the script with the account permissions of the user specified by User or Domain\User. The default is the permissions of the current logged on user on the computer issuing the command.
- **/p Password**··············Specifies the password of the user account that is specified in the /u parameter.
- **/fo {TABLE | LIST | CSV}**Specifies the format to use for the query output. Valid values are TABLE, LIST, and CSV. The default value is LIST.

Notes:

- Maximum paging file size is limited to available free disk space less the crashdump recovery settings for the boot drive.

PATH

Sets the command path in the PATH environment variable, which is the set of directories used to search for executable files.

Syntax:
    path [[%path%] [Drive:]Path [;...]]
Examples:
    The following command specifies that Windows XP is to search three directories to find external commands. The three paths for these directories are C:\User\Taxes, B:\User\Invest, and B:\Bin:
    path c:\user\taxes;b:\user\invest;b:\bin
Syntax Options:
    Used without parameters, path displays the current command path.
    [Drive:]Path ·················Specifies the drive and directory to set in the command path.
    ; ·················Separates directories in the command path.
    %path% ····Specifies Windows XP to append the command path to the existing set of directories listed in the PATH environment variable.

Notes:

• When used as the only parameter, ; deletes the existing command path value found in the PATH variable.

• When you include %path% in the syntax, Cmd.exe replaces it with the command path value found in the PATH variable, eliminating the need to manually enter these values at the command line. For more information about substituting environment variable values, see Command shell.

• The operating system always searches in the current directory first, before it searches the directories in the command path.

• You might have some files in the same directory that share the same file name but have different extensions. For example, you might have a file named Accnt.com that starts an accounting program and another file named Accnt.bat that connects your system to the accounting system network.

• The operating system searches for a file by using default file name extensions in the following order of precedence: .exe, .com, .bat, and .cmd. To run Accnt.bat when Accnt.com exists in the same directory, you must include the .bat extension at the command line.

• If you have two or more files in the command path that have the same file name and extension, Windows XP searches for the specified file name first in the current directory, and then it searches the directories in the command path in the order in which they are listed in PATH.

• If you place the path command in your Autoexec.nt file, it automatically appends the specified MS-DOS subsystem search path to the Windows XP search path every time you log on to your computer. Cmd.exe does not use the Autoexec.nt file. When started from a shortcut, Cmd.exe inherits the environment variables set in My Computer/Properties/Advanced/Environment.

PATHPING

Provides information about network latency and network loss at intermediate hops between a source and destination. Pathping sends multiple Echo Request messages to each router between a source and destination over a period of time and then computes results based on the packets returned from each router. Because pathping displays the degree of packet loss at any given router or link, you can determine which routers or subnets might be having network problems. Pathping performs the equivalent of the tracert command by identifying which routers are on the path. It then sends pings periodically to all of the routers over a specified time period and computes statistics based on the number returned from each.

Syntax:

    pathping [-n] [-h MaximumHops] [-g HostList] [-p Period] [-q NumQueries [-w Timeout] [-T] [-R] [TargetName]

Examples:
    The following example shows pathping command output:
    D:\>pathping -n corp1
    When pathping is run, the first results list the path. This is the same path that is shown using the tracert command. Next, a busy message is displayed for approximately 90 seconds (the time varies by hop count). During this time, information is gathered from all routers previously listed and from the links between them. At the end of this period, the test results are displayed.

In the sample report above, the This Node/Link, Lost/Sent = Pct and Address columns show that the link between 172.16.87.218 and 192.168.52.1 is dropping 13 percent of the packets. The routers at hops 2 and 4 also are dropping packets addressed to them, but this loss does not affect their ability to forward traffic that is not addressed to them. The loss rates displayed for the links, identified as a vertical bar (|) in the Address column, indicate link congestion that is causing the loss of packets that are being forwarded on the path. The loss rates displayed for routers (identified by their IP addresses) indicate that these routers might be overloaded.

Syntax Options:

Used without parameters, pathping displays help.

-n ·············Prevents pathping from attempting to resolve the IP addresses of intermediate routers to their names. This might expedite the display of pathping results.

-h MaximumHops ··········Specifies the maximum number of hops in the path to search for the target (destination). The default is 30 hops.

-g HostList Specifies that the Echo Request messages use the Loose Source Route option in the IP header with the set of intermediate destinations specified in HostList. With loose source routing, successive intermediate destinations can be separated by one or multiple routers. The maximum number of addresses or names in the host list is 9. The HostList is a series of IP addresses (in dotted decimal notation) separated by spaces.

-p Period···Specifies the number of milliseconds to wait between consecutive pings. The default is 250 milliseconds (1/4 second).

-q NumQueries ···············Specifies the number of Echo Request messages sent to each router in the path. The default is 100 queries.

-w TimeoutSpecifies the number of milliseconds to wait for each reply. The default is 3000 milliseconds (3 seconds).

-T ·············Attaches a layer-2 priority tag (for example, 802.1p) to the Echo Request messages that it sends to each of the network devices along the route. This helps to identify network devices that do not have layer-2 priority capability. This switch is used to test for Quality of Service (QoS) connectivity.

-R·············Determines whether each network device along the route supports the Resource Reservation Protocol (RSVP), which allows the host computer to reserve a specified amount of bandwidth for a data stream. This switch is used to test for Quality of Service (QoS) connectivity.

TargetName···················Specifies the destination, which is identified either by IP address or host name.

Notes:

• Pathping parameters are case-sensitive.

• To avoid network congestion, pings should be sent at a sufficiently slow pace.

• To minimize the effects of burst losses, do not send pings too frequently.

• When using the -p parameter, pings are sent individually to each intermediate hop. Because of this, the interval between two pings sent to the same hop is period multiplied by the number of hops.

• When using the -w parameter, multiple pings can be sent in parallel. Because of this, the amount of time specified in the Timeout parameter is not bounded by the amount of time specified in the Period parameter for waiting between pings.

• Enabling layer-2 priority on the host computer allows packets to be sent with a layer-2 priority tag, which can be used by layer-2 devices to assign a priority to the packet. Legacy devices that do not recognize layer-2 priority will discard these packets, since they appear to be malformed. This parameter helps identify network computer that are discarding these packets.

• An RSVP reservation message for a nonexistent session is sent to each network device on the route. If the device does not support RSVP, it returns an Internet Control Message Protocol (ICMP) Destination Unreachable-Protocol Unreachable message. If the device does support RSVP, it returns an RSVP Reservation Error message. Some devices might not return either of these messages. If this occurs, a time-out message is displayed.

• This command is available only if the Internet Protocol (TCP/IP) protocol is installed as a component in the properties of a network adapter in Network Connections

PAUSE

Suspends processing of a batch program and displays a message prompting the user to press any key to continue.

Syntax:

pause

Examples:

To create a batch program that prompts the user to change disks in one of the drives, type:

```
@echo off
:begin
copy a:*.*
echo Please put a new disk into drive A
pause
goto begin
```

In this example, all the files on the disk in drive A are copied to the current directory. After the displayed comment prompts you to place another disk in drive A, the pause command suspends processing so that you can change disks and then press any key to resume processing. This particular batch program runs in an endless loop. The goto BEGIN command sends the command interpreter to the begin label of the batch file. To stop this batch program, press CTRL+C and then Y.

Notes:

- When you run prompt command, the following message appears:
  Press any key to continue . . .

- If you press CTRL+C to stop a batch program, the following message appears:
  Terminate batch job (Y/N)?

- If you press Y (for yes) in response to this message, the batch program ends and control returns to the operating system. Therefore, you can insert the pause command before a section of the batch file you may not want to process. While pause suspends processing of the batch program, you can press CTRL+C and then Y to stop the batch program.

PBADMIN

Administers phone books.

Syntax:

pbadmin.exe /N PhoneBookName [/R RegionFilePath\RegionFileName]
[/P DataFilePath\DataFileName]

pbadmin.exe /I PhoneBookName /R RegionFilePath\RegionFileName

pbadmin.exe /I PhoneBookName /P DataFilePath\DataFileName

pbadmin.exe /O PhoneBookName ServerName UserName Password

pbadmin.exe /B PhoneBookName

Examples:

pbadmin.exe /N Awesome   *or*   pbadmin.exe /I Awesome /R C:\Temp\Region1.txt

Syntax Options:

Used without parameters, pbadmin starts Phone Book Administrator.

/N PhoneBookName ·······Creates a phone book (.mdb). The PhoneBookName parameter specifies the name of the file to create.

/I PhoneBookName ········Imports data into a phone book (.mdb) from a region (.txt) file or a phone book (.pbk or .txt) file. The PhoneBookName parameter specifies the phone book into which you want to import data. You must use the /R or the /P parameter in conjunction with the /I parameter.

/R RegionFilePath\RegionFileName ·····Specifies the location and the name of the region file you want to import into a phone book.

/P DataFilePath\DataFileName ··············Specifies the location and the name of the phone book file (.pbk or .txt) you want to import into a phone book.

/O PhoneBookName ServerName UserName Password
Configures options for a phone book. The PhoneBookName parameter specifies the name of the phone book for which you want to set options. The ServerName parame-

ter specifies the name of the server to which the phone book is published. The UserName parameter specifies a user account with FTP permissions on the Phone Book Service (PBS) server. The Password parameter specifies the password for the user account on the PBS server.

/B PhoneBookName ....Publishes a phone book. The PhoneBookName parameter specifies the name of the phone book to publish. Before you can use the /B parameter, you must configure the phone book with the /O parameter.

Notes:

• To create a phone book (.mdb), use this syntax: pbadmin.exe /N PhoneBookName [/R RegionFilePath\RegionFileName] [/P DataFilePath\DataFileName]

• To import data into a phone book from a region file, use this syntax: pbadmin.exe /I PhoneBookName /R RegionFilePath\RegionFileName

• To import data into a phone book from a phone book file (.pbk) or an appropriately formatted text file (.txt), use this syntax: pbadmin.exe /I PhoneBookName /P DataFilePath\DataFileName

• To configure publishing options for a phone book, use this syntax: pbadmin.exe /O PhoneBookName ServerName UserName Password

• To publish a phone book, use this syntax: pbadmin.exe /B PhoneBookName

• For pbadmin, the term "phone book" refers to a phone book (.mdb), and the term "phone book file" refers to a phone book file (.pbk).

• Command-line parameters are case-sensitive.

• A phone book name cannot consist of more than eight characters, cannot consist of all digits, and must not contain a space or any of the following symbols: ! , ; * = / \ : ? ' " < > | . & % { } [ ] @ ( ) ` ` ~

• If you specify a path, you must specify the full path. You cannot use spaces in the path to the phone book, to a phone book file, or to a region file.

• To use the pbadmin command, you must install Phone Book Administrator and then type the command from within the PBA directory. To install Phone Book Administrator, insert your Windows XP Professional or your Windows 2000 installation CD into your CD-ROM drive, and click Browse this CD. Open the VALUEADD folder, open the MSFT folder, open the MGMT folder, and open the PBA folder. Double-click PBAINST, and follow the instructions on your screen.

PENTNT

Detects floating point division error (if present) in the Pentium chip, disables floating point hardware, and turns on floating point emulation.

Syntax:

pentnt [-c] [-f] [-o]

Syntax Options:

-c ....Enables conditional emulation.

-f ....Enables forced emulation.

-o ....Disables forced emulation and reenables floating-point hardware if it is present.

Notes:

• Parameters used with this command must be prefixed with - (hyphen) rather than / (slash).

• Using the -c command-line option

• Floating-point emulation is forced on only if the system detects the Pentium processor floating-point division error at start time. If you select this parameter, you must restart the computer for the changes to take effect.

• Using the -f command-line option Floating-point hardware is disabled and floating-point emulation is always forced on, regardless of whether the system exhibits the Pentium processor floating-point division error. This parameter is useful for testing software emulators and for working around floating-point hardware defects known to the operating system. If you select this parameter, you must restart the computer for the changes to take effect.

• Using the -o command-line option If you select this parameter, you must restart the computer for the changes to take effect.

PERFMON

Allows you to open a Windows XP Performance console configured with settings files from Windows NT 4.0 version of Performance Monitor.

Syntax:

perfmon.exe [file_name] [/HTMLFILE:converted_file settings_file]

Examples:

Perfmon myfile_overview **or**
Perfmon myfile_overview /Commands:newfile_review oldfile_sample.pml

Syntax Options:

.exe··········Specifies the name of the file extension.

file_name··Specifies the name of the settings file.

/HTMLFILE:converted_file settings_file········Specifies the name of the converted files, and the name of the original Windows NT 4.0 settings file.

Notes:

• This procedure works for the following types of Windows NT 4.0 version of Performance Monitor settings files: chart (.pmc), report (.pmr), alert (.pma), and log (.pml).

• To display the Windows NT 4.0 settings file in System Monitor, the system temporarily converts the file for use with Windows XP System Monitor, then discards the converted version after the console starts. If you want to save the settings file for permanent use with System Monitor, type:

• Perfmon [file_name] [/HTMLFILE:converted_file settings_file]

• Where /HTMLFILE:converted_file is the name given to the converted file and settings_file is the name of the original Windows NT 4.0 settings file.

PING

Verifies IP-level connectivity to another TCP/IP computer by sending Internet Control Message Protocol (ICMP) Echo Request messages. The receipt of corresponding Echo Reply messages are displayed, along with round-trip times. Ping is the primary TCP/IP command used to troubleshoot connectivity, reachability, and name resolution.

Syntax:

ping [-t] [-a] [-n Count] [-l Size] [-f] [-i TTL] [-v TOS] [-r Count] [-s Count] [{-j HostList | -k HostList}] [-w Timeout] [TargetName]

Examples:

ping -a 10.0.99.221 **or** ping -n 10 -l 1000 10.0.99.221 **or** ping -r 4 10.0.99.221

Syntax Options:

Used without parameters, ping displays help.

-t ··············Specifies that ping continue sending Echo Request messages to the destination until interrupted. To interrupt and display statistics, press CTRL-BREAK. To interrupt and quit ping, press CTRL-C.

-a ··············Specifies that reverse name resolution is performed on the destination IP address. If this is successful, ping displays the corresponding host name.

-n Count····Specifies the number of Echo Request messages sent. The default is 4.

-l Size ·······Specifies the length, in bytes, of the Data field in the Echo Request messages sent. The default is 32. The maximum size is 65,527.

-f ··············Specifies that Echo Request messages are sent with the Don't Fragment flag in the IP header set to 1. The Echo Request message cannot be fragmented by routers in the path to the destination. This parameter is useful for troubleshooting path Maximum Transmission Unit (PMTU) problems.

-i TTL ·······Specifies the value of the TTL field in the IP header for Echo Request messages sent. The default is the default TTL value for the host. For Windows XP hosts, this is typically 128. The maximum TTL is 255.

-v TOS ·····Specifies the value of the Type of Service (TOS) field in the IP header for Echo Request messages sent. The default is 0. TOS is specified as a decimal value from 0 to 255.

-r Count ····Specifies that the Record Route option in the IP header is used to record the path taken by the Echo Request message and corresponding Echo Reply message. Each hop in the path uses an entry in the Record Route option. If possible, specify a Count that is equal to or greater than the number of hops between the source and destination. The Count must be a minimum of 1 and a maximum of 9.

-s Count ····Specifies that the Internet Timestamp option in the IP header is used to record the time of arrival for the Echo Request message and corresponding Echo Reply message for each hop. The Count must be a minimum of 1 and a maximum of 4.

-j HostList ·Specifies that the Echo Request messages use the Loose Source Route option in the IP header with the set of intermediate destinations specified in HostList. With loose source routing, successive intermediate destinations can be separated by one or multiple routers. The maximum number of addresses or names in the host list is 9. The host list is a series of IP addresses (in dotted decimal notation) separated by spaces.

-k HostList Specifies that the Echo Request messages use the Strict Source Route option in the IP header with the set of intermediate destinations specified in HostList. With strict source routing, the next intermediate destination must be directly reachable (it must be a neighbor on an interface of the router). The maximum number of addresses or names in the host list is 9. The host list is a series of IP addresses (in dotted decimal notation) separated by spaces.

-w Timeout Specifies the amount of time, in milliseconds, to wait for the Echo Reply message that corresponds to a given Echo Request message to be received. If the Echo Reply message is not received within the time-out, the "Request timed out" error message is displayed. The default time-out is 4000 (4 seconds).

TargetName····················Specifies the destination, which is identified either by IP address or host name.

Notes:

• You can use ping to test both the computer name and the IP address of the computer. If pinging the IP address is successful, but pinging the computer name is not, you might have a name resolution problem. In this case, ensure that the computer name you are specifying can be resolved through the local Hosts file, by using Domain Name System (DNS) queries, or through NetBIOS name resolution techniques.

• This command is available only if the Internet Protocol (TCP/IP) protocol is installed as a component in the properties of a network adapter in Network Connections

POPD

Changes the current directory to the directory stored by the pushd command.

Syntax:

popd

Examples:

You can use pushd and popd in a batch program to change the current directory from the one in which the batch program was run and then change it back. The following sample batch program shows how to do this:

```
@echo off
rem This batch file deletes all .txt files in a specified directory
pushd %1
del *.txt
popd
cls
echo All text files deleted in the %1 directory
```

Notes:

• Every time you use the pushd command, a single directory is stored for your use. However, you can store multiple directories by using the pushd command multiple times. The directories are stored sequentially in a virtual stack. If you use the pushd command once, the directory in which you use the command is placed at the bottom of the stack. If you use the command again, the second directory is placed on top of the first one. The process repeats every time you use the pushd command.

You can use the popd command to change the current directory to the directory most recently stored by the pushd command. If you use the popd command, the directory on the top of the stack is removed from the stack as the current directory is changed to that directory. If you use the popd command again, the next directory on the stack is removed.

• When command extensions are enabled, the popd command removes any drive-letter assignments created by pushd.

PRINT

Sends a text file to a printer.

Syntax:

print [/d:Printer] [Drive:][Path] FileName [...]

Examples:

print /d:LPT2 report.txt   or   print /d:\\coproom\printer1 c:\accounting\report.txt

Syntax Options:

/d:Printer···Specifies the printer on which you want to print the job. You can specify a local printer by specifying the port on your computer to which the printer is connected. Valid values for parallel ports are LPT1, LPT2, and LPT3. Valid values for serial ports are COM1, COM2, COM3, and COM4. You can also specify a network printer by its queue name (\\ServerName\ShareName). If you do not specify a printer, the print job is sent to LPT1.

Drive: ·······Specifies the logical or physical drive on which the file you want to print is located. This parameter is not required if the file you want to print is located on the current drive.

Path ·········Specifies where, on the drive, the file you want to print is located. This parameter is not required if the file you want to print is located in the current directory.

FileName [...] ···············Required. Specifies, by name, the file you want to print. You can include multiple files in one command.

Notes:

• A file can print in the background if you send it to a printer connected to a serial or parallel port on the local computer.

• Many programs have their own print commands. You should use the print command for a program to print files that you create with that program.

• You can perform many configuration tasks from the command line by using the mode command.

PRNCNFG.VBS

Configures or displays configuration information about a printer.

Syntax:

cscript prncnfg.vbs -g [-s RemoteComputer] -p PrinterName [-u UserName -w Password]

Example:

cscript prncnfg.vbs -g -s HRServer -p ColorPrinter_2

Syntax Options:

Used without parameters, prncnfg.vbs displays command-line help.

-g ·············Required. Specifies that you want to display configuration information about a printer.

-s RemoteComputer ······Specifies, by name, the remote computer that manages the printer about which you want to display information. If you do not specify a computer, the local computer is used.

-p PrinterName ···············Required. Specifies, by name, the printer about which you want to display information.

-u UserName -w Password ···················Specifies an account with permissions to connect by using Windows Management Instrumentation (WMI) services to the computer that hosts the printer about which you want to display information. All members of the Administrators group for that computer have these permissions, but the permissions can also be granted to other users. If you do not specify an account, you must be logged on under an account with these permissions for the command to work. For more information on WMI, see Related Topics.

Notes:

• This command starts a script that is located in the systemroot\system32 directory. You must type this command at a command prompt with that directory as the current directory, or you must type the full path to that directory at the beginning of the cscript command.

• If the information that you supply contains spaces, use quotation marks around the text (for example, "Computer Name").

To configure a printer

Syntax

cscript prncnfg.vbs -t [-s RemoteComputer] -p PrinterName [-u UserName -w Password]
[-r PortName] [-l Location] [-m Comment] [-h ShareName] [-f SeparatorText]
[-y DataType] [-st StartTime] [-ut EndTime] [-o Priority] [-i DefaultPriority] [{+ | -}shared] [{+
| -}direct] [{+ | -}published] [{+ | -}hidden] [{+ | -}rawonly] [{+ | -}queued] [{+ |
-}keepprintedjobs] [{+ | -}workoffline] [{+ | -}enabledevq] [{+ | -}docompletefirst][{+ |
-}enablebidi]

Example:

cscript prncnfg.vbs -t -s HRServer -p ColorPrinter_2 +keepprintedjobs

Syntax Options:

-t ....Required. Specifies that you want to configure a printer.

-s RemoteComputer ....Specifies, by name, the remote computer that manages the printer you want to configure. If you do not specify a computer, the printer is configured on the local computer.

-p PrinterName ....Required. Specifies, by name, the printer you want to configure.

-u UserName -w Password ....Specifies an account with permissions to connect by using Windows Management Instrumentation (WMI) services to the computer on which you want to configure a printer. All members of the Administrators group for that computer have these permissions, but the permissions can also be granted to other users. If you do not specify an account, you must be logged on under an account with these permissions for the command to work. For more information on WMI, see Related Topics.

-r PortName ....Specifies the port to which the printer is connected. If this is a parallel or a serial port, then use the ID of the port (for example, LPT1 or COM1). If this is a TCP/IP port, then use the port name that was specified when the port was added. For more information, see Related Topics.

-l Location·Specifies the printer location, such as "Copier Room."

-m Comment ....Specifies the comment string.

-h ShareName ....Specifies the share name.

-f SeparatorText ....Specifies a file that contains the text that appears on the separator page.

-y DataType ....Specifies the data types that the printer can accept. For more information on data types, see Related Topics.

-st StartTime ....Configures the printer for limited availability. Specifies the time of day after which the printer is available. If you send a document to a printer when it is unavailable, the document is held (spooled) until the printer becomes available. You must specify time as a 24-hour clock. For example, to specify 11 P.M., type 2300.

-ut EndTime ....Configures the printer for limited availability. Specifies the time of day after which the printer is no longer available. If you send a document to a printer when it is unavailable, the document is held (spooled) until the printer becomes available. You must specify time as a 24-hour clock. For example, to specify 11 P.M., type 2300.

-o Priority··Specifies a priority that the spooler uses to route print jobs. A print queue with a higher priority receives all its jobs before any queue with a lower priority.

-i DefaultPriority ....Specifies the default priority assigned to each print job.

{+ | -}shared ....Specifies whether this printer is shared on the network.

{+ | -}direct·Specifies whether the document should be sent directly to the printer without being spooled.

{+ | -}published...............Specifies whether this printer should be published in Active Directory. If you publish the printer, other users can search for it based on its location and capabilities, such as color printing and stapling.

{+ | -}hidden ....Reserved function.

{+ | -}rawonly···················Specifies whether only raw data print jobs can be spooled on this queue.

{+ | -}queued ....Specifies that the printer should not begin to print until after the last page of the document is spooled. The printing program is unavailable until the document has finished printing. However, using this option ensures that the whole document is available to the printer.

{+ | -}keepprintedjobs ······ Specifies whether the spooler should retain documents after they are printed. Enabling this option allows a user to resubmit a document to the printer from the print queue instead of from the printing program.

{+ | -}workoffline ············· Specifies whether you should be able to send print jobs to the print queue even if your computer is not connected to the network.

{+ | -}enabledevq ············· Specifies whether print jobs that do not match the printer setup (for example, PostScript files spooled to non-PostScript printers) should be held in the queue rather than being printed.

{+ | -}docompletefirst ······ Specifies whether the spooler should send to the appropriate queue print jobs with a lower priority that have completed spooling before sending to the same queue print jobs with a higher priority that have not completed spooling. If this option is enabled and no documents have completed spooling, the spooler will send larger documents before smaller ones. You should enable this option if you want to maximize printer efficiency at the cost of job priority. If this option is disabled, the spooler always sends higher priority jobs to their respective queues first.

{+ | -}enablebidi ··············· Specifies whether the printer sends status information to the spooler.

Notes:

• This command starts a script that is located in the systemroot\system32 directory. You must type this command at a command prompt with that directory as the current directory, or you must type the full path to that directory at the beginning of the cscript command.

• If the information that you supply contains spaces, use quotation marks around the text (for example, "Computer Name").

To change the name of a printer

Syntax

cscript prncnfg.vbs -x [-s RemoteComputer] -p PrinterName -z NewPrinterName
[-u UserName -w Password]

Example:

cscript prncnfg.vbs -x -s HRServer -p ColorPrinter_2 -z ColorPrinter_3

Syntax Options:

-x ·············· Required. Specifies that you want to change the name of a printer.

-s RemoteComputer ······· Specifies, by name, the remote computer that manages the printer you want to rename. If you do not specify a computer, the local computer is used.

-p PrinterName ·············· Required. Specifies the current printer name.

-z NewPrinterName ········ Required. Specifies the new printer name.

-u UserName -w Password ··················· Specifies an account with permissions to connect by using Windows Management Instrumentation (WMI) services to the computer that hosts the printer you want to rename. All members of the Administrators group for that computer have these permissions, but the permissions can also be granted to other users. If you do not specify an account, you must be logged on under an account with these permissions for the command to work. For more information on WMI, see Related Topics.

Notes:

• This command starts a script that is located in the systemroot\system32 directory. You must type this command at a command prompt with that directory as the current directory, or you must type the full path to that directory at the beginning of the cscript command.

• If the information that you supply contains spaces, use quotation marks around the text (for example, "Computer Name").

PRNDRVR.VBS

Adds, deletes, and lists printer drivers.

Syntax:

cscript prndrvr.vbs -a [-m DriverName] [-v {0 | 1 | 2 | 3}] [-e Environment]
[-s RemoteComputer] [-h Path] [-i FileName.inf] [-u UserName -w Password]

Example:

cscript prndrvr.vbs -a -m "Color Printer Driver 1" -v 3 -e "Windows NT x86"

Syntax Options:

Used without parameters, prndrvr.vbs displays command-line help for the prndrvr.vbs command.

-a ············· Required. Specifies that you want to install a driver.

-m DriverName ··············· Specifies, by name, the driver you want to install. Drivers are often named for the model of printer they support. See the printer documentation for more information.

-v {0 | 1 | 2 | 3}·············· Specifies the version of the driver you want to install. See the description of the -e Environment parameter for information on which versions are available for which environment. If you do not specify a version, the version of the driver appropriate for the version of Windows running on the computer on which you are installing the driver is installed.
Version 0 supports Windows 95, Windows 98, and Windows Millennium Edition.
Version 1 supports Windows NT 3.51.
Version 2 supports Windows NT 4.0.
Version 3 supports Windows XP and Windows 2000.

-e Environment ··············· Specifies the environment for the driver you want to install. If you do not specify an environment, the environment of the computer on which you are installing the driver is used. The following table lists the driver environments that are available and the versions that are available for each.

Environment	Available versions
"Windows NT x86"	1, 2, and 3
"Windows NT Alpha_AXP"	1 and 2
"Windows IA64"	3
"Windows NT R4000"	1
"Windows NT PowerPC"	1
"Windows 4.0"	0

-s RemoteComputer ······· Specifies the remote computer on which you want to install the driver. If you do not specify a computer, the driver is installed on the local computer.

-h Path······ Specifies the path to the driver file. If you do not specify a path, the path to the location from which Windows was installed is used.

-i FileName.inf ··············· Specifies the file name for the driver you want to install. If you do not specify a file name, ntprint.inf is used.

-u UserName -w Password ··············· Specifies an account with permissions to connect by using Windows Management Instrumentation (WMI) services to the computer on which you want to install the driver. All members of the Administrators group for that computer have these permissions, but the permissions can also be granted to other users. If you do not specify an account, you must be logged on under an account with these permissions for the command to work.

Notes:

• This command starts a script that is located in the systemroot\system32 directory. You must type this command at a command prompt with that directory as the current directory, or you must type the full path to that directory at the beginning of the cscript command.

• If the information that you supply contains spaces, use quotation marks around the text (for example, "Computer Name").

To delete a printer driver

Syntax:

cscript prndrvr.vbs -d [-s RemoteComputer] -m DriverName -v {0 | 1 | 2 | 3} -e Environment

[-u UserName -w Password]

Syntax Options:

-d ············· Required. Specifies that you want to delete a driver.

-s RemoteComputer ······· Specifies the remote computer from which you want to delete the driver. If you do not specify a computer, the driver is deleted from the local computer.

-m DriverName ·············Required. Specifies, by name, the driver you want to delete. Drivers are often named for the model of printer they support. See the printer documentation for more information.

-v {0 | 1 | 2 | 3}·············Required. Indicates the version of the driver to be deleted. See the description of the -e Environment parameter for information on which versions are available in which environment.
Version 0 supports Windows 95, Windows 98, and Windows Millennium Edition.
Version 1 supports Windows NT 3.51.
Version 2 supports Windows NT 4.0.
Version 3 supports Windows XP and Windows 2000.

-e Environment ·············Required. Specifies the environment for the driver you want to delete. The lists the driver environments that are available and the versions that are available for each.

Environment	Available versions
"Windows NT x86"	1, 2, and 3
"Windows NT Alpha_AXP"	1 and 2
"Windows IA64"	3
"Windows NT R4000"	1
"Windows NT PowerPC"	1
"Windows 4.0"	0

-u UserName -w Password ·············Specifies an account with permissions to connect by using Windows Management Instrumentation (WMI) services to the computer from which you want to delete the driver. All members of the Administrators group for that computer have these permissions, but the permissions can also be granted to other users. If you do not specify an account, you must be logged on under an account with these permissions for the command to work. For more information on WMI, see Related Topics.

To list the printer drivers on a computer

Syntax

cscript prndrvr.vbs -l [-s RemoteComputer] [-u UserName -w Password]

Syntax Options:

-l ··············Required. Specifies that you want to list all the drivers on a computer.

-s RemoteComputer ·······Indicates the remote computer whose drivers you want to list. If you do not specify a computer, drivers on the local computer are listed.

-u UserName -w Password ·············Specifies an account with permissions to connect by using Windows Management Instrumentation (WMI) services to the computer whose drivers you want to list. All members of the Administrators group for that computer have these permissions, but the permissions can also be granted to other users. If you do not specify an account, you must be logged on under an account with these permissions for the command to work. For more information on WMI, see Related Topics.

To delete all unused printer drivers from a computer

Syntax:

cscript prndrvr.vbs -x [-s RemoteComputer] [-u UserName -w Password]

Syntax Options:

-x ··············Required. Specifies that you want to delete all unused printer drivers from a computer.

-s RemoteComputer ·······Specifies the remote computer from which you want to delete drivers. If you do not specify a computer, drivers are deleted from the local computer.

-u UserName -w Password ·············Specifies an account with permissions to connect by using Windows Management Instrumentation (WMI) services to the computer from which you want to delete drivers. All members of the Administrators group for that computer have these permissions, but the permissions can also be granted to other users. If you do not specify an account, you must be logged on under an account with these permissions for the command to work. For more information on WMI, see Related Topics.

Pauses, resumes, cancels, and lists print jobs. Used without parameters, prnjobs.vbs displays command-line help for the prnjobs.vbs command.

To pause a print job

Syntax:

cscript prnjobs -z

[-s RemoteComputer] -p PrinterName -j JobNumber [-u UserName -w Password]

Example:

cscript prnjobs.vbs -z -s HRServer -p ColorPrinter -j 27

Syntax Options:

-z ·············Required. Specifies that you want to pause a print job.

-s RemoteComputer ·······Specifies, by name, the remote computer to which the print job you want to pause was sent. If you do not specify a computer, the local computer is used.

-p PrinterName ···············Required. Specifies, by name, the printer that would print the job you want to pause.

-j JobNumber ···················Required. Specifies, by ID number, the print job you want to pause.

-u UserName -w Password ·················Specifies an account with permissions to connect by using Windows Management Instrumentation (WMI) services to the computer to which the print job you want to pause was sent. All members of the Administrators group for that computer have these permissions, but the permissions can also be granted to other users. If you do not specify an account, you mfollowing tableust be logged on under an account with these permissions for the command to work. For more information on WMI, see Related Topics.

Notes:

• This command starts a script that is located in the systemroot\system32 directory. You must type this command at a command prompt with that directory as the current directory, or you must type the full path to that directory at the beginning of the cscript command.

• To display a list of print jobs and their ID numbers, use this command with the -l parameter.

• If the information that you supply contains spaces, use quotation marks around the text (for example, "Computer Name").

To resume a print job

Syntax:

cscript prnjobs -m [-s RemoteComputer] -p PrinterName -j JobNumber

[-u UserName -w Password]

Syntax Options:

-m ·············Required. Specifies that you want to resume a print job.

-s RemoteComputer ·······Specifies, by name, the remote computer to which the print job you want to resume was sent. If you do not specify a computer, the local computer is used.

-p PrinterName ···············Required. Specifies, by name, the printer that will print the job you want to resume.

-j JobNumber ···················Required. Specifies, by ID number, the print job you want to resume.

-u UserName -w Password ·················Specifies an account with permissions to connect by using Windows Management Instrumentation (WMI) services to the computer to which the print job you want to resume was sent. All members of the Administrators group for that computer have these permissions, but the permissions can also be granted to other users. If you do not specify an account, you must be logged on under an account with these permissions for the command to work. For more information on WMI, see Related Topics.

To cancel a print job

Syntax:

cscript prnjobs -x [-s RemoteComputer] -p PrinterName -j JobNumber
[-u UserName -w Password]

Syntax Options:

-x .... Required. Specifies that you want to cancel a print job.

-s RemoteComputer ·······Specifies, by name, the remote computer to which the job you want to cancel was sent. If you do not specify a computer, the local computer is used.

-p PrinterName .... Required. Specifies, by name, the printer that would print the job that you want to cancel.

-j JobNumber .... Required. Specifies, by ID number, the print job you want to cancel.

-u UserName -w Password .... Specifies an account with permissions to connect by using Windows Management Instrumentation (WMI) services to the computer to which the print job you want to cancel was sent. All members of the Administrators group for that computer have these permissions, but the permissions can also be granted to other users. If you do not specify an account, you must be logged on under an account with these permissions for the command to work. For more information on WMI, see Related Topics.

To list the print jobs in a print queue

Syntax:

cscript prnjobs -l [-s RemoteComputer] [-p PrinterName] [-u UserName -w Password]

Example:

cscript prnjobs.vbs -l -p ColorPrinter_2

Syntax Options:

-l .... Required. Specifies that you want to list all the print jobs in a print queue.

-s RemoteComputer ·······Specifies, by name, the remote computer that hosts the print queue whose jobs you want to list. If you do not specify a computer, the local computer is used.

-p PrinterName .... Specifies, by name, the printer whose print queue contains the jobs you want to list. If you do not specify a printer, then all jobs in all print queues are listed.

-u UserName -w Password .... Specifies an account with permissions to connect by using Windows Management Instrumentation (WMI) services to the computer that hosts the print queue whose jobs you want to list. All members of the Administrators group for that computer have these permissions, but the permissions can also be granted to other users. If you do not specify an account, you must be logged on under an account with these permissions for the command to work. For more information on WMI, see Related Topics.

PRNMNGR.VBS

Adds, deletes, and lists printers or printer connections, in addition to setting and displaying the default printer. Used without parameters, prnmngr.vbs displays command-line help for the prnmngr.vbs command.

To add a local printer

Syntax:

cscript prnmngr.vbs -a -p PrinterName [-s RemoteComputer] -m DriverName -r PortName
[-u UserName -w Password]

Example:

cscript prnmngr.vbs -a -p ColorPrinter_2 -m "Color Printer Driver1" -r lpt1:

Syntax Options:

-a .... Required. Specifies that you want to add a local printer.

-s RemoteComputer ·······Specifies, by name, the remote computer to which you want to add a local printer. If you do not specify a computer, the printer is added to the local computer.

-p PrinterName .... Required. Specifies, by name, the local printer that you want to add.

-m DriverName ·············· Required. Specifies, by name, the driver for the local printer you want to add. Drivers are often named for the model of printer they support. See the printer documentation for more information.

-r PortName ·············· Required. Specifies the port to which the printer is connected. If this is a parallel or a serial port, use the ID of the port (for example, LPT1 or COM1). If this is a TCP/IP port, use the port name that was specified when the port was added. For more information, see Related Topics.

-u UserName -w Password ·············· Specifies an account with permissions to connect by using Windows Management Instrumentation (WMI) services to the computer to which you want to add a local printer. All members of the Administrators group for that computer have these permissions, but the permissions can also be granted to other users. If you do not specify an account, you must be logged on under an account with these permissions for the command to work. For more information on WMI, see Related Topics.

Notes:

• This command starts a script that is located in the systemroot\system32 directory. You must type this command at a command prompt with that directory as the current directory, or you must type the full path to that directory at the beginning of the cscript command.

• If the information that you supply contains spaces, use quotation marks around the text (for example, "Computer Name").

To add a printer connection

Syntax:

cscript prnmngr.vbs -ac -p PrinterName

Syntax Options:

-ac ·············· Required. Specifies that you want to add a printer connection.

-p PrinterName ·············· Required. Specifies, by name, the printer for which you want to add a connection.

To delete a printer

Syntax:

cscript prnmngr.vbs -d -p PrinterName [-u UserName -w Password] [-s RemoteComputer]

Example:

cscript prnmngr.vbs -d -s HRServer -p ColorPrinter_2

Syntax Options:

-d ·············· Required. Specifies that you want to delete a printer.

-p PrinterName ·············· Required. Specifies, by name, the printer that you want to delete.

-u UserName -w Password ·············· Specifies an account with permissions to connect by using Windows Management Instrumentation (WMI) services to the computer from which you want to delete a printer. All members of the Administrators group for that computer have these permissions, but the permissions can also be granted to other users. If you do not specify an account, you must be logged on under an account with these permissions for the command to work. For more information on WMI, see Related Topics.

-s RemoteComputer ·············· Specifies, by name, the remote computer to which you want to add a local printer. If you do not specify a computer, the printer is added to the local computer.

To delete all of the printers from a computer

Syntax:

cscript prnmngr.vbs -x [-s RemoteComputer] [-u UserName] [-w Password]

Syntax Options:

-x ·············· Required. Specifies that you want to delete all printers from a computer.

-s RemoteComputer ·············· Specifies, by name, the remote computer from which you want to delete all printers. If you do not specify a computer, all printers are deleted from the local computer.

-u UserName -w Password ·············· Specifies an account with permissions to connect by using Windows Management Instrumentation (WMI) services to the computer from which you want to delete all printers. All members of the Administrators group for that computer have these permissions, but the permissions can also be granted to other users. If you do not specify an account, you must be logged on under an account with these permissions for the command to work. For more information on WMI, see Related Topics.

To display the default printer

Syntax:

cscript prnmngr.vbs -g

Syntax Options:

-g .... Required. Specifies that you want to display the default printer.

To set the default printer

Syntax:

cscript prnmngr.vbs -t -p PrinterName

Syntax Options:

-t .... Required. Specifies that you want to set the default printer.

-p PrinterName .... Required. Specifies, by name, the printer that you want to set as the default printer.

To list all of the printers for a computer

Syntax:

cscript prnmngr.vbs -l [-s RemoteComputer] [-u UserName -w Password]

Syntax Options:

-l .... Required. Specifies that you want to list all the printers for a computer.

-s RemoteComputer .... Specifies, by name, the remote computer for which you want to list printers. If you do not specify a computer, the printers added to the local computer are listed.

-u UserName -w Password .... Specifies an account with permissions to connect by using Windows Management Instrumentation (WMI) services to the computer for which you want to list printers. All members of the Administrators group for that computer have these permissions, but the permissions can also be granted to other users. If you do not specify an account, you must be logged on under an account with these permissions for the command to work. For more information on WMI, see Related Topics.

PRNPORT.VBS

Creates, deletes, and lists standard TCP/IP printer ports, in addition to displaying and changing port configuration.

Syntax:

cscript prnport.vbs -a -r PortName [-s RemoteComputer] -h IPAddress
[-u UserName -w Password] [-o {raw -n PortNumber | lpr}] [-q QueueName] [-m{e | d}]
[-i IndexName] [-y CommunityName] [-2{e | d}]

Syntax Options:

Used without parameters, prnport.vbs displays help for the prnport.vbs command.

-a .... Required. Specifies that you want to create a standard TCP/IP printer port.

-r PortName .... Required. Specifies the port to which the printer is connected.

-s RemoteComputer .... Specifies, by name, the remote computer to which you want to add the port. If you do not specify a computer, the port is added to the local computer.

-h IPAddress .... Required. Specifies the IP address you want to assign to the port.

-u UserName -w Password .... Specifies an account with permissions to connect by using Windows Management Instrumentation (WMI) services to the computer on which you want to create a standard TCP/IP printer port. All members of the Administrators group for that computer have these permissions, but the permissions can also be granted to other users. If you do not specify an account, you must be logged on under an account with these permissions for the command to work.

-o {raw -n PortNumber | lpr} ···············Specifies which protocol the port uses: TCP raw or TCP LPR. If you use TCP raw, specifies the port number for a TCP raw printer port. By default, this is port number 9100. For more information, see Related Topics. Most printers use TCP raw. On UNIX networks, printers often use TCP LPR. For more information about TCP LPR, see RFC 1179 at http://www.microsoft.com/resources/documentation/windows/xp/all/proddocs/en-us/copyright.mspx

-q QueueName ···············Specifies the queue name for a TCP raw port.

-m{e | d}····Specifies whether SNMP is enabled. The parameter e enables SNMP. The parameter d disables SNMP.

-i IndexName ···················Specifies the SNMP index, if SNMP is enabled. For more information, see RFC 1759 at http://www.microsoft.com/resources/documentation/windows/xp/all/proddocs/en-us/copyright.mspx

-y CommunityName ·······Specifies the SNMP community name, if SNMP is enabled. For more information, see Related Topics.

-2{e | d}·····Specifies whether double spools (also known as respooling) are enabled for TCP LPR ports. Double spools are necessary because TCP LPR must include an accurate byte count in the control file that is sent to the printer, but the protocol cannot get the count from the local print provider. Therefore, when a file is spooled to a TCP LPR print queue, it is also spooled as a temporary file in the system32 directory. TCP LPR determines the size of the temporary file and sends the size to the server running LPD. The parameter e enables double spools. The parameter d disables double spools.

Notes:

• This command starts a script that is located in the systemroot\system32 directory. You must type this command at a command prompt with that directory as the current directory, or you must type the full path to that directory at the beginning of the cscript command.

• If you want to change the configuration for a standard TCP/IP printer port after you create it, you can use the cscript prnport.vbs command with the -t parameter.

• If the information that you supply contains spaces, use quotation marks around the text (for example, "Computer Name").

To delete a standard TCP/IP printer port

Syntax:

cscript prnport.vbs -d -r PortName [-s RemoteComputer] [-u UserName -w Password]

Example:

cscript prnport.vbs -d -r IP_192.168.12.128 -s HRServer

Syntax Options:

-d ·············Required. Specifies that you want to delete a standard TCP/IP printer port.

-r PortName ···················Required. Specifies the standard TCP/IP printer port that you want to delete.

-s RemoteComputer ·······Specifies, by name, the remote computer from which to delete the port. If you do not specify a computer, the port is deleted from the local computer.

-u UserName -w Password ···················Specifies an account with permissions to connect by using Windows Management Instrumentation (WMI) services to the computer on which you want to delete a standard TCP/IP printer port. All members of the Administrators group for that computer have these permissions, but the permissions can also be granted to other users. If you do not specify an account, you must be logged on under an account with these permissions for the command to work.

To list all of the standard TCP/IP printer ports on a computer

Syntax:

cscript prnport.vbs -l [-s RemoteComputer] [-u UserName -w Password]

Example:

cscript prnport.vbs -l -s HRServer

Syntax Options:

-l ·············Required. Specifies that you want to list all standard TCP/IP printer ports on a computer.

-s RemoteComputer ·······Specifies, by name, the remote computer for which you want to list ports. If you do not specify a computer, the ports on the local computer are listed.

-u UserName -w Password ·············Specifies an account with permissions to connect by using Windows Management Instrumentation (WMI) services to the computer for which you want to list all standard TCP/IP printer ports. All members of the Administrators group for that computer have these permissions, but the permissions can also be granted to other users. If you do not specify an account, you must be logged on under an account with these permissions for the command to work.

To display the configuration of a standard TCP/IP printer port

Syntax:

cscript prnport.vbs -g -r PortName [-s RemoteComputer] [-u UserName -w Password]

Syntax Options:

-g ·············Required. Specifies that you want to display the configuration of a standard TCP/IP printer port.

-r PortName ·············Required. Specifies the port whose configuration you want to display.

-s RemoteComputer ·······Specifies, by name, the remote computer that hosts the port whose configuration you want to display. If you do not specify a computer, information is displayed for the port as it is configured on the local computer.

-u UserName -w Password ·············Specifies an account with permissions to connect by using Windows Management Instrumentation (WMI) services to the computer that hosts the port whose configuration you want to display. All members of the Administrators group for that computer have these permissions, but the permissions can also be granted to other users. If you do not specify an account, you must be logged on under an account with these permissions for the command to work.

To configure a standard TCP/IP printer port

Syntax:

cscript prnport.vbs -t -r PortName [-s RemoteComputer] [-o {raw -n PortNumber | lpr}] [-h IPAddress] [-q QueueName] [-m{e | d}] [-i IndexName] [-y CommunityName] [-2{e | d}] [-u UserName -w Password]

Syntax Options:

-t ·············Required. Specifies that you want to configure a standard TCP/IP printer port.

-r PortName ·············Required. Specifies the port to which the printer is connected.

-s RemoteComputer ·······Specifies, by name, the remote computer on which you want to configure the port. If you do not specify a computer, the port is configured on the local computer.

-o {raw -n PortNumber | lpr} ·············Specifies which protocol the port uses: TCP raw or TCP LPR. If you use TCP raw, specifies the port number for a TCP raw printer port. By default, this is port number 9100. For more information, see Related Topics. Most printers use TCP raw. On UNIX networks, printer ports often use TCP LPR. For more information about TCP LPR, see RFC 1179 at http://www.microsoft.com/resources/documentation/windows/xp/all/proddocs/en-us/copyright.mspx

-h IPAddress ·············Specifies, by IP address, the printer for which you want to configure the port.

-q QueueName ·············Specifies the queue name for a TCP raw port.

-m{e | d}····Specifies whether SNMP is enabled. The parameter e enables SNMP. The parameter d disables SNMP.

-i IndexName ·············Specifies the SNMP index, if SNMP is enabled. For more information, see RFC 1759 at http://go.microsoft.com/fwlink/?linkid=569%20

-y CommunityName ·······Specifies the SNMP community name, if SNMP is enabled. For more information, see Related Topics.

-2{e | d}····Specifies whether double spools (also known as respooling) are enabled for TCP LPR ports. Double spools are necessary because TCP LPR must include an accurate byte count in the control file that is sent to the printer, but the protocol cannot get the count from the local print provider. Therefore, when a file is spooled to a TCP LPR print queue, it is also spooled as a temporary file in the system32 directory. TCP LPR determines the size of the temporary file and sends the size to the server running LPD. The parameter e enables double spools. The parameter d disables double spools.

-u UserName -w Password ·············Specifies an account with permissions to connect by using Windows Management Instrumentation (WMI) services to the computer on which you want to configure a port. All members of the Administrators group for that computer have these permissions, but the permissions can also be granted to other users. If you do not specify an account, you must be logged on under an account with these permissions for the command to work.

PRNQCTL.VBS

Prints a test page, pauses or resumes a printer, and clears a printer queue. Used without parameters, prnqctl.vbs displays command-line help for the prnqctl.vbs command.

To pause printing

Syntax:

cscript prnqctl.vbs -z [-s RemoteComputer] -p PrinterName [-u UserName -w Password]

Example:

cscript prnqctl.vbs -z -s HRServer -p ColorPrinter_2

Syntax Options:

-z ··············Required. Specifies that you want to pause printing.

-s RemoteComputer ·······Specifies, by name, the remote computer to which the printer you want to pause is attached. If you do not specify a computer, the printer attached to the local computer is paused.

-p PrinterName ··············Required. Specifies, by name, the printer you want to pause.

-u UserName -w Password ·············Specifies an account with permissions to connect by using Windows Management Instrumentation (WMI) services to the computer that hosts the printer on which you want to pause printing. All members of the Administrators group for that computer have these permissions, but the permissions can also be granted to other users. If you do not specify an account, you must be logged on under an account with these permissions for the command to work.

Notes:

• This command starts a script that is located in the systemroot\system32 directory. You must type this command at a command prompt with that directory as the current directory, or you must type the full path to that directory at the beginning of the cscript command.

• If the information that you supply contains spaces, use quotation marks around the text (for example, "Computer Name").

To resume printing

Syntax:

cscript prnqctl.vbs -m [-s RemoteComputer] -p PrinterName [-u UserName -w Password]

Example:

cscript prnqctl.vbs -m -s HRServer -p ColorPrinter_2

Syntax Options:

-m ··············Required. Specifies that you want to resume printing.

-s RemoteComputer ·······Specifies, by name, the remote computer to which the printer you want to resume is attached. If you do not specify a computer, the printer attached to the local computer is resumed.

-p PrinterName ··············Required. Specifies, by name, the printer on which you want to resume printing.

-u UserName -w Password ·············Specifies an account with permissions to connect by using Windows Management Instrumentation (WMI) services to the computer that manages the printer on which you want to resume printing. All members of the Administrators group for that computer have these permissions, but the permissions can also be granted to other users. If you do not specify an account, you must be logged on under an account with these permissions for the command to work.

To print a test page

Syntax:

cscript prnqctl.vbs -e [-s RemoteComputer] -p PrinterName [-u UserName -w Password]

Syntax Options:

-e ··············Required. Specifies that you want to print a test page.

-s RemoteComputer ·······Specifies, by name, the remote computer to which the printer on which you want to print a test page is attached. If you do not specify a computer, the local computer is used.

-p PrinterName ···············Required. Specifies, by name, the printer on which you want to print a test page.

-u UserName -w Password ···················Specifies an account with permissions to connect by using Windows Management Instrumentation (WMI) services to the computer that manages the printer on which you want to print a test page. All members of the Administrators group for that computer have these permissions, but the permissions can also be granted to other users. If you do not specify an account, you must be logged on under an account with these permissions for the command to work.

To cancel all jobs spooled to a printer

Syntax:

cscript prnqctl.vbs -x [-s RemoteComputer] -p PrinterName [-u UserName -w Password]

Syntax Options:

-x ···············Required. Specifies that you want to cancel all jobs spooled to a printer.

-s RemoteComputer ·······Specifies, by name, the remote computer to which the printer for which you want to cancel all jobs is attached. If you do not specify a computer, the local computer is used.

-p PrinterName ···············Required. Specifies, by name, the printer for which you want to cancel all print jobs.

-u UserName -w Password ···················Specifies an account with permissions to connect by using Windows Management Instrumentation (WMI) services to the computer on which you want to cancel all print jobs. All members of the Administrators group for that computer have these permissions, but the permissions can also be granted to other users. If you do not specify an account, you must be logged on under an account with these permissions for the command to work.

PROMPT

Changes the Cmd.exe prompt. Used without parameters, prompt resets the command prompt to the default setting, the current drive letter followed by the current directory and a greater-than symbol (>).

Syntax:

prompt [text]

Examples:

prompt pg   *or*   prompt time is: t_date is: $d

Syntax Options:

text···········Specifies any text and information you want included in your system prompt.

Notes:

• You can customize the command prompt to display any text you want, including such information as the name of the current directory, the time and date, and the Windows XP version number.

• The following table lists the character combinations you can include instead of, or in addition to, one or more character strings in the text command-line option. The list includes a brief description of the text or information that each character combination adds to your command prompt.

Character	Description
$q	= (equal sign)
$$	$ (dollar sign)
$t	Current time
$d	Current date
$p	Current drive and path
$v	Windows XP version number
$n	Current drive
$g	> (greater-than sign)
$l	< (less-than sign)

Character	Description
$b	I (pipe)
$_	ENTER-LINEFEED
$e	ANSI escape code (code 27)
$h	Backspace (to delete a character that has been written to the prompt command line)
$a	& (ampersand)
$c	((left parenthesis)
$f	) (right parenthesis)
$s	space

• When command extensions are enabled (that is, the default) the prompt command supports the formatting characters listed in the following table.

Character	Description
$+	Zero or more plus sign (+) characters depending upon the depth of the pushd directory stack, one character for each level pushed.
$m	The remote name associated with the current drive letter or the empty string if current drive is not a network drive.

• If you include the $p character in the text parameter, your disk is read, after you enter each command, to determine the current drive and path. This can take extra time, especially for floppy disk drives.

PUSHD

Stores the name of the current directory for use by the popd command before changing the current directory to the specified directory.

Syntax:

pushd [Path]

Examples:

You can use the pushd command and the popd command in a batch program to change the current directory from the one in which the batch program was run and then change it back. The following sample batch program shows how to do this:

```
@echo off
rem This batch file deletes all .txt files in a specified directory
pushd %1
del *.txt
popd
cls
echo All text files deleted in the %1 directory
```

Syntax Options:

Path··········Specifies the directory to which the current directory should be changed. This command supports relative paths.

Notes:

• Every time you use the pushd command, a single directory is stored for your use. However, you can store multiple directories by using the pushd command multiple times. The directories are stored sequentially in a virtual stack. If you use the pushd command once, the directory in which you use the command is placed at the bottom of the stack. If you use the command again, the second directory is placed on top of the first one. The process repeats every time you use the pushd command.
You can use the popd command to change the current directory to the directory most recently stored by the pushd command. If you use the popd command, the directory on the top of the stack is removed from the stack as the current directory is changed to that directory. If you use the popd command again, the next directory on the stack is removed.

• If command extensions are enabled, the pushd command accepts either a network path or a local drive letter and path.

• If you specify a network path, the pushd command temporarily assigns the first unused drive letter (starting with Z:) to the specified network resource. The command then changes the current drive and directory to the specified directory on the newly assigned drive. If you use the popd command with command extensions enabled, the popd command removes the drive-letter assignation created by pushd.

XP Command: PUSHD   203

RASDIAL

You can automate the connection process for any Microsoft client by using a simple batch file and the rasdial command. The rasdial command starts a network connection by using a specified entry.

Syntax:

rasdial connectionname [username [password | *]] [/domain:domain]
[/phone:phonenumber] [/callback:callbacknumber] [/phonebook:phonebookpath]
[/prefixsuffix]

The rasdial command disconnects a network connection by using the following syntax:

rasdial [connectionname] /disconnect

Examples:

rasdial office   or   rasdial "office 2" /callback:555-0100   or   rasdial "EAST OFFICE" /d

Syntax Options:

None ········Used without options, rasdial displays the status of current connections.

connectionname ············Specifies an entry in the current .pbk file, located in the systemroot\System32\Ras folder. If the connection name contains spaces or special characters, enclose the connection name in quotation marks (").

The Rasphone.pbk file is used unless the Personal Phonebook option is selected. If the Personal Phonebook option is selected, the file username.pbk is used. The name is shown on the Rasphone title bar when Personal Phonebook/p is selected. Numbers are appended if name conflicts occur.

username [password | *]·Specifies a user name and password with which to connect. If an asterisk is used, the user is prompted for the password, but does not display the characters typed.

/domain:domain ············Specifies the domain the user account is located in.

If not present, the last value of the Domain field in the Connect To dialog box is used.

/phone:phonenumber ·····Substitutes the specified phone number for the entry's phone number in Rasphone.pbk.

/callback:callbacknumberSubstitutes the specified callback number for the entry's callback number in Rasphone.pbk.

/disconnect ··················Disconnects the specified entry.

/phonebook:phonebookpath ···············Specifies the path to the phonebook file. The default is systemroot\System32\Ras\username.pbk. You can specify a full path to the file.

/prefixsuffix ··················Applies the current TAPI location dialing settings to the phone number. These settings are configured in Telephony, which is located in Control Panel. This option is off by default.

Notes:

- The following Rasphone.exe features are not supported with rasdial:
- Entries that require Terminal mode user entry during the dial sequence.
- Operator-assisted or manual dialing.

RCP

Copies files between a Windows XP and a system running rshd, the remote shell service (daemon). Windows XP and Windows 2000 do not provide rshd service.

Syntax:

rcp [{-a | -b}] [-h] [-r] [Host][.User:] [Source] [Host][.User:] [Path\Destination]

Examples:

rcp filename remotecomputer: or   rcp filename remotecomputer:/directory/newfilename

Syntax Options:

Used without parameters, rcp displays help.

-a ···········Specifies ASCII transfer mode. This mode converts the end-of-line (EOL) characters to a carriage return for UNIX and a carriage return/line feed for computers. This is the default transfer mode.

-b ···········Specifies binary image transfer mode. No carriage return/line feed conversion occurs.

-h ·············Transfers source files that are marked with the hidden attribute to the Windows XP computer. Otherwise, hidden files are not copied.

-r ·············Recursively copies to the destination the contents of all subdirectories of the source.

Host ·········Specifies the local or remote host. If Host is specified as an IP address or if the host name contains dots (.), you must specify the user.

User·········Specifies the user name. If the user name is not specified, the name of the user who is currently logged on is used.

Source ·····Specifies the files to copy.

Path\Destination ·············Specifies the path relative to the logon directory on the remote host. Use the backslash (\), quotation mark ("), or apostrophe () escape characters in remote paths to use wildcard characters on the remote host. If multiple source files are specified, the destination is a directory.

Notes:

• The rcp command, a connectivity command, can also be used for third-party transfers. You can run the rcp command from a Windows XP computer to copy files between two other computers that are running rshd. The rshd daemon is available on UNIX computers, so the Windows XP computer can participate in a third-party transfer only as the system from which the commands are run.

• Both the Source and Path\Destination must be directories. However, you can use -r without recursion if the source is not a directory.

• If the file name does not begin with a forward slash (/) for UNIX or a backslash (\) for Windows XP, it is assumed to be relative to the current working directory. On Windows XP, this is the directory from which the command is run. On the remote system, it is the logon directory for the remote user. A period (.) indicates the current directory. You can use the backslash (\), quotation mark ("), or apostrophe () escape characters in remote paths as wildcard characters on the remote computer.

• The rcp command does not prompt for passwords. The current or specified user name must exist on the remote computer and allow remote command execution with rcp.

• The .rhosts file specifies which remote systems or users can access a local account using rsh or rcp. This file (or a Hosts equivalent) is required for access to a remote system using these commands. Both the rsh and rcp commands transmit the local user name to the remote system. The remote system uses this name and the IP address (usually resolved to a computer name) of the requesting system to determine whether access is granted. There is no provision for specifying a password to access an account using these commands.

• If the user is logged on to a domain, the primary domain controller must be available to resolve the logon name because it is not cached on the local computer. Because the user name is required as part of the rsh protocol, the command fails if it cannot be obtained.

• The .rhosts file is a text file in which each line is an entry. An entry consists of the local computer name, the local user name, and any comments about the entry. Each entry is separated by a tab or space, and comments begin with a pound sign (#), for example: computer5marie #This computer is in room 31A

• The .rhosts file must be in the user's home directory on the remote computer. For more information about the specific implementation of the .rhosts file on a remote computer, see the remote system documentation.

• Additionally, you can add your computer name to the /Etc/Hosts file on the remote computer. This allows the remote system to authenticate remote requests for your computer when you use the Windows XP TCP/IP utilities.

• Use the Computer.User parameters to use a user name other than the current one. If Computer.User is specified with Source, the .rhosts file on the remote computer must contain an entry for User, as follows: rcp host99.user7:file1 corp7.admin:file2

• If a computer name is supplied as a full domain name containing dots, a user name must be appended to the computer name, as previously described. This prevents the last part of the domain name from being interpreted as a user name, as follows: rcp domain-name1.user:user92 domain-name2.user:user7

• Remote processing is performed by a command that is run from the user logon shell on most UNIX systems. The .profile or .cshrc of the user is executed before parsing file

XP Command: RCP   205

names, and exported shell variables can be used (using the escape character or quotation marks) in remote file names.

• If you attempt to copy a number of files to a file rather than a directory, only the last file is copied. The rcp command cannot copy a file onto itself (the Source and Path/Destination cannot be the same).

• If you have logged onto the Windows XP Professional computer using a domain other than the local one, and the primary domain controller is unavailable, the command fails because rcp cannot determine the local user name. The same restriction applies to rsh.

• This command is available only if the Internet Protocol (TCP/IP) protocol is installed as a component in the properties of a network adapter in Network Connections

RECOVER

Recovers readable information from a bad or defective disk.

Syntax:
recover [Drive:][Path] FileName

Examples:
To recover the file Story.txt in the \Fiction directory in drive D:, type:
recover d:\fiction\story.txt

Syntax Options:
[Drive:][Path] FileName : Specifies the location and name of the file you want to recover.

Notes:
• The recover command reads a file sector by sector and recovers data from the good sectors. Data in bad sectors is lost.

• Limitation on [drive:][path]filename: You cannot use wildcards (* and ?) with the recover command. You must specify a file.

• Because all data in bad sectors is lost when you recover a file, you should recover files one at a time. You can use this method to edit each file and reenter missing information after you recover the file.

• Bad sectors reported by chkdsk were marked as "bad" when your disk was first prepared for operation. They pose no danger, and recover does not affect them.

Redirection Commands

Redirection Commands are used to redirect command input and output from the default location to a different location. There commands are also used in conjunction with Filter Commands (see page 135).

Syntax:
> ··············· Command output is written to a file or a device (such as a printer) instead of the default command prompt window. Default handle for > is 1

< ··············· Command input is read from a file instead of the keyboard

>> ·············· Command output is appended to the end of a file without deleting files contents

>& ··········· Command output is written from one location to a different location (&=handle)

<& ··········· Command input is read from one location and written to the output of another location. (&=handle)

| ··············· Reads output from one command and writes it to the input of another command.

Syntax Options:
STDIN handle ··············· &0, Keyboard input
STDOUT handle ··········· &1, Command Prompt window output
STDERR handle ··········· &2, Command Prompt window Error output
Undefined handles··········· &3...&9, Applications define these handles

Examples:
sort < sequoia.txt ···········sort and display the contents of the txt file
1 < &2 ·······························recirects error output to the Command Prompt window
dir > sequoia.txt ·············write a directory listing of the current folder to the txt file

dir > sequoia.txt > &1·····write a directory listing to the txt file and display in Command window

dir >> sequoia.txt ···········append a directory listing to the end of the existing txt file

ipconfig.exe >> log.txt 2 > &1....append ipconfig output to end of txt file and to Command Wind.

dir | sort > c:\sequoia.txt ·write a sorted directory listing to the sequoia.txt file

dir c:\winnt | more ···········write a directory listing of winnt one screen at a time to Com. Window

REG

Adds, changes, and displays registry subkey information and values in registry entries.

Caution: Incorrectly editing the registry may severely damage your system. Before making changes to the registry, you should back up any valued data on the computer.

Do not edit the registry directly unless you have no alternative. The registry editor bypasses standard safeguards, allowing settings that can degrade performance, damage your system, or even require you to reinstall Windows.

reg add

Adds a new subkey or entry to the registry.

Syntax:

reg add KeyName [/v EntryName|/ve] [/t DataType] [/s separator] [/d value] [/f]

Examples:

reg add \hklm\software\myco /v data /t reg_binary /d fe340ead   or
reg add "hkcu\software\microsoft\winmine" /v Name3 /t reg_sz /d Anonymous

Syntax Options:

KeyName··Specifies the full path of the subkey. For remote computers, include the computer name before the path of the subkey in the \\ComputerName\PathToSubkey format. Omitting ComputerName causes the operation to default to the local computer. Start the path with the appropriate subtree. The valid subtrees are HKLM, HKCU, HKCR, HKU, and HKCC.

/v EntryName··················Specifies the name of the entry to be added under the specified subkey.

/ve············Specifies that the entry that is added to the registry has a null value.

/t DataType ·····················Specifies the data type for the value of the entry. DataType can be one of the following:

REG_SZ
REG_MULTI_SZ
REG_DWORD_BIG_ENDIAN
REG_DWORD
REG_BINARY
REG_DWORD_LITTLE_ENDIAN
REG_LINK
REG_FULL_RESOURCE_DESCRIPTOR
REG_EXPAND_SZ

/s separator·····················Specifies the character used to separate multiple instances of data. Used when REG_MULTI_SZ is specified as the data type and more than one entry needs to be listed. If not specified, the default separator is \0.

/d value·····Specifies the value for the new registry entry.

/f ···············Adds the subkey or entry without asking for confirmation.

Notes:

• Subtrees cannot be added with this operation. This version of Reg does not ask for confirmation when adding a subkey.

• The following table lists the return values for the reg add operation.

Value ·······Description
0···········Success
1···········Failure

reg compare

Compares specified registry subkeys or entries.

Syntax:

reg compare KeyName1 KeyName2 [/v EntryName | /ve] {[/oa]|[/od]|[/os]|[on]} [/s]

Examples:

reg compare "hkcu\software\microsoft\winmine" "hkcu\software\microsoft\winmine" /od /s

Syntax Options:

KeyName··Specifies the full path of the subkey. For remote computers, include the computer name before the path of the subkey in the \\ComputerName\PathtoSubkey format. Omitting ComputerName causes the operation to default to the local computer. Start the path with the appropriate subtree. The valid subtrees are HKLM, HKCU, HKCR, HKU, and HKCC. If a remote computer is specified, you can use the HKLM and HKU subtrees only.

/v EntryName ················Compares a specific entry under the subkey.

/ve············Specifies that only entries that have no value will be compared.

{[/oa]|[/od]|[/os]|[on]}········Specifies how differences and matches are displayed. The default is /od.

Value ······Description

/oa············Specifies that all differences and matches are displayed. By default, only the differences are listed.

/od············Specifies that only differences are displayed. This is the default behavior.

/os············Specifies that only matches are displayed. By default, only the differences will be listed.

/on············Specifies that nothing is displayed. By default, only the differences will be listed.

/s Separator ················Compares all subkeys and entries.

Notes:

• The following table lists the return values for the reg compare operation.

Value ······Description

0············The comparison is successful and the result is identical.

1············The comparison failed.

2············The comparison is successful and differences were found.

reg copy

Copies a registry entry to a specified location in the local or remote computer.

Syntax:

reg copy KeyName1 KeyName2 [/s] [/f]

Examples:

reg copy "hkcu\software\microsoft\winmine" "hkcu\software\microsoft\winminebk" /s /f   *or*

reg copy "hkcu\software\microsoft\winminebk" "hkcu\software\microsoft\winmine" /s

Syntax Options:

KeyName1Specifies the full path of the subkey to copy. For remote computers, include the computer name before the path of the subkey in the \\ComputerName\PathToSubkey format. Omitting ComputerName causes the operation to default to the local computer. Start the path with the appropriate subtree. The valid subtrees are HKLM, HKCU, HKCR, HKU, and HKCC. If a remote computer is specified, you can use the HKLM and HKU subtrees only.

KeyName2Specifies the full path of the subkey destination. For remote computers, include the computer name before the path of the subkey in the \\ComputerName\PathToSubkey format. Omitting ComputerName causes the operation to default to the local computer. Start the path with the appropriate subtree. The valid subtrees are HKLM, HKCU, HKCR, HKU, and HKCC. If a remote computer is specified, you can use the HKLM and HKU subtrees only.

/s··············Copies all subkeys and entries under the specified subkey.

/f··············Copies the subkey without asking for confirmation.

Notes:

• This version of Reg does not ask for confirmation when copying a subkey.

• The following table lists the return values for the reg copy operation.

Value ·······Description
   0···········Success
   1···········Failure

reg delete

Deletes a subkey or entries from the registry.

Syntax:

reg delete KeyName [{/v EntryNamel/vel/va}] [/f]

Examples:

reg delete "hkcu\software\microsoft\winmine" /v Name1   *or*
reg delete "hkcu\software\microsoft\winmine" /v Time1

Syntax Options:

KeyName··Specifies the full path of the subkey. For remote computers, include the computer name before the path of the subkey in the \\ComputerName\PathToSubkey format. Omitting ComputerName causes the operation to default to the local computer. Start the path with the appropriate subtree. The valid subtrees are HKLM, HKCU, HKCR, HKU, and HKCC.

/v EntryName··················Deletes a specific entry under the subkey. If no entry is specified, then all entries and subkeys under the subkey will be deleted.

/ve···········Specifies that only entries that have no value will be deleted.

/va···········Deletes all entries under the specified subkey. Subkeys under the specified subkey are not deleted with this parameter.

/f ·············Deletes the existing registry subkey or entry without asking for confirmation.

Notes:

• The following table lists the return values for the reg delete operation.

Value ·······Description
   0···········Success
   1···········Failure

reg export

Creates a copy of specified subkeys, entries, and values into a file so that it can be transferred to other servers.

Syntax:

reg export KeyName FileName

Examples:

reg export "hkcu\software\microsoft\winmine" c:\data\regbackups\wmbkup.reg

Syntax Options:

KeyName··Specifies the full path of the subkey. The export operation works only with the local computer. Start the path with the appropriate subtree. The valid subtrees are HKLM, HKCU, HKCR, HKU, and HKCC.

FileName··Specifies the name and path of the file to be exported. The file must have a .reg extension.

Notes:

• The following table lists the return values for the reg export operation:

Value ·······Description
   0···········Success
   1···········Failure

reg import

Copies a file containing exported registry subkeys, entries, and values into the local computer's registry.

Syntax:

reg import FileName

Examples:

reg import "hkcu\software\microsoft\winmine" c:\data\regbackups\wmbkup.reg

Syntax Options:

    FileName··Specifies he name and path of the file that will be copied into the registry of the local computer. This file needs to be created beforehand with the reg export operation.

Notes:

- The following table lists the return values for the reg import operation:

Value ······· Description
    0············Success
    1············Failure

reg load

Writes saved subkeys and entries back to a different subkey in the registry. This is intended to be a temporary file that can be used for troubleshooting or editing registry entries.

Syntax:

    reg load KeyName FileName

Examples:

    reg load "hkcu\software\microsoft\winminebk2" wmbkup.hiv

Syntax Options:

    KeyName··Specifies the full path of the subkey. For remote computers, include the computer name before the path of the subkey in the \\ComputerName\PathToSubkey format. Omitting ComputerName causes the operation to default to the local computer. Start the path with the appropriate subtree. The valid subtrees are HKLM, HKCU, HKCR, HKU, and HKCC.

    FileName··Specifies the name and path of the file that will be loaded. This file must have been created with the reg save operation using a .hiv extension.

Notes:

- The following table lists the return values for the reg load operation:

Value ······· Description
    0············Success
    1············Failure

reg query

Returns a list of the next tier of subkeys and entries located under a subkey in the registry.

Syntax:

    reg query KeyName [{/v EntryName|/ve}] [/s]

Examples:

    reg query "hklm\system\currentcontrolset\control\session manager" /v maxstacktracedepth **or**
    reg query "hkcu\software\microsoft\winmine" /s

Syntax Options:

    KeyName··Specifies the full path of the subkey. For remote computers, include the computer name before the path of the subkey in the \\ComputerName\PathToSubkey format. Omitting ComputerName causes the operation to default to the local computer. Start the path with the appropriate subtree. The valid subtrees are HKLM, HKCU, HKCR, HKU, and HKCC. If a remote computer is specified, you can use the HKLM and HKU subtrees only.

    /v EntryName ··················Returns a specific entry and its value. This parameter only returns entries that are in the tier directly below the specified subkey. Entries that are located in subkeys under the current subkey will not be found. When EntryName is omitted, all entries under the subkey are returned.

    /ve············Specifies that only entries that have no value will be returned.

    /s···············Returns all subkeys and entries in all tiers. Without this parameter, only the next tier of subkeys and entries will be returned.

Notes:

- The following table lists the return values for the reg query operation:

Value ······· Description
    0············Success
    1············Failure

reg restore

Writes saved subkeys and entries back to the registry.

Syntax:

reg restore KeyName FileName

Examples:

reg restore "hkcu\software\microsoft\winmine" wmbkup.hiv

Syntax Options:

KeyName··Specifies the full path of the subkey. The restore operation works only with the local computer. Start the path with the appropriate subtree. The valid subtrees are HKLM, HKCU, HKCR, HKU, and HKCC.

FileName··Specifies the name and path of the file that will be written back to the registry. This file needs to be created beforehand with the reg save operation using a .hiv extension.

Notes:

• This operation is used to overwrite registry entries that have been edited. Before editing entries, save the parent subkey with the reg save operation. If the edit fails, restore the subkey with this operation.

• The following table lists the return values for the reg restore operation:

Value ········Description
0···········Success
1···········Failure

reg save

Saves a copy of specified subkeys, entries, and values of the registry in a specified file.

Syntax:

reg save KeyName FileName

Examples:

reg save "hkcu\software\microsoft\winmine" wmbkup.hiv

Syntax Options:

KeyName··Specifies the full path of the subkey. For remote computers, include the computer name before the path of the subkey in the \\ComputerName\PathToSubkey format. Omitting ComputerName causes the operation to default to the local computer. Start the path with the appropriate subtree. The valid subtrees are HKLM, HKCU, HKCR, HKU, and HKCC.

FileName··Specifies the name and path of the file that is created. If no path is specified, then the current path is used.

Notes:

• The following table lists the return values for the reg save operation.

Value ········Description
0···········Success
1···········Failure

reg unload

Removes a section of the registry that was loaded using the reg load operation.

Syntax:

reg unload KeyName

Examples:

reg unload "hkcu\software\microsoft\winminebk2"

Syntax Options:

KeyName··Specifies the full path of the subkey. For remote computers, include the computer name before the path of the subkey in the \\ComputerName\PathToSubkey format. Omitting ComputerName causes the operation to default to the local computer. Start the path with the appropriate subtree. The valid subtrees are HKLM, HKCU, HKCR, HKU, and HKCC.

Notes:

• The following table lists the return values for the reg unload operation.
Value ········Description

0···········Success
1···········Failure

• **Caution:** Incorrectly editing the registry may severely damage your system. Before making changes to the registry, you should back up any valued data on the computer.

• **Caution:** Do not edit the registry directly unless you have no alternative. The registry editor bypasses standard safeguards, allowing settings that can degrade performance, damage your system, or even require you to reinstall Windows. You can safely alter most registry settings by using the programs in Control Panel or Microsoft Management Console (MMC). If you must edit the registry directly, back it up first. Read the Registry Editor Help for more information.

• Using Reg directly edits the registry of local or remote computers. These changes can render the computers inoperable and cause the need for a new installation of the operating system. Instead of directly editing the registry, use Control Panel or Microsoft Management Console, whenever possible, to make changes to the registry.

• Some operations allow the viewing or configuration of registry entries on local or remote computers, while others allow only the configuration of local computers. Also, accessing the registry remotely might limit the parameters that you can use in an operation. Check the syntax for each operation to verify that it can be used on remote computers and to verify the parameters that can be used in that situation.

REGSVR32

This command-line tool registers .dll files as command components in the registry.

Syntax:

regsvr32 [/u] [/s] [/n] [/i:cmdline] dllname

Examples:

regsvr32 schmmgmt.dll

Syntax Options:

/u ·············Unregisters server.

/s ··············Specifies regsvr32 to run silently and to not display any message boxes.

/n ··············Specifies not to call DllRegisterServer. You must use this option with /i.

/i:cmdline ··Calls DllInstall passing it an optional [cmdline]. When used with /u, it calls dll uninstall.

dllname·····Specifies the name of the dll file that will be registered.

RELOG

Extracts performance counters from performance counter logs into other formats, such as text-TSV (for tab-delimited text), text-CSV (for comma-delimited text), binary-BIN, or SQL.

Syntax:

relog [FileName [filename ...]] [-a] [-c Path [path ...]] [-cf FileName] [-f {bin|csv|tsv|SQL}]
[-t value] [-o {output file | DSN!counter_log}] [-b M/d/yyyy [[hh:]mm:]ss]
[-e M/d/yyyy [[hh:]mm:]ss] [-config FileName] [-q]

Examples:

Relog c:\perflogs\daily_trace_log.blg -cf counter_file.txt -o c:\perflogs\reduced_log.csv -t 30 -f csv **or**
Relog c:\perflogs\daily_trace_log.blg -cf counter_file.txt -o c:\perflogs\reduced_log.blg -t 30

Syntax Options:

FileName [filename ...]····Specifies the pathname of an existing performance counter log. You can specify multiple input files.

-a ··············Appends output file instead of overwriting. This option does not apply to SQL format where the default is always to append.

-c Path [path ...] ··············Specifies the performance counter path to log. To specify multiple counter paths, separate them with a space and enclose the counter paths in quotation marks (for example, "CounterPath1 CounterPath2").

-cf FileName ··················Specifies the pathname of the text file that lists the performance counters to be included in a relog file. Use this option to list counter paths in an input file, one per line. Default setting is all counters in the original log file are relogged.

-f {bin|csv|tsv|SQL} ········Specifies the pathname of the output file format. The default format is bin. For a SQL database, the output file specifies the DSN!counter_log. You can specify the database location by using the ODBC manager to configure the DSN (Database System Name).

-t value ······Specifies sample intervals in "n" records. Includes every nth data point in the relog file. Default is every data point.

-o {output file | DSN\counter_log} ········Specifies the pathname of the output file or SQL database where the counters will be written.

-b M/d/yyyy hh[:mm[:ss]]·Specifies begin time for copying first record from the input file. Date and time must be in this exact format M/d/yyyy hh:mm:ss.

-e M/d/yyyy hh[:mm[:ss]]·Specifies end time for copying last record from the input file. Date and time must be in this exact format M/d/yyyy hh:mm:ss.

-config FileName ···········Specifies the pathname of the settings file that contains command-line parameters.

-q ···············Displays the performance counters and time ranges of log files specified in the input file.

Notes:

• The general format for counter paths is as follows:
[\\Computer\]object[parent/instance#index]\counter] where:
The parent, instance, index, and counter components of the format may contain either a valid name or a wildcard character. The computer, parent, instance, and index components are not necessary for all counters.

• You determine the counter paths to use based on the counter itself. For example, the LogicalDisk object has an instance index, so you must provide the #index or a wildcard. Therefore, you could use the following format: \LogicalDisk(*/*#*)*

• In comparison, the Process object does not require an instance index. Therefore, you could use the following format: \Process(*)\ID Process

• The following is a list of the possible formats:
\\machine\object(parent/instance#index)\counter
\\machine\object(parent/instance)\counter
\\machine\object(instance#index)\counter
\\machine\object(instance)\counter
\\machine\object\counter
\object(parent/instance#index)\counter
\object(parent/instance)\counter
\object(instance#index)\counter
\object(instance)\counter
\object\counter

• If a wildcard character is specified in the parent name, all instances of the specified object that match the specified instance and counter fields will be returned.

• If a wildcard character is specified in the instance name, all instances of the specified object and parent object will be returned if all instance names corresponding to the specified object match the wildcard character.

• If a wildcard character is specified in the counter name, all counters of the specified object are returned.

• Partial counter path string matches (for example, pro*) are not supported.

• Counter files are text files that list one or more of the performance counters in the existing log. Copy the full counter name from the log or the -q output in [\\Computer \ object [instance] \ counter] format. List one counter path on each line.

• When executed, Relog copies specified counters from every record in the input file, converting the format if necessary. Wildcard paths are allowed in the counter file.

• Use the -t parameter to specify that input files are inserted into output files at intervals of every nth record. By default, data is relogged from every record.

• You can specify that your output logs include records from before begin-time (-b) to provide data for counters that require computation values of the formatted value. The output file will have the last records from input files with timestamps less than the end-time (-e) parameter.

• Instrumentation (WMI) scripts, see Scripting Logs and Monitoring at http://www.microsoft.com/resources/documentation/windows/xp/all/proddocs/en-us/ntcmds.mspx

REM

Enables you to include comments (remarks) in a batch file or in your configuration files.

Syntax:

rem [comment]

Examples:

The following example shows a batch file that uses remarks for both explanations and vertical spacing:

```
@echo off
rem This batch program formats and checks new disks.
rem It is named Checknew.bat.
rem
echo Insert new disk in drive B.
pause
format b: /v
chkdsk b:
```

Suppose you want to include in your Config.nt file an explanatory comment before the prompt command. To do this, add the following lines to Config.nt:

```
rem Set prompt to indicate current directory
prompt $p$g
```

Syntax Options:

comment···Specifies any string of characters you want to include as a comment.

Notes:

- The rem command does not display comments on the screen. You must use the echo on command in your batch or Config.nt file to display comments on the screen.

- You cannot use a redirection character "(" or ")" or pipe (|) in a batch file comment.

- Although you can use rem without a comment to add vertical spacing to a batch file, you can also use blank lines. The blank lines are ignored when processing the batch program.

RENAME (REN)

Changes the name of a file or a set of files.

Syntax:

rename [Drive:][Path] filename1 filename2

ren [Drive:][Path] filename1 filename2

Examples:

Suppose you want to change the extensions of all the file names in the current directory that have the extension .txt; for example, you want to change the .txt extensions to .doc extensions. To make this change, type: ren *.txt *.doc

To rename a file or directory named Chap10 to Part10, type: ren chap10 part10

Syntax Options:

[Drive:][Path] filename1 ··Specifies the location and name of the file or set of files you want to rename.

filename2··Specifies the new name for the file. If you use wildcards (* and ?), filename2 specifies the new names for the files. You cannot specify a new drive or path when re-naming files.

Notes:

- You can rename all files matching the specified file name. You cannot use the rename command to rename files across drives or to move files to a different directory location.

- You can use wildcards (* and ?) in either file name parameter. If you use wildcards in filename2, the characters represented by the wildcards will be identical to the corresponding characters in filename1.

- If, for filename2, you specify a file name that already exists, rename displays the following message: Duplicate file name or file not found

REPLACE

Replaces files in the destination directory with files in the source directory that have the same name. You can also use replace to add unique file names to the destination directory.

Syntax:

replace [drive1:][path1] FileName [drive2:][path2] [/a] [/p] [/r] [/w]

replace [drive1:][path1] FileName [drive2:][path2] [/p] [/r] [/s] [/w] [/u]

Examples:

Suppose that several directories on drive C contain different versions of a file named Phones.cli, which contains client names and phone numbers. To replace all of these files with the latest version of the Phones.cli file from the disk in drive A, type: replace a:\phones.cli c:\ /s

To add new printer device drivers to a directory on drive C named Tools, which already contains several printer device-driver files for a word processor: replace a:*.prd c:\tools /a This command searches the current directory on drive A for any files that have the extension .prd and then adds these files to the Tools directory on drive C. Because the /a command-line option is included, replace adds only those files from drive A that do not exist on drive C.

Syntax Options:

[drive1:][path1] FileName ....Specifies the location and name of the source file or set of files.

[drive2:][path2] ....Specifies the location of the destination file. You cannot specify a file name for files you replace. If you specify neither a drive nor a directory, replace uses the current drive and directory as the destination.

/a ....Adds new files to the destination directory instead of replacing existing files. You cannot use this command-line option with the /s or /u command-line option.

/p ....Prompts you for confirmation before replacing a destination file or adding a source file.

/r ....Replaces read-only files as well as unprotected files. If you do not specify this command-line option but attempt to replace a read-only file, an error results and stops the replacement operation.

/w...............Waits for you to insert a disk before replace begins to search for source files. If you do not specify /w, replace begins replacing or adding files immediately after you press ENTER.

/s................Searches all subdirectories of the destination directory and replaces matching files. You cannot use the /s command-line option with the /a command-line option. The replace command does not search subdirectories specified in path1.

/u ....Replaces (updates) only those files on the destination directory that are older than those in the source directory. You cannot use the /u command-line option with the /a command-line option.

Notes:

• As replace adds or replaces files, the file names are displayed on the screen. After the replace command is finished, a summary line is displayed in one of the following formats:

nnn files added
nnn files replaced
no file added
no file replaced

• If you are using floppy disks and need to switch disks during the replace operation, you can specify the /w command-line option so that replace will wait for you to switch disks, as necessary.

• You cannot use the replace command to update hidden files or system files.

• The following list shows each exit code and a brief description of its meaning:

Exit code	Description
0	The replace command successfully replaced or added the files.
1	The replace command encountered an incorrect version of MS-DOS.
2	The replace command could not find the source files.
3	The replace command could not find the source or destination path.
5	The user does not have access to the files you want to replace.
8	There is insufficient system memory to carry out the command.
11	The user used the wrong syntax on the command line.

• You can use the errorlevel parameter on the if command line in a batch program to process exit codes returned by replace.

RESET SESSION

Enables you to reset (delete) a session from the terminal server.

Syntax:

reset session {SessionName|SessionID} [/server:ServerName] [/v]

Syntax Options:

SessionName ············The name of the session you want to reset. To determine the name of the session, use the query session command.

SessionID · The ID of the session to reset.

/server:ServerName········Specifies the terminal server containing the session you want to reset. Otherwise, the current terminal server is used.

/v············Displays information about the actions being performed.

Notes:

• You can always reset your own sessions, but you must have Full Control access permission to reset another user's session.

• Be aware that resetting a user's session without warning can result in loss of data at the session.

• You should reset a session only when it malfunctions or appears to have stopped responding.

• The /server parameter is required only if you use reset session from a remote server.

REXEC

Runs commands on remote computers running the Rexec service (daemon). The rexec command authenticates the user name on the remote computer before executing the specified command. Windows XP and Windows 2000 do not provide the Rexec service.

Syntax:

rexec [Host] [-l UserName] [-n] [Command]

Examples:

rexec vax1 -l admin1 telcon

Syntax Options:

Used without parameters, rexec displays help.

Host ·········Specifies the remote host (computer) on which to run Command by IP address or name.

-l UserName ··············Specifies the user name on the remote computer. If omitted, the user name of the user who is currently logged on is used.

-n ············Redirects the input of rexec to the NUL device. This prevents the display of the command results on the local computer.

Command·Specifies the command to run on the remote computer.

Notes:

• The rexec command prompts the user for a password and authenticates the given password on the remote computer. If the authentication succeeds, the command is run.

• The rexec command copies standard input to the remote command, standard output of the remote Command to its standard output, and the standard error of the remote command to its standard error. The rexec normally quits when the remote command quits.

• for redirection to occur on the remote computer, enclose redirection symbols in quotation marks (for example, ">"). If you do not use quotation marks, redirection occurs on the local computer. For example, the following command appends the remote file RemoteFile to the local file LocalFile:

rexec othercomputer cat remotefile > localfile

• The following command appends the remote file RemoteFile to the remote file OtherRemoteFile:

rexec othercomputer cat remotefile ">" otherremotefile

• You cannot run most interactive commands. For example, vi or emacs cannot be run by using rexec. You can, however, use telnet instead.

• This command is available only if the Internet Protocol (TCP/IP) protocol is installed as a component in the properties of a network adapter in Network Connections

RMDIR (RD)

Removes (that is, deletes) a directory.

Syntax:

rmdir [Drive:]Path [/s] [/q]

rd [Drive:]Path [/s] [/q]

Examples:

rmdir \user\smith   *or*   rmdir /s \user

Syntax Options:

[Drive:]Path ···············Specifies the location and name of the directory that you want to delete.

/s···············Removes the specified directory and all subdirectories including any files. Use /s to remove a tree.

/q ···············Runs rmdir in quiet mode. Deletes directories without confirmation.

Notes:

• The rmdir command, with different parameters, is available from the Recovery Console.

• You cannot delete a directory that contains files, including hidden or system files. If you attempt to do so, the following message appears:
The directory not empty

• Use the dir command to list hidden and system files, and the attrib command to remove hidden and system attributes from files. For more information, see Related Topics.

• If you insert a backslash (\) before the first directory name in path, the directory is treated as a subdirectory of the root directory, regardless of your current directory. If you do not insert a backslash before the first directory name in path, the directory is treated as a subdirectory of the current directory.

• You cannot use rmdir to delete the current directory. You must first change to a different directory (not a subdirectory of the current directory) and then use rmdir with a path. If you attempt to delete the current directory, the following message appears:
"The process cannot access the file because it is being used by another process."

ROUTE

Displays and modifies the entries in the local IP routing table.

Syntax:

route [-f] [-p] [Command [Destination] [mask Netmask] [Gateway] [metric Metric]] [if Interface]]

Examples:

route print   or   route print 10.*   *or*   route add 0.0.0.0 mask 0.0.0.0 192.168.12.1

Syntax Options:

Used without parameters, route displays help.

-f ···············Clears the routing table of all entries that are not host routes (routes with a netmask of 255.255.255.255), the loopback network route (routes with a destination of 127.0.0.0 and a netmask of 255.0.0.0), or a multicast route (routes with a destination of 224.0.0.0 and a netmask of 240.0.0.0). If this is used in conjunction with one of the commands (such as add, change, or delete), the table is cleared prior to running the command.

-p : When used with the add command, the specified route is added to the registry and is used to initialize the IP routing table whenever the TCP/IP protocol is started. By default, added routes are not preserved when the TCP/IP protocol is started. When used with the print command, the list of persistent routes is displayed. This parameter is ignored for all other commands. Persistent routes are stored in the registry location HKEY_LOCAL_MACHINE\SYSTEM\CurrentControlSet\Services\Tcpip\Parameters\PersistentRoutes.

Command·Specifies the command you want to run. The following table lists valid commands.

Command	Purpose
add	Adds a route.
change	Modifies an existing route.

Command	Purpose
delete	Deletes a route or routes.
print	Prints a route or routes.

Destination·················Specifies the network destination of the route. The destination can be an IP network address (where the host bits of the network address are set to 0), an IP address for a host route, or 0.0.0.0 for the default route.

mask Netmask··············Specifies the netmask (also known as a subnet mask) associated with the network destination. The subnet mask can be the appropriate subnet mask for an IP network address, 255.255.255.255 for a host route, or 0.0.0.0 for the default route. If omitted, the subnet mask 255.255.255.255 is used. Because of the relationship between the destination and the subnet mask in defining routes, the destination cannot be more specific than its corresponding subnet mask. In other words, there cannot be a bit set to 1 in the destination if the corresponding bit in the subnet mask is a 0.

Gateway ···Specifies the forwarding or next hop IP address over which the set of addresses defined by the network destination and subnet mask are reachable. For locally attached subnet routes, the gateway address is the IP address assigned to the interface that is attached to the subnet. For remote routes, available across one or more routers, the gateway address is a directly reachable IP address that is assigned to a neighboring router.

metric Metric··················Specifies an integer cost metric (ranging from 1 to 9999) for the route, which is used when choosing among multiple routes in the routing table that most closely match the destination address of a packet being forwarded. The route with the lowest metric is chosen. The metric can reflect the number of hops, the speed of the path, path reliability, path throughput, or administrative properties.

if Interface·Specifies the interface index for the interface over which the destination is reachable. For a list of interfaces and their corresponding interface indexes, use the display of the route print command. You can use either decimal or hexadecimal values for the interface index. For hexadecimal values, precede the hexadecimal number with 0x. When the if parameter is omitted, the interface is determined from the gateway address.

Notes:

• Large values in the metric column of the routing table are the result of allowing TCP/IP to automatically determine the metric for routes in the routing table based on the configuration of IP address, subnet mask, and default gateway for each LAN interface. Automatic determination of the interface metric, enabled by default, determines the speed of each interface and adjusts the metrics of routes for each interface so that the fastest interface creates the routes with the lowest metric. To remove the large metrics, disable the automatic determination of the interface metric from the advanced properties of the TCP/IP protocol for each LAN connection.

• Names can be used for Destination if an appropriate entry exists in the local Networks file stored in the systemroot\System32\Drivers\Etc folder. Names can be used for the gateway as long as they can be resolved to an IP address through standard host name resolution techniques such as Domain Name System (DNS) queries, use of the local Hosts file stored in the systemroot\system32\drivers\etc folder, and NetBIOS name resolution.

• If the command is print or delete, the Gateway parameter can be omitted and wildcards can be used for the destination and gateway. The Destination value can be a wildcard value specified by an asterisk (*). If the destination specified contains an asterisk (*) or a question mark (?), it is treated as a wildcard and only matching destination routes are printed or deleted. The asterisk matches any string, and the question mark matches any single character. For example, 10.*.1, 192.168.*, 127.*, and *224* are all valid uses of the asterisk wildcard.

• Using an invalid combination of a destination and subnet mask (netmask) value displays a "Route: bad gateway address netmask" error message. This error message appears when the destination contains one or more bits set to 1 in bit locations where the corresponding subnet mask bit is set to 0. To test this condition, express the destination and subnet mask using binary notation. The subnet mask in binary notation consists of a series of 1 bits, representing the network address portion of the destination, and a series of 0 bits, representing the host address portion of the destination. Check to determine whether there are bits in the destination that are set to 1 for the portion of the destination that is the host address (as defined by the subnet mask).

• The -p parameter is only supported on the route command for Windows NT 4.0, Windows 2000, Windows Millennium Edition, and Windows XP. This parameter is not supported by the route command for Windows 95 or Windows 98.

• This command is available only if the Internet Protocol (TCP/IP) protocol is installed as a component in the properties of a network adapter in Network Connections

RSH

Runs commands in Windows XP Professional, not in Windows XP Home.

Runs commands on remote computers running the RSH service or daemon. Windows XP and Windows 2000 do not provide an RSH service. An RSH service called Rshsvc.exe is provided with the Windows 2000 Server Resource Kit.

Syntax:

rsh [Host] [-l UserName] [-n] [Command]

Examples:

rsh vax1 -l admin1 telcon

Syntax Options:

Used without parameters, rsh displays help.

Host ·········· Specifies the remote host (computer) on which to run Command.

-l UserName ················· Specifies the user name to use on the remote computer. If omitted, the user name of the user who is currently logged on is used.

-n ·············· Redirects the input of rsh to the NUL device. This prevents the display of the command results on the local computer.

Command·Specifies the command to run.

Notes:

• The rsh command copies standard input to the remote Command, standard output of the remote Command to its standard output, and the standard error of the remote Command to its standard error. Rsh normally quits when the remote command quits.

• Enclose redirection symbols in quotation marks for redirection to occur on the remote computer (for example, ">"). If you do not use quotation marks, redirection occurs on the local computer. For example, the following command appends the remote file RemoteFile to the local file LocalFile:
rsh othercomputer cat remotefile > localfile

• The following command appends the remote file RemoteFile to the remote file OtherRemoteFile:
rsh othercomputer cat remotefile ">" otherremotefile

• When using a computer running Windows XP Professional that is logged on to a domain, the primary domain controller for the domain must be available to verify the user name or the rsh command fails.

• The .rhosts file typically permits network access on UNIX systems. The .rhosts file lists computer names and associated logon names that have access to remote computers. When you run rcp, rexec, or rsh commands remotely with a correctly configured .rhosts file, you do not need to provide logon and password information for the remote computer.

• The .rhosts file is a text file in which each line is an entry. An entry consists of the local computer name, the local user name, and any comments about the entry. Each entry is separated by a tab or space, and comments begin with a pound sign (#). For example:
host7 #This computer is in room 31A

• The .rhosts file must be in the user's home directory on the remote computer. For more information about the specific implementation of the .rhosts file on a remote computer, see the remote system documentation.

• This command is available only if the Internet Protocol (TCP/IP) protocol is installed as a component in the properties of a network adapter in Network Connections

RSM

Manages media resources using Removable Storage. Using the rsm command, you can run batch scripts for applications that do not currently support the Removable Storage API.

To allocate media from a media pool

Syntax:

rsm allocate /mmedia_pool_name /o{errunavail|new|next} {/l{g|f}logical_media_id |
/p{g|f}partition_id} [/lnlogical_media_name] [/ldlogical_media_description]
[/pnpartition_name] [/pdpartition_description] [/ttimeout] [/b]

Syntax Options:

/mmedia_pool_name ······Media are allocated from the specified media pool. This means that you will have allocated media in that pool.

/o ··············Permits the use of one of the parameters listed in the following table.

Value	Description
errunavail	Prevents the submission of an operator request for new media if none can be allocated with the specified constraints.
new	Allocates a partition that cannot be shared with another application. This can be used to reserve the second side of two-sided media.
next	Allocates the next side of media that was previously allocated using the new parameter.

/l{g|f}logical_media_id ·····Specifies the media to be allocated, using the logical media ID. You can use the GUID (with the lg command-line option), or the friendly name (with the lf command-line option). Logical_media_id specifies the next side of multi-sided media to allocate. This parameter is optional and must be used with the /o command-line option and the next parameter. After deallocating this media, the logical media ID is invalid.

/p{g|f}partition_id ··············Specifies the partition to be allocated, using the partition ID. You can use the GUID (with the pg command-line option), or the friendly name (with the pf command-line option). This parameter is optional and remains persistent even after the media is deallocated.

/lnlogical_media_name ···Specifies the media to be allocated, using the logical media name.

/ldlogical_media_description ················Specifies the media to be allocated, using the logical media description.

/pnpartition_name ··········Specifies the partition to be allocated, using the partition name.

/pdpartition_description ··Specifies the media partition to be allocated, using the partition description.

/ttimeout····Specifies the command timeout, in milliseconds. The default timeout value is infinite.

/b ··············Only the GUID for the allocate operation is displayed. This aids in scripting where you want to pass the output of one command to the next with minimal parsing.

Notes:

• You can use logical media names and side names can be used in other commands to specify media as the parameter to the /lf or /pf switch, respectively. If logical media names (which are friendly names) are not used with the allocate command, you can use only GUIDs in subsequent commands to specify logical media.

To create a media pool

Syntax :

rsm createpool /mmedia_pool_name /a{existing|always|new} [/t{g|f}media_pool_type_id]
[/d] [/r]

Syntax Options:

/mmedia_pool_name ······Specifies the name of the media pool to be created.

/a ··············Permits the use of one of the parameters listed in the following table.

Value	Description
existing	Opens the existing media pool or returns an error if the media pool specified does not exist.
always	Opens the existing media pool or creates a new media pool if not found.

Value	Description
new	Creates a new media pool or returns an error if the media pool specified already exists.

/tgmedia_pool_type_id ···Specifies the type of media the media pool will contain, using the GUID. The default type is a media pool that contains other media pools.

/tfmedia_pool_type_id ····Specifies the type of media the media pool will contain, using the friendly name. The default type is a media pool that contains other media pools.

/d ···············Permits the media pool to automatically draw media from the free media pool. If the /d switch is not included, the media pool will not be permitted to draw media from the free media pool.

/r ···············Permits the media pool to automatically return media to the free media pool. If the /r switch is not included, the media pool will not be permitted to return media to the free media pool.

To deallocate media
Syntax :

rsm deallocate /l{glf}logical_media_id | /p{glf}partition_id

Syntax Options:

/llogical_media_id ········Specifies the logical media to deallocate, using the GUID.

/lflogical_media_id ········Specifies the logical media to deallocate, using the friendly name.

/pgpartition_id ·············Specifies the media side to deallocate, using the GUID.

/pfpartition_id ··············Specifies the media side to deallocate, using the friendly name.

Notes:

• You can use the logical media name or the partition name to specify the logical media to deallocate only if one of these names were specified with the allocate command using the /ln or /pn switch respectively. Otherwise, you must specify either the logical media ID (LMID) or the partition ID (PARTID) instead.

To delete a media pool
Syntax :

rsm deletepool /mmedia_pool_name

Syntax Options:

/mmedia_pool_name ·····Specifies the name of the media pool to be deleted.

To dismount media from a drive
Syntax:

rsm dismount {/l{glf}logical_media_id | /p{glf}partition_id

rsm dismount [/o[deferred]]]}

Syntax Options:

/llogical_media_id ········Specifies the logical media to dismount, using the GUID.

/lflogical_media_id ········Specifies the logical media to dismount, using the friendly name.

/pgpartition_id ·············Specifies the media side to dismount, using the GUID.

/pfpartition_id ··············Specifies the media side to dismount, using the friendly name.

/o ···············When used with the optional deferred parameter, this optional switch marks the media as dismountable, but the media is kept in the drive. Subsequent mount commands can be completed normally. If not used, the media is dismounted from the drive immediately.

Notes:

• The logical media name or the partition name can be used to specify the logical media to dismount only if one of these names were specified with the allocate command using the /ln or /pn switch, respectively. Otherwise, you must specify either the logical media ID (LMID) or the partition ID (PARTID) instead.

To eject media from a library

The media to be ejected can be specified in one of three ways:

You can specify the physical media to eject using either the physical-media ID (PMID) or the physical media name.

You can eject the media in a specified slot within a specified library.

You can eject the media in a specified drive within a specified library.

Syntax:

rsm eject {/p{g|f}physical_media_id | /s{g|f}slot_id /l{g|f}library_id | /d{g|f}drive_id /l{g|f}library_id

rsm eject [/oeject_operation_id]

rsm eject [/a{start|stop|queue}]

rsm eject [/b]

Syntax Options:

/pgphysical_media_id ·····Specifies the physical media to eject, using the GUID.

/pfphysical_media_id ·····Specifies the physical media to eject, using the friendly name.

/sgslot_id ··Specifies the slot holding the media to eject, using the GUID.

/sfslot_id ···Specifies the slot holding the media to eject, using the friendly name.

/lglibrary_id ·····················Specifies the library containing the slot or drive from which to eject the media, using the GUID.

/lflibrary_id Specifies the library containing the slot or drive from which to eject the media, using the friendly name.

/dgdrive_idSpecifies the drive holding the media to eject, using the GUID.

/dfdrive_id·Specifies the drive holding the media to eject, using the friendly name.

/oeject_operation_id ·····Used to specify the GUID for the particular eject operation. The optional /o switch can be used in conjunction with the /a switch and the stop parameter to terminate a particular eject operation. This can also be used in conjunction with the /a switch and the start parameter to display the GUID of the particular eject operation.

/a ·············Permits the use of one of the parameters listed in the following table.

Value	Description
Start	The default, starts the eject operation immediately. The media is ejected until a timeout occurs, or unless another eject command is issued with the /a command-line option and the stop parameter. Such eject commands must also specify the eject operation GUID using the /o command-line option. The timeout parameter is specified in the library object (for all eject operations) for the library. To set this timeout parameter, you must use the Removable Storage API. Can also be used in conjunction with the /o switch to display the GUID of a particular eject operation.
Stop	Terminates the eject operation prior to a timeout expiring. The particular eject operation can be determined using the GUID displayed when the start parameter is used with the /a switch and the /o switch.
Queue	Queues the media for later ejection. This can be used for libraries with multi-slot inject/eject (IE) ports.

/b ·············Displays only the eject operation GUID for scripting purposes.

To eject media from an ATAPI changer

Syntax :

rsm ejectatapi /natapi_changer_number

Syntax Options:

/natapi_changer_numberSpecifies the changer number. Atapi_changer_number is the number found at the end of the string for the device name of the changer. For example, \\.\CdChanger0 has 0 as the ATAPI changer number.

Notes:

- Before you run this command, manually stop the ntmssvc service.

To inventory the media in a specified automated library

Syntax :

rsm inventory /l{g|f}library_id /a{full|fast|default|none|stop}

Syntax Options:

/lflibrary_id Specifies the library to inventory, using the friendly name.

/lglibrary_id ⋯⋯⋯⋯⋯⋯ Specifies the library to inventory, using the GUID.

/a ⋯⋯⋯⋯⋯ Required. Specifies the type of inventory operation to perform. The lists valid inventory operations.

Value	Description
Full	Performs a full on-media inventory of the library. Removable Storage mounts each tape or disk in the library and reads the on-media identifier.
Fast	Performs a bar code inventory, if the specified library has a bar code reader installed. If the library has no bar code reader, Removable Storage checks the storage slots and reads the on-media identifier on media in slots that were previously empty.
Default	Performs an inventory using the default method specified in the library's Properties dialog box.
None	Performs no inventory.
Stop	Stops the current inventory for the specified library, if one is being performed.

To mount media in the designated library

The logical media to be mounted can be specified using either the logical-media ID (LMID) or the logical media name.

Syntax:

rsm mount {/l{g|f}logical_media_id | /p{g|f}partition_id | [/s{g|f}slot_id /c{g|f}changer_id}

rsm mount [/d{g|f}drive_id]

rsm mount [/o{errunavail|drive|read|write|offline}

rsm mount [/r{normal|high|low|highest|lowest}]

rsm mount [/ttimeout]

Syntax Options:

/lflogical_media_id ⋯⋯⋯⋯ Specifies the logical media to mount, using the friendly name.

/pfpartition_id ⋯⋯⋯⋯⋯⋯ Specifies the media side to mount, using the friendly name.
/pgpartition_id

/lglogical_media_id ⋯⋯⋯⋯ Specifies the logical media to mount, using the GUID.

/cgchanger_id ⋯⋯⋯⋯⋯⋯ Specifies the changer that contains the media to be mounted, using the GUID. This can only be used in conjunction with the /sg switch and the slot GUID.

/cfchanger_id ⋯⋯⋯⋯⋯⋯ Specifies the changer that contains the media to be mounted, using the friendly name. This can be used only in conjunction with the /sg switch and the slot GUID.

/sgslot_id ⋯ Specifies the media slot that contains the media to be mounted, using the GUID. This can only be used in conjunction with the /cg switch and the changer GUID.

/sfslot_id ⋯ Specifies the media slot that contains the media to be mounted, using the friendly name. This can only be used in conjunction with the /cg switch and the changer GUID.

/dgdrive_id Specifies the particular drive on which to mount the applicable media, using the GUID. This parameter is optional, and must be used in conjunction with the /o switch and the drive parameter.

/dfdrive_id Specifies the particular drive on which to mount the applicable media, using the friendly name. This parameter is optional, and must be used in conjunction with the /o switch and the drive parameter.

/o ⋯⋯⋯⋯⋯ Permits the use of one of the parameters listed in the following table.

Value	Description
Errunavail	Generates an error if either the media or the drive is unavailable.

Value	Description
Drive	Specifies that a particular drive is to be mounted. This parameter is used in conjunction with the /d switch.
Read	Mounts the media for read access.
Write	Mounts the media for write access. If this parameter is used, completed media will not be mounted.
Offline	Generates an error if the media is offline.

/r ....Optionally specifies the mount order, or priority. Mount priority may also be specified using one of the listed parameters, normal (the default), high, low, highest, or lowest.

/t ....Optionally specifies the command timeout, in milliseconds. The default timeout is infinite.

Notes:

• When using the mount command, you can specify the media to be mounted using either the /l switch, the /p switch, or a combination of the /s switch and the /c switch.

To refresh a library, physical media, or all devices of a particular media type

This command causes a single poll of the target devices so that the Removable Storage database contains the current state of the device. This command can be useful after media insert or eject operations.

Syntax :

rsm refresh {/l{g|f}library_id | /p{g|f}physical_media_id | /tgmedia_type_id}

Syntax Options:

/gllibrary_id ....Specifies the library to refresh, using the GUID.

/fllibrary_id Specifies the library to refresh, using the friendly name.

/pgphysical_media_id ·····Specifies the physical media to refresh, using the GUID.

/pfphysical_media_id ······Specifies the physical media to refresh, using the friendly name.

/tgmedia_type_id ···········Specifies the media type to be refreshed. Only the GUID can be specified. This parameter can be used to refresh all removable media devices by specifying the GUID for the removable media. This GUID can be determined using the view command as follows: rsm view /tmedia_type /guiddisplay.

To display a list of media objects

Syntax:

rsm view /t{drive|library|changer|storageslot|iedoor|ieport|physical_media| media_pool|partition|logical_media|media_type|drive_type|librequest}

rsm view [/cgcontainer_id]

rsm view [/guiddisplay]

rsm view [/b]

Syntax Options:

/t {drive|library|changer|storageslot|iedoor|ieport|physical_media| media_pool|partition|logical_media|media_type|drive_type|librequest}
Displays a list of media objects of the specified type. When used without any parameter, the command displays a list of all media pools in the Removable Storage system (collection of libraries).

/cgcontainer_id ....Specifies the GUID for the object container. The type of container depends on the object type (parameter) specified with the /t switch. If the container ID is not specified, all instances of the applicable object type are displayed.

/guiddisplay.....................Displays both the GUID and the friendly name for objects.

/b ....Displays only the object GUID for scripting purposes.

Notes:

• If the /guiddisplay switch and the /b switch are not used, only the friendly names for objects are displayed.

RSM Notes:

• If a command succeeds, then the code ERROR_SUCCESS is returned. All commands that fail return an error code, which can be used for scripting purposes. The error code is either a system-defined error code or one of the error codes listed in the following table.

Error code	Description
536870913	Invalid arguments were specified. Frequently, this is caused by a space after an argument switch, for example, /t 50 instead of /t50.
536870914	Duplicate argument switches were specified. For example, the allocate command used with two /m switches.
536870915	No GUID matches the friendly name that was specified. Check capitalization because friendly names are case-sensitive.
536870916	An insufficient number of argument switches were specified. Check to see if a required switch is missing.
536870917	An invalid GUID was specified. Use the view command to determine the correct GUID for an object.
536870918	This is returned only by the ejectatapi command. Verify that the ATAPI changer is functioning correctly.

RUNAS

Allows a user to run specific tools and programs with different permissions than the user's current logon provides.

Syntax:

runas [{/profile | /noprofile}] [/env] [/netonly] [/smartcard] [/showtrustlevels] [/trustlevel] /user:UserAccountName program

Examples:

runas /user:localmachinename\administrator cmd   or
runas /user:companydomain\domainadmin "mmc %windir%\system32\compmgmt.msc"

Syntax Options:

/profile·······Loads the user's profile. /profile is the default.

/no profile··Specifies that the user's profile is not to be loaded. This allows the application to load more quickly, but it can also cause a malfunction in some applications.

/env···········Specifies that the current network environment be used instead of the user's local environment.

/netonly·····Indicates that the user information specified is for remote access only.

/smartcard Indicates whether the credentials are to be supplied from a smartcard.

/showtrustlevels ··············Lists the /trustlevel options.

/trustlevel··Specifies the level of authorization at which the application is to run. Use /showtrustlevels to see the trust levels available.

/user:UserAccountName·Specifies the name of the user account under which to run the program. The user account format should be user@domain or Domain\User.

program ····Specifies the program or command to run using the account specified in /user.

Notes:

• It is good practice for administrators to use an account with restrictive permissions to perform routine, nonadministrative tasks, and to use an account with broader permissions only when performing specific administrative tasks. To accomplish this without logging off and back on, log on with a regular user account, and then use the runas command to run the tools that require the broader permissions.

• The use of runas is not restricted to administrator accounts, although that is the most common use. Any user with multiple accounts can use runas to run a program, MMC console, or Control Panel item with alternate credentials.

• If you want to use the Administrator account on your computer, for the /user: parameter, type one of the following:
/user:AdministratorAccountName@ComputerName
/user:ComputerName\AdministratorAccountName

- If you want to use this command as a domain administrator, type one of the following:
/user:AdministratorAccountName@DomainName
/user:DomainName\AdministratorAccountName

- With the runas command, you can run programs (*.exe), saved MMC consoles (*.msc), shortcuts to programs and saved MMC consoles, and Control Panel items. You can run them as an administrator while you are logged on to your computer as a member of another group, such as the Users or Power Users group.

- You can use the runas command start any program, MMC console, or Control Panel item. As long as you provide the appropriate user account and password information, the user account has the ability to log on to the computer, and the program, MMC console, or Control Panel item is available on the system and to the user account.

- With the runas command, you can administer a server in another forest (the computer from which you run a tool and the server you administer are in different domains).

- If you try to start a program, MMC console, or Control Panel item from a network location using runas, it might fail because the credentials used to connect to the network share are different from the credentials used to start the program. The latter credentials may not be able to gain access to the same network share.

- Some items, such as the Printers folder and desktop items, are opened indirectly and cannot be started with the runas command.

- If the runas command fails, the Secondary Logon service might not be running or the user account you are using might not be valid. To check the status of the Secondary Logon service, in Computer Management, click Services and Applications, and then click Services. To test the user account, try logging on to the appropriate domain using the account.

SC

Communicates with the Service Controller and installed services. SC.exe retrieves and sets control information about services. You can use SC.exe for testing and debugging service programs. Service properties stored in the registry can be set to control how service applications are started at boot time and run as background processes. SC.exe parameters can configure a specific service, retrieve the current status of a service, as well as stop and start a service. You can create batch files that call various SC.exe commands to automate the startup or shutdown sequence of services. SC.exe provides capabilities similar to Services in the Administrative Tools item in Control Panel.

sc boot

Indicates whether the last boot should be saved as the last-known-good configuration.

Syntax:

sc [ServerName] boot [{bad|OK}]

Examples:

sc boot ok *or* sc boot bad

Syntax Options:

ServerName ·················Specifies the name of the remote server on which the service is located. The name must use the Universal Naming Convention (UNC) format ("\\myserver"). To run SC.exe locally, ignore this parameter.

[{bad|OK}]·Specifies whether the last boot was bad or whether it should be saved as the last-known-good boot configuration.

sc config

Modifies the value of a service's entries in the registry and in the Service Control Manager's database.

Syntax:

sc [ServerName] config [ServiceName] [type= {own|share|kernel|filesys|rec|adapt|interact type= {own|share}}] [start= {boot|system|auto|demand|disabled}] [error= {normal|severe|critical|ignore}] [binpath= BinaryPathName] [group= LoadOrderGroup] [tag= {yes|no}] [depend= dependencies] [obj= {AccountName|ObjectName}] [displayname= DisplayName] [password= Password]

Examples:

sc config NewService binpath= "ntsd -d c:\windows\system32\NewServ.exe"

Syntax Options:

ServerName ⋯⋯⋯⋯⋯ Specifies the name of the remote server on which the service is located. The name must use the Universal Naming Convention (UNC) format ("\\myserver"). To run SC.exe locally, ignore this parameter.

ServiceName ⋯⋯⋯⋯⋯ Specifies the service name returned by the getkeyname operation.

type= {own|share|kernel|filesys|rec|adapt|interact type= {own|share}}
Specifies the service type.

Value ⋯⋯⋯ Description

own ⋯⋯⋯⋯⋯ The service runs in its own process. It does not share an executable file with other services. This is the default.

share ⋯⋯⋯⋯ The service runs as a shared process. It shares an executable file with other services.

kernel ⋯⋯⋯⋯ Driver.

filesys ⋯⋯⋯⋯ File system driver.

rec ⋯⋯⋯⋯⋯ File system-recognized driver (identifies file systems used on the computer).

adapt ⋯⋯⋯⋯ Adapter driver (identifies hardware items such as keyboard, mouse, and disk drive).

interact ⋯⋯⋯⋯ The service can interact with the desktop, receiving input from users. Interactive services must be run under the LocalSystem account. This type must be used in conjunction with type= own or type= shared (for example, type= interact type= own). Using type= interact by itself will generate an invalid parameter error.

start= {boot|system|auto|demand|disabled}
Specifies the start type for the service.

Value ⋯⋯⋯ Description

boot ⋯⋯⋯⋯⋯ A device driver that is loaded by the boot loader.

system ⋯⋯⋯⋯ A device driver that is started during kernel initialization.

auto ⋯⋯⋯⋯⋯ A service that automatically starts each time the computer is restarted and runs even if no one logs on to the computer.

demand ⋯⋯⋯⋯ A service that must be manually started. This is the default value if start= is not specified.

disabled ⋯⋯⋯ A service that cannot be started. To start a disabled service, change the start type to some other value.

error= {normal|severe|critical|ignore} ⋯⋯ Specifies the severity of the error if the service fails to start during boot.

Value ⋯⋯⋯ Description

normal ⋯⋯⋯⋯ The error is logged and a message box is displayed informing the user that a service has failed to start. Startup will continue. This is the default setting.

severe ⋯⋯⋯⋯ The error is logged (if possible). The computer attempts to restart with the last-known-good configuration. This could result in the computer being able to restart, but the service may still be unable to run.

critical ⋯⋯⋯⋯ The error is logged (if possible). The computer attempts to restart with the last-known-good configuration. If the last-known-good configuration fails, startup also fails, and the boot process halts with a Stop error.

ignore ⋯⋯⋯⋯ The error is logged and startup continues. No notification is given to the user beyond recording the error in the Event Log.

binpath= BinaryPathName ⋯⋯⋯⋯⋯⋯ Specifies a path to the service binary file.

group= LoadOrderGroup Specifies the name of the group of which this service is a member. The list of groups is stored in the registry in the HKLM\System\CurrentControlSet\Control\ServiceGroupOrder subkey. The default is null.

tag= {yes|no} ⋯⋯⋯⋯⋯⋯ Specifies whether or not to obtain a TagID from the CreateService call. Tags are only used for boot-start and system-start drivers.

depend= dependencies ⋯⋯ Specifies the names of services or groups which must start before this service. The names are separated by forward slashes (/).

obj= {AccountName|ObjectName} ⋯⋯⋯⋯ Specifies a name of an account in which a service will run, or specifies a name of the Windows driver object in which the driver will run. The default is LocalSystem.

---

displayname= DisplayName ················Specifies a friendly, meaningful name that can be used in user-interface programs to identify the service to users. For example, the subkey name of one service is wuauserv, which is not helpful to the user, and the display name is Automatic Updates.

password= Password ·····Specifies a password. This is required if an account other than the LocalSystem account is used.

Notes:

• Without a space between a parameter and its value (for example, type= own, not type=own), the operation will fail.

sc continue

Sends a CONTINUE control request to a service in order to resume a paused service.

Syntax:

sc [ServerName] continue [ServiceName]

Examples:

sc continue tapisrv

Syntax Options:

ServerName ···················Specifies the name of the remote server on which the service is located. The name must use the UNC format ("\\myserver"). To run SC.exe locally, ignore this parameter.

ServiceName ···················Specifies the service name returned by the getkeyname operation.

Notes:

• Use the continue operation to resume a paused service.

sc control

Sends a CONTROL B to a service.

Syntax:

sc [ServerName] control [ServiceName]
{(paramchange|netbindadd|netbindremove|netbindenable|netbinddisable|UserDefinedCo ntrolB)}

Syntax Options:

ServerName ···················Specifies the name of the remote server on which the service is located. The name must use the UNC format ("\\myserver"). To run SC.exe locally, ignore this parameter.

ServiceName ···················Specifies the service name returned by the getkeyname operation.

{paramchange|netbindadd|netbindremove|netbindenable|netbinddisable|UserDefinedCon trolB} ····Specifies a control to send to a service.

sc create

Creates a subkey and entries for the service in the registry and in the Service Control Manager's database.

Syntax:

sc [ServerName] create [ServiceName] [type= {own|share|kernel|filesys|rec|adapt|interact type= {own|share}}] [start= {boot|system|auto|demand|disabled}] [error= {normal|severe|critical|ignore}] [binpath= BinaryPathName] [group= LoadOrderGroup] [tag= {yes|no}] [depend= dependencies] [obj= {AccountName|ObjectName}] [displayname= DisplayName] [password= Password]

Examples:

sc \\myserver create NewService binpath= c:\windows\system32\NewServ.exe *or*
sc create NewService binpath= c:\windows\system32\NewServ.exe type= share start= auto depend= "+TDI Netbios"

Syntax Options:

ServerName ···················Specifies the name of the remote server on which the service is located. The name must use the UNC format ("\\myserver"). To run SC.exe locally, ignore this parameter.

ServiceName ·············Specifies the service name returned by the getkeyname operation.

type= {own|share|kernel|filesys|rec|adapt|interact type= {own|share}}
Specifies the service type. The default is type= own.

Value ·······Description

own ·······The service runs in its own process. It does not share an executable file with other services. This is the default.

share ·······The service runs as a shared process. It shares an executable file with other services.

kernel·······Driver.

filesys ·······File system driver.

rec ···········File system recognized driver (identifies file systems used on the computer).

interact·······The service can interact with the desktop, receiving input from users. Interactive services must be run under the LocalSystem account. This type must be used in conjunction with type= own or type= shared (that is, type= interact type= own). Using type= interact by itself will generate an invalid parameter error.

start= {boot|system|auto|demand|disabled}
Specifies the start type for the service. The default start is start= demand.

boot ·········A device driver that is loaded by the boot loader.

system ·········A device driver that is started during kernel initialization.

auto ·········A service that automatically starts each time the computer is restarted and runs even if no one logs on to the computer.

demand ····A service that must be manually started. This is the default value if start= is not specified.

disabled ····A service that cannot be started. To start a disabled service, change the start type to some other value.

error= {normal|severe|critical|ignore} ····Specifies the severity of the error if the service fails to start during boot. The default is error= normal.

normal ·······The error is logged and a message box is displayed informing the user that a service has failed to start. Startup will continue. This is the default setting.

severe·······The error is logged (if possible). The computer attempts to restart with the last-known-good configuration. This could result in the computer being able to restart, but the service may still be unable to run.

critical ·······The error is logged (if possible). The computer attempts to restart with the last-known-good configuration. If the last-known-good configuration fails, startup also fails, and the boot process halts with a Stop error.

ignore ·······The error is logged and startup continues. No notification is given to the user beyond recording the error in the Event Log.

binpath= BinaryPathName·············Specifies a path to the service binary file. There is no default for binpath= and this string must be supplied.

group= LoadOrderGroup Specifies the name of the group of which this service is a member. The list of groups is stored in the registry in the HKLM\System\CurrentControlSet\Control\ServiceGroupOrder subkey. The default is null.

tag= {yes|no}·············Specifies whether or not to obtain a TagID from the CreateService call. Tags are only used for boot-start and system-start drivers.

depend= dependencies ··Specifies the names of services or groups that must start before this service. The names are separated by forward slashes (/).

obj= {AccountName|ObjectName} ·······Specifies a name of an account in which a service will run, or specifies a name of the Windows driver object in which the driver will run.

displayname= DisplayName ·············Specifies a friendly name that can be used by user-interface programs to identify the service.

password= Password ·····Specifies a password. This is required if an account other than LocalSystem is used.

Notes:

• Without a space between a parameter and its value (that is, type= own, not type=own), the operation will fail.

sc delete

Deletes a service subkey from the registry. If the service is running or if another process has an open handle to the service, then the service is marked for deletion.

Syntax:

sc [ServerName] delete [ServiceName]

Examples:

sc delete newserv

Syntax Options:

ServerName ················Specifies the name of the remote server on which the service is located. The name must use the UNC format ("\\myserver"). To run SC.exe locally, ignore this parameter.

ServiceName ···············Specifies the service name returned by the getkeyname operation.

Notes:

• Use Add or Remove Programs to delete DHCP, DNS, or any other built-in operating system services. Add or Remove Programs will not only remove the registry subkey for the service, but it will also uninstall the service and delete any shortcuts to the service.

sc description

Sets the description string for a service.

Syntax:

sc [ServerName] description [ServiceName] [Description]

Examples:

sc description newserv "Runs quality of service control."

Syntax Options:

ServerName ················Specifies the name of the remote server on which the service is located. The name must use the UNC format ("\\myserver"). To run SC.exe locally, ignore this parameter.

ServiceName ···············Specifies the service name returned by the getkeyname operation.

Description···············Specifies a description for the specified service. If no string is specified, the description of the service is not modified. There is no limit to the number of characters that can be contained in the service description.

sc enumdepend

Lists the services that cannot run unless the specified service is running.

Syntax:

sc [ServerName] enumdepend [ServiceName] [BufferSize]

Examples:

sc enumdepend rpcss 5690
sc enumdepend tapisrv

Syntax Options:

ServerName ················Specifies the name of the remote server on which the service is located. The name must use the UNC format ("\\myserver"). To run SC.exe locally, ignore this parameter.

ServiceName ···············Specifies the service name returned by the getkeyname operation.

BufferSize·Specifies the size (in bytes) of the enumeration buffer. The default is 1024 bytes.

Notes:

• If the buffer is not big enough, the enumdepend operation will output dependencies only partially, and will specify the additional buffer size required to output all dependencies. If the output is truncated, rerun the operation and specify the larger buffer size.

sc failure

Specifies what action to take upon failure of the service.

Syntax:

sc [ServerName] failure [ServiceName] [reset= ErrorFreePeriod] [reboot= BroadcastMessage] [command= CommandLine] [actions= FailureActionsAndDelayTime]

Examples:

sc failure msftpsvc reset= 30 actions= restart/5000   or
sc failure dfs reset= 60 command= c:\windows\services\restart_dfs.exe actions= run/5000

Syntax Options:

ServerName ·················Specifies the name of the remote server on which the service is located. The name must use the UNC format ("\\myserver"). To run SC.exe locally, ignore this parameter.

ServiceName ·················Specifies the service name returned by the getkeyname operation.

reset= ErrorFreePeriod ···Specifies the length of the period (in seconds) with no failures after which the failure count should be reset to 0. This parameter must be used in conjunction with the actions= parameter.

reboot= BroadcastMessage ·················Specifies the message to be broadcast upon failure of the service.

command= CommandLine ·················Specifies the command line to be run upon failure of the service.

actions= FailureActionsAndDelayTime ·Specifies the failure actions and their delay time (in milliseconds) separated by the forward slash (/). The following actions are valid: run, restart, and reboot. This parameter must be used in conjunction with the reset= parameter. Use actions= "" to take no action upon failure.

Notes:

• Not all services allow changes to their failure options. Some run as part of a service set.

• To run a batch file upon failure, specify cmd.exe Drive:\FileName.bat to the command= parameter, where Drive:\FileName.bat is the fully qualified name of the batch file.

• To run a VBS file upon failure, specify cscript drive:\myscript.vbs to the command= parameter, where drive:\myscript.vbs is the fully qualified name of the script file.

• It is possible to specify three different actions to the actions= parameter, which will be used the first, second, and third time a service fails.

• Without a space between a parameter and its value (that is, type= own, not type=own), the operation will fail.

sc getdisplayname

Gets the display name associated with a particular service.

Syntax:

sc [ServerName] getdisplayname [ServiceName] [BufferSize]

Examples:

sc getdisplayname clipsrv or sc getdisplayname tapisrv or sc getdisplayname sharedaccess

Syntax Options:

ServerName ·················Specifies the name of the remote server on which the service is located. The name must use the UNC format ("\\myserver"). To run SC.exe locally, ignore this parameter.

ServiceName ·················Specifies the service name returned by the getkeyname operation.

BufferSize·Specifies the size (in bytes) of the buffer. The default is 1024 bytes.

sc getkeyname

Gets the key name associated with a particular service, using the display name as input.

Syntax:

sc [ServerName] getkeyname [ServiceDisplayName] [BufferSize]

Examples:
   sc getkeyname "remote procedure call (rpc)" *or* sc getkeyname "internet connection sharing"

Syntax Options:
   ServerName ················Specifies the name of the remote server on which the service is located. The name must use the UNC format ("\\myserver"). To run SC.exe locally, ignore this parameter.
   ServiceDisplayName ······Specifies the display name of the service.
   BufferSize·Specifies the size (in bytes) of the buffer. The default is 1024 bytes.

Notes:
   • If the ServiceDisplayName contains spaces, use quotation marks around the text (that is, "Service Display Name").

sc interrogate

Sends an INTERROGATE control request to a service.

Syntax:
   sc [ServerName] interrogate [ServiceName]

Examples:
   sc interrogate sharedaccess *or* sc interrogate rpcss

Syntax Options:
   ServerName ················Specifies the name of the remote server on which the service is located. The name must use the UNC format ("\\myserver"). To run SC.exe locally, ignore this parameter.
   ServiceName ················Specifies the service name returned by the getkeyname operation.

Notes:
   • Sending INTERROGATE to a service causes the service to update its status with the Service Control Manager.

sc lock

Locks the Service Control Manager's database.

Syntax:
   sc [ServerName] lock

Examples:
   sc lock

Syntax Options:
   ServerName ················Specifies the name of the remote server on which the service is located. The name must use the UNC format ("\\myserver"). To run SC.exe locally, ignore this parameter.

Notes:
   • Locking the Service Control Manager's database prevents any services from starting. Use this if you want to make sure that a service will not be started after it has been stopped. This will allow you to take some action (for example, deleting the service) without interference.

   • Using the lock operation locks the Service Control Manager's database and then allows the database to be unlocked by typing u. You can also kill the process from which you locked the database.

sc pause

Sends a PAUSE control request to a service.

Syntax:
   sc [ServerName] pause [ServiceName]

Examples:
   sc pause tapisrv

Syntax Options:
   ServerName ················Specifies the name of the remote server on which the service is located. The name must use the UNC format ("\\myserver"). To run SC.exe locally, ignore this parameter.

ServiceName ·················Specifies the service name returned by the getkeyname operation.

Notes:

Use the pause operation to pause a service before shutting it down.

- Not all services can be paused.

- Not all services perform the same when paused. Some continue to service existing clients, but refuse to accept new clients. Others cease to service existing clients and also refuse to accept new ones.

sc qc

Queries the configuration information for a service.

Syntax:

sc [ServerName] qc [ServiceName] [BufferSize]

Examples:

sc qc \\myserver newsrvice   *or*   sc qc rpcss 248

Syntax Options:

ServerName ·················Specifies the name of the remote server on which the service is located. The name must use the UNC format ("\\myserver"). To run SC.exe locally, ignore this parameter.

ServiceName ·················Specifies the service name returned by the getkeyname operation.

BufferSize·Specifies the size (in bytes) of the buffer. The default is 1024 bytes.

Notes:

- The qc operation displays the following information about a service: SERVICE_NAME (service's registry subkey name), TYPE, ERROR_CONTROL, BINARY_PATH_NAME, LOAD_ORDER_GROUP, TAG, DISPLAY_NAME, DEPENDENCIES, and SERVICE_START_NAME.

- Administrators can use SC to determine the binary name of any service and find out if it shares a process with other services by typing the following at the command line:
sc qc ServiceName
SC can help match up services in the Services node of Microsoft Management Console (MMC) with processes in System Monitor. If the binary name is Services.exe, then the service shares the Service Controller process.
Services.exe starts all services. To conserve system resources, several Win32 services developed for Windows are written to share the Services.exe process. These services are not listed as separate processes in System Monitor or Task Manager. The same is true of Svchost.exe which is a service host process that many operating services share.

- There might not be a process for every Win32 service because third-party Win32 services can also be configured to share processes. SC can be used to get configuration information on these services. If a service does not share its process with other services, however, there will be a process for it in System Monitor when the service is running.
SC can be useful for developers of services because it provides more detailed and accurate information about services than Services.exe, which is included with Windows. Services.exe can determine whether a service is running, stopped, or paused. Although these tools are adequate for a debugged application that is running smoothly, the information they provide about a service being developed can be misleading. For example, a service that is starting is shown as started whether it is actually running or not.
SC implements calls to all Windows service control application programming interface (API) functions. Set the parameters to these functions by specifying them at the command line.
Using SC, you can query the service status and retrieve the values stored in the status structure fields. Services.exe cannot provide you with the complete status of a service, but SC shows the exact state of the service, as well as the last checkpoint number and wait hint. You can use the checkpoint as a debugging tool because it indicates how far the initialization progressed before the program stopped responding. SC also lets you specify the name of a remote computer so that you can call the service API functions or view the service status structures on a remote computer.

sc qdescription

Displays the description string of a service.

Syntax:

sc [ServerName] qdescription [ServiceName] [BufferSize]

Examples:

sc qdescription rpcss *or* sc qdescription rpcss 138

Syntax Options:

ServerName ··············Specifies the name of the remote server on which the service is located. The name must use the UNC format ("\\myserver"). To run SC.exe locally, ignore this parameter.

ServiceName ··············Specifies the service name returned by the getkeyname operation.

BufferSize·Specifies the size (in bytes) of the buffer. The default is 1024 bytes.

sc qfailure

Displays the actions that will be performed if the specified service fails.

Syntax:

sc [ServerName] qfailure [ServiceName] [BufferSize]

Examples:

sc qfailure rpcss *or* sc qfailure rpcss 20

Syntax Options:

ServerName ··············Specifies the name of the remote server on which the service is located. The name must use the UNC format ("\\myserver"). To run SC.exe locally, ignore this parameter.

ServiceName ··············Specifies the service name returned by the getkeyname operation.

BufferSize·Specifies the size (in bytes) of the buffer. The default is 1024 bytes.

Notes:

• The qfailure operation displays the following information about a service: SERVICE_NAME (service's registry subkey name), RESET_PERIOD, REBOOT_MESSAGE, COMMAND_LINE, and FAILURE_ACTIONS.

sc query

Obtains and displays information about the specified service, driver, type of service, or type of driver.

Syntax:

sc [ServerName] query [ServiceName] [type= {driver | service|all}] [type= {own | share | interact | kernel | filesys | rec | adapt}] [state= {active | inactive | all}] [bufsize= BufferSize] [ri= ResumeIndex] [group= GroupName]

Examples:

sc query *or* sc query messenger *or* sc query type= driver *or* sc query type= service

Syntax Options:

ServerName ··············Specifies the name of the remote server on which the service is located. The name must use the UNC format ("\\myserver"). To run SC.exe locally, ignore this parameter.

ServiceName ··············Specifies the service name returned by the getkeyname operation. This query parameter is not used in conjunction with other query parameters (other than ServerName).

type= {driver | service | all}··············Specifies what to enumerate. The default type is service.

Value ·······Description

driver ······Specifies that only drivers are enumerated.

service ······Specifies that only services are enumerated.

all···········Specifies that both drivers and services are enumerated.

type= {own | share | interact | kernel | filesys | rec | adapt} Specifies the type of services or type of drivers to enumerate.

Value ·······Description

---

own·········The service runs in its own process. It does not share an executable file with other services. This is the default.

share ·······The service runs as a shared process. It shares an executable file with other services.

interact······The service can interact with the desktop, receiving input from users. Interactive services must be run under the LocalSystem account.

kernel·······Driver.

filesys ······File system driver.

state= {active|inactive|all}·················Specifies the started state of the service for which to enumerate. The default state is active.

Value ·······Description

active ·······Specifies all active services.

inactive ····Specifies all paused or stopped services.

all·············Specifies all services.

bufsize= BufferSize·········Specifies the size (in bytes) of the enumeration buffer. The default size is 1024 bytes. Increase the size of the enumeration buffer when the display resulting from a query exceeds 1024 bytes.

ri= ResumeIndex·········Specifies the index number at which to begin or resume the enumeration. The default is 0. Use this parameter in conjunction with the bufsize= parameter when more information is returned by a query than the default buffer can display.

group= GroupName·······Specifies the service group to enumerate. The default is all groups.

Notes:

• Without a space between a parameter and its value (that is, type= own, not type=own), the operation will fail.

• The query operation displays the following information about a service: SER-VICE_NAME (service's registry subkey name), TYPE, STATE (as well as states which are not available), WIN32_EXIT_B, SERVICE_EXIT_B, CHECKPOINT, and WAIT_HINT.

• The type= parameter can be used twice in some cases. The first appearance of the type= parameter specifies whether to query services, drivers, or all. The second appearance of the type= parameter specifies a type from the create operation to further narrow a query's scope.

• When the display resulting from a query command exceeds the size of the enumeration buffer, a message similar to the following is displayed:
Enum: more data, need 1822 bytes start resume at index 79

• To display the remaining query information, rerun query, setting bufsize= to be the number of bytes and ri= to the specified index. For example, the remaining output would be displayed by typing the following at the command line:
sc query bufsize= 1822 ri= 79

sc queryex

Obtains and displays extended information about the specified service, driver, type of service, or type of driver.

Syntax:

sc [ServerName] queryex [type= {driver | service|all}] [type= {own | share | interact | kernel | filesys | rec | adapt}] [state= {active | inactive |

all}] [bufsize= BufferSize] [ri= ResumeIndex] [group= GroupName]

Examples:

sc queryex messenger   *or*   sc queryex group= ""

Syntax Options:

ServerName ··················Specifies the name of the remote server on which the service is located. The name must use the UNC format ("\\myserver"). To run SC.exe locally, ignore this parameter.

ServiceName ··················Specifies the service name returned by the getkeyname operation. This queryex parameter is not used in conjunction with any other queryex parameters except ServerName.

type= {driver|service|all}··Specifies what to enumerate. The default type is service.

Value ········Description

driver ········Specifies that only drivers are enumerated.

service ·····Specifies that only services are enumerated.

all············Specifies that both drivers and services are enumerated.

type= {own | share | interact | kernel | filesys | rec | adapt}
  Specifies the type of services or type of drivers to enumerate.

Value ········Description

own··········The service runs in its own process. It does not share an executable file with other services. This is the default.

share ········The service runs as a shared process. It shares an executable file with other services.

interact······The service can interact with the desktop, receiving input from users. Interactive services must be run under the LocalSystem account.

kernel········Driver.

filesys······File system driver.

state= {active|inactive|all}····················Specifies the started state of the service for which to enumerate. The default state is active.

Value ········Description

active ········Specifies all active services.

inactive ·····Specifies all paused or stopped services.

all·············Specifies all services.

bufsize= BufferSize········Specifies the size (in bytes) of the enumeration buffer. The default size is 1024 bytes.

ri= ResumeIndex ············Specifies the index number at which to begin or resume the enumeration. The default is 0.

group= GroupName········Specifies the service group to enumerate. The default is all groups.

Notes:

• Without a space between a parameter and its value (that is, type= own, not type=own), the operation will fail.

• The queryex operation displays the following information about a service: SERVICE_NAME (service's registry subkey name), TYPE, STATE (as well as states that are not available), WIN32_EXIT_B, SERVICE_EXIT_B, CHECKPOINT, WAIT_HINT, PID, and FLAGS.

• The type= parameter can be used twice in some cases. The first appearance of the type= parameter specifies whether to query services, drivers, or all. The second appearance of the type= parameter specifies a type from the create operation to further narrow a query's scope.

• When the display resulting from a queryex command exceeds the size of the enumeration buffer, a message similar to the following is displayed:
Enum: more data, need 2130 bytes start resume at index 75

• To display the remaining queryex information, rerun queryex, setting bufsize= to be the number of bytes and ri= to the specified index. For example, the remaining output would be displayed by typing the following at the command line:
sc queryex bufsize= 2130 ri= 75

sc querylock

Queries and displays the lock status for the Service Control Manager's database.

Syntax:

sc [ServerName] querylock

Syntax Options:

ServerName ·················Specifies the name of the remote server on which the service is located. The name must use the UNC format ("\\myserver"). To run SC.exe locally, ignore this parameter.

---

sc sdset

Sets a service's security descriptor using Service Descriptor Definition Language (SDDL).

Syntax:

sc [ServerName] sdset ServiceName ServiceSecurityDescriptor

Syntax Options:

ServerName ················Specifies the name of the remote server on which the service is located. The name must use the UNC format ("\\myserver"). To run SC.exe locally, ignore this parameter.

ServiceName ················Specifies the service name returned by the getkeyname operation.

ServiceSecurityDescriptor····················Specifies the service descriptor in SDDL.

Notes:

• For more information about SDDL, see "Security Descriptor Definition Language" at http://www.microsoft.com/resources/documentation/windows/xp/all/proddocs/en-us/ntcmds.mspx

sc sdshow

Displays a service's security descriptor using SDDL.

Syntax:

sc [ServerName] sdshow ServiceName

Examples:

sc sdshow rpcss

Syntax Options:

ServerName ················Specifies the name of the remote server on which the service is located. The name must use the UNC format ("\\myserver"). To run SC.exe locally, ignore this parameter.

ServiceName ················Specifies the service name returned by the getkeyname operation.

Notes:

• For more information about SDDL, see "Security Descriptor Definition Language" at http://www.microsoft.com/resources/documentation/windows/xp/all/proddocs/en-us/ntcmds.mspx

sc start

Starts a service running.

Syntax:

sc [ServerName] start ServiceName [ServiceArguments]

Examples:

sc start tapisrv

Syntax Options:

ServerName ················Specifies the name of the remote server on which the service is located. The name must use the UNC format ("\\myserver"). To run SC.exe locally, ignore this parameter.

ServiceName ················Specifies the service name returned by the getkeyname operation.

ServiceArguments ·········Specifies service arguments to pass to the service to be started.

sc stop

Sends a STOP control request to a service.

Syntax:

sc [ServerName] stop ServiceName

Examples

sc stop tapisrv

Syntax Options:

ServerName ·················Specifies the name of the remote server on which the service is located. The name must use the UNC format ("\\myserver"). To run SC.exe locally, ignore this parameter.

ServiceName ·················Specifies the service name returned by the getkeyname operation.

Notes:

• Not all services can be stopped.

SCHTASKS

Schedules commands and programs to run periodically or at a specific time. Adds and removes tasks from the schedule, starts and stops tasks on demand, and displays and changes scheduled tasks.

schtasks create

Creates a new scheduled task.

Syntax:

schtasks /create /tn TaskName /tr TaskRun /sc schedule [/mo modifier] [/d day] [/m month[,month...] [/i IdleTime] [/st StartTime] [/sd StartDate] [/ed EndDate] [/s computer [/u [domain\user /p password]] [/ru {[Domain\User | "System"} [/rp Password]] /?

Syntax Options:

/tn TaskName ·················Specifies a name for the task.

/tr TaskRun ·················Specifies the program or command that the task runs. Type the fully qualified path and file name of an executable file, script file, or batch file. If you omit the path, SchTasks.exe assumes that the file is in the Systemroot\System32 directory.

/sc schedule ·················Specifies the schedule type. Valid values are MINUTE, HOURLY, DAILY, WEEKLY, MONTHLY, ONCE, ONSTART, ONLOGON, ONIDLE.

Value	Description
MINUTE, HOURLY, DAILY, WEEKLY, MONTHLY	Specifies the time unit for the schedule.
ONCE	The task runs once at a specified date and time.
ONSTART	The task runs every time the system starts. You can specify a start date, or run the task the next time the system starts.
ONLOGON	The task runs whenever a user (any user) logs on. You can specify a date, or run the task the next time the user logs on.
ONIDLE	The task runs whenever the system is idle for a specified period of time. You can specify a date, or run the task the next time the system is idle.

/mo modifier ·················Specifies how often the task runs within its schedule type. This parameter is required for a MONTHLY schedule. This parameter is valid, but optional, for a MINUTE, HOURLY, DAILY, or WEEKLY schedule. The default value is 1.

Schedule type	Modifier	Description
MINUTE	1 - 1439	The task runs every n minutes.
HOURLY	1 - 23	The task runs every n hours.
DAILY	1 - 365	The task runs every n days.
WEEKLY	1 - 52	The task runs every n weeks.
MONTHLY	1 - 12	The task runs every n months.
LASTDAY	The task runs on the last day of the month.	
FIRST, SECOND, THIRD, FOURTH, LAST	Use with the /d day parameter to run a task on a particular week and day. For example, on the third Wednesday of the month.	

/d day········Specifies a day of the week or a day of a month. Valid only with a WEEKLY or MONTHLY schedule.

Schedule type	Day values
WEEKLY	Optional. Valid values are MON - SUN and * (every day). MON is the default.
MONTHLY	A value of MON - SUN is required when the FIRST, SECOND, THIRD, FOURTH, or LAST modifier (/mo) is used. A value of 1 - 31 is optional and is valid only with no modifier or a modifier of the 1 - 12 type. The default is day 1 (the first day of the month).

/m month[,month...]········Specifies a month of the year. Valid values are JAN - DEC and * (every month). The /m parameter is valid only with a MONTHLY schedule. It is required when the LASTDAY modifier is used. Otherwise, it is optional and the default value is * (every month).

/i IdleTime·Specifies how many minutes the computer is idle before the task starts. Type a whole number from 1 to 999. This parameter is valid only with an ONIDLE schedule, and then it is required.

/st StartTime ·················Specifies the time of day that the task starts in HH:MM:SS 24-hour format. The default value is the current local time when the command completes. The /st parameter is valid with MINUTE, HOURLY, DAILY, WEEKLY, MONTHLY, and ONCE schedules. It is required with a ONCE schedule.

/sd StartDate·················Specifies the date that the task starts in MM/DD/YYYY format. The default value is the current date. The /sd parameter is valid with all schedules, and is required for a ONCE schedule.

/ed EndDate··················Specifies the last date that the task is scheduled to run. This parameter is optional. It is not valid in a ONCE, ONSTART, ONLOGON, or ONIDLE schedule. By default, schedules have no ending date.

/s Computer ··················Specifies the name or IP address of a remote computer (with or without backslashes). The default is the local computer.

/u [domain\]user ···········Runs the command with the permissions of the specified user account. By default, the command runs with the permissions of the user logged on to the computer running SchTasks.

/p password ·················Specifies the password of the user account specified in the /u parameter. This parameter is required when the /u parameter is used.

/ru {[Domain\]User | "System"} ···············Runs the tasks with the permission of the specified user account. By default, the task runs with the permissions of the user logged on to the computer running SchTasks.

Value	Description
[Domain\]User	Specifies a user account.
"System" or ""	Specifies the NT Authority\System account, which is used by the operating system.

/rp Password··················Specifies the password of the user account that is specified in the /ru parameter. If you omit this parameter when specifying a user account, SchTasks.exe prompts you for the password and obscures the text you type. Tasks run with with permissions of the NT Authority\System account do not require a password and SchTasks.exe does not prompt for one.

Notes:

• The /u and /p command-line options are available only when you use /s. You must use /p with /u to provide the user's password.

• SchTasks.exe does not verify program file locations or user account passwords. If you do not enter the correct file location or the correct password for the user account, the task is created, but it does not run. Also, if the password for an account changes or expires, and you do not change the password saved in the task, then the task does not run.

• The NT Authority\System account does not have interactive logon rights. Users do not see and cannot interact with programs run with system permissions.

• Each task runs only one program. However, you can create a batch file that starts multiple tasks, and then schedule a task that runs the batch file.

• You can test a task as soon as you create it. Use the run operation to test the task and then check the SchedLgU.txt file (Systemroot\SchedLgU.txt) for errors.

schtasks create minute

Syntax:

schtasks /create /tn TaskName /tr TaskRun /sc minute [/mo {1 - 1439}] [/st StartTime] [/sd StartDate] [/ed EndDate] [/s computer [/u [domain\]user /p password]] [/ru {[Domain\]User | "System"} [/rp Password]]

Example:

To schedule a task to run every 20 minutes

The following command schedules a security script, Sec.vbs, to run every 20 minutes. Because the command does not include a starting date or time, the task starts 20 minutes after the command completes, and runs every 20 minutes thereafter whenever the system is running. Notice that the security script source file is located on a remote computer, but that the task is scheduled and executes on the local computer.
schtasks /create /sc minute /mo 20 /tn "Security Script" /tr \\central\data\scripts\sec.vbs
In response, SchTasks.exe displays a message explaining that the task will run with the permissions of the current user and requests the current user's password. When you enter the password, SchTasks.exe obscures the text you type.

The task will be created under current logged-in user name.
Please enter the password
****

Then, SchTasks.exe displays a message indicating that the task is scheduled:
SUCCESS: The Scheduled Task "Security Script" has successfully been created.
A query shows the task that the command scheduled:

TaskName	Next Run Time	Status
===	===	===
Security Script	10:50:00 AM , 4/4/2001	

schtasks create hourly

Syntax:

schtasks /create /tn TaskName /tr TaskRun /sc hourly [/mo {1 - 365}] [/st StartTime] [/sd StartDate] [/ed EndDate] [/s computer [/u [domain\]user /p password]] [/ru {[Domain\]User | "System"} [/rp Password]]

Example:

To schedule a command that runs every hour at five minutes past the hour

The following command schedules the MyApp program to run hourly beginning at five minutes past midnight. Because the /mo parameter is omitted, the command uses the default value for the hourly schedule, which is every (1) hour. If this command is issued after 12:05 A.M., the program will not run until the next day.
schtasks /create /sc hourly /st 00:05:00 /tn "My App" /tr c:\apps\myapp.exe

To schedule a command that runs every five hours

The following command schedules the MyApp program to run every five hours beginning on the first day of March 2001. It uses the /mo parameter to specify the interval and the /sd parameter to specify the start date. Because the command does not specify a start time, the current time is used as the start time.
schtasks /create /sc hourly /mo 5 /sd 03/01/2001 /tn "My App" /tr c:\apps\myapp.exe

schtasks create daily

Syntax:

schtasks /create /tn TaskName /tr TaskRun /sc daily [/mo {1 - 365}] [/st StartTime] [/sd StartDate] [/ed EndDate] [/s computer [/u [domain\]user /p password]] [/ru {[Domain\]User | "System"} [/rp Password]]

Example:

To schedule a task that runs every day

The following example schedules the MyApp program to run once a day, every day, at 8:00 A.M. until December 31, 2001. Because it omits the /mo parameter, the default interval of 1 is used to run the command every day.
schtasks /create /tn "My App" /tr c:\apps\myapp.exe /sc daily /st 08:00:00 /ed 12/31/2001

To schedule a task that runs every other day
The following example schedules the MyApp program to run every other day at 1:00 P.M. (13:00) beginning on December 31, 2001. The command uses the /mo parameter to specify an interval of two (2) days.
schtasks /create /tn "My App" /tr c:\apps\myapp.exe /sc daily /mo 2 /st 13:00:00 /sd 12/31/2001

schtasks create weekly

Syntax:
schtasks /create /tn TaskName /tr TaskRun /sc weekly [/d {MON - SUN | *}] [/mo {1 - 52}] [/st StartTime] [/sd StartDate] [/ed EndDate] [/s computer [/u [domain\]user /p password]] [/ru {[Domain\]User | "System"} [/rp Password]]

Example:

To schedule a task that runs every six weeks
The following command schedules the MyApp program to run on a remote computer every six weeks. The command uses the /mo parameter to specify the interval. It also uses the /s parameter to specify the remote computer and the /ru parameter to schedule the task to run with the permissions of the user's Administrator account. Because the /rp parameter is omitted, SchTasks.exe prompts the user for the Administrator account password.
Also, because the command is run remotely, all paths in the command, including the path to MyApp.exe, refer to paths on the remote computer.
schtasks /create /tn "My App" /tr c:\apps\myapp.exe /sc weekly /mo 6 /s Server16 /ru Admin01

To schedule a task that runs every other week on Friday
The following command schedules a task to run every other Friday. It uses the /mo parameter to specify the two-week interval and the /d parameter to specify the day of the week. To schedule a task that runs every Friday, omit the /mo parameter or set it to 1.
schtasks /create /tn "My App" /tr c:\apps\myapp.exe /sc weekly /mo 2 /d FRI

schtasks create monthly

Syntax:
General Monthly Schedule Syntax : schtasks /create /tn TaskName /tr TaskRun /sc monthly [/mo {FIRST | SECOND | THIRD | FOURTH | LAST | LASTDAY] [/d {MON - SUN | 1 - 31}] [/m {JAN - DEC[,JAN - DEC...] | *}] [/st StartTime] [/sd StartDate] [/ed EndDate] [/s computer [/u [domain\]user /p password]] [/ru {[Domain\]User | "System"} [/rp Password]]

Specific Week Syntax : schtasks /create /tn TaskName /tr TaskRun /sc monthly /mo {FIRST | SECOND | THIRD | FOURTH | LAST} /d {MON - SUN} [/m {JAN - DEC[,JAN - DEC...] | *}] [/st StartTime] [/sd StartDate] [/ed EndDate] [/s computer [/u [domain\]user /p password]] [/ru {[Domain\]User | "System"} [/rp Password]]

Lastday Syntax : schtasks /create /tn TaskName /tr TaskRun /sc monthly /mo LASTDAY /m {JAN - DEC[,JAN - DEC...] | *} [/st StartTime] [/sd StartDate] [/ed EndDate] [/s computer [/u [domain\]user /p password]] [/ru {[Domain\]User | "System"} [/rp Password]]

Specific Date Syntax : schtasks /create /tn TaskName /tr TaskRun /sc monthly /d {1 - 31} [/m {JAN - DEC[,JAN - DEC...] | *}] [/st StartTime] [/sd StartDate] [/ed EndDate] [/s computer [/u [domain\]user /p password]] [/ru {[Domain\]User | "System"} [/rp Password]]

Examples:

To schedule a task for the first day of every month

The following command schedules the MyApp program to run on the first day of every month. Because the default modifier is none (no modifier), the default day is day 1, and the default month is every month, the command does not need any additional parameters.

schtasks /create /tn "My App" /tr c:\apps\myapp.exe /sc monthly

To schedule a task for the last day of every month

The following command schedules the MyApp program to run on the last day of every month. It uses the /mo parameter to specify the last day of the month and the /m parameter with the wildcard character (*) to indicate that the program runs on the last day of every month.

schtasks /create /tn "My App" /tr c:\apps\myapp.exe /sc monthly /mo lastday /m *

To schedule a task that runs every three months

The following command schedules the MyApp program to run every three months. It uses the /mo parameter to specify the interval.

schtasks /create /tn "My App" /tr c:\apps\myapp.exe /sc monthly /mo 3

To schedule a task for the second Sunday of every month

The following command schedules the MyApp program to run on the second Sunday of every month. It uses the /mo parameter to specify the second week of the month and the /d parameter to specify the day.

schtasks /create /tn "My App" /tr c:\apps\myapp.exe /sc monthly /mo SECOND /d SUN

To schedule a task for the 15th days of May and June

The following command schedules the MyApp program to run on May 15 and June 15 at 3:00 PM (15:00). It uses the /d parameter to specify the date and the /m parameter to specify the months. It also uses the /st parameter to specify the start time.

schtasks /create /tn "My App" /tr c:\apps\myapp.exe /sc monthly /d 15 /m MAY,JUN /st 15:00:00

schtasks create once

Syntax:

schtasks /create /tn TaskName /tr TaskRun /sc once /st StartTime /sd StartDate [/s computer [/u [domain\]user /p password]] [/ru {[Domain\]User | "System"} [/rp Password]]

Example:

To schedule a task that runs one time

The following command schedules the MyApp program to run at midnight on January 1, 2002. It uses the /ru parameter to run the task with the permissions of the user's Administrator account and the /rp parameter to provide the password for the Administrator account.

schtasks /create /tn "My App" /tr c:\apps\myapp.exe /sc once /st 00:00:00 /sd 01/01/2002 /ru Admin23 /rp p@ssworD1

schtasks create onstart

Syntax:

schtasks /create /tn TaskName /tr TaskRun /sc onstart [/sd StartDate] [/s computer [/u [domain\]user /p password]] [/ru {[Domain\]User | "System"} [/rp Password]]

Example:

To schedule a task that runs every time the system starts

The following command schedules the MyApp program to run every time the system starts, beginning on March 15, 2001:

schtasks /create /tn "My App" /tr c:\apps\myapp.exe /sc onstart /sd 03/15/2001

schtasks create onlogon

Syntax:

schtasks /create /tn TaskName /tr TaskRun /sc onlogon [/sd StartDate] [/s computer [/u [domain\]user /p password]] [/ru {[Domain\]User | "System"} [/rp Password]]

Example:

To schedule a task that runs when a user logs on to a remote computer

The following command schedules a batch file to run every time a user (any user) logs on to the remote computer. It uses the /s parameter to specify the remote computer. Because the command is remote, all paths in the command, including the path to the batch file, refer to a path on the remote computer.

schtasks /create /tn "Start Web Site" /tr c:\myiis\webstart.bat /sc onlogon /s Server23

schtasks create onidle

Syntax:

schtasks /create /tn TaskName /tr TaskRun /sc onidle /iIdleTime [/sd StartDate] [/s computer [/u [domain\]user /p password]] [/ru {[Domain\]User | "System"} [/rp Password]]

Example:

To schedule a task that runs whenever the computer is idle

The following command schedules the MyApp program to run whenever the computer is idle. It uses the required /i parameter to specify that the computer must remain idle for ten minutes before the task starts.

schtasks /create /tn "My App" /tr c:\apps\myapp.exe /sc onidle /i 10

schtasks change

Changes one or more of the following properties of a task.

• The program that the task runs (/tr).
• The user account under which the task runs (/ru).
• The password for the user account (/rp).

Syntax:

schtasks /change /tn TaskName [/s computer [/u [domain\]user /p password]] [/tr TaskRun] [/ru Domain\]User | "System"] [/rp Password]

Syntax Options:

/tn TaskName : Identifies the task to be changed. Enter the task name.

/s Computer : Specifies the name or IP address of a remote computer (with or without backslashes). The default is the local computer.

/u [domain\]user : Runs the command with the permissions of the specified user account. By default, the command runs with the permissions of the user logged on to the computer running SchTasks.

/p password : Specifies the password of the user account specified in the /u parameter. This parameter is required when the /u parameter is used.

/tr TaskRun : Changes the program that the task run. Enter the fully qualified path and file name of an executable file, script file, or batch file. If you omit the path, SchTasks.exe assumes that the file is in the Systemroot\System32 directory. The specified program replaces the original program run by the task.

/ru [Domain\]User | "System" : Changes the user account for the task.

Value	Description
[Domain\]User	Specifies a user account.
"System" or ""	Specifies the NT Authority\System account, which is used by the operating system.

When you change the user account, you must also change the user password. If a command has an /ru parameter but not an /rp parameter, SchTasks.exe prompts for a new password and obscures the text you type.

Tasks run with permissions of the NT Authority\System account do not require a password and SchTasks.exe does not prompt for one.

/rp Password : Changes the account password for the task. Enter the new password.

Notes:

• Using the /s, /u, and /p command-line options
The /u and /p command-line options are available only when you use /s. You must use /p with /u to provide the user's password.

• The /tn and /s parameters identify the task. The /tr, /ru, and /rp parameters specify properties of the task that you can change.

• A command that uses the change operation must change at least one task property.

• The NT Authority\System account does not have interactive logon rights. Users do not see and cannot interact with programs run with system permissions.

Examples:

To change the program that a task runs

The following command changes the program that the Virus Check task runs from VirusCheck.exe to VirusCheck2.exe. This command uses the /tn parameter to identify the task and the /tr parameter to specify the new program for the task. (You cannot change the task name.)

schtasks /change /tn "Virus Check" /tr C:\VirusCheck2.exe

In response, SchTasks.exe displays the following success message:

SUCCESS: The parameter of the Scheduled Task "Virus Check" has been changed.

As a result of this command, the Virus Check task now runs VirusCheck2.exe.

To change the password for a remote task

The following command changes the password of the user account for the RemindMe task on the remote computer, Svr01. The command uses the /tn parameter to identify the task and the /s parameter to specify the remote computer. It uses the /rp parameter to specify the new password, p@ssWord3.

This procedure is required whenever the password for a user account expires or changes. If the password saved in a task is no longer valid, then the task does not run.

schtasks /change /tn RemindMe /s Svr01 /rp p@ssWord3

In response, SchTasks.exe displays the following success message:

SUCCESS: The parameter of the Scheduled Task "RemindMe" has been changed.

As a result of this command, the RemindMe task now runs under its original user account, but with a new password.

To change the program and user account for a task

The following command changes the program that a task runs and changes the user account under which the task runs. Essentially, it uses an old schedule for a new task. This command changes the Notepad task, which starts Notepad.exe every morning at 9:00 a.m., to start Internet Explorer instead.

The command uses the /tn parameter to identify the task. It uses the /tr parameter to change the program that the task runs and the /ru parameter to change the user account under which the task runs.

The /rp parameter, which provides the password for the user account, is omitted. You must provide a password for the account, but you can use the /rp parameter and type the password in clear text, or wait for SchTasks.exe to prompt you for a password, and then enter the password in obscured text.

schtasks /change /tn Notepad /tr "c:\program files\Internet Explorer\iexplore.exe" /ru DomainX\Admin01

In response, SchTasks.exe requests the password for the user account. It obscures the text you type, so the password is not visible.

Please enter the password for DomainX\Admin01: ********

Note that the /tn parameter identifies the task and that the /tr and /ru parameters change the properties of the task. You cannot use another parameter to identify the task and you cannot change the task name.

In response, SchTasks.exe displays the following success message:

SUCCESS: The parameter of the Scheduled Task "Notepad" has been changed.

As a result of this command, the RemindMe task now runs under its original user account, but with a new password.

To change a program to the System account

The following command changes the SecurityScript task so that it runs with permissions of the NT Authority\System account. It uses the /ru "" parameter to indicate the System account.

schtasks /change /tn SecurityScript /ru ""

In response, SchTasks.exe displays the following success message:

SUCCESS: The parameter of the Scheduled Task "SecurityScript" has been changed.

Because tasks run with System account permissions do not require a password, SchTasks.exe does not prompt for one.

Syntax Options:

/tn TaskName ·············· Identifies the task to be changed. Enter the task name.

/s Computer ·············· Specifies the name or IP address of a remote computer (with or without backslashes). The default is the local computer.

/u [domain\]user ··············Runs the command with the permissions of the specified user account. By default, the command runs with the permissions of the user logged on to the computer running SchTasks.

/p password ··················Specifies the password of the user account specified in the /u parameter. This parameter is required when the /u parameter is used.

/tr TaskRun ··················Changes the program that the task runs. Enter the fully qualified path and file name of an executable file, script file, or batch file. If you omit the path, SchTasks.exe assumes that the file is in the Systemroot\System32 directory. The specified program replaces the original program run by the task.

/ru [Domain\]User | "System"··············Changes the user account for the task.

Value	Description
[Domain\]User	Specifies a user account.
"System" or ""	Specifies the NT Authority\System account, which is used by the operating system.

When you change the user account, you must also change the user password. If a command has an /ru parameter but not an /rp parameter, SchTasks.exe prompts for a new password and obscures the text you type.

Tasks run with with permissions of the NT Authority\System account do not require a password and SchTasks.exe does not prompt for one.

/rp Password ··················Changes the account password for the task. Enter the new password.

Notes:

• The /u and /p command-line options are available only when you use /s. You must use /p with /u to provide the user's password.

• The /tn and /s parameters identify the task. The /tr, /ru, and /rp parameters specify properties of the task that you can change.

• A command that uses the change operation must change at least one task property.

• The NT Authority\System account does not have interactive logon rights. Users do not see and cannot interact with programs run with system permissions.

schtasks run

Starts a scheduled task immediately. The run operation ignores the schedule, but uses the program file location, user account, and password saved in the task to run the task immediately.

Syntax:

schtasks /run /tn TaskName [/s computer [/u [domain\]user /p password]] /?

Syntax Options:

/tn TaskName : Identifies the task. This parameter is required.

/s Computer : Specifies the name or IP address of a remote computer (with or without backslashes). The default is the local computer.

/u [domain\]user : Runs the command with the permissions of the specified user account. By default, the command runs with the permissions of the user logged on to the computer running SchTasks.

/p password : Specifies the password of the user account specified in the /u parameter. This parameter is required when the /u parameter is used.

Notes:

• Using the /s, /u, and /p command-line options
The /u and /p command-line options are available only when you use /s. You must use /p with /u to provide the user's password.

• Use this operation to test your tasks. If a task does not run, check the Task Scheduler Service transaction log, Systemroot\SchedLgU.txt, for errors.

• Running a task does not affect the task schedule and does not change the next run time scheduled for the task.

• To run a task remotely, the task must be scheduled on the remote computer. When you run it, the task runs only on the remote computer. To verify that a task is running on a remote computer, use Task Manager or the Task Scheduler transaction log, Systemroot\SchedLgU.txt.

Examples:

To run a task on the local computer

The following command starts the "Security Script" task.

schtasks /run /tn "Security Script"

In response, SchTasks.exe starts the script associated with the task and displays the following message:

SUCCESS: The Scheduled Task "Security Script" is running ......

To run a task on a remote computer

The following command starts the Update task on a remote computer, Svr01:

schtasks /run /tn Update /s Svr01

In this case, SchTasks.exe displays the following error message:

ERROR: Unable to run the Scheduled Task "Update".

To find the cause of the error, look in the Scheduled Tasks transaction log, C:\Windows\SchedLgU.txt on Svr01. In this case, the following entry appears in the log:

"Update.job" (update.exe) 3/26/2001 1:15:46 PM ** ERROR **

The attempt to log on to the account associated with the task failed, therefore, the task did not run.

The specific error is:

0x8007052e: Logon failure: unknown user name or bad password.

Verify that the task's Run-as name and password are valid and try again.

Apparently, the user name or password in the task is not valid on the system. The following schtasks /change command updates the user name and password for the Update task on Svr01:

schtasks /change /tn Update /s Svr01 /ru Administrator /rp PassW@rd3

After the change command completes, the run command is repeated. This time, the Update.exe program starts and SchTasks.exe displays the following message:

SUCCESS: The Scheduled Task "Update" is running......

Syntax Options:

/tn TaskName ················Identifies the task. This parameter is required.

/s Computer ···················Specifies the name or IP address of a remote computer (with or without backslashes). The default is the local computer.

/u [domain\]user ···········Runs the command with the permissions of the specified user account. By default, the command runs with the permissions of the user logged on to the computer running SchTasks.

/p password ···················Specifies the password of the user account specified in the /u parameter. This parameter is required when the /u parameter is used.

Notes:

• The /u and /p command-line options are available only when you use /s. You must use /p with /u to provide the user's password.

• Use this operation to test your tasks. If a task does not run, check the Task Scheduler Service transaction log, Systemroot\SchedLgU.txt, for errors.

• Running a task does not affect the task schedule and does not change the next run time scheduled for the task.

• To run a task remotely, the task must be scheduled on the remote computer. When you run it, the task runs only on the remote computer. To verify that a task is running on a remote computer, use Task Manager or the Task Scheduler transaction log, Systemroot\SchedLgU.txt.

schtasks end

Stops a program started by a task.

Syntax:

schtasks /end /tn TaskName [/s computer [/u [domain\]user /p password]] /?

Syntax Options:

/tn TaskName : Identifies the task that started the program. This parameter is required.

/s Computer : Specifies the name or IP address of a remote computer (with or without backslashes). The default is the local computer.

/u [domain\]user : Runs the command with the permissions of the specified user account. By default, the command runs with the permissions of the user logged on to the computer running SchTasks.

/p password : Specifies the password of the user account specified in the /u parameter. This parameter is required when the /u parameter is used.

Notes:

- Using the /s, /u, and /p command-line options

- The /u and /p command-line options are available only when you use /s. You must use /p with /u to provide the user's password.

- SchTasks.exe ends only the instances of a program started by a scheduled task. To stop other processes, use TaskKill, a tool included in Windows XP Professional.

Examples:

To end a task on a local computer

The following command stops the instance of Notepad.exe that was started by the My Notepad task:

schtasks /end /tn "My Notepad"

In response, SchTasks.exe stops the instance of Notepad.exe that the task started, and it displays the following success message:

SUCCESS: The Scheduled Task "My Notepad" has been terminated successfully.

To end a task on a remote computer

The following command stops the instance of Internet Explorer that was started by the InternetOn task on the remote computer, Svr01:

schtasks /end /tn InternetOn /s Svr01

In response, SchTasks.exe stops the instance of Internet Explorer that the task started, and it displays the following success message:

SUCCESS: The Scheduled Task "InternetOn" has been terminated successfully.

Syntax Options:

/tn TaskName ················Identifies the task that started the program. This parameter is required.

/s Computer ················Specifies the name or IP address of a remote computer (with or without backslashes). The default is the local computer.

/u [domain\]user ············Runs the command with the permissions of the specified user account. By default, the command runs with the permissions of the user logged on to the computer running SchTasks.

/p password ················Specifies the password of the user account specified in the /u parameter. This parameter is required when the /u parameter is used.

Notes:

- The /u and /p command-line options are available only when you use /s. You must use /p with /u to provide the user's password.

- SchTasks.exe ends only the instances of a program started by a scheduled task. To stop other processes, use TaskKill, a tool included in Windows XP Professional. For more information about TaskKill, see http://www.microsoft.com/resources/documentation/windows/xp/all/proddocs/en-us/taskkill.mspx

schtasks delete

Deletes a scheduled task.

Syntax:

schtasks /delete /tn {TaskName | *} [/f] [/s computer [/u [domain\]user /p password]] [/?]

Syntax Options:

/tn {TaskName | *} : Identifies the task being deleted. This parameter is required.

Value	Description
TaskName	Deletes the named task.
*	Deletes all scheduled tasks on the computer.

/f : Suppresses the confirmation message. The task is deleted without warning.

/s Computer : Specifies the name or IP address of a remote computer (with or without backslashes). The default is the local computer.

/u [domain\]user : Runs the command with the permissions of the specified user account. By default, the command runs with the permissions of the user logged on to the computer running SchTasks.

/p password : Specifies the password of the user account specified in the /u parameter. This parameter is required when the /u parameter is used.

Notes:

- Using the /s, /u, and /p command-line options

- The /u and /p command-line options are available only when you use /s. You must use /p with /u to provide the user's password.

- The delete operation deletes the task from the schedule. It does not delete the program that the task runs or interrupt a running program.

- The delete * command deletes all tasks scheduled for the computer, not just the tasks scheduled by the current user.

Examples:

To delete a task from the schedule of a remote computer

The following command deletes the "Start Mail" task from the schedule of a remote computer. It uses the /s parameter to identify the remote computer.
schtasks /delete /tn "Start Mail" /s Svr16
In response, SchTasks.exe displays the following confirmation message. To delete the task, type y. To cancel the command, type n:
WARNING: Are you sure you want to remove the task "Start Mail" (Y/N)? y
SUCCESS: The Scheduled Task "Start Mail" was successfully deleted.

To delete all tasks scheduled for the local computer

The following command deletes all tasks from the schedule of the local computer, including tasks scheduled by other users. It uses the /tn * parameter to represent all tasks on the computer and the /f parameter to suppress the confirmation message.
schtasks /delete /tn * /f
In response, SchTasks.exe displays the following success messages indicating that the only task scheduled, SecureScript, is deleted.
SUCCESS: The Scheduled Task "SecureScript" was successfully deleted.

Syntax Options:

/tn {TaskName | *}··········Identifies the task being deleted. This parameter is required.

Value	Description
TaskName	Deletes the named task.
*	Deletes all scheduled tasks on the computer.

/f ··············Suppresses the confirmation message. The task is deleted without warning.

/s Computer ····················Specifies the name or IP address of a remote computer (with or without backslashes). The default is the local computer.

/u [domain\]user ···············Runs the command with the permissions of the specified user account. By default, the command runs with the permissions of the user logged on to the computer running SchTasks.

/p password ····················Specifies the password of the user account specified in the /u parameter. This parameter is required when the /u parameter is used.

Notes:

- The /u and /p command-line options are available only when you use /s. You must use /p with /u to provide the user's password.

- The delete operation deletes the task from the schedule. It does not delete the program that the task runs or interrupt a running program.

- The delete * command deletes all tasks scheduled for the computer, not just the tasks scheduled by the current user.

schtasks query

Displays all tasks scheduled to run on the computer, including those scheduled by other users.

Syntax:

schtasks [/query] [/fo {TABLE | LIST | CSV}] [/nh] [/v] [/s computer [/u [domain\]user /p password]]

Syntax Options:

[/query] : The operation name is optional. Typing schtasks without any parameters performs a query.

/fo {TABLE | LIST | CSV} : Specifies the output format. TABLE is the default.

/nh : Omits column headings from the table display. This parameter is valid with the TA-BLE and CSV output formats.

/v : Adds advanced properties of the tasks to the display.
Queries using /v should be formatted as LIST or CSV.

/s Computer : Specifies the name or IP address of a remote computer (with or without backslashes). The default is the local computer.

/u [domain\]user : Runs the command with the permissions of the specified user account. By default, the command runs with the permissions of the user logged on to the computer running SchTasks.

/p password : Specifies the password of the user account specified in the /u parameter. This parameter is required when the /u parameter is used.

Notes:

- Using the /s, /u, and /p command-line options

- The /u and /p command-line options are available only when you use /s. You must use /p with /u to provide the user's password.

- The query operation lists all tasks scheduled for the computer, not just the tasks scheduled by the current user.

Examples:

To display the scheduled tasks on the local computer

The following commands display all tasks scheduled for the local computer. These commands produce the same result and can be used interchangeably.

schtasks
schtasks /query
In response, SchTasks.exe displays the tasks in the default, simple table format, as shown in the following table:

TaskName	Next Run Time	Status
===	===	===
Microsoft Outlook	At logon time	
SecureScript	14:42:00 PM , 2/4/2001	

To display advanced properties scheduled tasks

The following command requests a detailed display of the tasks on the local computer. It uses the /v parameter to request a detailed (verbose) display and the /fo LIST parameter to format the display as a list for easy reading. You can use this command to verify that a task you created has the intended recurrence pattern.

schtasks /query /fo LIST /v
In response, SchTasks.exe displays a detailed property list for all tasks. The following display shows the task list for a task scheduled to run at 4:00 A.M. on the last Friday of every month:

```
HostName: ·······  ............................RESKIT01
TaskName: ·······  ............................SecureScript
Next Run Time: ........................4:00:00 AM , 3/30/2001
Status: ·············  ........................Not yet run
Last Run Time:Never
Last Result: ·····0
Creator: ·······  ............................user01
Schedule: ·······  ............................At 4:00 AM on the last Fri of every month, starting
3/24/2001
Task To Run:···C:\WINDOWS\system32\notepad.exe
Start In: ·········  ............................notepad.exe
Comment: ·······  ............................N/A
Scheduled Task State:........................Enabled
Scheduled Type:............................Monthly
Modifier: ·········  ............................Last FRIDAY
Start Time: ·······  ............................4:00:00 AM
Start Date: ·······  ............................3/24/2001
End Date: ·······  ............................N/A
Days: ·············  ............................FRIDAY
```

Months:
JAN,FEB,MAR,APR,MAY,JUN,JUL,AUG,SEP,OCT,NOV,DEC
Run As User: ···RESKIT\user01
Delete Task If Not Rescheduled: ....Enabled
Stop Task If Runs X Hours and X Mins: 72:0
Repeat: Until Time: ....Disabled
Repeat: Duration:................................Disabled
Repeat: Stop If Still Running:...............Disabled
Idle: Start Time(For IDLE Scheduled Type): Disabled
Idle: Only Start If Idle for X Minutes: .....Disabled
Idle: If Not Idle Retry For X Minutes:.....Disabled
Idle: Stop Task If Idle State End: ....Disabled
Power Mgmt: No Start On Batteries: ......Disabled
Power Mgmt: Stop On Battery Mode: ...Disabled

To log tasks scheduled for a remote computer

The following command requests a list of tasks scheduled for a remote computer, and adds the tasks to a comma-separated log file on the local computer. You can use this command format to collect and track tasks that are scheduled for multiple computers. The command uses the /s parameter to identify the remote computer, Reskit16, the /fo parameter to specify the format and the /nh parameter to suppress the column headings. The > append symbol redirects the output to the task log, p0102.csv, on the local computer, Svr01. Because the command runs on the remote computer, the local computer path must be fully qualified.

schtasks /query /s Reskit16 /fo csv /nh > \\svr01\data\tasklogs\p0102.csv
In response, SchTasks.exe adds the tasks scheduled for the Reskit16 computer to the p0102.csv file on the local computer, Svr01.

Notes:

• SchTasks.exe performs operations similar to those in Scheduled Tasks in Control Panel. You can use either tool to create, delete, configure, or display scheduled tasks.

• Typing schtasks without any parameters performs a query.

• The user must be a member of the Administrators group on the computer that the command affects.

• To verify that a scheduled task ran or to find out why a scheduled task did not run, see the Task Scheduler service transaction log, Systemroot\SchedLgU.txt. This log records attempted runs initiated by all tools that use the service, including Scheduled Tasks and SchTasks.exe.

• On rare occasions, task files become corrupted. Corrupted tasks do not run. When you try to perform an operation on corrupted tasks, SchTasks.exe displays the following error message:
ERROR: The data is invalid.

• You cannot recover corrupted tasks. To restore the task scheduling features of the system, use SchTasks.exe or Scheduled Tasks to delete the tasks from the system and reschedule them.

• SchTasks.exe replaces At.exe, a tool included in previous versions of Windows.

SECEDIT

Configures and analyzes system security by comparing your current configuration to at least one template.

secedit /analyze

Syntax:

secedit /analyze /db FileName [/cfg FileName] [/log FileName] [/quiet]

Syntax Options:

/db FileName ················Required. Specifies the path and file name of a database that contains the stored configuration against which the analysis will be performed. If File-Name specifies a new database, the /cfg FileName command-line option must also be specified.

/cfg FileName ················Specifies the path and file name for the security template that will be imported into the database for analysis. This command-line option is only valid when used with the /db parameter. If this is not specified, the analysis is performed against any configuration already stored in the database.

/log FileName ················Specifies the path and file name of the log file for the process. If this is not provided, the default log file is used.

/quiet········Suppresses screen and log output. You can still view analysis results by using Security Configuration and Analysis.

secedit /configure

Configures system security by applying a stored template.

Syntax:

secedit /configure /db FileName [/cfg FileName] [/overwrite][/areas area1 area2...]
[/log FileName] [/quiet]

Syntax Options:

/db FileName ················Required. Provides the file name of a database that contains the security template that should be applied.

/cfg FileName ················Specifies the file name of the security template that will be imported into the database and applied to the system. This command-line option is only valid when used with the /db parameter. If this is not specified, the template that is already stored in the database is applied.

/overwrite··Specifies whether the security template in the /cfg parameter should overwrite any template or composite template that is stored in the database instead of appending the results to the stored template. This command-line option is only valid when the /cfg parameter is also used. If this is not specified, the template in the /cfg parameter is appended to the stored template.

/areas area1 area2... ······Specifies the security areas to be applied to the system. If an area is not specified, all areas are applied to the system. Each area should be separated by a space.

Area name	Description
SECURITYPOLICY	Local policy and domain policy for the system, including account policies, audit policies, and so on.
GROUP_MGMT	Restricted group settings for any groups specified in the security template
USER_RIGHTS	User logon rights and granting of privileges
REGKEYS	Security on local registry keys
FILESTORE	Security on local file storage
SERVICES	Security for all defined services

/log FileName ················Specifies the file name of the log file for the process. If it is not specified, the default path is used.

/quiet········Suppresses screen and log output.

secedit /export

Exports a stored template from a security database to a security template file.

Syntax:

secedit /export [/mergedpolicy] [/DB FileName] [/CFG FileName] [/areas area1 area2...]
[/log FileName] [/quiet]

Syntax Options:

/mergedpolicy ················Merges and exports domain and local policy security settings.

/db FileName ················Specifies the database file that contains the template that will be exported. If the name of a database file is not provided, the system policy database is used.

/db FileName ················Specifies the file name where the template should be saved.

/areas area1 area2... ······Specifies the security areas to be exported to a template. If an area is not specified, all areas are exported. Each area should be separated by a space.

Area name	Description
SECURITYPOLICY	Specifies local policy and domain policy for the system, including account policies, audit policies, and so on.
GROUP_MGMT	Specifies restricted group settings for any groups specified in the security template.
USER_RIGHTS	Specifies user logon rights and granting of privileges
REGKEYS	Specifies the security on local registry keys
FILESTORE	Specifies the security on local file storage
SERVICES	Specifies security for all defined services

/log FileName .... Specifies the file name of the log file for the process. If not specified, the default path is used.

/quiet .... Suppresses screen and log output.

secedit /validate

Validates the syntax of a security template to be imported into a database for analysis or application to a system.

Syntax

secedit /validate FileName

Syntax Options:

FileName ·· Specifies the file name of the security template you have created with Security Templates.

Notes:

• secedit /refreshpolicy has been replaced with gpupdate. For information on how to refresh security settings, see http://www.microsoft.com/resources/documentation/windows/xp/all/proddocs/en-us/refrgp.mspx

SET

Displays, sets, or removes environment variables.

Syntax:

set [[/a [expression]] [/p [variable=]] string]

Examples:

To set an environment variable named TEST^1, type: set testVar=test^^1

To set an environment variable named TEST&1, type: set testVar=test^&1

Set sets the variable value as everything following the equals sign (=). If you type:

set testVar="test^1"

You get the following result: testVar="test^1"

To set an environment variable named INCLUDE so that the string C:\Inc (the \Inc directory on drive C) is associated with it, type: set include=c:\inc

You can then use the string C:\Inc in batch files by enclosing the name INCLUDE with percent signs (%). For example, you might include the following command in a batch file so that you can display the contents of the directory associated with the INCLUDE environment variable:

dir %include%

When this command is processed, the string C:\Inc replaces %include%.

You can also use set in a batch program that adds a new directory to the PATH environment variable. For example:

```
@echo off
rem ADDPATH.BAT adds a new directory
rem to the path environment variable.
set path=%1;%path%
set
```

When command extensions are enabled (that is, the default) and you run set with a value, it displays the variables that match that value. For example, if you type set p at the command prompt, you get the following results:

```
Path=C:\WINNT\system32;C:\WINNT;C:\WINNT\System32\Wbem
PATHEXT=.COM;.EXE;.BAT;.CMD;.VBS;.VBE;.JS;.JSE;.WSF;.WSH
PROCESSOR_ARCHITECTURE=x86
```

```
PROCESSOR_IDENTIFIER=x86 Family 6 Model 8 Stepping 1, GenuineIntel
PROCESSOR_LEVEL=6
PROCESSOR_REVISION=0801
ProgramFiles=C:\Program Files
PROMPT=$P$G
```

Syntax Options:

Used without parameters, set displays the current environment settings.

/a ··············Sets string to a numerical expression that is evaluated.

/p ··············Sets the value of variable to a line of input.

variable·····Specifies the variable you want to set or modify.

string········Specifies the string you want to associate with the specified variable.

Notes:

- The set command, with different parameters, is available from the Recovery Console.

- The characters <, >, |, &, ^ are special command shell characters and must be either preceded by the escape character (^) or enclosed in quotation marks when used in string (that is, "StringContaining&Symbol"). If you use quotation marks to enclose a string containing one of the special characters, the quotation marks are set as part of the environment variable value.

- Use environment variables to control the behavior of some batch files and programs and to control the way Windows XP and the MS-DOS subsystem appears and works. The set command is often used in the Autoexec.nt file to set environment variables.

- When you type the set command alone, the current environment settings are displayed. These settings usually include the COMSPEC and PATH environment variables that are used to help find programs on disk. Two other environment variables used by Windows XP are PROMPT and DIRCMD.

- When you specify values for variable and string, the specified variable value is added to the environment and the string is associated with that variable. If the variable already exists in the environment, the new string value replaces the old string value.

- If you specify only a variable and an equal sign (without a string) for the set command, the string value associated with the variable is cleared (as if the variable is not there at all).

- The following table lists the operators supported for /a in descending order of precedence.

Operator	Operation performed
< >	Grouping
* / % + -	Arithmetic
< >	Logical shift
&	Bitwise AND
^	Bitwise exclusive OR
|	Bitwise OR
= *= /= %= += -= &= ^= |= <= >=	Assignment
,	Expression separator

- If you use logical (&& ||) or modulus (%) operators, enclose the expression string in quotation marks. Any non-numeric strings in the expression are considered environment variable names whose values are converted to numbers before being processed. If you specify an environment variable name that is not defined in the current environment, a value of zero is allotted, which allows you to do arithmetic with environment variable values without using the % to retrieve a value.

- If you run set /a from the command line outside of a command script, it displays the final value of the expression.

- Numeric values are decimal numbers unless prefixed by 0x for hexadecimal numbers or 0 for octal numbers. Therefore, 0x12 is the same as 18 is the same as 022. The octal notation can be confusing. For example, 08 and 09 are not valid numbers because 8 and 9 are not valid octal digits.

- You are not required to include a prompt string.

- Delayed environment variable expansion support has been added. This support is disabled by default, but you can enable or disable it by using cmd /v.

XP Command: SET   **253**

- When command extensions are enabled (that is, the default) and you run set alone, it displays all current environment variables. If you run set with a value, it displays the variables that match that value.

- When creating batch files, you can use set to create variables and use them in the same way that you would the numbered variables %0 through %9. You can also use the variables %0 through %9 as input for set.

- When you call a variable value from a batch file, enclose the value with percent signs (%). For example, if your batch program creates an environment variable named BAUD, you can use the string associated with BAUD as a replaceable parameter by typing %baud% at the command line.

SETLOCAL

Starts localization of environment variables in a batch file. Localization continues until a matching endlocal command is encountered or the end of the batch file is reached.

Syntax:

setlocal {enableextension | disableextensions} {enabledelayedexpansion | disabledelayedexpansion}

Examples:

You can localize environment variables in a batch file, as follows:
```
rem *******Begin Comment*************
rem This program starts the superapp batch program on the network,
rem directs the output to a file, and displays the file
rem in Notepad.
rem *******End Comment*************
@echo off
setlocal
path=g:\programs\superapp;%path%
call superapp>c:\superapp.out
endlocal
start notepad c:\superapp.out
```

Syntax Options:

enableextension ··········Enables the command extensions until the matching endlocal command is encountered, regardless of the setting prior to the setlocal command.

disableextensions ··········Disables the command extensions until the matching endlocal command is encountered, regardless of the setting prior to the setlocal command.

enabledelayedexpansion Enables the delayed environment variable expansion until the matching endlocal command is encountered, regardless of the setting prior to the setlocal command.

disabledelayedexpansion·····················Disables the delayed environment variable expansion until the matching endlocal command is encountered, regardless of the setting prior to the setlocal command.

Notes:

- When you use setlocal outside of a script or batch file, it has no effect.

- Use setlocal to change environment variables when you run a batch file. Environment changes made after you run setlocal are local to the batch file. Cmd.exe restores previous settings when it either encounters an endlocal command or reaches the end of the batch file.

- You can have more than one setlocal or endlocal command in a batch program (that is, nested commands).

- The setlocal command sets the ERRORLEVEL variable. If you pass either {enableextension | disableextensions} or {enabledelayedexpansion | disabledelayedexpansion}, the ERRORLEVEL variable is set to zero (0). Otherwise, it is set to one (1). You can use this in batch scripts to determine whether the extensions are available, for example:
```
verify other 2>nul
setlocal enableextensions
if errorlevel 1 echo Unable to enable extensions
```

- Because cmd does not set the ERRORLEVEL variable when command extensions are disabled, the verify command initializes the ERRORLEVEL variable to a nonzero value when you use it with an invalid argument. Also, if you use the setlocal command with arguments {enableextension | disableextensions} or {enabledelayedexpansion | disabledelayedexpansion} and it does not set the ERRORLEVEL variable to one (1), command extensions are not available.

SHIFT

Changes the position of batch parameters in a batch file.

Syntax:

shift

Examples:

The following batch file, Mycopy.bat, shows how to use shift with any number of batch parameters. It copies a list of files to a specific directory. The batch parameters are represented by the directory and file name arguments.

```
@echo off
rem MYCOPY.BAT copies any number of files
rem to a directory.
rem The command uses the following syntax:
rem mycopy dir file1 file2 ...
set todir=%1
:getfile
shift
if "%1"=="" goto end
copy %1 %todir%
goto getfile
:end
set todir=
echo All done
```

Notes:

• When command extensions are enabled (that is, the default), the shift command supports the /n command-line option, which tells the command to start shifting at the nth argument, where n can be a value from zero to eight. For example, SHIFT /2 would shift %3 to %2, %4 to %3, and so on, and leave %1 %1 unaffected.

• The shift command changes the values of the batch parameters %0 through %9 by copying each parameter into the previous one. In other words, the value of %1 is copied to %0, the value of %2 is copied to %1, and so on. This is useful for writing a batch file that performs the same operation on any number of parameters.

• You can also use the shift command to create a batch file that can accept more than 10 batch parameters. If you specify more than 10 parameters on the command line, those that appear after the tenth (%9) will be shifted one at a time into %9.

• Shift has no affect on the %* batch parameter.

• There is no backward shift command. After you carry out the shift command, you cannot recover the first batch parameter (%0) that existed before the shift.

SHUTDOWN

Allows you to shut down or restart a local or remote computer.

Syntax:

shutdown [{-l|-s|-r|-a)] [-f] [-m [\\ComputerName]] [-t xx] [-c "message"] [-d[u][p]:xx:yy]

Examples:

shutdown -r -f -m \\MyServer -t 60 -d up:125:1

Syntax Options:

Used without parameters, shutdown will logoff the current user.

-l ················Logs off the current user, this is also the default. -m ComputerName takes precedence.

-s ················Shuts down the local computer.

-r ················Reboots after shutdown.

-a ················Aborts shutdown. Ignores other parameters, except -l and ComputerName. You can only use -a during the time-out period.

-f ················Forces running applications to close.

-m [\\ComputerName] ·····Specifies the computer that you want to shut down.

-t xx ···········Sets the timer for system shutdown in xx seconds. The default is 20 seconds.

-c "message" ·············· Specifies a message to be displayed in the Message area of the System Shutdown window. You can use a maximum of 127 characters. You must enclose the message in quotation marks.

-d [u][p]:xx:yy ·············· Lists the reason code for the shutdown. The following table lists the different values.

Value	Description
u	Indicates a user code.
p	Indicates a planned shutdown code.
xx	Specifies the major reason code (0-255).
yy	Specifies the minor reason code (0-65536).

Notes:

• If you indicate a major and minor reason code, you must first define these reason codes on each computer for which you plan to use the particular reason. If the reason codes are not defined on the target computer, Event Viewer cannot log the correct reason text.

• Users can restart or shut down their own computers, administrators can also restart or shut down remote computers.

SIGVERIF

Analyzes all driver files to see if they are digitally signed by Microsoft.

Syntax
SIGVERIF

Examples:
SIGVERIF

Syntax Options:
Command Type and Version: External Command; WinXP only

SORT

Reads input, sorts data, and writes the results to the screen, to a file, or to another device

Syntax:
sort [/r] [/+n] [/m kilobytes] [/l locale] [/rec characters] [[drive1:][path1]filename1] [/t [drive2:][path2]] [/o [drive3:][path3]filename3]

[command |] sort [/r] [/+n] [/m kilobytes] [/l locale] [/rec characters]
[[drive1:][path1]filename1][/t [drive2:][path2]] [/o [drive3:][path3]filename3]

Examples:
Sorting a file
The following command reads the file Expenses.txt, sorts it in reverse order, and displays it on your screen: sort /r expenses.txt
Sorting the output from a command
To search a large file named Maillist.txt for the text "Jones," and to sort the results of the search, use the pipe (|) to direct the output of a find command to the sort command, as follows:
find "Jones" maillist.txt | sort
The command produces a sorted list of lines that contain the specified text.
Sorting keyboard input
To sort keyboard input and display the results alphabetically on the screen, you can first use the sort command with no parameters, as follows: sort
Then type the text you want sorted, pressing ENTER at the end of each line. When you have finished typing text, press CTRL+Z, and then press ENTER. The sort command displays the text you typed, sorted alphabetically.
You can also redirect sorted keyboard input to a file.

Syntax Options:
/r ·············· Reverses the sort order (that is, sorts from Z to A, and then from 9 to 0).

/+n ·············· Specifies the character position number, n, at which sort begins each comparison.

/m kilobytes ·············· Specifies the amount of main memory to use for the sort, in kilobytes (KB).

/l locale ·····Overrides the sort order of characters defined by the system default locale (that is, the language and Country/Region selected during installation).

/rec characters ················Specifies the maximum number of characters in a record, or a line of the input file (the default is 4,096, and the maximum is 65,535).

[drive1:][path1]filename1 Specifies the file to be sorted. If no file name is specified, the standard input is sorted. Specifying the input file is faster than redirecting the same file as standard input.

/t [drive2:][path2]·············Specifies the path of the directory to hold the sort command's working storage, in case the data does not fit in main memory. The default is to use the system temporary directory.

/o [drive3:][path3]filename3···················Specifies the file where the sorted input is to be stored. If not specified, the data is written to the standard output. Specifying the output file is faster than redirecting standard output to the same file.

Notes:

• In using the /+n command-line option, for example, /+3 indicates that each comparison should begin at the third character in each line. Lines with fewer than n characters collate before other lines. By default, comparisons start at the first character in each line.

• The memory used is always a minimum of 160 KB. If the memory size is specified, the exact specified amount (but at least 160 KB) is used for the sort, regardless of how much main memory is available.

• The default maximum memory size when no size is specified is 90 percent of available main memory if both the input and output are files, and 45 percent of main memory otherwise. The default setting usually gives the best performance.

• Currently, the only alternative to the default locale is the "C" locale, which is faster than natural language sorting and sorts characters according to their binary encodings.

• Unless you specify the command or FileName parameter, sort acts as a filter and takes input from the standard input (that is, usually from the keyboard, from a pipe, or from a file).

• You can use the pipe (|) symbol to direct data through the sort command from another command, or to direct the sort output to another command (for example, to the more command to display information one screen at a time). Using the less than symbol (<) or greater than symbol (>) to specify the input file or output file may not be very efficient; instead, specify the input file directly (as defined in the command syntax) and specify the output file using the /o parameter. This can be much faster, particularly with large files.

• The sort command does not distinguish between uppercase and lowercase letters.

• The sort command has no limit on file size.

• The sort program uses the collating-sequence table that corresponds to the Country/Region code and code-page settings. Characters greater than ASCII code 127 are sorted based on information in the Country.sys file or in an alternate file specified by the country command in your Config.nt file.

• If the sort fits in memory (that is, either the default maximum memory size or as specified by the /m parameter), the sort is performed in one pass. Otherwise, the sort is performed in two passes, such that the amounts of memory used for both the sort and merge passes are equal. When two passes are performed, the partially sorted data is stored in a temporary file on disk. If there is not enough memory to perform the sort in two passes, a run-time error is issued. If the /m command-line option is used to specify more memory than is truly available, performance degradation or a run-time error can occur.

START

Starts a separate Command Prompt window to run a specified program or command.

Syntax:

start ["title"] [/dPath] [/i] [/min] [/max] [{/separate | /shared}] [{/low | /normal | /high | /realtime | /abovenormal | belownormal}] [/wait] [/b] [FileName] [parameters]

Examples:

start myapp

Syntax Options:

Used without parameters, start opens a second command prompt window.

"title"················Specifies the title to display in Command Prompt window title bar.

/dPath·············Specifies the startup directory.
/i···················Passes the Cmd.exe startup environment to the new Command Prompt window.
/min ···············Starts a new minimized Command Prompt window.
/max ··············Starts a new maximized Command Prompt window.
/separate ········Starts 16-bit programs in a separate memory space.
/shared ···········Starts 16-bit programs in a shared memory space.
/low··············Starts an application in the idle priority class.
/normal ···········Starts an application in the normal priority class.
/high ··············Starts an application in the high priority class.
/realtime ·········Starts an application in the realtime priority class.
/abovenormal ··Starts an application in the abovenormal priority class.
/belownormal···Starts an application in the belownormal priority class.
/wait··············Starts an application and waits for it to end.
/b ·················Starts an application without opening a new Command Prompt window. CTRL+C handling is ignored unless the application enables CTRL+C processing. Use CTRL+BREAK to interrupt the application.
FileName·········Specifies the command or program to start.
parameters ······Specifies parameters to pass to the command or program.

Notes:

• You can run nonexecutable files through their file association by typing the name of the file as a command.

• When you run a command that contains a the string "CMD" as the first token without an extension or path qualifier, "CMD" is replaced with the value of the COMSPEC variable. This prevents users from picking up cmd from the current directory.

• When you run a 32-bit graphical user interface (GUI) application, cmd does not wait for the application to quit before returning to the command prompt. This new behavior does not occur if you run the application from a command script.

• When you run a command that uses a first token that does not contain an extension, Cmd.exe uses the value of the PATHEXT environment variable to determine which extensions to look for and in what order. The default value for the PATHEXT variable is: .COM;.EXE;.BAT;.CMD (that is, the syntax is the same as the PATH variable, with semicolons separating the different elements).

• When you search for an executable and there is no match on any extension, start searches directory name. If it does, start opens Explorer.exe on that path.

SUBST

Associates a path with a drive letter.

Syntax:

subst [drive1: [drive2:]Path]

subst drive1: /d

Examples:

To create a virtual drive Z for the path B:\User\Betty\Forms, type: subst z: b:\user\betty\forms

Now, instead of typing the full path, you can reach this directory by typing the letter of the virtual drive, followed by a colon, as follows: z:

Syntax Options:

Used without parameters, subst displays the names of the virtual drives in effect.

drive1:······Specifies the virtual drive to which you want to assign a path.

drive2:······Specifies the physical drive that contains the specified path (if different from the current drive).

Path ·········Specifies the path that you want to assign to a drive.

/d ············Deletes a virtual drive.

Notes:

• The following commands do not work, or should not be used, on drives used in the subst command:
chkdsk
diskcomp
diskcopy
format

label
recover

• The drive1 parameter must be within the range specified by the lastdrive command. If not, subst displays the following error message: Invalid parameter - drive1:

SYSTEM FILE CHECKER (SFC)

Scans and verifies the versions of all protected system files after you restart your computer.

Syntax:

sfc [/scannow] [/scanonce] [/scanboot] [/revert] [/purgecache] [/cachesize=x]

Syntax Options:

/scannow ··Scans all protected system files immediately.

/scanonce ·Scans all protected system files once.

/scanboot ··Scans all protected system files every time the computer is restarted.

/revert ·······Returns the scan to its default operation.

/purgecache ····················Purges the Windows File Protection file cache and scans all protected system files immediately.

/cachesize=x····················Sets the size, in MB, of the Windows File Protection file cache.

Notes:

• You must be logged on as a member of the Administrators group to run sfc.

• If sfc discovers that a protected file has been overwritten, it retrieves the correct version of the file from the %systemroot%\system32\dllcache folder, and then replaces the incorrect file.

• If the %systemroot%\system32\dllcache folder becomes corrupt or unusable, use sfc /scannow, sfc /scanonce, or sfc /scanboot to repair the contents of the Dllcache directory.

• Be sure to install the latest service pack from Microsoft after you have restored the files.

• SFC should be used as a last resort for WinXP users. Try rolling back to the most recent restore point to see if that fixes the files before using the SFC command.

SYSTEMINIFO

Displays detailed configuration information about a computer and its operating system, including operating system configuration, security information, product ID, and hardware properties, such as RAM, disk space, and network cards.

Syntax:

systeminfo[.exe] [/s Computer [/u Domain\User [/p Password]]] [/fo {TABLE|LIST|CSV}] [/nh]

Examples:

systeminfo.exe /s srvmain **or** systeminfo.exe /s srvmain /u maindom\hiropln

Syntax Options:

/s Computer ····················Specifies the name or IP address of a remote computer (do not use backslashes). The default is the local computer.

/u Domain\User··············Runs the command with the account permissions of the user specified by User or Domain\User. The default is the permissions of the current logged on user on the computer issuing the command.

/p Password····················Specifies the password of the user account that is specified in the /u parameter.

/fo {TABLE | LIST | CSV} Specifies the format to use for the output. Valid values are TABLE, LIST, and CSV. The default format for output is LIST.

/nh ····················Suppresses column headers in the output. Valid when the /fo parameter is set to TABLE or CSV.

Notes:

• Use this command to make an inventory of all computers on your network.

TASKKILL

Ends one or more tasks or processes. Processes can be killed by process ID or image name.

Syntax:

taskkill [/s Computer] [/u Domain\User [/p Pass-
word]]] [/fi FilterName] [/pid ProcessID] [/im ImageName] [/f][/t]

Examples:

taskkill /pid 1230 /pid 1241 /pid 1253 *or* taskkill /s srvmain /f /im notepad.exe

Syntax Options:

/s Computer ·················Specifies the name or IP address of a remote computer (do not use backslashes). The default is the local computer.

/u Domain\User ···········Runs the command with the account permissions of the user specified by User or Domain\User. The default is the permissions of the current logged on user on the computer issuing the command.

/p Password ···············Specifies the password of the user account that is specified in the /u parameter.

/fi FilterName ···············Specifies the types of process(es) to include in or exclude from termination. The following are valid filter names, operators, and values.

Name	Operators	Value
Hostname	eq, ne	Any valid string.
Status	eq, ne	RUNNING|NOT RESPONDING
Imagename	eq, ne	Any valid string.
PID	eg, ne, gt, lt, ge, le	Any valid positive integer.
Session	eg, ne, gt, lt, ge, le	Any valid session number.
CPUTime	eq, ne, gt, lt, ge, le	Valid time in the format of hh:mm:ss. The mm and ss parameters should be between 0 and 59 and hh can be any valid unsigned numeric value.
Memusage	eg, ne, gt, lt, ge, le	Any valid integer.
Username	eq, ne	Any valid user name ([Domain\]User).
Services	eq, ne	Any valid string.
Windowtitle	eq, ne	Any valid string.

/pid ProcessID ············Specifies the process ID of the process to be terminated.

/im ImageName ···········Specifies the image name of the process to be terminated. Use the wildcard (*) to specify all image names.

/f ···············Specifies that process(es) be forcefully terminated. This parameter is ignored for remote processes; all remote processes are forcefully terminated.

/t ···············Specifies to terminate all child processes along with the parent process, commonly known as a tree kill.

Notes:

• The wildcard character (*) is accepted only when specified along with the filters.

• Termination for remote processes will always be done forcefully regardless of whether the /f parameter is specified.

• Supplying a computer name to the HOSTNAME filter will cause a shutdown and all processes will be stopped.

• Use tasklist to determine the Process ID (PID) for the process to be terminated.

• Taskkill is a replacement for the Kill tool.

TASKLIST

Displays a list of applications and services with their Process ID (PID) for all tasks running on either a local or a remote computer.

Syntax:

tasklist[.exe] [/s computer] [/u domain\user [/p password]] [/fo {TABLE\|LIST\|CSV}]
[/nh] [/fi FilterName [/fi FilterName2 [...]]] [/m [ModuleName] \| /svc \| /v]

Examples:

tasklist /v /fi "PID gt 1000" /fo csv or tasklist /v /fi "STATUS eq running"

Syntax Options:

/s Computer ···············Specifies the name or IP address of a remote computer (do not use backslashes). The default is the local computer.

/u Domain\User ·············Runs the command with the account permissions of the user specified by User or Domain\User. The default is the permissions of the current logged on user on the computer issuing the command.

/p Password ··················Specifies the password of the user account that is specified in the /u parameter.

/fo {TABLE|LIST|CSV} ····Specifies the format to use for the output. Valid values are TABLE, LIST, and CSV. The default format for output is TABLE.

/nh ····························Suppresses column headers in the output. Valid when the /fo parameter is set to TABLE or CSV.

/fi FilterName ················Specifies the types of process(es) to include in or exclude from the query. The following table lists valid filter names, operators, and values.

Name	Operators	Value
Status	eq, ne	RUNNING|NOT RESPONDING
Imagename	eq, ne	Any valid string.
PID	eq, ne, gt, lt, ge, le	Any valid positive integer.
Session	eq, ne, gt, lt, ge, le	Any valid session number.
SessionName	eq, ne	Any valid string.
CPUTime	eq, ne, gt, lt, ge, le	Valid time in the format of hh:mm:ss. The mm and ss parameters should be between 0 and 59 and hh can be any valid unsigned numeric value.
Memusage	eq, ne, gt, lt, ge, le	Any valid integer.
Username	eq, ne	Any valid user name ([Domain\]User).
Services	eq, ne	Any valid string.
Windowtitle	eq, ne	Any valid string.
Modules	eq, ne	Any valid string.

/m [ModuleName] ···········Specifies to show module information for each process. When a module is specified, all the processes using that module are shown. When a module is not specified, all the processes for all the modules are shown. Cannot be used with the /svc or the /v parameter.

/svc ···························Lists all the service information for each process without truncation. Valid when the /fo parameter is set to TABLE. Cannot be used with the /m or the /v parameter.

/v ······························Specifies that verbose task information be displayed in the output. Cannot be used with the /svc or the /m parameter.

Notes:

- Tasklist is a replacement for the TList tool.

TCMSETUP

Sets up or disables the TAPI client.

Syntax:

tcmsetup [/q] [/x] /c Server1 [Server2...]

tcmsetup [/q] /c /d

Syntax Options:

/q ······························Prevents the display of message boxes.

/x ······························Specifies that connection-oriented callbacks will be used for heavy traffic networks where packet loss is high. When this parameter is omitted, connectionless callbacks will be used.

/c ······························Required. Specifies client setup.

Server1 ·····Required. Specifies the name of the remote server that has the TAPI service providers that the client will use. The client will use the service providers' lines and phones. The client must be in the same domain as the server or in a domain that has a two-way trust relationship with the domain that contains the server.

Server2...·Specifies any additional server or servers that will be available to this client. If you specify a list of servers is, use a space to separate the server names.

/d ······························Clears the list of remote servers. Disables the TAPI client by preventing it from using the TAPI service providers that are on the remote servers.

Notes:

- In order for TAPI to function correctly, you must run tcmsetup to specify the remote servers that will be used by TAPI clients.

- You must be in the Administrators group to run this command.

- Before a client user can use a phone or line on a TAPI server, the telephony server administrator must assign the user to the phone or line.

- The list of telephony servers that is created by this command replaces any existing list of telephony servers available to the client. You cannot use this command to add to the existing list.

TELNET COMMANDS

The telnet commands allow you to communicate with a remote computer that is using the Telnet protocol. You can run telnet without parameters in order to enter the telnet context, indicated by the Telnet prompt (telnet>). From the Telnet prompt, use the following commands to manage a computer running Telnet Client.

The tlntadmn commands allow you to remotely manage a computer running Telnet Server. These commands are run from the command prompt. Used without parameters, tlntadmn displays local server settings.

To switch from Telnet Client to command mode, at the Telnet prompt, press CTRL+]. To switch back to Telnet Client, press ENTER.

To start Telnet Client and to enter the Telnet prompt

Syntax:

telnet [\\RemoteServer]

Syntax Options:

\\RemoteServer ··············Specifies the name of the server to which you want to connect.

Notes:

- Used without parameters, telnet starts Telnet Client.

- When you are at the Telnet prompt, you must use Telnet commands.

To stop Telnet Client

Syntax:

quit

Notes:

- You can abbreviate this command to q.

To connect Telnet Client to a remote computer

Syntax:

open [\\RemoteServer] [Port]

Examples:

o redmond 44

Syntax Options:

\\RemoteServer ··············Specifies the name of the server that you want to manage. If you do not specify a server, the local server is assumed.

Port···········Specifies the port that you want to use. If you do not specify a port, the default port is assumed.

Notes:

- You can abbreviate this command to o.

To disconnect Telnet Client from a remote computer

Syntax:

close [\\RemoteServer]

Examples:

c redmond 44

Syntax Options:

\\RemoteServer ·············Specifies the name of the server that you want to manage. If you do not specify a server, the local server is assumed.

Notes:

- You can abbreviate this command to c.

To set Telnet Client options

Syntax:

set [\\RemoteServer] [ntlm] [localecho] [term {ansi | vt100 | vt52 | vtnt}] [escape Character] [logfile FileName] [logging] [bsasdel] [crlf] [delasbs] [mode {console | stream}] [?]

Syntax Options:

\\RemoteServer ·············Specifies the name of the server that you want to manage. If you do not specify a server, the local server is assumed.

ntlm···········Turns on NTLM authentication if it is available on the remote server.

localecho ··Turns on local echo.

term {ansi | vt100 | vt52 | vtnt}···············Sets the terminal to the specified type.

escape Character ···········Sets the escape character. The escape character can be a single character, or it can be a combination of the CTRL key plus a character. To set a control-key combination, hold down CTRL while you type the character that you want to assign.

logfile FileName···········Sets the file to be used for logging Telnet activity. The log file must be on your local computer. Logging begins automatically when you set this option.

logging······Turns on logging. If no log file is set, an error message appears.

bsasdel ·····Sets BACKSPACE to be sent as delete.

crlf···········Sets the new line mode, which causes the ENTER key to send 0x0D, 0x0A.

delasbs ·····Sets DELETE to be sent as backspace.

mode {console | stream}·Sets the mode of operation.

? ···············Allows you to view the complete syntax for this command.

Notes:

- To turn off an option that was previously set, at the Telnet prompt, type: unset [Option]

- To set the escape character, type: e Character

- On non-English versions of Telnet, the codeset Option is available. Codeset Option sets the current code set to an option, which can be any one of the following: Shift JIS, Japanese EUC, JIS Kanji, JIS Kanji (78), DEC Kanji, NEC Kanji. You should set the same code set on the remote computer.

To send Telnet Client commands

Syntax:

send [\\RemoteServer] [ao] [ayt] [esc] [ip] [synch] [?]

Syntax Options:

\\RemoteServer ·············Specifies the name of the server that you want to manage. If you do not specify a server, the local server is assumed.

ao··············Aborts output command.

ayt···········Sends an "Are you there?" command.

esc···········Sends the current escape character.

ip··············Interrupts the process command.

synch·········Performs the Telnet sync operation.

? ···············Allows you to view the complete syntax for this command.

To view the current settings for the Telnet client

Syntax:

display

Notes:

• The display command lists the currently operating parameters for the Telnet client. If you are in a Telnet session (in other words, if you are connected to a Telnet server), you can exit the Telnet session to modify the parameters by pressing CTRL+]. To return to the Telnet session, press ENTER.

To use tlntadmn commands at the command prompt

To administer a computer running Telnet Server

Syntax:

tlntadmn \\RemoteServer] [start] [stop] [pause] [continue]

Syntax Options:

\\RemoteServer ············Specifies the name of the server that you want to manage. If you do not specify a server, the local server is assumed.

start ··········Starts Telnet Server.

stop···········Stops Telnet Server.

pause·······Interrupts Telnet Server.

continue····Resumes Telnet Server.

Notes:

• You can remotely administer a computer running Telnet Server using the tlntadmn commands if both computers are running Windows XP. You can not use the tlntadmn commands to remotely administer a computer running Windows 2000 and Telnet Server from a computer that is running Windows XP.

To administer Telnet sessions

Syntax:

tlntadmn [\\RemoteServer] [-s] [-k{SessionID | all}] [-m {SessionID | all} "Message"]

Syntax Options:

\\RemoteServer ············Specifies the name of the server that you want to manage. If you do not specify a server, the local server is assumed.

-s ···············Displays active Telnet sessions.

-k{SessionID | all} ···········Terminates sessions. Type the session ID to terminate a specific session, or type all to terminate all sessions.

-m {SessionID | all} "Message"···············Sends a message to one or more sessions. Type the session ID to send a message to a specific session, or type all to send a message to all sessions. Type the message that you want to send between quotation marks (that is, "Message").

Notes:

• You can remotely administer a computer running Telnet Server using the tlntadmn commands if both computers are running Windows XP. You can not use the tlntadmn commands to remotely administer a computer running Windows 2000 and Telnet Server from a computer that is running Windows XP.

To set logging options on a computer running Telnet Server

Syntax:

tlntadmn [\\RemoteServer] config [auditlocation={eventlog | file | both}] [audit=[{+ | -}admin][{+ | -}user][{+ | -}fail]]

Examples:

tlntadmn config auditlocation=eventlog   or   tlntadmn config audit=+admin +fail

Syntax Options:

\\RemoteServer ············Specifies the name of the server that you want to manage. If you do not specify a server, the local server is assumed.

auditlocation={eventlog | file | both} ······Specifies whether to send event information to Event Viewer, to a file, or to both.

audit=[{+ | -}admin][{+ | -}user][{+ | -}fail]
Specifies which events you want to audit (administrative logon events, user logon events, or failed logon attempts). To audit events of a particular type, type a plus sign (+) before that event type. To stop auditing events of a particular type, type a minus sign (-) before that event type.

Notes:

• You can remotely administer a computer running Telnet Server using the tlntadmn commands if both computers are running Windows XP. You can not use the tlntadmn commands to remotely administer a computer running Windows 2000 and Telnet Server from a computer that is running Windows XP.

• If you specify where to send event information without specifying which type or types of information to audit, only information about administrative logon events will be audited and sent to the location that you specified.

To set the default domain on a computer running Telnet Server

Syntax:

tlntadmn [\\RemoteServer] config [dom=DomainName]

Examples:

tlntadmn config dom=Redmond

Syntax Options:

\\RemoteServer ·············Specifies the name of the server that you want to manage. If you do not specify a server, the local server is assumed.

dom=DomainName········Specifies the domain that you want to make the default domain.

Notes:

• You can remotely administer a computer running Telnet Server using the tlntadmn commands if both computers are running Windows XP. You can not use the tlntadmn commands to remotely administer a computer running Windows 2000 and Telnet Server from a computer that is running Windows XP.

To map the Alt key on a computer running Telnet Server

Syntax:

tlntadmn [\\RemoteServer] config [ctrlakeymap={yes | no}]

Syntax Options:

\\RemoteServer ·············Specifies the name of the server that you want to manage. If you do not specify a server, the local server is assumed.

ctrlakeymap={yes | no} ···Specifies whether you want Telnet Server to interpret CTRL+A as ALT. Type yes to map the shortcut key, or type no to prevent mapping.

Notes:

• You can remotely administer a computer running Telnet Server using the tlntadmn commands if both computers are running Windows XP. You can not use the tlntadmn commands to remotely administer a computer running Windows 2000 and Telnet Server from a computer that is running Windows XP.

• If you do not map the ALT key, Telnet Server does not send the ALT key to applications that might rely on that key.

To set the maximum number of connections on a computer running Telnet Server

Syntax:

tlntadmn [\\RemoteServer] config [maxconn=PositiveInteger]

Syntax Options:

\\RemoteServer ·············Specifies the name of the server that you want to manage. If you do not specify a server, the local server is assumed.

maxconn=PositiveInteger ·····················Sets the maximum number of connections. You must specify this number with a positive integer that is smaller than 10 million.

Notes:

• You can remotely administer a computer running Telnet Server using the tlntadmn commands if both computers are running Windows XP. You can not use the tlntadmn commands to remotely administer a computer running Windows 2000 and Telnet Server from a computer that is running Windows XP.

XP Commands

To set the maximum number of failed logon attempts on a computer running Telnet Server

Syntax:

tlntadmn [\\RemoteServer] config [maxfail=PositiveInteger]

Syntax Options:

\\RemoteServer ·············Specifies the name of the server that you want to manage. If you do not specify a server, the local server is assumed.

maxfail=PositiveInteger ··Sets the maximum number of failed logon attempts that a user is allowed. You must specify this number with a positive integer that is smaller than 100.

Notes:

• You can remotely administer a computer running Telnet Server using the tlntadmn commands if both computers are running Windows XP. You can not use the tlntadmn commands to remotely administer a computer running Windows 2000 and Telnet Server from a computer that is running Windows XP.

To set the mode of operation on a computer running Telnet Server

Syntax:

tlntadmn [\\RemoteServer] config [mode={console | stream}]

Syntax Options:

\\RemoteServer ·············Specifies the name for the server that you want to manage. If you do not specify a server, the local server is assumed.

mode={console | stream}Specifies the mode of operation.

Notes:

• You can remotely administer a computer running Telnet Server using the tlntadmn commands if both computers are running Windows XP. You can not use the tlntadmn commands to remotely administer a computer running Windows 2000 and Telnet Server from a computer that is running Windows XP.

To set the Telnet port on a computer running Telnet Server

Syntax:

tlntadmn [\\RemoteServer] config [port=IntegerValue]

Syntax Options:

\\RemoteServer ·············Specifies the name of the server that you want to manage. If you do not specify a server, the local server is assumed.

port=IntegerValue ··········Sets the Telnet port. You must specify the port with an integer smaller than 1,024.

Notes:

• You can remotely administer a computer running Telnet Server using the tlntadmn commands if both computers are running Windows XP. You can not use the tlntadmn commands to remotely administer a computer running Windows 2000 and Telnet Server from a computer that is running Windows XP.

To set the methods of authentication on a computer running Telnet Server

Syntax:

tlntadmn [\\RemoteServer] config [sec=[{+ | -}ntlm][{+ | -}passwd]]

Syntax Options:

\\RemoteServer ·············Specifies the name of the server that you want to manage. If you do not specify a server, the local server is assumed.

sec=[{+ | -}ntlm][{+ | -}passwd] ·············Specifies whether you want to use NTLM, a password, or both to authenticate logon attempts. To use a particular type of authentication, type a plus sign (+) before that type of authentication. To prevent using a particular type of authentication, type a minus sign (-) before that type of authentication.

Notes:

• You can remotely administer a computer running Telnet Server using the tlntadmn commands if both computers are running Windows XP. You can not use the tlntadmn commands to remotely administer a computer running Windows 2000 and Telnet Server from a computer that is running Windows XP.

• NTLM is the authentication protocol for transactions between two computers where one or both computers is running Windows NT 4.0 or an earlier version. In addition, NTLM is the authentication protocol for computers that are not participating in a domain, such as stand-alone servers and workgroups.

To set the time-out for idle sessions on a computer running Telnet Server

Syntax:

tlntadmn [\\RemoteServer] config [timeout=hh:mm:ss]

Syntax Options:

\\RemoteServer ·············Specifies the name of the server that you want to manage. If you do not specify a server, the local server is assumed.

timeout=hh:mm:ss ·········Sets the time-out period in hours, minutes, and seconds.

Notes:

• You can remotely administer a computer running Telnet Server using the tlntadmn commands if both computers are running Windows XP. You can not use the tlntadmn commands to remotely administer a computer running Windows 2000 and Telnet Server from a computer that is running Windows XP.

TFTP

Transfers files to and from a remote computer, typically a computer running UNIX, that is running the Trivial File Transfer Protocol (TFTP) service or daemon.

Syntax:

tftp [-i] [Host] [{get | put}] [Source] [Destination]

Examples:

tftp vax1 put users.txt users19.txt

Syntax Options:

Used without parameters, tftp displays help.

-i ···············Specifies binary image transfer mode (also called octet mode). In binary image mode, the file is transferred in one-byte units. Use this mode when transferring binary files. If -i is omitted, the file is transferred in ASCII mode. This is the default transfer mode. This mode converts the end-of-line (EOL) characters to an appropriate format for the specified computer. Use this mode when transferring text files. If a file transfer is successful, the data transfer rate is displayed.

Host ·········Specifies the local or remote computer.

put ···········Transfers the file Destination on the local computer to the file Source on the remote computer. Because the TFTP protocol does not support user authentication, the user must be logged onto the remote computer, and the files must be writable on the remote computer.

get ···········Transfers the file Destination on the remote computer to the file Source on the local computer.

Source ·····Specifies the file to transfer.

Destination·····················Specifies where to transfer the file. If Destination is omitted, it is assumed to have the same name as Source.

Notes:

• Specify put if transferring file FileTwo on the local computer to file FileOne on remote computer. Specify get if transferring file FileTwo on the remote computer to file FileOne on the remote computer.

• Windows XP or Windows 2000 do not provide a general purpose TFTP server. Windows 2000 provides a TFTP server service only to provide remote boot capabilities to Windows XP and Windows 2000 client computers.

• This command is available only if the Internet Protocol (TCP/IP) protocol is installed as a component in the properties of a network adapter in Network Connections

TIME

Displays or sets the system time.

Syntax:

time [/t] [/time] [hours:[minutes[:seconds[.hundredths]]][{A|P}]]

Examples:

time 13:36   *or*   time 1:36P

Syntax Options:

Used without parameters, time displays the system time and prompts you to enter a new time.

/t ·············Displays the current system time, without prompting you to enter a new time.

/time ··········Same as /t.

hours ········Specifies the hour. Valid values are in the range 0 through 23.

minutes ·····Specifies minutes. Valid values are in the range 0 through 59.

seconds ····Specifies seconds. Valid values are in the range 0 through 59.

hundredths···················Specifies hundredths of a second. Valid values are in the range 0 through 99.

{A | P} ·······Specifies A.M. or P.M. for the 12-hour time format. If you type a valid 12-hour time but do not type A or P, time uses A for A.M.

Notes:

- When using time without parameters, press ENTER to keep the same time.

- The /t command-line option is only available if command extensions are enabled (that is, the default). For more information about enabling and disabling command extensions, see cmd .

- If you specify the time in an invalid format the following message is displayed and the system then waits for you to enter the time in the correct format:
Invalid time
Enter new time:_

- You can change the time format by changing the setting in Date and Time in Control Panel. For just the MS-DOS subsystem, change the country setting in your Config.nt file. Depending on the Country/Region selected, time is displayed in the 12-hour format or the 24-hour format. If you are setting the time in the 12-hour format, specify P for hours after noon.

TITLE

Creates a title for the command prompt window.

Syntax:

title [string]

Examples:

To set the window title for a batch program, type:
rem This batch program updates the employee data:
cls
@echo off
title Updating Files
copy \\server\share*.xls c:\users\common*.xls
echo Files Updated.
title Command Prompt

Syntax Options:

string·········Specifies the title for the command prompt window.

Notes:

- To use the window title for batch programs, include the title command at the beginning of a batch program.

- Once set, the window title can be reset with the title command only.

TRACERPT

Processes event trace logs or real-time data from instrumented event trace providers and allows you to generate trace analysis reports and CSV (comma-delimited) files for the events generated.

Syntax:

tracerpt [FileName [filename ...]] [-o [FileName]] [-report [FileName]] [-rt session_name [session_name ...]] [-summary [FileName]] [-config [FileName]

Syntax Options:

FileName [filename ...]····Specifies the name of the file for the event trace session. You can specify multiple files.

-o [FileName] ················Specifies the name of the CSV (comma-delimited) file. If no files are specified, then the default is dumpfile.csv and not summary.txt.

-report [FileName]··········Specifies the name of the output report file. Default is work-load.txt.

-rt session_name [session_name ...] ····Gets data from the realtime data source. To use this option, include the event trace session.

-summary [FileName] ····Specifies name of output summary file. Default is summary.txt.

-config FileName ···········Specifies the pathname of the settings file that contains command line parameters. Use this to enter your command line options into a file.

Notes:

• Opening the dumpfile.csv format in Microsoft Excel allows you to view events in chronological order. The files include header records followed by comma-delimited text. The header fields are listed below:

Field	Description
TID	Thread identifier
Clock time	Event timestamp
Kernel (ms)	Processor time in kernel mode
User (ms)	Processor time in user mode
User data	Variable piece of header data based on the Managed Object Format (MOF) structure.
IID	Instance ID
PIID	Parent Instance ID

• To use the report option, you must include a "Windows kernel trace" file, and any other event trace file in your command line. You will receive an error message without this in your command line.

• When you use the -summary option, the following file is generated:

Files processed	list of files
Total buffers processed	N
Total events processed	N
Total events lost	N
Start time	dd MMM yyyy hh:mm:ss.ttt
End time	dd MMM yyyy hh:mm:ss.ttt
Elapsed time	N sec

• The contents of the setting file used with the -config option should have the following format:
[command_option]
value

where command_option is a command line option and value specifies its value. For example:
[o]
output.txt
[report]
report.txt
[summary]
summary.txt

• For more information about incorporating Tracerpt into your Windows Management Instrumentation (WMI) scripts, see Scripting Logs and Monitoring at http://www.microsoft.com/resources/documentation/windows/xp/all/proddocs/en-us/ntcmds.mspx

---

TRACERT

Determines the path taken to a destination by sending Internet Control Message Protocol (ICMP) Echo Request messages to the destination with incrementally increasing Time to Live (TTL) field values. The path displayed is the list of near-side router interfaces of the routers in the path between a source host and a destination. The near-side interface is the interface of the router that is closest to the sending host in the path.

Syntax:

tracert [-d] [-h MaximumHops] [-j HostList] [-w Timeout] [TargetName]

Examples:

tracert corp7.microsoft.com *or* tracert -d corp7.microsoft.com

Syntax Options:

Used without parameters, tracert displays help.

-d .... Prevents tracert from attempting to resolve the IP addresses of intermediate routers to their names. This can speed up the display of tracert results.

-h MaximumHops .... Specifies the maximum number of hops in the path to search for the target (destination). The default is 30 hops.

-j HostList · Specifies that Echo Request messages use the Loose Source Route option in the IP header with the set of intermediate destinations specified in HostList. With loose source routing, successive intermediate destinations can be separated by one or multiple routers. The maximum number of addresses or names in the host list is 9. The HostList is a series of IP addresses (in dotted decimal notation) separated by spaces.

-w Timeout Specifies the amount of time in milliseconds to wait for the ICMP Time Exceeded or Echo Reply message corresponding to a given Echo Request message to be received. If not received within the time-out, an asterisk (*) is displayed. The default time-out is 4000 (4 seconds).

TargetName........ Specifies the destination, identified either by IP address or host name.

Notes:

• This diagnostic tool determines the path taken to a destination by sending ICMP Echo Request messages with varying Time to Live (TTL) values to the destination. Each router along the path is required to decrement the TTL in an IP packet by at least 1 before forwarding it. Effectively, the TTL is a maximum link counter. When the TTL on a packet reaches 0, the router is expected to return an ICMP Time Exceeded message to the source computer. Tracert determines the path by sending the first Echo Request message with a TTL of 1 and incrementing the TTL by 1 on each subsequent transmission until the target responds or the maximum number of hops is reached. The maximum number of hops is 30 by default and can be specified using the -h parameter. The path is determined by examining the ICMP Time Exceeded messages returned by intermediate routers and the Echo Reply message returned by the destination. However, some routers do not return Time Exceeded messages for packets with expired TTL values and are invisible to the tracert command. In this case, a row of asterisks (*) is displayed for that hop.

• To trace a path and provide network latency and packet loss for each router and link in the path, use the pathping command.

• This command is available only if the Internet Protocol (TCP/IP) protocol is installed as a component in the properties of a network adapter in Network Connections

TREE

Graphically displays the directory structure of a path or of the disk in a drive.

Syntax:

tree [Drive:][Path] [/f] [/a]

Examples:

tree \ *or* tree c:\ /f | more *or* tree c:\ /f prn

Syntax Options:

Drive: ······· Specifies the drive that contains the disk for which you want to display the directory structure.

Path ········· Specifies the directory for which you want to display the directory structure.

/f ·············· Displays the names of the files in each directory.

/a ·············· Specifies that tree is to use text characters instead of graphic characters to show the lines linking subdirectories.

Notes:

- The structure displayed by tree depends upon the parameters you specify on the command line. If you do not specify a drive or path, tree displays the tree structure beginning with the current directory of the current drive.

TYPE

Displays the contents of a text file. Use the type command to view a text file without modifying it.

Syntax:

type [Drive:][Path] FileName

Examples:

type holiday.mar   *or*   type holiday.mar | more

Syntax Options:

[Drive:][Path] FileName ··Specifies the location and name of the file or files that you want to view. Separate multiple file names with spaces.

Notes:

- If you are using an NTFS drive and FileName contains spaces, use quotation marks around the text (that is, "File Name").

- If you display a binary file or a file created by a program, you may see strange characters on the screen, including formfeed characters and escape-sequence symbols. These characters represent control codes used in the binary file. In general, avoid using the type command to display binary files.

TYPEPERF

Writes performance counter data to the command window, or to a supported log file format. To stop Typeperf, press CTRL+C.

Syntax:

Typeperf [Path [path ...]] [-cf FileName] [-f {csv|tsv|bin}] [-si interval] [-o FileName] [-q [object]] [-qx [object]] [-sc samples] [-config FileName] [-s computer_name]

Examples:

typeperf "\Memory\Available bytes" "\processor(_total)\% processor time"   or
typeperf "\Process(Explorer)\Thread Count" -si 3 -o myfile.csv

Syntax Options:

- -c {Path [path ...] | -cf FileName}············Specifies the performance counter path to log. To list multiple counter paths, separate each command path by a space.
- -cf FileName ··················Specifies the file name of the file that contains the counter paths that you want to monitor, one per line.
- -f {csv|tsv|bin}··················Specifies the output file format. File formats are csv (comma-delimited), tsv (tab-delimited), and bin (binary). Default format is csv.
- -si interval [mm:] ss··Specifies the time between samples, in the [mm:] ss format. Default is one second.
- -o FileName ··················Specifies the pathname of the output file. Defaults to stdout.
- -q [object]··Displays and queries available counters without instances. To display counters for one object, include the object name.
- -qx [object]Displays and queries all available counters with instances. To display counters for one object, include the object name.
- -sc samples··················Specifies the number of samples to collect. Default is to sample until you press CTRL+C.
- -config FileName ··········Specifies the pathname of the settings file that contains command line parameters.
- -s computer_name··········Specifies the system to monitor if no server is specified in the counter path.

Notes:

- The general format for counter paths is as follows:
[\\Computer]\object[parent/instance#index]\counter] where:
The parent, instance, index, and counter components of the format may contain either a valid name or a wildcard character. The computer, parent, instance, and index components are not necessary for all counters.

• You determine the counter paths to use based on the counter itself. For example, the LogicalDisk object has an instance index, so you must provide the #index or a wildcard. Therefore, you could use the following format: \LogicalDisk(*/*#*)*

• In comparison, the Process object does not require an instance index. Therefore, you could use the following format: \Process(*)\ID Process

• The following is a list of the possible formats:
```
\\machine\object(parent/instance#index)\counter
\\machine\object(parent/instance)\counter
\\machine\object(instance#index)\counter
\\machine\object(instance)\counter
\\machine\object\counter
\object(parent/instance#index)\counter
\object(parent/instance)\counter
\object(instance#index)\counter
\object(instance)\counter
\object\counter
```

• If a wildcard character is specified in the parent name, all instances of the specified object that match the specified instance and counter fields will be returned.

• If a wildcard character is specified in the instance name, all instances of the specified object and parent object will be returned if all instance names corresponding to the specified index match the wildcard character.

• If a wildcard character is specified in the counter name, all counters of the specified object are returned.

• Partial counter path string matches (for example, pro*) are not supported.

• For counter path queries use this format Typeperf [{-q | -qx [\\Computer\] [object] [-o outputfile)}].

• Use the following command lines for complete queries:
Typeperf [\\Computer\]object[instance]\counter]
Typeperf -cf input file

• The contents of the setting file used with the -config option should have the following format:
[command_option]
value

where command_option is a command line option and value specifies its value. For example:
[-c]
\Windows\mypath
[-o]
report.csv
[-s]
mysystem

• For more information about incorporating Typeperf into your Windows Management Instrumentation (WMI) scripts, see Scripting Logs and Monitoring at http://www.microsoft.com/resources/documentation/windows/xp/all/proddocs/en-us/ntcmds.mspx

UNLODCTR

Removes Performance counter names and Explain text for a service or device driver from the system registry.

Syntax:

Unlodctr [\\ComputerName] DriverName

Examples:

unlodctr \\comp1 RSVP

Syntax Options:

[\\ComputerName] DriverName ··········Removes the Performance counter name settings and Explain text for driver or service DriverName from the Windows XP system registry. If you do not specify the ComputerName, Windows XP uses the local computer by default.

Notes:
  • If the information that you supply contains spaces, use quotation marks around the text (for example, "Computer Name").

VER

Displays the Windows XP version number.

Syntax:
  ver

VERIFY

Windows XP does not use this command. It is accepted only for compatibility with MS-DOS files.

VOL

Displays the disk volume label and serial number, if they exist. A serial number is displayed for a disk formatted with MS-DOS version 4.0 or later.

Syntax:
  vol [Drive:]

Syntax Options:
  Drive: ········Specifies the drive that contains the disk for which you want to display the volume label and serial number.

VSSADMIN

Displays current volume shadow copy backups and all installed shadow copy writers and providers in the command window.

Syntax:
  Vssadmin list {shadows [/set= [shadow copy set GUID]] | writers | providers}

Examples:
  vssadmin list providers

Syntax Options:
  list shadows [/set= [shadow copy set GUID]]
      Lists all shadow copies on the system, grouped by the Globally Unique Identifier (GUID) for the shadow copy set (a group of shadow copies created at the same time).
  list writers ·Lists the name, GUID, instance ID, and status of all installed shadow copy writers.
  list providers ···················Lists the name, type, GUID, and version of all installed shadow copy providers.

W32TM

A tool used to diagnose problems occurring with Windows Time

Syntax:
  {/config [/computer:ComputerName] [[/update] [/manualpeerlist:ListOfComputerNames]] [/syncfromflags:ListOfFlags]]|/monitor|/nttel/ntptel/registerl/resync [{:ComputerName] [/nowait]|[/rediscover}]|/tz|/unregister}

Examples:
  w32tm /tz

Syntax Options:
  /config [/computer:ComputerName] [[/update] [/manualpeerlist:ListOfComputerNames]] [/syncfromflags:ListOfFlags] ·············Adjusts the time settings on the local or target computer. Time synchronization peers can be set with the /manualpeerlist switch. Changes to configuration are not used by Windows Time unless the service is restarted or the /update switch is used. /syncfromflags can be used to set the types of sources used for synchronization, and can be set to either MANUAL to use the manual peer list or DOMHIER to synchronize from a domain controller.
  /monitor ····Monitors the target computer or list of computers.
  /ntte ·········Converts an NT system time into a readable format.
  /ntpte ·······Converts an NTP time into a readable format.
  /register ····Register to run as a service and add default configuration to the registry.
  /resync [{:ComputerName] [/nowait]|[/rediscover}]
      Resynchronize the clock as soon as possible, disregarding all accumulated error sta-

XP Command: VER   273

tistics. If no computer is specified, the local computer will resynchronize. The command will wait for resynchronization unless the /nowait switch is used. Currently used time resources will be used unless /rediscover is used, which will force redetection of network resourced before resynchronization.

/tz············Display the current time zone settings.

/unregister Unregister service and remove all configuration information from the registry.

Notes:

• This tool is designed for network administrators to use for diagnosing problems with Windows Time.

• For the Windows Time service to use the changed made with W32tm, it must be notified of the changes. To notify Windows Time, at the command prompt, type w32tm /config /update.

WINNT

Performs an installation of or upgrade to Windows XP. If you have hardware that is compatible with Windows XP, you can run winnt at a Windows 3.x or MS-DOS command prompt.

Syntax:

winnt [/s:SourcePath] [/t:TempDrive] [/u:answer file][/udf:ID [,UDB_file]]
[/r:folder][/rx:folder][/e:command][/a]

Syntax Options:

/s:SourcePath ···············Specifies the source location of the Windows XP files. The location must be a full path of the form x:\[Path] or \\server\share[\Path].

/t:TempDrive ·················Directs Setup to place temporary files on the specified drive and to install Windows XP on that drive. If you do not specify a location, Setup attempts to locate a drive for you.

/u:answer file ···············Performs an unattended Setup using an answer file. The answer file provides answers to some or all of the prompts that the end user normally responds to during Setup. If you use /u, you must also use /s.

/udf:ID [,UDB_file]···········Indicates an identifier (ID) that Setup uses to specify how a Uniqueness Database (UDB) file modifies an answer file (see /u). The UDB overrides values in the answer file, and the identifier determines which values in the UDB file are used. If no UDB_file is specified, Setup prompts you to insert a disk that contains the $Unique$.udb file.

/r:folder ·····Specifies an optional folder to be installed. The folder remains after Setup finishes.

/rx:folder ···Specifies an optional folder to be copied. The folder is deleted after Setup finishes.

/e:command ····················Specifies a command to be carried out just before the final phase of Setup.

/a ··············Enables accessibility options.

WINNT32

Performs an installation of or upgrade to Windows XP. You can run winnt32 at the command prompt on a computer running Windows 95, Windows 98, Windows Millennium Edition, Windows NT, Windows 2000, or Windows XP.

Syntax:

winnt32 [/checkupgradeonly] [/cmd:command_line] [/cmdcons]
[/copydir:{i386\ia64}\FolderName] [/copysource:FolderName] [/debug[Level]:[FileName]]
[/dudisable] [/duprepare:pathname] [/dushare:pathname] [/m:FolderName]
[/makelocalsource] [/noreboot] [/s:SourcePath] [/syspart:DriveLetter]
[/tempdrive:DriveLetter] [/udf:id [,UDB_file]] [/unattend[num]:[answer_file]]

Syntax Options:

/checkupgradeonly··········Checks your computer for upgrade compatibility with XP.

If you use this option with /unattend, no user input is required. Otherwise, the results are displayed on the screen, and you can save them under the file name you specify. The default file name is Upgrade.txt in the systemroot folder.

/cmd:command_line ·······Instructs Setup to carry out a specific command before the final phase of Setup. This would occur after your computer has restarted and after Setup has collected the necessary configuration information, but before Setup is complete.

/cmdcons··Installs the Recovery Console as a startup option on a functioning x86-based computer. The Recovery Console is a command-line interface from which you can perform tasks such as starting and stopping services and accessing the local drive (including drives formatted with NTFS). You can only use the /cmdcons option after normal Setup is finished.

/copydir:{i386|ia64}\FolderName···········Creates an additional folder within the folder in which the Windows XP files are installed. Folder_name refers to a folder that you have created to hold modifications just for your site. For example, for x86-based computers, you could create a folder called Private_drivers within the i386 source folder for your installation, and place driver files in the folder. Then you could type /copydir:i386\Private_drivers to have Setup copy that folder to your newly installed computer, making the new folder location systemroot\Private_drivers. You can use /copydir to create as many additional folders as you want.

/copysource:FolderNameCreates a temporary additional folder within the folder in which the Windows XP files are installed. Folder_name refers to a folder that you have created to hold modifications just for your site. For example, you could create a folder called Private_drivers within the source folder for your installation, and place driver files in the folder. Then you could type /copysource:Private_drivers to have Setup copy that folder to your newly installed computer and use its files during Setup, making the temporary folder location systemroot\Private_drivers. You can use /copysource to create as many additional folders as you want. Unlike the folders /copydir creates, /copysource folders are deleted after Setup completes.

/debug[Level]:[FileName]Creates a debug log at the level specified, for example, /debug4:Debug.log. The default log file is C:\systemroot\Winnt32.log, and the default debug level is 2. The log levels are as follows: 0 represents severe errors, 1 represents errors, 2 represents warnings, 3 represents information, and 4 represents detailed information for debugging. Each level includes the levels below it.

/dudisable ··Prevents Dynamic Update from running. Without Dynamic Update, Setup runs only with the original Setup files. This option will disable Dynamic Update even if you use an answer file and specify Dynamic Update options in that file.

/duprepare:pathname ····Carries out preparations on an installation share so that it can be used with Dynamic Update files that you downloaded from the Windows Update Web site. This share can then be used for installing Windows XP for multiple clients.

/dushare:pathname········Specifies a share on which you previously downloaded Dynamic Update files (updated files for use with Setup) from the Windows Update Web site, and on which you previously ran /duprepare:pathname. When run on a client, specifies that the client installation will make use of the updated files on the share specified in pathname.

/m:FolderName ················Specifies that Setup copies replacement files from an alternate location. Instructs Setup to look in the alternate location first, and if files are present, to use them instead of the files from the default location.

/makelocalsource············Instructs Setup to copy all installation source files to your local hard disk. Use /makelocalsource when installing from a CD to provide installation files when the CD is not available later in the installation.

/noreboot ··Instructs Setup to not restart the computer after the file copy phase of Setup is completed so that you can run another command.

/s:SourcePath ················Specifies the source location of the Windows XP files. To simultaneously copy files from multiple servers, type the /s:SourcePath option multiple times (up to a maximum of eight). If you type the option multiple times, the first server specified must be available, or Setup will fail.

/syspart:DriveLetter········On an x86-based computer, specifies that you can copy Setup startup files to a hard disk, mark the disk as active, and then install the disk into another computer. When you start that computer, it automatically starts with the next phase of Setup. You must always use the /tempdrive parameter with the /syspart parameter. You can start Winnt32 with the /syspart option on an x86-based computer running Windows NT 4.0, Windows 2000, or Windows XP. The computer cannot be running Windows 95, Windows 98, or Windows Millennium Edition.

/tempdrive:DriveLetter ····Directs Setup to place temporary files on the specified partition. For a new installation, Windows XP will also be installed on the specified partition. For an upgrade, the /tempdrive option affects the placement of temporary files only; the operating system will be upgraded in the partition from which you run winnt32.

/udf:id [,UDB_file]···········Indicates an identifier (id) that Setup uses to specify how a Uniqueness Database (UDB) file modifies an answer file (see the /unattend entry). The

UDB overrides values in the answer file, and the identifier determines which values in the UDB file are used. For example, /udf:RAS_user,Our_company.udb overrides settings specified for the RAS_user identifier in the Our_company.udb file. If no UDB_file is specified, Setup prompts the user to insert a disk that contains the \$Unique-\$.udb file.

/unattend ··Upgrades your previous version of Windows 98, Windows Millennium Edition, Windows NT 4.0, or Windows 2000 in unattended Setup mode. All user settings are taken from the previous installation, so no user intervention is required during Setup.

/unattend[num]:[answer_file]················Performs a fresh installation in unattended Setup mode. The specified answer_file provides Setup with your custom specifications. Num is the number of seconds between the time that Setup finishes copying the files and when it restarts your computer. You can use num on any computer running Windows 98, Windows Millennium Edition, Windows NT, Windows 2000, or Windows XP.

Using the /unattend command-line option to automate Setup affirms that you have read and accepted the Microsoft License Agreement for Windows XP. Before using this command-line option to install Windows XP on behalf of an organization other than your own, you must confirm that the end user (whether an individual, or a single entity) has received, read, and accepted the terms of the Microsoft License Agreement for Windows XP. OEMs may not specify this key on machines being sold to end users.

Notes:

• If you run winnt32 on an Itanium-based computer, the command can be run from the Extensible Firmware Interface (EFI) or from Windows XP (not from an earlier operating system). Also, on an Itanium-based computer, /cmdcons and /syspart are not available, and options relating to upgrades are also not available.

XCOPY

Copies files and directories, including subdirectories.

Syntax:

xcopy Source [Destination] [/w] [/p] [/c] [/v] [/q] [/f] [/l] [/g] [/d[:mm-dd-yyyy]] [/u] [/i] [/s [/e]] [/t] [/k] [/r] [/h] [/a|/m}] [/n] [/o] [/x] [/exclude:file1[+[file2]][+[file3]] [{/y|/-y}] [/z]

Examples:

• To copy all the files and subdirectories (including any empty subdirectories) from drive A to drive B, type: xcopy a: b: /s /e

• To include any system or hidden files in the previous example, add the /h command-line option as follows: xcopy a: b: /s /e /h

• To update files in the \Reports directory with the files in the \Rawdata directory that have changed since December 29, 1993, type: xcopy \rawdata \reports /d:12-29-1993

• To update all the files that exist in \Reports in the previous example, regardless of date, type:
xcopy \rawdata \reports /u

• To obtain a list of the files to be copied by the previous command (that is, without actually copying the files), type: xcopy \rawdata \reports /d:12-29-1993 /l > xcopy.out

• The file Xcopy.out lists every file that is to be copied.

• To copy the \Customer directory and all subdirectories to the directory \\Public\Address on network drive H:, retain the read-only attribute, and be prompted when a new file is created on H:, type: xcopy \customer h:\public\address /s /e /k /p

• To issue the previous command, ensure that xcopy creates the \Address directory if it does not exist, and suppress the message that appears when you create a new directory, add the /i command-line option as follows: xcopy \customer h:\public\address /s /e /k /p /i

• You can create a batch program to perform xcopy operations and use the batch if command to process the exit code if an error occurs. For example, the following batch program uses replaceable parameters for the xcopy source and destination parameters:

```
@echo off
rem COPYIT.BAT transfers all files in all subdirectories of
rem the source drive or directory (%1) to the destination rem drive or directory (%2)
xcopy %1 %2 /s /e
if errorlevel 4 goto lowmemory
if errorlevel 2 goto abort
if errorlevel 0 goto exit
```

```
:lowmemory
echo Insufficient memory to copy files or
echo invalid drive or command-line syntax.
goto exit
:abort
echo You pressed CTRL+C to end the copy operation.
goto exit
:exit
```

• To use this batch program to copy all files in the C:\Prgmcode directory and its subdirectories to drive B, type: copyit c:\prgmcode b:

• The command interpreter substitutes C:\Prgmcode for %1 and B: for %2, then uses
xcopy with the /e and /s command-line options. If xcopy encounters an error, the batch
program reads the exit code and goes to the label indicated in the appropriate IF
ERRORLEVEL statement, then displays the appropriate message and exits from the
batch program.

Syntax Options:

Source ······ Required. Specifies the location and names of the files you want to copy. This
parameter must include either a drive or a path.

Destination ······················· Specifies the destination of the files you want to copy. This parameter can include a drive letter and colon, a directory name, a file name, or a combination of these.

/w ············· Displays the following message and waits for your response before starting to
copy files: Press any key to begin copying file(s)

/p ············· Prompts you to confirm whether you want to create each destination file.

/c ·············· Ignores errors.

/v ·············· Verifies each file as it is written to the destination file to make sure that the
destination files are identical to the source files. Windows XP does not use this command. It is accepted only for compatibility with MS-DOS files.

/q ·············· Suppresses the display of xcopy messages.

/f ·············· Displays source and destination file names while copying.

/l ·············· Displays a list of files that are to be copied.

/g ·············· Creates decrypted destination files.

/d[:mm-dd-yyyy] ·············· Copies source files changed on or after the specified date only.
If you do not include a mm-dd-yyyy value, xcopy copies all Source files that are newer
than existing Destination files. This command-line option allows you to update files that
have changed.

/u ·············· Copies files from Source that exist on Destination only.

/i ··············· If Source is a directory or contains wildcards and Destination does not exist,
xcopy assumes destination specifies a directory name and creates a new directory.
Then, xcopy copies all specified files into the new directory. By default, xcopy prompts
you to specify whether Destination is a file or a directory.

/s ·············· Copies directories and subdirectories, unless they are empty. If you omit /s,
xcopy works within a single directory.

/e ·············· Copies all subdirectories, even if they are empty. Use /e with the /s and /t
command-line options.

/t ·············· Copies the subdirectory structure (that is, the tree) only, not files. To copy
empty directories, you must include the /e command-line option.

/k ·············· Copies files and retains the read-only attribute on destination files if present
on the source files. By default, xcopy removes the read-only attribute.

/r ·············· Copies read-only files.

/h ·············· Copies files with hidden and system file attributes. By default, xcopy does not
copy hidden or system files.

/a ·············· Copies only source files that have their archive file attributes set. /a does not
modify the archive file attribute of the source file. For information about how to set the
archive file attribute by using attrib, see Related Topics.

/m ·············· Copies source files that have their archive file attributes set. Unlike /a, /m turns
off archive file attributes in the files that are specified in the source. For information
about how to set the archive file attribute by using attrib, see Related Topics.

XP Command: XCOPY   **277**

/n ·············Creates copies by using the NTFS short file or directory names. /n is required when you copy files or directories from an NTFS volume to a FAT volume or when the FAT file system naming convention (that is, 8.3 characters) is required on the destination file system. The destination file system can be FAT or NTFS.

/o ·············Copies file ownership and discretionary access control list (DACL) information.

/x·············Copies file audit settings and system access control list (SACL) information (implies /o).

/exclude:filename1[+[filename2]][+[filename3]].....Specifies a list of files containing strings. List each string in a separate line in each file. If any of the listed strings match any part of the absolute path of the file to be copied, that file is then excluded from the copying process. For example, if you specify the string "\Obj\", you exclude all files underneath the Obj directory. If you specify the string ".obj", you exclude all files with the .obj extension.

/y·············Suppresses prompting to confirm that you want to overwrite an existing destination file. You can use /y in the COPYCMD environment variable. You can override this command by using -/y on the command line. By default, you are prompted to overwrite, unless you run copy from within a batch script.

/-y ·············Prompts to confirm that you want to overwrite an existing destination file.

/z·············Copies over a network in restartable mode. If you lose your connection during the copy phase (for example, if the server going offline severs the connection), it resumes after you reestablish the connection. /z also displays the percentage of the copy operation completed for each file.

Notes:

• Copying encrypted files to a volume that does not support EFS results in an error. Decrypt the files first or copy the files to a volume that does support EFS.

• To append files, specify a single file for destination, but multiple files for source (that is, by using wildcards or file1+file2+file3 format).

• If you omit Destination, the xcopy command copies the files to the current directory.

• If Destination does not contain an existing directory and does not end with a backslash (\), the following message appears:
Does destination specify a file name or directory name on the target (F = file, D = directory)?
Press F if you want the file or files to be copied to a file. Press D if you want the file or files to be copied to a directory.
You can suppress this message by using the /i command-line option, which causes xcopy to assume that the destination is a directory if the source is more than one file or a directory.

• The xcopy command creates files with the archive attribute set, whether or not this attribute was set in the source file.

• If you have a disk that contains files in subdirectories and you want to copy it to a disk that has a different format, use the xcopy command instead of diskcopy. Because the diskcopy command copies disks track by track, your source and destination disks must have the same format. The xcopy command does not have this requirement. Use xcopy unless you need a complete disk image copy.

• To process exit codes returned by xcopy, use the errorlevel parameter on the if command line in a batch program. For an example of a batch program that processes exit codes using if, see Related Topics. The following table lists each exit code and a description.

Exit code	Description
0	Files were copied without error.
1	No files were found to copy.
2	The user pressed CTRL+C to terminate xcopy.
4	Initialization error occurred. There is not enough memory or disk space, or you entered an invalid drive name or invalid syntax on the command line.
5	Disk write error occurred.

Chapter 6

Disk
Operating
System

DOS COMMANDS

Through MS-DOS® Version 6.22

This chapter is a concise general reference of DOS commands, <u>listed in alphabetic order regardless of command type!</u> In order to assist you in using the reference more effectively, a guide to conventions used in this chapter has been provided on page 284. A list of all DOS commands, grouped by command type, is located on page 281.

MS-DOS vs. PC-DOS

The following files contain the **D**isc **O**perating **S**ystem (DOS).

MS-DOS systems (most clones)
    MSDOS.SYS
    IO.SYS
    COMMAND.COM

PC-DOS systems (IBM)
    IBMBIO.COM
    IBMDOS.COM
    COMMAND.COM

These files (except COMMAND.COM) have attributes of "read only", "system" and "hidden" and are located in the root directory of the system's boot drive (hard drive or floppy drive). If any of these files are missing, the system will not start!

Despite the differences in these "operating system" files, most of the other commands prior to Version 6.0 use the same file names, e.g. both MS and PC use the FORMAT and FDISK programs to prepare a hard drive.

Due to space limitations, Sequoia Publishing is unable to provide information on commands for **PC**-DOS Versions 6.0, 6.1, and 6.3. Beginning with Version 6.0, Microsoft and IBM have taken radically different approaches to the commands supplied on the system disks, particularly the utility programs used for procedures such as disk repair and compression. We regret not being able to include these new PC-DOS commands, but we simply can't include the additional 100+ pages it would require. See page 280 for a list of the commands not covered.

DOS Commands, Drivers & Utilities

Operating System Files		The Following PC-DOS Version 6.0, 6.1, and 6.3 Files are Not Described in this Edition of Pocket PCRef	
Microsoft MSDOS files: Command.com Io.sys Msdos.sys	Label Recover Scandisk Subst Sys Unformat		Pcmata Pcmcs.sys Pcmcs.exe Pcmfdd Pcmfdd.exe Pcinfo Pcmmtd
IBM PCDOS files: Command.com Ibmbio.com Ibmdos.com	**Can Not Use While Running Windows** Append Defrag Emm386 Fastopen Memmaker Mscdex Nlsfunc Smartdrv Subst Vsafe	Cmosclk.sys Cpbackup Cpbdir Cpsched Datamon Drvlock E Eject Ibmavd Ibmavw Ibmavsp Installhigh Meutoini Mouse Pcformat	Pcmmtd.exe Pcmscd.exe Pcmscd Pcmvcd.386 Pendos Pendev.sys Qconfig Ramboost.exe Ramsetup Schedule Setup Umbcga.sys Umbems.sys Umbherc.sys Umbmono.sys Wnbackup Wnschedl
Can Not Use on a Network Chkdsk Diskcomp Diskcopy Fastopen Fdisk Format Join			

DOS Commands *(vertical side tab)*

External
(program file is
present on
drive)

Ados.com
Append.exe
Assign.com
Attrib.exe
Backinfo.exe
Backup.exe
Basic.exe
Basica.exe
Chkdsk.exe
Chkstate.sys
Command.com
Comp.exe
Country.sys
CV.com
Dblboot.bat
Dblspace.exe
Debug.exe
Defrag.exe
Deloldos.exe
Deltree.exe
Diskcomp.com
Diskcopy.com
Doskey.com
Dosshell.com
Dosshell.exe
Drvboot.bat
Drvspace.exe
Dvorak.sys
Edit.com
Edlin.exe
Emm386.exe
Exe2bin.exe
Expand.exe
Fasthelp.exe
Fastopen.exe
FC.exe
Fdisk.exe
Find.exe
Format.exe
Graftabl.com
Graphics.com
GW-Basic.exe
Help.com
Help.exe
Interlnk.exe
Intersvr.exe

Join.exe
Keyb.com
Keybxx.com
Label.exe
Link.exe
Loadfix.com
Mem.exe
Memmaker.exe
Mirror.com
Mode.com
More.com
Move.exe
Msav/Mwav.exe
Msbackup/
Mwbackup.exe
Mscdex.exe
Msd.com &.exe
Msherc.com
Nlsfunc.exe
Power.exe
Print.exe
Printfix.com
Qbasic.exe
Recover.exe
Replace.exe
Restore.exe
Scandisk.exe
Select.exe
Setup/
Busetup.exe
Setver.exe
Share.exe
Sizer.exe
Smartdrv.exe
Smartmon.exe
Sort.exe
Spatch.bat
Subst.exe
Sys.com
Tree.com
Truename.exe
Undelete/
Mwundel.exe
Unformat.com
Uninstal.exe
Vsafe.com
Wina20.386
Xcopy.exe

Internal
(program is
built into a Win-
dows system
file)

CD (Chdir)
Chcp
Chdir (CD)
Cls
Copy
Ctty
Date
Del (Erase)
Dir
Echo
Erase (Del)
Exit
For
LH(load high)
Loadhigh
MD (Mkdir)
Mkdir (MD)
Path
Prompt
RD (Rmdir)
Rem
Ren (Rename)
Rename (Ren)
Rmdir (RD)
Set
Time
Type
Ver
Verify
Vol

Config.sys

Ansi.sys
Break
Buffers
Command.com
Country.sys
Dblspace.sys
Device
Devicehigh
Display.sys
DOS
Driver.sys
Drivparm
Drvspace.sys

EGA.sys
Emm386.exe
Fastopen.exe
FCBS
Files
Himem.sys
Include
Install
Interlnk.exe
Kbdbuf.sys
Keyb.com/
Keyboard.sys
Lastdrive
Menucolor
Menudefault
Menuitem
Nlsfunc.exe
Numlock
Power.exe
Printer.sys
Ramdrive.sys/
Vdisk.sys
Rem
Setver.exe
Share.exe
Shell
Smartdrv.exe
Smartdrv.sys
Stacks
Submenu
Switchar
Switches

Batch
Commands

@
Break
Call
Choice.com
Echo
For
Goto
IF
Pause
Rem
Shift

DOS Commands

DOS History

DOS Type	Release Date	Command COM	io and ibmbio	msdos & ibmdos	Loaded System (if High)
PC 1.0	8-4-81	3,231	1,920	6,400	13,312
MS 1.0	---	---	---	---	---
PC 1.1	5-7-82	4,959	1,920	6,400	14,336
MS 1.25	---	---	---	---	---
Zenith		4,986	1,713	6,138	---
PC 2.0	3-8-83	17,792	4,608	17,152	40,960
MS 2.0	---	---	---	---	---
Wang 2.01	12-22-83	15,877	30,482(Bios)	17,521	---
PC 2.1	10-20-83	17,792	4,736	17,024	40,960
MS 2.11	---	---	---	---	---
?mfg	11-17-83	15,957	6,836	17,176	25,680
PC 2.11	11-17-83	---	---	---	---
PC 2.11	5-30-84	18,272	5,120	17,408	---
PCAT&T 2.11	6-5-85	15,957	6,917	17,176	---
MSSanyo2.11	9-83-84	16,117	5,164	17,019	---
MS 2.25	---	---	---	---	---
PC 3.0	8-14-84	22,042	8,964	27,920	60,416
MS 3.0	---	---	---	---	---
PC 3.1	3-7-85	23,210	9,564	27,760	62,464
MS 3.1	---	---	---	---	---
PC 3.2	12-30-85	23,791	16,369	28,477	69,632
MS 3.2	7-7-86	23,612	16,138	28,480	55,568
MS 3.21	5-1-87	---	---	---	---
ZenithMS 3.21	9-28-87	23,948	18,501	28,480	---
PC 3.3	3-17-87	25,307	22,100	30,159	78,848
MS 3.3	7-24-87	25,276	22,357	30,128	55,440
MS 3.3a	2-2-88	25,308	22,398	30,128	---
MS 4.0	10-6-88	---	---	---	---
PC 4.01	3-89	---	---	---	---
MS 4.01	11-30-88	---	---	---	---
MS 4.01a	4-7-89	37,557	33,337	37,376	73,232
PC 5.0	5-9-91	47,987	33,430	37,378	---
MS 5.0	4-9-91	33,430	37,394	47,845	62,576 (21,776)
PC 5.00.1a	2-28-92	48,006	33,446	37,378	---
PC 5.02	9-1-92	47,990	33,718	37,362	---
MS 6.0	3-10-93	52,925	40,470	38,138	63,065 (17,197)
IBM 6.1	6-29-93	52,589	40,964	38,138	---
PC 6.1	9-30-93	52,797	40,964	38,138	---
MS 6.2R0	9-30-93	54,619	40,566	38,138	63,085 (22,093)
MS 6.22	5-31-94	54,645	40,774	38,138	63,085 (25,037)
PC 6.3	12-31-93	54,654	40,758	37,174	---

ALL Microsoft support through DOS 6.22 ended 12-31-2001

NOTE: According to Microsoft, there were no official versions of MS-DOS prior to version 3.2. Prior to version 3.2, only OEM versions were sold with computers by the computer manufacturers. Slight variations in the sizes do occur, so use these as a general reference only.

DOS Commands

Product	Release Date	Microsoft Ends Support Date
Windows 1.01	11-85	12-31-01
Windows 2.0 (renamed Windows 286)	Fall 1987	12-31-01
Windows 386	Late 1987	12-31-01
Windows 3.0	5-22-90	12-31-01
Windows 3.1	4-6-92	12-31-01
Windows 3.11		12-31-01
Windows for Workgroups 3.1	4-6-92	12-31-01
Windows for Workgroups 3.11	12-31-93	12-31-01
Windows 95 Original	7-95	12-31-01
Service Pack 1 (Ver 4.00.95A)	12-31-95	
OSR2 (Ver 4.00.95B)	9-96	
OSR2.1		
OSR2.1 QFE		
OSR2.5 (Ver C) w/o USB support, IE4.0 req	2-98	
OSR2.5 IE4.0 required		
Windows 98	6-98	6-30-06
Service Pack 1	6-99	
Windows 98 SE (Second Edition)	6-10-99	6-30-06
Windows for Pen Computing 3.1	April 1992	
Windows CE		
Windows NT 3.1 (1st NT Version)	1994	?
Service Pack 3	10-20-94	
Windows NT 3.5	9-94	?
Service Pack 3	9-13-95	
Windows NT 3.51		?
Service Pack 1		
Service Pack 2		
Service Pack 3		
Service Pack 4	3-6-96	
Service Pack 5	9-19-96	
Windows NT 4.0	1996	6-30-03↓ (Workstation)
Service Pack 1		
Service Pack 2	12-14-96	
Service Pack 3	5-1-97	
Service Pack 4	10-16-98	
Service Pack 5	5-4-99	
Service Pack 6a	11-30-99	
Windows ME (Millennium Edition)	6-19-00	6-30-06
Windows 2000 (previously NT 5)	2-17-00	Current
Service Pack 1	7-31-00	
Service Pack 2	5-16-01	
Windows XP (Home & Professional)	10-25-01	Current
Service Pack 1	9-9-02	
Service Pack 1a	2-3-03	
Service Pack 2	8-6-2004	
Windows Server 2003	4-24-2003	Current
Windows Longhorn	2006	

DOS Commands

Command Notation and Syntax

Command descriptions in this chapter are based on the following notations and syntax:

COMMAND NAMES

Short Description: Long description

Syntax (double underlined is optional):

COMMAND   Drive: \Path /switches parameters

(Double underlined areas indicate optional parameters and switches)

Examples: Samples of the syntax and command layout

Syntax Options:

Drive:\Path .... Drive & Directory containing command.

/switches ...... *Switches* modify the way a command performs its particular function.

parameters .... Data (usually numeric) passed to the command when it's started.

Command Type and Version:

External command .... DOS commands stored as files on a disk. All externals end in .EXE, .COM or .SYS.

Internal command .... DOS commands contained in COMMAND.COM. These are loaded into the system on startup.

Batch command .... A script (text) file containing a sequence of commands to be run. The file always ends in .BAT

Config.sys command....... Script (text) file containing start-up system configuration information and device drivers.

Network command .... Will function on a network.

Introduced with Ver X.XX... The DOS version in which a command became available.

New commands added in DOS Versions 6.0 or 6.2:

ADOS.COM

Starts AccessDOS: AccessDOS contains a set of public domain MS-DOS extensions developed for persons with motion and hearing disabilities by the Univ of Wisconsin.

Syntax (double underlined is optional):

ADOS /a /c /L /m /x

Examples: ados /cos /c

Syntax options:

/a. . . . . Starts installation of AccessDOS.
/c. . . . . Runs in color mode.
/L. . . . . Runs in LCD mode.
/m . . . . Runs in monochrome mode.
/x. . . . . Runs in minimal mode.

Command Type and Version:

External command, Introduced with Ver 6.0. Available in the MS-DOS 6.0, 6.21, and 6.22 Supplemental disks.

Notes:

1. See the ADOS.TXT and AREADME.TXT files in the Supplemental disks for user information.

ANSI.SYS

A device driver loaded through CONFIG.SYS that allows the user to control the computer's display and keyboard. Once the ANSI.SYS driver has been loaded, ANSI escape code sequences can be used to customize both the display and keyboard. This was developed by the American National Standards Institute (ANSI).

Syntax (double underlined is optional):

DEVICE = Drive:\Path\ANSI.SYS /x /k /r

Examples: device=c:\dos\ansi.sys /x
If ANSI.SYS is loaded, try the following example for some enhancement of a color display:
    PROMPT $e[35;44;1m$pge[33;44;1m

Syntax Options:

Drive: . . . . Letter of drive containing *Path*.
\ *Path* . . . . Directory containing ANSI.SYS.
/x. . . . . Remaps 101-key keyboards so that the extended keys operate independently.
/k . . . . Extended keys on the 101-key keyboards will be ignored. This is particularly important on systems that do not accurately handle extended keyboard functions. Added in Ver 5.0

/r .... Used with screen-reading programs to adjust rate of line scrolling for easier reading. Version 6.2

Command Type and Version:
CONFIG.SYS command; Introduced with Ver 2.0

Notes:
1. The user has a lot of control over screen colors at the DOS level when the ANSI.SYS driver is loaded. See also PROMPT, p. 380.
2. The .SYS extension must be used in the syntax.
3. Using the Escape Code sequences is sometimes not an easy task. See PC Magazines book *DOS Power Tools, page 420,* for an example of how to write simple programs to send these codes.

ANSI escape sequences are a series of characters beginning with the ESCAPE (character 27) key, followed by open left bracket ([ ), followed by parameters sometimes, and ending with a letter or number. Note that the ending letter must be used in the correct upper or lower case format.

Parameters used in the escape sequences are as follows:

pl	Line number (decimal value)
pc	Column number (decimal value)
pn	Specifies parameter is numeric
ps	Specific decimal number for a function Multiple *ps* functions are separated with a ;

ANSI escape sequences:

ESC [pl ; pc H .... Moves cursor to a specific line (*pl* parameter) and column (*pc* parameter). If no *pl* or *pc* is specified, the cursor goes to the Home position.

ESC [pl ; pc f .... Functions same as **ESC [pl ; pc H**.

ESC [pn A ...... Moves Cursor Up *pn* number of lines. If cursor is on top line, ANSI.SYS ignores this sequence.

ESC [pn B ...... Moves Cursor Down *pn* number of lines. If the cursor is on the bottom line, ANSI.SYS ignores this sequence.

ESC [pn C ...... Moves Cursor Forward *pn* number of columns. If the cursor is at the farthermost right column, ANSI.SYS ignores this sequence.

ESC [pn D ...... Moves Cursor Backward *pn* number of lines. If the cursor is at the farthermost left column, ANSI.SYS ignores this sequence.

ESC [6n .... Reports status of selected device.

ESC [s .... Save Cursor Position. The cursor may be moved to the saved position by using the Restore Cursor sequence.

ESC [u .... Restore Cursor Position. Moves the cursor to the Save Cursor Position.

ESC [2 J .... Erase Display. Erases the screen and returns the cursor to the home position.

ESC [K .... Erase Line. Erases all characters from the cursor to the end of the line.

ESC [ps ; .. ; ps m Sets graphics functions (text attributes and foreground and background colors). Note:These functions stay active until a new set of parameters is issued with this command.

Text Attributes: All Attributes Off ... 0
Bold On.......... 1
Faint On.......... 2
Italic On.......... 3
Underscore .... 4 (Mono adapter only)
Blink On.......... 5
Rapid Blink On ... 6
Reverse Video On . 7
Concealed On..... 8

Colors	Foreground	Background
Black	30	40
Red	31	41
Green	32	42
Yellow	33	43
Blue	34	44
Magenta	35	45
Cyan	36	46
White	37	47

Example: Try using the following PROMPT command if you have a color monitor and ANSI.SYS has been loaded in CONFIG.SYS.

> PROMPT $e[35;44;1m$pge[33;44;1m

ESC [= *ps* **h** . . . . . Set Mode function. The active screen width and graphics mode type is changed with this sequence using the following values: ("mono" means monochrome).

Mode		Mode	
ps	(Graphics unless noted)	*ps*	(Graphics unless noted)
0	40 x 25 mono (text)	13	320 x 200 color
1	40 x 25 mono (text)	14	640 x 200 color (16 color)
2	80 x 25 mono (text)	15	640 x 350 mono (2 color)
3	80 x 25 color (text)	16	640 x 350 color (16 color)
4	320 x 200 (4-color)	17	640 x 480 mono (2 color)
5	320 x 200 mono	18	640 x 480 (16 color)
6	640 x 200 mono	19	320 x 200 color (256 color)
7	Enables line wrapping		

ESC [= *ps* **l** (l in the sequence to the left is a lower case **L**)

This sequence resets the Mode sequence described above. The *ps* parameter uses the same values as those shown in the Set Mode sequence above.

ESC [*code* **;** *string* **;...P** Redefine a specific keyboard key with a specific string of characters. *code* is one of the values in the ASCII Key Code table, on the next three pages, that represent keyboard keys or combinations of keys. Gray keys, keypad keys or codes shown in ( ) in the table may not function on some keyboards (try using the /x switch on the ANSI.SYS command line. *string* is either the decimal ASCII code for a single character (76 is the letter "C") or a string of characters in quotes ("<"). For example:

> ESC ["<" ; "+" p ESC ["+" ; "<" p
> ESC [60 ; 43 p ESC [43 ; 60 p

Both of the above sequences do the same task, they exchange the < and + keys. Note that it is not possible to alter the ALT and Caps Lock keys.

ASCII Key Codes for ANSI.SYS

Key	K means Key → K Code	SHIFT+K Code	CTRL+K Code	ALT+K Code
F1	0;59	0;84	0;94	0;104
F2	0;60	0;85	0;95	0;105
F3	0;61	0;86	0;96	0;106
F4	0;62	0;87	0;97	0;107
F5	0;63	0;88	0;98	0;108
F6	0;64	0;89	0;99	0;109
F7	0;65	0;90	0;100	0;110
F8	0;66	0;91	0;101	0;111
F9	0;67	0;92	0;102	0;112

DOS Commands

Key (K means Key →)	K Code	SHIFT+K Code	CTRL+K Code	ALT+K Code
F10	0;68	0;93	0;103	0;113
F11	0;133	0;135	0;137	0;139
F12	0;134	0;136	0;138	0;140
Home	0;71	55	0;119	—
Up Arrow	0;72	56	(0;141)	—
Page Up	0;73	57	0;132	—
Left Arrow	0;75	52	0;115	—
Right Arrow	0;77	54	0;116	—
End	0;79	49	0;117	—
Down Arrow	0;80	50	(0;145)	—
Page Down	0;81	51	0;118	—
Insert	0;82	48	(0;146)	—
Delete	0;83	46	(0;147)	—
Home (gray key)	224;71	224;71	224;119	224;151
Up Arrow (gray key)	224;72	224;72	224;141	224;152
Page Up (gray key)	224;73	224;73	224;132	224;153
Left Arrow (gray key)	224;75	224;75	224;115	224;155
Right Arrow (gray K)	224;77	224;77	224;116	224;157
End (gray key)	224;79	224;79	224;117	224;159
Down Arrow (gray key)	224;80	224;80	224;145	224;154
Page Down (gray key)	224;81	224;81	224;118	224;161
Insert (gray key)	224;82	224;82	224;146	224;162
Delete (gray key)	224;83	224;83	224;147	224;163
Print Screen	—	—	0;114	—
Pause/Break	—	—	0;0	—
Backspace	8	8	127	(0)
Tab	9	0;15	(0;148)	(0;165)
Null	0;3	—	—	—
A	97	65	1	0;30
B	98	66	2	0;48
C	99	66	3	0;46
D	100	68	4	0;32
Enter	13	—	10	(0;28)
E	101	69	5	0;18
F	102	70	6	0;33
G	103	71	7	0;34
H	104	72	8	0;35
I	105	73	9	0;23
J	106	74	10	0;36
K	107	75	11	0;37
L	108	76	12	0;38
M	109	77	13	0;50
N	110	78	14	0;49
O	111	79	15	0;24
P	112	80	16	0;25
Q	113	81	17	0;16
R	114	82	18	0;19
S	115	83	19	0;31
T	116	84	20	0;20
U	117	85	21	0;22
V	118	86	22	0;47
W	119	87	23	0;17
X	120	88	24	0;45
Y	121	89	25	0;21

ASCII Key Codes for ANSI.SYS (cont.)

Key	K means Key → K Code	SHIFT+K Code	CTRL+K Code	ALT+K Code
Z	122	90	26	0;44
1	49	33	—	0;120
2	50	64	0	0;121
3	51	35	—	0;122
4	52	36	—	0;123
5	53	37	—	0;124
6	54	94	30	0;125
7	55	38	—	0;126
8	56	42	—	0;127
9	57	40	—	0;128
0	48	41	—	0;129
− (minus sign)	45	95	31	0;130
= (equal sign)	61	43	—	0;131
[(left bracket)	91	123	27	0;26
] (right bracket)	93	125	29	0;27
\ (back slash)	92	124	28	0;43
; (semi-colon)	59	58	—	0;39
' (apostrophe)	39	34	—	0;40
, (comma)	44	60	—	0;51
. (period)	46	62	—	0;52
/ (forward slash)	47	63	—	0;53
` (accent)	96	126	—	(0;41)
ENTER (on keypad)	13	—	10	(0;166)
/ (on keypad)	47	47	(0;142)	(0;74)
* (on keypad)	42	(0;144)	(0;78)	—
− (on keypad)	45	45	(0;149)	(0;164)
+ (on keypad)	43	43	(0;150)	(0;55)
5 (on keypad)	(0;76)	53	(0;143)	—

APPEND.EXE

Sets directory search order : Searches specified directories on specified drives to locate files outside of the current directory that have extensions <u>other than</u> .COM, .EXE, or .BAT. *Use Caution!*

Syntax (double underlined is optional):

APPEND <u>Drive: \Path /X /E /Path:on or off ;</u>

Examples: APPEND /X /E
               APPEND C:\WORDDATA; D:\PFS
               APPEND ;

Syntax Options:

Drive: . . . . Letter of drive to be searched.

\Path . . . . Directory searched for data files.

/X :on or :off . . . Extends the DOS search path for specified
files when executing programs. Processes SEARCH FIRST,
FIND FIRST, and EXEC functions. :ON and :OFF, new to
Version 5.0, toggles this switch on and off.

/Path :on or :off	.If path is already included for a program file, :on tells program to also search in appended directories. Default= :on; added in DOS Ver 5.0
/E	Causes the appended path to be stored in the DOS environment and searched for there.
;	Use ";" to separate multiple Drive:\Path statements on one line. APPEND ; by itself will cancel the APPEND list.

Command Type and Version:
External command; Network; Introduced with Ver 3.2

Notes:
1. /X and /E switches can only be used the first time you use Append. The line following the APPEND /X /E line contains the Drive:\Path.
2. You can not use any paths on the same command line as /X & /E.
3. :ON and :OFF switches are valid for Ver 5.0 and later.
4. Do not use APPEND with Windows.

ASSIGN.COM

Assign disk drive: Instructs DOS to redirect disk operations on one drive to a different drive. Removed in DOS 6.0

Syntax (double underlined is optional):

ASSIGN <u>Source = Target</u> /status

Examples: ASSIGN A = B or ASSIGN A: = B:
            ASSIGN A = B B = C
            ASSIGN
            ASSIGN /status   ❺

Syntax Options:

ASSIGN	ASSIGN with no switch cancels redirected drive assignments and sets them back to their original drives.
Source	Letter(s) of source drive(s).
Target	Letter(s) of target drive(s). Starting with Version 5.0, a colon can be used with each assigned drive letter. For example; ASSIGN A: = B:
/Status	Lists current drive assignments. Ver 5.0.

Command Type and Version:
External command; Network; Introduced with Ver 2.0, Removed from Version 6.0, considered too dangerous. Available in the MS-DOS 6.0, 6.21, 6.22 Supplemental Disks.

Notes:
1. DO NOT use a colon after a drive letter in versions prior to 5.0.
2. FORMAT, DISKCOPY, DISKCOMP, BACKUP, JOIN, LABEL, RESTORE PRINT and SUBST cannot be used on ASSIGNed drives.

3. Be careful to reassign drives back to their original designations before running other programs.
4. If ASSIGN and APPEND are both used, the APPEND command must be used first.
5. See also the SUBST command.

ATTRIB.EXE

Changes or displays file attributes: Sets, displays or clears a file's read-only, archive, system, and hidden attributes. Removed in DOS Ver 6.0

Syntax (double underlined is optional):

ATTRIB +r-r +a-a +s-s +h-h Drive:\Path\Filename /s

Examples: ATTRIB wordfile.doc
             ATTRIB +r wordfile.doc
             ATTRIB +r d:\worddata*.* /s

Syntax Options:

Drive: . . . . Letter of drive containing \path\filename.
\Path . . . . Directory containing filename.
Filename . . . . . . Filename(s) of which attributes are to be
                        displayed or changed. Wildcards (? and *) can be used
                        for groups of files.
+ r . . . . Sets file to read-only.
− r . . . . Removes read-only attribute.
+ a . . . . Sets the archive file attribute.
− a . . . . Removes the archive file attribute.
+ s . . . . Sets file as a system file. Ver. 5
− s . . . . Removes system file attribute. Ver 5
+ h . . . . Sets file as a hidden file. Ver 5
− h . . . . Removes the hidden file attribute. Ver 5
 /s . . . . ATTRIB command processes files in the
                        current directory and its subdirectories.

Command Type and Version:

External command; Network; Introduced with Ver 3.0

Notes:

1. When the system or hidden attribute is set , the read-only and *archive* attrib-utes cannot be changed.
2. The *archive* attribute is used by the DOS BACKUP, RESTORE, and XCOPY commands when their **/m** switch is used and also the XCOPY command when the **/a** switch is used.

@ (at symbol)

Turns off the command echo function: In a batch file, placing the @ symbol at the start of a command line suppresses the echoed display of the command on the screen.

Syntax (double underlined is optional):

@ command

Examples: @xcopy a:*.* b:
               @ECHO off

Syntax Options:

command . . . . Any DOS command.

Command Type and Version:

Batch command; Introduced with Ver 3.3

Notes:

1. Useful in preventing the words ECHO OFF from displaying on the screen when ECHO OFF is used in a Batch file. This command is useful if all screen echos need to be turned off in a Batch file.
2. See also ECHO.

BACKINFO.EXE

MS-DOS utility: Allows viewing of files on a backup disk created by the DOS Version 3.3, 3.31, 4.0, 4.01, and 5.0 BACKUP command. Removed DOS Ver 6.0

Syntax (shaded area optional):

BACKINFO drive1:

Example: backinfo b:

Syntax options:

drive1: . . . . Drive containing the BACKUP disk.

Command Type and Version:

External command, Introduced with Ver 3.3.
Removed from Ver 6.0

BACKUP.EXE

Back up files: Backs up files from one drive to another drive. Source and target drives may be either hard disks or floppy disks. DOSV6 use MSBACKUP. Removed DOS Ver 6.0

Syntax (double underlined is optional):

BACKUP Source:\Path\Filename Target: /a /d:date /t:time
                             /f:size /L:LogDrive:\Path\Log /s /m

Examples: BACKUP C:*.* B: /s
               BACKUP C:\DATA*.* B: /s /L:C:\LOG

Syntax Options:

Source:\Path . . . Source drive & directory to be backed up.

Filename......	Filename (s) to be backed up. Use of Wild cards (? and *) is allowed.
Target:.......	Target drive for backed up files.
/s............	Backs up all files in *Source:\Path* and subdirectories under *Source:\Path*
/m...........	Backs up all files that have changed since the last backup (backup looks at the files archive attribute) and then turns off the files archive attribute.
/a............	Adds new backup files to the existing backup disk (existing files are not deleted.) If a backup was made with DOS 3.2 or earlier, the /a switch is ignored.
/d:date.......	Only files created or modified after *date* are backed up. The way *date* is written depends on COUNTRY.SYS settings.
/t:time........	Only files created or modified after *time* are backed up. The way *time* is written depends on COUNTRY.SYS settings. Always use the /d:date switch when /t:time is used.
/f:size........	Format backup disk to the following *size*: (*size* can also be with k or kb, e.g. 160 can be 160k or 160kb; or 1200 can be 1200k, 1200kb, 1.2, 1.2m or 1.2mb, etc.)

size	.	Disk size and type
160	....	160k single sided DD 5.25" disk
180	....	180k single sided DD 5.25" disk
320	....	320k double sided DD 5.25" disk
360	....	360k double sided DD 5.25" disk
720	....	720k double sided DD, 3.5" disk
1200	...	1.2meg double sided HD, 5.25"
1440	...	1.44meg double sided HD, 3.5"
2880	...	2.88meg double sided HD, 3.5" disk
(DD=Double Density, HD=High Density)		

/L:..........	Creates a log file during a specific backup operation.
Logdrive:\Path..	Drive & Directory where backup *Log* is to be sent.
Log.........	Text file log of a backup operation.

Command Type and Version:

External command; Network; Introduced with Ver 2.0
Removed from Version 6.0, replaced with MSBACKUP.
Available in the MS-DOS 6.0 and 6.22 Supplemental Disks.

Notes:

1. See also RESTORE, COPY, XCOPY, DISKCOPY, IF
2. The sequence number of a backup disk can be checked by doing a DIR of the backup disk (Valid for version after DOS 3.3)
3. BACKUP does not backup the 3 system files, COMMAND.COM, MSDOS.SYS (or IBMDOS.SYS) , and IO.SYS (or IBMBIO.SYS).
4. BACKUP/RESTORE commands are not compatible between pre DOS 5.0 version. DOS 5.0 will restore previous versions.
5. Do not use BACKUP when the ASSIGN, JOIN, or SUBST commands have been used.

6. When the IF ERRORLEVEL functions are used, BACKUP Exit Codes can be used to show why a backup failed (see IF):

Exit Code	Code Meaning
0	Successful backup
1	No files found to be backed up
2	File-sharing conflict, some files not backed up
3	BACKUP terminated by user with CTRL-C
4	Error terminated BACKUP procedure

7. Backup floppies are not readable by DOS, a special file format is used.

BASIC® and BASICA®

BASIC Computer Language: Depending on the system in use and version of DOS, it will run one of the BASIC interpreters (BASIC, BASICA, GW-BASIC, or QBASIC) and provide an environment for programming in the BASIC language. BASIC and BASICA are versions that were shipped with IBM® systems and were simply entry programs that started BASIC from the system's ROM. GW-BASIC is Microsoft's own version of BASIC that is shipped with MS-DOS versions through 4.01. For specifics on DOS 5.0/6.0 QBASIC, refer to page 381.

Syntax (double underlined is optional):

BASIC Filename

Examples: BASIC Test.bas
             BASICA

Syntax Options:

BASIC. . . . . BASIC without a filename just starts the BASIC Interpreter
Filename. . . . . . A program written in BASIC that is loaded and run when the BASIC interpreter starts. The files normally end with .BAS

Command Type and Version:

External command; Network; Introduced with Ver 1.0

Notes:

1. See also QBASIC and GW-BASIC.

BREAK

Turns on/off the DOS check for Control-C or Control-Break: Determines when DOS looks for a Ctrl-C or Ctrl-Break more frequently in order to stop a program.

Syntax (double underlined is optional):

BREAK on off

Examples: BREAK
             BREAK = ON (syntax for CONFIG.SYS)
             BREAK ON (syntax at DOS prompt)

Syntax Options:

BREAK	BREAK, with no switches or options, displays the current setting of BREAK.
ON	Tells DOS to check for Ctrl-C or Ctrl-Break from the keyboard, during disk reads and writes, and during screen and printer writes.
OFF	Tells DOS to check for Ctrl-C or Ctrl-Break from the keyboard only during screen and printer writes.

Command Type and Version:
Internal command; CONFIG.SYS and Batch command;
Introduced with Ver 2.0

Notes:
1. If BREAK is ON, your system will run slightly slower.
2. The default setting is BREAK=OFF.

BUFFERS

Sets number of disk buffers in memory: A disk buffer is a block of RAM memory that DOS uses to hold data while reading and writing data to a disk.

Syntax (double underlined is optional):

BUFFERS = X <u>,Y</u>

Examples: BUFFERS = 35
                 BUFFERS = 35,8

Syntax Options:

X . . . . The number of disk buffers allocated. The total may range from 1 to 99 for versions Ver 4.0 to 6.2x. Versions prior to 4.0 can be in the range from 2 to 255. Default values are as follows:

         Buffers. Drive Configuration

            2 . . . <128K RAM & 360k drive only
            3 . . . <128K RAM & Disks over 360K
            5 . . . 128K to 255K RAM
          10 . . . 256K to 511K RAM
          15 . . . 512K or more RAM

Y . . . . The number of secondary cache buffers. The total may range from 1 to 8, the default is 1.

Command Type and Version:
CONFIG.SYS command; Introduced with Ver 2.0

Notes:
1. Each buffer takes up approximately 532 bytes of RAM.
2. Standard buffer sizes should range from 20 to 30, unless more are required by a specific application (such as Dbase III Plus®)
3. If a disk cache program, such as SMARTDRV.SYS is used, the number of buffers can be set at 8 to 15 (sometimes lower).
4. In Ver 5.0, if DOS is in high memory, buffers are also in high mem.
5. The number of buffers (up to 35) significantly affects system speed; over 35, speed still increases but at much slower rate.

6. /X switch from earlier DOS versions is no longer available.

CALL

Calls a batch program: Starts one batch program from inside another batch program, without causing the initial batch program to stop.

Syntax (double underlined is optional):

CALL <u>Drive:\Path\</u> Filename <u>Parameters</u>

Examples: CALL C:\TEST %1

Syntax Options:
Drive: . . . . Letter of drive containing path.
\Path . . . . Path containing filename.
Filename . . . . . . Filename specifies name of the batch program to be
called. *Filename* must have a .BAT extension.
Parameters . . . . Specifies command-line information required by the batch
program, including switches, filenames, pass through pa-
rameters such as %1, and variables.

Command Type and Version:
Internal command; Batch; Introduced with Ver 3.3

Notes:
1. Any information that can be passed to a batch program can be contained
in the *Batch-parameters*, including switches, filenames, replaceable parameters %1 through %9, and variables such as % Parity %
2. Pipes and redirection symbols cannot be used with CALL.
3. If a recursive call (a program that calls itself) is created, an exit condition
must be provided or the two batch programs will loop endlessly.

CD or CHDIR

Change directory: Changes (moves) to another
directory or shows the name of the current directory path.

Syntax (double underlined is optional):

CD <u>Drive:\Path</u>

Examples: CD (displays current drive and directory)
CD D:\PFS (change to PFS directory on
D: drive)
CD\ (changes to root directory)

Syntax Options:
Drive: . . . . Drive containing the subdirectory to be changed. CD
does not move to Drive:, it remains on the current drive.
\Path . . . . Directory path name to be made current, if *Drive:* is the
current drive. If *Drive:* is not the current drive, *\Path* is simply
the active path on *Drive:* and the current drive and directory
remain unchanged. Pathname can be no longer than 63

characters and (\\) is to be used as the path's first character to
move to the root directory.

Command Type and Version:

Internal command; Network; Introduced with Ver 2.0

Notes:

1. When a drive letter is not specified, the current drive is assumed.
2. **CD ..** specifies move up one directory level.

CHCP

Change code page: Displays or changes the number of the active code page
for the command processor COMMAND.COM.

Syntax (double underlined is optional):

CHCP <u>ccc</u>

Examples: CHCP   (reports current *ccc* setting)
           CHCP 863

Syntax Options:

ccc . . . . These are the numbers that represent the prepared system
code pages defined by the COUNTRY.SYS command in
the CONFIG.SYS file. Valid code page numbers are as
follows:
437 . . . . United States
850 . . . . Multilingual (Latin I)
852 . . . . Slavic (Latin II)
860 . . . . Portuguese
863 . . . . Canadian-French
865 . . . . Nordic

Command Type and Version:

Internal command; Network; Introduced with Ver 3.3

Notes:

1. Once a specified code page has been selected, all programs that are
started will use that new code page.
2. NLSFUNC (national language support functions) must be installed before
a code page can be switched with CHCP.
3. MODE SELECT can also be used to change code pages.
4. See also DOS commands COUNTRY.SYS, NLSFUNC, DEVICE, and
MODE.

CHKDSK.EXE

Checks disk: Scans the disk and reports size, disk memory available, RAM available and checks for and corrects logical errors. A status report is displayed on screen.

Syntax (double underlined is optional):

CHKDSK <u>Drive:\Path\Filename</u> / f / v

Examples: CHKDSK C: / f
(If no Drive: is specified, the current drive is used.)

Syntax Options:

Drive:	Drive letter of the disk to be checked.
\Path	Directory path containing file to be checked.
Filename	Name of file to be checked by CHKDSK for fragmentation. Wildcards * & ? are allowed.
/ f	Fixes logical errors on the disk.
/ v	Verbose switch. Displays CHKDSK progress by listing each file in every directory as it is being checked.

Command Type and Version:

External command; Can NOT check a Network drive;
Introduced with Ver 1.0

Notes:

1. CHKDSK analyzes a disk's File Allocation Table (FAT) and file system. / f must be specified in order to fix errors. If / f is not used, CHKDSK reports the error, but does not fix the error, even if you answer yes to fixing the error at the CHKDSK prompt.
2. When CHKDSK / f finds an error, it asks if you want to convert the "lost clusters" to files. If you answer Yes, files in the form FILE0001.CHK are created and the lost areas dumped into those files. You must then determine if any valuable information is in that file. If they don't contain useful information, delete them.
3. Do not use CHKDSK from inside any other program, especially Windows.
4. Only logical errors are repaired by CHKDSK, not physical errors.
5. CHKDSK will not work when SUBST, JOIN or ASSIGN has been used.

CHKSTATE.SYS

CHKSTATE is used only by MemMaker to track the memory optimization process: During the memory optimization process, MemMaker adds CHKSTATE.SYS to the beginning of the CONFIG.SYS file. When the memory optimization process is complete, MemMaker automatically removes CHKSTATE.SYS. New in DOS Version 6.2

CHOICE.COM

Pauses the system and prompts the user to make a choice in a batch file:
This command can only be used in batch programs. New in DOS V6.0

Syntax (double underlined is optional):

CHOICE /C:keys /N /S /T:c,nn text

Syntax Options:

/C:keys . . . . Defines which keys are allowed in the prompt. The : is optional. Displayed keys are separated by commas and will be enclosed in [ ] brackets. Multiple keystroke characters are allowed. Default is [YN] (yes/no).

/N . . . . Prevents display of prompt, but the specified keys are still valid.

/S . . . . Specifies that CHOICE is case sensitive.

/T:c,nn . . . . . . Forces CHOICE to pause for nn seconds before defaulting to a specified key (c). nn can range from 0 to 99. The c key specified must be included in the /C:keys definition.

text . . . . Defines what text is displayed before the prompt. Quotation marks (" ") must be used if a "/ " character is included in the prompt. Default for CHOICE is no text displayed.

Command Type and Version:
Internal Batch command; Network; Introduced with Ver 6.0

Notes:
1. ERRORLEVEL 0 is returned if Control-C or Control-Break is pressed.

CLS

Clears or Erases Screen: All information is cleared from the DOS screen and the prompt and cursor is returned to the upper left corner of the screen.

Syntax:

CLS

Examples: CLS

Syntax Options:
None

Command Type and Version:
Internal command; Network; Introduced with Ver 2.0

Notes:
1. Screen colors set by ANSI.SYS will remain set.
2. If more than one video display is attached to the system, only the active display is cleared.
3. If ANSI.SYS is not loaded on the system, CLS will clear the screen to gray (or amber on an amber monitor, etc.) on black.

COMMAND.COM

Start a new DOS command processor: The command processor is responsible for displaying the prompt on the computer's display and contains all of the Internal DOS commands. It is also used to set variables such as environment size. Use the EXIT command to stop the new processor.

Syntax (double underlined is optional):

COMMAND <u>Drive:\Path\Device</u> <u>/ e:xxxx</u> <u>/ y</u> <u>/ c text</u> <u>/ k</u>

In CONFIG.SYS use the following:

SHELL = <u>Drive:\Path\</u> COMMAND.COM <u>/ e:xxxx</u> <u>/ p</u> <u>/ msg</u>

Examples: COMMAND /e:1024
(use the following in CONFIG.SYS with SHELL)
SHELL = Drive:\Path\COMMAND.COM /e:512 /p

Syntax Options:

Drive:\Path . . . . Drive and \Path of the command device. Must be included if COMMAND.COM is not located in the root directory.

\Device . . . . Device for command input or outpur (see the CTTY command on page 304).

/ e:xxxx . . . . Set environment size in bytes (xxxx). Default for Ver 5.0,6.0, and 6.2x = 256 bytes; default for versions before 5.0 is 160 bytes. Range is 160 to 32768 bytes.

/ p . . . . Makes the new command processor the permanent processor. Used only with SHELL command.

/ c text . . . . Forces the command processor to perform the commands specified by *text*. On completion, it returns to the primary command processor. Must be last switch on command line.

/ msg . . . . Causes error messages to be stored in memory. The */ p* switch must also be used when */ msg* is used.

/ k . . . . Execute a command, but after the command is executed, do not terminate the second COMMAND.COM that is running. Must be last switch on command line. In DOS 6.0

/ y . . . . Tells COMMAND.COM to step through files specified by the /c text or /k switches. In DOS Version 6.2

Command Type and Version:

External command;
CONFIG.SYS command when used with SHELL;
Introduced with Ver 1.0

Notes:

1. See also CTTY, EXIT and SHELL

2. Default environment sizes are commonly not large enough. Try setting the environment to 512 or 1024.

3. In Version 6.0, if DOS is unable to find COMMAND.COM, a warning message is issued that allows the user to "Enter correct name of Command In-

terpreter (e.g., C:\COMMAND.COM). This is a much improved error handling function and allows the system to complete the booting process.
4. Exercise caution when you are "messing around" with COMMAND.COM. It can get the user into some dangerous situations!
5. The SHELL command in CONFIG.SYS is the preferred method of increasing the environment size with the /e:xxxx switch.

COMP.EXE

Compare files: Compares the contents of two sets of disk files to see if they are the same or different. The comparison is made on a byte by byte basis. COMP displays filenames, locations and the differences found during the compare process. Removed in DOS Version 6.0

Syntax (double underlined is optional):

COMP <u>Drive1:\Path1\File1 Drive2:\Path2\File2 /d /a /L /n=xx /c</u>

| Examples: | COMP | (prompts for file locations) |
| | COMP C:\File1 D:\File2 /a | |

Syntax Options:

Drive1: Drive2: . . Letters of drives containing the file (s) to be compared.
\Path1 \Path2 . . Paths of files to be compared.
File1 File2 . . . . . Filenames to be compared. The names may be the same if they are in different locations. Wild cards (*?) are allowed.
/d. . . . . Displays file differences in decimal format, the default format is hexadecimal. Ver 5
/a. . . . . File differences displayed as characters. Ver 5.0
/L. . . . . Display Line numbers with different data instead of byte offsets. Ver 5.0
/n=xx. . . . . Compares the first number of lines (*xx*) in each file, even if files are different sizes. Ver 5.0
/c. . . . . Upper and lower case is ignored. Ver 5.0

Command Type and Version:

External command; Network; Introduced with Ver 1.0
Removed from Ver 6.0, replaced by FC.
Available on the MS-DOS 6.0, 6.21, and 6.22 Supplemental Disks.

Notes:

1. If the drive, path and filename information is not specific enough, COMP will prompt for the correct information
2. If more than 10 mismatches are found, COMP ends the compare.
3. See also DISKCOMP (for floppy disk comparisons) and FC.

COPY

Copies file(s) from one location to another: Files can also be combined (concatenated) using COPY.

Syntax (double underlined is optional):

COPY /y / -y /a /b Source /a /b+Source /a /b +..
        Target /a /b /v

Examples: COPY C:\Test*.* D:\Test2
              COPY Test1.txt + Text2.txt Test3.txt /a

Syntax Options:

Source . . . . Source Drive, Directory, and File(s) or Devices to be copied **from**.

Target . . . . Destination Drive, Directory, and File(s) or Devices being copied **to**.

/a . . . . Denotes an ASCII text file. If */a* precedes a filename, that file and all following files are treated as ASCII files until a */b* switch is encountered, then files that follow are considered to be binary files. If */a* follows a filename, it applies to all files before and after the */a* until a */b* switch is encountered, then files that follow are considered to be binary files.

/b . . . . Denotes a Binary file. If */b* precedes a filename, that file and all following files are treated as binary files until a */a* switch is encountered, then files that follow are considered to be ASCII files. If */b* follows a filename, it applies to all files before and after the */b* until a */a* switch is encountered, then files that follow are considered to be ASCII files. */b* forces copy to read exactly the number of bytes allocated to the file's size in the directory.

/v . . . . Verifies files were copied correctly.

/y . . . . Directs COPY to replace existing file without confirmation prompt. Confirmation prompt is default. In DOS Version 6.2

/-y . . . . Directs COPY to ask for confirmation prior to replacing existing files. Included in DOS Version 6.2

Command Type and Version:

Internal command; Network; Introduced with Ver 1.0

Notes:

1. COPY will only copy the contents of 1 directory. If a directory and its subdirectories need to be copied, use the XCOPY command.
2. COPY will not copy files 0 bytes in length, use XCOPY instead.
3. Both *Source* and *Destination* can be a device such as COM1: or LPT1:, however, when sending to *Destination*, if the */b* switch is used, all characters, including control codes, are sent to the device as data. If no switch is used, the data transfers as ASCII data and the transmitted control codes

may perform their special function on the device. For example, if a Ctrl + L
code is sent to a printer on LPT1:, the printer will form feed.

4. If Destination Filename is not specified, COPY will create a file with the
   same name and date and time of creation in the current directory (*Target*).
   If a file with the same name as *Filename* exists in the current directory,
   DOS will not copy the file and display an error message that says "File cannot be copied onto itself. 0 Files Copied."

5. If the + function is used to combine files, it is assumed that the files are
   ASCII files. Normally you should NOT combine binary files since the internal format of binary files may be different.

6. /v slows down the copy process. If a verify error occurs, the message is
   displayed on the screen.

7. In order to change the date and time of a file during the copy process,
   use the following syntax: **COPY /b Source + , ,**

8. See also DISKCOPY and XCOPY.

COUNTRY and COUNTRY.SYS

Country dependent information: Enables DOS to use international time,
date, currency, and case conversions.

Syntax (double underlined is optional):

COUNTRY= ccc ppp Drive:\Path \Filename

Examples: COUNTRY = 002

Syntax Options:

ccc . . . . Country code number. Default 001, USA
ppp . . . . Code page number.
Drive:\Path . . . . Drive & subdirectory containing *Filename*.
Filename. . . . . . . File containing country information.

Command Type and Version:

CONFIG.SYS; Introduced with Ver 3.0

Notes:

1. COUNTRY is put in CONFIG.SYS . If the *Drive:\Path\Filename* option is
   not used to specify which file contains country information, COUN-
   TRY.SYS must be in the root directory of the system's boot drive so that
   COUNTRY can retrieve the country data.

Country Code	Country or Language	Code Page	Time Format	Date Format
001	United States	437, 850	2:35:00.00p	06-30-1991
002	Canadian-French	863, 850	14:35:00,00	1991-06-30
003	Latin America	850, 437	2:35:00.00p	30/06/1991
031	Netherlands	850, 437	14:35:00,00	30-06-1991
032	Belgium	850, 437	14:35:00,00	30/06/1991
033	France	850, 437	14:35:00,00	30.06.1991
034	Spain	850, 437	14:35:00,00	30/06/1991
036	Hungary	852, 850	14:35:00,00	1991-06-30
038	Croatia\Slovenia\ Yugoslavia\Serbia	852, 850	14:35:00,00	1991-06-30

Country Code	Country or Language	Code Page	Time Format	Date Format
039	Italy	850, 437	14.35.00,00	30/06/1991
041	Switzerland	850, 437	14,35,00.00	30.06.1991
042	Czech Rep\Slovakia	852, 850	14:35:00.00	1991-06-30
044	United Kingdom	437, 850	14:35:00.00	30/06/1991
045	Denmark	850, 865	14.35.00.00	30-06-1991
046	Sweden	850, 437	14.35.00.00	1991-06-30
047	Norway	850, 865	14:35:00.00	30.06.1991
048	Poland	852, 850	14:35:00.00	1991-06-30
049	Germany	850, 437	14:35:00.00	30.06.1991
055	Brazil	850, 437	14:35:00.00	30/06/1991
061	Intl. English	437, 850	14:35:00.00	30-06-1991
351	Portugal	850, 860	14:35:00.00	30-06-1991
358	Finland	850, 437	14.35.00,00	30.06.1991

CTTY

Change to a remote console: Allows you to choose the device from which you issue commands. USE WITH CAUTION, you could lose control of your system!

Syntax (double underlined is optional):

CTTY Device

Examples: CTTY aux
             CTTY com1
             CTTY con

Syntax Options:

Device. . . . . Any valid DOS device for issuing commands. Examples include com1, com2, com3, com4, con, aux, prn (rare).

Command Type and Version:

Internal command; Network; Introduced with Ver 2.0

Notes:

1. *Device* refers to a character-oriented remote unit, or secondary terminal, that will be used for command input and output. This device name must be a valid MS/PC-DOS name, specifically, AUX, COM1, COM2, COM3, COM4, CON. The use of a colon after the device name is optional.
2. *ctty con* moves the input and output back to the main terminal (the local console screen and keyboard).
3. *When redirected, some programs that are designed to work with* the video display's control codes may not function correctly.
4. Other redirected IO or piping is not affected by CTTY.
5. CAUTION: the command CTTY NUL will disconnect the screen and keyboard !!!! Do not use unless the CTTY CON command is executed under some type of program control, such as a batchfile

CV.COM and CV.EXE

CV starts the CodeView program: CodeView is a debugging utility for programs written in C. Removed from DOS Version 6.2

Command Type and Version:
 External command, Introduced with Ver 5.0.
 Removed Ver. 6.2.
 Available in the MS-DOS 6.0, 6.21, & 6.22 Suppl. Disks.

Notes:
1. CAUTION- Using CodeView CV.EXE Versions 3.0 to 3.13 with a 80386 memory manager such as EMM386 may cause loss of data. This problem has been fixed in Version 3.14 of CodeView. To start CodeView Versions 3.0 to 3.13 safely, use CV.COM.
2. Use HIMEM.SYS Version 2.77 or later with CodeView.

DATE

Date: Change and /or display the system date. (Note: This does not reset the computer's battery powered clock if DOS 3.21 or earlier is used.)

Syntax (double underlined is optional):

DATE <u>month-day-year</u>

 Examples: **date mm-dd-yy** (for North America)
 Note: If COUNTRY in config.sys is set for a country other than a North American country, then the following syntax is used:
    DATE dd-mm-yy for Europe
    DATE yy-mm-dd for Far East

Syntax Description and Options:
 month . . . . One or two digit number (1 to 12)
 day . . . . One or two digit number (1 to 31). DOS knows the correct number of days in each month (28, 29, 30 or 31).
 year. . . . . Two or four digit number (80 to 99 – The 19 is assumed for 1980 to 1999).

Command Type and Version:
 Internal command; Network; Introduced with Ver 1.0

Notes:
1. You may separate the day, month and the year by the use of hyphens, periods or slashes.
2. If a system does not have an AUTOEXEC.BAT file in the root directory of the boot drive, the date and time functions are activated automatically when the system starts and the user is prompted for change or confirmation.
3. DOS has been programmed to change the year, month and day and adjusts the number of days in a month accordingly. DOS also knows which months have 28, 29, 30, or 31 days. DOS will issue errors if valid dates are not used.
4. Beginning with DOS 3.3, DATE and TIME both set the system's CMOS (battery powered) calendar (except in XT class systems)
5. See also TIME

DBLBOOT.BAT

Creates a bootable DBLSPACE floppy disk: Removed from DOS Ver 6.22

Syntax:

DBLBOOT drive1:

Syntax options:

drive1:. . . . . Drive containing floppy disk to be compressed.

Command Type and Version:

External command, Introduced with MS-DOS Ver 6.0.
Available in the MS-DOS 6.0, 6.21, and 6.22 Supplemental Disks; Removed in version 6.22.

Notes:

1. DBLBOOT works only on high-density floppy disks (1.44 or 1.2 MB).
2. DBLSPACE must be installed prior to using DBLBOOT.

DBLSPACE.EXE

Utility to compress both hard and floppy disk drives so that there is more available storage space on the drive: Once the .EXE program has been run, DBLSPACE.SYS must be included in CONFIG.SYS. *Many problems have been reported with the DOS 6.0 version of this program. USE WITH CAUTION or not at all, you could lose data on your drive!* New in DOS Verion 6.0 (DANGER); Removed from DOS Version 6.22

Syntax (double underlined is optional):

DBLSPACE /Automount /Chkdsk /Compress /Convstac
/Create /Defragment /Delete /Format
/Info /List /Mount /Ratio /Size /Unmount

Syntax Options:

/Automount	Automatically mount a compressed disk.
/ Chkdsk	Check the validity of a compressed disk's directory and FAT and report the status of the drive.
/ Compress	Start the compression process on a drive.
/ Convstac.	*Removed from DOS Ver 6.2:* Converts a Stacker compressed drive to a DBLSPACE compressed drive.
/ Create.	Creates a new compressed drive in the free space of an existing drive.
/ Defragment. . .	Defragment the files on an existing drive.
/ Delete	Remove a compressed drive.
/ Format	Format a compressed drive.
/ Info	Display detailed information on a compressed drive.
/ List	Display a list of both compressed and uncompressed drives on a system. It does not report network drives.
/ Mount	Mount a compressed drive.

/ Ratio	Display and change the estimated compression ratio of a compressed drive
/ Size.	Change the size of a compressed drive.
/ Uncompress . .	Uncompresses a drive compressed by DBLSPACE. DOS 6.2
/ Unmount	Unmount a compressed drive.

Command Type and Version:

External command; Introduced with Ver 6.0

Removed with Ver. 6.2, revision 2, and replaced by DRVSPACE.

Notes:

1. DBLSPACE can be run as a menu driven utility or with the command line switches listed under Syntax Options.
2. The maximum size of a DBLSPACE volume is 512 MB.
3. Default cluster size of a compressed volume is 8k.
4. When DBLSPACE.EXE is run, DBLSPACE.SYS is automatically placed in CONFIG.SYS as part of the installation process.
5. See Also DBLSPACE.SYS

DBLSPACE.SYS

Device driver that activates a compressed drive: DBLSPACE.SYS determines the final memory location of DBLSPACE.BIN, which provides access to the compressed drives. *Many problems have been reported with the DOS 6.0 version of this program. USE WITH CAUTION or not at all, you could lose data on your drive!* New in DOS Version 6.0 (DANGER); Removed from DOS Version 6.22.

Syntax (double underlined is optional):

DEVICE = <u>Drive:\Path\</u> DBLSPACE.SYS <u>/ Move / Nohma</u>

Examples: DEVICE = C:\DBLSPACE.SYS

It may also be loaded high using:
    DEVICEHIGH = C:\DBLSPACE.SYS / Move

Syntax Options:

Drive:\ Path . . .	Drive and Path of the DBLSPACE.SYS
/ Move.	Moves the DBLSPACE.BIN file to a different location in memory. By default it is loaded at the top of conventional memory. /Move moves it to the bottom of conventional memory. Note that if DEVICEHIGH is used, it can be moved to upper memory, thereby freeing up conventional memory.
/ Nohma	Tells DBLSPACE.SYS not to move DBLSPACE.BIN into high memory.

Command Type and Version:

CONFIG.SYS command; Introduced with Ver 6.0

Removed with Ver. 6.2, revision2, and replaced by DRVSPACE

Notes:

1. DBLSPACE can be run as a menu driven utility or with the command line switches listed under Syntax Options.
2. DBLSPACE.SYS is automatically inserted into CONFIG.SYS when the DBLSPACE.EXE installation program is run.
3. See also DBLSPACE.EXE and DEVICEHIGH.

DEBUG.EXE

Starts a debugging program: Debug is a program that provides a testing environment for binary and executable programs, i.e. all programs that have **.EXE** or **.COM** extensions . It is also commonly used to run executable programs that are in memory, such as a hard drive's setup program stored in ROM on a hard drive controller. The full use of DEBUG is beyond the scope of this book. Refer to books such as Microsoft's *DOS Manuals* or PC Magazine's *DOS Power Tools*.

Syntax (double underlined is optional):

There are two methods of starting DEBUG.

Method 1:

   DEBUG Drive:\Path\   Filename   Parameter

Method 2:

   DEBUG

Examples:
Method 1:   DEBUG   C:\test.exe
Method 2:   DEBUG   (run in command line mode)

Syntax Options:
Method 1:
   Drive:\Path . . . . Drive and Path of the executable *Filename* to be tested.
   Filename. . . . . . . Name of executable file to be tested.
   Parameter. . . . . . Command line information needed by *Filename*.
Method 2:
   Debug. . . . . Starts DEBUG in the command line mode where debug commands are given at the DEBUG hyphen prompt (–).

Command Type and Version:
   External command; Introduced with Ver 1.0
Debug Commands for Method 2:
Case makes no difference; *address* and *range* is in hex
   ? . . . . Display list of all DEBUG commands.
   A *address.* . . . . . Assemble 8086/8087/8088 mnemonics directly into memory at *address* (hex).
   C *range address* Compares contents of two memory blocks. *range* is the starting and ending address or starting address and length of Block 1 and *address* is the starting address of Block 2.

D range . . . . Dump (display) contents of memory with starting and ending addresses of *range*.

E address data . Enter data into memory starting at *address*. *data* is entered into successive bytes of memory.

F range data . . . Fill memory with *data* (hex or ASCII) in starting and ending addresses or starting address & length defined by *range*.

G=address bkp . Run program in memory starting at *address*. *bkp* defines 1 to 10 temporary breakpoints.

H hex1 hex2 . . . Does hexadecimal math on *hex1* & *hex2*. Two results are returned, first the sum of *hex1* and *hex2*; second, *hex1* minus *hex2*.

I port . . . . Read (input) & display 1 byte from *port*.

L address drive:start number . . . . . Load a file or specific drive sectors into memory. *address* is the memory location you want to load to. *drive* contains the sectors to be read. *start* is the hex value of the first sector to be read. *number* is the number of consecutive sectors to load.

M range address . . . Copies memory contents from the starting and ending address or starting address and length of *range*. *address* is the starting address of the destination.

N d:\path\file parameters . . . . Name the *drive:\path\filename* of an executable file for Debug *L* or *W*. Also used to specify *parameters* for the executable file. *N* by itself clears the current specification.

O port data . . . . Output *data* to a *port* (by address).

P=address value Run a loop, string instruction,subroutine, or software interrupt starting at *address* and for *value* number of instructions.

Q. . . . . Stop DEBUG without saving the file being tested. Returns to DOS.

R register. . . . . . Display or alter CPU (central processing units) *register*. *R* by itself displays contents of all registers.

S range data . . . Search for *data* at the beginning and ending address of *range*.

T=address value Trace instructions starting at *address* and for *value* number of instructions.

U range . . . . Unassemble code at the start & end address or start address & length of *range*.

W address drive:start number . . . . Write a file or specific drive sectors into memory. *address* is the memory location you want to write to. *drive* contains the sectors to be written. *start* is the hex value of the first sector to be written. *number* is the number of consecutive sectors to write.

XA count . . . . . . Allocate count number of 16k expanded memory pages.

XD handle . . . . . Deallocate a handle to expanded memory

XM Lpage Ppage handle . . . . Map a *Lpage* logical page of expanded
memory belonging to *handle*, to a *Ppage* physical page of
expanded memory.

XS. . . . . Display status info of expanded memory.

**DEBUG ERROR MESSAGES: BF=Bad Flag; BP=Too many breakpoints;
BR=Bad Register; DF=Double Flag**

DEFRAG.EXE

*Reorganizes or defragments a disk in order to optimize disk drive perfor-
mance.* New is DOS Version 6.0

Syntax (double underlined is optional):

DEFRAG Drive: /F /U /S:order /B /Skiphigh /LCD /BW
/GØ /A /H

Examples: DEFRAG C: /U /B

Syntax Options:

Drive:	Drive letter to be defragmented.
/ F	Insures that no empty disk space remains between files.
/ U	Leaves empty space, if any, between files.
/ S:order	Sort files in a specific sort *"order"*.
	N . . . . . In alphabetic order by name
	-N . . . . In reverse alphabetic name order
	E . . . . . In alphabetic order by extension
	-E . . . . In reverse alphabetic order by extension
	D . . . . . By date & time, earliest first
	-D . . . . By date & time, latest first
	S . . . . . By size, smallest first
	-S . . . . By size, largest first
/ B	Reboot system after DEFRAG is done.
/ Skiphigh	Load DEFRAG into conventional memory, instead of the default upper memory
/ LCD	Start DEFRAG in LCD color scheme mode.
/ BW	Start DEFRAG in black & white color mode.
/ GØ	Disable graphics mouse and character set.
/ A	Start DEFRAG in Automatic mode.
/ H	Moves hidden files.

Command Type and Version:

External command; Network; Introduced with Ver 6.0

Notes:

1. Do not use DEFRAG while Windows is running.

2. DEFRAG exit codes (ERRORLEVEL parameter) are:
   0   Successful deframentation.
   1   Internal error.

2	No free clusters, DEFRAG needs at least 1 free cluster.
3	Process aborted with CTRL+C by user.
4	General error.
5	Error occurred while reading a cluster.
6	Error occurred while writing a cluster.
7	Allocation error, correct using SCANDISK.
8	Memory error.
9	Insufficient memory for defragmentation.

DEL or ERASE

Delete or Erase: Deletes specified files from a directory.

Syntax (double underlined is optional):

DEL <u><u>Drive:\Path\</u></u> Filename <u><u>/p</u></u>

Examples: DEL *.*
           DEL *.exe
           DEL C:\budget\1990 /p
           ERASE C:\Bin*.dbf

Syntax Options:

Drive: . . . . Drive letter containing \Path
\Path . . . . Subdirectory containing \Filename
\Filename . . . . . Filename(s) to be deleted.
/P . . . . Screen prompts user for confirmation of the file(s) to be deleted.

Command Type and Version:

Internal command; Network; Introduced with Ver 1.0

Notes:

1. Use of wildcards * and ? is allowed. Use DEL *.* with caution, it will delete all files in the current directory. If you happen to be in the root directory of your boot drive when DEL *.* is used, COMMAND.COM,
   AUTOEXEC.BAT, CONFIG.SYS, etc will be deleted and the system will
   probably not start.
2. Files may be UNDELETED in DOS Versions 5.0, 6.0, and 6.2x..
3. See also RMDIR, MIRROR, and UNDELETE.

DELOLDOS.EXE

Directs DOS to delete the OLD_DOS directory: During setup (installation)
DOS moves any previous DOS version files to a directory called OLD_DOS.
The DELOLDOS command deletes the OLD_DOS directory and all contained
files. Removed from DOS Version 6.2

Syntax:

DELOLDOS

Examples: deloldos

Syntax options: None
Command Type and Version:

External command, Introduced Ver 6.0. Removed 6.2

Notes:
1. Deloldos should be the last step in the installation process for DOS Ver 6.0. When finished, DELOLDOS also deletes itself!

DELTREE.EXE

Deletes a directory and all the files and subdirectories that are in it: Exercise caution when using this command. New in DOS Version 6.0

Syntax (double underlined is optional):

DELTREE / Y Drive:\Path\Filename

Examples:　　DELTREE / Y A:*.*
　　　　　　　DELTREE / Y C:\DATA

Syntax Options:
Drive: . . . . Drive letter containing \Path
\ *Path* . . . . Subdirectory containing \Filename
\ *Filename*. . . . . Filename(s) to be deleted.
/ Y. . . . . Completes DELTREE without first prompting for confirmation of the deletion. Don't use this switch if you can avoid it.

Command Type and Version:
External command; Network; Introduced with Ver 6.0

Notes:
1. If a filename is not specified, all files and subdirectories in the Drive:\Path are deleted.
2. Wild card are supported in the filenames.
3. Attributes such as read only, system and hidden are ignored when a filename is specified.
4. See also DEL and RMDIR.

DEVICE

Loads a device driver into memory: Device drivers are loaded by way of CONFIG.SYS.

Syntax (double underlined is optional):

DEVICE = Drive:\Path\ Filename Parameters

Examples:　　DEVICE = C:\Dos\Himem.sys
　　　　　　　DEVICE = Smartdrv.sys 1024 512

Syntax Options:
Drive:\Path . . . . Drive and directory(s) containing *Filename*.
\Filename . . . . . Driver to be loaded.
Parameters . . . . Switches and/or parameters needed by the device driver.

Command Type and Version:
CONFIG.SYS command; Introduced with Ver 2.0

Notes:

1. Standard installable device drivers are: ANSI.SYS, DISPLAY.SYS, DRIVER.SYS, EGA.SYS, PRINTER.SYS, RAMDRIVE.SYS, EMM386.EXE, HIMEM.SYS, and SMARTDRV.SYS. SMARTDRV.SYS is in DOS 5.0 only, SMARTDRV.EXE replaced it first in Windows and then in DOS 6. Other device drivers, such as SETVER and DBLSPACE or DRVSPACE may also be loaded.

2. COUNTRY.SYS and KEYBOARD.SYS are files, not device drivers Do not try to load either of these files using the DEVICE command or your system will lock up and DOS will not be able to restart.

3. When new devices are purchased, such as a mouse or scanner,you will usually receive device driver software. Use DEVICE to install drivers, make certain that device driver is in the specified directory

4. Install third party console drivers before DISPLAY.SYS.

5. See also DEVICEHIGH.

DEVICEHIGH

Load a device driver into upper memory: After DOS=umb and HIMEM.SYS have been loaded in CONFIG.SYS, DEVICEHIGH makes it possible to load device drivers into the upper memory area. Loading devices high will free up conventional memory for other programs.

Syntax (double underlined is optional):

DEVICEHIGH = Drive:\Path\ Filename dswitch

or

DEVICEHIGH SIZE=hexsize Drive:\Path \Filename dswitch

The following version was introduced in DOS Version 6.0
DEVICEHIGH /L:(see below) / S Drive:\Path \Filename dswitch

Examples: DEVICEHIGH = C:\Filename.sys
              DEVICEHIGH SIZE=FF C:\Filename.sys

Syntax Options:

Drive:\Path . . . . Drive and Path of driver to be loaded high.
Filename. . . . . . . Device driver to be loaded high.
dswitch . . . . Command line switches required by the device driver being loaded.
SIZE= *hexsize* . Minimum number of bytes (in hex) that must be available for DEVICEHIGH to try to load a driver in high memory. Ver 5
/ L:*region1[,minsize1][;region2[,minsize2]* . . . (DOS Version 6.0)
              This switch specfies one or more memory regions into which to load a device driver. Normally, DOS loads the driver into the largest free UMB. / L allows a specific re-

gion to be selected. See your DOS manual for detailed information on using this switch.

/ S . . . . Use / S only in conjunction with / L. (DOS Version 6.0) / S shrinks the UMB to its minimum size while a driver is loading and therefore makes the most efficient use of memory.

Command Type and Version:
CONFIG.SYS command; Introduced with Ver 5.0
Updated with different switches in Ver 6.0

Notes:
1. DOS=umb and HIMEM.SYS must be loaded before DEVICE-HIGH in order to function. The following is typical in CONFIG.SYS:

    DEVICE = C:\HIMEM.SYS
    DOS = umb
    DEVICE = C:\DOS\EMM386.EXE
    DEVICEHIGH = C:\Filename.sys

As the example shows, EMM386.EXE or a comparable third-party product must be loaded before DEVICEHIGH will work. See DOS for more information.

2. If the driver being loaded high requires more high memory than is available, the system may lock-up. Use SIZE= to specify the memory required by the driver, after determining how much memory the driver normally takes by using MEM /DEBUG.
3. See also DOS, LOADHIGH, HIMEM.SYS and EMM386.
4. In MS-DOS Ver 6.0, see also MEMMAKER.

DIR

Directory: Displays the list of files and subdirectories within the current or a designated directory.

Syntax (double underlined is optional):

DIR Drive:\Path\Filename /p /w /a:attrib / o:sort /s /b /L /c (hd)

Examples: DIR or DIR *.* (wild cards are allowed)
              DIR *.exe /p

Syntax Options:

Drive:\Path . . . . Drive and subdirectory to be listed
\Filename . . . . . File name(s) and/or extension to display.
/ p . . . . Displays one screen of information, then pauses until any key is pressed.
/ w. . . . . Displays a wide screen list of files and subdirectories, but the file creation date & time, file size, and <DIR> subdirectory indicator are not shown.
/ a : attrib . . . . . Displays only files with *attrib* attributes: h=hidden, –h=not hidden, s=system, –s=not system, d=directories, –d=files,

---

a=files ready for archive, –a=files not changed, r=read only, –r=not read only. Introduced with Ver 5.0

/ o : sort. . . . . . . Displays by *sort* order: n=alphabetic by name, –n=reverse alphabetic, e=alphabetic by extension, –e=reverse extension alphabetic, d=earliest date/time 1st, –d=latest date/time 1st, s=smallest first, –s=largest 1st, g=group directories before files, –g=group directories after. Introduced with Ver 5.0

In DOS Ver 6.0, c=compression ratio (least compressed first), -c=compression ratio (most compressed first)

/ s . . . . Show all occurrences in both the current directory and all subdirectories below it. Introduced with Ver 5.0

/ b . . . . Displays directory 1 line at a time. Ver 5

/ L . . . . Displays unsorted names in lowercase. Introduced with Ver 5.0

/ c (hd) . . . . . . *Displays compression ratio. (DOS Version 6.0) The optional* (hd) switch displays compression ratio of DBLSPACE files based on cluster size of host drive. If / w or / b switches are used, / c (hd) is ignored.

Command Type and Version:
Internal command; Network; Introduced with Ver 1.0

Notes:
1. The date and time formats displayed by the *DIR* command will vary, depend-ing on which COUNTRY code is in CONFIG.SYS.
2. Place SET DIRCMD=/o /p in your Autoexec.bat file to force DIR to always sort and paginate the directory listing.

DISKCOMP.COM

Compares Disks: Compares the contents of the floppy disk in the Source drive to the contents of the floppy disk in the Target drive.

Syntax (double underlined is optional):

DISKCOMP <u>Source: Target: /1 /8</u>

Examples:
      DISKCOMP (first floppy disk drive is used)
      DISKCOMP A: B: /1

Syntax Options:
Source: . . . . Source drive containing one of the floppy disks to be compared.
Target: . . . . Target drive containing the other disk to be compared.
/ 1 . . . . Compares only the first side of disks.
/ 8 . . . . Compares first 8 sectors per track.

Command Type and Version:

External command; Not for network.
Introduced with Ver 1.0

Notes:

1. DISKCOMP must be used with identical size floppy disks. It cannot be used with a hard drive.
2. If a target drive is not specified, DISKCOMP uses the current drive.
3. DISKCOMP prompts you when to swap disks as necessary.
4. DISKCOMP cannot compare double-sided disk with single-sided disk, or double-density disk with high-density disk.
5. Do not use DISKCOMP on a drive that is affected by the ASSIGN, JOIN, or SUBST commands or DISKCOMP will display an error message. Do not use DISKCOMP on a network drive.
6. When using DISKCOMP to compare a disk made with the COPY command, although it is duplicate information, COPY may not put the information in the same location on the target disk and DISKCOMP will display an error message.
7. DISKCOMP exit codes are:
   - 0   Disks are the same.
   - 1   Disks are different.
   - 2   Process aborted with CTRL+C by user.
   - 3   Critical error.
   - 4   Initialization error.

DISKCOPY.COM

Copies disks: Copies entire contents of the disk (including the DOS system files) in the source drive onto the disk in the target drive.

Syntax (double underlined is optional):

DISKCOPY Source: Target: /1 / v /m

Examples:
     DISKCOPY   (current drive must be A: or B:)
     DISKCOPY A: B: /1
     DISKCOPY A: A: (prompts to change disks)

Syntax Options:

Source: . . . . The floppy disk to be copied.
Target: . . . . The floppy disk to be copied to.
/1 . . . . Copies one side of disk.
/ v . . . . Verifies that information is correctly copied.
                 Introduced with Ver 5.0
/ m   . . . . Forces the use of only conventional memory for interim storage. Introduced in DOS Version 6.2

Command Type and Version:

External command; Not for networks; Introduced Ver 1.0

Notes:

1. DISKCOPY must be used with identical size floppy disks only. It will not work with a hard disk.
2. If you do not enter a target drive, DOS uses the default drive as the target drive and DISKCOPY will overwrite all information that is on the target disk.
3. DISKCOPY will duplicate disk fragmentation from the source disk. Using the COPY command or the XCOPY command will give you a new disk that will be in sequential order and will not be fragmented.
4. DISKCOPY works only with removable (i.e. floppy) uncompressed disks.
5. DISKCOPY exit codes (ERRORLEVEL parameter) are:
   0   Successful copy.
   1   Nonfatal read/write error.
   2   Process aborted with CTRL+C by user.
   3   Critical error.
   4   Initialization error.

DISPLAY.SYS

Driver that supports code page switching for the display: Supported types include Mono, CGA, EGA (includes VGA), and LCD.

Syntax (double underlined is optional):

DEVICE = <u>Drive:\Path\</u> DISPLAY.SYS <u>CON:=(type, hwcp, (n,m))</u>

Examples:

    DEVICE = DISPLAY.SYS con:=(ega,437,2)

Syntax Options:

Drive:\Path . . . . Drive & directory containing DISPLAY.SYS
type . . . . Type of display adapter
hwcp . . . . The number assigned to a particular code page.
                    Choices are as follows:
                    437 . . . . United States
                    850 . . . . Multilingual (Latin I)
                    852 . . . . Slavic (Latin II)
                    860 . . . . Portuguese
                    863 . . . . Canadian-French
                    865 . . . . Nordic
n . . . . Number of code pages supported by the hardware: Range is 0 through 6, max for EGA is 6, LCD is 1.
m . . . . Number of subfonts supported by the hardware. Default=2 for EGA, 1 if LCD. If the *m* option is omitted, the parentheses around *n,m* can be omitted.

Command Type and Version:

CONFIG.SYS command; Introduced with Ver 3.3

Notes:

1. Code-page switching has no effect with monochrome and CGA display adapters.

2. If 3rd party console drivers are installed, make sure they are installed be-fore DISPLAY.SYS.

DOS

Forces DOS to keep a link with the upper memory area or to load itself into high memory: HIMEM.SYS must be loaded before DOS= can be used. DOS is useful in that it is part of the program set that frees up conventional memory.

Syntax (double underlined is optional):

DOS = high or low , umb or noumb

or

DOS = high or low, umb or noumb

Examples: DOS = high
              DOS = umb
              DOS = high, umb   or   DOS = umb, high

Syntax Options:

high . . . . Loads a portion of DOS into high memory.
low . . . . Forces DOS to stay in conventional mem.
umb . . . . Forces DOS to maintain link between high (upper) memory
                        & conventional memory
noumb . . . . Breaks the link between upper memory
                        and conventional memory.

Command Type and Version:

CONFIG.SYS command: Introduced with Ver 5.0

Notes:

1. See also DEVICEHIGH and LOADHIGH.
2. UMB must be used in order to load either DOS or drivers into upper memory. EMM386.EXE or a comparable third party product must be loaded and configured in order to provide upper memory blocks from ex-tended memory for DOS=UMB to work.
3. DOS can be placed anywhere in the CONFIG.SYS file.
4. UMB or NOUMB can be combined with HIGH or LOW in the same DOS = command line, see the example above.

DOSKEY.COM

Starts the DOSKEY program, which allows the user to edit command lines, create macros, and recall DOS commands:

Syntax (double underlined is optional):

DOSKEY /reinstall /bufsize=nnn /macros /history /insert
        /overstrike /macroname=text

Examples: DOSKEY   (start DOSKEY with defaults)
       DOSKEY / history > special.bat

Syntax Options:

/ reinstall . . . . . . Installs DOSKEY again. If DOSKEY is currently running, this command clears the buffer.

/ bufsize=nnn . . Sets the size of the buffer where DOSKEY store commands. Default=512 bytes, minimum=256 bytes.

/ macros or */m* . . Displays the current list of DOSKEY macros.

/ history or */h* . . Displays a list of all commands that were stored in memory.

/ insert . . . . Sets typing to insert mode (text is not overwritten as typing occurs)

/ overstrike . . . . Sets typing to overstrike mode (text <u>is</u> overwritten as typing occurs)

/ macroname=. . Name of file created to hold *text* macro.

text . . . . The commands and text to be recorded in the file named *macroname*.

Command Type and Version:

External command; Network; Introduced with Ver 5.0

Notes:

1. */macros* and */history* can be used with DOS redirection to a file. e.g. DOSKEY /macros > Macro.txt creates a text file list of macros.

2. DOSKEY is a very powerful program, see the Microsoft *Users Guide and Reference* for detailed comments and examples.

When DOSKEY is on, the following can be used to recall/edit commands from its command buffer:

Up Arrow . . . . . Recall command issued before currently displayed command.

Down Arrow. . . Recall command issued after the currently displayed command.

Page Up . . . . . Recall oldest command in current session.

Page Down . . . Recall most recent command in current session.

Left Arrow . . . . Moves cursor left one character.

Right Arrow . . . Moves cursor right one character.

Ctrl+Left Arrow Moves cursor left one word.

*Ctrl+Rght Arrow*Moves cursor right one word.

Home . . . . Moves cursor to start of line.

End . . . . Moves cursor to end of line.

Esc . . . . Clears the display command line.

F1 . . . . Copy one character from last command buffer to the command line.

F2 . . . . Look forward for the next key typed after pressing F2.

F3 . . . . Copies the remainder of the current template line at the current cursor position to the command line.

F4 . . . . Delete all characters of the current temp late line, up to but not including the character pressed after F4 is pressed

F5	Copy current line to template and clear command line
F6	Put Ctrl+Z (end of line marker) at the end of the current line.
F7	Displays all commands and numbers, beginning with the oldest, currently stored in the command buffer.
Alt+F7	Delete all commands in command buffer.
F8	Locate the most recently used command in the buffer that begins with a specific character(s). At the DOS prompt, simply type those beginning characters and then press *F8*.
F9	Display the command associated with a specific command line number in buffer.
Alt+F10	Delete all macros.

The following are special codes that can be used in creating macros. Code letters shown can be used in either upper or lower case.

$G	Redirect output (same as >) to a device other than the screen. e.g. a printer.
GG	Append output data (same as >>) to the end of a file instead of overwriting file.
$L	Redirect input (same as <) to read from a device other than the keyboard.
$B	Send output from macro to another command (same as I).
$T	Used to separate commands in either a macro or at the DOSKEY command line.
$$	Used to specify the $ character
$1 to *$9*	Batch parameters (similar to *%1*) for passing command line info to the macro when it is run.
$ *	A replaceable parameter similar to *$1* to *$9*, except that everything that is typed on the command line after *macroname* is substituted for the *$ ** in the macro.

Macros are run by simply typing the *macroname* at the DOS prompt, followed by any parameter info such as *$1* or *$**. If a macro is created that has the same name as a normal DOS command, the DOS command is started by typing a space and then the command name, whereas with the macro, simply type the *macroname* without a space preceding it.

DOSSHELL.COM & EXE

Starts the DOS graphical user interface shell:
Syntax (double underlined is optional):

DOSSHELL /t or /g :Res n /b

Examples: DOSSHELL / t
              DOSSHELL / g:m *or* DOSSHELL / g /b

Syntax Options:

/t	Directs DOSSHELL to start in text mode.
/g	Directs DOSSHELL to start in graphics mode
:Res	Screen resolution class. *l* (lowercase L) for Low, *m* for medium and *h* for high resolution.
n	If there is more than one resolution available in the *Res* category, *n* provides additional information concerning which category to use.*n* is hardware dependent.
/b	Starts DOSSHELL in black & white mode or the state /t or /g is in.

Command Type and Version:

External command; Network; Introduced with Ver 4.0

Notes:

1. If DOSSHELL has already been started, the screen resolution can be changed from the options menu.
2. DOSSHELL is very useful for such tasks as renaming subdirectories.

DRIVER.SYS

Defines a logical drive from an existing physical drive: A logical drive is simply a drive letter used to point to the actual physical drive. The new drive letter established by DRIVER.SYS is the next highest drive letter above the system's highest current drive.

Syntax (double underlined is optional):

DEVICE = Drive:\Path\ DRIVER.SYS /d:number /c / f:factor
                        /h:heads /s:sectors / t:tracks

Examples:

    DEVICE=C:\dos\driver.sys /d:1 /f:2 /h:2 /s:9 /t:80
    (above configures a 3.5" 720k floppy drive, if the last hard drive was drive
    E:, then the 3.5 inch would be designated as drive F:)

Syntax Options:

Drive:	Drive letter containing *Path*
Path	Subdirectory containing *DRIVER.SYS*
/d: number.	Specifies physical drive number. Values must be in the range of 0 to 127. Normally, Drive A=0, Drive B=1, etc.

/c	Specifies that the driver will be able to tell tell that the floppy disk drive door is open.
/ f: factor	Specifies type of drive. Default value= 2

Factor .	Description
0	160kb/180kb or 320kb/360kb
1	1.2 megabyte (Mb)
2	720kb (3.5 in. disk)
7	1.44Mb (3.5 in. disk)
9	2.88Mb (3.5 in.disk)

/h: heads	Specifies max. number of heads. Value for **heads** must be in the 1 to 99 range.
/s: sectors	Number of sectors per track, ranging in value from 1 to 99. The default varies according to the /f factor selected above. Normal values are 360kb and 720kb = 9 sectors, 1.44 meg = 18 sectors, 1.2 meg = 15 sectors and 2.8 meg = 36 sectors.
/t: tracks	Number of tracks per side on the block device, ranging from 1 to 999. Default values vary according to the /f factor selected above. Normal values are 360kb = 40 tracks, 720kb, 1.44 meg, and 1.2 meg = 80 tracks.

Command Type and Version:
CONFIG.SYS command; Introduced with Ver 3.2

Notes:
1. DRIVER.SYS is commonly used to set up a 3.5 inch floppy drive on a system that does not support 3.5 inch drives directly. Setting up external 3.5 inch drives is also common.
2. See also the DRIVEPARM command, it is used to modify existing parameters of a physical device.
3. DRIVER.SYS can not be used to define hard drives. If hard drive logical drive assignments need to be changed, see the SUBST command.
4. If two DRIVER.SYS command lines are used for the same physical drive, then two logical drive letters will be assigned to the single physical drive.
5. XT class systems, with standard floppy controllers, will still need either a special driver or special controller in order to recognize a 1.44 or 2.8 Mb 3.5 inch floppy or 1.2 Mb 5-1/4 inch floppy.

DRIVPARM

Defines block device parameters: DRIVPARM allows the default or original device driver settings to be overridden when DOS is started.

Syntax (double underlined is optional):

DRIVPARM = /d:number /c / f:factor /h:heads / i / n
           /s:sectors / t:tracks

Examples: DRIVPARM=/d:1 /c /f:2 /h:2 /s:9 /t:80
             (above configures a 3.5" 720k floppy drive)

Syntax Options:

/d: number	Specifies physical drive number. Numbers must be in the range of 0 to 255. Normally, Drive A=0, Drive B=1, etc.
/c	Specifies that the driver will be able to tell that the floppy disk drive door is open.
/f: factor	Specifies type of drive. Default value= 2

Factor	Description
0	160K/180K or 320K/360
1	1.2 megabyte (MB)
2	720K (3.5 in. disk)
5	Hard disk
6	Tape
7	1.44MB (3.5 in. disk)
8	Read/write optical disk
9	2.88MB (3.5 in.disk)

/h: heads	Specifies max. number of heads. Value for **heads** must be in the 1 to 99 range.
/i	In DOS Version 4, specifies an electronically-compatible 3.5 in. floppy disk drive. Use the / i switch if the ROM BIOS does not support 3.5 in. floppy disk drives.
/n	Non-removable block device.
/s: sectors	Number of sectors per track, ranging in value from 1 to 99. The default varies according to the /f factor selected above. Normal values are 360kb and 720kb = 9 sectors, 1.44 Mb = 18 sectors, 1.2 Mb = 15 sectors and 2.8 Mb = 36 sectors.
/t: tracks	Number of tracks per side on the block device, ranging from 1 to 999. Default values vary according to the /f factor selected above. Normal values are 360kb = 40 tracks, 720kb, 1.44 Mb, and 1.2 Mb = 80 tracks.

Command Type and Version:

CONFIG.SYS command; Introduced with Ver 3.2

Notes:

1. DRIVPARM is particularly useful in configuring 3.5 inch floppy drives.
2. Settings in DRIVPARM will override any settings specified for a device prior to the DRIVPARM command line.
3. Although DRIVPARM is listed as an option in DOS Ver 3.3, the command will not function in that version.
4. DRIVPARM does not create new logical drives, it can only modify existing physical drive parameters.
5. See also DRIVER.SYS

DRVBOOT.BAT

Creates a bootable DRVSPACE floppy disk: (New in DOS Ver 6.22)

Syntax:

DRVBOOT drive1:

Example: drvboot a:

Syntax options:

drive1: . . . . Drive containing floppy disk to be compressed.

Command Type and Version:

External command, Introduced with Ver 6.22.
Available in the MS-DOS 6.22 Supplemental Disks.

Notes:

1. DRVBOOT works only on high-density floppy disks (1.44 or 1.2 MB).
2. DRVSPACE must be installed prior to using DRVBOOT.

DRVSPACE.EXE

Directs DOS to compress hard drives or floppy disks or configure compressed files: (New in DOS Ver 6.22)

Syntax (double underlined is optional):

DRVSPACE (starts the interactive DriveSpace program)

Examples: DRVSPACE
               or
               DRVSPACE / task   (executes task command without
                              starting the DriveSpace program)

Example: DRVSPACE /create c: /newdrive=d: /reserve=50

Syntax for Task Command Options:

/compress drive1: /newdrive=drive2 /reserve=size /f

Directs DOS to compress files on an existing disk (hard drive, floppy, or other removable media).

    drive1: . . . . Specifies existing drive to compress.

    /compress or /com . . . . Compresses the floppy disk or hard drive specified by drive1:.

    /newdrive=drive2: or */new* ..Identifies the drive letter for the uncompressed drive. After compression, the drive will contain an existing compressed drive (drive1:) and a new uncompressed drive (newdrive).

    /reserve=size or */res* ....Size, in megabytes, of space to leave uncompressed. Space will be located on drive2:.

/f ....Suppresses display of the final DriveSpace screen and returns to command prompt.

/create drive1: /newdrive=drive2 /reserve=size /size=size
Directs DOS to create a new compressed drive in free space on an uncompressed drive. The new compressed drive will provide more storage
space than the amount of uncompressed storage it uses.

drive1:...........Specifies uncompressed existing drive containing space
to create new drive.

/create...........or /cr Creates a new compressed drive in free space on
the uncompressed drive specified by drive1:.

/newdrive=drive2: or /n.......Identifies the drive letter for the new compressed drive.

/reserve=size or /re .....Size, in megabytes, of space to leave uncompressed. Space will be located n drive2:. Can not use with
/size=size.

/size=size or /si ....Total size, in megabytes, of the compressed
volume file. Can not use with /reserve=size.

/defragment /f drive1:
Directs DOS to defragment the specified compressed drive.

drive1:...........Specifies existing compressed drive to defragment.

/defragment or def.......Defragments specified compressed drive.

/f ....Specifies full defragmentation of specified drive.

/delete drive1:
Directs DOS to delete selected compressed drive and erase associated
volume file.

drive1:...........Specifies drive to be deleted. Will not allow deletion of
drive c:.

/delete or /del ....Deletes the specified drive.

/format drive1:
Directs DOS to format selected compressed drive. Caution-A com-
pressed drive can not be unformatted after formatting using DRVSPACE
/FORMAT.

drive1:...........Specifies drive to be formated. Will not allow formatting of
drive c:.

/format or /f ...Formats the specified drive.

/info drive1:
Directs DOS to display information about selected compressed drive. Information includes free and unused space, name of compressed volume
file, and estimated and actual compression ratios. Command may be
used while Windows is running.

drive1:...........Specifies drive for which information is desired.

/format or /f ...Displays information for the specified drive.

/list

Directs DOS to list and describe, in brief terms, all available drives, except network and CD-ROM drives.

/list or /li ....Displays a list of all system drives, except CD-ROM or network drives.

/mount=nnn drive1: /newdrive=drive2

Directs DOS to create a reference between a compressed volume file (CVF) and a drive letter. DRVSPACE normally mounts compressed volume files automatically.

drive1: ....Specifies an existing drive containing the compressed volume file to be mounted. A drive must be specified.

/mount=ext or /mo=ext ....Directs DOS to mount the compressed volume file with the filename extension specified by ext.

/newdrive=drive2: or /new ..Identifies the drive letter for the new drive.

/ratio=r.r drive1: /all

Directs DOS to change the estimated compression ratio of the specified compressed drive. DOS uses the ratio to estimate the amount of free space the drive contains.

drive1: ....Specifies existing compressed drive to defragment.

/ratio=r.r or /ra=r.r........Changes the ratio of specified compressed drive. Ratios are allowed in the range from 1.0 to 16.0. If not specified, DOS sets the ratio to the average compression ratio for all compressed files on the drive.

/all ....Specifies a change of all mounted compressed drives. Do not use if a drive is specified using drive1.

/size=size1 /reserve=size2 drive1:

Directs DOS to enlarge or reduce the current size of a compressed drive. The command is used to free-up space on a drive or enlarge a compressed drive if ample free space is available.

drive1: ....Specifies the drive containing to be resized

/size=size1 or /si=size1 ......Changes the size of the drive specified by drive1: to size1 in megabytes. Can not be used with /reserve=size2.If neither switch is used, DOS will makes the compressed drive as small as possible.

/reserve=size2 or /res=size2......Size, in megabytes, of space to leave uncompressed. Can not use with /size=size1.

/uncompress drive1:

Directs DOS to uncompress files on an existing disk (hard drive, floppy, or other removable media). Uncompressing the last mounted drive also removes DRVSPACE.BIN from memory.

drive1: ....Specifies drive to uncompress.

/uncompress ....Uncompresses the floppy disk or hard drive specified
                    by drive1:

/unmount drive1:

Directs DOS to eliminate a previous reference between a compressed
volume file (CVF) and the specified drive. The unmounted drive is unavailable until again mounted. Drive c: can not be unmounted.

drive1: ....Specifies the drive to be unmounted. If no drive is speci-
                    fied DRVSPACE unmounts the current drive.
/unmount.......Directs DOS to unmount the specified drive.

Command Type and Version:
External command, Interactive
Introduced in MS-DOS Version 6.2, Revision 2.

Notes:
1. DRVSPACE is the Microsoft DOS Ver 6.2, Revision 2, replacement for
   DBLSPACE.
2. DRVSPACE requires 33Kb of memory to install.
3. DRVSPACE may slow down the speed of a system with a slow CPU.

DRVSPACE.SYS

*Device driver which directs DOS to move DRVSPACE.BIN to its final memory
location:* DRVSPACE.BIN provides DOS with access to compressed files. When
the computer is started, DOS loads DRVSPACE.BIN at the top of conventional
memory at the same time it loads other operating system functions; that is, prior to
executing the CONFIG.SYS and AUTOEXEC.BAT files. After processing the
CONFIG.SYS file, DOS moves DRVSPACE.BIN to the bottom of conventional
memory. Running DRVSPACE.SETUP adds a command for DRVSPACE.SYS to
the CONFIG.SYS file. New in DOS Version 6.22.

Syntax (double underlined is optional):

DEVICE   = DRVSPACE.SYS /move /nohma

DEVICEHIGH = DRVSPACE.SYS /move /nohma

Examples: DEVICE = DRVSPACE.SYS /move

Syntax Options:
/move . . . . Directs DOS to move DRVSPACE.BIN to its final memory
                        location.
/nohma . . . . Tells DRVSPACE.SYS not to move DRVSPACE.BIN into
                        high memory.

Command Type and Version:
External command, Introduced in Ver 6.2,revision 2.

DVORAK.SYS

Used with KEYB to provide an alternative to the standard QWERTY keyboard layout: New in DOS Version 6.0

Syntax (shaded area optional):

KEYB <u>nn,,drive1:\directory</u> \DVORAK.SYS

Example: KEYB rh,,d:\dos\dvorak.sys

Syntax Options:

drive1: . . . . Drive containing DVORAK.SYS.
\directory . . . . Directory containing DVORAK.SYS.
nn . . . . Designates keyboard configuration.
  dv = two-handed layout
  rh = right-handed layout
  lh = left-handed layout.

Command Type and Version:
  External command, Introduced with MS-DOS Ver 6.0.
  Available in the MS-DOS 6.0, 6.21, & 6.22 Supplemental Disks.

Notes:
1. To return to the U. S. standard keyboard press CTRL+ALT+F1.
2. To return to the Dvorak keyboard layout press CTRL+ALT+F2.

ECHO

Display a message or turn command echo feature on or off: When batch files are run, DOS usually displays (echoes) the name of the program being run to the display. This feature can be turned on or off with the ECHO command.

Syntax (double underlined is optional):

ECHO <u>Message | on | off</u>

Examples: ECHO off   or   ECHO on
              ECHO Enter program name to be run!

Syntax Options:
Message: . . . . . Text to be displayed on screen.
on . . . . Turn display echo on.
off . . . . Turn display echo off.

Command Type and Version:
  Internal and Batch command; Introduced with Ver 2.0

Notes:
1. Use the @ symbol in front of a batch file command in order to turn the screen echo function off.
2. NOTE: in DOS 6.0, ECHO. (with the period) on a command line will output a blank line. ECHO by itself displays ECHO status.

EDIT.COM

Starts MS-DOS Editor: EDIT is a full-screen text editor which can create, save, edit and print ASCII text files.

Syntax (double underlined is optional):

EDIT Drive:\Path \Filename /b /g /h /nohi

Examples: EDIT C:\Autoexec.bat

                EDIT D:\Bin\Test.bat /h

Syntax Options:

Drive:\Path. . . . Location of *Filename*.

\Filename . . . . . Name of ASCII text file to be edited.

/b. . . . . Editor displayed in black and white.

/g. . . . . Provides CGA monitors with the fastest screen update.

/h. . . . . Allows monitor to display maximum number of lines on the screen.

/nohi . . . . Normally, DOS uses a 16 color mode for monitors. This switch enables the use of 8 color monitors.

Command Type and Version:

External command; Network; Introduced with Ver 5.0

Notes:

1. QBASIC.EXE must be in the same directory as EDIT or included in the DOS path. If it is not, EDIT will not function.
2. Shortcut keys that are shown on the bottom line of the screen may not display properly. If this occurs, use the */b* and */nohi* switches.

EDLIN.EXE

Line oriented text editor: Edlin is an editor used to insert, change, copy, move and delete lines of text in an ASCII file. If a full screen editor is required, use EDIT (page 329). 24 lines of text can be displayed on the screen at one time. Removed in DOS Version 6.0

Syntax (double underlined is optional):

EDLIN Drive:\Path\ Filename /b

Examples: EDLIN Test *or* EDLIN C:\Autoexec.bat

Syntax Options:

Drive:\Path . . . . Drive and directory containing the file to be edited.

Filename. . . . . . File to be edited. If Edlin cannot find the file named *Filename*, it will automatically create the file in the specified *Drive:\Path* location.

/b . . . . Causes EDLIN to ignore Ctrl–Z (end of file character).

Command Type and Version:

External command; Network; Introduced with Ver 1.0

Removed from DOS Ver 6.0, use the EDIT command.

Available In the MS-DOS 6.0, 6.21, and 6.22 Supplemental Disks.

Notes:

1. Edlin can handle a maximum of 253 characters per line.
2. A full description of EDLIN is beyond the scope of this book. See a full DOS manual for additional details and instructions.
3. EDLIN uses an asterisk * prompt on a line by itself to ask for a command. If the * occurs after a line number, it indicates that that line number is the current line.

EDLIN Commands: (case doesn't matter)

Command	Description
?	Displays the list of EDLIN commands.
Line	Just typing a number, at the prompt, displays the text contained in that line #.
Ctrl–C	Exits user out of the insert (I) mode.
n A	Append n number of lines into memory from disk. Edlin will load till 75% of available memory is full.
L1,L2,L3,count C . . .	Copy a block of lines. L1=first line to copy, L2=last line to copy, L3=line before which EDLIN is to insert the block, count=number of times to copy.
L1, L2 D	Delete from line L1 to line L2.
E	Write current file to disk and stop EDLIN.
L1 I	Insert lines before line L1. Ctrl-C stops.
L1, L2 L	List (display) lines between L1 and L2.
L1, L2, L3 M . . . or L1,+n,L3 M . . .	Move a block of lines. L1=first line to move, L2=last line to move, L3=line before which EDLIN is to move the block, +n=include the next n lines.
L1, L2 P	Display all or part of the file one full screen of text at a time. L1=first line & L2=last line.
Q	Quit EDLIN without saving the current file to disk. Return to DOS.
L1,L2 ? R S1 S2 S3 . . .	Replace a block of lines with a string. L1=first line to replace, L2=last line to replace, ?=prompt user to confirm replacement, S1=string to be replaced, S2=Ctrl–Z separator, S3=string to replace S1.
L1,L2 ? S S1 . .	Search between L1 first line and L2 last line for string S1. ?=prompt user when string S1 is located.
L1 T D:\Path\Filename . . .	Transfer (merge) contents of a second file from disk into the current edited file. L1=line in current file before which user wants inserted file to be placed. D:\Path\Filename=name and directory location of file to be inserted into current file.
n W	Write n number of lines, starting at the first line, to disk.

EGA.SYS

When using Task Swapper with an EGA monitor, the EGA.SYS command saves and restores the display.

Syntax (double underlined is optional):

DEVICE = <u>Drive\path\</u> EGA.SYS

Examples: DEVICE=C:\Dos\EGA.SYS

Syntax Options:

Drive:\ Path . . . . Specifies the location of the EGA.SYS file.

Command Type and Version:

CONFIG.SYS command; Introduced with Ver 5.0

Notes:

1. To save memory when using a mouse on a system, install EGA.SYS before installing the mouse driver.

EMM386.EXE

Activates or deactivates expanded memory emulator for 80386 and higher systems: EMM386 is both a device driver loaded through CONFIG.SYS and an External command. It also enables or disables support of the Weitek coprocessor.

Syntax (double underlined is optional):

To load EMM386 initially in CONFIG.SYS:

Device= <u>Drive:\Path\</u> EMM386.EXE <u>on *or* off *or*</u>
<u>auto memory min=size w=on *or* w=off mx *or* frame = address</u>
<u>*or* /pmmm pn=address x=mm–nn i=mm–nn b=address</u>
<u>L=minXMS a=altregs h=handles d=nnn ram=mm-nn noems</u>
<u>novcpi highscan verbose win=mm-nn nohi rom=mm-nn</u>
<u>nomovexbda altboot</u>

To use EMM386 as an External command:
EMM386 <u>on *or* off *or* auto w=on *or* w=off /?</u>

Examples: Device=C:\EMM386.EXE noems
EMM386 on   (at DOS prompt)
EMM386   (at DOS prompt to show status)

Syntax Options:

Drive:\Path . . . . . Drive and directory containing EMM386

EMM386 . . . . At the DOS prompt this displays the current status of EMM386.

on . . . . Activates EMM386 driver. (default)

off . . . . Deactivates EMM386 driver.

auto . . . . Places EMM386 driver in auto mode, where expanded memory support is turned on when a program needs expanded memory.

memory . . . . kbytes of memory allocated to EMM386. Default=256, Range=16 to 32768, use multiples of 16. This memory is in addition to low-memory backfilling.

w=on.	Enable Weitek coprocessor support.
w=off.	Disable Weitek coprocessor support.
mx.	Address of page frame. Values for x can be 1 to 14 below. On systems with only 512k of memory, only 10 to 14 can be used.

1=C000 hex	8=DC00 hex
2=C400 hex	9=E000 hex
3=C800 hex	10=8000 hex
4=CC00 hex	11=8400 hex
5=D000 hex	12=8800 hex
6=D400 hex	13=8C00 hex
7=D800 hex	14=9000 hex

frame=*address* .	Specific page-frame segment address for base page. *address* can be C000h to E000h and 8000h to 9000h, in increments of 400h.
/pmmm	Address of page frame. *mmm* can range from C000h to E000h and 8000h to 9000h, in increments of 400h.
pn=mmm.	Specific segment address (*mmm*) of a specific page *n*. *n* can range from 0 to 255. *mmm* can range from 8000h to 9C00h and C000h to EC00h, in increments of 400h.
x=mm–nn	Excludes a range of segment addresses from EMS page use. *mm* and *nn* can both range from A000h to FFFFh, and are rounded off to the nearest 4k. x overrides i when two ranges overlap.
i=mm–nn.	Includes a range of segment addresses for EMS page or RAM use. *mm* and *nn* can both range from A000h to FFFFh, and are rounded off to the nearest 4k. x overrides i when two ranges overlap.
b=*address*	Lowest segment address that can be used for bank swapping of 16k EMS pages. Default=4000h, range=1000h to 4000h.
L=minXMS	Specifies that *minXMS* kbytes of extended memory will remain after EMM386 has been loaded. Default=0
a=*altregs*.	*altregs* number of fast alternate register sets are allocated to EMM386. Default=7, range=0 to 254. Each register uses an additional 400 bytes of memory.
h=*handles*	Number of handles EMM386 can have. Default=64, range=2 to 255.
d=*nnn*	Kbytes of memory reserved for buffered DMA (direct memory access). Default=16, range=16 to 256.
ram	Upper memory and expanded memory access is provided.
noems.	Upper memory access provided but not to expanded memory.
novcpi.	Disables VCPI application support. Used with /noems. DOS Version 6.2
highscan	Directs EMM386 to check availability of upper memory for UMB or EMS windows. DOS Ver 6.2
verbose or v . . .	Directs EMM386 to display error and/or status messages while loading. DOS Ver 6.2
Win=mm-nn . . .	Directs EMM386 to reserve the specified range of segment addresses for Windows. Values of mm and nn are

in the range A000h through FFFh, rounded down to the nearest 4 Kb boundary. The /x switch takes precedence over /win if overlap occurs. The /win switch takes precedence over /ram, /rom, or /i switches if overlap occurs. DOS Version 6.2

nohi. . . . . Forces EMM386 to load into convential memory thus increasing upper memory available for UMBs. DOS Ver 6.2

rom=mm-nn . . . Directs EMM386 to reserve the specified range of segment addresses for shadow RAM. Values of mm and nn are in the range A000h through FFFh, rounded down to the nearest 4 Kb boundary. DOS Ver 6.2

nomovexbda. . . Directs EMM386 to keep extended BIOS data in conventional memory. DOS Ver 6.2

altboot . . . . *Provides an alternate boot sequence for some computers with compatibility problems. Used if computer doesn't recognize Ctrl-Alt-Del. DOS Ver 6*

/ ? . . . . Help with command line switches.

Command Type and Version:

External and CONFIG.SYS command; Introduced with Ver 4.0

Notes:

1. HIMEM.SYS must be loaded before EMM386.EXE is loaded.
2. The .EXE extension of EMM386 <u>must</u> be used to load the driver.
3. The order of switches and parameters is not important.
4. Device=EMM386.EXE must precede DEVICEHIGH commands.
5. If enough memory is not available to set up a 64k page frame, the "Unable to set base address" error message will display.
6. DOS=umb must be used in CONFIG.SYS to provide access to the upper memory block.
7. See also DOS, HIMEM.SYS, DEVICEHIGH, and LOADHIGH.
8. Using EMM386.EXE and the Note 7 commands is a very complicated task. It is strongly recommended that the user spend a great deal of time with Microsoft's *MS-DOS 5.0 User's Guide and Refer.* earning about memory management and system optimization.

EXE2BIN.EXE

Converts an executable file to a binary file: Converting executable files (.EXE extension) to files with a binary format, is only useful to software developers and is of no value to general users. Removed from DOS Ver 6.0

Syntax (double underlined is optional):

EXE2BIN <u>Drive1:\Path1\</u> INfile <u>Drive2:\Path2\</u> OUTfile

Examples: EXE2BIN C:\Test.exe C:\test.bin

Syntax Options:

Drive1:\Path1 . . Drive and directory of input .EXE file.
Drive2:\Path2 . . Drive and directory of output binary file.

INfile . . . . Input .EXE file to be converted.
OUTfile . . . . Output binary file.

Command Type and Version:
External command; Introduced with Ver 1.0
Removed from DOS Ver 6.0
Available in the MS-DOS 6.0, 6.21, & 6.22 Supplemental Disks.

Notes:
1. EXE2BIN is not for the general computer user, only programmers.
2. Default extensions for INfile is .EXE and for OUTfile is .BIN.
3. INfile must have been produced by LINK & must not be packed
4. See also LINK

EXIT

Exits a secondary command processor and returns to the primary processor if one exists.

Syntax:

EXIT

Examples: EXIT

Syntax Options:
No options

Command Type and Version:
Internal; Network; Command processor function;
Introduced with Ver 2.0

Notes:
1. If a secondary command processor is not loaded (or /P is used with COMMAND.COM), the EXIT command will have no effect.
2. See Also COMMAND

EXPAND.EXE

Expands a compressed DOS file: Compressed files are not usable unless exanded. Use EXPAND to retrieve files from DOS installation or update disks.

Syntax (double underlined is optional):

EXPAND <u>Drive:\Path\</u> Filename Destination

Examples:
EXPAND B:\Dos\FIND.EX_ C:\Dos\FIND.EXE

Syntax Options:
Drive:\Path . . . . Specifies location and name of a compressed file to be expanded.
Filename . . . . . . File to be expanded.
Destination . . . . Target location where expanded files are to be placed. Destination can be a drive letter and colon, a filename, a

directory name <u>or</u> a combinaton. A destination filename
can only be used if a single compressed *Filename* is used.

Command Type and Version:

External command; Network; Introduced with Ver 5.0

Notes:

1. Wildcards (* and ?) **cannot** be used.
2. Compressed files, such as installation or update files, have a file extension which ends with an underscore character (_)
3. Although EXPAND is normally used by the DOS 5.0 Upgrade program to install all DOS 5.0 files, you can copy a single compressed file, such as FIND.EX_ , from an upgrade disk to the hard drive and EXPAND it for full use. A complete list of all files and what disk they are on is included in the file named PACKING.LST on upgrade disk 1 or 2.
4. One or more source filenames may be specified. Destination may include a filename only if a single source filename is specified. If no destination is specified, EXPAND prompts for it.

FASTHELP.EXE

Displays a list and gives a brief description of all DOS 6.0 commands: This command is a direct replacement for the DOS Ver 5.0 HELP. /? can be used in conjunction with other DOS commands to display the same help as FASTHELP would display for the same command. New in DOS Version 6.0

Syntax (double underlined is optional):

FASTHELP <u>command</u>

Examples: FASTHELP Chkdsk
                FASTHELP
                DISKCOPY /?

Syntax Options:

command . . . . . The particular DOS command that you want help about.
Command Type and Version:

External command; Network; Introduced with Ver 6.0

Notes:

1. FASTHELP without a command displays a list and brief description of all DOS 6.0 commands contained in the DOSHELP.HLP file.
2. Detailed information on DOS commands is available with the HELP command.
3. FASTHELP is a direct replacement for the DOS Ver 5.0 HELP command.

FASTOPEN.EXE

Fast opening of files: Decreases the amount of time to open frequently used files by keeping directory information in memory. FASTOPEN can be started at the DOS prompt or in either a Batch file or CONFIG.SYS. *DOS V4 is different, see manual.*

Syntax (double underlined is optional):

To start in a Batch file or at the DOS Prompt:
    FASTOPEN Drive1: = nnn Drive2:= nnn ... /x

To start in CONFIG.SYS use the following:
    Install=Drive:\Path\FASTOPEN.EXE
                    Drive1: = nnn Drive2:=nnn ... /x

Examples: FASTOPEN C:=97 /x
             Install=C:\DOS\FASTOPEN C:=97

Syntax Options:

Drive1: Drive2: . One or more drives FASTOPEN tracks.
nnn . . . . Number of files FASTOPEN can work with at the same time. The valid values are 10 through 999. 48 is the default.
/x. . . . . Creates the *name cache* in expanded memory rather than conventional memory. *name cache* is a buffer where names and locations of open files are stored.
Drive:\Path . . . . Drive and directory containing FASTOPEN.

Command Type and Version: Introduced with DOS Ver 3.3
External and CONFIG.SYS command; NOT for Network

Notes:
1. When placed in CONFIG.SYS, FASTOPEN.EXE must be used, not FASTOPEN without the extension.
2. FASTOPEN uses approximately 48 bytes of memory for each file that it tracks.
3. Deactivate FASTOPEN **BEFORE** disk compaction is used!!!!!
4. FASTOPEN works with hard drives only, not floppy drives.

FC.EXE

Compare two files and report the differences: FC reports the differences it finds between two files and displays them on screen. The comparison can be of ASCII or binary files.

Syntax (double underlined is optional):

FC /a /c /L /Lbx /n /t /w /nnn Drive1:\Path\ File1
    Drive2:\Path\ File2

or FC /b Drive1:\Path\ File1 Drive2:\Path\ File2

Examples: FC /a C:\DATA\Test.txt D:\Master.txt
             FC /b C:\DOS\MEM.EXE D:\UTIL\MEM2.EXE

Syntax Options:
Drive1\Path . . . Drive and directory of first file *(File1).*
Drive2\Path . . . Drive and directory of second file *(File2).*
File1 & File2 . . . The two files to be compared.

/a	Abbreviate ASCII comparison output, will only display first and last line of different block.
/c	Ignore upper/ lower case.
/L	Files compared in ASCII mode.
/Lbx	Set x lines of internal line buffer.
/n	During ASCII compare, displays line #s.
/t	Do not expand tabs to spaces. Default is to treat tabs as spaces with stops at every 8th position.
/w	During comparison, tabs and spaces are compressed. Also causes FC to ignore space that occurs at the beginning and end of lines.
/nnn	Set the number of consecutively matching lines before files are resynchronized.
/b	Files compared in binary mode. This is the default for all files ending in .EXE, .COM, .SYS, .OBJ, .LIB and .BIN.

Command Type and Version:

External command; Network; Introduced with Version 2.1

Notes:

1. See also COMP and DISKCOMP.
2. Use of wild cards (* or ?) is allowed.
3. For ASCII comparisons, the *File1* name is displayed, then the lines from *File1* that are different are displayed, then the first line to match in both files, then the *File2* name is displayed, then the lines from *File2* that are different, and finally, the first line to match in *File2*. FC uses a 100 line buffer to hold the lines being compared, if there are more than 100 lines of differences, FC cannot complete the comparison and issues a Resynch Failed error message.
4. For binary comparisons, the differences are reported on a single line as **xxxxxxxx: yy zz**, where xxxxxxxx is the hex address from the beginning of the file where the difference occurs. yy is the byte that is different in *File1* and zz is the byte that is different in *File2*. FC uses the same line buffer as Note 4 for binary comparisons, however if it runs out of memory, it will overlay portions of the memory until the comparison is completed.
5. FC is only available with MS-DOS®, not PC-DOS.

FCBS

Sets number of file control blocks that DOS can have open at the same time:

Syntax (double underlined is optional):

FCBS = x

Examples: FCBS = 10

Syntax Options:

x	File control blocks that DOS can have open at one time. Default = 4. Values can range from 1 through 255.

Command Type and Version:

CONFIG.SYS command; Introduced with Ver 3.0

Notes:
1. Normally, this command should only be used if a program specifically requires that FCBS be set to a specific value.
2. DOS may close a file opened earlier if there are not enough FCBs set aside.
3. The **,y** Syntax Option available in DOS Versions 4.01 and earlier, is no longer a valid option.

FDISK.EXE

Configures hard disk: After the low level format of a hard drive, FDISK is used to partition the drive for DOS. A series of menus are displayed to assist in the partitioning process. *Caution:* When a partition is deleted, all of the data stored on that partition is also deleted.

Syntax (double underlined is optional):

FDISK / status

Examples: FDISK

Syntax Options:

/ status . . . . *Display partition table info for hard drives installed in the system. DOS Version 6.0*

/ mbr . . . . Master boot record. Undocumented

Command Type and Version:

External command; Network, introduced with Ver 2.0

Notes:
1. Before DOS 3.3, FDISK did not create extended partitions or logical drives in the partitions. There could be only one DOS partition per drive. Until DOS 3.31 & 4.0, max size was 32Mb.
2. Using the FDISK command, you can accomplish the following:
   • Create a primary DOS partition on a hard drive.
   • Create an extended DOS partition on a hard drive.
   • Delete a partition on a hard drive.
   • Change the active partition on a hard drive.
   • Displays partition data for a hard drive.
   • Selects a different hard disk for partitioning.
3. Maximum partition size is 2 gigabytes.
4. In order to change the size of a partition, the partition must be deleted first, and a new partition created.
5. Drives formed by ASSIGN, SUBST, or JOIN cannot be partitioned with FDISK.
6. USE WITH CAUTION, backup hard drive data files before changing or deleting a partition.
7. The formatting of a hard drive for use by DOS is a three step process: Low level format, FDISK, then FORMAT. Note that IDE hard drives have been low level formatted at the factory, do not re-low level format these drives, only use FDISK then FORMAT.
8. See also FORMAT.

Sets the number of open files DOS can access.

Syntax:

FILES = nnn

Examples: FILES=20

Syntax Options:

nnn . . . . Number of files DOS can access, at one time, with valid
values ranging from 8-255. The Default is 8.

Command Type and Version:

CONFIG.SYS command; Introduced with Ver 2.0

Notes:

1. The standard value for files is FILES=20, however, many software packages, such as database managers, will require values in the range of 35
to 40. See the documentation for each program you wish to run and verify that your FILES= statement is not smaller than that required by the
program. It is all right if FILES= is larger than a program requires.

FIND.EXE

Looks for a text string in a file(s): Once the text string is located that FIND is
searching for, it displays those lines of text containing the text string.

Syntax (double underlined is optional):

FIND /v /c /n /i text Drive:\Path\ Filename

Examples: FIND /v /i "Dear Sir" C:\Test.doc
FIND "Dear Sir" Test.doc
FIND "Dear Sir" "Sincerely" "Help" C:\Test.doc

Syntax Options:

Drive:\Path . . . . Drive and directory containing *Filename*.
Filename. . . . . . File being searched for *Text*.
text . . . . Text string being searched for.
/ v . . . . Display lines that do not contain *Text*.
/ c . . . . Display line count of lines containing *Text*.
/ n . . . . File's line number containing *Text*.
/ i. . . . . Ignore upper/lower case during search. Ver 5.0

Command Type and Version:

External command; Network; Introduced with Ver 2.0

Notes:

1. Wild cards (* and ?) cannot be used in filenames being searched for by
FIND. See the FOR command for help in this area.
2. FIND ignores carriage returns, so *Text* must be a string that does not
contain any carriage returns.

3. If /c and /n are used together, the /n is disregarded.
4. If Filename is not specified, FIND will act as a filter for any standard device (keyboard, file, pipe, etc) and display those lines containing *Text*.
5. DOS provides three filter commands, FIND, MORE, and SORT.
6. /c /v used together will return count of lines that don't contain *Text*.

FOR

A logical batch command that runs a specific command for each file in a group: FOR can be run from inside a batch file or at the DOS prompt.

Syntax (double underlined is optional):

If used in a batch file, use the following:
FOR %%variable IN (set) DO command <u>cpar</u>

If used at the DOS prompt, use the following:
FOR %variable IN (set) DO command <u>cpar</u>

Examples:
FOR %T IN (*.doc, *.asc) DO DEL %T (deletes all .doc and .asc files in current directory)

Syntax Options:

%variable . . . . . Replaceable variable for use at the DOS prompt. The *variable* name can be any character(s) except the numbers 0 to 9. FOR replaces *variable* with each text string contained in *(set)* and runs *command* over and over until all are processed.

%%variable. . . . Same as *%variable*, except for use in batch files only.

(set) . . . . One or more files or text strings on which *command* is to operate. ( ) is required

command . . . . . Any DOS command to be run on each item listed in *(set)*.

cpar. . . . . Parameters for *command*.

Command Type and Version:
Batch and Internal command; Introduced with Ver 2.0

Notes:
1. FOR-IN-DO commands can't be nested on a single commandline.
2. Wild cards (* and ?) are allowed in *(set)*.
3. Multiple %variable names are allowed.

FORMAT.EXE

Format a floppy or hard disk: A disk must be formatted before DOS can recognize it.

Syntax (double underlined is optional):

There are 4 different syntax choices:

FORMAT Drive: /v:name /q /u /f:size /b /s /c

FORMAT Drive: /v:name /q /u /t:trak /n:sect /b /s /c

FORMAT Drive: /v:name /q /u /1 /4 /b /s /c

FORMAT Drive: /q /u /1 /4 /8 /b /s /c /autotest

Syntax Options:

Drive: . . . . Drive to be formatted. If no switches are used, the drive is
formatted according to its system drive type.

/v:name . . . . . . Assign the disk the volume label *name*. *name* can be up
to 11 characters long. If /v is not used, DOS will automatically prompt the user for a volume name when the format
process is finished. /v is not compatible with /8. See also
the VOL, DIR, and LABEL commands.

/q . . . . Quick format a disk by deleting the FAT (File Allocation
Table) and root directory. Only use this on disks that have
already been formatted. Ver 5.0

/u . . . . Unconditional format. Destroys all data and UNFORMAT
will not work. Use if read or write errors occur with this disk or
when a new disk is to be formatted. Ver. 5.0

/1 . . . . Format 1 side of floppy disk.

/4 . . . . Formats a DSDD (double-sided double-density) 5-1/4
inch, 360k floppy in a 1.2 m floppy drive. Warning: some
1.2m drives can not reliably do this format!

/8 . . . . Formats a 5-1/4 disk with 8 sectors per track. 8 sectors per track
are necessary for use with pre DOS 2.0 operating systems.

/f:size . . . . Floppy disk size. Use instead of /t and /n switches
if possible:

160, 160k or 160kb	160k SSDD, 5-1/4"
180, 180k or 180kb	180k SSDD, 5-1/4"
320, 320k or 320kb	320k DSDD, 5-1/4"
360, 360k or 360kb	360k DSDD, 5-1/4"
720, 720k, or 720kb	720k DSDD, 3.5"
1200, k, kb, 1.2, 1.2m, 1.2mb	1.2m DSHD, 5-1/4"
1440, k, kb, 1.44, 1.44m, 1.44mb	1.44m DSHD, 3.5"
2880, k, kb, 2.88, 2.88m, 2.88mb	2.88m DSEHD, 3.5"

/b . . . . Obsolete switch used to reserve space for the system files.
No longer generally used, retained for compatibility only.

/s . . . . Copies all 3 system files, [IO.SYS and MSDOS.SYS] or
[IBMBIO.COM and IBMDOS.COM] and COMMAND.COM
to the disk after formatting has finished. The
DBLSPACE.BIN file is also copied to the target drive (if
you are not using the DBLSPACE program, you can re-

move the hidden, system, read-only attributes from
DBLSPACE.BIN on the target disk and then delete it.)

/t:trak	Number of tracks on disk, must be used with the /n switch. Use /f:size switch if possible.
/n:sect	Number of sectors on disk, must be used with the /t switch. Use /f:size switch if possible.
/autotest	Bypasses prompts during formatting. Note that this is an un-documented command. DOS Version 6.0
/c	Retests for bad cluster. DOS Version 6.2

Command Type and Version:
External command; Introduced with Ver 1.0

Notes:

1. New floppy disks need only be formatted in order to make the disk use-able by DOS. Hard drives, however, require a 2 or 3 step format process which includes a low level format (Not on IDE drives), then partitioning with FDISK, and finally FORMAT.

2. If the /U switch is **not** used, UNFORMAT can unformat the disk. See also UNFORMAT

3. Format issues a warning when a hard drive is to be formatted.

4. Do not format Network drives or drives that have had ASSIGN, JOIN or SUBST used on the drive.

5. FORMAT /S and the DOS "SYS" command both copy the DBLSPACE.BIN file to the Target Disk.

6. FORMAT Exit codes are: 0 Successful FORMAT; 3 Aborted with Ctrl+C by user; 4 Fatal error other than 0,3, or 5
   5 No response to Proceed?

Directs DOS to process commands starting with the line after a specified label: Within a Batch program, when DOS finds the specified label, it processes the commands beginning with the next line after that label.

Syntax (shaded is optional):

GOTO Label

:Label

Examples:　　　GOTO Start

　　　　　　　Test.bat　　　　(bypassed by GOTO)

　　　　　　　:Start　　　　　(must begin with :)

Syntax Options:

Label. . . . . Directs DOS to a specific line in a batch file. Valid values for *Label* can include spaces but cannot include other separators, such as equal signs and semicolons. GOTO will recognize only the first 8 characters of the *Label* name. *Label*, on the GOTO command line, does not begin with a colon and it must have a matching *Label* line in the batch program. The *Label* line in the batch program must begin with a colon. You can also substitute an environment variable enclosed in percent signs, e.g. %RETURN%, for *Label*.

Command Type and Version:

Internal command; only used in a Batch program; Introduced with Ver 2.0

Notes:

1. A batch-program line beginning with a colon (:) is a label line, and will not be processed as a command. When the line begins with a (:) colon, DOS ignores any commands on that line.

GRAFTABL.COM

Allows a display to show extended characters in graphics mode from a specific code page: This command is required when a monitor is not able to display extended characters in graphics mode. (Most monitors do not need GRAFTABL.) Removed from DOS Version 6.0 and later.

Syntax (shaded is optional):

GRAFTABL nnn　　*or* GRAFTABL /status

Examples:

　　GRAFTABL 860　　　(Portuguese code page)

Syntax Options:

nnn . . . . Code page used to define extended characters.

　　　　　　　437. . . . United States

　　　　　　　850. . . . Multilingual

　　　　　　　852. . . . Slavic

/status .... Identifies current country code page.

Command Type and Version:
External command; Network; Introduced with Ver 3.0
Beginning with MS-DOS Ver 6.0, GRAFTABL is only available on
Microsoft's DOS Supplemental Disks.

Notes:
1. The active code page is not changed when GRAFTABL is run.
2. GRAFTABL uses approximately 1K of RAM.
3. GRAFTABL exit codes are as follows:
   0 Successful load of character set.
   1 Current character set replaced by new table.
   2 File error has occurred.
   3 Incorrect parameter, new table not loaded.
   4 Incorrect DOS version, 5.0 required.

GRAPHICS.COM

*Configures DOS so that Print Screen (Shift+Print Scrn) can print a graphics
screen to a printer. GRAPHICS supports CGA, EGA, and VGA display modes:*

Syntax (shaded is optional):
GRAPHICS Type Drive:\Path\ Filename /r /b /Lcd
                                    /pb:std or /pb:Lcd

Examples: GRAPHICS color4 /b

Syntax Options:

Type	Printer type (HP=Hewlett-Packard)
color1	IBM Color Printer with black ribbon
color4	IBM Color Printer with RGB ribbon
color8	IBM Color Printer with CMY ribbon
hpdefault	Any HP PCL printer
deskjet	HP DeskJet printer
graphics	IBM Graphics, Proprinter or Quietwriter
graphicswide ...	IBM Graphics Printer with 11 inch carriage
laserjet	HP LaserJet printer
laserjetii	HP LaserJet II printer
paintjet	HP PaintJet printer
quietjet	HP QuietJet printer
quietjetplus ...	HP QuietJet Plus printer
ruggedwriter ...	HP Rugged Writer printer
ruggedwriterwide	HP Rugged Writerwide printer
thermal	IBM PC-convertible Thermal Printer
thinkjet	HP ThinkJet printer

Drive:\Path	Drive and directory containing *Filename*.
Filename.	Printer profile where graphics screen is to be printed to. Default is GRAPHICS.PRO.
/r	Prints the image as white characters on a black background (black characters on a white background is the Default).
/b	Prints the background in color. (only color4 and color8 types are valid)
/Lcd	Prints image using an LCD screen aspect ratio instead of a CGA screen aspect ratio.
/pb:std	Sets printbox size. If this switch is used:
or /pb:Lcd . . .	you must check the GRAPHICS.PRO file and change each printbox line to *std* or *Lcd* so that it matches what you selected for */pb* :

Command Type and Version:

External command; Network; Introduced with Ver 2.0

Notes:

1. The GRAPHICS command does use a limited amount of conventional RAM when it is loaded.
2. Four shades of gray are printed if *color1* or *graphics* is in effect and the screen is in the 320x200 mode.
3. If a printer profile such as GRAPHICS.PRO is already loaded, and you wish to load a different .PRO file, the new .PRO must be smaller than the currently loaded .PRO. If it is larger, your system must be re-booted first in order for the larger profile to be loaded
4. Use the Graphics or Graphicswide printer types if the printer you are using is an Epson.
5. Supported displays include EGA and VGA.
6. See also PRINT
7. Do not use the /b switch in conjunction with the /r switch or with a black and white printer.

GW-BASIC®.EXE

BASIC language intrepreter: GW-BASIC® is Microsoft's own version of BA-SIC that shipped with MS–DOS versions prior to Ver 5.0. Starting with Ver 5.0, QBASIC is shipped with DOS.

Syntax (shaded is optional):

GWBASIC Drive:\Path\Filename < Input >> Output
/f:n /i /s:n /c:n /m:n,n /d

Examples:	GWBASIC	(starts BASIC)
	GWBASIC C:\BAS\test.bas /f:4 /d	

Syntax Options:

Drive:\Path	Drive and directory containing *Filename*.
Filename.	The BASIC program file to be run. The default file extension is .BAS

< *Input.*	Standard input is read from *Input* file.
> *Output*	Output is redirected to *Output* file or a device (screen, printer, etc)
>>	Causes *Output* to be appended.
/ f:n	Max number *n* of simultaneously open files while a BASIC program is running. Default is 3. / *i* must be used at the same time. Size requirement includes 194 bytes (File Control Block) plus 128 bytes (data buffer).
/ i.	Forces static allocation of memory for file operations.
/ s:nn.	Max record length *nn* for a file. Default is 128 bytes, maximum is 32,767 bytes.
/ c:nn.	Allocates *nn* bytes of Receive buffer and 128 bytes of Transmit buffer for RS-232 (serial) communications. /c:0 disables support. Defaults are 256 byte receive buffer and 128 byte transmit buffer for each RS-232 card.
/ m:x,y	Sets the highest memory location *x* and the maximum block size *y* in bytes. Block size is in multiples of 16.
/ d	Activates double-precision for the following functions: ATN, COS, EXP, LOG, SIN, SQR and TAN.

Command Type and Version:
External command; Network; Introduced with Ver 1.0

Notes:
1. See also BASIC, BASICA, and QBASIC.
2. Variables n, nn, x, and y listed above are all given in decimal values. If you wish to use hexadecimal values, precede the value with &H. If you wish to use octal values, precede the value with &O (O is the letter O, not zero).
3. A complete discussion of GW-BASIC is beyond the scope of this book. If you need information on GW-BASIC commands and how to program in BASIC, refer to Microsoft's manual on GW-BASIC or other texts on BASIC.
4. Different versions of GWBASIC were released and each needs to be run with its correct version of DOS.
5. Programs written in BASIC (IBM's version) may require small adjustments in order to run correctly under GW-BASIC

HELP.EXE - Version 5.0 only

Online information about MS-DOS version 5.0 commands:

Syntax (shaded is optional):

HELP command

Examples:	HELP	(brief description of commands)
	HELP chkdsk	
	DISKCOPY / ?	(see Note: 1 below)

Syntax Options:

Command..... Any specific DOS version 5.0 command on which more information is desired.

Command Type and Version:
External command; Network; Introduced with Ver 5.0
FASTHELP in Ver 6.0 is the same as HELP in Ver 5.0

Notes:
1. You can get online HELP in two ways. Either specify the name of the command on the HELP command line or type the command name and the /? switch at the command prompt.

HELP - Version 6.0 and 6.2x

Online information about MS-DOS Version 6.0 and 6.2x commands and a list of all DOS commands: The Ver 6.0 AND 6.2 information for HELP is much more detailed than FASTHELP or DOS Ver 5.0 HELP. New in DOS Version 6.0

Syntax (shaded is optional):
HELP command /B /G /H /nohi

   Examples: HELP   (List of commands)
                  HELP chkdsk
                  DISKCOPY / ?   (see Note: 1 below)

Syntax Options:
Command..... Any specific DOS version 6.0 command on which more information is desired.
/B .... Display in black-and-white mode.
/G .... Display in CGA color mode.
/H .... Display HELP with the maximum number of lines that the display supports.
/nohi .... Turn high-intensity display off.

Command Type and Version:
External command; Network; Introduced with Ver 6.0
FASTHELP in Ver 6.0 & 6.2x is the same as HELP in V5.0

Notes:
1. You can get online HELP in two ways. Either specify the name of the command on the HELP command line or type the command name and the /? switch at the command prompt.

HIMEM.SYS

Extended memory and HMA (high memory area) manager: HIMEM.SYS prevents programs from using the same memory locations at the same time.

Device= <u>Drive:\Path\</u> HIMEM.SYS /hmamin=m /numhandles=n

/int15=xxx /machine:xxx /a20control:on or off /shadowram:on

or <u>off</u> /cpuclock:on or <u>off</u> /EISA /verbose /test:on or <u>off</u>

Examples: Device=C:\Dos\HIMEM.SYS /test:off

Syntax Options:

Drive:\Path .... Drive and directory containing HIMEM.

/hmamin=m.... Minimum *m* kilobytes of memory a program must use before it can use the HMA. Default=0, Range=0 to 63. The
most efficient use of HMA is accomplished by setting m to
the amount of memory required by the program that uses
the most HMA.

/numhandles=n. Maximum number (*n*) of EMB (extended memory block)
handles that can be used at the same time. Each handle
uses 6 bytes of RAM. Default=32, Range=1 to 128.

/int15=xxx ..... *xxx* kilobytes of memory are assigned to the Interrupt 15h
interface. Programs must recognize VDisk headers in or-
der to use this switch.

/machine:xxx... Defines a specific A20 handler *xxx* to be used. Normally,
HIMEM automatically detects which A20 is to be used.
Default=1. If the required handler is not listed in the following table, see the README.TXT file in your DOS directory for additional information.

Number	Code	A20 handler
1	at	IBM PC/AT, Compuadd 386. JDR 386/33
2	ps2	IBM PS/2, Datamedia 386 /486, Unisys PowerPort
3	ptlcascade	Phoenix Cascade Bios
4	hpvectra	HP Vectra, A and A+
5	att6300plus	AT&T 6300 Plus
6	acer1100	Acer 1100
7	toshiba	Toshiba 1600,1200XE,5100
8	wyse	Wyse 12.5 MHz 286, Intel 361Z or 302, Hitachi HL500C
9	tulip	Tulip SX
10	zenith	Zenith ZBIOS
11	at1	IBM PC/AT
12	at2	IBM PC/AT (alt. delay)
12	css	CSS Labs
13	at3	IBM PC/AT (alt. delay)
13	philips	Philips
14	fasthp	HP Vectra
15	ibm7552	IBM 7552 Industrial Comp (Dos Version 6.0)
16	bullmicral	Bull Micral 60 (Dos Version 6.0)
17	dell	Dell XBIOS (Dos Version 6.0)

/a20control:on Off allows HIMEM.SYS to take control of

---

or /a20control:off   the A20 line only if A20 was off when HIMEM.SYS was
               loaded. Default=:on

/shadowram:on . If your system has Shadow RAM, :off
or /shadowram:off   switches the Shadow RAM off and returns control of
               that RAM to HIMEM. Default=:off if your system has less
               than 2 megabytes of RAM.

/cpuclock:on . . . If your system slows down when HIMEM.SYS is loaded,
               specifying :on might correct the problem. :on will slow
               down HIMEM.SYS.

/ EISA . . . . Used only on EISA systems to specify that HIMEM allo-
               cates all available extended memory. DOS Verion 6.0

/ verbose or / v HIMEM displays status and error messages while loading.
               Hold ALT key down during system startup to disable /verbose.
               DOS Version 6.0

/ test:on or :off. . Turns the HIMEM.SYS testing of all extended memory :on
               or :off during system startup.

Command Type and Version:
Config.sys command; Introduced with Ver 5.0

Notes:
1. Only one program at a time can use the high memory area.
2. HIMEM.SYS, or another XMS driver such as 386MAX or QEMM must be loaded before DOS can be loaded into HMA with the DOS=high command.
3. In most cases, command line switches do not need to be used.since the defaults are designed to work with most computer hardware.

IF

Performs a command based on the result of a condition in batch programs: If a conditional statement is true, DOS executes the command, if the condition is false, DOS ignores the command.

Syntax (shaded is optional):
Three syntax formats are valid:

    IF <u>not</u> errorlevel nnn *command*

    IF <u>not</u> string1==string2 *command*

    IF <u>not</u> exist filename *command*

Examples: IF errorlevel 3 goto end

Syntax Options:
not. . . . . The command is to be carried out only if the statement is false.

errorlevel nnn . . True only if the previous program executed by COM-
               MAND.COM had an exit code equal to or greater than *nnn*.

command . . . . . The specified command that DOS is to perform if the pre-
               ceding condition is met.

string1==string2 True, only if *string1* and *string2* are the same. The values of *string1* and *string2* can be literal strings or batch variables. Strings may not contain separators, such as commas, semicolons, spaces, etc.

exist *filename* . . True condition if *filename* exists.

Command Type and Version:
Internal command but only used in Batch programs;
Introduced with Ver 2.0

Notes:
1. The *errorlevel* parameter allows you to use exit codes as conditions. An exit code is returned to DOS whenever a programstops.
2. Use " " quotes around strings when comparing, it's safer.

INCLUDE

Includes the contents of one configuration block within another configuration block: This is one of five special CONFIG.SYS commands used to define multiple configurations. New in DOS Version 6.0

Syntax:
INCLUDE=blockname

Syntax Options:
blockname . . . . The name of the configuration block to be included.

Command Type and Version:
CONFIG.SYS command; Introduced with Ver 6.0

Notes:
1. See also MENUITEM, MENUDEFAULT, MENUCOLOR, and SUBMENU. These are the other four special CONFIG.SYS commands used to define multiple configurations.
2. Refer to your DOS 6.0 manual for more information on setting up the special multiple configuration menus.

INSTALL

Loads a memory-resident program when DOS is started: Use the INSTALL command to load FASTOPEN, KEYB, NLSFUNC, or SHARE in CONFIG.SYS.

Syntax (shaded is optional):
INSTALL = <u>Drive: \Path\</u> Filename <u>parameters</u>

Examples: INSTALL = C:\Dos\NLSFUNC

Syntax Options:
Drive:\Path . . . . Drive and directory containing *Filename.*

\Filename . . . . . Name of memory-resident program that you want to run.
Parameters . . . . Command parameters, if any, required by *Filename*.

Command Type and Version:
Config.sys command; Network; Introduced with Ver 4.0

Notes:
1. Less memory is used when you load a program with INSTALL instead of loading from the AUTOEXEC.BAT file since an environment for a program is not created by INSTALL .
2. Do not use INSTALL to load programs that use shortcut keys, environment variables, or require COMMAND.COM for error handling.
3. Not all programs will function properly if loaded with INSTALL.
4. See also FASTOPEN, KEYB, NLSFUNC, SHARE, CONFIG.SYS.

INTERLNK

Link computers to share resources:
INTERLNK.EXE must be installed as a device driver in the CONFIG.SYS file before the INTERLNK and INTERSVR commands can be run. New in DOS Version 6.0

Syntax (shaded is optional):
INTERLNK <u>client :</u> = <u>server :</u>

Examples: INTERLNK C: = F:

Syntax Options:
client : . . . . The drive letter of the client drive that is redirected to a drive on the server.
server : . . . . The drive letter on the server that will be redirected. If a letter is not specified, the client drive will no longer be redirected.

Command Type and Version:
External command; Network; Introduced with Ver 6.0

Notes:
1. See also INTERLNK.EXE and INTERSVR.
2. Note, the LASTDRIVE command may need to be used if drive letters greater than E are used.

INTERLNK.EXE

Link computers to share resources: New in DOS Version 6.0
INTERLNK.EXE must be installed as a device driver in the CONFIG.SYS file before the INTERLNK and INTERSVR commands can be run.

Syntax (shaded is optional):

Device= <u>Drive: \Path\</u> INTERLNK.EXE /drives:n /noprinter

/com:nladdress /lpt:nladdress /auto /noscan /low /baud:rate /v

Examples: Device=C:\ INTERLNK.EXE /drives:4

Syntax Options:

Drive:\Path . . . . Drive and directory containing the INTERLNK.EXE program.

/drives:n . . . . . . The number of redirected drives. Default is n=3. If n=0, only the printers are redirected.

/noprinter . . . . . No printers are to be redirected. Default is INTERLNK redirects all ports.

/com:nladdress Specifies that serial port *n* be used to transfer data. If *n* or the address is omitted, INTERLNK scans for the first available port. Default is INTERLNK redirects all ports.

/lpt:nladdress . . Specifies that parallel port n be used to transfer data. If *n* or the address is omitted, INTERLNK scans for the first available port. Default is INTERLNK redirects all ports.

/auto. . . . . INTERLNK.EXE is installed in memory only if *client* can make a connection when the *server* starts up. Default is INTERLNK is installed whether or not *server* is there.

/noscan . . . . . . INTERLNK.EXE driver is installed, but a connection between *client* & *server* is prevented.

/low . . . . INTERLNK.EXE forces driver to be loaded into conventional memory. Default is driver loaded into upper memory if it is available.

/baud:rate. . . . . Sets baud rate for com serial ports. Default=115200. Valid values are 9600, 19200, 38400, 57600, & 115200.

/v . . . . Used to resolve problems and conflicts between *com* and *lpt* ports and the computer's timer.

Command Type and Version:

CONFIG.SYS command; Network; Introduced Ver 6.0

Notes:

1. See also INTERSVR and INTERLNK the command.

INTERSVR.EXE

Starts the INTERLNK server so that resources can be shared between linked computers: New in DOS Version 6.0

INTERLNK.EXE must be installed as a device driver in the CONFIG.SYS file before the INTERLNK and INTERSVR commands can be run.

Syntax (shaded is optional):

INTERSVR <u>drive: /X=drive /lpt:nladdress /com:nladdress</u>

<u>/baud:rate /b /v /rcopy</u>

Examples: INTERSVR / rcopy

Syntax Options:

/X=drive	Specifies those drives that will not be redirected. Default is all drives are redirected.
/lpt:nladdress . .	Specifies that serial port n be used to transfer data. If *n* or the address is omitted, INTERLNK scans for the first available port. Default is INTERSVR scans all ports.
/com:nladdress	Specifies that serial port n be used to transfer data. If *n* or the address is omitted, INTERLNK scans for the first available port. Default is INTERSVR scans all ports.
/baud:rate.	Sets baud rate for com serial ports. Default=115200. Valid values are 9600, 19200, 38400, 57600, & 115200.
/b	Display stat screen in black-and-white.
/v	Used to resolve problems and conflicts between *com* and *lpt* ports and the computer's timer.
/rcopy.	Copies all INTERLNK files from one computer to another. Note that a full 7 wire null-modem serial cable must be installed on the *com* port and the DOS MODE command must be available.

Command Type and Version:

External command; Network; Introduced with Ver 6.0

Notes:

1. See also INTERLNK.EXE and INTERLNK.
2. If port numbers for com and lpt are not specified, INTERLNK will scan and select the first port it finds.

JOIN.EXE

Joins a disk drive to a specific directory on another disk drive: Once joined, DOS treats the directories and files of the first drive as the contents of the second drive and path. Removed from DOS Version 6.0 and later.

Syntax (shaded is optional):

Two syntax formats are valid:

JOIN <u>Drive1: Drive2:\Path</u>

JOIN <u>Drive: /d</u>

Examples: JOIN C: D:\Notes
JOIN C: D:\Notes\Bin (valid for DOS 5.0 only)

Syntax Options:

Drive1: . . . . Drive to be joined to *Drive2:\Path*.

DOS Commands

Drive2:\Path . . . Drive and Path to which you want to JOIN *Drive1:*.
Drive2:\Path must be empty and other than the root directory. With DOS Ver 5.0, you can JOIN to a subdirectory also, e.g. C:\Notes\Bin

Drive: . . . . Drive on which JOIN is to be canceled.

/d. . . . . Cancels the JOIN command.

Command Type and Version:
External command; Introduced with Ver 3.0
Removed from MS DOS Version 6.0, however, it is available on Microsoft's MS-DOS 6.0 and 6.2x Supplemental Disks.
Considered too dangerous to use.

Notes:
1. Once you use the JOIN command, Drive1: becomes invalid.
2. If a specified path already exists before using JOIN, that directory cannot be used while JOIN is in effect. The specified directory must be empty or the JOIN operation will be incomplete and an error message will be displayed.
3. Commands that do not work with drives formed by JOIN are: ASSIGN, BACKUP, CHKDSK, DISKCOMP, DISKCOPY, FDISK, FORMAT, LABEL, MIRROR, RECOVER, RESTORE, SYS.
4. Use JOIN without parameters to show a list of the currently joined drives.

KBDBUF.SYS

A device driver that sets the number of keystrokes stored in the keyboard buffer. DOS Version 6.0 and later.

Syntax (shaded is optional):

DEVICE = KBDBUF.SYS xxxx

Example: DEVICE = KBDBUF.SYS 200

Syntax Options (shaded is optional):

xxxx . . . . Designates the number of keystrokes held in the buffer. This number can range from 16 to 1024.

Command Type and Version:
CONFIG.SYS command
Introduced with MS-DOS Ver. 6.0
Available only on Microsoft's Supplemental Disks for MS-DOS Versions 6.0, 6.21 and 6.22.

KEYB.COM and KEYBOARD.SYS

Configures a keyboard for use with a specific language (installs alternate keyboard layout):

Syntax (shaded is optional):

If started in a batch file or at the DOS prompt:

KEYB xx,yyy,Drive:\Path\Filename /e / id:nn

If started in CONFIG.SYS:

install = Drive1:\Path1\KEYB.COM xx, yyy
                        Drive:\Path\Filename /e / id:nn

Examples: KEYB fr,850,437,C:\Dos\Keyboard.sys
install = C:\KEYB.COM fr , , C:\Dos\Keyboard.sys

Syntax Options:

xx	Keyboard code. See table on next page.
yyy	Code page. See table on next page.
Drive:\Path	Drive and directory containing Filename.
Filename.	Keyboard definition file. Default=KEYBOARD.SYS
/e.	Enhanced keyboard is being used. Ver5
/id:nn	Defines which keyboard is in use. See table on next page.
Drive1:\Path1 . .	Drive and directory containing KEYB.COM

Command Type and Version:

External command; Network; Introduced with Ver 3.3

Notes:

1. When KEYB is installed through CONFIG.SYS, KEYB.COM with the .COM must be used. See also the CHCP command.
2. The Code Page specified with yyy must already be loaded on your system before KEYB is used.
3. You can switch from the default keyboard configuration to the KEYB configuration by pressing Ctrl+Alt+F2. To switch to the default keyboard configuration, press Ctrl+Alt+F1
4. The following are KEYB exit codes:
   - 0 KEYB definition file loaded successfully.
   - 1 Invalid Keyboard Code, Code Page, or syntax.
   - 2 Bad or missing keyboard definition file.
   - 4 Communication error with CON device.
   - 5 Requested Code Page has not been prepared.

The following table lists xx, yyy, and nnn values for different countries and languages.

Country or language	Keyboard Code xx	Code Page yyy	Keyboard ID nnn
Belgium	be	850,437	
Brazil	br	850,437	
Canadian-French	cf	850,863	
Czech Republic	cz	852,850	
Denmark	dk	850,865	
Finland	su	850,437	
France	fr	850,437	120,189
Germany	gr	850,437	
Hungary	hu	852,850	
Italy	it	850,437	141,142

Latin America	la	850,437	
Netherlands	nl	850,437	
Norway	no	850,865	
Poland	pl	852,850	
Portugal	po	850,860	
Slovakia	sl	852,850	
Spain	sp	850,437	
Sweden	sv	850,437	
Switzerland (French)	sf	850,437	
Switzerland (German)	sg	850,437	
United Kingdom	uk	850,437	166,168
United States	us	850,437	
Yugoslavia	yu	852,850	

KEYBxx.COM

Loads a keyboard program for a specific country or keyboard type:

Syntax (shaded is optional):

KEYBxx

Examples: KEYBGR
          KEYBUK

Syntax Options:

xx . . . . Code for a specific keyboard type:

KEYBdv . . . . . Dvorak keyboard
KEYBfr . . . . . . France
KEYBgr . . . . . . Germany
KEYBit . . . . . . Italy
KEYBsp . . . . . Spain
KEYBuk . . . . . United Kingdom

Command Type and Version:

External command; Network; Introduced with Ver 3.0

Notes:

1. KEYBxx was discontinued after DOS version 3.2 and was replaced by KEYB.
2. Only one keyboard program can be loaded at a time.
3. You can switch from the default keyboard configuration to the KEYBxx configuration by pressing Ctrl+Alt+F2. To switch to the default keyboard configuration, press Ctrl+Alt+F1.
4. If you need to change from one keyboard type to another, restart the system after the changes have been made.

LABEL.EXE

Creates, changes or deletes the name or volume label of a disk: DOS displays the volume label and serial number, if it exists, as part of the directory listing.

Syntax (shaded is optional):

  LABEL <u>Drive: Label</u>

  Examples: LABEL
                  LABEL A: datadisc

Syntax Options:

Drive: . . . . Drive or diskette to be named.

Label. . . . . New volume label, up to 11 characters. A colon (**:**) must be
                              included between the drive letter and label, but <u>NO</u> space.

Command Type and Version:

  External command; Introduced with Ver 3.0

Notes:

1. Using the LABEL command without a label displays the following:
     Volume in Drive A is nnnnnnnnnnn; Volume Serial Number is nnnn-nnnn
     Volume Label (11 characters, ENTER for none)?
2. The Volume label cannot include tabs. Spaces are allowed, but consec-
    utive spaces may be treated as a single space.
3. **Do not** use the following characters in a volume label:
       * ? / \ | . , ; : + = [ ] ( ) & ^ < > "
4. LABEL is not case sensitive. (lower case is automatically converted to
    upper case.)
5. LABEL doesn't work on drives created by ASSIGN, JOIN or SUBST.

LASTDRIVE

Number of drives installed: By default, the last drive is the one *after* the last
drive used by your computer. DOS 4 and earlier it was E:

Syntax (shaded is optional):

  LASTDRIVE = param-   eter

  Examples: LASTDRIVE = F

Syntax Options:

parameter . . . . . A drive letter in the range of A through
                 Z to correspond to the number of logical drives installed.
                 Default is the drive after the last one used by the computer.

Command Type and Version:

  CONFIG.SYS command; Introduced with Ver 3.0

Notes:

1. Memory is allocated by DOS for each drive specified by LASTDRIVE there-
    fore, don't specify more drives than are necessary.

LINK.EXE

***8086 Object Linker that creates executable programs from Microsoft Macro
Assembler (MASM) object files:*** LINK is for the experienced programmer and is
not used by the general user. Removed from DOS Version 5.0

Syntax (shaded is optional):

LINK   (LINK prompts for file names, etc)

LINK object , execute , map , library options ;

Examples: LINK file /se:192 , , ;

Syntax Options:

object . . . . Object files to be linked together.
execute . . . . Name for created executable file.
map. . . . . Map listing file.
library . . . . Name(s) of library files to LINK.
options . . . . Options for the LINK program
; . . . . Terminates command line.

Command Type and Version:

External command; Introduced with Ver 1.0; Removed from Ver 5.0

Notes:

1. Further discussion of LINK is beyond the scope of Pocket PCRef.

LOADFIX.COM

Forces a program to load above the first 64k of conventional memory and then runs the program.

Syntax (shaded is optional):

LOADFIX Drive: \Path\ Filename parameters

Examples: LOADFIX C:\TEST.EXE

Syntax Options:

Drive:\Path\. . . . Drive and directory containing Filename.
Filename. . . . . . Name of program that you want to run.
Parameters . . . . Command parameters, if any, required by Filename.

Command Type and Version:

External command; Introduced with Ver 5.0

Notes:

1. Use LOADFIX when the error message "Packed file corrupt" is reported during the execution of a program.

LOADHIGH or LH

Loads programs into upper memory: Loading programs into upper memory frees up conventional memory for other programs. An upper memory manager such as EMM386 must be loaded first in order for LOADHIGH to function. LH and LOADHIGH are equivalent commands.

Syntax (shaded is optional):

LOADHIGH <u>Drive:\Path\</u> Filename <u>/L:region /s parameters</u>

Examples: LOADHIGH C:\Dos\doskey.com
                      LH C:\Dos\doskey.com

Syntax Options:

Drive:\Path. . . . Drive and directory containing *Filename*.

\Filename . . . . . Program to be loaded into high memory.

/L:region. . . . . . Load the device driver into a specific upper memory region.

/s . . . . Shrinks the upper-memory block (UMB) to minimum size while loading program. Used only with the */L:region* switch. Typically used only by MEMMAKER. Introduced in DOS Version 6.2

parameters . . . . Command line parameters required by *Filename*.

Command Type and Version:

Internal command; Network; Introduced with Ver 5.0

Notes:

1. DOS=umb must be included in your CONFIG.SYS in order for LOADHIGH to function.
2. HIMEM.SYS and EMM386.EXE must be loaded in CONFIG.SYS on a 386/486 system in order to provide upper memory management for 386/486 systems. (Programs such as 386MAX and QEMM will provide the same capabilities.)
3. If there is not enough upper memory to load a program, DOS will load the program into conventional memory (no notice is given).
4. See also DEVICEHIGH, DOS, HIMEM.SYS, and EMM386.
5. When LOADHIGH is used, it is typically placed in AUTOEXEC.BAT.
6. Use MEM © to see where programs are loaded.
7. Running MEMMAKER will automatically add all necessary LOADHIGH commands to AUTOEXEC.BAT.

MD or MKDIR

Makes a Directory: Creates a new subdirectory under the current directory (if no Drive:\Path is specified). A new subdirectory on a different drive or under a different path can also be created. MD and MKDIR are equivalent commands.

Syntax (shaded is optional):

MD <u>Drive:\Path\</u> subdirectory

Examples: MD contract
                    MKDIR contract
                    MD C:\contract\bin

Syntax Options:

Drive: . . . . Letter of drive for *subdirectory*.

\Path . . . . Path where subdirectory is to be made. If no path is speci-
                    fied, e.g. C:\ only, the new directory is made a subdirec-
                    tory under the root directory.

subdirectory . . . Name of the *subdirectory* being created.

Command Type and Version:

Internal command; Network; Introduced with Ver 2.0

Notes:

1. DOS will always assume that the MD command is on the current directory if no path is specified.
2. The maximum length of any path to the final subdirectory is 63 characters, including backslashes.

MEM.EXE

Display information about used and free system memory: Options are
available that will display items such as which programs are loaded, the order of
loaded programs, free memory, etc.

Syntax (shaded is optional):

MEM /program /page /a /c /d /f /m progname

Examples: MEM
             MEM /classify

Syntax Options:

MEM . . . . Without any switches, the status of
                    used and free memory is displayed.

/ program or / p . **DOS Version 4/5 only:** Displays the status of programs
                    currently loaded into memory. This switch can not be used
                    at the same time as /debug and /classify.

/ page or / p . . . **DOS Version 6 only.** Pauses display output after each
                    screen.

/ a . . . . Adds a line to the display stating the amount of memory
                    available in HMA (High Memory Area). In DOS Version 6.2

/ c or / classify . . Displays the status of all programs and
                    drivers currently loaded into conventional and upper mem-
                    ory. Other info, such as memory use and largest memory
                    blocks available are also displayed. This switch can not be
                    used at the same time as /program and /debug. Version 5.0

/ d or / debug . . Displays the status of programs and drivers currently
                    loaded into memory. This switch can not be used at the
                    same time as /program and /classify.

/ f or / free . . . . . Lists free regions in upper memory. / free can not be used
                    with other switches, except /module.

/m progname or /module progname . . . Display info on a particular program
                    loaded in memory. This switch can not be used with any
                    other switches except / page.

Command Type and Version:

External command; Network; Introduced with Ver 4.0

Notes:
1. Extended memory usage is displayed only if the installed system memory is 1 meg or greater. Only LIM 4.0 expanded memory use is displayed.
2. Total conventional memory=first 640k of RAM. Extended = mem above 1 meg. Expanded = bank switched LIM 4.0 memory.
3. If information is needed on hard drive available space, see the CHKDSK command.

MEMMAKER.EXE

Optimizes computer memory by moving device drivers and memory-resident programs (TSR's) into upper memory: The system must be either a 386 or 486 and have extended memory available. New in DOS Version 6.0

Syntax (shaded is optional):

MEMMAKER /b /batch /session /swap:drive /T /undo

/w:size1,size2

Examples: MEMMAKER
              MEMMAKER /undo

Syntax Options:

/ b . . . . Display in black-and-white mode. Use if there are problems with your monochrome monitor.

/ batch . . . . Run MEMMAKER in unattended mode. This forces acceptance of defaults at all prompts. If an error occurs during the process, MEMMAKER restores the original AUTOEXEC.BAT, CONFIG.SYS, and Windows SYSTEM.INI. Status messages and errors are reported in the MEMMAKER.STS file.

/ batch2 . . . . . . Completely automates the optimization process with absolutely no user intervention. No prompts, no pauses. Ver?

/ session . . . . . . This switch is only used by MEMMAKER during the optimizing process.

/ swap:drive . . . . Specifies the drive letter of the system startup drive, if it has changed since the system started up. (encountered with some disk swapping programs)

/ T . . . . If problems are encountered between MEMMAKER and an IBM Token Ring network, use this switch. It disables the Token-Ring detection function.

/ undo . . . . Forces MEMMAKER to undo the most recent changes it has made to the system. This switch is normally used if problems are encountered after MEMMAKER has been run and you wish the system to be returned to its original confituration.

/ w:size1,size2 . Sets the upper memory size reserved for Windows translation buffers. Windows needs two separate areas of up-
per memory for the buffers. size1 is the size of the first
area, size2 is the size of the second area. The default is
no buffers are created (/ w:0,0).

Command Type and Version:
External command; Introduced with Ver 6.0

Notes:
1. See also DEVICEHIGH and LOADHIGH.
2. **WARNING: Do not run this program if Windows is running!**
3. CHKSTATE.SYS is a CONFIG.SYS command line that is
   automatically created by MEMMAKER during the optimization
   process. At the end of the process, it is automatically removed
   from CONFIG.SYS.

MENUCOLOR

*Command line to set text and background colors for the DOS startup menu
in theCONFIG.SYS file:* The startup menu is a list of system configuration choices
that appear when your system is started. Each menu item is a set of CONFIG.SYS
commands and is called a "configuration block." See your DOS manual for details
of setting up and using the startup menu. New in DOS Version 6.0.

Syntax (shaded is optional):
  MENUCOLOR = X , Y

  Examples: MENUCOLOR 7, 9

Syntax Options:
X . . . . Sets menu text color. Valid values 0 to 15.
, Y . . . . Sets screen background color. Valid values are 0 to 15.
                Default=0 (black). Color Values:

0=Black	8=Gray
1=Blue	9=Bright blue
2=Green	10=Bright green
3=Cyan	11=Bright cyan
4=Red .	12=Bright red
5=Magenta	13=Bright magenta
6=Brown	14=Yellow
7=White	15=Bright white

            Note: colors 8 to 15 blink on some displays.

Command Type and Version:
CONFIG.SYS command; Network; Introduced with Ver 6.0

Notes:
1. See also MENUDEFAULT, MENUITEM, NUMLOCK, INCLUDE and
   SUBMENU. All are used by the startup menu.
2. Don't make X and Y the same number, text won't show!

MENUDEFAULT

Command line to set the default menu item for the DOS startup menu in CONFIG.SYS: The startup menu is a list of system configuration choices that appear when your system is started. Each menu item is a set of CONFIG.SYS commands and is called a "configuration block." See your DOS manual for details of setting up and using the startup menu. New in DOS Version 6.0.

Syntax (shaded is optional):

MENUDEFAULT = blockname , timeout

Examples: MENUDEFAULT = NET, 20

Syntax Options:

blockname . . . . Sets the default menu item. If no default is specified, item 1 is selected.

, timeout . . . . . . The number of seconds DOS waits before starting your computer with a default configuration.

Command Type and Version:

CONFIG.SYS command; Network; Introduced with Ver 6.0

Notes:

1. See also MENUCOLOR, MENUITEM, NUMLOCK, INCLUDE and SUBMENU. All are used by the startup menu.

MENUITEM

Command line to define a menu item for the DOS startup menu in CONFIG.SYS: The startup menu is a list of system configuration choices that appear when your system is started. Each menu item is a set of CONFIG.SYS commands and is called a "configuration block." See your DOS manual for details of setting up and using the startup menu. New in DOS Version 6.0.

Syntax (shaded is optional):

MENUITEM blockname , menutext

Examples: MENUITEM NET, Start your Network

Syntax Options:

blockname . . . . Defines a menu item on the startup menu. It is usable only within a menu block and there can be a maximum of nine menu items per menu. If DOS cannot find a specified name, the item will not appear on the startup menu. blockname can be up to 70 characters long but you cannot use spaces, \ (backslashes), / (forward slashes), commas, semicolons, equal signs or square brackets.

, menutext . . . . . Up to 70 characters of text to display for the menu item. If no text is given, DOS displays *blockname* as the menu item.

Command Type and Version:

CONFIG.SYS command; Network; Introduced with Ver 6.0

Notes:

1. See also MENUCOLOR, MENUDEFAULT, NUMLOCK, INCLUDE and SUBMENU. All are used by the startup menu.

MIRROR.COM

Records information about 1 or more disks for use by UNFORMAT and UNDELETE *commands*: Removed from DOS Version 6.0 and later.

Syntax (shaded is optional):

Three syntax formats are valid:

MIRROR Drives: /1 /Tdrive – entries . . .

MIRROR /u

MIRROR /partn

Examples: MIRROR /u
              MIRROR C: /Ta /Tc

Syntax Options:

Drives: . . . . The drive or drives to be MIRRORed.

/ 1 . . . . Instructs MIRROR to retain only the latest information about a disk. The default causes MIRROR to make a backup of existing information before new information is recorded.

/Tdrive – entries Loads a deletion–tracking program that maintains information so that the UNDELETE command can recover files. *drive* is required and is the drive to be MIRRORed. *entries* is optional and is the maximum number of entries in PCTRACKR.DEL (the deletion tracking file). *entries* can range from 1 to 999 and the *entries* defaults are as follows:

Disk Size	Default Entry	File Size
360k	25	5k
720k	50	9k
1.2 meg	75	14k
1.44 meg	75	14k
20 meg	101	18k
32 meg	202	36k
>32 meg	303	55k

/ u . . . . Unload and disable the deletion tracking program. If other memory resident programs have been loaded after MIRROR, the */u* switch will not function.

/ partn . . . . Save partitioning information for the UNFORMAT command. The information is saved on a floppy disk for use at a later time if partitions need to be rebuilt by UNFORMAT. The default drive to save the information to is A:, although a different drive can be specified at the prompt.

Command Type and Version:

External command; Network; Introduced with Ver 5.0

Removed from DOS Ver 6.0, functionally replaced by the UNDELETE / T command. MIRROR is available on Microsoft's MS-DOS Ver. 6.0,6.21, and 6.22 Supplemental Disks.

Notes:
1. If MIRROR is used without any switches, it saves information about the disk in the current drive.
2. Do not use MIRROR on any drive that has been redirected using the JOIN or SUBST commands. If ASSIGN is used, it must be used before MIRROR.
3. MIRROR saves a copy of a drive's FAT (file allocation table) and a copy of the drive's root directory. Since this information may change regularly, it is recommended that you use MIRROR regularly in order to maintain current information for UNFORMAT to use. It is recommended that MIRROR be placed in your AUTOEXEC.BAT file so that current information is saved every time your system is turned on or re-booted.
4. See also UNFORMAT and UNDELETE.
5. **DOS 6.0 Note:** MIRROR is still available from Microsoft as a supplemental disk, call them for details.

MODE.COM

Controls system devices such as display, serial ports, printer ports, and system settings: NOTE: Since there are many functions that MODE addresses, they will each be treated separately in the following pages.

Command Type and Version:
External command; Network; Introduced with Ver 1.0

MODE to Display Device Status

Syntax (shaded is optional):
MODE device /status

Examples:
> MODE   (Display status of all system devices)
> MODE con   (Display console status)
> MODE lpt1 /status

Syntax Options:
device . . . . Device for which status is requested.
/status or */sta* . . Displays status of redirected parallel printers.

Notes: None

MODE to Configure Printer

Configures parallel port printers: Ports that can be addressed include PRN, LPT1, LPT2, and LPT3. Printer types that can be configured are IBM compatibles and Epson compatibles.

Syntax (shaded is optional):

MODE Lptn : c , L , r

MODE Lptn : cols=c lines=L retry=r

Examples: MODE Lpt2:132,6

                  MODE Lpt1 cols=132 lines=8

Syntax Options:

Lptn. . . . . Parallel port to be configured.
                  Valid numbers for *n* are 1, 2, and 3.

c or *cols=* . . . . . Number of character columns per line.
                  Default=80, Values=80 or 132.

L or *lines=*. . . . . Number of vertical lines per inch.
                  Default=6, Values=6 or 8.

r or *retry=* . . . . . Type of retry if time-out error occurs. This option leaves a
                  memory resident piece of MODE in RAM. Valid *rs*' are:

    e . . . . Return busy port error from status check.

    b . . . . Return busy port "Busy" from status check.

    p . . . . Continue retry until printer accepts data.

    r . . . . Return "Ready" from busy port status check.

    n . . . . Disable retry (Default). "none" is also valid.

Notes:

1. *retry=b* is equivalent to the "p" parameter in earlier DOS versions
2. Ctrl+C will break out of a time-out loop.
3. PRN and LPT1 can be used interchangeably.
4. Do not use any *retry* options over a network.
5. The colon (:) with Lptn is optional.

MODE to Configure Serial Port

Configures a serial communications port: Ports that can be addressed include COM1, COM2, COM3, and COM4.

Syntax (shaded is optional):

MODE COMn : b , p , d , s , r

MODE COMn : baud=b parity=p data=d stop=s retry=r

Examples: MODE COM1:24,N,8,1

Syntax Options:

COM*n*. . . . . Asynchronous serial port to be configured. Valid values are
                  1, 2, 3, and 4.

b or *baud=* . . . . Transmission rate in bits per second. Only the first 2 digits
                  are required. Valid values are 11=110 baud, 15=150,
                  30=300, 60=600, 12=1200, 24=2400, 48=4800, 96=9600,
                  & 19=19,200 baud.

p or *parity=* . . . . Parity check. N=none, E=even, O=odd, M=mark,
                  S=space. Default=E

d or *data*= . . . . . Number of data bits in a character.
　　　　　　　　　　Valid values are 5, 6, 7, 8. Default=7

s or *stop*= . . . . . Number of stop bits for end of character. Valid values are
　　　　　　　　　　1, 1.5 or 2. Default=1 (Default at 110 baud=2)

r or *retry*= . . . . . Type of retry if time-out error occurs. This option leaves a
　　　　　　　　　　memory resident piece of MODE in RAM. Valid *rs'* are:

　　　e . . . . Return busy port error from status check.
　　　b . . . . Return busy port "Busy" from status check.
　　　p . . . . Continue retry until printer accepts data.
　　　r. . . . . Return "Ready" from busy port status check.
　　　n . . . . Disable retry (Default). "none" is also valid.

Notes:
1. If any parameters are omitted in the MODE statement, the most recent
   setting is used.
2. Do not use *retry* values over a network.
3. *retry=b* is equivalent to the "p" parameter in earlier DOS versions.

MODE to Redirect Printing

Redirects output from a parallel port to a serial port:

Syntax (shaded is optional):
　MODE L*ptm* : = COM*n* :

　Examples:　　MODE Lpt1: = COM1:
　　　　　　　　MODE Lpt1 = COM2

Syntax Options:
Lpt*m* . . . . The parallel port to be redirected.
　　　　　　　　　Valid *m* values are 1, 2, and 3.
COM*n* . . . . The serial port to be redirected to.
　　　　　　　　　Valid *n* values are 1, 2, 3, and 4.

Notes:
1. Following a redirection, the original output direction can be restored by
   typing MODE lpt*m* where m is the original printer port.

MODE to Set Device Code Pages

Selects, refreshes, prepares, or displays code page numbers for parallel
printers and the console:

Syntax (shaded is optional):

MODE device codepage prepare = <u>yyy Drive:\Path\Filename</u>

MODE device codepage select=yyy

MODE device codepage refresh

MODE device codepage /status

Examples:
```
MODE CON codepage prepare = 860
MODE LPT1 codepage /status
```

Syntax Options:

device . . . . Device to be affected. Valid values are CON, LPT1,
LPT2, and LPT3.

codepage prepare or cp prep.. . . . . Prepares the code page for the specific
device. Use codepage select after this command.

Drive:\Path\Filename Drive, directory and file containing code page information (.CPI files) needed to prepare a code page.

EGA.CPI . . . . . Enhanced graphics adapter or PS2

EGA2.CPI . . . . Similar to EGA.CPI, but with more   code pages.

4201.CPI . . . . . IBM Proprinters II and III, Model 4201
IBM Proprinters II & III, Model 4202

4208.CPI . . . . . IBM Proprinter X24E Model 4207
IBM Proprinter XL24E Model 4208

5202.CPI . . . . . IBM Quietwriter III Printer

LCD.CPI . . . . . IBM PC Convertible Liquid Crystal Disp.

ISO.CPI . . . . . . Complies with Part 3 of ISO 9241 spec

codepage select or cp sel Selects a code page for a specific device. cp prep
above must be run first.

codepage refresh or cp ref If a code page is lost, this command reinstates it.

codepage . . . . . When used alone, codepage displays the numbers of the
code pages that have been prepared for a specific device.

/status or /sta . . Displays the current code page numbers

Notes:

1. See also NLSFUNC and CHCP.
2. EGA.CPI and EGA2.CPI are shipped with DOS. All others are supplied
on Microsoft's MS-DOS Supplemental Disks.

MODE to Set Display Mode

Reconfigure or select active display adapter:

Syntax (shaded is optional):

MODE <u>adapter</u> , shift , t

MODE <u>adapter , n</u>

MODE CON <u>: cols=c lines=n</u>

Examples: MODE co80,r
MODE CON:cols=40 lines=43

Syntax Options:

adapter . . . . Display adapter category as follows:

40 or 80 . . . . Number of characters/line

bw40 or bw80 . . . . CGA (color graphics with color disabled.
Characters per line = 40 or 80

co40 or co80 . . . . . Color display with color
enabled. Characters per line = 40 or 80.

mono . . . . Monochrome display with 80 characters per line.

shift . . . . Shift CGA screen left or right. Valid values are L for left,
R for right.

t . . . . Starts a test pattern for screen alignment.

n . . . . Vertical lines per screen. Valid values are 25, 43, and 50.
ANSI.SYS must be loaded in CONFIG.SYS for this to work.

cols= . . . . Characters or columns per line. Valid values are 40 and 80.

lines= . . . . Vertical lines per screen. Valid values are 25, 43, and 50.
ANSI.SYS must be loaded in CONFIG.SYS for this to work.

Notes:

1. Some monitors do not support 43 and 50 vertical lines per screen.

MODE to Set Typematic Rate

Set the rate at which DOS repeats a character when a keyboard key is held down: Some keyboards do not recognize this command.

Syntax (shaded is optional):

MODE con <u>: rate= r delay= d</u>

Examples: MODE con : rate=20 delay=2

Syntax Options:

con or con: . . . . Keyboard

rate=*r* . . . . The rate that a character is repeated on the display when a
key is held down. *r* Default=20 for AT keyboards, Default=21
for PS2 keyboards. *r* Range = 1 to 32, which is equivalent to
the following: rate 1 = 2 characters per second (cps), 10 =
4.3 cps, 20 = 10 cps, 30 = 24 cps and 32 = 30 cps.

delay=*d* . . . . The amount of time, after a key is held down, before the repeat function activates. *d* Default=2, *d* valid values are 1, 2,
3 and 4 (equivalent to 0.25, 0.50, 0.75, and 1 second respectively). If a delay is specified, rate must also be specified.

Notes:
1. The keyboard must be an AT or PS/2 class or higher keyboard in order for this command to work.

MORE.COM

Displays output one screen at a time: MORE reads standard input from a pipe or redirected file and is typically used to view lengthy files. Each screen of information ends with the prompt -More- and you can press any key to view the next screen.

Syntax (shaded is optional):

MORE < <u>Drive: \Path\</u> Filename

or

command | MORE

Examples: MORE < C:\Data.txt
             DIR | MORE

Syntax Options:

Drive:\Path .... Drive and directory containing *Filename*.
Filename...... Name of file that supplies data to be displayed.
command ..... Name of command that supplies data to be displayed, for example, DIR

Command Type and Version:
External command; Network; Introduced with Ver 2.0

Notes:
1. When using the pipe (|) for redirection, you are able to use DOS commands, such as DIR, SORT, and TYPE with MORE, but the TEMP environment variable in AUTOEXEC.BAT should be set first.
2. MORE saves input information in a temporary file on disk until the data is ready to be displayed. If there is no room on the disk, MORE will not work. Also, if the current drive is a write-protected drive, MORE will return an error.

MOVE.EXE

Move files from one drive or directory to another: You can also move and rename complete directories, along with their files and subdirectories, to other drives or directories. **Warning:** DOS does not warn you if it is about to overwrite files with the same name. New in DOS Version 6.0.

Syntax (shaded is optional):

MOVE <u>/Y / -Y Drive: \Path\</u> Filename

<u>. Drive: \Path\</u> .... Filename Destination

Examples: Move c:\test.txt d:\temp\test.txt

Syntax Options:

/Y	Directs MOVE to replace existing files without a confirmation prompt. Started with DOS Version 6.2.
/-Y	Directs MOVE to ask for confirmation prior to replacing an existing file. (Default) Started with DOS Version 6.2.
Drive:\Path....	Drive and directory containing *Filename*.
Filename......	Name of file(s) that you want to move.
Destination	The new location of the file(s) being moved. This can be a drive, subdirectory, or combination of the two.

Command Type and Version:
External command; Network; Introduced with Ver 6.0

Notes:
1. If more than one file is being moved, the Destination must be a drive and subdirectory.

MSAV and MWAV.EXE

Microsoft Anti-Virus scanners for DOS (MSAV) and Windows (MWAV).

Syntax (shaded is optional): New in DOS Version 6.0

MSAV <u>Drive: /S /C /R /A /L /N /P /F /ss /video /IN /BW</u>

<u>/mono /LCD /FF /BF /NF /BT /NGM /LE /PS2</u>

Examples: MSAV C: /A /N /F

Syntax Options:

Drive:	Drive to be scanned. The Default is the current drive.
/S	Scan but do not remove viruses.
/C	Scan and remove viruses.
/R	Create a MSAV.RPT report that lists the number of files scaned, the number of viruses found, and the number of viruses removed. Default=no report.
/A	Scan all drives except A and B.
/L	Scan all logical drives except networks.
/N	Run in command mode, not graphical. Also, display contents of a MSAV.TXT file if it's present.
/P	Run in command line mode w/ switches.
/F	Do not display file names during scan.
/ss	Set screen display size:
	/25=25 lines, this is the default
	/28=28 lines, use with VGA
	/43=43 lines, use with EGA or VGA
	/50=50 lines, use with VGA
	/60=60 lines, use with VGA and Video7
/video........	Display list of valid video screen switches.
/IN	Run MSAV using a color scheme.
/BW	Run MSAV in black-and-white mode.
/mono	Run MSAV in monochrome mode.
/LCD	Run MSAV in LCD mode.

/ FF	Run MSAV in fast screen mode for CGA monitors. Screen quality is worse.
/ BF	Use computer BIOS to display video.
/ NF	Disable use of alternate screen fonts.
/ BT	Enable graphics mouse in Windows.
/ NGM	Use default mouse character instead of the graphics character.
/ LE	Switch left and right mouse buttons.
/ PS2	Reset mouse if the mouse cursor locks up or disappears.

Command Type and Version:
  External command; Network; Introduced with Ver 6.0

Notes:
1. MSAV is actually Central Point Software's Anti-Virus program which has been licensed to Microsoft.

MSBACKUP-MWBACKUP.EXE

Microsoft's menu driven program to backup and restore one or more files from one disk to another disk: This program is a replacement for BACKUP and RESTORE used in previous DOS versions. MSBACKUP is for DOS and MWBACKUP is for Windows. New in DOS Version 6.0.

Syntax (shaded is optional):
  MSBACKUP setup_file /BW /LCD /MDA

  Examples: MSBACKUP /BW

Syntax Options:
setup_file	Predefined setup that specifies which files to backup and the type of backup to be performed. MSBACKUP automatically creates this file if "save program settings". During the "save program" function, if no file name is specified, the file name DEFAULT.SET is used.
/ BW	Run screen in black-and-white mode.
/ LCD	Run screen in LCD mode.
/ MDA	Run screen in monochrome mode.

Command Type and Version:
  External command; Network; Introduced with Ver 6.0

Notes:
1. MSBACKUP does not support the use of tape backups.
2. Backups and catalog files are compatible between MSBACKUP and MWBACKUP.

MSCDEX.EXE

Microsoft's CD-ROM Extensions : MSCDEX is used in conjunction with the CD-ROM device driver that was shipped with the drive. It is normally executed in the AUTOEXEC.BAT file. New in DOS Version 6.0.

Syntax (shaded is optional):

MSCDEX /D:driver /D:driver2 . . . /E /K /S /V

/L:letter /M:number

Examples: MSCDEX /D:1

Syntax Options:

/D:driver . . . . . . Drive signature for the first CD-ROM drive. Typically this is MSCD0000. The drive signature must match that of the CD-ROM driver in CONFIG.SYS.

/D:driver2 . . . . . Drive signature of the second CD-ROM drive. Typically this is MSCD0001.

/E . . . . CD-ROM drive can use expanded memory, if available, to store sector buffers.

/K . . . . Provide Kanji support for CD-ROM.

/S . . . . Share CD-ROM on MS-NET network or Windows for workgroup servers.

/V . . . . Display MSCDEX memory stats when the program starts.

/L:letter . . . . . . Specifies drive letter for first CD-ROM. If more than one CD-ROM, DOS assigns the subsequent drive letters.

/M:number . . . . Specifies the number of sector buffers.

Command Type and Version:

External command; Network; Introduced with Ver 6.0

Notes:

1. Do not start MSCDEX after Windows has been started.

MSD.COM & .EXE

Microsoft's menu driven system diagnostics: This program provides detailed technical information about your system. New in DOS Version 6.0.

Syntax (shaded is optional):

MSD /I /B [/F drive:\path\filename] [/P drive:\path\filename]

[/S drive:\path\filename]

Examples: MSD
              MSD / B / I

Syntax Options:

/I . . . . Forces MSD to not initially detect hardware when it starts. This may be necessary if MSD is not running properly or locks up.

/B . . . . Run MSD in black-and-white mode.

drive:\path . . . . Drive and path where a MSD report file is to be written.

/F drive:\path\filename . . Prompts for a company, address, & phone to be written on the MSD report named *filename*.

/P drive:\path\filename . . Writes a complete MSD report to a file named *filename*.

DOS Commands

/ S drive:\path\filename. . Writes a summary MSD report to a file named
                              filename.

Command Type and Version:
  External command; Network; Introduced with Ver 6.0

Notes:
1. MSD has shipped with Windows for quite some time and is an excellent
   diagnostics tool.

MSHERC.COM

*Installs support for Qbasic graphics programs using the Hercules graph-
ics card:*

Syntax (shaded is optional):
  MSHERC / half

  Examples: MSHERC / half

Syntax Options:
  / half . . . . Use this switch if a color adapter card is also installed in
                       the system.

Command Type and Version:
  External command; Network; Introduced with Ver 5.0

NLSFUNC.EXE

National language support function, *loads country-specific information and
code-page switching:* Use NLSFUNC from either the command line or through
CONFIG.SYS.

Syntax (shaded is optional):
  At the DOS prompt:

  NLSFUNC Drive:\Path\ Filename

  If loaded through CONFIG.SYS:

  INSTALL = Drive1:\Path1\ NLSFUNC.EXE country

  Examples: NLSFUNC C:\Bin\Newcode.sys

Syntax Options:
  Drive:\Path . . . . Drive and directory containing *Filename*.
  Filename. . . . . . File containing country-specific information.
  Drive1:\Path1 . . Drive and directory containing NSLFUNC.
  country . . . . Same as *Filename*.

Command Type and Version:
  External & CONFIG.SYS command; Network; Introduced with Ver 3.3

Notes:

1. The COUNTRY command in CONFIG.SYS defines the default value for Drive:\Path \Filename. If there is no COUNTRY command in CONFIG.SYS, NLSFUNC looks for COUNTRY.SYS in the root directory of the start up drive.
2. See also CHCP and MODE.

NUMLOCK

Command line to set the NUM LOCK key to ON or OFF for the DOS startup menu in the CONFIG.SYS file: The startup menu is a list of system configuration choices that appear when your system is started. Each menu item is a set of CONFIG.SYS commands and is called a "configuration block." See your DOS manual for details of setting up and using the startup menu. New in DOS Version 6.0.

Syntax (shaded is optional):
NUMLOCK = <u>ON</u> or OFF

    Examples: NUMLOCK = ON

Syntax Options:
ON . . . . Turns NUM LOCK key on.
OFF . . . . Turns NUM LOCK key off.

Command Type and Version:
CONFIG.SYS command; Network; Introduced with Ver 6.0

Notes:
1. See also MENUDEFAULT, MENUITEM, MENUCOLOR, INCLUDE and SUBMENU. All are used by the startup menu.

PATH

Sets a directory search path: DOS uses the path command to search for executable files in specified directories. The default is the current working directory.

Syntax (shaded is optional):
PATH <u>Drive1: \Path1; Drive2: \Path2;...</u>

    Examples: PATH C:\ ;D:\ ;D:\Dos;D:\Utility\test
    PATH   (displays the current search path)
    PATH ;   (clears search-path settings other
                   than default setting (current directory)

Syntax Options:
Drive1: Drive2: Specifies drive letters to be included in the search path
\Path1 \Path 2 . Specifies directory (s) in the search path where DOS should look for files.
; . . . . Must be used to separate multiple *Drive:\Path* locations or if used as *Path ;* it clears search-path settings other than the default setting.

Command Type and Version:

Internal command; Network; Introduced with Ver 2.0

Notes:
1. The maximum number of characters allowed in the PATH statement is 127. See SUBST for ways to get around this limit. Also see the SET Path statement.
2. If files have the same name but different extensions, DOS searches for files in the following order: .COM, .EXE, .BAT.
3. If identical file names occur in different directories, DOS looks in the current directory first, then in locations specified in PATH in the order they are listed in the PATH statement.
4. A PATH command is usually included in the AUTOEXEC.BAT file so that it is issued at the time the system starts.

PAUSE

Pauses the processing of a batch file: Suspends processing of a batch file and prompts the user to press any key to continue.

Syntax (shaded is optional):
PAUSE

Examples: PAUSE

Syntax Options:
None

Command Type and Version:
Internal command; Only used in Batch Programs; Introduced with Ver 1.0

Notes:
1. Earlier versions of PAUSE indicated that a text comment could be inserted after PAUSE and the message would display when PAUSE ran, for example "PAUSE This is a test." This message function is not functional.
2. Ctrl+C or Ctrl Break will stop a Batch program while running or at pause

POWER

Reduces power consumption in a computer when applications and devices are idle: New in DOS Version 6.0. Once the POWER.EXE driver is loaded through the CONFIG.SYS file, POWER at the command line turns power on/off, reports status and sets conservation levels.

Syntax (shaded is optional):
POWER ADV[:MAX or REG or MIN] or STD or OFF

Examples: POWER (displays current settings)
              POWER OFF

Syntax Options:

ADV[:MAX or REG or MIN] . . . Conserves power when devices are idle.
MAX=maximum power conservation, REG=default, balance conservation with device performance, MIN=higher device performance is needed.

STD . . . . If the computer supports APM, STD conserves power. If not supported, it turns off the power.

OFF . . . . Turns off power management.

Command Type and Version:
External command;
Network; Introduced with Ver 6.0

Notes:
1. See also POWER.EXE.
2. If the computer does not support APM, using STD will disable the power completely.

POWER.EXE

Reduces power consumption in a computer when applications and devices are idle: New in DOS Version 6.0. This driver conforms to the Advanced Power Management (APM) specifications and is loaded through the CONFIG.SYS file.

Syntax (shaded is optional):

Device = <u>Drive:\Path\</u> POWER.EXE <u>ADV[:MAX or REG or MIN]</u>

or   <u>STD or OFF /low</u>

Examples: Device = POWER.EXE

Syntax Options:
Drive1\Path . . . Specifies the location of POWER.EXE

ADV[:MAX or REG or MIN] . . . Conserves power when devices are idle.
MAX=maximum power conservation, REG=default, balance conservation with device performance, MIN=higher device performance is needed.

STD . . . . If the computer supports APM, STD conserves power. If not supported, it turns off the power.

OFF . . . . Turns off power management.

/ low . . . . Loads driver into conventional memory, even if upper memory is available. The default is load into upper memory.

Command Type and Version:
CONFIG.SYS command; Network; Introduced with Ver 6.0

Notes:
1. See also POWER.
2. If the computer does not support APM, using STD will disable the power completely.

PRINT.EXE

Prints a text file to a line printer, in the background. Other DOS commands can be executed at the same time PRINT is running:

Syntax (shaded is optional):

PRINT /d:device /b:size /u:ticks1 /m:ticks2 /s:ticks3 /q:qsize /t

     Drive:\Path\ Filename ... /c /p

Examples: PRINT C:\Test.txt /c C:\test2.txt /p
                 PRINT /d:Lpt1 /u:25

Syntax Options:

/d:device	Name of printer device: **Parallel Ports:** Lpt1, Lpt2, Lpt3. **Serial Ports:** com1,com2, com3, com4. PRN and Lpt1 refer to the same parallel port. Default=PRN **/d must precede Filename.**
/b:size	Sets size (in bytes) of internal buffer. Default=512, Range=512 to 16384.
/u:ticks1.	Maximum number of clock ticks PRINT is to wait for a printer to become available. Default=1, Value Range=1 to 255.
/m:ticks2	Maximum number of clock ticks PRINT can take to print a character on printer. Default=2, Value Range=1 to 255.
/s:ticks3.	Maximum number of clock ticks allocated for background printing. Default=8, Value Range=1 to 255.
/q:qsize	Max number of files allowed in print queue. Default=10 Value Range=4 to 32.
/t	Removes files from the print queue.
Drive:\Path\Filename .	Location & Filename of file to be printed.
/c	Removes files from the print queue. Both the /c and /p switches can be used on the same command line. When the /c **precedes** the *Filenames* on the command line, it applies to all the files that follow until PRINT comes to a /p, in which case the /p switch applies to the file preceding the /p. When the /c switch **follows** the *Filenames*, it applies to the file that precedes the /c and all files that follow until PRINT comes to a /p switch.
/p	Adds files to the print queue. Both the /c and /p switches can be used on the same command line. When the /p **precedes** the *Filenames* on the command line, it applies to all the files that follow until PRINT comes to a /c, in which case the /c switch applies to the file preceding the /c. When the /p switch **follows** the *Filenames*, it applies to the file that precedes the /p and all files that follow until PRINT comes to a /c switch.

Command Type and Version:

External command; Introduced with Ver 2.0

Notes:

1. You can use the /d,/b,/u,/m,/s and /q switches only the first time you use PRINT. DOS must be restarted to use them again.

2. Use a program's own PRINT command to print files created with that program. PRINT only functions correctly with ASCII text.
3. Each queue entry includes a drive, directory and subdirectory and must not exceed 64 characters per entry.

PRINTER.SYS

Installable device driver that supports code-page switching for parallel ports PRN, LPT1, LPT2, and LPT3: Removed in DOS Version 6.0 and later.

Syntax (shaded is optional):

```
DEVICE = Drive:\Path\ PRINTER.SYS , hwcp , n
          LPTn = ( type          )
```

Examples:
DEVICE=C:\Dos\PRINTER.SYS LPT1:=(4201,437,2)

Syntax Options:

Drive:\Path . . . . Drive and directory containing PRINTER.SYS

LPT*n*. . . . . LPT1, LPT2, or LPT3

type . . . . Type of printer in use. Valid values for *type* and the printer represented by each value are as follows:

        4201 . . . IBM Proprinters II and III M.4201
                  IBM Proprinters II and III XL M.4202
        4208 . . . IBM Proprinters X24E M.4207
                  IBM Proprinters XL24E M.4208
        5202 . . . IBM Quietwriter III M.5202

hwcp . . . . Code-page supported by your hardware. DOS supports the following code pages:

        437 . . . . United States
        850 . . . . Multilingual (Latin I)
        852 . . . . Slavic (Latin II)
        860 . . . . Portuguese
        863 . . . . Canadian-French
        865 . . . . Nordic

n . . . . Number of additional code-pages.

Command Type and Version:
CONFIG.SYS command; Introduced with Ver 3.3. Removed in Ver. 6.0, however it is available from Microsoft on the MS-DOS 6.0, 6.21, and 6.22 Supplemental Disks

PRINTFIX.COM

Stops MS-DOS from Checking the status of the printer attached to the system: New in DOS Version 6.0.

Syntax:

PRINTFIX

Example: printfix

Syntax Options:
None

Command Type and Version:
External command, Introduced with Ver. 6.0
Available from Microsoft on the MS-DOS 6.0, 6.21, and 6.22 Supplemental Disks.

Notes:
1. Use only if printing problems occurred while installing MS-DOS 6.0, 6.21, or 6.22.

PROMPT

Change Prompt: Customizing prompt to display text or information and change color. Example: time or date, current directory or default drive.

Syntax (shaded is optional):

PROMPT Text $Characters

Examples: PROMPT pg (Most commonly used)
If ANSI.SYS is loaded and you have a color monitor, try the following for colors at the DOS level:
    PROMPT $e[35;44;1m$pge[33;44;1m

Syntax Options:

PROMPT . . . . . PROMPT by itself resets to default prompt.
Text . . . . *Text* can be any typed message.
$Characters . . . Type in special characters from the table below to create special prompts.

Typed character	displayed prompt
$q	The = character
$$	The $ sign
$t	Current time
$d	Current date
$p	Current drive and path
$v	DOS version number
$n	Current drive
$g	>Greater-than symbol
$l	<Less-than symbol
$b	(l) vertical bar
$_	Enter, first position of next line
$e	ASCII escape code (code 27)
$h	Backspace (deletes a prompts command line character)

Command Type and Version:
Internal command; Network; Introduced with Ver 2.0

Notes:
1. See also ANSI.SYS
2. The PROMPT command is typically inserted inAUTOEXEC.BAT

QBASIC®.EXE

Basic computer language: A program that reads instructions and interprets those instructions into executable computer code. A complete environment for programming in the Basic language is provided by the QBASIC program.

Syntax (shaded is optional):

QBASIC /b /editor /g /h /mbf /nohi /run Drive:\Path \Filename

Examples: QBASIC
              QBASIC C:\Qb\Bin\Test

Syntax Options:

Drive:\Path . . . . Drive and directory containing *Filename*.
\Filename . . . . . Name of file to load when QBASIC starts.
/b . . . . QBASIC is displayed in black and white.
/editor . . . . Invokes EDIT, DOS full-screen text Editor.
/g . . . . Fastest screen update of a CGA monitor.
/h . . . . Displays max. number of display lines.
/mbf . . . . Converts the resident functions MKS$, MKD$, CVS, and
                      CVD to MKSMBF$, MKDMBF$, CVSMBF, and CVDMBF.
/nohi . . . . Allows use of monitor without high-intensity video support.
                      COMPAQ laptop computers cannot use this switch.
/run . . . . The specified BASIC program is run before being displayed.

Command Type and Version:

External command; Network; Introduced with Ver 5.0

Notes:

1. QBASIC.EXE must be in the current directory, search path, or in same directory as EDIT.COM in order to use the DOS Editor.
2. Consecutive Basic programs can be run from a Batch file if the Basic system command and the /run switch is used.
3. If GW-BASIC programs need to be converted to QBASIC, read REMLINE.BAS in QBASIC's subdirectory.
4. If a monitor does not support shortcut keys, use */b* and */nohi*.

RAMDRIVE.SYS or VDISK.SYS

Creates a simulated hard disk from the system's RAM memory: RAM disks are much faster than hard disks but they are temporary (if the system shuts down, the data is lost).

Syntax (shaded is optional):

Device=Drive:\Path\ RAMDRIVE.SYS disksize sectorsize

numentry / e / a

Examples:

Device=C:\Dos\RAMDRIVE.SYS 4096 / a

Syntax Options:

Drive:\Path . . . . Drive & directory containing RAMDRIVE.SYS

disksize	Sets size of RAM disk in kilobytes. Valid sizes range from 4 to 32767.Default=64
sectorsize	Sets sector size in bytes. Valid sizes are 128, 256, and 512. Default=512. Do not change default if possible.
numentry	Sets the number of files and directories that the RAM disk's root directory can hold. Default=64, range=2 to 1024. If this parameter is used, *disksize* and *sectorsize* must also be set.
/ e	RAM disk uses extended memory. 4Kb minimum extended memory is needed. Default=uses conventional memory.
/a	RAM disk uses expanded memory. 4Kb minimum extended memory is needed. Default= uses conventional memory.

Command Type and Version:
CONFIG.SYS command; Introduced with Ver 3.1(Vdisk=3.0)

Notes:
1. Multiple RAM disks are allowed.
2. Always try to use */e* or */a* so that conventional RAM is not used.
3. A memory manager like HIMEM.SYS must be used if /e is used.
4. An expanded memory manager must be installed if /a is used.

RD or RMDIR

Removes a directory: You cannot delete a directory without first deleting its files and subdirectories. The directory must be empty except for the "." and ".." symbols which represent the directory itself and the parent directory. RD and RMDIR are equivalent commands.

Syntax (shaded is optional):
RD <u>Drive:</u> \Path

Examples: RD \Data
            RD \Data\Smith

Syntax Options:
Drive . . . . Drive containing *Path*.
\Path . . . . Directory to be deleted.

Command Type and Version:
Internal command; Network; Introduced with Ver 2.0

Notes:
1. Use DIR to list hidden and system files and ATTRIB to remove hidden and system file attributes in order to empty directory.
2. When a backslash (\) is used before the first directory name in *Path* DOS treats the directory as a subdirectory of the root directory. *Omit the backslash (\) before the first directory name and DOS treats the direc-tory as a subdirectory of the current directory.*
3. The directory being deleted cannot be the current directory and must be an empty directory.

RECOVER.EXE

Recovers readable information from a disk containing bad sectors: When CHKDSK reports bad sectors on a disk, use the RECOVER command to read a file, sector by sector, and recover data from the good sectors. Removed in DOS Version 6.0.

Syntax (shaded is optional):

RECOVER Drive:\Path\ Filename

Examples: RECOVER A:

Syntax Options:

Drive:\Path .... Drive and directory containing *Filename*.

\Filename ..... *Filename* to be recovered. If no *Filename* or *Path* is specified, the entire drive is recovered.

Command Type and Version:

External command; Introduced with Ver 2.0
Removed from Ver 6.0, deemed too dangerous.

Notes:

1. Wildcards (* and?) cannot be used with the RECOVER command.
2. When an entire disk is recovered, each file is placed in the root directory in a FILEnnnn.REC file. The 4 digit numbering sequence on each recovered file is as follows: FILE0001.REC, FILE0002, etc.
3. Since all data in bad sectors is lost when you recover a file, it is best to recover files one at a time, allowing you to edit each file and re-enter missing information.
4. If a drive was formed by the ASSIGN, JOIN or SUBST command, the RECOVER command will not work. It will not work with the BACKUP or RESTORE command since you must use RESTORE with backup files that you created with the BACKUP command.
5. RECOVER cannot recover files on a network drive.
6. If an entire drive is recovered, it is possible that some files will be lost, since the recovered files are written to the root directory and a limited number of files will fit in the root directory.
7. See also CHKDSK

REM

Allows use of remarks (comments) in a Batch file or in CONFIG.SYS: Any BATCH command or CONFIG.SYS line beginning with REM is ignored by DOS.

Syntax (shaded is optional):

REM Comment

Examples: REM begin files here

Syntax Options:

Comment ..... Line of text that you want to include as a comment.

Command Type and Version:

Internal command;
Batch command; Introduced with Ver 1.0
CONFIG.SYS command; Introduced with Ver 4.0

Notes:
1. ECHO ON must be used in the Batch or CONFIG.SYS file for a comment to be displayed.
2. REM can be used without a comment to add vertical spacing to a Batch file, but you can also use blank lines. Blank lines are ignored by DOS.
3. Do not use redirection characters (>or <) or pipe (I) in a Batch file comment.
4. a ";" can be used in place of REM in the WIN.INI file.

REN or RENAME

Renames a file(s): Changes the name(s) on all files matching a specified File-name. REN and RENAME are equivalent commands.

Syntax (shaded is optional):
  REN <u>Drive:\Path\</u> Filename1 Filename2

  Examples: REN C:\ data*.dbf *.db2

Syntax Options:
  Drive:\Path .... Drive and directory containing *Filename*.
  Filename1...... File(s) to be renamed.
  Filename2...... New name for file(s). You cannot rename Drive or Path.

Command Type and Version:
  Internal command; Network; Introduced with Ver 1.0

Notes:
1. The use of Wildcards (* and ?) are allowed.
2. You cannot duplicate a *Filename*.
3. See also LABEL, COPY and XCOPY.

REPLACE.EXE

Replaces files in the target drive with files from the source drive when the filenames are the same: If same name files are not on the target drive, the new files will be added to the target drive.

Syntax (shaded is optional):
  REPLACE <u>Source:\Path1\</u> Filename <u>Target:\Path2 /a /p /r /w</u>

  REPLACE <u>Source:\Path1\</u> Filename <u>Target:\Path2</u>

  <u>/p /r /s /w /u</u>

  Examples: REPLACE A:*.* C:\Test /a /s

Syntax Options:
  Source:\Path1 .. Source drive and directory containing *Filename*.
  Filename...... Name of source file.
  Target:\Path2 .. Location of the destination file(s).

/a.	Adds, instead of replacing, new files to the destination file. This switch **cannot** be used with /s or /u.
/p.	Prompts for confirmation before adding a source file or replacing the destination file.
/r.	Replaces read-only and unprotected files.
/s.	Searches subdirectories of the destination directory and replaces matching files with the source file. The /s switch **cannot** be used with /a.
/w	Waits for a disk to be inserted before REPLACE starts copying. If /w is not specified, REPLACE begins immediately.
/u.	Updates or replaces files in the destination directory that are older than files in the source directory.

Command Type and Version:
External command; Network; Introduced with Ver 3.2

Notes:
1. REPLACE issues a message concerning the number of files that have been added or replaced when the operation is complete.
2. Use /w if you need to change disks during REPLACE.
3. REPLACE does not function on system or hidden files.
4. REPLACE returns the following exit codes: (see IF errorlevel)
   - 0 Files successfully added or replaced
   - 2 Source files could not be found
   - 3 Source or destination path could not be found
   - 5 User does not have access to files being replaced
   - 8 Insufficient system memory to complete command
   - 11 Wrong command line syntax

RESTORE.EXE

Restores files that were backed up using the BACKUP command: The "backed up" and "restored to" disk types do not have to be identical. In Ver 6.0, RESTORE will only restore backups made with previous versions of DOS. It will **NOT** restore backups made with the Ver 6.0 or 6.2x MSBACKUP program!

Syntax (shaded is optional):
RESTORE Drive1: Drive2: \Path\ Filename /s /p /b:date /a:date
                                       /L:time /m /n /d

Examples: RESTORE A: C:*.* /s
              RESTORE B: D:\Data*.dbf /s / m

Syntax Options:
Drive1:	Drive on which backed-up files are stored.
Drive2:\Path . . .	Drive and directory to which backed-up files will be restored.
Filename.	Name(s) of backed-up file(s) to be restored.
/ s	Restores all subdirectories.
/ p	Prompts for permission to restore files that are read-only or files that have changed since last backup.

/b:*date*	Restores files changed or modified on or before a specified *date*.
/a :*date*.	Restores files changed or modified on or after a specified *date*.
/e:*time*	Restores files changed or modified at or earlier than a specified *time*.
/L :*time*.	Restores files changed or modified at or later than a specified *time*.
/m.	Restores only files changed or modified since the last backup.
/n	Restores files that no longer exist on the destination disk. (Drive2)
/d	Without restoring, /d displays a list of files on the backup disk that match names specified in *Filename*. Version 5.0

Command Type and Version:

External command; Network; Introduced with Ver 2.0

Notes:

1. RESTORE does not restore the system files (IO.SYS and MSDOS.SYS or IBMBIO.COM and IBMDOS.COM).
2. RESTORE will not function on drives that have been redirected with AS-SIGN, JOIN, or SUBST.
3. MS-DOS RESTORE Version 5.0 will restore backups made with all previous versions of BACKUP.
4. RESTORE returns the following exit codes: (see IF errorlevel)
   - 0 Files successfully restored
   - 1 Files to be restored could not be found
   - 3 RESTORE stopped by user Ctrl+C
   - 4 RESTORE ended in error.
5. BACKUP is not included in DOS Ver 6.0, see the MSBACKUP utility program.

SCANDISK.EXE

MS-DOS utility program to analyze and recover lost chains and lost clusters on hard or floppy disks to make more space available on these devices. SCANDISK also checks the surface of the disk for errors. Lost chains or lost clusters recovered by SCANDISK are saved in the root directory as files with a .CHK extension. The contents of each file can be examined using the MORE command or any text editor. The files can then be saved or deleted as needed. SCANDISK is an interactive program that steps the user through a series of options in order to scan and repair each selected drive. New in DOS Version 6.2.

Syntax (shaded is optional):

SCANDISK   Drive1: Drive2: Volume_Name

Drive:\Path\Filename /all /autofix /checkonly

/custom /fragment /mono /nosave /nosummary

/surface /undo Undo_Drive

Examples: SCANDISK C: /autofix
            SCANDISK /all
            SCANDISK /fragment C:\TEST\data

Syntax Options:

Drive: . . . . Identifies drive (disk) to scan.

Drive:\Path\Filename. . . . Identifies drive (disk), directory, and file to be checked for fragmentation

/all. . . . . Scan and repair all <u>local</u> drives.

/autofix . . . . Scan and repair without prompts.

/checkonly. . . . . Only scans the selected drives, no repairs are made. Can not be used with */custom* or */autofix*.

/custom. . . . . . . Scan and repair according to parameters set in SCANDISK.INI file. Can not be used with */autofix* or */checkonly*.

/fragment. . . . . . Check for fragmentation of files on selected drives. Individual directories and files may be indicated and wildcards may be used.

/mono . . . . Execute in monochrome mode.

/nosave. . . . . . . Scans automatically and deletes any lost chain or cluster. Can be used only with */autofix*. If */nosave* is left off, all lost chains and clusters will automatically be saved as .CHK files in the root directory of the drive being scanned.

/nosummary . . . Disables full-screen summary display. Full-screen summary display is the default setting for SCANDISK.

/surface. . . . . . . Scans for physical errors on disk.

Volume_Name . Name of unmounted compressed volume (compressed using either DRVSPACE or DBLSPACE) to be scanned and repaired.

/undo. . . . . Undo any repairs made by SCANDISK. Use a blank disk as the undo disk.

Undo_Drive. . . . Drive containing the current undo disk.

Command Type and Version:

External command, Interactive, NOT for Network; In DOS Version 6.2

Notes:

1. Do not use SCANDISK on CD-ROM drives, network drives, or drives created using ASSIGN, SUBST, JOIN, or INTERLNK.
2. Do not use SCANDISK on drives compressed using PC-DOS Ver 6.1.
3. All applications (including Windows) must be stopped before running SCANDISK or data may be lost.

4. Memory resident programs may need to be disabled in the
   AUTOEXEC.BAT and CONFIG.SYS files prior to running SCANDISK.
5. SCANDISK.INI file is a text file containing settings which determine how
   SCANDISK operates on start-up. Sections such as Environment and
   Custom contain the required settings. For more information see comments in the file.
6. SCANDISK is similar to CHKDSK but is more comprehensive in its analysis of a drive.
7. SCANDISK sets ERRORLEVEL to one of the following values upon return to the DOS prompt:
   0 - No problems detected.
   1 - Syntax error.
   2 - Unexpected termination due to an internal error or an
       out-of-memory error.
   3 - User exit prior to completion.
   4 - User exit during surface scan.
   254 - Disk problems found and all corrected.
   255 - Disk problems found but not all corrected.

SELECT.EXE

*Installs DOS on a new disk along with country specific information such
as time and date formats and collating sequences:* Select also formats the
target disk, creates CONFIG.SYS and AUTOEXEC.BAT on a new disk and
copies the source disk to the target disk. Removed from DOS Version 5.0.

Syntax (shaded is optional):

SELECT Source Target\Path yyy xx

Examples: SELECT B: A: 045 dk

Syntax Options:

Source . . . . Drive containing Information to be copied.
Target . . . . Drive containing disk onto which DOS is to be copied.
\Path . . . . Name of directory containing information to be copied.
yyy . . . . Country code. See COUNTRY Command.
nn . . . . Keyboard code. See KEYB Command.

Command Type and Version:

External command; Introduced with Ver 3.0
Removed from Version 5.0

Notes:

1. WARNING: SELECT is used to install DOS for the first time. Everything
   on the *target* disk is erased. SELECT is not available for use on Version
   5.0 and should be used with caution in earlier versions.
2. The *Source Drive* can be either Drive A:or Drive B:.
3. If a hard disk is used in the Target Drive, DOS will prompt for the correct
   internal label for that disk. If the wrong label is typed in, SELECT ends.

SET

Sets, removes or displays environment variables: SET is normally used in the AUTOEXEC.BAT file to set environment variables when the system starts. With DOS Ver 6.0, SET can be used in CONFIG.SYS.

Syntax (shaded is optional):
  SET <u>variable = string</u>

  Examples:
  SET   (displays current environment settings)
  SET TEMP=E:\Windows\Temp
  SET variable =   (clears *string* associated with *variable*)

Syntax Options:
variable. . . . . . . The *variable* to be set or modified.
string. . . . . Text *string* to be associated with *variable*.

Command Type and Version:
  Internal command; Network; Introduced with Ver 2.0

Notes:
1. If SET is used to define values for both *variable* and *string*, DOS adds *variable* to the environment and associates *string* with it. If *variable* already existed, the new *variable* replaces the old one.
2. In a Batch file, SET can be used to create variables that can be used in the same way as %1 through %9. In order to use the new variable, it must be enclosed with %, e.g. %variable%
3. The SET command uses memory from the environment space. If the environment space is too small, DOS will issue the error message "Out of Environment Space". See the SHELL command and COMMAND.COM for ways to increase environment space.
4. See also PATH, PROMPT, SHELL and DIR for additional information on environment variables.

SETUP and BUSETUP.EXE

Programs which initially install MS-DOS.

Syntax(shaded is optional):
  Initial installation from command prompt:
  drive1:SETUP: Example: a:setup

  Installation of certain utilities after initial installation from command line:
  drive1:SETUP: Example: a:setup <u>/e /f /u /i</u>

  Installation of certain utilities after initial installation by insertion of Setup disk and restart of computer:
  drive1:BUSETUP   Example: a:busetup <u>/e /u</u>

Syntax options:
drive1:. . . . . Drive containing the SETUP program.
/e. . . . . Install Anti-Virus, Backup, or Undelete after initial installations.

DOS Commands

DOS Commands

/f	If the system drive A is not compatible with the Setup disk, this switch makes a minimal installation of DOS by copying essential command files on a floppy disk which is compatible with drive A.
/u	Used when installing MS-DOS 6 with certain third-party disk-partitioning software.
/i	Causes Setup to skip automatic hardware detection.

Command Type and Version:

External command, Introduced with Version 5.0.

Notes:

1. See the README.TXT files with MS-DOS Versions 5.0, 5 Upgrade, 6.0, and 6.2 for more information.
2. Press F3 twice to exit Setup.

SETVER.EXE

Sets the DOS version number that is reported to a program by MS-DOS® 5.0: If a program will not run under Ver 5.0 and issues the error "Incorrect DOS Version," adding the program to the SETVER file may allow the program to run.

Syntax (shaded is optional):

To initially load the SETVER table in CONFIG.SYS

Device = <u>Drive:\Path\</u> SETVER.EXE

At DOS prompt or in Batch file:

SETVER <u>Drive:\Path\</u> (Displays current table)

SETVER <u>Drive:\Path</u> Filename v.vv

SETVER <u>Drive:\Path</u> Filename /delete /d /quiet

Examples: Device=C:\DOS\SETVER.EXE
SETVER C:\DOS (Displays current ver. table)
SETVER C:\DOS TEST.EXE 3.30
  (above adds TEST.EXE to the version table)
SETVER C:\DOS TEST.EXE /delete
  (above deletes TEST.EXE from the version table)

Syntax Options:

Drive:\Path	Drive and directory containing SETVER.
Filename	Program file to be added to version table. Must be a .EXE or .COM file. Wild cards are not allowed.
v.vv	The DOS version number that should be reported to the program when it is run.
/delete or */d*	Delete the version table entry for the *Filename* program.
/quiet	Hides the message normally displayed during the deletion process.

Command Type and Version:

External and CONFIG.SYS command; Network; Introduced with Ver 5.0

Notes:

1. When loaded in CONFIG.SYS, the .EXE extension of SETVER must be used.

2. In order for SETVER to function at the DOS prompt or in a Batch file it must first be loaded through CONFIG.SYS. SETVER is automatically added to CONFIG.SYS by the MS-DOS 5.0 setup program.

3. If you set a version number for your MS-DOS 5.0 COMMAND.COM, your system may not start.

4. If changes or additions or deletions are made to the SETVER table your system must be restarted in order for the changes to take effect.

5. If a program starts correctly after it has been added to the SETVER table, the program may still not run correctly under Ver 5.0 if a compatibility problem exists.

6. If a program is added to the SETVER table and the program name is already in the table, the new entry and version number will replace the existing entry.

7. The following SETVER exit codes can be used in conjunction with the IF errorlevel command to report completion and error codes:

   0 SETVER function completed successfully
   1 Invalid command switch.
   2 Invalid *Filename.*
   3 Insufficient system memory to complete command.
   4 Invalid version number (*v.vv*) format specified.
   5 Specified entry not currently in version table.
   6 SETVER could not find the SETVER.EXE file.
   7 Invalid drive specified.
   8 Too many command line parameters specified by user.
   9 Missing command line parameter.
   10 Error while reading SETVER.EXE file.
   11 Corrupt SETVER.EXE file.
   12 Specified SETVER.EXE file does not support a version table.
   13 Insufficient space in version table to add a new entry.
   14 Error detected while writing to the SETVER.EXE file.

SHARE.EXE

Program that installs file-sharing and locking capabilities on hard disk: The share command is installed through AUTOEXEC.BAT or CONFIG.SYS and is used by networking, multitasking under Windows, DOSSHELL, and others.

Syntax (shaded is optional):

In a Batch file or at the DOS prompt:

   SHARE / f:space /L:locks

In CONFIG.SYS:

   INSTALL = _Drive:\Path_ SHARE.EXE _/ f:space /L:locks_

Examples: SHARE / f:4096 /L:40
              INSTALL=C:\Dos\SHARE.EXE

Syntax Options:

Drive:\Path . . . . Drive and directory containing the SHARE.EXE file.

/f:space . . . . File space allocated in bytes for the DOS storage area used to record file-sharing information. Default=2048

/L:locks . . . . Number of files that are to be locked. Default=20

Command Type and Version:
  External command; Network; Introduced with Ver 3.0

Notes:
1. In CONFIG.SYS, the .EXE extension must be included with SHARE.EXE
2. SHARE allows DOS to check and verify all read and write requests from programs.
3. The average length of a file name and its Path is 20 bytes. Use that value when calculating the */f:space* switch.
4. Beginning with Ver 5.0, SHARE is no longer required to support drive partitions >32mb.

Specifies the name and location of a command interpreter, other than COM-MAND.COM: Include the SHELL command to CONFIG.SYS to add a different Command Interpreter.

Syntax (shaded is optional):
  SHELL = <u>Drive:\Path\</u> Filename parameters

  Examples:
    SHELL=C:\COMMAND.COM /e:1024 /p

Syntax Options:
Drive:Path . . . . . Drive and directory containing *Filename*.
\Filename . . . . . Command Interpreter to be used.
Parameters . . . . Command-line parameters or switches to be used with Command Interpreter.

Command Type and Version:
  CONFIG.SYS command; Introduced with Ver 2.0

Notes:
1. The SHELL command does not use or accept any switches, only the Command Interpreter uses switches .
2. The default Command Interpreter is COMMAND.COM.
3. SHELL must be used if the Command Interpreter is in a location other than the Root directory or if you need to change the environment size of COMMAND.COM.
4. **DOSSWAP** is the DOS Task Swapper and is used internally by the SHELL command. There are no switches for DOSSWAP and it should not be run from the DOS command line.

Allows a change in the position of replaceable command line parameters in a Batch file: Specifically, SHIFT copies the value of each replaceable parameter to the next lowest parameter (for example, %1 is copied to %0, %2 is copied to %1, etc).

Syntax:

SHIFT

Examples: SHIFT

Syntax Options:
None

Command Type and Version:

Internal command only used in Batch programs; Introduced with Ver 2.0

Notes:

1. Batch files, usually limited to ten parameters (%0 through %9) on the command line, can now use more than 10. This is made possible because if more than 10 parameters are used, those appearing after the 10th will be shifted one at a time into %9.

2. Once the parameters are shifted, they cannot be shifted back.

SIZER.EXE

SIZER is used only by MEMMAKER during the memory optimizing process. It is used to determine the size, in memory, of device drivers and memory resident programs. It is added automatically to AUTOEXEC.BAT or CONFIG.SYS in order to determine the memory size, and when MEMMAKER is finished, SIZER is automatically removed.

SMARTDRV.EXE

Directs DOS to create a disk cache in extended memory or conventional memory: The cache effectively increases the speed of all disk functions. The SMARTDRV command allows management of the cache created by SMARTDRV.EXE. New in DOS Version 6.0.

Syntax (shaded is optional):

SMARTDRV /x Drive: + or - /b:buffer size /c /e:element size
/f /initcachesize[wincachesize] / l /n /q /r /s /u / v

Example: SMARTDRV C-
             SMARTDRV / r

DEVICE = SMARTDRV.EXE /x Drive: + or - /b:buffer size
/e:element size /f /initcachesize[wincachesize]
/ l /n /q /r /s /u / v

Example: DEVICE = SMARTDRV.EXE C 1024 512
         DEVICE = SMARTDRV.EXE /q

DEVICE = SMARTDRV.EXE /Double buffer

DOS Commands

Drive: . . . . Identifies the drive (disk) that will use the cache. No specification allows all drives to use the cache. Ver 6.2 allows
the caching of CD_ROM drives.

+ or - . . . . Cache-type (read or write) is enabled or disabled for identified drive. With Ver 6.0, "+" allows both read and write cach-
ing for the disk, "-" allows no caching, no specification for a
floppy disk allows only read caching, and no specification for
a hard drive allows both read and write caching. With Ver
6.2, "+" allows both read and write caching for the disk, "-" allows no caching, no specification for a floppy disk, CD-ROM
drive, or drives created using INTERLINK allows only read
caching, and no specification for a hard drive allows both
read and write caching.

/b:buffer_size . . States the size of the read-ahead buffer. The buffer size
can be set to any multiple of the element_size. The default
size is 16 384 bytes (16K) which is twice the maximum
(default) element_size of 8192 bytes (8K).

/c. . . . . Directs SMARTDRV to clear the buffer by writing all data in
the cache to the cached disk. Use this switch before turning
off the computer to save the cached data to the disk.

/e: element_size States the size of cache that SMARTDRV moves at one
time. Element_ size(bytes) can be one of the following: 1024,
2048, 4096, or 8192 (default).

/f . . . . *Directs SMARTDRV to write data in the* cache to the disk
after completion of each command. This is the default setting.
Only in DOS Version 6.2 and later.

/initcachesize . . States size, in kilobytes, of the initial cache when
SMARTDRV starts and Windows is not active. If not
specified SMARTDRV sets initcachesize according to the
amount of extended memory available as follows:

Extended Memory	Initcachesize
below 1MB	All extended
1MB to 2MB	1MB
2MB to 4MB	1MB
4MB to 6MB	2MB
above 6MB	2MB

/ L . . . . Limits SMARTDRV to only conventional (low) memory, even if
extended memory (Upper Memory Blocks, UMB) is available.

/n . . . . Directs SMARTDRV to write data in the cache to disk only
when the system is idle. Only in DOS Version 6.2 and later.

/q. . . . . Directs SMARTDRV to load in the quiet mode with no messages on status or errors. Switch can not be used with /v.

/r. . . . . Restarts SMARTDRV after clearing all data from the current
cache to the cached disk.

/s. . . . . Status of SMARTDRV is displayed.

/u	Disables the loading of CD-ROM caching. Only in DOS Version 6.2 and later.
/v	Directs SMARTDRV to display messages on status or errors when loading. Default is to <u>not</u> display messages unless error conditions are encountered. Switch can not be used with /q.
/wincachesize. .	States, in kilobytes, the amount of cache that SMARTDRV will remove from initcachesize prior to starting Windows. If not specified SMARTDRV sets wincachesize according to the amount of extended memory available as follows:

Extended Memory	Wincachesize
below 1MB	0 (no cache)
from 1MB to 2MB	256KB
from 2MB to 4MB	512KB
from 4MB to 6MB	1MB
above 6MB	2MB

/x	Directs SMARTDRV to disable write-behind caching for all drives. Only in DOS Version 6.2 and later.
/Double_buffer.	Directs SMARTDRV to perform double buffering which is needed for compatibility with some hard-disk controllers.

Command Type and Version:

External Command or Device Driver

Introduced with Ver 6.0, and some Windows before that.

Notes:

1. Do not start or load SMARTDRV while Windows is running.
2. For CD drive to be cached SMARTDRV must load after MSCDEX.
3. MS-DOS LOADHIGH (LH) command can be used to load SMARTDRV high.
4. If the hard drive requires use of the double_buffer switch to perform properly, the double_buffer component of SMARTDRV must be loaded in conventional memory and the DEVICE command line for SMARTDRV must appear in the CONFIG.SYS file before the DEVICE command line for EMM386.
5. CONFIG.SYS must contain a DEVICE command which loads HIMEM.SYS or some other memory manager in order for SMARTDRV to use extended memory.
6. SMARTDRV is <u>not</u> an interactive program which steps the user through a series of screens.
7. If SMARTDRV is run without parameters being set, DOS will set up a disk cache using default parameters.

SMARTDRV.SYS

Creates a disk cache in extended or expanded memory: A disk cache can significantly increase the speed of any disk operations. Removed in DOS Version 6.0.

DOS Commands 395

Syntax (shaded is optional):
  DEVICE = Drive:\Path\ SMARTDRV.SYS initsize minsize /a

  Examples:
      DEVICE=C:\DOS\SMARTDRV.SYS 1024 512

Syntax Options:
Drive:\Path .... Drive & directory containing SMARTDRV.SYS
initsize........ Initial size of disk cache in kilobytes. Default=256;
                Range=128 to 8192. Size is rounded off to 16k blocks.
minsize .... Minimum size of disk cache in kilobytes. Default=no minimum
                size. This option is important to programs such as Windows,
                which can reduce the cache size as required for its own use.

/A...........

Command Type and Version:
  CONFIG.SYS command; Introduced with Ver 4.0
  Removed from MS-DOS Ver 6.0

Notes:
1. If no sizes are specified with SMARTDRV, then all available extended or expanded memory is allocated to the cache.
2. In order to use extended memory, HIMEM.SYS or another extended
   memory manager must be installed. HIMEM.SYS must precede
   SMARTDRV in CONFIG.SYS
3. On 80286 / 386 / 486 systems, extended memory is probably the best
   choice for SMARTDRV.
4. Do not use disk compaction programs while SMARTDRV is loaded.

SMARTMON.EXE

*Monitors SMARTDRV cache performance under Windows. Removed
from DOS 6.2*. New in DOS Version 6.0.

Command Type and Version:
  External command, Introduced in MS-DOS Ver 6.0. Removed from DOS 6.2

SORT.EXE

*A filtering program that reads the input, sorts the data and then writes the
results to a screen, file or another device:* The SORT command alphabetizes
a file, rearranges in ascending or descending order by using a collating table
based on Country Code and Code Page settings.

Syntax (shaded is optional):
SORT /r /+n < Drive1:\ Path1\ Filename1

> Drive2:\ Path2\ Filename2

command I SORT /r /+n > Drive2:\ Path2\ Filename2

Examples: SORT < C:\Data\Text.txt
           DIR I SORT > C:\Sortdata.txt

Syntax Options:
Drive1:\Path1\ .. Drive and directory containing *Filename*.
Filename1 . . . . . File containing data to be sorted.
\Drive2:\Path2\ . Drive and directory containing *Filename2*.
Filename2 . . . . . File in which to store sorted data.
Command . . . . . Specific command whose output is data to be sorted.
/r . . . . Reverses sorting order: Z to A and 9 to 0.
/+n . . . . Sorts according to character in column *n*.

Command Type and Version:
External command; Network; Introduced with Ver 2.0

Notes:
1. Use the pipe (I) or the less-than (<) to direct data through SORT from a command or filename. Before using a pipe for redirection, set the TEMP environment variable in AUTOEXEC.BAT
2. Specify the MORE command to display information one screen at a time. You are prompted to continue after one screen is shown.
3. SORT is not case sensitive.
4. Files as large as 64K can be accommodated by SORT.
5. ASCII characters with codes higher than 127 are sorted based on the system's configuration with COUNTRY.SYS.

SPATCH.BAT

Batch file needed to maintain compatibility between MS-DOS 6.0, 6.21, or 6.22 and the permanent swap file established by Windows Ver 3.0. New in DOS Version 6.0.

Command Type and Version:
External command, Introduced with MS-DOS Ver 6.0. Available on the MS-DOS 6.0, 6.21, and 6.22 Supplemental Disks.

STACKS

Supports the dynamic use of data stacks: The STACKS command is used in CONFIG.SYS.

Syntax:
STACKS = n,s

Examples: STACKS = 8, 512

Syntax Options:

n . . . . Defines the number of STACKS. Valid values for *n* are 0 and numbers in the range 8 to 64.

s . . . . Defines STACK size in bytes. Valid values for *s* are 0 and numbers in the range 32 to 512.

Command Type and Version:
CONFIG.SYS; Introduced with Ver 3.2

Notes:
1. Default setting for the STACKS command are as follows:

COMPUTER	STACKS
IBM PC, IBM PC/XT	0,0
IBM PC-PORTABLE	0,0
OTHER	9, 128

2. When the values for *n* and *s* are specified at 0, DOS allocates no stacks. If your computer does not seem to function properly when STACKS are set to 0, return to the default values.

SUBMENU

Command line to setup an item to display another set of choices for the DOS startup menu in CONFIG.SYS: The startup menu is a list of system configuration choices that appear when your system is started. Each menu item is a set of CONFIG.SYS commands and is called a "configuration block". See your DOS manual for details of setting up and using the startup menu. New in DOS Version 6.0.

Syntax (shaded is optional):

SUBMENU = blockname , menutext

Examples: SUBMENU = NET, Network Choices

Syntax Options:

blockname . . . . Sets the name of the associated menu block. The menu block must be defined somewhere else in the CONFIG.SYS file and can contain other menu definition commands. *Blockname* can be up to 70 characters but without spaces, backslashes, forward slashes, commas, semicolons, equal signs and square brackets.

, menutext . . . . . Text to be displayed for the menu item. If no text is defined, DOS displays the *blockname* as the menu item. menutext can be up to 70 characters long.

Command Type and Version:
CONFIG.SYS command; Network; Introduced with Ver 6.0

Notes:
1. See also MENUCOLOR, MENUITEM, NUMLOCK, INCLUDE and MENUDEFAULT. All are used by the startup menu.

SUBST.EXE

Substitutes a path with a drive letter: The SUBST command lets you use a drive letter (also known as a virtual drive) in commands as though it represents a physical drive.

Syntax (shaded is optional):

SUBST (Lists the virtual drives in effect)

SUBST Drive1: Drive2:\ Path

SUBST Drive1: /d (deletes virtual drive)

Examples:	SUBST
	SUBST R: B: \Data\Text.txt

Syntax Options:

Drive1: . . . . Virtual drive to which a path is assigned.
Drive2: . . . . Physical drive that contains the specified path.
\Path . . . . Path to be assigned to the virtual drive named *Drive1:*
/d . . . . Deletes the *Drive1:* virtual drive.

Command Type and Version:

External command; Introduced with Ver 3.1

Notes:

1. Commands that do not work on drives where SUBST has been used are as follows:

ASSIGN	DISKCOPY	RECOVER
BACKUP	FDISK	RESTORE
CHKDSK	FORMAT	SYS
DEFRAG	LABEL	UNDELETE /s
DISKCOMP	MIRROR	

2. A virtual drive letter must be included in the LASTDRIVE command in CONFIG.SYS.
3. Use SUBST rather than ASSIGN to ensure compatibility with future DOS versions.
4. If using drive letters higher than E, the LASTDRIVE command must also be used.
5. Do not use SUBST while Windows is running!

SWITCHAR

Changes the switch character: The forward slash, " / " is the standard switch character. SWITCHAR allows the user to choose another switch character.

Syntax (shaded is optional):

SWITCHAR= cc

Example: switchar = *

Syntax Options:

cc . . . . New switch character.

Command Type and Version:

CONFIG.SYS command, Introduced with Ver 2.0.
Removed Version 3.0.

SWITCHES

Forces enhanced keyboard to function like a conventional keyboard: This command is used in the CONFIG.SYS file.

Syntax (shaded is optional):

SWITCHES = /W /K /N /F

Examples: SWITCHES = / k

Syntax Options:

/ W . . . . If Windows 3.0 is used in enhanced mode and you have moved the WINA20.386 file, use this switch to tell DOS that the file has been moved.

/ K . . . . *Ignores extended keys on 101-key* keyboards. It forces COMMAND.COM to use an older BIOS call to read the keyboard , making it possible to use certain older TSRs that depend on the older call. Actually, this switch was introduced in DOS V4.0, but was undocumented. DOS Version 6.0 and later.

/ N . . . . *Disables the F5 and F8 keys so that you* cannot bypass startup commands. DOS Version 6.0 and later.

/ F . . . . *Skips the 2 second system delay after "Starting MS-DOS . . ."* is displayed during startup. DOS Version 6.0 and later.

Command Type and Version:

CONFIG.SYS command; Introduced with Ver 4.0

Notes:

1. Use the SWITCHES command when there is a program that does not properly interpret input from an enhanced keyboard. This command enables the enhanced keyboard to use conventional keyboard functions.
2. If SWITCHES=/k is used in a system that uses ANSI.SYS, be sure to also use the /k switch on the ANSI.SYS command.

SYS.COM

Copies the DOS system files (IO.SYS and MSDOS.SYS on MS-DOS systems or IBMBIO.COM and IBMDOS.COM on PC-DOS systems) and the Command Interpreter from one disk drive to another disk drive.

Syntax (shaded is optional):

SYS Drive1:\Path Drive2

Examples: SYS A: (current drive to drive A:)
          SYS D:\ A: (copy from disk in D: to A:)

Syntax Options:

Drive1:\Path . . . Drive and directory where system files are located. If a path is not specified, DOS searches the root directory. If a drive is not specified, DOS uses the current drive as the system files source drive.

Drive2: . . . . Drive to which system files are to be copied. These files can be copied to a root directory only.

Command Type and Version:
External command; Introduced with Ver 1.0

Notes:
1. The order in which the SYS command files are copied is as follows: IO:SYS, MSDOS.SYS and COMMAND.COM.
2. The two system files no longer need to be "contiguous" in Ver 5.0 In simple terms, this means that pre DOS 3.3 disks do not need to be reformatted in order to install the Ver 5.0 operating system.
3. The SYS command will not work on drives redirected by ASSIGN, JOIN or SUBST.
4. The SYS command does not work on Network drives.
5. See also DISKCOPY, which duplicated disks of the same size (including transfer of the operating system). See also COPY and XCOPY for information on copying all files except system and hidden files.
6. With **DOS 6.0**, DBLSPACE.BIN is also copied to the target drive.
7. Pre DOS 5.0 can only be SYS Drive1: DOS Version 6.0 and later.

TIME

Enter or change current system time: DOS uses the internal clock to update the directory with date and time when a file is created or changed.

Syntax (shaded is optional):

TIME Hours: Minutes: Seconds: Hundredths a or p

Examples:	TIME
	TIME 13:45 or TIME 1:45 p
	TIME 11:28p

Syntax Options:
Hours: . . . . Specifies the hour. One or two digit number with valid values from 0-23.
Minutes: . . . . . . Specifies the minute. One or two digit number with valid values from 0-59.
Seconds: . . . . . . Specifies the seconds. One or two digit number with valid values from 0-59.
Hundredths: . . . Specifies hundredths of a second. One or two digit number with valid values from 0-99.
a or p . . . . When a 12 hour time format is used instead of the 24 hour format, use **a** or **p** to specify A.M. or P.M. When a valid 12 hour time is entered and a parameter is not entered, *time* uses **a** (A.M.).

Command Type and Version:
Internal command; Network; Introduced with Ver 1.0

Notes:

1 Using *time* without parameters will display the current time and prompt
   you for a time change.
2. Use a colon (:) to separate hours, minutes, (seconds and hundred-ths of
   a second are optional), if as defined in COUNTRY, dependent information
   file for the United States.
3. With all versions of DOS 3.3 and later, the TIME command will update
   the system's battery powered clock (except XT-type systems.)

TREE.COM

Displays the directory structure of a path on a specific drive. See also DIR.

Syntax (shaded is optional):

   TREE Drive:\ Path / f /a

   Examples: TREE (all directories and subdirectories)
                 TREE \ (names of all subdirectories)
                 TREE D:\ /f | MORE
                 TREE D:\ /f > PRN

Syntax Options:
Drive:\Path . . . . Drive and directory containing disk for display of directory
                    structure.
/f. . . . . Displays file names in each directory.
/a . . . . Text characters used for linking lines, instead of graphic
                    characters. /a is used with code pages that do not sup-
                    port graphic characters and to send output to printers that
                    do not properly interpret graphic characters. DOS Version
                    4.0 and later.

Command Type and Version:
   External command; Network; Introduced with Ver 2.0

Notes:
1. The path structure displayed by the TREE command will depend upon
   the specified parameters on the command line.
2. The TREE command in MS-DOS 5.0 has been greatly enhanced.

TRUENAME

***Displays the TRUENAME of directories and logical drives created with AS-
SIGN, JOIN, and SUBST.***

Syntax (shaded if optional):
   TRUENAME drive1: \ path \filename

   Example: truename f:

Syntax options:
drive1:. . . . . Drive created by ASSIGN, JOIN, or SUBST.
\ path\ filename . Path and filename created by ASSIGN, JOIN, or SUBST.

Command Type and Version:

Internal command, Introduced with Ver 4.0.

TYPE

Screen display of a text file's contents: The TYPE command is used to view a text file without modifying it.

Syntax (shaded is optional):

TYPE <u>Drive:\ Path\</u> Filename

Examples: TYPE C:\Act\Receivbl.dat
              TYPE C:\Act\Receivbl.dat | MORE

Syntax Options:

Drive:\Path . . . . Drive and directory containing Filename.
\Filename . . . . . Name of text file to be viewed.

Command Type and Version:

Internal command; Network; Introduced with Ver 1.0.

Notes:

1. Avoid using the TYPE command to display binary files or files created using a program as you may see strange characters on the screen which represent control codes used in binary files.
2. Use DIR to find the name of a file and EDLIN or EDIT to change its contents.
3. When using the pipe (|) for redirection, set the TEMP environment variable in AUTOEXEC.BAT.
4. See also DIR and MORE.

UNDELETE / MWUNDEL.EXE

Recovers files that have been deleted with the DEL command: UNDELETE is the DOS version and MWUNDEL is the Windows version.

Syntax (shaded is optional):

UNDELETE <u>Drive:\Path\</u> Filename <u>/List or /all /purge:drive</u>

<u>/status /load [/dos or /dt or /ds] /sentry:drive</u>

<u>/tracker:drive-entries /unload</u>

Examples: UNDELETE /all
              UNDELETE C:\Data*.*

Syntax Options:

Drive:\Path . . . . Drive and directory containing *Filename*.
Filename. . . . . . File to be undeleted. By default, all files in the current directory will be undeleted. Wild cards * and ? are allowed.
/ List . . . . Lists all deleted files in *Drive:\Path* that can be undeleted, but doesn't undelete them.

/ all	Recovers all deleted files without a confirmation prompt. If the deletion tracking file is present, it is used, otherwise deleted file information is taken from the DOS directory. See Note: 3.
/ purge:drive	Deletes all files in the sentry directory on the specified *drive*. DOS Version 6.0 and later.
/ status	Displays the current UNDELETE protection level that is enabled. DOS Version 6.0 and later.
/ load	Load UNDELETE as memory resident, in order to track deleted files. DOS Version 6.0 and later.
/ unload	Unload the resident portion of the UNDELETE delete tracker. DOS Version 6.0 and later.
/ dos	Causes UNDELETE to ignore the deletion tracking file and recover only those files listed as deleted by DOS. A confirmation prompt occurs with each undelete.
/ ds	UNDELETE only files in /Sentry directory. DOS Version 6.0.
/ Sentry:drive	*Specify the drive to be used for delete sentry files.* DOS Version 6.0 and later.
/ dt	Causes UNDELETE to ignore the files listed as deleted by DOS and only recover those files listed in the deletion tracking file. A confirmation prompt occurs with each undelete.
/ Tracker:drive-entries	*Specify the drive to track deleted files on. The maximum number of deleted files to track can range from 1 to 999.* DOS Version 6.0 and later.

Command Type and Version:

External command; Introduced with Ver 5.0

Notes:

1. For best results, use MIRROR and the deletion tracking system.
2. When a file is recovered, it is assigned a # for the first character of its name, if a duplicate exists, another letter is selected, in order from the following list, until a unique filename is possible: #%&−1234567890AB CDEFGHIJKLMNOPQRSTUVWXYZ
3. If a switch is not specified with UNDELETE, the deletion tracking file is automatically used. If the deletion tracking file is not present, the DOS directory information is used. The deletion tracking system is much more accurate.
4. UNDELETE cannot undelete a directory.
5. UNDELETE cannot undelete a file if its directory has been deleted. A possible exception to this rule exists if the deleted directory was a main directory under the root directory and not a subdirectory of some other directory. If this is the case, see the UNFORMAT command. It is possible the directory and file can be saved. Use extreme caution with UNFORMAT and understand exactly what you are doing!!! If not used correctly, UNFORMAT can lose data and you might be worse off than when you started!

6. UNDELETE may not be able to recover a deleted file if data of any kind has been written to the disk since the file was deleted. If you accidentally delete a file, stop what you are doing immediately and run the UNDELETE program.
7. Some MIRROR commands from DOS 5.0 are included in the DOS 6.0 UNDELETE command.
8. See also the UNFORMAT command.

UNFORMAT.COM

Restores a disk that has been reformatted or restructured by the RE-COVER command: UNFORMAT can also rebuild disk partition tables that have been corrupted. Do not use UNFORMAT on a network drive.

Syntax (shaded is optional):
  UNFORMAT Drive: / J
  UNFORMAT Drive: / U / L / test / P
  UNFORMAT /partn / L

  Examples: UNFORMAT C: / J
                UNFORMAT A: / test

Syntax Options:

Drive: . . . . Drive containing disk to be unformatted.

/ J . . . . Check the file created by MIRROR for use with UNFORMAT to make sure it agrees with the system information. Use this switch only by itself. Removed from DOS Version 6.0.

/ U . . . . UNFORMAT a disk without using the MIRROR file. Removed from DOS Version 6.0.

/ L . . . . If /partn is not used, /L lists every file and directory found by UNFORMAT. Use if the MIRROR file is to be ignored. If /partn is used also, /L displays the complete partition table of the drive. Standard 512 byte sectors are assumed when the partition table size is displayed. ***Description for Version 5 ONLY.***

/ L . . . . Lists every file and subdirectory found by UNFORMAT. Default is to list only subdirectories and files that are fragmented. ***Description for Version 6.x ONLY.***

/ test . . . . Displays how UNFORMAT would rebuild information on the disk, but it does NOT unformat the disk. Use this switch only if you want UNFORMAT to ignore the MIRROR file. ***Description for Version 5 ONLY.***

/ test . . . . Displays how UNFORMAT would rebuild information on the disk, but it does NOT unformat the disk. ***Description for Version 6 ONLY.***

/ P . . . . Outputs messages to the LPT1 printer.

/ partn . . . . Rebuilds and restores a corrupted partition table of a hard drive. This switch will only work if MIRROR was run previously and the PARTNSAV.FIL file is available to UNFORMAT. Removed from DOS Version 6.0.

Command Type and Version:
External command; Introduced with Ver 5.0

Notes:

1. Although UNFORMAT is a very powerful tool, it can also do a lot of damage if not used correctly. BE CAREFUL!
2. UNFORMAT normally restores a disk based on MIRROR information. If disk information has changed since MIRROR was run, UNFORMAT may not be able to recover it. Use MIRROR frequently in order to assure an accurate restoration of the disk.
3. If FORMAT with its /u switch was used, UNFORMAT cannot restore the disk.
4. Per Microsoft's Ver 5.0 User's Guide: "The only case in which you would want to use a prior mirror file is the following: you use the MIRROR command, then the disk is corrupted, then you use the FORMAT command. If you use the MIRROR command and the FORMAT command after the disk is corrupted, the UNFORMAT command will not work. UNFORMAT searches the disk for the MIRROR file. Because UNFORMAT searches the disk directly, the disk does not have to be "readable" by MS-DOS for UNFORMAT to work. Do not use the FDISK command before using UNFORMAT; doing so can destroy information not saved by the MIRROR program."
5. If UNFORMAT does not use the MIRROR file, the restore will take much longer and be less reliable.
6. Without a MIRROR file, UNFORMAT cannot recover a file that is fragmented. It will recover what it can, then prompt for truncation of the file or delete the file.
7. If DOS displays the message "Invalid drive specification," the problem might be a corrupted disk partition table, which UNFORMAT can probably repair. In order to recover the disk partition table, the MIRROR file must be available.
8. When the /partn switch is used, you are prompted to insert a system disk in drive A: and press ENTER to restart. The restart will allow DOS to read the new partition table data. Once the system has been restarted, use UNFORMAT without the /partn switch to recover directories and the FAT (file allocation table).
9. See also UNDELETE, MIRROR, FORMAT, and FDISK.
10. In DOS Ver 5.0, the /p switch is not compatible with the /u switch.

UNINSTALL.EXE

Restores the previous version of DOS after the MS-DOS 6 is installed: Used in conjunction with the Uninstall Disk to protect files while MS-DOS 6 is installed. If problems occurs during installation, UNINSTALL can be used to restore the previous version of DOS. New in DOS Version 6.0.

Command Type and Version:
External command, Introduced with Version 6.0.

VER

Displays DOS version number: Type **ver** and the version number will display on the screen.

Syntax (shaded is optional):

VER /R

Examples: VER

Syntax Options:

/R . . . . Provides a more detailed report. DOS Version 6.0 and later.

Command Type and Version:
Internal command; Network; Introduced with Ver 2.0

VERIFY

Disk verification: Verifies that the files are written correctly to a disk.

Syntax (shaded is optional):

VERIFY on / off

Examples: VERIFY on

Syntax Options:

Verify . . . . **Verify** without an option will state whether verification is turned on or off.

on . . . . Forces DOS to confirm that information is being written correctly. The verify command will function until the system is rebooted or **verify off** is used.

off . . . . Turns verification off once it is on.

Command Type and Version:
Internal command; Network; Introduced with Ver 2.0

Notes:
1. When the VERIFY command is used, DOS verifies data as it is written to a disk. This will slow writing speed slightly.
2. COPY / V or XCOPY / V can also be used to verify that files are being copied correctly but on a case by case basis.
3. Verify does <u>not</u> perform a physical disk to disk comparison.

VOL

Displays disk Volume label: The VOL command displays the name of volume label given to a disk when it was formatted. DOS Version 4.0 and greater will also display a volume serial number.

Syntax (shaded is optional):

VOL <u>Drive:</u>

    Examples: VOL A: or VOL

Syntax Options:

VOL . . . . VOL, without options, displays the volume label and vol-
                 ume serial number of the disk in current drive.

Drive: . . . . Specifies the drive that contains the disk whose label is to
                 be displayed.

Command Type and Version:

Internal command; Network; Introduced with Ver 2.0
Volume serial numbers introduced with DOS Ver 4.0

Notes:

1. See also FORMAT and LABEL.

VSAFE.COM

Continuously monitors a system for viruses and displays a warning if it finds one: VSAFE is a memory resident program that uses approximately 22k of memory. See Windows Note below. New in DOS Version 6.0.

Syntax (shaded is optional):

VSAFE <u>/option + or - /NE /NX /A# /C# /N /D /U</u>

    Example: VSAFE / 2+ /NE /AV

Syntax Options:

/ option + or - . . Specifies how VSAFE looks for viruses. The + or - is used to
                 either turn on or turn off the option. Options are as follows:

1 - Warn of a formatting request. Default=On
2 - Warn if a program tries to stay resident. Default=Off
3 - Disable all disk writes. Default=Off
4 - Check executable files that DOS opens. Default=On
5 - Check for boot sector viruses. Default=On
6 - Warns if a program tries to write to the boot sector or
    partition table of a hard disk. Default=On
7 - Warns if a program tries to write to the boot sector or
    a floppy disk. Default=Off
8 - Warns if an attempt is made to modify an executable file. Default=Off

/ NE . . . . Prevents VSAFE from loading into expanded memory.

/ NX . . . . Prevents VSAFE from loading into extended memory.

/ A# . . . . Sets the VSAFE hot key as Alt plus the key specified by #.

/ C# . . . . Sets the VSAFE hot key as Ctrl plus the key specified by #.

/ N . . . . Enable network drive monitoring.

/ D . . . . Disable CRC checksumming.

/ U . . . . Unloads VSAFE from memory.

Command Type and Version:

External command; Network; Introduced with Ver 6.0

Notes:

1. If VSAFE is to be used when Windows 3.1 is running, you must include " load=MWAVTSR.EXE" in the WIN.INI file.

WINA20.386

The WINA20.386 file must be located in the root directory in order for Microsoft Windows Ver. 3.0 to run in enhanced mode. It is automatically placed in the root directory by MS-DOS during the installation process:

1. If the file is not in the root directory, you will receive the message "You must have the file WINA20.386 in the root of your boot drive to run Windows in Enhanced Mode."

2. WINA20.386 must remain in the root directory unless the SWITCHES /W command is used to tell DOS that it has been moved. You must also add a DEVICE command under the [386Enh] section of your Windows SYSTEM.INI file, which specifies where WINA20.386 is now located.

Command Type and Version:
   External command; Introduced with Ver 5.0

XCOPY.EXE

Copies files, directories, and subdirectories from one location to another location: XCOPY will not copy system or hidden files.

Syntax (shaded is optional):
   XCOPY Source Destination /a /d:date /e /m /p /s /v

/w /y /-y

   Examples: XCOPY C:\Dos*.* D:\Dos2\ /s

Syntax Options:

Source	Location and names of files to be copied.
Destination	Destination of the files to be copied.
/a	Copies *Source* files that have their archive file attributes set **without** modifying it.
/ d:date	Copies *Source* files that have been modified on or after a specific date.
/ e	Copies subdirectories even if empty.
/ m	Copies *Source* files that have their archive file attributes set and turns them off.
/ p	Prompts whether you want to create each destination file.
/ s	Copies directories and subdirectories, unless they are empty.
/ v	Verifies each file, as it is written, to confirm that the destination and source files are identical.
/ w	Displays "Press any key to begin copying file (s)," and waits for response before starting to copy files.

| / y . . . . | Directs XCOPY to replace existing files without a confirmation prompt. DOS Version 6.2 and later. |
| / -y . . . . | Directs XCOPY to ask for confirmation prior to replacing an existing file. Default. DOS Version 6.2 and later. |

Command Type and Version:

External command; Network; Introduced with Ver 3.2

Notes:

1. The default *Destination* is the current directory.
2. If the *Destination* subdirectory does not end with a "\", DOS will prompt you to find out if the subdirectory is a subdirectory or file.
3. XCOPY will not copy system or hidden files.
4. When a file is copied to *Destination*, the archive attribute is turned on, regardless of the file attribute in *Source*.
5. In order to copy between disks that are different formats, use XCOPY, not DISKCOPY, but remember that XCOPY does not copy the hidden or system files.
6. XCOPY exit codes are as follows: (see IF errorlevel)
   0 Files copied successfully
   1 Source files not found
   2 XCOPY stopped by user Ctrl+C
   4 One of the following errors ocurred:
      a. Initialization error
      b. Not enough disk space
      c. Insufficient memory available
      d. Invalid drive name
      e. Invalid syntax was used.
   5 Disk write error occurred.
7. When a files size is larger than 64k, use XCOPY instead of the COPY command.

Windows Keyboard Shortcuts 95-98-ME-NT-2K-XP

Keyboard Shortcuts

Keyboard Shortcuts

Keyboard Shortcuts for Microsoft Windows

Keystrokes	95	98	ME	NT	2K	XP	Action (for each Win version, X=valid shortcut, blank=untested, gray=invalid shortcut)
General							
ALT + DOWN ARROW	X	X	X	X	X	X	Display a drop-down list box
ALT + Enter					X	X	Displays properties dialogue box of selected item
ALT + ESC	X	X	X	X	X	X	Move forward through all open applications including minimized windows on the Taskbar
ALT + HYPHEN [-]		X	X	X	X	X	Display the System Menu for Multiple Document Interface (MDI) programs
ALT + M		X	X		X	X	When the focus is on the Taskbar or Desktop, minimize all windows and move the focus to the Desktop
ALT + S	X	X	X	X	X	X	Display Start Menu when no windows are open or applications selected on the Desktop. Use arrow keys to select menu commands. (Same as CTRL + ESC and WINKEY).
ALT + SHIFT + BACK SPACE	X			X			Redo the previously undone action
ALT + SPACEBAR	X	X	X	X	X	X	Display the current window's System Menu (aka Control Menu or Window menu, same as a LEFT CLICK on the program icon)
ALT + SPACEBAR + C				X	X	X	Close active window
ALT + SPACEBAR + N				X	X		Minimize active window
ALT + SPACEBAR + R					X		Change window from minimized to maximized
ALT + Underlined letter in menu name				X	X	X	Displays corresponding menu
ALT + SPACEBAR + Underlined Letter	X	X	X	X	X	X	Display the System Menu and activate menu item corresponding to the Underlined Letter
ARROW KEYS	X	X	X	X	X	X	Move between Taskbar buttons
CTRL + + (+ on the numeric keypad)				X	X	X	Autosize columns in Explorer
CTRL + A	X	X	X	X	X	X	Select all Items
CTRL + ALT + DELETE	X	X				X	Display the "Close Program" dialog box
CTRL + ALT + DELETE				X	X	X	Display the "Windows Security" dialog box
CTRL + C	X	X	X	X	X	X	Copies the selected item and moves it to the Clipboard (same as CTRL + INSERT)
CTRL + ESC	X	X	X	X	X	X	Display the Start Menu (same as WINKEY)
CTRL + ESC then ALT + M	X	X	X	X	X	X	Minimize all windows, return to desktop (same as WINKEY + M).
CTRL + ESC then ESC	X	X	X	X	X	X	Move the focus on the Taskbar so you can use TAB and then SHIFT + F10 for context menu
CTRL + F10	X	X	X	X	X	X	Switch focus to menu commands

Keyboard Shortcuts for Microsoft Windows

Keystrokes	95	98	ME	NT	2K	XP	Action (for each Win version, X=valid shortcut, blank=untested, gray=invalid shortcut)
CTRL + F4	X	X	X		X	X	Closes the active document in programs that allow you to have multiple documents open simultaneously
CTRL + G					X	X	Displays the Go To Folder dialog box
CTRL + SHIFT + (drag the file to the Desktop or a folder)		X	X				Create shortcut to selected item
CTRL + SHIFT + ARROW KEY	X	X	X	X	X	X	Highlight a block of text
CTRL + SHIFT + ESC		X	X	X	X	X	Display the "Task Manager" dialog box
CTRL + V	X	X	X	X	X	X	Paste the copied/cut item from the Clipboard (same as SHIFT + INSERT)
CTRL + X	X	X	X	X	X	X	Cut the selected item and move it to the Clipboard
CTRL + Z	X	X	X	X	X	X	Undo the last action (same as ALT + BACK SPACE)
DELETE	X	X	X	X	X	X	Delete
ESC	X	X	X	X	X	X	Cancel the current task
F1	X	X	X	X	X	X	Start the Help Program (same as WINKEY + F1)
F1			X		X		Start the Help and Support Center (same as WINKEY + F1)
F2	X	X	X	X	X	X	Rename an item
F3	X	X	X	X	X	X	Start the "find" tool (same as WINKEY + F)
F5	X	X	X	X	X	X	Refresh the contents of a window
F6	X	X	X	X	X	X	Move through screen elements in a window or on the Desktop
LEFT CLICK (on Application icon)						X	Display the current window's System Menu (aka Control Menu or Window menu, same as ALT + SPACEBAR)
NUM LOCK (hold down key for 5 seconds)		X	X		X	X	Opens a dialog box allowing you to enable ToggleKeys
NUM LOCK + ASTERISK on numeric keypad				X	X	X	Display all subfolders under selected folder
NUM LOCK + MINUS SIGN on numeric keypad				X	X	X	Collapse folder selected
PRINT SCREEN	X	X	X	X	X	X	Copy an image of the screen to the Clipboard
RIGHT CLICK	X	X	X	X	X	X	View Shortcut Menu for a selected item (same as SHIFT + F10)
SHIFT (while booting)	X	X	X	X			Boot to Safe Mode or bypass system files
SHIFT (while booting)				X			Boot to a "Select Boot Device Menu"
SHIFT (while inserting a CD)	X	X	X	X	X	X	Bypass AutoPlay when inserting a compact disc
SHIFT + ARROW KEY	X	X	X	X	X	X	Select more than one item in a window or on the Desktop, or select text within a document

Keyboard Shortcuts for Microsoft Windows

Keystrokes	95	98	ME	NT	2K	XP	Action (for each Win version, X=valid shortcut, blank=untested, gray=invalid shortcut)
SHIFT + CTRL + ESC				X	X	X	Launches Task Manager
SHIFT + DELETE	X	X	X	X	X	X	Delete an item immediately without placing it in the Recycle Bin
SHIFT + DOUBLE CLICK	X	X	X			X	Explore an object; if the object does not have an Explore command, this starts the default action (usually the Open command)
SHIFT + F8					X	X	Move without changing current selection when in extended selection list box
SHIFT + F10	X	X	X	X	X	X	View Shortcut Menu for a selected item (same as RIGHT CLICK)
SHIFT + SPACE					X	X	Extends the selection to the current item
Underlined Letter	X	X	X	X	X	X	Activate the Command represented by Underlined Letter

"Save As" or "Open" Dialog Box

	95	98	ME	NT	2K	XP	
BACK SPACE	X	X	X	X	X	X	Open a folder one level up if a folder is selected in the "Save As" or "Open" dialog box
CTRL + SHIFT + TAB	X	X	X	X	X	X	Move backward through category tabs
CTRL + TAB	X	X	X	X	X	X	Move forward through category tabs
F4	X	X	X	X	X	X	Open the "Save In" or "Look In" list
F5	X	X	X	X	X	X	Refresh the dialog box

Accessibility Options

(Note: To use Accessibility Options shortcut keys, the shortcut keys must be ENABLED)

	95	98	ME	NT	2K	XP	
LEFT ALT + LEFT SHIFT + NUM LOCK	X	X	X		X	X	Switch MouseKeys on and off
LEFT ALT + LEFT SHIFT + PRINT SCREEN	X	X	X		X	X	Switch High Contrast on and off (in NT 4.0, use Control Panel to select from different High Contrast schemes in the Appearance page under the Display Option)
NUM LOCK (press and hold for 5 seconds)	X	X	X	X	X	X	Switch ToggleKeys on and off
RIGHT SHIFT (press and hold for 8 seconds)	X	X	X	X	X	X	Switch FilterKeys on and off
SHIFT (press 5 times in quick succession)	X	X	X	X	X	X	Switch StickyKeys on and off

Control Panel

	95	98	ME	NT	2K	XP	
CTRL + A	X	X	X	X	X	X	Select All
CTRL + C	X	X	X	X	X	X	Copy
CTRL + V	X	X	X	X	X	X	Paste
CTRL + X	X	X	X	X	X	X	Cut
CTRL + Z	X	X	X	X	X	X	Undo

Desktop

Keyboard Shortcuts for Microsoft Windows						
Keystrokes	95	98	ME	NT	2K	XP	Action (for each Win version, X=valid shortcut, blank=untested, gray=invalid shortcut)
ANY LETTER	X	X	X	X	X	X	Move to icon on Desktop beginning with that letter
ARROW KEYS	X	X	X	X	X	X	Move between Desktop icons
F10			X				Opens between Desktop icons
F5	X	X		X			Opens the Shortcut Menu (same as RIGHT CLICK)
RIGHT CLICK	X	X	X	X	X	X	Move focus to My Computer
SHIFT + DOUBLE CLICK	X	X	X	X	X	X	Opens the Shortcut Menu (same as F10)
							Opens more than one application at a time
My Computer & Windows Explorer							
ALT + LEFT ARROW		X	X	X	X	X	Move backward to a previous view
ALT + RIGHT ARROW		X	X	X	X	X	Move forward to a previous view
BACK SPACE		X	X	X	X	X	View the folder one level up
SHIFT + (click the Close (X) button on the folder)		X	X	X	X	X	Close the selected folder and all of its parent folders
Desktop, My Computer, & Windows Explorer							
ALT + DOUBLE CLICK	X	X	X	X	X	X	View an item's properties (same as RIGHT CLICK, select "Properties"; same as ALT + ENTER)
ALT + ENTER	X	X	X	X	X	X	View an item's properties (same as RIGHT CLICK, select "Properties"; same as ALT + DOUBLE CLICK)
BACKSPACE		X	X	X	X	X	View the folder one level up
CTRL + (dragging a file to a folder)	X	X	X	X	X	X	Copy file
CTRL + A	X	X	X	X	X	X	Select all items
CTRL + RIGHT CLICK	X			X	X	X	Place alternative commands on the Context Menu (Open With)
CTRL + SHIFT + (drag the file to the Desktop or a folder)	X	X		X	X	X	Open a pull-up menu to move, copy, or create shortcut (for XP, right click and drag to get the menu, simply drag to create a shortcut.
F2	X	X		X	X	X	Rename an object (some objects can not be renamed)
F3	X	X		X	X	X	Display "Find: All Files" dialog box
F5	X	X		X	X	X	Refresh the contents of a window
RIGHT CLICK + N		X			X	X	Create a new folder or shortcut on the Desktop
RIGHT CLICK + W	X		X				Create a new folder or shortcut on the Desktop
SHIFT + (click the Close (X) button on the folder)		X				X	Close the selected folder and all its parent folders.

Keyboard Shortcuts for Microsoft Windows

Keystrokes	95	98	ME	NT	2K	XP	Action (for each Win version, X=valid shortcut, blank=untested, gray=invalid shortcut)
SHIFT + DELETE	X	X			X	X	Delete an item immediately without placing it in the Recycle Bin
Dialog Box							
ALT + Underlined Letter		X		X	X	X	Activate the command corresponding to Underlined Letter
ARROW KEYS		X		X	X	X	Select a button if the active option is a group of option buttons
BACKSPACE		X		X	X	X	Open a folder one level up if a folder is selected in the Save As or Open dialog box
CTRL + N	X	X	X		X	X	Display the "New" dialog box
CTRL + O	X	X	X		X	X	Display the "Open" dialog box
CTRL + PAGE DOWN	X	X		X	X	X	Move backward through tabs in a dialog box
CTRL + PAGE UP	X	X		X	X	X	Move forward through tabs in a dialog box
CTRL + S	X	X		X	X	X	Display the "Save" dialog box
CTRL + SHIFT + TAB	X	X	X	X	X	X	Move backward through tabs in a dialog box
CTRL + TAB	X	X	X	X	X	X	Move forward through tabs in a dialog box
ENTER	X	X	X	X	X	X	Carry out the command for the active option or button (same as LEFT CLICK)
ESC	X	X	X	X	X	X	Cancel current task (same as clicking the CANCEL button)
F1		X		X	X	X	Display Help on current dialog box item
F4		X			X	X	Display the "Save As" dialog box
F4					X	X	Display the items in the active list
F5					X	X	Refresh the "Save As" or "Open" dialog box
SHIFT + TAB	X	X		X	X	X	Move to previous control in dialog box
SPACEBAR	X	X		X	X	X	If the current controll is a button, clicks the button
SPACEBAR	X	X		X	X	X	If the current control is a check box, this toggles the check box
SPACEBAR	X	X		X	X	X	If the current control is an option, this selects the option
TAB	X	X		X	X	X	Move to next control in dialog box
Underlined Letter	X	X		X	X	X	Typing Underlined Letter moves cursor to corresponding field.
Open Application							
ALT + BACK SPACE	X	X		X	X	X	Undo the last action (same as CTRL + Z)
ALT + ESC	X						Display the Start Menu (same as clicking Start button)

Keyboard Shortcuts for Microsoft Windows

Keystrokes	95	98	ME	NT	2K	XP	Action (for each Win version, X=valid shortcut, blank=untested, gray=invalid shortcut)
ALT + ESC		X	X	X	X	X	Switches keyboard focus to the next application window, including minimized windows on the taskbar. Press ESC more than once to switch through successive windows and add SHIFT to reverse the direction.
ALT + F4	X	X	X		X	X	Close the active item or quit the active program
ALT + F6	X	X	X	X	X	X	Switch between multiple windows in the same program
ALT + HYPHEN [-]	X	X	X		X	X	Display the System Menu for MDI (Multiple Document Interface) program documents (same as LEFT CLICK on file icon on the Menu Bar)
ALT + PRINT SCREEN	X	X		X	X	X	Copy an image of the active window to the Clipboard
ALT + SHIFT + ESC		X		X	X	X	Move backward through all open applications including minimized windows on the Taskbar
ALT + SHIFT + TAB	X	X	X	X	X	X	Move backward through a list of open applications
ALT + SPACEBAR	X	X	X	X	X	X	Display the System Menu (same as ALT + HYPHEN [-] in Windows 95)
ALT + TAB	X	X	X	X	X	X	Switch to another window (hold ALT while repeatedly pressing TAB)
ALT + Underlined Letter	X	X	X	X	X	X	Activate the Menu Bar of the active window (same as F10) and opens the Menu represented by Underlined Letter
Application Key			X	X	X	X	Opens the shortcut menu for the active item (same as SHIFT + F10)
ARROW KEYS	X	X	X	X	X	X	Move between menu items.
ARROW KEYS	X	X	X	X	X	X	Move between characters in a text box
ARROW KEYS	X	X	X	X	X	X	Move between items in a list
BACK SPACE	X	X	X	X	X	X	Delete character to left of cursor
CTRL + 5				X	X	X	Set line spacing at 1.5 lines
CTRL + B	X	X	X	X	X	X	Activate Bold text
CTRL + BACK SPACE			X		X	X	Delete word to left of cursor
CTRL + C	X	X	X	X	X	X	Copy the selected item and move it to the Clipboard (same as CTRL + INSERT)
CTRL + DELETE			X		X	X	Delete word to right of cursor
CTRL + DOWN ARROW	X	X	X	X	X	X	Moves the insertion point to the beginning of the next paragraph
CTRL + END	X	X	X	X	X	X	Go to end of document
CTRL + F4	X	X	X	X	X	X	Close an open application or the active window
CTRL + F6		X		X	X	X	Switch to next document window in the active application

Keyboard Shortcuts for Microsoft Windows

Keystrokes	95	98	ME	NT	2K	XP	Action (for each Win version, X=valid shortcut, blank=untested, gray=invalid shortcut)
CTRL + HOME	X	X		X	X	X	Go to beginning of document
CTRL + I	X	X	X	X	X	X	Activate Italic text
CTRL + INSERT	X	X		X	X	X	Copy the selected item and move it to the Clipboard (same as CTRL + C)
CTRL + LEFT ARROW	X	X		X	X	X	Move cursor 1 item or word to the left
CTRL + N		X		X	X	X	Opens a new document
CTRL + O		X		X	X	X	Opens the Open dialog box
CTRL + P	X	X		X	X	X	Display the "Print" dialog box
CTRL + RIGHT ARROW	X	X		X	X	X	Move cursor 1 item or word to the right
CTRL + S	X	X		X	X	X	Opens the Save dialog box
CTRL + SHIFT + F6	X	X		X	X	X	Switch to previous document window in the active application
CTRL + TAB	X	X	X	X	X		Switch to the next child window of a Multiple Document Interface (MDI) application
CTRL + U	X	X	X	X	X	X	Activate Underline text
CTRL + UP ARROW	X	X	X	X	X	X	Move insertion point to the beginning of the previous paragraph
CTRL + V	X	X	X	X	X	X	Paste (move object from the Clipboard, same as SHIFT + INSERT)
CTRL + X	X	X	X	X	X	X	Cut (move object to the Clipboard, same as SHIFT + DELETE)
CTRL + Z	X	X	X	X	X	X	Undo last editing command (same as ALT + BACK SPACE)
DELETE	X	X	X	X	X	X	Delete selected item. If selected item is a file, move it to the Recycle Bin
DELETE + SHIFT			X	X	X	X	Delete selected item without moving to Recycle Bin
DOWN ARROW			X	X	X	X	When the Menu Bar is active, opens Menu Bar then moves focus down the menu
END	X	X	X	X	X	X	Go to end of current line
ENTER	X	X	X	X	X	X	When Menu Bar is active, opens menu or activates selected menu item
ESC	X	X	X	X	X	X	When Menu Bar is active, closes an open menu and returns focus to the menu title
F1	X	X	X	X	X	X	Display Help for the current application
F10	X	X	X	X	X	X	Activate the Menu Bar of the active window (same as ALT)
HOME	X	X	X	X	X	X	Go to beginning of current line
LEFT ARROW	X	X		X	X	X	When Menu Bar is active, moves focus left along Menu Bar
PAGE DOWN	X	X			X	X	Move down one screen
PAGE UP	X	X			X	X	Move up one screen

Keyboard Shortcuts for Microsoft Windows

Keystrokes	95	98	ME	NT	2K	XP	Action (for each Win version, X=valid shortcut, blank=untested, gray=invalid shortcut)
PRINT SCREEN	X	X			X	X	Copy entire screen to the Clipboard
RIGHT ARROW	X	X		X	X	X	When Menu Bar is active, moves focus right along Menu Bar
RIGHT CLICK	X	X	X	X	X	X	Display the Shortcut Menu for the active item (same as APPLICATION KEY or SHIFT + F10)
SHIFT + ALT + ESC	X	X		X	X	X	Switch to previous open application
SHIFT + ALT + TAB	X	X		X	X	X	Display a list of open applications. Holding down TAB key to move backward through the list; repeatedly pressing the TAB key displays open applications one at a time. Releasing the ALT key opens the selected application
SHIFT + CTRL + END	X	X		X	X	X	Select all text from the cursor to the end of document and moves cursor to end
SHIFT + CTRL + ESC		X	X	X	X	X	Launches Task Manager
SHIFT + CTRL + HOME	X	X		X	X	X	Select all text from the cursor back to the beginning of document and moves cursor to beginning
SHIFT + CTRL + LEFT ARROW	X	X		X	X	X	Select word immediately left of cursor
SHIFT + CTRL + RIGHT ARROW	X	X		X	X	X	Select word immediately right of cursor
SHIFT + DELETE	X	X		X	X	X	Cut (move object to the Clipboard, same as CTRL + X)
SHIFT + DOWN ARROW	X	X		X	X	X	Select one line of text from cursor location to end of the current line and from beginning of next line to the cursor location.
SHIFT + END	X	X		X	X	X	Highlight from current cursor position to end of line
SHIFT + F10	X	X		X	X	X	Display the Shortcut Menu for the active item (same as APPLICATION KEY or RIGHT-CLICK)
SHIFT + HOME	X	X	X	X	X	X	Highlight from current cursor position to beginning of line
SHIFT + INSERT	X	X		X	X	X	Paste the copied/cut item from the Clipboard (same as CTRL + V)
SHIFT + LEFT ARROW	X	X		X	X	X	Select one character immediately left of cursor
SHIFT + RIGHT ARROW	X	X		X	X	X	Select one character immediately right of cursor
SHIFT + RIGHT CLICK	X	X	X	X	X		Display a Shortcut Menu containing alternative commands
SHIFT + UP ARROW	X	X		X	X	X	Select one line of text from cursor location to beginning of the current line and from end of previous line to the cursor location.
Underlined Letter	X	X		X	X		Typing Underlined Letter selects corresponding command.
UP ARROW	X	X		X	X	X	When Menu Bar is active, moves focus up the menu

Keyboard Shortcuts

Keyboard Shortcuts for Microsoft Windows

Keystrokes	95	98	ME	NT	2K	XP	Action (for each Win version. X=valid shortcut, blank=untested, gray=invalid shortcut)
WINKEY + M				X	X	X	Minimizes all open windows (keyboard focus goes to the least recently selected icon on the desktop. Add SHIFT to expand previously opened windows and return focus to the most recently used application.

Windows Explorer

Keystrokes	95	98	ME	NT	2K	XP	Action
ALT + LEFT ARROW		X	X	X	X	X	Move backward to the previous folder
ALT + RIGHT ARROW		X	X	X	X	X	Move forward to the previous folder
BACK SPACE	X	X	X	X	X	X	View the folder one level up
CTRL + (dragging a file to a folder)	X	X	X	X	X	X	Copy file to folder
CTRL + A	X	X	X		X	X	Select all items in current window
CTRL + ARROW KEYS	X	X	X	X	X		Scroll without changing the selected file
CTRL + C	X	X		X	X	X	Copy
CTRL + DOUBLE CLICK (on a folder)	X						If you have more than one open window, this operation closes the active window
CTRL + DOUBLE CLICK (on a folder)	X			X			If you have only one window open, this operation opens a new window
CTRL + F				X	X	X	Opens the Find: All Files dialog box (same as F2, and WINKEY + F)
CTRL + G	X	X	X	X	X		Display the "Go To Folder" dialog box
CTRL + PLUS SIGN (+) + PLUS SIGN (+)	X	X	X	X			In Contents pane, automatically adjusts column width to view information in all columns
CTRL + SHIFT + (drag the file to the Desktop or a folder)	X	X	X	X	X	X	Create shortcut icon on the Desktop or in the folder
CTRL + V	X	X	X	X	X		Paste
CTRL + X	X	X	X	X	X		Cut
CTRL + Z	X	X	X	X	X	X	Undo last action or command
DELETE	X			X	X	X	Move a file or folder to the Recycle Bin
END				X	X	X	Display the bottom of the active window
F2	X	X	X	X	X	X	Highlight a file/folder name for renaming (same as two slow LEFT CLICKs)
F3	X	X	X	X	X	X	Display the "Find: All Files" dialog box (same as WINKEY + F)
F4	X	X	X	X			Display the "Go To A Different Folder" dialog box
F4					X	X	Display the Address Bar list
F5	X	X		X	X	X	Refresh the current window
F6	X	X		X	X	X	Move the focus between panes

Keyboard Shortcuts for Microsoft Windows

Keystrokes	95	98	ME	NT	2K	XP	Action (for each Win version, X=valid shortcut, blank=untested, gray=invalid shortcut)
HOME		X	X	X	X	X	Display the top of the active window
LEFT ARROW	X	X	X	X	X	X	Collapse the current selection if it is expanded; otherwise, go to the parent folder
ASTERICK [*] (on the Numeric Key Pad)	X	X	X		X	X	Expand everything under the current selection
MINUS SIGN [-] (on the Numeric Key Pad)	X	X	X	X	X	X	Collapse the current selection
PLUS SIGN [+] (on the Numeric Key Pad)	X	X	X	X	X	X	Expand the current selection
RIGHT ARROW	X	X	X	X	X	X	Expand the current selection if it is not expanded; otherwise, go to the first child folder
SHIFT + (click the Close (X) button on the folder)	X	X					Close the selected folder and all of its parent folders
SHIFT + CTRL + ESC				X	X	X	Launches Task Manager
SHIFT + DELETE	X	X			X	X	Delete a file/folder immediately without moving it to the Recycle Bin
SHIFT + DOUBLE CLICK	X	X			X	X	Open in a new Windows Explorer window
SHIFT + F10	X		X		X	X	Display the Shortcut Menu (aka Context Menu) for selected item (same as RIGHT-CLICK)
TAB	X	X		X	X	X	Switch between panes and the Toolbar (same as F6)
UP and DOWN ARROWS			X	X	X	X	Extends the selection to the current item
Internet Explorer							
ALT + A	X	X	X	X	X	X	Type the number of pages to be displayed
ALT + C	X	X	X	X	X	X	Closes print preview screen
ALT + D	X	X	X	X	X	X	Select text in the address bar
ALT + F	X	X	X	X	X	X	Specifies how frames are to be printed
ALT + P	X	X	X	X	X	X	Sets printing options
ALT + U	X	X	X	X	X	X	Change headers, footers, orientation, and margins for current page
ALT + Z	X	X	X	X	X	X	Zoom percentages displayed
ALT + END	X	X	X	X	X	X	Displays the last page to be printed
ALT + MINUS	X	X	X	X	X	X	Zoom Out
ALT + PLUS	X	X	X	X	X	X	Zoom In
ALT + HOME	X	X	X	X	X	X	Go to your Home page
ALT + LEFT ARROW	X	X	X	X	X	X	Go back to the previous page (same as BACKSPACE)

Keyboard Shortcuts

Keyboard Shortcuts for Microsoft Windows

Keystrokes	95	98	ME	NT	2K	XP	Action (for each Win version, X=valid shortcut, blank=untested, gray=invalid shortcut)
ALT + RIGHT ARROW	X	X	X	X	X	X	Go forward to the next page
BACKSPACE	X	X	X	X	X	X	Go back to the previous page (same as ALT + LEFT ARROW)
CTRL + A	X	X	X	X	X	X	Select all
CTRL + B	X	X	X	X	X	X	Open the "Organize Favorites" window
CTRL + C	X	X	X	X	X	X	Copy
CTRL + D	X	X	X	X	X	X	Add current web page to Favorites
CTRL + E	X	X	X	X	X	X	Open the "Search" box
CTRL + F	X	X	X	X	X	X	Find on this page
CTRL + F5	X	X	X	X	X	X	Refresh current web page even if time stamps are the same
CTRL + H	X	X	X	X	X	X	Open the "History" box
CTRL + I	X	X	X	X	X	X	Open the "Favorites" box
CTRL + L	X	X	X	X	X	X	Open a new web page (same as CTRL + O)
CTRL + N	X	X	X	X	X	X	Open a new browser window
CTRL + O	X	X	X	X	X	X	Open a new web page (same as CTRL + L)
CTRL + P	X	X	X	X	X	X	Print current page/frame
CTRL + R	X	X	X	X	X	X	Refresh current page/frame (same as F5)
CTRL + S	X	X	X	X	X	X	Save the current page
CTRL + TAB	X	X	X	X	X	X	Move forward between frames (same as F6)
CTRL + V	X	X	X	X	X	X	Paste
CTRL + W	X	X	X	X	X	X	Close the active Internet Explorer window
CTRL + X	X	X	X	X	X	X	Cut
CTRL + Enter	X	X	X	X	X	X	Places www. at the beginning and ".com" at the end in the address bar entry
CTRL + Click	X	X	X	X	X	X	Opens multiple folders in the Favorites or History bar.
CTRL + TAB	X	X	X	X	X	X	Move forward between frames
DOWN ARROW	X	X	X	X	X	X	Scroll toward the end of a document
END	X	X	X	X	X	X	Move to end of document
ENTER	X	X	X	X	X	X	Activate the selected link
ESC	X	X	X	X	X	X	Stop loading a page and display what has been loaded

Keyboard Shortcuts for Microsoft Windows

Keystrokes	95	98	ME	NT	2K	XP	Action (for each Win version, X=valid shortcut, blank=untested, gray=invalid shortcut)
F1	X	X	X	X	X	X	Start the Help program
F4		X	X		X	X	Displays the list of addresses you've typed in before
F5	X	X	X	X	X	X	Refresh current page (same as CTRL + R)
F6	X	X	X	X	X	X	Move forward between frames (same as CTRL + TAB)
F11		X	X		X	X	Toggle between full-screen and other views
HOME	X	X	X	X	X	X	Move to start of document
PAGE DOWN	X	X	X	X	X	X	Scroll toward end of document in larger increments
PAGE UP	X	X	X	X	X	X	Scroll toward start of document in larger increments
SHIFT + CTRL + TAB	X	X	X	X	X	X	Move backward between frames
SHIFT + F10	X	X	X	X	X	X	Display a shortcut menu for a link
SHIFT + TAB	X	X	X	X	X	X	Move backward through items on a web page
TAB	X	X	X	X	X	X	Move forward through items on a web page
UP ARROW	X	X	X	X	X	X	Scroll toward the start of a document

Microsoft Natural Keyboard and most Standard Keyboards with WinKey

Keystrokes	95	98	ME	NT	2K	XP	Action
APPLICATION KEY (aka MENU KEY)	X	X	X		X	X	Display the Shortcut Menu for the active item (same as RIGHT CLICK or SHIFT + F10). The APPLICATION KEY is to the right of the spacebar, looks like a menu with an arrow.
WINKEY	X	X	X		X	X	Display or hide the Start Menu (same as CTRL + ESC)
WINKEY + B						X	Move the focus to the Notification Area
WINKEY + BREAK	X	X	X		X	X	Display the "System Properties" dialog box
WINKEY + CTRL + F	X	X	X		X	X	Display the "Find: Computer" dialog box
WINKEY + CTRL + TAB	X	X	X		X	X	Move focus from Start Menu, to Quick Launch bar, to System Tray
WINKEY + D		X	X		X	X	Minimize all windows and show the Desktop, restore all windows
WINKEY + E	X	X	X		X	X	Open Windows Explorer
WINKEY + E				X			Open My Computer/Windows Explorer
WINKEY + F	X	X	X	X	X	X	Display the "Find: All Files" dialog box (same as F3)
WINKEY + F1	X	X	X	X	X	X	Open the Help Program (same as F1)
WINKEY + F1						X	Open the Windows Help and Support Center (same as F1)
WINKEY + L						X	Lock your computer if you are connected to a network domain

Keyboard Shortcuts for Microsoft Windows

Keystrokes	95	98	ME	NT	2K	XP	Action (for each Win version, X=valid shortcut, blank=untested, gray=invalid shortcut)
WINKEY + L		X	X			X	Switch users if you are not connected to a network domain
WINKEY + M	X	X	X	X	X	X	Minimize all open windows
WINKEY + R	X	X	X	X	X	X	Display the "Run" dialog box
WINKEY + S	X						Switch CAPS LOCK on and off
WINKEY + SHIFT + M	X	X	X	X	X	X	Undo Minimize/Restore all windows
WINKEY + SHIFT + TAB		X	X	X	X	X	Move focus to previous application on the Taskbar
WINKEY + SHIFT + TAB	X	X		X	X	X	Move through Taskbar buttons, press ENTER to open highlighted button
WINKEY + TAB					X	X	Display the "Utility Manager" dialog box
MS Natural Keyboard with Intellitype							
WINKEY + A	X	X	X	X	X	X	Display the "Accessibility Properties" dialog box
WINKEY + C	X	X	X	X	X	X	Display the "Control Panel" window
WINKEY + C	X	X	X	X	X	X	Display the "Mouse Properties" dialog box
WINKEY + I	X	X	X	X	X	X	Display the "Keyboard Properties" dialog box
WINKEY + K	X	X	X	X	X	X	Display the "Windows Logoff Feature" dialog box
WINKEY + L	X	X	X	X	X	X	Display the "Printers Folder" from Control Panel
WINKEY + P	X	X	X	X	X	X	Display a list of Microsoft IntelliType shortcut keys
WINKEY + SPACEBAR	X	X	X	X	X	X	Display the "Clipboard Viewer" dialog box
WINKEY + V	X	X	X	X	X	X	
Outlook							
CTRL + D	X	X	X	X	X	X	Delete an e-mail message, contact, calendar item, or task
CTRL + M	X	X	X	X	X	X	Check for new e-mail (same as F5)
CTRL + Q	X	X	X	X	X	X	Mark an e-mail message as read
CTRL + SHIFT + A	X	X	X	X	X	X	Start a new appointment
CTRL + SHIFT + B	X	X	X	X	X	X	Open the address book
CTRL + SHIFT + C	X	X	X	X	X	X	Start a new contact
CTRL + SHIFT + F	X	X	X	X	X	X	Display the "Advanced Find" dialog box
CTRL + SHIFT + I	X	X	X	X	X	X	Go to the Inbox
CTRL + SHIFT + K	X	X	X	X	X	X	Start a new task
CTRL + SHIFT + M	X	X	X	X	X	X	Start a new e-mail message

Keyboard Shortcuts for Microsoft Windows

Keystrokes	95	98	ME	NT	2K	XP	Action (for each Win version, X=valid shortcut, blank=untested, gray=invalid shortcut)
CTRL + SHIFT + O	X	X	X	X	X	X	Go to the Outbox
CTRL + SHIFT + Q	X	X	X	X	X	X	Start a new meeting request
F11	X	X	X	X	X	X	Make the Find a Contact box active
F5	X	X	X	X	X	X	Check for new e-mail (same as CTRL + M)
Printers							
CTRL + A	X	X	X		X	X	Select All
CTRL + C	X	X	X				Copy
CTRL + V	X	X	X				Paste
CTRL + X	X	X	X				Cut
CTRL + Z	X	X	X				Undo
Word							
ALT + F6	X					X	When Check Spelling As You Type is activated, moves to next error and opens context menu with suggested corrections
ALT + Underlined letter in a menu name	X	X	X	X	X	X	Display the corresponding menu
CTRL while dragging an item	X	X	X	X	X	X	Copy/move selected item
CTRL + B	X	X	X	X	X	X	Activate Bold text
CTRL + I	X	X	X	X	X	X	Activate Italic text
CTRL + SHIFT + GREATER THAN [>]	X	X	X	X	X	X	Increase selected Font by one size
CTRL + SHIFT + LESS THAN [<]	X	X	X	X	X	X	Decrease selected Font by one size
CTRL + U	X	X	X	X	X	X	Activate Underline text
CTRL + RIGHT ARROW	X	X	X	X	X	X	Move the insertion point to the beginning of the next word
CTRL + LEFT ARROW	X	X	X	X	X	X	Move the insertion point to the beginning of the previous word
CTRL + DOWN ARROW	X	X	X	X	X	X	Move the insertion point to the beginning of the next paragraph
CTRL + UP ARROW	X	X	X	X	X	X	Move the insertion point to the beginning of the previoous paragraph
CTRL + SHIFT with any of the arrow keys	X	X	X	X	X	X	Highlight a block of text
DELETE	X	X	X	X	X	X	Delete
F7	X	X	X	X	X	X	Spell check selected text and/or document
SHIFT with any of the arrow keys	X	X	X	X	X	X	Selects text within a document

Keyboard Shortcuts for Microsoft Windows

Keystrokes	95	98	ME	NT	2K	XP	Action (for each Win version, X=valid shortcut, blank=untested, gray=invalid shortcut)
SHIFT (while Word is loading)	X	X	X		X	X	Suppress the AutoExec macro
WordPad							
ALT + BACK SPACE	X	X	X	X	X	X	Undo last edit (same as CTRL + Z)
ALT + ENTER	X	X	X	X	X	X	Display object properties
ALT + F6	X	X	X	X	X	X	Switch between document and Find/Replace dialog box
CTRL + A	X	X	X	X	X	X	Select All
CTRL + C	X	X	X	X	X	X	Copy
CTRL + F	X	X	X	X	X	X	Find
CTRL + H	X	X	X	X	X	X	Replace
CTRL + N	X	X	X	X	X	X	Create a new file
CTRL + O	X	X	X	X	X	X	Open a file
CTRL + P	X	X	X	X	X	X	Print
CTRL + S	X	X	X	X	X	X	Save
CTRL + V	X	X	X	X	X	X	Paste
CTRL + X	X	X	X	X	X	X	Cut
CTRL + Z	X	X	X	X	X	X	Undo (same as ALT + BACK SPACE)
DELETE	X	X	X	X	X	X	Clear
F3	X	X	X	X	X	X	Find next
Paint							
CTRL + A	X			X		X	View Color Box
CTRL + A		X	X		X	X	Select All
CTRL + C	X	X	X	X	X	X	Copy
CTRL + E	X	X	X	X	X	X	Image Attributes
CTRL + F	X	X	X	X	X	X	View Bitmap
CTRL + I	X	X	X	X	X	X	Invert colors
CTRL + L	X			X			Select All
CTRL + L		X	X		X	X	View Color Box
CTRL + N	X	X	X	X	X	X	Start a new file

Keyboard Shortcuts for Microsoft Windows

Keystrokes	95	98	ME	NT	2K	XP	Action (for each Win version, X=valid shortcut, blank=untested, gray=invalid shortcut)
CTRL + O	X	X	X	X	X	X	Open an existing file
CTRL + P	X	X	X	X	X	X	Print
CTRL + R	X	X	X	X	X	X	Flip or rotate the image
CTRL + S	X	X	X	X	X	X	Save the file
CTRL + SHIFT + N	X	X	X	X	X	X	Clear image
CTRL + T	X	X	X	X	X	X	View Tool Box
CTRL + V	X	X	X	X	X	X	Paste
CTRL + W	X	X	X	X	X	X	Stretch or skew the image
CTRL + X	X	X	X	X	X	X	Cut
CTRL + Z	X	X	X	X	X	X	Undo
DELETE	X	X	X	X	X	X	Clear selection
F4	X	X	X	X	X		Repeat last edit command
Notepad							
CTRL + C	X	X	X	X	X	X	Copy
CTRL + V	X	X	X	X	X	X	Paste
CTRL + X	X	X	X	X	X	X	Cut
CTRL + Z	X	X	X	X	X	X	Undo
DELETE	X	X	X	X	X	X	Delete
F1	X	X	X	X	X	X	Help
F3	X	X	X	X	X	X	Find
F5	X	X	X	X	X	X	Insert time and date in document
Excel							
ALT + SHIFT + F1	X	X	X	X	X	X	Insert a New Worksheet
CTRL + 5	X	X	X	X	X	X	Strikethrough highlighted selection
CTRL + B	X	X	X	X	X	X	Activate Bold text
CTRL + F10	X	X	X	X	X	X	Maximize current window
CTRL + F6	X	X	X	X	X	X	Switch between open worksheets/windows
CTRL + F9	X	X	X	X	X	X	Minimize current window

Keyboard Shortcuts

Keyboard Shortcuts for Microsoft Windows

Keystrokes	95	98	ME	NT	2K	XP	Action (for each Win version, X=valid shortcut, blank=untested, gray=invalid shortcut)
CTRL + I	X	X	X	X	X	X	Activate Italic text
CTRL + P	X	X	X	X	X	X	Display the "Print" dialog box
CTRL + SEMICOLON [;]	X	X	X	X	X	X	Enters current Date
CTRL + SHIFT + SEMICOLON [:]	X	X	X	X	X	X	Enters current Time
CTRL + U	X	X	X	X	X	X	Activate Underlined text
F7	X	X	X	X	X	X	Spell check selected text and/or document
SHIFT + F5	X	X	X	X	X	X	Display "Find" dialog box
Front Page							
CTRL + ALT + NUMBER	X	X	X	X	X	X	Apply the Heading style corresponding to the number
CTRL + B	X	X	X	X	X	X	Activate Bold text
CTRL + E	X	X	X	X	X	X	Center a paragraph
CTRL + I	X	X	X	X	X	X	Activate Italic text
CTRL + INSERT	X	X	X	X	X	X	Enter Line Break
CTRL + L	X	X	X	X	X	X	Left align a paragraph
CTRL + PAGE DOWN	X	X	X	X	X	X	Move backward through Normal/HTML/Preview
CTRL + PAGE UP	X	X	X	X	X	X	Move forward through Normal/HTML/Preview
CTRL + R	X	X	X	X	X	X	Right aline a paragraph
CTRL + RIGHT or FRONT SLASH [/]	X	X	X	X	X	X	Display HTML tags
CTRL + SHIFT + N	X	X	X	X	X	X	Apply the Normal style
CTRL + U	X	X	X	X	X	X	Activate Underlined text
TAB	X	X	X	X	X	X	At the last row of a table will add a new row below the current row
Calculator, Scientific							
AMPERSAND [&]	X	X	X	X	X	X	Calculate bitwise AND (same as "And" button)
AT SYMBOL [@]	X	X	X	X	X	X	Calculate the square (x2) of the displayed number (same as "X^2" button)
CARET [^]	X	X	X	X	X	X	Calculate bitwise exclusive OR (same as "Xor" button)
CTRL + A	X	X	X	X	X	X	Calculate mean (average) of numbers in the Statistics Box (same as "Ave" button)
CTRL + D	X	X	X	X	X	X	Calculate standard deviation when population equals n-1 (same as "S" button)
CTRL + S	X	X	X	X	X	X	Turns on statistics mode and opens the Statistics Box (same as "Sta" button)

Keyboard Shortcuts for Microsoft Windows

Keystrokes	95	98	ME	NT	2K	XP	Action (for each Win version, X=valid shortcut, blank=untested, gray=invalid shortcut)
CTRL + T	X	X	X	X	X	X	Calculate sum of the numbers in the Statistics Box (same as "Sum" button)
ENTER	X	X	X	X	X	X	Calculate (same as "=" button)
EXCLAMATION POINT [!]	X	X	X	X	X	X	Calculate factorial of displayed number (same as "n!" button)
F2	X	X	X	X	X	X	For "decimal number system", set trigonometric input to degrees (same as "Degrees" button)
F2	X	X	X	X	X	X	For "hexadecimal, octal, or binary" number systems, show 32-bit representation of number (same as "Dword" button)
F3	X	X	X	X	X	X	For "decimal number system", set trigonometric input to radians (same as "Radians" button)
F3	X	X	X	X	X	X	For "hexadecimal, octal, or binary" number systems, show lower 16 bits of current number (same as "Word" button)
F4	X	X	X	X	X	X	For "decimal number system", set trigonometric input to gradients (same as "Gradients" button)
F4	X	X	X	X	X	X	For "hexadecimal, octal, or binary" number systems, show lower 8 bits of current number (same as "Byte" button)
F5	X	X	X	X	X	X	Convert displayed number to hexadecimal number system (same as "Hex" button)
F6	X	X	X	X	X	X	Convert displayed number to decimal number system (same as "Dec" button)
F7	X	X	X	X	X	X	Convert displayed number to octal number system (same as "Oct" button)
F8	X	X	X	X	X	X	Convert displayed number to binary number system (same as "Bin" button)
F9	X	X	X	X	X	X	Change sign of displayed number (same as "+/-" button)
H	X	X	X	X	X	X	Enable hyperbolic functions (same as "Hyp" button)
I	X	X	X	X	X	X	Enable inverse functions (same as "Inv" button)
INSERT	X	X	X	X	X	X	Enter displayed number into the Statistics Box (same as "Dat" button)
L	X	X	X	X	X	X	Calculate common (base 10) logarithms (same as "log" button)
LEFT PARENTHESIS [( ]	X	X	X	X	X	X	Start a new level of parentheses (same as "(" button)
LESS THAN [<]	X	X	X	X	X	X	Shift left a specified number of positions (same as "Lsh" button)
M	X	X	X	X	X	X	Set degrees to degree-minute-second format (same as "dms" button)
N	X	X	X	X	X	X	Calculate natural (base e) logarithms (same as "ln" button)
NUMBER SIGN [#]	X	X	X	X	X	X	Calculate the cube (x3) of the displayed number (same as "X^3" button)
O	X	X	X	X	X	X	Calculate cosine of displayed number (same as "cos" button)
P	X	X	X	X	X	X	Display value of pi (p) (3.1415.... same as "pi" button)

Keyboard Shortcuts for Microsoft Windows

Keystrokes	95	98	ME	NT	2K	XP	Action (for each Win version, X=valid shortcut, blank=untested, gray=invalid shortcut)
PERCENT [%]	X	X	X	X	X	X	Binary operator, display the modulus or remainder of x/y (same as "Mod" button)
R	X	X	X	X	X	X	Calculate reciprocal of displayed number (same as "1/x" button)
RIGHT PARENTHESIS [ )]	X	X	X	X	X	X	Close the current level of parentheses (same as ")" button)
S	X	X	X	X	X	X	Calculate sine of displayed number (same as "sin" button)
SEMICOLON [;]	X	X	X	X	X	X	Show integer portion of a decimal number (same as "Int" button)
T	X	X	X	X	X	X	Calculate tangent of displayed number (same as "tan" button)
TILDE [~]	X	X	X	X	X	X	Calculate bitwise inverse (same as "Not" button)
V	X	X	X	X	X	X	Toggle scientific notation on and off (same as "F-E" button)
VERTICAL BAR [	]	X	X	X	X	X	X	Calculate bitwise OR (same as "Or" button)
X	X	X	X	X	X	X	Set to scientific notation (same as "Exp" button)
Y	X	X	X	X	X	X	Calculate x raised to the yth power (xy) (same as "x^y" button)
Calculator, Standard and Scientific							
ASTERISK [*]	X	X	X	X	X	X	Multiply
BACK SPACE	X	X					Delete last digit of displayed number (same as "Back" button)
BACK SPACE			X	X	X	X	Delete last digit of displayed number (same as "Back Space" button)
CTRL + C	X	X	X	X	X	X	Copy
CTRL + L	X	X	X	X	X	X	Clear memory (same as "MC" button)
CTRL + M	X	X	X	X	X	X	Store displayed number in memory (same as "MS" button)
CTRL + P	X	X	X	X	X	X	Add displayed number to memory (same as "M+" button)
CTRL + R	X	X	X	X	X	X	Recall number stored in memory (same as "MR" button)
CTRL + V	X	X	X	X	X	X	Paste
ESC	X	X	X	X	X	X	Clear displayed number (same as "CE" button)
MINUS SIGN [-]	X	X	X	X	X	X	Subtract
PLUS SIGN [+]	X	X	X	X	X	X	Add
RIGHT or FRONT SLASH [/]	X	X	X	X	X	X	Divide

Chapter 8

Unix and Linux
Common Commands

This chapter is only meant to be a quick reference for 38 of the common Unix and Linux commands. Commands are listed alphabetically.

Command descriptions in this chapter are based on the following notations and syntax:

Command Name

Description of commands function

Syntax:

Command agreement [Optional items are enclosed in square brackets]

"agreement" is required and is typically a filename or directory

Syntax Options:

Option ....Options description

Examples:

Example.......Description of example

Notes:

• Additional information about the command or option

Unix & Linux

cal

Calendar containing months and year.

Syntax:

cal [month] [year]

Syntax Options:

month ....Month being requested.
Year................Year being requested.

Examples:

cal 05 2004 .....Display May, 2004 calendar.
cal...................Displays current month calendar.

cat

Read multiple files, modify and print.

Syntax:

cat filename [-n] [-b] [-u] [-s] [-v]

Syntax Options:

filename..........file(s) wanting to look at
-n ....Place line number prior to line output
-b ....Number lines. Omit numbers from blank lines.
-u ....Output not buffered. Default is buffered.
-s ....Silent concerning non-existent files.
-v ....Non-printing characters can be seen when printed. Tabs, new lines and form-feeds do not print.
-e ....$ character printed at end of line.
-t ....Tabs printed as ^I's. Formfeeds printed as ^L's.

Examples:

cat filename1.txt filename2.text> and filename3.txt
Combines filename1.txt and filename2.txt to make filename3.txt

Notes:

• If -v is used, -e and -t are ignored.

cd

Change working directory.

Syntax:

cd [name of directory sought]

Syntax Options:

directory..........Directory wanted.
cd.. ....Go back one directory if in UNIX shell.
cd- ....Go back one directory if in Korn shell.

Examples:

cd/Sequoia .....Finds Sequoia directory.
cd../Sequoia/help .....Go back 1 directory and open Sequoia/help.

cd../../Sequoia.....Go back 2 directories and open Sequoia.

chmod

Changes file's access restrictions.

Syntax:

chmod [-r] permissions filename

Syntax Options:

-r	Change file permission on subdirectories of directory you are currently accessing.
filename	File/Directory rights are associated with.
permissions	Specifies rights being granted.
u	User/owner of file
g	Group owner of file
o	Other
a	All
r	Read file
w	Write/edit file
x	Execute/run file as program

numeric permissions:

400	Owner read
040	Group read
004	Read by anyone
200	Owner written
020	Group written
002	Written by anyone
100	Owner executed
010	Group executed
001	Executed by anyone

Examples:

Every directory has 4 sets of permissions. Set 1 represents user, 2 represents group, 3 represents other and 4 represents all. A column looks like rwxrwxrwxrwx. The file owner can change the permission on the file two different ways using chmod command. Use either letter command or numeric permissions. To add permissions use + and to remove them use -.

1. ....Letter Command Example: File -rw--r--r--1 Jones book 476 Jan 10 09:42 series.html. To allow group Jones write ability type chmod g+w series.html. To remove read access from group type chmod g-r series.html.

2. ....Numeric Permissions Example: Each permission is assigned a numerical value. Read (4), write (2), and executable (1). Values are added together in each category. Permissions are changed by using 3 digit sequences - the first for owner, second for group and third for anyone. If you want the series.html file to be readable, writable, and executable for user, readable for group and writable for anyone type chmod 742 series.html. That would represent 400+200+100+040+0+0+0+002+0 totaling 742.

Unix & Linux

chown

Changes ownership of a file(s).

Syntax:

chown [-R] newowner file

Syntax Options:

filename..........File that access rights are being changed.
newowner.......Name of new owner
-R ....Change file permissions in subdirectories of current directory accessed.

Examples:

Change owner of sequoia_tree.html to cedar: chom cedar se-
quoia_tree.html

cp

Copies files/directories from one location to another.

Syntax:

cp [-l] [-r] currentfiles directory[/newfiles]

Syntax Options:

currentfiles......File being copied.
directory..........Name given to a new copy.
newfiles ....Place new files are going to be.
-l ....Prompt recei4ved before replacing file.
-r ....As directory is copied it copies subdirectories of directory
and makes new directory if not in existence.

Examples:

To copy file book.html into directory Sequoia type: cp book.html/Sequoia

Notes:

- If destination of file you are copying is existing file, then existing file is overwritten.
- If destination is an existing directory, file is copied into that directory.

date

Displays/sets date and time

Syntax:

date [-a] [-u] [-s datestr]

Syntax Options:

-a ....Adjusts time by fractions of a second.
-u ....Displays/sets date in Greenwich Mean Time. Bypasses
normal change to local time.
-s datestr ....Time and date set to this specified value.

Examples:

date ....Shows date/time of server in following format:
Sat May 1 12.15.20 MST 2004

date -s "05/01/2004 12:15:20"

Sets date to given information.
Date '+date: %m/%d/%y H:%M:%S'
Supply numeric string which is displayed as:
Date: 05/01/04
.........Time: 12:15:20

diff

Displays the differences of two given files

Syntax:

diff [-b] [-l] [-t] [-w] [-c] [-C] [-e] [-f] [-h] [-n] [-D string] [-l] [-r] [-s] [-S name] [filename1 filename2] [directoryname1 directoryname2]

Syntax Options:

-b ....Spacing differences ignored.
-l ....Case ignored.
-t ....TAB characters expanded in output lines.
-w ....Tabs and spaces ignored.
-c ....Shows differences listed in three lines of context.
-C ....Same as -c except with numbered lines of context.
-e ....Generates script of a, c and d commands which recreate filename2 from filename1. "Latest version" appears on output.
-f ....Produces similar script as -e but in reverse order.
-h ....Works on files of unlimited length. Chained stretches must be short and separated well.
-n ....Generates script like -e but in reverse order and has count of changed lines on each insert/delete command.
-D string ....Produces merged version of filename1 and filename2. C preprocessor controls included.
-l ....Creates output in long format. Text file(s) are piped through pr(1) to paginate it prior to diff.
-r ....Diff applied recursively to encountered subdirectories.
-s ....Reports identical files otherwise not recognized.
-S name ....Directory diff starts in middle, beginning with filename.
filename1 ....File one.
filename2 ....File two.
directoryname1 ·······Directory one.
directoryname2 ·······Directory two.

Examples:

diff directoryname1 directoryname2
Generates list of all line differences between the two directories.

echo

Screen displays information typed after echo.

Syntax:

echo [-n] text

Syntax Options:

-n ....New line not begun after echoed text.
text ....What will be displayed on screen.

Examples:

echo Sequoia Publishing ..Would return to Sequoia Publishing on screen.

exit

End current process and return to host home.

Syntax:

exit

Example:

If logged onto a remote host type "exit". Will be returned to your home host.

Notes:

• If exit does not respond, try Ctrl-D, bye, quit, lo or logout.

find

Locates file(s) that match given specifications. Minimum one pathname and one condition needed.

Syntax:

find pathname expressions

Syntax Options:

pathname ....Starting point path name.
-atime n ....True if file entered n days ago.
-cpio device ....Always true. Writes current file on device in cpio format.
-ctime n...........Locates file change n days ago, more than n (+n) or less than n (-n).
-depth ....Decends directory tree to work files first then parent directory.
-exec command ······True if at exit status executed command has a zero value. End of command must have an escaped semicolon.
-follow ....Symbolic links are followed. "Find" tracks directories visited so infinite loops are detected.
-fstype type .....Locates filesystem to which current file belongs if type type.
-group gname .Locates file belonging to group gname.
-inum n ....Locates file(s) having inode number n.
-links...............True when file has n links.
-local...............True when file system type is not remote type.
-ls ....Prints current pathname and associated statistics (inode #, size in kb, protection mode, # of hard links, user, group, size in bytes, modification time). If special file field will include major and minor device numbers.
-mount ....Restricts search to file system of specified directory.
-mtime n ....Locate file's data changed n days ago,(+n) or (-n) days ago.

Option	Description
-name pattern	Locates filename(s) that match pattern.
-ncpio device	Always true. Current file written on device in cpio -c format.
-newer file	Locate files that were modified more recently than argument file.
-nogroup	Locates file belonging to group not in the /etc/passwd file.
-nouser	Locates file belonging to user not in the /etc/passwd file.
-ok command	Same as -exec but user responds with y for command execution.
-perm [-]mode	Locates files which permissions match octal number [-] exactly. For example: 766 matches -rwx-rw-rw-.
-perm [-]onum	Using a [-] states only bits set in onum are compared with permissions.
-print	Current pathname prints.
-prune	Won't examine directories/files below pattern just matched.
-size n[c]	Locates file(s) with n blocks, or c, with n characters long.
-type c	Locates file type c. "c" is b (block style), c (character file), d (directory), D (door), f (plain file), l (symbolic link), p (pipe), or s (socket).
-user	Locates user files.
-xdev	Same as -mount primary.

Examples:

find -name 'Sequoia.htm'

> Locates all files in current directory named Sequoia.

find / -name 'Sequoia.htm'

> Locates all files in root and its subdirectories named Sequoia.

find -name 'Sequoia*'

> Locates any file beginning with Sequoia in current directory/subdirectory.

find -name '*' -size +256k..

> Locates any file larger than 256k.

find -mtime -4 -print

> Locate and print files modified in prior 4 days.

---

finger

Lists user(s) information.

Syntax:

finger [-b] [-f] [-h] [-i] [-l] [-m] [-p] [-q] [-s] [-w] [username]

Syntax Options:

Option	Description
-b	Omit long format print of users home directory and shell.
-f	Omit non-long format printout of header.
-h	Omit long format printout of .project file.
-i	Creates idle output format. Shows login name, terminal, login time and idle time.
-l	Long output format.
-m	Matches arguments on user name only.
-p	Omit .plan and .project from long format printout.

-q	Quick output format. Shows login name, terminal and login time.
-s	Short output format.
-w	Omit full name printed in short format printout.

Examples:

finger -b -p -bp

Displays information on user bp:

Login name:short Real life: Book Publisher

On since Aug 15 10:56:16 on pts/4 from domain bookpublisher.com

15 seconds idle time

Unread mail since Wed Aug 4 08:30:10 2004

grep

Locates and prints lines matching regular expressions in a file.

Syntax:

grep [-b] [-c] [-h] [-l] [-l] [-n] [-s] [-v] [-w] text filenames

Syntax Options:

-b	Begin line by block number on which it is located.
-c	Print count of matching lines
-h	Prints matched lines, not filenames. Used in multiple file searches.
-l	Ignores case distinctions.
-l	Shows matching files names, not individual matched lines.
-n	Prints line numbers before each line.
-s	Excludes error messages about unreadable/nonexistent files.
-v	Print lines that don't match pattern.
-w	Locates expressions as if surrounded by \< and />.
text	Searching within named text
filenames	File being searched.

Patterns used for searching:

.	Single character match.
*	Wild character.
{ }	Match characters within bracket.
^	Beginning of the line.
$	End of line.
\	Next character listed is taken serious.

Examples:

grep -c/bin/tcsh/etc/psswd......Locates # of users of tcsh

grep 'games'/trip/*.....Will find files in trip directory which use word 'games'. Output shown would be grep:/trip/solitaire: is a directory/trip/games.html. This states solitaire is a directory in trip that uses the word 'games'.

grep -c pattern files/grep:0......Find files not containing pattern.

halt

Stop computer.

Syntax:

halt [-l] [-n] [-q] [-y]

Syntax Options:

-l .... Stops message to be sent identifying who placed halt.
-n .... Stops sync before halt or reboot.
-q .... Immediate halt.
-y .... System halted. Occurs even if terminal is dial-up.

Examples:

halt .... Commands system to stop.

head

Default shows first 10 lines of a file.

Syntax:

head [-number\-n number] filename

Syntax Options:

-number .... # of lines to be listed.
-n number .... # of lines to be listed.
filename .... File lines to be listed from.

Examples:

head-20 sequoiafile.txt ...... Displays first 20 lines of sequoiafile.txt
grep '(303)' phone_list/head

Displays first 10 numbers with '303' area code.

kill

End or terminate process(s)

Syntax:

kill [-s] [-l] %pid

Syntax Options:

-s .... Designates signal name or number to send.
-l .... Write signal values supported by implementation.
pid .... Decimal integer designating a process or process group to be signaled. Or, a control job ID that designates a process group to be signaled.

Examples:

kill -s kill 100 - 150 ... Kills job 1 of 150.
kills -1 .... Terminate process immediately
kills -9 .... Forces an absolute end of process. Last resort.

less

Opposite of the more command.

Syntax:

less-?
less-help

less-V

less- - version

less[-+]aBcCdeEfFgGilJmMnNqQrRsSuUvwWX]

[-b space] [-h lines] [-j line] [-keyfile]

[-{oO} logfile] [pattern] [-P prompt] [-t tag]

[-T tagsfile] [-x tab,…] [-y lines] [-z lines]

[++]cmd] [-] [filename]…

Syntax Options:

-? or --help......Lists summary of commands less accepts.

-a or --search-skip-screen
    Search begins after last line displayed.

-bn or --buffers=n······Amount of buffer space 9in kilobytes) used by less
    for each file.

-B or --auto-buffers··Disables automatic allocation of buffers for pipes, so
    amount specified is used.

-c or --clear-screen ··Screen is redrawn from top.

-C or --Clear-screen·Screen cleared before repainted.

-d or --dumb....Cancels error message showing terminal is dumb.

-Dxcolor..........In MS-DOS, sets text display color.

-e or --quit-at-eof······Less automatically exits second time it is at
    end-of-file.

-E or --Quit-At-EOF··Less automatically exits first time it is at end-of-file.

-f or --force......Forces opening of non-regular files.

-F or --quit-if-one-screen
    Automatically exits if whole file fits on first screen.

g- or --hilite-search···Highlights the string last found in search command.
    Normally all strings highlighted.

-G or --Hilite-Search·Stops all highlighting of strings found by search com-
    mands.

-hn or --max-back-scroll+n
    Maximum number of lines to scroll backwards at once.

-I or --ignore-case ····Searches not case-sensitive. Will be case sensitive if
    uppercase letters in search pattern.

-I or --Ignore-Case ···Ignores case even if uppercase in search pattern.

-jn or --jump-target=n
    Line specified on screen where target line to be placed.

-J or --status-columns
    Status column displayed on left screen edge.

-kfilename or --lesskey-file=filename
    Less will open and read named file as a lesskey file.

-m or --long-prompt··Shows more-like prompt with percent of file read.

-M or --Long-Prompt Prompts even more verbosely than more.

-n or --line-numbers ·Line numbers not calculated.

-N or --Line-Numbers
    Each line in the display begins with a line number.

-ofilename or --log-file=filename
    When input from a pipe is copied to named file as it is
    viewed.

-Offilename or --LOG-FILE=filename
          Like -o except it overwrites existing file without confirma-
          tion.
-ppattern or --pattern=pattern
          Search at startup for first occurrence of pattern.
-Pprompt or --prompt=prompt
          Ability to tailor 3 prompt styles.
............-Ps followed by a string makes prompt short.
............-Pm changes default to medium prompt.
............-PM changes default to long prompt.
............-Ph changes help screen prompt
-q or --quiet or --silent
          Disables terminal bell to quiet operation.
-Q or --Quiet or --Silent
          Terminal bell never rings.
-r or --raw-control-chars
          "Raw" control characters displayed. Can't track screen ap-
          pearance.
-R or --Raw-Control-Chars
          Same as -r but keeps track of screen appearance.
-s or --squeeze-blank-lines
          Successive blank lines are printed as one line.
-S or --chop-long-lines
          Lines longer than screen width is chopped and discarded,
          not folded.
-ttag or --tag=tag ......Edit file containing that tag.
-Ttagsfile or --tag-file=tagsfile
          Use specified tags file.
-u or --underline-special
          Backspaces and carriage returns treated as printable char-
          acters.
-U or --Underline-Special
          Backspaces, tabs and carriage returns treated as printable
          characters.
-V or --version..........Less version number displayed
-w or --hilite-unread..First new line after a forward movement of a full page
          is highlighted.
-W or --HiLite-Unread
          Similar to -w, but highlights first new line after a forward
          movement command larger than one line.
-xn,.. or --tabs=n,.. ...Tab stops set to every n character. 'n's default 8.
-X or --no-init ..Stops termcap initialization and deinitialization strings from
          being sent to terminal.
--no-keypad ....Stops keypad initialization and deinitialization strings from
          being sent to terminal.
-yn or --max-forw-scroll=n
          'n' specifies amount of lines that can be scrolled forwards.
-[z]n or --window=n ···Sets default scrolling window size to 'n'lines.
-"cc or --quotes=cc···Filename quoting character changed.

Example:

less tree.txt .....Opens tree.txt in less.

lprm

Delete job(s) from printer's queue.

Syntax:

lprm [-P destination] [-] [request-ID] [user]

Syntax Options:

-P....................Printer's name.

-......................Delete's all jobs by specified user.

request-ID.......Deletes specific job specified by ID number.

user ....Specifies which jobs are associated with user.

Examples:

lprm -P techref 260 ..Removes ID #260 from techref destination.

ls

Displays contents of directories,

Syntax:

ls [-a] [-A] [-b] [-c] [-C] [-d] [-f] [-F] [-g] [-l] [-l] [-L] [-m] [-o] [-p] [-q] [-r] [-R] [-s] [t] [-u] [-x] [pathnames]

Syntax Options:

-a ....Displays all files.

-A....................Displays all files, but not the working and parent directories.

-b ....Non-printable characters printed in octal and alphabetic form.

-c ....Status change time of the i-node used for sorting and printing.

-C ....Output displayed as multi-column with data sorted down the columns.

-d ....Reports directory name but not contents.

-f ....Forces printing contents in order stored with no sorting.

-F ....Places a notation at end of each item: directories with a (/), doors (>),executable files (*), symbolic links (@),Fifo's (l), AF Unix address family sockets (=).

-g ....Similar to -l but owner not printed.

-l ....Prints i-node number for each file.

-l ....Displays long format listing.

-L ....With a symbolic link argument, list referenced file/directory and not link itself.

-m ....List files into a comma-separated stream output.

-n ....Similar to -l except owner and group ID numbers printed instead of names.

-o ....Similar to -l except group ID not printed.

-p ....All directories preceded by (/).

-q ....Display nonprinting characters as (?).

-r....................Display files in reverse order by name or time.
-R ....Include subdirectories contents.
-s ....File size printed in blocks for each entry.
-t ....Files sorted by modification time.
-u ....Files sorted by file access time.
-x ....Files listed in rows going across screen.
-1 ....Output displays 1 entry per line.
Pathname ....Directory/file listed.

Examples:

ls - 1d/cat /dog......List status of /cat and /dog directories.
Sequoia.com: [/tree]* ls -1......Will display files in directory and their permissions (filename, owner, group, size, date, time modified).

man

View command information online in Unix manual.

Syntax:

man [-] [-k keywords] topic

Syntax Options:

- ....View manual with no stopping.
-k keywords ....Searches all manuals for keywords.
topic................Finds manual for designated subject.

Examples:

man chmod.....Display help information on chmod command.
man -keyword dos ...Searches for manuals containing dos information.

mkdir

Create new directory(s).

Syntax:

mkdir directoryname

Syntax Options:

directoryname......Name of new directory being created.

Examples:

mkdir PCRef ...Create a new directory named PCRef.
Mkdir -m 444 storage ....Read-only 'storage' directory created.

Notes:

• User needs permission to write to parent directory.

more

File content displayed on terminal one screen at a time.

Syntax:

more [-c] [-d] [-e] [-f] [-l] [-l] [-n number] [-p command] [-r] [-s] [-t tagstring] [-u] [-w] [-lines] [+ linenumber] [+/ pattern] [file…]

Syntax Options:

-c .... Terminal clears and then repaints screen from top.
-d .... If unrecognized command is used, error message generated. Bell disabled.
-e .... Exit.
-f .... Count logical not screen lines. Long lines not folded.
-I .... Ignores case and performs pattern matching during search.
-l .... Form-feed (Ctrl-L) characters ignored.
-n number .... State line number per screen.
-p command .... Instead of scrolling, sort through each file by clearing window.
-r .... Control characters displayed in ^x form.
-s .... Multiple blank lines displayed as one.
-t tagstring ...... Tag specified in tagstring argument used to write screen.
-u .... Ignores underline characters.
-w .... Wait for keystrike to exit.
-lines .... Show number of lines indicated.
+linenumber .... Start up at linenumber.
filename .... Designated file.

Examples:

more +4 BoysPaper.txt ..... Command will display BoysPaper.txt file beginning on line 4. .
nroff tree I more -u ... Format tree document to screen without underlines.
More -cd book. Search through tree file in clear mode and show prompts.

mv

Move/rename file or directory.

Syntax:

mv [-f] [-I] oldfilename newfilename

Syntax Options:

-f .... File moved without prompt.
-I .... File movement creates prompt before overwriting another file.
oldfilename ..... File to be renamed.
newfilename ... New file name given.
filename .... Name of directory file is being moved to.

Examples:

mv john_smith.html john_taylor.html
Renaming john_smith.html to john_taylor.html and moving all contents of file to new file. Old file will not exist anymore.

passwd

Command to create or change user password.

Syntax:

passwd [-r\files\-r nis\-r nisplus] [-a] [-d\-l] [-e] [-f] [-g] [-h] [-n min] [-s] [-w] [-x] [-D] [name]

Syntax options:

-r.....................States which repository the operation is applied to.
-a.....................Displays password attributes.
-d.....................Login name not prompted for password.
-l......................Password entry locked for name.
-e.....................Login shell changed.
-f......................Expires password so user must change it at next login.
-g.....................Finger information changed.
-h.....................Home directory changed.
-n min ....Sets minimum number of days allowed between password changes for designated name.
-s.....................Password information displayed.
-w warn...........Sets a warning in x number of days for when the user's password expires.
-x max.............Sets maximum number of days password is valid for.

Examples:

passwd ....Pulls up 3 prompts allowing user to change password.

Notes:

• Privileged user or owner of password only ones who can make changes.

---

paste

Combine lines of files.

Syntax:

paste [-s] [-d char] file

Syntax Options:

-s ....Lines merged one file at a time.
-d list..............Columns separated with char instead of tab.
file..................Input file's pathname.

Examples:

man | paste --- Input in man pasted into 3 columns.
who | paste ----.........Users listed in 4 columns.

---

ps

Prints active process status.

Syntax:

ps [-a] [-A] [-c] [-d] [-e] [-f] [-j] [-l] [-L] [-P] [-y] [-g] [-n] [-o] [-p] [-s] [-t] [-u] [-U] [-G]

Syntax Options:

-a ....List frequently accessed process(es) information.
-A....................Display information on all processes.

-c	Display information showing scheduler properties in appropriate format.
-d	Do not show sessions leader in process information.
-e	Diplay information on all running processes.
-f	Full listing printed.
-j	Session and process group ID displayed.
-l	Long listing produced.
-L	Light weight process (lwp) information printed.
-P	Number of processors the lwp is connected to.
-y	RSS and Sz are long listed to report resident set size of process.
-g grplist	Display group leader's process data.
-n namelist	State alternative system name list instead of default.
-o format	Specifies format information is printed in.
-p proclist	Tells numbers of process data to be listed.
-s sidlist	States which session leader(s) information to be listed.
-t term	States terminal to which process data is to be listed.
-u uidlist	Tells which effective user's process data is to be listed.
-U uidlist	Tells which real user's process data is to be listed.
-G gidlist	States which real Group ID process data should be listed.
-ps	Display current running processes.

pwd

Display pathname of current working directory.

Syntax:

pwd

Examples:

pwd................May show location as /home/sequoia/employees_html

rlogin

Connects local terminal to remote host system.

Syntax:

flogin [-8] [-E] [-L] [-ec] [-l username] hostusername

Syntax Options:

-8	Use 8-bit input data path.
-E	No characters are interpreted as escape character.
-L	Run in litout mode.
-ec	Escape character specified as c.
-l username	Specifies remote login name.
hostusername	Remote machine.

Examples:

rlogin -l tree bush.com .....Allows user tree to login to remote host bush.

rm

A write permission user may remove a file from a directory.

Syntax:

rm [-f] [-i] [-R] [-r] [file]

Syntax Options:

-f ....Delete all files without prompt.
-i ....Receive prompt before deleting files.
-r/-R ....Delete directory, subdirectories and all contents.
file ....Filename targeted for removal.

Examples:

rm -f smithfile.txt .....smithfile.txt removed without prompt.
rm -r smith ......Remove smith directory.

rmdir

Delete directory. Not contents.

Syntax:

rmdir [-p] [-s] filename directory

Syntax Options:

-p ....Delete directories and associated parent directories.
-s ....Block printing of standard error message.
Directory ....Designated directory to be deleted.

Examples:

rmdir smith ......Removes smith directory.
rm -r smith ......Deletes smith directory even if there are associated files.

sleep

Idle for x amount of time before executing next command.

Syntax:

sleep time

Syntax Options:

time ....Number of seconds to wait.

Examples:

sleep 15 ....Wait 15 seconds prior to execution of next command.

su

Used by privileged user to login under another user name.

Syntax:

su [-] [user[arg]]

Syntax Options:

- ....Displayed as if user logged in instead of superuser.
user ....Name you want to login under.
arg ....Arguments needing to pass through su command.

Examples:

su - tree ....Superuser logs on as user tree with no environmental changes.

---

tail

Print last ten lines of designated file.

Syntax:

tail [+ number] [-l] [-b] [-c] [-r] [-f] [-c number] [-n number] [filename]

Syntax Options:

-l	Units of lines.
-b	Units of blocks.
-c	Units of bytes.
-r reverse	Prints file in reverse order.
-f follow	Program enters endless loop and doesn't terminate. Press Ctrl-C to end.
-c number	Decimal integer which sign tells location in the file to begin copying at. Measured in bytes.
	- ······Copying starts at file end
	+······Copying starts at beginning of file
	none·Copying starts at file end.
-n number	Starting location of file measured in lines. Similar to -c number.
filename	File to be displayed.

Examples:

tail smithfile.txt Display last 10 lines of smithfile.txt.

grep '\.str'file|tail -5....Display last 5 lines which have .str in them.

---

telnet

Protocol used to access remote systems.

Syntax:

telnet [-8] [-E] [-L] [-c] [-d] [-r] [-e escape_char] [-l user] [-n file] [host [port]] ....

Syntax Options:

-8	Use 8-bit input data path.
-E	No characters are interpreted as escape characters.
-L	Binary option negotiated on output since 8-bit data path specified.
-c	Blocks reading of user's telnetrc file.
-d	Initial debug toggle set at True.
-r	Escape character stated as ~ character.
-e escape_char	Set initial telnet escape character to esc_char.
-l user	If connecting to remote system that recognizes ENVIRON, send user to remote system as value for variable user.
-n file	Tracefile opened.

Examples:

telnet host.com ....Open telnet session to host.com domain.

whereis

Binary, source and manual page files located for specified command.

Syntax:

whereis [options] filename

Syntax Options:

-b .... Search for binaries only.
-m .... Search for manual sections only.
-s .... Search for sources only.
-u .... Search for unusual entries. Files with no documentation.
-B .... Limit/change areas searched for binaries.
-M .... Limit/change areas searched for manual sections.
-S .... Limit/change areas searched for sources.
-f .... Stop last directory list. Signal start of filenames.

Examples:

whereis /bin ....Locates directories where bin is stored.

which

Displays command location.

Syntax:

which [filename1]

Syntax Options:

filename1 ....File being searched for.

Examples:

which rlogin.....Locate rlogin command.

who

States user(s) logged onto system.

Syntax:

who [-a] [-b] [-d] [-H] [-l] [-m] [-nx] [-p] [-q] [-r] [-s] [-t] [-T] [-u] [am i] [file-name]

Syntax Options:

-a .... Process or named file.
-b .... Time and date of last reboot .
-d .... Lists processes that have expired.
-H .... Display output column headings above normal output.
-l .... Lookup host names of user waiting to login.
-m .... Information displayed on current terminal only.
-nx .... Specifies number of users listed per line.
-p .... Displays currently active processes.
-q .... List name and number of users logged on.

-r	Run-level of the init process.
-s	Name, time and line fields displayed.
-t	Displays last system clock change.
-T	Name, time, line and state field displayed.
-u	Users currently logged in and how long terminal has been idle.
am i	Username of the invoking user.

Examples:

$ who -uH ......An example of display is;

```
Name.....Line.....Time.................Idle.......Pid
Jim.........ttyp2....Nov 15 12:15.....10:25.....2410
Tim.........ttyp1....Nov 16 07:33................12046
```

From this one knows Jim's terminal has been idle for 10 hours, even though logged on. Tim's terminal is currently being used.

zcat

Uncompress and writes file to standard output.

Syntax:

zcat [-D] [-V] [v] filename

Syntax Options:

-D	Uncompress
-V	Displays version uncompressed.
-v	Identifies name of each uncompressed file.
filename	Compressed file name.

Examples:

zcat PCRef .....Will uncompress and display PCRef file.

Chapter 9

Å í û ≈ œ
π ∞ € ç
Ö ñ Ω ¿

ASCII and Numerics

Computer ASCII Codes

The following ASCII (**A**merican **S**tandard **C**ode for **I**nformation **I**nterchange) tables are used by most of the microcomputer industry. The codes occur in two sets: the "low–bit" set, from Dec 0 to Dec 127, and the "high–bit" set, from Dec 128 to Dec 255. The "low–bit" set is standard for almost all microcomputers but the "high–bit" set varies between the different computer brands. For instance, in the case of Apple computers and Epson printers, the "high–bit" set repeats the "low–bit" set except that the alphameric characters are italic. In the case of IBM and many other MSDOS systems, the "high–bit" set is composed of foreign language and box drawing characters and mathematic symbols.

Hex	Dec	Description	Abbr	Character		Control
00	0	Null	Null			Control @
01	1	Start Heading	SOH	☺		Control A
02	2	Start of Text	STS		☻	Control B
03	3	End of Text	ETX	♥		Control C
04	4	End Transmit	EOT		♦	Control D
05	5	Enquiry	ENQ	♣		Control E
06	6	Acknowledge	ACK		♠	Control F
07	7	Beep	BEL	•		Control G
08	8	Back space	BS		■	Control H
09	9	Horizontal Tab	HT	○		Control I
0A	10	Line Feed	LF		◙	Control J
0B	11	Vertical Tab	VT	♂		Control K
0C	12	Form Feed	FF		♀	Control L
0D	13	Carriage Ret.	CR	♪		Control M
0E	14	Shift Out	SO		♫	Control N
0F	15	Shift In	SI	☼		Control O
10	16	Device Link Esc	DUE		►	Control P
11	17	Dev Cont 1 X-ON	DC1	◄		Control Q
12	18	Dev Control 2	DC2		↕	Control R
13	19	Dev Cont 3 X-OFF	DC3	‼		Control S
14	20	Dev Control 4	DC4		¶	Control T
15	21	Negative Ack	NAK	§		Control U
16	22	Synchronous Idle	SON		▬	Control V
17	23	End Trans Block	ETB	↕		Control W
18	24	Cancel	CAN		↑	Control X
19	25	End Medium	EM	↓		Control Y
1A	26	Substitute	SUB		→	Control Z
1B	27	Escape	ESC	←		Control [
1C	28	Cursor Right	FS		└	Control \
1D	29	Cursor Left	GS	↔		Control]
1E	30	Cursor Up	RS		▲	Control ^
1F	31	Cursor Down	US	▼		Control _

ASCII-Numbers

Computer ASCII Codes

Hex	Dec	Character	Description
20	32		Space (SP)
21	33	!	Exclamation Point
22	34	"	Double Quote
23	35	#	Number sign
24	36	$	Dollar sign
25	37	%	Percent
26	38	&	Ampersand
27	39	'	Apostrophe
28	40	(	Left parenthesis
29	41	)	Right parenthesis
2A	42	*	Asterisk
2B	43	+	Plus sign
2C	44	,	Comma
2D	45	–	Minus sign
2E	46	.	Period
2F	47	/	Right or Front slash
30	48	0	Zero
31	49	1	One
32	50	2	Two
33	51	3	Three
34	52	4	Four
35	53	5	Five
36	54	6	Six
37	55	7	Seven
38	56	8	Eight
39	57	9	Nine
3A	58	:	Colon
3B	59	;	Semicolon
3C	60	<	Less than
3D	61	=	Equal sign
3E	62	>	Greater than
3F	63	?	Question mark
40	64	@	"at" symbol
41	65	A	Uppercase A
42	66	B	Uppercase B
43	67	C	Uppercase C
44	68	D	Uppercase D
45	69	E	Uppercase E
46	70	F	Uppercase F
47	71	G	Uppercase G
48	72	H	Uppercase H
49	73	I	Uppercase I
4A	74	J	Uppercase J
4B	75	K	Uppercase K
4C	76	L	Uppercase L

ASCII-Numbers

Computer ASCII Codes

Hex	Dec	Character	Description
4D	77	M	Uppercase M
4E	78	N	Uppercase N
4F	79	O	Uppercase O
50	80	P	Uppercase P
51	81	Q	Uppercase Q
52	82	R	Uppercase R
53	83	S	Uppercase S
54	84	T	Uppercase T
55	85	U	Uppercase U
56	86	V	Uppercase V
57	87	W	Uppercase W
58	88	X	Uppercase X
59	89	Y	Uppercase Y
5A	90	Z	Uppercase Z
5B	91	[	Left bracket
5C	92	\	Left or Back Slash
5D	93	]	Right bracket
5E	94	^	Caret
5F	95	_	Underline
60	96	`	Accent
61	97	a	Lowercase a
62	98	b	Lowercase b
63	99	c	Lowercase c
64	100	d	Lowercase d
65	101	e	Lowercase e
66	102	f	Lowercase f
67	103	g	Lowercase g
68	104	h	Lowercase h
69	105	I	Lowercase I
6A	106	j	Lowercase j
6B	107	k	Lowercase k
6C	108	l	Lowercase l
6D	109	m	Lowercase m
6E	110	n	Lowercase n
6F	111	o	Lowercase o
70	112	p	Lowercase p
71	113	q	Lowercase q
72	114	r	Lowercase r
73	115	s	Lowercase s
74	116	t	Lowercase t
75	117	u	Lowercase u
76	118	v	Lowercase v
77	119	w	Lowercase w
78	120	x	Lowercase x
79	121	y	Lowercase y

Computer ASCII Codes

Hex	Dec	Standard Character	Description
7A	122	z	Lowercase z
7B	123	{	Left brace
7C	124	|	Vertical line
7D	125	}	Right brace
7E	126	~	Tilde
7F	127	DEL	Delete

Hex	Dec	Standard Character	IBM Set	Standard Description
80	128	Null	ā	Null
81	129	SOH	ā	Start Heading
82	130	STS	Å	Start of Text
83	131	ETX	Å	End of Text
84	132	EOT	Å	End Transmit
85	133	ENQ	à	Enquiry
86	134	ACK	Å	Acknowledge
87	135	BEL	ā	Beep
88	136	BS	ā	Back Space
89	137	HT	ë	Horiz Tab
8A	138	LF	è	Line Feed
8B	139	VT	ï	Vertical Tab
8C	140	FF	î	Form Feed
8D	141	CR	ì	Carriage Return
8E	142	SO	Ä	Shift Out
8F	143	SI	Å	Shift In
90	144	DLE	É	Device Link Esc
91	145	DC1	æ	Device Cont 1 X-ON
92	146	DC2	Æ	Device Control 2
93	147	DC3	ô	Device Cont 3 X-OFF
94	148	DC4	ö	Device Control 4
95	149	NAK	ò	Negative Ack
96	150	SYN	û	Synchronous Idle
97	151	ETB	ù	End Transmit Block
98	152	CAN	ÿ	Cancel
99	153	EM	Ö	End Medium
9A	154	SUB	Ü	Substitute
9B	155	ESC	¢	Escape
9C	156	FS	£	Cursor Right
9D	157	GS	¥	Cursor Left
9E	158	RS	Pt	Cursor Up
9F	159	US	ƒ	Cursor Down
A0	160	Space	á	Space
A1	161	!	í	Italic Exclamation point
A2	162	"	ó	Italic Double quote
A3	163	#	ú	Italic Number sign
A4	164	$	ñ	Italic Dollar sign
A5	165	%	Ñ	Italic Percent
A6	166	&	ª	Italic Ampersand
A7	167	'	º	Italic Apostrophe

ASCII-Numbers

Computer ASCII Codes

Hex	Dec	Standard Character	IBM Set	Standard Description
A8	168	(	¿	Italic Left parenthesis
A9	169	)	⌐	Italic Right parenthesis
AA	170	*	¬	Italic asterisk
AB	171	+	½	Italic plus sign
AC	172	,	¼	Italic comma
AD	173	–	¡	Italic minus sign
AE	174	.	«	Italic period
AF	175	/	»	Italic right slash
B0	176	0		Italic Zero
B1	177	1		Italic One
B2	178	2		Italic Two
B3	179	3	│	Italic Three
B4	180	4	┤	Italic Four
B5	181	5	╡	Italic Five
B6	182	6	╢	Italic Six
B7	183	7	╖	Italic Seven
B8	184	8	╕	Italic Eight
B9	185	9	╣	Italic Nine
BA	186	:	║	Italic colon
BB	187	;	╗	Italic semicolon
BC	188	<	╝	Italic less than
BD	189	=	╜	Italic equal
BE	190	>	╛	Italic greater than
BF	191	?	┐	Italic question mark
C0	192	@	└	Italic "at" symbol
C1	193	A	┴	Italic A
C2	194	B	┬	Italic B
C3	195	C	├	Italic C
C4	196	D	─	Italic D
C5	197	E	┼	Italic E
C6	198	F	╞	Italic F
C7	199	G	╟	Italic G
C8	200	H	╚	Italic H
C9	201	I	╔	Italic I
CA	202	J	╩	Italic J
CB	203	K	╦	Italic K
CC	204	L	╠	Italic L
CD	205	M	═	Italic M
CE	206	N	╬	Italic N
CF	207	O	╧	Italic O
D0	208	P	╨	Italic P
D1	209	Q	╤	Italic Q
D2	210	R	╥	Italic R
D3	211	S	╙	Italic S
D4	212	T	╘	Italic T
D5	213	U	╒	Italic U
D6	214	V	╓	Italic V
D7	215	W	╫	Italic W
D8	216	X	╪	Italic X

Computer ASCII Codes

Hex	Dec	Standard Character	IBM Set	Description
D9	217	Y	⌐	Italic Y
DA	218	Z	Γ	Italic Z
DB	219	[	■	Italic left bracket
DC	220	\	■	Italic left or back slash
DD	221	]	▌	Italic right bracket
DE	222	^	▐	Italic caret
DF	223	—	▀	Italic underline
E0	224	'	α	Italic accent / alpha
E1	225	a	β	Italic a / beta
E2	226	b	Γ	Italic b / gamma
E3	227	c	π	Italic c / pi
E4	228	d	Σ	Italic d / sigma
E5	229	e	σ	Italic e / sigma
E6	230	f	μ	Italic f / mu
E7	231	g	γ	Italic g / gamma
E8	232	h	Φ	Italic h / phi
E9	233	i	θ	Italic i / theta
EA	234	j	Ω	Italic j / omega
EB	235	k	δ	Italic k / delta
EC	236	l	∞	Italic l / infinity
ED	237	m	Ø	Italic m / slashed zero
EE	238	n	∈	Italic n
EF	239	o	∩	Italic o
F0	240	p	≡	Italic p
F1	241	q	±	Italic q
F2	242	r	≥	Italic r
F3	243	s	≤	Italic s
F4	244	t	⌠	Italic t
F5	245	u	⌡	Italic u
F6	246	v	÷	Italic v
F7	247	w	≈	Italic w
F8	248	x	°	Italic x
F9	249	y	•	Italic y
FA	250	z	·	Italic z
FB	251	{	Ö	Italic left bracket
FC	252	l	n	Italic vertical line
FD	253	}	2	Italic right bracket
FE	254	~		Italic tilde
FF	255	Blank	Blank	Blank

Powers of 2

n	2^n	Hexadecimal
0	1	1
1	2	2
2	4	4
3	8	8
4	16	10
5	32	20
6	64	40
7	128	80
8	256	100
9	512	200
10	1024	400
11	2048	800
12	4096	1000
13	8192	2000
14	16384	4000
15	32768	8000
16	65536	10000
17	131072	20000
18	262144	40000
19	524288	80000
20	1048576	100000
21	2097152	200000
22	4194304	400000
23	8388608	800000
24	16777216	1000000
25	33554432	2000000
26	67108864	4000000
27	134217728	8000000
28	268435456	10000000
29	536870912	20000000
30	1073741824	40000000
31	2147483648	80000000
32	4294967296	100000000
33	8589934592	200000000
34	17179869184	400000000
35	34359738368	800000000
36	68719476736	1000000000
37	137438953472	2000000000
38	274877906944	4000000000
39	549755813888	8000000000
40	1099511627776	10000000000
41	2199023255552	20000000000
42	4398046511104	40000000000
43	8796093022208	80000000000
44	17592186044416	100000000000
45	35184372088832	200000000000
46	70368744177664	400000000000
47	140737488355328	800000000000
48	281474976710656	1000000000000
49	562949953421312	2000000000000
50	1125899906842624	4000000000000
51	2251799813685248	8000000000000
52	4503599627370496	10000000000000
53	9007199254740992	20000000000000
54	18014398509481984	40000000000000
55	36028797018963968	80000000000000
56	72057594037927936	100000000000000
57	144115188075855872	200000000000000
58	288230376151711744	400000000000000
59	576460752303423488	800000000000000
60	1152921504606846976	1000000000000000
61	2305843009213693952	2000000000000000
62	4611686018427387904	4000000000000000
63	9223372036854775808	8000000000000000
64	18446744073709551616	10000000000000000

Numeric Prefixes

Prefix	Abbreviation	Pronounce	Multiplier
yocto	y	yok-to	10^{-24}
zepto	z	zep-to	10^{-21}
atto	a	at–to	10^{-18}
femto	f	fem–to	10^{-15}
pico	p	pe–ko	10^{-12}
nano	n	nan–o	10^{-9}
micro	m	mi–kro	10^{-6}
milli	m	mil – l	10^{-3}
centi	c	sent–ti	10^{-2}
deci	d	des – I	10^{-1}
deka	da	dek–a	10^{1}
hecto	h	hek–to	10^{2}
kilo	k	kil-o	10^{3}
mega	M	meg–a	10^{6}
giga	G	gig–a	10^{9}
tera	T	ter–a	10^{12}
peta	P	pe–ta	10^{15}
exa	E	ex–a	10^{18}
zetta	Z	za-ta	10^{21}
yotta	Y	yot-ta	10^{24}
		octillion	10^{27}
		nonillion	10^{30}

Megabytes and Kilobytes

1 kilobyte = 2^{10} bytes = exactly 1,024 bytes

1 megabyte = 2^{20} bytes = exactly 1,048,576 bytes

1 gigabyte = 2^{30} bytes = 1 billion bytes

1 terabyte = 2^{40} bytes = 1 trillion bytes

1 petabyte = 2^{50} bytes = 1 quadrillion bytes

1 byte = 8 bits (bit is short for binary digit)

8 bit computers (such as the 8088)
    move data in 1 byte chunks

16 bit computers (such as the 80286 and 80386SX)
    move data in 2 byte chunks

32 bit computers (80386DX,80486,Pentium, Power PC)
    move data in 4 byte chunks

64 bit computers (such as the Alpha AXP)
    move data in 8 byte chunks

ASCII-Numbers

HEX to Decimal Conversion

Example: To convert the Hex number 1F7 to its decimal equivalent (Decimal 503), find 1F in the shaded left column of Hex numbers and follow the 1F row to the right, until it intersects the column with the *shaded* 7 at the top. The number at the intersection (503) is the decimal equivalent of Hex 1F7.

Standard Hex notation, using A through F to denote decimal values 10 through 15, is used in this table. ➡

↓ Hex→	0	1	2	3	4	5	6	7
00	0	1	2	3	4	5	6	7
01	16	17	18	19	20	21	22	23
02	32	33	34	35	36	37	38	39
03	48	49	50	51	52	53	54	55
04	64	65	66	67	68	69	70	71
05	80	81	82	83	84	85	86	87
06	96	97	98	99	100	101	102	103
07	112	113	114	115	116	117	118	119
08	128	129	130	131	132	133	134	135
09	144	145	146	147	148	149	150	151
0A	160	161	162	163	164	165	166	167
0B	176	177	178	179	180	181	182	183
0C	192	193	194	195	196	197	198	199
0D	208	209	210	211	212	213	214	215
0E	224	225	226	227	228	229	230	231
0F	240	241	242	243	244	245	246	247
10	256	257	258	259	260	261	262	263
11	272	273	274	275	276	277	278	279
12	288	289	290	291	292	293	294	295
13	304	305	306	307	308	309	310	311
14	320	321	322	323	324	325	326	327
15	336	337	338	339	340	341	342	343
16	352	353	354	355	356	357	358	359
17	368	369	370	371	372	373	374	375
18	384	385	386	387	388	389	390	391
19	400	401	402	403	404	405	406	407
1A	416	417	418	419	420	421	422	423
1B	432	433	434	435	436	437	438	439
1C	448	449	450	451	452	453	454	455
1D	464	465	466	467	468	469	470	471
1E	480	481	482	483	484	485	486	487
1F	496	497	498	499	500	501	502	503
20	512	513	514	515	516	517	518	519
21	528	529	530	531	532	533	534	535
22	544	545	546	547	548	549	550	551
23	560	561	562	563	564	565	566	567
24	576	577	578	579	580	581	582	583
25	592	593	594	595	596	597	598	599
26	608	609	610	611	612	613	614	615
27	624	625	626	627	628	629	630	631
28	640	641	642	643	644	645	646	647
29	656	657	658	659	660	661	662	663

HEX to Decimal Conversion

Large number conversion: (Up to five Hexidecimal digits) Find the fourth and fifth Hexidecimal significant digits in the following table and add their decimal equivalent to the value in the primary table. For example:

CB13F (Hex) = 786432 + 45056 + 319 = 831807 (Decimal)

Hex	Dec	Hex	Dec	Hex	Dec	Hex	Dec	Hex	Dec
1000	4096	7000	28672	D000	53248	40000	262144	A0000	655360
2000	8192	8000	32768	E000	57344	50000	327680	B0000	720896
3000	12288	9000	36864	F000	61440	60000	393216	C0000	786432
4000	16384	A000	40960	10000	65536	70000	458752	D0000	851968
5000	20480	B000	45056	20000	131072	80000	524288	E0000	917504
6000	24576	C000	49152	30000	196608	90000	589824	F0000	983040

↓Hex→	8	9	A	B	C	D	E	F
00	8	9	10	11	12	13	14	15
01	24	25	26	27	28	29	30	31
02	40	41	42	43	44	45	46	47
03	56	57	58	59	60	61	62	63
04	72	73	74	75	76	77	78	79
05	88	89	90	91	92	93	94	95
06	104	105	106	107	108	109	110	111
07	120	121	122	123	124	125	126	127
08	136	137	138	139	140	141	142	143
09	152	153	154	155	156	157	158	159
0A	168	169	170	171	172	173	174	175
0B	184	185	186	187	188	189	190	191
0C	200	201	202	203	204	205	206	207
0D	216	217	218	219	220	221	222	223
0E	232	233	234	235	236	237	238	239
0F	248	249	250	251	252	253	254	255
10	264	265	266	267	268	269	270	271
11	280	281	282	283	284	285	286	287
12	296	297	298	299	300	301	302	303
13	312	313	314	315	316	317	318	319
14	328	329	330	331	332	333	334	335
15	344	345	346	347	348	349	350	351
16	360	361	362	363	364	365	366	367
17	376	377	378	379	380	381	382	383
18	392	393	394	395	396	397	398	399
19	408	409	410	411	412	413	414	415
1A	424	425	426	427	428	429	430	431
1B	440	441	442	443	444	445	446	447
1C	456	457	458	459	460	461	462	463
1D	472	473	474	475	476	477	478	479
1E	488	489	490	491	492	493	494	495
1F	504	505	506	507	508	509	510	511
20	520	521	522	523	524	525	526	527
21	536	537	538	539	540	541	542	543
22	552	553	554	555	556	557	558	559
23	568	569	570	571	572	573	574	575
24	584	585	586	587	588	589	590	591
25	600	601	602	603	604	605	606	607
26	616	617	618	619	620	621	622	623
27	632	633	634	635	636	637	638	639
28	648	649	650	651	652	653	654	655
29	664	665	666	667	668	669	670	671

ASCII-Numbers

HEX to Decimal Conversion

↓ Hex→	0	1	2	3	4	5	6	7
2A	672	673	674	675	676	677	678	679
2B	688	689	690	691	692	693	694	695
2C	704	705	706	707	708	709	710	711
2D	720	721	722	723	724	725	726	727
2E	736	737	738	739	740	741	742	743
2F	752	753	754	755	756	757	758	759
30	768	769	770	771	772	773	774	775
31	784	785	786	787	788	789	790	791
32	800	801	802	803	804	805	806	807
33	816	817	818	819	820	821	822	823
34	832	833	834	835	836	837	838	839
35	848	849	850	851	852	853	854	855
36	864	865	866	867	868	869	870	871
37	880	881	882	883	884	885	886	887
38	896	897	898	899	900	901	902	903
39	912	913	914	915	916	917	918	919
3A	928	929	930	931	932	933	934	935
3B	944	945	946	947	948	949	950	951
3C	960	961	962	963	964	965	966	967
3D	976	977	978	979	980	981	982	983
3E	992	993	994	995	996	997	998	999
3F	1008	1009	1010	1011	1012	1013	1014	1015
40	1024	1025	1026	1027	1028	1029	1030	1031
41	1040	1041	1042	1043	1044	1045	1046	1047
42	1056	1057	1058	1059	1060	1061	1062	1063
43	1072	1073	1074	1075	1076	1077	1078	1079
44	1088	1089	1090	1091	1092	1093	1094	1095
45	1104	1105	1106	1107	1108	1109	1110	1111
46	1120	1121	1122	1123	1124	1125	1126	1127
47	1136	1137	1138	1139	1140	1141	1142	1143
48	1152	1153	1154	1155	1156	1157	1158	1159
49	1168	1169	1170	1171	1172	1173	1174	1175
4A	1184	1185	1186	1187	1188	1189	1190	1191
4B	1200	1201	1202	1203	1204	1205	1206	1207
4C	1216	1217	1218	1219	1220	1221	1222	1223
4D	1232	1233	1234	1235	1236	1237	1238	1239
4E	1248	1249	1250	1251	1252	1253	1254	1255
4F	1264	1265	1266	1267	1268	1269	1270	1271
50	1280	1281	1282	1283	1284	1285	1286	1287
51	1296	1297	1298	1299	1300	1301	1302	1303
52	1312	1313	1314	1315	1316	1317	1318	1319
53	1328	1329	1330	1331	1332	1333	1334	1335
54	1344	1345	1346	1347	1348	1349	1350	1351
55	1360	1361	1362	1363	1364	1365	1366	1367
56	1376	1377	1378	1379	1380	1381	1382	1383
57	1392	1393	1394	1395	1396	1397	1398	1399
58	1408	1409	1410	1411	1412	1413	1414	1415
59	1424	1425	1426	1427	1428	1429	1430	1431
5A	1440	1441	1442	1443	1444	1445	1446	1447
5B	1456	1457	1458	1459	1460	1461	1462	1463
5C	1472	1473	1474	1475	1476	1477	1478	1479
5D	1488	1489	1490	1491	1492	1493	1494	1495
5E	1504	1505	1506	1507	1508	1509	1510	1511
5F	1520	1521	1522	1523	1524	1525	1526	1527

ASCII-Numbers

HEX to Decimal Conversion

↓Hex→	8	9	A	B	C	D	E	F
2A	680	681	682	683	684	685	686	687
2B	696	697	698	699	700	701	702	703
2C	712	713	714	715	716	717	718	719
2D	728	729	730	731	732	733	734	735
2E	744	745	746	747	748	749	750	751
2F	760	761	762	763	764	765	766	767
30	776	777	778	779	780	781	782	783
31	792	793	794	795	796	797	798	799
32	808	809	810	811	812	813	814	815
33	824	825	826	827	828	829	830	831
34	840	841	842	843	844	845	846	847
35	856	857	858	859	860	861	862	863
36	872	873	874	875	876	877	878	879
37	888	889	890	891	892	893	894	895
38	904	905	906	907	908	909	910	911
39	920	921	922	923	924	925	926	927
3A	936	937	938	939	940	941	942	943
3B	952	953	954	955	956	957	958	959
3C	968	969	970	971	972	973	974	975
3D	984	985	986	987	988	989	990	991
3E	1000	1001	1002	1003	1004	1005	1006	1007
3F	1016	1017	1018	1019	1020	1021	1022	1023
40	1032	1033	1034	1035	1036	1037	1038	1039
41	1048	1049	1050	1051	1052	1053	1054	1055
42	1064	1065	1066	1067	1068	1069	1070	1071
43	1080	1081	1082	1083	1084	1085	1086	1087
44	1096	1097	1098	1099	1100	1101	1102	1103
45	1112	1113	1114	1115	1116	1117	1118	1119
46	1128	1129	1130	1131	1132	1133	1134	1135
47	1144	1145	1146	1147	1148	1149	1150	1151
48	1160	1161	1162	1163	1164	1165	1166	1167
49	1176	1177	1178	1179	1180	1181	1182	1183
4A	1192	1193	1194	1195	1196	1197	1198	1199
4B	1208	1209	1210	1211	1212	1213	1214	1215
4C	1224	1225	1226	1227	1228	1229	1230	1231
4D	1240	1241	1242	1243	1244	1245	1246	1247
4E	1256	1257	1258	1259	1260	1261	1262	1263
4F	1272	1273	1274	1275	1276	1277	1278	1279
50	1288	1289	1290	1291	1292	1293	1294	1295
51	1304	1305	1306	1307	1308	1309	1310	1311
52	1320	1321	1322	1323	1324	1325	1326	1327
53	1336	1337	1338	1339	1340	1341	1342	1343
54	1352	1353	1354	1355	1356	1357	1358	1359
55	1368	1369	1370	1371	1372	1373	1374	1375
56	1384	1385	1386	1387	1388	1389	1390	1391
57	1400	1401	1402	1403	1404	1405	1406	1407
58	1416	1417	1418	1419	1420	1421	1422	1423
59	1432	1433	1434	1435	1436	1437	1438	1439
5A	1448	1449	1450	1451	1452	1453	1454	1455
5B	1464	1465	1466	1467	1468	1469	1470	1471
5C	1480	1481	1482	1483	1484	1485	1486	1487
5D	1496	1497	1498	1499	1500	1501	1502	1503
5E	1512	1513	1514	1515	1516	1517	1518	1519
5F	1528	1529	1530	1531	1532	1533	1534	1535

ASCII-Numbers

HEX to Decimal Conversion

↓ Hex→	0	1	2	3	4	5	6	7
60	1536	1537	1538	1539	1540	1541	1542	1543
61	1552	1553	1554	1555	1556	1557	1558	1559
62	1568	1569	1570	1571	1572	1573	1574	1575
63	1584	1585	1586	1587	1588	1589	1590	1591
64	1600	1601	1602	1603	1604	1605	1606	1607
65	1616	1617	1618	1619	1620	1621	1622	1623
66	1632	1633	1634	1635	1636	1637	1638	1639
67	1648	1649	1650	1651	1652	1653	1654	1655
68	1664	1665	1666	1667	1668	1669	1670	1671
69	1680	1681	1682	1683	1684	1685	1686	1687
6A	1696	1697	1698	1699	1700	1701	1702	1703
6B	1712	1713	1714	1715	1716	1717	1718	1719
6C	1728	1729	1730	1731	1732	1733	1734	1735
6D	1744	1745	1746	1747	1748	1749	1750	1751
6E	1760	1761	1762	1763	1764	1765	1766	1767
6F	1776	1777	1778	1779	1780	1781	1782	1783
70	1792	1793	1794	1795	1796	1797	1798	1799
71	1808	1809	1810	1811	1812	1813	1814	1815
72	1824	1825	1826	1827	1828	1829	1830	1831
73	1840	1841	1842	1843	1844	1845	1846	1847
74	1856	1857	1858	1859	1860	1861	1862	1863
75	1872	1873	1874	1875	1876	1877	1878	1879
76	1888	1889	1890	1891	1892	1893	1894	1895
77	1904·	1905	1906	1907	1908	1909	1910	1911
78	1920	1921	1922	1923	1924	1925	1926	1927
79	1936	1937	1938	1939	1940	1941	1942	1943
7A	1952	1953	1954	1955	1956	1957	1958	1959
7B	1968	1969	1970	1971	1972	1973	1974	1975
7C	1984	1985	1986	1987	1988	1989	1990	1991
7D	2000	2001	2002	2003	2004	2005	2006	2007
7E	2016	2017	2018	2019	2020	2021	2022	2023
7F	2032	2033	2034	2035	2036	2037	2038	2039
80	2048	2049	2050	2051	2052	2053	2054	2055
81	2064	2065	2066	2067	2068	2069	2070	2071
82	2080	2081	2082	2083	2084	2085	2086	2087
83	2096	2097	2098	2099	2100	2101	2102	2103
84	2112	2113	2114	2115	2116	2117	2118	2119
85	2128	2129	2130	2131	2132	2133	2134	2135
86	2144	2145	2146	2147	2148	2149	2150	2151
87	2160	2161	2162	2163	2164	2165	2166	2167
88	2176	2177	2178	2179	2180	2181	2182	2183
89	2192	2193	2194	2195	2196	2197	2198	2199
8A	2208	2209	2210	2211	2212	2213	2214	2215
8B	2224	2225	2226	2227	2228	2229	2230	2231
8C	2240	2241	2242	2243	2244	2245	2246	2247
8D	2256	2257	2258	2259	2260	2261	2262	2263
8E	2272	2273	2274	2275	2276	2277	2278	2279
8F	2288	2289	2290	2291	2292	2293	2294	2295
90	2304	2305	2306	2307	2308	2309	2310	2311
91	2320	2321	2322	2323	2324	2325	2326	2327
92	2336	2337	2338	2339	2340	2341	2342	2343
93	2352	2353	2354	2355	2356	2357	2358	2359
94	2368	2369	2370	2371	2372	2373	2374	2375
95	2384	2385	2386	2387	2388	2389	2390	2391

HEX to Decimal Conversion

↓Hex→	8	9	A	B	C	D	E	F
60	1544	1545	1546	1547	1548	1549	1550	1551
61	1560	1561	1562	1563	1564	1565	1566	1567
62	1576	1577	1578	1579	1580	1581	1582	1583
63	1592	1593	1594	1595	1596	1597	1598	1599
64	1608	1609	1610	1611	1612	1613	1614	1615
65	1624	1625	1626	1627	1628	1629	1630	1631
66	1640	1641	1642	1643	1644	1645	1646	1647
67	1656	1657	1658	1659	1660	1661	1662	1663
68	1672	1673	1674	1675	1676	1677	1678	1679
69	1688	1689	1690	1691	1692	1693	1694	1695
6A	1704	1705	1706	1707	1708	1709	1710	1711
6B	1720	1721	1722	1723	1724	1725	1726	1727
6C	1736	1737	1738	1739	1740	1741	1742	1743
6D	1752	1753	1754	1755	1756	1757	1758	1759
6E	1768	1769	1770	1771	1772	1773	1774	1775
6F	1784	1785	1786	1787	1788	1789	1790	1791
70	1800	1801	1802	1803	1804	1805	1806	1807
71	1816	1817	1818	1819	1820	1821	1822	1823
72	1832	1833	1834	1835	1836	1837	1838	1839
73	1848	1849	1850	1851	1852	1853	1854	1855
74	1864	1865	1866	1867	1868	1869	1870	1871
75	1880	1881	1882	1883	1884	1885	1886	1887
76	1896	1897	1898	1899	1900	1901	1902	1903
77	1912	1913	1914	1915	1916	1917	1918	1919
78	1928	1929	1930	1931	1932	1933	1934	1935
79	1944	1945	1946	1947	1948	1949	1950	1951
7A	1960	1961	1962	1963	1964	1965	1966	1967
7B	1976	1977	1978	1979	1980	1981	1982	1983
7C	1992	1993	1994	1995	1996	1997	1998	1999
7D	2008	2009	2010	2011	2012	2013	2014	2015
7E	2024	2025	2026	2027	2028	2029	2030	2031
7F	2040	2041	2042	2043	2044	2045	2046	2047
80	2056	2057	2058	2059	2060	2061	2062	2063
81	2072	2073	2074	2075	2076	2077	2078	2079
82	2088	2089	2090	2091	2092	2093	2094	2095
83	2104	2105	2106	2107	2108	2109	2110	2111
84	2120	2121	2122	2123	2124	2125	2126	2127
85	2136	2137	2138	2139	2140	2141	2142	2143
86	2152	2153	2154	2155	2156	2157	2158	2159
87	2168	2169	2170	2171	2172	2173	2174	2175
88	2184	2185	2186	2187	2188	2189	2190	2191
89	2200	2201	2202	2203	2204	2205	2206	2207
8A	2216	2217	2218	2219	2220	2221	2222	2223
8B	2232	2233	2234	2235	2236	2237	2238	2239
8C	2248	2249	2250	2251	2252	2253	2254	2255
8D	2264	2265	2266	2267	2268	2269	2270	2271
8E	2280	2281	2282	2283	2284	2285	2286	2287
8F	2296	2297	2298	2299	2300	2301	2302	2303
90	2312	2313	2314	2315	2316	2317	2318	2319
91	2328	2329	2330	2331	2332	2333	2334	2335
92	2344	2345	2346	2347	2348	2349	2350	2351
93	2360	2361	2362	2363	2364	2365	2366	2367
94	2376	2377	2378	2379	2380	2381	2382	2383
95	2392	2393	2394	2395	2396	2397	2398	2399

ASCII-Numbers

HEX to Decimal Conversion

↓ Hex→	0	1	2	3	4	5	6	7
96	2400	2401	2402	2403	2404	2405	2406	2407
97	2416	2417	2418	2419	2420	2421	2422	2423
98	2432	2433	2434	2435	2436	2437	2438	2439
99	2448	2449	2450	2451	2452	2453	2454	2455
9A	2464	2465	2466	2467	2468	2469	2470	2471
9B	2480	2481	2482	2483	2484	2485	2486	2487
9C	2496	2497	2498	2499	2500	2501	2502	2503
9D	2512	2513	2514	2515	2516	2517	2518	2519
9E	2528	2529	2530	2531	2532	2533	2534	2535
9F	2544	2545	2546	2547	2548	2549	2550	2551
A0	2560	2561	2562	2563	2564	2565	2566	2567
A1	2576	2577	2578	2579	2580	2581	2582	2583
A2	2592	2593	2594	2595	2596	2597	2598	2599
A3	2608	2609	2610	2611	2612	2613	2614	2615
A4	2624	2625	2626	2627	2628	2629	2630	2631
A5	2640	2641	2642	2643	2644	2645	2646	2647
A6	2656	2657	2658	2659	2660	2661	2662	2663
A7	2672	2673	2674	2675	2676	2677	2678	2679
A8	2688	2689	2690	2691	2692	2693	2694	2695
A9	2704	2705	2706	2707	2708	2709	2710	2711
AA	2720	2721	2722	2723	2724	2725	2726	2727
AB	2736	2737	2738	2739	2740	2741	2742	2743
AC	2752	2753	2754	2755	2756	2757	2758	2759
AD	2768	2769	2770	2771	2772	2773	2774	2775
AE	2784	2785	2786	2787	2788	2789	2790	2791
AF	2800	2801	2802	2803	2804	2805	2806	2807
B0	2816	2817	2818	2819	2820	2821	2822	2823
B1	2832	2833	2834	2835	2836	2837	2838	2839
B2	2848	2849	2850	2851	2852	2853	2854	2855
B3	2864	2865	2866	2867	2868	2869	2870	2871
B4	2880	2881	2882	2883	2884	2885	2886	2887
B5	2896	2897	2898	2899	2900	2901	2902	2903
B6	2912	2913	2914	2915	2916	2917	2918	2919
B7	2928	2929	2930	2931	2932	2933	2934	2935
B8	2944	2945	2946	2947	2948	2949	2950	2951
B9	2960	2961	2962	2963	2964	2965	2966	2967
BA	2976	2977	2978	2979	2980	2981	2982	2983
BB	2992	2993	2994	2995	2996	2997	2998	2999
BC	3008	3009	3010	3011	3012	3013	3014	3015
BD	3024	3025	3026	3027	3028	3029	3030	3031
BE	3040	3041	3042	3043	3044	3045	3046	3047
BF	3056	3057	3058	3059	3060	3061	3062	3063
C0	3072	3073	3074	3075	3076	3077	3078	3079
C1	3088	3089	3090	3091	3092	3093	3094	3095
C2	3104	3105	3106	3107	3108	3109	3110	3111
C3	3120	3121	3122	3123	3124	3125	3126	3127
C4	3136	3137	3138	3139	3140	3141	3142	3143
C5	3152	3153	3154	3155	3156	3157	3158	3159
C6	3168	3169	3170	3171	3172	3173	3174	3175
C7	3184	3185	3186	3187	3188	3189	3190	3191
C8	3200	3201	3202	3203	3204	3205	3206	3207
C9	3216	3217	3218	3219	3220	3221	3222	3223
CA	3232	3233	3234	3235	3236	3237	3238	3239
CB	3248	3249	3250	3251	3252	3253	3254	3255

↓Hex→	8	9	A	B	C	D	E	F
96	2408	2409	2410	2411	2412	2413	2414	2415
97	2424	2425	2426	2427	2428	2429	2430	2431
98	2440	2441	2442	2443	2444	2445	2446	2447
99	2456	2457	2458	2459	2460	2461	2462	2463
9A	2472	2473	2474	2475	2476	2477	2478	2479
9B	2488	2489	2490	2491	2492	2493	2494	2495
9C	2504	2505	2506	2507	2508	2509	2510	2511
9D	2520	2521	2522	2523	2524	2525	2526	2527
9E	2536	2537	2538	2539	2540	2541	2542	2543
9F	2552	2553	2554	2555	2556	2557	2558	2559
A0	2568	2569	2570	2571	2572	2573	2574	2575
A1	2584	2585	2586	2587	2588	2589	2590	2591
A2	2600	2601	2602	2603	2604	2605	2606	2607
A3	2616	2617	2618	2619	2620	2621	2622	2623
A4	2632	2633	2634	2635	2636	2637	2638	2639
A5	2648	2649	2650	2651	2652	2653	2654	2655
A6	2664	2665	2666	2667	2668	2669	2670	2671
A7	2680	2681	2682	2683	2684	2685	2686	2687
A8	2696	2697	2698	2699	2700	2701	2702	2703
A9	2712	2713	2714	2715	2716	2717	2718	2719
AA	2728	2729	2730	2731	2732	2733	2734	2735
AB	2744	2745	2746	2747	2748	2749	2750	2751
AC	2760	2761	2762	2763	2764	2765	2766	2767
AD	2776	2777	2778	2779	2780	2781	2782	2783
AE	2792	2793	2794	2795	2796	2797	2798	2799
AF	2808	2809	2810	2811	2812	2813	2814	2815
B0	2824	2825	2826	2827	2828	2829	2830	2831
B1	2840	2841	2842	2843	2844	2845	2846	2847
B2	2856	2857	2858	2859	2860	2861	2862	2863
B3	2872	2873	2874	2875	2876	2877	2878	2879
B4	2888	2889	2890	2891	2892	2893	2894	2895
B5	2904	2905	2906	2907	2908	2909	2910	2911
B6	2920	2921	2922	2923	2924	2925	2926	2927
B7	2936	2937	2938	2939	2940	2941	2942	2943
B8	2952	2953	2954	2955	2956	2957	2958	2959
B9	2968	2969	2970	2971	2972	2973	2974	2975
BA	2984	2985	2986	2987	2988	2989	2990	2991
BB	3000	3001	3002	3003	3004	3005	3006	3007
BC	3016	3017	3018	3019	3020	3021	3022	3023
BD	3032	3033	3034	3035	3036	3037	3038	3039
BE	3048	3049	3050	3051	3052	3053	3054	3055
BF	3064	3065	3066	3067	3068	3069	3070	3071
C0	3080	3081	3082	3083	3084	3085	3086	3087
C1	3096	3097	3098	3099	3100	3101	3102	3103
C2	3112	3113	3114	3115	3116	3117	3118	3119
C3	3128	3129	3130	3131	3132	3133	3134	3135
C4	3144	3145	3146	3147	3148	3149	3150	3151
C5	3160	3161	3162	3163	3164	3165	3166	3167
C6	3176	3177	3178	3179	3180	3181	3182	3183
C7	3192	3193	3194	3195	3196	3197	3198	3199
C8	3208	3209	3210	3211	3212	3213	3214	3215
C9	3224	3225	3226	3227	3228	3229	3230	3231
CA	3240	3241	3242	3243	3244	3245	3246	3247
CB	3256	3257	3258	3259	3260	3261	3262	3263

ASCII-Numbers

HEX to Decimal Conversion

↓Hex→	0	1	2	3	4	5	6	7
CC	3264	3265	3266	3267	3268	3269	3270	3271
CD	3280	3281	3282	3283	3284	3285	3286	3287
CE	3296	3297	3298	3299	3300	3301	3302	3303
CF	3312	3313	3314	3315	3316	3317	3318	3319
D0	3328	3329	3330	3331	3332	3333	3334	3335
D1	3344	3345	3346	3347	3348	3349	3350	3351
D2	3360	3361	3362	3363	3364	3365	3366	3367
D3	3376	3377	3378	3379	3380	3381	3382	3383
D4	3392	3393	3394	3395	3396	3397	3398	3399
D5	3408	3409	3410	3411	3412	3413	3414	3415
D6	3424	3425	3426	3427	3428	3429	3430	3431
D7	3440	3441	3442	3443	3444	3445	3446	3447
D8	3456	3457	3458	3459	3460	3461	3462	3463
D9	3472	3473	3474	3475	3476	3477	3478	3479
DA	3488	3489	3490	3491	3492	3493	3494	3495
DB	3504	3505	3506	3507	3508	3509	3510	3511
DC	3520	3521	3522	3523	3524	3525	3526	3527
DD	3536	3537	3538	3539	3540	3541	3542	3543
DE	3552	3553	3554	3555	3556	3557	3558	3559
DF	3568	3569	3570	3571	3572	3573	3574	3575
E0	3584	3585	3586	3587	3588	3589	3590	3591
E1	3600	3601	3602	3603	3604	3605	3606	3607
E2	3616	3617	3618	3619	3620	3621	3622	3623
E3	3632	3633	3634	3635	3636	3637	3638	3639
E4	3648	3649	3650	3651	3652	3653	3654	3655
E5	3664	3665	3666	3667	3668	3669	3670	3671
E6	3680	3681	3682	3683	3684	3685	3686	3687
E7	3696	3697	3698	3699	3700	3701	3702	3703
E8	3712	3713	3714	3715	3716	3717	3718	3719
E9	3728	3729	3730	3731	3732	3733	3734	3735
EA	3744	3745	3746	3747	3748	3749	3750	3751
EB	3760	3761	3762	3763	3764	3765	3766	3767
EC	3776	3777	3778	3779	3780	3781	3782	3783
ED	3792	3793	3794	3795	3796	3797	3798	3799
EE	3808	3809	3810	3811	3812	3813	3814	3815
EF	3824	3825	3826	3827	3828	3829	3830	3831
F0	3840	3841	3842	3843	3844	3845	3846	3847
F1	3856	3857	3858	3859	3860	3861	3862	3863
F2	3872	3873	3874	3875	3876	3877	3878	3879
F3	3888	3889	3890	3891	3892	3893	3894	3895
F4	3904	3905	3906	3907	3908	3909	3910	3911
F5	3920	3921	3922	3923	3924	3925	3926	3927
F6	3936	3937	3938	3939	3940	3941	3942	3943
F7	3952	3953	3954	3955	3956	3957	3958	3959
F8	3968	3969	3970	3971	3972	3973	3974	3975
F9	3984	3985	3986	3987	3988	3989	3990	3991
FA	4000	4001	4002	4003	4004	4005	4006	4007
FB	4016	4017	4018	4019	4020	4021	4022	4023
FC	4032	4033	4034	4035	4036	4037	4038	4039
FD	4048	4049	4050	4051	4052	4053	4054	4055
FE	4064	4065	4066	4067	4068	4069	4070	4071
FF	4080	4081	4082	4083	4084	4085	4086	4087

HEX to Decimal Conversion

↓Hex→	8	9	A	B	C	D	E	F
CC	3272	3273	3274	3275	3276	3277	3278	3279
CD	3288	3289	3290	3291	3292	3293	3294	3295
CE	3304	3305	3306	3307	3308	3309	3310	3311
CF	3320	3321	3322	3323	3324	3325	3326	3327
D0	3336	3337	3338	3339	3340	3341	3342	3343
D1	3352	3353	3354	3355	3356	3357	3358	3359
D2	3368	3369	3370	3371	3372	3373	3374	3375
D3	3384	3385	3386	3387	3388	3389	3390	3391
D4	3400	3401	3402	3403	3404	3405	3406	3407
D5	3416	3417	3418	3419	3420	3421	3422	3423
D6	3432	3433	3434	3435	3436	3437	3438	3439
D7	3448	3449	3450	3451	3452	3453	3454	3455
D8	3464	3465	3466	3467	3468	3469	3470	3471
D9	3480	3481	3482	3483	3484	3485	3486	3487
DA	3496	3497	3498	3499	3500	3501	3502	3503
DB	3512	3513	3514	3515	3516	3517	3518	3519
DC	3528	3529	3530	3531	3532	3533	3534	3535
DD	3544	3545	3546	3547	3548	3549	3550	3551
DE	3560	3561	3562	3563	3564	3565	3566	3567
DF	3576	3577	3578	3579	3580	3581	3582	3583
E0	3592	3593	3594	3595	3596	3597	3598	3599
E1	3608	3609	3610	3611	3612	3613	3614	3615
E2	3624	3625	3626	3627	3628	3629	3630	3631
E3	3640	3641	3642	3643	3644	3645	3646	3647
E4	3656	3657	3658	3659	3660	3661	3662	3663
E5	3672	3673	3674	3675	3676	3677	3678	3679
E6	3688	3689	3690	3691	3692	3693	3694	3695
E7	3704	3705	3706	3707	3708	3709	3710	3711
E8	3720	3721	3722	3723	3724	3725	3726	3727
E9	3736	3737	3738	3739	3740	3741	3742	3743
EA	3752	3753	3754	3755	3756	3757	3758	3759
EB	3768	3769	3770	3771	3772	3773	3774	3775
EC	3784	3785	3786	3787	3788	3789	3790	3791
ED	3800	3801	3802	3803	3804	3805	3806	3807
EE	3816	3817	3818	3819	3820	3821	3822	3823
EF	3832	3833	3834	3835	3836	3837	3838	3839
F0	3848	3849	3850	3851	3852	3853	3854	3855
F1	3864	3865	3866	3867	3868	3869	3870	3871
F2	3880	3881	3882	3883	3884	3885	3886	3887
F3	3896	3897	3898	3899	3900	3901	3902	3903
F4	3912	3913	3914	3915	3916	3917	3918	3919
F5	3928	3929	3930	3931	3932	3933	3934	3935
F6	3944	3945	3946	3947	3948	3949	3950	3951
F7	3960	3961	3962	3963	3964	3965	3966	3967
F8	3976	3977	3978	3979	3980	3981	3982	3983
F9	3992	3993	3994	3995	3996	3997	3998	3999
FA	4008	4009	4010	4011	4012	4013	4014	4015
FB	4024	4025	4026	4027	4028	4029	4030	4031
FC	4040	4041	4042	4043	4044	4045	4046	4047
FD	4056	4057	4058	4059	4060	4061	4062	4063
FE	4072	4073	4074	4075	4076	4077	4078	4079
FF	4088	4089	4090	4091	4092	4093	4094	4095

ASCII-Numbers

Alphabet-DEC-HEX-EBCDIC

Hex	Dec	Alph	EBCDIC
00	0	Null	00
01	1	SOH	01
02	2	STX	02
03	3	ETX	03
04	4	EOT	37
05	5	ENQ	2D
06	6	ACK	2E
07	7	BEL	2F
08	8	BS	16
09	9	HT	05
0A	10	LF	25
0B	11	VT	0B
0C	12	FF	0C
0D	13	CR	0D
0E	14	SO	0E
0F	15	SI	0F
10	16	DLE	10
11	17	DC1	11
12	18	DC2	12
13	19	DC3	13
14	20	DC4	3C
15	21	NAK	3D
16	22	SYN	32
17	23	ETB	11
18	24	CAN	18
19	25	EM	19
1A	26	SUB	3F
1B	27	ESC	27
1C	28	FS	22
1D	29	GS	–
1E	30	RS	35
1F	31	US	–
20	32	space	40
21	33	!	5A
22	34	"	7F
23	35	#	7B
24	36	$	5B
25	37	%	6C
26	38	&	50
27	39	'	7D
28	40	(	4D
29	41	)	5D
2A	42	*	5C
2B	43	+	4E
2C	44	,	6B
2D	45	-	60
2E	46	.	4B
2F	47	/	61
30	48	0	F0
31	49	1	F1
32	50	2	F2
33	51	3	F3
34	52	4	F4
35	53	5	F5
36	54	6	F6
37	55	7	F7
38	56	8	F8
39	57	9	F9
3A	58	:	7A
3B	59	;	5E
3C	60	<	4C
3D	61	>	7E
3E	62	=	6E

Hex	Dec	Alph	EBCDIC
3F	63	?	6F
40	64	@	7C
41	65	A	C1
42	66	B	C2
43	67	C	C3
44	68	D	C4
45	69	E	C5
46	70	F	C6
47	71	G	C7
48	72	H	C8
49	73	I	C9
4A	74	J	D1
4B	75	K	D2
4C	76	L	D3
4D	77	M	D4
4E	78	N	D5
4F	79	O	D6
50	80	P	D7
51	81	Q	D8
52	82	R	D9
53	83	S	E2
54	84	T	E3
55	85	U	E4
56	86	V	E5
57	87	W	E6
58	88	X	E7
59	89	Y	E8
5A	90	Z	E9
5B	91	[	
5C	92	\	E0
5D	93	]	
5E	94	^	
5F	95	_	6D
60	96	`	–
61	97	a	81
62	98	b	82
63	99	c	83
64	100	d	84
65	101	e	85
66	102	f	86
67	103	g	87
68	104	h	88
69	105	i	89
6A	106	j	91
6B	107	k	92
6C	108	l	93
6D	109	m	94
6E	110	n	95
6F	111	o	96
70	112	p	97
71	113	q	98
72	114	r	99
73	115	s	A2
74	116	t	A3
75	117	u	A4
76	118	v	A5
77	119	w	A6
78	120	x	A7
79	121	y	A8
7A	122	z	A9
7B	123	{	C0
7C	124			6A
7D	125	}	D0
7E	126	~	A1
7F	127	DEL	07

Chapter 10

Hardware & Standards

See also "Wiring and Connectors" on page 517

Legacy PC Video Standards

Video Standard (year)	Mode	Horz x Vert Resolution (pixels)	Simultaneous Colors	Vert Freq Hz	Horz Freq kHz	Band Width MHz
MDA (1981)	Text	720x350	1	50Hz	18.43	16.257
HGC	Text	640x400	1	50	18.43	16.257
	Graph	720x348	1	50	"	"
CGA	Text	320x200	16	60	15.75	14.318
(1981)	Text	640x200	16	60	"	"
	Graph	320x200	4	60	"	"
	Graph	640x200	2	60	"	"
EGA Color	Text	640x350	16	60	15.75	14.318
(1985)	Graph	640x350	16	60	to	to
	Graph	320x200	16	60	21.85	16.257
	Graph	640x350	64	60	"	"
EGA Mono	Graph	640x350	1	50	"	"
MCGA	Text	320x400	16	70	31.50	25.175
(1987)	Text	640x400	16	70	"	"
	Graph	640x480	2	60	"	"
	Graph	320x200	256	70	"	"
VGA	Text	360x400	16	70	31.50	25.175
(1987)	Text	720x400	16	70	"	to
	Graph	640x350	16	70	"	28.322
	Graph	640x480	16	60	"	"
	Graph	640x480	2	60	"	"
	Graph	320x200	256	70	"	"
Super VGA	Graph	800x600	16	50,60	35,37	
(1989)	Graph	800x600	256	and	and	
	Graph	1024x768	16	72	60,80	
8514-A	Graph	1024x768	16	43.48	35.52	44.897
(1987)	Graph	640x480	256	60	31.5	"
256 color	Graph	1024x768	256	43.48	35.52	"
XGA	Graph	640x480	256	43.48	35.52	
(1990)	Graph	1024x768	256	43.48	"	
65536 color	Graph	640x480	65536	60	31.5	
	Text	1056x400	16	70	"	

Note: Most video cards built around the standards listed above are downward compatible and will function in the modes of the earlier standards. For example, most VGA cards will operate in all of the MDA, CGA, and EGA modes.

Video Standards

Abbreviations for the graphics standards defined on the previous page are as follows:

```
MDA . . . . . . Monochrome Display Adapter
HGC . . . . . . Hercules Graphics Card
CGA . . . . . . Color Graphics Adapter
EGA. . . . . . . Enhanced Graphics Adapter
```

PGA. . . . . . . Professional Graphics Adapter
MCGA . . . . . Multi Color Graphics Array
VGA. . . . . . . Video Graphics Array - digital - 640x480
8514-A. . . . . Video Graphics Array - analog
Super VGA . Super Video Graphics Array, VESA - 800x600
XGA. . . . . . . Extended Graphics Array - 1024x768
SXGA . . . . . Super Extended Graphics Array - 1280x1024
UXGA . . . . . Ultra Extended Graphics Array - 1600x1200
QXGA . . . . . Quantum Extended Graphics Array - 2048x1536

Number of Colors vs. Bits

Bits	Number of Colors
1 (Monochrome)	1
2	4
4	16
8	256
16 (High Color)	65536
24	16,777,216
32 (True Color)	4,294,967,296
36	68,719,476,736

Pixels are coded by assigning bits to the colors and as you can
see from the above table, the number of colors is dependent on
the number of bits per pixel. Video board memory limits the number of colors that a graphics adapter can store; for example, a
1024x768 adapter requires 786,432 bytes of memory in order to
display 256 colors. Needless to say, future video memory requirements will continue to grow. Consider that a 4096x3072 image
with 32 bit/pixel color will require nearly 50 Mb of video RAM. See
the table below.

Resolution and Bit Depth vs. Video Memory

Resolution	8 bit	16 bit	24 bit	32 bit
800x600	0.48 Mb	0.96 Mb	1.44 Mb	1.92 Mb
1024x768	0.79 Mb	1.58 Mb	2.37 Mb	3.16 Mb
1280x1024	1.31 Mb	2.62 Mb	3.93 Mb	5.24 Mb
1600x1200	1.92 Mb	3.84 Mb	5.76 Mb	7.68 Mb
2048x1536	3.16 Mb	6.32 Mb	9.48 Mb	12.64 Mb
4096x3072	12.6 Mb	25.3 Mb	37.9 Mb	50.6 Mb

Keyboard Scan Codes

Generally, expanded PC/XT, AT and PS/2 keyboard scan codes are converted to PC/XT standard scan codes prior to ROM BIOS ASCII Code conversion. Notable exceptions are the F11 and F12 keys, which generate new scan codes (see table below). Extended ASCII characters and some special "characters" are achieved by combining 2 or more key presses.

Shaded areas in the table represent keys and scan codes of the standard 84 key PC/XT keyboard, however, the "Key #" listed in column 1 of the table is not the correct Key # for the XT class keyboard. See your computer's keyboard documentation for verification of the correct Key # to Key Name assignments. AT Scan Codes are only relevant to AT class and PS/2 (Models 50 and above) computers.

Key # for 101 Keyboard	Key Name	XT scan codes Down • Up	AT hardware scan codes Down • Up
1	Esc	01 • 81	76 • F0 76
2	F1	3B • BB	05 • F0 05
3	F2	3C • BC	06 • F0 06
4	F3	3D • BD	04 • F0 04
5	F4	3E • BE	0C • F0 0C
6	F5	3F • BF	03 • F0 03
7	F6	40 • C0	0B • F0 0B
8	F7	41 • C1	83 • F0 83
9	F8	42 • C2	0A • F0 0A
10	F9	43 • C3	01 • F0 01
11	F10	44 • C4	09 • F0 09
12	F11	57 • D7	78 • F0 78
13	F12	58 • D8	07 • F0 07

Special Keys (expanded keyboards only)			
Key # for 101 Kbd	Key Name	XT scan codes Down • Up	AT hardware scan codes Down • U
14	**PrtScn / SysReq**		
14	–PRINT SCRN	E0 2A E0 37 • E0 B7 E0 AA	E0 12 E0 7C • E0 F0 7C E0 F0 12
14	–Sys Req (+ CTRL)	E0 37 • E0 B7	E0 7C • E0 F0 7C
14	–Sys Req (+ ALT)	54 • D4	84 • F0 84
15	ScrollLock	46 • C6	7E • F0 7E
16	**Pause / Break**		
16	–PAUSE (key alone) (No Auto Repeat)	E1 1D 45 E1 9D C5 • No Up Code	E1 14 77 E1 F0 14 F077 • No Up Code
16	–BREAK (+ CTRL) (No Auto Repeat)	E0 46 E0 C6 • No Up Code	E0 7E E0 F0 7E • No Up Code
31	**Insert Key**	E0 52 • E0 D2	E0 70 • E0 F0 70
31	–LEFT SHIFT case	E0 AA E0 52 • E0 D2 E0 2A	E0 F0 12 E0 70 • E0 F0 70 E0 12

Special Keys (expanded keyboards only)			
Key # for 101 Kbd	Key Name	XT scan codes Down • Up	AT hardware scan codes Down • U
31	–RIGHT SHIFT case	E0 B6 E0 52 • E0 D2 E0 36	E0 F0 59 E0 70 • E0 F0 70 E0 59
31	–NUM LOCK ON case	E0 2A E0 52 • E0 D2 E0 AA	E0 12 E0 70 • E0 F0 70 E0 F0 12
32	**Home**	E0 47 • E0 C7	E0 6C • E0 F0 6C
32	–LEFT SHIFT case	E0 AA E0 47 • E0 C7 E0 2A	E0 F0 12 E0 6C • E0 F0 6C E0 12
32	–RIGHT SHIFT case	E0 B6 E0 47 • E0 C7 E0 36	E0 F0 59 E0 6C • E0 F0 6C E0 59
32	–NUM LOCK ON case	E0 2A E0 47 • E0 C7 E0 AA	E0 12 E0 6C • E0 F0 6C E0 F0 12
33	**PageUp**	E0 49 • E0 C9	E0 7D • E0 F0 7D
33	–LEFT SHIFT case	E0 AA E0 49 • E0 C9 E0 2A	E0 F0 12 E0 7D • E0 F0 7D E0 12
33	–RIGHT SHIFT case	E0 B6 E0 49 • E0 C9 E0 36	E0 F0 59 E0 7D • E0 F0 7D E0 59
33	–NUM LOCK ON case	E0 2A E0 49 • E0 C9 E0 AA	E0 12 E0 7D • E0 F0 7D E0 F0 12
52	**Delete**	E0 53 • E0 D3	E0 71 • E0 F0 71
52	–LEFT SHIFT case	E0 AA E0 53 • E0 D3 E0 2A	E0 F0 12 E0 71 • E0 F0 71 E0 12
52	–RIGHT SHIFT case	E0 B6 E0 53 • E0 D3 E0 36	E0 F0 59 E0 71 • E0 F0 71 E0 59
52	–NUM LOCK ON case	E0 2A E0 53 • E0 D3 E0 AA	E0 12 E0 71 • E0 F0 71 E0 F0 12
53	**End**	E0 4F • E0 CF	E0 69 • E0 F0 69
53	–LEFT SHIFT case	E0 AA E0 4F • E0 CF E0 2A	E0 F0 12 E0 69 • E0 F0 69 E0 12
53	–RIGHT SHIFT case	E0 B6 E0 4F • E0 CF E0 36	E0 F0 59 E0 69 • E0 F0 69 E0 59
53	–NUM LOCK ON case	E0 2A E0 4F • E0 CF E0 AA	E0 12 E0 69 • E0 F0 69 E0 F0 12
54	**PageDown**	E0 51 • E0 D1	E0 7A • E0 F0 7A
54	–LEFT SHIFT case	E0 AA E0 51 • E0 D1 E0 2A	E0 F0 12 E0 7A • E0 F0 7A E0 12
54	–RIGHT SHIFT case	E0 B6 E0 51 • E0 D1 E0 36	E0 F0 59 E0 7A • E0 F0 7A E0 59
54	–NUM LOCK ON case	E0 2A E0 51 • E0 D1 E0 AA	E0 12 E0 7A • E0 F0 7A E0 F0 12
87	**UpArrow**	E0 48 • E0 C8	E0 75 • E0 F0 75
87	–LEFT SHIFT case	E0 AA E0 48 • E0 C8 E0 2A	E0 F0 12 E0 75 • E0 F0 75 E0 12

Special Keys (expanded keyboards only)			
Key # for 101 Kbd	Key Name	XT scan codes Down • Up	AT hardware scan codes Down • U
87	–RIGHT SHIFT case	E0 B6 E0 48 • E0 C8 E0 36	E0 F0 59 E0 75 • E0 F0 75 59
87	–NUM LOCK ON case	E0 2A E0 48 • E0 C8 E0 AA	E0 12 E0 75 • E0 F0 75 E0 12
97	LeftArrow	E0 4B • E0 CB	E0 6B • E0 F0 6B
97	–LEFT SHIFT case	E0 AA E0 4B • E0 CB E0 2A	E0 F0 12 E0 6B • E0 F0 6B E0 12
97	–RIGHT SHIFT case	E0 B6 E0 4B • E0 CB E0 36	E0 F0 59 E0 6B • E0 F0 6B E0 59
97	–NUM LOCK ON case	E0 2A E0 4B • E0 CB E0 AA	E0 12 E0 6B • E0 F0 6B E0 F0 12
98	DownArrow	E0 50 • E0 D0	E0 72 • E0 F0 72
98	–LEFT SHIFT case	E0 AA E0 50 • E0 D0 E0 2A	E0 F0 12 E0 72 • E0 F0 72 E0 12
98	–RIGHT SHIFT case	E0 B6 E0 50 • E0 D0 E0 36	E0 F0 59 E0 72 • E0 F0 72 E0 59
98	–NUM LOCK ON case	E0 2A E0 50 • E0 D0 E0 AA	E0 12 E0 72 • E0 F0 72 E0 F0 12
99	RightArrow	E0 4D • E0 CD	E0 74 • E0 F0 74
99	–LEFT SHIFT case	E0 AA E0 4D • E0 CD E0 2A	E0 F0 12 E0 74 • E0 F0 74 E0 12
99	–RIGHT SHIFT case	E0 B6 E0 4D • E0 CD E0 36	E0 F0 59 E0 74 • E0 F0 74 E0 59
99	–NUM LOCK ON case	E0 2A E0 4D • E0 CD E0 AA	E0 12 E0 74 • E0 F0 74 E0 F0 12

Alphanumeric Primary Keyboard Keys (Includes expanded keys)			
Key # for 101 Kbd	Key Name	XT scan codes Down • Up	AT hardware scan codes Down • Up
17	' ~ (accent, tilde)	29 • A9	0E • F0 0E
18	1 !	02 • 82	16 • F0 16
19	2 @	03 • 83	1E • F0 1E
20	3 #	04 • 84	26 • F0 26
21	4 $	05 • 85	25 • F0 25
22	5 %	06 • 86	2E • F0 2E
23	6 ^ (6, caret)	07 • 87	36 • F0 36
24	7 &	08 • 88	3D • F0 3D
25	8 * (8, asterisk)	09 • 89	3E • F0 3E
26	9 (	0A • 8A	46 • F0 46
27	0)	0B • 8B	45 • F0 45
28	– _ (dash, underline)	0C • 8C	4E • F0 4E
29	= + (equal, plus)	0D • 8D	55 • F0 55

Alphanumeric Primary Keyboard Keys (Includes expanded keys)			
Key # for 101 Kbd	Key Name	XT scan codes Down • Up	AT hardware scan codes Down • Up
30	Bkspace	0E • 8E	66 • F0 66
38	Tab	0F • 8F	0D • F0 0D
39	q Q	10 • 90	15 • F0 15
40	w W	11 • 91	1D • F0 1D
41	e E	12 • 92	24 • F0 24
42	r R	13 • 93	2D • F0 2D
43	t T	14 • 94	2C • F0 2C
44	y Y	15 • 95	35 • F0 35
45	u U	16 • 96	3C • F0 3C
46	i I	17 • 97	43 • F0 43
47	o O	18 • 98	44 • F0 44
48	p P	19 • 99	4D • F0 4D
49	[{	1A • 9A	54 • F0 54
50	] }	1B • 9B	5B • F0 5B
51	\	(backslash,bar)	2B • AB	5D • F0 5D
59	CapsLock	3A • BA	58 • F0 58
60	a A	1E • 9E	1C • F0 1C
61	s S	1F • 9F	1B • F0 1B
62	d D	20 • A0	23 • F0 23
63	f F	21 • A1	2B • F0 2B
64	g G	22 • A2	34 • F0 34
65	h H	23 • A3	33 • F0 33
66	j J	24 • A4	3B • F0 3B
67	k K	25 • A5	42 • F0 42
68	l L	26 • A6	4B • F0 4B
69	; : (semicolon,colon)	27 • A7	4C • F0 4C
70	' " (single quote,double)	28 • A8	52 • F0 52
71	Enter	1C • 9C	5A • F0 5A
75	Shift(left)	2A • AA	12 • F0 12
76	z Z	2C • AC	1A • F0 1A
77	x X	2D • AD	22 • F0 22
78	c C	2E • AE	21 • F0 21
79	v V	2F • AF	2A • F0 2A
80	b B	30 • B0	32 •
81	n N	31 • B1	31 • F0 31
82	m M	32 • B2	3A • F0 3A
83	, < (comma,less than)	33 • B3	41 • F0 41
84	. > (period,greater than)	34 • B4	49 • F0 49
85	/ ? (forward slash, ?)	35 • B5	4A • F0 4A
86	Shift(right)	36 • B6	59 • F0 59
92	Ctrl(left)	1D • 9D	14 • F0 14
93	Alt(left)	38 • B8	11 • F0 11

Alphanumeric Primary Keyboard Keys (Includes expanded keys)			
Key # for 101 Kbd	Key Name	XT scan codes Down • Up	AT hardware scan codes Down • Up
94	Space	39 • B9	29 • F0 29
95	Alt(right)	E0 38 • E0 B8	E0 11 • E0 F0 11
96	Ctrl(right)	E0 1D • E0 9D	E0 14 • E0 F0 14

Keypad Keys (Includes expanded keyboard layout)

Key # for 101 Kbd	Key Name	XT scan codes Down • Up	AT hardware scan codes Down • Up
34	NumLock	45 • C5	77 • F0 77
35	/	E0 35 • E0 B5	E0 4A • E0 F0 4A
35	–LEFT SHIFT case	E0 AA E0 35 • E0 B5 E0 2A	E0 F0 12 E0 4A • E0 F0 4A E0 12
35	–RIGHT SHIFT case	E0 B6 E0 35 • E0 B5 E0 36	E0 F0 59 E0 4A • E0 F0 4A E0 59
36	* (PrtSc 84 key)	37 • B7	7C • F0 7C
37	–	4A • C4	7B • F0 7B
55	Home 7	47 • C7	6C • F0 6C
56	UpArrow 8	48 • C8	75 • F0 75
57	PageUp 9	49 • C9	7D • F0 7D
58	+	4E • CE	79 • F0 79
72	LeftArrow 4	4B • CB	6B • F0 6B
73	5	4C • CC	73 • F0 73
74	RightArrow 6	4D • CD	74 • F0 74
88	End 1	4F • CF	69 • F0 69
89	DownArrow 2	50 • D0	72 • F0 72
90	PageDown 3	51 • D1	7A • F0 7A
91	Enter	E0 1C • E0 9C	E0 5A • E0 F0 5A
100	Ins 0	52 • D2	70 • F0 70
101	Del .	53 • D3	71 • F0 71

Resistor Color Codes

Color	1st Digit(A)	2nd Digit(B)	Multiplier©)	Tolerance(D)
Black	0	0	1	
Brown	1	1	10	1%
Red	2	2	100	2%
Orange	3	3	1,000	3%
Yellow	4	4	10,000	4%
Green	5	5	100,000	
Blue	6	6	1,000,000	
Violet	7	7	10,000,000	
Gray	8	8	100,000,000	
White	9	9	10⁹	
Gold			0.1 (EIA)	5%
Silver			0.01 (EIA)	10%
No Color				20%

Example: Red–Red–Orange = 22,000 ohms, 20%

Additional information concerning the Axial Lead resistor can be obtained if Band A is a wide band. Case 1: If only Band A is wide, it indicates that the resistor is wirewound. Case 2: If Band A is wide and there is also a blue fifth band to the right of Band D on the Axial Lead Resistor, it indicates the resistor is wirewound and flame proof.

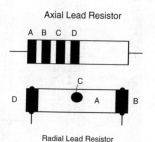

Axial Lead Resistor

Radial Lead Resistor

Paper Sizes

Paper Size	Standard	Millimeters	Inches
4A0	ISO	1,682 x 2,378	66.22 x 93.62
2A0	ISO	1,189 x 1,682	46.81 x 66.22
Eight Crown	UK	1,060 x 1,461	41.75 x 57.50
B0	ISO	1,000 x 1,414	39.37 x 55.67
Arch-E	Arch	914 x 1,219	36.00 x 48.00
SRA0	ISO	900 x 1,280	35.43 x 50.39
E (ANSI-E)	ANSI	864 x 1,118	34.00 x 44.00
RA0	ISO	860 x 1,220	33.86 x 48.03
A0	ISO	841 x 1,189	33.11 x 46.81
Quad Demy	UK	826 x 1,118	32.50 x 44.00
Quad Crown	UK	762 x 1,016	30.00 x 40.00
Antiquarian	UK	737 x 1,321	29.00 x 52.00
Double Princess	UK	711 x 1,118	28.00 x 44.00
B1	ISO	707 x 1,000	27.83 x 39.37
Double Elephant	UK	686 x 1,016	27.00 x 40.00
SRA1	ISO	640 x 900	25.20 x 35.43
RA1	ISO	610 x 860	24.02 x 33.86
Arch-D	Arch	610 x 914	24.00 x 36.00
A1	ISO	594 x 841	23.39 x 33.11
Double Demy	UK	572 x 889	22.50 x 35.00
D (ANSI-D)	ANSI	559 x 864	22.00 x 34.00
Imperial	UK	559 x 762	22.00 x 30.00
Princess	UK	546 x 711	21.50 x 28.00
B2	ISO	500 x 707	19.69 x 27.83
Demy	UK	470 x 584	18.50 x 23.00
Arch-C	Arch	457 x 610	18.00 x 24.00
SRA2	ISO	450 x 640	17.72 x 25.20
C (ANSI-C)	ANSI	432 x 559	17.00 x 22.00
RA2	ISO	430 x 610	16.93 x 24.02
A2	ISO	420 x 594	16.54 x 23.39
B3	ISO	353 x 500	13.90 x 19.69
Brief	UK	333 x 470	13.13 x 18.50
Arch-B	Arch	305 x 457	12.00 x 18.00
A3	ISO	297 x 420	11.69 x 16.54
B (ANSI-B)	ANSI	279 x 432	11.00 x 17.00
B4	ISO	250 x 353	9.84 x 13.90
Arch-A	Arch	229 x 305	9.00 x 12.00
Legal	US	216 x 356	8.50 x 14.00
A (ANSI-A)	ANSI	216 x 279	8.50 x 11.00
Demy Quarto	UK	216 x 273	8.50 x 10.75
Foolscap Folio	UK	210 x 333	8.25 x 13.13
A4	ISO	210 x 297	8.27 x 11.69
Crown Quarto	UK	184 x 242	7.25 x 9.50
B5	ISO	176 x 250	6.93 x 9.84
Foolscap Quarto	UK	165 x 206	6.50 x 8.13
Royal Octavo	UK	152 x 241	6.00 x 9.50
A5	ISO	148 x 210	5.83 x 8.27
Demy Octavo	US	140 x 216	5.50 x 8.50
Demy Octavo	US	137 x 213	5.38 x 8.38
-	US	127 x 178	5.00 x 7.00
B6	ISO	125 x 176	4.92 x 6.93
Crown Octavo	UK	121 x 181	4.75 x 7.13
A6	ISO	105 x 148	4.13 x 5.83
-	US	102 x 127	4.00 x 5.00
B7	ISO	88 x 125	3.46 x 4.92
-	US	76 x 127	3.00 x 5.00
A7	ISO	74 x 105	2.91 x 4.13
B8	ISO	62 x 88	2.44 x 3.46
A8	ISO	52 x 74	2.05 x 2.91
B9	ISO	44 x 62	1.73 x 2.44
A9	ISO	37 x 52	1.46 x 2.05
B10	ISO	31 x 44	1.22 x 1.73
A10	ISO	26 x 37	1.02 x 1.46

Abbreviations for the above table are: ANSI - American National Standards Institute;
Arch - Architects Standard, US; ISO - International Organization for Standardization;
UK-United Kingdom; US-United States

PC Memory Map

Address Range	Size	Description
00000-003FF	1K	Interrupt Vectors
00400-7FFFF	512K	Bios, DOS, 512K RAM Expansion
80000-9FFFF	128K	128K RAM Expansion (Top of 640K)
A0000-AFFFF	64K	EGA Video Buffer
B0000-B7FFF	32K	Monochrome & other screen buffers
B8000-BFFFF	32K	CGA and EGA Buffers
AT LIM Expanded Memory 64K page is between 768K and 896K		
C0000-C3FFF	16K	EGA Video Bios
C4000-C7FFF	16K	ROM Expansion Area
XT LIM Expanded Memory 64K page is between 800K and 960K		
C8000-CCFFF	20K	XT Hard Disk Controller Bios
CD000-CFFFF	12K	User PROM, Memory mapped I/O
D0000-DFFFF	64K	User PROM, normal LIM Location for Expanded Memory
E0000-EFFFF	64K	ROM expansion, I/O for XT
F0000-FDFFF	56K	ROM BASIC
FE000-FFFD9	8K	BIOS
FFFF0-FFFF4	4	1st Code run after system power on
FFFF5-FFFFC	8	BIOS Release Date
FFFFE-FFFFF	2	Machine ID (Top of 1 Meg RAM)
100000-FFFFFF	15Meg	AT Extended Memory

DMA Channels

XT 8 bit ISA Bus	
Channel	Function
0	Dynamic memory refresh
1	Unassigned or SDLC
2	Floppy disk controller
3	Hard disk controller
16 bit ISA, EISA, and MCA Bus	
Channel	Function
DMA Controller #1	
0	Dynamic memory refresh
1	Unassigned or SDLC
2	Floppy disk controller
3	Unassigned
DMA Controller #2	
4	First DMA Controller
5	Unassigned
6	Unassigned
7	Unassigned

PC Hardware Interrupts

Interrupt	Function
NMI	Non-Maskable Interrupt (Parity)
Interrupt Controller 1:	
IRQ0	System Timer Output, internal system use only
IRQ1	Keyboard controller, exclusively for keyboard input
IRQ2	XT – Available
	AT – Route to Interrupt Controller 2, IRQ8 to 15
IRQ3	Serial Port COM2: or COM4: or SDLC
IRQ4	Serial Port COM1: or COM3: or SDLC. On systems without a PS/2 mouse, this IRQ is almost always used for a serial mouse.
IRQ5	First choice IRQ for most sound cards. Can be used for Parallel Printer Port LPT2: Legacy: XT – Hard Disk Controller
IRQ6	Floppy Disk Controller, exclusive
IRQ7	Parallel Printer Port LPT1: or other devices that use parallel ports such as a Parallel Zip Drive.
Interrupt Controller 2 (AT/Pentium Only):	
IRQ8	Real Time Clock Timer, exclusive use
IRQ9	Open interrupt. Legacy: Software redirect to IRQ2 (Int Ø0A Hex)
IRQ10	Open interrupt
IRQ11	Open interrupt
IRQ12	Normally used for the PS/2 mouse. If no mouse, it is an open interrupt for other peripherals.
IRQ13	Reserved for the integrated floating point unit like the 80287 Math Coprocessor
IRQ14	Primary IDE hard disk controller; if no controller the IRQ is available for other devices.
IRQ15	Secondary IDE hard drive controller and some SCSI controllers

Serial/Com: Ports

Com: Port	PC / ISA IRQ / Address	PS2 / MCA IRQ / Address
1	4 / 03F8h	4 / 03F8h
2	3 / 02F8h	3 / 02F8h
3	4 / 03E8h*	3 / 3220h
4	3 / 02E8h*	3 / 3228h
5	not available	3 / 4220h
6	not available	3 / 4228h
7	not available	3 / 5220h
8	not available	3 / 5228h

* Note that some software and hardware products do not support the COM3: and COM4: addresses and interrupts

PC Hardware I/O Map

8088 Class Systems Address	Function
000–00F	DMA Controller (8237A)
020–021	Interrupt controller (8259A)
040–043	Timer (8253)
060–063	(8255A)
080–083	DMA page register (74LS612)
0A0–0AF	NMI – Non Maskable Interrupt
200–20F	Game Port Joystick controller
210–217	Expansion Unit
2E8–2EF	COM4: Serial Port (see page)
2F8–2FF	COM2: Serial Port
300–31F	Prototype Card
320–32F	Hard Disk
378–37F	Parallel Printer Port 1
380–38F	SDLC
3B0–3BF	MDA – Monochrome Adapter and printer
3D0–3D7	CGA – Color Graphics Adapter
3E8–3EF	COM3: Serial Port (see page)
3F0–3F7	Floppy Diskette Controller
3F8–3FF	COM1: Serial Port

80286 /386/486 Class Systems	
Address	**Function**
000–01F	DMA Controller #1 (8237A–5)
020–03F	Interrupt controller #1 (8259A)
040–05F	Timer (8254)
060–06F	Keyboard (8042)
070–07F	NMI – Non Maskable Interrupt & CMOS RAM
080–09F	DMA page register (74LS612)
0A0–0BF	Interrupt controller #2 (8259A)
0C0–0DF	DMA Controller #2 (8237A)
0F0–0FF	80287 Math Coprocessor
1F0–1F8	Hard Disk
200–20F	Game Port Joystick controller
258–25F	Intel Above Board
278–27F	Parallel Printer Port 2
2E8–2EF	COM4: Serial Port (see page)
2F8–2FF	COM2: Serial Port
300–31F	Prototype Card
378–37F	Parallel Printer Port 1
380–38F	SDLC or Bisynchronous Comm Port 2
3A0–3AF	Bisynchronous Comm Port 1
3B0–3BF	MDA – Monochrome Adapter
3BC–3BE	Parallel Printer on Monochrome Adapter
3C0–3CF	EGA – Reserved
3D0–3D7	CGA – Color Graphics Adapter
3E8–3EF	COM3: Serial Port (see page)
3F0–3F7	Floppy Diskette Controller
3F8–3FF	COM1: Serial Port

PC Software Interrupts

Address	Int #	Software Interrupt Name
000–003	0	Divide by zero
004–007	1	Single Step IRET
008–00B	2	NMI Non Maskable Interrupt
00C–00F	3	Breakpoint
010–013	4	Overflow IRET
014–017	5	Print Screen
018–01F	6	Reserved 018–01B and 01C–01F
020–023	8	Time of Day Ticker IRQ0
024–027	9	Keyboard IRQ1
028–02B	A	XT Reserved, AT IRQ2 direct to IRQ9
02C–02F	B	COM2 communications, IRQ3
030–033	C	COM1 communications, IRQ4
034–037	D	XT Hard disk, AT Parallel Printer, IRQ5
038–03B	E	Floppy Diskette, IRQ6
03C–03F	F	Parallel Printer 1, IRQ7, slave 8259, IRET
040–043	10	ROM Handler – Video
044–047	11	ROM Handler – Equipment Check
048–04B	12	ROM Handler – Memory Check
04C–04F	13	ROM Handler – Diskette I/O
050–053	14	ROM Handler – COMM I/O
054–057	15	XT Cassette, AT ROM Catchall Handlers
058–05B	16	ROM Handler – Keyboard I/O
05C–05F	17	ROM Handler – Printer I/O
060–063	18	ROM Handler – Basic Startup
064–067	19	ROM Handler – Bootstrap
068–06B	1A	ROM Handler – Time of Day
06C–06F	1B	ROM Handler – Keyboard Break
070–073	1C	ROM Handler – User Ticker
074–077	1D	ROM Pointer, Video Initialization
078–07B	1E	ROM Pointer, Diskette Parameters

Address	Int #	Software Interrupt Name
Ø7C–Ø7F	1F	ROM Pointer, Graphics Characters Set 2
Ø8Ø–Ø83	2Ø	DOS – Terminate Program
Ø84–Ø87	21	DOS – Function Call
Ø88–Ø8B	22	DOS – Program's Terminate Address
Ø8C–Ø8F	23	DOS – Program's Control–Break Address
Ø9Ø–Ø93	24	DOS – Critical Error Handler
Ø94–Ø97	25	DOS – Absolute Disk Read
Ø98–Ø9B	26	DOS – Absolute Disk Write
Ø9C–Ø9F	27	DOS – TSR Terminate & Stay Ready
ØAØ–ØFF	28–3F	DOS – Idle Loop, IRET
1ØØ–1Ø3	4Ø	Hard Disk Pointer–Original Floppy Handler
1Ø4–1Ø7	41	ROM Pointer, XT Hard Disk Parameters
1Ø8–1ØB	42–45	Reserved
1ØC–1ØF	46	ROM Pointer, AT Hard Disk Parameters
11Ø–17F	47–5F	Reserved
18Ø–19F	6Ø–67	Reserved for User (67 is Expanded Mem)
1AØ–1BF	68–6F	Not Used
1CØ–1C3	7Ø	AT Real Time Clock, IRQ8
1C4–1C7	71	AT Redirect to IRQ2, IRQ9, LAN Adapter 1
1C8–1CB	72	AT Reserved, IRQ1Ø
1CC–1CF	73	AT Reserved, IRQ11
1DØ–1D3	74	AT Reserved, IRQ12
1D4–1D7	75	AT 8Ø287 Error to NMI, IRQ13
1D8–1DB	76	AT Hard Disk, IRQ14
1DC–1DF	77	AT Reserved, IRQ15
1EØ–1FF	78–7F	Not Used
2ØØ–217	8Ø–85	Reserved for BASIC
218–21B	86	NetBIOS, Relocated Interrupt 18H
218–3C3	87–FØ	Reserved for BASIC Interpreter
3C4–3FF	F1–FF	Not Used

Modem Standards

V.xx Standards are international data communication standards defined by CCITT (Consultative Committee for International Telephone and Telegraph).

Standard	Description
V.13	Simulated half-duplex for synchronous networks.
V.21	300 bps, compatible with Bell 103. Mainly outside USA
V.22	1200 bps @ 600 baud, compatible with Bell 212A; full duplex; sync or async. Mainly outside USA
V.22bis	2400 bps with fall back to 1200 bps, compatible with Bell 212A and V.22; full duplex; sync or async. Used in the USA
V.23	1200 bps with 75 bps back channel for use in Europe
V.25	Provides autodialing capabilities to sync or async dial-up lines. Parallel interface.
V.25bis	Provides autodialing capabilities to sync or async dial-up lines. Serial interface.
V.29	Half-duplex, 9600bps, mostly used in fax.
V.32	4800 and 9600 bps with fall back to 4800; full duplex, sync or async. Automatically adjusts the transmission speed based on line quality. The first universal standard for 9600 bps modems.
V.32bis	14,400 with fall back to 12000, 9600 , 7200 and 4800 bps. Sync or async; full duplex. V.32bis incorporates "fastrain" in which it can automatically increase or decrease modem speed during operation.
V.32Turbo	19,200 bps modem
V.32Fast	or V.Fast, the 28,800 bps modem
V.33	14,400 or 12,000 bps sync transmission over 4 wire leased lines. Used in very high speed super computer environments. V.32bis provides the same capability but over 2 wire dial-up lines.
V.34	28,800 bps Standard approved in June 1994 and is the state-of-the-art protocol for high speed modem communications. It includes a 4-dimension 64 state trellis coding not found in the V.FC modems and also includes a V.8 high speed startup sequence. Standard is backward compatible with V.32 and V.32bis.
V.34bis	33,600 bps with a fallback to 31,200 bps
V.42	LAP-M (Link Access Protocol) Error Correction and support for MNP levels 1 to 4; falls back to MNP 1-4 if LAP-M is not available. Same transfer rate as V.34 but more reliable.
V.42bis	V.42 with intelligent data compression for data transfer rates of 34,000 bps and support for MNP5; compression up to 4:1.
V.44	With V.44 compliant modems at the ISP and the user, this provides Web page compression and increased speeds from fewer data packets.
V.FC or V.Fast	A class of modems incorporating some of the V.34 standards.
K56Flex	Proprietary 56k modem standard developed by Rockwell and Lucent Technologies
X2	Proprietary 3Com/US Robotics standard for 56k modems
V.90	The current standard for 56k modems adopted by the International Telecommunications Union. This standard is backward compatible with X2 and K56Flex. This is the fastest transmissions standard available for analog modems.
V.92	Same speed as V.90 but with reduced handshake time and an additional "on-hold" feature.

Bell Standards are USA data communication standards defined by Bell Labs and AT&T.

Standard	Description
Bell 103	300 bps, async, full duplex over 2 wire dial-up or leased lines. Comparable to V.21.
Bell 201B	2400 bps, sync, full duplex over 4 wire, half duplex over 2 wire dial-up lines. Comparable to V.26.
Bell 201C	Same as 201B but dial-up lines only.
Bell 208A	4800 bps, sync, full duplex over 4 wire leased line or half duplex over 2 wire leased line. Comparable to V.27
Bell 208B	Same as 208A but 2 wire dial-up lines only
Bell 212A	1200 bps, sync or async, full duplex over 2 wire leased or dial-up lines. Comparable to V.22.

MNP (Microcom Networking Protocol) Error Correction and Data Compression. In order to use MNP, the modems at both ends of the phone line must have the same MNP capability.

Standard	Description
MNP Level 1-4	Error correcting routines used to filter out line noise. It also reduces the size of data transferred by up to 20%, thereby speeding up transfers.
MNP Level 5	Conventional data compression of up to 2:1; useful for ASCII type files only not binary files like ZIP and ARC files. MNP 5 effectively doubles the baud rate of the transfer.

Hayes Compatible Modem Command Settings

Command	Function
	>>>>> Note: all commands are <u>not</u> available on all modems! <<<<<
+++	Default escape code, wait for modem to return state
A	Force answer mode; Immediate answer on ring
A /	Repeat last command line (Replaces AT)
AT	Attention code
Cn	n=Ø is Transmitter off, n=1 is on, (1=default)
Bn	n=Ø is CCITT answer tone, n=1 is US/Canada Tone
Dn	Dial telephone number
	n= Ø to 9 for phone numbers
	n= T is Touch Tone Dial, P is Pulse Dial
	n= R is Originate Only, n= , is Pause
	n= ! is xfer call to following extension
	n= " is dial letters that follow
	n= @ is Dial, Wait for answer, & continue
	n= ; is Return to command mode after dialing
En	n=Ø is no character echo in command state
	n=1 is echo all characters in command state
Fn	n=Ø is Half Duplex: n=1 if Full Duplex
Hn	n=Ø is On Hook (Hang Up), n=1 is Off Hook
	n=2 is Special Off Hook
In	n=Ø is Display product code, n=1 show Check Sum
	n=2 is show RAM test, n=3 is show call time length
	n=4 is show current modem settings
Kn	n=Ø at AT13 show last call length, n=1 show time
Ln	Speaker volume control: n=Ø or 1 is low volume
	n=2 is medium volume; n=3 is high volume
Mn	n=Ø is Speaker always off, n=2 is always on
	n=1 is Speaker on until carrier detected (default)
	n=3 is Speaker on during CONNECT sequence only
Nn	Auto data standard/speed adjust; n=Ø is connect at S37,
	n=1 auto data standard and speed adjust to match
On	n=Ø is return to on-line; n=1 is return to on-line & retain
Qn	n=Ø is send Result Codes; n=1 is do not send code
	n=2 is send result code only when originating call
SØ=n	n=Ø to 255 rings before answer (see switch 5)
S1=n	Counts rings from Ø to 255
S2=n	Set escape code character, n=Ø to 127, 43 default
S3=n	Set carriage return character, n=Ø to 127, 13 default
S4=n	Set line feed character, n=Ø to 127, 10 default
S5=n	Set backspace character, n=Ø to 127, 8 default
S6=n	Wait time for dial tone, n=2 to 255 seconds
S7=n	Wait time for carrier, n=2 to 255 seconds
S8=n	Set duration of "," pause character, n=Ø to 255 sec.
S9=n	Carrier detect response time, n=1 to 255 1/10 secs.
S10=n	Delay time carrier loss to hang-up, n=1 to 255 1/10 s.
S11=n	Duration & space of Touch Tones, n=50 to 255 ms.
S12=n	Escape code guard time, n=50 to 255 1/50 seconds
S13=n	UART Status Register Bit Mapped (reserved)
S14=n	Option Register, Product code returned by AT1Ø
S15=n	Flag Register (reserved)

Command	Function
S16=n	Self test mode. n=Ø is data mode (default), n=1 is Analog Loopback, n=2 is dial test, n=4 is Test Pattern, n=5 is Analog Loopback and Test Pattern
S18=n	Test timer for modem diagnostic tests
S37=n	Set line speed. Used in conjunction with Nn. n=Ø Attempt at speed of last AT command; n=1 to 3 attempt at 300bps; n=4 reserved; n=5 attempt 1200bps; n=6 attempt 2400bps; n=7 reserved; n=8 use 4800bps; n=9 use 9600; =10-12200bps; =11-14400bps; =12-7200
Sn ?	Send contents of Register n (Ø to 16) to Computer
Vn	n=Ø is send result codes as digits, n=1 is words
Wn	Protocol negotiation progress report; n=Ø is progress is not reported; n=1 is reported; n=2 is not reported but CONNECT XXXX message reports DCE speed
Xn	Send normal or extended result codes: n=Ø send basic set/blind dial; n=1 extended/blind dial; n=2 extended/dial tone; n=3 extended/blind & busy; n=4 extended/dial tone, busy
Yn	Long space disconnect: n=Ø is disabled; n=1 is enabled
Zn	Modem reset: n=Ø is power on; =1 to 3 user; =4 is factory
&Cn	n=Ø is DCD always active; n=1 active during connect
&Dn	n=Ø is DTR always ignored, =1 DTR causes return to command, =2 DTR disconnects; =3 disconnect/reset
&F	Get Factory Configuration
&Gn	n=Ø Disable Guard Tone, =1 is 550hz, =2 is 1800hz
&Kn	DTE: n=Ø is disable flow control, n=3 Enable RTS/CTS flow control; n=4 enable XON/XOFF flow control; n=5 enable transparent XON/XOFF flow control.
&Ln	n=Ø or 1 Speaker Volume Low, =2 medium, =3 high
&Mn	Communications mode (same as &Qn)
&Pn	n=Ø Pulse Make/Break Ratio USA 39% / 61% n=1 Pulse Make/Break Ratio UK 33% / 67%
&Qn	Communication mode: n=Ø is Async, Direct mode; n=4 modem issues OK result code; n=5 Error correction mode; n=6 Async, Normal mode; n=8 MNP; n=9 V.42 and V.42bis modes
&Rn	n=Ø is CTS tracks RTS, n=1 CTS always active
&Sn	n=Ø is DSR always active, n=1 DSR active at connect
&Tn	Test Commands: n=Ø end test, =1 local analog loopback, =3 local digital loopback, =4 enable Rmt digital loopback, =5 disable digital loopback, =6 request Rmt digital loop, =7 request Rmt dig loop & enter self test, =8 local analog loop & self test
&Vn	View current configuration
&W	Write Configuration to Memory
&Yn	n=Ø is Default is user configuration at NVRAM Ø ; n=1 default is user configuration at NVRAM location 1
&Zn=x	Store Phone Number "x" at location "n". n=0,1,2, or 3

UART Serial Chips

The UART (Universal Asynchronous Receiver-Transmitter) is the heart of a computer's serial port and it provides a parallel to serial and serial to parallel translation link between computer and modem. The chips listed below are made by Intel (INS) and National Semiconductor (NS).

INS8250
The original UART used in IBM's first PC serial port. It has slow access cycle delays and requires extra NOPS between CPU read-write cycles. Several bugs (one of which is an interrupt enable problem) are present in the chip but are not serious. The 8250 was replaced by the 8250A. Chip will not work properly at 9600 bps.

INS8250A and INS82C50A
This chip is an upgrade to the original 8250 and fixes some of the original bugs. The "A" series chip was designed to correct the bugs in conjunction with the PC and XT BIOS and is therefore not compatible with many software packages and other computer's. Avoid using this chip! Chip will not work properly at 9600 bps.

INS8250B
The final upgrade of the 8250 chip series in which the bugs of the first two versions have been repaired. This chip will work in PC and XT class systems; however, it may or may not function correctly in 80286 and higher systems. Chip will not work properly at 9600 bps.

NS16450 and NS16C450
A higher speed version of the 8250 chip. It was designed for 80286 and higher systems and may not work correctly in PC and XT class computers. A scratch register (#7) has been included. The OS2 operating system requires the 16450 or higher in serial ports. Maximum data rate is 38,400 bps.

NS16550
This chip is an upgrade to the 16450. It provides higher baud rates and a DMA interface. It does not support FIFO (first in - first out). It works well in 80286 and higher systems and the maximum data rate is 115,200 bps.

NS16550A
A higher speed version of the 16550 chip. It was designed for 80286 and higher systems. It allows multiple DMA access and has a built-in 16 character transmit and receive FIFO (first in - first out) buffer. The 16550A is currently the recommended UART for high speed data communications. Maximum data rate is 115,200 bps.

16750
A higher speed version of the 16550A but 100% compatible with the 16550. Has a 64 byte FIFO mode and an auto handshake mode.

16950
Very high data rates with no data loss or overrun errors. Has 128 byte input and 128 byte output FIFO buffer. Auto handshaking, Speeds up to 15 Mbaud in asynchronous mode.

CPU Specifications

CPU Type	Release Date	Max Mem Phys/Virt	Bus Int/Ext	Number of Transistors	Speeds MHz
Advanced Micro Devices (AMD)					
N80L286 (?)					10,12
AM386SX (?)	07-91	4Gb	32/16	161k	25,33,40
AM386DX (?)	03-91	4Gb	32/32	161k	25,33,40
AM486SX (doubler,?).	07-93	4Gb/64Tb	32/32	900k	33,40,25/50
AM486SXLV (3.3V)	07-93	4Gb/64Tb	32/32	900k	33
AM486DX (?)	?	4Gb/64Tb	32/32	1,300k	33, 40
AM486DX2 (doubler,?)	?	4Gb/64Tb	32/32	1,300k	25/50,33/66,40/80
AM486DX2 (doubler, 3.3V)	?	4Gb/64Tb	32/32	1,300k	100
AM486DXLV (3.3V)	?	4Gb/64Tb	32/32	1,300k	33
AM486DXL2 (doubler,?)	?	4Gb/64Tb	32/32	1,300k	25/50,33/66,40/80
AM486DXL4 (doubler,?)	?	4Gb/64Tb	32/32	1,300k	50/100
5x86 (3.3V)	12-95	4Gb/64Tb	32/32	1,300k	75
K5 (3.5V)	03-96	? / ?	64/64	4,300k	75,90,100,117,133
K6 (3.5V)	11-96	? / ?	64/64	8,800k	180,233,266,300
K6 MMX (2.9/3.2V)	4-97	? / ?	64/64	8,800k	166,200,233
K6 3D-Now MMX (?)	01-98	? / ?	64/64	9,300k	300,350
K6-II 3D-Now (?)	05-98	? / ?	64/64	9,300k	266,300,333,350, 366,380,400,450,475,500,533
Mobile K6-II (1.8V)	01-99	? / ?	64/64	9,300k	266,300,333
Mobile K6-II-P (2.2V)	03-99	? / ?	64/64	9,300k	350,366,380,400
K6-III-P (2V)	09-99	? / ?	64/64	21,300k	400,433,450
K6-II-P (2V)	09-99	? / ?	64/64	9,300k	433,450,475
Athlon (1.6/3.3V)	09-99	? / ?	? / ?	22,000k	550,600,650,700,750
Athlon (1.7/3V)	?	? / ?	? / ?	22,000k	800,850
Athlon (1.8/3.3V)	?	? / ?	? / ?	22,000k	900,950,1000
mobile K6-III+ (2V)	04-00	? / ?	? / ?	21,300k	450,475,500
mobile K6-II+ (2V)	04-00	? / ?	? / ?	9,300k	450,475,500
Duron (1.6V) (aka Morgan)	06-00	? / ?	? / ?	?	550,600,650,700,750, 800,850,900,950
Duron (1.75V) (aka Spitfire)	06-00	? / ?	? / ?	?	900,950,1000,1100,1200,1300
Athlon (1.70V) (Thunderbird)	06-00	? / ?	? / ?	?	650,700,750,800,850
Athlon (1.75V) (aka Thunderbird)	06-00	? / ?	? / ?	?	900,950,1000,1100, 1200,1300,1400
mobile Duron (1.4V)	01-01	? / ?	? / ?	?	600,700
mobile Duron (1.4V)	?	? / ?	? / ?	?	1000,1100,1200
mobile Athlon (?)	2Q-01	? / ?	? / ?	22,000k	1000
mobile Athlon 4 (?)	06-01	? / ?	? / ?	?	1000,1100,1200,1340,1400
Athlon MP (1.60V)	06-01	? / ?	? / ?	?	1400,1530,1600,1670,2000,2133
Athlon XP (1.7/2.5V)	09-01	4Gb/4Gb	32/32	37,500k	1340,1400,1470,1533, 1600,1670,1730
mobile Athlon XP (1.6/2.5V). (aka Palomino)	05-02	16Gb/4Gb	32/32	37,200k	1200,1270,1333,1340,1400, 1470,1533,1600,1667,1800
Opteron (1.55/2.5V) (aka SledgeHammer)	04-03	1Tb/256Tb	64/64	105,900k	800,1000,1200,1400 1600,1800,2000,2200,2400,2600
Athlon 64(1.55/2.5V) (aka ClawHammer)	09-03	1Tb/256Tb	64/64	105,900k	1400,1600,1800,2000, 2200,2400,2600
Athlon 64 FX(1.55/2.5V) (aka ClawHammer)	09-03	1Tb/256Tb	64/64	105,900k	1800,2200
Opteron HE (55Watt) (?) (aka Athens)	03-04	? / ?	64/64	?.	2000
Opteron EE (30Watt) (?) (aka Athens)	03-04	? / ?	64/64	?.	1400
Athlon 64(?). (aka Newcastle)	1H-04	? / ?	64/64	?.	?
Athlon 64(?). (aka Winchester)	2H-04	? / ?	64/64	?.	?
mobile Athlon 64(?) (aka Odessa)	2H-04	? / ?	64/64	?.	?
Athlon XP(?) (aka Paris)	2H-04	? / ?	64/64	?.	?
Athlon 64 FX(?) (aka San Diego)	2H-04	? / ?	64/64	?.	2700
dual processor Opteron (?) (aka Troy)	2H-04	? / ?	64/64	?.	?
Opteron (?) (aka Venus)	2H-04	? / ?	64/64	?.	?
mobile Athlon XP(?). (aka Dublin)	2H-04	? / ?	64/64	?.	?
Duron (?)	2005	? / ?	? / ?	?.	?

CPU Type	Release Date	Max Mem Phys/Virt	Bus Int/Ext	Number of Transistors	Speeds MHz
(aka Victoria)					
Athlon 64 FX(?)............	1H-05.	? / ?	64/64	?.	?
(aka Toledo)					
mobile Athlon 64(?)	1H-05.	? / ?	64/64	?.	?
(aka Oakville)					
Athlon XP(?)............	2H-05.	? / ?	64/64	?.	?
(aka Palermo)					
Opteron (?)............	2H-05.	? / ?	64/64	?.	?
(aka Egypt, K9)					
Opteron (?)............	2H-05.	? / ?	64/64	?.	?
(aka Italy, K9)					
Opteron (?)............	2H-05.	? / ?	64/64	?.	?
(aka Denmark, K9)					
mobile Athlon XP(?).	2H-05.	? / ?	64/64	?.	?
(aka Trinidad)					

Advanced Micro Devices - Upgrade Chips

CPU Type	Release Date	Max Mem Phys/Virt	Bus Int/Ext	Number of Transistors	Speeds MHz
AM186EM (?)............	09-94.	? / ?	16/16	?.	25,33,40
AM386EM (?)............	09-94.	? / ?	32/32	?.	25,33
AM486SE (3 or 5V)......	09-94.	? / ?	? / ?	?.	25,33

Alpha Processor, Inc.

CPU Type	Release Date	Max Mem Phys/Virt	Bus Int/Ext	Number of Transistors	Speeds MHz
Alpha 21164 (2.5V)......	1997	? / ?	64/64	?.	500,533,600,633,667
Alpha 21264 (2.3V)......	04-98.	? / ?	64/64	15,200k.	500,600

Centaur Technology – sold to Via Technologies in 1999.

Cyrix Corporation – sold to Via Technologies 1999.

CPU Type	Release Date	Max Mem Phys/Virt	Bus Int/Ext	Number of Transistors	Speeds MHz
CX486SLC (3 or 5V)......	04-92.	16Mb	32/16	600k.	20,25,33
CX486DLC (?)............	06-92.	4Gb/64Tb	32/32	600k.	25,33,40
CX486S (?)............	02-93.	4Gb/64Tb	32/16	?.	33,40
CX486DX (?)............	09-93.	4Gb/64Tb	32/32	?.	33,40,50
CX486DX2 (doubler,?)....	09-93.	4Gb/64Tb	32/32	?.	25/50,33/66
CX486SLC2 (doubler,?)...	10-93.	4Gb/64Tb	32/32	?.	25/50
CX486DXV (3V)............	?	4Gb/64Tb	32/32	?.	33
CX486DX2V (doubler, 3V)..	?	4Gb/64Tb	32/32	?.	25/50,33/66,40/80
5x86 (3.3V)............	07-95.	? / ?	32/64	2,000k.	100,120
6x86 (3.3V)............	10-95.	? / ?	32/64	3,000k.	100,110,120,133,150
6x86MX (3.3V)............	05-97.	? / ?	32/64	6,000k.	150,166,188,200,250,266
MediaGX (3.3V)............	02-97.	? / ?	64/64	2,400k.	120,133,150,166,
(Multimedia accelerator chip)					180,200,233

Cyrix Corporation - Upgrade Chips

CPU Type	Release Date	Max Mem Phys/Virt	Bus Int/Ext	Number of Transistors	Speeds MHz
CX486DRX2 (doubler,?) ...	08-93.	4Gb/64Tb	32/32	?.	16/32,20/40,25/50,33/66
CX486SRX2 (doubler,?) ...	10-93.	4Gb/64Tb	32/16	?.	20/40,25/50

Digital Equipment Corporation

(Merged with Compaq Computer Corp. in 1998. Compaq merged with HP in 2002.)

CPU Type	Release Date	Max Mem Phys/Virt	Bus Int/Ext	Number of Transistors	Speeds MHz
Alpha 21064 (3.3V)......	1992	16Gb/ ?	64/64	1,680k.	150,300
Alpha 21064A (3.3V).....	10-93.	16Gb/ ?	64/64	2,800k.	200,233,275,300
Alpha 21066 (3.3V)......	?	16Gb/ ?	64/64	1,750k.	166
Alpha 21066A (3.3V).....	01-95.	16Gb/ ?	64/64	1,750k.	100,233
Alpha 21164 (3.3V)......	1994	1Tb/8Tb	64/64	9,300k.	266,300,333,366,
					433,500,533,600
Alpha 21164A (3.3V).....	?	? / ?	? / ?	9,000k.	417
Alpha 21164PC (3.3V)....	03-97.	? / ?	? / ?	3,400k.	300,366,400,466,533
Alpha 21264 (2.3V) (aka EV6)	12-98.	16Gb/2.7Tb	64/64	15,200k.	500
Alpha 21264A(2.0V)(aka EV67)	2001	32Gb/2.7Tb	64/64	15,200k.	667,750,833
Alpha 21364 (?)(aka EV7)..	2002	1Tb/4Tb	64/64	100,000k.	1200
Alpha 21364A (?)(aka EV79)	2003.	? / ?	? / ?	100,000k.	1200+
Alpha 21464 (aka EV8) Cancelled 06-01					

Evergreen Technologies Inc. - Upgrade Chips

CPU Type	Release Date	Max Mem Phys/Virt	Bus Int/Ext	Number of Transistors	Speeds MHz
Rev To 486 (?)............	?	? / ?	? / ?	?.	25/50,25/75
Rev To DX4 (?)............	09-94.	? / ?	? / ?	?.	25/75,33/100,50/100
Evergreen 586 (?)........	?	? / ?	64/64	4,300k.	133
Evergreen PR166 (?)......	?	? / ?	64/64	3,000k.	150
Evergreen MxPro (?)......	09-97.	? / ?	64/64	8,800k.	180,200
Evergreen Spectra 333 (?)..	05-98.	? / ?	64/64	9,300k.	333
Evergreen Performa (?)....	?	? / ?	? / ?	?.	800,900,1000,1200,1400
Evergreen Performa III (?)..	?	? / ?	? / ?	?.	1000
Evergreen Performa 4 (?) ..	?	? / ?	? / ?	?.	2400,2500

CPU's

CPU Type	Release Date	Max Mem Phys/Virt	Bus Int/Ext	Number of Transistors	Speeds MHz

Exponential Technology, Inc.
(Out of business 1997 after Apple declined use of the X704 in its Power Mac line)

CPU Type	Release Date	Max Mem Phys/Virt	Bus Int/Ext	Number of Transistors	Speeds MHz
Exponential-X704 (?)	1998	? / ?	64/32	2,700k	410,533

Fujitsu Microelectronics, Inc.

CPU Type	Release Date	Max Mem Phys/Virt	Bus Int/Ext	Number of Transistors	Speeds MHz
TurboSPARC (3.3V)	09-96	? / ?	32/32	3,000k	160,170
SPARC64 GP (?)	?	? / ?	64/64	?	?
SPARC64-V (1.2V)	10-02	? / ?	64/64	191,000k	1080,1100,1300,
					1320,1350
dual-core SPARC64-VI (1.0-1.8V) 2H-05		? / ?	64/64	690,000k	2400+

Hewlett-Packard Company

CPU Type	Release Date	Max Mem Phys/Virt	Bus Int/Ext	Number of Transistors	Speeds MHz
PA-7100LC (3.3V)	1994	4Gb/ ?	32/32	800k	60,80,100
PA-7150 (3.3V)	12-93	? / ?	32/32	850k	125
PA-7200 (3.3V)	01-95	? / ?	32/32	1,260k	100,120
PA-7300LC (3.3V)	10-95	? / ?	32/32	9,200k	132,160,180
PA-8000 (3.3V)	03-96	? / ?	64/64	?	160,180
PA-8200 (3.3V)	03-97	? / ?	64/64	3,800k	200,220,240
PA-8500 (3.3V)	10-98	? / ?	64/64	140,000k	360,440
PA-8600 (?)	03-99	? / ?	64/64	140,000k	440,500,550
Itanium (with Intel) (2.1/3.3V)	5-01	? / ?	64/64	25,000k	733,800
(aka Merced or P7)					
PA-8700 (?)	08-01	? / ?	64/64	186,000k	650,750
Itanium 2 (with Intel) (?)	07-02	? / ?	64/64	221,000	900,1000
(aka McKinley)					
EV7 Alpha (?)	01-03	1Tb/4Tb	64/64	100,000k	1200
Itanium 2 (with Intel)(1.3V)	06-03	? / ?	64/64	410,000k	1300,1400,1500,1800
(aka Madison)					
dual-core PA-8800 (?)	02-04	? / ?	64/64	300,000k	800,900,1000
(aka Mako)					
PA-8900 (?)	2005	? / ?	64/64	?	1200
EV7z Alpha (?)	2005	? / ?	? / ?	?	?

Hitachi America, Ltd.

CPU Type	Release Date	Max Mem Phys/Virt	Bus Int/Ext	Number of Transistors	Speeds MHz
SH7702 (3.3V)	?	4Gb/ ?	? / ?	?	45
SH7708 (3.3V)	?	4Gb/ ?	? / ?	?	60

Integrated Device Technology (IDT)
(Microprocessor division acquired by Via Technologies, Inc. in 1999)

CPU Type	Release Date	Max Mem Phys/Virt	Bus Int/Ext	Number of Transistors	Speeds MHz
WinChip C6 (3.3V)	05-97	? / ?	? / ?	5,400k	180,200,225,240
WinChip C6+ (3.3V)	?	? / ?	? / ?	5,800k	266,300
WinChip 2 (?)	?	? / ?	? / ?	?	266,300
WinChip 2 3D (?)	?	? / ?	? / ?	?	?
WinChip 2+ (?)	?	? / ?	? / ?	?	?
WinChip 2+ NB (?)	?	? / ?	? / ?	?	?
WinChip 3 (?)	2Q-99	? / ?	? / ?	?	266,300
WinChip 4 (?)	4Q-99	? / ?	? / ?	?	400+

Intel Corporation - see detailed specs on page 506

CPU Type	Release Date	Max Mem Phys/Virt	Bus Int/Ext	Number of Transistors	Speeds MHz
8080 (?)	04-74	64Kb/ ?	8/8	6k	2
8086 (?)	06-78	1Mb	16/16	29k	5,8,10
8088 (?)	06-79	1Mb	16/8	29k	5,8
80286 (?)	02-82	16Mb/1Gb	16/16	134k	6,10,12
80386DX (?)	10-85	4Gb/64Tb	32/32	275k	16,20,25,33
80386SX (?)	06-88	16Mb/256Gb	32/16	275k	16,20,25,33
80486DX (3.3 or 5V)	04-89	4Gb/64Tb	32/32	1,200k	25,33,50
80386SL (3.3 or 5V)	10-90	4Gb/64Tb	32/16	855k	20,25
80486SX (3.3 or 5V)	04-91	4Gb/64Tb	32/32	1,185k/900k	16,20,25,33
80486DX2(doubler, 3.3/5V)	03-92	4Gb/64Tb	32/32	1,200k	25/50,33/66
80486SL (3.3 or 5V)	10-92	64Mb/64Tb	32/32	1,400k	20,25,33
Pentium (3.3 or 5V)	03-93	4Gb/64Tb	32/64	3,100k	60,66
80486DX4 (3.3 or 5V)	03-94	4Gb/64Tb	32/32	1,600k	75,100
Pentium (3.3 or 5V)	03-94	4Gb/64Tb	32/32	3,200k	75,90,100,120
Pentium (3.3 or 5V)	06-95	4Gb/64Tb	32/32	3,300k	133,150,166,200
Pentium Pro (3.3V)	10-95	64Gb/64Tb	32/32	5,500k	150,166,180,200
Pentium w/MMX (3.3 or 5V)	01-97	4Gb/64Tb	32/32	4,500k	166,200,233
Pentium II (?)	05-97	64Gb/64Tb	32/32	7,500k	233,266,300,333,350,400,450
mobile Pentium w/MMX (?)	09-97	68Gb/ ?	32/32	4,500k	200,233,266,300
Celeron (2.0V)	04-98	64Gb/64Tb	32/32	7,500k	266,300,333,366,400,433,466,500,533
mobile Pentium II (1.7V)	04-98	68Gb/64Tb	32/32	7,500k	233,266,300

CPU's

CPU Type	Release Date	Max Mem Phys/Virt	Bus Int/Ext	Number of Transistors	Speeds MHz
Pentium II Xeon (?)	06-98	64Gb/64Tb	32/32	7,500k	400,450,500
Celeron (1.5V)	08-98	64Gb/64Tb	32/32	19,000k	533,566,600
Celeron (1.65V)	?	64Gb/64Tb	32/32	19,000k	633,667,700,733,766,800
Celeron (1.70V)	?	64Gb/64Tb	32/32	19,000k	533,566,600,633, 667,700,733,766,800,850
mobile Celeron (1.6V)	01-99	64Gb/64Tb	32/32	18,900k	266,300,333,366,400,433,450, 466,500,550,600,650,700,750
mobile Pentium II (1.6V)	01-99	64Gb/64Tb	32/32	27,400k	266,300,333,366,400,433
Pentium III (2.0V)	02-99	64Gb/64Tb	32/32	9,500k	450,500,533,550,600
Pentium III Xeon (2.0V)	03-99	64Gb/64Tb	32/32	9,500k	500,550
mobile Pentium III (1.6/1.35V)	10-99	64Gb/ ?	32/32	28,000k	400,450,500,600,650, 700,750,800,850,900,1000
Pentium III (1.65V)	10-99	64Gb/ ?	32/32	28,000k	533,550,600,650,667, 700,733,750,800,850,866,933
Pentium III Xeon (2.8V)	05-00	64Gb/64Tb	32/32	9,500k	600,667,700,733, 800,866,900,933,1000
Pentium 4 (1.7V)	06-00	64Gb/ ?	32/32	42,000k	1300,1400,1500
Pentium 4 (1.75V)	06-00	64Gb/ ?	32/32	42,000k	1300,1400,1500,1600, 1700,1800,1900,2000
Pentium III (1.70V)	07-00	64Gb/ ?	32/32	28,000k	533,550,600,650,667,700, 733,750,800,850,866,933,1000
Celeron (1.75V)	11-00	64Gb/64Tb	32/32	19,000k	566,600,633,667,700,733, 766,800,850,900,950,1000,1100
ultra low voltage Pent. III (0.9V)	01-01	64Gb/?	32/32	9,500k	500,600,700
low voltage Pent. III (1.15V)	02-01	64Gb/?	32/32	9,500k	700,750,800
Xeon (1.70V)	5-01	64Gb/ ?	32/32	?	1400,1500,1700,2000
Itanium (with HP) (2.1/3.3V) (aka Merced or P7)	05-01	? / ?	64/64	25,000k	733,800
Pentium III (1.75V)	06-01	64Gb/ ?	32/32	28,000k	600,700,733,750,800,850, 866,900,933,1000,1100,1130
Pentium III (1.60V)	06-01	64Gb/ ?	32/32	28,000k	500,550
Celeron (1.475V)	07-01	64Gb/64Tb	32/32	19,000k	900,1000,1100,1200
mobile Celeron (1.15V)	10-01	64Gb/64Tb	32/32	19,000k	650,733,866,1000, 1066,1133,1200,1333
Pentium III (1.475V)	12-01	64Gb/ ?	32/32	28,000k	1000,1130,1200,1333
Celeron (1.50V)	01-02	64Gb/64Tb	32/32	19,000k	1200,1300
Pentium 4 (1.75V) (aka Northwood)	02-02	64Gb/ ?	32/32	55,000k	2000,2200,2260,2400,2530, 2800,3000,3060,3200,3400
Pentium III (1.45V)	02-02	64Gb/ ?	32/32	28,000k	1130,1260,1400
Xeon (1.75V)	02-02	64Gb/ ?	32/32	?	1800,2000,2200,2400
Xeon MP (1.7/3.3V)	03-02	64Gb/4Gb	32/32	?.	1400,1500,1600
Mobile Pentium 4 M (1.30V)	03-02	64Gb/ ?	32/32	?	1400,1500,1600,1700, 1800,1900,2000,2500
Timna (?) Cancelled 09-00.					
Itanium 2 (with HP) (1.5V) (aka McKinley)	07-02	? / ?	64/64	221,000k	900,1000
Celeron (1.75V)	05-02	64Gb/64Tb	32/32	42,000k	1700,1800
Pentium M (1.0/0.84V) (aka Banias)	03-03	? / ?	64/64	77,000k	900,1000,1100,1200, 1300,1400,1500,1600,1700
Xeon (1.75V)	03-03	64Gb/ ?	32/32	?	3000,3060
Celeron (?)	06-03	? / ?	? / ?	?	2000,2100,2200,2300 2400,2500,2600
Itanium 2 (with HP) (1.3V) (aka Madison)	06-03	? / ?	64/64	410,000k	1300,1400,1500,1800
Xeon MP (1.7/3.3V)	06-03	64Gb/4Gb	32/32	?	2000,2500,2800
Xeon DP (?)	07-03	? / ?	? / ?	?	3060
low-voltage Itanium 2 (1.1V) (aka Deerfield)	09-03	? / ?	64/64	410,000k	1000,1400
Pentium 4E (1.25/1.4V) (aka Prescott)	02-04	64Gb/ ?	32/32	125,000k	2800,3000,3200, 3400,3600
Pentium 4Extreme Edition (?)	02-04	64Gb/ ?	32/32	178,000k	2000,2200,2260,2400,2500, 2530,2600,2660,2800,3000,3060,3200,3400
Pentium 4 520, 530,540,550,560			32/32		2800,3000,3200,3400,3600
Celeron (?) (aka Prescott)	2Q-04	? / ?	? / ?	?	2530,2660,2800,3060
mobile Celeron(?) (aka Prescott)	2Q-04	? / ?	? / ?	?	2530,2660,2800,3060
Xeon DP (?). (aka Nocona)	2Q-04	? / ?	? / ?	?	3200,3600
Itanium 2 MP (?) (aka Madison 9M)	3Q-04	? / ?	? / ?	?	1500,1600,1700
Itanium 2 DP (?) (aka Fanwood)	3Q-04	? / ?	? / ?	?	1200,1400,1600

CPU Specifications

CPU Type	Release Date	Max Mem Phys/Virt	Bus Int/Ext	Number of Transistors	Speeds MHz
low-voltage Fanwood (?)	3Q-04	? / ?	? / ?	?	1200
mobile Pentium M (?) (aka Dothan)	4Q-04	? / ?	64/64	140,000k	1600,1700,1800,1900
Xeon MP (?) (aka Potomac)	2005	? / ?	? / ?	?	4000
Xeon DP (?) (aka Jayhawk)	2005	? / ?	? / ?	?	?
Dual-core Itanium 2(?) (aka Montecito)	2005	? / ?	64/64	1,000,000k	1600,1800
Dual-processor Millington (?)	2005	? / ?	64/64	?	?
Pentium M (?) (aka Jonah)	2005	? / ?	64/64	?	?
Shavano (or Chivano) (?)	2005	? / ?	64/64	?	2000,2200
Tejas (?) (aka Pentium V)	2005	? / ?	32/64	?	4200 to 9200
Mobile Merom (?)	2005	? / ?	? / ?	?	?
Conroe (?)	2006	? / ?	? / ?	?	?
Nehalem (?)	2006	? / ?	32/64	?	9200 to 10200
dual-core Xeon (?) (aka Tulsa)	2006	? / ?	? / ?	?	?
Mmulticore Gilo (?)	2006	? / ?	? / ?	?	?
Multicore Itanium 2 (?) (aka Tukwila, formerly called Tanglewood)	2007	? / ?	64/64	?	?
Dimona (?)	2007	? / ?	64/64	?	?

Intel Corporation - Upgrade Chips

CPU Type	Release Date	Max Mem Phys/Virt	Bus Int/Ext	Number of Transistors	Speeds MHz
SX2 Overdrive (3.3 or 5V)	?	4Gb/64Tb	32/32	?	50
DX2 Overdrive (?)	?	4Gb/64Tb	32/32	900k	40,50,66
DX4 Overdrive (?)	10-94	4Gb/64Tb	32/32	1,600k	63,83
Pentium Overdrive (?)	?	4Gb/64Tb	32/32	3,300k	120,133
Pent. Over. w/ MMX (3.3V)	?	? / ?	? / ?	?	125,150,166
Pentium II Overdrive (?)	07-98	? / ?	? / ?	?	300,333

International Business Machines Corporation (IBM)

CPU Type	Release Date	Max Mem Phys/Virt	Bus Int/Ext	Number of Transistors	Speeds MHz
80386SLC (?)	12-91	16Mb/	32/16	800k	16,20,25
80486SLC2 (doubler,?)	09-92	16Mb/	32/16	1,425k	20/40,25/50,33/66
80486SLC3 (tripler,?)	?	16Mb/	32/16	1,425k	25/75
BL486DX (doubler,?)	?	4Gb/64Tb	32/32	~1,400k	25/50,33/66,40/80,50/100
BL486DX2 (doubler,?)	?	4Gb/64Tb	32/32	~1,400k	25/50,33/66,40/80
BL486DXV (3.3V)	?	4Gb/64Tb	32/32	~1,400k	33,40
BL486DX2V (3.3V)	?	4Gb/64Tb	32/32	~1,400k	25/50,33/66,40/80
6x86 (3.3V)	?	? / ?	32/32	?	120,133,150
PowerPC 603 (3.3V)	?	? / ?	32/32	1,600k	66,80
PowerPC 603 (3.3V)	?	? / ?	32/32	2,500k	100
PowerPC 604 (3.3V)	10-94	? / ?	32/32	3,600k	100,120,133,150,166,180
PowerPC 603e (3.3V)	10-95	4Gb/4Pb	32/32	2,600k	150,166,180,200, 225,233,240,250
6x86MX (3.3V)	05-97	? / ?	32/32	?	150,165,188
PowerPC 604e (3.3V)	06-97	4Gb / ?	32/32	5,100k	160,180,200,225,233, 240,250,300,333,350
PowerPC 740 (2.5/3.3/3.7V)	?	4Gb/4Eb	32/32	6,350k	200,233,266,300,333, 366,400,466,500
PowerPC 750 (2.0/3.3V)	07-97	4Gb/4Eb	32/32	6,350k	200,233,250,266,275,300,333, 350,366,375,400,450,466,500
PowerPC 620 (3.3V)	?	? / ?	32/32	7,000k	?
Power 3 (?)	10-97	? / ?	64/64	?	500
PowerPC 750CX (1.8/2.5V)	?	4Gb/4Eb	32/32	20,000k	350,366,400,450, 466,500,550
PowerPC 750CXe (1.8/2.5V)	?	4Gb/4Eb	32/32	20,000k	400,500,600,667,700
PowerPC 750FX (1.40V)	04-02	4Gb/4Eb	32/64	38,000k	600,700,733,800
Power4 (1.5V)	12-01	? / ?	64/64	170,000k	1000,1100,1300
Power4+ (?)	11-02	? / ?	? / ?	184,000k	1200,1450,1500,1700
PowerPC 970 (1.3V)(aka G5)	06-03	? / ?	64/64	58,000k	1400,1600,1800,2000
PowerPC 970 FX (1.3V) (aka G5)	02-04	4Tb/ ?	64/64	58,000k+	2500,3000
Power5 (?)	2004	? / ?	? / ?	276,000k	1400 to 2000
multi-core Power5+ (?)	2005	? / ?	? / ?	?	2000 to 3000
Power6 (?)	2006	? / ?	? / ?	?	?
The Cell (with Sony for PlayStation 4)	2007	? / ?	? / ?	?	?

International Meta Systems, Inc.
(Chapter 11 bankruptcy in 1998.)

CPU Type	Release Date	Max Mem Phys/Virt	Bus Int/Ext	Number of Transistors	Speeds MHz
Meta 6000 (?)	01-98	? / ?	? / ?	?	225

CPU Type	Release Date	Max Mem Phys/Virt	Bus Int/Ext	Number of Transistors	Speeds MHz
Kingston Technology Company - Upgrade Chips					
SLC/Now! (?)	?	? / ?	32/32	?	20,25,50
486/Now! (?)	?	? / ?	? / ?	?	25,33
Lightning 486 (?)	?	? / ?	? / ?	?	66
MCMaster (?)	?	? / ?	? / ?	?	50,66
TurboChip 486 (?)	?	? / ?	? / ?	?	75,100
TurboChip 133 (?)	uses an AMD 5x86 processor				133
TurboChip 233 (?)	uses an Intel Pentium processor				233
TurboChip 366 (?)	uses an AMD-K6-II				166
TurboChip 400 (?)	uses an AMD-K6-II				400

Lenslet Labs (Ramat-Gan, Israel)
EnLight256 (40w) - 11-03 - Worlds first optical, laser-based digital signal processor.

CPU Type	Release Date	Max Mem Phys/Virt	Bus Int/Ext	Number of Transistors	Speeds MHz
MCST (Moscow, Russia)					
MCST-R80 (?)	1998	? / ?	? / ?	?	80
MCST-R150 (?)	2001	? / ?	? / ?	?	150
MCST-R500 (?)	2003	? / ?	? / ?	?	500
MCST-R1000 (?)	2003	? / ?	? / ?	?	1000
Elbrus (?)	2003	? / ?	? / ?	?	300
E2K (?)	2004	? / ?	? / ?	?	1200

CPU Type	Release Date	Max Mem Phys/Virt	Bus Int/Ext	Number of Transistors	Speeds MHz
MIPS Technologies, Inc.					
R2000 (?)	1986	? / ?	32/32	110k	8
R3000 (5V)	1988	? / ?	32/32	?	40
R6000 (?)	1991	? / ?	32/32	?	67
R4000 (?)	1992	? / ?	64/64	1,100k	100
R4400 (3.3V)	1992	64Gb/?	64/64	2,300k	150,200,250
R4200 (3.3V)	1993	? / ?	64/64	1,400k	80
R4600 (3.3V)	1994	? / ?	64/64	1,850k	133,150
R8000 (3.3V)	1994	? / ?	64/64	3,430k	75,90
R4300i (3.3V)	1995	? / ?	64/64	1,700k	100,133
R4700 (3.3V)	1995	? / ?	64/64	1,800k	175
R5000 (3.3V)	1996	? / ?	64/64	3,600k	180,200,250
R10000 (3.3V)	1996	? / ?	64/64	6,800k	150,175,200,275
R5000A (3.3V)	1997	? / ?	64/64	3,600k	?
RM7000 (?)	1997	? / ?	64/64	?	300
R12000 (3.3V)	1998	? / ?	64/64	?	300
H1 Series (?)	1999	? / ?	64/64	?	?
H2 Series (?)	2000	? / ?	64/64	?	?

CPU Type	Release Date	Max Mem Phys/Virt	Bus Int/Ext	Number of Transistors	Speeds MHz
Motorola Communications and Electronics, Inc.					
68020 (5V)	1985	? / ?	? / ?	?	25
68030 (5V)	?	? / ?	? / ?	270k	50
68040 (5V)	1989	? / ?	? / ?	1,200k	25
68060 (3.3V)	1993	? / ?	? / ?	2,400k	50
PowerPC 601 (3.6V)	1993	? / ?	32/64	2,800k	66,80,100
PowerPC 603 (3.3V)	1994	4Gb/4Pb	32/64	1,600k	50,66,80
PowerPC 604 (3.3V)	1994	4Gb/4Pb	32/64	3,600k	100,133,180
PowerPC 602 (3.3V)	1995	4Gb/4Pb	32/64	1,000k	66
PowerPC 603e (3.3V)	1995	4Gb/4Pb	32/64	2,600k	100,120,133,166, 180,200,250,275,300
PowerPC 620 (3.3V)	1995	1Tb/1Hb	64/64	7,000k	133,200
PowerPC 604e (3.3V)	1996	4Gb/4Pb	32/64	5,100k	180,200,225,233,250,300,350
PowerPC 630 (3.3V)	1997	? / ?	? / ?	?	600
PowerPC 740 (2.6/3.3V)	1998	4Gb/?	32/64	6,500k	200,233,266,300
PowerPC 750 (2.6/3.3V)	1998	4Gb/?	32/64	6,350k	200,233,266,300,333,366,400
PowerPC G3 (2.0V)	?	? / ?	32/32	6,500k	200 to 700
PowerPC G4 (1.8V)	?	? / ?	32/32	10,500k	350 to 550
(Motorola sold off its microprocessor division in 2003).					

CPU Type	Release Date	Max Mem Phys/Virt	Bus Int/Ext	Number of Transistors	Speeds MHz
NEC America, Inc.					
V3 (?)	03-84	1Mb	16/16	63k	8,10
V20 (?)	03-84	1Mb	16/8	63k	8,10
VR4100 (3.3V)	?	? / ?	64/64	?	40
VR4101 (3.3V)	?	? / ?	64/64	?	33
VR4300 (3.3V)	?	? / ?	64/64	?	100,133
VR4400 (3.3V)	?	? / ?	64/64	?	200,250
VR4400MC (3.3V)	?	? / ?	64/64	?	200
VR5000 (3.3V)	?	? / ?	64/64	?	150,180,200
VR10000 (2.6/3.3V)	?	? / ?	64/64	?	180,200,225,250
VR12000 (2.6/3.3V)	?	? / ?	64/64	?	300

CPU Type	Release Date	Max Mem Phys/Virt	Bus Int/Ext	Number of Transistors	Speeds MHz

NexGen, Inc.
(Company acquired by Advanced Micro Devices in 1995.)

CPU Type	Release Date	Max Mem Phys/Virt	Bus Int/Ext	Number of Transistors	Speeds MHz
Nx586 (?)	?	? / ?	32/32	3,500k	70,75,84,93

Philips Semiconductor

CPU Type	Release Date	Max Mem Phys/Virt	Bus Int/Ext	Number of Transistors	Speeds MHz
TriMedia TM-1000 (?)	07-97	? / ?	? / ?	5,500k	100,133,166
(Multimedia accelerator chip)

Rise Technology
(CPU technology sold to Silicon Integrated Systems 10-99.)

CPU Type	Release Date	Max Mem Phys/Virt	Bus Int/Ext	Number of Transistors	Speeds MHz
mP6 (3.3/2.8V)	03-99	? / ?	? / ?	?	166,233,266,333,366
iDragon mP6 IA (2.2/3.3V)	?	? / ?	? / ?	?	133,150,166,190,200, 238,250,285,300,333,350

Ross Technology, Inc. - Upgrade Chips
(Ross Technology closed down in 1998.)

CPU Type	Release Date	Max Mem Phys/Virt	Bus Int/Ext	Number of Transistors	Speeds MHz
hyperSPARC (5V)	1994	? / ?	32/32	1,500k	90,100,125,142,150,180,200
Viper (?)	1999	? / ?	64/64	?	?

SGS-Thomson Microelectronics

CPU Type	Release Date	Max Mem Phys/Virt	Bus Int/Ext	Number of Transistors	Speeds MHz
ST486DX (5V)	?	4Gb/ ?	32/32	?	33,40,50
ST486DX2 (doubler,5V)	?	4Gb/ ?	32/32	?	50,66,80
ST6x86 (3.3V)	?	? / ?	64/32	?	80,100,110,120,133,150
MPact R (3.3V)	04-97	? / ?	32	?	75
(Multimedia co-processor developed with Chromatic Research, Inc.)

Sun Microsystems, Inc.

CPU Type	Release Date	Max Mem Phys/Virt	Bus Int/Ext	Number of Transistors	Speeds MHz
Thunder I (5V)	1993	? / ?	32/32	6,000k	50
microSPARC-II (?)	1994	? / ?	32/32	2,300k	85,100
SuperSPARC-II (5V)	1995	? / ?	32/32	3,100k	75,90
UltraSPARC-I (1.9/3.3V)	10-95	? / ?	64/64	5,200k	143,167,182,200
UltraSPARC-II (3.3V)	10-95	? / ?	64/64	5,400k	250,300,330,360,400,450
UltraSPARC-IIi (3.3V)	10-96	? / ?	64/64	?	270,300,333,360,440,480
microSPARC-IIep (3.3V)	?	? / ?	32/32	?	100 to 125
UltraSPARC-III (1.7/1.5V)	1999	16Gb/ ?	64/64	29,000k	600,750,900
UltraSPARC-III Cu (1.7/1.5V)	07-01	16Gb/ ?	64/64	29,000k	600,750,900,1050,1200,1500
UltraSPARC-IIIi (?)	?	16Gb/ ?	64/64	87,500k	1000
dual-core UltraSPARC-IV (1.35V)	02-04	16Gb/ ?	64/64	66,000k	1050,1200,1500, 1600,2000
(aka Jaguar)					
UltraSPARC-IV+ (?)	2004	? / ?	64/64	?	?
(aka Panther)					
UltraSPARC-IV-? (?)	2004	? / ?	64/64	?	?
(aka Gemini)					
UltraSPARC-V (?)	2005	? / ?	64/64	?	1800,2100,2400,3000
UltraSPARC-VI (?)	2006	? / ?	64/64	?	?
(aka Niagara)					
UltraSPARC-VII (?)	2007	? / ?	64/64	?	?
(aka Rock)					

Texas Instruments, Inc.

CPU Type	Release Date	Max Mem Phys/Virt	Bus Int/Ext	Number of Transistors	Speeds MHz
TI486SXLC (3.3V)	?	16Mb/ ?	32/16	?	25,33
TX486SXLC (5V)	?	16Mb/ ?	32/16	?	33
TX486SXLC2 (doubler,5V)	?	16Mb/ ?	32/16	?	25/50
TX486SL (3.3V)	?	4Gb/ ?	32/32	?	33
TX486SL (5V)	?	4Gb/ ?	32/32	?	40
TX486SXL2 (doubler,3.3V)	?	4Gb/ ?	32/32	?	20/40
TX486SXL2 (doubler,5V)	?	4Gb/ ?	32/32	?	25/50

Texas Instruments, Inc. - Upgrade Chips

CPU Type	Release Date	Max Mem Phys/Virt	Bus Int/Ext	Number of Transistors	Speeds MHz
TI486SLC/E (5V)	?	16Mb/ ?	32/16	?	25,33
TI486SLC/E-V (3.3V)	?	16Mb/ ?	32/16	?	25
TI486DLC/E (5V)	?	4Gb/ ?	32/32	?	33,40
TI486DLC/E-V (3.3V)	?	4Gb/ ?	32/32	?	25,33

Transmeta Corporation

CPU Type	Release Date	Max Mem Phys/Virt	Bus Int/Ext	Number of Transistors	Speeds MHz
Crusoe TM3200 (1.5/3.3V)	01-00	? / ?	32/32	?	333,366,400
Crusoe TM5400 (1.2-1.6/3.3V)	01-00	? / ?	32/32	36,800k	500 to 700
Crusoe TM5600 (1.2-1.6/3.3V)	10-00	? / ?	32/32	36,800k	300 to 600
Crusoe TM5500 (0.9-1.3/3.3V)	06-01	? / ?	32/32	36,800k	667,700,733,800
Crusoe TM5800 (0.8-1.3/3.3V)	06-01	? / ?	32/32	36,800k	667,700,733,800,900,1000
Crusoe TM6000 (?)	2H-02	? / ?	? / ?	?	1000
Efficeon TM8600(?)	09-03	? / ?	? / ?	?	1000,1100,1200,1300

CPU Type	Release Date	Max Mem Phys/Virt	Bus Int/Ext	Number of Transistors	Speeds MHz
(aka Astro)					
Efficeon TM8800 (?)	2H-04	? / ?	? / ?	?	1400,1600,1800,2000

Trinity Works - Upgrade Chips

CPU Type	Release Date	Max Mem Phys/Virt	Bus Int/Ext	Number of Transistors	Speeds MHz
PowerStacker 5x86 (?)	?	? / ?	? / ?	?	64,80,100,133
PowerStacker for Pentium (?)	?	? / ?	? / ?	?	180,200

Via Technologies, Inc.

CPU Type	Release Date	Max Mem Phys/Virt	Bus Int/Ext	Number of Transistors	Speeds MHz
Via Cyrix III (1.9/3.3V)	02-00	4Gb/4Gb	32/32	11,300k	400,500,550,600
(aka Samuel I, C5A)					650,667,700,733,750,800
Via Cyrix III (1.6/3.3V)	03-01	4Gb/4Gb	32/32	15,800k	700,733,750,800
(aka Samuel II, C5B)					
Via Cyrix III (1.35V)	06-01	4Gb/4Gb	32/32	15,900k	800,850,866
(aka Ezra, C5C)					
Via Cyrix III (1.35/3.3V)	09-01	4Gb/4Gb	32/32	15,500k.	800,866,900,933
(aka Ezra-T, Samuel 3, C5M)					1000,1133
Via C3 (1.4/3.3V)	01-03	4Gb/4Gb	32/32	20,500k.	1000,1060,1130,
(aka Nehemiah, C5X)					1200,1400
Via Antaur mobile (1.25V)	07-03	? / ?	? / ?	20,400k	1000,1130,1200
Via C4 (?)	2H-04	? / ?	? / ?	?	2000+
(aka Ester, C5XL)					

Math Coprocessor Types

CPU Type	CoProcessor
8086,8088,V20 & V30	8087
80286	80287XL
80386SX & SL	80387SX
80386DX	80387DX
80486SX	80487SX
80486DX	Built In
Pentium - all versions are Built In	

CPU's

AMD CPU Identification

AMD 80L286
AT Class
6-10-12 MHz

AMD K5
PR75-PR133

AMD K6 MMX
PR166-233 MHz

AMD K6-2
266-450 MHz

CPU's

AMD K6-III
400-500 MHz

AMD 762
Socket A

AMD 766
Socket A

AMD Athlon
K7 (Classic)
Slot A CPU

AMD Duron
Socket A

AMD Athlon
Socket A

AMD Athlon XP
Socket A

AMD CPU Identification

AMD Opteron 64 - Socket 64

AMD Athlon 64 - Socket 64

AMD Athlon 64 FX - Socket 64FX

AMD Mobile Athlon 64
Front

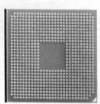

AMD Mobile Athlon 64
Back

CYRIX and VIA CPU Identification

Cyrix 486
25-80 MHz

Cyrix 586
100-120 MHz

Cyrix 6x86 M1
166-200 MHz

Cyrix 6x86 MX
150-266 MHz

Cyrix MII
300-350 MHz

Cyrix Media GX-MMX
120-233 MHz

Via C3
733-75- MHz

Via Apollo Pro
Socket 370

Via Apollo KT
Socket A

Intel CPU Identification

Intel 8088 - XT Class
5 and 8 MHz
(Gasp! do you remember
that far back!!!)

Intel 80386DX
16-20-25-33 MHz

Intel 80486DX2
25/50, 33/66 MHz

Intel Pentium P54C
75-200 MHz

Intel Pentium P55C
MMX 150-233 MHz

Intel Pentium III
500 MHz-1 GHz
Socket 370

Intel Pentium 3
1.13 Ghz-1.4Ghz
Socket 370

Intel Pentium 4
1.3-1.7 GHz
Socket 370

Intel Pentium 4
Socket 478

Intel Xeon
Socket 370

Intel Itanium

Intel CPU Form Factor Identification

S.E.C.C. Form Factor
Front side

Intel Pentium II
233-450 MHz
242 contacts

Intel Pentium II Xeon
Pentium III Xeon
330 contacts

S.E.C.C. Form Factor
Back side

Processor is completely
covered by a black plastic
shroud with an active heatsink
and fan. The gold finger
contacts are seated inside
the plastic housing.

S.E.C.C.2 Form Factor
Front side

Intel Pentium II
242 contacts

Intel Pentium III
450-550 MHz
242 contacts

S.E.C.C.2 Form Factor
Back side

Similar to the S.E.C.C. but
the goldfinger contacts are
exposed. Fan mounts with
4 pins that go through the
black plastic shroud and
circuit board.

Intel
Pentium III
Xeon
500-550 MHz

Intel CPU Form Factor Identification

S.E.P Form Factor
Front Side

Intel Celeron
242 contacts

S.E.P Form Factor
Back side

Processor is not completely
covered by the black plastic
shroud and circuit board is
visible from the bottom side.

Micro FC-BGA - front
pins (socket)
Mobile

Micro FC-BGA - back
pins (socket)
Mobile

MMC2 - front
pins (socket)
Mobile

Micro BGA2 - front
pins (socket)
Mobile

Micro BGA2 - back
pins (socket)
Mobile

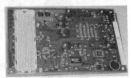

MMC2 - back
pins (socket)
Mobile

Intel CPU Form Factor Identification

FC-PGA - front
370 pins (socket 370)
Pentium III and Celeron

FC-PGA - back
370 pins (socket 370)
Pentium III and Celeron

PGA - front
603 pins (socket 603)
Xeon

FC-PGA2 - front
478 pins (socket 478)
Pentium 4

FC-PGA2 - back
478 pins (socket 478)
Pentium 4

PGA - back
603 pins (socket 603)
Xeon

FC-PGA2 - front
370 pins (socket 370)
Celeron

FC-PGA2 - back
370 pins (socket 370)
Celeron

PPGA - front
370 pins (socket 370)
Celeron

OOI - front
423 pins (socket 423)
Pentium 4

OOI - back
423 pins (socket 423)
Pentium 4

PPGA - back
370 pins (socket 370)
Celeron

CPU's

Intel CPU Form Factor Identification

FC-LGA4 - front
775 pins (socket 775)
Pentium 4 520,etc

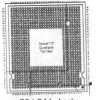

Socket 775
Quadrants
Top View

FC-LGA4 - back
775 pins (socket 775)
Pentium 4 520,etc

Intel Pentium CPU Specs

Intel sSpec Number	CPU Speed	Bus Speed	L2 Cache Size	Package Type
Intel Celeron D				
SL7C4	2.40G	533M	256K	478 pin PPGA
SL7C5	2.53G	533M	256K	478 pin PPGA
SL7C6	2.66G	533M	256K	478 pin PPGA
SL7C7	2.80G	533M	256K	478 pin PPGA
Intel Pentium 4 Extreme Edition				
SL7AA	3.20G	800M	2M	478 pin PPGA FC-PGA2
SL7CH	3.40G	800M	2M	478 pin PPGA
SL7GD	3.40G	800M	2M	775 pin PLGA
Intel Pentium 4				
SL4QD	1.30G	400M	256K	423 pin PPGA INT2
SL4SC	1.40G	400M	0K	423 pin PPGA INT2
SL4SF	1.30G	400M	0K	423 pin PPGA INT2
SL4SG	1.40G	400M	256K	423 pin PPGA INT2
SL4SH	1.50G	400M	256K	423 pin PPGA INT2
SL4TY	1.50G	400M	0K	423 pin PPGA INT2
SL4WS	1.40G	400M	256K	423 pin PPGA INT2
SL4WT	1.50G	400M	256K	423 pin PPGA INT2
SL4WU	1.60G	400M	256K	423 pin PPGA INT2
SL4WV	1.80G	400M	256K	423 pin PPGA INT2
SL4X2	1.40G	400M	256K	423 pin PPGA INT2
SL4X3	1.50G	400M	256K	423 pin PPGA INT2
SL4X4	1.60G	400M	256K	423 pin PPGA INT2
SL4X5	1.80G	400M	256K	423 pin PPGA INT2
SL57V	1.70G	400M	256K	423 pin PPGA INT2
SL57W	1.70G	400M	256K	423 pin PPGA INT2
SL59U	1.70G	400M	256K	478 pin PPGA FC-PGA2
SL59V	1.50G	400M	256K	FC-PGA2 478-pin
SL59X	1.70G	400M	256K	478 pin PPGA FC-PGA2
SL5FW	1.30G	400M	256K	423 pin PPGA INT2
SL5GC	1.30G	400M	256K	OOI 423-pin
SL5N7	1.40G	400M	0K	478 pin PPGA FC-PGA2
SL5N8	1.60G	400M	256K	478 pin PPGA FC-PGA2
SL5N9	1.70G	400M	256K	478 pin PPGA FC-PGA2
SL5SX	1.50G	400M	256K	423 pin PPGA INT3
SL5SY	1.70G	400M	256K	423 pin PPGA INT3
SL5SZ	2.00G	400M	256K	423 pin PPGA INT3
SL5TG	1.40G	400M	256K	478 pin PPGA FC-PGA2
SL5TJ	1.50G	400M	256K	478 pin PPGA FC-PGA2
SL5TK	1.70G	400M	256K	478 pin PPGA FC-PGA2
SL5TL	2.00G	400M	256K	478 pin PPGA FC-PGA2
SL5TN	1.50G	400M	0K	423 pin PPGA INT3
SL5TP	1.70G	400M	256K	423 pin PPGA INT3
SL5TQ	2.00G	400M	256K	423 pin PPGA INT3
SL5UE	1.40G	400M	0K	478 pin PPGA FC-PGA2
SL5UF	1.50G	400M	0K	478 pin PPGA FC-PGA2
SL5UG	1.70G	400M	256K	478 pin PPGA FC-PGA2
SL5UH	2.00G	400M	256K	478 pin PPGA FC-PGA2
SL5UJ	1.60G	400M	256K	478 pin PPGA FC-PGA2
SL5UK	1.80G	400M	256K	478 pin PPGA FC-PGA2
SL5UL	1.60G	400M	256K	423 pin PPGA INT3
SL5UM	1.80G	400M	256K	423 pin PPGA INT3
SL5US	1.60G	400M	256K	478 pin PPGA FC-PGA2
SL5UT	1.80G	400M	256K	478 pin PPGA FC-PGA2
SL5UV	1.80G	400M	256K	478 pin PPGA FC-PGA2
SL5UW	1.60G	400M	256K	478 pin PPGA FC-PGA2
SL5VH	1.60G	400M	256K	478 pin PPGA FC-PGA2
SL5VJ	1.80G	400M	256K	478 pin PPGA FC-PGA2
SL5VK	1.90G	400M	256K	478 pin PPGA FC-PGA2
SL5VL	1.60G	400M	256K	423 pin PPGA INT3
SL5VM	1.80G	400M	256K	423 pin PPGA INT3
SL5VN	1.90G	400M	256K	423 pin PPGA INT3
SL5WG	1.90G	400M	256K	478 pin PPGA FC-PGA2
SL5WH	1.90G	400M	256K	423 pin PPGA INT3
SL5YR	2.00G	400M	512K	478 pin PPGA FC-PGA2
SL5YS	2.20G	400M	512K	478 pin PPGA FC-PGA2
SL5ZT	2.00G	400M	512K	478 pin PPGA FC-PGA2
SL5ZU	2.20G	400M	512K	478 pin PPGA FC-PGA2
SL62P	1.80G	400M	512K	478 pin PPGA FC-PGA2
SL62Q	2.00G	400M	512K	478 pin PPGA FC-PGA2
SL62R	1.80G	400M	512K	478 pin PPGA FC-PGA2
SL62S	1.60G	400M	512K	478 pin PPGA FC-PGA2
SL62Y	1.50G	400M	256K	478 pin PPGA FC-PGA2
SL62Z	1.70G	400M	256K	478 pin PPGA FC-PGA2
SL63X	1.80G	400M	512K	478 pin PPGA FC-PGA2
SL65R	2.40G	400M	512K	478 pin PPGA FC-PGA2
SL668	1.60G	400M	512K	478 pin PPGA FC-PGA2
SL66Q	1.80G	400M	512K	478 pin PPGA FC-PGA2
SL66R	2.00G	400M	512K	478 pin PPGA FC-PGA2
SL66S	2.20G	400M	512K	478 pin PPGA FC-PGA2
SL66T	2.40G	400M	512K	478 pin PPGA FC-PGA2
SL679	1.60G	400M	256K	478 pin PPGA FC-PGA2
SL67A	1.70G	400M	256K	478 pin PPGA FC-PGA2
SL67B	1.80G	400M	256K	478 pin PPGA FC-PGA2
SL67C	1.90G	400M	256K	478 pin PPGA FC-PGA2
SL67R	2.40G	400M	512K	478 pin PPGA FC-PGA2
SL67Y	2.26G	533M	512K	478 pin PPGA FC-PGA2
SL67Z	2.40G	533M	512K	478 pin PPGA FC-PGA2
SL682	2.53G	533M	512K	478 pin PPGA FC-PGA2
SL683	2.26G	533M	512K	478 pin PPGA FC-PGA2

Intel sSpec Number	CPU Speed	Bus Speed	L2 Cache Size	Package Type
SL684	2.40G	533M	512K	478 pin PPGA FC-PGA2
SL685	2.53G	533M	512K	478 pin PPGA FC-PGA2
SL68Q	1.80G	400M	512K	478 pin PPGA FC-PGA2
SL68R	2.00G	400M	512K	478 pin PPGA FC-PGA2
SL68S	2.20G	400M	512K	478 pin PPGA FC-PGA2
SL68T	2.40G	400M	512K	478 pin PPGA FC-PGA2
SL6BA	1.50G	400M	256K	478 pin PPGA FC-PGA2
SL6BC	1.60G	400M	256K	478 pin PPGA FC-PGA2
SL6BD	1.70G	400M	256K	478 pin PPGA FC-PGA2
SL6BE	1.80G	400M	256K	478 pin PPGA FC-PGA2
SL6BF	1.90G	400M	256K	478 pin PPGA FC-PGA2
SL6D6	2.26G	533M	512K	478 pin PPGA FC-PGA2
SL6D7	2.40G	533M	512K	478 pin PPGA FC-PGA2
SL6D8	2.53G	533M	512K	478 pin PPGA FC-PGA2
SL6DU	2.26G	533M	512K	478 pin PPGA FC-PGA2
SL6DV	2.40G	533M	512K	478 pin PPGA FC-PGA2
SL6DW	2.53G	533M	512K	478 pin PPGA FC-PGA2
SL6DX	2.66G	533M	512K	478 pin PPGA FC-PGA2
SL6E6	1.80G	400M	512K	478 pin PPGA FC-PGA2
SL6E7	2.00G	400M	512K	478 pin PPGA FC-PGA2
SL6E8	2.20G	400M	512K	478 pin PPGA FC-PGA2
SL6E9	2.40G	400M	512K	478 pin PPGA FC-PGA2
SL6EB	2.50G	400M	512K	478 pin PPGA FC-PGA2
SL6EE	2.26G	533M	512K	478 pin PPGA FC-PGA2
SL6EF	2.40G	533M	512K	478 pin PPGA FC-PGA2
SL6EG	2.53G	533M	512K	478 pin PPGA FC-PGA2
SL6EH	2.66G	533M	512K	478 pin PPGA FC-PGA2
SL6ET	2.26G	533M	512K	478 pin PPGA FC-PGA2
SL6EU	2.40G	533M	512K	478 pin PPGA FC-PGA2
SL6EV	2.53G	533M	512K	478 pin PPGA FC-PGA2
SL6GQ	2.00G	400M	512K	478 pin PPGA FC-PGA2
SL6GR	2.20G	400M	512K	478 pin PPGA FC-PGA2
SL6GS	2.40G	400M	512K	478 pin PPGA FC-PGA2
SL6GT	2.50G	400M	512K	478 pin PPGA FC-PGA2
SL6GU	2.60G	400M	512K	478 pin PPGA FC-PGA2
SL6HB	2.60G	400M	512K	478 pin PPGA FC-PGA2
SL6HL	2.80G	533M	512K	478 pin PPGA FC-PGA2
SL6JJ	3.06G	533M	512K	478 pin PPGA FC-PGA2
SL6K6	2.40G	533M	512K	478 pin PPGA FC-PGA2
SL6K7	3.06G	533M	512K	478 pin PPGA FC-PGA2
SL6LA	1.80G	400M	512K	478 pin PPGA
SL6PB	2.26G	533M	512K	478 pin PPGA FC-PGA2
SL6PC	2.40G	533M	512K	478 pin PPGA FC-PGA2
SL6PD	2.53G	533M	512K	478 pin PPGA FC-PGA2
SL6PE	2.66G	533M	512K	478 pin PPGA FC-PGA2
SL6PF	2.80G	533M	512K	478 pin PPGA FC-PGA2
SL6PG	3.06G	533M	512K	478 pin PPGA FC-PGA2
SL6PK	2.00G	400M	512K	478 pin PPGA FC-PGA2
SL6PL	2.20G	400M	512K	478 pin PPGA FC-PGA2
SL6PM	2.40G	400M	512K	478 pin PPGA FC-PGA2
SL6PN	2.50G	400M	512K	478 pin PPGA FC-PGA2
SL6PP	2.60G	400M	512K	478 pin PPGA FC-PGA2
SL6PQ	1.80G	400M	512K	478 pin PPGA FC-PGA2
SL6Q7	2.26G	533M	512K	478 pin PPGA FC-PGA2
SL6Q8	2.40G	533M	512K	478 pin PPGA FC-PGA2
SL6Q9	2.53G	533M	512K	478 pin PPGA FC-PGA2
SL6QA	2.66G	533M	512K	478 pin PPGA FC-PGA2
SL6QB	2.80G	533M	512K	478 pin PPGA FC-PGA2
SL6QC	3.06G	533M	512K	478 pin PPGA FC-PGA2
SL6QL	1.80G	400M	512K	478 pin PPGA FC-PGA2
SL6QM	2.00G	400M	512K	478 pin PPGA FC-PGA2
SL6QN	2.20G	400M	512K	478 pin PPGA FC-PGA2
SL6QP	2.40G	400M	512K	478 pin PPGA FC-PGA2
SL6QQ	2.50G	400M	512K	478 pin PPGA FC-PGA2
SL6QR	2.60G	400M	512K	478 pin PPGA FC-PGA2
SL6RY	2.26G	533M	512K	478 pin PPGA FC-PGA2
SL6RZ	2.40G	533M	512K	478 pin PPGA FC-PGA2
SL6S2	2.53G	533M	512K	478 pin PPGA FC-PGA2
SL6S3	2.66G	533M	512K	478 pin PPGA FC-PGA2
SL6S4	2.80G	533M	512K	478 pin PPGA FC-PGA2
SL6S5	3.06G	533M	512K	478 pin PPGA FC-PGA2
SL6S6	1.80G	400M	512K	478 pin PPGA FC-PGA2
SL6S7	2.00G	400M	512K	478 pin PPGA FC-PGA2
SL6S8	2.20G	400M	512K	478 pin PPGA FC-PGA2
SL6S9	2.40G	400M	512K	478 pin PPGA FC-PGA2
SL6SA	2.50G	400M	512K	478 pin PPGA FC-PGA2
SL6SB	2.60G	400M	512K	478 pin PPGA FC-PGA2
SL6SH	2.40G	533M	512K	478 pin PPGA FC-PGA2
SL6SJ	2.53G	533M	512K	478 pin PPGA FC-PGA2
SL6SK	2.66G	533M	512K	478 pin PPGA FC-PGA2
SL6SL	2.80G	533M	512K	478 pin PPGA FC-PGA2
SL6SM	3.06G	533M	512K	478 pin PPGA FC-PGA2
SL6SN	1.80G	400M	512K	478 pin PPGA FC-PGA2
SL6SP	2.00G	400M	512K	478 pin PPGA FC-PGA2
SL6SR	2.40G	400M	512K	478 pin PPGA FC-PGA2
SL6WE	3.20G	800M	512K	478 pin PPGA
SL6WF	2.40G	800M	512K	478 pin PPGA FC-PGA2
SL6WG	3.20G	800M	512K	478 pin PPGA FC-PGA2
SL6WH	2.60G	800M	512K	478 pin PPGA FC-PGA2
SL6WJ	2.80G	800M	512K	478 pin PPGA FC-PGA2
SL6WK	3.00G	800M	512K	478 pin PPGA FC-PGA2
SL6WR	2.40G	800M	512K	478 pin PPGA FC-PGA2
SL6WS	2.60G	800M	512K	478 pin PPGA FC-PGA2
SL6WT	2.80G	800M	512K	478 pin PPGA FC-PGA2
SL6WU	3.00G	800M	512K	478 pin PPGA
SL6WZ	2.60G	400M	512K	478 pin PPGA
SL6Z3	2.40G	800M	512K	478 pin PPGA FC-PGA2
SL6Z5	2.80G	800M	512K	478 pin PPGA FC-PGA2
SL78Z	3.00G	800M	512K	478 pin PPGA
SL792	3.20G	800M	512K	478 pin PPGA
SL793	3.40G	800M	512K	478 pin PPGA
SL79B	2.40G	533M	512K	478 pin PPGA
SL79K	2.80G	800M	1M	478 pin PPGA
SL79L	3.00G	800M	1M	478 pin PPGA
SL7B8	3.20G	800M	1M	478 pin PPGA
SL7B9	3.40G	800M	1M	478 pin PPGA
SL7D8	2.80G	533M	1M	478 pin PPGA
SL7E8	2.40G	533M	1M	478 pin PPGA
SL7J5	2.80G	800M	1M	775 pin PLGA
SL7J6	3.00G	800M	1M	775 pin PLGA
SL7J7	3.20G	800M	1M	775 pin PLGA
SL7J8	3.40G	800M	1M	775 pin PLGA
SL7J9	3.60G	800M	1M	775 pin PLGA
SL7K9	2.80G	533M	1M	478 pin PPGA
SL7KC	3.20G	800M	1M	775 pin PLGA
SL7KJ	2.80G	800M	1M	775 pin PLGA
SL7KK	3.00G	800M	1M	775 pin PLGA
SL7KL	3.20G	800M	1M	775 pin PLGA
SL7KM	3.40G	800M	1M	775 pin PLGA
SL7KN	3.60G	800M	1M	775 pin PLGA
Intel Celeron				
SL27Z	300M	66M	none	S.E.P.P.
SL2QG	266M	66M	N/A	S.E.P.P.
SL2SY	266M	66M	N/A	S.E.P.P.
SL2TR	266M	66M	N/A	S.E.P.P.
SL2WM	300M	66M	128K	S.E.P.P.
SL2WN	333M	66M	128K	S.E.P.P.
SL2X8	300M	66M	none	S.E.P.P.
SL2Y2	300M	66M	none	S.E.P.P.
SL2YN	266M	66M	N/A	S.E.P.P.
SL2YP	300M	66M	none	S.E.P.P.
SL2Z7	300M	66M	N/A	S.E.P.P.
SL32A	300M	66M	128K	S.E.P.P.
SL32B	333M	66M	128K	S.E.P.P.
SL35Q	300M	66M	128K	PPGA
SL35R	333M	66M	128K	370 pin PPGA
SL35S	366M	66M	128K	370 pin PPGA
SL36A	300M	66M	128K	PPGA
SL36B	333M	66M	128K	PPGA
SL36C	366M	66M	128K	PPGA
SL376	366M	66M	128K	S.E.P.P.
SL37Q	366M	66M	128K	S.E.P.P.

Intel sSpec Number	CPU Speed	Bus Speed	L2 Cache Size	Package Type
SL37V	400M	66M	128K	S.E.P.P.
SL37X	400M	66M	128K	S.E.P.P.
SL39Z	400M	66M	128K	S.E.P.P.
SL3A2	466M	66M	128K	PPGA
SL3BA	433M	66M	128K	PPGA
SL3BS	433M	66M	128K	370 pin PPGA PPGA2
SL3EH	466M	66M	128K	PPGA
SL3FL	466M	66M	128K	370 pin PPGA PPGA2
SL3FY	500M	66M	128K	PPGA
SL3FZ	533M	66M	128K	PPGA
SL3LQ	500M	66M	128K	370 pin PPGA PPGA2
SL3PZ	533M	66M	128K	370 pin PPGA PPGA2
SL3VS	633M	66M	128K	FC-PGA
SL3W7	566M	66M	128K	FC-PGA
SL3W8	600M	66M	128K	FC-PGA
SL3W9	633M	66M	128K	FC-PGA
SL46S	533M	66M	128K	FC-PGA
SL46T	533M	66M	128K	370 pin PPGA
SL46U	600M	66M	128K	370 pin PPGA
SL48E	667M	66M	128K	370 pin PPGA
SL48F	700M	66M	128K	FC-PGA
SL4AB	466M	66M	128K	FC-PGA
SL4E6	700M	66M	128K	370 pin PPGA FC-PGA1
SL4NW	566M	66M	128K	370 pin PPGA
SL4NX	600M	66M	128K	370 pin PPGA
SL4NY	633M	66M	128K	370 pin PPGA
SL4NZ	667M	66M	128K	370 pin PPGA
SL4P2	733M	66M	128K	370 pin PPGA
SL4P3	733M	66M	128K	FC-PGA
SL4P6	766M	66M	128K	370 pin PPGA
SL4P7	733M	66M	128K	FC-PGA
SL4P8	700M	66M	128K	370 pin PPGA
SL4P9	667M	66M	128K	FC-PGA
SL4PA	633M	66M	128K	FC-PGA
SL4PB	600M	66M	128K	370 pin PPGA
SL4PC	766M	66M	128K	370 pin PPGA
SL4QF	766M	66M	128K	370 pin PPGA
SL4TF	800M	100M	128K	370 pin PPGA
SL52X	766M	66M	128K	370 pin PPGA
SL52Y	733M	66M	128K	370 pin PPGA
SL54P	800M	100M	128K	FC-PGA
SL54Q	850M	100M	128K	370 pin PPGA
SL55R	800M	100M	128K	FC-PGA
SL5EA	766M	66M	128K	FC-PGA
SL5EB	800M	100M	128K	370 pin PPGA
SL5EC	850M	100M	128K	370 pin PPGA
SL5GA	850M	100M	128K	370 pin PPGA
SL5GB	850M	100M	128K	370 pin PPGA
SL5LX	900M	100M	128K	370 pin PPGA
SL5MQ	900M	100M	128K	370 pin PPGA
SL5UZ	950M	100M	128K	370 pin PPGA
SL5V2	950M	100M	128K	370 pin PPGA
SL5VP	1.00G	100M	256K	370 pin PPGA
SL5VQ	1.10G	100M	256K	370 pin PPGA
SL5VR	1.30G	100M	256K	370 pin PPGA
SL5WA	900M	100M	128K	370 pin PPGA
SL5WB	850M	100M	128K	370 pin PPGA
SL5WC	800M	100M	128K	370 pin PPGA
SL5WW	800M	100M	128K	370 pin PPGA
SL5WX	850M	100M	128K	370 pin PPGA
SL5WY	900M	100M	128K	370 pin PPGA
SL5XQ	1.00G	100M	128K	370 pin PPGA
SL5XR	1.10G	100M	256K	370 pin PPGA
SL5XS	1.20G	100M	256K	370 pin PPGA
SL5XT	1.00G	100M	128K	370 pin PPGA
SL5XU	1.10G	100M	128K	370 pin PPGA
SL5Y5	1.20G	100M	256K	370 pin PPGA
SL5ZE	1.10G	100M	256K	370 pin PPGA
SL5ZF	1.00G	100M	256K	370 pin PPGA
SL5ZJ	1.30G	100M	256K	370 pin PPGA
SL633	900M	100M	128K	370 pin PPGA

Intel sSpec Number	CPU Speed	Bus Speed	L2 Cache Size	Package Type
SL634	950M	100M	128K	370 pin PPGA
SL635	1.00G	100M	128K	370 pin PPGA
SL64V	1.40G	100M	256K	370 pin PPGA
SL656	1.20G	100M	256K	370 pin PPGA
SL68C	1.70G	400M	128K	478 pin PPGA
SL68D	1.80G	400M	128K	478 pin PPGA
SL68F	2.00G	400M	128K	478 pin PPGA FC-PGA2
SL68G	1.40G	100M	256K	370 pin PPGA
SL68P	1.20G	100M	256K	370 pin PPGA
SL69Z	1.70G	400M	128K	478 pin PPGA
SL6A2	1.80G	400M	128K	478 pin PPGA
SL6C6	1.40G	100M	256K	370 pin PPGA
SL6C7	1.30G	100M	256K	370 pin PPGA
SL6C8	1.20G	100M	256K	370 pin PPGA
SL6CA	1.10G	100M	256K	370 pin PPGA
SL6CB	1.00G	100M	256K	370 pin PPGA
SL6HY	2.00G	400M	128K	478 pin PPGA
SL6JQ	1.00G	100M	256K	370 pin PPGA
SL6JR	1.10G	100M	256K	370 pin PPGA FC-PGA2
SL6JS	1.20G	100M	256K	370 pin PPGA
SL6JT	1.30G	100M	256K	370 pin PPGA
SL6JU	1.40G	100M	256K	370 pin PPGA
SL6JV	1.40G	100M	256K	370 pin PPGA
SL6LC	2.00G	400M	128K	478 pin PPGA
SL6RM	1.10G	100M	256K	370 pin PPGA
SL6RP	1.20G	100M	256K	370 pin PPGA
SL6RS	2.10G	400M	128K	478 pin PPGA
SL6RV	2.00G	400M	128K	478 pin PPGA
SL6RW	2.20G	400M	128K	478 pin PPGA
SL6SW	2.00G	400M	128K	478 pin PPGA
SL6SX	2.20G	400M	128K	478 pin PPGA
SL6SY	2.10G	400M	128K	478 pin PPGA
SL6T2	2.30G	400M	128K	478 pin PPGA FC-PGA2
SL6T3	2.30G	400M	128K	478 pin PPGA
SL6T5	2.30G	400M	128K	478 pin PPGA
SL6VR	2.00G	400M	128K	478 pin PPGA
SL6VT	2.20G	400M	128K	478 pin PPGA
SL6VU	2.40G	400M	128K	478 pin PPGA
SL6VV	2.60G	400M	128K	478 pin PPGA
SL6VY	2.00G	400M	128K	478 pin PPGA
SL6VZ	2.20G	400M	128K	478 pin PPGA
SL6W2	2.20G	400M	128K	478 pin PPGA
SL6W4	2.40G	400M	128K	478 pin PPGA
SL6W5	2.60G	400M	128K	478 pin PPGA
SL6WD	2.30G	400M	128K	478 pin PPGA
SL6XG	2.40G	400M	128K	478 pin PPGA FC-PGA2
SL6XJ	2.30G	400M	128K	478 pin PPGA
SL6ZY	2.50G	400M	128K	478 pin PPGA
SL72B	2.60G	400M	128K	478 pin PPGA
SL77S	2.70G	400M	128K	478 pin PPGA
SL77T	2.80G	400M	128K	478 pin PPGA
SL77U	2.70G	400M	128K	478 pin PPGA
SL77V	2.80G	400M	128K	478 pin PPGA
Intel Pentium III				
SL35D	450M	100M	512K	pin SECC2 OLGA1
SL35E	500M	100M	512K	S.E.C.C.2
SL364	450M	100M	512K	S.E.C.C.2
SL365	500M	100M	512K	S.E.C.C.2
SL37C	450M	- - -	512K	242 pin SECC2
SL37D	500M	100M	512K	S.E.C.C.2
SL3BN	533M	133M	512K	S.E.C.C.2
SL3CC	450M	100M	512K	S.E.C.C.2
SL3CD	500M	100M	512K	S.E.C.C.2
SL3E9	533M	- - -	512K	242 pin SECC2
SL3F7	550M	100M	512K	S.E.C.C.2
SL3FJ	550M	100M	512K	S.E.C.C.2
SL3H6	600M	100M	256K	S.E.C.C.2
SL3H7	600M	133M	256K	S.E.C.C.2
SL3JM	600M	100M	512K	S.E.C.C.2
SL3JP	600M	133M	512K	S.E.C.C.2
SL3JT	600M	100M	512K	S.E.C.C.2

Intel sSpec Number	CPU Speed	Bus Speed	L2 Cache Size	Package Type
SL3JU	600M	---	512K	242 pin SECC2
SL3KV	650M	100M	256K	S.E.C.C.2
SL3KW	667M	133M	256K	S.E.C.C.2
SL3N6	533M	133M	256K	S.E.C.C.2
SL3N7	550M	100M	256K	S.E.C.C.2
SL3NA	600M	---	256K	pin SECC2
SL3NB	600M	---	256K	pin SECC2
SL3ND	667M	---	256K	pin SECC2
SL3NL	600M	100M	256K	FC-PGA
SL3NM	650M	100M	256K	FC-PGA
SL3NR	650M	100M	256K	S.E.C.C.2
SL3Q9	500M	100M	256K	FC-PGA
SL3QA	500M	100M	256K	FC-PGA
SL3R2	500M	100M	256K	FC-PGA
SL3R3	500M	100M	256K	FC-PGA
SL3S9	700M	100M	256K	S.E.C.C.2
SL3SB	733M	133M	256K	S.E.C.C.2
SL3SX	533M	133M	256K	S.E.C.C.2
SL3SY	600M	---	256K	pin SECC2
SL3SZ	733M	133M	256K	pin SECC2
SL3T2	667M	133M	256K	FC-PGA
SL3T3	700M	100M	256K	FC-PGA
SL3T4	733M	133M	256K	FC-PGA
SL3V5	550M	---	256K	pin SECC2
SL3V6	750M	---	256K	pin SECC2
SL3V8	800M	---	256K	pin SECC2 OLGA1
SL3VA	533M	133M	256K	FC-PGA
SL3VB	600M	133M	256K	FC-PGA
SL3VC	533M	133M	256K	FC-PGA
SL3VF	533M	133M	256K	FC-PGA
SL3VG	600M	133M	256K	FC-PGA
SL3VH	600M	100M	256K	FC-PGA
SL3VJ	650M	100M	256K	FC-PGA
SL3VK	667M	133M	256K	FC-PGA
SL3VL	700M	100M	256K	FC-PGA
SL3VM	733M	133M	256K	FC-PGA
SL3VN	750M	100M	256K	FC-PGA
SL3WA	800M	133M	256K	S.E.C.C.2
SL3WC	750M	100M	256K	S.E.C.C.2
SL3XG	533M	133M	256K	S.E.C.C.2
SL3XH	550M	100M	256K	S.E.C.C.2
SL3XJ	600M	133M	256K	S.E.C.C.2
SL3XK	650M	100M	256K	S.E.C.C.2
SL3XL	667M	133M	256K	S.E.C.C.2
SL3XM	700M	100M	256K	S.E.C.C.2
SL3XN	733M	133M	256K	495 pin SECC2
SL3XP	750M	100M	256K	S.E.C.C.2
SL3XQ	800M	133M	256K	S.E.C.C.2
SL3XR	800M	100M	256K	S.E.C.C.2
SL3XS	533M	133M	256K	FC-PGA
SL3XT	600M	133M	256K	FC-PGA
SL3XU	600M	100M	256K	FC-PGA
SL3XV	650M	100M	256K	370 pin PPGA FC-PGA1
SL3XW	667M	133M	256K	370 pin PPGA
SL3XX	700M	100M	256K	370 pin PPGA
SL3XY	733M	133M	256K	370 pin PPGA
SL3XZ	750M	100M	256K	FC-PGA
SL3Y2	800M	133M	256K	370 pin PPGA
SL3Y3	800M	100M	256K	FC-PGA
SL43E	600M	100M	256K	S.E.C.C.2
SL43F	850M	100M	256K	S.E.C.C.2
SL43G	866M	100M	256K	S.E.C.C.2
SL43H	850M	100M	256K	370 pin PPGA
SL43J	866M	133M	256K	FC-PGA
SL446	500M	100M	256K	FC-PGA
SL448	933M	100M	256K	S.E.C.C.2
SL44G	550M	100M	256K	FC-PGA
SL44J	933M	133M	256K	370 pin PPGA
SL44W	533M	133M	256K	S.E.C.C.2
SL44X	550M	100M	256K	S.E.C.C.2
SL44Y	600M	100M	256K	S.E.C.C.2

Intel sSpec Number	CPU Speed	Bus Speed	L2 Cache Size	Package Type
SL44Z	600M	133M	256K	S.E.C.C.2
SL452	600M	100M	256K	S.E.C.C.2
SL453	667M	133M	256K	S.E.C.C.2
SL454	700M	100M	256K	S.E.C.C.2
SL455	733M	133M	256K	pin SECC2
SL456	700M	100M	256K	pin SECC2
SL457	800M	100M	256K	pin SECC2
SL458	850M	133M	256K	pin SECC2
SL45R	500M	100M	256K	FC-PGA
SL45S	533M	133M	256K	FC-PGA
SL45T	550M	100M	256K	FC-PGA
SL45U	600M	100M	256K	FC-PGA
SL45V	600M	133M	256K	FC-PGA
SL45W	650M	100M	256K	370 pin PPGA
SL45X	667M	133M	256K	FC-PGA
SL45Y	700M	100M	256K	370 pin PPGA
SL45Z	733M	133M	256K	370 pin PPGA
SL462	750M	100M	256K	370 pin PPGA
SL463	800M	100M	256K	370 pin PPGA
SL464	800M	133M	256K	FC-PGA
SL47M	800M	100M	256K	pin SECC2
SL47N	866M	133M	256K	S.E.C.C.2
SL47Q	933M	133M	256K	pin SECC2
SL47S	866M	133M	256K	S.E.C.C.2
SL48S	1.00G	133M	256K	S.E.C.C.2
SL49G	850M	100M	256K	370 pin PPGA
SL49H	866M	133M	256K	FC-PGA
SL49J	933M	133M	256K	FC-PGA
SL4BR	1.00G	133M	256K	495 pin SECC2
SL4BS	1.00G	100M	256K	S.E.C.C.2
SL4BT	933M	133M	256K	495 pin SECC2
SL4BV	866M	133M	256K	S.E.C.C.2
SL4BW	850M	100M	256K	495 pin SECC2
SL4BX	800M	133M	256K	495 pin SECC2 OLGA1
SL4BY	800M	100M	256K	S.E.C.C.2
SL4BZ	750M	100M	256K	S.E.C.C.2
SL4C2	733M	133M	256K	S.E.C.C.2
SL4C3	700M	100M	256K	495 pin SECC2
SL4C4	667M	133M	256K	S.E.C.C.2
SL4C5	650M	100M	256K	S.E.C.C.2
SL4C6	600M	133M	256K	S.E.C.C.2
SL4C7	600M	100M	256K	S.E.C.C.2
SL4C8	1.00G	133M	256K	370 pin PPGA
SL4C9	933M	133M	256K	370 pin PPGA
SL4CB	866M	133M	256K	370 pin PPGA
SL4CC	850M	100M	256K	370 pin PPGA
SL4CD	800M	133M	256K	FC-PGA
SL4CE	800M	100M	256K	370 pin PPGA
SL4CF	750M	100M	256K	370 pin PPGA
SL4CG	733M	133M	256K	370 pin PPGA
SL4CH	700M	100M	256K	FC-PGA
SL4CJ	667M	133M	256K	FC-PGA
SL4CK	650M	100M	256K	FC-PGA
SL4CL	600M	133M	256K	370 pin PPGA
SL4CM	600M	100M	256K	FC-PGA
SL4CX	733M	133M	256K	S.E.C.C.2
SL4FP	1.00G	133M	256K	S.E.C.C.2
SL4FQ	733M	133M	256K	S.E.C.C.2
SL4G7	800M	133M	256K	pin SECC2 OLGA1
SL4KD	733M	133M	256K	495 pin SECC2
SL4KE	750M	100M	256K	S.E.C.C.2
SL4KF	800M	133M	256K	495 pin SECC2
SL4KG	800M	133M	256K	S.E.C.C.2
SL4KH	850M	133M	256K	495 pin SECC2
SL4KJ	866M	133M	256K	pin SECC2 OLGA1
SL4KK	933M	133M	256K	pin SECC2
SL4KL	1.00G	100M	256K	495 pin SECC2
SL4M7	700M	100M	256K	FC-PGA
SL4M8	733M	133M	256K	FC-PGA
SL4M9	750M	100M	256K	FC-PGA
SL4MA	800M	100M	256K	370 pin PPGA

Intel sSpec Number	CPU Speed	Bus Speed	L2 Cache Size	Package Type
SL4MB	800M	133M	256K	370 pin PPGA
SL4MC	850M	100M	256K	FC-PGA
SL4MD	866M	133M	256K	FC-PGA
SL4ME	933M	133M	256K	FC-PGA
SL4MF	1.00G	133M	256K	370 pin PPGA
SL4SD	1.00G	100M	256K	370 pin PPGA
SL4Z2	850M	100M	256K	370 pin PPGA
SL4ZJ	866M	133M	256K	370 pin PPGA
SL4ZL	733M	133M	256K	370 pin PPGA
SL52P	800M	133M	256K	370 pin PPGA
SL52Q	933M	133M	256K	370 pin PPGA
SL52R	1.00G	133M	256K	370 pin PPGA
SL5B3	1.00G	133M	256K	370 pin PPGA
SL5BS	900M	100M	256K	FC-PGA
SL5BT	600M	133M	256K	370 pin PPGA
SL5DV	1.00G	133M	256K	370 pin PPGA
SL5DW	933M	133M	256K	370 pin PPGA
SL5DX	866M	133M	256K	370 pin PPGA
SL5FQ	1.00G	133M	256K	370 pin PPGA
SL5GN	1.20G	133M	256K	370 pin PPGA
SL5GQ	1.13G	133M	256K	370 pin PPGA
SL5GR	1.00G	133M	256K	370 pin PPGA
SL5LT	1.13G	133M	256K	370 pin PPGA
SL5LV	1.13G	133M	512K	370 pin PPGA
SL5LW	1.26G	133M	512K	370 pin PPGA
SL5PM	1.20G	133M	512K	370 pin PPGA
SL5PU	1.13G	133M	512K	370 pin PPGA
SL5QD	800M	133M	256K	370 pin PPGA
SL5QK	1.13G	133M	256K	370 pin PPGA
SL5QL	1.26G	133M	512K	370 pin PPGA
SL5QV	1.00G	100M	256K	370 pin PPGA
SL5QW	1.10G	100M	256K	370 pin PPGA
SL5U3	933M	133M	256K	FC-PGA2
SL5VX	1.33G	133M	256K	FC-PGA2
SL5XL	1.40G	133M	512K	370 pin PPGA
SL64W	1.40G	133M	256K	370 pin PPGA
SL657	1.40G	133M	512K	370 pin PPGA
SL69K	933M	133M	512K	479 pin H-PBGA
SL6BW	1.13G	133M	512K	370 pin PPGA
SL6BX	1.26G	133M	512K	370 pin PPGA
SL6BY	1.40G	133M	512K	370 pin PPGA
SL6HC	800M	133M	512K	479 pin H-PBGA
SL6QU	1.00G	133M	512K	479 pin H-PBGA
Intel Xeon				
SL4WX	1.40G	400M	256K	603 pin PPGA
SL4WY	1.50G	400M	256K	603 INT-mPGA
SL4XU	700M	100M	1M	330 pin SECC
SL4ZT	1.50G	400M	256K	603 pin PPGA
SL56G	1.40G	400M	256K	603 pin PPGA
SL56H	1.70G	400M	0K	603 pin PPGA INT2
SL56N	1.70G	400M	256K	603 pin PPGA
SL5TD	1.50G	400M	256K	603 pin PPGA
SL5TE	1.70G	400M	256K	603 pin PPGA
SL5TH	2.00G	400M	256K	603 pin PPGA
SL5U6	1.50G	400M	256K	603 pin PPGA
SL5U7	1.70G	400M	256K	603 pin PPGA
SL5UB	2.00G	400M	256K	603 pin PPGA
SL5Z8	1.80G	400M	512K	603 pin PPGA
SL5Z9	2.00G	400M	512K	603 pin PPGA
SL5ZA	2.20G	400M	512K	603 pin PPGA
SL622	1.80G	400M	512K	603 pin PPGA
SL623	2.00G	400M	512K	603 pin PPGA
SL624	2.20G	400M	512K	603 pin PPGA
SL65T	2.40G	400M	512K	603 pin PPGA
SL687	2.40G	400M	512K	603 pin PPGA
SL6EL	1.80G	400M	512K	603 pin PPGA
SL6EM	2.00G	400M	512K	603 pin PPGA
SL6EN	2.20G	400M	512K	603 pin PPGA
SL6EP	2.40G	400M	512K	603 pin PPGA
SL6EQ	2.40G	400M	512K	603 pin PPGA
SL6GD	2.40G	533M	512K	604 pin PPGA

Intel sSpec Number	CPU Speed	Bus Speed	L2 Cache Size	Package Type
SL6GF	2.66G	533M	512K	604 pin PPGA
SL6GG	2.80G	533M	512K	604 pin PPGA
SL6GH	3.06G	533M	512K	604 pin PPGA
SL6JX	1.80G	400M	512K	603 pin PPGA
SL6JY	2.00G	400M	512K	603 pin PPGA
SL6JZ	2.20G	400M	512K	603 pin PPGA
SL6K2	2.40G	400M	512K	603 pin PPGA
SL6K3	2.60G	400M	512K	603 pin PPGA
SL6M7	2.80G	400M	512K	603 pin PPGA
SL6MS	2.80G	400M	512K	603 pin PPGA
SL6NP	2.00G	533M	512K	604 pin PPGA
SL6NQ	2.40G	533M	512K	604 pin PPGA
SL6NR	2.66G	533M	512K	604 pin PPGA
SL6NS	2.80G	533M	512K	604 pin PPGA
SL6RQ	2.00G	533M	512K	604 pin PPGA
SL6RR	3.06G	533M	512K	604 pin PPGA
SL6VK	2.00G	533M	512K	604 pin PPGA
SL6VL	2.40G	533M	512K	604 pin PPGA
SL6VM	2.66G	533M	512K	604 pin PPGA
SL6VN	2.80G	533M	512K	604 pin PPGA
SL6VP	3.06G	533M	512K	604 pin PPGA
SL6VW	3.00G	400M	512K	603 pin PPGA
SL6W3	1.80G	400M	512K	603 pin PPGA
SL6W6	2.00G	400M	512K	603 pin PPGA
SL6W7	2.20G	400M	512K	603 pin PPGA
SL6W8	2.40G	400M	512K	603 pin PPGA
SL6W9	2.60G	400M	512K	603 pin PPGA
SL6WA	2.80G	400M	512K	603 pin PPGA
SL6WB	3.00G	400M	512K	603 pin PPGA
SL6X4	3.00G	400M	512K	603 pin PPGA INT3
SL6XL	2.00G	400M	512K	604 pin PPGA
SL6YM	2.00G	533M	512K	604 pin PPGA FC-PGA2
SL6YN	2.40G	533M	512K	604 pin PPGA
SL6YP	2.66G	533M	512K	604 pin PPGA
SL6YQ	2.80G	533M	512K	604 pin PPGA
SL6YR	3.06G	533M	512K	604 pin PPGA
SL6YS	1.80G	400M	512K	603 pin PPGA
SL6YT	2.00G	400M	512K	603 pin PPGA
SL6YU	2.20G	400M	512K	603 pin PPGA
SL6YV	2.40G	400M	512K	603 pin PPGA
SL6YW	2.60G	400M	512K	603 pin PPGA
SL6YX	2.80G	400M	512K	603 pin PPGA
SL6YY	3.00G	400M	512K	603 pin PPGA
SL6Z8	2.80G	400M	2M	603 pin PPGA
SL72C	2.00G	533M	512K	604 pin PPGA FC-PGA2
SL72D	2.40G	533M	512K	604 pin PPGA
SL72E	2.66G	533M	512K	604 pin PPGA
SL72F	2.80G	533M	512K	604 pin PPGA
SL72G	3.06G	533M	1M	604 pin PPGA
SL72Y	3.20G	533M	1M	604 pin PPGA
SL73K	2.00G	533M	512K	604 pin PPGA FC-PGA2
SL73L	2.40G	533M	512K	604 pin PPGA
SL73M	2.66G	533M	512K	604 pin PPGA
SL73N	2.40G	533M	512K	604 pin PPGA
SL73P	3.06G	533M	1M	604 pin PPGA
SL73Q	3.20G	533M	1M	604 pin PPGA
SL74T	2.40G	533M	512K	604 pin PPGA
SL74E	3.20G	533M	2M	604 pin PPGA
SL7BW	3.20G	533M	1M	604 pin PPGA
SL7D4	2.40G	533M	1M	604 pin PPGA
SL7D5	2.80G	533M	1M	604 pin PPGA
SL7DF	2.40G	533M	1M	604 pin PPGA
SL7DG	2.80G	533M	1M	604 pin PPGA
Intel Xeon MP				
SL5FZ	1.40G	400M	512K	603 pin PPGA
SL5G2	1.50G	400M	1M	603 pin PPGA
SL5G8	1.60G	400M	1M	603 pin PPGA
SL5RV	1.40G	400M	512K	603 pin PPGA
SL5RW	1.50G	400M	512K	603 pin PPGA
SL5S4	1.60G	400M	1M	603 pin PPGA
SL66Z	2.00G	400M	2M	603 pin PPGA

Intel sSpec Number	CPU Speed	Bus Speed	L2 Cache Size	Package Type
SL6GZ	1.50G	400M	1M	603 pin PPGA
SL6H2	1.90G	400M	1M	603 pin PPGA
SL6KB	1.50G	400M	1M	603 pin PPGA
SL6KC	1.90G	400M	1M	603 pin PPGA
SL6KD	2.00G	400M	2M	603 pin PPGA
SL6YJ	2.00G	400M	1M	603 pin PPGA
SL6YL	2.80G	400M	2M	603 pin PPGA
SL6Z2	2.50G	400M	1M	603 pin PPGA
SL6Z6	2.00G	400M	1M	603 pin PPGA
SL6Z7	2.50G	400M	1M	603 pin PPGA
SL79V	3.00G	400M	4M	603 pin PPGA
SL79Z	2.00G	400M	2M	603 pin PPGA
SL7A5	2.20G	400M	2M	603 pin PPGA
Intel Pentium III Xeon				
SL2XU	500M	100M	512K	S.E.C.C.
SL2XV	500M	100M	1024K	S.E.C.C.
SL2XW	500M	100M	2048K	S.E.C.C.
SL385	500M	100M	512K	S.E.C.C.
SL386	500M	---	1M	330 pin SECC
SL387	500M	100M	2048K	330 pin SECC
SL3BJ	600M	133M	256K	S.E.C.C.
SL3BK	600M	133M	256K	S.E.C.C.
SL3BL	667M	133M	256K	S.E.C.C.
SL3C9	500M	100M	512K	S.E.C.C.
SL3CA	500M	100M	1024K	S.E.C.C.
SL3CB	500M	---	2M	330 pin SECC
SL3CF	500M	100M	2048K	S.E.C.C.
SL3D9	550M	100M	512K	S.E.C.C.
SL3DA	500M	100M	1024K	S.E.C.C.
SL3DB	500M	100M	2048K	S.E.C.C.
SL3DC	667M	133M	256K	S.E.C.C.
SL3FK	550M	100M	512K	S.E.C.C.
SL3FR	550M	100M	512K	S.E.C.C.
SL3LM	550M	100M	512K	S.E.C.C.
SL3LN	550M	100M	1024K	S.E.C.C.
SL3LP	550M	100M	2048K	S.E.C.C.
SL3SF	733M	133M	256K	S.E.C.C.
SL3SG	733M	133M	256K	S.E.C.C.
SL3SS	600M	133M	256K	S.E.C.C.
SL3ST	667M	133M	256K	S.E.C.C.
SL3SU	733M	133M	256K	S.E.C.C.
SL3TW	550M	100M	1024K	S.E.C.C.
SL3U4	700M	100M	1024K	S.E.C.C.
SL3U5	700M	100M	1024K	S.E.C.C.
SL3V2	800M	133M	256K	S.E.C.C.
SL3V3	800M	133M	256K	S.E.C.C.
SL3VU	600M	133M	256K	S.E.C.C.
SL3WM	600M	133M	256K	S.E.C.C.
SL3WN	600M	133M	256K	S.E.C.C.
SL3WP	667M	133M	256K	S.E.C.C.
SL3WQ	667M	133M	256K	S.E.C.C.
SL3WR	733M	133M	256K	S.E.C.C.
SL3WS	733M	133M	256K	S.E.C.C.
SL3WT	800M	133M	256K	S.E.C.C.
SL3WU	800M	133M	256K	S.E.C.C.
SL3WV	866M	133M	256K	S.E.C.C.
SL3WW	866M	133M	256K	S.E.C.C.
SL3WX	933M	133M	256K	S.E.C.C.
SL3WY	933M	133M	256K	S.E.C.C.
SL3WZ	700M	100M	2048K	S.E.C.C.
SL3X2	700M	100M	2048K	S.E.C.C.
SL3Y4	550M	100M	512K	S.E.C.C.
SL49R	700M	100M	2M	330 pin SECC OLGA2
SL4GD	700M	100M	1024K	S.E.C.C.
SL4GE	700M	100M	1024K	S.E.C.C.
SL4GF	700M	100M	2048K	S.E.C.C.
SL4GG	700M	100M	2048K	S.E.C.C.
SL4H6	733M	133M	256K	S.E.C.C.
SL4H7	733M	133M	256K	495 pin SECC OLGA1
SL4H8	800M	133M	256K	S.E.C.C.
SL4H9	800M	133M	256K	495 pin SECC OLGA1

Intel sSpec Number	CPU Speed	Bus Speed	L2 Cache Size	Package Type
SL4HA	866M	133M	256K	S.E.C.C.
SL4HB	933M	133M	256K	495 pin SECC OLGA1
SL4HC	933M	133M	256K	495 pin SECC OLGA1
SL4HD	933M	133M	256K	495 pin SECC OLGA1
SL4HE	1.00G	133M	256K	495 pin SECC
SL4HF	1.00G	133M	256K	495 pin SECC
SL4PZ	866M	133M	256K	S.E.C.C.
SL4Q2	1.00G	133M	256K	495 pin SECC
SL4R9	933M	133M	256K	330 pin SECC2
SL4U2	933M	133M	256K	330 pin SECC2
SL4U3	933M	133M	256K	S.E.C.C.
Intel Pentium M				
SL6F5	1.40G	400M	1M	479 pin H-PBGA FC-BGA2
SL6F6	1.50G	400M	1M	479 pin H-PBGA FC-BGA2
SL6F7	1.60G	400M	1M	479 pin H-PBGA FC-BGA2
SL6F8	1.40G	400M	1M	478 pin PPGA FC-PGA2
SL6F9	1.50G	400M	1M	478 pin PPGA FC-PGA2
SL6FA	1.60G	400M	1M	478 pin PPGA FC-PGA2
SL6N4	1.30G	400M	1M	478 pin PPGA FC-PGA2
SL6N5	1.70G	400M	1M	478 pin PPGA FC-PGA2
SL6N8	1.30G	400M	1M	479 pin H-PBGA FC-BGA2
SL6N9	1.70G	400M	1M	479 pin H-PBGA FC-BGA2
SL6NB	1.20G	400M	1M	479 pin H-PBGA FC-BGA2
SL6NC	1.10G	400M	1M	479 pin H-PBGA FC-BGA2
SL6NJ	900M	400M	1M	479 pin H-PBGA FC
SL7EG	1.60G	400M	2M	478 pin PPGA
SL7EM	2.00G	400M	2M	478 pin PPGA
SL7EN	1.80G	400M	2M	478 pin PPGA
SL7EP	2.00G	400M	2M	478 pin PPGA
SL7GL	1.50G	400M	2M	478 pin PPGA
Intel Mobile Pentium 4				
SL723	2.40G	533M	512K	478 pin PPGA
SL724	2.66G	533M	512K	478 pin PPGA
SL725	2.80G	533M	512K	478 pin PPGA
SL726	3.06G	533M	512K	478 pin PPGA
SL77M	2.66G	533M	512K	478 pin PPGA
SL77N	2.80G	533M	512K	478 pin PPGA
SL77P	3.06G	533M	512K	478 pin PPGA
SL77R	3.20G	533M	512K	478 pin PPGA
SL7DS	2.80G	533M	1M	478 pin PPGA
SL7DT	3.06G	533M	1M	478 pin PPGA
SL7DU	3.20G	533M	1M	478 pin PPGA
Intel Mobile Pentium 4-M				
SL5YT	1.50G	400M	512K	478 pin PPGA FC-PGA2
SL5YU	1.60G	400M	512K	478 pin PPGA FC-PGA2
SL5Z7	1.70G	400M	512K	478 pin PPGA FC-PGA2
SL5ZH	1.40G	400M	512K	478 pin PPGA FC-PGA2
SL5ZW	1.40G	400M	512K	478 pin PPGA FC-PGA2
SL5ZX	1.50G	400M	512K	478 pin PPGA FC-PGA2
SL5ZY	1.60G	400M	512K	478 pin PPGA FC-PGA2
SL5ZZ	1.70G	400M	512K	478 pin PPGA FC-PGA2
SL65Q	1.80G	400M	512K	478 pin PPGA FC-PGA2
SL69D	1.80G	400M	512K	478 pin PPGA FC-PGA2
SL6CF	1.50G	400M	512K	478 pin PPGA FC-PGA2
SL6CG	1.60G	400M	512K	478 pin PPGA FC-PGA2
SL6CH	1.70G	400M	512K	478 pin PPGA FC-PGA2
SL6CJ	1.80G	400M	512K	478 pin PPGA FC-PGA2
SL6CK	1.90G	400M	512K	478 pin PPGA FC-PGA2
SL6CL	2.00G	400M	512K	478 pin PPGA FC-PGA2
SL6DE	1.90G	400M	512K	478 pin PPGA FC-PGA2
SL6DF	2.00G	400M	512K	478 pin PPGA FC-PGA2
SL6FF	1.60G	400M	512K	603 pin PPGA FC-PGA2
SL6FG	1.70G	400M	512K	478 pin PPGA FC-PGA2
SL6FH	1.80G	400M	512K	478 pin PPGA FC-PGA2
SL6FJ	1.90G	400M	512K	478 pin PPGA FC-PGA2
SL6FK	2.00G	400M	512K	478 pin PPGA FC-PGA2
SL6J5	2.20G	400M	512K	478 pin PPGA FC-PGA2
SL6K5	2.40G	400M	512K	478 pin PPGA FC-PGA2
SL6LR	2.20G	400M	512K	478 pin PPGA FC-PGA2
SL6LS	2.40G	400M	512K	478 pin PPGA FC-PGA2
SL6P2	2.50G	400M	512K	478 pin PPGA FC-PGA2
SL6V7	1.80G	400M	512K	478 pin PPGA FC-PGA2

CPU's

Intel sSpec Number	CPU Speed	Bus Speed	L2 Cache Size	Package Type
SL6V8	1.90G	400M	512K	478 pin PPGA FC-PGA2
SL6V9	2.00G	400M	512K	478 pin PPGA FC-PGA2
SL6VB	2.20G	400M	512K	478 pin PPGA FC-PGA2
SL6VC	2.40G	400M	512K	478 pin PPGA FC-PGA2
SL6WY	2.50G	400M	512K	478 pin PPGA FC-PGA2
Intel Mobile Celeron				
SL3AH	300M	66M	128K	BGA2
SL3C7	366M	66M	128K	BGA2
SL3C8	333M	66M	128K	BGA2
SL3DQ	266M	66M	128K	BGA2
SL3GQ	400M	66M	128K	BGA2
SL3GR	400M	66M	128K	Micro-PGA2
SL3HM	266M	66M	128K	Micro-PGA2
SL3HN	300M	66M	128K	Micro-PGA2
SL3HP	333M	66M	128K	Micro-PGA2
SL3HQ	366M	66M	128K	Micro-PGA2
SL3KA	433M	66M	128K	Micro-PGA2
SL3KB	433M	66M	128K	Micro-PGA2
SL3KC	466M	66M	128K	Micro-PGA2
SL3KD	466M	66M	128K	Micro-PGA2
SL3PC	500M	100M	128K	BGA2
SL3PD	450M	100M	128K	BGA2
SL3PE	500M	100M	128K	Micro-PGA2
SL3PF	450M	100M	128K	Micro-PGA2
SL3UL	500M	100M	128K	BGA2
SL3ZE	550M	100M	128K	BGA2
SL3ZF	500M	100M	128K	Micro-PGA2
SL43Q	500M	100M	128K	BGA2
SL43R	450M	100M	128K	Micro-PGA2
SL43T	450M	100M	128K	BGA2
SL43U	400M	100M	128K	Micro-PGA2
SL43W	400M	100M	128K	BGA2
SL43Z	500M	100M	128K	BGA2
SL45A	500M	100M	128K	BGA2
SL46Y	500M	100M	128K	495 pin PPGA FC-PGA1
SL4AD	650M	100M	128K	BGA2
SL4AE	600M	100M	128K	BGA2
SL4AP	600M	100M	128K	BGA2
SL4AR	500M	100M	128K	Micro-PGA2
SL4GU	700M	100M	128K	BGA2
SL4GX	700M	100M	128K	Micro-PGA2
SL4JC	450M	100M	128K	BGA2
SL4JD	500M	100M	128K	BGA2
SL4JE	550M	100M	128K	BGA2
SL4JF	600M	100M	128K	BGA2
SL4JG	650M	100M	128K	495 pin H-PBGA
SL4JS	450M	100M	128K	Micro-PGA2
SL4JT	500M	100M	128K	Micro-PGA2
SL4JU	500M	100M	128K	Micro-PGA2
SL4JV	600M	100M	128K	Micro-PGA2
SL4JW	650M	100M	128K	495 pin PPGA INT1
SL4MT	550M	100M	128K	Micro-PGA2
SL4MU	600M	100M	128K	495 pin PPGA FC-PGA1
SL4PT	450M	100M	128K	Micro-PGA2
SL4PV	500M	100M	128K	Micro-PGA2
SL4PW	600M	100M	128K	Micro-PGA2
SL4PX	650M	100M	128K	495 pin PPGA INT1
SL4PY	700M	100M	128K	495 pin PPGA INT1
SL4ZR	500M	100M	128K	BGA2
SL53C	750M	100M	128K	BGA2
SL53U	750M	100M	128K	BGA2
SL55Q	750M	100M	128K	495 pin PPGA
SL56P	750M	100M	128K	495 pin H-PBGA
SL56Q	750M	100M	128K	Micro-PGA2
SL57X	800M	100M	128K	BGA2
SL57Y	850M	100M	128K	BGA2
SL582	600M	100M	128K	BGA2
SL584	800M	100M	128K	Micro-PGA2
SL585	850M	100M	128K	Micro-PGA2
SL58K	750M	100M	128K	Micro-PGA2
SL5CB	800M	100M	128K	495 pin PPGA
SL5DS	600M	100M	128K	BGA2
SL5PX	900M	100M	128K	BGA2
SL5PY	900M	100M	128K	Micro-PGA2
SL5Q2	866M	133M	128K	Micro-FCBGA
SL5Q3	866M	133M	128K	Micro-FCPGA
SL5SK	933M	133M	128K	478 pin PPGA
SL5SP	733M	133M	128K	Micro-FCBGA
SL5SQ	800M	133M	128K	Micro-FCBGA
SL5SR	933M	133M	128K	Micro-FCBGA
SL5SS	733M	133M	128K	Micro-FCPGA
SL5ST	800M	133M	128K	Micro-FCPGA
SL5SU	933M	133M	128K	Micro-FCPGA
SL5T2	866M	133M	128K	478 pin PPGA
SL5T3	800M	133M	128K	478 pin PPGA
SL63F	650M	100M	256K	479 pin H-PBGA
SL63Z	1.20G	133M	256K	478 pin PPGA
SL642	1.13G	133M	256K	478 pin PPGA
SL643	1.06G	133M	256K	478 pin PPGA
SL64K	1.20G	133M	256K	478 pin PPGA
SL64L	1.13G	133M	256K	478 pin PPGA
SL64M	1.06G	133M	256K	478 pin PPGA
SL6AB	1.00G	133M	256K	478 pin PPGA
SL6B3	1.00G	133M	256K	479 pin H-PBGA
SL6B4	733M	133M	256K	479 pin H-PBGA
SL6FM	1.40G	400M	256K	478 pin PPGA
SL6FN	1.50G	133M	256K	478 pin PPGA
SL6HA	1.33G	133M	256K	478 pin PPGA
SL6J2	1.60G	400M	256K	478 pin PPGA
SL6J3	1.70G	400M	256K	478 pin PPGA
SL6J4	1.80G	400M	256K	478 pin PPGA
SL6M4	1.40G	400M	256K	478 pin PPGA
SL6M5	1.50G	400M	256K	478 pin PPGA
SL6QH	2.00G	400M	256K	478 pin PPGA
SL6VG	1.70G	400M	256K	478 pin PPGA
SL6VH	1.80G	400M	256K	478 pin PPGA
SL6VJ	2.00G	400M	256K	478 pin PPGA
SL6ZW	2.20G	400M	256K	478 pin PPGA
SL73Y	2.20G	400M	256K	478 pin PPGA
SL75J	2.40G	400M	256K	478 pin PPGA
Intel Mobile Pentium II				
SL2KH	266M	66M	512K	Mini-Cartridge
SL2KJ	266M	66M	512K	Mini-Cartridge
SL2RQ	233M	66M	512K	Mini-Cartridge
SL2RR	266M	66M	512K	Mini-Cartridge
SL2RS	300M	66M	512K	Mini-Cartridge
SL32M	266M	66M	256K	Mini-Cartridge
SL32N	300M	66M	256K	Mini-Cartridge
SL32P	333M	66M	256K	Mini-Cartridge
SL32Q	266M	66M	256K	BGA
SL32R	300M	66M	256K	BGA
SL32S	333M	66M	256K	BGA
SL36Z	366M	66M	256K	Mini-Cartridge
SL3AG	366M	66M	256K	BGA
SL3BW	400M	66M	256K	Micro-PGA
SL3DR	266M	66M	256K	BGA
SL3EM	400M	66M	256K	BGA
SL3HH	266M	66M	256K	Micro-PGA
SL3HJ	300M	66M	256K	Micro-PGA
SL3HK	333M	66M	256K	Micro-PGA
SL3HL	366M	66M	256K	Micro-PGA
SL3JW	400M	66M	256K	Mini-Cartridge
Intel Mobile Pentium III				
SL34Y	600M	100M	256K	BGA2
SL3DT	500M	100M	256K	BGA2
SL3DU	400M	100M	256K	BGA2
SL3DW	500M	100M	256K	Micro-PGA2
SL3KX	450M	100M	256K	BGA2
SL3LG	450M	100M	256K	Micro-PGA2
SL3PG	650M	100M	256K	BGA2
SL3PH	600M	100M	256K	BGA2
SL3PL	650M	100M	256K	Micro-PGA2
SL3PM	600M	100M	256K	Micro-PGA2

Intel sSpec Number	CPU Speed	Bus Speed	L2 Cache Size	Package Type
SL3RF	450M	100M	256K	Micro-PGA2
SL3RG	500M	133M	256K	495 pin PPGA
SL3TP	600M	133M	256K	495 pin PPGA
SL3TQ	650M	133M	256K	495 pin PPGA
SL3Z7	700M	100M	256K	BGA2
SL3Z8	700M	100M	256K	Micro-PGA2
SL43L	450M	100M	256K	BGA2
SL43N	450M	100M	256K	Micro-PGA2
SL43P	500M	100M	256K	Micro-PGA2
SL43X	650M	100M	256K	Micro-PGA2
SL442	650M	100M	256K	Micro-PGA2
SL443	600M	100M	256K	Micro-PGA2
SL44T	750M	100M	256K	Micro-PGA2
SL46V	600M	100M	256K	495 pin PPGA FC-PGA1
SL46W	650M	100M	256K	Micro-PGA2
SL479	500M	100M	256K	Micro-PGA2
SL4AG	850M	100M	256K	BGA2
SL4AH	850M	100M	256K	Micro-PGA2
SL4AK	800M	100M	256K	BGA2
SL4AS	750M	100M	256K	BGA2
SL4DL	700M	100M	256K	495 pin PPGA
SL4DM	750M	100M	256K	495 pin PPGA
SL4GH	600M	100M	256K	BGA2
SL4GT	800M	100M	256K	495 pin PPGA
SL4JM	600M	100M	256K	BGA2
SL4JQ	450M	100M	256K	Micro-PGA2
SL4JR	500M	100M	256K	Micro-PGA2
SL4JX	600M	100M	256K	Micro-PGA2
SL4JY	650M	100M	256K	Micro-PGA2
SL4JZ	700M	100M	256K	Micro-PGA2
SL4K2	750M	100M	256K	Micro-PGA2
SL4N3	1.06G	133M	512K	Micro-FCBGA
SL4PK	450M	100M	256K	Micro-PGA2
SL4PL	500M	100M	256K	Micro-PGA2
SL4PM	600M	100M	256K	Micro-PGA2
SL4PN	650M	100M	256K	Micro-PGA2
SL4PP	700M	100M	256K	495 pin PPGA
SL4PQ	750M	100M	256K	495 pin PPGA
SL4PR	800M	100M	256K	495 pin PPGA
SL4PS	850M	100M	256K	Micro-PGA2
SL4ZH	500M	100M	256K	BGA2
SL53L	850M	100M	256K	Micro-PGA2
SL53M	800M	100M	256K	Micro-PGA2
SL53P	750M	100M	256K	Micro-PGA2
SL53S	1.00G	100M	256K	495 pin PPGA
SL53T	900M	100M	256K	Micro-PGA2
SL547	850M	100M	256K	BGA2
SL548	800M	100M	256K	BGA2
SL54A	750M	100M	256K	BGA2
SL54F	1.00G	100M	256K	BGA2
SL56R	700M	100M	256K	BGA2
SL583	750M	100M	256K	BGA2
SL588	800M	100M	256K	Micro-PGA2
SL58M	750M	100M	256K	495 pin PPGA

Intel sSpec Number	CPU Speed	Bus Speed	L2 Cache Size	Package Type
SL58N	800M	100M	256K	495 pin PPGA
SL58P	850M	100M	256K	495 pin PPGA
SL58Q	900M	100M	256K	495 pin PPGA
SL58S	1.00G	100M	256K	495 pin PPGA
SL59H	900M	100M	256K	BGA2
SL59J	900M	100M	256K	Micro-PGA2
SL5AV	900M	100M	256K	495 pin PPGA
SL5CF	866M	133M	512K	478 pin PPGA
SL5CG	933M	133M	512K	478 pin PPGA
SL5CH	1.00G	133M	512K	478 pin PPGA
SL5CJ	1.06G	133M	512K	478 pin PPGA
SL5CK	1.13G	133M	512K	478 pin PPGA
SL5CL	1.20G	133M	512K	478 pin PPGA
SL5CN	866M	133M	512K	479 pin H-PBGA

Intel sSpec Number	CPU Speed	Bus Speed	L2 Cache Size	Package Type
SL5CP	933M	133M	512K	479 pin H-PBGA
SL5CQ	1.00G	133M	512K	479 pin H-PBGA FC-BGA2
SL5CR	1.06G	133M	512K	479 pin H-PBGA
SL5CS	1.13G	133M	512K	479 pin H-PBGA
SL5CT	1.20G	133M	512K	479 pin H-PBGA FC-BGA2
SL5N4	1.13G	133M	512K	478 pin PPGA
SL5N5	1.20G	133M	512K	478 pin PPGA
SL5PL	1.00G	133M	512K	478 pin PPGA
SL5QP	800M	133M	512K	479 pin H-PBGA
SL5QQ	800M	100M	512K	479 pin H-PBGA
SL5QR	750M	100M	512K	479 pin H-PBGA
SL5QS	733M	133M	512K	479 pin H-PBGA
SL5QT	700M	100M	512K	479 pin H-PBGA
SL5TB	1.00G	100M	512K	BGA2
SL5TF	1.00G	100M	256K	Micro-PGA2
SL5UB	866M	133M	512K	478 pin PPGA
SL5UC	933M	133M	512K	478 pin PPGA
SL637	1.26G	133M	512K	478 pin PPGA
SL68W	933M	133M	512K	479 pin H-PBGA
SL6A7	1.20G	133M	512K	478 pin PPGA
SL6A9	1.20G	133M	512K	478 pin PPGA
SL6AX	800M	133M	512K	479 pin H-PBGA
SL6AY	800M	100M	512K	479 pin H-PBGA
SL6CS	1.33G	133M	512K	479 pin H-PBGA

Intel Pentium II

Intel sSpec Number	CPU Speed	Bus Speed	L2 Cache Size	Package Type
SL264	233M	66M	512K	S.E.C.C.
SL265	266M	66M	512K	S.E.C.C.
SL28K	233M	66M	512K	S.E.C.C.
SL28L	266M	66M	512K	S.E.C.C.
SL28R	300M	66M	512K	S.E.C.C.
SL2HA	300M	66M	512K	S.E.C.C.
SL2HC	266M	66M	512K	S.E.C.C.
SL2HD	233M	66M	512K	S.E.C.C.
SL2KA	333M	66M	512K	S.E.C.C.
SL2MZ	300M	66M	512K	S.E.C.C.
SL2QA	233M	66M	512K	S.E.C.C.
SL2QB	266M	66M	512K	S.E.C.C.
SL2QC	300M	66M	512K	S.E.C.C.
SL2QF	333M	66M	512K	S.E.C.C.
SL2QH	333M	66M	512K	S.E.C.C.
SL2S5	350M	100M	512K	S.E.C.C.
SL2S6	350M	100M	512K	S.E.C.C.
SL2S7	400M	100M	512K	S.E.C.C.
SL2SF	350M	100M	512K	S.E.C.C.
SL2SH	400M	100M	512K	S.E.C.C.
SL2TV	333M	66M	512K	S.E.C.C.
SL2U3	350M	100M	512K	S.E.C.C.
SL2U5	400M	100M	512K	S.E.C.C.
SL2U6	400M	100M	512K	S.E.C.C.
SL2U7	450M	100M	512K	S.E.C.C.
SL2W7	266M	66M	512K	S.E.C.C.
SL2W8	300M	66M	512K	S.E.C.C.
SL2WB	450M	100M	512K	S.E.C.C.
SL2WY	333M	66M	512K	S.E.C.C.
SL2WZ	350M	100M	512K	S.E.C.C.
SL2YK	300M	66M	512K	S.E.C.C.
SL2YM	400M	100M	512K	S.E.C.C.
SL33D	266M	66M	512K	S.E.C.C.
SL356	350M	100M	512K	S.E.C.C.2
SL357	400M	100M	512K	S.E.C.C.2
SL358	450M	100M	512K	S.E.C.C.2
SL35V	300M	66M	512K	S.E.C.C.
SL36U	350M	100M	512K	S.E.C.C.2
SL37F	350M	100M	512K	S.E.C.C.2
SL37G	400M	100M	512K	S.E.C.C.2
SL37H	450M	100M	512K	S.E.C.C.2
SL38M	350M	100M	512K	S.E.C.C.
SL38N	400M	100M	512K	S.E.C.C.
SL38Z	400M	100M	512K	S.E.C.C.
SL3D5	400M	100M	512K	S.E.C.C.2

CPU's

Intel sSpec Number	CPU Speed	Bus Speed	L2 Cache Size	Package Type
SL3EE	400M	100M	512K	S.E.C.C.2
SL3F9	400M	100M	512K	S.E.C.C.2
SL3J2	350M	100M	512K	S.E.C.C.2
Intel Celeron M				
SL6N7	1.30G	400M	512K	478 pin PPGA FC-PGA2
SL6NM	1.30G	400M	512K	479 pin H-PBGA FC-BGA2
SL79S	1.20G	400M	512K	478 pin PPGA
SL79T	1.20G	400M	512K	479 pin H-PBGA
SL7DB	800M	400M	512K	479 pin H-PBGA
SL7ME	1.50G	400M	512K	478 pin PPGA
Intel Pentium II Xeon				
SL2NB	400M	100M	512K	S.E.C.C.
SL2RH	400M	100M	512K	S.E.C.C.
SL2XJ	450M	100M	512K	S.E.C.C.
SL2XK	450M	100M	1024K	S.E.C.C.
SL2XL	450M	100M	2048K	S.E.C.C.
SL33T	450M	100M	512K	S.E.C.C.
SL33U	400M	100M	1024K	S.E.C.C.
SL33V	400M	100M	2048K	S.E.C.C.
SL34H	400M	100M	512K	S.E.C.C.
SL34J	400M	100M	1024K	S.E.C.C.
SL354	450M	100M	512K	S.E.C.C.
SL35N	450M	100M	512K	S.E.C.C.
SL35P	450M	100M	1024K	S.E.C.C.
SL36W	450M	100M	512K	S.E.C.C.
Intel Pentium				
S106J	133M	66M	N/A	
SK079	75M	50M	N/A	TCP Mobile
SK086	120M	60M	N/A	Socket 5/7
SK089	75M	60M	N/A	TCP Mobile
SK090	90M	60M	N/A	TCP Mobile
SK091	75M	60M	N/A	SPGA
SK092	90M	60M	N/A	SPGA
SK098	133M	66M	N/A	Socket 5/7
SK106	133M	66M	N/A	Socket 5/7
SK107	133M	66M	N/A	Socket 5/7
SK110	120M	66M	N/A	Socket 5/7
SK113	120M	60M	N/A	TCP Mobile
SK118	120M	60M	N/A	TCP Mobile
SK119	75M	50M	N/A	TCP Mobile
SK120	90M	60M	N/A	TCP Mobile
SK121	100M	66M	N/A	TCP Mobile
SK122	75M	50M	N/A	SPGA
SK123	90M	60M	N/A	SPGA
SK124	100M	66M	N/A	SPGA
SL22M	120M	60M	N/A	Socket 5/7
SL22Q	133M	66M	N/A	Socket 5/7
SL24Q	200M	66M	N/A	Socket 7
SL24R	166M	66M	N/A	Socket 5/7
SL25H	200M	66M	N/A	Socket 7
SL25J	133M	66M	N/A	Socket 5/7
SL25L	133M	66M	N/A	Socket 5/7
SU031	90M	60M	N/A	Socket 5/7
SU032	100M	50M	N/A	Socket 5/7
SU033	120M	60M	N/A	Socket 5/7
SU038	133M	66M	N/A	Socket 5/7
SU070	75M	50M	N/A	Socket 5/7
SU071	150M	60M	N/A	Socket 5/7
Intel Pentium Pro				
SL22L	180M	60M	256K	PPGA
SL22S	180M	60M	256K	PPGA
SL22T	200M	66M	256K	CPGA
SL22U	180M	60M	256K	CPGA
SL22V	200M	66M	256K	CPGA
SL22X	166M	66M	512K	CPGA
SL22Z	200M	66M	512K	CPGA
SL23J	180M	60M	256K	CPGA
SL23K	200M	66M	256K	CPGA
SL23L	180M	66M	256K	CPGA
SL245	200M	66M	256K	CPGA
SL247	200M	66M	256K	CPGA

Intel sSpec Number	CPU Speed	Bus Speed	L2 Cache Size	Package Type
SL254	200M	66M	512K	CPGA
SL255	200M	66M	512K	CPGA
SL259	200M	66M	1024K	PPGA
SL25A	200M	66M	1024K	PPGA
SL2FJ	166M	66M	512K	CPGA
SU103	180M	60M	256K	PPGA
SU104	200M	60M	256K	CPGA
SY002	150M	60M	256K	CPGA
SY010	150M	60M	256K	CPGA
SY011	150M	60M	256K	CPGA
SY012	180M	60M	256K	CPGA
SY013	200M	66M	256K	CPGA
SY014	150M	60M	256K	CPGA
SY031	180M	66M	256K	CPGA
SY032	200M	66M	256K	CPGA
SY034	166M	66M	512K	CPGA
SY039	180M	60M	256K	CPGA
SY040	200M	66M	256K	CPGA
SY047	166M	66M	512K	CPGA
SY048	200M	66M	512K	CPGA
Intel Pentium with MMX Technology				
SL22F	166M	66M	N/A	TCP Mobile
SL22G	150M	66M	none	TCP Mobile
SL239	166M	66M	none	SPGA
SL23M	266M	66M	none	TCP Mobile
SL23P	266M	66M	none	TCP Mobile
SL23R	166M	66M	none	PPGA
SL23S	200M	66M	none	PPGA
SL23T	166M	66M	none	SPGA
SL23V	166M	66M	N/A	PPGA
SL23W	166M	66M	none	PPGA
SL23X	166M	66M	none	SPGA
SL23Z	166M	66M	none	PPGA
SL246	150M	66M	none	PPGA
SL25M	166M	66M	none	PPGA
SL25N	200M	66M	none	PPGA
SL26H	166M	66M	none	PPGA
SL26J	200M	66M	none	PPGA
SL26Q	166M	66M	none	PPGA
SL26T	166M	66M	none	TCP Mobile
SL26U	166M	66M	none	TCP Mobile
SL26V	166M	66M	none	SPGA
SL274	200M	66M	none	PPGA
SL27A	166M	66M	N/A	PPGA
SL27B	150M	66M	N/A	PPGA
SL27C	133M	66M	none	PPGA
SL27D	133M	66M	none	TCP Mobile
SL27H	166M	66M	none	PPGA
SL27J	166M	66M	none	SPGA
SL27K	166M	66M	none	PPGA
SL27S	233M	66M	none	PPGA
SL28P	200M	66M	none	TCP Mobile
SL28Q	233M	66M	none	TCP Mobile
SL293	233M	66M	N/A	PPGA
SL2BM	233M	66M	none	PPGA
SL2FP	166M	66M	none	PPGA
SL2FQ	200M	66M	none	PPGA
SL2HU	166M	66M	none	PPGA
SL2HX	166M	66M	none	SPGA
SL2N5	266M	66M	none	TCP Mobile
SL2N6	166M	66M	none	TCP Mobile
SL2RY	200M	66M	none	SPGA
SL2S9	200M	66M	none	SPGA
SL2WK	200M	66M	none	PPGA
SL2ZH	266M	66M	none	TCP Mobile
SL34N	300M	66M	none	TCP Mobile
SY059	166M	66M	none	PPGA
SY060	200M	66M	none	PPGA

Intel Pentium CPU Specs

AMD OPN (Ordering Part Number)	CPU Speed	Bus Speed	L2 Cache Size	Package Type
AMD Opteron				
OSA140CCO5AG	1.4G	800M	1M	940-Pin CµPGA
OSA140CEP5AK	1.4G	800M	1M	940-Pin CµPGA
OSA140CEP5AT	1.4G	800M	1M	940-Pin CµPGA
OSA142CCO5AG	1.6G	800M	1M	940-Pin CµPGA
OSA142CEP5AK	1.6G	800M	1M	940-Pin CµPGA
OSA142CEP5AT	1.6G	800M	1M	940-Pin CµPGA
OSA144CCO5AG	1.8G	800M	1M	940-Pin CµPGA
OSA144CEP5AG	1.8G	800M	1M	940-Pin CµPGA
OSA144CEP5AK	1.8G	800M	1M	940-Pin CµPGA
OSA144CEP5AT	1.8G	800M	1M	940-Pin CµPGA
OSA146CEP5AK	2.0G	800M	1M	940-Pin CµPGA
OSA146CEP5AT	2.0G	800M	1M	940-Pin CµPGA
OSA148CEP5AK	2.2G	800M	1M	940-Pin CµPGA
OSA148CEP5AT	2.2G	800M	1M	940-Pin CµPGA
OSA150CEP5AT	2.4G	800M	1M	940-Pin CµPGA
OSA240CCO5AH	1.4G	800M	1M	940-Pin CµPGA
OSA240CEP5AL	1.4G	800M	1M	940-Pin CµPGA
OSA240CEP5AU	1.4G	800M	1M	940-Pin CµPGA
OSA242CCO5AH	1.6G	800M	1M	940-Pin CµPGA
OSA242CEP5AL	1.6G	800M	1M	940-Pin CµPGA
OSA242CEP5AU	1.6G	800M	1M	940-Pin CµPGA
OSA244CCO5AH	1.8G	800M	1M	940-Pin CµPGA
OSA244CEP5AL	1.8G	800M	1M	940-Pin CµPGA
OSA244CEP5AU	1.8G	800M	1M	940-Pin CµPGA
OSA246CEP5AL	2.0G	800M	1M	940-Pin CµPGA
OSA246CEP5AU	2.0G	800M	1M	940-Pin CµPGA
OSA248CEP5AL	2.2G	800M	1M	940-Pin CµPGA
OSA248CEP5AU	2.2G	800M	1M	940-Pin CµPGA
OSA250CEP5AU	2.4G	800M	1M	940-Pin CµPGA
OSA340CCO5AI	1.4G	800M	1M	940-Pin CµPGA
OSA840CEP5AM	1.4G	800M	1M	940-Pin CµPGA
OSA840CEP5AV	1.4G	800M	1M	940-Pin CµPGA
OSA842CCO5AI	1.6G	800M	1M	940-Pin CµPGA
OSA842CEP5AM	1.6G	800M	1M	940-Pin CµPGA
OSA842CEP5AV	1.6G	800M	1M	940-Pin CµPGA
OSA844CCO5AI	1.8G	800M	1M	940-Pin CµPGA
OSA844CEP5AM	1.8G	800M	1M	940-Pin CµPGA
OSA844CEP5AV	1.8G	800M	1M	940-Pin CµPGA
OSA846CEP5AM	2.0G	800M	1M	940-Pin CµPGA
OSA846CEP5AV	2.0G	800M	1M	940-Pin CµPGA
OSA848CEP5AM	2.2G	800M	1M	940-Pin CµPGA
OSA848CEP5AV	2.2G	800M	1M	940-Pin CµPGA
OSA850CEP5AV	2.4G	800M	1M	940-Pin CµPGA
OSB140CSP5AT	1.4G	800M	1M	940-Pin CµPGA
OSB240CSP5AU	1.4G	800M	1M	940-Pin CµPGA
OSB840CSP5AV	1.4G	800M	1M	940-Pin CµPGA
OSK146CMP5AT	2.0G	800M	1M	940-Pin CµPGA
OSK246CMP5AU	1.8G	800M	1M	940-Pin CµPGA
OSK846CMP5AV	1.8G	800M	1M	940-Pin CµPGA
AMD Athlon 64 FX				
ADAFX51CEP5AK	2.2G	---	1M	940-Pin CµPGA
ADAFX51CEP5AT	2.2G	---	1M	940-Pin CµPGA
ADAFX53CEP5AT	2.4G	---	1M	940-Pin CµPGA
ADAFX53DEP5AS	2.4G	---	1M	939-Pin OµPGA
AMD Athlon 64				
ADA2800AEP4AX	1.8G	1600M	512K	754-Pin OµPGA
ADA3000AEP4AP	2.0G	1600M	512K	754-Pin OµPGA
ADA3000AEP4AR	2.0G	1600M	512K	754-Pin OµPGA
ADA3000AEP4AX	2.0G	1600M	512K	754-Pin OµPGA
ADA3200AEP4AX	2.0G	1600M	512M	754-Pin OµPGA
ADA3200AEP5AP	2.0G	1600M	1M	754-Pin OµPGA
ADA3200AEP5AR	2.0G	1600M	1M	754-Pin OµPGA
ADA3400AEP5AP	2.2G	1600M	1M	754-Pin OµPGA
ADA3400AEP5AR	2.2G	1600M	1M	754-Pin OµPGA
ADA3500DEP4AW	2.2G	1600M	512M	939-Pin OµPGA
ADA3700AEP5AR	2.4G	1600M	1M	754-Pin OµPGA
ADA3800DEP4AW	2.4G	1600M	512M	939-Pin OµPGA
AMD Athlon XP				
AX1500DMT3C	1333M	266M	256K	OPGA
AX1600DMT3C	1400M	266M	256K	OPGA
AX1700DMT3C	1467M	266M	256K	OPGA
AX1800DMT3C	1533M	266M	256K	OPGA
AX1900DMT3C	1600M	266M	256K	OPGA
AX2000DMT3C	1667M	266M	256K	OPGA
AX2100DMT3C	1733M	266M	256K	OPGA
AXDA1600DUT3C	1400M	266M	256K	OPGA
AXDA1700DLT3C	1467M	266M	256K	OPGA
AXDA1700DUT3C	1467M	266M	256K	OPGA
AXDA1800DLT3C	1533M	266M	256K	OPGA
AXDA1800DUT3C	1533M	266M	256K	OPGA

CPU's

AMD OPN (Ordering Part Number)	CPU Speed	Bus Speed	L2 Cache Size	Package Type
AXDA1900DLT3C	1600M	266M	256K	OPGA
AXDA2000DKT3C	1667M	266M	256K	OPGA
AXDA2000DUT3C	1667M	266M	256K	OPGA
AXDA2100DUT3C	1733M	266M	256K	OPGA
AXDA2200DKV3C	1800M	266M	256K	OPGA
AXDA2200DUV3C	1800M	266M	256K	OPGA
AXDA2400DKV3C	2000M	266M	256K	OPGA
AXDA2400DUV3C	2000M	266M	256K	OPGA
AXDA2500DKV4D	1833M	333M	512K	OPGA
AXDA2600DKV3C	2133M	266M	256K	OPGA
AXDA2600DKV3D	2083M	333M	512K	OPGA
AXDA2600DKV4D	1917M	333M	512K	OPGA
AXDA2700DKV3D	2167M	333M	256K	OPGA
AXDA2800DKV4D	2083M	333M	512K	OPGA
AXDA3000DKV4D	2167M	333M	512K	OPGA
AXDA3000DKV4E	2100M	400M	512K	OPGA
AXDA3200DKV4E	2200M	400M	512K	OPGA
AXDC2000DKV3C	1667M	266M	256K	OPGA
AXDC2200DKV3C	1800M	266M	256K	OPGA
AXDC2400DKV3C	2000M	266M	256K	OPGA
AMD Athlon MP				
AHX1000AMS3C	1000M	266M	256K	CPGA
AHX1200AMS3C	1200M	266M	256K	CPGA
AMP1500DMS3C	1333M	266M	256K	OPGA
AMP1600DMS3C	1400M	266M	256K	OPGA
AMP1800DMS3C	1533M	266M	256K	OPGA
AMP1900DMS3C	1600M	266M	256K	OPGA
AMP2000DMS3C	1667M	266M	256K	OPGA
AMP2100DMS3C	1733M	266M	256K	OPGA
AMSN2000DUT3C	1667M	266M	256K	OPGA
AMSN2200DKT3C	1800M	266M	256K	OPGA
AMSN2400DKT3C	2000M	266M	256K	OPGA
AMSN2600DKT3C	2133M	266M	256K	OPGA
AMSN2800DUT4C	2133M	266M	512K	OPGA
AMD Athlon				
A0650APT3B	650M	200M	256K	CPGA
A0700APT3B	700M	200M	256K	CPGA
A0750APT3B	750M	200M	256K	CPGA
A0800APT3B	800M	200M	256K	CPGA
A0850APT3B	850M	200M	256K	CPGA
A0900APT3B	900M	200M	256K	CPGA
A0950APT3B	950M	200M	256K	CPGA
A1000AMS3C	1000M	266M	256K	CPGA
A1000AMT3B	1000M	200M	256K	CPGA
A1000APT3B	1000M	200M	256K	CPGA
A1100AMS3B	1100M	200M	256K	CPGA
A1133AMS3C	1133M	266M	256K	CPGA
A1200AMS3B	1200M	200M	256K	CPGA
A1200AMS3C	1200M	266M	256K	CPGA
A1300AMS3B	1300M	200M	256K	CPGA
A1333AMS3C	1333M	266M	256K	CPGA
A1400AMS3B	1400M	200M	256K	CPGA
A1400AMS3C	1400M	266M	256K	CPGA
AMD-A0650MPR24BA	650M	200M	256K	---
AMD-A0700MPR24BA	700M	200M	256K	---
AMD-A0750MPR24BA	750M	200M	256K	---
AMD-A0800MPR24BA	800M	200M	256K	---
AMD-A0850MPR24BA	850M	200M	256K	---
AMD-A0900MMR24BA	900M	200M	256K	---
AMD-A0950MMR24BA	950M	200M	256K	---
AMD-A1000MMR24BA	1000M	200M	256K	---
AMD-K7100MNR53BA	1000M	200M	512K	---
AMD-K7500MTR51BA	500M	200M	512K	---
AMD-K7550MTR51BA	550M	200M	512K	---
AMD-K7550MTR51BB	550M	200M	512K	---
AMD-K7600MTR51BA	600M	200M	512K	---
AMD-K7600MTR51BC	600M	200M	512K	---
AMD-K7650MTR51BC	650M	200M	512K	---
AMD-K7650MTR51BC	650M	200M	512K	---
AMD-K7700MTR51BA	700M	200M	512K	---
AMD-K7700MTR51BC	700M	200M	512K	---

AMD OPN (Ordering Part Number)	CPU Speed	Bus Speed	L2 Cache Size	Package Type
AMD-K7750MTR52BA	750M	200M	512K	---
AMD-K7800MPR52BA	800M	200M	512K	---
AMD-K7850MPR52BA	850M	200M	512K	---
AMD-K7900MNR53BA	900M	200M	512K	---
AMD-K7950MNR53BA	950M	200M	512K	---
AMD Duron Model 3				
D0550AUT1B	550M	200M	64K	CPGA
D0600AUT1B	600M	200M	64K	CPGA
D0650AUT1B	650M	200M	64K	CPGA
D0700AUT1B	700M	200M	64K	CPGA
D0750AUT1B	750M	200M	64K	CPGA
D0800AUT1B	800M	200M	64K	CPGA
D0850AUT1B	850M	200M	64K	CPGA
D0900AUT1B	900M	200M	64K	CPGA
D0950AUT1B	950M	200M	64K	CPGA
AMD Duron Model 7				
DHD900AMT1B	900M	200M	64K	CPGA
DHD950AMT1B	950M	200M	64K	CPGA
DHD1000AMT1B	1000M	200M	64K	CPGA
DHD1100AMT1B	1100M	200M	64K	CPGA
DHD1200AMT1B	1200M	200M	64K	CPGA
DHD1300AMT1B	1300M	200M	64K	CPGA
AMD K6				
AMD-K6/200AFR	200M	---	---	321-pin CPGA
AMD-K6/233AFR	233M	---	---	321-pin CPGA
AMD-K6/266AFR	266M	---	---	321-pin CPGA
AMD-K6/300AFR	300M	---	---	321-pin CPGA
AMD K6-2				
AMD-K6-2/266AFR	266M	100M	---	321-pin CPGA
AMD-K6-2/300AFR	300M	100M	---	321-pin CPGA
AMD-K6-2/333AFR	333M	100M	---	321-pin CPGA
AMD-K6-2/350AFR	350M	100M	---	321-pin CPGA
AMD-K6-2/366AFR	366M	100M	---	321-pin CPGA
AMD-K6-2/380AFR	380M	100M	---	321-pin CPGA
AMD-K6-2/400AFQ	400M	100M	---	321-pin CPGA
AMD-K6-2/400AFR	400M	100M	---	321-pin CPGA
AMD-K6-2/450AFX	450M	100M	---	321-pin CPGA
AMD-K6-2/450AHX	450M	100M	---	321-pin CPGA
AMD-K6-2/475AFX	475M	100M	---	321-pin CPGA
AMD-K6-2/475AHX	475M	100M	---	321-pin CPGA
AMD-K6-2/500AFX	500M	100M	---	321-pin CPGA
AMD-K6-2/533AFX	533M	100M	---	321-pin CPGA
AMD-K6-2/550AGR	550M	100M	---	321-pin CPGA
AMD K6-III				
AMD-K6-III/400AFR	400M	100M	256K	321-pin CPGA
AMD-K6-III/400AHX	400M	100M	256K	321-pin CPGA
AMD-K6-III/450AFX	450M	100M	256K	321-pin CPGA
AMD-K6-III/450AHX	450M	100M	256K	321-pin CPGA

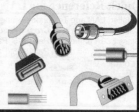

Chapter 11

Wiring and Pinouts

Quick Reference for LAN, Crossovers & Telephone

Detailed LAN and Telephone wiring is included on page 543

Cat 5 LAN Cable and Crossover Cable

Class 568A pair order: Pair1:4-5, Pair2:3-6, Pair3:1-2, Pair4:7-8 (ISDN)
Class 568B pair order: Pair1:4-5, Pair2:1-2, Pair3:3-6, Pair4:7-8 (Std Net)

EIA/TIA 568B RJ-45 Pin #	Signal	EIA/TIA 568B Color	RJ-45 Crossover Pin #	RJ-45 Crossover Signal
1 (Pair 2)	TX +	White/Orange	3	RX +
2 (Pair 2)	TX -	Orange/White or Orange	6	RX -
3 (Pair 3)	RX +	White/Green	1	TX +
4 (Pair 1)	Not used	Blue/White or Blue	4	Not used
5 (Pair 1)	Not used	White/Blue	5	Not used
6 (Pair 3)	RX -	Green/White or Green	2	TX -
7 (Pair 4)	Not used	White/Brown	7	Not used
8 (Pair 4)	Not used	Brown/White or Brown	8	Not used

Telephone Color Coding and Pair Assignment

Pair #	Line +	Line -	RJ12 6P6C "Line +" Pin #	RJ12 6P6C "Line -" Pin #
1	Green	Red	3	4
2	Black	Yellow	5	2
3	White	Blue	1	6

I/O Interfaces

Interface or Device	Max Speed Megabytes/Sec	Max # of Devices per Channel	Max Cable Length
ESDI			
Hard drive	3	2	Internal
Fibre Channel			
FC-AL, half duplex	100-200	126	6 miles
FC-AL, full duplex	200-400	126	6 miles
IDE/EIDE			

Note on wire length: minimum length is 10 inch, max 18 inch; minimum to first device is 5 inch, maximum is 12 inch; minimum to 2nd device is 5 inch, maximum 6 inch.

IDE/EIDE/ATAPI			
PIO Mode 0	3.3	2	18 inch
PIO Mode 1	5.2	2	18 inch
PIO Mode 2	8.3	2	18 inch
PIO Mode 3	11.1	2	18 inch
PIO Mode 4	16.7	2	18 inch
Ultra ATA/33 (16 bit data, 40pin plug/40 wire cable)	33	2	18 inch
Ultra ATA/66 (16 bit data, 40pin plug/80 wire cable)	66	2	18 inch
Ultra ATA/100 (16 bit data, 40pin plug/80 wire cable)	100	2	18 inch

Wiring & Pinout

Interface	Max Speed Megabytes/Sec	Max # of Devices per Channel	Max Cable Length
IEEE 1394			
1394-1995	12.5-50	63	14 ft
1394-FireWire & i.Link	12.5-50	63	14 ft
1394B	100-200	63	14 ft
Parallel			
Standard (12 foot length is a safer limit)	0.15	1	15 ft
IEEE-1284	3	1	30 ft
ECC (Extended Capability Port)	3	1	30 ft
EPP (Enhanced Parallel Port)	3	1	30 ft
SCSI			
SCSI-1	5	8	18 ft
Differential or LVD	5	8	75 ft
SCSI-2			
Fast, Fast Narrow	10	8	18 ft
Fast Wide, Wide	20	16	9 ft
Ultra Wide, 1 to 4 SCSI devices	40	16	9 ft
Ultra Wide, > 4 SCSI devices	40	16	4.5 ft
SCSI-3			
Ultra SCSI (Fast-20, Ultra Narrow)	20	8	9 ft
Ultra SCSI Differential	20	8	75 ft
Wide Ultra SCSI (Fast Wide 20)	40	16	9 ft
Wide Ultra SCSI Differential	40	16	75 ft
Ultra2 SCSI	40	8	36 ft
Wide Ultra2 SCSI (Fast 40)	80	16	36 ft
Ultra3 SCSI	80	8	36 ft
Wide Ultra3 SCSI (Fast-80DT)	160	16	36 ft
Ultra 160 (feature set of Ultra3SCSI)	160	16	36 ft
Ultra 320 (Ultra4)	320		36 ft
Serial			
16550 UART(115,200 bps)	0.015	1	50 ft
16570 UART(460.8 kbps)	0.06	1	10 ft
16590 UART(15 Mbps)	1.95	1	
V.35/RS449 values are heavily dependent on wire type and exact data rate; these are appx.			
V.35, RS449/422, RS530/422	0.056 to 0.064	1	4000 ft
V.35	0.224 to 0.256	1	3500 ft
V.35, RS449/422, RS530/422	0.896 to 1.024	1	1700 ft
RS449/422, RS530/422	0.224 to 0.256	1	1700 ft
RS449/422, RS530/422	0.896 to 1.024	1	350 ft
ST506/412			
Hard drive MFM & RLL	0.6 to 0.94	2	Internal
SSA (Serial Storage Architecture)			
Std 2 Channel System	20-40	128	75 ft
Token Ring			
Physical star, logical ring; Cat 3, RJ45 or IBM	4/16	72	1100/500
USB (Universal Serial Bus)			
USB 1.1 Low Speed	1.5	127	15 ft
USB 1.1 Full Speed	12	127	15 ft
USB 2.0	480		

Wiring & Pinout

Cable Length and Data Transmission Speed

Interface or Device	Max Speed Megabytes/Sec	Cable Type	Max Cable Length
Cable, Twisted Pair and Coax			
Cat 1 (old telephone standard)	obsolete	twisted pair	
Cat 2	4	twisted pair	
Cat 3 (minimum for data networks)	10	twisted pair	300 ft
Cat 4	16	twisted pair	300 ft
Cat 5 (most data today,shielded twisted pair=155mbps)	100	twisted pair	300 ft
Cat 5 Enhanced	100/1000	twisted pair	300 ft
Cat 6 (Patch cables for data, braided shield, two pair)		twisted pair	
Cat 8 (Flat cable, two twisted pair, under carpet standard)		twisted pair	
Cat 9 (Plenum cable, two twisted pair)		twisted pair	
Fiber Optic (8.3μ=single, 62.5-100μ=multi)	100 to 2Gbps	Fiber	6000 ft
RG-58 /U (50 ohm, solid copper wire core, max 30 taps per segment)		Coax	550 ft
RG-58 A/U (50 ohm, stranded copper wire core, max 30 taps)		Coax	550 ft
RG-58 C/U (50 ohm, stranded copper wire core, military version)		Coax	550 ft
RG-59 (75 ohm, cable TV)		Coax	
RG-6 (Satellite cable)		Coax	
RG-62 (93 ohm, ArcNet)		Coax	
RG-8 (50 ohm, thick ethernet, maximum 100 taps per segment)		Coax	1500 ft
RG-11 (75 ohm thick ethernet, maximum 100 taps per segment)		Coax	1500 ft
Token Ring (Cat 3, RJ45 or IBM DataConnnector)	4 or 16	UTP twisted pair	
Ethernet			
10Base-2 (Thinnet or Thin Ethernet)	10	RG-58 coax cable	550 ft
10Base-5 (Thinnet, N connector)	10	RG-58 coax cable	1500 ft
10Base-36 (multi-channel coax)	10	coax cable	11,000 ft
10Base-F (ethernet over optical fiber)	10	optical fiber	25 miles
10Base-FB (2 multi-mode, synchronous active hub)	10	2 optical fiber	25 miles
10Base-FL (2 fiber, asynchronous hub)	10	2 optical fiber	25 miles
10Base-FP (2 fiber, passive hub)	10	2 optical fiber	25 miles
10Base-T (Cat 3 twisted pair, RJ45)	10	UTP twisted pair	300 ft
10Broad-36 (3 channels of a cable TV system)	10	cable television	11,000 ft
10Gigabit (multimode fiber)	10 billion	optical fiber	900 ft
10Gigabit (single mode fiber)	10 billion	optical fiber	25 miles
100Base-FX (multimode fiber)	100	optical fibers	25 miles
100Base-T (Cat 5, RJ45)	100	UTP twisted pair	300 ft
100Base-T2 (2 pairs of Cat 3 or higher, unshielded)	100	UTP twisted pair	300 ft
100Base-T4 (4 pairs of Cat 3 or higher, unshielded)	100	UTP twisted pair	300 ft
100Base-TX (2 pairs of Cat 4 or higher, shielded)	100	UTP twisted pair	300 ft
1000Base-CX (2 pairs of 150 shielded cable)	1000	UTP twisted pair	300 ft
1000Base-LX (2 multimode; single mode longwave)	1000	2 optical fibers	25 miles
1000Base-SX (2 multimode; sinble mode shortwave)	1000	2 optical fibers	25 miles
1000Base-T (4 pairs of Cat 5 unshielded cable, RJ45)	1000	UTP twisted pair	300 ft

Wiring & Pinout

Parallel Printer Interface

Printer Pin Number	Signal Description	Function	Signal Direction at Printer
1	STROBE	Reads in the data	Input
2	DATA Bit 0	Data line	Input
3	DATA Bit 1	Data line	Input
4	DATA Bit 2	Data line	Input
5	DATA Bit 3	Data line	Input
6	DATA Bit 4	Data line	Input
7	DATA Bit 5	Data line	Input
8	DATA Bit 6	Data line	Input
9	DATA Bit 7	Data line	Input
10	ACKNLG	Acknowledge receipt of data	Output
11	Busy	Printer is busy	Output
12	Paper Empty	Printer out of paper	Output
13	SLCT	Online mode indicator	Output
14	Auto Feed XT		Input
15	Not Used	Not Used	
16	Signal ground	Signal ground	
17	Frame ground	Frame ground	
18	+5 volts	+5 volts	
19-30	Ground	Return signals of pins 1–12, twisted pairs.	
31	Input Prime or INIT	Resets printer, clears buffer & initializes	Input
32	Fault or Error	Indicates offline mode	Output
33	Signal ground	External ground	
34	Not Used	Not Used	
35	+5 Volts	+5 Volts (3.3 K-ohm)	
36	SLCT IN	TTL high level	Input

The above pinout is at the printer plug, computer side pinouts are on the next page. The "Parallel" or "Centronics" configuration for printer data transmission has become the de facto standard in the personal computer industry. This configuration was developed by a printer manufacturer (Centronics) as an alternative to serial data transmission. High data transfer rates are the main advantage of parallel and are attained by simultaneous transmission of all bits of a binary "word" (normally an ASCII code). Disadvantages of the parallel transfer are the requirement for 8 separate data lines and computer to printer cable lengths of less than 12 feet.

Centronics Amphenol 36 male connector for parallel interface

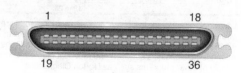

Parallel Pinouts @ Computer DB25 Systems

Computer Pin Number	Signal Description	Function	Signal Direction at Computer
1	STROBE	Reads in the data	Output
2	DATA Bit 0	Data line	Output
3	DATA Bit 1	Data line	Output
4	DATA Bit 2	Data line	Output
5	DATA Bit 3	Data line	Output
6	DATA Bit 4	Data line	Output
7	DATA Bit 5	Data line	Output
8	DATA Bit 6	Data line	Output
9	DATA Bit 7	Data line	Output
10	ACKNLG	Acknowledge receipt of data	Input
11	Busy	Printer is busy	Input
12	Paper Empty	Printer out of paper	Input
13	SLCT	Online mode indicator	Input
14	Auto Feed XT		Input
15	Fault or Error	Indicates offline mode	Input
16	Input Prime or INIT	Resets printer, clears buffer & initializes	Output
17	SLCT IN	TTL high level	Output
18-25	Ground	Return signals of pins 1–12, twisted pairs.	

Sub-D (DB25) male connector:

Loopback Diagnostic Plugs

Parallel-IBM DB25	Parallel-Other DB25	Serial-IBM DB25	Serial-Other DB25
1 to 13	2 to 15	1 to 7	2 to 3
2 to 15	3 to 13	2 to 3	4 to 5
10 to 16	4 to 12	4 to 5 to 8	6 to 8 to 20 to 22
11 to 17	5 to 10	6 to 11 to 20 to 22	
12 to 14	6 to 11	15 to 17 to 23	
		18 to 25	

Loopback plugs work in conjunction with various software diagnostics programs and are used to determine whether or not a parallel or serial port is functioning correctly. The plugs labeled "IBM" will work with the IBM Corporation Advanced Diagnostics software and those labeled as "Other" will work with a variety of other programs such as Norton Diagnostics.

Serial I/O Interfaces (RS232c)
Standard DB25 Pin Connector

Serial Pin Number	Signal Description	Function	Signal Direction at Device
1	FG	Frame ground	
2	TD	Transmit Data	Output
3	RD	Receive Data	Input
4	RTS	Request to Send	Output
5	CTS	Clear to Send	Input
6	DSR	Data Set Ready	Input
7	SG	Signal Ground	
8	DCD	Data Carrier Detect	Input
9	+V	+DC test voltage	Input
10	– V	– DC test voltage	Input
11	QM	Equalizer Mode	Input
12	(S)DCD	2nd Data Carrier Detect	Input
13	(S)CTS	2nd Clear to Send	Input
14	(S)TD	2nd Transmitted Data	Output
15	TC	Transmitter Clock	Input
16	(S)RD	2nd Received Data	Input
17	RC	Receiver Clock	Input
18	Not used	Not used	
19	(S)RTS	2nd Request to Send	Output
20	DTR	Data Terminal Ready	Output
21	SQ	Signal Quality Detect	Input
22	RI	Ring Indicator	Input
23		Data Rate Selector	Output
24	(TC)	External Transmitter Clk	Output
25	Not used	Not used	

DB25 male connector: see drawing on previous page.

IBM® Standard DB9 Pin Connector

Serial Pin Number	Signal Description	Function	Signal Direction at Device
1	DCD	Data Carrier Detect	Input
2	RD	Receive Data	Input
3	SD	Transmit Data	Output
4	DTR	Data Terminal Ready	Output
5	SG	Signal Ground	
6	DSR	Data Set Ready	Input
7	RTS	Request to Send	Output
8	CTS	Clear to Send	Input
9	RI	Ring Indicator	Input

Sub-D (DB9)male connector:

1   5

6   9

Wiring & Pinout

Notes On Serial Interfacing and Null Modem

Printers and asynchronous modems are relatively unsophisticated pieces of electronic equipment. Although all 25 pins of the Standard DB25 serial connector are listed 1 page back, only a few of the pins are needed for normal applications. The following list gives the necessary pins for each of the indicated applications.

1. "Dumb Terminals" – 1,2,3, & 7
2. Printers and asynchronous modems – 1,2,3,4,5,6,7,8, & 20
3. "Smart" & synchronous modems –1,2,3,4,5,6,7,8,13,14,15,17,20,22, & 24

Cable requirements also differ, depending on the particular hardware being used. The asynchronous modems normally use the 9 pin or 25 pin cables and are wired 1 to 1 (ie, pin 1 on one end of the cable goes to pin 1 on the other end of the cable.) Serial printers, however, have several wires switched in order to accommodate "handshaking" between computer and printer. The rewired junction is called a "Modem Eliminator" or "Null Modem". In the case of Standard DB25 the following are typical rewires:

Standard IBM PC DB25		Alternate IBM PC DB25	
at Computer	at Printer	at Computer	at Printer
1	1	1	1
3	2	3	2
2	3	2	3
8	4	20	5, 6 & 8
4	8	7	7
5 & 6	20	5, 6 & 8	20
20	5 & 6		
7	7		

Alternate PC to Terminal DB25		Alternate Hewlett-Packard DB25	
at PC	at Terminal	at Computer	at Printer
PC			
1	1	1	1
2	3	2	3
3	2	3	2
4	5	4 & 5	8
5	4	8	4 & 5
6 & 8	20	6	20
20	6 & 8	7 & 22	7 & 22
7	7	17	15
		11	12
		12	11
		15 & 24	17
		20	6

DB25 male connector

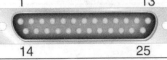

GPIB I/O Interface (IEEE-488)

The HPIB/GPIB/IEEE–488 standard is a very powerful interface developed originally by Hewlett–Packard (HP-IB). The interface has been adopted by a variety of groups, such as IEEE, and is known by names such as HP–IB, GPIB, IEEE–488 and IEC Standard 625–1 (outside the US). Worldwide use of this standard has come about due to its ease of use, handshaking protocol, and precisely defined function.

Information management is handled by three device types: Talkers, Listeners, and Controllers. Talkers send information, Listeners receive data, and Controllers manage the interactions. Up to 15 devices can be interconnected, but are usually located within 20 feet of the computer. Additional extenders can be used to access more than 15 devices. Devices can be set up in star, linear or other combinations and are easily set up using male/female stackable connectors.

GPIB 24 Line Bus		
Pin Description	Signal Function	Number
1	DATA I/O 1	Data line I/O bus
2	DATA I/O 2	Data line I/O bus
3	DATA I/O 3	Data line I/O bus
4	DATA I/O 4	Data line I/O bus
5	EIO	End or Identify
6	DAV	Data valid
7	NRFD	Not Ready For Data
8	NDAC	Data Not Accepted
9	SRQ	Service Request
10	IFC	Interface Clear
11	ATN	Attention
12	Shield	or wire ground
13	DATA I/O 5	Data line I/O bus
14	DATA I/O 6	Data line I/O bus
15	DATA I/O 7	Data line I/O bus
16	DATA I/O 8	Data line I/O bus
17	REN	Remote Enable
18	Ground	Ground
19	Ground	Ground
20	Ground	Ground
21	Ground	Ground
22	Ground	Ground
23	Ground	Ground
24	Logic Ground	Logic Ground

*Male Amphenol 24
for IEEE-488*

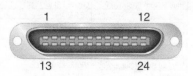

Analog Video Pinouts

Pin Number	Description - DB9 connector
Monochrome Display Adapter (MDA and HGC)	
1 & 2	Ground
3, 4, & 5	Not Used
6	+ Intensity
7	+ Video
8	+ Horizontal Drive
9	– Vertical Drive
Color Graphics Display Adapter (CGA)	
1 & 2	Ground
3	Red
4	Green
5	Blue
6	+ Intensity
7	Reserved
8	+ Horizontal Drive
9	– Vertical Drive
CGA Composite Video (RCA phono jack)	
1 (pin)	1.5 volt DC video signal
2 (shell)	Ground
Enhanced Graphics Adapter (EGA)	
1	Ground
2	Secondary Red
3	Red
4	Green
5	Blue
6	Secondary Green / Intensity
7	Secondary Blue / Monochrome
8	Horizontal Drive
9	Vertical Drive

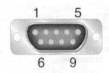

Sub-D (DB9) male connector

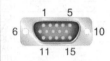

Sub-D High-Density 15 pin male connector

Video Graphics Array (VGA) - High-Density 15 pin connector			
Pin #	VGA - Standard	VGA - VESA DDC	Monochrome VGA
1	Red (Output)	Red (Output)	Not Used
2	Green (Output)	Green (Output)	Monochrome Video
3	Blue (Output)	Blue (Output)	Not Used
4	Reserved	Reserved	Not Used
5	Digital Ground	Digital Ground	Ground
6	Red Return (Input)	Ground Red	Key
7	Green Return (Input)	Ground Green	Monochrome Ground
8	Blue Return (Input)	Ground Blue	Not Used
9	Plug	+5 VDC	No Connection
10	Digital Ground	Sync Ground	Horizontal Sync Ground
11	Reserved	ID0 Monitor ID Bit 0	Not Used
12	Reserved	SCA - DDC serial data	Vertical Sync Ground
13	Horizontal Sync (Output)	Horizontal Sync (Output)	Horizontal Sync
14	Vertical Sync (Output)	Vertical Sync (Output)	Vertical Sync
15	Reserved	DDC Data Clock	No Connection

Digital Video

In the PC market, there are basically three different digital interface standards:

Standard	Owner	Signal Support	Specs
DVI	Digital Display Working Group (DDWG); supported by Intel www.ddwg.org	DVI and Analog VESA video P&D and DFP compatible	165 MHz x 1 6 channel, dual link 12 & 24 bit color 1920x1080 (HDTV)
DFP	Digital Flat Panel Group (DFP Group); VESA; supported by Compaq www.dfp-group.org	DFP only P&D compatible	165 MHz x 1 3 channel, single link 12 & 24 bit color 1280x1024 (SXGA)
P&D-A (formerly EVC)	Video Electronics Standards (VESA) www.vesa.org	EVA Analog VESA video USB IEEE 1394-1995	165 MHz x 1 3 channel, single link 12 & 24 bit color 1280x1024 (SXGA)

DVI Connectors

DVI-I (DVI digital & RGB analog)

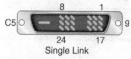
Single Link

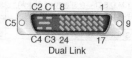
Dual Link

Pin#	Description	Pin#	Description
1	T.M.D.S DATA 2-	16	HOT PLUG DETECT
2	T.M.D.S DATA 2+	17	T.M.D.S DATA 0-
3	T.M.D.S DATA 2/4 SHIELD	18	T.M.D.S DATA 0+
4	T.M.D.S DATA 4- (not single link)	19	T.M.D.S DATA 0/5 SHIELD
5	T.M.D.S DATA 4+ (not single link)	20	T.M.D.S DATA 5- (not single link)
6	DDC CLOCK	21	T.M.D.S DATA 5+ (not single link)
7	DDC DATA	22	T.M.D.S CLOCK SHIELD
8	ANALOG VERT. SYNC	23	T.M.D.S CLOCK+
9	T.M.D.S DATA 1-	24	T.M.D.S CLOCK-
10	T.M.D.S DATA 1+		
11	T.M.D.S DATA 1/3 SHIELD	C1	ANALOG RED
12	T.M.D.S DATA 3- (not single link)	C2	ANALOG GREEN
13	T.M.D.S DATA 3+ (not single link)	C3	ANALOG BLUE
14	+5V POWER	C4	ANALOG HORZ SYNC
15	GROUND for +5V	C5	ANALOG Connon Ground Return

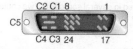

DVI-A (Analog)
Use above table less pins
3,4,5,9,10,11,12,13,19,20,21,22

DVI-D (DVI Digital ONLY)

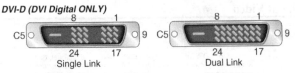

Single Link

Dual Link

Pin#	Description	Pin#	Description
1	T.M.D.S DATA 2-	16	HOT PLUG DETECT
2	T.M.D.S DATA 2+	17	T.M.D.S DATA 0-
3	T.M.D.S DATA 2/4 SHIELD	18	T.M.D.S DATA 0+
4	T.M.D.S DATA 4- (not single link)	19	T.M.D.S DATA 0/5 SHIELD
5	T.M.D.S DATA 4+ (not single link)	20	T.M.D.S DATA 5- (not single link)
6	DDC CLOCK	21	T.M.D.S DATA 5+ (not single link)
7	DDC DATA	22	T.M.D.S CLOCK SHIELD
8	ANALOG VERT. SYNC	23	T.M.D.S CLOCK+
9	T.M.D.S DATA 1-	24	T.M.D.S CLOCK-
10	T.M.D.S DATA 1+		
11	T.M.D.S DATA 1/3 SHIELD		
12	T.M.D.S DATA 3- (not single link)		
13	T.M.D.S DATA 3+ (not single link)		
14	+5V POWER		
15	GROUND for +5V	C5	ANALOG Connon Ground Return

DFP (Digital Flat Panel, old technology)

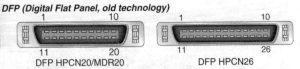

DFP HPCN20/MDR20

DFP HPCN26

Pin#	Description	Pin#	Description
1	Data TX1+	11	Data TX2+
2	Data TX1-	12	Data TX2-
3	SHIELD1	13	SHIELD2
4	SHIELDC	14	SHIELD0
5	Data TXC+	15	Data TX0+
6	Data TXC-	16	Data TX0-
7	GROUND	17	No Connection
8	+5V	18	HPD (Hot Plug Detect)
9	No Connection	19	DDC_DATA
10	No Connection	20	DDC_CLOCK

The HPCN26 connector shown above is listed in several sources but we could never locate a pinout table so it may not be a valid connector.

Digital Video (cont.)

P&D - (Plug & Display; formerly EVC)
Similar to DVI-I connector but is larger; used mostly in projectors; supports both analog and digital.

P&D-A (formerly EVC)
M1DA 30 pin connector

Pin#	Description	Pin#	Description
1	T.M.D.S DATA 2+	19	1394 VG
2	T.M.D.S DATA 2-	20	1394 VP
3	T.M.D.S DATA 2 RTN	21	T.M.D.S DATA 0-
4	SYNC RETURN	22	T.M.D.S DATA 0+
5	HORIZONTAL. SYNC TTL	23	T.M.D.S DATA 0 RETURN
6	VERTICAL. SYNC TTL	24	STEREO SYNC TTL
7	T.M.D.S CLOCK RETURN	25	DDC RETURN
8	CHARGING POWER INPUT+	26	DDC DATA SDA
9	1394 PAIR A, DATA	27	DDC CLOCK SCL
10	1394 PAIR A, DATA+	28	+5 VDC
11	T.M.D.S DATA 1+	29	1394 PAIR B, CLOCK+
12	T.M.D.S DATA 1-	30	1394 PAIR B, CLOCK-
13	T.M.D.S. DATA 1 RETURN	C1	RED VIDEO OUT
14	T.M.D.S CLOCK+	C2	GREEN VIDEO OUT
15	T.M.D.S CLOCK-	C3	PX CLOCK OUT
16	USB DATA+	C4	BLUE VIDEO OUT
17	USB DATA-	C5	COMMON GROUND RETURN
18	Firewire 1394 shield/charging power input-		

S-Video

Pin #	Description
1	Ground for Y
2	Ground for C
3	Intensity - luminance (Y)
4	Color - chrominance (©)
5	Ground for Composite Video (V)
6	No connection
7	Composite Video (V)

7 pin Mini-Din male connector

Light Pen Interface

Pin #	Description
1	– Light Pen Input
2	No connection
3	– Light Pen Switch
4	Chassis Ground
5	+5 Volts
6	+12 Volts

No standard connector, it can use Sub-DB9, USB, or proprietary connectors to a card in the computers slot.

Keyboard Plug - 5 Pin Din

Pin #	Description
1	Clock (TTL signal)
2	Data (TTL signal)
3	Not used
4	Ground
5	Power (+5 volt)

5 Pin Din male connector

Keyboard Plug - 6 Pin minidin

Pin #	Description
1	Data (TTL signal)
2	Not used
3	Ground
4	Power (+5 volt)
5	Clock (TTL signal)
6	Not used

6 Pin Mini-Din male connector

Mouse 9 Pin DB9-Shell

Pin #	Description
1	Not Used
2	Data
3	Clock
4	+5 Volt
5	Ground
6	Not Used
7	Enable Mouse
8	Mouse Ready

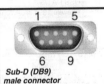

Sub-D (DB9) male connector

Mouse 6 Pin Mini Din

Pin #	Description
1	Data
2	Not Used
3	Signal Ground
4	+5 Volt
5	Clock
6	Not Used
Shell	

6 Pin Mini-Din male connector

S-Video

Mouse 9 Pin Microsoft Inport (Bus mouse)

Pin #	Description
1	+5 Volt
2	XA
3	XB
4	YA
5	YB
6	Switch 1
7	Switch 2
8	Switch 3
9	Signal Ground
Shell	Shield Ground

9 pin male connector, proprietary Microsoft

Game Control Cable

Joystick Signal Function	At Joystick	Direction Number	Signal Pin Description
1	+5 Volts	Supply voltage	Input
2	Button 1	Push Button 1	Output
3	Position 0	X Coordinate	Output
4	Ground	Ground	
5	Ground	Ground	
6	Position 1	Y Coordinate	Output
7	Button 2	Push Button 2	Output
8	+5 Volts	Supply voltage	Input
9	+5 Volts	Supply voltage	Input
10	Button 3	Push Button 3	Output
11	Position 2	X Coordinate	Output
12	Ground	Ground	
13	Position 3	Y Coordinate	Output
14	Button 4	Push Button 4	Output
15	+5 Volts	Supply voltage	Input

Sub-D (DB15) male connector:

Motherboard Battery Connector

Pin #	Description
1	Ground
2	Not used
3	Not used, or alignment key
4	+6 volt

Motherboard Speaker Connector

Pin #	Description
1	Audio
2	Alignment key
3	Ground
4	+5 volt

Disk Drive Power Plugs

Pin #	Description (4 pin molex)	Wire Color
1	+12 volt	Yellow
2	Ground	Black
3	Ground	Black
44	+5 volt	Red

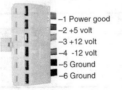

– 1 +12 volt
– 2 Ground
– 3 Ground
– 4 +5 volt

Hard & CDROM Drives -female

– 1 +12 volt
– 2 Ground
– 3 Ground
– 4 +5 volt

Floppy Drive-female

At Power Supply PS-8 Connector

Pin #	PS-8 (XT)	PS-8 (AT)	Wire Color
1	Power ground	Power good	Orange
2	Align Key	+5 volt	Red
3	+12 volt	+12 volt	Yellow
4	–12 volt	–12 volt	Blue
5	Ground	Ground	Black
6	Ground	Ground	Black

At Power Supply PS-9 Plug

Pin #	PS-9 (XT & AT)	Wire Color
1	Ground	Black
2	Ground	Black
3	–5 volt	White
4	+5 volt	Red
5	+5 volt	Red
6	+5 volt	Red

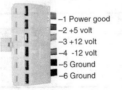

–1 Power good
–2 +5 volt
–3 +12 volt
–4 -12 volt
–5 Ground
–6 Ground

PS-8 Power Supply

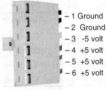

– 1 Ground
– 2 Ground
– 3 -5 volt
– 4 +5 volt
– 5 +5 volt
– 6 +5 volt

PS-9 Power Supply Plug

ATX Power Supply Plug

Pin #	Description	Wire Color
1	+3.3 V	Orange
2	+3.3 V	Orange
3	Ground	Black
4	+5.0 V	Red
5	Ground	Black
6	+5.0 V	Red
7	Ground	Black
8	Power Ok	Gray
9	+5 Vstand by	Violet
10	+12 V	Yellow
11	+3.3 V	Orange
12	−12.0 V	Blue
13	Ground	Black
14	Power Supply On	Green
15	Ground	Black
16	Ground	Black
17	Ground	Black
18	−5.0 V	White
19	+5.0 V	Red
20	+5.0 V	Red

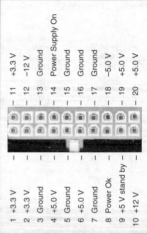

ATX 12Volt Power Supply Plug

Pin #	Description	Color
1	Ground	Black
2	Ground	Black
3	+12 VDC	Yellow
4	+12 VDC	Yellow

Female connector

4 +12 VDC −   − 3 +12 VDC

2 Ground −   − 1 Ground

AUX Auxiliary Power Plug

Pin #	Description	Wire Color
1	Ground	Black
2	Ground	Black
3	Ground	Black
4	+3.3 volt	Orange
5	+3.3 volt	Orange
6	+5 volt	Red

− 1 Ground

− 2 Ground

− 3 Ground

− 4 +5 volt

− 5 +5 volt

− 6 +5 volt

Female connector

EATX Power Supply 24 Pin - EATXPR1

Pin #	Description	Wire Color
1	+3.3 V	Orange
2	+3.3 V	Orange
3	Ground	Black
4	+5.0 V	Red
5	Ground	Black
6	+5.0 V	Red
7	Ground	Black
8	Power Ok	Gray
9	+5 Vstand by	Violet
10	+12 V	Yellow
11	+12 V	?
12	+3.3 V	?
13	+3.3 V	Orange
14	−12.0 V	Blue
15	Ground	Black
16	Power Supply On	Green
17	Ground	Black
18	Ground	Black
19	Ground	Black
20	−5.0 V	White
21	+5.0 V	Red
22	+5.0 V	Red
23	+5.0 V	?
24	Ground	?

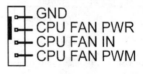

Fan Connectors

USB (Universal Serial Bus)

USB was developed in 1995 by the computer telecommunication industry members as an industry-standard for expanding PC's by adding peripheral devices. Its purpose is to make adding peripheral devices easy and low cost. USB is a cable bus that allows data exchange between your computer and external peripherals by using a standardized plug and port combination. Today, virtually all new PC's include a USB interface. Detailed information on USB is available at the **http://www.usb.org** website.

Windows Support

USB is supported by Microsoft Windows 95 OSR 2.1, Windows 98, Windows 98 Second Edition, Windows Millennium Edition (Windows ME), Windows 2000, and Windows XP. It is not supported by Windows versions earlier than Windows 95 OSR 2.1 and it is not supported by Windows NT. OSR 2.1 does no support all aspects of USB - see
 http://www.microsoft.com/hwdev/busbios/usbwin98.htm for details

USB Features

USB is hot-swappable and uses the plug-and-play interface to connect up to 127 devices at the same time to your computer. There are no IRQ conflicts, no DMA changes, and no hardware address changes (no jumpers). The operating system software will be able to identify the USB device when the device comes on line or goes off line. USB supports both isochronous and asynchronous data transfers.

USB 1.1 is the current version and it provides both a high-speed and low-speed mode. A comparison chart of I/O interface speeds is available on page 518. The following is a general summary of the two speed modes:

    Low Speed (1.5 Mbps) - unshielded cable
    Typical peripherals: keyboard, joystick, mouse, stylus, game peripherals.
    High Speed (12.0 Mbps) - shielded cable
    Typical peripherals: floppy drive, camera, modem, scanner, zip drive, video, imaging, broadband.

The latest USB specification is USB 2.0 (April 2000) and increases the available bandwidth to 480Mbps for high-speed devices. The increased bandwidth will be particularly useful for high-quality video conferencing cameras, high-resolution scanners, and high-density storage. As of mid 2001, USB 2.0 support will not be included in the RTM version of Windows XP because there is not a sufficient array of production-quality USB 2.0-conforming devices to test against.

Power Usage and Voltages

USB also distributes electrical power to the peripherals but the amount of power is limited, depending on the following:

    Bus-powered Hub - 100 mA maximum at power up and 500 mA at normal operation.
    Self-powered Hub - 100 mA maximum
    Low power, bus-powered functions - 100 mA maximum
    Self-powered functions - 100 mA maximum
    Suspended device - 0.5 mA maximum

Voltage supplied to the USB device must be in the range of 4.75V - 5.25V and the maximum voltage drop for a bus-powered hub is 0.35V. All USB devices must be able to send data at 4.4V, but only the low power functions have to work at this voltage. Voltage requirements for functions is 4.75V.
Universal Serial Bus Connector

USB Cables & Connectors
USB pinout for USB Type A and B connectors:

Pin #	Signal	Wire Color
1	Vcc, +5V DC	Red
2	D-, Data -	White
3	D+, Data +	Green
4	Ground	Black

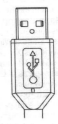

USB A-male connector with USB Logo

A-Male plug   B-Male plug

Mini USB Type B 5 Pin

Pin #	Signal
1	+5 VDC
2	-Data
3	+Data
4	No connection
5	Ground

Mini USB Type B male

Mini USB 4 Pin (could not find pinout by press time...)

Pin #	Signal
1	
2	
3	
4	

Mini USB 4 Pin male

A-male connector goes to the upstream port and connects to the hub or host computer.

B-male connector goes to the downstream port and connects to the peripheral device, such as a scanner

USB cables come in lengths between 0.5 (x feet) and 5.0 meters (15 feet). USB extension cables are available that have an A-female connector on one end and an A-male connector on the other, but be certain you do not exceed a total cable length of 5 meters. If you need a length beyond the 5 meter USB limitation, you can put up to 5 USB peripheral cables and 4 hubs in a daisy chain to reach out to a maximum of 25 meters (80 feet).

USB Cable length vs. wire gauge	
Gauge (AWG)	Maximum Length (meters)
28	0.81
26	1.31
24	2.08
22	3.33
20	5.0

Although USB cables have only 2 standard connectors, not all motherboards have the same USB pinouts on the header connector. Motherboard connectors can have 4, 5, 8, 10, and 16 pin headers but the manufacturer normally supplies an adapter cable to get to the A-female socket. Standard receptacle brackets on a modern motherboard are normally 2 x 4 pin, 1 x 10 pin, 2 x 5 pin, and 2 x 8 pin.

As with any "standard", there are always exceptions to the rules. In cases where the physical size of the B-male connector is too large to fit in a USB device, specialized tiny USB connectors are used. A typical example of this is where small digital cameras are equipped with a USB port for downloading pictures (the Olympus digital cameras use a tiny USB port that is only 5mm in width and is called the Mini USB.)

Wiring & Pinout

Firewire - IEEE-1394

Firewire was originally developed by Apple in 1955 and is a very fast, external bus for transferring data between devices. It is also referred to as IEEE1394 High Performance Serial Bus and is very similar to USB. FireWire devices are hot pluggable, which means they can be connected and disconnected any time, even with the power on. When a new FireWire device is connected to a computer, the operating system automatically detects it and prompts for the driver disk (thus the reference "plug-and-play"). Transfer rates of 400 Mbps (1394a) are the standard with 800 (1394b) and 1600 Mbps varients to follow shortly.

6 Pin IEEE 1394 Firewire

Pin #	Signal
1	Power
2	Ground
3	TPB -
4	TPB +
5	TPA -
6	TPA +

6 Pin FireWire, female

6 Pin FireWire, female

4 Pin IEEE 1394 Firewire

Pin #	Signal
1	TPB -
2	TPB +
3	TPA -
4	TPA +

4 Pin FireWire, female

4 Pin FireWire, female

Miscellaneous Network/Antenna Connectors

BNC on coax: LAN, video, antenna

N Type on coax, network, antennas, video

Twinax on coax, networks

TNC Cable: antenna

Miscellaneous Non-PC Connectors

Mac mouse or keyboard

Sun mouse or keyboard

Mac Localtalk (Appletalk, Mini Din 3

Mac serial port, Mini Din 8

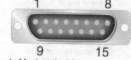

Apple Macintosh video

ADC Apple (proprietary) digital video

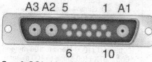

Sun & SGI video (13C3)

SGI Open LDI, MDR36

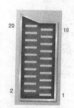

SCART : combined audio and video

Unshielded Twisted Pair (UTP) Voice/Data Cables

ANSI/TIA/EIA Category	IEC/ISO Class	Anixter Levels	Common Designation & Symbol	Maximum Bandwidth (MHz)	Wire Size (AWG)	Common Applications
8						Proposed
7	F	XP7	- - -	600	- - -	**Proposed** 10 Gigabit Ethernet
6e						Proposed
6	E	XP6	CAT6	250	24	**Twice the bandwidth of Cat 5e with lower signal-to-noise.** 1000BaseTX (1000 Mbps to 100 meters) 1000BaseT (1000 Mbps to 100 meters) 1000 Mbps ATM (to 160 meters) Gigabit Ethernet
5e	D	5e	CAT5e	100	24	**Tightly twisted pairs reduce crosstalk loss.** 1000BaseT (1000 Mbps to 100 meters) 100BaseTX (100 Mbps to 100 meters) 100BaseT (100 Mbps to 100 meters) Data to 100 Mbps Gigabit Ethernet Fast Ethernet
5	D	5	CAT5	100	24	**Currently most common cable in new installations.** 1000BaseT (1000 Mbps to 100 meters) 100BaseTX (100 Mbps to 100 meters) 100BaseT (100 Mbps to 100 meters) 10BaseT (10 Mbps to 100 meters) 100BaseT4 Data to 100 Mbps Gigabit Ethernet Fast Ethernet 155.52 Mbps ATM (to 150 meters) 51.84 Mbps ATM (to 160 meters) TP-PMD 100BaseVG-AnyLAN (to 100 meters)
4	- - -	- - -	CAT4	20	22 or 24	**Obsolete - no longer used** 10BaseT (10 Mbps to 100 meters) 1BaseT (1 Mbps to 500 meters) 100BaseT4 Data to 20 Mbps 16 Mbps token ring Ethernet 100BaseVG-AnyLAN (to 100 meters)

ANSI/TIA/EIA Category	IEC/ISO Class	Anixter Levels	Common Designation & Symbol	Maximum Bandwidth (MHz)	Wire Size (AWG)	Common Applications
3	C	3	CAT3	16	24	**Minimum standard for new installations** 100BaseT4 10BaseT (10 Mbps to 100 meters) 4 Mbps token ring Ethernet Data to 10 Mbps 155.52 Mbps ATM (to 100 meters) 51.84 Mbps ATM (to 100 meters) 25.6 Mbps ATM (to 100 meters) 100BaseVG-AnyLAN (to 100 meters) ISDN (basic rate) Voice telephone systems
2	B	2	- - -	1	22 or 24	**IBM Type 3** EIA-232 1Base5 Voice telephone systems 1.544 Mbps T1 4 Mbps token ring Data to 4 Mbps
1	A	1	- - -	100 kHz	22 or 24	**Pots - Plain Old Telephone Service** Alarm systems Voice only telephone systems Doorbell wire

Notes: Anixter Inc., 2301 Patriot Blvd., Glenview, IL 60025
Abbreviations: AF = The ATM Forum, ANSI = American National Standards Institute, ATM = asynchronous transfer mode, AWG = American Wire Gauge, EIA = Electronic Industries Alliance, ICEA = Insulated Cable Engineer's Association, IEC = International Electrotechnical Commission, ISDN = integrated services digital network, ISO = International Organization for Standardization, Mbps = megabits per second, MHz = mega-hertz = million Hertz, PHY = physical layer, TIA = Telecommunications Industry Association, TP-PMD = twisted-pair physical medium dependent, VG = voice grade

Wiring & Pinout

Jacks, Plugs and Modular Connectors

USOC (Uniform Service Ordering Codes) is defined in the US FCC, 47 CFR, Part 68 and determines what type of jack (RJ or Registered Jack) is used for a telephone circuit, how may pairs of wires are used, and to what the pairs of wires are connected. LAN wiring is defined by EIA/TIA (Electronics Industry Alliance/Telecommunications Industry Association) and uses the RJ45 connecter.

Modular Connector Pin Numbers
Male connectors

4 Position
Modular Connector.
Mostly analog
telephone

6 Position
Modular Connector.
Mostly analog
telephone

8 Position
Modular Connector
Telephone, LAN,
ISDN, RS232

10 Position
Modular Connector
Same width as 8 position connector

MMP or MMJ 6 Position Modified
Modular Connector
DEC Equipment

6 Pin Female on left
8 Pin Male on right

Pin 1

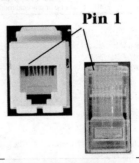

Telephone Wiring Configurations

USOC RJ11 (4-pin)	Pin Number			
	1	2	3	4
Line 1 - Tip (+)			X	
Line 1 - Ring (-)		X		

USOC RJ11 (6-pin)	Pin Number					
	1	2	3	4	5	6
Line 1 - Tip (+)				X		
Line 1 - Ring (-)			X			

USOC RJ11 (8-pin)	Pin Number							
	1	2	3	4	5	6	7	8
Line 1 - Tip (+)					X			
Line 1 - Ring (-)				X				

USOC RJ14 (4-pin)	Pin Number			
	1	2	3	4
Line 1 - Tip (+)			X	
Line 1 - Ring (-)		X		
Line 2 - Tip (+)	X			
Line 2 - Ring (-)				X

USOC RJ14 (6-pin)	Pin Number					
	1	2	3	4	5	6
Line 1 - Tip (+)				X		
Line 1 - Ring (-)			X			
Line 2 - Tip (+)		X				
Line 2 - Ring (-)					X	

USOC RJ14 (8-pin)	Pin Number							
	1	2	3	4	5	6	7	8
Line 1 - Tip (+)					X			
Line 1 - Ring (-)				X				
Line 2 - Tip (+)			X					
Line 2 - Ring (-)						X		

USOC RJ25 (6-pin)	Pin Number					
	1	2	3	4	5	6
Line 1 - Tip (+)				X		
Line 1 - Ring (-)			X			
Line 2 - Tip (+)		X				
Line 2 - Ring (-)					X	
Line 3 - Tip (+)	X					
Line 3 - Ring (-)						X

Telephone Wiring Configurations (cont.)

USOC RJ25 (8-pin)	Pin Number							
	1	2	3	4	5	6	7	8
Line 1 - Tip (+)					X			
Line 1 - Ring (-)				X				
Line 2 - Tip (+)			X					
Line 2 - Ring (-)						X		
Line 3 - Tip (+)		X						
Line 3 - Ring (-)							X	

USOC RJ31	Pin Number							
	1	2	3	4	5	6	7	8
Line 1 - Tip (+)								X
Line 1 - Ring (-)	X							
Network - Tip (+)					X			
Network - Ring (-)				X				

USOC RJ38	Pin Number							
	1	2	3	4	5	6	7	8
Line 1 - Tip (+)								X
Line 1 - Ring (-)	X							
Network - Tip (+)					X			
Network - Ring (-)				X				
Strap		X						
Strap							X	

USOC RJ41	Pin Number							
	1	2	3	4	5	6	7	8
Line 1 - Tip (+)					X			
Line 1 - Ring (-)				X				
PR Resistor							X	
PC Resistor								X
R-FLL	X							
T-FLL		X						
A or MI			X					
A1 or MIC						X		

USOC RJ45	Pin Number							
	1	2	3	4	5	6	7	8
Line 1 - Tip (+)					X			
Line 1 - Ring (-)				X				
PR Resistor							X	
PC Resistor								X
A or MI			X					
A1 or MIC						X		

Wiring & Pinout

USOC RJ61 (8-pin)	Pin Number							
	1	2	3	4	5	6	7	8
Line 1 - Tip (+)					X			
Line 1 - Ring (-)				X				
Line 2 - Tip (+)			X					
Line 2 - Ring (-)						X		
Line 3 - Tip (+)		X						
Line 3 - Ring (-)							X	
Line 4 - Tip (+)	X							
Line 4 - Ring (-)								X

Network Wiring Configurations

USOC 6P4C (6-pin)	Pin Number					
	1	2	3	4	5	6
Pair 1 - Tip (+)				X		
Pair 1 - Ring (-)			X			
Pair 2 - Tip (+)		X				
Pair 2 - Ring (-)					X	

USOC 6P6C (6-pin)	Pin Number					
	1	2	3	4	5	6
Pair 1 - Tip (+)				X		
Pair 1 - Ring (-)			X			
Pair 2 - Tip (+)		X				
Pair 2 - Ring (-)					X	
Pair 3 - Tip (+)	X					
Pair 3 - Ring (-)						X

USOC 8P8C (8-pin)	Pin Number							
	1	2	3	4	5	6	7	8
Pair 1 - Tip (+)					X			
Pair 1 - Ring (-)				X				
Pair 2 - Tip (+)			X					
Pair 2 - Ring (-)						X		
Pair 3 - Tip (+)		X						
Pair 3 - Ring (-)							X	
Pair 4 - Tip (+)								X
Pair 4 - Ring (-)	X							

Wiring & Pinout

Network Wiring Configurations (cont.)

USOC RJ48 (8-pin)	Pin Number							
	1	2	3	4	5	6	7	8
To Network - Tip (+)					X			
To Network - Ring (-)				X				
From Network - Tip (+)		X						
From Network - Ring (-)	X							

EIA/TIA-568-A (8-pin)	Pin Number							
	1	2	3	4	5	6	7	8
Pair 1 - Tip (+)					X			
Pair 1 - Ring (-)				X				
Pair 2 - Tip (+)			X					
Pair 2 - Ring (-)						X		
Pair 3 - Tip (+)	X							
Pair 3 - Ring (-)		X						
Pair 4 - Tip (+)							X	
Pair 4 - Ring (-)								X

EIA/TIA-568-B, WECO, AT&T, Bell 258A (8-pin)	Pin Number							
	1	2	3	4	5	6	7	8
Pair 1 - Tip (+)					X			
Pair 1 - Ring (-)				X				
Pair 2 - Tip (+)			X					
Pair 2 - Ring (-)						X		
Pair 3 - Tip (+)	X							
Pair 3 - Ring (-)		X						
Pair 4 - Tip (+)							X	
Pair 4 - Ring (-)								X

MMJ (DEC Wiring, RS423, 6-pin)	Pin Number					
	1	2	3	4	5	6
Pair 1 - Tip (+)		X				
Pair 1 - Ring (-)			X			
Pair 2 - Tip (+)					X	
Pair 2 - Ring (-)				X		
Pair 3 - Tip (+)	X					
Pair 3 - Ring (-)						X

Wiring & Pinout

Network Wiring Configurations (cont.)

Token Ring (4-wire Ethernet, 8-pin)	Pin Number							
	1	2	3	4	5	6	7	8
Pair 1 - Tip (+)					X			
Pair 1 - Ring (-)				X				
Pair 2 - Tip (+)			X					
Pair 2 - Ring (-)						X		

ANSI X3T9.5 TP-PMD (8-pin)	Pin Number							
	1	2	3	4	5	6	7	8
Pair 1 - Tip (+)	X							
Pair 1 - Ring (-)		X						
Pair 2 - Tip (+)							X	
Pair 2 - Ring (-)								X

10BaseT (4-wire Ethernet, 8-pin)	Pin Number							
	1	2	3	4	5	6	7	8
Pair 1 - Tip (+)	X							
Pair 1 - Ring (-)		X						
Pair 2 - Tip (+)			X					
Pair 2 - Ring (-)						X		

ISDN (ISO 8877:1987(E), 8-pin)	Pin Number							
	1	2	3	4	5	6	7	8
Power source 3 (+)	X							
Power source 3 (-)		X						
Transmit (+)			X					
Receive (+)				X				
Receive (-)					X			
Transmit (-)						X		
Power sink 2 (-)							X	
Power sink 2 (+)								X

Abbreviations: ANSI = American National Standards Institute, AT&T - American Telephone and Telegraph, DEC = Digital Equipment Company, EIA = Electronic Industries Alliance, ISDN = integrated services digital network, ISO = International Organization for Standardization, MMJ = modified modular jack, RJ = registered jack, RS423 = serial interface standard, TIA = Telecommunications Industry Association, TP-PMD = twisted pair - physical media dependent, USOC = universal service ordering code, WECO = WECO Electrical Connectors, Inc.

Wiring & Pinout

Optical Fiber Color Code

The follow table contains the standardized Optical Fiber Cable Color Codes under TIE/EIA-598. Colors are directly on the surface of the coated fiber or on the fiber's secondary coating.

Position	Color
1	Blue
2	Orange
3	Green
4	Brown
5	Slate
6	White
7	Red
8	Black
9	Yellow
10	Violet
11	Rose
12	Aqua

Telephone Wire Color Codes - Small Groups

AT&T established the following uniform wiring scheme to be used for individual telephone stations or terminals. The wiring scheme for standard 25 pair lines is included on the next page.

Pair Number	Wire Number	Solid Color	Stripe Color	Alternate Color	Pin Number
1	1	White	Blue	Green	4
1	2	Blue	White	Red	3
2	1	White	Orange	Black	2
2	2	Orange	White	Yellow	5
3	1	White	Green	White	1
3	2	Green	White	Blue	6

RG Coax Cable

Coax	OD Inches	Impedance ohms	Description
RG6/U	0.332	75	Broadband, CATV, satellite, HDTV, rated for higher frequencies than RG59 and gives better performance; F-Type connectors
RG6/U Quadshield	0.332	75	The new standard for DTV, CATV, SATV, HDTV; F-Type connectors
TG8/U	0.405	52	Thicknet
RG11/U	0.405	75	Backbone and runs > 545meters; F-Type connector
RG58	0.195	50	Thinnet network (A/U only), CATV
RG59	0.242	75	Basic analog CATV & CCTV, runs < 225 meters; BNC connectors
RG62	0.249	93	Older IBM or Arcnet networks

U = solid wire core; A/U = stranded wire core; C/U = Military spec

Wiring & Pinout

Telephone Wire Color Codes - 25 Pair

AT&T established the following uniform wiring scheme for 25 Pair blocks. Colors used for groups are white, red, black, yellow and violet. Colors used for Pairs within a Group are blue, orange, green, brown, and slate.

Pair Number	Wire Number	Solid Color	Stripe Color	Pin Number
1	1	White	Blue	26
1	2	Blue	White	1
2	1	White	Orange	27
2	2	Orange	White	2
3	1	White	Green	28
3	2	Green	White	3
4	1	White	Brown	29
4	2	Brown	White	4
5	1	White	Slate	30
5	2	Slate	White	5
6	1	Red	Blue	31
6	2	Blue	Red	6
7	1	Red	Orange	32
7	2	Orange	Red	7
8	1	Red	Green	33
8	2	Green	Red	8
9	1	Red	Brown	34
9	2	Brown	Red	9
10	1	Red	Slate	35
10	2	Slate	Red	10
11	1	Black	Blue	36
11	2	Blue	Black	11
12	1	Black	Orange	37
12	2	Orange	Black	12
13	1	Black	Green	38
13	2	Green	Black	13
14	1	Black	Brown	39
14	2	Brown	Black	14
15	1	Black	Slate	40
15	2	Slate	Black	15
16	1	Yellow	Blue	41
16	2	Blue	Yellow	16
17	1	Yellow	Orange	42
17	2	Orange	Yellow	17
18	1	Yellow	Green	43
18	2	Green	Yellow	18
19	1	Yellow	Brown	44
19	2	Brown	Yellow	19
20	1	Yellow	Slate	45
20	2	Slate	Yellow	20
21	1	Violet	Blue	46
21	2	Blue	Violet	21
22	1	Violet	Orange	47
22	2	Orange	Violet	22
23	1	Violet	Green	48
23	2	Green	Violet	23
24	1	Violet	Brown	49
24	2	Brown	Violet	24
25	1	Violet	Slate	50
25	2	Slate	Violet	25

Wiring & Pinout

Standard Copper Wire Specs

Gauge AWG	Solid or strands/ AWG	Outside Diameter		Circular Mils	Weight		Resistance	
		mm	Inch		kg/ km	lb/ 000ft	ohms/ km	ohms/ 1000ft
14	Solid	1.630	0.064	4110	18.50	12.40	8.6	2.6
	7/22	1.854	0.073	4480	20.18	13.53	7.6	2.3
	19/27	1.854	0.073	3830	17.25	11.56	8.9	2.7
	41/30	1.854	0.073	4100	18.45	12.37	8.3	2.5
	105/34	1.854	0.073	4168	18.77	12.58	8.2	2.5
16	Solid	1.290	0.051	2580	11.60	7.78	13.7	4.2
	7/24	1.524	0.060	2828	12.74	8.54	12.0	3.7
	65/34	1.499	0.059	2580	11.62	7.79	13.2	4.0
	26/30	1.499	0.059	2600	11.71	7.85	13.1	4.0
	19/29	1.473	0.058	2426	10.94	7.33	14.0	4.3
	105/36	1.499	0.059	2625	11.83	7.93	13.1	4.0
18	Solid	1.020	0.040	1620	7.32	4.91	21.8	6.6
	7/26	1.219	0.048	1770	7.98	5.35	19.2	5.9
	16/30	1.194	0.047	1600	7.20	4.83	21.3	6.5
	19/30	1.245	0.049	1900	8.56	5.74	17.9	5.5
	41/34	1.194	0.047	1627	7.32	4.91	20.9	6.4
	65/36	1.194	0.047	1625	7.31	4.90	21.0	6.4
20	Solid	0.813	0.032	1020	4.61	3.09	34.6	10.5
	7/28	0.965	0.038	1111	5.19	3.48	33.8	10.3
	10/30	0.889	0.035	1000	4.05	2.71	33.9	10.3
	19/32	0.940	0.037	1216	5.48	3.67	28.3	8.6
	26/34	0.914	0.036	1032	4.64	3.11	33.0	10.1
	41/36	0.914	0.036	1025	4.61	3.09	32.9	10.0
22	Solid	0.643	0.025	640	2.91	1.95	55.3	16.9
	7/30	0.762	0.030	700	3.16	2.12	48.4	14.8
	19/34	0.787	0.031	754	3.39	2.27	45.1	13.7
	26/36	0.762	0.030	650	2.93	1.96	52.3	15.9
24	Solid	0.511	0.020	404	1.82	1.22	89.4	27.2
	7/32	0.610	0.024	448	2.02	1.35	76.4	23.3
	10/34	0.582	0.023	397	1.79	1.20	85.6	26.1
	19/36	0.610	0.024	475	2.13	1.43	69.2	21.1
	41/40	0.582	0.023	384	1.73	1.16	84.0	25.6
26	Solid	0.409	0.016	256	1.14	0.76	143.0	43.6
	10/36	0.533	0.021	250	1.13	0.76	137.0	41.8
	19/38	0.508	0.020	304	1.37	0.92	113.0	34.4
	7/34	0.483	0.019	278	1.25	0.84	122.0	37.2
27	7/35	0.457	0.018	220	0.99	0.66	179.0	54.6
28	Solid	0.330	0.013	159	0.72	0.48	232.0	70.7
	7/36	0.381	0.015	175	0.79	0.53	213.0	64.9
	19/40	0.406	0.016	183	0.82	0.55	186.0	56.7
30	Solid	0.254	0.010	100	0.45	0.30	365.0	111.3
	7/38	0.305	0.012	112	0.50	0.34	339.0	103.3
	19/42	0.305	0.012	119	0.53	0.36	286.7	87.4
32	Solid	0.203	0.008	67	0.29	0.19	571.0	174.0
	7/40	0.203	0.008	67	0.30	0.20	538.0	164.0
	19/44	0.229	0.009	76	0.34	0.23	448.0	136.6
34	Solid	0.160	0.006	40	0.18	0.12	918.0	279.8
	7/42	0.192	0.008	44	0.20	0.13	777.0	236.8
36	Solid	0.127	0.005	25	0.11	0.08	1460.0	445.0
	7/44	0.152	0.006	28	0.13	0.08	1271.0	387.4

Chapter 12

Hard Drives

Hard Drive Interface Basics

The drive interface is a language that allows the drive to talk to the computer. There are two main types of interfaces, ATA (Advanced Technology Attachment) and SCSI (Small Computer System Interface.) ATA is more commonly know as the IDE interface. The following is a list of advantages of each type:

ATA/IDE / EIDE
1. Less expensive than SCSI
2. Easier to setup than SCSI
3. Does not require an additional controller card like SCSI

SCSI
1. SCSI has greater expandability than ATA and is capable of supporting up to 7 or 15 devices. ATA only allows 2 two devices per channel and most computers have only 2 ATA channels.
2. High end SCSI is faster than ATA.
3. SCSI Raid has better performance and better data security than ATA.

In general, the main factors that affect drive performance are transfer mode (ATA), signaling method (SCSI), bus width, bus speed, drive platter rotation speed, cache, and cable length.

ATA Transfer Modes

Transfer Mode	Data Transfer Rate in megabytes/second					
	Mode 0	Mode 1	Mode 2	Mode 3	Mode 4	Mode 5
PIO	3.3	5.2	8.3	11.1	16.7	–
Multicore DMA	4.2	13.3	16.7	–	–	–
Ultra DMA	16.7	25.0	33.3	44.4	66.7	100.0

SCSI Transceivers
The speed of SCSI devices is also controlled by which transceiver is used, single-ended (SE) or differential (HPD or LVD). SE is available for speeds below Ultra, HPD is available for Ultra2 and below, and LVD is available for Ultra2 and higher. SE was the original "standard" but as speeds increased, problems occurred with signal loss in cables. HPD was developed to take care of the cable problem but was more expensive than SE. LVD was developed as a low cost alternative to HPD and has longer cables than SE but shorter than HPD.

Until recently, SCSI was always the interface of choice due to it being faster and having larger drives available in both standard and Raid. With the advent of large, 10,000 RPM SATA drives, the gap has narrowed significantly and when the lower cost of ATA is factored into the equation, most individual and small business users will probably opt for SATA solutions.

Hard Drive Interface Standards & Specifications

Interface Type	Alternate Name	Max Data Rate (MB/sec)	Max Devices per Channel	Max Cable Length feet	Cable Connector Chart Number*
EIDE PIO Mode 0	IDE, ATA, ATA-1, obsolete	3.3	2	1.5	A
EIDE PIO Mode 1	IDE, ATA, ATA-1, obsolete	5.2	2	1.5	A
EIDE PIO Mode 2	IDE, ATA, ATA-1, obsolete	8.3	2	1.5	A
EIDE PIO Mode 3	IDE, Fast IDE, Fast ATA, ATA-2	11.1	2	1.5	A
EIDE PIO Mode 4	IDE, Fast IDE, Fast ATA, ATA-2, ATA-3,	16.7	2	1.5	A
Ultra ATA/33	IDE, Ultra ATA, Ultra DMA/33, ATA-4	33	2	1.5	A
Ultra ATA/66	IDE, Ultra DMA/66, ATA-5	66	2	1.5	B
Ultra ATA/100	IDE, Ultra DMA/100, ATA-6, ATA-7	100	2	1.5	B
Ultra ATA/133	IDE, Fast	133	2	1.5	B
Ultra SATA/1500	Serial ATA, SATA-1	187	1	3	C
SCSI	SCSI-1, 8-bit	5	8	18	D,E,F
Fast SCSI	SCSI-2, Fast Narrow SCSI, 8-bit	10	8	9	G
Fast Wide SCSI	SCSI-2 Wide, Wide SCSI, Fast-10, 16-bit	20	16	9	H
Ultra SCSI	SCSI-3, 16-bit	20	8	4.5	G
Ultra Wide SCSI	SCSI-3, Fast Wide 20, 16-bit	40	16	4.5	H
Ultra2 SCSI LVD	SCSI-3, SPI-2, 16-bit	40	8	36	H
Ultra2 Wide SCSI LVD	SCSI-3, Fast 40, 16-bit	80	16	36	H
Ultra 160/m SCSI LVD	SPI-3, Ultra3 SCSI, Ultra 160 SCSI, Fast-80DT, 16-bit	160	16	36	H,J
Ultra 320/m SCSI LVD	SPI-4, Ultra 320 SCSI	320	16	36	H,J

***See the next page for hard drive cable connector identification. See page 517 for interface wiring.**

Drive Connectors

Note: Sub-D and DB apply to the same connector.

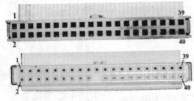
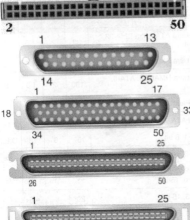

IDC40 (female): IDE, ATA and ATAPI drive connector. Show with 40 wire cable used on Ultra-ATA/33 and earlier interfaces.

IDC40 (female): IDE, ATA and ATAPI drive connector. Show with 80 wire cable used on Ultra-ATA/66 and later interfaces.

IDC50 (female): very common internal 8-bit SCSI-1 internal connector.

DB25 (male) used for SCSI-1. Also used on parallel ports, Zip Drives, scanners and Mac.

DB50 (male) used for SCSI-1 (primarily on Sun workstations)

Centronics 50 or CN50 (male) used for external SCSI-1 connections on a PC (also used by Telcos for non SCSI applications)

HPCN50 or Half Pitch Centronics 50 (male) is used on some docking stations for Notebooks and digital cameras:

HPCN60 or Half Pitch Centronics 60 (male) or HDCN60 used on IBS PS/2 and RS/6000 controllers:

Micro DB50 or Mini D50 or HPDB50 (male): used for SCSI-2, Fast SCSI, Fast Narrow SCSI, and Ultra SCSI (SCSI-3)

Drive Connectors (cont.)

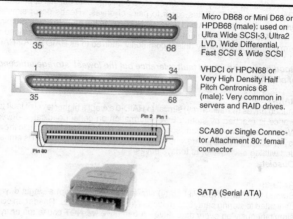

Micro DB68 or Mini D68 or HPDB68 (male): used on Ultra Wide SCSI-3, Ultra2 LVD, Wide Differential, Fast SCSI & Wide SCSI

VHDCI or HPCN68 or Very High Density Half Pitch Centronics 68 (male): Very common in servers and RAID drives.

SCA80 or Single Connector Attachment 80: femail connector

SATA (Serial ATA)

RAID Specifications

"RAID" is an acronym that stands for Redundant Array of Inexpensive Disks. Today, the "Inexpensive" is commonly changed to "Independent". RAID is a technology used to increase hard drive performance and/or provide hard drive fault-tolerance. The initial concept of RAID was developed in 1987 by Patterson, Gibson & Katz of the University of California.

There are five types of RAID disk array architectures, RAID-1 through RAID-5. RAID-0 is a sixth type that refers to a non-redundant array of drives. Today, RAID is available for both SCSI and EIDE drives and is a popular in I/O -intensive environments, particularly servers, like databases and imaging. "Hot Swap" configurations are readily available and allow the user to remove a defective drive in the RAID array without turning off the computer. RAID-0, -1 and -5 are the most commonly used configurations today.

RAID-0:

Striped disk drives with no data redundancy. Writes occur simultaneously on every drive. Reads occur simultaneously on every drive. A bad drive will cause the array to crash.

Best performance and worst fault tolerance.

RAID-1:
Mirrored (striped) array where drives store duplicate data but still appear as a single logical drive. Writes occur to pairs of drives. Reads occur simultaneously on every drive. A bad drive will NOT cause the array to crash. Striping is not used on a single pair of drives, however multiple pairs can be striped to form a single logical array (this is commonly referred to as RAID 0+1 or RAID 01.)
Good performance and fault tolerance but the lowest storage efficiency of all RAIDs.

RAID-2:
Striped drives (parallel array) similar to RAID-0 except a higher level of fault tolerance is reached by storing ECC information on certain dedicated drives. Writes span all drives. Reads span all drives. A bad drive will NOT cause the array to crash. RAID-2 is rarely used today because ECC information is embedded withing each sector of todays drives.
Obsolete.

RAID-3:
Striped drive array (parallel array) similar to RAID-2 except a single drive is dedicated to storing parity information. Writes span all drives. Reads can occur simultaneously on every data drive. A bad drive will NOT cause the array to crash. RAID-3 can perform only ONE I/O at a time, which limits its use to a single user system.
Good read performance, good fault tolerance, single user systems only.

RAID-4:
Striped drive array (parallel array) identical to RAID-3 except the stripe configuration causes records to be stored entirely on a single drive in the array. Every write must update the dedicated parity drive. Reads occur simultaneously on every data drive. A bad drive will NOT cause the array to crash.
Good multi-tasking but poor write performance, se RAID-5 instead.

RAID-5:
Striped drive array with evenly distributed parity information on all drives in the array. Multiple writes can be processed simultaneously but writes require parity to be updated. Reads occur simultaneously on every drive. A bad drive will NOT cause the array to crash. One drives worth of capacity is sacrificed for parity data. RAID-5 is a versatile array because it can be configured with either small or large stripes. RAID-5 parity groups can be striped together to appear as a single larger logical array (commonly referred to as RAID 0+5 or RAID-50).
Good read performance, good fault tolerance, good multi-user, mediocre write performance.

Hard Drive Manufacturers Directory

The following table is a general summary of companies that have manufactured and/or are still manufacturing hard drives. The number of models shown is based on data contained in this books Hard Drive Specifications table and Sequoia Publishing does not represent this summary as being exact. If you have information concerning the status of any of these companies, such as "XYZ Company went bankrupt in August, 1990" or "XYZ Company was bought by Q Company," please let us know so we can keep this section current. If a phone number is listed in the Status column, the company is in business.

Manufacturer	Status
Alps America	408-361-6400; No longer make hard drives.
Ampex	650-367-2011; No longer make hard drives.
Areal Technology, Inc	Out of Business
Atasi Technology, Inc	Out Of Business; Lipsig & Assoc provide support 408-733-1844
Aura Associates	Unknown.
BASF	See Emtech Data Corp
Brand Technologies	Out of Business
Bull (Evidian)	978-294-6000; No longer makes hard drives.
C.itoh Electronics, Inc	Unknown; Doing business as Itochu Tech; sold hard drive division to Y-E Data.
Cardiff	Out of Business.
Castlewood Systems, Inc.	408-956-2500
CDC	800-468-3472; See Seagate
Century Data (Systech Retail Systems	800-387-3262; Not a manufacturer.
CMI	Out of Business
CMS Enhancements, Inc	714-424-5520; Not a manufacturer. Ameriquest parent company
Cogito	Out of Business
Compaq	281-370-0670 (Hewlett Packard
Comport	Unknown
Conner Peripherals, Inc.	800-468-3472; Merged with Seagate Technology 2-5-96.
Core International	Unknown
Data Direct Networks	818-700-7676; Formerly Mega Drive Systems
Digital Equipment Corp.	800-282-6672 (Hewlett Packard)
Disc Tec	407-671-5500; Maker of removable-hard drives.
Disctron (Otari)	Out Of Business
DMA	Out of Business
Eloch	Unknown
Emtech Data Store Media	Unknown
Epson America	310-955-5300; No longer make hard drives.
Fuji Electric	510-438-9700; Do not manufacture hard drives in US.
Fujitsu America, Inc.	408-432-6333
Hewlett-Packard Co	Corporate: 800-282-6672.
Hitachi Global Storage Tech	914-332-5800 (Hitachi-IBM mergered)
Hyosung	Unknown
IBM Corp. (Storage Sys Div)	Merged into Hitachi Global Storage Tech
IMI	Unknown
Integral Peripherals	Out of Business; Product support by Mobile Storage Tech 408-935-8100
JCT	Unknown
JTS	Unknown
JVC	800-882-2345; No longer make hard drives.
Kalok Corporation	Out of Business
Kyocera Electronics, Inc.	Unknown; No longer make hard drives.
Lanstor	Unknown

Manufacturer	Status
Lapine	Unknown
Maxtor Corporation	408-432-1700; Sold XT product line to Sequel in 1992, acquired Quantum April 2001.
Mega Drive Systems	See Data Direct Network
Memorex	562-653-2800; No longer a manufacturer.
Micropolis Corp	Out of Business
Microscience Intl. Corp	Out of Business
Miniscribe Corporation	Out Of Business, Portions bought by Maxtor
Mitsubishi Electronics	714-220-2500
Mitsumi Electronics Corp.	408-970-0700; No longer make hard drives.
MMI	Unknown
NCL America	Unknown; No longer make hard drives.
NCR Corp	800-531-2222; No longer manufacture hard drives; call AT&T Global Info.
NEC Technologies Inc	Unknown
NEI	Unknown
Newbury Data	Unknown
NPL	Unknown
Okidata	856-235-2600
Olivetti	800-524-0799; Bought out by Wang Global
Optima Technology Corp	Unknown
Orca Technology Corp	Unknown
Otari	Out of Business
Pacific Magtron	408-956-8888; No longer make hard drives.
Panasonic	201-348-7000
Plus Development	408-894-4000; Bought Out By Quantum
Prairietek Corp	Unknown
Priam Corporation	Out Of Business; Lipsig & Assoc provide support 408-733-1844
Procom Technology	800-800-8600; Does not make drives, they Bundle
PTI (Peripheral Technology)	770-973-2156
Quantum Corporation	See Maxtor Corp, merged 402-01
Ricoh	800-955-3453; No longer make drives.
RMS	They say they have never made drives
Rodime Systems, Inc	Out of Business
Samsung	201-229-7000
Seagate Technologies	800-468-3472
Sequel, Inc	Unknown; Purchased XT model lines from Maxtor.
Shugart	Unknown, Intl Assembly Specialists
Siemens	Out of Business
Sony	408-432-1600
Storage Dimensions	Unknown
Syquest Technology	See Iomega and SYQT Inc
Tandon Computer Corp	Out of Business; Filed Chapter 11 Bankruptcy March 1993.
Tandy Corp	800-843-7422
Teac America, Inc.	323-726-0303; Do not manufacture HDD anymore
Texas Instruments	972-995-6611
Toshiba America, Inc.	212-596-0600
Tulin	Unknown
Vertex (see Priam)	Out Of Business; Lipsig & Assoc provide support 408-733-1844
Western Digital	949-672-7000
Xebec	Out of Business
Y-E Data America, Inc	No longer manufacture drives, they make heads. see yedata.com
Zentec	Unknown

===

Total Number of Drives ...... 6321 (Last edition was 5317)

Hard Drive Specifications and Table Syntax

The Hard Drive Specifications contained in the rest of this chapter is a comprehensive list of both current and legacy hard drives.

Telephone numbers for hard drive manufacturers are listed on the previous three pages and in the Phone Book (page 905).

The following are descriptions of the information contained in the hard drive tables that start on the next page.

Left hand page
1. Drive Model
2. Format Size MB . . Formatted drive size in megabytes (Mb)
3. Heads . . . . Number of data heads
4. Cyl . . . . Number of cylinders
5. Sect/Trac . . . . Number of sectors per track, V=Variable
6. Translate . . . . Head-Cyl-Sector/Track Translation. *UNIV is a Universal Translation where any drive setup can be used as long as the total translated sectors is less than total drive sectors (Total drive sectors=physical heads x physical cylinders x physical sectors per track)
7. RWC. . . . . Start Reduced Write Current cylinder
8. WPC. . . . . Start Write Precompensation cylinder
9. Form Factor . . . . . Physical diameter and height of drive 5.25HH, 3.5HH, 3.5/3H, 2.5
10. Power . . . . Power in watts that the drive consumes

Right hand page
1. Drive Model
2. Format Size MB . . Formatted drive size in megabytes (Mb)
3. Seek Time . . . . . . Avg. drive head access time, milliseconds
4. Interface . . . . Type of drive interface used ST412/506, ESDI, SCSI, IDE AT, IDE XT, EIDE
5. Encode . . . . Data encoding method used on drive MFM, 2,7RLL, 1,7 RLL, RLL ZBR, ERLL
6. Cache. . . . . Read ahead cache/buffer, in kilobytes (kb)
7. RPM . . . . Drive motor Revolutions Per Minute

PLEASE NOTE: The density of information in the hard drive table has made it necessary to conserve space by abbreviating kilobytes "kb" as "k".

Drive Model	Format Size MB	Head	Cyl	Sect/Trac	Translate H/C/S	RWC/WPC	Form Factor	Power Watts
ALPS AMERICA								
DR311C	106	2	2108	V		NA/NA	3.5 3H	
DR311D	106	2	2108	V		NA/NA	3.5 3H	
DR312C	212	4	2108	V		NA/NA	3.5 3H	
DR312D	212	4	2108	V		NA/NA	3.5 3H	
DRND-10A	11	2	615	17		616/616	3.5HH	
DRND-20A	21	4	615	17		616/616	3.5HH	
DRPO-20A	16	2	615	26		616/616	3.5HH	
DRPO-20D	16	2	615	26		616/616	3.5HH	
AMPEX								
PYXIS-13	11	4	320	17		132/132	5.25FH	
PYXIS-20	17	6	320	17		132/132	5.25FH	
PYXIS-27	22	8	320	17		132/132	5.25FH	
PYXIS-7	6	2	320	17		132/132	5.25FH	
AREAL TECHNOLOGY, INC								
A1080	1080					—/—	2.5 4H	
A120	132	4	1070	63	10/535/50	NA/NA	2.5 4H	
A130	130	2	1438	V	5/856/50	—/—	2.5 4H	
A180	183	4	1430	62	10/715/50	NA/NA	2.5 4H	
A260	260	4	1438	V	10/856/60	—/—	2.5 4H	
A270	270					—/—	2.5 4H	
A340	350	4	2120	V	12/950/60	—/—	2.5 4H	
A520	526	6	2120	V	16/1020/63	—/—	2.5 4H	
A540	540					—/—	2.5 4H	
A810	810					—/—	2.5 4H	
A85	86	2	1344	V		AUTO/AUTO	2.5 4H	
A90	92	2	1430	62	10/715/25	NA/NA	2.5 4H	
BP100 (never made)	105	2	1720	V		NA/NA	2.5 4H	
BP200 (never made)						—/—		
BP50 (never made)						—/—		
MD2050 (never made)	49	2	819	V		—/—	2.5 4H	
MD2060	62	2	1024	59	7/1024/17	NA/NA	2.5 4H	3
MD2065	62	2	1024			—/—	2.5 4H	
MD2080	81	2	1330	59	14/665/17	NA/NA	2.5 4H	
MD2085	86	2	1410	59	14/705/17	NA/NA	2.5 4H	
MD2100 (never made)	100	2	1638	V		—/—	2.5 4H	
ATASI TECHNOLOGY, INC								
3020	17	3	645	17		320/320	5.25FH	
3033	28	5	645	17		320/320	5.25FH	
3046	39	7	645	17		320/320	5.25FH	
3051	43	7	704	17		—/352	5.25FH	
3051+	44	7	733	17		—/368	5.25FH	
3053	44	7	733	17		350/368	5.25FH	
3075	67	8	1024	17		1025/1025	5.25FH	
3085	72	8	1024	17		—/512	5.25FH	
3128	128	8	1024	26		—/—	5.25FH	
519	159	15	1224	17		NA/NA	5.25FH	
519R	244	15	1224	26		NA/NA	5.25FH	
6120	1051	15	1925	71		NA/NA	5.25FH	24
638	338	15	1225	36		NA/NA	5.25FH	31
676	676	15	1632	54		NA/NA	5.25FH	31
7120	1034	15	1919	71		NA/NA	5.25FH	24
738	336	15	1225	36		NA/NA	5.25FH	31
776	668	15	1632	54		NA/NA	5.25FH	31
AURA ASSOCIATES								
AU126	125	4				—/—	1.8 4H	
AU211	211					NA/NA	1.8 4H	1.9
AU211S	211					NA/NA	1.8 4H	1.9
AU245	245					NA/NA	1.8 4H	1.9
AU245S	245					NA/NA	1.8 4H	1.9
AU43	42	2				—/—	1.8 4H	
AU63	42	2				—/—	1.8 4H	
AU85	85	4				—/—	1.8 4H	

Drive Model	Format Size MB	Seek Time	Interface	Encode	cache kb	RPM
ALPS AMERICA						
DR311C	106	13	IDE AT	1,7 RLL		
DR311D	106	13	SCSI-2	1,7 RLL		
DR312C	212	13	IDE AT	1,7 RLL		
DR312D	212	13	SCSI-2	1,7 RLL		
DRND-10A	11	60	ST412/506	MFM		
DRND-20A	21	60	ST412/506	MFM		
DRPO-20A	16	60	ST412/506	2,7 RLL		
DRPO-20D	16	60	ST412/506	2,7 RLL		
AMPEX						
PYXIS-13	11	90	ST412/506	MFM		
PYXIS-20	17	90	ST412/506	MFM		
PYXIS-27	22	90	ST412/506	MFM		
PYXIS-7	6	90	ST412/506	MFM		
AREAL TECHNOLOGY, INC						
A1080	1080		ATA Fast		128k	
A120	132	15	IDE AT	2,7-1,7RLL	32k	2981
A130	130	<15	IDE AT	1,7 RLL		2981
A180	183	17	IDE XT-AT	2,7 RLL	32k	2981
A260	260	<15	IDE AT	1,7 RLL		2981
A270	270		ATA Fast		128k	
A340	350	13	IDE AT	1,7 RLL		
A520	526	13	IDE AT	1,7 RLL		
A540	540		ATA Fast		128k	
A810	810		ATA Fast		128k	
A85	86	15	IDE	2,7 RLL		
A90	92	15	IDE XT-AT	2,7 RLL	32k	2981
BP100 (never made)	105	27	SCSI	2,7 RLL		
BP200 (never made)						
BP50 (never made)						
MD2050 (never made)	49	28		2,7 RLL		
MD2060	62	19	IDE AT	2,7 RLL	32k	1565
MD2065	62	<16	IDE AT	RLL		2504
MD2080	81	19	IDE AT	2,7 RLL	32k	1565
MD2085	86	19	IDE AT	2,7 RLL	32k	2504
MD2100 (never made)	100	29	SCSI	2,7 RLL		
ATASI TECHNOLOGY, INC						
3020	17		ST412/506	MFM		
3033	28	30	ST412/506	MFM		
3046	39	30	ST412/506	MFM		
3051	43	33	ST412/506	MFM		
3051+	44		ST412/506	MFM		
3053	44	27	ST412/506	MFM		
3075	67	27	ST412/506	MFM		
3085	72	27	ST412/506	MFM		
3128	128		ST412/506	2,7 RLL		
519	159	22	ST412/506	MFM		
519R	244	22	ST412/506	2,7 RLL		
6120	1051	14	ESDI	2,7 RLL		3600
638	338	18	ESDI			3600
676	676	16	ESDI	2,7 RLL		3600
7120	1034	14	SCSI	2,7 RLL		3600
738	336	18	SCSI			3600
776	668	16	SCSI			3600
AURA ASSOCIATES						
AU126	125	17	PCMCIA-ATA	1,7 RLL	32k	5400
AU211	211	13	ATA		128k	3448
AU211S	211	13	SCSI-2		128k	3448
AU245	245	13	ATA		128k	3448
AU245S	245	13	SCSI-2		128k	3448
AU43	42	17	IDE AT	1,7 RLL	32k	5400
AU63	42	17	PCMCIA-ATA	1,7 RLL	32k	5400
AU85	85	17	IDE AT	1,7 RLL	32k	5400

Drive Model	Format Size MB	Head	Cyl	Sect/Trac	Translate H/C/S	RWC/WPC	Form Factor	Power Watts
BASF								
6185	23	6	440	17		220/220	5.25FH	
6186	15	4	440	17		220/220	5.25FH	
6187	8	2	440	17		220/220	5.25FH	
6188-R1	10	2	612	17		—/—	5.25FH	
6188-R3	21	4	612	17		—/—	5.25FH	
BRAND TECHNOLOGIES								
9121A (never made)	107	5	1166	36	10/583/36	NA/NA	3.5HH	
9121E (never made)	107	5	1166	36		NA/NA	3.5HH	
9121S (never made)	107	5	1166	36		NA/NA	3.5HH	
9170A	150	7	1165	36	14/583/36	NA/NA	3.5HH	9
9170E	150	7	1166	36		NA/NA	3.5HH	11
9170S	150	7	1166	36		NA/NA	3.5HH	9
9220A	200	9	1209	36	16/401/61	NA/NA	3.5HH	9
9220E	200	9	1210	36		NA/NA	3.5HH	11
9220S	200	9	1210	36		NA/NA	3.5HH	9
BT8085	71	8	1024	17		NA/NA	5.25FH	
BT8128	109	8	1024	26		NA/NA	5.25FH	
BT8170E	142	8	1024	34		NA/NA	5.25FH	
BT8170S	142	8	1024	34		NA/NA	5.25FH	
BT9400A (never made)	400	6	1800	36	16/801/61	NA/NA	5.25FH	
BT9400S (never made)	400	6	1800	36		NA/NA	5.25FH	
BT9650A (never made)	650	10	1800	36	16/1024/63	NA/NA	5.25FH	
BT9650S (never made)	650	10	1800	36		NA/NA	5.25FH	
BULL								
D530	25	3	987	17		988/988	5.25FH	
D550	43	5	987	17		988/988	5.25FH	
D570	60	7	987	17		988/988	5.25FH	
D585	71	7	1166	17		1166/1166	5.25FH	
C.ITOH ELECTRONICS, INC								
SEE YE-DATA						—/—		
CALLUNA TECHNOLOGY, INC.								
105MB	105	4			4/828/31	—/—	1.8	
130MB	130	4			6/986/43	—/—	1.8	
170MB	170	4			8/923/45	—/—	1.8	
260MB	260	4			10/820/62	—/—	1.8	
520MB	520	4			16/1008/63	—/—	1.8	
85MB	85	4				—/—	1.8	
CT1040RM	1040	4				—/—	1.8	
CT260T2	260	1				—/—	1.8	
CARDIFF								
F3053	44	5	1024	17		—/—	3.5HH	
F3080E	68	5	1024	26		NA/NA	3.5HH	
F3080S	68	5	1024	26		NA/NA	3.5HH	
F3127E	109	5	1024	35		NA/NA	3.5HH	
F3127S	109	5	1024	35		NA/NA	3.5HH	
CDC								
94151-25 Wren II	25	3	921	19		—/—	5.25FH	
94151-27 Wren II	26	3	921	19		—/—	5.25FH	
94151-42 Wren II	42	5	921	19		—/—	5.25FH	
94151-44 Wren II	44	5	921	19		—/—	5.25FH	
94151-59 Wren II	59	7	921	19		—/—	5.25FH	
94151-62 Wren II	62	7	921	19		—/—	5.25FH	
94151-76 Wren II	76	9	921	19		—/—	5.25FH	
94151-80 Wren II	80	9	921	19		—/—	5.25FH	
94151-80SA Wren II	72	9	921	17		—/—	5.25FH	
94151-80SC Wren II	70	9	921	17		925/925	5.25FH	
94151-86 Wren II	72	9	925	17		697/697	5.25FH	
94155-021 Wren I	18	3	697	17		697/128	5.25FH	
94155-025 Wren I	24	4	697	17		698/128	5.25FH	
94155-028 Wren I	24	3	697	17		—/—	5.25FH	
94155-029 Wren I	25	3	925	17		—/—	5.25FH	

Drive Model	Format Size MB	Seek Time	Interface	Encode	cache kb	RPM
BASF						
6185	23	70	ST412/506	MFM		
6186	15	70	ST412/506	MFM		
6187	8	70	ST412/506	MFM		
6188-R1	10	70	ST412/506	MFM		
6188-R3	21	70	ST412/506	MFM		
BRAND TECHNOLOGIES						
9121A (never made)	107	16.5	IDE AT	2,7 RLL		
9121E (never made)	107	16.5	SCSI	2,7 RLL		
9121S (never made)	107	16.5	SCSI	2,7 RLL		
9170A	150	16.5	IDE AT	2,7 RLL	64k	
9170E	150	16.5	ESDI	2,7 RLL		3565
9170S	150	16.5	SCSI	2,7 RLL	64k	
9220A	200	16.5	IDE AT	2,7 RLL	64k	3565
9220E	200	16.5	ESDI	2,7 RLL		3565
9220S	200	16.5	SCSI	2,7 RLL	64k	
BT8085	71	25	ST412/506	MFM		
BT8128	109	25	ST412/506	2,7 RLL		
BT8170E	142	25	ESDI	2,7 RLL		
BT8170S	142	25	SCSI	2,7 RLL		
BT9400A (never made)	400	12	IDE AT	1,7 RLL		
BT9400S (never made)	400	12	SCSI-2	1,7 RLL		
BT9650A (never made)	650	12	IDE AT	1,7 RLL		
BT9650S (never made)	650	12	SCSI-2	1,7 RLL		
BULL						
D530	25		ST412/506	MFM		
D550	43		ST412/506	MFM		
D570	60		ST412/506	MFM		
D585	71		ST412/506	2,7 RLL		
C.ITOH ELECTRONICS, INC						
SEE YE-DATA						
CALLUNA TECHNOLOGY, INC.						
105MB	105	18	PCMCIA-ATA	1,7 RLL	32k	
130MB	130	16	PCMCIA-ATA	1,7 RLL	64k	
170MB	170	16	PCMCIA-ATA	1,7 RLL	64k	
260MB	260	16	PCMCIA-ATA	1,7 RLL	64k	
520MB	520	12	PCMCIA-ATA	1,7 RLL	128k	
85MB	85	18	PCMCIA-ATA	1,7 RLL	32k	
CT1040RM	1040	12	PCMCIA-ATA	1,7 RLL	128k	
CT260T2	260	12	PCMCIA-ATA	1,7 RLL	128k	
CARDIFF						
F3053	44	20	ST412/506	MFM		
F3080E	68	20	ESDI	2,7 RLL		
F3080S	68	20	SCSI	2,7 RLL		
F3127E	109	20	ESDI	2,7 RLL		
F3127S	109	20	SCSI	2,7 RLL		
CDC						
94151-25 Wren II	25					
94151-27 Wren II	26					
94151-42 Wren II	42					
94151-44 Wren II	44					
94151-59 Wren II	59					
94151-62 Wren II	62					
94151-76 Wren II	76					
94151-80 Wren II	80					
94151-80SA Wren II	72	38	SCSI			
94151-80SC Wren II	70	38	SCSI			
94151-86 Wren II	72	38	ST412/506	MFM		
94155-021 Wren I	18		ST412/506	MFM		
94155-025 Wren I	24		ST412/506	MFM		
94155-028 Wren I	24	28	ST412/506	MFM		
94155-029 Wren I	25	28	ST412/506	MFM		

Drive Model	Format Size MB	Head	Cyl	Sect/ Trac	Translate H/C/S	RWC/ WPC	Form Factor	Power Watts
94155-036 Wren I	31	5	733	17		697/128	5.25FH	
94155-037 Wren I	32	4	925	17		—/—	5.25FH	
94155-038 Wren I	31	5	733	17		734/0	5.25FH	
94155-048 Wren II	40	5	925	17		926/128	5.25FH	
94155-051 Wren II	43	5	989	17		990/128	5.25FH	
94155-057 Wren II	48	6	925	17		926/128	5.25FH	
94155-057P Wren II	48	6	925	17		926/128	5.25FH	
94155-067 Wren II	56	7	925	17		926/128	5.25FH	
94155-067P Wren II	56	7	925	17		926/128	5.25FH	
94155-077 Wren II	64	8	925	17		926/128	5.25FH	
94155-085 Wren II	71	8	1024	17		1025/128	5.25FH	
94155-085P Wren II	71	8	1024	17		1025/128	5.25FH	
94155-086 Wren II	72	9	925	17		926/128	5.25FH	
94155-087 Wren II	72	9	925	17		—/—	5.25FH	

Conversion Chart: Part I
Old CDC/Imprimis model # to new Seagate model

CDC/Imprimis ==>	Seagate	Seagate ==>	CDC/Imprimis
94155-135	ST4135R	ST1090A	94354-090
94155-85	ST4085	ST1090N	94351-090
94155-86	ST4086	ST1100	94355-100
94155-96	ST4097	ST1111A	94354-111
94161-182	ST4182N	ST1111E	94356-111
94166-182	ST4182E	ST1111N	94351-111
94171-350	ST4350N	ST1126A	94354-126
94171-376	ST4376N	ST1126N	94351-126
94181-385H	ST4385N	ST1133A	94354-133
94181-702	ST4702N	ST1133NS	94351-133S
94186-383	ST4383R	ST1150R	94355-150
94186-383H	ST4384E	ST1156A	94354-155
94186-442	ST4442E	ST1156E	94356-155
94191-766	ST4766N	ST1156N	94351-155
94196-766	ST4766E	ST1156NS	94351-155S
94204-65	ST274A	ST1162A	94354-160
94204-71	ST280A	ST1162N	94351-160
94204-74	ST274A	ST1186A	94354-186
94204-81	ST280A	ST1186NS	94351-186S
94205-51	ST253	ST1201A	94354-200
94205-77	ST279R	ST1201E	94356-200
94211-106	ST2106N	ST1201N	94351-200
94216-106	ST2106E	ST1201NS	94351-200S
94221-125	ST2125N	ST1239A	94354-239
94241-502	ST2502N	ST1239NS	94351-230S
94244-274	ST2274A	ST2106E	94216-106
94244-383	ST2383A	ST2106N	94211-106
94246-182	ST2182E	ST2125N	94221-125
94246-383	ST2383E	ST2182E	94246-182
94351-090	ST1090N	ST2274A	94244-274
94351-111	ST1111N	ST2383A	94244-383
94351-126	ST1126N	ST2383E	94246-383
94351-133S	ST1133NS	ST2502N	94241-502
94351-155	ST1156N	ST253	94205-51
94351-155S	ST1156NS	ST274A	94204-74
94351-160	ST1162N	ST274A	94204-65
94351-186S	ST1186NS	ST279R	94205-77
94351-200	ST1201N	ST280A	94204-81
94351-200S	ST1201NS	ST280A	94204-71
94351-230S	ST1239NS	ST4085	94155-85
94354-090	ST1090A	ST4086	94155-86

Drive Model	Format Size MB	Seek Time	Interface	Encode	cache kb	RPM
94155-036 Wren I	31		ST412/506	MFM		
94155-037 Wren I	32	28	ST412/506	MFM		
94155-038 Wren I	31	28	ST412/506	MFM		
94155-048 Wren II	40	28	ST412/506	MFM		
94155-051 Wren II	43	28	ST412/506	MFM		
94155-057 Wren II	48	28	ST412/506	MFM		
94155-057P Wren II	48	28	ST412/506	MFM		
94155-067 Wren II	56	28	ST412/506	MFM		
94155-067P Wren II	56	28	ST412/506	MFM		
94155-077 Wren II	56	38	ST412/506	MFM		
94155-085 Wren II	64	28	ST412/506	MFM		
94155-085P Wren II	71	28	ST412/506	MFM		
94155-086 Wren II	71	28	ST412/506	MFM		
94155-087 Wren II	72	28	ST412/506	MFM		
	72	38	ESDI			

Conversion Chart: Part II
Old CDC/Imprimis model # to new Seagate model

CDC/Imprimis	==>	Seagate		Seagate	==>	CDC/Imprimis
94354-111		ST1111A		ST4097		94155-96
94354-126		ST1126A		ST41200N		94601-12G/M
94354-133		ST1133A		ST41201J		97500-12G
94354-155		ST1156A		ST41201K		97509-12G
94354-160		ST1162A		ST4135R		94155-135
94354-186		ST1186A		ST41520N		97501-12G
94354-200		ST1201A		ST4182E		94166-182
94354-239		ST1239A		ST4182N		94161-182
94355-100		ST1100		ST4350N		94171-350
94355-150		ST1150R		ST4376N		94171-376
94356-111		ST1111E		ST4383E		94186-383
94356-155		ST1156E		ST4384E		94186-383H
94356-200		ST1201E		ST4385N		94181-385H
94601-12G/M		ST41200N		ST4442E		94186-442
94601-767H		ST4767N		ST4702N		94181-702
97100-80		ST683J		ST4766E		94196-766
97150-160		ST6165J		ST4766N		94191-766
97150-300		ST6315J		ST4767N		94601-767H
97150-340		ST6344J		ST6165J		97150-160
97150-500		ST6516J		ST6315J		97150-300
97200-1130		ST81123J		ST6344J		97150-340
97200-12G		ST81236J		ST6516J		97150-500
97200-23G		ST82272K		ST683J		97100-80
97200-25G		ST82500J		ST81123J		97200-1130
97200-368		ST8368J		ST81154K		97229-1150
97200-500		ST8500J		ST81236J		97200-12G
97200-736		ST8741J		ST81236K		97209-12G
97200-850		ST8851J		ST81236K		97201-12G
97201-12G		ST81236N		ST82105K		97289-21G
97201-25G		ST82500N		ST82272K		97200-23G
97201-368		ST8368N		ST82368K		97299-23G
97201-500		ST8500N		ST82500J		97200-25G
97201-736		ST8741N		ST82500K		97209-25G
97201-850		ST8851N		ST82500N		97201-25G
97209-12G		ST81236K		ST8368J		97200-368
97209-25G		ST82500K		ST8368N		97201-368
97229-1150		ST81154K		ST8500J		97200-500
97289-21G		ST82105K		ST8500N		97201-500
97299-23G		ST82368K		ST8741J		97200-736
97500-12G		ST41201J		ST8741N		97201-736
97501-12G		ST41520N		ST8851J		97200-850
97509-12G		ST41201K		ST8851N		97201-850

Hard Drives

Drive Model	Format Size MB	Head	Cyl	Sect/Trac	Translate H/C/S	RWC/WPC	Form Factor	Power Watts
94155-092 Wren II	77	9	989	17		—/-1.0	5.25FH	
94155-092P Wren II	77	9	989	17		—/128	5.25FH	
94155-096 Wren II	80	9	1024	17		—/—	5.25FH	
94155-120 Wren II	120	8	960	26		961/128	5.25FH	
94155-130 Wren II	122	9	1024	26		—/128	5.25FH	
94155-135 Wren II	115	9	960	26		961/128	5.25FH	
94156-048 Wren II	40	5	925	17		926/128	5.25FH	
94156-067 Wren II	56	7	925	17		926/128	5.25FH	
94156-086 Wren II	72	9	925	17		926/128	5.25FH	
94156-48 Wren II	40					—/—	5.25FH	
94156-67 Wren II	56					—/—	5.25FH	
94156-86 Wren II	72					—/—	5.25FH	
94161-086 Wren III	86	5	969	35		NA/NA	5.25FH	
94161-101 Wren III	84	5	969	34		NA/NA	5.25FH	
94161-103 Wren III	104	6	969	35		NA/NA	5.25FH	
94161-121 Wren III	121	7	969	35		NA/NA	5.25FH	
94161-138 Wren III	138	8	969	35		NA/NA	5.25FH	
94161-141 Wren III	118	7	969	35		NA/NA	5.25FH	
94161-151 Wren III	151	9	969	34		—/-1.0	5.25FH	
94161-155 Wren III	132	9	969	35		—/-1.0	5.25FH	
94161-156 Wren III	132	9	969	36		—/—	5.25FH	
94161-160 Wren III	160		969			NA/NA	5.25FH	
94161-182 Wren III	156	9	969	35		—/—	5.25FH	
94161-182M Wren III	160	9	969			—/-1.0	5.25FH	
94166-086 Wren III	86	5	969	35		NA/NA	5.25FH	
94166-101 Wren III	86	5	969	35		—/-1.0	5.25FH	
94166-103 Wren III	104	6	969	35		NA/NA	5.25FH	
94166-121 Wren III	107	6	969	36		—/-1.0	5.25FH	
94166-138 Wren III	138	8	969	35		NA/NA	5.25FH	
94166-141 Wren III	125	7	969	36		NA/NA	5.25FH	
94166-161 Compaq	160	9	969	36		NA/NA	5.25FH	
94166-161 Wren III	142	8	969	36		NA/NA	5.25FH	
94166-182 Wren III	161	9	969	36		NA/NA	5.25FH	
94171-300 Wren IV	300	9	1412			NA/NA	5.25FH	
94171-307 Wren IV	300	9	1412			NA/NA	5.25FH	
94171-327 Wren IV	300	9	1412			—/—	5.25FH	
94171-330 Wren IV	330					NA/NA	5.25FH	
94171-344 Wren IV	323	9	1549	V		NA/NA	5.25FH	
94171-350 Wren IV	307	9	1412	V		NA/NA	5.25FH	
94171-375 Wren IV	330	9	1549	V		NA/NA	5.25FH	
94171-376 Wren IV	330	9	1546	V		NA/NA	5.25HH	
94171-376D Wren IV	323	9	1549	V		—/—	5.25FH	
94181-383 Wren V	330	15	1224			NA/NA	5.25FH	
94181-385 Wren V	337	15	791	V		NA/NA	5.25FH	
94181-385D Wren V	337	15	791	V		NA/NA	5.25FH	
94181-385H Wren V	337	15	791	V		NA/NA	5.25FH	
94181-574 Wren V	574	15	1549	V		NA/NA	5.25FH	
94181-702 Wren V	613	15	1546	V		NA/NA	5.25FH	
94181-702D Wren V	601	15	1546	V		NA/NA	5.25FH	
94181-702M Wren V	613	15	1549			—/—	5.25FH	
94186-265 Wren V	234	9	1412	36		NA/NA	5.25FH	
94186-324 Wren V	278	11	1412	35		NA/NA	5.25FH	
94186-383 Wren V	338	7	1747	35		NA/NA	5.25FH	
94186-383H Wren V	338	7	1747	35		NA/NA	5.25FH	
94186-383S Wren V	338	13	1412	36		NA/NA	5.25FH	
94186-442 Wren V	380	15	1412	35		NA/NA	5.25FH	
94186-442S Wren V	390	15	1412	36		NA/NA	5.25FH	
94191-766 Wren VI	677	15	1632	54		NA/NA	5.25FH	
94191-766D Wren VI	677	15	1632	54		NA/NA	5.25FH	
94196-383 Wren VI	338	7	1747	54		NA/NA	5.25FH	
94196-766 Wren V	677	15	1632	54		NA/NA	5.25FH	
94204-051 Wren II	43	5	989	26		NA/NA	5.25HH	
94204-065 Wren II	63	5	948	26		NA/NA	5.25HH	
94204-071 Wren II	63	5	1032	27		NA/NA	5.25HH	
94204-074 Wren II	63	5	948	26		NA/NA	5.25HH	
94204-081 Wren II	71	5	1032	27		989/—	5.25FH	
94205-030 Wren II	26	3	989	17		990/128	5.25HH	
94205-041 Wren II	43	4	989	17				

Drive Model	Format Size MB	Seek Time	Interface	Encode	cache kb	RPM
94155-092 Wren II	77	38	ST412/506	MFM		
94155-092P Wren II	77	38	ST412/506	MFM		
94155-096 Wren II	80	28	ST412/506	MFM		
94155-120 Wren II	120	28	ST412/506	2,7 RLL		
94155-130 Wren II	122	28	ST412/506	RLL		
94155-135 Wren II	115	28	ST412/506	2,7 RLL		
94156-048 Wren II	40	28	ESDI	MFM		
94156-067 Wren II	56	28	ESDI	MFM		
94156-086 Wren II	72	28	ESDI	MFM		
94156-48 Wren II	40		ESDI	ST412/506		
94156-67 Wren II	56		ESDI	ST412/506		
94156-86 Wren II	72		ESDI	ST412/506		
94161-086 Wren III	86	16.5	SCSI	2,7 RLL		
94161-101 Wren III	84	16.5	SCSI	2,7 RLL		
94161-103 Wren III	104	16.5	SCSI	2,7 RLL		
94161-121 Wren III	121	16.5	SCSI	2,7 RLL		
94161-138 Wren III	138	16.5	SCSI	2,7 RLL		
94161-141 Wren III	118	16.5	SCSI	2,7 RLL		
94161-151 Wren III	151	16.5	SCSI	2,7 RLL		
94161-155 Wren III	132	17	SCSI	RLL		
94161-156 Wren III	132	17	SCSI	RLL		
94161-160 Wren III	160		SCSI	2,7 RLL		
94161-182 Wren III	156	16.5	SCSI	2,7 RLL		
94161-182M Wren III	160	17	SCSI	ZBR		
94166-086 Wren III	86	25	ESDI	RLL		
94166-101 Wren III	86	16.5	ESDI	2,7 RLL		
94166-103 Wren III	104	25	ESDI	RLL		
94166-121 Wren III	107	16.5	ESDI	2,7 RLL		
94166-138 Wren III	138	25	ESDI	RLL		
94166-141 Wren III	125	16.5	ESDI	2,7 RLL		
94166-161 Compaq	160		ESDI	2,7 RLL		
94166-161 Wren III	142		ESDI	2,7 RLL		
94166-182 Wren III	161	16.5	ESDI (10)	2,7 RLL		
94171-300 Wren IV	300	17	SCSI	RLL ZBR		
94171-307 Wren IV	300	17	SCSI	RLL ZBR		
94171-327 Wren IV	300	17	SCSI	RLL ZBR		
94171-330 Wren IV	330		SCSI	RLL ZBR		
94171-344 Wren IV	323	18	SCSI	RLL ZBR		
94171-350 Wren IV	307	16.5	SCSI	RLL ZBR		
94171-375 Wren IV	330	16	SCSI	RLL ZBR		
94171-376 Wren IV	330	17.5	SCSI	RLL ZBR		
94171-376D Wren IV	323		SCSI	RLL ZBR		
94181-383 Wren IV	330	18	SCSI	ZBR		
94181-385D Wren V	337		SCSI	RLL ZBR		
94181-385H Wren V	337	10.7	SCSI	RLL ZBR		
94181-574 Wren V	574	16	SCSI	RLL ZBR		
94181-702 Wren V	613	16.5	SCSI	RLL ZBR		
94181-702D Wren V	601		SCSI	RLL ZBR		
94181-702M Wren V	613	17	SCSI	ZBR		
94186-265 Wren V	234		ESDI (10)	2,7 RLL		
94186-324 Wren V	278		ESDI (10)	2,7 RLL		
94186-383 Wren V	338		ESDI (10)	2,7 RLL		
94186-383H Wren V	338		ESDI (10)	2,7 RLL		
94186-383S Wren V	338	19	SCSI	2,7 RLL		
94186-442 Wren V	380		ESDI (10)	2,7 RLL		
94186-442S Wren V	390	15	SCSI	2,7 RLL		
94191-766 Wren VI	677	15.5	SCSI	2,7 RLL		
94191-766D Wren VI	677		SCSI	2,7 RLL		
94196-383 Wren VI	338		ESDI (15)	2,7 RLL		
94196-766 Wren V	677		ESDI (15)	2,7 RLL		
94204-051 Wren II	43		IDE AT	2,7 RLL		
94204-065 Wren II	63		IDE AT	2,7 RLL		
94204-071 Wren II	63		IDE AT	2,7 RLL		
94204-074 Wren II	63	28	IDE AT	2,7 RLL		
94204-081 Wren II	71	28	IDE AT	2,7 RLL		
94205-030 Wren II	26		ST412/506	MFM		
94205-041 Wren II	43		ST412/506	MFM		

Drive Model	Format Size MB	Head	Cyl	Sect/Trac	Translate H/C/S	RWC/WPC	Form Factor	Power Watts
94205-051 Wren II	43	5	989	17		990/128	5.25HH	
94205-053 Wren II	43	5	1024	17		990/128	5.25HH	
94205-071 Wren II	43	5	989	26		990/128	5.25HH	
94205-075 Wren II	62	5	966	25		966/128	5.25HH	
94205-077 Wren II	66	5	989	26		—/—	5.25HH	
94208-062 Wren II	60	5	989	17		—/—	5.25HH	
94208-075 Wren II	66	5	989	26		NA/NA	5.25HH	
94208-106 Wren II	91		989			—/—	5.25HH	
94208-51 Wren II	43		989			—/—	5.25HH	
94208-91 Wren II	80		989			—/—	5.25HH	
94208-951 Wren II	42	5	989	17		990/128	5.25FH	
94211-086 Wren III	72	5	1024			—/—	5.25HH	
94211-091 Wren III	77	5	1024	17		970/970	5.25HH	
94211-106 Wren III	92	5	1024	35		NA/NA	5.25HH	
94211-106M Wren III	94	5	1024			1025/1025	5.25FH	
94211-209 Wren III	183	5	1547			1548/1548	3.5HH	
94216-106 Wren III	90	5	1024	34		NA/NA	5.25HH	
94221-125 Wren V	110	3	1544	V		NA/NA	5.25HH	
94221-169 Wren V	159	5	1310	V		NA/NA	5.25HH	
94221-190 Wren V	190	5	1547	V		NA/NA	5.25HH	
94221-209 Wren V	183	5	1544	V		NA/NA	5.25HH	
94241-383 Wren VI	338	7	1400	V		NA/NA	5.25HH	
94241-502 Wren VI		7	1765	V		NA/NA	5.25HH	
94241-502M Wren VI		7	1765	V		NA/NA	5.25HH	
94244-219 Wren VI	186	4	1747	54		1748/-1.0	5.25HH	
94244-274 Wren VI	233	5	1747	52		NA/NA	5.25HH	
94244-383 Wren VI	338	7	1747	54		NA/NA	5.25HH	
94246-182 Wren VI	161	4	1453	54		NA/NA	5.25HH	
94246-383 Wren VI	338	7	1747			NA/NA	5.25HH	
94311-136 Swift SL	120	5				NA/NA	3.5 3H	
94311-136S Swift SL	120	5	1247	36		NA/NA	3.5 3H	
94314-136 Swift SL	120	5				NA/NA	3.5HH	
94316-111 Swift	98	5		36		NA/NA	3.5HH	
94316-136 Swift SL	120	5		36		NA/NA	3.5 3H	
94316-155 Swift	138	7	1072	36		NA/NA	3.5HH	
94316-200 Swift	177	5		36		NA/NA	3.5HH	
94335-055 Swift SL	46	5				—/—	3.5HH	
94335-100 Swift	85	9	1072	17		—/—	3.5HH	
94335-150 Swift	128	9		26		—/—	3.5HH	
94351-090 Swift	80	5	1068			—/—	3.5HH	
94351-111 Swift	98	5	1068			NA/NA	3.5HH	
94351-126 Swift	111	7	1068	29		NA/NA	3.5HH	
94351-128 Swift	111	7	1068			NA/NA	3.5HH	
94351-133S Swift	117	5	1268	36		NA/NA	3.5HH	
94351-134 Swift	120	7	1268			—/—	3.5HH	
94351-135 Swift	121	6	1068			—/—	3.5HH	
94351-155 Swift	138	7	1068	36		NA/NA	3.5HH	
94351-155S Swift	138	7	1068	36		NA/NA	3.5HH	
94351-160 Swift	143	9	1068	29		NA/NA	3.5HH	
94351-172 Swift	177	9	1068	36		NA/NA	3.5HH	
94351-186S Swift	164	7	1268	36		NA/NA	3.5HH	
94351-200 Swift	178	7	1068	36		NA/NA	3.5HH	
94351-200S Swift	177	9	1068	36		NA/NA	3.5HH	
94351-230 Swift	210	9	1268	36		NA/NA	3.5HH	
94351-230S Swift	210	9	1268	36		NA/NA	3.5HH	
94354-090 Swift	80	5	102	29		—/-1.0	3.5HH	
94354-111 Swift	99	5	1072	36		NA/NA	3.5HH	
94354-126 Swift	111	7	1072	29		NA/NA	3.5HH	
94354-133 Swift	117	5	1272	36		NA/NA	3.5HH	
94354-155 Swift	138	7	1072	36		NA/NA	3.5HH	
94354-160 Swift	143	9	1072	29		NA/NA	3.5HH	
94354-186 Swift	164	7	1272	36		NA/NA	3.5HH	
94354-200 Swift	178	9	1072	36		NA/NA	3.5HH	
94354-230 Swift	204					—/—	3.5HH	
94354-239 Swift	211	9	1272	36		NA/NA	3.5HH	
94355-055 Swift II	46	5		17		—/—	3.5HH	
94355-100 Swift	84	9	1072	17		1073/300	3.5HH	

Drive Model	Format Size MB	Seek Time	Interface	Encode	cache kb	RPM
94205-051 Wren II	43	28	ST412/506	MFM		
94205-053 Wren II	43		ST412/506	MFM		
94205-071 Wren II	43		ST412/506	RLL		
94205-075 Wren II	62	28	ST412/506	RLL		
94205-077 Wren II	66	28	ST412/506	2,7 RLL		
94208-062 Wren II	60	28	COMPAQ	MFM		
94208-075 Wren II	66	30	IDE AT	2,7 RLL		
94208-106 Wren II	91		IDE AT			
94208-51 Wren II	43		IDE AT			
94208-91 Wren II	80		IDE AT			
94208-951 Wren II	42	28	COMPAQ	MFM		
94211-086 Wren III	72	18	SCSI	RLL		
94211-091 Wren III	77	18	SCSI	MFM		
94211-106 Wren III	92	18	SCSI	2,7 RLL		
94211-106M Wren III	94	18	SCSI	ZBR		
94211-209 Wren III	183	18	SCSI	ZBR		
94216-106 Wren III	90	18	ESDI (10)	2,7 RLL		
94221-125 Wren V	110	18	SCSI	RLL ZBR		
94221-169 Wren V	159	18	SCSI	RLL ZBR		
94221-190 Wren V	190	18	SCSI	RLL ZBR		
94221-209 Wren V	183	18	SCSI	RLL ZBR		
94241-383 Wren VI	338	14	SCSI	RLL ZBR		
94241-502 Wren VI			SCSI	RLL ZBR		
94241-502M Wren VI		16	SCSI(Mac)	RLL ZBR		
94244-219 Wren VI	186	16	AT	RLL		
94244-274 Wren VI	233	16	IDE AT	2,7 RLL		
94244-383 Wren VI	338	16	IDE AT	2,7 RLL		
94246-182 Wren VI	161	16	ESDI (20)	2,7 RLL		
94246-383 Wren VI	338	16	SCSI (20)	2,7 RLL		
94311-136 Swift SL	120	15	SCSI	2,7 RLL		
94311-136S Swift SL	120	15	SCSI-2	2,7 RLL		
94314-136 Swift SL	120	15	IDE AT	2,7 RLL		
94316-111 Swift	98	23	ESDI	2,7 RLL		
94316-136 Swift SL	120	15	ESDI	2,7 RLL		
94316-155 Swift	138	15	ESDI	2,7 RLL		
94316-200 Swift	177	15	ESDI	2,7 RLL		
94335-055 Swift SL	46	25	ST412/506	RLL		
94335-100 Swift	85	25	ST412/506	MFM		
94335-150 Swift	128	25	ST412/506	RLL		
94351-090 Swift	80	15	SCSI	RLL		
94351-111 Swift	98	15	SCSI	2,7 RLL		
94351-126 Swift	111	15	SCSI	2,7 RLL		
94351-128 Swift	111	15	SCSI	2,7 RLL		
94351-133S Swift	117	15	SCSI-2	2,7 RLL		
94351-134 Swift	120	15	SCSI	RLL		
94351-135 Swift	121	15	SCSI	RLL		
94351-155 Swift	138	15	SCSI	2,7 RLL		
94351-155S Swift	138	15	SCSI-2	2,7 RLL		
94351-160 Swift	143	15	SCSI	2,7 RLL		
94351-172 Swift	177	15	SCSI	2,7 RLL		
94351-186S Swift	164	15	SCSI-2	2,7 RLL		
94351-200 Swift	178	15	SCSI	2,7 RLL		
94351-200S Swift	177	15	SCSI-2	2,7 RLL		
94351-230 Swift	210	15	SCSI			
94351-230S Swift	210	15	SCSI-2	2,7 RLL		
94354-090 Swift	80	15	AT	RLL		
94354-111 Swift	99	15	IDE AT	2,7 RLL		
94354-126 Swift	111	15	IDE AT	2,7 RLL		
94354-133 Swift	117	15	IDE AT	2,7 RLL		
94354-155 Swift	138	15	IDE AT	2,7 RLL		
94354-160 Swift	143	15	IDE AT	2,7 RLL		
94354-186 Swift	164	15	IDE AT	2,7 RLL		
94354-200 Swift	178	15	IDE AT	2,7 RLL		
94354-230 Swift	204		IDE AT	2,7 RLL		
94354-239 Swift	211	15	IDE AT	2,7 RLL		
94355-055 Swift II	46	25	ST412/506	MFM		
94355-100 Swift	84	15	ST412/506	MFM		

Drive Model	Format Size MB	Head	Cyl	Sect/ Trac	Translate H/C/S	RWC/ WPC	Form Factor	Power Watts
94355-150 Swift	128	9	1072	26		1073/300	3.5HH	
94355-55 Swift	46					—/—	3.5HH	
94356-111 Swift	99	5	1072	36		NA/NA	3.5HH	
94356-155 Swift	138	7	1072	36		NA/NA	3.5HH	
94356-200 Swift	178	9	1072	36		NA/NA	3.5HH	
94601-12D Wren VII	1035	15	1931	V		NA/NA	5.25FH	
94601-12G Wren VII	1037	15	1937	V		NA/NA	5.25FH	
94601-12GM Wren VII	1037	15	1937	V		NA/NA	5.25FH	
94601-767H Wren VII	676	15	1356	V		NA/NA	5.25FH	
97155-036	30			17		—/—	8.0 FH	
9720-1123 Sabre	964	19				—/—	8.0 FH	
9720-1130 Sabre	1050	15	1635			—/—	8.0 FH	
9720-2270 Sabre	1948	19				—/—	8.0 FH	
9720-2500 Sabre	2145	19				—/—	8.0 FH	
9720-368 Sabre	368		1635			1218/1218	8.0 FH	
9720-500 Sabre	500	10	1217			1218/1218	8.0 FH	
9720-736 Sabre	736	15	1635			1636/1636	8.0 FH	
9720-850 Sabre	727	15	1381			1382/1382	8.0 FH	
97229-1150 Wren V	990	19				—/—	8.0 FH	
97501-15G Elite	1500	17				NA/NA	5.25FH	
97509-12G Elite	1050	17				—/—	5.25FH	
BJ7D5A/77731600	18	3	697	17		—/128	5.25FH	
BJ7D5A/77731601	18	3	697	17		—/128	5.25FH	
BJ7D5A/77731602	30	5	697	17		—/128	5.25FH	
BJ7D5A/77731603	30	5	697			—/128	5.25FH	
BJ7D5A/77731604	36	5	697			—/128	5.25FH	
BJ7D5A/77731605	30	5	697	17		—/128	5.25FH	
BJ7D5A/77731606	27			17		—/128	5.25FH	
BJ7D5A/77731607	18	3	697	17		—/128	5.25FH	
BJ7D5A/77731608	29	5	670	17		—/128	5.25FH	
BJ7D5A/77731609	30	5	697	17		—/128	5.25FH	
BJ7D5A/77731610	18	3	697	17		—/128	5.25FH	
BJ7D5A/77731611	30	5	697	17		—/128	5.25FH	
BJ7D5A/77731612	24	4	697	17		—/128	5.25FH	
BJ7D5A/77731613	31	5	733	17		—/128	5.25FH	
BJ7D5A/77731614	23	4	670	17		—/128	5.25FH	
BJ7D5A/77731615	24	4	697	17		—/128	5.25FH	
BJ7D5A/77731616	31	5	733	17		—/128	5.25FH	
BJ7D5A/77731617	30	5	697	17		—/128	5.25FH	
BJ7D5A/77731618	30	5	697	17		—/128	5.25FH	
BJ7D5A/77731619	30	5	697	17		—/128	5.25FH	
BJ7D5A/77731620	30	5	697	17		—/128	5.25FH	
Sabre 1123	964	19				—/—		
Sabre 1150	990	19				—/—		
Sabre 1230	1050	15	1635			—/—		
Sabre 2270	1948	19				—/—		
Sabre 2500	2145	19				—/—		
Sabre 368	368	10	1635			—/—		
Sabre 500	500	10	1217			—/—		
Sabre 736	741	15	1217			—/—		
Sabre 850	851	15	1635			—/—		

CENTURY DATA

Drive Model	Format Size MB	Head	Cyl	Sect/ Trac	Translate H/C/S	RWC/ WPC	Form Factor	Power Watts
CAST-10203E	55	3	1050	35		NA/NA	5.25FH	
CAST-10203S	55	3	1050	35		NA/NA	5.25FH	
CAST-10304E	75	4	1050	35		NA/NA	5.25FH	
CAST-10304S	75	4	1050	35		NA/NA	5.25FH	
CAST-10305E	94	5	1050	35		NA/NA	5.25FH	
CAST-10305S	94	5	1050	35		NA/NA	5.25FH	
CAST-14404E	114	4	1590	35		NA/NA	5.25HH	
CAST-14404S	114	4	1590	35		NA/NA	5.25HH	
CAST-14405E	140	5	1590	35		NA/NA	5.25HH	
CAST-14405S	140	5	1590	35		NA/NA	5.25HH	
CAST-14406E	170	6	1590	35		NA/NA	5.25HH	
CAST-14406S	170	6	1590	35		NA/NA	5.25HH	
CAST-24509E	258	9	1599	35		NA/NA	5.25FH	
CAST-24509S	258	9	1599	35		NA/NA	5.25FH	
CAST-24611E	315	11	1599	35		NA/NA	5.25FH	

Drive Model	Format Size MB	Seek Time	Interface	Encode	cache kb	RPM
94355-150 Swift	128	15	ST412/506	2,7 RLL		
94355-55 Swift	46		MFM			
94356-111 Swift	99	15	ESDI (10)	2,7 RLL		
94356-155 Swift	138	15	ESDI (10)	2,7 RLL		
94356-200 Swift	178	15	ESDI (10)	2,7 RLL		
94601-12D Wren VII	1035	15	SCSI	2,7 RLL		
94601-12G Wren VII	1037	15	SCSI	RLL ZBR		
94601-12GM Wren VII	1037	15	SCSI(Mac)	RLL ZBR		
94601-767H Wren VII	676	15	SCSI(Mac)	RLL ZBR		
97155-036	30		ST412/506	MFM		
9720-1123 Sabre	964	15	SMD	2,7 RLL		
9720-1130 Sabre	1050	15	SMD/SCSI	2,7 RLL		
9720-2270 Sabre	1948	12	SMD	2,7 RLL		
9720-2500 Sabre	2145	12	SMD/SCSI	2,7 RLL		
9720-368 Sabre	368	18	SMD/SCSI	2,7 RLL		
9720-500 Sabre	500	18	SMD/SCSI	2,7 RLL		
9720-736 Sabre	736	15	SMD/SCSI	2,7 RLL		
9720-850 Sabre	727	15	SMD/SCSI	2,7 RLL		
97229-1150 Wren V	990	15	IPI-2			
97501-15G Elite	1500	12	SCSI-2	RLL		
97509-12G Elite	1050	12	IPI-2			
BJ7D5A/77731600	18		ST412/506	MFM		
BJ7D5A/77731601	18		ST412/506	MFM		
BJ7D5A/77731602	30		ST412/506	MFM		
BJ7D5A/77731603	30		ST412/506	MFM		
BJ7D5A/77731604	36		ST412/506	MFM		
BJ7D5A/77731605	30		ST412/506	MFM		
BJ7D5A/77731606	27		ST412/506	MFM		
BJ7D5A/77731607	18		ST412/506	MFM		
BJ7D5A/77731608	29		ST412/506	MFM		
BJ7D5A/77731609	30		ST412/506	MFM		
BJ7D5A/77731610	18		ST412/506	MFM		
BJ7D5A/77731611	30		ST412/506	MFM		
BJ7D5A/77731612	24		ST412/506	MFM		
BJ7D5A/77731613	31		ST412/506	MFM		
BJ7D5A/77731614	23		ST412/506	MFM		
BJ7D5A/77731615	24		ST412/506	MFM		
BJ7D5A/77731616	31		ST412/506	MFM		
BJ7D5A/77731617	30		ST412/506	MFM		
BJ7D5A/77731618	30		ST412/506	MFM		
BJ7D5A/77731619	30		ST412/506	MFM		
BJ7D5A/77731620	30		ST412/506	MFM		
Sabre 1123	964	15				
Sabre 1150	990	15				
Sabre 1230	1050	15				
Sabre 2270	1948	12				
Sabre 2500	2145	12				
Sabre 368	368	18				
Sabre 500	500	18				
Sabre 736	741	15				
Sabre 850	851	15				

CENTURY DATA

Drive Model	Format Size MB	Seek Time	Interface	Encode	cache kb	RPM
CAST-10203E	55	28	ESDI	2,7 RLL		
CAST-10203S	55	28	SCSI	2,7 RLL		
CAST-10304E	75	28	ESDI	2,7 RLL		
CAST-10304S	75	28	SCSI	2,7 RLL		
CAST-10305E	94	28	ESDI	2,7 RLL		
CAST-10305S	94	28	SCSI	2,7 RLL		
CAST-14404E	114	25	ESDI	2,7 RLL		
CAST-14404S	114	25	SCSI	2,7 RLL		
CAST-14405E	140	25	ESDI	2,7 RLL		
CAST-14405S	140	25	SCSI	2,7 RLL		
CAST-14406E	170	25	ESDI	2,7 RLL		
CAST-14406S	170	25	SCSI	2,7 RLL		
CAST-24509E	258	18	ESDI	2,7 RLL		
CAST-24509S	258	18	SCSI	2,7 RLL		
CAST-24611E	315	18	ESDI	2,7 RLL		

Drive Model	Format Size MB	Head	Cyl	Sect/Trac	Translate H/C/S	RWC/WPC	Form Factor	Power Watts
CAST-24611S	315	11	1599	35		NA/NA	5.25FH	
CAST-24713E	372	13	1599	35		NA/NA	5.25FH	
CAST-24713S	372	13	1599	35		NA/NA	5.25FH	

CMI

Drive Model	Format Size MB	Head	Cyl	Sect/Trac	Translate H/C/S	RWC/WPC	Form Factor	Power Watts
CM3412	10	4	306	17		306/256	5.25FH	
CM3426	20	4	615	17		616/256	5.25FH	
CM5018H	15	2		17		—/—	5.25FH	
CM5205	4	2	256	17		128/128	5.25FH	
CM5206	5	2	306	17		307/256	5.25FH	
CM5410	8	4	256	17		128/128	5.25FH	
CM5412	10	4	306	17		307/128	5.25FH	
CM5616	14	6	256	17		257/257	5.25FH	
CM5619	16	6	306	17		307/128	5.25FH	
CM5826	20	8	306	17		—/—	5.25FH	
CM6213	11	2	640	17		641/256	5.25FH	
CM6426	22	4	615	17		—/300	5.25FH	
CM6426S	22	4	615	17		256/300	5.25FH	
CM6640	33	6	615	17		616/300	5.25FH	
CM7000	44	7	733	17		733/512	5.25FH	
CM7030	25	4	733	17		733/512	5.25FH	
CM7038	31	5	733	17		733/512	5.25FH	
CM7053	44	7	733	17		733/512	5.25FH	
CM7085	71	8	1024	17		1024/512	5.25FH	
CM7660	50	6	960	17		961/450	5.25FH	
CM7880	67	8	960	17		961/450	5.25FH	

CMS ENHANCEMENTS, INC

Drive Model	Format Size MB	Head	Cyl	Sect/Trac	Translate H/C/S	RWC/WPC	Form Factor	Power Watts
B1.0A1-U1	1281				16/2100/63	NA/NA	3.5 3H	
B340A4-U1	340				12/1010/55	NA/NA	3.5 3H	
B420A4-U1	425				16/1010/51	NA/NA	3.5 3H	
B540A4-U1	541				16/1023/63	NA/NA	3.5 3H	
B730A4-U1	731				16/1416/63	NA/NA	3.5 3H	
D20XT-OK	21	4	615	17		—/—	3.5HH	
D30XT-OK	32	4	615	26		—/—	3.5HH	
D40XT-OK	42	5	977	17		—/—	3.5HH	
F115ESD1-T	115	7	915	35		—/—	5.25FH	30
F150AT-CA	150	9	969	34		—/—	5.25FH	21
F150AT-WCA	151	9	969	34		—/—	5.25FH	21
F150EQ-WCA	151	9	969	34		—/—	5.25FH	20
F320AT-CA	320	15	1224	34		—/—	5.25FH	29
F70ESDI-T	73	7	583	35		—/—	5.25FH	30
H100286D-P	105	8	776	17		—/—	5.25HH	
H100386S-P	105	8	776	34		—/—	5.25HH	
H330E1 (PS Express)	330	7	1780	54		—/—	5.25HH	14
H340E1 (PS Express)	340	7	1780	54		—/—	5.25HH	14
H40M50-P	42	5	977	17		—/—	3.5HH	
H60286D-P	64	5	948	27		—/—	5.25HH	
H60SCSI-S	65	6	628	34		—/—	5.25HH	
H65M50-P	65	9	1024	17		—/—	3.5HH	
H80AT	84	9	1072	17		—/—	5.25HH	
H80SCSI-S	85	6	820	34		—/—	5.25HH	
HD20AT-S	21	4	615	17		—/—	5.25HH	
HD30AT-S	32	6	615	17		—/—	5.25HH	
HD40AT-S1	43	6	820	17		—/—	5.25HH	
K120M50Z-70P	125	8	925	33		—/—	3.5HH	
K20M25-WS	21	2	636	34		—/—	3.5HH	
K20M25/30-OK	21	4	615	17		—/—	3.5HH	
K20M25/30-WS	21	4	615	17		—/—	3.5HH	
K30M25/30-OK	32	6	615	17		—/—	3.5HH	
K30M25/30-WS	32	6	615	17		—/—	3.5HH	
K30M30E-P	31	4	615	25		—/—	3.5HH	
K40M25/30-WS	42	5	977	17		—/—	3.5HH	
K45M30286-ZS	48	6	615	26		—/—	3.5HH	
K50M50Z-70P	63	6	767	27		—/—	3.5HH	
K60M30286-ZS	61	5	921	26		—/—	3.5HH	
K80M25Z-30	84	9	1072	17		—/—	3.5HH	
K80M30286-WS	84	7	906	26		—/—	3.5HH	

Drive Model	Format Size MB	Seek Time	Interface	Encode	cache kb	RPM
CAST-24611S	315	18	SCSI	2,7 RLL		
CAST-24713E	372	18	ESDI	2,7 RLL		
CAST-24713S	372	18	SCSI	2,7 RLL		
CMI						
CM3412	10		ST412/506	MFM		
CM3426	20	85	ST412/506	MFM		
CM5018H	15	85	ST412/506	MFM		
CM5205	4		ST412/506	MFM		
CM5206	5	102	ST412/506	MFM		
CM5410	8	102	ST412/506	MFM		
CM5412	10	85	ST412/506	MFM		
CM5616	14	102	ST412/506	MFM		
CM5619	16	85	ST412/506	MFM		
CM5826	20	102	ST412/506	MFM		
CM6213	11	48	ST412/506	MFM		
CM6426	22	39	ST412/506	MFM		
CM6426S	22	39	ST412/506	MFM		
CM6640	33	39	ST412/506	MFM		
CM7000	44	42	ST412/506	MFM		
CM7030	25	42	ST412/506	MFM		
CM7038	31	42	ST412/506	MFM		
CM7053	44	42	ST412/506	MFM		
CM7085	71	42	ST412/506	MFM		
CM7660	50	28	ST412/506	MFM		
CM7880	67	28	ST412/506	MFM		
CMS ENHANCEMENTS, INC						
B1.0A1-U1	1281	10	IDE AT			4500
B340A4-U1	340	13	IDE AT			3600
B420A4-U1	425	13	IDE AT			3300
B540A4-U1	541	14	IDE AT			3600
B730A4-U1	731	11	IDE AT			4500
D20XT-OK	21	62	ST412/506	MFM		
D30XT-OK	32	62	ST412/506	2,7 RLL		
D40XT-OK	42	24	ST412/506	MFM		
F115ESD1-T	115	30	ESDI	2,7 RLL		
F150AT-CA	150	17	ESDI	2,7 RLL		
F150AT-WCA	151	17	ESDI	2,7 RLL		
F150EQ-WCA	151	17	ESDI	2,7 RLL		
F320AT-CA	320	18	ESDI	2,7 RLL		
F70ESDI-T	73	30	ESDI	2,7 RLL		
H100286D-P	105	25	IDE AT			
H100386S-P	105	25	IDE AT			
H330E1 (PS Express)	330	14	ESDI	2,7 RLL		
H340E1 (PS Express)	340	14	ESDI	2,7 RLL		
H40M50-P	42	24	ST412/506	MFM		
H60286D-P	64	29	IDE AT			
H60SCSI-S	65	28	SCSI			
H65M50-P	65	15	ST412/506	MFM		
H80AT	84	15	SCSI			
H80SCSI-S	85	28	SCSI			
HD20AT-S	21	65	ST412/506	MFM		
HD30AT-S	32	40	ST412/506	MFM		
HD40AT-S1	43	28	ST412/506	MFM		
K120M50Z-70P	125	23	MCA	2,7 RLL		
K20M25-WS	21	27	IDE AT			
K20M25/30-OK	21	62	ST412/506	MFM		
K20M25/30-WS	21	40	ST412/506	MFM		
K30M25/30-OK	32	62	ST412/506	MFM		
K30M25/30-WS	32	40	ST412/506	MFM		
K30M30E-P	31	39	IDE AT			
K40M25/30-WS	42	24	ST412/506	MFM		
K45M30286-ZS	48	28	SCSI			
K50M50Z/70P	63	27	MCA	2,7 RLL		
K60M30286-ZS	61	24	SCSI			
K80M25Z/30	84	15	ST412/506	MFM		
K80M30286-WS	84	24	SCSI			

Drive Model	Format Size MB	Head	Cyl	Sect/Trac	Translate H/C/S	RWC/WPC	Form Factor	Power Watts
LDSNECMS-20	20	4	575	32		—/—	3.5HH	
LDZE386-100	100	8	776	34		—/—	3.5HH	
PB340	340					NA/NA		1.0
PB520	520					NA/NA		1.2
PSExpress 150	150					—/—	5.25FH	21
PSExpress 320	320					—/—	5.25FH	21
Sentry 180	180	5	1546			—/—	5.25FH	
Sentry 300	290	9	1546			—/—	5.25FH	
Sentry 600	600	15	1546			—/—	5.25FH	
Sentry 90	90	5	1024			—/—	5.25FH	
COGITO								
CG906	5	2	306	17		128/128	5.25HH	
CG912	10	4	306	17		128/128	5.25HH	
CG925	21	4	612	17		307/307	5.25HH	
PT912	11	2	612	17		307/307	5.25HH	
PT925	21	4	612	17		307/307	5.25HH	
COMPAQ								
113640-001	43	2	1053	40		NA/NA	3.5HH	
113641-001	112	8	832	33		NA/NA	3.5HH	
115145-001	84	6	832	33		NA/NA	3.5HH	
115147-001	325	7	1744	52		NA/NA	5.25HH	
115158-001	651	15	1631	52		NA/NA	5.25FH	
115627-001	112	8	832	33		NA/NA	3.5HH	
115830-001	318	15	1220	34		NA/NA	5.25FH	
116562-001	123	4	1552	39		NA/NA	3.5HH	
116565-001	207	8	1336	38		NA/NA	3.5HH	
122136-001	60	2	1520	39		NA/NA	3.5HH	
123065-B22 (Hot-Plug)	9100					—/—	3.5 3H	
128417-B21 (Hot-Plug)	18210					—/—	3.5 3H	
128418-B22 (Hot-Plug)	18209					—/—	3.5 3H	
128419-B21 (Non-Plug)	18209					—/—	3.5 3H	
128420-B21 (Hot-Plug)	36419					—/—	3.5HH	
131067-001	510	12	1806	46		NA/NA	3.5HH	
131362-001	325	7	1744	52		NA/NA	5.25HH	
142018-001	1049	13	1974	56-96		—/—	3.5HH	
142216-001	2097	18	2626	68-108		—/—	3.5HH	
142671-B22 (Hot-Plug)	9100					—/—	3.5 3H	
142672-B21 (Non-Plug)	9100					—/—	3.5 3H	
142673-B22 (Hot-Plug)	18209					—/—	3.5 3H	
142674-B21 (Non-Plug)	18209					—/—	3.5 3H	
142676-B21 (Non-Plug)	36419					—/—	3.5HH	
146742-001	2097	18	2626	68-108		—/—	3.5HH	
146742-003	1049	13	1974	56-96		—/—	3.5HH	
146742-005	4293	21	3606	82-135		—/—	3.5HH	
146742-006	4293	21	3606	82-135		—/—	3.5HH	
146742-007	2097	11	3511	86-135		—/—	3.5HH	
147597-001	9100					—/—	3.5HH	
147598-001	18209.8					—/—	3.5HH	
159138-001	36419.5					—/—	3.5HH	
159764-B21	18GB					—/—	3.5 3H	
172492-002	421	4	2519	55-104	16/1010/51	—/—	3.5 3H	
172493-001	1083	6	3811	61-117	16/2100/63	—/—	3.5 3H	
172678-002	730	4	3658	64-128	16/1416/63	—/—	3.5 3H	
172874-001	541	4	2853	58-118	9/1926/61	—/—	3.5 3H	
176494-B21	72837					—/—	3.5HH	
176496-B22 (Hot-Plug)	36419					—/—	3.5 3H	
176497-B21 (Non-Plug)	36419					—/—	3.5 3H	
176498-B21 (Hot-Plug)	36419					—/—	3.5 3H	
188120-B22	9100					—/—	3.5 3H	
188122-B22 (Hot-Plug)	18209					—/—	3.5 3H	
191188-B21	18GB					—/—	3.5 3H	
191189-B21	36GB					—/—	3.5 3H	
196408-002	270	2	2853	58-118	14/944/40	—/—	3.5 3H	
199580-001	4293	21	3606	82-135		—/—	3.5HH	
199597-001	4293	21	3606	82-135		—/—	3.5HH	
199642-001	2097	11	3511	86-135		—/—	3.5HH	

Drive Model	Format Size MB	Seek Time	Interface	Encode	cache kb	RPM
LDSNECMS-20	20	28	IDE AT	2,7 RLL		
LDZE386-100	100	25	IDE AT			
PB340	340	12	SCSI-2	1,6 RLL	128k	4200
PB520	520	17	SCSI-2	1,7 RLL	128k	4500
PSExpress 150	150	17	ESDI	2,7 RLL		
PSExpress 320	320	15	ESDI	2,7 RLL		
Sentry 180	180	18	SCSI			
Sentry 300	290	16.5	SCSI			
Sentry 600	600	17	SCSI			
Sentry 90	90	18	SCSI			
COGITO						
CG906	5	93	ST412/506	MFM		
CG912	10	93	ST412/506	MFM		
CG925	21	93	ST412/506	MFM		
PT912	11	93	ST412/506	MFM		
PT925	21	93	ST412/506	MFM		
COMPAQ						
113640-001	43	29				
113641-001	112	25				
115145-001	84	25				
115147-001	325	19	ESDI			
115158-001	651	19	ESDI			
115627-001	112	25				
115830-001	318	18	ESDI			
116562-001	123	19				
116565-001	207	19			<T>	
122136-001	60	19				
123065-B22 (Hot-Plug)	9100	7.0	Ultra2SCSIW			7200
128417-B21 (Hot-Plug)	18210	5.2	UltraSCSI3W			1000
128418-B22 (Hot-Plug)	18209	5.2	Ultra2SCSIW			1000
128419-B21 (Non-Plug)	18209	5.5	Ultra2SCSIW			1000
128420-B21 (Hot-Plug)	36419	5.7	UltraSCSI3W			1000
131067-001	510	2				
131362-001	325	18	ESDI			
142018-001	1049	10	SCSI-2Fast			5400
142216-001	2097	9	SCSI-2Fast			6400
142671-B22 (Hot-Plug)	9100	5.0	Ultra3SCSIW			1000
142672-B21 (Non-Plug)	9100	5.0	Ultra3SCSIW			1000
142673-B22 (Hot-Plug)	18209	5.2	Ultra3SCSIW			1000
142674-B21 (Non-Plug)	18209	5.5	Ultra SCSI3			1000
142676-B21 (Non-Plug)	36419	5.7	Ultra SCSI3			1000
146742-001	2097	9	SCSI-2Fast			6400
146742-003	1049	10	SCSI-2Fast			5400
146742-005	4293	9	SCSI-2Fast			7200
146742-006	4293	9	SCSI-2FstW			7200
146742-007	2097	9	SCSI-2FstW			7200
147597-001	9100Mb	6.9	Ultra3SCSIW			7200
147598-001	18209.8Mb	6.9	Ultra3SCSIW			7200
159138-001	36419.5Mb	6.15	Ultra3SCSIW			1000
159764-B21	18GB	12	UL160SCSI			1000
172492-002	421	14	IDE AT		96k	3600
172493-001	1083	14	IDE AT		128k	4495
172678-002	730	11	IDE AT		96k	4500
172874-001	541	14	IDE AT		96k	3600
176494-B21	72837	12	Ultra3SCSIW			1000
176496-B22 (Hot-Plug)	36419	13	Ultra3SCSIW			1000
176497-B21 (Non-Plug)	36419	13	Ultra3SCSIW			1000
176498-B21 (Hot-Plug)	36419	16	Ultra3SCSIW			1000
188120-B22	9100	12	Ultra3SCSIW			1500
188122-B22 (Hot-Plug)	18209	12	Ultra3SCSIW			1500
191188-B21	18GB	8.2	UL160SCSI			1500
191189-B21	36GB	12	UL160SCSI			1500
196408-002	270	14	IDE AT		96k	1000
199580-001	4293	9	SCSI-2Fast			3600
199597-001	4293	9	SCSI-2FstW			7200
199642-001	2097	9	SCSI-2FstW			7200
						7200

Drive Model	Format Size MB	Head	Cyl	Sect/Trac	Translate H/C/S	RWC/WPC	Form Factor	Power Watts
201066-B21	40GB					—/—	3.5	3H
202352-B21 (Hot-Plug)	18209.3					—/—	3.5	3H
202353-B21	18209					—/—	3.5	3H
230534-B21	40GB					—/—	3.5	3H
231377-B21	20GB					—/—	3.5	3H
232432-B22 (Hot-Plug)	72837.2					—/—	3.5	3H
232617-B21 (Hot-Plug)	36419.2					—/—	3.5	3H
232916-B22 (Hot-Plug)	36419.2					—/—	3.5	3H
241139	6511	6	8895	170-28		—/—	5.25	
250020-B21	80GB					—/—	3.5	3H
250021-B21	120GB					—/—	3.5	3H
250022-B21	36GB					—/—	3.5	3H
250023-B21	72GB					—/—	3.5	3H
251974-B21	20GB					—/—	3.5	3H
262477	3227	6	5690	114-23		—/—	3.5	
269020-B21	18GB					—/—	3.5	3H
269021-B21	36GB					—/—	3.5	3H
269022-B21	73GB					—/—	3.5	3H
272577-001 (Hot-Plug)	4293					—/—	3.5	3H
272672-B21	18GB					—/—	3.5	3H
272673-B21	36GB					—/—	3.5	3H
272674-B21	146GB					—/—	3.5	3H
278424-B21	80GB					—/—	3.5	3H
286118	4018	8	5690	114-23		—/—	3.5	
286123	8038	4	11490	403-26		—/—	3.5	
291687-B21	73GB					—/—	3.5	3H
313706-B21 (Hot-Plug)	9100					—/—	3.5	3H
313756-B21 (Hot-Plug)	18209					—/—	3.5HH	
328938-B21 (Hot-Plug)	4290					—/—	3.5	3H
328939-B21 (Hot-Plug)	9100					—/—	3.5	3H
328939-B22 (Hot-Plug)	9100					—/—	3.5	3H
328941-B21 (Non-Plug)	4290					—/—	3.5	3H
328942-B21 (Non-Plug)	9100					—/—	3.5	3H
328943-B21 (Non-Plug)	18209					—/—	3.5HH	
336356-B21 (Hot-Plug)	4293					—/—	3.5	3H
336357-B21 (Hot-Plug)	9100					—/—	3.5	3H
336358-B21 (Hot-Plug)	18209					—/—	3.5HH	
336368-B21 (Non-Plug)	4293					—/—	3.5	3H
336369-B21 (Non-Plug)	9100					—/—	3.5	3H
336370-B21 (Non-Plug)	18209					—/—	3.5HH	
339506-B21 (Non-Plug)	4293					—/—	3.5	3H
339509-B21 (Non-Plug)	9100					—/—	3.5	3H
349513-B21 (Hot-Plug)	4290					—/—	3.5	3H
349514-B21 (Hot-Plug)	9100					—/—	3.5	3H
349525-B21 (Non-Plug)	4290					—/—	3.5	3H
349526-B21 (Non-Plug)	9100					—/—	3.5	3H
380588-B21	9100Mb					—/—	3.5HH	
380589-B21	18209.8Mb					—/—	3.5HH	
388143-B21 (Non-Plug)	18209					—/—	3.5	3H
388144-B22 (Hot-Plug)	18209					—/—	3.5	3H
400739-B21 (Hot-Plug)	18209					—/—	3.5	3H
400740-B21 (Hot-Plug)	36419					—/—	3.5HH	

COMPORT

Drive Model	Format Size MB	Head	Cyl	Sect/Trac	Translate H/C/S	RWC/WPC	Form Factor	Power Watts
2040	44	4	820	26		—/—	5.25HH	
2041	44	4	820	26		—/—	5.25HH	
2082	86	6	820	34		—/—	5.25HH	

CONNER PERIPHERALS, INC.

Drive Model	Format Size MB	Head	Cyl	Sect/Trac	Translate H/C/S	RWC/WPC	Form Factor	Power Watts
CFA1080A	1080	8		72-114		—/—	3.5	3H
CFA1080S	1080	8		72-114		—/—	3.5	3H
CFA1275A	1278	6			16/2479/63	—/—	3.5	3H
CFA1275S	1278	6				—/—	3.5	3H
CFA170A	172	2	2111	V		AUTO/AUTO	3.5 3H	
CFA170S	172	2	2111	67-91		—/—	3.5 3H	3
CFA2161A	2110	16	4095	63		—/—	3.5 3H	
CFA270A	270	2		72-114		—/—	3.5 3H	
CFA270S	270	2		72-114		—/—	3.5 3H	

Drive Model	Format Size MB	Seek Time	Interface	Encode	cache kb	RPM
201066-B21	40GB	8	UltraATA100			7200
202352-B21 (Hot-Plug)	18209.3	5.5	Ultra3SCSIW			1000
202353-B21	18209	5.5	Ultra3SCSIW			1000
230534-B21	40GB	8.5	ATA 100			7200
231377-B21	20GB	8.5	ATA 100			7200
232432-B22	72837.2	4.5	Ultra3SCSIW			1500
232617-B21 (Hot-Plug)	36419.2	5.7	Ultra3SCSIW			1500
232916-B22 (Hot-Plug)	36419.2	3.8	Ultra3SCSIW			1500
241139	6511	13	SCSI-3ULTRA		512k	3600
250020-B21	80GB	8	UltraATA100			7200
250021-B21	120GB	8	UltraATA100			7200
250022-B21	36GB	8.2	UL160SCSI			1500
250023-B21	72GB	12	UL160SCSI			1000
251974-B21	20GB	8	UltraATA100			7200
262477	3227	12	SCSI-3ULTRA		128k	4500
269020-B21	18GB	11	UL320 SCSI			1000
269021-B21	36GB	11	UL320 SCSI			1000
269022-B21	73GB	9.2	UL320 SCSI			1000
272577-001 (Hot-Plug)	4293	8.8	Ultra3SCSIW			7200
272672-B21	18GB	7	UL320 SCSI			1500
272673-B21	36GB	7	UL320 SCSI			1500
272674-B21	146GB	9.2	UL320 SCSI			1000
278424-B21	80GB	8.5	ATA 100			7200
286118	4018	12	SCSI-3ULTRA		128k	4500
286123	8038	12	SCSI-3ULTRA		128k	4000
291687-B21	73GB	6.7	UL320 SCSI			1500
313706-B21 (Hot-Plug)	9100	7.9	Ultra3SCSIW			7200
313756-B21 (Hot-Plug)	18209	8.0	Ultra3SCSIW			7200
328938-B21 (Hot-Plug)	4290	5.4	Ultra2 SCSI			1000
328939-B21 (Hot-Plug)	9100	5.4	Ultra2SCSIW			1000
328939-B22 (Hot-Plug)	9100	5.2	Ultra2SCSIW			1000
328941-B21 (Non-Plug)	4290	5.4	Ultra2 SCSI			1000
328942-B21 (Non-Plug)	9100	5.2	Ultra2SCSIW			1000
328943-B21 (Non-Plug)	18209	5.7	Ultra2 SCSI			1000
336356-B21 (Hot-Plug)	4293	5.4	SCSI3UltraW			1000
336357-B21 (Hot-Plug)	9100	5.4	SCSI3UltraW			1000
336358-B21 (Hot-Plug)	18209	5.7	SCSI3UltraW			1000
336368-B21 (Non-Plug)	4293	5.4	SCSI3UltraW			1000
336369-B21 (Non-Plug)	9100	5.4	SCSI3UltraW			1000
336370-B21 (Non-Plug)	18209	5.7	SCSI3UltraW			1000
339506-B21 (Non-Plug)	4293	8.8	SCSI3UltraW			7200
339509-B21 (Non-Plug)	9100	7.5	SCSI3UltraW			7200
349513-B21 (Hot-Plug)	4290	8.8	Ultra2 SCSI			7200
349514-B21 (Hot-Plug)	9100	7.9	Ultra2 SCSI			7200
349525-B21 (Non-Plug)	4290	7.5	Ultra2 SCSI			7200
349526-B21 (Non-Plug)	9100	7.1	Ultra2SCSIW			7200
380588-B21	9100Mb	5.4	Ultra3SCSIW			1000
380589-B21	18209.8Mb	5.7	Ultra3SCSIW			1000
388143-B21 (Non-Plug)	18209	7.0	Ultra3SCSIW			7200
388144-B22 (Hot-Plug)	18209	7.0	Ultra2SCSIW			7200
400739-B21 (Hot-Plug)	18209	6.9	Ultra3SCSIW			7200
400740-B21 (Hot-Plug)	36419	7.6	Ultra3SCSIW			7200

COMPORT

2040	44	35	ST412/506	2,7 RLL		
2041	44	29	IDE AT			
2082	86	29	SCSI			

CONNER PERIPHERALS, INC.

CFA1080A	1080	12	IDE AT	1,7 RLL	256k	4500
CFA1080S	1080	12	SCSI-2Fast	1,7 RLL	256k	4500
CFA1275A	1278	12	EIDE	1,7 RLL	256k	4500
CFA1275S	1278	12	SCSI-2	1,7 RLL	256k	4500
CFA170A	172	13	IDE	1,7 RLL	64k	
CFA170S	172	13	SCSI-2	1,7 RLL	64k	
CFA2161A	2110		IDE AT			4011
CFA270A	270	12	IDE AT	1,7 RLL	256k	4500
CFA270S	270	12	SCSI-2	1,7 RLL	256k	4500

Hard Drive Specs

Drive Model	Format Size MB	Head	Cyl	Sect/Trac	Translate H/C/S	RWC/WPC	Form Factor	Power Watts
CFA340A	343	4		67-91		NA/NA	3.5 3H	
CFA340S	343	4		67-91		NA/NA	3.5 3H	
CFA425A	426					—/—	3.5 3H	3.5
CFA425S	426					—/—	3.5 3H	3.5
CFA540A	541	4		72-114		—/—	3.5 3H	4
CFA540S	541	4		72-114		—/—	3.5 3H	4.0
CFA810A	810	6		72-114		—/—	3.5 3H	
CFA810S	810	6		72-114		—/—	3.5 3H	
CFA850A	852	4				—/—	3.5 3H	
CFA850S	852	4				—/—	3.5 3H	
CFL350A	350		2225		12/905/63	—/—	2.5 4H	
CFL420A	422	4	2393	V	16/818/63	—/—	2.5 4H	
CFN170A	168	4		47-72		—/—	2.5 4H	
CFN170S	168	4		47-72		—/—	2.5 4H	
CFN250A	252	6		47-72	16/489/63	—/—	2.5 4H	
CFN250S	252	6		47-72		—/—	2.5 4H	
CFN340A	344	6		53-89	16/667/63	—/—	2.5 4H	1.4
CFN340S	344	6		53-89		—/—	2.5 4H	1.4
CFP1060D	1062	8				—/—	3.5 3H	
CFP1060E	1062	8				—/—	3.5 3H	
CFP1060S	1062	8				—/—	3.5 3H	
CFP1060W	1062	8				—/—	3.5 3H	
CFP1080E (Filepro)	1080	6	3658	66-120		—/—	3.5 3H	3.75
CFP1080S (Filepro)	1080	6	3658	66-120		—/—	3.5 3H	3.75
CFP2105E	2147	10	3948	67-139		—/—	3.5 3H	5.7
CFP2105S	2147	10	3948	67-139		—/—	3.5 3H	5.7
CFP2105W	2147	10	3948	67-139		—/—	3.5 3H	5.7
CFP2107E (Filepro)	2147	10	4016	69-124		—/—	3.5 3H	8.9
CFP2107S (Filepro)	2147	10	4016	69-124		—/—	3.5 3H	8.9
CFP2107W (Filepro)	2147	10	4016	69-124		—/—	3.5 3H	8.9
CFP4207E (Filepro)	4294	20	4016	69-124		—/—	3.5HH	12.8
CFP4207S (Filepro)	4294	20	4016	69-124		—/—	3.5HH	12.8
CFP4207W (Filepro)	4294	20	4016	69-124		—/—	3.5HH	12.9
CFP4217C (Filepro)	4294		6028			NA/NA	3.5HH	
CFP4217E (Filepro)	4294		6028			NA/NA	3.5HH	
CFP4217S (Filepro)	4294		6028			NA/NA	3.5HH	
CFP4217W (Filepro)	4294		6028			NA/NA	3.5HH	
CFP4217WD (Filepro)	4294		6028			NA/NA	3.5HH	
CFP9117C (Filepro)	9100		6028			NA/NA	3.5HH	8.1
CFP9117E (Filepro)	9100		6028			NA/NA	3.5HH	8.1
CFP9117S (Filepro)	9100		6028			NA/NA	3.5HH	8.1
CFP9117W (Filepro)	9100		6028			NA/NA	3.5HH	8.1
CFP9117WD (Filepro)	9100		6028			NA/NA	3.5HH	8.1
CFS1060A	1060	16	2064	63		—/—	3.5 3H	
CFS1081A	1080	4	3930			—/—	3.5 3H	
CFS1275A	1275	6	3640		16/2479/63	—/—	3.5 3H	
CFS1276A	1275		4893			NA/NA	3.5 3H	3.5
CFS1621A	1620	6	3930			—/—	3.5 3H	
CFS2105S	2147	10	3948			—/—	3.5 3H	
CFS210A	213	2		68-107		—/—	3.5 3H	
CFS270A	270	2	2595		16/525/63	—/—	3.5 3H	
CFS420A	420	4		68-107	16/826/63	—/0	3.5 3H	
CFS425A	425	2	3687		16/826/63	—/—	3.5 3H	
CFS540A	540	4	3517		16/1050/63	—/—	3.5 3H	
CFS541A	540	2	3924			—/—	3.5 3H	
CFS635A	635	3	3640			—/—	3.5 3H	
CFS636A	635	2	4893			—/—	3.5 3H	3.5
CFS850A	850	4	3640		16/1652/63	—/—	3.5 3H	
CP1044 (Derringer)	42.6	2				NA/NA	2.5 4H	0.75
CP2020 (Kato)	21	2	653	32		NA/NA	2.5 4H	1.5
CP2022	20	2	653	32	4/615/17	NA/NA	3.5HH	
CP2024 (Kato)	21	2	653	32	4/615/17	NA/NA	2.5 4H	3
CP2031	30	2			4/411/38	NA/NA	2.5 4H	2.3
CP2034 (Pancho)	32	2	823	38	4/615/17	NA/NA	2.5 4H	1.3
CP2040	43	4	548	38		NA/NA	2.5 4H	
CP2044 (Pancho)	42	4	552	38	5/977/17	NA/NA	2.5 4H	
CP2048 (Pancho)					4/548/38	NA/NA	2.5 4H	2.3

Drive Model	Format Size MB	Seek Time	Interface	Encode	cache kb	RPM
CFA340A	343	13	IDE AT	1,7 RLL	64k	4011
CFA340S	343	13	SCSI-2	1,7 RLL	64k	4011
CFA425A	426	12	IDE AT	1,7 RLL	64k	4500
CFA425S	426	12	SCSI-2	1,7 RLL	64k	4500
CFA540A	541	12	IDE AT	1,7 RLL	256k	4500
CFA540S	541	12	SCSI-2Fast	1,7 RLL	256k	4500
CFA810A	810	12	IDE AT	1,7 RLL	256k	4500
CFA810S	810	12	SCSI-2Fast	1,7 RLL	256k	4500
CFA850A	852	12	IDE AT	1,7 RLL	256k	4500
CFA850S	852	12	SCSI-2	1,7 RLL	256k	4500
CFL350A	350	12	IDE AT	1,7 RLL	32k	3750
CFL420A	422	12	IDE AT	1,7 RLL	64k	3600
CFN170A	168	12	IDE AT	1,7 RLL	32k	4500
CFN170S	168	12	SCSI	1,7 RLL	32k	4500
CFN250A	252	12	IDE AT	1,7 RLL	32k	4500
CFN250S	252	12	SCSI	1,7 RLL	32k	4500
CFN340A	344	13	IDE AT	1,7 RLL	32k	4000
CFN340S	344	13	SCSI	1,7 RLL	32k	4000
CFP1060D	1062	9	SCSI-2Fast	1,7 RLL	512k	5400
CFP1060E	1062	9	SCSI	1,7 RLL	512k	5400
CFP1060S	1062	9	SCSI-2Fast	1,7 RLL	512k	5400
CFP1060W	1062	9	SCSI-2FstW	1,7 RLL	512k	5400
CFP1080E (Filepro)	1080	11	SCSI-2FstW	1,7 RLL	512k	5400
CFP1080S (Filepro)	1080	11	SCSI-2Fast	1,7 RLL	256k	5400
CFP2105E	2147	9	SCSI-2FstW	1,7 RLL	512k	5400
CFP2105S	2147	9	SCSI-2Fast	1,7 RLL	512k	5400
CFP2105W	2147	9	SCSI-2FstW	1,7 RLL	512k	5400
CFP2107E (Filepro)	2147	9	SCSI-2FstW	1,7 RLL	512k	7200
CFP2107S (Filepro)	2147	9	SCSI-2Fast	1,7 RLL	512k	7200
CFP2107W (Filepro)	2147	9	SCSI-2FstW	1,7 RLL	512k	7200
CFP4207E (Filepro)	4294	9.5	SCSI-2FstW	1,7 RLL	512k	7200
CFP4207S (Filepro)	4294	9.5	SCSI-2Fast	1,7 RLL	512k	7200
CFP4207W (Filepro)	4294	9.5	SCSI-2FstW	1,7 RLL	512k	7200
CFP4217C (Filepro)	4294	9	SSA		512k	7200
CFP4217E (Filepro)	4294	9	SCA		512k	7200
CFP4217S (Filepro)	4294	9	SCSI-3		512k	7200
CFP4217W (Filepro)	4294	9	SCSI-3Wide		512k	7200
CFP4217WD (Filepro)	4294	9	SCSI-3Wide		512k	7200
CFP9117C (Filepro)	9100	9	SSA	RLL 8,9	512k	7200
CFP9117E (Filepro)	9100	9	SCA	RLL 8,9	512k	7200
CFP9117S (Filepro)	9100	9	SCSI-3	RLL 8,9	512k	7200
CFP9117W (Filepro)	9100	9	SCSI-3Wide	RLL 8,9	512k	7200
CFP9117WD (Filepro)	9100	9	SCSI-3Wide	RLL 8,9	512k	7200
CFS1060A	1060		IDE AT			
CFS1081A	1080	14	IDE AT	1,7 RLL	64k	3600
CFS1275A	1275	14	IDE	1,7 RLL	64k	3600
CFS1276A	1275	14	ATA-2	1,7 RLL	64k	4500
CFS1621A	1620	14	IDE AT	1,7 RLL	64k	3600
CFS2105S	2147	9	SCSI-2Fast	1,7 RLL	512k	5400
CFS210A	213	14	IDE AT	1,7 RLL	32k	3600
CFS270A	270	14	IDE	1,7 RLL	32k	3400
CFS420A	420	14	IDE AT	1,7 RLL	32k	3600
CFS425A	425	14	IDE	1,7 RLL	64k	3600
CFS540A	540	14	IDE	1,7 RLL	64k	3600
CFS541A	540	14	IDE AT	1,7 RLL	64k	3600
CFS635A	635	14	IDE AT	1,7 RLL	64k	3600
CFS636A	635	13	ATA-2	1,7 RLL	64k	4500
CFS850A	850	14	IDE	1,7 RLL	64k	3600
CP1044 (Derringer)	42.6	19			32k	
CP2020 (Kato)	21	23	SCSI	2,7 RLL	8k	
CP2022	20	23	IDE AT	2,7 RLL		
CP2024 (Kato)	21	23	IDE AT	2,7 RLL	8k	3433
CP2031	30	19	ATA	2,7 RLL	32k	
CP2034 (Pancho)	32	19	IDE AT	2,7 RLL	32k	3433
CP2040	43	17	SCSI	2,7 RLL	32k	3486
CP2044 (Pancho)	42	19	IDE AT	2,7 RLL	32k	3486
CP2048 (Pancho)		19	ATA	2,7 RLL	32k	3486

Drive Model	Format Size MB	Head	Cyl	Sect/Trac	Translate H/C/S	RWC/WPC	Form Factor	Power Watts
CP2060	64	4	823	38		NA/NA	2.5 4H	
CP2064 (Pancho)	64	4	823	38		NA/NA	2.5 4H	
CP2084 (Pancho)	85	4	1096	38	8/548/38	NA/NA	2.5 4H	
CP2088	85	4		38	8/548/38	—/—	2.5 4H	1
CP2124 (Pancho)	120	4	1123	53	*UNIV T	NA/NA	2.5 4H	1.5
CP2250	253					NA/NA	2.5 4H	
CP2254 (Trigger)	253					NA/NA	2.5 4H	1.2
CP2304	209	8	1348	39	*UNIV T		3.5HH	
CP3000	42	2	1045	40	5/980/17	NA/NA	3.5 3H	
CP30060	60	2	1524	39		NA/NA	3.5 3H	
CP30064 (Hopi)	60	2	1524	39	4/762/39	NA/NA	3.5 3H	
CP30064H (Hopi)	60	2	1524	39	4/762/39	NA/NA	3.5 3H	
CP30069 (Hopi)	60	2	1524	39		NA/NA	3.5 3H	
CP30080	84	4	1053	39		NA/NA	3.5 3H	
CP30080E (Jaguar)	85	2	1806	46		NA/NA	3.5 3H	2.5
CP30081	85	4	1058	39	8/526/39	NA/NA	3.5 4H	
CP30084 (Hopi)	84	4	1053	39	8/526/39	NA/NA	3.5 3H	
CP30084E (Jaguar)	85	2	1806	46	4/903/46	NA/NA	3.5 3H	2.5
CP30100 (Hopi)	120	4	1522	39	8/762/39	NA/NA	3.5 3H	2.5
CP30101	122	4	1524	9		—/—	3.5 3H	
CP30101 (Hopi)	121	8	761	39	*UNIV T	NA/NA	3.5 3H	
CP30101G	122	4	1524	9	8/762/39		3.5 3H	
CP30104 (Hopi)	121	4	1524	39	8/762/39	NA/NA	3.5 3H	3.8
CP30104H (Hopi)	121	4	1524	39	8/762/39	NA/NA	3.5 3H	
CP30109 (Hopi)	120	4	1522	39		NA/NA	3.5 3H	3.8
CP30124	126	2		62	5/895/55	—/—	3.5 3H	
CP30170	172	2	2111	67-91		—/—	3.5 3H	3
CP30170E (Jaguar)	170	2	1806	46		NA/NA	3.5 3H	2.5
CP30174	172	2	2111	67-91		—/—	3.5 3H	3
CP30174E (Jaguar)	170	2	1806	46	8/903/46	NA/NA	3.5 3H	2.5
CP3020	21	2	636	33		NA/NA	3.5 3H	4.2
CP30200 (Cougar)	212	4	2124	49		NA/NA	3.5 3H	3.2
CP30201	212					—/—	3.5 3H	
CP30204 (Cougar)	212	4		49	16/683/38	NA/NA	3.5 3H	
CP3022	21	2	636	33	4/615/17	NA/NA	3.5 3H	
CP3023	21					—/—	3.5 3H	
CP3024	22	2	636	33	4/615/17	NA/NA	3.5 3H	4.2
CP30254	252	4	1985	62	10/895/55	NA/NA	3.5 3H	
CP30340	343	4		67-91		NA/NA	3.5 3H	
CP30344	343	4			16/665/63	NA/NA	3.5 3H	2.5
CP3040	40	2	1026	40		NA/NA	3.5 3H	4.2
CP3041	42	2	1047	40	5/977/17	NA/NA	3.5 3H	
CP3044	42	2	1047	40	5/977/17	NA/NA	3.5 3H	4.2
CP3045	40					—/—	3.5 3H	
CP30540	545	6	2243			—/—	3.5 3H	
CP30544	545	6	2243		16/989/63	—/—	3.5 3H	
CP3100	104	8	776	33		NA/NA	3.5HH	5.7
CP3101	104					—/—	3.5HH	
CP3102	104	8	776	33	*UNIV T	NA/NA	3.5HH	
CP3104	104	8	776	33	13/925/17	NA/NA	3.5HH	5.7
CP3106	104					—/—	3.5HH	
CP3111	107	8	832	33	*UNIV T	NA/NA	3.5HH	
CP3114	107	8	832	33	8/832/33	NA/NA	3.5HH	
CP31370	1372	14	2386			—/—	3.5HH	
CP31374 Baja	1372	14				NA/NA		6.2
CP3150	52	4	776	33		NA/NA	3.5HH	
CP3180	84	6	832	33		NA/NA	3.5HH	
CP3181	84	6	832	33		NA/NA	3.5HH	
CP3184	84	6	832	33	9/1024/17	NA/NA	3.5HH	
CP320	20	2	752	26		NA/NA	3.5 3H	
CP3200	209	8	1366	38		NA/NA	3.5HH	6.3
CP3200F	212	8	1366	38		NA/NA	3.5HH	4.2
CP3201I	215	8	1348	39	*UNIV T	NA/NA	3.5HH	
CP3204	209	8	1366	38	16/683/38	NA/NA	3.5HH	6.3
CP3204F	212	8	1366	38	16/683/38	NA/NA	3.5HH	6.3
CP3209F	212	8	1366	38	*UNIV T	NA/NA	3.5HH	
CP321	20	2	752	26	4/615/17	NA/NA	3.5 3H	

Drive Model	Format Size MB	Seek Time	Interface	Encode	cache kb	RPM
CP2060	64	19	SCSI	2,7 RLL	32k	3486
CP2064 (Pancho)	64	19	IDE AT	2,7 RLL	32k	3486
CP2084 (Pancho)	85	19	IDE AT	1,7 RLL	32k	3486
CP2088	85	19	IDE AT	1,7 RLL	32k	3486
CP2124 (Pancho)	120	26	IDE AT	1,7 RLL	32k	
CP2250	253	12	SCSI		32k	
CP2254 (Trigger)	253	12	ATA		32k	
CP2304	209	19	IDE AT	RLL		
CP3000	42	28	IDE AT	2,7 RLL	8k	3557
CP30060	60	19	SCSI	1,7 RLL		
CP30064 (Hopi)	60	19	IDE AT	1,7 RLL	64k	3400
CP30064H (Hopi)	60	19	IDE AT	1,7 RLL	32k	3400
CP30069 (Hopi)	60	19	MCA	1,7 RLL	64k	3399
CP30080 (Hopi)	84	19	SCSI	1,7 RLL	64k	3400
CP30080E (Jaguar)	85	17	SCSI	1,7 RLL	32k	3822
CP30081	85	19	IDE AT	2,7 RLL		
CP30084 (Hopi)	84	19	IDE AT	1,7 RLL	64k	3400
CP30084E (Jaguar)	85	17	IDE AT	1,7 RLL	32k	3822
CP30100 (Hopi)	120	19	SCSI	2,7 RLL	64k	3400
CP30101	122	19	IDE AT	2,7 RLL		
CP30101 (Hopi)	121	10	IDE AT	2,7 RLL		
CP30101G	122	19	IDE AT	2,7 RLL		
CP30104 (Hopi)	121	19	IDE AT	1,7 RLL	32k	3400
CP30104H (Hopi)	121	19	IDE AT	1,7 RLL	32k	3400
CP30109 (Hopi)	120	19	MCA	2,7 RLL	64k	3400
CP30124	126	14	IDE AT	1,7 RLL	32k	4542
CP30170	172	13	SCSI-2	1,7 RLL	64k	4011
CP30170E (Jaguar)	170	17	SCSI	1,7 RLL	32k	3833
CP30174	172	13	IDE AT	1,7 RLL	64k	4011
CP30174E (Jaguar)	170	17	IDE AT	1,7 RLL	32k	3833
CP3020	21	27	SCSI	2,7 RLL	8k	3575
CP30200 (Cougar)	212	12	SCSI-2	2,7 RLL	256k	4500
CP30201	212		IDE AT	2,7 RLL		
CP30204 (Cougar)	212	12	IDE AT	2,7 RLL	256k	4500
CP3022	21	27	IDE AT	2,7 RLL		
CP3023	21		IDE AT	2,7 RLL		
CP3024	22	27	IDE AT	2,7 RLL	8k	3575
CP30254	252	14	IDE AT	1,7 RLL	64k	4542
CP30340	343	13	SCSI-2	1,7 RLL	64k	4011
CP30344	343	13	ATA		64k	4500
CP3040	40	25	SCSI	2,7 RLL	8k	3557
CP3041	42	25	IDE AT	2,7 RLL		
CP3044	42	25	IDE AT	2,7 RLL	8k	3557
CP3045	40		IDE AT	2,7 RLL		
CP30540	545	10	SCSI-2Fast	1,7 RLL	256k	5400
CP30544	545	10	IDE AT	1,7 RLL	256k	5400
CP3100	104	25	SCSI	2,7 RLL	32k	3575
CP3101	104		IDE AT	2,7 RLL		
CP3102	104	25	IDE AT	2,7 RLL	16k	
CP3104	104	25	IDE AT	2,7 RLL	16k	3575
CP3106	104		IDE AT	2,7 RLL		
CP3111	107	25	IDE AT	2,7 RLL	16k	
CP3114	107	25	IDE AT	2,7 RLL		
CP31370	1372	10	SCSI-2Fast	1,7 RLL	256k	5400
CP31374 Baja	1372	11	ATA		256k	
CP3150	52	25	SCSI	2,7 RLL		
CP3180	84	25	SCSI	2,7 RLL	32k	3575
CP3181	84	25	IDE AT	2,7 RLL		
CP3184	84	25	IDE AT	2,7 RLL	32k	3575
CP320	20		SCSI	2,7 RLL		
CP3200	209	16	SCSI	2,7 RLL	64k	3485
CP3200F	212	16	SCSI	2,7 RLL	64k	3485
CP3201I	215	19	IDE AT	2,7 RLL		
CP3204	209	16	IDE AT	2,7 RLL		
CP3204F	212	16	IDE AT	2,7 RLL	64k	3485
CP3209F	212	16	IDE AT	2,7 RLL	64k	3485
CP321	20		IDE AT	2,7 RLL		

Drive Model	Format Size MB	Head	Cyl	Sect/ Trac	Translate H/C/S	RWC/ WPC	Form Factor	Power Watts
CP323	20	2	752	26	4/615/17	NA/NA	3.5 3H	
CP324	20	2	752	26	4/615/17	NA/NA	3.5 3H	
CP3304 (Summit)	340	8	1806	46	16/659/63	NA/NA	3.5HH	
CP3360 (Summit)	362	8	1807	49		NA/NA	3.5HH	6.7
CP3364 (Summit)	362	8	1808	49	16/702/63	NA/NA	3.5HH	6.7
CP340	42	4	788	26		NA/NA	3.5HH	4.25
CP341	42	4	805	26	5/977/17	NA/NA	3.5HH	
CP341I	42	4	805	26	5/977/17	NA/NA	3.5HH	
CP342	40	4	805	26	4/805/26	NA/NA	3.5HH	
CP343 (Zenith)	43	4	805		5/977/17	NA/NA	3.5HH	
CP344	43	4	805	26	5/977/17	NA/NA	3.5HH	4.25
CP346	42					—/—	3.5HH	
CP3500 (Summit)	510	12	1806	49		NA/NA	3.5HH	
CP3501	510	12	1806	46		Auto/Auto	3.5HH	
CP3504 (Summit)	510	12		48	16/987/63	NA/NA	3.5HH	
CP3505	510	12	1806	46		NA/NA	3.5HH	
CP3540 (Summit)	543	12	1807	49		NA/NA	3.5HH	6.7
CP3544 (Summit)	544	12	1808	49	16/1023/63	NA/NA	3.5HH	6.7
CP4021	20					—/—	3.5 4H	
CP4024 (Stubby)	21	2	627	34	4/615/17	NA/NA	3.5 4H	3.8
CP4041	42					—/—	3.5 4H	
CP4044 (Stubby)	43	2	1097	38	5/977/17	NA/NA	3.5 4H	1.5
CP4084 (Gator)	85	2	1806	46		NA/NA	3.5 4H	
CP5500	510	20	2034	50		NA/NA		11.1
CORE INTERNATIONAL								
3SHC230	230	5	1511	V		NA/NA	3.5HH	
AT115	115	7	968	35		—/—	5.25FH	60
AT145	58	7	968			—/—	5.25FH	
AT150	156	9	968	35		—/—	5.25FH	60
AT20	20	4	615	17		—/—	5.25FH	
AT26	26	3	988	17		—/—	5.25HH	
AT260	260	12	1212	35		—/—	5.25FH	68
AT30	32	5	733	17		—/—	5.25FH	
AT30R	49	5	733	26		—/—	5.25FH	
AT32	32	5	733	17		—/—	5.25HH	
AT32R	49	5	733	26		—/—	5.25HH	
AT40	40	5	924	17		—/—	5.25FH	
AT40F	40	4	564	35		—/—	5.25FH	60
AT40R	62	5	924	26		—/—	5.25FH	
ATPlus20	21	4	615	17		—/—	5.25HH	
ATPlus43	43	5	988	17		—/—	5.25HH	
ATPlus43R	66	5	988	26		—/—	5.25HH	
ATPlus44	44	7	733	17		—/—	3.5HH	
ATPlus44R	68	7	733	26		—/—	3.5HH	
ATPlus56	56	7	924	17		—/—	5.25FH	
ATPlus63	42	5	988	17		—/—	5.25FH	
ATPlus63R	65	65	988	26		—/—	5.25FH	
ATPlus72	73	9	924	17		—/—	5.25FH	
ATPlus72R	107	9	924	26		—/—	5.25FH	
ATPlus80	80	9	1024			—/—	3.5HH	
ATPlus80R	132	9	1024			—/—	3.5HH	
ATPlus82	82	5	968	35		—/—	5.25FH	60
HC100	101	15	379	35		—/—	5.25FH	
HC1000	1056	15	1787	77		NA/NA	5.25FH	
HC1000-20	1056	15	1787	77		—/—	5.25FH	71
HC1000S	1005	16	1918	64		—/—	5.25FH	62
HC150	150	7	1250	35		—/—	5.25HH	33
HC150FH	151	9	969	34		NA/NA	5.25FH	
HC150S	155	9	969	35		—/—	5.25FH	64
HC175	177	9	1072	35		—/—	5.25FH	
HC200	200	8			12/986/33	—/—	5.25FH	
HC230	230	5				NA/NA	3.5FH	
HC25	250					—/—	5.25FH	
HC260	260	12	1212	35		NA/NA	5.25FH	
HC310	325	7	1747	52		NA/NA	5.25HH	57
HC310S	330	8	1447	56		—/—	5.25FH	62
HC315-20	340	8	1447	57		—/—	5.25FH	63

Drive Model	Format Size MB	Seek Time	Interface	Encode	cache kb	RPM
CP323	20		ZENITH	2,7 RLL		
CP324	20		IDE AT	2,7 RLL		
CP3304 (Summit)	340		IDE AT	1,7 RLL		
CP3360 (Summit)	362	12	SCSI-2	2,7 RLL	256k	4500
CP3364 (Summit)	362	12	IDE AT	2,7 RLL	256k	4498
CP340	42	29	SCSI	2,7 RLL	1k	3600
CP341	42	29	IDE AT	2,7 RLL		
CP341I	42	29	IDE AT	2,7 RLL		
CP342	40	29	IDE AT	2,7 RLL		
CP343 (Zenith)	43	29	ZENITH			
CP344	43	29	IDE AT	2,7 RLL	8k	3600
CP346	42		IDE AT	2,7 RLL		
CP3500 (Summit)	510	12	SCSI	2,7 RLL	256k	3609
CP3501	510	12	IDE AT	2,7 RLL		
CP3504 (Summit)	510	12	IDE AT	2,7 RLL	256k	3828
CP3505	510	12	IDE AT	2,7 RLL		
CP3540 (Summit)	543	12	SCSI-2	2,7 RLL	256k	4500
CP3544 (Summit)	544	12	IDE AT	2,7 RLL	256k	4498
CP4021	20		IDE AT	2,7 RLL		
CP4024 (Stubby)	21	<29	IDE AT	2,7 RLL	8k	2913
CP4041	42		IDE AT	2,7 RLL		
CP4044 (Stubby)	43	<29	IDE AT	2,7 RLL	8k	
CP4084 (Gator)	85	19	IDE AT	2,7 RLL	32k	
CP5500	510	12	SCSI-2	RLL	512k	4498

CORE INTERNATIONAL

Drive Model	Format Size MB	Seek Time	Interface	Encode	cache kb	RPM
3SHC230	230	13	SCSI			
AT115	115	16	ESDI			3597
AT145	58	17	ST412/506	MFM		
AT150	156	16	ESDI	2,7 RLL		3597
AT20	20	20	ST412/506	MFM		
AT26	26	26	ST412/506	MFM		
AT260	260	25	ESDI			3524
AT30	32	21	ST412/506	MFM		
AT30R	49	21	ST412/506	2,7 RLL		
AT32	32	21	ST412/506	MFM		
AT32R	49	21	ST412/506	2,7 RLL		
AT40	40	26	ST412/506	MFM		
AT40F	40	10	ESDI			3597
AT40R	62	26	ST412/506	2,7 RLL		
ATPlus20	21	26	ST412/506	MFM		
ATPlus43	43	26	ST412/506	MFM		
ATPlus43R	66	26	ST412/506	2,7 RLL		
ATPlus44	44	26	ST412/506	MFM		
ATPlus44R	68	26	ST412/506	2,7 RLL		
ATPlus56	56	26	ST412/506	MFM		
ATPlus63	42	26	ST412/506	MFM		
ATPlus63R	65	26	ST412/506	2,7 RLL		
ATPlus72	73	26	ST412/506	MFM		
ATPlus72R	107	26	ST412/506	2,7 RLL		
ATPlus80	80	15	ST412/506	MFM		
ATPlus80R	132	15	ST412/506	2,7 RLL		
ATPlus82	82	16	ESDI			3597
HC100	101	9	ESDI			
HC1000	1056	14	ESDI (24)	2,7 RLL		
HC1000-20	1056	14	ESDI	2,7 RLL		3600
HC1000S	1005	15	SCSI	2,7 RLL		4002
HC150	150	17	ESDI	2,7 RLL		3600
HC150FH	151	16	ESDI (10)	2,7 RLL		
HC150S	155	16.5	SCSI	2,7 RLL		3597
HC175	177	14	ESDI	2,7 RLL		
HC200	200	16	IDE AT			
HC230	230	13	SCSI			
HC25	250		ESDI			
HC260	260	25	ESDI	2,7 RLL		
HC310	325	18	ESDI	2,7 RLL		3600
HC310S	330	16.5	SCSI	2,7 RLL		4002
HC315-20	340	17	ESDI	2,7 RLL		4002

Hard Drives

Drive Model	Format Size MB	Head	Cyl	Sect/Trac	Translate H/C/S	RWC/WPC	Form Factor	Power Watts
HC380	376	15	1412	35		—/—	5.25FH	
HC40	40	4	564	35		NA/NA	5.25FH	
HC650	658	15	1661	53		—/—	5.25FH	51
HC650S	663	16	1447	56		—/—	5.25FH	62
HC655-20	680	16	1447	57		—/—	5.25FH	63
HC90	91	5	969	35		NA/NA	5.25HH	
MC120	120	8	920	32		NA/NA	3.5HH	19
MC60	60	4	928	32		NA/NA	3.5HH	19
Optima 30	31	5	733	17		—/—	5.25HH	
Optima 30R	48	5	733	26		—/—	5.25HH	
Optima 40	41	5	963	17		—/—	5.25HH	
Optima 40R	64	5	963	26		—/—	5.25HH	
Optima 70	71	9	918	17		—/—	5.25HH	
Optima 70R	109	9	918	17		—/—	5.25HH	
Optima 80	80	9	1024	17		—/—	3.5HH	
Optima 80R	132	9	1024	26		—/—	3.5HH	

DIGITAL EQUIPMENT CORP.

Drive Model	Format Size MB	Head	Cyl	Sect/Trac	Translate H/C/S	RWC/WPC	Form Factor	Power Watts
Capella 3055	550					NA/NA	3H	
Capella 3110	1100					NA/NA	3H	
Capella 3221	2200					NA/NA	3H	
DSP3053L	535	4	3117			NA/NA	3.5 3H	
DSP3080	852					NA/NA	3H	
DSP3085	852	14		57		—/—	3.5HH	
DSP3105	1050	14		57		—/—	3.5HH	
DSP3107L	1070	8	3117			NA/NA	3.5 3H	
DSP3133L	1337	10	3117			NA/NA	3.5 3H	
DSP3160	1600	16				—/—	3.5HH	
DSP3210	2148	16				NA/NA	3.5HH	
DSP5300	3000	21				NA/NA	5.25FH	
DSP5350	3572	25				—/—	5.25FH	
DSP5400	4000	26				NA/NA	5.25FH	
DSRZ1BB-VW	2100					—/—	3.5FH	
DSRZ1CB-VW	4300					—/—	3.5FH	
DSRZ1CD-VW	4300					—/—	3.5 3H	
DSRZ1DB-VW	9100					—/—	3.5FH	
DSRZ1DF-VA	9100					—/—	3.5 3H	
DSRZ1DF-VW	9100					—/—	3.5 3H	
DSRZ1EF-VA	18200					—/—	3.5 3H	
DSRZ1EF-VW	18200					—/—	3.5 3H	
DSRZ26N-VZ	1050					—/—	3.5FH	
DSRZ28L-VA	2100					—/—	3.5FH	
DSRZ28M-VZ	2100					—/—	3.5FH	
DSRZ29L-VA	4300					—/—	3.5FH	
DSRZ40-VA	9100					—/—	3.5FH	
RZ26N-VA	1050					—/—	3.5FH	
RZ26N-VW	1050					—/—	3.5FH	
RZ28D-VA	2100					—/—	3.5FH	
RZ28D-VW	2100					—/—	3.5FH	
RZ28M-VA	2100					—/—	3.5FH	
RZ28M-VW	2100					—/—	3.5FH	
RZ29B-VA	4300					—/—	3.5FH	
RZ29B-VW	4300					—/—	3.5FH	
SP3430	4300	20				NA/NA	3.5HH	
VP3107	1075	5				NA/NA	3.5 3H	
VP3215	2150	10				NA/NA	3.5 3H	

DISC TEC

Drive Model	Format Size MB	Head	Cyl	Sect/Trac	Translate H/C/S	RWC/WPC	Form Factor	Power Watts
RHD-10000	10000	2			15/24832/63	—/—		0.85
RHD-120	130						3.5 3H	
RHD-1200	1440	4			16/2800/16	—/—		0.9
RHD-12000	12000	4			15/24832/63	—/—		0.85
RHD-14000	14130	10			16/16383/63	—/—		1.3
RHD-180	183					NA/NA	3.5 3H	
RHD-18000	18100	6			15/37248/63	—/—		0.95
RHD-20 (removable)	21	2	615	34		NA/NA	3.5 3H	
RHD-2000	2160	4			16/4200/16	—/—		0.9
RHD-20000	20000	4			15/49664/63	—/—		0.85

Drive Model	Format Size MB	Seek Time	Interface	Encode	cache kb	RPM
HC380	376	16	ESDI	2,7 RLL		
HC40	40	9	ESDI	2,7 RLL		
HC650	658	17	ESDI	2,7 RLL		3600
HC650S	663	16.5	SCSI			4002
HC655-20	680	17	ESDI	2,7 RLL		4002
HC90	91	16	ESDI	2,7 RLL		
MC120	120	23	MCA			3600
MC60	60	23	MCA			3600
Optima 30	31	21	ST412/506	MFM		
Optima 30R	48	21	ST412/506	2,7 RLL		
Optima 40	41	26	ST412/506	MFM		
Optima 40R	64	26	ST412/506	2,7 RLL		
Optima 70	71	26	ST412/506	MFM		
Optima 70R	109	26	ST412/506	2,7 RLL		
Optima 80	80	15	ST412/506	MFM		
Optima 80R	132	15	ST412/506	2,7 RLL		
DIGITAL EQUIPMENT CORP.						
Capella 3055	550	9	SCSI-2Fast			5400
Capella 3110	1100	9	SCSI-2Fast			5400
Capella 3221	2200	9	SCSI-2Fast			5400
DSP3053L	535	9.5	SCSI-2Fast	1,7 RLL	512k	5400
DSP3080	852	10	SCSI-2		512k	5400
DSP3085	852	9	SCSI-2Fast	1,7 RLL	512k	5400
DSP3105	1050	9	SCSI-2Fast	1,7 RLL	512k	5400
DSP3107L	1070	9.5	SCSI-2Diff	1,7 RLL	512	5400
DSP3133L	1337	9.5	SCSI-2Fast	1,7 RLL	512k	5400
DSP3160	1600	9.7	SCSI-2Fast	1,7 RLL	512k	5400
DSP3210	2148	9.5	SCSI-2Fast	1,7 RLL	1024k	5400
DSP5300	3000	12	SCSI-2Fast	1,7 RLL	512k	5400
DSP5350	3572	12	SCSI-2Fast	1,7 RLL	512k	5400
DSP5400	4000	12	SCSI-2Fast	1,7 RLL	1024k	5400
DSRZ1BB-VW	2100	9	SCSI-2FstW		512k	7200
DSRZ1CB-VW	4300	9	Ultra SCSI		512k	7200
DSRZ1CD-VW	4300	8.5	Ultra SCSI		512k	1000
DSRZ1DB-VW	9100	9	Ultra SCSI		512k	7200
DSRZ1DF-VA	9100	9	SCSI-2		1000k	7200
DSRZ1DF-VW	9100	8	SCSI-2		1000k	7200
DSRZ1EF-VA	18200	8	SCSI-2		1000k	7200
DSRZ1EF-VW	18200	8	SCSI-2		1000k	7200
DSRZ26N-VZ	1050	10	Ultra SCSI		480k	5400
DSRZ28L-VA	2100	9	Ultra SCSI		512k	7200
DSRZ28M-VZ	2100	10	Ultra SCSI		480k	5400
DSRZ29L-VA	4300	9	Ultra SCSI		512k	7200
DSRZ40-VA	9100	9	SCSI-2		512k	7200
RZ26N-VA	1050	14.5	SCSI-2Fast		480k	5400
RZ26N-VW	1050	14.5	SCSI-2FstW		480k	5400
RZ28D-VA	2100	12.2	SCSI-2Fast		480k	7200
RZ28D-VW	2100	12.2	SCSI-2FstW		480k	7200
RZ28M-VA	2100	14.5	SCSI-2Fast		480k	5400
RZ28M-VW	2100	14.5	SCSI-2FstW		480k	5400
RZ29B-VA	4300	12.2	SCSI-2Fast		1000k	7200
RZ29B-VW	4300	12.2	SCSI-2FstW		1000k	7200
SP3430	4300	9	SCSI-2Fast	1,7 RLL	2048k	7200
VP3107	1075	9	SCSI-2Fast	1,7 RLL	1024k	7200
VP3215	2150	9	SCSI-2Fast	1,7 RLL	1024k	7200
DISC TEC						
RHD-10000	10000	12			512k	4200
RHD-120	130	17	IDE AT	RLL		4200
RHD-1200	1440	13	IDE AT		128k	4200
RHD-12000	12000	12			512k	4200
RHD-14000	14130	13			460k	4900
RHD-180	183	14	IDE AT	RLL		
RHD-18000	18100	12			512k	4200
RHD-20 (removable)	21	23	IDE AT	RLL		
RHD-2000	2160	13			128k	4200
RHD-20000	20000	12			2048k	4200

Hard Drive Specs 585

Drive Model	Format Size MB	Head	Cyl	Sect/Trac	Translate H/C/S	RWC/WPC	Form Factor	Power Watts
RHD-210	210					NA/NA	3.5 3H	
RHD-25000	25300	10			15/62080/63	—/—		1.3
RHD-260	260					—/—	3.5 3H	
RHD-3000	30GB	4			15/74496/63	—/—	3.5 3H	0.95
RHD-30000	30GB	4			15/74496/63	—/—	3.5 3H	0.95
RHD-340	340					—/—	3.5 3H	
RHD-5000	5120	8			15/10592/63	—/—		1.3
RHD-520	520					—/—	3.5 3H	
RHD-60	62	2	1024	60		NA/NA	3.5 3H	
RHD-6000	6000	2			15/12416/63	—/—		0.85
RHD-80	81					NA/NA	3.5 3H	
RHD-8000	8100	10			16/15873/63	—/—		1.3

DISCTRON (OTARI)

Drive Model	Format Size MB	Head	Cyl	Sect/Trac	Translate H/C/S	RWC/WPC	Form Factor	Power Watts
D214	11	4	306	17		128/128	5.25FH	
D503	3	2	153	17		—/—	5.25FH	
D504	4	2	215	17		—/—	5.25FH	
D506	5	4	153	17		—/—	5.25FH	
D507	5	2	306	17		128/128	5.25FH	
D509	8	4	215	17		128/128	5.25FH	
D512	11	8	153	17		—/—	5.25FH	
D513	11	6	215	17		128/128	5.25FH	
D514	11	4	306	17		128/128	5.25FH	
D518	15	8	215	17		128/128	5.25FH	
D519	16	6	306	17		128/128	5.25FH	
D526	21	8	306	17		128/128	5.25FH	

DMA

Drive Model	Format Size MB	Head	Cyl	Sect/Trac	Translate H/C/S	RWC/WPC	Form Factor	Power Watts
306	11	2	612	17		612/400	5.25HH	

ELOCH

Drive Model	Format Size MB	Head	Cyl	Sect/Trac	Translate H/C/S	RWC/WPC	Form Factor	Power Watts
DISCACHE10	10	4	320	17		321/321	5.25FH	
DISCACHE20	20	8	320	17		321/321	5.25FH	

EPSON

Drive Model	Format Size MB	Head	Cyl	Sect/Trac	Translate H/C/S	RWC/WPC	Form Factor	Power Watts
HD560	21	4	615	17		615/300	5.25HH	
HD830	10	2	612	17		—/—	5.25HH	
HD850	10	4	306	17		—/—	5.25HH	
HD860	21	4	612	17		—/—	5.25HH	
HMD710	10	2	615	17		—/—	5.25HH	
HMD720	21	4	615	17		—/—	5.25HH	
HMD726A	21	4	615	32		—/—	3.5HH	
HMD755	21	2	615	34		—/—	5.25HH	
HMD765	42	4	615	34		—/—	5.25HH	
HMD976	69					—/—	3.5HH	

FUJI

Drive Model	Format Size MB	Head	Cyl	Sect/Trac	Translate H/C/S	RWC/WPC	Form Factor	Power Watts
FK301-13	10	4	306	17		307/128	3.5HH	
FK302-13	10	2	612	17		613/307	3.5HH	
FK302-26	21	4	612	17		613/307	3.5HH	
FK302-39	32	6	612	17		613/307	3.5HH	
FK303-52	40	8	615	17		—/616	3.5HH	
FK305-26	21	4	615	17		—/616	3.5HH	
FK305-26R	21		615	26		—/—	3.5HH	
FK305-39	32	6	615	17		—/616	3.5HH	3350
FK305-39R	32	4	615	26		—/616	3.5HH	
FK305-58	32	6	615	17		—/—	3.5HH	
FK305-58R	49	6	615	26		—/616	3.5HH	
FK308S-39R	45	6	615			—/—	3.5HH	
FK308S-58R	32	4	615	26		—/616	3.5HH	
FK309-26	21	4	615	17		—/616	3.5HH	
FK309-39R	32	4	615	26		—/616	3.5HH	
FK309S-50R	41	4	615			—/—	3.5HH	

FUJITSU AMERICA, INC.

Drive Model	Format Size MB	Head	Cyl	Sect/Trac	Translate H/C/S	RWC/WPC	Form Factor	Power Watts
Handy30-Data	30GB					—/—	4H	
Handy30-Video	30GB					—/—	4H	
Handy40-Data	40GB					—/—	4H	

Drive Model	Format Size MB	Seek Time	Interface	Encode	cache kb	RPM
RHD-210	210	19	IDE AT	RLL		
RHD-25000	25300	12			512k	5411
RHD-260	260	>14	IDE AT	RLL		
RHD-3000	30GB	12	IDE AT		2mb	4200
RHD-30000	30GB	12			2mb	4200
RHD-340	340	>14	IDE AT	RLL		
RHD-5000	5120	12			512k	4900
RHD-520	520	>14	IDE AT	RLL		
RHD-60	62	22	IDE AT	RLL		
RHD-6000	6000	12			512k	4200
RHD-80	81	16	IDE AT	RLL		
RHD-8000	8100	12			512k	4900

DISCTRON (OTARI)

D214	11		ST412/506	MFM		
D503	3		ST412/506	MFM		
D504	4		ST412/506	MFM		
D506	5		ST412/506	MFM		
D507	5		ST412/506	MFM		
D509	8		ST412/506	MFM		
D512	11		ST412/506	MFM		
D513	11		ST412/506	MFM		
D514	11		ST412/506	MFM		
D518	15		ST412/506	MFM		
D519	16		ST412/506	MFM		
D526	21		ST412/506	MFM		

DMA

306	11	170?	ST412/506	MFM		

ELOCH

DISCACHE10	10	65?	ST412/506	MFM		
DISCACHE20	20	65?	ST412/506	MFM		

EPSON

HD560	21	78	ST412/506	MFM		
HD830	10	93	ST412/506	MFM		
HD850	10		ST412/506	MFM		
HD860	21		ST412/506	MFM		
HMD710	10	78	ST412/506	MFM		
HMD720	21	78	ST412/506	MFM		
HMD726A	21	80	SCSI	2,7 RLL		
HMD755	21	80	ST412/506	2,7 RLL		
HMD765	42	80	ST412/506	2,7 RLL		
HMD976	69		SCSI			

FUJI

FK301-13	10	65	ST412/506	MFM		
FK302-13	10	65	ST412/506	MFM		
FK302-26	21	65	ST412/506	MFM		
FK302-39	32	65	ST412/506	MFM		
FK303-52	40	65?	ST412/506	MFM		
FK305-26	21	65	ST412/506	MFM		3350
FK305-26R	21	65	ST412/506	2,7 RLL		
FK305-39	32	65	ST412/506	MFM		
FK305-39R	32	65	ST412/506	2,7 RLL		3350
FK305-58	32	65	ST412/506	MFM		
FK305-58R	49	65	ST412/506	2,7 RLL		3350
FK308S-39R	45	65	SCSI	2,7 RLL		
FK308S-58R	32	65	ST412/506	2,7 RLL		
FK309-26	21	65	ST412/506	MFM		
FK309-39R	32	65	ST412/506	2,7 RLL		
FK309S-50R	41	45	SCSI	2,7 RLL		

FUJITSU AMERICA, INC.

Handy30-Data	30GB		USB2.0			4200
Handy30-Video	30GB		FireWire			4200
Handy40-Data	40GB		USB2.0			4200

Drive Model	Format Size MB	Head	Cyl	Sect/ Trac	Translate H/C/S	RWC/ WPC	Form Factor	Power Watts
Handy40-Video	40GB					—/—	4H	
Handy60-Data	60GB					—/—	4H	
Handy60-Video	60GB					—/—	4H	
M1603 SAU	540	3				—/—	3.5 3H	4.2
M1603 TAU	540	4				—/—	3.5 3H	
M1606 SAU	1080	6	3457	94		—/—	3.5 3H	4.2
M1606 TAU	1080	6				—/—	3.5 3H	
M1612 TAU	545	2	4133	85-153		—/—	3.5 3H	3.1
M1614 TAU	1090	4	4133	85-153		—/—	3.5 3H	3.1
M1623 TAU	1700	3				—/—	3.5 3H	4.5
M1624 TAU	2100	4				—/—	3.5 3H	4.5
M1636 TAU	1200	2				—/—	3.5 3H	4.5
M1638 TAU	2500	4				—/—	3.5 3H	4.5
M2225D	40	4	615	17		—/—	3.5HH	
M2225D2	20	4	615	17		—/—	3.5HH	
M2225DR	32	4	615	17		—/—	3.5HH	
M2226D	60	6	615	17		—/—	3.5HH	
M2226D2	30	6	615	17		—/—	3.5HH	
M2226DR	49	6	615	26		—/—	3.5HH	
M2227D	80	8	615	17		—/—	3.5HH	
M2227D2	42	8	615	17		—/—	3.5HH	
M2227DR	65	8	615	26		—/—	3.5HH	
M2230	5	2	320	17		320/180	5.25FH	
M2230AS	5	2	320	17		320/320	5.25FH	
M2230AT	5	2	320	17		320/320	5.25FH	
M2231	5	2	306	17		—/—	5.25FH	
M2233	10	4	320	17		320/128	5.25FH	
M2233AS	10	4	320	17		320/320	5.25FH	
M2233AT	10	4	320	17		320/320	5.25FH	
M2234	15	6	320	17		320/128	5.25FH	
M2234AS	15	6	306	17		320/320	5.25FH	
M2235	21	8	320	17		320/128	5.25FH	
M2235AS	20	8	320	17		320/320	5.25FH	
M2241AS	26	4	754	17		—/375	5.25FH	
M2241AS2	24	4	754	32		—/375	5.25FH	
M2242AS	45	7	754	17		754/375	5.25FH	
M2242AS2	43	7	754	17		—/—	5.25FH	
M2243AS	72	11	754	17		754/375	5.25FH	
M2243AS2	67	11	754	17		—/—	5.25FH	
M2243R	110	7	1186	26		—/—	5.25HH	
M2243T	68	7	1186	17		—/—	5.25HH	
M2244E	73	5	823	35		NA/NA	5.25FH	
M2244S	85U	5	823	65		NA/NA	5.25FH	
M2244SA	85U	5	823	35		NA/NA	5.25FH	
M2244SB	85U	5	823	19		NA/NA	5.25FH	
M2245E	120	7	823	35		NA/NA	5.25FH	
M2245S	120U	7	823	65		NA/NA	5.25FH	
M2245SA	120U	7	823	35		NA/NA	5.25FH	
M2245SB	120U	7	823	19		NA/NA	5.25FH	
M2246E	138	10	823	35		NA/NA	5.25FH	
M2246S	171U	10	823	65		NA/NA	5.25FH	
M2246SA	171U	10	823	35		NA/NA	5.25FH	
M2246SB	171U	10	823	19		NA/NA	5.25FH	
M2247E	285	7	1243	35		NA/NA	5.25FH	
M2247S	289	7	1243	65		NA/NA	5.25FH	
M2247SA	160	7	1243	36		NA/NA	5.25FH	
M2247SB	169	7	1243			NA/NA	5.25FH	
M2248E	266	11	1243	35		NA/NA	5.25FH	
M2248S	227	11	1243			NA/NA	5.25FH	
M2248SA	252	11	1243	36		NA/NA	5.25FH	
M2248SB	266	11	1243			NA/NA	5.25FH	
M2249E	334	15	1243	35		NA/NA	5.25FH	
M2249S	334	15	1243	35		NA/NA	5.25FH	
M2249SA	334	15	1243	35		NA/NA	5.25FH	
M2249SB	362	15	1243			NA/NA	5.25FH	
M2261E	321	8	1658			NA/NA	5.25FH	
M2261HA	357	8	1658	53		NA/NA	5.25FH	

Drive Model	Format Size MB	Seek Time	Interface	Encode	cache kb	RPM
Handy40-Video	40GB		FireWire			4200
Handy60-Data	60GB		USB2.0			4200
Handy60-Video	60GB		FireWire			4200
M1603 SAU	540	10	SCSI-2Fast	1,7 RLL	512k	5400
M1603 TAU	540	10	ATA-2	1,7 RLL	256k	5400
M1606 SAU	1080	10	SCSI-2Fast	1,7 RLL	512k	5400
M1606 TAU	1080	10	ATA-2	1,7 RLL	256k	5400
M1612 TAU	545	11	ATA-2	1,7 RLL	64k	4500
M1614 TAU	1090	11	ATA-2	PRML8,9	64k	4500
M1623 TAU	1700	10	ATA-2	PRML8,9		
M1624 TAU	2100	10	ATA-2	PRML	128k	5400
M1636 TAU	1200	10	ATA-2	PRML	128k	5400
M1638 TAU	2500	10	ATA-2	PRML	128k	5400
M2225D	40	40	ST412/506	MFM		
M2225D2	20	35	ST412/506	MFM		
M2225DR	32	35	ST412/506	2,7 RLL		
M2226D	60	40	ST412/506	MFM		
M2226D2	30	35	ST412/506	MFM		
M2226DR	49	35	ST412/506	2,7 RLL		
M2227D	80	40	ST412/506	MFM		
M2227D2	42	35	ST412/506	MFM		
M2227DR	65	35	ST412/506	2,7 RLL		
M2230	5	85	ST412/506	MFM		
M2230AS	5	27	ST412/506	MFM		3600
M2230AT	5	8	ST412/506	MFM		3600
M2231	5	85	ST412/506	MFM		
M2233	10	80	ST412/506	MFM		
M2233AS	10	27	ST412/506	MFM		3600
M2233AT	10	8	ST412/506	MFM		3600
M2234	15	8	ST412/506	MFM		3600
M2234AS	15	27	ST412/506	MFM		3600
M2235	21	85	ST412/506	MFM		3600
M2235AS	20	27	ST412/506	MFM		3600
M2241AS	26		ST412/506	MFM		
M2241AS2	24	30	ST412/506	MFM		
M2242AS	45	30	ST412/506	MFM		
M2242AS2	43	30	ST412/506	MFM		
M2243AS	72	30	ST412/506	MFM		
M2243AS2	67	30	ST412/506	MFM		
M2243R	110	25	ST412/506	2,7 RLL		
M2243T	68	25	ST412/506	MFM		
M2244E	73	25	ESDI	2,7 RLL		
M2244S	85U	25	SCSI	2,7 RLL		3600
M2244SA	85U	25	SCSI	2,7 RLL		3600
M2244SB	85U	25	SCSI	2,7 RLL		3600
M2245E	120	25	ESDI	2,7 RLL		
M2245S	120U	25	SCSI	2,7 RLL		3600
M2245SA	120U	25	SCSI	2,7 RLL		3600
M2245SB	120U	25	SCSI	2,7 RLL		3600
M2246E	138	25	ESDI	2,7 RLL		
M2246S	171U	25	SCSI	2,7 RLL		3600
M2246SA	171U	25	SCSI	2,7 RLL		3600
M2246SB	171U	25	SCSI	2,7 RLL		3600
M2247E	285	18	ESDI	1,7 RLL		
M2247S	289	18	SCSI	1,7 RLL		
M2247SA	160	18	SCSI	1,7 RLL		
M2247SB	169	18	SCSI	1,7 RLL		
M2248E	266	18	ESDI	1,7 RLL		
M2248S	227	18	SCSI	1,7 RLL		
M2248SA	252	18	SCSI	1,7 RLL		
M2248SB	266	18	SCSI	1,7 RLL		
M2249E	334	18	ESDI	1,7 RLL		
M2249S	334	18	SCSI	1,7 RLL		
M2249SA	334	18	SCSI	1,7 RLL		
M2249SB	362	18	SCSI	1,7 RLL		
M2261E	321	16	ESDI	1,7 RLL		
M2261HA	357	16	SCSI	1,7 RLL		

Drive Model	Format Size MB	Head	Cyl	Sect/ Trac	Translate H/C/S	RWC/ WPC	Form Factor	Power Watts
M2261S	321	8	1658			NA/NA	5.25FH	
M2261SA	415U	8	1658	53		NA/NA	5.25FH	
M2262E	448	11	1658			NA/NA	5.25FH	
M2262HA	476	11	1658	51		NA/NA	5.25FH	
M2262SA	476	11	1658	51		NA/NA	5.25FH	
M2263E	688	15	1658	53		NA/NA	5.25FH	
M2263HA	672	15	1658	53		NA/NA	5.25FH	
M2263S	650	15	1658	53		NA/NA	5.25FH	
M2266E	674	15	1658	53		NA/NA	5.25FH	
M2266H	953	15	1658			NA/NA	5.25FH	
M2266HA	1079	15	1658			NA/NA	5.25FH	
M2266HB	1140	15	1658			NA/NA	5.25FH	
M2266S	953	15	1658			NA/NA	5.25FH	
M2266SA	1079	15	1658	65		NA/NA	5.25FH	
M2266SB	1140	15	1658			NA/NA	5.25FH	
M2344KS	690	27	624	NA		NA/NA	8 FH	
M2372K	823	27	745			—/—		
M2372KS	823	27	745			—/—		
M2382K	1000	27	745			—/—		
M2382P	1000	27	745			—/—		
M2392K	2020	21	1916			—/—		
M2511A	128	1	9952	25		—/—	3.5 3H	
M2611H	46	2	1334	34		NA/NA	3.5HH	
M2611S	46	2	1334	68		NA/NA	3.5HH	
M2611SA	46	2	1334	34		NA/NA	3.5HH	8.9
M2611SB	46	2	1334	17		NA/NA	3.5HH	
M2611T	45	2	1334	33	4/667/33	NA/NA	3.5HH	8.9
M2612ES	90	4	1334			NA/NA	3.5HH	
M2612ESA	90	4	1334	34		NA/NA	3.5HH	
M2612ESB	90	4	1334			NA/NA	3.5HH	
M2612ET	90	4	1334	34	8/667/33	NA/NA	3.5HH	
M2612S	92	4	1334	34		NA/NA	3.5HH	
M2612SA	91	4	1334	33		NA/NA	3.5HH	10.4
M2612T	90	4	1334	33	8/667/33	NA/NA	3.5HH	8.9
M2613ES	139	6	1334			NA/NA	3.5HH	
M2613ESA	137	6	1334	34		NA/NA	3.5HH	
M2613ESB	139	6	1334			NA/NA	3.5HH	
M2613ET	137	6	1334	34	12/667/33	NA/NA	3.5HH	
M2613S	139	6	1334	34		NA/NA	3.5HH	
M2613SA	137	6	1334	34		NA/NA	3.5HH	10.4
M2613SB	139	6	1334	17		NA/NA	3.5HH	
M2613T	137	6	1334	34	12/667/33	NA/NA	3.5HH	10.4
M2614ES	185	8	1334			NA/NA	3.5HH	
M2614ESA	182	8	1334	34		NA/NA	3.5HH	
M2614ESB	185	8	1334			NA/NA	3.5HH	
M2614ET	180	8	1334	34	16/667/33	NA/NA	3.5HH	
M2614S	185	8	1334	34		NA/NA	3.5HH	
M2614SA	182	8	1334	34		NA/NA	3.5HH	10.4
M2614SB	186	8	1334	17		NA/NA	3.5HH	
M2614T	180	8	1334	34	16/667/33	NA/NA	3.5HH	10.4
M2615ES	52	2	1542	68		—/—	3.5 3H	
M2615ESA	52	2	1542	34		—/—	3.5 3H	
M2615ESB	52	2	1542	17		—/—	3.5 3H	
M2616ES	105	4	1542	68		NA/NA	3.5 3H	
M2616ESA	105	4	1542	34		—/—	3.5 3H	9.2
M2616ESB	105	4	1542	17		—/—	3.5 3H	
M2616ET	105	4	1542	34	8/771/33	NA/NA	3.5HH	
M2616SA	105	4	1542			NA/NA	3.5HH	7.2
M2616T	105	4	1542		8/771/33	NA/NA	3.5HH	7.2
M2617T	105	2	2010	40-64		—/—	3.5HH	Y
M2618T	210	4	2010	40-64		—/—	3.5HH	Y
M2621S	235	5	1435			NA/NA	3.5HH	
M2622F	293	7	1435			—/—	3.5HH	11
M2622FA	330	7	1435			—/—	3.5HH	
M2622H	330	7	1435			—/—	3.5HH	
M2622S	330	7	1153	80		NA/NA	3.5HH	
M2622SA	329	7	1429	56-70		NA/NA	3.5HH	

Drive Model	Format Size MB	Seek Time	Interface	Encode	cache kb	RPM
M2261S	321	16	SCSI	2,7 RLL		
M2261SA	415U		SCSI			
M2262E	448	16	ESDI	1,7 RLL		
M2262HA	476	16	SCSI	1,7 RLL		
M2262SA	476	16	SCSI	1,7 RLL		
M2263E	688	16	ESDI	1,7 RLL		
M2263HA	672	16	SCSI	1,7 RLL		3600
M2263S	650	16	SCSI	1,7 RLL		
M2266E	674	16	ESDI	1,7 RLL		
M2266H	953	14.5	SCSI	1,7 RLL		
M2266HA	1079	14.5	SCSI	1,7 RLL		3600
M2266HB	1140	14.5	SCSI	1,7 RLL		3600
M2266S	953	14.5	SCSI	1,7 RLL		3600
M2266SA	1079	14.5	SCSI	1,7 RLL		3600
M2266SB	1140	14.5	SCSI	1,7 RLL	256k	3600
M2344KS						
M2372K	690	16	SCSI/SMD	RLL		
M2372KS	823	16	HSMD	2,7 RLL		
M2382K	823	16	SCSI	2,7 RLL		
M2382P	1000	16	ESMD	1,7 RLL		
M2392K	1000	16	IPI	1,7 RLL		
M2511A	2020	12	ESMD	1,7 RLL		
M2611H	128	30	SCSI-2	1,7 RLL	256k	3600
M2611S	46	25	SCSI	1,7 RLL		
M2611SA	46	25	SCSI	1,7 RLL		
M2611SB	46	25	SCSI	1,7 RLL	24k	3490
M2611T	45	25	IDE AT	1,7 RLL	64k	3490
M2612ES	90	20	SCSI	1,7 RLL		
M2612ESA	90	20	SCSI	1,7 RLL		
M2612ESB	90	20	SCSI	1,7 RLL	24k	3490
M2612ET	90	20	IDE AT	1,7 RLL	64k	3490
M2612S	92	20	SCSI	1,7 RLL		3490
M2612SA	91	25	SCSI	1,7 RLL	24k	3490
M2612T	90	25	IDE AT	1,7 RLL	64k	3490
M2613ES	139	20	SCSI	1,7 RLL		
M2613ESA	137	20	SCSI	1,7 RLL		
M2613ESB	139	20	SCSI	1,7 RLL	24k	3490
M2613ET	137	20	IDE AT	1,7 RLL	64k	3490
M2613S	139	20	SCSI	1,7 RLL		3490
M2613SA	137	25	SCSI	1,7 RLL		3490
M2613SB	139	20	SCSI	1,7 RLL	24k	3490
M2613T	137	25	IDE AT	1,7 RLL		
M2614ES	185	20	SCSI	1,7 RLL	64k	3490
M2614ESA	182	20	SCSI	1,7 RLL		
M2614ESB	185	20	SCSI	1,7 RLL	24k	3490
M2614ET	180	20	IDE AT	1,7 RLL		
M2614S	185	20	SCSI	1,7 RLL		
M2614SA	182	25	SCSI	1,7 RLL		3490
M2614SB	186	20	SCSI	1,7 RLL	24k	3490
M2614T	180	20	IDE AT	1,7 RLL	64k	3490
M2615ES	52		SCSI	1,7 RLL		3490
M2615ESA	52		SCSI	1,7 RLL		3490
M2615ESB	52		SCSI	1,7 RLL		3490
M2616ES	105		SCSI	1,7 RLL		3490
M2616ESA	105	20	SCSI	1,7 RLL		3490
M2616ESB	105		SCSI	1,7 RLL	24k	3490
M2616ET	105		SCSI	1,7 RLL		3490
M2616SA	105	20	IDE AT	1,7 RLL	56k	3490
M2616S	105	20	SCSI	1,7 RLL	24k	3490
M2616T	105	20	IDE AT	1,7 RLL	64k	3490
M2617T	105		IDE AT	1,7 RLL		3490
M2618T	210		IDE AT	1,7 RLL		3490
M2621S	235	12	SCSI-2	1,7 RLL		
M2622F	293	12	SCSI	1,7 RLL		
M2622FA	330	12	SCSI-1/2	1,7 RLL		4400
M2622H	330		SCSI-2Diff	1,7 RLL	240k	4400
M2622S	330	12	SCSI-2	1,7 RLL		4400
M2622SA	329	12	SCSI-2	1,7 RLL	240k	4400

Drive Model	Format Size MB	Head	Cyl	Sect/ Trac	Translate H/C/S	RWC/ WPC	Form Factor	Power Watts
M2622T	326	7	1435		10/1013/63	NA/NA	3.5HH	12.5
M2623F	377	9	1429	V		NA/NA	3.5HH	
M2623FA	498	9	1435			—/—	3.5HH	
M2623H	425	9	1435	80		NA/NA	3.5HH	
M2623S	425	9	1153	80		NA/NA	3.5HH	
M2623SA	425	9	1429	64		NA/NA	3.5HH	
M2623T	420	9	1435		13/002/63	—/—	3.5HH	12.5
M2624F	461	6	1435			—/—	3.5HH	11
M2624FA	520	11	1435			—/—	3.5HH	
M2624H	520	11	1435			NA/NA	3.5HH	
M2624S	520	11	1463	63		NA/NA	3.5HH	
M2624SA	520	11	1429	64		NA/NA	3.5HH	
M2624T	513	11	1429	63	16/995/63	NA/NA	3.5HH	12.5
M2634S	120	3	1574	40-66		—/—	2.5 4H	1.75
M2634T	120	3	1574	40-66		—/—	2.5 4H	1.75
M2635S	160	4	1574	40-66		—/—	2.5 4H	1.75
M2635T	160	4	1569		8/620/63	—/—	2.5 4H	1.75
M2636S	200	5	1574	40-66		—/—	2.5 4H	1.75
M2636T	200	5	1574	40-66		—/—	2.5 4H	1.75
M2637S	240	6	1574	49		—/—	2.5 4H	
M2637SA	240	6	1574			—/—	FH	
M2637T	240	6	1569		8/930/63	—/—	2.5 4H	
M2637T	240	6	1574	49		—/—	2.5 4H	1.75
M2651SA	1400	16	1944	88		—/—	5.25FH	
M2652H	1628	20	1893	84		NA/NA	5.25FH	
M2652HA	1600	20	1944			NA/NA	FH	
M2652HD	1628	20	1893	84		NA/NA	5.25FH	
M2652P	1600	20	1893			NA/NA	FH	
M2652S	1628	20	1893	84		NA/NA	5.25FH	
M2652SA	1750	20	1944	88		—/—	5.25	
M2653	1400	15	2078	88		NA/NA	FH	
M2654HA	2000	21	2671			—/—	5.25FH	
M2654SA	2061	21	2170	88		—/—	8 FH	
M2671P	2640	15	2671			—/—	3.5 3H	
M2681SAU	264	3	2379			—/—	3.5 3H	3.0
M2681TAU	264	3	2379		11/977/48	—/—	3.5 3H	3.0
M2682SAU	350	4	2379	64-90		—/—	3.5 3H	
M2682TAU	352	4	2378	64-90	11/992/63	—/—	3.5 3H	3.0
M2684SAU	525	6	2379	74		—/—	3.5 3H	3.0
M2684TAU	525	6	2379		16/1024/63	—/—	3.5 3H	
M2691EHA	645	9	1818	V		NA/NA	3.5HH	
M2691EQ	756U	9	1831			—/—	3.5HH	12.1
M2691ER	756U	9	1831			—/—	3.5HH	
M2691ESA	645	9	1818	V		NA/NA	3.5HH	
M2692EQ	925U	11	1831			—/—	3.5HH	12.1
M2692ER	925U	11	1831			—/—	3.5HH	12.1
M2693EQ	1093U	13	1831			—/—	3.5HH	12.1
M2693ER	1093U	13	1831			—/—	3.5HH	
M2694EHA	1080	15	1818	V		NA/NA	3.5HH	
M2694EQ	1261U	15	1831			—/—	3.5HH	12.1
M2694ER	1261U	15	1831			—/—	3.5HH	
M2694ESA	1080	15	1818	V		NA/NA	3.5HH	
M2703S	260	3	2305			—/—	2.5 4H	1.45
M2703T	260	3	2305			—/—	2.5 4H	
M2704	260	3				—/—	2.5 4H	
M2704	350	4				—/—	2.5 4H	
M2704S	350	4	2305			—/—	2.5 4H	
M2704T	350	4				—/—	2.5 4H	
M2705	530	6				—/—	2.5 4H	
M2706	530	6				—/—	2.5 4H	
M2706S	530	6	2305			—/—	2.5 4H	
M2706T	530	6	2305			—/—	2.5 4H	
M2712TAM	540	1				—/—	2.5 4H	0.85
M2713TAM	1080	2				—/—	2.5 4H	0.85
M2714TAM	1080	2				—/—	3.5 3H	0.98
M2723	1200	3				—/—	3.5 3H	0.98
M2724	1600	4				—/—	3.5HH	
M2903	2100	14	3139			—/—	3.5HH	13.7

Drive Model	Format Size MB	Seek Time	Interface	Encode	cache kb	RPM
M2622T	326	12	IDE AT	1,7 RLL	240k	4400
M2623F	377	12	SCSI 1/2	1,7 RLL		4400
M2623FA	498	12	SCSI-1/2	1,7 RLL	240k	4400
M2623H	425		SCSI-2Diff	1,7 RLL		4400
M2623S	425		SCSI-2	1,7 RLL	240k	4400
M2623SA	425	12	SCSI-2	1,7 RLL	240k	4400
M2623T	420	12	IDE AT	1,7 RLL	240k	4400
M2624F	461	12	SCSI	1,7 RLL	240k	4400
M2624FA	520	12	SCSI-1/2	1,7 RLL	240k	4400
M2624H	520		SCSI-2Diff	1,7 RLL		4400
M2624S	520	12	SCSI-2	1,7 RLL	240k	4400
M2624SA	520	12	SCSI-2	1,7 RLL	240k	4400
M2624T	513	12	IDE AT	1,7 RLL	240k	4400
M2634S	120	14	SCSI-2	1,7 RLL	224k	4500
M2634T	120	14	IDE AT	1,7 RLL	224k	4500
M2635S	160	14	SCSI-2	1,7 RLL	224k	4500
M2635T	160	14	IDE AT	1,7 RLL	224k	4500
M2636S	200	14	SCSI-2	1,7 RLL	224k	4500
M2636T	200	14	IDE AT	1,7 RLL	224k	4500
M2637S	240	14	SCSI-2	1,7 RLL	224k	4500
M2637SA	240	14.5	SCSI-2	1,7 RLL	256	4500
M2637T	240	14	IDE AT	1,7 RLL	256k	4500
M2637T	240	14	IDE AT	1,7 RLL	256k	4500
M2651SA	1400	12	SCSI-2	1,7 RLL	224k	4500
M2652H	1628	11	SCSI-2	1,7 RLL	256k	5400
M2652HA	1600	11	SCSI-2Diff			5400
M2652HD	1628	11	SCSI-2Diff			5400
M2652P	1600	11	IPI-2	1,7 RLL		5400
M2652S	1628	11	SCSI-2			5400
M2652SA	1750	11	SCSI-2	1,7 RLL		5400
M2653	1400	12	SCSI-2Diff	1,7 RLL	256k	5400
M2654HA	2000	12	SCSI-2Diff			5400
M2654SA	2061	12	SCSI-2	1,7 RLL	256k	5400
M2671P	2640	12	IPI-2	1,7 RLL	256k	4340
M2681SAU	264	12	SCSI-2	1,7 RLL	256k	4500
M2681TAU	264	12	IDE AT	1,7 RLL	256k	4500
M2682SAU	350	12	SCSI-2	1,7 RLL	256k	4500
M2682TAU	352	12	IDE AT	1,7 RLL	256k	4500
M2684SAU	525	12	SCSI-2	1,7 RLL	256k	4500
M2684TAU	525	12	IDE AT	1,7 RLL	256k	4500
M2691EHA	645	10	SCSI-2	1,7 RLL	256k	5400
M2691EQ	756U	10	SCSI	1,7 RLL	512k	5400
M2691ER	756U	10	SCSI-2Diff	1,7 RLL	512k	5400
M2691ESA	645	10	SCSI-2	1,7 RLL	256k	5400
M2692EQ	925U	10	SCSI	1,7 RLL	512k	5400
M2692ER	925U	10	SCSI-2Diff	1,7 RLL	512k	5400
M2693EQ	1093U	10	SCSI	1,7 RLL	512k	5400
M2693ER	1093U	10	SCSI-2Diff	1,7 RLL	512k	5400
M2694EHA	1080	10	SCSI-2Diff	1,7 RLL	256k	5400
M2694EQ	1261U	10	SCSI	1,7 RLL	512k	5400
M2694ER	1261U	10	SCSI-2Diff	1,7 RLL	512k	5400
M2694ESA	1080	10	SCSI-2	1,7 RLL	512k	5400
M2703S	260	12	SCSI-2Fast	RLL	512k	5400
M2703T	260	12	ATA-2	RLL	512k	5400
M2704	260	12	SCSI		256k	5400
M2704S	350	12	SCSI-2Fast	RLL	256	5400
M2704T	350	12	ATA-2	RLL	512k	5400
M2705	350	12	SCSI		256k	5400
M2706	530	12	SCSI		256	5400
M2706S	530	12	SCSI-2Fast	RLL	512k	5400
M2706T	530	12	ATA-2	RLL	512k	5400
M2712TAM	540	12	ATA	PRML8,9	256k	5400
M2713TAM	1080	12	ATA	PRML8,9	128k	3634
M2714TAM	1080	12	ATA	PRML8,9	128k	3634
M2723	1200	12	ATA-3	PRML8,9	128k	3634
M2724	1600	12	ATA-3	PRML	128k	4000
M2903	2100	10.5	SCSI-2FstW	PRML	128k	4000
				RLL	512k	5400

Drive Model	Format Size MB	Head	Cyl	Sect/ Trac	Translate H/C/S	RWC/ WPC	Form Factor	Power Watts
M2903	2110	13	3150			—/—	3.5HH	
M2903HA	2110	13	3150			—/—	3.5HH	
M2903HB	2110	13	3150			—/—	3.5HH	
M2903HX	2110	13	3150			—/—	3.5HH	
M2903JA	2110	13	3150			—/—	3.5HH	
M2903JB	2110	13	3150			—/—	3.5HH	
M2903JX	2110	13	3150			—/—	3.5HH	
M2903KA	2110	13	3150			—/—	3.5HH	
M2903KB	2110	13	3150			—/—	3.5HH	
M2903KX	2110	13	3150			—/—	3.5HH	
M2903QA	2110	13	3150			—/—	3.5HH	
M2903QB	2110	13	3150			—/—	3.5HH	
M2903QX	2110	13	3150			—/—	3.5HH	
M2903RA	2110	13	3150			—/—	3.5HH	
M2903RB	2110	13	3150			—/—	3.5HH	
M2903RX	2110	13	3150			—/—	3.5HH	
M2903SA	2110	13	3150			—/—	3.5HH	
M2903SB	2110	13	3150			—/—	3.5HH	
M2903SX	2110	13	3150			—/—	3.5HH	13.7
M2909	3100	20	3139			—/—	3.5HH	
M2909	3100	19	3150			—/—	3.5HH	
M2909HA	3100	19	3150			—/—	3.5HH	
M2909HB	3100	19	3150			—/—	3.5HH	
M2909HX	3100	19	3150			—/—	3.5HH	
M2909JA	3100	19	3150			—/—	3.5HH	
M2909JB	3100	19	3150			—/—	3.5HH	
M2909JX	3100	19	3150			—/—	3.5HH	
M2909KA	3100	19	3150			—/—	3.5HH	
M2909KB	3100	19	3150			—/—	3.5HH	
M2909KX	3100	19	3150			—/—	3.5HH	
M2909QA	3100	19	3150			—/—	3.5HH	
M2909QB	3100	19	3150			—/—	3.5HH	
M2909QX	3100	19	3150			—/—	3.5HH	
M2909RA	3100	19	3150			—/—	3.5HH	
M2909RB	3100	19	3150			—/—	3.5HH	
M2909RX	3100	19	3150			—/—	3.5HH	
M2909SA	3100	19	3150			—/—	3.5HH	
M2909SB	3100	19	3150			—/—	3.5HH	
M2909SX	3100	19	3150			—/—	3.5HH	
M2914	2100	7				—/—	3.5HH	13.7
M2915	2100	15	3018			—/—	3.5HH	13.7
M2915HA	2100	15	3018			—/—	3.5HH	13.7
M2915HB	2100	15	3018			—/—	3.5HH	13.7
M2915HX	2100	15	3018			—/—	3.5HH	13.7
M2915JA	2100	15	3018			—/—	3.5HH	13.7
M2915JB	2100	15	3018			—/—	3.5HH	13.7
M2915JX	2100	15	3018			—/—	3.5HH	13.7
M2915KA	2100	15	3018			—/—	3.5HH	13.7
M2915KB	2100	15	3018			—/—	3.5HH	13.7
M2915KX	2100	15	3018			—/—	3.5HH	13.7
M2915QA	2100	15	3018			—/—	3.5HH	13.7
M2915QB	2100	15	3018			—/—	3.5HH	13.7
M2915QX	2100	15	3018			—/—	3.5HH	13.7
M2915RA	2100	15	3018			—/—	3.5HH	13.7
M2915RB	2100	15	3018			—/—	3.5HH	13.7
M2915RX	2100	15	3018			—/—	3.5HH	13.7
M2915SA	2100	15	3018			—/—	3.5HH	13.7
M2915SB	2100	15	3018			—/—	3.5HH	13.7
M2915SX	2100	15	3018			—/—	3.5HH	
M2927	1100	4				—/—	3.5HH	15.5
M2932	2170	10	3422			—/—	3.5HH	15.5
M2934	4350	19	3422			—/—	3.5HH	15
M2948S	8800	18	5751			—/—	3.5HH	15
M2949S	9100	18	5772			—/—	3.5 3H	10
M2952S	2200	5	5565			—/—	3.5 3H	10
M2954S	4400	9	5565			—/—	3.5HH	
MAA3182	18200	19	9040			—/—		

Drive Model	Format Size MB	Seek Time	Interface	Encode	cache kb	RPM
M2903	2110	9.8	SCSI-2	8,9 RLL	512k	5400
M2903HA	2110	9.8	SCSI-2Diff	8,9 RLL	512k	5400
M2903HB	2110	9.8	SCSI-2Diff	8,9 RLL	1024k	5400
M2903HX	2110	9.8	SCSI-2Diff	8,9 RLL	256k	5400
M2903JA	2110	9.8	SCSI-2Fast	8,9 RLL	512k	5400
M2903JB	2110	9.8	SCSI-2Fast	8,9 RLL	1024k	5400
M2903JX	2110	9.8	SCSI-2Fast	8,9 RLL	256k	5400
M2903KA	2110	9.8	SCSI-2Diff	8,9 RLL	512k	5400
M2903KB	2110	9.8	SCSI-2Diff	8,9 RLL	1024k	5400
M2903KX	2110	9.8	SCSI-2Diff	8,9 RLL	256k	5400
M2903QA	2110	9.8	SCSI-2FstWd	8,9 RLL	512k	5400
M2903QB	2110	9.8	SCSI-2FstWd	8,9 RLL	1024k	5400
M2903QX	2110	9.8	SCSI-2FstWd	8,9 RLL	256k	5400
M2903RA	2110	9.8	SCSI2FstWdD	8,9 RLL	512k	5400
M2903RB	2110	9.8	SCSI2FstWdD	8,9 RLL	1024k	5400
M2903RX	2110	9.8	SCSI2FstWdD	8,9 RLL	256k	5400
M2903SA	2110	9.8	SCSI-2Fast	8,9 RLL	512k	5400
M2903SB	2110	9.8	SCSI-2Fast	8,9 RLL	1024k	5400
M2903SX	2110	9.8	SCSI-2Fast	8,9 RLL	256k	5400
M2909	3100	10.5	SCSI-2FstW	RLL	512k	5400
M2909	3100	9.8	SCSI-2	8,9 RLL	512k	5400
M2909HA	3100	9.8	SCSI-2Diff	8,9 RLL	512k	5400
M2909HB	3100	9.8	SCSI-2Diff	8,9 RLL	1024k	5400
M2909HX	3100	9.8	SCSI-2Diff	8,9 RLL	256k	5400
M2909JA	3100	9.8	SCSI-2Fast	8,9 RLL	512k	5400
M2909JB	3100	9.8	SCSI-2Fast	8,9 RLL	1024k	5400
M2909JX	3100	9.8	SCSI-2Fast	8,9 RLL	256k	5400
M2909KA	3100	9.8	SCSI-2Diff	8,9 RLL	512k	5400
M2909KB	3100	9.8	SCSI-2Diff	8,9 RLL	1024k	5400
M2909KX	3100	9.8	SCSI-2Diff	8,9 RLL	256k	5400
M2909QA	3100	9.8	SCSI-2FstWd	8,9 RLL	512k	5400
M2909QB	3100	9.8	SCSI-2FstWd	8,9 RLL	1024k	5400
M2909QX	3100	9.8	SCSI-2FstWd	8,9 RLL	256k	5400
M2909RA	3100	9.8	SCSI2FstWdD	8,9 RLL	512k	5400
M2909RB	3100	9.8	SCSI2FstWdD	8,9 RLL	1024k	5400
M2909RX	3100	9.8	SCSI2FstWdD	8,9 RLL	256k	5400
M2909SA	3100	9.8	SCSI-2Fast	8,9 RLL	512k	5400
M2909SB	3100	9.8	SCSI-2Fast	8,9 RLL	1024k	5400
M2909SX	3100	9.8	SCSI-2Fast	8,9 RLL	256k	5400
M2914	2100	9	SCSI-2FstW		512k	7200
M2915	2100	9.8	SCSI-2FstW	RLL	512k	7200
M2915HA	2100	9.8	SCSI-2Diff	RLL	512k	7200
M2915HB	2100	9.8	SCSI-2Diff	RLL	1024k	7200
M2915HX	2100	9.8	SCSI-2Diff	RLL	256k	7200
M2915JA	2100	9.8	SCSI-2Fast	RLL	512k	7200
M2915JB	2100	9.8	SCSI-2Fast	RLL	1024k	7200
M2915JX	2100	9.8	SCSI-2Fast	RLL	256k	7200
M2915KA	2100	9.8	SCSI-2Diff	RLL	512k	7200
M2915KB	2100	9.8	SCSI-2Diff	RLL	1024k	7200
M2915KX	2100	9.8	SCSI-2Diff	RLL	256k	7200
M2915QA	2100	9.8	SCSI-2FstWd	RLL	512k	7200
M2915QB	2100	9.8	SCSI-2FstWd	RLL	1024k	7200
M2915QX	2100	9.8	SCSI-2FstWd	RLL	256k	7200
M2915RA	2100	9.8	SCSI2FstWdD	RLL	512k	7200
M2915RB	2100	9.8	SCSI2FstWdD	RLL	1024k	7200
M2915RX	2100	9.8	SCSI2FstWdD	RLL	256k	7200
M2915SA	2100	9.8	SCSI-2Fast	RLL	512k	7200
M2915SB	2100	9.8	SCSI-2Fast	RLL	1024k	7200
M2915SX	2100	9.8	SCSI-2Fast	RLL	256k	7200
M2927	1100	10.5	SCSI-2FstW		512k	5400
M2932	2170	11	SCSI-2Fast	RLL	510k	7200
M2934	4350	11	SCSI-2Fast	RLL	510k	7200
M2948S	8800	10	SCSI-2FstW	PR4ML	512k	7200
M2949S	9100	10	SCSI-2FstW	RLL 0,4,4	512k	7200
M2952S	2200	8	SCSI-2FstW	RLL 8,9	512k	7200
M2954S	4400	8	SCSI-2FstW	RLL 8,9	512k	7200
MAA3182	18200	9	Ultra2 LVD	PRML8,9	512k	7200

Drive Model	Format Size MB	Head	Cyl	Sect/Trac	Translate H/C/S	RWC/WPC	Form Factor	Power Watts
MAB3045	4550	5	8490			—/—	3.5 3H	
MAB3091 SB	9100	10				—/—		11
MAC3045	4550	5	8690	156-24		—/—	3.5 3H	14.0
MAC3045	4550	5	8690	156-24		—/—	3.5 3H	14.0
MAC3045	4550	5	8690	156-24		—/—	3.5 3H	14.0
MAC3091	9100	10	8690	156-24		—/—	3.5 3H	14.0
MAC3091	9100	10	8690	156-24		—/—	3.5 3H	14.0
MAC3091	9100	10	8690	156-24		—/—	3.5 3H	14.0
MAD3363	36400	19	10200	274-45		—/—	3.5HH	9.5
MAE3091	9100	4		281-42		—/—	3.5 3H	8.0
MAE3091LC	9100	4				—/—	3.5 3H	8.0
MAE3091LP	9100	4				—/—	3.5 3H	8.0
MAE3182	18200	8	12010	281-42		—/—	3.5 3H	8.0
MAE3182LC	18200	8				—/—	3.5 3H	8.0
MAE3182LP	18200	8				—/—	3.5 3H	8.0
MAF3364	36400	19	10200	281-42		—/—	3.5HH	14.5
MAF3364FC	36400	19				—/—	3.5HH	14.5
MAF3364LC	36400	19				—/—	3.5HH	14.5
MAF3364LP	36400	19				—/—	3.5HH	14.5
MAG3091	9100	5	9866	278-42		—/—	3.5 3H	10.5
MAG3091FC	9100	5				—/—	3.5 3H	10.5
MAG3091LC	9100	5				—/—	3.5 3H	10.5
MAG3091LP	9100	5				—/—	3.5 3H	10.5
MAG3182	18200	10	9866	278-42		—/—	3.5 3H	10.5
MAG3182FC	18200	10				—/—	3.5 3H	10.5
MAG3182LC	18200	10				—/—	3.5 3H	10.5
MAG3182LP	18200	10				—/—	3.5 3H	10.5
MAH3091	9100	2	17700			—/—	3.5 3H	6.0
MAH3091MC	9100	2				—/—	3.5 3H	6.0
MAH3091MP	9100	2				—/—	3.5 3H	6.0
MAH3182	18200	4	17700			—/—	3.5 3H	6.0
MAH3182MC	18200	4				—/—	3.5 3H	2.4
MAH3182MP	18200	4				—/—	3.5 3H	2.4
MAJ3091MC	9100	3				—/—	3.5 3H	5.4
MAJ3091MP	9100	3				—/—	3.5 3H	5.4
MAJ3182MC	18200	5				—/—	3.5 3H	6.0
MAJ3182MP	18200	5				—/—	3.5 3H	6.0
MAJ3364MC	36400	10	14792	369-57		—/—	3.5 3H	7.8
MAJ3364MP	36400	10	14792	369-57		—/—	3.5 3H	7.8
MAK3091	9100	3	15000			—/—	3.5 3H	8.0
MAK3091	9100	3	15000			—/—	3.5 3H	8.0
MAK3182	18200	5	15000			—/—	3.5 3H	9.0
MAK3182	18200	5	15000			—/—	3.5 3H	9.0
MAK3364	36400	10	15000			—/—	3.5 3H	11.0
MAK3364	36400	10	15000			—/—	3.5 3H	11.0
MAM3184MC	18.4GB	4	18650	399-51		—/—	3.5 3H	7.8
MAM3184MP	18.4GB	4	18650	399-51		—/—	3.5 3H	7.8
MAM3367MC	36.7GB	4	18650	399-51		—/—	3.5 3H	7.8
MAM3367MP	36.7GB	4	18650	399-51		—/—	3.5 3H	7.8
MAN3184MC	18.4GB	2	29884			—/—	3.5 3H	7
MAN3184MP	18.4GB	2	29884			—/—	3.5 3H	7
MAN3367FC	36.7GB	4	29884			—/—	3.5 3H	7.5
MAN3367MC	36.7GB	4	30200	432-73		—/—	3.5 3H	8.4
MAN3367MP	36.7GB	4	29884			—/—	3.5 3H	7.5
MAN3735FC	73.5GB	4	29932	432-73		—/—	3.5 3H	10.2
MAN3735MC	73.5GB	8	29884			—/—	3.5 3H	9.5
MAN3735MP	73.5GB	8	29884			—/—	3.5 3H	9.5
MAP3147FC	147GB	8	48000			—/—	3.5 3H	11.5
MAP3147NC	147GB	8	48000			—/—	3.5 3H	9.5
MAP3147NP	147GB	8	48000			—/—	3.5 3H	9.5
MAP3367	36.7GB	2	48000			—/—	3.5 3H	5.8
MAP3367	36.7GB	2	48000			—/—	3.5 3H	
MAP3735FC	73.5GB	4	48000			—/—	3.5 3H	8.6
MAP3735NC	73500					—/—	3.5 3H	6.6
MAP3735NP	73.5GB	4	48000			—/—	3.5 3H	6.6
MAS3184NC	18.4GB	2	29680			—/—	3.5 3H	7.5
MAS3184NP	18.4GB	2	29680			—/—	3.5 3H	7.5

FUJITSU AMERICA, INC.

Drive Model	Format Size MB	Seek Time	Interface	Encode	cache kb	RPM
MAB3045	4550	8.5	SCSI-2	PRML8,9	512k	7200
MAB3091 SB	9100	16	ULSCSI40FST	PRML	512k	7200
MAC3045	4550	7.5	Ultra SCSI	PRML8,9	512k	1003
MAC3045	4550	7.5	Ultra2 LVD	PRML8,9	512k	1003
MAC3045	4550	7.5	FC-AL	PRML8,9	512k	1003
MAC3091	9100	7.5	FC-AL	PRML8,9	512k	1003
MAC3091	9100	7.5	Ultra2 LVD	PRML8,9	512k	1003
MAC3091	9100	7.5	Ultra SCSI	PRML8,9	512k	1003
MAD3363	36400	5.5	Ultra2 SCSI	16/17 EPR4	2048k	7200
MAE3091	9100	7.0	Ultra2 SCSI	16/17 EPR4	2048k	7200
MAE3091LC	9100	7.0	Ultra2 SCSI	EPR4ML 16,17	2048k	7200
MAE3091LP	9100	7.0	Ultra2 SCSI	EPR4ML 16,17	2048k	7200
MAE3182	18200	7.0	Ultra2 SCSI	16/17 EPR4	2048k	7200
MAE3182LC	18200	7.0	Ultra2 SCSI	EPR4ML 16,17	2048k	7200
MAE3182LP	18200	7.0	Ultra2 SCSI	EPR4ML 16,17	2048k	7200
MAF3364	36400	5.5	Ultra2 SCSI	16/17 EPR4	2048k	1002
MAF3364FC	36400	5.5	Ultra2 SCSI	EPR4ML 16,17	2048k	1002
MAF3364LC	36400	5.5	Ultra2 SCSI	EPR4ML 16,17	2048k	1002
MAF3364LP	36400	5.5	Ultra2 SCSI	EPR4ML 16,17	2048k	1002
MAG3091	9100	5.0	Ultra2 SCSI	16/17 EPR4	2048k	1002
MAG3091FC	9100	5.0	UL2SCSIFCAL	EPR4ML 16,17	2048k	1002
MAG3091LC	9100	5.0	UL2LVDSCSI	EPR4ML 16,17	2048k	1002
MAG3091LP	9100	5.0	UL2LVDSCSI	EPR4ML 16,17	2048k	1002
MAG3182	18200	5.0	Ultra2 SCSI	16/17 EPR4	2048k	1002
MAG3182FC	18200	5.0	UL2SCSIFCAL	EPR4ML 16,17	2048k	1002
MAG3182LC	18200	5.0	UL2LVDSCSI	EPR4ML 16,17	2048k	1002
MAG3182LP	18200	5.0	UL2LVDSCSI	EPR4ML 16,17	2048k	1002
MAH3091	9100	6.8	Ultra SCSI3	EPR4ML 32/34	4096k	7200
MAH3091MC	9100	6.8	U160/SCA-2	MEEPRML32/34	4096k	7200
MAH3091MP	9100	6.8	Ultra 160	MEEPRML32/34	4096k	7200
MAH3182	18200	6.8	Ultra SCSI3	EPR4ML 32/34	4mb	7200
MAH3182MC	18200	6.8	U160/SCA-2	MEEPRML32/34	4096k	7200
MAH3182MP	18200	6.8	Ultra 160	MEEPRML32/34	4096k	7200
MAJ3091MC	9100	4.7	U160/SCA-2	MEEPRML32/34	4096k	1002
MAJ3091MP	9100	4.7	Ultra 160	MEEPRML32/34	4096k	1002
MAJ3182MC	18200	4.7	U160/SCA-2	MEEPRML32/34	4096k	1002
MAJ3182MP	18200	4.7	Ultra 160	MEEPRML32/34	4096k	1002
MAJ3364MC	36400	4.7	U160/SCA-2	MEEPRML32/34	4096k	1002
MAJ3364MP	36400	4.7	Ultra 160	MEEPRML32/34	4096k	1002
MAK3091	9100	5.2	UL3SCSIWD	MEPR4 32/34	4mb	1002
MAK3091	9100	5.2	FC-AL	MEPR4 32/34	4mb	1002
MAK3182	18200	5.2	FC-AL	MEPR4 32/34	4mb	1002
MAK3182	18200	5.2	UL3SCSIWD	MEPR4 32/34	4mb	1002
MAK3364	36400	5.2	UL3SCSIWD	MEPR4 32/34	4mb	1002
MAK3364	36400	5.2	FC-AL	MEPR4 32/34	4mb	1002
MAM3184MC	18.4GB	3.5	U160/SCA-2	EEPRML32,34	8mb	1500
MAM3184MP	18.4GB	3.5	U160/68-pnW	EEPRML32,34	8mb	1500
MAM3367MC	36.7GB	3.5	U160/SCA-2	EEPRML32,34	8mb	1500
MAM3367MP	36.7GB	3.5	U160/68pnW	EEPRML32,34	8mb	1500
MAN3184MC	18.4GB	4.5	SCA-2	MEEPRML32/34	8mb	1002
MAN3184MP	18.4GB	4.5	68-pin wide	MEEPRML32/34	8mb	1002
MAN3367FC	36.7GB	4.5	SCA-2	MEEPRML32/34	8mb	1002
MAN3367MC	36.7GB	4.5	U160/SCA-2	MEEPRML32/34	8mb	1002
MAN3367MP	36.7GB	4.5	68-pin wide	MEEPRML32/34	8mb	1002
MAN3735FC	73.5GB	4.5	FC-AL2/SCA2	MEEPRML32/34	8mb	1002
MAN3735MC	73.5GB	4.5	SCA-2	MEEPRML32/34	8mb	1002
MAN3735MP	73.5GB	4.5	68-pin wide	MEEPRML32/34	8mb	1002
MAP3147FC	147GB	4.5	FC-AL2/40pn	MEEPRML32/34	8mb	1002
MAP3147NC	147GB	4.5	SCA-2	MEEPRML32/34	8mb	1002
MAP3147NP	147GB	4.5	UL320 SCSI	MEEPRML32/34	8mb	1002
MAP3367	36.7GB	4.5	UL320 SCSI	MEEPRML32/34	8mb	1002
MAP3367	36.7GB	4.5	FC-AL2/40pn	MEEPRML32/34	8mb	1002
MAP3735FC	73.5GB	4.5	FC-AL2/40pn	MEEPRML32/34	8mb	1002
MAP3735NC	73500	4.5	SCA-2	32/34 NPV2	8mb	1002
MAP3735NP	73.5GB	4.5	UL320 SCSI	MEEPRML32/34	8mb	1002
MAS3184NC	18.4GB	3.5	SCA-2	MEEPRML32/34	8mb	1500
MAS3184NP	18.4GB	3.5	UL320 SCSI	MEEPRML32/34	8mb	1500

Drive Model	Format Size MB	Head	Cyl	Sect/Trac	Translate H/C/S	RWC/WPC	Form Factor	Power Watts
MAS3367NC	36.7GB	4	29680			—/—	3.5 3H	8.5
MAS3367NP	36.7GB	4	29680			—/—	3.5 3H	8.5
MAS3735NC	73.5GB	8	29680			—/—	3.5 3H	11.5
MAS3735NP	73.5GB	8	29680			—/—	3.5 3H	11.5
MAT3 147GB	147GB					—/—	3.5 3H	
MAT3 300GB	300GB					—/—	3.5 3H	
MAT3 73GB	73GB					—/—	3.5 3H	
MAU 147GB	147GB					—/—	3.5 3H	
MAU 36GB	36GB					—/—	3.5 3H	
MAU 73GB	73GB					—/—	3.5 3H	
MHA2021	2160	4				—/—	2.5 3H	0.88
MHA2032	3240	6				—/—	2.5 3H	0.88
MHB2021	2160	4				—/—	2.5 4H	0.88
MHB2032	3240	6				—/—	2.5 4H	0.88
MHC2020AT	4090	6	7229			—/—	2.5 4H	0.81
MHC2040AT	4090	6	7230			—/—	2.5 4H	
MHD2021AT	2160	3	7289			—/—	2.5 4H	0.91
MHD2021AT	3250	4	7317			—/—	2.5 4H	0.91
MHE2043AT	4320	4	8647	180-31		—/—	2.5 4H	0.95
MHE2064AT	6400	6	8647	180-31		—/—	2.5 4H	0.95
MHF2021AT	2160	2	8467	180-31		—/—	2.5 4H	0.95
MHF2043AT	4320	4	8467	180-31		—/—	2.5 4H	0.95
MHG2102AT	10000	6	8647			—/—	2.5 4H	0.95
MHH2032AT	3200	2	8647			—/—	2.5 4H	0.95
MHH2048AT	4800	3	8647			—/—	2.5 4H	0.95
MHH2064AT	6400	4	8647			—/—	2.5 4H	0.95
MHJ2181AT	18100	6	14784			—/—	2.5 4H	0.95
MHK2060AT	6000	2	14784			—/—	2.5 4H	0.95
MHK2090AT	9000	3	14784			—/—	2.5 4H	0.95
MHK2120AT	12000	4	14784			—/—	2.5 4H	0.95
MHL2300AT	30000	6	19936	363-62		—/—	2.5 4H	0.28
MHM2100AT	10000	2	19936	363-62		—/—	2.5 4H	0.25
MHM2150AT	15000	3	19936	363-62		—/—	2.5 4H	0.25
MHM2200AT	20000	4	19936	363-62		—/—	2.5 4H	0.25
MHN2100AT	10GB	2	28416			—/—	2.5 4H	0.75
MHN2150AT	15GB	2	28416			—/—	2.5 4H	0.75
MHN2200AT	20GB	3	28416			—/—	2.5 4H	0.75
MHN2300AT	30GB	4	28416			—/—	2.5 4H	0.75
MHR2010AT	10GB	1				—/—	2.5 4H	
MHR2020AT	20GB	2				—/—	2.5 4H	
MHR2030AT	30GB	3				—/—	2.5 4H	
MHR2040AT	40GB	4				—/—	2.5 4H	
MHS2020AT	20GB	2				—/—	2.5 4H	0.65
MHS2030AT	30GB	2				—/—	2.5 4H	0.65
MHS2040AT	40GB	3				—/—	2.5 4H	0.65
MHS2060AT	60GB	4				—/—	2.5 4H	0.65
MHT-BH 40GB	40GB					—/—	2.5 4H	
MHT-BH 60GB	60GB					—/—	2.5 4H	
MHT-BH 80GB	80GB					—/—	2.5 4H	
MHT2020AT	20GB					—/—	2.5 4H	
MHT2030AT	30GB					—/—	2.5 4H	0.65
MHT2040AH	40GB					—/—	2.5 4H	0.85
MHT2040AT	40GB					—/—	2.5 4H	
MHT2060AH	60GB					—/—	2.5 4H	0.85
MHT2060AT	60GB					—/—	2.5 4H	
MHT2080AH	80GB					—/—	2.5 4H	0.85
MHT2080AT	80GB					—/—	2.5 4H	0.65
MPA3017AT	1750	2	8713	132-25		—/—	3.5 3H	4.4
MPA3026AT	2620	3	8713	132-25		—/—	3.5 3H	4.4
MPA3035AT	3500	4	8713	132-25		—/—	3.5 3H	4.4
MPA3043AT	4370	5	8713	132-25		—/—	3.5 3H	4.4
MPA3052AT	5250	6	8713	132-25		—/—	3.5 3H	4.4
MPB3021AT	2160	2	8983	168-30		—/—	3.5 3H	3.7
MPB3032AT	3240	3	8983	168-30		—/—	3.5 3H	4.0
MPB3043AT	4320	4	8983	168-30		—/—	3.5 3H	
MPB3052AT	5240	5	8983	168-30		—/—	3.5 3H	4.5
MPB3064AT	6480	6	8983	168-30		—/—	3.5 3H	

Drive Model	Format Size MB	Seek Time	Interface	Encode	cache kb	RPM
MAS3367NC	36.7GB	3.5	SCA-2	MEEPRML32/34	8mb	1500
MAS3367NP	36.7GB	3.5	UL320 SCSI	MEEPRML32/34	8mb	1500
MAS3735NC	73.5GB	3.5	UL320 SCSI	MEEPRML32/34	8mb	1500
MAS3735NP	73.5GB	3.5	SCA-2	MEEPRML32/34	8mb	1500
MAT3 147GB	147GB		U320/FC		8mb	1000
MAT3 300GB	300GB		U320/FC		8mb	1000
MAT3 73GB	73GB		U320/FC		8mb	1000
MAU 147GB	147GB		U320/FC		8mb	1500
MAU 36GB	36GB		U320/FC		8mb	1500
MAU 73GB	73GB		U320/FC		8mb	1500
MHA2021	2160	13	ATA-3	PRML	128k	4000
MHA2032	3240	13	ATA-3	PRML	128k	4000
MHB2021	2160	13	ATA-3	PRML	128k	4000
MHB2032	3240	13	ATA-3	PRML	128k	4000
MHC2020AT	4090	13	ATA-3	PRML	512k	4000
MHC2040AT	4090	13	ATA-3	EPR4ML	512k	4000
MHD2021AT	2160	13	ATA-3	PRML		4000
MHD2032AT	3250	13	ATA-3	PRML		4000
MHE2043AT	4320	13	ATA-4	16/17 EPR4	512k	4200
MHE2064AT	6400	13	ATA-4	16/17 EPR4	512k	4200
MHF2021AT	2160	13	ATA-4	16/17 EPR4	512k	4200
MHF2043AT	4320	13	ATA-4	16/17 EPR4	512k	4200
MHG2102AT	10000	13	ATA-4		512k	4200
MHH2032AT	3200	13	ATA-4	EPR4ML 16,17	512k	4200
MHH2048AT	4800	13	ATA-4	EPR4ML 16,17	512k	4200
MHH2064AT	6400	13	ATA-4	EPR4ML 16,17	512k	4200
MHJ2181AT	18100	13	ATA-5	MEEPRML	512k	4200
MHK2060AT	6000	13	ATA-5	MEEPRML	512k	4200
MHK2090AT	9000	13	ATA-5	MEEPRML	512k	4200
MHK2120AT	12000	13	ATA-5	MEEPRML	512k	4200
MHL2300AT	30000	12	ATA-5	MEEPRML16/17	2mb	4200
MHM2100AT	10000	12	ATA-5	MEEPRML16/17	2mb	4200
MHM2150AT	15000	12	ATA-5	MEEPRML16/17	2mb	4200
MHM2200AT	20000	12	ATA-5	MEEPRML16/17	2mb	4200
MHN2100AT	10GB	12	ATA-5	MEEPRML16/17	2mb	4200
MHN2150AT	15GB	12	ATA-5	MEEPRML16/17	2mb	4200
MHN2200AT	20GB	12	ATA-5	MEEPRML16/17	2mb	4200
MHN2300AT	30GB	12	ATA-5	MEEPRML16/17	2mb	4200
MHR2010AT	10GB	12	ATA-5	MEEPRML48/50	2mb	4200
MHR2020AT	20GB	12	ATA-5	MEEPRML48/50	2mb	4200
MHR2030AT	30GB	12	ATA-5	MEEPRML48/50	2mb	4200
MHS2020AT	40GB	12	ATA-5	MEEPRML48/50	2mb	4200
MHS2030AT	20GB	12	ATA-6	MEEPRML48/50	2mb	4200
MHS2040AT	30GB	12	ATA-6	MEEPRML48/50	2mb	4200
MHS2060AT	40GB	12	ATA-6	MEEPRML48/50	2mb	4200
	60GB	12	ATA-6	MEEPRML48/50	2mb	4200
MHT-BH 40GB	40GB		SATA II			5400
MHT-BH 60GB	60GB		SATA II			5400
MHT-BH 80GB	80GB		SATA II			5400
MHT2020AT	20GB	12	ATA-6	MEEPRML32/34	2mb	4200
MHT2030AT	30GB	12	ATA-6			4200
MHT2040AH	40GB	12	ATA-6			5400
MHT2040AT	40GB	12	ATA-6		8mb	4200
MHT2060AH	60GB	12	ATA-6	MEEPRML32/34	2mb	5400
MHT2060AT	60GB	12	ATA-6		8mb	4200
MHT2080AH	80GB	12	ATA-6	MEEPRML32/34	2mb	5400
MHT2080AT	80GB	12	ATA-6		8mb	4200
MPA3017AT	1750	10	ATA-3	PRML8,9	128k	5400
MPA3026AT	2620	10	ATA-3	PRML8,9	128k	5400
MPA3035AT	3500	10	ATA-3	PRML8,9	128k	5400
MPA3043AT	4370	10	ATA-3	PRML8,9	128k	5400
MPA3052AT	5250	10	ATA-3	PRML8,9	128k	5400
MPB3021AT	2160	10	ATA-3	PRML8,9	256k	5400
MPB3032AT	3240	10	ATA-3	PRML8,9	256k	5400
MPB3043AT	4320	10	ATA-3	PRML8,9	256k	5400
MPB3052AT	5240	10	ATA-3	PRML8,9	256k	5400
MPB3064AT	6480	10	ATA-3	PRML8,9	256k	5400

Drive Model	Format Size MB	Head	Cyl	Sect/ Trac	Translate H/C/S	RWC/ WPC	Form Factor	Power Watts
MPC3032AT	3240	2	11116	192-33		—/—	3.5 3H	3.4
MPC3043AT	4320	3	11116	192-33		—/—	3.5 3H	3.8
MPC3045AH	4500	4	10424	162-24		—/—	3.5 3H	4.5
MPC3064AT	6480	4	11116	192-33		—/—	3.5 3H	3.8
MPC3065AH	6500	6	10424	162-24		—/—	3.5 3H	4.5
MPC3084AT	8450	6	11116	192-33		—/—	3.5 3H	4.2
MPC3096AT	9740	6	11116	192-33		—/—	3.5 3H	4.2
MPC3102AT	10200	6	11116	192-33		—/—	3.5 3H	4.2
MPD3043AT	4300	2	13033	222-40		—/—	3.5 3H	3.3
MPD3064AT	6400	3	13033	222-40		—/—	3.5 3H	3.7
MPD3084AT	8400	4	13033	222-40		—/—	3.5 3H	3.7
MPD3091AH	9100	4				—/—	3.5 3H	5.5
MPD3108AT	10800	5	13033	222-40		—/—	3.5 3H	4.2
MPD3129AT	12900	6	13033	222-40		—/—	3.5 3H	4.2
MPD3130AT	13000	6	13033	222-40		—/—	3.5 3H	3.8
MPD3137AH	13700	6	12555	250-40		—/—	3.5 3H	5.9
MPD3173AT	17300	8	13033	222-40		—/—	3.5 3H	4.6
MPD3182AH	18200	8	12555	250-40		—/—	3.5 3H	6.3
MPE3043AE	4340	1	17301	334-57		—/—	3.5 3H	3.3
MPE3064AT-AL	6480	2	15264	301-50		—/—	3.5 3H	3.4
MPE3084AE	8450	2	17301	334-57		—/—	3.5 3H	3.3
MPE3084AE	17340	4	17301	334-57		—/—	3.5 3H	3.6
MPE3102AH	10200	3	15871	295-50		—/—	3.5 3H	3.0
MPE3102AT	10240	2	18719	352-62		—/—	3.5 3H	3.7
MPE3102AT-AL	10240	3	15264	301-50		—/—	3.5 3H	3.7
MPE3136AH	13600	4	15871	295-50		—/—	3.5 3H	3.7
MPE3136AT-AL	13660	4	15264	301-50		—/—	3.5 3H	3.0
MPE3153AT	15360	3	18719	352-62		—/—	3.5 3H	4.1
MPE3170AT-AL	17080	5	16348	286-50		—/—	3.5 3H	3.6
MPE3173AE	4300		17301	334-57		—/—	3.5 3H	5.7
MPE3204AH	20400	6	15871	295-50		—/—	3.5 3H	3.5
MPE3204AT	20480	6	18719	352-62		—/—	3.5 3H	4.1
MPE3204AT-AL	20490	6	16348	286-50		—/—	3.5 3H	6.4
MPE3273AH	27300	8	15871	295-50		—/—	3.5 3H	4.6
MPE3273AT-AL	27320	8	16348	286-50		—/—	3.5 3H	5.5
MPF3102AH	10240	2				—/—	3.5 3H	3.5
MPF3102AT	10240	2				—/—	3.5 3H	5.5
MPF3153AH	15360	3				—/—	3.5 3H	5.5
MPF3153AT	15360	3				—/—	3.5 3H	3.5
MPF3204AH	20480	4				—/—	3.5 3H	5.5
MPF3204AT	20480	4				—/—	3.5 3H	3.5
MPG3102AH	10200	2	19424	352-60		—/—	3.5 3H	6.1
MPG3102AT-E	10200	1	30784	441-79		—/—	3.5 3H	6.1
MPG3153AH	15300	3	19424	352-60		—/—	3.5 3H	6.4
MPG3204AH	20400	4	19424	352-60		—/—	3.5 3H	6.4
MPG3204AH-E	20400	2	30784	456-73		—/—	3.5 3H	6.1
MPG3204AT-E	20400	2	30784	441-79		—/—	3.5 3H	6.1
MPG3307AH	30700	4				—/—	3.5 3H	
MPG3307AH-E	30700	4	30784	336-60		—/—	3.5 3H	6.1
MPG3307AH-E	30700	2	28928	357-63		—/—	3.5 3H	6.1
MPG3307AT	20400					—/—	3.5 3H	
MPG33204AH	40900	4	30784	456-73		—/—	3.5 3H	6.1
MPG3409AH-E	40900	4	30784	441-79		—/—	3.5 3H	6.1
MPG3409AT-E								

HEWLETT-PACKARD CO

Drive Model	Format Size MB	Head	Cyl	Sect/ Trac	Translate H/C/S	RWC/ WPC	Form Factor	Power Watts
230534-B21	40GB					—/—	3.5 3H	
23568-B22	72837Mb					—/—	3.5 3H	
23568-B23	72837Mb					—/—	3.5 3H	
236205-B22	36419.2Mb					—/—	3.5 3H	
236205-B23	36419.2Mb					—/—	3.5 3H	
238590-B22	36GB					—/—	3.5 3H	
238590-B23	36GB					—/—	3.5 3H	
238921-B22	72837Mb					—/—	3.5 3H	
238921-B22	36419.2Mb					—/—	3.5 3H	
238921-B23	72837Mb					—/—	3.5 3H	
238921-B23	36419.2Mb					—/—	3.5 3H	
271832-B21	36.4GB					—/—	3.5 3H	
278424-B21	80GB					—/—	3.5 3H	

Drive Model	Format Size MB	Seek Time	Interface	Encode	cache kb	RPM
MPC3032AT	3240		ATA-3	PRML16,17	256k	5400
MPC3043AT	4320		ATA-3	PRML16,17	256k	5400
MPC3045AH	4500	9	ATA-3	PRML8,9	512k	7200
MPC3064AT	6480		ATA-3	PRML16,17	256k	5400
MPC3065AH	6500	9	ATA-3	PRML8,9	512k	7200
MPC3084AT	8450		ATA-3	PRML16,17	256k	5400
MPC3096AT	9740		ATA-3	PRML16,17	256k	5400
MPC3102AT	10200		ATA-3	PRML16,17	256k	5400
MPD3043AT	4300	9.5	ATA-4	16/17 EPR4	512k	5400
MPD3064AT	6400	9.5	ATA-4	16/17 EPR4	512k	5400
MPD3084AT	8400	9.5	ATA-4	16/17 EPR4	512k	5400
MPD3091AH	9100	9	ATA-4		512k	7200
MPD3108AT	10800	9.5	ATA-4		512k	5400
MPD3129AT	12900	9.5	ATA-4	16/17 EPR4	512k	5400
MPD3130AT	13000	9.5	ATA-4	16/17 EPR4	512k	5400
MPD3137AH	13700	9	ATA-4		512k	7200
MPD3173AT	17300	9.5	ATA-4	16/17 EPR4	512k	5400
MPD3182AH	18200	9	ATA-4		512k	7200
MPE3043AE	4340	10.5	ATA-4		512k	7200
MPE3064AT-AL	6480	10.5	ATA-4		512k	5400
MPE3084AE	8450	10.5	ATA-4		512k	5400
MPE3084AE	17340	10.5	ATA-4		512k	5400
MPE3102AH	10200	9.5	ATA-4		512k	5400
MPE3102AT	10240	10.5	ATA-5		2mb	7200
MPE3102AT-AL	10240	10.5	ATA-4		512k	5400
MPE3136AH	13000	9.5	ATA-4		512k	5400
MPE3136AT-AL	13660	10.5	ATA-4		2mb	7200
MPE3153AT	15360	10.5	ATA-5		512k	5400
MPE3170AT-AL	17080	10.5	ATA-4		512k	5400
MPE3173AE	4300	9.5	ATA-4		512k	5400
MPE3204AH	20400	9.5	ATA-4	EPR4ML 48/51	512k	5400
MPE3204AT	20480	10.5	ATA-5		2mb	7200
MPE3204AT-AL	20490	10.5	ATA-4		512k	5400
MPE3273AH	27300	9.5	ATA-4		512k	5400
MPE3273AT-AL	27320	10.5	ATA-4		2mb	7200
MPF3102AH	10240	8.5	ATA-5		512k	5400
MPF3102AT	10240	8.5	ATA-5		2mb	7200
MPF3153AH	15360	8.5	ATA-5	EPR4ML 48,51	512k	5400
MPF3153AT	15360	8.5	ATA-5		2mb	7200
MPF3204AH	20480	8.5	ATA-5	EPR4ML 48,51	512k	5400
MPF3204AT	20480	8.5	ATA-5		2mb	7200
MPG3102AH	10200	9.5	ATA-5	EPR4ML 48,51	512k	5400
MPG3102AT-E	10200	9.5	ATA-5	EPR4ML 48,52	2mb	7200
MPG3153AH	15300	8.5	ATA-5	EPR4ML 48,51	512k	5400
MPG3204AH	20400	9.5	ATA-5	EPR4ML 48,51	2mb	7200
MPG3204AH-E	20400	9.5	ATA-5	EPR4ML 48,51	2mb	7200
MPG3204AT-E	20400	9.5	UltraATA100	EPR4ML 48,52	512k	5400
MPG3307AH	30700	9.5	Ultra ATA		2mb	7200
MPG3307AH-E	30700	9.5	ATA-5	EPR4ML 48,51	2mb	7200
MPG3307AT	30700	9.5	ATA-5	EPR4ML 48,52	512k	5400
MPG33204AH	20400	9.5	UltraATA100			7200
MPG3409AH-E	40900	9.5	ATA-5	EPR4ML 48,51	2mb	7200
MPG3409AT-E	40900	9.5	ATA-5	EPR4ML 48,52	512k	5400

HEWLETT-PACKARD CO

Drive Model	Format Size MB	Seek Time	Interface	Encode	cache kb	RPM
230534-B21	40GB	8.5	ATA 100			7200
23568-B22	72837Mb	5.1	FC-AL 2Gb			1500
23568-B23	72837Mb	5.1	FC-AL 2Gb			1500
236205-B22	36419.2Mb	0.3	FC-AL 2Gb			1500
236205-B23	36419.2Mb	0.3	FC-AL 2Gb			1500
238590-B22	36GB	5.4	FC-AL2GB			1500
238590-B23	36GB	5.4	FC-AL2GB			1000
238921-B22	72837Mb	5.4	FC-AL 2Gb			1000
238921-B22	36419.2Mb	5.4	FC-AL 2Gb			1000
238921-B23	72837Mb	5.4	FC-AL 2Gb			1000
238921-B23	36419.2Mb	5.4	FC-AL 2Gb			1000
271832-B21	36.4GB	5.4	UL320 SCSI			1000
278424-B21	80GB	8.5	ATA 100			7200

Drive Model	Format Size MB	Head	Cyl	Sect/ Trac	Translate H/C/S	RWC/ WPC	Form Factor	Power Watts
286713-B22	36.4GB					—/—	3.5	3H
286714-B22	72.8GB					—/—	3.5	3H
286716-B22	146.8GB					—/—	3.5	3H
286775-B22	18.2GB					—/—	3.5	3H
286776-B22	36.4GB					—/—	3.5	3H
286778-B22	72837.2					—/—	3.5	3H
293556-B22	146.8Mb					—/—	3.5	3H
293556-B23	146.8Mb					—/—	3.5	3H
293568-B22	72GB					—/—	3.5	3H
293568-B23	72GB					—/—	3.5	3H
332751-B21	72.8GB					—/—	3.5	3H
349237-B21	80GB					—/—	3.5	3H
349238-B21	160GB					—/—	3.5	3H
349239-B21	250GB					—/—	3.5	3H
366486-B21	160GB					—/—	3.5	3H
A6060B	36GB					—/—	3.5	3H
A7195A	40GB					—/—	3.5	3H
A7214B	73GB					—/—	3.5	3H
A7836A	36GB					—/—	3.5	3H
A9647A	120GB					—/—	3.5	3H
A9647A	146GB					—/—	3.5	3H
A9648A	250GB					—/—	3.5	3H
AA612A	36GB					—/—	3.5	3H
AA613A	73GB					—/—	3.5	3H
AA614A	146GB					—/—	3.5	3H
AA616A	36GB					—/—	3.5	3H
AA617A	73GB					—/—	3.5	3H
DC180A	40GB					—/—	3.5	3H
DC181A	80GB					—/—	3.5	3H
DC189A	160GB					—/—	3.5	3H
DC516A	250GB					—/—	3.5	3H
DE705A	36GB					—/—	3.5	3H
DE706A	74GB					—/—	3.5	3H
DS702A	80GB					—/—	3.5	3H
DU962A	160GB					—/—	3.5	3H
DX760A	250GB					—/—	3.5	3H
HP97501A	10	2	698	28	8/142/17	—/—	3.5HH	
HP97501B	20	2	1400	28	8/288/17	—/—	3.5HH	
HP97530E	136	4				NA/NA	5.25FH	
HP97530S	204	6				NA/NA	5.25FH	
HP97532D	215	4	1643	64*V		NA/NA	5.25FH	
HP97532E	215	4	1643	64		NA/NA	5.25FH	
HP97532S	215	4	1643	64		NA/NA	5.25FH	
HP97532T	215	4	1643	64		NA/NA	5.25FH	
HP97533D	323	6	1643	64		NA/NA	5.25FH	
HP97533E	323	6	1643	64		NA/NA	5.25FH	
HP97533S	323	6	1643	64		NA/NA	5.25FH	
HP97533T	323	6	1643	64		NA/NA	5.25FH	
HP97536D	646	12	1643	64		NA/NA	5.25FH	
HP97536E	646	12	1643	64		NA/NA	5.25FH	
HP97536S	646	12	1643	64		NA/NA	5.25FH	
HP97536SP	320					—/—	5.25FH	
HP97536SX	322					—/—	5.25FH	
HP97536T	646	12	1643	64		NA/NA	5.25FH	
HP97536TA	320					—/—	5.25HH	
HP97544D	331	8	1447	56		NA/NA	5.25FH	
HP97544E	337	8	1447	56		NA/NA	5.25FH	
HP97544P	331	8	1447	56		NA/NA	5.25FH	
HP97544S	331	8	1447	56		—/—	5.25FH	
HP97544SA	331					NA/NA	5.25FH	
HP97544T	331	8	1447	56		NA/NA	5.25FH	
HP97548D	663	16	1447	56		NA/NA	5.25FH	
HP97548E	675	16	1447	56		NA/NA	5.25FH	
HP97548P	663	16	1447	56		NA/NA	5.25FH	
HP97548S	663	16	1447	56		—/—	5.25FH	
HP97548SZ	663					NA/NA	5.25FH	
HP97548T	663	16	1447	56		NA/NA	5.25FH	

Drive Model	Format Size MB	Seek Time	Interface	Encode	cache kb	RPM
286713-B22	36.4GB	4.9	UL320 SCSI			1000
286714-B22	72.8GB	4.9	UL320 SCSI			1000
286716-B22	146.8GB	4.9	UL320 SCSI			1000
286775-B22	18.2GB	3.8	UL320 SCSI			1500
286776-B22	36.4GB	3.8	UL320 SCSI			1500
286778-B22	72837.2	3.8	UL320 SCSI			1500
293556-B22	146.8Mb	4.9	FC-AL 2Gb			1000
293556-B23	146.8Mb	4.9	FC-AL 2Gb			1000
293568-B22	72GB	11	FC			1500
293568-B23	72GB	11	FC			1500
332751-B21	72.8GB	4.9	UL320 SCSI			1000
349237-B21	80GB	9	SATA			7200
349238-B21	160GB	9	SATA			7200
349239-B21	250GB	10	SATA			7200
366486-B21	160GB	10	ATA 100			7200
A6060B	36GB	4.5	UL320 SCSI			1000
A7195A	40GB	9.0	UltraATA100		2mb	7200
A7214A	73GB	3.8	UL320 SCSI			1500
A7836A	36GB	3.7	UL320 SCSI			1500
A9647A	120GB	9.0	UltraATA100		2mb	7200
A9647A	146GB	4.9	UL320 SCSI			1000
A9648A	250GB	9.0	UltraATA100		8mb	7200
AA612A	36GB	4.5	UL320 SCSI			1000
AA613A	73GB	4.9	UL320 SCSI			1000
AA614A	146GB	4.9	UL320 SCSI			1000
AA616A	36GB	3.7	UL320 SCSI			1500
AA617A	73GB	3.8	UL320 SCSI			1500
DC180A	40GB	9.0	UltraATA100		2mb	7200
DC181A	80GB	9.0	UltraATA100		2mb	7200
DC189A	160GB	9.0	UltraATA100		2mb	7200
DC516A	250GB	9.0	UltraATA100		8mb	7200
DE705A	36GB	5.2	ESATA		8mb	1000
DE706A	74GB	4.5	ESATA		8mb	1000
DS702A	80GB	9.3	SATA		8mb	7200
DU962A	160GB	9.3	SATA		8mb	7200
DX760A	250GB	9.0	SATA		8mb	7200
HP97501A	10	75		MFM		
HP97501B	20			MFM		
HP97530E	136	18	ESDI	2,7 RLL		
HP97530S	204	18	SCSI	2,7 RLL		
HP97532D	215	17	SCSI	2,7 RLL	16k	3348
HP97532E	215	17	ESDI (10)	2,7 RLL	16k	3348
HP97532S	215	17	SCSI	2,7 RLL	16k	3348
HP97532T	215	17	SCSI	2,7 RLL	16k	3348
HP97533D	323	17	SCSI	2,7 RLL	16k	3348
HP97533E	323	17	ESDI	2,7 RLL	16k	3348
HP97533S	323	17	SCSI	2,7 RLL	16k	3348
HP97533T	323	17	SCSI	2,7 RLL	16k	3348
HP97536D	646	17	SCSI	2,7 RLL	16k	3348
HP97536E	646	17	ESDI	2,7 RLL	16k	3348
HP97536S	646	17	SCSI	2,7 RLL	16k	3348
HP97536SP	320		SCSI	2,7 RLL		
HP97536SX	322		SCSI	2,7 RLL		
HP97536T	646	17	SCSI	2,7 RLL	16k	3348
HP97536TA	320		SCSI	2,7 RLL		
HP97544D	331	16	SCSI	2,7 RLL	64k	4002
HP97544E	337	17	ESDI	2,7 RLL	64k	4002
HP97544P	331	17	SCSI-2	2,7 RLL	64k	4002
HP97544S	331	16	SCSI	2,7 RLL	64k	4002
HP97544SA	331		SCSI	2,7 RLL		
HP97544T	331	17	SCSI-2	2,7 RLL	64k	4002
HP97548D	663	16	SCSI	2,7 RLL	64k	4002
HP97548E	675	17	ESDI	2,7 RLL	64k	4002
HP97548P	663	17	SCSI-2	2,7 RLL	64k	4002
HP97548S	663	16	SCSI	2,7 RLL	64k	4002
HP97548SZ	663		SCSI	2,7 RLL		
HP97548T	663	17	SCSI-2	2,7 RLL	64k	4002

Drive Model	Format Size MB	Head	Cyl	Sect/ Trac	Translate H/C/S	RWC/ WPC	Form Factor	Power Watts
HP97549P	1001	16	1911	64		NA/NA	5.25FH	
HP97549T	1001	16	1911	69		NA/NA	5.25FH	
HP97556	786					—/—	5.25FH	
HP97556E	688	11	1697	72		NA/NA	5.25FH	
HP97556P	677	11	1670	72		NA/NA	5.25FH	
HP97556T	677	11	1670	72		NA/NA	5.25FH	
HP97558E	1084	15	1962	72		NA/NA	5.25FH	
HP97558P	1069	15	1935	72		NA/NA	5.25FH	
HP97558T	1069	15	1935	72		NA/NA	5.25FH	
HP97560	1300					—/—	5.25FH	
HP97560E	1374	19	1962	72		NA/NA	5.25FH	
HP97560P	1355	19	1935	72		NA/NA	5.25FH	
HP97560T	1355	19	1935	72		NA/NA	5.25FH	
HPC2233 ATA	238	5	1546	V	16/462/63	NA/NA	3.5HH	
HPC2233S	234	5	1546	V		NA/NA	3.5HH	
HPC2234 ATA	334	7	1546	V	16/647/63	NA/NA	3.5HH	
HPC2234S	328	7	1546	V		NA/NA	3.5HH	
HPC2235A	429					NA/NA	FH	11.6
HPC2235S	422	9	1546	V		NA/NA	3.5HH	
HPC2244	566	7	2051	79		—/—	3.5HH	
HPC2245	728	9	2051	79		—/—	3.5HH	
HPC2246	890	11	2051	79		—/—	3.5HH	
HPC2247	1052	13	1981	56-96		NA/NA	3.5HH	
HPC2247D	1052	13	1981	56-96		NA/NA	3.5HH	
HPC2247SE	1052	13	1981	56-96		NA/NA	3.5HH	
HPC2247W	1052	13	1981	56-96		NA/NA	3.5HH	
HPC2270S	320					—/—	5.25FH	
HPC2271S	663					—/—	5.25FH	
HPC2490D	2100	18	2582	68-108		—/—	3.5HH	16
HPC2490SE	2100	18	2582	68-108		—/—	3.5HH	
HPC2490W	2100	18	2582	68-108		—/—	3.5HH	
HPC3007	1370		2255			NA/NA	FH	
HPC3009	1792		2255			NA/NA	FH	
HPC3010	2003					NA/NA	FH	
HPC3013A	21	3	700		4/615/17	—/—	1.3 4H	
HPC3014A	42	4	786			—/—	1.3 4H	
HPC3031A	21	3				—/—	1.3 4H	
HPC3323D	1050	7	2910	72-120		NA/NA	3.5 3H	
HPC3323SE	1050	7	2910	72-120		NA/NA	3.5 3H	
HPC3323W	1050	7	2910	72-120		NA/NA	3.5 3H	
HPC3324	1050	9	3703	100		—/—	3.5 3H	
HPC3325A	2170	9	3610	100-14		—/—	3.5 3H	7.5
HPC3335 ATA	429	9	1546	V		NA/NA	3.5HH	
HPC3550	2000					—/—	3.5HH	
HPC3555	1000					—/—	3.5HH	
HPC3653A	8700	20	5371	124-17		—/—	3.5HH	12
HPC3724D	1200	5	3610	100-14		NA/NA	3.5 3H	7.6
HPC3724S	1200	5	3610	100-14		NA/NA	3.5 3H	7.5
HPC3724W	1200	5	3610	100-14		NA/NA	3.5 3H	7.6
HPC3725D	2170	9	3610	100-14		—/—	3.5 3H	7.6
HPC3725S	2170	9	3610	100-14		—/—	3.5 3H	7.5
HPC3725W	2170	9	3610	100-14		—/—	3.5 3H	7.6
HPC5270A	1084	4		91-155		—/—	3.5HH	3.64
HPC5271A	1626	6		91-155		—/—	3.5HH	3.64
HPC5272A	1336	4		94-162		—/—	3.5 3H	4.4
HPC5273A	2004	6		94-162		—/—	3.5 3H	4.4
HPC5273AK	1336	4		94-162		—/—	3.5 3H	4.40
HPC5280A	1084	4		91-155		—/—	3.5 3H	3.64
HPC5281A	1626	6		91-155		—/—	3.5 3H	3.64
HPC5283A	2004	6		94-162		—/—	3.5 3H	4.4
HPC5421SK	8700	20	5371	124-17		—/—	3.5HH	12
HPC5421TK	8700	20	5371	124-17		—/—	3.5HH	12
HPC5435A	1336	4		94-162		—/—	3.5 3H	4.4
HPC5435AK	1300					—/—	3.5 3H	4.4
HPC5436AK	2004	6		94-162		—/—	3.5 3H	4.40
HPC6516A	4200					—/—	3.5 3H	
HPC6517A	9100					—/—	3.5 3H	

Drive Model	Format Size MB	Seek Time	Interface	Encode	cache kb	RPM
HP97549P	1001	17	SCSI-2	2,7 RLL	128k	4002
HP97549T	1001	17	SCSI-2	2,7 RLL	128k	4002
HP97556	786			2,7 RLL		
HP97556E	688	14	ESDI	2,7 RLL	128k	4002
HP97556P	677	14	SCSI-2	2,7 RLL	128k	4002
HP97556T	677	14	SCSI-2	2,7 RLL	128k	4002
HP97558E	1084	14	ESDI	2,7 RLL	128k	4002
HP97558P	1069	14	SCSI-2	2,7 RLL	128k	4002
HP97558T	1069	14	SCSI-2	2,7 RLL	128k	4002
HP97560	1300		SCSI-2	2,7 RLL		
HP97560E	1374	14	ESDI	2,7 RLL	128k	4002
HP97560P	1355	14	SCSI-2	2,7 RLL	128k	4002
HP97560T	1355	14	SCSI-2	2,7 RLL	128k	4002
HPC2233 ATA	238	12.6	IDE AT	2,7 RLL	64k	3600
HPC2233S	234	12	SCSI-2	2,7 RLL	64k	3600
HPC2234 ATA	334	12.6	IDE AT	2,7 RLL	64k	3600
HPC2234S	328	12	SCSI-2	2,7 RLL	64k	3600
HPC2235A	429	13	ATA			
HPC2235S	422	12	SCSI-2	2,7 RLL	64k	3600
HPC2244	566	10	SCSI-2	1,7 RLL	256k	5400
HPC2245	728	10	SCSI-2	1,7 RLL	256k	5400
HPC2246	890	10	SCSI-2	1,7 RLL	256k	5400
HPC2247	1052	10	SCSI-2	1,7 RLL	256k	5400
HPC2247D	1052	10	SCSI-2Diff	1,7 RLL	256k	5400
HPC2247SE	1052	10	SCSI-2	1,7 RLL	256k	5400
HPC2247W	1052	10	SCSI-2FstW	1,7 RLL	256k	5400
HPC2270S	320		SCSI			
HPC2271S	663		SCSI			
HPC2490D	2100	9	SCSI-2Diff			6400
HPC2490SE	2100	9	SCSI			6400
HPC2490W	2100	9	SCSI-2FstW			6400
HPC3007	1370	12	SCSI-2		256k	5400
HPC3009	1792	12	SCSI-2		256k	5400
HPC3010	2003	12	SCSI-2		256k	5400
HPC3013A	21	15	IDE AT	1,7 RLL		
HPC3014A	42	18	IDE			5310
HPC3031A	21	18	IDE			5310
HPC3323D	1050	9.5	SCSI-2Diff		512k	5400
HPC3323SE	1050	9.5	SCSI-2		512k	5400
HPC3323W	1050	9.5	SCSI-2Diff		512k	5400
HPC3324	1050	9.5	SCSI-2	1,7 RLL	512k	5400
HPC3325A	2170	10.5	SCSI-2	PRML	512k	5400
HPC3335 ATA	429	12.6	IDE AT	2,7 RLL	64k	3600
HPC3550	2000		SCSI-2FstW			
HPC3555	1000		SCSI-2FstW			
HPC3653A	8700	9	SE SCSI	PRML	512k	7200
HPC3724D	1200	9.5	SCSI-2Diff			5400
HPC3724S	1200	9.5	SCSI-2			5400
HPC3724W	1200	9.5	SCSI-2FstW			5400
HPC3725D	2170	9.5	SCSI-2Diff			5400
HPC3725S	2170	9.5	SCSI-2			5400
HPC3725W	2170	9.5	SCSI-2Diff			5400
HPC5270A	1084	<12	EIDE/ATA-2		128k	4480
HPC5271A	1626	<12	EIDE/ATA-2		128k	4480
HPC5272A	1336	<12	EIDE/AT		64k	4480
HPC5273A	2004	<12	EIDE/AT	1,7 RLL	64k	4480
HPC5273AK	1336	<12	EIDE/ATA-2	1,7 RLL	128k	4480
HPC5280A	1084	<12	EIDE		128k	4480
HPC5281A	1626	<12	EIDE		128k	4480
HPC5283A	2004	<12	EIDE/AT	1,7 RLL	128k	4480
HPC5421SK	8700	8.7	SE SCSI	PRML	512k	7200
HPC5421TK	8700	8.7	SE SCSI-2W	PRML	512k	7200
HPC5435A	1336	<12	EIDE/AT	1,7 RLL	64k	4480
HPC5435AK	1300	<12	EIDE	1,7 RLL	64k	4480
HPC5436AK	2004	<12	EIDE/ATA-2	1,7 RLL	128k	4480
HPC6516A	4200	7.5	Ultra Wide		384k	7200
HPC6517A	9100	7.5	Ultra Wide		384k	7200

Drive Model	Format Size MB	Head	Cyl	Sect/Trac	Translate H/C/S	RWC/WPC	Form Factor	Power Watts
HPC6526A (rackable)	4200					—/—	3.5 3H	
HPC6527A (rackable)	9100					—/—	3.5 3H	
HPC6534A	4500					—/—	3.5 3H	
HPC6535A (rackable)	4500					—/—	3.5 3H	
HPC6536A	9100					—/—	3.5 3H	
HPC6537A (rackable)	9100					—/—	3.5 3H	
HPC6538A	18200					—/—	3.5 3H	
HPC6539A (rackable)	18200					—/—	3.5 3H	
HPC6544A (rackable)	18200					—/—		
HPC6545A (rackable)	18200					—/—		
HPD1296A	21	4	615	17		0/300	5.25HH	
HPD1297A	42	6	820	17		—/—	5.25HH	
HPD1660A	340	8	1457	57		NA/NA	5.25HH	
HPD1661A	680	16	1457	57		NA/NA	5.25HH	
HPD1674A	108	6	820	40		—/—	5.25FH	
HPD1675A	155	6	820	40		—/—	5.25FH	
HPD1676A	310	6	820	40		—/—	5.25FH	
HPD1697A	240	4	1800		8/930/63	—/—	3.5 3H	
HPD2076B	1050					—/—		
HPD2077A	2100	8				—/—	3.5 3H	
HPD2389A	540					—/—	3.5	
HPD3340A	2100					—/—		
HPD3341A	4200					—/—		
HPD4884A	2130	5				—/—	3.5 3H	
HPD4910A	4260	5				—/—	3.5 3H	
HPD4911A	9100	10				—/—	3.5 3H	
HPD4956A	4260	10				—/—	3.5 3H	
HPD4963A	4260	6				—/—	3.5 3H	

HITACHI AMERICA

Drive Model	Format Size MB	Head	Cyl	Sect/Trac	Translate H/C/S	RWC/WPC	Form Factor	Power Watts
DK211A-51	510	6				NA/NA	2.5 4H	2.0
DK211A-54	540	16	1047	63	16/1047/63	NA/NA	2.5 4H	
DK211A-68	680				16/1384/60	—/—	2.5 4H	
DK211C-51	510	6				NA/NA	2.5 4H	
DK212A-10	1080	8				—/—	2.5 4H	2.0
DK212A-81	810	8				—/—	2.5 4H	2.0
DK213A-13	1350	10	2605			—/—	2.5 4H	1.3
DK213A-18	1800				16/3491/63	—/—	2.5 4H	
DK221A-34	340	4			16/692/60	NA/NA	2.5 4H	2.0
DK222A-27	270	2				—/—	2.5 4H	2.0
DK222A-54	540	4				—/—	2.5 4H	2.0
DK223A-11	1080				16/2095/63	—/—	2.5 4H	
DK223A-81	810	6	2605			—/—	2.5 4H	1.1
DK224A-14	1440				16/2792/63	—/—	2.5 4H	
DK225A-14	1440	16	4188	63	16/2792/63	—/—	2.5 4H	
DK225A-21	2160				16/4188/63	—/—	2.5 4H	
DK226A-21	2160	2				—/—	2.5 4H	2.35
DK226A-21U	2160	2				—/—	2.5 4H	2.35
DK226A-32	3240				16/6282/63	—/—	2.5 4H	
DK226A-32U	3240				16/6282/63	—/—	2.5 4H	
DK227A-41	4090					—/—	2.5 4H	
DK227A-50	5020					—/—	2.5 4H	
DK228A-65	6490	3				—/—	2.5 4H	2.3
DK229A-10	10000	3				—/—	2.5 4H	
DK229A-10U	10000	3				—/—	2.5 4H	
DK22AA-18	18140					—/—	2.5	
DK237A-32	3240					—/—	2.5 4H	0.95
DK237A-32	3240	2				—/—	2.5 4H	0.95
DK237A-32U	3240	2				—/—	2.5 4H	0.75
DK238A-32	3250	2				—/—	2.5 4H	0.75
DK238A-32U	3250	2				—/—	2.5 4H	0.75
DK238A-43	4327	2			15/8944/63	—/—	2.5 4H	0.75
DK238A-43U	4330	2				—/—	2.5 4H	0.75
DK239A-48	4870	2				—/—	2.5 4H	
DK239A-65	6490	2				—/—	2.5 4H	0.75
DK239A-65U	6490	2				—/—	2.5 4H	0.75
DK23AA-12	12070					—/—	2.5 4H	
DK23AA-60	6010					—/—	2.5 4H	

Drive Model	Format Size MB	Seek Time	Interface	Encode	cache kb	RPM
HPC6526A (rackable)	4200	7.5	Ultra Wide		384k	7200
HPC6527A (rackable)	9100	7.5	Ultra Wide		384k	7200
HPC6534A	4500	7.5	Ultra2SCSIW		1mb	1002
HPC6535A (rackable)	4500	7.5	Ultra2SCSIW		1mb	1002
HPC6536A	9100	7.5	Ultra2SCSIW		4mb	1002
HPC6537A (rackable)	9100	7.5	Ultra2SCSIW		4mb	1002
HPC6538A	18200	7.5	Ultra2SCSIW		4mb	7200
HPC6539A (rackable)	18200	7.5	Ultra2SCSIW		4mb	7200
HPC6544A (rackable)	18200	7.5	Ultra2SCSIW		4mb	1000
HPC6545A (rackable)	18200	7.5	Ultra2SCSIW		4mb	1000
HPD1296A	21	65	ST412/506	MFM		
HPD1297A	42	65	ST412/506	MFM		
HPD1660A	340	16	ESDI (15)	2,7 RLL	64k	
HPD1661A	680	16	ESDI (15)	2,7 RLL	64k	
HPD1674A	108	40	ST412/506	MFM		
HPD1675A	155	40	ESDI (15)	2,7 RLL		
HPD1676A	310	40	ESDI (15)	2,7 RLL		
HPD1697A	240	17	IDE AT	1,7 RLL		
HPD2076B	1050	10.5	SCSI-2Fast		256k	5400
HPD2077A	2100	10.5	SCSI-2Fast		256k	5400
HPD2389A	540	14	IDE AT			3600
HPD3340A	2100	8.4	SCSI-2		512k	5400
HPD3341A	4200	8.4	SCSI-2		512k	5400
HPD4884A	2130	12	SCSI-2		128k	4500
HPD4910A	4260	8.3	SCSI-2		384k	7200
HPD4911A	9100	8.3	SCSI-2		384k	7200
HPD4956A	4260	9.5	SCSI-2		512k	7200
HPD4963A	4260	9	SCSI-2		512k	5400

HITACHI AMERICA

Drive Model	Format Size MB	Seek Time	Interface	Encode	cache kb	RPM
DK211A-51	510	12.6	IDE AT		64k	4464
DK211A-54	540	12	ATA		64k	4464
DK211A-68	680	12	IDE AT		64k	4464
DK211C-51	510	12.6	SCSI-2Fast		512k	
DK212A-10	1080	12	EIDE/ATA-2	PRML8,9	64k	4464
DK212A-81	810	12	EIDE/ATA-2	PRML8,9	64k	4464
DK213A-13	1350	12	ATA-2	PRML8,9	128k	4464
DK213A-18	1800	12	ATA-2		128k	4464
DK221A-34	340	12.6	IDE AT		64k	4464
DK222A-27	270	12	EIDE/ATA-2	PRML8,9	64k	4464
DK222A-54	540	12	EIDE/ATA-2	PRML8,9	64k	4464
DK223A-11	1080	12	ATA-2		128k	4464
DK223A-81	810	12	ATA-2	PRML8,9	128k	4464
DK224A-14	1440	12	ATA-2		128k	4464
DK225A-14	1440	12	ATA-3		128k	4464
DK225A-21	2160	12	ATA-2 Fast		128k	4464
DK226A-21	2160	12	ATA-3		128k	4000
DK226A-21U	2160	12	Ultra DMA		128k	4000
DK226A-32	3240	12	ATA-3		128k	4000
DK226A-32U	3240	12	Ultra DMA		128k	4000
DK227A-41	4090	12	ATA-3	EPRML 16,17	512k	
DK227A-50	5020	12	ATA-3		512k	
DK228A-65	6490	12	ATA-4		512k	4200
DK229A-10	10000	12	ATA-4		512k	4200
DK229A-10U	10000	12	Ultra DMA		512k	4200
DK22AA-18	18140	12	ATA-5	PRML	512k	4200
DK237A-32	3240	12	ATA-3	EPRML 16,17	512k	
DK237A-32	3240	12	ATA-3		512k	4000
DK237A-32U	3240	12	Ultra DMA		512k	4000
DK238A-32	3250	12	ATA-4		512k	4200
DK238A-32U	3250	12	Ultra DMA		512k	4200
DK238A-43	4327	12	ATA-4		512k	4200
DK238A-43U	4330	12	Ultra DMA		512k	4200
DK239A-48	4870	12	ATA-4	PRML	512k	4200
DK239A-65	6490	12	ATA-4		512k	4200
DK239A-65U	6490	12	Ultra DMA		512k	4200
DK23AA-12	12070	12	ATA-5	PRML	512k	4200
DK23AA-60	6010	12	ATA-5	PRML	512k	4200

Drive Model	Format Size MB	Head	Cyl	Sect/Trac	Translate H/C/S	RWC/WPC	Form Factor	Power Watts
DK23AA-90	9040	1				—/—	2.5 4H	
DK23BA-10	10.06GB	1				—/—	2.5 4H	
DK23BA-20	20GB	1				—/—	2.5 4H	
DK23BA-60	6.01GB	1				—/—	2.5 4H	
DK23CA-10	10.056GB	1				—/—	2.5 4H	
DK23CA-15	15.103GB	1				—/—	2.5 4H	
DK23CA-20	20.003GB	1				—/—	2.5 4H	
DK23CA-30	30.005GB	1				—/—	2.5 4H	
DK23CA-75	7.501GB	1				—/—	2.5 4H	
DK23DA-10F	10GB					—/—	2.5 4H	
DK23DA-20F	20GB					—/—	2.5 4H	
DK23DA-30F	30GB					—/—	2.5 4H	
DK23DA-40F	40GB					—/—	2.5 4H	
DK23EA-30	30.005GB	2	42091			—/—	2.5 4H	
DK23EA-40	40.007GB	3	42091			—/—	2.5 4H	
DK23EA-60	60.011GB	4	42091			—/—	2.5 4H	
DK23EB-20	20GB	2				—/—	2.5 4H	
DK23EB-40	40.007GB	4	32081			—/—	2.5 4H	
DK23FB-20	20GB	2				—/—	2.5 4H	1.10
DK23FB-40	40GB	3				—/—	2.5 4H	1.10
DK23FB-60	60GB	4				—/—	2.5 4H	1.10
DK301-1	10	4	306	17		—/—	3.5HH	
DK301-2	15	6	306	17		—/—	3.5HH	
DK312C-20	209	9	1076	38		—/—	3.5HH	
DK312C-25	251	11	1076	38		—/—	3.5HH	
DK314C-41	419	14		17		—/—	3.5HH	
DK315C-10	1000	11				NA/NA	3.5HH	
DK315C-11	1100	15				NA/NA	3.5HH	
DK315C-14	1400	15				NA/NA	3.5HH	
DK318H-91	9100	20				—/—	3.5HH	0.8
DK31H-18	18200					—/—	3.5	
DK31AH-36LC	36800	10	11767			—/—	3.5HH	12.6
DK31AH-36LW	36800	10	11767			—/—	3.5HH	12.6
DK31CJ-72FC	73900					—/—	3.5HH	
DK31CJ-72NC	73900					—/—	3.5HH	
DK31CJ-72NW	73900					—/—	3.5HH	
DK325C-57	573	6	2458	75		NA/NA	5.25HH	
DK326C-10	1050	8				NA/NA	3.5 3H	9.5
DK326C-10WD	1050	7				NA/NA	3.5 3H	9.5
DK326C-6	601	4				NA/NA	3.5 3H	
DK326C-6WD	601	4				NA/NA	3.5 3H	
DK328C-10	1050	3				—/—	3.5 3H	9.5
DK328C-21	2100	5				—/—	3.5 3H	9.5
DK328C-43	4300	10				—/—	3.5 3H	9.5
DK328H-43	4370	10				—/—	3.5 3H	0.5
DK329H-91	9100					—/—	3.5	
DK32AH-18LC	18400	5	11767			—/—	3.5 3H	8.1
DK32AH-18LW	18400	5	11767			—/—	3.5 3H	8.1
DK32AH-91	9100	3	11767			—/—	3.5 3H	8.1
DK32CJ-18FC	18400					—/—	3.5 3H	
DK32CJ-18MC	18400					—/—	3.5 3H	
DK32CJ-18MW	18400					—/—	3.5 3H	
DK32CJ-36FC	36900					—/—	3.5 3H	
DK32CJ-36MC	36900	12				—/—	3.5 3H	
DK32CJ-36MW	36900	12				—/—	3.5 3H	
DK32CJ-72	73900					—/—	3.5FH	
DK32CJ-72	73900					—/—	3.5FH	
DK32DJ-18FC	18.4GB	3				—/—	3.5 3H	
DK32DJ-18MC	18.4GB	3				—/—	3.5 3H	
DK32DJ-18MW	18.4GB	3				—/—	3.5 3H	
DK32DJ-36FC	36.9GB	3				—/—	3.5 3H	
DK32DJ-36MC	36.9GB	3				—/—	3.5 3H	
DK32DJ-36MW	36.9GB	3				—/—	3.5 3H	
DK32DJ-72FC	73.9GB	5				—/—	3.5 3H	
DK32DJ-72MC	73.9GB	5				—/—	3.5 3H	
DK32DJ-72MW	73.9GB	5				—/—	3.5 3H	
DK32EJ-14FC	147.8GB					—/—	3.5 3H	

Drive Model	Format Size MB	Seek Time	Interface	Encode	cache kb	RPM
DK23AA-90	9040	12	ATA-5	PRML	512k	4200
DK23BA-10	10.06GB	12	ATA-5	MEEPRML	512k	4200
DK23BA-20	20GB	12	ATA-5	MEEPRML	512k	4200
DK23BA-60	6.01GB	12	ATA-5	MEEPRML	512k	4200
DK23CA-10	10.056GB	12	ATA-5	MEEPRML	512k	4200
DK23CA-15	15.103GB	12	ATA-5	MEEPRML	512k	4200
DK23CA-20	20.003GB	12	ATA-5	MEEPRML	512k	4200
DK23CA-30	30.005GB	12	ATA-5	MEEPRML	512k	4200
DK23CA-75	7.501GB	12	ATA-5	MEEPRML	512k	4200
DK23DA-10F	10GB	13	ATA-5		2mb	4200
DK23DA-20F	20GB	13	ATA-5		2mb	4200
DK23DA-30F	30GB	13	ATA-5		2mb	4200
DK23DA-40F	40GB	13	ATA-5		2mb	4200
DK23EA-30	30.005GB	13	ATA-5	MEEPRML	2mb	4200
DK23EA-40	40.007GB	13	ATA-5	MEEPRML	2mb	2048
DK23EA-60	60.011GB	13	ATA-5	MEEPRML	2mb	2048
DK23EB-20	20GB	13	ATA-5	ME2PRML	2mb	2048
DK23EB-40	40.007GB	13	ATA-5	MEEPRML	2mb	5400
DK23FB-20	20GB	13	ATA-5		8mb	5400
DK23FB-40	40GB	13	ATA-5		8mb	5400
DK23FB-60	60GB	13	ATA-5		8mb	5400
DK301-1	10	85	ST412/506	MFM		
DK301-2	15	85	ST412/506	MFM		
DK312C-20	209	17	SCSI	2,7 RLL		3600
DK312C-25	251	17	SCSI	2,7 RLL		3600
DK314C-41	419	17	SCSI	2,7 RLL		3600
DK315C-10	1000	11.8	SCSI-2Fast		64k	
DK315C-11	1100	11	SCSI-2Fast		256k	4500
DK315C-14	1400	11	SCSI-2Fast		256k	4500
DK318H-91	9100	9	Ultra SCSI		256k	7200
DK319H-18	18200	7.5	Ultra SCSI	PRML	512k	7200
DK31AH-36LC	36800	7	Ultra2 SCSI		512k	7200
DK31AH-36LW	36800	7	Ultra2SCSIW		2mb	7200
DK31CJ-72FC	73900	5.7	FC-AL		2mb	1002
DK31CJ-72NC	73900	5.7	Ultra 160		4mb	1002
DK31CJ-72NW	73900	5.7	UL160SCSIW		4mb	1002
DK325C-57	573	12	SCSI-2	1,7 RLL	4mb	1002
DK326C-10	1050	9.8	SCSI-2Fast		448k	6300
DK326C-10WD	1050	9.8	SCSI-2FstW		448k	6300
DK326C-6	601	<10	SCSI-2Fast		448k	
DK326C-6WD	601	<10	SCSI-2FstW		448k	
DK328C-10	1050	9.8	SE SCSI-2F		512k	5400
DK328C-21	2100	9.8	SE SCSI-2D		512k	5400
DK328C-43	4300	9.8	SE SCSI-2F		512k	5400
DK328H-43	4370	9	Ultra SCSI		512k	7200
DK329H-91	9100	7.5	Ultra SCSI	PRML	512k	7200
DK32AH-18LC	18400	6.8	Ultra2 SCSI		2mb	7200
DK32AH-18LW	18400	6.8	Ultra2SCSIW		2mb	7200
DK32AH-91	9100	6.8	Ultra2 LVD	PRML	2mb	7200
DK32CJ-18FC	18400	6.0	FC-AL	PRML	4mb	1002
DK32CJ-18MC	18400	6.0	UL160SCSI	PRML	4mb	1002
DK32CJ-18MW	18400	6.0	UL160SCSIW	PRML	4mb	1002
DK32CJ-36FC	36900	6.0	FC-AL	PRML	4mb	1002
DK32CJ-36MC	36900	6.0	UL160SCSI	PRML	4mb	1002
DK32CJ-36MW	36900	6.0	UL160SCSIW	PRML	4mb	1002
DK32CJ-72	73900	6.5	UL160SCSIS	PRML	4mb	1002
DK32CJ-72	73900	6.5	FC-AL	PRML	4mb	1002
DK32DJ-18FC	18.4GB	4.9	FC-AL	MEEPRML	16mb	1002
DK32DJ-18MC	18.4GB	4.9	Ultra 160	MEEPRML	16mb	1002
DK32DJ-18MW	18.4GB	4.9	UL320 SCSI	MEEPRML	16mb	1002
DK32DJ-36FC	36.9GB	4.9	FC-AL	MEEPRML	16mb	1002
DK32DJ-36MC	36.9GB	4.9	Ultra 160	MEEPRML	16mb	1002
DK32DJ-36MW	36.9GB	4.9	UL320 SCSI	MEEPRML	16mb	1002
DK32DJ-72FC	73.9GB	4.9	FC-AL	MEEPRML	16mb	1002
DK32DJ-72MC	73.9GB	4.9	Ultra 160	MEEPRML	16mb	1002
DK32DJ-72MW	73.9GB	4.9	UL320 SCSI	MEEPRML	16mb	1002
DK32EJ-14FC	147.8GB	4.9	FC 2Gb		16mb	1002

Drive Model	Format Size MB	Head	Cyl	Sect/Trac	Translate H/C/S	RWC/WPC	Form Factor	Power Watts
DK32EJ-14NC	147.8GB					—/—	3.5 3H	
DK32EJ-14NW	147.8GB					—/—	3.5 3H	
DK32EJ-36FC	36.9GB					—/—	3.5 3H	
DK32EJ-36NC	36.9GB					—/—	3.5 3H	
DK32EJ-36NW	36.9GB					—/—	3.5 3H	
DK32EJ-72FC	73.9GB					—/—	3.5 3H	
DK32EJ-72NC	73.9GB					—/—	3.5 3H	
DK32EJ-72NW	73.9GB					—/—	3.5HH	
DK3E1T-91	9200	9					5.25HH	
DK503-2	10					—/—	5.25HH	
DK505-2	21	4	615	17		—/—	5.25FH	
DK511-3	29	5	699	17		—/300	5.25FH	
DK511-5	41	7	699	17		—/300	5.25FH	
DK511-8	67	10	823	17		—/400	5.25FH	
DK512-12	94	7	823			NA/NA	5.25FH	
DK512-17	134	10	823			NA/NA	5.25FH	
DK512-8	67	5	823			NA/NA	5.25FH	
DK512C-12	94	7	823			—/—	5.25FH	
DK512C-17	134	10	819	35		—/—	5.25FH	
DK512C-8	67	5	823			—/—	5.25FH	
DK512S-17	143					—/—	5.25FH	
DK514-38	330	14	903	51		NA/NA	5.25FH	
DK514C-38	322	14	898	50		—/—	5.25FH	
DK514S-38	332					—/—	5.25FH	
DK515-12	1229	15		69		NA/NA	5.25FH	
DK515-78	673	14	1361	69		—/—	5.25FH	
DK515C-78	670	14	1356	69		—/—	5.25FH	
DK515C-78D	673	14	1361	69		NA/NA	5.25FH	
DK515S-78	673	14				—/—	5.25FH	
DK516-12	1230	15	1787			—/—	5.25FH	
DK516-15	1320	15	2235			NA/NA	5.25FH	
DK516C-16	1340	15	2172			—/—	5.25FH	
DK517C-26	2000	14				NA/NA	5.25FH	
DK517C-37	2900	21				NA/NA	5.25FH	
DK521-5	51	6	823	17		—/NONE	5.25HH	
DK522-10	91	6	823	36		NA/NA	5.25HH	
DK522C-10	87	6	819	35		—/—	5.25FH	
DK524	173	6	1105			—/—	5.25HH	
DK524C-20	169	6	1105	51		—/—	5.25HH	

HITACHI GLOBAL STORAGE TECHNOLOG

Drive Model	Format Size MB	Head	Cyl	Sect/Trac	Translate H/C/S	RWC/WPC	Form Factor	Power Watts
Deskstar &k80	40GB	1				—/—	3.5 3H	4.7
Deskstar 180GXP	60GB	2				—/—	3.5 3H	
Deskstar 180GXP	80GB	3				—/—	3.5 3H	
Deskstar 180GXP	120GB	4				—/—	3.5 3H	
Deskstar 180GXP	180GB	6				—/—	3.5 3H	
Deskstar 7K250 120GB	120GB	3				—/—	3.5 3H	5.0
Deskstar 7K250 120GB	120GB	3				—/—	3.5 3H	5.0
Deskstar 7K250 120GB	120GB	3				—/—	3.5 3H	5.6
Deskstar 7K250 160GB	160GB	4				—/—	3.5 3H	5.0
Deskstar 7K250 160GB	160GB	4				—/—	3.5 3H	5.0
Deskstar 7K250 160GB	160GB	4				—/—	3.5 3H	5.6
Deskstar 7K250 250GB	250GB	6				—/—	3.5 3H	5.0
Deskstar 7K250 250GB	250GB	6				—/—	3.5 3H	5.6
Deskstar 7K250 40GB	40GB	1				—/—	3.5 3H	5.0
Deskstar 7K250 80GB	80GB	2				—/—	3.5 3H	5.0
Deskstar 7K250 80GB	80GB	2				—/—	3.5 3H	5.6
Deskstar 7K400	400GB	5				—/—	3.5 3H	9
Deskstar 7K400	400GB	10				—/—	3.5 3H	9.6
Deskstar 7K80	80GB	2				—/—	3.5 3H	4.7
Endurastar J4K20	20GB	2				—/—	2.5 4H	1.8
Endurastar N4K20	20GB	2				—/—	2.5 4H	1.8
HDS722512VLAT20	120GB	3				—/—	3.5 3H	5.0
HDS722512VLAT80	120GB	3				—/—	3.5 3H	5.0
HDS722512VLSA80	120GB	3				—/—	3.5 3H	5.6
HDS722516VLAT20	160GB	4				—/—	3.5 3H	5.0
HDS722516VLAT80	160GB	4				—/—	3.5 3H	5.0
HDS722516VLSA80	160GB	4				—/—	3.5 3H	5.6

Drive Model	Format Size MB	Seek Time	Interface	Encode	cache kb	RPM
DK32EJ-14NC	147.8GB	4.9	UL320 SCSI		16mb	1002
DK32EJ-14NW	147.8GB	4.9	UL320SCSIWD		16mb	1002
DK32EJ-36FC	36.9GB	4.9	FC 2Gb		16mb	1002
DK32EJ-36NC	36.9GB	4.9	UL320 SCSI		16mb	1002
DK32EJ-36NW	36.9GB	4.9	UL320SCSIWD		16mb	1002
DK32EJ-72FC	73.9GB	4.9	FC 2Gb		16mb	1002
DK32EJ-72NC	73.9GB	4.9	UL320 SCSI		16mb	1002
DK32EJ-72NW	73.9GB	4.9	UL320SCSIWD		16mb	1002
DK3E1T-91	9200	5	Ultra2 SCSI		512k	1203
DK503-2		10		MFM		
DK505-2	21	85	ST412/506	MFM		
DK511-3	29	30	ST412/506	MFM		
DK511-5	41	26	ST412/506	MFM		
DK511-8	67	23	ST412/506	MFM		3600
DK512-12	94	23	ESDI	2,7 RLL		3600
DK512-17	134	23	ESDI	2,7 RLL		3482
DK512-8	67	23	ESDI	2,7 RLL		3482
DK512C-12	94	23	SCSI	2,7 RLL		3482
DK512C-17	134	23	SCSI	2,7 RLL		
DK512C-8	67	23	SCSI	2,7 RLL		
DK512S-17	143		SMD-E			
DK514-38	330	16	ESDI	2,7 RLL		3600
DK514C-38	322	16	SCSI	2,7 RLL		3600
DK514S-38	332		SMD-E			3600
DK515-12	1229	14	ESDI	2,7 RLL		
DK515-78	673	16	ESDI	2,7 RLL		3600
DK515C-78	670	16	SCSI	2,7 RLL		3600
DK515C-78D	673	16	SCSI	2,7 RLL		3600
DK515S-78	673	16	E-SMD			3600
DK516-12	1230	14	ESDI			
DK516-15	1320	14	ESDI			3600
DK516C-16	1340	14	SCSI	2,7 RLL		3600
DK517C-26	2000	12	SCSI-2			3600
DK517C-37	2900	12	SCSI-2Fast		512k	
DK521-5	51	25	ST412/506	MFM		
DK522-10	91	25	ESDI	2,7 RLL		
DK522C-10	87	25	SCSI	2,7 RLL		3600
DK524	173	25	ESDI			3600
DK524C-20	169	25	SCSI-2	2,7 RLL		3600

HITACHI GLOBAL STORAGE TECHNOLOG

Drive Model	Format Size MB	Seek Time	Interface	Encode	cache kb	RPM
Deskstar &k80	40GB	8.8	ATA 100		2mb	7200
Deskstar 180GXP	60GB	8.5	ATA-6		8mb	7200
Deskstar 180GXP	80GB	8.5	ATA-6		8mb	7200
Deskstar 180GXP	120GB	8.5	ATA-6		8mb	7200
Deskstar 180GXP	180GB	8.5	ATA-6		8mb	7200
Deskstar 7K250 120GB	120GB	8.5	ATA ULTR100		2mb	7200
Deskstar 7K250 120GB	120GB	8.5	ATA ULTR100		8mb	7200
Deskstar 7K250 120GB	120GB	8.5	SATA/1.5GBs		8mb	7200
Deskstar 7K250 160GB	160GB	8.5	ATA ULTR100		2mb	7200
Deskstar 7K250 160GB	160GB	8.5	ATA ULTR100		8mb	7200
Deskstar 7K250 160GB	160GB	8.5	SATA/1.5GBs		8mb	7200
Deskstar 7K250 250GB	250GB	8.5	ATA ULTR100		8mb	7200
Deskstar 7K250 250GB	250GB	8.5	SATA/1.5GBs		8mb	7200
Deskstar 7K250 40GB	40GB	8.5	ATA ULTR100		2mb	7200
Deskstar 7K250 80GB	80GB	8.5	ATA ULTR100		2mb	7200
Deskstar 7K250 80GB	80GB	8.5	SATA/1.5GBs		2mb	7200
Deskstar 7K400	400GB	8.5	UltraATA100		8mb	7200
Deskstar 7K400	400GB	8.5	SATA		8mb	7200
Deskstar 7K80	80GB	8.8	ATA 100		8mb	7200
Endurastar J4K20	20GB	13	ATA-5		2mb	7200
Endurastar N4K20	20GB	13	ATA-5		8mb	4172
HDS722512VLAT20	120GB	8.5	ATA ULTR100		8mb	4172
HDS722512VLAT80	120GB	8.5	ATA ULTR100		2mb	7200
HDS722512VLSA80	120GB	8.5	SATA/1.5GBs		8mb	7200
HDS722516VLAT20	160GB	8.5	ATA ULTR100		8mb	7200
HDS722516VLAT80	160GB	8.5	ATA ULTR100		2mb	7200
HDS722516VLSA80	160GB	8.5	SATA/1.5GBs		8mb	7200

Drive Model	Format Size MB	Head	Cyl	Sect/ Trac	Translate H/C/S	RWC/ WPC	Form Factor	Power Watts
HDS722525VLAT80	250GB	6				—/—	3.5 3H	5.0
HDS722525VLSA80	250GB	6				—/—	3.5 3H	5.6
HDS722540VLAT20	40GB	1				—/—	3.5 3H	5.0
HDS722580VLAT20	80GB	2				—/—	3.5 3H	5.0
HDS722580VLSA80	80GB	2				—/—	3.5 3H	5.6
HDS724040KLAT80	400GB	5				—/—	3.5 3H	9
HDS724040KLSA80	400GB	10				—/—	3.5 3H	9.6
HDS728040PLAT20	40GB	1				—/—	3.5 3H	4.7
HDS728080PLAT20	80GB	2				—/—	3.5 3H	4.7
HTA422020F9ATJ0	20GB	2				—/—	2.5 4H	1.8
HTA422020F9ATN0	20GB	2				—/—	2.5 4H	1.8
HTC424020F7AT00	20GB	2				—/—	2.5 4H	0.33
HTC424040F9AT00	40GB	4				—/—	2.5 4H	0.33
HTE726040M9AT00	40GB	4				—/—	2.5 4H	2.0
HTE726060M9AT00	60GB	4				—/—	2.5 4H	2.0
HTS424020M9AT00	20GB	1				—/—	2.5 4H	0.85
HTS424030M9AT00	30GB	2				—/—	2.5 4H	0.85
HTS424040M9AT00	40GB	2				—/—	2.5 4H	0.85
HTS428030F9AT00	30GB	2				—/—	2.5 4H	1.65
HTS428040F9AT00	40GB	2				—/—	2.5 4H	1.65
HTS428060F9AT00	60GB	3				—/—	2.5 4H	1.65
HTS428080F9AT00	80GB	4				—/—	2.5 4H	1.65
HTS548020M9AT00	20GB	1				—/—	2.5 4H	1.3
HTS548040M9AT00	40GB	2				—/—	2.5 4H	1.3
HTS548060M9AT00	60GB	3				—/—	2.5 4H	1.3
HTS548080M9AT00	80GB	4				—/—	2.5 4H	1.3
HTS726060M9AT00	60GB	4				—/—	2.5 4H	1.3
HTS726060M9ATX0	60GB	4				—/—	2.5 4H	2.0
HUS103014FL3600	147GB	5				—/—	3.5 3H	8.5
HUS103014FL3800	147GB	5				—/—	3.5 3H	8.5
HUS103014FLF210	147GB	5				—/—	3.5 3H	10.8
HUS103030FL3600	300GB	10				—/—	3.5 3H	11.2
HUS103030FL3800	300GB	10				—/—	3.5 3H	11.2
HUS103030FLF210	300GB	10				—/—	3.5 3H	13.4
HUS103036FL3600	36.7GB	2				—/—	3.5 3H	7.0
HUS103036FL3800	36.7GB	2				—/—	3.5 3H	7.0
HUS103036FLF210	36.7GB	2				—/—	3.5 3H	9.2
HUS103073FL3600	73.4GB	3				—/—	3.5 3H	8.0
HUS103073FL3800	73.4GB	3				—/—	3.5 3H	8.0
HUS103073FLF210	73.4GB	3				—/—	3.5 3H	10.3
HUS157336EL3600	36.9GB	5				—/—	3.5 3H	10
HUS157336EL3800	36.9GB	5				—/—	3.5 3H	10
HUS157336ELF200	36.9GB	5				—/—	3.5 3H	12
HUS157373EL3600	73.9GB	10				—/—	3.5 3H	12
HUS157373EL3800	73.9GB	10				—/—	3.5 3H	12
HUS157373ELF200	73.9GB	10				—/—	3.5 3H	14
IC25N010ATCS04	10GB	1				—/—	2.5 4H	0.85
IC25N010ATCX04	10GB	1				—/—	2.5 4H	
IC25N020ATCS04	20GB	2				—/—	2.5 4H	0.85
IC25N020ATCS05	20GB	2				—/—	2.5 4H	1.3
IC25N020ATCX04	20GB	2				—/—	2.5 4H	
IC25N020ATMR04	20GB	1				—/—	2.5 4H	0.85
IC25N030ATCS04	30GB	3				—/—	2.5 4H	0.95
IC25N030ATCX04	30GB	3				—/—	2.5 4H	
IC25N030ATMR04	30GB	2				—/—	2.5 4H	0.85
IC25N040ATCS04	40GB	4				—/—	2.5 4H	0.95
IC25N040ATCS05	40GB	4				—/—	2.5 4H	1.3
IC25N040ATCX04	40GB	4				—/—	2.5 4H	
IC25N040ATMR04	40GB	2				—/—	2.5 4H	0.85
IC25N060ATMR04	60GB	3				—/—	2.5 4H	0.95
IC25N080ATMR04	80GB	4				—/—	2.5 4H	0.95
IC25T060ATCS05	60GB	8				—/—	2.5 4H	1.3
IC25T060ATCX05	60GB	8				—/—	2.5 4H	1.3
IC35L018F2DY10	18.3GB	2				—/—	3.5 3H	6.8
IC35L018UCDY10	18.3GB	2				—/—	3.5 3H	5.9
IC35L018UCPR15	18.4GB	8				—/—	3.5 3H	11
IC35L018UWDY10	18.3GB	2				—/—	3.5 3H	5.9

Drive Model	Format Size MB	Seek Time	Interface	Encode	cache kb	RPM
HDS722525VLAT80	250GB	8.5	ATA ULTR100		8mb	7200
HDS722525VLSA80	250GB	8.5	SATA/1.5GBs		8mb	7200
HDS722540VLAT20	40GB	8.5	ATA ULTR100		2mb	7200
HDS722580VLAT20	80GB	8.5	ATA ULTR100		2mb	7200
HDS722580VLSA80	80GB	8.5	SATA/1.5GBs		8mb	7200
HDS724040KLAT80	400GB	8.5	UltraATA100		8mb	7200
HDS724040KLSA80	400GB	8.5	SATA		8mb	7200
HDS728040PLAT20	40GB	8.8	ATA 100		2mb	7200
HDS728080PLAT20	80GB	8.8	ATA 100		2mb	7200
HTA422020F9ATJ0	20GB	13	ATA-5		8mb	4172
HTA422020F9ATN0	20GB	13	ATA-5		8mb	4172
HTC424020F7AT00	20GB	15	ATA-5	ME2PRML	2mb	4200
HTC424040F9AT00	40GB	15	ATA-5	ME2PRML	2mb	4200
HTE726040M9AT00	40GB	10	ATA-6		8mb	7200
HTE726060M9AT00	60GB	10	ATA-6		8mb	7200
HTS424020M9AT00	20GB	12	ATA-6		2mb	4200
HTS424030M9AT00	30GB	12	ATA-6		2mb	4200
HTS424040M9AT00	40GB	12	ATA-6		2mb	4200
HTS428030F9AT00	30GB	13	ATA-6	PRML	2mb	4200
HTS428040F9AT00	40GB	13	ATA-6	PRML	2mb	4200
HTS428060F9AT00	60GB	13	ATA-6	PRML	8mb	4200
HTS428080F9AT00	80GB	13	ATA-6	PRML	8mb	4200
HTS548020M9AT00	20GB	12	ATA-6	PRML	8mb	5400
HTS548040M9AT00	40GB	12	ATA-6	PRML	8mb	5400
HTS548060M9AT00	60GB	12	ATA-6	PRML	8mb	5400
HTS548080M9AT00	80GB	12	ATA-6	PRML	8mb	5400
HTS726060M9AT00	60GB	10	ATA-6		8mb	7200
HTS726060M9ATX0	60GB	10	ATA-6		8mb	7200
HUS103014FL3600	147GB	4.5	UL320 SCSI		8mb	1002
HUS103014FL3800	147GB	4.5	UL320 SCSI		8mb	1002
HUS103014FLF210	147GB	4.5	FC 2Gb		16mb	1002
HUS103030FL3600	300GB	4.7	UL320 SCSI		8mb	1002
HUS103030FL3800	300GB	4.7	UL320 SCSI		8mb	1002
HUS103030FLF210	300GB	4.7	FC 2Gb		16mb	1002
HUS103036FL3600	36.7GB	4.3	UL320 SCSI		8mb	1002
HUS103036FL3800	36.7GB	4.3	UL320 SCSI		8mb	1002
HUS103036FLF210	36.7GB	4.3	FC-AL2GB		16mb	1002
HUS103073FL3600	73.4GB	4.3	UL320 SCSI		8mb	1002
HUS103073FL3800	73.4GB	4.3	UL320 SCSI		8mb	1002
HUS103073FLF210	73.4GB	4.3	FC 2Gb		16mb	1002
HUS157336EL3600	36.9GB	3.9	UL320 SCSI	ME2PRML		1503
HUS157336EL3800	36.9GB	3.9	UL320 SCSI	ME2PRML		1503
HUS157336ELF200	36.9GB	3.9	FC-AL2GB	ME2PRML		1503
HUS157373EL3600	73.9GB	3.9	UL320 SCSI	ME2PRML		1503
HUS157373EL3800	73.9GB	3.9	UL320 SCSI	ME2PRML		1503
HUS157373ELF200	73.9GB	3.9	FC-AL2GB	ME2PRML		1503
IC25N010ATCS04	10GB	12	ATA-5		2mb	4200
IC25N010ATCX04	10GB	12	ATA-5		2mb	4200
IC25N020ATCS04	20GB	12	ATA-5		2mb	4200
IC25N020ATCS05	20GB	12	ATA-5		8mb	5400
IC25N020ATCX04	20GB	12	ATA-5		2mb	4200
IC25N020ATMR04	20GB	12	ATA-6		2mb	4200
IC25N030ATCS04	30GB	12	ATA-5		2mb	4200
IC25N030ATCX04	30GB	12	ATA-5		2mb	4200
IC25N030ATMR04	30GB	12	ATA-6		2mb	4200
IC25N040ATCS04	40GB	12	ATA-5		2mb	4200
IC25N040ATCS05	40GB	12	ATA-5		8mb	5400
IC25N040ATCX04	40GB	12	ATA-5		2mb	4200
IC25N040ATMR04	40GB	12	ATA-6		2mb	4200
IC25N060ATMR04	60GB	12	ATA-6		8mb	4200
IC25N080ATMR04	80GB	12	ATA-6		8mb	4200
IC25T060ATCS05	60GB	12	ATA-5		2mb	5400
IC25T060ATCX05	60GB	12	ATA-5		2mb	5400
IC35L018F2DY10	18.3GB	4.7	FC-AL2GB		8mb	1000
IC35L018UCDY10	18.3GB	4.7	UL160SCSI		8mb	1000
IC35L018UCPR15	18.4GB	3.4	UL160SCSI		4mb	1500
IC35L018UWDY10	18.3GB	4.7	UL320 SCSI		8mb	1000

Drive Model	Format Size MB	Head	Cyl	Sect/ Trac	Translate H/C/S	RWC/ WPC	Form Factor	Power Watts
IC35L018UWPR15	18.4GB	8				—/—	3.5 3H	11
IC35L036F2DY10	36.7GB	3				—/—	3.5 3H	7.9
IC35L036UCDY10	36.7GB	3				—/—	3.5 3H	7.0
IC35L036UCPR15	36.7GB	12				—/—	3.5 3H	13.5
IC35L036UWDY10	36.7GB	3				—/—	3.5 3H	7.0
IC35L036UWPR15	36.7GB	12				—/—	3.5 3H	13.5
IC35L060AVV207-0	60GB	2				—/—	3.5 3H	
IC35L073F2DY10	73.4	6				—/—	3.5 3H	8.6
IC35L073UCDY10	73.4	6				—/—	3.5 3H	7.7
IC35L073UWDY10	73.4	6				—/—	3.5 3H	7.7
IC35L090AVV207-0	80GB	3				—/—	3.5 3H	
IC35L120AVV207-0	120GB	4				—/—	3.5 3H	
IC35L146F2DY10	146.8GB	6				—/—	3.5 3H	11.1
IC35L146UCDY10	146.8GB	12				—/—	3.5 3H	10.2
IC35L146UWDY10	146.8GB	12				—/—	3.5 3H	10.2
IC35L180AVV207-1	180GB	6				—/—	3.5 3H	
Travelstar 40GN 10GB	10GB	1				—/—	2.5 4H	0.85
Travelstar 40GN 10GB	10GB	1				—/—	2.5 4H	
Travelstar 40GN 20GB	20GB	2				—/—	2.5 4H	0.85
Travelstar 40GN 20GB	20GB	2				—/—	2.5 4H	
Travelstar 40GN 30GB	30GB	3				—/—	2.5 4H	0.95
Travelstar 40GN 30GB	30GB	3				—/—	2.5 4H	
Travelstar 40GN 40GB	40GB	4				—/—	2.5 4H	0.95
Travelstar 40GN 40GB	40GB	4				—/—	2.5 4H	
Travelstar 40GNX 20GB	20GB	2				—/—	2.5 4H	1.3
Travelstar 40GNX 40GB	40GB	4				—/—	2.5 4H	1.3
Travelstar 4K80 30GB	30GB	2				—/—	2.5 4H	1.65
Travelstar 4K80 40GB	40GB	2				—/—	2.5 4H	1.65
Travelstar 4K80 60GB	60GB	3				—/—	2.5 4H	1.65
Travelstar 4K80 80GB	80GB	4				—/—	2.5 4H	1.65
Travelstar 5K80 20GB	20GB	1				—/—	2.5 4H	1.3
Travelstar 5K80 40GB	40GB	2				—/—	2.5 4H	1.3
Travelstar 5K80 60GB	60GB	3				—/—	2.5 4H	1.3
Travelstar 5K80 80GB	80GB	4				—/—	2.5 4H	1.3
Travelstar 60GH	60GB	8				—/—	2.5 4H	1.3
Travelstar 60GH	60GB	8				—/—	2.5 4H	1.3
Travelstar 7K60	60GB	4				—/—	2.5 4H	1.3
Travelstar 80GN 20GB	20GB	1				—/—	2.5 4H	0.85
Travelstar 80GN 30GB	30GB	2				—/—	2.5 4H	0.85
Travelstar 80GN 40GB	40GB	2				—/—	2.5 4H	0.85
Travelstar 80GN 60GB	60GB	3				—/—	2.5 4H	0.95
Travelstar 80GN 80GB	80GB	4				—/—	2.5 4H	0.95
Travelstar C4K40 20GB	20GB	2				—/—	2.5 4H	0.33
Travelstar C4K40 40GB	40GB	4				—/—	2.5 4H	0.33
Travelstar E7K60	60GB	4				—/—	2.5 4H	2.0
Travelstar E7K60 40GB	40GB	4				—/—	2.5 4H	2.0
Travelstar E7K60 60GB	60GB	4				—/—	2.5 4H	2.0
Ultrastar 10K300 147GB	147GB	5				—/—	3.5 3H	8.5
Ultrastar 10K300 147GB	147GB	5				—/—	3.5 3H	8.5
Ultrastar 10K300 147GB	147GB	5				—/—	3.5 3H	10.8
Ultrastar 10K300 300GB	300GB	10				—/—	3.5 3H	11.2
Ultrastar 10K300 300GB	300GB	10				—/—	3.5 3H	13.4
Ultrastar 10K300 300GB	300GB	10				—/—	3.5 3H	11.2
Ultrastar 10K300 36.7G	36.7GB	2				—/—	3.5 3H	7.0
Ultrastar 10K300 36.7G	36.7GB	2				—/—	3.5 3H	7.0
Ultrastar 10K300 36.7G	36.7GB	2				—/—	3.5 3H	9.2
Ultrastar 10K300 73.4G	73.4GB	3				—/—	3.5 3H	8.0
Ultrastar 10K300 73.4G	73.4GB	3				—/—	3.5 3H	8.0
Ultrastar 10K300 73.4G	73.4GB	3				—/—	3.5 3H	10.3
Ultrastar 15K73 36.9GB	36.9GB	5				—/—	3.5 3H	12
Ultrastar 15K73 36.9GB	36.9GB	5				—/—	3.5 3H	10
Ultrastar 15K73 36.9GB	36.9GB	5				—/—	3.5 3H	10
Ultrastar 15K73 73.9GB	73.9GB	10				—/—	3.5 3H	14
Ultrastar 15K73 73.9GB	73.9GB	10				—/—	3.5 3H	12
Ultrastar 15K73 73.9GB	73.9GB	10				—/—	3.5 3H	12
Ultrastar 36Z15 18.4GB	18.4GB	8				—/—	3.5 3H	11
Ultrastar 36Z15 18.4GB	18.4GB	8				—/—	3.5 3H	11

Drive Model	Format Size MB	Seek Time	Interface	Encode	cache kb	RPM
IC35L018UWPR15	18.4GB	3.4	UL160SCSI		4mb	1500
IC35L036F2DY10	36.7GB	4.7	FC-AL2GB		8mb	1000
IC35L036UCDY10	36.7GB	4.7	UL160SCSI		8mb	1000
IC35L036UCPR15	36.7GB	4.2	UL160SCSI		4mb	1500
IC35L036UWDY10	36.7GB	4.7	UL320 SCSI		8mb	1000
IC35L036UWPR15	36.7GB	4.2	UL160SCSI		4mb	1500
IC35L060AVV207-0	60GB	8.5	ATA-6		8mb	7200
IC35L073F2DY10	73.4	4.7	FC-AL2GB		8mb	1000
IC35L073UCDY10	73.4	4.7	UL160SCSI		8mb	1000
IC35L073UWDY10	73.4	4.7	UL320 SCSI		8mb	1000
IC35L090AVV207-0	80GB	8.5	ATA-6		8mb	7200
IC35L120AVV207-0	120GB	8.5	ATA-6		8mb	7200
IC35L146F2DY10	146.8GB	4.7	FC-AL2GB		8mb	1000
IC35L146UCDY10	146.8GB	4.7	UL160SCSI		8mb	1000
IC35L146UWDY10	146.8GB	4.7	UL320 SCSI		8mb	1000
IC35L180AVV207-1	180GB	8.5	ATA-6		8mb	7200
Travelstar 40GN 10GB	10GB	12	ATA-5		2mb	4200
Travelstar 40GN 10GB	10GB	12	ATA-5		2mb	4200
Travelstar 40GN 20GB	20GB	12	ATA-5		2mb	4200
Travelstar 40GN 20GB	20GB	12	ATA-5		2mb	4200
Travelstar 40GN 30GB	30GB	12	ATA-5		2mb	4200
Travelstar 40GN 30GB	30GB	12	ATA-5		2mb	4200
Travelstar 40GN 40GB	40GB	12	ATA-5		2mb	4200
Travelstar 40GN 40GB	40GB	12	ATA-5		2mb	4200
Travelstar 40GNX 20GB	20GB	12	ATA-5		8mb	5400
Travelstar 40GNX 40GB	40GB	12	ATA-5		8mb	5400
Travelstar 4K80 30GB	30GB	13	ATA-6	PRML	2mb	4200
Travelstar 4K80 40GB	40GB	13	ATA-6	PRML	2mb	4200
Travelstar 4K80 60GB	60GB	13	ATA-6	PRML	8mb	4200
Travelstar 4K80 80GB	80GB	13	ATA-6	PRML	8mb	4200
Travelstar 5K80 20GB	20GB	12	ATA-6	PRML	8mb	5400
Travelstar 5K80 40GB	40GB	12	ATA-6	PRML	8mb	5400
Travelstar 5K80 60GB	60GB	12	ATA-6	PRML	8mb	5400
Travelstar 5K80 80GB	80GB	12	ATA-6	PRML	8mb	5400
Travelstar 60GH	60GB	12	ATA-5		2mb	5400
Travelstar 60GH	60GB	12	ATA-5		2mb	5400
Travelstar 7K60	60GB	10	ATA-6		8mb	7200
Travelstar 80GN 20GB	20GB	12	ATA-6		2mb	4200
Travelstar 80GN 30GB	30GB	12	ATA-6		2mb	4200
Travelstar 80GN 40GB	40GB	12	ATA-6		2mb	4200
Travelstar 80GN 60GB	60GB	12	ATA-6		8mb	4200
Travelstar 80GN 80GB	80GB	12	ATA-6		8mb	4200
Travelstar C4K40 20GB	20GB	15	ATA-5	ME2PRML	2mb	4200
Travelstar C4K40 40GB	40GB	15	ATA-5	ME2PRML	2mb	4200
Travelstar E7K60	60GB	10	ATA-6		8mb	7200
Travelstar E7K60 40GB	40GB	10	ATA-6		8mb	7200
Travelstar E7K60 60GB	60GB	10	ATA-6		8mb	7200
Ultrastar 10K300 147GB	147GB	4.5	UL320 SCSI		8mb	1002
Ultrastar 10K300 147GB	147GB	4.5	UL320 SCSI		8mb	1002
Ultrastar 10K300 147GB	147GB	4.5	FC 2Gb		16mb	1002
Ultrastar 10K300 300GB	300GB	4.7	UL320 SCSI		8mb	1002
Ultrastar 10K300 300GB	300GB	4.7	UL320 SCSI		8mb	1002
Ultrastar 10K300 300GB	300GB	4.7	FC 2Gb		16mb	1002
Ultrastar 10K300 36.7G	36.7GB	4.3	UL320 SCSI		8mb	1002
Ultrastar 10K300 36.7G	36.7GB	4.3	UL320 SCSI		8mb	1002
Ultrastar 10K300 36.7G	36.7GB	4.3	FC-AL2GB		16mb	1002
Ultrastar 10K300 73.4G	73.4GB	4.3	UL320 SCSI		8mb	1002
Ultrastar 10K300 73.4G	73.4GB	4.3	UL320 SCSI		8mb	1002
Ultrastar 10K300 73.4G	73.4GB	4.3	FC 2Gb		16mb	1002
Ultrastar 15K73 36.9GB	36.9GB	3.9	FC-AL2GB	ME2PRML		1503
Ultrastar 15K73 36.9GB	36.9GB	3.9	UL320 SCSI	ME2PRML		1503
Ultrastar 15K73 36.9GB	36.9GB	3.9	UL320 SCSI	ME2PRML		1503
Ultrastar 15K73 73.9GB	73.9GB	3.9	FC-AL2GB	ME2PRML		1503
Ultrastar 15K73 73.9GB	73.9GB	3.9	UL320 SCSI	ME2PRML		1503
Ultrastar 15K73 73.9GB	73.9GB	3.9	UL320 SCSI	ME2PRML		1503
Ultrastar 36Z15 18.4GB	18.4GB	3.4	UL160SCSI		4mb	1500
Ultrastar 36Z15 18.4GB	18.4GB	3.4	UL160SCSI		4mb	1500

Hard Drive Specs

Drive Model	Format Size MB	Head	Cyl	Sect/ Trac	Translate H/C/S	RWC/ WPC	Form Factor	Power Watts
Ultrastar 36Z15 36.7GB	36.7GB	12				—/—	3.5 3H	13.5
Ultrastar 36Z15 36.7GB	36.7GB	12				—/—	3.5 3H	13.5

HYOSUNG

Drive Model	Format Size MB	Head	Cyl	Sect/ Trac	Translate H/C/S	RWC/ WPC	Form Factor	Power Watts
HC8085	71	8	1024	17		NA/NA	5.25FH	
HC8128	109	8	1024	26		NA/NA	5.25FH	
HC8170E	150	8	1024	36		NA/NA	5.25FH	

IBM

Drive Model	Format Size MB	Head	Cyl	Sect/ Trac	Translate H/C/S	RWC/ WPC	Form Factor	Power Watts
06H3370	2250					—/—	3.5 3H	
06H3372	2250					—/—	3.5 3H	
06H5709	4510					—/—	3.5HH	
06H5710	5318					—/—	3.5HH	
06H6111	1080	2				—/—	3.5 3H	
06H6740	2255					—/—	3H	8.9
06H6741	4510					—/—	3.5HH	
06H6742	4512					—/—	3.5HH	13.3
06H6749	5318					—/—	3.5HH	
06H6750	5318					—/—	3.5HH	
06H7141	540					—/—	3.5 3H	
06H7142	540					—/—	3.5 3H	
06H8558	540					—/—	3.5 3H	
06H8724	1700	2				—/—	3.5 3H	
06H8891	1080					—/—	3.5 3H	
07H0386	125	3				—/—	3.5 3H	
07H0387	2250	5				—/—	3.5 3H	
07H0834	4510	10				—/—	3.5HH	
07H1124	2160	3				—/—	3.5 3H	
07H1128	2160	3				—/—	3.5 3H	
07H2689	9100	18				—/—	3.5HH	
32G3796	2000					—/—	3.5 3H	
32G4194	245					—/—	3.5 3H	
32G4195	340					—/—	3.5 3H	
32G4196	527					—/—	3.5 3H	
32G4198	1000					—/—	3.5 3H	
32G4199	105					—/—	FH	
32G4336	2000					—/—	3.5HH	
32G4338	2880					—/—	3.5 3H	
3513364	364					—/—	HH	15
3513527	527					—/—	HH	15
70G7164	1000					—/—	3.5 3H	
70G7424	170	2	2233			—/—	3.5 3H	12.6
70G8480	170	2	2111			—/—	3.5 3H	6.5
70G8481	340	4	2111			—/—	3.5 3H	6.5
70G8486	527					—/—	3.5 3H	15.7
70G8487	270					—/—	3.5 3H	15.7
70G8488	364					—/—	3.5 3H	15.7
70G8491	540	7	2466			—/—	3.5 3H	4.5
70G8492	1052	6				—/—	3.5 3H	7.28
70G8493	2014	16				—/—	3.5HH	9.75
70G8494	2014	16				—/—	3.5HH	9.75
70G8495	40					—/—	FH	
70G8499	1440					—/—	3.5 3H	
70G8500	1440					—/—	5.25HH	
70G8511	728	4	3875			—/—	3.5 3H	15.7
70G8512	1000	5				—/—	3.5 3H	7.02
70G8847	270					—/—	3.5 3H	
70G8848	364					—/—	3.5 3H	15.7
70G8849	527					—/—	3.5 3H	15.7
70G8850	728					—/—	3.5 3H	15.7
70G9743	1000					—/—	3.5 3H	
71G0666	1000	5				—/—	3.5 3H	7.02
71G6550	170	2	2111			—/—	3.5 3H	6.5
76H2687	4512	9				—/—	3.5 3H	
76H2689	9100	18				—/—	3.5 3H	
76H7246	4200	6				—/—	3.5 3H	
82G5926	270					—/—	3.5 3H	15.7
82G5927	364					—/—	3.5 3H	15.7

Drive Model	Format Size MB	Seek Time	Interface	Encode	cache kb	RPM
Ultrastar 36Z15 36.7GB	36.7GB	4.2	UL160SCSI		4mb	1500
Ultrastar 36Z15 36.7GB	36.7GB	4.2	UL160SCSI		4mb	1500

Drive Model	Format Size MB	Seek Time	Interface	Encode	cache kb	RPM
HC8085	71	25	ST412/506			
HC8128	109	25	ST412/506			
HC8170E	150	25	ESDI			

Drive Model	Format Size MB	Seek Time	Interface	Encode	cache kb	RPM
06H3370	2250	7.5	SCSI-2Fast		512k	7200
06H3372	2250	7.5	SCSI-2FstW		512k	7200
06H5709	4510	8	SCSI-2FstW		512k	7200
06H5710	5318	8	SCSI-2FstW		512k	5400
06H6111	1080	10.5	ATA-2		512k	5400
06H6740	2255	8	SCSI-2Diff			7200
06H6741	4510	8	SCSI-2Fast		512k	7200
06H6742	4512	8	SCSI-2Diff			7200
06H6749	5318	8	SCSI-2Diff			5400
06H6750	5318	8	SCSI-2Diff			5400
06H7141	540	12	ATA-2		128k	4500
06H7142	540	12	ATA-2		128k	4500
06H8558	540	12	SCSI-2Fast		128k	4500
06H8724	1700	12	ATA-2		128k	4500
06H8891	1080	10.5	SCSI-2Fast		512k	4500
07H0386	125	8.5	SCSI-2FstW			7200
07H0387	2250	8.5	SCSI-2FstW			7200
07H0834	4510	8.5	SCSI-2FstW			7200
07H1124	2160	8.5	SCSI-2Fast		512k	5400
07H1128	2160	8.5	Ultra SCSIW		512k	5400
07H2689	9100	8.5	Ultra Wide		512k	7200
32G3796	2000	9.5	SCSI-2FstW		512k	5400
32G4194	245	15	IDE AT			
32G4195	340	14	IDE AT			
32G4196	527	9	IDE AT			
32G4198	1000	8.6	SCSI-2Fast		512k	5400
32G4199	105	15	PCMCIA			
32G4336	2000	9.5	SCSI-2Fast		512k	5400
32G4338	2880	94	AT BUS			
3513364	364	12	PCMCIA			
3513527	527	12	PCMCIA			
70G7164	1000	8.6	SCSI-2Fast		512k	5400
70G7424	170	14	IDE AT		96k	3322
70G8480	170	13	SCSI-2Fast		64k	4011
70G8481	340	13	SCSI-2		64k	4011
70G8486	527	12	IDE AT		96k	4500
70G8487	270	12	IDE AT		96k	4500
70G8488	364	12	IDE AT		96k	4500
70G8491	540	8.5	SCSI-2Fast		256k	6300
70G8492	1052	8.6	SCSI-2Fast		512k	5400
70G8493	2014	9.5	SCSI-2Fast		512k	5400
70G8494	2014	9.5	SCSI-2FstW		512k	5400
70G8495	40	18	PCMCIA			
70G8499	1440	94	IDE AT			
70G8500	1440	94	IDE AT			
70G8511	728	12	IDE AT		96k	4500
70G8512	1000	8.5	IDE AT		512k	5400
70G8847	270	12	IDE AT		96k	4500
70G8848	364	12	IDE AT		96k	4500
70G8849	527	12	IDE AT		96k	4500
70G8850	728	12	IDE AT		96k	4500
70G9743	1000	8	SCSI-2FstW		512k	5400
71G0666	1000	8.5	IDE AT		512k	5400
71G6550	170	13	SCSI-2Fast		64k	4011
76H2687	4512	7.5	Ultra Wide		512k	7200
76H2689	9100	8.5	Ultra Wide		512k	7200
76H7246	4200	9.5	ATA-3 Fast		128k	5400
82G5926	270	12	IDE AT		96k	4500
82G5927	364	12	IDE AT		96k	4500

Drive Model	Format Size MB	Head	Cyl	Sect/Trac	Translate H/C/S	RWC/WPC	Form Factor	Power Watts
82G5928	540					—/—	3.5 3H	
82G5929	1000	5				—/—	3.5 3H	7.02
82G5930	270					—/—	3.5 3H	15.7
82G5931	364					—/—	3.5 3H	15.7
82G5932	540					—/—	3.5 3H	15.7
82G5933	728					—/—	3.5 3H	15.7
82G6106	527					—/—	3.5 3H	15.7
92F0428	1052	6				—/—	3.5 3H	7.28
92F0440	2014	16				—/—	3.5HH	9.75
94G2413	1052	6				—/—	3.5 3H	7.28
94G2439	270					—/—	3.5 3H	15.7
94G2440	364					—/—	3.5 3H	15.7
94G2441	540					—/—	3.5 3H	15.7
94G2442	728					—/—	3.5 3H	15.7
94G2644	270					—/—	3.5 3H	15.7
94G2645	364					—/—	3.5 3H	15.7
94G2646	540					—/—	3.5 3H	15.7
94G2647	728					—/—	3.5 3H	
94G2649	1120					—/—	3.5 3H	
94G2650	2250					—/—	3.5 3H	
94G2651	4510					—/—	3.5HH	
94G3052	1120					—/—	3.5 3H	
94G3054	2250					—/—	3.5 3H	
94G3055	2250					—/—	3.5 3H	8.9
94G3056	2255					—/—	3.5HH	
94G3057	4510					—/—	3.5HH	
94G3059	5318					—/—	3.5 3H	
94G3183	1080	2				—/—	3.5 3H	
94G3184	1080	2				—/—	3.5 3H	
94G3186	1080	2				—/—	3.5 3H	
94G3187	1080	2				—/—	3.5 3H	
94G3192	2250					—/—	3.5 3H	
94G3193	2250					—/—	3.5 3H	
94G3195	4510					—/—	3.5HH	
94G3196	4510					—/—	3.5HH	
94G3197	5318					—/—	3.5HH	
94G3198	4510					—/—	3H	8.9
94G3199	2255					—/—	3.5HH	13.3
94G3200	4512					—/—	3.5HH	
94G3201	5318					—/—	3H	8.9
94G3203	2255					—/—	3.5HH	13.3
94G3204	4512					—/—	3.5HH	
94G3205	5318					—/—	3.5HH	
94G3787	5318					—/—	3.5HH	
94G3794	5318					—/—	3.5HH	
94G4196	527					—/—	3.5 3H	

IBM CORP. (STORAGE SYS DIV)

Drive Model	Format Size MB	Head	Cyl	Sect/Trac	Translate H/C/S	RWC/WPC	Form Factor	Power Watts
0661-371	326	14	949	48		NA/NA	3.5HH	
0661-371	325	14	949	48		—/—	3.5HH	
0661-437	467					NA/NA	3.5HH	
0661-467	412	14	1199	48		—/—		
0661-467	406	14	1199	48		—/—	3.5FH	
0661-467R	400	14	1199	48		—/—	3.5 3H	
0662-A10	1052	6				—/—	3.5 3H	7.26
0662-S12	1062	6				—/—	3.5 3H	10.3
0662-S1D	1052					NA/NA	3.5 3H	7.26
0662-SW1	1062	6				—/—	3.5 3H	7.26
0662-SWD	1062	6				—/—	3.5HH	
0663-E12	1044	14				—/—	3.5HH	
0663-E15	1206	16				—/—	3.5FH	
0663-E15R	1206	13	2463	66		—/—	3.5HH	
0663-H11	868	13	2051	66		NA/NA	3.5HH	
0663-H12	1004	15	2051	66		NA/NA	3.5HH	
0663-L08	623	9	2051	66		NA/NA	3.5HH	
0663-L11	868	13	2051	66		NA/NA	3.5FH	
0663-L12R	1004	15	2051	66		NA/NA	3.5FH	
0663-W2H	2412	15				—/—	5.25FH	

Drive Model	Format Size MB	Seek Time	Interface	Encode	cache kb	RPM
82G5928	540	12	ATA-2		128k	4500
82G5929	1000	8.5	IDE AT		512k	5400
82G5930	270	12	SCSI-2Fast		96k	4500
82G5931	364	12	SCSI-2Fast		96k	4500
82G5932	540	12	SCSI-2Fast		96k	4500
82G5933	728	12	SCSI-2Fast		96k	4500
82G6106	527	12	IDE AT		96k	4500
92F0428	1052	8.6	SCSI-2Fast		512k	5400
92F0440	2014	9.5	SCSI-2Fast		512k	5400
94G2413	1052	8.6	SCSI-2Fast		512k	5400
94G2439	270	12	SCSI-2Fast		96k	4500
94G2440	364	12	SCSI-2Fast		96k	4500
94G2441	540	12	SCSI-2Fast		96k	4500
94G2442	728	12	SCSI-2Fast		96k	4500
94G2644	270	12	SCSI-2Fast		96k	4500
94G2645	364	12	SCSI-2Fast		96k	4500
94G2646	540	12	SCSI-2Fast		96k	4500
94G2647	728	12	SCSI-2Fast		96k	4500
94G2649	1120	6	SCSI-2FstW		512k	7200
94G2650	2250	7	SCSI-2FstW		512k	7200
94G2651	4510	8	SCSI-2FstW		512k	7200
94G3052	1120	6.9	SCSI-2FstW		512k	7200
94G3054	2250	7.5	SCSI-2Fast		512k	7200
94G3055	2250	7.5	SCSI-2FstW		512k	7200
94G3056	2255	7.5	SCSI-2FstW		512k	7200
94G3057	2255	7.5	SCSI-2FstW		512k	7200
94G3059	4510	8	SCSI-2FstW		512k	7200
94G3183	5318	8	SCSI-2FstW		512k	5400
94G3184	1080	10.5	ATA-2		512k	5400
94G3186	1080	10.5	SCSI-2Fast		512k	5400
94G3187	1080	10.5	ATA-2		512k	5400
94G3192	1080	10.5	SCSI-2Fast		512k	5400
94G3193	2250	7.5	SCSI-2Fast		512k	7200
94G3195	2250	7.5	SCSI-2FstW		512k	7200
94G3196	4510	8	SCSI-2FstW		512k	7200
94G3197	4510	8	SCSI-2FstW		512k	7200
94G3198	5318	8	SCSI-2FstW		512k	5400
94G3199	4510	8	SCSI-2FstW		512k	7200
94G3200	2255	7.5	SCSI-2Diff		512k	7200
94G3201	4512	8	SCSI-2Diff		512k	7200
94G3203	5318	8	SCSI-2Diff		512k	5400
94G3204	2255	7.5	SCSI-2Diff		512k	7200
94G3205	4512	8	SCSI-2Diff		512k	7200
94G3787	5318	8	SCSI-2Diff		512k	5400
94G3794	5318	8	SCSI-2Fast		512k	5400
94G4196	527	8	IDE AT		512k	5400

IBM CORP. (STORAGE SYS DIV)

Drive Model	Format Size MB	Seek Time	Interface	Encode	cache kb	RPM
0661-371	326	12.5	SCSI-2		64k	
0661-371	325	12	SCSI-2	RLL	64k	4316
0661-437	467		SCSI			
0661-467	412	11.5	SCSI-2		128k	
0661-467	406	11	SCSI-2		128k	4316
0661-467R	400	11	SCSI-2		128k	4316
0662-A10	1052	10	IDE AT		512k	5400
0662-S12	1062	10	SCSI-2Fast		512k	5400
0662-S1D	1052	10	SCSI-2FstD		512k	5400
0662-SW1	1062	10	SCSI-2FstW		512k	5400
0662-SWD	1062	10	SCSI-2FstW		512k	5400
0663-E12	1044	11	SCSI-2Fast		256k	4317
0663-E15	1206	11	SCSI-2Fast		256k	4317
0663-E15R	1206	11	SCSI-2		256k	4317
0663-H11	868	11	SCSI-2		256k	4316
0663-H12	1004	11	SCSI-2	RLL	256k	4316
0663-L08	623	9.8	SCSI-2	RLL	256k	4316
0663-L11	868	11	SCSI-2		256k	
0663-L12R	1004	11	SCSI-2	RLL	256k	4316
0663-W2H	2412	9	SCSI-2Fast	RLL	256k	4317

Drive Model	Format Size MB	Head	Cyl	Sect/ Trac	Translate H/C/S	RWC/ WPC	Form Factor	Power Watts
0664-CSH	4027	38	2328	211		—/—	5.25FH	23
0664-DSH	4027	32				—/—	5.25FH	
0664-ESH	4027	38	2328	211		—/—	5.25FH	23
0664-FSH	4027	32				—/—	5.25FH	
0664-M1H	2013	16				—/—	3.5HH	
0664-N1H	2013	16				—/—	3.5HH	
0664-P1S	1741	15	2304			—/—	3.5HH	
0665-38	31	5	733	17		NA/NA	5.25FH	
0665-53	44	7	733	17		NA/NA	5.25FH	
0667-61	52	5	582	35		NA/NA	5.25FH	
0667-85	73	7	582	35		NA/NA	5.25FH	
0669-133	133					—/—	5.25FH	
0671-315/S	315					—/—	5.25FH	
0671-S11	234	11	1224	34		NA/NA	5.25FH	
0671-S15	319	15	1224	34		NA/NA	5.25FH	
0681-1000	865	20	1458	58		NA/NA	5.25FH	
0681-500	476	11	1458	58		NA/NA	5.25FH	
115MB	118	7	915	36		—/—	5.25	
120MB	120	8	920	32		—/—	5.25FH	
120MB	120	8	920	32		—/—	5.25FH	
1430	21	4	615	17		320/128	5.25FH	
1431	31	5	733	17		733/733	5.25FH	
1470	31	5	733	17		733/733	5.25FH	
1471	31	5	733	17		733/733	5.25FH	
170MB	170					—/—	3H	
20MB	21	4	612	17		—/306	5.25FH	
20MB PS/2	21	4	612	17		—/—	3.5FH	
245MB	245					—/—	4H	
30MB	31	4	615	25		—/300	5.25FH	
314MB	319	15	1225	34		—/—	5.25FH	
340MB	340					—/—	3H	
44MB	44	7	733	17		—/300	5.25FH	
527MB	527					—/—	3.5 3H	
540MB	540	7	2466			—/—	3.5 3H	4.5
60MB	60	6	762	26		—/—	5.25FH	
70MB	75	7	583	36		—/—	5.25FH	
DADA 25400	5400	5	9280			—/—	4H	1.85
DADA 26480	6480	6	9280			—/—	4H	1.85
DALA 3540	540	2	4892		16/1049/63	—/—	3.5 3H	2.6
DALA 3540	528				16/1049/63	—/—	3.5 3H	2.6
DALS 3540	541	2				—/—	3.5 4H	
DAQA 32160	2160	4	6911			—/—	3.5 3H	2.7
DAQA 33240	3240	6	6911			—/—	3.5 3H	3.3
DARA 206000	6000	2	17088			—/—	2.5 4H	1.85
DARA 209000	9000	3	17088			—/—	2.5 4H	1.85
DARA 212000	12000	4	17088			—/—	2.5 4H	1.85
DARA 215000	15100	5	17088			—/—	2.5 4H	1.85
DARA 218000	18100	6	17088			—/—	2.5 4H	1.85
DARA 225000	25300	10	16064			—/—	2.5 4H	2.0
DBCA 203240	3200	2	11648			—/—	2.5 4H	1.85
DBCA 204860	4800	3	11648			—/—	2.5 4H	1.85
DBCA 206480	6400	4	11648			—/—	2.5 4H	1.85
DBOA 2360	360	2	3478		16/700/63	—/—	2.5 4H	
DBOA 2528	528				16/1024/63	—/—	2.5 4H	0.95
DBOA 2540	540	3	3478		16/1050/63	—/—	2.5 4H	0.95
DBOA 2720	722	4	3478		16/1400/63	—/—	3.5 3H	3.5
DCAA 32880	2880	4	8210			—/—	3.5 3H	3.5
DCAA 33610	3610	5	8210			—/—	3.5 3H	3.5
DCAA 34330	4330	6	8210			—/—	3.5 3H	3.42
DCAS 32160	2160	3	8120			—/—	3.5 3H	3.42
DCAS 34330	4330	6	8120			—/—	3.5 3H	11.2
DCHC 34550	4550	9				—/—	3.5FH	
DCHC 38700	8700	18				—/—	3.5HH	15.6
DCHC 39100	9100	18				—/—	3.5 3H	11.2
DCHS 34550	4550	9				—/—	3.5FH	
DCHS 38700	8700	18				—/—	3.5FH	
DCHS 39100	9100	18				—/—	3.5HH	15.6

Drive Model	Format Size MB	Seek Time	Interface	Encode	cache kb	RPM
0664-CSH	4027	11	SCSI-2Fast			5400
0664-DSH	4027	<11	SCSI-2Fast			5400
0664-ESH	4027	11	SCSI-2Fast			5400
0664-FSH	4027	<11	SCSI-2Fast			5400
0664-M1H	2013	11	SCSI-2Fast		512k	5400
0664-N1H	2013	11	SCSI-2FstW		512k	5400
0664-P1S	1741	11	IPI-2			5400
0665-38	31	40	ST412/506	MFM		
0665-53	44	40	ST412/506	MFM		
0667-61	52	30	ESDI	RLL		
0667-85	73	30	ESDI			
0669-133	133		ESDI			
0671-315/S	315		ESDI			
0671-S11	234	21.5	SCSI			
0671-S15	319	21.5	SCSI			
0681-1000	865	13	SCSI			
0681-500	476	13	SCSI	RLL		
115MB	118	28	ESDI	RLL		
120MB	120	23	ST412/506	MFM		
120MB	120	23	ST412/506	MFM		
1430	21	80	ST412/506	MFM		
1431	31	40	ST412/506	MFM		
1470	31	40	ST412/506	MFM		
1471	31	40	ST412/506	MFM		
170MB	170	15	IDE AT		128k	4500
20MB	21		ST412/506	MFM		
20MB PS/2	21	80	ST412/506	MFM		
245MB	245	15	IDE AT			
30MB	31		ST412/506	MFM		
314MB	319	23	ESDI			
340MB	340	15	IDE AT		128k	4500
44MB	44		ST412/506	MFM		
527MB	527	9	IDE AT			
540MB	540	9	SCSI-2		256k	6300
60MB	60	27	ST412/506	MFM		
70MB	75	30	ESDI			
DADA 25400	5400	12	ATA-4		512k	4200
DADA 26480	6480	12	ATA-4		512k	4200
DALA 3540	540	12	ATA-2		128k	4500
DALA 3540	528	12	ATA-2		128k	4500
DALS 3540	541	12	SCSI-2Fast		64k	4500
DAQA 32160	2160	9.5	ATA-3		128k	5400
DAQA 33240	3240	9.5	ATA-3		128k	5400
DARA 206000	6000	12	ATA-4		512k	4200
DARA 209000	9000	12	ATA-4		512k	4200
DARA 212000	12000	12	ATA-4		512k	4200
DARA 215000	15100	12	ATA-4		512k	4200
DARA 218000	18100	12	ATA-4		512k	4200
DARA 225000	25300	12	ATA-4		512k	4200
DBCA 203240	3200	13	ATA-4		512k	5400
DBCA 204860	4800	13	ATA-4		512k	4200
DBCA 206480	6400	13	ATA-4		512k	4200
DBOA 2360	360	13	ATA-2		32k	4000
DBOA 2528	528	13	ATA-2		64k	4000
DBOA 2540	540	13	ATA-2		32k	4000
DBOA 2720	722	13	ATA-2		64k	4000
DCAA 32880	2880	9.5	ATA-3	PRML	128k	5400
DCAA 33610	3610	9.5	ATA-3	PRML	128k	5400
DCAA 34330	4330	9.5	ATA-3	PRML	128k	5400
DCAS 32160	2160	8.5	SCSI-3Ultra	PRML	512k	5400
DCAS 34330	4330	8.5	SCA-2	PRML	512k	5400
DCHC 34550	4550	7.5	SSA	PRML	512k	7200
DCHC 38700	8700	9	SSA		512k	7200
DCHC 39100	9100	7.5	SSA		512k	7200
DCHS 34550	4550	7.5	SCSI-2FstW	PRML	512k	7200
DCHS 38700	8700	9	IPI-2		512k	7200
DCHS 39100	9100	7.5	SCSI-3Fst20	PRML	512k	7200

Drive Model	Format Size MB	Head	Cyl	Sect/Trac	Translate H/C/S	RWC/WPC	Form Factor	Power Watts
DCMS 310800	10800	20				—/—	3.5FH	
DCRA 22160	2160				16/4200/63	—/—	2.5 4H	1.1
DCXA 208100	8100	5	11968			—/—	2.5 4H	1.85
DCXA 210000	10000	6	11968			—/—	2.5 4H	1.85
DCYA 214000	14100	10	11136			—/—	2.5 4H	1.3
DDLA 21215	1215	3	5120			—/—	2.5 4H	1.85
DDLA 21620	1620	4	5120			—/—	2.5 4H	1.85
DDRS 34560	4500	5	8420			—/—	3.5 3H	5.3
DDRS 34560	4500	5	8420			—/—	3.5 3H	5.3
DDRS 39130	9100	10	8420			—/—	3.5 3H	5.3
DDRS 39130	9100	10	8420			—/—	3.5 3H	5.3
DDYD-DDYF 9.1GB	9100	3				—/—	3.5 3H	8.5
DDYS-DDYF 18.3GB	18300	6				—/—	3.5 3H	9.7
DDYS-DDYF 18.3GB	18300	6				—/—	3.5 3H	9.7
DDYS-DDYF 36.6GB	36700	12				—/—	3.5 3H	12.9
DDYS-DDYF 36.7GB	36700	12				—/—	3.5 3H	12.9
DDYS-DDYF 9.1GB	9100	3				—/—	3.5 3H	8.5
Deskstar 10GP 10.1GB	10100	6	13085			—/—	3H	3.4
Deskstar 10GXP 10.1GB	10100	7	13085			—/—	3H	6.9
Deskstar 120GXP 102GB	102GB					—/—		
Deskstar 120GXP 120GB	123GB					—/—		
Deskstar 120GXP 20GB	20GB					—/—		
Deskstar 120GXP 41GB	41GB					—/—		
Deskstar 120GXP 61GB	61GB					—/—		
Deskstar 120GXP 82GB	82GB					—/—		
Deskstar 13GP 13.5GB	13500	8	13085			—/—		3H 3.4
Deskstar 14GXP 10.1GB	10GB	7	13085			—/—		3H 6.9
Deskstar 14GXP 12.9GB	13GB	8	13085			—/—		3H 6.9
Deskstar 14GXP 14.4GB	14GB	10	13085			—/—		3H 6.9
Deskstar 16GP 10.1GB	10GB	6	13085			—/—		3H 3.4
Deskstar 16GP 12.9GB	12900	8	13085			—/—		3H 4.9
Deskstar 16GP 13.5GB	13500	8		181-30	16/16383/63	—/—	3.5 3H	
Deskstar 16GP 16.8GB	16800	10	13085			—/—		3H 4.9
Deskstar 16GP 3.2GB	3200	2	13085			—/—		3H 3.4
Deskstar 16GP 4.3GB	4300	3	13085			—/—		3H 3.4
Deskstar 16GP 6.4GB	6400	4	13085			—/—		3H 3.4
Deskstar 16GP 8.4GB	8400	5	13085			—/—		3H 3.4
Deskstar 1700AT	1700	2				—/—	3.5 3H	
Deskstar 22GXP 13.5GB	13500	6	15012			—/—	3.5 3H	5.2
Deskstar 22GXP 18.0GB	18000	8	15012			—/—	3.5 3H	6.9
Deskstar 22GXP 22.0GB	22000	10	15012			—/—	3.5 3H	6.9
Deskstar 22GXP 9.1GB	9100	4	15012			—/—	3.5 3H	5.2
Deskstar 25GP 10.1GB	10100	4	15302			—/—	3.5 3H	3.4
Deskstar 25GP 15.2GB	15200	6	15302			—/—	3.5 3H	3.4
Deskstar 25GP 20.3GB	20300	8	15302			—/—	3.5 3H	4.9
Deskstar 25GP 25.0GB	25000	10	15302			—/—	3.5 3H	4.9
Deskstar 3	2160					—/—	3.5 3H	
Deskstar 34GXP 13.6GB	13600	4	17494			—/—	3.5 3H	6.9
Deskstar 34GXP 20.5GB	20500	6	17494			—/—	3.5 3H	5.2
Deskstar 34GXP 27.3GB	27300	8	17494			—/—	3.5 3H	6.9
Deskstar 34GXP 34.2GB	34200	10	17494			—/—	3.5 3H	6.9
Deskstar 37GP 15.0GB	15000	4	17688			—/—	3.5 3H	4.9
Deskstar 37GP 22.5GB	22500	6	17688			—/—	3.5 3H	3.7
Deskstar 37GP 30.0GB	30000	8	17688			—/—	3.5 3H	4.9
Deskstar 37GP 37.5GB	37500	10	17688			—/—	3.5 3H	4.9
Deskstar 4 3.61GB	3610	5	8210			—/—	3.5 3H	3.5
Deskstar 4 4.33GB	4330	6	8210			—/—	3.5 3H	3.5
Deskstar 40GV 10GB	1027					—/—	3H	
Deskstar 40GV 20GB	20000	2	34326			—/—	3H	
Deskstar 40GV 30GB	30000	3	34326			—/—	3H	
Deskstar 40GV 40GB	40000	4	34326			—/—	3H	
Deskstar 5 EIDE	4200	6				—/—	3.5 3H	
Deskstar 5 EIDE	6400					—/—	3.5 3H	
Deskstar 5 EIDE	4860	6	8209			—/—	3.5 3H	4.7
Deskstar 540AT	540					—/—	3.5 3H	
Deskstar 60GXP 20GB	20.57GB	2				—/—	3.5 3H	6.7
Deskstar 60GXP 30GB	30GB					—/—	3.5 3H	6.7

Drive Model	Format Size MB	Seek Time	Interface	Encode	cache kb	RPM
DCMS 310800	10800	9	SCSI-2FstW		512k	5400
DCRA 22160	2160	12	IDE AT		96k	4200
DCXA 208100	8100	12	ATA-4		512k	4200
DCXA 210000	10000	12	ATA-4		512k	4200
DCYA 214000	14100	12	ATA-4		512k	4900
DDLA 21215	1215	13	ATA-3	PRML	128k	4000
DDLA 21620	1620	13	ATA-3	PRML	128k	4000
DDRS 34560	4500	7.5	SCA-2	PRML16,17	512k	7200
DDRS 34560	4500	7.5	SCA-2FstW	PRML16,17	512k	7200
DDRS 39130	9100	7.5	Ultra SCSI3	PRML16,17	512k	7200
DDRS 39130	9100	7.5	Ultra2 SCSI	PRML16,17	512k	7200
DDYD-DDYF 9.1GB	9100	4.9	UL160SCSI		4mb	1000
DDYS-DDYF 18.3GB	18300	4.9	UL160SCSI		4mb	1000
DDYS-DDYF 18.3GB	18300	4.9	FC-AL		4mb	1000
DDYS-DDYF 36.7GB	36700	4.9	UL160SCSI		4mb	1000
DDYS-DDYF 36.7GB	36700	4.9	FC-AL		4mb	1000
DDYD-DDYF 9.1GB	9100	4.9	FC-AL		4mb	1000
Deskstar 10GP 10.1GB	10GB	9.5	ATA-4	PRML	512k	5400
Deskstar 10GXP 10.1GB	10GB	9.5	ATA-4	PRML	512k	7200
Deskstar 120GXP102GB	10GB	8.5	ATA/100			7200
Deskstar 120GXP120GB	123GB	8.5	ATA/100			7200
Deskstar 120GXP 20GB	21GB	8.5	ATA/100			7200
Deskstar 120GXP 41GB	41GB	8.5	ATA/100			7200
Deskstar 120GXP 61GB	61GB	8.5	ATA/100			7200
Deskstar 120GXP 82GB	82GB	8.5	ATA/100			7200
Deskstar 13GP 13.5GB	13500	9.5	ATA-4	PRML	512k	5400
Deskstar 14GXP 10.1GB	10100	9.5	ATA-4	PRML	512k	7200
Deskstar 14GXP 12.9GB	12900	9.5	ATA-4	PRML	512k	7200
Deskstar 14GXP 14.4GB	14400	9.5	ATA-4	PRML	512k	7200
Deskstar 16GP 10.1GB	10100	9.5	ATA-4	PRML	512k	5400
Deskstar 16GP 12.9GB	12900	9.5	ATA-4	PRML	512k	5400
Deskstar 16GP 13.5GB	13500	9.5	ATA-4	PRML	512k	5400
Deskstar 16GP 16.8GB	16800	9.5	ATA-4	PRML	512k	5400
Deskstar 16GP 3.2GB	3200	9.5	ATA-4	PRML	512k	5400
Deskstar 16GP 4.3GB	4300	9.5	ATA-4	PRML	512k	5400
Deskstar 16GP 6.4GB	6400	9.5	ATA-4	PRML	512k	5400
Deskstar 16GP 8.4GB	8400	9.5	ATA-4	PRML	512k	5400
Deskstar 1700AT	1700	12	ATA-2		128k	4500
Deskstar 22GXP 13.5GB	13500	9.0	ATA-4		2mb	7200
Deskstar 22GXP 18.0GB	18000	9.0	ATA-4		2mb	7200
Deskstar 22GXP 22.0GB	22000	9.0	ATA-4		2mb	7200
Deskstar 22GXP 9.1GB	9100	9.0	ATA-4		2mb	7200
Deskstar 25GP 10.1GB	10100	9	ATA-4		512k	5400
Deskstar 25GP 15.2GB	15200	9	ATA-4		512k	5400
Deskstar 25GP 20.3GB	20300	9.0	ATA-4		2mb	5400
Deskstar 25GP 25.0GB	25000	9.0	ATA-4		2mb	5400
Deskstar 3	2160	9.5	EIDE		128k	5400
Deskstar 34GXP 13.6GB	13600	9	ATA-4		2mb	7200
Deskstar 34GXP 20.5GB	20500	9	ATA-4		2mb	7200
Deskstar 34GXP 27.3GB	27300	9	ATA-4		2mb	7200
Deskstar 34GXP 34.2GB	34200	9	ATA-4		2mb	7200
Deskstar 37GP 15.0GB	15000	9	ATA-4		2mb	5400
Deskstar 37GP 22.5GB	22500	9	ATA-4		512k	5400
Deskstar 37GP 30.0GB	30000	9	ATA-4		2mb	5400
Deskstar 37GP 37.5GB	37500	9	ATA-4		2mb	5400
Deskstar 4 3.61GB	3610	9.5	ATA-3	PRML	128k	5400
Deskstar 4 4.33GB	4330	9.5	ATA-3	PRML	128k	5400
Deskstar 40GV 10GB	1027	9.5	ATA		512k	5400
Deskstar 40GV 20GB	20000	9.5	ATA		512k	5400
Deskstar 40GV 30GB	30000	9.5	ATA		512k	5400
Deskstar 40GV 40GB	40000	9.5	ATA		512k	5400
Deskstar 5 EIDE	4200	9.5	ATA-3 Fast		128k	5400
Deskstar 5 EIDE	6400	9.5	EIDE			7200
Deskstar 5 EIDE	4860	9.5	ATA-3 Fast		512k	5400
Deskstar 540AT	540	12	ATA-2		128k	4500
Deskstar 60GXP 20GB	20.57GB	8.5	ATA/100		2mb	7200
Deskstar 60GXP 30GB	30GB	8.5	ATA/100		2mb	7200

Drive Model	Format Size MB	Head	Cyl	Sect/Trac	Translate H/C/S	RWC/WPC	Form Factor	Power Watts
Deskstar 60GXP 40GB	41.17GB	4				—/—	3.5 3H	6.7
Deskstar 60GXP 60GB	61.49GB	6				—/—	3.5 3H	6.7
Deskstar 6GP 6.4GB	6400	4	13085				3H	3.4
Deskstar 75GXP 15GB	15000	2	27724			—/—	3H	
Deskstar 75GXP 20GB	20000	3	27724			—/—	3H	
Deskstar 75GXP 30GB	30000	4	27724			—/—	3H	
Deskstar 75GXP 45GB	45000	6	27724			—/—	3H	
Deskstar 75GXP 60GB	60000	8	27724			—/—	3H	
Deskstar 75GXP 75GB	75000	10	27724			—/—	3H	
Deskstar 8 4.3GB	4330	4		154-26	16/16383/63	—/—	3.5 3H	
Deskstar 8 6.4GB	6480	6		154-26	16/16383/63	—/—	3.5 3H	
Deskstar 8 8.4GB	8400	8			16/16383/63	—/—	3.5 3H	
Deskstar 8GP 8.4GB	8400	5	13085			—/—	3H	3.4
Deskstar XP 1.	1080	4				—/—	3.5 3H	
DFHC 31080	1126	4				—/—	3.5 3H	
DFHC 32160	2255	8				—/—	3.5 3H	
DFHC 32160	2255	8				—/—	3.5 3H	
DFHC 34320	4512	16				—/—	3.5HH	
DFHC 34320	4512	16				—/—	3.5HH	
DFHC C4x	4510	16				—/—	3.5 3H	1.26
DFHS 31080 S1F	1126	4				—/—	3.5 3H	
DFHS 32160	2255	8				—/—	3.5 3H	
DFHS 32160 S2D	2255					—/—	3.5 3H	8.9
DFHS 32160 S2F	2250					—/—	3.5 3H	
DFHS 32160 S2W	2250					—/—	3.5 3H	
DFHS 34320	4512	16				—/—	3.5HH	
DFHS 34320 S4D	4512					—/—	3.5HH	13.3
DFHS 34320 S4F	4510					—/—	3.5HH	
DFHS 34320 S4W	4510					—/—	3.5HH	
DFMS 31080	1320	4				—/—	3.5 3H	
DFMS 32160	2325	8				—/—	3.5 3H	
DFMS 32600	2657	8				—/—	3.5 3H	
DFMS 34320	4320	13				—/—	3.5HH	
DFMS 351AV	5106	16				—/—	3.5HH	
DFMS 35250	5318	16				—/—	3.5HH	
DFMS 35250 S5D	5318					—/—	3.5HH	
DFMS 35250 S5F	5318					—/—	3.5HH	
DFMS 35250 S5W	5318					—/—	3.5HH	
DGHL 39110	9100	10				—/—	3.5 4H	9.2
DGHS 318200	18200	20				—/—	3.5 3H	13.1
DGHS 39110	9100	10				—/—	3.5 4H	9.2
DGHS 39110	9100	10				—/—	3.5 4H	9.2
DGHU 39110	9100	10				—/—	3.5 4H	9.2
DGVS 39110	9100	12				—/—		16.5
DHAA 2270	270	2	2788		16/524/63	—/—	2.5 4H	4.7
DHAA 2344	344	3	2788			—/—	2.5 4H	4.7
DHAA 2405	405	3	2788		16/785/63	—/—	2.5 4H	4.7
DHAA 2540	540	4	2788		16/1047/63	—/—	2.5 4H	4.7
DHAS 2270	270	2	2788			—/—	2.5 4H	4.7
DHAS 2344	344	3	2788			—/—	2.5 4H	4.7
DHAS 2405	405	3	2788			—/—	2.5 4H	4.7
DHAS 2540	540	4	2788			—/—	2.5 4H	4.7
DHEA 34330	4330	5	8209			—/—	3.5 3H	4.7
DHEA 34331	4330	4		154-26	16/16383/63	—/—	3.5 3H	
DHEA 34860	4860	6	8209			—/—	3.5 3H	4.7
DHEA 34860	4860	8	8209			—/—	3.5 3H	4.7
DHEA 36480	6480	8	8209			—/—	3.5 3H	4.7
DHEA 36481	6480	6		154-26	16/16383/63	—/—	3.5 3H	4.7
DHEA 38451	8450	8	9784			—/—	3.5 3H	
DJAA 31270	1270				16/2480/63	—/—	3.5 3H	
DJAA 31700	1700				16/3308/63	—/—	3.5 3H	
DJNA 351010	10100	4	15302			—/—	3.5 3H	3.4
DJNA 351520	15200	6	15302			—/—	3.5 3H	3.4
DJNA 352030	20300	8	15302			—/—	3.5 3H	4.9
DJNA 352500	25000	10	15302			—/—	3.5 3H	4.9
DJNA 370910	9100	4	15012			—/—	3.5 3H	5.2
DJNA 371350	13500	6	15012			—/—	3.5 3H	5.2

Drive Model	Format Size MB	Seek Time	Interface	Encode	cache kb	RPM
Deskstar 60GXP 40GB	41.17GB	8.5	ATA/100		2mb	7200
Deskstar 60GXP 60GB	61.49GB	8.5	ATA/100		2mb	7200
Deskstar 6GP 6.4GB	6400	9.5	ATA-4	PRML	512k	5400
Deskstar 75GXP 15GB	15000	8.5	ATA		2mb	7200
Deskstar 75GXP 20GB	20000	8.5	ATA		2mb	7200
Deskstar 75GXP 30GB	30000	8.5	ATA		2mb	7200
Deskstar 75GXP 45GB	45000	8.5	ATA		2mb	7200
Deskstar 75GXP 60GB	60000	8.5	ATA		2mb	7200
Deskstar 75GXP 75GB	75000	8.5	ATA		2mb	7200
Deskstar 8 4.3GB	4330	9.5	IDE			5400
Deskstar 8 6.4GB	6480	9.5	IDE			5400
Deskstar 8 8.4GB	8400	9.5	IDE			5400
Deskstar 8GP 8.4GB	8400	9.5	ATA-4	PRML	512k	5400
Deskstar XP 1.	1080	10.5	ATA-2	PRML	512k	5400
DFHC 31080	1126	9	SSA		512k	7200
DFHC 32160	2255	9	SSA		512k	7200
DFHC 32160	2255	9	SSA		512k	7200
DFHC 34320	4512	9	SSA		512k	7200
DFHC 34320	4512	9	SSA		512k	7200
DFHC C4x	4510	8	SSA			7200
DFHS 31080 S1F	1126	9	SCSI-2 F/FW		512k	7200
DFHS 32160	2255	9	SCSI-2 F/FW		512k	7200
DFHS 32160 S2D	2255	7.5	SCSI-2Diff		512k	7200
DFHS 32160 S2F	2250	7.5	SCSI-2Fast		512k	7200
DFHS 32160 S2W	2250	7.5	SCSI-2FstW		512k	7200
DFHS 34320	4512	9.5	SCSI-2 F/FW		512k	7200
DFHS 34320 S4D	4512	8	SCSI-2Diff		512k	7200
DFHS 34320 S4F	4510	8	SCSI-2Fast		512k	7200
DFHS 34320 S4W	4510	8	SCSI-2FstW		512k	7200
DFMS 31080	1320	7	SCSI-2Fast		512k	5400
DFMS 32160	2325	9	SCSI-2Fast		512k	5400
DFMS 32600	2657	9	SCSI-2Fast		512k	5400
DFMS 34320	4320	9.5	SCSI-2Fast		512k	5400
DFMS 351AV	5106	9.5	SCSI-2 F/W		512k	5400
DFMS 35250	5318	9.5	SCSI-2Fast		512k	5400
DFMS 35250 S5D	5318	8	SCSI-2Diff		512k	5400
DFMS 35250 S5F	5318	8	SCSI-2Diff		512k	5400
DFMS 35250 S5W	5318	8	SCSI-2FstW		512k	5400
DGHL 39110	9100	6.5	FC-AL	RLL 16,17	1000k	7200
DGHS 318200	18200	6.5	SCA-2FstWd	RLL 16,17	1000k	7200
DGHS 39110	9100	6.5	SSA	RLL 16,17	1000k	7200
DGHS 39110	9100	6.5	SCA-2FstWd	RLL 16,17	1000k	7200
DGHU 39110	9100	6.5	SCA-2FstWd	RLL 16,17	1000k	7200
DGVS 39110	9100	6.3	ULSCSI40FST	PRML	1mb	1000
DHAA 2270	270	14	IDE AT		32k	3800
DHAA 2344	344	14	IDE AT		32k	3800
DHAA 2405	405	14	IDE AT		32k	3800
DHAA 2540	540	14	IDE AT		32k	3800
DHAS 2270	270	14	SCSI-2Fast		32k	3800
DHAS 2344	344	14	SCSI-2Fast		32k	3800
DHAS 2405	405	14	SCSI-2Fast		32k	3800
DHAS 2540	540	14	SCSI-2Fast		32k	3800
DHEA 34330	4330	9.5	ATA-3	PRML	512k	5400
DHEA 34331	4330	9.5	IDE			5400
DHEA 34860	4860	9.5	ATA-3	PRML	512k	5400
DHEA 34860	4860	9.5	ATA-3 Fast		512k	5400
DHEA 36480	6480	9.5	ATA-3	PRML	512k	5400
DHEA 36481	6480	9.5	IDE			5400
DHEA 38451	8450	9.5	ATA-3	PRML	512k	5400
DJAA 31270	1270	12	IDE		96k	4500
DJAA 31700	1700	12	IDE		96k	4500
DJNA 351010	10100	9	ATA-4		512k	5400
DJNA 351520	15200	9	ATA-4		512k	5400
DJNA 352030	20300	9.0	ATA-4		2mb	5400
DJNA 352500	25000	9.0	ATA-4		2mb	5400
DJNA 370910	9100	9.0	ATA-4		2mb	7200
DJNA 371350	13500	9.0	ATA-4		2mb	7200

Drive Model	Format Size MB	Head	Cyl	Sect/Trac	Translate H/C/S	RWC/WPC	Form Factor	Power Watts
DJNA 371800	18000	8	15012			—/—	3.5 3H	6.9
DJNA 372200	22000	10	15012			—/—	3.5 3H	6.9
DJSA 205000	5000	1	22784			—/—	2.5 4H	
DJSA 210000	10000	2	22784			—/—	2.5 4H	
DJSA 220000	20000	4	22784			—/—	2.5 4H	
DJSA 230000	30000	6	22784			—/—	2.5 4H	
DJSA 232000	32000	8	21664			—/—	2.5 4H	
DKLA 22160	2160	2	9280			—/—		4.7
DKLA 23240	3240	3	9280			—/—		4.7
DKLA 24320	4320	4	9280			—/—		4.7
DLGA 22690	2690	7	5120		16/5216/63	—/—	2.5 4H	2.0
DLGA 23080	3080	7	5120		16/5968/63	—/—	2.5 4H	2.0
DMCA 21080	1080	3	4975		16/2100/63	—/—	2.5 4H	1.7
DMCA 21440	1440	4	4975		16/2800/63	—/—	2.5 4H	1.7
DMDM 10170	170	2				—/—	3H	
DMDM 10340	340					—/—	3H	
DMVS 18	18300	10				—/—		11.5
DMVS 36	36700	20				—/—		17.4
DMVS 9	9100	5				—/—		10.0
DNEF 309170	9100	5	11347			—/—	3.5 3H	8.3
DNEF 318350	18200	10	11347			—/—	3.5 3H	9.9
DNES 309170	9100	5	11347			—/—	3.5 3H	5.3
DNES 318350	18200	10	11347			—/—	3.5 3H	6.9
DORS 32160	2160	3				—/—	3.5 3H	3.9
DPEA 30540	540				16/1050/63	—/—	3.5 3H	2.7
DPEA 30810	812				16/1574/63	—/—	3.5 3H	
DPEA 31080	1083				16/2100/63	—/—	3.5 3H	17.5
DPES 30540	540	4	4896			—/—	3.5 3H	17.5
DPES 30810	810	4	4896			—/—	3.5 3H	17.5
DPES 31080	1080	4	4896			—/—	3.5 3H	17.5
DPLA 24480	4480	7	6976			—/—	2.5 4H	2.0
DPLA 25120	5120	8	6976			—/—	2.5 4H	2.0
DPRA 20810	810	16	1572	63		—/—	2.5 4H	1.3
DPRA 21215	1215	16	2358	63		—/—	2.5 4H	1.3
DPRS 20810	810					—/—	2.5 4H	1.6
DPRS 21215	1215	16	2358	63		—/—	2.5 4H	1.3
DPSS 309170	9100	3				—/—	3.5 3H	8.9
DPSS 318350	18300	5				—/—	3.5 3H	8.9
DPSS 336950	36900	10				—/—	3.5 3H	8.9
DPTA 351500	15000	4	17688			—/—	3.5 3H	4.9
DPTA 352250	22500	6	17688			—/—	3.5 3H	3.7
DPTA 353000	30000	8	17688			—/—	3.5 3H	4.9
DPTA 353750	37500	10	17688			—/—	3.5 3H	4.9
DPTA 371360	13600	4	17494			—/—	3.5 3H	6.9
DPTA 372050	20500	6	17494			—/—	3.5 3H	5.2
DPTA 372730	27300	8	17494			—/—	3.5 3H	6.9
DPTA 373420	34200	10	17494			—/—	3.5 3H	6.9
DRHL 36L	36400	20	11275			—/—	3.5HH	13.1
DRHS 36D	36400	20	11275			—/—	3.5HH	13.1
DRHS 36V	36400	20	11275			—/—	3.5HH	13.1
DRVS 09D	9100	10	7065			—/—	3.5 3H	10.1
DRVS 18D	18200	20	7065			—/—	3.5HH	16.3
DRVS 18LV	18200	20	7065			—/—	3.5HH	16.3
DSAA 3270	270					—/—	3.5 3H	15.7
DSAA 3360	364					—/—	3.5 3H	15.7
DSAA 3540	548	3	3875			—/—	3.5 3H	15.7
DSAA 3720	720	3	3875			—/—	3.5 3H	15.7
DSAS 3270	270					—/—	3.5 3H	15.7
DSAS 3360	364					—/—	3.5 3H	15.7
DSAS 3540	548	4	3875			—/—	3.5 3H	15.7
DSAS 3720	720	4	3875			—/—	3.5 3H	15.7
DSCM 10340	340					—/—		
DSCM 10512	512					—/—		
DSCM 11000	1000					—/—		
DSOA 20540	540				16/1050/63	—/—	2.5 4H	1.7
DSOA 20810	810				16/1575/63	—/—	2.5 4H	1.7
DSOA 21080	1080				16/2100/63	—/—	2.5 4H	1.7

Drive Model	Format Size MB	Seek Time	Interface	Encode	cache kb	RPM
DJNA 371800	18000	9.0	ATA-4		2mb	7200
DJNA 372200	22000	9.0	ATA-4		2mb	7200
DJSA 205000	5000	12	ATA-5		512k	4200
DJSA 210000	10000	12	ATA-5		512k	4200
DJSA 220000	20000	12	ATA-5		2048k	4200
DJSA 230000	30000	12	ATA-5		2048k	4200
DJSA 232000	32000	12	ATA-5		2048k	5411
DKLA 22160	2160	12	ATA-4		512k	4200
DKLA 23240	3240	12	ATA-4		512k	4200
DKLA 24320	4320	12	ATA-4		512k	4200
DLGA 22690	2690	12	ATA-3	PRML	128k	4900
DLGA 23080	3080	12	ATA-3	PRML	128k	4900
DMCA 21080	1080	13	ATA-3	PRML	128k	4000
DMCA 21440	1440	13	ATA-3	PRML	128k	4000
DMDM 10170	170	15	IDE AT		128k	4500
DMDM 10340	340	15	IDE AT		128k	4500
DMVS 18	18300	4.9	Ultra 160	RLL 16,17	2mb	1000
DMVS 36	36700	5.4	Ultra2 SCSI	RLL 16,17	2mb	1000
DMVS 9	9100	4.9	Ultra 160	RLL 16,17	2mb	1000
DNEF 309170	9100	7.0	FC-AL		2mb	7200
DNEF 318350	18200	7.0	FC-AL		2mb	7200
DNES 309170	9100	7.0	Ultra SCSI		2mb	7200
DNES 318350	18200	7.0	Ultra SCSI		2mb	7200
DORS 32160	2160	8.5	SCSI-3Ultra		512k	5400
DPEA 30540	540	10.5	ATA-2		448k	5400
DPEA 30810	812	10.5	IDE AT		448k	5400
DPEA 31080	1083	10.5	ATA-2		448k	5400
DPES 30540	540	10.5	SCSI-2Fast		512k	5400
DPES 30810	810	10.5	SCSI-2Fast		512k	5400
DPES 31080	1080	10.5	SCSI-2Fast		512k	5400
DPLA 24480	4480	12	ATA-3	PRML	512k	4900
DPLA 25120	5120	12	ATA-3	PRML	512k	4900
DPRA 20810	810	12	ATA-2		64k	4900
DPRA 21215	1215	12	ATA-2		64k	4900
DPRS 20810	810	12	SCSI-2		64k	4900
DPRS 21215	1215	12	SCSI-2		64k	4900
DPSS 309170	9100	6.8	UL160SCSI		4mb	7200
DPSS 318350	18300	6.8	UL160SCSI		4mb	7200
DPSS 336950	36900	6.8	UL160SCSI		4mb	7200
DPTA 351500	15000	9	ATA-4		2mb	5400
DPTA 352250	22500	9	ATA-4		512k	5400
DPTA 353000	30000	9	ATA-4		2mb	5400
DPTA 353750	37500	9	ATA-4		2mb	5400
DPTA 371360	13600	9	ATA-4		2mb	7200
DPTA 372050	20500	9	ATA-4		2mb	7200
DPTA 372730	27300	9	ATA-4		2mb	7200
DPTA 373420	34200	9	ATA-4		2mb	7200
DRHL 36L	36400	7.5	FC-AL	RLL 16,17	4mb	7200
DRHS 36D	36400	7.5	SSA	RLL 16,17	4mb	7200
DRHS 36V	36400	7.5	Ultra2 LVD	RLL 16,17	4mb	7200
DRVS 09D	9100	5.6	SSA	16,17 RLL	4mb	1002
DRVS 18D	18200	6.5	SSA	16,17 RLL	4mb	1002
DRVS 18LV	18200	6.5	Ultra2 LVD	16,17 RLL	4mb	1002
DSAA 3270	270	12	IDE AT		96k	4500
DSAA 3360	364	12	IDE AT		96k	4500
DSAA 3540	548	12	ATA-2		128k	4500
DSAA 3720	720	12	ATA-2		128k	4500
DSAS 3270	270	12	SCSI-2Fast		96k	4500
DSAS 3360	364	12	SCSI-2Fast		96k	4500
DSAS 3540	548	12	SCSI-2Fast		128k	4500
DSAS 3720	720	12	SCSI-2Fast		128k	4500
DSCM 10340	340	12	CF+		128k	3600
DSCM 10512	512	12	CF+		128k	3600
DSCM 11000	1000	12	CF+		128k	3600
DSOA 20540	540	13	IDE AT		128k	4000
DSOA 20810	810	13	IDE AT		128k	4000
DSOA 21080	1080	13	IDE AT		128k	4000

Drive Model	Format Size MB	Head	Cyl	Sect/Trac	Translate H/C/S	RWC/WPC	Form Factor	Power Watts
DTCA 23240	3240	5	6976			—/—	2.5 4H	1.85
DTCA 24090	4090	6	6976			—/—	2.5 4H	1.85
DTLA 305010	1027						3H	
DTLA 305020	20000	2	34326			—/—	3H	
DTLA 305030	30000	3	34326			—/—	3H	
DTLA 305040	40000	4	34326			—/—	3H	
DTLA 307015	15000	2	27724			—/—	3H	
DTLA 307020	20000	2	27724			—/—	3H	
DTLA 307030	30000	4	27724			—/—	3H	
DTLA 307045	45000	6	27724			—/—	3H	
DTLA 307060	60000	8	27724			—/—	3H	
DTLA 307075	75000	10	27724			—/—	3H	
DTNA 21800	1800	5	4928			—/—	2.5 4H	1.85
DTNA 22160	2160	6	4928			—/—	2.5 4H	1.85
DTTA 350320	3200	2	13085			—/—	3H	3.4
DTTA 350430	4300	3	13085			—/—	3H	3.4
DTTA 350640	6400	4	13085			—/—	3H	3.4
DTTA 350840	8400	5	13085			—/—	3H	3.4
DTTA 351010	10100	6	13085			—/—	3H	4.9
DTTA 351290	12900	8	13085			—/—	3H	4.9
DTTA 351350	13500	8	13085			—/—	3H	3.4
DTTA 351680	16800	10	13085			—/—	3H	4.9
DTTA 371010	10100	7	13085			—/—	3H	6.9
DTTA 371290	12900	8	13085			—/—	3H	6.9
DTTA 371440	14400	10	13085			—/—	3H	6.9
DTZN 0810SP	8000	10				—/—		2.0
DTZN 1000TP	10000	6				—/—		1.85
DVAA 2810	810	6	2788		16/1571/63	—/—	2.5 4H	4.7
DVAA 2810	810				16/1571/63	—/—	2.5 4H	1.2
DVAS 2810	810	6	2788			—/—	2.5 4H	4.7
DYKA 22160	2160	3	8128			—/—	2.5 4H	2.3
DYKA 23240	3240	4	8128			—/—	2.5 4H	2.3
DYLA 26480	6480	8	8320			—/—	2.5 4H	1.3
DYLA 27900	7900				15/16383/63	—/—	2.5 4H	
DYLA 28100	8100	10	8320			—/—	2.5 4H	1.3
H1172-S2	172	2	2264			—/—	2.5 4H	4.7
H2172-A2	172	2	2264			Auto/Auto	2.5 4H	4.7
H2172-S2	172	2	2264			Auto/Auto	2.5 3H	4.7
H2258-A3	258	3	2264			—/—	2.5 4H	4.7
H2258-S3	258	3	2264			—/—	2.5 4H	4.7
H2344-A4	344	4	2264			—/—	2.5 4H	4.7
H2344-S4	344	4	2264			—/—	2.5 4H	4.7
H3133-A2	133	2	2420		15/1023/17	—/—	3.5 3H	
H3171-A2	171	2	2420		10/984/34	—/—	3.5 3H	
H3256-A3	256	3	2420		16/872/36	—/—	3.5 3H	
H3342-A4	342	4	2420		16/872/48	—/—	3.5 3H	
IC25N006ATDA04	6GB	1				—/—	2.5 4H	0.85
IC25N010ATCS04	10GB	1				—/—	2.5 4H	0.85
IC25N010ATDA04	10GB	2				—/—	2.5 4H	0.85
IC25N015ATDA04	15GB	2				—/—	2.5 4H	0.85
IC25N020ATCS04	20GB	1				—/—	2.5 4H	0.85
IC25N020ATCS05	20GB	2				—/—	2.5 4H	1.3
IC25N020ATD	20GB	3				—/—	2.5 4H	1.85
IC25N030ATCS04	30GB	2				—/—	2.5 4H	065
IC25N030ATDA04	30GB	4				—/—	2.5 4H	1.85
IC25N040ATCS04	40GB	2				—/—	2.5 4H	065
IC25N040ATCS05	40GB	4				—/—	2.5 4H	1.3
IC25T006ATDA04	6GB	1				—/—	2.5 4H	0.85
IC25T010ATDA04	10GB	2				—/—	2.5 4H	0.85
IC25T015ATDA04	15GB	2				—/—	2.5 4H	0.85
IC25T048ATDA05	48GB	8				—/—	2.5 4H	1.3
IC25T060ATCS05	60GB	4				—/—	2.5 4H	1.3
IC25T060ATCX05	60GB	4				—/—	2.5 4H	1.3
IC35L009F2D210	9.17GB	2				—/—	3.5 3H	5.6
IC35L009UCD210	9.17GB	2				—/—	3.5 3H	5.6
IC35L009UWD210	9.17GB	12				—/—	3.5 3H	9.5
IC35L009UWD210	9.17GB	2				—/—	3.5 3H	5.6

Drive Model	Format Size MB	Seek Time	Interface	Encode	cache kb	RPM
DTCA 23240	3240	13	ATA-3	PRML	512k	4000
DTCA 24090	4090	13	ATA-3	PRML	512k	4000
DTLA 305010	1027	9.5	ATA		512k	5400
DTLA 305020	20000	9.5	ATA		512k	5400
DTLA 305030	30000	9.5	ATA		512k	5400
DTLA 305040	40000	9.5	ATA		512k	5400
DTLA 307015	15000	8.5	ATA		2mb	7200
DTLA 307020	20000	8.5	ATA		2mb	7200
DTLA 307030	30000	8.5	ATA		2mb	7200
DTLA 307045	45000	8.5	ATA		2mb	7200
DTLA 307060	60000	8.5	ATA		2mb	7200
DTLA 307075	75000	8.5	ATA		2mb	7200
DTNA 21800	1800	13	ATA-3	PRML	128k	4000
DTNA 22160	2160	13	ATA-3	PRML	128k	4000
DTTA 350320	3200	9.5	ATA-4	PRML	512k	5400
DTTA 350430	4300	9.5	ATA-4	PRML	512k	5400
DTTA 350640	6400	9.5	ATA-4	PRML	512k	5400
DTTA 350840	8400	9.5	ATA-4	PRML	512k	5400
DTTA 351010	10100	9.5	ATA-4	PRML	512k	5400
DTTA 351290	12900	9.5	ATA-4	PRML	512k	5400
DTTA 351350	13500	9.5	ATA-4	PRML	512k	5400
DTTA 351680	16800	9.5	ATA-4	PRML	512k	5400
DTTA 371010	10100	9.5	ATA-4	PRML	512k	7200
DTTA 371290	12900	9.5	ATA-4	PRML	512k	7200
DTTA 371440	14400	9.5	ATA-4	PRML	512k	7200
DTZN 0810SP	8000	12	PCMCIA		512k	
DTZN 1000TP	10000	12	PCMCIA		512k	
DVAA 2810	810	14	IDE AT		32k	3800
DVAA 2810	810	14	IDE AT	1,7 RLL	32k	3800
DVAS 2810	810	14	SCSI-2Fast		32k	3800
DYKA 22160	2160	13	ATA-3	PRML	128k	4200
DYKA 23240	3240	13	ATA-3	PRML	128k	4200
DYLA 26480	6480	12	ATA-3	PRML	512k	4900
DYLA 27900	7900	12	EIDE	PRML	459k	4900
DYLA 28100	8100	12	ATA-3	PRML	512k	4900
H1172-S2	172	14	SCSI		32k	3800
H2172-A2	172	14	IDE AT		32k	3800
H2172-S2	172	14	SCSI-2		32k	3800
H2258-A3	258	14	IDE AT		32k	3800
H2258-S3	258	14	SCSI		32k	3800
H2344-A4	344	14	IDE AT		32k	3800
H2344-S4	344	14	SCSI		32k	3800
H3133-A2	133	14	IDE AT		96k	3600
H3171-A2	171	14	IDE AT		96k	3600
H3256-A3	256	14	IDE AT		96k	3600
H3342-A4	342	14	IDE AT		96k	3600
IC25N006ATDA04	6GB	12	ATA-5	PRML		4200
IC25N010ATCS04	10GB	12	ATA-5	PRML	2mb	4200
IC25N010ATDA04	10GB	12	ATA-5	PRML		4200
IC25N015ATDA04	15GB	12	ATA-5	PRML		4200
IC25N020ATCS04	20GB	12	ATA-5	PRML	2mb	4200
IC25N020ATCS05	20GB	12	ATA-5		8192k	5400
IC25N020ATD	20GB	12	ATA-5	PRML	2048k	4200
IC25N030ATCS04	30GB	12	ATA-5	PRML	2mb	4200
IC25N030ATDA04	30GB	12	ATA-5	PRML	2048k	4200
IC25N040ATCS04	40GB	12	ATA-5	PRML	2mb	4200
IC25N040ATCS05	40GB	12	ATA-5		8192k	5400
IC25T006ATDA04	6GB	12	ATA-5	PRML		4200
IC25T010ATDA04	10GB	12	ATA-5	PRML		4200
IC25T015ATDA04	15GB	12	ATA-5	PRML		4200
IC25T048ATDA05	48GB	12	ATA-5	PRML	2048k	5400
IC25T060ATCS05	60GB	12	ATA-5	PRML	2mb	5400
IC25T060ATCX05	60GB	12	ATA-5	PRML	2mb	5400
IC35L009F2D210	9.17GB	4.9	FC-AL2		4096k	1000
IC35L009UCD210	9.17GB	4.9	UL160SCSI		4096k	1000
IC35L009UWD210	9.17GB	4.9	UL160SCSIW		4096k	1000
IC35L009UWD210	9.17GB	4.9	UL160SCSIW		4096k	1000

Drive Model	Format Size MB	Head	Cyl	Sect/ Trac	Translate H/C/S	RWC/ WPC	Form Factor	Power Watts
IC35L018F2D210	18.3GB	3				—/—	3.5 3H	6.7
IC35L018F2DY10 18.3GB	18.3GB	2				—/—	3.5 3H	6.8
IC35L018UCD210	18.3GB	3				—/—	3.5 3H	6.7
IC35L018UCDY10 18GB	18.3GB	2				—/—	3.5 3H	5.9
IC35L018UCPR15	18.35GB	8				—/—	3.5 3H	11
IC35L018UWD210	18.3GB	3				—/—	3.5 3H	6.7
IC35L018UWDY10 18GB	18.3GB	2				—/—	3.5 3H	5.9
IC35L018UWPR15	18.4GB	8				—/—	3.5 3H	11
IC35L018XCPR15	18.35GB	8				—/—	3.5 3H	11
IC35L018XWPR15	18.4GB	8				—/—	3.5 3H	11
IC35L020AVER07	20.57GB	2				—/—	3.5 3H	6.7
IC35L020AVVA07	20.57GB					—/—		
IC35L030AVER07	30GB					—/—	3.5 3H	6.7
IC35L036F2D210	36.7GB	6				—/—	3.5 3H	7.4
IC35L036F2DY10 36GB	36.7GB	3				—/—	3.5 3H	7.0
IC35L036UCD210	36.7GB	6				—/—	3.5 3H	7.4
IC35L036UCDY10	36.7GB	3				—/—	3.5 3H	7.0
IC35L036UCPR15	36.7GB	12				—/—	3.5 3H	13.5
IC35L036UWD210	36.7GB	6				—/—	3.5 3H	7.4
IC35L036UWDY10	36.7GB	3				—/—	3.5 3H	7.0
IC35L036UWPR15	36.7GB	12				—/—	3.5 3H	13.5
IC35L036XCPR15	36.7GB	12				—/—	3.5 3H	13.5
IC35L036XWPR15	36.7GB	12				—/—	3.5 3H	13.5
IC35L040AVER07	41.17GB	4				—/—	3.5 3H	6.7
IC35L040AVVA07	41.17GB					—/—		
IC35L060AVER07	61.49GB	6				—/—	3.5 3H	6.7
IC35L060AVVA07	61.49GB					—/—		
IC35L073F2D210	73.41GB	12				—/—	3.5 3H	9.5
IC35L073F2DY10 73GB	73.4GB	6				—/—	3.5 3H	8.6
IC35L073UCD210	73.41GB	12				—/—	3.5 3H	9.5
IC35L073UCDY10 73GB	73.4GB	6				—/—	3.5 3H	7.7
IC35L073UWD210	73.41GB	12				—/—	3.5 3H	9.5
IC35L073UWDY10 73GB	73.4GB	6				—/—	3.5 3H	7.7
IC35L080AVVA07	82.34GB					—/—		
IC35L100AVVA07	102GB					—/—		
IC35L120AVVA07	123.52GB					—/—		
IC35L146F2DY10 146GB	146GB	12				—/—	3.5 3H	11.1
IC35L146UCDY10 146GB	146GB	12				—/—	3.5 3H	
IC35L146UWDY10 146GB	146GB	12				—/—	3.5 3H	
MicroDrive 1GB	1000					—/—		
MicroDrive 340MB	340					—/—		
MicroDrive 512MB	512					—/—		
Travelstar 10E	10000	6				—/—		1.85
Travelstar 10E	10000	6				—/—		1.85
Travelstar 10GT 10.0G	10000	6	11968			—/—	2.5 4H	1.85
Travelstar 10GT 8.1GB	8100	5	11968			—/—	2.5 4H	1.85
Travelstar 12GN 12.0GB	12000	4	17088			—/—	2.5 4H	1.85
Travelstar 12GN 6.0GB	6000	2	17088			—/—	2.5 4H	1.85
Travelstar 12GN 9.0GB	9000	3	17088			—/—	2.5 4H	1.85
Travelstar 14GS 14.1GB	14100	10	11136			—/—	2.5 4H	1.3
Travelstar 15GN 10GB	10GB	2				—/—	2.5 4H	0.85
Travelstar 15GN 15GB	15GB	2				—/—	2.5 4H	0.85
Travelstar 15GN 6GB	6GB	1				—/—	2.5 4H	0.85
Travelstar 18GT 15.1GB	15100	5	17088			—/—	2.5 4H	1.85
Travelstar 18GT 18.1GB	18100	6	17088			—/—	2.5 4H	1.85
Travelstar 20GN 10GB	10000	2	22784			—/—	2.5 4H	
Travelstar 20GN 20GB	20000	4	22784			—/—	2.5 4H	
Travelstar 20GN 5GB	5000	1	22784			—/—	2.5 4H	
Travelstar 25GS	25300	10	16064			—/—	2.5 4H	2.0
Travelstar 30GN	30GB	4				—/—	2.5 4H	1.85
Travelstar 30GN	20GB	3				—/—	2.5 4H	1.85
Travelstar 30GT	30000	6	22784			—/—	2.5 4H	
Travelstar 32GH	32000	8	21664			—/—	2.5 4H	
Travelstar 3GN 2.16GB	2160	3	8128			—/—	2.5 4H	2.3
Travelstar 3GN 3.24GB	3240	4	8128			—/—	2.5 4H	2.3
Travelstar 3LP	1080	3	4975		16/2100/63	—/—	2.5 4H	1.7
Travelstar 3LP	1440	4	4975		16/2800/63	—/—	2.5 4H	1.7

Drive Model	Format Size MB	Seek Time	Interface	Encode	cache kb	RPM
IC35L018F2D210	18.3GB	4.9	FC-AL2		4096k	1000
IC35L018F2DY10 18.3GB	18.3GB	4.9	FC-AL2GB		8192k	1000
IC35L018UCD210	18.3GB	4.9	UL160SCSI		4096k	1000
IC35L018UCDY10 18GB	18.3GB	4.9	UL160SCSI		8192k	1000
IC35L018UCPR15	18.35GB	4.9	UL160SCSI		4096k	1500
IC35L018UWD210	18.35GB	3.4	UL160SCSI		4096k	1500
IC35L018UWDY10 18GB	18.3GB	4.9	UL160SCSIW		4096k	1000
IC35L018UWPR15	18.4GB	4.7	UL320 SCSI		8192k	1000
IC35L018XCPR15	18.35GB	3.4	UL160SCSIW		4096k	1500
IC35L018XWPR15	18.4GB	3.4	UL320 SCSI		4096k	1500
IC35L020AVER07	20.57GB	8.5	ATA/100		2mb	7200
IC35L020AVVA07	20.57GB	8.5	ATA/100			7200
IC35L030AVER07	30GB	8.5	ATA/100		2mb	7200
IC35L036F2D210	36.7GB	4.9	FC-AL2		4096k	1000
IC35L036F2DY10 36GB	36.7GB	4.7	FC-AL2		8192k	1000
IC35L036UCD210	36.7GB	4.9	UL160SCSI		4096k	1000
IC35L036UCDY10	36.7GB	4.7	UL160SCSI		8mb	1000
IC35L036UCPR15	36.7GB	4.2	UL160SCSI		4096k	1500
IC35L036UWD210	36.7GB	4.9	UL160SCSIW		4096k	1000
IC35L036UWDY10	36.7GB	4.7	UL320 SCSI		8mb	1000
IC35L036UWPR15	36.7GB	4.2	UL160SCSIW		4096k	1500
IC35L036XCPR15	36.7GB	4.2	UL320SCSI		4096k	1500
IC35L036XWPR15	36.7GB	4.2	UL320SCSIW		4096k	1500
IC35L040AVER07	41.17GB	8.5	ATA/100		2mb	7200
IC35L040AVVA07	41.17GB	8.5	ATA/100			7200
IC35L060AVER07	61.49GB	8.5	ATA/100		2mb	7200
IC35L060AVVA07	61.49GB	8.5	ATA/100			7200
IC35L073F2D210	73.41GB	4.9	FC-AL2		4096k	1000
IC35L073F2DY10 73GB	73.4GB	4.7	FC-AL2		8192k	1000
IC35L073UCD210	73.41GB	4.9	UL160SCSI		4096k	1000
IC35L073UCDY10 73GB	73.4GB	4.7	U160/80pin		8192k	1000
IC35L073UWD210	73.41GB	4.9	UL160SCSIW		4096k	1000
IC35L073UWDY10 73GB	73.4GB	4.7	UL320 SCSI		8192k	1000
IC35L080AVVA07	82.34GB	8.5	ATA/100			7200
IC35L100AVVA07	102GB	8.5	ATA/100			7200
IC35L123AVVA07	123.52GB	8.5	ATA/100			7200
IC35L146F2DY10 146GB	146GB	4.7	FC-AL2GB		8mb	1000
IC35L146UCDY10 146GB	146GB	4.7	UL160SCSI		8mb	1000
IC35L146UWDY10 146GB	146GB	4.7	UL320 SCSI		8mb	1000
MicroDrive 1GB	1000	12	CF+		128k	3600
MicroDrive 340MB	340	12	CF+		128k	3600
MicroDrive 512MB	512	12	CF+		128k	3600
Travelstar 10E	10000	12	PCMCIA		512k	
Travelstar 10E	10000	12	PCMCIA		512k	
Travelstar 10GT 10.0G	10000	12	ATA-4		512k	4200
Travelstar 10GT 8.1GB	8100	12	ATA-4		512k	4200
Travelstar 12GN 12.0GB	12000	12	ATA-4		512k	4200
Travelstar 12GN 6.0GB	6000	12	ATA-4		512k	4200
Travelstar 12GN 9.0GB	9000	12	ATA-4		512k	4200
Travelstar 14GS 14.1GB	14100	12	ATA-4		512k	4900
Travelstar 15GN 10GB	10GB	12	ATA-5	PRML		4200
Travelstar 15GN 15GB	15GB	12	ATA-5	PRML		4200
Travelstar 15GN 5GB	6GB	12	ATA-5	PRML		4200
Travelstar 18GT 15.1GB	15100	12	ATA-4		512k	4200
Travelstar 18GT 18.1GB	18100	12	ATA-4		512k	4200
Travelstar 20GN 10GB	10000	12	ATA-5		512k	4200
Travelstar 20GN 20GB	20000	12	ATA-5		2048k	4200
Travelstar 20GN 5GB	5000	12	ATA-5		512k	4200
Travelstar 25GS	25300	12	ATA-5		512k	5400
Travelstar 30GN	30GB	12	ATA-5	PRML	2048k	4200
Travelstar 30GN	20GB	12	ATA-5	PRML	2048k	4200
Travelstar 30GT	30000	12	ATA-5		2048k	4200
Travelstar 32GH	32000	12	ATA-5		2048k	5411
Travelstar 3GN 2.16GB	2160	13	ATA-3	PRML	128k	4200
Travelstar 3GN 3.24GB	3240	13	ATA-3	PRML	128k	4200
Travelstar 3LP	1080	13	ATA-3	PRML	128k	4000
Travelstar 3LP	1440	13	ATA-3	PRML	128k	4000

Drive Model	Format Size MB	Head	Cyl	Sect/Trac	Translate H/C/S	RWC/WPC	Form Factor	Power Watts
Travelstar 3XP	2690	7	5120		16/5216/63	—/—	2.5 4H	2.0
Travelstar 3XP	3080	7	5120		16/5968/63	—/—	2.5 4H	2.0
Travelstar 40GN 10GB	10GB	1				—/—	2.5 4H	0.85
Travelstar 40GN 20GB	20GB	1				—/—	2.5 4H	0.85
Travelstar 40GN 30GB	30GB	2				—/—	2.5 4H	065
Travelstar 40GN 40GB	40GB	2				—/—	2.5 4H	065
Travelstar 40GNX 20GB	20GB	2				—/—	2.5 4H	1.3
Travelstar 40GNX 40GB	40GB	4				—/—	2.5 4H	1.3
Travelstar 48GH	48GB	8				—/—	2.5 4H	1.3
Travelstar 4GN 2.16GB	2160	2	9280			—/—		4.7
Travelstar 4GN 3.24GB	3240	3	9280			—/—		4.7
Travelstar 4GN 4.32GB	4320	4	9280			—/—		4.7
Travelstar 4GT 3.2GB	3240	5	6976			—/—	2.5 4H	1.85
Travelstar 4GT 4.0GB	4090	6	6976			—/—	2.5 4H	1.85
Travelstar 5GS 4.4GB	4480	7	6976			—/—	2.5 4H	2.0
Travelstar 5GS 5.1GB	5120	8	6976			—/—	2.5 4H	2.0
Travelstar 60GH	60GB	4				—/—	2.5 4H	1.3
Travelstar 60GH	60GB	4				—/—	2.5 4H	1.3
Travelstar 6GN 3.2GB	3200	2				—/—	2.5 4H	1.85
Travelstar 6GN 4.8GB	4800	3	11648			—/—	2.5 4H	1.85
Travelstar 6GN 6.4GB	6400	4	11648			—/—	2.5 4H	1.85
Travelstar 6GT 5.4GB	5400	5	9280			—/—	4H	1.85
Travelstar 6GT 6.48GB	6480	6	9280			—/—	4H	1.85
Travelstar 8E	8000	10				—/—		2.0
Travelstar 8GS 6.48GB	6480	8	8320			—/—	2.5 4H	1.3
Travelstar 8GS 7.9GB	7900				15/16383/63	—/—	2.5 4H	
Travelstar 8GS 8.10GB	8100	10	8320			—/—	2.5 4H	1.3
Ultrastar 146Z10 146GB	146GB	12				—/—	3.5 3H	
Ultrastar 146Z10 146GB	146GB	12				—/—	3.5 3H	
Ultrastar 146Z10 146GB	146GB	12				—/—	3.5 3H	11.1
Ultrastar 146Z10 18GB	18.3GB	2				—/—	3.5 3H	5.9
Ultrastar 146Z10 18GB	18.3GB	2				—/—	3.5 3H	5.9
Ultrastar 146Z10 18GB	18.3GB	2				—/—	3.5 3H	6.8
Ultrastar 146Z10 36GB	36.7GB	3				—/—	3.5 3H	7.0
Ultrastar 146Z10 36GB	36.7GB	3				—/—	3.5 3H	7.0
Ultrastar 146Z10 36GB	36.7GB	3				—/—	3.5 3H	7.0
Ultrastar 146Z10 73GB	73.4GB	6				—/—	3.5 3H	7.7
Ultrastar 146Z10 73GB	73.4GB	6				—/—	3.5 3H	7.7
Ultrastar 146Z10 73GB	73.4GB	6				—/—	3.5 3H	8.6
Ultrastar 18ES 18.2GB	18200	10	11347			—/—	3.5 3H	6.9
Ultrastar 18ES 18.2GB	18200	10	11347			—/—	3.5 3H	9.9
Ultrastar 18ES 9.1GB	9100	5	11347			—/—	3.5 3H	5.3
Ultrastar 18ES 9.1GB	9100	5	11347			—/—	3.5 3H	8.3
Ultrastar 18LZX 18.3GB	18300	10				—/—		11.5
Ultrastar 18LZX 9.1GB	9100	5				—/—		10.0
Ultrastar 18XP 18.2GB	18200	20				—/—	3.5HH	13.1
Ultrastar 18XP 18.2GB	18200	20				—/—	3.5HH	13.1
Ultrastar 18XP 18.2GB	18200	20				—/—	3.5HH	13.1
Ultrastar 18XP 18.2GB	18200	20				—/—	3.5HH	13.1
Ultrastar 18ZX 18.2GB	18200	20	7065			—/—	3.5HH	16.3
Ultrastar 18ZX 18.2GB	18200	20	7065			—/—	3.5HH	16.3
Ultrastar 18ZX 18.2GB	18200	20	7065			—/—	3.5HH	16.3
Ultrastar 2ES 2.1GB	2160	3	8120			—/—	3.5 3H	3.42
Ultrastar 2ES 4.3GB	4330	6	8120			—/—	3.5 3H	4.05
Ultrastar 2XP 4.51GB	4512	9				—/—	3.5 3H	
Ultrastar 2XP 9.1GB	9100	18				—/—	3.5 3H	
Ultrastar 36LP 18.3GB	18300	5				—/—	3.5 3H	8.9
Ultrastar 36LP 36.9GB	36900	10				—/—	3.5 3H	8.9
Ultrastar 36LP 9.1GB	9100	3				—/—	3.5 3H	8.9
Ultrastar 36LZX 18.3GB	18300	6				—/—	3.5 3H	9.7
Ultrastar 36LZX 18.3GB	18300	6				—/—	3.5 3H	9.7
Ultrastar 36LZX 36.7GB	36700	12				—/—	3.5 3H	12.9
Ultrastar 36LZX 36.7GB	36700	12				—/—	3.5 3H	12.9
Ultrastar 36LZX 9.1GB	9100	3				—/—	3.5 3H	8.5
Ultrastar 36LZX 9.1GB	9100	3				—/—	3.5 3H	8.5
Ultrastar 36XP 36.4GB	36400	20	11275			—/—	3.5HH	13.1
Ultrastar 36XP 36.4GB	36400	20	11275			—/—	3.5HH	13.1

Drive Model	Format Size MB	Seek Time	Interface	Encode	cache kb	RPM
Travelstar 3XP	2690	12	ATA-3	PRML	128k	4900
Travelstar 3XP	3080	12	ATA-3	PRML	128k	4900
Travelstar 40GN 10GB	10GB	12	ATA-5	PRML	2mb	4200
Travelstar 40GN 20GB	20GB	12	ATA-5	PRML	2mb	4200
Travelstar 40GN 30GB	30GB	12	ATA-5	PRML	2mb	4200
Travelstar 40GN 40GB	40GB	12	ATA-5	PRML	2mb	4200
Travelstar 40GNX 20GB	20GB	12	ATA-5		8192k	5400
Travelstar 40GNX 40GB	40GB	12	ATA-5		8192k	5400
Travelstar 48GH	48GB	12	ATA-5	PRML	2048k	5400
Travelstar 4GN 2.16GB	2160	12	ATA-4		512k	4200
Travelstar 4GN 3.24GB	3240	12	ATA-4		512k	4200
Travelstar 4GN 4.32GB	4320	12	ATA-4		512k	4200
Travelstar 4GT 3.2GB	3240	13	ATA-3	PRML	512k	4000
Travelstar 4GT 4.0GB	4090	12	ATA-3	PRML	512k	4000
Travelstar 5GS 4.4GB	4480	12	ATA-3	PRML	512k	4900
Travelstar 5GS 5.1GB	5120	12	ATA-3	PRML	512k	4900
Travelstar 60GH	60GB	12	ATA-5	PRML	2mb	5400
Travelstar 60GH	60GB	12	ATA-5	PRML	2mb	5400
Travelstar 6GN 3.2GB	3200	13	ATA-4		512k	4200
Travelstar 6GN 4.8GB	4800	13	ATA-4		512k	4200
Travelstar 6GN 6.4GB	6400	13	ATA-4		512k	4200
Travelstar 6GT 5.4GB	5400	12	ATA-4		512k	4200
Travelstar 6GT 6.48GB	6480	12	ATA-4		512k	4200
Travelstar 8E	8000	12	PCMCIA		512k	
Travelstar 8GS 6.48GB	6480	12	ATA-3	PRML	512k	4900
Travelstar 8GS 7.9GB	7900	12	EIDE	PRML	459k	4900
Travelstar 8GS 8.10GB	8100	12	ATA-3	PRML	512k	4900
Ultrastar 146Z10 146GB	146GB	4.7	UL320 SCSI		8mb	1000
Ultrastar 146Z10 146GB	146GB	4.7	UL160SCSI		8mb	1000
Ultrastar 146Z10 146GB	146GB	4.7	FC-AL2GB		8mb	1000
Ultrastar 146Z10 18GB	18.3GB	4.7	UL320 SCSI		8192k	1000
Ultrastar 146Z10 18GB	18.3GB	4.7	UL160SCSI		8192k	1000
Ultrastar 146Z10 18GB	18.3GB	4.7	FC-AL2GB		8mb	1000
Ultrastar 146Z10 36GB	36.7GB	4.7	FC-AL2		8192k	1000
Ultrastar 146Z10 36GB	36.7GB	4.7	UL320 SCSI		8mb	1000
Ultrastar 146Z10 36GB	36.7GB	4.7	UL160SCSI		8mb	1000
Ultrastar 146Z10 73GB	73.4GB	4.7	UL320 SCSI		8192k	1000
Ultrastar 146Z10 73GB	73.4GB	4.7	U160/80pin		8192k	1000
Ultrastar 146Z10 73GB	73.4GB	4.7	FC-AL2		8192k	1000
Ultrastar 18ES 18.2GB	18200	7.0	Ultra SCSI		2mb	7200
Ultrastar 18ES 18.2GB	18200	7.0	FC-AL		2mb	7200
Ultrastar 18ES 9.1GB	9100	7.0	Ultra SCSI		2mb	7200
Ultrastar 18ES 9.1GB	9100	7.0	FC-AL		2mb	7200
Ultrastar 18LZX 18.3GB	18300	4.9	Ultra 160	RLL 16,17	2mb	1000
Ultrastar 18LZX 9.1GB	9100	4.9	Ultra 160	RLL 16,17	2mb	1000
Ultrastar 18XP 18.2GB	18200	6.5	SCA-2FstWd	RLL 16,17	1000k	7200
Ultrastar 18XP 18.2GB	18200	6.5	SCA-2FstWD	RLL 16,17	1000k	7200
Ultrastar 18XP 18.2GB	18200	6.5	SSA	RLL 16,17	1000k	7200
Ultrastar 18XP 18.2GB	18200	6.5	FC-AL	RLL 16,17	1000k	7200
Ultrastar 18ZX 18.2GB	18200	6.5	Ultra2 LVD	16,17 RLL	4mb	1002
Ultrastar 18ZX 18.2GB	18200	6.5	SSA	16,17 RLL	4mb	1002
Ultrastar 18ZX 18.2GB	18200	6.5	FC-AL	16,17 RLL	4mb	1002
Ultrastar 2ES 2.1GB	2160	8.5	SCSI-3ULTRA	PRML	512k	5400
Ultrastar 2ES 4.3GB	4330	8.5	SCSI-3ULTRA	PRML	512k	5400
Ultrastar 2XP 4.51GB	4512	7.5	Ultra Wide		512k	7200
Ultrastar 2XP 9.1GB	9100	7.5	Ultra Wide		512k	7200
Ultrastar 36LP 18.3GB	18300	6.8	UL160SCSI		4mb	7200
Ultrastar 36LP 36.9GB	36900	6.8	UL160SCSI		4mb	7200
Ultrastar 36LP 9.1GB	9100	6.8	UL160SCSI		4mb	7200
Ultrastar 36LZX 18.3GB	18300	4.9	UL160SCSI		4mb	1000
Ultrastar 36LZX 18.3GB	18300	4.9	FC-AL		4mb	1000
Ultrastar 36LZX 36.7GB	36700	4.9	UL160SCSI		4mb	1000
Ultrastar 36LZX 36.7GB	36700	4.9	FC-AL		4mb	1000
Ultrastar 36LZX 9.1GB	9100	4.9	UL160SCSI		4mb	1000
Ultrastar 36LZX 9.1GB	9100	4.9	FC-AL		4mb	1000
Ultrastar 36XP 36.4GB	36400	7.5	Ultra2 LVD	RLL 16,17	4mb	7200
Ultrastar 36XP 36.4GB	36400	7.5	SSA	RLL 16,17	4mb	7200

Hard Drive Specs

Drive Model	Format Size MB	Head	Cyl	Sect/Trac	Translate H/C/S	RWC/WPC	Form Factor	Power Watts
Ultrastar 36XP 36.4GB	36400	20	11275			—/—	3.5HH	13.1
Ultrastar 36Z15 18.4GB	18.4GB	8				—/—	3.5 3H	11
Ultrastar 36Z15 18.4GB	18.4GB	8				—/—	3.5 3H	11
Ultrastar 36Z15 36.7GB	36.7GB	12				—/—	3.5 3H	13.5
Ultrastar 36Z15 36.7GB	36.7GB	12				—/—	3.5 3H	13.5
Ultrastar 36ZX	36700	20						17.4
Ultrastar 72ZX DDHF	73.4	22				—/—	3.5HH	16.9
Ultrastar 72ZX DDHS	73.4	22				—/—	3.5HH	16.9
Ultrastar 73LZX 18.3GB	18.3GB	3				—/—	3.5 3H	6.7
Ultrastar 73LZX 18.3GB	18.3GB	3				—/—	3.5 3H	6.7
Ultrastar 73LZX 18.3GB	18.3GB	3				—/—	3.5 3H	6.7
Ultrastar 73LZX 36.7GB	36.7GB	6				—/—	3.5 3H	7.4
Ultrastar 73LZX 36.7GB	36.7GB	6				—/—	3.5 3H	7.4
Ultrastar 73LZX 36.7GB	36.7GB	6				—/—	3.5 3H	7.4
Ultrastar 73LZX 73.4GB	73.41GB	12				—/—	3.5 3H	9.5
Ultrastar 73LZX 73.4GB	73.41GB	12				—/—	3.5 3H	9.5
Ultrastar 73LZX 73.4GB	73.41GB	12				—/—	3.5 3H	9.5
Ultrastar 73LZX 9.17GB	9.17GB	2				—/—	3.5 3H	5.6
Ultrastar 73LZX 9.17GB	9.17GB	2				—/—	3.5 3H	5.6
Ultrastar 73LZX 9.17GB	9.17GB	2				—/—	3.5 3H	5.6
Ultrastar 9ES 4.5GB	4500	5	8420			—/—	3.5 3H	5.3
Ultrastar 9ES 9.0GB	9100	10	8420			—/—	3.5 3H	5.3
Ultrastar 9LP 9.1GB	9100	10				—/—	3.5 4H	9.2
Ultrastar 9LP 9.1GB	9100	10				—/—	3.5 4H	9.2
Ultrastar 9LP 9.1GB	9100	10				—/—	3.5 4H	9.2
Ultrastar 9LP 9.1GB	9100	10				—/—	3.5 4H	9.2
Ultrastar 9LZX 9.1GB	9100	10	7065			—/—	3.5 3H	10.1
Ultrastar 9LZX 9.1GB	9100	10	7065			—/—	3.5 3H	10.1
Ultrastar 9LZX 9.1GB	9100	10	7065			—/—	3.5 3H	10.1
Ultrastar 9ZX 9.1GB	9100	12				—/—	3.5HH	16.5
Ultrastar Ultra 2.16S	2160	3				—/—	3.5 3H	
Ultrastar XP 2.25GB	2250	4				—/—	3.5 3H	
Ultrastar XP 4.51GB	4510	8				—/—	3.5HH	
WD-12	10	4	306	17		296/296	5.25FH	
WD-2120	126	4	1248	50		—/—	2.5 4H	
WD-240	42	2	1120	38		NA/NA	2.5 4H	
WD-240	43	2	1122	38		NA/NA	2.5 4H	
WD-240	42	2	1120	38		—/—	2.5 4H	
WD-25	20	8	306	17		296/296	5.25FH	
WD-25A	20					—/—	5.25FH	
WD-25R	20					—/—	2.5 4H	
WD-280	85	4	1120	38		NA/NA	3.5FH	
WD-3158	120	8	920	32		—/—	3.5HH	
WD-3158(PS2/70)	120					NA/NA	3.5HH	
WD-3160	163	8	1021	39		—/—	3.5HH	
WD-325	21	4	615	17		—/—	3.5HH	
WD-325K	20					—/—	3.5HH	
WD-325N(PS2/50)	21					—/—	3.5HH	
WD-325Q(PS2/30)	21					—/—	3.5HH	
WD-336P(PS2/30E)	31					—/—	3.5HH	
WD-336R(PS2/50Z)	31					—/—	3.5HH	
WD-380	81	4	1021	39		NA/NA	3.5HH	
WD-380S(PS2/70)	81					—/—	3.5HH	
WD-387(PS2/70)	60	4	928	32		NA/NA	3.5HH	
WD-387T(PS2/70)	60					—/—	3.5HH	
WD-L320(PS2/30E)	20					—/—	3.5HH	
WD-L330P(PS2/30E)	30					—/—	3.5HH	
WD-L330R(PS2/70)	30					—/—	3.5HH	
WD-L40	41	2	1038	39		NA/NA	3.5HH	
WD-L40S(PS2/70)	41	2	1038	39		NA/NA	3.5HH	
WDA-2120R	126	4	1243	50		—/—	2.5 3H	1.2
WDA-240	43	2	1122	38		NA/NA	2.5 4H	
WDA-260	63	2	1248	50		—/—	2.5 4H	
WDA-2120	87	4	1122	38		NA/NA	2.5 4H	
WDA-3160	81	4	1021	39		NA/NA	3.5HH	
WDA-380	81	4	1021	39		NA/NA	3.5HH	
WDA-L160	171	4	1923	44	8/966/44	—/—	3.5 4H	

Drive Model	Format Size MB	Seek Time	Interface	Encode	cache kb	RPM
Ultrastar 36XP 36.4GB	36400	7.5	FC-AL	RLL 16,17	4mb	7200
Ultrastar 36Z15 18.4GB	18.4GB	3.4	UL160SCSI		4096k	1500
Ultrastar 36Z15 18.4GB	18.4GB	3.4	UL160SCSIW		4096k	1500
Ultrastar 36Z15 36.7GB	36.7GB	4.2	UL160SCSI		4096k	1500
Ultrastar 36Z15 36.7GB	36.7GB	4.2	UL160SCSIW		4096k	1500
Ultrastar 36ZX	36700	5.4	Ultra2 SCSI	RLL 16,17	2mb	1000
Ultrastar 72ZX DDHF	73.4	5.3	FC-AL		16mb	1000
Ultrastar 72ZX DDHS	73.4	5.3	UL160SCSI		16mb	1000
Ultrastar 73LZX 18.3GB	18.3GB	4.9	UL160SCSI		4096k	1000
Ultrastar 73LZX 18.3GB	18.3GB	4.9	UL160SCSIW		4096k	1000
Ultrastar 73LZX 18.3GB	18.3GB	4.9	FC-AL2		4096k	1000
Ultrastar 73LZX 36.7GB	36.7GB	4.9	UL160SCSI		4096k	1000
Ultrastar 73LZX 36.7GB	36.7GB	4.9	UL160SCSIW		4096k	1000
Ultrastar 73LZX 36.7GB	36.7GB	4.9	FC-AL2		4096k	1000
Ultrastar 73LZX 73.4GB	73.41GB	4.9	UL160SCSI		4096k	1000
Ultrastar 73LZX 73.4GB	73.41GB	4.9	UL160SCSIW		4096k	1000
Ultrastar 73LZX 73.4GB	73.41GB	4.9	FC-AL2		4096k	1000
Ultrastar 73LZX 9.17GB	9.17GB	4.9	UL160SCSI		4096k	1000
Ultrastar 73LZX 9.17GB	9.17GB	4.9	UL160SCSIW		4096k	1000
Ultrastar 73LZX 9.17GB	9.17GB	4.9	FC-AL2		4096k	1000
Ultrastar 9ES 4.5GB	4500	7.5	SCA-2FstW	PRML16,17	512k	7200
Ultrastar 9ES 9.0GB	9100	7.5	Ultra SCSI3	PRML16,17	512k	7200
Ultrastar 9LP 9.1GB	9100	6.5	SCA-2FstWd	RLL 16,17	1000k	7200
Ultrastar 9LP 9.1GB	9100	6.5	SCA-2FstWD	RLL 16,17	1000k	7200
Ultrastar 9LP 9.1GB	9100	6.5	SSA	RLL 16,17	1000k	7200
Ultrastar 9LP 9.1GB	9100	6.5	FC-AL	RLL 16,17	1000k	7200
Ultrastar 9LZX 9.1GB	9100	5.6	Ultra2 SCSI	16,17 RLL	4mb	1002
Ultrastar 9LZX 9.1GB	9100	5.6	FC-AL	16,17 RLL	4mb	1002
Ultrastar 9LZX 9.1GB	9100	5.6	SSA	16,17 RLL	4mb	1002
Ultrastar 9ZX 9.1GB	9100	6.3	ULSCSI40FST	PRML	1mb	1002
Ultrastar Ultra 2.16S	2160	8.5	Ultra SCSIW		512k	5400
Ultrastar XP 2.25GB	2250	7.5	SCSI-2Fast		512k	7200
Ultrastar XP 4.51GB	4510	8	SCSI-2Fast		512k	7200
WD-12	10		ST412/506	MFM		3600
WD-2120	126	16	IDE AT	RLL		3600
WD-240	42	19	MCA			3600
WD-240	43	19	MCA			3600
WD-240	42	19	MCA			3600
WD-25	20		ST412/506	MFM		3600
WD-25A	20		ST412/506	MFM		3600
WD-25R	20		ST412/506	MFM		
WD-280	85	17	MCA			3600
WD-3158	120	23	MCA			
WD-3158(PS2/70)	120		MCA			
WD-3160	163	16	MCA			
WD-325	21	88	MCA			
WD-325K	20		ST412/506	MFM		
WD-325N(PS2/50)	21		MCA			
WD-325Q(PS2/30)	21		MCA			
WD-336P(PS2/30E)	31		MCA			
WD-336R(PS2/50Z)	31		MCA			
WD-380	81	16	MCA			
WD-380S(PS2/70)	81		MCA			
WD-387(PS2/70)	60	23	MCA			
WD-387T(PS2/70)	60		MCA			
WD-L320(PS2/30E)	20		MCA			
WD-L330P(PS2/30E)	30		MCA			
WD-L330R(PS2/70)	30		MCA			
WD-L40	41	17	MCA			
WD-L40S(PS2/70)	41	17	MCA			
WDA-2120R	126	16	IDE AT			3600
WDA-240	43	19	IDE AT			3600
WDA-260	63	16	IDE AT			3600
WDA-280	87	19	IDE AT			3600
WDA-3160	81	16	IDE AT			
WDA-380	81	16	IDE AT			
WDA-L160	171	16	IDE AT			3600

Drive Model	Format Size MB	Head	Cyl	Sect/ Trac	Translate H/C/S	RWC/ WPC	Form Factor	Power Watts
WDA-L40	41	2	1040	39		NA/NA	3.5 3H	
WDA-L42	42	2	1067	39		NA/NA	3.5 3H	
WDA-L80	85	2	1923	44		—/—	3.5 4H	
WDS-240	43	2	1120	38		NA/NA	2.5 4H	
WDS-260	63	2	1248	50		—/—	2.5 4H	
WDS-280	85	4	1120	38		—/—	2.5 4H	
WDS-3100	104	2	1990	44		NA/NA	3.5 4H	
WDS-3160	163	8	1021	39		NA/NA	3.5HH	
WDS-3168	160					—/—	3.5HH	
WDS-3200	209	4	1990	44		—/—	3.5 4H	
WDS-380	81	4	1021	39		NA/NA	3.5HH	
WDS-387	80					—/—	3.5HH	
WDS-L160	171	4	1923	44		—/—	3.5 4H	
WDS-L40	41	2	1038	39		NA/NA	3.5 3H	
WDS-L42	42	2	1066	39		NA/NA	3.5 3H	
WDS-L80	85	2	1923	44		NA/NA	3.5 4H	

IMI

Drive Model	Format Size MB	Head	Cyl	Sect/ Trac	Translate H/C/S	RWC/ WPC	Form Factor	Power Watts
5006	5	2	306	17		307/214		
5007	5	2	306	17		—/—	5.25FH	
5012	10	4	306	17		307/214		
5018	15	6	306	17		307/214		
5021H	15			17		—/—	5.25FH	
7720	20			17		—/—		
7740	40			17		—/—		

INTERGRAL PERIPHERALS

Drive Model	Format Size MB	Head	Cyl	Sect/ Trac	Translate H/C/S	RWC/ WPC	Form Factor	Power Watts
105 (Viper)	105	4				—/—	1.8 IN	
170 (Viper)	171	4				—/—	1.8 IN	
1820 (Mustang)	21	2	615			NA/NA	1.8	
1842 (Stingray)	42	3				NA/NA	1.8	
1862	64	3		V		NA/NA		
2100	1000	6			16/1900/63	NA/NA	2.5 4H	
260 (Viper)	262	4				—/—	1.8 IN	
340 (Viper)	341	4				—/—	1.8 IN	

IOMEGA CORPORATION

Drive Model	Format Size MB	Head	Cyl	Sect/ Trac	Translate H/C/S	RWC/ WPC	Form Factor	Power Watts
HDD 120GB ATA Internal	120GB	4				—/—	3.5 3H	
HDD 120GB USB	120GB					—/—	3.5 3H	
HDD 120GB USB/FIREWIRE	120GB					—/—	3.5FH	
HDD 20GB FIREWIRE	20GB					—/—	3.5FH	
HDD 20GB USB	20GB					—/—	3.5FH	
HDD 250GB ATA Internal	250GB	6				—/—	3.5 3H	7.0
HDD 250GB USB	250GB					—/—	3.5FH	
HDD 250GB USB/FIREWIRE	250GB					—/—	3.5FH	
HDD 30GB FIREWIRE	30GB					—/—	3.5FH	
HDD 30GB USB	30GB					—/—	3.5FH	
HDD 40GB FIREWIRE	40GB					—/—	3.5FH	
HDD 40GB USB	40GB					—/—	3.5FH	
HDD 40GB USB/FIREWIRE	40GB					—/—	3.5FH	
HDD 60GB USB/FIREWIRE	60GB					—/—	3.5FH	
HDD 80GB FIREWIRE EXT	80GB					—/—	3.5FH	
HDD 80GB USB External	80GB					—/—	3.5FH	
HDD 80GB USB/FIREWIRE	80GB					—/—	3.5FH	
Jaz 1GB Ext SCSI PC/Mc	1070					—/—	3.5FH	
Jaz 1GB Int SCSI PC	1070					—/—	3.5FH	
Jaz 2GB Ext SCSI PCMac	2000					—/—	3.5FH	
Jaz 2GB Int PCMAC	2002					—/—		
Zip 100 Atapi/IDE	100					—/—	3.5 3H	
Zip 100 PP	100					—/—		
Zip 100 SCSI	100					—/—		
Zip 100 USB	100					—/—		
Zip 250 Atapi/IDE	250					—/—	3.5 3H	
Zip 250 PP	250					—/—		3
Zip 250 SCSI	250					—/—	3.5 3H	
Zip 250 USB	250					—/—		

Drive Model	Format Size MB	Seek Time	Interface	Encode	cache kb	RPM
WDA-L40	41	17	IDE AT	2,7 RLL		
WDA-L42	42	17	IDE AT	2,7 RLL		
WDA-L80	85	16	SCSI-2			
WDS-240	43	19	SCSI			3600
WDS-260	63	16	SCSI-2			3600
WDS-280	85	17	SCSI-2			3600
WDS-3100	104	12	SCSI-2			
WDS-3160	163	16	SCSI-2		32k	4320
WDS-3168	160		SCSI			
WDS-3200	209	12	SCSI-2		32k	4320
WDS-380	81	16	SCSI-2			
WDS-387	80		SCSI			
WDS-L160	171	16	SCSI-2			
WDS-L40	41	17	SCSI-2			3600
WDS-L42	42	17	SCSI-2			
WDS-L80	85	16	SCSI-2			3600

IMI

5006	5	27	ST412/506	MFM		
5007	5	85	ST412/506	MFM		
5012	10	27	ST412/506	MFM		
5018	15	27	ST412/506	MFM		
5021H	15	85	ST412/506	MFM		
7720	20	85	ST412/506	MFM		
7740	40	85	ST412/506	MFM		

INTERGRAL PERIPHERALS

105 (Viper)	105	15	PCMCIA-ATA	1,7 RLL	32k	4500
170 (Viper)	171	12	PCMCIA-ATA	1,7 RLL	32k	4500
1820 (Mustang)	21	18	IDE AT	1,7 RLL		
1842 (Stingray)	42	18	IDE AT	1,7 RLL		
1862	64	18	IDE AT	1,7 RLL		
2100	1000	12	ATA-2	1,7 RLL	128k	4200
260 (Viper)	262	12	PCMCIA-ATA	1,7 PRML	32k	4500
340 (Viper)	341	12	PCMCIA-ATA	1,7 PRML	32k	4500

IOMEGA CORPORATION

HDD 120GB ATA Internal	120GB	8.5	ATA-6			
HDD 120GB USB	120GB	8.9	USB2.0		8mb	7200
HDD 120GB USB/FIREWIRE	120GB		USB2/FIREWR		8mb	7200
HDD 20GB FIREWIRE	20GB		FireWire			4200
HDD 20GB USB	20GB		USB2.0			4200
HDD 250GB ATA Internal	250GB	8.5	ATA ULTR100			7200
HDD 250GB USB	250GB	8.9	USB2.0		8mb	7200
HDD 250GB USB/FIREWIRE	250GB		USB2/FIREWR		8mb	7200
HDD 30GB FIREWIRE	30GB		FireWire			4200
HDD 30GB USB	30GB		USB2.0			4200
HDD 40GB FIREWIRE	40GB		FireWire			5400
HDD 40GB USB	40GB		USB2.0			5400
HDD 40GB USB/FIREWIRE	40GB		USB2/FIREWR			5400
HDD 60GB USB/FIREWIRE	60GB		USB2/FIREWR			4200
HDD 80GB FIREWIRE EXT	80GB		FireWire			7200
HDD 80GB USB External	80GB		USB2.0			7200
HDD 80GB USB/FIREWIRE	80GB		USB2/FIREWR			7200
Jaz 1GB Ext SCSI PC/Mc	1070	10-12	SCSI-2		256k	
Jaz 1GB Int SCSI PC	1070	10-12	SCSI-2		256k	5394
Jaz 2GB Ext SCSI PCMac	2000	15.5	Ultra SCSI		512k	
Jaz 2GB Int PCMAC	2002	10	Ultra SCSI		512k	5394
Zip 100 Atapi/IDE	100	20-29	IDE		16k	2941
Zip 100 PP	100	29	ParallelPor		32k	2941
Zip 100 SCSI	100	20-29	SCSI		16k	2941
Zip 100 USB	100	29	USB		16k	2941
Zip 250 Atapi/IDE	250		EIDE			
Zip 250 PP	250	29	ParallelPor		32k	2941
Zip 250 SCSI	250	29	SCSI		16k	2941
Zip 250 USB	250	>40	USB			

Drive Model	Format Size MB	Head	Cyl	Sect/Trac	Translate H/C/S	RWC/WPC	Form Factor	Power Watts
Zip 750 Atapi	750					—/—	3.5 4H	
Zip 750 FireWire	750					—/—	2.5 4H	
Zip 750 USB	750					—/—	2.5 4H	

JCT (SEE MAXCARD)

Drive Model	Format Size MB	Head	Cyl	Sect/Trac	Translate H/C/S	RWC/WPC	Form Factor	Power Watts
100	5			17		—/—	5.25HH	
1000	5			17		—/—	5.25HH	
1005	7			17		—/—	5.25HH	
1010	14			17		—/—	5.25HH	
105	5	2	306	17		—/—	5.25HH	
110	14			17		—/—	5.25HH	
120	20			17		—/—	5.25HH	

JTS CORPORATION

Drive Model	Format Size MB	Head	Cyl	Sect/Trac	Translate H/C/S	RWC/WPC	Form Factor	Power Watts
C1700-2AF	1700	4	3312			—/—	3.5 3H	3.39
C2000-2AF	2000	4	3882			—/—	3.5 3H	3.39
C2500-3AF	2500	6	4970			—/—	3.5 3H	3.39
C3000-3AF	3000	6	5824			—/—	3.5 3H	3.39
Champ Family	1000	4	5050			—/—	3.5 4H	3.0
Champ Family	1300	6	5050			—/—	3.5 4H	3.0
Champ Family	1700	6	5050			—/—	3.5 4H	3.0
Champ Family	2000	6	5050			—/—	3.5 4H	3.0
N1080-2AR	1080	4	4032				3.0	1.1
N1440-3AR	1440	6	4032				3.0	1.3
N1620-3AR	1620	6	4032			—/—	3.0	1.3
N2160-3AR	2160	6	4435				3.0	

JVC COMPANIES OF AMERICA

Drive Model	Format Size MB	Head	Cyl	Sect/Trac	Translate H/C/S	RWC/WPC	Form Factor	Power Watts
JD-3842HA	21	2	436	48		—/—	3.5 3H	
JD-3848HA	43	4	436	48		—/—	3.5 3H	
JD-E2042M	42	2	973	43		NA/NA	2.5 4H	3.7
JD-E2085M	85	4	973	43		NA/NA	2.5 4H	4.5
JD-E2825P(A)	21	2	581	36		—/—	3.5 4H	3.6
JD-E2825P(S)	21	2	581	36		—/—	3.5 4H	3.6
JD-E2825P(X)	21	2	581	36		—/—	3.5 4H	3.6
JD-E2850P(A)	42	3	791	35		—/—	3.5 4H	3.7
JD-E2850P(S)	42	3	791	35		—/—	3.5 4H	3.7
JD-E2850P(X)	42	3	791	35		—/—	3.5 4H	3.7
JD-E3824TA	21	2	436	48		—/—	3.5 3H	
JD-E3848HA	42	4	436	48		—/—	3.5 3H	
JD-E3848P(A)	42	2	862	48		—/—	3.5 4H	6
JD-E3848P(S)	42	2	862	48		—/—	3.5 4H	6
JD-E3848P(X)	42	2	862	48		—/—	3.5 4H	6
JD-E3896P(A)	84	4	862	48		—/—	3.5 4H	3.6
JD-E3896P(S)	84	4	862	48		—/—	3.5 4H	3.6
JD-E3896P(X)	84	4	862	48		—/—	3.5 4H	3.6
JD-E3896V(A)	84	4	862	48		NA/NA	3.5 3H	
JD-E3896V(S)	84	4	862	48		NA/NA	3.5 3H	
JD-E3896V(X)	84	4	862	48		NA/NA	3.5 3H	
JD-F2042M	42	2	973	43		NA/NA	2.5 4H	3.7

KALOK CORPORATION

Drive Model	Format Size MB	Head	Cyl	Sect/Trac	Translate H/C/S	RWC/WPC	Form Factor	Power Watts
KL1000	105	6	978	35		—/—	3.5HH	
KL3100	105	6	820	48/35		NA/NA	3.5HH	10
KL3120	121	6	820	55/40	6/979/35	NA/NA	3.5HH	10
KL320	21	4	615	17	6/981/40	616/300	3.5HH	
KL330	33	4	615	26		617/617	3.5HH	
KL332	40	4	615			—/—	3.5HH	
KL340	43	6	820	17		—/—	3.5HH	
KL341	42	4	676	31		—/—	3.5HH	
KL342	43	4	676	31		—/—	3.5HH	
KL343	43	4	676	31		645/645	3.5HH	10
KL360	66	6	820	26		—/—	3.5HH	
KL360	85	6	820			—/—	3.5HH	
KL381	84	6	815	34		—/—	3.5HH	
KL383	84	6	815	34	6/815/33	NA/NA	3.5 4H	2.5
P3250	251	4	2048	80	16/961/32	NA/NA	3.5 4H	2.5
P3360	362	4	791	56	16/791/56	NA/NA	3.5 4H	
P3540	540	4	1024	63		NA/NA	3.5 4H	

Drive Model	Format Size MB	Seek Time	Interface	Encode	cache kb	RPM
Zip 750 Atapi	750		Atapi			
Zip 750 FireWire	750		FireWire			
Zip 750 USB	750		USB2.0			
JCT (SEE MAXCARD)						
100	5	110	ST412/506	MFM		
1000	5	110	Commodore	MFM		
1005	7	110	Commodore	MFM		
1010	14	130	Commodore	MFM		
105	5	110	ST412/506	MFM		
110	14	130	ST412/506	MFM		
120	20	100	ST412/506	MFM		
JTS CORPORATION						
C1700-2AF	1700	<12	EIDE/ATA-3		256k	5400
C2000-2AF	2000	<12	EIDE/ATA-3		256k	5400
C2500-3AF	2500	<12	EIDE/ATA-3		256k	5400
C3000-3AF	3000	<12	EIDE/ATA-3		256k	5400
Champ Family	1000	<14	EIDE	1,7 RLL	128k	4500
Champ Family	1300	<14	EIDE	1,7 RLL	128k	4500
Champ Family	1700	<14	EIDE	1,7 RLL	128k	4500
Champ Family	2000	<14	EIDE	1,7 RLL	128k	4500
N1080-2AR	1080	<14	EIDE/ATA-3		128k	4103
N1440-3AR	1440	<14	EIDE/ATA-3		128k	4103
N1620-3AR	1620	<14	EIDE/ATA-3		128k	4103
N2160-3AR	2160	<14	EIDE/ATA-3		128k	4103
JVC COMPANIES OF AMERICA						
JD-3842HA	21	28		2,7 RLL		
JD-3848HA	43	29		2,7 RLL		
JD-E2042M	42	16	IDE AT	1,7 RLL	32k	3118
JD-E2085M	85	16	IDE AT	1,7 RLL	32k	3118
JD-E2825P(A)	21	25	IDE AT	2,7 RLL		3109
JD-E2825P(S)	21	25	SCSI	2,7 RLL		3109
JD-E2825P(X)	21	25	IDE XT	2,7 RLL		3109
JD-E2850P(A)	42	25	IDE AT	2,7 RLL	32k	3109
JD-E2850P(S)	42	25	SCSI	2,7 RLL	32k	3109
JD-E2850P(X)	42	25	IDE XT	2,7 RLL	32k	3109
JD-E3824TA	21	28		2,7 RLL		
JD-E3848HA	42	29		2,7 RLL		
JD-E3848P(A)	42	25	IDE AT	2,7 RLL		2332
JD-E3848P(S)	42	25	SCSI	2,7 RLL		2332
JD-E3848P(X)	42	25	IDE XT	2,7 RLL		2332
JD-E3896P(A)	84	25	IDE AT	2,7 RLL		3109
JD-E3896P(S)	84	25	SCSI	2,7 RLL		3109
JD-E3896P(X)	84	25	IDE XT	2,7 RLL		3109
JD-E3896V(A)	84	25	IDE AT	2,7 RLL		
JD-E3896V(S)	84	25	SCSI	2,7 RLL		
JD-E3896V(X)	84	25	IDE XT	2,7 RLL		
JD-F2042M	42	16	IDE AT	1,7 RLL	32k	3118
KALOK CORPORATION						
KL1000	105	25	IDE AT	2,7 RLL	32k	3662
KL3100	105	19	IDE AT	2,7 RLL		3662
KL3120	121	19	IDE AT	2,7 RLL		3663
KL320	21	40	ST412/506	MFM		3600
KL330	33	40	ST412/506	2,7 RLL		3600
KL332	40	48	MCA	2,7 RLL		
KL340	43	25	ST412/506	MFM		
KL341	43	33	SCSI	2,7 RLL	8k	3375
KL342	42	30	MCA	2,7 RLL		
KL343	43	28	IDE AT	2,7 RLL	8k	3375
KL360	66	25	ST412/506	2,7 RLL		
KL381	85	25	SCSI	2,7 RLL		
KL383	84	25	IDE AT	2,7 RLL		
P3250	251	16.5	IDE AT	1,7 RLL	128k	3600
P3360	362	16.5	IDE AT	1,7 RLL	128k	3600
P3540	540	16.5	IDE AT	1,7 RLL	128k	4200

Drive Model	Format Size MB	Head	Cyl	Sect/Trac	Translate H/C/S	RWC/WPC	Form Factor	Power Watts
P5-125(A)	125	2	2048			NA/NA		
P5-125(S)	125	2	2048			NA/NA		
P5-250(A)	251	4	2048			NA/NA		
P5-250(S)	251	4	2048			NA/NA		

KYOCERA ELECTRONICS, INC.

Drive Model	Format Size MB	Head	Cyl	Sect/Trac	Translate H/C/S	RWC/WPC	Form Factor	Power Watts
KC20A	21	4	615	17		—/—	3.5HH	
KC20B	21	4	615	17		—/—	3.5HH	
KC30A	33	4	615	26		—/—	3.5HH	
KC30B	33	4	615	26		—/—	3.5HH	
KC40GA	40	2	1075	17	4/577	33/—	3.5HH	
KC80C	87	8	787	28		NA/NA	3.5HH	
KC80GA	78	4	1069	36	8/577/33	NA/NA	3.5HH	

LANSTOR

Drive Model	Format Size MB	Head	Cyl	Sect/Trac	Translate H/C/S	RWC/WPC	Form Factor	Power Watts
LAN-115	15		918	17		—/NONE		
LAN-140	8		1024	34		—/NONE		
LAN-180	8		1024	26		—/NONE		
LAN-64	8		1024	17		—/NONE		

LAPINE

Drive Model	Format Size MB	Head	Cyl	Sect/Trac	Translate H/C/S	RWC/WPC	Form Factor	Power Watts
LT10	10	2	615	17		616/—	3.5HH	
LT100 (not verified)	10					—/—	3.5HH	
LT20	20	4	615	17		616/—	3.5HH	
LT200	20	4	614	17		615/—	3.5HH	
LT2000	20	4	614	17		615/—	3.5HH	
LT300	32	4	614	17		615/—	3.5HH	
LT3065	10	4	306	17		306/128	3.5HH	
LT3512	10	4	306	17		306/128	3.5HH	
LT3522	10	4	306	17		307/—	3.5HH	
LT3532	32	4	614	26		—/615	3.5HH	
LT4000 (not verified)	40					—/—	3.5HH	
Titan 20	21	4	615	17		—/—	3.5HH	
Titan 30	21	4	615			—/—	3.5HH	

MAXTOR CORPORATION

Drive Model	Format Size MB	Head	Cyl	Sect/Trac	Translate H/C/S	RWC/WPC	Form Factor	Power Watts
250837	837	5		66-132		—/—	2.5 4H	
250840	840	5		43-67		—/—	2.5 4H	
25084A	80	2		43-67	16/569/18	NA/NA	2.5 4H	
251005	1005	6		66-132		—/—	2.5 4H	
251010	1010	6		66-132		—/—	2.5 4H	
25128A	128	4	1092	NA	14/1024/17	NA/NA	2.5 4H	2.2
251340	1340	8		66-132		—/—	2.5 4H	
251350	1350	8		66-132	16/2616/63	—/—	2.5 4H	
25252A	252	6			16/569/54	—/—	2.5 4H	
25252S	251	6		67		NA/NA	2.5 4H	
2585A	85	4	1092	NA	10/981/17	NA/NA	2.5 4H	2.2
2585S (never made)	85	4	1092	V		NA/NA	2.5 4H	
2B004H1	4GB	1	8184		16/16383/63	—/—		
2B006H1	6GB	1	13328		16/16383/63	—/—		
2B008H1	8GB	1	16351		16/16383/63	—/—		
2B010H1	10GB	1	19386		16/16383/63	—/—		
2B015H1	15GB	1	29104		16/16383/63	—/—		
2B020H1	20GB	1	38792		16/16383/63	—/—		
2F020J0	20GB				16/16383/63	—/—	3.5 4H	
2F020L0	20GB				16/16383/63	—/—	3.5 4H	
2F030J0	30GB				16/16383/63	—/—	3.5 4H	
2F030L0	30GB				16/16383/63	—/—	3.5 4H	
2F040J0	40GB				16/16383/63	—/—	3.5 4H	
2F040L0	40GB				16/16383/63	—/—	3.5 4H	
2R010H1	10000				16/16383/63	—/—	3.5 4H	4.0
2R015H1	15000				16/16383/63	—/—	3.5 4H	4.0
3000DV	60GB					—/—		
3000DV 80GB	80GB					—/—	3.5	
3000LE	40GB					—/—		
3000LE 120GB	120GB					—/—	3.5	
3000LE 40GB	40GB					—/—	3.5	
3000LS 40GB	40GB					—/—	3.5	

Drive Model	Format Size MB	Seek Time	Interface	Encode	cache kb	RPM
P5-125(A)	125	17	IDE AT	1,7 RLL		
P5-125(S)	125	17	SCSI-2	1,7 RLL		
P5-250(A)	251	17	IDE AT	1,7 RLL		
P5-250(S)	251	17	SCSI-2	1,7 RLL		

KYOCERA ELECTRONICS, INC.

Drive Model	Format Size MB	Seek Time	Interface	Encode	cache kb	RPM
KC20A	21	65	ST412/506	MFM		
KC20B	21	62	ST412/506	MFM		
KC30A	33	65	ST412/506	2,7 RLL		
KC30B	33	62	ST412/506	2,7 RLL		
KC40GA	40	28	IDE AT	2,7 RLL		
KC80C	87	28	SCSI	2,7 RLL		
KC80GA	78	23	IDE AT	2,7 RLL		

LANSTOR

Drive Model	Format Size MB	Seek Time	Interface	Encode	cache kb	RPM
LAN-115						
LAN-140						
LAN-180						
LAN-64						

LAPINE

Drive Model	Format Size MB	Seek Time	Interface	Encode	cache kb	RPM
LT10	10	27	ST412/506	MFM		
LT100 (not verified)	10	85	ST412/506			
LT20	20		ST412/506	MFM		
LT200	20	65	ST412/506	MFM		
LT2000	20		ST412/506	MFM		
LT300	32		ST412/506	2,7 RLL		
LT3065	10	65	ST412/506	2,7 RLL		
LT3512	10	65	ST412/506	2,7 RLL		
LT3522	10	27	ST412/506	MFM		
LT3532	32	65	ST412/506	2,7 RLL		
LT4000 (not verified)	40	27	SCSI			
Titan 20	21		ST412/506	MFM		
Titan 30	21			RLL?		

MAXTOR CORPORATION

Drive Model	Format Size MB	Seek Time	Interface	Encode	cache kb	RPM
250837	837	14	IDE AT	1,7 RLL	64k	4464
250840	840	12	IDE AT	1,7 RLL	128k	4247
25084A	80	12	IDE AT	1,7 RLL	128k	4247
251005	1005	14	IDE AT	1,7 RLL	64k	4464
251010	1010	14	IDE AT	1,7 RLL	64k	4464
25128A	128	14	IDE AT	1,7 RLL		3600
251340	1340	14	IDE AT	1,7 RLL	64k	4464
251350	1350	13	IDE AT	1,7 RLL	64k	4464
25252A	252	12	IDE AT	1,7 RLL	64k	4247
25252S	251	12	SCSI	1,7 RLL	128k	4247
2585A	85	14	IDE AT	1,7 RLL		3600
2585S (never made)	85	15	SCSI	1,7 RLL		3600
2B004H1	4GB	12	UltraATA100		2mb	5400
2B006H1	6GB	12	UltraATA100		2mb	5400
2B008H1	8GB	12	UltraATA100		2mb	5400
2B010H1	10GB	12	UltraATA100		2mb	5400
2B015H1	15GB	12	UltraATA100		2mb	5400
2B020H1	20GB	12	UltraATA100		2mb	5400
2F020J0	20GB	12	ATA/133		2mb	5400
2F020L0	20GB	12	ATA/133		2mb	5400
2F030J0	30GB	12	ATA/133		2mb	5400
2F030L0	30GB	12	ATA/133		2mb	5400
2F040J0	40GB	12	ATA/133		2mb	5400
2F040L0	40GB	12	ATA/133		2mb	5400
2R010H1	10000	15	EIDE		2mb	5400
2R015H1	15000	15	EIDE		2mb	5400
3000DV	60GB		FireWire			7200
3000DV 80GB	80GB		ATA		2mb	7200
3000LE	40GB		USB2.0			5400
3000LE 120GB	120GB		USB2.0		2mb	5400
3000LE 40GB	40GB		USB2.0		2mb	5400
3000LS 40GB	40GB	12	USB2.0		2mb	5400

Drive Model	Format Size MB	Head	Cyl	Sect/ Trac	Translate H/C/S	RWC/ WPC	Form Factor	Power Watts
3000LS 60GB	60GB					—/—	3.5	
3000XT 160GB	160GB					—/—	3.5	
30510H1	5121				16/16383/63	—/—	3.5 3H	5.5
3053	44	5	1024	17		1024/512	5.25HH	12.4
30680H1	6448				16/16383/63	—/—	3.5 3H	5.5
30768H1	7683				16/16383/63	—/—	3.5 3H	5.5
30768U1	7683	1			16/16383/63	—/—	3.5 3H	4.9
30840H2	8455				16/16383/63	—/—	3.5 3H	5.5
30840U2	8400	1			16/16383/63	—/—	3.5 3H	4.9
3085	68	7	1170	17		1170/512	5.25HH	13.5
31024H1	10245				16/16383/63	—/—	3.5 3H	5.5
31024H2	9770				16/16383/63	—/—	3.5 3H	5.5
31024U2	10240	1			16/16383/63	—/—	3.5 3H	4.9
3130E	112	5	1250	36		1251/512	5.25HH	
3130S	112	5	1255	35		1256/512	5.25HH	18
31369H2	13020				16/16383/63	—/—	3.5 3H	5.5
31535H2	15367				16/16383/63	—/—	3.5 3H	5.5
31536H2	15367				16/16383/63	—/—	3.5 3H	5.5
31536U2	15367	2			16/16383/63	—/—	3.5 3H	4.9
3180E	150	7	1250	35		1251/512	5.25HH	18
3180S	153	7	1255	36		1256/512	5.25HH	18
32049H2	20491				16/16383/63	—/—	3.5 3H	5.5
32049H3	19541				16/16383/63	—/—	3.5 3H	5.5
32049U3	20490	3			16/16383/63	—/—	3.5 3H	4.9
32305H3	23051				16/16383/63	—/—	3.5 3H	5.5
32305U3	23050	1			16/16383/63	—/—	3.5 3H	4.9
33073H3	30736				16/16383/63	—/—	3.5 3H	5.5
33073H4	29311				16/16383/63	—/—	3.5 3H	5.5
33073U4	30735	4			16/16383/63	—/—	3.5 3H	4.9
3380	338	15	1224	NA		NA/NA	5.25FH	
34098H4	40982				16/16383/63	—/—	3.5 3H	5.5
34610H6	45020				16/16383/63	—/—	3.5 3H	5.5
36147H8	60022				16/16383/63	—/—	3.5 3H	5.5
4A160J0	160GB					—/—	3.5 3H	
4D020H1	20GB	1				—/—	3.5 3H	3.75
4D040H2	40GB	2				—/—	3.5 3H	3.75
4D060H3	60GB	3				—/—	3.5 3H	3.75
4D080H4	80GB	4				—/—	3.5 3H	3.75
4G120J6	120GB	6				—/—	3.5 3H	3.75
4G160J8	120GB	8				—/—	3.5 3H	3.75
4K020H1	20GB	1				—/—	3.5 3H	3.75
4K040H2	40GB	2				—/—	3.5 3H	3.75
4K060H3	60GB	3				—/—	3.5 3H	3.75
4K080H4	80GB	4				—/—	3.5 3H	3.75
4R060J0	60GB				16/16383/63	—/—	3.5 3H	
4R060L0	60GB				16/16383/63	—/—	3.5 3H	
4R080J0	80GB				16/16383/63	—/—	3.5 3H	
4R080L0	80GB				16/16383/63	—/—	3.5 3H	
4R120L0	80GB				16/16383/63	—/—	3.5 3H	
4R160J0	80GB				16/16383/63	—/—	3.5 3H	
4R160L0	80GB				16/16383/63	—/—	3.5 3H	
4W010H1	10GB	1			16/16383/63	—/—	3.5 3H	4
4W015H1	15GB	1			16/16383/63	—/—	3.5 3H	4
4W020H2	20GB	2			16/16383/63	—/—	3.5 3H	4
4W030H2	30GB	2				—/—	3.5 3H	4
4W040H3	40GB	3				—/—	3.5 3H	4
4W060H4	60GB	4				—/—	3.5 3H	4
4W080H6	80GB	6				—/—	3.5 3H	4
4W100H6	100GB	6				—/—	3.5 3H	4
5000DV 120GB	120GB					—/—		
5000DV 160GB	160GB					—/—		
5000DV 200GB	200GB					—/—		
5000DV 200GB FW	200GB					—/—		
5000LE 80GB	80GB					—/—		
5000XT 250G	250GB					—/—		
51023H2	10.2GB	2	19852		16/16383/63	—/—	3.5 3H	6.6
51024H2	10240	2			16/16383/63	—/—	3.5 3H	6.6

Drive Model	Format Size MB	Seek Time	Interface	Encode	cache kb	RPM
3000LS 60GB	60GB	12	USB2.0		2mb	5400
3000XT 160GB	160GB		UltraATA133		2mb	5400
30510H1	5121	9.5	ATA5/DMA100		512k	5400
3053	44	25	ST412/506	MFM		3600
30680H1	6448	9.5	ATA5/DMA100		512k	5400
30768H1	7683	9.5	ATA5/DMA100		512k	5400
30768U1	7683	9.5	ATA5/UDMA66		512k	5400
30840H2	8455	9.5	ATA5/DMA100		512k	5400
30840U2	8400	9.5	ATA5/UDMA66		512k	5400
3085	68	22	ST412/506	MFM		3600
31024H1	10245	9.5	UltraATA100		2mb	5400
31024H2	9770	9.5	ATA5/DMA100		512k	5400
31024U2	10240	9.5	ATA5/UDMA66		512k	5400
3130E	112	17	ESDI	2,7 RLL		3600
3130S	112	17	SCSI	2,7 RLL		3600
31369H2	13020	9.5	ATA5/DMA100		512k	5400
31535H2	15367	9.5	UltraATA100		2mb	5400
31536H2	15367	9.5	ATA5/DMA100		512k	5400
31536U2	15367	9.5	ATA5/UDMA66		512k	5400
3180E	150	17	ESDI	2,7 RLL		3600
3180S	153	17	SCSI	2,7 RLL		3600
32049H2	20491	9.5	UltraATA100		2mb	5400
32049H3	19541	9.5	ATA5/DMA100		512k	5400
32049U3	20490	9.5	ATA5/UDMA66		512k	5400
32305H3	23051	9.5	ATA5/DMA100		512k	5400
32305U3	23050	9.5	ATA5/UDMA66		512k	5400
33073H3	30736	9.5	UltraATA100		2mb	5400
33073H4	29311	9.5	ATA5/DMA100		512k	5400
33073U4	30735	9.5	ATA5/UDMA66		512k	5400
3380	338	27	SCSI	RLL		3600
34098H4	40982	9.5	UltraATA100		2mb	5400
34610H6	45020	9.5	ATA5/DMA100		512k	5400
36147H8	60022	9.5	ATA5/DMA100		512k	5400
4A160J0	160GB	12.6	Ultra ATA		2mb	5400
4D020H1	20GB	9.6	Ultra ATA		2mb	5400
4D040H2	40GB	9.6	Ultra ATA		2mb	5400
4D060H3	60GB	9.6	Ultra ATA		2mb	5400
4D080H4	80GB	9.6	Ultra ATA		2mb	5400
4G120J6	120GB	12	Ultra ATA		2mb	5400
4G160J8	120GB	12	Ultra ATA		2mb	5400
4K020H1	20GB	9.6	Ultra ATA		2mb	5400
4K040H2	40GB	9.6	Ultra ATA		2mb	5400
4K060H3	60GB	9.6	Ultra ATA		2mb	5400
4K080H4	80GB	9.6	Ultra ATA		2mb	5400
4R060J0	60GB	12.6	ATA/133		2mb	5400
4R060L0	60GB	12.6	ATA/133		2mb	5400
4R080J0	80GB	12.6	ATA/133		2mb	5400
4R080L0	80GB	12.6	ATA/133		2mb	5400
4R120L0	80GB	12.6	ATA/133		2mb	5400
4R160J0	80GB	12.6	ATA/133		2mb	5400
4R160L0	80GB	12.6	ATA/133		2mb	5400
4W010H1	10GB	10.5	UltraATA100		2mb	5400
4W015H1	15GB	10.5	UltraATA100		2mb	5400
4W020H2	20GB	10.5	UltraATA100		2mb	5400
4W030H2	30GB	10.5	Ultra ATA		2mb	5400
4W040H3	40GB	10.5	Ultra ATA		2mb	5400
4W060H4	60GB	10.5	Ultra ATA		2mb	5400
4W080H6	80GB	10.5	Ultra ATA		2mb	5400
4W100H6	100GB	10.5	Ultra ATA		2mb	5400
5000DV 120GB	120GB	9	UltraATA133		2mb	7200
5000DV 160GB	160GB	9.3	USB2/FIREWR		8mb	7200
5000DV 200GB	200GB	9	UltraATA133		8mb	7200
5000DV 200GB FW	200GB	9.3	FireWire		8mb	7200
5000LE 80GB	80GB	9.3	USB2.0		2mb	7200
5000XT 250G	250GB	12.6	USB2.0		2mb	5400
51023H2	10.2GB	8.7	UltraATA100		2mb	7200
51024H2	10240	9	ATA5/DMA100		2mb	7200

Drive Model	Format Size MB	Head	Cyl	Sect/Trac	Translate H/C/S	RWC/WPC	Form Factor	Power Watts
51024U2	10245	2				—/—	3.5 3H	6.6
51369H2	13.6GB	2	26310		16/16383/63	—/—	3.5 3H	6.6
51369H3	13690	3			16/16383/63	—/—	3.5 3H	6.6
51536H2	15.3GB	2	29777		16/16383/63	—/—	3.5 3H	6.6
51536H3	15360	3			16/16383/63	—/—	3.5 3H	6.6
51536U3	15367	3				—/—	3.5 3H	6.6
52049H3	20.4GB	3	39704		16/16383/63	—/—	3.5 3H	6.6
52049H4	20490	4			16/16383/63	—/—	3.5 3H	6.6
52049U4	20490	4				—/—	3.5 3H	6.6
52732H6	27320	6			16/16383/63	—/—	3.5 3H	6.6
53073H4	30.7GB	4	59554		16/16383/63	—/—	3.5 3H	6.6
53073U6	30735	6				—/—	3.5 3H	6.6
53076H6	30760	6			16/16383/63	—/—	3.5 3H	6.6
536DX 100GB	100GB	6				—/—	3.5 3H	4
536DX 10GB	10GB	1			16/16383/63	—/—	3.5 3H	4
536DX 15GB	15GB	1			16/16383/63	—/—	3.5 3H	4
536DX 20GB	20GB	2			16/16383/63	—/—	3.5 3H	4
536DX 30GB	30GB	2				—/—	3.5 3H	4
536DX 40GB	40GB	3				—/—	3.5 3H	4
536DX 60GB	60GB	4				—/—	3.5 3H	4
536DX 80GB	80GB	6				—/—	3.5 3H	4
54098H6	40.9GB	6	79408		16/16383/63	—/—	3.5 3H	6.6
54098H8	40980	8			16/16383/63	—/—	3.5 3H	6.6
54098U8	40981	8				—/—	3.5 3H	6.6
541DX DMA 100 10GB	10GB	1	19386		16/16383/63	—/—		
541DX DMA 100 15GB	15GB	1	29104		16/16383/63	—/—		
541DX DMA 100 20GB	20GB	1	38792		16/16383/63	—/—		
541DX DMA 100 4GB	4GB	1	8184		16/16383/63	—/—		
541DX DMA 100 6GB	6GB	1	13328		16/16383/63	—/—		
541DX DMA 100 8GB	8GB	1	16351		16/16383/63	—/—		
54610H6	46.1GB	6	89331		16/16383/63	—/—	3.5 3H	6.6
5A250J0	250GB	8			16/16383/63	—/—	3.5 3H	
5A300J0	300GB	8			16/16383/63	—/—	3.5 3H	
5T010H1	10GB	1			16/16383/63	—/—	3.5 3H	6.7
5T020H2	20GB	2			16/16383/63	—/—	3.5 3H	6.7
5T030H3	30GB	3			16/16383/63	—/—	3.5 3H	6.7
5T040H4	40GB	4			16/16383/63	—/—	3.5 3H	6.7
5T060H6	60.5GB	6			16/16383/63	—/—	3.5 3H	6.7
6E020L0	20GB				16/16383/63	—/—	3.5 3H	
6E030L0	30GB				16/16383/63	—/—	3.5 3H	
6E040L0	40GB				16/16383/63	—/—	3.5 3H	
6L020J1	20GB	1				—/—	3.5 3H	7.4
6L020L1	20GB	1				—/—	3.5 3H	7.4
6L040J2	40GB	2				—/—	3.5 3H	7.4
6L040L2	40GB	2				—/—	3.5 3H	7.4
6L060J3	60GB	3				—/—	3.5 3H	7.4
6L060L3	60GB	3				—/—	3.5 3H	7.4
6L080J4	80GB	4				—/—	3.5 3H	7.4
6L080L4	80GB	4				—/—	3.5 3H	7.4
6Y060L0	60GB				16/16383/63	—/—	3.5 3H	
6Y060M0	60GB				16/16383/63	—/—	3.5 3H	
6Y080L0	80GB				16/16383/63	—/—	3.5 3H	
6Y080M0	80GB				16/16383/63	—/—	3.5 3H	
6Y080P0	80GB				16/16383/63	—/—	3.5 3H	
6Y120L0	120GB				16/16383/63	—/—	3.5 3H	
6Y120M0	120GB				16/16383/63	—/—	3.5 3H	
6Y120P0	120GB				16/16383/63	—/—	3.5 3H	
6Y160L0	160GB				16/16383/63	—/—	3.5 3H	
6Y160M0	160GB				16/16383/63	—/—	3.5 3H	
6Y160P0	160GB				16/16383/63	—/—	3.5 3H	
6Y200M0	160GB				16/16383/63	—/—	3.5 3H	
6Y200P0	160GB				16/16383/63	—/—	3.5 3H	
7040A	41	2	1155	36	5/981/17	NA/NA	3.5 3H	3.6
7040S	42	2	1155	36		NA/NA	3.5 3H	
7060A	65	2	1498	NA	16/467/17	NA/NA	3.5 3H	
7060S	60	2	1498	42		NA/NA	3.5 3H	
7080A	85	4	1166	36	10/981/17	NA/NA	3.5 3H	3.7

Drive Model	Format Size MB	Seek Time	Interface	Encode	cache kb	RPM
51024U2	10245	9.0	ATA5/UDMA66		2mb	7200
51369H2	13.6GB	8.7	UltraATA100		2mb	7200
51369H3	13690	9	ATA5/DMA100		2mb	7200
51536H2	15.3GB	8.7	UltraATA100		2mb	7200
51536H3	15360	9	ATA5/DMA100		2mb	7200
51536U3	15367	9.0	ATA5/UDMA66		2mb	7200
52049H3	20.4GB	8.7	UltraATA100		2mb	7200
52049H4	20490	9	ATA5/DMA100		2mb	7200
52049U4	20490	9.0	ATA5/UDMA66		2mb	7200
52732H6	27320	9	ATA5/DMA100		2mb	7200
53073H4	30.7GB	8.7	UltraATA100		2mb	7200
53073U6	30735	9.0	ATA5/DMA66		2mb	7200
53076H6	30760	9	ATA5/DMA100		2mb	7200
536DX 100GB	100GB	10.5	Ultra ATA		2mb	5400
536DX 10GB	10GB	10.5	UltraATA100		2mb	5400
536DX 15GB	15GB	10.5	UltraATA100		2mb	5400
536DX 20GB	20GB	10.5	UltraATA100		2mb	5400
536DX 30GB	30GB	10.5	UltraATA100		2mb	5400
536DX 40GB	40GB	10.5	Ultra ATA		2mb	5400
536DX 60GB	60GB	10.5	Ultra ATA		2mb	5400
536DX 80GB	80GB	10.5	Ultra ATA		2mb	5400
54098H6	40.9GB	8.7	UltraATA100		2mb	7200
54098H8	40980	9	ATA5/DMA100		2mb	7200
54098U8	40981	9.0	ATA5/UDMA66		2mb	7200
541DX DMA 100 10GB	10GB	12	UltraATA100		2mb	5400
541DX DMA 100 15GB	15GB	12	UltraATA100		2mb	5400
541DX DMA 100 20GB	20GB	12	UltraATA100		2mb	5400
541DX DMA 100 4GB	4GB	12	UltraATA100		2mb	5400
541DX DMA 100 6GB	6GB	12	UltraATA100		2mb	5400
541DX DMA 100 8GB	8GB	12	UltraATA100		2mb	5400
54610H6	46.1GB	8.7	UltraATA100		2mb	7200
5A250J0	250GB	10	ATA/133		2mb	5400
5A300J0	300GB	10	ATA/133		2mb	5400
5T010H1	10GB	8.7	UltraATA100		2mb	7200
5T020H2	20GB	8.7	UltraATA100		2mb	7200
5T030H3	30GB	8.7	UltraATA100		2mb	7200
5T040H4	40GB	8.7	UltraATA100		2mb	7200
5T060H6	60.5GB	8.7	UltraATA100		2mb	7200
6E020L0	20GB	10	ATA/133		2mb	7200
6E030L0	30GB	10	ATA/133		2mb	7200
6E040L0	40GB	10	ATA/133		2mb	7200
6L020J1	20GB	8.5	UltraATA133		2mb	7200
6L020L1	20GB	8.5	UltraATA133		2mb	7200
6L040J2	40GB	8.5	UltraATA133		2mb	7200
6L040L2	40GB	8.5	UltraATA133		2mb	7200
6L060J3	60GB	8.5	UltraATA133		2mb	7200
6L060L3	60GB	8.5	UltraATA133		2mb	7200
6L080J4	80GB	8.5	UltraATA133		2mb	7200
6L080L4	80GB	8.5	UltraATA133		2mb	7200
6Y060L0	60GB	9.4	ATA/133		2mb	7200
6Y060M0	60GB	9.4	SATA/150		8mb	7200
6Y080L0	80GB	9.4	ATA/133		2mb	7200
6Y080M0	80GB	9.4	SATA/150		8mb	7200
6Y080P0	80GB	9.4	ATA/133		8mb	7200
6Y120L0	120GB	9.4	ATA/133		2mb	7200
6Y120M0	120GB	9.4	SATA/150		8mb	7200
6Y120P0	120GB	9.4	ATA/133		8mb	7200
6Y160L0	160GB	9.4	ATA/133		8mb	7200
6Y160M0	160GB	9.4	SATA/150		8mb	7200
6Y160P0	160GB	9.4	ATA/133		8mb	7200
6Y200M0	160GB	9.4	SATA/150		8mb	7200
6Y200P0	160GB	9.4	ATA/133		8mb	7200
7040A	41	17	IDE AT	1,7 RLL	32k	3703
7040S	42	17	SCSI	1,7 RLL	32k	3600
7060A	65	15	IDE AT	1,7 RLL		3600
7060S	60	15	SCSI	1,7 RLL		3600
7080A	85	17	IDE AT	1,7 RLL	32k	3703

Drive Model	Format Size MB	Head	Cyl	Sect/ Trac	Translate H/C/S	RWC/ WPC	Form Factor	Power Watts
7080S	85	4	1166	36		NA/NA	3.5 3H	
71000A	1002	3			16/1946/63	—/—	3.5 3H	4.4
71050A	1000	5		77-124	16/2045/63	—/—	3.5 3H	4.4
71050S	1000	5		77-124		—/—	3.5 3H	
71084A	1084	4	4136	91-155	16/2105/63	NA/NA	3.5 3H	4.4
71084AP	1084	4	4136	91-155	16/2105/63	NA/NA	3.5 3H	4.4
7120A	125	4	1498	NA	16/936/17	NA/NA	3.5 3H	4.5
7120S	125	4	1498	42		NA/NA	3.5 3H	4.5
71260A	1200	4		77-124	16/2448/63	—/—	3.5 3H	
71260AP	1260	5	4136	91-155	16/2632/63	NA/NA	3.5 3H	4.4
71260S	1200	4				—/—	3.5 3H	
7131A	125	2	2096		8/1002/32	NA/NA	3.5 3H	
71336A	1336	4	4721		16/2595/63	—/—	3.5 3H	4.4
71336AP	1336	4	4721		16/2595/63	—/—	3.5 3H	4.4
71350A	1350	4			16/2624/63	—/—	3.5 3H	4.5
71350AP	1350	4			16/2624/63	—/—	3.5 3H	4.5
7135AV	135	1		72-123	13/966/21	—/—	3.5 3H	
71626A	1626	6	4136	91-155	16/3158/63	NA/NA	3.5 3H	4.4
71626AP	1626	6	4136	91-155	16/3158/63	NA/NA	3.5 3H	4.4
71670A	1670	5	4721		16/3224/63	—/—	3.5 3H	4.4
71670AP	1670	5	4721		16/3224/63	—/—	3.5 3H	4.4
71687AP	1687	5			16/3280/63	—/—	3.5 3H	4.5
7170A	171	4	1281	48-72	10/984/34	—/—	3.5 3H	
	172	2		V	15/866/26	—/—	3.5 3H	
7171A						—/—	3.5 3H	
72004A	2004	6	4721		16/3893/63	—/—	3.5 3H	4.4
72004AP	2004	6	4721		16/3893/63	—/—	3.5 3H	4.4
72025AP	2025	6			16/3936/63	—/—	3.5 3H	
7213A	213	4	1690	42	16/683/38	NA/NA	3.5 3H	3.5
7213S	213	4	1690	42		NA/NA	3.5 3H	3.5
7245A	234	4		48-72	16/967/31	—/—	3.5 3H	
7245S	245	4		48-72		—/—	3.5 3H	
72577AP	2577	8			16/4996/63	—/—	3.5 3H	4.5
72700AP	2700	8			16/5248/63	—/—	3.5 3H	4.5
7270AV	270	2		72-123	11/959/50	—/—	3.5 3H	
7273A	273	3		V	16/1012/33	—/—	3.5 3H	
7290A	290	4		60-96		NA/NA	3.5 3H	
7290S	290	4				—/—	3.5 3H	
7345A	345	4			15/790/57	—/—	3.5 3H	
7345S	345	4				—/—	3.5 3H	
7405A	4051				16/989/50	—/—	3.5 3H	3.9
7405AV	405	3		72-123	16/989/50	—/—	3.5 3H	
7420AV	420	3		72-123	16/1046/63	—/—	3.5 3H	
7425AV	425	2	3721	76-144	16/1000/52	NA/NA	3.5 3H	3.26
7540AV	540	4		72-123	16/1046/63	—/—	3.5 3H	
7541A	541	2	4136	91-155	16/1052/63	NA/NA	3.5 3H	4.4
7541AP	541	2	4136	91-155	16/1052/63	NA/NA	3.5 3H	4.4
7546A	547	4		V	16/1024/63	—/—	3.5 3H	
7546S	547	4		V		—/—	3.5 3H	
7668A	668	2	4721		16/1297/63	—/—	3.5 3H	4.4
7668AP	668	2	4721		16/1297/63	—/—	3.5 3H	4.4
7850AV	850	4	3721	76-144	16/1648/63	NA/NA	3.5 3H	3.52
7Y250M0	250GB	6			16/16383/63	—/—	3.5 3H	
7Y250P0	250GB	6			16/16383/63	—/—	3.5 3H	
8051A	41	4	745	26	5/981/17	NA/NA	3.5HH	8
8051S	40	4	793	28		NA/NA	3.5HH	
80875A2	875	2			16/1700/63	—/—	3.5 3H	4.52
81080A3	1080	3			16/2100/63	—/—	3.5 3H	4.52
81081A2	1081	2			16/2100/63	—/—	3.5 3H	3.95
81275A3	1275	3			16/2480/63	—/—	3.5 3H	4.52
81280A2	1280	2			16/2481/63	—/—	3.5 3H	4.5
81312A3	1312	3			16/2548/63	—/—	3.5 3H	4.52
81620A3	1550	3			16/3150/63	—/—	3.5 3H	3.95
81630A4	1630	4			16/3168/63	—/—	3.5 3H	4.52
81750A2	1750	2			15/3618/63	—/—	3.5 3H	4.6
81750A4	1750	4			16/3400/63	—/—	3.5 3H	4.52
81750D2	1750	2			15/3618/63	—/—	3.5 3H	4.6
82100A4	2100	4			16/4092/63	—/—	3.5 3H	3.95

Drive Model	Format Size MB	Seek Time	Interface	Encode	cache kb	RPM
7080S	85	17	SCSI	1,7 RLL	32k	3600
71000A	1002	12	IDE AT	1,7 RLL		
71050A	1000	12	EIDE	1,7 RLL	256k	4500
71050S	1000	12	SCSI	1,7 RLL	256k	4500
71084A	1084	12	IDE AT	1,7 RLL	64k	4480
71084AP	1084	12	IDE AT	1,7 RLL	128k	4480
7120A	125	15	IDE AT	1,7 RLL	64k	3600
7120S	125	15	SCSI	1,7 RLL	64k	3600
71260A	1200	12	EIDE	1,7 RLL	256k	4500
71260AP	1260	12	IDE AT	1,7 RLL	128k	4480
71260S	1200	14	ATA-2	1,7 RLL	256k	4500
7131A	125	14	IDE AT	1,7 RLL	64k	3551
71336A	1336	<12	IDE AT	1,7 RLL	64k	4480
71336AP	1336	<12	IDE AT	1,7 RLL	128k	4480
71350A	1350	<12	IDE AT	1,7 RLL	64k	4480
71350AP	1350	<12	IDE AT	1,7 RLL	128k	4480
7135AV	135	12	IDE AT	1,7 RLL	32k	3551
71626A	1626	12	IDE AT	1,7 RLL	64k	4480
71626AP	1626	12	IDE AT	1,7 RLL	128k	4480
71670A	1670	<12	IDE AT	1,7 RLL	64k	4480
71670AP	1670	<12	IDE AT	1,7 RLL	128k	4480
71687AP	1687	<12	IDE AT	1,7 RLL	128k	4480
7170A	171	15	IDE AT	1,7 RLL	64k	3551
7171A	172	14	IDE AT	1,7 RLL	64k	3551
72004A	2004	<12	IDE AT	1,7 RLL	64k	4480
72004AP	2004	<12	IDE AT	1,7 RLL	128k	4480
72025AP	2025	<12	IDE AT	1,7 RLL	128k	4480
7213A	213	15	IDE AT	1,7 RLL	64k	3551
7213S	213	15	SCSI	1,7 RLL	64k	3551
7245A	234	15	IDE AT	1,7 RLL	64k	3551
7245S	245	15	SCSI	1,7 RLL	64k	3551
72577AP	2577	<12	IDE AT	1,7 RLL	128k	4480
72700AP	2700	<12	IDE AT	1,7 RLL	128k	4480
7270AV	270	12	IDE AT	1,7 RLL	32k	3551
7273A	273	12	IDE AT	1,7 RLL	256k	4500
7290A	290	14	IDE AT	1,7 RLL	64k	3551
7290S	290	14	SCSI	1,7 RLL	64k	3551
7345A	345	14	IDE AT	1,7 RLL	64k	3551
7345S	345	14	SCSI	1,7 RLL	64k	3551
7405A	4051	12	IDE AT	1,7 RLL	32k	3551
7405AV	405	12	IDE AT	1,7 RLL	32k	3551
7420AV	420	12	IDE AT	1,7 RLL	32k	3551
7425AV	425	12	IDE AT	1,7 RLL	64k	3551
7540AV	540	12	IDE AT	1,7 RLL	32k	3551
7541A	541	12	IDE AT	1,7 RLL	64k	4480
7541AP	541	12	IDE AT	1,7 RLL	128k	4480
7546A	547	12	IDE AT	1,7 RLL	256k	4500
7546S	547	12	SCSI	1,7 RLL	256k	4500
7668A	668	<12	IDE AT	1,7 RLL	64k	4480
7668AP	668	<12	IDE AT	1,7 RLL	128k	4480
7850AV	850	12	IDE AT	1,7 RLL	64k	3551
7Y250M0	250GB	9	SATA/150		8mb	7200
7Y250P0	250GB	9	PATA/133		8mb	7200
8051A	41	28	IDE AT	2,7 RLL	32k	3484
8051S	40	28	SCSI	2,7 RLL		3600
80875A2	875	12	EIDE	1,7 RLL	128k	4480
81080A3	1080	12	ATA-3	1,7 RLL	128k	4480
81081A2	1081	11	ATA-3	1,7 RLL	256k	4480
81275A3	1275	12	IDE AT	1,7 RLL	128k	4480
81280A2	1280	10	ATA-3	RLL 8,9	256k	5400
81312A3	1312	12	EIDE	1,7 RLL	128k	4480
81620A3	1550	11	ATA-3	RLL 8,9	256k	4480
81630A4	1630	10	IDE AT	1,7 RLL	128k	4480
81750A2	1750	10	ATA-4	RLL 8,9	256k	5200
81750A4	1750	12	EIDE	1,7 RLL	128k	4480
81750D2	1750	10	ATA-4	RLL 8,9	256k	5200
82100A4	2100	11	ATA-3	RLL 8,9	256k	4480

Drive Model	Format Size MB	Head	Cyl	Sect/Trac	Translate H/C/S	RWC/WPC	Form Factor	Power Watts
82160A4	2160	4			16/4185/63	—/—	3.5 3H	4.5
82160D2	2160	2			15/4465/63	—/—	3.5 3H	4.0
82187A5	2187	5			16/4248/63	—/—	3.5 3H	4.52
82400A4	2400	4			16/4708/63	—/—	3.5 3H	4.5
82559A4	2559	4			16/4960/63	—/—	3.5 3H	4.5
82560A3	2560	3			15/5292/63	—/—	3.5 3H	4.6
82560A4	2560	4			16/4962/63	—/—	3.5 3H	4.5
82560D3	2560	3			15/5292/63	—/—	3.5 3H	4.6
82561D3	2441				16/2559/63		3.5 3H	
82577A6	2577	6			16/5000/63	—/—	3.5 3H	4.52
82580A5	2580	5			16/5004/63	—/—	3.5 3H	3.95
82625A6	2625	6			16/5100/63	—/—	3.5 3H	4.52
83062A7	3062	7			16/5948/63	—/—	3.5 3H	4.52
83200A5	3200	5			16/6296/63	—/—	3.5 3H	4.5
83200A6	3200	6			15/6296/15	—/—	3.5 3H	4.5
83200A8	3200	8			16/6218/63	—/—	3.5 3H	4.52
83201A6	3201	6			16/6218/63	—/—	3.5 3H	3.95
83202A6	3202	6			15/6296/63	—/—	3.5 3H	4.5
83209A5	3209	5			16/6218/63	—/—	3.5 3H	4.5
83240A4	3240	4			16/6696/63	—/—	3.5 3H	4.6
83240D3	3240	3			15/6697/63	—/—	3.5 3H	4.0
83240D4	3240	4			15/6696/63	—/—	3.5 3H	4.6
83500A4	3500	4			15/7237/63	—/—	3.5 3H	4.52
83500A8	3500	8			16/6800/63	—/—	3.5 3H	4.6
83500D4	3500	4			15/7237/63	—/—	3.5 3H	4.6
83840A6	3840	6			16/7441/63	—/—	3.5 3H	4.5
84000A6	4000	6			16/7763/63	—/—	3.5 3H	4.5
84004A8	4004	8			16/7758/63	—/—	3.5 3H	4.5
84200A8	4200	8			16/8184/63	—/—	3.5 3H	4.5
8425S	21	4	612	17		616/128	3.5HH	13
84320A5	4320	5			15/8928/63	—/—	3.5 3H	4.6
84320A8	4320	8			16/8400/63	—/—	3.5 3H	3.95
84320D4	4320	4			15/8930/63	—/—	3.5 3H	4.6
84320D5	4320	5			15/8928/63	—/—	3.5 3H	4.6
85120A8	5120	8			16/9924/63	—/—	3.5 3H	4.5
85121A8	5121	8			15/10585/63	—/—	3.5 3H	4.5
85210D6	5210	6			15/10856/63	—/—	3.5 3H	4.6
85250A6	5250	6			15/10856/63	—/—	3.5 3H	4.6
85250D6	5210	6			15/10856/63	—/—	3.5 3H	4.6
85400D5	5493	5			15/11162/63	—/—	3.5 3H	
86480A8	6480	8			15/13392/63	—/—	3.5 3H	4.6
86480D6	6480	6			15/13395/63	—/—	3.5 3H	4.6
86480D8	6480	8			15/13392/63	—/—	3.5 3H	4.6
87000A8	7000	8			15/14475/63	—/—	3.5 3H	4.6
87000D8	7000	8			15/14475/63	—/—	3.5 3H	4.6
88400D8	8400	8			16/16278/63	—/—	3.5 3H	4.0
8B036J0	36.7GB	2				—/—	3.5 3H	7.3
8B036L0	36.7GB	2				—/—	3.5 3H	7.3
8B073J0	73.4GB	4				—/—	3.5 3H	8.2
8B073L0	73.4GB	4				—/—	3.5 3H	8.2
8B146J0	146.9GB	8				—/—	3.5 3H	11
8B146L0	146.9GB	8				—/—	3.5 3H	11
8C018J0	18.4GB	2				—/—	3.5 3H	7.2
8C018L0	18.4GB	2				—/—	3.5 3H	7.2
8C036J0	36.7GB	4				—/—	3.5 3H	9.4
8C036L0	36.7GB	4				—/—	3.5 3H	9.4
8C073J0	73.4GB	8				—/—	3.5 3H	11
8C073L0	73.4GB	8				—/—	3.5 3H	11
90250D2	2559				16/4960/63	—/—	3.5	
90256D2	2560	2			16/4960/63	—/—	3.5 3H	3.9
90288D2	2880	2			16/5583/63	—/—	3.5 3H	3.9
90320D2	3240				15/6697/63	—/—	3.5	
90340D2	3400	2		269-32	16/6588/63	—/—	3.5 3H	4.4
90340D3	4311				15/8912/63	—/—	3.5	
90431U1	4310	1			16/16383/63	—/—	3.5 3H	4.7
90432D2	4320	2		230-38	16/8374/63	—/—	3.5 3H	4.1
90432D3	4320	3			16/8374/63	—/—	3.5 3H	3.9

Drive Model	Format Size MB	Seek Time	Interface	Encode	cache kb	RPM
82160A4	2160	10	ATA-3	RLL 8,9	256k	5400
82160D2	2160	9.7	ATA-4	16,17 RLL	256k	5200
82187A5	2187	12	EIDE	1,7 RLL	128k	4480
82400A4	2400	10	ATA-3	RLL 8,9	256k	5400
82559A4	2559	10	ATA-3	RLL 8,9	256k	5400
82560A3	2560	10	ATA-4	RLL 8,9	256k	5200
82560A4	2560	10	ATA-3	RLL 8,9	256k	5400
82560D3	2560	10	ATA-4	RLL 8,9	256k	5200
82561D3	2441		EIDE	8,9 RLL	256k	5200
82577A6	2577	12	IDE AT	1,7 RLL	128k	4480
82580A5	2580	11	ATA-3	RLL 8,9	256k	4480
82625A6	2625	12	EIDE	1,7 RLL	128k	4480
83062A7	3062	12	EIDE	1,7 RLL	128k	4480
83200A5	3200	10	ATA-3	RLL 8,9	256k	5400
83200A6	3200	10	ATA-3	RLL 8,9	256k	5400
83200A8	3200	12	EIDE	1,7 RLL	128k	4480
83201A6	3201	11	ATA-3	RLL 8,9	256k	4480
83202A6	3202	10	ATA-3	RLL 8,9	256k	5400
83209A5	3209	10	ATA-3	RLL 8,9	256k	5400
83240A4	3240	10	ATA-4	RLL 8,9	256k	5200
83240D3	3240	9.7	ATA-4	16,17 RLL	256k	5200
83240D4	3240	10	ATA-4	RLL 8,9	256k	5200
83500A4	3500	10	ATA-4	RLL 8,9	256k	5200
83500A8	3500	12	EIDE	1,7 RLL	128k	4480
83500D4	3500	10	ATA-4	RLL 8,9	256k	5200
83840A6	3840	10	ATA-3	RLL 8,9	256k	5400
84000A6	4000	10	ATA-3	RLL 8,9	256k	5400
84004A8	4004	10	ATA-3	RLL 8,9	256k	5400
84200A8	4200	10	ATA-3	RLL 8,9	256k	5400
8425S	21	68	SCSI	MFM		3600
84320A5	4320	10	ATA-4	RLL 8,9	256k	5200
84320A8	4320	11	ATA-3	RLL 8,9	256k	5200
84320D4	4320	10	EIDE	RLL 8,9	256k	4480
84320D5	4320	10	ATA-4	RLL 8,9	256k	5200
85120A8	5120	10	ATA-3	RLL 8,9	256k	5200
85121A8	5121	10	ATA-3	RLL 8,9	256k	5400
85210D6	5210	10	ATA-4	RLL 8,9	256k	5200
85250A6	5250	10	ATA-4	RLL 8,9	256k	5200
85250D6	5210	10	ATA-4	RLL 8,9	256k	5200
85400D5	5493	9.7	EIDE	8,9 RLL	256k	5200
86480A8	6480	10	ATA-4	RLL 8,9	256k	5200
86480D6	6480	10	EIDE	RLL 8,9	256k	5200
86480D8	6480	10	ATA-4	RLL 8,9	256k	5200
87000A8	7000	10	ATA-4	RLL 8,9	256k	5200
87000D8	7000	10	ATA-4	RLL 8,9	256k	5200
88400D8	8400	9.7	ATA-4	16,17 RLL	256k	5200
8B036J0	36.7GB	4.8	U320SCSISCA		8mb	1000
8B036L0	36.7GB	4.3	UL320SCSIWD		8mb	1000
8B073J0	73.4GB	4.8	U320SCSISCA		8mb	1000
8B073L0	73.4GB	4.3	UL320SCSIWD		8mb	1000
8B146J0	146.9GB	4.9	U320SCSISCA		8mb	1000
8B146L0	146.9GB	4.4	UL320SCSIWD		8mb	1000
8C018J0	18.4GB	3.6	U320SCSISCA		8mb	1500
8C018L0	18.4GB	3.2	UL320SCSIWD		8mb	1500
8C036J0	36.7GB	3.6	U320SCSISCA		8mb	1500
8C036L0	36.7GB	3.2	UL320SCSIWD		8mb	1500
8C073J0	73.4GB	3.8	U320SCSISCA		8mb	1500
8C073L0	73.4GB	3.4	UL320SCSIWD		8mb	1500
90250D2	2559	9	EIDE		256k	5400
90256D2	2560	9	ATA-4	PRML	252k	5400
90288D2	2880	9	ATA-4	PRML	252k	5400
90320D2	3240	9	EIDE		256k	5400
90340D2	3400	9	ATA-4	16/17 EPR4	256k	5400
90430D2	4311	9	EIDE		256k	5400
90431U1	4310	9.5	ATA5/UDMA66		512k	5400
90432D2	4320	9	ATA-4/EIDE	PRML	512k	5400
90432D3	4320	9	ATA-4	PRML	252k	5400

Drive Model	Format Size MB	Head	Cyl	Sect/Trac	Translate H/C/S	RWC/WPC	Form Factor	Power Watts
90500D4	5003				16/9695/63	—/—	3.5	
90510D3	5100	3		269-32	16/9882/63	—/—	3.5 3H	4.4
90510D4	5122	5			16/9925/63	—/—	3.5 3H	3.9
90576D4	5760	4			16/11166/63	—/—	3.5 3H	3.9
90625D5	6254				16/12119/63	—/—	3.5	
90640D4	6481				15/13395/63	—/—	3.5	
90640D4	6448				15/13328/63	—/—	3.5	
90640E4	6480	3		230-38	16/12556/63	—/—	3.5 3H	4.1
90648D3	6480	5			16/12555/63	—/—	3.5 3H	3.9
90648D5	6500	2		266-46	16/16383/63	—/—	3.5 3H	5.3
90650U2	6510				16/16383/63	—/—	3.5 3H	4.9
90651U2	6800	4		269-32	16/13176/63	—/—	3.5 3H	4.4
90680D4	6800				16/16383/63	—/—	3.5 3H	5.3
90680U2						—/—	3.5 3H	7.2
90683U2	6831	2				—/—	3.5 3H	4.7
90684U2	6840	2			16/16383/63	—/—	3.5 3H	3.9
90720D5	7200	5			16/13957/63	—/—	3.5	
90750D6	7505				16/14542/63	—/—	3.5	
90840D5	8438				16/16383/63	—/—	3.5 3H	3.9
90840D6	8400	6			16/16276/63	—/—	3.5	
90840D7	8400				16/16277/63	—/—	3.5	
90840E5	8438				16/16383/63	—/—	3.5 3H	4.9
90841U2	8410				16/16383/63	—/—	3.5 3H	4.1
90845D4	8455	4		230-38	16/16383/63	—/—	3.5 3H	4.4
90845D5	8450	5				—/—	3.5 3H	4.4
90845D54	8455	5		269-32		—/—	3.5 3H	3.9
90845D6	8455	6			16/16383/63	—/—	3.5 3H	4.7
90845U2	8450				16/16383/63	—/—	3.5 3H	5.3
90845U3	8455	3		266-46		—/—	3.5 3H	
90864D6	8644				16/16383/63	—/—	3.5 3H	
90871U2	8710	2			16/16383/63	—/—	3.5 3H	4.7
90875D7	8756				16/16966/63	—/—	3.5	
90910D8	9106				16/17645/63	—/—	3.5	
90913U2	9130				16/16383/63	—/—	3.5 3H	4.7
91000D8	10007	8			16/19390/63	—/—	3.5	
91008D7	10080	7			16/19540/63	—/—	3.5 3H	3.9
91010D6	10110				16/19590/63	—/—	3.5	
91010E6	10005				16/19386/63	—/—	3.5	4.4
91020D6	10200	6		269-32	16/19765/63	—/—	3.5 3H	5.3
91020U3	10209	3		266-46	16/16383/63	—/—	3.5 3H	4.9
91021U1	10210				16/16383/63	—/—	3.5 3H	4.7
91021U2	10245	2				—/—	3.5 3H	5.3
91023U2	10240				16/16383/63	—/—	3.5 3H	7.0
91024D4	10240	4		240-40		—/—	3.5 3H	4.7
91024U2	10245	2			16/16383/63	—/—	3.5 3H	7.2
91024U3	10246	3				—/—	3.5 3H	4.1
91080D8	10800	5		230-38	16/20928/63	—/—	3.5 3H	3.9
91152D8	11520	8			16/22332/63	—/—	3.5 3H	4.4
91190D7	11900	7			16/23059/63	—/—	3.5	
91202D8	12020				16/23291/63	—/—	3.5	
91202E8	12020				16/23291/63	—/—	3.5 3H	4.7
91301U3	13010	3			16/16383/63	—/—	3.5 3H	4.1
91303D6	13030	6		230-38	16/25249/63	—/—	3.5	
91350D8	13520				16/26197/63	—/—	3.5	
91350E8	13520				16/26197/63	—/—	3.5 3H	4.4
91360D8	13600	8		269-32	16/26353/63	—/—	3.5 3H	5.3
91360U4	13613	4		266-46	16/16383/63	—/—	3.5 3H	4.9
91361U3	13610				16/16383/63	—/—	3.5 3H	4.7
91362U3	13620	4				—/—	3.5 3H	7.2
91366U4	13662	4				—/—	3.5 3H	4.7
91369U3	13698	3			16/16383/63	—/—	3.5 3H	4.1
91512D7	15120	7		230-38	16/29298/63	—/—	3.5 3H	4.9
91531U3	15367	3			16/16383/63	—/—	3.5 3H	7.0
91536D6	15360	6		240-40		—/—	3.5 3H	5.5
91536H2	15367	2				—/—	3.5 3H	5.3
91536U2	15360				16/16383/63	—/—	3.5 3H	4.7
91536U3	15360	4			16/16383/63	—/—	3.5 3H	5.3
91700U5	17000				16/16383/63	—/—	3.5 3H	5.3

Drive Model	Format Size MB	Seek Time	Interface	Encode	cache kb	RPM
90500D4	5003	9	EIDE			7200
90510D3	5100	9	ATA-4	16/17 EPR4	256k	5400
90510D4	5122	9	ATA-4	PRML	252k	5400
90576D4	5760	9	ATA-4	PRML	252k	5400
90625D5	6254	9	EIDE			7200
90640D4	6481	9	EIDE		256k	5400
90640E4	6448	9	EIDE		256k	5400
90648D3	6480	9	ATA-4/EIDE	PRML	512k	5400
90648D5	6480	9	ATA-4	PRML	252k	5400
90650U2	6500	9	ATA-4		2mb	5400
90651U2	6510	9.5	ATA5/UDMA66		2mb	5400
90680D4	6800	9	ATA-4	16/17 EPR4	256k	5400
90680U2	6800	9	ATA-4		2mb	5400
90683U2	6831	9.0	ATA5/UDMA66		2mb	7200
90684U2	6840	9.0	ATA5/UDMA66		2mb	5400
90720D5	7200	9	ATA-4	PRML	252k	5400
90750D6	7505	9	EIDE			7200
90840D5	8438	9	EIDE		256k	5400
90840D6	8400	9	ATA-4	PRML	252k	5400
90840D7	8400	9	EIDE			7200
90840E5	8438	9	EIDE		256k	5400
90841U2	8410	9.5	ATA5/UDMA66		2mb	5400
90845D4	8455	9	ATA-4/EIDE	PRML	512k	5400
90845D54	8450	9	ATA-4	16/17 EPR4	256k	5400
90845D5	8455	9	ATA-4		256k	5400
90845D6	8455	9	ATA-4	PRML	252k	5400
90845U2	8450	9.0	ATA5/UDMA66		2mb	5400
90845U3	8455	9	ATA-4		2mb	5400
90864D6	8644	9	EIDE	8,9 RLL	256k	5400
90871U2	8710	9.5	ATA5/UDMA66		512k	5400
90875D7	8756	9	EIDE			7200
90910D8	9106	9	EIDE			7200
90913U2	9130	9.0	ATA5/UDMA66		2mb	5400
91000D8	10007	9	EIDE	PRML	512k	7200
91008D7	10080	9	ATA-4	PRML	252k	5400
91010D6	10110	9	EIDE		256k	5400
91010E6	10005	9	EIDE		256k	5400
91020D6	10200	9	ATA-4	16/17 EPR4	256k	5400
91020U3	10209	9	ATA-4		2mb	5400
91021U1	10210	9.5	ATA5/UDMA66		2mb	5400
91021U2	10245	9.5	ATA5/UDMA66		512k	5400
91023U2	10240	9.0	ATA5/UDMA66		2mb	5400
91024D4	10240	9.0	EIDE	PRML	512k	7200
91024U2	10245	9.0	ATA5/UDMA66		2mb	5400
91024U3	10246	9.0	ATA5/UDMA66		2mb	7200
91080D5	10800	9	ATA-4/EIDE	PRML	512k	5400
91152D8	11520	9	ATA-4	PRML	252k	5400
91190D7	11900	9	ATA-4	16/17 EPR4	256k	5400
91202D8	12020	9	EIDE		256k	5400
91202E8	12020	9	EIDE		256k	5400
91301U3	13010	9.5	ATA5/UDMA66		512k	5400
91303D6	13030	9	ATA-4/EIDE	PRML	512k	5400
91350D8	13520	9	EIDE		256k	5400
91350E8	13520	9	EIDE		256k	5400
91360D8	13600	9	ATA-4	PRML	256k	5400
91360U4	13613	9	ATA-4		2mb	5400
91361U3	13610	9.5	ATA5/UDMA66		2mb	5400
91362U3	13620	9.0	ATA5/UDMA66		2mb	5400
91366U4	13662	9.0	ATA5/UDMA66		2mb	7200
91369U3	13698	9.0	ATA5/UDMA66		2mb	5400
91512D7	15120	9	ATA-4/EIDE	PRML	512k	5400
91531U3	15367	9.5	ATA5/UDMA66		2mb	5400
91536D6	15360	9.0	EIDE	PRML	512k	7200
91536H2	15367	9.0	ATA5/UDMA66		2mb	5400
91536U3	15360	9.0	ATA5/UDMA66		2mb	5400
91536U3	15360	9.0	ATA5/UDMA66		2mb	5400
91700U5	17000	9	ATA-4		2mb	5400

Drive Model	Format Size MB	Head	Cyl	Sect/Trac	Translate H/C/S	RWC/WPC	Form Factor	Power Watts
91707U5	17078	5				—/—	3.5 3H	7.2
91728D8	17280	8		230-38	16/33483/63	—/—	3.5 3H	4.1
91731U4	17310				16/16383/63	—/—	3.5 3H	4.9
91741U4	17410	4			16/16383/63	—/—	3.5 3H	4.7
91826U4	18264	4				—/—	3.5 3H	4.7
91862U6	18260	6			16/16383/63	—/—	3.5 3H	4.7
92040U6	20419	6		266-46	16/16383/63	—/—	3.5 3H	5.3
92041U4	20490	4				—/—	3.5 3H	4.7
92041U4	20410				16/16383/63	—/—	3.5 3H	4.9
92048D8	20480	8		240-40		—/—	3.5 3H	7.0
92049U3	20490				16/16383/63	—/—	3.5 3H	4.7
92049U4	20490	4			16/16383/63	—/—	3.5 3H	7.2
92049U6	20493	6				—/—	3.5 3H	5.5
92305H3	23051	3			16/16383/63	—/—	3.5 3H	5.3
92305U3	20490				16/16383/63	—/—	3.5 3H	5.3
92380U7	23800				16/16383/63	—/—	3.5 3H	4.9
92561U5	25610				16/16383/63	—/—	3.5 3H	4.9
92562U5	25620	8		266-46	16/16383/63	—/—	3.5 3H	5.3
92720U8	27226	8		266-46		—/—	3.5 3H	7.2
92732U8	27325	8			16/16383/63	—/—	3.5 3H	4.7
92739U6	27396	6			16/16383/63	—/—	3.5 3H	4.9
93071U6	30710				16/16383/63	—/—	3.5 3H	5.3
93073H4	30735	4				—/—	3.5 3H	5.3
93073U4	25620				16/16383/63	—/—	3.5 3H	4.7
93073U6	30735	6			16/16383/63	—/—	3.5 3H	4.9
93076U6	30760	8			16/16383/63	—/—	3.5 3H	4.7
93652U8	36529	8				—/—	3.5 3H	5.3
9380E	338	15	1224	36		NA/512	5.25FH	18
9380S	336	15	1218	36		NA/512	5.25FH	18
94091U8	40910				16/16383/63	—/—	3.5 3H	4.9
94098U8	40980	8			16/16383/63	—/—	3.5 3H	4.7
94610H6	46103	6				—/—	3.5 3H	5.5
94610U6	30760	6			16/16383/63	—/—	3.5 3H	5.5
96147H6	61473				16/16383/63	—/—	3.5 3H	5.5
96147H8	61471	8	119108			—/—		5.5
96147U8	61470	8			16/16383/63	—/—	3.5 3H	5.5
9780E	676	15	1661	53		NA/512	5.25FH	22
9780S	676	15	1661	53		166/512	5.25FH	22
98196H8	81964				16/16383/63	—/—	3.5 3H	5.5
A01A160	160GB					—/—		
A01A160	160GB					—/—		
A01A200	200GB					—/—		
A01A200	200GB					—/—		
A01A250	250GB					—/—		
A01A250	250GB					—/—		
A01B080	80GB					—/—		
A01B120	120GB					—/—		
A01C250	250GB					—/—		
Atlas 10K III 18.4	18400	2				—/—	3.5 3H	7.5
Atlas 10K III 36.7	36700	4				—/—	3.5 3H	9.5
Atlas 10K III 73.4	73400	8				—/—	3.5 3H	10.0
Atlas 10K IV 146.9	146.9GB	8				—/—	3.5 3H	11
Atlas 10K IV 146.9	146.9GB	8				—/—	3.5 3H	11
Atlas 10K IV 36.7	36.7GB	2				—/—	3.5 3H	7.3
Atlas 10K IV 36.7	36.7GB	2				—/—	3.5 3H	7.3
Atlas 10K IV 73.4	73.4GB	4				—/—	3.5 3H	8.2
Atlas 10K IV 73.4	73.4GB	4				—/—	3.5 3H	8.2
Atlas 15K 18.4	18.4GB	2				—/—	3.5 3H	7.2
Atlas 15K 18.4	18.4GB	2				—/—	3.5 3H	7.2
Atlas 15K 36.7	36.7GB	4				—/—	3.5 3H	9.4
Atlas 15K 36.7	36.7GB	4				—/—	3.5 3H	9.4
Atlas 15K 73.4	73.4GB	8				—/—	3.5 3H	11
Atlas 15K 73.4	73.4GB	8				—/—	3.5 3H	11
B01D300	300GB					—/—		
B01D300	300GB					—/—		
D540X ATA100 20GB	20GB	1				—/—	3.5 3H	3.75
D540X ATA100 20GB	20GB	1				—/—	3.5 3H	3.75

Drive Model	Format Size MB	Seek Time	Interface	Encode	cache kb	RPM
91707U5	17078	9.0	ATA5/UDMA66			7200
91728D8	17280	9	ATA-4/EIDE	PRML	2mb	5400
91731U4	17310	9.5	ATA5/UDMA66		512k	5400
91741U4	17410	9.5	ATA5/UDMA66		2mb	5400
91826U4	18264	9.0	ATA5/UDMA66		512k	5400
91862U4	18260	9.0	ATA5/UDMA66		2mb	5400
92040U6	20419	9	ATA-4		2mb	5400
92041U4	20490	9.5	ATA5/UDMA66		512k	5400
92041U4	20410	9.5	ATA5/UDMA66		2mb	5400
92048D8	20480	9.0	EIDE	PRML	512k	7200
92049U3	20490	9.0	ATA5/UDMA66		512k	5400
92049U4	20490	9.0	ATA5/UDMA66		2mb	5400
92049U6	20493	9.0	ATA5/UDMA66		2mb	5400
92305H3	23051	9.0	ATA5/UDMA66		2mb	7200
92305U3	20490	9.0	ATA5/UDMA66		2mb	5400
92380U7	23800	9	ATA-4		2mb	5400
92561U5	25610	9.5	ATA5/UDMA66		2mb	5400
92562U5	25620	9.0	ATA5/UDMA66		2mb	5400
92720U8	27226	9	ATA-4		2mb	5400
92732U8	27325	9.0	ATA5/UDMA66		2mb	5400
92739U6	27396	9.0	ATA5/UDMA66		2mb	7200
93071U6	30710	9.5	ATA5/UDMA66		2mb	5400
93073H4	30735	9.0	ATA5/UDMA66		2mb	5400
93073U4	25620	9.0	ATA5/UDMA66		2mb	5400
93073U6	30735	9.0	ATA5/UDMA66		2mb	5400
93076U6	30760	9.0	ATA5/UDMA66		2mb	5400
93652U8	36529	9.0	ATA5/UDMA66		2mb	5400
9380E	338	16	ESDI	2,7 RLL		3600
9380S	336	16	SCSI	2,7 RLL		3600
94091U8	40910	9.5	ATA5/UDMA66		2mb	5400
94098U8	40980	9.0	ATA5/UDMA66		2mb	5400
94610H6	46103	9.0	ATA5/UDMA66		2mb	5400
94610U6	30760	9.0	ATA5/UDMA66		2mb	5400
96147H6	61473	9.0	ATA Fast		2mb	5400
96147H8	61471	9.0	UltraDMA/66		2mb	5400
96147U8	61470	9.0	ATA5/UDMA66		2mb	5400
9780E	676	17	ESDI	1,7 RLL		3600
9780S	676	17	SCSI	1,7 RLL		3600
98196H8	81964	9.0	ATA Fast			3600
A01A160	160GB	9.3	FireWire		2mb	5400
A01A160	160GB	9.3	USB2.0		8mb	7200
A01A200	200GB	9.3	USB2.0		8mb	7200
A01A200	200GB	9.3	FireWire		8mb	7200
A01A250	250GB	9.3	FireWire		8mb	7200
A01A250	250GB	9.3	USB2.0		8mb	7200
A01B080	80GB	9.3	USB2.0		2mb	7200
A01B120	120GB	9.3	USB2.0		8mb	7200
A01C250	250GB	9.3	FireWire		8mb	7200
Atlas 10K III 18.4	18400	4.5	UL320 SCSI	PRML50/52	8mb	1000
Atlas 10K III 36.7	36700	4.5	UL320 SCSI	PRML50/52	8mb	1000
Atlas 10K III 73.4	73400	4.5	UL320 SCSI	PRML 50/52	8mb	1000
Atlas 10K IV 146.9	146.9GB	4.4	UL320SCSIWD		8mb	1000
Atlas 10K IV 146.9	146.9GB	4.9	UL320SCSIWD		8mb	1000
Atlas 10K IV 36.7	36.7GB	4.3	U320SCSISCA		8mb	1000
Atlas 10K IV 36.7	36.7GB	4.8	U320SCSISCA		8mb	1000
Atlas 10K IV 73.4	73.4GB	4.3	UL320SCSIWD		8mb	1000
Atlas 10K IV 73.4	73.4GB	4.8	U320SCSISCA		8mb	1000
Atlas 15K 18.4	18.4GB	3.2	U320SCSISCA		8mb	1500
Atlas 15K 18.4	18.4GB	3.6	U320SCSISCA		8mb	1500
Atlas 15K 36.7	36.7GB	3.2	U320SCSISCA		8mb	1500
Atlas 15K 36.7	36.7GB	3.6	UL320SCSIWD		8mb	1500
Atlas 15K 73.4	73.4GB	3.4	UL320SCSIWD		8mb	1500
Atlas 15K 73.4	73.4GB	3.8	U320SCSISCA		8mb	1500
B01D300	300GB	10	USB2.0		2mb	5400
B01D300	300GB	10	FireWire		2mb	5400
D540X ATA100 20GB	20GB	9.6	Ultra ATA		2mb	5400
D540X ATA100 20GB	20GB	9.6	Ultra ATA		2mb	5400

Drive Model	Format Size MB	Head	Cyl	Sect/Trac	Translate H/C/S	RWC/WPC	Form Factor	Power Watts
D540X ATA100 40GB	40GB	2				—/—	3.5 3H	3.75
D540X ATA100 40GB	40GB	2				—/—	3.5 3H	3.75
D540X ATA100 60GB	60GB	3				—/—	3.5 3H	3.75
D540X ATA100 60GB	60GB	3				—/—	3.5 3H	3.75
D540X ATA100 80GB	80GB	4				—/—	3.5 3H	3.75
D540X ATA100 80GB	80GB	4				—/—	3.5 3H	3.75
D540X ATA133 120GB	120GB	6				—/—	3.5 3H	3.75
D540X ATA133 160GB	120GB	8				—/—	3.5 3H	
DiamondMax 16 60GB	60GB				16/16383/63	—/—	3.5 3H	
DiamondMax Plus8 20GB	20GB				16/16383/63	—/—	3.5 3H	
DiamondMax Plus8 30GB	30GB				16/16383/63	—/—	3.5 3H	
DiamondMax Plus8 40GB	40GB				16/16383/63	—/—	3.5 3H	
DiamondMax Plus9 120GB	120GB				16/16383/63	—/—	3.5 3H	
DiamondMax Plus9 120GB	120GB				16/16383/63	—/—	3.5 3H	
DiamondMax Plus9 120GB	120GB				16/16383/63	—/—	3.5 3H	
DiamondMax Plus9 160GB	160GB				16/16383/63	—/—	3.5 3H	
DiamondMax Plus9 160GB	160GB				16/16383/63	—/—	3.5 3H	
DiamondMax Plus9 160GB	160GB				16/16383/63	—/—	3.5 3H	
DiamondMax Plus9 200GB	160GB				16/16383/63	—/—	3.5 3H	
DiamondMax Plus9 200GB	160GB				16/16383/63	—/—	3.5 3H	
DiamondMax Plus9 60GB	60GB				16/16383/63	—/—	3.5 3H	
DiamondMax Plus9 60GB	60GB				16/16383/63	—/—	3.5 3H	
DiamondMax Plus9 80GB	80GB				16/16383/63	—/—	3.5 3H	
DiamondMax Plus9 80GB	80GB				16/16383/63	—/—	3.5 3H	
DiamondMax Plus9 80GB	80GB				16/16383/63	—/—	3.5 3H	
DiamondMax16 120GB	80GB				16/16383/63	—/—	3.5 3H	
DiamondMax16 160GB	80GB				16/16383/63	—/—	3.5 3H	
DiamondMax16 160GB	80GB				16/16383/63	—/—	3.5 3H	
DiamondMax16 60GB	60GB				16/16383/63	—/—	3.5 3H	
DiamondMax16 80GB	80GB				16/16383/63	—/—	3.5 3H	
DiamondMax16 80GB	80GB				16/16383/63	—/—	3.5 3H	
EXT4175	149	7	1224	34		NA/NA	5.25FH	
EXT4280	234	11	1224	36		NA/NA	5.25FH	
EXT4380	319	15	1224	34		NA/NA	5.25FH	
FireBall3 20GB	20GB				16/16383/63	—/—	3.5 4H	
FireBall3 20GB	20GB				16/16383/63	—/—	3.5 4H	
FireBall3 30GB	30GB				16/16383/63	—/—	3.5 4H	
FireBall3 30GB	30GB				16/16383/63	—/—	3.5 4H	
FireBall3 40GB	40GB				16/16383/63	—/—	3.5 4H	
FireBall3 40GB	40GB				16/16383/63	—/—	3.5 4H	
G01J010	60GB					—/—	3.5	
G01J040	40GB					—/—	3.5	
G01J060	60GB					—/—	3.5	
LXT100A	90						3.5HH	
LXT100S	96	8	733	32		NA/NA	3.5HH	
LXT200A	191	7	1320	NA	15/816/32	NA/NA	3.5HH	10
LXT200S	207	7	1320	33,53		NA/NA	3.5HH	10
LXT213A	203	7	1320	NA	16/683/38	NA/NA	3.5HH	
LXT213S	213	7	1320	34-56		NA/NA	3.5HH	
LXT340A	340	7	1560	47-72	16/654/63	NA/NA	3.5HH	11
LXT340S	340	7	1560	47-72		NA/NA	3.5HH	11
LXT437A (never made)	437	9	1560	V	16/842/63	NA/NA	3.5HH	
LXT437S (never made)	437	9	1560	V		NA/NA	3.5HH	
LXT50S	48	4	733	32		NA/NA	3.5HH	11
LXT535A	535	11	1024	63	16/1024/36	NA/NA	3.5HH	11
LXT535S	535	11	1560	47-72		NA/NA	3.5HH	
MobileMax 105MB	105	4	1254	28-50		—/—	1.8 4H	
MobileMax 131MB	131	4	1254	28-50		—/—	2.8 4H	
MobileMax 171MB	171	4	1254	28-50		—/—	1.8 4H	
MobileMax 262MB	262					—/—	3.5 4H	
MX9217SDN	2170	9		100-14		—/—	3.5 3H	7.6
MX9217SDW	2170	9		100-14		—/—	3.5 3H	7.6
MX9217SSN	2170	9		100-14		—/—	3.5 3H	7.6
MX9217SSW	2170	9		100-14		NA/NA	3.5 3H	7.6
MXT1240S	1240	15	2512	NA		NA/NA	3.5HH	13
MXT540AL	547	7	2466		16/1024/63	NA/NA	3.5 3H	12
MXT540SL	547	7	2466	NA		NA/NA	3.5 3H	12

Drive Model	Format Size MB	Seek Time	Interface	Encode	cache kb	RPM
D540X ATA100 40GB	40GB	9.6	Ultra ATA		2mb	5400
D540X ATA100 40GB	40GB	9.6	Ultra ATA		2mb	5400
D540X ATA100 60GB	60GB	9.6	Ultra ATA		2mb	5400
D540X ATA100 60GB	60GB	9.6	Ultra ATA		2mb	5400
D540X ATA100 80GB	80GB	9.6	Ultra ATA		2mb	5400
D540X ATA100 80GB	80GB	9.6	Ultra ATA		2mb	5400
D540X ATA133 120GB	120GB	12	Ultra ATA		2mb	5400
D540X ATA133 160GB	120GB	12	ATA/133		2mb	5400
DiamondMax 16 60GB	60GB	12.6	ATA/133		2mb	5400
DiamondMax Plus8 20GB	20GB	10	ATA/133		2mb	7200
DiamondMax Plus8 30GB	30GB	10	ATA/133		2mb	7200
DiamondMax Plus8 40GB	40GB	10	ATA/133		2mb	7200
DiamondMax Plus9 120GB	120GB	9.4	ATA/133		2mb	7200
DiamondMax Plus9 120GB	120GB	9.4	ATA/133		8mb	7200
DiamondMax Plus9 120GB	120GB	9.4	SATA/150		8mb	7200
DiamondMax Plus9 160GB	160GB	9.4	ATA/133		2mb	7200
DiamondMax Plus9 160GB	160GB	9.4	ATA/133		8mb	7200
DiamondMax Plus9 160GB	160GB	9.4	SATA/150		8mb	7200
DiamondMax Plus9 200GB	160GB	9.4	ATA/133		8mb	7200
DiamondMax Plus9 200GB	160GB	9.4	SATA/150		8mb	7200
DiamondMax Plus9 60GB	60GB	9.4	ATA/133		2mb	7200
DiamondMax Plus9 60GB	60GB	9.4	SATA/150		8mb	7200
DiamondMax Plus9 80GB	80GB	9.4	ATA/133		2mb	7200
DiamondMax Plus9 80GB	80GB	9.4	ATA/133		8mb	7200
DiamondMax Plus9 80GB	80GB	9.4	SATA/150		8mb	7200
DiamondMax16 120GB	80GB	12.6	ATA/133		2mb	5400
DiamondMax16 160GB	80GB	12.6	ATA/133		2mb	5400
DiamondMax16 160GB	80GB	12.6	ATA/133		2mb	5400
DiamondMax16 60GB	60GB	12.6	ATA/133		2mb	5400
DiamondMax16 80GB	80GB	12.6	ATA/133		2mb	5400
DiamondMax16 80GB	80GB	12.6	ATA/133		2mb	5400
EXT4175	149	27	ESDI	RLL		3600
EXT4280	234	27	ESDI	RLL		3600
EXT4380	319	27	ESDI	RLL		3600
FireBall3 20GB	20GB	12	ATA/133		2mb	5400
FireBall3 20GB	20GB	12	ATA/133		2mb	5400
FireBall3 30GB	30GB	12	ATA/133		2mb	5400
FireBall3 30GB	30GB	12	ATA/133		2mb	5400
FireBall3 40GB	40GB	12	ATA/133		2mb	5400
FireBall3 40GB	40GB	12	ATA/133		2mb	5400
G01J010	60GB	12	USB2.0		2mb	5400
G01J040	40GB	12	USB2.0		2mb	5400
G01J060	60GB	12	USB2.0		2mb	5400
LXT100A	90		IDE AT	1,7 RLL		3600
LXT100S	96	27	SCSI	2,7 RLL		3600
LXT200A	191	15	IDE AT	1,7 RLL		3600
LXT200S	207	15	SCSI	1,7 RLL		3600
LXT213A	203	15	IDE AT	1,7 RLL	32k	3600
LXT213S	213	15	SCSI-2	1,7 RLL	32k	3600
LXT340A	340	15	IDE AT	2,7 RLL	128k	3600
LXT340S	340	15	SCSI	2,7 RLL	128k	3600
LXT437A (never made)	437	13	IDE AT	2,7 RLL		3600
LXT437S (never made)	437	13	SCSI	2,7 RLL		3600
LXT50S	48	27	SCSI	2,7 RLL		3600
LXT535A	535	12	IDE AT	2,7 RLL	128k	3600
LXT535S	535	13	SCSI	2,7 RLL	128k	3600
MobileMax 105MB	105	19	PCMCIA-ATA	1,7 RLL	31k	4464
MobileMax 131MB	131	19	PCMCIA-ATA	1,7 RLL	31k	4464
MobileMax 171MB	171	19	PCMCIA-ATA	1,7 RLL	31k	4464
MobileMax 262MB	262		PCMCIA-ATA	1,7 RLL		
MX9217SDN	2170	10.5	SE SCSI-2D	1,7 RLL	512k	5400
MX9217SDW	2170	10.5	SE SCSI-2DW	1,7 RLL	512k	5400
MX9217SSN	2170	10.5	SE SCSI-2	1,7 RLL	512k	5400
MX9217SSW	2170	10.5	SE SCSI-2W	1,7 RLL	512k	5400
MXT1240S	1240	9	SCSI-2Fast	1,7 RLL		6300
MXT540AL	547	9	IDE AT	1,7 RLL		6300
MXT540SL	547	9	SCSI-2Fast	1,7 RLL		6300

Drive Model	Format Size MB	Head	Cyl	Sect/Trac	Translate H/C/S	RWC/WPC	Form Factor	Power Watts
P0-12S Panther	1045	15	1632	61-103		NA/NA	5.25FH	26
P1-08E (never made)	696	9	1778	85		NA/NA	5.25FH	
P1-12E (never made)	1051	15	1778	77		NA/NA	5.25FH	
P1-13E (never made)	1160	15	1778			NA/NA	5.25FH	
P1-16E (never made)	1331	19	1778			NA/NA	5.25FH	
P1-17E (never made)	1470	19	1778	85		NA/NA	5.25FH	
P1-17S Panther	1503	19	1778	70-101		NA/NA	5.25FH	26
R01J080	80GB					—/—		
RXT-800HD	786					—/—	5.25HH	
RXT-800HS	786					—/—	5.25HH	
RXT-800S	786					—/—	5.25HH	
S01J250	250GB					—/—		
T01J120	120GB					—/—		
T01P160	160GB					—/—		
T01P200	200GB					—/—		
T01P200 200GB	200GB					—/—		
T01P200 200GB	200GB					—/—		
X01FWRA160	160GB					—/—	3.5	
X01USB2040	40GB					—/—	3.5	
X01USB2120	120GB					—/—	3.5	
XT1050	38	5	902	17		NA/NA	5.25FH	
XT1065	52	7	918	17		NA/NA	5.25FH	
XT1085	71	8	1024	17		NA/NA	5.25FH	28
XT1105	84	11	918	17		NA/NA	5.25FH	
XT1120R	105	8	1024	25		NA/NA	5.25FH	28
XT1140	119	15	918	17		NA/NA	5.25FH	28
XT1240R	196	15	1024	25		NA/NA	5.25FH	28
XT2085	72	7	1224	17		NA/NA	5.25FH	
XT2140	113	11	1224	17		NA/NA	5.25FH	
XT2190	159	15	1224	17		NA/NA	5.25FH	28
XT3170	146	9	1224	26		NA/NA	3.5FH	35
XT3280	244	15	1224	26		NA/NA	5.25FH	
XT3380	319	15	1224	34		NA/NA	5.25FH	35
XT4170E	157	7	1224	35/36	16	NA/NA	5.25FH	27
XT4170S	157	7	1224	35-36		NA/NA	5.25FH	27
XT4175	234	11	1224	34		NA/NA	5.25FH	
XT4230E	203	9	1224	35/36		NA/NA	5.25FH	27
XT4280SF	338	15	1224	36		NA/NA	5.25FH	
XT4380E	338	15	1224	36		NA/NA	5.25FH	27
XT4380S	338	15	1224	NA		NA/NA	5.25FH	27
XT81000E	889	15	1632	71		NA/NA	5.25FH	
XT8380E	361	8	1632	53-54		NA/NA	5.25FH	35
XT8380EH	360	8	1632	54		NA/NA	5.25FH	27
XT8380S	361	8	1632	NA		NA/NA	5.25FH	35
XT8380SH	360	8	1632	NA		NA/NA	5.25FH	27
XT8610E	541	12	1632	53-54		NA/NA	5.25FH	
XT8702S	616	15	1490	NA		NA/NA	5.25FH	
XT8760E	676	15	1632	53-54		NA/NA	5.25FH	27
XT8760EH	676	15	1632	54		NA/NA	5.25FH	27
XT8760S	670	15	1632	NA		NA/NA	5.25FH	27
XT8760SH	670	15	1632	NA		NA/NA	5.25FH	27
XT8800E	694	15	1274	54		NA/NA	5.25FH	
Y01FWRA080	80GB					—/—	3.5	

MEGA DRIVE SYSTEMS

Drive Model	Format Size MB	Head	Cyl	Sect/Trac	Translate H/C/S	RWC/WPC	Form Factor	Power Watts
M1-105	105	4	1219			—/—	3.5HH	4.5
M1-120	122	2	1818			—/—	3.5HH	5.0
M1-240	245	4	1818			—/—	3.5HH	5.0
M1-52	52	2	1219			—/—	3.5HH	4.5
MH-1G	1050	13	1974			—/—	3.5HH	10.5
MH-340	338	9	1100			—/—	3.5HH	9.0
MH-425	426	9	1520			—/—	3.5HH	9.0
MH-535	525	9	1476			—/—	3.5HH	9.5
P105	103	6	1019	33		NA/NA	3.5HH	
P120	120	5	1123			NA/NA	3.5HH	
P170	168	7	1123			NA/NA	3.5HH	
P210	210	7	1156			NA/NA	3.5HH	
P320	320	15	886			NA/NA	3.5HH	

Drive Model	Format Size MB	Seek Time	Interface	Encode	cache kb	RPM
P0-12S Panther	1045	13	SCSI-2	RLL	256k	3600
P1-08E (never made)	696	12	ESDI	RLL		3600
P1-12E (never made)	1051	13	ESDI	RLL		3600
P1-13E (never made)	1160	13	ESDI	RLL		3600
P1-16E (never made)	1331	13	ESDI	RLL		3600
P1-17E (never made)	1470	13	ESDI	RLL		3600
P1-17S Panther	1503	13	SCSI-2	RLL		3600
R01J080	80GB	9.3	USB2.0		256k	3600
RXT-800HD	786		SCSI		2mb	7200
RXT-800HS	786		SCSI			
RXT-800S	786		SCSI			
S01J250	250GB	12.6	USB2.0			
T01J120	120GB	9	UltraATA133		2mb	5400
T01P160	160GB	9.3	USB2/FIREWR		2mb	7200
T01P200	200GB	9.3	USB2.0		8mb	7200
T01P200 200GB	200GB	9.3	USB2.0		8mb	7200
T01P200 200GB	200GB	9	UltraATA133		8mb	7200
X01FWRA160	160GB	9.3	FireWire		8mb	7200
X01USB2040	40GB		UltraATA133		2mb	5400
X01USB2120	120GB		USB2.0		2mb	5400
XT1050	38	30	ATA		2mb	5400
XT1065	52	30	ST412/506	MFM		3600
XT1085	71	28	ST412/506	MFM		3600
XT1105	84	27	ST412/506	MFM		3600
XT1120R	105	27	ST412/506	2,7 RLL		3600
XT1140	119	27	ST412/506	MFM		3600
XT1240R	196	27	ST412/506	2,7 RLL		3600
XT2085	72	30	ST412/506	MFM		3600
XT2140	113	30	ST412/506	MFM		3600
XT2190	159	29	ST412/506	MFM		3600
XT3170	146	30	SCSI	RLL		3600
XT3280	244	30	SCSI	RLL		3600
XT3380	319	27	SCSI	RLL		3600
XT4170E	157	14	ESDI	1,7 RLL		3600
XT4170S	157	14	SCSI	1,7 RLL		3600
XT4175	234	27	ESDI	RLL		3600
XT4230E	203	16	ESDI	1,7 RLL		3600
XT4280SF	338	16	SCSI	1,7 RLL		3600
XT4380E	338	16	ESDI	1,7 RLL		3600
XT4380S	338	16	SCSI	1,7 RLL		3600
XT81000E	889	16	ESDI	1,7 RLL		3600
XT8380E	361	16	ESDI	1,7 RLL		3600
XT8380EH	360	13	ESDI	1,7 RLL		3600
XT8380S	361	14	SCSI	1,7 RLL		3600
XT8380SH	360	14	SCSI	1,7 RLL		3600
XT8610E	541	16	ESDI	1,7 RLL	256k	3600
XT8702S	616	17	SCSI	1,7 RLL		3600
XT8760E	676	16	ESDI	1,7 RLL		3600
XT8760EH	676	14	ESDI	1,7 RLL		3600
XT8760S	670	16	SCSI	1,7 RLL		3600
XT8760SH	670	14	SCSI	1,7 RLL		3600
XT8800E	694	14	ESDI	1,7 RLL	256k	3600
Y01FWRA080	80GB		ATA		2mb	7200

MEGA DRIVE SYSTEMS

Drive Model	Format Size MB	Seek Time	Interface	Encode	cache kb	RPM
M1-105	105	17	SCSI	2,7 RLL	64k	3662
M1-120	122	16	SCSI	1,7 RLL	256k	4306
M1-240	245	16	SCSI	1,7 RLL	256k	4306
M1-52	52	17	SCSI	2,7 RLL	64k	3662
MH-1G	1050	10	SCSI	1,7 RLL	256k	5400
MH-340	338	13	SCSI	1,7 RLL	64k	4412
MH-425	426	14	SCSI	1,7 RLL	64k	4412
MH-535	525	14	SCSI	1,7 RLL	256k	4412
P105	103	19	SCSI	2,7 RLL		
P120	120	14	SCSI	1,7 RLL		
P170	168	14	SCSI	1,7 RLL		
P210	210	14	SCSI	1,7 RLL		
P320	320	12.5	SCSI	1,7 RLL		

Drive Model	Format Size MB	Head	Cyl	Sect/Trac	Translate H/C/S	RWC/WPC	Form Factor	Power Watts
P42	42	3	834	33		NA/NA	3.5HH	
P425	426	9	1512			NA/NA	3.5HH	
P84	84	6	834	33		NA/NA	3.5HH	
MEMOREX								
321	5	2	320	17		321/128	5.25FH	
322	10	4	320	17		321/128	5.25FH	
323	15	6	320	17		321/128		
324	20	8	320	17		321/128		
450	10	2	612	17		321/350		
512	25	3	961	17		321/480		
513	41	5	961	17		321/480		
514	58	7	961	17		961?/480		
MICROPOLIS CORP								
1050 AV LT	1000	9	2360	V		—/—	3.5FH	
1302	20	3	830	17		831/831	5.25FH	29
1303	35	5	830	17		831/831	5.25FH	29
1304	40	6	830	17		831/831	5.25FH	29
1323	35	4	1024	17		1025/1025	5.25FH	29
1323A	44	5	1024	17		1025/1025	5.25FH	29
1324	53	6	1024	17		1025/1025	5.25FH	29
1324A	62	7	1024	17		1025/1025	5.25FH	29
1325	71	8	1024	17		1025/1025	5.25FH	29
1325CT	71		1024	17		1025/1025	5.25FD	29
1333	35	4	1024	17		1025/1025	5.25FH	29
1333A	44	5	1024	17		1025/1025	5.25FH	29
1334	53	6	1024	17		1025/1025	5.25FH	29
1334A	62	7	1024	17		1025/1025	5.25FH	29
1335	71	8	1024	17		—/—	5.25FH	
1352	32	2	1024	36		NA/NA	5.25FH	
1352A	41	3	1024	36		NA/NA	5.25FH	32
1353	75	4	1024	36		NA/NA	5.25FH	32
1353A	94	5	1024	36		NA/NA	5.25FH	32
1354	113	6	1024	36		NA/NA	5.25FH	32
1354A	131	7	1024	36		NA/NA	5.25FH	32
1355	150	8	1024	36		—/—	5.25FH	
1372A	52		1024	36		1017/1017	5.25FH	35
1373	72	4	1024	36		1017/1017	5.25FH	35
1373A	91	5	1024	36		1017/1017	5.25FH	35
1374	109	6	1024	36		—/—	5.25HH	
1374-6	135	6	1245	36		1017/1017	5.25FH	35
1374A	127	7	1024	36		1017/1017	5.25FH	35
1375	145	8	1024	36		NA/NA	5.25FH	
1516-10S	678	10	1840	72		NA/NA	5.25FH	
1517-13	922	13	1925	72		—/—	5.25FH	
1517-14	981	14	1925	71		—/—	5.25FH	
1517-15	1051	15	1925	71		—/—	5.25FH	24
1518	1346					NA/NA	5.25FH	
1518-14	993	14	1925	72		NA/NA	5.25FH	24
1518-15	1341	15	2104	83		—/—	5.25FH	24
1528	1342	15	2100	84		NA/NA	5.25FH	24
1528-15	1342	15	2100	84		—/—	5.25FH	
1528-15D	1300					NA/NA	5.25FH	
1538	871	15	1669	68		NA/NA	5.25FH	24
1538-15	910	15	1669	71		NA/NA	5.25FH	24
1548-15	1748	15	2112	V		NA/NA	5.25FH	
1554-07	157	7	1224	36		NA/NA	5.25FH	
1555-08	180	8	1224	36		NA/NA	5.25FH	
1555-09	203	9	1224	36		NA/NA	5.25FH	
1556-10	225	10	1224	36		NA/NA	5.25FH	
1556-11	248	11	1224	36		NA/NA	5.25FH	
1557-12	270	12	1224	36		NA/NA	5.25FH	
1557-13	293	13	1224	36		1225/1225	5.25FH	
1557-14	315	14	1224	36		1225/1225	5.25FH	
1557-15	338	15	1224	36		—/—	5.25FH	24
1558	338		1224	36		NA/NA	5.25FH	
1558-13	293	14	1224	36		NA/NA	5.25FH	

Drive Model	Format Size MB	Seek Time	Interface	Encode	cache kb	RPM
P42	42	19	SCSI	2,7 RLL		
P425	426	12	SCSI	1,7 RLL		
P84	84	19	SCSI	2,7 RLL		

MEMOREX

321	5		ST412/506	MFM		
322	10		ST412/506	MFM		
323	15		ST412/506	MFM		
324	20		ST412/506	MFM		
450	10		ST412/506	MFM		
512	25		ST412/506	MFM		
513	41		ST412/506	MFM		
514	58		ST412/506	MFM		

MICROPOLIS CORP

1050 AV LT	1000	10	SCSI-2Fast	MZR	512k	5400
1302	20	30	ST412/506	MFM		3600
1303	35	30	ST412/506	MFM		3600
1304	40	30	ST412/506	MFM		3600
1323	35	28	SP412/506	MFM		3600
1323A	44	28	ST412/506	MFM		3600
1324	53	28	ST412/506	MFM		3600
1324A	62	28	ST412/506	MFM		3600
1325	71	28	ST412/506	MFM		3600
1325CT	71	28	ST412/506	MFM		3600
1333	35	28	ST412/506	MFM		3600
1333A	44	28	ST412/506	MFM		3600
1334	53	28	ST412/506	MFM		3600
1334A	62	28	ST412/506	MFM		3600
1335	71	28	ST412/506	MFM		3600
1352	32	23	ESDI	2,7 RLL		
1352A	41	23	ESDI	2,7 RLL		
1353	75	23	ESDI	2,7 RLL		3600
1353A	94	23	ESDI	2,7 RLL		3600
1354	113	23	ESDI	2,7 RLL		3600
1354A	131	23	ESDI	2,7 RLL		3600
1355	150	23	ESDI	2,7 RLL		3600
1372A	52		SCSI	2,7 RLL		
1373	72	23	SCSI	2,7 RLL		3600
1373A	91	23	SCSI	2,7 RLL		3600
1374	109	23	SCSI	2,7 RLL		3600
1374-6	135	16	SCSI	2,7 RLL		3600
1374A	127	23	SCSI	2,7 RLL		3600
1375	145	23	SCSI	2,7 RLL		3600
1516-10S	678	14	ESDI	2,7 RLL		
1517-13	922	14	ESDI	2,7 RLL		
1517-14	981	14	ESDI	2,7 RLL		
1517-15	1051	14	ESDI	2,7 RLL		
1518	1346	14.5	ESDI	1,7 RLL		
1518-14	993	14	ESDI	2,7 RLL		
1518-15	1341	14	ESDI	2,7 RLL		3600
1528	1342	14.5	SCSI-2		256k	3600
1528-15	1342	14	SCSI-2			3600
1528-15D	1300		SCSI-2Diff			3600
1538	871		ESDI	1,7 RLL		3600
1538-15	910	15	ESDI	2,7 RLL		3600
1548-15	1748	14	SCSI-2		256k	3600
1554-07	157	18	ESDI	2,7 RLL		3600
1555-08	180	18	ESDI	2,7 RLL		3600
1555-09	203	18	ESDI	2,7 RLL		3600
1556-10	225	18	ESDI	2,7 RLL		3600
1556-11	248	18	ESDI	2,7 RLL		3600
1557-12	270	18	ESDI	2,7 RLL		3600
1557-13	293	18	ESDI	2,7 RLL		3600
1557-14	315	18	ESDI	2,7 RLL		3600
1557-15	338	18	ESDI	2,7 RLL		3600
1558	338	19	ESDI	2,7 RLL		3600
1558-13	293	18	ESDI	2,7 RLL		3600

Drive Model	Format Size MB	Head	Cyl	Sect/Trac	Translate H/C/S	RWC/WPC	Form Factor	Power Watts
1558-14	315	14	1224	36		NA/NA	5.25FH	
1558-15	338	15	1224	36		NA/NA	5.25FH	32
1560-8S	389	8	1632	54		—/—	5.25FH	
1564-07	315	7	1224	54		NA/NA	5.25FH	
1565-08	360	8	1224	54		NA/NA	5.25FH	
1565-09	406	9	1224	54		NA/NA	5.25FH	
1566-10	451	10	1224	54		NA/NA	5.25FH	
1566-11	496	11	1224	54		NA/NA	5.25FH	
1567-12	541	12	1632	54		NA/NA	5.25FH	
1567-13	586	13	1224	54		NA/NA	5.25FH	
1567-14	631	14	1632	54		—/—	5.25FH	
1568	676		1632	54		—/—	5.25FH	24
1568-13	586		1632	54		—/—	5.25FH	24
1568-14	631	14	1632	54		NA/NA	5.25FH	29
1568-15	676	15	1632	54		NA/NA	5.25FH	29
1574-07	155	7	1224	36		NA/NA	5.25FH	
1575-08	177	8	1224	36		NA/NA	5.25FH	
1575-09	199	9	1224	36		NA/NA	5.25FH	
1576-10	221	10	1224	36		1224/1224	5.25FH	
1576-11	243	11	1224	36		1224/1224	5.25FH	
1577-12	265	12	1224	36		1224/1224	5.25FH	
1577-13	287	13	1224	36		1224/1224	5.25FH	
1578	331		1224	36		1224/1224	5.25FH	24
1578-14	310	14	1224	36		1224/1224	5.25FH	32
1578-15	332	15	1224	36		1224/1224	5.25FH	32
1585-8S	344	8	1628	54		—/—	5.25FH	
1586-11	490	11	1628	54		1632/1632	5.25FH	
1587-12	540	12	1628	54		1632/1632	5.25FH	
1587-13	579	13	1628	54		1632/1632	5.25FH	
1587-13	585	13	1628	54		NA/NA	5.25FH	
1588	668					—/—	5.25FH	24
1588-14	624	14	1628	54		1632/1632	5.25FH	
1588-15	667	15	1632	54		1632/1632	5.25FH	28
1588T-15	676	15	1632	54		NA/NA	5.25FH	
1596-10S	668	10	1834	72		1835/1835	5.25FH	
1597-13	909	13	1919	72		1835/1835	5.25FH	
1598	1034					—/—	5.25FH	24
1598-14	979	14	1919	72		1920/1920	5.25FH	
1598-15	1034	15	1928	71		1920/1920	5.25FH	30
1624	667	7	2089	V		Auto/Auto	5.25HH	
1624-7	667	7	2112			NA/NA	5.25HH	14
1653-4	92	4	1249	36		NA/NA	5.25HH	14
1653-5	115	5	1249	36		NA/NA	5.25HH	14
1653-6	138	6	1249			—/—	5.25HH	
1654	161		1249	36		—/—	5.25HH	14
1654-6	138	6	1249	36		NA/NA	5.25HH	14
1654-7	161	7	1249	36		NA/NA	5.25HH	14
1663-4	197	4	1780	54		NA/NA	5.25HH	
1663-5	246	5	1780	54		NA/NA	5.25HH	
1664	345		1780	54		—/—	5.25HH	14
1664-6	295	6	1780	54		NA/NA	5.25HH	
1664-7	344	7	1780	54		NA/NA	5.25HH	14
1670-4	90	4	1245	36		—/—	5.25HH	
1670-5	90		1245	36		—/—	5.25HH	
1670-6	112		1245	36		—/—	5.25HH	
1670-7	135		1245	36		—/—	5.25HH	
1673-4	90	4	1249	36		1250/1250	5.25HH	15
1673-5	112	5	1249	36		1250/1250	5.25HH	15
1674	158		1249	36		—/—	5.25HH	14
1674-6	135	6	1249	36		1250/1250	5.25HH	15
1674-7	157	7	1249	36		1250/1250	5.25HH	15
1683-4	193	4	1776	54		1777/1777	5.25HH	
1683-5	242	5	1776	54		1777/1777	5.25HH	
1684	340		1776	54		—/—	5.25HH	14
1684-6	291	6	1776	54		1777/1777	5.25HH	
1684-7	339	7	1780	54		1777/1777	5.25HH	15
1743-5	112	5	1140	28		NA/NA	3.5HH	

Drive Model	Format Size MB	Seek Time	Interface	Encode	cache kb	RPM
1558-14	315	18	ESDI	2,7 RLL		
1558-15	338	18	ESDI	2,7 RLL		3600
1560-8S	389	16	ESDI	2,7 RLL		3600
1564-07	315	18	ESDI	2,7 RLL		
1565-08	360	18	ESDI	2,7 RLL		3600
1565-09	406	18	ESDI	2,7 RLL		3600
1566-10	451	18	ESDI	2,7 RLL		3600
1566-11	496	18	ESDI	2,7 RLL		3600
1567-12	541	18	ESDI	2,7 RLL		3600
1567-13	586	18	ESDI	2,7 RLL		3600
1567-14	631	16	ESDI	2,7 RLL		3600
1568	676	16	ESDI	2,7 RLL		3600
1568-13	586	16	ESDI	2,7 RLL		3600
1568-14	631	16	ESDI	2,7 RLL		3600
1568-15	676	16	ESDI	2,7 RLL		3600
1574-07	155	16	SCSI	2,7 RLL		3600
1575-08	177	16	SCSI	2,7 RLL		3600
1575-09	199	16	SCSI	2,7 RLL		3600
1576-10	221	16	SCSI	2,7 RLL		3600
1576-11	243	16	SCSI	2,7 RLL		3600
1577-12	265	16	SCSI	2,7 RLL		3600
1577-13	287	16	SCSI	2,7 RLL		3600
1578	331	16	SCSI		64k	
1578-14	310	16	SCSI	2,7 RLL		3600
1578-15	332	16	SCSI	2,7 RLL		3600
1585-8S	344	16	SCSI	2,7 RLL		
1586-11	490	16	SCSI	2,7 RLL		
1587-12	540	16	SCSI	2,7 RLL		
1587-13	579	16	SCSI	2,7 RLL		
1587-13	585	16	SCSI	2,7 RLL		
1588	668	16	SCSI	2,7 RLL	256k	
1588-14	624	16	SCSI	2,7 RLL		
1588-15	667	16	SCSI	2,7 RLL		
1588T-15	676	16	SCSI	2,7 RLL		3600
1596-10S	668	14	SCSI	2,7 RLL		
1597-13	909	14	SCSI	2,7 RLL		
1598	1034	14.5	SCSI-2	2,7 RLL	256k	
1598-14	979	14	SCSI	2,7 RLL		
1598-15	1034	14	SCSI-2	2,7 RLL		3600
1624	667	15	SCSI-2			
1624-7	667	15	SCSI-2Fast			3600
1653-4	92	16	ESDI	2,7 RLL		3600
1653-5	115	16	ESDI	2,7 RLL		3600
1653-6	138		ESDI	2,7 RLL		
1654	161	16	ESDI	2,7 RLL		
1654-6	138	16	ESDI	2,7 RLL		3600
1654-7	161	16	ESDI	2,7 RLL		3600
1663-4	197	14	ESDI	2,7 RLL		
1663-5	246	14	ESDI	2,7 RLL		
1664	345	15	ESDI	2,7 RLL		
1664-6	295	14	ESDI	2,7 RLL		
1664-7	344	14	ESDI	2,7 RLL		3600
1670-4	90	16	SCSI			
1670-5	90		SCSI			
1670-6	112		SCSI			
1670-7	135		SCSI			
1673-4	90	16	SCSI	2,7 RLL		3600
1673-5	112	16	SCSI	2,7 RLL		3600
1674	158	16	SCSI	2,7 RLL		
1674-6	135	16	SCSI	2,7 RLL		3600
1674-7	157	16	SCSI	2,7 RLL		3600
1683-4	193	14	SCSI	2,7 RLL		
1683-5	242	14	SCSI	2,7 RLL		
1684	340	15	SCSI	2,7 RLL		
1684-6	291	14	SCSI	2,7 RLL		
1684-7	339	14	SCSI	2,7 RLL		3600
1743-5	112	15	IDE AT	2,7 RLL		

Drive Model	Format Size MB	Head	Cyl	Sect/Trac	Translate H/C/S	RWC/WPC	Form Factor	Power Watts
1744-6	135	6	1140	28		NA/NA	3.5HH	
1744-7	157	7	1140	28		NA/NA	3.5HH	
1745-8	180	8	1140	28		NA/NA	3.5HH	
1745-9	202	9	1140	28		—/—	3.5HH	
1760 AV LT	1700	15	2360	V		1141/1141	3.5HH	
1773-5	112	5	1140	28		1141/1141	3.5HH	
1774-6	135	6	1140	28		1141/1141	3.5HH	
1774-7	157	7	1140	28		1141/1141	3.5HH	
1775-8	180	8	1140	28		1141/1141	3.5HH	
1775-9	202	9	1140	28		1141/1141	3.5HH	
1908-15	1381	15	2112	V		NA/NA	5.25FH	24
1924-21	2100	21	2267	V		NA/NA	5.25FH	30
1924D	2100		2267	V		—/—	5.25FH	30
1926	2158	15				NA/NA	5.25FH	
1926-15	2158	15	2772	V		—/—	5.25FH	
1936	3022	21	2759	V		NA/NA	5.25FH	
1936-21	3022	21	2772	V		NA/NA	5.25FH	
1936AV	3022	21	2759	V		NA/NA	5.25FH	
1936D	3022	21	2759	V		NA/NA	5.25FH	
1991	9091	27	4446	V		—/—	5.25FH	30
1991AV	9090	27	4477	V		—/—	5.25FH	30
1991W	9090	27	4477	V		—/—	5.25FH	30
1991WAV	9090	27	4477	V		—/—	5.25FH	30
2100	512	15	2759			NA/NA	5.25FH	
2105(A)	560	8	1745	V	16/1084/63	NA/NA	3.5HH	
2105(S)	560	8	1745	V		NA/NA	3.5HH	
2105-15	560	15	1747	V		NA/NA	3.5FH	
2105A-15	560	15	1747	V		NA/NA	3.5FH	
2108(A)	666	10	1745	V		NA/NA	3.5HH	
2108(S)	666	10	1745	V		NA/NA	3.5HH	
2112(A)	1050	15	1745	V	16/2034/63	NA/NA	3.5HH	
2112(D)	1050	15	1744	V		NA/NA	5.25FH	
2112(S)	1050	15	1745	V		NA/NA	3.5HH	
2112-15	1050	15	1747	V		NA/NA	3.5HH	12
2112-DW	1050	15	1745	V		NA/NA	3.5HH	15.5
2112A-15	1050	15	1747	V		NA/NA	3.5HH	12
2121(A)				V		NA/NA	3.5FH	
2121(S)				V		NA/NA	5.25FH	
2205	585	5	2360			NA/NA	3.5HH12.25	
2205A	542	5				NA/NA	3.5FH	
2207	701	9	2360	V		NA/NA	3.5FH12.25	
2210	1056	9	2360	V		NA/NA	3.5FH12.25	
2210 AV	1000	9	2360	V		—/—	3.5HH	
2210A	976	9	2360			NA/NA	3.5FH	
2210AV	1056	9	2360			NA/NA	3.5FH	
2210WD	1056	9	2360	V		—/—	3.5FH	
2217	1765	15	2360	V		NA/NA	3.5FH12.25	
2217 AV	1700	15	2360	V		—/—	3.5HH	
2217A	1626	15				NA/NA	3.5FH	
2217AV	1765	15				NA/NA	3.5FH	
2217WD	1765		2360	V		—/—	3.5FH	
3020	512	21	2759			NA/NA	5.25FH	
3221	2050		3956	V		—/—	3.5HH	14
3221AV	2050		3956	V		—/—	3.5HH	14
3243	4294	19	4124	V		—/—	3.5HH	14
3243AV	4290	19	4081			NA/NA	3.5HH	16
3243S	4294	19	3957	V		—/—	3.5HH	14
3243W	4294	19	3956	V		—/—	3.5HH	14
3243WAV	4294	19	3957	V		NA/NA	3.5HH	16
3243WD	4294	19	3956	V		—/—	3.5FH	16
3243WDAV	4294	19	3956	V		—/—	3.5FH	16
3387NS	8700		4811	V		—/—	3.5FH	14
3387SS	8700		4811	V		—/—	3.5FH	14
3387WS	8700		4811	V		—/—	3.5FH	14
3391AV	9103		4811	V		—/—	3.5HH	14
3391NS	9103		4811	V		—/—	3.5HH	14
3391SS	9103		4811	V		—/—	3.5HH	14

Drive Model	Format Size MB	Seek Time	Interface	Encode	cache kb	RPM
1744-6	135	15	IDE AT	2,7 RLL		
1744-7	157	15	IDE AT	2,7 RLL		
1745-8	180	15	IDE AT	2,7 RLL		
1745-9	202	15	IDE AT	2,7 RLL		
1760 AV LT	1700	10	SCSI-2Fast	MZR	512k	5400
1773-5	112	15	SCSI	2,7 RLL		
1774-6	135	15	SCSI	2,7 RLL		
1774-7	157	15	SCSI	2,7 RLL		
1775-8	180	15	SCSI	2,7 RLL		
1775-9	202	15	SCSI	2,7 RLL		
1908-15	1381	11	SCSI-2Fast			5400
1924-21	2100	12	SCSI-2Fast			5400
1924D	2100	12	SCSI-2Fast			5400
1926	2158	13	SCSI-2Fast		512k	5400
1926-15	2158	13	SCSI-2			5400
1936	3022	12	SCSI-2Fast		256k	5400
1936-21	3022	11.5	SCSI-2	2,7 RLL		5400
1936AV	3022	13	SCSI-2Fast	MZR	256k	5400
1936D	3022	12	SCSI-2Fast		256k	5400
1991	9091	12	SCSI-2Fast		512k	5400
1991AV	9090	12	SCSI-2Fast	MZR	512k	5400
1991W	9090	12	SCSI-2FstW	MZR	512k	5400
1991WAV	9090	12	SCSI-2FstW	MZR	512k	5400
2100			SCSI-2Fast		512k	5400
2105(A)	512	13	SCSI-2Fast		512k	5400
2105(S)	560	10	IDE AT	RLL		
2105-15	560	10	SCSI-2	RLL		
2105A-15	560	10	SCSI-2Fast			5400
2108(A)	560	10	IDE AT			5400
2108(S)	666	10	IDE AT	RLL		
2112(A)	666	10	SCSI-2	RLL		
2112(D)	1050	10	IDE AT	RLL		
2112(S)	1050	10	SCSI-2Diff			
2112-15	1050	10	SCSI-2	RLL		
2112-DW	1050	10	SCSI-2Fast	RLL		5400
2112A-15	1050	10	SCSI-2FstW	RLL		5400
2121(A)	1050	10	IDE AT	RLL		5400
2121(S)		10	IDE AT	RLL		
2205		10	SCSI-2	RLL		
2205A	585	10	SCSI-2Fast			5400
2207	542	10	IDE AT		512k	5400
2210	701	10	SCSI-2Fast		512k	5400
2210 AV	1056	10	SCSI-2Fast		512k	5400
2210A	1000		SCSI-2Fast	MZR	512k	5400
2210AV	976	10	IDE AT		512k	5400
2210WD	1056	10	SCSI-2Fast		512k	5400
2217	1056	10	SCSI-2FstW			5400
2217 AV	1765	10	SCSI-2Fast			5400
2217A	1700		SCSI-2Fast	MZR	512k	5400
2217AV	1626	10	IDE AT		512k	5400
2217WD	1765	10	SCSI-2Fast		512k	5400
3020	1765	10	SCSI-2FstW			5400
3221	512	13	SCSI-2Fast		512k	5400
3221AV	2050	9	SCSI-2Fast			7200
3243	2050	9	SCSI-2Fast			7200
3243AV	4294	8.5	SCSI-2Fast			7200
3243S	4290	9	SCSI-2Fast	MZR	512k	7200
3243W	4294	9	SCSI-2Fast		512k	7200
3243WAV	4294	9	SSA-SCSI		512k	7200
3243WD	4294	9	SCSI-2FstW	MZR	512k	7200
3243WDAV	4294	9	SCSI-2FstW	MZR	512k	7200
3387NS	4294	9	SCSI-2Diff		512k	7200
3387SS	8700	8	SCSI-2Diff		512k	7200
3387WS	8700	8	Ultra SCSI3			7200
3391AV	8700	8	Ultra SCSI3			7200
3391NS	9103	8	Ultra SCSI3			7200
3391SS	9103	8	Ultra SCSI3		2mb	7200
	9103	8	Ultra SCSI3			7200
			SCSI-3Wide		2mb	7200

Drive Model	Format Size MB	Head	Cyl	Sect/Trac	Translate H/C/S	RWC/WPC	Form Factor	Power Watts
3391WAV	9103		4811	V		—/—	3.5HH	14
3391WD	9103		4811	V		—/—	3.5HH	14
3391WS	9103		4811	V		—/—	3.5HH	14
3418NS	18250		7308	V		—/—	3.5 3H	14
3418SS	18250		7308	V		—/—	3.5 3H	14
3418WS	18250		7308	V		—/—	3.5 3H	14
3420AV	20270		7308	V		—/—	3.5 3H	14
3420WAV	20270		7308	V		—/—	3.5 3H	14
4110	1052	9				NA/NA	3.5 3H	
4110	1052		2415	V		—/—	3.5 3H	7.0
4110A	1057			V	16/1024/63	—/—	3.5 3H	8.25
4210	1000			V		—/—	3.5 3H	
4221	2050		4150	V		—/—	3.5 3H	11
4221AV	2050	9	4050			NA/NA	3.5 3H	10.5
4221W	2050	9	4150	V		NA/NA	3.5 3H	10.25
4221WAV	2050	9	4150			NA/NA	3.5 3H	10.5
4221WD	2050	9	4050			NA/NA	3.5 3H	10.5
4221WDAV	2050	9	4150	V		—/—	3.5 3H	10.5
4341NS	4130		4811	V		—/—	3.5 3H	10
4341SS	4130		4811	V		—/—	3.5 3H	10
4341WS	4130		4811	V		—/—	3.5 3H	10
4345AV	4550		4811	V		—/—	3.5 3H	10
4345NS	4550		4811	V		—/—	3.5 3H	10
4345SD	4550		4811	V		—/—	3.5 3H	10
4345SS	4550		4811	V		—/—	3.5 3H	10
4345WAV	4550		4811	V		—/—	3.5 3H	10
4345WD	4550		4811	V		—/—	3.5 3H	11
4345WS	4550		4811	V		—/—	3.5 3H	10
4421	2147		4050	V		—/—	3.5 3H	7.5
4421AV	2050		4050	V		—/—	3.5 3H	7.5
4525A	2500	4	6807		16/4884/63	—/—	3.5 3H	5.0
4540A	4000	6	6807		16/7847/63	—/—	3.5 3H	5.0
4550A	5000	8	6807		16/9768/63	—/—	3.5 3H	5.0
4691AV	9100		7308	V		—/—	3.5 3H	10
4691NS	9100		7308	V		—/—	3.5 3H	10
4691SS	9100		7308	V		—/—	3.5 3H	10
4691WAV	9100		7308	V		—/—	3.5 3H	10
4691WS	9100		7308	V		—/—	3.5 3H	10
4721NS	2100		6565	V		—/—	3.5 3H	5.5
4743NS	4300		6565	V		—/—	3.5 3H	5.5
4743SS	4300		6565	V		—/—	3.5 3H	5.5
4743WS	4300		6565	V		—/—	3.5 3H	5.5

MICROSCIENCE INTERNATIONAL COR

Drive Model	Format Size MB	Head	Cyl	Sect/Trac	Translate H/C/S	RWC/WPC	Form Factor	Power Watts
4050	44	5	1024	17		1025/1025	3.5HH	
4060	67	5	1024	26		—/—	3.5HH	
4070	62	7	1024	17		—/—	3.5HH	
4090	93	7	1024	26		—/—	3.5HH	
5040	45	3	855	35		NA/NA	3.5HH	
5070	76	5	855	35		NA/NA	3.5HH	
5070-20	86	5	960	35		NA/NA	3.5HH	
5100	110	7	855	36		NA/NA	3.5HH	
5100-20	120	7	960	35		NA/NA	3.5HH	
5160	159	7	1271	35		NA/NA	3.5HH	
6100	110	7	855	36		NA/NA	3.5HH	
7040	47	3	855	36		NA/NA	3.5HH	
7070-20	86	5	960	35		NA/960	3.5HH	
7100	100	7	855	36		NA/NA	3.5HH	
7100-20	120	7	960	35		NA/960	3.5HH	
7100-21	121	5	1077	44		NA/992	3.5HH	
7200	200	7	1277	44		—/—	3.5HH	
7400	304	8	1904			NA/NA	3.5HH	
8040	42	2	1024	40		NA/NA	3.5 3H	
8040MLC 48-000	42	2	1024	40		NA/NA	3.5 3H	
8080	85	2	1768	47		NA/NA	3.5 3H	
8200	152	4	1904			NA/NA	3.5 3H	
FH21200	1062	15	1921	72		NA/NA	5.25FH	33
FH21600	1418	15	2147	86		NA/NA	5.25FH	33

Drive Model	Format Size MB	Seek Time	Interface	Encode	cache kb	RPM
3391WAV	9103	8	SCSI-3Wide		2mb	7200
3391WD	9103	8	SCSI-3Wide			7200
3391WS	9103	8	Ultra SCSI3			7200
3418NS	18250	8	Ultra SCSI3			7200
3418SS	18250	8	SCSI-3Wide			7200
3418WS	18250	8	SCSI-3Wide			7200
3420AV	20270	8	Ultra SCSI3		2mb	7200
3420WAV	20270	8	SCSI-3Wide		2mb	7200
4110	1052	8.5	SCSI-2Fast		512k	5400
4110	1052	8.5	SCSI-2Fast			5400
4110A	1057	8.5	IDE AT		512k	5400
4210	1000		SCSI-2			7200
4221	2050	9	SCSI-2Fast		512k	7200
4221AV	2050	9	SCSI-2Fast	MZR	512k	7200
4221W	2050	9	SCSI-2FstW	MZR	512k	7200
4221WAV	2050	9	SCSI-2FstW	MZR	512k	7200
4221WD	2050	9	SCSI-2Diff	MZR	512k	7200
4221WDAV	2050	9	SCSI-2Diff	MZR	512k	7200
4341NS	4130	8	Ultra SCSI3			7200
4341SS	4130	8	SCSI-3Wide			7200
4341WS	4130	8	SCSI-3Wide			7200
4345AV	4550	8	Ultra SCSI3			7200
4345NS	4550	8	Ultra SCSI3		2mb	7200
4345SD	4550	8	SCSI-3Wide			7200
4345SS	4550	8	SCSI-3Wide			7200
4345WAV	4550	8	SCSI-3Wide		2mb	7200
4345WD	4550	8	SCSI-3Wide			7200
4345WS	4550	8	SCSI-3Wide			7200
4421	2147	9	SCSI-2Fast		512k	5400
4421AV	2050	9	SCSI-2Fast			5400
4525A	2500	10.5	EIDE	PRML		5200
4540A	4000	10.5	EIDE	PRML		5200
4550A	5000	10.5	EIDE	PRML		5200
4691AV	9100	7.9	Ultra SCSI3		2mb	7200
4691NS	9100	7.9	Ultra SCSI3		2mb	7200
4691SS	9100	7.9	SCSI-3Wide		2mb	7200
4691WAV	9100	7.9	SCSI-3Wide		2mb	7200
4691WS	9100	7.9	SCSI-3Wide		2mb	7200
4721NS	2100		Ultra SCSI3			5400
4743NS	4300	10	Ultra SCSI3			5400
4743SS	4300	10	Ultra SCSI3			5400
4743WS	4300	10	SCSI-3Wide			5400

MICROSCIENCE INTERNATIONAL COR

Drive Model	Format Size MB	Seek Time	Interface	Encode	cache kb	RPM
4050	44	18	ST412/506	MFM		
4060	67	18	ST412/506	2,7 RLL		
4070	62	18	ST412/506	MFM		
4090	93	18	ST412/506	2,7 RLL		
5040	45	18	ESDI	2,7 RLL		
5070	76	18	ESDI	2,7 RLL		
5070-20	86	18	ESDI	2,7 RLL		
5100	110	18	ESDI	2,7 RLL		
5100-20	120	18	ESDI	2,7 RLL		
5160	159	18	ESDI	2,7 RLL		
6100	110	18	SCSI	2,7 RLL		
7040	47	18	IDE AT	2,7 RLL		
7070-20	86	18	IDE AT	2,7 RLL		
7100	100	18	IDE AT	2,7 RLL		
7100-20	120	18	IDE AT	2,7 RLL		3600
7100-21	121	18	IDE AT	2,7 RLL		
7200	200	18	IDE AT	2,7 RLL		
7400	304	15	IDE AT	2,7 RLL		
8040	42	25	IDE AT	2,7 RLL		
8040MLC 48-000	42	25	IDE AT	2,7 RLL		
8080	85	17	IDE AT	2,7 RLL		
8200	152	16	IDE AT	2,7 RLL		
FH21200	1062	14	ESDI	2,7 RLL		3600
FH21600	1418	14	ESDI	2,7 RLL		3600

Drive Model	Format Size MB	Head	Cyl	Sect/Trac	Translate H/C/S	RWC/WPC	Form Factor	Power Watts
FH2414	366	8	1658	54		NA/NA	5.25FH	
FH2777	687	15	1658	54		NA/NA	5.25FH	30
FH31200	1062	15	1921	72		NA/NA	5.25FH	33
FH31600	1418	15	2147	86		NA/NA	5.25FH	33
FH3414	366	8	1658	54		NA/NA	5.25FH	
FH3777	687	15	1658	54		NA/NA	5.25FH	30
HH1050	44	5	1024	17		1025/1025	5.25HH	
HH1060	65	5	1024	26		1025/1025	5.25HH	
HH1075	62	7	1024	17		1025/1025	5.25HH	
HH1080	65	5	1024	26		—/—	5.25HH	
HH1090	80	7	1314	17		1315/1315	5.25HH	
HH1095	95	7	1024	26		1025/1025	5.25HH	
HH1120	122	7	1314	26		1315/1315	5.25HH	
HH2012	10	4	306	17		—/—	5.25HH	
HH2120	128	7	1024	35		NA/NA	5.25HH	
HH2160	160	7	1276	35		NA/NA	5.25HH	
HH312	10	4	306	17		307/307	5.25HH	
HH3120	121	5	1314	36		—/—	5.25HH	
HH315	10	4	306	17		307/307	5.25HH	
HH3160	170	7	1314	36		—/—	5.25HH	
HH325	21	4	612	17		613/613	5.25HH	
HH330	32	4	612	26		613/613	5.25HH	
HH612	10	4	306	17		307/307	5.25HH	
HH625	21	4	612	17		613/613	5.25HH	
HH712	10	2	612	17		613/613	5.25HH	
HH712A	10	2	612	17		—/—	5.25HH	
HH725	21	4	612	17		613/613	5.25HH	
HH738	32	4	612	26		613/613	5.25HH	
HH825	21	4	615	17		616/616	5.25HH	
HH830	33	4	615	26		616/616	5.25HH	

MINISCRIBE CORPORATION

Drive Model	Format Size MB	Head	Cyl	Sect/Trac	Translate H/C/S	RWC/WPC	Form Factor	Power Watts
1006	5	2	306	17		307/128	5.25FH	
1012	10	4	306	17		307/128	5.25FH	
2006	5	2	306	17		307/128	5.25FH	
2012	10	4	306	17		307/128	5.25FH	
3006	5	2	306	17		613/128	5.25HH	
3012	10	2	612	19		1024/512	5.25HH	12.4
3053	44	5	1024	17		1170/512	5.25HH	13.5
3085	68	7	1170	17		NA/NA	5.25HH	
3085E	72	3	1270	36		NA/NA	5.25HH	
3085S	72	3	1255	125		1251/512	5.25HH	
3130E	112	5	1250	36		1256/512	5.25HH	18
3130S	112	5	1255	35		1251/512	5.25HH	18
3180E	150	7	1250	35		1256/512	5.25HH	18
3180S	153	7	1255	36		NA/NA	5.25HH	
3180SM	161	7	1250	36		NA/NA	5.25HH	
3212	10	2	612	17		613/128	5.25HH	18.6
3212 Plus	11	2	615	17		613/128	5.25HH	18.6
3412	10	4	306	17		307/128	5.25HH	
3425	20	4	615	17		616/128	5.25HH	14.5
3425 Plus	20	4	615	17		616/128	5.25HH	18.6
3425S	21	4	612	17		615/128	5.25HH	
3438	32	4	615	26		616/128	5.25HH	14.5
3438 Plus	32	4	615	26		616/128	5.25HH	18.6
3650	40	6	809	17		819/128	5.25HH	18.1
3650F	42	6	809	17		810/128	5.25HH	
3650R	64	6	809	26		809/128	5.25HH	
3675	63	6	809	26		810/128	5.25HH	
4010	8	2	480	17		481/128	5.25FH	
4020	16	4	480	17		481/128	5.25FH	
5330	25	6	480	17		481/128	5.25FH	
5338	32	6	612	17		613/306	5.25FH	
5440	32	8	480	17		481/128	5.25FH	
5451	43	8	612	17		613/306	5.25FH	
6032	26	3	1024	17		1024/512	5.25FH	18
6053	44	5	1024	17		1024/512	5.25FH	18
6074	62	7	1024	17		1025/512	5.25FH	

Drive Model	Format Size MB	Seek Time	Interface	Encode	cache kb	RPM
FH2414	366	14	ESDI	2,7 RLL		
FH2777	687	14	ESDI	2,7 RLL		
FH31200	1062	14	SCSI	2,7 RLL		3600
FH31600	1418	14	SCSI	2,7 RLL		3600
FH3414	366	14	SCSI	2,7 RLL		3600
FH3777	687	14	SCSI	2,7 RLL		3600
HH1050	44	28	ST412/506	MFM		
HH1060	65	28	ST412/506	2,7 RLL		
HH1075	62	28	ST412/506	MFM		
HH1080	65	28	ST412/506	2,7 RLL		
HH1090	80	28	ST412/506	MFM		
HH1095	95	28	ST412/506	2,7 RLL		
HH1120	122	28	ST412/506	2,7 RLL		
HH2012	10		ST412/506	MFM		
HH2120	128	28	ESDI (10)	2,7 RLL		
HH2160	160	28	ESDI (10)	2,7 RLL		
HH312	10	65	ST412/506	MFM		
HH3120	121	28	SCSI	2,7 RLL		
HH315	10	65	ST412/506	MFM		
HH3160	170	28	SCSI	2,7 RLL		
HH325	21	80	ST412/506	MFM		
HH330	32	105	ST412/506	2,7 RLL		
HH612	10	85	ST412/506	MFM		
HH625	21	65	ST412/506	MFM		
HH712	10	105	ST412/506	MFM		
HH712A	10	75	ST412/506	MFM		
HH725	21	105	ST412/506	MFM		
HH738	32	105	ST412/506	MFM		
HH825	21	65	ST412/506	2,7 RLL		
HH830	33	65	ST412/506	2,7 RLL		

MINISCRIBE CORPORATION

Drive Model	Format Size MB	Seek Time	Interface	Encode	cache kb	RPM
1006	5	179	ST412/506	MFM		
1012	10	179	ST412/506	MFM		
2006	5	93	ST412/506	MFM		
2012	10	85	ST412/506	MFM		
3006	5		ST412/506	MFM		
3012	10	155	ST412/506	MFM		
3053	44	25	ST412/506	MFM		
3085	68	22	ST412/506	MFM		3600
3085E	72	17	ESDI	2,7 RLL		3600
3085S	72	17	SCSI	2,7 RLL		
3130E	112	17	ESDI	2,7 RLL		3600
3130S	112	17	SCSI	2,7 RLL		3600
3180E	150	17	ESDI	2,7 RLL		3600
3180S	153	17	SCSI	2,7 RLL		3600
3180SM	161	17	SCSI(Mac)	RLL		
3212	10	85	ST412/506	MFM		
3212 Plus	11	53	ST412/506	MFM		3600
3412	10	60	ST412/506	MFM		3600
3425	20	85	ST412/506	MFM		
3425 Plus	20	53	ST412/506	MFM		3600
3425S	21	68	SCSI	MFM		3600
3438	32	85	ST412/506	2,7 RLL		
3438 Plus	32	53	ST412/506	2,7 RLL		3600
3650	40	61	ST412/506	MFM		3600
3650F	42	46	ST412/506	MFM		3600
3650R	64	61	ST412/506	2,7 RLL		3600
3675	63	61	ST412/506	2,7 RLL		3600
4010	8	133	ST412/506	MFM		
4020	16	133	ST412/506	MFM		
5330	25	27	ST412/506	MFM		
5338	32	27	ST412/506	MFM		
5440	32	27	ST412/506	MFM		
5451	43	27	ST412/506	MFM		
6032	26	28	ST412/506	MFM		
6053	44	28	ST412/506	MFM		3600
6074	62	28	ST412/506	MFM		3600

Drive Model	Format Size MB	Head	Cyl	Sect/Trac	Translate H/C/S	RWC/WPC	Form Factor	Power Watts
6079	68	5	1024	26		1024/512	5.25FH	18
6085	71	8	1024	17		1024/512	5.25FH	18
6128	109	8	1024	26		1024/512	5.25FH	18
6170E	130	8	1024	34		NA/NA	5.25FH	
6212	10	2	612	17		613/128	5.25FH	
7040A	40	2	1159	36	5/981/17	981/512	3.5 3H	9.5
7040S	40	2	1156	36		NA/NA	3.5 3H	
7060A	65	2	1516	42	7/1024/17	NA/NA	3.5 3H	
7060S	65	2	1516	42		NA/NA	3.5 3H	
7080A	81	4	1159	36	10/981/17	981/512	3.5 3H	9.5
7080S	81	4	1156	36		NA/NA	3.5 3H	
7120A	131	2	1516	85	14/1024/17	NA/NA	3.5 3H	
7120S	131	2	1516	85		NA/NA	3.5 3H	
7426	21	4	612	17		613/613	3.5HH	
8051A	41	4	745	26	4/745/28	746/128	3.5HH	8
8051S	43	4	745	26		746/128	3.5HH	8
80SC-MFM	21	4	615	17		—/—	3.5HH	14
80SC-RLL	33	4	615	26		—/—	3.5HH	14
8212	10	2	615	17		616/128	3.5HH	9.9
8225	20	2	771	26		772/128	3.5HH	10.7
8225A	21	2	747	28	4/615/17	NA/NA	3.5HH	12
8225AT	20	2	747	28		748/128	3.5HH	12
8225S	21	2	804	26		805/128	3.5HH	13
8225XT	20	2	805	26		806/128	3.5HH	10
8412	10	4	306	17		307/128	3.5HH	
8425	21	4	615	17		616/128	3.5HH	12
8425F	20	4	615	17		616/128	3.5HH	12.5
8425S	21	4	612	17		616/128	3.5HH	13
8425XT	20	4	615	17		616/128	3.5HH	12
8434F	32	4	615	26		616/128	3.5HH	
8438	31	4	615	26		616/128	3.5HH	10
8438 Plus	31	4	615	26		615/128	5.25HH	
8438F	32	4	615	26		616/128	5.25HH	12.5
8438XT	31	4	615	26		NA/NA	3.5HH	10
8450	39	4	771	26		772/128	3.5HH	10.7
8450AT	42	4	745	28		746/128	3.5HH	12
8450S	42	4	804	26		805/128	3.5HH	13
8450XT	42	4	805	26		806/128	3.5HH	12
9000E	338	15	1224	36		NA/NA	5.25FH	
9000S	347	15	1220	36		NA/NA	5.25FH	
9230	203	9	1224	34		0/512	5.25FH	
9230E	203	9	1224	36		NA/NA	5.25FH	
9230S	203	9	1224	36		NA/NA	5.25FH	
9380E	338	15	1224	36		NA/512	5.25FH	18
9380S	336	15	1218	36		NA/512	5.25FH	18
9380SM	319	15	1218			NA/NA	5.25FH	
9424E	360	8	1661			NA/NA	5.25FH	
9424S	355	8	1661			NA/NA	5.25FH	
9780E	676	15	1661	53		NA/512	5.25FH	22
9780S	676	15	1661	53		166/512	5.25FH	22

MITSUBISHI ELECTRONICS

Drive Model	Format Size MB	Head	Cyl	Sect/Trac	Translate H/C/S	RWC/WPC	Form Factor	Power Watts
M2860-1	21			17		—/—		
M2860-2	50			17		—/—		
M2860-3	85			17		—/—		
MR335	69	7	743	26		—/—	3.5HH	
MR521	10	2	612	17		—/—	5.25HH	
MR522	20	4	612	17		—/300	5.25HH	
MR5310E	65	5	977	26		NA/NA	5.25HH	
MR533	24	3	971	17		—/NONE	5.25HH	
MR535	42	5	977	17		300/300	5.25HH	
MR535-U00	42	5	977	17		300/300	5.25HH	
MR535R	65	5	977	26		NA/NA	5.25HH	
MR535S	85	5	977	34		NA/NA	5.25HH	
MR537S	65	5	977	26		NA/NA	5.25HH	

MITSUMI ELECTRONICS CORP.

Drive Model	Format Size MB	Head	Cyl	Sect/Trac	Translate H/C/S	RWC/WPC	Form Factor	Power Watts
HD2509AA	92	4		>52		—/—	2.5 4H	

Drive Model	Format Size MB	Seek Time	Interface	Encode	cache kb	RPM
6079	68	28	ST412/506	2,7 RLL		3600
6085	71	28	MFM			3600
6128	109	28	ST412/506	2,7 RLL		3600
6170E	130	28	ESDI	RLL		
6212	10	27	ST412/506	MFM		
7040A	40	19	IDE AT	1,7 RLL	32k	3703
7040S	40	19	SCSI	RLL		
7060A	65	15	IDE AT	1,7 RLL		
7060S	65	15	SCSI	1,7 RLL		
7080A	81	19	IDE AT	1,7 RLL		
7080S	81	19	SCSI	1,7 RLL	32k	3703
7120A	131	15	IDE AT	1,7 RLL		
7120S	131	15	SCSI	1,7 RLL		
7426	21	28	ST412/506	MFM		
8051A	41	28	IDE AT	2,7 RLL	32k	3484
8051S	43	28	SCSI	2,7 RLL	32k	3484
80SC-MFM	21	68	ST412/506	MFM		3600
80SC-RLL	33	68	ST412/506	2,7 RLL		3600
8212	10	68	ST412/506	MFM		3600
8225	20	68	ST412/506	2,7 RLL		3600
8225A	21		IDE	2,7 RLL		3600
8225AT	20	40	IDE AT	2,7 RLL		3600
8225S	21	68	SCSI	2,7 RLL		3600
8225XT	20	68	IDE XT	2,7 RLL		3600
8412	10	50	ST412/506	MFM		3600
8425	21	68	ST506/412	MFM		3600
8425F	20	40	ST412/506	MFM		3600
8425S	21	68	SCSI	MFM		3600
8425XT	20	68	IDE XT	MFM		3600
8434F	32	40	ST412/506	RLL		3600
8438	31	68	ST412/506	RLL		3600
8438 Plus	31	55	ST412/506	2,7 RLL		3600
8438F	32	40	ST412/506	2,7 RLL		3600
8438XT	31	68	IDE XT	2,7 RLL		3600
8450	39	45	ST412/506	RLL		3600
8450AT	42	40	IDE AT	2,7 RLL		3600
8450S	42	45	SCSI	2,7 RLL		3600
8450XT	42	68	IDE XT	2,7 RLL		3600
9000E	338	16	ESDI			
9000S	347	16	SCSI			
9230	203	16	ESDI			
9230E	203	16	ESDI	RLL		
9230S	203	16	SCSI	RLL		
9380E	338	16	ESDI	2,7 RLL		
9380S	336	16	SCSI	2,7 RLL		3600
9380SM	319	16	SCSI(Mac)	RLL		
9424E	360	17	ESDI	2,7 RLL		
9424S	355	17	SCSI	2,7 RLL		
9780E	676	17	ESDI	1,7 RLL		3600
9780S	676	17	SCSI	1,7 RLL		3600

MITSUBISHI ELECTRONICS

Drive Model	Format Size MB	Seek Time	Interface	Encode	cache kb	RPM
M2860-1	21		ST412/506	MFM		
M2860-2	50		ST412/506	MFM		
M2860-3	85		ST412/506	MFM		
MR335	69	20	ST412/506	MFM		
MR521	10	85	ST412/506	MFM		
MR522	20	85	ST412/506	MFM		
MR5310E	65	28	ESDI	2,7 RLL		
MR533	24		ST412/506	MFM		
MR535	42	28	ST412/506	MFM		3600
MR535-U00	42	28	ST412/506	MFM		
MR535R	65	28	ST412/506	2,7 RLL		3600
MR535S	85	28	SCSI	2,7 RLL		
MR537S	65	28	SCSI	2,7 RLL		

MITSUMI ELECTRONICS CORP.

Drive Model	Format Size MB	Seek Time	Interface	Encode	cache kb	RPM
HD2509AA	92	16	IDE AT	1,7 RLL	32k	3600

Hard Drive Specs **669**

Drive Model	Format Size MB	Head	Cyl	Sect/Trac	Translate H/C/S	RWC/WPC	Form Factor	Power Watts
HD2513AA	130	4		>52		—/—	2.5 4H	
MMI								
M106	5	2	306	17		—/128	3.5HH	
M112	10	4	306	17		—/128	3.5HH	
M125	20	8	306	17		—/128	3.5HH	
M212	10	4	306	17		—/128	5.25HH	
M225	20	8	306	17		—/128	5.25HH	
M306	5	2	306	17		—/128	5.25HH	
M312	10	4	306	17		—/128	5.25HH	
M325	20	8	306	17		—/128	5.25HH	
M350	42	8	612	17		—/288	5.25HH	
NCL AMERICA								
SEE BRAND TECHNOLOGIES						—/—		
NCR CORP								
6091-5101	323	9				NA/NA	5.25	
6091-5301	675	15				NA/NA	5.25	
H6801-STD1-03-17	53	7	872	17		—/650	3.5HH	
H6801-STD1-07-17	45	3	868	34		NA/NA	3.5HH	
H6801-STD1-10-17	104	8	776	33		NA/NA	3.5HH	
H6801-STD1-12-17	42	2	1047	40		NA/NA	3.5 3H	
H6801-STD1-46-46	21	4	615	17		616/128	3.5HH	
H6801-STD1-47-46	71	8	1024	17		1025/128	5.25FH	
H6801-STD1-47-46	121	7	969	35		1025/128	5.25FH	
NEC TECHNOLOGIES INC								
D1711	42	2				—/—	4H	
D1731	85	4				—/—	4H	
D3126	21	4	615	17		616/256	3.5HH	
D3126H	21					—/—	3.5HH	
D3142	42	8	642	17		—/—	3.5HH	
D3146H	40	8	615	17		—/—	3.5HH	
D3661	118	7	915	36		NA/NA	3.5HH	
D3713	345	16	670	63		—/—	3.5 3H	1.8
D3717	540	4	2924			—/—	3.5 3H	
D3724	426	2			16/827/63	—/—	3.5 3H	1.8
D3725-351	730	4	3493		16/1416/63	—/—	3.5 3H	
D3725-351	730	4			16/1416/63	—/—	3.5 3H	3.6
D3725-501	540	2			16/1048/63	—/—	3.5 3H	1.8
D3725-540	540	2			16/1416/63	NA/NA	3.5 3H	1.8
D3727	1083	6	3493		16/2100/63	NA/NA	3.5 3H	1.8
D3735	45	2	1084	41	4/542/41	—/—	3.5 3H	4
D3741	40					—/—	3.5HH	
D3743	540	2			16/1048/63	—/—	3.5 3H	
D3745-301	1080	4			16/2096/63	NA/NA	3.5 3H	4.0
D3745-351	1080	4			16/2096/63	—/—	3.5 3H	4.0
D3747	1620	6	3678			—/—	3.5 3H	1.8
D3755	105	4	1250	41	8/625/41	—/—	3.5 3H	4
D3756	105					—/—	3.5HH	
D3761	114	7	915	35	7/915/35	—/—	3.5HH	
D3781	425	9	1464	63	9/1464/63	—/—	3.5HH	8.5
D3817	540	4				—/—	3.5 3H	
D3825	730	4				—/—	3.5 3H	3.5
D3825	1083	6				—/—	3.5 3H	3.6
D3827	1083	6				—/—	3.5 3H	
D3835	45	2	1084	41		—/—	3.5 3H	4
D3841	45	8	440	25		—/—	3.5HH	
D3843	540	2				—/—	3.5 3H	
D3845	1080	4				—/—	3.5 3H	4.0
D3847	1620	6				—/—	3.5 3H	4.0
D3855	105	4	1250	41		—/—	3.5 3H	4
D3856	105					—/—	3.5HH	
D3861	114	7	915	35		—/—	3.5HH	
D3881	425	9	1464	63		—/—	3.5HH	8.5
D3896	2160	9				—/—	3.5 3H	12.4
D5114	5	2	306	17		—/—	5.25HH	

Drive Model	Format Size MB	Seek Time	Interface	Encode	cache kb	RPM
HD2513AA	130	16	IDE AT	1,7 RLL	32k	3600
MMI						
M106	5	75	ST412/506	MFM		
M112	10	75	ST412/506	MFM		
M125	20	75	ST412/506	MFM		
M212	10	75	ST412/506	MFM		
M225	20	75	ST412/506	MFM		
M306	5	75	ST412/506	MFM		
M312	10	75	ST412/506	MFM		
M325	20	75	ST412/506	MFM		
M350	42	75	ST412/506	MFM		
NCL AMERICA						
SEE BRAND TECHNOLOGIES						
NCR CORP						
6091-5101	323	27	SCSI	2,7 RLL		
6091-5301	675	25	SCSI	2,7 RLL		
H6801-STD1-03-17	53	28	ST412/506	MFM		
H6801-STD1-07-17	45	18	IDE AT	2,7 RLL		
H6801-STD1-10-17	104	25	IDE AT	2,7 RLL		
H6801-STD1-12-17	42	25	IDE AT	2,7 RLL		
H6801-STD1-46-46	21	68	ST412/506	MFM		
H6801-STD1-47-46	71	28	ST412/506	MFM		
H6801-STD1-47-46	121	16	ESDI (10)	2,7 RLL		
NEC TECHNOLOGIES INC						
D1711	42	19	IDE/PCMCIA	1,7 RLL	32k	5400
D1731	85	19	IDE/PCMCIA	1,7 RLL	32k	5400
D3126	21	85	ST412/506	MFM		
D3126H	21		ST412/506	MFM		
D3142	42	28	ST412/506	MFM		
D3146H	40	35	ST412/506	MFM		
D3661	118	20	ESDI (10)	2,7 RLL		
D3713	345	12	IDE		64k	
D3717	540	12	IDE AT	1,7 RLL	96k	4500
D3724	426	14	IDE	PRML 8,9	256k	4500
D3725-351	730	11	IDE AT	1,7 RLL	128k	4090
D3725-351	730	11	IDE AT	1,7 RLL	128k	4090
D3725-501	540	11	IDE	1,7RLL		4090
D3725-540	540	11	IDE AT	1,7 RLL	128k	4090
D3727	1083	11	IDE AT	1,7 RLL	128k	4090
D3735	45	25	IDE AT	1,7 RLL		3456
D3741	40		IDE AT			
D3743	540	11	IDE	PRML 8,9	128k	4500
D3745-301	1080	11	IDE	PRML 8,9	128k	4500
D3745-351	1080	11	IDE	PRML 8,9	128k	4500
D3747	1620	11	IDE AT	PRML	128k	4500
D3755	105	25	IDE AT	1,7 RLL		3456
D3756	105		IDE AT			
D3761	114	20	IDE AT	2,7 RLL		
D3781	425	15	IDE AT	1,7 RLL	64k	3600
D3817	540	12	SCSI-2	1,7 RLL	96k	4500
D3825	730	11	SCSI-2	1,7 RLL	64k	4090
D3825	1083	11	SCSI-2	1,7 RLL	32k	4090
D3827	1083	11	SCSI-2	1,7 RLL	64k	4090
D3835	45	25	SCSI	1,7 RLL		3456
D3841	45	28	SCSI	1,7 RLL		
D3843	540	11	SCSI-2	PRML 8,9	64k	4500
D3845	1080	11	SCSI-2	PRML	64k	4500
D3847	1620	11	SCSI-2	PRML8,9	64k	4500
D3855	105	25	SCSI	1,7 RLL		3456
D3856	105		SCSI			
D3861	114	20	SCSI	2,7 RLL		
D3881	425	15	SCSI	1,7 RLL	64k	3600
D3896	2160	9	SCSI-2	1,7 RLL	1024k	7200
D5114	5		ST412/506	MFM		

Drive Model	Format Size MB	Head	Cyl	Sect/ Trac	Translate H/C/S	RWC/ WPC	Form Factor	Power Watts
D5124	10	4	309	17		310/310	5.25HH	
D5126	20	4	612	17		613/NONE	5.25HH	
D5126H	21	4	612	17		613/NONE	5.25HH	
D5146	40	8	615	17		616/NONE	5.25HH	
D5146H	42	8	615	17		616/NONE	5.25HH	
D5392	1322	16		17		—/—	5.25FH	
D5452	71	10	823	17		—/—	5.25FH	
D5652	143	10	823	34		NA/NA	5.25FH	
D5655	140	7	1224	35		NA/NA	5.25FH	
D5662	300	15	1224	35		NA/NA	5.25FH	
D5682	664	15	1633	53		NA/NA	5.25FH	32
D5862	301	15	1224	53		NA/NA	5.25FH	
D5882	664	15	1633	53		—/—	5.25FH	32
D5892	1404	19	1678	86		—/—	5.25FH	
D5S2100A	2111	4			16/4092/63	—/—	3.5 3H	
DSE1700A	1706	4			16/3306/63	—/—	3.5 3H	
DSE2010A	2010	6			16/3900/63	—/—	3.5 3H	
DSE2100A	2100	5			16/4092/63	—/—	3.5 3H	
DSE2550A	2550	6			16/4960/63	—/—	3.5 3H	
EPP-340	340					—/—		
EPP-540	540					—/—		
FZ110A ZIP	100					—/—	2.5 4H	

NEI

Drive Model	Format Size MB	Head	Cyl	Sect/ Trac	Translate H/C/S	RWC/ WPC	Form Factor	Power Watts
RD3127	10	2	612	17		—/—	5.25	
RD3255	20	4	612	17		—/—	5.25	
RD4127	10	4	306	17		—/—	5.25	
RD4255	20	8	306	17		—/—	5.25	

NEWBURY DATA

Drive Model	Format Size MB	Head	Cyl	Sect/ Trac	Translate H/C/S	RWC/ WPC	Form Factor	Power Watts
NDR1065	55	7	918	17		—/—	5.25FH	
NDR1085	71	8	1024	17		—/NONE	5.25FH	
NDR1105	87	11	918	17		—/NONE	5.25FH	
NDR1140	120	15	918	17		—/NONE	5.25FH	
NDR2085	74	7	1224	17		1224/1224	5.25FH	
NDR2140	117	11	1224	17		1224/1224	5.25FH	
NDR2190	160	15	1224	17		—/NONE	5.25FH	
NDR3170S	146	9	1224	26		NA/NA	5.25FH	
NDR320	21	4	615	17		—/NONE	5.25FH	
NDR3280S	244	15	1224	26		—/—	5.25FH	
NDR3380S	319	15	1224	34		NA/NA	5.25FH	
NDR340	42	8	615	17		—/NONE	3.5FH	
NDR4175	179	7	1224	36		NA/NA	5.25FH	
NDR4380	338	15	1224	36		NA/NA	5.25FH	
NDR4380S	319	15	1224	34		—/—	5.25FH	
Penny 340	42	8	615	17		615/615	5.25HH	

NPL

Drive Model	Format Size MB	Head	Cyl	Sect/ Trac	Translate H/C/S	RWC/ WPC	Form Factor	Power Watts
4064	5			17		—/—	5.25FH	
4127	10			17		—/—	5.25FH	
4191S	15			17		—/—	5.25FH	
4255	20			17		—/—	5.25FH	
4362	30			17		—/—	5.25FH	
NP02-13	11	4	320	17		NA/0	5.25FH	
NP02-26A/26S	22	4	640	17		NA/0	5.25FH	
NP02-52A	44	8	640	17		NA/640	5.25FH	
NP03-20	16	6	306	17		NA/0	3.5FH	
NP04-13T	10	6		17		—/—	5.25FH	
NP04-55	45	7	754	17		NA/0	5.25FH	
NP04-85	72	11	754	17		NA/0	3.5HH	

OKIDATA

Drive Model	Format Size MB	Head	Cyl	Sect/ Trac	Translate H/C/S	RWC/ WPC	Form Factor	Power Watts
OD526	31	4	640	26		651/651	5.25HH	
OD540	51	6	640	26		651/651	5.25HH	

OLIVETTI

Drive Model	Format Size MB	Head	Cyl	Sect/ Trac	Translate H/C/S	RWC/ WPC	Form Factor	Power Watts
HD662/11	10	2	612	17		—/—	5.25HH	
HD662/12	20	4	612	17		—/—	5.25HH	

Drive Model	Format Size MB	Seek Time	Interface	Encode	cache kb	RPM
D5124	10	80	ST412/506	MFM		
D5126	20	80	ST412/506	MFM		
D5126H	21	40	ST412/506	MFM		
D5146	40	40	ST412/506	MFM		
D5146H	42	40	ST412/506	MFM		
D5392	1322	14	IPI-2			
D5452	71		ST412/506	MFM		
D5652	143	23	ESDI	2,7 RLL		
D5655	140	18	ESDI	2,7 RLL		
D5662	300	18	ESDI	2,7 RLL		
D5682	664	16	ESDI	RLL 1,7		
D5862	301	18	SCSI			3600
D5882	664	16	SCSI	1,7 RLL		
D5892	1404	14	SCSI	1,7 RLL		3600
D5S2100A	2111	11	IDE	PRML8,9		
DSE1700A	1706	11	IDE	PRML 8,9	64k	5200
DSE2010A	2010	11	IDE	PRML 8,9	128k	5200
DSE2100A	2100	11	IDE	PRML 8,9	128k	5200
DSE2550A	2550	11	IDE	PRML 8,9	128k	5200
EPP-340	340		ParallelPor		128k	5200
EPP-540	540		ParallelPor			
FZ110A ZIP	100	29	ATAPI		32k	2941

NEI

Drive Model	Format Size MB	Seek Time	Interface	Encode	cache kb	RPM
RD3127	10		ST412/506	MFM		
RD3255	20		ST412/506	MFM		
RD4127	10		ST412/506	MFM		
RD4255	20		ST412/506	MFM		

NEWBURY DATA

Drive Model	Format Size MB	Seek Time	Interface	Encode	cache kb	RPM
NDR1065	55	25	ST412/506	MFM		
NDR1085	71	26	ST412/506	MFM		
NDR1105	87	25	ST412/506	MFM		
NDR1140	120	25	ST412/506	MFM		
NDR2085	74		ST412/506	MFM		
NDR2140	117		ST412/506	MFM		
NDR2190	160	28	ST412/506	MFM		
NDR3170S	146	28	SCSI	2,7 RLL		
NDR320	21		ST412/506	MFM		
NDR3280S	244	28	SCSI	2,7 RLL		
NDR3380S	319	28	SCSI	2,7 RLL		
NDR340	42	40	ST412/506	MFM		
NDR4175	179	28	ESDI	2,7 RLL		
NDR4380	338	28	ESDI	2,7 RLL		
NDR4380S	319	28	SCSI	RLL		
Penny 340	42		ST412/506	MFM		

NPL

Drive Model	Format Size MB	Seek Time	Interface	Encode	cache kb	RPM
4064	5		ST412/506	MFM		
4127	10		ST412/506	MFM		
4191S	15		ST412/506	MFM		
4255	20		ST412/506	MFM		
4362	30		ST412/506	MFM		
NP02-13	11	95	ST412/506	MFM		
NP02-26A/26S	22	40	ST412/506	MFM		
NP02-52A	44	40	ST412/506	MFM		
NP03-20	16	85	ST412/506	MFM		
NP04-13T	10	85	ST412/506	MFM		
NP04-55	45	35	ST412/506	MFM		
NP04-85	72	35	ST412/506	MFM		

OKIDATA

Drive Model	Format Size MB	Seek Time	Interface	Encode	cache kb	RPM
OD526	31	85	ST412/506	2,7 RLL		
OD540	51	85	ST412/506	2,7 RLL		

OLIVETTI

Drive Model	Format Size MB	Seek Time	Interface	Encode	cache kb	RPM
HD662/11	10	27	ST412/506	MFM		
HD662/12	20	27	ST412/506	MFM		

Drive Model	Format Size MB	Head	Cyl	Sect/ Trac	Translate H/C/S	RWC/ WPC	Form Factor	Power Watts
XM3220	21	4	612	17		NA/128	3.5HH	
XM5210	10	2	612	17		—/—	5.25HH	
XM5220/2	20	4	612	17		—/—	5.25FH	
XM5221	21	4	615	17		NA/256	5.25HH	
XM5340	42	6	820	17		256/256	5.25HH	
XM5360	42	6	820	17		128/128	5.25HH	
XM563-12	10					—/—	5.25FH	

OPTIMA TECHNOLOGY CORP

Drive Model	Format Size MB	Head	Cyl	Sect/ Trac	Translate H/C/S	RWC/ WPC	Form Factor	Power Watts
Concorde 1050	990	15				NA/NA	5.25	24
Concorde 1350	1342					NA/NA	5.25	36
Concorde 23	22130					—/—	5.25FH	35
Concorde 23W	22130					—/—	5.25FH	35
Concorde 635	640	14				NA/NA	5.25	36
Concorde 9000	8669					NA/NA	5.25FH	
Concorde 9000W	8669					NA/NA	5.25FH	
Diskovery 1000	1001					NA/NA	3.5 4H	
Diskovery 1000	2040					NA/NA	3.5 4H	
Diskovery 130	137					NA/NA	5.25	10
Diskovery 1800DHW	1763					NA/NA	3.5HH	
Diskovery 200	200					NA/NA	5.25	12
Diskovery 2100W	2040					NA/NA	3.5 4H	
Diskovery 325	321					NA/NA	5.25	14
Diskovery 40	45					NA/NA	5.25	9
Diskovery 4100	4095					NA/NA	3.5HH	
Diskovery 4100W	4095					NA/NA	3.5HH	
Diskovery 420	416	8				NA/NA	5.25	14
Diskovery 500	520					NA/NA	3.5 4H	
Diskovery 9000	8683					—/—	3.5HH	20
Diskovery 9000W	8683					—/—	3.5HH	20
MiniPak 100	104	4				NA/NA	3.5HH	
MiniPak 1000	1001					NA/NA	3.5 4H	
MiniPak 200	209	8				NA/NA	3.5HH	
MiniPak 2100	2040					NA/NA	3.5 4H	
MiniPak 2100	2040					NA/NA	3.5 4H	
MiniPak 300	320					NA/NA	3.5HH	
MiniPak 40	45					NA/NA	3.5HH	9.2
MiniPak 4100	4095					NA/NA	3.5HH	
MiniPak 500	520					NA/NA	3.5 4H	

ORCA TECHNOLOGY CORP

Drive Model	Format Size MB	Head	Cyl	Sect/ Trac	Translate H/C/S	RWC/ WPC	Form Factor	Power Watts
320A	370	9				NA/NA	3.5HH	
320S	370	9				NA/NA	3.5HH	
400A	470	9				NA/NA	3.5HH	
400S	470	9				NA/NA	3.5HH	
760E	760	15	1564			NA/NA	5.25	
760S	760	15	1564			NA/NA	5.25	

OTARI

SEE DISCTRON						—/—		

PACIFIC MAGTRON

Drive Model	Format Size MB	Head	Cyl	Sect/ Trac	Translate H/C/S	RWC/ WPC	Form Factor	Power Watts
MT3050	50	2	1062	46		—/—	5.25HH	
MT3100	100	4	1062	46		—/—	5.25HH	
MT4115E	115	4	1597			—/—	5.25HH	
MT4115S	115	4	1597			—/—	5.25HH	
MT4140E	140	5	1597			—/—	5.25HH	
MT4140S	140	5	1597			—/—	5.25HH	
MT4170E	170	6	1597			—/—	5.25HH	
MT4170S	170	6	1597			—/—	5.25HH	
MT5760E	676	15	1632	54		NA/NA	5.25FH	
MT5760S	673	15	1632	54		NA/NA	5.25FH	
MT6120S	1050	15	1927	71		NA/NA	5.25FH	

PANASONIC

Drive Model	Format Size MB	Head	Cyl	Sect/ Trac	Translate H/C/S	RWC/ WPC	Form Factor	Power Watts
JU116	20	4	615	17		616/616	3.5HH	
JU128	42	7	733	17		734/734	3.5HH	

Drive Model	Format Size MB	Seek Time	Interface	Encode	cache kb	RPM
XM3220	21	85	ST412/506	MFM		
XM5210	10	65	ST412/506	MFM		
XM5220/2	20	85	ST412/506	MFM		
XM5221	21	40	ST412/506	MFM		
XM5340	42	40	ST412/506	MFM		
XM5360	42	40	ST412/506			
XM563-12	10		ST412/506	MFM		

OPTIMA TECHNOLOGY CORP

Drive Model	Format Size MB	Seek Time	Interface	Encode	cache kb	RPM
Concorde 1050	990	15	SCSI	2,7 RLL		
Concorde 1350	1342	14	SCSI	2,7 RLL		
Concorde 23	22130	13.2	Ultra SCSI			
Concorde 23W	22130	13.2	Ultra Wide			
Concorde 635	640	16	SCSI	2,7 RLL		
Concorde 9000	8669	11	SCSI-2Fast	2,7 RLL		5400
Concorde 9000W	8669	11	SCSI-2FstW	2,7 RLL		5400
Diskovery 1000	1001	9	SCSI-2Fast	2,7 RLL		5400
Diskovery 1000	2040	8	SCSI-2Fast	2,7 RLL		5400
Diskovery 130	137	20	SCSI	2,7 RLL		
Diskovery 1800DHW	1763	8	SCSI-2FstW	2,7 RLL		
Diskovery 200	200	15	SCSI	2,7 RLL		
Diskovery 2100W	2040	8	SCSI-2FstW	2,7 RLL		7200
Diskovery 325	321	14	SCSI	2,7 RLL		
Diskovery 40	45	25	SCSI	2,7 RLL		
Diskovery 4100	4095	8	SCSI-2Fast	2,7 RLL		7200
Diskovery 4100W	4095	8	SCSI-2FstW	2,7 RLL		7200
Diskovery 420	416	16	SCSI	2,7 RLL		
Diskovery 500	520	12	SCSI-2Fast	2,7 RLL		5411
Diskovery 9000	8683	9	Ultra SCSI	2,7 RLL		
Diskovery 9000W	8683	9	Ultra Wide			
MiniPak 100	104	25	SCSI	2,7 RLL		
MiniPak 1000	1001	9	SCSI-2Fast	2,7 RLL		5400
MiniPak 200	209	20	SCSI	2,7 RLL		
MiniPak 2100	2040	8	SCSI-2Fast	2,7 RLL		7200
MiniPak 2100	2040	8	SCSI-2FstW	2,7 RLL		7200
MiniPak 300	320	13	SCSI	2,7 RLL		
MiniPak 40	45	25	SCSI	2,7 RLL		
MiniPak 4100	4095	8	SCSI-2Fast	2,7 RLL		7200
MiniPak 500	520	12	SCSI-2Fast	2,7 RLL		5411

ORCA TECHNOLOGY CORP

Drive Model	Format Size MB	Seek Time	Interface	Encode	cache kb	RPM
320A	370	12	IDE AT	2,7 RLL		
320S	370	12	SCSI	2,7 RLL		
400A	470	12	IDE AT	2,7 RLL		
400S	470	12	SCSI	2,7 RLL		
760E	760	14	ESDI	2,7 RLL		
760S	760	14	SCSI	2,7 RLL		

OTARI
SEE DISCTRON

PACIFIC MAGTRON

Drive Model	Format Size MB	Seek Time	Interface	Encode	cache kb	RPM
MT3050	50	20	IDE AT	2,7 RLL		
MT3100	100	20	IDE AT	2,7 RLL		
MT4115E	115	16	ESDI	2,7 RLL		
MT4115S	115	16	SCSI	2,7 RLL		
MT4140E	140	16	ESDI	2,7 RLL		
MT4140S	140	16	SCSI	2,7 RLL		
MT4170E	170	16	ESDI	2,7 RLL		
MT4170S	170	16	SCSI	2,7 RLL		
MT5760E	676	14	ESDI (15)	1,7 RLL		
MT5760S	673	14	SCSI	1,7 RLL		
MT6120S	1050	14	SCSI	1,7 RLL		

PANASONIC

Drive Model	Format Size MB	Seek Time	Interface	Encode	cache kb	RPM
JU116	20	85	ST412/506	MFM		
JU128	42	35	ST412/506	MFM		

Drive Model	Format Size MB	Head	Cyl	Sect/ Trac	Translate H/C/S	RWC/ WPC	Form Factor	Power Watts
PLUS DEVELOPMENT								
HardCard 20	21	4	615	17		NA/NA	3.5	3H
HardCard 40	42	8	612	17		NA/NA	3.5	3H
HardCard II-40	40	5	925	17		NA/NA	3.5	3H
HardCard II-80	80	10	925	17		NA/NA	3.5	3H
HardCard II-XL105	105	15	806	17		—/—	CARD	3H
HardCard II-XL50	52	10	601	17		—/—	CARD	3H
Impulse 105AT/LP	105	16	755	17	16/755/17	—/—	3.5	3H
Impulse 105S	105	6	1019			—/—	3.5	3H
Impulse 105S/LP	105	4	1056			—/—	3.5HH	
Impulse 120AT	120	5	1123	42	9/814/32	—/—	3.5HH	
Impulse 120S	120	5	1123	42		—/—	3.5HH	
Impulse 170AT	169	7	1123	42	10/966/34	—/—	3.5HH	
Impulse 170S	169	7	1123	42		—/—	3.5HH	
Impulse 210AT	174	7	1156	42	13/873/36	—/—	3.5HH	
Impulse 210S	174	7	1156	42		—/—	3.5HH	
Impulse 330AT	331					—/—	3.5HH	
Impulse 330S	331					—/—	3.5HH	
Impulse 40AT	41	5	965	17	5/968/17	NA/NA	3.5HH	
Impulse 40S	42	3	834			—/—	3.5HH	
Impulse 425AT	425					—/—	3.5HH	
Impulse 425S	425					—/—	3.5HH	
Impulse 52AT/LP	52	8	751	17	8/751/17	—/—	3.5	3H
Impulse 52S/LP	52	2				—/—	3.5	3H
Impulse 80AT	83	10	965	17	6/611/17	NA/NA	3.5HH	
Impulse 80AT/LP	85	16	616	17	6/611/17	—/—	3.5	3H
Impulse 80S	84	6	918			—/—	3.5HH	
Impulse 80S/LP	85	4				—/—	3.5	3H
PRAIRIETEK CORP								
Prairie 120	21	2	615	34		—/—	2.5	4H
Prairie 140	42	4	615	34		NA/NA	2.5	4H
Prairie 220A	20	4	612	16		—/—	2.5	3H
Prairie 220S	20	4	612	16		—/—	2.5	3H
Prairie 240	42	4	615	34		—/—	2.5	3H
Prairie 242A	42	4	615	34		NA/NA		
Prairie 242S	42	4	615	34		NA/NA		
Prairie 282A	82	4		34		NA/NA		
Prairie 282S	82	4		34		NA/NA		
PRIAM CORPORATION								
3504	32	4	820	26		—/—	3.5HH	
502	46	7	755	17		756/756	5.25FH	
504	46	7	755	17		756/756	5.25FH	
514	117	11	1224	17		—/—	5.25FH	
519	160	15	1224	17		1225/1225	5.25FH	
519	244	11	1224	26		—/—	5.25FH	
617	153	7	1225			NA/NA	5.25FH	
628	241	11	1225			NA/NA	5.25FH	
638	329	15	1225			NA/NA	5.25FH	
717	153	7	1225			1226/1226	5.25FH	
728	241	11	1225			1226/1226	5.25FH	
738	329	15	1225			1226/1226	5.25FH	
ID/ED040	42	5	987	17		—/—	5.25FH	
ID/ED045	50	5	1166	17		—/—	5.25FH	
ID/ED060	62	7	1018	17		—/—	5.25FH	
ID/ED062	71	7	1166	17		—/—	5.25FH	
ID/ED075	74	5	1166	25		—/—	5.25FH	
ID/ED100	122	7	1314	26		—/—	5.25FH	
ID/ED1000	1046	15	1919	71		—/—	5.25FH	
ID/ED120	121	7	1024	33		NA/NA	5.25FH	
ID/ED130	159	15	1224	17		—/—	5.25FH	
ID/ED150	160	7	1276	35		NA/NA	5.25HH	
ID/ED160	158	7	1225	36		NA/NA	5.25FH	
ID/ED230	235	15	1224	25		—/—	5.25FH	
ID/ED240	243	15	1220	26		—/—	5.25FH	
ID/ED250	248	11	1225	36		NA/NA	5.25FH	

Drive Model	Format Size MB	Seek Time	Interface	Encode	cache kb	RPM
PLUS DEVELOPMENT						
HardCard 20	21	40	IDE AT	2,7 RLL		
HardCard 40	42	40	IDE AT	2,7 RLL		
HardCard II-40	40	25	IDE AT	2,7 RLL		
HardCard II-80	80	25	IDE AT	2,7 RLL		
HardCard II-XL105	105	17	IDE AT	2,7 RLL		
HardCard II-XL50	52	17	IDE AT	2,7 RLL		
Impulse 105AT/LP	105	17	IDE AT	2,7 RLL		
Impulse 105S	105	19	SCSI-2	2,7 RLL		
Impulse 105S/LP	105	17	SCSI-2	2,7 RLL		
Impulse 120AT	120	15	IDE AT	1,7 RLL		3605
Impulse 120S	120	15	SCSI-2	1,7 RLL		3605
Impulse 170AT	169	15	IDE AT	1,7 RLL		3605
Impulse 170S	169	15	SCSI-2	1,7 RLL		3605
Impulse 210AT	174	15	IDE AT	1,7 RLL		3605
Impulse 210S	174	15	SCSI-2	1,7 RLL		3605
Impulse 330AT	331	14	IDE AT	1,7 RLL		
Impulse 330S	331	14	SCSI-2	1,7 RLL		
Impulse 40AT	41	19	IDE AT	2,7 RLL		3660
Impulse 40S	42	19	SCSI-2	2,7 RLL		3660
Impulse 425AT	425	14	SCSI-2	1,7 RLL		
Impulse 425S	425	14	SCSI-2	1,7 RLL		
Impulse 52AT/LP	52	17	IDE AT	2,7 RLL		3660
Impulse 52S/LP	52	17	SCSI-2	2,7 RLL		
Impulse 80AT	83	19	IDE AT	2,7 RLL		3660
Impulse 80AT/LP	85	17	IDE AT	2,7 RLL		3660
Impulse 80S	84	19	SCSI-2	2,7 RLL		3660
Impulse 80S/LP	85	17	SCSI-2	2,7 RLL		
PRAIRIETEK CORP						
Prairie 120	21	23	IDE AT	2,7 RLL		
Prairie 140	42	23	IDE AT	2,7 RLL		
Prairie 220A	20	28	IDE AT	2,7 RLL		
Prairie 220S	20	28	SCSI	2,7 RLL		
Prairie 240	42	28	IDE AT	2,7 RLL		
Prairie 242A	42	23	IDE XT-AT	2,7 RLL		
Prairie 242S	42	23	SCSI	2,7 RLL		
Prairie 282A	82	28	IDE AT	2,7 RLL		
Prairie 282S	82	23	SCSI	2,7 RLL		
PRIAM CORPORATION						
3504	32	27	ST412/506	2,7 RLL		
502	46	22	ST412/506	MFM		
504	46	22	ST412/506	MFM		
514	117	22	ST412/506	MFM		
519	160	22	ST412/506	MFM		
519	244	22	ST412/506	2,7 RLL		
617	153	20	ESDI	2,7 RLL		
628	241	20	ESDI	2,7 RLL		
638	329	20	SCSI	2,7 RLL		
717	153	20	SCSI	2,7 RLL		
728	241	20	SCSI	2,7 RLL		
738	329	20	SCSI	2,7 RLL		
ID/ED040	42	23	ST412/506	MFM		
ID/ED045	50	23	ST412/506	MFM		
ID/ED060	62	30	ST412/506	MFM		
ID/ED062	71	23	ST412/506	MFM		
ID/ED075	74	23	ST412/506			
ID/ED100	122	15	ST412/506	2,7 RLL		
ID/ED1000	1046	14	SCSI			
ID/ED120	121	28	ESDI	2,7 RLL		
ID/ED130	159	13	ST412/506	MFM		
ID/ED150	160	28	ESDI	2,7 RLL		
ID/ED160	158	18	ESDI	2,7 RLL		
ID/ED230	235	11	ST412/506			
ID/ED240	243	28	ST412/506	2,7 RLL		
ID/ED250	248	18	ESDI			

Drive Model	Format Size MB	Head	Cyl	Sect/ Trac	Translate H/C/S	RWC/ WPC	Form Factor	Power Watts
ID/ED660	675	15	1628	54		—/—	5.25FH	
ID100	103	7	1166	25			5.25FH	
ID1000	1034	15	1919	71		NA/NA	5.25FH	
ID110	119	7	1024	33		NA/NA	5.25FH	
ID120	132	15	1224	17		—/—	5.25FH	
ID130	158	7	1276	35		NA/NA	5.25FH	
ID150	158	7	1218	36		—/—	5.25FH	
ID160	156	7	1225	36		NA/NA	5.25FH	
ID160H	157	7	1225	36		—/—	5.25FH	
ID20	25	3	987	17		—/—	5.25FH	
ID230	233	15	1224	25		NA/NA	5.25FH	
ID250	246	11	1225	36		—/—	5.25FH	
ID330	339	15	1218	36		NA/NA	5.25FH	
ID330D	337	15	1225	36		—/—	5.25FH	
ID330E	337	15	1218	36		—/—	5.25FH	
ID330E-PS/2	330	15	1195	36		NA/NA	5.25FH	
ID330S	338	15	1225	36		—/—	5.25FH	
ID340H	340	7	1218	36		—/—	5.25FH	
ID40	42	5	987	17		—/—	5.25FH	
ID40AT	40	5	1018	17		—/—	5.25FH	
ID45	44	5	1018	17		—/—	5.25FH	
ID45H	44	5	1024	17		—/—	5.25HH	
ID60	59	7	987	17		—/—	5.25FH	
ID60AT	59	7	987	17		—/—	5.25FH	
ID62	62	7	1166	17		—/—	5.25FH	
ID660	660	15	1632	54		NA/NA	5.25FH	
ID75	73	5	1166	25		—/—	5.25FH	
V130	39	3	987	26		988/988	5.25FH	
V150	42	5	987	17		988/988	5.25FH	
V160	50	5	1166	17		1167/1167	5.25FH	
V170	60	7	987	17		988/988	5.25FH	
V170R	91	7	987	26		988/988	5.25FH	
V185	72	7	1166	17		1167/1167	5.25FH	
V519	159	15	1224	17		—/NONE	5.25FH	
PROCOM TECHNOLOGY								
ATOM-AT1300	1350					—/—	2.5 4H	
ATOM-AT1302	1350					—/—	2.5 4H	
ATOM-AT2001	2160					—/—	2.5 4H	
ATOM-AT3000	3050					NA/NA	2.5 4H	
ATOM-AT340	340					—/—		
ATOM-AT4000	4090				16/7944/63	—/—		
ATOM-AT500	528					—/—	2.5 4H	
ATOM-AT5000	5020				16/10380/63	—/—		
ATOM-AT6000	6480				15/13424/63	—/—		
ATOM-AT800	811					—/—	2.5 4H	
ATOM-AT8000	8100				16/15880/63	—/—		
ATOMlite-523	520				16/1008/63	—/—		
BRAVOPAQ120	124	14	1024	17		—/—	3.5HH	
BRAVOPAQ40	42	5	977	17		—/—	3.5HH	
Hiper 145	150	8	1024	36		—/—	5.25FH	
Hiper 155	160	9	966	36		—/—		
Hiper 20	21	4	615	17		—/—		
Hiper 30	33	4	615	26		—/—		
Hiper 330	337	15	1224	36		—/—	5.25FH	
Hiper 380	388	16	755	63		—/—	5.25FH	
Hiper 48	48	6	615	26		—/—		
Hiper/II 155	157	64	150	32		—/—	5.25FH	
Hiper/II 380	383	64	365	32		—/—	5.25FH	
Hiper/II 65	65	9	925	17		—/—	5.25FH	
MD100	104	64	102	32		—/—	3.5	
MD1003 (external)	1080	4	4826	116		—/—		
MD120	122					—/—	FH	
MD18000W	18000				10/8419/63	—/—	HH	
MD18010L	18000				20/7065/63	—/—		
MD20	21	64	21	32		—/—		
MD200	209	32	200	32		—/—	3.5	
MD2003 (external)	2160	5	2149	148		—/—	3.5	
MD2103 (external)	2147	11	3711	86-125		—/—		

Drive Model	Format Size MB	Seek Time	Interface	Encode	cache kb	RPM
ID/ED660	675	16	SCSI			
ID100	103	15	ST412/506	2,7 RLL		
ID1000	1034	14	ESDI			
ID120	119	28	ESDI	2,7 RLL		
ID130	132	13	ST412/506	MFM		
ID150	158	28	ESDI	2,7 RLL		
ID160	158	28	SCSI			
ID160H	156	28	ESDI	2,7 RLL		
ID20	25	23	ST412/506	MFM		
ID230	233	11	ST412/506	2,7 RLL		
ID250	246	18	ESDI	2,7 RLL		
ID330	339	18	SCSI	2,7 RLL		
ID330D	337	18	ESDI	2,7 RLL		
ID330E	337	18	ESDI	2,7 RLL		
ID330E-PS/2	330	18	PS/2	2,7 RLL		
ID330S	338	18	SCSI	2,7 RLL		
ID340H	340	14	ESDI	2,7 RLL		
ID40	42	23	ST412/506	MFM		
ID40AT	40	23	ST412/506	MFM		
ID45	44	23	ST412/506	MFM		
ID45H	44	25	ST412/506	MFM		
ID60	59	30	ST412/506	MFM		
ID60AT	59	23	ST412/506	MFM		
ID62	62	23	ST412/506	MFM		
ID660	660	16	ESDI	2,7 RLL		
ID75	73	23	ST412/506	2,7 RLL		
V130	39		ST412/506	2,7 RLL		
V150	42			MFM		
V160	50			MFM		
V170	60	28	ST412/506	MFM		
V170R	91	28	ST412/506	MFM		
V185	72	28	ST412/506	MFM		
V519	159	20		MFM		
PROCOM TECHNOLOGY						
ATOM-AT1300	1350	13	ATA-2		128k	4200
ATOM-AT1302	1350	13	ATA-2		128k	4200
ATOM-AT2001	2160	13	ATA-2		128k	4200
ATOM-AT3000	3050	13	ATA-2		128k	4852
ATOM-AT340	340	16	IDE		120k	
ATOM-AT4000	4090	12	ATA-3		512k	4000
ATOM-AT500	528	13	IDE		128k	
ATOM-AT5000	5020	12	ATA-3		512k	4000
ATOM-AT6000	6480	13	ATA-3		512k	4200
ATOM-AT800	811	13	IDE		128k	
ATOM-AT8000	8100	12	ATA-3		512k	4900
ATOMlite-523	520	12	PCMCIAType3		128k	4800
BRAVOPAQ120	124	19	IDE AT	RLL		
BRAVOPAQ40	42	25	IDE AT	RLL		
Hiper 145	150	23	ESDI			
Hiper 155	160	16.5	SCSI	RLL		
Hiper 20	21	40	ST412/506	MFM		
Hiper 30	33	28	ST412/506	RLL		
Hiper 330	337	18	ESDI			
Hiper 380	388	16	SCSI	RLL		
Hiper 48	48	28	ST412/506	RLL		
Hiper/II 155	157	16.5	ESDI	RLL		
Hiper/II 380	383	16	ESDI	RLL		
Hiper/II 65	65	28	ST412/506	MFM		
MD100	104	18	SCSI	RLL		
MD1003 (external)	1080	12.5	SCSI-2Fast		128k	5376
MD120	122	17	SCSI	RLL		
MD18000W	18000	7	Ultra Wide		1792k	7200
MD18010L	18000	6.5	Ultra2 SCSI		4000k	1000
MD20	21	28	SCSI	RLL		
MD200	209	18	SCSI	RLL		
MD2003 (external)	2160	8.5	SCSI-2Fast		448k	5400
MD2103 (external)	2147	9	SCSI-2Fast		512k	7200

Drive Model	Format Size MB	Head	Cyl	Sect/Trac	Translate H/C/S	RWC/WPC	Form Factor	Power Watts
MD2103W (external)	2100					—/—		3.5
MD240	245					—/—		3.5
MD30	30	64	30	32		—/—		
MD320	337	64	317	32		—/—		
MD36000L	36000				20/11494/63	—/—		HH
MD420	442	64	415	32		—/—		3.5 3H
MD4300W	4500				5/8419/63	—/—		FH
MD4303 (external)	4350					—/—		3.5HH
MD4303W (external)	4294					—/—		3.5
MD45	45	64	45	32		—/—		
MD544 (external)	541	2	4901	108		—/—		3.5
MD80	83	64	80	32		—/—		
MD9100W	9100				10/8419/63	—/—		FH
MD9103	9100					—/—		
MD9103W	9100					—/—		
MTD1000	1037	64	989	32		—/—		
MTD1350	1420					—/—		
MTD1900	1900					—/—		
MTD2000	2040					—/—		
MTD2800	2800					—/—		
MTD320-10	337	64	317	32		—/—		
MTD585	601	64	573	32		—/—		
MTD650	676	64	650	32		—/—		
MTD9000 (external)	9090					—/—		
PAT100	110	14	535	29		—/—		3.5HH
PAT40	42	4	805	26		—/—		5.25HH
PH.D20	21	4	615	17		—/—		3.5HH
PH.D2520	21	4	615	17		—/—		3.5HH
PH.D2545	45	7	733	17		—/—		3.5HH
PH.D30	33	4	615	26		—/—		3.5HH
PH.D30-CE	33	4	615	26		—/—		3.5HH
PH.D3020	21	4	615	17		—/—		3.5HH
PH.D45	45	7	773	17		—/—		3.5HH
PH.D48	49	6	615	26		—/—		3.5HH
PH.D5045	45	7	773	17		—/—		3.5HH
PIRA 100	101	8	776	33		—/—		3.5HH
PIRA 120	124	14	1024	17		—/—		3.5HH
PIRA 200	210	12	954	36		—/—		3.5HH
PIRA 40	42	5	977	17		—/—		3.5HH
PIRA 50-120	210	14	1024	36		—/—		3.5HH
PIRA 50-200	210	12	954	36		—/—		3.5HH
PIRA 50-270	270					—/—		3.5HH
PIRA 50-340	340					—/—		3.5HH
PIRA 50-420	420					—/—		3.5HH
PIRA 55-270	270					—/—		
PIRA 55-340	340					—/—		
PIRA 55-420	420					—/—		
PR-IDE1000	1080					—/—		3H
PR-IDE1200	1200					—/—		
PR-IDE13500	13500				15/16383/63	—/—		
PR-IDE1600	1629					—/—		
PR-IDE16800	16800					—/—		
PR-IDE2000	2113					—/—		
PR-IDE20000	20000				16/16383/63	—/—		3H
PR-IDE210	210				15/16383/63	—/—		3H
PR-IDE25000	25000					—/—		3H
PR-IDE270	270				16/6296/63	—/—		
PR-IDE3000	3200					—/—		3H
PR-IDE340	340					—/—		3H
PR-IDE420	420					—/—		3H
PR-IDE4300U	4300				16/8400/63	—/—		
PR-IDE500	510					—/—		3H
PR-IDE6400U	6400				16/12592/63	—/—		
PR-IDE800	800					—/—		3H
PR-IDE8400	8400				16/16383/63	—/—		
PROPAQ/N100	101	8	776	33		—/—		3.5HH
PROPAQ/N120-19	124	14	1024	17		—/—		3.5HH

Drive Model	Format Size MB	Seek Time	Interface	Encode	cache kb	RPM
MD2103W (external)	2100	8	SCSI-2FstW			7200
MD240	245	17	SCSI	RLL		
MD30	30	28	SCSI	RLL		
MD320	337	12	SCSI	RLL		
MD36000L	36000	7.5	Ultra2 SCSI		4000k	7200
MD420	442	14	SCSI	RLL		
MD4300W	4500	7.5	Ultra Wide		384k	7200
MD4303	4350	8	SCSI-2Fast		512k	7200
MD4303W (external)	4294	8	SCSI-2FstW		1024k	7200
MD45	45	12	SCSI	RLL		
MD544 (external)	541	12	SCSI-2Fast			
MD80	83	24	SCSI	RLL	64k	5400
MD9100W	9100	7.5	Ultra Wide		384k	7200
MD9103	9100	9	Ultra SCSI		2024k	7200
MD9103W	9100	9	WIDE SCSI		2024k	7200
MTD1000	1037	15	SCSI	RLL ZBR		
MTD1350	1420	15	SCSI	RLL ZBR		
MTD1900	1900	12.9	SCSI	RLL ZBR		
MTD2000	2040	11	SCSI-2Fast	RLL ZBR		
MTD2800	2800	11	SCSI-2Fast	RLL ZBR		5400
MTD320-10	337	10.7	SCSI	RLL ZBR		5400
MTD585	601	16.5	SCSI	RLL ZBR		
MTD650	676	15.5	SCSI	RLL ZBR		
MTD9000 (external)	9090	11	SCSI-2Fast		1024k	
PAT100	110	15	IDE AT	RLL		
PAT40	42	25	IDE AT	RLL		
PH.D20	21	40	ST412/506	MFM		
PH.D2520	21	40	ST412/506	MFM		
PH.D2545	45	25	ST412/506	MFM		
PH.D30	33	28	ST412/506	RLL		
PH.D30-CE	33	28	ST412/506	RLL		
PH.D3020	21	40	ST412/506	MFM		
PH.D45	45	25	ST412/506	MFM		
PH.D48	49	28	ST412/506	RLL		
PH.D5045	45	25	ST412/506	MFM		
PIRA 100	101	25	IDE AT			
PIRA 120	124	18	IDE AT	RLL		
PIRA 200	210	15	IDE AT	RLL		
PIRA 40	42	28	IDE AT	RLL		
PIRA 50-120	210	19	IDE AT	RLL		
PIRA 50-200	210	15	IDE AT	RLL		
PIRA 50-270	270	14	IDE AT	RLL		
PIRA 50-340	340	15	IDE AT	RLL		
PIRA 50-420	420	14	IDE AT	RLL		
PIRA 55-270	270	14	IDE			
PIRA 55-340	340	14	IDE			
PIRA 55-420	420	14	IDE			
PR-IDE1000	1080	14	ATA-2		128k	3800
PR-IDE1200	1200	10	IDE			
PR-IDE13500	13500	8.5	ATA-4		464k	5400
PR-IDE1600	1629	12	ATA-2		128k	4480
PR-IDE16800	16800	8.5	Ultra ATA		464k	5400
PR-IDE2000	2113	10.5	ATA-2		256k	5400
PR-IDE20000	20000	9	Ultra ATA-4		2048k	5400
PR-IDE210	210	14	IDE			
PR-IDE25000	25000	9	Ultra ATA-4			
PR-IDE270	270	14	IDE		2048k	5400
PR-IDE3000	3200	9.5	Ultra ATA		256k	5400
PR-IDE340	340	12	IDE			
PR-IDE420	420	14	IDE			
PR-IDE4300U	4300	8.5	Ultra ATA-3		476k	5400
PR-IDE500	510	12	IDE			
PR-IDE6400U	6400	8.5	Ultra ATA-3		476k	5400
PR-IDE800	800	12	IDE			
PR-IDE8400	8400	8.5	Ultra ATA-3		476k	5400
PROPAQ/N100	101	25	IDE AT	RLL		
PROPAQ/N120-19	124	19	IDE AT	RLL		

Drive Model	Format Size MB	Head	Cyl	Sect/Trac	Translate H/C/S	RWC/WPC	Form Factor	Power Watts
PROPAQ/N185-15	189	12	1023	33		—/—	3.5HH	
PROPAQ/N40	40	4	805	26		—/—	3.5HH	
PROPAQ/N40N	40	6	560	26		—/—	3.5HH	
PROPAQ/S100	101	8	776	33		—/—	3.5HH	
PROPAQ/S120-19	124	14	1024	17		—/—	3.5HH	
PROPAQ/S185-15	189	12	1023	33		—/—	3.5HH	
PROPAQ/S40	40	4	805	26		—/—	3.5HH	
PROPAQ/S40N	40	6	560	26		—/—	3.5HH	
PROPAQ100	101	8	776	33		—/—	3.5HH	
PROPAQ120-19	124	14	1024	17		—/—	3.5HH	
PROPAQ185-15	189	12	1023	33		NA/NA	3.5HH	
PROPAQ185-15	189	5				—/—	3.5HH	
PROPAQ40	40	4	805	26		—/—	3.5HH	
PROPAQ40N	40	6	560	26		—/—	3.5HH	
PROTON 523	520					—/—		
SI100	104	64	102	32		—/—	5.25FH	
SI1000	1037	64		32		NA/NA	5.25	
SI1000/S5	1037	8				—/—	3.5 3H	
SI1003	1080	4	4826	116		—/—	3.5 3H	
SI1003/C	1080	4	4826	116		—/—	FH	
SI18000W/C	18000				10/8419/63	—/—		
SI18000W/HST	18000				10/8419/63	—/—		
SI18000W/HST2	18000				10/8419/63	—/—	HH	
SI18010L/C	18000				20/7065/63	—/—		
SI18010W/HST	18000				20/7065/63	—/—		
SI200	209	64	200	32		NA/NA	3.5HH	
SI200/PS3	209	4				—/—	3.5 3H	
SI2003	2160	5	2149	148		—/—	3.5 3H	
SI2003/C	2160	5	2149	148		—/—	3.5 3H	
SI2103	2147	11	3711	86-125		—/—	3.5 3H	
SI2103/C	2147	11	3711	86-125		—/—	3.5 3H	
SI2103W/C	2100					—/—	5.25FH	
SI320-10	337	64	317	32		—/—	5.25FH	
SI320H	331	64	339	32		—/—	HH	
SI36000L/C	36000				20/11494/63	—/—		
SI36000W/HST	36000				20/11494/63	—/—	5.25FH	
SI420H	435	64	415	32		—/—	3H	
SI4300/C	4500	84	63		5/8419/63	—/—		
SI4300/HST	4500				5/8419/63	—/—	3H	
SI4300W/C	4500				5/8419/63	—/—		
SI4300W/HST	4500				5/8419/63	—/—		
SI4300W/HST2	4300				5/8419/63	—/—	3.5HH	
SI4303	4350	10	5288	165		—/—	3.5HH	
SI4303/C	4350	10	5288	165		—/—		
SI4303W/C	4300					—/—	3.5 3H	
SI45	48	64	45	32		—/—	3.5 3H	
SI544	541	2	4901	108		—/—	5.25FH	
SI544/C	544	2	4901	108		—/—		
SI585	601	64	415	32		NA/NA	5.25	
SI585/PS5	601	8				NA/NA	5.25	
SI585/S5	601	8				—/—	5.25FH	
SI650	662	64	632	32		—/—		
SI80	83	64	80	32		—/—	5.25FH	
SI9000/S5	9090					—/—	3H	
SI9100/C	9100				10/8419/63	—/—		
SI9100/HST	9100				10/8419/63	—/—	3H	
SI9100W/C	9100				10/8419/63	—/—		
SI9100W/HST	9100				10/8419/63	—/—		
SI9100W/HST2	9100				10/8419/63	—/—		
SI9103	9100	20	5273	153-23		—/—		
SI9103W	9100	20	5273	153-23		—/—		
SI9103W/C	9100	20	5273	153-23		—/—		

PTI (PERIPHERAL TECHNOLOGY)

Drive Model	Format Size MB	Head	Cyl	Sect/Trac	Translate H/C/S	RWC/WPC	Form Factor	Power Watts
PL100 Turbo	105	4				NA/NA	3.5HH	
PL200 Turbo	210	7				NA/NA	3.5HH	
PL32 Turbo	320	14				NA/NA	3.5HH	
PT225	21	4	615	17		—/—	3.5HH	

Drive Model	Format Size MB	Seek Time	Interface	Encode	cache kb	RPM
PROPAQ/N185-15	189	15	IDE AT	RLL		
PROPAQ/N40	40	25	IDE AT	RLL		
PROPAQ/N40N	40	25	IDE AT	RLL		
PROPAQ/S100	101	25	IDE AT	RLL		
PROPAQ/S120-19	124	19	IDE AT	RLL		
PROPAQ/S185-15	189	15	IDE AT	RLL		
PROPAQ/S40	40	25	IDE AT	RLL		
PROPAQ/S40N	40	25	IDE AT	RLL		
PROPAQ/S100	101	25	IDE AT	RLL		
PROPAQ120-19	124	19	IDE AT	RLL		
PROPAQ185-15	189	15	IDE AT	RLL		
PROPAQ185-15	189		IDE AT	RLL		
PROPAQ40	40	25	IDE AT	RLL		
PROPAQ40N	40	25	IDE AT	RLL		
PROTON 523	520	12	PCMCIA-ATA			
SI100	104	18	SCSI	RLL		
SI1000	1037	15	SCSI	RLL		
SI1000/S5	1037	15	SCSI			
SI1003	1080	12	SCSI-2Fast		128k	5376
SI1003/C	1080	12	SCSI-2Fast		128k	5376
SI18000W/C	18000	7	Ultra Wide		1792k	7200
SI18000W/HST	18000	7	SCSI-2Fast		1792k	7200
SI18000W/HST2	18000	7	Ultra Wide		1792k	7200
SI18010L/C	18000	6.5	Ultra2 SCSI		4000k	1000
SI18010W/HST	18000	6.5	Ultra Wide		4000k	1000
SI200	209	18	SCSI	RLL		
SI200/PS3	209	18	SCSI	2,7 RLL		
SI2003	2160	8.5	SCSI-2Fast			5400
SI2003/C	2160	8.5	SCSI-2Fast			5400
SI2103	2147	9	SCSI-2Fast		512k	7200
SI2103/C	2147	9	SCSI-2Fast		512k	7200
SI2103W/C	2100	8	SCSI-2FstW			7200
SI320-10	337	10.7	SCSI	RLL		
SI320H	331	14	SCSI	RLL		
SI36000L/C	36000	7.5	Ultra2 SCSI		4000k	7200
SI36000W/HST	36000	7.5	Ultra Wide		4000k	7200
SI420H	435	16	SCSI	RLL		
SI4300/C	4500	7.5	Ultra SCSI		384k	7200
SI4300/HST	4500	7.5	Ultra SCSI		384k	7200
SI4300W/C	4500	7.5	Ultra Wide		384k	7200
SI4300W/HST	4500	7.5	Ultra Wide		384k	7200
SI4300W/HST2	4300	7.5	Ultra Wide		384k	7200
SI4303	4350	8	SCSI-2Fast		512k	7200
SI4303/C	4350	8	Ultra SCSI		512k	7200
SI4303W/C	4300	8	SCSI-2FstW		1024k	7200
SI45	48	28	SCSI	RLL		
SI544	541	12	SCSI-2Fast		64k	5400
SI544/C	544	12	SCSI-2Fast		64k	5400
SI585	601	16.5	SCSI	RLL		
SI585/PS5	601	17	SCSI			
SI585/S5	601	17	SCSI			
SI650	662	15.5	SCSI	RLL		
SI80	83	24	SCSI	RLL		
SI9000/S5	9090	11	SCSI-2Fast		1024k	
SI9100/C	9100	7.5	Ultra SCSI		384k	7200
SI9100/HST	9100	7.5	Ultra SCSI		384k	7200
SI9100W/C	9100	7.5	Ultra Wide		384k	7200
SI9100W/HST	9100	7.5	Ultra Wide		384k	7200
SI9100W/HST2	9100	7.5	Ultra Wide		384k	7200
SI9103	9100	9	Ultra SCSI		2024k	7200
SI9103W	9100	9	SCSI WIDE		2024k	7200
SI9103W/C	9100	9	WIDE SCSI		2024k	7200
PTI (PERIPHERAL TECHNOLOGY)						
PL100 Turbo	105	19	SCSI	2,7 RLL		
PL200 Turbo	210	19	SCSI	2,7 RLL		
PL32 Turbo	320	12	SCSI	2,7 RLL		
PT225	21	35	ST412/506	MFM		

Hard Drive Specs **683**

Drive Model	Format Size MB	Head	Cyl	Sect/ Trac	Translate H/C/S	RWC/ WPC	Form Factor	Power Watts
PT234	28	4	820	17		—/—	3.5HH	
PT238A	32	4	615	26		NA/NA	3.5HH	
PT238R	32	4	615	26		—/—	3.5HH	
PT238S	32	4	615	26		—/—	3.5HH	
PT251A	51	4	820	26		—/—	3.5HH	
PT251R	44	4	820	26		—/—	3.5HH	
PT251S	44	4	820	26		—/—	3.5HH	
PT338	32	6	615	17		—/—	3.5HH	
PT351	42	6	820	17		—/—	3.5HH	
PT357A	49	6	615	26		—/—	3.5HH	
PT357R	49	6	615	26		—/—	3.5HH	
PT357S	49	6	615	26		—/—	3.5HH	
PT376A	65	6	820	26		NA/NA	3.5HH	
PT376R	65	6	820	26		—/—	3.5HH	
PT376S	65	6	820	26		—/—	3.5HH	
PT4102A	87	8	820	26		—/—	3.5HH	
PT4102R	87	8	820	26		—/—	3.5HH	
PT4102S	87	8	820	26		—/—	3.5HH	
PT468	57	8	820	17		—/—	3.5HH	
QUANTUM CORPORATION								
Atlas 10K 18.2	18200	12				—/—	3.5 3H	12.0
Atlas 10K 36.4	36400	24				—/—	3.5 3H	12.0
Atlas 10K 9.1	9100	6				—/—	3.5 3H	12.0
Atlas 10K II 18.4	18400	6				—/—	3.5 3H	9.7
Atlas 10K II 36.7	36700	10				—/—	3.5 3H	10
Atlas 10K II 73.4	73400	20				—/—	3.5FH	14.3
Atlas 10K II 9.2	9200	3				—/—	3.5 3H	9.7
Atlas 10K III 18.4	18400	2				—/—	3.5 3H	7.5
Atlas 10K III 36.7	36700	4				—/—	3.5 3H	9.5
Atlas 10K III 73.4	73400	8				—/—	3.5 3H	10.0
Atlas II XP32275	2275	5			V	—/—	3.5 3H	7.6
Atlas II XP34550	4550	10			V	—/—	3.5 3H	9
Atlas II XP39100	9100	20			V	—/—	3.5HH	12
Atlas III 18.2S	18200	20				—/—	3.5HH	
Atlas III 18.2S	18200	20				—/—	3.5HH	
Atlas III 18.2S	18200	20				—/—	3.5HH	
Atlas III 4.5S	4550	5				—/—	3.5 3H	
Atlas III 4.5S	4550	5				—/—	3.5 3H	
Atlas III 4.5S	4550	5				—/—	3.5 3H	
Atlas III 9.1S	9100	10				—/—	3.5 3H	
Atlas III 9.1S	9100	10				—/—	3.5 3H	
Atlas III 9.1S	9100	10				—/—	3.5 3H	
Atlas IV 18.2	18200	8				—/—	3.5 3H	8.0
Atlas IV 36.4	36400	16				—/—	3.5 3H	8.0
Atlas IV 9.1	9100	4				—/—	3.5 3H	8.0
Atlas V 18.3	18300	4				—/—	3.5 3H	9.0
Atlas V 36.7	36700	8				—/—	3.5 3H	9.0
Atlas V 9.1	9100	2				—/—	3.5 3H	9.0
Atlas XP31070S	1075	5		80-134		—/—	3.5 3H	7.6
Atlas XP32150S	2150	10		80-134		—/—	3.5 3H	9
Atlas XP34300S	4350	20		80-134		—/—	3.5HH	12
Bigfoot 1275	1275	2		144-23	16/2492/63	—/—	5.25 4H	4.0
Bigfoot 2.1	2110	4		149-27		—/—	5.25 4H	4.0
Bigfoot 2550	2550	4		144-23	16/4994/63	—/—	5.25 4H	4.0
Bigfoot CY 2.1	2111	2			16/4092/63	—/—	5.25 3H	5.75
Bigfoot CY 4.3	4335	4			15/8960/63	—/—	5.25 3H	5.75
Bigfoot CY 6.4	6510	6			15/13456/63	—/—	5.25 3H	5.75
Bigfoot TS 12.7	12720	4			16/16384y/6	—/—	5.25	5.75
Bigfoot TS 19.2	19292	6			16/16384y/6	—/—	5.25	5.75
Bigfoot TS 6.4	6418	2			15/13264/63	—/—	5.25	5.75
Bigfoot TS 8.4	8455	3			16/16384y/6	—/—	5.25	5.75
Bigfoot TX 12.0	12056	6			16/23361/63	—/—	5.25	7.6
Bigfoot TX 4.0	4018				15/8306/63	—/—	5.25	7.6
Bigfoot TX 6.0	6028				15/12459/63	—/—	5.25	7.6
Bigfoot TX 8.0	8037				15/15574/63	—/—	5.25	7.6
Capella VP31110S	1108	4		97-149		—/—	3.5 3H	5.8
Capella VP32210S	2216	8		97-149		—/—	3.5 3H	6.3

Drive Model	Format Size MB	Seek Time	Interface	Encode	cache kb	RPM
PT234	28	35	ST412/506	MFM		
PT238A	32	35	IDE AT	2,7 RLL		
PT238R	32	35	ST412/506	2,7 RLL		
PT238S	32	35	SCSI	2,7 RLL		
PT251A	51	35	IDE AT	2,7 RLL		
PT251R	44	35	ST412/506	2,7 RLL		
PT251S	44	35	SCSI	2,7 RLL		
PT338	32	35	ST412/506	MFM		
PT351	42	35	ST412/506	MFM		
PT357A	49	35	IDE AT	2,7 RLL		
PT357R	49	35	ST412/506	2,7 RLL		
PT357S	49	35	SCSI	2,7 RLL		
PT376A	65	35	IDE AT	2,7 RLL		
PT376R	65	35	ST412/506	2,7 RLL		
PT376S	65	35	SCSI	2,7 RLL		
PT4102A	87	35	IDE AT	2,7 RLL		
PT4102R	87	35	ST412/506	2,7 RLL		
PT4102S	87	35	SCSI	2,7 RLL		
PT468	57	35	ST412/506	MFM		

QUANTUM CORPORATION

Drive Model	Format Size MB	Seek Time	Interface	Encode	cache kb	RPM
Atlas 10K 18.2	18200	5	Ultra2	PRML24/25	2000k	1000
Atlas 10K 36.4	36400	5.5	Ultra SCSI	PRML24/25	2000k	1000
Atlas 10K 9.1	9100	5	Ultra 160/m	PRML24/25	2000k	1000
Atlas 10K II 18.4	18400	4.7	UL 160 SCSI	PRML	8mb	1000
Atlas 10K II 36.7	36700	4.7	UL 160 SCSI	PRML	8mb	1000
Atlas 10K II 73.4	73400	5.2	UL 160 SCSI	PRML	8mb	1000
Atlas 10K II 9.2	9200	4.7	UL 160 SCSI	PRML	8mb	1000
Atlas 10K III 18.4	18400	4.5	UL320 SCSI	PRML 50/53	8mb	1000
Atlas 10K III 36.7	36700	4.5	UL320 SCSI	PRML 50/53	8mb	1000
Atlas 10K III 73.4	73400	4.5	UL320 SCSI	PRML 50/53	8mb	1000
Atlas II XP32275	2275	8	SCSI-3	1,7 RLL	512k	7200
Atlas II XP34550	4550	8	SCSI-3	1,7 RLL	512k	7200
Atlas II XP39100	9100	8	SCSI-3	1,7 RLL	1024k	7200
Atlas III 18.2S	18200	7.5	ULTRA 2 LVD	PRML16,17	1024k	7200
Atlas III 18.2S	18200	7.5	FC	PRML16,17	1024k	7200
Atlas III 18.2S	18200	7.5	UL SE SCSI3	PRML16,17	1024k	7200
Atlas III 4.5S	4550	7.5	UL SE SCSI3	PRML16,17	1024k	7200
Atlas III 4.5S	4550	7.5	FC	PRML16,17	1024k	7200
Atlas III 4.5S	4550	7.5	Ultra 2 LVD	PRML16,17	1024k	7200
Atlas III 9.1S	9100	7.5	FC	PRML16,17	1024k	7200
Atlas III 9.1S	9100	7.5	UL SE SCSI3	PRML16,17	1024k	7200
Atlas III 9.1S	9100	7.5	ULTRA 2 LVD	PRML16,17	1024k	7200
Atlas IV 18.2	18200	6.9	Ultra2	PRML24/25	2000k	7200
Atlas IV 36.4	36400	7.9	Ultra SCSI	PRML24/25	2000k	7200
Atlas IV 9.1	9100	6.9	Ultra 160/m	PRML24/25	2000k	7200
Atlas V 18.3	18300	6.3	UL 160 SCSI	PRML24,25	4mb	7200
Atlas V 36.7	36700	6.3	UL 160 SCSI	PRML24,25	4mb	7200
Atlas V 9.1	9100	6.3	UL 160 SCSI	PRML24,25	4mb	7200
Atlas XP31070S	1075	8	SCSI-2Fast	1,7 RLL	1024k	7200
Atlas XP32150S	2150	8	SCSI-2Fast	1,7 RLL	1024k	7200
Atlas XP34300S	4350	8	SCSI-2Fast	1,7 RLL	1024k	7200
Bigfoot 1275	1275	15.5	ATA-2 Fast	PRML16,17	128k	3600
Bigfoot 2.1	2110	15.5	ATA-2 Fast	PRML16,17	128k	3600
Bigfoot 2550	2550	15.5	ATA-2 Fast	PRML16,17	128k	3600
Bigfoot CY 2.1	2111	<12	ATA-2 Fast		128k	3600
Bigfoot CY 4.3	4335	<14	ATA-2 Fast		128k	3600
Bigfoot CY 6.4	6510	<14	ATA-2 Fast		128k	3600
Bigfoot TS 12.7	12720	10.5	Ultra ATA		512k	4000
Bigfoot TS 19.2	19292	10.5	Ultra ATA		512k	4000
Bigfoot TS 6.4	6418	10.5	Ultra ATA		512k	4000
Bigfoot TS 8.4	8455	10.5	Ultra ATA		512k	4000
Bigfoot TX 12.0	12056	12	Ultra ATA	PRML	128k	4000
Bigfoot TX 4.0	4018	12	Ultra ATA		128k	4000
Bigfoot TX 6.0	6028	12	Ultra ATA		128k	4000
Bigfoot TX 8.0	8037	12	Ultra ATA		128k	4000
Capella VP31110S	1108	9	SCSI-2Fast	1,7 RLL	1024k	5400
Capella VP32210S	2216	9	SCSI-2Fast	1,7 RLL	1024k	5400

Drive Model	Format Size MB	Head	Cyl	Sect/Trac	Translate H/C/S	RWC/WPC	Form Factor	Power Watts
Daytona 127AT	127	2		54-92	9/677/41	NA/NA	2.5 4H	
Daytona 127S	127	2		54-92		NA/NA	2.5 4H	
Daytona 170AT	256	3		54-92	10/538/62	NA/NA	2.5 4H	
Daytona 170S	170	3		54-92		NA/NA	2.5 4H	
Daytona 256AT	256	4		54-92	11/723/63	NA/NA	2.5 4H	
Daytona 256S	256	4		54-92		NA/NA	2.5 4H	
Daytona 341AT	341	6		54-92	15/1011/44	NA/NA	2.5 4H	
Daytona 341S	341	6		54-92		NA/NA	2.5 4H	
Daytona 514AT	514	8		54-92	16/996/63	NA/NA	2.5 4H	
Daytona 514S	514	8		54-92		NA/NA	2.5 4H	
DSP3053LS	535	4		59-119		—/—	3.5 3H	7.5
DSP3107LS	1070	8		59-119		—/—	3.5 3H	8.5
DSP3133LS	1337	10		59-119		—/—	3.5 3H	9.5
DSP3210S	2148	16		59-119		—/—	3.5HH	9.8
ELS127AT	127	3	1536	V	16/919/17	NA/NA	3.5 3H	
ELS127S	127	3	1536	V		NA/NA	3.5 3H	
ELS170AT	170	4	1536	V	15/1011/22	NA/NA	3.5 3H	
ELS170S	170	4	1536	V		NA/NA	3.5 3H	
ELS42AT	42	1	1536	V	5/968/17	NA/NA	3.5 3H	
ELS42S	42	1	1536	V		NA/NA	3.5 3H	
ELS85AT	85	2	1536	V	10/977/17	NA/NA	3.5 3H	
ELS85S	85	2	1536	V		NA/NA	3.5 3H	
Empire 1080S	1080	8				—/—	3.5 3H	
Empire 1400S	1400	8		72-137		—/—	3.5HH	8.2
Empire 2100S	2100	12		72-137		—/—	3.5HH	9.6
Empire 540S	540	4				NA/NA	3.5 3H	
Empire II VP32181S	2180	5				—/—	3.5 3H	
Empire II VP34360S	4360	10				—/—	3.5HH	
Empire II VP39100S	9100	20	3115	86-126		—/—	2.5 4H	1.0
Europa 1080AT	1080	8		66-110	15/2362/60	—/—	2.5 4H	1.0
Europa 540AT	540	4		66-110	15/1179/60	—/—	2.5 4H	1.0
Europa 810AT	810	6		66-110	15/1771/63	—/—	3.5 3H	4.0
Fireball 1080AT	1089	4		88-177	16/2112/63	—/—	3.5 3H	4.0
Fireball 1080S	1093	4		88-177		—/—	3.5 3H	3.8
Fireball 1280AT	1280	4		95-177	16/2484/63	—/—	3.5 3H	3.8
Fireball 1280S	1280	4		95-177		—/—	3.5 3H	3.5
Fireball 540AT	544	2		88-177	16/1056/63	—/—	3.5 3H	3.5
Fireball 540S	545	2		88-177		—/—	3.5 3H	
Fireball 640AT	640	2		95-177	16/1244/63	—/—	3.5 3H	
Fireball 640S	640	2		95-177		—/—	3.5 3H	
Fireball CR 12.7	12700				9/14848/63	—/—	3.5 3H	6.2
Fireball CR 4.3	4310	3			15/13328/63	—/—	3.5 3H	6.2
Fireball CR 6.4	6448	4			16/16383/63	—/—	3.5 3H	6.2
Fireball CR 8.4	8455	6			16/16383/63	—/—	3.5 3H	
Fireball CX 10.2	10275	3			16/16383/63	—/—	3.5 3H	6.2
Fireball CX 13.0	13020	4			16/16383/63	—/—	3.5 3H	
Fireball CX 20.4	20553	6			16/16383/63	—/—	3.5 3H	
Fireball CX 6.4	6448	2			9/14158/63	—/—	3.5 3H	
Fireball EL 10.2	10262	8			16/19885/63	—/—	3.5 3H	6.0
Fireball EL 2.5	2564	2			15/5300/63	—/—	3.5 3H	6.0
Fireball EL 5.1	5130	4			15/10602/63	—/—	3.5 3H	6.0
Fireball EL 7.6	7696	6			15/15907/63	—/—	3.5 3H	6.0
Fireball EX 10.2	10262	6			16/19885/63	—/—	3.5 3H	6.0
Fireball EX 12.7	12750	8			16/24704/63	—/—	3.5 3H	6.0
Fireball EX 3.2	3228	2			16/6256/63	—/—	3.5 3H	6.0
Fireball EX 5.1	5130	3			15/10602/63	—/—	3.5 3H	6.0
Fireball EX 6.4	6448	4			15/13328/63	—/—	3.5 3H	6.0
Fireball Plus AS 10.2	10273	1			15/16383/63	—/—	3.5 3H	7.5
Fireball Plus AS 20.5	20547	2			16/16383/63	—/—	3.5 3H	7.5
Fireball Plus AS 30.0	30020	3			16/16383/63	—/—	3.5 3H	7.5
Fireball Plus AS 40.0	40027	4			16/16383/63	—/—	3.5 3H	7.5
Fireball Plus AS 60.0	60040	6			16/16383/63	—/—	3.5 3H	7.5
Fireball Plus KA 13.6	13699	6			16/16383/63	—/—	3.5 3H	7.5
Fireball Plus KA 18.2	18216	8			15/13328/63	—/—	3.5 3H	7.5
Fireball Plus KA 6.4	6449	3			16/16383/63	—/—	3.5 3H	7.5
Fireball Plus KA 9.1	9132	4			16/16383/63	—/—	3.5 3H	7.5
Fireball Plus KX 10.2	10273	3			16/16383/63	—/—	3.5 3H	7.5

Drive Model	Format Size MB	Seek Time	Interface	Encode	cache kb	RPM
Daytona 127AT	127	17	IDE AT	1,7 RLL	96k	4500
Daytona 127S	127	17	SCSI-2	1,7 RLL	96k	4500
Daytona 170AT	256	17	IDE AT	1,7 RLL	96k	4500
Daytona 170S	170	17	SCSI-2	1,7 RLL	96k	4500
Daytona 256AT	256	17	IDE AT	1,7 RLL	96k	4500
Daytona 256S	256	17	SCSI-2	1,7 RLL	96k	4500
Daytona 341AT	341	17	IDE AT	1,7 RLL	96k	4500
Daytona 341S	341	17	SCSI-2	1,7 RLL	96k	4500
Daytona 514AT	514	17	IDE AT	1,7 RLL	96k	4500
Daytona 514S	514	17	SCSI-2	1,7 RLL	96k	4500
DSP3053LS	535	9.5	SCSI-2Fast	1,7 RLL	512k	5400
DSP3107LS	1070	9.5	SCSI-2Fast	1,7 RLL	512k	5400
DSP3133LS	1337	9.5	SCSI-2Fast	1,7 RLL	512k	5400
DSP3210S	2148	9.5	SCSI-2Fast	1,7 RLL	1024k	5400
ELS127AT	127	17	IDE AT	1,7 RLL	32k	3663
ELS127S	127	17	SCSI	1,7 RLL	32k	3663
ELS170AT	170	17	IDE AT	1,7 RLL	32k	3663
ELS170S	170	17	SCSI	1,7 RLL	32k	3663
ELS42AT	42	19	IDE AT	2,7 RLL		
ELS42S	42	19	SCSI	2,7 RLL		
ELS85AT	85	17	IDE XT	2,7 RLL		
ELS85S	85	17	SCSI	2,7 RLL		
Empire 1080S	1080	9.5	SCSI-3		512k	5400
Empire 1400S	1400	11	SCSI-3Fast	PRML0,4,4	512k	5400
Empire 2100S	2100	11	SCSI-3Fast	PRML0,4,4	512k	5400
Empire 540S	540	9.5	SCSI-3		512k	5400
Empire II VP32181S	2180	9	SCSI-3	PRML	512k	5400
Empire II VP34360S	4360	9	SCSI-3	PRML	512k	5400
Empire II VP39100S	9100	9	SCSI-3	PRML	512k	5400
Europa 1080AT	1080	14	ATA-2 Fast	PRML	128k	3800
Europa 540AT	540	14	ATA-2 Fast	PRML	128k	3800
Europa 810AT	810	14	ATA-2 Fast	PRML	128k	3800
Fireball 1080AT	1089	12	ATA-2 Fast	PRML16,17	128k	5400
Fireball 1080S	1093	12	SCSI-3	PRML	128k	5400
Fireball 1280AT	1280	12	ATA-2 Fast	PRML16,17	128k	5400
Fireball 1280S	1280	12	SCSI-3	PRML16,17	128k	5400
Fireball 540AT	544	12	ATA-2	PRML	128k	5400
Fireball 540S	545	12	SCSI-3	PRML	128k	5400
Fireball 640AT	640	12	ATA-2 Fast	PRML16,17	128k	5400
Fireball 640S	640	12	SCSI-3	PRML16,17	128k	5400
Fireball CR 12.7	12700	9.5	ULTRA ATA66			5400
Fireball CR 4.3	4310	9.5	ULTRA ATA66			5400
Fireball CR 6.4	6448	9.5	ULTRA ATA66		512k	5400
Fireball CR 8.4	8455	9.5	ULTRA ATA66		512k	5400
Fireball CX 10.2	10275	9.5	Ultra ATA66		512k	5400
Fireball CX 13.0	13020	9.5	Ultra ATA66		512k	5400
Fireball CX 20.4	20553	9.5	Ultra ATA66		512k	5400
Fireball CX 6.4	6448	9.5	Ultra ATA66		512k	5400
Fireball EL 10.2	10262	9.5	Ultra ATA	PRML	512k	5400
Fireball EL 2.5	2564	9.5	Ultra ATA		512k	5400
Fireball EL 5.1	5130	9.5	Ultra ATA		512k	5400
Fireball EL 7.6	7696	9.5	Ultra ATA		512k	5400
Fireball EX 10.2	10262	9.5	Ultra ATA		512k	5400
Fireball EX 12.7	12750	9.5	Ultra ATA		512k	5400
Fireball EX 3.2	3228	9.5	Ultra ATA		512k	5400
Fireball EX 5.1	5130	9.5	Ultra ATA		512k	5400
Fireball EX 6.4	6448	9.5	Ultra ATA		512k	5400
Fireball Plus AS 10.2	10273	8.5	UltraATA100		2mb	7200
Fireball Plus AS 20.5	20547	8.5	UltraATA100		2mb	7200
Fireball Plus AS 30.0	30020	8.5	UltraATA100		2mb	7200
Fireball Plus AS 40.0	40027	8.5	UltraATA100		2mb	7200
Fireball Plus AS 60.0	60040	8.5	UltraATA100		2mb	7200
Fireball Plus KA 13.6	13699	8.5	ULTRA ATA66		512k	7200
Fireball Plus KA 18.2	18216	8.5	ULTRA ATA66		512k	7200
Fireball Plus KA 6.4	6449	8.5	ULTRA ATA66		512k	7200
Fireball Plus KA 9.1	9132	8.5	ULTRA ATA66		512k	7200
Fireball Plus KX 10.2	10273	8.5	ATA-4		512k	7200

Hard Drive Specs 687

Drive Model	Format Size MB	Head	Cyl	Sect/Trac	Translate H/C/S	RWC/WPC	Form Factor	Power Watts
Fireball Plus KX 13.6	13698	4			16/16383/63	—/—	3.5 3H	7.5
Fireball Plus KX 20.5	20547	6			16/16383/63	—/—	3.5 3H	7.5
Fireball Plus KX 27.3	27397	8			16/16383/63	—/—	3.5 3H	7.5
Fireball Plus KX 6.8	6849	2			15/13328/63	—/—	3.5 3H	7.5
Fireball Plus LM 10.2	10273	2			15/16383/63	—/—	3.5 3H	6.9
Fireball Plus LM 15.0	15020	3			16/16383/63	—/—	3.5 3H	6.9
Fireball Plus LM 20.5	20547	4			16/16383/63	—/—	3.5 3H	6.9
Fireball Plus LM 30.0	30020	6			16/16383/63	—/—	3.5 3H	6.9
Fireball SE 2.1AT	2111	2			16/4092/63	—/—	3.5 3H	
Fireball SE 2.1S	2111	2				—/—	3.5 3H	
Fireball SE 3.2AT	3228	3			16/6256/63	—/—	3.5 3H	
Fireball SE 3.2S	3228	3				—/—	3.5 3H	
Fireball SE 4.3AT	4310	4			9/14848/63	—/—	3.5 3H	
Fireball SE 4.3S	4310	4				—/—	3.5 3H	
Fireball SE 6.4AT	6448	6			15/13328/63	—/—	3.5 3H	
Fireball SE 6.4S	6448	6				—/—	3.5 3H	
Fireball SE 8.4AT	8455	8			16/16383/63	—/—	3.5 3H	
Fireball SE 8.4S	8455	8				—/—	3.5 3H	
Fireball ST 1.6	1614	2			16/3128/63	—/—	3.5 3H	6.0
Fireball ST 2.1	2111	3				—/—	3.5 3H	6.0
Fireball ST 3.2AT	3228	4			16/6256/63	—/—	3.5 3H	6.0
Fireball ST 3.2S	3228	4				—/—	3.5 3H	6.0
Fireball ST 4.3AT	4310	6			9/14848/63	—/—	3.5 3H	6.0
Fireball ST 4.3S	4310	6				—/—	3.5 3H	6.0
Fireball ST 6.4AT	6448	8			15/13328/63	—/—	3.5 3H	6.0
Fireball ST 6.4S	6448	8				—/—	3.5 3H	6.0
Fireball TM 1.0	1089	2		104-23	16/2112/63	—/—	3.5 3H	3.8
Fireball TM 1.2AT	1281	2		104-23	16/2484/63	—/—	3.5 3H	3.8
Fireball TM 1.2S	1281	2		104-23		—/—	3.5 3H	3.8
Fireball TM 2.1AT	2111	4		104-23	16/4092/63	—/—	3.5 3H	3.8
Fireball TM 2.1S	2111	4		104-23		—/—	3.5 3H	3.8
Fireball TM 2.5AT	2564	4		104-23	16/4969/63	—/—	3.5 3H	3.8
Fireball TM 3.2AT	3216	5		104-23	16/6232/63	—/—	3.5 3H	3.8
Fireball TM 3.2S	3216	5		104-23		—/—	3.5 3H	3.8
Fireball TM 3.8AT	3860	6		104-23	16/7480/63	—/—	3.5 3H	3.8
Fireball.lct08 13.0	13021	3			16/25392/63	—/—	3.5 3H	5.0
Fireball.lct08 17.3	17362	4			16/33863/63	—/—	3.5 3H	5.0
Fireball.lct08 26.0	26043	6			16/50298/63	—/—	3.5 3H	5.0
Fireball.lct08 4.3	4340	1			9/15049/63	—/—	3.5 3H	5.0
Fireball.lct08 8.4	8681	2			16/16931/63	—/—	3.5 3H	5.0
Fireball.lct10 10.2	10262	2			16/16383/63	—/—	3.5 3H	5.0
Fireball.lct10 15.0	15020	3			16/16383/63	—/—	3.5 3H	5.0
Fireball.lct10 20.4	20416	4			16/16383/63	—/—	3.5 3H	5.0
Fireball.lct10 30.04	30020	6			16/16383/63	—/—	3.5 3H	5.0
Fireball.lct10 5.1	5121	1			15/10585/63	—/—	3.5 3H	5.0
Fireball.lct15 10.0	15020				16/16383/63	—/—	3.5 3H	
Fireball.lct15 20.4	20416				16/16383/63	—/—	3.5 3H	
Fireball.lct15 30.0	30020				16/16383/63	—/—	3.5 3H	
Fireball.lct15 7.5	4510				15/14552/63	—/—	3.5 3H	
Fireball.lct20 10.0	10262	1			16/16383/63	—/—	3.5 3H	5.0
Fireball.lct20 20.0	20416	2			16/16383/63	—/—	3.5 3H	5.0
Fireball.lct20 30.0	30020	3			16/16383/63	—/—	3.5 3H	5.0
Fireball.lct20 40.0	40027	4			16/16383/63	—/—	3.5 3H	5.0
Godrive 120AT	127	4	1097	V	13/731/26	NA/NA	2.5 3H	
Godrive 120S	127	4	1097	V		NA/NA	2.5 3H	
Godrive 40AT	43	2	957		6/820/17	—/—	2.5 4H	4.5
Godrive 40S	43	2	957			—/—	2.5 4H	4.5
Godrive 60AT	63	2	1097	V	9/526/26	NA/NA	2.5 3H	
Godrive 60S	63	2				NA/NA	2.5 4H	
Godrive 80AT	84	2		NA	10/991/17	NA/NA	2.5 4H	
Godrive 80S	84	2				NA/NA	2.5 4H	
Godrive GLS127AT	127	3			9/677/41	NA/NA	2.5	
Godrive GLS127S	127	3				NA/NA	2.5	
Godrive GLS170AT	170	4			10/538/62	NA/NA	2.5	
Godrive GLS170S	170	4				NA/NA	2.5	
Godrive GLS256AT	256	6			11/723/63	NA/NA	2.5	
Godrive GLS256S	256	6				NA/NA	2.5	

Drive Model	Format Size MB	Seek Time	Interface	Encode	cache kb	RPM
Fireball Plus KX 13.6	13698	8.5	ATA-4		512k	7200
Fireball Plus KX 20.5	20547	8.5	ATA-4		512k	7200
Fireball Plus KX 27.3	27397	8.5	ATA-4		512k	7200
Fireball Plus KX 6.8	6849	8.5	ATA-4		512k	7200
Fireball Plus LM 10.2	10273	8.5	ATA-4		2mb	7200
Fireball Plus LM 15.0	15020	8.5	ATA-4		2mb	7200
Fireball Plus LM 20.5	20547	8.5	ATA-4		2mb	7200
Fireball Plus LM 30.0	30020	8.5	ATA-4		2mb	7200
Fireball SE 2.1AT	2111	9.5	ULTRA ATA		128k	5400
Fireball SE 2.1S	2111	9.5	Ultra SCSI3		128k	5400
Fireball SE 3.2AT	3228	9.5	ULTRA ATA		128k	5400
Fireball SE 3.2S	3228	9.5	ULTRA SCSI3		128k	5400
Fireball SE 4.3AT	4310	9.5	ULTRA ATA		128k	5400
Fireball SE 4.3S	4310	9.5	ULTRA SCSI3		128k	5400
Fireball SE 6.4AT	6448	9.5	ULTRA ATA		128k	5400
Fireball SE 6.4S	6448	9.5	ULTRA SCSI3		128k	5400
Fireball SE 8.4AT	8455	9.5	ULTRA ATA		128k	5400
Fireball SE 8.4S	8455	9.5	ULTRA SCSI3		128k	5400
Fireball ST 1.6	1614	<10	ULTRA ATA		128k	5400
Fireball ST 2.1	2111	<10	ULTRA SCSI3		128k	5400
Fireball ST 3.2AT	3228	<10	ULTRA ATA		128k	5400
Fireball ST 3.2S	3228	<10	ULTRA SCSI3		128k	5400
Fireball ST 4.3AT	4310	<10	ULTRA ATA		128k	5400
Fireball ST 4.3S	4310	<10	ULTRA SCSI3		128k	5400
Fireball ST 6.4AT	6448	<10	ULTRA ATA		128k	5400
Fireball ST 6.4S	6448	<10	ULTRA SCSI3		128k	5400
Fireball TM 1.0	1089	12	ATA-2 Fast	PRML16,17	128k	4500
Fireball TM 1.2AT	1281	12	ATA-2 Fast	PRML16,17	128k	4500
Fireball TM 1.2S	1281	12	ULTRA SCSI3	PRML16,17	128k	4500
Fireball TM 2.1AT	2111	10.5	ULTRA ATA	PRML16,17	128k	4500
Fireball TM 2.1S	2111	10.5	ULTRA SCSI3	PRML16,17	128k	4500
Fireball TM 2.5AT	2564	10.5	ULTRA ATA	PRML16,17	128k	4500
Fireball TM 3.2AT	3216	10.5	ULTRA ATA	PRML16,17	128k	4500
Fireball TM 3.2S	3216	10.5	ULTRA SCSI3	PRML16,17	128k	4500
Fireball TM 3.8AT	3860	10.5	ULTRA ATA	PRML16,17	128k	4500
Fireball.lct08 13.0	13021	9.5	Ultra ATA66		512k	5400
Fireball.lct08 17.3	17362	9.5	Ultra ATA66		512k	5400
Fireball.lct08 26.0	26043	9.5	Ultra ATA66		512k	5400
Fireball.lct08 4.3	4340	9.5	Ultra ATA66		512k	5400
Fireball.lct08 8.4	8681	9.5	Ultra ATA66		512k	5400
Fireball.lct10 10.2	10262	8.9	Ultra ATA66		512k	5400
Fireball.lct10 15.0	15020	8.9	Ultra ATA66		512k	5400
Fireball.lct10 20.4	20416	8.9	Ultra ATA66		512k	5400
Fireball.lct10 30.04	30020	8.9	Ultra ATA66		512k	5400
Fireball.lct10 5.1	5121	8.9	Ultra ATA66		512k	5400
Fireball.lct15 15.0	15020	12	UltraATA/33		512k	7200
Fireball.lct15 20.4	20416	12	UltraATA/33		512k	7200
Fireball.lct15 30.0	30020	12	UltraATA/33		512k	7200
Fireball.lct15 7.5	4510	12	UltraATA/33		512k	7200
Fireball.lct20 10.0	10262	12	UltraATA100		128k	
Fireball.lct20 20.0	20416	12	UltraATA100		128k	
Fireball.lct20 30.0	30020	12	UltraATA100		128k	
Fireball.lct20 40.0	40027	12	UltraATA100		128k	
Godrive 120AT	127	17	IDE AT	1,7 RLL	32k	
Godrive 120S	127	17	SCSI	1,7 RLL	32k	
Godrive 40AT	43	19	IDE AT	1,7 RLL	32k	
Godrive 40S	43	19	SCSI	1,7 RLL	32k	
Godrive 60AT	63	19	IDE AT	1,7 RLL		
Godrive 60S	63	17	SCSI	1,7 RLL		
Godrive 80AT	84	19	IDE AT	1,7 RLL		
Godrive 80S	84	17	SCSI	1,7 RLL		
Godrive GLS127AT	127	17	IDE AT		128k	
Godrive GLS127S	127	17	SCSI-2		128k	
Godrive GLS170AT	170	17	IDE AT		128k	
Godrive GLS170S	170	17	SCSI-2		128k	
Godrive GLS256AT	256	17	IDE AT		128k	
Godrive GLS256S	256	17	SCSI-2		128k	

Drive Model	Format Size MB	Head	Cyl	Sect/Trac	Translate H/C/S	RWC/WPC	Form Factor	Power Watts
Godrive GLS85AT	85	2			10/722/23	NA/NA	2.5	
Godrive GLS85S	85	2				NA/NA	2.5	
Godrive GRS160AT	169	4			10/966/34	NA/NA	2.5	
Godrive GRS160S	169	4				NA/NA	2.5	
Godrive GRS80AT	84	2		45-73	5/966/34	NA/NA	2.5 4H	
Godrive GRS80S	84	2				NA/NA	2.5	
GrandPrix XP32140S	2140	10				—/—	3.5HH	
GrandPrix XP32151S	2150	10		118		—/—	3.5HH	10
GrandPrix XP34280S	4280	20				—/—	3.5HH	
GrandPrix XP34301S	4300	20		118		—/—	3.5HH	14
HardCard EZ 42	42	5	977	17		NA/NA		
Lightning 365AT	366	2		61-128	12/976/61	NA/NA	3.5 3H	
Lightning 365S	365	2		64-128		NA/NA	3.5 3H	
Lightning 540AT	541	4		61-128	16/1120/59	NA/NA	3.5 3H	
Lightning 540S	541	3		64-128		NA/NA	3.5 3H	
Lightning 730AT	731	4		61-128	16/1416/63	NA/NA	3.5 3H	
Lightning 730S	732	4		54-128		NA/NA	3.5 3H	
Maverick 270AT	271	2		58-118	14/944/40	NA/NA	3.5 3H	
Maverick 270S	271	2		58-118		NA/NA	3.5 3H	
Maverick 540AT	541	4		58-118	16/1049/63	NA/NA	3.5 3H	
Maverick 540S	542	4		58-118		NA/NA	3.5 3H	
Pioneer SG 1.0	1082	2			16/2097/63	—/—	3.5 3H	3.7
Pioneer SG 2.1	2111	4			16/4092/63	—/—	3.5 3H	3.7
Prodrive 525S	525	6	2446	NA		NA/NA	3.5HH	
Prodrive 100E	103					NA/NA	3.5HH	
Prodrive 1050S	1050	12	2442	NA		NA/NA	3.5HH	
Prodrive 105AT	104	4	1219	17	16/755/17	NA/NA	3.5HH	9
Prodrive 105S	105	6	1019			—/—	3.5HH	9
Prodrive 120AT	120	5	1123		9/814/32	NA/NA	3.5HH	12
Prodrive 120S	120	5	1123			NA/NA	3.5HH	12
Prodrive 1225S	1225	14	2444	NA		NA/NA	3.5HH	
Prodrive 145E	145					NA/NA	3.5HH	
Prodrive 160AT	168	4	839			NA/NA	3.5 4H	
Prodrive 160S	168	4	839			NA/NA	3.5 4H	
Prodrive 170AT	168	7	1123		10/968/34	NA/NA	3.5HH	12
Prodrive 170S	168	7	1123			—/—	3.5HH	12
Prodrive 1800S	1800	14				NA/NA	3.5HH	
Prodrive 210AT	209	7	1156		13/873/36	NA/NA	3.5HH	12.6
Prodrive 210S	210	7	1156			—/—	3.5HH	11.4
Prodrive 330AT	331	7	1156			—/—	3.5HH	11.4
Prodrive 330S	331	7	1156		5/965/17	NA/NA	3.5HH	9
Prodrive 40AT	42	3	834			—/—	3.5HH	9
Prodrive 40S	42	3	834			NA/NA	3.5HH	
Prodrive 425AT	426	9	1520	V	16/1021/51	NA/NA	3.5HH	11.8
Prodrive 425S	426	9				—/—	3.5HH	11.8
Prodrive 700S	700	8	2443	NA		NA/NA	3.5HH	
Prodrive 80AT	84	6	834	35	10/965/17	NA/NA	3.5HH	9
Prodrive 80S	84	6	834	35		NA/NA	3.5HH	9
Prodrive LPS105AT	105	4	1219		16/755/17	NA/NA	3.5 3H	5.5
Prodrive LPS105S	105	4	1219			—/—	3.5 3H	5.5
Prodrive LPS120AT	122	2			5/901/53	NA/NA	3.5 3H	
Prodrive LPS120S	122	2	1818			—/—	3.5 3H	
Prodrive LPS127AT	128	2		65-91	16/919/17	NA/NA	3.5 3H	
Prodrive LPS127S	127	2				NA/NA	3.5 3H	
Prodrive LPS170AT	171	2		52-91	15/1011/22	NA/NA	3.5 3H	
Prodrive LPS170S	170	2				NA/NA	3.5 3H	
Prodrive LPS210AT	211	2		55-104	15/723/38	NA/NA	3.5 3H	
Prodrive LPS240AT	245	4			13/723/51	NA/NA	3.5 3H	
Prodrive LPS240S	245	4	1818	V	13/723/51	NA/NA	3.5 3H	
Prodrive LPS270AT	270	2		V	14/944/40	NA/NA	3.5 3H	
Prodrive LPS270S	270	2				NA/NA	3.5 3H	
Prodrive LPS340AT	342	4			15/1011/44	NA/NA	3.5 3H	
Prodrive LPS340S	342	4				NA/NA	3.5 3H	
Prodrive LPS420AT	420	4		55-104	16/1010/51	NA/NA	3.5 3H	
Prodrive LPS525AT	525	6			16/1017/63	NA/NA	3.5 3H	
Prodrive LPS525S	525	6				NA/NA	3.5 3H	
Prodrive LPS52AT	52	2	1219		8/751/17	NA/NA	3.5 3H	5.5

Drive Model	Format Size MB	Seek Time	Interface	Encode	cache kb	RPM
Godrive GLS85AT	85	17	IDE AT		128k	
Godrive GLS85S	85	17	SCSI-2		128k	
Godrive GRS160AT	169	17	IDE AT		32k	
Godrive GRS160S	169	17	SCSI		32k	
Godrive GRS80AT	84	17	IDE AT	1,7 RLL	32k	
Godrive GRS80S	84	17	SCSI		32k	3600
GrandPrix XP32140S	2140	9	SCSI-3Fast		512k	7200
GrandPrix XP32151S	2150	10	SCSI-3	PRML0,4,4	512k	7200
GrandPrix XP34280S	4280	9	SCSI-3Fast		512k	7200
GrandPrix XP34301S	4300	10	SCSI-3	PRML0,4,4	512k	7200
HardCard EZ 42	42		IDE AT			
Lightning 365AT	366	11	IDE AT	1,7 RLL	128k	4500
Lightning 365S	365	11	SCSI-2	1,7 RLL	128k	4500
Lightning 540AT	541	11.5	IDE AT	1,7 RLL	128k	4500
Lightning 540S	541	11.5	SCSI-2	1,7 RLL	128k	4500
Lightning 730AT	731	11.5	IDE AT	1,7 RLL	128k	4500
Lightning 730S	732	11.5	SCSI-2	1,7 RLL	128k	4500
Maverick 270AT	271	14	IDE AT	1,7 RLL	128k	3600
Maverick 270S	271	14	SCSI-2	1,7 RLL	128k	3600
Maverick 540AT	541	14	IDE AT	1,7 RLL	128k	3600
Maverick 540S	542	14	SCSI-2	1,7 RLL	128k	3600
Pioneer SG 1.0	1082	12	ATA-2 Fast		64k	4500
Pioneer SG 2.1	2111	12	ATA-2 Fast		64k	4500
Prodrie 525S	525		SCSI			
Prodrive 100E	103	19	ESDI	2,7 RLL		
Prodrive 1050S	1050	10	SCSI		512k	4500
Prodrive 105AT	104	17	IDE AT	2,7 RLL		
Prodrive 105S	105	19	SCSI	2,7 RLL	64k	
Prodrive 120AT	120	15	IDE AT	1,7 RLL	64k	3605
Prodrive 120S	120	15	SCSI	1,7 RLL	64k	
Prodrive 1225S	1225	10	SCSI		512k	4500
Prodrive 145E	145	19	ESDI			
Prodrive 160AT	168	19	IDE AT	1,7 RLL		
Prodrive 160S	168	19	SCSI	1,7 RLL		
Prodrive 170AT	168	15	IDE AT	1,7 RLL	56k	3605
Prodrive 170S	168	15	SCSI	1,7 RLL	64k	
Prodrive 1800S	1800	10	SCSI		512k	4500
Prodrive 210AT	209	15	IDE AT	1,7 RLL	56k	3605
Prodrive 210S	210	15	SCSI	1,7 RLL	64k	3606
Prodrive 330AT	331	14	IDE AT	1,7 RLL	64k	3606
Prodrive 330S	331	14	SCSI	1,7 RLL	64k	
Prodrive 40AT	42	19	IDE AT	2,7 RLL	64k	
Prodrive 40S	42	19	SCSI	2,7 RLL	64k	
Prodrive 425AT	426	14	IDE AT	1,7 RLL	56k	3606
Prodrive 425S	426	14	SCSI	1,7 RLL	64k	3606
Prodrive 700S	700	10	SCSI		512k	4500
Prodrive 80AT	84	19	IDE AT	2,7 RLL	64k	
Prodrive 80S	84	19	SCSI	2,7 RLL	64k	
Prodrive LPS105AT	105	17	IDE AT	2,7 RLL	64k	
Prodrive LPS105S	105	17	SCSI	2,7 RLL	64k	
Prodrive LPS120AT	122	16	IDE AT	1,7 RLL	256k	
Prodrive LPS120S	122	16	SCSI	1,7 RLL	256k	4306
Prodrive LPS127AT	128	14	IDE AT	1,7 RLL	128k	3600
Prodrive LPS127S	127	14	SCSI-2	1,7 RLL	128k	3600
Prodrive LPS170AT	171	14	IDE AT	1,7 RLL	128k	3600
Prodrive LPS170S	170	14	SCSI-2	1,7 RLL	128k	3600
Prodrive LPS210AT	211	15	IDE AT	1,7 RLL	128k	3600
Prodrive LPS240AT	245	16	IDE AT	1,7 RLL	256k	4306
Prodrive LPS240S	245	17	SCSI	1,7 RLL	256k	4306
Prodrive LPS270AT	270	14	IDE AT	1,7 RLL	128k	3600
Prodrive LPS270S	270	12	SCSI-2	1,7 RLL	128k	4500
Prodrive LPS340AT	342	12	IDE AT		128k	3600
Prodrive LPS340S	342	12	SCSI-2		128k	3600
Prodrive LPS420AT	420	13	IDE AT	1,7 RLL	128k	3600
Prodrive LPS525AT	525	10	IDE AT		512k	4500
Prodrive LPS525S	525	10	SCSI		512k	4500
Prodrive LPS52AT	52	17	IDE AT	2,7 RLL	64k	

Drive Model	Format Size MB	Head	Cyl	Sect/Trac	Translate H/C/S	RWC/WPC	Form Factor	Power Watts
Prodrive LPS52S	52	2	1219			—/—	3.5 3H	5.5
Prodrive LPS540AT	541	4		V	16/1120/59	NA/NA	3.5 3H	
Prodrive LPS540S	541	4				NA/NA	3.5 3H	
Prodrive LPS80AT	85				16/616/17	NA/NA	3.5 3H	
Prodrive LPS80S	86	4				NA/NA	3.5 3H	
Saturn VP31080S	1080	5				—/—	3.5 3H	0.2
Saturn VP32170S	2170	10				—/—	3.5 3H	0.26
Sirocco 1700AT	1700	4		90-180	16/3309/63	NA/NA	3.5 3H	
Sirocco 1700S	1700	4		90-180		NA/NA	3.5 3H	
Sirocco 2550AT	2550	6		90-180	16/4969/63	NA/NA	3.5 3H	
Sirocco 2550S	2550	6		90-180		NA/NA	3.5 3H	
Trailblazer 420AT	422	2		76-141	16/1010/51	—/—	3.5 3H	3.3
Trailblazer 420S	425	2		76-141		—/—	3.5 3H	3.3
Trailblazer 635AT	636	3		76-141	16/1234/63	—/—	3.5 3H	3.3
Trailblazer 635S	636	3		76-141		—/—	3.5 3H	3.3
Trailblazer 850AT	850	4		76-141	16/1647/63	—/—	3.5 3H	3.3
Trailblazer 850S	852	4		76-141		—/—	3.5 3H	3.3
Viking 2.1S	2180	4				—/—	3.5 3H	
Viking 4.3S	4360	8				—/—	3.5 3H	
Viking II 4.5 1-98	4550	5				—/—	3.5 3H	7.0
Viking II 4.5 1-98	4550	5				—/—	3.5 3H	7.0
Viking II 9.1 1-98	9100	10				—/—	3.5 3H	9.0
Viking II 9.1 1-98	9100	10				—/—	3.5 3H	9.0

RICOH

Drive Model	Format Size MB	Head	Cyl	Sect/Trac	Translate H/C/S	RWC/WPC	Form Factor	Power Watts
RH5130	10	2	612	17		613/400		
RH5260	10	2	615	17		—/—		
RH5261	10	2	612	17		—/—		
RH5500	100	2	1285	76		NA/NA	5.25HH	
RS9150AR	100	2	1285	76		NA/NA	5.25HH	

RMS

Drive Model	Format Size MB	Head	Cyl	Sect/Trac	Translate H/C/S	RWC/WPC	Form Factor	Power Watts
RMS503	2.5	2	153	17		77/77	5.25	
RMS506	5	4	153	17		77/77	5.25	
RMS509	8	6	153	17		77/77	5.25FH	
RMS512	10	8	153	17		77/77	5.25	

RODIME SYSTEMS, INC

Drive Model	Format Size MB	Head	Cyl	Sect/Trac	Translate H/C/S	RWC/WPC	Form Factor	Power Watts
Cobra 1000E (Mac)	1000					—/—		30
Cobra 110AT	110	4				—/—	3.5HH	
Cobra 210AT	210	5				—/—	3.5HH	
Cobra 330E (Mac)	330					—/—		30
Cobra 40AT	40	2	1170	36	4/585/36	—/—	3.5HH	
Cobra 650E (Mac)	650					—/—		30
Cobra 80AT	80	4	1159	36	8/579/36	—/—	3.5HH	
RO101	6	2	192	17		96/192	5.25HH	
RO102	12	4	192	17		96/192	5.25HH	
RO103	18	6	192	17		96/192	5.25HH	
RO104	24	8	192	17		96/192	5.25HH	
RO200	11	4	320	17		—/132	5.25FH	
RO201	5	2	321	17		132/300	5.25FH	
RO201E	11	2	640	17		264/300	5.25FH	
RO202	10	4	321	17		132/300	5.25FH	
RO202E	21	4	640	17		264/300	5.25FH	
RO203	15	6	321	17		132/300	5.25FH	
RO203E	32	6	640	17		264/300	5.25FH	
RO204	21	8	320	17		132/300	5.25FH	
RO204E	43	8	640	17		264/300	5.25FH	
RO251	5	2	306	17		307/307	5.25HH	
RO252	11	4	306	17		64/128	5.25HH	
RO3045	37	5	872	17		873/—	3.5HH	
RO3055	45	6	872	17		873/—	3.5HH	
RO3055A	49					—/—	3.5HH	
RO3055T	45	3	1053	26		NA/NA	3.5HH	
RO3057S	45	5	680			—/—	3.5HH	
RO3058A	45	3	868	17	3/868/34	—/—	3.5HH	
RO3058T	45	3	868	17		—/—	3.5HH	
RO3059A	46	2	1216	17		—/—	3.5HH	

Drive Model	Format Size MB	Seek Time	Interface	Encode	cache kb	RPM
Prodrive LPS52S	52	17	SCSI	2,7 RLL	64k	
Prodrive LPS540AT	541	14	IDE AT	1,7 RLL	128k	3600
Prodrive LPS540S	541	12	SCSI-2	1,7 RLL	128k	4500
Prodrive LPS80AT	85		IDE AT			
Prodrive LPS80S	86	19	SCSI	2,7 RLL		
Saturn VP31080S	1080	8.5	SCSI-2	1,7 RLL	512k	5400
Saturn VP32170S	2170	8.5	SCSI-3Fast	1,7 RLL	512k	5400
Sirocco 1700AT	1700	11	ATA-2	PRML16,17	128k	4500
Sirocco 1700S	1700	11	SCSI-2	PRML16,17	128k	4500
Sirocco 2550AT	2550	11	ATA-2	PRML16,17	128k	4500
Sirocco 2550S	2550	11	SCSI-3	PRML16,17	128k	4500
Trailblazer 420AT	422	14	ATA-2 Fast	1,7 RLL	128k	4500
Trailblazer 420S	425	14	SCSI-2Fast	1,7 RLL	128k	4500
Trailblazer 635AT	636	14	ATA-2 Fast	1,7 RLL	128k	4500
Trailblazer 635S	636	14	SCSI-3	1,7 RLL	128k	4500
Trailblazer 850AT	850	14	ATA-2 Fast	1,7 RLL	128k	4500
Trailblazer 850S	852	14	SCSI-2Fast	1,7 RLL	128k	4500
Viking 2.1S	2180	8.5	Ultra SCSI3	1,7 RLL	128k	4500
Viking 4.3S	4360	8.5	Ultra SCSI3		512k	7200
Viking II 4.5 1-98	4550	8	ULTRA 2 LVD	PRML16,17	512k	7200
Viking II 4.5 1-98	4550	8	UL SE SCSI3	PRML16,17	512k	7200
Viking II 9.1 1-98	9100	8	UL SE SCSI3	PRML16,17	512k	7200
Viking II 9.1 1-98	9100	8	ULTRA 2 LVD	PRML16,17	512k	7200

RICOH

Drive Model	Format Size MB	Seek Time	Interface	Encode	cache kb	RPM
RH5130	10	85	ST412/506	MFM		
RH5260	10	85	ST412/506	MFM		
RH5261	10	85	SCSI	MFM		
RH5500	100	25	SCSI	2,7 RLL		
RS9150AR	100	25	SCSI	2,7 RLL		

RMS

Drive Model	Format Size MB	Seek Time	Interface	Encode	cache kb	RPM
RMS503	2.5		ST412/506	MFM		
RMS506	5		ST412/506	MFM		
RMS509	8		ST412/506	MFM		
RMS512	10		ST412/506	MFM		

RODIME SYSTEMS, INC

Drive Model	Format Size MB	Seek Time	Interface	Encode	cache kb	RPM
Cobra 1000E (Mac)	1000	15	SCSI			
Cobra 110AT	110	19	IDE AT	2,7 RLL	45k	3600
Cobra 210AT	210		IDE AT	2,7 RLL		
Cobra 330E (Mac)	330	14.5	SCSI			
Cobra 40AT	40	19	IDE AT	2,7 RLL	45k	3600
Cobra 650E (Mac)	650	16.5	SCSI	2,7 RLL		
Cobra 80AT	80	20	IDE AT	2,7 RLL	45k	3600
RO101	6		ST412/506	MFM		
RO102	12		ST412/506	MFM		
RO103	18	55	ST412/506	MFM		
RO104	24		ST412/506	MFM		
RO200	11		ST412/506	MFM		
RO201	5	85	ST412/506	MFM		
RO201E	11	55	ST412/506	MFM		
RO202	10	85	ST412/506	MFM		
RO202E	21	55	ST412/506	MFM		
RO203	15	85	ST412/506	MFM		
RO203E	32	55	ST412/506	MFM		
RO204	21	85	ST412/506	MFM		
RO204E	43	55	ST412/506	MFM		
RO251	5	85	ST412/506	MFM		
RO252	11	85	ST412/506	MFM		
RO3045	37	28	ST412/506	MFM		
RO3055	45	28	ST412/506	MFM		
RO3055A	49		IDE AT	2,7 RLL		
RO3055T	45		SCSI	RLL		
RO3057S	45	28	SCSI	2,7 RLL		
RO3058A	45	18	IDE AT	2,7 RLL		
RO3058T	45	18	SCSI	2,7 RLL		
RO3059A	46	18	IDE AT	2,7 RLL		

Drive Model	Format Size MB	Head	Cyl	Sect/Trac	Translate H/C/S	RWC/WPC	Form Factor	Power Watts
RO3059T	46	2	1216	34		—/—	3.5HH	
RO3060R	50	2	1216	17		—/—	3.5HH	
RO3065	53	7	872	17		—/650	3.5HH	
RO3070S	71					—/—	3.5HH	
RO3075R	59	6	750			—/650	3.5HH	
RO3085R	69	7	750			—/650	3.5HH	
RO3085S	69	7	750			—/650	3.5HH	
RO3088A	75	5	868	34	5/868/34	—/—	3.5HH	
RO3088T	75	5	868	34		—/—	3.5HH	
RO3089A	70	3	1216	34		—/—	3.5HH	
RO3089T	70	3	1216	34		—/—	3.5HH	
RO3090T	75	5	1053	28		NA/NA	3.5HH	
RO3095A	80	3	1216	34	5/923/34	—/—	3.5HH	
RO3099A	80	4	1030		15/614/17	NA/NA	3.5HH	
RO3099AP	80	4	1030		15/614/17	NA/NA	3.5HH	
RO3128A	105	7	868	34		—/—	3.5HH	
RO3128T	105	7	868	17		—/—	3.5HH	
RO3129A	105	5	1090			—/—	3.5HH	
RO3129T	105	5	1090	17		—/—	3.5HH	
RO3130S	105	7	1047	30		—/—	5.25HH	
RO3130T	105	7	1053	28		NA/NA	5.25HH	
RO3135A	112	7	923	34	7/923/34	—/—	3.5HH	
RO3139A	112	5	1168	17	15/861/17	—/—	3.5HH	
RO3139AP	112	5	1168		15/861/17	NA/NA	3.5HH	
RO3139S	112	5	1148			NA/NA	3.5HH	
RO3139TP	112	5	1148			NA/NA	3.5HH	
RO3258TS	210					—/—	3.5HH	
RO3259A	210				15/976/28	—/—	3.5HH	
RO3259AP	212	9	1235		15/990/28	NA/NA	3.5HH	
RO3259T	210					—/—	3.5HH	
RO3259TP	210	9	1148	V		NA/NA	3.5HH	
RO3259TS	210	9	1216			NA/NA	3.5HH	
RO351	5	2	306	17		307/307	3.5HH	
RO352	11	4	306	17		64/128	3.5HH	
RO365	21	4	612	17		613/613	3.5HH	
RO5040S	38	3		17		—/—	5.25HH	
RO5065	63	5		17		—/—	5.25HH	
RO5075E	65	3	1224	35		NA/NA	5.25HH	
RO5075S	76					—/—	5.25HH	
RO5078S	62	3	1224	33		NA/NA	5.25HH	
RO5090	89	7	1224	17		—/—	5.25HH	
RO5095R	81	5	1224	26		NA/NA	5.25HH	
RO5125-1F2	106	5	1219	34		NA/NA	5.25HH	
RO5125E	106	5	1224	34		—/—	5.25HH	
RO5125S	106	5	1219	34		NA/NA	5.25HH	
RO5128S	103	5	1224	33		NA/NA	5.25HH	
RO5130R	114	7	1224	26		—/—	5.25FH	
RO5178S	144	7	1219			—/—	5.25HH	
RO5180-1F2	148	7	1219	34		NA/NA	5.25HH	
RO5180E	149	7	1224	34		—/—	5.25HH	
RO5180S	144	7	1219	34		—/—	5.25HH	
RO652	20	4	306	33		NA/NA	3.5HH	
RO652A	20					—/—	3.5HH	
RO652B	20	4	306	33		—/—	3.5HH	
RO752	20	4	306	33		NA/NA	5.25HH	
RO752A	25					—/—	5.25HH	

SAMSUNG

Drive Model	Format Size MB	Head	Cyl	Sect/Trac	Translate H/C/S	RWC/WPC	Form Factor	Power Watts
ACB20811A (Rel. 10-96)	810					—/—	2.5	
ACE21021A (Rel. 10-96)	1020					—/—	2.5	
MP0302H	30GB					—/—	2.5 4H	0.85
MP0402H	40GB					—/—	2.5 4H	0.85
MP0603H	60GB					—/—	2.5 4H	0.85
MP0804H	80GB					—/—	2.5 4H	0.85
PLS30424A	420				16/823/63	—/—	3.5 3H	
PLS30540A	547	3			16/1024/63	—/—	3.5 3H	
PLS30730A	731	4				—/—	3.5 3H	
PLS30850A	731	4				—/—	3.5 3H	

Drive Model	Format Size MB	Seek Time	Interface	Encode	cache kb	RPM
RO3059T		46	18	SCSI	2,7 RLL		
RO3060R		50	28	ST412/506	2,7 RLL		
RO3065		53	28	ST412/506	MFM		
RO3070S		71	28	SCSI	2,7 RLL		
RO3075R		59	28	ST412/506	2,7 RLL		
RO3085R		69	28	ST412/506	2,7 RLL		
RO3085S		69	28	SCSI	2,7 RLL		
RO3088A		75	18	IDE AT	2,7 RLL		
RO3088T		75	18	SCSI	2,7 RLL		
RO3089A		70	18	IDE AT	2,7 RLL		
RO3089T		70	18	SCSI	2,7 RLL		
RO3090T		75		SCSI	2,7 RLL		
RO3095A		80	18	IDE AT	2,7 RLL		
RO3099A		80	19	IDE AT	2,7 RLL		
RO3099AP		80	19	IDE AT	2,7 RLL		
RO3128A		105	18	IDE AT	2,7 RLL		
RO3128T		105	18	SCSI	2,7 RLL		
RO3129A		105	18	IDE AT	2,7 RLL		
RO3129T		105	18	SCSI	2,7 RLL		
RO3130S		105	22	SCSI	2,7 RLL		
RO3130T		105	22	SCSI	2,7 RLL		
RO3135A		112	19	IDE AT	2,7 RLL		
RO3139A		112	18	IDE AT	2,7 RLL		
RO3139AP		112	18	IDE AT	2,7 RLL		
RO3139S		112	18	SCSI			
RO3139TP		112		SCSI	RLL ZBR		
RO3258TS		210		SCSI			
RO3259A		210	18	IDE AT	2,7 RLL		
RO3259AP		212		IDE AT			
RO3259T		210	18	SCSI	2,7 RLL		
RO3259TP		210		SCSI	2,7 RLL		
RO3259TS		210	18	SCSI	2,7 RLL		
RO351		5	85	ST412/506	MFM		
RO352		11	85	ST412/506	MFM		
RO365		21		ST412/506	MFM		
RO5040S		38	28	SCSI	MFM		
RO5065		63	28	ST412/506	MFM		
RO5075E		65	28	ESDI			
RO5075S		76	28	SCSI			
RO5078S		62		SCSI			
RO5090		89	28	ST412/506	MFM		
RO5095R		81		ST412/506	2,7 RLL		
RO5125-1F2		106	18	SCSI	2,7 RLL		
RO5125E		106	18	ESDI	2,7 RLL		
RO5125S		106	28	SCSI	2,7 RLL		
RO5128S		103		SCSI			
RO5130R		114	28	ST412/506	2,7 RLL		
RO5178S		144	19	SCSI	2,7 RLL		
RO5180-1F2		148	19	SCSI	2,7 RLL		
RO5180E		149	18	ESDI	2,7 RLL		
RO5180S		144	28	SCSI	2,7 RLL		
RO652		20	85	SCSI	2,7 RLL		
RO652A		20	85	SCSI			
RO652B		20	85	SCSI	2,7 RLL		
RO752		20	85	SCSI			
RO752A		25	85	SCSI			

SAMSUNG

Drive Model	Format Size MB	Seek Time	Interface	Encode	cache kb	RPM
ACB20811A (Rel. 10-96)	810	12	ATA-2 Fast			
ACE21021A (Rel. 10-96)	1020	12	ATA-2 Fast			
MP0302H	30GB	12	ATA-7		8mb	5400
MP0402H	40GB	12	ATA-7		8mb	5400
MP0603H	60GB	12	ATA-7		8mb	5400
MP0804H	80GB	12	ATA-7		8mb	5400
PLS30424A	420	11	EIDE			
PLS30540A	547	11	IDE AT			
PLS30730A	731	11	IDE AT		256k	4500
PLS30850A	731	11	IDE AT		256k	4500
					256k	4500

Drive Model	Format Size MB	Head	Cyl	Sect/Trac	Translate H/C/S	RWC/WPC	Form Factor	Power Watts
PLS30850S	731	4	3868	72-132		—/—	3.5 3H	
PLS30854A	850	4	3868		16/1647/63	—/—	3.5 3H	3.2
PLS30854S	850	4	3868	VAR		—/—	3.5 3H	
PLS31084A	1080	5	3840	72-144	16/2093/63	—/—	3.5 3H	1.6
PLS31084S	1080	5	3840	72-144	16/2093/63	—/—	3.5 3H	1.6
PLS31100A	1100	6				—/—	3.5 3H	
PLS31100S	1100	6				—/—	3.5 3H	
PLS31274A	1273	5	3844	72-132	16/2466/63	—/—	3.5 3H	2.8
PLS31274S	1273	5	3844	72-132		—/544	3.5 3H	2.8
SHD2040N	44	4	820	26	4/820/63	—/544	3.5HH	
SHD2041	47	4	820	28		NA/NA	3.5HH	
SHD30280A	280	2	2768	72-120	10/869/63	NA/NA	3.5HH	
SHD30420A	421	3	2768	72-120	16/856/60	—/—	3.5 3H	3
SHD30560A	561	4	2768	72-120	16/1086/63	—/—	3.5 3H	3.0
SHD30560A	528	4			16/1024/63	—/—	3.5 3H	3.0
SHD3061A	60	2	1478	40	7/993/17	NA/NA	3.5 3H	
SHD3062A	121	4	1479	40	15/927/17	NA/NA	3.5 3H	4
SHD3101A	105				8/766/33	NA/NA	3.5 3H	
SHD3101B	105	4	1282	40		NA/NA	3.5 3H	
SHD3121A	125	2	1956	79	16/615/25	—/—	3.5 3H	
SHD3122A	251	4	1956	79	15/937/35	—/—	3.5 3H	
SHD3122S	251	4	1956	79		—/—	3.5 3H	
SHD3171A	178	2			8/968/45	—/—	3.5 3H	
SHD3172A	356	4	2223	96	16/968/45	—/—	3.5 3H	
SHD3172S	356	4	2223	96		—/—	3.5 3H	
SHD3201S	212	7	1376			—/—	3.5 3H	
SHD3202S	212	7	1376	43		NA/NA	3.5HH	
SHD3210S	212	7	1376	43		NA/NA	3.5HH	
SHD3211A	213	2	2570	55-95	8/1002/52	—/—	3.5 3H	3.2
SHD3212A	426				16/1002/52	NA/NA	3.5HH	
SHD3272A	545	4				—/—		
SHD3272S	545	4				—/—		
SP0401N	40GB					—/—	3.5 3H	7
SP0802N	80GB					—/—	3.5 3H	7
SP0812C	80GB					—/—	3.5 3H	7.7
SP0812N	80GB					—/—	3.5 3H	7
SP0914D	9100	4	12354	240-40		—/—	3.5 3H	6.0
SP1001H	10GB	1				—/—	3.5 3H	6.0
SP1203N	120GB					—/—	3.5 3H	5.5
SP1213C	120GB					—/—	3.5 3H	7.7
SP1213N	120GB					—/—	3.5 3H	7
SP1366D	13650	6	12354	240-40		—/—	3.5 3H	6.0
SP1604N	160GB					—/—	3.5 3H	7
SP1614C	160GB					—/—	3.5 3H	7.7
SP1828D	18200	8	12354	240-40		—/—	3.5 3H	6.0
SP2001H	20GB	1				—/—	3.5 3H	5.8
SP2002H	20GB	2				—/—	3.5 3H	6.0
SP3003H	30GB	2				—/—	3.5 3H	6.0
SP4002H	40GB	2				—/—	3.5 3H	5.8
SP4004H	40GB	4				—/—	3.5 3H	6.0
SP6003H	60GB	3				—/—	3.5 3H	5.8
SP8004H	80GB	4				—/—	3.5 3H	
STG31271A	1280	4			16/2483/63	—/—	3.5 3H	
STG31601A	1610				16/3104/63		3.5	
SV0211N	20GB					—/—	2.5 4H	5.5
SV0221H	20GB					—/—	3.5 3H	4.5
SV0221N	20GB					—/—	2.5 4H	6.1
SV0311N	30GB					—/—	2.5 4H	4.6
SV0322A	3200	2			9/11024/63	—/—	3.5 3H	5.4
SV0401H	40GB					—/—	3.5 3H	4.6
SV0401N	40GB					—/—	2.5 4H	5.5
SV0411N	40GB					—/—	2.5 4H	4.6
SV0431D	4300	1				—/—	3.5 3H	
SV0432A	4300	2			15/8912/63	—/—	3.5 3H	6.7
SV0432D	4300	2	12257	231-40		—/—	3.5 3H	4.1
SV0511D	5100	1				—/—	3.5 3H	
SV0602H	60GB					—/—	3.5 3H	4.5

Drive Model	Format Size MB	Seek Time	Interface	Encode	cache kb	RPM
PLS30850S	731	11	SCSI		256k	4500
PLS30854A	850	11	EIDE	1,7 RLL	256k	4500
PLS30854S	850	11	SCSI-2Fast	1,7 RLL	256k	4500
PLS31084A	1080	11	ATA-2	1,7 RLL	256k	4500
PLS31084S	1080	11	SCSI-2	1,7 RLL	256k	4500
PLS31100A	1100	11	IDE AT		256k	4500
PLS31100S	1100	11	SCSI		256k	4500
PLS31274A	1273	11	ATA-2	1,7 RLL	256k	4500
PLS31274S	1273	11	SCSI-2	1,7 RLL	256k	4500
SHD2040N	44	39	ST412/506	2,7 RLL		3568
SHD2041	47	29	IDE AT	2,7 RLL		3525
SHD30280A	280	12	ATA	1,7 RLL		3600
SHD30420A	421	12	IDE AT	1,7 RLL	64k	3600
SHD30560A	561	12	IDE AT	1,7 RLL	128k	3600
SHD30560A	528	12	IDE AT	1,7 RLL	128k	3600
SHD3061A	60	16	IDE AT	1,7 RLL	128k	3600
SHD3062A	121	16	IDE AT	1,7 RLL		
SHD3101A	105	19	IDE AT	1,7 RLL		
SHD3101B	105	19	IDE AT	1,7 RLL	32k	3600
SHD3121A	125	16	IDE AT	1,7 RLL	32k	3600
SHD3122A	251	16	IDE AT	1,7 RLL	64k	3600
SHD3122S	251	16	SCSI	1,7 RLL	64k	3600
SHD3171A	178	13	IDE AT	1,7 RLL	64k	3600
SHD3172A	356	13	IDE AT	1,7 RLL	64k	3600
SHD3172S	356	13	SCSI	1,7 RLL	64k	3600
SHD3201S	212	16	SCSI	1,7 RLL	64k	3600
SHD3202S	212	16	SCSI			
SHD3210S	212	16	SCSI	1,7 RLL		
SHD3211A	213	13	IDE AT	1,7 RLL	64k	3600
SHD3212A	426	13	ATA	1,7 RLL	128k	
SHD3272A	545	12	IDE AT	1,7 RLL	256k	4510
SHD3272S	545	12	SCSI-2Fast	1,7 RLL	256k	4510
SP0401N	40GB	8.9	ATA-7		2mb	7200
SP0802N	80GB	8.9	ATA-7		2mb	7200
SP0812C	80GB	8.9	SATA/1.0		2mb	7200
SP0812N	80GB	8.9	ATA-7		80mb	7200
SP0914D	9100	9	ATA4FstEIDE	16/17 EPR4	8mb	7200
SP1001N	10GB	8.9	UltraATA100		1024k	7200
SP1203N	120GB	8.9	ATA-7		2mb	7200
SP1213C	120GB	8.9	SATA/1.0		20mb	5400
SP1213N	120GB	8.9	ATA-7		80mb	7200
SP1366D	13650	9	ATA4FstEIDE	16/17 EPR4	8mb	7200
SP1604N	160GB	8.9	ATA-7		1024k	7200
SP1614C	160GB	8.9	SATA/1.0		2mb	7200
SP1828D	18200	9	ATA4FstEIDE	16/17 EPR4	80mb	7200
SP2001H	20GB	8.9	UltraATA100		1024k	7200
SP2002H	20GB	9.0	UltraATA100		2mb	7200
SP3003H	30GB	9.0	UltraATA100		2mb	7200
SP4002H	40GB	8.9	UltraATA100		2mb	7200
SP4004H	40GB	9.0	UltraATA100		2mb	7200
SP6003H	60GB	8.9	UltraATA100		2mb	7200
SP8004H	80GB	8.9	UltraATA100		2mb	7200
STG31271A	1280	12	ATA-2 Fast		128k	4500
STG31601A	1610	12	ATA-2 Fast		128k	4500
SV0211N	20GB	8.9	ATA-7		20mb	5400
SV0221H	20GB	8.9	UltraATA100		2mb	5400
SV0221N	20GB	11	UltraATA133		2mb	5400
SV0311H	30GB	10	ATA-6		20mb	5400
SV0322A	3200	10	Ultra ATA	16/17 EPR4	512k	5400
SV0401H	40GB	10	ATA-6		2mb	5400
SV0401N	40GB	8.9	ATA-7		20mb	5400
SV0411N	40GB	11	UltraATA133		2mb	5400
SV0431D	4300	8.5	ATA-4 Fast		512k	5400
SV0432A	4300	9.5	Ultra ATA	16/17 EPR4	512k	5400
SV0432D	4300	9.5	EIDE	16/17 EPR4	512k	5400
SV0511D	5100	8.5	Ultra DMA66		512k	5400
SV0602H	60GB	9.0	UltraATA100		2mb	5400

Drive Model	Format Size MB	Head	Cyl	Sect/Trac	Translate H/C/S	RWC/WPC	Form Factor	Power Watts
SV0612N	60GB					—/—	3.5 3H	7
SV0643A	6400	3			15/13328/63	—/—	3.5 3H	6.7
SV0644A	6400	4			15/13232/63	—/—	3.5 3H	5.8
SV0682D	6800	2				—/—	3.5 3H	4.3
SV0761D	7600	1				—/—	3.5 3H	4.0
SV0802N	80GB					—/—	3.5 3H	5.5
SV0813H	80GB					—/—	3.5 3H	4.5
SV0842D	8400	2				—/—	3.5 3H	
SV0844A	8400	4			16/16383/63	—/—	3.5 3H	6.7
SV0844D	8400	4	12257	231-40		—/—	3.5 3H	4.1
SV1021D	10200	1				—/—	3.5 3H	4.0
SV1021H	10200	1				—/—	3.5 3H	4.0
SV1022D	10200	2				—/—	3.5 3H	3.3
SV1022D	10200	2				—/—	3.5 3H	
SV1023D	10200	3				—/—	3.5 3H	4.3
SV1203H	120GB					—/—	3.5 3H	
SV1204H	120GB					—/—	3.5 3H	4.5
SV1296A	12900	6			16/25038/63	—/—	3.5 3H	6.7
SV1296D	12900	6	12257	231-40		—/—	3.5 3H	4.1
SV1363D	13600	3				—/—	3.5 3H	
SV1363D	13600	3				—/—	3.5 3H	4.3
SV1364D	13600	4				—/—	3.5 3H	4.0
SV1532D	15300	2				—/—	3.5 3H	3.3
SV1533D	15300	3				—/—	3.5 3H	
SV1533D	15300	3				—/—	3.5 3H	
SV1604N	160GB					—/—	3.5 3H	
SV1705D	17000	5				—/—	3.5 3H	4.3
SV1824D	18200	4				—/—	3.5 3H	
SV2001H	20GB	1				—/—	3.5 3H	
SV2002H	20GB					—/—	3.5 3H	
SV2042D	20400	2				—/—	3.5 3H	4.0
SV2042H	20400	2				—/—	3.5 3H	4.0
SV2043D	20400	3				—/—	3.5 3H	4.0
SV2044D	20400	4				—/—	3.5 3H	3.3
SV2044D	20400	4				—/—	3.5 3H	
SV2046D	20400	6				—/—	3.5 3H	4.3
SV3002H	30GB	2				—/—	3.5 3H	3.3
SV3063D	30600	3				—/—	3.5 3H	4.0
SV3063D	30600	3				—/—	3.5 3H	4.0
SV3064D	30600	4				—/—	3.5 3H	4.0
SV4002H	40GB	2				—/—	3.5 3H	4.8
SV4003H	40GB	3				—/—	3.5 3H	3.3
SV4084D	40800	4				—/—	3.5 3H	4.0
SV4084H	40800	4				—/—	3.5 3H	4.0
SV6003H	60GB	3				—/—	3.5 3H	4.8
SV6004H	60GB	4				—/—	3.5 3H	3.3
SV8004H	80GB	4				—/—	3.5 3H	4.8
SW0212A	2100	2			16/4092/63	—/—	3.5 3H	3.1
SW0323A	3200	3			16/6248/63	—/—	3.5 3H	3.1
SW0434A	4300	4			15/8896/63	—/—	3.5 3H	3.1
TBR31080A	1080	4			16/2092/63	—/—	3.5 3H	
TBR31080S	1080	4			16/2092/63	—/—	3.5 3H	
TBR31081A	1080	4	4308		16/2093/63	—/—		
TBR31081S	1080	4	4308			—/—		
TBR31084A	1080				16/2092/63	—/—		
VA34323A	4300	4			15/8938/63	—/—	3.5 3H	6.2
VA38454A	8400				16/16383/63	—/—	3.5 3H	6.2
VG31702A	1700					—/—	3.5 3H	
VG32163A	2100	2			16/4192/63	—/—	3.5 3H	5.6
VG32502A	2550					—/—	3.5 3H	
VG33243A	3245					—/—	3.5 3H	
VG33402A	3400	4			16/6591/63	—/—	3.5 3H	
VG34202A	4250	5				—/—		
VG34323A	4300	4			9/14896/63	—/—	3.5 3H	5.6
VG34324A	4300	3			9/14896/63	—/—	3.5 3H	5.6
VG35102A	5100	6				—/—		
VG35403A	5403					—/—	3.5 3H	
VG36483A	6495	6				—/—	3.5 3H	

Drive Model	Format Size MB	Seek Time	Interface	Encode	cache kb	RPM
SV0612N	60GB	8.9	ATA-7		2mb	7200
SV0643A	6400	9.5	Ultra ATA	16/17 EPR4	512k	5400
SV0644A	6400	10	Ultra ATA	16/17 EPR4	512k	5400
SV0682D	6800	9.5	ATA-4 Fast		512k	5400
SV0761D	7600	9	UltraDMA/66		512k	5400
SV0802N	80GB	8.9	ATA-7		20mb	5400
SV0813H	80GB	8.9	UltraATA100		2mb	5400
SV0842D	8400	8.5	ATA-4 FAST		512k	5400
SV0844A	8400	9.5	Ultra ATA	16/17 EPR4	512k	5400
SV0844D	8400	9.5	EIDE	16/17 EPR4	512k	5400
SV1021D	10200	9	UltraDMA/66		512k	5400
SV1021H	10200	9.0	UltraDMA/66		512k	5400
SV1022D	10200	8.5	ATA-5 FAST		512k	5400
SV1022D	10200	8.5	Ultra DMA66		512k	5400
SV1023D	10200	9.5	ATA-4 Fast		512k	5400
SV1203D	120GB	8.9	ATA-7		2mb	5400
SV1204H	120GB	8.9	UltraATA100		2mb	5400
SV1296A	12900	9.5	Ultra ATA	16/17 EPR4	512k	5400
SV1296D	12900	9.5	EIDE	16/17 EPR4	512k	5400
SV1363D	13600	8.5	ATA-4 Fast		512k	5400
SV1364D	13600	9.5	ATA-4 Fast		512k	5400
SV1532D	15300	9	UltraDMA/66		512k	5400
SV1533D	15300	8.5	ATA-5 FAST		512k	5400
SV1533D	15300	8.5	Ultra DMA66		512k	5400
SV1604N	160GB	8.9	ATA-7		2mb	5400
SV1705D	17000	9.5	ATA-4 Fast		512k	5400
SV1824D	18200	8.5	ATA-4 Fast		512k	5400
SV2001H	20GB	8.9	UltraATA100		2mb	5400
SV2002H	20GB	9	UltraATA100		2mb	5400
SV2042H	20400	9	UltraDMA/66		512k	5400
SV2042H	20400	9	UltraDMA/66		512k	5400
SV2043D	20400	9	UltraDMA/66		512k	5400
SV2044D	20400	8.5	ATA-5 FAST		512k	5400
SV2044D	20400	8.5	Ultra DMA66		512k	5400
SV2046D	20400	9.5	ATA-4 Fast		512k	5400
SV3002H	30GB	9	UltraATA100		512k	5400
SV3063D	30600	9	UltraDMA/66		512k	5400
SV3063H	30600	9	UltraDMA/66		512k	5400
SV3064D	30600	9	UltraDMA/66		512k	5400
SV4002H	40GB	8.9	UltraATA100		2mb	5400
SV4003H	40GB	9	UltraATA100		512k	5400
SV4084D	40800	9	UltraDMA/66		512k	5400
SV4084H	40800	9	UltraDMA/66		512k	5400
SV6003H	60GB	8.9	UltraATA100		2mb	5400
SV6004H	60GB	9	UltraATA100		512k	5400
SV8004H	80GB	8.9	UltraATA100		2mb	5400
SW0212A	2100	11	Ultra ATA	16/17 EPR4	512k	5400
SW0323A	3200	11	Ultra ATA	16/17 EPR4	512k	5400
SW0434A	4300	11	Ultra ATA	16/17 EPR4	512k	5400
TBR31080A	1080	9	ATA-2 Fast		256k	5400
TBR31080S	1080	9	SCSI		256k	5400
TBR31081A	1080	9	ATA-2 Fast	1,7 RLL	256k	5400
TBR31081S	1080	9	SCSI-2Fast	1,7 RLL	256k	5400
TBR31084A	1080	11	IDE AT	1,7 RLL		
VA34323A	4300	10	Ultra ATA	16/17 EPR4	512k	5400
VA38454A	8400	10	EIDE	16/17 EPR4	512k	5400
VG31702A	1700	10	ATA			
VG32163A	2100	10	Ultra ATA	16/17 EPR4	512k	5400
VG32502A	2550	10	IDE AT			
VG33243A	3245	10	IDE AT			
VG33402A	3400	11	IDE AT		128k	5400
VG34202A	4250	11			128k	5400
VG34323A	4300	10	Ultra ATA	16/17 EPR4	128k	5400
VG34324A	4300	10	Ultra ATA	16/17 EPR4	512k	5400
VG35102A	5100	11			128k	5400
VG35403A	5403	10	EIDE/AT	PRML		
VG36483A	6495	10	EIDE/AT	PRML	512k	5400

Drive Model	Format Size MB	Head	Cyl	Sect/Trac	Translate H/C/S	RWC/WPC	Form Factor	Power Watts
VG36483A	6400	6			15/13424/63	—/—	3.5 3H	5.6
VG38404A	8400	6			15/17360/63	—/—	3.5 3H	6.2
WA31083A	1080				16/2094/63	—/—		
WA31273A	1279				16/2480/63	—/—		
WA32162A	2160				16/4186/63	—/—		
WA32163A	2162				16/4190/63	—/—		
WA32543A	2560				16/4962/63	—/—		
WA33203A	3200				16/6202/63	—/—		
WN310816A	1080	3	4563				3.5 3H	3.3
WN310820A	1080	2	6022		16/2093/63		3.5 3H	3.3
WN312016A	1207	3	5389		16/2340/63		3.5 3H	3.3
WN312021A	1207	2	6077		16/2340/63		3.5 3H	3.3
WN31271A	1200	3	5525				3.5 3H	3.3
WN31273A	1270	2	6333		16/2464/63		3.5 3H	3.3
WN316025A	1620	3	5891		16/3121/63		3.5 3H	3.3
WN31603A	1611				16/3121/63			
WN321010S	2160	6	5588				3.5 3H	3.5
WN32103U	2160	4	6333				3.5 3H	3.5
WN321620A	2160	6	6022		16/4186/63		3.5 3H	3.5
WN32162U	2160	4	5909				3.5 3H	7.5
WN32163A	2160				16/4186/63			
WN32163U	2160	4	6746	101-19				
WN32543A	2540	4	6331		16/4924/63		3.5 3H	3.6
WN33203A	3175	5	6331				3.5 3H	3.6
WN33203A	3240	6	6132				3.5 3H	3.3
WN332420A	3810	6	6712				3.5 3H	3.5
WN33813A	4000	6					3.5 3H	
WN34003A	4000	6				—/—	3.5 3H	
WN34003U	4300	6				—/—	3.5 3H	5.0
WN34324U	1610	4	5589		16/3121/63		3.5 3H	3.5
WNR31601A	2104	6			16/4077/63		3.5 3H	
WNR32100A	2060	5	5589				3.5 3H	3.5
WNR32101A	2415	6			16/4681/63		3.5 3H	
WNR32501A	1600	2			16/3140/63		3.5 3H	3.7
WU31605A	2160				16/4186/63		3.5 3H	3.5
WU32163A	2100	3			16/4186/63		3.5 3H	3.5
WU32165A	2541				16/4924/63			
WU32543A	2550				16/4924/63		3.5 3H	3.5
WU32553A	3200	4			16/6280/63		3.5 3H	3.5
WU33205A	4320				16/8372/63	—/—		
WU34324A	4319				15/8928/63	—/—		
WU34325A								

SEAGATE TECHNOLOGIES

Drive Model	Format Size MB	Head	Cyl	Sect/Trac	Translate H/C/S	RWC/WPC	Form Factor	Power Watts
Barracuda 36ES	18400	2	29850	768		—/—	3.5 3H	6.25
Barracuda 36ES	18400	2	29850			—/—	3.5 3H	6.25
Barracuda 36ES	36.9GB	4	29851			—/—	3.5 3H	7.0
Barracuda 36ES	36.9GB	4	29851			—/—	3.5 3H	7.0
Barracuda 36ES	18.4GB	2	29851			—/—	3.5 3H	6.2
Barracuda 36ES	18.4GB	2	29851			—/—	3.5 3H	6.2
Barracuda 36ES2	36.9GB	2	56332			—/—	3.5 3H	9.0
Barracuda 36ES2	36.9GB	2	56332			—/—	3.5 3H	9.0
Barracuda 5400.1	40GB	1			16/16383/63	—/—	2.5 4H	4.5
Barracuda 5400.1	40GB	1			16/16383/63	—/—	2.5 4H	4.5
Barracuda 7200.7 120GB	120GB	3			16/16383/63	—/—	3.5 3H	7.5
Barracuda 7200.7 160GB	160GB	4			16/16383/63	—/—	3.5 3H	7.5
Barracuda 7200.7 40GB	40GB	1			16/16383/63	—/—	3.5 3H	7.5
Barracuda 7200.7 80GB	80GB	2			16/16383/63	—/—	3.5 3H	7.5
Barracuda 7200.7 80GB	80GB	2			16/16383/63	—/—	3.5 3H	7.5
Barracuda 7200.7 PLUS	120GB	3			16/16383/63	—/—	3.5 3H	7.5
Barracuda 7200.7 PLUS	160GB	4			16/16383/63	—/—	3.5 3H	7.5
Barracuda 7200.7 PLUS	200GB	4			16/16383/63	—/—	3.5 3H	7.5
Barracuda 7200.7 PLUS	200GB	4			16/16383/63	—/—	3.5 3H	7.5
Barracuda 7200.7 SATA	80GB	2			16/16383/63	—/—	3.5 3H	7.0
Barracuda 7200.7 SATA	80GB	2			16/16383/63	—/—	3.5 3H	7.5
Barracuda 7200.7 SATA	120GB	3			16/16383/63	—/—	3.5 3H	7.0
Barracuda 7200.7 SATA	120GB	3			16/16383/63	—/—	3.5 3H	7.5
Barracuda 7200.7 SATA	160GB	4			16/16383/63	—/—	3.5 3H	7.0
Barracuda 7200.7 SATA	160GB	4			16/16383/63	—/—	3.5 3H	7.5

Drive Model	Format Size MB	Seek Time	Interface	Encode	cache kb	RPM
VG36483A	6400	10	Ultra ATA	16/17 EPR4	512k	5400
VG38404A	8400	10	Ultra ATA	16/17 EPR4	512k	5400
WA31083A	1080	11	IDE AT			
WA31273A	1279	11	IDE AT			
WA32162A	2160	11	IDE AT			
WA32163A	2162	11	IDE AT			
WA32543A	2560	11	IDE AT			
WA33203A	3200	11	IDE AT			
WN310816A	1080	11	ATA-2 Fast	PRML8,9	128k	5400
WN310820A	1080	<10	ATA-2 Fast	RLL 8,9	128k	4500
WN312016A	1207	11	ATA-2 Fast	RLL 8,9	128k	4500
WN312021A	1207	10	ATA-2 Fast	RLL 8,9	128k	4500
WN311273A	1200	11	ATA-2 Fast	PRML8,9	128k	5400
WN312273A	1270	11	ATA-2 Fast	RLL 8,9	128k	4500
WN316025A	1620	10	ATA-2 Fast	RLL 8,9	128k	4500
WN31603A	1611	10	IDE AT		128k	5400
WN321010S	2160	11	SCSI-2Fast	PRML8,9	128k	5400
WN32103U	2160	9.5	SCSI3Fast20	8,9 PR4	512k	5400
WN321620A	2160	<10	ATA-2 Fast	RLL 8,9	128k	5400
WN32162U	2160	9.5		RLL 8,9	512k	5400
WN32163A	2160	10	IDE AT			
WN32163U	2160	11	SCSI3Fast20			
WN32543A	2540	11	ATA-2 Fast	RLL 8,9	128k	5400
WN33203A	3175	10	ATA-2 Fast	RLL 8,9	128k	5400
WN332420A	3240	10	ATA-2 Fast	PRML8,9	128k	4500
WN33813A	3810	10	ATA-2 Fast	PRML8,9	128k	5400
WN34003A	4000	10	ATA-2 Fast	RLL 8,9	128k	5400
WN34003U	4000	10	Ultra SCSI	RLL 8,9	128k	5400
WN34324U	4300	10	Ultra SCSI	8,9 PR4	512k	5400
WNR31601A	1610	11	ATA-2 Fast	RLL 8,9	128k	5400
WNR32100A	2104	11			128k	5400
WNR32101A	2060	11	ATA-2 Fast	RLL 8,9	128k	5400
WNR32501A	2415	11	ATA-2 Fast	PRML	128k	5400
WU31605A	1600	11	Ultra ATA	16/17 EPR4	128k	5400
WU32163A	2160	11	IDE AT		128k	5400
WU32165A	2100	11	Ultra ATA	16/17 EPR4	128k	5400
WU32543A	2541	11	IDE AT		128k	5400
WU32553A	2550	11	IDE AT			
WU33205A	3200	11	Ultra ATA	16/17 EPR4	128k	5400
WU34324A	4320	11	IDE AT			
WU34325A	4319	9.7	IDE AT			

SEAGATE TECHNOLOGIES

Drive Model	Format Size MB	Seek Time	Interface	Encode	cache kb	RPM
Barracuda 36ES	18400	8.5	Ultra SCSI	EPRML	2048k	7200
Barracuda 36ES	18400	8.5	Ultra SCSI	EPRML	2048k	7200
Barracuda 36ES	36.9GB	8.5	Ultra 160	EPRML	2mb	7200
Barracuda 36ES	36.9GB	8.5	UL160SCSIW	EPRML	2mb	7200
Barracuda 36ES	18.4GB	8.5	Ultra 160	EPRML	2mb	7200
Barracuda 36ES	18.4GB	8.5	UL160SCSIW	EPRML	2mb	7200
Barracuda 36ES2	36.9GB	9.25	UL160SCSIW	EPRML	2048k	7200
Barracuda 36ES2	36.9GB	9.25	50-pin	EPRML	2048k	7200
Barracuda 5400.1	40GB	12.5	UltraATA100	GPRML 96/102	2mb	5400
Barracuda 5400.1	40GB	12.5	UltraATA100	GPRML 96/102	2mb	5400
Barracuda 7200.7 120GB	120GB	8.5	UltraATA100	EPRML16,17	2mb	7200
Barracuda 7200.7 160GB	160GB	8.5	UltraATA100	EPRML16,17	2mb	7200
Barracuda 7200.7 40GB	40GB	8.5	UltraATA100	EPRML16,17	2mb	7200
Barracuda 7200.7 80GB	80GB	8.5	UltraATA100	EPRML16,17	2mb	7200
Barracuda 7200.7 80GB	80GB	8.5	UltraATA100	EPRML16,17	2mb	7200
Barracuda 7200.7 PLUS	120GB	8.5	UltraATA100	EPRML16,17	8mb	7200
Barracuda 7200.7 PLUS	160GB	8.5	UltraATA100	EPRML16,17	8mb	7200
Barracuda 7200.7 PLUS	200GB	8.5	UltraATA100	EPRML16,17	8mb	7200
Barracuda 7200.7 PLUS	200GB	8.5	UltraATA100	EPRML16,17	8mb	7200
Barracuda 7200.7 SATA	80GB	8.5	SATA/150	EPRML16,17	8mb	7200
Barracuda 7200.7 SATA	80GB	8.5	SATA/150	EPRML16,17	8mb	7200
Barracuda 7200.7 SATA	120GB	8.5	SATA/150	EPRML16,17	8mb	7200
Barracuda 7200.7 SATA	120GB	8.5	SATA/150	EPRML16,17	8mb	7200
Barracuda 7200.7 SATA	160GB	8.5	SATA/150	EPRML16,17	8mb	7200
Barracuda 7200.7 SATA	160GB	8.5	SATA/150	EPRML16,17	8mb	7200

Drive Model	Format Size MB	Head	Cyl	Sect/Trac	Translate H/C/S	RWC/WPC	Form Factor	Power Watts
Barracuda 7200.7 SATA	200GB	4			16/16383/63	—/—	3.5 3H	7.0
Barracuda 7200.7 SATA	40GB	1			16/16383/63	—/—	3.5 3H	7.5
Barracuda 9LP	9100	10				—/—	3.5 3H	
Barracuda ATA IV 20GB	20GB	1			16/16383/63	—/—	3.5 3H	8.0
Barracuda ATA IV 40GB	40GB	2			16/16383/63	—/—	3.5 3H	8.0
Barracuda ATA IV 60GB	60GB	3			16/16383/63	—/—	3.5 3H	8.0
Barracuda ATA IV 80GB	80GB					—/—	3.5 3H	
Cheetah 10K.6	36.7GB	8	49854			—/—	3.5 3H	7.5
Cheetah 10K.6	36.7GB	8	49854			—/—	3.5 3H	7.7
Cheetah 10K.6	36.7GB	8	49854			—/—	3.5 3H	7.5
Cheetah 10K.6	146.8GB	8	49854			—/—	3.5 3H	11
Cheetah 10K.6	146.8GB	8	49854			—/—	3.5 3H	10.8
Cheetah 10K.6	146.8GB	8	49854			—/—	3.5 3H	10.8
Cheetah 10K.6	73.4GB	8				—/—	3.5 3H	9.2
Cheetah 10K.6	73.4GB	8				—/—	3.5 3H	9
Cheetah 10K.6	73.4GB	8				—/—	3.5 3H	9
Cheetah 10K.6	73.4GB	8				—/—	3.5 3H	9
Cheetah 15K.3	18.4GB	2				—/—	3.5 3H	9
Cheetah 15K.3	18.4GB	2				—/—	3.5 3H	9
Cheetah 15K.3	18.4GB	2				—/—	3.5 3H	10
Cheetah 15K.3	36.7GB	4				—/—	3.5 3H	10
Cheetah 15K.3	36.7GB	4				—/—	3.5 3H	10
Cheetah 15K.3	36.7GB	4				—/—	3.5 3H	12
Cheetah 15K.3	18.4GB	8				—/—	3.5 3H	12
Cheetah 15K.3	18.4GB	8				—/—	3.5 3H	12
Cheetah 15K.3	18.4GB	8				—/—	3.5 3H	8.5
Cheetah 36ES	18.4GB	2	19036			—/—	3.5 3H	8.5
Cheetah 36ES	18.4GB	2	19036			—/—	3.5 3H	8.5
Cheetah 36ES	36.9GB	4	19036			—/—	3.5 3H	8.5
Cheetah 36ES	36.9GB	4	19036			—/—	3.5 3H	8.5
Cheetah 36ES	36.9GB	4	19036			—/—	3.5 3H	8.5
Cheetah 36ES	36.9GB	4	19036			—/—	3.5 3H	8.0
Cheetah 36XL	18.352GB	4	19036	471		—/—	3.5 3H	8.0
Cheetah 36XL	18.352GB	4	19036	471		—/—	3.5 3H	9.6
Cheetah 36XL	36.704GB	8	19036	471		—/—	3.5 3H	9.6
Cheetah 36XL	36.704GB	8	19036			—/—	3.5 3H	7.5
Cheetah 36XL	9.176GB	2	19036	471		—/—	3.5 3H	7.5
Cheetah 36XL	9.176GB	2	19036	471		—/—	3.5 3H	9.3
Cheetah 73LP	36.7GB	4	29550			—/—	3.5 3H	11.0
Cheetah 73LP	73.4GB	8	29550			—/—	3.5 3H	9.9
Cheetah 73LP	73.4GB	8	29550			—/—	3.5 3H	9.9
Cheetah 73LP	73.4GB	8	29550			—/—	3.5 3H	9.9
Cheetah X15	18.35GB	10	10377	345		—/—	3.5 3H	10.7
Cheetah X15	18.4GB	10	18497			—/—	3.5 3H	10.5
Cheetah X15	18.4GB	4	18497			—/—	3.5 3H	11.5
Cheetah X15	18.4GB	4	18497			—/—	3.5 3H	10.5
Cheetah X15	36.7GB	8	18497			—/—	3.5 3H	11.5
Cheetah X15	36.7GB	8	18497			—/—	3.5 3H	11.5
Cheetah X15	36.7GB	8	18497			—/—	3.5 3H	11.5
Elite12G	1050	17				—/—	5.25FH	
Medalist 10230	10200	6			16/16383/63	—/—	3.5 3H	4.5
Medalist 10231	10200	6			16/16383/63	—/—	3H	5.5
Medalist 12930	12900	6			16/16383/63	—/—	3.5 3H	5.5
Medalist 13030	13000	6			16/16383/63	—/—	3.5 3H	4.5
Medalist 13640	13600	8			16/16383/63	—/—	3H	5.5
Medalist 17240	17200	8			16/16383/63	—/—	3.5 3H	5.5
Medalist 17240	17200	8				—/—	3.5 3H	
Medalist 2140	2100				16/6296/63	—/—	3.5 3H	4.5
Medalist 3210	3200	2			15/8894/63	—/—	3H	5.5
Medalist 4310	4300	2			15/8894/63	—/—	3.5 3H	5.5
Medalist 4310	4300	2			16/13228/63	—/—	3.5 3H	4.5
Medalist 6422	6400	4			16/16383/63	—/—	3H	5.5
Medalist 8420	8400	4			16/16383/63	—/—	3.5 3H	5.5
Medalist 8420	8400	4				—/—	3H	
Medalist Pro 9140	9100					—/—		
Sabre1123	964	19				—/—	8.0 FH	
Sabre1150	990	19				—/—	8.0 FH	

Drive Model	Format Size MB	Seek Time	Interface	Encode	cache kb	RPM
Barracuda 7200.7 SATA	200GB	8.5	SATA/150	EPRML16,17	8mb	7200
Barracuda 7200.7 SATA	40GB	8.5	UltraATA100	EPRML16,17	2mb	7200
Barracuda 9LP	9100	7.1	Ultra2 SCSI	PRML	1mb	7200
Barracuda ATA IV 20GB	20GB	9	UltraATA100	EPRML16,17		7200
Barracuda ATA IV 40GB	40GB	9	UltraATA100	EPRML16,17		7200
Barracuda ATA IV 60GB	60GB	9.5	UltraATA100	EPRML16,17		7200
Barracuda ATA IV 80GB	80GB	9.5	UltraATA100			7200
Cheetah 10K.6	36.7GB	4.7	UL320 SCSI			1000
Cheetah 10K.6	36.7GB	4.7	FC			1000
Cheetah 10K.6	36.7GB	4.7	UL320 SCSI			1000
Cheetah 10K.6	146.8GB	4.7	FC			1000
Cheetah 10K.6	146.8GB	4.7	UL320 SCSI			1000
Cheetah 10K.6	146.8GB	4.7	UL320 SCSI			1000
Cheetah 10K.6	73.4GB	4.7	FC			1000
Cheetah 10K.6	73.4GB	4.7	UL320 SCSI			1000
Cheetah 10K.6	73.4GB	4.7	UL320 SCSI			1000
Cheetah 15K.3	18.4GB	3.6	UL320 SCSI	EPRML		1500
Cheetah 15K.3	18.4GB	3.6	UL320 SCSI	EPRML		1500
Cheetah 15K.3	18.4GB	3.6	FC	EPRML		1500
Cheetah 15K.3	36.7GB	3.6	FC	EPRML		1500
Cheetah 15K.3	36.7GB	3.6	UL320 SCSI	EPRML		1500
Cheetah 15K.3	36.7GB	3.6	UL320 SCSI	EPRML		1500
Cheetah 15K.3	18.4GB	3.6	FC	EPRML		1500
Cheetah 15K.3	18.4GB	3.6	UL320 SCSI	EPRML		1500
Cheetah 15K.3	18.4GB	3.6	UL320 SCSI	EPRML		1500
Cheetah 36ES	18.4GB	5.2	UL320 SCSI	EPRML 32,34	4096k	1000
Cheetah 36ES	18.4GB	5.2	UL320 SCSI	EPRML 32,34	4096k	1000
Cheetah 36ES	36.9GB	5.2	UL320 SCSI	EPRML	4096k	1000
Cheetah 36ES	36.9GB	5.2	UL320 SCSI	EPRML	4096k	1000
Cheetah 36ES	36.9GB	6	80-pin	EPRML32,34	4096k	1000
Cheetah 36ES	36.9GB	6	80-pin	EPRML32,34		1000
Cheetah 36XL	18.352GB	5.4	Ultra 160	EPR4 32,34	4096k	1002
Cheetah 36XL	18.352GB	5.4	Ultra 160	EPR4 32,34	4096k	1002
Cheetah 36XL	36.704GB	5.4	Ultra 160	EPR4 32,34	4096k	1002
Cheetah 36XL	36.704GB	5.4	Ultra 160	EPR4 32,34	4096k	1002
Cheetah 36XL	9.176GB	5.4	Ultra 160	EPR4 32,34	4096k	1002
Cheetah 36XL	9.176GB	5.4	Ultra 160	EPR4 32,34	4096k	1002
Cheetah 73LP	36.7GB	4.6	FC	EPR4	4096k	1000
Cheetah 73LP	73.4GB	4.9	FC	EPR4	4096k	1000
Cheetah 73LP	73.4GB	4.9	Ultra 160	EPR4	4096k	1000
Cheetah 73LP	73.4GB	4.9	Ultra 160	EPR4	16384	1000
Cheetah X15	18.35GB	3.9	FC	EPRML	4096k	1500
Cheetah X15	18.4GB	3.6	UL320 SCSI	EPRML	8192k	1500
Cheetah X15	18.4GB	3.6	FC	EPRML	8192k	1500
Cheetah X15	18.4GB	3.6	UL320 SCSI	EPRML	8192k	1500
Cheetah X15	36.7GB	3.6	UL320 SCSI	EPRML	8192k	1500
Cheetah X15	36.7GB	3.6	FC	EPRML		1500
Cheetah X15	36.7GB	3.6	UL320 SCSI	EPRML	8192k	1500
Elite12G	1050	12	SMD	RLL		
Medalist 10230	10200	9.5	Ultra ATA	EPR4 (16/17)	512k	5400
Medalist 10231	10200	9	Ultra ATA	EPR4(16/17)	512k	5400
Medalist 12930	12900	9	Ultra ATA	EPRML 16,17	512k	5400
Medalist 13030	13000	9	Ultra ATA	EPRML 16,17	512k	5400
Medalist 13640	13600	9.5	Ultra ATA	EPRML 16,17	512k	5400
Medalist 17240	17200	9	Ultra ATA	EPR4(16/17)	512k	5400
Medalist 17240	17200	9	Ultra ATA	EPRML 16,17	512k	5400
Medalist 2140	2100		EIDE		256k	5400
Medalist 3210	3200	9.5	Ultra ATA	EPRML 16,17	256k	5400
Medalist 4310	4300	9	Ultra ATA	EPR4(16/17)	512k	5400
Medalist 4310	4300	9	Ultra ATA	EPRML 16,17	512k	5400
Medalist 6422	6400	9.5	Ultra ATA	EPRML 16,17	256k	5400
Medalist 8420	8400	9	Ultra ATA	EPR4(16/17)	512k	5400
Medalist 8420	8400	9	Ultra ATA	EPRML 16,17	512k	5400
Medalist Pro 9140	9100		Ultra ATA	PRML	512k	7200
Sabre1123	964	15	SMD	RLL		
Sabre1150	990	15	IPI-2	RLL		

Drive Model	Format Size MB	Head	Cyl	Sect/ Trac	Translate H/C/S	RWC/ WPC	Form Factor	Power Watts
Sabre1230	1050	15	1635			—/—	8.0 FH	
Sabre2270	1948	19				—/—	8.0 FH	
Sabre2500	2145	19				—/—	8.0 FH	
Sabre368	368	10	1635			—/—	8.0 FH	
Sabre500	500	10	1217			—/—	8.0 FH	
Sabre736	741	15	1217			—/—	8.0 FH	
Sabre850	851	15	1635			—/—	8.0 FH	
ST1057A	53	3	1024	17	6/1024/17	NA/NA	3.5HH	9
ST1057N	49	3	940	34		NA/NA	3.5HH	9
ST1090A	79	5	1072	29	16/335/29	NA/NA	3.5HH	
ST1090N	79	5	1068	29		NA/NA	3.5HH	
ST1096N	84	7	906	26		NA/NA	3.5HH	9
ST1100	83	9	1072	17		1073/1073	3.5HH	
ST1102A	89	5	1024	17	10/1024/17	NA/NA	3.5HH	9
ST1102N	84	5	965	34		—/—	3.5HH	9
ST1106R	91	7	977	26		NA/NA	3.5HH	
ST1111A	98	5	1072	36	10/536/36	NA/NA	3.5HH	
ST1111E	98	5	1072	36		NA/NA	3.5HH	
ST1111N	98	5	1068	36		NA/NA	3.5HH	
ST1200N	1054	15	1872	73		—/—	3.5HH	
ST11200ND	1050	15	1877			—/—	3.5HH	
ST11201N (never made)	1054	15	1872	73		—/—	3.5HH	
ST11201ND	1050	15	1877			—/—	3.5HH	
ST1126A	111	7	1072	29	16/469/29	NA/NA	3.5HH	
ST1126N	107	7	1068	29		NA/NA	3.5HH	
ST1133A	117	5	1272	36	10/636/36	NA/NA	3.5HH	
ST1133NS	113	5	1268	36		NA/NA	3.5HH	9
ST1144A	131	7	1024	32	15/1001/17	—/—	3.5HH	9
ST1144N	126	7		32		NA/300	3.5HH	
ST1150R	128	9	1072	26		NA/NA	3.5HH	
ST1156A	138	7	1072	36	14/536/36	NA/NA	3.5HH	
ST1156E	138	7	1072	36		NA/NA	3.5HH	
ST1156N	138	7	1068	36		NA/NA	3.5HH	
ST1156NS	138	7	1068	36		—/—	3.5HH	
ST1162A	143	9	1072	29	16/603/29	NA/NA	3.5HH	
ST1162N	138	9	1068	29		NA/NA	3.5HH	
ST11700N	1430	13	2626			—/—	3.5HH	
ST11700ND	1430	13	2626			—/—	3.5HH	
ST11701N	1430	13	2626			—/—	3.5HH	
ST11701ND	1430	13	2626			—/—	3.5HH	
ST11750N	1437		2756			—/—	3.5HH	
ST11750ND	1437		2756			—/—	3.5HH	
ST11751N	1437		2756			—/—	3.5HH	
ST11751ND	1437		2756			—/—	3.5HH	
ST1181677FCV	181.6GB	12	24247			—/—	3.5HH	10.3
ST1181677LCV	181.6GB	24	24247			—/—	3.5HH	9.95
ST1181677LWV	181.6GB	24	24247			—/—	3.5HH	9.95
ST118202FC	18200	24	6962			—/—	3.5HH	
ST118202LC	18200	24	6962			—/—	3.5HH	
ST118202LW	18200	24	6962			—/—	3.5HH	
ST118273FC	18200	20				—/—	3.5HH	15
ST118273LC	18200	20				—/—	3.5HH	13
ST118273LW	18200	20				—/—	3.5HH	13
ST118273N	18200	20				—/—	3.5HH	13
ST118273W	18200	20				—/—	3.5HH	13
ST118273WC	18200	20				—/—	3.5HH	13
ST118273WD	18200	20				—/—	3.5HH	13
ST1186A	164	7	1272	36	12/742/36	NA/NA	3.5HH	
ST1186NS	159	7	1268	36		NA/NA	3.5HH	
ST11900N	1700	15	2621	83		NA/NA	3.5HH	
ST11900NC	1700	15	2621	83		NA/NA	3.5HH	
ST11900ND	1700	15	2621	83		NA/NA	3.5HH	
ST11900W	1700	15	2621	83		NA/NA	3.5HH	
ST11900WC	1700	15	2621	83		NA/NA	3.5HH	
ST11900WD	1700	15	2621	83		NA/NA	3.5HH	
ST11950N	1690	15	2706	81		NA/NA	3.5HH	
ST11950ND	1690					NA/NA	3.5HH	

Drive Model	Format Size MB	Seek Time	Interface	Encode	cache kb	RPM
Sabre1230	1050	15	SMD/SCSI	RLL		
Sabre2270	1948	12	SMD	RLL		
Sabre2500	2145	12	SMD/SCSI	RLL		
Sabre368	368	182	SMD/SCSI	RLL		
Sabre500	500	18	SMD/SCSI	RLL		
Sabre736	741	15	SMD/SCSI	RLL		
Sabre850	851	15	SMD/SCSI	RLL		
ST1057A	53	19	IDE AT	RLL ZBR	8/32k	3528
ST1057N	49	19	SCSI-2	2,7 RLL	8/32k	3528
ST1090A	79	15	IDE AT	2,7 RLL		3600
ST1090N	79	15	SCSI	RLL		3600
ST1096N	84	20	SCSI	2,7 RLL	8k	3600
ST1100	83	15	ST412/506	MFM		3600
ST1102A	89	15	IDE AT	RLL ZBR	8k	3528
ST1102N	84	19	SCSI-2	RLL ZBR	8/32k	3528
ST1106R	91	24	ST412/506	RLL		3600
ST1111A	98	15	IDE AT	2,7 RLL		3600
ST1111E	98	15	ESDI (10)	2,7 RLL		3600
ST1111N	98	15	SCSI	RLL		3600
ST11200N	1054	11	SCSI-2Fast	RLL ZBR	256k	5411
ST11200ND	1050	11	SCSI-2Fast	1,7 RLL	256k	5400
ST11201N (never made)	1054	10	SCSI-2Fast	ZBR,1,7RLL	256k	5411
ST11201ND	1050	10	SCSI-2FstWD	1,7 RLL	256k	5400
ST1126A	111	15	IDE AT	2,7 RLL	32k	3600
ST1126N	107	15	SCSI	RLL	64k	3600
ST1133A	117	15	IDE AT	2,7 RLL	64k	3600
ST1133NS	113	15	SCSI	RLL		3600
ST1144A	131	19	IDE AT	RLL ZBR	32k	3528
ST1144N	126	19	SCSI-2	RLL ZBR	8/32k	3528
ST1150R	128	15	ST412/506	RLL		3600
ST1156A	138	15	IDE AT	2,7 RLL		3600
ST1156E	138	15	ESDI	RLL		3600
ST1156N	138	15	SCSI	RLL		3600
ST1156NS	138	15	SCSI-2	2,7 RLL		3600
ST1162A	143	15	IDE AT	2,7 RLL	32k	3600
ST1162N	138	15	SCSI	2,7 RLL	64k	3600
ST11700N	1430	9	SCSI-2Fast	1,7 RLL	256k	5400
ST11700ND	1430	10	SCSI-2Fast	1,7 RLL	256k	5400
ST11701N	1430	9	SCSI-2FstW	1,7 RLL	256k	5400
ST11701ND	1430	10	SCSI-2FstW	1,7 RLL	256k	5400
ST11750N	1437	8	SCSI-2Fast	1,7 RLL	1024k	7200
ST11750ND	1437	9	SCSI-2Fast	1,7 RLL	1024k	7200
ST11751N	1437	8	SCSI-2Fast	1,7 RLL	1024k	7200
ST11751ND	1437	9	SCSI-2Fast	1,7 RLL	1024k	7200
ST1181677FCV	181.6GB	7.4	FC	EPR4		7200
ST1181677LCV	181.6GB	8.2	80-pin	EPR4	16384	7200
ST1181677LWV	181.6GB	8.2	68-pin	EPR4		7200
ST118202FC	18200	5.7	FC	8,9 PR4	1024k	1000
ST118202LC	18200	5.7	Ultra2 SCSI	8,9 PR4	1024k	1000
ST118202LW	18200	5.7	Ultra2 SCSI	8,9 PR4	1024k	1000
ST118273FC	18200	7.1	FiberChanel	16/17 EPR4	1024k	7200
ST118273LC	18200	7.1	Ultra2 SCSI	16/17 EPR4	1024k	7200
ST118273LW	18200	7.1	Ultra2 SCSI	16/17 EPR4	1024k	7200
ST118273N	18200	7.1	Ultra SCSI	16/17 EPR4	512k	7200
ST118273W	18200	7.1	Ultra SCSI	16/17 EPR4	512k	7200
ST118273WC	18200	7.1	SCA-2	16/17 EPR4	512k	7200
ST118273WD	18200	7.1	Ultra2 SCSI	16/17 EPR4	1024k	7200
ST1186A	164	15	IDE AT	2,7 RLL	32k	3600
ST1186NS	159	15	SCSI	2,7 RLL	64k	3600
ST11900NC	1700	10	SCSI-2Fast	1,7 RLL		5411
ST11900NC	1700	10	SCSI-2Fast	1,7 RLL		5411
ST11900ND	1700	10	SCSI-2Fast	1,7 RLL		5411
ST11900W	1700	10	SCSI-2FstW	RLL ZBR		5411
ST11900WC	1700	10	SCSI-2FstW	RLL ZBR		5411
ST11900WD	1700	10	SCSI-2FstW	RLL ZBR		5411
ST11950N	1690	9	SCSI-2Fast	RLL ZBR	1024k	7200
ST11950ND	1690	9	SCSI-2Fast		1024k	7200

Drive Model	Format Size MB	Head	Cyl	Sect/Trac	Translate H/C/S	RWC/WPC	Form Factor	Power Watts
ST11950W	1690	15	2706	81		NA/NA	3.5HH	
ST11950WD	1690					NA/NA	3.5HH	
ST1201A	177	9	1072	36	9/804/48	NA/NA	3.5HH	
ST1201E	177	9	1072	36		NA/NA	3.5HH	
ST1201N	172	9	1068	36		—/—	3.5HH	
ST1201NS	177	9	1068	36		NA/NA	3.5HH	
ST1239A	211	9	1272	36	14/817/36	NA/NA	3.5HH	
ST1239NS	204	9	1268	36		NA/NA	3.5HH	
ST124	21	4	615	17		616/616	3.5HH	8
ST12400N	2148	19	2621	83		NA/NA	3.5HH	
ST12400NC	2148	19	2621	83		NA/NA	3.5HH	
ST12400ND	2100	19	2626			—/—	3.5HH	
ST12400ND	2148	19	2621	83		NA/NA	3.5HH	
ST12400W	2148	19	2621	84		NA/NA	3.5HH	
ST12400WC	2148	19	2621	84		NA/NA	3.5HH	
ST12400WD	2148	19	2621	84		NA/NA	3.5HH	
ST12401N	2100	19	2626			NA/NA	3.5HH	
ST12401ND	2100	19	2626			—/—	3.5HH	
ST12450W	1849	18	2710	149		NA/NA	3.5HH	
ST12450WD	1781					NA/NA	3.5HH	
ST125-0	21	4	615	17		NA/NA	3.5HH	8
ST125-1	21	4	615	17		NA/NA	3.5HH	8
ST12550N	2139	19	2707	81		NA/NA	3.5HH	
ST12550ND	2139		2756			NA/NA	3.5HH	
ST12550W	2139	19	2707	81		NA/NA	3.5HH	
ST12550WD	2139		2756			NA/NA	3.5HH	
ST12551N	2100		2756			—/—	3.5HH	
ST12551ND	2100		2756			—/—	3.5HH	
ST125A-0	21	4	404	26	4/615/17	NA/NA	3.5HH	8
ST125A-1	21	4	404	26	4/615/17	NA/NA	3.5HH	8
ST125N-0	21	4	407	26		NONE/NA	3.5HH	8
ST125N-1	21	4	407	26		NA/NA	3.5HH	8
ST125R	21.5	4	404	26		—/—	3.5HH	
ST1274A	230	4	407	26	4/407/26	—/—	3.5HH	
ST136403FC	36400	24	9772			—/—	3.5HH	
ST136403FCV	36400	24	9772			—/—	3.5HH	
ST136403LC	36400	24	9772			—/—	3.5HH	
ST136403LCV	36400	24	9772			—/—	3.5HH	
ST136403LW	36400	24	9772			—/—	3.5HH	
ST136403LWV	36400	24	9772			—/—	3.5HH	
ST136475FC	36400	20	11737			—/—	3.5HH	
ST136475LC	36400	20	11737			—/—	3.5HH	
ST136475LW	36400	20	11737			—/—	3.5HH	
ST137R	33	4	615	26		—/—	3.5HH	
ST138-0	32	6	615	17		NA/NA	3.5HH	8
ST138-1	32	6	615	17		NA/NA	3.5HH	8
ST138A-0	32	4	604	26	6/615/17	NA/NA	3.5HH	8
ST138A-1	32	4	604	26	6/615/17	NA/NA	3.5HH	8
ST138N-0	32	4	615	26		NA/NA	3.5HH	8
ST138N-1	32	4	615	26		NA/NA	3.5HH	8
ST138R-0	32	4	615	26		NA/NA	3.5HH	8
ST138R-1	32	4	615	26		NA/NA	3.5HH	8
ST1400A	331	7	1475	NA	12/1018/53	NA/NA	3.5HH	9.1
ST1400N	331	7	1476	62		NA/NA	3.5HH	
ST1401A	340	9	1132		15/726/61	NA/NA	3.5HH	9.1
ST1401N	338	9	1100	66		NA/NA	3.5HH	
ST14207N Cayman	4294	20	4016	104		NA/NA	3.5HH	12.8
ST14207W Cayman	4294	20	4016	104		NA/NA	3.5HH	12.8
ST14209N Cayman	4295	20	3999	104		NA/NA	3.5HH	12.8
ST14209W Cayman	4295	20	3999	104		NA/NA	3.5HH	12.8
ST1480A	426	9	1474	NA	15/895/62	NA/NA	3.5HH	9.1
ST1480N	426	9	1476	62		NA/NA	3.5HH	9.1
ST1480NV	426	9	1478	V		NA/NA	3.5HH	
ST1481N	426	9	1476	62		NA/NA	3.5HH	
ST150176FC	50100	22	12024			—/—	3.5HH	
ST150176LC	50100	22	12024			—/—	3.5HH	
ST150176LW	50100	22	12024			—/—	3.5HH	

Drive Model	Format Size MB	Seek Time	Interface	Encode	cache kb	RPM
ST11950W	1690	9	SCSI-2FstW	RLL ZBR	1024k	7200
ST11950WD	1690	9	SCSI-2FstW		1024k	7200
ST1201A	177	15	IDE AT	2,7 RLL	32k	3600
ST1201E	177	15	ESDI (10)	2,7 RLL		3600
ST1201N	172	15	SCSI	2,7 RLL		3600
ST1201NS	177	15	SCSI-2	2,7 RLL	64k	3600
ST1239A	211	15	IDE AT	2,7 RLL	32k	3600
ST1239NS	204	15	SCSI-2	2,7 RLL	64k	3600
ST124	21	40	ST412/506	MFM		3600
ST12400N	2148	9	SCSI-2Fast	RLL ZBR	256k	5411
ST12400NC	2148	9	SCSI-2Fast	RLL ZBR	256k	5411
ST12400ND	2100	9	SCSI-2Fast	1,7 RLL	256k	5400
ST12400ND	2148	9	SCSI-2Fast	RLL ZBR	256k	5411
ST12400W	2148	10.5	SCSI-2FstW	RLL ZBR	256k	5411
ST12400WC	2148	10.5	SCSI-2FstW	RLL ZBR	256k	5411
ST12400WD	2148	10.5	SCSI-2FstW	RLL ZBR	256k	5411
ST12401N	2100	9	SCSI-2FstW	1,7 RLL	256k	5411
ST12401ND	2100	10	SCSI-2Fast	1,7 RLL	256k	5400
ST12450W	1849	9	SCSI-2FstW	1,7RLL,ZBR	1024k	7200
ST12450WD	1781	9	SCSI-2FstW	1,7RLL,ZBR	1024	7200
ST125-0	21	40	ST412/506	MFM		3600
ST125-1	21	28	ST412/506	MFM		3600
ST12550N	2139	8	SCSI-2Fast	1,7 RLL	1024k	7200
ST12550ND	2139	9	SCSI-2Fast	1,7 RLL	1024k	7200
ST12550W	2139	9	SCSI-2FstW	1,7RLL,ZBR	1024k	7200
ST12550WD	2139	9	SCSI-2FstW		1024k	7200
ST12551N	2100	8	SCSI-2Fast	1,7 RLL	1024k	7200
ST12551ND	2100	9	SCSI-2Fast	1,7 RLL	1024k	7200
ST125A-0	21	40	IDE AT	RLL	2k	3600
ST125A-1	21	28	IDE AT	RLL	2k	3600
ST125N-0	21	40	SCSI	RLL	2k	3600
ST125N-1	21	28	SCSI	RLL	2k	3600
ST125R	21.5		ST412/506	2,7 RLL		
ST1274A	230	18	IDE AT	2,7 RLL		
ST136403FC	36400	5.7	FC	16/17 PR4	1024k	1000
ST136403FCV	36400	5.7	FC	16/17 PR4	1024k	1000
ST136403LC	36400	5.7	Ultra2 SCSI	16/17 PR4	1024k	1000
ST136403LCV	36400	5.7	Ultra2 SCSI	16/17 PR4	1024k	1000
ST136403LW	36400	5.7	Ultra2 SCSI	16/17 PR4	1024k	1000
ST136403LWV	36400	5.7	Ultra2 SCSI	16/17 PR4	1024k	1000
ST136475FC	36400	7.4	FC	8,9 PR4	1024k	7200
ST136475LC	36400	7.4	Ultra2 SCSI	8,9 PR4	1024k	7200
ST136475LW	36400	7.4	Ultra2 SCSI	8,9 PR4	1024k	7200
ST137R	33	40	ST412/506	2,7 RLL		
ST138-0	32	40	ST412/506	MFM	2k	3600
ST138-1	32	28	ST412/506	MFM	2k	3600
ST138A-0	32	40	IDE AT	2,7 RLL	2k	3600
ST138A-1	32	28	IDE AT	2,7 RLL	2k	3600
ST138N-0	32	40	SCSI	2,7 RLL	2k	3600
ST138N-1	32	28	SCSI	2,7 RLL	2k	3600
ST138R-0	32	40	ST412/506	2,7 RLL	2k	3600
ST138R-1	32	28	ST412/506	2,7 RLL	2k	3600
ST1400A	331	14	IDE AT	1,7 RLL	64k	4412
ST1400N	331	14	SCSI-2	1,7RLL,ZBR	64k	4412
ST1401A	340	12	IDE AT	1,7 RLL	64k	4412
ST1401N	338	12	SCSI-2	1,7RLL,ZBR	64k	4412
ST14207N Cayman	4294	9	SCSI-2Fast	1,7 RLL	512k	7200
ST14207W Cayman	4294	9	SCSI-2FstW	1,7 RLL	512k	7200
ST14209N Cayman	4295	9	Ultra SCSI	1,7 RLL	512k	7200
ST14209W Cayman	4295	9	Ultra SCSIW	1,7 RLL	512k	7200
ST1480A	426	14	IDE AT	ZBR	64k	4412
ST1480N	426	14	SCSI-2	ZBR	64k	4412
ST1480NV	426	14	SCSI-2	1,7 RLL	64k	4412
ST1481N	426	14	SCSI-2Fast	ZBR,1,7RLL	64k	4412
ST150176FC	50100	7.4	FC	16/17 PR4	1024k	7200
ST150176LC	50100	7.4	Ultra2 SCSI	16/17 PR4	1024k	7200
ST150176LW	50100	7.4	Ultra2 SCSI	16/17 PR4	1024k	7200

Drive Model	Format Size MB	Head	Cyl	Sect/Trac	Translate H/C/S	RWC/WPC	Form Factor	Power Watts
ST151	42	5	977	17		NA/NA	3.5HH	8
ST15150DC	4294	21	3711			NA/NA	3.5HH	12.5
ST15150FC	4294	21	3711			NA/NA	3.5HH	18.4
ST15150N	4294	21	3711	81		NA/NA	3.5HH	12.5
ST15150ND	4294	21	3711			NA/NA	3.5HH	12.5
ST15150W	4294	21	3711			NA/NA	3.5HH	12.5
ST15150WC	4294	21	3711			NA/NA	3.5HH	12.5
ST15150WD	4294	21	3711			NA/NA	3.5HH	12.5
ST15230DC	4294	19	3892			NA/NA	3.5HH	9
ST15230N	4294	19	3892			NA/NA	3.5HH	9
ST15230ND	4294	19	3892			NA/NA	3.5HH	9
ST15230W	4294	19	3892			NA/NA	3.5HH	9
ST15230WC	4294	19	3892			NA/NA	3.5HH	9
ST15230WD	4294	19	3892			NA/NA	3.5HH	9
ST15320N	4294					—/—	3.5HH	
ST157A-0	45	6	560	26	7/733/17	NA/NA	3.5HH	9
ST157A-1	45	6	560	26	7/733/17	NA/NA	3.5HH	9
ST157N-0	49	6	615	26		NA/NA	3.5HH	9
ST157N-1	49	6	615	26		NA/NA	3.5HH	9
ST157R-0	49	6	615	26		NA/NA	3.5HH	8
ST157R-1	49	6	615	26		NA/NA	3.5HH	8
ST1581N	525	9	1476	77		NA/NA	3.5HH	
ST173404FC	73400	24	14100			—/—	3.5HH	16.5
ST173404FCV	73400	24	14100			—/—	3.5HH	15.7
ST173404LC	73400	24	14100			—/—	3.5HH	15.7
ST173404LCV	73400	24	14100			—/—	3.5HH	15.7
ST173404LW	73400	24	14100			—/—	3.5HH	15.7
ST173404LWV	73400	24	14100			—/—	3.5HH	15.7
ST177N	60	5	921	26		NA/NA	3.5HH	9
ST1830N	702	13	1325			—/—	3.5HH	
ST18771DC	8700	20	5333			NA/NA	3.5HH	12.4
ST18771FC	8700	20	5333			NA/NA	3.5HH	16.4
ST18771N	8700	20	5333			NA/NA	3.5HH	12.4
ST18771ND	8700	20	5333			NA/NA	3.5HH	12.4
ST18771W	8700	20	5333			NA/NA	3.5HH	12.4
ST18771WC	8700	20	5333			NA/NA	3.5HH	12.4
ST18771WD	8700	20	5333			NA/NA	3.5HH	12.4
ST19101DC	9100	16	6526			—/—	3.5HH	20.7
ST19101FC	9100	16	6526			—/—	3.5HH	20.7
ST19101N	9100	16	6526			—/—	3.5HH	20.7
ST19101W	9100	16	6526			—/—	3.5HH	20.7
ST19101WC	9100	16	6526			—/—	3.5HH	20.7
ST19101WD	9100	16	6526			—/—	3.5HH	20.7
ST19171DC	9100	20	5274			—/—	3.5	13
ST19171FC	9100	20	5274			—/—	3.5	13
ST19171N	9100	20	5274			—/—	3.5	13
ST19171W	9100	20	5274			—/—	3.5	13
ST19171WC	9100	20	5274			—/—	3.5	13
ST19171WD	9100	20	5274			—/—	3.5	13
ST1950N	803	13	1575			—/—	3.5	
ST1980N	860	13	1730	74		NA/NA	3.5	
ST1980NC	860	13	1730			NA/NA	3.5	
ST1980ND	860	13	1730			—/—	3.5	
ST206	5	2	306	17		307/128	5.25FH	
ST2106E	89	5	1024	34		NA/NA	5.25FH	
ST2106N	91	5	1022	36		NA/NA	5.25FH	
ST2106NM	94	5	1022	35		NA/NA	5.25FH	
ST212	10	4	306	17		307/128	5.25FH	
ST2125N	107	3	1544	45		NA/NA	5.25FH	
ST2125NM	107	3	1544	45		NA/NA	5.25FH	
ST2125NV	107	3	1544	45		NA/NA	5.25FH	
ST213	10	2	615	17		616/300	5.25FH	14
ST2182E	160	4	1453	54		NA/NA	5.25FH	
ST2209N	179	5	1544	45		NA/NA	5.25FH	
ST224N	21	2				—/—	5.25FH	
ST225	21	4	615	17		None/300	5.25FH	14.8
ST225N	21	4	615	17		NA/NA	5.25FH	16

Drive Model	Format Size MB	Seek Time	Interface	Encode	cache kb	RPM
ST151	42	24	ST412/506	MFM		3600
ST15150DC	4294	9	SCSI-2Diff	1,7 RLL	1024k	7200
ST15150FC	4294	9	FC	1,7 RLL	1024k	7200
ST15150ND	4294	9	SCSI-2Diff	1,7 RLL	1024k	7200
ST15150ND	4294	9	SCSI-2Diff	1,7 RLL	1024k	7200
ST15150NW	4294	9	SCSI-2FstW	1,7 RLL	1024k	7200
ST15150WC	4294	9	SCSI-2FstW	1,7 RLL	1024k	7200
ST15150WD	4294	9	SCSI-2Diff	1,7 RLL	1024k	7200
ST15230DC	4294	10	SCSI-2FstW	ZBR,1,7RLL	512k	5411
ST15230N	4294	9	SCSI-2Fast	1,7 RLL	512k	5411
ST15230ND	4294	9	SCSI-2Fast	1,7 RLL	512k	5411
ST15230W	4294	10	SCSI-2FstW	ZBR,1,7RLL	512k	5411
ST15230WC	4294	10	SCSI-2FstW	ZBR,1,7RLL	512k	5411
ST15230WD	4294	10	SCSI-2FstW	ZBR,1,7RLL	512k	5411
ST15320N	4294	10	ASA-2			5400
ST157A-0	45	40	IDE AT	2,7 RLL	2k	3600
ST157A-1	45	28	IDE AT	2,7 RLL	2k	3600
ST157N-0	49	40	SCSI	2,7 RLL	2k	3600
ST157N-1	49	28	SCSI	2,7 RLL	2k	3600
ST157R-0	49	40	ST412/506	2,7 RLL	2k	3600
ST157R-1	49	28	ST412/506	2,7 RLL	2k	3600
ST1581N	525	14	SCSI-2Fast	RLL ZBR	64k	4412
ST173404FC	73400	5.6	FC	NPV	4096k	1000
ST173404FCV	73400	5.6	FC	NPV	16384	1000
ST173404LC	73400	5.6	UL160SCSI	NPV	16384	1000
ST173404LCV	73400	5.6	UL160SCSI	NPV	16384	1000
ST173404LW	73400	5.6	UL160SCSI	NPV	16384	1000
ST173404LWV	73400	5.6	UL160SCSI	NPV	16384	1000
ST177N	60	24	SCSI	RLL	8k	3600
ST1830N	702		SCSI-2Fast	ZBR,1,7RLL	256k	4535
ST18771DC	8700	9	ULTRA SCSI	PRML0,6,6	512k	7200
ST18771FC	8700	9	FC	PRML0,6,6	512k	7200
ST18771N	8700	9	ULTRA SCSI	PRML0,6,6	512k	7200
ST18771ND	8700	9	ULTRA SCSI	PRML0,6,6	512k	7200
ST18771W	8700	9	ULTRA SCSI	PRML0,6,6	512k	7200
ST18771WC	8700	9	ULTRA SCSI	PRML0,6,6	512k	7200
ST18771WD	8700	9	ULTRA SCSI	PRML0,6,6	512k	7200
ST19101DC	9100	8	Ultra SCSI	PRML0,4,4	512k	1003
ST19101FC	9100	8	FC	PRML0,4,4	1024k	1003
ST19101N	9100	8	Ultra SCSI	PRML0,4,4	512k	1003
ST19101W	9100	8	Ultra SCSI	PRML0,4,4	512k	1003
ST19101WC	9100	8	Ultra SCSI	PRML0,4,4	512k	1003
ST19101WD	9100	8	Ultra SCSI	PRML0,4,4	512k	1003
ST19171DC	9100	9	FC-AL	PRML0,4,4	512k	7200
ST19171FC	9100	9	FC-AL	PRML0,4,4	512k	7200
ST19171N	9100	9	Ultra SCSI	PRML0,4,4	512k	7200
ST19171W	9100	9	FC-AL	PRML0,4,4	512k	7200
ST19171WC	9100	9	FC-AL	PRML0,4,4	512k	7200
ST19171WD	9100	9	FC-AL	PRML0,4,4	512k	7200
ST1950N	803		SCSI-2Fast	ZBR,1,7RLL	256k	4535
ST1980N	860	10	SCSI-2Fast	ZBR1,7RLL	256k	5411
ST1980NC	860	11	SCSI-2Fast		256k	5400
ST1980ND	860	11	SCSI-2Fast	1,7 RLL	256k	5400
ST206	5		ST412/506	MFM		
ST2106E	89	18	ESDI (10)	2,7 RLL		3600
ST2106N	91	18	SCSI	2,7 RLL	32k	3600
ST2106NM	94	18	SCSI	2,7 RLL	32k	3600
ST212	10	65	ST412/506	MFM		3600
ST2125N	107	18	SCSI	ZBR,2,7RLL	32k	3600
ST2125NM	107	18	SCSI	ZBR,2,7RLL	32k	3600
ST2125NV	107	18	SCSI	ZBR,2,7RLL	32k	3600
ST213	10	65	ST412/506	MFM		3600
ST2182E	160	16	ESDI (15)	2,7 RLL		3600
ST2209N	179	18	SCSI	ZBR,2,7RLL	32k	3600
ST224N	21	70	SCSI	2,7 RLL		3600
ST225	21	65	ST412/506	MFM		3600
ST225N	21	65	SCSI	MFM		3600

Drive Model	Format Size MB	Head	Cyl	Sect/Trac	Translate H/C/S	RWC/WPC	Form Factor	Power Watts
ST225R	21	2	667	31		NA/NA	5.25HH	14.8
ST2274A	241	5	1747	54	16/536/55	NA/NA	5.25HH	
ST2383A	338	7	1747	54	16/737/56	NA/NA	5.25HH	
ST2383E	338	7	1747	54		NA/NA	5.25HH	
ST2383N	332	7	1261	74		NA/NA	5.25HH	
ST2383ND	332	7	1261	NA		NA/NA	5.25HH	
ST2383NM	332	7	1261	NA		NA/NA	5.25HH	
ST238R	32	4	615	26		NA/NA	5.25HH	14.8
ST2502N	435	7	1755	NA		NA/NA	5.25HH	
ST2502ND	435	7	1765	NA		NA/NA	5.25HH	
ST2502NM	435	7	1765	NA		NA/NA	5.25HH	
ST2502NV	435	7	1765	NA		NA/NA	5.25HH	
ST250N	42	4	667			NA/NA	5.25HH	14.8
ST250R	42	4	667	31		NA/NA	5.25HH	12
ST251-0	42	6	820	17		NA/NA	5.25HH	12
ST251-1	42	6	820	17		NA/NA	5.25HH	13
ST251N-0	43	4	820	26		NA/NA	5.25HH	13
ST251N-1	43	4	820	26		NA/NA	5.25HH	11
ST251R	43	4	820	26		NA/NA	5.25HH	9.7
ST252	42	6	820	17		NA/128	5.25HH	
ST253	43	5	989	17		NA/NA	5.25HH	
ST274A	65	5	948	26	8/940/17	NA/NA	5.25HH	
ST277N-0	65	6	820	26		NA/NA	5.25HH	13
ST277N-1	65	6	628	34		NA/NA	5.25HH	13
ST277R-0	65	6	820	26		NA/NA	5.25HH	12
ST277R-1	65	6	820	26		NA/NA	5.25HH	12
ST278R	65	6	820	26		NA/128	5.25HH	9.7
ST279R	65	5	989	26		NA/NA	5.25HH	
ST280A	71	5	1032	26	10/516/27	NA/NA	5.25HH	13
ST296N	85	6	820	34		NA/NA	3.5 3H	4
ST3025A	21	1	615	17	2/808/26	NA/NA	3.5 3H	4
ST3025N	21	1	1616	26		NA/NA	3.5 3H	
ST3051A	43	6	820	17	6/820/17	NA/NA	3.5 3H	4
ST3057A	53	*	1024	17		NA/NA	3.5 3H	4
ST3057N	49	3	940	34		NA/NA	3.5 3H	4
ST3096A	90	10	1024	17	8/836/26	NA/NA	3.5 3H	5.1
ST3096N	84	3	1024	35		NA/NA	3.5 3H	5.1
ST310014ACE	10GB	1			16/16383/63	—/—	2.5 4H	4.5
ST31010A	1082	2			16/2098/63	NA/NA	3.5 3H	3.8
ST31012A	1082	2			16/2098/63	NA/NA	3.5 3H	3.8
ST310210A	10200	2			16/16383/63	—/—	3.5 3H	7
ST310211A	10000	1			16/16368/63	—/—	3.5 3H	4.8
ST310212A	10200	2			16/16383/63	—/—	3.5 3H	3.5
ST310215A	10200	1			16/16383/63	—/—	3.5 3H	
ST310216A	10.2GB	2			16/16383/63	—/—	3.5 3H	7
ST310220A	10200	3			16/16383/63	—/—	3.5 3H	
ST310230A	10200	6			16/16383/63	—/—	3.5 3H	4.5
ST310231A	10200	6			16/16383/63	—/—	3H	5.5
ST310232A	10242	3			16/16383/63	—/—	3.5 3H	5.5
ST310240A	10200	4				—/—	3.5 3H	4.9
ST31051N	1060	4	4176			NA/NA	3.5 3H	6.3
ST31051W	1060	4	4176			NA/NA	3.5 3H	6.3
ST31051WC	1060	4	4176			NA/NA	3.5 3H	6.3
ST31055N	1060	4	4176			—/—	3.5 3H	
ST31055W	1060	4	4176			—/—	3.5 3H	
ST31055WC	1060	4	4176			—/—	3.5 3H	
ST31060A	1065	6	3640		16/2064/63	NA/NA	3.5 3H	3.5
ST31060N	1062	8	2757	94		NA/NA	3.5 3H	6.6
ST31060W	1062	8	2757	94		NA/NA	3.5 3H	6.6
ST31080N	1080	6	3658	96		NA/NA	3.5 3H	3.75
ST31081A	1081	8	3924		16/2097/63	—/—	3.5 3H	3.9
ST31082A	1082				4/2097/63	—/—	3.5 3H	4.0
ST3120020A	120GB	4				—/—	3.5 3H	9.5
ST3120022A	120GB	3			16/16383/63	—/—	3.5 3H	7.5
ST3120022AS	120GB	3			16/16383/63	—/—	3.5 3H	7.5
ST3120023A	120GB	4			16/16383/63	—/—	3.5 3H	9.5
ST3120023AS	120GB	4			16/16383/63	—/—	3.5 3H	9.5

Drive Model	Format Size MB	Seek Time	Interface	Encode	cache kb	RPM
ST225R	21	70	ST412/506	2,7 RLL		3000
ST2274A	241	16	IDE AT	2,7 RLL	32k	3600
ST2383A	338	16	IDE AT	2,7 RLL	32k	3600
ST2383E	338	16	ESDI	2,7 RLL		3600
ST2383N	332	14	SCSI	ZBR,2,7RLL	64k	3600
ST2383ND	332	14	SCSI	RLL ZBR	64k	3600
ST2383NM	332	14	SCSI	RLL ZBR	64k	3600
ST238R	32	65	ST412/506	RLL		3600
ST2502N	435	16	SCSI	ZBR,2,7RLL	64k	3600
ST2502ND	435	16	SCSI	RLL ZBR	64k	
ST2502NM	435	16	SCSI	RLL ZBR	64k	
ST2502NV	435	16	SCSI	RLL ZBR	64k	
ST250N	42	70	SCSI	2,7 RLL		
ST250R	42	70	ST412/506	2,7 RLL		3600
ST251-0	42.	40	ST412/506	MFM		3600
ST251-1	42	28	ST412/506	MFM		3600
ST251N-0	43	40	SCSI	RLL		3600
ST251N-1	43	28	SCSI	RLL		3600
ST251R	43	40	ST412/506	2,7 RLL		3600
ST252	42	40	ST412/506	MFM		3600
ST253	43	28	ST412/506	MFM		3600
ST274A	65	29	IDE AT	RLL		3600
ST277N-0	65	40	SCSI	RLL		3600
ST277N-1	65	28	SCSI	RLL	2k	3600
ST277R-0	65	40	ST412/506	2,7 RLL	2k	3600
ST277R-1	65	28	ST412/506	2,7 RLL		3600
ST278R	65	40	ST412/506	2,7 RLL		3600
ST279R	65	28	ST412/506	RLL		3600
ST280A	71	29	IDE AT	RLL		3600
ST296N	85	28	SCSI	2,7 RLL		3600
ST3025A	21	19	IDE AT	2,7 RLL	8/32k	3600
ST3025N	21	19	SCSI-2	2,7 RLL	8/32k	3600
ST3051A	43	16	IDE AT	2,7 RLL	32k	3211
ST3057A	53	19	IDE AT	2,7 RLL	8/32k	3600
ST3057N	49	19	SCSI-2	2,7 RLL	8/32k	3600
ST3096A	90	14	IDE AT	2,7 RLL	32k	3211
ST3096N	84	20	SCSI-2	2,7 RLL	8/32k	3528
ST310014ACE	10GB	12.7	UltraATA100	GPRML96/102	2mb	5400
ST31010A	1082	12.5	ATA-2 Fast	1,7 RLL	128k	4500
ST31012A	1082	12.5	Ultra ATA-3	1,7 RLL	128k	4500
ST310210A	10200	8.2	UltraATA/66	EPRML 16,17	2mb	7200
ST310211A	10000	8.9	UltraATA100	EPRML 16,17		5400
ST310212A	10200	8.9	UltraATA/66	EPRML 24,26	512k	5400
ST310215A	10200	8.9	UltraATA100	EPRML 16,17	4160k	2048
ST310216A	10.2GB	8.2	UltraATA100	EPRML16,17		7200
ST310220A	10200	8	Ultra ATA66	EPRML 16,17	512k	7200
ST310230A	10200	9.5	Ultra ATA	EPRML 16,17	512k	5400
ST310231A	10200	9	Ultra ATA	EPR4(16/17)	512k	5400
ST310232A	10242	9	Ultra ATA-4	EPRML 16,17	512k	5400
ST310240A	10200	11	Ultra ATA	16/17 EPR4	128k	5400
ST31051N	1060	10.5	SCSI-3Fast	RLL 0,4,4	256k	5411
ST31051W	1060	10.5	SCSI-3Fast	RLL 0,4,4	512k	5411
ST31051WC	1060	10.5	SCSI-3Fast	RLL 0,4,4	512k	5411
ST31055N	1060	9	Ultra SCSI	RLL 0,4,4	256k	5411
ST31055W	1060	9	Ultra SCSI	RLL 0,4,4	512k	5411
ST31055WC	1060	9	Ultra SCSI	RLL 0,4,4	512k	5411
ST31060A	1065	14	ATA	RLL ZBR	64k	3600
ST31060N	1062	9	SCSI-2Fast	1,7 RLL	512k	5400
ST31060W	1062	9	SCSI-2FstW	1,7 RLL	512k	5400
ST31080N	1080	11	SCSI-2Fast	1,7 RLL	256k	5400
ST31081A	1081	14	ATA	1,7 RLL	64k	3600
ST31082A	1082	12.5	ATA-3	1,7 RLL	64k	4500
ST3120020A	120GB	9.4	UltraATA100	EPRML16,17	1mb	5400
ST3120022A	120GB	8.5	UltraATA100	EPRML16,17	2mb	7200
ST3120022AS	120GB	8.5	SATA/150	EPRML16,17	8mb	7200
ST3120023A	120GB	9.4	UltraATA100	EPRML16,17	2mb	7200
ST3120023AS	120GB	9.4	SATA/150	EPRML16,17	8mb	7200

Drive Model	Format Size MB	Head	Cyl	Sect/Trac	Translate H/C/S	RWC/WPC	Form Factor	Power Watts
ST3120024A	120GB	4			16/16383/63	—/—	3.5 3H	9.5
ST3120025ACE	120GB	3				—/—	3.5 3H	7.5
ST3120026A	120GB	3			16/16383/63	—/—	3.5 3H	7.5
ST3120026AS	120GB	3			16/16383/63	—/—	3.5 3H	7.0
ST3120029A	120GB					—/—	3.5 3H	
ST31200N	1052	9	2700	84		NA/NA	3.5 3H	
ST31200NC	1052					NA/NA	3.5 3H	
ST31200ND	1052	9	2626			NA/NA	3.5 3H	
ST31200W	1052	9	2700	84		NA/NA	3.5 3H	
ST31200WC	1052	9	2700	84		NA/NA	3.5 3H	
ST31200WD	1052	9	2700	84		NA/NA	3.5 3H	
ST3120A	107	12	1024	NA	12/1024/17	NA/NA	3.5 3H	5.1
ST31210A	1083	6	3876		16/2099/63	—/—	3.5 3H	2.75
ST31220A	1083	6	3876		16/2099/63	NA/NA	3.5 3H	2.75
ST31230DC	1050	5	3892			NA/NA	3.5 3H	6.3
ST31230N	1050	5	3892			NA/NA	3.5 3H	6.3
ST31230NC	1050	5	3898			NA/NA	3.5 3H	
ST31230ND	1050	5	3892			NA/NA	3.5 3H	6.3
ST31230W	1050	5	3892			NA/NA	3.5 3H	6.3
ST31230WC	1050	5	3898			NA/NA	3.5 3H	6.3
ST31230WD	1050	5	3898			NA/NA	3.5 3H	6.3
ST31231N	1060	5	3992			NA/NA	3.5 3H	6
ST3123A	106	2			12/1024/17	NA/NA	3.5 3H	
ST31250N	1021	5	3711	107		NA/NA	3.5 3H	6.8
ST31250ND	1021	5	3711			NA/NA	3.5 3H	6.8
ST31250W	1021	5	3711			NA/NA	3.5 3H	6.8
ST31250WC	1021	5	3711			NA/NA	3.5 3H	6.8
ST31250WD	1021	5	3711			NA/NA	3.5 3H	6.8
ST31270A	1283	6	3876		16/2485/63	NA/NA	3.5 3H	2.75
ST31274A	1279	6	3659		16/2479/63	NA/NA	3.5 3H	3.9
ST31275A	1275	6	3640		16/2477/63	NA/NA	3.5 3H	3.5
ST31276A	1281	4	4893		16/2482/63	NA/NA	3.5 3H	3.5
ST31277A	1281	4			16/2482/63	NA/NA	3.5 3H	4.0
ST312930A	12900	6			16/16383/63	—/—	3H	5.5
ST313021A	13000	3			16/16368/63	—/—	3.5 3H	
ST313021A	13000	3			16/16368/63	—/—	3.5 3H	3.5
ST313030A	13000	6			16/16383/63	—/—	3.5 3H	5.5
ST313032A	13000	6			16/8354/63	—/—	3.5 3H	
ST313620A	13600	4			16/16383/63	—/—	3.5 3H	
ST313640A	13600	8			16/16383/63	—/—	3.5 3H	4.5
ST3144A	130	15	1001	17	15/1001/17	NA/NA	3.5 3H	
ST3145A	130	2				NA/NA	3.5 3H	
ST3146807FC	146.8GB	8	49854			—/—	3.5 3H	11
ST3146807LC	146.8GB	8	49854			—/—	3.5 3H	10.8
ST3146807LW	146.8GB	8	49854			—/—	3.5 3H	10.8
ST315310A	15300	2			16/16383/63	—/—	3.5 3H	
ST315311A	15000	2			16/16383/63	—/—	3.5 3H	4.8
ST315320A	15300	4			16/16383/63	—/—	3.5 3H	7
ST315323A	13000	3			16/16368/63	—/—	3.5 3H	3.5
ST315324A	15300	3			16/16383/63	—/—	3.5 3H	7
ST3160021A	160GB	4			16/16383/63	—/—	3.5 3H	7.5
ST3160021AS	160GB	4			16/16383/63	—/—	3.5 3H	7.5
ST3160022ACE	160GB	4				—/—	3.5 3H	7.5
ST3160023A	160GB	4			16/16383/63	—/—	3.5 3H	7.5
ST3160023AS	160GB	4			16/16383/63	—/—	3.5 3H	7.0
ST31621A	1621	6	3924		16/3146/63	NA/NA	3.5 3H	3.9
ST31640A	1625		4834		16/3150/63	NA/NA	3.5 3H	3.5
ST31720A	1700	2			16/3306/63	—/—	3.5 3H	4.0
ST31721A	1704	4			16/3303/63	NA/NA	3.5 3H	3.8
ST317221A	17200	2			16/16368/63	—/—	3.5 3H	3.5
ST31722A	1704	4			16/3303/63	NA/NA	3.5 3H	3.8
ST317240A	17200	8			16/16383/63	—/—	3H	5.5
ST317240A	17200	8			16/16383/63	—/—	3.5 3H	5.5
ST317242A	17200	8			16/16383/63	—/—		5.5
ST318203FC	18200	12	9772			—/—	3.5 3H	
ST318203FCV	18200	12	9772			—/—	3.5 3H	
ST318203LC	18200	12	9772			—/—	3.5 3H	

Drive Model	Format Size MB	Seek Time	Interface	Encode	cache kb	RPM
ST3120024A	120GB	9.4	UltraATA100	EPRML16,17	8mb	7200
ST3120025ACE	120GB		UltraATA100			7200
ST3120026A	120GB	8.5	UltraATA100	EPRML16,17	8mb	7200
ST3120026AS	120GB	8.5	SATA/150	EPRML16,17	8mb	7200
ST3120029A	120GB	9.4	UltraATA100	EPRML16,17	2mb	7200
ST31200N	1052	10	SCSI-2Fast		256k	5411
ST31200NC	1052	10.5	SCSI-2Fast	ZBR,1,7RLL	256k	5400
ST31200ND	1052	10	SCSI-2Fast		256k	5400
ST31200W	1052	10.5	SCSI-2FstW	1,7 RLL	256k	5411
ST31200WC	1052	10.5	SCSI-2FstW	ZBR,1,7RLL	256k	5411
ST31200WD	1052	10.5	SCSI-2FstW	ZBR,1,7RLL	256k	5411
ST3120A	107	15	IDE AT			5411
ST31210A	1083	11.5	AT	RLL ZBR	32k	3211
ST31220A	1083	12	ATA-2 Fast	1,7 RLL	256k	5400
ST31230DC	1050	10.5	SCSI-2Diff	1,7 RLL	256k	4500
ST31230N	1050	10.5	SCSI-2Fast	1,7 RLL	512k	5411
ST31230NC	1050	10.5	SCSI-2Fast	1,7 RLL	512k	5411
ST31230ND	1050	10.5	SCSI-2Fast	ZBR,1,7RLL		5411
ST31230W	1050	10.5	SCSI-2FstW	1,7 RLL	512k	5411
ST31230WC	1050	10.5	SCSI-2FstW	1,7 RLL	512k	5411
ST31230WD	1050	10.5	SCSI-2FstW	1,7 RLL	512k	5411
ST31231N	1060	10.5	SCSI-2Diff	1,7 RLL	512k	5411
ST3123A	106	10	SCSI-2Fast	RLL ZBR	256k	5411
ST31250N	1021	9	IDE AT	ZBR,1,7RLL	32k	3811
ST31250ND	1021	9	SCSI-2Fast	1,7 RLL	512k	7200
ST31250W	1021	9	SCSI-2FstW	1,7 RLL	512k	7200
ST31250WC	1021	9	SCSI-2FstW	1,7 RLL	512k	7200
ST31250WD	1021	9	SCSI-2Diff	1,7 RLL	512k	7200
ST31270A	1021	9	SCSI-2Diff	1,7 RLL	512k	7200
ST31274A	1283	12	ATA	RLL ZBR	256k	4500
ST31275A	1279	12	ATA	RLL ZBR	256k	4500
ST31276A	1275	14	ATA	RLL ZBR	64k	3600
ST31277A	1281	12	ATA	RLL ZBR	64k	4500
ST312930A	1281	12.5	ATA-2 Fast	1,7 RLL	128k	4500
ST313021A	12900	9	Ultra ATA	EPR4(16/17)	512k	5400
ST313021A	13000	9	UltraATA66	EPRML 24/26	512k	5400
ST313030A	13000	8.9	UltraATA/66	EPRML 24,26	512k	5400
ST313032A	13000	9	Ultra ATA	EPRML 16,17	512k	5400
ST313620A	13000	9	UltraATA/66	EPRML 16,17	512k	5400
ST313640A	13600	8	Ultra ATA66	EPRML 16,17	512k	7200
ST3144A	13600	9.5	Ultra ATA	EPRML 16,17	512k	5400
ST3145A	130	16	IDE AT	2,7 RLL	32k	3211
ST3146807FC	130	16	IDE AT	1,7 RLL		3811
ST3146807LC	146.8GB	4.7	FC			1000
ST3146807LW	146.8GB	4.7	UL320 SCSI			1000
ST315310A	146.8GB	4.7	UL320 SCSI			1000
ST315311A	15300	8.9	UltraATA100	EPRML 16,17	4160k	2048
ST315320A	15000	8.9	UltraATA100	EPRML 16,17		5400
ST315323A	15300	8.2	UltraATA/66	EPRML 16,17	2096k	7200
ST315324A	13000	8.9	UltraATA/66	EPRML 24,26	512k	5400
ST3160021A	15300	8.2	UltraATA100	EPRML16,17		7200
ST3160021AS	160GB	8.5	UltraATA100	EPRML16,17	2mb	7200
ST3160021ACE	160GB	8.5	SATA/150	EPRML16,17	8mb	7200
ST3160023A	160GB		UltraATA100			7200
ST3160023AS	160GB	8.5	UltraATA100	EPRML16,17	8mb	7200
ST31621A	160GB	8.5	SATA/150	EPRML16,17	8mb	7200
ST31640A	1621	14	ATA	RLL ZBR	64k	3600
ST31720A	1625	10	ATA-2 FAST	1,7 RLL	256k	5400
ST31721A	1700	12	ATA-2	1,7 RLL	128k	4500
ST317221A	1704	12.5	ATA-2 Fast	1,7 RLL	128k	4500
ST31722A	17200	8.9	UltraATA/66	EPRML 24,26	512k	5400
ST317240A	1704	12.5	Ultra ATA-3	1,7 RLL	128k	4500
ST317240A	17200	9	Ultra ATA	EPR4(16/17)	512k	5400
ST317242A	17200	9	Ultra ATA	EPRML 16,17	512k	5400
ST318203FC	17200	9	Ultra ATA66	EPRML 16,17	512k	5400
ST318203FCV	18200	5.2	FC	16/17 PR4	1024k	1000
ST318203LC	18200	5.2	FC	16/17 PR4	1024k	1000
	18200	5.2	Ultra2 SCSI	16/17 PR4	1024k	1000

Drive Model	Format Size MB	Head	Cyl	Sect/ Trac	Translate H/C/S	RWC/ WPC	Form Factor	Power Watts
ST318203LCV	18200	12	9772			—/—	3.5 3H	
ST318203LW	18200	12	9772			—/—	3.5 3H	
ST318203LWV	18200	12	9772			—/—	3.5 3H	
ST318233LCV	18200	12	9772			—/—	3.5 3H	
ST318233LWV	18200	12	9772			—/—	3.5 3H	
ST318275FC	18200	10	11737			—/—	3.5 3H	
ST318275LC	18200	10	11737			—/—	3.5 3H	
ST318275LW	18200	10	11737			—/—	3.5 3H	
ST318304FC	18400	6	14100			—/—	3.5 3H	12.5
ST318304FCV	18400	6	14100			—/—	3.5 3H	12.5
ST318404FC	18400	6	14384			—/—	3.5 3H	
ST318404LC	18400	6	14384			—/—	3.5 3H	
ST318404LW	18400	6	14384			—/—	3.5 3H	
ST318405LC	18.352GB	4	19036	471		—/—	3.5 3H	8.0
ST318405LW	18.352GB	4	19036	471		—/—	3.5 3H	8.0
ST318406LC	18.4GB	2	19036			—/—	3.5 3H	8.5
ST318406LW	18.4GB	2	19036			—/—	3.5 3H	8.5
ST318416N	18400	6	14384			—/—	3.5 3H	
ST318416W	18400	6	14384			—/—	3.5 3H	6.25
ST318417N	18400	2	29850	768		—/—	3.5 3H	6.25
ST318417W	18400	2	29850			—/—	3.5 3H	8
ST318418NW	18.4GB	2	26435			—/—	3.5 3H	
ST318426LC	18400	6	14384			—/—	3.5 3H	
ST318426LW	18400	6	14384			—/—	3.5 3H	
ST318432LC	18.4GB	4	18497			—/—	3.5 3H	10.5
ST318432LW	18.4GB	4	18497			—/—	3.5 3H	10.3
ST318436LC	18400	6	14384			—/—	3.5 3H	
ST318436LCV	18400	6	14384			—/—	3.5 3H	
ST318436LW	18400	6	14384			—/—	3.5 3H	
ST318436LWV	18400	6	14384			—/—	3.5 3H	
ST318437LC	18.4GB	2	29851			—/—	3.5 3H	6.2
ST318437LW	18.4GB	2	29851			—/—	3.5 3H	6.2
ST318438LW	18.4GB	2	26435			—/—	3.5 3H	9
ST318446LC	18.4GB	2	19036			—/—	3.5 3H	8.5
ST318446LW	18.4GB	2	19036			—/—	3.5 3H	8.5
ST318451FC	18400	10	10377			—/—	3.5 3H	12.5
ST318451FC	18400	10	10377			—/—	3.5 3H	
ST318451FCV	18400	10	10377			—/—	3.5 3H	12.5
ST318451FCV	18400	10	10377			—/—	3.5 3H	
ST318451LC	18400	10	10377			—/—	3.5 3H	11
ST318451LC	18400	10	10377			—/—	3.5 3H	
ST318451LCV	18400	10	10377			—/—	3.5 3H	11
ST318451LCV	18400	10	10377			—/—	3.5 3H	
ST318451LW	18400	10	10377			—/—	3.5 3H	11
ST318451LW	18400	10	10377			—/—	3.5 3H	
ST318451LWV	18400	10	10377			—/—	3.5 3H	11
ST318451LWV	18400	10	10377			—/—	3.5 3H	
ST318452FC	18.35GB	10	10377	345		—/—	3.5 3H	10.7
ST318452FC	18.4GB	10	18497			—/—	3.5 3H	11.5
ST318452LC	18.4GB	4	18497			—/—	3.5 3H	10.5
ST318452LW	18.4GB	4	18497			—/—	3.5 3H	10.5
ST318453FC	18.4GB	2				—/—	3.5 3H	9
ST318453LC	18.4GB	2				—/—	3.5 3H	9
ST318453LW	18.4GB	2				NA/NA	3.5 3H	9
ST31930N	1700	7	3898			NA/NA	3.5 3H	
ST31930ND	1700	7	3898			NA/NA	3.5 3H	
ST3195A	170	4			10/981/34	—/—	3.5 3H	
ST3200021A	200GB	4			16/16383/63	—/—	3.5 3H	7.5
ST320011A	20GB	1			16/16383/63	—/—	3.5 3H	8.0
ST320014A	20GB	1			16/16383/63	—/—	2.5 4H	4.5
ST3200822A	200GB	4			16/16383/63	—/—	3.5 3H	7.5
ST3200822AS	200GB	4			16/16383/63	—/—	3.5 3H	7.0
ST320410A	20GB	1			16/16383/63	—/—	3.5 3H	5
ST320413A	20000	2			16/16383/63	—/—	3.5 3H	4.8
ST320414A	20000	2			16/16383/63	—/—	3.5 3H	
ST320420A	20400	4			16/16383/63	—/—	3.5 3H	7
ST320423A	20400	4			16/16368/63	—/—	3.5 3H	3.5

Drive Model	Format Size MB	Seek Time	Interface	Encode	cache kb	RPM
ST318203LCV	18200	5.2	Ultra2 SCSI	16/17 PR4	1024k	1000
ST318203LW	18200	5.2	Ultra2 SCSI	16/17 PR4	1024k	1000
ST318203LWV	18200	5.2	Ultra2 SCSI	16/17 PR4	1024k	1000
ST318233LCV	18200	5.2	UI 160 SCSI	16/17 PR4	1024k	1000
ST318233LW	18200	5.2	UI 160 SCSI	16/17 PR4	1024k	1000
ST318233LWV	18200	5.2	UI 160 SCSI	16/17 PR4	1024k	1000
ST318275FC	18200	6.9	FC	16/17 EPR4	1024k	7200
ST318275LC	18200	6.9	Ultra2 SCSI	16/17 EPR4	1024k	7200
ST318275LW	18200	6.9	Ultra2 SCSI	8,9 PR4	1024k	7200
ST318304FC	18400	5.2	FC		4096k	1000
ST318304FCV	18400	5.2	FC		4096k	1000
ST318404FC	18400	5.2	FC		16384	1000
ST318404LC	18400	5.2	UL160SCSI	NPV		1000
ST318404LW	18400	5.2	UL160SCSI	NPV		1000
ST318405LC	18.352GB	5.4	Ultra 160	EPR4 32,34	4096k	1002
ST318405LW	18.352GB	5.4	Ultra 160	EPR4 32,34	4096k	1002
ST318406LC	18.4GB	5.2	UL320 SCSI	EPRML 32,34	4096k	1000
ST318406LW	18.4GB	5.2	UL320 SCSI	EPRML 32,34	4096k	1000
ST318416N	18400	5.9	Ultra SCSI	EPRML		7200
ST318416W	18400	5.9	Ultra SCSI	EPRML		7200
ST318417N	18400	8.5	Ultra SCSI	EPRML	2048k	7200
ST318417W	18400	8.5	Ultra SCSI	EPRML	2048k	7200
ST318418NW	18.4GB	8	50-pin	EPRML	2048k	7200
ST318426LC	18400	5.9	UL160SCSI	EPRML		7200
ST318426LW	18400	5.9	UL160SCSI	EPRML		7200
ST318432LC	18.4GB	4.2	UL320 SCSI	EPRML		1500
ST318432LW	18.4GB	4.2	UL320 SCSI	EPRML		1500
ST318436LC	18400	5.9	UL160SCSI	EPRML		7200
ST318436LCV	18400	5.9	UL160SCSI	EPRML		7200
ST318436LW	18400	5.9	UL160SCSI	EPRML		7200
ST318436LWV	18400	5.9	UL160SCSI	EPRML		7200
ST318437LC	18.4GB	8.5	Ultra 160	EPRML	2mb	7200
ST318437LW	18.4GB	8.5	UL160SCSIW	EPRML	2mb	7200
ST318438LW	18.4GB	8	68-pin	EPRML	2048k	7200
ST318446LC	18.4GB	6	80-pin	EPRML32,34		1000
ST318446LW	18.4GB	6	80-pin	EPRML32,34		1000
ST318451FC	18400	3.9	FC 2Gb	NPV	4mb	1500
ST318451FCV	18400	3.9	FC	NPV	4096k	1500
ST318451FCV	18400	3.9	FC 2Gb	NPV	16mb	1500
ST318451FCV	18400	3.9	FC	NPV	16348	1500
ST318451LC	18400	3.9	UL160SCSIW	NPV	4mb	1500
ST318451LC	18400	3.9	UL160SCSI	NPV	4096k	1500
ST318451LCV	18400	3.9	UL160SCSIW	NPV	16mb	1500
ST318451LCV	18400	3.9	UL160SCSI	NPV	16384	1500
ST318451LW	18400	3.9	UL160SCSIW	NPV	4mb	1500
ST318451LWV	18400	3.9	UL160SCSIW	NPV	4096k	1500
ST318451LWV	18400	3.9	UL160SCSI	NPV	16mb	1500
ST318451LWV	18400	3.9	UL160SCSI	NPV	16384	1500
ST318452FC	18.35GB	3.9	FC	EPRML	8192k	1500
ST318452FC	18.4GB	3.6	FC	EPRML	8192k	1500
ST318452LC	18.4GB	3.6	UL320 SCSI	EPRML	8192k	1500
ST318452LW	18.4GB	3.6	UL320 SCSI	EPRML	8192k	1500
ST318453FC	18.4GB	3.6	FC	EPRML		1500
ST318453LC	18.4GB	3.6	UL320 SCSI	EPRML		1500
ST318453LW	18.4GB	3.6	UL320 SCSI	EPRML		1500
ST31930N	1700	10.5	SCSI-2Fast	ZBR,1,7RLL		5411
ST31930ND	1700	10.5	SCSI-2Fast	ZBR,1,7RLL		5411
ST3195A	170	16	IDE AT	ZBR,1,7RLL	64k	3811
ST3200021A	200GB	8.5	UltraATA100	EPRML16,17	8mb	7200
ST320011A	20GB	9	UltraATA100	EPRML16,17		7200
ST320014A	20GB	12.7	UltraATA100	GPRML96/102	2mb	5400
ST3200822A	200GB	8.9	UltraATA100	EPRML16,17	8mb	7200
ST3200822AS	200GB	8.5	SATA/150	EPRML16,17	8mb	7200
ST320410A	20GB	8.9	UltraATA100	GPRML	2000	5400
ST320413A	20000	8.9	UltraATA100	EPRML 16,17		5400
ST320414A	20000	8.9	UltraATA100	EPRML 16,17	4160k	2048
ST320420A	20400	8.2	UltraATA/66	EPRML 16,17	2096k	7200
ST320423A	20400	8.9	UltraATA/66	EPRML 24,26	512k	5400

Drive Model	Format Size MB	Head	Cyl	Sect/Trac	Translate H/C/S	RWC/WPC	Form Factor	Power Watts
ST320424A	20GB	4			16/16368/63	—/—	3.5 3H	7
ST320430A	20400	6			16/16383/63		3.5 3H	
ST32105N Cayman	2147	10	3948	106		NA/NA	3.5 3H	6.2
ST32105W Cayman	2147	10	3948	106		NA/NA	3.5 3H	6.2
ST32107N Cayman	2147	10	3999	104		NA/NA	3.5 3H	9.1
ST32107W Cayman	2147	10	3999	104		NA/NA	3.5 3H	9.1
ST32109N	2147	10	3999	104		—/—	3.5 3H	9.1
ST32109W	2147	10	3999			—/—	3.5 3H	9.1
ST32110A	2100	1			16/4092/63	—/—	3.5 3H	4.9
ST32112A	2.16GB	1				—/—	3.5 3H	3.1
ST3211A	213	2	2388		16/685/38	NA/NA	3.5 3H	3.8
ST32120A	2111	4			16/4092/63	NA/NA	3.5 3H	3.8
ST32122A	2100	4			16/4092/63	—/—	3.5 3H	4.4
ST32132A	2113	6			6/4095/63	—/—	3.5 3H	3.2
ST32140A	2113	8	4834		16/4200/63	—/—	3.5 3H	4.7
ST32151N	2148	8	4176			NA/NA	3.5 3H	6
ST32151W	2148	8	4176			NA/NA	3.5 3H	6
ST32151WC	2148	8	4176			NA/NA	3.5 3H	6
ST32155N	2148	8	4176			—/—	3.5 3H	
ST32155W	2148	8	4176			—/—	3.5 3H	
ST32155WC	2148	8	4176			—/—	3.5 3H	
ST32161A	2147	8	4474		16/4095/63	NA/NA	3.5 3H	5.0
ST32171DC	2150	6	5178			NA/NA	3.5 3H	8.8
ST32171FC	2150	6	5178			NA/NA	3.5 3H	8.9
ST32171N	2150	6	5178			NA/NA	3.5 3H	8.9
ST32171ND	2150	6	5178			NA/NA	3.5 3H	8.9
ST32171W	2150	6	5178			NA/NA	3.5 3H	8.9
ST32171WC	2150	6	5178			NA/NA	3.5 3H	8.9
ST32171WD	2150	6	5178			NA/NA	3.5 3H	8.9
ST32271DC	2260	6	5178			—/—	3.5 3H	8.8
ST32271N	2260	6	5178			—/—	3.5 3H	8.8
ST32271W	2260	6	5178			—/—	3.5 3H	8.8
ST32271WC	2260	6	5178			—/—	3.5 3H	8.8
ST32271WD	2260	6	5178			—/—	3.5 3H	8.8
ST32272DC	2260	4	6311			—/—	3.5 3H	
ST32272N	2260	4	6311			—/—	3.5 3H	
ST32272W	2260	4	6311			—/—	3.5 3H	
ST32272WC	2260	4	6311			—/—	3.5 3H	
ST32272WD	2260	4	6311			NA/NA	3.5 3H	
ST3240A	211	2				NA/NA	3.5 3H	6.5
ST32430DC	2147	9	3892			NA/NA	3.5 3H	6.5
ST32430N	2147	9	3892			NA/NA	3.5 3H	
ST32430NC	2147	9	3898			NA/NA	3.5 3H	6.5
ST32430ND	2147	9	3898			NA/NA	3.5 3H	6.5
ST32430W	2147	9	3892			NA/NA	3.5 3H	6.5
ST32430WC	2147	9	3892			NA/NA	3.5 3H	6.5
ST32430WD	2147	9	3892			NA/NA	3.5 3H	
ST3243A	214	4	1024	34	12/1024/34	NA/NA	3.5 3H	
ST3250A	213	2			12/1024/34		3.5 3H	4.2
ST32510A	2557	2			16/4956/63	—/—	3.5 3H	4.5
ST32520A	2500	2			15/4888/63	—/—	3.5 3H	
ST32530A	2558	6			16/4958/63	NA/NA	3.5 3H	4.5
ST32531A	2557	6			6/4956/63	—/—	3.5 3H	4.8
ST32532A	2557	6			16/4956/63	NA/NA	3.5 3H	8.8
ST32550DC	2147	11	3711	V		NA/NA	3.5 3H	8.8
ST32550N	2147	11	3711	V		NA/NA	3.5 3H	8.8
ST32550ND	2147	11	3711	V		NA/NA	3.5 3H	
ST32550W	2147	11	3510	108		NA/NA	3.5 3H	8.8
ST32550WC	2147	11	3711	V		NA/NA	3.5 3H	8.8
ST32550WD	2147	11	3711	V		NA/NA	3.5 3H	8.8
ST325A,X	21	2	615	17	4/615/17	NA/NA	3.5HH	1.8
ST325N	21	2	654	32		NA/NA	3.5HH	2.7
ST325X	21	2	615	17		NA/NA	3.5HH	2
ST3270A	271	2	2595		14/600/63	NA/NA	3.5 3H	3.8
ST3271A	265	2	2805		10/977/53	NA/NA	3.5 3H	
ST327240A	27000	8				—/—	3.5 3H	

Drive Model	Format Size MB	Seek Time	Interface	Encode	cache kb	RPM
ST320424A	20GB	8.2	UltraATA100	EPRML16,17		7200
ST320430A	20400	8	Ultra ATA66	EPRML 16,17	512k	7200
ST32105N Cayman	2147	9.5	SCSI-2Fast	1,7 RLL	512k	5400
ST32105W Cayman	2147	9.5	SCSI-2FstW	1,7 RLL	512k	5400
ST32107N Cayman	2147	8.5	SCSI-2Fast	1,7 RLL	512k	7200
ST32107W Cayman	2147	8.5	SCSI-2FstW	1,7 RLL	512k	7200
ST32109N	2147	8.5	SCSI-2Fast	1,7 RLL	512k	7200
ST32109W	2147	8.5	SCSI-2FstWd	1,7 RLL	512k	7200
ST32110A	2100	11	Ultra ATA	EPRML16,17	128k	5400
ST32112A	2.16GB	10.5	UltraATA/66	EPRML16,17	256k	5400
ST3211A	213	14	ATA	RLL ZBR	32k	3600
ST32120A	2111	12.5	ATA-2 Fast	1,7 RLL	128k	4500
ST32122A	2100	12	Ultra ATA	2/3(1,7)RLL	128k	4500
ST32132A	2113	12.5	ATA-3	PRML0,12,8	128k	4500
ST32140A	2113	10	ATA-2 Fast	1,7 RLL	128k	5400
ST32151N	2148	10.5	SCSI-3Fast	RLL 0,4,4	256k	5411
ST32151W	2148	10.5	SCSI-3Fast	RLL 0,4,4	512k	5411
ST32151WC	2148	10.5	SCSI-3Fast	RLL 0,4,4	512k	5411
ST32155N	2148	9	Ultra SCSI	RLL 0,4,4	256k	5411
ST32155W	2148	9	Ultra SCSI	RLL 0,4,4	512k	5411
ST32155WC	2148	9	Ultra SCSI	RLL 0,4,4	512k	5411
ST32161A	2147	10.5	ATA	RLL ZBR	128k	5400
ST32171DC	2150	9	ULTRA SCSI	PRML	512k	7200
ST32171FC	2150	9	FC-AL	PRML	512k	7200
ST32171N	2150	9	ULTRA SCSI	PRML	512k	7200
ST32171ND	2150	9	ULTRA SCSI	PRML	512k	7200
ST32171W	2150	9	ULTRA SCSI	PRML	512k	7200
ST32171WC	2150	9	ULTRA SCSI	PRML	512k	7200
ST32171WD	2150	9	ULTRA SCSI	PRML	512k	7200
ST22271DC	2260	9	Ultra SCSI	PRML	512k	7200
ST22271N	2260	9	Ultra SCSI	PRML	512k	7200
ST22271W	2260	9	Ultra SCSI	PRML	512k	7200
ST22271WC	2260	9	Ultra SCSI	PRML	512k	7200
ST22271WD	2260	9	Ultra SCSI	PRML	512k	7200
ST32272DC	2260	9	Ultra SCSI	PRML	512k	7200
ST32272N	2260	9	Ultra SCSI	PRML	512k	7200
ST32272W	2260	9	Ultra SCSI	PRML	512k	7200
ST32272WC	2260	9	Ultra SCSI	PRML	512k	7200
ST32272WD	2260	9	Ultra SCSI	PRML	512k	7200
ST32240A	211	8	IDE AT	RLL ZBR	120k	3811
ST32430DC	2147	10.5	SCSI-2Fast	1,7 RLL	512k	5411
ST32430N	2147	10.5	SCSI-2Fast	1,7 RLL	512k	5411
ST32430NC	2147	10.5	SCSI-2Fast	ZBR,1,7RLL		5411
ST32430ND	2147	10.5	SCSI-2Diff	1,7 RLL		5411
ST32430W	2147	10.5	SCSI-2FstW	ZBR,1,7RLL	512k	5411
ST32430WC	2147	10.5	SCSI-2FstW	1,7 RLL	512k	5411
ST32430WD	2147	10.5	SCSI-2Diff	1,7 RLL	512k	5411
ST3243A	214	16	IDE AT	ZBR,1,7RLL	32k	3811
ST3250A	213	15	IDE AT	ZBR,1,7RLL	120k	3811
ST32510A	2557	12.5	Ultra ATA-3	PRML16,17	128k	5400
ST32520A	2500	13	Ultra ATA	EPRML16,17	256k	5400
ST32530A	2558	10.5	ATA	ZBR PRML	128k	5376
ST32531A	2557	12	ATA-3	1,7 RLL	128k	5400
ST32532A	2557	12.5	Ultra ATA-3	1,7 RLL	128k	4500
ST32550DC	2147	8	SCSI-2Diff	1,7 RLL	512k	7200
ST32550N	2147	8	SCSI-2Fast	1,7 RLL	512k	7200
ST32550ND	2147	8	SCSI-2Diff	1,7 RLL	512k	7200
ST32550W	2147	8	SCSI-2FstW	RLL ZBR	512k	7200
ST32550W	2147	8	SCSI-2FstW	1,7 RLL	512k	7200
ST32550WC	2147	8	SCSI-2FstW	1,7 RLL	512k	7200
ST32550WD	2147	8	SCSI-2Diff	1,7 RLL	512k	7200
ST325A,X	21	28	IDE AT	ZBR,2,7RLL	8/32k	3048
ST325N	21	28	SCSI	2,7 RLL	2k/8k	3600
ST325X	21	45	IDE XT	2,7 RLL	8/32k	3600
ST3270A	271	15	ATA	RLL ZBR	32k	3400
ST3271A	265	10.5	ATA	RLL ZBR	256k	4500
ST327240A	27000	8	Ultra ATA66	EPRML 16,17	512k	7200

Hard Drives

Hard Drive Specs   717

Drive Model	Format Size MB	Head	Cyl	Sect/Trac	Translate H/C/S	RWC/WPC	Form Factor	Power Watts
ST328040A	28000	8			16/16383/63	—/—		6.8
ST3283A	245				14/978/35	NA/NA	3.5 3H	
ST3283N	248	5	1691	57		NA/NA	3.5 3H	
ST3285N	248	3	1691			NA/NA	3.5 3H	
ST3290A	260				15/1001/34	NA/NA	3.5 3H	
ST3291A	272	4			14/761/50	NA/NA	3.5 3H	
ST3295A	273	2			14/761/50	NA/NA	3.5 3H	9.5
ST330012A	30GB	1				—/—	3.5 3H	5
ST330610A	30GB	2			16/16383/63	—/—	3.5 3H	
ST330620A	30000	3			16/16383/63	—/—	3.5 3H	4.8
ST330621A	30000	4			16/16383/63	—/—	3.5 3H	7
ST330630A	30600	6			16/16383/63	—/—	3.5 3H	
ST330631A	30GB	6			16/16383/63	—/—	3.5 3H	4.5
ST33210A	3200	2			16/6296/63	—/—	3.5 3H	4.3
ST33220A	3227	4			16/6253/63	NA/NA	3.5 3H	4.9
ST33221A	3200	2			16/6253/63	—/—	3.5 3H	3.3
ST33223A	3249	3			16/6296/63	—/—	3.5 3H	4.8
ST33230A	3227	6				—/—	3.5 3H	5.4
ST33232A	3200	6			16/6253/63	—/—	3.5 3H	4.5
ST33240A	3227	8			8/6253/63	—/—	3.5 3H	4.5
ST3360706LC	36.9GB	4	19036			—/—	3.5 3H	8.5
ST336605FC	36.7GB	4	29550			—/—	3.5 3H	9.3
ST336607FC	36.7GB	8	49854			—/—	3.5 3H	7.7
ST336607LC	36.7GB	8	49854			—/—	3.5 3H	7.5
ST336607LW	36.7GB	8	49854			—/—	3.5 3H	7.5
ST336704FC	36700	12	14100			—/—	3.5 3H	
ST336704FCV	36700	12	14100			—/—	3.5 3H	
ST336704LC	36700	12	14100			—/—	3.5 3H	
ST336704LCV	36700	12	14100			—/—	3.5 3H	
ST336704LW	36700	12	14100			—/—	3.5 3H	
ST336704LWV	36700	12	14100			—/—	3.5 3H	
ST336705LC	36.704GB	8	19036	471		—/—	3.5 3H	9.6
ST336705LW	36.704GB	8	19036			—/—	3.5 3H	9.6
ST336706LC	36.9GB	4	19036			—/—	3.5 3H	8.5
ST336706LW	36.9GB	4	19036			—/—	3.5 3H	8.5
ST336732LC	36.7GB	8	18497			—/—	3.5 3H	
ST336732LW	36.7GB	8	18497			—/—	3.5 3H	
ST336737LC	36.9GB	4	29851			—/—	3.5 3H	7.0
ST336737LW	36.9GB	4	29851			—/—	3.5 3H	7.0
ST336746LC	36.9GB	4	19036			—/—	3.5 3H	8.5
ST336746LW	36.9GB	4	19036			—/—	3.5 3H	8.5
ST336752FC	36.7GB	8	18497			—/—	3.5 3H	11.5
ST336752LC	36.7GB	8	18497			—/—	3.5 3H	11.5
ST336752LW	36.7GB	8	18497			—/—	3.5 3H	11.5
ST336753FC	36.7GB	4				—/—	3.5 3H	10
ST336753LC	36.7GB	4				—/—	3.5 3H	10
ST336753LW	36.7GB	4				—/—	3.5 3H	10
ST336918N	36.9GB	2	56332			—/—	3.5 3H	9.0
ST336938LW	36.9GB	2	56332			—/—	3.5 3H	9.0
ST3385A	340	5	767	62	14/767/62	NA/NA	3.5 3H	
ST3390A	341				14/768/62	NA/NA	3.5 3H	
ST3390N	344	3	2676	83		NA/NA	3.5 3H	
ST3391A	341	4			14/768/62	NA/NA	3.5 3H	
ST340012A	40GB	2			16/16383/63	—/—	3.5 3H	9.5
ST340014A	40GB	1			16/16383/63	—/—	3.5 3H	7.5
ST340014AS	40GB	1			16/16383/63	—/—	3.5 3H	7.5
ST340015A	40GB	1			16/16383/63	—/—	2.5 4H	4.5
ST340015ACE	40GB	1			16/16383/63	—/—	2.5 4H	4.5
ST340016A	40GB	2			16/16383/63	—/—	3.5 3H	8.0
ST340017A	40GB	2			16/16383/63	—/—	3.5 3H	9.5
ST340810A	40GB	2			16/16383/63	—/—	3.5 3H	5
ST340810ACE	40GB	2			16/16383/63	—/—	3.5 3H	5
ST340823A	40000	4			16/16383/63	—/—	3.5 3H	4.8
ST340824A	40000	4			16/16383/63	—/—	3.5 3H	
ST3420A	427	4	2388		16/826/63	NA/NA	3.5 3H	3.8
ST34217N	4294	10	6028			—/—	3.5 3H	8.1
ST34217W	4294	10	6028			—/—	3.5 3H	8.1

Drive Model	Format Size MB	Seek Time	Interface	Encode	cache kb	RPM
ST328040A	28000	8	Ultra ATA66	EPRML 16,17	512k	7200
ST3283A	245	12	IDE AT	RLL ZBR	128k	4500
ST3283N	248	12	SCSI-2Fast	RLL ZBR	128k	4500
ST3285N	248	12	SCSI-2Fast	ZBR,1,7RLL	128k	4500
ST3290A	260	16	IDE AT	1,7 RLL		3811
ST3291A	272	13	IDE AT	ZBR,1,7RLL	120k	3811
ST3295A	273	14	IDE AT	1,7 RLL	120k	3811
ST330012A	30GB	9	UltraATA100	EPRML16,17		5400
ST330610A	30GB	8.9	UltraATA100	EPRML16,17	1mb	5400
ST330620A	30000	8.9	UltraATA100	GPRML	2000	5400
ST330621A	30000	8.9	UltraATA100	EPRML 16,17	4160k	2048
ST330630A	30600	8.2	UltraATA/66	EPRML 16,17	2096k	7200
ST330631A	30GB	8.2	UltraATA100	EPRML16,17		7200
ST33210A	3200	9.5	Ultra ATA	EPRML 16,17	256k	5400
ST33220A	3227	11	Ultra ATA-3	PRML16,17	128k	4490
ST33221A	3200	11	Ultra ATA	EPRML16,17	128k	5400
ST33223A	3249	13	Ultra ATA-3	PRML16,17	128k	4500
ST33230A	3227	12.5	ATA-2 Fast	1,7 RLL	128k	4500
ST33232A	3200	12	Ultra ATA	2/3(1,7)RLL	128k	4500
ST33240A	3227	12	ATA-3	1,7 RLL	128k	4500
ST3360706LC	36.9GB	4.2	UL320 SCSI	EPRML		1000
ST336605FC	36.7GB	4.6	FC	EPR4	4096k	1000
ST336607FC	36.7GB	4.7	FC			1000
ST336607LC	36.7GB	4.7	UL320 SCSI			1000
ST336607LW	36.7GB	4.7	UL320 SCSI			1000
ST336704FC	36700	5.2	FC	NPV		1000
ST336704FCV	36700	5.2	FC	NPV		1000
ST336704LC	36700	5.2	UL160SCSI	NPV		1000
ST336704LCV	36700	5.2	UL160SCSI	NPV		1000
ST336704LW	36700	5.2	UL160SCSI	NPV		1000
ST336704LWV	36700	5.2	UL160SCSI	NPV		1000
ST336705LC	36.704GB	5.4	Ultra 160	EPR4 32,34	4096k	1002
ST336705LW	36.704GB	5.4	Ultra 160	EPR4 32,34	4096k	1002
ST336706LC	36.9GB	5.2	UL320 SCSI	EPRML	4096k	1000
ST336706LW	36.9GB	5.2	UL320 SCSI	EPRML	4096k	1000
ST336732LC	36.7GB	4.2	UL320 SCSI	EPRML		1000
ST336732LW	36.7GB	4.2	UL320 SCSI	EPRML		1000
ST336737LC	36.9GB	8.5	Ultra 160	EPRML	2mb	7200
ST336737LW	36.9GB	8.5	UL160SCSIW	EPRML	2mb	7200
ST336746LC	36.9GB	6	80-pin	EPRML32,34		7200
ST336746LW	36.9GB	6	80-pin	EPRML32,34		1000
ST336752FC	36.7GB	3.6	FC	EPRML	8192k	1500
ST336752LC	36.7GB	3.6	UL320 SCSI	EPRML	8192k	1500
ST336752LW	36.7GB	3.6	UL320 SCSI	EPRML	8192k	1500
ST336753FC	36.7GB	3.6	FC	EPRML		1500
ST336753LC	36.7GB	3.6	UL320 SCSI	EPRML		1500
ST336753LW	36.7GB	3.6	UL320 SCSI	EPRML		1500
ST336918N	36.9GB	9.25	50-pin	EPRML	2048k	7200
ST336938LW	36.9GB	9.25	UL160SCSIW	EPRML	2048k	7200
ST3385A	340	12	IDE AT	ZBR,1,7RLL	256k	4500
ST3390A	341	12	IDE AT	1,7 RLL		4500
ST3390N	344	12	SCSI-2Fast	ZBR,1,7RLL	256k	4500
ST3391A	341	14	IDE AT	ZBR,1,7RLL	120k	3811
ST340012A	40GB	9	UltraATA100	EPRML16,17	1mb	5400
ST340014A	40GB	8.5	UltraATA100	EPRML16,17	2mb	7200
ST340014AS	40GB	8.5	UltraATA100	EPRML16,17	2mb	7200
ST340015A	40GB	12.5	UltraATA100	GPRML 96/102	2mb	5400
ST340015ACE	40GB	12.5	UltraATA100	GPRML 96/102	2mb	5400
ST340016A	40GB	9	UltraATA100	EPRML16,17		7200
ST340017A	40GB	9	UltraATA100	EPRML16,17	2mb	7200
ST340810A	40GB	8.9	UltraATA100	GPRML	2000	5400
ST340810ACE	40GB	8.9	UltraATA100	GPRML	2mb	5400
ST340823A	40000	8.9	UltraATA100	EPRML 16,17		5400
ST340824A	40000	8.9	UltraATA100	EPRML 16,17	4160k	2048
ST3420A	427	14	ATA	RLL ZBR	32k	3600
ST34217N	4294	9	Ultra SCSI	8,9RLL	512k	7200
ST34217W	4294	9	Ultra SCSI	8,9RLL	512k	7200

Drive Model	Format Size MB	Head	Cyl	Sect/Trac	Translate H/C/S	RWC/WPC	Form Factor	Power Watts
ST34217WC	4294	10	6028			—/—	3.5 3H	8.1
ST34217WD	4294	10	6028			—/—	3.5 3H	8.1
ST3425A	425	2	3687		16/839/62	NA/NA	3.5 3H	3.0
ST34310A	4300	2			15/8894/63		3H	5.5
ST34310A	4300	2			15/8894/63		3.5 3H	5.5
ST34311A	4327	2			15/8944/63		3.5 3H	3.1
ST34311A	2163	1			16/4192/63		3.5 3H	3.1
ST34312A	4311	2			16/8354/63		3.5 3H	5.5
ST34312A	4300	2			16/8354/63		3.5 3H	
ST34313A	4300	1			15/8944/63		3.5 3H	
ST34313A	4300	1			15/8944/63		3.5 3H	3.5
ST34321A	4300	2			15/8894/63		3.5 3H	4.9
ST34323A	4311	4			15/8912/63		3.5 3H	3.3
ST34340A	4303	8			8/8894/63		3.5 3H	4.8
ST34342A	4300	8			15/8894/63		3.5 3H	5.4
ST34371DC	4350	10	5288			NA/NA	3.5 3H	10
ST34371FC	4350	10	5288			NA/NA	3.5 3H	10
ST34371N	4350	10	5288			NA/NA	3.5 3H	10
ST34371ND	4350	10	5288			NA/NA	3.5 3H	10
ST34371W	4350	10	5288			NA/NA	3.5 3H	10
ST34371WC	4350	10	5288			NA/NA	3.5 3H	10
ST34371WD	4350	10	5288			NA/NA	3.5 3H	10
ST34501DC	4550	8	6526			—/—	3.5 3H	12
ST34501FC	4550	8	6526			—/—	3.5 3H	15.5
ST34501FC	4550	8	6526			—/—	3.5 3H	12
ST34501N	4550	8	6526			—/—	3.5 3H	12
ST34501W	4550	8	6526			—/—	3.5 3H	12
ST34501WC	4550	8	6526			—/—	3.5 3H	12
ST34501WD	4550	8	6526			—/—	3.5 3H	12
ST34502FC	4550	6				—/—	3.5 3H	10.5
ST34502LC	4550	6				—/—	3.5 3H	10.5
ST34502LW	4550	6				—/—	3.5 3H	10.5
ST34520A	4550	4			15/9408/63	—/—	3.5 3H	11.0
ST34520LC	4550	4	9006			—/—	3.5 3H	
ST34520LW	4550	4	9006			—/—	3.5 3H	
ST34520N	4550	4	9006			—/—	3.5 3H	11.0
ST34520W	4550	4	9006			—/—	3.5 3H	11.0
ST34520WC	4550	4	9006			—/—	3.5 3H	11.0
ST34555N	4550	8	6311	176		NA/NA	3.5 3H	8.8
ST34555W	4550	8	6311	176		NA/NA	3.5 3H	8.8
ST34571DC	4550					—/—	3.5 3H	
ST34571FC	4550					—/—	3.5 3H	
ST34571N	4550					—/—	3.5 3H	
ST34571W	4550					—/—	3.5 3H	
ST34571WD	4550					—/—	3.5 3H	
ST34572DC	4550	8	6311			—/—	3.5 3H	8.8
ST34572N	4550	8	6311			—/—	3.5 3H	8.8
ST34572W	4550	8	6311			—/—	3.5 3H	8.8
ST34572WC	4550	8	6311			—/—	3.5 3H	8.8
ST34572WD	4550	8	6311			—/—	3.5 3H	8.8
ST34573FC	4550	5				—/—	3.5 3H	12
ST34573LC	4550	5				—/—	3.5 3H	10
ST34573LW	4550	5				—/—	3.5 3H	10
ST34573N	4550	5				—/—	3.5 3H	10
ST34573W	4550	5				—/—	3.5 3H	10
ST34573WC	4550	5				—/—	3.5 3H	10
ST34573WD	4550	5				—/—	3.5 3H	10
ST3491A	428	4			15/899/62	NA/NA	3.5 3H	1.8
ST3500A	426	7	1547		15/895/62	NA/NA	3.5 3H	
ST3500N	426	7	1547	V		NA/NA	3.5 3H	
ST35040A	5008	8	6536		15/10352635	NA/NA	3.5 3H	7.3
ST35120A	5121	4			15/10585/63	—/—	3.5 3H	4.2
ST35130A	5121	6			15/10585/63	NA/NA	3.5 3H	4.3
ST351A,X	43	2	820	17		NA/NA	3.5 3H	2
ST352A,X	42	2		17	5/980/17	NA/NA	3.5 3H	
ST3541A	541	2	3925		16/1048/63	NA/NA	3.5 3H	2.5
ST3543A	542	4	2574		16/1050/63	NA/NA	3.5 3H	3.9

SEAGATE TECHNOLOGIES

Drive Model	Format Size MB	Seek Time	Interface	Encode	cache kb	RPM
ST34217WC	4294	9	Ultra SCSI	8,9RLL	512k	7200
ST34217WD	4294	9	Ultra SCSI	8,9RLL	512k	7200
ST3425A	425	14	ATA	RLL ZBR	64k	3600
ST34310A	4300	9	Ultra ATA	EPR4(16/17)	512k	5400
ST34310A	4300	9	Ultra ATA	EPRML 16,17	512k	5400
ST34311A	4327	10.5	Ultra ATA-3	EPRML 16,17	256k	5400
ST34311A	2163	10.5	Ultra ATA-3	EPRML 16,17	256k	5400
ST34312A	4311	9	Ultra ATA-4	EPRML 16,17	512k	5400
ST34312A	4300	9	Ultra ATA66	EPRML 16,17	512k	5400
ST34313A	4300	9	Ultra ATA66	EPRML 24,26	256k	5400
ST34313A	4300	8.9	UltraATA/66	EPRML 24,26	256k	5400
ST34321A	4300	11	Ultra ATA	EPRML16,17	128k	5400
ST34323A	4311	13	Ultra ATA-3	PRML16,17	128k	4500
ST34340A	4303	12	ATA-3	1,7 RLL	128k	4500
ST34342A	4300	12	Ultra ATA	2/3(1,7)RLL	128k	4500
ST34371DC	4350	9	ULTRA SCSI	RLL 0,4,4	512k	7200
ST34371FC	4350	9	FC-AL	RLL 0,4,4	512k	7200
ST34371N	4350	9	ULTRA SCSI	RLL 0,4,4	512k	7200
ST34371ND	4350	9	ULTRA SCSI	RLL 0,4,4	512k	7200
ST34371W	4350	9	ULTRA SCSI	RLL 0,4,4	512k	7200
ST34371WC	4350	9	ULTRA SCSI	RLL 0,4,4	512k	7200
ST34371WD	4350	9	ULTRA SCSI	RLL 0,4,4	512k	7200
ST34501DC	4550	7.5	Ultra SCSI	PRML0,4,4	512k	1003
ST34501FC	4550	7.5	FC	PRML0,4,4	1024k	1003
ST34501FC	4550	7.5	FiberChanel	PRML0,4,4	512k	1003
ST34501W	4550	7.5	Ultra SCSI	PRML0,4,4	512k	1003
ST34501WC	4550	7.5	Ultra SCSI	PRML0,4,4	512k	1003
ST34501WD	4550	7.5	Ultra SCSI	PRML0,4,4	512k	1003
ST34502FC	4550	5.4	FC	8/9 PR4	1024	1002
ST34502LC	4550	5.4	Ultra2 SCSI	8/9 PR4	1024	1002
ST34502LW	4550	5.4	Ultra2 SCSI	8/9 PR4	1024	1002
ST34520A	4550	9.5	Ultra ATA	EPRML16,17	512	7200
ST34520LC	4550	9.5	Ultra2 SCSI	EPRML 16,17		7200
ST34520LW	4550	9.5	Ultra2 SCSI	EPRML 16,17		7200
ST34520N	4550	9.5	Ultra SCSI3	EPRML16,17	512k	7200
ST34520W	4550	9.5	Ultra SCSI3	EPRML16,17	512k	7200
ST34520WC	4550	9.5	SCA-2	EPRML16,17	512k	7200
ST34555N	4550	9.1	Ultra SCSI	ZBR PRML	512k	7200
ST34555W	4550	9.1	Ultra SCSIW	ZBR PRML	512k	7200
ST34571DC	4550	8.8	SCSI-2Diff			7200
ST34571FC	4550	8.8	FC-AL			7200
ST34571N	4550	8.8	Ultra SCSI			7200
ST34571W	4550	8.8	Ultra SCSI			7200
ST34571WD	4550	8.8	SCSI-2Diff			7200
ST34572DC	4550	9	Ultra SCSI	PRML	512k	7200
ST34572N	4550	9	Ultra SCSI	PRML	512k	7200
ST34572W	4550	9	Ultra SCSI	PRML	512k	7200
ST34572WC	4550	9	Ultra SCSI	PRML	512k	7200
ST34572WD	4550	9	Ultra SCSI	PRML	512k	7200
ST34573FC	4550	7.1	FiberChanel	16/17 EPR4	1024	7200
ST34573LC	4550	7.1	Ultra2 SCSI	16/17 EPR4	1024	7200
ST34573LW	4550	7.1	Ultra2 SCSI	16/17 EPR4	1024	7200
ST34573N	4550	7.1	Ultra SCSI	16/17 EPR4	512k	7200
ST34573W	4550	7.1	Ultra SCSI	16/17 EPR4	512k	7200
ST34573WC	4550	7.1	Ultra SCSI	16/17 EPR4	512k	7200
ST34573WD	4550	7.1	Ultra2 SCSI	16/17 EPR4	1024	7200
ST3491A	428	14	ATA Fast	ZBR,1,7RLL	120k	3811
ST3500A	426	10	AT BUS	RLL ZBR	256k	4535
ST3500N	426	11	SCSI-2Fast	ZBR,1,7RLL	240k	4535
ST35040A	5008	10	ATA-2 Fast	PRML8,9	512k	5397
ST35120A	5121	12.5	Ultra ATA-3	PRML16,17	12kk	5400
ST35130A	5121	11	Ultra ATA-3	PRML16,17	128k	4490
ST351A,X	43	28	IDE AT	2,7 RLL	32k	3048
ST352A,X	42	28	AT/XT	ZBR,2,7RLL		3048
ST3541A	541	14	ATA	RLL ZBR	64k	3600
ST3543A	542	14	ATA	RLL ZBR	64k	3600

Drive Model	Format Size MB	Head	Cyl	Sect/Trac	Translate H/C/S	RWC/WPC	Form Factor	Power Watts
ST3544A	540	4	2805		16/1048/63	NA/NA	3.5 3H	4.0
ST3550A	452	5	1018	62	14/1018/62	NA/NA	3.5 3H	
ST3550N	456	5	2126	83		NA/NA	3.5 3H	
ST360012A	60GB	2			16/16383/63	—/—	3.5 3H	9.5
ST360014A	60GB	2				—/—	3.5 3H	7.5
ST360014A	60GB	2			16/16383/63	—/—	3.5 3H	9.5
ST360015A	60GB	2			16/16383/63	—/—	3.5 3H	7.5
ST360015AS	60GB	2			16/16383/63	—/—	3.5 3H	5
ST360020A	60GB	3			16/16383/63	—/—	3.5 3H	
ST360021A	60GB	2				—/—	3.5 3H	
ST3600A	528	7	1872		16/1024/63	NA/NA	3.5 3H	
ST3600N	525	7	1872	79		NA/NA	3.5 3H	
ST3600ND	525	7	1872			NA/NA	3.5 3H	
ST360210A	60GB	2			16/16383/63	—/—	3.5 3H	
ST3610N	535	7	1872	79		NA/NA	3.5 3H	
ST3610NC	535					NA/NA	3.5 3H	
ST3610ND	535	7	1872			NA/NA	3.5 3H	
ST3620N	545	5	2700	78		NA/NA	3.5 3H	
ST3620NC	545	5	2700	78		NA/NA	3.5 3H	
ST3620ND	545	5	2700	78		NA/NA	3.5 3H	
ST3620W	546	5	2700	78		NA/NA	3.5 3H	
ST3630A	631	4			16/1223/63	NA/NA	3.5 3H	1.86
ST3635A	635	3	3640		16/1238/63	NA/NA	3.5 3H	3.5
ST3636A	640	2	4893		16/1241/63	NA/NA	3.5 3H	
ST36421A	6449	3			15/13330/63	—/—	3.5 3H	3.1
ST36422A	6400	4			16/13328/63	—/—	3.5 3H	4.5
ST36450A	6448	10	6536		15/13328/63	NA/NA	3.5 3H	7.8
ST36451A	6448	10	6536		15/13328/63	NA/NA	3.5 3H	7.8
ST36530A	6500	6			15/13456/63	—/—	3.5 3H	11.0
ST36530N	6550	6				—/—	3.5 3H	11.0
ST36530W	6550	6				—/—	3.5 3H	11.0
ST36530WC	6550	6				—/—	3.5 3H	11.0
ST36531A	6505	6			15/13446/63	NA/NA	3.5 3H	5.8
ST36540A	6505	8			15/13446/63	NA/NA	3.5 3H	4.3
ST3655A	528	5			16/1024/63	NA/NA	3.5 3H	2.5
ST3655N	545	5	2393	89		NA/NA	3.5 3H	
ST3660A	545				16/1057/63	NA/NA	3.5 3H	1.9
ST36810A	6800	2			15/14123/63	—/—	3.5 3H	9.2
ST373307FC	73.4GB	8				—/—	3.5 3H	9
ST373307LC	73.4GB	8				—/—	3.5 3H	9
ST373307LW	73.4GB	8				—/—	3.5 3H	11.0
ST373405FC	73.4GB	8	29550			—/—	3.5 3H	9.9
ST373405LC	73.4GB	8	29550			—/—	3.5 3H	9.9
ST373405LCV	73.4GB	8	29550			—/—	3.5 3H	9.9
ST373405LW	73.4GB	8	29550			—/—	3.5 3H	12
ST373453FC	18.4GB	8				—/—	3.5 3H	12
ST373453LC	18.4GB	8				—/—	3.5 3H	12
ST373453LW	18.4GB	8				—/—	3.5 3H	4.2
ST37630A	7682	6			15/15878/63	—/—	3.5 3H	
ST3780A	722	4	3876		16/1399/63	NA/NA	3.5 3H	
ST380011A	80GB	2			16/16383/63	—/—	3.5 3H	7.5
ST380011AS	80GB	2			16/16383/63	—/—	3.5 3H	7.5
ST380012ACE	80GB	2				—/—	3.5 3H	7.5
ST380013A	80GB	2			16/16383/63	—/—	3.5 3H	7.5
ST380013AS	80GB	2			16/16383/63	—/—	3.5 3H	7.0
ST380015A	80GB	3			16/16383/63	—/—	3.5 3H	
ST380020A	80GB	4			16/16383/63	—/—	3.5 3H	5
ST380020ACE	80GB	4			16/16383/63	—/—	3.5 3H	5
ST380021A	80GB					—/—	3.5 3H	
ST380022A	80GB	3			16/16383/63	—/—	3.5 3H	9.5
ST380023A	80GB	3			16/16383/63	—/—	3.5 3H	9.5
ST380023AS	80GB	3			16/16383/63	—/—	3.5 3H	7.5
ST380024A	80GB	3			16/16368/63	—/—	3.5 3H	
ST38410A	8400	2			16/16368/63	—/—	3.5 3H	3.5
ST38410A	8400	2			16/16383/63	—/—	3H	5.5
ST38420A	8400	4			16/16383/63	—/—	3.5 3H	5.5
ST38420A	8400	4			16/16383/63	—/—	3.5 3H	
ST38421A	8400	4			16/16368/63	—/—	3.5 3H	

Drive Model	Format Size MB	Seek Time	Interface	Encode	cache kb	RPM
ST3544A	540	12	ATA	RLL ZBR	256k	4500
ST3550A	452	12	IDE AT	ZBR,1,7RLL	256k	4500
ST3550N	456	12	SCSI-2Fast	ZBR,1,7RLL	256k	4500
ST360012A	60GB	9	UltraATA100	EPRML16,17	1mb	5400
ST360014A	60GB	8.5	UltraATA100	EPRML16,17	2mb	7200
ST360015A	60GB	9	UltraATA100	EPRML16,17	2mb	7200
ST360015AS	60GB	9	SATA	EPRML16,17	8mb	7200
ST360020A	60GB	8.9	UltraATA100			5400
ST360021A	60GB	9.5	UltraATA100		2mb	7200
ST3600A	528	11	IDE AT	1,7 RLL	256k	4535
ST3600N	525	12	SCSI-2Fast	ZBR,1,7RLL	256k	4467
ST3600ND	525	12	SCSI-2Fast	1,7 RLL	256k	5400
ST360210A	60GB	9.0	UltraATA100	EPRML16,17	2mb	7200
ST3610N	535	12	SCSI-2Fast	1,7 RLL	256k	5400
ST3610NC	535	12	SCSI-2Fast	ZBR,1,7RLL	256k	5400
ST3610ND	535	12	SCSI-2Fast			5400
ST3620N	545	10.5	SCSI-2Fast	1,7 RLL	256k	5400
ST3620NC	545	10.5	SCSI-2Fast	ZBR,1,7RLL	256k	5411
ST3620ND	545	10.5	SCSI-2Fast	ZBR,1,7RLL	256k	5411
ST3620W	546	10	SCSI-2FstW	ZBR,1,7RLL	256k	5411
ST3630A	631	14	ATA	RLL ZBR	256k	5411
ST3635A	635	14	ATA	RLL ZBR	120k	3811
ST3636A	640	12.5	ATA	RLL ZBR	64k	3600
ST36421A	6449	10.5	Ultra ATA-3	PRML16,17	256k	4500
ST36422A	6400	9.5	Ultra ATA	EPRML 16,17	256k	5400
ST36450A	6448	10	ATA-2 Fast	PRML8,9	512k	5397
ST36451A	6448	10	Ultra ATA-3	PRML8,9	512k	5397
ST36530A	6500	9.5	Ultra	EPRML16,17	512k	7200
ST36530N	6550	9.5	Ultra SCSI3	EPRML16,17	512k	7200
ST36530W	6550	9.5	Ultra SCSI3	EPRML16,17	512k	7200
ST36530WC	6550	9.5	SCA-2	EPRML16,17	512k	7200
ST36531A	6505	10.5	Ultra ATA-3	PRML16,17	128k	5400
ST36540A	6505	11	Ultra ATA-3	PRML16,17	128k	4490
ST3655A	528	12	IDE AT	1,7 RLL	256k	4500
ST3655N	545	12	SCSI-2Fast	ZBR,1,7RLL		4500
ST3660A	545	14	ATA Fast	1,7 RLL	120k	3811
ST36810A	6800	8	Ultra ATA66	EPRML 16,17	512k	7200
ST373307FC	73.4GB	4.7	FC			1000
ST373307LC	73.4GB	4.7	UL320 SCSI			1000
ST373307LW	73.4GB	4.7	UL320 SCSI			1000
ST373405FC	73.4GB	4.9	FC	EPR4	4096k	1000
ST373405LC	73.4GB	4.9	Ultra 160	EPR4	4096k	1000
ST373405LCV	73.4GB	4.9	Ultra 160	EPR4	16384	1000
ST373405LW	73.4GB	4.9	Ultra 160	EPR4	4096k	1000
ST373453FC	18.4GB	3.6	FC	EPRML		1500
ST373453LC	18.4GB	3.6	UL320 SCSI	EPRML		1500
ST373453LW	18.4GB	3.6	UL320 SCSI	EPRML		1500
ST37630A	7682	12.5	Ultra ATA-3	PRML16,17	128k	5400
ST3780A	722	14	IDE AT	RLL ZBR	256k	4500
ST380011A	80GB	8.5	UltraATA100	EPRML16,17	2mb	7200
ST380011AS	80GB	8.5	SATA/150	EPRML16,17	8mb	7200
ST380012ACE	80GB		UltraATA100			
ST380013A	80GB	8.5	UltraATA100	EPRML16,17	2mb	7200
ST380013AS	80GB	8.5	SATA/150	EPRML16,17	8mb	7200
ST380015A	80GB	9.4	UltraATA100	EPRML16,17	2mb	7200
ST380020A	80GB	8.9	UltraATA100	GPRML		5400
ST380020ACE	80GB	8.9	UltraATA100	GPRML	2mb	5400
ST380021A	80GB	9.5	UltraATA100			7200
ST380022A	80GB	9.4	UltraATA100	EPRML16,17	1mb	5400
ST380023A	80GB	9.4	UltraATA100	EPRML16,17	2mb	7200
ST380023AS	80GB	9.4	SATA/150	EPRML16,17	2mb	7200
ST380024A	80GB	9.4	UltraATA100	EPRML16,17	8mb	7200
ST38410A	8400	9	Ultra ATA66	EPRML 24/26	512k	5400
ST38410A	8400	9	UltraATA/66	EPRML 24,26	512k	5400
ST38420A	8400	9	Ultra ATA	EPR4(16/17)	512k	5400
ST38420A	8400	9	UltraATA	EPRML 16,17	512k	5400
ST38421A	8400	10.5	Ultra ATA66	EPRML 16,17	256k	5400

Drive Model	Format Size MB	Head	Cyl	Sect/Trac	Translate H/C/S	RWC/WPC	Form Factor	Power Watts
ST38422A	8622	4			16/16383/63	—/—	3.5 3H	5.5
ST3850A	850	4			16/1648/63	NA/NA	3.5 3H	1.86
ST3851A	850	4	3640		16/1654/63	NA/NA	3.5 3H	3.5
ST3852A	850	1			16/1653/63	—/—	3.5 3H	4
ST3853A	852	4	3659		16/1652/63	NA/NA	3.5 3H	3.9
ST38630A	8606	6			16/16383/63	—/—	3.5 3H	5.5
ST38641A	8606	8			16/16383/63	NA/NA	3.5 3H	5.8
ST39102FC	9100	12				—/—	3.5 3H	13.7
ST39102LC	9100	12				—/—	3.5 3H	13.7
ST39102LW	9100	12				—/—	3.5 3H	13.7
ST39103FC	9100	6	9772			—/—	3.5 3H	
ST39103FCV	9100	6	9772			—/—	3.5 3H	
ST39103LC	9100	6	9772			—/—	3.5 3H	
ST39103LCV	9100	6	9772			—/—	3.5 3H	
ST39103LW	9100	6	9772			—/—	3.5 3H	
ST39103LWV	9100	6	9772			—/—	3.5 3H	
ST39133LCW	9100	6	9772			—/—	3.5 3H	
ST39133LWV	9100	6	9772			—/—	3.5 3H	
ST39140A	9100	8			16/16383/63	—/—	3.5 3H	11
ST39140LC	9100	8	9006			—/—	3.5 3H	
ST39140LW	9100	8	9006			—/—	3.5 3H	11.0
ST39140N	9100	8	9006			—/—	3.5 3H	11.0
ST39140W	9100	8	9006			—/—	3.5 3H	11.0
ST39140WC	9100	8	9006			—/—	3.5 3H	12
ST39173FC	9190	10				—/—	3.5 3H	10
ST39173LC	9190	10				—/—	3.5 3H	10
ST39173LW	9190	10				—/—	3.5 3H	10
ST39173N	9190	10				—/—	3.5 3H	10
ST39173W	9190	10				—/—	3.5 3H	10
ST39173WC	9190	10				—/—	3.5 3H	10
ST39173WD	9190	10				—/—	3.5 3H	10
ST39175FC	9100	5	11737			—/—	3.5 3H	
ST39175LC	9100	5	11737			—/—	3.5 3H	
ST39175LW	9100	5	11737			—/—	3.5 3H	
ST39204FC	9200	3	14384			—/—	3.5 3H	
ST39204LC	9200	3	14384			—/—	3.5 3H	
ST39204LW	9200	3	14384			—/—	3.5 3H	
ST39205LC	9.176GB	2	19036	471		—/—	3.5 3H	7.5
ST39205LW	9.176GB	2	19036	471		—/—	3.5 3H	7.5
ST39216N	9200	3	14384			—/—	3.5 3H	6.5
ST39216W	9200	3	14384			—/—	3.5 3H	6.5
ST39226LC	9200	3	14384			—/—	3.5 3H	6.5
ST39226LW	9200	3	14384			—/—	3.5 3H	6.5
ST39236LC	9200	3	14384			—/—	3.5 3H	6.5
ST39236LCV	9200	3	14384			—/—	3.5 3H	6.5
ST39236LW	9200	3	14384			—/—	3.5 3H	6.5
ST39236LWV	9200	3	14384			—/—	3.5 3H	6.5
ST4026	20	4	615	17		NA/NA	5.25FH	25
ST4038	31	5	733	17		NA/300	5.25FH	25
ST4038N	30	5	733			NA/NA	5.25FH	
ST4051	40	5	977	17		NA/NA	5.25FH	25
ST4053	44	5	1024	17		NA/NA	5.25FH	23
ST406	5	2	306	17		NA/128	5.25FH	
ST4077N	67	5	1024	26		1025/1025	5.25FH	25
ST4077R	65	5	1024	26		1025/1025	5.25FH	25
ST4085	71	8	1024	17		NA/NA	5.25FH	
ST4086	72	9	925	17		NA/NA	5.25FH	
ST4096	80	9	1024	17		NA/NA	5.25FH	23
ST4096N	83	4				—/—	5.25FH	25
ST4097	80	9	1024	17		NA/NA	5.25FH	22
ST410800N	9090	27	4925	133		NA/NA	5.25FH	22
ST410800ND	9090	27	4925	133		NA/NA	5.25FH	22
ST410800W	9090	27	4925	133		NA/NA	5.25FH	23
ST410800WD	9090	27	4925	133		NA/NA	5.25FH	23
ST41097J	1097	17	2101			NA/NA	5.25FH	
ST412	10	4	306	17		307/128	5.25FH	
ST41200N	1037	15	1931	71		NA/NA	5.25FH	

Drive Model	Format Size MB	Seek Time	Interface	Encode	cache kb	RPM
ST38422A	8622	9	Ultra ATA-4	PRML16,17	512k	5400
ST3850A	850	14	ATA	1,7 RLL	120k	3811
ST3851A	850	14	ATA	RLL ZBR	64k	3600
ST3852A	850	12	ATA-2	1,7 RLL	128k	4500
ST3853A	852	12	ATA	RLL ZBR	256k	4500
ST38630A	8606	9.5	Ultra ATA-3	PRML16,17	256k	4500
ST38641A	8606	10.5	Ultra ATA-3	PRML16,17	256k	5400
ST39102FC	9100	5.4	FiberChanel	8/9 PR4	1024	1002
ST39102LC	9100	5.4	Ultra2 SCSI	8/9 PR4	1024	1002
ST39102LW	9100	5.4	Ultra2 SCSI	8/9 PR4	1024	1002
ST39103FCV	9100	5.2	FC	16/17 PR4	1024k	1000
ST39103LC	9100	5	FC	16/17 PR4	1024k	1000
ST39103LCV	9100	5.2	Ultra2 SCSI	16/17 PR4	1024k	1000
ST39103LW	9100	5.2	Ultra2 SCSI	16/17 PR4	1024k	1000
ST39103LWV	9100	5.2	Ultra2 SCSI	16/17 PR4	1024k	1000
ST39133LCW	9100	5.2	Ultra2 SCSI	16/17 PR4	1024k	1000
ST39133LWV	9100	5.2	UI160SCSI	16/17 PR4	1024k	1000
ST39140A	9100	9.5	Ultra ATA	EPRML16,17	512k	7200
ST39140LC	9100	9.5	Ultra2 SCSI	EPRML16,17		7200
ST39140LW	9100	9.5	Ultra2 SCSI	EPRML16,17		7200
ST39140N	9100	9.5	Ultra SCSI3	EPRML16,17		7200
ST39140W	9100	9.5	Ultra SCSI3	EPRML16,17	512k	7200
ST39140WC	9100	9.5	SCA-2	EPRML16,17	512k	7200
ST39173FC	9190	7.1	FiberChanel	16/17 EPR4	1024k	7200
ST39173LC	9190	7.1	Ultra2 SCSI	16/17 EPR4	1024k	7200
ST39173LW	9190	7.1	Ultra2 SCSI	16/17 EPR4	1024k	7200
ST39173N	9190	7.1	Ultra SCSI	16/17 EPR4	512k	7200
ST39173W	9190	7.1	Ultra SCSI	16/17 EPR4	512k	7200
ST39173WC	9190	7.1	SCA-2	16/17 EPR4	512k	7200
ST39173WD	9190	7.1	Ultra2 SCSI	16/17 EPR4		7200
ST39175FC	9100	6.9	FC	16/17 EPR4		7200
ST39175LC	9100	6.9	Ultra2 SCSI	16/17 EPR4	1024k	7200
ST39175LW	9100	6.9	Ultra2 SCSI	16/17 EPR4	1024k	7200
ST39204FC	9200	5.2	FC	NPV		1000
ST39204LC	9200	5.2	FC	NPV		1000
ST39204LW	9200	5.2	UL160SCSI	NPV		1000
ST39205LC	9.176GB	5.4	Ultra 160	EPR4 32,34	4096k	1002
ST39205LW	9.176GB	5.4	Ultra 160	EPR4 32,34	4096k	1002
ST39216N	9200	5.9	Ultra SCSI	EPRML		7200
ST39216W	9200	5.9	Ultra SCSI	EPRML		7200
ST39226LC	9200	5.9	UI160SCSI	EPRML		7200
ST39226LW	9200	5.9	UI160SCSI	EPRML		7200
ST39236LC	9200	5.9	UI160SCSI	EPRML		7200
ST39236LCV	9200	5.9	UI160SCSI	EPRML		7200
ST39236LW	9200	5.9	UI160SCSI	EPRML		7200
ST39236LWV	9200	5.9	UI160SCSI	EPRML		7200
ST4026	20	40	ST412/506	MFM		3600
ST4038	31	40	ST412/506	MFM		3600
ST4038N	30		SCSI			
ST4051	40	40	ST412/506	MFM		3600
ST4053	44	28	ST412/506	MFM		3600
ST406	5	85	ST412/506	MFM		3600
ST4077N	67	28	SCSI	2,7 RLL		
ST4077R	65	28	ST412/506	2,7 RLL		
ST4085	71	28	ST412/506	MFM		3600
ST4086	72	28	ST412/506	MFM		3600
ST4096	80	28	ST412/506	MFM		3600
ST4096N	83	17	SCSI			
ST4097	80	28	ST412/506	MFM		3600
ST410800N	9090	12	SCSI-2Fast	1,7 RLL	1024k	5400
ST410800ND	9090	12	SCSI-2Fast	1,7 RLL	1024k	5400
ST410800W	9090	12	SCSI-2FstW	1,7 RLL	1024k	5400
ST410800WD	9090	12	SCSI-2FstW	1,7 RLL	1024k	5400
ST41097J	1097	11	SMD-O/E	2,7 RLL		5400
ST412	10	85	ST412/506	MFM		
ST41200N	1037	15	SCSI-2	1,7RLL,ZBR	256k	3600

Drive Model	Format Size MB	Head	Cyl	Sect/Trac	Translate H/C/S	RWC/WPC	Form Factor	Power Watts
ST41200ND	1037	15	1931	NA		NA/NA	5.25FH	
ST41200NM	1037	15	1931	NA		NA/NA	5.25FH	
ST41200NV	1037	15	1931	NA		NA/NA	5.25FH	
ST41201J	1200U	17	2101			NA/NA	5.25FH	
ST41201K	1200U	17	2101	NA		NA/128	5.25FH	
ST4135R	115	9	960	26		NA/NA	5.25FH	25
ST4144N	122	9	1024	26		NA/NA	5.25FH	23
ST4144R	122	9	1024	26		NA/NA	5.25FH	37
ST41520N	1370	17	2101	NA		NA/NA	5.25FH	37
ST41520ND	1370	17	2101	NA		NA/NA	5.25FH	37
ST41600N	1370	17	2101	NA		NA/NA	5.25FH	37
ST41600ND	1370	17	2101	NA		NA/NA	5.25FH	37
ST41601N	1370	17	2101	V		NA/NA	5.25FH	
ST41601ND	1370	17	2101	V		NA/NA	5.25FH	
ST41650N	1415	15	2107	87		NA/NA	5.25FH	
ST41650ND	1415	15	2107	NA		NA/NA	5.25FH	
ST41651N	1415	15	2107	87		NA/NA	5.25FH	
ST41651ND	1415	15	2107	NA		NA/NA	5.25FH	
ST41800K	1986U	18	2627	NA		NA/NA	5.25FH	
ST4182E	151	9	969	34		NA/NA	5.25FH	
ST4182N	155	9	967	36		NA/NA	5.25FH	
ST4182NM	155	9	967	36		307/128	5.25FH	
ST419	15	6	306	32		NA/NA	5.25FH	
ST4192E	169	8	1147	36		1148/1148	5.25FH	25
ST4192N	168	8	1147	36		NA/NA	5.25FH	
ST42000N,ND	1792	16	2627	83		NA/NA	5.25FH	
ST42100N	1900	15	2573	96		—/—	5.25FH	22
ST423451N	23.2	28	6876	237		—/—	5.25FH	22
ST423451W	23.2	28	6876	237		—/—	5.25FH	22
ST423451WD	23.2	28	6876	237		NA/NA	5.25FH	
ST42000N,ND	2129	19	2627	83		307/128	5.25FH	
ST425	20	8	306	17		NA/NA	5.25FH	40
ST43200K	3386u	20	2738			NA/NA	5.25FH	
ST43200N	3338			NA		NA/NA	5.25FH	30
ST43400N	2912	21	2738	99		NA/NA	5.25FH	30
ST43400ND	2912	21	2738	99		NA/NA	5.25FH	30
ST43401N	2912	21	2738			NA/NA	5.25FH	30
ST43401ND	2912	21	2738			NA/NA	5.25FH	30
ST43402N	2912	21	2738	99		NA/NA	5.25FH	
ST43402ND	2912	21	2738	99		NA/NA	5.25FH	
ST4350N	300	9	1412	46		NA/NA	5.25FH	
ST4350NM	307	9	1412	NA		NA/NA	5.25FH	
ST4376N	330	9	1549	45		NA/NA	5.25FH	
ST4376NM	330	9	1549	NA		NA/NA	5.25FH	
ST4376NV	330	9	1549	NA		NA/NA	5.25FH	
ST4383E	319	13	1412	34		NA/NA	5.25FH	
ST4384N	319	15	1224	34		NA/NA	5.25FH	
ST4385N	330	15	791	55		NA/NA	5.25FH	
ST4385NM	330	15	791	NA		NA/NA	5.25FH	
ST4385NV	330	15	791	NA		NA/NA	5.25FH	
ST4442E	368	15	1412	34		NA/NA	5.25FH	
ST446452W	4700	28	9996			—/—	5.25FH	22.8
ST4702N	601	15	1546	50		NA/NA	5.25FH	
ST4702NM	601	15	1546	NA		NA/NA	5.25FH	
ST4766E	664	15	1632	53		NA/NA	5.25FH	
ST4766N	676	15	1632	54		NA/NA	5.25FH	
ST4766NM	663		1632	54		NA/NA	5.25FH	
ST4766NV	663		1632	54		NA/NA	5.25FH	
ST4767E	676	15	1399	63		NA/NA	5.25FH	
ST4767N	665	15	1356	64		NA/NA	5.25FH	
ST4767ND	665	15	1356	64		NA/NA	5.25FH	
ST4767NM	665	15	1356	64		NA/NA	5.25FH	
ST4767NV	665	15	1356	64		NA/NA	5.25FH	
ST4769E	631	15	1552	53		128/128	3.5 4H	
ST506	5	4	153	17		NA/NA	3.5 4H	3.0
ST51080A	1080	4	4771		16/2114/63	—/—	2.5 4H	
ST51080N	1000							

Drive Model	Format Size MB	Seek Time	Interface	Encode	cache kb	RPM
ST41200ND	1037	15	SCSI-2	RLL ZBR	256k	
ST41200NM	1037	15	SCSI-2	RLL ZBR	256k	
ST41200NV	1037	15	SCSI-2	RLL ZBR	256k	
ST41201J	1200U	11	SMD-O/E	2,7 RLL		5400
ST41201K	1200U	11	IPI-2	2,7 RLL		5400
ST4135R	115	28	ST412/506	RLL		3600
ST4144N	122	28	SCSI	2,7 RLL		
ST4144R	122	28	ST412/506	2,7 RLL		3600
ST41520N	1370	11	SCSI-2	ZBR,2,7RLL	48k	5400
ST41520ND	1370	11	SCSI-2	ZBR	48k	5400
ST41600N	1370	11	SCSI-2	ZBR,2,7RLL	48k	5400
ST41600ND	1370	11	SCSI-2	ZBR	48k	5400
ST41601N	1370	11	SCSI-2Fast	ZBR,2,7RLL	256k	5400
ST41601ND	1370	11	SCSI-2Fast	2,7 RLL	256k	5400
ST41650N	1415	15	SCSI-2	ZBR,1,7RLL	256k	3600
ST41650ND	1415	15	SCSI-2Diff	RLL ZBR	256k	
ST41651N	1415	15	SCSI-2Diff	ZBR,1,7RLL	256k	3600
ST41651ND	1415	15	SCSI-2Diff	1,7 RLL	256k	
ST41800K	1986U	11	IPI-2	2,7 RLL		5400
ST4182E	151	16	ESDI	RLL		3600
ST4182N	155	16	SCSI	2,7 RLL	32k	3600
ST4182NM	155	16	SCSI	2,7 RLL	32k	3600
ST419	15	85	ST412/506	MFM		
ST4192E	169	17	ESDI	2,7 RLL		
ST4192N	168	17	SCSI	2,7 RLL		
ST42000N,ND	1792	11	SCSI-2Fast	ZBR,2,7RLL		5400
ST42100N	1900	13	SCSI-2FstW	ZBR,1,7RLL	256k	3600
ST423451N	23.2	13	Ultra SCSI	PRML0,4,4	2048k	5400
ST423451W	23.2	13	Ultra SCSI	PRML0,4,4	2048k	5400
ST423451WD	23.2	13	Ultra SCSI	PRML0,4,4	2048k	5400
ST42400N,ND	2129	11	SCSI-2Fast	ZBR,2,7RLL	512k	5400
ST425	20		ST412/506	MFM		
ST43200K	3386u	11	IPI-2	1,7 RLL	512k	5400
ST43200N	3338	11	IPI-2	RLL ZBR		5400
ST43400N	2912	11	SCSI-2Fast	1,7 RLL	512k	5400
ST43400ND	2912	11	SCSI-2Fast	1,7 RLL	512k	5400
ST43401N	2912	11	SCSI-2FstW	1,7 RLL	512k	5400
ST43401ND	2912	11	SCSI-2FstW	1,7 RLL	512k	5400
ST43402N	2912	11	SCSI-2 2POR	ZBR,1,7RLL	2048k	5400
ST43402ND	2912	11	SCSI-2 2POR	ZBR,1,7RLL	394k	5400
ST4350N	300	16	SCSI	ZBR,2,7RLL	32k	3600
ST4350NM	307	16	SCSI	RLL ZBR	32k	
ST4376N	330	17	SCSI	ZBR,2,7RLL	32k	3600
ST4376NM	330	17	SCSI	RLL ZBR	32k	
ST4376NV	330	17	SCSI	RLL ZBR	32k	
ST4383E	319	18	ESDI	2,7 RLL		3600
ST4384E	319	14	ESDI	2,7 RLL		3600
ST4385N	330	10	SCSI	ZBR,2,7RLL	32k	3600
ST4385NM	330	10	SCSI	RLL ZBR	32k	
ST4385NV	330	10	SCSI	RLL ZBR	32k	
ST4442E	368	16	ESDI	RLL		3600
ST446452W	4700	13.2	Ultra Wide	ZBR PRML	4096k	5400
ST4702N	601	16	SCSI	ZBR,2,7RLL	32k	5400
ST4702NM	601	16	SCSI	RLL ZBR	32k	
ST4766E	664	16	ESDI (15)	RLL		3600
ST4766N	676	15	SCSI	RLL	32k	3600
ST4766NM	663	15	SCSI	2,7 RLL	32k	
ST4766NV	663	15	SCSI	2,7 RLL	32k	
ST4767E	676	11	ESDI (24)	1,7 RLL		4800
ST4767N	665	11	SCSI-2	ZBR,1,7RLL	256k	4800
ST4767ND	665	11	SCSI-2	RLL ZBR	256k	4800
ST4767NM	665	11	SCSI-2	RLL ZBR	256k	4800
ST4767NV	665	11	SCSI-2	RLL ZBR	256k	4800
ST4769E	631	14	ESDI	1,7 RLL		4800
ST506	5	85	ST412/506	MFM		
ST51080A	1080	10	ATA-2 Fast	1,7 RLL	256k	5400
ST51080N	1000		SCSI			

Drive Model	Format Size MB	Head	Cyl	Sect/Trac	Translate H/C/S	RWC/WPC	Form Factor	Power Watts
ST51270A	1282	4	5414		16/2485/63	NA/NA	3.5 4H	3.5
ST52160A	2113	4			16/4095/63	—/—	3.5 3H	3.2
ST52160C	2170	4	6536	161		—/—	3.5 4H	8.0
ST52160N	2170	4	6536			—/—	3.5 4H	8
ST52160WC	2170	4	6536	161			3.5 4H	
ST52520A	2560	4			16/4970/63	—/—	3.5 4H	3.2
ST5540A	541	2	4834		16/1050/63	NA/NA	3.5 4H	
ST5660A	545	4	3420		16/1057/63	NA/NA	3.5 4H	
ST5660N	545	4	3420	77		NA/NA	3.5 4H	
ST5660NC	545	4		77		NA/NA	3.5 4H	
ST5850A	855	4	4085		16/1656/63	NA/NA	3.5 4H	3.0
ST5851A	854	4	4834		16/1656/63	NA/NA	3.5 4H	3.36
ST6165J	165	10	823			—/—	8	
ST6315J	315	19	823			—/—	9	
ST6344J	344	24	711			—/—	9	
ST6515J	516	24	711			—/—	9	
ST6515K	516u	24	711			—/—	9	
ST6515J	516	24	711			—/—	9	
ST683J	83	5	823				8	
ST7050P	42	2				NA/NA	1.8 4H	
ST706	5	2	306	17		307/128	5.25FH	
ST81123J	1123U	15	1635			—/—	8	
ST81154K	1154U	14	1635			—/—	8	
ST81236J	1236	15	1635			—/—	8	
ST81236K	1236	15	1635			—/—	8	
ST81236N	1056	15	1635	NA		NA/NA	8	
ST82030J	2030U	19	2120			—/—	8	
ST82030K	2030U	19	2120			—/—	8	
ST82038J	2038U	19	2611			—/—	8	
ST82105K	2105U	16	2611			—/—	8	
ST82272J	2272U	19	2611			—/—	8	
ST82368K	2368U	18	2611			—/—	8	
ST82500J	2500	19	2611			—/—	8	
ST82500K	2500 (U)	19	2611			—/—	8	
ST82500N	2140U	19	2611	NA		NA/NA	8	
ST83050K	3050U	18	2655	NA		NA/NA	8	
ST83050N	3050U	18	2655	NA		NA/NA	8	
ST83073J	3073u	19	2655			NA/NA	8 FH	
ST83220K	3220U	19	2655	NA		NA/NA	8	
ST8368J	368U	10	1217			—/—	8 FH	
ST8368N	316	10	1217	NA		NA/NA	8	
ST8500J	500U	10	1217			—/—	8	
ST8500N	427	10	1217	NA		NA/NA	8	
ST8741J	741U	15	1635			—/—	8	
ST8741N	637	15	1635	NA		NA/NA	8	
ST8851J	851	15	1381			—/—	8	
ST8851K	851	15	1381			—/—	8	
ST8851N	727	15	1381			NA/NA	8	
ST8885N	727			NA		NA/NA	8	
ST9025A	21	4	1024		4/615/17	NA/NA	2.5 4H	3
ST9051A	43	4	654	32	6/820/17	NA/NA	2.5 4H	3
ST9052A	42	16	1024	63	5/980/17	—/—	2.5 4H	
ST9077A	64	4	802	39	11/669/17	NA/NA	2.5 4H	8
ST9080A	64	2		38	4/823/38	NA/NA	2.5 4H	
ST9096A	85	4		34	10/980/17	NA/NA	2.5 4H	8
ST9100A	85					NA/NA	2.5 4H	
ST9100AG	85	2		63	14/748/16	NA/NA	2.5 4H	
ST91080A	1083	6			16/2100/63	NA/NA	2.5 4H	0.9
ST91350AG	1350				16/2616/63	—/—	2.5 4H	0.9
ST9140AG	127	4			15/980/17	NA/NA	2.5 4H	
ST91420A	1442	4			16/2794/63	NA/NA	2.5 4H	1.0
ST91430A	1449	6			16/2808/63	NA/NA	2.5 4H	0.9
ST9144A	128	6			15/980/17	NA/NA	2.5 4H	
ST9145A	128	4	1463		15/980/17	NA/NA	2.5 4H	0.8
ST9145AG	127	4	1463		15/980/17	NA/NA	2.5 4H	0.7
ST9150AG	131	2			13/419/47	NA/NA	2.5 4H	
ST91685AG	1680				8/3256/63	—/—	2.5 4H	1.2

Drive Model	Format Size MB	Seek Time	Interface	Encode	cache kb	RPM
ST51270A	1282	10.5	ATA	RLL ZBR	128k	5376
ST52160A	2113	11	ATA-2 Fast	PRML	128k	5400
ST52160C	2170	12	Ultra SCSI3	2BR PRML	256k	5397
ST52160N	2170	12	Ultra SCSI	2BR PRML	128k	5400
ST52160WC	2170	12	Ultra SCSI3	2BR PRML	256k	5400
ST52520A	2560	11	ATA-2 Fast	PRML	128k	5400
ST5540A	541	10.5	ATA	RLL ZBR	128k	5376
ST5660A	545	12	IDE AT	1,7 RLL		4500
ST5660N	545	12	SCSI-2Fast	ZBR,1,7RLL		4500
ST5660NC	545	12	SCSI-2Fast	ZBR,1,7RLL	256k	4500
ST5850A	855	11	ATA-2 Fast	1,7 RLL	256k	5400
ST5851A	854	10.5	ATA	RLL ZBR	128k	5376
ST6165J	165	30	SMD	2,7 RLL		3600
ST6315J	315	20	SMD-E	MFM		3600
ST6344J	344	18	SMD-O/E	MFM		3600
ST6515J	516	18	SMD	2,7 RLL		3600
ST6515K	516u	18	IPI-2	2,7 RLL		3600
ST6516J	516	18	SMD-E	2,7 RLL		3600
ST683J	83	30	SMD	2,7 RLL		3600
ST7050P	42	18	PCMCIA/ATA	1,7 RLL	32k	3545
ST706	5		ST412/506	MFM		
ST81123J	1123U	15	SMD-E	2,7 RLL		3600
ST81154K	1154U	15	IPI-2	2,7 RLL		3600
ST81236J	1236	15	SMD-E	2,7 RLL		3600
ST81236K	1236	15	IPI-2	2,7 RLL		3600
ST81236N	1056	15	SCSI	2,7 RLL		3600
ST82030J	2030U	11	SMD-O/E	2,7 RLL		3600
ST82030K	2030U	11	IPI-2	2,7 RLL		3600
ST82038J	2038U	12	SMD-E	2,7 RLL		3600
ST82105K	2105U	12	IPI-2	2,7 RLL		3600
ST82272J	2272U	12	SMD-E	2,7 RLL		3600
ST82368K	2368U	12	IPI-2	2,7 RLL		
ST82500J	2500	12	SMD-E	2,7 RLL		3600
ST82500K	2500 (U)	12	IPI-2	2,7 RLL		3600
ST82500N	2140	12	SCSI	2,7 RLL		3600
ST83050K	3050U	12	IPI-2	1,7 RLL		4365
ST83050N	3050U	12	IPI-2	1,7 RLL		4365
ST83073J	3073u	12	SMD-O/E	1,7 RLL		4235
ST83220K	3220U	12	IPI-2	1,7 RLL		4365
ST8368J	368U	18	SMD-E	2,7 RLL		3600
ST8368N	316	18	SCSI	2,7 RLL		3600
ST8500J	500U	18	SMD-E	2,7 RLL		3600
ST8500N	427	18	SCSI	2,7 RLL		3600
ST8741J	741U	15	SMD-E	2,7 RLL		3600
ST8741N	637	15	SCSI	2,7 RLL		3600
ST8851J	851	15	SMD-E	2,7 RLL		3600
ST8851K	851	15	IPI-2	2,7 RLL		3600
ST8851N	727	12	SCSI	2,7 RLL		3600
ST8885N	727	15	SCSI			
ST9025A	21	<20	IDE AT	2,7 RLL		3631
ST9051A	43	<20	IDE AT	2,7 RLL	32k	3631
ST9052A	42	16	IDE AT	2,7 RLL	32k	3450
ST9077A	64	19	IDE AT	2,7 RLL	32k	3546
ST9080A	64	16	IDE AT	ZBR,2,7RLL	32k	3449
ST9096A	85	16	IDE AT	ZBR,2,7RLL	64k	3450
ST9100A	85	16	IDE AT		120k	
ST9100AG	85	16	IDE AT	ZBR,1,7RLL	120k	3545
ST91080A	1083	12	ATA-3	PRML8,9	103k	4508
ST91350AG	1350	12	ATA-2 Fast	RLL ZBR	103k	4508
ST9140AG	127	16	IDE AT	ZBR,1,7RLL	120k	3545
ST91420A	1442	12	ATA-3	PRML16,17	103k	4508
ST91430A	1449	12	ATA-3	PRML16,17	103k	4508
ST9144A	128	16	IDE AT	ZBR,2,7RLL	64k	3450
ST9145A	128	16	AT BUS	RLL ZBR	32k	3449
ST9145AG	127	16	IDE AT	ZBR,2,7RLL	32k	3449
ST9150AG	131	16	IDE AT	ZBR,1,7RLL	120k	3980
ST91685AG	1680	12	ATA-2 Fast	RLL ZBR	103k	4508

Drive Model	Format Size MB	Head	Cyl	Sect/ Trac	Translate H/C/S	RWC/ WPC	Form Factor	Power Watts
ST9190AG	171	4			16/873/24	NA/NA	2.5 4H	
ST92011A	20GB	1			16/16383/63	—/—	2.5 4H	
ST92120AG	2167	3			16/4200/63	—/—	2.5 4H	1.0
ST92130A	2163	6			16/4191/63	NA/NA	2.5 4H	1.0
ST92255AG	2250				10/4360/63	—/—	2.5 4H	1.2
ST9235AG	209	6	985	32	13/985/32	NA/NA	2.5 4H	
ST9235N	209	13	985	NA		NA/NA	2.5 4H	
ST9240AG	210	4			8/988/52	NA/NA	2.5 4H	0.73
ST9252N	252	6	1339			—/—	3.5 4H	1.0
ST92811A	20GB	1			16/16383/63	—/—	2.5 4H	
ST9295AG	261	16	1024	63		—/—	2.5 4H	
ST9295N (never made)	250N	NA	NA			—/—	2.5 4H	
ST9300AG	262	4			15/569/60	NA/NA	2.5 4H	0.73
ST93230AG	3253	5			16/6304/63	—/—	2.5 4H	1.0
ST9342A	345	6	1598		16/667/63	NA/NA	2.5 4H	1.0
ST9352A	350	4	2225		12/905/63	—/—	2.5 4H	0.85
ST936701FC	36.7GB	2	51052			—/—	2.5 4H	6.5
ST936701LC	36.7GB	2	51052			—/—	2.5 4H	4.8
ST9385AG	341	6			16/934/51	NA/NA	2.5 4H	0.9
ST94011A	40GB	2			16/16383/63	—/—	2.5 4H	
ST94030AG	4099	6			16/7944/16	—/—	2.5 4H	1.0
ST9420AG	420				16/988/32	—/—	2.5 4H	0.9
ST9422A	421	4	2393		16/816/63	NA/NA	2.5 4H	0.85
ST94811A	40GB	2			16/16383/63	—/—	2.5 4H	
ST9546A	540	6			16/1047/63	NA/NA	2.5 4H	1.3
ST9550AG	455	6			16/942/59	NA/NA	2.5 4H	
ST9655AG	524	6			14/1016/63	NA/NA	2.5 4H	1.03
ST973401FC	73GB	4	51052			—/—	2.5 4H	6.8
ST973401LC	73GB	4	51052			—/—	2.5 4H	5.1
ST9810AG	811	4			16/1572/63	NA/NA	2.5 4H	0.9
ST9816AG	810				16/1571/63	NA/NA	2.5 4H	1.3
ST9840AG	840	4			16/1628/63	NA/NA	3.5 4H	0.82
U Series X 10	10GB	1			16/16383/63	—/—	2.5 4H	4.5
U Series X 20	20GB	1			16/16383/63	—/—	2.5 4H	4.5

SEQUEL, INC

Drive Model	Format Size MB	Head	Cyl	Sect/ Trac	Translate H/C/S	RWC/ WPC	Form Factor	Power Watts
5300	3000	21		V		—/—	5.25FH	
5350	3572	25		V		—/—	5.25FH	
5400	4000	26		V		NA/NA	5.25FH	
EXT4175	149	7	1224	34		NA/NA	5.25FH	
EXT4280	234	11	1224	36		NA/NA	5.25FH	
EXT4380	319	15	1224	34		NA/NA	5.25FH	
XT1050	38	5	902	17		NA/NA	5.25FH	
XT1065	52	7	918	17		NA/NA	5.25FH	
XT1085	71	8	1024	17		NA/NA	5.25FH	28
XT1105	84	11	918	17		NA/NA	5.25FH	
XT1120R	105	8	1024	25		NA/NA	5.25FH	28
XT1140	119	15	918	17		NA/NA	5.25FH	28
XT1240R	196	15	1024	25		NA/NA	5.25FH	28
XT2085	72	7	1224	17		NA/NA	5.25FH	
XT2140	113	11	1224	17		NA/NA	5.25FH	
XT2190	159	15	1224	17		NA/NA	5.25FH	28
XT3170	146	9	1224	26		—/—	5.25FH	
XT3280	244	15	1224	26		—/—	5.25FH	
XT3380	319	15	1224	34		—/—	5.25FH	
XT4170E	157	7	1224	35/36	16	NA/NA	5.25FH	27
XT4170S	157	7	1224	35-36		NA/NA	5.25FH	27
XT4380E	338	15	1224	36		NA/NA	5.25FH	27
XT4380S	338	15	1224	36		NA/NA	5.25FH	27
XT8380E	361	8	1632	53-54		NA/NA	5.25FH	35
XT8380S	361	8	1632	54		NA/NA	5.25FH	35
XT8760E	676	15	1632	53-54		NA/NA	5.25FH	27
XT8760EH	676	15	1632	54		NA/NA	5.25FH	27
XT8760S	670	15	1632	NA		NA/NA	5.25FH	27
XT8760SH	670	15	1632	NA		NA/NA	5.25FH	27
XT8800E	694	15	1274	54		NA/NA	5.25FH	

SHUGART

Drive Model	Format Size MB	Seek Time	Interface	Encode	cache kb	RPM
ST9190AG	171	16	IDE AT	ZBR,1,7RLL	120k	3545
ST92011A	20GB	12	UltraATA100	RLL0,11	2mb	5400
ST92120AG	2167	12	Ultra ATA	ZBR PRML	128k	4500
ST92130A	2163	12	ATA-3	PRML16,17	103k	4508
ST92255AG	2250	12	ATA-2 Fast		103k	4508
ST9235AG	209	16	IDE AT	RLL ZBR	64k	3449
ST9235N	209	16	SCSI	ZBR,2,7RLL	64k	3449
ST9240AG	210	16	ATA Fast	ZBR,1,7RLL	120k	3980
ST9252N	252	12	SCSI	1,7 RLL	32k	4500
ST92811A	20GB	12	UltraATA100	RLL0,11	8mb	5400
ST9295AG	261	16	IDE AT	2,7 RLL	120k	3450
ST9295N (never made)	250	16	SCSI	2,7 RLL	64k	3450
ST9300AG	262	16	ATA Fast	ZBR,1,7RLL	120k	3980
ST93230AG	3253	12	Ultra ATA	ZBR PRML	128k	4500
ST9342A	345	13	ATA	RLL ZBR	32k	4000
ST9352A	350	12	ATA	RLL ZBR	32k	3750
ST936701FC	36.7GB	4.1	FC		8mb	1000
ST936701LC	36.7GB	4.1	UL320 SCSI		8mb	1000
ST9385AG	341	16	ATA Fast	ZBR,1,7RLL	120k	3980
ST94011A	40GB	12	UltraATA100	RLL0,11	2mb	5400
ST94030AG	4099	12	Ultra ATA	EPRML 16,17	128k	4500
ST9420AG	420	16	ATA-2 Fast		120k	4500
ST9422A	421	12	ATA	RLL ZBR	64k	3600
ST94811A	40GB	12	UltraATA100	RLL0,11	8mb	5400
ST9546A	540	16	ATA	RLL ZBR	120k	4500
ST9550AG	455	16	IDE AT	ZBR,1,7RLL	120k	3980
ST9655AG	524	16	ATA Fast	ZBR,1,7RLL	120k	3980
ST973401FC	73GB	4.1	FC		8mb	1000
ST973401LC	73GB	4.1	UL320 SCSI		8mb	1000
ST9810AG	811	16	ATA	PRML8,9	120k	3968
ST9816AG	810	16	ATA-2 Fast		120k	4500
ST9840AG	840	14	ATA	PRML8,9	107k	4500
U Series X 10	10GB	12.7	UltraATA100	GPRML96/102	2mb	5400
U Series X 20	20GB	12.7	UltraATA100	GPRML96/102	2mb	5400

SEQUEL, INC

Drive Model	Format Size MB	Seek Time	Interface	Encode	cache kb	RPM
5300	3000	12	SCSI-2FstW	1,7 RLL	512	5400
5350	3572	12	SCSI-2FstW	1,7 RLL	512k	5400
5400	4000	12	SCSI-2FstW	1,7 RLL	1024k	5400
EXT4175	149	27	ESDI	RLL		3600
EXT4280	234	27	ESDI	RLL		3600
EXT4380	319	27	ESDI	RLL		3600
XT1050	38	30	ST412/506	MFM		3600
XT1065	52	30	ST412/506	MFM		3600
XT1085	71	28	ST412/506	MFM		3600
XT1105	84	27	ST412/506	MFM		3600
XT1120R	105	27	ST412/506	2,7 RLL		3600
XT1140	119	27	ST412/506	MFM		3600
XT1240R	196	27	ST412/506	2,7 RLL		3600
XT2085	72	30	ST412/506	MFM		3600
XT2140	113	30	ST412/506	MFM		3600
XT2190	159	29	ST412/506	MFM		3600
XT3170	146	30	SCSI	RLL		3600
XT3280	244	30	SCSI			3600
XT3380	319	27	SCSI			3600
XT4170E	157	14	ESDI	1,7 RLL		3600
XT4170S	157	14	SCSI	1,7 RLL		3600
XT4380E	338	16	ESDI	1,7 RLL		3600
XT4380S	338	16	SCSI	1,7 RLL		3600
XT8380E	361	16	ESDI	1,7 RLL		3600
XT8380S	361	14	SCSI	1,7 RLL		3600
XT8760E	676	16	ESDI	1,7 RLL		3600
XT8760EH	676	16	ESDI	1,7 RLL		3600
XT8760S	670	16	SCSI	1,7 RLL		3600
XT8760SH	670	14	SCSI	1,7 RLL	256k	3600
XT8800E	694	14	ESDI	1,7 RLL		3600

SHUGART

Drive Model	Format Size MB	Head	Cyl	Sect/Trac	Translate H/C/S	RWC/WPC	Form Factor	Power Watts
1002	5			17		—/—	8.0 FH	
1004	10			17		—/—	8.0 FH	
1006	30					—/—	8.0	
4004	14			17		—/—		
4008	29			17		—/—	14.0	
4100	56			17		—/—		
604	5	4	160	17		128/128	5.25FH	
606	7	6	160	17		128/128	5.25FH	
612	10	4	306	17		307/128	5.25FH	
706	6	2	320	17		321/128	5.25FH	
712	10	4	320	17		321/128	5.25FH	
725	20					—/—	5.25HH	

SIEMENS

Drive Model	Format Size MB	Head	Cyl	Sect/Trac	Translate H/C/S	RWC/WPC	Form Factor	Power Watts
1200	174	8	1216	35		NA/NA	5.25FH	
1300	261	12	1216	35		NA/NA	5.25FH	
2200	174	8	1216			NA/NA	5.25FH	
2300	261	12	1216	35		NA/NA	5.25FH	
4410	322	11	1100	52		NA/NA	5.25FH	
4420	334	11	1100	54		NA/NA	5.25FH	
5710	655	15				NA/NA	5.25FH	
5720	655	15				NA/NA	5.25FH	
5810	777	16				NA/NA	5.25FH	
5820	777	16				NA/NA	5.25FH	
6200	1200					NA/NA	5.25FH	
7520	655	15				NA/NA	5.25FH	

SONY

Drive Model	Format Size MB	Head	Cyl	Sect/Trac	Translate H/C/S	RWC/WPC	Form Factor	Power Watts
2020A	20					—/—	3.5HH	
2040A	40					—/—	3.5HH	
3080L	80					—/—	3.5HH	
SRD2040Z	42	4	624			—/—	3.5 3H	
SRD3040C	42.9					—/—	3.5 3H	4.9
SRD3040Z	42.9					—/—	3.5 3H	4.5
SRD3080C	85.8					—/—	3.5 3H	5.9
SRD3080Z	85.8					—/—	3.5 3H	5.5

STORAGE DIMENSIONS

Drive Model	Format Size MB	Head	Cyl	Sect/Trac	Translate H/C/S	RWC/WPC	Form Factor	Power Watts
AT100	109	8	1024	26		—/NONE		
AT1000S	1000	15				NA/NA		
AT100S	105	15				NA/NA	3.5HH	
AT120	119	15	918	17		NA/NA	5.25HH	
AT133	133	15	1024	17		—/NONE		
AT140	142	8	1024	34		—/NONE		
AT155E	158	9	1224	36		—/—	5.25FH	
AT155S	156	9	1224	36		—/—	5.25FH	
AT160	160	15	1224	17		—/NONE	5.25FH	
AT200	204	15	1024	26		—/NONE	3.5HH	
AT200S	204	7				—/—	3.5HH	
AT320S	320	15	1224	36		—/—	5.25FH	
AT335E	338	15	1224	36		—/—	5.25FH	
AT40	44	5	1024	17		—/NONE		
AT650E	651	15	1632	54		—/—	5.25FH	
AT650S	651	15	1632	54		—/—	5.25FH	
AT70	70			17		—/—	5.25FH	
CDASM-1051F	1000					—/—	3.5	
CDASM-2105F	2100					—/—	3.5	
CDASM-4005F	4300					—/—	3.5	
DMH-A02W	2100					—/—	3.5	
DMH-A04W	4300					—/—	3.5	
DMH-B02W	2100					—/—	3.5	
DMH-B04W	4300					—/—	3.5	
DMH-B09W	9100					—/—	3.5	
LAN1050F	1050					—/—	3.5	
LAN2101F	2101					—/—	3.5	
LAN2105F	2105					—/—	3.5	
LAN4005	4300					—/—	3.5	
LAN9000F	9000					—/—	5.25FH	

Hard Drives

Drive Model	Format Size MB	Seek Time	Interface	Encode	cache kb	RPM
1002	5		ST412/506	MFM		
1004	10		ST412/506	MFM		
1006	30		ST412/506	MFM		
4004	14		ST412/506	MFM		
4008	29		ST412/506	MFM		
4100	56		ST412/506	MFM		
604	5	27	ST412/506	MFM		
606	7	27	ST412/506	MFM		
612	10	27	ST412/506	MFM		
706	6	27	ST412/506	MFM		
712	10	27	ST412/506	MFM		
725	20		ST412/506	MFM		

SIEMENS

Drive Model	Format Size MB	Seek Time	Interface	Encode	cache kb	RPM
1200	174	25	ESDI	2,7 RLL		
1300	261	25	ESDI	2,7 RLL		
2200	174	25	ESDI	2,7 RLL		
2300	261	25	ESDI	2,7 RLL		
4410	322	18	ESDI	2,7 RLL		
4420	334	16	ESDI	2,7 RLL		
5710	655	16	SCSI	2,7 RLL		
5720	655	16	ESDI	2,7 RLL		
5810	777	18	SCSI	2,7 RLL		
5820	777	18	ESDI	2,7 RLL		
6200	1200	14	SCSI	2,7 RLL		
7520	655	16	SCSI	2,7 RLL		

SONY

Drive Model	Format Size MB	Seek Time	Interface	Encode	cache kb	RPM
2020A	20		SCSI			
2040A	40		SCSI			
3080L	80		SCSI			
SRD2040Z	42	29	SCSI			3600
SRD3040C	42.9	18	IDE AT		64k	2975
SRD3040Z	42.9	18	SCSI		8k	2975
SRD3080C	85.8	18	IDE AT		64k	2975
SRD3080Z	85.8	18	SCSI		8k	2975

STORAGE DIMENSIONS

Drive Model	Format Size MB	Seek Time	Interface	Encode	cache kb	RPM
AT100	109		ST412/506	2,7 RLL		
AT1000S	1000		SCSI			
AT100S	105	19	SCSI	2,7 RLL		
AT120	119	26	ST412/506	MFM		
AT133	133		ST412/506	MFM		
AT140	142					
AT155E	158	14	ESDI	2,7 RLL		
AT155S	156	17	SCSI	2,7 RLL		
AT160	160	28	ST412/506	MFM		
AT200	204		ST412/506	2,7 RLL		
AT200S	204	16	SCSI	2,7 RLL		
AT320S	320	17	SCSI	2,7 RLL		
AT335E	338	16	ESDI	2,7 RLL		
AT40	44		ST412/506	MFM		
AT650E	651	16	ESDI	2,7 RLL		
AT650S	651	16	SCSI	2,7 RLL		
AT70	70	27	ST412/506	MFM		
CDASM-1051F	1000	9.5	SCSI-2Fast			5400
CDASM-2105F	2100	8.5	SCSI-2Fast			7200
CDASM-4005F	4300	8.5	SCSI-2Fast			7200
DMH-A02W	2100	9.5	SCSI-2Fast			5400
DMH-A04W	4300	9.5	SCSI-2Fast			5400
DMH-B02W	2100	8.5	SCSI-2FstW			7200
DMH-B04W	4300	8.5	SCSI-2FstW			7200
DMH-B09W	9100	9	SCSI-2FstW			7200
LAN1050F	1050	9.5	SCSI-2Fast			5400
LAN2101F	2101	9	SCSI-2Fast			5400
LAN2105F	2105	8.5	SCSI-2Fast			7200
LAN4005	4300	8.5	SCSI-2Fast			7200
LAN9000F	9000	11.5	SCSI-2Fast			5400

Drive Model	Format Size MB	Head	Cyl	Sect/Trac	Translate H/C/S	RWC/WPC	Form Factor	Power Watts
MAC-195	195	7				NA/NA	3.5HH	
PS155E	156	9	1224	36		—/—	5.25FH	
PS155S	156	9	1224	36		—/—	5.25FH	
PS320S	320	15	1224	36		—/—	5.25FH	
PS335E	338	15	1224	36		—/—	5.25FH	
PS650S	651	15	1632	16		—/—	5.25FH	
XT100	109	8	1024	26		—/NONE		
XT120	119	15	1024	17		—/NONE		
XT200	204	15	1024	26		—/NONE		
XT40	44	5	1024	17		—/NONE		
XT70	71	8	1024	17		—/NONE		

SYQUEST TECHNOLOGY

Drive Model	Format Size MB	Head	Cyl	Sect/Trac	Translate H/C/S	RWC/WPC	Form Factor	Power Watts
EZ135 (removable)	135					—/—	3.5 3H	2.0
EZ135 (removable)	135					—/—	3.5 3H	2.0
EZ230 (removable)	230					—/—	3.5 3H	
EZ230 (removable)	230	1	4092			—/—	3.5 3H	2.25
SparQ 1GB (removable)	1008					—/—	3.5	
SparQ 1GB (removable)	1008					—/—	3.5	
SQ105 (removable)	105					—/—	3.5 3H	1.75
SQ1080 (removable)	80					—/—	1.8	
SQ200	200					—/—	5.25HH	
SQ225F	20			17		—/—	5.25HH	
SQ270 (removable)	270					—/—	3.5 3H	1.75
SQ306F	5			17		—/—	5.25HH	
SQ306R	5	2	306	17		—/—	5.25HH	
SQ306RD	5	2	306	17		307/307	5.25HH	
SQ3105 (removable)	105	2			16/420/32	—/—	3.5 3H	1.5
SQ312	10	2	615	17		—/—	5.25HH	
SQ312RD	10	2	615	17		616/616	5.25HH	
SQ319	10	2	612	17		—/—	5.25HH	
SQ325	21	4	612	17		612/612	5.25HH	
SQ325F	20	4	615	17		616/616	5.25HH	
SQ3270 (removable)	256	2			16/1024/32	—/—	3.5 3H	1.5
SQ338F	30	6	615	17		616/616	5.25HH	
SQ340AF	38	6	640	17		616/616	5.25HH	
SQ5110C (removable)	89					—/—	5.25HH	
SQ5200C (removable)	200					—/—	5.25HH	
SQ555 (removable)	44					—/—	5.25HH	
SQ88	88					—/—	3.5HH	
SYJET 1.3 (removeable)	1300					—/—	3.5HH	
SYJET 1.5 (removeable)	1500					—/—	3.5HH	
SYJET 1.5 (removeable)	1500					—/—	3.5HH	
SYJET 650 (removeable)	650					—/—	3.5HH	

TANDON COMPUTER CORPORATION

Drive Model	Format Size MB	Head	Cyl	Sect/Trac	Translate H/C/S	RWC/WPC	Form Factor	Power Watts
TM2085	74	9	1004	17		1005/1005	5.25FH	
TM2128	115	9	1004	26		1005/1005	5.25FH	
TM2170	154	9	1344	26		1345/1345	5.25FH	
TM244	41	4	782	26		783/783	3.5HH	
TM246	62	6	782	26		783/783	3.5HH	
TM251	5	2	306	17		—/—	5.25	
TM252	10	4	306	17		307/307	5.25HH	
TM261	10	2	615	17		616/616	5.25	
TM262	21	4	615	17		616/616	3.5HH	
TM262R	20	2	782	26		783/783	3.5HH	
TM264	41	4	782	26		783/783	3.5HH	
TM3085	71	8	1024	17		1024/1024	5.25	
TM3085R	105	8	1024	26		1024/1024	5.25	
TM344	41	4	782	26		783/783	3.5HH	
TM346	62	6	782	26		783/783	3.5HH	
TM361	10	2	615	17		616/616	5.25	
TM362	20	4	615	17		616/616	5.25	
TM362R	20	2	782	26		783/783	3.5HH	
TM364	41	4	782	26		783/783	3.5HH	
TM501	5	2	306	17		128/153	5.25FH	
TM502	10	4	306	17		128/153	5.25FH	
TM503	15	6	306	17		128/153	5.25FH	

Drive Model	Format Size MB	Seek Time	Interface	Encode	cache kb	RPM
MAC-195	195	15	SCSI	2,7 RLL		
PS155E	156	14	ESDI	2,7 RLL		
PS155S	156	14	SCSI	2,7 RLL		
PS320S	320	16	SCSI	2,7 RLL		
PS335E	338	15	ESDI	2,7 RLL		
PS650S	651	15	SCSI	2,7 RLL		
XT100	109		ST412/506	2,7 RLL		
XT120	119		ST412/506	MFM		
XT200	204		ST412/506	2,7 RLL		
XT40	44		ST412/506	MFM		
XT70	71		ST412/506	MFM		

SYQUEST TECHNOLOGY

Drive Model	Format Size MB	Seek Time	Interface	Encode	cache kb	RPM
EZ135 (removable)	135	13	SCSI-2	1,7 RLL	64k	3600
EZ135 (removable)	135	13	ATA-2	1,7 RLL	64k	3600
EZ230 (removable)	230	13.5	SCSI			
EZ230 (removable)	230	13.5	EIDE			
SparQ 1GB (removable)	1008	12	EIDE		32k	3600
SparQ 1GB (removable)	1008	12	Parall Port		512k	
SQ105	105	14.5	IDE AT		512k	
SQ1080 (removable)	80	16	PCMCIA-ATA		64k	3600
SQ200	200	18				5400
SQ225F	20	99			64k	
SQ270	270	13.5	IDE AT	MFM		
SQ306F	5	99	ST412/506		128k	3600
SQ306R	5	99	ST412/506	MFM		
SQ306RD	5	99	ST412/506	MFM		
SQ3105 (removable)	105	14.5	ATA-2	MFM	64k	3600
SQ312	10	80	ST412/506	1,7 RLL		
SQ312RD	10	80	ST412/506	MFM		
SQ319	10	80	ST412/506	MFM		
SQ325	21	80	ST412/506	RLL		
SQ325F	20	99	ST412/506	MFM		
SQ3270 (removable)	256	13.5	ATA-2	MFM	128k	3600
SQ338F	30	80	ST412/506	1,7 RLL		
SQ340AF	38	80	ST412/506	MFM		
SQ5110C (removable)	89	20	SCSI-2	MFM		
SQ5200C (removable)	200	18	SCSI-2		64k	3220
SQ555 (removable)	44	20	SCSI-2		64k	3220
SQ88	88	20			64k	3220
SYJET 1.3 (removeable)	1300	<11	SCSI		32k	
SYJET 1.5 (removeable)	1500	12	SCSI-2		256k	5400
SYJET 1.5 (removeable)	1500	12	EIDE		512k	
SYJET 650 (removeable)	650	<11	SCSI		512k	
					256k	5400

TANDON COMPUTER CORPORATION

Drive Model	Format Size MB	Seek Time	Interface	Encode	cache kb	RPM
TM2085	74	25	SCSI	MFM		
TM2128	115	25	SCSI	2,7 RLL		
TM2170	154	25	SCSI	2,7 RLL		
TM244	41	37	ST412/506	2,7 RLL		
TM246	62	37	ST412/506	2,7 RLL		
TM251	5		ST412/506	MFM		
TM252	10	85	ST412/506	MFM		
TM261	10		ST412/506	MFM		
TM262	21	65	ST412/506	MFM		
TM262R	20	85	ST412/506	2,7 RLL		
TM264	41	85	ST412/506	2,7 RLL		
TM3085	71	35	ST412/506	MFM		
TM3085R	105	35	ST412/506	2,7 RLL		
TM344	41	35	ST412/506	2,7 RLL		
TM346	62	35	ST412/506	2,7 RLL		
TM361	10	27	ST412/506	MFM		
TM362	20	85	ST412/506	MFM		
TM362R	20	85	ST412/506	2,7 RLL		
TM364	41	85	ST412/506	2,7 RLL		
TM501	5	85	ST412/506	MFM		
TM502	10	85	ST412/506	MFM		
TM503	15	85	ST412/506	MFM		

Drive Model	Format Size MB	Head	Cyl	Sect/Trac	Translate H/C/S	RWC/WPC	Form Factor	Power Watts
TM601	3					—/—	5.25FH	
TM602S	5	4	153	17		128/128	5.25FH	
TM602SE	12		153	17		—/—	5.25FH	
TM603S	10	6	153	17		128/128	5.25FH	
TM603SE	12	6	230	17		128/128	5.25FH	
TM702	20	4	615	26		616/616	5.25FH	
TM702AT	21	4	615	17		616/616	5.25FH	
TM703	30	5	733	17		734/734	5.25FH	
TM703AT	31	5	733	17		733/733	5.25FH	
TM703C	25	17	733			—/—	5.25FH	
TM705	41	5	962	17		—/NONE	5.25FH	
TM755	42	5	981	17		982/982	5.25FH	

TANDY CORP

Drive Model	Format Size MB	Head	Cyl	Sect/Trac	Translate H/C/S	RWC/WPC	Form Factor	Power Watts
25-1045	28					—/—	3.5HH	
25-1046	43	4	782	27		NA/NA	3.5HH	7
25-4130	100	4	1219			NA/NA	3.5HH	

TEAC AMERICA, INC.

Drive Model	Format Size MB	Head	Cyl	Sect/Trac	Translate H/C/S	RWC/WPC	Form Factor	Power Watts
SD150	10	4	306	17		—/—	5.25	
SD240	43	2	1000	42		NA/NA	2.5	2
SD260	63	2	1226	50		NA/NA	2.5	2
SD3105A	105	4	1282	40	8/641/40	NA/NA	3.5 3H	4.7
SD3105S	105	4	1282	40		NA/NA	3.5 3H	4.7
SD3210A	215	4	1695	62	8/847/62	NA/NA	3.5 3H	
SD3210S	215	4	1695	62		NA/NA	3.5 3H	
SD3240	245	4	1930		8/965/62	—/—	3.5 3H	
SD3250N (removable)	252					NA/NA	5.25HH	
SD3360N (removable)	363					NA/NA	5.25HH	
SD340A	43	2	1050	40	4/525/40	NA/NA	3.5 3H	11.9
SD340HA	43	2	1050	40		NA/NA	3.5 3H	11.9
SD340HS	43	2	1050	40		—/—	3.5 3H	11.9
SD340S	43	2	1050	40		NA/NA	3.5 3H	11.9
SD3540N (removable)	540					NA/NA	5.25HH	
SD380	86	4	1025	40	8/965/62	NA/300	3.5 3H	11.9
SD380HA	86	4	1050	40		NA/NA	3.5 3H	11.9
SD380HS	86	4	1050	40		—/—	3.5 3H	11.9
SD380S	86	4	1050	40		—/—	3.5 3H	11.9
SD510	10	4	306	17		128/128	5.25FH	
SD520	20	4	615	17		128/128	5.25FH	
SD540	40	8	615	17		—/—	5.25FH	

TEXAS INSTRUMENTS

Drive Model	Format Size MB	Head	Cyl	Sect/Trac	Translate H/C/S	RWC/WPC	Form Factor	Power Watts
525-122	20					—/—	5.25FH	
DB260	212	8				NA/NA	3.5HH	
DB380	333	15				64/64	5.25FH	
TI5	5	4	153	17		64/64	5.25FH	

TOSHIBA AMERICA, INC.

Drive Model	Format Size MB	Head	Cyl	Sect/Trac	Translate H/C/S	RWC/WPC	Form Factor	Power Watts
2.0GB 0.85-INCH HDD	2GB	1				—/—	1.8	
4.0GB 0.85-INCH HDD	4GB	2				—/—	1.8	
HDD1212	2000	2			16/3900/63	—/—	1.8	
HDD1232	5027	2			15/10390/63	—/—	1.8	
HDD1242	5007	2			15/10350/63	—/—	2.5 4H	
HDD1262	10GB	2			15/23080/63	—/—		
HDD1285	15GB	2			16/16383/63	—/—	1.8	
HDD1324	10014	2			15/20700/63	—/—	1.8 4H	0.7
HDD1364	20GB	4			16/16383/63	—/—		
HDD1384	30GB	4			16/16383/63	—/—	1.8	
HDD1524	40GB	4			16/16383/63	—/—*	1.8	0.6
HDD2130	2100	2			16/4200/63	—/—	4H	0.85
HDD2131	2160	2			16/4200/63	—/—	2.5 4H	
HDD2132	3250	3			16/6004/63	—/—	2.5 4H	
HDD2133	3200	2			16/6004/63	—/—	2.5 4H	
HDD2134	4320	4			15/8944/63	—/—	2.5 4H	0.85
HDD214	6007	2			15/12416/63	—/—	2.5 4H	0.85
HDD2143	6491	4			15/8944/63	—/—	2.5 4H	
HDD2144	6400					—/—	2.5 4H	

Drive Model	Format Size MB	Seek Time	Interface	Encode	cache kb	RPM
TM601	3		ST412/506	MFM		
TM602S	5	85	ST412/506	MFM		
TM602SE	12		ST412/506	MFM		
TM603S	10		ST412/506	MFM		
TM603SE	12		ST412/506	MFM		
TM702	20	27	ST412/506	MFM		
TM702AT	21	27	ST412/506	MFM		
TM703	30	40	ST412/506	MFM		
TM703AT	31	40	ST412/506	MFM		
TM703C	25		ST412/506	MFM		
TM705	41		ST412/506	MFM		
TM755	42	27	ST412/506	MFM		

TANDY CORP

Drive Model	Format Size MB	Seek Time	Interface	Encode	cache kb	RPM
25-1045	28	28	IDE XT			
25-1046	43	28	IDE XT	2,7 RLL		
25-4130	100	17	IDE XT	2,7 RLL		

TEAC AMERICA, INC.

Drive Model	Format Size MB	Seek Time	Interface	Encode	cache kb	RPM
SD150	10		ST412/506	MFM		
SD240	43	19	IDE AT	1,7 RLL	32k	3600
SD260	63	19	IDE AT	1,7 RLL	32k	3600
SD3105A	105	19	IDE AT	2,7 RLL	64k	3600
SD3105S	105	19	SCSI	2,7 RLL	64k	3600
SD3210A	215	17	IDE AT	1,7 RLL	65k	3600
SD3210S	215	17	SCSI	1,7 RLL	63k	3600
SD3240	245	17	IDE AT	1,7 RLL	64k	3600
SD3250N (removable)	252	17	IDE			3600
SD3360N (removable)	363	17	IDE			3600
SD340A	43	23	IDE AT	2,7 RLL	64k	2358
SD340HA	43	19	IDE AT	2,7 RLL		2358
SD340HS	43	19	SCSI	2,7 RLL		2358
SD340S	43	23	SCSI	2,7 RLL	28k	2358
SD3540N (removable)	540	11	IDE			4201
SD380	86	22	IDE AT	2,7 RLL		2358
SD380HA	86	19	IDE AT	2,7 RLL		2358
SD380HS	86	19	SCSI	2,7 RLL		2358
SD380S	86	22	SCSI	2,7 RLL		2358
SD510	10	27	ST412/506	MFM		
SD520	20	27	ST412/506	MFM		
SD540	40	40				3600

TEXAS INSTRUMENTS

Drive Model	Format Size MB	Seek Time	Interface	Encode	cache kb	RPM
525-122	20		ST412/506	MFM		
DB260	212	16	SCSI			
DB380	333	16	SCSI	MFM		
TI5	5	27	ST412/506	MFM		

TOSHIBA AMERICA, INC.

Drive Model	Format Size MB	Seek Time	Interface	Encode	cache kb	RPM
2.0GB 0.85-INCH HDD	2GB					3600
4.0GB 0.85-INCH HDD	4GB					3600
HDD1212	2000	15	ATA/Card II		256k	4200
HDD1232	5027	15	ATA (1-5)		256k	3990
HDD1242	5007	15	ATA (1-5)		1024k	4200
HDD1262	10GB	15	ATA-2/3/4/5		512k	4200
HDD1285	15GB	15	ATA-5		512k	4200
HDD1324	10014	15	ATA (1-5)		1024k	4200
HDD1364	20GB	15	ATA-2/3/4/5		512k	4200
HDD1384	30GB	15	ATA-5		512k	4200
HDD1524	40GB	15	ATA (2-5)		512k	4200
HDD2130	2100	13	ATA-4		512k	4200
HDD2131	2160	13	ATA-4		512k	
HDD2132	3250	13	ATA-4		512k	4200
HDD2133	3200	13	ATA-4		512k	4200
HDD2134	4320	13	ATA-4		512k	4200
HDD214	6007	13	ATA-4		1024k	4200
HDD2143	6491	13	ATA-4		512k	4200
HDD2144	6400	13	ATA-4		1024k	4200

Drive Model	Format Size MB	Head	Cyl	Sect/Trac	Translate H/C/S	RWC/WPC	Form Factor	Power Watts
HDD2146	6000	2			15/12416/63	—/—		
HDD2149	12000	4			16/16383/63	—/—	2.5 4H	0.85
HDD2151	10056	2			16/16383/63	—/—	2.5 4H	
HDD2152	10056	2			16/16383/63	—/—		
HDD2154	20003	4			15/12416/63	—/—	2.5 4H	
HDD2155	6007	2			16/16383/63	—/—	2.5 4H	
HDD2158	20GB	3			16/16383/63	—/—	2.5 4H	
HDD2164	20GB	2			16/16383/63	—/—	2.5 4H	
HDD2166	40GB	4			16/16383/63	—/—	2.5 4H	
HDD2168	20GB				16/16383/63	—/—	2.5 4H	
HDD2169	30GB	3			16/16383/63	—/—	2.5 4H	
HDD2170	40GB	4			16/16383/63	—/—	2.5 4H	
HDD2171	20.0039GB	2			16/16383/63	—/—	2.5 4H	1.05
HDD2171	40GB	4			16/16383/63	—/—	2.5 4H	
HDD2172	30.0056GB	3			16/16383/63	—/—	2.5 4H	
HDD2173	40.0078GB	4			16/16383/63	—/—		
HDD2181	30GB	2			16/16383/63	—/—	2.5 4H	
HDD2182	40GB	3			16/16383/63	—/—	2.5 4H	
HDD2183	60.0116GB	4			16/16383/63	—/—		
HDD2184	60GB	4			16/16383/63	—/—	2.5 4H	1.05
HDD2187	20GB	2			16/16383/63	—/—	2.5 4H	0.9
HDD2188	80GB	4			16/16383/63	—/—	2.5 4H	0.9
HDD2190	40GB	2			16/16383/63	—/—	2.5 4H	
HDD2193	40GB	4			16/16383/63	—/—	2.5 4H	1.05
HDD2326	126	2	812		8/812/38	NA/NA	2.5 4H	
HDD2336	131	2			8/842/38	—/—	2.5 4H	
HDD2338	213	4			16/684/38	NA/NA	2.5 4H	
HDD2339	262	4	841		16/842/38	NA/NA	2.5 4H	
HDD2512	353	4		63	16/682/63	NA/NA	2.5 4H	0.9
HDD2514	543	4			16/1030/63	NA/NA	2.5 4H	0.9
HDD2517	815	6			16/1579/63	NA/NA	2.5 4H	0.9
HDD2522	352	4	2050			—/—	2.5 4H	0.9
HDD2524	543	4	2920			—/—	2.5 4H	0.9
HDD2612	1350	10			16/2633/63	NA/NA	2.5 4H	1.4
HDD2616	2160	10			16/4200/63	—/—	2.5 4H	
HDD2619	3008				16/6409/63	—/—	2.5 4H	1.6
HDD2710	1080	5			16/2100/63	—/—	2.5 4H	
HDD2712	1350					—/—	2.5 4H	
HDD2712	1440	6			16/2800/63	—/—	2.5 4H	0.9
HDD2712	1350	6			16/2633/63	—/—	2.5 4H	
HDD2712	1440	4			16/2800/63	—/—	3.5 3H	0.9
HDD2714	2160	6			16/4200/63	—/—	2.5 4H	
HDD2716	2160	4			16/4200/63	—/—	2.5 4H	0.9
HDD2718	2160	4			16/2100/63	—/—	2.5 4H	0.9
HDD2731	1085	6			16/4200/63	—/—	2.5 4H	
HDD2910	2160	4			16/4200/63	—/—	2.5 4H	0.9
HDD2912	3250	6			16/5850/63	—/—	2.5 4H	
HDD2914	4090	6			16/7944/63	—/—	4H	0.9
HDD2918	6490	6			15/13424/63	—/—		
HDD2932	10050	6			16/16383/63	—/—	3.5 3H	
HDD2934	18100	6			16/16383/63	—/—	2.5 4H	0.5
HDD2A02	100GB	4				—/—	2.5 4H	
MK1001MAV	1080	5			16/2100/63	—/—	1.8 4H	0.7
MK1002GAH	10014	4			15/20700/63	—/—	2.5 4H	0.9
MK1002MAV	1085	6			16/2100/63	—/—		
MK1003GAL	10GB	2			15/23080/63	—/—	2.5 4H	
MK1011GAV	10050	6			16/16383/63	—/—	2.5 4H	
MK1016GAP	10056	2				—/—		
MK1016GAP	10056	2			16/16383/63	—/—	2.5 4H	
MK1017GAP	10056	2			16/16383/63	—/—	2.5 4H	0.5
MK1031GAS	100GB	4				—/—	3.5 3H	
MK1034FC	107	4	1345		8/664/39	—/—	2.5 4H	
MK1122FC	43	2	977		5/988/17	—/—	2.5 4H	0.85
MK1214GAP	12000	4			16/16383/63	—/—	3.5HH	
MK130	53	7	733			—/—	2.5 4H	
MK1301MAV	1350	6			16/2633/63	—/—	3.5HH	
MK132FA	18					—/—	3.5HH	
MK133FA	30					—/—		

TOSHIBA AMERICA, INC.

Drive Model	Format Size MB	Seek Time	Interface	Encode	cache kb	RPM
HDD2146	6000	13	ATA-2/3/4		256k	4200
HDD2149	12000	13	ATA-4		1024k	4200
HDD2151	10056	13	ATA-2/3/4		1024k	4200
HDD2152	10056	13	ATA-2/3/4		1024k	4200
HDD2154	20003	13	ATA-2/3/4		1024k	4200
HDD2155	6007	13	ATA-2/3/4		256k	4200
HDD2158	20GB	13	ATA-2/3/4/5		2mb	4200
HDD2164	20GB	13	ATA-2/3/4/5		2mb	4200
HDD2166	40GB	13	ATA-2/3/4/5		2mb	4200
HDD2168	20GB	12	ATA-2/3/4/5		2mb	4200
HDD2169	30GB	12	ATA-5		2mb	4200
HDD2170	40GB	12	ATA-2/3/4/5		2mb	4200
HDD2171	20.0039GB	12	ATA-2/3/4/5		16384	5400
HDD2171	40GB	12	ATA-5		16mb	5400
HDD2172	30.0056GB	12	ATA-5		16384	5400
HDD2173	40.0078GB	12	ATA-2/3/4/5		16384	5400
HDD2181	30GB	12	ATA-5		2mb	4200
HDD2182	40GB	12	ATA-5		2mb	4200
HDD2183	60.0116GB	12	ATA-2/3/4/5		2048k	4200
HDD2184	60GB	12	ATA-5		16mb	5400
HDD2187	20GB	12	ATA-5		2mb	4200
HDD2188	80GB	12	ATA-6		8mb	4200
HDD2190	40GB	12	ATA-6		8mb	4200
HDD2193	40GB	12	ATA-6		16mb	5400
HDD2326	126	15	IDE AT		128k	3600
HDD2336	131	13	IDE AT		128k	4000
HDD2338	213	13	IDE AT		128k	4000
HDD2339	262	13	IDE AT		128k	4200
HDD2512	353	13	ATA-2		128k	4200
HDD2514	543	13	ATA-2		128k	4200
HDD2517	815	13	ATA-2		128k	4200
HDD2522	352	13	SCSI-2	1,7 RLL	128k	4200
HDD2524	543	13	SCSI-2	8,9RLL	128k	4200
HDD2612	1350	13	ATA-2		128k	4200
HDD2616	2160	13	ATA-2		128k	
HDD2619	3008	13	ATA-2		128k	4852
HDD2710	1080	13	ATA-2		128k	4200
HDD2712	1350	13	ATA-2		128k	
HDD2712	1440	13	ATA-2		128k	4200
HDD2712	1350	13	ATA-2 Fast	PRML	128k	4200
HDD2714	1440	13	ATA-2		128k	4200
HDD2716	2160	13	ATA-3		128k	4200
HDD2718	2160	13	ATA-4		128k	4200
HDD2731	1085	13	ATA-2		128k	4200
HDD2910	2160	13	ATA-4		128k	
HDD2912	3250	13	ATA-4		512k	4200
HDD2914	4090	13	ATA-4		512k	4200
HDD2918	6490	13	ATA-4		512k	4200
HDD2932	10050	13	ATA-4		512k	4200
HDD2934	18100	13	ATA-2		1024k	4200
HDD2A02	100GB	12	ATA-6		8mb	4200
MK1001MAV	1080	13	ATA-2		128k	4200
MK1002GAH	10014	15	ATA (1-5)		1024k	4200
MK1002MAV	1085	13	ATA-2		128k	4200
MK1003GAL	10GB	15	ATA-2/3/4/5		512k	4200
MK1011GAV	10050	13	ATA-4		512k	4200
MK1016GAP	10056	13	ATA			4200
MK1016GAP	10056	13	ATA-2/3/4		1024k	4200
MK1017GAP	10056	13	ATA-2/3/4		1024k	4200
MK1031GAS	100GB	12	ATA-6		8mb	4200
MK1034FC	107	16	IDE AT	2,7 RLL	64k	3414
MK1122FC	43	23	IDE AT	2,7 RLL	32k	3600
MK1214GAP	12000	13	ATA-4		1024k	4200
MK130	53	25	ST412/506	MFM		
MK1301MAV	1350	13	ATA-2 Fast	PRML	128k	4200
MK132FA	18		ST412/506	MFM		
MK133FA	30		ST412/506	MFM		

Drive Model	Format Size MB	Head	Cyl	Sect/Trac	Translate H/C/S	RWC/WPC	Form Factor	Power Watts
MK134FA	44	7	733	17		—/—	3.5HH	
MK134FA(R)	65	7	733	26		—/—	3.5HH	
MK1401MAV	1440	6			16/2800/63	—/—	2.5 4H	0.9
MK1403MAN	1440	4			16/2800/63	—/—	3.5 3H	0.9
MK1422FCV	86	2	988		10/988/17	—/—	2.5 4H	
MK1504GAL	15GB	2			16/16383/63	—/—	1.8	
MK1517GAP	15100	2				—/—	2.5 4H	
MK1522FCV	126	2	812		8/812/38	NA/NA	2.5 4H	
MK153FA	74	5	830	35		NA/NA	5.25FH	
MK153FA-I	74	5	830	35		NA/NA	5.25FH	
MK153FB	76	5	830	35		—/—	5.25FH	
MK154FA	104	7	830	35		NA/NA	5.25FH	
MK154FA-I	104	7	830	35		NA/NA	5.25FH	
MK154FB	106	7	830	35		—/—	5.25FH	
MK156FA	148	10	830	35		NA/NA	5.25FH	
MK156FB	152	10	830	35		—/—	5.25FH	
MK158FA	173u	10	830			—/—	5.25FH	
MK1624FCV	213	4			16/684/38	NA/NA	2.5 4H	
MK1722FCV	131	2			8/842/38	—/—	2.5 4H	
MK1724FCV	262	4	841		16/842/38	NA/NA	2.5 4H	
MK1814GAV	18100	6			16/16383/63	—/—	3.5 3H	
MK1824FBV	352	4	2050		16/16383/63	—/—	2.5 4H	0.9
MK1824FCV	353	4		63	16/682/63	NA/NA	2.5 4H	0.9
MK182FB	83	5	823			—/—	8.00 FH	
MK184FB	116	7	823			—/—	8.00 FH	
MK186FB	166	10	823			—/—	8.00 FH	
MK1924FBV	543	4	2920			—/—	2.5 4H	0.9
MK1924FCV	543	4			16/1030/63	NA/NA	2.5 4H	0.9
MK1926FBV	815	6	2920			—/—	2.5 4H	0.9
MK1926FCV	815	6			16/1579/63	NA/NA	2.5 4H	0.9
MK2001MPL	2000	2			16/3900/63	—/—	1.8	
MK2003GAH	20GB	2			16/16383/63	—/—	1.8	0.6
MK2004GAL	20GB	2				—/—	1.8	1.4
MK2016GAP	20003	4				—/—	2.5 4H	
MK2016GAP	20003	4			16/16383/63	—/—	2.5 4H	
MK2017GAP	20GB	3			16/16383/63	—/—	2.5 4H	
MK2018GAP	20GB	2			16/16383/63	—/—	2.5 4H	
MK2018GAS	20GB				16/16383/63	—/—	2.5 4H	
MK2019GAX	20.0039GB	2			16/16383/63	—/—	2.5 4H	
MK2023GAS	20GB	2			16/16383/63	—/—	2.5 4H	0.9
MK2024FC	86	4	977	43	10/988/17	NA/NA	2.5 4H	
MK2101MAN	2160	10			16/4200/63	—/—	2.5 4H	1.4
MK2103MAV	2160	6			16/4200/63	—/—	2.5 4H	
MK2104MAV	2160	4			16/4200/63	—/—	2.5 4H	0.9
MK2105MAT	2160	4			16/2100/63	—/—	2.5 4H	
MK2105MAV	2160	4			16/4200/63	—/—	2.5 4H	
MK2109MAT	2100	2			16/4200/63	—/—	4H	0.85
MK2110MAT	2160					—/—	2.5 4H	
MK2110MAV	2160	2			16/4200/63	—/—	2.5 4H	
MK2124FC	130	4	934	55	16/934/17	NA/NA	2.5 4H	
MK2224FB	213	4	1560	83		NA/NA	2.5 4H	1.0
MK2224FC	213	4	684		16/684/38	NA/NA	2.5 4H	
MK2326FB	340	6	1830	74		NA/NA	2.5 4H	1.0
MK2326FC	340	6			14/969/49	NA/NA	2.5 4H	
MK2326FCH	340					—/—	2.5 4H	
MK232FB	45	3	845	35		—/—	3.5HH	10
MK232FBS	45	3	845	35		—/—	3.5HH	
MK232FC	45	3	845	35		NA/NA	3.5HH	
MK233FB	75	5	845	35		—/—	3.5HH	10
MK234FB	106	7	845	35		—/—	3.5HH	10
MK234FBS	106	7	845	35		—/—	3.5HH	
MK234FC	106	7	845	35	7/845/35	—/—	3.5HH	10
MK234FCH	106	7	845	35	7/845/35	—/—	3.5HH	
MK2428FB	524	8	1920	83		NA/NA	2.5 4H	1.4
MK2428FC	524	8		63	16/1016/63	NA/NA	2.5 4H	
MK250FA	382	10	1224	35		NA/NA	5.25FH	
MK250FB	382	10	1224	35		NA/NA	5.25FH	

Drive Model	Format Size MB	Seek Time	Interface	Encode	cache kb	RPM
MK134FA	44	25	ST412/506	MFM		3600
MK134FA(R)	65	23	ST412/506	2,7 RLL		
MK1401MAV	1440	13	ATA-2		128k	4200
MK1403MAN	1440	13	ATA-2		128k	4200
MK1422FCV	86	15	IDE AT		32k	3600
MK1504GAL	15GB	15	ATA-5		512k	4200
MK1517GAP	15100	13	ATA-5		2048k	4200
MK1522FCV	126	15	IDE AT		128k	3600
MK153FA	74	23	ESDI	2,7 RLL		3600
MK153FA-I	74	23	ESDI	2,7 RLL		
MK153FB	76	23	SCSI	2,7 RLL	32k	3600
MK154FA	104	23	ESDI	2,7 RLL		3600
MK154FA-I	104	23	ESDI	2,7 RLL		
MK154FB	106	23	SCSI	2,7 RLL	32k	3600
MK156FA	148	23	ESDI	2,7 RLL		
MK156FB	152	23	SCSI	2,7 RLL	32k	3600
MK158FA	173u	23	ESDI	2,7 RLL		3600
MK1624FCV	213	13	IDE AT		128k	4000
MK1722FCV	131	13	IDE AT		128k	4000
MK1724FCV	262	12	IDE AT		128k	4000
MK1814GAV	18100	13	ATA-2		1024k	4200
MK1824FBV	352	13	SCSI-2	1,7 RLL	128k	4200
MK1824FCV	353	13	ATA-2		128k	4200
MK182FB	83	18	SMD/CMD	2,7 RLL		3600
MK184FB	116	18	SMD/CMD	2,7 RLL		3600
MK186FB	166	18	SMD/CMD	2,7 RLL		3600
MK1924FBV	543	13	SCSI-2	8,9RLL	128k	4200
MK1924FCV	543	13	ATA-2		128k	4200
MK1926FBV	815	13	SCSI-2	8,9RLL	128k	4200
MK1926FCV	815	13	ATA-2		128k	4200
MK2001MPL	2000	15	ATA/Card II		256k	4200
MK2003GAH	20GB	15	ATA-2/3/4/5		512k	4200
MK2004GAL	20GB	15	ATA-5		2mb	4200
MK2016GAP	20003	13	ATA			4200
MK2016GAP	20003	13	ATA-2/3/4		1024k	4200
MK2017GAP	20GB	13	ATA-2/3/4/5		2mb	4200
MK2018GAP	20GB	13	ATA-2/3/4/5		2mb	4200
MK2018GAS	20GB	12	ATA-2/3/4/5		2mb	4200
MK2019GAX	20.0039GB	12	ATA-2/3/4/5		16384	5400
MK2023GAS	20GB	12	ATA-5		2mb	4200
MK2024FC	86	19	IDE AT	2,7 RLL	32k	3600
MK2101MAN	2160	13	ATA-2	PRML	128k	4200
MK2103MAV	2160	13	ATA-3		128k	4200
MK2104MAV	2160	13	ATA-4		128k	4200
MK2105MAT	2160	13	ATA-4		128k	4200
MK2105MAV	2160	13	ATA-4		128k	
MK2109MAT	2100	13	ATA-4		512k	4200
MK2110MAT	2160	13	ATA-4		512k	
MK2110MAV	2160	13	ATA-3		512k	4200
MK2124FC	130	17	IDE AT	2,7 RLL	32k	3600
MK2224FB	213	12	SCSI-2Fast		128k	4000
MK2224FC	213	12	IDE AT		128k	4000
MK2326FB	340	12	SCSI-2Fast		128k	4200
MK2326FC	340	12	IDE AT		128k	4200
MK2326FCH	340		IDE AT			
MK232FB	45	25	SCSI			3600
MK232FBS	45	19	SCSI	2,7 RLL		
MK232FC	45	25	IDE AT	2,7 RLL		
MK233FB	75	25	SCSI	2,7 RLL		3600
MK234FB	106	25	SCSI	2,7 RLL		3600
MK234FBS	106	19	SCSI	2,7 RLL		
MK234FC	106	25	IDE AT	2,7 RLL		3600
MK234FCH	106	25	IDE AT	2,7 RLL		
MK2428FB	524	12	SCSI-2Fast		512k	4000
MK2428FC	524	12	IDE AT		512k	4000
MK250FA	382	18	ESDI	2,7 RLL		
MK250FB	382	18	SCSI	2,7 RLL		

Drive Model	Format Size MB	Head	Cyl	Sect/ Trac	Translate H/C/S	RWC/ WPC	Form Factor	Power Watts
MK2526FB	528					—/—	2.5	
MK2526FC	528	6		63	16/1023/63	NA/NA	2.5 4H	
MK2528FB	704					—/—	2.5	
MK2528FC	704	8			16/1365/63	NA/NA	2.5 4H	
MK253FA	162					—/—	5.25FH	
MK253FB	158					—/—	5.25FH	
MK254FA	227					—/—	5.25FH	
MK254FB	221					—/—	5.25FH	
MK256FA	325					—/—	5.25FH	
MK256FB	316					—/—	5.25FH	
MK256FB	315					—/—	2.5 4H	
MK2616	2160	10				—/—	2.5 4H	
MK2628FC	811	8			16/1571/63	NA/NA	2.5 4H	1.3
MK2712	1350					—/—	2.5	
MK2720FC	1350	10			16/2633/63	NA/NA	2.5 4H	1.4
MK2728FB	1080					—/—	2.5	
MK2728FC	1080	8			16/1579/63	—/—	2.5 4H	1.4
MK286FC	374	11	823			—/—	8.00 FH	
MK288FC	510	15	823			—/—	8.00 FH	
MK3003MAN	3008				16/16383/63	—/—	2.5 4H	1.6
MK3004GAH	30GB	4			16/16383/63	—/—	1.8	
MK3017GAP	30000	4				—/—	2.5 4H	
MK3018GAS	30GB	3			16/16383/63	—/—	2.5 4H	
MK3019GAX	40.0078GB	4			16/16383/63	—/—	2.5 4H	
MK3019GAX	30.0056GB	3			16/16383/63	—/—	2.5 4H	
MK3021GAS	30GB	2			16/16383/63	—/—	2.5 4H	
MK3205MAV	3250	6			16/5850/63	—/—	2.5 4H	0.9
MK3209MAT	3250	3			16/6004/63	—/—	2.5 4H	
MK3212MAT	3200	2			16/6004/63	—/—	2.5 4H	
MK3303	3300					—/—	2.5 4H	
MK355FA	405	9	1661	53		—/—	5.25FH	3.0
MK355FB	405	9	1661	53		—/—	5.25FH	3.0
MK356FA	495					—/—	5.25FH	
MK358FA	675	15	1661	53		—/—	5.25FH	3.0
MK358FB	675	15	1661	53		—/—	5.25FH	3.0
MK388FA	720	15	1162			—/—	8.00 FH	
MK4004GAH	40GB	4			16/16383/63	—/—	1.8	0.6
MK4006MAV	4090	6			16/7944/63	—/—	2.5 4H	
MK4018GAP	40GB	4			16/16383/63	—/—	2.5 4H	
MK4018GAS	40GB	4			16/16383/63	—/—	2.5 4H	
MK4019GAX	40GB	4			16/16383/63	—/—	2.5 4H	1.05
MK4021GAS	40GB	3			16/16383/63	—/—	2.5 4H	
MK4025GAS	40GB	2			16/16383/63	—/—	2.5 4H	
MK4026GAX	40GB	2			16/16383/63	—/—	2.5 4H	1.05
MK4309MAT	4320	4			15/8944/63	—/—	2.5 4H	0.85
MK4310MAT	4300	4			15/8944/63	—/—	2.5 4H	
MK438FB	900	11	1980			NA/NA	3.5HH	10
MK5002MAL	5007	2			15/10350/63	—/—	2.5 4H	
MK5002MPL	5007	2			15/10390/63	—/—	1.8	
MK537FB	1064	13	1980	NA		NA/NA	3.5HH	10
MK538FB	1230	15	1980	NA		NA/NA	3.5HH	10
MK53FA	36	5	830	17		—/512	5.25FH	
MK53FA(M)	36	5	830	17		830/512	5.25FH	
MK53FA(R)	43	5	830	26		831/831	5.25FH	
MK53FB	36	5	830	17		830/512	5.25FH	
MK53FB(M)	36	5	830	17		831/831	5.25FH	
MK53FB(R)	64	5	830	26		830/512	5.25FH	
MK53FB-I	36	5	830	17		831/512	5.25FH	
MK54FA(M)	60	7	830	17		831/831	5.25FH	
MK54FA(R)	90	7	830	26		830/512	5.25FH	
MK54FB(M)	60	7	830	17		831/831	5.25FH	
MK54FB(R)	90	7	830	26		830/512	5.25FH	
MK54FB-I	50	7	830	17		NA/NA	5.25FH	
MK556FA	152	10	830			831/831	5.25FH	
MK56FA(M)	86	10	830	17		—/512	5.25FH	
MK56FA(R)	129	10	830	26		830/512	5.25FH	
MK56FB(M)	86	10	830	17			5.25FH	

Drive Model	Format Size MB	Seek Time	Interface	Encode	cache kb	RPM
MK2526FB	528	12	SCSI-2		128k	
MK2526FC	528	13	IDE AT		128k	4200
MK2528FB	704	12	SCSI-2		128k	
MK2528FC	704	13	IDE AT		128k	4200
MK253FA	162		ESDI			
MK253FB	158		SCSI			
MK254FA	227		ESDI			
MK254FB	221		SCSI			
MK256FA	325		ESDI			
MK256FB	316		SCSI			
MK256FB	315		SCSI			
MK2616	2160	13	ATA-2		128k	4200
MK2628FC	811	13	ATA-2		128k	4200
MK2712	1350	13	ATA-2		128k	4200
MK2720FC	1350	13	ATA-2		128k	4200
MK2728FB	1080	12	SCSI-2		128k	
MK2728FC	1080	13	ATA-2		128k	4200
MK286FC	374	18	HSMD	2,7 RLL		3600
MK288FC	510	18	HSMD	2,7 RLL		3600
MK3003MAN	3008	12	ATA-2/3		128k	4852
MK3004GAH	30GB	15	ATA-5		512k	4200
MK3017GAP	30000	13	ATA-5		2048k	4200
MK3018GAS	30GB	12	ATA-5		2mb	4200
MK3019GAX	40.0078GB	12	ATA-2/3/4/5		16384	5400
MK3019GAX	30.0056GB	12	ATA-2/3/4/5		16384	5400
MK3021GAS	30GB	12	ATA-5		2mb	4200
MK3205MAV	3250	13	ATA-4		512k	4200
MK3209MAT	3250	13	ATA-4		512k	4200
MK3212MAT	3200	13	ATA-4		512k	4200
MK3303	3300	13	ATA-3			4852
MK355FA	405	16	ESDI	1,7 RLL	64k	3600
MK355FB	405	16	SCSI	2,7 RLL	64k	3600
MK356FA	495		SCSI	RLL		
MK358FA	675	16	ESDI	1,7 RLL	64k	3600
MK358FB	675	16	SCSI-2	2,7 RLL	64k	
MK388FC	720	18	HSMD	2,7 RLL		3600
MK4004GAH	40GB	15	ATA (2-5)		2mb	4200
MK4006MAV	4090	13	ATA-4		512k	4200
MK4018GAP	40GB	13	ATA-2/3/4/5		2mb	4200
MK4018GAS	40GB	12	ATA-2/3/4/5		2mb	4200
MK4019GAX	40GB	12	ATA-5		16mb	5400
MK4021GAS	40GB	12	ATA-5		2mb	4200
MK4025GAS	40GB	12	ATA-6		8mb	4200
MK4026GAX	40GB	12	ATA-6		16mb	5400
MK4309MAT	4320	13	ATA-4		512k	4200
MK4310MAT	4300	13	ATA-4		512k	4200
MK438FB	900	12	SCSI-2	1,7 RLL	512k	
MK5002MAL	5007	15	ATA (1-5)		1024k	4200
MK5002MPL	5027	15	ATA (1-5)		256k	3990
MK537FB	1064	12	SCSI-2	1,7 RLL	512k	
MK538FB	1230	12	SCSI-2	1,7 RLL	512k	
MK53FA	36	30	ST412/506	MFM		
MK53FA(M)	36	25	ST412/506	MFM		
MK53FA(R)	43	30	ST412/506	2,7 RLL		
MK53FB	36	25	ST412/506	MFM		
MK53FB(M)	36	25	ST412/506	MFM		
MK53FB(R)	64	25	ST412/506	2,7 RLL		
MK53FB-I	36	25	ST412/506	MFM		
MK54FA(M)	60	25	ST412/506	MFM		
MK54FA(R)	90	25	ST412/506	2,7 RLL		
MK54FB(M)	60	25	ST412/506	MFM		
MK54FB(R)	90	25	ST412/506	2,7 RLL		
MK54FB-I	50	25	ST412/506	MFM		
MK556FA	152	23	ESDI			
MK56FA(M)	86	30	ST412/506	MFM		
MK56FA(R)	129	30	ST412/506	2,7 RLL		
MK56FB(M)	86	25	ST412/506	MFM		

Drive Model	Format Size MB	Head	Cyl	Sect/Trac	Translate H/C/S	RWC/WPC	Form Factor	Power Watts
MK56FB(R)	129	10	830	26		831/831	5.25FH	
MK56FB-I	72	10	830	17		830/512	5.25FH	
MK6014MAP	6007	2			15/12416/63	—/—	2.5 4H	0.85
MK6015GAP	6007	2				—/—	2.5 4H	
MK6015MAP	6000	2			15/12416/63	—/—	2.5 4H	
MK6017MAP	6007	2			15/12416/63	—/—		
MK6021GAS	60.0116GB	4			16/16383/63	—/—	2.5 4H	1.05
MK6022GAX	60GB	4			16/16383/63	—/—	4H	0.9
MK6409MAV	6490	6			15/13424/63	—/—	2.5 4H	
MK6411MAT	6400	4			15/13424/63	—/—	2.5 4H	
MK6412MAT	6491	4			15/8944/63	—/—	2.5 4H	
MK6414MAP	6400					—/—	2.5 4H	
MK72PC	72	10	830	17			3.5HH	
MK72PCR	109	10	830	26			3.5HH	
MK8025GAS	80GB	4			16/16383/63	—/—	2.5 4H	0.9
MK8028GAS	80GB	4			16/16383/63	—/—	2.5 4H	
MKM0351E	36	5	830	17		830/512	5.25FH	
MKM0351J	36	5	830	17		830/512	5.25FH	
MKM0352E	50	7	830	17		—/512	5.25FH	
MKM0352J	50	7	830	17		—/512	5.25FH	
MKM0353E	72	10	830	17		830/512	5.25FH	
MKM0353J	72	10	830	17		830/512	5.25FH	
MKM0363A	74	5	830	35		NA/NA	5.25FH	
MKM0363J	74	5	830	35		NA/NA	5.25FH	
MKM0364A	104	7	830	35		NA/NA	5.25FH	
MKM0364J	104	7	830	35		NA/NA	5.25FH	
MKM0381E	36	5	830	17		830/512	5.25FH	
MKM0381J	36	5	830	17		830/512	5.25FH	
MKM0382E	50	7	830	17		—/512	5.25FH	
MKM0382J	50	7	830	17		—/512	5.25FH	
MKM0383E	72	10	830	17		830/512	5.25FH	
MKM0383J	72	10	830	17		830/512	5.25FH	

TULIN

Drive Model	Format Size MB	Head	Cyl	Sect/Trac	Translate H/C/S	RWC/WPC	Form Factor	Power Watts
TL213	10	2	640	17		656/656	5.25HH	
TL226	22	4	640	17		656/656	5.25HH	
TL238	22	4	640	17		—/NONE	5.25HH	
TL240	33	6	640	17		656/656	5.25HH	
TL258	32	6	640	17		—/NONE	5.25HH	
TL326	22	4	640	17		641/641	5.25HH	
TL340	33	6	640	17		641/641	5.25HH	

VERTEX (SEE PRIAM)
—/—

WESTERN DIGITAL

Drive Model	Format Size MB	Head	Cyl	Sect/Trac	Translate H/C/S	RWC/WPC	Form Factor	Power Watts
PhD1000	1083					—/—	3.0 4H	
PhD1400	1400					—/—	3.0 4H	
PhD2100	2168					—/—	3.0 4H	
Piranha 105A	1104	4				NA/NA	3.5HH	
Piranha 105S	1104	4				NA/NA	3.5HH	
Piranha 210A	210					—/—	3.5HH	
Piranha 210S	210					—/—	3.5HH	
WD1000AB	100GB					—/—	3.5 3H	
WD1000BB	100030	6			16/16383/63	—/—	3.5 3H	
WD1000JB	100030	4			16/16383/63	—/—	3.5 3H	
WD1000JB	100GB					—/—	3.5 3H	
WD100AA	10005				16/16383/63	—/—	3.5 3H	
WD100EB	10005	1			16/16383/63	—/—	3.5 3H	5.32
WD102AA	10262	3			16/16383/63	—/—	3.5 3H	6.18
WD102BA (Caviar)	10254	2			16/16383/63	—/—	3.5 3H	6.9
WD102BA (Expert)	10255	3			16/16383/63	—/—	3.5 3H	6.9
WD102BARTL	10255	3			16/16383/63	—/—	3.5 3H	6.9
WD1200AB	120GB					—/—	3.5 3H	
WD1200BB	120034	6			16/16383/63	—/—	3.5 3H	
WD1200JB	120GB					—/—	3.5 3H	
WD1200JD	120GB	3				—/—	3.5 3H	9.5
WD1200LB	120034	6			16/16383/63	—/—	3.5 3H	

Drive Model	Format Size MB	Seek Time	Interface	Encode	cache kb	RPM
MK56FB(R)	129	25	ST412/506	2,7 RLL		
MK56FB-I	72	25	ST412/506	MFM		
MK6014MAP	6007	13	ATA-4			4200
MK6015GAP	6007	13	ATA		1024k	4200
MK6015MAP	6000	13	ATA-2/3/4		256k	4200
MK6017MAP	6007	13	ATA-2/3/4		256k	4200
MK6021GAS	60.0116GB	12	ATA-2/3/4/5		2048k	4200
MK6022GAX	60GB	12	ATA-5		16mb	5400
MK6409MAV	6490	13	ATA-4			4200
MK6411MAT	6400	13	ATA-4		512k	4200
MK6412MAT	6491	13	ATA-4		512k	4200
MK6414MAP	6400	13	ATA-4		512k	4200
MK72PC	72	25	ST412/506	MFM	1024k	4200
MK72PCR	109	25	ST412/506	2,7 RLL		
MK8025GAS	80GB	12	ATA-6			
MK8028GAS	80GB	12	ATA-6		8mb	4200
MKM0351E	36	25	ST412/506	MFM	8mb	4200
MKM0351J	36	25	ST412/506	MFM		
MKM0352E	50	30	ST412/506	MFM		
MKM0352J	50	30	ST412/506	MFM		
MKM0353E	72	25	ST412/506	MFM		
MKM0353J	72	25	ST412/506	MFM		
MKM0363A	74	23	ESDI	2,7 RLL		
MKM0363J	74	23	SCSI	2,7 RLL		
MKM0364A	104	23	ESDI	2,7 RLL		
MKM0364J	104	23	ESDI	2,7 RLL		
MKM0381E	36	25	ST412/506	MFM		
MKM0381J	36	25	ST412/506	MFM		
MKM0382E	50	30	ST412/506	MFM		
MKM0382J	50	30	ST412/506	MFM		
MKM0383E	72	25	ST412/506	MFM		
MKM0383J	72	25	ST412/506	MFM		

TULIN

Drive Model	Format Size MB	Seek Time	Interface	Encode	cache kb	RPM
TL213	10	27	ST412/506	MFM		
TL226	22	85	ST412/506	MFM		
TL238	22		ST412/506	MFM		
TL240	33	85	ST412/506	MFM		
TL258	32		ST412/506	MFM		
TL326	22	40	ST412/506	MFM		
TL340	33	40	ST412/506	MFM		

VERTEX (SEE PRIAM)

WESTERN DIGITAL

Drive Model	Format Size MB	Seek Time	Interface	Encode	cache kb	RPM
PhD1000	1083	14	PCMIDE		128k	4536
PhD1400	1400	14	PCMIDE		256k	4000
PhD2100	2168	14	PCMIDE		256k	4000
Piranha 105A	1104	15	IDE AT	2,7 RLL		
Piranha 105S	1104	15	SCSI	2,7 RLL		
Piranha 210A	210		IDE AT			
Piranha 210S	210		SCSI			
WD1000AB	100GB	8.9	UltraATA100		2mb	5400
WD1000BB	100030	8.9	EIDE		2mb	7200
WD1000JB	100030	8.9	EIDE		8mb	7200
WD1000JB	100GB	8.9	EIDE		8mb	7200
WD100AA	10005	9.5	EIDE			
WD100EB	10005	12.1	EIDE	PRML16,17	2mb	5400
WD102AA	10262	9.5	EIDE	PRML16,17	2mb	5400
WD102BA (Caviar)	10254	9	EIDE	PRML16,17	2mb	7200
WD102BA (Expert)	10255	9	EIDE	PRML	2mb	7200
WD102BARTL	10255	9	EIDE	PRML	2mb	7200
WD1200AB	120GB	8.9	UltraATA100		2mb	5400
WD1200BB	120034	8.9	EIDE		2mb	7200
WD1200JB	120GB	8.9	EIDE		8mb	7200
WD1200JD	120GB	8.9	SATA		8mb	7200
WD1200LB	120034	8.9	EIDE		2mb	7200

Drive Model	Format Size MB	Head	Cyl	Sect/Trac	Translate H/C/S	RWC/WPC	Form Factor	Power Watts
WD135AA	13520				16/16383/63	—/—	3.5 3H	6.18
WD136AA	13601	4			16/16383/63	—/—	3.5 3H	6.9
WD136BA	13676	3			16/16383/63	—/—	3.5 3H	
WD136BARTL	13676	4			16/16383/63	—/—	3.5 3H	
WD140	40					—/—	3.5 3H	
WD153AA (Caviar)	15393	3			16/16383/63	—/—	3.5 3H	6.18
WD153BA (Caviar)	15382	3			16/16383/63	—/—	3.5 3H	7.1
WD1600AB	160GB	6			16/16383/63	—/—	3.5 3H	6.0
WD1600B008-RNx	160GB					—/—	3.5 3H	
WD1600BB	160GB					—/—	3.5 3H	
WD1600JB	160GB	4				—/—	3.5 3H	9.5
WD1600JD	160GB					—/—	3.5 3H	
WD172AA	17247	5			16/16383/63	—/—	3.5 3H	6.18
WD1800BB	200GB					—/—	3.5 3H	
WD1800JB	180GB					—/—	3.5 3H	
WD1800LB	200GB					—/—	3.5 3H	
WD181AA	18134	4			16/16383/63	—/—	3.5 3H	6.18
WD183FG-00AS	18310	8	13614			—/—	3.5 3H	
WD183FH-00AS	18310	8	13614			—/—	3.5 3H	
WD183FN-00AS	18310	8	13614			—/—	3.5 3H	
WD2000B002-RNx	200GB					—/—	3.5 3H	
WD2000BB	200GB					—/—	3.5 3H	
WD2000JB	200GB				16/16383/63	—/—	3.5 3H	
WD2000JBRTL	200GB					—/—	3.5 3H	9.5
WD2000JD	200GB	5				—/—	3.5 3H	
WD2000LB	200GB					—/—	3.5 3H	
WD200AB	20020	2			16/16383/63	—/—	3.5 3H	7.5
WD200BB	20020	2			16/16383/63	—/—	3.5 3H	7.5
WD200BBRTL	20525	2			16/16383/63	—/—	3.5 3H	5.32
WD200EB	20020	2			16/16383/63	—/—	3.5 3H	6.18
WD205AA (Caviar)	20520	6			16/16383/63	—/—	3.5 3H	6.9
WD205BA	20525				16/16383/63	—/—	3.5 3H	
WD205BARTL	20525	6			16/16383/63	—/—	3.5 3H	
WD2120	125					—/—	3.5 3H	
WD2500BB	250GB	6			16/16383/63	—/—	3.5 3H	
WD2500JB	250GB					—/—	3.5 3H	
WD2500JD	250GB	6				—/—	3.5 3H	9.5
WD262	20	4	615	17		616/616	3.5HH	
WD272AA (Caviar)	27201	6			16/16383/63	—/—	3.5 3H	6.18
WD273BA	27373				16/16383/63	—/—	3.5 3H	6.9
WD280	80					—/—	3.5 3H	
WD300A001	30020	4			16/16383/63	—/—	3.5 3H	7.1
WD300AB	30020	2			16/16383/63	—/—	3.5 3H	7.5
WD300BB	30020	3			16/16383/63	—/—	3.5 3H	7.5
WD300BBRTL	30758	3			16/16383/63	—/—	3.5 3H	
WD300EB	30020	3			16/16383/63	—/—	3.5 3H	6.18
WD307AA (Caviar)	30758	6			16/16383/63	—/—	3.5 3H	
WD307AARTL	30758	6			16/16383/63	—/—	3.5HH	
WD344R	40	4	782	26		783/783	3.5 3H	9.25
WD360GD	36.7GB					—/—	3.5HH	
WD362	20	4	615	17		616/616	3.5HH	
WD382R	20	2	782	26		783/783	3.5HH	
WD383R	30	4	615	26		616/616	3.5HH	
WD384R	40	2	782	26		783/783	3.5HH	
WD400AB	40021	3			16/16383/63	—/—	3.5 3H	7.1
WD400BB	40021	4			16/16383/63	—/—	3.5 3H	7.5
WD400BBRTL	40804	4			16/16383/63	—/—	3.5 3H	
WD400EB	40020	2			16/16383/63	—/—	3.5 3H	5.4
WD400EB	40GB	2				—/—	3.5 3H	
WD400JB	40GB					—/—	3.5 3H	9.5
WD400JD	40GB	1				—/—	3.5 3H	
WD43AA (Caviar)	4311	1			16/8356/63	—/—	3.5 3H	6.18
WD450AA (Caviar)	45020	6			16/16383/63	—/—	3.5 3H	6.18
WD514400	14400					—/—	3.5 3H	
WD544R	40	4	782	26		783/783	3.5HH	
WD562-5	21	4	615	17		—/—	3.5HH	
WD582R	20	2	782	26		783/783	3.5HH	

Drive Model	Format Size MB	Seek Time	Interface	Encode	cache kb	RPM
WD135AA	13520	9.5				5400
WD136AA	13601	9.5	EIDE		2mb	7200
WD136BA	13676	9	EIDE	PRML16,17	2mb	7200
WD136BARTL	13676	9.0	IDE AT	PRML		
WD140	40		EIDE		2mb	5400
WD153AA (Caviar)	15393	9.5	EIDE	PRML16,17	2mb	7200
WD153BA (Caviar)	15382	8.9	USB2.0	PRML16,17	2mb	5400
WD1600AB	160GB	8.9	UltraATA100		2mb	7200
WD1600B008-RNx	160GB	8.9	EIDE		2mb	7200
WD1600BB	160GB	8.9	SATA		8mb	7200
WD1600JB	160GB	8.9	EIDE		8mb	7200
WD1600JD	160GB	8.9	UltraATA100		2mb	5400
WD172AA	17247	9.5	EIDE	PRML16,17	2mb	7200
WD1800BB	200GB	8.9	EIDE		8mb	7200
WD1800JB	180GB	8.9	UltraATA100		2mb	5400
WD1800LB	200GB	8.9	EIDE	PRML16,17	2mb	7200
WD181AA	18134	9.5	Ultra2 SCSI	EPR4 0,6,8	2mb	1003
WD183FG-00AS	18310	6.6	Ultra2 SCSI	EPR4 0,6,8	2mb	1003
WD183FH-00AS	18310	6.6	Ultra2 SCSI	EPR4 0,6,8	2mb	1003
WD183FN-00AS	18310	6.6	FireWire		2mb	7200
WD2000B002-RNx	200GB	8.9	UltraATA100		2mb	7200
WD2000BB	200GB	8.9	UltraATA100		8mb	7200
WD2000JB	200GB	8.9	EIDE		8mb	7200
WD2000JBRTL	200GB	4.2	SATA		8mb	7200
WD2000JD	200GB	8.9	UltraATA100		2mb	7200
WD2000LB	200GB	8.9	EIDE		2mb	5400
WD200AB	20020	9.5	EIDE	PRML16,17	2mb	7200
WD200BB	20020	8.9	EIDE	PRML16,17	2mb	7200
WD200BBRTL	20525	8.9	EIDE	PRML16,17	2mb	5400
WD200EB	20020	12	EIDE	PRML16,17	2mb	5400
WD205AA (Caviar)	20520	9.5	EIDE		2mb	7200
WD205BA	20525	9	EIDE	PRML	2mb	7200
WD205BARTL	20525	9	IDE AT			
WD2120	125		EIDE		2mb	7200
WD2500BB	250GB	8.9	EIDE		8mb	7200
WD2500JB	250GB	8.9	SATA		8mb	7200
WD2500JD	250GB	8.9	ST412/506	MFM		
WD262	20	80	EIDE	PRML16,17	2mb	5400
WD272AA (Caviar)	27201	9.5	EIDE		2mb	7200
WD273BA	27373	9	IDE AT			
WD280	80		FireWire		2mb	5400
WD300A001	30020	9.5	EIDE		2mb	5400
WD300AB	30020	12	EIDE	PRML16,17	2mb	7200
WD300BB	30020	8.9	EIDE	PRML16,17	2mb	7200
WD300BBRTL	30758	8.9	EIDE	PRML16,17	2mb	5400
WD300EB	30020	12.1	EIDE	PRML16,17	2mb	5400
WD307AA (Caviar)	30758	9.5	EIDE	PRML16,17	2mb	5400
WD307AARTL	30758	9.5	ST412/506	2,7 RLL		
WD344R	40	40	SATA		8mb	1000
WD360GD	36.7GB	5.2	ST412/506	MFM		
WD362	20	80	ST412/506	2,7 RLL		
WD382R	20	85	ST412/506	2,7 RLL		
WD383R	30	85	ST412/506	2,7 RLL		
WD384R	40	85	EIDE	PRML16,17	2mb	5400
WD400AB	40021	12	EIDE	PRML16,17	2mb	7200
WD400BB	40021	8.9	EIDE	PRML16,17	2mb	7200
WD400BBRTL	40804	8.9	EIDE		2mb	5400
WD400EB	40020	12.4	EIDE		2mb	5400
WD400EB	40GB	12.8	EIDE		8mb	7200
WD400JB	40GB	8.9	SATA		8mb	7200
WD400JD	40GB	8.9	EIDE	PRML16,17	2mb	5400
WD43AA (Caviar)	4311	9.5	EIDE	PRML16,17	2mb	5400
WD450AA (Caviar)	45020	9.5	EIDE			
WD514400	14400	9.5	ST412/506	2,7 RLL		
WD544R	40	40	ST412/506	MFM		
WD562-5	21	80	ST412/506	2,7 RLL		
WD582R	20	85				

Western Digital

Drive Model	Format Size MB	Head	Cyl	Sect/Trac	Translate H/C/S	RWC/WPC	Form Factor	Power Watts
WD583R	30	4	615	26		616/616	3.5HH	
WD584R	40	4	782	26		783/783	3.5HH	
WD600A001	60022	4			16/16383/63	—/—	3.5 3H	
WD600AB	60022	4			16/16383/63	—/—	3.5 3H	7.1
WD600ABRTL	60022	4			16/16383/63	—/—	3.5 3H	7.25
WD600BB	60022	5			16/16383/63	—/—	3.5 3H	
WD600BBRTL	60022	5			16/16383/63	—/—	3.5 3H	
WD600EB	60GB					—/—	3.5 3H	
WD600JB	60GB					—/—	3.5 3H	
WD600JD	60GB	2				—/—	3.5 3H	9.5
WD64AA	6448	2			15/13328/63	—/—	3.5 3H	6.18
WD68AA	6800				16/13176/63	—/—	3.5 3H	6.9
WD68BA	6833				16/13240/63	—/—	3.5 3H	7.9
WD740GD	74GB	4				—/—	3.5 3H	
WD800AB	80026	6			16/16383/63	—/—	3.5 3H	7.25
WD800BB	80026	6			16/16383/63	—/—	3.5 3H	
WD800BBRTL	80026	6			16/16383/63	—/—	3.5 3H	
WD800EB	80GB					—/—	3.5 3H	
WD800JB	80GB					—/—	3.5 3H	
WD800JB	80GB					—/—	3.5 3H	
WD800JD	80GB	2				—/—	3.5 3H	9.5
WD84AA (Caviar)	8455	2			16/16383/63	—/—	3.5 3H	
WD91FG-00AS	9150	4	13614			—/—	3.5 3H	
WD91FH-00AS	9150	4	13614			—/—	3.5 3H	
WD91FN-00AS	9150	4	13614			—/—	3.5 3H	
WD93018-A	21					—/—	3.5HH	
WD93020-XE1	20	4	615	17		NA/NA	3.5HH	
WD93023-A	21					—/—	3.5HH	
WD93024-A	21	2	782	27	4/615/17	NA/NA	3.5HH	
WD93024-X	21	2	782	27		NA/NA	3.5HH	
WD93028-A	21	2	782	27	4/615/17	NA/NA	3.5HH	
WD93028-AD	21	2	782	27		NA/NA	3.5HH	
WD93028-X	21	2	782	27		NA/NA	3.5HH	
WD93034-X	32	3	782	27		NA/NA	3.5HH	
WD93038-X	32	3	782	27		NA/NA	3.5HH	
WD93044-A	43	4	782	27	5/977/17	NA/NA	3.5HH	
WD93044-X	43	4	782	27		NA/NA	3.5HH	
WD93048-X	40	4	782	27		NA/NA	3.5HH	
WD93048-AD	43	4	782	27		NA/NA	3.5HH	
WD93048-X	43	4	782	27		NA/NA	5.25HH	
WD95024-A	21	2	782	27	4/615/17	783/783	3.5HH	6.9
WD95024-X	21	2	782	27		NA/NA	5.25HH	
WD95028-A	20	2	782	27		783/783	3.5HH	
WD95028-AD	21	2	782	27		NA/NA	5.25HH	
WD95028-X	20	2	782	27		783/783	3.5HH	6.9
WD95034-X	32	3	782	27		NA/NA	5.25HH	
WD95038-X	30	3	782	27		783/783	5.25HH	
WD95044-A	43	4	782	27	4/782/27	783/783	3.5HH	6.9
WD95044-X	43	4	782	27	4/782/27	783/783	5.25HH	
WD95048-X	40	4	782	27	4/782/27	NA/NA	5.25HH	
WD95048-AD	43	4	782	27	4/782/27	NA/NA	5.25HH	
WD95048-X	40	4	782	27	4/782/27	NA/NA	5.25HH	
WDAB130 (Tidbit)	31	5	733	17	4/916/17	734/734	2.50 4H	
WDAB140	42	4	1390		5/980/17	—/—	2.5 4H	
WDAB260 (Tidbit)	62	4	1020	17		NA/NA	2.5 4H	
WDAC11000	1056	16	2046	63		—/—		
WDAC11200	1282				16/2484/63		3.5 3H	5.1
WDAC11600 (Caviar)	1624	2			16/3148/63		3.5 3H	5.3
WDAC1210 (Caviar)	170	2	2233	56-96	6/1010/55	NA/NA	3.5 3H	3
WDAC1210 (Caviar)	212	2	2720	55-99	12/989/35	NA/NA	3.5 3H	
WDAC12100 (Caviar)	2111	2			16/4092/63		3.5 3H	5.35
WDAC12500	2560				16/4960/63	—/—	3.5 3H	
WDAC1270 (Caviar)	270	2			12/917/48	—/—	3.5 3H	
WDAC13200	3249		3249		16/6296/63	—/—	3.5 3H	
WDAC1365 (Caviar)	364	2			16/708/63	—/—	3.5 3H	
WDAC140 (Caviar)	42	2	1082	39	5/980/17	NA/NA	3.5 3H	
WDAC14200	4224				16/8184/63	—/—	3.5 3H	

Drive Model	Format Size MB	Seek Time	Interface	Encode	cache kb	RPM
WD583R	30	85	ST412/506	2,7 RLL		
WD584R	40	85	ST412/506	2,7 RLL		
WD600A001	60022	9.5	FireWire			
WD600AB	60022	12	EIDE		2mb	5400
WD600ABRTL	60022	12	EIDE	PRML16,17	2mb	5400
WD600BB	60022	10.9	EIDE	PRML16,17	2mb	5400
WD600BBRTL	60022	10.9	EIDE	PRML16,17	2mb	7200
WD600EB	60022	10.9	EIDE	PRML16,17	2mb	7200
WD600JB	60GB	13	EIDE		2mb	5400
WD600JD	60GB	8.9	EIDE		8mb	7200
WD64AA	60GB	8.9	SATA		8mb	7200
WD68AA	6448	9.5	EIDE		2mb	
WD68BA	6800	9.5				
WD740GD	6833	9	EIDE		2mb	7200
WD800AB	74GB	4.5	ESATA		8mb	1000
WD800BB	80026	9.5	EIDE		2mb	5400
WD800BBRTL	80026	10.9	EIDE	PRML16,17	2mb	7200
WD800EB	80026	10.9	EIDE	PRML16,17	2mb	7200
WD800JB	80GB	13	EIDE		2mb	5400
WD800JB	80GB	8.9	UltraATA100		8mb	7200
WD800JD	80GB	8.9	EIDE		8mb	7200
WD84AA (Caviar)	80GB	8.9	SATA		8mb	7200
WD91FG-00AS	8455	9.5	EIDE	PRML16,17	8mb	7200
WD91FH-00AS	9150	7.9	Ultra FstWd	EPR4 0,6,8	2mb	5400
WD91FN-00AS	9150	7.9	Ultra FstWd	EPR4 0,6,8	2mb	1003
WD93018-A	9150	7.9	UltraNarrow	EPR4 0,6,8	2mb	1003
WD93020-XE1	21		IDE AT			1003
WD93023-A	20	85	IDE XT	2,7 RLL		
WD93024-A	21		IDE AT			
WD93024-X	21	28	IDE AT	2,7 RLL		
WD93028-A	21	39	IDE XT	2,7 RLL	1k	
WD93028-AD	21	70	IDE AT	2,7 RLL		
WD93028-X	21	69	IDE AT	2,7 RLL		
WD93034-X	21	70	IDE XT	2,7 RLL		
WD93038-X	32	39	IDE AT	2,7 RLL	1k	
WD93044-A	32	70	IDE XT	2,7 RLL		
WD93044-X	43	28	IDE AT	2,7 RLL	640k	
WD93048-A	43	39	IDE AT	2,7 RLL	1k	
WD93048-AD	40	69	IDE AT	2,7 RLL		
WD93048-X	43	69	IDE AT	2,7 RLL		
WD95024-A	43	70	IDE XT	2,7 RLL		
WD95024-X	21	28	IDE AT	2,7 RLL		
WD95028-A	21	39	IDE AT	2,7 RLL	1k	
WD95028-AD	20	70	IDE XT	2,7 RLL		
WD95028-X	21	69	IDE AT	2,7 RLL		
WD95034-X	20	70	IDE XT	2,7 RLL		
WD95038-X	32	39	IDE AT	2,7 RLL	1k	
WD95044-A	30	70	IDE XT	2,7 RLL		
WD95044-X	43	28	IDE AT	2,7 RLL	1k	
WD95048-A	43	39	IDE AT	2,7 RLL		
WD95048-AD	40	70	IDE AT	2,7 RLL		
WD95048-X	43	70	IDE XT	2,7 RLL		
WDAB130 (Tidbit)	31	19	IDE AT-XT	2,7 RLL	32k	
WDAB140	42	16	IDE	2,7 RLL		
WDAB260 (Tidbit)	62	19	IDE XT-AT	2,7 RLL		
WDAC11000	1056	<12	EIDE			
WDAC11200	1282	11	EIDE		256k	5200
WDAC11600 (Caviar)	1624	11	EIDE	GCR 8,9PRML	256k	5400
WDAC1170 (Caviar)	170	13	IDE AT	1,7 RLL	32k	3322
WDAC1210 (Caviar)	212	13	IDE AT	1,7 RLL	64k	3314
WDAC12100 (Caviar)	2111	9.5	EIDE	GCR 8,9PRML	256k	5400
WDAC12500	2560	9.5	EIDE			
WDAC1270 (Caviar)	270	11	IDE AT			
WDAC13200	3249	9.5			64k	4500
WDAC1365 (Caviar)	364	10	IDE AT			
WDAC140 (Caviar)	42	18	IDE AT	2,7 RLL	64k	4500
WDAC14200	4224	9.5			32k	

Drive Model	Format Size MB	Head	Cyl	Sect/Trac	Translate H/C/S	RWC/WPC	Form Factor	Power Watts
WDAC1425 (Caviar)	427	2			16/827/63	—/—	3.5 3H	
WDAC14300 (Caviar)	4311	2			15/8912/63	—/—	3.5 3H	6.18
WDAC160 (Caviar)	62	7	1024	17	7/1024/17	1023/1023	3.5 3H	
WDAC172AA	17248				16/16383/63	—/—	3.5 3H	5.1
WDAC21000 (Caviar)	1083	4			16/16383/63	—/—	3.5 3H	
WDAC210200	10262				16/16383/63	—/—	3.5 3H	5
WDAC2120 (Caviar)	125	8	872	35	8/872/35	872/872	3.5 3H	5.1
WDAC21200 (Caviar)	1282	4			16/2484/63	—/—	3.5 3H	5.1
WDAC21600 (Caviar)	1625	4			16/3148/63	NA/NA	3.5 3H	5
WDAC2170 (Caviar)	171	4	1584	48-56	6/1010/55	NA/NA	3.5 3H	
WDAC21700	1707	16	3308	63		NA/NA	3.5 3H	5
WDAC2200 (Caviar)	213	4	1971	48-56	12/989/35	NA/NA	3.5 3H	5.1
WDAC22000	2000				16/3876/63	—/—	3H	5.1
WDAC22100	2112				16/4092/63	—/—	3.5 3H	12
WDAC2250 (Caviar)	256	3	2233	56-96	9/1010/55	NA/NA	3.5 3H	5.1
WDAC22500	2559				16/4960/63	—/—	3.5 3H	5.3
WDAC23200 (Caviar)	3249	4			16/6296/63	—/—	3.5 3H	3
WDAC2340 (Caviar)	341	4	2233	56-96	12/1010/55	NA/NA	3.5 3H	
WDAC2420 (Caviar)	425	4	2720	55-99	15/989/56	NA/NA	3.5 3H	5.35
WDAC24300 (Caviar)	4311	4			15/8912/63	—/—	3.5 3H	
WDAC25100	5163				15/10672/63	—/—	3.5 3H	
WDAC2540 (Caviar)	540	3			16/1048/63	NA/NA	3.5 3H	
WDAC26200	6226				15/12868/63	—/—	3.5 3H	
WDAC2635 (Caviar)	640	3			16/1240/63	—/—	3.5 3H	6.18
WDAC26400 (Caviar)	6448	4			15/13328/63	—/—	3.5 3H	
WDAC2700 (Caviar)	730	4			16/1416/63	—/—	3.5 3H	6
WDAC280 (Caviar)	85	10	980	17	10/980/17	NA/NA	3.5 3H	
WDAC28200	8292				16/16067/63	—/—	3.5 3H	6.18
WDAC28400 (Caviar)	8455	4			16/16383/63	—/—	3.5 3H	4.6
WDAC2850 (Caviar)	854	4			16/1654/63	—/—	3.5 3H	6.9
WDAC29100	9115	4			16/16383/63	—/—	3.5 3H	
WDAC31000 (Caviar)	1084	6			16/2100/63	—/—	3.5 3H	6.18
WDAC310100 (Caviar)	10141	6			16/16383/63	—/—	3.5 3H	6.18
WDAC310100 (Caviar)	10414	6			16/16383/63	—/—	3.5 3H	6.18
WDAC310200 (Caviar)	10262	5			16/16383/63	—/—	3.5 3H	
WDAC31200 (Caviar)	1282	6			16/2484/63	—/—	3.5 3H	6.18
WDAC313000 (Caviar)	13020	6			16/16383/63	—/—	3.5 3H	7.3
WDAC313500	13578	6			16/16383/63	—/—	3.5 3H	
WDAC315300	15377				16/16383/63	—/—		5.1
WDAC31600 (Caviar)	1625	6			16/3148/63	—/—	3.5 3H	
WDAC3210 (Caviar)	1250					NA/NA	3H	
WDAC32100 (Caviar)	2112	5			16/4092/63	NA/NA	3.5 3H	5.1
WDAC32500 (Caviar)	2560	6			16/4960/63	NA/NA	3.5 3H	5.1
WDAC33100 (Caviar)	3166				16/6296/63	—/—	3.5 3H	5.2
WDAC33200 (Caviar)	3249	5			16/7752/63	—/—	3H	5.2
WDAC34000	4001				16/8184/63	—/—	3H	
WDAC34200	4224				15/8896/63	—/—	3.5 3H	5.6
WDAC34300	4304				15/10672/63	—/—	3.5 3H	5.6
WDAC35100	5163				15/13328/63	—/—	3.5 3H	5.35
WDAC36400	6449	6			16/16383/63	—/—		
WDAC38400	8455				16/16383/63	—/—	3.5 3H	6.9
WDAC418000	18042	8			16/16383/63	—/—	3.5 3H	
WDAC420400 (Caviar)	20416	8			16/16383/63	—/—	3.5 3H	
WDAC514400	14400				16/16383/63	—/—		
WDAC516800	16800				16/16383/63	—/—		
WDAH260 (Tidbit)	62	4	1024	17	7/1024/17	NA/NA	2.5 4H	
WDAH280	86	4	1390	V	10/980/17	NA/NA	2.5 4H	
WDAL1100	100					—/—	2.5 4H	
WDAL2120	120	15	1001	17	8/872/35	NA/NA	2.5 3H	
WDAL2170	170					—/—	2.5 4H	
WDAL2200	200					—/—	2.5 4H	
WDAL2540	541	4			16/1048/63	—/—	2.5 4H	
WDAP2120 (Piranha)	125	8	872	35		NA/NA	3.5 3H	
WDAP4200 (Piranha)	212	8	1280	41	12/987/35	NA/NA	3.5H	
WDCU140	42	2	1050	30-50	5/980/17	NA/NA	1.8 4H	
WDE18300-0048	18310	12	10601			—/—	3.5 3H	
WDE18300-0049	18310	12	10601			—/—	3.5 3H	

Drive Model	Format Size MB	Seek Time	Interface	Encode	cache kb	RPM
WDAC1425 (Caviar)	427	10	IDE AT		64k	4500
WDAC14300 (Caviar)	4311	9.5	EIDE	PRML16,17	512k	5400
WDAC160 (Caviar)	62	17	IDE AT	2,7 RLL		
WDAC172AA	17248	9.0				3605
WDAC21000 (Caviar)	1083	<11	EIDE		128k	
WDAC210200	10262	9				5200
WDAC2120 (Caviar)	125	15	IDE AT	2,7 RLL	32k	
WDAC21200 (Caviar)	1282	<11	EIDE		128k	5200
WDAC21600 (Caviar)	1625	12	EIDE		128k	5200
WDAC2170 (Caviar)	171	14	IDE AT	2,7 RLL	32k	3652
WDAC21700	1707	<12				
WDAC2200 (Caviar)	213	14	IDE AT	2,7 RLL	64k	3652
WDAC22000	2000	11	EIDE		256k	5200
WDAC22100	2112	12	EIDE		128k	5200
WDAC2250 (Caviar)	256	13	IDE AT	1,7 RLL	64k	3322
WDAC22500	2559	11	EIDE		256k	5200
WDAC23200	3249	11	EIDE	GCR 8,9PRML	256k	5400
WDAC2340 (Caviar)	341	13	IDE AT	1,7 RLL	128k	3322
WDAC2420 (Caviar)	425	13	IDE AT	1,7 RLL	128k	3314
WDAC24300 (Caviar)	4311	9.5	EIDE	GCR 8,9PRML	256k	5400
WDAC25100	5163	9.5				
WDAC2540 (Caviar)	540	11	IDE AT		64k	4500
WDAC26200	6226	9.5				
WDAC2635 (Caviar)	640	10	IDE AT		64k	4500
WDAC26400	6448	9.5	EIDE	PRML16,17	512k	5400
WDAC2700 (Caviar)	730	10	IDE AT		64k	4500
WDAC280 (Caviar)	85	17	IDE AT	2,7 RLL	32k	3595
WDAC28200	8292	9.5				
WDAC28400 (Caviar)	8455	9.5	EIDE	PRML16,17	512k	5400
WDAC2850 (Caviar)	854	10	EIDE		64k	4500
WDAC29100	9115	9.0	EIDE	PRML	2mb	7200
WDAC31000 (Caviar)	1084	10	IDE AT		128k	4500
WDAC310100 (Caviar)	10141	9.5	EIDE	PRML16,17	512k	5400
WDAC310100 (Caviar)	10414	9.5	EIDE	PRML16,17	512k	5400
WDAC310200 (Caviar)	10262	9.5	EIDE	PRML16,17	512k	5400
WDAC31200 (Caviar)	1282	10	IDE AT		64k	4500
WDAC313000 (Caviar)	13020	9.5	EIDE	PRML16,17	512k	5400
WDAC313500	13578	9.0	EIDE		2mb	7200
WDAC315300	15377	9				
WDAC31600 (Caviar)	1625	<11	EIDE		128k	5200
WDAC3210 (Caviar)	1250	13	IDE		128k	4500
WDAC32100 (Caviar)	2112	<12	EIDE		128k	5200
WDAC32500 (Caviar)	2560	<12	EIDE		128k	5200
WDAC33100 (Caviar)	3166	<12	EIDE		128k	5200
WDAC33200 (Caviar)	3249	11.5	EIDE	GCR 8,9PRML	128k	5200
WDAC34000	4001	11.5	EIDE		256k	5200
WDAC34200	4224	12			256k	5200
WDAC34300	4304	11	EIDE		256k	5400
WDAC35100	5163	11	EIDE		256k	5400
WDAC36400	6449	9.5	EIDE	PRML	256k	5400
WDAC38400	8455	9.5				
WDAC418000	18042	9.0	EIDE	PRML	2mb	7200
WDAC420400 (Caviar)	20416	9.0	EIDE	PRML	2mb	5400
WDAC514400	14400	9.5				
WDAC516800	16800	9.5				
WDAH260 (Tidbit)	62	19	IDE XT-AT	2,7 RLL		
WDAH280	86	19	IDE XT-AT	2,7 RLL		3383
WDAL1100	100	17	IDE AT			
WDAL2120	100	17	IDE AT		32k	
WDAL2170	120	<16	IDE AT	2,7 RLL		
WDAL2200	170	16	IDE AT		32k	
WDAL2540	200	17	IDE AT		32k	
WDAP2120 (Piranha)	541	13	EIDE		128k	4500
WDAP2120 (Piranha)	125	15	IDE AT	2,7 RLL		3605
WDAP4200 (Piranha)	212	14	IDE AT	2,7 RLL	64k	
WDCU140	42	19	PCMCIA-ATA	1,7 RLL	32k	4503
WDE18300-0048	18310	6.9	Ultra2 LVD	0,6,8 EPR4	2mb	7200
WDE18300-0049	18310	6.9	Ultra LVD-W	0,6,8 EPR4	2mb	7200

Drive Model	Format Size MB	Head	Cyl	Sect/Trac	Translate H/C/S	RWC/WPC	Form Factor	Power Watts
WDE18300-AV0038	18310	12	10601			—/—	3.5 3H	
WDE18300-AV0039	18310	12	10601			—/—	3.5 3H	
WDE18310-0040	18310	8	13614			—/—	3.5 3H	
WDE18310-0042	18310	8	13614			—/—	3.5 3H	
WDE18310-0050	18310	8	13614			—/—	3.5 3H	
WDE18310-0051	18310	8	13614			—/—	3.5 3H	
WDE18310-0052	18310	8	13614			—/—	3.5 3H	
WDE18310-0053	18310	8	13614			—/—	3.5 3H	
WDE18310-AV0041	18310	8	13614			—/—	3.5 3H	
WDE18310-AV0043	18310	8	13614			—/—	3.5 3H	
WDE2170-0003	2170					—/—	3.5	
WDE2170-0007	2170					—/—	3.5	
WDE2170-0008	2170					—/—	3.5	
WDE2170-0023	2170					—/—	3.5	
WDE4360-0003	4360					—/—	3.5	
WDE4360-0007	4360					—/—	3.5	
WDE4360-0008	4360					—/—	3.5	
WDE4360-0023	4360					—/—	3.5	
WDE4550	4550	6				—/—	3.5 3H	7.6
WDE9100-0003 (50-pin)	9105	12				—/—	3.5 3H	9.2
WDE9100-0007 (68-pin)	9105	12				—/—	3.5 3H	9.2
WDE9100-0008 (80-pin)	9105	12				—/—	3.5 3H	9.2
WDE9100-0016 (68-pin)	9105	12				—/—	3.5 3H	9.2
WDE9100-0017 (80-pin)	9105	12				—/—	3.5 3H	9.2
WDE9150-0040 (68-pin)	9150	4	13614			—/—	3.5 3H	
WDE9150-0042 (80-pin)	9150	4	13614			—/—	3.5 3H	
WDE9150-0050 (68-pin)	9150	4	13614			—/—	3.5 3H	
WDE9150-0051 (68-pin)	9150	4	13614			—/—	3.5 3H	
WDE9150-0052 (80-pin)	9150	4	13614			—/—	3.5 3H	
WDE9150-0053 (80-pin)	9150	4	13614			—/—	3.5 3H	
WDE9150-AV0041(68-pin)	9150	4	13614			—/—	3.5 3H	
WDE9150-AV0043(80-pin)	9150	4	13614			—/—	3.5 3H	
WDE9180-0048 (68-pin)	9150	6	10601			—/—	3.5 3H	
WDE9180-0049 (80-pin)	9150	6	10601			—/—	3.5 3H	
WDE9180-AV0038(68-pin)	9150	6	10601			—/—	3.5 3H	
WDE9180-AV0039(80-pin)	9150	6	10601			—/—	3.5 3H	
WDMI130-44 (44 PIN)	31	2	920	33		NA/NA	3.5 3H	
WDMI130-72 (72 PIN)	30	2	928	32		NA/NA	3.5 3H	
WDMI4120-72 (72 PIN)	125	2	925	33		NA/NA	3.5 3H	
WDSC8320 (Condor)	320	14	949	48		NA/NA	3.5HH	12
WDSC8400 (Condor)	400	15	1199	48		NA/NA	3.5HH	
WDSP2100 (Piranha)	104	4	1265	41		NA/NA	3.5HH	
WDSP4200 (Piranha)	209	8	1265	41		NA/NA	3.5HH	
WDTM262R (Tandon)	20	2	782	26		783/783	3.5HH	
WDTM364 (Tandon)	41	4	782	26		783/783	3.5HH	
WDXB1200BB	120GB					—/—	3.5HH	
WDXB1600JB	160GB					—/—	3.5HH	
WDXB2000JB	200GB					—/—	3.5 3H	
WDXB2500JB	250GB					—/—	3.5 3H	
WDXC1200BB	120GB					—/—	3.5HH	
WDXC1200JB	120GB					—/—	3.5HH	
WDXC2000BB	200GB					—/—	3.5HH	
WDXC2500JB	250GB					—/—	3.5HH	
WDXC800BB	80GB					—/—	3.5HH	
WDXF1600JB	160GB					—/—	3.5HH	
WDXF2000JB	200GB					—/—	3.5HH	
WDXF2000JB	200GB					—/—	3.5HH	
WDXF2500JB	250GB					—/—	3.5HH	
WDXF2500JB	250GB					—/—	3.5HH	
WDXU1200BB	120GB					—/—	3.5HH	
WDXU1600BB	160GB					—/—	3.5HH	
WDXU800BB	80GB					—/—	3.5HH	

XEBEC

Drive Model	Format Size MB	Head	Cyl	Sect/Trac	Translate H/C/S	RWC/WPC	Form Factor	Power Watts
OWL I	25	4				—/—	5.25HH	
OWL II	38	4				—/—	5.25HH	
OWL III	52	4				—/—	5.25HH	
XE3100	105	6	979	35		—/—		

Drive Model	Format Size MB	Seek Time	Interface	Encode	cache kb	RPM
WDE18300-AV0038	18310	6.9	Ultra Fast	0,6,8 EPR4	4mb	7200
WDE18300-AV0039	18310	6.9	Ultra FastW	0,6,8 EPR4	4mb	7200
WDE18310-0040	18310	6.2	Ultra2 SCSI	EPR4 0,6,8	2mb	1003
WDE18310-0042	18310	6.2	Ultra2 SCSI	EPR4 0,6,8	2mb	1003
WDE18310-0050	18310	6.2	Ultra 160	EPR4 0,6,8	2mb	1003
WDE18310-0051	18310	6.2	Ultra 160	EPR4 0,6,8	8mb	1003
WDE18310-0052	18310	6.2	Ultra 160	EPR4 0,6,8	2mb	1003
WDE18310-0053	18310	6.2	Ultra 160	EPR4 0,6,8	8mb	1003
WDE18310-AV0041	18310	6.2	Ultra2 LVD	EPR4 0,6,8	8mb	1003
WDE18310-AV0043	18310	6.2	Ultra2 LVD	EPR4 0,6,8	8mb	1003
WDE2170-0003	2170	8	UltraFast	PRML	512k	7200
WDE2170-0007	2170	8	UltraFastW	PRML	512k	7200
WDE2170-0008	2170	8	SCA-2	PRML	512k	7200
WDE2170-0023	2170	8	Ultra FstDf	PRML	512k	7200
WDE4360-0003	4360	8	UltraFast	PRML	512k	7200
WDE4360-0007	4360	8	UltraFastW	PRML	512k	7200
WDE4360-0008	4360	8	SCA-2	PRML	512k	7200
WDE4360-0023	4360	8	Ultra FstDf	PRML	512k	7200
WDE4550	4550	7.8	Ultra2 SCSI	PRML	512k	7200
WDE9100-0003 (50-pin)	9105	7.9	ULSCSIFST	PRML	512k	7200
WDE9100-0007 (68-pin)	9105	7.9	ULSCSIFstWD	PRML	512k	7200
WDE9100-0008 (80-pin)	9105	7.9	SCA-2	PRML	512k	7200
WDE9100-0016 (68-pin)	9105	7.9	ULSCSIFstWD	PRML	512k	7200
WDE9100-0017 (80-pin)	9105	7.9	SCA-2	PRML	1000k	7200
WDE9150-0040 (68-pin)	9150	6.2	Ultra2 SCSI	EPR4 0,6,8	1000k	7200
WDE9150-0042 (80-pin)	9150	6.2	Ultra2 SCSI	EPR4 0,6,8	2mb	1003
WDE9150-0050 (68-pin)	9150	6.2	Ultra2 SCSI	EPR4 0,6,8	2mb	1003
WDE9150-0051 (68-pin)	9150	6.2	Ultra2 SCSI	EPR4 0,6,8	2mb	1003
WDE9150-0052 (80-pin)	9150	6.2	Ultra2 SCSI	EPR4 0,6,8	8mb	1003
WDE9150-0053 (80-pin)	9150	6.2	Ultra2 SCSI	EPR4 0,6,8	2mb	1003
WDE9150-AV0041(68-pin)	9150	6.2	Ultra2 SCSI	EPR4 0,6,8	8mb	1003
WDE9150-AV0043(80-pin)	9150	6.2	Ultra2 SCSI	EPR4 0,6,8	8mb	1003
WDE9180-0048 (68-pin)	9150	6.9	Ultra2 SCSI	EPR4 0,6,8	8mb	1003
WDE9180-0049 (80-pin)	9150	6.9	Ultra2 SCSI	EPR4 0,6,8	2mb	7200
WDE9180-AV0038(68-pin)	9150	6.9	Ultra2 SCSI	EPR4 0,6,8	2mb	7200
WDE9180-AV0039(80-pin)	9150	6.9	Ultra2 SCSI	EPR4 0,6,8	4mb	7200
WDMI130-44 (44 PIN)	31	19	MCA	RLL	4mb	7200
WDMI130-72 (72 PIN)	30	19	MCA	RLL		
WDMI4120-72 (72 PIN)	125	23	MCA	2,7 RLL		
WDSC8320 (Condor)	320	12	SCSI-2	1,7 RLL	64k	4316
WDSC8400 (Condor)	400	16	SCSI-2	1,7 RLL	128k	4316
WDSP2100 (Piranha)	104	14	SCSI-2	2,7 RLL	64k	
WDSP4200 (Piranha)	209	14	SCSI-2	2,7 RLL	64k	
WDTM262R (Tandon)	20	85	ST412/506	2,7 RLL		
WDTM364 (Tandon)	41	85	ST412/506	2,7 RLL		
WDXB1200BB	120GB	8.9	FireWire		2mb	7200
WDXB1600JB	160GB	8.9	FireWire		8mb	7200
WDXB2000JB	200GB	8.9	FireWir/USB		8mb	7200
WDXB2500JB	250GB	8.9	FireWir/USB		8mb	7200
WDXC1200BB	120GB	8.9	FireWire		2mb	7200
WDXC1200JB	120GB	8.9	FireWire		8mb	7200
WDXC2000BB	200GB	8.9	FireWire		2mb	7200
WDXC2500JB	250GB	8.9	FireWire		8mb	7200
WDXC800BB	80GB	8.9	FireWire		2mb	7200
WDXF1600JB	160GB	8.9	FireWire		8mb	7200
WDXF2000JB	200GB	8.9	FireWire		8mb	7200
WDXF2000JB	200GB	8.9	FireWire		8mb	7200
WDXF2500JB	250GB	8.9	FireWire		8mb	7200
WDXF2500JB	250GB	8.9	FireWire		8mb	7200
WDXU1200BB	120GB	8.9	USB2.0		2mb	7200
WDXU1600BB	160GB	8.9	USB2.0		2mb	7200
WDXU800BB	80GB	8.9	USB2.0		2mb	7200

XEBEC

Drive Model	Format Size MB	Seek Time	Interface	Encode	cache kb	RPM
OWL I	25	55	SCSI	MFM		
OWL II	38	40	SCSI	MFM		
OWL III	52	38	SCSI	MFM		
XE3100	105		IDE AT			

Drive Model	Format Size MB	Head	Cyl	Sect/ Trac	Translate H/C/S	RWC/ WPC	Form Factor	Power Watts
Y-E DATA AMERICA, INC								
YD3042	43	4	788	28		789/789	3.5HH	12
YD3081B	45	2	1057	42		NA/NA	3.5HH	
YD3082	87	8	788	28		789/789	3.5HH	12
YD3082B	90	4	1057	42		NA/NA	3.5HH	
YD3083B	136	6	1057	42		NA/NA	3.5HH	
YD3084B	181	8	1057	42		NA/NA	3.5HH	
YD3161B	45	2	1057	42		NA/NA	3.5 3H	
YD3162B	90	4	1057	42		NA/NA	3.5 3H	
YD3181B	45	2	1057	42		NA/NA	3.5 3H	
YD3182B	90	4	1057	42		NA/NA	3.5HH	
YD3530	32	5	731	17		732/732	3.5HH	
YD3540	42	7	733	32		732/732	3.5HH	12
YD3541	45	8	731	15		732/732	3.5HH	12
ZENTEC								
DRACO	518	6	2142	V		—/—	3.5 3H	
ZH3100(A)	86					NA/NA	3.5HH	
ZH3100(S)	86					NA/NA	3.5HH	
ZH3140(A)	121					NA/NA	3.5HH	
ZH3140(S)	121					—/—	3.5 3H	
ZM3180	170					—/—	3.5 3H	
ZM3272	260	4	2076	55		—/—	3.5 3H	
ZM3360	340					—/—	3.5 3H	
ZM3540	518					—/—	3.5 3H	
ZQ2140	126	4	1410	44		—/—	2.5 4H	

Drive Model	Format Size MB	Seek Time	Interface	Encode	cache kb	RPM
Y-E DATA AMERICA, INC						
YD3042	43	28	SCSI	2,7 RLL		
YD3081B	45	28	SCSI	2,7 RLL		
YD3082	87	28	SCSI	2,7 RLL		
YD3082B	90	28	SCSI	2,7 RLL		
YD3083B	136	28	SCSI	2,7 RLL		
YD3084B	181	28	SCSI	2,7 RLL		
YD3161B	45	19	IDE AT	2,7 RLL		
YD3162B	90	19	IDE AT	2,7 RLL		
YD3181B	45	19	SCSI	2,7 RLL		
YD3182B	90	19	SCSI	2,7 RLL		
YD3530	32	26	ST412/506	MFM		
YD3540	42	29	ST412/506	MFM		3600
YD3541	45	29	SCSI	2,7 RLL		3600
ZENTEC						
DRACO	518	12	SCSI-2Fast	1,7 RLL	512k	4200
ZH3100(A)	86	20	IDE AT			
ZH3100(S)	86	20	SCSI			
ZH3140(A)	121	20	IDE AT			
ZH3140(S)	121	20	SCSI			
ZM3180	170	12	IDE AT			
ZM3272	260	13	IDE AT	1,7 RLL	64k	3600
ZM3360	340	12	IDE AT			
ZM3540	518	12	IDE AT			
ZQ2140	126	18	IDE AT	1,7 RLL	32k	3600

Standard 286/386/486 Hard Disk Types

Hard Drives

Drive Type	# of Cylinders	# of Heads	Write Precomp	Land Zone	Size in Megabytes
1	306	4	128	305	10
2	615	4	300	615	21
3	615	6	300	615	31
4	940	8	512	940	63
5	940	6	512	940	47
6	615	4	65535	615	21
7	462	8	256	511	31
8	733	5	65535	733	31
9	900	15	65535	901	112
10	820	3	65535	820	21
11	855	5	65535	855	36
12	855	7	65535	855	50
13	306	8	128	319	21
14	733	7	65535	733	43
15	0	0	0	0	0
16	612	4	0	663	21
17	977	5	300	977	41
18	977	7	65535	977	57
19	1024	7	512	1023	60
20	733	5	300	732	31
21	733	7	300	732	43
22	733	5	300	733	31
23	306	4	0	336	10
24	698	7	300	732	42
25	615	4	0	615	21
26	1024	4	65535	1023	34
27	1024	5	65535	1023	43
28	1024	8	65535	1023	68
29	512	8	256	512	34
30	615	2	615	615	10
31	732	7	300	732	44
32	1023	5	65535	1023	44
33	306	4	0	340	10
34	976	5	488	977	42
35	1024	9	1024	1024	77
36	1024	5	512	1024	43
37	830	10	65535	830	69
38	823	10	256	824	68
39	615	4	128	664	21
40	615	8	128	664	41
41	917	15	65535	918	114
42	1023	15	65535	1024	127
43	823	10	512	823	68
44	820	6	65535	820	41
45	1024	8	65535	1024	68
46	925	9	65535	925	69
47	699	7	256	700	41

Note: Drive types over #24 vary between computer manufacturers

Chapter 13

CD & DVD Drive Specifications

Introduction to Optical Media

Note: For information on drive interfaces see page 554 and for interface pinouts, see page 517.

Optical Media is a form of data storage in which a laser reads and writes (except early analog devices) the information to a disk. As with many things in the computer world, it is easy to forget the short period of time in which these technologies have been used. We have included the following Historical Time Line for your "entertainment".

Year	Description
1958	First optical disk (videodisk) was invented by David Paul Gregg.
1961	First patent for videodisk; an analog video optical disk. Subsequently, MCA purchased Gregg's company and patent in the early 1960's.
1965	James Russell invented the compact digital disk. 22 patents
1970	Russell: first digital to optical recording and playback system
1978	MCA Discovision released the first consumer Optical disc player.
1980	Russell manufactured the first CD disk player
1982	Sony & Phillips released first audio CD format called CD-DA
1994	DVD introduced: Super Disk (SD) and Multimedia CD (MMCD)
1996	Single standard DVD technology converged

Optical Media Comparison

Drive Type	Optical Media Description
CD or CD-Audio	CD player, Audio CD, read only
CD-ROM	Compact Disk-Read Only Memory. Includes CD-ROM, CD-R, Audio CD, and Photo CD
CD-ROM Multiread	Compact Disk-Read Only Memory Multiread. Includes CD-ROM, CD-R, CD-RW, Photo CD and CD-I
CD-R	Compact Disk-Recordable. Reads CD-ROM and CD-R and in some cases can read CD-RW disks.
CD-RW	Compact Disk Rewritable. Reads CD-ROM, CD-R, and CD-RW. Writes and rewrites CD-RW disks.
DVD-ROM	Digital Versatile Disc-Read Only Memory. High-capacity data storage medium similar to CD-ROM in its recording technology, backward compatible with CD-ROM. Uses MPEG-2 to compress video. Most DVD-ROM players can read DVD-R,+R,-RW, & +RW
DVD-Audio	Audio DVD, read only

CD & DVD

Drive Type	Optical Media Description
DVD-Video	Digital storage medium for feature-length motion pictures. Unlike DVD-ROMs, the Digital-Video format includes a Content Scrambling System (CSS) to prevent users from copying discs
DVD-RAM	Digital Versatile Disc-Random Access Memory, A DVD Forum standard. Reads all CD media and DVD ROM. Reads, writes, and fast rewrites DVD-RAM media. A highly reliable media with estimated 30-year data life and can be rewritten over 100,000 times. It incorporates error correction and defect management, comes in a cartridge sleeve. and does not require special software to write to the media (it is accessed like a floppy or hard drive). DVD-RAM is NOT a magneto-optical medium like CD-R, it uses "phase change" technology. Media is more expensive than DVD-R and +R.
DVD-R	Digital Versatile Disc Read Only Memory, A DVD Forum standard, can write to only one layer of the disc. DVD-RG is the general public version and DVD-RA is an authoring version used for mastering DVD video.
DVD-RW	Digital Versatile Disc Rewritable, A DVD Forum standard, can be rewritten about 1,000 times, can write to only one layer of the disc
DVD+R	Digital Versatile Disc Read Only Memory, supported by the Alliance (Sony, Philips, HP, Dell, Ricoh, Yamaha, and Microsoft), can write to multiple disc layers
DVD+RW	Digital Versatile Disc Rewritable, supported by the Alliance (Sony, Philips, HP, Dell, Ricoh, Yamaha, and Microsoft), can be rewritten about 1,000 times, +RW writes faster than DVD-RAM, can write to multiple disc layers
HD-DVD	High Definition-Digital Versatile Disc; generic term, specific formats include Blu-Ray and AOD
Blu-Ray	An HD-DVD format developed by Sony, Samsung, Sharp, Thomson, Hitachi, Matsushita, Pioneer and Philips, and Mitsubishi. Rewritable Blue-violet laser technology that provides data transfer rates of 36Mbps and disks hold up to 27GB of data on a single-sided single layer disc.
AOD	An HD-DVD format developed jointly by Toshiba and NEC. Rewritable Blue-violet laser technology that supports up to 20GB of data on a single-sided single layer disc.

CD & DVD

Optical Media Data Rates

Drive Speed	Data Transfer Rate MB/s	Disc write time CD=650MB:DVD=4.37GB
CD 1x	0.153	71 min.
CD 2x	0.307	35 min.
CD 3x	0.460	24 min.
CD 4x	0.614	18 min.
CD 6x	0.921	12 min.
CD 8x	1.228	9 min.
CD 10x	1.536	7 min.
CD 12x	1.843	6 min.
CD 16x	2.457	4 min.
CD 18x	2.764	4 min.
CD 24x	3.686	3 min.
CD 32x	4.915	2 min.
CD 100x	15.360	0.7 min.
CD CAV drives (12x - 24x)	1.843 - 3.686	5.8 to 2.9 min.
DVD 1x	1.32	53 min.
DVD 2x	2.64	27 min.
DVD 4x	5.28	14 min.
DVD 5x	6.60	11 min.
DVD 6x	7.93	9 min.
DVD 8x	10.57	7 min.
DVD 10x	13.21	6 min.
DVD 16x	21.13	4 min.

CD & DVD

CD/DVD Drive Manufacturers

The following table is a general summary of companies that have manufactured and/or are still manufacturing CD-ROM drives. If you have information concerning the status of any of these companies, such as "XYZ Company went bankrupt in August, 1990" or "XYZ Company was bought by Q Company," please let us know so we can keep this section current. If a phone number is listed in the Status column, the company is in business.

Manufacturer	Phone
Acer America	408-432-6200
ACS Innovation, Inc.	408-566-0900
Addonics Technology	408-433-3899
Aiwa America Inc.	201-512-3600
Alps Electric, Inc.	408-361-6400
(Stopped manufacturing CD-ROM's in 1995)	
Apple Computer	408-996-1010
BTC (Behavior Tech Computer Corp.)	510-657-3956
CD Technology	Unknown
Chinon America	See Tech Media?
Creative Labs, Inc.	408-428-6600
Delta Microsystems	Unknown
Denon America	Unknown
Diamond Multimedia (Sonic Blue)	541-967-2450
Digital Equipment Corp	508-841-3111
(Supported by Compaq Computer)	
Digital Video Systems, Inc.	408-392-0268
Fidelity International Tech	732-417-2230
Funai Electric Co., Ltd.	408-330-6000
Goldstar Electronics Intern'l	800-752-0900
Hewlett-Packard Co	301-670-4300 or 800-752-0900
Hi-Val (Iomagic)	714-953-3000
Hitachi America, Ltd.	800-448-2244
IBM	800-772-2227
Iomega	801-332-1000
JVC	714-816-6500
LaCie	503-844-4503
Laser Magnetic Storage	See Plasmon
Lite-On Inc.	408-946-4873
Mashusta	201-348-7000
Micro Design International	407-677-8333
Micro Solutions	815-756-3411
Mitsumi Electronics Corp	408-970-0700
Nakamichi America Corp	Unknown
NEC Technologies	800-632-4636
NewCom, Inc.	Out of business
Nomai, USA	33-(0)2 33 89 16 50 (France)
(Acquired by Iomega in July 1998)	
Ocean Information Systems (Denco Mfg)	408-487-3279

Manufacturer	Status
Optical Access Intern'l (See Prime Array Syst, sold 7-99)	....
Optics Storage	65-3823100 (Japan)
Panasonic Communications	800-742-8086
Panasonic Computer Peripherals	201-348-7000
Peripheral Land	Unknown
Philips Electronics	212-536-0500
Pinnacle Micro, Inc.	949-635-3000
Pioneer Communications	201-327-6400
Pioneer New Media Tech, Inc.	310-952-2111
Plasmon Data, Inc.	952-946-4100
Plextor	800-475-3986
Prime Array Systems	800-433-5133
Procom Technology	949-852-1000
Ricoh Corp	408-432-8800
Samsung Electronics America	201-229-7000
Sanyo Electric	81-64 432 949 (Japan)
Severn Companies	301-794-9680
Smart and Friendly	Out of business
Sony Corp	201-930-1000
Sun Microsystems	650-960-1300
Teac America, Inc.	323-726-0303
Tech Media	Unknown
Texel	Unknown
Todd Enterprises	516-777-8633
Toshiba America	212-596-0600
Wearnes Systems Tech, inc.	Unknown
Yamaha Corp.	714-522-9227
Young Minds Inc.	909-335-1350

Total number CD/DVD Drives = 1817 (last year 1522)

CD-ROM Drive Syntax and Notation

The following are descriptions of the information contained in the CD-ROM tables. Telephone numbers for manufacturers are in the Phone Book chapter (page 905)

1. Drive Type .... CD-ROM=Read only CD-ROM
   CD-R=Write once CD-ROM
   CD-RW=Rewritable CD-ROM
   DVD=Digital Versatile Disk
   DVD-R=Write once; DVD Forum
       Versions: A=Authoring; G=General
   DVD+R=Write once; DVD+RW; Alliance
   DVD-RAM=Rewritable from DVD Forum and
       Panasonic (primarily Apple computers)
   DVD-ROM=Read only
   DVD-RW=Rewritable; DVD Forum
   DVD+RW=Rewritable from the
       DVD+RW; Alliance
   DVD-Video=DVD for home movie players
   Changer=multi disk CD-ROM

2. Speed .... Drive speed, for example "32X".
   1X is defined as the speed of audio CDs, so 32X is 32 times faster than audio speed. In actuality, a drive rated at 32X maximum and the average is approximately 8X.

3. Interface .... Type of communication interface between the computer and drive

4. Buffer .... Size of memory buffer in drive. More provides better performance.

5. Discs .... Number of discs the drive holds

6. Loader .... Type of disc carrier. Magazine, Tray, Caddy (including brand of caddy, if available)

7. Plug & Play .... If indicated, drive is Plug & Play.
   Note: Many of the listed drives are Plug & Play, but could not be verified so they are not listed as Plug & Play.

8. Internal/External ·· Internal=mounted inside computer
   External=mounted in an external drive case.

Sequoia needs your help! If you have specifications on new or obsolete CD-ROM drives, please send them to us so that we can include them in future editions of this book.

CD/DVD Drive Specifications

Manufacturer Model	Drive Type	Drive Speed	Drive Interface	# Discs & Loader	Internal-External	Buffer
Acer, Inc.						
CD-612A	CDROM	12X	IDE	1 disc Tray	Internal	128k
CD-620A	CDROM	20X	E-IDE/ATAPI	1 disc	Internal	128k
CD-624A	CDROM	24X	E-IDE/ATAPI	1 disc	Internal	128k
CD-632A	CDROM	32X	EIDE/ATAPI	1 disc	Internal	128k
CD-636A	CDROM	36X	EIDE/ATAPI	1 disc	Internal	128k
CD-640A	CDROM	40X	EIDE/ATAPI	1 disc	Internal	128k
CD-640P	CDROM	40X	EIDE/ATAPI	1 disc	Internal	128k
CD-648P	CDROM	48X	EIDE/ATAPI	1 disc	Internal	128k
CD-650P	CDROM	50X	EIDE/ATAPI	1 disc	Internal	128k
CD-652P	CDROM	52X	EIDE/ATAPI	1 disc	Internal	128k
CD-656A	CDROM	56X	EIDE/ATAPI	1 disc	Internal	128k
CD-912E	CDROM	12X	E-IDE/ATAPI	1 disc	Internal	128k
CD-916 E	CDROM	16X	ATAPI IDE	1 disc Tray	Internal	
CD-916E	CDROM	16X	Atapi IDE	1 disc Tray	Internal	128k
CD-920E	CDROM	20X	ATAPI IDE	1 disc Tray	Internal	128k
CD-924E	CDROM	24X	ATAPI IDE	1 disc Tray	Internal	128k
CD-RW 6206A	CD-RW	6Xr/4Xrw	EIDE/ATAPI	disc	Internal	512k
CRW-1032A	CD-RW	32Xr/10Xw/4Xrw	EIDE/ATAPI	1 disc		4Mb
CRW-1208A	CD-RW	32Xr/12Xw/8Xrw	EIDE/ATAPI	1 disc		2Mb
CRW-1610A	CD-RW	40Xr/16Xw/10Xrw	EIDE/ATAPI	1 disc		2Mb
CRW-1832A	CD-RW	32Xr/10Xw/8Xrw	EIDE/ATAPI	1 disc		4Mb
CRW-2010A	CD-RW	40Xr/20Xw/10Xrw	EIDE/ATAPI	1 disc		2Mb
CRW-2410A	CD-RW	40Xr/24Xw/10Xrw	EIDE/ATAPI	1 disc		2Mb
CRW-4232A	CD-RW	32Xr/4Xw/2Xrw	EIDE/ATAPI	1 disc	Internal	2Mb
CRW-4406EU	CD-RW	6Xr/4Xw/4Xrw	USB 1.0	1 disc	External	2Mb
CRW-4432A	CD-RW	32Xr/4Xrw	EIDE/ATAPI	1 disc	Internal	1Mb
CRW-620	CDROM	6XR/2XW	SCSI-2	1 disc	Internal	1Mb
CRW-6206A	CDROM	6Xr/2Xw	EIDE/ATAPI	1 disc	Internal	512k
CRW-6406EU	CD-RW	6Xr/6Xw/4Xrw	USB 1.1	1 disc	External	2Mb
CRW-6424MU	CD-RW	24Xr/4Xw/4Xrw	USB 1.1	1 disc	External	2Mb
CRW-6432A	CD-RW	32Xr/6Xw/4Xrw	EIDE/ATAPI	disc	Internal	2Mb
CRW-8432A	CD-RW	32Xr/8Xw/4Xrw	EIDE/Atapi	1 disc	Internal	8Mb
CRW-8432IA	CD-RW	32Xr/8Xw/4Xrw	EIDE/Atapi	1 disc	Internal	2MB
CRW-8824MM	CD-RW	24Xr/8Xw/4Xrw	USB 1.1	1 disc	External	2MB
DV-605A	DVD-ROM		EIDE/ATAPI	1 disc	Internal	128k
DVD-606A	DVD-ROM	128kb	E-IDE/Atapi	1 disc	Internal	
DVP 1040A	DVD-ROM	10Xdvd/40Xcdrom	EIDE/Atapi	1 disc	Internal	512kb
DVP 1640A	DVD-ROM	16Xdvd/40Xcdrom	EIDE/ATAPI	1 disc	Internal	512kb
DVP 1648A	DVD-ROM	16Xdvd/48Xcd	EIDE/ATAPI	1 disc	Internal	512kb
SDV-8032EP	DVD-ROM	8Xdvd/32Xcdrom	CARDBUS	1 disc	External	512kb
ACS Innovation, Inc.						
COMPRO 32X	CDROM	32X	IDE/ATAPI	1 disc Tray		128k
COMPRO 40X	CD-ROM	40X	IDE/ATAPI	1 disc Tray	Internal	128k
COMPRO CD-RW 12432	CD-RW	32Xr/12Xw/4Xrw	SCSI-3	1 disc Tray		2Mb
COMPRO CD-RW 4416i	CD-RW	16Xr/4Xrw	EIDE/ATAPI	1 disc Tray	Internal	2Mb
COMPRO CD-RW 4416s	CD-RW	16Xr/4Xw	SCSI	1 disc Tray	2Mb	16Xr/4Xrw
COMPRO CD-RW 4420-NB	CD-RW	20Xr/4Xw/4Xrw	EIDE/ATAPI	1 disc Tray		2Mb
COMPRO CD-RW 4432	CD-RW	32Xr/4Xw/4Xrw	EIDE/ATAPI	1 disc Tray	Internal	2Mb
COMPRO CD-RW 7040	CD-RW	32Xr/4Xrw	EIDE/ATAPI	1 disc Tray	Internal	2Mb
COMPRO CD-RW 7585	CD-RW	32Xr/8Xw/4Xrw	EIDE/ATAPI	1 disc Tray	Internal	2Mb
COMPRO CD-RW 7586	CD-RW	32Xr/8Xw/4Xrw	EIDE/ATAPI	1 disc Tray	Internal	2Mb
COMPRO CD-RW 8424s	CD-RW	24Xr/8Xw/4Xrw	SCSI-3	1 disc Tray		4Mb
COMPRO CD-RW 8432	CD-RW	32Xr/8Xw/4Xrw	EIDE/ATAPI	1 disc Tray		2Mb
COMPRO CD-RW 8824s	CD-RW	24Xr/8Xw/8Xrw	SCSI-3	1 disc Tray		4Mb
COMPRO CDR-7501-INT	CD-R	4X	Adaptec SCS	disc Tray	Internal	1Mb
COMPRO CDR-7502B	CDROM	8XR/4XW	SCSI	1 disc		1Mb
COMPRO CDR-7503	CDROM	20X	SCSI-2	1 disc		2Mb
COMPRO CDR-7582	CDROM	8Xr/4Xw	EIDE/ATAPI	1 disc	Internal	1Mb
COMPRO CR-585B	CDROM	24X	IDE/ATAPI	1 disc Tray	Internal	128k
COMPRO CR-594	CDROM	48X	IDE/ATAPI	1 disc Tray	Internal	128k
COMPRO DVP-126	DVD-ROM	8Xcdrom/4Xrec	SCSI-2	1 disc		
COMPRO LMD-584	CDROM	12X	IDE/ATAPI	1 disc		128k
COMPRO SR-8586	DVD-ROM	16Xdvd/48Xcdrom	EIDE/ATAPI	1 disc Tray		512kb
Addonics Technology						
AEMCDRW24XCB	CD-RW	40Xr/24Xw/10Xrw	PCMCIA	1 disc Slot	Mobile	2Mb
AEMCDRW24XFW	CD-RW	40Xr/24Xw/10Xrw	FireWire	1 disc Slot	Mobile	2Mb
AEMCDRW24XUM	CD-RW	40Xr/24Xw/10Xrw	USB 2.0	1 disc Slot	Mobile	2Mb
AEMCDRW32XCB	CD-RW	40Xr/24Xw/10Xrw	PCMCIA	1 disc	Mobile	2Mb
AEMCDRW32XFW	CD-RW	40Xr/32Xw/12Xrw	FireWire	1 disc	Mobile	2Mb
AEMCDRW32XUM	CD-RW	40Xr/24Xw/10Xrw	USB 2.0	1 disc	Mobile	2Mb
AEMCDRW8XCB	CD-RW	32Xr/8Xw/4Xrw	PCMCIA	1 disc Slot	Mobile	2Mb
AEMCDRW8XUM	CD-RW	32Xr/8Xw/4Xrw	USB 2.0	1 disc Slot	Mobile	2Mb

Manufacturer Model	Drive Type	Drive Speed	Drive Interface	# Discs & Loader	Internal-External	Buffer
AEMDVRW12XCB	DVD/CD-RW	8dvd32r12w8rw	PCMCIA	1 disc	External	2Mb
AEMDVRW12XFW	DVD/CD-RW	8dvd32r12w8rw	FireWire	1 disc	External	2Mb
AEMDVRW12XUM	DVD/CD-RW	8dvd32r12w8rw	USB 2.0	1 disc	External	2Mb
AEMDVRW20XCB	DVD/CD-RW	12dvd40r20w10rw	PCMCIA	1 disc	External	2Mb
AEMDVRW20XFW	DVD/CD-RW	12dvd40r20w10rw	FireWire	1 disc	External	2Mb
AEMDVRW20XUM	DVD/CD-RW	12dvd40r20w10rw	USB 2.0	1 disc	External	2Mb
AEMDVRW8XCB	DVD/CD-RW	8dvd32r8w4rw	PCMCIA	1 disc	External	2Mb
AEMDVRW8XFW	DVD/CD-RW	8dvd32r8w4rw	FireWire	1 disc	External	2Mb
AEMDVRW8XUM	DVD/CD-RW	8dvd32r8w4rw	USB 2.0	1 disc	External	2Mb
AEPCDRW16X	CDRW	24Xr/16Xw/10Xrw	PCMCIA	1 disc	Portable	2Mb
AEPCDRW16XUM	CDRW	24Xr/16Xw/10Xrw	USB 2.0	1 disc		2Mb
AEPCDRW16XFW	CDRW	24Xr/16Xw/10Xrw	FireWire	1 disc		2Mb
AEPCDRW4X	CDRW	20Xr/4Xw/4Xrw	PCMCIA	1 disc		2Mb
AEPCDRW4XUM	CDRW	20Xr/4Xw/4Xrw	USB 2.0	1 disc Slot		2Mb
AEPCDRW4XUM	CDRW	20Xr/4Xw/4Xrw	FireWire	1 disc		2Mb
AEPCDRW8X	CDRW	24Xr/8Xw/4Xrw	PCMCIA	1 disc		2Mb
AEPCDRW8XUM	CDRW	24Xr/8Xw/4Xrw	USB 2.0	1 disc		2Mb
AEPCDRW8XUM	CDRW	24Xr/8Xw/4Xrw	FireWire	1 disc		2Mb
AEPDVD2K8X24	PocketDVD	8Xdvd/24Xcd	PCMCIA	1 disc Slot		128k
AEPDVD2K8X24FW	PocketDVD	8Xdvd/24Xcd	FireWire	1 disc		128k
AEPDVD2K8X24UM	PocketDVD	8Xdvd/24Xcd	USB 2.0	1 disc		128k
AEPDVRW888CB	DVD/CD-RW	8dvd/24r/8w/8rw	PCMCIA	1 disc	Mobile	2Mb
AEPDVRW888FW	DVD/CD-RW	8dvd/24r/8w/8rw	FireWire	1 disc	Mobile	2Mb
AEPDVRW888UM	DVD/CD-RW	8dvd/24r/8w/8rw	USB 2.0	1 disc	Mobile	2Mb
AERWCOP24XCB	CD-RW/COP	40Xr/24Xw/10Xrw	CardBus	1 disc	External	
AERWCOP24XFW	CD-RW/COP	40Xr/24Xw/10Xrw	FireWire	1 disc	External	
AERWCOP24XUM	CD-RW/COP	40Xr/24Xw/10Xrw	USB 2.0	1 disc	External	
Mobile 12X10X32	CD-RW	32Xr/12Xw/10Xrw	ATAPI PCMCI	1 disc	Mobile	2Mb
Mobile 16X10X40	CD-RW	40Xr/16Xw/10Xrw	ATAPI PCMCI	1 disc	Mobile	2Mb
Mobile 2X2X6	CDROM	6Xr/2Xrw	ATAPI PCMCI	1 disc	Mobile	8Mb
Mobile 4X4X16	CD-RW	16Xr/4Xrw	ATAPI PCMCI	1 disc	Mobile	1Mb
Mobile 8X4X32	CD-RW	32Xr/8Xw/4Xrw	ATAPI PCMCI	1 disc	Mobile	2Mb
PCD4X4	CDROM	4X		disc		
PCD6X	CDROM	6X		disc		
PCDS6X	CDROM	6X		disc		
PocketCD	CDROM	20X	PCMCIA	1 disc Tray	Portable	128k
PocketCD	CDROM	32X	PCMCIA	1 disc Tray	Portable	
PocketCD	CDROM	24X	PCMCIA	1 disc Tray	Portable	
PocketCD-RW 20X4X4X	CD-RW	20Xr/4Xw/4Xrw	PCMCIA	1 disc		2Mb
PocketCD-RW 24X8X4X	CD-RW	24Xr/8Xw/4Xrw	PCMCIA	1 disc		2Mb
PocketCD98	CDROM	24X	PCMCIA	1 disc Tray	Portable	128k
PocketDVD 2X	DVD-ROM	2Xdvd/20Xcdrom	PCMCIA	1 disc Tray	Portable	512k
PocketDVD 4X	DVD-ROM	4Xdvd/24Xcdrom	CardBus/PCM	1 disc Tray	External	128kb
PocketDVD 8X	DVD-ROM	8Xdvd/24Xcdrom	CardBus/PCM	1 disc Tray	External	128kb

Aiwa America Inc.

ACD-630	CDROM	4X		3 disc		256KB

Alps Electric (USA), Inc

Alps 4X Internal	CDROM-cha	4X	EIDE	4 disc Mag	Internal	128KB
CD544C	CDROM-cha	4X	EIDE	4 disc Mag		128k

Altec Lansing Technologies Inc

AMC2800	CDROM	8X	PC Card	1 disc	External	

Apple Computer

AppleCD SC	CDROM	1X	SCSI	1 disc Sony Caddy	External	64k

APS Tech

4.7 DVD-RAM Ext SCSI Pro2	DVD-RAM	20Xcd/2Xdvd	SCSI-3		External	1Mb
CD-RW 16X10X40 FireWire Plus	CD-RW	40Xr/16Xw/10Xrw	IEEE1394USB	1 disc		2Mb
CD-RW 16X10X40 SCSI Pro2	CD-RW	40Xr/16Xw/10Xrw	Ultra SCSI	1 disc Tray		2Mb
CD-RW 24X10X40 FireWire Plus	CD-RW	40Xr/24Xw/10Xrw		disc		
CD-RW 4X4X32 USB Pro2	CD-RW	32Xr/4Xw/4Xrw	USB	1 disc		2Mb
CD-RW 8X4X32 FireWire Plus	CD-RW	32Xr/8Xw/4Xrw	IEEE1394USB	1 disc Tray		4Mb
CD-RW 8X4X32 SCSI Pro2	CD-RW	32Xr/8Xw/4Xrw		1 disc		

Behavior Tech Computer Corp

BCD 10X	CDROM	10X	EIDE	1 disc Tray	Internal	256k
BCD 16X	CDROM	16X	EIDE	1 disc Tray	Internal	256k
BCD 20X	CDROM	20X	EIDE	1 disc Tray	Internal	256k
BCD 24X	CDROM	24X	EIDE	1 disc Tray	Internal	256k
BCD 32X	CDROM	32X	ATAPI/IDE	1 disc Tray	Internal	256k
BCD 36X	CDROM	36X	EIDE	1 disc Tray	Internal	
BCD 40X	CDROM	40X	EIDE	1 disc Tray	Internal	256k
BCD 44X	CDROM	44X	IDE/ATAPI	1 disc Tray	Internal	256k
BCD 48SB	CDROM	48X	E-IDE/Atapi	1 disc Tray	Internal	128kb
BCD 50SB	CDROM	50X	E-IDE/Atapi	1 disc Tray	Internal	128kb
BCD 52X	CDROM	52X	E-IDE/Atapi	1 disc Tray	Internal	128kb

Manufacturer Model	Drive Type	Drive Speed	Drive Interface	# Discs & Loader	Internal-External	Buffer
BCD 56X	CDROM	56X	E-IDE/Atapi	1 disc Tray	Internal	128kb
BCD 739	CDROM	8X	EIDE	1 disc Tray	Internal	128k
BCD 8X	CDROM	8X	EIDE	1 disc Tray		256k
BCE 1281E	CD-RW	32Xr/12Xw/8Xrw	EIDE/ATAPI	1 disc Tray		2Mb
BCE 1610IM	CD-RW	40Xr/16Xw/10Xrw	EIDE/ATAPI	1 disc Tray		2Mb
BCE 2410IM	CD-RW	40Xr/32Xw/10Xrw	EIDE/ATAPI	1 disc Tray		2Mb
BCE 3212IM	CD-RW	32Xr/4Xw/4Xrw	EIDE/ATAPI	1 disc Tray	Internal	2Mb
BCE 432IE	CD-RW		EIDE/ATAPI	1 disc Tray	Internal	
BCE 621E	CD-RW	6Xr/2Xrw	EIDE	1 disc Tray	Internal	
BCE 62PE	CD-RW	6Xr/2Xrw	IDE/ATAPI	1 disc Tray	Internal	
BCE 833IE	CD-RW	32Xr/8Xw/4Xrw	EIDE/ATAPI	1 disc Tray	Internal	2Mb
BCO 4816IM	DVD/CD-RW	16Xdvd/cd48Xr48	EIDE/ATAPI	1 disc Tray	Internal	2mb
BDV 108A	DVD-ROM	32Xcd8Xdvd	EIDE/ATAPI	1 disc		512kb
BDV 212B	DVD-ROM	40Xcd/12Xdvd	EIDE/ATAPI	1 disc		256kb
BDV 316B	DVD-ROM	16Xdvd/48Xcd	EIDE/ATAPI	1 disc		512kb

CD Technology

Manufacturer Model	Drive Type	Drive Speed	Drive Interface	# Discs & Loader	Internal-External	Buffer
CD T3501 Porta-Drive	CDROM	4X	SCSI	1 disc	External	256k
CD T4100 Porta-Drive	CDROM	2X	SCSI	1 disc	Portable	64k
CD-T3201MAC	CDROM	2X	SCSI	1 disc Sony Caddy	External	64k
CD-T3201MCA	CDROM	2X	SCSI	1 disc Sony Caddy	External	64k
CD-T3201PC	CDROM	2X	SCSI	1 disc Sony Caddy	External	64k

Chinon America

Manufacturer Model	Drive Type	Drive Speed	Drive Interface	# Discs & Loader	Internal-External	Buffer
CDA-535	CDROM	2X	SCSI	1 disc Caddy		320k
CDS-430	CDROM	1X	Non-SCSI Pa	1 disc Tray	External	32k
CDS-435	CDROM	2X		1 disc Tray	Internal	
CDS-525	CDROM	2X	SCSI	1 disc Tray	Internal	64k
CDS-535	CDROM	2X	SCSI-2	1 disc Tray	Internal	256k
CDS-545	CDROM	2X	EIDE	1 disc	Internal	128k
CDX-431	CDROM	1X	SCSI	1 disc Sony Caddy	External	32k
CDX-535	CDROM	2X	SCSI	1 disc Caddy	Internal a	320k

Compaq

Manufacturer Model	Drive Type	Drive Speed	Drive Interface	# Discs & Loader	Internal-External	Buffer
217053-B21	DVD-ROM	4X	EIDE/Atapi	1 disc Tray	Internal	512k
223312-001	CDROM	12X	SCSI-2	disc	Internal	128k
264007-B21	DVD-ROM	8Xdvd/24Xcd	EIDE/Atapi	1 disc Tray	Internal	256k
295545-B21	CDROM	24X	IDE/ATAPI	1 disc Slot	Internal	128k
295888-B21	CDROM	8X	IDE/ATAPI	1 disc Tray		128k
388481-B21	DVD-ROM	8Xdvd	EIDE/ATAPI	1 disc Tray	Internal	512k

Creative Labs, Inc.

Manufacturer Model	Drive Type	Drive Speed	Drive Interface	# Discs & Loader	Internal-External	Buffer
Blaster CD 24X	CDROM	24X	EIDE	1 disc Tray	Internal	256k
Blaster CD 32X	CDROM	32X	EIDE	disc Tray	Internal	
Blaster CD 48X	CDROM	48X	EIDE	disc Tray	Internal	
Blaster CD 4X	CDROM	4X	IDE	1 disc		256k
Blaster CD 52X	CDROM	52X	EIDE/ATAPI	1 disc Tray	Internal	128kb
Blaster CD 6X	CDROM	6X	IDE	1 disc		256k
Blaster CD 8X	CDROM	8X	IDE	1 disc	Internal	
Blaster CD-RW 12/10/32	CD-RW	32Xr/12Xw/10Xrw	ATAPI	1 disc Tray	Internal	2Mb
Blaster CD-RW 24/10/4	CD-RW	24Xr/10Xw/4Xrw	USB 1.0	1 disc	External	2Mb
Blaster CD-RW 4224	CD-RW	24Xr/4Xw/2Xrw	Atapi	1 disc Tray	Internal	2Mb
Blaster CD-RW 6424	CD-RW	24Xr/6Xw/4Xrw		1 disc Tray	Internal	2Mb
Blaster CD-RW 8432	CD-RW	32Xr/8Xw/4Xrw		1 disc Tray	Internal	2Mb
CD 1220E	CDROM	12X	IDE/ATAPI	1 disc Tray	Internal	256k
CD 1220S	PC-DVD RA	2Xdvd	SCSI	disc Tray		2Mb
CD 1620E	CDROM	16X	IDE/ATAPI	1 disc Tray	Internal	256k
CD 200	CDROM	2X	Creative/MK	disc Tray	Internal	64k
CD 220E	CDROM	2X	Creative/MK	disc Tray	Internal	64k
CD 2422E	CDROM	24X	IDE/ATAPI	1 disc Tray	Internal	512k
CD 3230E	CDROM	32X	IDE/ATAPI	1 disc Tray	Internal	256kb
CD 3620E	CDROM	36X	Toshiba IDE	1 disc Tray		256k
CD 400T	CDROM	4X	IDE/ATAPI	1 disc Tray	Internal	256k
CD 420E	CDROM	4X	Creative PC	disc	External	256k
CD 420P	CDROM	4X	Creative PC	disc	External	256k
CD 4820E	CDROM	48X	IDE	1 disc Tray	Internal	256kb
CD 4830E	CDROM	48X	Atapi	1 disc Tray	Internal	128kb
CD 620E	CDROM	8X	IDE/ATAPI	1 disc Tray	Internal	256k
CD 820E	CDROM	8X	IDE	1 disc Tray	Internal	
CD 948E	CDROM	48X	SCSI-2	1 disc Caddy		512k
CDR 2000	CDROM	2X	NEC SCSI	1 disc Tray		64k
CDR 210	CDROM	4X	NEC IDE/ATA	1 disc Tray		256k
CDR 271	CDROM	4X	NEC IDE/ATA-1	1 disc Tray		128k
CDR 272	CDROM	4X	NEC IDE/ATA-1	1 disc Tray		128k
CDR 273	CDROM	4X	NEC IDE/ATA	1 disc Tray		256k
CDR 4210	CD-R	4Xr/2Xw	SCSI-2	1 disc Tray		256k
CDR 510	CDROM	3X	NEC SCSI	1 disc Tray		256k
CDR 7730	CDROM	4X	IDE/ATAPI	disc Tray	Internal	128k
CDU 33A	CDROM	2X	Sony interf	1 disc Tray		64k

Manufacturer Model	Drive Type	Drive Speed	Drive Interface	# Discs & Loader	Internal-External	Buffer
CDU 75E	CDROM	4X	Sony IDE/AT	1 disc Tray		256k
CR 521	CDROM	1X	Creative/Pa	1 disc Caddy	Internal	64k
CR 523	CDROM	1X	Creative/Pa	1 disc Caddy	Internal	64k
CR 531	CDROM	1X	Creative/Pa	1 disc Caddy	Internal	64k
CR 563	CDROM	2X	Creative/MK	disc Tray		64k
CR 574	CDROM	4X	MKE IDE/ATA	1 disc Tray		256k
CR 581	CDROM	4X	MKE IDE/ATA	1 disc Tray		128k
CR 583	CDROM	8X	IDE/ATAPI	1 disc Tray		128k
CR 585B	CDROM	24X	IDE	1 disc Tray		128k
CR 586-B	CDROM	32X	IDE	1 disc Tray		256k
CR 587B	CDROM	24X	IDE/ATAPI	1 disc Tray		128k
CRMC FX-120T	CDROM	12X	IDE/ATAPI	1 disc Tray		256k
DVD-2240E	DVD-ROM	2Xdvd/20Xcdrom	IDE/ATAPI	1 disc Tray		512k
DVD-6240E	DVD-ROM	6Xdvd/24Xcdrom	IDE	1 disc Tray	Internal	512k
GCD R580B	CDROM	8X	IDE/ATAPI	1 disc Tray		128k
PC-DVD Encore 12X	DVD-ROM	12Xdvd/40Xcdrom	IDE	1 disc Tray	Internal	512kb
PC-DVD Encore 5X	DVD-ROM	5Xdvd/32Xcdrom		1 disc Tray	Internal	512k
PC-DVD Encore 6X	DVD-ROM	6Xdvd/24Xcdrom	IDE	1 disc Tray	Internal	512kb
PC-DVD Encore 8X	DVD-ROM	8Xdvd/40Xcdrom		1 disc Tray	Internal	512kb
PC-DVD Encore Dxr2	DVD-ROM	2Xdvd/32Xcdrom	IDE	1 disc Tray	Internal	256k
PC-DVD Ovation 12X	DVD-ROM	12Xdvd/40Xcdrom	IDE	1 disc Tray	Internal	
PC-DVD Ovation 16X	DVD-ROM	16Xdvd/48Xcdrom		1 disc Tray	Internal	512k
PC-DVD RAM	DVD-RAM	2Xdvd/20Xcdrom	IDE	1 disc Tray	Internal	
PC-DVD RAM 5.2GB	DVD-RAM	2Xdvd/20Xcdrom	SCSI-2/Fast	1 disc Tray	Internal	2Mb
PC-DVD X2	DVD-ROM	2Xdvd/16Xcdrom	SCSI-2 Fast	1 disc Tray	Internal	2Mb
SCR 830	CDROM	8X	IDE/ATAPI	1 disc Tray		512k
SR 8581	DVD CDROM	1Xdvd/6Xcdrom	IDE/ATAPI	1 disc Tray		128k
Vibra 24X	CDROM	24X	IDE	1 disc Tray	Internal	256k

Delta Microsystems

SS-600C	CDROM	1X	SCSI	1 disc Sony Caddy External		8k

Denon America

DRD-253M	CDROM	1X	SCSI	1 disc Sony Caddy External		32k
DRD-253S	CDROM	1X	SCSI	1 disc Sony Caddy External		32k

Digital Equipment Company

24X CD/FD Combo	CDROM/FD	24X		1 disc		

Digital Equipment Company

32 MAX Atapi	CDROM	32X	Atapi	1 disc		
PowerFile C200	DVD/CD			200 disc		
RRD40 w/controller	CDROM	1X	SCSI 4 Driv	1 disc Philips Ca External		2k
RRD40 Slave	CDROM	1X	Qbus	1 disc Philips Ca External		2k
RRD40 Slave SCSI	CDROM	1X	SCSI	1 disc Philips Ca External		2k
RRD40 w/controller	CDROM	1X	Qbus 4 Driv	1 disc Philips Ca External		2k
RRD46-VA	CDROM	12X	SCSI	1 disc Tray	Internal	
RRD46-VU	CDROM	12X	SCSI	1 disc Tray	Internal	
RRD47	CDROM	32X	SCSI	1 disc Tray	Internal	

Digital Video Systems, Inc.

12832	CD-RW	32Xr/12Xw/8Xrw	EIDE/ATAPI	1 disc		2Mb
5.2X DVD	DVD-ROM	5.2Xdvd/32Xcdro	EIDE/ATAPI	disc	Internal	512k
6.2X DVD-ROM	DVD-ROM	6.2Xdvd/32Xcdro	EIDE/ATAPI	1 disc	Internal	512k
CD-20	CDROM	20X	Parallel Po	disc	External	
CD-24	CDROM	24X	Parallel Po	disc	External	
CD-32	CDROM	32X	Parallel Po	disc	External	
CD-R 4x12e	CD-R	12Xr/4Xw	SCSI-2	1 disc Tray	External	1Mb
CD-R 4x12i	CD-R	12Xr/4Xw	SCSI-2	1 disc Tray	Internal	1Mb
CD-RW 2x6i	CD-RW	6Xr/2Xw	IDE/ATAPI	1 disc Tray	Internal	1Mb
CD-RW 2x6p	CD-RW	6Xr/2Xw	EPP Paralle	disc Tray	External	1Mb
DSL-710A	DVD Loadr	dvd2Xcd4X	ATAPI	1 disc		512k
DSR-1600H	DVD-ROM	16Xdvd	EIDE/ATAPI			256k

DynaTek Automation Sys, Inc

CDM400	CDROM	4Xr/4Xw	SCSI	1 disc	Internal	512k

Fidelity Int'l Technologies

TCD4X-P	CDROM	4X	Parallel SC	disc Tray	External	
TCD6X-P	CDROM	6X	Parallel SC	1 disc Tray	External	

Funai Electric Co., Ltd.

E2420	CDROM	2X	ISA	1 disc Tray	Internal	
E2450	CDROM	2X	ISA	1 disc Tray	Internal	
E2550UA	CDROM	2X	Creative/MK	1 disc Tray	Internal	64k
E2620UA	CDROM	6X		1 disc Tray	Internal	
E2650	CDROM	6X	IDE/ATAPI	1 disc Tray	Internal	
E2720UA	CDROM	4X		1 disc Tray	Internal	

Manufacturer Model	Drive Type	Drive Speed	Drive Interface	# Discs & Loader	Internal-External	Buffer
E2750UA	CDROM	4X	IDE/ATAPI	1 disc Tray	Internal	128k
E2800UA	CDROM	2X	Creative/MK	1 disc Tray	Internal	64k
E2820	CDROM	8X		1 disc Tray	Internal	
E2850	CDROM	8X	IDE/ATAPI	1 disc Tray	Internal	
E2920	CDROM	16X		1 disc Tray	Internal	
E2950UA	CDROM	16X		1 disc Tray	Internal	
E2960	CDROM	16X	IDE/ATAPI	1 disc Tray	Internal	

Goldstar Electronics Int'l, In

GCD-R320B	CDROM	2X	SCSI	1 disc Tray	Internal	64k
GCD-R540B	CDROM	4X	IDE/ATAPI	1 disc Tray	Internal	128k
GCD-R56B	CDROM	6X	IDE	1 disc Tray	Internal	
GCD-R580B	CDROM	8X	EIDE	1 disc Tray	Internal	256k

Hewlett-Packard Company

CD-2807A	CDROM	32X	SCSI-2	disc		512k
CD-2896A	CDROM	4X	IDE/ATAPI	1 disc Tray	Internal	256k
CD-2989A	CDROM	32X	SCSI-2	disc	External	256k
CD-4020i	CDROM wri	4xrd/2xrec	SCSI-2	1 disc Tray	Internal	1Mb
CD-6020ep	CDROM wri	6Xrd/2Xrec	parallel SC	1 disc Tray	External	1Mb
CD-6020es	CDROM wri	6XRd/2Xrec	SCSI-2	1 disc Tray	External	1Mb
CD-6020i	CDROM wri	6XRd/2Xrec	SCSI-2	1 disc Tray	Internal	1Mb
CD-6100/600/A	CDROM	1X	HP-1B (IEEE	1 disc Philips Ca	External	12k
CD-7110e	CD-RW	2X/2X/6X	Parallel Po	1 disc Tray	External	1Mb
CD-7110i	CD-RW	2X/2X/6X	IDE	1 disc Tray	Internal	1Mb
CD-7200e	CD-RW	6Xr/2Xw	Parallel	1 disc Tray	External	1Mb
CD-7200i	CD-RW	6Xr/2Xw	EIDE/ATAPI	1 disc Tray	Internal	1Mb
CD-7570i	CD-RW	24Xr/4Xw	EIDE/ATAPI	1 disc Tray	Internal	1Mb
CD-8100i	CDROM	24Xr/4Xw	EIDE/ATAPI	disc Tray	Internal	1Mb
CD-8110i	CD-RW	24Xr/4Xw	EIDE/ATAPI	disc Tray	Internal	1Mb
CD-9500i	CD-RW	32Xr/10Xw/4Xw	EIDE/ATAPI	1 disc Tray	Internal	4Mb
CD-9510i	CD-RW	32Xr/10Xw/4Xw	SCSI-2	1 disc Tray	Internal	4Mb
CD-9600se	CD-RW	32Xr/12Xw/8Xw	EIDE/ATAPI	1 disc Tray	Internal	4Mb
CD-9600si	CD-RW	32Xr/12Xw/8Xw	SCSI-2	1 disc Tray	Internal	4Mb
CD-9700i	CD-RW	40Xr/16Xw/10Xrw	EIDE/ATAPI	1 disc Tray	Internal	8Mb
CD-9710i	CD-RW	40Xr/16Xw/10Xrw	EIDE/ATAPI	1 disc Tray	Internal	8Mb
CD-9900ci	CD-RW/DVD	32Xr/12X/10X/8X	IDE	1 disc Tray	Internal	2Mb
CD-Writer Plus 7500e	CD-RW	6Xr/2Xrw	IEEE1284 co	1 disc Tray	External	1Mb
CD-Writer Plus 7500i	CD-RW	6Xr/2Xrw	IEEE1284 co	1 disc Tray	Internal	1Mb
CD-Writer Plus 7510E	CD-RW	6Xr/2Xrw	IEEE1284 co	1 disc Tray	External	1Mb
CD-Writer Plus 7550i	CD-RW	24Xr/2Xw/2Xrw	Atapi/EIDE	1 disc Tray	Internal	1Mb
CD-Writer Plus 7570i	CD-RW	24Xr/2Xw/2Xrw	Atapi/EIDE	1 disc Tray	Internal	1Mb
CD-Writer Plus 8200e	CD-RW	6Xr/4Xw	USB	1 disc Tray	External	2Mb
CD-Writer Plus 8200i	CD-RW	24Xr/4Xw/4Xrw	Atapi/EIDE	1 disc Tray	Internal	2Mb
CD-Writer Plus 8210i	CD-RW	24Xr/4Xw/4Xrw	Atapi/EIDE	1 disc Tray	Internal	2Mb
CD-Writer Plus 8250i	CD-RW	24Xr/4Xw/4Xrw	EIDE/ATAPI	1 disc Tray	Internal	4Mb
CD-Writer Plus 9100i	CD-RW	32Xr/8Xw/4Xrw	EIDE/ATAPI	1 disc Tray	Internal	4Mb
CD-Writer Plus 9110i	CD-RW	32Xr/8Xw/4Xrw	EIDE/ATAPI	1 disc Tray	Internal	4Mb
CD-Writer Plus 9200e	CD-RW	32Xr/8Xw/4Xrw	SCSI-2	1 disc Tray	External	4Mb
CD-Writer Plus 9200i	CD-RW	32Xr/8Xw/4Xrw	SCSI-2	1 disc Tray	Internal	4Mb
CD-Writer Plus 9210e	CD-RW	32Xr/8Xw/4Xrw	SCSI-2	1 disc Tray	External	4Mb
CD-Writer Plus 9210i	CD-RW	32Xr/8Xw/4Xrw	SCSI-2	1 disc Tray	Internal	4Mb
CD-Writer Plus 9300i	CD-RW	32Xr/10Xw/4Xrw	IDE	1 disc Tray	Internal	4Mb
CD-Writer Plus 9310i	CD-RW	32Xr/10Xw/4Xrw	IDE	1 disc Tray	Internal	4Mb
CD-Writer Plus M820e	CD-RW	20Xr/4Xw/4Xrw	PCMCIA	1 disc Top Ld	External	2Mb
cd12	CD-RW	32Xr/12Xw/10Xrw	IDE	1 disc Tray	Internal	
cd16	CD-RW	40Xr/16Xw/10Xrw	IDE	1 disc Tray	Internal	
cd24	CD-RW	40Xr/24Xw/10Xrw	IDE	1 disc Tray	Internal	
cd4	CD-RW	4X4X6X6	USB		External	
DVD 100i	DVDRW	2.4dvd32r12w10	IDE/ATAPI	1 disc Tray	Internal	2Mb
DVD 200e	DVDRW	2.4dvd/32/12/10	USB 2.0	1 disc Tray	External	
DVD 200i	DVD+RW	2.4dvd/32/12/10	IDE/ATAPI	1 disc Tray	Internal	2Mb
DVD Writer 3100	DVD-RW			disc		

Hi-Val

12X10X32	CD-RW	32Xr/12Xw/10Xrw	EIDE/ATAPI	1 disc Tray		
16X	CDROM-Cha	16X	EIDE	5 disc Direct Ld	External	
16X HotPort	CDROM	16X	IDE	1 disc Tray	External	
16X10X40	CD-RW	40Xr/16Xw/10Xrw	EIDE/ATAPI	1 disc Tray	Internal	
24X	CDROM	24X	IDE/ATAPI	1 disc Tray	External	128k
24X MAX EIDE	CDROM	24X	EIDE	1 disc Slot	External	
24X MAX SCSI	CDROM	24X	SCSI	1 disc Tray	Internal	128kb
24X(Portable)	CDROM	24X	PCMCIA Type	1 disc Tray	External	
24X10X40	CD-RW	40Xr/24Xw/10Xrw	EIDE/ATAPI	1 disc Tray	Internal	
24X10X40	CD-RW	40Xr/24Xw/10Xrw	USB 2.0	1 disc Tray	External	
2X24X2 Ritestore Gold EIDE	CD-RW	24Xr/2Xw/2Xrw	EIDE	1 disc Dbl Float T	Internal	2Mb
2X6 EPP	CD-R	2Xrec/6Xp	EPP to IDE	1 disc	External	1Mb
2X6 HotPort	CD-R	2Xrec/6Xpl	EIDE/ATAPI	1 disc Tray	External	1Mb
2X8	CD-R	2Xw/6Xr	EIDE/ATAPI	1 disc	Internal	1Mb
2X8 EPP	CD-R	2Xrec/8Xpl	EPP to EIDE	1 disc Tray	External	1Mb

Manufacturer Model	Drive Type	Drive Speed	Drive Interface	# Discs & Loader	Internal-External	Buffer
2X8 HotPort	CD-R	2Xrec/8Xpl	IDE	1 disc Tray	External	1Mb
32X MAX	CDROM	32X	EIDE	1 disc Slot	Internal	
32X Pioneer EasyLoad	CDROM	32X	EIDE	1 disc Slot	Internal	
32X10X40	CD-RW	40Xr/32Xw/10Xrw	EIDE/ATAPI	1 disc Tray	Internal	2Mb
36X MAX	CDROM	36X	EIDE	1 disc Tray	Internal	
4.8X DVD-ROM	DVD-ROM	4.8Xdvd/32Xcd-r	EIDE	1 disc Tray	Internal	256k
40X MAX	CDROM	40X	EIDE	1 disc Tray	Internal	
40X SCSI	CDROM	40X	SCSI	1 disc Tray	Internal	
45X EIDE	CDROM	45X	EIDE	1 disc Tray	Internal	128kb
48X EIDE	CDROM	48X	EIDE	1 disc Tray	Internal	512kb
4X4X16 EIDE	CD-RW	16Xr/4Xw/4Xrw	EIDE	1 disc Tray	Internal	2Mb
4X4X16 SCSI	CD-RW	16Xr/4Xw/4Xrw	SCSI-2	1 disc Tray	Internal	2Mb
4X4X24	CD-RW	24X	EIDE	1 disc Tray	Internal	2Mb
4X4X32	CD-RW	32X	EIDE	1 disc Tray	Internal	2Mb
4X4X6	CD-RW	6Xr/4Xw/4Xrw	USB 1.0	1 disc Tray	External	2Mb
4X8 IDE	CD-R	4Xw/8Xr	IDE/ATAPI	1 disc Tray	Internal	
50X EIDE	CDROM	50X	Atapi/EIDE	1 disc Tray	Internal	128kb
52X EIDE	CDROM	52X	EIDE	1 disc Tray	Internal	512kb
56X Max	CDROM	56X	EIDE	1 disc Tray	Internal	512kb
6X24 SCSI	CD-R	24Xr/6Xw	SCSI	1 disc Tray	Internal	
6X2X2X	CD-RW	6Xr/2Xw/2Xrw	EIDE/ATAPI	1 disc Tray	Internal	2Mb
HDVD10AS-00R	DVD-ROM	10Xdvd	EIDE/ATAPI	1 disc Tray	Internal	1Mb
HDVD10X-00R	DVD-ROM	10Xdvd	EIDE	1 disc Slot	Internal	
HDVD12A-16R	DVD-ROM	12Xdvd/40Xcd	EIDE	1 disc		512k
HDVD16A-16R	DVD-ROM	16Xdvd/40Xcd	EIDE	1 disc		512k
HDVD6S-00R	DVD-ROM	6Xdvd	SCSI	1 disc	Internal	
HDVD6X-00R	DVD-ROM	6Xdvd	EIDE	1 disc	Internal	
HDVD8X-00R	DVD-ROM	8Xdvd	EIDE	1 disc	Internal	
HDVDR-00R	DVD-RAM		SCSI	1 disc Tray	Internal	2Mb
HV6200	CD-RW	6Xr/2Xw	SCSI -2	1 disc Tray	Internal	1Mb
True40X40	CDROM	40X	EIDE/ATAPI	1 disc Tray	Internal	2048k

Hitachi America, Ltd.

Manufacturer Model	Drive Type	Drive Speed	Drive Interface	# Discs & Loader	Internal-External	Buffer
CDR-1503S	CDROM			disc	External	
CDR-1520S	CDROM			disc	External	
CDR-1700S	CDROM		SCSI	1 disc	Internal	
CDR-1750S	CDROM		SCSI	1 disc	Internal	
CDR-1900S	CDROM		SCSI	1 disc	Internal	
CDR-1950S	CDROM	2X	Hitachi Bus	1 disc Caddy	External	128k
CDR-2500S	CDROM	2X	SCSI-2	1 disc Caddy	External	256k
CDR-3500	CDROM			disc	External	
CDR-3600	CDROM			disc	Internal	
CDR-3650	CDROM			disc	Internal	
CDR-3700	CDROM			disc		
CDR-3750	CDROM			disc	Internal	
CDR-6700	CDROM			disc		
CDR-6750	CDROM	2X	Hitachi Bus	1 disc Caddy	Internal	128k
CDR-7730	CDROM	2X	SCSI-2	1 disc Caddy	Internal	256k
CDR-7830	CDROM	4X	IDE/ATAPI	1 disc Tray	Internal	256k
CDR-7930	CDROM	8X	IDE		disc	
CDR-8130	CDROM	16X	EIDE/ATAPI	1 disc Tray	Internal	
CDR-8230	CDROM	20X	EIDE/ATAPI	disc		128k
CDR-8235	CDROM	24X	EIDE/ATAPI	1 disc Tray	Internal	128k
CDR-8330	CDROM	24X	EIDE/ATAPI	disc		128k
CDR-8335	CDROM	24X	EIDE/ATAPI	1 disc Tray	Internal	128k
CDR-8430	CDROM	32X	EIDE/ATAPI	disc 1	Internal	
CDR-8435	CDROM	32X	EIDE/ATAPI	disc		128k
GD-1000	DVD-ROM	8X	EIDE/ATAPI	1 disc Tray	Internal	256k
GD-2000	DVD-ROM	2Xdvd/20Xcav cd	EIDE/ATAPI	1 disc	Internal	512k
GD-2500 BV	DVD-ROM	4Xdvd/24Xcdrom	EIDE/ATAPI	1 disc	Internal	512k
GD-2500 BX	DVD-ROM	6Xdvd/24Xcdrom	EIDE/ATAPI	disc	Internal	512k
GD-5000	DVD-ROM	8Xdvd/40Xcd	EIDE/ATAPI	1 disc	Internal	512k
GD-7000	DVD-ROM	8Xdvd	EIDE/ATAPI	1 disc	Internal	512k
GD-7500	DVD-ROM	12Xdvd	EIDE/ATAPI	1 disc	Internal	512k
GD-8000	DVD-ROM	16Xdvd	EIDE/ATAPI	1 disc	Internal	512k
GF-1000	DVD-RAM		ATAPI		Internal	
GF-1050	DVD-RAM	2.76dvd-rom/1.3	Fast SCSI-2	1 disc Tray	Internal	1Mb
GF-2000	DVD-RAM	12Xdvd	SCSI	1 disc	Internal	2MB
GF-2050	DVD-RAM	12Xdvd	UltraSCSI	1 disc	Internal	2MB

Hitachi New Media

Manufacturer Model	Drive Type	Drive Speed	Drive Interface	# Discs & Loader	Internal-External	Buffer
CD-MAC	CDROM	1X	SCSI	1 disc Sony Caddy	External	64k
CDR-1503BZ	CDROM	1X	Non-SCSI Pa	1 disc Tray	External	32k
CDR-1503S	CDROM	1X	Non-SCSI Pa	1 disc Tray	External	32k
CDR-1600	CDROM	1X	Non-SCSI Pa	1 disc Sony Caddy	External	32k
CDR-1600SY	CDROM	1X	Non-SCSI Pa	1 disc Sony Caddy	External	32k
CDR-1600SZ	CDROM	1X	Non-SCSI Pa	1 disc Sony Caddy	External	32k
CDR-1650	CDROM	1X	SCSI	1 disc Sony Caddy	External	64k

Hitachi Sales Corporation

Manufacturer Model	Drive Type	Drive Speed	Drive Interface	# Discs & Loader	Internal-External	Buffer
CDR-1503S-MC	CDROM	1X	Non-SCSI Pa	1 disc Tray	External	8k
CDR-1503S-PC	CDROM	1X	Non-SCSI Pa	1 disc Tray	External	32k

IBM

Manufacturer Model	Drive Type	Drive Speed	Drive Interface	# Discs & Loader	Internal-External	Buffer
24X/4X/2X	CD-RW	24Xr/4Xw/2Xrw	EIDE	1 disc	Internal	1Mb
2X Internal SCSI	CDROM	2X	SCSI-2	1 disc Tray	Internal	256k
32X Internal IDE	CDROM	32X	IDE	1 disc Tray	Internal	128k
4X CD External SCSI	CDROM	4X	SCSI-2	1 disc Tray	External	256k
4X PCMCIA	CDROM	4X	PCMCIA Type	disc	External	128k
4X PCMCIA Stereo	CDROM	4X	PCMCIA Type	disc	External	128k
6X Internal IDE	CDROM	6X	IDE	1 disc Tray	Internal	
7210 Model 015 External	CDROM		SCSI-2	1 disc Tray	External	
7210 Model 020 External	CDROM	32X	SCSI-2	1 disc Tray	External	256k
Ext CD-ROM Drive	CDROM	1X	SCSI	1 disc Sony Caddy External		64k
IDE 16XMAX	CDROM	16X	IDE/ATAPI	1 disc Tray	Internal	128k
PS/2 Ext CD-ROM Drive	CDROM	1X	SCSI	1 disc Sony Caddy External		64k
SCSI 8X	CDROM	8X	SCSI-2	1 disc Tray	Internal	256k
SCSI 8X External	CDROM	8X	SCSI-2	1 disc Tray	External	256k
TP 2X DVD	DVD-ROM	2Xdvd/16Xcdrom	ATAPI	1 disc	Internal	
TP 365X/XD 8X Int IDE	CDROM	8X	IDE/ATAPI	1 disc	Internal	128k
TP 380/385 8X IDE	CDROM	8X	IDE/ATAPI	1 disc	Internal	128k
TP 600 24X-10X Int IDE	CDROM	24X	IDE	1 disc	Internal	256k
TP 760/765 20X-8X IDE	CDROM	20X	ATAPI	1 disc	Internal	128k
TP 770 24X-10X Int	CDROM	24X	IDE	1 disc	Internal	128k
TP DVD Ultraslim	DVD-ROM	20Xcdrom	ATAPI	1 disc	Internal	512k

Imation Corp

Manufacturer Model	Drive Type	Drive Speed	Drive Interface	# Discs & Loader	Internal-External	Buffer
IMR080020ES	CD-R	20Xr/8Xw	SCSI	1 disc	External	4Mb
IMR080020IS	CD-R	20Xr/4Xw	SCSI	1 disc	Internal	4Mb
IMW040420EA	CD-RW	20Xr/4Xw/4Xrw	EIDE/Atapi	1 disc	External	2Mb
IMW040420IA	CD-RW	20Xr/4Xw/4Xrw	EIDE/atapi	1 disc	Internal	2Mb

Iomega

Manufacturer Model	Drive Type	Drive Speed	Drive Interface	# Discs & Loader	Internal-External	Buffer
31025	CD-RW	32Xr/8Xw/4Xrw	ATAPI		Internal	
31120	CD-RW	32Xr/12Xw/10Xrw	ATAPI		Internal	
31429	CD-RW	40Xr/16Xw/10Xrw	ATAPI		Internal	
CD-RW 24X10X40	CD-RW	40Xr/24Xw/10Xrw	USB		Internal	2MB
Predator 32X8X4X	CD-RW	32Xr/8Xw/4Xrw	IEEE1394	1 disc	Portable	
ZipCD 650	CD-RW	24Xr/4Xrw	EIDE/Atapi	1 disc	Internal	2Mb
ZipCD 650 10X10X32	CD-RW	32Xr/12Xw/4Xrw	ATAPI	1 disc	Internal	2mb
ZipCD 650 12X4X32	CD-RW	32Xr/12Xw/4Xrw	ATAPI	1 disc	Internal	1.8mb
ZipCD 650 4X4X24	CD-RW	24Xr/4Xw/4Xrw	ATAPI	1 disc	Internal	2mb
ZipCD 650 4X4X6	CD-RW	6Xr/4Xw/4Xrw	USB	1 disc	Internal	2mb
ZipCD 650 6X4X24X4	DVD	4dvd/24r/6w/4rw	ATAPI	1 disc	Internal	1.8mb
ZipCD 650 8X4X32	CD-RW	32Xr/8Xw/4Xrw	ATAPI	1 disc	Internal	2mb

JVC Company of America

Manufacturer Model	Drive Type	Drive Speed	Drive Interface	# Discs & Loader	Internal-External	Buffer
JVC CD-R50S	CD-R	4Xr/4Xrec	SCSI-2	1 disc Tray		1 Mb
JVC CD-R55S	CD-R	12Xr/4Xrec	SCSI-2	1 disc Tray		1 Mb
JVC CDR-100	CDROM	4Xr/4Xw/4Xrec	SCSI-2	1 disc Caddy	Internal	512k
JVC MC-1100	CDROM Lib		SCSI-2	100 disc Slot		
JVC MC-1200	CDROM Lib	32X	SCSI-2	200 disc Slot	External	256k
JVC MC-1600	CDROM Lib	32X	SCSI-2	600 disc Slot	External	256k
JVC MC-2100	CD/DVD Li	32Xcd	SCSI-2	100 disc Slot		
JVC MC-2200	CDROM Lib		SCSI-2	200 disc Slot		
JVC MC-2600	CDROM Lib		SCSI-2	600 disc Slot		
JVC MC-7100	DVD-RAM L	4-1Xdvd-ram	SCSI-2	100 disc Mag SI External		1Mb
JVC MC-7200	DVD-RAM L	6-1Xdvd-ram	SCSI-2	200 disc Mag SI External		1Mb
JVC MC-7600	DVD-RAM L	6-1Xdvd-ram	SCSI-2	600 disc Cart SI External		1Mb
JVC MC-D104U	DVD-ROM	4Xdvd/24Xcdrom	SCSI-2	1 disc	Internal	512k
JVC MC-D18U	CDROM	8X	SCSI-2	1 disc	Internal	256k
JVC MC-D32U	CDROM	32X	Ultra SCSI	1 disc	Internal	512k
JVC MC-R12U	CD-R	4Xr/2Xw	SCSI-2	1 disc	Internal	512k
JVC MC-R14U	CD-R	12X/4Xw	SCSI-2	1 disc	Internal	1 Mb
JVC MC-R200U	DVD-RAM	1Xdvd-ram	SCSI-2	disc	Internal	1Mb
MC-2000	DVD/CDJuk			disc		
Personal RomMaker	CDROM-Rec	2X	SCSI-2	1 disc Caddy		1Mb
XR-R100	CDROM	1X	SCSI	1 disc JVC Caddy	External	24k
XR-RW2224	CD-R/RW	24Xr/8Xw/2Xrw	ATAPI	1 disc Tray	Internal	2Mb
XR-RW4224	CD-R/RW	24Xr/4Xw/2Xrw	ATAPI	1 disc Tray	Internal	2Mb
XR-RW4424	CD-R/RW	24Xr/4Xw/4Xrw	ATAPI	1 disc Tray	Internal	2Mb
XR-W1001	CD-R	1Xr/1Xrec	SCSI-2	1 disc Caddy	Internal	64k
XR-W2001	CD-R	2Xr/2Xrec	SCSI-2	1 disc Caddy	Internal	1 Mb
XR-W2010	CD-R	4Xr/2Xrec	SCSI-2	1 disc Tray	Internal	1 Mb
XR-W2020	CD-R	6Xr/2Xrec	SCSI-2	1 disc Tray	Internal	1 Mb
XR-W2022	CD-R	6Xr/2Xw	SCSI-2	1 disc		1 Mb
XR-W2040	CD-R	6Xr/2Xrec/2Xrw	SCSI-2	1 disc Tray		1Mb
XR-W2042	CD-RW	6Xr/2Xw	SCSI-2	1 disc Tray		1Mb

Manufacturer Model	Drive Type	Drive Speed	Drive Interface	# Discs & Loader	Internal-External	Buffer
XR-W2080	CD-R	24Xr/2Xrec/2Xrw	ATA/ATAPI-4	1 disc Tray	Internal	2 Mb
XR-W4082	CD-R/RW	24Xr/4Xw/2Xrw	ATAPI	1 disc Tray	Internal	2Mb

L G Electronics USA Inc

CED-8040B	CD-RW	8Xr/2Xrw/4Xw	EIDE/ATAPI	1 disc Tray	Internal	2Mb
CED-8041B	CD-RW	8Xr/2Xrw/4Xw	EIDE/ATAPI	1 disc Tray	Internal	2Mb
CED-8042B	CD-RW	24X/4Xw	Atapi/EIDE	1 disc Tray	Internal	2Mb
CED-8080B	CD-RW	32X/8Xw/4Xw	EIDE/ATAPI	1 disc Tray	Internal	2Mb
CED-8083B	CD-RW	32X/4Xw/4Xrw	EIDE/ATAPI	1 disc Tray	Internal	2Mb
CED-8120B	CD-RW	32Xr/12Xw/8Xrw	EIDE/ATAPI	1 disc Tray	Internal	8Mb
CRD-8160B	CDROM	16X		1 disc Tray1	Internal	128k
CRD-8161B	CDROM	16X		1 disc Slot	Internal	128k
CRD-8240B	CDROM	24X	IDE	1 disc Tray	Internal	128k
CRD-8241B	CDROM	24X	IDE	1 disc Slot	Internal	128k
CRD-8320B	CDROM	32X	EIDE/ATAPI	1 disc Tray	Internal	128k
CRD-8322B	CDROM	32X	EIDE/ATAPI	1 disc Slot	Internal	128k
CRD-8400B	CDROM	40X	EIDE/ATAPI	1 disc Tray	Internal	128k
CRD-8480B	CDROM	48X	Atapi/EIDE	1 disc Tray	Internal	128k
CRD-8480C	CDROM	48X	EIDE/ATAPI	1 disc Tray	Internal	128k
CRD-8480M	CDROM	48X	EIDE/ATAPI	1 disc Tray	Internal	128k
CRD-8481B	CDROM	48X	EIDE/ATAPI	1 disc Tray	Internal	128k
CRD-8482B	CDROM	48X	EIDE/ATAPI	1 disc Tray	Internal	128k
CRD-8520B	CD-RW	52X	EIDE/ATAPI	1 disc Tray	Internal	128k
CRD-8521B	CD-RW	52X	EIDE/ATAPI	1 disc Tray	Internal	128k
CRD-8522B	CD-RW	52X	EIDE/ATAPI	1 disc Tray	Internal	128k
CRN-8240E	CDROM	24X	EIDE/ATAPI	1 disc Tray	Portable	128k
DAD-8020B	DVDRAM/RW		EIDE/ATAPI	1 disc Tray	Internal	
DRD-8080B	DVD-ROM	8Xdvd/36Xcdrom	Atapi 2.8/E	1 disc Tray	Internal	512k
DRD-810B	DVD-ROM	1Xdvd/8Xcdrom	ATAPI 2.6	1 disc Tray	Internal	512k
DRD-8120B	DVD-ROM	12Xdvd/40Xcdrom	EIDE/ATAPI	1 disc Tray	Internal	512kb
DRD-8160B	DVD-ROM	16Xdvd/48Xcd	EIDE/ATAPI	1 disc Tray	Internal	512k
GCC-4120B	DVD/CD-RW	8X/32X/12X/8X	EIDE/ATAPI	1 disc Tray	Internal	2Mb
GCE-8160B	CD-RW	40Xr/16Xw/10Xrw	EIDE/ATAPI	1 disc Tray	Internal	2Mb
GCE-8240B	CD-RW	40Xr/24Xw/10Xrw	EIDE/ATAPI	1 disc Tray	Internal	8Mb
GCE-8320B	CD-RW	40Xr/32Xw/10Xrw	EIDE/ATAPI	1 disc Tray	Internal	8Mb
GCR-8521B	CD-ROM	52X	EIDE/ATAPI	1 disc Tray	Internal	128k

LaCie

16X/10X/40X IEEE 1394	CD-RW	40Xr/16Xw/10Xrw	FireWire	1 disc Tray	Internal	8Mb
16X/10X/40X IEEE 1394 (burn)	CD-RW	40Xr/16Xw/10Xrw	FireWire	1 disc Tray	Internal	8Mb
24X/10X/40X CD-RW	CD-RW	40Xr/24Xw/10Xrw	USB 2.0	1 disc Tray		2Mb
2X/2X/6X	CD-RW	6Xr/2Xw/2Xrw	SCSI-2	1 disc Tray		1Mb
2X/6X	CD-R	6Xr/2Xw	SCSI-2	1 disc Caddy		512k
32X10X40X	CD-RW	40Xr/32Xw/10Xrw	USB 2.0	1 disc Tray		2Mb
40X IDE	CDROM	40X	Atapi	1 disc Tray		128kb
40X SCSI	CDROM	40X	SCSI-2	1 disc Tray	External	512kb
4X/12X	CD-R	12Xr/4Xw	SCSI-2	1 disc Tray		1Mb
4X/4X/16X	CD-RW	16Xr/4Xw/4Xrw	SCSI-2	1 disc Tray		1Mb
4X/6X	CD-R	6Xr/4Xw	SCSI-2	1 disc Tray		2Mb
4X/8X	CD-R	8Xr/4Xw	SCSI-2	1 disc Tray		1Mb
6/24X	CD-R	24Xr/6Xw	SCSI-2	1 disc Tray		2Mb
6X/4X/16X	CD-RW	16Xr/6Xw/4Xrw	SCSI-2	1 disc Tray	Internal	2Mb
8X/4X/32X IEEE 1394	CD-RW	32Xr/8Xw/4Xrw	FireWire	1 disc Tray		2Mb
CDC32	CDROM	32X	SCSI-2	1 disc Tray		512kb
CDR 820 8X/20X	CD-R	20Xr/8Xw	SCSI-2	1 disc Tray		2Mb
CDRW-8220 (8X/2X/20X)	CD-RW	20Xr/8Xrec/2Xrw	SCSI-2	1 disc Tray		2Mb
DVD-R 4.7GB	DVD-R	6Xdvd/24Xcd	FireWire	1 disc Tray		2Mb
DVD-RW 4.7GB	DVD-RW	4Xdvd/24Xcd	FireWire	1 disc Tray		2Mb
DVDAH52	DVD-RAM		SCSI-2	1 disc		
DVDAM52	DVD-RAM		SCSI-2	1 disc		
PocketCD-RW 16X10X24	CD-RW	24Xr/16Xw/10Xrw	IEEE 1394	1 disc Tray	Portable	2Mb
PocketCD-RW 8X8X24X	CD-RW	24Xr/8Xw/8Xrw	IEEE 1394	1 disc Tray	Portable	2Mb
SCSI 40X	CDROM	40X	SCSI-2	1 disc Tray		128kb
SCSI Dupli 40X	CDROM	40X	SCSI-2	1 disc Tray		512kb
SCSI DVD-RAM	DVD-RAM		SCSI-2, fas	1 disc Front End T		2Mb
UCB 4X/2X/8X	CD-RW	8Xr/4Xw/2Xrw	USB	1 disc Tray		2Mb
USB 2X/2X/6X	CDROM	6Xr/2Xw/2Xrw	USB	1 disc Tray		1Mb

Laser Magnetic Storage

CM121	CDROM	1X	Serial	1 disc Philips Ca External		2k
CM131	CDROM	1X	SCSI	1 disc Philips Ca External		2k
CM206	CDROM		AT	1 disc Tray	Internal	
CM215	CDROM		SCSI	1 disc Tray	Internal	
CM221	CDROM	1X	Serial	1 disc Philips Ca External		2k
CM231	CDROM	1X	SCSI	1 disc Philips Ca External		64k

Lite-On Technology

10X ATAPI DVD-ROM	DVD-ROM	10Xdvd/40Xcdrom	EIDE/ATAPI	1 disc		
12X/4X/32X	CD-RW	32X/12Xw/4Xrw	SCSI-3	1 disc	Internal	

Manufacturer Model	Drive Type	Drive Speed	Drive Interface	# Discs & Loader	Internal-External	Buffer
16X ATAPI DVD-ROM	DVD-ROM	16Xdvd/48Xcdrom	EIDE/ATAPI	disc		
24Xmax ATAPI	CDROM	24X	ATAPI/EIDE	1 disc	Internal	
24Xmax Slim-Type			ATAPI	1 disc	Internal	
2W24R	CD-RW		ATAPI	1 disc	Internal	
2W6R ATAPI CD-RW	CD-RW	6Xr/2Xw	ATAPI/EIDE	1 disc	Internal	
32Xmax ATAPI	CDROM	32X	ATAPI/EIDE	1 disc Flot Loader	Internal	
36Xmax ATAPI	CDROM	36X	ATAPI/EIDE	1 disc	Internal	
4X ATAPI DVD	DVD-ROM	4Xdvd	ATAPI	1 disc	Internal	
8X/4X/32X	CD-RW		EIDE/ATAPI	1 disc	Internal	
LSD-081	DVD-ROM	8Xdvd/24Xcd	EIDE/ATAPI	1 disc Tray		
LSD-082	DVD-ROM	8Xdvd/24Xcd	EIDE/ATAPI	1 disc Slot		
LTD-061	DVD-ROM	6Xdvd/32Xcd	EIDE/ATAPI	1 disc Tray		
LTD-102	DVD-ROM	10Xdvd/40Xcd	EIDE/ATAPI	1 disc Tray		
LTD-122	DVD-ROM	12Xdvd/40Xcd	EIDE/ATAPI	1 disc Tray		
LTD-163	DVD-ROM	16Xdvd/48Xcd	EIDE/ATAPI	1 disc Tray		
LTD-165	DVD-ROM	16Xdvd/48Xcd	EIDE/ATAPI	1 disc Tray		
LTN-222 12X	CDROM	12X	ATAPI/EIDE	1 disc	Internal	256k
LTN-262 16X	CDROM	16X	ATAPI/EIDE	1 disc	Internal	256k
LTN-323	CDROM	32X	ATAPI/EIDE	1 disc		
LTN-382	CDROM	40X	ATAPI/EIDE	1 disc Float Loade	Internal	
LTN-403	CDROM	40X	ATAPI/EIDE	1 disc		
LTN-483	CDROM	48X	ATAPI/EIDE	1 disc		
LTN-485S	CDROM	48X	EIDE/ATAPI	1 disc Tray		
LTN-486S	CDROM	48X	ATAPI/EIDE	1 disc	Internal	
LTN-525	CDROM	52X	EIDE/ATAPI	1 disc Tray		
LTN-526	CD-RW	32Xr/8Xw/4Xrw	EIDE/ATAPI	1 disc Tray		2Mb
LTR-0841	CD-RW	32Xr/16Xw/10Xrw	EIDE/ATAPI	1 disc Tray		2Mb
LTR-12101B	CD-RW	32Xr/16Xw/10Xrw	EIDE/ATAPI	1 disc Tray		2Mb
LTR-12102B	CD-RW	32Xr/16Xw/10Xrw	EIDE/ATAPI	1 disc Tray		2Mb
LTR-12102C	CD-RW	32Xr/16Xw/10Xrw	EIDE/ATAPI	1 disc Tray		2Mb
LTR-1240	CD-RW	32Xr/12Xw/4Xrw	SCSI-3	1 disc Tray		
LTR-16101B	CD-RW	40Xr/16Xw/10Xrw	EIDE/ATAPI	1 disc Tray		2Mb
LTR-16102B	CD-RW	40Xr/16Xw/10Xrw	EIDE/ATAPI	1 disc Tray		2Mb
LTR-16102C	CD-RW	40Xr/16Xw/10Xrw	EIDE/ATAPI	1 disc Tray		2Mb
LTR-24102B	CD-RW	40Xr/24Xw/10Xrw	EIDE/ATAPI	1 disc Tray		2Mb
LTR-24103S	CD-RW	40Xr/24Xw/10Xrw	EIDE/ATAPI	1 disc Tray		2Mb
LTR-32123S	CD-RW	40Xr/32Xw/12Xrw	EIDE/ATAPI	1 disc Tray		2Mb
LTR-40125S	CD-RW	48Xr/40Xw/12Xrw	EIDE/ATAPI	1 disc Tray		2Mb
LTR-511	CD-R/RW	6Xr/2Xw	ATAPI/EIDE	1 disc	Internal	
LTV-023	DVD-ROM	5Xdvd/15Xcd	EIDE	1 disc Tray	External	
LXR-24101A	CD-RW	40Xr/24Xw/10Xrw	EIDE/ATAPI	1 disc	External	2Mb
LXR-40122A	CD-RW	40Xr/40Xw/12Xrw	USB 2.0	1 disc	External	

Memorex

Manufacturer Model	Drive Type	Drive Speed	Drive Interface	# Discs & Loader	Internal-External	Buffer
48X CD-ROM	CDROM	48X	EIDE	1 disc	Internal	128k
6XDVD/32XCDROM	DVD/CDROM	6Xdvd/32Xcd	ATAPI/EIDE	1 disc	Internal	
CD-RW 12x4x32	CD-RW	32Xr/12Xw/4Xrw	ATAPI/EIDE	1 disc	Internal	2Mb
CD-RW 4206	CD-RW	6Xr/4Xw/2Xrw	ATAPI/EIDE	1 disc	Internal	2Mb
CD-RW 4224	CD-RW	24Xr/4Xw/2Xrw	ATAPI/EIDE	1 disc	Internal	2Mb
CD-RW 8220	CD-RW	20Xr/8Xw/2Xrw	SCSI-3	1 disc	Internal	2Mb

Micro Design International

Manufacturer Model	Drive Type	Drive Speed	Drive Interface	# Discs & Loader	Internal-External	Buffer
10X DVD-ROM	DVD-ROM	10Xdvd/40Xcdrom	EIDE/ATAPI	1 disc Slot		512k
22120	CD-R Juke	8Xr/4Xw		120 disc	External	
32X/10X/4X	CD-R	32Xr/10Xw/4Xrw	IDE	1 disc Tray	Internal	512k
4120	CDROM Juk	4 24X		120 disc	External	
42240	CD-R Juke	8Xr/4Xw		240 disc	External	
42480	CD-R Juke	8Xr/4Xw		480 disc	External	
600 DX4	CDROM	4X	SCSI-2	1 disc	Internal	256k
600C LaserBank	CDROM	1X	SCSI	1 disc Sony Caddy Ext.		None
6240	CDROM Juk	6 24X		240 disc	External	
6480	CDROM Juk	6 24X		480 disc	External	
CD-Express Library	CDROM Juk	4 12X	SCSI-2	150 disc Mags/S		
CD12X	CDROM	12X	SCSI-2	1 disc Tray		256k
CD32X	CDROM	32X	SCSI-2	1 disc Slot		128k
CD36X	CDROM	36X	SCSI-2	1 disc Slot	Internal	128k
CD48X	CDROM	48X	EIDE/ATAPI	1 disc Slot	Internal	128k
CD5.16	CDROM-cha	16X	SCSI-2	5 disc Slot		256k
CD52X	CDROM	52X	EIDE/ATAPI	1 disc	Internal	128k
CD5X7	CDROM		SCSI-2	disc		256k
SCSI Express	CDROM-cha	8X	SCSI-2	1 disc Slot	External	256k
UV-DVD6X2	DVD-ROM	2.6DVD/20Xcdrom	SCSI-2	1 disc Slot		512k
UV-DVD8X10	DVD-ROM		SCSI-2	1 disc Tray		256k

Micro Solutions

Manufacturer Model	Drive Type	Drive Speed	Drive Interface	# Discs & Loader	Internal-External	Buffer
167550	CD-ROM		PC Parallel	1 disc	Portable	128k
167700	CD-ROM		PC Parallel	1 disc	Portable	128k
181100	CD-ROM		PC Parallel	1 disc	Portable	128k
181150	CD-ROM		Par or Card	1 disc	Portable	128k
181200	CD-ROM		PC Parallel	1 disc	Portable	128k

CD & DVD

Manufacturer Model	Drive Type	Drive Speed	Drive Interface	# Discs & Loader	Internal-External	Buffer
185100	CD-RW	20Xr/4Xw/4Xrw	PC Parallel	1 disc	Portable	2Mb
185150	CD-RW	24Xr/8Xw/8Xrw	PC Parallel	1 disc	Portable	2Mb
186100	CD-RW	16Xw/10Xrw	USB 2.0	1 disc	Portable	
190130	CD-RW	8Xr/4Xw	PC parallel	1 disc	External	2Mb
191100	CD-RW	20Xr/4Xw/4Xrw	PC parallel	1 disc	External	2Mb
192100	CD-RW	24Xr/4Xw/4Xrw	PC parallel	1 disc	External	2Mb
193200	CD-RW	32Xr/4Xw/8Xrw	PC parallel	1 disc	External	2Mb
193250	CD-RW	32Xr/8Xw/8Xrw	PC parallel	1 disc	External	2Mb
194200	CD-RW	40Xr/32Xw/10Xrw	PC parallel	1 disc	External	2Mb
195200	CD-RW	40Xr/32Xw/10Xrw	PC parallel	1 disc	External	
24X Backpack Bantam	CDROM	24X	PC Parallel	1 disc Tray		128k
32X Backpack	CDROM	32X	ParalledI P	1 disc Tray		256k
8X Bantam Backpack	CDROM	8X	Parallel Po	1 disc Tray		256k
Backpack Bantam CD-RW	CD-RW	20Xr/4Xw/4Xrw	PC Parallel	1 disc	Portable	2Mb
Backpack CD-RW	CD-RW	8Xr/4Xw	PC parallel	1 disc	External	2Mb
Backpack pd/cd	CDROM	4X	PC parallel	1 disc	External	128k

Mitsumi Electronics Corp

32X max	CDROM	32X	IDE/ATAPI	1 disc Tray		256k
40X	CDROM	40X	IDE/ATAPI		Internal	256k
48X Max	CD-ROM	48X	EIDE/ATAPI	1 disc Tray	Internal	128k
4X4X24 IDE	CD-RW	24Xr/4Xw/4Xrw	Atapi/EIDE		Internal	2Mb
4X8 CD-R	CD-R	8Xr/4Xrec	Atapi/EIDE			2mb
CR-2600TE	CD-R	6Xr/2Xw	EIDE/ATAPI	1 disc Tray	Internal	1 MB
CR-2801TE	CD-R	2X	EIDE/ATAPI	1 disc Tray	Internal	512k
CR-4801TE	CD-R	4Xrec/8Xp	EIDE/ATAPI	1 disc Tray	Internal	2 MB
CR-4802TE	CD-R	8Xr/4Xw/2Xrw	EIDE/ATAPI	1 disc Tray	Internal	2Mb
CR-4802TU	CD-RW	8Xr/4Xw/2Xrw	USB	1 disc Tray	External	2Mb
CR-4804TE	CD-RW	24Xr/4Xrw	EIDE/ATAPI	1 disc Tray	Internal	2mb
CR-4824TU	CD-RW	8Xr/4Xrw	USB	1 disc Tray	External	2mb
CRMC-FX001D	CDROM	2X	16 bit Prop			32k
FX120	CDROM	12X	ATAPI IDE	1 disc Tray	Internal	256k
FX1200	CDROM	12X	IDE/ATAPI	1 disc Tray	Internal	256k
FX1600	CDROM	16X	IDE/ATAPI	1 disc Tray	Internal	256k
FX240	CDROM	12X/24X	EIDE	disc Caddyless		
FX2400	CDROM	24X	IDE/ATAPI	1 disc Tray	Internal	256k
FX3200	CDROM	32X	IDE/ATAPI	1 disc Tray	Internal	256k
FX320S	CDROM	32X	IDE/ATAPI	1 disc Tray	Internal	256k
FX3210S	CDROM	32X	IDE/ATAPI	1 disc Tray	Internal	
FX400	CDROM	4X	IDE/ATAPI	1 disc Tray	Internal	
FX4010M	CDROM	40X	IDE/ATAPI	1 disc Tray	Internal	128k
FX4830	CDROM	48X	IDE/ATAPI	1 disc Tray	Internal	
FX600S	CDROM	6X	EIDE	1 disc Tray	Internal	128k
FX800	CDROM	8X	IDE/ATAPI	1 disc Tray	Internal	256k
FXN01DE	CDROM	2X	ATAPI/IDE	1 disc Tray		
SR243	CDROM	24X	IDE/ATAPI	1 disc		

Nakamichi America Corp

MJ-4.4	CDROM-Cha	4X	EIDE		External	128k
MJ-4.8s	CDROM-Cha	8X	SCSI-2	4 disc Slot	Internal	256k
MJ-5.16	CDROM-C	16X	EIDE/ATAPI	5 disc Direct Load		128k
MJ-5.16si	CDROM-C	16X	SCSI-2	5 disc Direct Load		256k

NEC Technologies

CDR-1350A	CDROM	6X	EIDE Interf	2 disc	Internal	128k
CDR-1400A	CDROM		IDE	1 disc		128k
CDR-1410A	CDROM		SCSI-2	disc		256k
CDR-1450	CDROM	8X	EIDE Interf	2 disc	Internal	128k
CDR-1460A	CDROM	8X	SCSI	disc Integrated Internal		256k
CDR-1600A	CDROM		EIDE	disc		128k
CDR-1610A	CDROM		SCSI-2	1 disc		256k
CDR-1800A	CDROM		EIDE	disc		128k
CDR-1801A	CDROM		IDE/ATAPI	disc		128k
CDR-1810A	CDROM		SCSI-2	disc		256k
CDR-1900A	CDROM		IDE/ATAPI	disc		128k
CDR-1901A	CDROM		IDE/ATAPI	disc		128k
CDR-1910A	CDROM		SCSI-2	disc		256k
CDR-210	CDROM	2X	SCSI	1 disc Tray	Internal	64k
CDR-211	CDROM	2X		disc		
CDR-222S	CDROM	4X	EIDE	1 disc	Internal	
CDR-25	CDROM	1X	SCSI-1	1 disc	Portable	64k
CDR-250	CDROM	2X	IDE	1 disc Tray	Internal	256k
CDR-250DX	CDROM	2X	IDE	1 disc Tray	Internal	256k
CDR-251	CDROM		IDE	disc		
CDR-260	CDROM	2X	EIDE	1 disc		
CDR-271	CDROM	4X	IDE/ATAPI	disc Tray		256k
CDR-272	CDROM		IDE	disc		
CDR-273I	CDROM	4X	IDE	1 disc	Internal	
CDR-3 Intersect	CDROM	1X	SCSI	1 disc Top Load External		2k
CDR-300 (MAC)	CDROM	2X	SCSI	1 disc Tray	External	256k

Manufacturer Model	Drive Type	Drive Speed	Drive Interface	# Discs & Loader	Internal-External	Buffer
CDR-3000A	CDROM		IDE/ATAPI	disc		128k
CDR-3460A	CDROM	8X	SCSI	1 disc Integrated	External	256k
CDR-35	CDROM	1X	SCSI-1	1 disc	Portable	64k
CDR-36	CDROM	1X	SCSI-1	1 disc	Portable	64k
CDR-36M	CDROM	1X	SCSI-1	1 disc	Portable	64k
CDR-37	CDROM	2X	SCSI-1	1 disc Top Load	Internal	64k
CDR-38	CDROM	3X	SCSI-2	1 disc Top Load	Internal	256k
CDR-400	CDROM	3.3X	SCSI-2	1 disc Top Load	Internal	256k
CDR-401	CDROM		EIDE	disc		128k
CDR-4400A	CDROM		EIDE	disc		128k
CDR-500	CDROM	3X	SCSI-2	1 disc	Internal a	256k
CDR-501	CDROM	4X	SCSI-2	1 disc Cartridge	Internal	256k
CDR-502	CDROM	6X	SCSI-2	1 disc Cartridge	Internal	256k
CDR-510	CDROM	4X	SCSI	1 disc Tray	Internal	256k
CDR-511	CDROM	4X	SCSI	1 disc Caddy	Internal	256k
CDR-600	CDROM	4X	SCSI-2	1 disc Caddy	Internal	256k
CDR-601	CDROM	6X	SCSI-2	1 disc Cartridge	Internal	256k
CDR-602	CDROM	6X	SCSI-2	1 disc Cartridge	Internal a	256k
CDR-7 Intersect	CDROM	1X	SCSI	1 disc Sony Caddy	External	64k
CDR-72	CDROM	1X	SCSI-1	1 disc	External	64k
CDR-73	CDROM	1X	SCSI-1	1 disc	External	64k
CDR-73M	CDROM	1X	SCSI-1	1 disc	External	64k
CDR-74	CDROM	2X	SCSI	1 disc Caddy	External	2X
CDR-74-1	CDROM	256k	SCSI	1 disc	External	
CDR-77	CDROM	1X	SCSI-1	1 disc	Internal	64k
CDR-80	CDROM	1X	SCSI-1	1 disc	Internal	64k
CDR-82	CDROM	1X	SCSI-1	1 disc	Internal	64k
CDR-83	CDROM	1X	SCSI-1	1 disc	Internal	64k
CDR-83M	CDROM	2X	SCSI-1	1 disc	Internal	64k
CDR-84	CDROM	2X	SCSI	1 disc Caddy	Internal	256k
CDR-84-1	CDROM	4X	SCSI-2/SCSI	1 disc Cartridge	External	256k
CDR-900	CDROM-C	4X	EIDE	4 disc Direct Feed	Internal	
CDR-C251		128KB				
CDR-c301	CDROM-cha	2X	SCSI-2	7 disc Drawer	External	64k
CDR-C302	CDROM-Cha	4X	SCSI-2	2 disc Drawer	External	128k
MultiCDR	CD-R	2Xw/20Xp	EIDE/ATAPI	1 disc Tray	Internal	1 Mb
MultiSpin 2Vi	CDROM-Cha	2X	IDE	7 disc Drawer	External	64k
MultiSpin 2Xc	CDROM	2X	SCSI-2	1 disc Caddy	Internal	256k
MultiSpin 2Xe	CDROM	2X	SCSI	1 disc Caddy	Internal	256k
MultiSpin 2Xi	CDROM	2X	SCSI	1 disc Top Load	Internal	64k
MultiSpin 2Xp	CDROM	2X	SCSI	1 disc Caddy	Internal	256k
MultiSpin 3Xe	CDROM	3X	SCSI	1 disc	Internal	
MultiSpin 3Xi	CDROM	3X	SCSI-2	1 disc	Internal	256k
MultiSpin 3Xp Plus	CDROM	3.3X	SCSI-2	1 disc Tray	Internal	256k
MultiSpin 4X4	CDROM	4X	EIDE	1 disc Slot	Internal	128k
MultiSpin 4Xc	CDROM-Ch	4X	SCSI-2	7 disc Drawer	External	128k
MultiSpin 4Xi	CDROM	4X	SCSI-2	1 disc Caddy	Internal	256k
MultiSpin 6V	CDROM	6X	EIDE	1 disc Tray	Internal	128k
MultiSpin 6Xe	CDROM	6X	SCSI-2	1 disc Cartridge	Internal	256k
MultiSpin 6Xi	CDROM	6X	SCSI-2	1 disc Cartridge	Internal	256k
MultiSpin 8V	CDROM	8X	ATAPI 2.5	1 disc Tray	Internal	128k
MultiSpin 8Xe	CDROM	8X	SCSI-2	1 disc Tray	External	256k
MultiSpin 8Xi	CDROM	8X	SCSI-2	1 disc Tray	Internal	256k

NewCom, Inc.

Manufacturer Model	Drive Type	Drive Speed	Drive Interface	# Discs & Loader	Internal-External	Buffer
CDRW622 CopyCat	CD-RW	2Xrec/6Xr	IDE/ATAPI	1 disc	Internal	1M
Cinema II Plus DVD	DVD-ROM	2Xdvd/20Xc		disc		
NewCom 10X	CDROM	10X	IDE/ATAPI	1 disc	Internal	
NewCom 12X	CDROM	12X	IDE/ATAPI	1 disc	Internal	
NewCom 16X	CDROM	16X	IDE/ATAPI	1 disc	Internal	
NewCom 20X	CDROM	20X	IDE/ATAPI	1 disc	Internal	
NewCom 24X	CDROM	24X	EIDE/ATAPI	1 disc	Internal	
NewCom 32X	CDROM	32X	EIDE/ATAPI	1 disc	Internal	
NewCom 6X	CDROM	6X	IDE/ATAPI	1 disc	Internal	
NewCom 8X	CDROM	8X	IDE/ATAPI	1 disc	Internal	
Zzap CD-R	CD-R	4Xr/2Xrec	SCSI-2	1 disc	Internal	1Mb

Nomai USA

Manufacturer Model	Drive Type	Drive Speed	Drive Interface	# Discs & Loader	Internal-External	Buffer
680R.W.	CD-ReWrit	6Xr/2Xw	AdvanSys UI	1 disc Tray	Internal a	512k
750.c	CD-ReWrit		Fast SCSI-2	1 disc Cartridge		512k

Ocean Information Systems, Inc

Manufacturer Model	Drive Type	Drive Speed	Drive Interface	# Discs & Loader	Internal-External	Buffer
CDR-688	CDROM	8X	EIDE/ATAPI	1 disc Tray	Internal	256k
CDR-810	CDROM	10X	EIDE/ATAPI	1 disc Tray	Internal	256k
CDR-812	CDROM	12X	EIDE/ATAPI	1 disc Tray	Internal	256k
CDR-820	CDROM	20X	EIDE/ATAPI	1 disc Tray	Internal	256k
CDR-824	CDROM	24X	EIDE/ATAPI	1 disc Tray	Internal	256k
RW260	CDROM	6Xr/2Xw	EIDE/ATAPI	1 disc Tray	Internal	1M

Manufacturer Model	Drive Type	Drive Speed	Drive Interface	# Discs & Loader	Internal-External	Buffer
Optical Access International						
Access CD	CDROM	1X	SCSI	1 disc Philips Ca	External	64k
Optics Storage						
Mach 5111	DVD-ROM	24X	IDE/ATAPI	1 disc Tray	Internal	256k
Maverick 8424	CDROM	12X	Fast SCSI-2	1 disc Tray	External	256k
Maverick 8622 (EIDE)	CDROM	12X	EIDE	1 disc Tray	Internal	256k
Maverick 8622 (SCSI)	CDROM	12X	Fast SCSI-2	1 disc Tray	Internal	256k
Maverick 8623	CDROM	12X	IDE/ATAPI	1 disc Tray	Internal	256k
Maverick 8831	CDROM	16X	IDE/ATAPI	1 disc Tray	Internal	128k
Maverick 8841	CDROM	16X	IDE/ATAPI	1 disc Tray	Internal	128k
Pacific Digital						
121032ei	CD-RW	32Xr/12Xw/10Xrw	EIDE/ATAPI	1 disc	Internal	2Mb
161040ei	CD-RW	40Xr/16Xw/10Xrw	EIDE/ATAPI	1 disc	Internal	2Mb
161040USB	CD-RW	40Xr/16Xw/10Xrw	USB-2	1 disc	External	2Mb
16X DVD-ROM	DVD-ROM	16Xdvd/40Xcd	EIDE/ATAPI	1 disc	Internal	512kb
2224ei	CD-RW	24Xr/2Xw/2Xrw	IDE/ATAPI	1 disc	Internal	2Mb
226ei	CD-RW	6Xr/2Xw/2Xrw	IDE/ATAPI	1 disc	Internal	1Mb
241040ei	CD-RW	40Xr/24Xw/10Xrw	EIDE/ATAPI	1 disc	Internal	2Mb
241040USB	CD-RW	40Xr/24Xw/10Xrw	USB-2	1 disc	External	2Mb
428ei	CD-RW	8Xr/4Xw/2Xrw	IDE/ATAPI	1 disc	Internal	512kb
428USB	CD-RW	8Xr/4Xw/2Xrw	USB	1 disc	External	2Mb
4416si	CD-RW	16Xr/4Xw/4Xrw	SCSI-2	1 disc	Internal	2Mb
4424ei	CD-RW	24Xr/4Xw/4Xrw	IDE/ATAPI	1 disc	Internal	2Mb
448USB	CD-RW	8Xr/4Xw/4Xrw	USB	1 disc	External	2Mb
8824ei	CD-RW	24Xr/8Xw/8Xrw	EIDE/ATAPI	1 disc	Internal	4Mb
8824si	CD-RW	24Xr/8Xw/8Xrw	SCSI-3	1 disc	Internal	4Mb
8832ei	CD-RW	32Xr/8Xw/8Xrw	EIDE/ATAPI	1 disc	Internal	2Mb
DVD-R/RAM	DVD-RAM	2Xdvdram/24Xcd	EIDE/ATAPI	1 disc	Internal	1Mb
Panasonic Communications						
CD-616P	CDROM	16X	E-IDE/ATAPI	1 disc Tray	Internal	128k
KXL-783A	CDROM	8X	PCMCIA	1 disc Tray	Portable	128k
KXL-807A	CDROM	20X	ATAPI	1 disc	Portable	128k
KXL-810A	CDROM	20X	PCMCIA	disc	Portable	
KXL-D720	CDROM		PCMCIA	1 disc Tray	Portable	128k
KXL-D721	CDROM	2X		disc		
KXL-D740	CDROM	4X	PC Card Typ	1 disc Tray	Portable	128k
KXL-D742	CDROM	4X	PCMCIA	1 disc Tray	Portable	128k
KXL-D745	CDROM	4X	PCMCIA Typl	1 disc Tray	Portable	128k
KXL-RW10A	CD-R/RW	20Xr/4Xw/4Xrw	SCSI-2	1 disc	Portable	2Mb
LF-1000	PD/CDROM	4X	SCSI-2	1 disc Tray	External	256k
LF-1004	PD/CDROM	4X	SCSI-2	1 disc Tray	Internal	256k
LF-1007AD	PD/CDROM	24X	Fast SCSI-2	1 disc Cartridge	Internal	640k
LF-1600A	PD/CDROM	20X	Fast SCSI-2	1 disc Cartridge		640k
LF-D101U	DVD-RAM	20X	Fast SCSI-2	1 disc Cartridge	Internal	2Mb
LF-D102U	DVD-RAM	2Xdvd/20Xcd	SCSI-2	1 disc	External	2Mb
LF-D103U	DVD-RAM	2Xdvd/20Xcdrom	Fast SCSI-2	disc	External	2Mb
LF-D201U	DVD-RAM	6Xdvd/24Xcdrom	SCSI-2	1 disc	Internal	1Mb
LF-D211V	DVD-RAM	6Xdvd/24Xcd	ATAPI	1 disc	Internal	1Mb
LF-D291N	DVD-RAM	6Xdvd/24Xcd	SCSI-2	1 disc	Internal	1Mb
LF-D311	DVD-RAM	6Xdvd/24Xcd	SCSI-2	1 disc	Internal	1Mb
LF-J100	CDROM Lib	4X	SCSI-2	100 disc	External	
LF-J50	CDROM Lib	4X	SCSI-2	50 disc	External	
LK-MC501B	CDROM		SCSI	disc	External	
LK-MC501S	CDROM		SCSI	disc	Internal	
LK-MC509S	CDROM	2X	SCSI	disc	External	
LK-MC521B	CDROM		AT BUS	disc	External	
LK-MC521S	CDROM		AT BUS	disc	External	
LK-MC579BP	CDROM	2X	EIDE/ATAPI	1 disc Tray	Internal	
LK-MC604S	CDROM	4.5X	SCSI	1 disc Tray	External	256k
LK-MC605BP	CDROM	4X	SCSI	1 disc Disk	Internal	
LK-MC605S	CDROM	4X	SCSI	1 disc Tray	External	
LK-MC606BP	CDROM	24X	SCSI	1 disc Tray	Internal	256k
LK-MC608BP	CDROM	8X	SCSI	1 disc Tray	External	256k
LK-MC608S	CDROM	8X	SCSI	1 disc Tray	Internal	256k
LK-MC682BP	CDROM	32X	IDE	1 disc Tray	Internal	256k
LK-MC684BP	CDROM	4.5X	EIDE/ATAPI	1 disc Tray	Internal	256k
LK-MC686BP	CDROM	24X	ATAPI	1 disc Tray	Internal	
LK-MC688BP	CDROM	8X	IDE/ATAPI	1 disc Tray	Internal	128k
LK-MW602BP	CDROM	2Xw/4Xrd	SCSI-2	disc 1		256k
SQ-TC500N Big 5	CDROM-Cha	4X	EIDE/ATAPI	5 disc Tray	Internal	256k
SQ-TC510N	CDROM-Cha	10X	EIDE/ATAPI	5 disc Tray	Internal	
SQ-TC512N	CDROM-Cha	12X	EIDE/ATAPI	5 disc Tray	Internal	
SQ-TC520N	CDROM-Cha	20X	EIDE/ATAPI	5 disc Tray		128k
Panasonic Computer Peripheral						
Big 5	CDROM-Cha	10X	ATAPI/IDE	5 disc Tray	Internal	128k

Manufacturer Model	Drive Type	Drive Speed	Drive Interface	# Discs & Loader	Internal-External	Buffer
LK-MV8581BP	DVD-ROM		ATAPI	disc	Internal	
Peripheral Land						
PLI CD-ROM	CDROM	1X	SCSI	1 disc Sony Caddy	External	64k
Phillips Electronics						
2.5x8xDVD+RW	DVD/RW	2.5Xdvd/8Xrw	EIDE/ATAPI	disc	Internal	
CDD 2000/12	CD-R	4Xr/2Xw	SCSI	1 disc Tray	Internal	1Mb
CDD 2000/20	CD-R	4Xr/2Xw	SCSI	1 disc Tray	Internal	1Mb
CDD 2600	CDROM	6Xr/2Xw	SCSI-2	1 disc Tray	Internal	1Mb
CDD 300	CDROM	2X	IDE/ATAPI	1 disc Tray	Internal	256k
CDD 3600	CD-R	6Xr/2Xw	SCSI-2	1 disc Tray	Internal	1Mb
CDD 3610	CD-R	6Xr/2Xw	EIDE	1 disc Tray	Internal	1Mb
CDD 3801	CD-RW	24Xr	EIDE/ATAPI	1 disc Tray	Internal	
CDD 4201	CD-RW	24Xr/4Xrw	EIDE/ATAPI	1 disc Tray	Internal	2Mb
CDD 521	CDROM		SCSI	1 disc Caddy		
CDD 522	CDROM	6X	SCSI-2	1 disc	Internal	1 Mb
CM405	CDROM	2X	SCSI-2	1 disc	Internal	
CM425	CDROM	2X	SCSI-2	1 disc	External	
DRD 5200	CDROM/DVD	24X/2XDVD	ATAPI/IDE	1 disc Tray	Internal	256k
DRD 5420	DVD-ROM	6Xr		disc		
OmniWriter 12	CD-RW	2X/2X/6X	ATAPI	1 disc Tray	Internal	1Mb
OmniWriter 20	CD-RW	2X/2X/6X	SCSI	1 disc Tray	Internal	1Mb
OmniWriter 40	CD-RW	2X/2X/6X	SCSI	1 disc Tray	External	1Mb
PCA 202 CD (Europe)	CDROM	20X	ATAPI/IDE	1 disc	Internal	128k
PCA 243 CD (Europe)	CDROM	24X	ATAPI/IDE	1 disc	Internal	128k
PCA 363RW 6X/2X/2X	CD-RW	6Xr/2Xw/2Xrw	ParalelPort	1 disc	External	1Mb
PCA 52CR	CDROM	5X	ATAPI/IDE	1 disc	Internal	128k
PCA 532DK	DVD-ROM	32X	IDE/ATAPI	disc	Internal	256k
PCA 62CR	CDROM	6X	IDE	1 disc	Internal	256k
PCA 80SC	CDROM	8X	SCSI-2	1 disc	Internal	
PCDV 104K	DVD-ROM	10Xdvd/XCdrom	IDE/ATAPI	1 disc	Internal	512k
PCDV 104R	DVD-ROM	10Xdvd/40Xcdrom	IDE/ATAPI	1 disc	Internal	512k
PCRW 1208	CD-RW	36Xr/12Xw/8Xrw	EIDE/ATAPI	1 disc	Internal	
PCRW 2010	CD-RW	40Xr/20Xw/10Xrw	EIDE/ATAPI	1 disc	Internal	2Mb
PCRW 404K	CD-RW	32Xr/4Xw/4Xrw	EIDE/ATAPI	1 disc	Internal	2Mb
PCRW 463K	CD-RW	5Xr/4Xw/4Xrw	USB	1 disc	External	2Mb
PCRW 464K	CD-RW	16Xr/4Xw/4Xrw	PCMCIA	1 disc	External	2Mb
PCRW 804K	CD-RW	32Xr/8Xw/4Xrw	EIDE/ATAPI	1 disc Tray	Internal	2Mb
Pinnacle Micro, Inc.						
10Xtreme	CDROM	10X	IDE	1 disc	Internal	
Flex 5.2GB DVD-RAM	DVD-RAM		SCSI-2	disc Cartridge	Int/Ext	1Mb
Flex Cinema	DVD Video		SCSI-2	disc	External	1 Mb
RCD 1000	CDROM-Rec	2X	SCSI-1	1 disc Caddy	External	1Mb
RCD 202	CDROM		SCSI	1 disc Caddy	External	
RCD 4X12 Ext Mac Pro	CDROM	4Xw/12Xr	SCSI-2	1 disc	External	256k
RCD 4X12 Ext PC Pro	CDROM	4Xw/12Xr	SCSI-2	1 disc	External	256k
RCD 4X12 Int PC Pro	CDROM	4Xw/12Xr	SCSI-2	1 disc	Internal	256k
RCD 4X4 Int IPCA	CDROM	4Xw/4Xr	SCSI-2	1 disc Tray	Internal	256k
RCD 5020	CD-R	2X	SCSI-2	1 disc Tray	Internal	1Mb
RCD 5040	CDROM	4X	SCSI	1 disc	Internal	
RCD 5040	CD-R	4Xp/2Xrec	SCSI-2	1 disc Caddy	Internal	512k
RCD 6X24 Ext Mac Pro	CDROM	24Xr/6Xw	SCSI-2	1 disc	External	2Mb
RCD 6X24 Ext PC Pro	CD-R	24Xr/6Xw	SCSI-2	1 disc	External	2Mb
RCD 6X24 Int PC Pro	CD-R	24Xr/6Xw	SCSI-2	1 disc	Internal	2Mb
RCD 6X24 IPC	CD-R	24Xr/8Xw	SCSI-2 Fast	1 disc Tray	Internal	4Mb
RCD 8X24 MAC	CD-R	24Xr/8Xw	SCSI-2 Fast	1 disc Tray	External	4Mb
RCD 8X24 PC	CD-R	24Xr/8Xw	SCSI-2 Fast	1 disc Tray	External	4Mb
RCD 8X24 UNIX	CD-R	24Xr/8Xw	SCSI-2 Fast	1 disc Tray	Ext.	4Mb
RW 426	CD-R	6Xr/4Xrec	SCSI-2	1 disc Tray	External	2Mb
RW 4432	CD-RW	32Xr/4Xw/4Xrw	IEEE 1394	1 disc Tray	External	2Mb
RW 448U	CD-RW	8Xr/4Xw/4Xrw	USB	1 disc Tray	External	2Mb
Pioneer New Media Tech, Inc						
12X Internal ATAPI	CDROM	12X	ATAPI	1 disc	Internal	128k
12X Internal SCSI	CDROM	12X	SCSI-2	1 disc	Internal	128k
DR-504S	CDROM	32X	ATAPI	1 disc Slot	Internal	128k
DR-506S	CDROM	32X	SCSI	1 disc Slot	Internal	128k
DR-544	CDROM	32X	ATAPI/IDE	1 disc Slot	Internal	128k
DR-566	CDROM	32X	SCSI	1 disc Slot	Internal	128k
DR-704S	CDROM	36X	ATAPI	1 disc Slot	Internal	128k
DR-706S	CDROM	36X	SCSI-2	1 disc Slot		128k
DR-714	CDROM	36X	ATAPI	1 disc Slot	Internal	128k
DR-744	CDROM	36X	ATAPI	1 disc Tray	Internal	128k
DR-766	CDROM	36X	SCSI-2	1 disc Tray	Internal	128k
DR-914	CDROM	40X	ATAPI	1 disc Tray	Internal	
DR-944	CDROM	40X	ATAPI (Ultr	1 disc Tray	Internal	128k
DR-966	CDROM	40X	Ultra SCSI	1 disc Tray	Internal	128k

Manufacturer Model	Drive Type	Drive Speed	Drive Interface	# Discs & Loader	Internal-External	Buffer
DR-A04S	CDROM	32X	ATAPI	1 disc Slot		128k
DR-A14S	CDROM	36X	ATAPI	1 disc Slot		128kb
DR-R7181	CD-R	24Xr/8Xw		1 disc	Internal	4Mb
DR-U06S	CDROM	32X	SCSI-2	1 disc Slot		
DR-U10X	CDROM	10X	SCSI-2	1 disc		
DR-U1124X	CDROM	4.4X	SCSI-2	1 disc Tray	Internal	128k
DR-U16S	CDROM	36X	SCSI-2	1 disc Slot		128kb
DRJ-5004x	CDROM Juk	4.4X	SCSI-2	500 disc 4 Cartridge		
DRM-1004V40 Jukebox	DVD-ROM J		SCSI-2	100 disc magazine sl External		
DRM-1004X10/40/R21	CDROM JUK	2.5Xdvd/20Xcd	SCSI-2	100 disc Mail Slot Internal		
DRM-1804X	CDROM-Juk	4X	SCSI	18 disc 3 Cartridge External		
DRM-5002R2W	CDROM rec	2 4Xr/2 4X		500 disc	Internal	
DRM-5003R1W	CDROM rec	3 4X read/		500 disc	Internal	
DRM-5004X	CDROM rec	4 4X read	SCSI-3	500 disc		
DRM-600X	CDROM	1X	SCSI-2	6 disc 6 Disc Mag External		512k
DRM-602X	CDROM	2X	SCSI-2	6 disc Mag		256k
DRM-604X	CDROM	4X	SCSI-2	6 disc 6 Disc Mag Internal		128k
DRM-624X	CDROM cha	4.4X	SCSI-2	6 disc Mag	Internal a	128k
DRM-6324X	CDROM-cha	24X	SCSI 2	6 disc Mag disc Internal		
DRM-7000 FlexLibrary	DVD-ROM L		SCSI-2	720 disc 50 Disc Mag External		
DVD-101	DVD-ROM		ATAPI	1 disc Tray		512kb
DVD-102	DVD-ROM	2.6DVD/24X	ATAPI	disc Slot		512kb
DVD-103S	DVD-ROM	6Xdvd/32Xcdrom	ATA/ATAPI-4	1 disc Slot		512kb
DVD-104S	DVD-ROM	10Xdvd/40Xcdrom	ATA/ATAPI-4	1 disc Slot	Internal	512kb
DVD-105S	DVD-ROM	16Xdvd/40Xcdrom	ATA/ATAPI-4	1 disc Slot		512kb
DVD-106S	DVD	16Xdvd/40Xcdrom	ATA/ATAPI5	1 disc Slot/Tray		256kb
DVD-113	DVD-ROM	6Xdvd/32Xcdrom	ATA/ATAPI-4	1 disc Tray		512kb
DVD-114	DVD-ROM	10Xdvd, 40Xcdro	ATA/Atapi-4	1 disc Tray		512kb
DVD-115	DVD-ROM	16Xdvd/40Xcdrom	ATA/ATAPI-4	1 disc Tray		512kb
DVD-116	DVD-ROM		ATAPI	1 disc Tray		256kb
DVD-116	DVD	16Xdvd/40Xcd	ATA/ATAPI5	1 disc Tray		256kb
DVD-301	DVD-ROM	1Xdvd/10Xdrom	SCSI	1 disc Tray	Internal	
DVD-302	DVD-ROM	2.6X/20XCD	SCSI-2	1 disc Tray		512kb
DVD-303S	DVD-ROM	6Xdvd/32Xcdrom	SCSI-2	1 disc Slot	Internal	512kb
DVD-304S	DVD-ROM	10Xdvd/40Xcdrom	SCSI-2	1 disc Slot		512kb
DVD-305S	DVD-ROM		SCSI	1 disc Tray		512kb
DVD-A01	DVD-ROM		ATAPI	1 disc Tray		512kb
DVD-A02	DVD-ROM	2.6DVD/24X	ATAPI	disc Slot	Internal	512kb
DVD-A03S	DVD-ROM	6Xdvd/32Xcdrom	ATAPI	1 disc Slot	Internal	512kb
DVD-A04X	DVD-ROM	10Xdvd/40Xcdrom	ATA/ATAPI-4	1 disc Slot	Internal	512kb
DVD-A05S	DVD-ROM	16Xdvd/40Xcdrom	ATA/ATAPI-4	1 disc Slot	Internal	512kb
DVD-A06S	DVD	16Xdvd/40Xcd	ATA/ATAPI5	1 disc Slot/Tray		512k
DVD-D7361	DVD-ROM	6Xdvd/32Xcd		1 disc	Internal	256kb
DVD-R7211	DVD-R Wri	2Xr/1Xw		disc	Internal	8Mb
DVD-ROM Jukebox	DVD-ROM J	4 2.5Xdvd/20Xcd	SCSI-2	100 disc Mail Slot		
DVDS101	DVD-R		SCSI-2	1 disc Tray		4Mb
DVD-U01	DVD-ROM		SCSI-2	1 disc		512kb
DVD-U02	DVD-ROM	2.6X/20XCD	SCSI	1 disc Slot		512kb
DVD-U03S	DVD-ROM	6Xdvd/32Xcdrom	SCSI	1 disc		512kb
DVD-U04S	DVD-ROM	10Xdvd	SCSI-2	1 disc		
DVD-U05S	DVD-ROM		SCSI	1 disc Tray		512kb
DVR-103	DVD-R/RW	2Xdvd/8Xcdr/4rw	ATAPI	1 disc		2Mb
DVR-104	DVD-R/RW	2Xdvd/8Xcdr/4rw	ATAPI	1 disc		2Mb
DVR-A03	DVD-ROM	4Xdvd/24Xcdrom	ATA/ATAPI-5	1 disc		2Mb
DVR-A04	DVD-ROM	6Xdvd/24Xcdrom	ATAPI	1 disc Tray		2Mb
DVR-S101	DVD-Recor		SCSI-2	1 disc		
DVR-S201	DVD-ROM	2Xr/1Xw	SCSI-2	1 disc Tray		4Mb
DW-S114X	CD-R	4X	SCSI	1 disc Tray	External	1Mb
Super 10X Atapi	CDROM	10X	ATAPI	1 disc	Internal	128k
Super 10X SCSI	CDROM	10X	SCSI-2	1 disc	Internal	128k

Plasmon Data, Inc.

Manufacturer Model	Drive Type	Drive Speed	Drive Interface	# Discs & Loader	Internal-External	Buffer
CDR-4220	CD-R	4X	SCSI	1 disc Tray	External	1Mb
CDR-4240(Afterburner)	CD-R	2Xw/4Xr	EIDE	1 disc Tray	External	1Mb
D120-22	CD-R Libr	2 8Xcdrom/2 2X		120 disc Slot		
D120-40	CDROM Lib	4 8X		120 disc Slot		
D120-P4	PD/CD Lib	4 6Xpd/cd drive		120 disc Slot		
D240-42	CD-R Libr	4 8Xcdrom/2 2X		240 disc Slot		
D240-60	CDROM Lib	6 8X		240 disc Slot		
D240-P6	PD/CD Lib	6 6Xpd/cd drive		120 disc Slot		
D480-42	CD-R Libr	4 8Xcdrom/ 2 2X		480 disc Slot		
D480-60	CDROM Lib	6 8X		480 disc Slot		
D480-P6	CDROM	6 6Xpd/cd drive		480 disc Slot		
PD2000e	CDROM	4X	SCSI	1 disc	External	
RF4102	CDROM-Rec	2X	SCSI-2	1 disc Tray		128k

Plextor

Manufacturer Model	Drive Type	Drive Speed	Drive Interface	# Discs & Loader	Internal-External	Buffer
12/20PleX	CDROM	12X/20X	SCSI	1 disc Caddyless External		
12PleX	CDROM	12X	SCSI	1 disc Caddy-Tray Int.		512k
6PleX	CDROM	6X	SCSI-2	1 disc Caddy	Internal	256k

CD & DVD Drives

Manufacturer Model	Drive Type	Drive Speed	Drive Interface	# Discs & Loader	Internal-External	Buffer
8PleX	CDROM	8X	SCSI	1 disc Caddy	Internal	256k
DM-3020	CDROM		SCSI-1	1 disc Caddy	Internal	64k
DM-3021	CDROM		SCSI-2	1 disc Caddy	Internal	64k
DM-3024	CDROM	2X	SCSI-2	1 disc Caddy	Internal	64k
DM-3028	CDROM	2X	SCSI-2	1 disc Caddy	Internal	64k
DM-5020	CDROM		SCSI-1	1 disc Caddy	External	64k
DM-5021	CDROM		SCSI-2	1 disc Caddy	External	64k
DM-5024	CDROM		SCSI-2	1 disc Caddy	External	64k
DM-5028	CDROM		SCSI-2	1 disc Caddy	External	64k
PlexCombo 20/10/40-12A	DVD/CDRW	12xdvd/40Xcd	EIDE/ATAPI4	1 disc Tray	Internal	2Mb
PlexWriter 12/10/32A	CD-RW	32Xr/12Xw/10Xrw	EIDE/ATAPI4	1 disc Tray	Internal	2Mb
PlexWriter 12/10/32S	CD-RW	32Xr/12Xw/10Xrw	Ultra SCSI	1 disc Tray	External	4Mb
PlexWriter 12/10/32S	CD-RW	32Xr/12Xw/10Xrw	Ultra SCSI	1 disc Tray	External	4Mb
PlexWriter 12/4/32	CD-RW	32Xr/12Xw/4Xrw	Ultra SCSI	1 disc Tray	External	4Mb
PlexWriter 16/10/40A	CD-RW	40Xr/16Xw/10Xrw	EIDE/ATAPI4	1 disc Tray	Internal	2Mb
PlexWriter 24/10/40A	CD-RW	40Xr/24Xw/10Xrw	USB 2.0	1 disc Tray	External	2Mb
PlexWriter 4/12	CD-R	12Xr/4Xw	Fast SCSI	1 disc Caddy	External	1Mb
PlexWriter 40/12/40A	CD-RW	40Xr/40Xw/12Xrw	EIDE/ATAPI	1 disc Tray	Internal	4Mb
PlexWriter 8/2/20	CD-RW	20Xr/8Xrec/2Xrw	Fast SCSI	1 disc Tray	Int/Ext	4Mb
PlexWriter 8/20	CD-R	20Xr/8Xrec	SCSI	disc	Internal	4Mb
Plexwriter 8/4/32	CD-RW	32Xr/8Xw/4Xrw	ATAPI4/EIDE	1 disc Tray	Internal	2Mb
Plexwriter 8/4/24U	CD-RW	24Xr/8Xw/8Xrw	USB 2.0	1 disc	External	2Mb
PlexWriter RW 4/2/20	CD-RW	20Xr/4Xw	Fast SCSI	1 disc	External	2Mb
PX-12CS	CDROM	12X	Fast SCSI B	1 disc Caddy	Internal	512k
PX-12CSe	CDROM	12X	SCSI-2	1 disc Caddy	External	512k
PX-12CSe/ISA	CDROM	12X	SCSI-2	1 disc Caddy	External	512k
PX-12CSi	CDROM	12X	SCSI	1 disc Caddy	Internal	512k
PX-12TSe	CDROM	12X	SCSI-2	1 disc Caddy	External	512k
PX-12TSe/MAC	CDROM	12X	SCSI-2	1 disc Tray	External	512k
PX-12TSe/PCI	CDROM	12X	SCSI-2	1 disc Caddy	External	512k
PX-12TSi	CDROM	12X	Fast SCSI B	1 disc Tray	Internal	512k
PX-12TSi/ISA	CDROM	12X	SCSI-2; 16-	1 disc Tray	Internal	512k
PX-12TSi/PCI	CDROM	12X	SCSI-2; 32-	1 disc Tray	Internal	512k
PX-20TSe	CDROM	20X	Fast SCSI	1 disc Tray	External	512k
PX-20TSi	CDROM	20X	Fast SCSI	1 disc Tray	Internal	512k
PX-20TSi/e	CDROM	12/20X	Fast SCSI	1 disc Tray	External	512k
PX-320A	DVD/CDRW	12xdvd/40Xcd	EIDE/ATAPI4	1 disc Tray	Internal	2Mb
PX-32CSe	CDROM	32X	SCSI-2	1 disc Caddy	External	512k
PX-32CSe/ISA	CDROM	32X	SCSI-2; 16-	1 disc Caddy	External	512k
PX-32CSe/MAC	CDROM	32X	SCSI-2	1 disc Caddy	External	512k
PX-32CSe/PCI	CDROM	32X	SCSI-2; 32-	1 disc Caddy	External	512k
PX-32CSe/PCMCIA	CDROM	32X	Ultra SCSI	1 disc Caddy	External	512k
PX-32CSi/e	CDROM	32X/14X	Ultra SCSI	1 disc Caddy	Internal	512k
PX-32CSi/ISA	CDROM	32X	Ultra SCSI	1 disc Caddy	Internal	512k
PX-32CSi/PCI	CDROM	32X	Ultra SCSI	1 disc Caddy	Internal	512k
PX-32TSe	CDROM	32X	SCSI-2	1 disc Tray	External	512k
PX-32TSe/ISA	CDROM	32X	SCSI-2, 16-	1 disc Tray	External	512k
PX-32TSe/MAC	CDROM	32X	SCSI-2	1 disc Tray	External	512k
PX-32TSi/e	CDROM	32X	Ultra SCSI	1 disc Tray	Internal	512k
PX-32TSi/ISA	CDROM	32X	Ultra SCSI	1 disc Tray	Internal	512k
PX-32TSi/PCI	CDROM	32X	Ultra-SCSI	1 disc Tray	Internal	512k
PX-40TSi/e	CDROM	40X	Ultra SCSI	1 disc Tray	Internal	512k
PX-40TSUWi/e	CDROM	40X	Wide Ultra	1 disc Tray	Internal	512k
PX-43CE	CDROM	4.5X	SCSI-2	1 disc Caddy	Internal	256k
PX-43CH	CDROM	4X	SCSI BUS	1 disc Caddy	Internal	1Mb
PX-43CS	CDROM	4.5X	SCSI	1 disc Caddy	Internal	256k
PX-45CE	CDROM	4.5X	SCSI-2	1 disc Caddy	External	256k
PX-45CH	CDROM	4X	SCSI-BUS	1 disc Caddy	External	1Mb
PX-45CS	CDROM	4.5X	SCSI-2	1 disc Caddy	External	256k
PX-63CS	CDROM	6X	Adaptec SCS	1 disc Caddy	Internal	256k
PX-65CS	CDROM	6X	Adaptec SCS	1 disc Caddy	External	256k
PX-83CS	CDROM	8X	Fast SCSI-2	1 disc Caddy	Internal	256k
PX-85CS	CDROM	8X	Fast SCSI-2	1 disc Caddy	External	256k
PX-J2200 MegaPleX	CDROM Juk	2.8X	SCSI-2	200 disc	Internal	256k
PX-J2200-IXS	CDROM Juk	2.8X	SCSI-2	200 disc	External	256k
PX-R24CS	CD-R	2Xrec/4Xr	SCSI-2	1 disc Caddy	Internal	512k
PX-R24CSe	CD-R	2Xrec/4Xr	SCSI-2	1 disc Tray	External	256k
PX-R412CE	CD-RW	20X	SCSI-2	1 disc Caddy/Tray	External	2Mb
PX-R412CE/ISA	CD-RW	12X	Fast SCSI-2	1 disc Caddy	External	2Mb
PX-R412CE/PCI	CD-RW	12X	Fast SCSI-2	1 disc Caddy	External	2Mb
PX-R412CE/PCMCIA	CD-RW	12X	Fast SCSI-2	1 disc Caddy	External	2Mb
PX-R412CE/SW	CD-RW	12X	Fast SCSI-2	1 disc Caddy	External	2Mb
PX-R412CI/e	CD-RW	4Xrec/12Xr	Fast SCSI	1 disc Caddy	External	2Mb
PX-R412CI/ISA	CD-RW	4Xrec/12Xr	SCSI-2; 16-	1 disc Caddy	Internal	2Mb
PX-R412CI/PSI	CD-RW	4Xrec/12Xr	SCSI-2; 32-	1 disc Caddy	Internal	2Mb
PX-R412CI/SW	CD-RW	4Xrec/12Xr	Fast SCSI-2	1 disc Caddy	Internal	2Mb
PX-R820Ti/e 8/20max	CD-R	20Xr/8Xrec	Fast SCSI	1 disc Tray	Internal	4Mb
PX-W1210TA/SW	CD-RW	32Xr/12Xw/10Xw	EIDE/ATAPI4	1 disc Tray	Internal	2Mb
PX-W1210TS/SW	CD-RW	32Xr/12Xw/10Xrw	Ultra SCSI	1 disc Tray	Internal	4Mb

CD & DVD

Manufacturer Model	Drive Type	Drive Speed	Drive Interface	# Discs & Loader	Internal-External	Buffer
PX-W1210TSE/SW	CD-RW	32Xr/12Xw/10Xrw	Ultra SCSI	1 disc Tray	External	4Mb
PX-W1610TA/SW	CD-RW	16Xr/16Xw/10Xrw	EIDE/ATAPI4	1 disc Tray	Internal	2Mb
PX-W2410TU/SW	CD-RW	40Xr/24Xw/10Xrw	USB 2.0	1 disc Tray	External	4Mb
PX-W4220/e	CD-RW	4Xrec/20Xr	Fast SCSI	1 disc Tray	Internal	2Mb
PX-W8220Ti/e	CDROM	20Xr/8Xrec/2Xrw	Fast SCSI	1 disc Tray	Internal	4Mb
PX-W8432Ti	CD-RW	32Xr/8Xw/4Xrw	ATAPI4/EIDE	1 disc Tray	Internal	4Mb
UltraPlex	CDROM	32X	Ultra SCSI	1 disc Caddy	Internal	512k
UltraPleX 40MAX	CDROM	40X	UltraSCSI	1 disc Tray	Internal	512k
UltraPleX Wide	CDROM	40X	Wide Ultra	disc		512k

Procom Technology

Manufacturer Model	Drive Type	Drive Speed	Drive Interface	# Discs & Loader	Internal-External	Buffer
4X/4X/16X CDRW	CD-RW	16Xr/4Xw/4Xrw	Fast SCSI-2	1 disc Tray	Internal	2Mb
5X DVD IDE	DVD-ROM	5Xdvd/32Xcdrom	IDE	1 disc Tray	Internal	
5X DVD SCSI	DVD-ROM	5Xdvd/32Xcdrom	SCSI	1 disc Tray	Internal	
8X	CDROM	8X	SCSI	1 disc Caddy	Internal	
CCA-35E1	CDROM Juk	16X	SCSI-2	35 disc		256k
CCA-70E1	CDROM Juk	16X	SCSI-2	70 disc		256k
CD/DVD Force	DVD-ROM L	16Xcdrom	SCSI-2	disc Tray		128k
DR07001	DVD-ROM	1Xdvd	SCSI-2	1 disc Tray	Internal	512dvd
DR08001	DVD-ROM	1Xdvd/8Xcd	EIDE/ATAPI	1 disc Tray	Internal	256k
MCD 4X	CDROM	4X	SCSI-2	1 disc Tray	Internal	256k
MCD 650 MAC	CDROM	1X	SCSI	1 disc Procom Cad External		None
MCD 650 XT/AT/MCA	CDROM	1X	SCSI	1 disc Procom Cad Ext.	Internal	None
PCDR 2X/6X	CD-R	6Xr/2Xrec	SCSI	1 disc Tray	Internal	1 Mb
PCDR 4X/12X	CD-R	12Xr/4Xrec	Fast SCSI-2	1 disc Tray	Internal	1 Mb
PCDR 4X/24X	CD-R	24Xr/4Xrec	Fast SCSI-2	1 disc Tray	Internal	2Mb
PCDR 6X/24X	CD-R	24Xr/6Xrec	SCSI-2	1 disc Tray	Internal	2Mb
PCDR 800	CD-R	24Xr/8Xw	SCSI-2 Wide	1 disc Tray	Internal	2Mb

Ricoh Corporation

Manufacturer Model	Drive Type	Drive Speed	Drive Interface	# Discs & Loader	Internal-External	Buffer
MP-6200A	CD-RW	2Xw/6Xr	IDE/ATAPI	1 disc	Internal	1Mb
MP-6200S	CD-RW	6Xr/2Xw	SCSI-2	1 disc	External	2Mb
MP-6200S	CD-RW	6Xr/2Xw	SCSI-2	1 disc	Internal	2Mb
MP-7040A	CD-R/CD-R	20Xr/4Xrec	EIDE/ATAPI	disc	Internal	2Mb
MP-7060A	CD-RW/CDR	24Xr/6Xw/4Xrw	ATAPI/EIDE	1 disc	Internal	2Mb
MP-7060S	CD-RW/CDR	24Xr/6Xw/4Xrw	SCSI-2	1 disc	Internal	2Mb
MP-7060SE	CD-RW/CDR	24Xr/6Xw/4Xrw	SCSI-2	1 disc	External	2Mb
MP-7063A	CD-RW	32Xr/6Xw/4Xrw	ATAPI/EIDE	1 disc	Internal	2Mb
MP-7080A	CD-RW	32Xr/8Xw/4Xrw	ATAPI/EIDE	1 disc	Internal	4Mb
MP-7083A	CD-RW	32Xr/8Xw/8Xrw	ATAPI/EIDE	1 disc	Internal	2mb
MP-7120A	CD-RW	32Xr/8Xw/10Xrw	ATAPI/EIDE	1 disc Tray	Internal	4mb
MP-7125A	CD-R/RW	32Xr/12Xcdr/10X	ATAPI/EIDE	1 disc Tray	Internal	4Mb
MP-7200A	CD-RW	40Xr/20Xcdr/10X	ATAPI/EIDE	1 disc Tray	Internal	2Mb
MP-8040SE	CD-RW	20Xr/4Xw	SCSI-2	1 disc	External	2Mb
MP-9060A	CD-RW/DVD	24Xr/6Xw/4Xrw	ATAPI	1 disc Tray	Internal	2Mb
MP-9120A	CD-RW	32Xr/12Xw/10Xrw	ATAPI/EIDE	1 disc Tray	Internal	2mb
MP-7320A	CD-R/RW	40X/32Xw/10Xrw	EIDE/ATAPI	1 disc Tray	Internal	8Mb
MP-9200A	CDR-RW	40Xr/20Xw/10Xrw	ATAPI/EIDE	disc	Internal	2Mb
RO-1420C	CDROM	4Xr/2Xw	SCSI-2	1 disc Caddy	Internal	1Mb
RS-1060C	CD-R	2Xr/2Xw	SCSI	1 disc Caddy		512k

Samsung Electronics America

Manufacturer Model	Drive Type	Drive Speed	Drive Interface	# Discs & Loader	Internal-External	Buffer
DVD-905	CDROM			disc		
MR-A02B	DVD-RAM/R	6Xdvd/24Xcd	EIDE/ATAPI	1 disc Tray	Internal	1Mb
SC-140	CDROM	40X	EIDE/ATAPI	1 disc Tray	Internal	128k
SC-148C	CDROM	48X	EIDE/ATAPI	1 disc Tray	Internal	128k
SC-152L	CDROM	52X	EIDE/ATAPI	1 disc Tray	Internal	128k
SCR-1231	CDROM		ATAPI	1 disc Tray	Internal	256k
SCR-1638	CDROM	16X	EIDE/ATAPI	1 disc Tray	Internal	128k
SCR-2030	CDROM	24X	EIDE/ATAPI	1 disc Tray	Internal	512k
SCR-2430	CDROM	24X	EIDE/ATAPI	1 disc Tray	Internal	512k
SCR-2431	CDROM	24X	EIDE/ATAPI	1 disc Tray	Internal	512k
SCR-2437	CDROM	10X/24X	EIDE/ATAPI	1 disc Tray	Internal	256k
SCR-2438 (Slim)	CDROM	24X	EIDE/ATAPI	1 disc Tray	Internal	256k
SCR-3230	CDROM	12.8X/32X	EIDE/ATAPI	1 disc Tray	Internal	512k
SCR-3231	CDROM	32X	EIDE/ATAPI	1 disc Tray	Internal	512k
SCR-3232	CDROM	32X	EIDE/ATAPI	1 disc Tray	Internal	128k
SCR-630	CDROM	4X	ATAPI/EIDE	1 disc Tray	Internal	256k
SCR-631	CDROM		EIDE/ATAPI	1 disc Tray	Internal	128k
SCR-830	CDROM			disc		
SCR-831	CDROM		ATAPI	1 disc Tray	Internal	256k
SCW-230	CD-RW	6Xr/2Xw	EIDE/ATAPI	1 disc Tray	Internal	512k
SD-604	DVD-ROM	5Xdvd/32Xcd-rom	EIDE/ATAPI	1 disc Tray	Internal	512k
SD-606	DVD-ROM	32Xcd	EIDE/ATAPI	1 disc Tray	Internal	512k
SD-608	DVD-ROM	8Xdvd/40Xcdrom	EIDE/ATAPI	1 disc Tray	Internal	64k
SD-612	DVD-ROM	12Xdvd/40Xcdrom	EIDE/ATAPI	1 disc Tray	Internal	512k
SD-616T	DVD-ROM	16Xdvd/48Xcd	EIDE/ATAPI	1 disc Tray	Internal	512k
SDR-430	DVD-ROM		EIDE/ATAPI	1 disc Tray	Internal	512k
SM-304	DVD-ROM	4Xdvd/24Xcd/4Xw	EIDE/ATAPI	1 disc Tray	Internal	2Mb
SM-308	CD-RW/DVD	32x/8x/4x/8xdvd	EIDE/ATAPI	1 disc Tray	Internal	2mb

Manufacturer Model	Drive Type	Drive Speed	Drive Interface	# Discs & Loader	Internal-External	Buffer
SM-316B	DVD/CD-RW	12Xdvd/40/16/10	EIDE/ATAPI	1 disc Drawer	Internal	2mb
SN-124P	CDROM	24X	EIDE/ATAPI	1 disc Drawer	Internal	128k
SN-132	CDROM	32X	EIDE/ATAPI	1 disc Drawer	Internal	128k
SN-308B	DVD/CORW	8Xdvd/24X/8X/8X	EIDE/ATAPI	1 disc Tray	Internal	2Mb
SN-608	DVD-ROM	8Xdvd/24Xcd	EIDE/ATAPI	1 disc Tray	Internal	512k
SW-204	CD-RW	24Xr/4Xrec	EIDE/ATAPI	1 disc Tray	Internal	2048k
SW-206	CD-RW	32Xr/6Xw/4Xrw	EIDE/ATAPI	1 disc Tray	Internal	4096k
SW-207	CD-RW	32Xr/6Xw/4Xrw	EIDE/ATAPI	1 disc Tray	Internal	2048k
SW-208	CD-RW	32Xr/6Xw/4Xrw	EIDE/ATAPI	1 disc Tray	Internal	4096k
SW-212	CD-RW	32Xr/12Xrec/8Xrw	EIDE/ATAPI	1 disc		8mb
SW-216B	CD-RW	32Xr/16Xw/10Xrw	EIDE/ATAPI	1 disc		2Mb
SW-224B	CD-RW	40Xr/24Xw/10Xrw	EIDE/ATAPI	1 disc		2Mb
SW-408	CD-RW	32Xr/8Xrec/8Xrw	EIDE/ATAPI	1 disc Tray	Internal	2mb

Sanyo Electric

Manufacturer Model	Drive Type	Drive Speed	Drive Interface	# Discs & Loader	Internal-External	Buffer
C3G	CDROM	4X	EIDE	1 disc Caddy		256k
CRD-254SH	CDROM	4X	SCSI	1 disc Drawer		256k
ROM 3000 U	CDROM	1X	Non-SCSI Pa	1 disc Sony Caddy Ext		32k
ROM 3001 U	CDROM	1X	Non-SCSI Pa	1 disc Sony Caddy Ext		32k

Severn Companies

Manufacturer Model	Drive Type	Drive Speed	Drive Interface	# Discs & Loader	Internal-External	Buffer
SC-922 Gemini	CDROM	1X	Non-SCSI Pa	1 disc Sony Caddy Ext.		None

Smart and Friendly

Manufacturer Model	Drive Type	Drive Speed	Drive Interface	# Discs & Loader	Internal-External	Buffer
CD Pocket RW	CD-RW	20Xr/4Xw/4Xrw	PCMCIA	1 disc Tray	External	2Mb
CD Rocket 8X	CDROM	8Xw/20Xp	SCSI-2	1 disc Tray	Internal a	2Mb
CD Rocket Mach 12	CD-R	32Xr/12Xw/4Xrw	Ultra SCSI	1 disc Tray	Internal a	4Mb
CD SpeedWriter Deluxe	CDROM	12Xr/4Xw	SCSI-2	1 disc Tray	External	1Mb
CD SpeedWriter Internal	CDROM	12Xr/4Xw	SCSI-2	1 disc Tray	Internal	1Mb
CD SpeedWriter Plus External	CD-RW	24Xr/4Xw/2Xrw	SCSI-2	1 disc Tray	External	2Mb
CD SpeedWriter Plus Internal	CD-RW	24Xr/4Xw/2Xrw	Atapi	1 disc Tray	Internal	2Mb
CD TurboWriter RW External	CD-RW	24Xr/6Xw/4Xrw	SCSI-2	1 disc Tray	External	2 Mb
CD TurboWriter RW Internal	CD-RW	24Xr/6Xw/4Xrw	Atapi	1 disc Tray	Internal	2 Mb
CD-R 1002	CDROM	2Xr/2Xrec	SCSI-2	1 disc Caddy	External	1Mb
CD-R 1004	CDROM		SCSI-2	1 disc Caddy		512k
CD-R 2000	CD-R	2X	SCSI-2	1 disc	Internal	2 Mb
CD-R 2006 Plus	CDROM-rec	2Xrec/6Xr	SCSI-2	1 disc		1 Mb
CD-R 4000	CDROM	4X	SCSI-2	1 disc Caddy	Internal	512k
CD-R 4006	CDROM	6Xr/4Xw	SCSI-2	1 disc Tray	Internal	2Mb
CD-R 8020	CD-R	20Xp/8Xw	SCSI-2	1 disc Tray	Internal	1Mb
CD-RW 226 Plus External	CDROM	2X	SCSI-2	1 disc Tray	External	1Mb
CD-RW 226 Plus Internal	CDROM	2X	SCSI-2	1 disc Tray	Internal	1Mb
CD-RW 426 Deluxe	CDROM	6Xr/4Xw	EIDE	1 disc Tray	Internal	2Mb
CD-RW 426 Deluxe External	CDROM	6Xr/4Xw	SCSI-2	1 disc Tray	External	2Mb
CDJ 20016	CDROM Juk	20 disc Slot			External	256k
CDJ 28016	CDROM Juk	8X	SCSI-1	35 disc	External	256k
CDJ 35016	CDROM Juk	16X		4 disc Slot	External	256k
CDJ 4008	CDROM Juk	8X	SCSI-2	5 disc Slot	Internal	
CDJ 5016 SAF047	CDROM Juk	16X	SCSI-2	5 disc Slot	External	
CDJ 70016	CDROM Juk	16X		70 disc		256k
CDJ 7004	CDROM Juk	4X		7 disc Slot	External	128k
SAF1201 CD Mach 12 External	CD-R	32Xr/12Xw/4Xrw	Ultra SCSI	1 disc Tray	External	4Mb
SAF1202 CD Mach 12 Internal	CD-R	32Xr/12Xw/4Xrw	Ultra SCSI	1 disc Tray	Internal	4Mb
SAF757 CD Rocket SE Int	CD-R	20Xr/8Xw	SCSI-2	1 disc Tray	Internal	2Mb
SAF758 CD TurboWriter RW	CD-RW	24Xr/6Xw/4Xw	Atapi	1 disc Tray	Internal	2Mb
SAF759 CD TurboWriter RW	CD-RW	24Xr/6Xw/4Xrw	SCSI-2	1 disc Tray	External	2Mb
SAF768	CD-RW	24Xr/4Xw/4Xrw	PCMCIA	1 disc Tray	External	2Mb
SAF780	CDR	6Xr/4Xw	SCSI-2	1 disc Caddy	Internal	2Mb
SAF781	CDR	6Xr/4Xw	SCSI-2	1 disc Caddy	External	2Mb
SAF783	CD-R	12Xr/4Xw	SCSI-2	1 disc Tray	Internal	1Mb
SAF785	CDROM	12Xr/4Xw	SCSI-2	1 disc Tray	External	1Mb
SAF788	CD-R	16Xp/4Xw	SCSI-2	1 disc Tray	Internal	2Mb
SAF789	CD-R	16Xp/4Xw	SCSI-2	1 disc Tray	External	2Mb
SAF791 CD Rocket External	CD-R	20Xr/8Xw	SCSI-2	1 disc Tray	External	2Mb
SAF792	CDROM	24Xp/2Xw	EIDE	1 disc Tray	Internal	2Mb
SAF793 CD Rocket Internal	CD-R	20Xr/8Xw	SCSI-2	1 disc Tray	Internal	2Mb
SAF794	CD-R	24Xp/6Xw	SCSI-2	1 disc Tray	External	2Mb
SAF795	CD-R	24Xp/6Xw	SCSI-2	1 disc Tray	Internal	2Mb
SAF796 CD Rocket Internal	CD-R	20Xr/8Xw/2Xrw	SCSI-2	1 disc Tray	Internal	2Mb
SAF797 CD Rocket RW External	CD-R	20Xp/8Xw/2Xrw	Atapi	1 disc Tray	External	2Mb
SAF798	CD-RW	24Xr/4Xw/2Xrw	SCSI-2	1 disc Tray	External	2Mb
SAF799	CD-RW	24Xr/4Xw/2Xrw	SCSI-2	1 disc Tray	External	2Mb

Sony Corporation

Manufacturer Model	Drive Type	Drive Speed	Drive Interface	# Discs & Loader	Internal-External	Buffer
CDL-1100	CDROM Lib	2 12X	SCSI-2	100 disc Slot	External	
CDL-1100-20	CDROM Lib	2 12X	SCSI-2	100 disc Slot	External	64kb
CDL-1100-22H	CDROM Lib	2 12X	SCSI-2 FAST	100 disc Slot	External	64kb
CDL-1100-23M	CDROM Lib	2 12X	SCSI-2	100 disc Slot	External	64kb

Manufacturer Model	Drive Type	Drive Speed	Drive Interface	# Discs & Loader	Internal-External	Buffer
CDL-1100-40	CDROM Lib	2 24X	SCSI-2 FAST	100 disc Slot	External	64kb
CDL-2100-22B	CDROM	2 12X	SCSI-2	125 disc Slot	External	1 Mb
CDL-2200-22B	CDROM Lib	4 12X	SCSI-2	225 disc Slot	External	1 Mb
CDU-111	CDROM	8X	IDE (ATAPI)	1 disc Tray	Internal	128k
CDU-311-10	CDROM	8X	IDE (ATAPI)	1 disc Tray	Internal	128k
CDU-311-20	CDROM	8X	IDE (ATAPI)	1 disc Tray	Internal	256k
CDU-31A-02	CDROM	2X	Sony BUS	1 disc Tray	Internal	128k
CDU-31A-03	CDROM	2X	Sony BUS	1 disc Tray	Internal	64k
CDU-31A-LL/L	CDROM Lib			6 disc Tray	Internal	64k
CDU-31A-LL/N	CDROM Lib			6 disc Tray	Internal	64k
CDU-33A	CDROM			3 disc Tray	Internal	64k
CDU-415	CDROM	2X	Sony BUS	1 disc Tray	Internal	64k
CDU-510	CDROM	8X-12X	SCSI	1 disc Tray	Internal	256k
CDU-511	CDROM	13.6X	IDE/ATAPI	1 disc Caddy	Internal	
CDU-531	CDROM		Sony BUS	1 disc Caddy	Internal	128k
CDU-535	CDROM		Sony BUS	1 disc Caddy	Internal	8k
CDU-541	CDROM		Sony BUS	1 disc Caddy	External	8k
CDU-55E	CDROM	2X	SCSI-2 BUS	1 disc Tray	Internal	64k
CDU-55S	CDROM	2.4X	ATAPI	1 disc Tray	External	256k
CDU-561	CDROM	2X	SCSI-2	1 disc Caddy	Internal	256k
CDU-571	CDROM	13.6X	SCSI-2 BUS	1 disc Caddy	Internal	256k
CDU-6100	CDROM	1X	IDE/ATAPI	1 disc Slot	Internal	128k
CDU-6101	CDROM	1X	Non-SCSI Pa	1 disc Sony Caddy	External	8k
CDU-611	CDROM	24X	IDE/ATAPI	1 disc Tray	Internal	256k
CDU-6110	CDROM	1X	SCSI	1 disc Sony Caddy	External	8k
CDU-6111	CDROM	1X	SCSI	1 disc Sony Caddy	External	8k
CDU-625	CDROM	24X	IDE	1 disc Caddy	Internal	
CDU-6511	CDROM	2X	SCSI-2	1 disc Caddy	Internal	
CDU-6811	CDROM	2X	SCSI-2	1 disc Tray	Internal	256k
CDU-701	CDROM	32X	EIDE/ATAPI	disc	Caddy	External	128k
CDU-7101	CDROM	1X	Non-SCSI Pa	1 disc Sony Caddy	External	8k
CDU-711	CDROM	32X	EIDE	1 disc Caddy	Internal	256k
CDU-7201	CDROM		Sony BUS	1 disc Tray	External	8k
CDU-7205/N	CDROM		Sony BUS	1 disc Tray	External	8k
CDU-7211	CDROM		SCSI BUS	1 disc Tray	External	64k
CDU-7305	CDROM Lib		Sony BUS	6 disc Tray	External	64k
CDU-7305-3A	CDROM		Sony BUS	1 disc	External	64k
CDU-7511	CDROM	2X	SCSI-2	1 disc Tray	External	256k
CDU-75E	CDROM	4X	IDE	1 disc Tray	Internal	256k
CDU-76E	CDROM	4X	ATAPI (Mode	1 disc Tray	Internal	256k
CDU-77E	CDROM	4X	SCSI-2	1 disc Tray	Internal	256k
CDU-7811	CDROM	2X	IDE (ATAPI)	1 disc Tray	Internal	128k
CDU-8003	CDROM	2X	SCSI-2 BUS	1 disc Caddy	External	256k
CDU-920S	CDROM-R	2X	SCSI	1 disc Caddy	Internal	1Mb
CDU-9211S	CDROM-Rec	2X	SCSI-2	1 disc Caddy	Internal	1Mb
CDU-921S	CDROM-R	2X	SCSI-2	1 disc Caddy	Internal	1Mb
CDU-924S	CD-R	4Xr/2Xw	Single-ende	1 disc Caddy		1Mb
CDU-926S	CDROM	4Xr/2Xw	Single-ende	1 disc Caddy		512k
CDU-928E	CDROM-R	6Xr, 2Xw	Single-ende	1 disc Tray		512k
CDU-928E/C	CD-R	8X	IDE/ATAPI	1 disc Tray	Internal	512k
CDU-928E/H	CD-R	2Xw/8Xr	IDE/ATAPI	1 disc Caddy	Internal	512k
CDU-948S/C	CDROM	2Xw/8Xr	IDE/ATAPI	1 disc Caddy	Internal	512k
CDU-948S/CH	CDROM	4Xw/8Xr	SCSI-2	1 disc Caddy	Internal	
CDW-900E	CDROM-rec	2X	SCSI	1 disc Caddy	Internal	
CRX-100E/CH	CD-RW	4Xrec/24Xr	IDE/ATAPI	disc 1	Internal	1Mb
CRX-100E/X	CD-RW	6Xr/4Xrec/2Xrw	USB	1 disc	Internal	1Mb
CRX-100E/X2	CD-RW	6Xr/4Xrec/2Xrw	USB	1 disc Tray	External	1Mb
CRX-10U/A2	CD-RW	6Xr/4Xrec	USB	1 disc	Portable	8Mb
CRX-120E/C	CD-RW	24X/4Xrec/4Xrw	EIDE	1 disc	Internal	
CRX-120E/X	CD-RW	24X/4Xrec		1 disc	Internal	
CRX-140E/CH	CD-RW	32X/8Xw/4Xrw	EIDE/ATAPI	1 disc Tray	Internal	2Mb
CRX-140E/CH2	CD-RW	32X/8Xw/4Xrw	EIDE/ATAPI	1 disc Tray	Internal	4Mb
CRX-140S/C	CD-RW	32X/8Xw/4Xrw	SCSI-2	1 disc Tray	Internal	4Mb
CRX-145E/XI	CD-RW	32X/10Xw/4Xrw	EIDE/ATAPI	1 disc Tray	Internal	4Mb
CRX-145E/XH	CD-RW	32X/10Xw/4Xrw	IEEE 1394	1 disc Tray	External	4Mb
CRX-145S/C	CD-RW	32X/10Xw/4Xrw	SCSI-2	1 disc Tray	Internal	4Mb
CRX-145S/XS	CD-RW	32X/8Xw/4Xrw	SCSI-2	1 disc Tray	External	4Mb
CRX-1600L/A2	CD-RW	32X/12Xrec/8Xw	IEEE 1394	1 disc Tray	External	4Mb
CRX-160E/A1	CD-RW	32X/12Xrec/8Xw	EIDE/ATAPI	1 disc	Internal	4Mb
CRX-168B/A1	CD-RW	40X/16Xrec/10w	EIDE/ATAPI	1 disc	Internal	8Mb
CRX-1750L/A2	CD-RW	40X/24Xw/10Xrw	IEEE 1394	1 disc Tray	External	8Mb
CRX-1750U/A2	CD-RW	40X/24Xw/10Xrw	USB 2.0	1 disc Tray	External	2Mb
CRX-175A2/C1	CD-RW	40X/24Xw/10Xrw	EIDE	1 disc	Internal	
CRX-185A1/C1	CD-RW	40X/32Xw/10Xrw	EIDE/ATAPI	1 disc	Internal	2Mb
CRX-200E/A1	CD-RW	32X/12Xrec/8Xw	EIDE/ATAPI	1 disc	Internal	
CRX-75L/A2	CD-RW	24X/8Xw/4Xrw	IEEE 1394	1 disc	Internal	8Mb
CRX-85U/A2	DVD/CD-RW	8X/24X/20X/8X	USB 2.0	1 disc	Portable	4Mb
CSD-760E	CDROM	4X	ATAPI (Mode	1 disc Tray	External	8Mb
CSD-760S	CDROM	4X	SCSI-II	1 disc Tray	Internal	256k
CSD-7611M	CDROM	4X	SCSI-II	1 disc Tray	External	256k

CD & DVD

Manufacturer Model	Drive Type	Drive Speed	Drive Interface	# Discs & Loader	Internal-External	Buffer
CSD-76SB	CDROM	4X	SCSI-II	1 disc Tray	Internal	256k
CSD-880E	CDROM	8X	IDE/ATAPI	1 disc Tray	Internal	256k
CSD-88EN	CDROM	8X	IDE (ATAPI)	1 disc Tray	Internal	1M
CSP-920S	CDROM	2X	SCSI-2	1 disc Caddy	External	1M
CSP-9211S	CD-R	2X	SCSI-2	3 disc Caddy	Internal	1Mb
CSP-940S	CD-R	2X	SCSI	5 disc Caddy	Internal	1Mb
CSP-9411S	CD-R	2Xw/6Xr	Single-ende	1 disc	Internal	512k
CSP-960S	CD-R	2Xw/6Xr	Single-ende	1 disc	Internal	512k
CSP-9611H	CD-R	2Xw/6Xr	Single-ende	1 disc	External	512k
DDU100E/C	DVD-ROM	1XDVD/8XCD	IDE/ATAPI	1 disc	Internal	512k
DDU100E/N	DVD-ROM	1XDVD/8XCD	IDE/ATAPI	1 disc	Internal	512k
DDU220E/H	DVD-ROM	5Xdvd/24Xc	EIDE/ATAPI	disc Tray		2Mb
DRU120A	DVD+RW/CD	8Xdvd/32Xcd	IDE/ATAPI	1 disc		
DVD220	DVD-ROM		DVD/24X	disc		
PRD-250WN	CDROM	4X	SCSI-2 to P	1 disc Slot	External	128k
PRD-650WN	CDROM	6X	SCSI-2	1 disc Tray	Portable	128k

Sun Microsystems

Manufacturer Model	Drive Type	Drive Speed	Drive Interface	# Discs & Loader	Internal-External	Buffer
Sun CD 64k	CDROM	1X	SCSI	1 disc Sony Caddy	External	

Teac America, Inc.

Manufacturer Model	Drive Type	Drive Speed	Drive Interface	# Discs & Loader	Internal-External	Buffer
4X24	CDR	24Xr/4Xrec	Fast SCSI-2	1 disc Tray	Int/Ext	2Mb
6X24X4	CD-R	24Xr/6Xrec/4Xw	Fast SCSI-2	1 disc Tray	Int/Ext	2Mb
8X24	CDR	24Xr/8Xw	Fast SCSI-2	1 disc Tray	Int/Ext	4Mb
CD-210PU	CDROM	10X	USB	1 disc Tray	External	128k
CD-211PE(Portable)	CDROM	10X	PCMCIA Type	1 disc Clam Shell	External	128k
CD-220E	CDROM	20X	IDE/ATAPI	1 disc	Internal	
CD-224E	CDROM	24X	IDE/ATAPI	1 disc	Internal	
CD-224PE	CDROM	24X	PCMCIA	1 disc	Portable	
CD-28L	CDROM	8X	IDE/ATAPI	1 disc	Internal	128k
CD-316E	CDROM	16X	IDE/ATAPI	1 disc Drawer	Internal	128k
CD-36E	CDROM	8X	ATAPI	1 disc Drawer	Internal	128k
CD-38E	CDROM	8X	IDE/ATAPI	1 disc	Internal	128k
CD-40E	CDROM	2X	IDE/ATAPI	1 disc Tray	Internal	128k
CD-44E	CDROM	4X	SCSI-2	1 disc Caddy	Internal	64k
CD-50	CDROM	2X	SCSI-2	1 disc Tray	Internal	128k
CD-512E	CDROM	12X	IDE/ATAPI	1 disc Tray	Internal	512k
CD-512S	CDROM	12X	SCSI-2	1 disc Tray	Internal	128k
CD-516E	CDROM	16X	IDE/ATAPI	1 disc Tray	Internal	512k
CD-516S	CDROM	16X	SCSI-2	1 disc Tray	Internal	128k
CD-524E	CDROM	24X	ATAPI	1 disc Tray	Internal	128k
CD-532E	CDROM	32X	IDE/ATAPI	1 disc Tray	Internal	512k
CD-532S	CDROM	32X	Ultra SCSI	1 disc Tray	Internal	512k
CD-540	CDROM	40X	IDE/Atapi	1 disc Tray	Internal	128k
CD-55A	CDROM	4X	Teac AT Int	1 disc Tray	Internal	64k
CD-56E	CDROM	6X	IDE/ATAPI	1 disc Tray	Internal	256k
CD-56S	CDROM	6X	SCSI-2	1 disc Tray	Internal	256k
CD-58E	CDROM	8X	IDE/ATAPI	1 disc Tray	Internal	128k
CD-58S	CDROM	8X	SCSI-2	1 disc Tray	Internal	128k
CD-C68E	CDROM cha	8X	IDE/ATAPI	6 disc Direct Load	Internal	128k
CD-R50S	CD-R	4Xr/4Xw	Fast SCSI-2	1 disc Tray	Internal	1Mb
CD-R55S	CD-R	12Xr/4Xw	Fast SCSI-2	1 disc Tray	Internal	1Mb
CD-R55S	CD-R	12Xr/4Xw	Fast SCSI-2	1 disc Tray	External	
CD-W512E	CD-RW	32Xr/12Xw/10Xrw	IDE/Atapi	1 disc Tray	Internal	4Mb
CD-W516E	CD-RW	40Xr/16Xw/10Xrw	IDE/ATAPI	1 disc Tray	Internal	2Mb
CD-W524E	CD-RW	40Xr/24Xw/10Xrw	IDE/ATAPI	1 disc Tray	Internal	8Mb
CD-W540E	CD-RW	48Xr/40Xw/12Xrw	IDE/ATAPI	1 disc Tray	Internal	2Mb
CD-W54E	CD-RW	32Xr/4Xr/4Xw	IDE/Atapi	1 disc Tray	Internal	2Mb
CD-W54E/USB	CD-RW	6Xr/4Xrec/4Xrw	USB	1 disc Tray	External	2Mb
CD-W58E	CD-RW	32Xr/8Xw/8Xrw	IDE/ATAPI	1 disc Tray	Internal	
DV-22E	DVD-ROM			disc		
DV-28PE/KIT	DVD-ROM	8Xdvd/24Xcdrom	PCMCIA	1 disc Tray	Portable	
MC-1200	CDROM	8X	SCSI-2	200 disc 4 Mag	External	256k
MC-1600	CDROM	8X	SCSI-2	600 disc 12 Mag	External	256k
SuperQuad CF506A 4X	CDROM	4X	AT	1 disc Tray	Internal	64k

Texel

Manufacturer Model	Drive Type	Drive Speed	Drive Interface	# Discs & Loader	Internal-External	Buffer
DM 3024	CDROM	2X	SCSI	1 disc Caddy	Internal	64k
DM 3028	CDROM	2X	SCSI	1 disc Caddy	Internal	64k
DM 5000 LM	CDROM	1X	SCSI	1 disc Sony Caddy	External	64k
DM 5000 LS	CDROM	1X	SCSI	1 disc Sony Caddy	External	64k
DM 5028	CDROM	2X	SCSI-2	1 disc Caddy	External	64k

Todd Enterprises

Manufacturer Model	Drive Type	Drive Speed	Drive Interface	# Discs & Loader	Internal-External	Buffer
TCDR-3000	CDROM	1X	Non-SCSI Pa	1 disc Sony Caddy	External	32k
TCDR-3004	CDROM	1X	Non-SCSI Pa	1 disc Sony Caddy	External	32k
TCDR-6000	CDROM	1X	Non-SCSI Pa	1 disc Sony Caddy	External	32k

Manufacturer Model	Drive Type	Drive Speed	Drive Interface	# Discs & Loader	Internal-External	Buffer
Toshiba America						
CD400T	CDROM	4X	IDE/ATAPI	1 disc Tray	Internal	256k
SD-C2002	DVD-ROM			disc		
SD-C2102	DVD-ROM	2.4dvd/20Xcdrom	ATAPI	1 disc	Internal	256k
SD-C2202	DVD-ROM	24Xcdrom	ATAPI	1 disc	Internal	
SD-C2302	DVD-ROM	6Xdvd/24Xcdrom	Atapi	1 disc	Internal	128k
SD-C2402	DVD-ROM	8Xdvd/24Xcdrom	Atapi	1 disc	Internal	128k
SD-C2502	DVD-ROM	24Xcdrom	Atapi	1 disc	Internal	128k
SD-C2512	DVD-ROM	8Xdvd/24Xcd	Atapi	1 disc	Internal	512k
SD-M1102	DVD-ROM	2Xdvd/24Xcdrom	ATAPI	1 disc	Internal	256k
SD-M1201	DVD-ROM	32Xcdrom	SCSI	1 disc	Internal	
SD-M1202	DVD-ROM	4.8dvd/32Xcdrom	ATAPI	1 disc	Internal	256k
SD-M1212	DVD-ROM	32Xcdrom/6Xdvd	ATAPI	1 disc	Internal	
SD-M1302	DVD-ROM	8Xdvd/40Xcdrom	Atapi	1 disc		256k
SD-M1401	DVD-ROM		SCSI	1 disc		128k
SD-M1402	DVD-ROM	12Xdvd/40Xcdrom	Atapi	1 disc		128k
SD-M1502	DVD-ROM	48Xcdrom	Atapi	1 disc Tray		128k
SD-M1612	DVD-ROM	16Xdvd/48Xcd	Atapi	1 disc	Internal	512k
SD-R1002	CD-RW/DVD	4Xdvd/24Xcdrom	EIDE/ATAPI	1 disc	Internal	2Mb
SD-R1102	CD-RW/DVD	8Xdvd/32r/8rw/8	EIDE/ATAPI	1 disc	Internal	2Mb
SD-R1202	CD-RW/DVD	12Xdvd/40r/10rw	Atapi	1 disc	Internal	2Mb
SD-R2002	CD-RW/DVD	6Xdvd/24r/4rw/4	EIDE/ATAPI	1 disc	Internal	2Mb
SD-R2102	CD-RW/DVD	8Xdvd/24r/8rw/8	Atapi	1 disc	Internal	2Mb
SD-W1001	DVD-RAM		SCSI-2	disc		
SD-W1002	DVD-RAM	16Xcdrom	ATAPI	1 disc	Internal	
SD-W1101	DVD-RAM	2Xdvd/16Xcdrom	SCSI-2	1 disc Cartridges	Internal	
SD-W1111	DVD-RAM		SCSI	1 disc	Internal	2Mb
SD-W2002	DVD-RAM	24Xcd	ATAPI	1 disc	Internal	8Mb
SR-C8002	CDR/CD-RW	24Xr/8Xw/8Xrw	Atapi	1 disc	Internal	2Mb
SR-C8102	CDR/CD-RW	24Xr/16Xw/10Xrw	Atapi	1 disc	Internal	2Mb
TXM-3401E	CDROM	2X	SCSI-2	1 disc	External	256k
TXM-3401P	CDROM	2X	SCSI-2	1 disc	Portable	256k
TXM-3501A4	CDROM	4X	SCSI	disc Caddy		
TXM-3501E	CDROM	4X	SCSI-2	1 disc Caddy	External	256k
TXM-3601D	CDROM	4X	SCSI-2	1 disc	Internal	
TXM-3701D	CDROM	6.7X	SCSI-2	1 disc Tray	External	256k
TXM-3801F1	CDROM	15X	SCSI-2	1 disc Tray	External	256k
TXM-4101L	CDROM		SCSI-2	1 disc Tray	External	
TXM-5201D	CDROM	3.4X	SCSI-2	1 disc	External	256k
TXM-5701F1	CDROM	12X	SCSI	1 disc	External	256k
TXM-6201F1	CDROM	24X	SCSI	1 disc	External	
XM-1402B	CDROM	6X		disc		
XM-1502B	CDROM	11X	ATAPI	1 disc Tray	Internal	128k
XM-1602B	CDROM	20X	ATAPI	1 disc Tray	Internal	128k
XM-1702B	CDROM		ATAPI	1 disc Tray	Internal	128k
XM-1802B	CDROM	24X	EIDE/ATAPI	1 disc	Internal	128k
XM-1902B	CDROM	24X	EIDE/ATAPI	1 disc	Internal	128k
XM-2402B	CDROM	11X	ATAPI	1 disc Tray	Internal	128k
XM-3201A1-MAC	CDROM	2X	SCSI	1 disc Sony Caddy	External	-64k
XM-3201A1-PCF	CDROM	2X	SCSI	1 disc Sony Caddy	External	-65k
XM-3201A1-PS2	CDROM	2X	SCSI	1 disc Sony Caddy	External	-64k
XM-3401B	CDROM	2X	SCSI-2	1 disc Caddy	Internal	256k
XM-3501B	CDROM	4X	SCSI-2	1 disc Caddy	Internal	256k
XM-3501E	CDROM	4X	SCSI	1 disc	External	
XM-3601D1	CDROM	4.5X	SCSI	1 disc	External	
XM-3701	CDROM	6.7X	SCSI-2	1 disc Tray	External	256k
XM-3701B	CDROM	6.7X	SCSI-2	1 disc Tray	Internal	256k
XM-3801B	CDROM	15X	SCSI-2	1 disc Tray	Internal	256k
XM-4100A	CDROM	2X	SCSI-2	1 disc Tray	Portable	-64k
XM-4101B	CDROM	2X	SCSI-2	1 disc Tray	Internal	-64k
XM-5071	CDROM	12X	SCSI	1 disc	Internal	
XM-5100-A-MAC	CDROM	2X	SCSI	1 disc Tray	External	-64k
XM-5100-A-PCF	CDROM	2X	SCSI	1 disc Tray	External	-64k
XM-5100-A-PS2	CDROM	2X	SCSI	1 disc Tray	External	-64k
XM-5201B	CDROM	3.4X	SCSI-2	1 disc Tray	Internal	256k
XM-5302B	CDROM	4X	ATAPI/IDE	1 disc Tray	Internal	256k
XM-5401	CDROM	4X	SCSI-2	1 disc Tray	Internal	256k
XM-5402	CDROM	4X	IDE/ATAPI	1 disc Tray	Internal	256k
XM-5522	CDROM	6X	ATAPI	1 disc Tray	Internal	128k
XM-5602	CDROM	8X	ATAPI	1 disc Tray	Internal	256k
XM-5701B	CDROM	12X	SCSI-2	1 disc Tray	Internal	256k
XM-5702B	CDROM	12X	ATAPI	1 disc Tray	Internal	256k
XM-6002B	CDROM	16X	EIDE/ATAPI	1 disc Tray	Internal	256k
XM-6102B	CDROM	12-24X	ATAPI	1 disc	Internal	256k
XM-6201B	CDROM	32X	SCSI-2	1 disc Tray	Internal	256k
XM-6201F1	CDROM	32X	SCSI-2	1 disc Tray	External	256k
XM-6202B	CDROM	32X	EIDE/ATAPI	1 disc Tray	Internal	256k
XM-6302B	CDROM	32X	EIDE/ATApi	1 disc	Internal	256k
XM-6401B	CDROM	40X	EIDE/ATAPI	1 disc	Internal	256k
XM-6402B	CDROM	32X	EIDE/ATAPI	1 disc	Internal	128k

Manufacturer Model	Drive Type	Drive Speed	Drive Interface	# Discs & Loader	Internal-External	Buffer
XM-6502B	CDROM	40X	EIDE/ATAPI	1 disc Tray	Internal	128k
XM-6602B	CDROM	40X	EIDE/ATAPI	1 disc Tray	Internal	128k
XM-6702B	CDROM	48X	EIDE/ATAPI	1 disc Tray	Internal	128k
XM-7002B	CDROM	24X	EIDE/ATAPI	1 disc Tray	Internal	128k
XM-7102B	CDROM	32X	Atapi	1 disc Tray	Internal	128k

Verbatim

Manufacturer Model	Drive Type	Drive Speed	Drive Interface	# Discs & Loader	Internal-External	Buffer
CD-RW 2x2x6 Mac Ext	CD-RW	6Xr/2Xrw	SCSI-2	1 disc Tray	External	1 Mb
CD-RW 2x2x6 PC Ext	CD-RW	6Xr/2Xrw	SCSI-2	1 disc Tray	External	1 Mb
CD-RW 2x2x6 PC Int	CD-RW	6Xr/2Xrw	SCSI-2	1 disc Tray	Internal	1 Mb
CD-RW 2x2x6e	CD-RW	6Xr/4Xrw	SCSI	1 disc	External	
CD-RW 4420a	CD-RW	20Xr/4Xrw	ATAPI/EIDE	1 disc Tray	Internal	2Mb
CDR 4x12	CD-R	12Xr/4Xw	Fast SCSI-2	1 disc Tray	Internal	1Mb
MCA CDVR	CD-R	4Xr/2Xw	SCSI-2	disc	Internal	1 Mb

Wearnes Peripherals Intl

Manufacturer Model	Drive Type	Drive Speed	Drive Interface	# Discs & Loader	Internal-External	Buffer
CDD-1020	CDROM	10X	IDE	1 disc Tary	Internal	256k
CDD-120	CDROM	2X	IDE/ATAPI	1 disc Tray		256k
CDD-240	CDROM	4X	IDE	1 disc	Internal	256k
CDD-320	CDROM	6X	IDE	1 disc Tray	Internal	256k
Multi-Taskin' CDD-1620	CDROM	16X	EIDE/ATAPI	1 disc Tray		128k

Workstatin Solutions

Manufacturer Model	Drive Type	Drive Speed	Drive Interface	# Discs & Loader	Internal-External	Buffer
OFS-CD	CDROM	1X	SCSI	1 disc Sony Caddy Ext.		None

Yamaha Systems Tech, Inc.

Manufacturer Model	Drive Type	Drive Speed	Drive Interface	# Discs & Loader	Internal-External	Buffer
CDR100	CDROM	2X	SCSI-2	1 disc Caddy	Internal	512k
CDR100-Recordable	CD-R	4X	SCSI-2	1 disc Caddy	Internal	512k
CDR102	CDROM	2X	SCSI-2	1 disc Caddy	Internal	512k
CDR400	CD-R	6Xr/4Xrw	SCSI-2	1 disc Tray	Internal	2Mb
CDR400AT	CD-R	1Xrec/6Xr	SCSI-2	1 disc Tray	Internal	2Mb
CDR400TI	CDROM	6Xr/4Xrw	SCSI-2	1 disc Tray	Internal	256k
CDR401	CD-R	4Xr/2Xw	EIDE/ATAPI	1 disc Tray	Internal	2Mb
CRW2100EZ	CD-RW	40Xr/16Xw/10Xrw	EIDE	1 disc Tray	Internal	8Mb
CRW2100FXZ	CD-RW	40Xr/16Xw/10Xrw	IEEE 1394	1 disc Tray	External	8Mb
CRW2100SXZ	CD-RW	40Xr/16Xw/10Xrw	SCSI-3	1 disc Tray	External	8Mb
CRW2100SZ	CD-RW	40Xr/16Xw/10Xrw	SCSI-3	1 disc Tray	Internal	8Mb
CRW2200EZ	CD-RW	40Xr/20Xw/10Xrw	EIDE	1 disc Tray	Internal	8Mb
CRW2200FXZ	CD-RW	40Xr/20Xw/10Xrw	IEEE 1394	1 disc Tray	External	8Mb
CRW2200SXZ	CD-RW	40Xr/20Xw/10Xrw	UltraSCSI3	1 disc Tray	External	8Mb
CRW2200SZ	CD-RW	40Xr/20Xw/10Xrw	ULSCSI/EIDE	1 disc Tray	Internal	8Mb
CRW2200UXZ	CD-RW	40Xr/20Xw/10Xrw	USB 2.0	1 disc Tray	External	8Mb
CRW216E	CD-RW	16Xr/2Xrw	EIDE	1 disc	Internal	1Mb
CRW2216EZ	CD-RW	16Xr/2Xrw/2Xrw	EIDE	1 disc Tray	Internal	1Mb
CRW2260TIPC	CD-RW	6Xr/2Xw/2Xrw	SCSI-2	1 disc		1Mb
CRW3200EZ	CD-RW	40Xr/24Xw/10Xrw	EIDE/ATAPI	1 disc Tray	Internal	8Mb
CRW3200FXZ	CD-RW	40Xr/24Xw/10Xrw	IEEE1394	1 disc Tray	External	8Mb
CRW3200SXZ	CD-RW	40Xr/24Xw/10Xrw	UltraSCSI3	1 disc Tray	External	8Mb
CRW3200SZ	CD-RW	40Xr/24Xw/10Xrw	SCSI3/EIDE	1 disc Tray	Internal	8Mb
CRW3200UXZ	CD-RW	40Xr/24Xw/10Xrw	USB 2.0	1 disc Tray	External	8Mb
CRW4001	CD-RW	2Xw/6Xr	EIDE/ATAPI	1 disc Tray	Internal	2MB
CRW4260	CDROM	6X	SCSI-2	1 disc Tray	External	2Mb
CRW4260TI	CDROM	6X	SCSI-2	1 disc Tray	Internal	256k
CRW4260TIPC	CD-RW	6Xr/4Xw/2Xrw	SCSI-2	1 disc	Internal	2Mb
CRW4260TXPM	CD-RW	6Xr/4Xw/2Xrw	SCSI-2	1 disc	External	2Mb
CRW4261TIPC	CD-RW	6Xr/4Xw/2Xrw	EIDE	1 disc	Internal	2Mb
CRW4416E	CD-RW	16Xr/4Xrw	EIDE	1 disc Tray	Internal	2Mb
CRW4416S	CD-RW	16Xr/4Xrw	Fast SCSI-2	1 disc Tray	Internal	2Mb
CRW4416SXZ	CD-RW	16Xr/4Xw/4Xrw	SCSI-2	1 disc Tray	External	2Mb
CRW6416S	CD-R	16Xr/4Xw	Fast SCSI-2	1 disc Tray	Internal	2Mb
CRW6416SXZ	CD-RW	16Xr/6Xw/4Xrw	SCSI-2	1 disc Tray	External	2Mb
CRW6416SZ	CD-RW	16Xr/6Xw/4Xrw	SCSI-2	1 disc Tray	Internal	2Mb
CRW70	CD-RW	24Xr/12Xw/8Xrw	USB 2.0	1 disc Tray		8Mb
CRW8424EZ	CD-RW	24Xr/8Xw/4Xrw	EIDE/ATAPI	1 disc Tray	Internal	4Mb
CRW8424SXZ	CD-RW	24Xr/8Xw/4Xrw	SCSI-3	1 disc Tray	External	4Mb
CRW8424SZ	CD-RW	24Xr/8Xw/4Xrw	SCSI-3	1 disc Tray	Internal	4Mb
CRW8824EZ	CD-RW	24Xr/8Xw/8Xrw	EIDE/ATAPI	1 disc Tray	Internal	4Mb
CRW8824FXZ	CD-RW	24Xr/8Xw/8Xrw	IEEE 1394	1 disc Tray	External	4Mb
CRW8824SXZ	CD-RW	24Xr/8Xw/8Xrw	SCSI-3	1 disc Tray	External	4Mb
CRW8824SZ	CD-RW	24Xr/8Xw/8Xrw	SCSI-3	1 disc Tray	Internal	4Mb

Young Minds

Manufacturer Model	Drive Type	Drive Speed	Drive Interface	# Discs & Loader	Internal-External	Buffer
CDR 100 XA	CDROM Juk	2X	SCSI	100 disc 2 Cartridge		
Kubik 240	CDROM Juk	4 12Xcdrom/4 12	SCSI	disc Mailbox Slo		
NSM Mercury 20	CDROM Juk	2 4X	SCSI	150 disc 3 Cartridge		
NSM Mercury 40	CDROM Juk	4 4X	SCSI	150 disc 3 Cartridge		
YMI Dual Drv for Sun	CDROM	1X	SCSI	2 disc Sony Caddy	External	64k
YMI Single Drv	CDROM	1X	SCSI	1 disc Sony Caddy	External	64k

Magneto Optical Drive Specifications

Magneto Optical Drive Manufacturers

The following table is a general summary of companies that have manufactured and/or are still manufacturing MO drives. If you have information concerning the status of any of these companies, such as "XYZ Company went bankrupt in August, 1990" or "XYZ Company was bought by Q Company," please let us know so we can keep this section current. If a phone number is listed in the Status column, the company is in business. Telephone numbers for drive manufacturers are also listed in the Phone Book chapter of this book. (page 905)

Manufacturer	Phone
Adaptec	408-945-8600
APS Technologies	800-395-5871
Digital Equipment Corp	800-282-6672 Supported by Compaq Computer
Epson America, Inc.	562-981-3840
Fujitsu America, Inc.	408-432-6333
Hewlett-Packard Co	301-670-4300 or 800-752-0900
Hitachi America, Ltd.	800-448-2244
IBM	800-772-2227
Maxoptix	510-353-9700
Maxtor Corporation	303-678-2700
Most, Inc.	714-898-9400
Olympus America, Inc.	631-844-5520
OR Computer Systems PTE Ltd	Unknown
Pinnacle Micro, Inc.	949-635-3000
Pioneer New Media Tech, Inc.	800-444-6784
Plasmon Data, Inc.	952-946-4100
Quantum Corporation	See Maxtor; merged 4-2-01
Sony Corp	201-930-1000
Teac America, Inc.	323-726-0303
Verbatim Corp.	704-547-6500

Total number of Magneto Optical Drives = 403 (last year - 396)

Magneto Optical Drive Syntax and Notation

The following are descriptions of the information contained in the MO drive tables.

1. Drive Size	Formatted drive size in megabytes
2. Media Type	Size and type of disk media
3. Discs	Number of discs the drive holds
4. Interface	Type of communication interface between the computer and drive
5. Encoding	Data encoding method used on drive: 1,7RLL, 2,7RLL, etc.
6. Form Factor	Physical diameter and height (in inches) of drive 5.25HH, 3.5HH, 3.5/3H, 2.5, etc.
7. Xfer Rate	The rate, in megabytes/second, that data can move to and from the drive.
8. RPM	Drive motor Revolutions Per Minute, larger number=faster drive
9. Cache Size	Read ahead cache/buffer. More provides better performance.

Sequoia needs your help! If you have specifications on new or obsolete MO drives, please send them to us so that we can include them in future editions of this book.

Magneto Optical

Manufacturer	Drive Size Form Factor	Media Type Xfer Rate	#Disks RPM	Interface Cache	Factor Encoding
ADAPTEC					
2940	—	—	—	SCSI-2	—
	—	—	—	—	
APS TECHNOLOGIES					
PRO 640MB MAC	606Mb	—	—	SCSI-2	—
		—	3600	2mb	
PRO 640MB PC	606Mb	—	—	SCSI-2	—
	3.5	—	3600	2mb	
DIGITAL EQUIPMENT CORP					
RW545-UA	—	—	—	—	—
	—	—	—	—	
RW546-ZA	—	—	—	—	—
	—	—	—	—	
RW551-UA	—	—	—	—	—
	—	—	—	—	
RW551-ZC	—	—	—	—	—
	—	—	—	—	
RW552-UA	—	—	—	—	—
	—	—	—	—	
RW552-UB	—	—	—	—	—
	—	—	—	—	
RW552-ZF	—	—	—	—	—
	—	—	—	—	
RW555-ZF	—	—	—	—	—
	—	—	—	—	
RW557-UA	—	—	—	—	—
	—	—	—	—	
RW557-ZF	—	—	—	—	—
	—	—	—	—	
RWZ53-FA	—	—	—	—	—
	—	—	—	—	
RWZ53-VA	—	—	—	—	—
	—	—	—	—	
RWZ53-VU	—	—	—	—	—
	—	—	—	—	
EPSON AMERICA, INC.					
OMD-5010	128Mb	—	—	SCSI	—
	3.5HH	7.6Mb/s	3600	256k	
OMD-6020	128Mb	—	—	SCSI	2,7 RLL
	3.5 3H	3.8Mb/s	3600	500k	
OMD-6020	230Mb	—	—	SCSI	2,7 RLL
	3.5 3H	3.8Mb/s	3600	500k	
FUJITSU AMERICA, INC.					
DynaMO 1300FE	1300Mb	3.5-inch MO	—	IEEE 1394	1,7 RLL
	3.5	5.9Mb/s	4500	512k	
DynaMO 1300SD	128Mb	90mm MO	—	SCSI-2	1,7 RLL
	—	10Mb/s	4500	2048k	
DynaMO 1300SD	230Mb	90mm MO	—	SCSI-2	1,7 RLL
	—	10Mb/s	4500	2048k	
DynaMO 1300SD	540Mb	90mm MO	—	SCSI-2	1,7 RLL
	—	10Mb/s	4500	2048k	
DynaMO 1300SD	640Mb	90mm MO	—	SCSI-2	1,7 RLL
	—	10Mb/s	4500	2048k	
DynaMO 1300SD	1283Mb	90mm MO	—	SCSI-2	1,7 RLL
	—	10Mb/s	3214	2048k	
DynaMO 1300SF	1300Mb	90mm MO	—	Ultra SCSI	1,7 RLL
	3.5	5.9	4500	2mb	
DynaMO 1300SFUSB	1300Mb	90mm MO	—	USB 1.1	1,7 RLL
	3.5	5.9	4500	2mb	
DynaMO 1300SZI	1300Mb	90mm MO	—	Ultra SCSI	1,7 RLL
	—	5.9Mb/s	4500	2mb	

Manufacturer	Drive Size / Form Factor	Media Type / Xfer Rate	#Disks RPM	Interface / Cache Factor	Encoding
DynaMO 230	230Mb / 3.5 3H	90mm MO / 2.1Mb/s	3600	SCSI-2 / 237k	2,7 RLL
DynaMO 230	128Mb / 3.5 3H	90mm MO / 1.1Mb/s	3600	SCSI-2 / 237k	2,7 RLL
DynaMO 230 IDE	128Mb	90mm MO / 1.6Mb/s	2700	EIDE/ATA-2 / 128k	2,7 RLL
DynaMO 230 IDE	230Mb	90mm MO / 1.6Mb/s	2700	EIDE/ATA-2 / 128k	2,7 RLL
DynaMO 230 PCMCIA	128Mb	90mm MO / 1.6Mb/s	2700	PCMCIA-ATA / 128k	2,7 RLL
DynaMO 230 PCMCIA	230Mb	90mm MO / 1.6Mb/s	2700	PCMCIA-ATA / 128k	2,7 RLL
DynaMO 640	128Mb	90mm MO / 3.9Mb/s	3600	SCSI-2 / 512k	2-7 RLLC
DynaMO 640	230Mb	90mm MO / 3.9Mb/s	3600	SCSI-2 / 512k	2-7 RLLC
DynaMO 640	540Mb	90mm MO / 3.9Mb/s	3600	SCSI-2 / 512k	1-7 RLLC
DynaMO 640	640Mb	90mm MO / 3.9Mb/s	3600	SCSI-2 / 512k	1-7 RLLC
DynaMO 640 Parallel	230Mb	90mm MO / 3.9Mb/s	3600	SCSI / 512k	2-7 RLLC
DynaMO 640 Parallel	540Mb	90mm MO / 3.9Mb/s	3600	SCSI / 512k	2-7 RLLC
DynaMO 640 Parallel	640Mb	90mm MO / 3.9Mb/s	3600	SCSI / 512k	1-7 RLLC
DynaMO 640AI	230Mb / 3.5	MO / 3.9Mb/s	3600	ATAPI / 512k	
DynaMO 640AI	128Mb / 3.5	MO / 3.9Mb/s	3600	ATAPI / 512k	
DynaMO 640AI	540Mb / 3.5	MO / 3.9Mb/s	3600	ATAPI / 512k	
DynaMO 640AI	640Mb / 3.5	MO / 3.9Mb/s	3600	ATAPI / 512k	
DynaMO 640FE	640Mb / 3.5	3.5-inch MO / 3.9Mb/s	3600	IEEE 1394 / 512k	2,7 RLL
DynaMO 640FE	540Mb / 3.5	3.5-inch MO / 2.1Mb/s	3600	IEEE 1394 / 512k	RLL 2,7
DynaMO 640FE	230Mb / 3.5	3.5-inch MO / 2.1Mb/s	3600	IEEE 1394 / 512k	2,7 RLL
DynaMO 640FE	128Mb / 3.5	3.5-inch MO / 1.1Mb/sec	3600	IEEE 1394 / 512k	2,7 RLL
DynaMO 640SD	128Mb	90mm MO / 10Mb/s	3600	SCSI-2 / 2048k	2-7 RLLC
DynaMO 640SD	230Mb	90mm MO / 10Mb/s	3600	SCSI-2 / 2048k	2-7 RLLC
DynaMO 640SD	540Mb	90mm MO / 10Mb/s	3600	SCSI-2 / 2048k	1-7 RLLC
DynaMO 640SD	640Mb	90mm MO / 10Mb/s	3600	SCSI-2 / 2048k	1-7 RLLC
DynaMO 640SE	643Mb / 3.5	90mm MO / 3.9Mb/sec	3600	SCSI-2 / 2mb	1-7 RLLC
DynaMO 640SE	538Mb / 3.5	90mm MO / 3.9Mb/s	3600	SCSI-2 / 2mb	1-7 RLLC
DynaMO 640SE	230Mb / 3.5	90mm MO / 2.1Mb/s	3600	SCSI-2 / 2mb	2-7 RLLC
DynaMO 640SE	128Mb / 3.5	90mm MO / 1.09Mb/s	3600	SCSI-2 / 2mb	2-7 RLLC
DynaMO 640SF	640Mb / 3.5	3.5-inch MO / —	4558	Ultra SCSI / 2mb	—
DynaMO 640SFUSB	640Mb / 3.5	90mm MO / —	3600	USB 1.1 / 2mb	2,7 RLL
DynaMO 640SZI	540Mb / 3.5	MO /	3600	SCSI-2	

Magneto Optical Drive Specs

Manufacturer	Drive Size / Form Factor	Media Type / Xfer Rate	#Disks / RPM	Interface / Cache Factor	Encoding
DynaMO 640SZI	640Mb / 3.5	MO / 3.9Mb/s	— / 3600	SCSI-2 / 2mb	
DynaMO 640SZI	230Mb / 3.5	MO / 3.9Mb/s	— / 3600	SCSI-2 / 2mb	
DynaMO 640SZI	128Mb / 3.5	MO / 3.9Mb/s	— / 3600	SCSI-2 / 2mb	
DynaMO 640USB	128Mb / 3.5	MO / 3.9Mb/s	— / 3600	USB / 2mb	
DynaMO 640USB	230Mb / 3.5	MO / 3.9Mb/s	— / 3600	USB / 2mb	
DynaMO 640USB	540Mb / 3.5	MO / 3.9Mb/s	— / 3600	USB / 2mb	
DynaMO 640USB	640Mb / 3.5	MO / 3.9Mb/s	— / 3600	USB / 2mb	
IFD-230B	230Mb / 3.5 3H	90mm MO / 2.1Mb/s	— / 3600	SCSI-2 / 237k	2-7 RLLC
IFD-230B	128Mb / 3.5 3H	90mm MO / 2.1Mb/s	— / 3600	SCSI-2 / 237k	2-7 RLLC
M2511A	128Mb / 3.5 3H	O-ROM / 1.09Mb/s	— / 3600	SCSI-2 / 256k	—
M2512A	128Mb / 3.5 3H	90mm MO / 1.1Mb/s	— / 3600	SCSI-2 / 237k	2,7 RLL
M2512A	230Mb / 3.5 3H	90mm MO / 2.1Mb/s	— / 3600	SCSI-2 / 237k	2,7 RLL
M2512EXT	230Mb / 3.5 3H	90mm MO / 2.1Mb/s	— / 3600	SCSI-2 / 237k	2-7 RLLC
M2512EXT	128Mb / 3.5 3H	90mm MO / 2.1Mb/s	— / 3600	SCSI-2 / 237k	2-7 RLLC
M2513A	640Mb / 3.5 3H	90mm MO / 3.9Mb/s	— / 3600	SCSI-2 / 512k	1-7 RLLC
M2513A	540Mb / 3.5 3H	90mm MO / 3.9Mb/s	— / 3600	SCSI-2 / 512k	1-7 RLLC
M2513A	230Mb / 3.5 3H	90mm MO / 2.1Mb/s	— / 3600	SCSI-2 / 512k	2-7 RLLC
M2513A	128Mb / 3.5 3H	90mm MO / 1.09Mb/s	— / 3600	SCSI-2 / 512k	2-7 RLLC
M2522A1	36000Mb / 5.25	5.25-inch MO / 1-2Mb/s	28 / 3000	SCSI-2 / —	—
M2522A2	33000Mb / 5.25	5.25-inch MO / 1-2Mb/s	28 / 3000	SCSI-2 / —	—
M2522B2	101000Mb / 5.25	5.25-inch MO / 1-2Mb/s	78 / 3000	SCSI-2 / —	—
M2522B3	101000Mb / 5.25	5.25-inch MO / 1-2Mb/s	78 / 3000	SCSI-2 / —	—
M2522B4	110000Mb / 5.25	5.25-inch MO / 1-2Mb/s	78 / 3000	SCSI-2 / —	—
M2522B4	110000Mb / 5.25	5.25-inch MO / 1-2Mb/s	78 / 3000	SCSI-2 / —	—
M2522B5	110000Mb / 5.25	5.25-inch MO / 1-2Mb/s	78 / 3000	SCSI-2 / —	—
M2531A1	8580Mb / 3.5	MO / 10Mb/s	35 / 3600	SCSI-2 / 530k	
M2531A2	8580Mb / 3.5	MO / 10Mb/s	35 / 3600	SCSI-2 / 530k	
M2531B1	8050Mb / 3.5	MO / 5Mb/s	35 / 3600	SCSI-2 / 530k	
M2531B2	8050Mb / 3.5	MO / 5Mb/s	35 / 3600	SCSI-2 / 530k	
M2532B2	2200Mb / —	90mm MO / 3.9Mb/s	— / 3600	SCSI-2 / 2mb	
M2541B	128Mb / 3.5 3H	3.5-inch MO / 1.6Mb/s	— / 2700	EIDE / 128k	

Manufacturer	Drive Size Form Factor	Media Type Xfer Rate	#Disks RPM	Interface Cache Factor	Encoding
M2541B	230Mb	3.5-inch MO	—	EIDE	—
	3.5 3H	1.6Mb/s	2700	128k	
M2541S	230Mb	90mm MO	—	PCMCIA-ATA	—
	3.5	1.6Mb/s	2700	128k	
M2541S	128Mb	90mm MO	—	PCMCIA-ATA	—
	3.5	0.8Mb/s	2700	128k	
MCA3064AP	640Mb	90mm MO	—	ATAPI-4	1-7 RLLC
	3.5 3H	3.9Mb/s	3600	512k	
MCA3064AP	540Mb	90mm MO	—	ATAPI-4	1-7 RLLC
	3.5 3H	3.9Mb/s	3600	512k	
MCA3064AP	230Mb	90mm MO	—	ATAPI-4	2-7 RLLC
	3.5 3H	3.9Mb/s	3600	512k	
MCA3064AP	128Mb	90mm MO	—	ATAPI-4	2-7 RLLC
	3.5 3H	3.9Mb/s	3600	512k	
MCB3064SS	128Mb	90mm MO	—	SCSI-2	2-7 RLLC
	3.5 3H	1.3Mb/s	4300	2mb	
MCB3064SS	230Mb	90mm MO	—	SCSI-2	2-7 RLCC
	3.5 3H	2.5Mb/s	4300	2mb	
MCB3064SS	540Mb	90mm MO	—	SCSI-2	1-7 RLCC
	3.5 3H	4.7Mb/s	4300	2mb	
MCB3064SS	640Mb	90mm MO	—	SCSI-2	1-7 RLCC
	3.5 3H	4.7Mb/s	4300	2mb	
MCC3064AP	128Mb	90mm MO	—	ATAPI	2-7 RLCC
	3.5 3H	1.09Mb/s	3600	2mb	
MCC3064AP	230Mb	90mm MO	—	ATAPI	2-7 RLCC
	3.5 3H	2.1Mb/s	3600	2mb	
MCC3064AP	540Mb	90mm MO	—	ATAPI	1-7 RLCC
	3.5 3H	3.9Mb/s	3600	2mb	
MCC3064AP	640Mb	90mm MO	—	ATAPI	1-7 RLCC
	3.5 3H	3.9Mb/s	3600	2mb	
MCC3064SS	128Mb	90mm MO	—	SCSI-2	2-7 RLCC
	3.5 3H	1.09Mb/s	3600	2mb	
MCC3064SS	230Mb	90mm MO	—	SCSI-2	2-7 RLCC
	3.5 3H	1.09Mb/s	3600	2mb	
MCC3064SS	540Mb	90mm MO	—	SCSI-2	1-7 RLCC
	3.5 3H	3.9Mb/s	3600	2mb	
MCC3064SS	640Mb	90mm MO	—	SCSI-2	1-7 RLCC
	3.5 3H	3.9Mb/s	3600	2mb	
MCD3130SS	128Mb	90mm MO	—	SCSI-2	1,7 RLL
	—	10Mb/s	4500	2048k	
MCD3130SS	230Mb	90mm MO	—	SCSI-2	1,7 RLL
	—	10Mb/s	4500	2048k	
MCD3130SS	540Mb	90mm MO	—	SCSI-2	1,7 RLL
	—	10Mb/s	4500	2048k	
MCD3130SS	640Mb	90mm MO	—	SCSI-2	1,7 RLL
	—	10Mb/s	4500	2048k	
MCD3130SS	1283Mb	90mm MO	—	SCSI-2	1,7 RLL
	—	10Mb/s	3214	2048k	
MCE3064SS	128Mb	90mm MO	—	Ultra SCSI	2-7 RLLC
	—	20Mb/s	4558	2mb	
MCE3064SS	230Mb	90mm MO	—	Ultra SCSI	2-7 RLLC
	—	20Mb/s	4558	2mb	
MCE3064SS	540Mb	90mm MO	—	Ultra SCSI	1-7 RLLC
	—	20Mb/s	4558	2mb	
MCE3064SS	640Mb	90mm MO	—	Ultra SCSI	1-7 RLLC
	—	20Mb/s	4558	2mb	
MCE3130AP	128Mb	90mm MO	—	IDE	—
	3.5	16Mb/s	4558	2mb	
MCE3130AP	230Mb	90mm MO	—	IDE	—
	3.5	16Mb/s	4558	2mb	
MCE3130AP	540Mb	90mm MO	—	IDE	—
	3.5	16Mb/s	4558	2mb	
MCE3130AP	640Mb	90mm MO	—	IDE	—

Manufacturer	Drive Size / Form Factor	Media Type / Xfer Rate	#Disks / RPM	Interface / Cache Factor	Encoding
	3.5	16Mb/s	4558	2mb	
MCE3130AP	1300Mb	90mm MO		IDE	
	3.5	16Mb/s	4558	2mb	
MCE3130SS	128Mb	90mm MO		SCSI	
	3.5	20Mb/s	3214	2mb	
MCE3130SS	230Mb	90mm MO		SCSI	
	3.5	20Mb/s	3214	2mb	
MCE3130SS	540Mb	90mm MO		SCSI	
	3.5	20Mb/s	3214	2mb	
MCE3130SS	640Mb	90mm MO		SCSI	
	3.5	20Mb/s	3214	2mb	
MCE3130SS	1300Mb	90mm MO		SCSI	
	3.5	20Mb/s	3214	2mb	
MCF3064SS	128Mb	90mm MO		Ultra SCSI	2-7 RLLC
	3.5 3H	1.09Mb/s	3600	2mb	
MCF3064SS	230Mb	90mm MO		Ultra SCSI	2-7 RLLC
	3.5 3H	2.1Mb/s	3600	2mb	
MCF3064SS	540Mb	90mm MO		Ultra SCSI	1-7 RLLC
	3.5 3H	3.9Mb/s	3600	2mb	
MCF3064SS	640Mb	90mm MO		Ultra SCSI	1-7 RLLC
	3.5 3H	3.9Mb/s	3600	2mb	
MCJ3230AP	2300Mb	90mm MO		IDE	
	3.5 3H	8Mb/s	5455	8mb	
MCJ3230AP	1300Mb	90mm MO		IDE	
	3.5 3H	8Mb/s	5455	8mb	
MCJ3230AP	640Mb	90mm MO		IDE	
	3.5 3H	8Mb/s	5455	8mb	
MCJ3230AP	540Mb	90mm MO		IDE	
	3.5 3H	8Mb/s	5455	8mb	
MCJ3230AP	230Mb	90mm MO		IDE	
	3.5 3H	8Mb/s	5455	8mb	
MCJ3230AP	128Mb	90mm MO		IDE	
	3.5 3H	8Mb/s	5455	8mb	
MCJ3230SS	128Mb	90mm MO		SCSI	
	3.5 3H	8Mb/s	5455	8mb	
MCJ3230SS	230Mb	90mm MO		SCSI	
	3.5 3H	8Mb/s	5455	8mb	
MCJ3230SS	540Mb	90mm MO		SCSI	
	3.5 3H	8Mb/s	5455	8mb	
MCJ3230SS	640Mb	90mm MO		SCSI	
	3.5 3H	8Mb/s	5455	8mb	
MCJ3230SS	1300Mb	90mm MO		SCSI	
	3.5 3H	8Mb/s	5455	8mb	
MCJ3230SS	2300Mb	90mm MO		SCSI	
	3.5 3H	8Mb/s	5455	8mb	
MDB3064SS	640Mb	MO		SCSI-2	
	—	—	3600	2mb	
MDD3064AP	640Mb	3.5-inch MO		ATAPI-4	
	3.5	—	3600	512k	
MDE3130SS	1300Mb	3.5-inch MO		SCSI-2	
	—	—	3210	2mb	
MDF3130EE	1300Mb	3.5-inch MO		IEEE 1394	1,7 RLL
	3.5	—	3214	2mb	
MDF3130EE	640MBMb	3.5-inch MO		IEEE 1394	1,7 RLL
	3.5	—	4500	2mb	
MDF3130EE	540MBMb	3.5-inch MO		IEEE 1394	1,7 RLL
	3.5	—	4500	2mb	
MDF3130EE	230Mb	3.5-inch MO		IEEE 1394	1,7 RLL
	3.5	—	4500	2mb	
MDG3130SS	1300Mb	3.5-inch MO		Ultra SCSI	
	3.5	—	3214	2mb	
MDG3130SS	640Mb	3.5-inch MO		Ultra SCSI	
	3.5	—	4558	2mb	

Manufacturer	Drive Size / Form Factor	Media Type / Xfer Rate	#Disks / RPM	Interface / Cache Factor	Encoding
MDG3130SS	540Mb	3.5-inch MO	—	Ultra SCSI	—
	3.5	—	4558	2mb	
MDG3130SS	230Mb	3.5-inch MO	—	Ultra SCSI	
	3.5	—	4558	2mb	
MicroMO 230	230Mb	90mm MO	—	PCMCIA-ATA	
	3.5	1.6Mb/s	2700	128k	
MicroMO 230	128Mb	90mm MO	—	PCMCIA-ATA	
	3.5	0.8Mb/s	2700	128k	
MiniEddy-2	2200Mb	90mm MO	—	SCSI-2	
	3.5	3.9Mb/s	3600	2mb	
MOcity	128Mb	90mm MO	—	SCSI-2	2-7 RLLC
	3.5 3H	2.1Mb/s	3600	237k	
MOcity	230Mb	90mm MO	—	SCSI-2	2-7 RLLC
	3.5 3H	2.1Mb/s	3600	237k	

HEWLETT-PACKARD CO

Manufacturer	Drive Size / Form Factor	Media Type / Xfer Rate	#Disks / RPM	Interface / Cache Factor	Encoding
120T	114400Mb	5.25-inch MO	88	SCSI-2	
	—	5Mb/s	2400	512k	
200T	187200Mb	5.25-inch MO	144	SCSI-2	
	—	5Mb/s	2400	512k	
20XT	20800Mb	5.25-inch MO	16	SCSI-2	
	—	5Mb/s	2400	512k	
40T	40000Mb	5.25-inch MO	32	SCSI-2	
	—	5Mb/s	2400	512k	
C1716C	650Mb	5.25-inch MO	—	SCSI-2	
	5.25	5Mb/s	2400	512k	
C1716T	1300Mb	5.25-inch MO	—	SCSI-2	
	5.25	5Mb/s	2400	512k	
HP SureStore 1200ex	1200000Mb	—	—	SCSI-2	PRML
	5.25FH	4.6Mb/s	3000	2mb	
HP SureStore 1200mx	1164000Mb	MO	128	—	
HP SureStore 125ex	125000Mb	—	—	SCSI-2	PRML
	—	—	3000	2mb	
HP SureStore 125ex	125000Mb	—	—	LVDS	PRML
	—	4.6Mb/s	3000	2mb	
HP SureStore 1300t	1300Mb	5.25-inch MO	—	SCSI-2	
	—	5Mb/s	2400	512k	
HP SureStore 160ex	166400Mb	—	—	SCSI-2	PRML
	—	4.6Mb/s	3000	2mb	
HP SureStore 220mx	218400Mb	MO	—	—	
	5.25				
HP SureStore 320ex	320Mb	—	—	SCSI-2	PRML
	—	4.6Mb/s	3000	2mb	
HP SureStore 330mx	291200Mb	MO	32	—	
	5.25				
HP SureStore 400ex	395Mb	—	—	SCSI-2	PRML
	—	4.6Mb/s	3000	2mb	
HP SureStore 5200ex	5200Mb	MO	1	SCSI-2	PRML
	5.25FH	4.6Mb/s	3000	2mb	
HP SureStore 660ex	665000Mb	MO	—	SCSI-2	PRML
	5.25FH	4.6Mb/s	3000	2mb	
HP SureStore 660mx	582400Mb	MO	64	—	
HP SureStore 700mx	691600Mb	—	76	—	
HP SureStore 80ex	83Mb	—	—	SCSI-2	PRML
	—	4.6Mb/s	3000	2mb	
HP SureStore 9100mx	9100Mb	MO	—	—	
	5.25				

HITACHI AMERICA

Manufacturer	Drive Size / Form Factor	Media Type / Xfer Rate	#Disks / RPM	Interface / Cache Factor	Encoding
A-6967-S180 (Novell)	363Mb	—	—	SCSI-2	
	5.25	10Mb/s	—	—	

Manufacturer	Drive Size Form Factor	Media Type Xfer Rate	#Disks RPM	Interface Cache Factor	Encoding
A-6967-S180 (Unix)	363Mb	—	—	SCSI-2	—
	5.25	10Mb/s	—	—	
A-6967-S48 (Novell)	97Mb	—	—	SCSI-2	—
	5.25	10Mb/s	—	—	
A-6967-S48 (Unix)	97Mb	—	—	SCSI-2	—
	5.25	10Mb/s	—	—	
OD112-L1	644Mb	—	1	SCSI	—
	5.25	—	—	—	
OD152S	2000Mb	—	—	SCSI-2	—
	5.25	3Mb/s	—	—	
OD172DOW	2600Mb	MO	—	SCSI-2	—
	5.25	3.37Mb/s	—	1mb	
OD321-1	7000Mb	—	1	SCSI	—
	—	—	—	—	
OD321-2	7000Mb	—	1	SCSI	—
	—	—	—	—	
OL112	30000Mb	—	—	SCSI	—
	5.25	—	—	—	
OL152-180	363Mb	—	—	SCSI-2	—
	5.25	5Mb/s	—	—	
OL152-192	388Mb	—	—	SCSI-2	—
	5.25	5Mb/s	—	—	
OL152-48	97Mb	—	—	SCSI-2	—
	5.25	5Mb/s	—	—	
OL152-60	121Mb	—	—	SCSI-2	—
	5.25	5Mb/s	—	—	
OL321-22	329000Mb	—	—	SCSI	—
	—	—	—	—	
OL321-32	448000Mb	—	—	SCSI	—
	—	—	—	—	
OLF321-5	560000Mb	—	—	SCSI	—
	—	—	—	—	
OU321-1	7000Mb	—	1	SCSI	—
	—	—	—	—	
IBM CORP					
0632-CHA	1300Mb	MO,CCW	—	SCSI-2	—
	5.25HH	5Mb/s	3500	1mb	
0632-CHB	1300Mb	MO,CCW	—	SCSI-2	—
	5.25HH	5Mb/s	3500	1mb	
0632-CHC	1300Mb	MO,CCW	—	SCSI-2	—
	5.25HH	5Mb/s	2400	1mb	
MD3125B	127Mb	MO,O-ROM	—	SCSI	2,7 RLL
	3.5 3H	7.25Mb/s	3000	256k	
MTA-3127	127Mb	MO,O-ROM	—	SCSI-2	2-7 RLLC
	3.5 3H	—	3000	243k	
MTA-3230	230Mb	MO,O-ROM	—	SCSI-2	2-7 RLLC
	3.5 3H	5Mb/s	3600	243k	
MAXOPTIX					
640se	540Mb	MO	—	SCSI-2	—
	3.5	10Mb/s	3600	512k	
640si	230Mb	MO	—	SCSI-2	—
	3.5	10Mb/s	3600	512k	
640spe	640Mb	MO	—	SCSI-2	—
	3.5	10Mb/s	3600	512k	
MX6126	655000Mb	MO,CCW,LIMDOW	126	Ultra SCSI	—
	—	—	—	8mb	
MX620	104000Mb	MO,CCW,LIMDOW	20	Ultra SCSI	—
	—	—	—	8mb	
MX6202	1050000Mb	MO,CCW,LIMDOW	202	Ultra SCSI	—
	—	—	—	8mb	
MX6278	1450000Mb	MO,CCW,LIMDOW	278	Ultra SCSI	—
	—	—	—	8mb	

Manufacturer	Drive Size / Form Factor	Media Type / Xfer Rate	#Disks / RPM	Interface / Cache Factor	Encoding
MX640	208000Mb / —	MO,CCW,LIMDOW	40	Ultra SCSI / 8mb	—
T3-1300	1300Mb / —	—	—	—	—
T3-1304	1300Mb / FH	—	—	—	—
T4-1300	—	—	—	—	—
T4-2600	2600Mb / HH	—	—	—	—
T5-2600	2600Mb / HH	MO,CCW,LIMDOW / 20Mb/s	3868	Ultra SCSI / 4mb	—
T5-2600	2300Mb / —	MO,CCW,LIMDOW / 20Mb/s	3868	Ultra SCSI / 4mb	—
T5-2600	1300Mb / —	MO,CCW / 20Mb/s	3649	Ultra SCSI / 4mb	—
T5-2600	1200Mb / —	MO,CCW / 20Mb/s	3649	Ultra SCSI / 4mb	—
T5-2600	1000Mb / —	MO,CCW / 20Mb/s	4325	Ultra SCSI / 4mb	—
T5-2600	900Mb / —	MO,CCW / 20Mb/s	4325	Ultra SCSI / 4mb	—
T5-2600	650Mb / —	MO,CCW / 20Mb/s	4325	Ultra SCSI / 4mb	—
T5-2600	600Mb / —	MO,CCW / 20Mb/s	4325	Ultra SCSI / 4mb	—
T6-5200	5200Mb / HH	MO,CCW / 20Mb/s	2996	Ultra SCSI / 8mb	—
T6-5200	4800Mb / —	MO,CCW / 20Mb/s	2996	Ultra SCSI / 8mb	—
T6-5200	4100Mb / —	MO,CCW / 20Mb/s	2996	Ultra SCSI / 8mb	—
T6-5200	2600Mb / —	MO,CCW,LIMDOW / 20Mb/s	2996	Ultra SCSI / 3868	—
T6-5200	2300Mb / —	MO,CCW,LIMDOW / 20Mb/s	2996	Ultra SCSI / 3868	—
T6-5200	1300Mb / —	MO,CCW / 20Mb/s	3649	Ultra SCSI / 3868	—
T6-5200	1200Mb / —	MO,CCW / 20Mb/s	3649	Ultra SCSI / 3868	—
T6-5200	1000Mb / —	MO,CCW / 20Mb/s	4325	Ultra SCSI / 3868	—
T6-5200	900Mb / —	MO,CCW / 20Mb/s	4325	Ultra SCSI / 3868	—
T6-5200	650Mb / —	MO,CCW / 20Mb/s	4325	Ultra SCSI / 3868	—
T6-5200	600Mb / —	MO,CCW / 20Mb/s	4325	Ultra SCSI / 3868	—

MAXTOR CORPORATION

Manufacturer	Drive Size / Form Factor	Media Type / Xfer Rate	#Disks / RPM	Interface / Cache Factor	Encoding
ESP5047	475Mb / 5.25	— / 10Mb/s	—	SCSI-2Fast	—
ESP5095	5095Mb / 5.25	— / 10Mb/s	—	SCSI-2Fast	—
RXD-HD	2500Mb / HH	— / 1.25Mb/s	—	SCSI	—
RXT-800HS	393Mb / HH	— / 1.25Mb/s	—	SCSI	—
RXT-800HS	786Mb / HH	— / 1.25Mb/s	—	SCSI	—
Tahiti II	644Mb / HH	— / 6.8Mb/s	—	SCSI	—
Tahiti II	1020Mb / HH	— / 6.8Mb/s	—	SCSI	—

Manufacturer	Drive Size / Form Factor	Media Type / Xfer Rate	#Disks / RPM	Interface / Cache Factor	Encoding
MOST, INC.					
RMD-5300-S	384Mb	MO,O-ROM	—	SCSI-2	—
	3.5	5Mb/s	2400	256k	
OLYMPUS AMERICA INC.					
MOS320	230Mb	MO	—	SCSI	
	3.5	—	—	—	
MOS330E	230Mb	MO	—	SCSI	
	3.5	—	—	—	
MOS331E14	230Mb	MO	—	SCSI	
	3.5	—	—	—	
MOS3380S	640Mb	MO	1	SCSI-2	
	3.5	6.5	6000	2mb	
MOS3381S	1300Mb	MO	1	SCSI-2	
	3.5	6.8	6000	2mb	
MOS3390S	640Mb	MO	1	USB 1.1	
	3.5	1.5	3000	2mb	
MOS350S	640Mb	MO	1	SCSI-2	
	3.5	—	4335	2mb	
MOS351S	640mbMb	MO	1	SCSI-2	
	3.5	6.7	3600	2mb	
MOS362S	640Mb	MO	1	SCSI-2	
	3.5	—	4643	2mb	
MOS363S	640Mb	MO	1	SCSI-2	
	3.5	—	3869	2mb	
MOS540E	2600Mb	MO	—	SCSI	
	5.25	—	—	—	
Power MO 640	640Mb	MO	1	SCSI-2	
	3.5	—	4335	2mb	
PowerMO 2600/VAR	2600Mb	—	—	—	
	—	—	3600	—	
SYS.230 (MAC)	230Mb	—	—	SCSI-2	
	3.5	—	4200	256k	
SYS.230 (PC)	230Mb	—	—	SCSI-2	
	3.5	—	4200	—	
TURBO LE 640 MO	640mbMb	MO	1	SCSI-2	
	3.5	6.7	3600	2mb	
TURBO MO 640 II	640Mb	MO	1	SCSI-2	
	3.5	—	3869	2mb	
TURBO MO 640S II	640Mb	MO	1	SCSI-2	
	3.5	—	4643	2mb	
TURBO MO 640S III	640Mb	MO	1	SCSI-2	
	3.5	—			
TURBO MO mini	640Mb	MO	1	USB 1.1	
	3.5	1.5	3000	2mb	
TURBO MO MO133S1S	1300Mb	MO	1	SCSI-2	
	3.5	6.8	6000	2mb	
TURBO MO MO646S1S	640Mb	MO	1	SCSI-2	
	3.5	6.5	6000	2mb	
OR COMPUTER SYSTEM PTE LTD (EASYSTOR)					
EMO-1300	1300Mb	MO	—	SCSI-2	
	—	5Mb/s	3000	1mb	
EMO-2600H	2600Mb	MO	—	SCSI-2	
	—	5Mb/s	3000	1mb	
PINNACLE MICRO, INC.					
APEX 4.2	4200Mb	—	—	SCSI-2Fast	—
	—	—	—	1mb	
APEX 4.6	4600Mb	MO	2	SCSI-1	PWMRLL1,7
	5.25	3.5Mb/s	2400	1mb	
APEX 4.6	2607Mb	MO	—	SCSI-1	PWMRLL1,7
	5.25	4.3Mb/s	3755	1mb	
APEX 4.6	2023Mb	MO	—	SCSI-1	PWMRLL1,7
	5.25	4.3Mb/s	3755	1mb	

Manufacturer	Drive Size Form Factor	Media Type Xfer Rate	#Disks RPM	Interface Cache Factor	Encoding
Peak 104/1	104GBMb	MO	20	SCSI-2	—
	—	—	3300	4mb	
Peak 104/2	104GBMb	MO	20	SCSI-2	—
	—	—	3300	4mb	
Peak 1340/2	1340GBMb	MO	258	SCSI-2	—
	—	—	3300	4mb	
Peak 1340/4	1340GBMb	MO	258	SCSI-2	—
	—	—	3300	4mb	
Peak 1340/6	1340GBMb	MO	258	SCSI-2	—
	—	—	3300	4mb	
Peak 165/2	166GBMb	MO	32	SCSI-2	—
	—	—	3300	4mb	
Peak 270/2	270GBMb	MO	52	SCSI-2	—
	—	—	3300	4mb	
Peak 540/2	540GBMb	MO	104	SCSI-2	—
	—	—	3300	4mb	
Peak 540/4	540GBMb	MO	104	SCSI-2	—
	—	—	3300	4mb	
Peak 810/2	810GBMb	MO	156	SCSI-2	—
	—	—	3300	4mb	
Peak 810/4	810GBMb	MO	156	SCSI-2	—
	—	—	3300	4mb	
Peak 810/6	810GBMb	MO	156	SCSI-2	—
	—	—	3300	4mb	
Ultra 5.2	5200Mb	MO,CCW	2	SCSI-2	—
	5.25	2.9Mb/s	2996	8mb	
Ultra 5.2	4100Mb	MO,CCW	—	SCSI-2	—
	5.25	2.9Mb/s	2996	8mb	
Ultra 5.2	4800Mb	MO,CCW	—	SCSI-2	—
	5.25	2.9Mb/s	2996	8mb	
Ultra 5.2	2600Mb	MO,CCW,LIMDOW	—	SCSI-2	—
	5.25	2.9Mb/s	3868	8mb	
Ultra 5.2	2300Mb	MO,CCW,LIMDOW	—	SCSI-2	—
	5.25	2.9Mb/s	3868	8mb	
Ultra 5.2	1300Mb	MO,CCW	—	SCSI-2	—
	5.25	2.9Mb/s	3649	8mb	
Ultra 5.2	1200Mb	MO,CCW	—	SCSI-2	—
	5.25	2.9Mb/s	3649	8mb	
Ultra 5.2	1000Mb	MO,CCW	—	SCSI-2	—
	5.25	2.9Mb/s	4325	8mb	
Ultra 5.2	900Mb	MO,CCW	—	SCSI-2	—
	5.25	2.9Mb/s	4325	8mb	
Ultra 5.2	650Mb	MO,CCW	—	SCSI-2	—
	5.25	2.9Mb/s	4325	8mb	
Ultra 5.2	600Mb	MO,CCW	—	SCSI-2	—
	5.25	2.9Mb/s	4325	8mb	

PIONEER NEW MEDIA TECH

Manufacturer	Drive Size Form Factor	Media Type Xfer Rate	#Disks RPM	Interface Cache Factor	Encoding
DD-M5101	1300Mb	5.25-inch WORM	—	SCSI	—
	5.25HH	—	1800	—	
DD-S5101	1300Mb	5.25-inch WORM	—	SCSI	—
	5.25	5.94Mb/s	1800	—	
DD-U5101	1300Mb	5.25-inch WORM	—	SCSI	—
	5.25FH	5.94Mb/s	1800	—	
DDJ-U5105	—	5.25-inch WORM	—	SCSI	—
	5.25	—	1800	256k	
DE-H7101	—	MO	—	—	—
DE-H7101	—	—	—	SCSI-2	—
	—	—	—	—	
DE-H9101	1700Mb	—	—	SCSI-2	—
	—	—	—	—	
DE-S7001	—	MO	—	SCSI	—
	5.25	5.94Mb/s	1800	—	

Manufacturer	Drive Size / Form Factor	Media Type / Xfer Rate	#Disks RPM	Interface Cache Factor	Encoding
DE-SH7101	—	MO	—	SCSI	—
DE-SH9101	1.7GBMb / 5.25	MO	—	SCSI	—
DE-U7001	— / 5.25FH	MO / 5.94Mb/s	1800	SCSI / 256k	—
DE-UH7101	654Mb / 5.25HH	MO / 2.4Mb/s	2400	SCSI-2 / 64k	—
DE-UH9101	1700Mb / 5.25	MO	—	SCSI-2	—
DE-UH9101	1700Mb / 5.25	MO	—	SCSI-2	—
DEJ-U7001	— / 5.25	5.94Mb/s	1800	SCSI	—

PLASMON DATA, INC.

Manufacturer	Drive Size / Form Factor	Media Type / Xfer Rate	#Disks RPM	Interface Cache Factor	Encoding
DW260e	2600Mb / 5.25HH	WORM,LIMDOW / 4Mb/s	3600	4mb	—
DW260i	2600Mb / 5.25HH	WORM,LIMDOW / 4Mb/s	3600	4mb	—
G104 Library	950GBMb / 5.25HH	MO	104	SCSI-3 / 8mb	—
G164 Library	1.5TBMb / 5.25HH	MO	164	SCSI-3 / 8mb	—
G238 Library	2.2TBMb / 5.25HH	MO	238	SCSI-3 / 8mb	—
G438 Library	4.0TBMb / 5.25HH	MO	104	SCSI-3 / 8mb	—
G638 Library	5.8TBMb / 5.25HH	MO	638	SCSI-3 / 8mb	—
G64 Library	580GBMb / 5.25HH	MO	64	SCSI-3 / 8mb	—
M104J-260	270000Mb / 5.25	MO / 4Mb/s	104 / 3600	SCSI-2 / 1mb	—
M156J-260	405000Mb / 5.25	MO / 4Mb/s	156 / 3600	SCSI-2 / 1mb	—
M20J-260	52000Mb / 5.25	MO / 4Mb/s	20 / 3600	SCSI-2 / 1mb	—
M258J-260	670000Mb / 5.25	MO / 4Mb/s	258 / 3600	SCSI-2 / 1mb	—
M32J-260	83000Mb / 5.25	MO / 4Mb/s	32 / 3600	SCSI-2 / 1mb	—
M52J-260	135000Mb / 5.25	MO / 4Mb/s	52 / 3600	SCSI-2 / 1mb	—
MOD 520 5.2	5200Mb	—	3300	SCSI-2 / 4mb	—
MOD 910e 9.1	9100Mb / 6	MO	3300	SCSI-2 / 8mb	—
MOD 910i 9.1	9100Mb / 6	MO	3300	SCSI-2 / 8mb	—

QUANTUM CORPORATION

Manufacturer	Drive Size / Form Factor	Media Type / Xfer Rate	#Disks RPM	Interface Cache Factor	Encoding
ESP5011	118Mb / 5.25	— / 10Mb/s	—	SCSI-2Fast	—
ESP510	510Mb / 5.25	— / 10Mb/s	—	SCSI-2Fast	—
ESP530	267Mb / 5.25	— / 10Mb/s	—	SCSI-2Fast	—
ESP540	428Mb / 5.25	— / 10Mb/s	—	SCSI-2Fast	—
ESP580	856Mb / 5.25	— / 10Mb/s	—	—	—
RU3026	268Mb / 3.5HH	— / 30	—	SCSI-3	—

Magneto Optical

Manufacturer	Drive Size / Form Factor	Media Type / Xfer Rate	#Disks / RPM	Interface / Cache Factor	Encoding
RU3053	536Mb	—	—	SCSI-3	—
	3.5HH	30		—	
RU3107-V	1070Mb	—		SCSI-3	
	3.5HH	30	—		
RU3160-V	1600Mb	—		SCSI-3	
	3.5HH	30	—		
RU5107	1072Mb	—	—	SCSI-3	—
	5.25FH	30		—	
RU5210	2100Mb	—		SCSI-3	
	5.25FH	30	—		
RU5320	3200Mb	—		SCSI-3	
	5.25FH	30	—		
SONY					
MDM111	140Mb	MO		SCSI	
	—	1.5Mb/s	—	—	
Optical Express	—			SCSI-2	
	—	—	3600	—	
OSL-2000	26000Mb	MO		SCSI-2	
	5.25	5Mb/s	—	—	
OSL-2001	26000Mb	MO		SCSI-2	
	5.25	2.4Mb/s	20 3600	—	
RMO-S350	128Mb	3.5-inch MO		SCSI	
	3.5	7.25Mb/s	3000	64k	
RMO-S550	650Mb	MO		SCSI	
	5.25	1.2Mb/s	2400	64k	
RMO-S550	594Mb	MO		SCSI	
	5.25	6.8Mb/s	2400	64k	
RMO-S551/DD	5200Mb	—		SCSI-2	
	—	—	3600		
RMO-S551/S	5200Mb	MO		SCSI-2Fast	1,7 RLL
	5.25	5.07Mb/s	3300	4mb	
RMO-S561/S	9100Mb	MO		SCSI-2	
	5.25	6Mb/s	3300	8mb	
RMO-S561/S	9100Mb	MO		SCSI-2	
	5.25	6Mb/s	3600	8mb	
RMO-S570	1300Mb	MO		SCSI-2	
	5.25	5Mb/s	3000	1mb	
RMO-S594/DWPS	2600Mb	MO		SCSI-2Fast	1,7 RLL
	5.25	4Mb/s	3600	4mb	
SMO-E301F	128Mb	MO,O-ROM		SCSI-2	
	3.5HH	7.25Mb/s	3000	256k	
SMO-E501	650Mb	—		SCSI	
	5.25FH	1.2Mb/s	2400	64k	
SMO-E502	650Mb	—		SCSI	
	5.25FH	3Mb/s	2400	256k	
SMO-E511	650Mb	—		SCSI	
	5.25FH	1.2Mb/s	2400	64k	
SMO-F521	1300Mb	5.25-inch MO		SCSI-2	
	5.25HH	2Mb/s	3000	1mb	
SMO-F531	1300Mb	5.25-inch MO		SCSI-2	
	5.25HH	2.4Mb/s	3600	4mb	
SMO-F541	2600Mb	MO		SCSI-2Fast	
	5.25	4Mb/s	3600	1mb	
SMO-F541-40	1300Mb	—		SCSI-2	
	5.25		—	4mb	
SMO-F541-40	2600Mb	—		SCSI-2	
	5.25		—	4mb	
SMO-F541-40	2300Mb	—		SCSI-2	
	5.25		—	4mb	
SMO-F541-40	1200Mb	—		SCSI-2	
	5.25		—	4mb	
SMO-F541/DW	2600Mb	MO		SCSI-2Fast	
	5.25	4Mb/s	3600	1mb	

Magneto Optical

Manufacturer	Drive Size Form Factor	Media Type Xfer Rate	#Disks RPM	Interface Cache Factor	Encoding
SMO-F544	2600Mb	—	—	SCSI	—
	5.25	—	3600	4mb	
SMO-F544/DW	2600Mb	—	—	SCSI-2Fast	—
	5.25	4Mb/s	3600	4mb	
SMO-F551	5200Mb	MO	—	SCSI-2Fast	1,7 RLL
	5.25	5.07Mb/s	3300	4mb	
SMO-F551S	5200Mb	MO	—	SCSI-2Fast	—
	5.25	5.07Mb/s	3600	4mb	
SMO-P301	128Mb	—	—	SCSI-2	—
	3.5HH	4Mb/s	3000	64k	
SMO-S501	650Mb	—	—	—	—
SMO-S531	1300Mb	5.25-inch MO	—	SCSI-2	—
	5.25HH	2.4Mb/s	3600	4mb	
SMO-S551	5200Mb	MO	—	SCSI-2Fast	—
	5.25	5Mb/s	3300	4mb	
SMO-S561	9.1GBMb	MO	1	—	—
	5.25	—	3600	8mb	
WDD-901	—	MO	—	SCSI-2	—
WDD-930-01	6550Mb	MO	—	SCSI-2	—
	—	—	1080	256k	
WDD-931	—	MO	—	SCSI-2	—
	—	—	1080	8mb	
TEAC					
OD-3000	127Mb	90mm MO	—	SCSI-2	—
	3.5HH	7.25Mb/s	3000	128k	
VERBATIM CORP					
1X MO	650Mb	MO	—	Ultra SCSI	—
	5.25	20Mb/s	4325	4mb	
1X MO	600Mb	MO	—	Ultra SCSI	—
	5.25	20Mb/s	4325	4mb	
2X MO	1300Mb	MO	—	Ultra SCSI	—
	5.25	20Mb/s	4325	4mb	
2X MO	1200Mb	MO	—	Ultra SCSI	—
	5.25	20Mb/s	4325	4mb	
3X MO	2000Mb	MO	—	Ultra SCSI	—
	5.25	—	—	4mb	
3X MO	1700Mb	MO	—	Ultra SCSI	—
	5.25	—	—	4mb	
4X MO	2600Mb	MO	—	Ultra SCSI	—
	5.25	20Mb/s	3868	4mb	
4X MO	2300Mb	MO	—	Ultra SCSI	—
	5.25	20Mb/s	3868	4mb	
5200 5.2GB	5200Mb	—	—	Ultra SCSI	—
	5.25	—	—	4mb	
8X MO	5200Mb	MO	—	Ultra SCSI	—
	5.25	20Mb/s	2942	4mb	
8X MO	4800Mb	MO	—	Ultra SCSI	—
	5.25	20Mb/s	2942	4mb	
8X MO	4100Mb	—	—	Ultra SCSI	—
	5.25	—	2942	4mb	
MCA2600 2.6GB	2600Mb	—	—	SCSI-2Fast	—
	—	—	3000	—	
MCA4600 4.6GB	4600Mb	MO	—	SCSI-2Fast	—
	—	—	—	1mb	
MCA5200 5.2GB	5200Mb	—	—	Ultra SCSI	—
	5.25FH	—	—	4mb	
MCA5200S 5.2GB	5200Mb	MO	—	Ultra SCSI	—
	—	—	—	4mb	
MCA640	640Mb	—	—	SCSI-2	—
	—	—	3600	—	

Chapter 15

Tape Drive Specifications

Tape Drive Manufacturers

The following table is a general summary of companies that have manufactured and/or are still manufacturing tape drives. If you have information concerning the status of any of these companies, such as "XYZ Company went bankrupt in August, 1990" or "XYZ Company was bought by Q Company", please let us know so we can keep this section current. If a phone number is listed in the Status column, the company is in business. Telephone for drive manufacturers are also listed in the Phone Book chapter of this book. (page 905)

Manufacturer	Status
Aiwa America	800-289-2492
Benchmark Storage (acquired by Quantum 12-2002)	408-432-1700
Certance (name changed from Seagate RSS 2-1996)	714-641-1230
Compaq	281-370-0670
Conner Peripherals	800-468-3472 (Seagate)
Dynatek Automation	+44 (0) 1962844000 (UK)
Exabyte	303-442-4333
Fujitsu	408-432-6333
Hewlett-Packard	650-857-1501
IBM Corp	408-256-1600
Iomega	888-446-6342
M4 Data Inc. (acquired by Pintree Peripherals 12-2002)	
Micro Solutions	815-754-4500
Qualstar Corp (Vinastar Corp bought all tapes 6-2003)	866-743-7827
Quantum	408-432-1700 (Maxtor)
Seagate Technologies	800-468-3472
Sony	408-432-1600
StorageTek	303-673-5151
Tandberg Data	858-726-0277
Teac America	323-726-0303
Tecmar Technologies (Wangtek)	No longer manufactures; see Overland Storage for support info.

Total number of Tape Drives = 459 (last year = 265)

Tape Drive Syntax and Notation

The following are descriptions of the information contained in the Tape drive tables.

1. Interface	Type of communication interface between the computer and drive
2. Capacity	The Average COMPRESSED capacity of the drive, which is normally assumed to be about twice the non-compressed capacity
3. Speed	The rate in Mb/second that the taped drive is able to back up data.
4. Tape	The type of tape accepted by the drive.
5. Tape Example	A specific tape number example used by the drive.
6. Note	Specific model information, tape lengths and miscellaneous notes.

Sequoia needs your help! If you have specifications on new or obsolete Tape drives, please send them to us so that we can include them in future editions of this book.

Tape Drive Specs by Model

Aiwa America

Model	Interface	Capacity	Speed
GD-8000	SCSI-2	40GB	
Tape: DDS-2 Note: Tapelength120m			
TD-801			
Tape: QD2080/QD2120			
TD-802			
Tape: QD2080/QD2120			
TD-803			
Tape: QD2080/QD2120			
TD-811			
Tape: QD2080(QIC80)/QD2120(QIC80)			
TD-811B			
Tape: QD2080(QIC80)/QD2120(QIC80)			
TD-P250			
Tape: QD2080(QIC80)/QD2120(QIC80)			
TD-P3200	ParallelPort	1.6GB	2Mb/sec
Tape: Travan TR-3			
TD-S1600	FloppyDisk	800Mb	1Mb/sec
Tape: Travan TR-2			
TD-S3200	FloppyDisk	1.6GB	1Mb/sec
Tape: Travan TR-3			

Benchmark Storage In

Model	Interface	Capacity	Speed
DLT1	WideUltraSCSI	40GB	3Mb/sec
Tape: DLT Tape: Bevchmark DLTtapeIV			
Valusmart Tape 160		160GB	
Tape: DLT			
Valusmart Tape 80	WideUltraSCSI	40GB	3Mb/sec
Tape: DLT Tape: Benchmark DLTtapeIV			

Certance

Model	Interface	Capacity	Speed
CD144LW1U-S	Ultra2-LVDS	144GB	
Tape: DAT72 Tape: CDM72			
CD72LW1U-S	Ultra2-LVDS	72GB	
Tape: DAT72 Tape: CDM72			
CD72LWE-S	Ultra2-LVDS	72GB	
Tape: DAT72 Tape: CDM72			
CD72LWE-TSS	Ultra2-LVDS	72GB	
Tape: DAT72 Tape: CDM72			
CD72LWH-S	Ultra2-LVDS	72GB	
Tape: DAT72 Tape: CDM72			
CD72LWH-TSS	Ultra2-LVDS	72GB	
Tape: DAT72 Tape: CDM72			
CDL432LW2U-S	Ultra2-LVDS	432GB	
Tape: DAT72 Tape: CDM72			
CDL432LWEF-S	Ultra2-LVDS	432GB	
Tape: DAT72 Tape: CDM72			
CDL432LWF-Q	Ultra2-LVDS	432GB	
Tape: DAT72 Tape: CDM72			
CDL432LWF-S	Ultra2-LVDS	432GB	
Tape: DAT72 Tape: CDM72			
CDL864LW2U-S	SCSI LVD	864GB	
Tape: DAT72 Tape: CDM72			
CL400LW2U-SS	UL160SCSI	400GB	

Model	Interface	Capacity	Speed
Tape Number:	Notes and/or Tape Example:		
Tape: Ultrium 2	Tape: CLM400-5		
CL400LWEF-S	UL160SCSI	400GB	
Tape: Ultrium 2	Tape: CLM400-5		
CL400LWF-Q	UL160SCSI	400GB	
Tape: Ultrium 2	Tape: CLM400-5		
CL400LWF-S	UL160SCSI	400GB	
Tape: Ultrium 2	Tape: CLM400-5		
CL800LW2U-SS	UL160SCSI	400GB	
Tape: Ultrium 2	Tape: CLM400-5		
CLL3200LWEF-S	UL160SCSI	400GB	
Tape: Ultrium 2	Tape: CLM400-20		
CP31001-160-S	UL160SCSI	160GB	
Tape: DDS-4,DAT72	Tape: CDM72		
CP3100R1-320-S	UL160SCSI	320GB	
Tape: DDS-4,DAT72	Tape: CDM72		
CP3101D-160-S	UL160SCSI	160GB	
Tape: DDS-4,DAT72	Tape: CDM72		
CP3101R1-160-S	UL160SCSI	160GB	
Tape: DDS-4,DAT72	Tape: CDM72		

Compaq

Model	Interface	Capacity	Speed
157766-B21	SCSI-2Fast20/WideLVD	50GB	
Tape: 8mm 170-230 AME	Tape: 152841-001 Note: TapeLength755ft/230m		
157767-001	SCSI-2Fast20/WideLVD	50GB	
Tape: 8mm 170-230 AME	Tape: 152841-001 Note: TapeLength755ft/230m		
157769-B21	Ultra2-LVDS	20GB	
Tape: 20GB DDS-4	Tape: 152842-001 Note: tapelength492ft/125m		
157770-001	Ultra2-LVDS	20GB	
Tape: 20GB DDS-4	Tape: 152842-001 Note: tapelength492ft/125m		
242520-B21		35GB	4Mb/sec
Tape: DLT	Tape: Compaq DLT 295194-B21 Note: tapelength1800ft		
242521-B21		35GB	4Mb/sec
Tape: DLT	Tape: Compaq 295194-B21 Note: tapelength1800ft		
295353-B22		4GB	
Tape: 4GB DDS-2	Tape: 137611-001 Note: tapelength393ft/120m		
295480-B22	SCSI	4GB	
Tape: 4GB SLR	Tape: 295842-B21 Note: tapelengt1500ft/457m		
295513-B22	Fast SCSI-2	12GB	
Tape: 12GB DDS-3	Tape: 295515-B21 Note: tapelength410ft/125m		
340743-B21	SCSI-2	20GB	
Tape: DLT IV	Tape: CompIII 0.5in,1100Ft;CompIVI .5in,1700ft		
340744-B21	SCSI-2	20GB	
Tape: DLT IV	Tape: CompIII 0.5in,1100Ft;CompIVI .5in,1700ft		
386		150Mb	
Tape: QD6150			
388504-B21	SCSI-2Fst/Wd68pin	35GB	
Tape: 8mm 170-230m AME	Tape: 402371-B21		
388507-001	SCSI-2Fst/Wd68pin	35GB	
Tape: 8mm 170-230m AME	Tape: 402371-B21		

Conner Peripherals

Model	Interface	Capacity	Speed
TapeStor 3200	FloppyDisk	1.6GB	2Mb/sec

Dynatek

Model	Interface	Capacity	Speed
AIT2500	SCSI-2	25GB	3Mb/sec
AIT2500SD-SM9	SCSI-2	25GB	3Mb/sec
AIT5000	SCSI-2	50GB	3Mb/sec

Tape Drives

Tape Drive Manufacturer			
Model······················Interface··············		Capacity ·········Speed	
Tape Number: Notes and/or Tape Example:			

Model	Interface	Capacity	Speed
AIT5000SD-SM9 ··················SCSI-2 ··················		50GB ··········	3Mb/sec
DAT12000 ··········		12GB ··········	
Tape: DDS-3			
DAT12000HD-SS9 ··········		12GB ··········	
Tape: DDS-3			
DAT2000 ··········			
Tape: DG90M/60M			
DAT20000 ··········		20GB ··········	
Tape: DDS-4			
DAT20000HD-SS9 ··········		20GB ··········	
Tape: DDS-4			
DAT4000 ··········			
Tape: DG90M/60M			
DAT8000 ··········		4GB ··········	
Tape: DDS-2			
DAT8000HD-SS9 ··········		4GB ··········	
Tape: DDS-2			
DLT2000 ··········		15GB ··········	
Tape: DLT			
DLT2000QD ··········		15GB ··········	
Tape: DLT			
DLT4000 ··········		20GB ··········	1.5Mb/sec
Tape: DLT			
DLT4000QD-SM9 ··········		20GB ··········	1.5Mb/sec
Tape: DLT			
DLT7000 ··········		35GB ··········	5Mb/sec
Tape: DLT			
DLT7000QD-SM9 ··········		35GB ··········	5Mb/sec
Tape: DLT			

Ecrix

Model	Interface	Capacity	Speed
VXA-1 IDE ··················IDE ··················		33GB ··········	3MB/sec
VXA-1 V10 ··················SCSI-2 ··················		20GB ··········	
Tape: VXA			
VXA-1 V17 ··················SCSI-2 ··················		33GB ··········	
Tape: VXA			
VXA-1 V6 ··················SCSI-2 ··················		12GB ··········	
Tape: VXA			

Exabyte

Model	Interface	Capacity	Speed
Eagle TR-3 ··················IDE ··················			
Tape: QIC (quarter inch) Tape: QW-3020XLF			
Eagle TR-4i ··················IDE ··················			
Tape: Travan Tape: MC3000XL			
Eliant 820 ··················SCSI 1 ··················		7GB ··········	
Tape: 8mm			
Enspire NS8 ··················SCSI ··················		4GB ··········	514Kb/sec
Tape: Travan Tape: TR-4 Travan Mini			
EXB-10(i) ··········			
Tape: QG112M/54M/15M			
EXB-10CHS ··········			
Tape: QG112M/54M/15M			
EXB-120 ··········			
Tape: QG112M/54M/15M			
EXB-120CHS ··········			
Tape: QG112M/54M/15M			
EXB-1500 ··········			

Model	Interface	Capacity	Speed
Tape Number: Notes and/or Tape Example:			
EXB-2501/c			
EXB-4200/c			
Tape: 4mm DDS			
EXB-60			
Tape: QG112M/54M/15M			
EXB-8200	SCSI		1.5Mb/sec
Tape: 8mm	Tape: QG112M/54M/15M		
EXB-8200SX			
Tape: QG112M/54M/15M			
EXB-8205	SCSI	5GB	500Kb/sec
Tape: 8mm	Tape: QG112M/54M/15M		
EXB-8205XL			
Tape: QGD160M/112M/54M/15M			
EXB-8500	SCSI	10GB	1Mb/sec
Tape: 8mm	Tape: QG112M/54M/15M		
EXB-8500c	SCSI	5GB	1Mb/sec
Tape: 8mm	Tape: QG112M/54M/15M		
EXB-8505	SCSI	10GB	1Mb/sec
Tape: 8mm	Tape: QG112M/54M/15M		
EXB-8505XL			
Tape: QGD160M/112M/54M/15M			
EXB-8700	SCSI	7GB	500Kb/sec
Tape: 8mm	Tape: 160mXL		
Mammoth	Fast SCSI-2	20GB	3Mb/sec
Tape: 8mm			
Mammoth-2 (M2)	LVD	60GB	12Mb/sec
Tape: 8mm	Tape: Exabyte 75m,150m,225m AME		
Mammoth-2 (M2)	FC	60GB	12Mb/sec
Tape: 8mm	Tape: Exabyte 75m,150m,225m AME		
Mammoth-LT	LVD	14GB	2Mb/sec
Tape: 8mm	Tape: 125m AME		
VXA-1 Firewire	FireWire/IEEE1394	33GB	
Tape: VXA	Tape: V17,V10,V6		
VXA-1 LVD 33GB	SCSI Ultra2LVD	33GB	
Tape: VXA	Tape: V17,V10,V6		
VXA-1 LVD 66GB	SCSI Ultra2LVD	66GB	
Tape: VXA	Tape: V17,V10,V6		
VXA-2 Packet LVD	SCSI Ultra2LVD	80GB	
Tape: VXA	Tape: V23,V17,V10,V6		
VXA-2 PacketFireWire	FireWire/IEEE1394	80GB	
Tape: VXA	Tape: V23,V17,V10,V6		

Fujitsu

Model	Interface	Capacity	Speed
M2481A	SCSI-2	200MB	1.5mb/sec
Tape: 1/2in Cartridge			
M2481B	SCSI-2	200MB	3mb/sec
Tape: 1/2in Cartridge			
M2483B	SCSI-2	200Mb	3mb/sec
Note: Rack Mount			
M2483B-1	SCSI-2	200Mb	3mb/sec
Note: w/autoloader			
M2483H	SCSI-2	600Mb	3mb/sec
Note: Rack mount			
M2483H-1	SCSI-2	600Mb	3mb/sec
Note: Rack mount w/autolod			
M2485B	SCSI-2	200Mb	3mb/sec
Note: Desktop			

Model	Interface	Capacity	Speed
Tape Number:	Notes and/or Tape Example:		
M2485B-1	SCSI-2	200Mb	3Mb/sec
Note: desktop w/autoloader			
M2485H	SCSI-2	600Mb	3Mb/sec
Note: Desktop			
M2485H-1	SCSI-2	600Mb	3Mb/sec
Note: Desktop w/autoload			
M2488C	SCSI-2	1.2GB	3Mb/sec
Tape: writes 36 track Note: tapelength545ft			
M2488E	SCSI-2	1.2GB	3Mb/sec
Tape: reads and writes 36 track Note: tapelength545ft			
M8100A	SCSI U/W	16Mb	13.5Mb/sec
Tape: 1/2 in Tape: 3590			

Hewlett-Packard

Model	Interface	Capacity	Speed
12000e Autoloader	SCSI-2	24Gb	1Mb/sec
Tape: 4mm DDS			
157766-B22	Ultra2-LVDS	50GB	
Tape: AIT-1 Tape: Q1997A			
157767-002	Ultra2-LVDS	50GB	
Tape: AIT-1 Tape: Q1997A			
215487-b21	Ultra2-LVDS	50GB	
Tape: AIT-1 Tape: Q1997A			
216884-B21	Ultra2-LVDS	35GB	
Tape: AIT-1 Tape: Q1997A			
216885-001	Ultra2-LVDS	35GB	
Tape: AIT-1 Tape: Q1997A			
216886-b21	Ultra2-LVDS	35GB	
Tape: AIT-1 Tape: Q1997A			
246627-B22	IDE/ATAPI	35GB	
Tape: AIT-1 Tape: Q1997A			
249160-001	Ultra2-LVDS	100GB	
Tape: AIT-3 Tape: Q1999A			
249161-B21	Ultra2-LVDS	100GB	
Tape: AIT-3 Tape: Q1999A			
249189-B21	Ultra2-LVDS	100GB	
Tape: AIT-3 Tape: Q1999A			
3R-A2392-AA	Ultra2-LVDS	35GB	
Tape: AIT-1 Tape: Q1997A			
88780	SCSI	40MB	
Tape: 9 Track			
88781A	SCSI	40MB	
Tape: 9 Track			
AIT 100GB	Ultra2-LVDS	100GB	
Tape: AIT-3 Tape: Q1999A			
AIT 35GB IDE	IDE/ATAPI	35GB	
Tape: AIT-1 Tape: Q1997A			
AIT 35GB LVD	Ultra2-LVDS	35GB	
Tape: AIT-1 Tape: Q1997A			
AIT 50GB LVD	Ultra2-LVDS	50GB	
Tape: AIT-1 Tape: Q1997A			
DAT24e	Ultra2SCSI	12GB	1.5Mb/sec
Tape: DDS-3 Tape: C5707A/C5708A Note: HPC1556D			
DAT24eU	Ultra2SCSI	12GB	1.5Mb/sec
Tape: DDS-3 Tape: C5707A/C5708A Note: HPC5653C			
DAT24i	Ultra2SCSI	12GB	1.5Mb/sec
Tape: DDS-3 Tape: C57-7A/C5708A Note: HPC1555D			
DAT40e	UltraWideLVD/SESCSI2	20GB	3Mb/sec

Tape Drives

Tape Drive Manufacturer

Model	Interface	Capacity	Speed
Tape Number: Notes and/or Tape Example:			
Tape: DDS-3	Tape: C5708A Note: Q1555A		
DAT40h	UltraWideLVD/SESCSI2	20GB	3Mb/sec
Tape: DDS-3,DDS-4	Tape: C5708A,C5718A Note: Q1546A		
DAT40i	UltraWideLVD/SESCSI2	20GB	3Mb/sec
Tape: DDS-3,DDS-4	Tape: C5708A,C5718A Note: Q1553A		
DAT72e	WideUltraSCSILVD	36GB	3Mb/sec
Tape: DAT72,DDS-3,DDS-4	Tape: C8010A,C5708A,C5718A Note: Q1527A		
DAT72h	WideUltraSCSILVD	36GB	3Mb/sec
Tape: DAT72,DDS-3,DDS-4	Tape: C8010A,C5708A,C5718A Note: Q1529A		
DAT72i	WideUltraSCSILVD	36GB	3Mb/sec
Tape: DAT72,DDS-3,DDS-4	Tape: C8010A,C5708A,C5718A Note: Q1525A		
DAT8e	SCSI-2	4GB	
Tape: DDS-2	Tape: C5706A Note: HPC1529K		
DAT8eU	SCSI-2	4GB	
Tape: DDS-2	Tape: C5706A Note: HPC1552D		
DAT8i	SCSI-2	4GB	
Tape: DDS-2	Tape: C5706A Note: HPC1528K		
DLT 80	SCSI-2FstWd	40GB	
Tape: DLTTapeIV	Tape: C5141F		
DLT 80e	WideUltraSCSI2LVD	40GB	6Mb/s
Tape: DLT5	Tape: DLT4000,DLT1,DLTvs80 Note: HPC7503A		
DLT 80i	WideUltraSCSI2LVD	40GB	6Mb/s
Tape: DLT5	Tape: DLT4000,DLT1,DLTvs80 Note: HPC7504A		
DLT VS80	WideUltraSCSI2LVD	40GB	
Tape: DLT(digital linear)	Tape: DLTTape IV,DLT1,DLT4000 Note: C5141F		
HPC1528K	SCSI-2	4GB	
Tape: DDS-2	Tape: C5706A Note: DAT8i		
HPC1529K	SCSI-2	4GB	
Tape: DDS-2	Tape: C5706A Note: DAT8e		
HPC1533	SCSI-2	24Gb	1Mb/sec
Tape: 4mm DDS	Tape: Sony DGD120MA		
HPC1537			
Tape: 4mm DDS	Tape: DDS-3		
HPC1552D	SCSI-2	4GB	
Tape: DDS-2	Tape: C5706A Note: DAT8eU		
HPC1555D	Ultra2SCSI	12GB	10Mb/sec
Tape: DDS-3	Note: DAT24i		
HPC1556D	Ultra2SCSI	12GB	10Mb/sec
Tape: DDS-3	Note: DAT24e		
HPC5653C	Ultra2SCSI	12GB	10Mb/sec
Tape: DDS-3	Note: DAT24eU		
HPC7400A	Ultra2/WdSCSI	100GB	15Mb/sec
Note: Ultrium 230i			
HPC7401A	Ultra2/WdSCSI	100GB	15Mb/sec
Note: Ultrium 230e			
HPC7420A	Ultra2SCSI	100GB	7.5Mb/sec
Tape: Ultrium 1	Note: Ultrium 215i		
HPC7421A	Ultra2SCSI	100GB	7.5Mb/sec
Tape: Ultrium 1	Note: Ultrium 215e		
HPC7421A	Ultra2SCSI	100GB	7.5Mb/sec
Tape: Ultrium 1	Note: Ultrium 215e for UX		
HPC7470A	Ultra2/WdSCSI	100GB	15Mb/sec
Note: Ultrium 230m			
HPC7492A	Ultra2SCSI	100GB	7.5Mb/sec
Tape: Ultrium 1	Note: Ultrium 215m		
HPC7503A	WideUltraSCSI2LVD	40GB	

Tape Drives

Tape Drive Manufacturer Model	Interface	Capacity	Speed
Tape Number: Notes and/or Tape Example:			
Tape: DLT	Tape: DLT4000,DLT1,DLTvs80 Note: DLT vs80e		
HPC7504A	WideUltraSCSI2LVD	40GB	
Tape: DLT	Tape: DLT4000,DLT1,DLTvs80 Note: DLT vs80i		
SDLT 220	Ultra2-LVDS	110GB	
SDLT 320	Ultra2-LVDS	160GB	
Tape: SDLT1	Tape: C7980A		
T1000	FloppyDisk	400Mb	1Mb/sec
T1000e	ParallelPort	400Mb	1Mb/sec
Ultrium 215e	Ultra2SCSI	100GB	7.5Mb/sec
Tape: Ultrium 1	Tape: HPC7421A		
Ultrium 215i	Ultra2SCSI	100GB	7.5Mb/sec
Tape: Ultrium 1	Tape: HPC7420A		
Ultrium 215m	Ultra2SCSI	100GB	7.5Mb/sec
Tape: Ultrium 1	Tape: HPC7492A		
Ultrium 230e	Ultra2/WdSCSI	100GB	15Mb/sec
Tape: Ultrium 1	Tape: HPC7401A		
Ultrium 230i	Ultra2/WdSCSI	100GB	15Mb/sec
Tape: Ultrium 1	Tape: HPC7400A		
Ultrium 230m	Ultra2/WdSCSI	100GB	15Mb/sec
Tape: Ultrium 1	Tape: HPC7470A		
Ultrium 460e	Ultra3SCSIW	200GB	30Mb/sec
Tape: Ultrium 2	Tape: C7972A,Q15120A		
Ultrium 460i	Ultra3SCSIW	200GB	30Mb/sec
Tape: Ultrium 2	Tape: C7972A,Q1518A		

Ibm Corp.

	Interface	Capacity	Speed
3580-H23	UL160SCSI	200GB	15Mb/sec
Tape: Ultrium 2	Tape: IBM Ultrium 08L9870		
3580-L23	Ultra2/WdSCSI	200GB	15Mb/sec
Tape: Ultrium 2	Tape: IBM Ultrium 08L9120		
3590	SCSI-2	30GB	
Tape: 05H4434			
3592 J1A	FC	60GB	
Tape: Cartridge	Tape: 18P7534,IBM3592		
3592 J1A	FC	300GB	
Tape: Cartridge	Tape: 18P7534,IBM3592		
3660			
Tape: QD6150			
3850			
Tape: QD300XL/P			
3851			
Tape: QD300XL/P			
5100			
Tape: QD300XL/P			
5110			
Tape: QD300XL/P			
5150			
Tape: QD300XL/P			
5363			
Tape: QD6150			
5550		45Mb	
Tape: QD300XL/P			
6110			
Tape: QD300XL/P			
6157-1			
Tape: QD300XL/P			

Tape Drive Manufacturer Model	Interface	Capacity	Speed
Tape Number: Notes and/or Tape Example:			
6157-2			
Tape: QD6150			
7205	SCSI-2DIFF	35GB	5Mb/sec
Tape: 1/2-in DLT tape-IV Tape: 35L1119			
7206 110	SCSI-2	12GB	1Mb/sec
Tape: 4mm DDS-3 Tape: 4mm 125-meter #59H3465			
7206 220	LVD/SEWD ULSCSI-2	20GB	3Mb/sec
Tape: 4mm DDS-4 Tape: 59H4456			
7206 336	LVD	36GB	
Tape: DAT72,4mm Tape: 18P7912			
7206-VX2	SCSI-2	20GB	
Tape: 8mm Tape: 19P4876,19P4877,19P4878			
7207 122	SCSI-2	4GB	380kb/sec
Tape: Quarter-Inch Cartridge Tape: 59H3660			
7207 330	SCSI-2	30GB	
Tape: Quarter-Inch Cartridge Tape: 19P4209			
7208 341	SCSI	20GB	3Mb/sec
Tape: 8mmAME;8mm MP Tape: 8mm 170-meter AME part #59H2678			
7208 342	SCSI	20GB	3Mb/sec
Tape: 8mm AME; 8mm MP Tape: 8mm 170-meter AME #59H2678			
7208 345	SCSI Ultra2LVD	60GB	12Mb/sec
Tape: 8mm AME Tape: 225 meter AME;18P6485-60GB			
8723	Ultra2/WdSCSI	100GB	
Tape: Ultrium LTO Tape: IBM 08L9120			

Iomega

1600LTO	WideUltraSCSI2LVD	800GB	
Tape: LTO-1			
6400LTO	UL160SCSI-3LVD	3.2TB	
Tape: Ultrium 2			
640VS	WideUltraSCSI2LVD	320GB	
Tape: VS80,DLT-IV			
Ditto 1700	ParallelPort	835MB	2Mb/sec
Tape: QW-3020XLW			
Ditto 250	ParallelPort	120MB	1Mb/sec
Tape: DC2080,DC2120			
Ditto 2GB	ParallelPort	1GB	1Mb/sec
Tape: Iomega 2GB			
Ditto 420	ParallelPort	210MB	1Mb/sec
Tape: QW-5122F/QW5122XL			
Ditto 850	ParallelPort	420MB	1Mb/sec
Tape: QD-3010XLW			
Ditto Easy 3200	ParallelPort	1600MB	2Mb/sec
Tape: TR-3,TR-2 Tape: QW-3020XLW,QW-3010XLW			
Ditto Easy 800	ParallelPort	400Mb	1Mb/sec
Ditto Easy 800	ParallelPort	400MB	1Mb/sec
Tape: QIC-80,QW-5122,TR-1			
Ditto Max	ParallelPort	5GB	36Mb/sec
Tape: Iomega 10GB			

Jvc

8436	SCSIFSTWD	800MB	

Lacie

106994	SCSI Wide LVD	160GB	
Tape: SDLT			
107986	SCSI Wide LVD	500GB	

Tape Drive Manufacturer Model	Interface	Capacity	Speed
Tape Number: Notes and/or Tape Example:			
Tape: S-AIT			
300909	SCSI U/W	50GB	
Tape: AIT-2			
300910	SCSI U/W	100GB	
Tape: AIT-3			

M4 Data Inc

9906G	SCSI		
Tape: 9 Track			
9906P	SCSI		
Tape: 9 Track			
9914	SCSI		
Tape: 9 Track			
9914V	SCSI		
Tape: 9 Track			
M490E	SCSI-2FstWd	800MB	
Tape: 18 Track Tape: ANSI 3480,3490			

Micro Solutions

Backpack 800T	ParallelPort	400Mb	1Mb/sec
Backpack 800TD	ParallelPort		1Mb/sec

Ncr

3445			
Tape: QD6320/QD6525			
6091			
Tape: QD6150			
6091-2500			
Tape: QD90M/60M			
7200			
Tape: QD300XLP			
8100			
Tape: QD300XLP			
8130			
Tape: QD300XLP			
8150			
Tape: QD300XLP			
9100			
Tape: QD600A			
9300			
Tape: QD600A			

Olivetti

M24			
Tape: QD2040			
M28			
Tape: QD2040			
M30			
Tape: QD300XL/P			
M380		60Mb	
Tape: QD600A/QD300XL/P			
M380		150Mb	
Tape: QD6150			
M40			
Tape: QD300XL/P			
M54			
Tape: QD300XL/P			

Model	Interface	Capacity	Speed
Tape Number: Notes and/or Tape Example:			
M60			
Tape: QD300XL/P			
M64			
Tape: QD300XL/P			
M70			
Tape: QD300XL/P			

Optima Technology

Model	Interface	Capacity	Speed
110L Autoloader	Ultra2-LVDS	1024GB	
Tape: Ultrium LTO			
AIT-2	UltraSCSI	50GB	
Tape: 8mm	Tape: SDX2-50C,SDX-135C,SDX-T3C		
DLT	LVD	110GB	
Tape: SDLT			

Panasonic

Model	Interface	Capacity	Speed
WB-A111			
Tape: QD2040			
WB-A113			
Tape: QD2040			

Procom Technology

Model	Interface	Capacity	Speed
IDAT 1300			
Tape: DG90M/60M			
MDAT 1300			
Tape: DG90M/60M			
MDAT 1300/E	SCSI		
Tape: DG60M			
MDAT 1300/M			
Tape: DG60M			
PT40			
Tape: QD2040			
PXT40-250			
Tape: QD2040			
PXT40-500			
Tape: QD2040			

Qualstar Corporation

Model	Interface	Capacity	Speed
3402	SCSI-2		
Tape: 9 Track			
3404	SCSI-2		
Tape: 9 Track			
3404S	SCSI-2		
Tape: 9 Track			
3404SD	SCSI-2DIFF		
Tape: 9 Track			
3410	SCSI	270MB	
Tape: 9 Track			
3412	SCSI		
Tape: 9 Track			
3412S	SCSI-2		
Tape: 9 Track			
3412SD	SCSI-2DIFF		
Tape: 9 Track			
3414	SCSI		
Tape: 9 Track			
3414S	SCSI-2		

Tape Drives

Tape Drive Manufacturer

Model	Interface	Capacity	Speed
Tape Number: Notes and/or Tape Example:			
Tape: 9 Track			
3414SD	SCSI-2DIFF		
Tape: 9 Track			
3418	SCSI		
Tape: 9 Track			
3418S	SCSI-2		
Tape: 9 Track			
3418SD	SCSI-2DIFF		
Tape: 9 Track			
DLT4000	SCSI-2	20GB	1.5Mb/sec
Tape: DLT	Tape: DLTtapeIII,DLTtapeIIIxt,DLTtapeIV		
DLT6101	SCSI-2	70GB	
Tape: DLT(digital linear)			
DLT7000	SCSI-2	35GB	5Mb/sec
Tape: DLT	Tape: DLTtapeIII,DLTtapeIIIxt,DLTtapeIV		

Quantum

Model	Interface	Capacity	Speed
DLT VS160	UL160SCSI2	80GB	
Tape: DLT1	Tape: DLT VS1		
DLT VS80	WideUltraSCSI2	40GB	
Tape: DLTTapeIV	Tape: DLT4000		
DLT1	WideUltraSCSI	40GB	3Mb/sec
Tape: DLTTape IV			
DLT2000XT	SCSI-2	15GB	1.25Mb/sec
Tape: DLT tape IIIXT,III			
DLT4000	SCSI-2Fast	20GB	1.5Mb/sec
Tape: DLT IV,IIIXT,III			
DLT7000	SCSI-2Fast	35GB	5Mb/sec
Tape: DLT IV,IIIXT,III			
DLT8000	SCSI-2Fst/WD/LVD/HVD	40GB	6Mb/sec
Tape: DLT IV,IIIXT,III			
SDLT 320	LVD	160GB	
Tape: SDLT	Tape: SuperDLT Tape I		
SDLT 600	LVD	300GB	
Tape: SDLT	Tape: SuperDLT Tape I		
SDLT220	Ultra2SCSI,LVD,HVD	110GB	11Mb/sec
Tape: SDLT	Tape: Super DLTTape I		

Seagate Technologies

Model	Interface	Capacity	Speed
STA150000W-S	SCSI-2FstWd	25GB	3Mb/sec
Tape: 16K MIC	Note: Tapelength170M		
STA250000W-S	SCSI-2FstWd	25GB	3Mb/sec
Tape: 16K MIC	Note: Tapelength170M		
STA4200000W-S	SCSI-2FstWd	100GB	3Mb/sec
Tape: 16K MIC	Note: Tapelength170M		
STA6200000W-S	SCSI-2FstWd	100GB	3Mb/sec
Tape: 16K MIC	Note: Tapelength170M		
STA650000W-S	SCSI-2FstWd	25GB	3Mb/sec
Tape: 16K MIC	Note: Tapelength170M		
STD124000N	SCSI-2	2600	
Tape: DDS-3			
STD18000N		2000	
Tape: DDS-2			
STD224000N-RFT	SCSI-2	12GB	1100kb/sec
Tape: DDS-3	Tape: Seagate STMD24G Note: Tapelength125M		
STD224000N-RYT	SCSI-2	12GB	
Tape: DDS-3	Tape: Seagate STMD24,STDM8		

Model	Interface	Capacity	Speed
Tape Number:	Notes and/or Tape Example:		
STD224000N-S	SCSI-2	12GB	
Tape: DDS	Tape: Seagate STMD24G		
STD224000N-SB	SCSI-2	12GB	1100kb/sec
Tape: DDS-2,DDS-3	Tape: STMD24G Note: Tapelength125M		
STD24000N-SB	SCSI-2	2GB	550kb/sec
Tape: DDS-3	Tape: Seagate 32000 Note: Tapelength90M		
STD2401LW-R	Ultra2SCSI	20GB	
Tape: DDS-4	Tape: Seagate STDM40		
STD2401LW-RY	68-PinA	20GB	
Tape: DDS-4	Tape: Seagate STDM40,STDM24,STDM8		
STD2401LW-S	68-Pin-A	20GB	
Tape: DDS-4	Tape: Seagate STDM40,STDMCL,STDM24,STDM8		
STD28000N-RFT	SCSI-2	4GB	550kb/sec
Tape: DDS-2	Tape: Seagate 34000 Note: Tapelength120m		
STD28000N-SB	SCSI-2	4GB	550kb/sec
Tape: DDS-2	Tape: Seagate 34 Note: Tapelength120M		
STD496000N-S	SCSI-2	48GB	
Tape: DDS-3	Tape: STMD24G		
STD496000N-SB	SCSI-2	48GB	1100kb/sec
Tape: DDS-2,DDS-3	Note: Tapelength125M		
STD624000N-RFT	SCSI-2	12GB	1100kb/sec
Tape: DDS-3	Tape: Seagate STMD24G Note: Tapelength125M		
STD624000N-RYT	50-PinA	12GB	
Tape: DDS-3	Tape: Seagate STMD24, STDM8		
STD624000N-S	SCSI-2	12GB	
Tape: DDS	Tape: Seagate STMD24G		
STD624000N-SB	SCSI-2	12GB	1100kb/sec
Tape: DDS-2,DDS-3	Tape: STMD24G Note: Tapelength125M		
STD64000N-SB	SCSI-2	2GB	550kb/sec
Tape: DDS-DC	Tape: Seagate 32000 Note: Tapelength90M		
STD6401LW-R	Ultra2SCSI	20GB	
Tape: DDS-4	Tape: Seagate STDM40		
STD6401LW-RY	Ultra2SCSI	40GB	
Tape: DDS-4	Tape: STDM40		
STD6401LW-S	LVD	20GB	
Tape: DDS-4	Tape: Seagate STDM40,STDMCL,STDM24,STDM8		
STD68000N-RFT	SCSI-2	4GB	550kb/sec
Tape: DDS-2	Tape: Seagate 34000 Note: Tapelength120m		
STD68000N-SB	SCSI-2	4GB	550kb/sec
Tape: DDS-2	Tape: Seagate 34 Note: Tapelength120M		
STD696000N-SB	SCSI-2	48GB	1100kb/sec
Tape: DDS-2,DDS-3	Note: Tapelength125M		
STDL42401LW-K	Ultra2SCSI	120GB	
Tape: DDS-4	Tape: Seagate STDM40		
STDL42401LW-KY	Ultra2SCSI	120GB	
Tape: DDS-4	Tape: Seagate STDM40,STDM24,STDM8		
STDL42401LW-S	Ultra2SCSI	120GB	
Tape: DDS	Tape: Seagate STDM40		
STDL62401LW-K	Ultra2SCSI	120GB	
Tape: DDS-4	Tape: Seagate STDM40		
STDL62401LW-KY	Ultra2SCSI	120GB	
Tape: DDS-4	Tape: Seagate STDM40,STDM24,STDM8		
STDL62401LW-S	Ultra2SCSI	120GB	
Tape: DDS-4	Tape: Seagate STDM40		
STL496000N-S	SCSI-2	48GB	
Tape: DDS-3	Tape: STDM24,STDMCL,STDM8		

Tape Drives

Tape Drive Manufacturer Model	Interface	Capacity	Speed
Tape Number: Notes and/or Tape Example:			
STL696000N-S	SCSI-2	48GB	
Tape: DDS-3	Tape: STDM24,STDMCL,STDM8		
STT220000A-M	Atapi	10GB	
Tape: Travan 20/NS20,TR-5	Tape: Seagate STTM20		
STT220000A-RFT	Atapi	10GB	1000kb/sec
Tape: Travan 20	Tape: Seagate8000TR4,SonyQW-3080XLF		
STT220000N-M	SCSI-2	10GB	
Tape: Travan 20/NS20,TR-5	Tape: Seagate STTM20		
STT220000N-MC	SCSI-2	10GB	
Tape: Travan 20/NS20,TR-5	Tape: Seagate STTM20		
STT220000N-RCVT	SCSI-2	10GB	2000kb/sec
Tape: Travan 20	Tape: Seagate8000TR4,SonyQW-3080XLF		
STT220000N-RFT	SCSI-2	10GB	
Tape: Travan 20	Tape: Seagate STMT20G		
STT22000A-M	Atapi	4GB	1000kb/sec
Tape: Travan 20	Tape: Seagate8000TR4		
STT22000N-MC	SCSI-2	10GB	2000kb/sec
Tape: Travan 20	Tape: Seagate 8000TR4		
STT2401A-M	Atapi	20GB	
Tape: Travan			
STT2401A-S	Atapi	20GB	
Tape: Travan			
STT28000A-M	Atapi	4GB	600kb/sec
Tape: Travan 8	Tape: Seagate8000TR4,4000QT,SonyQW3080XLF		
STT28000A-RFT	Atapi	4GB	600kb/sec
Tape: 3M Travan 8	Tape: Seagate8000TR4,4000QT,SonyQW-3080XLF		
STT28000N-M	SCSI-2	4GB	600kb/sec
Tape: Travan 8	Tape: Seagate8000TR4,4000QT,SonyQW3080XLF		
STT28000N-MC	SCSI-2	4GB	1200kb/sec
Tape: Travan 8/NS8,TR-4	Tape: Seagate8000TR4,4000QT,SonyQW3080XLF		
STT28000N-RCVT	SCSI-2	4GB	1200kb/sec
Tape: 3M Travan 8	Tape: Seagate8000TR4,4000QT,SonyQW-3080XLF		
STT28000N-RFT	SCSI-2	4GB	600kb/sec
Tape: 3M Travan 8	Tape: Seagate8000TR4,4000QT,SonyQW-3080XLF		
STT3401A-ED	Atapi/IDE	40GB	
Tape: Travan 40	Tape: CTM40		
STT3401A-EY	Atapi/IDE	40GB	
Tape: Travan 40	Tape: CTM40		
STT3401A-RD	Atapi/IDE	40GB	
Tape: Travan 40	Tape: CTM40		
STT3401A-RY	Atapi/IDE	40GB	
Tape: Travan 40	Tape: CTM40		
STT496000N-S	SCSI-2	48GB	
Tape: DDS	Tape: Seagate STMD24G		
STT6201U-A	USB	10GB	
Tape: Travan 20	Tape: Seagate STTM20		
STT6201U-E	USB	10GB	
Tape: Travan 20	Tape: Seagate STTM20		
STT6201U-R	USB	10GB	
Tape: Travan 20	Tape: Seagate STTM20		
STT6201U2	USB	10GB	
Tape: Travan 20			
STT6201U2-E	USB	10GB	
Tape: Travan 20			
STT6201U2-R	USB2.0	30MB	
Tape: Travan 20	Tape: STMT20G		

Tape Drive Manufacturer

Model	Interface	Capacity	Speed
Tape Number:	Notes and/or Tape Example:		
STT6401U2	USB2.0	20GB	
Tape: Travan			
STT6401U2-E	USB2.0	20GB	
Tape: Travan			
STT6401U2-R	USB2.0	20GB	
Tape: Travan40/Travan20/TR5	Tape: STTM40G		
STT681U-A	USB	4GB	
Tape: Travan 8GB	Tape: Seagate STTM8		
STT681U-E	USB	4GB	
Tape: Travan 8GB	Tape: Seagate STTM8		
STT681U-R	USB	4GB	
Tape: Travan 8GB	Tape: Seagate STTM8		
STT696000N-S	SCSI-2	48GB	
Tape: DDS	Tape: Seagate STMD24G		
STU42001LW-K	Ultra2SCSI	100GB	
Tape: Ultrium 1	Tape: Seagate STUM200		
STU42001LW-S	Ultra2SCSI	100GB	
Tape: Ultrium 1	Tape: STUM200		
STU42001WD-S	UltraSCSI	100GB	
Tape: Ultrium 1	Tape: STUM200		
STU62001LW-K	Ultra2SCSI	100GB	
Tape: Ultrium 1	Tape: Seagate STUM200		
STU62001LW-S	Ultra2SCSI	100GB	
Tape: Ultrium 1	Tape: STUM200		
STU62001WD-S	UltraSCSI	100GB	
Tape: Ultrium 1	Tape: STUM200		
STUL620001LW-K	Ultra2SCSI	1100GB	
Tape: STUM200A			
STUL816001LW-K	Ultra2-LVDS	1600GB	
Tape: Ultrium LTO	Tape: STUM200A		
STUL816001LW-S	Ultra2-LVDS	1600GB	
Tape: Ultrium LTO	Tape: STUM200A		

Sony

Model	Interface	Capacity	Speed
AITE130UL	USB2.0	50GB	
Tape: AIT-2	Tape: SDX2-50C		
AITE90-UL	USB2.0	35GB	
Tape: AIT-1	Tape: SDX1-35C		
SDT-10000	DDS-4		
Tape: 4mm DDS	Tape: DDS-4		
SDT-11000BM	WideUltraSCSI	20GB	14Mb/s
Tape: DDS-4			
SDT-11000PB	WideUltraSCSI	20GB	14Mb/s
Tape: DDS-4			
SDT-2000	SCSI-2	2GB	183kb/sec
Tape: DDS	Note: Tapelength90m		
SDT-4000	SCSI-2	2GB	183-366kb/sec
Tape: DDS	Note: Tapelength90m		
SDT-5000	SCSI-2	4GB	
Tape: DDS-2	Note: Tapelength120m		
SDT-5200	SCSI-2	4GB	
Tape: DDS-2	Note: Tapelength120m		
SDT-7000BM	SCSI-2Fast/Narrow	4GB	5.0Mb/s
Tape: DDS-2			
SDT-7000PB DDS2 INT	SCSI-2Fast/Narrow	4GB	
Tape: DDS-2			
SDT-9000BM	SCSI-2Fast/Narrow	12GB	5.0Mb/s

Tape Drive Manufacturer Model	Interface	Capacity	Speed
Tape Number: Notes and/or Tape Example:			
Tape: DDS-3			
SDT-9000PB	SCSI-2Fast/Narrow	12GB	5.0Mb/s
Tape: DDS-3			
SDT-D11000ME DDS4EXT	WideUltraSCSI	20GB	14Mb/s
Tape: DDS-4			
SDT-D11000PB DDS4EXT	WideUltraSCSI	20GB	14Mb/s
Tape: DDS-4			
SDT-D7000ME	SCSI-2Fast/Narrow	4GB	5.0Mb/s
Tape: DDS-2			
SDT-D7000PB	SCSI-2Fast/Narrow	4GB	5.0Mb/s
Tape: DDS-2			
SDT-D9000ME	SCSI-2Fast/Narrow	12GB	5.0Mb/s
Tape: DDS-3			
SDT-D9000PB DDS3 EXT	SCSI-2Fast/Narrow	12GB	
Tape: DDS-3			
SDX-300C/BM AIT1 INT	SCSI-2FstWd	35GB	4Mb/s
Tape: AIT-1			
SDX-300C/TB AIT1 INT	SCSI-2FstWd	35GB	4Mb/s
Tape: AIT-1			
SDX-500C/BM AIT2 INT	WideUltraSCSI	50GB	
Tape: AIT-2			
SDX-510C/L	HDV		
Tape: AIT-2			
SDX-S300C/TB AIT1 EX	SCSI-2FstWd	35GB	4Mb/s
Tape: AIT-1			
SDX-S500C/BM AIT2 EX	WideUltraSCSI	50GB	
Tape: AIT-2			
SDX-S500C/TB AIT2 EX	WideUltraSCSI	50GB	
Tape: AIT-2			
SDX-S500C/TB AIT2INT	WideUltraSCSI	50GB	
Tape: AIT-1,AIT-2			

Storagetek

LTO GEN 1	Ultra2SCSI	100GB	
Tape: Ultrium LTO			
LTO GEN 2	Ultra3SCSI	200GB	
Tape: Ultrium 2			
T9840A	UltraSCSI	20GB	10Mb/sec
T9840B	FC	20GB	19Mb/sec
Tape: StorageTek 9840			
T9840C	FC	40GB	
T9940A	UltraSCSI	60GB	10Mb/sec
Tape: QIC (quarter inch)			
T9940B	FC	200GB	
Tape: QIC (quarter inch)			

Summit Memory System

SE120	FloppyDisk		
Tape: Summit DC2000,DC2080,DC2120			
SE250	FloppyDisk		
Tape: Summit DC2080,DC2120			

Tandberg Data

DLT VS160	UL160SCSI	110GB	
Tape: DLTTapeIV			
DLT VS80	SCSI	40GB	6Mb/sec
Tape: DLTtapeIV			

Tape Drives

Tape Drive Manufacturer

Model	Interface	Capacity	Speed
Tape Number: Notes and/or Tape Example:			
DLT1	SCSI	40GB	3Mb/sec
Tape: DLTtape IV			
DLT4000	SCSI	20GB	
DLT7000	SCSI	35GB	
DLT8000	SCSI	40GB	
Tape: DLTtapeIV			
NS20 Pro	SCSI	10GB	
Tape: Travan			
SDLT220	Ultra2-LVDS	110GB	
Tape: SDLT			
SDLT320	SCSI	160GB	
Tape: SDLT-1			
SLR100	Ultra2/WdSCSI	50GB	5Mb/sec
Tape: SLR Tape: SLR60			
SLR140	WideUltraSCSI	70GB	6Mb/sec
Tape: SLR Tape: SLRtape40,50,60,75,100			
SLR2	SCSI-2	525Mb	
SLR24	SCSI-3	12GB	1.2Mb/sec
SLR3	SCSI-2	1.2GB	
SLR32	SCSI-3	12GB	
SLR4	SCSI-2	2.5GB	
SLR40	Ultra2/WdSCSI	20GB	3Mb/sec
SLR5	SCSI-2	4GB	
Tape: QIC (quarter inch) Tape: qic2gb/1000/525			
SLR50	SCSI-3	25GB	2Mb/s
Tape: SLR			
SLR60	Ultra2/WdSCSI	30GB	4Mb/sec
Tape: SLR Tape: SLRtape60			
SLR7	Ultra2-LVDS	20GB	3Mb/sec
Tape: SLR Tape: SLR5			
SLR75	Ultra2/WdSCSI	38GB	4Mb/sec
Tape: SLR Tape: SLRtape40,50,60			

Teac America

Model	Interface	Capacity	Speed
Combo 700	FloppyDisk	340Mb	1Mb/sec
Tape: QIC-3010-MC Tape: 3M MC3000XL,PIMAT Note: Tapelength400ft			
FT-3008TR	FloppyDisk	400Mb	
Tape: Travan TR-1 Tape: QIC-Wide,CD2102XL,XIMAT			
FT-3010	FloppyDisk	340Mb	1Mb/sec
Tape: QIC-3030-MC Tape: MC3000XL Note: Tapelength400ft			
FT-3020	FloppyDisk	1.4GB	
MT-01F	SCSI		
MT-01N			
Tape: QDE2560			
MT-20			
Tape: QD300XL/P			
MT-40			
Tape: QD300XL/P			
Super Tape 1600	FloppyDisk	800Mb	1Mb/sec
Tape: Travan TR-2 Tape: QIC-Wide,MC3000XL PIMAT			

Tecmar Technologies

Model	Interface	Capacity	Speed
3100	SCSI-1	2GB	
Tape: DAT Tape: WangDAT 811147 Note: Tapelength90m			
3100SE	SCSI-1	2GB	
Tape: DAT Tape: WangDAT 811147 Note: Tapelength90m			

Tape Drives

Tape Drive Manufacturer Model	Interface	Capacity	Speed
Tape Number:	Notes and/or Tape Example:		
3200	SCSI-2	2GB	
Tape: DAT	Tape: WangDAT 811147 Note: Tapelength90m		
3200SE	SCSI-2	2GB	
Tape: DAT	Tape: WangDAT 811147 Note: Tapelength90m		
3400	SCSI-2	4GB	
Tape: DDS-2	Tape: WangDAT 811148 Note: Tapelength120m		
3400SE	SCSI-2	4GB	
Tape: DDS-2	Tape: WangDAT 811148 Note: Tapelength120m		
51000HT	SCSI-2	1.2GB	17.1Mb/min
Tape: QIC	Tape: DC9120		
5150ES	SCSI-2	250Mb	6.75Mb/min
Tape: QIC	Tape: DC6250		
52000HT	SCSI	2.5GB	
Tape: QIC (quarter inch)	Tape: DC6525,DC9120,DC9250		
5525ES	SCSI-2	525Mb	12Mb/min
Tape: QIC	Tape: DC6525		
6200HS	SCSI-2	2GB	
Tape: 4mm DAT			
9000	SCSI-2	10GB	
E51000HT	SCSI-2	1.2GB	17.1Mb/min
Tape: QIC	Tape: DC9120		
E52000HT	SCSI	2.5GB	
Tape: QIC (quarter inch)	Tape: DC9250		
E5525ES	SCSI-2	525Mb	12Mb/min
Tape: QIC	Tape: DC6525		
ETS420C	SCSI-2	4GB	
Tape: QIC (quarter inch),Travan 4			
NS20	SCSI-2	10GB	1Mb/sec
NS8	SCSI-2	4GB	
Tape: QIC (quarter inch)			
TS3900E-D01	SCSI	12GB	
Tape: DAT (digital audio tape)	Tape: 125M DAT 205391		
TS3900I-D01	SCSI	12GB	
Tape: DAT (digital audio tape)	Tape: 125M DAT 205391		
TS420C (Internal)	SCSI-2	4GB	
Tape: QIC (quarter inch),Travan 4			
TS420Se-D01	SCSI-2Fast	4GB	
Tape: TR4	Tape: QTT400-005		
TS420Si-D01	SCSI-2Fast	4GB	
Tape: TR4	Tape: QTT400-005		
TS420Si-D12	SCSI-2Fast	4GB	
Tape: TR4	Tape: QTT400-005		
TS520SI-D01	SCSI	10GB	
Tape: Travan			

Chapter 16

Floppy Drive Specifications

Many thanks to Bottom Line Industries, 9556 Cozycroft Ave, Chatsworth, California, 91311, (818) 700-1922, (800) 344-6044 for providing Sequoia with additional floppy drive information included in this chapter. If you need to have a floppy or hard drive rebuilt or would like to purchase a rebuilt floppy or hard drive, Bottom Line Industries is an excellent source!

Floppy Drives

Floppy Drive Manufacturers

The following table is a general summary of companies that have manufactured and/or are still manufacturing floppy drives. If you have information concerning the status of any of these companies, such as "XYZ Company went bankrupt in August, 1990" or "XYZ Company was bought by Q Company", please let us know so we can keep this section current. If a phone number is listed in the Status column, the company is in business.

Floppy Manufacturer	Status
Alps	408-361-6400
Aurora Tech	508-588-6110
Bachelor	Unknown
BASF	800-343-4600 (Changed Name to Emtech Data Store Media)
Burroughs	Unknown
Calcomp (CalGraph Tech)	Unknown
Canon	949-753-4000
C.D.C	Unknown
Century Data (Systech Retail Systems)	800-387-3262; Not a manufacturer
Chinon (Tech Media)	Unknown
Citizen	Unknown
Emtech Corp	Unknown
Epson	562-290-4000
Fuji	510-438-9700; Do not manufacture floppy or hard drives anymore.
Fujitsu	888-664-0672; Do not manufacture floppy or hard drives anymore.
Hewlett Packard	800-22-5547
Hi-Tech (China)	886-773-3555
Hitachi	914-332-5800
IBM	914-765-1900
Imation	651-704-4000
Iomega	801-332-1000
JVC	714-816-6500 Never manufactured floppy drives
MFE	Unknown
MPI	708-460-0555
Maple Tech	Unknown
Matsushita	Unknown
Memorex	Unknown
Micropolis	Out of Business

Floppy Drives

Floppy Manufacturer	Status
Mitac	510-656-3333 (merged with Synnex on 4-2-02)
Mitsubishi	403-730-5900 (don't manufacture floppy drives anymore)
Mitsumi	408-970-0700
NEC	800-632-4636
Newtronic	Unknown
Okidata	800-654-3282
Olivetti	Out of Business
Pacific Rim	Out of Business
Panasonic	866-462-5138
Persci	Unknown
Pertec	Unknown
Phillips (Plasmon)	719-593-7900
Qume (WYSE Tech)	800-800-9973
Remex	Unknown
Samsung	201-229-7000
Sanyo (Japan)	81-64-432-949
Seiko	408-546-0670; Never manufactured floppy drives
Shugart	Out of Business, see Seagate
Siemans	Out of Business
Sierra, Inc	Unknown
Sony	201-930-1000
Tandon	Filed Chapter 11 bankruptcy 9-95; See Sierra, Inc for support
Teac Corp.	323-727-4860
Tec	Unknown
Tech Media	Unknown
Tecmate	Unknown
Texas Peripherals	Unknown
Toshiba	949-583-3000
Victor	Unknown
Weltec	Unknown
World Storage	Unknown
WYSE Tech	800-800-9973
Y-E Data	847-887-7540

General Floppy Drive Specs

Formatted Capacity	Sides	Tracks	Sectors	Byte	Media Type*	Media Agent
5-1/4 inch diameter						
160 kb**	1	40	8	FE	SSDD	Ferrite
180 kb**	1	40	9	FC	SSDD	Ferrite
320 kb**	2	40	8	FF	DSDD	Ferrite
360 kb	2	40	9	FD	DSDD	Ferrite
1.2 Mb	2	80			DSQD	Ferrite
1.2 Mb	2	80	15	F9	DSHD	Cobalt
3-1/2 inch diameter						
720 kb	2	80	9	F9	DSDD	Cobalt
1.44 Mb	2	80	18	F0	DSHD	Cobalt
2.8 Mb	2	80	36	F0	DSEHD	Barium

* SS = Single Sided, DS=Double Sided
  DD = Double Density
  HD = High Density
  QD = Quad Density (now obsolete)
  EHD or ED = Extra High Density

** Obsolete drives

Maximum Entries in the Root Directory:
  5-1/4 DD and 3.5 DD = 112 Entries
  5-1/4 HD and 3.5 HD = 224 Entries
  3.5 EHD = 240 Entries

All floppy drives currently produced rotate at 300 RPM, except for the 1.2Mb, 5-1/4 HD drives, which rotate at 360 RPM.

All floppy drives are formatted at 512 Bytes Per Sector.

Floppy disks have 2 FATs, 12 Bit Type

Sequoia needs your help! If you have specifications on new or obsolete floppy drives, please send them to us for future editions of this book.

Floppy Drives

Floppy Drive Specs By Model

Manufacturer	Model Number	Width (Inch)	Height (Inch)	Format Capacity	Media Density
Alps	413(PS2)	3.50	Half	720kb	DSDD
	713(PS2)	3.50	Half	1.44Mb	DSHD
	723	3.50	Third	1.44Mb	DSHD
	723(PS2)	3.50	Half	1.44Mb	DSHD
	2124	5.25	Half	180kb	SSDD
	2124A	5.25	Full	360kb	DSDD
	2624-BKI	5.25	Half	360kb	DSDD
	DF328N	3.50	Qtr	2.88Mb	DSHD
	DF354H	3.50	1.0	1.44Mb	DSHD
	DF354N	3.50	1.0	1.44Mb	DSHD
	DFC 222 B02A,01A	5.25	Half	360kb	DSDD
	DFC 222A05A	5.25	Half	360kb	DSDD
	DFC 642 B01B	5.25	Half	1.2Mb	DSDD
Aurora Tech	FD350(SCSI)	3.50	Half		
	FD525(SCSI)	5.25	Half		
Bachelor	FD-104	5.25	Half	360kb	DSDD
BASF	6106	5.25	Full	180kb	SSDD
	6128	5.25	Half	360kb	DSDD
	6138	5.25	Half	720kb	DSDD
Burroughs	B9489-1	8.00	Full	1.6Mb	DSDD
Calcomp	142	8.00	Full	800kb	SSDD
	143	8.00	Full	1.6Mb	DSDD
Canon	221	5.25	Half	720kb	DSDD
	530	5.25	Half	720kb	DSDD
	531	5.25	Half	360kb	DSDD
	3361	3.50	Qtr	1.44Mb	DSHD
	5201	5.25	Half	360kb	DSDD
	5501	5.25	Third	1.2Mb	DSDD
	5511	5.25/3.5	Half	1.2/1.44Mb	DUAL
C.D.C.	9404	8.00	Full	800kb	SSDD
	9406-3	8.00	Full	800kb	SSDD
	9406-4	8.00	Full	1.6Mb	DSDD
	9408	5.25	Full	180kb	SSDD
	9409	5.25	Full	360kb	DSDD
	9409T	5.25	Full	720kb	DSQD
	9428	5.25	Half	360kb	DSDD
	9428-01	5.25	Half	180kb	SSDD
	9428-02	5.25	Half	360kb	DSDD
	9429	5.25	Half	720kb	DSQD
	9429-01	5.25	Half	360kb	SSQD
	BR8B1A	5.25	Full	360kb	DSDD
Century Data	140	8.00	Full	800kb	SSDD
Chinon	506-L	5.25	Half	1.2Mb	DSDD
	C354	3.50	Half	720kb	DSDD
	FP357	3.50	Half	1.4Mb	DSHD
	FR506	5.25	Full	1.2Mb	DSHD
	FX354	3.50	1.0	720kb	DSDD
	FZ357	3.50	1.0	1.4Mb	DSHD
	FZ358	3.50	1.0	1.4mb	DSHD
	FZ502	5.25	Half	360kb	DSDD
	FZ506	5.25	Full	1.2Mb	DSHD
	C359	3.50	Half	1.4Mb	DSHD
	F,FZ,C502	5.25	Half	360kb	DSDD
	C506	5.25	Half	1.2Mb	DSHD
Citizen	OSDA-01D	3.50	Third	720kb	DSQD
	OSDA-14A	3.50	Third	1.44Mb	DSHD
	OSDA-39D	3.50	Third	1.44Mb	DSDD

Floppy Drive Specs By Model

Manufacturer	Model Number	Width (Inch)	Height (Inch)	Format Capacity	Media Density
	OSDA-51B	3.50	Third	1.44Mb	DSHD
	OSDA-52B	3.50	Third	1.44Mb	DSHD
	OSDA-53B	3.50	Third	1.44Mb	DSHD
	OSDA-77D	3.50	Third	720kb	DSQD
	OSDA-81F	3.50	Half	1.44Mb	DSHD
	OSDA-90E-U	3.50	Third	720kb	DSQD
	OPDB-22A	3.50	Half	720kb	DSQD
	OSDD-05B	3.50	Third	720kb	DSQD
	OSDD-57	3.50	Third	720kb	DSQD
	OSDD-57B	3.50	Third	720kb	DSQD
	U1DA-14A	3.50	Qtr	1.44Mb	DSHD
	V1DA-10A	3.50	Qtr	1.44Mb	DSHD
	V1DA-27A	3.50	Qtr	1.44Mb	DSHD
	V1DA-31B	3.50	Qtr	1.44Mb	DSHD
	V9DA-55A	3.50	Qtr	1.44Mb	DSHD
	V9DA-55B	3.50	Qtr	1.44Mb	DSHD
	V9DA-71B	3.50	Qtr	1.44Mb	DSHD
Compaq	LS-120	3.50		1.44/120Mb	
Digital	PBXRX-AA	3.50	1.0	1.44Mb	DSHD
	PBXRX-AB	3.50	1.0	1.44Mb	DSHD
	FR-PC7XR-AA	3.50		1.44Mb	DSHD
	FR-PC7XR-BA	5.25		1.2Mb	DSHD
Emtech Corp (See BASF)					
Epson	170-SMD	3.50	Half	400kb	SSDD
	180	3.50	Half	720kb	DSDD
	200P-053	3.50	Half	720kb	DSDD
	200P-055	3.50	Half	720kb	DSDD
	200P-073	3.50	Half	720kb	DSDD
	280	3.50	Half	720kb	DSDD
	300	3.50	Third	1.44Mb	DSHD
	340	3.50	Third	1.44Mb	DSHD
	400 W/FRAME	3.50	Third	1.44Mb	DSHD
	400P-4	3.50	Third	1.44Mb	DSHD
	500	5.25	Half	360kb	DSDD
	521	5.25	Half	360kb	DSDD
	521L	5.25	Half	360kb	DSDD
	621L	5.25	Half	360kb	DSDD
	700/800	5.25/3.5		1.2/1.44Mb	DUAL
	1000	3.50	Third	1.44Mb	DSHD
	1000P	3.50	Qtr	1.44Mb	DSHD
	DYO-211	3.50	Half	1.44Mb	DSHD
	DYO-212	3.50	Half	1.44Mb	DSHD
	SD-321	5.25	Third	360kb	DSDD
	SD-520	5.25	Half	360kb	DSDD
	SD-521	5.25	Half	360kb	DSDD
	SD-581	5.25	Half		
	SD-621L	5.25	Half	328kb	DSDD
	SD-680L	5.25	Half	1.02Mb	DSHD
	SMD-1040	3.50	0.7	1.44Mb	DSHD
	SMD-1060	3.50	0.7	2.8Mb	DSEHD
	SMD-1340	3.50	1.0	1.44Mb	DSHD
	SMD-340	3.50	1.0	1.47Mb	DSHD
	SMD-349	3.50	Half	1.4Mb	DSHD
	SMD-380	3.50	1.0	656kb	DSDD
	SMD-389	3.50	Half	720kb	DSDD
	SMD-400P-4	3.50	Third	1.44Mb	DSHD
Fuji/Toshiba	FDD4206AOK	3.50	Half	720kb	DSDD
	FDD421GOK	3.50	1.0	720kb	DSDD
	FDD5452BOK	5.25	Half	360kb	DSDD

Floppy Drive Specs By Model

Manufacturer	Model Number	Width (Inch)	Height (Inch)	Format Capacity	Media Density
	FDD6471LOK	5.25	Half	360kb	DSDD
	FDD6474H1	5.25	Half	360kb	DSDD
Fujitsu	2551 A08	5.25	Half	360kb	DSDD
	2552K	5.25	Half	720kb	DSDD
	2553A,K	5.25	Half	1.2Mb	DSHD
	2553 K03B	5.25	Half	1.2Mb	DSHD
	2554	5.25	Half	720kb	DSQD
	M2537K	3.50	Third	1.44Mb	DSHD
	N02B-0112-B001	3.50	Half	720kb	DSDD
	N02B-0112-B201	3.50	Half	720kb	DSDD
Hewlett Packard	OmniB 800	3.50		1.44Mb	DSHD
	J455-3	5.25	Half	360kb	DSDD
	J475-1	5.25	Half	1.2Mb	DSQD
Hi-Tech	548-25	5.25	Half	180kb	SSDD
	548-50	5.25	Half	360kb	DSDD
	548-A	5.25	Half	360kb	DSDD
	596-10	5.25	Full	720kb	DSQD
Hi-Val	H055-R	3.50		1.44Mb	DSHD
Hitachi	HFD 305S	5.25	Half	360kb	SSDD
	FD532EIU	5.25	Half	2.4Mb	DSHD
	FDD412A	5.25	Half	1.2Mb	DSDD
IBM	0384-002	5.25	Full	360kb	DSDD
Imation	SuperDisk (LS120)	3.50	1.0	120Mb	Propr.
	51122-01946	3.50	Half	720kb	DSDD
	51122-01946	3.50	Half	1.44Mb	DSHD
	51122-16217	3.50	1.0	720kb	DSDD
	51122-16217	3.50	1.0	1.44Mb	DSHD
JVC	MDP-100	5.25	Half	720kb	DSQD
	SS01JG	5.25	Half	360kb	DSDD
Maple Tech	MT-502	5.25	Half	360kb	DSQD
Matsushita	EME-263TL	3.50	Qtr	1.44Mb	DSHD
	EME-278T	3.50	Qtr	1.44Mb	DSHD
	EME-278TA	3.50	Qtr	1.44Mb	DSHD
Memorex	651	8.00	Full	1.2Mb	DSDD
MFE	M700	8.00	Full	1.6Mb	DSDD
	M750	8.00	Full	1.6Mb	DSDD
Micropolis	1006-4N	5.25	Full	720kb	DSQD
	1015-2	5.25	Full	360kb	SSDD
	1015-4	5.25	Full	720kb	DSQD
	1015-6	5.25	Full	720kb	DSQD
	1016-2	5.25	Full	360kb	DSDD
	1115-4	5.25	Full	720kb	DSQD
	1115-5	5.25	Full	360kb	SSDD
	1115-6	5.25	Full	720kb	DSQD
	1117-6	5.25	Full	720kb	DSQD
Microsolutions	Backpack	3.50		1.44Mb	DSHD
Mitac	MC-490	5.25	Half	360kb	DSDD
Mitsubishi (Model numbers may start with MF)					
	2894	8.00	Full	1.6Mb	DSDD
	2894-63	8.00	Full	1.6Mb	DSDD
	2896	8.00	Half	1.6Mb	DSDD
	2896-63	8.00	Half	1.6Mb	DSDD
	353AF	3.50	Half	720kb	DSDD
	353B-12	3.50	Half	720kb	DSDD

Floppy Drive Specs By Model

Manufacturer	Model Number	Width (Inch)	Height (Inch)	Format Capacity	Media Density
	353B-82	3.50	Third	720kb	DSDD
	353B,C	3.50	Half	720kb	DSDD
	353C	3.50	Third	720kb	DSDD
	353-12	3.50	Third	720kb	DSDD
	355A,B,C	3.50	1.0	1.4Mb	DSHD
	355B-52	3.50	Half	1.44Mb	DSHD
	355B-82UF	3.50	Half	1.44Mb	DSHD
	355BA-82UF/W51/4	3.50	Half	1.44Mb	DSHD
	355BA-88UF/W51/4	3.50	Half	1.44Mb	DSHD
	355B-88UF	3.50	Half	1.44Mb	DSHD
	355C-12	3.50	Third	1.44Mb	DSHD
	355C-215	3.50	Third	1.44Mb	DSHD
	355C-222	3.50	Third	1.44Mb	DSHD
	355C-258MC	3.50	Third	1.44Mb	DSHD
	355C-352	3.50	Third	1.44Mb	DSHD
	355C-37/W51/4	3.50	Third	1.44Mb	DSHD
	355C-526	3.50	Third	1.44Mb	DSHD
	355C-58UF	3.50	Third	1.44Mb	DSHD
	355C599MA(PS2)	3.50	Half	1.4Mb	DSHD
	355C599MB(PS2)	3.50	Half	1.4Mb	DSHD
	355C599MR4(PS2)	3.50	Half	1.4Mb	DSHD
	355C599MQ4(PS2)	3.50	Half	1.4Mb	DSHD
	355C599MQ41(PS2)	3.50	Half	1.4Mb	DSHD
	355C-82UF/W51/4	3.50	Half	1.44Mb	DSHD
	355C-88UF/W51/4	3.50	Half	1.44Mb	DSHD
	355F258	3.50	Third	1.4Mb	DSHD
	355F3250MG	3.50	1.0	1.44Mb	DSHD
	355F3250UG	3.50	Full	1.44Mb	DSHD
	355F3252UG	3.50	Full	1.44Mb	DSHD
	355F3258UG	3.50	Full	1.44Mb	DSHD
	355H-120MG	3.50	Half	1.44Mb	DSHD
	355H-212MG	3.50	Half	1.44Mb	DSHD
	355H-218MG	3.50	Half	1.44Mb	DSHD
	355H-240MG	3.50	Half	1.44Mb	DSHD
	355H-242MG	3.50	Half	1.44Mb	DSHD
	355H-248MG	3.50	Half	1.44Mb	DSHD
	355W99M1(PS2)	3.50	Half	1.4Mb	DSHD
	355W99M2(PS2)	3.50	Half	1.4Mb	DSHD
	355W99M3(PS2)	3.50	Half	1.4Mb	DSHD
	355W99WI(PS2)	3.50	Half	1.4Mb	DSHD
	356F-250UG	3.50	Full	2.8Mb	DSHD
	356F-252UG	3.50	Full	2.8Mb	DSHD
	356F-258UG	3.50	Full	2.8Mb	DSHD
	357G	3.5	1.0	1.44Mb	DSHD
	357H	3.5	Half	1.44Mb	DSHD
	4851	5.25	Half	360kb	DSDD
	4852	5.25	Full	720kb	DSQD
	4853	5.25	Half	720kb	DSQD
	4854	5.25	Half	1.2Mb	DSDD
	501A	5.25	Half	360kb	DSDD
	501B	5.25	Half	360kb	DSDD
	501C	5.25	Half	360kb	DSDD
	503	5.25	Half	720kb	DSQD
	504A	5.25	Half	1.2Mb	DSHD
	504B	5.25	Half	1.2Mb	DSQD
	504C	5.25	Half	1.2Mb	DSQD
	504S	5.25	Half	1.2Mb	DSQD
	LS-120	3.50	Full	1.44Mb	DSHD
Mitsumi					
	D352E	3.50	1.0	1.44Mb	DSHD
	D353F2	3.50	Half	1.44Mb	DSHD
	D353F2E	3.50	Half	1.44Mb	DSHD

Floppy Drive Specs By Mode

Manufacturer	Model Number	Width (Inch)	Height (Inch)	Format Capacity	Media Density
	D353F3	3.50	.5 inch	1.44Mb	DSHD
	D353FUE	3.50	1.0	1.44Mb	DSHD
	D353G	3.50	Half	1.44Mb	DSHD
	D353GU	3.50	Third	1.44Mb	DSHD
	D353M3	3.50	1.0	1.44Mb	DSHD
	D353P3	3.50		1.44Mb	DSHD
	D353T3	3.50	1.0	1.44Mb	DSHD
	D353T5	3.50	Full	1.44Mb	DSHD
	D353T7	3.50		1.44Mb	DSHD
	D358F2	3.50	Half	1.2Mb	DSQD
	D358F3	3.50	.5 inch	1.2Mb	DSQD
	D358P3	3.50		1.2Mb	DSQD
	D358T3	3.50	1.0	1.2Mb	DSQD
	D359C	3.50	Qtr	1.44Mb	DSHD
	D359F2	3.50	Half	1.44Mb	DSHD
	D359F2E	3.50	Half	1.44Mb	DSHD
	D359F3	3.50	.5 inch	1.44Mb	DSHD
	D359G	3.50	Half	1.44Mb	DSHD
	D359M3	3.50	1.0	1.44Mb	DSHD
	D359P3	3.50		1.44Mb	DSHD
	D359T2	3.50	Third	1.44Mb	DSHD
	D359T3	3.50	Third	1.44Mb	DSHD
	D359T5	3.50	Third	1.44Mb	DSHD
	D359T7	3.50	Full	1.44Mb	DSHD
	D503	5.25	Half	360kb	DSDD
	D509V	5.25	Half	1.2Mb	DSQD
	D509V3	5.25		1.2Mb	DSQD
	D509V5	5.25	Full	1.2Mb	DSQD
	D539W	5.25/3.5	Half	1.2/1.44Mb	DUAL
	DP119F2	3.50	Full	1.44Mb	DSHD
MPI	501	5.25	Half	180kb	SSDD
	502B	5.25	Half	360kb	DSDD
	51M	5.25	Full	180kb	SSDD
	51S	5.25	Full	180kb	SSDD
	52M	5.25	Full	360kb	DSDD
	52S	5.25	Full	360kb	DSDD
	91M	5.25	Full	360kb	SSQD
	92M-002	5.25	Full	720kb	DSQD
	B101M-S	5.25	Full	180kb	SSQD
	B102M-S	5.25	Full	360kb	DSQD
	B51S	5.25	Full	180kb	SSDD
	B52S	5.25	Full	360kb	DSDD
	B91S	5.25	Full	360kb	SSQD
	B92M	5.25	Full	720kb	DSQD
	B92S	5.25	Full	720kb	DSQD
NEC	1035	3.50	Half	720kb	DSDD
	1036A	3.50	Third	720kb	DSDD
	1037A	3.50	Third	720kb	DSDD
	1053	5.25	Half	360kb	DSDD
	1055	5.25	Half	720kb	DSQD
	1137H	3/50	Third	1.44Mb	DSHD
	1155C	5.25	Half	1.2Mb	DSQD
	1157C	5.25	Half	1.2Mb	DSQD
	1158C	5.25	Third	1.2Mb	DSHD
	1165A	8.00	Half	1.6Mb	DSDD
	1165FQ	8.00	Half	1.6Mb	DSDD
	5138A	3.50	Third	1.44Mb	DSHD
	FD1035	3.50	Half	720kb	DSDD
	FD1138H	3.50	.75	1.44Mb	DSHD
	FD1139H	3.50	0.6	1.44Mb	DSHD
	FD1148H	3.50	0.78	1.44Mb	DSHD

Floppy Drive Specs By Model

Manufacturer	Model Number	Width (Inch)	Height (Inch)	Format Capacity	Media Density
	FD1155C	5.25	1.6	1.2Mb	DSQD
	FD1157C	5.25	1.6	1.2Mb	DSQD
	FD1158C	5.25	1.6	1.2Mb	DSQD
	FD1165F	8.00	Half	1.6Mb	DSDD
	FD1165H	8.00	Half	1.6Mb	DSDD
	FD1165S	8.00	Half	1.6Mb	DSDD
	FD1177C	5.25	1.6	1.2Mb	DSHD
	FD1231H	3.50	1.0	1.44Mb	DSHD
	FD1238H	3.50	0.5	1.44Mb	DSHD
	FD1335H	3.50	1.0	1.44Mb	DSHD
	FD5839H	5.25/3.5	1.63	1.2/1.44Mb	DUAL
	UF0002	3.50	Half	1.44Mb	DSHD
Newtronic	D357	3.50	Third	720kb	DSDD
Okidata	3305	5.25	Half	360kb	DSDD
	3305BU	5.25	Third	360kb	DSDD
	3305U	5.25	Half	360kb	DSDD
	3315B	5.25	Half	360kb	DSDD
Olivetti	4311	5.25	Half	360kb	DSDD
	4311-3	5.25	Half	360kb	DSDD
Pacific Rim	P35	3.50	1.0	1.44Mb	DSHD
	U1.2	5.25	Half	1.2Mb	DSHD
	U1.44	3.50		1.44Mb	DSHD
	U4	3.50	1.0	2.88Mb	DSEHD
	U720	3.50		720kb	DSDD
	U360	5.25	Half	360kb	DSDD
Panasonic	253	3.50	Third	720kb	DSDD
	257	3.50	Third	1.44Mb	DSHD
	257 W/FRAME	3.50	Third	1.44Mb	DSHD
	455 (-5=bk,-7=gr)	5.25	Half	360kb	DSDD
	465	5.25	Half	720kb	DSQD
	475	5.25	Half	1.2Mb	DSQD
	551	5.25	Half	360kb	DSDD
	595	5.25	Half	1.2Mb	DSQD
	FD32MB	3.50	Ext.	32Mb	DSHD
Persci	277(6N)	8.00	Full	1.2Mb	SSDD
	299	8.00	Full	2.0Mb	DSDD
Pertec	FD200	5.25	Full	180kb	SSDD
	FD250	5.25	Full	360kb	DSDD
	FD400	8.00	Full	800Kb	SSDD
	FD410	8.00	Full	800kb	SSDD
	FD500	8.00	Full	800kb	SSDD
	FD510	8.00	Full	800kb	DSDD
	FD511	8.00	Full	800kb	SSDD
	FD514-U2	8.00	Full	800kb	SSDD
	FD650	8.00	Full	1.6Mb	DSDD
Phillips	3121		Half	360kb	SSDD
	3132	5.25	Half	360kb	DSDD
	3133	5.25	Half	720kb	DSDD
	3134	5.25	Half	1.0Mb	DSDD
Qume	142	5.25	Half	360kb	DSDD
	242	8.00	Half	1.6Mb	DSDD
	542	5.25	Full	360kb	DSDD
	841	8.00	Full	800kb	DSDD
	842	8.00	Full	1.6Mb	DSDD
	DT/5	5.25	Full	360kb	DSDD
	DT/8	8.00	Full	1.6Mb	DSDD
Remex	RFD 2000	8.00	Full	800kb	SSDD

Floppy Drive Specs By Model

Manufacturer	Model Number	Width (Inch)	Height (Inch)	Format Capacity	Media Density
	RFD 4000	8.00	Full	1.6Mb	DSDD
	RFD 480	5.25	Half	360kb	DSDD
Richoh	5100	5.25	Half	720kb	DSQD
	RF8160	8.00	Half	1.6Mb	DSDD
Samsung	SFD500K	5.25	Half	360kb	DSDD
	SFD-560DT	5.25	Half	1.2Mb	DSHD
	SFD-321DT	3.50	Half	1.44Mb	DSHD
Sanyo	500C	5.25	Half	360kb	DSDD
	FDA5200	5.25	Half	360kb	DSDD
Seiko	8640	5.25	Full	640kb	DSDD
Shugart	SA200	5.25	Half	180kb	SSDD
	SA210	5.25	Half	360kb	DSDD
	SA215	5.25	Half	180kb	DSDD
	SA300	3.50	Half	360kb	SSDD
	SA390	5.25	Full	180kb	SSDD
	SA400	5.25	Full	180kb	SSDD
	SA400L	5.25	Full	180kb	SSDD
	SA410	5.25	Full	360kb	SSQD
	SA450	5.25	Full	360kb	DSDD
	SA455	5.25	Half	360kb	DSDD
	SA460	5.25	Full	720kb	DSQD
	SA465	5.25	Half	720kb	DSQD
	SA475	5.25	Half	1.2Mb	DSQD
	SA551	5.25	Half	360kb	DSDD
	SA561	5.25	Half	720kb	DSQD
	SA800-1	8.00	Full	800kb	SSDD
	SA800-1R	8.00	Full	800kb	SSDD
	SA800-2	8.00	Full	800k	SSDD
	SA800-2R	8.00	Full	800kb	SSDD
	SA800-4	8.00	Full	800kb	SSDD
	SA801	8.00	Full	800kb	SSDD
	SA801-R	8.00	Full	800kb	SSDD
	SA810	8.00	Half	800kb	SSDD
	SA850	8.00	Full	1.6Mb	DSDD
	SA850R	8.00	Full	1.6Mb	DSDD
	SA851	8.00	Full	1.6Mb	DSDD
	SA851R	8.00	Full	1.6Mb	DSDD
	SA860	8.00	Half	1.6Mb	DSDD
	SA860-1	8.00	Half	1.6Mb	DSDD
	SA900-1	8.00	Full	800kb	SSSD
	SA901	8.00	Full	800kb	SSSD
Siemans	FDD100-5	5.25	Full	180kb	SSDD
	FDD100-8	8.00	Full	800kb	SSDD
	FDD220-8	8.00	Full	800kb	SSDD
	FDD121-5	5.25	Full	360kb	SSDD
	FDD196-5	5.25	Full	360kb	SSDD
	FDD221-5	5.25	Full	360kb	DSDD
Sony	120-04	3.50	Third	1.44Mb	DSHD
	17W	3.50	Third	1.44Mb	DSHD
	17W-5PF	3.50	Third	1.44Mb	DSHD
	17W-10/W51/4	3.50	Third	1.44Mb	DSHD
	17W-34/W51/4	3.50	Third	1.44Mb	DSHD
	17W-42/W51/4	3.50	Third	1.44Mb	DSHD
	17W-55	3.50	Half	1.44Mb	DSHD
	17W-90	3.50	Third	1.44Mb	DSHD
	17W-WFP	3.50	Third	1.44Mb	DSHD
	40W-00(PS2)	3.50	Third	2.8Mb	DSHD
	40W-9E	3.50	Third	2.8Mb	DSHD

Floppy Drive Specs By Model

Manufacturer	Model Number	Width (Inch)	Height (Inch)	Format Capacity	Media Density
	40W-15	3.50	Half	2.8Mb	DSHD
	40W-KO	3.50	Half	2.8Mb	DSHD
	420-6	3.50	Third	1.44Mb	DSHD
	53	3.50	Third	1.44Mb	DSHD
	53W	3.50	Third	720kb	DSQD
	63W	3.50	Third	720kb	DSQD
	73W	3.50	3Qtr	1.44Mb	DSHD
	73W-34D/W51/4	3.50	3Qtr	1.44Mb	DSHD
	77W(PS2)	3.50	Third	1.44Mb	DSHD
	HIFD	3.50	?	1.44Mb	DSHD
	MFD51W	3.50	Third	800kb	DSQD
	MPR17W	3.50	1.0		
	MPF82E	3.50	1.0	1.44Mb	DSHD
	MPF88E	3.50	1.0	720kb	DSDD
	MPF88E	3.50	1.0	1.44Mb	DSHD
	MPF320	3.50	Half	1.44Mb	DSHD
	MPF40W	3.50	1.0	2.88Mb	DSHD
	MPF420	3.50	1.0	1.44Mb	DSHD
	MPF520	3.50	1.0	1.44Mb	DSHD
	MPF920	3.50	1.0	1.44Mb	DSHD
	MPF920-Z	3.50	1.0	1.44Mb	DSHD
	MSFD-20U	3.50	1.0	1.44Mb	DSHD
Tandon	TM100-1A	5.25	Full	180kb	SSDD
	TM100-2A	5.25	Full	360kb	DSDD
	TM100-3	5.25	Full	360kb	SSQD
	TM100-3M	5.25	Full	360kb	SSQD
	TM100-4	5.25	Full	720kb	DSQD
	TM100-4A	5.25	Full	720kb	DSQD
	TM101-2	5.25	Full	360kb	DSDD
	TM101-3	5.25	Full	360kb	SSQD
	TM101-4	5.25	Full	720kb	DSQD
	TM50-1	5.25	Half	180kb	SSDD
	TM50-2	5.25	Half	360kb	DSDD
	TM55-1	5.25	Half	180kb	SSDD
	TM55-2	5.25	Half	360kb	DSDD
	TM55-4	5.25	Half	720kb	DSQD
	TM65-1L	5.25	Half	180kb	SSDD
	TM65-2L	5.25	Half	360kb	DSDD
	TM65-4	5.25	Half	720kb	DSQD
	TM65-8	5.25	Half	1.2Mb	DSQD
	TM75-2	5.25	Half	360kb	DSDD
	TM75-8	5.25	Half	1.2Mb	DSQD
	TM848-1	8.00	Half	800kb	SSDD
	TM848-1E	8.00	Half	800kb	SSDD
	TM848-2	8.00	Half	1.6Mb	DSDD
	TM848-2E	8.00	Half	1.6Mb	DSDD
	TM965-2	5.25	Full	360kb	DSDD
Teac	35F	3.50	Half	720kb	DSDD
	35FN	3.50	Half	720kb	DSDD
	35HFN	3.50	Third	1.44Mb	DSHD
	50A	5.25	Full	180kb	SSDD
	53B	5.25	Half	360kb	DSDD
	54B	5.25	Half	360kb	DSDD
	55A	5.25	Half	180kb	SSDD
	55B	5.25	Half	360kb	DSDD
	55BR	5.25	Half	360kb	DSDD
	55BV	5.25	Half	360kb	DSDD
	55E	5.25	Half	360kb	DSDD
	55FR	5.25	Half	720kb	DSQD
	55FV	5.25	Half	720kb	DSDD
	55G	5.25	Half	1.2Mb	DSHD

Floppy Drive Specs By Model

Manufacturer	Model Number	Width (Inch)	Height (Inch)	Format Capacity	Media Density
	55GFR	5.25	Half	1.2Mb	DSQD
	55GR	5.25	Half	1.2Mb	DSHD
	55GS (SCSI)	5.25	Half	1.2Mb	DSHD
	55GV	5.25	Half	1.2Mb	DSQD
	55GVF	5.25	Half	1.2Mb	DSQD
	135FN	3.50	Third	720kb	DSDD
	135HF	3.50	Third	1.44Mb	DSHD
	135HFN	3.50	Third	720kb	DSDD
	155GF	5.25	1.0	1.2Mb	DSHD
	235F	3.50	Third	720kb	DSDD
	235GF	3.50	1.0	1.6Mb	DSDD
	235HF	3.50	Third	1.44Mb	DSHD
	235HG	3.50	Third	1.44Mb	DSHD
	235HS (SCSI)	3.50	1.0	1.44Mb	DSHD
	235J	3.50	1.0	2.88Mb	DSEHD
	235JS (SCSI)	3.50	1.0	2.88Mb	DSEHD
	334	3.50	1.0	1.44Mb	DSHD
	335F	3.50	0.75	720kb	DSDD
	335HF	3.50	0.75	1.44Mb	DSHD
	335HS (SCSI)	3.50	0.75	1.4Mb	DSHD
	335J	3.50	0.75	2.88Mb	DSEHD
	335JS (SCSI)	3.50	0.75	2.88Mb	DSEHD
	505	5.25/3.5	Half	1.2/1.44Mb	DSHD
	05HF-030	3.50	Third	1.44Mb	DSHD
	05HF-532U	3.50	Third	1.44Mb	DSHD
	CF506A	3.50	Full	1.44Mb	DSHD
	FD-04	5.25	Half	1.44Mb	
	FD-05	5.25	Half	1.44Mb	
	FD-05GF	3.50	Half	1.44Mb	DSDD
	FD-05HF	3.50	Half	720kb	DSHD
	FD-05HG	3.50	Half	1.44Mb	DSDD
	FD-235GS	3.50	1.0	1.44Mb	DSDD
	HiFD	3.50	1.0	1.44Mb	DSHD
Tec	FB501	5.25	Half	180kb	SSDD
	FB503	5.25	Half	360kb	DSDD
	FB504	5.25	Half	720kb	DSQD
Tecmate	1103	5.25	Half	3.3Mb	DSDD
Texas Peripherals					
	10-5355-001	5.25	Full	180kb	SSDD
Toshiba	0202A	5.25	Full	720kb	DSQD
	0242A	5.25	Half	360kb	DSDD
	0401GR	5.25	Half	360kb	DSDD
	0801GR	5.25	Half	1.2Mb	DSDD
	0802GR	5.25	Half	1.2Mb	DSHD
	352TH	3.50	Third	720kb	DSQD
	3527H	3.50	Third	720kb	DSDD
	3527TH	3.50	Third	720kb	DSQD
	3561GR	3.50	Third	1.44Mb	DSHD
	3564	3.50	Third	1.44Mb	DSHD
	3567	3.50	Third	1.44Mb	DSHD
	4210	3.50	Third	720kb	DSDD
	4202-AOK	3.50	Third	720kb	DSDD
	4207-AOK	3.50	1.0	720kb	DSQD
	4207-AOK	3.50	Third	720kb	DSDD
	4261	3.50	Third	720kb	DSQD
	4449-AOZ(PS2)	3.50	Half	720kb	DSQD
	5401	5.25	Half	360kb	DSDD
	5406	5.25	Half	360kb	DSDD
	5426	5.25	Half	360kb	DSDD
	5451	5.25	Half	360kb	DSDD

Floppy Drives

Floppy Drive Specs By Model

Manufacturer	Model Number	Width (Inch)	Height (Inch)	Format Capacity	Media Density
	5454	5.25	Half	360kb	DSDD
	5471	5.25	Half	360kb	DSDD
	5472	5.25	Half	360kb	DSDD
	5474	5.25	Half	360kb	DSDD
	5629	5.25	Half	720kb	DSQD
	5861	5.25	Half	1.2Mb	DSHD
	5862	5.25	Half	1.2Mb	DSHD
	5863	5.25	Half	1.2Mb	DSHD
	5881	5.25	Half	1.2Mb	DSHD
	5882	5.25	Half	1.2Mb	DSQD
	6371	5.25	Half	360kb	DSDD
	6374	5.25	Half	360kb	DSDD
	6379R3B	5.25	Half	360kb	DSDD
	6471	5.25	Half	360kb	DSDD
	6474-T2P	5.25	Half	360kb	DSDD
	6782	5.25	Half	1.2Mb	DSHD
	6784	5.25	Half	1.2Mb	DSHD
	6881	5.25	Half	1.2Mb	DSHD
	6882	5.25	Half	1.2Mb	DSHD
	6890	5.25	Half	1.2Mb	DSHD
	M48D-12	5.25	Half	360kb	DSDD
	ND-04	5.25	Half	360kb	DSDD
	ND-08	5.25	Half	1.2Mb	DSHD
	ND-352T,S	3.50	1.0	720kb	DSDD
	ND-354A	3.50	1.0	720kb	DSDD
	ND-356	3.50	Third	1.44Mb	DSHD
	ND-3565-A	3.50	Third	1.44Mb	DSHD
	ND-3571	3.50	1.0	2.88Mb	DSEHD
	PD-211	3.50	1.0	2.88Mb	DSEHD
Victor	TM100-3	5.25	Full	360kb	SSQD
	TM100-4	5.25	Full	720kb	DSQD
Weltec	M16-A22	5.25	Half	1.0Mb	DSDD
	M16-P12	5.25	Half	720kb	DSDD
	M-16-R12	5.25	Half	1.0Mb	DSDD
	M16-R12/910	5.25	Half	720kb	DSDD
	M48D-1	5.25	Half	360kb	DSDD
	M48D-14	5.25	Half	360kb	DSDD
	N96-12	5.25	Half	720kb	DSDD
World Storage	FD100-5	5.25	Full	180kb	SSDD
	FD100-8	8.00	Full	800kb	SSDD
	FD200-5	5.25	Full	360kb	DSDD
	FD200-8	8.00	Full	1.6Mb	DSDD
YE-Data	YD180	8.00	Half	1.6Mb	DSDD
	YD280	5.25	Full	720kb	DSQD
	YD380	5.25	Half	1.2Mb	DSHD
	YD380B	5.25	Half	1.2Mb	DSHD
	YD380C	5.25	Half	1.2Mb	DSHD
	YD580	5.25	Half	360kb	DSDD
	YD580B	5.25	Half	360kb	DSDD
	YD701	3.50	Third	1.44Mb	DSHD
	YD701(PS2)	3.50	Third	1.44Mb	DSHD
	YD702D	3.50	1.0	1.44Mb	DSHD
	YD702J	3.50	0.5	1.44Mb	DSHD
	YD-8Y12	3.50	Half	1.44Mb	DSHD
	YD-8U12	3.50	Half	720kb	DSDD
	YD-8U10	3.50	Half	1.44Mb	DSHD
	YD-8U10	3.50	Half	720kb	DSDD
	YD-8U14	3.50	Half	720kb	DSDD
	YD-8U14	3.50	Half	1.44Mb	DSHD

Chapter 17

Miscellaneous References

Country Domain Extensions

Ext	Country	Ext	Country	Ext	Country
.ac	United Kingdom academic inst.	.ch	Switzerland	.gh	Ghana
.ad	Andorra	.ci	Cote D'Ivoire (Ivory Coast)	.gi	Gibraltar
.ae	United Arab Emirates			.gl	Greenland
		.ck	Cook Islands	.gm	Gambia
.af	Afghanistan	Ext	Country	.gn	Guinea
.ag	Antigua & Barbuda	.cl	Chile	.gp	Guadeloupe (French)
.ai	Anguilla	.cm	Cameroon		
.al	Albania	.cn	China	.gq	Equatorial Guinea
.am	Armenia	.co	Colombia	.gr	Greece
.an	NetherlandsAntilles	.cr	Costa Rica	.gs	Unrestricted**
.ao	Angola	.cs	Czechoslovakia (former)	.gt	Guatemala
.aq	Antarctica			.gu	Guam
.ar	Argentina	.cu	Cuba	.gw	Guinea-Bissau
.as	American Samoa	.cv	Cape Verde	.gy	Guyana
.at	Austria	.cx	Christmas Island	.hk	Hong Kong
.au	Australia	.cy	Cyprus	.hm	Heard & McDonald Islands
.aw	Aruba	.cz	Czech Republic		
.az	Azerbaijan	.de	Germany	.hn	Honduras
.ba	Bosnia-Herzegovina	.dj	Djibouti	.hr	Croatia
		.dk	Denmark	.ht	Haiti
.bb	Barbados	.dm	Dominica	.hu	Hungary
.bd	Bangladesh	.do	DominicanRepublic	.id	Indonesia
.be	Belgium	.dz	Algeria	.ie	Ireland
.bf	Burkina Faso	.ec	Ecuador	.il	Israel
.bg	Bulgaria	.ee	Estonia	.in	India
.bh	Bahrain	.eg	Egypt	.io	British Indian Ocean Territory
.bi	Burundi	.eh	Western Sahara		
.bj	Benin	.er	Eritrea	.iq	Iraq
.bm	Bermuda	.es	Spain	.ir	Iran
.bn	Brunei Darussalam	.et	Ethiopia	.is	Iceland
.bo	Bolivia	.fi	Finland	.it	Italy
.br	Brazil	.fj	Fiji	.jm	Jamaica
.bs	Bahamas	.fk	Falkland Islands (Malvinas)	.jo	Jordan
.bt	Bhutan			.jp	Japan
.bv	Bouvet Island	.fm	Micronesia	.ke	Kenya
.bw	Botswana	.fo	Faroe Islands	.kg	Kyrgyzstan
.by	Belarus	.fr	France	.kh	Cambodia
.bz	Unrestricted**	.fx	France(Metropoli-tan)	.kj	Kiribati
.ca	Canada			.km	Comoros
.cc	Unrestricted**	.ga	Gabon	.kn	Saint Kitts & Nevis
.cf	Central African Republic	.gb	Great Britain	.kp	Korea (North)
		.gd	Grenada	.kr	Korea (South)
.cg	Congo	.ge	Georgia	.kw	Kuwait
		.gf	French Guiana	.ky	Cayman Islands

Ext	Country
.kz	Kazakhstan
.la	Laos
.lb	Lebanon
.lc	Saint Lucia
.li	Liechtenstein
.lk	Sri Lanka
.lr	Liberia
.ls	Lesotho
.lt	Lithuania
.lu	Luxembourg
.lv	Latvia
.ly	Libya
.ma	Morocco
.mc	Monaco
.md	Moldova
.mg	Madagascar
.mh	Marshall Islands
.mk	Macedonia
.ml	Mali
.mm	Maynamar
.mn	Mongolia
.mo	Macau
.mp	Northern Mariana Islands
.jq	Martinique
.mr	Mauritania
.ms	Unrestricted**
.mt	Malta
.mu	Mauritius
.mv	Maldives
.mw	Malawi
.mx	Mexico
.my	Malaysia
.mz	Mozambique
.na	Namibia
.nc	New Caledonia (French)
.ne	Niger
.nf	Norfolk Island
.ng	Nigeria
.ni	Nicaragua
.nl	Netherlands
.no	Norway
.np	Nepal
.nr	Nauru
.nt	Neutral Zone

Ext	Country
.nu	Niue
.nz	New Zealand
.om	Oman
.pa	Panama
.pe	Peru
.pf	Polynesia (French)
.pg	Papua New Guinea
.ph	Philipines
.pk	Pakistan
.pl	Poland
.pm	Saint Pierre & Miquelon
.pn	Pitcairn
.pr	Puerto Rico
.pt	Portugal
.py	Paraguay
.pw	Palau
.qa	Qatar
.re	Reunion
.ro	Romania
.ru	RussianFederation
.rw	Rwanda
.sa	Saudi Arabia
.sb	Solomon Islands
.sc	Seychelles
.sd	Sudan
.se	Sweden
.sg	Singapore
.sh	Saint Helena
.si	Slovenia
.sj	Svalbard & Jan Mayen Islands
.sk	Slovak Republic
.sl	Sierra Leone
.sm	San Marino
.sn	Senegal
.so	Somalia
.sr	Suriname
.st	Sao Tome & Principe
.su	USSR (former)
.sv	El Salvador
.sy	Syria
.sz	Swaziland
.tc	Unrestricted**
.td	Chad

Ext	Country
.tf	French Southern Territories
.tg	Togo
.th	Thailand
.tj	Tajikistan
.tk	Tokelau
.tm	Turkmenistan
.tn	Tunisia
.to	Tonga
.tp	East Timor
.tr	Turkey
.tt	Trinidad & Tobago
.tv	Tuvalu
.tw	Taiwan
.tz	Tanzania
.ua	Ukraine
.ug	Uganda
.uk	United Kingdom
.um	US Minor Outlying Islands
.us	United States
.uy	Uruguay
.uz	Uzbekistan
.va	Vatican City State
.vc	Saint Vincent & the Grenadines
.ve	Venezuela
.vg	Unrestricted**
Ext	Country
.vi	Virgin Islands (USA)
.vn	Vietnam
.vu	Vanuatu
.wf	Wallis & Futuna Islands
.ws	Unrestricted**
.ye	Yemen
.yt	Mayotte
.yu	Yugoslavia
.za	South Africa
.zm	Zambia
.zr	Zaire
.zw	Zimbabwe

**Unrestricted: originally for a country but now available to anyone.

Emoticons

Emoticons are a combination of ASCII characters designed to show an emotional state in plain text messages. Usually, emoticons are constructed to be viewed by tilting your head left so the right side of the emoticon is at the bottom of the "glyph." The emoticon was invented by Scott E. Fahlman on September 19, 1982 when he posted a message posted on the Carnegie Mellon University bulletin board and suggested "for joke markers use :-)" Today, the most common emoticons are the basic smiley face :-) and the basic frowney face :-(

Emoticon	Description	Emoticon	Description
=):-)=	Abraham Lincoln	?(	Black eye
->-	Airline tickets going cheap	?-(	Black eye
* :-o	Alarmed!	:-{}	Blowing a kiss
(..)	Alienated	*^_^*	Blushing
%-}	Amused	: [	Bored, sad
0:-)	Angel	: I	Bored, sad
O :-)	Angel	%-6	Brain-dead
O:-)	Angel	:-[#]	Braces
(:&	Angry	(:-...	Broken heart
(:-&	Angry	:-#I	Bushy mustache
>:-<	Angry	*<I<I<I=	Christmas tree
}: [	Angry, frustrated	:-)	Classic smiley
:-(	Angry, or got a black eye	*-=I8-D	Clown
>:-(	Annoyed	:^)	Clowning
:-Y	Aside comment	:~)	Cold (runny nose)
I-I	Asleep	:-~)	Cold (runny nose)
II	Asleep	:-~I	Cold (runny nose)
(I	Asleep	Q:-)	College graduate
:C	Astonished	%-(	Confused
:-C	Astonished	:~/	Confused
8-O	Astonished	:,(	Crying
@==	Atomic bomb	:.(	Crying
~:o	Baby	:\'	Crying
][	Back to back	:\'(	Crying
(::():::)	Bandaid, meaning comfort	:\'-(	Crying
:<=	Beard	:~~(	Crying
~==	Begins a flame (inflammatory message)	;(	Crying
		@.'v	Curly hair
=^D	Big grin	%-)	Dazed or silly
I-D	Big laugh	8-#	Death
(:-D	Big mouth; Blabbermouth	(8=X	Death (skull & cross-bones)
:-k	Biting lip		
I-(	Black eye	:-I :-I	Deja vu

Emoticon	Description
]:->	Devil
<:>	Devilish expression
<:->	Devilish expression
>-)	Devilish wink
:e	Disappointed
:-e	Disappointed
:3-<	Dog
:-)'	Drooling; Dribbling
<:-(	Dunce
<:|	Dunce
<:-|	Dunce
(:|	Egghead
~:\	Elvis
~:-\	Elvis
5:-)	Elvis
_/	Empty glass
~~:-(	Especially hot flame message
*^o^*	Exciting
:-6	Exhausted
}{	Face to face
>-	Female
O+	Female
(O—<	Fishy
~:-(	Flame message
:-')	Flu; or has a cold
[:|	Frankenstein
[:-|	Frankenstein
8-[	Frayed nerves; overwrought
P*	French kiss
<=-O	Frightened
*<(:')	Frosty the Snowman
:-(	Frown
\-/	Full glass
>-<	Furious
>:-<	Furious
:	Fuzzy
(: (	Ghost
^ ^ ^	Giggles
:-[>	Goatee
l-{	Good grief!
%+{	Got beat up
:+(	Got punched in the nose
'!	Grim (profile)
8^|	Grim

Emoticon	Description
%\	Hangover
]:-)	Happy devil
:^D	Happy, approving
:,-)	Happy, they're crying
d :-o	Hats off to you!
:{	Having a hard time
:X	Hear no evil
:-d~	Heavy smoker
:-p~	Heavy smoker
^5	High five
(8(l)	Homer
[]	Hug
[[ ]]	Hug Insert a name in the brackets of the one who is being hugged, as: [[Marcia]]
{{ }}	Hug; the one whose name is in the brackets is being hugged Example: {{MJ}}
()	Hugging
(( )):**	Hugs and kisses
%-}	Humorous or ironic
%-\	Hung over
IOHO	In Our Humble Opinion
:-I	Indifferent, bored or disgusted
%*}	Inebriated
8	Infinity
<:-)	Innocently asking dumb question
%-{	Ironic
(@ @)	Joking?, You're
X-(	Just died
(@ @)	Kidding!, You're
(:-*	Kiss
*	Kiss
.*	Kiss
:-*	Kiss
:x	Kiss
:-x	Kiss, or My lips are sealed
=^*	Kisses
:-(l)	Kiss, a big
+<ll-)	Knight
:-D	Laughing
%-(l)	Laughing out loud
:,-D	Laughing so much they're crying

Emoticon	Description
/\/\/\	Laughter
(-:	Left-handed smile, or smiley from the southern hemisphere
:———}	Liar
:-9	Licking lips
:-?	Licking lips, or tongue in cheek
:-+	Lipstick, too much
~=	Lit candle, indicating a flame (inflammatory message)
>:)	Little devil
((()))	Lots of hugging (initials or a name can be put in the middle of the one being hugged)
:( )	Loudmouth, talks all the time; or shouting
>:-<	Mad
:-	Male
O->	Male
)-:::-(	Married
>:-)	Mischievous devil
:-}	Mischievous smile
:-/	Mixed up
+<:-I	Monk or nun
/\	Mountain
/_/\	Mountain range
= X	My lips are sealed
:-X	My lips are sealed; or a kiss
:-#	My lips are sealed; or someone wearing braces
~~:[	Net flame
{}	No comment
:/i	No smoking
:/)	Not funny
:-j	One-sided smile
:-l	One-sided smile
:-O	Open-mouthed, surprised
:-l	Pondering, or impartial
+:-)	Priest
:-l 8( )-	Pregnant
%(l:-)	Propeller-head
!-)	Proud of black eye
l-	Puckered up for a kiss
:-><	Puckered up to kiss
=:-)	Punk, or hosehead
:-k	Puzzlement
`:-)	Raised eyebrow
+<:-)	Religious leader
:**:	Returning kiss
[:]	Robot
[:l]	Robot
7:)	Ronald Reagan
7:^)	Ronald Reagan
@}->—	Rose
12x@>—> ——	Roses, a dozen
@>—>——	Rose, long-stemmed
: (	Sad
M:-)	Salute
*<:-)	Santa Claus
*<l:-)	Santa Claus, or a clown
(:-(	Scared
!#!^*&:-)	Schizophrenic
:-@	Screaming
M-)	See no evil
M-), :X, :-M	See no evil, hear no evil, speak no evil
:`-(	Shedding a tear
#:-o	Shocked
8-o	Shocked
(o_o)	Shocked
*-)	Shot to death
:-V	Shouting
*(H-)	Skier, downhill
l(	Sleepy (on late night email message)
l-(	Sleepy, struggling to stay awake, or sleeping badly
:)	Smile
:->	Smile of happiness or sarcasm
:-{}	Smile with moustache
:-{)}	Smile with moustache and beard
(:-)	Smiley variation
:-]	Smiling blockhead; also sarcasm
:-,	Smirk
:-Q~	Smoking
~~8}	Snake

Emoticon	Description
~~8}	Snake
=====:}	Snake
:-\'l	Sniffles
l^o	Snoring
-=	Snuffed candle to end a flame message
:-M	Speak no evil
[:-]	Square head
'T	Straight face (profile), keeping a
O 8-)	Starry-eyed angel
O8-)	Starry-eyed angel
~ :-(	Steaming mad
:-f	Sticking out tongue
:P	Sticking out tongue
:-P	Sticking out tongue
:-p	Sticking tongue out
:-r	Sticking tongue out
-/-	Stirring up trouble
(@_@)	Stunned
:-)o->	Suit and tie
B:-)	Sunglasses on head
= O	Surprised
8-(	Surprised!
:-o	Surprised look, or yawn
:-@%$#	Swearing
:\'-)	Tears of happiness
&-(	Tearful
+O:-)	The Pope
(:>-<	Thief
2B|^2B	To be or not to be
:-Q	Tongue hanging out in disgust, or a smoker
-)	Tongue in cheek
:-J	Tongue in cheek
:-&	Tongue-tied
(:-	Unsmiley
(:-(	Unsmiley
:-t	Unsmiley
:-[	Unsmiling blockhead; also criticism
:-||	Very angry
>:->	Very mischievous devil
(:-\	Very sad
:-<	Very sad
:-c	Very unhappy

Emoticon	Description
[:-)	Wearing a Walkman
:-@	What?
:>	What?
:-s	What?!
8-l	Wide-eyed surprise
8)	Wide-eyed, or wearing glasses
8-)	Wide-eyed, or wearing glasses
;)	Wink
;-P	Wink with a raspberry
;-)	Winkey
;-D	Winking and laughing
>->	Winking devil
(o)(-)	Winking eyes
\')	Winky
\'-)	Winky
#-)	Wiped out, partied all night
-=#:-)	Wizard
8 :-)	Wizard
$-)	Won the lottery, or money on the brain
%-l	Worked all night
8-]	Wow!
:-/	Wry face
}-)	Wry smile
:-i	Wry smile or half-smile
l-O	Yawn
:-(0)	Yelling
>=^ P	Yuck
8-P	Yuck!

File Name Extensions

Windows file names have two parts, the file name to the left of the period and the extension (or suffix) to the right of the period. Originally, DOS and the FAT 16 limited the file name to 8 characters and the extension to 3 characters . . . this was known as the 8.3 file naming convention. Beginning with Windows 95, Microsoft implimented a long file name structure and mixed-case Unicode file names.

Today, there are over 15,000 file types in use and since there is no central registry, there are many dlplicates (the same extension for different file types). The File Name Extension table included in this section contains about 200 of the more common File Types. Detailed information on specific extensions can be obtained from through the following web site: http://filext.com

Please note: we have included the words "Potentially Dangerous" in the Program Description field below for those file extensions that can contain malicious program code. Files with these extensions can be easily attached to an email and if executed or opened, can do severe damage to your system. Designating an extension as "Potentially Dangerous does NOT mean that it is always bad, it simply means that it can be bad. For example, the Windows operating system comes with many legitimate ".exe" files because they are valid executable applications but you would not normally receive an email from someone that contained a .exe file attachment. When in doubt, always check with the person sending you the email before you do anything with these "Potentially Dangerous" file types.

File extensions that are very safe include the following: gif, jpg, jpeg, tif, tiff, mpg, mpeg, mp3 and wave.

Extension	File Type and Program Description
ADE	Microsoft Access Project Extension (Potentially Dangerous)
ADP	Microsoft Access Project (Potentially Dangerous)
AIF	Audio Interchange File used with SGI and Macintosh applications.
ANI	Animated cursors used in Microsoft Windows.
API	Application Program Interface.
ART	Clipart.
ASC	ASCII text file.
ASM	Assembler code.
ASP	Microsoft Active Server Page.
ASX	Windows Media Audio or Video shortcut (Potentially Dangerous)
AVI	Audio/Video Interleaved used for Windows based movies.
BAK	Backup Files.
BAS	BASIC programming language sourcecode. (Potentially Dangerous)
BAT	MS-DOS batch file. (Potentially Dangerous)

Extension	File Type and Program Description
BFC	Briefcase document used in Windows.
BIN	Binary File.
BIN	MacBinary-encoded files.
BMP	Bitmap format.
BUD	Backup Disk for Quicken by Intuit.
BZ2	Bzip2-compressed files.
C	C source file.
CAB	Cabinet file, Microsoft installation archive
CAT	Security Catalog file.
CBL	Cobol code.
CBT	Computer Based Training.
CDA	Compact Disc Audio Track.
CDT	Corel Draw Template file.
CFML	ColdFusion Markup Language.
CGI	Common Gateway Interface. Web based programs and scripts.
CHM	Compiled HTML Help files used by Windows. (Potentially Dangerous)
CLASS	Javascript Class file.
CLP	Windows Clipboard file.
CMD	Dos Command File. (Potentially Dangerous)
COM	Command File. (Potentially Dangerous)
CPL	Control Panel Extension (Potentially Dangerous)
CPP	C++ programming language source code.
CSS	Cascading Style Sheet. Creates a common style reference for a set of web pages.
CSV	Comma Separated Values format.
CMF	Corel Metafile.
CRT	Security Certificate (Potentially Dangerous)
CUR	Cursor in Microsoft Windows.
DAO	Registry Backup file for Windows registry.
DAT	Data file.
DD	Compressed Archive by Macintosh DiskDoubler.
DEV	Device Driver.
DIC	Dictionary file.
DIR	Macromedia Director file.
DLL	Dynamic Linked Library. Microsoft application file. (Potentially Dangerous)

Extension	File Type and Program Description
DOC	Document format for Word Perfect and Microsoft Word.
DOT	Microsoft Word Template.
DRV	Device Driver.
DS	TWAIN Data source file.
DUN	Dial-up networking configuration file.
DWG	Autocad drawing.
DXF	Autocad drawing exchange format file.
EMF	Enhanced Windows Metafile.
EML	Microsoft Outlook e-mail file.
EPS	Encapsulated PostScript supported by most graphics programs.
EPS2	Adobe PostScript Level II Encapsulated Postscript.
EXE	DOS based executable file which is also known as a program. (Potentially Dangerous)
FFL	Microsoft Fast Find file.
FFO	Microsoft Fast Find file.
FLA	Macromedia Flash movie format.
FNT	Font file.
GIF	Graphics Interchange Format that supports animation. Created by CompuServe and used primarily for web use.
GID	Windows global index. Contains the index information used by "Help" in Windows.
GRP	Microsoft Program Manager Group.
GZ	Unix compressed file.
HEX	Macintosh binary hex(binhex) file.
HLP	Standard help file. (Potentially Dangerous)
HT	HyperTerminal files.
HTA	HTML Applications (runs app from HTML document) (Potentially Dangerous)
HQX	Macintosh binary hex(binhex) file.
HTM	Hyper Text Markup. This markup language is used for web design.
HTML	Hyper Text Markup Language. This markup language is used for web design.
ICL	Icon Library File.
ICM	Image Color Matching profile.
ICO	Microsoft icon image.
INF	Information file used in Windows.
INI	Initialization file used in Windows. (Potentially Dangerous)
INS	Internet Naming Service (Potentially Dangerous)

Extension	File Type and Program Description
ISP	Internet communication settings (Potentially Dangerous)
JAR	Java Archive. A compressed java file format.
JPEG	Compression scheme supported by most graphics programs and used predominantly for web use.
JPG	More common extension for JPEG described above.
JS	JavaScript File (Potentially Dangerous)
JSE	JavaScript Encoded Script File (Potentially Dangerous)
LAB	Microsoft Excel mailing labels.
LGO	Windows 9x startup logo.
LIT	eBooks in Microsoft Reader format.
LNK	Windows 9x shortcut file. (Potentially Dangerous)
LOG	Application log file.
LSP	Autocad(visual) lisp program.
MAQ	Microsoft Access Query.
MAR	Microsoft Access Report.
MDB	Microsoft Access DataBase File. (Potentially Dangerous)
MDE	Microsoft Access DataBase File. (Potentially Dangerous)
MDL	Rose model file. Opens with Visual Modeler or Rational Rose.
MDT	Microsoft Access Add-In Data (Potentially Dangerous)
MDW	Microsoft Access Workgroup Information (Potentially Dangerous)
MDZ	Microsoft Access Wizard program (Potentially Dangerous)
MID	MIDI music file.
MOD	Microsoft Windows 9.x kernel module.
MOV	Quicktime movie.
MP3	MPEG Audio Layer 3.
MPEG	Animation file format.
MPP	Microsoft Project File.
MSC	Microsoft Common Console Document (Potentially Dangerous)
MSG	Microsoft Outlook message file.
MSG	Fidonet messages.
MSI	Windows Installer Package (Potentially Dangerous)
MSP	Windows Installer Patch (Potentially Dangerous)
MST	Visual Test Source File (Potentially Dangerous)
NCF	Netware command File.
NLM	Netware loadable Module.
O	Object file, used by linkers.

Extension	File Type and Program Description
OCX	ActiveX Control: A component of the Windows environment.
OGG	Ogg Vorbis digitally encoded music file.
OST	Microsoft Exchange/Outlook offline file.
PAK	WAD file that contains information about levels, settings, maps, etc for Quake and Doom.
PCD	Photo CD Image or Microsoft Visual Test compiled script (Potentially Dangerous)
PCL	Printer Control Language file. PCL is a Page Description Language developed by HP.
PCT	Macintosh drawing format.
PDF	Portable Document File by Adobe. Viewable in a web browser or with Adobe Acrobat.
PDF	Printer Description File. Provides printer support for certain applications.
PDR	Port driver for windows 95. It is actually a virtual device driver (vxd).
PHP	Web page that contains a PHP script.
PHTML	Web page that contains a PHP script.
PIF	Program Information File (Potentially Dangerous)
PIF	Vector graphics GDF file(IBM Mainframe)
PIF	Macintosh Compressed archive
PL	Perl source code file. (Potentially Dangerous)
PM	Perl Module. (Potentially Dangerous)
PM3	PageMaker 3.0 document.
PM4	PageMaker 4.0 document.
PM5	PageMaker 5.0 document.
PM6	PageMaker 6.0 document.
PNG	Portable Network Graphic file.
POL	System Policy file for Windows NT.
POT	Microsoft PowerPoint design template.
PPD	PostScript Printer description file used in Macintosh and Windows operating systems to provide printer specific features to a driver.
PPS	Microsoft PowerPoint slide show.
PPT	Microsoft PowerPoint presentation(default extension).
PRN	A print file created as the result of "printing to file".
PS	PostScript file.
PSD	Native Adobe Photoshop format.
PSP	Paint Shop Pro image.
PST	Personal Folder File for Microsoft Outlook.

Extension	File Type and Program Description
PUB	Microsoft Publisher document.
PWL	Windows Password list file.
QIF	Quicken Import file.
RAM	RealAudio Metafile.
RAR	RAR compressed archive created by Eugene Roshall.
RAW	Raw File Format.
REG	Registry file that contains registry settings. (Potentially Dangerous)
RM	RealAudio video file.
RPM	RedHat Package Manager.
RSC	Standard resource file.
RTF	Rich Text Format.
SCF	Windows Explorer command (Potentially Dangerous)
SCR	Screen Saver file. (Potentially Dangerous)
SCT	Windows Script Component (Potentially Dangerous)
SEA	Self-extracting archive for Macintosh Stuffit files.
SGML	Standard Generalized Markup Language.
SH	Unix shell script.
SHB	Shortcut into a document (Potentially Dangerous)
SHS	Shell Scrap Obmect (Potentially Dangerous)
SHTML	HTML file that supports Server Side Includes(SSI).
SIT	Compressed Macintosh Stuffit files.
SMD	SEGA mega drive ROM file.
SVG	Adobe scalable vector graphics file.
SWF	Shockwave Flash file by Macromedia.
SWP	DOS swap file.
SYS	Windows system file used for hardware configuration or drivers.
TAR	Unix Tape Archive.
TGA	Targa bitmap.
TIFF	Tagged Image File Format. Universal graphics format supported
TMP	Windows temporary file.
TTF	True Type font.
TXT	Text Format.
UDF	Uniqueness Definition File. Used for Windows unattended installations.
URL	Uniform Resource Locator (Internet Shortcut) (Potentially Dangerous)
UUE	UU-encoded file.

Extension	File Type and Program Description
VB	Visual Basic File (Potentially Dangerous)
VBE	Visual Basic Script Encoded Script (Potentially Dangerous)
VBS	Visual Basic Script File(Potentially Dangerous)
VBX	Microsoft Visual basic extension.
VM	Virtual Memory file.
VXD	Windows 9x virtual device driver.
WAV	Waveform sound file.
WMF	Windows Metafile (graphics format).
WS	Windows Script File (Potentially Dangerous)
WSC	Windows Script Component (Potentially Dangerous)
WSF	Windows Script File (Potentially Dangerous)
WSH	Windows Scripting Host Settings file (Potentially Dangerous)
WSZ	Winamp Skin.
XCF	The GIMP's native image format.
XIF	Wang imaging file. Wang Image Viewer comes with Windows 95/2000.
XIF	Xerox Image file (same as TIFF).
XIF	Image file eXtended by ScanSoft is similar to TIFF and is a Pagis application format.
XLS	Microsoft Excel Spreadsheet.
XLT	Microsoft Excel Template.
XML	Extensible markup language.
XSL	XML style sheet.
ZIP	Compressed Zip archive.

Chapter 18

Glossary and Acronyms

This chapter contains over 2700 definitions or acronyms or computer related terms. If you find a mistake or an omission, please let us know and we will fix it! See page 2 of this book for contact information.

10Base5 ....IEEE StarLAN standard for networks at 10 Mbps, maximum segment length of 500 meters, using baseband transmission.

10Base2 ....IEEE Ethernet standard using thin (50 ohm) coaxial cable. Operates at 10 Mbps, uses baseband transmission, maximum cable segment length of 185 meters. Also known as ThinEthernet, ThinNet or ThinWire.

10Base5 ....IEEE Ethernet standard using thick coaxial cable. Maximum data transfer speed is 10 Mbps, maximum cable length is 500 meters, uses baseband transmission. Also known as ThickEthernet, ThickNet or ThickWire.

10BaseF ....IEEE Ethernet standard using fiber optic cable at 10 Mbps. Maximum cable length to 5 kilometers.

10BaseFB ....IEEE Ethernet standard using two multi-mode fiber optic cables at 10 Mbps. Uses baseband transmission. Maximum cable length up to 2 kilometers.

10BaseFL ....IEEE Ethernet standard using fiber optic cables at 10 Mbps. Uses baseband transmission. Maximum cable length up to 2 kilometers.

10BaseFP ....IEEE Ethernet standard using fiber optic cable at 10 Mbps. Uses baseband transmission. Maximum cable length up to 1 kilometer.

10BaseT ....IEEE Ethernet standard using UTP cable. Uses baseband transmission. Transmission speed depends on the grade of the cable, maximum transmission speed is 10 Mbps, maximum length is 100 meters.

10Broad-36 ....IEEE Ethernet standard using multi-channel, broadband coaxial cable. Operates at 10 Mbps, uses broadband transmission, maximum cable segment length of 1000 meters.

100BaseFX ....IEEE Fast Ethernet standard. Transmission speeds to 100Mbps. Used with fiber optic cable. Uses baseband transmission. Maximum cable length up to 2000 meters.

100BaseT ....IEEE Fast Ethernet standard. Transmission speeds to 100Mbps. Uses baseband transmission. Maximum cable length up to 100 meters.

100BaseT4 ....IEEE Fast Ethernet standard. Transmission speeds to 100Mbps. Uses 4 pairs of catagory3 or higher UTP cable. Uses baseband transmission. Maximum cable length up to 100 meters.

100BaseTX ....IEEE Fast Ethernet standard. Transmission speeds to 100Mbps. Used with 2 pairs of catagory5 UTP cable. Uses baseband transmission. Maximum cable length up to 100 meters.

100BaseVG	Ethernet standard using Voice Grade (VG) cable (UTP or STP cable) at 100 Mbps using baseband transmission (IBM and AT&T).
100 block	Telephone terminal block with 4 rows of 25-pair connections.
1000BaseCX	IEEE Gigabit Ethernet standard at transmission speeds to 1000Mbps. Used with coaxial cable. Maximum cable length is 25 meters.
1000BaseFX	IEEE Gigabit Ethernet standard at transmission speeds to 1000Mbps. Used with fiber optic cable. Maximum cable length is 100 meters.
1000BaseLX	IEEE Gigabit Ethernet standard at transmission speeds to 1000Mbps. Used with fiber optic cable. Maximum cable length is either 550 or 3000 meters depending on cable.
1000BaseSX	IEEE Gigabit Ethernet standard at transmission speeds to 1000Mbps. Used with fiber optic cable. Maximum cable length is either 260 or 525 meters depending on cable.
1000BaseT	IEEE Gigabit Ethernet standard at transmission speeds to 1000Mbps. Uses catagory5 UTP. Maximum cable length is 100 meters.
1000BaseTX	IEEE Gigabit Ethernet standard at transmission speeds to 1000Mbps. Used with 2 pairs of catagory5, 5e or 6 UTP cable. Maximum cable length is 100 meters.
2B1Q	2 Binary 1 Quaternary
4GL	4" Generation Programming Language
66 block	Telephone terminal block with 4 columns of 50 pins each.
AA	Auto Answer
AAA	Authentication, Authorization and Accounting
AAB	All-to-All Broadcast
AAL	ATM Adaption Layer: Asynchronous Transfer Mode Adaption Layer
AAMOF	Text messaging abbreviation for "As a matter of fact".
AAP	Applications Access Point
	Text messaging abbreviation for "Always a pleasure".
AAR	Text messaging abbreviation for "At any rate".
AARP	AppleTalk Address Resolution Protocol (Apple)
AAS	All-to-All Scatter
	Text messaging abbreviation for "Alive and smiling".
AASP	ASCII Asynchronous Support Package: American Standard Code for Information Interchange Asynchronous Support Package
AAT	Average Access Time
AAUI	Apple Attachment Unit Interface (Apple)
AB Box	A hardware switch for switching between two devices on one port used to switch from A to B or one device to another.
ABEND	Abnormal End: When an application program ends earlier then expected due to some error - often something which the programmer had not considered.
ABI	Application Binary Interface
ABIOS	Advanced BIOS: Advanced Basic Input/Output System
ABIST	Automatic Built In Self-Test
ABLE	Adaptive Battery Life Extender
ABR	Available Bit Rate
ABS	Address Book Synchronization
ABT	Abort
ABTS	ASCII Block Terminal Services: American Standard Code for Information Interchange Block Terminal Services
.ac	URL domain name, site is associated with an academic institution e.g. www.utexas.ac (domain name, Internet).
AC-3	Audio coding system (Dolby Digital).
AC'97	Audio Codec '97: Audio component specification that defines a high-quality 20-bit audio architecture for the PC (Intel).
ACAP	Application Configuration Access Protocol (TCP/IP)
ACC	Accumulator
Access	Rights granted to a network user.
Access line	Cable connecting an end-user to a network, aka local loop or last mile.
Access network	The part of a PSTN that connects Access nodes to subscribers.
Access nodes	Points in the Access network where individual Access lines are concentrated into feeder lines.
Access number	The telephone number dialed by a modem to connect to an ISP.

Access time	The amount of time it takes the computer to request data and for the data to be transferred to the computer. The access time is determined by latency, the seek time and command overhead.
ACCU	Association of C and C++ Users
ACD	Automatic Call Distribution
ACDI	Asynchronous Communications Device Interface
ACE	Access Control Encryption
	Access Control Entry
	Automatic Computing Engine
ACF	Access Control Field
ACH	Automated Clearing House
ACIAS	Automated Calibration Interval Analysis System
ACIS	American Committee for Interoperable Systems
ACK	Acknowledgment
ACL	Access Control List
ACM	Audio Compression Manager (Microsoft)
	Association for Computing Machinery
	Address Complete Message
ACMS	Application Control Management System
ACP	Ancillary Control Program
	Auxiliary Control Process (TCP/IP)
ACPI	Advanced Configuration and Power Interface
ACR	Allowed Cell Rate
Acronym	A word which is composed of the initial letter or letters from a series of words.
ACS	Access
	Anti-curl System
	Access Control Set
	Access Control System
	Asynchronous Communication Server
ACSE	Association Control Service Element
ACSL	Advanced Continuous Simulation Language: A simulation language developed in 1980.
Activate	In Windows, to make a window the Active Window by clicking on it (Microsoft).
Active filter	A filter circuit that includes an amplifier.
Active-matrix display	Technology used in high-quality flat-panel displays.
Active window	In Windows, the front-most window on the desktop. The window which accepts any keyboard input (Microsoft).
ActiveX	A Microsoft API, that is similar to Java in that it helps developers create interactive content and is used primarily on the Internet (Microsoft).
ACTS	Automated Computer Time Service
ACTT	Advanced Communication and Timekeeping Technology
Actuator	The motor in a hard drive that controls the read/write head movement by making the access arm move from the center to the edge of the platters.
ACU	Automatic Calling Unit
A/D	Analog to Digital
AD	Active Directory (Microsoft)
ADA	Automatic Data Acquisitions
	An object-oriented language developed by the US Department of Defense in 1978 and named after Augusta Ada Byron, Countess of Lovelace.
ADB	Apple Desktop Bus (Apple)
ADC	Adaptive Data Compression Protocol (Hayes)
	Analog to Digital Converter: A device that converts analog signals to digital.
ADCCP	Advanced Data Communication Control Procedure
	Advanced Data Communication Control Protocol
ADD	Automatic Document Detection
Address	Computers: The hexadecimal number representing a unique bit location in memory.
	Internet: Three address types are in common use, E-mail address, IP address, and URLs.

Address book	An E-mail utility that contains frequently used E-mail addresses.
Address mark	A number assigned to each possible head position so that the disk drive control circuit knows the location of the head assembly.
ADF	Automatic Document Feeder
	Automatically Defined Function
ADI	AutoCAD/AutoDesk Device Interface
ADL	Address Data Latch
ADLAT	Adaptive Lattice Filter
ADLC	Asynchronous Data Link Control: A protocol for connecting remote terminals asynchronously.
	Adaptive Data Lossless Compression
ADMACS	Apple Document Management And Control System (Apple)
ADMD	Administrative Management Domain
ADN	Advanced Digital Network
	Text messaging abbreviation for "Any day now".
ADO	ActiveX Data Objects (Microsoft)
ADP	Automatic Data Processing
ADPCM	Adaptive Differential Pulse Code Modulation
ADR	Address
ADS	Application Development Solutions
	Automatic Distribution System
ADSC	Adobe Document Structuring Conventions (Adobe)
	Address Status Changed
ADSI	Analog Display Services Interface (Bellcore)
	Active Directory Service Interface (Microsoft)
ADSL	Asymmetric Digital Subscriber Line: 1.5 Mbps to 8 Mbps downstream, 16 Mbps to 640 Mbps upstream.
ADSL Forum	Asymmetric Digital Subscriber Line Forum: Industry group developing and defining xDSL standards.
ADSP	AppleTalk Data Stream Protocol (Apple)
ADT	Abstract Data Type
ADU	Automatic Dialing Unit
AE	Above or Equal
AEAP	Text messaging abbreviation for "As early as possible".
AEB	Analog Expansion Bus
AEC	Architecture, Engineering, Construction
AEP	AppleTalk Echo Protocol (Apple)
.aero	URL designation for entities related to the aviation community(domain name, Internet).
AES	Advanced Encryption Standard
AESA	ATM End System Address: Asynchronous Transfer Mode End System Address
AFA	Accelerated File Access
AFAIK	Text messaging abbreviation for "As far as I know".
AFC	Automatic Font Change
	Automatic Frequency Control
AFD	Automatic File Distribution
AFDW	Active Framework for Data Warehousing
AFI	Authority and Format Identifier
AFII	Association for Font Information Interchange
AFK	Text messaging abbreviation for "Away from keyboard".
AFP	Advanced Function Presentation
	AppleTalk Filing Protocol (Apple)
AFS	Andrew File System Protocol
AFTP	Anonymous File Transfer Protocol
AGA	Advanced Graphics Adapter
AGC	Automatic Gain Control
AGP	Accelerated Graphics Port: An interface specification that enhances 3D graphics (Intel).
	Advanced Graphics Port
AGRAS	Antiglare-Antireflective-Antistatic
AGU	Address Generation Unit
AH	IP Authentication Header: Internet Protocol Authentication Header (Internet)

AHCI	Advanced Host Controller Interface (Intel)
AHS	Automated Highway Systems
AI	Analog Input
	Artificial Intelligence
AI44	Alpha-Index 4-4: A surface video subtype that has a value of 8 bits per pixel.
AIA	Applications Integration Architecture
AIC	AIXwindows Interface Composer (IBM, UNIX)
AIF	Audio Interchange Format
AIFF	Audio Interchange File Format
AIIM	Association for Information and Image Management
AIM	America Online Instant Messaging (AOL)
AIN	Advanced Intelligent Network
AIR	Architecture Implementation Review
AIS	Automated Identification System
AISB	Association of Imaging Service Bureaus
	Text messaging abbreviation for "As it should be".
AISP	Association of Information Systems Professionals
AIT	Advanced Intelligent Tape
AIX	Advanced Interactive Executive (IBM, UNIX)
AIXwindows	Advanced Interactive Executive **windows**: A graphical user interface environment (IBM, UNIX).
AKA	Text messaging abbreviation for "Also known as".
ALC	Arithmetic and Logic Circuits
	Automatic Level Control
ALE	Address Latch Enable
Algol	**Algo**rithmic language: A block-structured programming language developed in 1958 by John Backus.
Algorithm	Programming or mathematics: A term for a procedure or formula for solving a problem.
Alias	An alternate name.
ALICE	Artificial Linguistic Computer Entity: An open source, natural language chat robot that relies on AI for human interaction.
AIML	Artificial Intelligence Markup Language: An XML-compliant programming language for chat bots.
ALINK	Active **Link** (HTML)
ALIWEB	Archie Like Indexing in the **Web**
ALN	Asynchronous Learning Network
Alpha	First internal stages of tests on pre-released software.
Alphanumeric	A character set of letters, numbers, punctuation marks and symbols.
ALT	Alternate
ALU	Arithmetic Logic Unit
Always on	Telephone connection that is always connected.
AMA	Automatic Message Accounting
AMANDDA	Automated Messaging **and** Directory Assistance
AMD	Active Matrix Display
AMI	Alternate Mark Inversion
AML	ACPI Machine Language: **A**dvanced **C**onfiguration and **P**ower **I**nterface Machine Language
AMMA	Advanced Memory Management Architecture
AMP	Asynchronous Multi-Processing
	Asymmetric Multi-Processing
	Amphenol: Manufacturer of various electrical connectors and plugs.
	Amplifier
	Analog Mobile Phone
	Advanced Mobile Phone
AMPS	Advanced Mobile Phone Service
AMR	Audio Modem Riser (Intel)
AMTA	American Mobile Telecommunications Association
Analog	The use of variable voltage in electrical signals to represent data.
Anchor	A synonym for hyperlink.
ANCOVA	Analysis of **Cova**riance
ANDF	Architecture-Neutral Distribution Format
ANI	Automatic Number Identification

Glossary

Animated GIF	A collection of GIF images, presented one after the other, each picture slightly different from the previous to create the illusion of movement.
ANN	Artificial Neural Network
ANNA	Annotated ADA: An extended version of the ADA programming language.
Anonymous FTP	An FTP site not requiring the user's specific User ID & password is called an Anonymous FTP Site.
ANOVA	Analysis of Variance
ANSI	American National Standards Institute. A voluntary US business group that sets standards for the computer industry.
Anti-Virus software	Utility programs that search computers for well-known viruses and remove any that are found.
ANX	Automotive Network Exchange
AO	Analog Output
AOCE	Apple Open Collaboration Environment (Apple)
AO/DI	Always On/Dynamic ISDN: Always On/Dynamic Integrated Services Digital Network
AODV	—Ad hoc On-demand Distance Vector Routing (TCP/IP)
AOE	Application Operating Environment
AOL	America Online: The worlds largest ISP.
AOS	Add Or Subtract
AOTA	Text messaging abbreviation for "All of the above".
AP	Access Point
A/P	Accounts Payable
APA	Adaptive Packet Assembly
	— All Points Addressable
	— Arithmetic Processing Accelerator
APAR	Authorized Program Analysis Report
APAREN	Address Parity Enable (IBM)
APC	Asynchronous Procedure Call (Microsoft)
APCUG	Association of PC User Groups
APEX	Application Exchange (TCP/IP)
API	Application Programming Interface: Pre-programmed modules that can be used by a programmer to create a software application consistent with a given operating system.
APIC	Advanced Programmable Interrupt Controller (Intel)
APIPA	Automatic Private IP Addressing: Automatic Private Internet Protocol Addressing
APIS	Advanced Passenger Information System
APL	A Programming Language: A mathematical programming language created in 1960 at IBM by Kenneth E. Inverson.
APM	Advanced Power Management (IBM)
APNIC	Asia-Pacific Network Information Center (Internet)
APOP	Authenticated Post Office Protocol (TCP/IP)
APPC	Advanced Program to Program Communications (IBM)
APPI	Advanced Peer-to-Peer Internetworking
AppleScript	A command or scripting language developed by Apple Computer in 1993 for the Macintosh (Apple).
Applet	A small JAVA language program that can be embedded in Web pages.
AppleTalk	Apple Computer's Network Operating System (Apple)
Application	See Software.
APPN	Advanced Peer-to-Peer Networking (IBM)
Apps	Applications, see Software.
APRP	Adaptive Pattern Recognition Processing
APS	Advanced Photo System
	— Asynchronous Protocol Specification
APSE	ADA Programming Support Environment
APT	Address Pass Through
	— Automatically Programmed Tools
A/R	Accounts Receivable
ARA	AppleTalk Remote Access (Apple)
ARAG	Antireflective-Antiglare
ARAS	Antireflective-Antistatic

ARCA	Advanced RISC Computing Architecture: Advanced Reduced Instruction Set Computing Computing Architecture
Archie	A program to find files on the Internet which can transfer using FTP.
Archive	A backup copy of data kept for security or audit.
ARCnet	Attached Resource Computer Network
Areal density	Also called bit density is calculated by multiplying bits per inch by tracks per inch. Tells how much data can be stored into an area of medium. The range is about 2 kilobits per square inch for old drives up to 100 gigabits per square inch for the newest drives.
ARL	Adjusted Ring Length
ARLL	Advanced Run Length Limited: Little used variation of RLL also known as RLL 3,9.
ARM	Advanced RISC Machine (processor)
	Asynchronous Response Mode
	Annotated Reference Manual
ARMA	Association of Records Managers and Administrators
ARP	Address Resolution Protocol (Internet)
.arpa	High-level domain name for ARPANet sites (domain name, Internet).
ARPA	Advanced Research Projects Agency
ARPANet	Advanced Research Projects Agency Network: Forerunner of the World Wide Web, developed in 1969 by the US Department of Defense.
ARPC	Asynchronous RPC: Asynchronous Remote Procedure Call
ARPL	Adjust Requested Privilege Level
ARQ	Automatic Repeat Request
ARTA	Apple Real Time Architecture (Apple)
ARTIC	A Real Time Interface Coprocessor
ARTS	Asynchronous Remote Takeover Server
ARTT	Asynchronous Remote Takeover Terminal
ARU	Audio Response Unit
AS	Autonomous System
AS3AP	ANSI SQL Standard Scalable and Portable: American National Standards Institute Structured Query Language Standard Scalable and Portable
ASAI	Adjunct Switch Application Interface
ASAP	Text messaging abbreviation for "As soon as possible".
	Automatic Switching And Processing
ASCC	Automatic Sequence Controlled Calculator
ASCII	American Standard Code for Information Interchange: A standard for representing text as binary numbers. A code set of 128 characters. The first 32 characters are control codes & the remaining 96 are upper & lower case letters, numbers, punctuation marks & special characters.
ASF	Advanced Streaming Format (Microsoft)
	Active Streaming Format (Microsoft)
	Automatic Sheet Feeder
ASIC	Application-Specific Integrated Circuit
ASIT	Advanced Security and Identification Technology
ASL	Adaptive Speed Leveling
	ACPI Source Language: Advanced Configuration and Power Interface Source Language
A/S/L	Text messaging abbreviation for "Age/sex/location".
ASLM	Apple Shared Library Manager (Apple)
ASLS	Analog Single Line Station
ASMP	Asymmetric Multiprocessing
ASN	Abstract Syntax Notation
	Autonomous System Number
ASN.1	Abstract Syntax Notation 1
ASO	Automated Systems Operations
ASP	Active Server Pages (Microsoft)
	— Application Service Provider
	— Association of Shareware Professionals
	— AppleTalk Session Protocol (Apple)
Aspect ratio	Ratio of a monitor screen width to height, 640X480 equals an aspect ratio of 4:3.

ASPI	**A**dvanced **S**CSI **P**rogramming **I**nterface: **A**dvanced **S**mall **C**omputer **S**ystem **I**nterface **P**rogramming **I**nterface (Adaptec)
ASP.Net	**A**pplication **S**ervice **P**rovider **Net**work: Next generation ASP (Microsoft)
ASPS	**A**dvanced **S**ignal **P**rocessing **S**ystem
ASR	**A**ddress **S**pace **R**egister
	Automatic **S**end-**R**eceive
	Automatic **S**peech **R**ecognition
Assembler	A compiler that reduces assembly language code to machine language.
Assembly language	
	A programming language that is one step from machine language.
Astable	Unstable, opposite of stable.
AS/U	**A**dvanced **S**erver for **U**NIX (UNIX)
ASVD	**A**nalog **SVD**: **A**nalog **S**imultaneous **V**oice and **D**ata
Asymmetric	Opposite of symmetric.
ASYNC	**Async**hronous
Asynchronous	Data sent in parallel mode without a clock pulse, one character at a time.
AT	**A**dvanced **T**echnology
	Automatic **T**ransmission
	Text messaging abbreviation for "At your terminal".
AT&T	**A**merican **T**elephone and **T**elegraph
ATA	**A**dvanced **T**echnology **A**ttachment: An IDE type standard for accessing the hard disk.
ATA-2	An improved ATA product, also called Fast ATA, which increased performance.
ATA-3	An improved ATA product which increased performance.
ATA66	ATA at 66 MBps maximum transfer rate .
ATA/100	ATA at 100 MBps maximum transfer rate.
ATA/133	ATA at 133 MBps maximum transfer rate.
ATAPI	**A**dvanced **T**echnology **A**ttachment **P**acket **I**nterface: Used for peripherals like CD-ROM drives and tape drives.
ATE	**A**utomated **T**est **E**quipment
ATG	**A**dvanced **T**echnology **G**roup
	Address **T**ranslation **G**ateway (DEC)
ATL	**A**ctive **T**emplate **L**ibrary
ATM	**A**dobe **T**ypeface **M**anager (Adobe)
	Asynchronous **T**ransfer **M**ode (network)
	Text messaging abbreviation for "At the moment".
ATM Forum	Industry group that develops and defines ATM standards.
ATMP	**A**scend **T**unnel **M**anagement **P**rotocol (TCP/IP)
ATP	**A**ppleTalk **T**ransaction **P**rotocol (Apple)
ATPS	**A**ppleTalk **P**rinting **S**ervices (Apple)
ATR	**A**utomatic **T**erminal **R**ecognition
ATS	**A**pple **T**erminal **S**ervices (Apple)
	Administrative **T**erminal **S**ystem
Attack	An act to subvert a system's security protocol.
ATTN	**Att**ention
ATTRIB	**Attrib**ute
ATU-C	**A**DSL **T**ermination **U**nit - **C**entral Office: **A**symmetric Digital Subscriber Line Termination Unit - Central Office
ATU-R	**A**DSL **T**ermination **U**nit – **R**emote: **A**symmetric Digital Subscriber Line Termination Unit – Remote
ATX	**A**dvanced **T**echnology E**x**tended: A specification for a motherboard including audio & video (Intel).
Audio scrubbing	Process for locating a particular section within an audio file or tape.
AUDIT	**A**utomated Data **I**nput **T**erminal
AUI	**A**ttachment **U**nit **I**nterface
	Autonomous **U**nit **I**nterface
AUP	**A**cceptable **U**se **P**olicy (Internet)
AURP	**A**ppleTalk **U**pdate-based **R**outing **P**rotocol (Apple)
Authentication	Verification of a user or process identity (Network).
Authorization	Process used to access a network resource (Network).
AUTO	**Auto**matic

Autochanger	A mass storage device that can change the media it uses, normally a backup device, also called a Juke Box.
Autoexec.bat	A batch file normally located in the C Drive Root Directory which executes when the PC is started.
AutoFont support	Printer technology that supplies width information for fonts (Hewlett Packard).
Auto parking	When power to a hard drive is shut off, the motor forces the read/write head away from data on the disk and sends it to a special landing zone to be held.
Autoresponder	A program on a mail server that automatically replies to e-mails.
Autorun	Process that allows that starts a CD or DVD upon insertion (Microsoft).
A/UX	UNIX for the Macintosh (Apple).
AUX	Auxiliary
AV	Audio/Video
AVA	Audio Visual Authoring
Avatar	An icon, in a cyberspace system, that represents a real person.
	Name for a super user account on a UNIX system, also called root.
AVC	Audio-Visual Connection
AVD	Alternating Voice and Data
Average latency	For a hard drive, a measurement of how much time it takes for a bit of data to rotate under the head (approximately 8.4 milliseconds for most drives).
AVG	Average
AVI	Audio Visual Interleave (Microsoft)
AVR	Automatic Voice Recognition
AVS	Age Verification Service
AVT	Applied Voice Technology
AWE	Advanced Wave Effects
AWG	American Wire Gage
AWK	A pattern scanning and processing programming language for UNIX developed in 1988 and named for its authors Alfred V. Aho, Peter J. Weinberger and Brian W. Kernighan.
AWT	Abstract Window Toolkit (JAVA)
AX	Architecture Extended
AX.25	Amateur X.25: Packet radio: Layer 2 protocol for digital communications over radio waves (TCP/IP).
AYEC	Text messaging abbreviation for "At your earliest convenience".
AYSOS	Text messaging abbreviation for "Are you stupid or something".
AZERTY	Standard European keyboard, see QWERTY.
B/F	Background/Foreground
	Text messaging abbreviation for "Boyfriend".
B2B	Business to (2) Business (Internet)
B2X	Binary to (2) Hexadecimal
B3ZS	Binary 3 Zero Substitution
B4	Text messaging abbreviation for "Before".
B4N	Text messaging abbreviation for "Bye for now".
B6ZS	Binary 6 Zero Substitution
B8ZS	Binary 8 Zero Suppression
	Bipolar 8 Zero Suppression
	Bipolar 8 Zero Substitution
Backbone	Top level of a network; the central connection (Network)
Backplane	A circuit board used to support other circuit boards.
BACP	Bandwidth Allocation Control Protocol
BAK	Binary Adaptation Kit
	Text messaging abbreviation for "Back at keyboard".
BAL	Basic Assembly Language
BALUN	Balanced Unbalanced (device)
BAM	Boyan Action Module
Bandwidth	Refers to the amount of data that can be sent through a network or modem connection, usually measured in bits per second.
Bank	Slot/group of slots on the motherboard that holds the memory chips.
	Memory in a computer.
BAP	Bandwidth Allocation Protocol
BAPI	Business Application Programming Interface

Baseband	Digital transmission in which the wire carries only one channel at a time.
BASH	Bourne Again Shell (UNIX)
BASIC	Beginner's All-purpose Symbolic Instruction Code: A block-structured programming language developed in 1963 at Dartmouth College by John Kemeney and Thomas Kurtz.
BASM	Built-In Assembler
BAT	Block Address Translation
Batch file	A file that runs without user intervention, see Autoexec.bat.
BAU	Text messaging abbreviation for "Business as usual".
Baud	Measure of data transmission speed, in bits per second (bps), for a modem. Named after the French engineer Jean Maurice Emile Baudot.
BBIAF	Text messaging abbreviation for "Be back in a few".
BBIAM	Text messaging abbreviation for "Be back in a minute".
BBL	Text messaging abbreviation for "Be back later".
BBS	Bulletin Board System
	Text messaging abbreviation for "Be back soon".
BC	Text messaging abbreviation for "Because".
BCAI	Byte Count After Index
BCAST	Broadcast (Novell)
BCC	Block Check Character
	Blind Carbon Copy
BCD	Binary-Coded Decimal
BCL	Batch Command Language
BCN	Beacon
BCNU	Text messaging abbreviation for "Be seeing you".
BCP	Best Current Practice
	Bulk Copy Program
	Bridging Control Protocol
BCPL	Basic Computer Programming Language
BCR	Byte Count Register
BCS	Bar Code Sorter
BDA	BIOS Data Area: Basic Input/Output System Data Area
BDC	Backup Domain Controller
BDE	Borland Database Engine
BDLS	Bidirectional Loop Switching
BDOS	Basic Disk Operating System
BDR	Bus Device Request
BE	Below or Equal
BECN	Backward Explicit Congestion Notification
BEDO	Burst Extended Data Out
Bell 103	Telecommunication protocol at 300 bps, full duplex.
Bell 212A	Telecommunication protocol at 1200 bps, full duplex.
BER	Basic Encoding Rules
	Bit Error Rate
	Bit Error Ratio
BERT	Bit Error Rate Test
	Bit Error Rate Tester
Beta	Pre-release version of software.
Bezel	Cover for the front of the hard drive.
BF	Bad Flag
	Text messaging abbreviation for "Best friend".
BFF	Binary File Format
BFI	Bytes From Index
BFN	Text messaging abbreviation for "Bye for now".
BFT	Binary File Transfer
BFTP	Batch FTP: Batch File Transfer Protocol (TCP/IP)
BGA	Ball Grid Array
BGCOLOR	Background Color (HTML)
BGE	Branch if Greater or Equal
BGMP	Border Gateway Multicast Protocol
BGP	Border Gateway Protocol (TCP/IP)
BGP-4	Border Gateway Protocol version 4
BGT	Branch if Greater Than

BHI	Branch if Higher
BHIS	Branch if Higher or Same
BI	Binary Input
BICC	Bearer Independent Call Control Protocol (SS7)
BiDi	Bi-Directional
Bi-directional	A path for data flow in two directions.
BIFET	Bipolar Field Effect Transistor
BIFF	Binary Interchange File Format
BIF-L	Bi(f)phase Level
BIM	Beginning of Information Marker
BINAC	Binary Automatic Computer
Binary code	Basic computer language, composed of a series of 0s and 1s, that is interpreted by a computer into numbers, letters, punctuation marks, and symbols.
Binary number	The base 2 mathematics system of counting — only two digits of 1 and 0 (or the mechanical or electrical status of on and off).
BIND	Berkeley Internet Name Domain
BINHEX	Binary Hexadecimal
BIOS	Basic Input/Output System: The operating system for microcomputers that controls the input and output. It tells the drive controller to put the information being sent to a specific drive, in a certain cylinder and into a certain sector. It also allows the computer to communicate with peripherals.
BIP-RZ	Bipolar Return to Zero
BIS	Business Information System
B-ISDN	Broadband ISDN: Broadband Integrated Services Digital Network: Transmission rates to 1.5 Mbps over fiber optic cable.
BIST	Built In Self-Test
BISUP	B-ISDN User Part: Broadband Integrated Services Digital Network User Part (SS7)
BiSYNC	See BSYNC.
Bit	An information storage unit (8 bits = 1 byte).
	Binary Digit
Bit cell	The length of track used to store 1 bit.
Bit density	See Areal density.
Bitmap	A graphic file format: A map of dots or bits that looks like a picture.
BITNET	Because It's Time Network
BIU	Bus Interface Unit
.biz	URL designation for businesses(domain name, Internet).
BKSP	Backspace
BL	Backlit
BLAST	Blocked Asynchronous Transmission Protocol
BLE	Branch if Less or Equal
BLER	Block Error
BLK	Block
BLNT	Text messaging abbreviation for "Better luck next time".
BLOB	Binary Large Object
Block	A group of bytes that is equal to 1 physical sector of data.
Blog	Internet term for "Web Log", refers to a list of journal entries posted on a Web page.
BLOS	Branch if Lower Or Same
Bluetooth	A wireless communication technology.
BM&Y	Text messaging abbreviation for "Between me and you".
BMI	Branch if Minus
BMIC	Bus Master Interface Controller
BMP	Basic Mapping Support
	Batch Message Processing Program
	Burst Mode Protocol (Novell)
BMT	Biel Mean Time: See Internet time, referenced to meridian at Biel, Switzerland.
BNC	Bayonet Neill Concelman: Connector used with coaxial cable.
BNE	Branch if Not Equal
BNF	Backus Naur Form
	Backus Normal Form

BNS	Backbone Network Service
BnZS	Bipolar with n Zero Substitution
BO	Binary Output
BoB	Break-out Box
BOC	Basic Operator Console
BOF	Beginning Of File
BOL	Text messaging abbreviation for "Best of luck".
BOM	Basic Online Memory
	Beginning of Message
BOND	Bandwidth on Demand
Bookmark	A stored URL link to a Web page.
Boolean	Logic used by computers to determine if a statement is true or false.
Boot	To start up a computer. See Cold boot or Warm boot.
Boot disk	A backup disk containing essential files for operating system start-up.
BOOTP	Bootstrap Protocol (TCP/IP)
Boot virus	See Virus.
BOPS	Billion Operations Per Second
BOS	Basic Operating System
BOT	Beginning of Table
	Beginning of Tape
	Robot
	Automated software, executes a sequence of commands after receiving a signal.
Bounce	Return of a piece of undeliverable e-mail.
BP	Base Pointer
BPB	BIOS Parameter Block: Basic Input/Output System Parameter Block
BPDU	Bridge Protocol Data Unit
BPI	Bits per Inch: Measurement of bit density.
B Picture	Bidirectionally-coded Picture
BPL	Branch if Plus
BPS	Bits Per Second: Measurement indicating speed of data processes.
	Bytes Per Second
BPSK	Binary Phase Shift Keying Modulation
BPV	BiPolar Violation
BR	Bad Register
BRB	Text messaging abbreviation for "Be right back".
BRGC	Binary Reflected Gray Code
BRI	Basic Rate Interface: See ISDN-BRI.
Bridge	A device that physically connects two network segments.
	A simple way to separate or connect LANs.
	Software that allows data access by a program that cannot read native files.
	Software that translates files from one computer platform to another.
	Software that translates files from one application to another.
Broadband	Digital transmission in which the wire carries more than one channel at a time.
Brouter	Bridge router: A device that serves as a bridge, a router or both.
Browser	A World Wide Web client. An information retrieval tool.
Browsing	Exploring The Web.
BRT	Text messaging abbreviation for "Be right there".
BRZ	See BIP-RZ.
BS	Backspace
BSAM	Basic Sequential Access Method
BSC	Binary Synchronous Communication
BSCS	Bachelor of Science in Computer Science (degree)
BSF	Bit Scan Forward
BSI	British Standards Institute
BSM	Basic Storage Module
BSP	Bulk Synchronous Parallelism
BSR	Bit Scan Reverse
BSRAM	Burst Static RAM: Burst Static Random Access Memory
BSS	Block Started by Symbol
	Basic Service Set
	Base Station Subsystem

	Broadband Switching System
	Broadcasting-Satellite System
BSY	Busy
BSYNC	Binary Synchronous Communications Protocol
BT	Bit Test
BTA	Text messaging abbreviation for "But then again".
BTAM	Basic Telecommunications Access Method
BTB	Branch Target Buffer
BTC	Bit Test and Complement
BTDT	Text messaging abbreviation for "Been there, done that".
BTOA	Binary to ASCII
BTP	Batch Transfer Program
BTR	Bit Test and Reset
BTS	Bit Test and Set
BTW	Text messaging abbreviation for "By the way".
BU	Branch Unit
Buddy list	A utility that helps you stay in contact with people you frequently interact with online.
BUF	Buffer
Buffer	Part of the RAM that holds data temporarily; data that is going from one device to another.
Bug	Computer malfunction due to either a software or hardware error.
Burn	Writing data to a CD or DVD.
BUS	Broadcast and Unknown Server
Bus	The main communication path in a computer consisting of all the parallel wires to which the memory, the CPU, and all input/output devices are connected.
Bus clock speed	The speed in megahertz at which the I/O bus runs.
Bus mouse	A mouse attached to the bus not via a serial port but through a special card on the motherboard.
Bus width	Number of data bits that can be accessed simultaneously.
BVH	Base Video Handler
BWM	Block-Write Mode
Byte	Binary element string.
	The memory space required to store one character, usually 8 bits. [8 bits (storage unit) plus one parity = 1 byte]
C	A block-structured programming language developed between 1972 and 1978 at Bell Labs by D.M. Ritchie, B.W. Kernighan and K. Thompson.
C#	Pronounced "see-sharp": An object-oriented hybrid of several programming languages including C, C++ and Visual Basic developed in 1999 by Microsoft.
C++	An object-oriented programming language derived from C. Developed by Bjarne Stoustrup at Bell Labs in 1985.
CA	Certification Authority
CAB	Cabinet. A Windows file type containing compressed pieces of the operating system. Used during Windows installation (Microsoft).
Cable modem	A modem attached to a cable TV system to provide high-speed Internet access.
Cache	A small fast memory used to store frequently accessed data or instructions.
Cache memory	Caching: A temporary storage area between the computer's CPU and its main RAM. Its purpose is to increase the speed of data transfer by decreasing repetition.
CAD	Computer Aided Design
CAD-CAM	Computer Aided Drawing-Computer Aided Manufacturing
CADD	Computer Aided Design and Drafting
CAM	Common Access Method
CAN	Campus Area Network
CAP	Carrierless Amplitude and Phase
	Capacitor
Capacity	The number of hard disk megabytes available.
CAPI	Computer Assisted Personal Interviewing
	Common ISDN Application Programming Interface

Carriage assembly ·Holds the hard disk roller bearings and read/write heads.

CAS	Column Address Strobe
	Content Addressed Storage
CAV	Constant Angular Velocity
CBR	Constant Bit Rate
CBT	Core Based Trees Multicast Routing Architecture (TCP/IP)
CC	Carbon Copy
CCB	Context Control Block
CCD	Charge Coupled Device
CCITT	Comite Consultatif International Telegraphique et Telephonique (International Telegraph and Telephone Consultative Committee): See ITU.
CCL	Connection Control Language
	Cursor Control Language
ccTLD	country code Top-Level Domain (Internet)
CCTV	Closed Circuit TeleVision
CD - ROM	Compact Disc - Read Only Memory
CD	Carrier Detect
	Compact Disc
CDDI	Copper Data Distribution Interface
CDFS	CD - ROM File System: Compact Disc- Read Only Memory File System
CDMA	Code Division Multiple Access
CDO	Collaboration Data Object
CDP	Cisco Discovery Protocol (Cisco)
CDPD	Cellular Digital Packet Data
CDV	Compressed Digital Video: Video files are compressed to enable them to be transmitted from A to B on the Internet quickly.
CEBus	Consumer Electronics Bus
CERN	Centre Europeene por la Recherche Nucleaire: The European Laboratory for Particle Physics. The originators of the HTTP and HTML concepts.
CERT	Computer Emergency Response Team
CF	Compact Flash
CFDP	Coherent File Distribution Protocol (TCP/IP)
CGA	Color Graphics Adapter. A CGA Monitor can display 640 X 200 pixels using 2 different colors or 320 X 200 pixels using 4 colors.
CGI	Common Gateway Interface: Programming scripts used to perform basic functions such as counting the number of times a Web Page is accessed.
CGM	Computer Graphics Metafile
CGMP	Cisco Group Management Protocol (Cisco)
CHAP	Challenge Handshake Authorization Protocol
Chargen	Character Generator (TCP/IP)
Chat	Communicating with others via the Internet by typing text into a message box.
Chat room	A Web site where you can have a real time chat with other members.
Checksum	A simple error detection scheme.
Chip	A thin wafer of semiconductor containing miniature electric circuits.
Chipset	Term used to describe the architecture of an IC.
Chmod	Change mode (UNIX)
CHS	Cylinders, Heads, Sectors Per Track: The three parameters used to determine a hard drive capacity (physical = actual number; logical = translation).
CI	Calling Indicator: One of four calling signal tones, part of the V.8 protocol.
	Customer Installation
	Component Instrumentation
CICS	Customer Information Control System
CID	Client Identifier
CIDR	Classless Inter-Domain Routing
CIF	Common Intermediate Format
CIFS	Common Internet File System: Microsoft standard for sharing Internet files (Microsoft).
CIS	CompuServe Information Service

	Computer Information Systems
	Card Information Structure
CISC	Complex Instruction Set Computing: A microprocessor architecture.
CIX	Commercial Internet Exchange
CLDAP	Connection-less Lightweight **DAP**: Connection-less Lightweight X.500 Directory Access Protocol (TCP/IP)
CLEC	Competitive Local Exchange Carrier
CLI	Common Language Infrastructure: An international standard proposed in 2000 by Microsoft, Hewlett-Packard and Intel. It allows programs written in a variety of program languages and executed on different platforms.
Client	The software that allows users the ability to retrieve information from the Internet and World Wide Web.
Client server model	A network configuration: A server is linked to a number of clients.
CLNP	Connectionless-mode Network Protocol
Cluster	Allocation Unit: A small group of sectors that is allocated by the system when disk space is needed.
CLV	Constant Linear Velocity
CMA	Circular Mil Area: A unit of measurement, area of a wire.
CMIIW	Text messaging abbreviation for "Correct me if I'm wrong".
CMIL	Circular Mil: A unit of measurement for area of a wire.
CMIP	Common Management Information Protocol
CMIS	Common Management Information Services
CMOL	**CMIP** over LLC: Common Management Information Protocol over Logical Link Control
CMON	Text messaging abbreviation for "Come on".
CMOS	Complementary Metal - Oxide Semiconductor: A type of memory chip that uses only small amounts of electric power.
CMOT	**CMIP** over TCP/IP: Common Management Information Protocol over Transmission Control Protocol/Internet Protocol
CMP	Cellular Multi-Processing
CMYK	Cyan Magenta Yellow Black: Model for combining the primary colors.
CNE	Certified Novell Engineer (Novell)
	Certified Network Engineer
CNG	Calling: An 1100 Hz, 0.5 second tone sent out every 3.5 seconds by Fax machines.
CNR	Communicating and Networking Riser
	Carrier-to-Noise Ratio
CO	Central Office
COAST	Cache on A Stick: Level 2 cache memory.
Coax	Coaxial cable
COB	Text messaging abbreviation for "Close of business".
COBOL	Common Business-Oriented Language: A high-level business-oriented programming language developed by CODASYL in 1960.
CODASYL	Conference on Data Systems Languages: A volunteer organization founded by the US Department of Defense in 1957 that developed Cobol.
Codec	Coder-decoder
COE	Component Object Model (Microsoft)
Cold boot	Restarting a computer from the power-off mode.
Cold start	See Cold boot.
Collision	A network error. Occurs on when two nodes transmit at the same time.
.com	URL designation for commercial organizations(domain name, Internet).
COM	Component Object Model
COM 1	1st serial port on a PC, normally used for a mouse or a modem.
COM 2	2nd serial port on a PC, normally used for a mouse or a modem.
COM 3	3rd serial port on a PC, normally used for a mouse or a modem.
COM 4	4th serial port on a PC, normally used for a mouse or a modem.
Command interpreter	
	A DOS program that executes commands entered at the DOS prompt.
Compile	Validates instructions entered into a text file & converts them into instructions that the operating system can understand.
Compiler	An application that translates program commands into machine language.

Compression	A technique to reduce the size of a file. See Data Compression.
CONP	Connection-Oriented Network Protocol
Controller	The link between the disk and the computer program. A printed circuit board that takes bits of data and converts them into bytes and words.
Conventional memory	
	The first 640 kilobytes of memory.
Cookie	A file that is written to your hard disk when you access certain Web pages.
.coop	URL designation for bona fide cooperatives and cooperative service organizations(domain name, Internet).
COPS	Common Open Policy Service (TCP/IP)
CORBA	Common Object Request Broker Architecture
CPAN	Comprehensive PERL Archive Network
CPC	Calling Party Control
	Cost Per Click
	Constant Point Calculation
CPE	Customer Provided Equipment
	Customer Premise Equipment
	Central Processing Equipment
CPI	Characters Per Inch: Number of characters that will print in one horizontal inch.
CPL	Characters Per Line
CPLD	Complex Programmable Logic Device
CPS	Characters Per Second: A measure of how fast a printer can print.
CPSUI	Common Property Sheet User Interface
CPU	Central Processing Unit: The primary microprocessor in the computer.
Craker	See Hacker.
CRANE	Common Reliable Accounting for Network Element Protocol (TCP/IP)
Crash	A computer problem with software or hardware that causes information loss or computer malfunction.
CRC	Cyclic Redundancy Check: A computer protection scheme that checks for corrupt data.
CRL	Certificate Revocation List
CR-LDP	Constraint-based LDP: Constraint-based Label Distribution Protocol (Internet)
CRM	Customer Relationship Management
Cron	A program that executes commands automatically at a pre-set time/date (UNIX).
CRT	Cathode Ray Tube
CSA	Carrier Service Area
	Connection and Streaming Architecture
	Canadian Standards Association
CSMA/CD	Carrier Sense Multiple Access / Collision Detection
CSN	Card Select Number
CSP	Cryptographic Service Provider
CSS	Cascading Style Sheets
	Content Scrambling System
CSTN	Color Super-Twist Nematic
CSU	Channel Service Unit
CTCP	Client-To-Client Protocol
CTERM	Command Terminal (DEC)
CTS	Clear To Send
	Computer Telephony Solution (IBM)
	Customer Telephone System
CTT	Character Translation Table
CU	Text messaging abbreviation for "See you."
CUA	Text messaging abbreviation for "See you later".
CUL	Text messaging abbreviation for "See you later".
CUL8R	Text messaging abbreviation for "See you later".
Cursor	A character, usually blinking, displayed on a computer monitor that shows you where the next action or operation will take place.
CWYL	Text messaging abbreviation for "Chat with you later".
CXML	Commerce XML: Commerce Extensible Markup Language
CYA	Text messaging abbreviation for "See ya".

Cyberspace	Describes the virtual world of computers, the Internet, also used to refer to the global network of computers.
Cylinder	Each platter on a hard disk has tracks on it. They are numbered (starting with "0") from the outside edge in. When you stack the platters on top of each other (as in a 4-platter hard disk), the tracks that line up with each other and have the same number are called a cylinder.
CYO	Text messaging abbreviation for "See you online".
DAC	Digital to Analog Converter. A device which converts digital information to analog.
DACL	Discretionary Access Control List
Daemon	A process that lies dormant in the background (UNIX).
Daisy chain	Method to connect (like beads on a string) more than one drive to a controller.
DAP	Directory Access Protocol (DEC)
DASD	Direct Access Storage Device (IBM)
DAT	Digital Audio Tape
	Dynamic Address Translation
Database	Structured data, such as a table of lines and columns. Software for organizing information.
Data compression	A term used for data that is altered by a software program and is subsequently stored in a smaller space.
Daytime	Daytime Protocol: Returns current time and day in ASCII format (TCP/IP).
dB	deciBel
	dataBase
DB9	A D-series telephone cable connector.
DB15	A D-series telephone cable connector.
DB25	A D-series telephone cable connector.
DBMS	Database Management System
DBCS	Double-Byte Character Set
DBS	Direct Broadcast Satellite
DC	Device Context
	Domain Controller
DCAP	Data Link Switching Client Access Protocol (TCP/IP)
DCB	Directory Control Block
DCC	Direct Cable Connection
	Data Communication Channel
	Data Country Code
DCD	Data Carrier Detect
DCE	Data Communication Equipment
	Data Circuit-Terminating Equipment (X.25)
DCOM	Distributed Component Object Model
DCT	Discrete Cosine Transform
DDB	Device Dependent Bitmap
	Differentiated Definition Block
DDC	Display Data Channel
DDCMP	Digital Data Communications Message Protocol (DEC)
DDE	Dynamic Data Exchange
DDI	Device Driver Interface
DDL	Data Definition Language
DDP	Datagram Delivery Protocol (AppleTalk, Apple)
DDR	Double Data Rate
Dead reckoning	A type of hard drive mechanism used in early PCs that makes the read/write heads go to a predetermined position.
Debug	Locate and fix hardware defects or software malfunctions.
DEC	Digital Equipment Corporation (now part of Hewlett-Packard)
DECnet	Set of network communication protocols developed by DEC in 1975.
Default	A preset value for some option in a computer program.
Defragment	Hard disk maintenance operation to recover disk space.
DEGT	Text messaging abbreviation for "Don't even go there".
DELPHI	A programming language derived from Turbo Pascal developed by Borland in 1995.
DES	Data Encryption Standard: Standard developed by IBM & NIST in 1976 that uses 64-bit blocks and a 56-bit key.

Glossary

Desktop	In Windows, the main directory of the user <u>interface</u>, it contains <u>icons</u> that <u>link</u> the user to applications, files and folders (Microsoft).
Device driver	Software that allows the PC to control hardware devices.
Device manager	System to monitor and control devices making up the computer (Windows).
DFS	Distributed File System
DHCP	Dynamic Host Configuration Protocol: A standard method for assigning dynamic IP addresses to computers on a network (TCP/IP).
DHCPv6	Dynamic Host Configuration Protocol for IPv6
DHTML	Dynamic HyperText Markup Language: A programming language (Internet).
DIAG	Diagnostic Responder (Novell)
Dialog box	A tool within a graphical user interface through which a user communicates with and gives commands to the software.
Dial-up connection	A temporary connection between two computers via a telephone line, normally using a modem.
Diameter	Diameter Base Protocol (TCP/IP)
DIB	Device Independent Bitmap
Dicode-NRZ	Di-code Non-Return to Zero
DICT	Dictionary Server Protocol (TCP/IP)
DID	Direct Inward Dialing
	Device Identifier
	Digital Identification
Differential	A type of hard drive developed as an option to single-ended SCSI to increase bus length.
DiffServ	Differentiated Services (Internet)
Digerati	Digital literati: The digital elite.
Digitize	Transforming analog information to digital information.
DIKU	Text messaging abbreviation for "Do I know you".
DIMM	Dual In-line Memory Module: Memory chips that are soldered onto plugs.
DIN	Deutsches Institut fur Normung: The German national standards organization.
DIP	Dual Inline Package
	Digital Image Processing
DIP switch	Tiny switches built into a circuit board.
Dir	See Directory.
Directory	A list of files stored on a storage device.
DirectX	APIs used by Windows to allow application programs direct access to hardware features, especially graphics accelerators (Microsoft).
DIRID	Directory Identifier
DIRQL	Device Interrupt Request Level
DIS	Distributed Interactive Simulation (TCP/IP)
Discard	A debugging tool using UDP and TCP port 9 (TCP/IP).
Disk cache	A temporary storage area for data between the RAM and disk drive which allows for faster data retrieval.
DISL	Dynamic Inter-Switch Link Protocol
DIVX	Digital Video Express
DIXIE	Dixie Protocol: A DAP for small servers like PC's and Macintoshes (TCP/IP).
D/L	Text messaging abbreviation for "Download".
DLC	Data Link Control (IBM)
	Digital Loop Carrier
	Dynamic Load Control
	Distributed Loop Carrier
DLL	Dynamic Linked Library: A library of program subroutines which can be shared between applications (Microsoft).
DLS	Data-Link Switching (TCP/IP)
DLSw	Data-Link Switching (IBM)
DMA	Direct Memory Access: A method that increases speed of transfer of data between peripherals and RAM by data going from memory to peripherals without the use of the CPU.

DMI	Desktop Management Interface: Software for managing the PCs within a network from a central PC.
DMSP	Distributed Mail System Protocol (TCP/IP)
DMT	Discrete Multi-Tone: Technical foundation for all ADSL variations.
DMTF	Desktop Management Task Force
DNA	Digital Network Architecture (DEC)
DNIC	Data Network Identification Code (X.25)
DNS	Domain Name Service
	Domain Name System (TCP/IP)
DO	Device Object
DOCSIS	Data Over Cable Service Interface Specification (ITU Recommendation J.112)
DOM	Document Object Model
Domain	An IP address or set of IP addresses that comprise a domain.
Domain name	Name that identifies a Web site.
Dongle	Security key.
	Ethernet card adapter for laptops.
DOS	Disk Operating System: A term used by computer manufacturers as a name for various operating systems (i.e., MS-DOS by Microsoft for the 16-bit microcomputers).
Dot pitch	A measure, in millimeters, of the distance between pixels displayed on the monitor. The smaller the distance, the higher the possible screen resolution.
Download	Receiving a file from another computer.
DPC	Deferred Procedure Call
DPI	Dots Per Inch: A measure of the quality of a printer. More dots per inch generally mean a higher quality printed image.
DPMS	Display Power Management Signaling
DPSK	Differential Phase Shift Keying Modulation
DQDB	Distributed Queue Dual Bus
DQMOT	Text messaging abbreviation for "Don't quote me on this".
Drag	An action performed using the mouse. Hold down a mouse button and move the object under the cursor to a new location on screen.
DRAM	Dynamic RAM: Dynamic Random Access Memory
DRAP	Data-Link Switching Remote Access Protocol (TCP/IP)
DRARP	Dynamic RARP: Dynamic Reverse ARP: Dynamic Reverse Address Resolution Protocol (TCP/IP)
Driver	A small file that helps a computer communicate with a hardware device.
Drive type	A code number assigned to a disk drive that indicates a standard configuration of CHS.
DRM	Digital Rights Management
Drop-down menu	In Windows, a menu that opens vertically displaying context-related options (Microsoft).
DRP	DECnet Routing Protocol (DEC)
DS	Distribution System
DSDT	Differentiated System Description Table
DSL	Digital Subscriber Line
DSLAM	DSL Access Multiplexer: Digital Subscriber Line Access Multiplexer
DSN	Data Source Name
DSP	Digital Signal Processor
DSR	Data Set Ready
DSS	Digital Satellite System
	Decision Support System
DSSS	Direct Sequence Spread Spectrum, a modulation scheme
DSTN	Double Layer Super Twisted Nematic: A type of LCD display, most commonly used in laptop computers.
DSTP	Data Space Transfer Protocol (Internet)
DSU	Data Service Unit
	Digital Switching Unit
	Digital Service Unit
DSVD	Digital Simultaneous Voice and Data
DTCP	Dynamic Tunnel Configuration Protocol (TCP/IP)
DTD	Document Type Definition

DTE	Data Terminal Equipment (X.25)
DTM	Dynamic Synchronous Transfer Mode
DTMF	Dual-Tone Multi-Frequency
DTP	Desktop Publishing
	Dynamic Trunking Protocol (Cisco)
DTR	Data Terminal Ready
	Data Transfer Rate: Measurement indicating how fast the controller reads a file once it finds it. Usually recorded as bits per second or bytes per second.
DTS	Text messaging abbreviation for "Don't think so".
DUAL	Diffusing Update Algorithm
Dual scan display	An LCD used in laptop computers.
DUN	Dial-Up Networking
DUP	Data User Part (SS7)
Duplex	The ability to send and receive data & voice at the same time, also called full duplex.
DV	Digital Video
DVD	Digital Video Disc or Digital Versatile Disc: A high capacity storage device for video and other processes that require removable data storage.
DVDROM	Digital Video Disk Read Only Media
DVI	Digital Video Interface
DVMRP	Distance Vector Multicast Routing Protocol (TCP/IP)
Dvorak	A speed-typing keyboard layout. See QWERTY and AZERTY.
DVR	Digital Video Recorder
DWDM	Dense Wavelength Division Multiplexing
Dynaset	Dynamic Interactive Data Set: Database technology that selects and sorts specific records.
EA	Extended Attribute
EAP	Extensible Authentication Protocol
EBCDIC	Extended Binary Coded Decimal Interchange Code
EBKAC	Text messaging abbreviation for "Error between keyboard and chair".
E-book	Electronic book: A hand-held, electronic device that allows a person to view digital reading materials.
ECC	Error Correction Code: Allows computer to detect and correct any pattern of errors in a sector.
Echo	A debugging tool that uses UDP and TCP port 7 (TCP/IP).
ECMA	European Computer Manufacturers Association: A non-profit industry association founded in 1961.
ECMAScript	European Computer Manufacturers Association Script: A scripting programming language based on JavaScript and JScript adopted by ECMA in 1999.
E-commerce	Electronic commerce: Business using services such as the Internet.
ECP	Enhanced Communication Port: A technology to improve I/O for parallel ports.
	Extended Capabilities Port
	Enhanced Capabilities Port
ECS	Extended Character Set
	Enhanced Chip Set
	Emergency Calling Service
EDGE	Enhanced Data for GSM Evolution: Enhanced Data for Global System for Mobile Communications Evolution
EDI	Electronic Data Interchange: A standard to transmit documents.
EDID	Extended Display Identification Data
Editor	See Text editor.
EDO	Extended Data Out
EDO RAM	Extended Data Out Random Access Memory
EDP	Electronic Data Processing
.edu	URL designation for educational institution(domain name, Internet).
Edutainment	Educational material presented in an entertaining way via computer.
EEPROM	Electrically Erasable Programmable Read - Only Memory
EFF	Electronic Frontier Foundation
EFI	Extensible Firmware Interface
E-form	Electronic form

EGA	Enhanced Graphics Adapter: An EGA Monitor displays 640 X 350 pixels using 16, colors from a table of 64 colors.
EGP	Exterior Gateway Protocol (TCP/IP)
EHCI	Enhanced Host Controller Interface (Intel)
EIA	Electronic Industries Alliance
EIDE	Enhanced IDE: Enhanced Integrated Drive Electronics: Interface for home machines, internal hard drives and CD-ROM drives based on ATA-2 and ATAPI standards.
EIFFEL	An object-oriented programming language developed by Bertrand Meyer of Interactive Software Engineering in 1986. Named for Gustave Eiffel designer of the Eiffel Tower. Based on SIMULA.
EIGRP	Enhanced Interior Gateway Routing Protocol (TCP/IP)
EIRP	Effective Isotropic Radiated Power
EISA	Extended Industry Standard Architecture
EMA	Text messaging abbreviation for "E-mail address".
E-mail	Electronic mail
Embedded servo system	
	Servo data is embedded with data on every cylinder.
EMF	Enhanced Metafile
EMI	Electro-Magnetic Interference
Emoticon	A cluster of punctuation marks used in internet communications to give emotional context to what is written. Looks like a face with a certain kind of expression. See Page 838.
EMS	Expanded Memory Specification: A technique that allows DOS to use more than 1 megabyte of main memory.
EMSD	Efficient Mail Submission and Delivery Protocol (TCP/IP)
Encoding schemes	The two hard drive types are MFM and RLL.
Encryption	Coding or scrambling of information transmitted between secure Web sites.
EOD	Text messaging abbreviation for "End of day".
EOF	End of File
EOL	End of Line
	End of Life
	End of List
EOM	Text messaging abbreviation for "End of message".
EOS	ECC on SIMM: Error Correction Code on Single In-line Memory Module
EP	Error Protocol (XNS)
E-paper	Electronic paper (IBM)
EPIC	Explicitly Parallel Instruction Computing (Intel)
EPP	Enhanced Parallel Port: IEEE 1284 standard that supports data transfer rates of up to 1 Mbps.
	Extensible Provisioning Protocol (TCP/IP)
EPROM	Erasable Programmable Read - Only Memory
EPS	Encapsulated PostScript
ESD	Electronic Software Distribution
ESDI	Enhanced Small Device Interface: A controller that evolved from ST412/ST506 interface in 1983. The clock-data separator is on the drive in the ESDI whereas it is on the controller in the ST 412/ST506. Therefore, the encoding and decoding is done on the drive, which allows for increased capacities and faster communication. It has a data transfer rate of 10-24 megabits/second.
ES-IS	End-System to Intermediate System
ESMTP	Extended Simple Mail Transfer Protocol (TCP/IP)
ESN	Electronic Serial Number
	Electronic Security Number
ESP	Encapsulating Security Payload (Internet)
	Enhanced Serial Port: A standard that supports data transfer rates of up to 921.6 Kbps.
ESRO	Efficient Short Remote Operations Protocol (TCP/IP)
ESS	Extended Service Set
	Electronic Switching System
ETFTP	Enhanced Trivial File Transfer Protocol (TCP/IP)

Ethernet	A LAN that was developed by Xerox to transmit data at a rate of 10 megabits per second.
Ethernet card	A circuit board attached to the motherboard to which a network cable can be attached.
EtherTalk	AppleTalk IEEE 802.3 Ethernet interface standard (Apple).
ETSI	European Telecommunications Standards Institute
EUDC	End-User Defined Characters
Exabyte	1,152,921,504,606,846,976 bytes; 1,024 petabyte.
Expanded memory manager	
	A program that allows DOS to utilize the expanded memory.
E-zine	Electronic magazine
F2F	Text messaging abbreviation for "Face to face".
FACS	Firmware ACPI Control Structure: Firmware Advanced Configuration and Power Interface Control Structure
FADT	Fixed ACPI Description Table: Fixed Advanced Configuration and Power Interface Description Table
FANP	Flow Attribute Notification Protocol (Toshiba)
FAQ	Frequently Asked Questions (Internet)
Fast Ethernet	Ethernet LAN at 100 Mbps (IEEE 802.3u). See 100BaseT, 100BaseTX, 100BaseT4, 100BaseFX.
Fast SCSI	A designation of the SCSI-2 specification indicates a double speed transmission of 10 MB/s versus the SCSI-2 transfer rate of 5MB/s.
Fast Wide SCSI	SCSI using a 16-bit bus, supports data transfer speeds of 20 MBps.
FAT	File Allocation Table: Tells what clusters are allocated to what files and their availability.
FAT16	File Allocation Table - 16 bit: An improvement to the FAT system.
FAT32	File Allocation Table - 32 bit: An improvement to the FAT system, supports up to 2 terabytes of hard disk storage.
FBM	Text messaging abbreviation for "Fine by me".
FC-AL	Fiber Channel-Arbitrated Loop
FCB	File Control Block
FCC	Federal Communications Commission
FCI	Flux Changes per Inch: In RLL: 1 FCI = 1.5 BPI, in MFM: 1 FCI = 1BPI.
FCIP	Fiber Channel over Internet Protocol
FCP	Fiber Channel Protocol
FD	Floppy Disk
FDC	Floppy Disk Controller
FDDI	Fiber Distributed Data Interface: A network standard for transmitting data via fiber optic cables.
FDM	Frequency Division Multiplexing
FDO	Functional Device Object
FEC	Forward Error Correction
FEP	Front End Processor
FET	Field Effect Transistor
FEXT	Front End Cross (x) Talk
	Far End Cross (x) Talk
FFDI	Fiber Distributed Data Interface
FFDT	FFDI Full Duplex Technology: Fiber Distributed Data Interface Full Duplex Technology
FHSS	Frequency Hopping Spread Spectrum, a modulation scheme
Fiber-optic cable	Cable made up of filaments of glass that can carry beams of light
Fiber optics	Data transmission using light through glass fiber cable.
FiDO	See Filter DO.
FIF	Fractal Interchange Format
FIFO	First In First Out
File virus	See Virus.
Filter DO	Filter Device Object
Firewall	A combination of hardware & software to keep unauthorized users from accessing information within a computer system.
FireWire®	The IEEE 1394 high-speed interface for Apple computers. Original interface could transfer data at 400 Mbps, FireWire 800 supports data transfer rates of 800 Mbps (Apple).
Firmware	Software stored in ROM (half way between hardware and software).
FISH	Text messaging abbreviation for "First in, still here".

FITB	Text messaging abbreviation for "Fill in the blanks".
Flame	Internet term for inappropriate harsh online commentary.
Flash	Refers to Macromedia's Web animation technology.
Flash memory	See Flash RAM
Flash RAM	Quickly accessed RAM memory sometimes used instead of a hard drive.
Floating point calculation	A mathematical method used to perform calculations needing a high degree of accuracy.
Floppy disk	Mass storage device, 3-1/2 inch square, 1.44 MB of storage.
Flops	**Flo**ating-**p**oint **o**perations per **s**econd: A measure of computer computational speed, one floating-point operations per second.
Flux	Magnetic impulses on the disk surface.
FM Encoding	**F**requency **M**odulation **Encoding**: Archaic way of encoding data which was replaced by MFM encoding.
FMT	Filtered Multi-tone
FOAF	Text messaging abbreviation for "Friend of a friend".
FOIRL	Fiber Optic Inter-Repeater Link
FOMCL	Text messaging abbreviation for "Falling off my chair laughing".
Format	A process that prepares a memory device for data storage.
Formatting	Records header data (sector number, head and cylinder address) on a disk so it is ready to be read or written to.
Form factor	The physical external size of a hard drive platter(desk top usually 3.5 inches or 5.25 inches; portable and lap tops usually 2.5 inches).
FORTRAN	**For**mula **tran**slator: The oldest high-level programming language, developed in 1954 by John Backus and others at IBM.
Forum	A topic-focused discussion area.
FOS	Text messaging abbreviation for "Father over shoulder".
FOURCC	Four Character Code
FPGA	Field Programmable Gate Array
FPM	Fast Page Mode
FPU	Floating Point Unit
FQDN	Fully Qualified Domain Name (Internet)
FRAD	Frame Relay Access Device
	Frame Relay Assembler/ Disassembler
Freeware	Like Shareware but it's free.
FS	File System
FSAN	Full-Service Access Network
FSB	Front Side Bus
FSCTL	File System Control Code
FSK	Frequency Shift Keying Modulation
FTAM	File Transfer Access and Management
FTP	File Transfer Protocol: A method of transferring files to/from remote computers (TCP/IP).
FTTC	Fiber To The Curb
FTTH	Fiber To The Home
Full duplex	See Duplex.
Full-height drive	A drive with the following physical parameters: 3.25 inch height, 8.00 inch depth, and 5.75 inch width.
Function	A Function has input & output parameters and is similar to a repeatable subroutine.
FWIW	Text messaging abbreviation for "For what it's worth".
FYEO	Text messaging abbreviation for "For your eyes only".
FYI	Text messaging abbreviation for "For your information".
G2G	Text messaging abbreviation for "Got to go".
G2R	Text messaging abbreviation for "Got to run".
G.922.2	See G.lite ADSL.
GA	Text messaging abbreviation for "Go ahead".
GAL	Text messaging abbreviation for "Get a life".
Game port	An I/O port for devices such as joysticks that are used to play computer games.
GARP	Generic Attribute Registration Protocol (Internet)
GART	Graphics Address Remapping Table
Gateway	Software or hardware that connects networks together.

GAWK	GNU **AWK**: An extended version of the AWK programming language written by the Gnu Project. See AWK and Gnu Project.
GB	See Gigabyte.
	Text messaging abbreviation for "Goodbye".
GbE	See Gigabit Ethernet.
Gbps	Gigabits per second.
GBU	Text messaging abbreviation for "God bless you".
GDI	Graphics Device Interface
G/F	Text messaging abbreviation for "Girlfriend".
GFI	Text messaging abbreviation for "Go for it".
	General Format Identifier (X.25)
Gflops	**Giga**flops. **Giga** **f**loating **p**oint **o**perations **p**er **s**econd
GG	Text messaging abbreviation for "Gotta go".
	Text messaging abbreviation for "Good game".
GGP	Gateway to Gateway Protocol (TCP/IP)
GHz	Gigahertz
GIAR	Text messaging abbreviation for "Give it a rest".
GIF	Graphics Interchange Format: The most common type of compressed image file used on the Internet, limited to 256 colors.
Gigabit Ethernet	Ethernet at 1000 Mbps (IEEE 802.3). See 1000BaseCX, 1000BaseFX, 1000BaseLX, 1000BaseSX, 1000BaseT, 1000BaseTX.
Gigabyte	A unit of storage equal to 1,073,741,824 bytes or approximately 1,000 megabytes.
GIGO	Text messaging abbreviation for "Garbage in, garbage out".
GIS	Geographic Information Systems
GL	Text messaging abbreviation for "Good luck".
GL/HF	Text messaging abbreviation for "Good luck, have fun".
G.lite	See G.lite ADSL
G.lite ADSL	A moderate rate ADSL: Data rates from 500 Kbps to 1.5 Mbps. Governed by ITU G.992.2.
GLM	General Linear Model
GLNG	Text messaging abbreviation for "Good luck next game".
GMRP	GARP Multicast Registration Protocol: **G**eneric **A**ttribute **R**egistration Protocol **M**ulticast **R**egistration **P**rotocol (Internet)
GMTA	Text messaging abbreviation for "Great minds think alike".
GNN	Global Network Navigator
GNU	Gnu's Not UNIX
GNU Project	**G**nu's **N**ot **U**NIX **Project**: A UNIX-compatible software system developed by the Free Software Foundation founded in 1985 by Richard Stallman of MIT to write and disseminate free, open-source software.
GOI	Text messaging abbreviation for "Get over it".
GOL	Text messaging abbreviation for "Giggling out loud".
Gopher	A text based distributed information system developed at the University of Minnesota.
.gov	URL designation for non-military government organizations(domain name, Internet).
GPD	Generic Printer Description
GPF	General Protection Fault: A general protection fault occurs if exclusive memory is accessed by another program (Microsoft).
GPRS	**G**eneral **P**acket **R**adio **S**ervice
	General **P**acket **R**adio **S**ystem
GPS	Global Positioning System
GPU	Graphics Processing Unit
GR8	Text messaging abbreviation for "Great".
GR&D	Text messaging abbreviation for "Grinning, running and ducking".
GRE	Generic Routing Encapsulation (Internet)
GREP	Global Regular Expression Print
Groupware	Software that enables groups of people to work together.
G.SHDSL	See SHDSL.
GSM	**G**lobal **S**ystem for **M**obile Communications
GSS-API	Generic Security Service Application Programming Interface
GSTN	General Switched Telephone Network
GTG	Text messaging abbreviation for "Got to go".
GTLD	Global Top-Level Domain (Internet)

GTRM	Text messaging abbreviation for "Going to read mail".
GTT	Glyph Translation Table
GUI	Graphical User Interface
GUID	Global Universal Identifier
	Globally Unique Identifier
GVRP	GARP VLAN Registration Protocol: Generic Attribute Registration Protocol Virtual Local Area Network Registration Protocol (Internet)
GW-BASIC	Gee-Whiz BASIC: A dialect of BASIC (Microsoft)
H.263	An ITU standard for video compression.
H.323	A set of ITU standards for audiovisual data transmission.
H.324	An ITU standard for videoconferencing over POTS.
Hacker	A person who tries to gain unauthorized access to a computer system or network.
HAGN	Text messaging abbreviation for "Have a good night".
HAGO	Text messaging abbreviation for "Have a good one".
HAL	Hardware Abstraction Layer
Half duplex	The transmission of data one direction at a time.
Half-height drive	A drive with the following physical parameters: 1.625 inch height, 4.0 or 8.0 inch depth, and 4.0 or 5.75 inch width.
HAND	Text messaging abbreviation for "Have a nice day".
Handle	Names people use to identify themselves in online chat (Internet).
Hard disk	Mass storage device, current models hold 15 to 200 GB.
Hard drive	See Hard disk.
Hardware	Components (both physical and mechanical) of a computer system, including the circuit boards, chips, monitor, disk drives, keyboard, modem, and printer.
Hardware RAID	Hardware Redundant Array of Inexpensive Disks: Using dedicated hardware to control the array.
HBA	Host Bus Adapter
HCI	Host Controller Interface (Intel)
	Human-Computer Interaction
HCL	Hardware Compatibility List
HCMOS	High Speed Complementary Metal-Oxide Semiconductor
HCT	Hardware Compatibility Test
HD	See High density.
HDC	Hard Disk Controller
HDD	Hard Disk Drive
HDEV	Handle to a Device Object
HDIS	Network Driver Interface Specification
HDLC	High Level Data Link Control (X.25)
HDML	Handheld Device Markup Language
HDSL	High Bit-Rate Digital Subscriber Line: Speeds of 1.5 Mbps or 2.048 Mbps, two or three wire pairs.
	High Data-rate DSL
	High-Speed DSL
HDSL2	High Bit-Rate Digital Subscriber Line 2: Speeds of 1.5 Mbps or 2.048 Mbps, one wire pair.
HDX	Half Duplex
Head	The part of the hard disk that reads and writes data on the platters -usually 1 read/write head per each side of a platter (i.e., 2 platters = 4 heads). [Three types: composition, monolithic and thin film.]
Head crash	Catastrophic failure that occurs when the hard drive read head touches the disk platter surface causing damage. A crash usually occurs because loose particles get between the head and the rotating disk platter.
Head parking	See Auto Parking.
HEL	Hardware Emulation Layer
Hex	See Hexadecimal.
Hexadecimal	The base 16 numbering system. The decimal numbers 10 to 15 are represented by the letters A to F. 10 hexadecimal is equivalent to 16 decimal.
HF	Text messaging abbreviation for "Have fun".
HFC	Hybrid Fiber Coaxial Cable
HFS	Hierarchical File System

HHIS	Text messaging abbreviation for "Head hanging in shame".
HID	Human Interface Device
High density	The amount of disk storage capacity.
High level language	A programming language that is somewhat independent of the type of computer platform it is executed on.
History list	A list of document titles and URLs of recently visited Web pages which are kept in memory.
Hit	Internet term for an access made to a Web page (Internet).
HMA	High Memory Area: The first 64 Kilobytes of Extended Memory (Microsoft).
HMP	Host Monitoring Protocol (TCP/IP)
HOAS	Text messaging abbreviation for "Hold on a second".
Home page	The top level document of a Web Site (Internet).
HomePNA	Home Phoneline Networking Alliance
	Home Phoneline Network Adapter
Host	An Internet service provider or Internet server (Internet).
Host adapter card	A printed circuit board (card) added to a microcomputer to add a connector port.
Hostname	Hostname Server Protocol (TCP/IP)
Hot JAVA	A Web browser which can display "executable content" written in the JAVA Programming Language.
Hotspots	Exact monitor screen positions where mouse clicks result in a particular event occurring.
HPA	High Performance Addressing
HPGL	Hewlett Packard Graphics Language: Programming language (Hewlett Packard).
HPIB	Hewlett Packard Interface Bus (Hewlett Packard)
HPNA	See HomePNA.
HPPCL	Hewlett Packard Printer Control Language (Hewlett Packard)
HP-UX	Hewlett Packard UNIX (Hewlett Packard)
HREF	Hypertext Reference
HRU	Text messaging abbreviation for "How are you".
HSB	Hue Saturation Brightness
HSCSD	High Speed Circuit Switched Data
HSRP	Hot Standby Routing Protocol (TCP/IP)
HSSI	High Speed Serial Interface
HTH	Text messaging abbreviation for "Hope this helps".
HTML	HyperText Markup Language: A programming language, a subset of SGML (Internet).
HTTP	HyperText Transport Protocol: Communication protocol used by WWW servers (TCP/IP).
HTTPS	HyperText Transfer Protocol Secure: Communication protocol used by WWW servers when passwords are required.
Hub	A hardware device used to network computers.
HWID	Hardware Identifier
Hyperlink	A link in a given document to information within another document. These links are usually represented by highlighted words or images. The user has the option to underline these hyperlinks.
Hypermedia	Richly formatted documents containing a variety of information types, such as textual, image, movie, and audio. These information types are easily found through hyperlinks.
Hypertext	Text which contains links to additional information. Hypertext can be clicked with a mouse.
I2C	Inter-Integrated Circuit
I2O	Intelligent Input/Output
IA44	Index-Alpha 4-4: A video surface subtype that has a value of 8 bits per pixel.
IAB	Internet Architecture Board: An advisory group within the ISOC.
IAC	Text messaging abbreviation for "In any case".
IAD	Integrated Access Device
IANAL	Text messaging abbreviation for "In am not a lawyer".
IAP	Internet Access Provider
	Internet Access Point

IARP	See InARP.
IB	Text messaging abbreviation for "I'm back".
I-biz	Internet business(z)
IC	Integrated circuit
	Text messaging abbreviation for "I see".
ICANN	Internet Corporation for Assigned Names and Numbers: International organization responsible for managing and coordinating the Domain Name System.
ICAP	Internet Content Adaptation Protocol (TCP/IP)
ICBW	Text messaging abbreviation for "It could be worse".
ICD	Installable Client Driver
ICE	Intelligence Concept Extraction
ICEA	Insulated Cable Engineer's Association
ICM	Image Color Management
ICMP	Internet Control Message Protocol (TCP/IP)
ICMPv6	ICMP version 6: Internet Control Message Protocol version 6 (TCP/IP)
I-commerce	Internet commerce: Business using the Internet. See E-commerce.
Icon	Introduced in 1984 by Apple. A symbol on a computer screen that represents an object, file or program on the hard drive. (Apple)
ICP	Internet Cache Protocol (TCP/IP)
ICPv2	Internet Cache Protocol version 2 (TCP/IP)
ICQ	Text messaging abbreviation for "I seek you"
ICS	Internet Connection Sharing
IDCT	Inverse Discrete Cosine Transform
IDE	Integrated Drive Electronics: The most commonly used hard drive interface in which you do not need a controller card because the RLL or MFM controller is built into the drive and plugs directly into the motherboard. [Three types: XT IDE (8-bit); AT (ATA) IDE (16-bit); MCA IDE (16-bit) -basically an advanced RLL used on high capacity (>500Mb) drives are connected.
	Integrated Device Electronics
	Imbedded Drive Electronics
	Integrated Development Environment (Borland)
	Interface Design Enhancement
IDK	Text messaging abbreviation for "I don't know".
IDN	International Data Number (X.25)
IDP	Internet Datagram Protocol (XNS)
IDPR	Inter Domain Policy Routing Protocol (TCP/IP)
IDRP	Inter Domain Routing Protocol
IDSL	ISDN Digital Subscriber Line: Integrated Services Digital Network Digital Subscriber Line, speeds of 144 Kbps.
	Internet Digital Subscriber Line
IDT	Interrupt Dispatch Table
IDTS	Text messaging abbreviation for "I don't think so".
IE	Internet Explorer (Microsoft)
IEC	Inter-Exchange Carrier
	International Electrotechnical Commission
IEEE	Institute of Electrical and Electronics Engineers
IEEE 802.1	IEEE standard related to networks.
IEEE 802.2	IEEE standard related to the old OSI Reference Model.
IEEE 802.3	IEEE standard specific to Ethernet networks.
IEEE 802.4	IEEE standard specific to token-bus networks.
IEEE 802.5	IEEE standard for token-ring networks.
IEEE 802.6	IEEE standard for Metropolitan Area Networks.
IEEE 1394	IEEE standard interface for audio-video devices and computer peripherals, either a 4-pin or 6-pin type (aka FireWire® by Apple, i.Link® by Sony).
IETF	Internet Engineering Task Force: A volunteer subgroup of IAB concentrating on technical Internet issues.
iFCP	Internet Fiber Channel Protocol (TCP/IP)
IFMP	Ipsilon Flow Management Protocol (TCP/IP)
I-Frame	Information frame (X.25)
IG2R	Text messaging abbreviation for "I got to run".

IGAP	IGMP for User Authentication Protocol (TCP/IP): Internet Group Management Protocol for User Authentication Protocol (TCP/IP)
IGMP	Internet Group Management Protocol (TCP/IP)
IGP	Interior Gateway Protocol
IGRP	Interior Gateway Routing Protocol (TCP/IP)
IHTML	Inline HTML: Inline HyperText Markup Language: A powerful server-side language.
IIC	See I2C.
IID	Instance Identifier
IIO	See I2O.
IIOP	Internet Inter-ORB Protocol: Internet Inter-Object Request Broker Protocol (Microsoft)
IIRC	Text messaging abbreviation for "If I remember correctly".
IIS	Internet Information Server (Microsoft)
IKE	Internet Key Exchange Protocol (TCP/IP)
ILBL8	Text messaging abbreviation for "I'll be late".
ILEC	Incumbent Local Exchange Carrier
ILU	Text messaging abbreviation for "I love you".
ILY	Text messaging abbreviation for "I love you".
ILYT	Text messaging abbreviation for "I love you too".
IM	Instant Message
IMA	Interactive Multimedia Association
IMA-ADPCM	Interactive Multimedia Association Adaptive Differential Pulse Code Modulation
Image map	A graphic image divided into hotspot areas each of which hyperlink to web pages.
IMAP	Internet Message Access Protocol: Conceived at Stanford University in 1986 (TCP/IP).
	Internet Mail Access Protocol
IMAP2	Internet Message Access Protocol version 2: 1987, included UNIX (TCP/IP).
IMAP2bis	Internet Message Access Protocol version 2 with MIME support: 1991 (TCP/IP).
IMAP3	Internet Message Access Protocol version 3: 1991 (TCP/IP).
IMAP4	Internet Message Access Protocol version 4: 1994 (TCP/IP).
IMAP4rev1	Internet Message Access Protocol version 4 revision 1: 1997 (TCP/IP).
IME	Input Method Editor
IMHO	Text messaging abbreviation for "In my humble opinion".
IMM	Input Method Manager
IMNSHO	Text messaging abbreviation for "In my not so humble opinion".
IMO	Text messaging abbreviation for "In my opinion".
IMP	Interface Message Processors
IMPP	Instant Messaging and Presence Protocol
INAL	Text messaging abbreviation for "I'm not a lawyer".
INAP	Intelligent Network Application Protocol
InARP	Inverse ARP: Inverse Address Resolution Protocol (Internet)
Index	A list that points to other information.
Index pulse	The start point for each disk track.
Index time	A measurement of the time it takes for a disk platter to make one revolution.
.info	URL designation for information sites(domain name, Internet).
In-line image	A graphic image that is displayed with an HTML document.
Input device	A device that allows input of information to a computer. Devices can include keyboard, stylus and tablet, mouse or microphone.
.int	URL designation for international organizations(domain name, Internet).
Interface	Components that provide communication between computer devices.
Interleave	Makes a hard drive read data slower by renumbering the sectors and allowing the CPU to read six sectors in only one rotation. [PC/XT interleave = 3 or 4 -PC/AT interleave = 1 or 2 -XT interleave = 3.]
Internet	A international computer network of networks that connect government, academic and business institutions.

Internet time	A global Internet time concept marketed by Swatch based on beats. The day is divided into 1000 beats, each beat equals 1 minute 26.4 seconds. Referenced to time in Biel, Switzerland, home of Swatch.
InterNIC	The company that manages Domain Name registration. Alliance between Network Solutions, Inc; AT&T and the National Science Foundation.
Intranet	A internal Internet type service.
I/O	Input/Output: The input is the data that is imported into the computer for it to process through an input device (i.e., keyboard). The output is the end result information the computer generates and which is displayed on a terminal, printout, disks, etc.
IOCHRDY	Input/Output Channel Ready: The CPU sends this signal to a peripheral to notify it that more resources are ready for transfer [Intel].
IOCTL	Input/Output Control
IOTP	Internet Open Trading Protocol
IOW	Text messaging abbreviation for "In other words".
IP	Internet Protocol version 4: 32 bit IP Addresses
IP Address	Internet Protocol **Address**: A unique number used to represent a computer on the Internet. All Internet computers have a unique IP Address. The format of the IP Address is 4 series of 1 to 3 digits separated by dots e.g. 123.456.789.987.
IPC	Interprocess Communication
IPCP	Internet Protocol version 4 Control Protocol (Internet)
IPD	Internal Pointing Device
IPDC	IP Device Control: Internet Protocol Device Control
IPI	Intelligent Peripheral Interface: High-bandwidth hard disk drive or tape drive interface at rates between 3 and 25 Mbps.
I Picture	Intra-coded **Picture**
IPL	Initial Program Load
IPNG	Internet Protocol Next Generation: See **IPv6**. (Internet)
IPP	Internet Printing Protocol (TCP/IP)
IPPCP	IP Payload Compression Protocol: Internet Protocol Payload Compression Protocol (TCP/IP)
IPsec	IP Security Architecture: Internet Protocol Security Architecture (Internet)
IPv4	See IP.
IPv6	Internet Protocol version 6: 128 bit IP Addresses (Internet).
IPv6CP	Internet Protocol version 6 Control Protocol (Internet)
IPX	Internetwork Packet Exchange (Novell)
IRB	I/O Request Block
IRC	See IRCP.
IRCP	Internet Relay Chat Protocol: The Internet "CB" radio. (TCP/IP)
IRDA	Infrared Data Association
IRDP	Internet Router Discovery Protocol
IRL	Text messaging abbreviation for "In real life".
IRMC	Text messaging abbreviation for "I rest my case".
IRP	I/O Request Packet
IRQ	Interrupt Request Line
IRQL	Interrupt Request Level
IRTF	Internet Research Task Force: A sub group of the IAB that considers strategic Internet issues.
IRTP	Internet Reliable Transaction Protocol (TCP/IP)
IS	Information System
	Interrupt Status
	Interim Standard
	International Standard
ISA	Industry Standard Architecture: PC, XT and AT systems use these types of 8 and 16 bit expansion slots.
ISAKMP	Internet Security Association and Key Management Protocol (TCP/IP)
ISAM	Indexed Sequential Access Method: Used to locate specific records stored on a hard drive.
iSCSI	Internet SCSI: Internet Small Computer System Interface (TCP/IP)
ISDN	Integrated Services Digital Network: A fast digital telephone service.

ISDN BRI	ISDN Basic Rate Interface: Integrated Services Digital Network Basic Rate Interface: Two 64-Kbps B-channels and one D-channel.
ISDN PRI	ISDN Primary Rate Interface: Integrated Services Digital Network Primary Rate Interface: Twenty-three B-channels and one D-channel.
ISDN TA	ISDN Terminal Adapter: Integrated Services Digital Network Terminal Adapter
IS-IS	Intermediate System to Intermediate System
ISL	Inter-Switch Link Protocol (Cisco)
iSNS	Internet Storage Name Service
ISO	International Organization for Standardization
ISOC	Internet Society: A worldwide standards organization, sponsors the IAB.
Isochronous data transfer	
	The type of data transfer that is sent at a fixed rate and is matched to a clock. Used with video-audio connections to devices such as a TV.
ISO-IP	ISO Internetworking Protocol: International Organization for Standardization Internetworking Protocol
ISO/OSI	International Organization for Standardization/Open System Interconnect
ISO-PP	ISO Presentation Protocol: International Organization for Standardization Presentation Protocol
ISO-SP	ISO Session Protocol: International Organization for Standardization Session Protocol
ISO-TP	ISO Transport Protocol: International Organization for Standardization Transport Protocol
ISP	Internet Service Provider: A company that provides access from your computer to the Internet.
ISR	Interrupt Service Routine
ISUP	ISDN User Part: Integrated Services Digital Network User Part (SS7)
ISV	Independent Software Vendor
IT	Information Technology
ITOT	ISO Transport Service on Top of TCP: International Organization for Standardization Transport Service on Top of Transmission Control Protocol
ITU	International Telecommunication Union: Based in Geneva, sets international standards for telecommunications, formerly called the CCITT.
ITU-T	International Telecommunication Union – Telecommunication Standardization Sector
ITU V.xx	See V.xx.
IUA	ISDN User Adaptation Layer: Integrated Services Digital Network User Adaptation Layer (TCP/IP)
IUSS	Text messaging abbreviation for "If you say so".
IVR	Interactive Voice Response
IXC	Inter-Exchange Carrier
IYKWIM	Text messaging abbreviation for "If you know what I mean".
IYO	Text messaging abbreviation for "In your opinion".
IYSS	Text messaging abbreviation for "If you say so".
J2EE	JAVA 2 Platform Enterprise Edition
J2ME	JAVA 2 Platform Micro Edition
J2SE	JAVA 2 Platform Standard Edition
JAC	Text messaging abbreviation for "Just a second".
JAS	Text messaging abbreviation for "Just a second".
JAVA	An interpreted, object-oriented program language developed by Sun Microsystems in 1995 that can be run on most computers, making it well suited for the WWW.
JavaScript	A programming language for developing client Internet applications embedded in an HTML page, similar to Common Gateway Interface (CGI) programs, developed by Brendan Eich at Netscape Communications in 1994.
JAXB	JAVA Architecture for XML Binding: JAVA Architecture for Extensible Markup Language Binding (JAVA)
JAXP	JAVA API for XML Processing: JAVA Application Programming Interface for Extensible Markup Language Processing (JAVA)

Glossary

JAXR	JAVA API for XML Registries: JAVA Application Programming Interface for Extensible Markup Language Registries (JAVA)
JAX-RPC	JAVA API for XML-based RPC: JAVA Application Programming Interface for Extensible Markup Language-based Remote Procedure Call Protocol (JAVA)
JCL	Job Control Language
JEDEC	Joint Electron Device Engineering Council: Now called the JEDEC Solid State Technology Association.
JIC	Text messaging abbreviation for "Just in case".
JIK	Text messaging abbreviation for "Just in case".
JJA	Text messaging abbreviation for "Just joking around".
JK	Text messaging abbreviation for "Just kidding".
J/K	Text messaging abbreviation for "Just kidding".
JMO	Text messaging abbreviation for "Just my opinion".
JP	Text messaging abbreviation for "Just playing".
JPEG	Joint Photographic Experts Group
JScript	Microsoft's implementation of ECMAScript (Microsoft).
JSP	JAVA Server Page (JAVA)
Jumper	A small metal connector used to alter hardware configurations.
JVM	JAVA Virtual Machine (JAVA)
JYO	Text messaging abbreviation for "Just your opinion".
K56flex	Modem chipset to allow 56 Kbps over POTS (Rockwell). See V.90.
KBC	Keyboard Controller
Kbps	Kilobits per second: A unit used to measure data transfer rate.
KCMIL	1000 CMIL: 1000 Circular Mil: A unit of measurement for area of a wire, also see CMIL.
Kerberos	A network authentication protocol written at MIT (TCP/IP).
Kermit	A Columbia University program to transfer files between computers (TCP/IP).
Kernel	The software heart of the operating system.
Keystroke	Typing one character on a keyboard.
Kilobyte	1,024 bytes, or 8,192 bits
KISS	Text messaging abbreviation for "Keep it simple stupid".
KIT	Text messaging abbreviation for "Keep in touch".
KLOC	Thousand (kilo) Lines of Code
KNIM	Text messaging abbreviation for "Know what I mean".
KOTC	Text messaging abbreviation for "Kiss on the cheek".
KQML	Knowledge Query and Manipulation Language: Part of the ARPA Knowledge Sharing Effort.
L2F	Layer 2 Forwarding (TCP/IP)
L2TP	Layer 2 Tunneling Protocol (TCP/IP)
L3F	Layer 3 Forwarding (TCP/IP)
L3TP	Layer 3 Tunneling Protocol (TCP/IP)
L8R	Text messaging abbreviation for "Later".
LAN	Local Area Network
Landing zone	The part of the disk used as a safe area for head parking when the power is off.
LANE	LAN Emulation: Local Area Network Emulation
LANE-NNI	LAN Emulation-Network to Network Interface: Local Area Network Emulation-Network to Network Interface
LANE-UNI	LAN Emulation-User to Network Interface: Local Area Network Emulation-User to Network Interface
LAP	Link Access Procedure
LAPB	Link Access Procedure Balanced (X.25)
LAPD	Link Access Protocol on the D Channel (X.25)
LAPF	Link Access Protocol for Frame-mode Bearer Services
LAPM	Link Access Protocol for Modems
Laptop	A portable PC.
LAT	Local Area and Transport Protocol (DEC)
LATA	Local Access and Transport Area
Latency	The amount of time (in milliseconds) it takes the platter of a hard drive to make a half revolution.
	The amount of time (in milliseconds) it takes a packet of data to move across a network connection.

LAVC	Local Area VAX Cluster (DEC)
LBA	Logical Block Address: Method of accessing the disk via a logical sector number which points to a location on a drive instead of using CHS information.
LBN	Logical Block Number
LCD	Liquid Crystal Display: A low power display, used in Laptops.
LCI	Logical Channel Identifier (X.25)
LCID	Locale Identifier Code
LCP	Link Control Protocol
LD	Text messaging abbreviation for "Later dude".
	Text messaging abbreviation for "Long distance".
LDAP	Lightweight Directory Access Protocol (TCP/IP)
LDP	Label Distribution Protocol (TCP/IP)
	Loader-Debugger Protocol (TCP/IP)
LEC	Local Exchange Carrier
	LAN Emulation Client: Local Area Network Emulation Client
LED	Light Emitting Diode: A solid state electronic device that gives off light when an electric current is present.
Level 1 cache	Fast memory which is part of the processor itself.
Level 2 cache	Cache Memory mounted on the Motherboard.
LFAP	Lightweight Flow Admission Protocol (TCP/IP)
LFN	Long File Name
LID	Language Identifier
LIFO	Last In First Out
LILO	Last In Last Out
Link	See Hyperlink.
LINUX	An open source, UNIX-based operating system developed by Linus Torvalds.
LISP	List processor: A high-level programming language for artificial intelligence developed in 1956 by John McCarthy at MIT.
ListServ	List Server: An Internet program used to subscribe to a mailing list.
LLAP	LocalTalk Link Access Protocol (AppleTalk, Apple)
LLC	Logical Link Control (IEEE 802.2)
LLC2	Logical Link Control 2: Second implementation of LLC.
LMAO	Text messaging abbreviation for "Laughing my ass off".
LMDS	Local Multipoint Distribution Service
LMTP	Local Mail Transfer Protocol (TCP/IP)
LOC	Lines of Code
Login	A combination of information, usually a user ID and password, that authenticates a network users identity.
LOL	Text messaging abbreviation for "Laughing out loud".
LOM	LAN on Motherboard: Local Area Network on Motherboard (Intel)
LOS	Line of Sight
	Loss of Signal
Low-level format	This step connects the drive and controller once physical installation is finished. [XT system - use DOS' debug utility -80 x 86 system - use 80 x 86 advanced diagnostics -IDS system] Caution - A low-level format is usually done at the factory.
LPC	Low Pin Count Bus
LPD	Line Printer Daemon
LPP	Lightweight Presentation Protocol
LPR	Line Printer Remote Protocol (TCP/IP)
LPT	Line Printer Terminal
LS-120	Laser Storage 120-MB: High-capacity floppy disk drive by Imation Corporation.
LSA	Local Security Authority
LT	LaGrande Technology
LTM	Text messaging abbreviation for "Laugh to myself".
LTNS	Text messaging abbreviation for "Long time no see".
LU	Logical Unit (IBM)
LUID	Locally Unique Identifier
Luminance	The brightness of a screen image.
LUN	Logical Unit Number: The units number on a daisy chain. It equals the SCSI ID number.

LYLAB	Text messaging abbreviation for "Love you like a brother".
LYLAS	Text messaging abbreviation for "Love you like a sister".
LZW	Lempel-Ziv-Welch compression algorithm, developed by J. Ziv, A. Lempel and Terry Welch.
M8	Text messaging abbreviation for "Mate".
MAC	Media Access Control (DEC)
	Mandatory Access Control
	Medium Access Control (DEC)
	Message Authentication Code
MACL	Mandatory Access Control List
Mac OS	Operating system used on Apple Macintosh computers. (Apple)
Macro	A memorized series of commands carried out at the request of the user.
Macro virus	See Virus.
MADCAP	Multicast Address Dynamic Client Allocation Protocol (TCP/IP)
Mainframe	An ultra-high-performance computer designed for intense computing.
MAN	Metropolitan Area Network
MAP	Media Access Procedure
	Mobile Application Part (SS7)
	Maintenance Analysis Procedures
	Manufacturing Automation Protocol
MAPI	Mail Application Interface
MARS	Multicast Address Resolution Server
MASC	Multicast Address-Set Claim Protocol (TCP/IP)
MASM	Macro Assembler
MATIP	Mapping of Airline Traffic over IP: Mapping of Airline Traffic over Internet Protocol (TCP/IP)
MAU	Multi-station Access Unit
Mb	Megabit
MB	See Megabyte.
MBCS	Multibyte Character Set
MBGP	Multiprotocol BGP: Multiprotocol Border Gateway Protocol
MBps	Megabytes per second
MBR	Multiple Bit Rate
MB/s	See MBps.
MBS	Maximum Burst Size
Mbus	Message Bus (TCP/IP)
MCA	Micro Channel Architecture: A type of bus introduced in 1987 that is used in most PS/2 models (IBM).
MCB	Map Control Block
MCD	Miniclient Driver
MCI	Multimedia Command Interface: A method for controlling multimedia devices [Windows].
MCL	Motion Control Language (Logosol)
MCM	Multi-Carrier Modulation
MCP	Microsoft Certified Professional (Microsoft)
MCSE	Microsoft Certified System Engineer (Microsoft)
MCT	Modem Compatibility Test
MCU	Microcontroller Unit
MDA	Monochrome Display Adapter
MDF	Main Distribution Frame
MDI	Multiple Document Interface
MDL	Memory Descriptor List
Megabyte	A unit of measure for data storage containing 1,048,576 bytes (1,024 x 1,024).
Megaco	See MGCP.
Megahertz	One million cycles per second: Measure of transmission rate.
Memory	The part of computer where information is stored.
MEMS	Micro-Electro-Mechanical Systems
Menu	A list of options.
Menu bar	In Windows, a bar across the top of the current window (Microsoft).
Merge	Combining two or more files of identical format into a single file.
Meta tag	In HTML, a tag used to store information about a Web page but not displayed in a Web browser (Internet).

MFC	Microsoft Foundation Classes (Microsoft)
MFD	Multifunction Device
MFM	Modified Frequency Modulation
MFM encoding	Modified Frequency Modulation **encoding**: The data encoding method that decreases bit cell size by omitting each clock pulse associated with a bit cell (except those cells holding 0) so that data is stored evenly on a platter. The standard MFM has 17 SPT and 512 bytes per sector.
MGA	Monochrome Graphics Adapter
MGCP	Multimedia Gateway Control Protocol (TCP/IP)
MHz	See Megahertz.
MIB	Management Information Base
MICR	Magnetic Ink Character Recognition
Microprocessor	The semiconductor chip at the heart of all computers, also called a processor.
MIDI	Musical Instrument Digital Interface: A sound standard for computers.
.mil	URL designation for military government organizations (domain name, Internet).
Mil	Unit of linear measurement equal to 0.001 inch.
MIME	Multipurpose Internet Mail Extension: A method of identifying files such that the first packet of information received by a client, contains information about the type of file the server has sent. For example text, audio, movie, postscript, word document, etc.
MIPS	Million Instructions Per Second
Mirror	See Mirror site.
Mirror site	A server providing identical file downloads as a main site (Internet).
MIS	Management Information Services
	Management Information System
	Multimedia Information Sources
MIT	Massachusetts Institute of Technology
MLD	Multicast Listener Discovery for IPv6 (TCP/IP)
MLP	Multilink Procedure (X.25)
MLPPP	Multilink PPP: Multilink Point to Point Protocol
MMA	MIDI Manufacturers Association: Musical Instrument Digital Interface Manufacturers Association
MMC	Multimedia Card
	Multimedia Commands
MMDS	Multipoint Microwave Distribution System
	Multi-channel Multipoint Distribution Service
	Multimedia Data Services
MMJ	Modified Modular Jack
MMP	Multichassis Multilink PPP: Multichassis Multilink Point to Point Protocol
MMX	Multimedia Extensions
MNP	Microcom Networking Protocol (Microcom)
Mobile IP	Mobile Internet Protocol (TCP/IP)
Modem	Modulator / Demodulator: A device that converts electronic signals from analog to digital or digital to analog.
MODULA	A programming language developed by Niklaus Wirth (inventor of PASCAL) at the Swiss Federal Institute of Technology in 1978 as a replacement for PASCAL.
MODULA-2	Second iteration of MODULA by Niklaus Wirth at the Swiss Federal Institute of Technology in 1980.
MODULA-3	Third iteration of MODULA by Luca Cardelli and others at Olivetti and DEC in 1988.
MOP	Maintenance Operations Protocol (DEC)
MORF	Text messaging abbreviation for "Male or female".
MOS	Metal Oxide Semiconductor
	Text messaging abbreviation for "Mother over shoulder".
Mosaic	The original Web browser, developed at the National Center for Supercomputing Applications at the University of Illinois.
MOSPF	Multicast OSPF: Multicast Open Shortest Path First Routing Protocol (TCP/IP)
Motherboard	A computer's main printed circuit board.

Mouse	A pointing device for controlling cursor position and action on the screen.
MOV	Metal Oxide Varistor
MP	Multilink Protocol
MP3	MPEG-1 Audio Layer-3: Moving Picture Experts Group-1 Audio Layer-3: A compressed audio file format.
MPC	Multimedia PC Council
MPDL	Music Parameter Description Language
MPEG	Moving Picture Experts Group
MPEG1	First generation full motion video compression scheme, resolution of 352 x 240 pixels at 30 frames per second.
MPEG2	Second generation full motion video compression scheme, resolution of 720 x 480 pixels at 30 frames per second.
MPEG4	Fourth generation full motion video compression scheme.
MPEG7	Seventh generation full motion video compression scheme.
MPL	Multi-agent Robot Language
	Maximum Packet Lifetime (XNS)
MPLS	Multi-protocol Layer Switching (TCP/IP)
MPOA	Multi-protocol over ATM: Multi-protocol over Asynchronous Transfer Mode
MPP	Message Posting Protocol (TCP/IP)
MPR	Multi-protocol Router
MPTU	Multi-protocol Tenant Unit
MSCS	Microsoft Cluster Server (Microsoft)
MS-DOS	Microsoft Disk Operating System (Microsoft)
MSDP	Multicast Source Discovery Protocol (TCP/IP)
MSN	Microsoft Network (Microsoft)
MTBF	Mean Time Between Failures: Measurement of time (in power-on hours) a drive should last between hardware failures.
MTD	Memory Technology Driver
MTP	Message Transfer Part (SS7)
	Multicast Transport Protocol (TCP/IP)
	Mail Transfer Protocol (TCP/IP)
MTP-2	Message Transfer Part Level 2 (SS7)
MTP-3	Message Transfer Part Level 3 (SS7)
MTSO	Mobile Telephone Switching Office
MTT	Multi-transaction Timer
MTTR	Mean Time to Restore: The average time to repair or service a drive.
Multimedia	A presentation of video, audio, graphics, text & animation by computers & software.
MultiPPP	See MLPP.
Multitasking	Multitasking operating system performs more than one task at a time, using Context Switching, Cooperative and Time-slice multitasking.
MUMPS	Massachusetts General Hospital Utility Multi-programming System: A programming language for databases developed in the hospital's animal lab by Octo Barnett in 1969.
MUPDATE	Mailbox Update Distributed Mailbox Database Protocol (TCP/IP)
.museum	URL designation for the museum community (domain name, Internet).
MUSM	Text messaging abbreviation for "Miss you so much".
MUX	Multiplexer
MVL	Multiple Virtual Line
MYOB	Text messaging abbreviation for "Mind your own business".
MZAP	Multicast-Scope Zone Announcement Protocol
N00B	Text messaging abbreviation for "Newbie".
NAK	Negative Acknowledgment
.name	URL designation for individuals (domain name, Internet).
NAP	National Attachment Point: Exchange points that enable data to be exchanged between ISPs. The 4 USA locations are: New York, Chicago, Washington, DC, and San Francisco.
NARP	NBMA Address Resolution Protocol: Non-broadcast, Multi Access Address Resolution Protocol (TCP/IP)
Narrow	Term used to indicate a SCSI device for a 8-bit data path.
NAS	Network Attached Storage
	Network Application Support (DEC)

	Network Access Server
	NetNews Administration System(TCP/IP)
NAT	Network Address Translation
NAU	Network Addressable Unit (IBM)
NAWK	New AWK: A new version of the AWK programming language.
NBD	Text messaging abbreviation for "No big deal".
NBMA	Non-broadcast, Multi Access
NBP	Name Binding Protocol (AppleTalk, Apple)
NBSS	NetBIOS Session Service: Network Basic Input/Output Services Session Service
NCP	Network Control Program
	Network Control Panel
	Network Control Processor
	Network Control Protocol
	NetWare Core Protocol (Novell)
	Not Copy Protected
NCSA	National Center for Supercomputing Applications
	National Computer Security Association
NCSA Mosaic	See Mosaic.
NDIS	Network Driver Interface Specification
	Network Device Interface Specification
NDMP	Network Data Management Protocol
NDS	NetWare Directory Services (Novell)
NE1000	Ethernet standard for 8-bit NICs.
NE2000	Ethernet standard for 16-bit NICs.
NEBS	Network Equipment Building Standards
.net	URL designation for networks (domain name, Internet).
NetBEUI	NetBIOS Extended User Interface: Network Basic Input/Output Services Extended User Interface
NetBIOS	Network Basic Input/Output Services
NetBLT	Network Block Transport (TCP/IP)
Netiquette	Generally acceptable rules of online behavior associated with the Internet.
NetWare	Novell Network Operating System (Novell)
Network	A group of two or more interconnected computers.
Newbie	A new user of any technology, a newcomer.
Newsgroup	A Internet group focused on a common discussion topic (Internet).
NEXT	Near End Cross (X) Talk
NFILE	New File Protocol (TCP/IP)
NFM	Text messaging abbreviation for "None for me".
	Text messaging abbreviation for "Not for me".
NFS	Network File System (TCP/IP)
NHRP	Next Hop Resolution Protocol
NIC	Network Interface Card
NICE	Network Information and Control Exchange (DEC)
NID	Network Interface Device
NIMBY	Text messaging abbreviation for "Not in my back yard".
NIS	Network Information Services
NIST	National Institute of Standards and Technology
NLM	NetWare Loadable Module (Novell)
NLS	National Language Support
NLSP	NetWare Link Services Protocol (Novell)
NLT	Text messaging abbreviation for "No later than".
NM	Text messaging abbreviation for "Nothing much".
	Text messaging abbreviation for "Never mind".
NMH	Text messaging abbreviation for "Not much here".
NMI	Non-maskable Interrupt
NMS	Network Management System (Novell)
NNI	Network to Network Interface
NNTP	Network News Transfer Protocol (TCP/IP)
Node	Any device connected to a network.
NOS	Network Operating System
NOYB	Text messaging abbreviation for "None of your business".
NP	Text messaging abbreviation for "No problem".

NRN	Text messaging abbreviation for "No reply necessary".
	Text messaging abbreviation for "No response necessary".
NRZ	Non-return to Zero: The data-encoding strategy where a pattern of pulses is converted into half pulses without any information loss.
NRZ-I	Non-return to Zero Inverse
NRZ-L	Non-return to Zero Level
NRZ-M	Non-return to Zero Mark
NRZ-S	Non-return to Zero Space
NS BASIC	A version of BASIC for handheld devices.
NSP	Network Service Provider
	Network Service Protocol (DEC)
NTFS	NT File System (Microsoft)
NTP	Network Time Protocol (TCP/IP)
NTSC	National Television System Committee (US)
NVP	Network Voice Protocol (TCP/IP)
NVRAM	Non-volatile Random Access Memory
NVS	Text messaging abbreviation for "Not very smart".
NW	Text messaging abbreviation for "No way".
OBERON	A programming language developed by Niklaus Wirth and Jurg Gutknecht at the Swiss Federal Institute of Technology in 1985 as an object-oriented language based on MODULA.
OBERON-2	Second iteration of OBERON.
OBMC	Overlapped Block Motion Compensation: Part of the H.263 standard.
OC	Optical Carrier. See OC-x.
OC-1	Optical Carrier - 1: Optical carrier at 51.84 Mbps. See OC-x.
OC-3	Optical Carrier - 3: Optical carrier at 155.52 Mbps. See OC-x.
OC-6	Optical Carrier - 6: Optical carrier at 311.04 Mbps. See OC-x.
OC-9	Optical Carrier - 9: Optical carrier at 466.56 Mbps. See OC-x.
OC-12	Optical Carrier -12: Optical carrier at 622.08 Mbps. See OC-x.
OC-24	Optical Carrier -24: Optical carrier at 1.24416 Gbps. See OC-x.
OC-48	Optical Carrier -48: Optical carrier at 2.48832 Gbps. See OC-x.
OCR	Optical Character Recognition
Octal	A Base 8 numbering system. 10 in octal is equivalent to 8 in decimal.
OC-x	Optical Carrier - Speed (x): The base speed unit found in SONET technology. Speed increases in increments of 51.84 Mbps, so OC-1 is 51.84 Mbps and OC-6 is 331.04 Mbps (6 times 51.84).
ODBC	Open Database Connectivity: A Windows interface used by application programs to access databases (Microsoft).
ODETTE-FTP	ODETTE File Transfer Protocol: Organization for Data Exchange by Tele-Transmission in Europe File Transfer Protocol (TCP/IP)
OEM	Original Equipment Manufacturer: Term which refers to company that makes a product and sells it to a reseller.
OEMCP	OEM Code Page: Original Equipment Manufacturer Code Page
OGL	See OpenGL
OIC	Text messaging abbreviation for "Oh, I see".
OLE	Object Linking and Embedding: Information created in one application program can be displayed in another application program.
OLSR	Optimized Link State Routing Protocol (TCP/IP)
OMG	Object Management Group
	Text messaging abbreviation for "Oh, my goodness".
OMW	Text messaging abbreviation for "On my way".
OO	Text messaging abbreviation for "Over and out".
OOH	Text messaging abbreviation for "Out of here".
OOP	Object Oriented Programming
OOTD	Text messaging abbreviation for "One of these days".
OpenGL	Open Graphics Library: A 2-D and 3-D graphics language (Silicon Graphics).
Open HCI	Open Host Controller Interface (Intel)
Open source	Software whose original source code has been released to the general public to be developed openly.
Operating System	Computer software that communicates with system hardware.
OPX	Off Premise Extension
ORB	Object Request Broker (Microsoft)
.org	URL designation for non-profit organizations (domain name, Internet).

OS	See Operating System.
OS/2	Operating System/2 (IBM)
OS/2 Warp	Operating System/2 with built-in Internet and Network support (IBM).
OSD	On Screen Display
	Open Source Development
	On Software Description
	On Software Distribution
OSDL	Open Source Development Labs
OSI	Open System Interface
	Open System Interconnect
	Open Switching Interval
OSP	Outside Plant
OSPF	Open Shortest Path First Routing Protocol (TCP/IP)
OTB	Text messaging abbreviation for "Off to bed".
OTL	Text messaging abbreviation for "Out to lunch".
OTOH	Text messaging abbreviation for "On the other hand".
OTP	Text messaging abbreviation for "On the phone".
OTTOMH	Text messaging abbreviation for "Off the top of my head".
OTW	Text messaging abbreviation for "Off to work".
OUI	Organizational Unique Identifier
PABX	Private Automatic Branch Exchange
Packet	A unit of information.
PAD	Packet Assembler/Disassembler (X.25)
PAL	Phase Alternation Line
Palm	Hand-held computer.
Page impression	Occurs every time a Web Page is displayed by someone using the Internet.
PAN	Personal Area Network
PAP	Password Authentication Protocol
	Printer Access Protocol (AppleTalk, Apple)
Parallel port	A device that transmits data to peripherals 8 bits at a time instead of 1 bit at a time as a serial port does. Usually designated as LPT1, LPT2, etc.
Parity	Computer error recognition method where there is a 9th bit that accompanies every byte in a system RAM; therefore, if a bit is stored or read wrong the parity will be wrong so the PC realizes there is an error.
Parse	To break text up into smaller parts.
Partition	Sector of a hard drive, divides the physical hard drive into logical volumes, maximum of 4 partitions per disk.
PASCAL	A high-level programming language developed by Niklaus Wirth at the Swiss Federal Institute of Technology in 1970 and named for the 17th century French mathematician Blaise Pascal.
PBX	Private Branch Exchange
PC	Personal Computer
PCB	Printed Circuit Board
PCD	Plotter Characterization Data
PCI	Peripheral Component Interconnect: A bus used with most Pentium and 486 systems (Intel).
	Personal Computer Interface
PCI-X	PCI Extended: Peripheral Component Interconnect Extended
PCL	Printer Control Language: A page description language developed by Hewlett Packard. See HPPCL (Hewlett Packard).
PCM	Pulse Code Modulation
PCmail	See DMSP.
PCMCIA	Personal Computer Memory Card International Association: An industry group that sets standards for the interconnection between plug-in modules and electronic systems.
PCOS	Personal Computer Operating System (IBM)
PCR	Processor Control Region
	Peak Cell Rate
PCS	Personal Communications Service
	Personal Communications System
PCT	Private Communication Technology
PDA	Personal Digital Assistant

PDC	Primary Domain Controller
PDEV	Physical Device
PDF	Portable Document Format (Adobe)
PDL	Page Description Language: A programming language for the printed page that describes the layout and content of the page.
PDN	Public Data Network
PDO	Physical Device Object
PDQ	Text messaging abbreviation for "Pretty darn quick".
PDU	Protocol Data Unit (DEC)
Pel	See Pixel.
PEP	Packet Exchange Protocol (XNS)
Peripheral	The equipment attached to the computer (i.e., modem, printer).
PERL	Practical Extraction and Report Language: An interpretive scripting programming language for processing text (UNIX) developed by Larry Wall in 1987.
Petabyte	A unit of measure for data storage, approximately a thousand terabytes.
Petaflops	A measure of computer computational speed, a thousand-trillion floating-point operations per second.
PFC	Personal Filing Cabinet
PFN	Page Frame Number
PGAWK	A profiling version of the AWK programming language.
PGM	Pragmatic General Multicast Protocol (TCP/IP)
PHP	Personal Home Page: An HTML-embedded Web scripting language, also known as PHP: Hypertext Preprocessor.
	PHP Hypertext Preprocessor: An open-source, server-side HTML-embedded scripting language based on PERL designed by Rasmus Lerdorf in 1994.
PIM	Personal Information Manager: An application program to manage daily activities.
	Protocol Independent Multicast (TCP/IP)
PIM-DM	Protocol Independent Multicast-Dense Mode (TCP/IP)
PIM-SM	Protocol Independent Multicast-Sparse Mode (TCP/IP)
PINE	Program for Internet News and E-mail
Ping	A test to see if a computer on the Internet is working.
PING	Packet Internet Groper: A program for communications testing between Internet computers.
PIO	Parallel Input/Output
	Programmed Input/Output
	Processor Input/Output: Data transfer between memory and peripherals by an input/output command without communicating with the hard drive.
Pitch	See CPI.
Pixel	Pic(x)ture element or Picture element: The smallest element of information that programs can display or print.
PJL	Printer Job Language (Hewlett-Packard)
PKI	Public Key Infrastructure
PKUnzip	A DOS based data decompression utility (PKWare).
PKZip	A DOS based data compression utility (PKWare).
PLA	Programmable Logic Array
Plated thin film disks	
	A magnetic disk memory media whose surface is coated with metallic alloy instead of oxide.
Platter	A part of the hard disk which is usually made of aluminum alloy (sometimes ceramic or glass) and has data recorded on it - usually between 2-8 platters per hard disk - but can be a maximum of 14. Each platter on a hard disk contains tracks.
PLD	Programmable Logic Device
PLL	Phase Lock Loop
	Phase Locked Loop
PLMK	Text messaging abbreviation for "Please let me know".
PLP	Packet Layer Protocol (X.25)

PL/SQL	Procedural Language / SQL: Procedural Language / Structured Query Language: An extended SQL by Oracle Corporation based upon ADA (Oracle).
Plug-in	A software add-on that adds functionality to a program.
Plug and Play	A concept of automatically adding and configuring new components to a computer (Microsoft).
Plug and Play SCSI	See SCAM.
PLZ	Text messaging abbreviation for "Please".
PM	Power Management
PME	Power Management Event
PMFI	Text messaging abbreviation for "Pardon me for interrupting".
PMFJI	Text messaging abbreviation for "Pardon me for jumping in".
PNG	Portable Network Graphic
PNNI	Private Network-to-Network Interface
PnP	Plug and Play: See Plug and Play
PNP	Plug and Play: See Plug and Play
POAHF	Text messaging abbreviation for "Put on a happy face".
PON	Passive Optical Network
POP	Post Office Protocol (TCP/IP)
	Point of Presence
POP2	Post Office Protocol version 2 (TCP/IP)
POP3	Post Office Protocol version 3 (TCP/IP)
Pop-up menu	In Windows, a menu that opens vertically or horizontally displaying context-related options (Microsoft).
Port	Internet port: A number that indicates which protocol an Internet server uses.
	Hardware port: A hardware plug where devices can be attached to a computer.
	Port or Porting: Editing a program's code so that it can run on another platform.
Portal	A Web page with user selected information and links for easily repeated access to the Internet.
POS	Text messaging abbreviation for "Parent over shoulder".
POSIX	Portable Operating System Interface for UNIX (UNIX)
POST	Power-On Self Test: The series of system tests that the BIOS runs at power-up where errors are recognized and reported with an error message or a beep sound stating everything checks out "okay."
PostScript	A page description language developed by John Warnock and others at Adobe Systems in 1982 (Adobe).
POTS	Plain Old Telephone Service
PPD	PostScript Printer Description
PPDN	Public Packet-switched Data Network
PPGA	Plastic Pin Grid Array
P Picture	Predictive-coded Picture
PPL	Text messaging abbreviation for "People".
PPM	Pages Per Minute: The rate at which a printer can print.
PPP	Point to Point Protocol: A standard for using a modem & telephone line to connect to the Internet using TCP/IP (Internet).
PPPoA	Point to Point Protocol over ATM: Point to Point Protocol over Asynchronous Transfer Mode (Internet)
PPPoE	Point to Point Protocol over Ethernet (Internet)
PPTP	Point to Point Tunneling Protocol (TCP/IP)
PQ	Priority Queuing
PRI	Primary Rate Interface: See ISDN PRI.
Primary cache	Level 1 cache.
.pro	URL designation for certified professionals such as doctors, engineers, accounts, etc. (domain name, Internet).
PROLOG	Programming logic: A high-level programming language for artificial intelligence created by Alain Colmerauer in 1972.
Program	A series of instructions processed by a computer.
Program language	A set of standardized rules used to instruct a computer to execute specific operations.
PROM	Programmable Read - Only Memory

Glossary

Protocol	A standard set of rules & conditions for a process that performs a function.
Proxy server	Often a security function controlling access to a main server.
PRW	Text messaging abbreviation for "Parents are watching".
	Text messaging abbreviation for "People are watching".
PSD	Power Spectral Density
PSE	Packet-Switching Exchange (X.25)
PSDT	Persistent System Description Table
PSN	Packet Switched Network (X.25)
	Processor Serial Number
	Private Switched Network
PSTN	Public Switched Telephone Network
PTE	Page Table Entry
PTI	Packet Type Identifier (X.25)
PTL	Text messaging abbreviation for "Praise the Lord".
PTP	Performance Transparency Protocol (TCP/IP)
PTT	Post, Telephone and Telegraph
PU	Text messaging abbreviation for "That stinks".
PUA	Private Use Area
Puck	An input device, like a mouse, with a magnifying glass with cross-hairs.
Pull-down menu	See Pop-up menu.
Pulse	An older method of telephone ringing now often replaced by a tone system.
Push technology	An Internet technology that sends information to users before they request it.
PVC	Permanent Virtual Circuit (X.25)
PWDGEN	Password Generator Protocol (TCP/IP)
PWS	Personal Web Server (Microsoft)
PXE	Pre-boot Execution Environment
PXT	Text messaging abbreviation for "Please explain that".
PYTHON	An interpreted, interactive, object-oriented programming language developed in 1991 by Guido van Rossum and named for the television show Monty Python's Flying Circus.
QAM	Quadrature Amplitude Modulation
QBASIC	Quick BASIC: The version of the BASIC language that shipped with DOS and Windows95.
QBE	Query By Example: A search method used by search engines.
QCIF	Quarter Common Intermediate Format
QEMM	Quarterdeck Extended Memory Manager
QIC	Quarter-Inch Cartridge: A standard for tape drives.
QIC 11	Quarter-Inch Cartridge 11: 4 track, 45 MB, DC600A tape.
QIC 24	Quarter-Inch Cartridge 24: 9 track, 60 MB, DC600A tape.
QIC 120	Quarter-Inch Cartridge 120: 15 track, 125 MB, DC6150 tape.
QIC 150	Quarter-Inch Cartridge 150: 18 track, 150 MB, DC6150 tape.
QIC 525	Quarter-Inch Cartridge 525: 26 track, 525 MB, DC6525 tape.
QIC 1000	Quarter-Inch Cartridge 1000: 30 track, 1.0 GB, DC9100 tape.
QIK	Text messaging abbreviation for "Quick".
QLLC	Qualified LLC: Qualified Logical Link Control (IBM, IEEE 802.2)
QoS	Quality of Service
QPSK	Quadrature Phase Shift Keying Modulation
QTM	Quadratic Texture Mapping
QTVR	QuickTime Virtual Reality (Apple)
Queue	A list of operations waiting to be processed by a computer.
QuickTime	A method of storing movie and audio files in a digital format.
QWERTY	A term used to describe a standard keyboard because the first six keys on the left end of the first row are Q-W-E-R-T-Y.
QXGA	Quantum Extended Graphics Array
RA-ADSL	See RADSL.
RAD	Rapid Application Development
Radial	Attaching multiple drives to a controller.
RADIUS	Remote Authentication Dial-In User Service (TCP/IP)
	Remote Access Dial-In User Service
	Remote Authorization Dial-In User Service

Glossary

RADSL	Rate Adaptive Asymmetric Digital Subscriber Line: Asymmetric service, speeds of 600 Kbps to 8 Mbps downstream, 128 Kbps to 1 Mbps upstream, with simultaneous voice service.
RAID	Redundant Array of Inexpensive Disks: Method of combining two or more drives together to obtain more speed or better data protection. The four major types of RAID are striping, mirroring, parity using another disk for error protection, and parity using several disks for error protection. The hard drives are placed in a central cabinet as modules.
RAM	Random Access Memory: A short-term data storage area where information is placed prior to being stored on the disk so that it can be accessed at an instant by the microprocessor.
RAMDAC	Random Access Memory Digital-to-Analog Converter
RAP	Internet Route Access Protocol (TCP/IP)
RAPI	Remote API: Remote Application Programming Interface (Microsoft)
RARP	Reverse ARP: Reverse Address Resolution Protocol (TCP/IP)
RAS	Remote Access Server (Microsoft)
	Remote Access Service (Microsoft)
	Row Address Select
	Row Address Strobe
	Remote Announcing System
	Random Access Storage
RBOC	Regional Bell Operating Company
RBSM	Text messaging abbreviation for "Reply by snail mail".
RDBMS	Relational Database Management System
RDP	Reliable Data Protocol (TCP/IP)
RDR	Redirector
	Remote Data Recovery
RDRAM	Rambus Dynamic Random Access Memory
Recalibrate	A disk drive function to return heads to track zero.
Registry	The database for configuration information about installed software. It consists of six parts: HKEY_User, HKEY_Current_User, HKEY_Current_Configuration, HKEY_Classes_Root, HKEY_Local_Machine and HKEY_Dyn_Data (Microsoft).
REN	Ringer Equivalence Number
Resolution	A term describing how many pixels can be displayed (monitor) or printed (printer).
REXX	Restructured Extended Executor: A block-structured, scripting procedural language developed by Mike Cowlishaw in 1979 at IBM UK Laboratories and included with IBM operating systems (IBM).
RF	Radio Frequency
RFC	Request For Comments
RG	Radio Grade: Grade for coaxial cable.
RG6	75 ohm coaxial cable.
RG8	50 ohm coaxial cable.
RG9	75 ohm coaxial cable.
RG11	75 ohm coaxial cable.
RG58	50 ohm coaxial cable.
RG59	75 ohm coaxial cable.
RG174	50 ohm coaxial cable.
RGB	Red Green Blue
RGMP	Router-Port Group Management Protocol
Ribbon cable	A flat electrical cable of parallel wires.
RIFF	Resource Interchange File Format
RIMM	Rambus Inline Memory Module
Ring	The telephone wire carrying the negative charge.
Ring network	A LAN in which all nodes are connected in a closed loop.
RIP	Remote Imaging Protocol
	Raster-Image Processor
	Routing Information Protocol (XNS)
RIPng	RIP for IPv6: Remote Imaging Protocol for Internet Protocol version 6 (TCP/IP)
RIPX	Routing Information Protocol Exchange (Novell)
RISC	Reduced Instruction Set Computing: A microprocessor architecture.
RJ	Registered Jack: Designation for telephone jacks. See Page 517.

Glossary

RJ-11	Registered Jack - 11: Telephone jack. See Page 517.
RJ-45	Registered Jack - 45: Telephone jack. See Page 517.
RL	Text messaging abbreviation for "Real life".
RLE	Run Length Encoded
RLL	Run Length Limited: A type of hard-disk controller that increases storage by 50% over MFM by creating 25 or 26 sectors per track (instead of the usual 17 sectors per track) by decreasing level of data-checking information that is stored on disk. RLL-types are RLL 1,7: 25% larger capacity than MFM encoding; RLL 2,7: 50% larger capacity than MFM encoding; and RLL 3,9 which doubles the storage capacity over MFM encoding. RLL 3,9 is also called ARLL.
RLOGIN	Remote Login (TCP/IP)
RLP	Resource Location Protocol (TCP/IP)
RMA	Return Material Authorization
— Return to Manufacturer Authorization	
RMCP	Remote Mail Checking Protocol (TCP/IP)
RME	Text messaging abbreviation for "Rolling my eyes".
RMI	Remote Method Invocation (Sun)
— Remote Messaging Interface	
RMON	Remote Monitoring
RNA	Remote Network Access
RNDIS	Remote NDIS: Remote Network Driver Interface Specification
RNP	Text messaging abbreviation for "Really nice person".
ROFL	See ROTFL.
ROM	Read-Only Memory
Root directory	The master directory of the hard or floppy disk that holds FAT and operating system boot files.
ROP	Raster Operation
— RISC Operation: Reduced Instruction Set Computing Operation	
— Remote Operation	
ROSE	Remote Operation Service Element
Rotational speed	Media spin rate which is usually 3,500 RPM for 5.25 inch or 3.5 inch Winchester drives.
ROTFL	Text messaging abbreviation for "Rolling on the floor laughing".
Router	A hardware device that routes data from a LAN to another network connection.
RPC	Remote Procedure Call Protocol (Sun)
RPG	Report Program Generator: A database or text-based programming language developed by IBM in 1965 for punch card machines (IBM).
RS-232	An industry standard for the transmission of data.
RSDP	Root System Description Pointer
RSDT	Root System Description Table
RSIP	Realm Specific IP: Realm Specific Internet Protocol (TCP/IP)
RSN	Text messaging abbreviation for "Real soon now".
RSoP	Resultant Set of Policy (Microsoft)
RSSI	Receive Signal Strength Indication
RSVP	Resource Reservation Protocol (TCP/IP)
RSVP-TE	RSVP-Traffic Engineering: Resource Reservation Protocol-Traffic Engineering
RT	Remote Terminal
— Real Time	
— RISC Technology: Reduced Instruction Set Computing Technology	
— Run Time	
RTCP	RTP Control Protocol: Real-time Transport Control Protocol (TCP/IP)
RTF	Rich Text Format: A standardized text file format (Microsoft).
RTFM	Text messaging abbreviation for "Read the flipping manual".
RTL	Run-Time Library
RTL routines	Run-Time Library routines
RTMP	Routing Table Maintenance Protocol (AppleTalk, Apple)
RTP	Real Time Transport Protocol (TCP/IP)
RTS	Request To Send
RTS/CTS	Request To Send/Clear To Send
RTSE	Reliable Transfer Service Element

Glossary

RTSP	Real Time Streaming Protocol (TCP/IP)
RTS threshold	Request To Send **threshold**: Packet size that controls the RTS/CTS transaction.
RUDP	Reliable **UDP**: Reliable User Datagram Protocol
Runtime	Term used by programmers to indicate that a program is running.
Runtime error	An error that occurs while the program is running.
RWC	Reduced Write Current: The input signal that lessens the degree of write current at the drive head.
RWhois	Referral **Whois** Protocol (TCP/IP)
RZ	Return to Zero
RZ-AMI	Return to Zero - Alternate Mark Inversion
S56KDS	Switched **56** Kbps Digital Service
SA-400 interface	Industry standard floppy interface.
SAAJ	SOAP with Attachments API for JAVA: Simple Object Access Protocol with Attachments Application Programming Interface for JAVA (JAVA)
SACL	System Access Control List
SACRED	Securely Available Credentials (TCP/IP)
SAF	Security Authentication Facility
	— Support Automation Framework (Microsoft)
	— Service Access Facility (Sun)
SAM	Serial Access Memory
	— Single Application Mode (Microsoft)
	— Sequential Access Method
	— Security Account Manager (Microsoft)
	— Synchronous Access Mode
SAMI	Synchronized Accessible Media Interchange: An XML-based language.
SAML	Security Assertion Markup Language
SAN	Storage Area Network
	— System Area Network
SAP	Secondary Audio Program (NTSC)
	Service Access Point (DEC)
	Service Advertising Protocol (Novell)
	Session Announcement Protocol (Internet)
SAS	Serial Attached SCSI: Serial Attached Small Computer System Interface
SBC	Single Board Computer
SBCS	Single-Byte Character Set
SBS	Smart Battery Specification (Intel, Duracell, Energizer, Fujitsu, et al)
	Small Business Server (Microsoft)
	Small Business Suite (Novell)
SBST	Smart Battery Subsystem Table
SBP	Serial Bus Protocol
SCA	Single Connector Attachment: Way to connect drive modules to the cabinet in SCSI RAID systems.
Scalable	Expandable software & hardware.
SCAM	SCSI Configuration Automatically: Small Computer System Interface Configuration Automatically
SCCP	Skinny Client Control Protocol (Internet)
	Signaling Connection Control Part (SS7)
SCI	System Control Interrupt
	Supply Chain Intelligence
	Scalable Coherent Interface
	Serial Communications Interface
SCP	Save Cursor Position
	Service Control Point
	System Control Program
	System Control Process
	System Control Protocol
	Session Control Protocol (DEC)
SCR	Sustained Cell Rate
Screen name	A term specific to AOL that denotes the name of the user.
Script	A series of program instructions.
SCSI	Small Computer System Interface: A standard bus developed in 1970s by Shugart for high-speed connections to peripherals. A SCSI allows

up to seven peripherals to communicate in a daisy-chain with a PC, does most of the interfacing, and uses a wide ribbon cable and 50-pin connector.

SCSI-1 .... SCSI using an 8-bit bus, supports data transfer speeds of 4 MBps.
SCSI-2 .... A bus that can carry 32 bits because it has a wider cable than the SCSI-1 and this allows data to transfer twice as fast.
SCSI-3 .... SCSI using a 16-bit bus, supports data transfer speeds of 40 MBps.
SCTP .... Stream Control Transmission Protocol (TCP/IP)
SDE .... Secure Data Exchange
SDDV .... Standard Definition Digital Video
SDH .... Synchronous Digital Hierarchy
SDK .... Software Development Kit (Microsoft)
SDLC .... Synchronous Data Link Control
SDP .... Session Description Protocol (Internet)
SDRAM .... Synchronous DRAM: Synchronous Dynamic Random Access Memory
SDRP .... Source Demand Routing Protocol (TCP/IP)
SDSL .... Symmetric Digital Subscriber Line: Two-way speeds of 768 Kbps.
— Single-line Digital Subscriber Line
Search engine .... Internet services for finding Web sites with particular information.
SECAM .... Sequentiel Couleur avec Memoire (Sequential Color with Memory): Video color standard used in parts of Europe.
Secondary cache .... A term for Level 2 Cache.
Sector .... A chunk of stored data that is one section of track.
Sector header .... The address portion of a sector that holds three numbers: head, cylinder and physical sector numbers.
Sector sparing .... Method of decreasing the capacity of a drive by decreasing the number of sectors on each track by one and then putting defect information on it.
Seek .... Radial movement of the heads to a specific cylinder or track address.
Seek time .... Time required for the heads to move between current location and where needed data is stored on the track.
SEH .... Structured Exception Handling
Send .... Message Send Protocol version 2 (TCP/IP)
SEQUEL .... Structured English Query Language: Original SQL developed by IBM in the mid-70s (IBM).
SER .... Serialization (Novell)
Serial transmission .... Sending signals one after another over a single wire, like moving beads on a string.
Server .... A computer that serves information and software to the Internet community.
SES .... Solution Exchange Standard
SFD .... SCSI Filter Driver: Small Computer System Interface Filter Driver
— Start Frame Delimiter
SFF .... Small Form Factor
SFP .... System File Protection (Windows)
S-frame .... Supervisory frame (X.25)
SFTP .... Simple FTP: Simple File Transfer Protocol (TCP/IP)
SGML .... Standard Generalized Markup Language: An international standard, an encoding scheme for creating textual information.
SGMP .... Simple Gateway Monitoring Protocol (TCP/IP)
SGRAM .... Synchronous Graphics Random Access Memory
Shareware .... Software that you can try for free but pay for if you used on a regular basis.
SHDSL .... Symmetric High-bit Rate Digital Subscriber Loop: Data rates from 192 Kbps to 2.32 Mbps.
Shout .... Text messaging term for sending text in all Upper Case.
S-HTTP .... Secure HTTP: See HTTPS.
SICNR .... Text messaging abbreviation for "Sorry I could not resist".
SID .... Server Identifier
— Service Identifier
— Security Identifier
— Stream Identifier
— System Identifier
— Subsystem Identifier

— Serial Input Data
— Station Identification (AT&T)

SIFT/UFT ················· Sender-Initiated File Transfer/Unsolicited File Transfer Protocol
(TCP/IP)
SIG ····························· Special Interest Group
SIG2R ························ Text messaging abbreviation for "Sorry I've got to run".
SIGTR ························ Text messaging abbreviation for "Sorry I've got to run".
SIMD ························· Single Instruction Multiple Data (Intel)
SIMM ························· Single Inline Memory Module: A small circuit board that holds memory
chips.
SIMULA ····················· An object-oriented programming language developed in 1962 by
Ole-Johan Dahl and Kristen Nygaard at the Norwegian Computing
Center.
Single-ended ·········· There is a significant difference between the signal and the ground in
this type of signal transmission.
SIP ··························· Single In-line Package
— Session Initiation Protocol (TCP/IP)
SIR ···························· Serial Infrared (Hewlett-Packard)
SIS ···························· Text messaging abbreviation for "Snickering in silence".
SIT ···························· Special Information Tone
Site ··························· A group of associated Web pages.
Skin ·························· Programming term referring to a program's user interface and how it
appears to the user.
SKIP ························· Simple Key Management for Internet Protocols (TCP/IP)
Slack space ············ Area at the end of a cluster that does not have data stored in it.
SLAP ························ Text messaging abbreviation for "Sounds like a plan".
Slashdot ·················· Term referring to the effect of Internet traffic volume on a server. A
server has been "slashdotted" if a sudden traffic volume increase
causes the server to be unreachable.
SLDRAM ··················· Synchronous Link DRAM: Synchronous Link Dynamic Random Access
Memory
SLDSL ······················ See SDSL.
SLIP ·························· Serial Line IP: Serial Line Internet Protocol (Internet)
SLP ··························· Service Location Protocol (TCP/IP)
— See SLIP.
SMALLTALK ············· An object-oriented programming language developed at Xerox Corpo-
ration by Alan Kay and the Xerox Software Concepts Group in 1972
(Xerox).
SMART ······················ Self-Monitoring Analysis And Reporting Technology (Microsoft)
SMB ·························· Server Message Block Protocol (IBM)
SMBIOS ···················· System Management BIOS: System Management Basic Input/Output
System
SMBP ························ See SMB.
SMBus ······················ System Management Bus
SMD ·························· Surface Mount Device
SMDS ························ Switched Multimegabit Data Service
SMHID ······················ Text messaging abbreviation for "Scratching my head in disbelief".
SMI ··························· System Management Interrupt
— Structure of Management Information
— Static Memory Interface
S/MIME ····················· Secure/Multipurpose Internet Mail Extension
SMP ·························· Symmetric Multiprocessor
— Simple Management Protocol
— Symmetric Multiprocessing
SMPTE ······················ Society of Motion Picture and Television Engineers
SMPTE time code ··· Society of Motion Picture and Television Engineers time code
SMS ·························· Short Message Service (Microsoft)
— Systems Management Server (Microsoft)
SMT ·························· Surface-Mount Technology
SMTP ························ Simple Mail Transfer Protocol (TCP/IP)
SMUX ························ SNMP Multiplexing Protocol: Simple Network Management Protocol
Multiplexing Protocol (TCP/IP)
SNA ·························· Systems Network Architecture (IBM)
SNAP ························ Sub-network Access Protocol (Internet)

Snail mail	Postal Service Mail
SNMP	**S**imple **N**etwork **M**anagement **P**rotocol (TCP/IP)
SNPP	**S**imple **N**etwork **P**aging **P**rotocol (TCP/IP)
SNPPv2	**S**imple **N**etwork **P**aging **P**rotocol **v**ersion **2** (TCP/IP)
SNPPv3	**S**imple **N**etwork **P**aging **P**rotocol **v**ersion **3** (TCP/IP)
SNR	**S**ignal-to-**N**oise **R**atio
SNTP	**S**imple **N**etwork **T**ime **P**rotocol (TCP/IP)
SO	**S**ervice **O**ffice
— Serial Output	
SOAP	**S**imple **O**bject **A**ccess **P**rotocol (Microsoft)
SOCKS	**S**ocket **S**erver **P**rotocol (TCP/IP)
SO/CO	**S**ervice **O**ffice/**C**entral **O**ffice
Software	A computer program, also known as an Application.
Software RAID	**Software R**edundant **A**rray of **I**nexpensive **D**isks: Using software to control the array.
SoHo	**S**mall **O**ffice **H**ome **O**ffice
SOMY	Text messaging abbreviation for "Sick of me yet".
SONET	**S**ynchronous **O**ptical **Net**work
SOTMG	Text messaging abbreviation for "Short of time, must go".
Source code	HTML code for a Web Page.
SP	**S**ervice **P**atch
— Stack Page	
— Service Pack (IBM & Microsoft)	
— Stack Pointer	
— Service Provider	
— Signaling Point	
Spam	Nuisance Internet e-mail advertising sent to many users.
SPI	**S**ervice **P**rovider **I**nterface
— SCSI Parallel Interface: Small Computer System Interface Parallel Interface	
— Security Parameter Index	
— Stateful Packet Inspection	
SPID	**S**ervice **P**rofile **Id**entifier
Spider	An automated search engine information gathering program that collects Web page data.
Spindle	Hub structure to which disks are attached. It is controlled by signals that cause the hub structure to rotate the platters at a constant speed.
Spindle motor	Motor that makes the platters spin at a usual rate of 3,600 RPM (some models at 4,800 -7,200 RPM).
Spindle motor ground strap	
	Older model hard drives have this strap attached to the circuit board which is used to press against the spindle motor to decrease static and sometimes causes a scraping or high pitched drive noise that can be eliminated by oiling.
Splitter	A device designed to use one connection as two.
SPK	Text messaging abbreviation for "Speak".
SPLD	**S**imple **P**rogrammable **L**ogic **D**evice
SPOT	**S**mart **P**ersonal **O**bject **T**echnology (Microsoft)
SPP	**S**equenced **P**acket **P**rotocol (XNS)
SPST	Text messaging abbreviation for "Same place, same time".
SPX	**S**equenced **P**acket E**x**change (Novell)
SQL	**S**tructured **Q**uery **L**anguage: A standardized language for database queries created by IBM in 1979 (IBM).
SRAM	**S**tatic **RAM**: Static Random Access Memory
SRB	**S**CSI **R**equest **B**lock: Small Computer System Interface Request Block
— Service Request Block	
— Stream Request Block	
— Source-Route Bridge	
SRTCP	**S**ecure **RTP** **C**ontrol **P**rotocol: Secure Real-time Transport Protocol Control Protocol (TCP/IP)
SRTP	**S**ecure **RTP**: Secure Real-time Transport Protocol (TCP/IP)
SRY	Text messaging abbreviation for "Sorry".
SS	Text messaging abbreviation for "So sorry".
SS7	**S**ignaling **S**ystem **7**: ITU protocol for offloading PSTN data for broadband communications.

Glossary

SSDD	Text messaging abbreviation for "Same stuff, different day".
SSDT	**S**econdary **S**ystem **D**escription **T**able
SSE	**S**treaming **S**IMD **E**xtensions: **S**treaming **S**ingle **I**nstruction **M**ultiple **D**ata **E**xtensions
SSH	**S**ecure **Sh**ell Protocol (Internet)
SSI	**S**erver **S**ide **I**nclude
— Small-Scale Integration (Microsoft)	
— Single System Image	
— Signal Strength Indicator	
— Synchronous Serial Interface	
SSID	**S**ervice **S**et **Id**entifier
SSINF	Text messaging abbreviation for "So stupid it's not funny".
SSL	**S**ecure **S**ockets **L**ayer
SSP	**S**witch-to-**S**witch **P**rotocol (TCP/IP)
ST	Internet **St**ream Protocol (TCP/IP)
ST506/ST412	A standard interface developed in 1980 by Seagate Technologies where the controller mechanism is on the controller card and is used with MFM drives smaller than 152 Mb or RLL drives less than 233Mb (Seagate).
Stack	A type of data structure, a means of storing information in a computer.
STATSRV	**Stat**istics **S**er**v**er Protocol (TCP/IP)
STB	**S**et-top **B**ox
Step	An increase or decrease of the head positioning arm so that the head can move in or out one track.
Stepper motor actuator	
	Moves the heads back and forth over the platters by rotating the motor a step at a time.
Step pulse	Controller pulse that tells the stepper motor to start a step operation.
STI	**St**ill **I**mage Architecture (Microsoft)
Stiction	Name for the most common type of hard drive failure which occurs when the drive heads get stuck to the platter causing the drive to stick and not turn.
STM	**S**ynchronous **T**ransfer **M**ode
STP	**S**hielded **T**wisted **P**air
— Spanning Tree Protocol (DEC)	
— Signal Transfer Point	
STR8	Text messaging abbreviation for "Straight".
Streaming	Technology that allows multimedia files to begin play-back before downloading is complete.
STU-C	SDSL **T**ermination **U**nit - **C**entral Office: **S**ymmetric **D**igital **S**ubscriber **L**ine **T**ermination **U**nit - **C**entral Office
STUN	**S**imple **T**raversal of **U**DP Through **N**AT (TCP/IP): **S**imple **T**raversal of **U**ser **D**atagram **P**rotocol Through **N**etwork **A**ddress **T**ranslators (TCP/IP)
STU-R	SDSL **T**ermination **U**nit – **R**emote: **S**ymmetric **D**igital **S**ubscriber **L**ine **T**ermination **U**nit – **R**emote
STW	Text messaging abbreviation for "Search The Web".
Stylus and tablet	An input device using a pen-shaped stylus to draw on the tablet.
SUITM	Text messaging abbreviation for "See you in the morning".
SUL	Text messaging abbreviation for "See you later".
Surf	Internet term for exploring Web sites, also known as Surfing.
SVC	**S**witched **V**irtual **C**ircuit (X.25)
SVD	**S**imultaneous **V**oice and **D**ata
SVGA	**S**uper **V**ideo **G**raphics **A**rray
SVID	**S**ubsystem **V**endor **Id**entifier
— System V Interface Definition (UNIX)	
S-Video	**S**uper **Video**: Method for transmitting video data over cable using two signals, one for color (chrominance, C) and one for brightness (luminance, Y).
Swatch Internet time	
	See Internet time.
SYL	Text messaging abbreviation for "See you later".
Synchronous data:	Data sent with a clock pulse.
Syntax	A set of programming language grammar rules for code.

SysOp	**Sys**tem **Op**erator
System disk	A floppy disk formatted with basic operating system startup information to initialize a computer.
Systray	**Sys**tem **tray**: A collection of icons located on the right side of the Windows toolbar.
T1	A trunk telephone line for Internet service; 24 voice channels, 1.544 Mbps.
T1c	A trunk telephone line for Internet service; 48 voice channels, 3.152 Mbps.
T2	A trunk telephone line for Internet service; 96 voice channels, 6.312 Mbps.
T3	A trunk telephone line for Internet service; 672 voice channels, 44.736 Mbps.
T4	A trunk telephone line for Internet service; 4032 voice channels, 274.760 Mbps.
TA	**T**erminal **A**dapter: See ISDN TA.
TACACS	**T**erminal **A**ccess **C**ontroller **A**ccess **C**ontrol **S**ystem (TCP/IP)
TAFN	Text messaging abbreviation for "That's all for now".
Tag	An HTML term for codes that tell the Web browser how to display image and text information.
TAL	Text messaging abbreviation for "Thanks a lot".
TALI	**T**ransport **A**dapter **L**ayer **I**nterface
TAM	Text messaging abbreviation for "Tomorrow a.m.".
Tape drive	A data-backup, removable mass storage device that uses magnetic tape.
TAPI	**T**elephony **A**pplication **P**rogramming **I**nterface
TB	See Terabyte.
TBD	Text messaging abbreviation for "To be determined".
TBH	Text messaging abbreviation for "To be honest".
TBRPF	**T**opology **B**roadcast Based on **R**everse-**P**ath **F**orwarding Protocol (TCP/IP)
TC	**T**elecommunications **C**loset
	— **T**ransmission **C**onvergence
	— **T**raffic **C**ontrol
	— **T**est **C**ontrol
	— **T**ransmission **C**ontrol
	— Text messaging abbreviation for "Take care".
TCAP	**T**ransaction **C**apabilities **A**pplication **P**art (SS7)
TCL	**T**ool **C**ommand **L**anguage: An interpreted, scripting language developed by John Ousterhout at the University of California in Berkeley in 1990. Now distributed free by Sun Microsystems.
TCL/TK	**T**ool **C**ommand **L**anguage / **T**ool **K**it: A version of TCL that includes a graphical tool kit.
TCM	**T**rellis **C**oded **M**odulation
TCP	**T**ransmission **C**ontrol **P**rotocol
TC-PAM	**T**rellis **C**oded - **P**ulse **A**mplitude **M**odulation
TCP/IP	**T**ransmission **C**ontrol **P**rotocol/**I**nternet **P**rotocol: A set of rules for data transmission.
TDD	**T**elecommunications **D**evices for the **D**eaf
TDI	**T**ransport **D**river **I**nterface
TDM	**T**ime **D**ivision **M**ultiplexing
TDMA	**T**ime **D**ivision **M**ultiple **A**ccess
TEB	**T**hread **E**nvironment **B**lock
TELCO	**Tel**ephone **Co**mpany
TELNET	TCP/IP **T**erminal **E**mulation Protocol: Transmission Control Protocol/Internet Protocol Terminal Emulation Protocol (TCP/IP)
Template	A file that serves as a starting point for a new document.
Terabyte	A unit of measure for data storage. 1024 gigabytes = 2^{40} bytes = 1,099,511,627,776 bytes = approximately 1 trillion bytes.
Teraflops	A measure of computer computational speed, a trillion floating-point operations per second.
Terminating resistors	
	aka **Terminator**: Circuitry added at the end of the bus which absorbs

	reflected signals, improves data integrity and/or provides an electrical signal termination for the controller.
Text editor	A simple word processing program that can be used to type and edit text.
TFT	Thin-Film Transistor: A technology used in the screens of laptop computers.
TFTP	Trivial File Transfer Protocol (TCP/IP)
TGIF	Text messaging abbreviation for "Thank God it's Friday".
TGT	Ticket Granting Ticket
THD	Total Harmonic Distortion
THD+N	Total Harmonic Distortion plus Noise
The Web	See World Wide Web.
Thumbnail	Small images representing a larger image file (Windows).
THX	Text messaging abbreviation for "Thanks".
TIA	Telecommunications Industry Association — Text messaging abbreviation for "Thanks in advance".
TIAD	Text messaging abbreviation for "Tomorrow is another day".
TID	Target Identifier
TIES	Time Independent Escape Sequence
TIFF	Tag Image File Format: A file format used for storing image files.
Tip	The telephone wire carrying the positive charge.
TLB	Translation Look-aside Buffer
TLK2UL8R	Text messaging abbreviation for "Talk to you later".
TLS	Transport Layer Security Protocol (Internet)
TMI	Text messaging abbreviation for "Too much information".
TMKBC	Trusted Mobile Keyboard Controller
TMux	Transport Multiplexing Protocol (TCP/IP)
TMWFI	Text messaging abbreviation for "Take my word for it".
TNEF	Transport Neutral Encapsulation Format
TNSTAAFL	Text messaging abbreviation for "There's no such thing as a free lunch".
TNT	Transparent Network Transport
Token	Networking: A series of bits that circulate on a token-ring network. — Programming: A single element of a programming language. — Security systems: A card that displays an ID code used to log onto a network.
Token ring	A network configuration defined in IEEE 802.5.
TokenTalk	AppleTalk token ring interface (Apple).
ToS	Terms of Service
TP	Twisted Pair
	Transaction Processing
TPI	Tracks Per Inch: Measures track density.
TP/IX	The Next Internet: Also called TCP/IP version 7
TPM	Text messaging abbreviation for "Tomorrow p.m.".
	Trusted Platform Module
TP-PMD	Twisted Pair-Physical Media Dependent
TPTB	Text messaging abbreviation for "The powers that be".
TR	Token Ring
	Technical Report
	Terminal Ready
Track	The circular rings of data on the surface of the HD platters.
Transfer rate:	How much data moves to the motherboard from the drive per unit of time.
TRIP	Telephony Routing over IP: Telephony Routing over Internet Protocol (TCP/IP)
Trojan horse:	See Virus.
TSAPI	Telephone Server Application Programming Interface
TSP	TAPI Service Provider: Telephony Application Programming Interface Service Provider
	Traveling Salesman Problem
	Telephony Service Provider
	Time-Stamp Protocol (TCP/IP)
TSR	Terminate and Stay Resident
TSTB	Text messaging abbreviation for "The sooner the better".

TTFN	Text messaging abbreviation for "Ta ta for now".
TTFNY	Text messaging abbreviation for "Ta ta for now ya'll".
TTL	Time To Live
	Transistor-Transistor Logic
TTTT	Text messaging abbreviation for "These things take time".
TTY	Teletype
TTYL	Text messaging abbreviation for "Talk to you later".
TTYS	Text messaging abbreviation for "Talk to you soon".
TU	Text messaging abbreviation for "Thank you".
TUP	Telephone User Part (SS7)
TURTLE	A constraint imperative programming language from the Gnu Project.
TWAIN	Technology Without An Interesting Name: An image capture API for scanners and digital cameras.
TWIP	Twentieth of a Point
TxD	Transmit (x) Data
TY	Text messaging abbreviation for "Thank you".
TYT	Text messaging abbreviation for "Take your time".
TYVM	Text messaging abbreviation for "Thank you very much".
UADSL	Universal Asymmetrical Digital Subscriber Line
UART	Universal Asynchronous Receiver / Transmitter
UAS	User Account System
UBR	Unspecified Bit Rate
UDF	Universal Disk Format
UDMA	Ultra Direct Memory Access
UDP	User Datagram Protocol (TCP/IP)
UDSL	Unidirectional Digital Subscriber Line
UFM	Unidrv Font Metrics
U-frame	Unnumbered frame (X.25)
UGTBK	Text messaging abbreviation for "You've got to be kidding".
UHCI	Universal Host Controller Interface (Intel)
UI	User Interface
UKTR	Text messaging abbreviation for "You know that's right".
U/L	Text messaging abbreviation for "Upload".
ULS	User Location Service
Ultra 2 SCSI	SCSI using an 8-bit bus supports data transfer speeds of 40 MBps.
Ultra ATA	ATA at 33 MBps maximum transfer rate.
Ultra DMA	Ultra Direct Memory Access: Data transfer technology between a hard drive and memory, maximum burst rate is 33.3 MBps (Quantum & Intel).
Ultra SCSI	SCSI using an 8-bit bus supports data transfer speeds of 20 MBps.
Ultra Wide SCSI	See SCSI-3.
UMA	Unified Memory Architecture
	Upper Memory Area
UMB	Upper Memory Block
UMD	User-Mode Driver
UML	Unified Modeling Language: A graphical programming language for object-oriented software development standardized by the Object Management Group (OMG).
UMSP	Unified Memory Space Protocol (TCP/IP)
UMTS	Universal Mobile Telecommunications System
UNC	Universal Naming Convention: A filename format used to specify the location of resources on a LAN.
UNE	Unbundled Network Element
UNI	User Network Interface
Unidrv	Universal Printer Driver (Microsoft)
UNIQID	Unique Device Identifier
UNI-RZ	Uni-polar Return to Zero
UNIX	Main multitasking operating system program used by Internet host computers, developed in the late-60s at Bell Labs.
Upload	Sending a file from your computer to another computer.
UPnP	Universal Plug and Play: See Plug and Play.
UPNP	Universal Plug and Play: See Plug and Play.
UPS	Uninterruptible Power Supply
UR	Text messaging abbreviation for "You are".

	......Text messaging abbreviation for "You're".
URB	......USB Request Block: **U**niversal Serial Bus **R**equest **B**lock
URI	......**U**niversal **R**esource **I**dentifier
URL	......**U**niform **R**esource **L**ocator: The Internet address to a web page.
USB	......**U**niversal **S**erial **B**us: An interface for keyboards, modems, digital cameras and other devices.
USBD	......**U**niversal **S**erial **B**us **D**evice
UseNet	......See Newsgroup.
USN	......**U**pdate **S**equence **N**umber
USOC	......**U**niversal **S**ervice **O**rdering **C**ode
UTP	......**U**nshielded **T**wisted **P**air: See Page 517
UUCP	......UNIX to UNIX Copy (TCP/IP)
UUID	......**U**niversally **U**nique **Id**entifier
UUNET	......UNIX to UNIX Network
UV	......Text messaging abbreviation for "Unpleasant visual".
V.17	......ITU-T standard for full-duplex, 2-wire fax transmissions at 14.4 Kbps.
V.19	......ITU-T standard for modems for parallel data transmission.
V.21	......ITU-T standard for full-duplex transmissions at 300 bps over GSTN using FSK modulation.
V.22	......ITU-T standard for full-duplex transmissions at 1200 bps over GSTN using DPSK modulation.
V.22bis	......V.22-2nd version: ITU-T standard for full-duplex modems at speeds up to 2400 bps over GSTN using asynchronous QAM.
V.23	......ITU-T standard for 600/1200 baud half-duplex modems over GSTN using FSK modulation.
V.25	......ITU-T standard for synchronous and asynchronous automatic dialing and control.
V.26	......ITU-T standard for 2400bps modem for 4-wire leased telephone-type circuits.
V.26bis	......V.26-2nd version: ITU-T standard for 2400/1200 bps modem for GSTN.
V.26ter	......V.26-3rd version: ITU-T standard for 2400 bps full-duplex modem for GSTN.
V.27	......ITU-T standard for 4800 bps modems over leased telephone-type circuits.
V.27bis	......V.27-2nd version: ITU-T standard for half-duplex modems at speeds of 4800/2400 bps over leased telephone-type circuits.
V.27ter	......V.27-3rd version: ITU-T standard for full-duplex modems at speeds of 4800/2400 bps over GSTN.
V.29	......ITU-T standard for half-duplex & fax modems at speeds of 1200, 2400, 4800, or 9600 bps.
V.32	......ITU-T standard for full-duplex 2-wire modems at speeds up to 9600 bps asynchronous TCM or 4800 bps asynchronous QAM over GSTN.
V.32bis	......V.32-2nd version: V.32 protocol extended to speeds up to 14.4 kbps asynchronous TCM or 4800 bps asynchronous QAM.
V.32ter	......V.32-3rd version: V.32 protocol extended to speeds of 21.6 kbps asynchronous TCM, 19.2 kbps synchronous TCM or 4800 bps asynchronous QAM.
V.33	......ITU-T standard for full-duplex modems at speeds up to 14400 bps
V.34	......ITU-T standard for full-duplex modems at speeds up to 28.8 kbps asynchronous TCM, also called V-Fast.
V.34bis	......V.34-2nd version: ITU-T standard for full-duplex modems at speeds up to 33.6 kbps.
V.36	......ITU-T standard for synchronous data transmission modems using 60 to 108 kHz group band circuits.
V.37	......ITU-T standard for synchronous data transmission modems at 72kbps using 60 to 108 kHz group band circuits.
V.61	......ITU-T standard for simultaneous voice plus data modems at rates of 4800 bps for voice plus data and 14400bps for data only.
V.90	......ITU-T standard for full-duplex modems at speeds up to 56 kbps downstream and up to 33.6 kbps upstream over PSTN.
V.91	......ITU-T standard for speeds up to 64000 bps over 4-wire circuit switched connections.
V.150	......ITU-T standard for modem-over-IP networks.
V.250	......ITU-T standard for serial asynchronous automatic dialing and control.

V.xx	Generic form for the ITU-T V standards. See individual standard.
VA	Video Acceleration
	Virtual Address
	Visual Age (IBM)
Van Jacobson	A TCP header compression protocol that improves TCP/IP performance over low speed (300 to 19,200 bps) serial links.
VAR	Value Added Reseller
VAX	Virtual Address Extension: A computer architecture developed by Digital Equipment Corporation (DEC).
VB	See Visual BASIC.
VBA	Visual BASIC for Applications
VBE	VESA BIOS Extension: Video Electronics Standards Association Basic Input/Output System Extension
VBI	Vertical Blanking Interval
VBN	Virtual Block Number
VBR	Variable Bit Rate
VBScript	Visual BASIC Scripting Edition: A scripting version of the BASIC language developed by Microsoft in 1995 (Microsoft).
VBX	Visual BASIC Extension
VC	Virtual Circuit
	Virtual Channel
	Video Control
	Volume Control
VCACHE	A 32-bit protected-mode cache driver (Microsoft).
VCB	Volume Control Block
VCI	Virtual Channel Identifier
	Virtual Circuit Identifier
	Virtual Circuit Interconnect
VCOMM	A 32-bit protected-mode communications driver (Microsoft).
VDM	Virtual DOS Machine
	Video Display Metafile
VDMA	Virtual DMA: Virtual Direct Memory Access
VDSL	Very High Bit-rate Digital Subscriber Line: Speeds of 12.9 Mbps to 52.8 Mbps.
VEMMI	Versatile Multimedia Interface (TCP/IP)
Veronica	Very Easy Rodent-Oriented Net-wide Index to Computerized Archives. Software that searches for file names on Gopher servers.
VESA	Video Electronics Standards Association
V-Fast	See V.34.
VFAT	Virtual File Allocation Table
VG	Voice Grade
VGA	Video Graphics Array
VIB	Volume Information Block
VID	Vendor Identifier
Virtual memory	Swap files that are used to supplement RAM with hard drive space.
Virtual split	Logical split of the disk drive.
Virus	Small, malicious program that negatively impacts the health of your computer. Viruses include boot virus, file virus, macro virus, Trojan horse, and worm.
Visual BASIC	An advanced dialect of BASIC developed by Microsoft in 1987 to facilitate creation of Windows-based programs (Microsoft).
Visual C++	A C++ application development tool created by Microsoft in 1993 (Microsoft).
VLAN	Virtual LAN: Virtual Local Area Network (Internet)
VLB	VESA Local Bus: Video Electronics Standards Association Local Bus
VLIW	Very Large Instruction Word
VLM	Very Large Memory
VLSI	Very Large Scale Integration
VM	Virtual Machine
VMCB	Volume Map Control Block
VME	Versa Module Eurocard
VME64	Versa Module Eurocard 64-bit: A 64-bit extension of the VMEbus.
VMEbus	Versa Module Eurocard bus: A 32-bit bus developed by Motorola and others. Widely used by over 300 manufacturers worldwide.

Glossary

VMR	Video Mixing Renderer
VMTP	Versatile Message Transaction Protocol (TCP/IP)
VODSL	Voice over Digital Subscriber Line
Voice-coil actuator	Controls coil movement to and from a magnet, resulting in sound from the speaker cone.
VoIP	Voice over Internet Protocol
VPB	Volume Parameter Block
VPE	Video Port Extension
	Visual Programming Environment
VPI	Virtual Path Identifier
VpicD	Virtual Programmable Interrupt Controller Device
VPID	Virtual Path Identifier
VPN	Virtual Private Network
VR	Virtual Reality
VRAM	Video Random Access Memory
VRML	Virtual Reality Modeling Language: A programming language used to build 3D pages on the Internet (Silicon Graphics).
	Virtual Reality Markup Language: Original name for Virtual Reality Modeling Language
VRP	Video Request Packet
VRRP	Virtual Router Redundancy Protocol (TCP/IP)
VSAM	Virtual Storage Access Method
VToA	Voice Telephony over ATM: Voice Telephony over Asynchronous Transfer Mode
VTP	VLAN Trunking Protocol: Virtual Local Area Network Trunking Protocol (Internet)
	Virtual Terminal Protocol
VxD	Virtual Extended Driver
	Virtual (x) Device Driver
VXML	Voice XML: Voice Extensible Markup Language: A joint effort between AT&T, IBM, Lucent Technologies and Motorola; XTML uses voice-recognition to browse The Web.
W3	See World Wide Web.
W3C	World Wide Web Consortium
W3O	World Wide Web Organization
WAIS	Wide Area Information Server: An Internet information service database.
WAM	Text messaging abbreviation for "Wait a minute".
WAN	Wide Area Network
WAN2TLK	Text messaging abbreviation for "Want to talk".
WAP	Wireless Application Protocol
Warm boot	Restarting a computer from the power-on mode.
WAYF	Text messaging abbreviation for "Were are you from".
W/B	Text messaging abbreviation for "Write back".
WB	Text messaging abbreviation for "Welcome back".
WBEM	Web-based Enterprise Management
WCCP	Web Cache Coordination Protocol
WDDX	Web Distributed Data Exchange
WDL	Windows Driver Library (Microsoft)
WDM	Windows Driver Model (Microsoft)
WDMCSA	WDM Connection and Streaming Architecture: Windows Driver Model Connection and Streaming Architecture (Microsoft)
WDOG	Watchdog (Novell)
WebCam	A video camera attached to a computer that takes and sends live images to a Web browser.
WebDAV	Web-based Distributed Authoring and Versioning (TCP/IP)
Webmaster	The person responsible for maintaining a Web site.
Web page	The heart of the World Wide Web, these documents are written in HTML and are translated by a Web browser.
Web site	A collection of Web pages.
WEP	Wired Equivalent Privacy
WFP	Windows File Protection (Microsoft)
White paper	Articles that explain certain technologies or products.
Whois	Who is: An Internet Access Protocol.

WIA	Windows Image Acquisition (Microsoft)
Wide SCSI	Term used to indicate a SCSI device for a 16-bit data path and which requires a 68-pin cable. Can transmit twice as much data as Narrow SCSI.
Wide Ultra 2 SCSI	SCSI using a 16-bit bus, supports data transfer speeds of 80 MBps.
Wi-Fi	Wireless Fidelity: Wireless data transfer based on one of the Wi-Fi Alliance's 802.11 standards.
WIIFM	Text messaging abbreviation for "What's in it for me".
Win32	See Win32 API.
Win32 API	Windows 32-bit API: API for developing 32-bit applications, used in Windows 95, Windows 98, Windows NT, and Windows XP (Microsoft).
Winchester drive	Non-removable hard drive originally used in early PCs.
Windows	An operating system for PCs (Microsoft).
WINS	Windows Internet Naming Service (Microsoft)
WinSock	Windows Sockets (Microsoft)
Wizard	A part of a program that guides the user through required steps.
WK	Text messaging abbreviation for "Week".
WKD	Text messaging abbreviation for "Weekend".
WLAN	Wireless LAN: Wireless Local Area Network (IEEE 802.11)
WLL	Wireless Local Loops
WMA	Windows Media Audio (Microsoft)
WMDM	Windows Media Device Manager (Microsoft)
WMF	Windows Metafile Format (Microsoft)
WMI	Windows Management Instrumentation (Microsoft)
WML	Wireless Markup Language
WMP	Windows Media Player (Microsoft)
WOMBAT	Text messaging abbreviation for "Waste of money, brains and time".
World Wide Web = WWW = W3 = The Web	A distributed hypertext based information system conceived at CERN to provide its user community an easy way to access global information.
Worm	See Virus.
Worm drive	Write Once Read Memory: A removable media optical drive that writes data to the drive once (cannot be changed), but can be read many times.
WP	Write Precompensation: Helps with bit crowding when using high density data on a small cylinder.
W-PBX	Wireless PBX: Wireless Private Branch Exchange
WPS	Windows Printing System (Microsoft)
	Workplace Shell (OS2)
WRUD	Text messaging abbreviation for "What are you doing".
WSD	WinSock Direct: Windows Sockets Direct (Microsoft)
WSDL	Web Services Description Language: A joint effort between Ariba, IBM and Microsoft to develop an XML-formatted language to describe Web service capabilities.
WSL	Working Set List
WSP	WinSock Proxy: Windows Sockets Proxy (Microsoft)
WTF	Text messaging abbreviation for "What the f**k.
WTG	Text messaging abbreviation for "Way to go".
WTH	Text messaging abbreviation for "What the heck".
WTMWU	Text messaging abbreviation for "What's the matter with you".
WTT	Text messaging abbreviation for "Want to talk".
WU?	Text messaging abbreviation for "What's up".
WUCIWUG	Text messaging abbreviation for "What you see is what you get".
WUF	Text messaging abbreviation for "Were are you from".
WWJD	Text messaging abbreviation for "What would Jesus do".
WWW	See World Wide Web.
WWYC	Text messaging abbreviation for "Write when you can".
WYLEI	Text messaging abbreviation for "When you least expect it".
WYSIWYG	What You See Is What You Get
X2	Modem technology for transmitting at 56 Kbps over POTS (US Robotics now 3Com). See V.90.
X.21bis	Physical layer protocol (X.21)
X.25	ITU-T packet-switching protocol for LANs.

X.400	ITU-T protocol for E-mail.
X.500	An extension to ITU-T X.400 that defines addressing formats.
XA	Extended Architecture
XBM	**X B**it **M**ap: A simple image format. XBMs only appear in black and white and you will find them inline in HTML documents
xDSL	Extended Digital Subscriber Line
XGA	Extended Graphics Array
XMI	**XML M**etadata **I**nterchange: Extensible Markup Language Metadata Interchange
XMIT	**(x) T**ransmitter
XML	Extensible Markup Language: A flexible subset of SGML aimed at Web site developers (Java).
Xmodem	File transfer protocol, 1977, 128 byte data block, checksum error detection.
Xmodem 1k	File transfer protocol, 1 kilobyte data block, CRC.
Xmodem CRC	File transfer protocol, 128 byte data block, CRC.
XMS	Extended Memory Specification
XNS	Xerox Network Systems (Xerox)
XOFF	**XMIT off: (x) T**ransmitter **off**
XON	**XMIT on: (x) T**ransmitter **on**
XOT	**X.**25 over TCP: **X.**25 over Transmission Control Protocol
XSDT	Extended System Description Table
XSL	Extensible Style Language
XSP	Extensible Server Pages (JAVA)
XT	Extended Technology
XTP	Express Transfer Protocol
X-Window	**X-Window** Systems Protocol (UNIX)
YAHOO	**Y**et **A**nother **H**ierarchical **O**fficious **O**racle: An Internet search engine.
YBS	Text messaging abbreviation for "You'll be sorry".
Y/C Video	See S-Video.
YGBKM	Text messaging abbreviation for "You gotta be kiddin' me".
YMMV	Text messaging abbreviation for "Your mileage may vary".
Ymodem	An asynchronous file transfer protocol, 1 kilobyte data block, CRC.
Ymodem-G	An asynchronous file transfer protocol, 1 kilobyte data block, hardware error correction.
YW	Text messaging abbreviation for "You're welcome".
ZAW	Zero Administration Windows (Microsoft)
ZBR	Zone Bit Recording: Formatting done at the factory where the sector per track depends on the cylinder circumference.
Z-CAV	Zoned Constant Angular Velocity
ZCHS	Zone, Cylinder, Head and Sector
ZDL	Zero Delay Lockout
ZIF	Zero Insertion Force
Zine	See E-zine.
ZIP	See PKZip (PKWare).
	Zone Information Protocol (AppleTalk, Apple)
ZIPI	An MPDL by Keith McMillen, David Wessel and Matthew Wright.
Zmodem	An asynchronous file transfer protocol, 512 byte data block, CRC, automatic reconnection.
ZV	Zoomed Video
ZVP	**ZV** Port: Zoomed Video Port

Chapter 19

PC Industry
Phone Directory

Anyone who has worked on a directory before knows that they can be a nightmare to keep error free and current. This directory is no exception. If you find errors, changes, additions, etc, please fax them to us at 303-932-1800 or send an email to: info@sequoiapublishing.com

The following has been included for each company if it was available:

Company Name...City, State: Main Phone
   Secondary Entry (such as product line)...........Phone
Tech Phone:.. Toll Free Phone:
Fax: .... Fax on Demand:
Wide Site Address:

01 Communique Laboratory Inc ······················ **Mississauga, ON: (905) 795-2888**
Tech:(905) 795-8166   Toll Free:(800) 668-2185
Web Page: http://www.01com.com

1776 Inc ··· **Los Angeles, CA: (310) 215-1776**
Tech:(310) 215-1776   Toll Free:(800) 661-6959
Web Page: http://www.1776soft.com

1mage Software inc ··· **Englewood, CO: (303) 773-1424**
Toll Free:(800) 844-1468
Web Page: http://www.1mage.com

1st Class Software ··· **Georgetown, ON: (905) 302-9988**
Tech:(905) 302-9988
Web Page: http://www.1st-class-software.com

1st Vision ··· **Andover, MA: (949) 361-0350**
Tech:(978) 474-0044
Web Page: http://www.1stvision.com

20/20 Software (see Symantec Corp)

3Com Corp ··· **Malborough, MA: (508) 323-5000**
Tech:(800) 876-3266   Toll Free:(800) 638-3266
Web Page: http://www.3com.com

3Com Corp ··· **Santa Clara, CA: (408) 326-5000**
Toll Free:(800) 638-3266
Web Page: http://www.3com.com
Channel Development ····································· (952) 820-3153
Toll Free:(800) 847-6972
Home Connect Products ································ (847) 262-3700
Web Page: http://www.3com.com
Palm Computing (see Palm Inc)
Tech Support ·· (847) 262-0770
Tech:(800) 527-8677
U.S. Robotics
Tech:(888) 428-9450   Toll Free:(888) 428-9450
Web Page: http://www.3com.com

3D Realms Entertainment ································ **Garland, TX: (972) 278-5655**
Toll Free:(800) 337-3256
Web Page: http://www.3drealms.com

3D Systems Inc ·· **Valencia, CA: (661) 295-5600**
Toll Free:(888) 337-9786
Web Page: http://www.3dsystems.com

3D Visions (see Visual Numerics)
3D.com (see Strata Software)
3Dfx Interactive (see Nvidia)
Web Page: http://www.3dfx.com

3Dlabs Inc ··· **Madison, AL: (256) 319-1100**
Tech:(800) 464-3348   Toll Free:(877) 286-1185
Web Page: http://www.3dlabs.com

3DO Company, The (Chapter 11) ···················· **Redwood City, CA:**
Web Page: http://www.3do.com

3DTV Corp ··· **Springfield, OR: (415) 680-1678**
Web Page: http://www.3dmagic.com

3M Data Storage Products Div ······················· **Saint Paul, MN: (651) 733-1110**
Tech:(800) 328-9438   Toll Free:(800) 328-6276
Web Page: http://www.mmm.com

3M Touch Systems ··· **Methuen, MA: (978) 659-9000**
Tech:(978) 659-9200   Toll Free:(866) 407-6666
Web Page: http://www.microtouch.com

3M Visual Systems ··· **Austin, TX: (800) 328-1371**
Toll Free:(800) 328-1371
Web Page: http://www.3m.com/meetings

3R Technologies ·· **River Edge, NJ: (201) 498-9460**
Tech:(866) 378-3247   Toll Free:(888) 541-9971

Web Page: http://www.3rtechnologies.com

4D Inc .... San Jose, CA: (408) 557-4600
Tech:(800) 881-3466   Toll Free:(800) 881-3466
Web Page: http://www.4d.com

4Translation Inc .... Lone Tree, CO: (303) 683-5084
Tech:(888) 777-9531   Toll Free:(888) 777-9531
Web Page: http://www.4translation.com

6 .... Redmond, WA: (425) 861-5858
Tech:(425) 861-5858   Toll Free:(800) 861-5858
Web Page: http://www.avocent.com

7th Level Inc (see Learn2.com)

7th Street.com (see Learn2.com)

8 X 8 Inc .... Santa Clara, CA: (408) 727-1885
Web Page: http://www.netergynet.com

A Bit Better Corporation .... Los Altos, CA: (650) 948-4766
Web Page: http://www.bitbetter.com

A-Prompt Corp .... Whitehall, PA: (610) 770-9204
Toll Free:(800) 478-9515
Web Page: http://www.aprompt.com

A2ia Corp .... New York City, NY: (917) 237-0390
Web Page: http://www.a2ia.com
V-Com Technology .... (909) 986-0966
Web Page: http://www.a4tech.com

Aaeon Electronics Inc .... Hazlet, NJ: (732) 203-9300
Web Page: http://www.aaeon.com

Aardvark Software Inc .... New York, NY: (212) 327-1964
Toll Free:(800) 482-2742
Web Page: http://www.aardsoft.com

Aavid Thermalloy .... CONCORD, NH: (603) 224-9988
Web Page: http://www.thermalloy.com

Abacus Acct. Systems (see Exchequer)

Abacus Software Inc .... Grand Rapids, MI: (616) 698-0330
Tech:(616) 698-0330   Toll Free:(800) 451-4319
Web Page: http://www.abacuspub.com

Abaton (see Everex Systems)

Abbeon Cal .... Santa Barbara, CA: (805) 966-0810
Toll Free:(800) 922-0977
Web Page: http://www.abbeon.com

Abbott Systems Inc .... Pleasantville, NY: (914) 747-4201
Toll Free:(800) 552-9157
Web Page: http://www.abbottsys.com

Abbyy USA .... Fremont, CA: (510) 226-6717
Web Page: http://www.abbyyusa.com

Ability Systems Corp .... Roslyn, PA: (215) 657-4338
Web Page: http://www.abilitysystems.com

ABIT Computer Corp .... Fremont, CA: (510) 623-0500
Tech:(510) 492-0968
Web Page: http://www.abit-usa.com

ABL Electronics Inc (see APC Cable)

Able Software Co .... Lexington, MA: (781) 862-2804
Web Page: http://www.ablesw.com

Abra Cadabra Software (see Best! Soft)

Abracadata Ltd. (800) 451-4871
Tech:(541) 342-3030   Toll Free:(800) 451-4871
Web Page: http://www.abracadata.com

Abracon .... Aliso Viejo, CA: (949) 448-7070
Web Page: http://www.abracon.com

ABS Imaging Systems Inc .... Silverdale, PA: (212) 258-1229
Toll Free:(800) 355-2271

Web Page: http://www.absimaging.com

Absolute Battery (see Acme Battery)

Absolute Software ·· Bellevue, WA: (604) 730-9851
Tech:(888) 771-7790   Toll Free:(800) 220-0733
Web Page: http://www.absolute.com

Accelio Corp (see Adobe Systems)

Access Micro Prod (see All Ameri. Semi)

Access Softek ·· Sunnyvale, CA: (408) 746-4990
Toll Free:(800) 667-6383
Web Page: http://www.softek.com

AccessData Corp ·· Orem, UT: (801) 377-5410
Tech:(801) 377-5622   Toll Free:(800) 574-5199
Web Page: http://www.accessdata.com

Acclaim Entertainment Inc ·· Glen Cove, NY: (516) 656-5000
Tech:(516) 759-7800
Web Page: http://www.acclaim.com

Accolade Inc (see Infogrames Ent.)

Accom Inc ··· Menlo Park, CA: (650) 328-3818
Web Page: http://www.accom.com

AccountMate Software Corp ··· Novato, CA: (415) 883-8873
Tech:(415) 883-1019   Toll Free:(800) 877-8896
Web Page: http://www.accountmate.com

Accrue Software Inc (see Datanautics, Inc.)

Accton Technology Corp ··· San Jose, CA: (408) 452-8900
Tech:(408) 452-8080   Toll Free:(800) 926-9288
Web Page: http://www.accton.com

Accu-Med Services ··· Milford, OH: (888) 350-4100
Tech:(800) 777-9144   Toll Free:(800) 423-7650
Web Page: http://www.accu-med.com

Accu-Sort Systems Inc ··· Telford, PA: (215) 723-0981
Toll Free:(800) 227-2633
Web Page: http://www.accusort.com

Acculogic Inc ·· San Diego, CA: (858) 530-8170
Toll Free:(800) 697-8378
Web Page: http://www.acculogic.com

Accurate Research (see Homework Help.com)

Accurite Technologies Inc ··· Fremont, CA: (510) 668-4900
Web Page: http://www.accurite.com

Accusentry ·· Marietta, GA: (770) 850-1700
Web Page: http://www.accusentry.com

Accusoft Corp ·· Northborough, MA: (508) 351-9092
Toll Free:(800) 525-3577
Web Page: http://www.accusoft.com

Accutek Inc. (see IEC Electronics Corp)

ACE Contact manager (see Go Ace)

Acecad Inc ·· Exton, PA: (610) 280-9840
Tech:(831) 655-9911   Toll Free:(800) 676-4223
Web Page: http://www.acecad.com

Acer America Corp ·· San Jose, CA: (408) 432-6200
Tech:(800) 445-6495   Toll Free:(800) 733-2237
Web Page: http://www.acer.com/aac
Customer Support ·· (800) 938-2237
Toll Free:(800) 445-6495
Support ··· (800) 816-2237
Tech:(800) 816-2237
Web Page: http://www.acersupport.com

Acer Communications & Multimedia ······································· San Jose, CA: (888) 723-2238
Tech:(909) 569-0699   Toll Free:(800) 452-2237
Web Page: http://www.acerperipherals.com

Aces Research Inc ································· **Fremont, CA: (510) 683-8855**
Tech:(510) 661-2093
Web Page: http://www.acesxprt.com

Acheeve Inc ···································· **Dallas, TX: (972) 556-0030**
Toll Free:(888) 693-8388
Web Page: http://www.acheeve.com

Aci US Inc (see 4D Inc)

ACL Staticide ····························· **Elk Grove Village, IL: (847) 981-9212**
Tech:(847) 981-9212   Toll Free:(800) 782-8420
Web Page: http://www.aclstaticide.com

Acma Computers Inc ··························· **Fremont, CA: (510) 623-1212**
Tech:(800) 786-8998   Toll Free:(800) 786-6888
Web Page: http://www.acma.com

Acme Battery Co ····························· **Hamilton, ON: (905) 545-4454**
Toll Free:(877) 549-4454
Web Page: http://www.absolutebattery.com

Acme Electric Corp
  Aerospace Division ···························· (480) 894-6864
  Web Page: http://www.acmeelec.com
  Electronics Division ···························· (716) 968-2400
  Toll Free:(800) 325-5848
  Web Page: http://www.acmeelec.com
  Power Distribution Products ···················· (910) 738-1121
  Tech:(910) 738-4251   Toll Free:(800) 334-5214
  Web Page: http://www.acmeelec.com

Acodisc CD and DVD Data Recovery ·········· **San Diego, CA: (619) 640-0065**
Web Page: http://www.acodisc.com

Acomdata ···································· **Pomona, CA: (909) 348-0680**

Acorn Computers (see Text 100 Corp.)

Acroprint Time Recorder Co ···················· **Raleigh, NC: (919) 872-5800**
Tech:(919) 872-4449   Toll Free:(800) 334-7190
Web Page: http://www.acroprint.com

ACT Networks Inc (see Clarent)

Actel Corp ································ **Mountain View, CA: (650) 318-4200**
Tech:(800) 262-1060   Toll Free:(800) 262-1060
Web Page: http://www.actel.com

Acterna ···································· **Germantown, MD: (301) 353-1560**
Tech:(800) 622-5515   Toll Free:(866) 228-3762
Web Page: http://www.acterna.com

Acterna Corp (Out of Business)

ACTion Imaging Solutions (see Colortrac Ltd)

Actiontec Electronics Inc ····················· **Sunnyvale, CA: (408) 752-7700**
Tech:(408) 752-7714   Toll Free:(800) 797-1001
Web Page: http://www.actiontec.com

Active Arts (see ImageBuilder Software)

Active Voice Corp ····························· **Seattle, WA: (206) 441-4700**
Tech:(800) 284-3575   Toll Free:(800) 284-3575
Web Page: http://www.activevoice.com

ActiveLight ································· **Poulsbo, WA: (360) 779-8490**
Tech:(800) 557-2796   Toll Free:(800) 557-2796
Web Page: http://www.activelight.com

Activision ································ **Santa Monica, CA: (310) 255-2000**
Tech:(310) 255-2050   Toll Free:(800) 477-3650
Web Page: http://www.activision.com

Acton Research Corp ··························· **Acton, MA: (978) 263-3584**
Web Page: http://www.acton-research.com

Actuate Software Corp ······················ **San Francisco, CA: (650) 837-2000**
Tech:(800) 914-2259   Toll Free:(888) 422-8828
Web Page: http://www.actuate.com

Acucorp Inc ···································· San Diego, CA: (858) 689-4500
   Tech:(800) 399-7220   Toll Free:(800) 262-6585
   Web Page: http://www.acucobol.com

Acuscape ·· Glendora, CA: (626) 963-3699
   Web Page: http://www.acuscape.com

Adam.com ·· Atlanta, GA: (770) 980-0888
   Web Page: http://www.adam.com

Adaptec Inc ···································· Milpitas, CA: (408) 945-8600
   Tech:(408) 934-7274   Toll Free:(800) 959-7274
   Web Page: http://www.adaptec.com
   Customer Service ································· (408) 957-2550
   Raid & Fibre Channel ···························· (321) 207-2000

Adaptive Micro-Ware Inc ················ Fort Wayne, IN: (260) 489-0046
   Web Page: http://www.adaptivemicro.com

Adaptive Optics Associates ·········· Cambridge, MA: (617) 806-1400
   Web Page: http://www.adaptiveoptics.com

Adaptive Solutions Inc (see KoFile Inc)

Adax Inc ··· Berkeley, CA: (510) 548-7047
   Web Page: http://www.adax.com

ADC Access Products ···················· Portland, OR: (503) 643-1681
   Tech:(800) 232-5879   Toll Free:(800) 733-5511
   Web Page: http://www.adc.com

ADC Fibermux corp (see ADC Access Prod.)

ADC Kentrox ································· Hillsboro, OR: (503) 350-6007
   Tech:(503) 643-1681   Toll Free:(800) 733-5511
   Web Page: http://www.kentrox.com

ADC Telecommunications ············· Eden Prairie, MN: (952) 938-8080
   Tech:(800) 366-3889   Toll Free:(800) 366-3891
   Web Page: http://www.adc.com

Adco Circuits ······························ Rochester Hills, MI: (248) 820-4677
   Tech:(248) 829-4677
   Web Page: http://www.adcocircuits.com

Addlogix ·· Irvine, CA: (800) 344-6921
   Tech:(949) 341-0888   Toll Free:(800) 344-6921
   Web Page: http://www.addlogix.com

Addonics Technologies Corp ··········· San Jose, CA: (408) 433-3899
   Tech:(408) 433-3855   Toll Free:(800) 787-8580
   Web Page: http://www.addonics.com

Addtron Technology Co. Ltd. (Unknown)

Adept Computer Solutions Inc ········· San Diego, CA: (858) 792-4664
   Tech:(858) 597-1776   Toll Free:(800) 578-6277
   Web Page: http://www.streetwizard.com

Adept Technology ·························· Livermore, CA: (925) 245-3400
   Tech:(408) 434-5000   Toll Free:(800) 232-3378
   Web Page: http://www.adept.com

Adesso Inc ···································· Culver City, CA: (310) 645-3746
   Tech:(626) 912-9071
   Web Page: http://www.adessoinc.com

Adexis ··· Columbus, OH: (614) 431-8000
   Toll Free:(800) 945-6245
   Web Page: http://www.adexisstorage.com

ADI Systems Inc ···························· Newark, CA: (510) 795-6200
   Tech:(877) 792-7234   Toll Free:(800) 228-0530
   Web Page: http://www.adiusa.com

Adjile Systems ····························· Sacramento, CA: (916) 338-7660
   Toll Free:(800) 347-7621
   Web Page: http://www.adjile.com

Adobe Systems Inc ·························· San Jose, CA: (408) 536-6000
   Tech:(800) 833-6687   Toll Free:(800) 628-2320

Web Page: http://www.adobe.com

Adobe Systems Inc ··· **Seattle, WA: (206) 675-7000**
Acrobat ·· (206) 675-6304
  Tech:(206) 675-6304   Toll Free:(800) 272-3623
Active Share ··· (206) 675-6319
Adobe Store ·· (888) 724-4508
  Toll Free:(888) 724-4508
After Effects ··· (206) 675-6310
  Tech:(206) 675-6310   Toll Free:(800) 685-3504
Ares Font Utilities (support on web)
  Web Page: http://www.adobe.com
ATM ·· (206) 675-6306
  Tech:(206) 675-6306   Toll Free:(800) 685-4148
Customer First Services ································· (800) 685-3652
Dimensions ·· (206) 675-6316
  Tech:(206) 675-6316   Toll Free:(800) 685-3505
File Utilities (see Inso Corp)························· (312) 692-5300
  Web Page: http://www.inso.com
Font Chameleon (discontinued)
Font Folio ·· (206) 675-6306
FontFiddler (discontinued)
FontHopper (discontinued)
FontMinder (discontinued)
FontMonger (discontinued)
FrameMaker ·· (206) 675-6312
  Toll Free:(800) 843-7263
FrameMaker + SGML ······································ (206) 675-6315
  Toll Free:(800) 843-7263
FrameViewer ··· (206) 675-6353
  Toll Free:(800) 843-7263
Gallery Effects (see Photo Shop)
Go Live ··· (206) 675-6321
  Toll Free:(800) 685-3612
Illustrator ·· (206) 675-6307
  Toll Free:(800) 649-3875
Image Club Products (see EyeWire Inc)
  Web Page: http://www.eyewire.com
ImageReady ·· (206) 675-6370
ImageStyler (Discontinued)
InDesign ·· (206) 675-6311
  Toll Free:(800) 562-3623
InfoPublisher (support on web)
  Web Page: http://www.adobe.com
Intellidraw (discontinued)
Live Motion ·· (206) 675-6325
  Toll Free:(800) 967-7853
PageMaker ··· (206) 675-6301
  Toll Free:(800) 422-3623
PageMill (Discontinued)
Persuasion (support on web)
PhotoDeluxe Business Edition ························ (206) 675-6371
  Toll Free:(800) 238-5972
PhotoDeluxe Home Edition ···························· (206) 675-6309
  Toll Free:(800) 888-6293
Photoshop ··· (206) 675-6303
  Toll Free:(800) 492-3623
Photoshop Elements ······································ (206) 675-6358
Photostyler (discontinued)
Pre Sales Adobe Products ······························ (800) 685-3505
Premiere ·· (206) 675-6305
  Toll Free:(888) 724-4507
Press Ready ··· (206) 675-6320

Toll Free:(800) 323-1722
Printer Drivers ·· (206) 675-6314
Streamline ···(206) 675-6317
Type ··(206) 675-6306
Toll Free:(800) 682-3623
Type Reunion ···(206) 675-6206
Web Workgroup Server ···(206) 675-6321
ADPI ·· **Troy, OH: (937) 339-2241**
Toll Free:(800) 758-1041
Web Page: http://www.adpi.com
ADS Technologies ·································· **Cerritos, CA: (562) 926-1928**
Tech:(562) 926-4338   Toll Free:(800) 888-5244
Web Page: http://www.adstech.com
Adtec Inc ····································· **Nashville, TN: (615) 256-6619**
Web Page: http://www.adtecinc.com
Adtran ······································ **Huntsville, AL: (256) 963-8000**
Tech:(888) 423-8726   Toll Free:(800) 923-8726
Web Page: http://www.adtran.com
Advan International Corp ························· **Fremont, CA: (510) 490-1005**
Tech:(888) 786-1688   Toll Free:(888) 786-1688
Web Page: http://www.advancorp.com
Advanced Computer & Network Corp ··············· **Pittsburgh, PA: (412) 683-9010**
Tech:(888) 686-2262   Toll Free:(800) 213-2667
Web Page: http://www.acnc.com
Advanced Computer Innovations ··················· **Pittsford, NY: (585) 383-1939**
Tech:(585) 383-1939
Web Page: http://www.acii.com
Advanced Data Capture Corp ······················ **Concord, MA: (978) 287-5558**
Tech:(800) 300-3584   Toll Free:(800) 500-9173
Web Page: http://www.adc-barcode.com
Advanced Digital Info. Corp. (ADIC) ·············· **Redmond, WA: (425) 881-8004**
Tech:(800) 827-3822   Toll Free:(800) 336-1233
Web Page: http://www.adic.com
Advanced Digital Systems (see ADS Tech)
Advanced Graphics Software Inc ·················· **Encinitas, CA: (760) 634-8360**
Toll Free:(800) 795-4754
Web Page: http://www.slidewrite.com
Advanced Gravis (see Gravis)
Advanced Illumination ························· **Rochester, VT: (802) 767-3830**
Web Page: http://www.advill.com
Advanced Innovative Marketing (see ASI)
Advanced Logic Res. (see Gateway Resell)
Advanced Matrix Technology Inc ·················· **Camarillo, CA: (805) 388-5799**
Tech:(800) 476-2450   Toll Free:(800) 215-9192
Web Page: http://www.amtprinters.com
Advanced Media Services ························· **Salem, NH: (603) 898-7500**
Toll Free:(800) 466-0813
Web Page: http://www.amsstorage.com
Advanced Micro Devices ························· **Sunnyvale, CA: (408) 732-2400**
Tech:(408) 749-3060   Toll Free:(800) 538-8450
Web Page: http://www.amd.com
Advanced Recognition Technologies ·············· **Lawrenceville, GA: (678) 376-5959**
Web Page: http://www.artrecognition.com
Advanced Research Instruments ················· **Wheat Ridge, CO: (303) 463-5500**
Web Page: http://www.aricorp.com
Advanced RISC Machines (see ARM Ltd)
Advanced Software (see Prairie Group)
Advanced Storage Concepts Inc ·················· **Galveston, TX: (409) 744-2129**
Tech:(409) 744-2129

Phone Directory

Web Page: http://www.advstor.com

Advanced Video Technology(see TFS)

Advanced Visual Systems ································· **Waltham, MA: (781) 890-4300**
Tech:(800) 428-7001   Toll Free:(800) 728-1600
Web Page: http://www.avs.com

AdvanSystem Product (see ConnectCom)

Advantage Memory ·················· **Rancho Santa Margarita, CA: (949) 453-8111**
Tech:(949) 288-4262   Toll Free:(800) 245-5299
Web Page: http://www.advantagememory.com

Advantech Technologies ······························ **Irvine, CA: (949) 789-7178**
Tech:(800) 866-6008   Toll Free:(800) 557-6813
Web Page: http://www.advantech.com

Advent Software Inc ··························· **San Francisco, CA: (415) 543-7696**
Toll Free:(800) 727-0605
Web Page: http://www.advent.com

AEC Management (see AEC Software)

AEC Software ···································· **Sterling, VA: (703) 450-1980**
Tech:(703) 450-2318   Toll Free:(800) 346-9413
Web Page: http://www.aecsoft.com

Aegis Electronics Group ·························· **Carlsbad, CA: (760) 729-2026**
Toll Free:(800) 362-3447
Web Page: http://www.aegis-elec.com

AEI North America ···························· **Skaneateles, NY: (315) 217-0164**
Web Page: http://www.aeinorthamerica.com

AER Energy Resources Inc ························· **Smyrna, GA: (770) 433-2127**
Toll Free:(800) 769-3720
Web Page: http://www.aerenergy.com

Aerocomm Inc ································· **Lenexa, KS: (913) 492-2320**
Tech:(913) 492-2320   Toll Free:(800) 492-2320
Web Page: http://www.aerocomm.com

Aeronics Inc ································· **Austin, TX: (512) 258-2303**
Tech:(512) 258-2303   Toll Free:(800) 824-8578
Web Page: http://www.aeronics.com

Aerotech ································· **Pittsburgh, PA: (412) 963-7470**
Web Page: http://www.aerotechinc.com

Affinity Industries Inc ·························· **Ossipee, NH: (603) 539-3600**
Tech:(603) 539-5005   Toll Free:(800) 238-8581
Web Page: http://www.affinitychillers.com

Affinity Systems ····························· **Rochester, NY: (585) 482-0150**
Toll Free:(877) 278-9444
Web Page: http://www.affsys.com

AgData ·································· **Gridley, CA: (530) 846-6203**
Toll Free:(888) 327-6257
Web Page: http://www.agdata.com

Agfa Corp ····························· **Ridgefield Park, NJ: (201) 440-2500**
Tech:(800) 879-2432   Toll Free:(800) 926-2432
Web Page: http://www.agfaus.com
Technical Imaging ····························· (864) 421-1600
Tech:(888) 557-6100   Toll Free:(877) 777-2432
Web Page: http://www.agfamedical.com

Agfa Monotype ···························· **Wilmington, MA: (978) 284-7201**
Tech:(978) 284-7122   Toll Free:(800) 424-8973
Web Page: http://www.monotype.com

Agile Networks Inc (see Lucent Tech)

Agilent Technologies ·························· **San Jose, CA: (408) 654-8675**
Toll Free:(800) 235-0312
Web Page: http://www.agilent.com

Agilent Technologies ·························· **Palo Alto, CA: (650) 752-5000**
Web Page: http://www.agilent.com

Communication Solutions ································ (800) 829-4444
  Web Page: http://www.agilent.com
Semiconductor Products ······················· (408) 654-8675
  Toll Free:(800) 235-0312
  Web Page: http://www.agilent.com
Ahern Communications Corp ············· Quincy, MA: (617) 471-1100
  Tech:(617) 471-1100   Toll Free:(800) 451-5067
  Web Page: http://www.aherncorp.com
AHT ·· Victor, NY: (716) 742-2200
  Tech:(716) 742-2200   Toll Free:(888) 248-2487
  Web Page: http://www.aht.com
AHT Advanced HiTech Corp ············· El Segundo, CA: (310) 615-1870
  Tech:(877) 330-0868   Toll Free:(877) 330-0868
  Web Page: http://www.aht.com
Aim Tech (see Asymetrix Learning Systems)
Aiptek Inc ·· Irvine, CA: (949) 585-9600
  Web Page: http://www.aiptek.com
AIST Inc ·· Bellingham, WA: (360) 527-1489
  Tech:(360) 594-4250   Toll Free:(866) 924-2478
  Web Page: http://www.aistinc.com
AITech International ························· San Jose, CA: (408) 570-0000
  Web Page: http://www.aitech.com
Aiwa America Inc. ······························· Mahwah, NJ: (201) 512-3600
  Tech:(877) 876-4765   Toll Free:(800) 289-2492
  Web Page: http://www.aiwa.com
AJA Video Systems ······················· Grass Valley, CA: (530) 274-2048
  Toll Free:(800) 251-4224
  Web Page: http://www.aja.com
Alacron ·· Nashua, NH: (603) 891-2750
  Web Page: http://www.alacron.com
Aladdin Knowledge Systems Inc ········· New York, NY: (212) 564-5678
  Toll Free:(800) 223-4277
  Web Page: http://www.aks.com
Aladdin Soft Secur. (see Aladdin Knowl)
Aladdin Systems Inc ····················· Watsonville, CA: (831) 761-6200
  Tech:(831) 761-6200   Toll Free:(888) 245-1723
  Web Page: http://www.aladdinsys.com
Alaris Inc ·· Fremont, CA: (510) 770-5700
  Tech:(510) 770-5766
  Web Page: http://www.alaris.com
Alberta Printed Circuits LTD ················· Calgary, AB: (403) 250-3406
  Tech:(403) 250-3406
  Web Page: http://www.apcircuits.com
Alcatel Internetworking ···················· Calabasas, CA: (818) 878-4507
  Tech:(800) 995-2696   Toll Free:(800) 999-9526
  Web Page: http://www.ind.alcatel.com
Aldridge Co, The ······························· Houston, TX: (713) 403-9150
  Tech:(281) 368-0166
  Web Page: http://www.aldridge.com
Aldus Corp (see Adobe Systems Inc)
Alexander LAN Inc ······························· Nashua, NH: (603) 880-8800
  Tech:(603) 880-8800
  Web Page: http://www.alexander.com
Alfred Publishing ······························· Van Nuys, CA: (818) 891-5999
  Web Page: http://www.alfredpub.com
Algor Inc ·· Pittsburgh, PA: (412) 967-2700
  Toll Free:(800) 482-5467
  Web Page: http://www.algor.com
Alias Wavefront ································· Atlanta, GA: (404) 367-9949

Toll Free:(866) 226-8859
Web Page: http://www.aliaswavefront.com

Alien Skin Software ·· **Raleigh, NC: (919) 832-4124**
Toll Free:(888) 921-7546
Web Page: http://www.alienskin.com

AlienWare Corp ·· **Miami, FL: (305) 251-9797**
Toll Free:(866) 287-6727
Web Page: http://www.alienware.com

Align Mark ·· **Maitland, FL: (800) 682-4587**
Tech:(800) 682-4587
Web Page: http://www.alignmark.com

ALK Technologies ··· **Princeton, NJ: (609) 252-8197**
Tech:(609) 252-8191   Toll Free:(888) 872-8768
Web Page: http://www.alk.com

Alki Software Corp ··· **Seattle, WA: (206) 286-2600**
Tech:(206) 286-2780   Toll Free:(800) 669-9673
Web Page: http://www.alki.com

All American Semi ··· **San Jose, CA: (408) 441-1300**
Toll Free:(800) 573-2727
Web Page: http://www.allamerican.com

All Components Inc ·· **Farmers Branch, TX: (972) 233-0203**
Tech:(972) 233-0203   Toll Free:(800) 334-4637
Web Page: http://www.allcomponents.com

Allaire Corp (see Macromedia)

Allegiant (Out of Business)

Allegro New Media (see SBT Accounting Sys)

Allegro Systems Ltd (Out of Business)

Allen Communications ·· **Salt Lake City, UT: (801) 537-7800**
Tech:(800) 515-2626   Toll Free:(800) 325-7850
Web Page: http://www.mentergy.com

Allen Systems Group ·· **Naples, FL: (239) 435-2200**
Tech:(800) 354-3578   Toll Free:(800) 932-5536
Web Page: http://www.asg.com

Alliance Computer Services ·· **Mesa, AZ: (480) 898-0100**
Web Page: http://www.alliance-comp.com

Alliance Research (see ORA Electronics)

Allied Telesyn International ·· **Bothell, WA: (425) 487-8880**
Tech:(800) 428-4835   Toll Free:(800) 424-4284
Web Page: http://www.alliedtelesyn.com

AllMicro (see ForeFront Direct)

Allsop Inc. ·· **Bellingham, WA: (360) 734-9090**
Tech:(360) 734-9090   Toll Free:(800) 426-4303
Web Page: http://www.allsop.com

Almo Corp ·· **Philadelphia, PA: (215) 698-4000**
Tech:(215) 698-6099
Web Page: http://www.almo.com

ALOS Micrographics Corporation ································ **Montgomery, NY: (845) 457-4400**
Tech:(845) 457-4400   Toll Free:(800) 431-7105
Web Page: http://www.alosusa.com

Alpha Innotech Corp ··· **San Leandro, CA: (510) 483-9620**
Tech:(800) 823-0404   Toll Free:(800) 795-5556
Web Page: http://www.alphainnotech.com

Alpha Microsystems (see Alphaserv.com)

Alpha Software Corp ·· **Burlington, MA: (781) 229-4500**
Tech:(781) 229-9497   Toll Free:(800) 451-1018
Web Page: http://www.alphasoftware.com

Alpha Technologies Inc ·· **Bellingham, WA: (360) 647-2360**
Web Page: http://www.alpha-us.com

AlphaBlox Corp ·· **Mountain View, CA: (650) 526-1700**

Tech:(650) 526-1700   Toll Free:(888) 256-9669
Web Page: http://www.alphablox.com

Alpharel Inc (see Altris Software Inc)

Alphaserv.com (see Network Query Lang.)

Alps Electric USA .... San Jose, CA: (408) 361-6400
Tech:(888) 805-3587
Web Page: http://www.alps.com

ALR Inc (see Gateway 2000 Inc/Reseller)

Alta Technology (see Linux Networx)

Altair Engineering .... Troy, MI: (248) 614-2400
Tech:(248) 614-2425
Web Page: http://www.altair.com

AltaVista Software (see Compaq)

Altec Lansing .... Milford, PA: (570) 296-4434
Tech:(800) 258-3288   Toll Free:(866) 570-5702
Web Page: http://www.altecmm.com

Altek Corp .... Silver Spring, MD: (301) 572-2555
Tech:(301) 572-2555
Web Page: http://www.altek.com

Altera Corp .... San Jose, CA: (408) 544-7000
Tech:(408) 544-8767   Toll Free:(800) 767-3753
Web Page: http://www.altera.com

Altex Computers & Electronics .... Corpus Christi, TX: (361) 814-8882
Toll Free:(800) 531-5369
Web Page: http://www.altex.com

Altex Computers & Electronics .... San Antonio, TX: (210) 637-3200
Tech:(210) 637-3200   Toll Free:(800) 531-5369
Web Page: http://www.altex.com

Austin .... (512) 832-9131
Toll Free:(800) 531-5369
Web Page: http://www.altex.com

Dallas .... (972) 267-8882
Toll Free:(800) 531-5369
Web Page: http://www.altex.com

San Antonio .... (210) 499-4201
Toll Free:(800) 531-5369
Web Page: http://www.altex.com

Altia Inc .... Colorado Springs, CO: (719) 598-4299
Web Page: http://www.altia.com

Altigen .... Fremont, CA: (510) 252-9712
Toll Free:(888) 258-4436
Web Page: http://www.altigen.com

Altima Technologies Inc .... Glen Ellyn, IL: (630) 790-0500
Web Page: http://www.altimatech.com

Altris Software (see Spescom Software)

Altura XL LLC .... Alpharetta, GA: (770) 625-0000
Toll Free:(800) 241-3946
Web Page: http://www.alturaxl.com

Alvarion .... Carlsbad, CA: (760) 431-9880
Tech:(760) 517-3100
Web Page: http://www.alvarion.com

Alventive Inc (see BlueSky Solutions LLC)

Always Technology Corp (Out of Business)

AM Communications .... Quakerstown, PA: (215) 538-8700
Toll Free:(800) 248-9004
Web Page: http://www.amcomm.com

Amain Electronics Co .... Simi Valley, CA: (775) 825-6001
Web Page: http://www.amain.com

Amanda Company, The .... San Diego, CA: (800) 410-2745

Tech:(203) 744-0537   Toll Free:(800) 410-2745
Web Page: http://www.taa.com

Amateur Electronic Supply ··· Milwaukee, WI: (414) 358-0333
Tech:(414) 358-4087   Toll Free:(800) 558-0411
Web Page: http://www.aesham.com

Amazon Imaging ·· Simi Valley, CA: (800) 469-1686
Toll Free:(800) 469-1686
Web Page: http://www.amazonimaging.com

Amber Wave Systems (see 3Com)

Amdahl Corp (see Fujitsu IT Holdings)

Amdek Corp (see Wyse Technology)

AmDocs ··· San Jose, CA: (408) 965-7000
Web Page: http://www.amdocs.com

American Altec ·· Princeton, NJ: (609) 452-1555

American Bible Society ··· New York, NY: (212) 408-1200
Tech:(212) 408-1200   Toll Free:(800) 322-4253
Web Page: http://www.americanbible.org

American Business Info (see infoUSA)

American Business System ································· Chelmsford, MA: (978) 250-9600
Tech:(978) 250-9600   Toll Free:(800) 356-4034
Web Page: http://www.abs-software.com

American Cybernetics ·· Tempe, AZ: (480) 968-1945
Tech:(480) 968-1945   Toll Free:(800) 899-0100
Web Page: http://www.amcyber.com

American Digital Cartography Inc ····················· Appleton, WI: (920) 733-6678
Tech:(920) 733-6678   Toll Free:(800) 236-7973
Web Page: http://www.adci.com

American Fibertek Inc ··· Somerset, NJ: (732) 302-0660
Web Page: http://www.americanfibertek.com

American Fundware ································· Greenwood Village, CO: (303) 756-3030
Toll Free:(800) 551-4458
Web Page: http://www.fundware.com

American Megatrends Inc ·· Norcross, GA: (770) 246-8600
Tech:(770) 246-8645   Toll Free:(800) 828-9264
Web Page: http://www.ami.com

American Ntl Standards Institute ································· New York, NY: (212) 642-4900
Web Page: http://www.ansi.org/

American Power Conversion ································· Hunt Valley, MD: (410) 584-2700
Tech:(410) 584-2738   Toll Free:(800) 726-0610
Web Page: http://www.apcc.com

American Power Conversion Corp ··············· West Kingston, RI: (401) 789-5735
Tech:(800) 555-2725   Toll Free:(800) 788-2208
Web Page: http://www.apcc.com

American Small Bus Comp (see ViaGrafix)

American Software Inc ·· Atlanta, GA: (404) 261-4381
Tech:(404) 264-5296   Toll Free:(800) 726-2946
Web Page: http://www.amsoftware.com

Amerinex Applied Imaging ··· Amherst, MA: (413) 253-1282
Web Page: http://www.aai.com

AmeriQuest Technologies ································· Warminster, PA: (267) 280-0430
Toll Free:(800) 223-7087
Web Page: http://www.ameriquest.com

Amicus Networks Inc ·· Austin, TX: (512) 418-8828
Tech:(512) 531-3400   Toll Free:(800) 419-0150
Web Page: http://www.amicus.com

Amitech ·· Fairfax, VA: (703) 591-7800
Web Page: http://www.amitech.com

AmNet Computers ··· Baltimore, MD: (443) 919-2000
Web Page: http://www.amnet-comp.com

AMP Inc (see Tyco Electronics)

Ampex Corp ··· **Redwood City, CA: (650) 367-2011**
Tech:(650) 367-4111   Toll Free:(800) 227-8402
Web Page: http://www.ampex.com

Amptron International Inc ······························ **City Of Industry, CA: (626) 912-5205**
Tech:(626) 912-5789
Web Page: http://www.amptron.com

ANA Tech (see ACTion Imaging Solutions)

Analog & Digital Peripherals ································· **Troy, OH: (937) 339-2241**
Toll Free:(800) 758-1041
Web Page: http://www.adpi.com

Analog Data Conversion ······································ **Peabody, MA: (800) 237-2200**
Toll Free:(800) 237-2200
Web Page: http://www.analogic.com/dcp

Analog Devices Inc ·· **Norwood, MA: (781) 329-4700**
Tech:(800) 426-2564   Toll Free:(800) 262-5643
Web Page: http://www.analog.

Analog Way ·· **New York, NY: (212) 269-1902**
Web Page: http://www.analogway.com

Analogic Corp ··· **Peabody, MA: (978) 977-3000**
Toll Free:(800) 237-2200
Web Page: http://www.analogic.com

Analogic Data Conversion ··································· **Wakefield, MA: (978) 977-3000**
Web Page: http://www.analogic.com/dcp

Ancor Communications (see QLogic)

Andataco (see nStor Technologies)

Anderson Inv. Soft. (see Investor Soft)

Andrea Electronics Corp ····································· **Melville, NY: (800) 442-7787**
Tech:(800) 707-5779   Toll Free:(800) 442-7787
Web Page: http://www.andreaelectronics.com

Andrew Corp ·· **Orland Park, IL: (708) 349-3300**
Tech:(800) 458-2820   Toll Free:(800) 255-1479
Web Page: http://www.andrew.com

Andromeda Research ··· **Milford, OH: (513) 831-9708**
Web Page: http://www.arlabs.com

Andromeda Software ··· **Thousand Oaks, CA: (805) 379-4109**
Web Page: http://www.andromeda.com

Andromedia (see Macromedia)

Andyne Computing Ltd (see Hummingbird)

Angenieux ·· **Totowa, NJ: (973) 812-4326**
Web Page: http://www.angenieux.com

ANGOSS Software Corp ······································· **Toronto, ON: (416) 593-1122**
Tech:(416) 593-2417
Web Page: http://www.angoss.com

AniCom Inc (see Animated Communications)

Animated Communications ··································· **Chapel Hill, NC: (919) 967-2890**
Toll Free:(800) 949-4559
Web Page: http://www.3dchor.com

Animated Image Systems (see AIST Inc)

Anna Technology ··· **Poway, CA: (858) 435-2000**
Toll Free:(800) 462-1042
Web Page: http://www.annatechnology.com

Annex.com Inc ·· **Encino, CA: (818) 761-2100**
Tech:(818) 761-2100   Toll Free:(800) 462-6639
Web Page: http://www.annex.com

Ansoft Corp ··· **Pittsburgh, PA: (412) 261-3200**
Tech:(412) 261-3200
Web Page: http://www.ansoft.com

Antec Inc ·· Fremont, CA: (510) 770-1200
Tech:(800) 222-6832   Toll Free:(888) 542-6832
Web Page: http://www.antec-inc.com

Antex Electronics Corp ································ Gardena, CA: (800) 338-4231
Tech:(310) 532-3092   Toll Free:(800) 338-4231
Web Page: http://www.antex.com

Anthem Technology Sys (see Arrow Elec.)

Anthro Corp ·· Tualatin, OR: (503) 691-2556
Toll Free:(800) 325-3841
Web Page: http://www.anthro.com

Anton/Bauer ·· Shelton, CT: (203) 929-1100
Tech:(800) 541-1667   Toll Free:(800) 422-3473
Web Page: http://www.antonbauer.com

Aonix ·· San Diego, CA: (858) 657-0860
Tech:(858) 457-2700   Toll Free:(800) 972-6649
Web Page: http://www.aonix.com

AOpen America Inc ····································· San Jose, CA: (510) 489-8928
Tech:(510) 489-8928   Toll Free:(888) 852-6736
Web Page: http://www.aopenusa.com

APA Cables & Networks ····························· Plymouth, MN: (763) 476-6866
Toll Free:(800) 422-2537
Web Page: http://www.apacn.com

APC (see American Power Conversion)

Apcom Systems (see Applied Computer Sys)

Aperture Tech Inc ·· Stamford, CT: (203) 357-0800
Tech:(800) 342-9022   Toll Free:(800) 346-6828
Web Page: http://www.aperture.com

Apertus Technologies (see Carleton)

Apex Data Inc (see Smart Modular Tech.)

Apex Inc (see Avocent)

Apex Software (see Component One)

Apex Voice Communications Inc ·················· Sherman Oaks, CA: (818) 379-8400
Tech:(818) 379-8400
Web Page: http://www.apexvoice.com

Apexx Technology (see eSoft Inc)

Apian Software ··· Seattle, WA: (206) 547-5321
Tech:(206) 547-8392   Toll Free:(800) 237-4565
Web Page: http://www.apian.com

Apogee Instruments ···································· Auburn, CA: (530) 888-0500
Tech:(530) 888-0500
Web Page: http://www.ccd.com

Apogee Software (see 3DRealms)

Apogee Software Inc ···································· Campbell, CA: (408) 369-9001
Toll Free:(800) 854-6705
Web Page: http://www.apogee.com

Appian Graphics ··· Redmond, WA: (425) 882-2020
Tech:(800) 422-7369   Toll Free:(800) 727-7426
Web Page: http://www.appian.com

Application Techniques Inc ·························· Pepperell, MA: (978) 433-5201
Tech:(978) 433-8464   Toll Free:(800) 433-5201
Web Page: http://www.screencapture.com

Applied Computer Sciences Inc ··················· Dublin, OH: (614) 717-1855
Web Page: http://www.appcs.com

Applied Computer Systems ························· Sunnyvale, CA: (408) 744-0001
Toll Free:(888) 422-0867
Web Page: http://www.apcom.com

Applied Information Systems Inc ·················· Chapel Hill, NC: (800) 334-5510
Tech:(919) 942-7801   Toll Free:(800) 334-5510
Web Page: http://www.ais.com

Applied Integration ·· Tucson, AZ: (520) 743-3095
  Web Page: http://www.appliedi.com
Applied Micro Circuits Corp ··············· San Diego, CA: (800) 840-6055
  Tech:(800) 840-6055
  Web Page: http://www.amcc.com
Applied Microsystems Corp ·················· Redmond, WA: (425) 882-2000
  Tech:(800) 275-4262   Toll Free:(800) 426-3925
  Web Page: http://www.amc.com
Applied Scientific Instrumentation ···········Eugene, OR: (541) 461-8181
  Toll Free:(800) 706-2284
  Web Page: http://www.asiimaging.com
Applied Testing and Technology ············Los Gatos, CA: (408) 399-1930
  Web Page: http://www.aptest.com
Applix Inc·· Westboro, MA: (508) 870-0300
  Tech:(800) 827-7549   Toll Free:(800) 827-7549
  Web Page: http://www.applix.com
Appro International Inc ·························· Milpitas, CA: (408) 941-8100
  Toll Free:(800) 927-5464
  Web Page: http://www.appro.com
Approach Software (see Lotus Develop)
Apricorn Inc ··· Poway, CA: (858) 513-2000
  Tech:(800) 458-5448   Toll Free:(800) 458-5448
  Web Page: http://www.apricorn.com
APS Technologies (see LaCie)
Apsylog Inc (see Peregrine Systems)
AR Industries (see Road Warrior Int.)
Arabesque Software (see NetManage)
Araize (see DS Design)
Arc Media.com··································· Getzville, NY: (416) 410-4429
  Web Page: http://www.arcmedia.com
Arcada Software (see Seagate Software)
Architext ·· San Antonio, TX: (210) 490-2240
  Web Page: http://www.architext.com
Archive Software (see Seagate Software)
Archos Technology······························· Irvine, CA: (949) 609-1400
  Web Page: http://www.archos.com
Archtek America Corp ···················· City Of Industry, CA: (626) 330-3600
  Web Page: http://www.archtek.com
Arco Computer Products Inc················· Hollywood, FL: (954) 925-2688
  Tech:(954) 925-7347   Toll Free:(800) 458-1666
  Web Page: http://www.arcoide.com
Arcom Control Systems ····················· Kansas City, MO: (913) 549-1000
  Toll Free:(888) 941-2224
  Web Page: http://www.arcomcontrol.com
ArcSoft Inc ·· Fremont, CA: (510) 440-9901
  Tech:(510) 440-9901   Toll Free:(800) 762-8657
  Web Page: http://www.arcsoft.com
Ardent Software (see Informix Software)
Areal Technology Inc (Out of Business)
Arescom Inc ··· Fremont, CA: (510) 445-3638
  Toll Free:(888) 575-4736
  Web Page: http://www.arescom.com
Argent Software······································ Farmington, CT: (860) 674-1700
  Web Page: http://www.argent.com
Argus Camera ·· Inverness, IL: (847) 228-5300
  Web Page: http://www.arguscamera.com
Arista Group ·· Hauppauge, NY: (631) 435-0200
  Tech:(800) 274-7824   Toll Free:(800) 274-7824

Web Page: http://www.aristagroup.com

Aristo Computers (see Cable E Commerce)

Aristosoft (see Software Made Simple)

Arm Computer Inc ·· **San Jose, CA: (408) 964-2500**
Tech:(408) 964-2555   Toll Free:(888) 824-5709
Web Page: http://www.armcomputer.com

ARM Ltd ·· **Los Gatos, CA: (408) 579-2200**
Tech:(408) 579-2200
Web Page: http://www.arm.com

Arnet Corp (see Digi International)

Arrow Electronics Inc ·································· **Melville, NY: (516) 391-1300**
Tech:(877) 237-8621   Toll Free:(800) 359-3580
Web Page: http://www.arrowelectronics.com
CMS Distribution Group ···································(408) 441-4050
Toll Free:(888) 263-7720
Semiconductor Group ····································(516) 391-1300
Tech:(408) 453-1200   Toll Free:(800) 777-2776
Zeus Electronics ··(914) 701-7400
Toll Free:(800) 524-4735

Arrowfield International Inc ························· **Tustin, CA: (714) 669-0101**
Toll Free:(800) 227-9628
Web Page: http://www.arrowfieldinc.com

Art Today ·· **Tucson, AZ: (520) 881-8101**
Tech:(520) 881-2310   Toll Free:(800) 482-4567
Web Page: http://www.arttoday.com

Artec (see Artronix Technology)

Artecon Inc (see Dot Hill)

Artel Video Systems Inc ························· **Boxborough, MA: (978) 263-5775**
Tech:(800) 225-0228   Toll Free:(800) 225-0228
Web Page: http://www.artel.com

Artemis ·· **Boulder, CO: (303) 531-3159**
Tech:(800) 777-7100   Toll Free:(800) 477-6648
Web Page: http://www.artemispm.com

Artesyn Tech ·· **Madison, WI: (608) 831-5500**
Tech:(800) 327-1251   Toll Free:(800) 356-9602
Web Page: http://www.artesyn.com

Artic Technologies Intl ································· **Troy, MI: (248) 588-7370**
Tech:(248) 588-1425
Web Page: http://www.artictech.com

Articulate Sys. (see Lernout & Hauspie)

Artisoft Inc ·· **Cambridge, MA: (617) 354-0600**
Tech:(617) 491-2944   Toll Free:(800) 914-9985
Web Page: http://www.artisoft.com

Artist Graphics Inc (see Comtrol Corp)

Artronix Technology ····································· **Brea, CA: (714) 854-7738**
Tech:(714) 854-7750
Web Page: http://www.artecusa.com

Arts & Letters ·· **Carrollton, TX: (972) 661-8960**
Tech:(888) 853-9292   Toll Free:(800) 752-9057
Web Page: http://www.arts-letters.com

Asaca Corp ·· **Golden, CO: (303) 278-1111**
Toll Free:(800) 423-6347
Web Page: http://www.asaca.com

Asante Technologies ································· **San Jose, CA: (408) 435-8388**
Tech:(800) 622-7464   Toll Free:(800) 662-9686
Web Page: http://www.asante.com

Ascend Comm. (see Lucent Internetworking)

Ascent Solutions Inc ····························· **Miamisburg, OH: (937) 847-2374**
Tech:(937) 847-2687

Web Page: http://www.asizip.com

ASCII Group Inc, The ··· Bethesda, MD: (301) 718-2600
Toll Free:(800) 394-2724
Web Page: http://www.ascii.com

Ashby Industries ··· Oklahoma City, OK: (405) 722-1705
Toll Free:(800) 927-4297
Web Page: http://www.ashbyindustries.com

Ashlar Inc ··· Austin, TX: (512) 250-2186
Tech:(800) 877-2745   Toll Free:(800) 877-2745
Web Page: http://www.ashlar.com

Ashton-Tate (see Inprise Corp)

ASI ··· Fremont, CA: (510) 226-8000
Web Page: http://www.asi2000.com

ASIC Northwest Inc ··· Powell Butte, OR: (541) 923-3755
Web Page: http://www.asicnw.com

Asint North America ··· Ann Arbor, MI: (734) 677-0840
Toll Free:(877) 767-8862
Web Page: http://www.asintgroup.com

askSam Systems ··· Perry, FL: (850) 584-6590
Tech:(850) 584-6590   Toll Free:(800) 800-1997
Web Page: http://www.asksam.com

ASP Computer Product (see Cables To Go)

Aspect Software Engineer (see Microsoft)

Aspen Systems Inc ··· Wheat Ridge, CO: (303) 431-4606
Tech:(800) 992-9242   Toll Free:(800) 992-9242
Web Page: http://www.aspsys.com

Aspen Technology Inc ··· Cambridge, MA: (617) 949-1000
Tech:(281) 584-4357   Toll Free:(888) 996-7100
Web Page: http://www.aspentec.com

Aspro ··· Mississauga, ON: (905) 712-2131
Web Page: http://www.aspro.com

Association for Computing Machinery ··· New York, NY: (212) 869-7440
Tech:(212) 626-0500   Toll Free:(800) 342-6626
Web Page: http://www.acm.org

Astea International Inc ··· Horsham, PA: (215) 682-2500
Tech:(215) 682-2288   Toll Free:(800) 347-7334
Web Page: http://www.astea.com

Astec America Inc ··· Carlsdad, CA: (760) 930-4600
Tech:(760) 757-1880   Toll Free:(888) 412-7832
Web Page: http://www.astec.com

Astec Standard Power (see Astec America)

Astoria Software ··· San Mateo, CA: (650) 357-7477
Web Page: http://www.astoriasoftware.com

Astound Inc ··· Los Altos, CA: (650) 623-0803
Tech:(416) 207-0868   Tech:(877) 278-6863
Web Page: http://www.astound.com

ASUSTek Computer Intl ··· Newark, CA: (510) 739-3777
Web Page: http://www.asus.com

Asymetrix Corp (see Asymetrix Learning)

Asymetrix Learning (see Click To Learn)

AT&T IP Services ··· San Diego, CA: (858) 812-5000
Toll Free:(888) 237-3638
Web Page: http://www.cerf.net

AT&T Wireless Services Inc ··· Kirkland, WA: (800) 888-7600
Tech:(800) 888-7600
Web Page: http://www.attws.com

Atcom Info (see Case Software Solutions)

ATI Technologies Inc ··· Markham, ON: (905) 882-2600
Tech:(905) 882-2626

Web Page: http://www.atitech.com

Atlantic Cable Technology (800) 642-8816
Toll Free:(800) 642-8816
Web Page: http://www.atlanticcable.com

Atlas Business Solutions .... Fargo, ND: (701) 235-5226
Toll Free:(800) 874-8801
Web Page: http://www.abs-usa.com

Atlus Co .... Irvine, CA: (949) 788-0455
Tech:(949) 788-0353
Web Page: http://www.atlus.com

Atmel .... San Jose, CA: (408) 441-0311
Web Page: http://www.atmel.com

Atrium Software .... Phoenix, AZ: (602) 912-5762
Web Page: http://www.atrium-software.com

Atronics International Inc .... Fremont, CA: (510) 656-8400
Toll Free:(800) 488-7776
Web Page: http://www.atronics.com

Attachmate Corp .... Bellevue, WA: (425) 644-4010
Tech:(800) 688-3270   Toll Free:(800) 426-6283
Web Page: http://www.attachmate.com

Attain (Out of Business)

Attar Software USA .... Newbury Port, MA: (978) 465-5111
Toll Free:(800) 456-3966
Web Page: http://www.attar.com

Attrasoft .... Savannah, GA: (912) 484-1717
Tech:(912) 897-1717
Web Page: http://www.attrasoft.com

Audio Video Supply .... San Diego, CA: (858) 565-1101
Toll Free:(800) 284-2288
Web Page: http://www.avsupply.com

Audiovox Communications .... Hauppauge, NY: (631) 233-3300
Tech:(631) 231-6051   Toll Free:(800) 229-1235
Web Page: http://www.audiovox.com

Aura Networks .... Merrimack, NH: (603) 880-1833
Tech:(800) 952-6227   Toll Free:(877) 526-2278
Web Page: http://www.auranetinc.com

Aurora Technologies .... Brockton, MA: (508) 588-6110
Tech:(508) 588-6110
Web Page: http://www.auroratech.com

AUSCAN Software Limited .... Toronto, ON: (416) 651-4037
Tech:(705) 434-1239
Web Page: http://www.interlog.com/~rjp/auscan.html

Auspex Systems Inc (see GlassHouse Tech)

Austin James Inc (see MadeToOrder.com)

Austin-Hayne (see SuccessFactors.com)

Authentica Inc .... Lexington, MA: (781) 487-2600
Web Page: http://www.authentica.com

Authentium .... Palm Beach Gardens, FL: (561) 575-3200
Toll Free:(800) 423-9147
Web Page: http://www.authertuim.com

Auto-trol Technology Corp .... Denver, CO: (303) 452-4919
Toll Free:(800) 233-2882
Web Page: http://www.auto-trol.com

Auto.Des.Sys Inc .... Columbus, OH: (614) 488-8838
Web Page: http://www.autodessys.com

Autodesk Inc .... San Rafael, CA: (415) 507-5000
Tech:(415) 507-4600   Toll Free:(800) 538-6401
Web Page: http://www.autodesk.com

Autograph Intl Inc .... San Jose, CA: (408) 282-7880

Web Page: http://www.augrin.com

Automatic Answer, The (see Amanda Co)

Autoquant Imaging Inc ··· Watervliet, NY: (518) 276-2138
Web Page: http://www.aqi.com

AutoTester Inc ·· Dallas, TX: (214) 368-1196
Tech:(214) 368-8276   Toll Free:(800) 328-1196
Web Page: http://www.autotester.com

Avalan Technology (see Computer Assoc)

Avalon Hill Game (see Hasbro)

Avanti Technology Inc ·· Austin, TX: (512) 335-1168
Tech:(512) 335-1168   Toll Free:(800) 638-1168
Web Page: http://www.avanti-tech.com

Avatar/DCA (see Attachmate)

Avax International ··· Erin, ON: (519) 833-2900
Toll Free:(800) 443-4542
Web Page: http://www.avax.com

Avcom Technologies Inc ·· Silver Spring, MD: (703) 442-9220
Web Page: http://www.avcom.com

AVer Media ·· Milipitas, CA: (408) 263-3828
Tech:(408) 942-2121   Toll Free:(800) 863-2332
Web Page: http://www.avermedia.com

Avery Dennison Consumer Service Center ···················· Brea, CA: (972) 389-3699
Tech:(972) 389-3699   Toll Free:(800) 462-8379
Web Page: http://www.avery.com

Avesta Tech (see Visual Networks Tech)

Avid Technology ·· Tewsbury, MA: (978) 640-3425
Tech:(800) 800-2843   Toll Free:(800) 949-2843
Web Page: http://www.avid.com

Avistar Systems ··· Redwood Shores, CA: (650) 610-2900
Tech:(650) 610-2961   Toll Free:(800) 803-0153
Web Page: http://www.avistar.com

Avnet Inc ·· Phoenix, AZ: (480) 643-2000
Toll Free:(800) 408-8353
Web Page: http://www.avnet.com

Avocent ·· Huntsville, AL: (256) 430-4000
Tech:(866) 286-2368   Toll Free:(800) 793-3758
Web Page: http://www.cybex.com

Avocet Systems Inc ·· Rockport, ME: (207) 236-9055
Tech:(207) 236-6010   Toll Free:(800) 448-8500
Web Page: http://www.avocetsystems.com

Avtek Systems ·· Sterling, MA: (978) 422-3466
Web Page: http://www.pspdigital.com

Award Software (See Phoenix Technologies)

Aware Inc ··· Bedford, MA: (781) 276-4000
Web Page: http://www.aware.com

Axent Tech (see Symantec Corp)

Axis Communications Inc ··································· Chelmsford, MA: (978) 614-2000
Tech:(978) 614-3000   Toll Free:(800) 444-2947
Web Page: http://www.axis.com

Axis Systems Inc ·· Sunnyvale, CA: (408) 588-2000
Tech:(408) 588-2000
Web Page: http://www.axiscorp.com

Axonix Corp ·· Salt Lake City, UT: (801) 521-9797
Tech:(800) 866-9797   Toll Free:(800) 866-9797
Web Page: http://www.axonix.com

AXS-One Inc ··· Rutherford, NJ: (201) 935-3400
Tech:(800) 328-7660   Toll Free:(800) 828-7660
Web Page: http://www.axs-one.com

Axtel Inc ··· Vista, CA: (760) 477-2200

Web Page: http://www.axtel.com

Aydin Displays ··· Birdsboro, PA: (610) 404-7400
Tech:(866) 367-2934
Web Page: http://www.aydindisplays.com

Az-Tech Software ·· Richmond, MO: (816) 776-2700
Tech:(816) 776-2700
Web Page: http://www.az-tech.com

Azerty Inc ··· Orchard Park, NY: (716) 662-0200
Tech:(800) 755-8800   Toll Free:(800) 888-8080
Web Page: http://www.azerty.com

Aztech Labs Inc ··· Fremont, CA: (510) 683-9800
Web Page: http://www.aztech.com

Aztek Inc ··· Lake Forest, CA: (949) 770-8787
Toll Free:(800) 472-7455
Web Page: http://www.aztek.com

Azure Tech (see GN Nettest Group)

B & B Electronics Mfg Co ··· Ottawa, IL: (815) 433-5100
Web Page: http://www.bb-elec.com

B & L Associates Inc ··· Needham Heights, MA: (781) 444-1404
Web Page: http://www.bandl.com

B&H Photo-Video ··· New York, NY: (212) 444-5000
Tech:(212) 239-7765   Toll Free:(800) 221-5743
Web Page: http://www.bhphotovideo.com

B&H Photo-Video (212) 444-6615
Toll Free:(800) 606-6969
Web Page: http://www.bhphotovideo.com

B.C. Software Inc (see Final Draft)

B.E. Meyers & Co Inc ··· Redmond, WA: (425) 881-6648
Toll Free:(800) 327-5648
Web Page: http://www.bemeyers.com

BackWeb Technologies ··· San Jose, CA: (408) 933-1700
Tech:(408) 933-1800   Toll Free:(800) 863-0100
Web Page: http://www.backweb.com

BakBone Software Inc ··· San Diego, CA: (858) 450-9009
Toll Free:(877) 939-2663
Web Page: http://www.bakbone.com

Balboa Software ··· Scottsdale, AZ: (480) 632-1901
Tech:(408) 632-1901   Toll Free:(800) 763-8542
Web Page: http://www.balboa-software.com

Baler Software Corp (see Tech Tools)

Ball Aerospace & Technologies Corp ··································· Boulder, CO: (303) 939-6100
Web Page: http://www.ballaerospace.com

BancTec ··· Irving, TX: (972) 341-4000
Toll Free:(800) 226-2832
Web Page: http://www.banctec.com

Banner Blue Software (see Broderbund)

Banner Engineering Inc ··· Minneapolis, MN: (763) 544-3164
Tech:(800) 809-7043   Toll Free:(888) 373-6767
Web Page: http://www.bannerengineering.com

Banyan Systems (see ePresence)

Baranti Group Inc ··· Markham, ON: (905) 479-0148
Toll Free:(888) 844-5485
Web Page: http://www.baranti.com

Barbanel Design ··· Leominster, MA: (978) 840-4100

Barbey Electronics ··· Reading, PA: (610) 376-7451
Tech:(610) 376-7451   Toll Free:(800) 822-2251
Web Page: http://www.barbeyele.com

Barco Display Systems ··· Duluth, GA: (678) 475-8105
Tech:(678) 475-8000

Web Page: http://www.barco.com/display

Barco Graphics ··· Vadalia, OH: (937) 454-1721

Barco Projection Systems Inc ···················· Kennesaw, GA: (770) 218-3200
Web Page: http://www.barco.com

Barr Systems Inc ···································· Gainesville, FL: (352) 491-3100
Toll Free:(800) 227-7797
Web Page: http://www.barrsystems.com

BASF Corp ··· Mount Olive, NJ: (973) 426-2600
Toll Free:(800) 526-1072
Web Page: http://www.basf.com

BASF Magnetics (see Emtech Data)

Basler Vision Technologies ···························· Exton, PA: (610) 280-0171
Web Page: http://www.baslerweb.com

Bason Computer Inc ································· Chatsworth, CA: (818) 727-9054
Tech:(818) 725-9704   Toll Free:(800) 238-4453
Web Page: http://www.basoncomputer.com

Bate Tech Software Inc. (see Ixchange)

Batteries Direct ···································· Parkersburg, WV: (304) 428-2296
Tech:(304) 428-2296   Toll Free:(800) 666-2296
Web Page: http://www.batteryking.com

Battery Express (see Fullers Wholesale)

Battery Technology Inc (BTI) ················· City Of Industry, CA: (626) 336-6878
Tech:(800) 982-8284   Toll Free:(800) 982-8284
Web Page: http://www.batterytech.com

Bay Networks (see Nortel Networks)

Baydel ··· San Jose, CA: (408) 383-7472
Tech:(408) 383-7474
Web Page: http://www.baydel.com

Bayer Corp. (see Agfa Compugraphics)

Baystate Tech (see Cadkey Corp)

BayWare Inc (see Transparent Language)

BBN Inc. (see GTE Internetworking)

BCAM Int. Inc. (out of business)

BCD Associates ······························· Oklahoma City, OK: (405) 843-4574
Toll Free:(800) 223-6734
Web Page: http://www.bcdusa.com

BE Inc (See Palm Inc)

BEA Systems Inc ···································· San Jose, CA: (408) 570-8000
Tech:(408) 743-4070   Toll Free:(800) 817-4232
Web Page: http://www.beasys.com

Beagle Software ································· Minneapolis, MN: (612) 370-1091
Toll Free:(877) 845-2549
Web Page: http://www.beaglesoft.com

Beatnik ··· San Mateo, CA: (650) 295-2300
Web Page: http://www.mixman.com

BeatWare Inc ····································· Redwood City, CA: (650) 556-7900
Web Page: http://www.beatware.com

Beckman Industrial (see Wavetek)

BEI Corp (see Ultra Bac)

Beiley Software Inc ··································· Phoenix, AZ: (480) 705-0129
Web Page: http://www.beiley.com

Belden Wire And Cable ···························· Richmond, IN: (765) 983-5200
Tech:(765) 983-5200   Toll Free:(800) 235-3361
Web Page: http://www.belden.com

Belkin Components ·································· Compton, CA: (310) 898-1100
Tech:(800) 223-5546   Toll Free:(800) 223-5546
Web Page: http://www.belkin.com

Bell & Howell Scanners ····························· Wheeling, IL: (847) 675-7600

Toll Free:(800) 722-6495
Web Page: http://www.bellhowell.com
Bell Microproducts ··· San Jose, CA: (408) 451-9400
Toll Free:(800) 800-1513
Web Page: http://www.bellmicro.com
Belmont Distributing (see Almo Corp)
Bencher Inc ··· Antioch, IL: (847) 838-3195
Web Page: http://www.bencher.com
Benefit Software Inc ······································· Santa Barbara, CA: (805) 568-0240
Tech:(800) 533-8801   Toll Free:(800) 533-1388
Web Page: http://www.bsiweb.com
Bennet-Tec Information Systems Inc ···························· Jericho, NY: (516) 997-5596
Tech:(516) 997-5596
Web Page: http://www.bennet-tec.com
Bentley Systems Inc ······································· Exton, PA: (610) 458-5000
Toll Free:(800) 236-8539
Web Page: http://www.bentley.com
BERG Electronics Corp ······································· Etters, PA: (800) 237-2374
Toll Free:(800) 237-2374
Web Page: http://www.bergelect.com
Berkeley Systems Inc (see Sierra)
Berkshire Products ······································· Suwanee, GA: (770) 271-0088
Web Page: http://www.berkprod.com
Bernstein & Assoc. (see Mind IQ)
Bescor Video ······································· Farmingdale, NY: (631) 420-1717
Toll Free:(800) 645-7182
Web Page: http://www.bescor.com
Best Data Products Inc ······································· Chatsworth, CA: (818) 773-9600
Tech:(818) 773-9600
Web Page: http://www.bestdata.com
Best Power (see PowerWare)
Best Programs Inc. (see Best Software)
Best Software Inc ······································· Irvine, CA: (949) 753-1222
Tech:(800) 944-5481   Toll Free:(800) 854-3415
Web Page: http://www.sota.com
Business Works Division ······································· (916) 791-7730
Tech:(800) 447-5700   Toll Free:(800) 447-5700
Web Page: http://www.sage.com
DacEasy Division ······································· (972) 732-7500
Tech:(972) 248-0205   Toll Free:(800) 322-3279
Web Page: http://www.sota.com
Best US Holdings ······································· Dallas, TX: (972) 818-3900
Tech:(972) 713-0259   Toll Free:(800) 835-6244
Web Page: http://www.telemagic.com
Best! Software ······································· Reston, VA: (703) 709-5200
Tech:(800) 331-8514   Toll Free:(800) 368-2405
Web Page: http://www.bestsoftware.com
HR Products Group ······································· (727) 579-1111
Tech:(727) 579-1111   Toll Free:(800) 424-9392
Web Page: http://www.bestsoftware.com
Best! Ware Inc (see MYOB US Inc)
Bethesda Softworks ······································· Rockville, MD: (301) 926-8300
Tech:(301) 963-2002   Toll Free:(800) 677-0700
Web Page: http://www.bethsoft.com
Better Light Inc ······································· San Carlos, CA: (650) 631-3680
Web Page: http://www.betterlight.com
Bi-Tronics ······································· Hawthorne, NY: (914) 592-1800
Toll Free:(800) 666-0996
Web Page: http://www.bi-tronics.com

Bible Research Systems (see BRS)

Biblesoft ·· Seattle, WA: (206) 824-8360
Tech:(206) 870-1463   Toll Free:(800) 877-0778
Web Page: http://www.biblesoft.com

Bidali Software ·· Roseville, CA: (967) 683-3153
Web Page: http://www.bidali.com

Big Storage ·· San Francisco, CA: (415) 845-2240
Toll Free:(800) 864-3789
Web Page: http://www.bigstorage.com

Bindview Development ·· Houston, TX: (713) 561-4000
Tech:(800) 813-5867   Toll Free:(800) 813-5869
Web Page: http://www.bindview.com

Binuscan ·· Hartsdale, NY: (914) 682-3144
Web Page: http://www.binuscan.com

Bio-Imaging Research Inc ······································ Newtown, PA: (267) 757-3000
Web Page: http://www.bio-imaging.com

Bio-Rad ··· Hercules, CA: (510) 741-1000
Tech:(510) 724-7000   Toll Free:(800) 424-6723
Web Page: http://www.bio-rad.com

Birmy Graphics (see iProof Systems)

Biscom Inc ··· Chelmsford, MA: (978) 250-8355
Tech:(978) 250-8355   Toll Free:(800) 477-2472
Web Page: http://www.biscom.com

Bitflow Inc ··· Woburn, MA: (781) 932-2900
Web Page: http://www.bitflow.com

BitShop ·· College Park, MD: (301) 345-6789
Toll Free:(888) 467-8447
Web Page: http://www.bitshop.com

Bitstream Inc ·· Cambridge, MA: (617) 497-6222
Tech:(617) 497-7514   Toll Free:(800) 522-3668
Web Page: http://www.bitstream.com

Bittware Research Systems ·································· Concord, NH: (603) 226-0404
Web Page: http://www.bittware.com

Biz Base Inc (see ACE Contact Manager)

Black Belt Systems ·· Glasgow, MT: (406) 228-8945
Tech:(406) 228-8944   Toll Free:(800) 888-3979
Web Page: http://www.blackbeltsystems.com

Black Box Corp ·· Lawrence, PA: (724) 746-5500
Tech:(724) 746-5565   Toll Free:(877) 877-2269
Web Page: http://www.blackbox.com

Black Diamond Software ·· Ridgefield, CT: (203) 431-9600
Tech:(203) 431-9600   Toll Free:(877) 977-8865
Web Page: http://www.blackdiamondsoftware.com

Black Dog Communications ·································· Morgan Hill, CA: (408) 782-7448
Web Page: http://www.blackdogcommunications.com

Black Ice Software Inc ·· Amherst, NH: (603) 673-1019
Tech:(603) 673-1019
Web Page: http://www.blackice.com

Blackbaud Inc ·· Charleston, SC: (800) 468-8996
Tech:(866) 267-3378   Toll Free:(800) 443-9441
Web Page: http://www.blackbaud.com

BLAST Inc ·· Pittsboro, NC: (919) 545-2535
Toll Free:(800) 242-5278
Web Page: http://www.blast.com

Blastronix ·· Angels Camp, CA: (209) 795-0738
Web Page: http://www.blastronix.com

Blizzard Entertainment ··· Irvine, CA: (949) 955-0283
Tech:(949) 955-1382   Toll Free:(800) 953-7669
Web Page: http://www.blizzard.com

Blue Lance Software Inc ···································Houston, TX: (713) 680-1187
  Toll Free:(800) 856-2583
  Web Page: http://www.bluelance.com
Blue Ocean Software Inc (see Intuit, Inc.)
Blue Phoenix ··Cary, NC: (919) 380-5100
  Toll Free:(800) 400-9087
  Web Page: http://www.bluephoenixsolutions.com
Blue Sky Software (see eHelp Corp)
Blue Squirrel ···Sandy, UT: (801) 352-1551
  Toll Free:(800) 403-0925
  Web Page: http://www.bluesquirrel.com
Blue Willow Inc (see Sequoia Publishing)
Bluebird Systems (see Open Text Corp)
BlueSky Solutions LLC ·························Harrison City, PA: (724) 744-2299
  Web Page: http://www.alventive.com
Bluestone Software (see Hewlett-Packard)
BMC Software Inc ···································Houston, TX: (713) 918-8800
  Tech:(800) 537-1813   Toll Free:(800) 841-2031
  Web Page: http://www.bmc.com
BMDP Statistical Software (see SPSS)
Boeckeler Instruments ·······························Tucson, AZ: (520) 745-0001
  Web Page: http://www.boeckler.com
Bogen Photo Corp ···································Ramsey, NJ: (201) 818-9500
  Tech:(212) 695-8166
  Web Page: http://www.bogenphoto.com
Bokler Software Corp ·······························Huntsville, AL: (256) 539-9901
  Web Page: http://www.bokler.com
Boland Communications ·······················Mission Viejo, CA: (949) 367-9911
Borland International (see Inprise Corp)
BORLAND USA / Inprise Corp ·················Scotts Valley, CA: (831) 431-1000
  Tech:(888) 588-2230   Toll Free:(800) 457-9527
  Web Page: http://www.borland.com
  Development Support·······························(831) 431-1000
  Tech:(800) 457-9527   Toll Free:(800) 457-9527
  Web Page: http://www.borland.com/devsupport
Bose Corp (800) 999-2673
  Tech:(800) 367-4008   Toll Free:(800) 999-2673
  Web Page: http://www.bose.com
Bottomline Technologies ·························Portsmouth, NH: (603) 436-0700
  Tech:(800) 243-2528   Toll Free:(800) 839-9029
  Web Page: http://www.bottomline.com
Boundless Technologies ·························Hauppauge, NY: (631) 342-7400
  Tech:(800) 231-5445   Toll Free:(800) 231-5445
  Web Page: http://www.boundless.com
Box Hill Systems Corp (see dot Hill)
Boxer Software ···································Scottsdale, AZ: (602) 485-1635
  Tech:(602) 485-1635   Toll Free:(800) 982-6937
  Web Page: http://www.boxersoftware.com
Boxx Technologies Inc ·······························Austin, TX: (512) 835-0400
  Toll Free:(877) 877-2699
  Web Page: http://www.boxxtech.com
Bradmark Technologies Inc ·························Houston, TX: (800) 621-2808
  Toll Free:(800) 621-2808
  Web Page: http://www.bradmark.com
Brain-Storm Technologies Inc ···········North Hollywood, CA: (818) 760-7974
  Tech:(818) 760-7974
  Web Page: http://www.mindtech.com
Braintech inc ·······································N. Vancouver, BC: (604) 988-6440
  Web Page: http://www.braintech.com

Bravo Communications Inc ························· San Jose, CA: (408) 297-8700
Tech:(408) 297-8700   Toll Free:(800) 366-0297
Web Page: http://www.bravobravo.com

Breece Hill Tech (see MaxOptic Corp)

BreezeCom (see Alvarion)

Brick Computer Company, The ····················· Ipswich, MA: (978) 356-1228
Tech:(978) 356-1229   Toll Free:(800) 843-2742
Web Page: http://www.ergo-computing.com

Brighter Child Interactive ······················· Worthington, OH: (614) 430-3021
Toll Free:(888) 283-2246
Web Page: http://www.brighterchild.com

Brightwork Development (see McAfee East)

Brilliant Digital Entertainment ················· Woodland Hills, CA: (818) 615-1500
Web Page: http://www.brilliantdigital.com

Brio Software (see Hyperion Solutions)

Bristol Technology Inc ··························· Danbury, CT: (203) 798-1007
Web Page: http://bristol.com

BroadVision ····································· Waltham, MA: (781) 290-0710
Tech:(800) 688-5151   Toll Free:(800) 955-5323
Web Page: http://www.ileaf.com

BroadVision ····································· Redwood City, CA: (650) 542-5100
Tech:(800) 688-5151   Toll Free:(800) 269-9375
Web Page: http://www.broadvision.com

Broadxent ······································· Milpitas, CA: (408) 262-1277
Tech:(408) 719-5100
Web Page: http://www.broadxent.com

Broderbund ····································· Novato, CA: (415) 382-4400
Tech:(319) 247-3333   Toll Free:(800) 521-6263
Web Page: http://www.learningco.com
  Customer Service ······························ (319) 247-3325
  Toll Free:(800) 395-0277
  Educational Software ·························· (800) 821-5895
  Parsons Technology ···························· (319) 395-9626
  Tech:(319) 247-3333   Toll Free:(800) 779-6000
  Web Page: http://www.broderbund.com

Brooks Automation Inc ·························· Salt Lake City, UT: (801) 322-2069
Tech:(801) 736-3201
Web Page: http://www.autosoft.com

Brooktrout Technology ·························· Needham, MA: (781) 449-4100
Tech:(800) 268-7688   Toll Free:(800) 268-7688
Web Page: http://www.brooktrout.com

Brother International ··························· Somerset, NJ: (800) 284-4357
Toll Free:(800) 284-4357
Web Page: http://www.brother.com

Brother International ··························· Bridgewater, NJ: (908) 704-1700
Tech:(800) 276-7746   Toll Free:(800) 276-7746
Web Page: http://www.brother.com
  Accessories ··································· (888) 879-3232
  Toll Free:(888) 879-3232
  Web Page: http://www.brother.com
  Fax/Multi-function Machine ··················· (800) 284-4329
  Tech:(800) 276-7746   Toll Free:(800) 284-4329
  Web Page: http://www.brother.com
  Machine Tools ································· (847) 718-9500
  Web Page: http://www.brother.com
  Mobile Computing ······························ (800) 284-1937
  Toll Free:(800) 284-1937
  Web Page: http://www.brother.com

BRS ··· Austin, TX: (512) 251-7541
Tech:(512) 251-7541   Toll Free:(800) 423-1228

Web Page: http://www.brs-inc.com

BSDI ·· Concord, CA: (925) 674-0783
Tech:(800) 872-4977
Web Page: http://www.bsdi.com

BT Syntegra ··· Arden Hills, MN: (651) 415-4401
Tech:(651) 482-6736
Web Page: http://www.btsyntegra.com

BTC (Behavior Tech Computer Corp) ············ Freemont, CA: (510) 657-3956
Web Page: http://www.btcusa.com

Buerg Software And Computers ·················· Petaluma, CA: (707) 778-1811
Toll Free:(800) 442-8374
Web Page: http://www.buerg.com

Buhl Industries ························· South Hackensack, NJ: (201) 296-0600
Toll Free:(800) 631-0868
Web Page: http://www.buhl-ind.com

BulletProof Corp ······························ Ft Lauderdale, FL: (954) 828-9400
Toll Free:(800) 505-0105
Web Page: http://www.bulletproof.com

Bullseye Disc ····································· Portland, OR: (503) 233-2313
Toll Free:(800) 652-7194
Web Page: http://www.cd-rom-works.com

Bungie Software (see Microsoft)

Burr-Brown Corp (see Texas Instruments)

Bus-Tech Inc ····································· Burlington, MA: (800) 284-3172
Tech:(781) 272-8200   Toll Free:(800) 284-3172
Web Page: http://www.bustech.com

Business Forecast Systems Inc ·················· Belmont, MA: (617) 484-5050
Web Page: http://www.forecastpro.com

Business Resource Software (see BRS)

BusLogic Inc (see Mylex Corp)

Bytex Corp ··· Milford, MA: (508) 422-9422
Tech:(800) 227-1145   Toll Free:(800) 227-1145
Web Page: http://www.bytex.com

C&M Corp ··· Wauregan, CT: (860) 774-4812
Web Page: http://www.cm-corp.com

C-Cor Electronics ····························· State College, PA: (814) 238-2461
Toll Free:(800) 233-2267
Web Page: http://www.c-cor.com

Cable Connection ································· Los Gatos, CA: (408) 395-6700
Web Page: http://www.cable-connection.com

Cable E Commerce (see Kewill)

Cables To Go (CTG) ······························ Dayton, OH: (937) 224-8646
Tech:(800) 506-9607   Toll Free:(800) 826-7904
Web Page: http://www.cablestogo.com

Cabletron Systems (see Enterasys Network)

CABLExpress ····································· Syracuse, NY: (315) 476-3000
Tech:(315) 476-3100   Toll Free:(800) 913-9467
Web Page: http://www.cablexpress.com

Caci Products ····································· San Diego, CA: (619) 542-5228
Toll Free:(877) 663-3746
Web Page: http://www.caciasL.com

Cactus Development Company Inc ·················· Austin, TX: (512) 453-1251
Tech:(512) 453-1251   Toll Free:(800) 336-9444
Web Page: http://www.cactusdevelopment.com

Cadco ··· Garland, TX: (800) 877-2288
Tech:(972) 271-3651   Toll Free:(800) 877-2288
Web Page: http://www.cadcosystems.com

Cadence Design Systems Inc ····················· San Jose, CA: (408) 943-1234
Tech:(877) 237-4911   Toll Free:(800) 746-6223

Web Page: http://www.cadence.com

CadKey Corp (see Kubotek USA Inc.)

CADRE Tech (see Sterling Software)

Caere Corp (see Scan Soft Inc)

Caffeine Software Inc (Out of Business)

Cais Software Solutions (see Cisco Systems)

CakeWalk Music Software ·· Boston, MA: (617) 423-9004
  Toll Free:(888) 225-3925
  Web Page: http://www.cakewalk.com

Cal Comp Inc (see CalGraph Tech)

Calculus Inc ·· Menlo Park, CA: (650) 854-3130

Caldera Inc ··· Lindon, UT: (888) 465-4689
  Tech:(801) 765-4999   Toll Free:(800) 850-7779
  Web Page: http://www.caldera.com

Calera Recognition Systems (see Caere)

CalGraph Technology Services Inc ························· Fullerton, CA: (714) 578-9292
  Tech:(714) 578-9292   Toll Free:(800) 225-2667
  Web Page: http://www.calgraphinc.com

Calico Technology Inc (see Pivotal Corp)

California Software Products Inc ····················· San Clememte, CA: (949) 498-9300
  Web Page: http://www.calsw.com

Caligari Corporation ··· Mountain View, CA: (650) 390-9600
  Tech:(650) 390-9600   Toll Free:(800) 351-7620
  Web Page: http://www.caligari.com

Caliper Corp ·· Newton, MA: (617) 527-4700
  Tech:(617) 527-8617
  Web Page: http://www.caliper.com

Callware Technologies ································· Salt Lake City, UT: (801) 937-6800
  Tech:(801) 984-6230   Toll Free:(800) 888-4226
  Web Page: http://www.callware.com

Cambridge Research & Instrumentation ················· Woburn, MA: (781) 935-9099
  Tech:(781) 935-3388   Toll Free:(888) 372-1242
  Web Page: http://www.cri-inc.com

Cambridge Soundworks ···································· Andover, MA: (978) 623-4400
  Toll Free:(800) 367-4434
  Web Page: http://www.cambridgesoundworks.com

Cambridge Technology ······························· Cambridge, MA: (617) 441-0600
  Web Page: http://www.camtech.com

Campbell Services Inc (see Open Text)

Canary Communications ····································· Morgan Hill, CA: (408) 465-2277
  Toll Free:(800) 883-9201
  Web Page: http://www.canarycom.com

Candle Corp ·· El Segundo, CA: (310) 535-3600
  Tech:(310) 535-3636   Toll Free:(800) 328-1811
  Web Page: http://www.candle.com

Canoga Perkins Corp ······································· Chatsworth, CA: (818) 718-6300
  Tech:(818) 718-6300   Toll Free:(800) 360-6642
  Web Page: http://www.canoga.com

Canon USA Inc ······································· Lake Success, NY: (516) 488-6700
  Tech:(800) 423-2366   Toll Free:(800) 828-4040
  Web Page: http://www.usa.canon.com
  Broadcast Equipment ···································· (201) 816-2900
    Web Page: http://www.usa.canon.com
  Custom Integrated Technology Inc ··············· (757) 881-6300
    Web Page: http://www.usa.canon.com
  Industrial Resource Technologies Inc ············· (804) 695-7000
    Web Page: http://www.usa.canon.com
  Business Solutions Inc ···································· (708) 706-3400
    Web Page: http://www.solutions.canon.com

Business Solutions Inc ···································· (310) 217-3000
  Web Page: http://www.solutions.canon.com
Business Solutions Inc ···································· (609) 387-8700
  Web Page: http://www.solutions.canon.com
Business Solutions Inc ···································· (212) 850-1000
  Web Page: http://www.usa.canon.com
C. S. Polymer Inc ·· (757) 249-5500
  Web Page: http://www.usa.canon.com
Canon Business Machines ····························· (714) 556-4700
  Web Page: http://www.usa.canon.com
Canon Information Systems ··························· (949) 856-7100
  Web Page: http://www.usa.canon.com
Canon Software America ······························· (516) 327-2270
  Web Page: http://www.usa.canon.com
Canon Virginia Inc ··· (757) 881-6000
  Web Page: http://www.usa.canon.com
Consumer Products ··· (714) 438-3000
  Tech:(800) 423-2366   Toll Free:(800) 423-2366
  Web Page: http://www.usa.canon.com/consumer
Consumer Products ··· (800) 828-4040
  Tech:(800) 423-2366   Toll Free:(800) 652-2666
Government Marketing Division ···················· (703) 807-3400
  Web Page: http://www.usa.canon.com
Regional Office ·· (949) 753-4000
  Web Page: http://www.usa.canon.com
Regional Office ·· (732) 521-7000
  Web Page: http://www.usa.canon.com
Regional Office ·· (630) 250-6200
  Web Page: http://www.usa.canon.com
Regional Office ·· (972) 409-7800
  Web Page: http://www.usa.canon.com
Regional Office ·· (770) 849-7700
  Web Page: http://www.usa.canon.com
Regional Office ·· (808) 522-5930
  Web Page: http://www.usa.canon.com
Regional Office ·· (408) 468-2000
South Tech Inc ·· (804) 443-8000
  Web Page: http://www.usa.canon.com
Technical Support ·· (800) 828-4040
  Tech:(757) 413-2848   Toll Free:(800) 423-2366
Canon Visual Communication Systems··············Lake Success, NY: (516) 488-6700
  Web Page: http://www.usa.canon.com
Canopus Corp ··San Jose, CA: (408) 954-4500
  Tech:(408) 954-4506   Toll Free:(888) 899-3348
  Web Page: http://www.justedit.com
Canto Software ··San Francisco, CA: (415) 495-6545
  Web Page: http://www.canto.com
Canyon Software ··San Rafael, CA: (415) 453-9779
  Tech:(415) 453-9779   Toll Free:(800) 280-3691
  Web Page: http://www.canyonsw.com
CAP Automation··Fort Worth, TX: (817) 560-8139
  Tech:(817) 560-7007   Toll Free:(800) 826-5009
  Web Page: http://www.capauto.com
Capital Business Systems······························Forest Hills, NY: (718) 268-1417
  Web Page: http://www.capitalbusiness.com
Capital Computing Services····························Raleigh, NC: (919) 749-6656
  Web Page: http://www.capitalcomputing.com/
Capital Equipment Corp ··································Bedford, NH: (603) 472-1068
  Toll Free:(800) 234-4232
  Web Page: http://www.cec488.com
Capsoft Development Corp (see LexisNexis)

Captaris ·· Bellevue, WA: (425) 455-6000
  Toll Free:(800) 678-1097
  Web Page: http://www.captaris.com
Captaris ··· Tucson, AZ: (520) 320-7000
  Tech:(520) 320-7070
  Web Page: http://www.rightfax.com
Captiva Software Corp ·· San Diego, CA: (858) 320-1000
  Web Page: http://www.captivasoftware.com
Caravelle Networks (see Avesta Tech)
Cardexpert Technology Inc ·· Fremont, CA: (510) 252-1118
  Web Page: http://www.gainward.com/us.htm
Cardiff Software Inc (see Verity)
Carl Zeiss Inc ·· Thornwood, NY: (914) 681-7815
  Web Page: http://www.zeiss.com
Cartesia Software (see Map Resources)
Cartridges USA ·· Las Vegas, NV: (888) 866-3787
  Toll Free:(888) 866-3787
  Web Page: http://www.cartridgesusa.com
Casady & Greene (Out of Business)
Cascade (see Ascend Communications)
Case Logic Inc ·· Longmont, CO: (303) 652-1000
  Tech:(877) 227-3347   Toll Free:(800) 925-8111
  Web Page: http://www.caselogic.com
Case Software (see Cais Software)
Casio Inc ··· Dover, NJ: (973) 361-5400
  Tech:(800) 962-2746   Toll Free:(800) 634-1895
  Web Page: http://www.casio.com
  Cassiopeia ···(888) 204-7765
  Digital Cameras & Printers ···(800) 435-7732
  Manuals ···(973) 252-7570
  Product Support ···(973) 442-5707
    Toll Free:(800) 634-1895
  Repair Center ···(201) 329-9030
Castelle ·· Morgan Hill, CA: (408) 852-8000
  Tech:(408) 852-8080   Toll Free:(800) 289-7555
  Web Page: http://www.castelle.com
Cataline Technologies Inc ··· Natick, MA: (508) 651-0715
  Web Page: http://www.catalina-tech.com
Catenary Systems Inc ··· St Louis, MO: (314) 962-7833
  Tech:(314) 962-7833
  Web Page: http://www.catenary.com
Cayenne Soft (see Sterling Software)
Cayman Systems (see Netopia)
CBC America Corp ·· Commack, NY: (631) 864-9700
  Toll Free:(800) 422-6707
  Web Page: http://www.cbcamerica.com
CBT Systems (see Smart Force)
CCOM Information (see Lucent Tech)
CCS America Inc ·· Waltham, MA: (781) 899-2494
  Web Page: http://www.ccsamerica.com
CD Associates Inc (Unknown)
CD Dimensions Inc ·· Old Saybrook, CT: (860) 395-6396
  Toll Free:(888) 395-6396
  Web Page: http://www.cddimensions.com
CD International Inc ··· Kennebunk, ME: (207) 985-6370
  Tech:(207) 985-6442   Toll Free:(877) 985-6370
  Web Page: http://www.cdcomputer.com
CD-Rom Strategies (see DV Studio Inc)

CD-Rom Works Inc (see Bullseye Disc)

CDB Systems Inc ··································· Boulder, CO: (303) 444-7071
Tech:(303) 417-0639
Web Page: http://www.cdbsystems.com

CDC Solutions (see Liquent)

CE Software ································· West Des Moines, IA: (515) 221-1801
Tech:(515) 221-1803   Toll Free:(800) 523-7638
Web Page: http://www.cesoft.com

Cedar Technologies (see Rimage)

Celco ···································· Rancho Cucamonga, CA: (909) 481-4648
Web Page: http://www.celco.com

Celestica Inc ······································· Canada, : (416) 448-5800
Web Page: http://www.celestica.com

Center Span Comm. (see Guillemot)

Centerline Development Systems Inc ·················· Needham, MA: (781) 444-8000
Tech:(781) 444-8000   Toll Free:(800) 669-2687
Web Page: http://www.centerline.com

Centillion Digital Systems ······················ Indianapolis, IN: (317) 262-4896
Toll Free:(800) 262-9160
Web Page: http://www.centilliondigital.com

Centon Electronics Inc ···························· Aliso Viejo, CA: (949) 855-9111
Tech:(800) 234-9292   Toll Free:(800) 836-1986
Web Page: http://www.centon.com

Central Data Corp (see Digi Int.)

Central Point Software (see Symantec)

CentrePoint Technologies ························· Ottawa, ON: (613) 725-2980
Toll Free:(888) 332-9322
Web Page: http://www.ctrpoint.com

Centron Software Inc ···························· Pinehurst, NC: (910) 215-5708
Toll Free:(800) 848-2424
Web Page: http://www.centronsoftware.com

Centrum Business (see Scott Systems)

Centura Software (see M-Brain)

Century Microelectronics Inc ······················· Santa Clara, CA: (408) 748-7788
Web Page: http://www.century-micro.com

Century Software Inc ····························· Salt Lake City, UT: (801) 268-3088
Tech:(800) 877-3088   Toll Free:(800) 877-3088
Web Page: http://www.censoft.com

CEO Software Inc ································· Tucson, AZ: (520) 296-7577
Toll Free:(877) 236-7638
Web Page: http://www.ceosoft.com

Certus (see Symantec)

CFS Media Services ······························· Oak Park, MI: (248) 548-0025
Web Page: http://www.cfsmedia.com

CH Products ···································· Vista, CA: (760) 598-2518
Tech:(760) 598-7833   Toll Free:(800) 240-7282
Web Page: http://www.chproducts.com

Chaco Communications (see Andromedia)

Chain Store Guide Info Serv (CSGIS) ················ Tampa, FL: (813) 627-6800
Tech:(800) 252-9793   Toll Free:(800) 778-9794
Web Page: http://www.csgis.com

ChainTech-Excel Computer Inc ····················· Fremont, CA: (510) 656-3648
Web Page: http://www.chaintech.com.tw

Champion Business Systems Inc (see RedWing)

Charles River Media ······························· Hingham, MA: (781) 740-0400
Toll Free:(800) 382-8505
Web Page: http://www.charlesriver.com

Chase Research (see Perle Systems)

Chatsworth Products Inc ....Westlake Village, CA: (818) 735-6100
    Toll Free:(800) 834-4969
    Web Page: http://www.chatsworth.com
Check Point Software Technologies Inc ....Redwood City, CA: (650) 628-2000
    Tech:(817) 606-6600
    Web Page: http://www.checkpoint.com
CheckFree ....Norcross, GA: (678) 375-3000
    Tech:(888) 212-9342   Toll Free:(800) 297-3180
    Web Page: http://www.checkfree.com
CheckMark Software ....Fort Collins, CO: (970) 225-0522
    Tech:(970) 225-0387   Toll Free:(800) 444-9922
    Web Page: http://www.checkmark.com
Chemtronics (see ITW Chemtronics)
Cherry Corp ....Waukegan, IL: (847) 662-9200
    Toll Free:(800) 510-1689
    Web Page: http://www.cherrycorp.com
Cheyenne Software (see Computer Assoc.)
Chicago Map Corp (see Undertow Software)
Chicago-Soft Ltd ....Hanover, NH: (603) 643-4002
    Web Page: http://www.chicago-soft.com
    Customer Support Center ....(773) 282-4777
    Web Page: http://www.chicago-soft.com
Chinon America (see Tech Media)
ChipChat Technology Group ....Dearborn, MI: (313) 565-4000
    Tech:(313) 565-4000
    Web Page: http://www.chipchat.com
Chipcom Corp (see 3Com Corp)
Chips And Technologies Inc (see Intel)
ChipSoft Inc (see Intuit)
Chori America Inc ....New York, NY: (212) 642-0403
    Toll Free:(800) 445-4233
    Web Page: http://www.chori-america.com
Chorus Systems (see Sun Microsystems)
Chroma Graphics Inc ....San Bruno, CA: (650) 827-4700
    Tech:(650) 685-6806   Toll Free:(888) 824-7662
    Web Page: http://www.chromagraphics.com
Chrystal Software (see Astoria Software)
Chuck Atkinson (see CAP Automation)
Ci Design ....Anaheim, CA: (714) 646-0111
    Toll Free:(800) 576-5487
    Web Page: http://www.ci-design.com
Cidco Inc (see EarthLink)
Cimmetry Systems Inc ....Cambridge, MA: (514) 735-3219
    Tech:(514) 735-9941   Toll Free:(800) 361-1904
    Web Page: http://www.cimmetry.com
Cincinnati Electronics ....Mason, OH: (513) 573-6744
    Tech:(513) 573-6100   Toll Free:(800) 852-5105
    Web Page: http://www.cinele.com
Cincinnati Industrial Automation ....Erlanger, KY: (859) 371-5070
    Toll Free:(800) 758-1141
    Web Page: http://www.ciaviston.com
Cincom Systems Inc ....Cincinnati, OH: (513) 612-2769
    Tech:(513) 612-2769   Toll Free:(800) 224-6266
    Web Page: http://www.cincom.com
Cipher Data Products (see Overland Data)
Ciprico Inc ....Plymouth, MN: (763) 551-4000
    Tech:(763) 551-4131   Toll Free:(800) 727-4669
    Web Page: http://www.ciprico.com

Circle.com (see Euro RSCG 4D)

Circuit Technology Inc .... Holly Springs, NC: (919) 552-3434
   Web Page: http://www.smt-network.com

Cirque Corp .... Salt Lake City, UT: (801) 467-1100
   Tech:(801) 467-1100   Toll Free:(800) 454-3375
   Web Page: http://www.cirque.com

Cirrus Logic Inc .... Fremont, CA: (510) 623-8300
   Tech:(512) 912-3555   Toll Free:(888) 937-2787
   Web Page: http://www.cirrus.com

Cisco Systems .... San Jose, CA: (408) 526-4000
   Tech:(800) 553-2447   Toll Free:(800) 553-6387
   Web Page: http://www.cisco.com

Citadel Computer Sys (see Citadel Tech)

Citadel Technology .... Dallas, TX: (214) 520-9292
   Tech:(800) 325-3587   Toll Free:(888) 824-8233
   Web Page: http://www.citadel.com

Citation Computer Systems Inc .... Chesterfield, MO: (314) 579-7900
   Toll Free:(800) 325-1382
   Web Page: http://www.cita.com

Citizen America Corp .... Irvine, CA: (949) 428-3700
   Tech:(800) 556-7660   Toll Free:(800) 556-7660

Service Center .... (310) 781-1460
   Tech:(800) 843-8270   Toll Free:(800) 421-6516
   Web Page: http://www.cbma.com

Citrix Systems Inc .... Ft. Lauderdale, FL: (954) 267-3000
   Tech:(800) 424-8749   Toll Free:(800) 437-7503
   Web Page: http://www.citrix.com

Clarent Corp (see Verso)

Clariion (see EMC Corp)

Clarion Software (see Top Speed Corp)

Claris Corp (see Filemaker Inc)

Clarity International .... Portland, OR: (503) 535-8056
   Web Page: http://www.clarity.com

Clark Development Comp (Out of Business)

Clark Wire & Cable .... Mundelein, IL: (847) 949-9944
   Toll Free:(800) 222-5348
   Web Page: http://www.clarkwc.com

Clary Corp .... Monrovia, CA: (626) 359-4486
   Tech:(800) 551-6111   Toll Free:(800) 442-5279
   Web Page: http://www.clary.com

Classic PIO Partners .... Pasadena, CA: (626) 564-8106
   Tech:(626) 564-8106   Toll Free:(800) 370-2746
   Web Page: http://www.classicpartners.com

Classic Software Inc .... Cincinnati, OH: (513) 232-6764
   Tech:(513) 232-6764   Toll Free:(800) 677-2952
   Web Page: http://www.classicsoftware.com

Clear Software (see SPSS Inc)

Clearpoint Enterprises Inc .... Hopkinton, MA: (508) 544-9694
   Tech:(800) 253-2778   Toll Free:(800) 253-2778
   Web Page: http://www.clearpoint.com

Clemex Technologies .... Longueuil, QC: (450) 651-6573
   Toll Free:(888) 651-6573
   Web Page: http://www.clemex.com

Cleo Communications (see Interface Sys)

Cleo Products Group .... Loves Park, IL: (815) 654-8110
   Tech:(800) 233-2536   Toll Free:(800) 233-2536
   Web Page: http://www.cleo.com

Click2Learn.com (see SumTotal)

Clickable Software (see Virtual Pub)

Clickaction Inc (see Elibrium Inc)

Client/Server Connection ································· San Diego, CA: (858) 571-7156
  Toll Free:(866) 876-6160
  Web Page: http://www.cscl.com

Cliffs Notes (see Hungry Minds)

Clinton Electronics Corp ····························· Loves Park, IL: (815) 633-1444
  Web Page: http://www.cec-displays.com

Clover Systems ·· Laguna Hills, CA: (949) 582-8010
  Web Page: http://www.cloversystems.com

CMD Technology Inc ····································· Irvine, CA: (949) 454-0800
  Tech:(949) 454-0800   Toll Free:(800) 426-3832
  Web Page: http://www.cmd.com

CMH Software ··· Libby, MT: (406) 293-4977
  Tech:(406) 293-3616   Toll Free:(800) 680-7638
  Web Page: http://www.cmhsoftware.com

CMI Software (406) 549-0171
  Web Page: http://www.cmisoftware.com

CMP Media Inc ··· San Francisco, CA: (415) 947-6000
  Web Page: http://www.cmp.com

CMS Enhancements (see CMS Peripherals)

CMS Peripherals ··· Costa Mesa, CA: (714) 424-5520
  Tech:(800) 555-1671   Toll Free:(800) 327-5773
  Web Page: http://www.cmsperipheralsinc.com

CNC Software Inc ·· Tolland, CT: (860) 875-5006
  Web Page: http://www.mastercam.com

CNet Shopper ·· New York, NY: (212) 503-3800
  Toll Free:(800) 274-6384
  Web Page: http://shopper.cnet.com

CNet Technology Inc ···································· Milpitas, CA: (408) 934-0800
  Tech:(408) 934-0800   Toll Free:(800) 486-2638
  Web Page: http://www.cnetusa.com

CNF Inc ·· Palo Alto, CA: (503) 450-2000
  Web Page: http://www.cnf.com

CNT / Inrange Technologies ··························· Minneapolis, MN: (763) 268-6000
  Toll Free:(800) 752-8061
  Web Page: http://www.cnt.com

Coastal Optical Systems ······························ West Palm Beach, FL: (561) 881-7400
  Web Page: http://www.coastalopt.com

Coastcom Corp ·· Alameda, CA: (510) 523-6000
  Tech:(800) 385-4689   Toll Free:(800) 433-3433
  Web Page: http://www.coastcom.com

Cobalt Microserver (see Cobalt Networks)

Cobalt Networks (see Sun Microsystems)

Cobra Electronics ······································ Chicago, IL: (773) 889-3087
  Web Page: http://www.cobra.com

Coconut Computing (see ITU Engineering)

Coda Music Technology ································· Eden Prairie, MN: (952) 937-9611
  Tech:(952) 937-9703   Toll Free:(800) 843-2066
  Web Page: http://www.codamusic.com

Codenell Tech (see Dbas Codenell)

Codonics Imaging Division ····························· Middleburg Heights, OH: (440) 243-1198
  Toll Free:(800) 444-1198
  Web Page: http://www.codonics.com

Cogent Data Tech Inc (see Adaptec)

Cognex Corp ··· Natick, MA: (508) 650-3000
  Tech:(508) 650-6300
  Web Page: http://www.cognex.com

Cognitive Technology Corp ·············· Corte Madera, CA: (415) 945-0700
  Toll Free:(800) 599-4440
  Web Page: http://www.ocr.com
Cognos Corporation ·············· Burlington, MA: (781) 229-6600
  Tech:(613) 228-7900   Toll Free:(800) 426-4667
  Web Page: http://www.cognos.com
Cohu Electronics Division ·············· San Diego, CA: (858) 277-6700
  Web Page: http://www.cohu-cameras.com
Cole-Parmer Instrument ·············· Vernon Hills, IL: (847) 549-7600
  Toll Free:(800) 323-4340
  Web Page: http://www.coleparmer.com
Colorado Memory (see Hewlett-Packard)
ColorAge Inc (see Splash Technology)
Colorgraphic Communications Corp ·············· Atlanta, GA: (770) 455-3921
  Tech:(770) 455-3921   Toll Free:(877) 943-3843
  Web Page: http://www.www.colorgraphic.com
Colorspan Inc ·············· Eden Prairie, MN: (952) 944-9330
  Tech:(800) 925-0563   Toll Free:(800) 477-7714
  Web Page: http://www.colorspan.com
Colorspan Inc ·············· Eden Prairie, MN: (952) 944-4040
  Tech:(952) 944-4040   Toll Free:(800) 925-0563
  Web Page: http://www.colorspan.com
Colortrac Ltd US ·············· Golden, CO: (303) 973-6722
  Web Page: http://www.colortrac.com
Columbia Data Products Inc ·············· Altamonte Springs, FL: (407) 869-6700
  Tech:(407) 869-6700   Toll Free:(800) 613-6288
  Web Page: http://www.cdp.com
Columbia University Kermit Software ·············· New York, NY: (212) 854-3703
  Tech:(212) 854-5126
  Web Page: http://www.columbia.edu/kermit
Com Com Systems ·············· Clearwater, FL: (727) 725-3200
  Web Page: http://www.comcom.net
Com Squared Systems Inc ·············· Norcross, GA: (770) 734-5300
  Tech:(800) 523-4875   Toll Free:(800) 592-3766
  Web Page: http://www.comsquared.com
Com-Kyle Inc (Unknown)
Comark Corp ·············· Medfield, MA: (508) 359-8161
  Toll Free:(800) 280-8522
  Web Page: http://www.comarkcorp.com
Comark Inc (see Insight)
Command Communications Inc ·············· Englewood, CO: (303) 792-0890
  Tech:(800) 288-6794   Toll Free:(800) 288-3491
  Web Page: http://www.command-comm.com
Command Software Systems Inc(see Authentium)
Command Technology Corp ·············· Scottsdale, AZ: (480) 585-3868
  Toll Free:(800) 336-3320
  Web Page: http://www.commandtechnology.com
Commax Technologies Inc ·············· San Jose, CA: (408) 327-8990
  Tech:(408) 327-8990
  Web Page: http://www.commax.com
Common Ground Software (see Hummingbird)
CommTouch Software Inc ·············· Mountain View, CA: (650) 864-2000
  Toll Free:(888) 283-6245
  Web Page: http://www.commtouch.com
Communications Specialities ·············· Hauppauge, NY: (631) 273-0404
  Web Page: http://www.commspecial.com
Compaq Computer Corp (see Hewlett Packard)
Compatible Systems (see Cisco Systems)
Compex Inc ·············· Anaheim, CA: (714) 630-7302

Tech:(714) 630-5451   Toll Free:(800) 279-8891
Web Page: http://www.cpx.com

Compex Technology Inc (see Kenpax)

Compix Inc ....Cranberry Township, PA: (724) 772-5277
Web Page: http://www.cimaging.net

Compix Media Inc ....Torrance, CA: (310) 320-8937
Web Page: http://www.compixmedia.com

Complete PC, The (see Boca Research)

Component One ....Pittsburgh, PA: (412) 681-4343
Tech:(412) 681-4738   Toll Free:(800) 858-2739
Web Page: http://www.componentone.com

Compsee Inc ....Mount Gilead, NC: (910) 439-6141
Tech:(910) 439-6141   Toll Free:(800) 628-3888
Web Page: http://www.compsee.com

Compu-Teach ....Redmond, WA: (425) 885-0517
Tech:(800) 448-3224   Toll Free:(800) 448-3224
Web Page: http://www.compu-teach.com

CompuCable Mfg. Group (see Addlogix)

CompuCover Inc ....Fort Walton Beach, FL: (850) 862-4448
Toll Free:(800) 874-6391
Web Page: http://www.compucover.com

Compulink Laserfiche Inc ....Long Beach, CA: (562) 988-1688
Toll Free:(800) 985-8533
Web Page: http://www.laserfiche.com

CompuMart ....Corpus Christi, TX: (361) 992-6400
Toll Free:(800) 864-1155
Web Page: http://www.compumart.com

Compus Learning ....San Diego, CA: (858) 587-0087
Tech:(800) 678-1412   Toll Free:(800) 247-1380
Web Page: http://www.compasslearning.com

CompUSA Inc ....Dallas, TX: (800) 266-7872
Tech:(800) 266-7872   Toll Free:(800) 266-7872
Web Page: http://www.compusa.com

Computalabel International ....Newburyport, MA: (978) 462-0993
Web Page: http://www.computalabel.com

Computational Mechanics (see Altier Eng)

Computer Aided Business Solutions ....Golden, CO: (800) 800-2227
Tech:(303) 279-1868   Toll Free:(800) 800-2227
Web Page: http://www.cabs-cad.com

Computer Associates ....Islandia, NY: (631) 342-5224
Tech:(631) 342-4100   Toll Free:(800) 225-5224
Web Page: http://www.cai.com
License Key/Authorization Code ....(800) 338-6720
Toll Free:(800) 338-6720

Computer Connections ....Westwood, MA: (781) 320-3600
Web Page: http://www.computerconnect.com

Computer Conversions Inc ....San Diego, CA: (858) 746-3000
Toll Free:(800) 328-2911
Web Page: http://www.computer-conversions.com

Computer Corp of America ....Framingham, MA: (508) 270-6666
Web Page: http://www.cca-int.com

Computer Discount Warehouse (CDW) .... Vernon Hills, IL: 847.465.6000
Toll Free:800-750-4239
Web Page: http://www.cdw.com

Computer Dynamics ....Greenville, SC: (864) 627-8800
Web Page: http://www.cdynamics.com

Computer Expressions Inc ....Philadelphia, PA: (215) 487-7700
Toll Free:(800) 443-8278
Web Page: http://www.compexpress.com

Phone Directory

Computer Friends Inc ·· Portland, OR: (503) 626-2291
   Tech:(503) 626-2291   Toll Free:(800) 547-3303
   Web Page: http://www.cfriends.com

Computer Industry Almanac ···································· Arlington Heights, IL: (847) 758-3687
   Web Page: http://www.c-i-a.com

Computer Intelligence (see ZD Market)

Computer Knacks Inc ·· Shrewsbury, NJ: (732) 530-0262
   Tech:(732) 530-0262

Computer Modules Inc ·· San Diego, CA: (858) 613-1818
   Web Page: http://www.computermodules.com

Computer Network Technology Corp ····························· Minneapolis, MN: (763) 268-6000
   Toll Free:(800) 638-8324
   Web Page: http://www.cnt.com

Computer Parts Unlimited (see CPU Mart)

Computer Peripherals Unlimited ···································· Flagstaf, AZ: (800) 278-3480
   Tech:(928) 526-2261   Toll Free:(800) 278-3480
   Web Page: http://www.cpuinc.com

Computer Products Plus (see Road Warrior)

Computer Prompting and Captioning ····························· Rockville, MD: (301) 738-8487
   Toll Free:(800) 977-6678
   Web Page: http://www.cpcweb.com

Computer Recognition Systems Inc ····························· Cambridge, MA: (617) 491-7665
   Web Page: http://www.as-its.com

Computer Review ·· Gloucester, MA: (978) 283-2100
   Web Page: http://www.computerreview.com

Computer Shopper (see CNet Shopper)

Computer Station Corp ·· Houston, TX: (713) 777-6860
   Tech:(713) 777-6860
   Web Page: http://www.computerstationcorp.com

Computer Support (see Arts & Letters)

Computer System Products ···································· Plymouth, MN: 763-476-6866
   Tech:800-422-2537   Toll Free:800-422-2537
   Web Page: http://www.csp.com

Computer Technology Review (see RKG Int)

ComputerPREP Inc ·· Phoenix, AZ: (602) 275-7700
   Toll Free:(800) 228-1027
   Web Page: http://www.computerprep.com

Computers for Marketing Corp ····························· San Francisco, CA: (415) 777-0470
   Tech:(415) 777-2922
   Web Page: http://www.cfmc.com

ComputerTrend Systems (see Premio Comp)

Computhink ·· Lombard, IL: (630) 705-9050
   Toll Free:(800) 988-4465
   Web Page: http://www.computhink.com

Computone Corp (see Altura XL)

Computopia ·· Warwick, RI: (401) 732-5588
   Web Page: http://www.computopia.com

Computron Software (see AXS-One Inc)

Compuware Corp ·· Detroit, MI: (313) 227-7300
   Tech:(248) 737-7700   Toll Free:(800) 538-7822
   Web Page: http://www.compuware.com

Compuware NuMega ·· Nashua, NH: (603) 578-8400
   Tech:(888) 686-3427   Toll Free:(800) 468-6342
   Web Page: http://www.numega.com

Comrex Corp ·· Devens, MA: (978) 784-1776
   Tech:(978) 263-1800   Toll Free:(800) 237-1776
   Web Page: http://www.comrex.com

Comstor Inc ·· Broomfield, CO: (303) 222-4747

Tech:(800) 654-6311   Toll Free:(800) 543-6098
Web Page: http://www.comstor.com

Comtech Publishing ·· Reno, NV: (775) 825-9000
Tech:(775) 825-9000
Web Page: http://www.accutek.com/comtech

Comtrol Corp ·· Minneapolis, MN: (763) 494-4100
Tech:(763) 494-4100   Toll Free:(800) 926-6876
Web Page: http://www.comtrol.com

Concentric Data (see Wall Data)

Concept Software ··· St. Charles, MO: (636) 720-3800
Web Page: http://www.softwarekey.com

Concord Communications ································ Marlboro, MA: (508) 460-4646
Tech:(888) 832-4340   Toll Free:(800) 851-8725
Web Page: http://www.concord.com

Concurrent Computer Corp ······························· Duluth, GA: (678) 258-4000
Toll Free:(877) 978-7363
Web Page: http://www.ccur.com

Condre Inc ·· Eden Prairie, MN: (952) 294-4900
Toll Free:(866) 500-3472
Web Page: http://www.condre.com

Conduant Corp ··· Longmont, CO: (303) 485-2721
Tech:(303) 485-5104   Toll Free:(888) 497-7327
Web Page: http://www.conduant.com

Conexant Systems Inc ··································· Red Bank, NJ: (732) 345-7500
Toll Free:(888) 855-4562
Web Page: http://www.conexant.com

Connect Tech Inc ··· Guelph, ON: (519) 836-1291
Tech:(519) 836-1291   Toll Free:(800) 426-8979
Web Page: http://www.connecttech.com

ConnectCom Solutions (see Initio Corp)

Connectix Corp ··· San Mateo, CA: (650) 571-5100
Tech:(970) 304-9533   Toll Free:(800) 950-5880
Web Page: http://www.connectix.com

Connector Resources Unlimited Inc ············· Vancouver, WA: (360) 86-1741
Tech:(360) 816-1772   Toll Free:(800) 260-9800
Web Page: http://www.cruinc.com

ConnectSoft Inc (see Vogo Networks)

Connectworks ··· Belmont, CA: (650) 637-8702
Web Page: http://www.connectworks.com

Conner Peripherals Inc (see Seagate)

Conner Tape Products (see Seagate)

Conrac Corp ·· Baldwin Park, CA: (626) 480-0095
Web Page: http://www.conrac.com

Consilium Inc ··· Santa Clara, CA: (408) 727-5555
Tech:(408) 986-3827   Toll Free:(800) 726-7400
Web Page: http://www.consilium.com

Consistency Point Technologies Inc ············· Morgan Hill, CA: (408) 778-0715
Web Page: http://www.cpt.com

Consumer Electronics Manufacturers ············· Arlington, VA: (703) 907-7600
Tech:(703) 907-7681
Web Page: http://www.cemacity.org

Contact East ·· North Andover, MA: (978) 682-2000
Tech:(888) 866-5487   Toll Free:(888) 925-2960
Web Page: http://www.contacteast.com

Contour Design Inc ······································· Windham, NH: (603) 893-4556
Tech:(603) 893-4556   Toll Free:(800) 462-6678
Web Page: http://www.contourdesign.com

Control Data Sys. (see Syntegra)

Control Technology Inc ·································· Knoxville, TN: (865) 584-0440

Toll Free:(800) 537-8398
Web Page: http://www.controltechnology.com
Convergent Media Systems ································· Alpharetta, GA: **(770) 369-9000**
Web Page: http://www.convergent.com
Conversay ··· Redmond, WA: **(425) 895-1800**
Toll Free:(888) 487-4373
Web Page: http://www.conversay.com
Cooke Corp ··· Auburn Hills, MI: **(248) 276-8820**
Web Page: http://www.cookecorp.com
Copia International Ltd ································· Naperville, IL: **(630) 388-6900**
Tech:(630) 388-6964   Toll Free:(800) 689-8898
Web Page: http://www.copia.com
Coptech Inc ··· Woburn, MA: **(781) 935-2679**
Toll Free:(800) 934-1560
Web Page: http://www.coptechinc.com
Coptervision ·· Van Nuys, CA: **(818) 781-3003**
Tech:(818) 781-3003
Web Page: http://www.coptervision.com
CopyPro Inc ·· Concord, CA: **(925) 689-1200**
Toll Free:(800) 887-9906
Web Page: http://www.copypro.com
Cordin Co ··· Salt Lake City, UT: **(801) 972-5272**
Web Page: http://www.cordin.com
Core Technology Corp ··································· Lansing, MI: **(517) 627-1521**
Toll Free:(800) 338-2117
Web Page: http://www.ctc-core.com
Coreco ·· Billerica, MA: **(978) 670-2000**
Web Page: http://www.coreco.com
Corel Corporation ··· Ottawa, ON: **(888) 267-3548**
Tech:(613) 274-0500   Toll Free:(800) 772-6735
Web Page: http://www.corel.com
  Automated Support ··································· (877) 422-6735
  Toll Free:(877) 422-6735
  Business Development ································ (613) 728-8200
  French ·· (613) 274-0505
  Micrografx Inc ·· (469) 232-1000
  Tech:(469) 232-1100   Toll Free:(888) 744-1210
  Web Page: http://www.micrografx.com
  Novell Customer Response Center ············· (888) 321-4272
  Tech:(800) 858-4000   Toll Free:(888) 321-4272
  Web Page: http://www.novell.com
  Personal Sales ······································ (800) 772-6735
  Premium Service ····································· (613) 728-6807
  Professional Service ································ (877) 864-7446
  Solution Partners ··································· (613) 274-0503
  Support ·· (888) 267-3548
  Toll Free:(877) 702-6735
  Tech Support ··· (613) 274-0500
  Tech:(613) 274-0500   Toll Free:(877) 662-6735
  Web Page: http://www.corel.com/support
Corex Technologies Corp ······························ Cambridge, MA: **(617) 492-4200**
Tech:(800) 942-6739   Toll Free:(800) 942-6739
Web Page: http://www.cardscan.com
Cornerstone Peripherals Technology ················· Fremont, CA: **(510) 580-8900**
Tech:(888) 338-6490   Toll Free:(800) 562-2552
Web Page: http://www.bigmonitors.com
Cornerstone Solutions Group Inc ····················· St. Louis, MO: **(314) 469-9910**
Web Page: http://www.csgsolutions.com
Corning Cable Systems ································· Hickory, NC: **(828) 901-5000**
Tech:(800) 743-2675   Toll Free:(800) 743-2671

Web Page: http://www.corningcablesystems.com

Corollary Inc (see Intel)

Corporate Disk Company ···Woodale, IL: (630) 616-0700
Toll Free:(800) 634-3475
Web Page: http://www.disk.com

Cosmi Corp ···Ranch Dominguez, CA: (310) 886-3510
Web Page: http://www.cosmi.com

CoStar Corp (see Dymo-CoStar Corp)

Cougar Mountain Software Inc ··Boise, ID: (208) 375-4455
Tech:(800) 727-0656   Toll Free:(800) 388-3038
Web Page: http://www.cougarmtn.com

Covey Leadership (see Franklin Covey)

Cox Automation Systems ··West Chicago, IL: (630) 293-9470
Web Page: http://www.coxautomation.com

Cox Technologies ···Belmont, NC: (704) 825-8146
Tech:(800) 283-8033   Toll Free:(800) 848-9865
Web Page: http://www.coxtec.com

CPU Mart ··Simi Valley, CA: (805) 306-2500
Tech:(800) 758-4640   Toll Free:(800) 644-4494
Web Page: http://www.cpumart.com

CR Technology (see Photondynamics)

Cranel Imaging ···Columbus, OH: (614) 431-8000
Toll Free:(888) 732-1233
Web Page: http://www.cranelimaging.com

Cray Research (see Silicon Graphics)

Creative Labs Inc ··Milpitas, CA: (408) 428-6600
Tech:(405) 742-6655   Toll Free:(800) 998-1000
Web Page: http://us.creative.com

Creative Multimedia (see Dataware Tech)

Creative Wonders (see Learning Co)

Creoscitex ··Billerica, MA: (781) 275-5150
Toll Free:(800) 472-2727
Web Page: http://www.creoscitex.com

Crestron Electronics ··Rockleigh, NJ: (201) 767-3400
Tech:(888) 273-7876   Toll Free:(800) 237-2041
Web Page: http://www.crestron.com

CRI Inc ···Woburn, MA: (781) 935-9099
Toll Free:(800) 383-7924
Web Page: http://www.cross.com

Cross Pen Computing Group ··Lincoln, RI: (401) 333-1200
Toll Free:(800) 282-7676
Web Page: http://www.cross.com

Crosstalk Communication (see Attachmate)

Crosswise Corp (see Java News Inc)

Crowley Micrographics Inc ···Frederick, MD: (301) 631-6825
Web Page: http://www.crowleymicrographics.com

Crucial Technology ··Meridian, ID: (208) 363-5911
Tech:(800) 336-8916   Toll Free:(800) 932-4995
Web Page: http://www.crucial.com
Business Memory Upgrade
Corporate Memory Upgrade
Customer Service ···(208) 363-5790
Tech:(800) 336-8915
Web Page: http://www.crucial.com
Federal Government
State, Local, Education ···(888) 363-4166
VAR/Reseller Memory Upgrade

Cruse Digital Equipment ···Oak Ridge, NJ: (973) 208-7289
Web Page: http://www.crusedigital.com

Crystal Decisions Inc ·· San Jose, CA: (604) 681-3435
   Toll Free:(800) 877-2340
   Web Page: http://www.crystaldecisions.net

Crystal Services (see Seagate Software)

CS Electronics ·· Irvine, CA: (949) 475-9100
   Web Page: http://www.scsi-cables.com

CSS Laboratories Inc ·· Irvine, CA: (949) 852-8161
   Tech:(800) 966-2771   Toll Free:(800) 852-2680
   Web Page: http://www.csslabs.com

Ctec Photonics ·· Madesto, CA: (209) 529-2555
   Web Page: http://www.ctecphotonics.com

CTI/VTEK ··· Tracy, CA: (209) 839-2990
   Toll Free:(888) 777-8835
   Web Page: http://www.cti-vtek.com

CTX International Inc ·································· City Of Industry, CA: (626) 709-1000
   Tech:(800) 888-2012   Toll Free:(800) 282-2205
   Web Page: http://www.ctxintl.com
   Desktop & notebook ·· (626) 709-1045
   Web Page: http://www.ctxintl.com
   Monitor ·· (800) 266-1491
   Toll Free:(800) 888-2012
   Web Page: http://www.ctxintl.com

CTX Opto Inc (see Optoma Technology)

Cubix Corp ·· Carson City, NV: (775) 888-1000
   Tech:(800) 953-0205   Toll Free:(800) 829-0550
   Web Page: http://www.cubix.com

CUC International (see Sierra On-Line)

Cuda Fiberoptics ·· Jacksonville, FL: (904) 737-7611
   Toll Free:(877) 677-2832
   Web Page: http://www.cuda.com

Current Technology ··· Richmond, VA: (804) 236-3300
   Toll Free:(800) 238-5000
   Web Page: http://www.currenttechnology.com

Curtis Computer Products (merged w/ Esselte)·······Melville, NY: (631) 675-5700
   Toll Free:(800) 645-6051
   Web Page: http://www.esselte.com/curtis

Curtis Inc ·· Minneapolis, MN: (763) 404-9081
   Toll Free:(800) 245-3171
   Web Page: http://www.mncurtis.com

Curtis Manufacturing Co (see Rolodex)

Curtis Mathes (see uniView Technologies)

CUseeME Networks (see First Virtual Comm.)
   Web Page: http://www.fvc.com

Cutting Edge ··· La Mesa, CA: (619) 667-7888
   Tech:(619) 667-7896   Toll Free:(800) 257-1666
   Web Page: http://www.cuttedge.com

Cvision Technologies ··· Queens, NY: (718) 793-5572
   Toll Free:(866) 871-7304
   Web Page: http://www.cvisiontech.com

Cway Software ·· Hatfield, PA: (215) 953-1102
   Web Page: http://www.cway.com

CXR ·· Fremont, CA: (510) 657-8810
   Tech:(800) 537-5762   Toll Free:(800) 537-5762
   Web Page: http://www.cxr.com

Cyber Acoustics ··· Vancouver, WA: (360) 883-0333
   Tech:(360) 883-0333
   Web Page: http://www.cyber-acoustics.com

Cyber Optics ·· Portland, OR: (503) 495-2200
   Toll Free:(800) 366-9131

Phone Directory

Web Page: http://www.imagenation.com

Cyber Optics Corp ···································· Minneapolis, MN: (763) 542-5003
Toll Free:(800) 526-2540
Web Page: http://www.cyberoptics.com

Cyberguard Corp ································ Fort Lauderdale, FL: (954) 958-3900
Tech:(954) 958-3898   Toll Free:(800) 666-4273
Web Page: http://www.cyberguardcorp.com

Cyberlink ··· Fremont, CA: (510) 668-0118
Web Page: http://www.gocyberlink.com

CyberMedia Inc (see Network Associates)

Cybernet Systems Corp ································ Ann Arbor, MI: (734) 668-2567
Tech:(734) 668-2567
Web Page: http://www.cybernet.com

CyberOptics Semiconductor / Imagenation ···· Beaverton, OR: (503)495-2200
Toll Free:(800) 366-9131
Web Page: http://www.imagenation.com

CyberPower Systems ································· Shakopee, MN: (952) 403-9500
Tech:(877) 297-6937   Toll Free:(877) 297-6937
Web Page: http://www.cyberpowersystems.com

Cybex Computer (see Avocent)

Cyborg Systems Inc ································ Lincolnshire, IL: (847) 295-5000
Web Page: http://www.cyborg.com

Cyclone Microsystems ···························· New Haven, CT: (203) 786-5536
Web Page: http://www.cyclone.com

Cycolor ·· Miamisburg, OH: (937) 428-1900
Toll Free:(888) 292-6567
Web Page: http://www.cycolor.com

Cykic Software ·· San Diego, CA: (619) 459-8799
Web Page: http://www.cykic.com

CyLink Corp ··· Belcamp, MD: (410) 931-7500
Web Page: http://www.cylink.com

Cyma Systems Inc ·· Tempe, AZ: (480) 303-2962
Tech:(480) 303-2962   Toll Free:(800) 292-2962
Web Page: http://www.cyma.com

Cypress Research (see Aveo)

Cypress Semiconductor Corp ······················ San Jose, CA: (408) 943-2600
Tech:(408) 943-2821   Toll Free:(800) 858-1810
Web Page: http://www.cypress.com

Cyrano Inc ··· Newburyport, MA: (978) 462-0737
Tech:(978) 462-0737   Toll Free:(800) 714-4900
Web Page: http://www.cyrano.com

Cyrix Corp (see Via Technologies)

C£ram Software Inc. / IT Designs USA Inc ···· Santa Clara, CA: (408) 387-8111
Toll Free:(866) 41-CURAM
Web Page: http://www.curamsoftware.com

D&VP Corp ·· Bountiful, UT: (801) 519-0500
Toll Free:(800) 561-2345
Web Page: http://www.dandvp.com

D-Link Systems Inc ······························· Fountain Valley, CA: (949) 788-0805
Tech:(949) 598-8150   Toll Free:(800) 326-1688
Web Page: http://www.dlink.com

da Vinci Systems Inc ······························ Coral Springs, FL: (954) 688-5600
Web Page: http://www.davsys.com

Da-Lite Screen ··· Warsaw, IN: (574) 267-8101
Toll Free:(800) 622-3737
Web Page: http://www.da-lite.com

DacEasy Inc (see Sage Software)

Dage-MTI Inc ··· Michigan City, IN: (219) 872-5514
Web Page: http://www.dagemti.com

Daige Inc ··· Albertson, NY: (516) 621-2100
   Toll Free:(800) 645-3323
   Web Page: http://www.daige.com
Daikin (see Sonic Solutions)
Daitron Inc ·· Wilsonville, OR: (503) 682-7560
   Toll Free:(888) 324-8766
   Web Page: http://www.daitron.com
Dalbani Corp of America··· Miami, FL: (305) 716-1016
   Toll Free:(800) 325-2264
   Web Page: http://www.dalbani.com
Dalco Electronics ·· Springboro, OH: (937) 743-8042
   Tech:(800) 543-2526   Toll Free:(800) 445-5342
   Web Page: http://www.dalco.com
   Maxim Integrated Products, Inc.························(408)737-7600
   Web Page: http://www.maxim-ic.com
Dalsa ··· Waterloo, Ontario, : (519) 886-6000
   Web Page: http://www.dalsa.com
Danpex Corp·· San Jose, CA: (408) 434-1688
   Tech:(888) 432-6739   Toll Free:(800) 452-1551
   Web Page: http://www.danpex.com
Dantz Development Corp··· Orinda, CA: (925) 948-9000
   Toll Free:(888) 777-8997
   Web Page: http://www.dantz.com
Dariana Software (see E-Ware)
Dart Communications··· Rome, NY: (315) 339-8040
   Toll Free:(866) 383-3278
   Web Page: http://www.dart.com
Data Access Corp·· Miami, FL: (305) 238-0012
   Tech:(305) 232-3142   Toll Free:(800) 451-3539
   Web Page: http://www.daccess.com
Data Assist Inc·· Columbus, OH: (614) 888-8088
   Tech:(800) 326-8088   Toll Free:(800) 326-8088
   Web Page: http://www.data.assist.com
Data Assurance ·· Waltham, MA: (781) 890-0110
   Web Page: http://www.datassociates.com
Data Base Access Systems Inc ························· Mountain Lakes, NJ: (973) 335-0800
   Web Page: http://www.dbasinc.com
Data Becker Corp································ Needham Heights, MA: (617) 614-0600
   Web Page: http://www.databecker.com
data by Acxiom ·· Danvers, MA: (402) 537-6180
   Tech:(402) 537-6181
   Web Page: http://www.acxiom.com
Data Code Inc··· Orlando, FL: (407) 352-5215
   Toll Free:(800) 762-1480
   Web Page: http://www.datacode.com
Data Conversion Laboratory ·························· Fresh Meadows, NY: (718) 357-8700
   Web Page: http://www.dclab.com
Data Direct Networks ·· Chatsworth, CA: (818) 700-7600
   Tech:(818) 700-7676   Toll Free:(800) 322-4744
   Web Page: http://www.megadrive.com
Data Distributing ·· Santa Cruz, CA: (831) 457-3537
   Toll Free:(800) 635-6779
   Web Page: http://www.datadistributing.com
Data Fellows (see F Secure Inc)
Data General Corp·· Westborough, MA: (508) 898-5000
   Tech:(800) 344-3577   Toll Free:(800) 328-2436
   Web Page: http://www.dg.com
Data I/O Corp··· Redmond, WA: (425) 881-6444
   Tech:(800) 247-5700   Toll Free:(800) 426-1045

Web Page: http://www.data-io.com

Data I/O Corp ·· **Redmond, WA: (425) 881-6444**
Tech:(800) 332-8246   Toll Free:(800) 735-6070
Web Page: http://www.dataio.com

Pervasive Software Inc ································· (512) 231-6000
Toll Free:(800) 287-4383
Web Page: http://www.pervasive.com

Data Pro Accounting Software ···················· **St Petersburg, FL: (727) 803-1500**
Tech:(727) 803-1500
Web Page: http://www.dpro.com

Data Race (see IP Axess)

Data Storage Marketing (see Comstor)

Data Techniques Inc ································· **Burnsville, NC: (828) 682-4111**
Tech:(828) 682-0161   Toll Free:(800) 955-8015
Web Page: http://www.data-tech.com

Data Technology Corp (DTC) ······················ **Sunnyvale, CA: (408) 745-9320**
Web Page: http://www.dtc.com

Data Translation Inc ······························· **Marlboro, MA: (508) 481-3700**
Toll Free:(800) 525-8528
Web Page: http://www.datx.com

Data Watch Corp ································· **Lowell, MA: (978) 441-2200**
Tech:(978) 441-2200   Toll Free:(800) 988-4739
Web Page: http://www.datawatch.com

Data-Ray Corp ································· **Brea, CA: (714) 987-1988**
Web Page: http://www.data-ray.com

Database Access Systems Inc ·················· **Mountain Lakes, NJ: (973) 335-0800**
Web Page: http://www.dbasinc.com

DataCal Corp ································· **Gilbert, AZ: (480) 813-3100**
Tech:(800) 459-7931   Toll Free:(800) 223-0123
Web Page: http://www.datacal.com

Datacube Inc ································· **Danvers, MA: (978) 777-4200**
Web Page: http://www.datacube.com

DataEase Int (see MultiWare Inc)

Datalight Inc ································· **Bothell, WA: (425) 951-8086**
Toll Free:(800) 221-6630
Web Page: http://www.datalight.com

Datalux Corp ································· **Winchester, VA: (540) 723-4602**
Toll Free:(888) 811-0650
Web Page: http://www.datalux.com

Datamar Systems ································· **El Cajon, CA: (619) 579-8244**
Web Page: http://www.datamar.com

DataMirror Corp ································· **Markham, ON: (905) 415-0310**
Tech:(905) 415-5199   Toll Free:(800) 362-5955
Web Page: http://www.datamirror.com

Datanautics, Inc. ································· **Santa Clara, CA: (408) 350-1300**
Web Page: http://www.datanautics.com

DataPlay Inc ································· **San Francico, CA: (415) 252+2000**
Web Page: http://www.dataplay.com

Datapoint Corp ································· **San Antonio, TX: (210) 614-9977**
Web Page: http://www.datapointusa.com

Dataproducts Corp (see Hitachi Koki)

Dataquest Int (see Gartner Group)

Dataram Corp ·················· **West Windsor Township, NJ: (609) 799-0071**
Tech:(800) 599-0071   Toll Free:(800) 328-2726
Web Page: http://www.dataram.com

Datashield Unison (see Tripp Lite)

Datasouth Computer Corp ······················ **Charlotte, NC: (704) 523-8500**
Tech:(800) 476-2450   Toll Free:(800) 476-2120
Web Page: http://www.datasouth.com

DataSpec (see ORA Electronics)
Datastor ··· Garden Grove, CA: (714) 895-6676
  Toll Free:(800) 777-6621
  Web Page: http://www.dstor.com
Datastorm Tech (see Symantec)
Datastream Systems Inc ································· Greenville, SC: (864) 422-5001
  Tech:(800) 365-6775   Toll Free:(800) 955-6775
  Web Page: http://www.dstm.com
DataTech Software Inc ································· Harrisburg, PA: (717) 652-4344
  Tech:(717) 652-4344   Toll Free:(800) 556-7526
  Web Page: http://www.quickandeasy.com
DataViews Corp ···································· Foxborough, MA: (508) 698-3322
  Web Page: http://www.gefanucautomation.com
DataViz Inc ·· Milford, CT: (203) 268-0030
  Tech:(203) 874-0085   Toll Free:(800) 733-0030
  Web Page: http://www.dataviz.com
Dataware Technologies (see Open text)
Datawatch ·· Lowell, MA: (978) 441-2200
  Tech:(978) 988-9700   Toll Free:(800) 445-3311
  Web Page: http://www.datawatch.com
Datel Inc ·· Mansfield, MA: (508) 339-3000
  Toll Free:(800) 233-2765
  Web Page: http://www.datel.com
Datum Inc (merged Symmetricon)····················San Jose, CA: (408) 433-0910
  Web Page: http://www.symmetricom.com
Dauphin Technology Inc ································· Palatine, IL: (847) 358-4406
  Tech:(847) 358-4406
  Web Page: http://www.dauphintech.com
David Systems Inc (see 3Com Corp)
Davidson & Assoc. (see Knowledge Adven)
DAX Archiving Solutions ··························· Laguna Hills, CA: (949) 348-8250
  Toll Free:(800) 341-1050
  Web Page: http://www.daxarchiving.com
Day Runner ·· Fullerton, CA: (714) 680-3500
  Tech:(800) 643-9923   Toll Free:(800) 232-9786
  Web Page: http://www.dayrunner.com
Dayna Communications (see Intel)
Dazzle Multimedia (see Pinnacle Systems)
Db-Tech Inc (see WebSci Technologies)
Dbas Codenoll (see Data Base Access)
DCA Inc ·· Cushing, OK: (918) 225-0346
  Web Page: http://www.dcainc.com
DCA/IRMA (see Attachmate)
Deadly Games ·· Eden Praire, MN: (631) 537-6060
  Tech:(631) 537-6060
  Web Page: http://www.deadlygames.com
DEC (see Compaq Computer Corp)
Decisioneering Inc ································· Denver, CO: (303) 534-1515
  Tech:(800) 373-5885   Toll Free:(800) 289-2550
  Web Page: http://www.decisioneering.com
DecisionOne Corp ································· Frazer, PA: (800) 767-2876
  Toll Free:(800) 767-2876
  Web Page: http://www.decisionone.com
Decisive Tools ·· Denver, CO: (303) 757-7115
  Toll Free:(800) 732-9414
  Web Page: http://www.decisivetools.com
Deerfield.com ·· Gaylord, MI: (989) 732-8856
  Web Page: http://www.deerfield.com

Definitive Software (see Decisive Tools)

Delkin Devices Inc ··· Poway, CA: (858) 391-1234
Toll Free:(800) 637-8087
Web Page: http://www.delkin.com

Dell Computer Corp ··· Round Rock, TX: (512) 338-4400
Tech:(800) 624-9896　　　　　　Toll Free:(800) 289-3355
Web Page: http://www.dell.com

Dell Computer Corp (800) 999-3355
Toll Free:(800) 915-3355
　Education ··· (800) 626-8286
　Tech:(877) 499-3355　　　　　Toll Free:(800) 626-8286
　Government ··· (800) 416-3355
　Toll Free:(800) 416-3355
　Web Page: http://www.dell.com/statestore
　Health Care Systems ···································· (888) 264-7788
　Tech:(800) 293-3492　　　　　Toll Free:(888) 583-3355
　Home Office ·· (800) 274-3355
　Tech:(800) 915-3355　　　　　Toll Free:(800) 274-3355
　Information ··· (800) 917-3355
　Toll Free:(800) 274-3355

DeLorme Mapping Corp ····································· Yarmouth, ME: (207) 846-7051
Toll Free:(800) 561-5105
Web Page: http://www.delorme.com

Delphi Internet Service ··· Troy, MI: (248) 813-2000
Web Page: http://www.delphi.com

Delrina Software (see Symantec)

Deltec (see Exide Electronics)

Deltek Systems Inc ··· Herndon, VA: (703) 734-8606
Tech:(703) 734-8606　　　　　　Toll Free:(800) 456-2009
Web Page: http://www.deltek.com

Denco Manufacturing Corp ···································· San Jose, CA: (408) 487-3209
Web Page: http://www.ocean-usa.com

Deneba Software ·· Miami, FL: (305) 596-5644
Tech:(305) 596-5644
Web Page: http://www.deneba.com

Derivation Systems ··· Carlsbad, CA: (760) 431-1400
Web Page: http://www.derivation.com

Desaware ··· Campbell, CA: (408) 377-4770
Web Page: http://www.desaware.com

DeScribe Inc (Out of Business)

Design Intelligence Inc ··· Nocross, GA: (770) 209-3770
Web Page: http://www.design-intelligence.com

Design Science Inc ·· Long Beach, CA: (526) 433-0685
Toll Free:(800) 827-0685
Web Page: http://www.dessci.com

DesignCAD (see ViaGrafix)

DesignCAD.com ·· Pryor, OK: (918) 825-4844
Tech:(918) 825-4844　　　　　　Toll Free:(800) 233-3223
Web Page: http://www.designcad.com

Desktop Video Systems ·· Lenexa, KS: (913) 782-7888
Toll Free:(800) 662-6901
Web Page: http://www.desktopvideosystems.com

Develcon Electronics Ltd ·· Toronto, ON: (416) 385-1390
Web Page: http://www.develcon.com

Devont Software Inc ·· Spring, TX: (281) 754-4203
Web Page: http://www.devont.com

DFI Inc ·· Sacramento, CA: (916) 568-1234
Tech:(916) 568-1234　　　　　　Toll Free:(800) 909-4334
Web Page: http://www.dfiusa.com

Dia-Nielsen .... Moorestown, NJ: (856) 642-9700
  Tech:(856) 642-9700   Toll Free:(800) 893-6361
  Web Page: http://www.diapens.thomasregister.com
DiagSoft Inc (see Sykes)
Dialogic Corp (see Intel Corp)
Diamond Audio Technology Inc .... Chandler, AZ: (480) 813-6200
  Web Page: http://www.diamondaudio.com
Diamond Comp (see Diamond Multimedia)
Diamond Flower Electric (see DFI Inc)
Diamond Multimedia (see Sonicblue)
Diamond Systems .... Newark, CA: (510) 456-7800
  Web Page: http://www.diamondsystems.com
Diaquest Inc .... Emeryville, CA: (510) 547-4544
  Web Page: http://www.diaquest.com
Diehl Graphsoft (see Nemetschek N.A.)
Diffraction Limited .... Ottawa, Ontario, : (613) 225-2732
  Web Page: http://www.cyanogen.com
Digi International .... Minnetonka, MN: (952) 912-3444
  Tech:(952) 912-3456   Toll Free:(877) 912-3444
  Web Page: http://www.dgii.com
Digi-Botics .... Addison, TX: (972) 417-1100
  Web Page: http://www.digibotics.com
Digi-Data Corp .... Columbia, MD: (410) 730-6880
  Web Page: http://www.digidata.com
Digi-Key Corporation .... Thief River Falls, MN: (218) 681-6674
  Toll Free:(800) 344-4539
  Web Page: http://www.digikey.com
Digiboard Inc (see Digi International)
Digicom Systems (see Broadxent)
Digidesign .... Daly City, CA: (650) 731-6300
  Tech:(650) 731-6100   Toll Free:(800) 333-2137
  Web Page: http://www.digidesign.com
Digilog Inc .... Willow Grove, PA: (215) 830-9400
  Toll Free:(800) 344-4564
  Web Page: http://www.digilog.com
Digimarc Corp .... Tualatin, OR: (503) 885-9699
  Toll Free:(800) 344-4627
  Web Page: http://www.digimarc.com
Digimation Inc .... St Rose, LA: (504) 468-7898
  Tech:(504) 468-3372   Toll Free:(800) 854-4496
  Web Page: http://www.digimation.com
Digisette .... New Vernon, NJ: (973) 455-7084
  Web Page: http://www.digisette.com
Digit Head (see Invario Network Eng.)
Digital Asset Man. (see Think Direct)
Digital Audio Labs .... Chanhassen, MN: (952) 401-7700
  Web Page: http://www.digitalaudio.com
Digital Design Inc .... Cedar Grove, NJ: (973) 857-0900
  Toll Free:(800) 967-7746
  Web Page: http://www.genesisinkjet.com
Digital Dynamics .... Scotts Valley, CA: (831) 438-4444
  Toll Free:(800) 765-1288
  Web Page: http://www.digitaldynamics.com
Digital Equipment Corp (see Compaq)
Digital Fountain .... Fremont, CA: (510) 284-1400
  Tech:(510) 284-1591   Toll Free:(866) 344-3686
  Web Page: http://www.digitalfountain.com
Digital Impact Inc .... San Mateo, CA: (650) 356-3400

Tech:(650) 372-2110   Toll Free:(800) 491-9320
Web Page: http://www.digitalimpact.com

Digital Instrumentation Tech .... Los Alamos, NM: (505) 662-1459
Web Page: http://www.dit.com

Digital Persona .... Redwood City, CA: (650) 261-6070
Toll Free:(877) 378-2738
Web Page: http://www.digitalpersona.com

Digital Projection Inc .... Kennesaw, GA: (770) 420-1365
Tech:(770) 420-1350
Web Page: http://www.digitalprojection.com

Digital Storage .... Lewis Center, OH: (800) 232-3475
Toll Free:(800) 232-3475
Web Page: http://www.digitalstorage.com

Digital Video Camera Co .... Austin, TX: (512) 301-9564
Web Page: http://www.dvcco.com

Digital Video Systems .... Palo Alto, CA: (650) 322-8108
Web Page: http://www.dvsystems.com

Digital Vision (see Focus Enhancement)

Digital Wisdom .... Tapahannock, VA: (804) 443-9000
Toll Free:(800) 800-8560
Web Page: http://www.digiwis.com

Digitech Systems .... Greenwood Village, CO: (888) 374-3569
Toll Free:(888) 374-3569
Web Page: http://www.digitechsystems.com

Digivision .... San Diego, CA: (858) 571-4700
Web Page: http://www.digivision.com

Dimension Technologies .... Rochester, NY: (585) 436-3530
Web Page: http://www.dti3d.com

Dimensional Insight Inc .... Burlington, MA: (781) 229-9111
Web Page: http://www.dimins.com

Direct Data .... St Louis, MO: (314) 994-9591
Web Page: http://www.direct-data.com

Direct Network Services .... Littleton, MA: (978) 952-6000
Web Page: http://www.directnetserv.com

Directed Perception .... Burlingame, CA: (650) 342-9399
Web Page: http://www.dperception.com

Dirt Cheap Drives .... Dickinson, TX: (281) 534-4140
Tech:(281) 534-6292   Toll Free:(800) 786-1186
Web Page: http://www.dirtcheapdrives.com

DISC Inc .... Santa Clara, CA: (408) 350-1200
Tech:(408) 350-1200
Web Page: http://www.disc-storage.com

Disc Tec .... Orlando, FL: (407) 671-5500
Web Page: http://www.disctec.com

Discovision Associates .... Irvine, CA: (949) 660-5000
Web Page: http://www.discovision.com

Discreet .... San Francisco, CA: (415) 547-2000
Tech:(800) 869-3504   Toll Free:(800) 225-7904
Web Page: http://www.discreet.com

DiscsDirect.com .... Montreal, Quebec, : (514) 393-1616
Toll Free:(800) 869-3504
Web Page: http://www.discsdirect.com

Disney Interactive .... Burbank, CA: (818) 841-3326
Tech:(800) 228-0988   Toll Free:(800) 900-9234
Web Page: http://www.disney.com

DisplayMate Technologies Corp .... Amherst, NH: (603) 672-8500
Toll Free:(800) 932-6323
Web Page: http://www.displaymate.com

Displaytech .... Longmont, CO: (303) 772-2191

Toll Free:(800) 397-8124
Web Page: http://www.displaytech.com

Distinct Corp ··· San Jose, CA: (408) 445-3270
Tech:(408) 445-3270
Web Page: http://www.distinct.com

Distributed Processing (see Adaptec)

Diversified Engineering ··· Orange, CT: (203) 799-7875
Web Page: http://www.diversifiedengineering.net

Diversified Software Systems ································· Morgan Hill, CA: (408) 778-9914
Web Page: http://www.dssi-jcl.com

Diversified Systems Group Inc ······························· Redmond, WA: (425) 947-1500
Toll Free:(800) 255-3142
Web Page: http://www.dsgi.com

Diversified Technologies ·· Folsom, CA: (916) 616-0591
Web Page: http://www.d-technologies.com

Diversified Technology ·· Ridgeland, MS: (601) 856-4121
Toll Free:(800) 443-2667
Web Page: http://www.dtims.com

DLT Tape (see Quantum Corp)

DMA (see Symantec)

Dobbs-Stanford (see Grandtec USA)

DocuCorp Intl ·· Dallas, TX: (214) 891-6500
Tech:(800) 818-7778   Toll Free:(800) 735-6620
Web Page: http://www.docucorp.com

DocuLex Inc ·· Winter Haven, FL: (863) 297-3691
Web Page: http://www.doculex.com

DocuMagix Inc (see E Fax)

Document Sciences Corp ·· Carlsbad, CA: (760) 602-1400
Tech:(760) 602-1500
Web Page: http://www.docscience.com

Documentum Inc ·· Pleasanton, CA: (925) 600-6800
Tech:(925) 600-6860
Web Page: http://www.documentum.com

DocuWare ··· Newburgh, NY: (845) 563-9045
Toll Free:(888) 565-5907
Web Page: http://www.docuware.com

Dolan-Jenner Industries ··· Lawrence, MA: (978) 681-8000
Toll Free:(800) 833-4237
Web Page: http://www.dolan-jenner.com

Dolch Computer Systems ·· Fremont, CA: (510) 661-2220
Tech:(800) 995-7579   Toll Free:(877) 347-4938
Web Page: http://www.dolch.com

Dolphin Systems Inc ··· Alton, ON: (519) 942-0344
Web Page: http://www.dolphinsys.com

Dome Imaging Systems ··· Waltham, MA: (781) 895-1155
Web Page: http://www.domeimaging.com

Doremi Labs Inc ·· Burbank, CA: (818) 562-1101
Web Page: http://www.doremilabs.com

Dot Hill ··· Carlsbad, CA: (760) 931-5500
Tech:(877) 368-7924   Toll Free:(800) 872-2783
Web Page: http://www.artecon.com

Dotronix Inc ·· New Brighton, MN: (651) 633-1742
Toll Free:(800) 720-7218
Web Page: http://www.dotronix.com

Double Click ··· Toronto, ON: (416) 369-1100
Tech:(800) 793-6320
Web Page: http://www.mediasynergy.com

dpiX LLC ·· Palo Alto, CA: (650) 842-9960
Web Page: http://www.dpix.com

DPS Inc ·· **Indianapolis, IN: (317) 574-4300**
   Toll Free:(800) 654-4689
   Web Page: http://www.dpslink.com

DPS Software Group ······································· **Florence, KY: (859) 371-5533**
   Toll Free:(800) 775-3314
   Web Page: http://www.dps.com

DPT (see Adaptec)

Dr. Solomon's Soft (see Network Assoc)

Dragon Systems Inc (see ScanSoft)

Drastic Technologies ···································· **Toronto, ON: (416) 255-5636**
   Tech:(800) 830-5184
   Web Page: http://www.drastictech.com

Dream Home Source ······································ **Portland, OR: (503) 452-8664**
   Tech:(503) 452-8664   Toll Free:(800) 447-0027
   Web Page: http://www.dreamhomesource.com

Dream Theater ································· **Westlake Village, CA: (818) 661-1109**
   Web Page: http://www.dreamtheater.com

Dreamworks Interactive ····························· **Los Angeles, CA: (425) 635-7134**
   Tech:(425) 635-7134
   Web Page: http://www.dreamworks.com

DRS Technologies ······································· **Parsippany, NJ: (973) 898-1500**
   Web Page: http://www.drs.com

DS Design ·· **Cary, NC: (919) 319-1770**
   Toll Free:(800) 745-4037
   Web Page: http://www.dsdesign.com

DS Design (see Araize)

DSP Architectures Inc ································· **Vancouver, WA: (360) 573-4084**
   Web Page: http://www.dsparchitectures.com

DSP Development Corp ·································· **Newton, MA: (617) 969-0185**
   Toll Free:(800) 424-3131
   Web Page: http://www.dadisp.com

DSP Group Inc ·· **Santa Clara, CA: (408) 986-4300**
   Web Page: http://www.dspg.com

Dukane Corporation ··································· **Saint Charles, IL: (630) 584-2300**
   Web Page: http://www.dukane.com

Duncantech Inc ··· **San Diego, CA: (858) 481-8182**
   Toll Free:(800) 462-4307
   Web Page: http://www.duncantech.com

Dundas Software Ltd ····································· **Toronto, ON: (416) 467-5100**
   Tech:(416) 467-9100   Toll Free:(800) 463-1492
   Web Page: http://www.dundas.com

Durand Interstellar Inc ······························· **Los Gatos, CA: (408) 356-3886**
   Web Page: http://www.interstellar.com

Duxbury Systems Inc ··································· **Westford, MA: (978) 692-3000**
   Web Page: http://www.duxburysystems.com

DV Studio Inc ··· **Santa Ana, CA: (714) 241-7901**
   Web Page: http://www.dv-studio.com

DVC Co ·· **Austin, TX: (512) 301-9564**
   Web Page: http://www.dvcco.com

DVO Enterprises ·· **Alpine, UT: (801) 492-1290**
   Toll Free:(888) 462-6656
   Web Page: http://www.dvo.com

DVS Digital Video ······································ **Glendale, CA: (818) 241-8680**
   Web Page: http://www.digitalvideosystems.com

DVT Corp ·· **Norcross, GA: (770) 449-4960**
   Web Page: http://www.dvtsensors.com

Dy4Systems ··· **Leesburg, VA: (703) 779-7800**
   Tech:(703) 779-4754
   Web Page: http://www.dy4.com

Dymo-CoStar Corp ··· Greenwich, CT: (203) 661-9700
  Tech:(203) 588-2500   Toll Free:(800) 426-7827
  Web Page: http://www.dymo-costar.com

Dynacomp Inc ··· Livonia, NY: (315) 549-7168
  Web Page: http://www.dynacomp.com

Dynalink Technologies ··· Westmont, QC: (514) 489-3007
  Tech:(514) 489-3007
  Web Page: http://www.dynalinktech.com

Dynamic Control Systems ··· Huntingburg, IN: (812) 683-8213
  Web Page: http://www.dynamiccontrol.com

Dynamic Displays Inc ··· Eau Claire, WI: (715) 835-9440
  Toll Free:(800) 793-6862
  Web Page: http://www.dynamicdisplay.com

Dynamic Graphics ··· Peoria, IL: (309) 688-8800
  Toll Free:(800) 255-8800
  Web Page: http://www.dgusa.com

Dynasty Technologies Inc ··· Houston, TX: (281) 582 0020
  Web Page: http://www.dynasty.com

Dynatech Computer Power (see SL Waber)

Dynatran (see Accu-Med Northwest)
C/S Engineering &
Development, LLC ··· (253) 857-2180
  Tech:(253) 857-2180   Toll Free:(800) 247-1431
  Web Page: http://www.csdevel.com

e-Media ··· San Diego, CA: (858) 453-0333
  Web Page: http://www.e-media.com

e-Media Vision inc ··· Fremont, CA: (510) 445-6370
  Web Page: http://www.emvusa.com

E-mu Systems Inc ··· Scottsvalley, CA: (831) 438-1921
  Tech:(831) 438-1921
  Web Page: http://www.emu.com

E-Z Legal Forms Inc ··· Deerfield Beach, FL: (954) 480-8933
  Toll Free:(800) 822-4566
  Web Page: http://www.e-zlegal.com

Eagle Point Software Corp ··· Dubuque, IA: (563) 556-8392
  Tech:(800) 477-0909   Toll Free:(800) 678-6565
  Web Page: http://www.eaglepoint.com

Eagle Technology ··· Lexington, KY: (800) 432-4541
  Toll Free:(800) 432-4541
  Web Page: http://www.eagleone.com

EarthLink (877) 946-6774
  Tech:(888) 829-8466   Toll Free:(800) 327-8454
  Web Page: http://www.earthlink.com

Eastern Systems Inc ··· Westborough, MA: (508) 366-3223
  Web Page: http://www.easternsystems.com

Eastman Kodak Co (see Kodak)
Document Imaging ··· (716) 724-4000
  Web Page: http://www.kodak.com/go/businessimaging
Image Sensor Solutions ··· (716) 722-4385
  Web Page: http://www.kodak.com/go/imagers

Eastman Software Inc ··· Billerica, MA: (978) 313-7000
  Tech:(800) 970-5209   Toll Free:(800) 229-2973
  Web Page: http://www.eastmansoftware.com

Easy Software Products ··· Hollywood, MD: (301) 373-9600
  Tech:(301) 373-9600
  Web Page: http://www.easysw.com

Eccentric Software ··· Seattle, WA: (800) 436-6758
  Tech:(206) 760-9547   Toll Free:(800) 436-6758
  Web Page: http://www.eccentricsoftware.com

Echo Digital Audio Corp·····················Carpinteria, CA: (805) 684-4593
  Tech:(805) 684-4593
  Web Page: http://www.echoaudio.com
Echo Management Group·····················Conway, NH: (603) 447-8600
  Toll Free:(800) 635-8209
  Web Page: http://www.echoman.com
EchoMail Inc·····················Cambridge, MA: (617) 354-8585
  Toll Free:(888) 354-8585
  Web Page: http://www.interactive.com
Eclipse Tech Inc (see Stellar Winds)
ECRM·····················Tewksbury, MA: (978) 851-0207
  Toll Free:(800) 537-3276
  Web Page: http://www.ecrm.com
Edge Systems·····················Naperville, IL: (630) 810-9669
  Web Page: http://www.edge.com
Edify Corp·····················Santa Clara, CA: (408) 982-2000
  Tech:(800) 723-3439   Toll Free:(800) 944-0056
  Web Page: http://www.edify.com
Edimax Computer Co·····················Santa Clara, CA: (408) 496-1105
  Tech:(408) 988-6092   Toll Free:(800) 652-6776
  Web Page: http://www.edimax.com
Edmark Corp (see River Deep)
Edmund Industrial Optics·····················Barrington, NJ: (856) 573-6250
  Tech:(856) 573-6852   Toll Free:(800) 363-1992
  Web Page: http://www.edmundoptics.com
EDP Systems Services Inc·····················Lynwood, WA: (425) 771-3796
  Tech:(800) 827-4055   Toll Free:(800) 827-4055
  Web Page: http://www.abarcode.com
EDS·····················Plano, TX: (972) 605-6557
  Toll Free:(800) 566-9337
  Web Page: http://www.eds.com
EDS Unigraphics (see Unigraphics)
Educational Resources·····················Elgin, IL: (800) 860-7004
  Toll Free:(800) 860-9008
  Web Page: http://www.edresources.com
EDUCORP Multimedia (see Crimson Multi.)
EEPD North America·····················Sunrise, FL: (954) 331-8128
  Web Page: http://www.eepd.com
EFA Corp of America·····················Fremont, CA: (510) 979-2130
  Tech:(510) 979-2121
  Web Page: http://www.efacorp.com
EFI Electronics Corp·····················Salt Lake City, UT: (801) 977-9009
  Toll Free:(800) 877-1174
  Web Page: http://www.efinet.com
Egghead.com·····················Menlo Park, CA: (800) 344-4323
  Toll Free:(800) 344-4323
  Web Page: http://www.egghead.com
eHelp Corp·····················San Francisco, CA: (415) 252-2000
  Toll Free:(800) 470-7211
  Web Page: http://www.ehelp.com
Intel Network Systems·····················(514) 745-5500
  Web Page: http://www.shiva.com
Eicon Networks Corporation)
Eidos Interactive·····················San Francisco, CA: (415) 547-1200
  Tech:(415) 547-1244
  Web Page: http://www.eidosinteractive.com
Eigentech Inc·····················Marlton, NJ: (856) 985-9185
  Toll Free:(800) 676-8689
  Web Page: http://www.eigentech.com

Eiger Labs Inc ·· Newark, CA: (510) 739-0900
  Web Page: http://www.eigerlabs.com
Eizo Nanao Technologies Inc ····································· Cypress, CA: (562) 431-5011
  Toll Free:(800) 800-5202
  Web Page: http://www.eizo.com
Elan Software (see Goldmine Software)
Elcom Intl ·· Norwood, MA: (781) 440-3333
  Toll Free:(800) 713-3993
  Web Page: http://www.elcominternational.com
Electric Image ·· San Antonio, TX: (830) 438-4955
  Web Page: http://www.electricimage.com
Electrim Corp ·· Princeton, NJ: (609) 683-5546
  Toll Free:(800) 683-5546
  Web Page: http://www.electrim.com
Electro-Optical Tech Inc ··· Falls Church, VA: (571) 633-0744
  Web Page: http://www.garlic.com/biz
Electrohome Display Sys ··· Kitchener, ON: (519) 749-3120
  Web Page: http://www.electrohome.com
Electroimage Corp ··· Great Neck, NY: (516) 773-4305
  Web Page: http://www.electroimage.com
Electronic Arts ··· San Mateo, CA: (650) 572-2787
  Tech:(650) 572-2787   Toll Free:(800) 448-8822
  Web Page: http://www.ea.com
Electronic City ·· Burbank, CA: (818) 842-5275
  Web Page: http://www.electroniccity.com
Electronic Data Systems Corp (EDS) ····················· Plano, TX: (972) 604-6000
  Tech:(972) 605-6000   Toll Free:(800) 566-9337
  Web Page: http://www.eds.com
Electronic Energy Control Inc ··································· Columbus, OH: (614) 464-4470
  Tech:(614) 464-4470   Toll Free:(800) 842-7714
  Web Page: http://www.eeci.com
Electronix Corp ·· Fairborn, OH: (937) 878-9878
  Tech:(937) 878-1828   Toll Free:(800) 223-3205
  Web Page: http://www.electronix.com
Electrophysics Corp ·· Fairfield, NJ: (973) 882-0211
  Web Page: http://www.electrophysicscorp.com
Electrosonic ·· Minneapolis, MN: (952) 931-7500
  Toll Free:(800) 328-6202
  Web Page: http://www.electrosonic.com
Elgar Corp ··· San Diego, CA: (858) 450-0085
  Tech:(858) 458-0250   Toll Free:(800) 733-5427
  Web Page: http://www.elgar.com
Elibrium ··· Menlo Park, CA: (650) 345-8067
  Tech:(650) 345-1036   Toll Free:(800) 325-0834
  Web Page: http://www.elibrium.com
Elite Products ·· Wheeling, WV: (304) 277-2952
  Toll Free:(800) 372-7377
  Web Page: http://www.miniwhiteboards.com
Elitegroup Computer System (ECS) ······················· Fremont, CA: (510) 226-7333
  Tech:(510) 226-7333
  Web Page: http://www.ecsusa.com
Elmo Manufacturing Corp ··· Plainview, NY: (516) 501-1400
Elo TouchSystems Inc ·· Fremont, CA: (510) 739-5016
  Tech:(800) 557-1458   Toll Free:(800) 356-8682
  Web Page: http://www.elotouch.com
Elsa Inc ··· San Jose, CA: (408) 961-4600
  Tech:(408) 961-4600   Toll Free:(800) 272-3572
  Web Page: http://www.elsa.com
Eltron International Inc ··· Camarillo, CA: (805) 579-1800

Toll Free:(800) 344-4003
Web Page: http://www.eltron.com

eMachines ·· Irvine, CA: (801) 401-1419
Tech:(801) 401-1419   Toll Free:(800) 362-2446
Web Page: http://www.emachines.com

Emblem Interactive ·································· Miami, FL: (305) 649-1207
Tech:(305) 541-4331   Toll Free:(800) 323-8324
Web Page: http://www.embleminteractive.com

EMC Corp ·· Hopkinton, MA: (508) 435-1000
Toll Free:(800) 672-7729
Web Page: http://www.emc.com

EMC Corp ·· McLean, VA: (703) 970-5818
Toll Free:(866) 283-8841
Web Page: http://www.emc.com

Emerald Systems (see NCE Storage)

Empire Imaging Systems ···················· Plattsburgh, NY: (800) 280-5980
Web Page: http://www.empireimaging.com

Empire Interactive ······························ San Francisco, CA: (415) 439-4854
Tech:(415) 439-4859   Toll Free:(800) 216-9706
Web Page: http://www.empireinteractive.com

Empix Imaging Inc ······························ Mississauga, ON: (905) 820-2944
Tech:(905) 820-3369   Toll Free:(888) 933-6749
Web Page: http://www.empix.com

Empress Software Inc ·························· Greenbelt, MD: (301) 220-1919
Tech:(301) 220-1919   Toll Free:(866) 626-8888
Web Page: http://www.empress.com

Emtech DataStoreMedia ······················ Billerica, MA: (800) 343-4600
Tech:(800) 708-6334   Toll Free:(800) 343-4600
Web Page: http://www.emtech.com

Emulex ··· Costa Mesa, CA: (714) 662-5600
Tech:(714) 513-8270   Toll Free:800-EMULEX3
Web Page: http://www.emulex.com

Encad ·· San Diego, CA: (858) 452-0882
Tech:(877) 362-2387   Toll Free:(800) 453-6223
Web Page: http://www.encad.com

Encore Computer (see Encore Realtime)

Encore Realtime Computing ················· Melbourne, FL: (321) 473-1008
Web Page: http://www.encore.com

Encore Software ································· Gardena, CA: (310) 768-1800
Tech:(310) 719-2890   Toll Free:(800) 507-1375
Web Page: http://www.encoresoftware.com

Endl Publications ······························· Saratoga, CA: (408) 867-6642
Tech:(408) 867-6630
Web Page: http://www.rahul.net/endl

Enerdyne ·· El Cajon, CA: (877) 363-7396
Web Page: http://www.enerdyne.com

Engineering Design Team ····················· Beaverton, OR: (503) 690-1234
Web Page: http://www.edt.com

Enhance 3000 (see Street Technology)

Enhance Memory Prod (see Enhance 3000)

Enhanced Software Technologies Inc ····· Phoenix, AZ: (602) 470-1115
Tech:(602) 470-1333   Toll Free:(800) 998-8649
Web Page: http://www.estinc.com

Enlight Corp ·· Santa Fe Springs, CA: (562) 781-9898
Toll Free:(877) 696-8899
Web Page: http://www.enlightcorp.com

Ensco Inc ··· Falls Church, VA: (703) 321-9000
Toll Free:(800) 367-2682
Web Page: http://www.ensco.com

Ensemble Designs Inc ························· Grass Valley, CA: (530) 478-1830
  Tech:(530) 478-1830
  Web Page: http://www.ensembledesigns.com

Enseo ··· Richardson, TX: (972) 234-2513
  Web Page: http://www.enseo.com

ENSONIQ Corp (see E-mu Systems)

Entegrity Solutions ····························· Nashua, NH: (603) 882-1306
  Toll Free:(800) 525-4343
  Web Page: http://www.entegrity.com

Enterasys Network ······························ Andover, MA: (978) 684-1000
  Toll Free:(877) 801-7082
  Web Page: http://www.cabletron.com

Entercept Security Technologies ········ Santa Clara, CA: (800) 338-8754
  Toll Free:(800) 338-8754
  Web Page: http://www.entercept.com

Enterprise Corporation International ········ West Des Moines, IA: (515) 282-4490
  Toll Free:(800) 842-5788
  Web Page: http://www.ecicorp.com

Entrega Technologies (see Xircom)

Envelope Manager Software ················ Palo Alto, CA: (650) 321-2640
  Tech:(800) 576-3279   Toll Free:(800) 576-3279
  Web Page: http://www.envmgr.com

Environmental Systems Research Inst ········ Redlands, CA: (888) 377-4575
  Toll Free:(800) 447-9778
  Web Page: http://www.esri.com

Envision Product Design ····················· Anchorage, AK: (907) 563-1141
  Web Page: http://www.envisionproductdesign.com

EO (see AT&T)

EOS Systems ······································· Vancouver, BC: (604) 732-6658
  Web Page: http://www.photomodeler.com

EPC Laboratories Inc ···························· Danvers, MA: (978) 777-1996
  Web Page: http://www.epclabs.com

Epicor Software Corp ····························· Irvine, CA: (949) 585-4000
  Toll Free:(800) 999-1809
  Web Page: http://www.epicor.com

Epilogue Technology (see Windriver)

Epix Inc ··· Buffalo Grove, IL: (847) 465-1818
  Web Page: http://www.epixinc.com

Epox International Inc ···························· La Habra, CA: (714) 680-0898
  Web Page: http://www.epox.com

ePresence (merged Unisys)

Epson America Inc ································ Torrance, CA: (800) 338-2349
  Tech:(310) 782-2600   Toll Free:(800) 289-3776
  Web Page: http://www.epson.com

Epson America Inc ······························ Long Beach, CA: (562) 981-3840
  Tech:(800) 922-8911   Toll Free:(800) 463-7766
  Accessories ···································· (800) 873-7766
  Web Page: http://www.epsonsupplies.com
  OEM ··· (562) 290-5304
  Tech Support ································· (562) 276-1300
  Tech:(310) 782-2600

Epson Electronics America ···················· San Jose, CA: (408) 922-0200
  Toll Free:(800) 228-3964
  Web Page: http://www.eea.epson.com

Epson Factory Automation Robotics ········· Carson, CA: (562) 290-5910
  Tech:(310) 517-7869
  Web Page: http://www.robots.epson.com

Equilibrium Inc ·································· Sausalito, CA: (415) 892-3700
  Web Page: http://www.equilibrium.com

Equinox Systems Inc ·· Sunrise, FL: (954) 746-9000
  Tech:(954) 746-9000   Toll Free:(800) 275-3500
  Web Page: http://www.equinox.com
Equisys Inc ·· Alpharetta, GA: (770) 772-7201
  Tech:(770) 946-9149
  Web Page: http://www.equisys.com
Erdas Inc ··· Atlanta, GA: (404) 248-9000
  Toll Free:(877) 463-7327
  Web Page: http://www.erdas.com
Ergo Computing (see Brick Computer Co)
Ergo Tech Int. (see G2X Software)
Ergotron Inc ··· St. Paul, MN: (800) 888-8458
  Toll Free:(800) 888-8458
  Web Page: http://www.ergotron.com
Ericsson Datacom Inc ·· Santa Barbara, CA: (805) 685-4455
  Tech:(800) 666-7308   Toll Free:(800) 444-7854
  Web Page: http://www.ericsson.com
Ericsson WebCom Inc ·· Menlo Park, CA: (650) 324-6100
  Tech:(650) 210-9434
  Web Page: http://www.ericsson-webcom.com
Erim Intl Inc ··· Ann Arbor, MI: (734) 994-1200
  Web Page: http://www.erim-int.com
Esker Inc ··· Madison, WI: (608) 828-6000
  Toll Free:(800) 368-5283
  Web Page: http://www.esker.com
Esker Inc ··· Stillwater, OK: (405) 533-5500
  Toll Free:(800) 343-7070
  Web Page: http://www.esker.com
eSoft Inc ··· Broomfield, CO: (303) 444-1600
  Tech:(877) 754-2986   Toll Free:(888) 903-7638
  Web Page: http://www.esoft.com
ESRI (see Environmental Sys. Research)
ESS Technology Inc ·· Fremont, CA: (510) 492-1088
  Web Page: http://www.esstech.com
Essential Data Inc ··· Oregon House, CA: (530) 692-2459
  Toll Free:(800) 795-4756
  Web Page: http://www.cdduplicators.com
Essential Software ·· Westborough, MA: (508) 366-3888
  Tech:(800) 729-3553
  Web Page: http://www.ardentsoftware.com
eSupport.com ··· North Andover, MA: (978) 686-6468
  Tech:(978) 686-2204   Toll Free:(800) 800-2467
  Web Page: http://www.esupport.com
eSynch/Kissco ··· Santa Ana, CA: (714) 258-1900
  Tech:(714) 258-1900   Toll Free:(888) 833-1228
  Web Page: http://www.kissco.com
Etak Inc (see TeleAtlas)
Etech ··· Charlotte, NC: (704) 554-1919
  Web Page: http://www.etechcad.com
eTek International ·· Aurora, CO: (303) 369-4456
  Toll Free:(800) 888-6894
  Web Page: http://www.etek.net
eTesting Labs ··· Morrisville, NC: (919) 380-2800
  Tech:(919) 380-2837   Toll Free:(877) 619-9259
  Web Page: http://www.etestinglabs.com
Euresys Inc ·· Itasca, IL: (630) 250-2300
  Toll Free:(866) 387-3797
  Web Page: http://www.euresys.com
Euro RSCG 4D ·· New York, NY: (212) 886-2000

Tech:(212) 886-2063
Web Page: http://www.euroscg4d.com

Eurologic Systems ··· Foxborough, MA: (978) 266-9224
Toll Free:(800) 231-4070
Web Page: http://www.eurologic.com

Europa Software (see RuleSpace)

Evans & Sutherland ·· Salt Lake City, UT: (801) 588-1000
Tech:(801) 588-1088   Toll Free:(800) 582-4375
Web Page: http://www.es.com

Everex Systems ·· Fremont, CA: (510) 498-1111
Tech:(510) 252-7773   Toll Free:(800) 383-7391
Web Page: http://www.everex.com

Evergreen Technologies Inc ································· Corvallis, OR: (541) 757-0934
Tech:(541) 757-7341   Toll Free:(888) 380-7111
Web Page: http://www.evertech.com

Evex Analytical ··· Princeton, NJ: (609) 252-9192
Web Page: http://www.evex.com

Evolution Computing ·· Phoenix, AZ: (480) 967-8633
Tech:(480) 967-6967   Toll Free:(800) 874-4028
Web Page: http://www.fastcad.com

Evolutionary Technologies ··· Austin, TX: (512) 383-3000
Toll Free:(800) 392-2983
Web Page: http://www.eti.com

Ex Machina Inc (see Air Media)

Exabyte Corp ··· Boulder, CO: (303) 442-4333
Tech:(303) 417-7792   Toll Free:800-EXABYTE
Web Page: http://www.exabyte.com

Exact Software ··· Andover, MA: (978) 474-4900
Web Page: http://exactamerica.com

Exar Corp ··· Fremont, CA: (510) 668-7000
Web Page: http://www.exar.com

Exceller Software Corp ·· Cincinnati, OH: (513) 792-9555
Tech:(513) 792-9555
Web Page: http://www.exceller.com

Excelon Corp (see Object Design)

Exchequer Software Inc (see Intellisol)

Excite (see Architext)

Executive Software ··· Burbank, CA: (818) 771-1600
Toll Free:(800) 829-6468
Web Page: http://www.execsoft.com

Exide Electronics (see Powerware)

EXP Computer ·· Hickville, NY: (516) 942-0507
Tech:(909) 595-2046   Toll Free:(800) 397-6922
Web Page: http://www.expnet.com

Expert Software (see Activision)

ExperTelligence Inc ··· Santa Barbara, CA: (805) 962-2558
Web Page: http://www.expertelligence.com

ExperVision Inc ··· Fremont, CA: (510) 623-7071
Tech:(510) 623-7177   Toll Free:(800) 732-3897
Web Page: http://www.expervision.com

Express Systems Inc (see WRQ)

Extended Systems Inc ··· Boise, ID: (208) 322-7575
Toll Free:(800) 235-7576
Web Page: http://www.extendsys.com

Extensis ··· Portland, OR: (503) 274-2020
Tech:(503) 274-7030   Toll Free:(800) 796-9798
Web Page: http://www.extensis.com

Extreme CCTV ·· Burnaby, BC, : (604) 420-7711
Toll Free:(888) 409-2288

Web Page: http://www.extremecctv.com

Extron USA / Inline Inc(see Extron) ·················· Anaheim, CA: (714) 491-1500
Toll Free:(800) 633-9876
Web Page: http://www.extron.com

Eyewire Inc ······································· Seattle, WA: (206) 925-5000
Toll Free:(800) 661-9410
Web Page: http://www.eyewire.com

Ezonics Corp ······································· Pleasanton, CA: (925) 468-0818
Web Page: http://www.ezonics.com

F Secure inc ······································· San Jose, CA: (408) 938-6700
Tech:(408) 938-6700   Toll Free:(888) 432-8233
Web Page: http://www.datafellows.com

Fabius Software Systems ····················· Mission Viejo, CA: (800) 632-2487
Tech:(949) 888-1685   Toll Free:(800) 632-2487
Web Page: http://www.fabius.com

Facet Corp ······································· Plano, TX: (972) 985-9901
Tech:(877) 322-3846   Toll Free:(800) 235-9901
Web Page: http://www.facetcorp.com

Fairchild Semiconductor ····················· Portlan, ME: 207-775-8100
Toll Free:800-341-0392
Web Page: http://www.fairchildsemi.com

Faircom Corp ······································· Columbia, MO: (573) 445-6833
Tech:(573) 445-6833   Toll Free:(800) 234-8180
Web Page: http://www.faircom.com

Fairhaven Software ····························· New Bedford, MA: (508) 994-6400
Toll Free:(800) 582-4747
Web Page: http://www.fairsoft.com

Falcon Safety Products Inc ···················· Somerville, NJ: (908) 707-4900
Web Page: http://www.falconsafety.com

Falcon Software Inc ···················· Victoria, British Columbia, : (250) 480-1311
Tech:(250) 480-1322   Toll Free:(800) 707-1311
Web Page: http://www.falconsoftware.com

Farallon Computing (see Netopia)

FARGO Electronics ······························· Eden Prairie, MN: (952) 941-9470
Tech:(952) 941-0050   Toll Free:(800) 459-5636
Web Page: http://www.fargo.com

Farpoint Technologies Inc ····················· Morrisville, NC: (919) 460-4551
Tech:(919) 460-1887   Toll Free:(800) 645-5913
Web Page: http://www.fpoint.com

Fast Color.Com ······························· Sinking Springs, PA: (610) 678-8035
Tech:(610) 678-8035   Toll Free:(800) 899-2595
Web Page: http://www.fastcolor.com

Fast Point Technologies ······················· Stanton, CA: (714) 484-6300
Toll Free:(800) 962-3900
Web Page: http://www.fastpoint.com

FastComm Communications Corp ·················· Dulles, VA: (703) 318-7750
Tech:(703) 318-4350   Toll Free:(800) 521-2496
Web Page: http://www.fastcomm.com

Faulkner Information Services ················· Pennsauken, NJ: (856) 662-2070
Toll Free:(800) 843-0460
Web Page: http://www.faulkner.com

FaxBack Inc ······································· Tigard, OR: (503) 645-1114
Toll Free:(800) 329-2225
Web Page: http://www.faxback.com

Fedco Electronics Inc ·························· Fond Du Lac, WI: (920) 922-6490
Tech:(800) 542-9761   Toll Free:(800) 542-9761
Web Page: http://www.fedcoelectronics.com

FedWorld Info Network ····························· Springfield, VA: (703) 605-6000
Toll Free:(800) 553-6847
Web Page: http://www.fedworld.gov

Feith Systems & Software ·· Ft Washington, PA: (215) 646-8000
  Web Page: http://www.feith.com
Fellowes ·· Itasca, IL: (630) 893-1600
  Tech:(888) 335-8324   Toll Free:(800) 955-0959
  Web Page: http://www.fellowes.com
FGS (see Symantec)
Fiber Options(Branch of GE) ································· Corvallis,, OR: (800) 469-1676
  Tech:(877) 342-3732   Toll Free:(800) 469-1676
  Web Page: http://www.geindustrial.com
Fibermux (see ADC Kentrox)
Fiberoptic Systems Inc ·· Simi Valley, CA: (805) 583-2088
  Toll Free:(800) 995-8016
  Web Page: http://www.fibopsys.com
Ficomp ·· Colmar, PA: (215) 997-2600
  Web Page: http://www.ficomp.com
Ficus Systems (Out of Business)
Fifth Generation Sys (see Symantec)
Filemaker Inc ·· Santa Clara, CA: (408) 987-7000
  Tech:(408) 727-9004   Toll Free:(800) 325-2747
  Web Page: http://www.filemaker.com
FileNet Corp ··· Kirkland, WA: (425) 893-7000
  Tech:(800) 624-4877   Toll Free:(800) 345-3638
  Web Page: http://www.filenet.com
FileNET Corp(see FileNet)
Final Draft Inc ·· Calabasas, CA: (818) 995-8995
  Toll Free:(800) 231-4055
  Web Page: http://www.finaldraft.com
Financial Navigator Int'l ·· Mountain View, CA: (650) 962-0300
  Tech:(650) 962-8510   Toll Free:(800) 468-3636
  Web Page: http://www.finnav.com
Firefox Inc (see FTP Software Inc)
First Floor Inc (see Calico Technology)
First International Computer Inc ······························ Fremont, CA: (510) 252-7777
  Tech:(510) 252-8888
  Web Page: http://www.fica.com
First Logic ·· La Cross, WI: (608) 782-5000
  Tech:(888) 788-9004   Toll Free:(888) 215-6442
  Web Page: http://www.firstlogic.com
First Things First (see Visionary Soft)
First Vision ··· Andover, MA: (978) 474-0044
  Web Page: http://www.1stvision.com
Firstwave Technologies Inc ······································ Atlanta, GA: (770) 431-1200
  Tech:(770) 431-1200   Toll Free:(800) 540-6061
  Web Page: http://www.firstwave.net
Fitnesoft Inc ··· Orem, UT: (801) 221-7777
  Tech:(801) 221-7708
  Web Page: http://www.fitnesoft.com
FJW Optical Systems Inc ··· Palatine, IL: (847) 358-2500
  Web Page: http://www.findrscope.com
Flagship Systems Inc ··· Burnaby (Vancouver), B.C., : (604) 294-1070
  Web Page: http://www.flagshipsystems.com
FlexiInternational Software ······································ Shelton, CT: (203) 925-3040
  Tech:(800) 353-9443   Toll Free:(800) 353-9492
  Web Page: http://www.flexi.com
Flir Systems Inc ·· N. Billerica, MA: (978) 901-8000
  Toll Free:(800) 464-6372
  Web Page: http://www.flir.com
Flonetwork (see Double Click)

Fluke ··· Phoenix, AZ: (602) 952-6400
  Tech:(800) 638-3497   Toll Free:(800) 253-7813
  Web Page: http://www.microtest.com

Fluke Corporation ·· Everett, WA: (425) 347-6100
  Tech:(888) 993-5853   Toll Free:(800) 443-5853
  Web Page: http://www.fluke.com

Focus Enhancements ·· Campbell, CA: (408) 866-8300
  Web Page: http://www.focusinfo.com

Foley Hi-Tech Systems (Out of Business)

Folio Corp (see Open Market)

Folsom Research Inc ······································ Rancho Cordova, CA: (916) 859-2500
  Toll Free:(888) 414-7226
  Web Page: http://www.folsom.com

Fong Kai USA, Inc ·· Richardson, TX: (972) 644-1584
  Toll Free:(888) 644-1584
  Web Page: http://www.fkusa.com

Fore Systems (see Marconi Comm.)

Forefront Direct (see Smart Certify)

Foresight Imaging ··· Lowell, MA: (978) 458-4624
  Web Page: http://www.foresightimaging.com

Foresight Resources Corp (see Autodesk)

FormGen Inc (see GT Interactive)

Forte Inc ·· Carlsbad, CA: (760) 431-6460
  Toll Free:(800) 441-7635
  Web Page: http://www.forteinc.com

Fortel ·· Chantilly, VA: (703) 563-3000
  Toll Free:(877) 744-4854
  Web Page: http://www.fortel.com

Fotec Inc ·· Medford, MA: (781) 396-6155
  Tech:(617) 396-6155   Toll Free:(800) 537-8254
  Web Page: http://www.fotec.com

Four Star Systems (see Lan Star)

Fourth Shift Corp ·· Minneapolis, MN: (612) 851-1500
  Tech:(800) 342-5675   Toll Free:(800) 232-4563
  Web Page: http://www.fs.com

Fractal Design Corp (see Metacreations)

Frame Technology (see Adobe Systems)

Franklin Covey ·· Salt Lake City, UT: (801) 975-1776
  Tech:(801) 975-9999   Toll Free:(800) 654-1776
  Web Page: http://www.franklinquest.com

Franklin Electronic Publishers ······················· Burlington, NJ: (800) 266-5626
  Tech:(609) 386-8997   Toll Free:(800) 266-5626
  Web Page: http://www.franklin.com

Frederick Engineering Inc ····················· Linthicum Heights, MD: (410) 789-7890
  Tech:(410) 789-7890   Toll Free:(888) 866-9001
  Web Page: http://www.fetest.com

FreeGate Corp (see Tut Systems)

Front Range Solutions ································ Colorado Springs, CO: (719) 531.500
  Toll Free:(800) 776.7889
  Web Page: http://www.frontrange.com

Front Range Solutions Inc ······························· Denver, CO: (800) 693-2508
  Toll Free:(800) 743-6238
  Web Page: http://www.ixchange.com

Front Step(see MAPICS, Inc.) ······················· Alpharetta, GA: (678) 319-8000
  Web Page: http://www.frontstep.com

Frontier Technologies ·· Mequon, WI: (262) 243-5190
  Tech:(262) 243-5190
  Web Page: http://www.frontiertech.com

Fry's Electronics ·· Palo Alto, CA: (650) 496-6000
   Web Page: http://www.FrysElectronics.com
Frye Computer (see Seagate)
FSI Automation ··· Bothell, WA: (425) 486-3444
   Web Page: http://www.fsiautomation.com
FSR Inc ·· W. Paterson, NJ: (973) 785-4347
   Toll Free:(800) 332-3771
   Web Page: http://www.fsrinc.com
FTP Software (see NetManage)
Fuji Photo Film ·· Elmsford, NY: (800) 755-3854
   Web Page: http://www.fujifilm.com
Fujikura America ··· Marietta, GA: (770) 956-7200
   Web Page: http://www.fujikura.com
Fujinon Inc ··· Wayne, NJ: (973) 633-5600
   Web Page: http://www.fujinon.com
Fujitsu America Inc ·· San Jose, CA: (408) 432-1300
   Web Page: http://www.fai.fujitsu.com
Fujitsu America Inc (see HAL Comp Systems)
   Customer Assistance Center ·····················(800) 654-0715
   Technical Assistance Center ·····················(800) 242-3227
Fujitsu Component America Inc ····························· Sunnyvale, CA: (408) 745-4900
   Web Page: http://www.fujitsu.takamisawa.com
Fujitsu Compound Semiconductor inc ··················· San Jose, CA: (408) 232-9500
   Web Page: http://www.fcsi.fujitsu.com
Fujitsu Computer Packaging Technologies ·············· San Jose, CA: (408) 943-7700
   Web Page: http://www.fcpt.com
Fujitsu Computer Products ·································· San Jose, CA: (408) 432-6333
   Tech:(800) 591-5924   Toll Free:(800) 626-4686
   Web Page: http://www.fcpa.fujitsu.com
Fujitsu General America Inc ································· Fairfield, NJ: (973) 575-0380
   Toll Free:(888) 888-3424
   Web Page: http://www.fujitsugeneral.com
Fujitsu ICL ·· Dallas, TX: (972) 716-8300
   Tech:(800) 345-0845   Toll Free:(800) 538-8716
   Web Page: http://www.ftxs.fujitsu.com
Fujitsu Internet Service ·· San Jose, CA:
   Web Page: http://www.fai.fujitsu.com
Fujitsu IT Holdings Inc ···································· Sunnyvale, CA: (408) 746-6000
   Tech:(800) 638-1764   Toll Free:(800) 538-8460
   Web Page: http://www.amdahl.com
Fujitsu Laboratories of America Inc ····················· Sunnyvale, CA: (408) 530-4500
   Web Page: http://www.fujitsu.com/FLA
Fujitsu Media Devices of America Inc ····················· San Jose, CA: (408) 437-8900
   Toll Free:(888) 437-8900
   Web Page: http://www.fujitsumedia.com
Fujitsu Microelectronics Inc ································ San Jose, CA: (800) 866-8608
   Toll Free:(800) 866-8608
   Web Page: http://www.fujitsumicro.com
Fujitsu Network Communications Inc ···················· Richardson, TX: (972) 690-6000
   Tech:(800) 873-3822   Toll Free:(800) 777-3278
   Web Page: http://www.fnc.fujitsu.com
Fujitsu PC Corp ·· Santa Clara, CA: (408) 982-9500
   Tech:(901) 259-5790   Toll Free:(888) 466-8434
   Web Page: http://www.fujitsupc.com
Fujitsu Systems Business of America ···················· Santa Clara, CA: (408) 988-8012
   Toll Free:(877) 240-3557
   Web Page: http://www.fsba.com
Fujitsu Technology Solutions Inc ························· Sunnyvale, CA: (877) 905-3644
Fujitsu Ten Corp of America ···································· Torrance, CA: (310) 327-2151

Tech:(800) 233-2216   Toll Free:(800) 237-5413
Web Page: http://www.eclipse-web.com

Full Armor ·· Boston, MA: (617) 457-8100
Tech:(617) 457-8100
Web Page: http://www.fullarmor.com

Full Time Software (see Legato Systems)

Fuller's Wholesale (see Batteries Direct)

Funai Corp ··· Teterboro, NJ: (201) 288-2063
Tech:(201) 288-2666   Toll Free:(800) 966-3862
Web Page: http://www.funai-corp.com

Funai Electric Silicon Valley ······························ Santa Clara, CA: (408) 330-6000
Web Page: http://www.funaiusa.com

Funk Software Inc ·· Cambridge, MA: (617) 497-6339
Tech:(617) 491-6503   Toll Free:(800) 828-4146
Web Page: http://www.funk.com

Future Domain Corp (see Adaptec)

Future Thinking (see Precision Power)

FutureSoft ·· Houston, TX: (281) 496-9400
Tech:(281) 588-6868   Toll Free:(800) 989-8908
Web Page: http://www.fse.com

FutureTense (see Open Market Inc)

Futurus Corp (see Novell Corporation)

FWB Software LLC ··· Newark, CA: (510) 894-0727
Web Page: http://www.fwb.com

G & A Imaging ··· Alpharetta, GA: (678) 366-5030
Toll Free:(888) 772-7601
Web Page: http://www.ga-imaging.com

G.V.C. (see Gentec Marketing)

G2X Software ··· New York, NY: (212) 741-1720
Toll Free:(800) 289-9801
Web Page: http://www.g2x.com

G7 Productivity Systems ································· San Diego, CA: (858) 613-6686
Toll Free:(800) 303-2620
Web Page: http://www.g7ps.com

Gadzoox Networks Inc ···································· San Jose, CA: (408) 360-4950
Toll Free:(888) 423-3222
Web Page: http://www.gadzoox.com

GAI-Tronics Corp ··· Mohnton, PA: (610) 777-1374
Tech:(800) 492-1212   Toll Free:(800) 492-1212
Web Page: http://www.gai-tronics.com

Galacticomm Inc (see netVillage.com)

Gammalink (see Dialogic Gammalink)

Garmin International ······································· Olathe, KS: (913) 397-8200
Toll Free:(800) 800-1020
Web Page: http://www.garmin.com

Gartner Group ·· San Jose, CA: (408) 468-8000
Tech:(408) 748-1111   Toll Free:(800) 419-3282
Web Page: http://www.gartner.com

Gates Arrow ·· Greenville, SC: (800) 332-2222
Toll Free:(800) 332-2222
Web Page: http://www.gatesarrow.com

Gates Arrow ·· Duluth, GA: (770) 623-3430
Tech:(800) 927-6824   Toll Free:(800) 428-3732

Gateway 2000 Inc ·· North Sioux City, SD: (605) 232-2000
Tech:(800) 846-2301   Toll Free:(800) 846-2000
Web Page: http://www.gateway.com
Automated Troubleshooting Service ··············(800) 846-2118
Toll Free:(800) 846-2118
Business Technical Support Center ··············(605) 232-2191

Toll Free:(877) 485-1464
Customer Service ··(800) 846-5259
Tech:(800) 444-4257   Toll Free:(800) 846-2302
Gateway Direct ··(949) 454-3200
Toll Free:(800) 235-4425
Gateway.net ···(888) 874-7681
Home Networks Solutions ······················(877) 485-1465
International Technical Support ············(605) 232-2191
TDD ··(800) 846-1778
Toll Free:(800) 846-1778

Gateway Electronics·································**Saint Louis, MO: (314) 427-6116**
Tech:(800) 669-5810   Toll Free:(800) 669-5810
Web Page: http://www.gatewayelex.com

Gazelle Systems (see GTM Software)

GCC Technologies····································**Bedford, MA: (781) 276-8620**
Tech:(781) 276-8620   Toll Free:(800) 422-7777
Web Page: http://www.gcctech.com

GE Information Services ···················**Gaithersburg, MD: (301) 340-4000**
Tech:(800) 560-4347   Toll Free:(800) 334-2255
Web Page: http://www.geis.com

Gear Software ···**Tequesta, FL: (561) 575-4327**
Toll Free:(800) 423-9147
Web Page: http://www.gearsoftware.com

GemStone Systems Inc ··························**Beaverton, OR: (503) 533-3000**
Web Page: http://www.gemstone.com

General DataComm Inc ························**Naugatuck, CT: (203) 729-0271**
Web Page: http://www.gdc.com

General Interactive (see EchoMail)

General Magic Inc ·································**Sunnyvale, CA: (408) 774-4000**
Toll Free:(800) 468-4342
Web Page: http://www.genmagic.com

General Nanotechnology ·······················**Berkeley, CA: (303) 444-8193**
Web Page: http://www.gennano.com

General Signal (see Inrange Tech)

General Software····································**Bellevue, WA: (425) 576-8300**
Tech:(425) 576-8300   Toll Free:(800) 850-5755
Web Page: http://www.gensw.com

General Technology Corp ·················**Albuquerque, NM: (505) 345-5591**
Web Page: http://www.gt-corp.com

General Video Corp······························**Quackertown, PA: (215) 536-1900**
Toll Free:(800) 482-0075
Web Page: http://www.gvcusa.com

General Vision··**Petaluma, CA: (707) 765-6150**
Web Page: http://www.general-vision.com

Generic Software (see AutoDesk)

Genesis Microchip Corp ··························**Alviso, CA: (408) 262-6599**
Web Page: http://www.gnss.com

Genicom Corp ··**Chantilly, VA: (703) 633-8700**
Tech:(540) 949-1031   Toll Free:(800) 436-4266
Web Page: http://www.genicom.com

Genicom Enterprising Service Solutions ·······**Chantilly, VA: (703) 633-8700**
Tech:(800) 848-8855   Toll Free:(800) 436-4266
Web Page: http://www.genicom.com

Genovation Inc ··**Irvine, CA: (949) 833-3355**
Tech:(949) 833-3355   Toll Free:(800) 822-4333
Web Page: http://www.genovation.com

Gensym Corp··**Burlington, MA: (781) 265-7100**
Web Page: http://www.gensym.com

Gentec Marketing ······································**Concord, ON: (905) 738-9300**

Tech:(905) 738-5736
Web Page: http://www.gvc.ca/

Geocomp Corp ··· Boxborough, MA: (978) 635-0012
Tech:(978) 635-0012
Web Page: http://www.geocomp.com

Geographic Data Technology Inc ·················· Lebanon, NH: (603) 643-2815
Tech:(800) 331-7881   Toll Free:(800) 331-7881
Web Page: http://www.geographic.com

GeoWorks ·· Dallas, TX: (214) 661-7479
Web Page: http://www.geoworks.com

Getronics ·· Billerica, MA: (978) 625-5000
Toll Free:(800) 225-0654
Web Page: http://www.getronics.com/us

Getty Images ·· New York, NY: (646) 613-4000
Tech:(877) 438-8966   Toll Free:(800) 462-4379
Web Page: http://www.photodisc.com

GFI Fax & Voice USA ······································· Cary, NC: (919) 388-3397
Tech:(919) 388-3900   Toll Free:(888) 243-4329
Web Page: http://www.gfifax.com

Gibson Musical ·· Nashville, TN: (800) 444-2766
Toll Free:(877) 999-4199
Web Page: http://www.opcode.com

Gibson Research Corp ·································· Laguna Hills, CA: (949) 348-7100
Toll Free:(800) 736-0637
Web Page: http://www.grc.com

GigaByte Technology Co Ltd ············· City Of Industry, CA: (626) 854-9334
Tech:(626) 854-9338
Web Page: http://www.giga-byte.com

GigaTrend Inc ·· Carlsbad, CA: (760) 931-9122
Tech:(760) 931-9122   Toll Free:(800) 743-4442
Web Page: http://www.gigatrend.com

GITI ·· Piscataway, NJ: (732) 271-4200
Web Page: http://www.giti.com

Glare Guard ··· St Paul, MN: (866) 273-9088
Toll Free:(866) 273-9088
Web Page: http://www.glareguard.com

GlassHouse Technologies ······························ Framingham, MA:
Tech:(508) 879-5729
Web Page: http://www.glasshouse.com

Glidecam Industries Inc ································· Plymouth, MA: (508) 830-1414
Tech:(800) 600-2011   Toll Free:(800) 949-2089
Web Page: http://www.glidecam.com

Global Computer Supply ································· Compton, CA: (310) 603-2266
Tech:(800) 227-1246   Toll Free:(888) 845-6225
Web Page: http://www.globalcomputer.com

Global Computer Supply ································· Fletcher, OH: (937) 368-2309
Tech:(937) 368-3862   Toll Free:(800) 445-2015
Web Page: http://www.globalcomputer.com

Global Engineering Documents ····················· Englewood, CO: (303) 397-7956
Toll Free:(800) 854-7179
Web Page: http://global.ihs.com

Global Graphics Software ······························ Centreville, VA: (703) 266-9588
Web Page: http://www.globalgraphics.com

Global Payment Sys (see National Data)

Global Streams ··· St. Louis, MO: (314) 997-5100
Toll Free:(800) 788-7205
Web Page: http://www.globalstreams.com

Global Technologies Group ····························· Arlington, VA: (703) 486-0500
Web Page: http://www.gtgi.com

Global Village Comm. (see Boca Global)
Globalink Inc (see Lernout & Hauspie)
Globe Manufacturing Inc ··· Mountainside, NJ: (908) 232-7306
   Tech:(908) 232-7301   Toll Free:(800) 227-3258
   Web Page: http://www.akstamping.com
Globecomm Systems ·· Hauppauge, NY: (631) 231-9800
   Web Page: http://www.globecommsystems.com
Globelle Inc (see Tech Data)
Globetrotter Software ··· Santa Clara, CA: (408) 743-8600
   Web Page: http://www.globetrotter.com
Glyph Technologies ·· Ithaca, NY: (607) 275-0345
   Web Page: http://www.glyphtech.com
GN Nettest (see NetTest Inc)
Go Ahead Software Inc ·· Bellevue, WA: (425) 453-1900
   Web Page: http://www.goahead.com
Goal Semiconductor Inc ·· Montreal, QC: (514) 871-2447
   Toll Free:(800) 943-4625
   Web Page: http://www.goalasic.com
Gold Disk Inc (see Astound Inc)
Gold Standard Multimedia Inc ·································· Tampa, FL: (813) 258-4747
   Toll Free:(800) 375-0943
   Web Page: http://www.gsm.com
Golden Bow Systems ··· San Diego, CA: (619) 298-9349
   Tech:(800) 284-3269   Toll Free:(800) 284-3269
   Web Page: http://www.goldenbow.com
Golden Software ··· Golden, CO: (303) 279-1021
   Tech:(303) 279-1021   Toll Free:(800) 972-1021
   Web Page: http://www.goldensoftware.com
GoldenRam ··· Irvine, CA: (949) 460-9000
   Tech:(800) 546-9124   Toll Free:(800) 222-8861
   Web Page: http://www.goldenram.com
Goldmine Software (see Front Range Sol.)
GoldStar USA (see LG Electronics USA)
Gordon Instruments Inc ··· Orchard Park, NY: (716) 662-5353
   Toll Free:(800) 333-2672
   Web Page: http://www.gordon-instruments.com
Gradient Tech. (see Entegrity Solutions)
Graftek Imaging ·· Austin, TX: (512) 416-1099
   Toll Free:(800) 441-2118
   Web Page: http://www.graftek.com
Grand Junction Network (see Cisco Sys)
Grandtec USA ··· Dallas, TX: (214) 366-3496
   Tech:(214) 956-0447   Toll Free:(800) 856-0777
   Web Page: http://www.grandtec.com
Granite Communications Inc ······································ Amherst, NH: (603) 881-8666
   Web Page: http://www.gcicom.com
Graphic Simulations Corp ·· Dallas, TX: (972) 386-7575
   Web Page: http://www.graphsim.com
GraphOn Corp ··· Morgan Hill, CA: (603) 225-3525
   Toll Free:(800) 472-7466
   Web Page: http://www.graphon.com
GraphPad Software ·· San Diego, CA: (858) 259-5770
   Web Page: http://www.graphpad.com
Graphsoft (see Diehl Graphsoft Inc)
Graphx.com ··· Woburn, MA: (781) 932-0430
   Web Page: http://www.graphx.com
Gravis ··· San Mateo, CA: (605) 572-2700
   Web Page: http://www.gravis.com

Great Falls Computer (see Microtec)
Great Plains (see Microsoft Great Plains)
Great Wave Software ··Scotts Valley, CA: (800) 423-1144
  Tech:(800) 423-1144   Toll Free:(800) 423-1144
  Web Page: http://www.greatwave.com
Greenleaf Software ···Dallas, TX: (214) 349-3005
  Tech:(972) 267-1662   Toll Free:(800) 523-9830
  Web Page: http://www.gleaf.com
Greentree Technologies ··································Hauppauge, NY: (631) 234-6544
  Toll Free:(800) 257-7708
  Web Page: http://www.green-tree.com
Greenview Data ···Ann Arbor, MI: (734) 996-1300
  Toll Free:(800) 458-3348
  Web Page: http://www.vedit.com
Gretag Lab Systems ·······································Englewood, CO: (303) 754-0200
  Toll Free:(877) 574-3662
  Web Page: http://www.gretag.com
Gretag Macbeth ···New Windsor, NY: (845) 565-7660
  Toll Free:(800) 622-2384
  Web Page: http://www.gretagmacbeth.com
Griffin Technologies/DBS ·····························Lawrence, KS: (785) 832-1623
  Tech:(785) 832-1623   Toll Free:(800) 986-6578
  Web Page: http://www.griftech.com
Grolier Interactive Inc ··································Danbury, CT: (877) 667-4420
  Toll Free:(800) 621-1115
  Web Page: http://www.grolier.com
Group 1 Software ···Lanham, MD: (301) 731-2300
  Tech:(800) 367-6950   Toll Free:(888) 413-6763
  Web Page: http://www.g1.com
Group Logic Inc···Arlington, VA: (703) 528-1555
  Tech:(703) 528-1555   Toll Free:(800) 476-8781
  Web Page: http://www.grouplogic.com
Gruber Industries Inc ·····································Phoenix, AZ: (602) 863-2655
  Toll Free:(800) 658-5883
  Web Page: http://www.gruber.com
Gryphon Soft. (see Knowledge Adventure)
GSI Inc (see Pacific Digital)
GT Interactive (see Infogrames)
GT Software Inc ···Atlanta, GA: (404) 253-1300
  Tech:(800) 765-4348   Toll Free:(800) 765-4348
  Web Page: http://www.gtsoftware.com
GTCO Corp ···Columbia, MD: (410) 381-6688
  Tech:(800) 458-5888   Toll Free:(800) 344-4723
  Web Page: http://www.gtco.com
GTM Software···West Jordan, UT: (801) 446-8226
  Web Page: http://www.shopsite.com/gtm
GTVideo Productions ······································Dillion, CO: (970) 468-1084
  Web Page: http://www.gtvideo.com
Gupta Corp (see Centura Software Corp)
Gupta Technology ···Redwood Shores, CA: (650) 596-3400
  Tech:(888) 523-6887   Toll Free:(800) 444-8782
  Web Page: http://www.centurasoft.com
Gurley Precision Instruments ··································Troy, NY: (518) 272-6300
  Web Page: http://www.gurley.com
Guru Software Corp (see G1 Business App)
GVC Technologies Inc (see MaxTech GVC)
Gvox ··· Westfield, NJ:
  Web Page: http://www.gvox.com
GW Instruments Inc ································Somerville, MA: (617) 625-4096

Web Page: http://www.gwinst.com

Gyration Inc ·· Saratoga, CA: (408) 973-7070
Toll Free:(800) 316-5432
Web Page: http://www.gyration.com

H45 Technology Inc ···································· Mountain View, CA: (650) 961-9114
Tech:(800) 373-8181
Web Page: http://www.h45.com

HAHT Commerce ··· Gaithersburg, MD: (301) 340-4000
Toll Free:(800) 560-4347
Web Page: http://www.haht.com

Hamamatsu Corp ··· Bridgewater, NJ: (908) 231-0960
Toll Free:(800) 524-0504
Web Page: http://www.usa.hamamatsu.com

Handspring Inc ·· Mountain View, CA: (650) 230-5000
Tech:(877) 426-3777   Toll Free:(888) 565-9393
Web Page: http://www.handspring.com

HandySoft Corp ··· Vienna, VA: (703) 442-5600
Toll Free:(800) 753-9343
Web Page: http://www.handysoft.com

Hansol Multitech ·· Cerritos, CA: (562) 809-8005
Toll Free:(800) 344-5631
Web Page: http://www.hansol-us.com

Harbinger Corp (see Peregrine Systems)

Harbor Electronics ······································ Santa Clara, CA: (408) 988-6544
Web Page: http://www.harbor-electronics.com

Harlequin (see Global Graphics Software)

Harmonic ·· Sunnyvale, CA: (408) 542-2500
Toll Free:(800) 788-1330
Web Page: http://www.harmonicinc.com

Harmony Computers ···································· Brooklyn, NY: (718) 692-3232
Tech:(877) 427-6669   Toll Free:(800) 441-1144
Web Page: http://www.shopharmony.com

Harnel Case Mfrs ·· Grand Rapids, MI: (616) 452-4522
Toll Free:(800) 756-5522
Web Page: http://www.harnelcase.com

Harris Computer Systems (see Concurrent)

Harris Corp ··· Melbourne, FL: (321) 727-9100
Tech:(321) 727-9207   Toll Free:(800) 442-7747
Web Page: http://www.harris.com

Harte-Hanks Market Intelligence ············· La Jolla, CA: (858) 450-1667
Tech:(800) 645-5795   Toll Free:(800) 854-8409
Web Page: http://www.zdintelligence.com

Hasbro ·· Pawtucket, RI: (401) 431-8697
Tech:(800) 242-7276   Toll Free:(888) 836-7025
Web Page: http://www.hasbro.com

Hauppauge Computer Works Inc ·············· Hauppauge, NY: (631) 434-1600
Tech:(631) 434-3197   Toll Free:(800) 443-6284
Web Page: http://www.hauppauge.com

HavenTree Software Ltd (see SPSS Inc)

Hayes Microcomputer (see Zoom Tele.)

HDC Computer (see WRQ)

HDS Network Systems (see Neoware)

Heathkit Educational Systems ·················· Benton Harbor, MI: (269) 925-6000
Toll Free:(800) 253-0570
Web Page: http://www.heathkit.com

Helix Software Co. (see Network Assoc)

Heroix Corp ··· Newton, MA: (617) 527-1550
Toll Free:(800) 229-6500
Web Page: http://www.heroix.com

Heurikon Corp (see Artesyn Technologies)

Heuris .... St. Louis, MO: (323) 201-2705
   Web Page: http://www.heuris.com
Hewlett-Packard .... Santa Clara, CA: (800) 752-0900
   Toll Free:(800) 752-0900
   Web Page: http://www.hp.com
Hewlett-Packard .... Palo Alto, CA: (650) 857-1501
   Toll Free:(800) 752-0900
   Web Page: http://www.hp.com
Hewlett-Packard .... Greeley, CO: (970) 350-5608
   Web Page: http://www.hp.com/go/optical
   Advantage Center .... (800) 637-7740
   Award Center .... (800) 728-9665
   Bluestone Software .... (856) 727-4600
      Tech:(856) 778-7900
      Web Page: http://www.bluestone.com
   Customer Care .... (208) 323-2551
      Tech:(970) 635-1000   Toll Free:(877) 283-4684
      Web Page: http://www.hp.com/go/support
   DeskJet/DeskWriter .... (208) 344-4131
   EESof Design Technology .... (800) 473-3763
      Toll Free:(800) 473-3763
   Fax Back .... (800) 231-9300
      Toll Free:(800) 231-9300
   Handheld Products .... (970) 392-1001
      Toll Free:(800) 443-1254
   HP Shopping.com .... (888) 999-4747
   Information Storage Group .... (970) 635-1500
      Toll Free:(800) 826-4111
      Web Page: http://www.hp.com/go/storage_support
   NetServer Products .... (800) 322-4772
      Toll Free:(800) 533-1333
      Web Page: http://www.hp.com/go/netserver
   Parts .... (800) 227-8164
      Toll Free:(800) 227-8164
   Software Drivers .... (208) 323-2551

Hi-Val .... Irvine, CA: (949) 707-4800
   Tech:(949) 707-4888
   Web Page: http://www.hival.com
Hifn Inc .... Los Gatos, CA: (408) 399-3500
   Web Page: http://www.hifn.com
Higher Ground Diagnostics Inc .... Lawrenceville, GA: (770) 997-8410
   Web Page: http://www.uglyware.com
Highland Technology .... San Francisco, CA: (415) 753-5814
   Web Page: http://www.highlandtechnology.com
Hilgraeve Inc .... Monroe, MI: (734) 243-0576
   Tech:(734) 243-0576   Toll Free:(800) 826-2760
   Web Page: http://www.hilgraeve.com
Hitachi America .... Brisbane, CA: (650) 589-8300
   Toll Free:(800) 448-2244
   Web Page: http://www.hitachi.com
Hitachi America .... Los Angeles, CA: (310) 286-0243
   Home Electronics .... (770) 457-9160
      Tech:(800) 241-6558   Toll Free:(800) 981-2588
      Web Page: http://www.hitachi.com/tv
   Home Electronics .... (619) 661-0227
   Literature Distribution Center .... (800) 285-1601
      Toll Free:(800) 285-1601
   Monitors .... (781) 461-8300
      Tech:(800) 536-6721   Toll Free:(800) 441-4832
      Web Page: http://www.hitachidisplays.com

Power & Industrial ·· (914) 631-0600
  Tech:(914) 332-5800
  Web Page: http://www.hitachi.com
Hitachi Cable ·· Manchester, NH: (603) 669-4347
  Toll Free:(800) 772-0116
  Web Page: http://www.hcm.hitachi.com
Hitachi Cable ·· New Albany, IN: (812) 945-9011
  Tech:(812) 945-9011
Hitachi Computer Products ·························· Santa Clara, CA: (206) 429-3972
  Toll Free:(800) 555-6820
  Web Page: http://www.hitachipc.com
Hitachi Data Systems ······························ Santa Clara, CA: (408) 970-1000
  Toll Free:(800) 555-6820
  Web Page: http://www.hds.com
Hitachi Denshi America ···························· Woodbury, NY: (516) 921-7200
  Web Page: http://www.hdal.com
Hitachi Digital Graphics ···························· San Jose, CA: (408) 392-9650
  Web Page: http://www.hitachidigital.com
Hitachi Instruments ································ San Jose, CA: (408) 432-0520
  Toll Free:(800) 548-9001
  Web Page: http://www.hii.hitachi.com
Hitachi Internetworking ···························· Santa Clara, CA: (408) 588-3119
  Tech:(408) 588-3119
  Web Page: http://www.internetworking.hitachi.com
Hitachi Koki Imaging Solutions ·················· Simi Valley, CA: (805) 578-4000
  Tech:(805) 578-4455   Toll Free:(800) 887-8848
  Web Page: http://www.hitachi-hkis.com
Hitachi Semiconductor ···························· San Jose, CA: (408) 433-1990
  Web Page: http://www.hitachi.com/semiconductor
Hitachi Software (see Quadrasis)
Hitachi Software Engineering ·················· South San Francisco, CA: (650) 615-9600
  Toll Free:(888) 615-9600
  Web Page: http://www.hitachi-soft.com
Hitachi Software Global Technology ············ Westminster, CO: (303) 466-9255
  Toll Free:(800) 447-2579
  Web Page: http://www.hsgt.com
Hitachi Telecom ·································· Norcross, GA: (770) 446-8820
  Web Page: http://www.hitel.com
Hitech Control Systems ·························· Green Bay, WI: (920) 465-4600
  Web Page: http://www.hitech-inc.com
HNC Software ·································· San Deigo, CA: (858) 799-8000
  Web Page: http://www.hncs.com
Holometrics ·································· Escondido, CA: (760) 743-2747
Holotek ·································· Henrietta, NY: (716) 321-6000
  Web Page: http://www.holotek.com
HomeStyles Publishing & Marketing ············ St Paul, MN: (651) 602-5000
  Tech:(888) 447-1946   Toll Free:(888) 626-2026
  Web Page: http://www.homestyles.com
Homework Help.com ······························ Sunnyvale, CA: (408) 441-2122
  Toll Free:(800) 799-8802
  Web Page: http://www.homeworkhelp.com
Honeywell Inc ·································· Morristown, NJ: (973) 455-2000
  Toll Free:(800) 707-4555
  Web Page: http://www.honeywell.com
  Aerospace ·································· (602) 365-4980
    Tech:(602) 365-2180   Toll Free:(800) 421-2133
  Customer response ································ (612) 951-1000
    Toll Free:(800) 328-5111
Hooleon Corp ·································· Cottonwood, AZ: (928) 634-7515

Tech:(928) 634-7515   Toll Free:(800) 937-1337
Web Page: http://www.hooleon.com
Hopkins Imaging Systems ·· Duarte, CA: (626) 305-8833
Web Page: http://www.hopkinsimaging.com
Hopkins Technology ·· Hopkins, MN: (952) 931-9376
Tech:(800) 397-9211   Toll Free:(800) 397-9211
Web Page: http://www.hoptechno.com
Horita ·· Mission Viejo, CA: (949) 489-0240
Web Page: http://www.horita.com
Horizon Imaging ·· College Place, WA: (509) 525-1168
Web Page: http://www.horizonimaging.com
Horizons Tech. (see Titan Systems)
Hot Door Inc ·· Laguna Beach, CA: (530) 274-0626
Toll Free:(888) 236-9540
Web Page: http://www.hotdoor.com
Hot Office Tech. (Out of Business)
Houghton Mifflin Int. (see Sunburst Tech)
Houston Instrument (see CalComp)
Howtek Inc ·· Nashua, NH: (603) 882-5200
Web Page: http://www.howtek.com
HP (see Hewlett-Packard)
HP Marketing Corp ·· Pine Brook, NJ: (973) 808-9010
Toll Free:(800)735-4373
Web Page: http://www.hpmarketingcorp.com
HP Santa Barbara
Web Page: http://www.transoftnetworks.com
HREF Tools Corp ·· Santa Rosa, CA: (707) 581-1828
Web Page: http://www.href.com
HSC Software (see MetaCreations)
HT Electronics ·· Fremont, CA: (510) 438-6556
Web Page: http://www.hte-inc.com
Hughes Network Systems ·· Germantown, MD: (301) 212-7950
Tech:BELOW
Web Page: http://www.hns.com
HumanCAD Systems Inc (Out of Business)
Hummingbird ·· Toronto, Ontario, : (416) 496-2200
Toll Free:(877) 359-4866
Web Page: http://www.hummingbird.com
Hummingbird Communications ·· Mountain View, CA: (650) 917-2360
Tech:(650) 917-7300   Toll Free:(800) 598-3821
Web Page: http://www.hummingbird.com
Humongous Entertainment(see Atari Entertainm
Hyland Software ·· Westlake, OH: (440) 788-5000
Tech:(440) 788-5600
Web Page: http://www.onbase.com
Hynix Semiconductor ·· San Jose, CA: (408) 232-8000
Web Page: http://www.hynix.com
Hyperformix Inc ·· Austin, TX: (512) 328-5544
Toll Free:(800) 759-6333
Web Page: http://www.hyperformix.com
Hyperion Solutions
Web Page: http://www.hyperion.com
Hyperion Solutions Corporation ·· Sunnyvale, CA: (408) 744-9500
Toll Free:(800) 286-8000
Web Page: http://www.hysoft.com
Hyundai Electronics America (800) 568-0060
I Touch Communications Now MRV Communication Chatsworth, CA: (818) 7730900
Tech:(800) 435-7997   Toll Free:(800) 338-5316

Web Page: http://www.mrv.com

i-Chips Technology/Jepico America, Inc ·············· Santa Clara, CA: (408) 844-0530
Toll Free:(866) 392-4447
Web Page: http://www.i-chipstech.com

I-Cube ··· Glen Bumie, MD: (410) 987-5555
Toll Free:(888) 774-2823
Web Page: http://www.i-cubeinc.com

I/O Magic Corp ··· Irvine, CA: (949) 707-4800
Tech:(949) 808-4888
Web Page: http://www.iomagic.com

I/O Software Inc ··· Riverside, CA: (909) 222-7600
Web Page: http://www.iosoftware.com

I2 Technologies ·· Dallas, TX: (800) 800-3288
Tech:(888) 428-4984   Toll Free:(588) 926-9286
Web Page: http://www.i2.com

I2S - The Line Scan Co ································· Niskayuna, NY: (518) 374-3045
Web Page: http://www.i2s-linescan.com

Iambic Software ·· Sunnyvale, CA: (408) 736-2022
Tech:(408)736-2022
Web Page: http://www.iambic.com

iAnywhere ·· Dublin, CA: 519-883-6898
Toll Free:800-801-2069
Web Page: http://www.ianywhere.com

Ibex Tech (see Castelle Ibex Tech)

IBM Corporation ·· Austin, TX: (800) 426-7282
Tech:(800) 426-7282   Toll Free:(877) 426-6006
Web Page: http://www.ibm.com

IBM Corporation ·· Atlanta, GA: (404) 238-7000
Tech:(800) 426-7282
Web Page: http://www.ibm.com

IBM Corporation (800) 426-2255
Tech:(800) 426-4968   Toll Free:(800) 426-2255

IBM Corporation ··································· White Plains, NY: (800) 426-4968
Toll Free:(888) 846-8426
Web Page: http://www.ibm.com

AIX Systems Support Center	(817) 962-6000
Toll Free:(800) 426-7378	
Ambra	(800) 426-7378
APL products & Services	(800) 426-7378
Aptiva	(800) 426-3377
Tech:(919) 517-2800	
Web Page: http://www.direct.ibm.com	
Authorized Dealer Locator	(800) 447-4700
Bulletin Board System	(919) 517-0001
Business Partners Support Operations	(800) 624-6875
Chemicals Hotline	(800) 426-4333
Customer Support Center	(800) 426-4968
Easy Options Technical Support	(800) 426-7378
General Inquires	(800) 426-7378
Hardware Service	(800) 426-7378
IBM PC	(800) 426-7378
IBM TalkLink Customer Support Center	(800) 426-7378
Toll Free:(800) 426-7378	
IBM Teach	(888) 220-3343
Web Page: http://www.can.ibm.com/edu	
Independence Series Product Info	(800) 426-4832
Information Center	(914) 288-3000
Web Page: http://www.ibm.com	
Informix Software	(800) 426-7378
Toll Free:(800) 426-7378	
Web Page: http://www.informix.com	

Integrated Technology	(888) 426-4343
Toll Free:(888) 426-4343	
Integrateed Technologies	(888) 426-4343
Intellistation	(800) 426-7378
Ispirati	(800) 426-7378
Learnout Hauspie	(800) 426-7378
Toll Free:(800) 426-7378	
Web Page: http://www.dragonsystems.com	
Lotus	(800) 426-7378
Maintenance, Parts & Warranty	(800) 426-7378
Monitors	(800) 426-7378
NBA Helpdesk	(800) 426-7378
NetVista	(800) 426-7378
Network Station	(507) 286-6366
Web Page: http://www.pc.ibm.com	
Networking Support Line	(888) 787-7678
Web Page: http://www.networking.ibm.com	
OEM Support Group	(800) 426-7378
Options By IBM	(800) 426-7378
OS/400	(800) 426-7378
Toll Free:(800) 426-7378	
Partner Line	(770) 863-2048
Tech:(800) 426-9990 Toll Free:(800) 426-9990	
Web Page: http://www.developer.ibm.com	
PC Company	(800) 426-7235
Personal Systems Help Center	(888) 787-7478
Printing Systems	(800) 358-6661
Toll Free:(800) 426-7378	
Web Page: http://www.printers.ibm.com	
S/390	(800) 426-7378
Shop IBM	(888) 746-7426
Software & Publication Support	(800) 879-2755
Software Service Support	(800) 426-7378
Tech:(800) 426-7378	
Think Pad	(800) 426-7378
Tivoli	(800)848-6548
Tech:(800) 848-6548	
Voice Recognition	(800) 426-7378
Toll Free:(800) 426-7378	
Windows NT	(800) 426-7378
Work Pad	(800) 426-7378
Toll Free:(800) 426-7378	
IC Systems (see Cyber Cash)	
Icom America Inc	Bellevue, WA: (425) 454-8155
Tech:(425) 454-7619	
Web Page: http://www.icomamerica.com	
Iconovex Corp	Hopkins, MN: (952) 930-4675
Tech:(952) 930-4675	
Web Page: http://www.iconovex.com	
ICVerify Inc	Oakland, CA: (800) 666-5777
Toll Free:(800) 900-6133	
Web Page: http://www.icverify.com	
Ideal Engineering	Surry, BC: (604) 000-0000
Web Page: http://www.idealeng.com	
Ideal Scanners & Systems	Rockville, MD: (301) 468-0123
Toll Free:(800) 764-3325	
Web Page: http://www.ideal.com	
IDS Software	Diamond Bar, CA: (909) 396-6472
Web Page: http://www.idssoftware.com	
IDX Systems Corp	Burlington, VT: (802) 862-1022
Toll Free:(888) 439-6584	

Web Page: http://www.idx.com

IEC ·· Commerce City, CO: (303) 288-5000
Toll Free:(800) 765-4432
Web Page: http://www.iec.net

IEC Electronics Corp. ···································· Newark, NY: (315) 331-7742
Web Page: http://www.iec-electronics.com

IEEE Computer (Now Tech Depot) ············ Trumbull, CT: (800) 721-8344
Toll Free:(800) 721-8344
Web Page: http://www.techdepot.com

iEntertainment Network ··································· Cary, NC: (919) 678-8301
Web Page: http://www.iencentral.com

iGo Corp ··· Scottsdale, AZ: (800) 588-4593
Tech:(800) 474-7593   Toll Free:(888) 205-0093
Web Page: http://www.igo.com

iiyama North America ·································· Warminster, PA: (215) 682-9050
Toll Free:(800) 594-7480
Web Page: http://iiyama.com

Ikegami Electronics ··· Maywood, NJ: (201) 368-9171
Web Page: http://www.ikegami.com

Ikon Office Solutions ··· Malvern, PA: (610) 296-8000
Toll Free:(888) 456-6457
Web Page: http://www.ikon.com

Interface Technical Training ····················· (602) 266-9029
Toll Free:(888) 456-6457
Web Page: http://www.midak.com

Ilford ··· Paramus, NJ: (201) 265-6000
Web Page: http://www.ilford.com

Illinois Lock Co ·· Wheeling, IL: (847) 537-1800
Tech:(800) 733-3907   Toll Free:(800) 733-3907
Web Page: http://www.illinoislock.com

Illumination Technologies ···················· East Syracuse, NY: (315) 463-4673
Toll Free:(800) 738-4297
Web Page: http://www.illuminationtech.com

Illustra Information Tech (see Informix)

ILog Inc ·· Mountain View, CA: (775) 881-2800
Toll Free:(800) 367-4564
Web Page: http://www.ilog.com

ILY Enterprise ·· Santa Fe Springs, CA: (562) 801-2888
Toll Free:(888) 742-5459
Web Page: http://www.ily.com

Image Club Graphics (see Eyewire Inc)

Image Graphics Inc ··· Shelton, CT: (203) 926-0100
Toll Free:(888) 464-6243
Web Page: http://www.igraph.com

Image Peak Systems ·· Berthoud, CO: (303) 774-8769
Web Page: http://www.imagepeak.com

Image Power Inc ··· Vancouver, BC: (604) 268-9988
Web Page: http://www.imagepower.com

Image Processing Solutions Inc ············ North Reading, MA: (978) 276-0094
Web Page: http://www.ipsimaging.com

Image Solutions ·· Whippany, NJ: (973) 560-0404
Web Page: http://www.imagesolutions.com

Image Systems Corp ··· Minnetonka, MN: (952) 935-1171
Web Page: http://www.imagesystemscorp.com

Image Video ·· Scarborough, ON: (416) 750-8872
Web Page: http://www.imagevideo.com

Image-In (see Hi-Image)

ImageBuilder Software Inc ····························· Portland, OR: (503) 684-5151
Web Page: http://www.imagebuilder.com

Imagination Software(Out Of Business) (

Imagine Products ··· Carmel, IN: (317) 843-0706
    Web Page: http://www.imagineproducts.com

Imaging Automation ··· Bedford, MA: (603) 471-9325
    Web Page: http://www.imagingauto.com

Imaging Business Machine ······························· Birmingham, AL: (205) 439-7100
    Tech:(205) 956-4071
    Web Page: http://www.ibml.com

Imaging Research Inc ····································· St. Catherines, ON: (905) 688-2040
    Toll Free:(866) 818-1199
    Web Page: http://www.imagingresearch.com

Imaging Source, The ·· Charlotte, NC: (704) 370-0110
    Toll Free:(877) 462-4772
    Web Page: http://www.theimagingsource.com

Imaging Technologies Corp ······························· San Diego, CA: (858) 487-8944
    Tech:(858) 207-6521   Toll Free:(800) 756-0556
    Web Page: http://www.itec.net

iManage Inc(see Interwoven)

Imation Publishing Software ······························· Oakdale, MN: (888) 466-3456
    Toll Free:(888) 466-3456
    Web Page: http://www.imation.com

IMC Networks ··· Foothill Ranch, CA: (949) 465-3000
    Tech:(800) 624-1070
    Web Page: http://www.imcnetworks.com

Immersion Corp ·· San Jose, CA: (408) 467-1900
    Web Page: http://www.immersion.com

Impact Computer CO ··· Marlton, NJ: 856-596-8050
    Toll Free:(800) 444-1585
    Web Page: http://www.willow.com

Impediment Inc ··· Marshfield, MA: (781) 834-3800
    Web Page: http://www.impediment.com

Impression Products Inc ····································· Fremont, CA: (888) 532-7878
    Tech:(888) 532-7878
    Web Page: http://www.impression-brand.com

Improvision Inc ··· Lexington, MA: (781) 402-0134
    Tech:(781) 402-0211
    Web Page: http://www.improvision.com

IMS Island Microsystems ································· Campbell River, BC: (250) 286-0624
    Web Page: http://www.islandmicro.com

IMSI Software ··· Novato, CA: (415) 257-4000
    Tech:(415) 878-4000   Toll Free:(800) 833-8082
    Web Page: http://www.imsisoft.com

In-Sync ··· Bethesda, MD: (301) 656-1700
    Toll Free:(800) 864-7272
    Web Page: http://www.in-sync.com

InContext Systems Inc (see Pervasive)

Independent Technology Service ··························· Simi Valley, CA: (805) 526-1555
    Toll Free:(800) 342-3475
    Web Page: http://www.i-t-s.com

Indiana Cash Drawer Co ····································· Shelbyville, IN: (317) 398-6643
    Tech:(800) 227-4832   Toll Free:(800) 227-4379
    Web Page: http://www.icdpos.com

Individual Software Inc ····································· Pleasanton, CA: (925) 734-6767
    Tech:(800) 331-3313   Toll Free:(800) 822-3522
    Web Page: http://www.individualsoftware.com

Infinite Technologies (see Captaris)

Infinity Photo-Optical ·· Boulder, CO: (303) 440-4544
    Web Page: http://www.infinity-usa.com

Info Access Inc (see Stellent)

Info. Cybernetics (see General Inter.)

InFocus ·· Wilsonville, OR: (503) 685-8888
Tech:(503) 685-7244   Toll Free:(800) 294-6400
Web Page: http://www.infocus.com

InfoGold American Multisystems ···················· Milpitas, CA: (408) 945-2296
Tech:(800) 879-8818   Toll Free:(800) 888-6615
Web Page: http://www.infogold.com

Infogrames ·· Plymouth, MN: (212) 726-6500
Tech:(425) 398-3051
Web Page: http://www.infogrames.com

Infogrames Entertainment Inc ······················· San Jose, CA: (408) 212-7800
Web Page: http://www.infogrames.net

InfoMagic Inc(Out of Business)

Informatics Inc ··· Plano, TX: (972) 881-5500
Web Page: http://www.informatics-inc.com

Information Builders Inc ··························· New York, NY: (212) 736-4433
Tech:(800) 736-6130   Toll Free:(800) 969-4636
Web Page: http://www.ibi.com

Informative Graphics Corp ······················· Scottsdale, AZ: (602) 971-6061
Tech:(602) 971-6061   Toll Free:(800) 398-7005
Web Page: http://www.infograph.com

Informix Software (see Essential Soft)

Inforonics Inc ·· Littleton, MA: (978) 698-6400
Tech:(978) 698-6390
Web Page: http://www.inforonics.com

Infotel Distributing ·· Fletcher, OH: (888) 728-8599
Tech:(800) 262-6622   Toll Free:(888) 728-8599
Web Page: http://www.infoteldistributing.com

infoUSA Inc ··· Omaha, NE: (402) 930-3500
Tech:(402) 593-4515   Toll Free:(800) 321-0869
Web Page: http://www.lookupusa.com

InfoVision Technologies Inc ························ Westboro, MA: (508) 366-3660
Tech:(508) 366-3660   Toll Free:(800) 277-9600
Web Page: http://www.ivtinc.com

Infowave Wireless Messaging ···················· Burnaby, BC: (604) 473-3600
Tech:(604) 473-3700   Toll Free:(800) 663-6222
Web Page: http://www.infowave.net

Infragistics ·· Cranbury, NJ: (609) 448-2000
Tech:(631) 753-0985   Toll Free:(800) 231-8588
Web Page: http://www.infragistics.com

Infragistics Dev. Lab ······································ Melville, NY: (631) 753-0985
Tech:(631) 753-0985
Web Page: http://www.infragistics.com

Ingram Micro ··· Santa Ana, CA: (714) 566-1000
Tech:(800) 445-5066   Toll Free:(800) 274-4800
Web Page: http://www.ingrammicro.com

Inherent.com Inc ·· Portland, OR: (503) 224-6751
Tech:(503) 224-6751
Web Page: http://www.inherent.com

Initio Corp ··· Sunnyvale, CA: (800) 994-6484
Tech:(800) 540-3360   Toll Free:(800) 994-6484
Web Page: http://www.initio.com

Inmagic Software ··· Woburn, MA: (781) 938-4444
Tech:(781) 938-4442   Toll Free:(800) 229-8398
Web Page: http://www.inmagic.com

Inmark Development (see RogueWave)

Inner Media ·· Hollis, NH: (603) 465-3216
Tech:(603) 465-2696   Toll Free:(800) 962-2949
Web Page: http://www.innermedia.com

Innomedia Inc ··· Milpitas, CA: (408) 432-5400
   Tech:(408) 432-5400   Toll Free:(888) 251-6250
   Web Page: http://www.innomedia.com

Innovation Advertising & Design ····················Essex Junction, VT: (802) 879-1164
   Toll Free:(800) 255-0562
   Web Page: http://www.ad-art.com

Innovative Electronics Corp (see IEC)

Innovative Quality Soft (out of business)

Innovative Software (see Phoenix Tech)

Innovision Optics ··Santa Monica, CA: (310) 453-4866
   Web Page: http://www.innovision-optics.com

Inprise Corp (Out of Business)

Inprise Corp (Out of Business)

Inprise Corp (Out of Business)

Insci Corp ··· Westboro, MA: (508) 870-4000
   Tech:(800) 546-6600
   Web Page: http://www.insci.com

Inset Systems (see Quarterdeck Office)

Insight Development Corp ····································San Ramone, CA: (925) 244-2000
   Tech:(925) 244-2000   Toll Free:(800) 825-4115
   Web Page: http://www.insightdev.com

Insight Software Solutions ································Kaysville, UT: (801) 928-5009
   Web Page: http://www.wintools.com

Insignia Solutions ··Fremont, CA: (510) 360-3700
   Toll Free:(800) 848-7677
   Web Page: http://www.insignia.com

Inspiration Software Inc ····································Portland, OR: (503) 297-3004
   Tech:(800) 877-4292   Toll Free:(800) 877-4292
   Web Page: http://www.inspiration.com

InstallShield Software Corp ····························Schaumburg, IL: (847) 466-4000
   Tech:(847) 413-2896   Toll Free:(800) 374-4353
   Web Page: http://www.installshield.com

InStranet Inc ··· New York, NY: (312) 629-4580
   Toll Free:(877) 932-5826
   Web Page: http://www.instranet.com

Instrument Technology ··Westfield, MA: (413) 562-3606
   Web Page: http://www.scopes.com

Int'l Electronic Research (IERC) ····················Burbank, CA: (818) 842-7277
   Web Page: http://www.ctscorp.com/ierc

Int. Communications Assoc. (CTS) ···················Elkhart, IN: (574) 293-7511
   Web Page: http://www.ctscorp.com

Integral Per. (see Mobile Storage Tech)

Integral Technologies ···Indianapolis, IN: (317) 845-9242
   Web Page: http://www.integraltech.com

Integral Vision ···Farmington Hills, MI: (248) 471-2660
   Web Page: http://www.iv-usa.com

Integrated Computer Solution ··························Cambridge, MA: (617) 621-0060
   Tech:(617) 621-0060
   Web Page: http://www.ics.com

Integrated Device Technology ··························Santa Clara, CA: (509) 727-6116
   Tech:(408) 654-6420   Toll Free:(800) 345-7015
   Web Page: http://www.idt.com

Integrated Info. Tech (see 8 X 8)

Integrated Management Concepts ··················Thousand Oaks, CA: (805) 778-1629
   Web Page: http://www.intgconcepts.com

Integrated Systems (see Wind River)

Intel Corp ···Hillsboro, OR: (503) 696-8080
   Tech:(541) 850-5365   Toll Free:(800) 538-3373

Web Page: http://www.intel.com
Intel Corp ·· Chandler, AZ: (480) 554-8080
Intel Corp ·· Dupont, WA: (253) 371-8080
Intel Corp ·· Rio Rancho, NM: (505) 893-7000
Intel Corp Corporate Headquarters ···················· Santa Clara, CA: (408) 765-8080
  Toll Free:(800) 628-8686
  Web Page: http://www.intel.com
Dialogic Corp ·· (973) 993-3000
  Tech:(800) 755-4444   Toll Free:(800) 329-4727
  Web Page: http://www.dialogic.com
Microprocessor & Overdrive Processor ········ (916) 377-7000
  Tech:(916) 377-7000
Motherboards & Servers ······························ (800) 468-3548
  Toll Free:(800) 404-2284
Support Center ·· (916) 377-7000
  Web Page: http://www.support.intel.com
Intelidata Technology ·································· Reston, VA: (703) 259-3000
  Tech:(800) 337-0440   Toll Free:(800) 878-1053
  Web Page: http://www.intelidata.com
Intelitool Inc ··· Richmond, VA: (800) 955-7621
  Toll Free:(800) 955-7621
  Web Page: http://www.intelitool.com
Intelliquis International ······························ Draper, UT: (801) 307-0080
  Toll Free:(800) 590-0809
  Web Page: http://www.intelliquis.com
Intellisol International (Out of Business)
InterActive Inc (Out of Business)
Interactive magic (see iEntertainment)
Interactive Software Engineering ···················· Goleta, CA: (805) 685-1006
  Web Page: http://www.eiffel.com
InterActual Technologies Inc ························· San Jose, CA: (408) 436-6700
  Web Page: http://www.interactual.com
InterCon Systems (see Ascend)
Interex Inc ··· Sunnyvale, CA: (408) 747-0227
  Tech:(800) 468-3739
  Web Page: http://www.interex.com
Interface Group, The ···································· Washington, DC: (202) 861-0500
  Web Page: http://www.interfacevideo.com
Intergraph Corp ·· Huntsville, AL: (256) 730-2000
  Tech:(800) 633-7248   Toll Free:(800) 345-4856
  Web Page: http://www.intergraph.com
Interleaf Inc (see BroadVision)
Interlink Electronics ···································· Camarillo, CA: (805) 484-8855
  Tech:(805) 484-1331   Toll Free:(800) 340-1331
  Web Page: http://www.interlinkelec.com
International Data Sciences ·························· Warwick, RI: (401) 737-9900
  Tech:(800) 437-3282   Toll Free:(800) 437-3282
  Web Page: http://www.idsdata.com
International Software Engineering ·················· Marquette, MI: (906) 228-7800
  Tech:(906) 228-6500   Toll Free:(800) 472-6727
  Web Page: http://www.haja.com
Internet Content Rating Association ················ Washington, DC: (202) 654-4229
  Web Page: http://www.rsac.org
Internet Solutions (see Learning Co)
Interphase Corp ·· Plano, TX: (214) 654-5000
  Toll Free:(800) 327-8638
  Web Page: http://www.iphase.com
Interplay Productions
Interse Corp (see Microsoft)

Intershop Communications ························· San Francisco, CA: (415) 229-0100
   Tech:(415) 844-1500   Toll Free:(800) 736-5197
   Web Page: http://www.intershop.com

Intersolv (see Merant)

Interwoven ························· Sunnyvale, CA: (408) 774-2000
   Tech:(408) 530-5800   Toll Free:(888) 468-3796
   Web Page: http://www.interwoven.com

Intex Solutions Inc ························· Needham, MA: (781) 449-6222
   Tech:(781) 449-6222
   Web Page: http://www.intex.com

IntraNetics.com ························· Woburn, MA: (781) 932-0960
   Toll Free:(888) 932-2600
   Web Page: http://www.intranetics.com

IntraServer Technology (see LSI Logic)

Intrusion.com ························· Richardson, TX: (972) 664-8090
   Toll Free:(888) 637-7770
   Web Page: http://www.intrusion.com

Intuit Inc ························· Mountain View, CA: (650) 944-6000
   Toll Free:(800) 446-8848
   Web Page: http://www.intuit.com
   Quick Books ························· (520) 901-3220
   Toll Free:(800) 246-8848
   Quicken ························· (520) 901-3220
   Toll Free:(800) 811-8766
   Turbo Tax ························· (520) 901-3220
   Toll Free:(800) 440-3279

Intuitive Manufacturing Systems Inc ························· Kirkland, WA: (425) 821-0740
   Toll Free:(877) 549-2149
   Web Page: http://www.mrp9000.com

Invado (Out of Business)

Invario Network Engineers ························· Arlington, VA: (703) 528-0101
   Tech:(703) 524-0101
   Web Page: http://www.invario.net

Invensys Power Systems ························· Foxboro, MA: (508) 543-8750
   Toll Free:(800) 854-2658
   Web Page: http://www.invensys.com

Invensys Power Systems ························· Raleigh, NC: (919) 872-3020
   Toll Free:(800) 554-3448
   Web Page: http://www.invensys.com
   Traders Press, Inc. ························· (864) 298-0222
   Toll Free:(800) 927-8222
   Web Page: http://www.investorsoftware.com

Invisco ························· Manhatten Beach, CA:
   Web Page: http://www.invisco.com

Invisible Software (Out of Business)

Inxight ························· Sunnyvale, CA: (408) 738-6200
   Toll Free:(888) 414-4949
   Web Page: http://www.inxight.com

IO Industries ························· London, ON: (519) 663-9570
   Web Page: http://www.ioindustries.com

IOMEGA Corp ························· San Diego, CA: (858) 314-7000
   Web Page: http://www.iomega.com

IONA Technologies ························· Waltham, MA: (781) 902-8000
   Web Page: http://www.iona.com

IOTech Inc ························· Cleveland, OH: (440) 439-4091
   Toll Free:(888) 714-3272
   Web Page: http://www.iotech.com

Ipedo Inc ························· Redwood City, CA: (650) 306-4000
   Web Page: http://www.ipedo.com

IPIX .... Oak Ridge, TN: (865) 482-3000
  Toll Free:(888) 909-4749
  Web Page: http://www.ipix.com
iProof Systems Inc .... Satellite Beach, FL: (321) 777-3910
  Web Page: http://www.iproofsystems.com
Ipswitch Inc .... Lexington, MA: (781) 676-5700
  Tech:(781) 676-5784   Toll Free:(800) 793-4825
  Web Page: http://www.ipswitch.com
IQ Software (see Information Advantage)
IQ Technologies Inc (see Smart Cable)
Iridian Technologies .... Moorestown, NJ: (856) 222-9090
  Toll Free:(866) 474-3426
  Web Page: http://www.iridiantech.com
Irwin Magnetic Systems (see Conner)
ISDN*tek .... San Gregorio, CA: (650) 712-3000
  Web Page: http://www.isdntek.com
ISI ResearchSoft .... Carlsbad, CA: (760) 438-5526
  Tech:(800) 722-1227   Toll Free:(800) 722-1227
  Web Page: http://www.risinc.com
ISI Researchsoft .... Berkeley, CA: (510) 559-8592
  Tech:(510) 559-8592   Toll Free:(800) 722-1227
  Web Page: http://www.isiresearchsoft.com
Island Software .... Folsom, CA: (916) 454-3742
  Toll Free:(800) 255-4499
  Web Page: http://www.islandsoft.com
Isogon Corp .... New York, NY: (212) 376-3200
  Tech:(212) 237-6326
  Web Page: http://www.isogon.com
Isomedia .... Redmond, WA: (425) 869-5411
  Tech:(877) 638-9277   Toll Free:(800) 468-3939
  Web Page: http://www.isomedia.com
ISRA Vision Systems/Insight Integration .... Lansing, MI: (517) 887-8878
  Web Page: http://www.isravision.com
Isys/Odyssey Development Inc .... Greenwood Village, CO: (303) 689-9998
  Web Page: http://www.isysdev.com
IT Bridge Int .... Santa Clara, CA: (408) 737-7878
  Toll Free:(800) 444-7300
  Web Page: http://www.itbridge.com
ITAC Systems Inc .... Garland, TX: (972) 494-3073
  Tech:(800) 533-4822   Toll Free:(800) 533-4822
  Web Page: http://www.mousetrak.com
ITI Software .... Montreal, QC: (514) 597-1692
  Web Page: http://www.iti-logiciel.com
ITK Telecommunications (see Digi Int.)
iTouch Communications / MRV .... Chatsworth, CA: (818) 773-0900
  Tech:(800) 435-7997   Toll Free:(800) 435-7997
  Web Page: http://www.mrv.com
ITT Pomona Electronics .... Pomona, CA: (909) 469-2900
  Tech:(909) 469-2900
  Web Page: http://www.ittpomona.com
ITW Chemtronics Inc .... Kennesaw, GA: (770) 424-4888
  Tech:(800) 424-9300   Toll Free:(800) 645-5244
  Web Page: http://www.chemtronics.com
IVI Publishing (see On Health Network)
IVP Inc .... Woodinville, WA: (425) 483-9669
  Web Page: http://www.ivpvision.com
IVP Inc(this branch no longer open)
iWill USA Corporation .... Irvine, CA: (949) 753-5488
  Web Page: http://www.iwillusa.com

Ixchange (see Front Range Solutions)

J & K Imaging ································· Marietta, GA: (770) 984-1212
Web Page: http://www.jkimaging.com

J & R Electronics Inc ··················· New York, NY: (212) 238-9000
Tech:(212) 238-9080   Toll Free:(800) 221-3191
Web Page: http://www.jandr.com

J-Mark Computer Corp ················· San Dimas, CA: (909) 305-8800
Tech:(909) 305-8800
Web Page: http://www.j-mark.com

J. River Inc ···························· Minneapolis, MN: (612) 677-8200
Tech:(612) 339-2521
Web Page: http://www.jriver.com

Jade Computer ·························· Torrence, CA: (310) 370-7474
Toll Free:(800) 421-5500
Web Page: http://www.jadecomputer.com

JAI Pulnix Inc ························ Sunnyvale, CA: (408) 747-0300
Tech:(800) 445-5444   Toll Free:(800) 445-5444
Web Page: http://www.jai.com

Jameco Electronics ···················· Belmont, CA: (650) 592-8097
Tech:(800) 536-4316   Toll Free:(800) 831-4242
Web Page: http://www.jameco.com

Janna Systems (see Siebel Systems)

Jasc Inc ···························· Eden Prairie, MN: (952) 934-8888
Tech:(952) 930-9171   Toll Free:(800) 622-2793
Web Page: http://www.jasc.com

Jaton Video Cards ····················· Milpitas, CA: (408) 942-9888
Tech:(408) 934-9369

Java News Inc ························ Santa Cruz, CA: (831) 459-9060
Tech:(831) 459-9060
Web Page: http://www.crosswise.com

JDA Software Group ··················· Scottsdale, AZ: (480) 308-3000
Toll Free:(888) 441-1532
Web Page: http://www.jdasoftware.com

JDI Technologies ····················· Calabasas, CA: (818) 884-4351
Web Page: http://www.jditechnologies.com

JDI Technologies ······················ Fremont, CA: (510) 249-1120
Web Page: http://www.jditechnologies.com

JDR Microdevices ····················· San Jose, CA: (408) 494-1400
Tech:(800) 538-5002   Toll Free:(800) 538-5000
Web Page: http://www.jdr.com

JE Software

Jems Data Unlimited ··················· Salem, NH: (603) 896-6319
Toll Free:(800) 838-5367
Web Page: http://www.jemsdata.com

Jensen Tools Inc ······················ Phoenix, AZ: (602) 453-3169
Toll Free:(800) 426-1194
Web Page: http://www.jensentools.com

Jeol USA ····························· Peabody, MA: (978) 535-5900
Tech:(978) 536-2320
Web Page: http://www.jeol.com

JES Hardware Solutions Inc (305) 597-3980
Toll Free:(800) 482-1866
Web Page: http://www.jescdrom.com

Jet Fax Inc (see E Fax)

JetForm (see Accelio Corp)

Jetta International Inc ··············· Monmouth Junction, NJ: (732) 329-9651
Tech:(732) 329-9651   Toll Free:(800) 445-3882
Web Page: http://www.jetta.com

JIAN ······························· Mill Valley, CA: (650) 254-5600

Tech:(650) 254-5600   Toll Free:(800) 346-5426
Web Page: http://www.jianusa.com

Jinco Computers ·· San Gabriel, CA: (626) 309-1108
Toll Free:(800) 253-2531
Web Page: http://www.jinco.com

JKN Electronics Inc ·· Bellingham, MA: (508) 966-2721
Web Page: http://www.jknelectronics.com

JL Chatcom Inc (see Chatcom Inc)

JL Cooper Electronics ··· El Segundo, CA: (310) 322-9990
Tech:(310) 322-9990
Web Page: http://www.jlcooper.com

Jobs.com ··· Irving, TX: (972) 444-0300
Toll Free:(888) 562-7266
Web Page: http://www.jobs.com

Jobscope Corp ··· Greenville, SC: (800) 443-5794
Toll Free:(800) 443-5794
Web Page: http://www.jobscope.com

Jostens Learning (see Compus Learning)

JP Software Inc ··· Chestertown, MD: (410) 810-8818
Web Page: http://www.jpsoft.com

JPA Electronics Supply (see i-Chips)

Judson Rosebush Company ································· New York, NY: (212) 581-3000
Web Page: http://www.rosebush.com

Jukebox Information Systems ······························· Hayward, CA: (510) 441-2211
Web Page: http://www.jbis.com

JVC ·· Irvine, CA: (973) 315-5000
Web Page: http://www.jvc.com
  Consumer Information Center ·························(800) 252-5722
  Toll Free:(800) 252-5722
  Web Page: http://www.jvcservice.com
  Digital Storage Systems ································(714) 816-6500
  Web Page: http://www.jvcinfo.com
  Disc America ···(205) 556-7111
  Toll Free:(800) 677-5518
  Web Page: http://www.jvcdiscusa.com
  Professional Products Company ·················(973) 315-5000
  Tech:(973) 317-5000   Toll Free:(800) 582-5825
  Professional Products Repair Department ·····(973) 396-1200
  Toll Free:(800) 526-5308
  Professional Products Service ·····················(714) 229-8016
  Service & Engineering ··································(713) 935-9331
  Web Page: http://www.jvcservice.com
  Service & Engineering Company ··················(770) 339-2582
  Web Page: http://www.jvcservice.com
  Service & Engineering Company ··················(781) 376-9100
  Web Page: http://www.jvcservice.com
  Service & Engineering Company ··················(630) 851-7855
  Web Page: http://www.jvcservice.com
  Service & Engineering Company ··················(808) 833-5828
  Web Page: http://www.jvcservice.com
  Service & Engineering Company ··················(954) 472-1960
  Web Page: http://www.jvcservice.com
  Service & Engineering Company ··················(973) 808-9279
  Tech:(973) 396-1000
  Web Page: http://www.jvcservice.com

K-Par Archiving Software ······································ Princeton, NJ: (403) 264-8311
Tech:(403) 264-8311
Web Page: http://www.k-par.com

K-Space Associates ··· Ann Arbor, MI: (734) 668-4644
Web Page: http://www.k-space.com

K-Talk Communications .... Columbus, OH: (614) 488-8818
Web Page: http://www.ktalk.com

K2 Micro Systems .... Pewaukee, WI: (262) 695-8373
Web Page: http://www.k2micro.com

Kadak Products Ltd .... Vancouver, BC: (604) 734-2796
Tech:(604) 734-2796
Web Page: http://www.kadak.com

Kaidan Inc .... Feasterville, PA: (215) 364-1778
Web Page: http://www.kaidan.com

Kallix Corp .... Westford, MA: (978) 392-9642
Web Page: http://www.kallix.com

Kalpana (see Cisco Systems)

Kandu Software Corp .... Warm Springs, VA: (540) 839-3488
Tech:(540) 839-3491   Toll Free:(800) 579-2244
Web Page: http://www.kandusoftware.com

Kanguru Solutions / Interactive Media Corp .... Millis, MA: (888) 526-4878
Toll Free:(888) 526-4878
Web Page: http://www.kanguru.com

Kanisa Inc .... Cupertino, CA: (408) 863-5800
Web Page: http://www.kanisa.com

Kappa Opto-Electronics .... Monrovia, CA: (626) 256-4343
Web Page: http://www.kappa.de

Kay Elemetrics Corp .... Lincoln Park, NJ: (973) 628-6200
Tech:(973) 628-6200
Web Page: http://www.kayelemetrics.com

KBM Group .... Silver Spring, MD: (301) 587-7333
Web Page: http://www.kbmgroup.com

KDS USA (Korea Data Systems) .... Garden Grove, CA: (714) 379-5599
Tech:(800) 283-1311   Toll Free:(800) 237-9988
Web Page: http://www.kdsusa.com

Keithly Instruments .... Cleveland, OH: (440) 248-0400
Tech:(800) 348-0033   Toll Free:(800) 552-1115
Web Page: http://www.keithly.com

Kensington Technology Group .... San Mateo, CA: (650) 572-2700
Tech:(800) 535-4242   Toll Free:(800) 280-8318
Web Page: http://www.kensington.com

Kent Marsh Ltd (see Citadel Technology)

Kenwood Technologies inc .... San Jose, CA: (562) 483-8740
Web Page: http://www.kenwoodtech.com

Kenyon Laboratories .... Essex, CT: (860) 767-3235
Toll Free:(800) 253-4681
Web Page: http://www.ken-lab.com

MediaLive .... (451) 905-2300
Web Page: http://www.medialiveinternational.com

Key Power Inc .... South Plainfield, NJ: (908) 755-8000
Web Page: http://www.keypower.com

Key Source International .... Oakland, CA: (800)562-5000
Toll Free:(800) 722-6066
Web Page: http://www.ksikeyboards.com

Key Tronic Corp .... Spokane, WA: (509) 928-8000
Tech:(509) 927-5273   Toll Free:(800) 262-6006
Web Page: http://www.keytronic.com

Keyfile Corp (see Lexign)

Keystone Automation Inc .... Stillwater, MN: (651) 439-4268
Toll Free:(800) 328-4827
Web Page: http://www.keystoneautomation.com

Keystone Learning Systems (see Planetlearn) .... Portland, ME: (888) 277-6556
Web Page: http://www.Planetlearn.com

Keytronics Corp .... Spokane, WA: (509) 928-8000

Tech:(800) 266-6006   Toll Free:(800) 266-6006
Web Page: http://www.keytronic.com

Keyware Technologies .... Woburn, MA: (781) 933-1311
Toll Free:(888) 539-9273
Web Page: http://www.keyware.com

Keywest Technology Inc .... Lenexa, KS: (913) 492-4666
Toll Free:(800) 331-2019
Web Page: http://www.keywesttechnology.com

Khameleon Software .... Tampa, FL: (813) 223-4148
Toll Free:(800) 655-6598
Web Page: http://www.designdatasys.com

Khoral Research Inc .... Albuquerque, NM: (505) 837-6500
Web Page: http://www.khoral.com

Kidasa Software Inc .... Austin, TX: (512) 328-0167
Tech:(512) 328-0168   Toll Free:(800) 765-0167
Web Page: http://www.kidasa.com

KidSoft L.L.C. (see AbleSoft MMI)

Kinesis Corp .... Bothell, WA: (425) 402-8100
Tech:(425) 402-8100   Toll Free:(800) 454-6374
Web Page: http://www.kinesis-ergo.com

Kinetix (see Discreet)

Kingston Technologies .... Fountain Valley, CA: (714) 435-2600
Tech:(714) 435-2639   Toll Free:(877) 546-4786
Web Page: http://www.kingston.com

Kinyo Co Inc .... La Puente, CA: (626) 333-3711
Toll Free:(800) 735-4696
Web Page: http://www.kinyo.com

Kiss Software (see eSynch/Kissco)

KL Group (see Sitraka)

Knowledge Adventure .... Glendale, CA: (818) 246-4400
Tech:(818) 246-4811   Toll Free:(800) 757-7707
Web Page: http://www.knowledgeadventure.com

Knowledge Based Systems Inc .... College Station, TX: (979) 260-5274
Web Page: http://www.kbsi.com

Knowledge Garden Inc .... Lake Worth, FL: (561) 963-7195
Web Page: http://www.kgarden.com

Knowledge Quest .... Laguna Beach, CA: (949) 376-8150
Tech:(949) 376-8150
Web Page: http://www.knowledgequest.com

KnowledgePoint Software .... Petaluma, CA: (707) 762-0333
Tech:(707) 762-0333   Toll Free:(800) 727-1133
Web Page: http://www.knowledgepoint.com

Knozall Systems Inc .... Casa Grande, AZ: (520) 876-5357
Web Page: http://www.knozall.com

Kodak Co .... Rochester, NY: (866) 352-4367
Tech:(800) 235-6325   Toll Free:(800) 242-2424
Web Page: http://www.kodak.com

Business Imaging .... (800) 243-8811
Toll Free:(800) 243-8811

DANKA Office Imaging .... (585) 784-0982
Toll Free:(800) 255-3434
Web Page: http://www.kodak.com

Digital Imaging .... (585) 726-7260
Tech:(585) 726-7260   Toll Free:(800) 235-6325

Health Imaging (Dental) .... (585) 724-5631
Toll Free:(800) 933-8031
Web Page: http://www.kodak.com

Health Imaging (Medical Products) .... (716) 724-9362
Toll Free:(800) 336-4722
Web Page: http://www.kodak.com

Information Center .... (585) 724-4000
  Toll Free:(800) 242-2424
  Web Page: http://www.kodak.com
Professional Motion Imaging .... (800) 621-3456
  Toll Free:(800) 621-3456
  Web Page: http://www.kodak.com
Scientific Imaging Systems .... (203) 786-5657
  Tech:(877) 747-4357   Toll Free:(800) 225-5352
  Web Page: http://www.kodak.com
Kofax Image Products .... Irvine, CA: (949) 727-1733
  Tech:(949) 727-1733   Toll Free:(888) 563-2901
  Web Page: http://www.kofax
KoFile Inc .... Rochester, NY: (585) 424-1950
  Tech:(800) 482-6277   Toll Free:(800) 482-6277
  Web Page: http://www.kofile.com
Kom Inc .... Nashua, NH: (888) 556-6462
  Toll Free:(800) 668-1777
  Web Page: http://www.komnetworks.com
Konami Of America Inc .... Buffalo Grove, IL: (847) 215-5100
  Tech:(650) 654-5687
  Web Page: http://www.konami.com
Konexx Unlimited Systems Corp .... San Diego, CA: (858) 622-1400
  Tech:(858) 622-1400   Toll Free:(800) 275-6354
  Web Page: http://www.konexx.com
Konica Business Technologies .... Windsor, CT: (800) 456-6422
  Web Page: http://www.konicabt.com
Konica Camera Repair .... Mahwah, NJ: (201) 574-4000
  Tech:(888) 756-6422   Toll Free:(800) 285-6422
  Web Page: http://www.konica.com
Konica Graphic Imaging USA .... Glen Cove, NY: (800) 227-2948
  Web Page: http://www.konica.com/kgi
Konica Medical Imaging Inc .... Wayne, NJ: (800) 934-1034
  Web Page: http://www.konicamedical.com
Konica Photo Imaging .... Englewood Cliffs, NJ: (201) 574-4000
  Tech:(888) 756-6422   Toll Free:(800) 285-6422
  Web Page: http://www.konica.com
Konica Photo Imaging .... Scarborough, ME: (207) 883-7200
  Tech:(800) 509-9022   Toll Free:(800) 283-0653
  Web Page: http://www.konica.com
Kopin Corp .... Taunton, MA: (508) 824-6696
  Web Page: http://www.kopin.com
Koss Corp .... Milwaukee, WI: (414) 964-5000
  Tech:(800) 558-8305   Toll Free:(800) 872-5677
  Web Page: http://www.koss.com
KTI Networks .... Houston, TX: (713) 266-3891
  Web Page: http://www.ktinet.com
Kubotek USA, Inc. .... Malborough, MA: (508) 229-2020
  Toll Free:(800) 372-3872
  Web Page: http://www.cadkey.com
Kurta (see Altek Corp)
Kwery .... Bellevue, WA: (800) 285-9379
  Toll Free:(800) 285-9379
  Web Page: http://www.kwery.com
Kyocera Electronics Inc .... Somerset, NJ: (732) 560-3400
  Tech:(800) 459-6329   Toll Free:(800) 232-6797
  Web Page: http://www.kyocera.com
L3 Communications (see Microdyne)
LA Computer .... Torrance, CA: (310) 533-7177
  Web Page: http://www.lacomp.com

LAB Tech ·· Andover, MA: (978) 470-0099
  Tech:(800) 879-5228   Toll Free:(800) 879-5228
  Web Page: http://www.labtech.com
Labtec Enterprises Inc (702) 269-3612
  Toll Free:(800) 732-3053
  Web Page: http://www.labtec.com
Labtronics Inc ·· Guelph, ON: (519) 767-1061
  Web Page: http://www.labtronics.com
LaCie Limited ··· Hillsboro, OR: (503) 844-4500
  Tech:(503) 844-4503   Toll Free:(800) 999-1179
  Web Page: http://www.lacie.com
Lan Star ··· Houston, TX: (713) 790-0333
  Tech:(281) 829-2448   Toll Free:(800) 474-3947
  Web Page: http://www.fourstarsystems.com
Lancast Inc (see Aura Networks)
Landmark Research (see Quarterdeck Sel)
LandWare Inc ··· Oradell, NJ: (201) 261-7944
  Toll Free:(800) 526-3977
  Web Page: http://www.landware.com
Lanier ··· Dayton, OH: (800) 432-9787
  Tech:(800) 432-9787
Lanier Worldwide Inc ·· Atlanta, GA: (770) 496-9500
  Web Page: http://www.lanier.com
LANshark Systems (see Linux Unlimited)
Lantronix ··· Irvine, CA: (949) 453-3990
  Tech:(800) 422-7044   Toll Free:(800) 422-7055
  Web Page: http://www.lantronix.com
Lapis Technologies (see Focus Enhance)
Laplink.com ··· Kirkland, WA: (425) 952-6000
  Web Page: http://www.laplink.com
Larscom Inc ·· Newark, CA: (510) 492-0800
  Toll Free:(888) LARSCOM
  Web Page: http://www.larscom.com
Laser Age (see Cartridges USA)
Laser Design Inc ·· Minneapolis, MN: (952) 884-9648
  Web Page: http://www.laserdesign.com
Laser Magnetic Stor.(see Philips Mag.)
Laser Master Tech (see Colorspan Corp)
Laser Printer Accessories (see PCPI)
Laser Publishing Group ·· El Sobrante, CA: (510) 222-0199
  Web Page: http://www.lp-group.com
LaserCard Systems Corp ·· Mountain View, CA: (650) 969-4428
  Web Page: http://www.lasercard.com
LaserMedia (see ActFit.com Inc)
LaserTools Corp (out of business)
Lasiris (see Stockard Yale)
Lattice Incorporated ·· Wheaton, IL: (630) 949-3250
  Toll Free:(800) 444-4309
  Web Page: http://www.lattice.com
Lava Computer Mfg. Inc ··· Toronto, ON: (416) 674-5942
  Toll Free:(800) 241-5282
  Web Page: http://www.lavalink.com
Lawson Software ·· Minneapolis, MN: (651) 767-7000
  Toll Free:(800) 477-1357
  Web Page: http://www.lawson.com
Lazarus Data Recovery ·· San Francisco, CA: (415) 495-5556
  Toll Free:(800) 341-3282
  Web Page: http://www.lazarus.com

Phone Directory

LCD Lighting Inc · **Orange, CT: (203) 795-1520**
Web Page: http://www.lcdl.com

Lead Technologies Inc · **Charlotte, NC: (704) 332-5532**
Tech:(704) 372-9681   Toll Free:(800) 637-4699
Web Page: http://www.leadtools.com

Leader Technologies · **Newport Beach, CA: (949) 757-1787**
Web Page: http://www.leadertech.com

Leadtek Research · **Fremont, CA: (510) 490-8076**
Web Page: http://www.leadtek.com

Learn Technologies Interactive · · · · · · · · · · · · · · · · · **New York, NY: (212) 334-2225**
Tech:(212) 219-2522   Toll Free:(888) 292-5584
Web Page: http://www.learntech.com

Learn2.com · **White Plains, NY: (914) 682-4300**
Tech:(800) 842-4723   Toll Free:(888) 231-9327
Web Page: http://www.learn2.com

Learned-Mahn (see Global Payment Sys)

Learning Company, The · **Fremont, CA: (510) 792-2101**
Tech:(319) 247-3333   Toll Free:(800) 409-1497

LearnIT Corp · **Gainesville, FL: (352) 375-6655**
Toll Free:(800) 352-4806
Web Page: http://www.learnitcorp.com

LearnKey Inc · **St George, UT: (435) 674-9733**
Tech:(435) 674-0037   Toll Free:(800) 865-0165
Web Page: http://www.learnkey.com

Leco Corp · **St Joseph, MI: (269) 985-5496**
Toll Free:(800) 292-6141
Web Page: http://www.leco.com

Legacy Storage Systems Corp · · · · · · · · · · · · · · · · · · **Markham, ON: (905) 475-1077**
Tech:(905) 475-1380   Toll Free:(800) 361-5685
Web Page: http://www.storageflex.com

Legato · **Orem, UT: (801) 223-3100**
Tech:(801) 223-3104   Toll Free:(888) 808-4622
Web Page: http://www.vinca.com

Legato Systems · **Mountain View, CA: (650) 812-6000**
Tech:(650) 812-6032   Toll Free:(888) 853-4286
Web Page: http://www.legato.com

Legato Systems · **Cincinnati, OH: (513) 579-0455**
Toll Free:(888) 724-6736
Web Page: http://www.legato.com

Legi-Tech (see Statenet)

Leica Microsystems inc · **Bannockburn, IL: (847) 405-0123**
Toll Free:(800) 248-0123
Web Page: http://www.leica-microsystems.com

Leitch Inc · **Chesapeake, VA: (757) 548-2300**
Toll Free:(888) 231-9673
Web Page: http://www.leitch.com

Lenel Systems International Inc · · · · · · · · · · · · · · · · · · **Pittsford, NY: (585) 248-9720**
Web Page: http://www.lenel.com

Leo Electronics Inc · **Torrance, CA: (310) 372-5872**
Web Page: http://www.excess.com

Lernout & Hauspie · **Peabody, MA: (978) 977-2000**
Web Page: http://www.lhsl.com

Leutrek Vision Inc · **Burlington, MA: (781) 238-0213**
Web Page: http://www.leutrek.com

Level 8 Systems · **Berkeley, CA: (510) 704-2000**
Tech:(510) 528-2900   Toll Free:(800) 763-0050
Web Page: http://www.starquest.com

Leviton Voice & Data · **Bothell, WA: (425) 486-2222**
Tech:(800) 722-2082   Toll Free:(800) 722-2082

Web Page: http://www.levitontelcom.com

Lexar Media ·· Fremont, CA: (510) 413-1200
Tech:(510) 413-1275
Web Page: http://www.lexarmedia.com

Lexign ·· Nashua, NH: (603) 883-3800
Toll Free:(800) 453-9345
Web Page: http://www.lexign.com

Lexington Technology Inc ·· Irvine, CA: (949) 428-7888
Tech:(949) 428-7870   Toll Free:(888) 432-3683
Web Page: http://www.lexingtontech.com

LexisNexis ·· Dayton, OH: (937) 865-6800
Toll Free:(800) 253-5624
Web Page: http://www.lexisnexis.com

LexJet Direct ·· Sarasota, FL: (941) 330-1210
Toll Free:(800) 453-9538
Web Page: http://www.lexjet.com

Lexmark Direct (800) 438-2468

Lexmark International Inc ·· Lexington, KY: (859) 232-2000
Tech:(800) 553-9457   Toll Free:(800) 258-8575
Web Page: http://www.lexmark.com

LG Electronics USA Inc ·· Englewood Cliffs, NJ: (201) 816-2000
Tech:(800) 243-0000   Toll Free:(800) 243-0000
Web Page: http://www.lgeus.com

li

Liant Software Corp ·· Framingham, MA: (508) 872-8700
Web Page: http://www.liant.com
Sales ·· (512) 343-1010
Tech:(512) 343-1010   Toll Free:(800) 349-9222
Web Page: http://www.liant.com/
Software Serv ·· (512) 371-7028
Web Page: http://www.liant.com/
Technical Support ·· (512) 502-9074
Tech:(512) 343-1010

Liberty Systems (see Resale World.com)

Liebert Corp ·· Columbus, OH: (614) 888-0246
Tech:(800) 543-2378   Toll Free:(800) 222-5877
Web Page: http://www.liebert.com

Lifeboat (see Programmers Paradise)

Lifestyle Software Group ·· St. Augustine, FL: (904) 794-7070
Web Page: http://www.lifeware.com

Light Gain Corp ·· Gainsville, GA: (770) 654-7191

Light Source Computer (see X-Rite)

Lighten Inc (see Advance Planning)

Ligos Technology ·· San Francisco, CA: (415) 249-0100
Web Page: http://www.ligos.com

like "j & r*"

Likeminds Inc (see Andromedia)

Lilly Software Associates Inc ·· Hampton, NH: (603) 926-9696
Web Page: http://www.visualmfg.com

Lind Electronics ·· Minneapolis, MN: (952) 927-6303
Toll Free:(800) 697-3702
Web Page: http://www.lindelectronics.com

Lindo Systems inc ·· Chicago, IL: (312) 988-7422
Tech:(312) 988-9421   Toll Free:(800) 441-2378
Web Page: http://www.lindo.com

Linguist's Software ·· Edmunds, WA: (425) 775-1130
Tech:(425) 775-1130
Web Page: http://www.linguistsoftware.com

Link Instruments Inc ·· Fairfield, NJ: (973) 808-8990

Web Page: http://www.linkinstruments.com

Link Technologies (see Wyse Technology)

Linksys Group Inc ·· Irvine, CA: (949) 261-1288
Tech: (949) 261-1288   Toll Free: (800) 546-5797
Web Page: http://www.linksys.com

Lino Color ··· Hauppauge, NY: (703) 903-0254
Tech: (703) 903-0254   Toll Free: (888) 546-6265
Web Page: http://www.linocolor.com

Linos Photonics ·· Milford, MA: (508) 478-6200
Web Page: http://www.linos.com

Linos Photonics Inc (see file 4171)

Linux Networx ·· Bluffdale, UT: (877) 505-5694
Toll Free: (877) 505-LNXI
Web Page: http://www.linuxnetworx.com

Linux Unlimited ·· Gahanna, OH: (614) 416-4111
Tech: (614) 416-4111
Web Page: http://www.lanshark.com

Liquent ·· Fort Washington, PA: (215) 619-6000
Toll Free: (800) 515-3777
Web Page: http://www.cdcsolutions.com

Lite-On Manufacturing Services ···························· Tucson, AZ: (520) 294-5450
Web Page: http://www.lmsus.com

Lite-On Technology ·· Milipitas, CA: (408) 946-4873
Tech: (408) 935-5353
Web Page: http://www.liteontc.com

Live Picture (see MGI Software)

Live Pix Company (see MGI Software)

Lixi Inc ·· Downers Grove, IL: (630) 620-4646
Web Page: http://www.lixi.com

LizardTech ·· Seattle, WA: (206) 652-5211
Web Page: http://www.lizardtech.com

LM Intelligent Library Systems ···························· Sunnyvale, CA: (408) 743-7871
Web Page: http://www.lmils.com

LMG ·· Orlando, FL: (407) 850-0505
Toll Free: (800) 226-3100
Web Page: http://www.lmg.net

Locus Computing (see Platinum Tech)

Logical Co, The ·· Cottage Grove, OR: (541) 942-3610
Web Page: http://www.u-master.com

Logitech Inc ·· Fremont, CA: (510) 795-8500
Tech: (702) 269-3457   Toll Free: (800) 231-7717
Web Page: http://www.logitech.com

Lone Wolf Software ·· Cambridge, ON: (519) 624-1236
Web Page: http://www.lwolf.com

Loral Skynet Satellite Services ···························· Bedminster, NJ: (908) 470-2300
Toll Free: (800) 242-2422
Web Page: http://www.loralskynet.com

Lotus Development Corp (see IBM)

LSC Inc ·· Eagan, MN: (651) 554-1500
Tech: (651) 482-5683   Toll Free: (800) 650-2337
Web Page: http://www.lsci.com

LSI Logic Corp ·· Milpitas, CA: (408) 433-8000
Tech: (800) 574-4286   Toll Free: (866) 574-5741
Web Page: http://www.lsilogic.com

LucasArts Entertainment ···························· San Rafael, CA: (415) 507-4545
Tech: (415) 507-4545   Toll Free: (888) 532-4263
Web Page: http://www.lucasarts.com

Lucent Parts Sales Center ···························· Murray Hill, NJ: (908) 508-8080
Toll Free: (888) 582-3686

Web Page: http://www.lucent.com

Lucent Technologies .... Murray Hill, NJ: **(908) 582-8500**
Toll Free:(888) 458-2368
Web Page: http://www.lucent.com
   Consumer Products .... (800) 222-3111
   Tech:(800) 344-0223
   DNS Global Services .... (888) 384-3763
   Toll Free:(888) 384-3763
   Web Page: http://www.lucent.com
   Internetworking Systems .... (650) 318-1000
   Web Page: http://www.lucent.com
   Octel Messaging Division .... (408) 321-2000
   Web Page: http://www.octel.com

Luminex .... Riverside, CA: **(909) 781-4100**
Toll Free:(888) 586-4639
Web Page: http://www.luminex.com

Luna Imaging Inc .... Culver City, CA: **(310) 452-8370**
Toll Free:(800) 452-5862
Web Page: http://www.luna-imaging.com

Lura Tech Inc ....
Redwood City, CA: **(650) 326-8829**
Web Page: http://www.luratech.com

LynuxWorks .... San Jose, CA: **(408) 979-3900**
Tech:(408) 979-3900   Toll Free:(800) 255-5969
Web Page: http://www.lynx.com

Lynx Real-Time Systems (see LynuxWorks)

Lytec Systems Inc .... Gilbert, AZ: **(800) 735-1991**
Tech:(800) 895-6700   Toll Free:(800) 735-1991
Web Page: http://www.lytec.com

M-Brain (see Gupta Technology)

MA Laboratories Inc .... San Jose, CA: **(408) 941-0808**
Tech:(408) 941-0808
Web Page: http://www.malabs.com

Mabry Software Inc .... Stanwood, WA: **(360) 629-9278**
Toll Free:(800) 996-2279
Web Page: http://www.mabry.com

Mackie Designs Inc .... Woodinville, WA: **(425) 487-4333**
Tech:(800) 898-3211   Toll Free:(800) 258-6883
Web Page: http://www.mackie.com

Macmillan New Media (see Electro Press)

Macola Software (see Exact Software)

Macro 4 .... Parsippany, NJ: **(973) 402-8000**
Tech:(800) 866-6224   Toll Free:(800) 766-6224
Web Page: http://www.macro4.com

Macro Enter Corp .... Boca Raton, FL: **(561) 395-9996**
Toll Free:(800) 622-7568
Web Page: http://www.macroenter.com

Macromedia Inc .... San Francisco, CA: **(415) 252-2000**
Tech:(415) 252-9080   Toll Free:(800) 888-9335
Web Page: http://www.macromedia.com
   Allaire Corp .... (617) 761-2000
   Tech:(617) 219-2000   Toll Free:(888) 939-2545
   Web Page: http://www.allaire.com

Macronix Inc .... Milpitas, CA: **(408) 453-8088**
Web Page: http://www.macronix.com

Macrovision .... Sunnyvale, CA: **(408) 743-8600**
Web Page: http://www.macrovision.com

Madge.connect .... Livonia, MI: **(209) 830-1257**
Tech:(209) 830-1257
Web Page: http://www.madge.com

Madison Cable ·· Worcester, MA: (508) 752-2884
   Tech:(508) 752-2884   Toll Free:(877) 623-4766
   Web Page: http://www.madisoncable.com

MAG InnoVision Inc ·· Garden Grove, CA: (714) 799-3899
   Tech:(714) 379-6290
   Web Page: http://www.maginnovision.com

Magee Enterprises Inc ·· Norcross, GA: (770) 446-6611
   Tech:(770) 446-6611
   Web Page: http://www.magee.com

Magenta Research Group ·· Brookfield, CT: (203) 740-0592
   Web Page: http://www.magenta-research.com

Magic Software Enterprises ·· Irvine, CA: (949) 250-1718
   Toll Free:(800) 345-6244
   Web Page: http://www.magic-sw.com

Magic Solutions (see Network Associates)

Magix Entertainment Corp ·· Miami Beach, FL: (305) 695-6363
   Web Page: http://www.magix.net

Magnavox (see Philips)

Magnetic Shield Corp ·· Bensenville, IL: (630) 766-7800
   Toll Free:(888) 766-7800
   Web Page: http://www.magnetic-shield.com

Mailer's Software ·· Rancho Santa Margarita, CA: (949) 589-5200
   Toll Free:(800) 800-6245
   Web Page: http://www.800mail.com

Mainstay ·· Camarillo, CA: (805) 484-9400
   Tech:(805) 484-9400   Toll Free:(800) 362-2605
   Web Page: http://www.mstay.com

Maintenance Troubleshooting ·· Newark, DE: (302) 738-0532
   Toll Free:(800) 755-7672
   Web Page: http://www.mtroubleshooting.com

Management Systems Designers ·· Vienna, VA: (703) 281-7440
   Tech:(703) 281-7451
   Web Page: http://www.msdinc.com

Manatron Inc ·· Portage, MI: (616) 567-2900
   Toll Free:(866) 471-2900
   Web Page: http://www.manatron.com

MangoSoft Corp ·· Westborough, MA: (508) 871-7300
   Tech:(508) 861-0212   Toll Free:(888) 886-2646
   Web Page: http://www.mango.com

Manhattan Electric Cable ·· Manchester, CT: (800) 228-6322
   Toll Free:(800) 228-6322
   Web Page: http://www.manhattancdt.com

Mannesmann Tally (see Tally Printer)

Mansfield Software Group Inc ·· Storrs, CT: (860) 429-8402
   Tech:(860) 429-8402   Toll Free:(800) 479-8639
   Web Page: http://www.kedit.com

Manugistics Inc ·· Rockville, MD: (301) 255-5000
   Toll Free:(877) 331-0728
   Web Page: http://www.manugistics.com

Map Resources ·· Lambertville, NJ: (609) 397-1611
   Tech:(609) 397-1611   Toll Free:(800) 334-4291
   Web Page: http://www.mapresources.com

MapInfo ·· Troy, NY: (518) 285-6000
   Toll Free:(800) 327-8627
   Web Page: http://www.mapinfo.com

Marcan Inc ·· Bellevue, WA: (425) 635-7477
   Toll Free:(800) 635-7477
   Web Page: http://www.marcan.com

Marconi Applied Technologies ·· Elmsford, NY: (914) 592-6050

Toll Free:(800) 342-5338
Web Page: http://www.eev.com

Marconi Communications ·· **Greensboro, NC: (336) 545-7300**
Web Page: http://www.marconi.com

Mark Of The Unicorn Inc ······································ **Cambridge, MA: (617) 576-2760**
Tech:(617) 576-3066
Web Page: http://www.motu.com

MarketArts (see Window on Wallstreet)

Marshall Electronics ·· **El Segundo, CA: (310) 333-0606**
Web Page: http://www.Marshall.com

Marshall Industries (see Avnet Inc)

Mass Multimedia Inc ··· **Colorado Springs, CO: (719) 593-7500**
Toll Free:(800) 348-8610
Web Page: http://www.touchscreens.com

Masterclips Graphics (see IMSI Software)

MasterSoft Inc (see Adobe Systems)

MathSoft Inc ··· **Cambridge, MA: (617) 444-8000**
Tech:(617) 444-8102   Toll Free:(800) 628-4223
Web Page: http://www.mathsoft.com

MathWorks Inc, The ··· **Natick, MA: (508) 647-7000**
Tech:(508) 653-1415
Web Page: http://www.mathworks.com

Matrox ··· **Dorval, PQ: (514) 685-2630**
Tech:(514) 822-6061   Toll Free:(800) 804-6243
Web Page: http://www.matrox.com/video

Mattel Inc ··· **El Segundo, CA: (310) 252-2000**
Toll Free:(800) 524-8697
Web Page: http://www.mattelmedia.com

Max Levy Autograph Inc ······································· **Philadelphia, PA: (215) 842-3675**
Toll Free:(800) 798-3675
Web Page: http://www.maxlevy.com

Maxell Corp Of America ·· **Fair Lawn, NJ: (201) 794-5900**
Tech:(201) 377-5887   Toll Free:(800) 533-2836
Web Page: http://www.maxell.com
CD-ROM/DVD Replication ······························(619) 661-6600
Consumer Relations ······································(800) 525-2797
Toll Free:(800) 525-2797
Data Storage Group ·······································(888) 262-9355
Toll Free:(888) 262-9355

Maxi Switch (see Lite-On Mfg)

Maximized Software ·· **Mill Valley, CA: (415) 383-1389**
Toll Free:(888) 629-7638
Web Page: http://www.maximized.com

Maximum Strategy (see Sun Microsystems)

Maxis Software ··· **Walnut Creek, CA: (925) 933-5630**
Tech:(650) 628-4311
Web Page: http://www.simcity.com

MaxOptic Corp ··· **Boulder, CO: (303) 449-2673**
Tech:(800) 848-3092   Toll Free:(800) 953-0550
Web Page: http://www.maxoptic.com

Maxoptix Corp ··· **Fremont, CA: (510) 353-9700**
Tech:(800) 848-3092   Toll Free:(800) 848-3092
Web Page: http://www.maxoptix.com

Maxspeed Corp ··· **Palo Alto, CA: (650) 856-8818**
Tech:(800) 877-7998   Toll Free:(800) 877-7998
Web Page: http://www.maxspeed.com

Maxtor Corp ··· **Longmont, CO: (303) 678-2015**
Toll Free:(800) 262-9867
Web Page: http://www.maxtor.com

Maynard Electronic (see Seagate)

McAfee Associates (see Network Assoc)

McAfee.com .... Sunnyvale, CA: (408) 992-8100
Tech:(408) 992-8599   Toll Free:(888) 847-8766
Web Page: http://www.mcafee.com

McCabe & Associates Inc .... Warwick, RI: (401) 384-6180
Toll Free:(800) 638-6316
Web Page: http://www.mccabe.com

McData .... Broomfield, CO: (720) 558-8000
Toll Free:(800) 752-4572
Web Page: http://www.mcdata.com

MCM Electronics .... Centerville, OH: (937) 434-0031
Tech:(800) 824-8324   Toll Free:(800) 543-4330
Web Page: http://www.mcmelectronics.com

MCS Product (see Micro Computer System)

MD & I Corp .... El Monte, CA: (626) 442-8899
Toll Free:(800) 619-8899
Web Page: http://www.mdinotebook.com

MDL Corp .... Bellevue, WA: (425) 788-4849
Toll Free:(800) 800-3766
Web Page: http://www.mdlcorp.com

Mead School & Office Products .... Dayton, OH: (937) 495-6323
Web Page: http://www.meadweb.com

Measurement Computing Corp .... Middleboro, MA: (508) 946-5100
Web Page: http://www.measurementcomputing.com

MECA Software LLC (see Concentrex Inc)

MECC (see Learning Company, The)

Mechanical Dynamics Inc (see MSC Software)

Medea .... Tustin, CA: (949) 852-8511
Toll Free:(800) 525-9217
Web Page: http://www.medea.com

Medea Corp .... West Lake Village, CA: (818) 880-0303
Web Page: http://www.medea.com

Media 100 .... Marlboro, MA: (508) 460-1600
Tech:(800) 773-1770   Toll Free:(800) 922-3220
Web Page: http://www.media100.com

Media Cybernetics LP .... Silver Spring, MD: (301) 495-3305
Web Page: http://www.mediacy.com

Media Source Inc .... Marrietta, GA: (800) 588-3827
Tech:(800) 356-2553   Toll Free:(800) 241-8857
Web Page: http://www.mediasource.com

Media Synergy (see Flonetwork)

Media-X Systems Inc .... Ottawa, ON: (613) 722-9990
Toll Free:(888) 722-9990
Web Page: http://www.media-x.com

Media4 Productions Inc .... West Des Moines, IA: (515) 225-7409
Tech:(515) 225-7409   Toll Free:(800) 528-7440
Web Page: http://www.media4.com

MediaBin .... Atlanta, GA: (404) 264-8000
Tech:(800) 437-2285   Toll Free:(800) 437-2285
Web Page: http://www.mediabin.com

MediaForm Inc .... Exton, PA: (610) 458-9200
Tech:(610) 458-9200   Toll Free:(800) 220-1215
Web Page: http://www.mediaform.com

Mediascape Corp .... Southfield, MI: (248) 945-1100
Web Page: http://www.mediascape.com

Mediatechnics Systems Inc .... Sutter Creek, CA: (209) 267-1567
Toll Free:(800) 474-8996
Web Page: http://www.mediatechnics.com

Mediatrix Peripherals Inc ·································· Sherbrooke, PQ: (819) 829-8749
   Tech:(819) 829-8749   Toll Free:(800) 820-8749
   Web Page: http://www.mediatrix.com
Medical Manager ··· Tampa, FL: (813) 287-2990
   Toll Free:(800) 222-7701
   Web Page: http://www.medicalmanager.com
Mega Drive Sys (see Data Direct Network)
Mega Haus ··· Dickinson, TX: (281)534-6292
   Toll Free:(800)786-1157
   Web Page: http://www.megahaus.com
Megahertz Corp (see 3Com)
Megatel Computer Corp ······················ Glen Williams, Ontario, : (905) 873-9988
   Web Page: http://www.megatel.ca
Megavision ·· Columbus, NE: (402) 562-5904
   Web Page: http://www.megavision.com
Melissa Data Corp ····························· Rancho Santa Margarita, CA: (949) 589-5200
   Toll Free:(800) 635-4772
   Web Page: http://www.melissadata.com
Memorex (see Memtek)
Memtek Products Inc ··························· Santa Fe Springs, CA: (562) 906-2800
   Tech:(310) 891-1680   Toll Free:(800) 919-3647
   Web Page: http://www.memtek.com
Mentalix Inc ··· Plano, TX: (972) 423-9377
   Web Page: http://www.mentalix.com
Mentat Inc ··· Los Angeles, CA: (310) 208-2650
   Toll Free:(888) 463-6828
   Web Page: http://www.mentat.com
Mentor Electronics (see Qualtek Electr)
Mentor Graphics Corp ························· Wilsonville, OR: (503) 685-7000
   Tech:(800) 592-2210   Toll Free:(800) 547-3000
   Web Page: http://www.mentor.com
Mentor Graphics Corporation / Innoveda Inc ··········· Wilsonville, OR: (508) 685-8000
   Tech:(800) 547.3000   Toll Free:(800) 592-2210
   Web Page: http://www.mentor.com
Merant(see Data Direct)
   Web Page: http://www.datadirect.com
Merant(see Serena Solution)
   Web Page: http://www.serena.com
Mercron Inc ·· Richardson, TX: (972) 690-6565
   Web Page: http://www.mercron.com
Mercury Computer Systems ··················· Chelmsford, MA: (978) 256-1300
   Toll Free:(800) 229-2006
   Web Page: http://www.mc.com
Mercury Interactive Corp ······················ Mountain View, CA: (650) 603-5200
   Web Page: http://www.mercury.com
Mergent Int. (see Utimaco Safeware)
Meridian Data (see Quantum Corp)
Meridian Software Inc ··························· Raleigh, NC: (919) 518-1070
   Web Page: http://www.meridian-software.com
Merisel ·· El Segundo, CA: (310) 615-3080
   Tech:(800) 462-5241   Toll Free:(800) 637-4735
   Web Page: http://www.merisel.com
Meritec ·· Painesville, OH: (440) 354-3148
   Toll Free:(888) 637-4832
   Web Page: http://www.meritec.com
Merritt Computer Products Inc ··············· Dallas, TX: (214) 339-0753
   Tech:(214) 339-0753
Meta Communications ··························· Iowa City, IA: (319) 337-8599
   Toll Free:(800) 771-6382

Web Page: http://www.meta-comm.com

Meta Software Corp ·· Cambridge, MA: (617) 576-6920
Toll Free:(800) 227-4106
Web Page: http://www.metasoftware.com

MetaCard Corp ··· Boulder, CO: (303) 447-3936
Web Page: http://www.metacard.com

Metacreations Corp (see Viewpoint)

Metafile Infomation Systems ··· Rochester, MN: (507) 286-9232
Tech:(800) 222-4096   Toll Free:(800) 638-2445
Web Page: http://www.metafile.com

Metagraphics Software Corp ··· Woodinville, WA: (425) 844-1110
Toll Free:(800) 332-1550
Web Page: http://www.metagraphics.com

Metaphase Technologies ·· St. Louis, MO: (314) 721-0700
Web Page: http://www.metaphase.com

MetaStorm ··· Severna Park, MD: (410) 647-9691
Tech:(801) 434-9595
Web Page: http://www.metastorm.com

MetaTools Inc (see Viewpoint)

Methode Electronics Inc ·· Chicago, IL: (708) 867-6777
Web Page: http://www.methode.com

Metrics Technology Inc ··· Albuquerque, NM: (505) 761-9630
Toll Free:(800) 398-1490
Web Page: http://www.metricstech.com

Metrix Inc ·· Waukesha, WI: (262) 717-6500
Tech:(262) 798-7900   Toll Free:(800) 543-2130
Web Page: http://www.metrix-inc.com

Metromedia Fiber Network ·· White Plains, NY: (914) 421-6700
Tech:(877) 479-7378   Toll Free:(877) 748-3002
Web Page: http://www.mfn.com

Metrowerks Corp ··· Austin, TX: (512) 996-5300
Web Page: http://www.metrowerks.com

MGE UPS ··· Costa Mesa, CA: (714) 557-1636
Tech:(800) 438-7373   Toll Free:(800) 523-0142
Web Page: http://www.mgeups.com

MGI Software Corp (see Roxio)

Micah Development Corp (see Full Armor)

Micom Comm. (see Nortel Networks)

Micro 2000 Inc ··· Glendale, CA: (818) 547-0125
Toll Free:(800) 864-8008
Web Page: http://www.micro2000.com

Micro Accessories Inc ··· Fremont, CA: (510) 226-6310
Tech:(510) 226-6310   Toll Free:(800) 777-6687
Web Page: http://www.micro-a.com

Micro Center Order ·· Hilliard, OH: (800) 634-3478
Toll Free:(800) 634-3478
Web Page: http://www.microcenterorder.com

Micro Computer Cable Company ··· Taylor, MI: (800) 421-0402
Toll Free:(800) 421-0402
Web Page: http://www.microccc.com

Micro Computer Systems ·· Irving, TX: (214) 262-3530
Web Page: http://www.mcsdallas.com

Micro Design International Inc ·· Lake Mary, FL: (407) 472-6000
Toll Free:(800) 228-0891
Web Page: http://www.mdi.com

Micro Electronics Inc ··· Seekonk, MA: (508) 761-9161
Web Page: http://www.micro-strip.com

Micro Exchange Corp ·· Wayne, NJ: (973) 872-1200
Toll Free:(800) 284-9296

Web Page: http://www.microexch.com

Micro Firmware Inc .... **Norman, OK: (405) 321-8333**
Tech:(888) 472-2467   Toll Free:(800) 767-5465
Web Page: http://www.firmware.com

Micro Focus (see Merant)

Micro Focus Group .... **Mountain View, CA: (650) 938-3700**
Toll Free:(877) 772-4450
Web Page: http://www.microfocus.com

Micro House (see EarthWeb Inc)

Micro Integration (see Iceweb.net)
Web Page: http://www.iceweb.net

Micro Logic Corp .... **Midland Park, NJ: (201) 447-6991**
Tech:(201) 447-8954
Web Page: http://www.miclog.com

Micro Sense Inc .... **Leucadia, CA: (760) 632-8623**
Tech:(800) 544-4252   Toll Free:(800) 544-4252
Web Page: http://www.microsense.com

Micro Solutions Inc .... **Dekalb, IL: (815) 756-3411**
Tech:(815) 754-4500   Toll Free:(800) 890-7227
Web Page: http://www.micro-solutions.com

Micro Star Software .... **Carlsbad, CA: (760) 931-4949**
Tech:(760) 931-4955   Toll Free:(800) 777-4228
Web Page: http://www.micro-star-usa.com

Micro Warehouse (see Warehouse.com)

Micro-Pace Inc .... **Champaign, IL: (217) 356-1884**
Tech:(217) 356-8949
Web Page: http://www.micro-pace.com

MicroBiz Corp .... **Upper Saddle River, NJ: (201) 512-0900**
Web Page: http://www.microbiz.com

Microboards Technology .... **Chanhassen, MN: (952) 556-1600**
Tech:(952) 556-1639   Toll Free:(800) 646-8881
Web Page: http://www.microboards.com

Microchip Technology Inc .... **Chandler, AZ: (480) 792-7627**
Tech:(480) 792-7627   Toll Free:(800) 437-2767
Web Page: http://www.microchip.com

Microcom Corp .... **Lewis Center, OH: (740) 548-6262**
Toll Free:(800) 642-7626
Web Page: http://www.microcomcorp.com

Microcomputer Systems Inc .... **Baton Rouge, LA: (225) 769-2154**
Web Page: http://www.microcomputersystems.com

Microdyne Corp
L3 Communications .... (352) 687-4633
Tech:(800) 265-2821   Toll Free:(800) 874-4633
Web Page: http://telemetry.microdyne.com

Microdyne Outsourcing .... **Torrance, CA: (800) 792-6567**

Micrografx Inc (see Corel)

MicroHelp Inc .... **Newport News, VA: (757) 873-6707**
Web Page: http://www.microhlp.com

Microimage Video Systems .... **Boyertown, PA: (610) 754-6800**
Web Page: http://www.mivs.com

Microimages Inc .... **Lincoln, NE: (402) 477-9554**
Web Page: http://www.microimages.com

Microleague Int Sftr(Out of Business)

Microleague Multimedia (see Ablesoft)

Microlite Corp .... **Aliquippa, PA: (724) 375-6711**
Tech:(888) 257-3343   Toll Free:(800) 992-2827
Web Page: http://www.microlite.com

Microm Technologies Solutions .... **Oklahoma City, OK: (405) 789-9000**
Web Page: http://www.microm.net

MicroMedium Inc (see TrainerSoft.com)
Micron Electronics (see MicronPC.com)
Micron Technology .... Boise, ID: (208) 368-3900
Tech:(208) 368-4000   Toll Free:(800) 828-0416
Web Page: http://www.micron.com
MicroNet Technology .... Torrance, CA: (310) 320-7272
Tech:(949) 453-6060   Toll Free:(800) 800-3475
Web Page: http://www.micronet.com
Micronics Comp. (see Diamond Multimedia)
MicronPC.com .... Boise, ID: (208) 368-4000
Tech:(888) 349-6972   Toll Free:(800) 964-2766
Web Page: http://www.micron.com
MicronPC.com (see SpecTek)
Microplex Systems Ltd .... Port Coquitlam, BC: (604) 468-2444
Toll Free:(800) 665-7798
Web Page: http://www.microplex.com
Micropolis Corp (Out of Business)
Microprose Software .... Alameda, CA: (800) 832-4958
Web Page: http://www.microprose.com
MicroQuill .... Kirkland, WA: (425) 827-7200
Web Page: http://www.microquill.com
MicroRidge Systems Inc .... Sunriver, OR: (541) 593-3500
Tech:(541) 593-1656
Web Page: http://www.microridge.com
Microscan .... Renton, WA: (425) 226-5700
Tech:(800) 251-7711   Toll Free:(800) 762-1149
Web Page: http://www.microscan.com
MicroSearch .... Houston, TX: (713) 988-2818
Toll Free:(888) 299-5060
Web Page: http://www.microsearch.com
Microsoft Corporation .... Redmond, WA: (425) 882-8080
Tech:(800) 936-3500   Toll Free:(800) 426-9400
Web Page: http://www.microsoft.com
3D Movie Maker (see Home & Personal Use)
500 Nations (see Home & Personal Use)
Access (see Developer Issues)
Web Page: http://www.microsoft.com/access
Actimates (see Home & Personal Use)
Web Page: http://www.microsoft.com/hardware/actimates
Active X SDK (see Developer Issues)
Age of Empires (see Home & Personal Use)
Web Page: http://www.microsoft.com/games/empires
Ancient Lands (see Home & Personal Use)
Arcade (see Games & Multimedia)
Art Gallery (see Home & Personal Use)
Asherons Call (see games & multimedia)
Automap (see Home & Personal Use)
Back Office Server (see IT Professional)
Web Page: http://www.microsoft.com/backofficeserver
Ballpoint (see Desktop Sys. & Hardware)
Barney (see games & Multimedia)
Baseball 3D (see Games & Multimedia)
Web Page: http://www.microsoft.com/games/sports/baseball
Basic (see Developer Issues)
Basic Mouse (see Desktop Sys. & Hardware)
Beethoven (see Home & Personal Use)
Beyond the Limit (see Games & Multimedia)
Bookshelf (see Home & Personal Use)
Web Page: http://bookshelf.msn.com/na
Business Systems Products (see IT Pro.)

C++ (see Developer Issues)
Canada Office Support ································ (905) 568-2294
Canada Personal Operating Systems Support ············· (905) 568-4494
Canada Product Support ································ (905) 568-3503
CART Precision Racing (see Home & Personal Use)
  Web Page: http://www.microsoft.com/games/precisionracing
CD Sampler (see Home & Personal Use)
Certificate Server (see IT Professional)
Certified Partners ································ (888) 677-9444
Chat (see Home & Personal Use)
  Web Page: http://www.microsoft.com/ie/chat
Cinemania (see Games & Multimedia)
Close Combat (see Games & Multimedia)
  Web Page: http://www.microsoft.com/games/closecombat
Combat Flight Simulator (see Games)
  Web Page: http://www.microsoft.com/games/combatfs
Commerce Server (see IT Professional)
Commercial Internet System (see IT Pro.)
  Web Page: http://www.microsoft.com/mcis
Complete Baseball Guide (see Games)
Complete Basketball (see Games)
Complete Do-It-Yourself Guide (see Games)
Complete Gardening (see Games & Multi.)
Composer Collection (see Games)
Conference Server (see IT Professional)
Cordless Phone (see Desktop Sys. & Hard.)
  Web Page: http://www.microsoft.com/phone
Countdown (see Home & Personal)
Creative Writer (see Games & Multimedia)
  Web Page: http://www.microsoft.com/kids/creativewriter
Crimewave (see Home & Personal)
Dangerous Creatures (see Games & Multi.)
Deadly Tide (see Games & Multimedia)
Desktop Applications ································ (425) 454-2030
  Tech:(425) 635-7056   Toll Free:(800) 936-5700
Desktop Applications ································ (425) 454-2030
Desktop System & Hardware ················ (425) 635-7040
Developer Issues ································ (425) 635-7050
  Tech:(800) 936-5500   Toll Free:(800) 936-5800
Developer Network (see Developer Issues)
  Web Page: http://msdn.microsoft.com/subscriptions
Device Driver Kit (see Developer Issues)
Dinosaurs (see Games & Multimedia)
Dogs (see Games & Multimedia)
DSS-80 Speakers (see Desktop Sys. & Hard.)
  Web Page: http://www.microsoft.com/hardware
EasyBall (see Desktop Sys. & Hard.)
  Web Page: http://microsoft.com/hardware/mouse/easyball
Electronic Forms Designer (see IT Pro.)
Encarta (see Games & Multimedia)
Entertainment Pack (see Games & Multi.)
Excel (see Home & Personal Use)
Excel SDK (see Developer Issues)
Exchange (see IT Professional)
  Web Page: http://www.microsoft.com/exchange
Expedia (see Games & Multimedia)
  Web Page: http://www.microsoft.com/expedia
Explorapedia (see Games & Multimedia)
Fighter Ace (Games & multimedia)
Fine Artist (see Games & Multimedia)
Flight Simulator (see Games & Multimedia)
  Web Page: http://www.microsoft.com/games/fsim

Midtown Madness (see Games & Multimedia)
Money (see Desktop Applications)
  Web Page: http://www.microsoft.com/money
Monster Truck Madness (see Games & Multi.)
Motocross Madness (see Games & Multimedia)
Mouse (see Desktop Sys. & Hardware)
Mozart (see Games & Multimedia)
MS-DOS (see Home & Personal Use)
MSN Internet Access ···(877) 635-7019
  Web Page: http://support.microsoft.com/support
Multimedia Products (see Home & Personal)
Musical Instruments (see Games & Multi.)
My Personal Tutor (see Games & Multi.)
  Web Page: http://www.microsoft.com/kids
Natural Keyboard (see Desktop Sys. & Hard.)
  Web Page: http://www.microsoft.com/hardware
NBA Full Court Press (see Games & Multi.)
NetMeeting (see Home & Personal Use)
  Web Page: http://www.microsoft.com/netmeeting
NetShow (see IT Professional)
News Server (see IT Professional)
Nickelodeon 3D Movie Maker
Oceans (see Games & Multimedia)
ODBC (see IT Professional)
  Web Page: http://www.microsoft.com/data/odbc
OEM ··(800) 936-2197
Office (see Home & Personal)
Open EIS (see Home & Personal Use)
Outlook (see Home & Personal Use)
  Web Page: http://microsoft.com/office/outlook
Outwars (see Games & Multimedia)
Personal Operating Systems (Canada) ·········(905) 568-4494
Personal Tutor Series (see Games & Mutli.)
Personal Web Server (see Home & Personal)
Personal Web Server NT (see IT Pro.)
PhotoDraw (see Desktop Applications)
  Web Page: http://www.microsoft.com/office/photodraw
Picture It! (see Desktop Applications)
  Web Page: http://www.microsoft.com/pictureit
Platform SDK (see IT Professional)
Plus! (see Desktop Applications)
Pocket Series (see IT Professional)
PowerPoint (see Desktop Applications)
  Web Page: http://www.microsoft.com/office/powerpoint
Premiere & Alliance Support ·······················(800) 936-3100
Preschool Workshop (see Games & Multi.)
Product Analyzer ·······································(425) 635-7179
Product Support Services (Canada) ··············(905) 568-3503
Productivity Pack (see Desktop Applications)
Profit ··(800) 723-3333
Project (see Desktop Applications)
  Web Page: http://www.microsoft.com/project
Proofing Tools (see Desktop Applications)
Proxy Server (see IT Professional)
  Web Page: http://www.microsoft.com/proxy
Publisher (see Home & Personal Use)
  Web Page: http://www.microsoft.com/publisher
Publisher Commercial Printers ····················(425) 635-3142
Purchase Tech Support ······························(800) 936-3500
Puzzle Collection (see Games & Multi.)
QuickBasic (see Developer Issues)
QuickC (see Developer Issues)

Web Page: http://msdn.microsoft.com/vstudio
Visual Test (see Developer Issues)
Visual Tools (see Developer Issues)
Vizact (see IT Professional)
Vxtreme Client (see Home & Personal Use)
Vxtreme Server (see IT Professional)
Web Publishing Wizard (see Desktop Apps)
Wheel Mouse (see Desktop Sys. & Hardware)
Web Page: http://microsoft.com/products/hardware
Windows (see Home & Personal Use)
Windows 95 ··· (800) 936-5700
Windows 98 ··· (425) 635-7222
Windows Based Terminal Server (see IT Pro.)
Windows CE (see Developer Issues)
Web Page: http://www.microsoft.com/windowsce
Windows Entertainment Products (see Games)
Windows for Workgroups (see Home & Personal)
Windows ME ·· (425) 635-3311
Windows NT Server (see IT Professional)
Web Page: http://microsoft.com/ntserver
Windows Sound System (see Desktop Sys.)
Wine Guide (see Games & Multimedia)
Word (see Desktop Apps.)
Web Page: http://www.microsoft.com/office
Works (see Desktop Apps.)
World of Flight (see Games & Multimedia)
Write (see Desktop Applications)
Visio (see IT Professional)

Microsoft Great Plains Bus. Solutions ··················· Fargo, ND: (701) 281-0555
Tech:(701) 281-6500   Toll Free:(800) 456-0025
Web Page: http://www.GPS.com

Microsoft Great Plains Bus. Solutions ············· Manchester, NH: (603) 641-0200
Toll Free:(800) 678-6336
Web Page: http://www.greatplains.com

MicroSolutions ··· De Kalb, IL: (815) 756-3411
Tech:(815) 754-4500   Toll Free:(800) 890-7227
Web Page: http://www.micro-solutions.com

Microspeed Inc ··· El Cajon, CA: (619) 448-2888
Tech:(619) 448-2888   Toll Free:(800) 232-7888
Web Page: http://www.microspeed.com

Microspot USA (see Macro Enter Corp)

Microstar Laboratories Inc ······························· Bellevue, WA: (425) 453-2345
Web Page: http://www.mstarlabs.com

Microstar Software (see Open text)

MicroStrategy Inc ··· McLean, VA: (703) 848-8600
Tech:(703) 848-8700
Web Page: http://www.microstrategy.com

MicroSynergy ··· Irvine, CA: (949) 477-1700
Toll Free:(888) 877-6777
Web Page: http://www.burncd.com

Microsystems (see Learning Co)

MicroSystems Development Tech ························ San Jose, CA: (408) 280-1226
Tech:(408) 280-1226
Web Page: http://www.msd.com

MicroTac Soft. (see Lernout & Hauspie)

Microtec (see Mentor Graphics Corp)

Microtech International (see Zio Corp)

Microtech Systems ··· Belmont, CA: (650) 596-1900
Toll Free:(800) 223-3693
Web Page: http://www.microtech.com

Zio Corporation .... (408) 544-2700
  Web Page: http://www.microtechint.com
Microtek .... Carson, CA: (310) 687-5800
  Tech:(310) 687-5940
  Web Page: http://www.microtekusa.com
Microtest Inc (see Fluke)
Microtouch Systems (see 3M Touch)
MicroUnity Systems Engineering .... Santa Clara, CA: (408) 734-8100
  Web Page: http://www.microunity.com
MicroVideo Learning Systems .... New York, NY: (800) 231-4021
  Tech:(212) 777-9595   Toll Free:(800) 231-4021
  Web Page: http://www.microvideo.com
MicroVision Development Inc .... Carlsbad, CA: (760) 438-7781
  Tech:(760) 438-0305   Toll Free:(800) 998-4555
  Web Page: http://www.mvd.com
Microware Education (see IT Bridge)
Microware Systems Corp .... Des Moines, IA: (515) 223-8000
  Tech:(515) 224-0458   Toll Free:(800) 475-9000
  Web Page: http://www.microware.com
MicroWarehouse .... Lakewood, NJ: (800) 796-4239
  Web Page: http://www.warehouse.com
Microwave Filter Company Inc .... East Syracuse, NY: (800) 448-1666
  Tech:(315) 438-4700   Toll Free:(800) 448-1666
  Web Page: http://www.microwavefilter.com
MicroWay Inc .... Plymouth, MA: (508) 746-7341
  Tech:(508) 746-7341
  Web Page: http://www.microway.com
MicroWest Software Systems .... San Diego, CA: (619) 280-0440
  Toll Free:(800) 969-9699
  Web Page: http://www.microwst.com
Midak (see Ikon)
MIDI Solutions Inc .... Vancouver, BC: (604) 794-3013
  Tech:(604) 794-3013   Toll Free:(800) 561-6434
  Web Page: http://www.midisolutions.com
Midway Games .... Chicago, IL: (773) 961-2222
  Tech:(903) 874-2683
  Web Page: http://www.midway.com
Midwest Computer Works .... Buffalo Grove, IL: (847) 215-9900
  Toll Free:(800) 659-5400
  Web Page: http://www.mcworks.com
Midwest Micro (see Global Computer)
MII .... Birdsboro, PA: (610) 323-2825
  Tech:(610) 582-9450   Toll Free:(800) 835-8766
  Web Page: http://www.miipgt.com
Mijenix Corp (see Ontrack/Mijenix)
Milan Technology (see Digi Lan Connect)
Miles Spicer (see Open Doors Software)
MilesTek .... Denton, TX: (940) 484-9400
  Toll Free:(800) 524-7444
  Web Page: http://www.milestek.com
Milgo Solutions (see Nextira)
Miller Freeman (see CMP Media)
Mind IQ .... Norcross, GA: (770) 248-0442
  Toll Free:(800) 511-5299
  Web Page: http://www.mindiq.com
Mind Path Technologies (see Proxima)
Mindplay .... Tucson, AZ: (520) 888-1800
  Toll Free:(800) 221-7911

Web Page: http://www.mindplay.com
Mindscape (see Learning Co)
Minerva Networks ·· Santa Clara, CA: (408) 567-9400
 Web Page: http://www.minervanetworks.com
Ministor Peripherals (Out of Business)
Minitab Inc ·· State College, PA: (814) 238-3280
 Tech:(814) 231-2682   Toll Free:(800) 448-3555
 Web Page: http://www.minitab.com
Minolta Advance Technology ·································· Goshen, NY: (845) 294-8400
 Web Page: http://www.minolta.com
Minolta Business Solutions ·································· Mahwah, NJ: (201) 512-5800
 Web Page: http://www.minoltambs.com
Minolta Corp ·· Ramsey, NJ: (201) 825-4000
 Web Page: http://www.minoltausa.com
 Information Systems ·································· (201) 512-5800
 Web Page: http://www.misi.minolta.com
 Instrument Systems ·································· (201) 529-6060
 Toll Free:(888) 473-2656
 Web Page: http://www.minolta.com
 QMS ·· (251) 633-4301
 Tech:(877) 778-2687   Toll Free:(888) 264-6658
 Web Page: http://www.minoltaqms.com
Minolta Systems Laboratory ·································· San Jose, CA: (408) 383-0477
 Web Page: http://www.minolta.com
Minuteman UPS ·· Carrollton, TX: (972) 446-7363
 Toll Free:(800) 238-7272
 Web Page: http://www.minutemanups.com
Mips Dataline (see G7 Productivity)
MIPS Group ·· Mountain View, CA: (650) 567-5000
 Web Page: http://www.mips.com
Miramar Systems ·· Santa Barbara, CA: (805) 966-2432
 Tech:(805) 965-5161   Toll Free:(800) 862-2526
 Web Page: http://www.miramarsys.com
Miros Inc (see eTrue Inc)
Misco Power Up (see Global Computer)
Mitac Industrial Corp ·· Fremont, CA: (510) 656-5288
 Toll Free:(800) 648-2295
 Web Page: http://www.mitacinds.com
Mitel Corp ·· Kanata, ON: (613) 592-2122
 Tech:(613) 592-2122   Toll Free:(800) 648-3579
 Web Page: http://www.mitel.com
Mitsubishi Digital Electronics America ············ Irvine, CA: (949) 465-6000
 Tech:(949) 465-6435   Toll Free:(800) 332-2119
 Web Page: http://www.mitsubishi-tv.com
Mitsubishi Electric Automation Inc ············ Vernon Hills, IL: (847) 478-2100
 Web Page: http://www.meau.com
Mitsubishi Electronics America ·················· Cypress, CA: (714) 220-2500
 Toll Free:(800) 843-2515
 Web Page: http://www.mitsubishielectric-usa.com
 Electronic Device Group ·································· (408) 730-5900
 Web Page: http://www.angleview.com
 Mobile Computing Division ·································· (888) 445-5250
 Toll Free:(888) 445-5250
 Web Page: http://www.mitsubishi-mobile.com
Mitsubishi International Corp ·················· New York, NY: (212) 605-2000
 Web Page: http://www.micusa.com
Mitsubishi Wireless Communications ············ Markham, Ontario, : (905) 475-7728
 Web Page: http://www.mitsubishiwireless.com
Mitsui Advanced Media Inc ·················· Colorado Springs, CO: (719) 262-2400

Web Page: http://www.mitsuiadv.com

Mitsumi Electronics Corp ·················· Irving, TX: (972) 550-7300
Toll Free:(800) 648-7864
Web Page: http://www.mitsumi.com

Mitten Software Corp ·················· Long Lake, MN: (952) 745-4941
Toll Free:(800) 825-5461
Web Page: http://www.mittensoftware.com

Mixman Technologies (see Beatnik)

MKS (Mortice Kern Systems) ·················· Waterloo, ON: (519) 884-2251
Tech:(519) 884-2270   Toll Free:(800) 265-2797
Web Page: http://www.mks.com

MKS (Mortice Kern Systems) ·················· Lombard, IL: (630) 495-2108
Tech:(800) 633-1235   Toll Free:(800) 633-6298
Web Page: http://www.mks.com

Mnemonics Inc ·················· Mont Laurel, NJ: (856) 234-0970
Web Page: http://www.mnemonicsinc.com

Mobility Electronics ·················· Scottsdale, AZ: (480) 596-0061
Web Page: http://www.mobilityelectronics.com

Mobius Management Systems ·················· Rye, NY: (914) 921-7200
Tech:(914) 921-7400   Toll Free:(800) 235-4471
Web Page: http://www.mobius-inc.com

Modgraph Inc ·················· Woburn, MA: (781) 938-4488
Web Page: http://www.modgraph.com

Molex Inc ·················· Lisle, IL: (630) 969-4550
Web Page: http://www.molex.com

Molloy Group (see ServiceWare)

Monaco Systems ·················· Andover, MA: (978) 749-9944
Web Page: http://www.monacosystems.com

Monolith Productions ·················· Kirkland, WA: (425) 739-1500
Web Page: http://www.lith.com

Monotype Systems Inc ·················· Rolling Meadows, IL: (847) 427-8800
Web Page: http://www.monoexpress.com

Monotype Typography (see AGFA Monotype)

Monster Cable ·················· Brisbane, CA: (415) 840-2000
Web Page: http://www.monstercable.com

Moon Valley Software ·················· Grover Beach, CA: (805) 994-1040
Web Page: http://www.moonvalley.com

Moritex USA Inc ·················· San Jose, CA: (408) 363-2100
Toll Free:(877) 261-2100
Web Page: http://www.moritexusa.com

Mortice Kern Systems Inc (see MKS)

Most Significant Bits Inc ·················· Avon, OH: (440) 934-1385
Tech:(440) 934-1397   Toll Free:(800) 755-4619
Web Page: http://www.msbcd.com

Motion Analysis Inc ·················· Eugene, OR: (541) 342-3440
Toll Free:(800) 935-3440
Web Page: http://www.maimaging.com

Motorola Computer Group ·················· Tempe, AZ: (800) 759-1107
Tech:(602) 438-5720   Toll Free:(800) 624-6745
Web Page: http://www.mcg.mot.com
Modem Support Center ·················· (800) 221-4380
Toll Free:(800) 221-4380
Semiconductor Products Sector ·················· (256) 922-4000
Web Page: http://www.mot.com
Vangard Manage Solutions ·················· (508) 261-4000
Toll Free:(800) 544-0062
Web Page: http://www.motorola.com/networking

Mouser Electronics ·················· Mansfield, TX: (817) 804-3888
Tech:(800) 346-6873   Toll Free:(800) 346-6873

Web Page: http://www.mouser.com

MPC Computer ·· **Nampa, ID: (208) 368-4400**
Tech:(208) 893-3434   Toll Free:877-894-5693
Web Page: http://www.buympc.com

MRO Software ·· **Bedford, MA: (781) 280-2000**
Tech:(866) 669-6764   Toll Free:(877) 762-9466
Web Page: http://www.mro.com

MSC Software Corp ·· **Santa Ana, CA: (714) 540-8900**
Toll Free:(800) 328-4672
Web Page: http://www.mscsoftware.com

Msoft ·· **Woodland Hills, CA: (818) 716-7081**
Web Page: http://www.serversound.com

MSR Development ··· **Encinitas, CA: (760) 633-3900**
Web Page: http://www.msrdev.com

MSS Computer Systems ···················· **Edmonton, Alberta, : (780) 486-0493**
Web Page: http://www.superclerk.com

MTI Technology Corp ·· **Tustin, CA: (714) 481-7800**
Tech:(800) 366-4684   Toll Free:(800) 999-9684
Web Page: http://www.mti.com

Muddy Shoes Software LLC(see Newvo Design)

Multi-Tech Systems Inc ································· **Mounds View, MN: (763) 785-3500**
Tech:(800) 972-2439   Toll Free:(800) 328-9717
Web Page: http://www.multitech.com

Multiactive Software Inc(now Maximizer) ············· **Vancouver, BC, : (604) 601-8000**
Tech:(604) 899-3838   Toll Free:(888) 577-7809
Web Page: http://www.maximizer.com

Multiactive Software Inc(location closed) ··································· **Duluth, :**

Multimedia 2000 ·· **Seattle, WA: (206) 622-5530**
Web Page: http://www.m-2k.com

Multimedia Learning (see Align Mark)

Musitek ·· **Ojai, CA: (805) 646-8051**
Tech:(805) 646-5841   Toll Free:(800) 676-8055
Web Page: http://www.musitek.com

Mustang Software (see Avaya Comm.)

Mustek Inc ·· **Irvine, CA: (949) 790-3800**
Tech:(949) 788-3600   Toll Free:(800) 468-7835
Web Page: http://www.mustek.com

Mutech Inc ··· **Billerica, MA: (978) 663-2400**
Web Page: http://www.mutech.com

Mutoh America ·· **Phoenix, AZ: (480) 968-7772**
Web Page: http://www.mutoh.com

My Software Co (see Elibrium)

Mylex Corp (see LSI Logic)

MYOB US Inc ·· **Rockaway, NJ: (973) 586-2200**
Tech:(973) 586-2325   Toll Free:(800) 322-6962
Web Page: http://www.myob.com

Myriad Logic / Mercury Computer Systems ··········· **Chelmsford, MA: (978) 256-1300**
Web Page: http://www.mc.com

Mystic River Software ···································· **Burlington, MA:**
Web Page: http://www.mysticriver.com

n Software Inc ··································· **Research Triangle Park, NC: (919) 402-0590**
Tech:(919) 402-0590   Toll Free:(800) 225-4190
Web Page: http://www.nsoftware.com

Nac Image Technology ·· **Simi Valley, CA: (805) 584-8862**
Toll Free:(800) 969-2711
Web Page: http://www.nacinc.com

NAG (Numeric Algorithms Group) ·················· **Downers Grove, IL: (630) 971-2337**
Tech:(630) 971-2345
Web Page: http://www.nag.com

Nakamichi America Corp ·· **Singapore, : (65) 6221 0010**
  Web Page: http://www.nakamichi.com
Nanao USA Corp (see EIZO Nanao Tech Inc)
Nanosystems(see ISRA VISION SYSTEMS INC)
Napersoft Inc ··· **Naperville, IL: (630) 420-1515**
  Web Page: http://www.napersoft.com
National Assoc. Of Service Managers ······················ **Milwaukee, WI: (414) 466-6060**
  Web Page: http://www.nasm.com
National Computer Dist (see AmeriQuest)
National Computer Systems(see Pearson NCS) ···· **Bloomington, MN: (800) 328-6172**
  Tech:(800) 338-5544   Toll Free:(800) 336-3426
  Web Page: http://www.ncs.com
National Data Corp (see NDC Health)
National Graphic Supply ·· **Albany, NY: (800) 223-7130**
  Toll Free:(800) 223-7130
  Web Page: http://www.ngscorp.com
National Instruments ·· **Austin, TX: (512) 794-0100**
  Tech:(512) 683-0100
  Web Page: http://www.natinst.com
National Parts Depot (800) 227-8274
  Toll Free:(800) 227-8274
National Semi Conductor ······································ **Santa Clara, CA: (408) 721-5000**
  Toll Free:(800) 272-9959
  Web Page: http://www.national.com
National Technical Info Service ······························ **Springfield, VA: (703) 605-6000**
  Tech:(703) 605-6585   Toll Free:(800) 553-6847
  Web Page: http://www.ntis.gov
Natural intelligence (see Circle.com)
  Business Solutions)
  Web Page: http://www.microsoft.com/businesssolutions/default
Navitar ·· **Rochester, NY: (585) 359-4000**
  Toll Free:(800) 828-6778
  Web Page: http://www.navitar.com
Nbase-Xyplex (see I Touch Comm.)
NCE Computer Group ··· **El Cajon, CA: (619) 212-3000**
  Tech:(800) 767-2587   Toll Free:(800) 562-1600
  Web Page: http://www.ncegroup.com
NCR Corp ··· **Dayton, OH: (937) 445-1936**
  Tech:(800) 262-7782   Toll Free:(800) 225-5627
  Web Page: http://www.ncr.com
NCR Microelectronics (see LSI Logic)
NDC Communications (see SOHOware)
NDC Health ··· **Atlanta, GA: (404) 728-2000**
  Tech:(404) 728-2000   Toll Free:(800) 778-6711
  Web Page: http://www.ndchealth.com
Neam Co ··· **Boston, MA: (800) 937-1300**
  Toll Free:(800) 937-1300
  Web Page: http://www.neamco.com
NEBS Software ·· **Groton, MA: (800) 225-6380**
  Tech:(800) 225-9540   Toll Free:(800) 225-9540
  Web Page: http://www.nebs.com
NEC America Inc ··· **Irving, TX: (214) 262-2000**
  Web Page: http://www.necus.com
NEC Business Network Solutions Inc ···························· **Irving, TX: (214) 262-6000**
  Web Page: http://www.necbns.com
NEC Computers Inc ··· **Santa Clara, CA: (800) 632-4525**
  Toll Free:(800) 632-4525
  Web Page: http://www.nec-computers.com
NEC Electronics Inc ··· **Santa Clara, CA: (408) 588-6000**

Web Page: http://www.necel.com
Semiconductors··(408) 588-6000
  Tech:(800) 366-9782   Toll Free:(800) 366-9782
  Web Page: http://www.necel.com
  NEC Solutions (America), Inc.)

NEC Technologies Inc(see NEC Solutions) ······· Rancho Cordov, CA: (916) 463-7000
  Toll Free:(800) 632-4636
  Web Page: http://www.necsam.com

NEC USA Inc··· New York, NY: (212) 326-2400
  Toll Free:(800) 338-9549
  Web Page: http://www.necus.com

Needhams Electronics··· Sacramento, CA: (916) 924-8037
  Web Page: http://www.needhams.com

Nemetschek N.A.··· Columbia, MD: (410) 290-5114
  Tech:(410) 290-8050   Toll Free:(888) 646-4223
  Web Page: http://www.nemetschek.net

Neo-Core(now Xpriori)······························· Colorado Springs, CO: (719) 527-1315
  Web Page: http://www.xpriori.com

NeoMagic Corp··· Santa Clara, CA: (408) 988-7020
  Web Page: http://www.neomagic.com

Neoware··· King Of Prussia, PA: (610) 277-8300
  Tech:(800) 437-1551   Toll Free:(800) 437-1551
  Web Page: http://www.neoware.com

Net Acquire ·· Kirkland, WA: (425) 576-0822
  Toll Free:(888) 675-1122
  Web Page: http://www.realtimeint.com

Net Objects Inc··· Jacksonville, FL: (877) 729-8625
  Toll Free:(877) 729-8625
  Web Page: http://www.netobjects.com

NET Silicon Inc··· Waltham, MA: (781) 647-1234
  Toll Free:(800) 243-2333
  Web Page: http://www.netsilicon.com

Net USA Inc·· Highland, IN: (219) 934-9042
  Toll Free:(800) 266-5906
  Web Page: http://www.net-usa-inc.com

net-linx PS·· Sacramento, CA: (916) 830-2400
  Web Page: http://www.nxps.com

Net.com··· Fremont, CA: (510) 713-7300
  Tech:(703) 948-1999   Toll Free:(800) 234-4638
  Web Page: http://www.net.com

net.Genesis Corp(now SPSS Inc)··· Chicago, IL: (312) 651-3000
  Toll Free:(800) 525-4980
  Web Page: http://www.netgen.com

Net2Net (see Visual Networks Broadband)

Netaccess (see Brooktrout Tech.)

Netegrity Inc·· Waltham, MA: (781) 890-1700
  Tech:(781) 890-1700   Toll Free:(800) 325-9870
  Web Page: http://www.netegrity.com

Netergy Networks (see 8 X 8 Inc)

NETg·· Naperville, IL: (630) 369-3000
  Tech:(877) 561-6384   Toll Free:(800) 265-1900
  Web Page: http://www.netg.com

Netgear Inc·· Santa Clara, CA: (408) 907-8000
  Tech:(800) 211-2069   Toll Free:(888) 638-4327
  Web Page: http://www.netgear.com

NetIQ Corp··· San Jose, CA: (408) 856-3000
  Toll Free:(888) 323-6768
  Web Page: http://www.netiq.com

Netis Technology Inc··· Milpitas, CA: (408) 263-0368

Phone Directory

Tech:(408) 263-0395
Web Page: http://www.netistech.com

NetManage ·· **Cupertino, CA: (408) 973-7171**
   Tech:(800) 786-2202   Toll Free:(800) 352-3270
   Web Page: http://www.netmanage.com/
   35 New England Business Center·············(978) 685-4000
   Web Page: http://www.netmanage.com

Netopia·· **Billerica, MA: (978) 262-1700**
   Marketplace Tower·······························(510) 420-7400
   Web Page: http://www.netopia.com

NetPro Computing·································· **Phoenix, AZ: (620) 346-3600**
   Tech:(620) 346-3670   Toll Free:(800) 998-5090
   Web Page: http://www.netpro.com

Netrix (see Nex Networks)

Netscape Communications Corp ···············**Mountain View, CA: (650) 254-1900**
   Toll Free:(800) 411-0707
   Web Page: http://www.netscape.com

NetSilicon Inc·································· **Waltham, MA: (781) 647-1234**
   Tech:(781) 647-1234   Toll Free:(800) 243-2333
   Web Page: http://www.netsilicon.com

NetTest Inc·································· **Utica, NY: (315) 266-5000**
   Toll Free:(800) 443-6154
   Web Page: http://www.gnnettest.com

NetTest Inc (see NetTest)
   Web Page: http://www.gnnettest.com

netViz Corp·································· **Gaithersburg, MD: (581) 486-4411**
   Tech:(888) 832-4340   Toll Free:(800) 827-1856
   Web Page: http://www.netviz.com

Netwave Tech (see Bay Networks)

Network Appliance·································· **Sunnyvale, CA: (408) 822-6000**
   Tech:(408) 822-4700   Toll Free:(888) 463-8277
   Web Page: http://www.netapp.com
   Magic Solutions (now Remedy)················(800) 966-9695
   Tech:(800) 338-8754   Toll Free:(800) 966-2442
   Web Page: http://www.remedy.com
   McAfee··(800) 338-8754
   Tech:(972) 963-8000   Toll Free:(800) 338-8754
   Web Page: http://www.mcafee.com
   McAfee Software Division·······················(800) 338-8754
   Tech:(972) 963-8000   Toll Free:(800) 338-8754
   Web Page: http://www.nai.com
   PGP··(888) 747-3011
   Sniffer··(800) 338-8754
   Tech:(800) 338-8754

Network Communications Corp···············**Bloomington, MN: (763) 862-8744**
   Tech:(763) 862-8744
   Web Page: http://www.netcommcorp.com

Network Computing Devices ······················ **Portland, OR: (503) 431-8600**
   Web Page: http://www.ncd.com

Network Controls Intl Inc·························· **Charlotte, NC: (704) 527-4357**
   Tech:(704) 527-4357
   Web Page: http://www.nci-inc.com

Network General Corp (see Network Assoc)

Network Software Associates(see ASG Software

Network Wizards·································· **Menlo Park, CA: (650) 326-2060**
   Web Page: http://www.nw.com

Network-1 Security Solutions (Out of Bus.)

NeuralWare Inc ·································· **Carnegie, PA: (412) 278-6280**
   Tech:(412) 278-6289   Toll Free:(888) 963-8766
   Web Page: http://www.neuralware.com

Neuro Logic Systems ·· Camarillo, CA: (805) 389-5435
  Web Page: http://www.touch-dvd.com

Nevrona Designs ·· Chandler, AZ: (480) 491-5492
  Toll Free:(888) 776-4765
  Web Page: http://www.nevrona.com

New England Photoconductor ································· Norton, MA: (508) 285-5561
  Toll Free:(888) 727-7273
  Web Page: http://www.nepcorp.com

New Soft America Inc ·· Fremont, CA: (510) 445-8600
  Tech:(510) 445-8616
  Web Page: http://www.newsoftinc.com

New Vision Technology Inc ····················· Incline Village, NV: (775) 832-3860
  Web Page: http://www.3d-web.com

New World Computing Inc (see 3DO)

NewCom Inc (out of business)
  Eidon a division of Newell Rubbermaid ········· (800) 446-5652
  Toll Free:(800) 827-5055

NewGen Imaging Sys (see Imaging Tech)

Newpoint (see Power Sentry)

Newport Corp ·· Irvine, CA: (949) 863-3144
  Toll Free:(800) 222-6440
  Web Page: http://www.newport.com

Newport Systems (see Cisco Systems)

NewTek ··· San Antonio, TX: (210) 370-8000
  Tech:(210) 341-8444   Toll Free:(800) 862-7837
  Web Page: http://www.newtek.com

NewWave Technologies Inc ···························· Gaithersburg, MD: (301) 948-5222
  Toll Free:(800) 536-5222
  Web Page: http://www.newwavetech.com

NexGen Inc (see Advanced Micro Devices)

Nexpress Solutions ·· Rochester, NY: (585) 253-5224
  Toll Free:(877) 446-3977
  Web Page: http://www.nexpress.com

Next Page ·· Draper, UT: (801) 748-4400
  Toll Free:(800) 543-6546
  Web Page: http://www.nextpage.com

Nextgrid Inc (see Power Kinetics)

Nextira ·· Houston, TX: (800) 324-2222
  Toll Free:(800) 324-2222
  Web Page: http://www.nextiraone.com

NHC Communications ···································· Mount Royal, QC: (514) 735-2741
  Tech:(514) 734-4326   Toll Free:(888) 831-2077
  Web Page: http://www.nhc.com

Nikon Inc ·· Melville, NY: (631) 547-4200
  Tech:(800) 645-6678   Toll Free:(800) 526-4566
  Web Page: http://www.nikonusa.com
  Digital Imaging ·· (631) 547-4200
  Toll Free:(800) 645-6689
  Web Page: http://www.nikonusa.com

Nimax Inc ··· San Diego, CA: (858) 452-2220
  Tech:(858) 452-2220   Toll Free:(800) 876-4629
  Web Page: http://www.nimax.com

Nintendo of America ··· Redmond, WA: (800) 255-3700
  Toll Free:(800) 255-3700
  Web Page: http://www.nintendo.com

Nippon Pulse America ·· Radford, VA: (540) 633-1677
  Web Page: http://www.nipponpulse.com

Nirvana Systems Inc ·· Austin, TX: (512) 345-2566
  Tech:(512) 345-2592   Toll Free:(800) 880-0338

Web Page: http://www.nirv.com

Nisus Software Inc .... Solana Beach, CA: (858) 481-1477
Tech:(858) 481-1584   Toll Free:(800) 890-3030
Web Page: http://www.nisus.com

Niwot Networks .... Longmont, CO: (303) 772-8664
Toll Free:(800) 657-3278
Web Page: http://www.niwot.com

Nlynx/Decision Data .... Austin, TX: (512) 301-8000
Tech:(888) 659-6967   Toll Free:(800) 328-2696
Web Page: http://www.nlynx.com

NMB Technologies Inc .... Chatsworth, CA: (818) 341-3355
Web Page: http://www.nmbtech.com

Noesis Vision Inc .... Montreal, QC: (514) 846-0009

Nohau Corp .... Campbell, CA: (408) 866-1820
Toll Free:(888) 886-6428
Web Page: http://www.nohau.com

Nokia Americas .... Irving, TX: (972) 894-5000
Tech:(800) 483-7952   Toll Free:(888) 665-4228
Web Page: http://www.nokia.com

Nolo.com .... Berkeley, CA: (510) 549-1976
Tech:(510) 549-4660   Toll Free:(800) 728-3555
Web Page: http://www.nolo.com

Nombas Inc .... Medford, MA:
Web Page: http://www.nombas.com

NoRad Corp .... Los Angeles, CA: (323) 937-1562
Web Page: http://www.noradcorp.com

Norpix .... Montreal, PC: (514) 846-0009
Web Page: http://www.norpix.com

Nortech Systems .... Merrifield, MN: (218) 765-3151
Web Page: http://www.nortechsys.com/intercon

Nortel Networks Inc .... Santa Clara, CA: (408) 495-2400
Toll Free:(800) 466-7835
Web Page: http://www.nortelnetworks.com

Nortel Networks Inc .... Richardson, TX: (972) 684-1000
Tech:(800) 466-7835   Toll Free:(800) 667-8437
Web Page: http://www.nortelnetworks.com

Micom Communications Corp .... (805) 583-8600
Tech:(800) 466-7835
Web Page: http://www.micom.com

North American Coating Laboratories .... Cleveland, OH: (440) 442-9277
Toll Free:(866) 216-6225
Web Page: http://www.nacl.com

North Edge Software (see Sage USA Inc)

Northrop Grumman .... Herndon, VA: (703) 713-4000
Web Page: http://www.northropgrummanit.com

Norton-Lambert Corp .... Santa Barbara, CA: (805) 964-6767
Tech:(805) 964-6767
Web Page: http://www.norton-lambert.com

Nova Development Corp .... Calabasas, CA: (818) 591-9600
Web Page: http://www.novadevelopment.com

Novadigm Inc .... Mahwah, NJ: (201) 512-1000
Tech:(201) 512-7800   Toll Free:(800) 626-6682
Web Page: http://www.novadigm.com

NovaLogic Inc .... Calabasas, CA: (818) 880-1997
Web Page: http://www.novalogic.com

Novarra Inc .... Arlington Hts, IL: (847) 368-7800
Toll Free:(800) 490-9557
Web Page: http://www.novarra.com

Novastor Corporation .... Simi Valley, CA: (805) 579-6700

Tech:(805) 579-6700
Web Page: http://www.novastor.com

Novell Corporation ··· **Provo, UT: (801) 861-4000**
  Tech:(800) 858-4000   Toll Free:(800) 638-9273
  Web Page: http://www.novell.com

Novell Corporation ··· **San Jose, CA: (408) 961-1021**
  DeveloperNet ·· (801) 861-5281
  Tech:(801) 861-5544   Toll Free:(800) 733-9673
  Web Page: http://developer.novell.com
  Education ··· (800) 233-3382
  Tech:(801) 861-3382   Toll Free:(800) 233-3382
  Evaluation Software Program ······································ 0
  Hibbert Group ··· (303) 297-1634
  Toll Free:(800) 377-4136
  Support Connection ··· (800) 858-4000
  Toll Free:(800) 858-4000

Novellus ··· **San Jose, CA: (408) 943-9700**
  Web Page: http://www.novellus.com

Now Software (see Qualcomm)

nStor Technologies ··· **Carlsbad, CA: (760) 683-2500**
  Web Page: http://www.nstor.com

nStor Technologies ··· **San Diego, CA: (760) 683-2500**
  Web Page: http://www.nstor.com

Nuclear Associates ··· **Hicksville, NY: (516) 870-0100**
  Toll Free:(888) 466-8257
  Web Page: http://www.cardinal.com
  National Instruments ··· (512) 683-0100
  Web Page: http://www.ni.com

Number Nine Visual (see S3 Inc.)

Numega Tech. (see Compuware NuMega)

Numeridex Inc ··· **Wheeling, IL: (847) 541-8840**
  Tech:(800) 328-0727   Toll Free:(800) 323-7737
  Web Page: http://www.numeridex.com

Numonics Corp ··· **Montgomeryville, PA: (215) 362-2766**
  Toll Free:(800) 523-6716
  Web Page: http://www.numonics.com

Nur America Inc ·· **Moonachie, NJ: (210) 708-2100**
  Web Page: http://www.nur.com

NVIDIA Corp ··· **Santa Clara, CA: (408) 486-2000**
  Web Page: http://www.nvidia.com

Nview Corp
  Web Page: http://www.nview.com
  NSGDatacom, Inc ·· (703) 793-2000
  Web Page: http://www.netrix.com

Nxtwave Communications ··································· **Langhorne, PA: (267) 757-1100**
  Tech:(949) 585-1800
  Web Page: http://www.nsgdata.com

O'Reilly and Associates Inc ······························· **Sebastopol, CA: (707) 829-0515**
  Toll Free:(800) 998-9938
  Web Page: http://www.oreilly.com

Oak Technology(see Zoran) ································ **Sunnyvale, CA: (408) 796-2260**
  Web Page: http://www.zoran.com

Oberon Software (see On Display)

Object Design (see Excelon Corp)

Object Design(see Progress Software)

Object Management Group ·································· **Needham, MA: (781) 444-0404**
  Web Page: http://www.omg.org

Object/FX ·· **Minneapolis, MN: (866) 900-2002**
  Web Page: http://www.objectfx.com

ObjectSpace Inc(seeRecursion Software, Inc.)

Observera ···································· Chantilly, VA: (703) 378-3153
  Toll Free:(800) 444-6905
  Web Page: http://www.observera.com

Oce-USA Inc ···································· Chicago, IL: (773) 714-8500
  Toll Free:(877) 803-2621
  Web Page: http://www.oceusa.com

Ocean Group (see Denco Manufacturing)

Ocean Info Systems (see Denco Mfg.)

Ocean Isle Soft (see Stac Software)
  JDS Uniphase ···································· (707) 545-6440
  Tech:(800) 545-6254   Toll Free:(800) 545-6254
  Web Page: http://www.ocli.com

Octave Systems Inc ···································· Campbell, CA: (408) 866-8424
  Toll Free:(800) 626-8539
  Web Page: http://www.octave.com

Octel Communications (see Lucent Tech)

ODS Networks (see Intrusion.com)

Odyssey Computing Inc ···································· San Diego, CA: (858) 623-3310
  Toll Free:(800) 965-7224
  Web Page: http://www.odysseyinc.com

Oem Sales ···································· West Lynn, MA: (781) 595-8300
  Toll Free:(877) 595-8300
  Web Page: http://www.oem-sales.com

OKI Network Technologies ···································· Sunnyvale, CA: (408) 737-6477
  Tech:(408) 737-6401   Toll Free:(800) 641-8909
  Web Page: http://www.okint.com

Oki Semiconductor ···································· Sunnyvale, CA: (408) 720-1900
  Web Page: http://www.okisemi.com

Oki Telecom ···································· Suwanee, GA: (678) 482-9640
  Toll Free:(800) 554-3112
  Web Page: http://www.oki.com

Okidata Americas ···································· Mt. Laurel, NJ: (856) 235-2600
  Tech:(800) 634-0089   Toll Free:(800) 654-3282
  Web Page: http://www.okidata.com

Okino Computer Graphics ···································· Mississauga, ON: (905) 672-9328
  Toll Free:(888) 336-5466
  Web Page: http://www.okino.com

Okna Corp (Out of Business)

Olitec America(no USA information)

Olympus America Inc ···································· Melville, NY: (631) 844-5000
  Tech:(800) 622-6372   Toll Free:(800) 798-2777
  Web Page: http://www.olympusamerica.com
  Consumer Products ···································· (800) 347-4027
  Diagnostic Systems
  Toll Free:800-798-2777
  Digital Cameras ···································· (888) 553-4448
  Toll Free:888-553-4448
  Digital Tech Support
  Toll Free:(888) 553-4448
  Surgical Products
  Toll Free:800-798-2777

Omega Research Inc (see Trade Station)

Omega.com ···································· Stamford, CT: (203) 359-1660
  Tech:(800) 848-4286   Toll Free:(800) 622-2378
  Web Page: http://www.omega.com

Omni Data Systems ···································· Wildwood, MO: (636) 273-6800
  Tech:(636) 273-6720   Toll Free:(800) 766-2449
  Web Page: http://www.omni1.com

Omnicomp Systems(Out of Business)

OmniMedia ·· **Mendham, NJ: (908) 879-3244**
Web Page: http://www.omedia.com

Omniprint Inc (see Digital Design Inc)

OmniRim Solutions ································ **Seattle, WA: (604) 685-4111**
Toll Free:(866) 666-4746
Web Page: http://www.omnirim.com

Omnitrend ·· **Burlington, CT: (860) 673-8910**
Tech:(860) 673-8910
Web Page: http://www.omnitrend.com

Omnivision Technologies ···················· **Sunnyvale, CA: (408) 733-3030**
Tech:(408) 542-3000
Web Page: http://www.ovt.com

Omron Advanced Systems Inc ·············· **Santa Clara, CA: (408) 727-6644**
Web Page: http://www.omron.com

Omron Electronics Inc ·························· **Schamburg, IL: (847) 285-7011**
Toll Free:(800) 556-6766
Web Page: http://www.omron.com/oei

On Display (see Vignette)

On Technology Corp (see Symantec)

OneOnOne Computer Training ·············· **Addison, IL: (800) 424-8668**
Tech:(800) 424-8668   Toll Free:(800) 424-8668
Web Page: http://www.oootraining.com

OnHealth Network (see Web MD)

OPS Inc. ·· **(303) 741-5641**
Toll Free:(800) 445-4824
Web Page: http://www.powersupply.com
Only put a name here if 2 or more records ····· **(111) 111-1111**
Tech:(333) 333-3333   Toll Free:(222) 222-2222

Ontar Corp ·· **N. Andover, MA: (978) 689-9622**
Web Page: http://www.ontar.com

Ontario Systems ·································· **Muncie, IN: (765) 751-7000**
Toll Free:(800) 283-3227
Web Page: http://www.ontariosystems.com

Ontrack Computer (see Ontrack Data Int.)

Ontrack Data International ···················· **Eden Prairie, MN: (952) 937-5161**
Tech:(952) 937-2121   Toll Free:(800) 872-2599
Web Page: http://www.ontrack.com

Opcode Systems (see Gibson Musical)

Open Connect Systems Inc ·················· **Dallas, TX: (972) 484-5200**
Tech:(972) 888-0420   Toll Free:(800) 551-5881
Web Page: http://www.openconnect.com

Open Doors Software ···························· **San Diego, CA: (850) 755-2868**
Toll Free:(800) 923-8463
Web Page: http://www.opendoors.com

Open Market (see Next Page)

Open Route Networks (see Nex Networks)

Open Systems Inc ································ **Shakopee, MN: (952) 403-5700**
Tech:(800) 582-5000   Toll Free:(800) 328-2276
Web Page: http://www.osas.com

Open Text Inc ·· **Livonia, MI: (734) 542-5955**
Tech:(519) 888-9933   Toll Free:(800) 559-5955
Web Page: http://www.opentext.com

Open TV ·· **San Franisco, CA: (415) 962-5000**
Web Page: http://www.opentv.com

Optelecom ·· **Germantown, MD: (301) 444-2200**
Tech:(301) 444-2273   Toll Free:(800) 293-4237
Web Page: http://www.optelecom.com

Opteon Corp ·· **Cambridge, MA: (617) 520-6658**

Web Page: http://www.opteontech.com

Optern(Out 0f Business)

OPTi Inc ································· Mountain View, CA: (650) 625-8787
Web Page: http://www.opti.com

Optibase Inc ···························· Mountain View, CA: (650) 230-2400
Tech:(650) 903-4900   Toll Free:(800) 451-5101
Web Page: http://www.optibase.com

Optical Cable Corp ····························· Roanoke, VA: (800) 622-7711
Tech:(540) 265-0690   Toll Free:(800) 622-7711
Web Page: http://www.occfiber.com

Optical Data Systems (see ODS Networks)

Optical Electronics Inc ························· Tucson, AZ: (520) 889-8811
Web Page: http://www.oei-az.com

Optical Image Technology ················ State College, PA: (814) 238-0038
Web Page: http://www.opticaltech.com

Optical Laser Inc ························ Huntington Beach, CA: (800) 776-9215
Toll Free:(800) 776-9215
Web Page: http://www.opticallaser.com

Opticom Technologies ························ Vancouver, BC: (604) 682-2265

Optika Imaging Systems Inc (see Stellebt)

Optima Technology Corp ··························· Irvine, CA: (949) 476-0515
Web Page: http://www.optimatech.com

Optio Software ······························· Alpharetta, GA: (770) 576-3500
Web Page: http://www.optiosoftware.com

Optiquest (see Viewsonic)

Opto-Knowledge Systems ······················ Torrance, CA: (310) 371-4445
Web Page: http://www.techexpo.com/opto-knowledge

Optoma Technology Inc ························· Milpitas, CA: (408) 383-3700
Toll Free:(888) 289-6786
Web Page: http://www.optomausa.com

Optronics ······································ Goleta, CA: (805) 968-3568
Toll Free:(800) 796-8909
Web Page: http://www.optronics.com

EmFast ······································· (866) 436-3278
Web Page: http://www.facsys.com

ORA Electronics (Out of Business)

Oracle Corp ·························· Redwood Shores, CA: (650) 506-7000
Tech:(800) 223-1711   Toll Free:(800) 542-1170
Web Page: http://www.oracle.com

Orad ·· New York, NY: (212) 931-6723
Web Page: http://www.orad-ny.com

Orange Micro Inc ···························· Anaheim, CA: (714) 779-2772
Tech:(714) 779-2772
Web Page: http://www.orangemicro.com

Orbit Enterprises Inc ························ Glen Ellyn, IL: (800) 767-6724
Tech:(630) 469-3405   Toll Free:(800) 767-6724
Web Page: http://www.digitize.com

Orchid Tech (see Diamond Multimedia)

Oregon Micro Systems ························ Beaverton, OR: (503) 629-8081
Toll Free:(800) 707-8111
Web Page: http://www.omsmotion.com

Origin Instruments ·························· Grand Prairie, TX: (972) 606-8740
Web Page: http://www.orin.com

Origin Systems Inc ······························· Austin, TX: (512) 434-4263
Tech:(512) 434-4357   Toll Free:(800) 245-4525
Web Page: http://www.origin.ea.com

OriginLab Corp ·························· Northampton, MA: (800) 969-7720
Tech:(415) 586-2013   Toll Free:(800) 969-7720
Web Page: http://www.originlab.com

Ornetix Network Prod. (see Store Logic)
OSC (see Macromedia)
Osicom (see NETsilicon)
Ositech Communications·······································Guelph, Ontario, : (519) 836-8063
  Tech:(800) 563-2386   Toll Free:(888) 674-8324
  Web Page: http://www.ositech.com
OTC (see Output Tech Corp)
OTG Software Inc (see LEGATO Software) ·········Mountain View, CA: (650) 210-7000
  Tech:(877) 534-2867
  Web Page: http://www.legato.com
Output Technology Corp (OTC)································Spokane, WA: (509) 536-0468
  Tech:(509) 533-1268   Toll Free:(800) 468-8788
  Web Page: http://www.output.com
Overland Data Inc···San Diego, CA: (858) 571-5555
  Tech:(858) 571-5555   Toll Free:(800) 729-8725
  Web Page: http://www.overlanddata.com
P.I. Engineering Inc ···Williamston, MI: (517) 655-5523
  Tech:(517) 655-5523   Toll Free:(800) 628-3185
  Web Page: http://www.piengineering.com
Pacific Digital Corp···Irvine, CA: (949) 252-1111
  Tech:(888) 999-0732   Toll Free:(888) 333-6732
  Web Page: http://www.1pdc.com
Pacific Image Communications Inc ·····················S Pasadena, CA: (626) 441-2533
  Web Page: http://www.supervoice.com
Pacific Magtron Inc··Milpitas, CA: (408) 956-8888
  Tech:(408) 956-8888
  Web Page: http://www.pacmag.com
Pacific Microelectronics (see Net USA)
Packard Bell/NEC (888) 410-6303
Page Digital Inc··Englewood, CO: (800) 569-1122
  Toll Free:(800) 569-1122
  Web Page: http://www.pagedigital.com
Paladin Tools···Oilville,, VA: (804) 550-1121
  Toll Free:(800) 272-8665
  Web Page: http://www.paladin-tools.com
Palindrome Corp (see Seagate Software)
Palisade Corp···Newfield, NY: (607) 277-8000
  Toll Free:(800) 432-7475
  Web Page: http://www.palisade.com
Palm Inc··Milpitas, CA: (408) 503-7000
  Web Page: http://www.palmone.com
Palm Inc (Out of Business)
Palo Alto Software··Eugene, OR: (541) 683-6162
  Tech:(888) 752-6776   Toll Free:(800) 229-7526
  Web Page: http://www.palo-alto.com
Panacea (see Spacetec IMC)
Panamax··Petaluma, CA: (707) 283-5900
  Toll Free:(800) 472-5555
  Web Page: http://www.panamax.com
Panasonic Broadcast & Television System ···········Los Angeles, CA: (323) 436-3500
  Toll Free:(800) 222-0741
  Web Page: http://www.panasonic.com/broadcast
Panasonic Computer Per. (see Mashuta)
Panasonic Computer Solutions Co (800) 662-3537
  Toll Free:(800) 662-3537
Panasonic Document Imaging Co··························Secaucus, NJ: (201) 392-6280
  Web Page: http://www.panasonic.com/scanners
Panasonic Industrial Co···Milpitas,, CA: (408) 945-5600

Phone Directory

Battery Division .... (877) 726-2228
   Toll Free:(877) 726-2228
Battery Sales Group .... (877) 726-2228
Broadcast & Digital Systems .... (800) 526-6610
Business Equipment
Computer Peripherals .... (800) 726-2797
   Tech:(800) 346-4768
Customer Call Center .... (800) 211-7262
   Toll Free:(800) 211-7262
Document Imaging Company .... (800) 843-0080
   Toll Free:(800) 742-8086
Fax Diagnostic .... (800) 435-7329
   Toll Free:(800) 435-7329
Information Systems .... (847) 468-4600
Tech Support Center .... (888) 744-2424
Wireless Products .... (800) 414-4408
   Toll Free:(800) 414-4408
Panasonic Security/Digital Imaging .... Secaucus, NJ: (201) 392-6674
   Toll Free:(800) 528-6747
   Web Page: http://www.panasonic.com/mv
Panasonic Services Company (253) 395-7343
   Toll Free:(800) 833-9626
   Web Page: http://www.panasonic.com
   Computer & Systems .... (800) 742-8086
      Tech:(800) 843-0080   Toll Free:(800) 742-8086
      Web Page: http://www.panasonic.com
   Repairs .... (847) 468-5100
Panda Software USA .... Glendale, CA: (818) 543-6901
   Web Page: http://www.pandasoftware.com
Pantheon (see Zip2 Corp)
PaperClip Software Inc .... Hasbrouck Heights, NJ: (201) 329-6300
   Tech:(201) 329-6300   Toll Free:(800) 929-3503
   Web Page: http://www.paperclip.com
Paperless Corp .... Richardson, TX: (972) 235-4008
   Web Page: http://www.paperlesscorp.com
Paracel Inc .... Pasadena, CA: (626) 744-2000
   Tech:(626) 744-2000   Toll Free:(888) 727-2235
   Web Page: http://www.paracel.com
Paradigm Software (see Work Wise Soft)
Paradise (see Western Digital Corp)
Paradise Innovations (see SciTech)
Paradise Software Inc .... Manalapan, NJ: (732) 446-7009
   Web Page: http://www.paradise.com
Paradyne .... Largo, FL: (727) 530-2000
   Tech:(727) 530-2340   Toll Free:(800) 805-9493
   Web Page: http://www.paradyne.com
Paragon imaging .... Woburn, MA: (781) 937-9800
   Tech:(800) 937-4544   Toll Free:(800) 671-9890
   Web Page: http://www.paragon.com
Paragraph International (see PhatWare)
Parallax Inc .... Rocklin, CA: (916) 624-8333
   Tech:(916) 624-8333   Toll Free:(888) 512-1024
   Web Page: http://www.parallaxinc.com
Parametric Technology Corp .... Needham, MA: (781) 370-5000
   Tech:(781) 370-5260   Toll Free:(800) 477-6435
   Web Page: http://www.ptc.com
Parascript .... Boulder, CO: (303) 381-3100
   Toll Free:(888) 772-7478
   Web Page: http://www.parascript.com
Parc Place Digitalk (see Object Share)

Parsons Technology (see Learning Co)

Parts Now Inc ·· Madison, WI: (608) 276-8688
Toll Free:(800) 886-6688
Web Page: http://www.partsnowinc.com

Parvus ·· Salt Lake City, UT: (801) 483-1533
Web Page: http://www.parvus.com

Patton & Patton Software Corp ····················· Tucson, AZ: (520) 888-6500
Tech:(520) 888-6500   Toll Free:(800) 525-0082
Web Page: http://www.patton-patton.com

Patton Electronics Co ······························· Gaithersburg, MD: (301) 975-1000
Tech:(301) 975-1007
Web Page: http://www.patton.com

Paul Mace Software Inc ······································· Ashland, OR: (541) 488-2322
Tech:(541) 488-2322   Toll Free:(800) 944-0191
Web Page: http://www.pmace.com

PC America ·· Congers, NY: (845) 267-3500
Toll Free:(800) 722-6374
Web Page: http://www.pcamerica.com

PC Checks & Supplies (Now Checks Tomorrow) ······ Birmingham, AL: (800)467-0714
Toll Free:(800)467-0714
Web Page: http://www.checkstomorrow.com

PC Concepts Inc ·· San Fernando, CA: (818) 837-9495
Web Page: http://www.igsco.ne

PC Connection ·· Merrimack, NH: (603) 355-6005
Toll Free:(888) 213-0607
Web Page: http://www.pcconnection.com

PC Docs (see Hummingbird)

PC Doctor ··· Reno, NV: (775) 336-4000
Web Page: http://www.ws.com

PC Dynamics Inc ·· Oak Park, CA: (818)889-1741
Toll Free:(800) 888-1741
Web Page: http://www.pcdynamics.com

PC Guardian ··· San Rafael, CA: (415) 459-0190
Tech:(800) 440-0419   Toll Free:(800) 288-8126
Web Page: http://www.pcguardian.com

PC Power & Cooling Inc ··· Carlsbad, CA: (760) 931-5700
Tech:(760) 931-5700   Toll Free:(800) 722-6555
Web Page: http://www.pcpowercooling.com

PC-Kwik Corp (see Micro Design)

PC411 Inc (see Digital Asset Manage)

PCMCIA ··· San Jose, CA: (408) 433-2273
Web Page: http://www.pc-card.com

PCPI Tech (see Imaging Tech Corp)

PCPortable.com ··· Marlboro, NJ: (732) 780-9696
Web Page: http://www.pcportable.com

PDC Solutions Inc ··· King Of Prussia, PA: (610) 265-3300
Toll Free:(800) 654-4732
Web Page: http://www.pdc.com

PDE Technology Corp ·· Garden Grove, CA: (714) 799-1704
Web Page: http://www.pdetechnology.com

Peachtree Software ··· Norcross, GA: (770) 724-4000
Tech:(800) 336-1420   Toll Free:(800) 247-3224
Web Page: http://www.peachtree.com

Peerless Industries Inc ··· Melrose Park, IL: (708) 865-8870
Web Page: http://www.peerlessindustries.com

Pegasus Disk Technologies ······························· San Ramon, CA: (925) 314-1800
Tech:(925) 314-1800
Web Page: http://www.pegasus-ofs.com

Pegasus Imaging Corp ·· Tampa, FL: (813) 875-7575

Toll Free:(800) 875-7009
Web Page: http://www.imagn.com
Pelikan Inc (see NuKote International)
Pen Magic Soft (see Pivotal Graphics)
Pendragon Software Corp ·· Libertyville, IL: (847) 816-9660
Web Page: http://www.pendragonsoftware.com
Penn Camera ·· Beltsville, MD: (301) 210-7366
Web Page: http://www.penncamera.com
Penril Datability Net (see Hayes Corp)
Pentafour Software Solutions ·· Cerritos, CA: (562) 467-1141
Web Page: http://www.pentafourss.com
Pentax Technologies Corp ·· Golden, CO: (303) 460-1659
Tech:(303) 460-1820   Toll Free:(800) 543-6144
Web Page: http://www.pentaxtech.com
Pentax/Cosmicar Lens ·· Golden, CO: (303) 728-0255
Toll Free:(800) 877-0155
Web Page: http://www.pentax.com
Pentek ·· Upper Saddle River, NJ: (201) 818-5900
Web Page: http://www.pentek.com
People Soft / J. D. Edwards ·· Pleasanton, CA: (925) 225-3000
Toll Free:(800) 380-7638
Web Page: http://www.jdedwards.com
PeopleSoft ·· Pleasanton, CA: (925) 225-3000
Tech:(800) 477-5738   Toll Free:(888) 773-8277
Web Page: http://www.peoplesoft.com
Perceptive Solutions Inc ·· Duncanville, TX: (972) 298-4847
Tech:(214) 954-1774
Web Page: http://www.psidisk.com
Peregrine Systems ·· San Diego, CA: (858) 481-5000
Toll Free:(800) 638-5231
Web Page: http://www.peregrine.com
Peregrine Systems ·· San Diego, CA: (858) 481-5000
Toll Free:(800) 638-5231
Web Page: http://www.peregrine.com
PerfectData Corp ·· Simi Valley, CA: (805) 581-4000
Toll Free:(800) 973-7332
Web Page: http://www.perfectdata.com
Peripheral Enhancements Corp ···································· Ada, OK: (580) 310-6504
Toll Free:(800) 259-6565
Web Page: http://www.peripheral.com
Peripheral Imaging Corp ·· San Jose, CA: (408) 428-0123
Toll Free:(877) 756-5135
Web Page: http://www.p-imaging.com
Peripheral Repair Corp ·· Chatsworth, CA: (800) 627-3475
Toll Free:(800) 627-3475
Web Page: http://www.drive-experts.com
Perisol Technology ·· Santa Clara, CA: (408) 748-8306
Web Page: http://www.perisol.com
Perkin Elmer Optoelectronics ···································· Fremont, CA: (510) 748-8306
Toll Free:(800) 775-6786
Web Page: http://www.perkinelmer.com
Perle Systems inc ·· Nashville, TN: (615) 872-0770
Toll Free:(800) 467-3753
Web Page: http://www.perle.com
Perseus Development Corp ·· Braintree, MA: (781) 848-8100
Toll Free:(877) 737-7387
Web Page: http://www.perseusdevelopment.com
Persoft Inc (see Esker Inc)
Persona Technologies (see Monster Cable)

Phone Directory

Personal Tex Inc ·· San Francisco, CA: (415) 296-7550
  Toll Free:(800) 808-7906
  Web Page: http://www.pctex.com

Personal Training Systems (see CBT Sys)

Personics Corp (see Data Watch Corp)

Pervasive Software ·· Austin, TX: (512) 231-6000
  Toll Free:(800) 287-4383
  Web Page: http://www.pervasive.com

Pesa Switching Systems ·· Melville, NY: (631) 845-5020
  Toll Free:(800) 328-1008
  Web Page: http://www.pesa.com

Pesa Switching Systems ·· Huntsville, AL: (256) 726-9200
  Toll Free:(800) 323-7372
  Web Page: http://www.pesa.com

PFU Systems Inc ·· Santa Clara, CA: (408) 236.3000
  Web Page: http://www.pfusystems.com

Pharos Systems ·· East Rochester, NY: (585) 249-8999
  Tech:(877) 848-0397   Toll Free:(888) 864-7768
  Web Page: http://www.pharos.com

Phase 1 Technology Corp ··· Deer Park, NY: (631) 254-2600
  Toll Free:(800) 683-0068
  Web Page: http://www.phase1tech.com

Phase One ·· Melville, NY: (631) 547-8900
  Web Page: http://www.phaseone.com

PhatWare Corp ·· Mountain View, CA: (650) 559-5600
  Web Page: http://www.phatware.com

PHD - Pro Help Desk (see Computer Assoc)

Philips Consumer Electronics Corp ·································· Knoxville, TN: (865) 521-4316
  Tech:(865) 525-9516   Toll Free:(800) 326-6586
  Web Page: http://www.philips.com

Philips Electronics ··· New York, NY: (212) 536-0500
  Web Page: http://www.philipsusa.com

Philips Laser Magnetic Storage (see Plasmon)

Philips Magnavox (800) 531-0039
  Toll Free:(800) 531-0039
  Web Page: http://www.philipsusa.com
  Consumer Electronics ·· (865) 521-4316
    Tech:(865) 525-0234
    Web Page: http://www.magnavox.com
  Customer Care Center ·· (800) 531-0039
    Toll Free:(800) 531-0039
  Factory Service
    Toll Free:(800) 531-0039
  Laser Magnetic Storage ·· (719) 593-7900
    Tech:(719) 593-4393   Toll Free:(800) 777-5674
    Web Page: http://www.philipslms.com
  Repair Center Locations
    Toll Free:(800) 531-0039

Philtek Power ··· Blaine, WA: (360) 323-7252
  Toll Free:(800) 727-4877
  Web Page: http://www.philtek.com

Phoenix Imaging Machine Vision ···································· Livonia, MI: (248) 476-4200
  Web Page: http://www.phoeniximaging.com

Phoenix Technologies ··· Norwood, MA: (781) 551-5000
  Tech:(781) 551-4000   Toll Free:(800) 677-7300
  Web Page: http://www.phoenix.com

Phoenix Technologies ··· Milpitas, CA: (408) 570-1000
  Toll Free:(800) 677-7305
  Web Page: http://www.phoenix.com

Photo Channel Networks Inc ·· Vancouver BC, : (604) 893-8955

Web Page: http://www.photochannel.com

Photo-Sonics Inc ···················· Burbank, CA: (818) 842-2141
Web Page: http://www.photosonics.com

Photobit Corp ···················· Pasadena, CA: (626) 685-5100
Web Page: http://www.micron.com

Photodex corp ···················· Austin, TX: (512) 419-7000
Toll Free:(800) 377-4686
Web Page: http://www.photodex.com

PhotoDisc Inc (see Getty Images)

Photographic Solutions ···················· Onset, MA: (508) 759-2322
Toll Free:(800) 637-3212
Web Page: http://www.photosol.com

Photon Technology Intl ···················· Lawrenceville, NJ: (609) 896-0310
Toll Free:(877) 784-4349
Web Page: http://www.pti-nj.com

Photon Visions Systems Inc (Out of Business)

Photondynamics ···················· San Jose, CA: (408) 226-9900
Web Page: http://www.photondynamics.com

Photron USA ···················· San Diego, CA: (858) 684-3555
Toll Free:(800) 585-2129
Web Page: http://www.photron.com

Physician Micro Systems Inc ···················· Seattle, WA: (206) 441-2400
Toll Free:(800) 770-7674
Web Page: http://www.pmsi.com

Physimetrics ···················· Roswell, GA: (770) 642-6858
Web Page: http://www.physimetrics.com

Phytec America ···················· Bainbridge Island, WA: (206) 780-9047
Toll Free:(800) 278-9913
Web Page: http://www.phytec.com

Pictron Corp ···················· San Jose, CA: (408) 777-8111
Web Page: http://www.pictron.com

PictureTel Corp (see PolyCom Inc)

Piiceon ···················· Fremont, CA: (510) 252-0266
Toll Free:(800) 366-2983
Web Page: http://www.piiceon.com

Piller Inc ···················· Middletown, NY: (845) 355-5000
Tech:(800) 338-7781   Toll Free:(800) 597-6937
Web Page: http://www.piller.com

Pinnacle Data Systems Inc ···················· Columbus, OH: (614) 748-1150
Web Page: http://www.pinnacle.com

Pinnacle Micro Inc (Division of EZ Systems) ···················· Santa Ana, CA: (714) 662-4959
Web Page: http://www.pinnaclemicro.com

Pinnacle Systems ···················· Mountain View, CA: (650) 526-1600
Tech:(650) 237-1800   Toll Free:(888) 484-3366
Web Page: http://www.pinnaclesys.com

Pioneer Electronics ···················· Long Beach, CA: (800) 421-1404
Toll Free:(800) 872-4159
Web Page: http://www.pioneerelectronics.com

Pioneer New Media Technologies ···················· Long Beach, CA: (310) 835-7980
Web Page: http://www.pioneerelectronics.com

Pitney Bowes ···················· Stamford, CT: (230) 356-5000
Toll Free:(800) 574-8639
Web Page: http://www.pitneybowes.com

Pivar Computing Services Inc ···················· Buffalo Grove, IL: (847) 478-8000
Toll Free:(800) 266-8378
Web Page: http://www.pivar.com

Pivotal Corp ···················· Vancouver, B.C., : (604) 699-8000
Toll Free:(877) 748-6825
Web Page: http://www.pivotal.com

Pivotal Graphics Inc (Out of Business)

Pixar Animation Studios ························· **Emeryville, CA: (510) 752-3000**
Tech:(800) 937-3179   Toll Free:(800) 888-9856
Web Page: http://www.pixar.com

Pixel Translations ····························· **San Jose, CA: (408) 441-2200**
Tech:(408) 441-2260   Toll Free:(800) 749-4310
Web Page: http://www.pixeltranslations.com

Pixelink ···························· **Ottawa, ON, : (613) 247-1211**
Toll Free:(888) 484-8262
Web Page: http://www.pixelink.com

Pixelink Corp ·························· **Hudson, MA: (978) 562-4803**
Toll Free:(800) 222-2787
Web Page: http://www.pixelinkcorp.com

PixelTools Corp ······················· **Cupertino, CA: (408) 374-5327**
Web Page: http://www.pixeltools.com

Pixelvision Inc(Out of Business)

Pixelworks ···························· **Tualatin, OR: (503) 454-1750**
Web Page: http://www.pixelworks.com

Pixera Corp ···························· **Los Gatos, CA: (408) 341-1800**
Toll Free:(888) 474-9372
Web Page: http://www.pixera.com

Pixie Technologies (Out of Business)

PixTech (Out of Business)

PK Electronics (see Nextgrid Inc)

PKware Inc ··························· **Brown Deer, WI: (414) 354-8699**
Tech:(414) 354-8699
Web Page: http://www.pkware.com

Planettechnology ······················· **Evansville, IN: (800) 443-8594**
Toll Free:(800) 443-8594
Web Page: http://www.planettechnology.com

Plantronics Inc ······················· **Santa Cruz, CA: (831) 458-7700**
Tech:(831) 426-5858   Toll Free:(800) 544-4660
Web Page: http://www.plantronics.com

Plasmaco (see Panasonic) ················· **Highland, NY: (845) 883-6800**

Plasmon IDE Inc ······················· **Englewood, CO: (720) 873.2500**
Toll Free:(800) 451.6845
Web Page: http://www.plasmon.com

Platinum Software (see Epicor Soft.)

Platinum Technology (see Computer Assoc.)

Play Inc (see Global Streams)

Play Pro Software Inc ···················· **Santa Clara, CA: (408) 969-0800**
Web Page: http://www.playprosoft.com

Plextor ···························· **Fremont, CA: (510) 440-2000**
Toll Free:(800) 886-3935
Web Page: http://www.plextor.com

Plexus Software ······················· **Santa Clara, CA: (408) 748-4300**
Toll Free:(800) 999-5910
Web Page: http://www.plx.com

Plotworks Inc ························· **Ramona, CA: (858) 457-5090**
Web Page: http://www.plotworks.com

Plus and Minus Software Corp ··············· **Houston, TX: (713) 465-5645**
Tech:(877) 465-5645
Web Page: http://www.plusandminus.com

Plus Development Corp (see Quantum Corp)

PNY Electronics ······················· **Parsippany, NJ: (973) 515-9700**
Tech:(800) 234-4597   Toll Free:(800) 234-4597
Web Page: http://www.pny.com

Poet Software (see Versant Corp.)

Point 4 Data Corporation ························· Coasta Mesa, CA: (714) 755-6550
  Web Page: http://www.point4data.com
Point Grey Research ····························· Vancouver, BC: (604) 730-9937
  Web Page: http://www.ptgrey.com
PointCast Inc (see EntryPoint)
PointOfSale.com ································ Richland, WA: (509) 375-0598
  Toll Free:(888) 430-1685
  Web Page: http://www.pointofsale.com
Polaris Industries ······························ Norcross, GA: (678) 405-6080
  Toll Free:(800) 308-4204
  Web Page: http://www.polarisusa.com
Polaroid Corporation ···························· Waltham, MA: (781) 386-2000
  Tech:(800) 343-5000   Toll Free:(800) 343-5000
  Web Page: http://www.polaroid.com
Polhemus Inc ·································· Colchester, VT: (802) 655-3159
  Tech:(802) 655-3159   Toll Free:(800) 357-4777
  Web Page: http://www.polhemus.com
Polycom Inc ··································· Andover, MA: (978) 292-5000
  Tech:(800) 874-2835   Toll Free:(800) 765-9266
  Web Page: http://www.polycom.com
Polycom Inc ··································· Milpitas, CA: (408) 526-9000
  Tech:(408) 474-2050   Toll Free:(800) 765-9266
  Web Page: http://www.polycom.com
Polygon Inc ··································· Saint Louis, MO: (314) 787-0431
  Web Page: http://www.polygon.com
Polywell Computers Inc ·························· San Francisco, CA: (650) 871-3920
  Tech:(650) 887-3921   Toll Free:(800) 999-1278
  Web Page: http://www.polywell.com
Popkin Software & Systems ······················ New York, NY: (646) 346-8500
  Toll Free:(800) 732-5227
  Web Page: http://www.popkin.com
Port Inc (see Targus)
Portable Graphics (see Template Graph)
Portrait Displays Inc ··························· Pleasanton, CA: (925) 227-2700
  Web Page: http://www.portrait.com
POSitive Software (see PointOfSale.com)
Power Kinetics (located in the UK)
  Web Page: http://www.powerkinetics.com
Power Sentry ·································· Plymouth,, MN: (763) 557-8889
  Toll Free:(800) 852-4312
  Web Page: http://www.powersentry.com
Power Solutions Inc ···························· Roslyn Heights, NY: (516) 484-6689
  Web Page: http://www.powersolutions.com
  Verticent ································ (813) 226-2600
  Tech:(813) 229-8808   Toll Free:(800) 251-8449
  Web Page: http://www.powercerv.com
Powercom America Inc ·························· Fullerton, CA: (714) 525-8889
  Toll Free:(800) 666-8931
  Web Page: http://www.powercom-usa.com
Powercore Inc (see CE Software)
PowerFile ···································· Los Gatos, CA: (408) 969-7123
  Tech:(408) 354-6313   Toll Free:(866) 838-3669
  Web Page: http://www.powerfile.com
PowerLeap ··································· Branchburg, NJ: (908) 431-1973
  Toll Free:(866) 757 2537
  Web Page: http://www.powerleap.com
PowerProduction Software ························ Los Gatos, CA: (408) 297-7250
  Tech:(408) 297-7227   Toll Free:(800) 457-0383
  Web Page: http://www.powerproduction.com

PowerQuest Corp (see Symantec)
Powersoft Corp (see Sybase Inc)
PowerWare ·· Raleigh, NC: (919) 872-3020
  Toll Free:(800) 356-5794
  Web Page: http://www.powerware.com
Powerware (see Invensys Power Systems)
PowerWay Inc ····································· Indianapolis, IN: (317) 598-1760
  Toll Free:(800) 488-3227
  Web Page: http://www.powerwayinc.com
Poynting Products Inc ··························· Oak Park, IL: (708) 704-6310
  Web Page: http://www.poynting.com
PPT Vision ······································ Eden Prairie, MN: (952) 996-9500
  Web Page: http://www.pptvision.com
Prairie Group ································ West Des Moines, IA: (515) 225-3720
  Tech:(515) 225-4122
  Web Page: http://www.prgrsoft.com
Precision Instruments Inc ························· Knoxville, TN: (865) 558-4967
  Web Page: http://www.precision-instruments.com
Precision Powerhouse ··························· Minneapolis, MN: (612) 333-9111
  Web Page: http://www.power-house.com
Premenos Corp (see Peregrine Systems)
Premier Mounts ··································· Anaheim, CA: (800) 368-9700
  Toll Free:(800) 368-9700
  Web Page: http://www.premiermounts.com
Premio Computer ··························· City Of Industry, CA: (626) 839-3100
  Tech:(800) 568-6388   Toll Free:(800) 677-6477
  Web Page: http://www.premiopc.com
Prep Software ····································· Dallas, TX: (877) 283-3684
  Toll Free:(877) 283-3684
  Web Page: http://www.prepsoftware.com
Prescience (see Waterloo Maple Software)
Previo Inc (see Altiris Inc) ······················ San Diego, CA: (858) 794-4300
  Tech:(877) 977-3846   Toll Free:(800) 305-7822
  Web Page: http://www.previo.com
Primary Image ···································· Orlando, FL: (407) 382-7100
  Tech:(407) 540-1252   Toll Free:888-670-3233
  Web Page: http://www.primary-image.com
Primavera Systems Inc ······················ Bala Cynwyd, PA: (610) 667-8600
  Tech:(610) 668-3030   Toll Free:(800) 423-0245
  Web Page: http://www.primavera.com
PrimeArray Systems Inc ······················ Chelmsford, MA: (978) 654-6250
  Toll Free:(800) 433-5133
  Web Page: http://www.primearray.com
Primera Technology ···························· Plymouth, MN: (763) 475-6676
  Tech:(763) 475-6669   Toll Free:(800) 797-2772
  Web Page: http://www.primeratechnology.com
Princeton Digital ·································· Irvine, CA: (714) 619-8000
  Toll Free:(800) 747-6249
  Web Page: http://www.princetongraphics.com
Princeton Diskette Co ····················· Pt. Pleasant Beach, NJ: (732) 892-6136
  Tech:(732) 892-5655   Toll Free:(800) 426-0247
  Web Page: http://www.princetondisc.com
Princeton Gamma-Tech Inc ······················ Rocky Hill, NJ: (609) 924-7310
  Tech:609-924-8981
  Web Page: http://www.pgt.com
Princeton Review ································· New York, NY: (212) 874-8282
  Toll Free:(800) 273-8439
  Web Page: http://www.review.com
Printcafe Software Inc ·························· Pittsburgh, PA: (412) 456-1141

Phone Directory

Web Page: http://www.printcafe.com

Printer Works, The ··· Hayward, CA: (510) 670-2700
Tech:(425) 558-4549   Toll Free:(800) 832-1400
Web Page: http://www.printerworks.com

Printronix Inc ··· Irvine, CA: (800) 665-6210
Tech:714-368-2686   Toll Free:(800) 854-6463
Web Page: http://www.printronix.com

Pro CD Inc (see data by Acxiom)

Process Software Corp ································· Framingham, MA: (508) 879-6994
Tech:(508) 879-6994   Toll Free:(800) 722-7770
Web Page: http://www.process.com

Procom Technology ··· Irvine, CA: (949) 852-1000
Tech:(800) 800-8600   Toll Free:(800) 800-8600
Web Page: http://www.procom.com

Procomp USA Inc ·· Columbus, OH: (614) 272-0202
Toll Free:(800) 850-8649
Web Page: http://www.procomp.com

Professional Marketing Services ·················· Chandler, AZ: (480) 940-5400
Web Page: http://www.promarketinc.com

Programmer's Paradise Inc ······················· Shrewsbury, NJ: (732) 389-8950
Toll Free:(800) 445-7899
Web Page: http://www.programmers.com

Progress Software Corp ································· Bedford, MA: (781) 280-4000
Tech:(781) 280-4999   Toll Free:(800) 477-6473
Web Page: http://www.progress.com

Progressive Networks (see Real Networks)

Prometheus Products (Out of Business)

Promise Technology Inc ································· Milpitas, CA: (408) 228-6300
Toll Free:(800) 888-0245
Web Page: http://www.promise.com

Promptus Communications Inc ···················· Portsmouth, RI: (401) 683-6100
Web Page: http://www.promptus.com

ProSoft Corp ··· Dallas, TX:

Prostar Interactive MediaWorks ················ Vancouver, BC: (604)742-2930
Tech:(604) 273-4099   Toll Free:866-742-2930
Web Page: http://www.minicat.com

Proteon Inc (see Open Route Networks)

ProtoView Development (see Infragistics)

Provantage Corp ······································· North Canton, OH: (330) 494-8715
Tech:(330) 494-8715   Toll Free:(800) 336-1166
Web Page: http://www.provantage.com

Proview Technology ································· Garden Grove, CA: (714) 799-3899
Web Page: http://www.proview.net

ProVUE Development ···························· Huntington Beach, CA: (714) 841-7779
Tech:(714) 841-8779   Toll Free:(800) 966-7878
Web Page: http://www.provue.com

ProWorks ··· Corvalis, OR: (541) 752-9885
Web Page: http://www.proworks.com

Proxim Inc ·· Sunnyvale, CA: (408) 731-2700
Toll Free:(800) 229-1630
Web Page: http://www.proxim.com

Proxim IncThis location closed)

Proxima Corp (see In Focus)

PSI Integration (see Diamond Multimedia)

Psygnosis Ltd (see Sony Interactive)

PTFS Inc ·· Bethesda, MD: (301) 654-8088
Web Page: http://www.ptfs.com

Publishing Perfection ···································· Waukesha, WI: (262) 717-0600

Toll Free:(800) 782-5974
Web Page: http://www.publishingperfection.com

Pulnix America Inc ·· Sunnyvale, CA: (408) 747-0300
Tech:(408) 747-0300   Toll Free:(800) 445-5444
Web Page: http://www.pulnix.com

Pulse Digital ·· New York, NY: (212) 387-8800
Web Page: http://www.pulsedigital.com

Pulse Instruments ··· Torrance, CA: (310) 515-5330
Web Page: http://www.pulseinstruments.com
   Intellisync ··· (408) 321-7650
   Tech:(970) 351-6038   Toll Free:(800) 248-2795
   Web Page: http://www.intellisync.com

Punch! Software ··· Kansas City, MO: (816) 891-0025
Toll Free:(800) 365-4832
Web Page: http://www.punchsoftware.com

Q Imaging ·· Burnaby, BC: (604) 708-5061
Web Page: http://www.qimaging.com

QAD Inc ·· Carpinteria, CA: (805) 684-6614
Tech:(856) 273-8868   Toll Free:(888) 766-3495
Web Page: http://www.qad.com

Qantel Technologies Inc ····································· Hayward, CA: (510) 731-2080
Toll Free:(800) 666-3686
Web Page: http://www.qantel.com

QDI Computer ··· Fremont, CA: (510) 668-4933
Web Page: http://www.qdigrp.com

QLogic ··· Aliso Viejo, CA: (949) 389-6000
Tech:(952) 932-4040   Toll Free:(800) 662-4471
Web Page: http://www.qlogic.com
   Ancor Communications ································· (952) 932-4000
   Tech:(952) 932-4040   Toll Free:(800) 662-4471
   Web Page: http://www.qlogic.com

QMS Inc (see Konica Minolta) ······························ Mobile, AL: (251) 633-4300
Toll Free:(800) 523-2696
Web Page: http://www.minolta-qms.com

QNX Software Systems Ltd ································· Ottawa, ON: (613) 591-0931
Tech:(800) 363-9001   Toll Free:(800) 676-0566
Web Page: http://www.qnx.com
   Digital Peripheral Solutions Inc.) ··············· (714) 998-3440
   Tech:(714) 998-7113
   Web Page: http://www.qps-inc.com

Quadralay Corp (see Webworks.com)

Quadrasis ·· Waltham, MA: (781) 768-5911
Toll Free:(888) 569-3803
Web Page: http://www.quadrasis.com

Quadtel Corp (see Phoenix Technologies)

Qualcomm Inc ·· San Diego, CA: (858) 587-1121
Tech:(858) 658-1913
Web Page: http://www.qualcomm.com

Qualitas Inc ·· Shepherdstown, WV:
Web Page: http://www.qualitas.com

Quality America Inc ··· Tucson, AZ: (520) 722-6154
Tech:(800) 722-6154   Toll Free:(800) 643-9889
Web Page: http://www.qualityamerica.com

QualityLogic ·· Moorpark, CA: (805) 531-9030
Tech:(805) 531-9030   Toll Free:(800) 436-6292
Web Page: http://www.qualitylogic.com

Qualix Group (see Full Time Software)

Qualstar Corp ·· Simi Valley, CA: (805) 583-7744
Tech:(877) 444-1744   Toll Free:(888) 814-3975
Web Page: http://www.qualstar.com

Phone Directory

Qualtec Data Prod (see Curtis Computer)
Qualtek Electronic Corp ·· Mentor, OH: (440) 951-3300
   Tech:(440) 951-3300   Toll Free:(888) 258-3468
   Web Page: http://www.qualtekusa.com
Quantegy Inc ··· Opelika, AL: (334) 745-7643
   Toll Free:(800) 752-0732
   Web Page: http://www.quantegy.com
Quantitative Imaging (see Qimaging) ··················· Burnaby, B.C., : (604) 708-5061
   Web Page: http://www.qimaging.com
Quantum 3D ·· San Jose, CA: (408) 361-9999
   Web Page: http://www.quantum3d.com
Quantum Corp ··· San Jose, CA: (408) 944-4000
   Tech:(888) 827-3378   Toll Free:(800) 677-6268
   Web Page: http://www.quantum.com
   DLT Tape ·· (719) 536-5000
   Toll Free:(800) 677-6268
   Web Page: http://www.quantum.com
Quantum Data Inc ··· Elgin, IL: (847) 888-0450
   Toll Free:(888) 252-6133
   Web Page: http://www.quantumdata.com
Quark Inc ·· Denver, CO: (303) 894-8888
   Tech:(303) 894-8899   Toll Free:(800) 676-4575
   Web Page: http://www.quark.com
Quarter-Inch Cartridge Dr Stds ················· Santa Barbara, CA: (805) 687-7755
   Web Page: http://www.qic.org
Quarterdeck Corp (see Symantec Corp)
Quarton USA Co ·· San Antonio, TX: (210) 735-0280
   Toll Free:(800) 520-8435
   Web Page: http://www.quarton.com
Quercus Systems ·· Pacific Grove, CA: (831) 372-7399
   Toll Free:(800) 440-5944
   Web Page: http://www.quercus-sys.com
Quest Software ·· Toronto, ON: (416) 594-1026
   Tech:(800) 709-2947   Toll Free:(800) 663-4723
   Web Page: http://www.quest.com
Quest Software ··· Irvine, CA: (949) 754-8000
   Web Page: http://www.quest.com
Quick Eagle Networks ·· Sunnyvale, CA: (408) 745-6200
   Tech:(408) 745-4200   Toll Free:(888) 280-5465
   Web Page: http://www.quickeagle.com
QuickLogic Corp ··· Sunnyvale, CA: (408) 990-4000
   Web Page: http://www.quicklogic.com
Quicknet Technologies Inc ································· San Francisco, CA: (415) 864-5225
   Web Page: http://www.quicknet.net
QuickShot Technology Inc ······································· El Monte, CA: (626) 810-3890
   Tech:(626) 810-9550
   Web Page: http://www.quickshot.com
Quickstream ·· Colorado Springs, CO: (719) 520-1878
   Web Page: http://www.quickstream.com
Quill Corp ·· Palatine, IL: (800) 789-1331
   Tech:(800) 789-0041   Toll Free:(800) 982-3400
   Web Page: http://www.quillcorp.com
Qume (see Wyse Technology)
Qume Corp (see Data Technology)
Quvis Inc ··· Topeka, KS: (785) 272-3656
   Toll Free:(800) 554-8116
   Web Page: http://www.quvis.com
Quyen Systems (see netViz Corp)
QVS East ·· Romulus, MI: (734) 641-6700

Web Page: http://www.qvs.com

QVS West .... Las Vegas, NV: (702) 228-3670
  Web Page: http://www.qvs.com

Rabbit Software (see Tangram)

Racal Data Group (see Milgo Solutions)

Rackmount Equipment.com .... Atlanta, GA: (770) 491-1131
  Toll Free:(800) 959-3525
  Web Page: http://www.rackmountequipment.com

Racore Technology Corp .... West Valley City, UT: (801) 973-9779
  Web Page: http://www.racore.com

RAD Data Communications .... Mahwah, NJ: (201) 529-1100
  Tech:(201) 529-1100   Toll Free:(800) 444-7234
  Web Page: http://www.rad.com/usa

Rad technologies .... Mahwah, NJ: (201) 529-1100
  Tech:(877) 523-8105   Toll Free:(800) 444-7234
  Web Page: http://www.radusa.com

Radio Shack .... Fort Worth, TX: (817) 415-3700
  Toll Free:(800) 843-7422
  Web Page: http://www.radioshackcorporation.com

Radio Shack (see Tandy Corp)
  Radio Shack Customer Relations ....(817) 415-3200
    Web Page: http://www.radioshackcorporation.com
  Radio Shack Product Support Center ....(800) 843-7422
    Toll Free:(800) 843-7422
    Web Page: http://www.radioshack.com
  RadioShack.com
    Toll Free:(800) 442-7221
    Web Page: http://www.radioshack.com

RadioLan .... San Jose, CA: (408) 365-6200
  Tech:(408) 365-7675   Toll Free:(866) 272-3465
  Web Page: http://www.radiolan.com

Radisys Corp .... Hillsboro, OR: (503) 615-1100
  Tech:(503) 615-1640   Toll Free:(800) 950-0044
  Web Page: http://www.radisys.com

Radius Inc (see Digital Origin)

Radstone Technology Corp .... Woodcliff Lake, NJ: (201) 391-2700
  Toll Free:(800) 368-2738
  Web Page: http://www.radstone.com

Radvision Inc .... Fair Lawn, NJ: (201) 689-6300
  Web Page: http://www.radvision.com

RAG Electronics (see Test Equity)

Rail Systems Center .... Mount Vernon, PA: (412) 751-8470
  Web Page: http://www.lm.com/~urichard/rsc_1.htm

Raima Corp (see Centura Software)

Rainbow Mt. View (see Elan Computer)

Rainbow Technologies (merged SafeNet Inc) .... Irvine, CA: (949) 450-7300
  Web Page: http://www.rainbow.com

Rambus Inc .... Los Altos, CA: (650) 947-5000
  Web Page: http://www.rambus.com

Ramp Networks(see Nokia)

Rancho Technology Inc. .... Rancho Cucamonga, CA: (909) 987-3966
  Web Page: http://www.rancho.com

Rand McNally .... Skokie, IL: (800) 333-0136
  Tech:(847) 982-0944   Toll Free:(800) 234-0679
  Web Page: http://www.randmcnally.com

Rand Software (see Extended Systems)

Raosoft Inc .... Seattle, WA: (206) 525-4025
  Tech:(206) 525-4025
  Web Page: http://www.raosoft.com

Raritan Computer Inc ··· Somerset, NJ: (732) 764-8886
   Toll Free:(800) 724-8090
   Web Page: http://www.raritan.com

Raster OPS (see TrueVision)

Rational Software Corp (see IBM Rational) ················· Cupertino, CA: (408) 863-9900
   Tech:(800) 863-4000   Toll Free: (800) 426-7378
   Web Page: http://www-306.ibm.com/software/rational/

Raxco Software Inc ·· Gaithersburg, MD: (301) 527-0803
   Tech:(800) 836-3844   Toll Free:(800) 546-9728
   Web Page: http://www.raxco.com

Ray Dream (see MetaCreations)

Rayovac Corp ··· Madison, WI: (608) 275-3340
   Toll Free:(800) 237-7000
   Web Page: http://www.rayovac.com

Raytheon ·· Waltham, MA: (781) 862-6600
   Web Page: http://www.raytheon.com

Read Soft Inc ·· Metairie, CA: (888) 732-3763
   Toll Free:(888) 732-3763
   Web Page: http://www.readsoft.com

Ready-To-Run Software Inc ··························· North Chelmsford, MA: (978) 251-5400
   Toll Free:(800) 743-1723
   Web Page: http://www.rtr.com

Real 3D (see Intel)

Real Time Devices Inc ·· State College, PA: (814) 234-8087
   Web Page: http://www.rtdusa.com

Real Time Integration (see Net Acquire)

Reality Online (see Reuters)

Reality Tech (see Reuters)

RealNetworks Inc ·· Seattle, WA: (206) 674-2700
   Tech:(206) 674-2650   Toll Free:(800) 444-8011
   Web Page: http://www.realnetworks.com

Realviz ·· San Francisco, CA: (415) 615-9800
   Web Page: http://www.realviz.com

RealWorld Corp (see Great Plains)

Reasoning Systems Inc ·· Mountain View, CA: (650) 316-4400
   Web Page: http://www.reasoning.com

Recital Corp ··· Beverly, MA: (978) 921-5594
   Toll Free:(800) 873-7443
   Web Page: http://www.recital.com

Recognition Research Inc ·· Blacksburg, VA: (540) 961-6500
   Web Page: http://www.recognitionresearch.com

Recognition Systems Inc ·· Campbell, CA: (408) 341-4100
   Toll Free:(866) 861-2480
   Web Page: http://www.handreader.com

Recoton(see Thompson Inc.)

Red Hat Software Inc ·· Raleigh, NC: (919) 754-3700
   Tech:(800) 454-5502   Toll Free:(888) 733-4281
   Web Page: http://www.redhat.com

Red Wing Business Systems Inc ····························· Red Wing, MN: (651) 388-1106
   Toll Free:(800) 732-9464
   Web Page: http://www.redwingsoftware.com

Red-Hawk Inc ··· Milpitas, CA: (408) 945-1800
   Toll Free:(800) 989-4295
   Web Page: http://www.red-hawk.com

RedCreek Communications (see SonicWall)

Redlake MASD ··· San Diego, CA: (858) 481-8182
   Tech:(800) 854-7006   Toll Free:(800) 453-1223
   Web Page: http://www.redlake.com

Redstorm Entertainment ······················· Morrisville, NC: (919) 460-1776
  Tech:(919) 460-9778
  Web Page: http://www.redstorm.com
Relay Technology (see NetManage)
Reliable Communications Inc (see Relcomm) ········ Angelscamp, CA: (209) 736-0421
  Tech:(800) 222-0042   Toll Free:(800) 222-2810
  Web Page: http://www.relcomm.com
Relisys (see Advanced Innovative)
REMco Software Inc ······························· Dickinson, ND: (701) 456-5700
  Tech:(800) 501-2626   Toll Free:(800) 432-5009
  Web Page: http://www.remcosoftware.com
Remote Control Intl (see Telemagic)
Repeat-O-Type Mfg. Corp ························· Englewood, NJ: (201) 735-0232
  Toll Free:(800) 288-3330
  Web Page: http://www.repeatotype.com
Reply Corp (see Digital Origin)
Resale World.com ································ Orlando, FL: (407) 297-9448
  Tech:(800) 785-4800   Toll Free:(800) 858-1758
  Web Page: http://www.resaleworld.com
Research Info Sys (see ISI ResearchSoft)
Research Systems Inc ····························· Boulder, CO: (303) 786-9900
  Tech:(303) 413-3920
  Web Page: http://www.rsinc.com
Responsive Soft (see Westing Software)
Responsive Software ····························· Trinidad, CA: (415) 459-4744
  Tech:(707) 677-1960   Toll Free:(800) 669-4611
  Web Page: http://www.responsivesoftware.com
ReSTAR Inc ···································· Glastonbury, CT: (860) 657-3099
  Tech:(860) 657-3099   Toll Free:(800) 331-8307
  Web Page: http://www.restar.com
Restrac Inc(now Webhire Inc.) ·················· Lexington, MA: (781) 869-5000
  Tech:(781) 869-6000
  Web Page: http://www.webhire.com
Retix (see Sonoma Systems)
Revelation Software Inc ························· Westword, NJ: (201) 594-1422
  Tech:(800) 262-4747   Toll Free:(800) 262-4747
  Web Page: http://www.revelation.com
Rexon Data Storage (see Tecmar Tech)
RFF Electronics ································ Loveland, CO: (970) 663-5767
  Tech:(970) 663-5767
  Web Page: http://www.rff.com
RGB Spectrum ································· Alameda, CA: (510) 814-7000
  Web Page: http://www.rgb.com
Rhode Island Soft Systems Inc ················· Woonsocket, RI: (401) 767-3106
  Tech:(401) 767-3106   Toll Free:(800) 959-7477
  Web Page: http://www.risoftsystems.com
RIAS Corporation (Out of Business)
Ricoh Corp ·································· West Caldwell, NJ: (973) 882-2000
  Toll Free:(800) 637-4264
  Web Page: http://www.ricoh-usa.com
  Business Systems ···························(714) 891-9397
  Tech:(800) 351-2144   Toll Free:(800) 776-9484
  Web Page: http://www.ricoh-socal.com
  Business Systems ···························(973) 808-4484
  Tech:(973) 276-2500
  CD-R, CD-RW & Media Products ··················(877) 742-6479
  Toll Free:(877) 742-6479
  Web Page: http://www.ricohdms.com
  Consumer Products ···························(775) 352-1600

Toll Free:(800) 225-1899
Digital Cameras ································· (909) 890-9039
  Web Page: http://www.ricohzone.com
Electronic Devices ······························ (408) 432-8800
  Web Page: http://www.ricoh-usa.com
Network Office Appliances ·················· (408) 346-4500
  Tech:(888) 742-6466   Toll Free:(888) 742-6466
  Web Page: http://www.ecabinet.net
Peripheral Products ···························· (408) 432-8800
  Tech:(800) 955-3453   Toll Free:(800) 955-3453
Scanners ··· (714) 259-1310
  Toll Free:(800) 955-3453

Ricoh Electronics Inc ···················· Tustin, CA: (714) 566-2500

RightFax Inc (see Captaris)

Rimage Corp ················· Minneapolis, MN: (952) 944-8144
  Tech:(952) 946-0004   Toll Free:(800) 445-8288
  Web Page: http://www.rimage.com

Rinda Technologies Inc ·············· Chicago, IL: (773) 736-6633
  Web Page: http://www.rinda.com

Ring King Visibles (see Curtis Computer)

Ringdale Inc ···················· Georgetown, TX: (512) 288-9080
  Toll Free:(888) 288-9080
  Web Page: http://www.ringdale.com

Ripcord Games ················ Santa Clara, CA: (888) 774-6918
  Web Page: http://www.ripcordgames.com

Riser Bond Instruments ··············· Mahwah, NJ: (201) 848-8070
  Toll Free:(800) 688-8377
  Web Page: http://www.riserbond.com

Rising Edge Technologies ·············· Herndon, VA: (703) 471-8108
  Web Page: http://www.risingedge.com

River Deep The Learning Company ········· Novato, CA: (415) 763-4700
  Toll Free:(800) 691-2986
  Web Page: http://www.riverdeep.net

River Run Software Group Inc ········· Greenwich, CT: (203) 532-0500
  Web Page: http://www.riverrun.com

Rivers Edge Corp ·················· Cedar Park, TX: (512) 219-7768
  Web Page: http://www.riversedge.com

RKG Interactive ·············· Redondo Beach, CA: (310) 376-9500
  Web Page: http://www.rkgi.com

RLM Group ················ East Brunswick, NJ: (732) 448-3200
  Toll Free:(888) 756-1688
  Web Page: http://www.rlmgroup.com

RNS Inc (see Osicom)

Road Warrior International (see iGO Product)

Robocom Systems Inc ·············· Masapequa, NY: (516) 795-5100
  Toll Free:(800) 795-5100
  Web Page: http://www.robocom.com

Rockwell Automation ·············· Milwaukee, WI: (414) 382-1261
  Tech:(414) 382-2000
  Web Page: http://www.rockwellautomation.com

Rockwell Semiconductor (see Conexant)

Rockwell Software Inc ·············· Milwaukee, WI: (414) 382-8300
  Tech:(440) 646-5800
  Web Page: http://www.software.rockwell.com

RogueWave Software ·············· Boulder, CO: (303) 473-9118
  Tech:(800) 404-4767   Toll Free:(888) 442-9641
  Web Page: http://www.roguewave.com

ROI Systems Inc (see Epicor)

Roland Corp US ·················· Los Angeles, CA: (323) 890-3700

Web Page: http://www.rolandus.com

Roland Digital Group ···················· Irvine, CA: (949) 727-2100
Tech:(800) 542-2307   Toll Free:(800) 542-2307
Web Page: http://www.rolanddga.com
Name change to Ronald A Massa Associates ··········· (781) 383-2100
Web Page: http://www.rmassa.com

Rolodex (see Franklin Electronic Pub.)

Roper Scientific ···················· Tucson, AZ: (520) 889-9933
Web Page: http://www.roperscientific.com

Rorke Data Inc. ···················· Eden Prairie, MN: (952) 829-0300
Toll Free:(800) 328-8147
Web Page: http://www.rorke.com

Roscor Corp ···················· Mount Prospect, IL: (847) 299-8080
Web Page: http://www.roscor.com

Rose Electronics ···················· San Jose, CA: (408) 943-0200
Toll Free:(800) 632-4789
Web Page: http://www.rose-elec.com

Rosetta Technologies ···················· Tampa, FL: (813) 623-6205
Toll Free:(800) 937-4224
Web Page: http://www.rosettatechnologies.com

Ross Computer Systems Inc ···················· New York, NY: (212) 221-7677
Tech:(317) 877-7677
Web Page: http://www.rossusa.com

Ross Systems ···················· Atlanta, GA: (770) 351-9600
Web Page: http://www.rossinc.com

Ross Technology Inc (Out of Business)

Roxio ···················· Santa Clara, CA: (408) 367-3100
Tech:(905) 482-5200   Toll Free:(800) 518-2432
Web Page: http://www.roxio.com

Roxio ···················· Richmond Hill, ON: (905) 764-7000
Tech:(905) 764-7291
Web Page: http://www.roxio.com

RSA Security Inc ···················· San Mateo, CA: (650) 295-7600
Tech:(877) 772-4900   Toll Free:(800) 782-5453
Web Page: http://www.rsasecurity.com

RSA Security Inc ···················· Bedford, MA: (781) 515-5010
Tech:(800) 995-5095   Toll Free:(877) 772-4900
Web Page: http://www.rsasecurity.com

RTI-Research Tech Intl ···················· Lincolnwood, IL: (847) 677-3000
Toll Free:(800) 323-7520
Web Page: http://www.rtico.com

RuleSpace ···················· Portland, OR: (503) 290-5100
Tech:(503) 290-5100
Web Page: http://www.rulespace.com

Rupp Technology Corporation ···················· Miami, FL: (305) 969-5923
Tech:(305) 254-6290   Toll Free:(800) 844-7775
Web Page: http://www.rupp.com

RVSI ···················· Nashua, NH: (603) 598-8400
Toll Free:(800) 729-9888
Web Page: http://www.rvsi.com

RVSI Northeast Robotics ···················· Weare, NH: (603) 529-2385
Web Page: http://www.ncrlite.com

Rybs Electronics Inc ···················· Superior, CO: (303) 499-2076
Tech:(720) 319-1969
Web Page: http://www.rybs.com

S.H. Pierce & Co ···················· Cambridge, MA: (617) 338-2222
Web Page: http://www.posterworks.com

S3 Incorporated (see Sonicblue)
Saber Software (see Network Associates)

Safe Harbor Computers ·· Waukesha, WI: (262) 548-8120
  Tech:(262) 548-8157   Toll Free:(800) 544-6599
  Web Page: http://www.sharbor.com
SAG Electronics ·· Cambridge, MA: (978) 683-0339
  Toll Free:(800) 488-4724
  Web Page: http://www.sagelectronics.com
Sage Software (see Best Software)
Sage US Holdings (see Best US Holdings)
Sager Electronics ··· Hingham, MA: (781) 740-2300
  Toll Free:(800) 724-3780
  Web Page: http://www.sager.com
SAI Inc (see Microleague Multimedia)
SAI Systems International ··· Shelton, CT: (230) 929-0790
  Tech:(230) 929-0790   Toll Free:(877) 724-4748
  Web Page: http://www.saisystems.com
SAIC ··· San Diego, CA: (858) 826-6000
  Toll Free:(800) 430-7629
  Web Page: http://www.saic.com
Saitek Industries ·· Torrance, CA: (310) 212-5412
  Tech:(310) 972-9930
  Web Page: http://www.saitekusa.com
Sales Partner Systems ··· Ormond Beach, FL: (386) 672-8434
  Web Page: http://www.spsi.com
SalesLogix ··· Scottsdale, AZ: (480) 368-3700
  Tech:(480) 607-9738   Toll Free:(800) 643-6400
  Web Page: http://www.saleslogix.com
Sampo Technology Inc ··· Norcross, GA: (770) 449-6220
  Tech:(770) 449-6220
  Web Page: http://www.sampotech.com
Samsung America Inc ··· La Mirada, CA: (562) 802-2211
  Toll Free:(800) 726-7864
  Web Page: http://www.samsungla.com
Samsung Camera ··· Secaucus, NJ: (201) 902-0347
  Toll Free:(800) 762-7746
  Web Page: http://www.samsungcamerausa.com
Samsung Electronic America ··· Ledgewood, NJ: (201) 229-4000
  Tech:(201) 229-4000   Toll Free:(800) 726-7864
  Web Page: http://www.samsungelectronics.com
  Consumer Electronics ··· (201) 229-4000
  Tech:(973) 601-6000   Toll Free:(800) 726-7864
  Web Page: http://www.samsungusa.com
Samsung Information Systems America ······························· San Jose, CA: (408) 544-5400
  Toll Free:(800) 726-7864
Samsung Semiconductor Inc ·· San Jose, CA: (408) 544-4000
  Web Page: http://www.samsungusa.com
Samsung Telecommunications America ·································· Richardson, TX: (972) 761-7000
  Toll Free:(888) 987-4357
  Web Page: http://www.samsungusa.com
Sanchez Computer Associates ·· Malvern, PA: (610) 296-8877
  Web Page: http://www.sanchez.com
SanDisk Corp ·· Sunnyvale, CA: (408) 542-0500
  Tech:(408) 542-0405   Toll Free:(866) 726-3475
  Web Page: http://www.sandisk.com
Santa Cruz Operations (see Tarantella)
Santa Fe Software (see ACE Contact Man.)
Santorini Consult & Design (Out of Business)
Sanyo Fisher Co ··· Chadsworth, CA: (818) 998-7322
  Web Page: http://www.sanyoservice.com
Sanyo Semiconductor Corp (201) 825-8080

Web Page: http://www.sanyo.com

SAP America Inc ···································· Newton Square, PA: (610) 661-1000
Toll Free:(888) 777-1727
Web Page: http://www.sap.com

Saperion Inc ·· Newton, MA: (781) 899-1228
Web Page: http://www.saperion.com

Sarnoff Corp ··· Princeton, NJ: (609) 734-2000
Web Page: http://www.sarnoff.com

Saros Corp (see Filenet Corp)

SAS Institute Inc ·· Cary, NC: (919) 677-8000
Tech:(919) 677-8008   Toll Free:(800) 727-0025
Web Page: http://www.sas.com

Savin Corp ··· Stamford, CT: (203) 967-5000
Web Page: http://www.savin.com

Sax.net ··· Eugene, OR: (541) 344-2235
Toll Free:(800) 645-3729
Web Page: http://www.sax.net

Scala Inc ··· Calabasas, CA: (818) 878-6950
Tech:(888) 444-5867   Toll Free:(888) 967-2252
Web Page: http://www.scala.com

Scala North America Inc (Epicer Scala) ········· Heathrow, FL: (407) 333-8829
Toll Free:(888) 722-5241
Web Page: http://www.scala.net

Scan-Optics Inc ····································· Manchester, CT: (860) 645-7878
Toll Free:(800) 745-6001
Web Page: http://www.scanoptics.com

Scanalytics Inc ··· Fairfax, VA: (703) 208-2230
Web Page: http://www.scanalytics.com

Scanport Inc ··· Industry, CA: (310) 687-5757
Tech:(310) 687-5755
Web Page: http://www.scanport.com

ScanSoft Inc ··· Peabody, MA: (978) 977-2000
Toll Free:(800) 654-1187
Web Page: http://www.scansoft.com

Scantron Corp ·· Irvine, CA: (800) 722-6876
Tech:(800) 445-3141   Toll Free:(800) 722-6876
Web Page: http://www.scantron.com

Sceptre Technologies Inc ··············· City Of Industry, CA: (626) 369-3698
Tech:(888) 523-3815   Toll Free:(800) 788-2878
Web Page: http://www.sceptretech.com

SCH Technologies (see Legato Systems)

Scholastic Inc ·· New York, NY: (212) 343-6100
Toll Free:(800) 724-6527
Web Page: http://www.scholastic.com

Schott-Fostec ··· Auburn, NY: (315) 255-2791
Web Page: http://www.schott-fostec.com

Scientific & Eng. Soft. (see Hyperformix)

Scientific Imaging Technologies ··············· Tigard, OR: (503) 431-7100
Web Page: http://www.site-inc.com

Scientific Vision Systems ···················· Carlsbad, CA: (760) 929-8133
Web Page: http://www.svsimaging.com

Scion Corp ··· Frederick, MD: (301) 695-7870
Web Page: http://www.scioncorp.com

SciTech Software Inc ································· Chico, CA: (530) 894-8400
Tech:(530) 894-8400   Toll Free:(800) 486-4823
Web Page: http://www.scitechsoft.com

Scitor Corp ··· Herndon, VA: (703) 961-4079
Web Page: http://www.scitor.com

SCO (see Santa Cruz Operations)

Scopus Technology (see Siebel)

Scott Systems ··· **Carlsbad, CA: (800) 996-6777**
  Toll Free:(800) 996-6777
  Web Page: http://www.scottsystems.com

Screen Scan Systems ···································· **West Salem, WI: (608) 786-0300**
  Toll Free:(800) 843-9377
  Web Page: http://www.screenscan.com

Screenplay Systems ··· **Glendale, CA: (818) 843-6557**
  Tech:(818) 843-7819   Toll Free:(800) 847-8679
  Web Page: http://www.screenplay.com

SDC Information Systems ······························· **Naperville, IL: (630) 235-7112**
  Web Page: http://www.mmorph.com

Seagate Software (see Veritas Software)

Seagate Technology ···································· **Scotts Valley, CA: (831) 438-6550**
  Tech:(800) 732-4283   Toll Free:(800) 468-3472
  Web Page: http://www.seagate.com
  Disc Drive Products ··· 0
    Toll Free:(800) 468-3472
  Pre-Sales Support (Disc) ··· 405-324-4730
    Toll Free:(877) 271-3285
  Pre-Sales Support (Tape) ·· (714) 641-2500
    Toll Free:(800) 626-6637
  SeaFone - Automated Self-Help Services
    Toll Free:(800) 732-4283
  Tape Drive Products (IDE/SCSI)
    Tech:(800) 732-4283   Toll Free:(800) 468-3472
  Tape Drive Products (Internal/External)
    Toll Free:(800) 468-3472

Seagull Scientific Systems ···························· **Bellevue, WA: (425) 641-1408**
  Tech:(425) 641-1408   Toll Free:(800) 758-2001
  Web Page: http://www.seagullscientific.com

Sealevel Systems ··· **Liberty, SC: (864) 843-4343**
  Tech:(864) 843-4343
  Web Page: http://www.sealevel.com

Seanix Technology Corp ······························· **Richmond, BC: (604) 303-2900**
  Tech:(888) 252-1197   Toll Free:(800) 867-2649
  Web Page: http://www.seanix.com

Seattle Lab ··· **Anaheim, CA: 714-695-1000**
  Web Page: http://www.seattlelab.com

Second Nature Software Inc ······················· **Vancouver, WA: (360) 737-4170**
  Tech:(360) 737-4170
  Web Page: http://www.secondnaturecd.com

Securaplane Technologies ································· **Tucson, AZ: (520) 297-0844**
  Web Page: http://www.securaplane.com

Secure Computing ······································· **San Jose, CA: (408) 918-6100**
  Tech:(800) 379-4944   Toll Free:(800) 692-5625
  Web Page: http://www.securecomputing.com

Secure-It Inc ··································· **East Longmeadow, MA: 413-525-7039**
  Toll Free:(800) 451-7592
  Web Page: http://www.secure-it.com

Security Dynamics (see RSA Security)

SEEC Inc ··· **Pittsburgh, PA: (412) 893-0300**
  Tech:412-893-0369   Toll Free:(800) 682-7332
  Web Page: http://www.seec.com

Seek Systems ··· **Woodinville, WA: (425) 806-7335**
  Toll Free:(800) 790-7335
  Web Page: http://www.seeksystems.com

Sega Dreamcast Inc ································· **San Francisco, CA: (800) 872-7342**
  Tech:(866) 734-2638   Toll Free:(800) 872-7342
  Web Page: http://www.sega.com

Segue Software Inc ·· **Lexington, MA: (781) 402-1000**
  Tech:(800) 922-3771   Toll Free:(800) 287-1329
  Web Page: http://www.segue.com

Seiko Instruments USA ·· **Torrance, CA: (310) 517-7700**
  Web Page: http://www.seiko-instruments-usa.com
  Business & Home Office Products ··················310-517-7700
    Tech:(800) 757-1011   Toll Free:(800) 688-0817
    Web Page: http://www.siibusinessproducts.com
  Consumer Products ···(310) 517-7810
    Toll Free:(800) 873-4508
  Electronic Componets Division ······················310-517-7771
    Web Page: http://seiko.usa.ecd.com
  Fiber Optic Connectors ·································(310) 517-8113
    Web Page: http://www.siifiber.com
  Micro Printers ···(310) 517-7778
    Toll Free:(800) 553-6570
    Web Page: http://www.siiprinters.com

Semicaps Inc ·· **San Jose, CA: (408) 452-8898**
  Web Page: http://www.semicaps.com

SemWare Corp ··· **Kennesaw, GA: 678-355-9810**
  Toll Free:(800) 467-3692
  Web Page: http://www.semware.com

Senior Products Inc ·· **East Hanover, NJ: (973) 884-1755**
  Toll Free:(800) 755-2201
  Web Page: http://www.sensorprod.com

Sensors Unlimited Inc ··· **Princeton, NJ: (609) 520-0610**
  Web Page: http://www.sensorsinc.com

Sensory Co ·· **Tigard, OR: (503) 684-8008**
  Tech:(503) 684-8073
  Web Page: http://www.sensory.com

Sensytech Imaging Group ·· **Ann Arbor, MI: (734) 769-5649**
  Toll Free:(800) 275-8207
  Web Page: http://www.sensytech.com

Sentech America ··· **Carrollton, TX: 972-481-9223**
  Toll Free:(877) 736-8324
  Web Page: http://www.sentechamerica.com

Sequent Computer Systems (see IBM)

Sequoia Publishing ·· **Littleton, CO: (303) 932-1400**
  Toll Free:(888) 932-1500
  Web Page: http://www.sequoiapublishing.com

Ser Solutions Inc ··· **Dulles, VA: (703) 948-5500**
  Toll Free:(800) 274-5676
  Web Page: http://www.sersolutions.com

Serif Inc ··· **Amherst, NH: (603) 889-8650**
  Tech:(603) 886-6642   Toll Free:(800) 557-3743
  Web Page: http://www.serif.com

Serome Technology (see dialpad.com)

Server Technology Inc ·· **Reno, NV: (775) 284-2000**
  Tech:(800) 835-1515   Toll Free:(800) 835-1515
  Web Page: http://www.servertech.com

Service 2000 (see Kennsco Inc)

Service News Mag. (see United Pub.)

ServiceWare ··· **Pittsburg, PA: 412-222-4450**
  Toll Free:(800) 572-5748
  Web Page: http://www.serviceware.com

Set Enterprises Inc ·· **Fountain Hills, AZ: (480) 837-3628**
  Tech:(480) 837-3628   Toll Free:(800) 351-7765
  Web Page: http://www.setgame.com

Severn Companies Inc ··· **Laurel, MD: (301) 776-2400**
  Tech:(301) 776-2400   Toll Free:800-327-6589

Web Page: http://www.severn.com

SGI (see Silicon Graphics)

SGS-Thomson (see STMicroelectronics)

Shaffstall Corp ·· **Indianapolis, IN: (317) 842-2077**
Tech:(317) 842-2077   Toll Free:(800) 357-6250
Web Page: http://www.shaffstall.com

Shape Electronics Inc ··· **Addison, IL: (630) 620-8394**
Tech:(630) 620-8394   Toll Free:(800) 367-5811

Shapeware (Out of Business)

Sharp Electronics Corp ·· **Mahwah, NJ: (201) 529-8200**
Tech:(800) 237-4277   Toll Free:(800) 237-4277
Web Page: http://www.sharp-usa.com

Sharp Electronics Corp ·············· **Huntington Beach, CA: (714) 903-4600**
Web Page: http://www.sharpsdi.com
National Service and Parts Center ··············(630) 226-2400
Toll Free:(800) 237-4277
Web Page: http://www.sharp-usa.com
Sharp Labs of America ·······························(360) 817-8400
Sharp Latin American Group ····················(305) 264-2277
Sharp Microelectronics ·····························(360) 834-8700
Tech:877-343-2181
Web Page: http://www.sharpsma.com
Southeastern Regional Office ··················(770) 513-6449
Web Page: http://www.sharp-usa.com
Western Regional Office ···························(714) 903-4600
Web Page: http://www.sharpsdi.com

Sharp Manufacturing Company ······················· **Memphis, TN: (901) 795-6510**
Web Page: http://www.sharp-usa.com

Shearwater Technology (out of bussiness) ··············· **Littleton, MA: (978) 486-9716**
Web Page: http://www.shearwatertech.com

Sheridan Software (see Infragistics)

Sherwood America ··· **Cerritos, CA: 562-741-0960**
Tech:800-962-3203   Toll Free:(800) 777-8755
Web Page: http://www.sherwoodamerica.com

Shin-ho Electronics & Communications (310) 323-8377

Shinko Technologies Inc ··· **Hayward, CA: (510) 259-0292**
Toll Free:(800) 997-4465
Web Page: http://www.shinkotech.com

Shiva Corp (see Intel Network Systems)

Shuttle Computer Group ······················ **City Of Industry, CA: (626) 820-9000**
Web Page: http://www.shuttlegroup.com

Side-Eight Software ·· **Garden Grove, CA: (714) 892-0770**
Tech:800-325-0604   Toll Free:(800) 356-3316
Web Page: http://www.side8.com

Siebel Systems Inc ·· **San Mateo, CA: 650-295-5000**
Web Page: http://www.siebel.com

Siebel Systems Inc ··· **San Mateo, CA: (650) 295-5000**
Toll Free:(800) 647-4300
Web Page: http://www.siebel.com

Siemens Medical Solutions ································· **Malvern, PA: 610-448-4500**
Web Page: http://www.siemensmedical.com

Siemon Co ·· **Watertown, CT: (860) 945-4200**
Tech:(860) 945-4385
Web Page: http://www.siemon.com

Sienna Imaging(location closed) ···················· **Englewood, CO: (303) 754-0200**
Web Page: http://www.siennaimaging.com

Sierra ·· **Bellevue, WA: (425) 649-9800**
Tech:310-649-8033   Toll Free:(800) 757-7707
Web Page: http://www.sierra.com

Sierra Imaging Inc(out of business) ·················· **Scotts Valley, CA: (831) 461-2070**
Tech:(831) 430-5465   Toll Free:(877) 446-2439
Web Page: http://www.sierraimaging.com
Sierra Wireless inc ···································· **Richmond, BC: (604) 231-1100**
Tech:(604) 232-1488   Toll Free:(877) 231-1144
Web Page: http://www.sierrawireless.com
Sightech Vision Systems ····························· **San Jose, CA: (408)282-3779**
Toll Free:800-992-4188
Web Page: http://www.sightech.com
Sigma Data ·· **New London, NH: (603) 526-6909**
Tech:(603) 526-7100   Toll Free:(800) 446-4525
Web Page: http://www.sigmadata.com
Sigma Designs Inc ···································· **Milpitas, CA: (408) 262-9003**
Tech:408-957-9866   Toll Free:(800) 845-8086
Web Page: http://www.sigmadesigns.com
SIIG ·· **Fremont, CA: (510) 657-8688**
Tech:(510) 353-7542
Web Page: http://www.siig.com
Silent Witness (888) 289-2288
Tech:(800) 893-9513   Toll Free:(888) 289-2288
Silicon Graphics Inc ································· **Mountain View, CA: (650) 960-1980**
Tech:(800) 800-4744   Toll Free:(800) 800-7441
Web Page: http://www.sgi.com
Silicon Image ·· **Sunnyvale, CA: (408) 616-4000**
Web Page: http://www.siimage.com
SilverStream Software(seeNovell) (888) 823-9700
Toll Free:(888) 823-9700
Silvon Software Inc ···································· **Westmont, IL: (630) 655-3313**
Tech:(630) 655-6371   Toll Free:(800) 874-5866
Web Page: http://www.silvon.com
Simple Technology Inc ································ **Santa Ana, CA: (949) 476-1180**
Toll Free:(800) 367-7330
Web Page: http://www.simpletech.com
Sinar Bron Imaging ··································· **Edison, NJ: (908) 754-5800**
Toll Free:(800) 456-0203
Web Page: http://www.sinarbron.com
Sirsi Corp ·· **St Louis, MO: (314) 432-1100**
Toll Free:(800) 325-0888
Web Page: http://www.sirsi.com
Skill soft ·· **Nashua, NH: 603-324-3000**
Toll Free:877-545-5763
Web Page: http://www.skillsoft.com
SkiSoft Publishing Corp ····························· **Lexington, MA: (781) 863-1876**
Web Page: http://www.skisoft.com
Sky Computers Inc ···································· **Chelmsford, MA: (978) 250-1920**
Toll Free:800-486-1920
Web Page: http://www.skycomputers.com
Skyeye Corp ··· **Wellesley, MA: (781) 237-6806**
Web Page: http://www.skyeye.com
Skyline Tools Imaging ·································· **Woodland Hills, CA: (818) 346-4200**
Toll Free:(800) 404-3832
Web Page: http://www.skylinetools.com
SL Waber Inc ·· **Mount Laurel, NJ: (856-727-1500**
Web Page: http://www.slindustries.com
Smart and Friendly (Out of Business)
Smart Cable Co ·· **Tacoma, WA: (253) 474-9967**
Toll Free:(800) 752-6526
Web Page: http://www.smart-cable.com
Smart Modular Technologies ························ **Fremont, CA: (510) 623-1231**

Tech:(510) 249-1605   Toll Free:(800) 841-2739
Web Page: http://www.smartm.com

Smart Sound Software ·· **Northridge, CA: 818-920-9122**
Toll Free:(800) 454-1900
Web Page: http://www.smartsound.com

Smart Storage Inc(see Legato Systems)

Smart Technologies ·· **Calgary, AB: (403) 245-0333**
Tech:866-518-6791   Toll Free:(888) 427-6278
Web Page: http://www.smarttech.com

SmartCertify Direct ·· **Clearwater, FL: (727) 724-8994**
Tech:(727) 725-2755   Toll Free:800-475-5831
Web Page: http://www.smartcertify.com

Smarterkids.com ·· **Needham, MA: (800) 293-9314**
Tech:(800) 293-9314   Toll Free:(800) 293-9314
Web Page: http://www.smarterkids.com

SMC Networks ·· **Irvine, CA: 949-679-8000**
Toll Free:(800) 762-4968
Web Page: http://www.smc.com

SMC Networks (see Accton Technology)

Smead Software Solutions ·· **Hastings, MN: (651) 438-2061**
Tech:800-800-6131   Toll Free:800-216-3832
Web Page: http://www.smeadsoftware.com

Smith Corona ·· **Cortland, NY: (607) 753-6611**
Toll Free:(800) 448-1018
Web Page: http://www.smithcorona.com

Smith Micro Software Inc ·· **Aliso Viejo, CA: (949) 362-5800**
Tech:(949) 362-5810   Toll Free:(800) 964-7674
Web Page: http://www.smithmicro.com

SMS Data Products Group Inc ·· **McLean, VA: (703) 709-9898**
Tech:(800) 331-1767   Toll Free:(800) 331-1767
Web Page: http://www.sms.com

SMS Technology ·· **San Diego, CA: (858) 587-6900**
Tech:(858) 587-6900   Toll Free:(800) 821-4822
Web Page: http://www.smstech.com

Snell & Wilcox Inc ·· **Santa Clara, CA: (408) 260-1000**
Web Page: http://www.snellwilcox.com

Snow International Corp ·· **Clearwater, FL: (727) 784-6699**
Web Page: http://www.snowsoft.com

Snowbound Software ·· **Watertoion, MA: (617) 607-2000**
Toll Free:(866) 630-9495
Web Page: http://www.snowbnd.com

SNX ·· **New York, NY: (718) 499-6293**
Tech:(718) 369-2944   Toll Free:(800) 447-9639
Web Page: http://www.snx.com

Socket Communications ·· **Newark, CA: (510) 744-2700**
Tech:(510) 744-2720   Toll Free:(800) 552-3300
Web Page: http://www.socketcom.com

Soffront Software Inc ·· **Fremont, CA: (510) 413-9000**
Toll Free:(800) 763-3766
Web Page: http://www.soffront.com

Soft Automation ·· **Milford, MI: 248-685-8179**
Web Page: http://www.soft-automation.com

Soft Imaging System Corp ·· **Lakewood, CO: (303) 234-9270**
Toll Free:(888) 346-3747
Web Page: http://www.soft-imaging.com

Soft Velocity ·· **Pompano Beach, FL: (954) 785-4555**
Tech:(954) 785-4556   Toll Free:800-207-4562
Web Page: http://www.softvelocity.com

Softarc (see Centrinity)

Softbank Comdex (see ZD Comdex)

Softbite International ·· Aurea, IL: 630-566-8400
Web Page: http://www.softbite.com

SoftCad International ·· Walnut Creek, CA: (925) 974-3398
Tech:(800) 763-8223   Toll Free:(800) 763-8223
Web Page: http://www.softcad.com

Softdesk Retail Products (see Autodesk)

Softel vdm Inc ·· Punta Gorda, FL: (941) 505-8600
Web Page: http://www.softelvdm.com

Softimage ··· Montreal, ON: (514) 845-1636
Web Page: http://www.softimage.com

Softkey International (see Learning Co)

SofTouch Systems Inc ·· Oklahoma City, OK: (405) 728-1902
Tech:(405) 703-8080   Toll Free:(800) 944-3036
Web Page: http://www.softouch.com

Softronics Inc ··· Colorado Springs, CO: (719) 593-9540
Toll Free:(800) 225-8590
Web Page: http://www.softronics.com

Softsource ·· Bellingham, WA: (360) 676-0999
Toll Free:800-877-1875
Web Page: http://www.softsource.com

SoftTalk Inc (see Callware Tech)

Software & Information Industry ································ Washington, DC: (202) 289-7442
Tech:(202) 289-7442   Toll Free:(800) 388-7478
Web Page: http://www.siia.net

Software 602 Inc ··· Jacksonville, FL: (904) 642-5400
Toll Free:(888) 468-6602
Web Page: http://www.software602.com

Software Architects Inc ·· Bothell, WA: (425) 487-0122
Web Page: http://www.softarch.com

Software Business Tech (see SBT)

Software Directions Inc ·· Palo Alto, CA: 650-329-1287
Web Page: http://www.softwaredirections.com

Software FX Inc ·· Boca Raton, FL: (561) 999-8888
Tech:(561) 392-2023   Toll Free:800-392-4278
Web Page: http://www.softwarefx.com

Software Interphase Inc ·· Foster, RI: (401) 397-4540
Web Page: http://www.sinterphase.com

Software Labs, The ·· Redmond, WA: (425) 653-2432
Tech:(425) 869-6729
Web Page: http://www.softwarelabs.com

Software Marketing (see Learning Co)

Software Pub. (see Software & Info)

Software Pub. Corp (see Vizacom Inc)

Software Science Inc ·· San Rafael, CA: 415-479-7288
Tech:(415) 479-7286
Web Page: http://www.softsci.com

Software Spectrum Inc ·· Garland, TX: (972) 840-6600
Toll Free:(800) 624-0503
Web Page: http://www.swspectrum.com

Software Technology (see Savoir Tech)

Software Toolworks (see Mindscape)

SOHOware ··· Santa Clara, CA: (408) 565-9888
Tech:(888) 785-8222   Toll Free:(800) 632-1118
Web Page: http://www.sohoware.com

Sola Hevi Duty ·· Rosemont, IL: 847-268-6000
Tech:(800) 289-7652   Toll Free:(800) 377-4384
Web Page: http://www.sol-hevi-duty.com

Solectek Accessories ···················· San Diego, CA: (858) 450-1220
   Tech:(800) 437-1518   Toll Free:(800) 437-1518
   Web Page: http://www.solectek.com

Solidex (see Unitech Industries)

Solidworks Corp ·························· Concord, MA: (978) 371-5011
   Toll Free:(800) 693-9000
   Web Page: http://www.solidworks.com

Solltech Inc ······························ Oakdale, IA: (319) 335-4702
   Web Page: http://www.geocities.com/solltech

Solomon Software(see microsoft bussiness)
   Tech:888-477-7989
   Web Page: http://www.microsoft.com/bussinessloutions

Solsource Computers (see Osage Systems)

Sonic (see Fast Color.Com)

Sonic Foundry ·························· Madison, WI: (608) 443-1600
   Tech:(608) 256-5555   Toll Free:877-783-7987
   Web Page: http://www.sonicfoundry.com

Sonic Solutions ························ Novato, CA: (415) 893-8000
   Tech:(415) 893-7000   Toll Free:(888) 766-4297
   Web Page: http://www.sonic.com

Sonic Systems (see SonicWall)

Sonicblue(out of bussiness) ······· Santa Clara, CA: (408) 588-8000
   Tech:(408) 588-8585   Toll Free:(800) 468-5846
   Web Page: http://www.sonicblue.com

SonicWall Inc ························· Sunnyvale, CA: (408) 745-9600
   Tech:(888) 557-6642   Toll Free:(888) 777-1476
   Web Page: http://www.sonicwall.com

Sonoma Systems (see Nortel Networks)

Sony Electronics ····················· Park Ridge, NJ: (201) 930-1000
   Tech:(888) 476-6972
   Web Page: http://www.sony.com

Sony Electronics ····················· San Jose, CA: (408) 432-1600
   Accessory and Parts ······················· (800) 488-7669
      Toll Free:(800) 488-7669
   Broadcast & Professional ·················· (201) 833-5300
      Toll Free:(800) 538-7550
   Broadcast & Professional ·················· (630) 773-6037
   Broadcast & Professional ·················· (714) 229-4133
   Broadcast & Professional ·················· (800) 686-7669
      Tech:(800) 883-6817
   Computer Entertainment ··················· (650) 655-8000
   Computer Peripheral ······················ (800) 326-9551
      Tech:(800) 597-5649
      Web Page: http://www.ita.sel.sony.com/support
   Computer Products ························· (408) 922-0699
      Toll Free:(800) 352-7669
      Web Page: http://www.sony.com/technology
   Customer Information Services ·············· (800) 222-7669
      Tech:(800) 882-3891   Toll Free:(800) 222-7669
      Web Page: http://www.sony.com
   Magic Link Personal Communicator ········· (800) 556-2442
      Toll Free:(800) 556-2442
   Mavica Digital Camera ····················· (888) 449-7669
   Media Solutions
      Web Page: http://www.sony.com
   National Support Center ··················· (770) 263-8016
   Out of Warranty Support ··················· (800) 766-9236
      Web Page: http://www.sony.com
   PlayStation ······························· (800) 345-7669
      Tech:(800) 697-7266   Toll Free:(800) 345-7669

Web Page: http://www.playstation.com
Sony Style ··· (888) 595-8246
Web Page: http://www.sonystyle.com/vaio
Technical Response Center ························· (408) 435-8910
Sony Precision Technology ························· Lake Forest, CA: (949) 770-8400
Toll Free:888-327-7669
Web Page: http://www.sonypt.com
Sophos ··· Lynnfield, MA: (781) 973-0110
Toll Free:(888) 767-4679
Web Page: http://www.sophos.com
Sound Source Int. (see TDK Mediactive)
Sound Vision Inc ··· Framingham, MA: (508) 358-9000
Web Page: http://www.soundvisioninc.com
Soundblaster (see Creative Labs)
SourceMate Info (see AccountMate Soft)
Southland Micro Systems ··························· Irvine, CA: (949) 380-1958
Tech:(949) 380-9876   Toll Free:(800) 255-4200
Web Page: http://www.southlandmicro.com
Southpeak Interactive(out of Bussiness)·········· Midlothian, VA: (804) 379-8404
Tech:(800) 732-5818   Toll Free:(800) 774-6183
Web Page: http://www.southpeak.com
Soyo Group··· Ontario, CA: 909-292-2500
Web Page: http://www.soyousa.com
Spacetec IMC (see Labtec 3D)
Spalding Software ·· Norcross, GA: (770) 449-0594
Tech:(770) 449-0594
Web Page: http://www.spaldingsoft.com
SPARC International Inc ······························ Campbell, CA: (408) 364-3000
Web Page: http://www.sparc.com
SpartaCom Inc ·· Tucson, AZ: (520) 670-7100
Toll Free:(800) 846-9726
Web Page: http://www.spartacom.com
Special Optics ··· Wharton, NJ: (973) 366-7289
Web Page: http://www.specialoptics.com
Specialix (see Perle Specialix Inc)
Specialized Products Co ······························ Southlake, TX: (817) 329-6647
Tech:(800) 866-5353   Toll Free:(800) 866-5353
Web Page: http://www.specialized.net
Specialty Bulb Co ·· Bohemia, NY: (631) 589-3393
Toll Free:(800) 331-2852
Web Page: http://www.bulbspecialists.com
Spectragraphics (see SMS Technology)
Spectral Instruments ··································· Tucson, AZ: (520) 884-8821
Web Page: http://www.specinst.com
Spectrum HoloByte (see Microprose Soft)
Spectrum Signal Processing ························· Burnaby, BC: (604) 421-6422
Tech:(604) 421-5422   Toll Free:(800) 663-8986
Web Page: http://www.spectrumsignal.com
Spectrum Software ······································· Sunnyvale, CA: (408) 738-4387
Web Page: http://www.spectrum-soft.com
Spescom Software ·· San Diego, CA: (858) 625-3000
Tech:(800) 633-6784   Toll Free:858-410-6876
Web Page: http://www.altris.com
Spicer ··· Westlake, OH: (440) 899-1818
Web Page: http://www.spicer.com
Spinnaker Software (see Learning Co)
Splash of Color ·· Richardson, TX: (972) 437-5733
Toll Free:(800) 441-9064
Web Page: http://www.splashofcolor.com

Sprague Magnetics ·· Sylmar, CA: (818) 364-1800
  Tech:(800) 553-8712   Toll Free:(800) 553-8712
  Web Page: http://www.sprague-magnetics.com

SPSS (once showcase corp) ·· Chicago, IL: (312) 651-3000
  Tech:312-651-3410   Toll Free:(800) 829-3555
  Web Page: http://www.spss.com

SPSS Inc ·· Chicago, IL: (312) 651-3000
  Tech:312-651-3410   Toll Free:(800) 521-1337
  Web Page: http://www.spss.com

Spyglass Open TV (see Open TV)

SSA Global / Infinium Software ·· Chicago, IL: (312) 258-6000
  Tech:(312) 474-7400   Toll Free:(800) 997-9014
  Web Page: http://www.ssaglobal.com

Stac Electronics (see Previo Inc)

Stac Software Inc (see Previo Inc)

Staffware(see Tibco inc)

Stallion Technologies Inc/ Lantronix Co ····························· Soquel, CA: (831) 477-0440
  Toll Free:(800) 347-7979
  Web Page: http://www.stallion.com

Stampede Technologies Inc ·· Dayton, OH: (937) 291-5035
  Tech:(937) 291-5035   Toll Free:(800) 763-3423
  Web Page: http://www.stampede.com

Standard Microsystems Corp (see SMC)

Standford Computer Optics ·· Berkeley, CA: (510) 527-3516
  Web Page: http://www.stanfordcomputeroptics.com

Star Media Systems (see DPS Software)

Star Micronics America ··· Edison, NJ: (732) 623-5500
  Toll Free:(800) 782-7636
  Web Page: http://www.starmicronics.com

Star Tech Computer Products ··· Groveport, OH: (519) 455-9675
  Tech:(519) 455-4931   Toll Free:(800) 265-1844
  Web Page: http://www.startechcomp.com

Starbase Corp (see Borland USA)

Stardock ·· Livonia, MI: (734) 762-0687
  Web Page: http://www.stardock.com

Starfish Software(out of bussiness) ·································· Scotts Valley, CA: (831) 461-5800
  Tech:(970) 522-4610
  Web Page: http://www.starfishsoftware.com

Starquest (see Level 8 systems)

State of the Art (see Sage Software)

Statenet ·· Sacramento, CA: (916) 444-0840
  Tech:(916) 444-0840   Toll Free:(800) 726-4566
  Web Page: http://www.statenet.com

StatSoft Inc ··· Tulsa, OK: (918) 749-1119
  Toll Free:918-749-1119
  Web Page: http://www.statsoft.com

STB Electrical Test Equipment Inc ····································· Auburn, CA: (530) 823-5111
  Toll Free:(800) 888-7898
  Web Page: http://www.stbinc.com

STB Systems Inc (see 3D Fx Interactive)

Steinberg North America (out of bussiness) ···························· Chatsworth, CA: (818) 678-5100
  Tech:(818) 678-5100

Stellent Inc ··· Eden Prairie, MN: (952) 903-2000
  Tech:952-903-2020   Toll Free:877-332-9567
  Web Page: http://www.stellent.com

Stellent(location closed) ··· Bellevue, WA: (425) 201-1915
  Tech:(425) 201-1916   Toll Free:(800) 344-9737
  Web Page: http://www.stellent.com

Stellent, Inc. / INSO Corporation ················ **Eden Prairie, MN: (952) 903-2000**
  Tech:952-903-2020   Toll Free:877-332-9567
  Web Page: http://www.stellent.com

Stereographics Corp ································ **San Rafael, CA: (415) 459-4500**
  Toll Free:(800) 783-2660
  Web Page: http://www.stereographics.com

Sterling Commerce (see Xcellenet)

Sterling Software (see Computer Assoc.)

STI Certified ····································· **Fremont, CA: (510) 226-9074**
  Toll Free:(800) 274-3475
  Web Page: http://www.sticertified.com

STMicroelectronics ································ **Phoenix, AZ: (602) 485-6100**
  Tech:(602) 485-6100
  Web Page: http://www.st.com

STMicroelectronics ································ **Lexington, MA: (781) 861-2650**
  Tech:(781) 861-2664
  Web Page: http://www.stmicroelectronics.com

Stocker Yale ···································· **Montreal, QC: (514) 335-1005**
  Toll Free:(800) 814-9552
  Web Page: http://www.stockeryale.com

StockerYale Inc ·································· **Salem, NH: (603) 893-8778**
  Toll Free:(800) 843-8011
  Web Page: http://www.stockeryale.com

Stonehouse Technologies Inc ···················· **Dallas, TX: (972) 581-7300**
  Tech:(972) 581-7303
  Web Page: http://www.stonehouse.com

Storage Computer Corp ·························· **Nashua, NH: (603) 880-3005**
  Web Page: http://www.storage.com

Storage Concepts (see Medea)

Storage Dimensions (see Dot Hill)

Storage Technology Corporation ·················· **Louisville, CO: (303) 673-5151**
  Tech:800-525-0369   Toll Free:(800) 786-7835
  Web Page: http://www.stortek.com

Storcomm ······································ **Jacksonville, FL: (904) 731-1289**
  Toll Free:(888) 731-0731
  Web Page: http://www.storcomm.com

Stradis ·· **Atlanta, GA: (404) 320-0110**
  Web Page: http://www.stradis.com

Strata Inc (see 3D.com)

Strata Software ·································· **Saint George, UT: (435) 628-5218**
  Tech:(435) 628-9751   Toll Free:(800) 678-7282
  Web Page: http://www.strata.com

Strategic Mapping (see Software Support)

Strategic Networks (see ZD Labs)

Strategic Simulations (see Mindscape)

Strategic Studies Group ························· **Tucson, AZ: (641) 396-2184**
  Web Page: http://www.ssgus.com

Stratus Technologies ···························· **Maynard, MA: (978) 461-7000**
  Tech:(978) 461-7100   Toll Free:(800) 634-2122
  Web Page: http://www.stratus.com

c/o Information Today Inc. ························ **(917) 523-4562**
  Toll Free:(800) 319-4756
  Web Page: http://www.streamingmedia.com

Streaming21 ···································· **Los Gatos, CA: (408) 866-8080**
  Web Page: http://www.streaming21.com

Street Electronics (see Echo Speech)

Street Technology ································ **Tarzana, CA: (818) 757-2300**
  Toll Free:(877) 966-7372
  Web Page: http://www.street-technology.com

Streetwise Software .... Santa Monica, CA: (310) 829-7827
Tech:(310) 998-3361   Toll Free:(800) 743-6765
Web Page: http://www.swsoftware.com

Stromberg LLC .... Lake Mary, FL: (407) 333-3282
Tech:(407) 333-7376   Toll Free:(800) 787-6623
Web Page: http://www.stromberg.com

Structured Software (see Facet Corp)

Structured Software Ser. (see Vergetech)

Successfactors Inc .... San Mateo, CA: (650) 645-2000
Tech:(800) 846-6503   Toll Free:(800) 809-9920
Web Page: http://www.successfactors.com

Summagraphics Corp (see Cal Comp)

Summit Software Co .... Jamesville, NY: (315) 445-9000
Tech:(315) 445-9000
Web Page: http://www.summsoft.com

SumTotal .... Mountain View, CA: (650) 934-9500
Toll Free:(866) 768-6825
Web Page: http://www.sumtotalsytems.com

Sun Gard EPI .... Wayne, RI: (484) 582-2000
Toll Free:(800) 468-7483
Web Page: http://www.sungard.com

Sun Microsystems .... Mountain View, CA: (650) 960-1300
Tech:(800) 872-4786   Toll Free:(800) 555-9786
Web Page: http://www.sun.com

Sun Microsystems .... Palo Alto, CA: (650) 960-1300
Toll Free:(800) 872-4786
Web Page: http://www.sun.com

Sun Microsystems .... Santa Clara, CA: (650) 960-1300
Toll Free:(800) 555-9786
 Cobalt Networks
  Web Page: http://www.sun.com
 Computer Systems .... (800) 786-0404
  Web Page: http://www.sun.com
 Developer Connection .... (800) 945-6111
  Toll Free:(800) 945-6111
  Web Page: http://www.sun.com
 Education Services .... (303) 464-4097
  Toll Free:(800) 422-8020
  Web Page: http://www.sun.com
 Java Advanced Imaging .... (650) 786-0529
  Toll Free:(800) 786-7638
  Web Page: http://www.java.sun.com
 Software .... (800) 786-7638
  Web Page: http://www.sun.com
 Sun Professional Services
  Web Page: http://www.sun.com
 Technical Service Support .... (800) 872-4786
  Toll Free:(800) 872-4786
  Web Page: http://www.sun.com

Sunburst Technology .... Elgin, IL: (914) 747-3310
Tech:(800) 338-3457   Toll Free:(800) 338-3457
Web Page: http://www.sunburst.com

Suncom Technologies Inc (Out of Business)

Sunex .... Carlsbad, CA: (760) 602-0988
Web Page: http://www.sunex.com

Sungard Banking Systems-Tiger .... New York, NY: (212) 363-5600
Toll Free:(800) 468-7483
Web Page: http://www.sungard.com

Sunrise Imaging .... Tustin, CA: (714) 505-1144
Tech:(714) 505-1144   Toll Free:(800) 734-6241

Web Page: http://www.sunriseimaging.com

SunSoft (see Sun Microsystems Computer)

Superbase Developers Inc ································ Huntington, NY: (631) 757-3110
Tech:(415) 499-8396   Toll Free:(800) 315-7944
Web Page: http://www.superbase.com

Supercircuits ··· Liberty Hill, TX: (512) 260-0333
Toll Free:(800) 335-9777
Web Page: http://www.supercircuits.com

Superdups ·· Salem, NH: (800) 617-3877
Toll Free:(800) 617-3877
Web Page: http://www.superdups.com

Supermac Technology (see Digital Origin)

Supermicro ·· San Jose, CA: (408) 503-8000
Tech:(408) 503-8000
Web Page: http://www.supermicro.com

Supra Corp (see Diamond Multimedia)

SurfControl ······································· Westborough, MA: (831) 440-2500
Tech:(831) 440-2700   Toll Free:(800) 368-3366
Web Page: http://www.surfcontrol.com

Surveyor Corp······································ San Luis Obiso, CA: (805)784-0925
Web Page: http://www.surveyorcorp.com

Suse Inc ·· San Francisco, CA: (415) 591-6620
Toll Free:(888) 875-4689
Web Page: http://www.suse.com

Susteen Inc ··· Irvine, CA: (949) 341-0007
Tech:(949) 789-8200
Web Page: http://www.susteen.com

Sutter Instrument································ Novato, CA: (415) 883-0128
Web Page: http://www.sutter.com

Swfte International (see Expert Soft.)

Sybase Inc ··· Dublin, CA: (925) 236-5000
Toll Free:(800) 879-2273
Web Page: http://www.sybase.com

Sydex Inc·· Eugene, OR: (541) 683-6033
Web Page: http://www.sydex.com

Sykes ·· Tampa, FL: (813) 274-1000
Toll Free:(800) 867-9537
Web Page: http://www.sykes.com

Symantec Corp·································· Cupertino, CA: (408) 253-9600
Tech:(408) 517-8000   Toll Free:(800) 441-7234
Web Page: http://www.symantec.com

Symantec Corp·································· Beaverton, OR: (503) 690-4700
20/20 Software ································(203) 316-5500
Tech:(203) 316-5501   Toll Free:(800) 745-6052
Web Page: http://www.twenty.com

ACT! ··(408) 368-3799
Customer Operations ···················(541) 335-5000
Tech:(888) 727-8671   Toll Free:(800) 441-7234
Web Page: http://www.symantec.com

Fax Back ··(800) 554-4403
Toll Free:(800) 554-4403

IBM Anti Virus (no phone support)
Web Page: http://service.symantec.com

Norton ··(310) 453-4600
Toll Free:(800) 927-4017
Web Page: http://www.norton.com

Norton Diskdoubler Pro (no phone supp.)
Web Page: http://service.symantec.com

pcAnywhere (no phone support)
Web Page: http://service.symantec.com

Priority Support ···························· (541) 335-7000
  Web Page: http://www.symantec.com
TalkWorks (no phone support)
  Web Page: http://service.symantec.com
Technical Support ···························· (800) 927-4021
  Toll Free:(800) 339-1136
WebCompass (no phone support)
  Web Page: http://service.symantec.com
Symbios Logic (see LSI Logic)
Symbol Technologies Inc···························· Holtsville, NY: (631) 738-2400
  Tech:(631) 738-5200   Toll Free:(800) 722-6234
  Web Page: http://www.symbol.com
Symco Inc···························· Stirling, NJ: (908) 647-6262
  Web Page: http://www.symcoinc.com
Synchronics···························· Memphis, TN: (901) 761-1166
  Tech:(800) 852-8755   Toll Free:(800) 852-5852
  Web Page: http://www.synchronics.com
Synergy Software···························· Reading, PA: (610) 779-0522
  Tech:(610) 779-0522   Toll Free:(800) 876-8376
  Web Page: http://www.synergy.com
Synergy Solutions (see Artisoft)
Synergystex International···························· Brunswick, OH: (330) 225-3112
  Web Page: http://www.synergystex.com
Synex (see SNX)
Synopsys Inc···························· Mountain View, CA: (650) 584-5000
  Tech:(800) 245-8005   Toll Free:(800) 541-7737
  Web Page: http://www.synopsys.com
SynOptics Commun (see Nortel Networks)
Syqt Inc (Out of Business)
SyQuest Technology (Out of Business)
Syracuse Language Systems (Out of Business)
Sys Technology···························· Cypress, CA: (714) 821-3900
  Tech:(714) 821-3900   Toll Free:(800) 613-9963
  Web Page: http://www.sys.com
SysKonnect···························· Sunnyvale, CA: (408) 222-2500
  Web Page: http://www.syskonnect.com
Sysper Technologies Inc···························· San Jose, CA:
  Web Page: http://www.sysper.com
Syspro Impact Software Inc···························· Costa Mesa, CA: (714) 437-1000
  Tech:(714) 437-1000   Toll Free:(800) 369-8649
  Web Page: http://www.sysprousa.com
Systech···························· Cranbury, NJ: (609) 395-8400
  Toll Free:(800) 847-7123
  Web Page: http://www.systech-tips.com
System Integrators (see net-linx PS)
System Software Associates···························· Chicago, IL: (312) 258-6000
  Toll Free:(800) 997-9014
  Web Page: http://www.ssax.com
Systems Compatibility (see INSO)
SystemSoft Corp···························· Newton,, MA: (617) 614-4315
  Tech:(800) 796-0088
  Web Page: http://www.systemsoft.com
Systium Technologies···························· Minneapolis, MN: (612) 788-0923
  Web Page: http://www.systium.com
Systran Corp···························· Dayton, OH: (937) 252-5601
  Toll Free:(800) 252-5601
  Web Page: http://www.systran.com
Sytron Corp (see Seagate Software)
SyVox Corp···························· Boulder, CO: (303) 938-1110

Web Page: http://www.genesta.com

T.A.L. Technologies Inc ·· **Philadelphia, PA: (215) 496-0222**
    Tech:(215) 496-0322   Toll Free:(800) 722-6004
    Web Page: http://www.taltech.com

T.M.C. (Out of Bussiness)

T.S. Solutions (888) 447-8484
    Toll Free:(888) 447-8484
    Web Page: http://www.ts-solutions.com

T/Maker Company (see Broderbund)

T/R Systems ··· **Norcross, GA: (770) 448-9008**
    Toll Free:(888) 487-7462
    Web Page: http://www.trsystems.com

TAC Systems Inc (Out of Business)

Tadiran Batteries ································ **Port Washington, NY: (516) 621-4980**
    Toll Free:(800) 537-1368
    Web Page: http://www.tadiranbat.com

Tadpole Cycle ··· **Carlsbad, CA: (760) 929-0992**
    Tech:(800) 734-7030
    Web Page: http://www.tadpolerdi.com

Tallgrass Technologies (see Exabyte)

Tally Genicom ·· **Kent, WA: (425) 251-5500**
    Toll Free:(800) 426-4813
    Web Page: http://www.tally.com

TalonSoft Inc ·· **White Marsh, MD: (410) 933-9191**
    Tech:(410) 933-9191
    Web Page: http://www.talonsoft.com

Talyon Software Corp (see Plus & Minus)

Tandberg Data Inc ·· **Poway, CA: (858) 726-1800**
    Toll Free:(800) 826-3237
    Web Page: http://www.tandberg.com

Tandem Computers Inc. (see Compaq)

Tandon Information Solutions ···························· **Simi Valley, CA: (805) 582-3200**
    Web Page: http://www.tandoninfo.com

Tangent Computers Inc ······························· **Burlingame, CA: (800) 342-9388**
    Tech:(650) 399-8324
    Web Page: http://www.tangent.com

Tangram Enterprise Solutions (see Opsware) (408) 744-7770
    Web Page: http://www.opsware.com

Tarantella ·· **Santa Cruz, CA: (831) 427-7222**
    Tech:(800) 995-9806   Toll Free:(888) 831-9700
    Web Page: http://www.tarantella.com

Targus ··· **Anaheim, CA: (714) 765-5555**
    Tech:(877) 482-7487
    Web Page: http://www.targus.com

Tarian Software Corp (see IBM) ··································· **Fairfax, VA:**

Tatung Company Of America ···················· **Long Beach, CA: (310) 637-2105**
    Tech:(310) 637-2105   Toll Free:(800) 827-2850
    Web Page: http://www.tatungusa.com

Tatung Science & Technology ························ **Fremont, CA: (510) 687-9688**
    Tech:(510) 687-9688   Toll Free:(800) 659-5902
    Web Page: http://www.tsti.com

TCSI Corp/Rocket Software ···························· **Alameda, CA: (510) 749-8500**
    Web Page: http://www.tcsi.com

TDA/IPC ·· **Bothell, WA: (425) 402-7000**
    Tech:(425) 402-7000   Toll Free:(800) 624-2101
    Web Page: http://www.ipc-software.com

TDA/WINK Data Products (see TDA/IPC)

TDK Corp of America ···································· **Mount Prospect, IL: (847) 803-6100**
    Toll Free:(888) 835-6646

Web Page: http://www.component.tdk.com

TDK Electronics Corp .... Garden City, NY: (516) 535-2600
Tech:(800) 835-8273   Toll Free:(800) 835-8273
Web Page: http://www.tdk.com

TDK Mediactive (location closed)

TDK Semiconductor .... Irvine, CA: (714) 508-8800
Web Page: http://www.tsc.tdk.com

TEAC America Inc .... Montebello, CA: (323) 726-0303
Tech:(323) 727-4860
Web Page: http://www.teac.com

Team Systems Inc .... Santa Clara, CA: (408) 720-8877
Web Page: http://www.team-systems.com

Tech Data Corp .... Clearwater, FL: (727) 539-7429
Tech:(800) 553-7976   Toll Free:(800) 237-8931
Web Page: http://www.techdata.com

Tech Online .... Bedford, MA: (781) 266-5000
Toll Free:(877) 472-7882
Web Page: http://www.techonline.com

Tech Tools (see Alacrity Systems Inc)

TechAmerica (see Tandy/RadioShack.com)

Techni-Tool Inc .... Worcester, PA: (610) 825-4990
Tech:(866) 885-3266   Toll Free:(800) 832-4866
Web Page: http://www.techni-tool.com

Techniquip .... Pleasanton, CA: (925) 251-9030
Toll Free:(888) 414-0789
Web Page: http://www.techniquip.com

Technology Concepts (Out of Business)

TechSmith Corp .... Okemos, WI: (517) 381-2300
Toll Free:(800) 517-3001
Web Page: http://www.techsmith.com

Tecra Tool .... Denver, CO: (303) 338-9224
Tech:(800) 284-0808   Toll Free:(800) 284-0808
Web Page: http://www.tecratools.com

TEI Imaging Solutions .... Portsmouth, NH: (603) 431-3624
Toll Free:(800) 370-8663
Web Page: http://www.tei-imaging.com

Tekelec .... Calabasas, CA: (818) 880-5656
Tech:(888) 628-5521   Toll Free:(800) 835-3532
Web Page: http://www.tekelec.com

Teknowledge Corp .... Palo Alto, CA: (650) 424-0500
Web Page: http://www.teknowledge.com

TekSoft Inc .... Scottsdale, AZ: (408) 367-0132
Tech:(480) 367-0132
Web Page: http://www.teksoft.com

Tektronix .... Beaverton, OR: (503) 627-7111
Tech:(800) 833-9200   Toll Free:(800) 835-9433
Web Page: http://www.tek.com

Telco Systems .... Foxboro, MA: (781) 551-0300
Tech:(800) 227-0937   Toll Free:(800) 221-2849
Web Page: http://www.telco.com

Teldar Corp .... Gilbert, AZ: (480) 988-7902
Web Page: http://www.teldar.com

TeleAdapt Inc .... San Jose, CA: (408) 350-1440
Toll Free:(877) 835-3232
Web Page: http://www.teleadaptusa.com

TeleAtlas .... Menlo Park, CA: (650) 328-3825
Tech:(800) 765-0555   Toll Free:(800) 765-0555
Web Page: http://www.teleatlas.com

Telebit Corp (see ITK Telecomm)

Telebyte Technology ·· Greenlawn, NY: (631) 423-3232
  Toll Free:(800) 835-3298
  Web Page: http://www.telebyteusa.com
Telecast Fiber Systems Inc ································ Worcester, MA: (508) 754-4858
  Web Page: http://www.telecast-fiber.com
Telect Inc ·· Liberty Lake, WA: (509) 926-6000
  Tech:(888) 821-4856   Toll Free:(800) 551-4567
  Web Page: http://www.telect.com
Telemagic (see Sage US Holdings)
Telemate.net Software (see Verso Tech)
  Web Page: http://www.verso.com
Telemetrics Inc ·· Mahwah, NJ: (201) 848-9818
  Web Page: http://www.telemetricsinc.com
Telesensory Corporation ································· Sunnyvale, CA: (408) 616-8700
  Tech:(800) 286-8484   Toll Free:(800) 227-8418
  Web Page: http://www.telesensory.com
TeleType Co Inc ·· Boston, MA: (617) 542-6220
  Tech:(888) 835-3897   Toll Free:(800) 717-4478
  Web Page: http://www.teletype.com
Televideo Inc ·· San Jose, CA: (408) 954-8333
  Tech:(408) 955-7711   Toll Free:(800) 345-6050
  Web Page: http://www.televideo.com
Telex Communications ······································· Burnsville, MN: (952) 884-4051
  Web Page: http://www.telex.com
Telex Communications Inc ··································· Burnsville, MN: (952) 884-4051
  Web Page: http://www.telex.com
Teltone Corp ·· Bothell, WA: (425) 487-1515
  Toll Free:(800) 426-3926
  Web Page: http://www.teltone.com
Teltron Technologies Inc ··································· Birdsboro, PA: (610) 582-9450
  Toll Free:(800) 835-8766
  Web Page: http://www.teltrontech.com
Template Graphics Software ·································· San Diego, CA: (858) 457-5359
  Tech:(800) 428-7588   Toll Free:(800) 544-4847
  Web Page: http://www.tgs.com
Ten X Technology ·· Austin, TX: (512) 918-9182
  Toll Free:(800) 922-9050
  Web Page: http://www.tenx.com
Tenex Systems Inc ······································· King Of Prussia, PA: (610) 239-9988
  Tech:(877) 327-1219   Toll Free:(800) 295-3975
  Web Page: http://www.tenexsys.com
TenXpert Technologies Inc ·································· Austin, TX: (512) 346-6944
  Web Page: http://www.tenxpert.com
Teradyne ·· Boston, MA: (617) 482-2700
  Web Page: http://www.teradyne.com
TeraTech Inc ·· Rockville, MD: (301) 424-3903
  Toll Free:(800) 447-9120
  Web Page: http://www.teratech.com
Test Equity ·· Thousand Oaks, CA: (805) 498-9933
  Toll Free:(800) 950-3457
  Web Page: http://www.testequity.com
Texas Instruments ·· Dallas, TX: (972) 995-6611
  Toll Free:(800) 336-5236
  Web Page: http://www.ti.com
Texas Instruments ·· San Jose, CA: (408) 894-9000
  Web Page: http://www.ti.com
Texas Instruments ·· Dallas, TX: (972) 995-2011
  Web Page: http://www.ti.com
  Customer Support Line ······························· (972) 917-8324

Toll Free:(800) 842-2737
Factory Repair Center
Product Information Center ·························(972) 644-5580
Toll Free:(800) 477-8924
Software Upgrades ·····································(972) 293-5050

Texas Memory Systems Inc ································Houston, TX: (713) 266-3200
Tech:(713) 266-3200
Web Page: http://www.texmemsys.com

Texas Micro (see Radisys)

TFS (Three-Five Systems, Inc.) ···························Tempe, AZ: (602) 389-8600
Web Page: http://www.tfsc.com

The Other Guys ··Olympia, WA: (360) 943-5118
Toll Free:(800) 789-4897
Web Page: http://www.togi.com

Themis Computer ···Fremont, CA: (510) 252-0870
Web Page: http://www.themis.com

Theos Software Corp ·······························Walnut Creek, CA: (925) 935-1118
Toll Free:(800) 600-5660
Web Page: http://www.theos-software.com

Thermo Cidtec ···Liverpool, NY: (315) 451-9410
Web Page: http://www.cidtec.com

Thermo Electron ··Waltham, MA: (781) 622-1000
Toll Free:(877) 843-7668
Web Page: http://www.thermo.com

Think Direct Marketing.com (Out of Business)

Think Peak Inc ··Apex, NC: (919) 414-6653
Web Page: http://www.thinkpeak.com

Thinkstream Inc ···Tigard, OR: (503) 968-1656
Tech:(503) 968-1656
Web Page: http://www.thinkstream.com

Thomas Computer Corporation ·····················Orlando, FL: (407) 855-2020
Toll Free:(800) 621-3906
Web Page: http://www.thomascomputer.com

Thomas Electronics ·······································Wayne, NJ: (973) 696-5200
Web Page: http://www.thomaselectronics.com

Thomas-Conrad Corp (see Compaq)

THQ Inc ··Calabasas, CA: (818) 591-1310
Tech:(818) 871-5000
Web Page: http://www.thq.com

Three D Graphics ·····································Los Angeles, CA: (310) 231-3330
Toll Free:(800) 913-0008
Web Page: http://www.threedgraphics.com

ThrustMaster (see Center Span Comm.)

Tibco Inc ···Palo Alto, CA: (650) 846-1000
Toll Free:(800) 420-8450
Web Page: http://www.tibco.com

Tier Two (see Open Text Corp)

Tiffen Company, The ····································Hauppauge, NY: (631) 273-2500
Tech:(800) 593-3331   Toll Free:(800) 645-2522
Web Page: http://www.tiffen.com

Tiger Direct Inc ···Miami, FL: (305) 415-2200
Tech:(888) 335-4062   Toll Free:(800) 879-1597
Web Page: http://www.tigerdirect.com

Tiger Systems (see Sungard Banking)

TigerSoftware (see Tiger Direct Inc)

Timberline Software ···································Beaverton, OR: (503) 690-6775
Tech:(800) 858-7098   Toll Free:(800) 628-6583
Web Page: http://www.timberline.com

Time Motion Tools ·······································Poway, CA: (858) 679-0303

Tech:(858) 679-0303   Toll Free:(800) 779-8170
Web Page: http://www.timemotion.com

Time Value Software ··· Irvine, CA: (949) 727-1800
 Toll Free:(800) 426-4741
 Web Page: http://www.tvalue.com

Timeline ··· Bellevue, WA: (425) 822-3140
 Tech:(425) 822-9034
 Web Page: http://www.timeline.com

Timeslips Corp (see Sage U.S. Inc)

Timeslips Inc ·· Norcross, GA: (770 492-6414
 Toll Free:(800) 285-0999
 Web Page: http://www.timeslips.com

TimeTrak Systems Inc ·· Port Huron, MI: (810) 984-1313
 Toll Free:(888) 484-6387
 Web Page: http://www.timetrak.com

Timex Corp ·· North Little Rock, AR: (800) 448.4639
 Toll Free:(800) 448.4639
 Web Page: http://www.timex.com

Tir Systems ··· Burnaby, BC, BC: (604) 294 8477
 Toll Free:(800) 663-2036
 Web Page: http://www.tirsys.com

Titan Systems ·· Billercia, MA: (978) 663-6600
 Web Page: http://www.horizons.com

Titan Systems Corp ·· San Diego, CA: (858) 552-9500
 Tech:(858) 527-6100   Toll Free:(800) 621-8474
 Web Page: http://www.titan.com

Titan Systems Corp ·· Melbourne, FL: (321) 727-0660
 Toll Free:(800) 622-8554
 Web Page: http://www.titan.com/dbasystems

Titan Tool Supply Inc ·· Buffalo, NY: (716) 873-9907
 Web Page: http://www.titantoolsupply.com

Tivoli Systems (see IBM) ·· Austin, TX: (888) 839-9289
 Toll Free:(888) 839-9289
 Web Page: http://www.tivoli.com

TKO Media Inc ·· El Monte, CA: (626) 350-1520
 Web Page: http://www.tko-media.com

TMS Sequoia ·· Stillwater, OK: (405) 377-0880
 Toll Free:(800) 944-7654
 Web Page: http://www.tmsinc.com

Todd Enterprises ·· Plainview, NY: (516) 777-8633
 Tech:(800) 643-4351   Toll Free:(800) 445-8633
 Web Page: http://www.toddent.com

Tokina Industrial Inc ·· Medford, NY: (631) 289-5700
 Toll Free:(888) 486-5462
 Web Page: http://www.tokina-usa.com

Toko America ·· Mt Prospect, IL: (847) 297-0070
 Toll Free:(800) 745-8656
 Web Page: http://www.toko.com

Tool Kit Specialists (see Com-Kyle)

Top Image Systems ·· Wakefield, MA: (866) 254 5105
 Web Page: http://www.topimagesystems.com

Top Microsystems Corp ·· Santa Clara, CA: (408) 980-9813
 Toll Free:(800) 827-8721
 Web Page: http://www.topmicro.com

Top Speed (see Soft Velocity)

Toray Industries ·· San Mateo, CA: (650) 341-7152
 Tech:(650) 341-7152
 Web Page: http://www.toray.com

Torque Systems Inc ·· San Francisco, CA: (415) 225-1926

Phone Directory

Web Page: http://www.torque.com

Toshiba America .... **New York, NY: (212) 596-0600**
Web Page: http://www.toshiba.com
Business Solutions .... (949) 462-6000
Tech:(973) 316-2700   Toll Free:(800) 950-4373
Computer Systems Division .... (800) 867-4422
Toll Free:(800) 867-4422
Web Page: http://www.csd.toshiba.com
Consumer Products .... (973) 628-8000
Toll Free:(800) 631-3811
Web Page: http://www.toshiba.com/tacp
Disk Product Repair Center .... (510) 651-6798
Electronic Components .... (949) 455-2000
Web Page: http://www.toshiba.com/taec
Facsimile Product Support .... (800) 777-8068
Tech:(800) 777-8068
Imaging Systems .... (978) 251-0877
Web Page: http://www.cameras.toshiba.com
In Touch Center .... (800) 457-7777
Tech:(800) 457-7777   Toll Free:(800) 457-7777
Web Page: http://pcsupport.toshiba.com
Information Systems .... (949) 583-3000
Tech:(973) 316-2700
Web Page: http://www.toshiba.com
Medical Systems Inc .... (714) 730-5000
Network Products Division .... (949) 461-4840
Tech:(949) 583-3223
Web Page: http://internet.toshiba.com
Shop Toshiba .... (800) 959-4100
Toll Free:(800) 867-4422
Toshiba International Corp .... **Houston, TX: (713) 466-0277**
Toll Free:(800) 231-1412
Toshiba Storage Devices .... **Irvine, CA: (949) 457-0777**
Tech:(503) 615-4364
Web Page: http://www.toshiba.com/taecdpd
Tosoh USA Inc .... **Grove City, OH: (614) 539-8622**
Toll Free:(866) 844-6953
Web Page: http://www.tosoh.com
Total Management (see Planettechnology)
Totally Hip Software Inc .... **Vancouver, BC: (604) 685-6525**
Tech:(604) 685-0984
Web Page: http://www.totallyhip.com
Touch Stone Software .... **North Andover, MA: (978) 686-6468**
Web Page: http://www.touchstone-sc.com
Touchstone Software (see Smith Micro)
TouchWave Inc (see Ericsson WebCom)
Tower Technology .... **Boston, MA: (617) 236-5500**
Tech:(800) 954-1329   Toll Free:(888) 733-5500
Web Page: http://www.towertechnology.com
Trade Station Technologies .... **Plantation, FL: (954) 652-7000**
Toll Free:(800) 556-2022
Web Page: http://www.tradestation.com
TrainerSoft.com .... **Boston, MA: (617) 897.6800**
Web Page: http://www.outstart.com
Transcend Information Inc .... **Orange, CA: (714) 921-2000**
Tech:(714) 921-2000   Toll Free:(800) 886-5590
Web Page: http://www.transcendusa.com
TransEra Corp .... **Orem, UT: (801) 224-6550**
Web Page: http://www.transera.com
Transition Networks Inc .... **Minneapolis, MN: (952) 941-7600**

Tech:(800) 260-1312   Toll Free:(800) 526-9267
Web Page: http://www.transition.com

Transoft Networks (see Hewlett Packard)

Transparent Language Inc..Merrimack, NH: (603) 262-6300
Toll Free:(888) 245-1829
Web Page: http://www.transparent.com

Transtech Parallel Systems..Ithaca, NY: (607) 272-5494
Web Page: http://www.transtech-dsp.com

Trantor Systems Ltd (see Adaptec)

Traquair Data Systems...Ithaca, NY: (607) 266-6000
Web Page: http://www.traquair

Traveling Software (see Laplink.com)

Trax Softworks Inc...Los Angeles, CA: (805) 649-5800
Toll Free:(800) 367-8729
Web Page: http://www.traxsoft.com

Trellix Corp...Concord, MA: (978) 318-7200
Tech:(978) 318-7256
Web Page: http://www.trellix.com

Trend Micro Inc...Cupertino, CA: (408) 257-1500
Tech:(877) 268-4847   Toll Free:(800) 228-5651
Web Page: http://www.trendmicro.com

Trenton Technology Inc...Gainsville, GA: (770) 287-3100
Tech:(800) 875-6031   Toll Free:(800) 875-6031
Web Page: http://www.trentonprocessors.com

Tri-Star Computer (see Tri Cad/Cam Syst.)............Phoenix, AZ: (602) 333-1600
Toll Free:(800) 800-1714
Web Page: http://www.tristar.com

Tri-Tel Communications Inc..Salt Lake City, UT: (801) 265-9292
Web Page: http://www.tritel.com

Tribe Computer (see Zoom Telephonics)

Tricor Systems Inc..Elgin, IL: (847) 742-5542
Web Page: http://www.tricor-systems.com

Tricord Systems Inc (see Adaptec)............................Milpitas, CA: (408) 945-8600
Web Page: http://www.adaptec.com

Trident Microsystems Inc...Sunnyvale, CA: (408) 991-8800
Web Page: http://www.tridentmicro.com

Trident Software..Sausalito, CA: (415) 332-0188
Web Page: http://www.tridentsoft.com

TriGem America Corporation.......................................Foothill Ranch, CA: (949) 460-5900
Tech:(949) 580-3676
Web Page: http://www.trigem-usa.com

Continuous Computing...(858) 882-8800
Web Page: http://www.ccpu.com

TriniTech Inc...Largo, FL: (727) 442-8882
Tech:(727) 647-3742
Web Page: http://www.pcanalyzer.com

Tripp Lite Worldwide...Chicago, IL: (773) 869-1111
Tech:(773) 869-1234
Web Page: http://www.tripplite.com

Trius Inc...North Andover, MA: (978) 794-9377
Web Page: http://www.triusinc.com

Trompeter Electronics..Westlake Village, CA: (818) 707-2020
Toll Free:(800) 982-2629
Web Page: http://www.trompeter.com

Troy Wireless...Santa Ana, CA: (949) 250-3280
Web Page: http://www.troygroup.com

TrueArc Inc (see Documentum Worldwide)..............Pleasanton, CA: (925) 600-6800
Web Page: http://www.truearc.com

Truevision (see Pinnacle Systems)

Trumatch Inc .... Southampton, NY: (800) 878-9100
  Toll Free:(800) 878-9100
  Web Page: http://www.trumatch.com

TSI Power Corp .... Antigo, WI: (715) 623-0636
  Toll Free:(800) 874-3160
  Web Page: http://www.tsipower.com

TSLI Technical Services & Logistics Inc .... Simi Valley, CA: (805) 581-0163
  Toll Free:(800) 286-0651
  Web Page: http://www.tsli.com

TT Systems Corp .... Baltimore, MD: (410) 244 1150
  Web Page: http://www.ttsystemsinc.com

Tucker Electronics .... Garland, TX: (214) 348-8800
  Toll Free:(877) 667-6044
  Web Page: http://www.tucker.com

Tulin Technology (see Computer Review)

Turbolinux .... Palm Springs, CA: (760) 318-0495
  Web Page: http://www.turbolinux.com

Turbopower Software Comp. (Out of Business)

Turtle Beach Systems (see Voyetra)

Tut Systems .... Lake Oswego, OR: (503) 594-1400
  Toll Free:(800) 998-4888
  Web Page: http://www.tutsys.com

TV One Multimedia Solutions .... Erlanger, KY: (859) 282-7303
  Toll Free:(800) 721-4044
  Web Page: http://www.tvone.com

Twain Working Group (831) 338-8042
  Web Page: http://www.twain.org

Twelve Tone Sys (see Cake Walk Music)

TwinBridge Software Corp .... Monterey Park, CA: (323) 263-3926
  Tech:(323) 263-5931   Toll Free:(888) 650-8899
  Web Page: http://www.twinbridge.com

Twinhead Corp .... Fremont, CA: (510) 492-0828
  Toll Free:(800) 995-8946
  Web Page: http://www.twinhead.com

Tyan Computer Corp .... Fremont, CA: (510) 651-8868
  Tech:(510) 440-8808
  Web Page: http://www.tyan.com

Tyco Electronics .... Harrisburg, PA: (717) 564-0100
  Tech:(800) 526-0721   Toll Free:(800) 522-6752
  Web Page: http://www.amp.com

Typhoon Software .... Santa Barbara, CA: (805) 966-7633
  Web Page: http://www.typhoon.com

TYX Corp .... Reston, VA: (703) 264-1080
  Toll Free:(800) 321-7297
  Web Page: http://www.tyx.com

U-Tron Technologies Inc (Out of Business)

Ubisoft Inc .... San Francisco, CA: (415) 547-4000
  Tech:(415) 547-4028   Toll Free:(800) 824-7638
  Web Page: http://www.ubisoft.com

Ulead Systems Inc .... Torrance, CA: (310) 896-6388
  Tech:(310) 896-6391   Toll Free:(800) 858-5323
  Web Page: http://www.ulead.com

Ultima International (see Artec)

Ultimatte Corp .... Chatsworth, CA: (818) 993-8007
  Web Page: http://www.ultimatte.com

Ultra Bac .... Bellevue, WA: (425) 644-6000
  Tech:(425) 644-6000
  Web Page: http://www.ultrabac.com

Ultra-X Inc .... Santa Clara, CA: (408) 261-7090

Tech:(909) 946-8321 Toll Free:(800) 722-3789
Web Page: http://www.ultra-x.com

Ultravolt ·· Ronkonkoma, NY: (631) 471-4444
Toll Free:(800) 948-7693
Web Page: http://www.ultravolt.com

UMAX Technologies Inc ···································· Dallas, TX: (214) 342-9799
Tech:(214) 739-1915
Web Page: http://www.umax.com
Service Repair Center ···································· (214) 739-1968

Undertow Software Inc ···································· Channahon, IL: (815) 521-9950
Toll Free:(800) 257-9244
Web Page: http://www.undertowsoftware.com

Underware (see Numega Labs)

Unibrain Inc ·· San Ramon, CA: (925) 866-3000
Web Page: http://www.unibrain.com

Unicore Software (see eSupport.com)

Uniden America Corp ······································ Fort Worth, TX: (817) 858-3300
Tech:(888) 686-4336 Toll Free:(800) 235-3874
Web Page: http://www.uniden.com

Unigraphics Solutions (see EDS)

Unimark Inc ·· Lenexa, KS: (913) 649-2424
Tech:(913) 649-2232 Toll Free:(800) 255-6356
Web Page: http://www.unimark.com

UniPress Software Inc ···································· Edison, NJ: (800) 222-0550
Tech:(732) 287-2100 Toll Free:(800) 222-0550
Web Page: http://www.unipress.com

Unison Information Systems ····························· Natick, MA: (508) 655-4049
Toll Free:(800) 846-3472
Web Page: http://www.unisoninfo.com

Unison Software Inc (see Tivoli Systems)

Unisys Corp ··· Farmington, NY: (716) 924-0480
Tech:(800) 328-0440 Toll Free:(800) 874-8647
Web Page: http://www.unisys.com

Unitech Industries ··· Tempe, AZ: (480) 303-9853
Tech:(480) 303-9853
Web Page: http://www.unitech-industries.com

United Media ··· Anaheim, CA: (714) 777-4510
Web Page: http://www.unitedmediainc.com

United Publications ·· Yarmouth, ME: (207) 846-0600
Web Page: http://www.ccnews.com

United Visual ··· Itasca, IL: (630) 467-1500
Toll Free:(800) 226-1131
Web Page: http://www.unitedvisual.com

Unitron Inc ·· Bohemia, NY: (631) 589-6666
Web Page: http://www.unitronusa.com

Univ. Research & Develop. (Out of Business)

Univel (see Novell)

Universal Imaging Corp ···································· Downingtown, PA: (610) 873-5610
Web Page: http://www.universal-imaging.com

Universal Technical Systems ···························· Rockford, IL: (800) 435-7887
Tech:(815) 963-2220 Toll Free:(800) 435-7887
Web Page: http://www.uts.com

Universe Kogaku America ································ Oyster Bay, NY: (516) 624-2444
Web Page: http://www.ukaoptics.com

uniView Technologies (Out of Business)

Unixware (see Novell)

Unwired Technology ·· Plainview, NY: (516) 293-6900
Web Page: http://www.un-wired.com

Up Software .... San Francisco, CA: (800) 959-8208
  Tech:(415) 921-4691   Toll Free:(800) 959-8208
  Web Page: http://www.upsoftware.com

UrLabs Inc (see Symantec Corp)

US Design .... Columbia, MD: (410) 381-3000
  Toll Free:(800) 622-8732
  Web Page: http://www.usdesign.com

US Robotics .... Schamburg, IL: (847) 874-2000
  Tech:(866) 287-7669   Toll Free:(877) 710-0884
  Web Page: http://www.usr.com/home.asp

US Robotics Inc (see 3Com)
  Analog ··· (801) 401-1141
  ISDN ·· (801) 401-1142
  Wireless & Network ································· (801) 401-1143

USA Flex (see Comark Inc)

Utah Scientific Inc .... Salt Lake City, UT: (801) 575-8801
  Tech:(801) 575-3247   Toll Free:(800) 447-7204
  Web Page: http://www.utahscientific.com

Utimaco Safeware .... Worcester, MA: (508) 799-4333
  Toll Free:(800) 688-1199
  Web Page: http://www.utimaco.com

Utobia Corp (Out of Business)

V Communications Inc .... San Jose, CA: (408) 965-4000
  Tech:(408) 965-4018   Toll Free:(800) 648-8266
  Web Page: http://www.v-com.com

V-One Corp .... GermanTown, MD: (301) 515-5200
  Tech:(888) 220-8663   Toll Free:(800) 495-8663
  Web Page: http://www.v-one.com

Varatouch Technology Inc ···························· El Dorado Hills, CA: (916) 941 0744
  Web Page: http://www.varatouch.com

Variant Microsystems ·· Fremont, CA: (510) 440-2870
  Toll Free:(800) 827-4268
  Web Page: http://www.variantusa.com

Varta Batteries ·· Madison, WI: (608) 275-3340
  Toll Free:(800) 237-7000
  Web Page: http://www.varta.com

Vartech Inc (Out of Business)

Vasco Data Security ·· Oakbrook Terrace, IL: (630) 932-8844
  Tech:(630) 495-0279
  Web Page: http://www.vasco.com

Vaytek Inc·· Fairfield, IA: (641) 472-2227
  Web Page: http://www.vaytek.com

VBrick Systems ··· Wallingford, CT: (203) 265-0044
  Toll Free:(866) 827-4251
  Web Page: http://www.vbrick.com

Vela Research Inc ·· Clearwater, FL: (727) 507-5300
  Toll Free:(800) 231-1349
  Web Page: http://www.vela.com

Venetica Corp ·· Charlotte, NC: (704) 926-3000
  Web Page: http://www.venetica.com

Ventura Software (see Corel)

VenturCom Inc ··· Waltham, MA: (781) 647-3000
  Web Page: http://www.vci.com

Verbatim Corp ·· Charlotte, NC: (704) 547-6500
  Tech:(800) 538-8589
  Web Page: http://www.verbatim.com

Verbex Voice Systems (see Voxware)

Vergetech ·· Dallas, TX: (972) 386-3372
  Web Page: http://www.vergetech.com

VeriFone ·· Santa Clara, CA: (408) 330-6300
Tech:(408) 330-6390
Web Page: http://www.verifone.com

VeriSign Inc ·· Mountain View, CA: (650) 961-7500
Tech:(888) 642-9675   Toll Free:(888) 883-9770
Web Page: http://www.verisign.com

Veritas Soft. (see Crystal Decisions)

Verity Inc ·· Sunnyvale, CA: (408) 541-1500
Tech:(403) 294-1107
Web Page: http://www.verity.com

Verity Systems ·· Placerville, CA: (530) 626-9363
Toll Free:(800) 642-5151
Web Page: http://www.veritysystems.com

Vermont Creative Software ·· Richford, VT: (802) 848-7589
Tech:(802) 848-7731   Toll Free:(800) 848-1248
Web Page: http://www.vtsoft.com

Versant Object Technology ·· Fremont, CA: (510) 789-1500
Toll Free:(800) 837-7268
Web Page: http://www.versant.com

Versitron ·· Newark, DE: (302) 894-0699
Toll Free:(800) 537-2296
Web Page: http://www.versitron.com

Verso Technologies ·· Atlanta, GA: (678) 589-3500
Web Page: http://www.verso.com

Vertex Interactive ·· Poramus, NJ: (973) 777-3500
Tech:(973) 777-3500
Web Page: http://www.vertex.com

Vertisoft Systems (see Symantec)

VESA Standards (see Video Electronic)

Vexcel Corp ·· Boulder, CO: (303) 444-0094
Web Page: http://www.vexcel.com

Vhsage Technology ·· Littleton, MA: (978) 952-2200

ViaGrafix (see DesignCAD.com)

Victory Enterprises Tech ·· Austin, TX: (512) 450-0801
Toll Free:(800) 727-3475
Web Page: http://www.victoryent.com

Vidar Systems Corp ·· Herndon, VA: (703) 471-7070
Toll Free:(800) 471.7226
Web Page: http://www.vidar.com

Video Display Corp ·· Tucker, GA: (770) 938-2080
Toll Free:(800) 241-5005
Web Page: http://www.videodisplay.com

Video Electronic Standards Assn ·· Milpitas, CA: (408) 957-9270
Web Page: http://www.vesa.org

Video Instruments ·· Xenia, OH: (937) 376-4361
Toll Free:(800) 962-8905
Web Page: http://www.videoinstruments.com

Video Scope Intl ·· Dulles, VA: (703) 437-5534
Web Page: http://www.videoscopeintl.com

Videodiscovery Inc ·· Seattle, WA: (206) 285-5400
Tech:(800) 548-3472   Toll Free:(800) 548-3472
Web Page: http://www.videodiscovery.com

Videolabs Inc (see ClearOne) ·· Salt Lake City, UT: (801) 975-7200
Toll Free:(800) 945-7730
Web Page: http://www.clearone.com

Videology Imaging Solutions Inc ·· Grenville, RI: (401) 949-5332
Web Page: http://www.videologyinc.com

Videomail Inc ·· Sunnyvale, CA: (408) 492-1500
Web Page: http://www.videomail.com

Phone Directory

Videomedia ···················· Athol, ID: (208) 755-4561
  Web Page: http://www.videomedia.com
Videonics Inc (see Focus Enhancements)
Videotex Systems ···················· Dallas, TX: (972) 231-9200
  Toll Free:(800) 888-4336
  Web Page: http://www.videotexsystems.com
Videx Inc ···················· Corvallis, OR: (541) 758-0521
  Web Page: http://www.videx.com
ViewCast Corp ···················· Dallas, TX: (972) 488-7200
  Toll Free:(800) 540-4119
  Web Page: http://www.viewcast.com
Viewpoint ···················· New York, NY: (212) 201-0800
  Web Page: http://www.viewpoint.com
Viewpoint Digital (Out of Business)
ViewSonic Corp ···················· Walnut, CA: (909) 444-8888
  Tech:(909) 688-6688   Toll Free:(800) 888-8583
  Web Page: http://www.viewsonic.com
Vignette ···················· Austin, TX: (512) 741-4300
  Toll Free:(888) 608-9900
  Web Page: http://www.vignette.com
Viisage Technology ···················· Billerica, MA: (978) 952-2200
  Web Page: http://www.viisage.com
Viking Components ···················· Rancho Santa Margarita, CA: (949) 643-7255
  Tech:(949) 888-6087   Toll Free:(800) 338-2361
  Web Page: http://www.vikingcomponents.com
Viking Software Services ···················· Tulsa, OK: (918) 491-6144
  Toll Free:(800) 324-0595
  Web Page: http://www.vikingsoft.com
Vinca Corp (see Legato)
Vinten Inc ···················· Valley Cottage, NY: (845) 268-0100
  Web Page: http://www.vinten.com
VIO North America ···················· Roseland, NJ: (973) 535-6080
  Web Page: http://www.vio-dgn.com
Virage Inc ···················· San Francisco, CA: (415) 243-9955
  Web Page: http://www.virage.com
Vireo Software (see Compuware NuMega)
Virgin Interactive Ent. (out of business)
  Web Page: http://www.vie.com
Virtual Publisher (see Web Site Pros)
Virtual Tech (see Virtual Comtech)
Virtus Corp ···················· Cary, NC: (919) 467-9700
  Web Page: http://www.virtus.com
Visara ···················· Morrisville, NC: (919) 882-0200
  Tech:(919) 882-0206
  Web Page: http://www.visara.com
Visible Light ···················· Winter Springs, FL: (800) 596-4494
  Toll Free:(800) 596-4494
  Web Page: http://www.visiblelight.com
Visicon Inspection Tech ···················· Napa, CA: (707) 259-1300
  Web Page: http://www.visicontech.com
Visio Corp (see Microsoft)
Vision Computers Inc ···················· Norcross, GA: (770) 840-0015
  Tech:(770) 840-9249   Toll Free:(800) 886-4466
  Web Page: http://www.visioncomputers.com
Vision Identics Systems Inc ···················· Mamaroneck, NY: (914) 381-2625
  Toll Free:(800) 750-8840
  Web Page: http://www.visionid.com
Vision Imaging (see Advanced Media)

Vision Machines·····································North Reading, MA: (978) 276-3465
   Web Page: http://www.vision-machines.com
Vision Research Inc·····································Wayne, NJ: (973) 696-4500
   Toll Free:(800) 737-6588
   Web Page: http://www.visiblesolutions.com
Visionary Networks·····································Portland, OR: (503) 246-6200
   Tech:(503) 246-6200
Visionary Solutions·····································Carpentaria, CA: (805) 566-5811
   Web Page: http://www.vsicam.com
Visioneer·····································Pleasanton, CA: (925) 251-6300
   Tech:(925) 251-6397
   Web Page: http://www.visioneer.com
Visionics·····································Jersey City, NJ: (201) 332-9213
Visionshape·····································Placentia, CA: (714) 792-3612
   Toll Free:(800) 962-3585
   Web Page: http://www.visionshape.com
Visual Applications·····································Sarasota, FL: (941) 924-1989
   Web Page: http://www.visapp.com
Visual Business Systems (see Graphx)
Visual Circuits·····································Minneapolis, MN: (763) 571-7588
   Toll Free:(800) 250-5533
   Web Page: http://www.visualcircuits.com
Visual Networks Broadband Tech Grp·····································Seattle, WA: (301) 296-2300
   Tech:(301) 296-2300
   Web Page: http://www.net2net.com
Visual Numeric Inc·····································Westminster, CO: (303) 379-3040
   Tech:(303) 379-3033
   Web Page: http://www.vni.com
Visual Numerics·····································San Ramon, CA: (925) 415-8300
   Web Page: http://www.vni.com
Visual Solutions Inc·····································Houston, TX: (713) 784-3131
   Tech:(713) 954-6439   Toll Free:(800) 222-4675
   Web Page: http://www.vissim.com
Vital Image Technology·····································Auga Dulce, CA: 661-268-8600
   Toll Free:888-611-5211
   Web Page: http://www.vitalimage.com
Vitana Corp (see Pixelink)
Vitec Multimedia·····································Duluth, GA: 678-580-3165
   Web Page: http://www.vitecmm.com
Vivitar Corp·····································Oxnard, CA: 805-988-0463
   Web Page: http://www.vivitar.com
Vivo Software (see Real Networks Inc)
VMark Software (see Ardent Software Inc)
VocalTec Inc·····································Fort Lee, NJ: (201) 228-7000
   Tech:(201) 228-7101
   Web Page: http://www.vocaltec.com
Voice It Worldwide Inc (see VXI Corp)
Voice Pilot (Out of bussiness)·····································Miami, FL: (305) 412-8217
   Toll Free:(877) 864-2374
   Web Page: http://www.voicepilot.com
Voicenet·····································Ivyland, PA: (215) 674-9290
   Tech:(888) 647-4373   Toll Free:(800) 835-5710
   Web Page: http://www.voicenet.com
Volpi Mfg. USA·····································Auburn, NY: (315) 255-1737
   Toll Free:(800) 688-6574
   Web Page: http://www.volpiusa.com
Voxware Inc·····································Lawrenceville, NJ: (609) 514-4100
   Tech:(888) 483-7239   Toll Free:(888) 483-7239
   Web Page: http://www.voxware.com

Voyager Co (see Learn Technologies)

Voyetra Turtle Beach Inc ·································· Yonkers, NY: (914) 966-0600
Tech:(914) 966-2150   Toll Free:(800) 233-9377
Web Page: http://www.voyetra-turtle-beach.com

VR Toolbox ·································· Pittsburgh, PA: (412) 767-4947
Toll Free:(877) 878-6657
Web Page: http://www.vrtoolbox.com

VTech Industries ·································· Arlington Hights, IL: 847-400-3600
Toll Free:800-521-2010
Web Page: http://www.vtech.com

Vtel Corp ·································· Austin, TX: 512-821-7000
Tech:(800) 835-5266   Toll Free:(800) 299-8835
Web Page: http://www.vtel.com

VXI Corp ·································· Rollinsford, NH: (800) 742-8588
Tech:(800) 742-8588   Toll Free:(800) 742-8588
Web Page: http://www.vxicorp.com

Wacom Technology Corp ·································· Vancouver, WA: (360) 896-9833
Tech:(800) 922-6613   Toll Free:(800) 922-9348
Web Page: http://www.wacom.com

Walker Interactive Systems ·································· San Francisco, CA: (415) 495-8811
Tech:(415) 495-3013
Web Page: http://www.walker.com

Walker Richer & Quinn Inc (see WRQ)

Wall Data Inc (see NetManage)

Walnut Creek CDROM (see BSDI)

Wam Net ·································· Bloomington, MN: 952-852-4800
Tech:888-638-6771
Web Page: http://www.wamnet.com

Wang Global (see Getronics)

Wang Laboratories (see Getronics)

Wangtek/WangDAT (see Tecmar Tech)

Ward Systems Group ·································· Frederick, MD: (301) 662-7950
Web Page: http://www.wardsystems.com

Warehouse.com (see MicroWarehouse)

Warever Corp(Out of Bussiness) ·································· Draper, UT: (801) 572-2555
Tech:(801) 572-8923   Toll Free:(800) 766-7229
Web Page: http://www.actionplus.com

Warrantech Corp ·································· Bedford, TX: 817-785-6601
Toll Free:800-833-8801
Web Page: http://www.warrantech.com

Wasatch Computer Technology ·································· Salt Lake City, UT: (801) 575-8043
Tech:(800) 683-8214   Toll Free:(800) 894-1544
Web Page: http://www.wasatchinc.com

WatchSoft Inc ·································· Houston, TX: (281) 282-0188
Tech:(888) 709-2824   Toll Free:(888) 709-2824
Web Page: http://www.watchsoft.com

Waterford Group(out of bussiness) ·································· Campbell, CA: (408) 374-8450
Web Page: http://www.thewaterfordgroup.com

Watergate Software (see PC Doctor)

Waterloo Maple Software ·································· Waterloo, ON: (519) 747-2373
Tech:(519) 747-2505   Toll Free:(800) 267-6583
Web Page: http://www.maplesoft.com

Wave Technologies ·································· Chicago, IL: 773-380-7200
Toll Free:(888) 204-6143
Web Page: http://www.wavetech.com

WaveMetrics Inc ·································· Lake Oswego, OR: (503) 620-3001
Web Page: http://www.wavemetrics.com

Wavetek, Wandel, Golter. (see Acterna)

Wayzata Technology Inc (Out of Business)

Web MD ···································· Elmwood Dark, NJ: 201-703-3401
 Web Page: http://www.webmd.com

Web Site Pros (904) 680-6600
 Toll Free:(888) 218-5863
 Web Page: http://www.websitepros.com

WebCo International (see RuleSpace)

WebGear Inc(Out of Bussiness) ···················· San Jose, CA: (925) 551-5099
 Web Page: http://www.webgear.com

WebManage (see Network Appliance)

WebMaster Inc ····································· Santa Clara, CA: (408) 345-1800
 Web Page: http://www.webmaster.com

WebSci Technologies(Out of bussiness) ······· Monmouth Junction, NJ: (732) 329-900
 Web Page: http://www.websci.com

WebTrends Corp ···································· Portland, OR: (503) 294-7025
 Tech:(503) 223-3023
 Web Page: http://www.webtrends.com

Webworks.com ····································· Austin, TX: (512) 719-3399
 Tech:(512) 719-3399
 Web Page: http://www.webworks.com

WEN Technology Corp ······························ Yonkers, NY: (800) 377-4936
 Toll Free:(800) 377-4936
 Web Page: http://www.wentech.com

Westbrook Technologies Inc ·················· Branford, CT: (203) 483-6666
 Tech:(203) 483-6666   Toll Free:(800) 949-3453
 Web Page: http://www.filemagic.com

Westech Optical Corp(out of bussiness) ··············· Penfield, NY: (716) 377-2490

Western Digital Corp ······························ Lake Forest, CA: (949) 672-7000
 Tech:(800) 275-4932   Toll Free:(800) 832-4778
 Web Page: http://www.wdc.com

Western Micro Tech (see Software Tech)

Western Scientific Inc ····························· San Diego, CA: (858) 565-6699
 Toll Free:(800) 443-6699
 Web Page: http://www.wsm.com

Western Telematic Inc ····························· Irvine, CA: (949) 586-9950
 Tech:(888) 280-7227   Toll Free:(800) 854-7226
 Web Page: http://www.wti.com

Westing Software (see Responsive Soft.)

Westwood Studio (see Virgin Interactive)

WexTech Systems ·································· Elmsford, NY: 914-592-2400
 Toll Free:(800) 939-8324
 Web Page: http://www.wextech.com

Where?Media Inc ·································· St Johns, NF: (709) 753-6334
 Tech:(866) 753-6366   Toll Free:(866) 753-6334
 Web Page: http://www.wheremedia.com

White Electronic Designs ························ Phoenix, AZ: (602) 437-1520
 Web Page: http://www.whiteedc.com

White Pine Software (see CUseeME)

Whittaker Xyplex (see nbase-Xyplex)

Wholesale Computer Exchange ····················· Monroe, CT: (203) 459-8222
 Web Page: http://www.wholesalecomputer.com

Wilcom Products ·································· Laconia, NH: (603) 524-2622
 Toll Free:(800) 222-1898
 Web Page: http://www.wilcominc.com

WildCard Technologies (see PureData)

Williams Advanced Materials/Pure Data ············ Buffalo, NY: (716) 837-1000
 Web Page: http://www.williams-adv.com

Willies Computer Software (WCSC) ···················· Kingwood, TX: (281) 360-4232

Tech:(281) 360-3187   Toll Free:(800) 966-4832
Web Page: http://www.wcscnet.com

WinBook 614-777-2802
Tech:800-468-1225   Toll Free:800-468-1633
Web Page: http://www.winbookcorp.com

Wind River .... **Alameda, CA: (408) 542-1500**
Tech:(800) 872-4977   Toll Free:800-545-9463
Web Page: http://www.isi.com

Wind2 Software Inc .... **Fort Collins, CO: (970) 482-7145**
Tech:(970) 482-7152   Toll Free:(800) 779-4632
Web Page: http://www.wind2.com

Windata (see Direct Network Services)

Window on Wallstreet (see Trade Station)

Windsoft International Inc .... **Orlando, FL: (407) 355-0800**
Toll Free:(800) 542-4455
Web Page: http://www.windsoft.net

Windsor Technologies Inc .... **San Rafael, CA: (415) 456-2200**
Tech:(415) 456-2200
Web Page: http://www.windsortech.com

Wingra Technologies Inc .... **Madison, WI: 608-662-4400**
Web Page: http://www.wingra.com

Winnov .... **Sunnyvale, CA: (408) 744-9777**
Web Page: http://www.winnov.com

WinSoft Corp .... **Santa Ana, CA: (714) 444-4844**
Toll Free:(877) 946-7638
Web Page: http://www.winsoft.com

WinStation .... **Moses Lake, WA: (509) 765-7759**
Toll Free:(800) 243-3475
Web Page: http://www.winstation.com

Winstation Systems Corp .... **Moses Lake, WA: (509) 765-7759**
Tech:(800) 243-3475   Toll Free:(800) 243-3475
Web Page: http://www.winstation.com

Winsted Corp .... **Minneapolis, MN: (952) 944-9050**
Toll Free:(800) 447-2257
Web Page: http://www.winsted.com

Winsystems Inc .... **Arlington, TX: (817) 274-7553**
Web Page: http://www.winsystems.com

Wintek Corp .... **Lafayette, IN: 765-742-8428**
Tech:(765) 742-8428   Toll Free:(800) 742-6809
Web Page: http://www.wintek.com

Wintriss Engineering Corp .... **San Diego, CA: (858) 550-7300**
Toll Free:(800) 550-7300
Web Page: http://www.weco.com

WinWay Corp .... **Folsom, CA: (916) 965-7878**
Tech:(916) 965-7878   Toll Free:(800) 494-6929
Web Page: http://www.winway.com

Wise Solutions Inc .... **Plymouth, MI: (734) 456-2100**
Tech:(734) 456-2600   Toll Free:(800) 554-8565
Web Page: http://www.wise.com

Wizard Works Group (see Infogrames)

Wizardware LLC .... **Carlsbad, CA: 760-729-1514**
Web Page: http://www.wizardware.com

Wizzard Software Corp .... **Pittsburgh, PA: (412) 621-0902**
Toll Free:(800) 721-7701
Web Page: http://www.wizzardsoftware.com

Wolfram Research Inc .... **Champaign, IL: (217) 398-0700**
Tech:(217) 398-6500   Toll Free:(800) 965-3726
Web Page: http://www.wolfram.com

Woll2Woll Software .... **Livermore, CA: (925) 371-1663**

Web Page: http://www.woll2woll.com

Wollongong (see Attachmate)

Wonderware Corp .... Lake Forest, CA: (949) 727-3200
Tech:(949) 727-3299
Web Page: http://www.wonderware.com

WordStar Int (see Learning Co)

Wordstar USA (see Learning Co)

Work Wise Software .... Bellevue, WA: (425) 822-3140
Toll Free:(800) 588-7632
Web Page: http://www.workwise

World Software Corp .... Ridgewood, NJ: (201) 444-3228
Tech:(201) 444-3290   Toll Free:(800) 962-6360
Web Page: http://www.worldox.com

Worldcomm Sys (see Globecomm Systems)

Worth Data .... Santa Cruz, CA: (831) 458-9938
Toll Free:(800) 345-4220
Web Page: http://www.barcodehq.com

WRQ .... Seattle, WA: (206) 217-7500
Tech:(206) 217-7000   Toll Free:(800) 872-2829
Web Page: http://www.wrq.com

Wyatt River Software (see Rainbow Tech)

Wyndstone Specialty Products .... Wheeling, IL: (847) 808-9487
Web Page: http://www.wyndstone.com

Wyse Technology .... San Jose, CA: (408) 473-1200
Toll Free:(800) 438-9973
Web Page: http://www.wyse.com

X Consortium (see Open Group)

X-10 Wireless Technology Inc .... Seattle, NJ: (800) 675-3044
Web Page: http://www.x10.com

X-Rite Inc .... Grandville, MI: (616) 534-7663
Toll Free:800-248-9748
Web Page: http://www.xrite.com

Xaar .... Schamburg, IL: (847) 470-2088
Tech:(847) 490-2088
Web Page: http://www.xaar-usa.com

Xante Corp .... Mobile, AL: (251) 473-6502
Toll Free:(800) 926-8839
Web Page: http://www.xante.com

XcelleNet Inc (see Sterling Commerce)

Xebec (Out of Business)

Xecom Inc .... Milpitas, CA: 408-942-2200
Web Page: http://www.xecom.com

Xedar Corp .... Boulder, CO: (303) 443-6441
Web Page: http://www.xedar.com

Xerox Corp .... Rochester, NY: (716) 423-5090
Tech:(800) 822-2979   Toll Free:(800) 275-9376
Web Page: http://www.xerox.com
Customer & Product Safety .... (800) 828-6571
Toll Free:(800) 828-6571
Customer Education & Registration .... (800) 445-5554
Toll Free:(800) 445-5554
Documentation/Software Services .... (800) 327-9753
Toll Free:(800) 428-2995
Engineering Equipment .... (800) 937-8255
Environment, Health & Safety .... (800) 828-6571
Toll Free:(800) 828-6571
Fax Back .... (800) 979-9709
Font & Forms Services .... (310) 333-6311
Toll Free:(800) 445-3668

Headquarters .... (203) 968-3000
  Toll Free:(800) 334-6200
Manuels & Documentation .... (800) 327-9753
  Toll Free:(800) 327-9753
Mobile doc .... (650) 813-7044
Office Printing .... (800) 835-6100
  Tech:(503) 682-7377   Toll Free:(800) 835-6100
Parts .... (800) 828-5881
Printer Support .... (800) 835-6100
Scanning/Image Capture .... (888) 362-8462
ScanSoft .... (970) 526-0019
Service Calls .... (800) 828-9090
Special Projects Services .... (800) 734-6856
  Toll Free:(800) 734-6856
Supplies .... (800) 822-2200
Support .... (800) 821-2797
Team Xerox .... (800) 832-6979
  Toll Free:(800) 832-6979
Xerox Foundation .... (203) 968-3333
Xerox Omnifax .... Austin, TX: (512) 719-5566
  Tech:(800) 693-6664   Toll Free:(800) 221-8330
  Web Page: http://www.omnifax.com
Xicor Inc .... Milpitas, CA: (408) 432-8888
  Tech:(408) 954-1627
  Web Page: http://www.xicor.com
Xilinx Software .... San Jose, CA: (408) 559-7778
  Tech:408-559-7114   Toll Free:800-255-7778
  Web Page: http://www.xilinx.com
Xing Technology Corp (see Real.com)
Xiotech .... Eden Prairie, MN: (952) 983-3000
  Tech:(800) 734-4716   Toll Free:(866) 472-6764
  Web Page: http://www.xiotech.com
Xircom Inc (Part Of Intel) .... Thousand Oaks, CA: (800) 438-4526
  Toll Free:(800) 438-4526
  Web Page: http://www.xircom.com
Xirlink .... San Jose, CA: (408) 474-0494
  Tech:(408) 474-0494   Toll Free:(800) 928-8008
  Web Page: http://www.xirlink.com
Xmetal 866-793-1542
  Web Page: http://www.xmetal.com
XmlCities Inc .... Milpitas, CA: (408) 934-7878
  Web Page: http://www.xmlcities.com
Xtend Micro Products (see IGO) .... Corona Del Mar, CA: (949) 221-8025
  Toll Free:(800) 232-9836
  Web Page: http://www.XtendMicro.com
XTree Company (see Symantec Corp)
Xybernaut Corp .... Fairfax, VA: 703-631-6925
  Toll Free:(888) 992-3777
  Web Page: http://www.xybernaut.com
Xybion Electronic Systems .... Cedar Knolls, NJ: 973-538-5111
  Web Page: http://www.xybion.com
XyEnterprise .... Reading, MA: (781) 756-4400
  Tech:(800) 925-1269
  Web Page: http://www.xyvision.com
Xylan Corp (see Alcatel Internetworking)
Xylogics Inc (see Nortel Networks)
Xyntek Inc .... Yardley, PA: (215) 493-7091
  Web Page: http://www.xyntekinc.com
Xyplex (see I Touch Communications)
Xyris Software Inc .... Brooklyn, NY: 718-388-0962

Web Page: http://www.xyris.com

Yahoo! Inc ·· Sunnyvale, CA: (408) 731-3300
Tech:(408) 349-3300
Web Page: http://www.yahoo.com

Yamaha Corporation Of America ····················· Buena Park, CA: (714) 522-9011
Tech:(714) 522-9000   Toll Free:(800) 889-2624
Web Page: http://www.yamaha.com

Yamaha Corporation(Out of bussiness) ················· San Jose, CA: (714) 522-9227
Tech:(888) 926-2426
Web Page: http://www.yamahayst.com

Young Minds Inc ··· Colton, CA: 909-426-4860
Toll Free:(800) 964-4964
Web Page: http://www.ymi.com

Z-Code Software (see Net Manage)

Z-Ram (see Camintonn Z-Ram)

Zachariah & Lundbergh ······························ Marco Island, FL: 239-642-9622
Web Page: http://www.zlvideo.com

Zapex Technologies(Out of Bussiness) ········· Mountain View, CA: (650) 930-1300
Toll Free:(888) 254-2380
Web Page: http://www.zapex.com

ZD Events (see Key 3 Media Group)

ZD Labs (see eTesting Labs)

ZD Market Intel. (see Harte-Hanks)

Zebra Technologies ··· Vernon Hills, IL: (847) 634-6700
Tech:(847) 634-7000   Toll Free:(800) 423-0422
Web Page: http://www.zebra.com

Zedcor (see Art Today)

Zeh Software ··· Houston, TX: (281) 589-7757
Web Page: http://www.zeh.com

Zenith Data Systems (Comptek Systems) ····················· Dalls, TX: 214-503-6500
Web Page: http://www.zdsparts.com

Zenith Electronics Corp ······························· Lincolnshire, IL: (847) 391-7000
Toll Free:877-993-6484
Web Page: http://www.zenith.com
National Parts and Accessories ·····················973-330-5056
Tech:(330) 593-3364   Toll Free:(888) 393-6484

Zenographics Inc ··· Irvine, CA: (949) 737-4500
Tech:(800) 566-7468   Toll Free:(800) 366-7494
Web Page: http://www.zeno.com

Zeos International (see Micron PC)

Zephyr Development Corp ································· Houston, TX: (800) 966-3270
Tech:(713) 623-0089   Toll Free:(800) 966-3270
Web Page: http://www.zephyrcorp.com

ZH Computer Inc ··· Minneapolis, MN: (952) 844-0915
Web Page: http://www.zhcomputer.com

Zilog Inc ··· San Jose, CA: (408) 558-8500
Web Page: http://www.zilog.com

Zio Soft.com (408) 778-6500
Tech:(408) 778-7101
Web Page: http://www.ziosoft.com

Zitel Corp (see Fortel)

Zmation Inc ··· Portland, OR: (503) 253-8871
Web Page: http://www.zmation.com

Zombie Virtual Reality Studios ························· Seattle, WA: (206) 623-9655
Web Page: http://www.zombie.com

Zoom Telephonics Inc ······································· Boston, MA: (800) 631-3116
Tech:(561) 997-9686   Toll Free:(800) 666-6191
Web Page: http://www.zoomtel.com

Zoran Corp ·· Santa Clara, CA: (408) 919-4111
  Web Page: http://www.zoran.com
ZSoft Corp (see Learning Co)
Zydacron ·· Manchester, NH: (603) 647-1000
  Web Page: http://www.zydacron.com
ZyLAB International Inc ···························· Germantown, MD: (301) 428-0045
  Tech:(301) 428-0045   Toll Free:(800) 544-6339
  Web Page: http://www.zylab.com
ZyPCom Inc ·· Hayward, CA: (510) 783-2501
  Tech:(510) 783-2501
  Web Page: http://www.zypcom.com
ZyXEL Communications Inc ························· Placentia, CA: (714) 632-0882
  Tech:(714) 632-0882   Toll Free:(800) 255-4101
  Web Page: http://www.zyxel.com
Zzyzx Peripherals ······································ San Diego, CA: (858) 558-7800
  Toll Free:(800) 377-6151
  Web Page: http://www.zzyzx.com

Main Index

Index

Index

Index

Index

Index

Index

Index

Index